Introduction to Programming Using Visual Basic 5.0

An Integrated Visual/Procedural Approach

Gary Bronson

Fairleigh Dickinson University

P-65

Scott/Jones, Inc. Publishers
P.O.B. 696
El Granada, CA 94018
Voice: 650-726-2436
Fax: 650-726-4693
E-mail: scotjones2@aol.com
Web page: http://www.scottjonespub.com

Introduction to Programming Using Visual Basic 5.0: An Integrated Visual/Procedural Approach
Gary Bronson

ISBN: 1881991-47-4

Text Design and Composition: Bob Jones
Production Management: Heather Bennett
Book Manufacturing: Malloy Lithographing, Inc.

987   XY

A Word About Trademarks

All product names identified in this book are trademarks or registered trademarks of their respective companies. We have used the names in an editorial fashion only, and to the benefit of the trademark owner, with no intention of infringing the trademark. ActiveX, Microsoft, Visual Basic, Windows, and Word are trademarks of Microsoft Corporation. DEC, VAX, and VMX are trademarks of Digital Equipment Corporation. IBM and Lotus are trademarks of International Business Machines. INTEL is a trademark of Intel Corporation. WordPerfect is a trademark of Corel Corporation.

Additional Titles of Interest from Scott/Jones

C Through Objects
by John Connely

Problem Solving with C
by Jacqueline A. Jones and Keith Harrow

Assembly Language for the IBM PC, Second Edition
QuickStart in C++
by William B. Jones

Advanced Visual Basic
by Kip Irvine

C by Discovery, Second Edition
by L. S. Foster

The DOS 6 Coursebook
Visual Basic Programming
QuickStart in Visual Basic
The Visual Basic 5 Coursebook
by Forest Lin

Visual Basic with Business Applications, Second Edition
by Mark Simkin

The Access Guidebook: A Short Course
The Access Guidebook: A Full Course
by Maggie Trigg and Phyllis Dobson

The Windows 95 Textbook, Standard Edition
The Windows 95 Textbook, Extended Edition
A Short Course in Windows 95
by Stewart Venit

Table of Contents ▬▬▬▬▬▬

Preface

Visual Basic® has emerged as the preeminent programming language for Windows® based applications. A major reason for this is that Visual Basic® provides a rather complete set of visual objects, such as Command buttons, Labels, Text boxes, and Picture boxes, that can easily be assembled into a working graphical user interface (GUI—pronounced Goo-eey) and integrated into a Microsoft® Windows® operating system environment. From both a teaching and learning viewpoint, Visual Basic requires familiarity with three elements, only one of which is common to traditional programming languages such as Basic, Pascal, and C. These are

- The new visual objects required in creating a Windows-based graphical user interface;
- The new concept of event-based programming, where the user, rather than the programmer, determines the sequence of operations that is to be executed; and
- The traditional concept of procedural program code.

The major objective of this textbook is to introduce each of these elements, within the context of sound programming principles, in a manner that is accessible to the beginning programmer.

Thus, the basic requirement of this text is that all topics be presented in a clear and unambiguous manner. In addition to the basic material, a set of breadth topics and practical programming techniques that are known and used by all professional programmers, such as creating Splash screens and realistic menu systems, is included as extra material for those students who are ready for this additional material.

Prerequisites

In using this text no prerequisites are assumed. A short Chapter 1 briefly presents computer literacy material for those who need this background. The large numbers of examples and exercises used in the text are drawn from everyday experience and business fields. Thus, an instructor may choose applications and select a topic presentation that matches students' experience for a particular course emphasis.

Distinctive Features

Writing Style. I firmly believe that for a textbook to be useful it must provide a clearly defined supporting role to the leading role of the professor. Once the professor sets the stage, however, the textbook must encourage, nurture, and assist the student in acquiring and owning the material presented in class, To do this, the text must be written in a manner that makes sense to the student. Thus, first and foremost, I feel that the writing style used to convey the concepts presented is the most important and distinctive aspect of this text.

Flexibility. To be an effective teaching resource, this text is meant to provide a flexible tool that each professor can use in a variety of ways, depending on *how many* programming concepts and programming techniques are to be introduced in a single course, and *when* each is to be introduced. This is accomplished by partitioning the text into three parts and providing Looking Further sections at the end of each chapter.

Part I. Excluding Chapter 1, which presents basic computer literacy material, Part I presents the fundamental visual and procedural elements of Visual Basic. While presenting this basic material, much of the enrichment material presented in the Looking Further sections can be introduced as desired. For example, the material on Forms Design (Section 3.9) and Creating Menu Systems (Section 11.8) can be introduced almost any time after Chapter 3. In addition, many professors find that student interest is heightened by introducing the animation and graphics material in Chapter 11 immediately after the introductory material in Chapter 2.

Parts II and III. Once Part I is completed, the material in Parts II and III can be covered in any order. For example, in a more traditional introduction to programming type of course, Part I would be followed by Chapter 8. However, if a requirement is that the course must emphasize database applications, Part I could just as easily be followed by Chapter 9. In a third instance, if the course is to have a more theoretical slant, Part I can be immediately followed by Chapter 12. In each of these cases, a "pick-and-choose" approach to the Looking Further sections can be applied, as these topics are appropriate to the overall course structure and emphasis. Thus, regardless of what the decision is, this book provides a flexible means of customizing a course around the central core topics presented in Part I. This flexibility of topic introduction is illustrated by the following topic dependency chart.

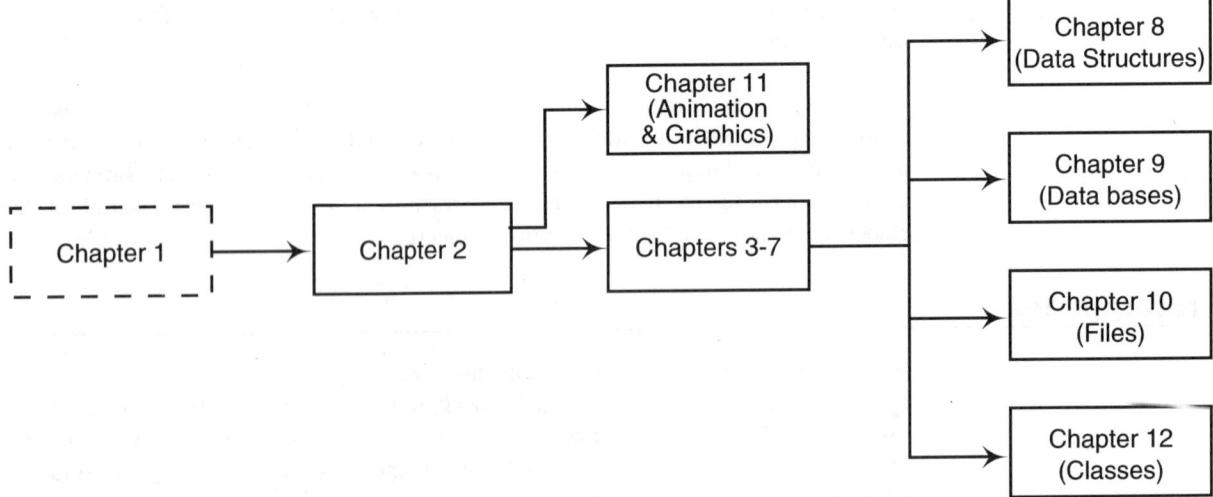

Software Engineering. Although this is primarily an introductory Visual Basic text, as opposed to a CS1 introductory programming book, the text is meant to familiarize students with the fundamentals of software engineering, from both a procedural and object-oriented viewpoint. This process begins in Section 1.2 with the formal introduction of the software development cycle and is a thread maintained throughout the text. In some instances, this conceptual material can be skipped. For example, a course could omit Chapter 1 entirely and begin with Chapter 2. Similarly, in a strictly language-oriented course, the introductory section on repetition statements (Section 8.1), which presents the concepts of both pre- and posttest loops, might be omitted. The same is true of the database theory presented in Section 9.1. In most cases, however, the more general programming aspects are interwoven within the text's main language component precisely because the text is meant to both introduce and strengthen the why as well as the how of programming.

Program Testing. Every single Visual Basic program in this text has been successfully entered and executed using Microsoft Visual Basic Version 5.0. A source diskette of all programs is included with the text. This will permit students to both experiment and extend the existing programs and more easily modify them, as required by a number of end-of-section exercises.

Pedagogical Features

To facilitate the goal of making Visual Basic accessible in a first-level course, the following pedagogical features have been incorporated into the text.

End of Section Exercises. Almost every section in the book contains numerous and diverse skill-builder and programming exercises. In addition, solutions to selected odd-numbered exercises are provided on the disk included with the text.

Pseudocode Descriptions. Pseudocode is stressed throughout the text. Flowchart symbols are presented, but are used only in visually presenting flow-of-control constructs.

Common Programming Errors and Chapter Review. Each chapter ends with a section on common programming errors and a review of the main topics covered in that chapter.

Looking Further Sections. Given the many different emphases that can be applied in teaching Visual Basic, a number of basic and enrichment topics have been included. These sections range from such basic material as using the Help facility to additional topics, such as defining error types and using the Wizards. The purpose of these sections is to provide flexibility as to the choice of which topics to present and the timing of when to present them.

Programmers' Notes. These shaded boxes are meant primarily as a reference for commonly used tasks, such as creating a new project, saving a project, and successfully navigating through the integrated development environment (IDE), the Programmers' Notes are also used to highlight programming techniques and provide additional concept material.

Laboratory Exercises. These longer programming projects should extend and reinforce the principles in the textbook. They appear at the end of each of the three parts, that is, following chapters 7, 10, and 12.

Appendices and Supplements

An expanded set of appendices is provided. These include appendices on keywords, operator precedence, ANSI codes, additional controls, and Object Linking and Embedding (OLE). In addition, a disk containing source code to all applications presented in the text and solutions to selected odd-numbered exercises is packaged with the text.

Acknowledgments

This book began as an idea. It became a reality only due to the encouragement, skills, and efforts supplied by many people. I would like to acknowledge their contribution. First, I would like to thank Richard Jones, my editor at Scott/Jones Publishing Company. In addition to his continuous faith and encouragement, his ideas and partnership were instrumental in creating this text. I also am very grateful to Linda Utter of Scott/Jones for her handling of numerous scheduling and review details that permitted me to concentrate on the actual writing of the text. In addition, I would like to express my gratitude to the following individual reviewers.

Ben Acton
Montgomery College

Dennis Benincasa
Macomb Community College

Sid Brounstein
Montgomery College

Jan Buttermore
Riverside Community College

John Hay
Valencia Community College

Lee Hunt
Collin County Community College

Harold Kollmeier
Franklin Pierce College

Mark Lattanzi
James Madison University

Hseuh-Ming Tommy Lu
Delaware Technical College

Matt McCaskill
Brevard Community College

Jim Moore
Indiana University-Purdue University

George Novacky
University of Pittsburgh

Merrill Parker
Chattanooga State Technical Community College

Margaret Anne Pierce
Georgia Southern University

James L. Richards
Bemidji State University

Ethel Schuster
Simmons College

Jeffrey Scott
Blackhawk Technical College

John Sharlow
Eastern Connecticut State University

Robert Signorile
Boston College

B.J. Sineath
Forsyth Technical Community College

Milton Smith
Texas Tech University

Marianne Stefanski
Triton College

Cherie Stevens
South Florida Community College

Sharon Stewart
Howard Community College

Ken Strukel
Hibbing Community College

Melinda White
Santa Fe Community College

Each of these individuals supplied extremely detailed and constructive reviews of both the original manuscript and a number of revisions. Their suggestions, attention to detail, and comments were extraordinarily helpful to me as the manuscript evolved and matured through the editorial process.

Once the review process was completed, the task of turning the final manuscript into a textbook depended on many people other than myself. For this I especially want to thank the production and copy editor, Heather Bennett, and the compositor, Bob Jones. The dedication of these people was incredible and very important to me. I am also very appreciative of the suggestions and work of the assistant promotion manager at Scott/Jones, Hazel Dunlap.

Special acknowledgment goes to Mark Lattanzi, of James Madison University, who graciously supplied the material that formed the Laboratory Exercises in the text, and Cherie Stevens of South Florida Community College, who provided extra insight into various topics used throughout the text.

I would also like to gratefully acknowledge the encouragement and support of Fairleigh Dickinson University. Specifically, this includes the positive academic climate provided by the university and the direct encouragement and support of my dean, Dr. Paul Lerman, and my chairperson, Professor Ron Heim. Without their support, this text could not have been written.

Finally, I deeply appreciate the patience, understanding, and love provided by my friend, wife, and partner, Rochelle.

Gary Bronson
1998

Dedicated to Rochelle, Jeremy, David, and Matthew

Part I
Fundamentals

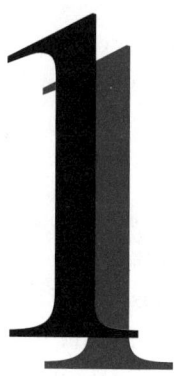

1 Introduction to Computers and Programming

1.1 Introduction to Programming

A computer, such as the modern notebook shown in Figure 1-1, is a machine made of physical components that are collectively referred to as *hardware*. In this regard, a computer is the same as any other machine composed of physical elements, such as an automobile or lawn mower. Like these other machines, a computer must be turned on and then driven, or controlled, to do the task it was meant to do. How this gets done is what distinguishes computers from other types of machinery.

In an automobile, for example, control is provided by the driver, who sits inside of and directs the car. In a computer, the driver is a set of instructions, called a *program*. More formally, a computer program is defined as a self-contained set of instructions used to

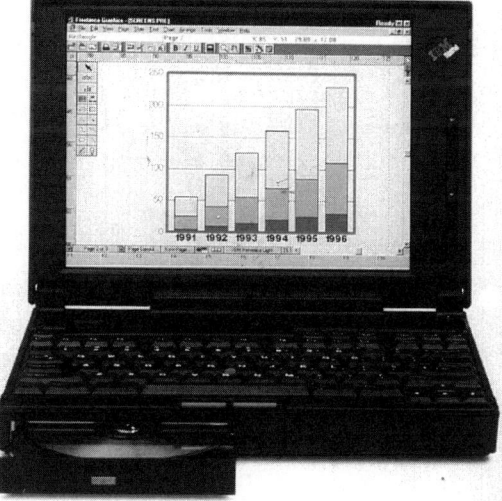

Figure 1-1

An IBM ThinkPad Notebook Computer

operate a computer to produce a specific result. Another term for a program or set of programs is *software*, and we will use both terms interchangeably throughout the text.

Historically, the first recorded attempt at creating a general purpose calculating machine controlled by externally supplied instructions was by Charles Babbage in England, in 1822. The set of instructions for this machine, which Babbage called an analytical engine, was developed by

Figure 1-2

*Charles Babbage's
Analytical Engine*

Ada Byron, the daughter of the poet, Lord Byron. Thus, Ada Byron is sometimes considered the world's first programmer.

Although Babbage's machine was not successfully built in his lifetime, the first practical realization of his idea was achieved in 1946 with the ENIAC (Electrical Numerical Integrator and Computer) at the University of Pennsylvania in 1946. ENIAC, which was based on work done previously by Dr. John V. Atanasoff and Clifford Berry at Iowa State University in 1937, was not a stored program computer, where the instructions directing its operation are inside the machine. Rather, ENIAC depended on externally connected wires to direct its operation. This meant that reprogramming ENIAC to alter its operation required changing the external wiring.

The final goal of storing both the raw data and the instructions directing its manipulation within the computer's memory was realized in 1949 at the University of Cambridge. Here the EDSAC (Electronic Delayed Storage Automatic Computer) became the first commercially produced computer to permit instructions stored inside the computer's memory to direct and control the machine's operation. With EDSAC, the theory of a computer program as a stored sequence of instructions, to be executed in order, became a reality that made modern computing possible.

First and Second Generation (Low-Level) Languages

Once the goal of a stored program was achieved, the era of programming languages began. The instructions used in EDSAC initiated the first generation of such languages, which were also referred to as *machine languages*. These languages consist of a sequence of instructions represented as binary numbers such as

```
11000000 00000001 00000010
11110000 00000010 00000011
```

Each new computer type, even including modern desktop and notebook computers, can only be operated by a machine-language program that is compatible with the computer's internal processing hardware. The difference in the processing hardware of early computers, such as IBM, Univac, and Sperry-Rand, meant that each manufacturer had its own machine language. This same situation is still present today and explains why machine-language programs that operate on Intel-based machines, such as IBM personal computers (PCs),

Figure 1-3

*Assembly Programs
Must be Translated*

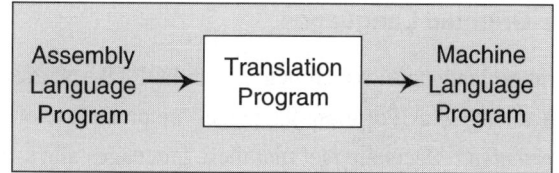

cannot run on Motorola-based Sun computers or Apple Macintoshes. As you might expect, it is very tedious and time consuming to write machine-language programs.

One of the first advances in programming was the replacement of machine-language binary codes with abbreviated words, such as ADD, SUB, and MUL, to indicate the desired operation, and both decimal numbers and labels to indicate the location of the data. For example, using these words and decimal values, the previous two machine-language instructions might be written:

```
ADD 1, 2
MUL 2, 3
```

Programming languages that use this type of symbolic notation are referred to as *assembly languages.* Assembly languages formally comprise the *second generation* of computer languages. Since computers can only execute machine-language programs, the set of instructions contained within an assembly-language program must be translated into machine language before it can be executed on a computer (Figure 1-3). Translator programs that translate assembly-language programs into machine-language programs are known as *assemblers.*

Both first-generation machine languages and second-generation assembly languages are referred to as *low-level languages.* Low-level languages are, by definition, machine dependent, in that programs written in a low-level language can only be run on a particular type of computer. This is because low-level languages all use instructions that are directly tied to specific processing hardware. Such programs do, however, permit using special features of a particular computer and generally execute at the fastest possible levels.

Third and Fourth Generation (High-Level) Languages

With the commercial introduction of the FORTRAN[1] in 1957, the third generation of languages began.This new generation of computer languages initiated the era of high-level languages. The term *high level* refers to the fact that the programs written in these languages can be translated to run on a variety of computer types, unlike the low-level languages that are restricted to a particular computer type. If a high-level program is going to be run on an IBM computer, for example, a translator program would produce an IBM machine-language program for execution. Similarly, if the program were to be run on another type of computer, an appropriate specific translator would be used. We are still in the era of high-level languages. Figure 1-4 illustrates the relationship and evolution of programming languages. As shown, both third and fourth generation languages are considered high-level languages. Additionally, as illustrated, third generation languages include both procedure-oriented and object-oriented languages.

---

[1] FORTRAN is an acronym for FORMula TRANslation.

Procedure-Oriented Languages

Third generation languages, which began with FORTRAN, grew rapidly to include COBOL, BASIC, Pascal, and C. All of these languages are procedure-oriented languages. The term *procedure-oriented* reflects the fact that these languages allow programmers to concentrate on the procedures they are using to solve a problem without regard for the specific hardware that will ultimately run the program. Unlike low-level languages that permitted only one mathematical operation per instruction, a single procedural language instruction can permit many such operations to be performed. For example, an instruction in a procedure-oriented high-level language to add two numbers and multiply the result by a third number could appear as

```
answer = (first + second) * third
```

Typically, a group of such statements are combined together to create a logically consistent set of instructions, called a procedure, that is used to produce one specific result. A complete program is then composed of multiple procedures that together fulfill a desired programming objective.

Until the early 1980s, all new programming languages were predominately high-level procedure-oriented languages. Programs written in these languages are typically produced by following the steps shown in Figure 1-5. Here the programmer first plans what the program will do. The required instructions are then entered into the computer using a text-editing program and stored together as a file, which is referred to as the *source program* or *source file*. The source program is then translated into machine language by a translator program and subsequently run on a computer. The final machine-language program is referred to as an *executable program*, or *executable*, for short.

Translation into a machine-language program is accomplished in two ways. When each statement in a high-level language source program is translated individually and executed immediately, the programming language is referred to as an *interpreted language,* and the program doing the translation is called an *interpreter*.

When all of the statements in a source program are translated before any one statement is executed, the programming language used is

Figure 1-4

The Evolution of Programming Languages

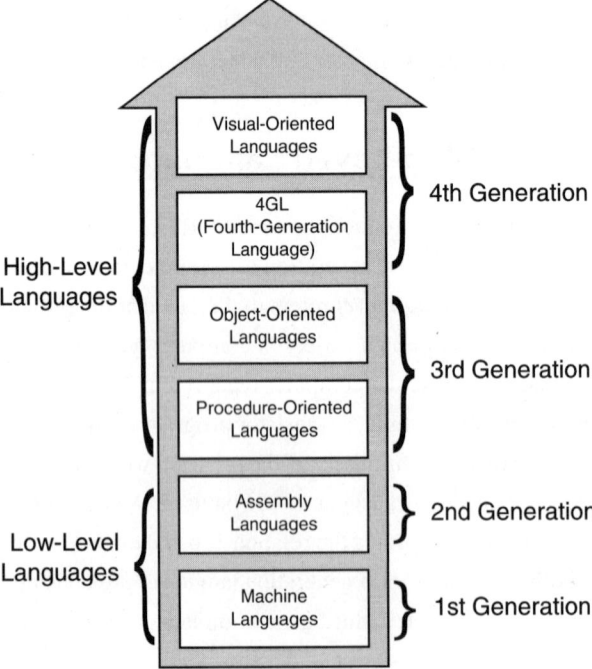

Figure 1-5

Traditional Procedural Programming Steps to Create a Program

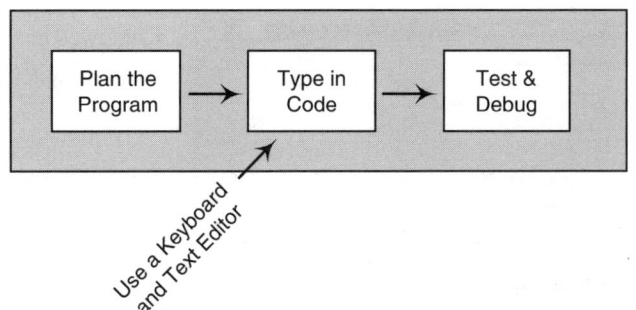

called a *compiled language*. In this case, the program doing the translation is called a *compiler*. Both compiled and interpreted versions of a language can exist, although one typically predominates. For example, although compiled versions of the original BASIC language exist, BASIC is predominately an interpreted language, as is Visual Basic. Similarly, although C is predominately a compiled language, interpreted versions of C do exist.

Although all high-level source programs must still be translated into machine code to run on a computer, the steps required to produce a program (shown in Figure 1-5) have changed dramatically over the last few years, with the introduction of a new type of high-level languages. Languages of this new type are referred to as both *object-oriented* and *event-driven*.

Object-Oriented Languages

Although high-level languages represented a major advancement over their low-level counterparts, the procedural aspect of high-level languages did pose some problems. One of these was the difficulty of reusing procedural programs for new or similar applications without extensive revision, retesting, and revalidation. The second and more fundamental reason for disenchantment with procedural-based programming was its incompatibility with graphical screens and windowed applications. Programming multiple windows on the same graphical screen is virtually impossible using standard procedural programming techniques.

The reason for this is that the major procedural languages were developed before the advent of graphical user interfaces. Because the standard input and output devices prior to the 1980s all used character-based text, such as that produced by a standard keyboard and printer, procedural languages were geared to the input, processing, and output of text characters and not to the creation of graphical images such as those shown in Figure 1-6. At a minimum, a new way of constructing and then interacting with such images was required.

Figure 1-6

A Multiwindowed Screen

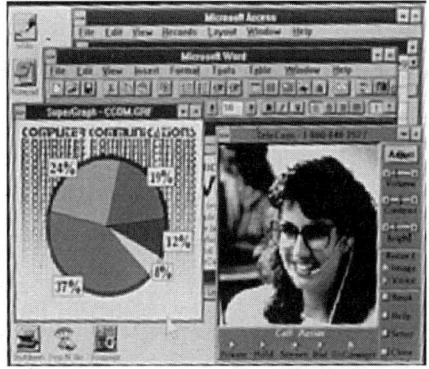

The solution to producing programs that efficiently manipulate graphical screens and provide reusable windowing code was found in artificial intelligence and simulation programming techniques. Artificial intelligence offered extensive research on geometrical object specification and recognition. Simulation provided considerable background in representing items as objects with well-defined interactions between them. This object-based paradigm[2] fitted well in a graphical

---

[2] A paradigm is a way of thinking about or doing something.

Figure 1-7

The Screen Image of an Executing Visual Basic Program

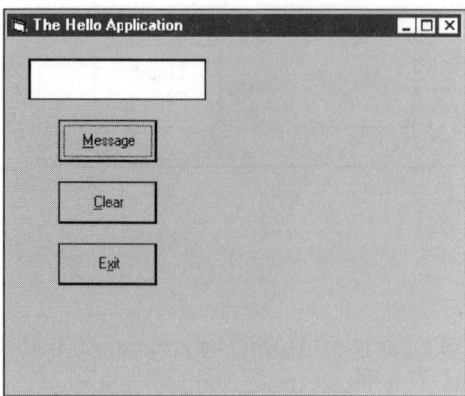

windowed environment, where each window could be specified as a self-contained object.

An object is also well suited to a programming representation because it can be specified by two basic characteristics: a current *state*, which defines how the object appears at the moment, and a behavior, which defines how the object reacts to external inputs. To make this more meaningful, consider the screen image reproduced in Figure 1-7.

Figure 1-7 was produced by a very simple Visual Basic Program—one, in fact, that we will write in the next chapter. This screen is an example of a graphical user interface (GUI, pronounced "goo-eey"); it provides a graphical way for the user to interact with the program. Examining Figure 1-7 a bit closer reveals that it contains five objects, four of which the user can interact with directly. The first object is the window itself, which includes the caption (or title), `The Hello Application`, and three buttons, the Close, Maximize, and Minimize buttons in the top right corner.

Within the window illustrated in Figure 1-7 are four basic objects: three Command buttons and one Text box. Each of the Command buttons has its own caption, `Message`, `Clear`, and `Exit`, respectively. The Text box currently contains no text. In object-oriented terms, the three Command buttons and the single Text box are objects that have been placed on a form when the program was being designed and developed. When the program is run, producing the image shown in Figure 1-7, the form becomes a window. Each object in the window is defined by a set of properties that determine where and how that object appears. The most obvious properties of the Command buttons are their position on the screen and their captions; each of these properties was set by the programmer.

Events

The most noticeable difference between procedure-based and object-based programs is the manner in which the user interacts with a running program. Take another look at Figure 1-7. Here the user has a number of options. He or she can choose to click on any of the internal Command buttons, in any sequence, or on one of the buttons on the top line of the window itself. For the moment, let us only concern ourselves with the three Command buttons labeled Message, Clear, and Exit. Selecting any one of these buttons constitutes an event. As a practical matter, a user-initiated event can be triggered in one of the following three ways:

- By placing the mouse pointer over a Command button and clicking the left mouse button (clicking means pushing and releasing the left mouse button);
- By simultaneously holding down the [ALT] key and pressing one of the underlined letters (this is called "activating a hot key"); or
- By pressing the [TAB] key until the desired button is highlighted with a dotted line and then pressing the [ENTER] key.

The control that is highlighted with the dotted line is said "to have the focus." (As shown in Figure 1-7 the M̲essage button has the focus, so pressing [ENTER] will activate this control.)

Once an event is triggered by a user, which in this case is done by simply selecting and activating one of the three button controls in the window, program instructions take over. If the programmer has written instructions for a user-activated event, some processing will take place; otherwise, no processing occurs. For the program shown on Figure 1-7,there are three events for which code has been written. If the user activates the M̲essage Command button, the message "Hello There World!" is displayed in the Text box. Clicking on the C̲lear Command button clears the text area of the Text box, while clicking on the Ex̲it Command button results in a beep and termination of the program.

Notice that the sequence of events, that is, which actions are taken and in what order, is controlled by the user. The user can click any one of three Command buttons, in any order, or even run a different Windows program while the Visual Basic program is executing. This user determination of which event will take place next, as the program is running, is quite a different approach than the traditional procedure-based programming paradigm. In a procedure-based program, the decisions as to which actions can be taken and in what order are controlled by the programmer when the program is being designed.

Unfortunately, an event-based user graphical interface such as that illustrated in Figure 1-7 does not eliminate the need for all procedural code. The programmer must still provide the code to appropriately process the events triggered by the user. From a design standpoint then, the construction of an object-based program proceeds using the steps shown in Figure 1-8.

Figure 1-8

The Steps in Developing an Object-Based Program

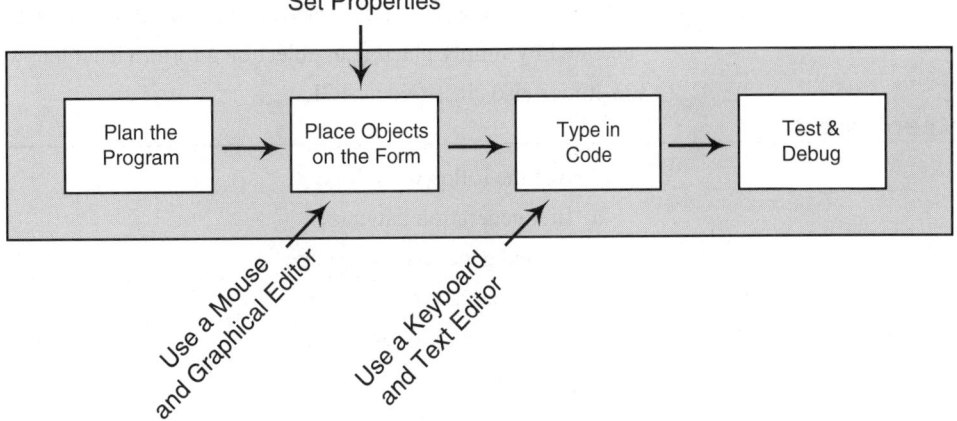

The revolutionary aspect of programming languages such as Visual Basic is that they provide a basic set of objects that can be placed on a form while a program is being developed. This is done within an integrated design environment that makes creating the graphical interface quite easy. Thus, in using Visual Basic, the programmer does not have to be concerned either with writing the code for producing the graphical objects or with recognizing when certain events, such as "the mouse was clicked on the Command button," actually occur. Once the desired objects are selected and placed on the form, Visual Basic takes care of creating the object and recognizing appropriate object events. Programming languages that permit the programmer to manipulate graphical objects directly, without requiring the programmer to provide the necessary code to support selected objects and their interface, are sometimes referred to as Visual Languages. Visual Basic is an example of a Visual Language. Using such a language, however, still requires programmer responsibility for

1. Initially selecting and placing objects on a form when the program is being developed; and
2. Writing and including procedural code to correctly processes events that can be triggered by a user's interaction with the program's objects when the program is run.

An example of a classic object-oriented language, without the visual programming interface, is C++. The visual language equivalent of C++ is Visual C++. One of the major differences between Visual Basic and Visual C++ is that Visual Basic provides the ability to place existing objects into a program, while Visual C++ also provides the ability to create new objects.

Finally, sitting between object-oriented languages and visual languages in Figure 1-4 are a group of languages referred to as *4GLs*. These were the initial fourth generation languages (hence, 4GL) that permitted users to access and format information without writing any procedural code. For example, in a 4GL, both a programmer and user could type the following English-like command to produce a formatted report with the desired information:

```
List the name, starting date, and salary for all employees who
have more than 20 years of service
```

In a 4GL, this request for information causes the program to produce the actual code for satisfying the request without any programmer intervention. Since a similar type of operation occurs in visual languages, where the code for each object is automatically generated by simply placing an object on a form, visual languages such as Visual Basic are sometimes also classified as 4GLs.

Exercises 1.1

1. Define the following terms:
   a. first generation language
   b. second generation language
   c. third generation language
   d. fourth generation language
   e. high-level language
   f. low-level language

g. machine language

h. assembly language

i. assembler

j. interpreter

k. compiler

l. object

m. event

n. graphical user interface

o. procedure-oriented language

p. object-oriented language

2. Describe the accomplishments of the following people:

a. Charles Babbage

b. Ada Byron

3. a. Describe the difference between high and low-level languages.

b. Describe the difference between procedure-oriented and object-oriented languages.

4. Describe the similarities and differences between procedure and object-oriented languages

5. a. To be classified as a fourth generation language (4GL), the language must provide a specific capability. What is this capability?

b. Must a 4GL provide the ability to create event-driven programs?

1.2 Problem Solution and Software Development

Problem solving has become a way of life in modern society because as society has become more complex, so have its problems. Issues such as solid waste disposal, global warming, international finance, pollution, and nuclear proliferation are relatively new, yet solutions to these problems now challenge our best technological and human capabilities.

Most problem solutions require considerable planning and forethought if the solution is to be appropriate and efficient. For example, imagine trying to construct a cellular telephone network or create an inventory management system for a department store by trial and error. Such a solution would be expensive at best, disastrous at worst, and practically impossible.

Creating a program is no different, because a program is a solution developed for a particular problem. First you must determine what the problem is and what method will be used to solve it. Each field of study has its own name for the systematic approach to solving problems. In science and engineering the approach is referred to as the *scientific method*, while in quantitative analysis, it is called the *systems approach*.

The technique used by professional software developers for understanding the problem that is being solved and for creating an effective and appropriate software solution is called the *software development procedure*. This procedure, as illustrated in Figure 1-9, consists of three overlapping phases:

- Development and Design,
- Documentation, and
- Maintenance.

As a discipline, *software engineering* is concerned with creating readable, efficient, reliable, and maintainable programs and systems, and uses the software development procedure to achieve this goal.

Figure 1-9

The Three Phases of Program Development

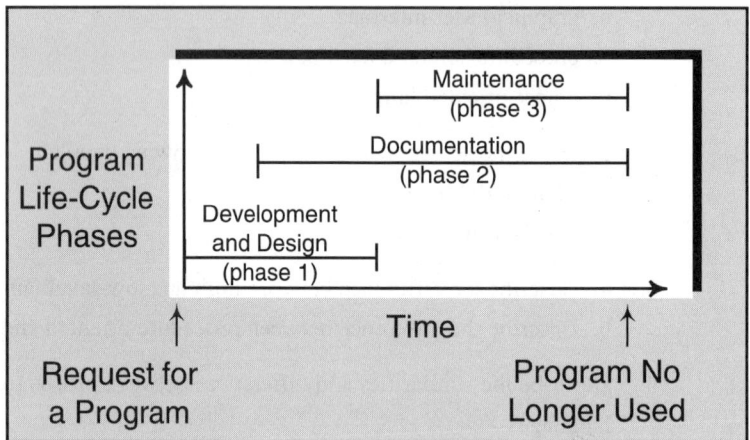

Phase I: Development and Design

This phase begins with either a statement of a problem or a specific request for a program, which is referred to as a *program requirement*. Once a problem has been stated or a specific request for a program solution has been made, the development and design phase begins. This phase consists of the four well-defined steps illustrated in Figure 1-10 and summarized below.

1. Analyze the Problem

This step ensures that we clearly define and understand the problem. The determination that the problem is clearly defined is only made when the person doing the analysis understands what outputs are required and what inputs will be needed. To accomplish this, the analyst

Figure 1-10

The Development and Design Steps

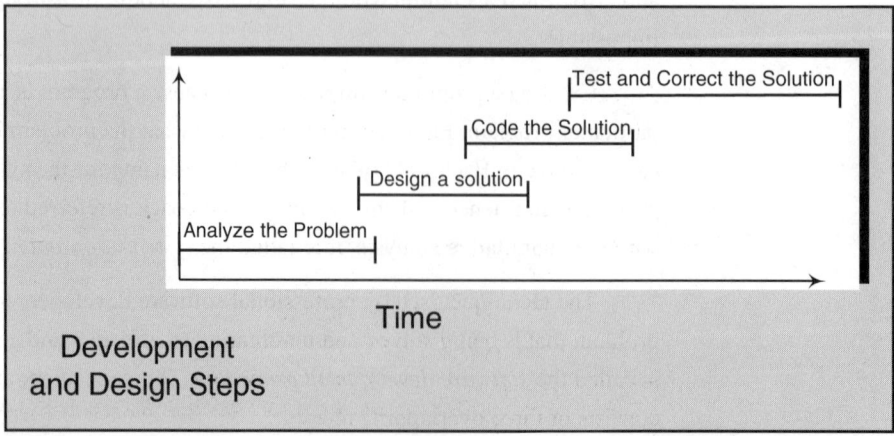

must have an understanding of how inputs can be used to produce the desired output. For example, assume that you receive the following assignment:

We need a program to provide information about student grades.

—- Management

A simple analysis reveals that it is not a well-defined problem because we do not know exactly what output information is required. Therefore, it would be a major mistake to begin immediately writing a program to solve it. To clarify and define the problem statement your first step should be to ask "Management" to define exactly what information is needed (the outputs) and what data will be provided (the inputs). If it is unclear how to obtain the required outputs from the given inputs, a more in-depth analysis may be required. This typically means obtaining more background information about the problem or application. It also frequently entails doing one or more hand calculations to ensure that you understand the inputs and how they must be combined to achieve the desired output.

2. Develop a Solution

In this step, we determine and select a solution for the problem. An acceptable and complete solution is typically refined from the preliminary solution identified in the analysis step. This solution must be checked to ensure that it correctly produces the desired outputs, typically by doing one or more hand calculations, if they were not already done in the analysis step.

Sometimes the selected solution is quite easy, and sometimes it is quite complex. For example, the solution to determining the dollar value of the change in one's pocket or determining the area of a rectangle is quite simple and consists of a simple calculation. The construction of an inventory tracking and control system for a department, however, is clearly more complex.

3. Program the Solution

This step, which is also referred to as implementing the solution, consists of translating the solution into a usable application. In Visual Basic, it means constructing a graphical user interface (GUI) and providing the necessary computer instructions, which are referred to as *code*.

4. Test and Correct the Application

As its name suggests, this step requires testing the completed application to ensure that it does, in fact, provide a solution to the problem. Any errors found during the tests must be corrected.

Listed in Table 1-1 is the relative amount of effort typically expended on each of these four development and design steps in large commercial programming projects. As this listing demonstrates, programming is not the major effort in this phase.

Table 1-1	
Step	**Effort**
Analyze the Problem	10%
Develop a Solution	20%
Program the Solution	20%
Test the Application	50%

Many new programmers have trouble because they spend the majority of their time writing the program, without spending sufficient time understanding the problem or designing an appropriate solution. In this regard, it is worthwhile to remember the programming proverb: "It is impossible to construct a successful application for a problem that is not fully understood." A somewhat equivalent and equally valuable proverb is "The sooner you start programming an application, the longer it usually takes to complete."

Phase II: Documentation

In practice, most programmers forget many of the details of their own programs a few months after they have finished working on them. If they or other programmers must subsequently make modifications to a program, much valuable time can be lost figuring out just how the original program works. Good documentation prevents this from happening.

For every problem solution, there are five elements in complete documentation:

1. Initial Application Description,
2. Description of Modification and Changes,
3. Well-Commented Code Listing,
4. Sample Test Runs, and
5. A User's Manual.

The documentation phase formally begins in the design phase and continues into the maintenance phase.

Phase III: Maintenance

Maintenance includes the correction of newly found errors and the addition of new features and modifications to existing applications. Figure 1-11 illustrates the relative proportion of time spent on maintenance as compared to development and design of a typical program.

Using the data provided in Figure 1-11, we see that the maintenance of existing programs currently accounts for approximately 75 percent of all programming costs.

Figure 1-11

Maintenance is the Predominant Software Cost

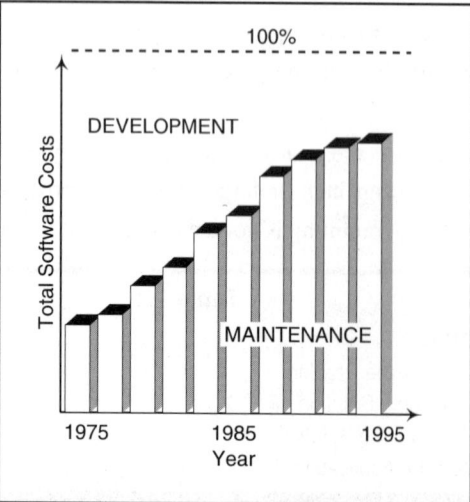

Students generally find this strange because they are accustomed to solving one problem and moving on to a different one. Commercial and scientific fields, however, do not operate this way. In these fields, one application or idea is typically built on a previous one, and may require months or years of work. This is especially true in programming. Once an application is written, which may take weeks or months, maintenance may continue for years as new features are needed. Advances in technology such as communication, networking, fiber optics, and new graphical displays constantly demand updated software products.

How easily a program can be maintained (corrected, modified, or enhanced) is related to the ease with which the program can be read and understood, which is directly related to the quality of its development and design.

A Closer Look at Phase I

Because the majority of this text is concerned with Phase I of the software development procedure, we elaborate further on the four steps required for this phase. The use of these steps forms the central focus of our work in creating useful programming solutions.

Step 1: Analyze the Problem

Countless hours have been spent writing computer programs that either have never been used or have caused considerable animosity between programmer and user because the

Figure 1-12

Six Individual Shapes

programmer did not produce what the user needed or expected. Successful programmers understand and avoid this by ensuring that the problem is clearly defined. This is the first step in creating an application and the most important, because it determines the specifications for a final solution. If the requirements are not fully and completely understood before programming begins, the results are almost always disastrous.

Imagine designing and building a house without fully understanding the architect's specifications. After the house is completed, the architect tells you that a bathroom is required on the first floor, where you have built a wall between the kitchen and the dining room. In addition, that particular wall is one of the main support walls for the house and contains numerous pipes and electrical cables. In this case, adding one bathroom requires a rather major modification to the basic structure of the house.

Experienced programmers understand the importance of analyzing and understanding a program's requirements before programming the solution. Most have, in the past, constructed programs that later had to be entirely dismantled and redone. The following exercise should give you a sense of this experience.

Figure 1-12 illustrates the outlines of six individual shapes from a classic children's puzzle. Assume that as one or more shapes are given, starting with shapes A and B, an easy-to-describe figure must be constructed.

Figure 1-13

Typical First Figure

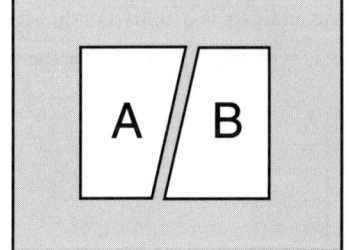

Typically, shapes A and B are initially arranged to obtain a square, as illustrated in Figure 1-13. Next, when shape C is considered, it is usually combined with the existing square to form a rectangle, as illustrated in Figure 1-14. Then, when pieces D and E are added, they

Figure 1-14

Typical Second Figure

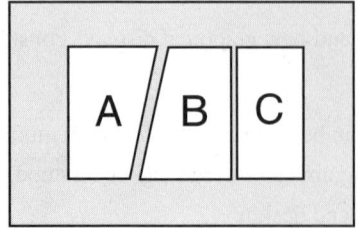

are usually arranged to form another rectangle, which is placed alongside the existing rectangle to form a square, as shown in Figure 1-15.

The process of adding new pieces onto the existing structure is identical to constructing a program and then adding to it as each subsequent requirement is understood, rather than completely analyzing the problem before undertaking to solve it. The problem arises when the program is almost finished and a requirement is added that does not fit easily into the established pattern. For example, assume that the last shape (shape F - see Figure 1-16) must now be added. This last piece does not fit into the existing pattern that has been constructed. In order to include this piece with the others, the pattern must be completely dismantled and restructured.

Unfortunately, many programmers structure their programs in the same sequential manner used to construct Figure 1-15. Rather than

Figure 1-15

Typical Third Figure

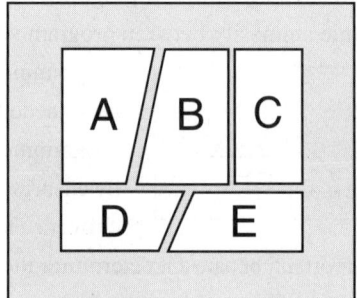

taking the time to understand the complete set of requirements, new programmers frequently start designing a solution based on understanding only a small subset of the total requirements. Then, when a subsequent requirement does not fit the existing program structure, the programmer is forced to dismantle and restructure either parts or all of the application.

Now, let's approach the problem of creating a figure from another view. If we started by arranging the first set of pieces as a parallelogram, all the pieces could be included in the final figure, as illustrated in Figure 1-17.

It is worthwhile observing that the piece that caused us to dismantle the first figure (Figure 1-15) actually sets the pattern for the final figure illustrated in Figure 1-17. This is often the case with programming requirements. The requirement that seems to be the least clear is frequently the one that determines the main interrelationships of the program. It is worthwhile to include and understand all the known requirements before beginning a solution. In sum, before any solution is attempted the analysis step must be completed.

The person performing the analysis must initially take a broad perspective, see all of the pieces, and understand the main purpose of what the program or system is meant to achieve. The key to success here, which ultimately determines the success of the final program, is to determine the main purpose of the system as seen by the person or organization making the request. For large applications, the analysis is usually conducted by a systems analyst. For smaller applications, the analysis is typically performed by the programmer.

Figure 1-16

The Last Piece

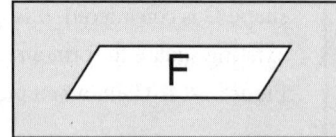

Regardless of how the analysis is done, or by whom, at its conclusion there should be a clear understanding of

- What the system or program must do,
- What reports or outputs must be produced, and
- What inputs are required to create the desired outputs.

Step 2: Designing and Developing a Solution

Once the problem is clearly understood, a solution can be developed. In this regard the programmer is in a position similar to that of an architect who must draw up the plans for a house: the house must conform to certain specifications and meet the needs of its owner but can be designed and built in many possible ways. So too for a program.

Figure 1-17

Including All the Pieces

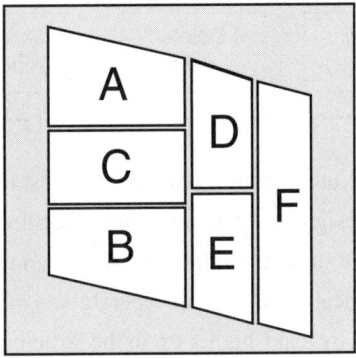

For small applications the solution may be simple, consisting of only a few calculations. More typically, the initial solution must be refined and organized into smaller subsystems, with specifications for how the subsystems will interface with each other. To achieve this goal, describing the solution starts at the highest level (top-most) requirement and proceeds downwards through the parts that must be constructed to achieve this requirement. To make this more meaningful, consider that a computer program is required to track the number of parts in inventory. The required output for this program is a description of all parts carried in inventory and the number of units of each item in stock; the given inputs are the initial inventory quantity of each part, the number of items sold, the number of items returned, and the number of items purchased.

Figure 1-18

First-Level Structure Diagram

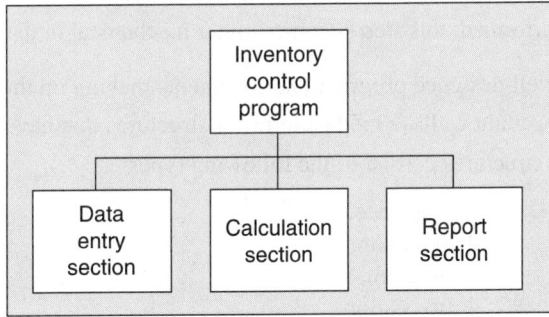

For these specifications, a designer could initially organize the requirements for the program into the three sections illustrated in Figure 1-18. This is called a *first-level structure diagram,* because it represents the first overall structure of the program selected by the designer.

Once an initial structure is developed, it is refined until the tasks indicated in the boxes are completely defined. For example, both the data entry and report subsections shown in Figure 1-18 would be further refined as follows: the data entry section certainly must include provisions for entering the data. Since it is the system designer's responsibility to plan for contingencies and human error, provisions must also be made for changing incorrect data after an entry has been made and for deleting a previously entered value altogether. Similar subdivisions for the report section can also be made. Figure 1-19 illustrates a second-level structure diagram for an inventory tracking system that includes these further refinements.

Figure 1-19

*Second-Level Refinement
Structure Diagram*

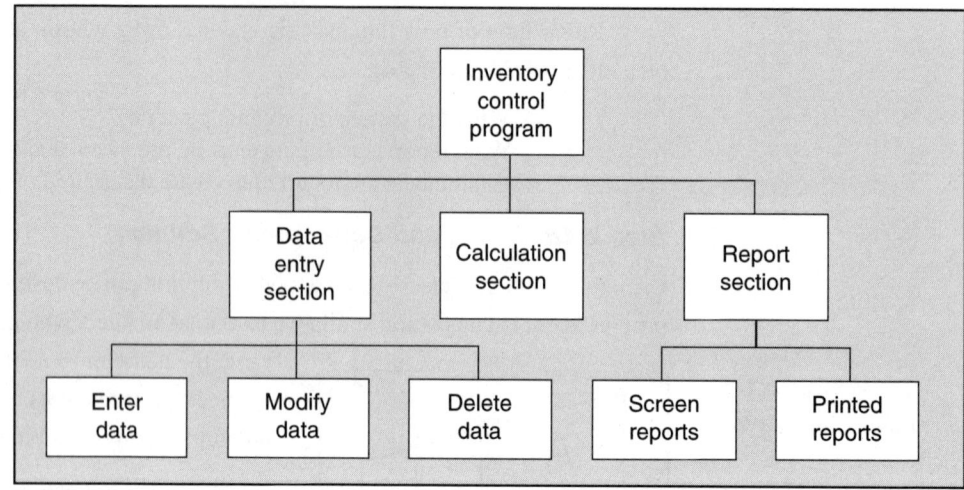

The process of refining a solution continues until the smallest requirement is included within the solution. Notice that the design produces a treelike structure where the levels branch out as we move from the top of the structure to the bottom. When the design is complete, each task designated in a box is typically coded with separate sets of instructions that are executed as they are called upon by tasks higher up in the structure.

Step 3: Program the Solution

Programming the solution involves translating the chosen design solution into a computer program. In Visual Basic this means creating all of the necessary graphical user interfaces and providing procedural code. If the analysis and solution steps have been correctly performed, this step becomes rather mechanical in nature.

In a well-designed program, the statements making up the procedural code will conform to certain well-defined patterns, or structures that have been defined in the solution step. These structures consist of the following types:

1. Sequence,
2. Selection,
3. Iteration, and
4. Invocation.

Sequence defines the order in which instructions within each event procedure are executed by the program. The specification of which instruction comes first, which comes second, and so on, is essential if the procedure is to achieve a well-defined purpose.

Selection provides the capability to make a choice between different operations, depending on the result of some condition. For example, the value of a number can be checked before a division is performed. If the number is not zero, it can be used as the denominator of a division operation, otherwise the division will not be performed and the user will be issued a warning message.

Repetition, which is also referred to as looping and iteration, allows the same operation to be repeated based on the value of a condition. For example, grades might be repeatedly entered and added until a negative grade is entered. In this case the entry of a negative grade is the condition that signifies the end of the repetitive input and addition of grades. At that point, the calculation of an average for all the grades entered could be performed.

Invocation involves invoking, or summoning into action, a set of procedural code as it is needed. For example, in response to a user-initiated action, such as clicking a button, an event procedure is called into action, or invoked.

Step 4: Test and Correct the Solution

The purpose of testing is to verify that a program works correctly and actually fulfills its requirements. In theory, testing would reveal all existing program errors (in computer terminology, a program error is called a *bug*[3]). In practice, this would require checking all possible combinations of statement execution. Because of the time and effort required, this is usually an impossible goal (we illustrate why in Section 5.8).

Since exhaustive testing is not feasible for most programs, different philosophies and methods of testing have evolved. At its most basic level, however, testing requires a conscious effort to ensure that a program works correctly and produces meaningful results. This means that careful thought must be given to what the test is meant to achieve and the data that will be used in it. If testing reveals an error (bug), the process of debugging, which includes locating, correcting, and verifying the correction, can be initiated. It is important to realize that although testing may reveal the presence of an error, it does not necessarily guarantee the absence of one. Thus, the fact that a test revealed one bug does not prove that another one is not lurking somewhere else in the program.

Backup

Although not part of the formal design and development process, it is critical to make and keep backup copies of your work at each step of the programming process. This becomes your recovery of last resort in the event of an unforeseen system crash or an unexpected loss of your original work.

Exercises 1.2

1. a. List and describe the four steps required in the development and design stage of an application.
    b. In addition to development and design stage, what are the other two stages required in producing a program and why are they required?

2   A note from your department head, Ms. R. Karp says:

    Solve our inventory problems.

    —R. Karp

    a. What should be your first task?
    b. How would you accomplish this task?
    c. Assuming everyone cooperates, how long do you think it would take to complete this task?

---

[3] The derivation of this term is rather interesting. When a program stopped running on the MARK I, at Harvard University in September 1945, Grace Hopper traced the malfunction to a dead insect that had gotten into the electrical circuits. She recorded the incident in her logbook at 15:45 hours as "Relay #70.... (moth) in relay. First actual case of bug being found."

3. Program development is only one phase in the overall software development procedure. Assume that documentation and maintenance require 60 percent of the software effort in designing a system, and using Table 1-2, determine the amount of effort required for initial program coding as a percentage of total software effort.

4. Many people requesting a program or system for the first time consider programming to be the most important aspect of program development. They feel that they know what they need and think that the programmer can begin programming with minimal time spent in analysis. As a programmer, what pitfalls can you envision in working with such people?

5. Many first-time computer users try to contract with programmers for a fixed fee (total amount to be paid is fixed in advance). What is the advantage to the user in having this arrangement? What is the advantage to the programmer in having this arrangement? What are some disadvantages to both user and programmer?

6. Many programmers prefer to work on an hourly rate basis. Why do you think this is so? Under what conditions would it be advantageous for a programmer to give a client a fixed price for the programming effort?

7. Experienced users generally want a clearly written statement of programming work to be done, including a complete description of what the program will do, delivery dates, payment schedules, and testing requirements. What is the advantage to the user in requiring this? What is the advantage to a programmer in working under this arrangement? What disadvantages does this arrangement have for both user and programmer?

8. Assume that a computer store makes, on average, 15 sales per day. Assuming that the store is open six days a week and that each sale requires an average of 100 characters, determine the minimum storage that the system must have to keep all sales records for a two year period.

9. Assume that you are creating a sales recording system for a client. Each sale input to the system requires that the operator type in a description of the item sold, the name and address of the firm buying the item, the value of the item, and a code for the person making the trade. This information consists of a maximum of 300 characters. Estimate the time it would take for an average typist to input 200 sales. (**Hint**: To solve this problem you must make an assumption about the number of words per minute that an average typist can type and the average number of characters per word.)

10. Most commercial printers for personal computers can print at a speed of 165 characters per second. Using such a printer, determine the time it would take to print out a complete list of 10,000 records. Assume that each record consists of 300 characters.

1.3 Introduction to Modularity

One key feature of a well-designed program is its modular structure. In programming, the term *structure* has two interrelated meanings. The first refers to the program's overall construction, which is the topic of this section. The second refers to the form used to carry out individual tasks within a program, which is the topic of Chapters 5 and 6. In relation to the first meaning, programs whose structure consists of interrelated screens and tasks, arranged in a logical and easily understandable order to form an integrated and complete unit, are referred to as *modular programs*. Not surprisingly, it has been found that modular programs are noticeably easier to develop, correct, and modify than programs constructed otherwise. This is because modular programs permit each screen and its associated procedural code to be tested and modified without disturbing other modules and procedural code in the application.

Figure 1-20

A Sample Opening Screen

In a modular application each part of the application is designed and developed to perform a clearly defined and specific function. For example, the first screen presented to a user might include a company logo and a choice of buttons that will activate other screens, as shown in Figure 1-20. Depending on which button the user clicks, either another screen will appear or some specific task will be accomplished. Each subsequent screen or task would also be designed to produce a clearly understandable and useful result.

Not surprisingly, the segments used to construct a modular application are referred to as *modules*. In Visual Basi,c modules that contain both the visual parts of a program, that is the screens seen by a user, and the code associated with objects on the screen, are called *form modules*. For each screen in your Visual Basic application you will have one form module. Thus, if your program has five screens, for example, it will contain five form modules. Each form module is given a unique name and is stored in version 5.0 as an individual ASCII text file with the extension suffix .frm.

Figure 1-21

An Application With Three Modules

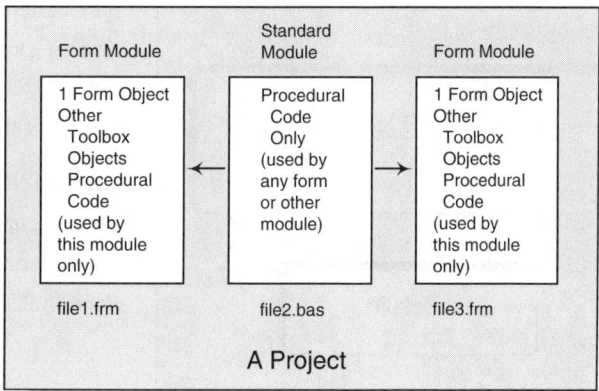

The procedural code that performs actual data processing tasks is most commonly executed in program units called *procedures* and *functions*. Most user-written procedures are stored directly within form modules because they contain the code associated with objects, such as buttons, that are on a screen.

Procedural code that will be used by more than one form module, however, must be stored in special code-only modules. Two types of code-only modules exist, *standard* and *class modules*. Figure 1-21 illustrates the interrelationships for an application consisting of two screens and one standard module. As shown, each screen is stored using its own form module, which also contains procedures and functions that can only be used by the screen described in the module. Code that is to be shared between the two screens is stored on the standard module. Initially, we will concentrate on single-screen applications that, by definition, are stored in a single form module.

Procedural Code

Figure 1-22

A Procedural Unit Accepts Data, Operates on the Data, and Produces a Result

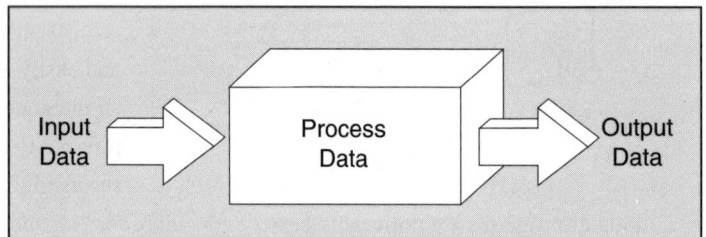

Functions and procedures, both of which contain Visual Basic language instructions, are essentially small procedural program units in their own right that must be capable of receiving data, operating on the data, and producing a result (see Figure 1-22). Typically, a function or procedure performs a single and limited task required by the larger application of which it is a part. We shall learn and use both of these unit types in our work, with initial emphasis on procedures.

It is useful to think of both types of program units, functions and procedures, as small machines that transform the data they receive into a finished product. For example, Figure 1-23 illustrates a program unit that accepts three numbers, computes their average, and displays the result.

All procedures have the same structure, which is described in detail in Section 2.3.

Figure 1-23

A Procedural Unit that Averages Three Numbers

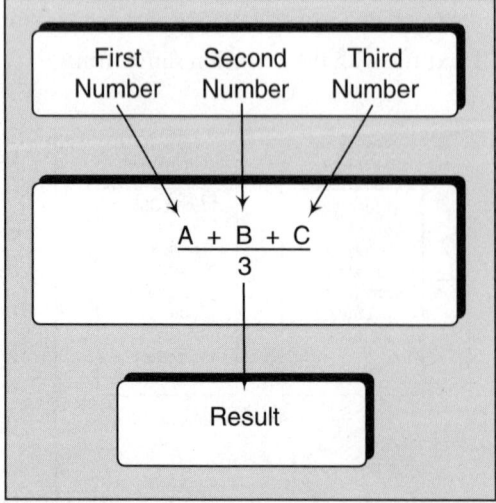

A particular type of procedure, one that we will be working with extensively, is an *event procedure*. This is a procedure called into operation, by either a system- or user-initiated event (see Section 1.1), such as the clicking of the mouse or the loading of a screen.

In Visual Basic, event procedures are designated solely by their event names, and are described in detail in Section 2.3.

Exercises 1.3

1. Describe what information is contained in a form module.

2. Describe the relationship between the information contained in a form module and that contained in a standard module.

3. List two types of programming units that are used to contain procedural code.

4. What is an event procedure?

5. Assuming that cmdMessage is the name of a button on a screen, determine what events cause the following procedures to execute:

   a. `Private Sub cmdMessage_Click()`
   b. `Private Sub cmdMessage_DblClick()`

   Note: Most projects, both programming and nonprogramming, can usually be structured into smaller subtasks or units of activity, each of which can be assigned to an individual user screen or window. The development of each screen can often be delegated to a different person, so that when all the screens and their associated tasks are finished and integrated, the application is complete. For Exercises 7 through 10, determine a set of screens and tasks that could be used for the application. Be aware that there are many possible solutions for each exercise. The only requirement is that the set of screens and their associated tasks, when taken together, completes the required application. The purpose of these exercises is to have you consider the different ways applications can be structured. Although there is no one correct solution to each problem, there are incorrect solutions and solutions that are better than others. An incorrect solution is one that does not fully solve the problem. One solution is better than another if it more clearly or easily allows a user to operate the application.

6. An inventory application needs to be written that must provide for inputting product data, such as where in the warehouse the product is located and its quantity, for deducting amounts when a product is shipped, and for generating reports, such as quantity on hand and quantity sold for all products.

7. A calculation program needs to be written that determines the area of a rectangle.

8. A billing application needs to be written that provides the user with three options: one is to enter the items that are to be billed, one to list all the bills prepared on any given day, and one to list the twenty most recent billed amounts to any given customer.

9. a. A national medical testing laboratory desires a computer system to prepare its test results. The system must be capable of creating each day's results. Additionally, the laboratory wants the ability to retrieve and output a printed report of all results that meet certain criteria; for example, all results obtained for a particular doctor, or all results obtained for hospitals in a particular state. Determine three or four major screens into which this system could be separated.

   b. Suppose someone enters incorrect data for a particular test result, a fact which is discovered after the data has been entered and stored by the system. What additional screen and processing are needed to correct this problem? Discuss why this capability might or might not be required by most applications.

   c. Assume that a user can alter or change data that has been incorrectly entered and stored. Discuss the need for including an "audit trail" that would allow for a later reconstruction of the changes made, when they were made, and who made them.

1.4 Algorithms

Before the body of any event procedure is written, the programmer must clearly understand what data he or she needs to use, the desired result, and the steps required to produce this result. This procedure or solution is an algorithm. More precisely, an *algorithm* is defined as a step-by-step sequence of instructions that must terminate and describes how data is processed to produce desired outputs.

Only after we clearly understand the data we will be using and select an algorithm (the specific steps required to produce the desired result) can any coding begin. Seen in this light, writing an event procedure is simply translating a selected algorithm into a language the computer can use.

To illustrate an algorithm, we shall consider a simple problem. Assume a procedure that must calculate the sum of all whole numbers from 1 through 100. Figure 1-24 illustrates three methods we could use to find the required sum. Each method constitutes an algorithm.

Figure 1-24

Summing the Numbers 1 through 100

Method 1. Columns: Arrange the numbers from 1 to 100 in a column and add them.

```
         1
         2
         3
         4
         .
         .
        98
        99
      +100
      ─────
      5050
```

Method 2. Groups: Arrange the numbers in convenient groups that sum 100. Multiply the number of groups by 100 and add in any unused numbers.

```
 0  +  100  =  100  ┐
 1  +   99  =  100  │   50 groups
 2  +   98  =  100  │
 3  +   97  =  100  │
                    │         (50 x 100) + 50 = 5050
    .   .    .   .  │
    .   .    .   .  │
    .   .    .   .  │
49  +   51  =  100  ┘
50  +    0  =   50
                        One used number
```

Method 3. Formula: Use the formula

$$\text{Sum} = \frac{n(a + b)}{2}$$

where

n = number of terms to be added
a = first number to be added (1)
b = last number to be added (100)

$$\text{Sum} = \frac{100(1+100)}{2} = 5050$$

Clearly, most people would not bother to list the possible alternatives in a detailed step-by-step manner, as we have done here, and then select one of the algorithms to solve the problem. But then, most people do not think algorithmically; they think intuitively. For example, if you had to change a flat tire on your car, you would not think of all the steps required, you would simply change the tire or call someone else to do the job. This is an example of intuitive thinking.

Unfortunately, computers do not respond to intuitive commands. A general statement such as "add the numbers from 1 to 100" means nothing to a computer, because the computer can only respond to algorithmic commands written in an acceptable language such as Visual Basic. To program a computer successfully, you must clearly understand this difference between algorithmic and intuitive commands. You cannot tell a computer to change a tire or to add the numbers from 1 through 100. Instead, you must give the computer a detailed step-by-step set of instructions that, collectively, forms an algorithm. For example, the set of instructions

```
Set n equal to 100
Set a = 1
Set b equal to 100
                  n(a + b)
Calculate sum = ──────────
                     2

Print the sum
```

constitutes a detailed method, or algorithm, for determining the sum of the numbers from 1 through 100. Notice that these instructions are not a Visual Basic procedure. Unlike a procedure, which must be written in a language the computer can respond to, an algorithm can be written or described in various ways. When English-like phrases are used to describe the algorithm (the processing steps), as in this example, the description is called *pseudocode*. When mathematical equations are used, the description is called a

Figure 1-25

Flowchart Symbols

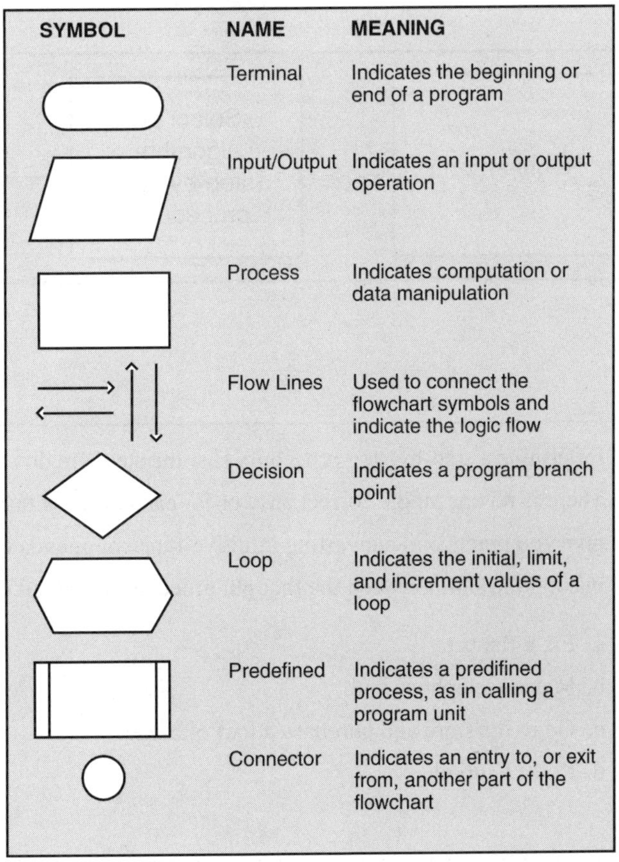

SYMBOL	NAME	MEANING
	Terminal	Indicates the beginning or end of a program
	Input/Output	Indicates an input or output operation
	Process	Indicates computation or data manipulation
	Flow Lines	Used to connect the flowchart symbols and indicate the logic flow
	Decision	Indicates a program branch point
	Loop	Indicates the initial, limit, and increment values of a loop
	Predefined	Indicates a predifined process, as in calling a program unit
	Connector	Indicates an entry to, or exit from, another part of the flowchart

Figure 1-26

*Flowchart for
Calculating the Average
of Three Numbers*

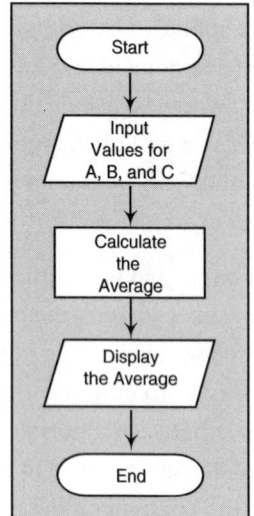

formula. When diagrams that employ the symbols shown in Figure 1-25 are used, the description is referred to as a *flowchart.* Figure 1-26 illustrates the use of these symbols in depicting an algorithm for determining the average of three numbers.

Because flowcharts are cumbersome to revise and can easily support unstructured programming practices, they have fallen out of favor with professional programmers, while the use of pseudocode to express the logic of algorithms has gained acceptance. An example of pseudocode for describing the steps needed to compute the average of three numbers is

Input the three numbers into the computer's memory
Calculate the average by adding the numbers and dividing the sum by three
Display the average

Only after an algorithm has been selected and the programmer understands the required steps can the algorithm be written using computer-language statements. The writing process is called *coding* the algorithm, which is the third step in our program development procedure (see Figure 1-27).

Figure 1-27

Coding an Algorithm

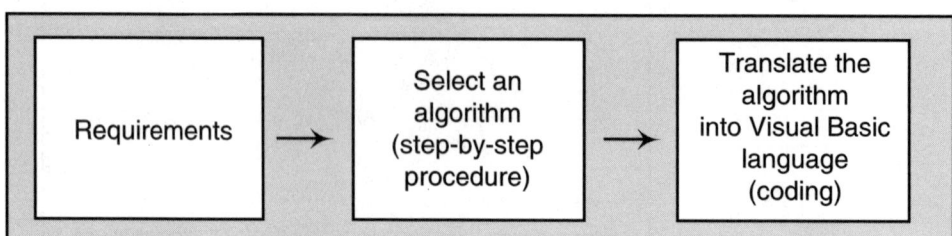

Exercises 1.4

1. Determine a step-by-step procedure (list the steps) to do the following tasks. (**Note:** There is no one single correct answer for each of these tasks. The exercise is designed to give you practice in converting intuitive-type commands into equivalent algorithms and making the shift between the thought processes involved in the two types of thinking.)

   a. Fix a flat tire.

   b. Make a telephone call.

   c. Go to the store and purchase a loaf of bread.

   d. Roast a turkey.

Figure 1-28

*A Simple
Paint-by-Number Figure*

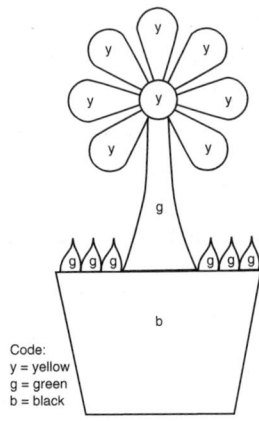

Code:
y = yellow
g = green
b = black

2. a. Determine the six possible step-by-step procedures (list the steps) to paint the flower shown in Figure 1-28, with the restriction that each color must be completed before a new color can be started. (**Hint:** one of the algorithms is *Use Yellow first, Green second, Black last.*)

   b. Which of the six painting algorithms (series of steps) is best if we are limited to using one paintbrush and that we know there is no turpentine to clean the brush.

3. Determine and write an algorithm (list the steps) to interchange the contents of two cups of liquid. Assume that a third cup is available to hold the contents of either cup temporarily. Each cup should be rinsed before any new liquid is poured into it.

4. Write a detailed set of instructions, in English, to calculate the dollar amount of money in a piggybank that contains *h* half-dollars, *q* quarters, *n* nickels, *d* dimes, and *p* pennies.

5. Write a set of detailed, step-by-step instructions, in English, to find the smallest number in a group of three integers.

6. a. Write a set of detailed, step-by-step instructions, in English, to calculate the change remaining from a dollar after a purchase is made. Assume that the cost of goods purchased is less than a dollar. The change received should consist of the smallest number of coins possible.

   b. Repeat Exercise 6a but assume the change is to be given only in pennies.

7. a. Write an algorithm to locate the first occurrence of the name *JONES* in a list of names arranged in random order.

   b. Discuss how you could improve your algorithm for Exercise 7a. if the list of names was arranged in alphabetical order.

8. Write an algorithm to determine the total occurrences of the letter *e* in any sentence.

9. Determine and write an algorithm to sort four numbers into ascending (from lowest to highest) order.

1.5 Common Programming Errors and Problems

The most common errors associated with the material presented in this chapter are

1. A major programming error made by most beginning programmers is the rush to create and run an application before fully understanding what is required, including the algorithms that will be used to produce the desired result. A symptom of this haste to get a program entered into the computer is the lack of any documentation or even a program outline. Many problems can be caught just by checking the selected algorithm written in pseudocode.

2. A second major error is not backing up a program. Almost all new programmers make this mistake until they lose a program that has taken considerable time to code.

3. The third error made by many new programmers is not understanding that computers respond only to explicitly defined algorithms. Telling a computer to add a group of numbers is quite different than telling a friend to add the numbers. The computer must be given, in a programming language, the precise instructions for performing any operation.

1.6 Chapter Review

Key Terms

algorithm	high-level language	repetition
analysis	low-level language	secondary storage
assembler	machine language	selection
assembly language	object-oriented	sequence
coding	procedure-oriented	software
compiler	programming	software development procedure
development and design	programming language	software engineering
documentation	pseudocode	software maintenance
hardware	refinement	testing

Summary

1. The first recorded attempt at creating a self-operating computational machine was by Charles Babbage in 1822.

2. The ENIAC (Electrical Numerical Integrator and Computer) was the first working digital computer. It became operational in 1946 and depended on externally connected wires to direct its operation. The internal design of ENIAC was based on work done previously by Dr. John V. Atanasoff and Clifford Berry at Iowa State University in 1937.

3. The EDSAC (Electronic Delayed Storage Automatic Computer) became the first commercially produced computer to permit instructions stored inside the computer's memory to direct and control the machine's operation. Prior to this computers used external wiring to direct their operation.

4. Programming languages come in a variety of forms and types. Machine-language programs contain the binary codes that can be executed by a computer. Assembly languages permit the use of symbolic names for mathematical operations and memory addresses. Machine and assembly languages are referred to as *low-level languages*.

5. *High-level languages* are written using instructions that resemble a natural language, such as English, and can be run on a variety of computer types. Compiler languages require a compiler to translate the program into machine code, while interpreter languages require an interpreter to do the translation.

6. *Procedure-oriented* languages consist of a series of procedures that direct the operation of a computer.

7. *Object-oriented* languages permit the use of objects within a program. Each object is defined by its properties, such as size and color.

8. *Event-based* programs execute program code depending on what events occur, which in turn depends on what the user does.

9. GUIs are graphical user interfaces that provide the user with objects that recognize events, such as clicking a mouse.

10. An *algorithm* is a step-by-step sequence of instructions that describes how a computation is to be performed.

1.7 Looking Further: Computer Hardware

All computers, from large supercomputers costing millions of dollars to smaller desktop personal computers, must perform a minimum set of functions and provide the capability to

1. Accept input;
2. Display output;
3. Store information in a logically consistent format (traditionally binary);
4. Perform arithmetic and logic operations on either the input or stored data; and
5. Monitor, control, and direct the overall operation and sequencing of the system.

Figure 1-30 illustrates the computer hardware components that support these capabilities. These physical components are collectively referred to as *hardware*.

Memory Unit

This unit stores information in a logically consistent format. Typically, both instructions and data are stored in memory, usually in separate and distinct areas.

Each computer contains memory of two fundamental types: RAM and ROM. *RAM*, which is an acronym for *Random Access Memory*, is usually volatile, which means that whatever is stored there is lost when the computer's power is turned off. Your programs and data are stored in RAM while you are using the computer. The size of a computer's RAM memory is usually specified in terms of how many bytes of RAM are available to the user. Most personal computer (PC) memories currently consist of between one and 32 million bytes. A million bytes is called a megabyte, or MB, for short.

ROM, which is an acronym for *Read Only Memory*, contains fundamental instructions that cannot be lost or changed by the casual computer user. These instructions include those necessary for loading anything else into the machine when it is first turned on and any other instructions that need to be permanently accessible when the computer is turned on. ROM is *non-volatile*; its contents are not lost when the power goes off.

Figure 1-29

Basic Hardware Units of a Computer

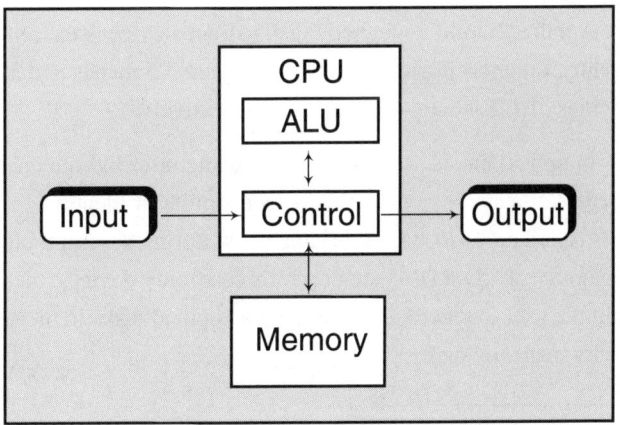

Control Unit

The control unit directs and monitors the overall operation of the computer. It keeps track of where in memory the next instruction resides, issues the signals needed to both read data from and write data to other units in the system, and executes all instructions.

Arithmetic and Logic Unit (ALU)

The ALU performs all the arithmetic and logic functions—addition, subtraction, comparison, and so forth—provided by the system.

Input/Output (I/O) Unit

This unit provides access to and from the computer. It is the interface to which peripheral devices such as keyboards, cathode ray screens, and printers are attached.

Secondary Storage

Because RAM memory in large quantities is still relatively expensive and volatile, it is not practical as a permanent storage area for programs and data. Secondary or auxiliary storage devices are used for this purpose. Although data has been stored on punched cards, paper tape, and other media in the past, virtually all secondary storage is now done on magnetic tape, magnetic disks, and optical storage media.

The surfaces of magnetic tapes and disks are coated with a material that can be magnetized by a write head, and the stored magnetic field can be detected by a read head. Current tapes are capable of storing thousands of characters per inch of tape, and a single tape may store up to hundreds of megabytes. Tapes, by nature, are sequential storage media, which means that they allow data to be written or read in one sequential stream from beginning to end. Should you desire access to a block of data in the middle of the tape, you must scan all preceding data on the tape to find the block you want. Because of this tapes are primarily used for mass backup of the data stored on large-capacity disk drives.

A more convenient method of rapidly accessing stored data is provided by a *direct access storage device (DASD)*, where any one file or program can be written or read independent of its position on the storage medium. The most popular DASD in recent years has been the magnetic disk. A *magnetic hard disk* consists of either a single rigid platter or several platters that spin together on a common spindle. A movable access arm positions the read/write heads over, but not quite touching, the recordable surfaces.

Another common magnetic disk storage device is the removable *floppy diskette*. Currently, the most popular sizes for these are 3.5 inches and 5.25 inches in diameter, with capacities of 1.2 and 1.44 megabytes, respectively.

In optical media, data is stored by using laser light to change the reflective surface properties of a single removable diskette similar or identical to an audio compact disk. The disk is called a *CD-ROM* and is capable of storing several thousand megabytes[4]. Although the majority of CD-ROMs are currently read-only devices, methods are coming into use that permit the user to record, erase, and reuse optical disks in the same manner as a very high capacity magnetic disk.

---

[4] A thousand megabytes is referred to as a gigabyte.

Hardware Evolution

In the first commercially available computers of the 1950s, all hardware units were built using relays and vacuum tubes. The resulting computers were extremely large pieces of equipment, capable of making thousands of calculations per second, and costing millions of dollars. With the introduction of transistors in the 1960s, both the size and cost of computer hardware were reduced. The transistor was approximately one-twentieth the size of its vacuum tube counterpart. The transistors' small size allowed manufacturers to combine the ALU with the control unit. This combined unit is called the *central processing unit (CPU)*. The combination of the ALU and control units into one CPU made sense because a majority of control signals generated by a program are directed to the ALU in response to arithmetic and logic instructions within the program. Combining the ALU with the control unit simplified this interface and provided improved processing speed.

The mid-1960s saw the introduction of integrated circuits (ICs), which resulted in still another significant reduction in the space required to produce a CPU. Initially, integrated circuits were manufactured with up to 100 transistors on a single one-centimeter-square chip of silicon. Such devices are referred to as small-scale integrated (SSI) circuits.

Current versions of these chips contain from hundreds of thousands to over a million transistors and are referred to as very large scale integrated (VLSI) chips. VLSI chip technology has provided the means of transforming the giant computers of the 1950s into today's desktop models. The individual units required to form a computer (CPU, memory, and I/O) are now all manufactured on individual VLSI chips, respectively, and the single-chip CPU is referred to as a *microprocessor*. Figure 1-30 illustrates how these chips are connected internally within current personal computers, such as IBM-PCs.

Figure 1-30

VLSI Chip Connections for a Desktop Computer

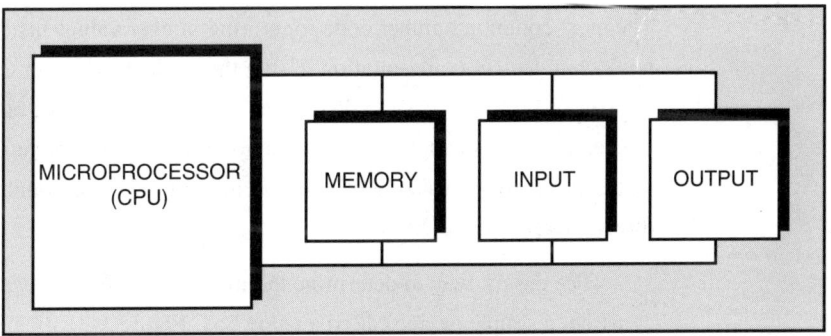

Concurrent with the remarkable reduction in computer hardware size has been an equally dramatic decrease in cost and increase in processing speeds. Equivalent computer hardware that cost over a million dollars in 1950 can now be purchased for less than five hundred dollars. If the same reductions occurred in the automobile industry, for example, a Rolls-Royce could now be purchased for ten dollars! The processing speeds of current computers have also increased by a factor of a thousand over their 1950s predecessors; the computational speeds of current machines are now measured in both millions of instructions per second (MIPS) and billions of instructions per second (BIPS).

Bits and Bytes

It would have been very convenient if a computer stored numbers and letters inside its memory and arithmetic and logic units the way that people do. The number *126*, for example, would then be stored as 126, and the letter *A* stored as the letter A. Unfortunately, this is not the case.

The smallest and most basic data item in a computer is called a bit. Physically, a bit is really a switch that can be either open or closed. By convention, the open and closed positions of each switch are represented as a 0 and a 1, respectively.

A single bit that can represent the values 0 and 1, by itself, has limited usefulness. All computers, therefore, group a set number of bits together, both for storage and transmission. The grouping of eight bits to form a larger unit is an almost universal computer standard. Such groups are commonly referred to as bytes. A single byte consisting of eight bits, where each bit is either a 0 or 1, can represent any one of 256 distinct patterns. These consist of the pattern 00000000 (all eight switches open) to the pattern 11111111 (all eight switches closed), and all possible combinations of 0s and 1s in between. Each of these patterns can be used to represent either a letter of the alphabet; other single characters, such as a dollar sign, comma, etc.; a single digit; or numbers containing more than one digit. The patterns of 0s and 1s used to represent letters, single digits, and other single characters are called *character codes* (one such code, called the ANSI code, is presented in Section 3.1). The patterns used to store numbers are called *number codes*, one of which is presented below.

Two's Complement Numbers

The most common number code for storing integer values inside a computer is called the *two's complement* representation. Using this code, the integer equivalent of any bit pattern, such as 10001101, is easy to determine and can be found for either positive or negative integers, with no change in the conversion method. For convenience we will assume byte-sized bit patterns consisting of a set of eight bits each, although the procedure carries directly over to larger bit patterns.

The easiest way to determine the integer represented by each bit pattern is first to construct a simple device called a value box. Figure 1-31 illustrates such a box for a single byte. Mathematically, each value in the box illustrated in Figure 1-31 represents an increasing power of two. Since two's complement numbers must be capable of representing both positive and negative integers, the leftmost position, in addition to having the largest absolute magnitude, also has a negative sign.

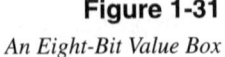

Figure 1-31
An Eight-Bit Value Box

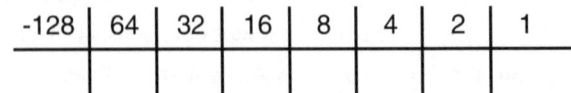

-128	64	32	16	8	4	2	1

Introduction to Visual Basic

-128	64	32	16	8	4	2	1
1	0	0	0	1	1	0	1

Figure 1-32

Converting 10001101 to a Base 10 Number

$-128 + 0 + 0 + 0 + 8 + 4 + 0 + 1 = -115$

Conversion of any binary number, for example 10001101, simply requires inserting the bit pattern in the value box and adding the values having ones under them. Thus, as illustrated in Figure 1-32, the bit pattern 10001101 represents the integer number -115.

The value box can also be used in reverse, to convert a base 10 integer number into its equivalent binary bit pattern. Some conversions, in fact, can be made by inspection. For example, the base 10 number -125 is obtained by adding 3 to -128. Thus, the binary representation of -125 is 10000011, which equals -128 + 2 + 1. Similarly, the two's complement representation of the number 40 is 00101000, which is 32 plus 8.

Although the value box conversion method is deceptively simple, the method is directly related to the underlying mathematical basis of two's complement binary numbers. The original name of the two's complement code was the weighted-sign code, which correlates directly to the value box. As the name *weighted sign* implies, each bit position has a weight, or value, of two raised to a power and a sign. The signs of all bits except the leftmost bit are positive and the sign of the leftmost bit is negative.

In reviewing the value box, it is evident that any two's complement binary number with a leading 1 represents a negative number, and any bit pattern with a leading 0 represents a positive number. Using the value box it is easy to determine the largest positive and negative values it can store. The greatest negative value that can be stored in a single byte is the decimal number -128, which has the bit pattern 10000000. Any other nonzero bit will simply add a positive amount to the number. A positive number must have a 0 as its leftmost bit. From this you can see that the largest positive eight-bit two's complement number is 01111111 or 127.

Words

One or more bytes may themselves be grouped into larger units, called *words*, which facilitate faster and more extensive data access. For example, retrieving a word consisting of four bytes from a computer's memory results in more information than that obtained by retrieving a word consisting of a single byte. Such a retrieval is also considerably faster than four individual byte retrievals. This increase in speed and capacity, however, is achieved by an increase in the computer's cost and complexity.

Early personal computers, such as the Apple IIe and Commodore machines, internally stored and transmitted words consisting of single bytes. AT&T 6300 and IBM-PC/XTs use word sizes consisting of two bytes, while Digital Equipment, Data General, and Prime minicomputers store and process words consisting of four bytes each. Supercomputers, such as the CRAY-1 and Control Data 7000, use six- and eight-byte words, respectively.

Table 1-2 Integer Values and Word Size

Word	Maximum Integer Value	Minimum Integer Value
1 Byte	127	-128
2 Bytes	32,767	-32,768
4 Bytes	2,147,483,647	-2,147,483,648

The number of bytes in a word determines the maximum and minimum values that can be represented by that word. Table 1-2 lists these values for one-, two-, and four-byte words (each of the values listed can be derived using eight-, 16-, and 32-bit value boxes, respectively).

In addition to representing integer values, computers must also store and transmit numbers containing decimal points, which are mathematically referred to as real numbers. The codes used for real numbers are more complex than those used for integers, but still depend on a two's complement type of representation.

Introduction to Visual Basic

In this chapter we begin our journey into learning both the fundamentals of programming and Visual Basic. First we examine the two elements required by every practical Visual Basic program: the screens and instructions seen by the user and the "behind the scenes" processing done by the program. We then present the basic design windows that you must be familiar with to produce such programs. Finally, we show you how to use these design windows to create the graphical user interface, or GUI, and then add processing instructions.

2.1 Elements of a Visual Basic Application

Visual Basic was initially introduced in 1991 as the first programming language that directly supported programmable graphical user interfaces using language supplied objects. Version 2.0 appeared in 1992, followed by Version 3.0 in 1993. Version 4.0, introduced in 1995, provided the additional capability of creating user-defined objects, and unlike earlier versions that created 16-bit machine code (see Section 1.7), each edition of Version 4 allowed the creation of 32-bit code.[1] Thus, Visual Basic 4 applications could achieve a Windows 95 look and feel.

On March 19, 1997, Microsoft announced the commercial introduction of Version 5.0. The major enhancements provided by this version were an improved design environment, an

---

[1] The Professional and Enterprise editions also permitted the construction of 16-bit code, while the Standard edition could only produce 32-bit code.

improved debugging environment, and the introduction of ActiveX support. From a practical standpoint, the term ActiveX has a number of different meanings (see Appendix F). Fundamentally, however, ActiveX is a programming technology that permits cross use of any ActiveX component by any programming language that supports the technology. This means that an ActiveX component created in Visual Basic can be used within a C++ environment that supports ActiveX. Additionally, complete ActiveX programs can be transferred across the Internet and executed by different computers connected to the Internet. Like earlier versions, Version 5.0 also permits integration and control of Microsoft Excel, Access, and Word applications directly from within a Visual Basic program.

Visual Basic Version 5.0 comes in three commercial editions, named the Learning Edition, Professional Edition, and Enterprise Edition. A fourth edition, the Control Creation Edition, which is limited to creating ActiveX controls, is available for downloading from the Internet, and is not available in retail stores. Only the Learning, Professional, and Enterprise editions will be discussed in this text. Essentially, we will be describing the Professional Edition, but will point out the differences between this and the other editions as we proceed. Henceforth, when the term Visual Basic Version 5.0 is used in the text, it will describe the common features of the Learning, Professional, and Enterprise editions only.

From a programming viewpoint Visual Basic Version 5.0 is an object-based program-ming language that consists of two fundamental parts, a visual part and a language part.[2] The visual part of the language consists of a set of objects, while the language part consists of a high-level procedural programming language.

The two elements of the language, the visual part and the programming language part, are used together to create applications. An application is simply a Visual Basic program that can be run under the Windows operating system. The term *application* is frequently used in preference to the word *program* for two reasons: one, it is the term selected by Microsoft to designate any program that can be run under its Windows Operating System (all versions) and two, it is used to avoid confusion with older procedural programs that consisted entirely of a language element. Thus, for our purposes we can express the elements of a Visual Basic application this way:

Visual Basic Application = Object-Based Visual Part + Procedural-Based Language Part

Thus, learning to create Visual Basic applications requires being very familiar with both elements, visual and language.

---

[2] An object-oriented programming language is one that not only uses objects but provides the additional ability to create new object types from existing types, using features called inheritance and polymorphism. Prior to Version 4.0, Visual Basic did not provide the abitlity to create new object types, and the term object-based effectively denoted that the language was a consumer, or user of objects, rather than a creator of them. Although Versions 4.0 and 5.0 do provide the ability to create new object types, since they do not provide a true inheritance feature, they cannot be classified as object-oriented and are instead, still referred to as object-based languages.

The Visual Element

From a user's standpoint, the visual part of an application is provided by the window. This is the graphical interface that allows the user to see the inputs and outputs provided by the application. This user interface is referred to as the graphical user interface (GUI). From a programmer's perspective the graphical user interface is constructed from a set of objects placed on a form when the program is being developed. For example, consider Figure 2-1, which shows how a particular application would look to the user. From a programmer's viewpoint, the application shown in Figure 2-1 is based on the design form shown in Figure 2-2.

Figure 2-1

*A User's View
of an Application*

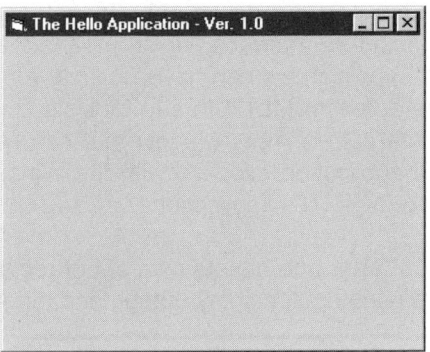

On this form, which is itself a Visual Basic object, the programmer can place various objects. When an application is run the form becomes a window that provides the background for the various objects placed on the form by the programmer. The objects on the window become the controls used to direct program events. Let's take a moment to look at the objects provided in common by all three Visual Basic editions. When Visual Basic is started one of the windows that it supplies is called the object toolbox. The standard object toolbox, which is provided by all three editions of Visual Basic and is illustrated in Figure 2-3, contains the objects we will use in constructing each graphical user interface.

Figure 2-2

*The Design Form on Which
Figure 2-1 is Based*

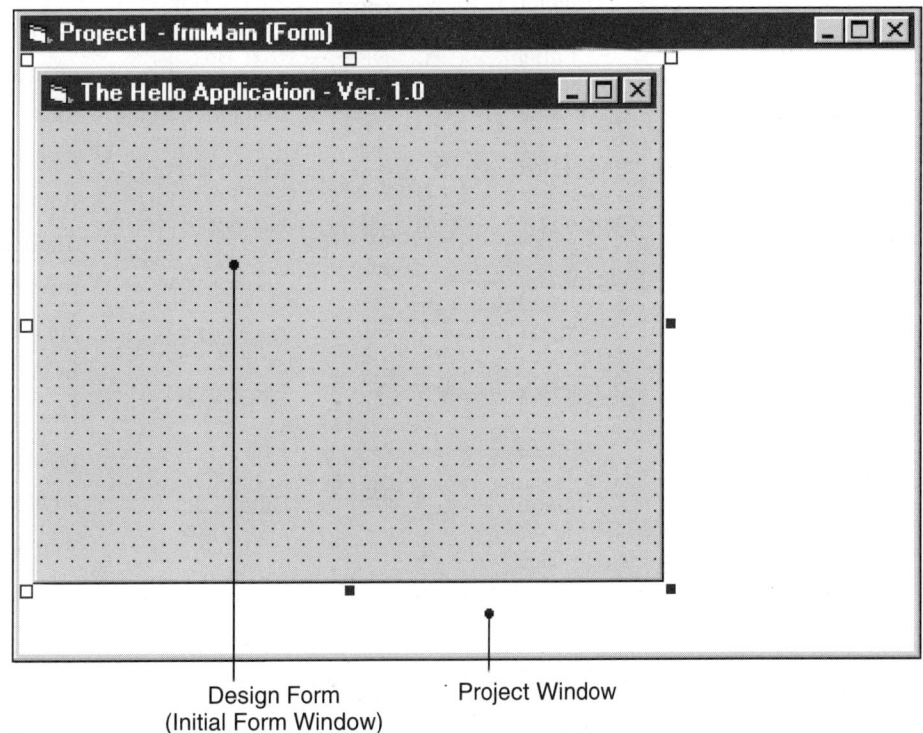

Design Form
(Initial Form Window)

Project Window

Programmers' Notes

Forms and Controls

A *form* is a container upon which controls are placed during the design of an application. When an application is executed, the form becomes either a window or dialog box. Forms can be of two types, SDI or MDI. The acronym SDI stands for Single Document Interface, which means that only one window at a time can be displayed by an application. SDI applications can have multiple windows, but only one window at a time can be viewed by a user. The acronym MDI refers to Multiple Document Interface, which means the application consists of a single "parent" or main window that can contain multiple "child" or internal windows. For example, the Notepad application supplied with the Windows operating system is an SDI application, while Excel and Access are both MDI applications.

A *control* is an object that can be placed on a form, and has its own set of recognized properties, methods, and events. Controls are used to receive user input, display output, and trigger event procedures.

Surprisingly, a majority of applications can be constructed using a minimal set of the objects provided by the standard object toolbox. This minimal set consists of the Label, Text box, Picture, and Command button objects. The next set of objects frequently found in applications include the Check box, Option button, List box, and Combo box. Finally, the Timer and Picture box can be used for constructing interesting moving images across the window. Table 2-1 lists these object types and describes what each object is used for. It is the purpose of the remaining sections of the text to more thoroughly introduce you to all of the objects in the toolbox, with special emphasis on the three objects (Label, Text box, and Command button) that you will use in almost every application you develop.

In addition to the basic set of controls provided in the standard toolbox by all three Visual Basic editions, an extended set of controls is provided within each edition. These added controls, which were referred to as OCXs in Version 4, are referred to as ActiveX controls in Version 5.[3] Specifically, the Learning, Professional, and Enterprise editions provide 8, 20, and 21 additional ActiveX controls, respectively, that can be included

Figure 2-3

The Standard Object Toolbox

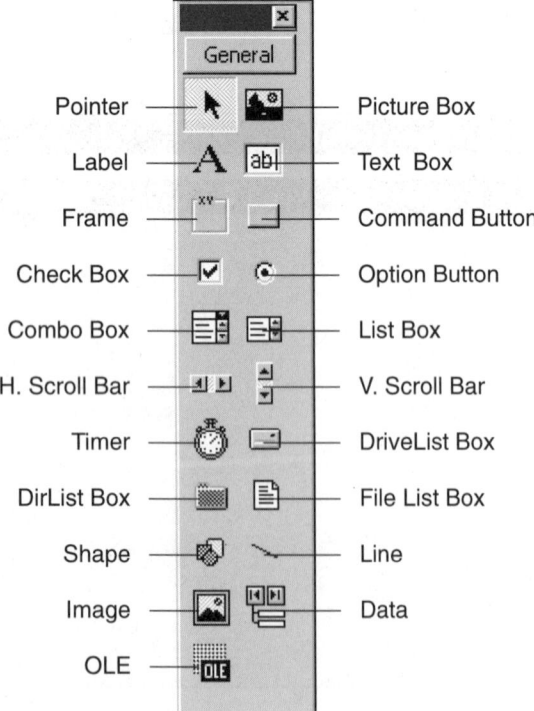

Pointer	Picture Box
Label	Text Box
Frame	Command Button
Check Box	Option Button
Combo Box	List Box
H. Scroll Bar	V. Scroll Bar
Timer	DriveList Box
DirList Box	File List Box
Shape	Line
Image	Data
OLE	

---

[3]The term OCX comes from the fact that each such control is stored in a separate file that has a `.ocx` extension. This extension name was retained in Version 5, and the terms ActiveX control and OCX control are effectively synonyms.

　　　　　　　　　　　　　　　　　　　　　　　　　　　Introduction to Visual Basic

Table 2-1 Fundamental Object Types and Their Uses

Object Type	Use
Label	Create text that a user cannot directly change.
Text Box	Enter or display data.
Picture Box	Display text or graphics.
Command Button (also called a push-button)	Initiate an action, such as a display or calculation.
Check Box	Select one option from two mutually exclusive options.
Option Button (also called a radio-button)	Select one option from a group of mutually exclusive options.
List Box	Display a list of items from which one can be selected.
Combo Box	Display a list of items from which one can be selected plus permit users to type the value of the desired item.
Image	Display a text or graphics with fewer options than a Picture box.
Timer	Create a timer to automatically initiate program actions.

within the object toolbox. For a greater number of objects, either for special purpose applications or to enhance standard applications, third-party ActiveX controls can be purchased.[4]

Don't be overwhelmed by all of the available controls. At a minimum you will always have the objects provided by the standard toolbox available to you, and these are the ones we will be working with. Once you learn how to place the standard control objects on a form you will also understand how to place the additional objects, because every object used in a Visual Basic application, whether it is selected from a standard, extended, or third party object toolbox, is placed on a form in the same simple manner. Similarly, each and every object contains two basic characteristics: properties and methods.

An object's *properties* define its state, which is simply how the object appears on the screen. For example, the properties of a Text box include the location of the Text box on the form, the color of the box (the background color), the color that text will be displayed in the box (the foreground color), and whether it is read-only or can also be written to by the user.

Methods are pre-defined procedures that are supplied with the object for performing specific tasks. For example, you can use a method to move an object to a different location or change its size.

Additionally, each object recognizes certain actions. For example, a Command button recognizes when the mouse pointer is pointing to it and the left mouse button is clicked. These types of actions, as we have seen, are referred to as *events*. In our example we would say that the Command button recognizes the mouse-click event. Once an event is activated, however, we must write our own procedures to do something in response to the event. This is where the language element of Visual Basic comes into play.

---

[4]The term *third-party* stems from the following: The first party is considered the supplier of the Visual Basic package (Microsoft, Borland, etc.). The second party is the applications developer (the programmer). The third party is the supplier of any additional software or tools used in the application.

The Language Element

Before the advent of graphical user interfaces, computer programs consisted entirely of a sequence of instructions, and programming was the process of writing these instructions in a language that the computer could respond to. The set of instructions and rules that could be used to construct a program was called a programming language. Frequently, the word *code* was used to designate the instructions contained within a program. With the advent of graphical user interfaces the need for code (program instructions) has not gone away—rather it forms the basis for responding to the events taking place on the GUI. Figure 2-4 illustrates the interaction between an event and program code.

As illustrated in Figure 2-4, an event, such as clicking the mouse on a Command button, sets in motion a sequence of occurrences. If code has been written for the event, the code is executed, otherwise the event is ignored. This is, of course, the essence of graphical user interfaces and event-driven applications—the selection of which code is executed depends on what events occur, which ultimately depends on what the user does. The code, however, must still be written by the programmer.

The Visual Basic programming language is a high-level language that supports all of the procedural programming features found in most other modern languages. These include statements to perform calculations, as well as statements that permit repetitive instruction execution, and statements to select between two or more alternatives.

With these basics in mind, it is now time to create our first Visual Basic application. In the next section we introduce the Visual Basic programming environment and create an application that uses a single object, the form itself. We will then add additional objects and code to create a more complete Visual Basic application.

Figure 2-4

An Event "Triggers" the Initiation of a Procedure

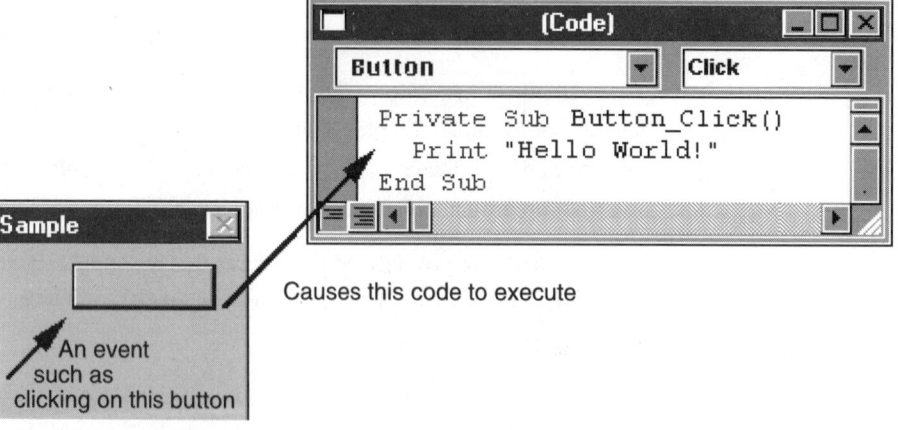

Exercises 2.1

1. List the two elements of a Visual Basic Application.

2. What is the purpose of a GUI and what elements does a user see in a GUI?.

3. What does a Visual Basic toolbox provide?

4. Name and describe the use of the four most commonly used toolbox objects.

5. When an application is run, what does a design form become?

6. What gets executed when an event occurs?

2.2 Getting Started in Visual Basic

It's now time to begin designing and developing Visual Basic programs. To do this you will have to bring up the opening Visual Basic screen and understand the basic elements of the Visual Basic development environment. To bring up the opening Visual Basic screen either double-click on the Visual Basic icon (see Figure 2-5), which is typically located within the Visual Basic Group, or, if you have a shortcut to Visual Basic on the desktop, double-click on this icon.

When you first launch the Professional edition of Visual Basic, the New Project dialog box shown in Figure 2-6 will appear. This dialog consists of three tabs, named New, Existing, and Recent, respectively. Clicking on the Existing tab brings up a standard Windows 95 file Dialog box, which permits you to retrieve a previously saved Visual Basic program. Clicking on the Recent tab permits you to chose from a list of the most recently accessed Visual Basic programs.[5] The New tab, which is shown in Figure 2-6, provides you with a choice of nine project types, which are listed in Table 2-2 (*page 43*). In this text we will primarily be concerned with the first three project types listed in this table.

The major similarities and differences between the three Visual Basic editions can be discerned by viewing their New Project dialogs. As shown in Figure 2-7, the Learning Edition provides only the first three project types listed in Table 2-2. In addition, the Learning Edition provides only eight additional ActiveX controls, in contrast to the 20 additional controls provided by the Professional Edition. The Learning Edition does, however, provide an interactive CD-based learning program that is not included with either of the two other editions.

Figure 2-5

The Visual Basic Icon within the Visual Basic Group

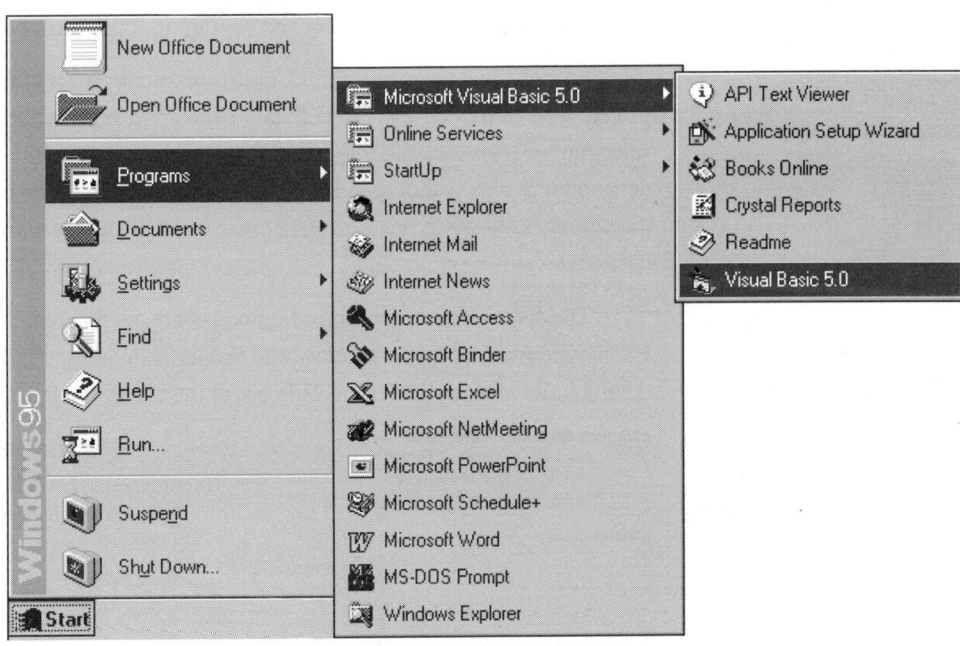

_____
[5]Currently, the maximum size of this list is 99 items.

Figure 2-6

The Professional Edition's New Project Dialog

Most Recently Used Projects Tab

Saved Projects Tab

New Projects Tab

Project Type Icons

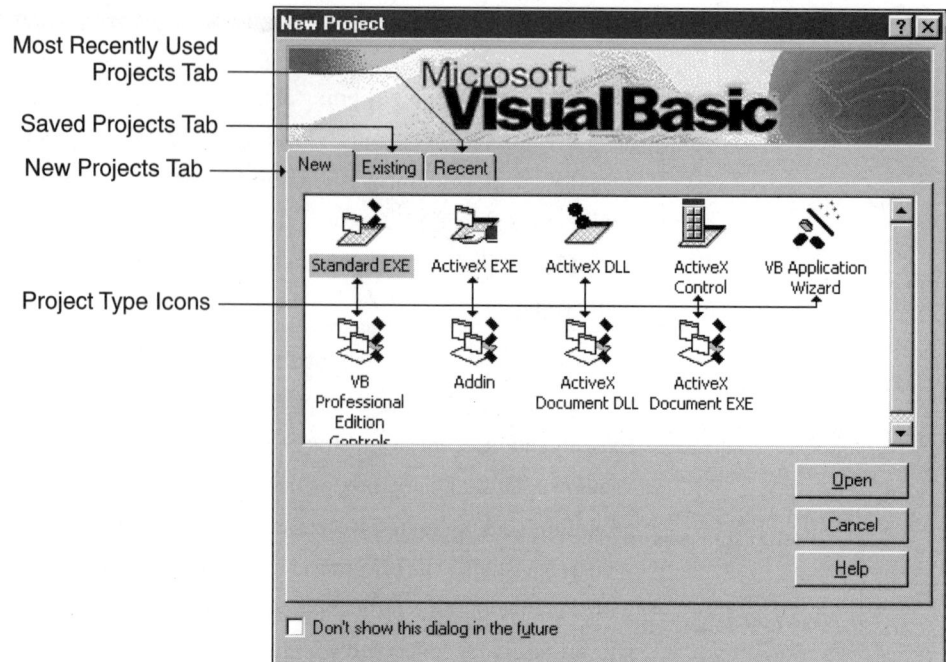

As shown in Figure 2-8, the Enterprise Edition provides the same nine project types as the Professional Edition. The only difference within these project types is that the Enterprise Edition provides an additional ActiveX control, named the Remote Data Object (RDO) control, that can be used for remote data access. Additionally, the Enterprise Edition provides support for reduced instruction set computers (RISC), and comes with three additional CD-ROMs that contain programs for building structured query language (SQL— pronounced both as S-Q-L and Sequel) servers, source code managers, visual database tools, and development tools for developing and testing multiplatform based programs.

Initially, and throughout most of this textbook, we will select the Standard EXE project type from the New Project dialog shown in Figures 2-6 through 2-8. Making this selection will bring up the Integrated Development Environment or IDE, which has the development screen shown in Figure 2-9 (*page 44*). Don't be upset if you do not see all of the windows shown in this figure, because we will shortly show you how to produce the desired development screen.

The five windows shown in Figure 2-9 are, as marked, the Toolbox window, the Initial Form window, the Project window, the Properties window, and the Form Layout window. Additionally, directly under the Title bar at the top of the figure, are a Menu bar and a

Figure 2-7

The Learning Edition's New Project Dialog

Figure 2-8

The Enterprise Edition's New Project Dialog

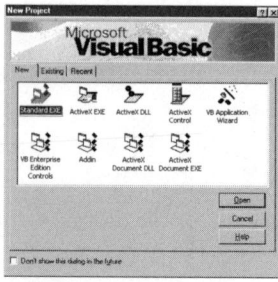

Table 2-2 The Professional Edition's Nine Available Project Types

Project Type	Purpose
1 Standard EXE	This provides a standard toolbox (see Figure 2-3), which is common to all three Visual Basic editions and is used to create a standard Visual Basic program. Since the 21 controls provided in the standard toolbox are built-in controls, this toolbox loads at the highest speed possible.
2 VB Professional Edition Controls	This provides the standard toolbox's built-in controls plus 20 more Active X controls that can be automatically added into the toolbox. Since ActiveX controls are stored as external files, selecting this option takes more time for the toolbox to load.[6]
3 VB Application Wizard	This provides a skeleton program containing the essential elements that can then be used as the foundation for a completed program.
4 ActiveX Controls	This provides the means of creating additional ActiveX controls, similar to the ones that are provided in the VB Professional Edition. These new controls can be used in a Visual Basic program or any programming language that supports ActiveX technology (see Section 10.8 for instructions to create an ActiveX control).
5 ActiveX EXE	This is used to create a Visual Basic program that can be called from another Visual Basic program, but always runs as a separate executable program. The program that calls the ActiveX EXE program is referred to as a *client*, while the called ActiveX EXE program is referred to as a *server*. In prior versions the server ActiveX program was referred to as an OLE Automation executable program (see Appendix F).
6 ActiveX DLL	This is used to create a Visual Basic program that can be called from another Visual Basic program, but becomes linked into the calling program and always runs as part of the same process in which the calling program is running. The program that calls the ActiveX DLL program is referred to as a *client*, while the called ActiveX DLL program is referred to as a *server*. In prior versions this was referred to as an OLE Automation DLL (see Appendix F).
7 ActiveX Document EXE	This is used to create an executable program that can be run as an Internet Web page document.
8 Document DLL	This is used to create a dynamically linked program that can be run as an Internet Web page document.
9 AddIn	This provides the ability to include any ActiveX EXE and DLL program (Document or non-Document) that alters the design environment provided by Visual Basic.

Toolbar, which should not be confused with the Toolbox window. Table 2-3 (*page 45*) provides a description of these components. Before examining each component in depth, it will be useful to consider the Integrated Development Environment (IDE) as a whole and how it uses standard Windows 95 keyboard and mouse techniques.

The IDE as a Windows Workspace

The IDE (pronounced as both I-D-E, and IDEE) is an acronym for the Integrated Development Environment. It consists of three main components, which are the form and module development secion, a code editor, and a debugger. In the normal course of developing a Visual Basic program, you will use each of these components. Initially, however, we will work with IDE's form and module development section, which is the screen shown in Figure 2-9. This screen is a typical Windows 95 MDI window. The term MDI is an acronym for Multiple Document Interface, which means the window consists of a single "parent" or main window that can contain multiple "child" (internal) windows. This is the same type of interface presented by both Excel and Access, each of which is an example of an MDI application.

---

[6] By default, the additional controls are strored with a `.ocx` extension in the Windows/System directory.

As a windows based application, each child window within the overall parent window, as well as the parent window itself, can be resized and closed in the same manner as all Windows 95 windows. Thus, to close a window you can double-click on the X in the upper right-hand corner of each window. Similarly, each window can be resized by first moving the mouse pointer to a window's border. Then, when the pointer changes to a double-headed arrow, click and drag the border in the desired direction. With one exception, each window can be moved by simply clicking the mouse within the window's Title bar, and then dragging the window to the desired position on the screen. The one exception is when a window is docked onto another window.

In Visual Basic Version 5.0, windows can be aligned and attached to other windows, which ensures that each such window remains visible and accessible. This alignment and attachment of two or more windows is referred to as *docking*. It is extremely useful because windows that are docked together always remain visible and are never hidden behind any other window, tool, or menu bar.

If you need to see more of a particular docked window, simply resize one of its borders. If you resize a side border that is common to all of the docked windows, the complete set of windows will be resized; otherwise, if you resize a border separating two windows, the increase in size of one of the docked windows will be made at the expense of its immediately attached neighbor, and the overall size of the complete set of docked windows remains the same. When dealing with a docked window border, the cursor will appear as shown between the Properties and Layout windows in Figure 2-9.

Figure 2-9

The Integrated Development Environment's Initial Screen

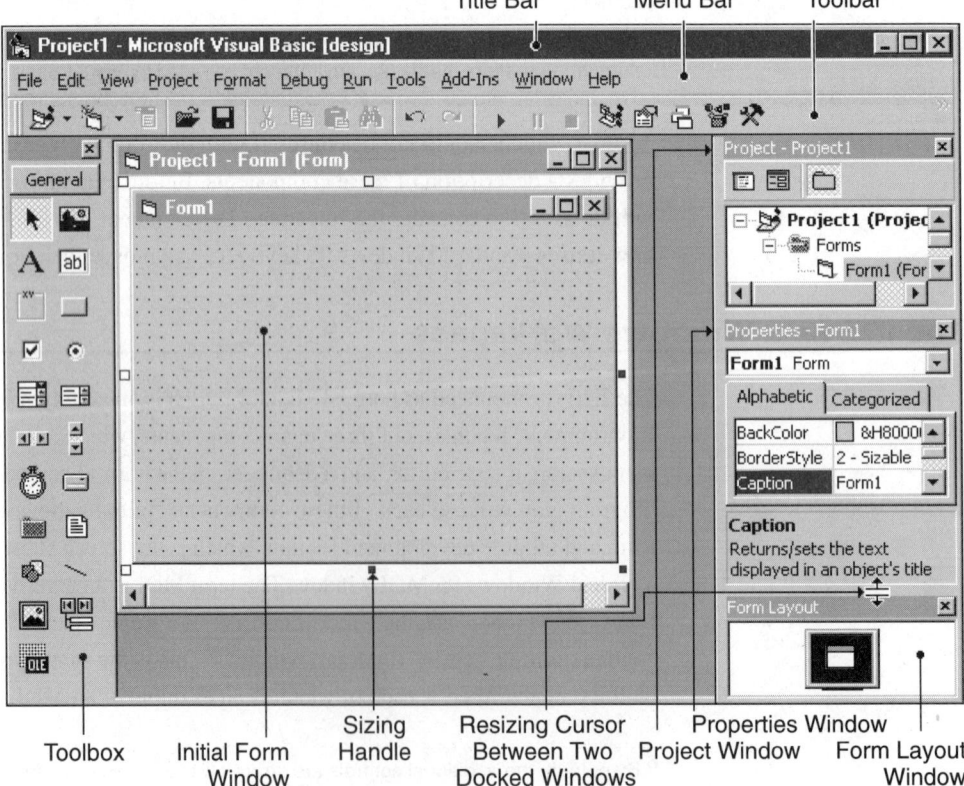

Title Bar   Menu Bar   Toolbar

Toolbox   Initial Form Window   Sizing Handle   Resizing Cursor Between Two Docked Windows   Project Window   Properties Window   Form Layout Window

Introduction to Visual Basic

Table 2-3 Initial Development Screen Components

Component	Description
Title Bar	The colored bar at the top edge of a window that contains the window's name.
Menu Bar	Contains the names of the menus that can be used with the currently active window. The menu bar can be modified but cannot be deleted from the screen.
Toolbar	Contains icons, also called buttons, that provide quick access to commonly used Menu Bar commands. Clicking a Toolbar button carries out the designated action represented by that button.
Toolbox	Contains a set of objects that can be placed on a Form window to produce a graphical user interface (GUI).
Initial Form	The form upon which controls are placed to produce a graphical user interface (GUI). By default, this form becomes the first window that is displayed when a program is executed. This default can be changed by selecting the Properties item within the Project submenu.
Properties	Lists the property settings for the selected form or control and permits changes to each setting to be made. Properties, which are characteristics of an object, such as its size, name, and color, can be viewed and altered either from an alphabetical or category listing.
Project	Displays a hierarchical list of projects and all of the items contained in a project. Also referred to as both the Project Resource Window and the Project Explorer.
Form Layout	Provides a visual means of setting the Initial Form window's position on the screen when a program is executed.

Windows may by docked and undocked in a variety of ways. The simplest method is to click the right mouse button within a selected window (as with all windows, a window is selected by clicking within it, in which case its Title bar typically changes color from gray to blue), which will bring up a menu similar to the one shown in Figures 2-10a and 2-10b. Menus that are displayed using the right mouse button are referred to as both *context menus* and *context sensitive menus*, because what is displayed by the menu depends on (i.e., is sensitive to) the context in which the menu is activated. Practically, this means that the displayed menu depends on which window is active and where in a particular window the right mouse is clicked.[7] For example, the context menu shown in Figure 2-10a was obtained by clicking the right mouse button on the Title bar of the Properties window shown in Figure 2-9, while the menu shown in Figure 2-10b was obtained by right-clicking within the Properties window itself. As shown in both figures, the Dockable item has been checked, indicating that the window is in a dockable state. Simply clicking on this item will deselect it, and permit the window to be moved about the screen independent of any other window. In general, a context menu simply provides shortcuts to frequently performed actions for the designated portion of a window in which the menu is activated.

Figure 2-10a

Context Sensitive Menus Illustrating the Dockable Property

Figure 2-10b

---

[7] More correctly, context sensitive menus are activated by the *secondary mouse button*, which is usually the right button. The *primary mouse button*, which is typically the left button, is the button configured for Windows' click and double-click operations.

Figure 2-11

Visual Basic's Menu Bar

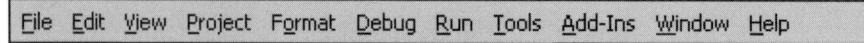

File   Edit   View   Project   Format   Debug   Run   Tools   Add-Ins   Window   Help

A more comprehensive manner of both selecting and determining the set of dockable windows is to use the Menu bar (see Figure 2-11). Initially, in fact, the Menu bar is the most important item on the screen, because you can use it to tailor the IDE environment to your particular needs and liking. This includes bringing up any of the windows that are missing from the screen, adding controls to the toolbar, or making specific windows dockable and undockable.

For example, you can both determine which windows are dockable and then make your selections by using the Options item from within the Menu bar's Tools submenu (see Figure 2-12). This will bring up the Options dialog. By selecting the Docking tab, as shown in Figure 2-13, you can easily check all of the windows that you want to be docked.

Figure 2-12

The Tools Submenu

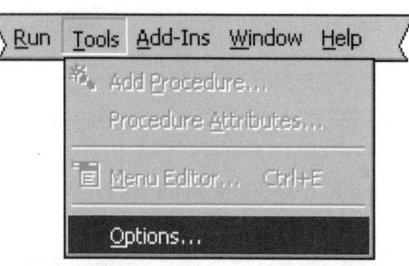

Run   Tools   Add-Ins   Window   Help

Add Procedure...

Procedure Attributes...

Menu Editor...   Ctrl+E

Options...

More commonly, you will use the Menu bar when you have finished working on a current program and want to start a completely new program. In this case you would choose the File item from menu bar, which will bring up the File submenu illustrated in Figure 2-14. From this menu you can save the current project using the Save Project option and then click on the New Project command and a New Project dialog will appear. To access an existing program you can also use the Menu bar File item, except you would then select the Open Project command to reopen a previously saved program. Similarly, these two options can also be activated by clicking on the first and second icons, respectively, on the Toolbar located immediately under the Menu bar.

Once a program has been opened, you can always use the Menu bar's View item to display any windows you need. For example, if either the Properties or Toolbox windows are not visible on the development screen, select the View item from the Menu bar. This will bring up the Views submenu illustrated in Figure 2-15. From this submenu click on either the Properties or Toolbars items to bring up the desired window. Notice in Figure 2-15 that all of Visual Basic's windows are listed in the View submenu.

Figure 2-13

The Options Dialog

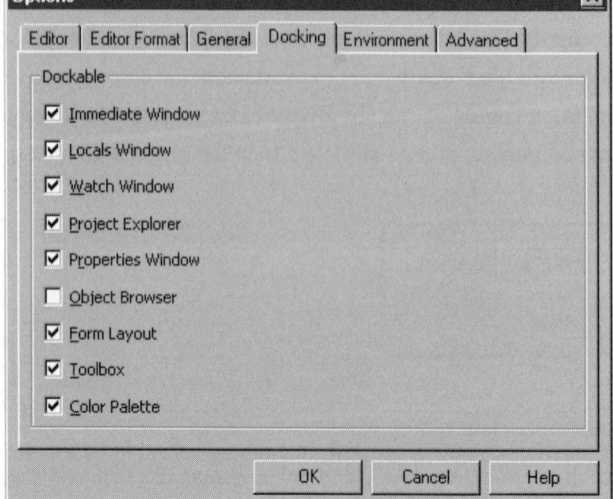

Options

Editor | Editor Format | General | Docking | Environment | Advanced

Dockable

☑ Immediate Window

☑ Locals Window

☑ Watch Window

☑ Project Explorer

☑ Properties Window

☐ Object Browser

☑ Form Layout

☑ Toolbox

☑ Color Palette

OK   Cancel   Help

In a similar manner, you use the Menu bar to add or delete any of the ActiveX controls provided with your edition to the Toolbox. To do this, select the Components item from the Project menu, as shown in Figure 2-16. (The Project menu is new with version 5.0, and replaces the Insert menu found in all earlier versions.) Selecting the Components item will bring up a component selection

Figure 2-14
The File Submenu

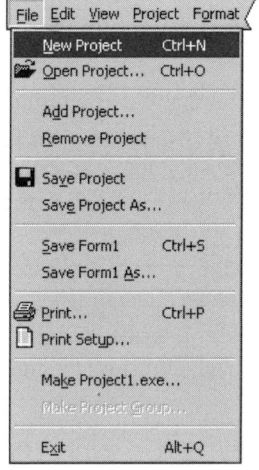

Figure 2-15
The View Submenu

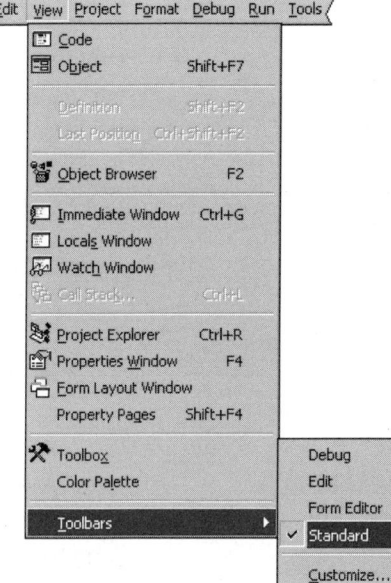

Figure 2-16
The Project Submenu

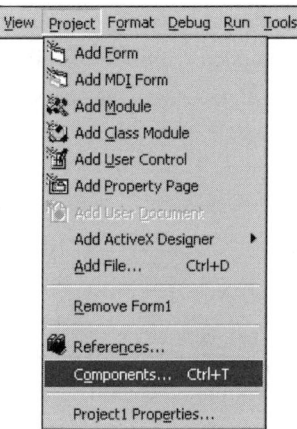

dialog, from which you can check the desired additional controls that you want added to the toolbox.

Having taken a quick tour through how the Menu bar is used to configure the development screen provided by Visual Basic, make sure that you begin with the initial development screen shown in Figure 2-17, which is the same as Figure 2-9 with the Form Layout window closed. We choose to close this window for the convenience of having more room to display the Properties window. If any additional windows appear on the screen, close them by clicking the window's close button (the box with the X in the upper right corner); the window does

not have to be active to do this.

Figure 2-17
The Basic Development Screen

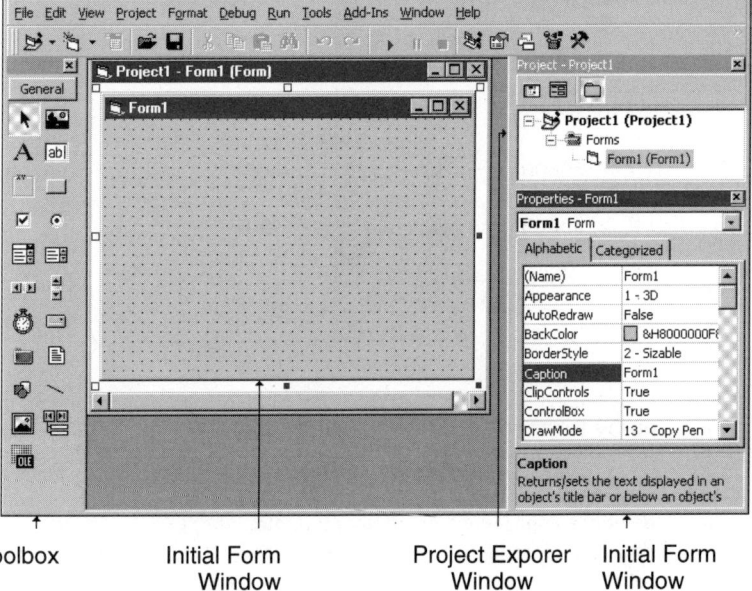

Toolbox   Initial Form Window   Project Exporer Window   Initial Form Window

Notice that the caption within the top title bar of the screen shown in Figure 2-17 contains the words Microsoft Visual Basic [design]. The word [design] in the top Title bar caption is important because it tells us that we are in the design phase of a Visual Basic program. It is in this phase that every Visual Basic application is designed and developed. At any point within our development we can run the program and see how it will looks to the user.

Once the basic design windows are available, creating a Visual Basic application in the design phase requires the following three steps:

1. Create the graphical user interface (GUI).
2. Set the properties of each object on the interface.
3. Write the code.

The foundation of creating the graphical user interface (Step 1) is the Initial Form window. It is on this design form that we place various objects to produce the interface that we want our users to see when the program is executed. When the program is run, the design form becomes a window and the objects that we place on the design form become visual controls that are used to input data, display output, and activate events. The objects that we can place on the design form are contained within the Toolbox shown in Figure 2-13. For convenience, this standard object Toolbox, which was previously introduced in Section 2.1, is reproduced as Figure 2-18.[8]

Figure 2-18

The Standard Object Toolbox

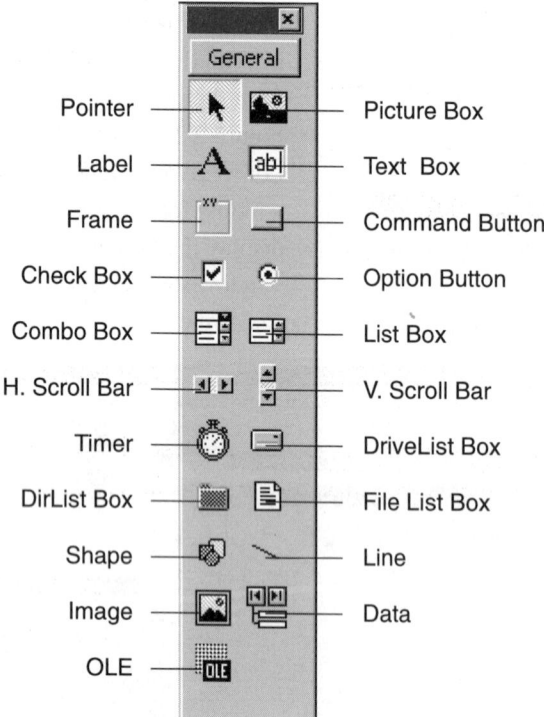

Pointer — Picture Box
Label — Text Box
Frame — Command Button
Check Box — Option Button
Combo Box — List Box
H. Scroll Bar — V. Scroll Bar
Timer — DriveList Box
DirList Box — File List Box
Shape — Line
Image — Data
OLE

Again, don't be confused by the available objects. Simply realize that Visual Basic provides a basic set of object types that can be selected to produce a graphical user interface. It is the purpose of the remaining sections of this book to explain, in detail, what these objects represent and how to design a Visual Basic application using them. To give you an idea of how simple it is to design such an interface, however, move the mouse pointer to the Command button object on the Toolbox (this is the third object shown in Figure 2-18's right-hand column). Notice that a boxed label, called a ToolTip, pops up with the text `CommandButton`.[9] Here, the ToolTip simply provides the name of the pointed to icon. Now double-click

---

[8] By default, all of the Toolbox's control objects are placed within the **General** tab. By right-clicking on this tab a context-sensitive menu will appear that provides the means of creating additional Toolbox tabs. Since you can copy objects between tabs (or use the mouse to drag and drop objects between tabs), you can use these additional tabs to customize your Toolbox. Thus, for example, you might keep your most commonly used controls within the **General** tab window, all controls connected with database applications on another tab, etc.

[9] By default, Visual Basic displays ToolTips. This feature, however, can be turned on or off from within the **General** tab of the Tools menu Options item.

Introduction to Visual Basic

Programmers' Notes

Bringing Up the Basic Design Windows

To create a Visual Basic Program you will need the following three windows: the Toolbox window for selecting objects, a Form window for placing objects, and a Properties window for altering an object's properties. In addition, you should initially have the Project window visible. If any of these windows are in the background, you may click on them to activate and bring them to the foreground, or you may use the following procedures:

For a Form window:
For a new project, first select File from the Menu bar and then select New Project from the submenu (or use the hot-key sequence [Alt]+[F], then [N]). This will bring up a new Form window.
For an existing project, select File from the menu bar and then select Open Project from the submenu (or use the hot-key sequence [Alt]+[F], then [O]). This will bring up a Project window. Then, either
- Double-click on the Form icon to view the existing form, or
- Select the Object submenu item from the View menu bar item, or
- Press the [Shift] and [F7] ([Shift]+[F7]) keys at the same time.

For a Toolbox window:
To either activate an existing Toolbox window or bring one up, if it is not on the screen, either:
- Select View and then Toolbox , or
- Use the hot-key sequence [Alt]+[V] and then press the [X] key ([Alt]+[V] / [X]).

For a Properties window:
To activate an existing Properties window or bring one up, if it is not on the screen, either:
- Select View and then Properties Window, or
- Use the hot-key sequence [Alt]+[V], and then press the [W] key ([Alt]+[V]/ [W]), or
- Press the [F4] function key.

For a Project window:
To activate an existing Properties window or bring one up, if it is not on the screen, either:
- Select View and then Project Explorer, or
- Use the hot-key sequence [Alt]+[V] and then press the [P] key ([Alt]+[V] / [P]), or
- Press the [Ctrl] and [R] keys ([Ctrl] +[R]) at the same time.

the Command button icon. Notice that a Command button object appears on the form. Placing any object from the Toolbox onto a form is this simple. For now, however, click on the newly created Command button within the form and press the Delete key to remove it.

Setting an Object's Properties

As we have already discovered, all objects have properties. These define where on the form the object will appear (the object's vertical and horizontal position relative to the left hand corner of the form), the color of the object, its size, and various other attributes. To gain an understanding of these properties, we will now examine the most basic object in Visual Basic, which is the form itself. Like any other object, the form has properties that define how it will appear as a window when the program is run. As an introduction to the ease with which properties are set, we will first explore these form properties. To do this make sure you have a basic design screen (see Figure 2-17).

Figure 2-19

The Properties Window

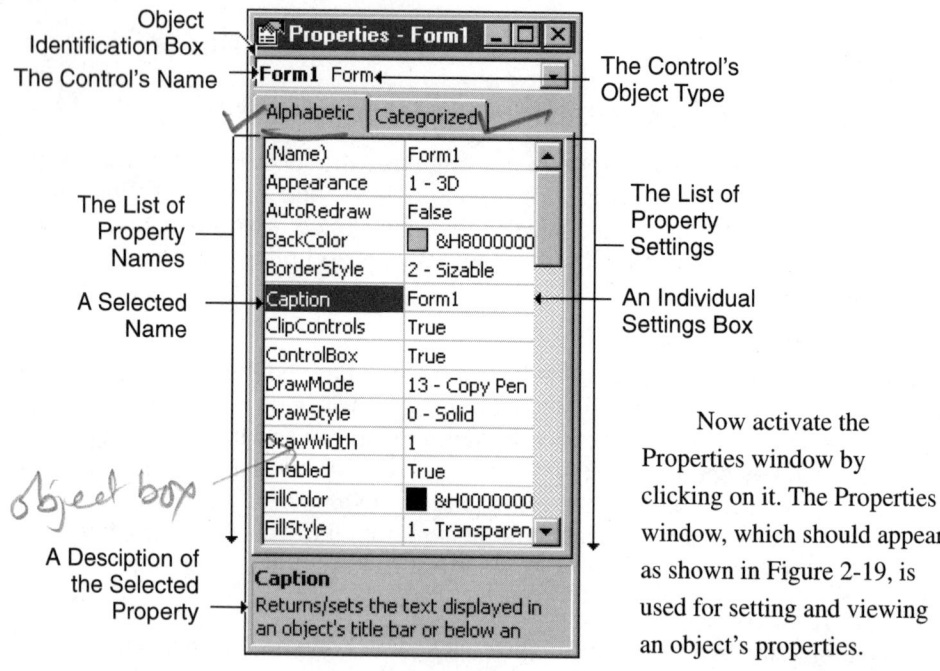

The List of
Property
Names

A Selected
Name

object box

A Desciption of
the Selected
Property

Now activate the
Properties window by
clicking on it. The Properties
window, which should appear
as shown in Figure 2-19, is
used for setting and viewing
an object's properties.

A new feature of the
Properties window, introduced in Version 5.0, is the addition of the two tabs shown in
Figure 2-19. Using the appropriate tab, properties can be viewed either alphabetically, as is the
case in Figure 2-19, or by category. In the alphabetical list however, the **Name** property is
always listed first. This is done strictly for convenience, for the name of each control should
be changed for every control that is placed on a form. In the categorical list, individual
properties are grouped according to appearance, font, position, behavior, etc.

No matter which tab is used, the first box within a Properties window is the *Object
Identification box*, located immediately under the window's Title bar. This box lists the
name of the object and its object type. In Figure 2-19 the name of the form is `Form1`
and its type is `Form`.

The two columns within the Properties window identify individual object properties.
The column on the left is the properties list, which provides the names of all the properties
of the object named in the object box. The column to the right is the settings list, which
provides the current value assigned to the property on the left. A currently selected property
is highlighted. For example, the **Caption** property is highlighted in Figure 2-19. The value
assigned to a highlighted property can be changed directly in the property settings list.

Take a moment now and, using the keyboard arrows, move down the Properties
window. Observe that each property is highlighted as it is selected, and that the description
of the highlighted property is displayed in the description box at the bottom of the window.[10]
Now move back until the **Name** property at the top of the alphabetical list is highlighted, as
shown in Figure 2-20. The name Form1, shown in the figure, is the default name Visual
Basic gives to the first form object provided for a new program. If a second form were used,
it would be given the default name `Form2`, the third form would be named `Form3`, and so on.

---

[10] The description box can be toggled on or off by clicking the right mouse button from within the
Properties window. This will produce the context sensitive menu previously shown in Figure 2-10b.

Figure 2-20

Setting the Name Property

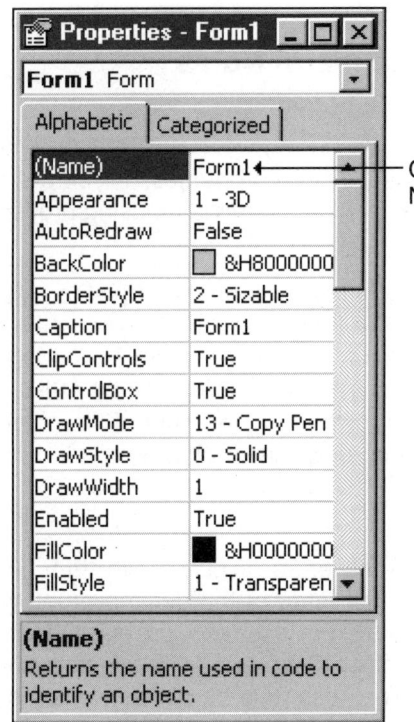

Change the Name Here

The Name Property

There is nothing inherently wrong with keeping the default name that Visual Basic provides for each form and object you use. Good programming practice, however, dictates that all form and other object names be more descriptive and convey some idea about what the object is used for. The names permissible for all objects, of which a form is one, are also used to name other elements in the Visual Basic programming language, and are collectively referred to as *identifiers*. Identifiers can be made up of any combination of letters, digits, or underscores (_) selected according to the following rules:

1. The first character of an identifier must be a letter.
2. Only letters, digits or underscores may follow the initial letter. Blank spaces, special characters, and punctuation marks are not allowed; use the underscore or capital letters to separate words in an identifier consisting of multiple words.
3. An identifier can be no longer than 200 characters.
4. An identifier should not be a keyword. (A *keyword* is a word that is set aside by the language for a special purpose. [11]

Table 2-4 contains a list of Visual Basic's most commonly encountered keywords and a complete list of keywords is provided in Appendix A.[12]

Table 2-4 Common Keywords

Boolean	Date	For	LostFocus	Property	Sub
Byte	DblClick	GotFocus	MouseDown	Public	Switch
Call	Dim	If	MouseMove	Rem	Then
Case	Do	Integer	MouseUp	Single	Variant
Click	Double	Let	Me	Static	Wend
Const	Else	Lxong	Next	Stop	While
Currency	End	Loop	Object	String	

---

[11]Unlike those in most other programming languages, not all of Visual Basic's keywords are restricted. A *restricted* keyword, which is referred to in other languages as a *reserved* word, is a Visual Basic keyword that is set aside by the language for a specific purpose and can only be used for that purpose. Examples of restricted keywords are **If**, **Else**, and **Loop**. The keyword **Click**, for example, is not restricted. In general, it is good programming practice to use keywords, restricted or not, only for their intended purpose.

[12]Although each keyword is capitalized, Visual Basic is case insensitive. A *case insensitive* language does not differentiate between uppercase and lowercase letters. Thus, the keyword **Sub**, for example, can be typed as sub, SUB, or sUB. Visual Basic will recognize each of these spellings and automatically convert all of them to the keyword **Sub.**

```
┌─────────────────────────────────────────────────────────────────┐
│                                                                   │
│                      Programmers' Notes                           │
│                                                                   │
```

The Properties Window

The Properties window is where you set an object's initial properties. These are the properties the object will exhibit when the application is first run. They can be altered later, using procedural code.

To Activate the Properties Window:

To activate a particular object's Properties window, first click on the object to select it, and then press the [F4] function key. For a new project, first select File from the menu bar and then select New Project from the submenu You can also Select View and then Properties Window (or use the hot-key sequence [Alt]+[V], then [W]). This will activate the Properties window for the currently active object. Once the Properties window is active, clicking the down-facing arrowhead to the right of the object identification box (immediately under the Title bar) will activate a drop-down list that can be used to select any form object, including the form itself.

To Move to a Specific Property:

First make sure that the Properties window is active. To quickly move through the Properties window, press the [Ctrl] and [Shift] keys together with the first letter of the desired property. This will move you directly to the next property beginning with this letter. For example, pressing the [Ctrl], [Shift], and [C] key together will place you directly on the Caption property. Continuing with this sequence will cycle you through all the properties beginning with C. This sequence can also be used in place of the [F4] function key to activate the Properties window.

At any time you can cursor up or down through the properties by using the up and down arrow keys or simply clicking on the desired property with the mouse.

Using these rules the convention followed by Visual Basic programmers is to provide forms and other objects with a name beginning with a standard three letter prefix to identify the object type, followed by a descriptive name for the specific object. The standard three letter prefix used for all forms is `frm` (Appendix B contains the complete list of prefixes used for all of the object types provided in the Toolbox window). Additionally, in this text we will use the descriptive name `Main` to describe the first form used in each Visual Basic Program we create. Thus, our first form will always be given the name `frmMain`. To assign this name to our current form, do the following:

If the Name property is not already highlighted, either click on the name property, arrow to this property in the Properties window, or press the [Ctrl], [Shift], and [N] keys at the same time. (This is a fast way to get to the first property name beginning in N. Continuing this combination of key strokes will cycle you through all the property names beginning in N. This shortcut can be used with any other letter). Change the name to `frmMain` by directly typing in the settings list to the right of the **Name** property. The name change takes effect when you either press the [Enter] key, move to another property, or activate another object.

The Caption Property

While a form's name property is important to the programmer when developing an application, it is the form's **Caption** property that is important to the user when a program is run. This is because it is the caption that the user sees within the a window's Title bar when an application is executing.

Programmers' Notes

The Form Layout Window

A new feature provided with Version 5.0 is the Form Layout window, which is used to place the initial form at its desired position on the screen each time an application is executed. By clicking inside the form contained within the Form Layout window's monitor screen, and then dragging the resulting four-headed arrow, you can visually set the initial form's startup position. From a properties standpoint, what is being set is the form's **Top** and **Left** property values, which can also be set manually from within the Properties window. The Form Layout window is especially useful if your application uses two or more forms, because you can use the window to visually arrange the forms onscreen exactly as you want them to appear when the application is executed. This window can also be used to preview form window locations at varying monitor resolutions.

To activate an existing Form Layout window or bring one up, if it is not on the screen, either

- Select <u>V</u>iew and then Form Layout window, or
- Use the hot-key sequence Alt + V and then press the F key (Alt + V / F).

To change the **Caption** property select this property from the Properties window. To do this, make sure the Properties window is selected and try the shortcut method of pressing the Shift, Ctrl, and C keys at the same time. This will take you to the first property name beginning in a C, which happens to be the **Caption** property (continued pressing of this key combination will simply cycle you through all property names beginning with the letter C). Now change the caption to read

```
The Hello Application - Version 1 (pgm2-1).
```

Notice that as you type the caption in the settings box, it automatically appears both in the settings section of the Properties window and directly on the Title bar of the form itself. If the caption is larger than the space shown in the settings box, as is the case in Figure 2-21, the caption will scroll as you type it in. When you have changed the caption, the design screen should appear as shown in Figure 2-21.

Figure 2-21

The Design Screen after the Caption Change

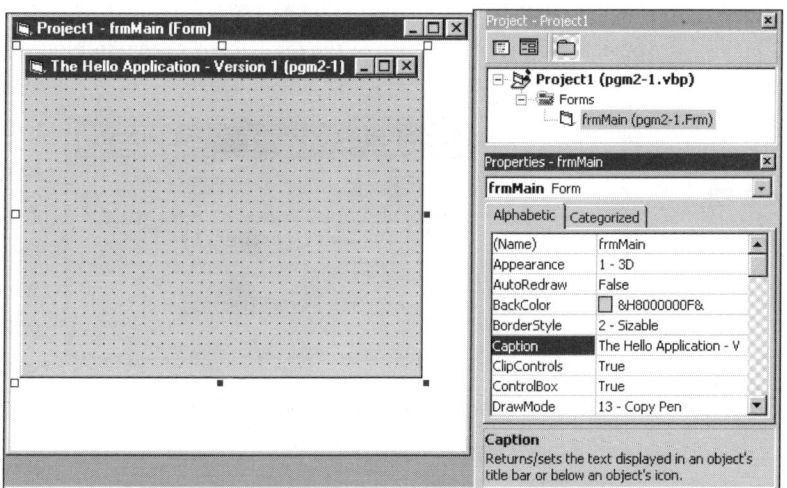

Before we leave the Properties window to run our application, let's take a moment more to see how properties that have restricted values can also be changed.

Both the **Name** and **Caption** properties were changed by simply typing in new values. Certain properties, however, have a fixed set of available values. For example, the **Appearance** property, which determines whether the object will appear flat or raised can only have the values 0-Flat or 1-3D. Similarly, the **FontName** property, which determines the type of font used for an object's displayed text, such as its caption, can only be selected from a list of available fonts. Likewise, the **BackColor** and **ForeColor** Properties, which determine the background color and the color of text displayed in the foreground, can only be selected from a predefined pallet of colors. When one of these properties is selected either a down-facing arrowhead property button (▼) or an ellipsis (…) property button will appear to the right of the selected setting. Clicking on this button will show you the available settings. A selection is then made by clicking on the desired value. In the case of colors, a palette of available colors is displayed, and clicking on a color sets the numerical code for the chosen color as the property's value.

The Project Window

The Project window, which is also referred to as the *Project Resource window* and the *Project Explorer* displays a hierarchical list of projects and all of the current items contained in a project, as shown in Figure 2-22. As files are added or removed from a project, Visual Basic will reflect all of your changes within the displayed hierarchical tree.

The hierarchical tree uses the same folder tree structure found in Windows 95, which means that you can expand and contract tree sections by clicking on plus (+) and minus (–) symbols, respectively. As always, sections of the tree that are hidden from view due to the size of the window can be displayed using the attached scroll bars.

The Project window is extremely useful in providing a visual picture of what files are in a project and in providing a rapid means of accessing, copying, and deleting files associated with a project. For example, if a form object is not displayed on the design screen, you can make it visible by double-clicking on the desired form object from within the hierarchical tree. In a similar manner you can expand a folder, or bring up both code and visible objects by clicking on one of the three icons shown in Figure 2-22. You can also use standard windows drag-and-drop techniques to copy files between folders shown within the Project window. We will have much more to say about the Project window later in this chapter where we will use it to recall saved projects.

For now, however, two further items relating to the Project

Figure 2-22

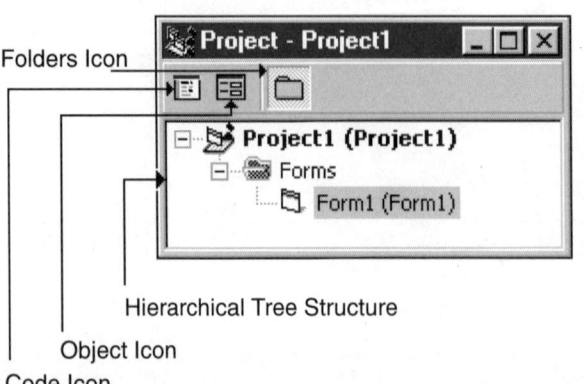

Folders Icon

Hierarchical Tree Structure

Object Icon

Code Icon

window are worth noting. First, the names given to each project added to the Project window are, by default selected as follows: the first project in the window is named `Project1`, the second project is named `Project2`, and so on. These names can be changed by either selecting the General tab from within the Properties option of the Project submenu, or selecting the Properties option from the context menu that is displayed by right-clicking on a project item within the Project window. In this text we will only use the Project window to work on one project at a time, and will always accept the default name (Project1). Having two or more projects visible at the same time is useful when debugging multiple projects that interface with one another, such as a client/server application (see Appendix F).

Finally, it is worth noting that the first two items in the View menu, Code and Object, have the same icons displayed in the Project window shown in Figure 2-22. Thus, both code and objects can be displayed by using either the View menu or the Project window.

Running an Application

At any time during program development you can run your program using one of the following four methods:

1. Select the Run Menu and select Start.
2. Use the hot-key sequence [Alt]+[R], then press the [S] key.
3. Press the [F5] function key.
4. Click the Run button on the Menu toolbar at the top of screen.

If you do this now for Program 2-1, the program will appear as shown in Figure 2-23.

Notice that when the program is run, the form becomes a standard window. Thus, even though we have not placed any object on our form or added any code to our program, we can manipulate the window using standard window techniques. Thus, you can click on the Maximize or Minimize buttons, move or resize the window, and close the application by clicking on the Close (X) button.

A nice feature of Visual Basic is that you can run your program at any point within its development process. This permits you to check both the look of the graphical user interface and the operation of any code that you write, while the program is being developed, rather than at the end of the design. As you write more involved programs it is a good idea to get into the habit of checking program features, by running the program, as the features are added.

Figure 2-23

The Form as a Window When the Application is Run

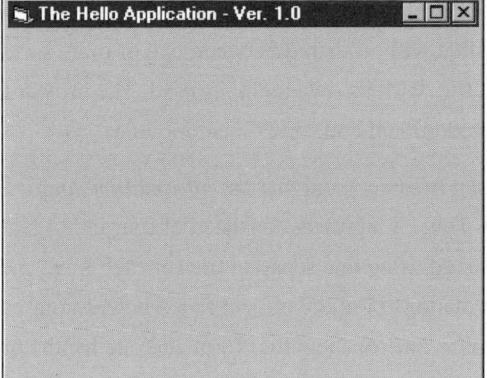

To clearly distinguish between when a program is being developed and when it is being executed, Visual Basic uses the terms design-time and run-time. *Design-time* is defined as the time when a Visual Basic application is being developed. During design-time objects are placed on a

---

Programmers' Notes

Running an Application

While creating a Visual Basic application, you can run the application at any time using any of the following procedures:

1. Select the Run Menu and select Start.
2. Use the hot-key sequence Alt+R, then press the S key (Alt+R/ S).
3. Press the F5 function key.
4. Click on the run icon (the icon with the right-facing arrow head) on the Toolbar. (If the Toolbar is not visible, select it from the View menu.)

When you have completed your development and want to make a stand-alone executable version of the application that can be launched by clicking on its icon from within a Windows 95 program group, use the procedure presented in Appendix G.

---

form, their initial properties are set, and program code is written. *Run-time* is defined as the time a program is running. During run-time each form becomes a window, and the windows and controls respond to events, such as a mouse-click, by invoking the appropriate procedural code. Run-time can be initiated directly from design-time by pressing the F5 function key (or by any of the other methods listed in the accompanying Programmers' Notes on Running an Application). Although in this section we have changed object properties at design-time, we will see in Section 2.4 that an object's properties can also be changed at run-time.

Saving and Recalling a Project

In the next section we will add three Command buttons and one Text box to our form. Then, in Section 2.4, we will complete our application by adding program code. Before doing so, however, let's make sure you can save and then retrieve the work completed so far.

Unlike our current program, which consists of a single form module, a program can consist of many form modules, additional modules containing program code, and third-party supplied objects. A *form module* contains the data for a single form, information for each object placed on the form (in this case there are none), all event code related to these objects, and any general code related to the form as a whole. A *code module* contains procedural code (no objects) that will be shared between two or more form modules. This is the reason a separate project file, with its own name, is used. The project file keeps track of all form modules, and any additional code and object modules.

It is important to understand that *the information contained in each module is saved as an individual file*. Thus, if a project consisted of four individual forms, the application as a whole would be saved using one separate file for each form and an additional project file to save general information about the project as a whole. In our case the application will be saved using two files, one for the initial form and one for the project as a whole.

Figure 2-24

The Save File Dialog Box

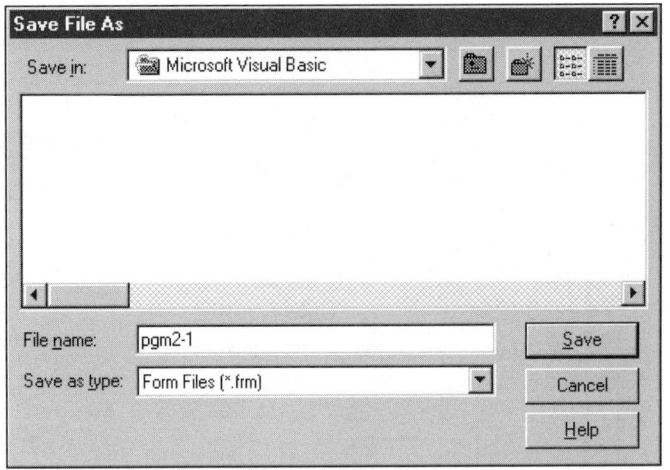

To save an application, first select the File menu and then select Save Project. At this point a dialog box similar to the one illustrated in Figure 2-24 will appear.

In response to the Save File dialog box illustrated in Figure 2-24, verify the directory where you want the form saved and enter the name of the file that will be used to save the form. In this case use the file name pgm2-1, which is the name of the file we used to store this form on the enclosed source-code diskette, or any other valid file name you prefer. After completing the input data for the Save File dialog box, press the OK Command button. Doing so will create a file named pgm2-1.frm (the extension suffix .frm is automatically provided by Visual Basic) and cause the Save As Project dialog box illustrated in Figure 2-25 to appear.

For this project, type in the name pgm2-1 (the name we used to store the project file on the diskette packaged with this text) as the project file's name, or any other valid file name, and press the OK Command button. Doing this will save the project information in a file named pgm2-1.vbp. Again the extension suffix .vbp is automatically appended by Visual Basic.[13] Thus, you will now have saved two files—one named pgm2-1.frm, that contains all information related to the form, including the form itself, any objects placed on the form, and any code connected with these objects or the form, and a second file named pgm2-1.vbp, which contains information about the project as a whole. This second file lists all of the forms (in this case there is only one) and other modules (in this case there are none) that make up the complete project. Both of these files are automatically created in Version 5.0 as ASCII text files that can be examined using an ASCII text editor or displayed using the DOS TYPE command.

Figure 2-25

The Save Project As Dialog Box

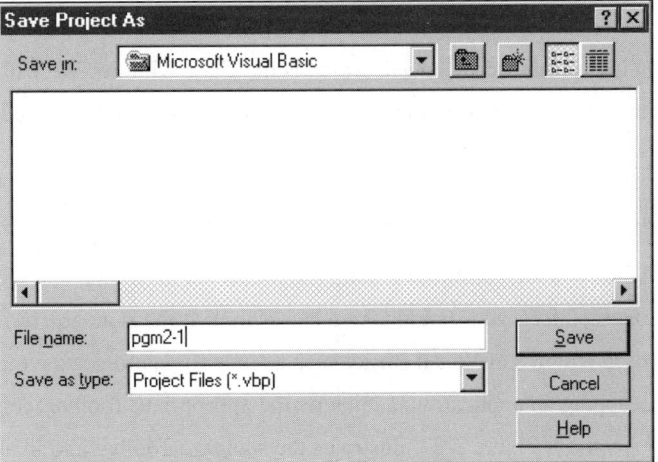

To retrieve a project, select Open Project from the File menu, at which point an Open Project dialog box similar to the

---

[13]Prior to Version 4.0, project files were automatically saved with a .mak extension.

Figure 2-26

The Open Project Dialog Box

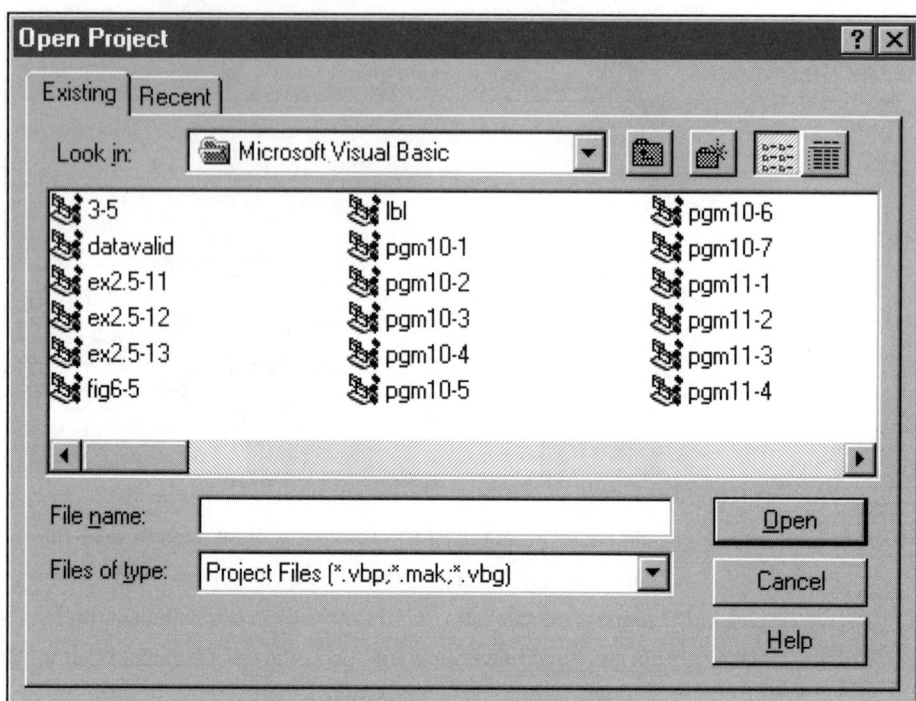

one shown in Figure 2-26 is displayed. As shown in this figure, you can either select an existing project using the Existing tab, or select a recently accessed project using the Recent tab. These two tabs provide the same information displayed by the equivalent New Project dialog tabs when Visual Basic is first launched (see Figures 2-6 to 2-8 on page 42). From either of these tabs, choose the desired project, which in our case is named `pgm2-1.vbp`. When you make your selection a design screen similar to the one previously shown as Figures 2-9 and 2-17 will appear.

If the design screen opened by Visual Basic does not display the Initial Form window, either double-click on the Form icon within the Project Explorer window or select this icon and click on the Object icon (see Figure 2-22). Notice that the Project Explorer window has a Code icon (again, see Figure 2-22). Clicking on this button produces the last basic design window that we will need, which is the Code window. We will make use of this window in the next section. For now, save the project and close the Visual Basic application.

Using the Toolbar

Once you are comfortable with the Menu bar items and can see how they operate and interconnect, you should take a closer look at the standard Toolbar. For the most commonly used features of Visual Basic, such as opening a project, saving a project, and running or stopping an application, a click on the appropriate Toolbar icon performs the desired operation. Figure 2-27 illustrates the standard Toolbar and identifies the icons that you will use as you progress in designing Visual Basic applications. To make sure the standard Toolbar is visible, simply select the Toolbar item from the View menu. When this item is

Figure 2-27

Visual Basic's Standard Toolbar

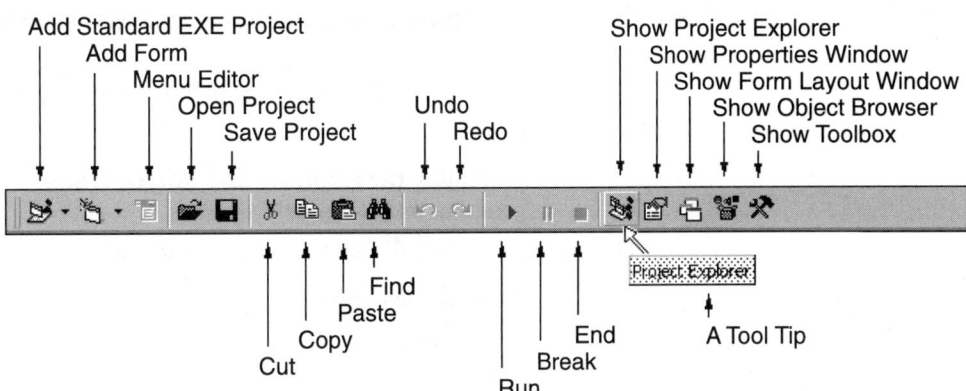

selected a menu listing the available toolbars is displayed. Make sure that a check mark (✓) appears to the left of the Standard item. For your immediate use, the most useful standard Toolbar buttons are represented by the Open Project, Save Project, Run, and End icons.

Exercises 2.2

1. Describe the difference between design-time and run-time.

2. a. What are the three windows that should be visible during an application's design?

   b. What are the steps for bringing up each of the windows listed in your answer to Exercise 2a?

   c. In addition to the three basic design windows, what two additional windows may also be visible on the design screen?

3. What two form properties should be changed for every application?

4. What does a form become during run-time?

5. List the steps for creating a Visual Basic application.

6. a. List the rules that must be followed when naming a Visual Basic object.

   b. What is the three-letter prefix that should be used in every form's name?

7. Determine the number of properties that a form object has. (**Hint**: activate a form's Property window and count the properties.)

8. a. Design a Visual Basic application that consists of a single form with the caption `Test Form`. The form should have no Minimize button and no Maximize button, but should contain a Close button. (**Hint**: locate these properties in the Properties window and change their values from *True* to *False*).

   b. Run the application you designed in Exercise 8a.

9. By looking at the screen how can you tell whether an application is in design-time or run-time mode?

2.3 Adding an Event Procedure

In the previous section we completed the first two steps required in constructing a Visual Basic application:

1. Creating the graphical user interface, and
2. Setting initial object properties.

It now remains to finish the application by completing the third step:

3. Adding procedural code.

At this point our simple application, `pgm2-1`, produces a blank window when it is executed. If you click anywhere on the window, nothing happens. This is because no event procedures have been included for the form. We will complete this application by providing a mouse-click event procedure that displays a message whenever the application is running and the mouse is clicked anywhere on the application's window.

In a well-designed program each procedure consists of a set of instructions necessary to complete a well-defined task. Although a procedure can be initiated in a variety of ways, a procedure that is executed (that is called into action, or *invoked)* when an event occurs is referred to as an *event procedure*. The general structure of an event procedure is illustrated in Figure 2-28.

Figure 2-28

The Structure of an Event Procedure

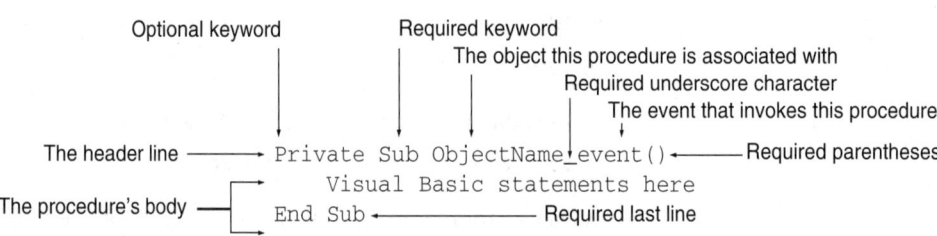

The first line of a procedure is always a header line. A *header line* begins with the optional keyword **Private**[14] and must contain the keyword **Sub** (this comes from the word Subprogram, the name of procedures in earlier versions of Basic), the name of the procedure and a set of parentheses. For event procedures the name must consist of an object identification, an underscore character, (_), and a valid event for the object. If the object is the form itself, the object name Form is used. For example, the header line `Private Sub Form_Click()` denotes an event procedure that will be activated when the mouse is clicked on the form. As was previously described in Section 1.3, the parentheses at the end of a header line are used for transmitting data to and from the procedure when it is invoked. Data transmitted in this fashion are referred to as *arguments* of the procedure. A set of parentheses with no intervening spaces, such as `()`, denotes that no data will be transmitted as arguments when the procedure is executed. The last line of each procedure consists of the keywords **End Sub**.

---

[14]The significance of the keyword **Private** is explained in Chapter 7.

Statements following the program header line, up to and includ[ing] statement, as illustrated on Figure 2-28, are collectively referred to a[s] body. The *body* of the procedure determines what the unit does. Ever[y] must conform to certain rules, which collectively are called the langu[age] each statement in the unit's body resides on a line by itself, although a single statement can continue across a maximum of 10 lines.[15] Multiple statements are allowed in Visual Basic but must be separated by colons (:).

For a form's mouse-click event, the required procedure's structure is

```
Private Sub Form_Click()
   Visual Basic statements in here
End Sub
```

The first and last lines of a procedure, consisting of the header line and terminating body line **End Sub**, are referred to as the procedure's *template*. As shown in Figure 2-29, event procedure templates need not be manually typed because they are automatically provided in Visual Basic's Code window.

Before activating the Code window, we need to decide what Visual Basic statements will be included in the body of our event procedure. In this section we present two ways for easily displaying an output message: the **MsgBox** statement and the **Print** method.

Figure 2-29

The Code Window, Showing a Click Event Procedure Template

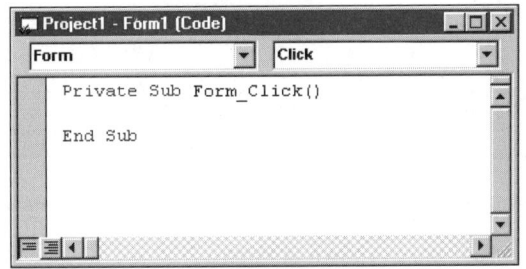

The MsgBox Statement

Visual Basic provides over 200 different statements and built-in functions for constructing event procedures. The first statement we will use is the **MsgBox** statement.[16] The name of this statement is derived from the term Message Box, and its purpose is to display a box on the window with a user supplied message inside. For example, the boxes illustrated in Figure 2-30 were all created using the **MsgBox** statement. The general form of a **MsgBox** statement is

MsgBox "*message*", *type*, "*title*"

Although numerous types of pre-defined message boxes are available, for now we will limit ourselves to the four types listed in Table 2-5.

---

[15] To continue a statement on the next line requires terminating the current line with a space followed by and underscore character (_).

[16] Strictly speaking, the MsgBox statement is a Visual Basic 3.0 statement that is supported in Version 5.0. After variables are introduced in Section 3.2, which will enable us to handle a function's return value, we will always use a MsgBox() function instead of a MsgBox statement.

Table 2-5 MsgBox Types		
Type	**Icon**	**Example**
vbExclamation	Exclamation Point	Figure 2-30a
vbQuestion	Question Mark	Figure 2-30b
vbInformation	The Letter I	Figure 2-30c
vbCritical	The Letter X	Figure 2-30d

For example, the statement

```
MsgBox "Hello World!",vbExclamation, "Sample"
```

produced the message box shown in Figure 2-30a. Notice that the message `Hello World!` is included within the box, and the title at the top of the box is `Sample`. The exclamation icon included within the box is produced by the **vbExclamation** type used in the statement. (**vbExclamation** is a symbolic constant provided by Visual Basic, which is described in detail in Section 4.3). The icons shown in Figures 2-30b through 2-30d are **vbQuestion**, **vbInformation**, and **vbCritical** types, respectively. Thus, Figure 2-30b was produced by the statement

```
MsgBox "Hello World!", vbQuestion, "Sample".
```

Figure 2-30

Message Boxes

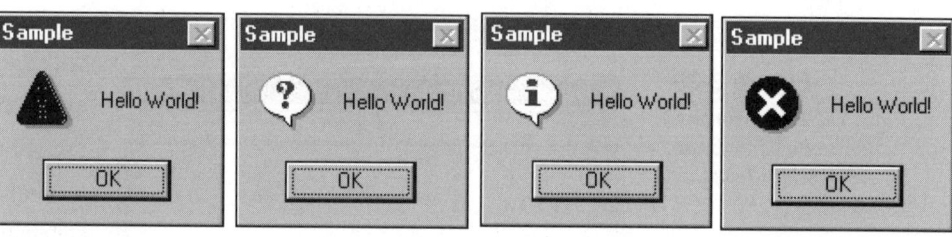

(a) vbExclamation   (b) vbQuestion   (c) vbInformaton   (d) vbCritical

The message boxes shown in Figure 2-30 are all special cases of a more general type of box referred to as dialog boxes. A *dialog box* is any box that appears which requires the user to supply additional information to complete a task. In the case of the message boxes illustrated in Figure 2-30, the required additional information is simply that the user must either click the OK box or push the Enter key to permit the application to continue.

Messages, such as those displayed in message boxes, are called *strings* in Visual Basic. A *string* consists of a string of characters made up of letters, numbers, and special characters, such as the exclamation point. The beginning and end of a string of characters are marked by double quotes ("string in here").

Figure 2-31

The frmMain Form at Design Time

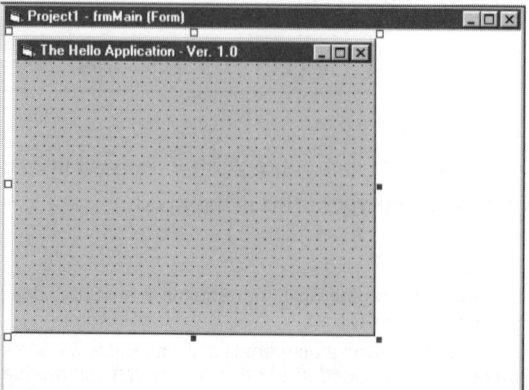

Except for messages within double quotes and certain specific cases that will be noted as they occur, Visual Basic ignores all white space, where *white space* refers to any combination of blank spaces and tabs. Therefore, blank spaces may be freely inserted within a statement to improve its appearance. For example, both of the following statements produce the same result when typed.

```
MsgBox "Hello World!",   vbExclamation,  "Sample"
MsgBox "Hello World!",vbExclamation,"Sample"
```

Now let's attach a **MsgBox** statement to our form so that the statement will be executed when the mouse is clicked. The required procedure is

```
Private Sub Form_Click()
   MsgBox "Hello World!", vbExclamation, "Sample"
End Sub
```

To enter this code, first make sure that you are in design mode and have a form named frmMain showing on the screen, as illustrated in Figure 2-31.

To bring up the Code window, do any one of the following:

- If the Code window is visible, click on it.
- Double-click anywhere on the Form window.
- Select the Code option from the View menu.
- Press the F7 function key anywhere on the design form.
- Select the Code icon from the Project window.

Any of these actions will bring up the Code window shown in Figure 2-32.

The title of the Code window is frmMain; the object identification box should display Form and the procedure identification box should display Load. This indicates that the current object is the Form and the event procedure is Load. Notice that a template for the Form_Load procedure is automatically supplied within the Code window. The two buttons at the bottom of Figure 2-32, are new with Version 5.0. Pressing the Procedure View button activates the option where only one procedure at a time can be viewed, which was the default provided in all versions prior to 5.0. Pressing the Module View button displays all procedures and declarations that have been written, with each procedure separated by a line. When the Code window is not large enough to display either all procedures or even all of a single procedure, the scroll bars can be used to bring in sections of code within the visible window area.

When you have the Code window shown in Figure 2-32 visible, click on the down facing arrowhead (▼) to the right of the procedure identification box. This will produce the window shown in Figure 2-33. Here the drop-down list can be scrolled to provide all of the events associated with the selected object.

Figure 2-32

The Code Window

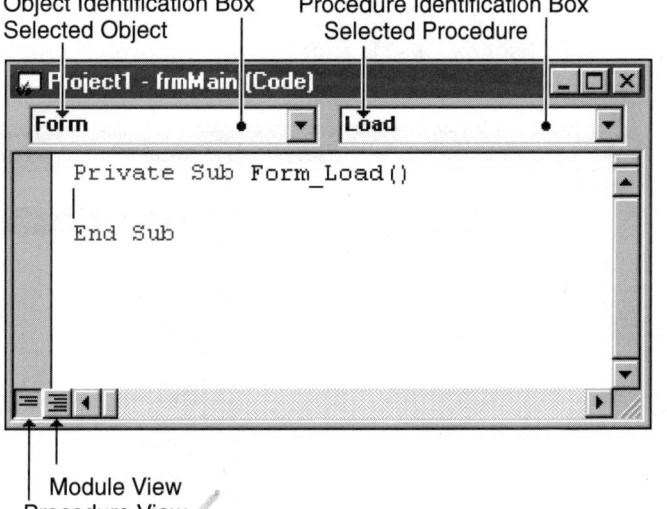

Object Identification Box
Selected Object

Procedure Identification Box
Selected Procedure

Module View
Procedure View

Programmers' Notes

Activating the Code Window

To activate the Code window, use one of the following procedures:

1. If the Code window is visible, click on it.
2. Double-click anywhere on the design form.
3. Select the <u>C</u>ode item from the <u>V</u>iew menu .
4. Press the F7 key.
5. Select the <u>C</u>ode icon from the Project window.

To select the **Click** procedure do any of the following:

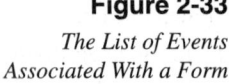

* Use the list's scroll bar until the word **Click** is visible, and then click on this keyword.
* Use the up-arrow cursor key to highlight the word **Click**, and press Enter.
* Press the Ctrl+Shift+C keys together to move directly to **Click**, and press Enter.

Any of these actions will make the Code window appear as shown in Figure 2-34.

Notice in Figure 2-34 that the Module View button has been selected (lower left-hand side of the figure). This selection has the effect of showing all code associated with the form, with lines used to separate code sections. For now, ignore the first line of code, Option Explicit, which is explained in Section 3-2. Clicking on the Procedure View button effectively hides this code by making only the **Click** event procedure immediately visible.

When you have gotten the Code window to look like the one shown in Figure 2-34, type in the line

```
MsgBox "Hello World!", vbExclamation, "Sample"
```

between the header line Private Sub Form_Click() and the terminating line End Sub that are automatically entered in the Code window. When this is completed, the procedure should be

```
Private Sub Form_Click()
   MsgBox "Hello World!", vbExclamation, "Sample"
End Sub
```

Figure 2-33

The List of Events Associated With a Form

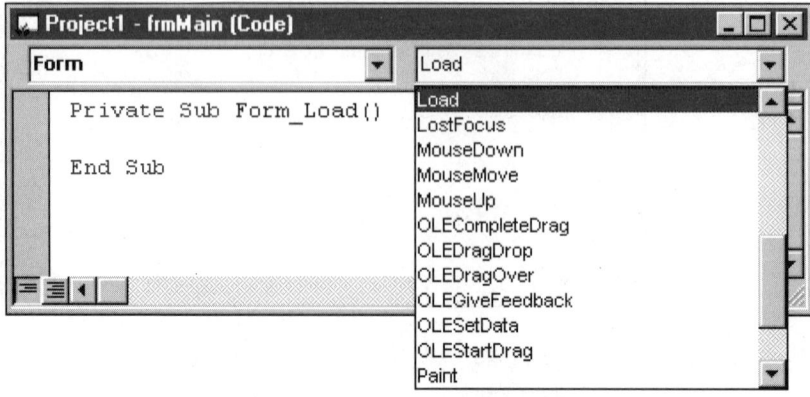

Figure 2-34

The Code Window for the Form_Click Event Procedure

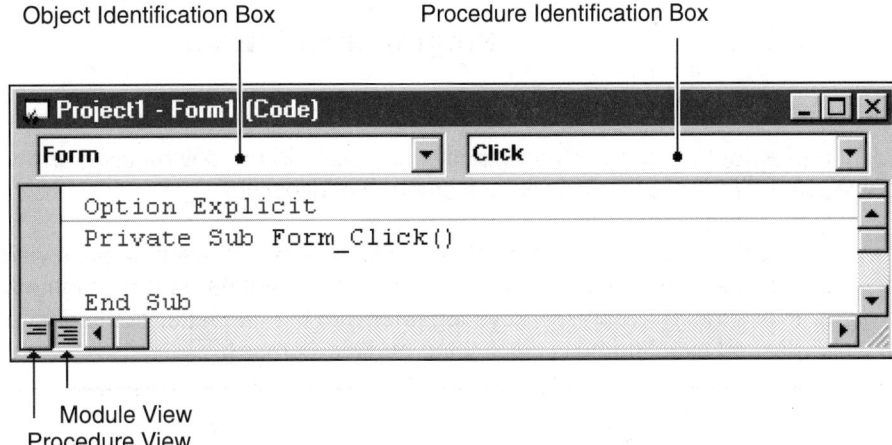

Object Identification Box   Procedure Identification Box

Module View
Procedure View

Notice that we have indented the single Visual Basic statement using two spaces.

Figure 2-35

The Initial Run-Time Application Window

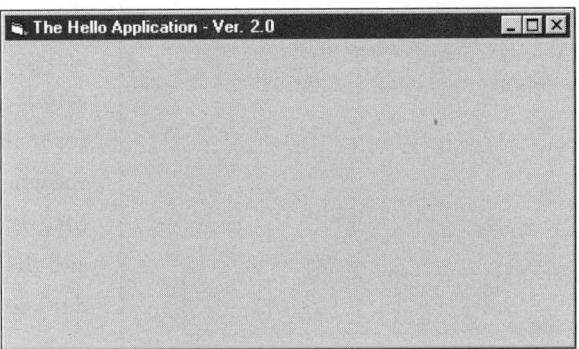

Although this is not required, indentation is a sign of good programming practice. Here it permits the statements within the procedure to be easily identified.

Our event procedure is now complete and you can close the Code and Project windows. When you run the program, the application should appear as shown in Figure 2-35. Clicking anywhere on the window will create the window shown in Figure 2-36. To remove the message box, press either the escape [Esc] or [Enter] key, or click on the OK Command button. Save the application by naming the form file pgm2-2.frm and the project file pgm2-2.Vbp.

Figure 2-36

The Effect of the Mouse Click Event

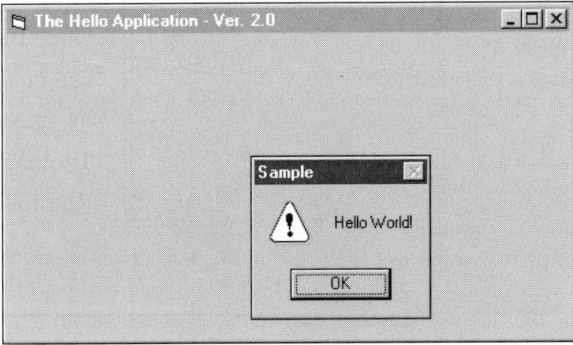

Correcting Errors

If you incorrectly type the message box statement in your procedure, the code window with this procedure will automatically be displayed with the incorrect statement highlighted when the program is run. For example, if you inadvertently spell **MsgBox** as MsgBx, the window shown in Figure 2-37a will appear when you click the mouse (assuming both the project and form files were saved using the file name pgm2-2). If you then click OK in the message box (or press [Enter]), the caption at the top of the window will change from

---

Programmers' Notes

Selecting a Procedure from the Code Window

To select a procedure from the Code window, first click on the down-facing arrow head (▼) at the right of the procedure identification box. Then use one of the following:

1. Use the drop-down list's scroll bar until the desired event name is visible and then click it.
2. Use the arrow cursor keys until the desired event name is highlighted and then press (Enter).
3. Press the (Ctrl) and (Shift) keys together with the first letter of the desired event's name until the desired event name is highlighted and then press (Enter).

```
pgm2-2 - Microsoft Visual Basic [run]
```
to
```
pgm2-2 - Microsoft Visual Basic [break]
```

Figure 2-37a

Notification of an Error

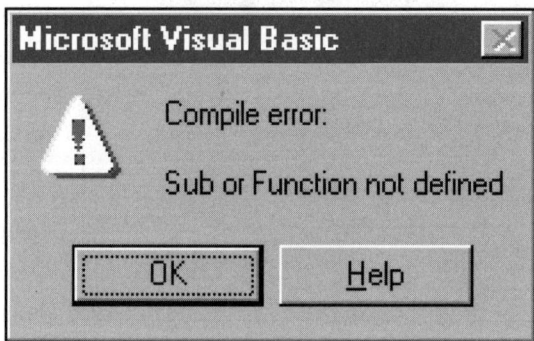

and the Code window will be activated as shown in Figure 2-37b for making code changes. As shown, in this figure, the invalid MsgBx keyword is highlighted and the header line of the procedure containing the invalid line of code is both highlighted and pointed to by an arrow in the left margin of the Code window. Once the correction is made you can change back to run mode by pressing (F7), clicking the Toolbar's Run icon, or using the Run menu item.

Figure 2-37b

Identification of the Invalid Statement and its Procedure

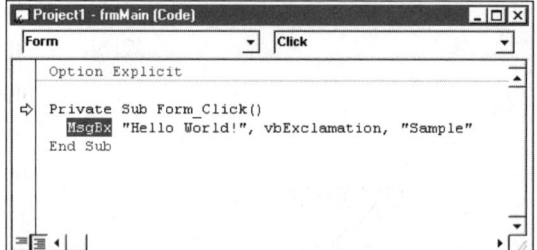

The Print Method

Currently you have been introduced to objects, their properties, and events. The last item you will need to be familiar with is an object's methods. A *method* is a built-in procedure that is an integral part of an object, like a property, but is used to perform a specific action on the object.

Two such methods that are connected to a form object are named **Print** and **Cls**. The **Print** method, as its name suggests, is a method that prints data provided to it, onto an object. For example, if the message "Hello World!" is given to a **Print** method that

---

Introduction to Visual Basic

Programmers' Notes

Code Editor Options:

The editor provided with Visual Basic 5.0 provides a number of options that are very useful when you are entering code into the Code window. These include:

Color Coded Instructions:
The Visual Basic Editor displays procedural code in a variety of user-selected colors. By default, the following color selections are used:

- Keywords—Blue
- Comments—Green
- Errors—Red
- Other Text—Black

These default colors can be changed from within the Editor Format tab in the Tools' menu Option dialog box.

Completing a Word:
Once you have entered enough characters for Visual Basic to identify a work, you can have the Editor complete the word. This option can be activated by pressing the Ctrl+Spacebar keys or by selecting it from the context menu that is displayed when the right-mouse button is clicked from inside the Code window.

Quick Syntax Information:
If you are trying to complete a statement, such as a MsgBox statement, and forget the required syntax, you can ask the editor to provide it. This option can be activated by pressing the Ctrl+I keys, by selecting the Auto Quick Info from within the Editor tab in the Tools' menu Option dialog box, or by selecting it from the context menu that is displayed when the right-mouse button is clicked from inside the Code window.

---

is attached to a form, this message will be printed (displayed) on the window generated by the form. The general syntax of the **Print** method is

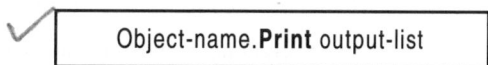

Object-name.**Print** output-list

The name to the left of the required period identifies the object, while the name to the right of the period identifies the method. Any data provided to the method is listed to the right of the method name, and is separated from the name by at least one space. For example, if frmMain is the name of a form, the statement

```
frmMain.Print "Hello World!"
```

will display the message "Hello World!" on the form. In addition to forms, the **Print** method can be applied to Picture boxes, Debug windows, and the printer. For example, if picShow is the name of a Picture box, the statement picShow.Print "Here I am" will cause the text Here I am to be displayed in the Picture box.

A useful option to using the **Print** method is that, if the object name is omitted, the display will always default to the current form. Thus, the statements

```
frmMain.Print "Hello World!"  and  Print "Hello World!"
```

---

are equivalent. In this text we will always use the shorter statement, so remember when you see it, and know that in using it we are printing to a form.

To see how this statement is used in practice, simply replace the MsgBox statement in the form's click event procedure with a **Print** statement so that the procedure is

```
Private Sub Form_Click()
    Print " Hello World!"
End Sub
```

When you run the program and click on the mouse now, the application window shown in Figure 2-38 will appear.

Although the form's click-event procedure displays only a single message, we can add additional **Print** statements within the procedure to display more than one message. See if you can read the following click-event procedure and determine what it does.

```
Private Sub Form_Click()
    Print "    Welcome to the Guess a Number Game Program"
    Print "I will think of a number between 1 and 100"
    Print "    You will have seven tries to guess the number"
    Print "After each guess I will tell you if you were "
    Print "    Either high, low, or guessed the correct number"
    Print "Have fun and good luck"
End Sub
```

When this click event is activated, the following will be displayed on the form:

```
    Welcome to the Guess a Number Game Program
I will think of a number between 1 and 100
    You will have seven tries to guess the number
After each guess I will tell you if you were
    Either high, low, or guessed the correct number
Have fun and good luck
```

As you might have guessed, each **Print** statement in the event procedure subroutine causes a new line to be displayed. Since the procedure has six **Print** statements, six individual lines are produced. In each case the message in the **Print** statement is displayed exactly as it appears within the enclosing double quotes, including spaces. Thus, the leading spaces in the first, third, and sixth messages are retained in the displayed output.

Figure 2-38

An Application Using the Print Method

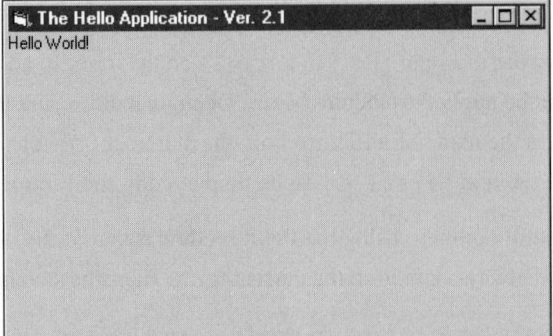

Also notice the sequence in which the statements in the event procedure are executed. The procedure begins with the header line and continues sequentially, statement by statement, until the **End Sub** statement is encountered. The statements within the body of

this procedure are executed sequentially, with each **Print** statement producing a separate line of output.

Altering the placement of any of the **Print** statements in the event procedure automatically alters the display on the form. For example, if the statements in the procedure are written in the order shown below,

```
Private Sub Form_Click()
    Print "Have fun and good luck"
    Print "I will think of a number between 1 and 100"
    Print "    You will have seven tries to guess the number"
    Print "After each guess I will tell you if you were "
    Print "    Either high, low, or guessed the correct number"
    Print "    Welcome to the Guess a Number Game Program"
End Sub
```

the following sequence of messages would be produced:

```
Have fun and good luck
I will think of a number between 1 and 100
    You will have seven tries to guess the number
After each guess I will tell you if you were
    Either high, low, or guessed the correct number
    Welcome to the Guess a Number Game Program
```

Although this set of messages have used only letters, this is not required in Visual Basic. Messages can contain any characters, including lowercase letters, percent signs (%), ampersands (&), exclamation points (!), and any other symbol supported by Visual Basic. All of these characters are allowed within messages because Visual Basic attributes no significance to them, other than to store and display the characters exactly as they appear in the message. Messages can even include double quotes by using two double quotes in succession. For example, the message "They said ""Hello"" to me" produces the output:

```
They said "Hello" to me
```

Finally, it is possible to use the **Print** statements with no output. For example, the statement

```
Print
```

causes a blank line to be displayed. Thus, the sequence of statements

```
    Print "The greeting of the day"
    Print
    Print "for January 1st is"
    Print
    Print "Happy New Year!"
```

causes the following double spaced screen display:

```
The greeting of the day

for January 1st is

Happy New Year!
```

As we have seen, when no object name is used, the **Print** method defaults to the current form, which permitted us to use the abbreviated statement,

```
Print "Hello World!"
```

in place of the longer statement, `frmMain.print "Hello World!"`. Another style you may also encounter is the use of the question mark in place of the keyword **Print**, which saves having to type in the whole word **Print**. For example, each of the following statements produces the same effect in displaying the message `Hello World!` on the window named frmMain:

```
Print "Hello World!"
? "Hello World!"
frmMain.Print "Hello World!"
frmMain.? "Hello World!"
```

Certainly, if a lot of typing is involved in a program or you are trying to quickly test the effect of a **Print** statement, the question mark is advantageous. When the question mark is typed in the Code Window it is automatically converted to the word **Print** by the Visual Basic editor when you press the (Enter) key or move to another line. In this text, however, we will always type the method name, **Print**, and only include an object name if we are not printing to the form. Thus, when you see the **Print** keyword by itself, you will know we are referring to the form.

The Cls Method

Notice that each time you generate the click event in our latest version of the Hello Application (which is stored on the enclosed diskette as `Pgm2-2a`) by clicking the mouse on the run-time window, the message `Hello World!`, shown in Figure 2-38, is printed again. For example, if you click the mouse five times, the message appears five times. This is because each click is a unique event that triggers the **Print** method.

At this stage you might want to provide a user with a way of clearing the window. Fortunately, a method named **Cls** exists for removing all data displayed by the **Print** method. For example, to clear the form named `frmMain`, the statement `Cls` can be used. If we attach this statement to the double-click mouse event (use the Code window), the event procedure becomes:

```
Private Sub Form_DblClick()
   Cls
End Sub
```

Now when you run your application each mouse click will display the message `Hello World!` and each double-click will clear the window of all printed messages. In addition to forms, the **Cls** method can be applied to other objects, such as Picture boxes and the Debug windows. When applied to these other objects, the **Cls** method must be preceded by the object's name. For example, if `picShow` is the name of a Picture box object, the statement `picShow.Cls` is required to clear the Picture box. When no object name is provided the **Cls** method refers to the current window. As with the **Print** method, however, a form name may also be used. Thus, in our application where the form's name is `frmMain`, the statements `Cls` and `frmMain.Cls` are equivalent, and both clear the window of any printed messages.

Exercises 2.3

1. Define the following terms:
   a. event procedure
   b. dialog box
   c. method
   d. header line
   e. argument
   f. template

2. a. What window do you use to enter the code for an event procedure?
   b. List two ways of activating the window you listed as the answer for Exercise 2a.

3. a. Assume that you have created a project with a form named `frmMain` that contains two Command buttons named `cmdButton1` and `cmdButton2`. Write the header line that is required for each object's click-event procedures.
   b. Write the template that will be supplied by Visual Basic for the `cmdButton1` click-event procedure.

4. Using the Code window determine how many event procedures are associated with a form.

5. Design and run the application presented in this section using the **MsgBox** statement in the form's click-event procedure.

6. a. Design and run the application presented in this section using the **Print** method in the form's click event procedure and the **Cls** method in the form's double-click event procedure.
   b. For the project designed in Exercise 6a. change the form's **Font** property to **MS Serif** in a 12-point size. Do this by first selecting the **Font** property and then click on the ellipsis (…) to the right of the settings box. Also change the form's **ForeColor** property to red. Do this by selecting the **ForeColor** property, clicking on the down arrow head (▼) to the right of the setting box, and then clicking on the red box. Now run the application.

7. Design and run a Visual Basic application that uses the **Print** method to print your name on one line, your street address on a second line, and your city, state, and zip code on a third line of the window when you click the mouse. (**Hint**: you will need three **Print** method statements in your event procedure.)

8. Design and run a Visual Basic application that prints the following verse in a window when a user clicks the mouse. By double-clicking the mouse the verse should be cleared from the window.

```
Computers, computers everywhere
    as far as I can see
I really, really like these things,
    Oh joy, O joy for me!
```

2.4 Adding Controls

Although the application presented in the previous section is useful in introducing the basic design-time windows needed for developing Visual Basic applications, it is not a very useful application in itself. To make it such we will have to add additional objects and event procedures to the form. Adding objects to the form creates the final graphical interface that the user will see and interact with when the program is run. Adding event procedures to the objects then brings them "alive," so that when they are selected something actually happens. In this section we present the basic method of placing objects on a form, and in the next section we will attach specific event procedures to these objects.

Objects placed on a form are formally referred to as *controls*. The controls consist of the objects that are selected from the Toolbox and placed on the form. Placing objects on a form is quite simple, and the same method is used for all objects. Thus, after placing one object on the form you have learned the method for placing any Toolbox object on a form.

The simplest procedure is to double-click on the desired toolbox object. This causes an object of the selected type to be automatically placed on the form. Once this is done you can change its size and position, and set any additional properties, such as its name, caption, or color. These later properties are modified from within the Properties window, and determine how the object appears when it is first displayed during run-time.

By far the most commonly used Toolbox objects are the Command button, Text box, Label, and Picture box. For our second application we will use the first two of these object types, the Command button and Text box, to create the design-time interface shown in Figure 2-39.

Figure 2-39

Program 2-3's Interface

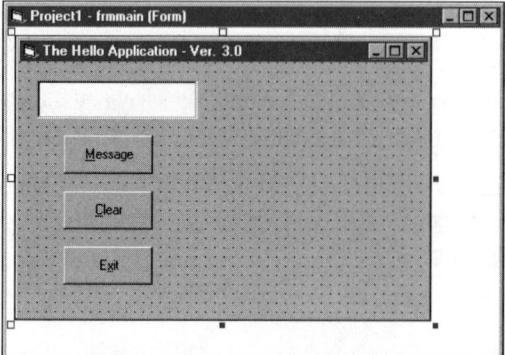

To start our third project either select <u>N</u>ew Project from the <u>F</u>ile menu or press the Alt+F keys followed by the N key (Alt+F/N). Then change the **Name** property of the form to frmMain and change its **Caption** property to The Hello Program.

Adding a Command Button

To place a Command button on the form, double-click on the Command button icon. This icon is the second icon in the toolbox's right column and consists of a rectangle with rounded corners. Double-clicking on this icon causes a Command button with eight small squares, referred to as *sizing handles*, to be placed in the middle of the form, as shown in Figure 2-40. The fact that the sizing handles are showing indicates that the object is *active*, which means that it can be moved, resized, and have its other properties changed. Only one object can be active at a time. To deactivate the currently active object, use the mouse to click anywhere outside of it. Clicking on another object will activate this other object, while clicking on an area of the form where no object is located activates the form object itself.

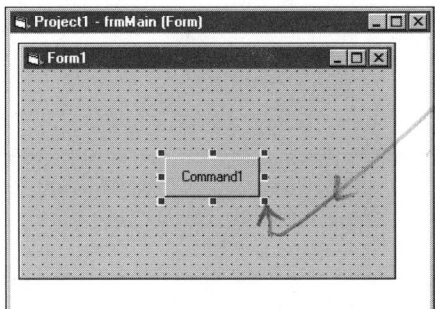

Figure 2-40

The First Command Button Placed on the Form

The active object, which should now be the Command button just placed on the form, can be moved by placing the mouse pointer anywhere inside the object (but not on the sizing handles), holding down the mouse's left button, and dragging the object to its desired new position. Do this now and place this first Command button in the position of the Message button shown in Figure 2-39. Your form should now look like the one shown in Figure 2-41.

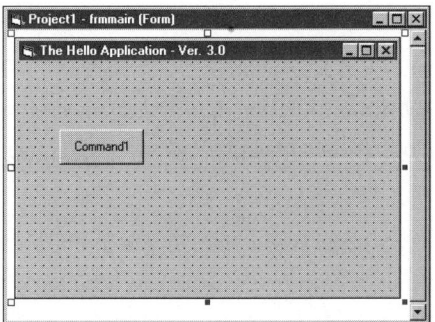

Figure 2-41

The Final Placement of the First Command Button

Once you have successfully placed the first Command button on the form, either use the same procedure to place two more Command buttons in the positions shown in Figure 2-42, or use the alternative procedure given in the Programmers' Notes box on page 74. Included in this box are additional procedures for resizing, moving, and deleting an object.

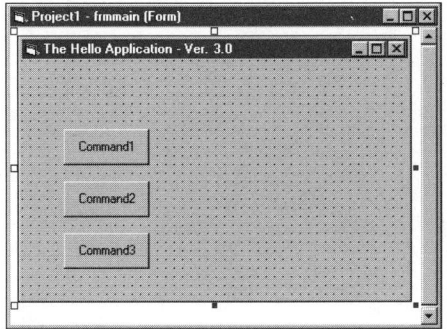

Figure 2-42

Placement of Three Command Buttons on the Form

Programmers' Notes

Creating and Deleting Objects

To Add an Object:
Double-click on the desired object in the Toolbox. Doing this places a pre-sized object on the form.

Or, click on the desired object in the Toolbox and then move the mouse pointer onto the form. When the mouse pointer moves onto the form, it will change to a crosshair cursor. Hold the left mouse button down when the crosshairs are in the desired position for any corner of the object and drag the mouse diagonally away from this corner, in any direction, to generate the opposite corner. When the object is the desired size, release the left mouse button.

To Resize an Object:
Activate the object by clicking inside of it. Place the mouse pointer on one of the sizing handles. This will cause the mouse pointer to change to a double-sided arrow (<—>) Hold the left mouse button down and move the mouse in the direction of either arrow head. Release the mouse button when the desired size is reached.

To Move an Object:
Whether the object is active or not, place the mouse pointer inside of the object and hold down the left mouse button. Drag the object to the desired position and then release the mouse button.

To Delete an Object:
Activate the object by clicking inside of it, and then press the Del key.

Adding a Text Box

Text boxes can be used for both entering data and displaying results. In our current application we will use a Text box for displaying a message when one of the form's Command buttons is clicked.

The Text box icon is the second icon in the toolbox's first column. A Text box object is placed on a form in the same way we placed the three Command button objects: that is, by simply double-clicking on the Text box icon. If you happen to double-click the wrong icon, simply activate it and press the Del key to remove it. Once you have placed a Text box on the form, move and resize it so it appears as shown in Figure 2-43.

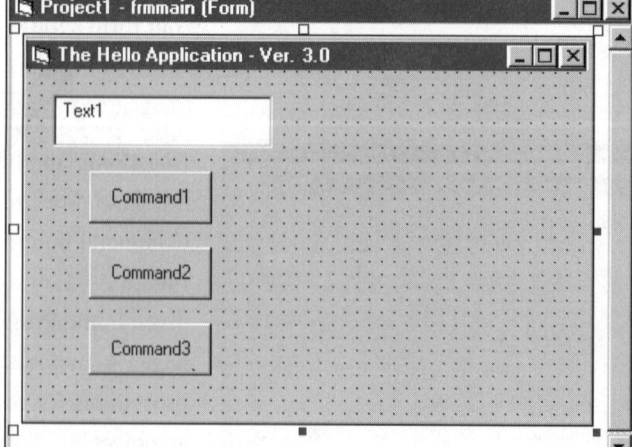

Figure 2-43

Placement of the Text Box

Table 2-6 Program 2-3's Initial Property Settings

Object	Property	Setting
Form1	Name	frmMain
	Caption	The Hello Program - Ver. 3.0
Command1	Name	cmdMessage
	Caption	&Message
Command2	Name	cmdClear
	Caption	&Clear
Command3	Name	cmdExit
	Caption	E&xit
Text1	Name	txtDisplay
	Text	(blank)

practice

Setting the Initial Object Properties

At this point we have assembled all of the form controls that are required for our application. We still need to change the names of these objects from their default names and set the captions of the Command buttons to those previously shown in Figure 2-39. After that, we can add the code so that each Command button performs its designated task when it is clicked. So let's change the initial properties of our four objects to make them appear as shown in Figure 2-39. Table 2-6 lists the desired property settings for each object, including the form.

Before we set the properties listed in Table 2-6, two comments are in order. The first concerns the ampersand (&) symbol included in the captions of all of the Command buttons. This symbol should be typed exactly as shown. Its visual effect is to cause the character immediately following it to be underlined. Its operational effect is to create an *accelerator key*. An accelerator key, which is also referred to as a *hot-key sequence* (or hot key, for short), is simply a keyboard short cut for a user to make a selection. When used with a Command button it permits the user to activate that button by simultaneously pressing the [Alt] key with the underlined letter key, rather than by clicking with the mouse or by first selecting the **Command** button and then pressing the [Enter] key.

ampersand &

The second comment concerns the **Text** property and its setting, which is the last entry in Table 2-6. Unlike Command buttons, Text boxes do not have captions. They do, however, have a property called **Text**. The setting of this property determines what text will be displayed in the Text box. As shown in Figure 2-42 the initial data shown in the Text box is Text1, which is the default value for this property. The term (blank) means that we will set this value to a blank.

Also note that, although we are setting the initial properties for all of the objects at the same time, this is not necessary. We are doing so here to show the various settings in one place. In practice we could just as easily have set each object's properties immediately after it was placed on the form.

Recall from the Programmers' Notes box on page 52 that a Properties window can be activated in a variety of ways: by pressing the [F4] function key or by selecting Properties from the View menu (which can also be obtained by the hot-key sequence [Alt]+[V], followed by [W]). Now, however, we have four objects on the design screen, which include the form, three Command buttons, and a Text box. To select the properties for a particular object, you can use any of the options listed in the Programmers' Notes box on page 52.

The simplest method is to first activate the desired object by clicking on it, and then press either the [F4] function key or the hot-key sequence, [Ctrl]+[Shift] + the first letter of the desired property. For example, if a Command button is active, pressing [Ctrl]+[Shift]+[N] will place the cursor at the **Name** property for the activated control. Because an object is automatically activated just after it is placed on a form, these two methods are particularly useful for immediately changing the object's properties. This sequence of adding an object and immediately changing its properties is preferred by many programmers.

An alternative method is to bring up the Properties window for the currently active object, no matter what it is, and then click on the downward facing arrowhead key (▼) to the right of the object's name (see Figure 2-44). The drop-down list that appears contains the names of all objects associated with the form. Clicking on the desired object name in the list both activates the desired object and brings up its Properties window. This method is particularly handy when changing the properties of a group of objects, by sequencing through them after all objects have been placed on the form. Using either of these methods, alter the initial properties to those listed in Table 2-6.

At this stage, you should have the design screen shown in Figure 2-44. Within the context of a complete program development we have achieved the first two steps in our three-step process:

1. Create the graphical user interface.
2. Set the properties of each object on the interface.

Figure 2-44

Changing Properties Settings

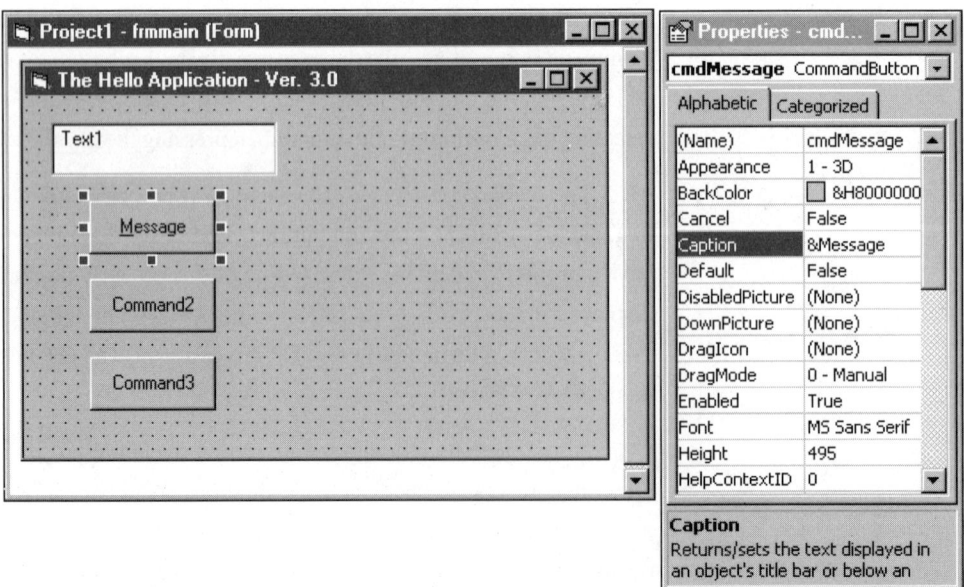

Introduction to Visual Basic

We will complete the third and final step of writing the code in the next section. Before doing so, however, run the application by pressing the F5 function key. Although clicking on any of the Command buttons produces no effect (precisely because we have not yet attached any code to these buttons), we can use the application to introduce two important concepts connected with any form: focus and tab sequence.

Looking at the Focus and Tab Sequence

When an application is run and a user is looking at the form, only one of the form's controls will have *input focus*, or focus, for short. The control with focus is the object that will be affected by pressing a key or clicking the mouse. For example, when a Command button has the focus, its caption will be surrounded by a dotted rectangle, as shown in Figure 2-45. Similarly, when a Text box has the focus, a solid cursor appears on the box, indicating that the user can type in data.

An object can only receive focus if it is capable of responding to user input either through the keyboard or mouse. Thus, such controls as labels, lines, and rectangles can never receive the focus. In order to actually get the focus a control must have its **Enabled**, **Visible**, and **TabStop** properties set to **True**. By enabling an object you permit it to respond to user-generated events, such as pressing a key or clicking a mouse, while the **Visible** property determines whether an object will actually be visible on the window during run-time (it is always available for view during design-time). A **True** **TabStop** setting forces a tab stop for the object, while a **False** value causes the object to be skipped over in the tab stop sequence. As the default settings for all three properties is **True**, they do not usually have to be checked for normal tab operation. A control capable of receiving focus, such as a Command button, can get the focus in one of three ways:

Figure 2-45

A Command Button With and Without Focus

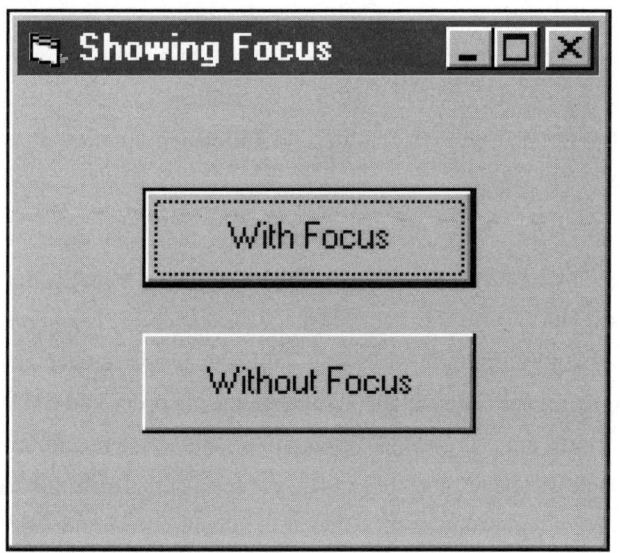

1. A user clicks the mouse directly on the object.
2. A user presses the tab key until the object gets the focus.
3. The code activates the focus.

Programmers' Notes

Activating the Properties Window for a Specific Object

1. Activate the object by clicking on it, and then press the [F4] function key.
2. Activate the object by clicking on it, and then press [Ctrl]+[Shift]+ the first letter of property you want to change.
3. Activate the Properties window for the currently selected object or form, whatever it may be, either by pressing the [F4] key or selecting the Properties option from the Windows menu ([Alt]+[V]/[W]). Then change to the desired object from within the Properties window. Do this by clicking on the underlined down-arrow to the right of the object's name and then selecting the desired object from the drop-down list.

To see how the first method operates, press the [F5] function key to execute the Hello Program (pgm2-3). Once the program is executing, click on any of the form objects. As you do, notice how the focus shifts. If any object does not respond, go back to the design stage and make sure that the object's **Enabled** property is set to **True**. Now press the tab key a few times and see how the focus shifts from control to control. The sequence in which the focus shifts from control to control as the tab key is pressed is called the *tab sequence*. This sequence is initially determined by the order in which controls are placed on the form. For example, assume you first create Command buttons named cmdCom1, cmdCom2, and cmdCom3, respectively, and then create a Text box named txtText1. When the application is run, the cmdCom1 button will have the focus. As you press the [Tab] key, focus will shift to the cmdCom2 button, then to the cmdCom3 button, and finally to the Text box. Thus, the tab sequence is cmdCom1 to cmdCom2 to cmdCom3 to txtText1. (This assumes that each control has its **Enabled**, **Visible**, and **TabStop** properties all set to **True**, which permits the object to receive focus.)

The default tab order obtained as a result of placing controls on the form can be altered by modifying an object's **TabIndex** value. Initially, the first control placed on a form is assigned a **TabIndex** value of 0, the second object is assigned a **TabIndex** value of 1, and so on. Controls that do not have a **TabIndex** property, such as lines and rectangles, are not assigned a **TabIndex** value. To change the tab order you simply have to change an object's **TabIndex** value and Visual Basic will renumber the remaining objects in a logical order. For example, if you have six objects on the form with **TabIndex** values from 0 to 5, and change the object with value 3 to a value of 0, the objects with initial values of 0, 1, and 2 will have their values automatically changed to 1, 2, and 3, respectively. Similarly, if you change the object with a **TabIndex** value of 2 to 5, the objects with initial values of 3, 4, and 5 will all have their values automatically reduced by one. Thus, the sequence from one object to another remains the same for all objects, except for the insertion or deletion of the altered object. If, however, you ever get confused, simply reset the complete sequence in the desired order by manually starting with a **TabIndex** value of 0 and then assigning values in the desired order. A control whose **TabStop** property has been set to **False** maintains its **TabIndex** value, but is simply skipped for the next object in the tab sequence.

The Format Menu Option[17]

The Format menu option, which is new with Version 5.0, provides the ability to align and move selected controls as a unit, as well as lock controls and make selected controls the same size. This is a great help in constructing a consistent look on a form that contains numerous controls. In this section we will see how this menu option is used.

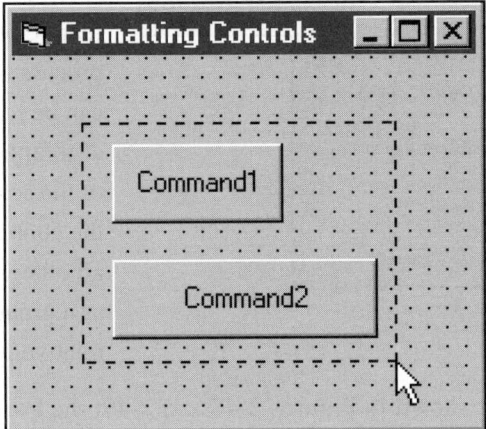

Figure 2-46

Preparing Two Controls for Formatting

As a specific example using the Format menu, consider Figure 2-46, which shows two command controls on a design form. To both align and make both controls the same size, the first operation that you must perform is to select the desired controls. This can be done by clicking on the form and dragging the resulting dotted line to enclose all of the controls you wish to format, as is illustrated on the figure, or by holding the Shift key down and clicking on the desired controls.

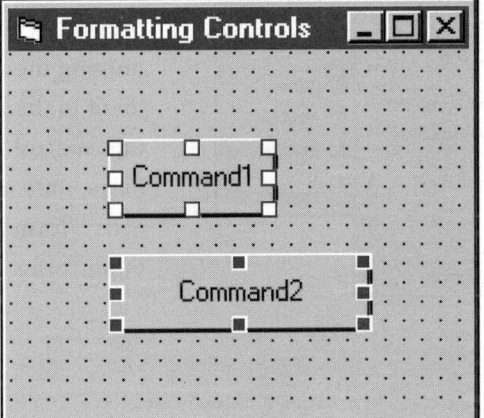

Figure 2-47

Locating the Defining Control

Once you have selected the desired controls for formatting, the last selected object will appear with solid grab handles. For example, in Figure 2-47 this is the lower Command control. The solid grab handles designate the control that is the *defining control*. It is this control that sets the pattern for both sizing and aligning the other selected controls. If this control is not the defining control you want, simply select another by clicking on it.

Having selected the desired defining control, click on the Format menu bar item and then select the desired format option. For example, Figure 2-48 illustrates the selection for making all controls within the dotted lines the same size. Within this submenu, you have the choice of making either the width, height, or both dimensions of all controls equal to the defining control's respective dimensions. The choice shown in this figure sets all selected controls equal in both width and height to the defining control.

In addition to sizing controls, you may also want to align a group of controls within a form. Figure 2-49 illustrates the options provided for the Align submenu. As shown, controls may be aligned in seven different ways, the first six of which are aligned relative to the position of the defining control. Choosing anyone of these first six options will move all

---

[17]This topic may be omitted on first reading with no loss of subject continuity.

Figure 2-48

Making Controls the Same Size

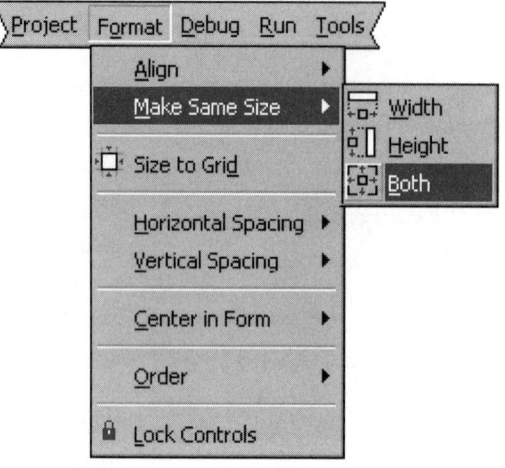

other selected controls in relation to the defining control; the position of the defining control *is not* altered.

An additional and very useful feature of the format selection process is that all selected controls can be moved as a unit. This is accomplished by clicking within one of the selected controls and dragging the control. As the control is dragged, all other selected controls will move, as a group, while maintaining their relative positions to each other.

Finally, as shown in Figures 2-48 and 2-49, the Format menu provides a number of other format choices, all of which are rather self-evident in their effect,

Figure 2-49

Aligning Controls to the Defining Control

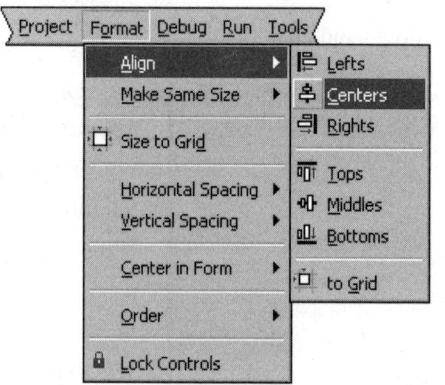

except perhaps for the Lock Control. This control locks all controls on the form in their current positions and prevents you from inadvertently moving them once you have placed them in their desired positions. Since this control works on a form-by-form basis, only controls on the currently active form are locked, and controls on other forms are unaffected.

Exercises 2.4

1. Determine how many initial properties can be set for a Command control. (**Hint**: Activate the Code window for a form that has a Command control and count the available procedures.)

2. Determine how many initial properties can be set for a Text box control.

3. Determine if a Label has a **Caption** or a **TabStop** property.

4. What is the difference between the **Name** and **Caption** properties?

5. How is a hot (accelerator) key created for a Command button?

6. Create a Command button named `cmdInput` having a **Caption** setting of Values.

Introduction to Visual Basic

7. Create a Command button named `cmdDisplay` having the **Caption** setting of <u>D</u>isplay.

8. Assume that one Command button has a **Caption** setting of `Message`, and a second Command button has a **Caption** setting of `Display`. Determine what happens when the hot-key sequence ⒶⓁⓉ+Ⓐ is pressed twice. Do this by creating the two Command buttons and running the program.

9. Create a Text box named `txtOne` that has a red foreground color and a blue background color. The initial text displayed in the box should be `Welcome to Visual Basic`. (**Hint**: Use the **ForeColor** and **BackColor** properties; click on the ellipses (...) to bring up the available colors.)

10. Create a Text box named `txtTwo` that has a blue foreground color and a gray background color. The initial text displayed in the box should be `High-Level Language`. (**Hint**: Use the **ForeColor** and **BackColor** properties - click on the ellipses (...) to bring up the available colors.)

11. What are the three ways that an object can receive focus?

12. To receive focus in the tab sequence, what three properties must be set to **True**?

13. a. Create a graphical user interface that contains two Command buttons and two Text boxes. The names of these controls should be `cmdOne`, `cmdTwo`, `txtFirst`, and `txtSecond`. Set the tab sequence so that tab control goes from `txtFirst` to `txtSecond` to `cmdOne` to `cmdTwo`.

    b. For the tab sequence established in Exercise 13a., set the **TabStop** property of `cmdOne` to **False** and determine how the tab sequence is affected. What was the effect on the other objects' **TabIndex** values?

    c. For the tab sequence established in Exercise 13a., set the **TabStop** property of `cmdOne` to **True** and its **Visible** property to **False**. What is the run-time tab sequence now? Did these changes affect any object's **TabIndex** Values?

    d. For the tab sequence established in Exercise 13a., set the **TabStop** property of `cmdOne` to True, its **Visible** property to **True**, and its **Enabled** property to **False**. What is the run-time tab sequence now? Did these changes affect any object's **TabIndex** values?

    e. Change the tab sequence so that focus starts on `txtFirst`, and then goes to `cmdOne`, `txtSecond`, and finally `cmdTwo`. For this sequence what are the values of each object's **TabIndex** property?

14. a. Does setting a Command control's **TabStop** property to **False** ensure that it cannot receive focus?

    b. Does setting a Text box control's **TabStop** property to **False** ensure that it cannot receive focus?

For exercises 16-19 create the interfaces shown in each figure.

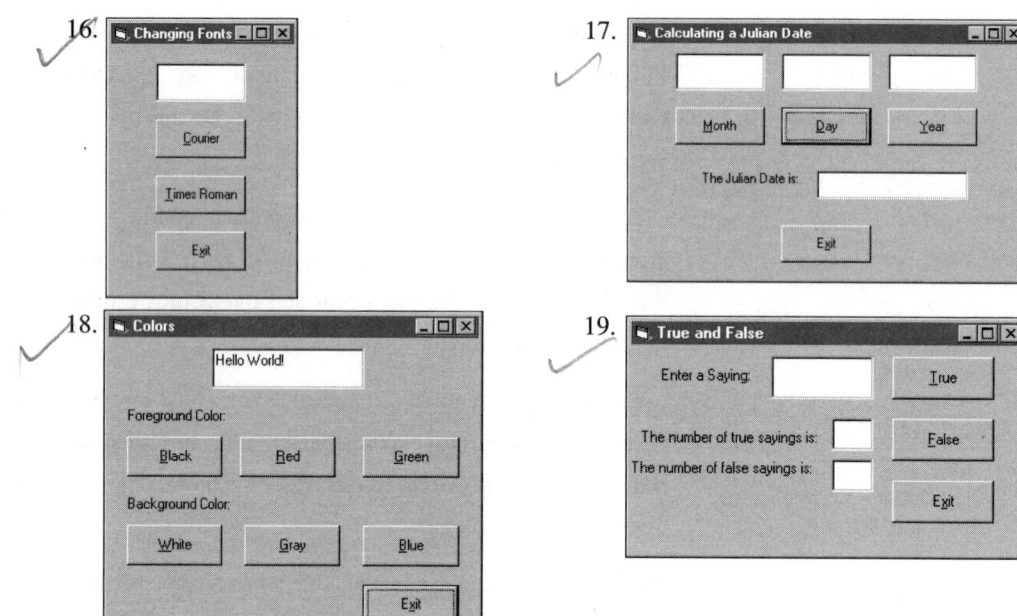

2.5 Adding Additional Event Procedures

Now that we have added four objects to Program 2-3 (The Hello Application, Ver. 3.0, shown in Figure 2-44), we will need to supply these objects with event code. Although each object can have many events associated with it, one of the most commonly used events is the clicking of a Command button. For our Hello Application we will initially create three such mouse-click event procedures, each of which will be activated by clicking on one of the three Command buttons. Two of these event procedures will be used to change the text displayed in the Text box, and the last will be used to exit the program.

To change an object's property value while a program is running, a statement having the form

> Object.Property = value

is used. The term to the left of the equal sign identifies the desired object and property. For example, `cmdMessage.Name` refers to the **Name** property of the control named `cmdMessage`, and `txtDisplay.Text` refers to the **Text** property of the control named `txtDisplay`. The period between the object's name and its property is required. The value to the right of the equal sign provides the new setting for the designated property. For example, the statement `cmdMessage.Enabled = True` would set the **Enabled** property of the `cmdMessage` control to **True**. For our program we want to display the text `Hello World!` when the Command button named `cmdMessage` is clicked. This requires the statement

```
txtDisplay.Text = "Hello World!"
```

to be executed for the click event of the `cmdMessage` control. Notice that this statement will change a property of one object, the Text box, using an event procedure associated with another object, a Command button. Now let's attach this code to the `cmdMessage`

Figure 2-50

The Code Window

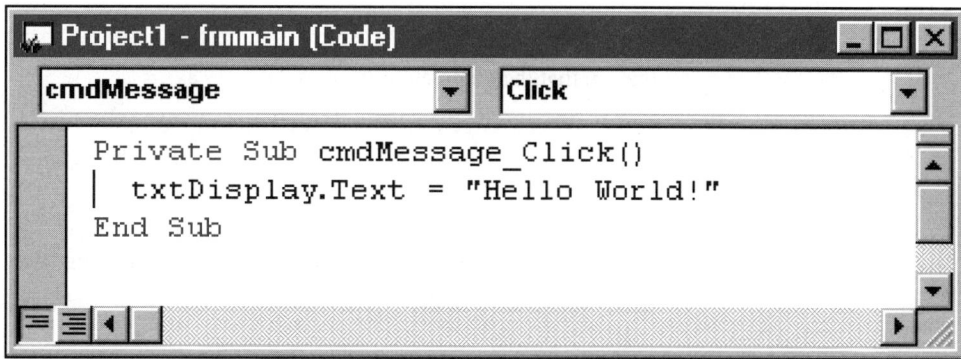

button so that it is activated when this control is clicked. The required event procedure code is

```
Private Sub cmdMessage_Click()
  txtDisplay.Text =  "Hello World!"
End Sub
```

To enter this code, double-click on the cmdMessage control. (Make sure you have the design form illustrated in Figure 2-39 on the screen.) This will bring up the Code window shown in Figure 2-50. As always, the template for the desired event is automatically supplied for you, requiring you to complete the procedure's body with your own code. You might also notice that the keywords **Private**, **Sub**, and **End** are displayed in a different color than the procedure's name.[18]

The object identification box should display cmdMessage and the procedure identification box should display Click. This indicates that the current object is the cmdMessage

Figure 2-51

The Code Window Object List

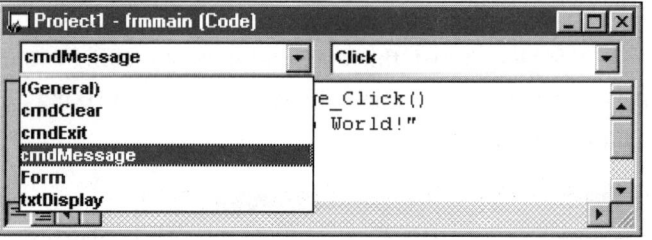

control and that the procedure we are working on is for the **Click** event. If either of these boxes do not contain the correct data, click on the down-facing arrow head to the right of the box and then select the desired object and procedure. Note that when you click on the arrow head to the right of the object identification box, a drop-down list appears as shown in Figure 2-51, which lists all of the form's objects, including the form itself, and the term **(General)**. **General** procedures are those that can be invoked by any and all of the form's procedures. To create a general procedure you must write your own procedure header line and body, which is the topic of Chapter 7.

When the Code window looks like the one shown in Figure 2-51, type in the line

```
txtDisplay.Text = "Hello World!"
```

---

[18]Typically, the color for keywords (automatically supplied when a keyword is typed) is blue. This Keyword Text property can, however, be changed by selecting it within the Editor tab of the Options submenu in the Tools menu.

between the header line, `Private Sub cmdMessage_Click()`, and terminating **End Sub** line, so that the complete procedure appears as

```
Private Sub cmdMessage_Click()
  txtDisplay.Text = "Hello World!"
End Sub
```

Notice that we have indented the statement using two spaces. A space has also been placed around the equal sign. This is not required but is included for readability.

After your procedure is completed, press the F5 function key to run the

Figure 2-52

The Interface Produced by Clicking the Message Button

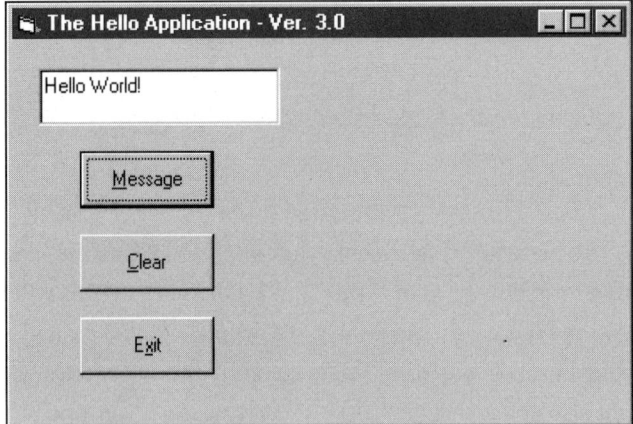

program. When the program is running activate the `cmdMessage` control by clicking on it with the mouse, tabbing to it and pressing the Enter key, or using the hot-key combination Alt + M. When either of these actions is done, your screen should appear as shown in Figure 2-52.

Being able to run and test an event procedure immediately after you have written it, rather than having to check each feature after the whole application is completed, is one of the nice features of Visual Basic. You should get into the habit of doing this as you develop your own programs.

Now let's finish this application by attaching event code to the click events of the remaining two Command buttons, and then fixing a minor problem with the Text box control.

Figure 2-53

The Code Window for the cmdClear Click Event

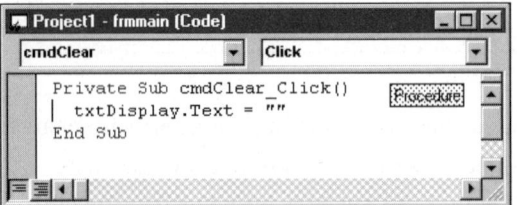

Bring up the Code window for the `cmdClear` button by double-clicking on this control after you have terminated program execution and are back in design mode. When the Code window looks like the one shown in Figure 2-53, add the single line

```
txtDisplay.Text = ""
```

between the procedures header and terminating lines.

When this is completed, the procedure should be

```
Private Sub cmdClear_Click()
  txtDisplay.Text = ""
End Sub
```

Figure 2-54

*The Initial
Run Time Window*

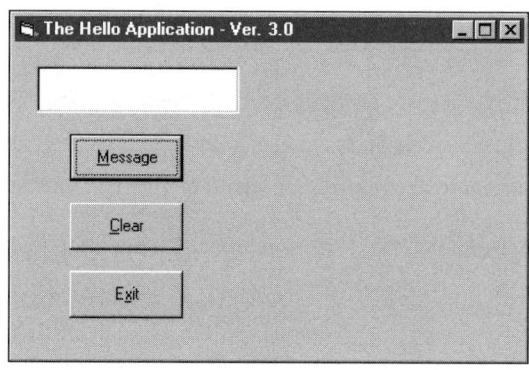

The string `" "`, with no spaces, is called the *empty string*. This string consists of no characters. Setting the **Text** property of the Text box to this string value will have the effect of clearing the Text box of all text. Note that a value such as `"    "`, which consists of one or more blank spaces, will also clear the Text box. A string with one or more blank spaces, however, is not an empty string, which is defined as a string having *no* characters.

When this procedure is completed, use the arrow to the right of the object identification box in the Code window to switch to the `cmdExit` control. (You can, of course, also double-click on the `cmdExit` control to bring up the Code window.) The event procedure for this event should be

```
Private Sub cmdExit_Click()
    Beep
    End
End Sub
```

Beep is an instruction that causes the computer to make a short beeping sound, while the keyword **End** terminates an application.

You are now ready to run the application by pressing the F5 function key. Running the application should initially produce the window shown in Figure 2-54. Notice that when the program is first run, focus is on the `cmdMessage` button and the Text box is empty. The empty Text box occurs because we set this control's **Text** property to a blank during design-time. Similarly, focus is on the `cmdMessage` box because this was the first control added to the form (its **TabIndex** value is 0).

Now click on the <u>M</u>essage control. Doing so will activate the `cmdMessage_Click()` procedure and display the message shown in Figure 2-55.

Figure 2-55

*The Run Time Window after
the Message Button is Clicked*

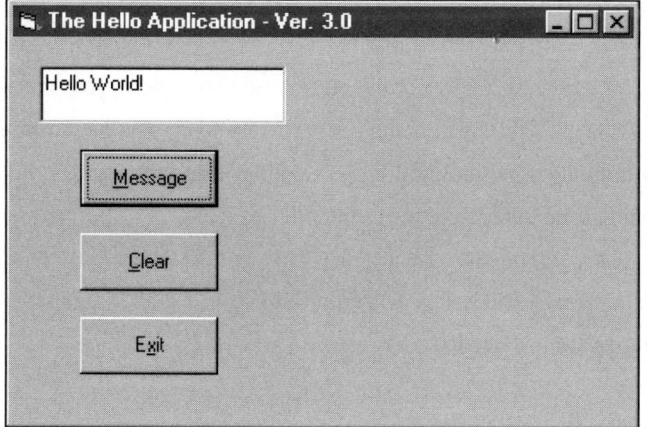

Clicking the <u>C</u>lear button invokes the `cmdClear_Click()` procedure, which clears the Text box, while clicking the E<u>x</u>it button invokes the `cmdExit_Click()` procedure. This procedure causes a short beep and terminates program execution.

Comments

Comments are explanatory remarks made within a program. When used carefully, comments can be very helpful in clarifying what a complete program is about, what a specific group of statements is meant to accomplish, or what one line is intended to do.

Comments are indicated by using either the apostrophe or the keyword **Rem**, which is short for Remark.

For example,

```
Rem this is a comment
' this is a comment
' this program calculates a square root
```

are all comment lines.

Comments, with one exception, can be placed anywhere within a program and have no effect on program execution. Visual Basic ignores all comments—they are there strictly for the convenience of anyone reading the program. The one exception is that comments cannot be included at the end of a statement that is itself continued on the next line.

A comment can always be written either on a line by itself or on the same line as a program statement that is not continued on the next line. When written on a line by itself, either an apostrophe or the keyword **Rem** may be used. When a comment is written on the same line as a program statement, the comment must begin with an apostrophe. In all cases a comment only extends to the end of the line it is written on. For example, the following event procedure illustrates the use of comments.

```
Rem This is the click event procedure associated with the Exit Command button
        Private Sub cmdExit_Click()    ' this is the header line
            Beep ' this causes a short beep
            End  ' this ends the application
        End Sub
```

In no case can a comment extend for more than one line. If you need to create multiline comments, each line must begin with either an apostrophe or the **Rem** keyword.

Typically, many comments are required when using nonstructured programming languages. These comments are necessary to clarify the purpose of either the program itself or individual sections and lines of code within the program. In Visual Basic, the program's inherent modular structure is intended to make the program readable, making the use of extensive comments unnecessary. However, if the purpose of a procedure or any of its statements is still not clear from its structure, name, or context, include comments where clarification is needed.

Statement Categories

You will have many statements at your disposal in constructing Visual Basic event procedures. All statements, however, belong to one of two broad categories: executable statements and nonexecutable statements. An *executable statement* causes some specific action to be performed by the compiler or interpreter. For example, a **MsgBox** statement or a statement that tells the computer to add or subtract a number is an executable statement. A nonexecutable statement is a statement that describes some feature of either the program or its data but does not cause the computer to perform any action. An example of a nonexecutable statement is a comment statement. As the various Visual Basic statements are introduced in the upcoming sections, we will point out which ones are executable and which are nonexecutable.

A Closer Look at the Text Box Control

Text boxes form a major part of almost all Visual Basic Programs, because they can be used for both input and output purposes. For example, run Program 2-3 (see Figure 2-54) again, but this time click on the Text box. Notice that a cursor appears in the Text box. At this point, you can type in any text you like, directly from the keyboard. The text you enter will stay in the box until you click on one of the Command buttons, which will either change the text to `Hello World!`, clear the box of all text, or terminate the program.

Since we have constructed the program essentially to use the Text box for output display purposes only, we would like to alter the operation of the Text box so that a user cannot enter data into the box. To do this we will set the box's click event to immediately set focus on one of the Command buttons. The following procedure accomplishes this:

```
Private Sub txtDisplay_Click()
   cmdMessage.SetFocus
End Sub
```

Enter this procedure now in the Text box's Code window. When you first bring up the Code window, for the Text box object (either press the Shift+F4 keys or use the View menu), the Code window may appear as shown in Figure 2-56. If this happens, click on the arrow to the right of the procedure identification box and select the **Click** event.

SetFocus, like **Print**, is a method. In this case, **SetFocus** is a method that sets the focus on its object.[19] Thus, when a user clicks on the Text box, it will trigger the `txtDisplay_Click()` procedure which in turn will call the `cmdMessage` **SetFocus** method. This method will set the focus on the Message Command button.

---

[19]An alternative solution is to set the Locked property of the text box to True. With this property set to True, the text box is locked from receiving any input and effectively becomes a read-only box. It still, however, can be clicked on and receive focus.

Programmers' Notes

Using the Object Browser window

To activate the Object Browser window:
    1. Select Object Browser from the View menu, or
    2. Press the F2 function key.

To activate a Code window from the Object Browser Window:
    1. Double-click on the desired object in the Classes box.
    2. Double-click on the desired event procedure in the Members box.

To cycle through each event code procedure in a Code window:
    1. Press the Ctrl + ↓ keys, or
    2. Press the Ctrl + ↑ keys.

Before leaving the Text box, two additional features should be mentioned. First, it is worthwhile noting that when you initially entered characters into the box, before we deactivated it for input, the entered characters were actually accepted as a string of text. This is always true of a Text box—all data entered or displayed is considered a string. As we will see in the next chapter, when we want to use a Text box to input a number, such as 12356, we will have to check carefully that a string representing an invalid number, such as 123a56, is not inadvertently entered. This type of validation is necessary because the Text box does not filter out unwanted characters from an input or displayed string. Finally, since we are only using the Text box for output, we could have used a Picture box instead. Picture boxes are very similar to Text boxes, except they cannot be used for input. Although we will use Picture boxes in the future for output-only display, we introduced the Text box here because it is one of the most widely used control objects.

Figure 2-56

The Code Window

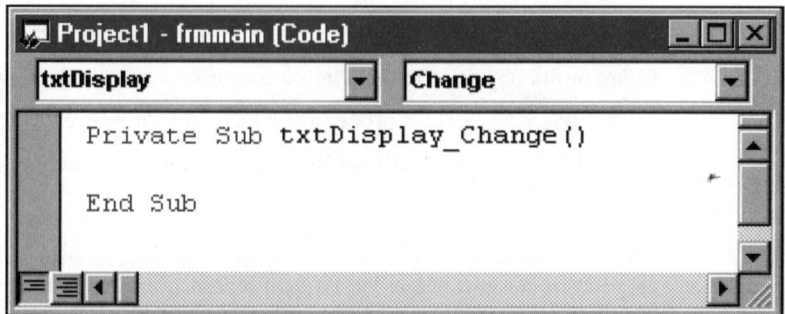

Viewing All Your Procedures at Once

As you add controls and event procedures to an application, it becomes increasingly convenient to be able to get a listing of all the procedures and controls in a central place. Such a listing is possible using the Object Browser. This browser is obtained either by selecting Object Browser from the <u>V</u>iew menu or by pressing the [F2] function key anywhere during design-time. Figure 2-57 shows the Object Browser window for pgm2-3.

Notice that the **Classes** box contains a list of modules, which in our case includes frmMain and the **Members** box contains a list of all methods and procedures currently available. In addition, procedures for which code has been written are highlighted in bold.

To view or edit any single event procedure, simply double-click on the desired procedure in the box. Once any Code window is active you can sequentially cycle through each event procedure by pressing the [Ctrl] and [↓] keys together. This will cause the next procedure to be displayed. To reverse the sequence, simply press the [Ctrl] and [↑] keys. These are the hot-key combinations for Next Procedure and Previous Procedure, respectively, from the Code window.

Figure 2-57

The Object Browser Window

Exercises 2.5

1. a. Determine the number of events that can be associated with a Command button.
      (**Hint**: create a Command button and use the Code window to view its various events.)
   b. List the event names for each event that can be associated with a Command button.

2. Repeat Exercise 1a. for a Text box.

3. Repeat Exercise 1a. for a Label

4. Repeat Exercise 1a. for a Picture box.

5. List the objects and the events that the following procedures refer to:
   a. `Private Sub cmdDisplay_Click()`
   b. `Private Sub cmdBold_LostFocus()`
   c. `Private Sub txtInput_GotFocus()`
   d. `Private Sub txtOutput_LostFocus()`

6. Using the following correspondence:

Event Name	Event
Click	Click
DblClick	Double-click
GotFocus	Got focus
LostFocus	Lost focus

   a. Write the header line for the double-click event associated with a Label control named `lblFirstName`.
   b. Write the header line for the click event associated with a Picture box named `picID`.
   c. Write the header line for the lost-focus event of a Text box named `txtLastName`.
   d. Write the header line for the got-focus event of a Text box named `txtAddress`.

7. Write instructions that will display the following message in a Text box named `txtTest`:
   a. `Welcome to Visual Basic`
   b. `Now is the time`
   c. `12345`
   d. `4 * 5 is 20`
   e. `Vacation is Near`

8. Determine the event associated with the Command button `cmdDisplay` and what is displayed in the Text box named `txtOut`, for each of the following procedures:

   a.
   ```
   Private Sub cmdDisplay_Click()
      txtOut.Text = "As time goes by"
   End Sub
   ```
   = As time goes by

   b.
   ```
   Private Sub cmdDisplay_GotFocus()
      txtOut.Text = "456"
   End Sub
   ```
   456

   c.
   ```
   Private Sub cmdDisplay_LostFocus()
      txtOut.Text = "Play it again Sam"
   End Sub
   ```
   Blank.

   d.
   ```
   Private Sub cmdDisplay_GotFocus()
      txtOut.Text = "          "
   End Sub
   ```
   blank.

9. a. Four properties that can be set for a Text box are named **FontBold**, **FontItalic**, **FontName**, and **FontSize**. What do you think these properties control?

   b. What display do you think the following procedure produces when the Command button `cmdOne` is clicked?

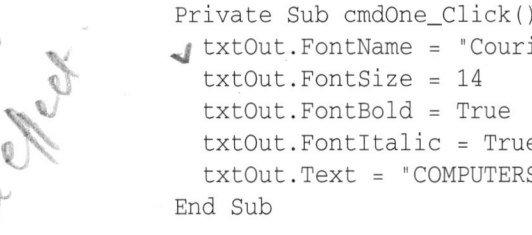

```
Private Sub cmdOne_Click()
   txtOut.FontName = "Courier"
   txtOut.FontSize = 14
   txtOut.FontBold = True
   txtOut.FontItalic = True
   txtOut.Text = "COMPUTERS"
End Sub
```

10. Enter and run the Program 2-1.

   For exercises 11 through 13, create the given interface and initial properties. Then complete the application by writing code to produce the stated task.

11.

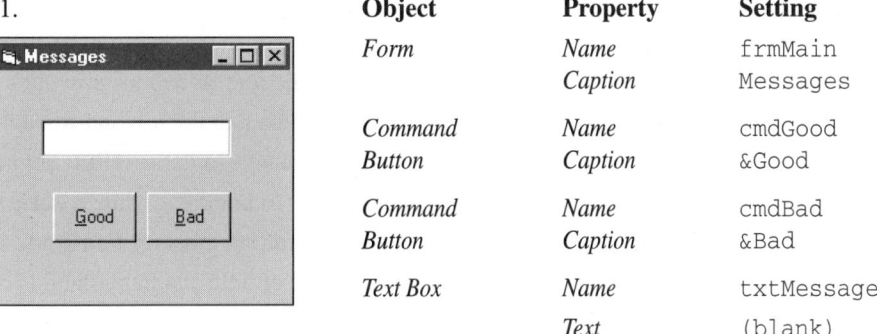

Object	Property	Setting
Form	*Name*	frmMain
	Caption	Messages
Command Button	*Name*	cmdGood
	Caption	&Good
Command Button	*Name*	cmdBad
	Caption	&Bad
Text Box	*Name*	txtMessage
	Text	(blank)

When a user clicks the Good button, the message `Today is a good day!` should appear in the Text box, and when the Bad button is clicked, the message `I'm having a bad day today!` should be displayed.

12.

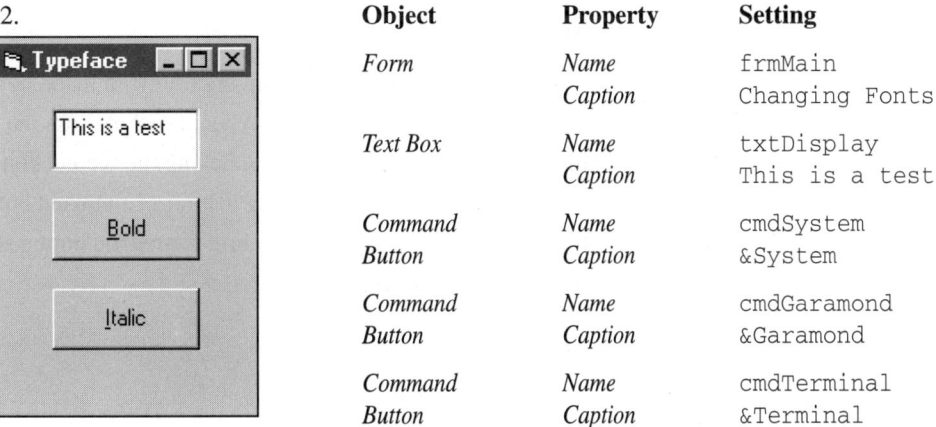

Object	Property	Setting
Form	*Name*	frmMain
	Caption	Changing Fonts
Text Box	*Name*	txtDisplay
	Caption	This is a test
Command Button	*Name*	cmdSystem
	Caption	&System
Command Button	*Name*	cmdGaramond
	Caption	&Garamond
Command Button	*Name*	cmdTerminal
	Caption	&Terminal

When the first Command button is clicked, the text in the Text box should change to a System font, when the second Command button is clicked, the text should change to a Garamond font (if your system does not have a Garamond font, select a font that you do have available), and when the third Command button is clicked, the text should change to a Terminal font. (**Hint**: the statement `txtDisplay.FontName = "System"` will change the text in the Text box to a System font.)

13.

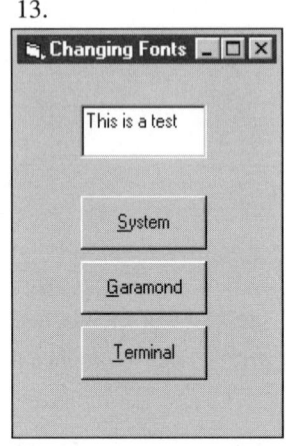

Object	Property	Setting
Form	*Name*	`frmMain`
	Caption	`Typeface`
Command	*Name*	`cmdBold`
Button	*Caption*	`&Bold`
Command2	*Name*	`cmdItalic`
Button	*Caption*	`&Italic`
Text box	*Name*	`txtDisplay`
	Text	`This is a test`

By clicking on the Text box, the user should be able to enter any desired text in nonboldface and nonitalic font. When the user clicks on the <u>B</u>old button, the text in the Text box should change to boldface, and when the user clicks on the <u>I</u>talic button, the text should change to italic. (**Hint**: Setting the Text property **FontBold** to **True** changes the font to boldface, while a **False** value removes boldface. Similarly, a **True** value for the property **FontItalic** sets Italic and a **False** value removes it. The removal of bold and italic should be accomplished when the Text box gets the focus.)

14. Write a Visual Basic application having three Command buttons and one Text box that is initially blank. Clicking the first Command button should produce the message `See no evil`. Clicking the second Command button should produce the message `Hear no evil`, and clicking the third Command button should produce the message `Speak no evil` in the Text box.

15. Write a Visual Basic Program having four Command buttons and one Text box with the initial message `Hello World`. When the user clicks the first Command button, the message should change to bold. Clicking the second button should change the text to a nonbold state. Similarly, clicking the third Command button should italicize the Text box message, and clicking the fourth Command button should ensure that the message is not italicized. (**Hint**: See Exercise 13.)

2.6 Common Programming Errors and Problems

One of the most frustrating problems for students learning Visual Basic is not being able to locate all of the elements needed to create an application. This usually means that either the Form, object Toolbox, or Properties window are missing from the design screen. To bring up the Form, either retrieve an existing project or select New Project from the File menu (hot-key sequence [Alt]+[F], then [N]). To bring up the object Toolbox or the Properties window, select the View option from the menu bar and then select the desired window.

A common error made by beginning programmers is forgetting to save a project at periodic intervals at design-time. Although you can usually get away without periodic saves, every experienced programmer knows the agony of losing work due to a variety of mistakes or an unexpected power outage. To avoid this, you should develop the habit of periodically saving your work.

Finally, the most consistently troublesome error occurs when you do not change a form or object's name immediately when you begin working with it. *Changing a name after you have added event code detaches the object from the code.* This occurs because the event code procedure name is based on the object's name at the time when the code is entered. The event-code doesn't become lost, it just becomes a **General** procedure (accessed via the Code window), because it is no longer attached to an existing object. After you locate the event code as a **General** procedure, you can either rename the procedure to the object's new name or copy and paste the code into the new object's event template.

2.7 Chapter Review

Key Terms

accelerator key	event	**MsgBox**
Cls	executable statement	nonexecutable statement
code module	focus	**Print**
Code window	form	properties
Command button	form module	run-time
comment	graphical user interface	sizing handles
controls	hot key	string
design screen	identifier	Text box
design-time	Label	Toolbar
dialog box	menu bar	Toolbox
empty string	methods	

Summary

1. In an object-based language the programmer uses pre-existing object types, while an object-oriented language permits creation of new object types and provides features called inheritance and polymorphism. Although Visual Basic does provide the means of creating new objects, since it does not provide a true inheritance feature, it is still classified as an object-based language.

2. Event-based programs execute program code depending on what events occur, which depends on what the user does.

3. GUIs are graphical user interfaces that provide the user with objects that recognize events, such as clicking a mouse.

4. An *application* is any program that can be run under a Windows Operating System.

5. The term *design-time* refers to the period of time when a Visual Basic application is being developed.

6. The term *run-time* refers to the period of time when an application is executing.

7. A Visual Basic program consists of a visual part and a language part. The visual part is provided by the objects used in the design of the graphical user interface, while the language part consists of procedural code.

8. The basic steps in developing a Visual Basic program are
   a. Create the graphical user interface.
   b. Set the properties of each object on the interface.
   c. Write procedural code.

9. A form is used during design-time to create a graphical user interface for a Visual Basic application. At run-time the form becomes a window.

10. The most commonly placed objects on a form are Command buttons, Labels, Text boxes, and Picture boxes.

11. Each object placed on a form has a **Name** property. Form names should begin with the prefix `frm`, Text boxes should be given a name beginning in `txt`, and Command buttons a name beginning in `cmd`. Identifiers must be chosen according to the following rules:
   a. The first character of the name must be a letter.
   b. Only letters, digits or underscores may follow the initial letter. Blank spaces, special characters, and punctuation marks are not allowed; use the underscore or capital letters to separate words in an identifier consisting of multiple words.
   c. An identifier can be no longer than 200 characters in Versions 4.0 and 5.0 (40 in Version 3.0).
   d. An identifier should not be a keyword.

2.8 Looking Further: The Help Facility

No matter how experienced you become at using Visual Basic, there will be times when you'll need some help either in performing a particular task, looking up the exact syntax of a statement, or finding the parameters required by a built-in function. While you are programming it is frequently very convenient to use Visual Basic's on-line help facility to find the answers to these questions. The on-line help facility provides immediate on-screen information about Visual Basic and is an extremely powerful programming aid. It can be accessed at any time by selecting the Help menu option, which displays the initial Help menu shown in Figure 2-58.

Figure 2-58

The Help Menu Options

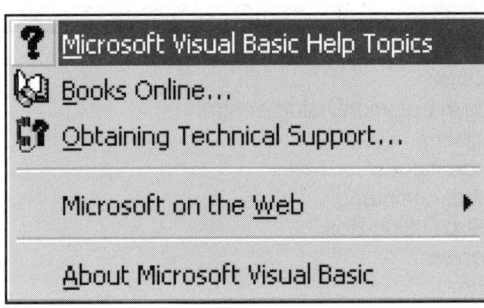

The most useful of the options shown in Figure 2-58 is the first option, which is highlighted in the figure. When you select this option, the Help Topics dialog box illustrated in Figure 2-59 is activated.

As indicated in Figure 2-59, the Index tab is active. The remaining two tabs, Contents and Find, can also be activated by clicking on them. Initially, and throughout your Visual Basic programming career, you will find the Index tab the most frequently used of the three tabs.

The Index tab is useful because it operates much like an index in a book, with one major improvement. In a book, after looking up the desired topic, you must manually turn to the referenced page or pages. In the on-line help facility, this look-up and display is automatic once you indicate the desired topic. Selection of the topic is accomplished by double-

Figure 2-59

The Help Topics Dialog Box

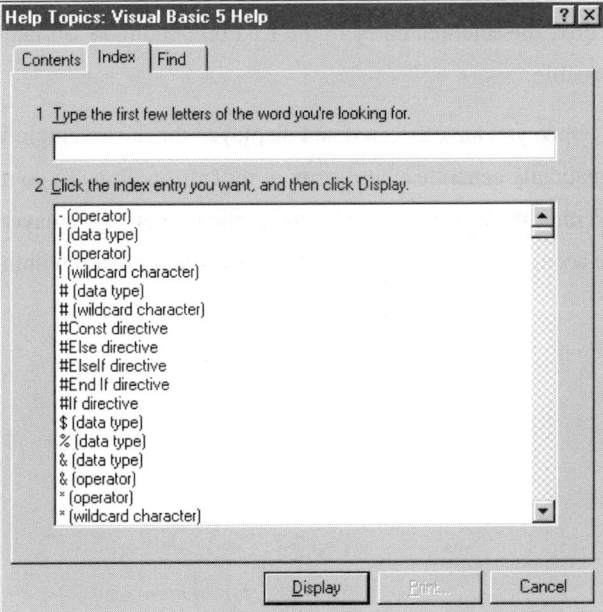

clicking on a topic shown in the index entry List box. If the topic you desire is not shown, simply type the topic's name in the first Text box. This will highlight the item in the index entry list box. Another means of locating the desired entry is to use the scroll bar to the right of the index entry box and manually move through each item.

Figure 2-60

The Indexed Help Tab with a Typed User Entry

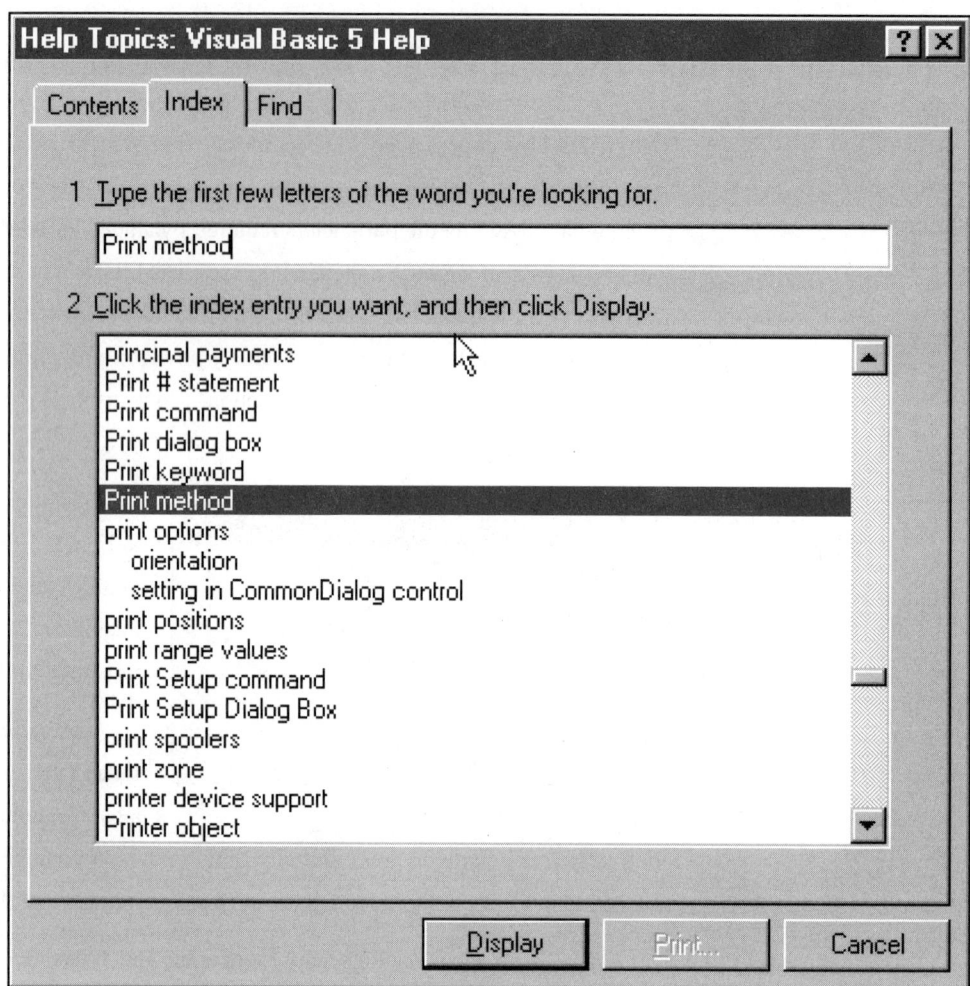

For example, in Figure 2-60, the topic `Print method` has been typed in the first Text box, and the List box entry for this topic has been selected. As each letter is typed in the Text box, the selected entry in the List box changes to match the input letters as closely as possible.

Once you have selected and displayed the desired topic in on-line help, you can automatically generate a hard copy of the information. To do this, select the Print Topic item from either the Options menu button at the top of the displayed information or the context menu accessed by clicking the right-mouse button from within the displayed information.

Data and Operations

3.1 Data Values and Arithmetic Operations

3.2 Variables and Declaration Statements

3.3 Assignment Statements

3.4 Using Intrinsic Functions

3.5 Common Programming Errors and Problems

3.6 Chapter Review

3.7 Looking Further: Basics of Forms Design

Visual Basic programs can process different types of data in different ways. For example, calculating the a company's income tax requires mathematical computations on numerical data, while sorting a list of names requires comparison operations using alphabetic data. In this chapter we introduce Visual Basic's elementary data types and the procedural operations that can be performed on them, with emphasis on numerical and string data.

3.1 Data Values and Arithmetic Operations

Visual Basic distinguishes between a number of fundamental types of data, such as integers, real numbers, character strings, boolean, date, currency, and so on. Table 3-1 lists all of the fundamental types recognized in Version 5.0, including their storage size and range of values (if you are unfamiliar with the concept of a byte, review Section 1.7). In this section we introduce the numerical, string, and boolean types. The remaining types are introduced in later sections.

Integer Values

An integer value in Visual Basic is any positive or negative number without a decimal point. Examples of valid integer values are

> 6   -12   +35   1000   186   -25821   +42

As these examples illustrate, integer constants, which are frequently referred to as integer numbers, or integers, for short, may either be signed (have a leading + or - sign) or unsigned (no leading + or - sign). No commas, decimal points, or special symbols, such as the dollar sign, are allowed. Examples of invalid integer constants are

> $187.62   3,532   4.   8,634,941   2,371.98   +7.0

Table 3-1 Fundamental Visual Basic Data Types

Type	Bytes of Storage	Range of Values
Byte	1	0 to 255
Integer	2	-32768 to 32767
Long	4	-2,147,483,648 to 2,147,483,647
Single 4		-3.402823E38 to -1.401298E-45 and +1.401298E-45 to +3.402823E38
Double 8		-1.79769313486232E308 to -4.94065645841247E-324 and +4.94065645841247E-324 to +1.79769313486232E308
String	1 per character	0 to approximately 65,500 characters (0 to 2E32 on 32-bit systems)
Boolean	2	True or False
Currency	8	-922337203685477.5808 to +922337203685477.5807
Date	8	January 1, 100 to December 31, 9999 (also includes space for the time as hours, minutes, and seconds)
Object	4	Any object reference
Variant (with numbers)	16	Any numeric value up to a Double.
Variant (with characters)	22+1 per character	0 to approximately 2 billion.

An integer constant can be any integer value between -32768, which is the smallest (most negative) value, to +32767, which is the largest (most positive) value. These values are defined by the 2-byte storage size required for all integers.[1]

Sometimes, larger integer numbers are required than those supported by the memory allocations shown in Table 3-1. For example, many financial applications use dates, such as 7/12/96. Notice in Table 3-1 that Visual Basic's Date type requires eight bytes of storage for each date, which is large enough to store both a date and a time. If a program must use and store many dates, where the time is not needed, the dates can be stored in a simple manner using integers. This is done by converting each date into an integer number representing the number of days from the turn of the century. This scheme makes it possible to store and sort dates, using a single integer number for each date. Unfortunately, for dates after 1987, the number of days from the turn of the century is larger than the maximum of 32,767 allowed by an integer.

To accommodate real application requirements such as this, Visual Basic provides for long integer values, which are referred to as Longs. A Long integer requires only four bytes of storage and can store integer values ranging from approximately - 2 billion to + 2 billion.

---

[1] It is interesting to note that in all cases the magnitude of the most negative integer allowed is always one more than the magnitude of the most positive integer. This is due to the method most commonly used to represent integers, called the two's complement representation. For an explanation of the two's complement representation, see Section 1.7.

Floating Point Values

A floating point value, which is also called a real number, is any signed or unsigned number having a decimal point. Examples of floating point values are

$$+10.625 \quad 5. \quad -6.2 \quad 3251.92 \quad 0.0 \quad 0.33 \quad -6.67 \quad +2.$$

Notice that the numbers 5., 0.0, and +2. are classified as floating point numbers, while the same numbers written without a decimal point (5, 0, +2) would be integer values. As with integer values, special symbols, such as the dollar sign and the comma, are not permitted in real numbers. Examples of invalid real numbers are

$$5,326.25 \quad 24 \quad 123 \quad 6,459 \quad \$10.29$$

Visual Basic supports two different categories of floating point numbers: single and double. The name single is derived from the term *single precision number* and *double* from *double precision number*. The difference between these two types of numbers is the amount of storage allocated for each type. Visual Basic requires a double precision number to use twice the amount of storage than that of a single precision number. In practice this means that a single precision constant in Visual Basic retains six decimal digits to the right of the decimal point and double precision constants retain fourteen digits.

Exponential Notation

Floating point numbers can be written in exponential notation, which is similar to scientific notation and is commonly used to express both very large and very small numbers in a compact form. The following examples illustrate how numbers with decimals can be expressed in exponential and scientific notation.

Decimal Notation	Exponential Notation	Scientific Notation
1625.	1.625E3	1.625×10^3
63421.	6.3421E4	6.3421×10^4
.00731	7.31E-3	7.31×10^{-3}
.000625	6.25E-4	6.25×10^{-4}

In exponential notation, the letter *E* stands for exponent. The number following the *E* represents a power of 10 and indicates the number of places the decimal point should be moved to obtain the standard decimal value. The decimal point is moved to the right if the number after the *E* is positive, or moved to the left if the number after the *E* is negative. For example, the E3 in the number 1.625E3 means to move the decimal place three places to the right, so that the number becomes 1625. The E-3 in the number 7.31E-3 means move the decimal point three places to the left, so that 7.31E-3 becomes .00731. Expressing a floating point number using exponential notation, using an *E* to denote the exponent, causes the number to be stored as a single precision value. Using a *D* in place of the *E* forces the number to be stored as a double precision value. In the absence of an explicit specification, the number is stored as a Variant type.

String Values

The third basic data value recognized by Visual Basic is a string value. Other names used for string values are messages, strings, and string literals. Strings were introduced in the previous chapter. To review, a string value consists of one or more characters enclosed within double quotes. Examples of valid character constants are

```
"A"
"**&!##!!"
"$3,256.22"
"25.68"
"VELOCITY"
"HELLO THERE WORLD!"
```

Table 3-2 The ANSI Uppercase Letter Codes			
Letter	ANSI Code	Letter	ANSI Code
A	01000001	N	01001110
B	01000010	O	01001111
C	01000011	P	01010000
D	01000100	Q	01010001
E	01000101	R	01010010
F	01000110	S	01010011
G	01000111	T	01010100
H	01001000	U	01010101
I	01001001	V	01010110
J	01001010	W	01010111
K	01001011	X	01011000
L	01001100	Y	01011001
M	01001101	Z	01011010

The number of characters within a string is the length of the value. For example, the length of the string value `"$3,256.22"` is nine and the length of the string constant `"A"` is one. Should it be required to include a double quote within a string constant, two double quotes are used. For example, the string `"They said ""Hello"" to me"` is a string of length 23 consisting of the characters

```
They(space)said(space)"Hello"(space)to(space)me
```

String constants are typically represented in a computer using the ANSI codes. ANSI, pronounced AN-SEE, is an acronym for American National Standards Institute. This code assigns individual characters to a specific pattern of 0s and 1s. Table 3-2 lists the correspondence between bit patterns and the uppercase letters of the alphabet used by the ANSI code.

Using Table 3-2, we can determine how the string constant `"SMITH"`, for example, is stored inside the computer. Using the ANSI code, this sequence of characters requires five bytes of storage (one byte for each letter) and would be stored as illustrated in Figure 3-1.

Figure 3-1

The Letters SMITH Stored Inside a Computer

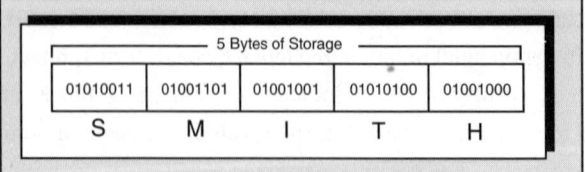

Boolean Values

There are only two boolean data values in Visual Basic. These values are the constants

True   False

The words **True** and **False** are restricted keywords in Visual Basic.

Boolean data is useful in programming because all programming languages have the ability to select a course of action based on the state of a programmer-specified condition.

Any condition has one of two possible outcomes—either the condition is satisfied or it is not. In computer terms a condition that is satisfied is considered to be **True** and a condition that is not satisfied is considered to be **False**. The two boolean constants in Visual Basic correspond to these outcomes and are used extensively in programs that incorporate decision-making statements.

Numeric Operations

Integers and real numbers may be added, subtracted, multiplied, divided, and raised to a power. The symbols for performing these and other numeric operations in Visual Basic are listed in Table 3-3.

Each of these numeric operators is referred to as a *binary operator* because it requires two operands to operate on. A *simple numeric expression* consists of a numeric binary operator connecting two arithmetic operands and has the syntax

Table 3-3 Visual Basic's Numeric Operators	
Operator	**Operation**
+	Addition
–	Subtraction
*	Multiplication
/	Division
\	Integer Division
^	Exponentiation (raising to a power)
Mod	Return a remainder

```
operand operator operand
```

Examples of simple numeric expressions are

```
6 + 2
17 - 5
12.75 + 9.3
0.06 * 14.8
26.7 / 3.03.1416 ^ 2
```

The spaces around the arithmetic operators in these examples are inserted strictly for clarity and may be omitted without affecting the value of the expression.

The value of any numeric expression can be displayed using either a **Print** or **MsgBox** statement. For example, the value of the expression 0.06 * 14.8 can be displayed on a form using the statement

```
Print 0.06 * 14.8
```

Here the expression, with no surrounding double quotes, is included directly in the **Print** statement. When this statement is executed, the indicated multiplication is performed and the output 0.888 is displayed on the form.

In addition to calculating and displaying the value of an expression, a **Print** statement can also include a message. For example, the **Print** statement

```
Print "The value of the expression 0.06 * 14.8 is"; 0.06 * 14.8
```

contains two items that will be printed directly on the form. The first item is a message, which is enclosed in double quotes, and the second item is an arithmetic expression. When an arithmetic expression is used, the **Print** method displays the numerical result of the expression. Positive numeric values are displayed with a single leading and trailing space, while negative values display a negative sign instead of the leading space. The semicolon between items causes Visual Basic to print one item immediately after another. Event Procedure 3-1 illustrates this statement within the context of a complete `Form_Click` event procedure.

Event Procedure 3-1

```
Private Sub Form_Click()
    Print "The value of the expression 0.06 * 14.8 is"; 0.06 * 14.8
End Sub
```
because it is " "

When this event procedure is executed the display produced on the screen is

```
The value of the expression .06 * 14.8 is  0.888
```

Notice that the space between items is produced by the leading space that Visual Basic always uses for positive numbers.

See if you can determine what output is produced by the Event Procedure 3-2:

Event Procedure 3-2

```
Private Sub Form_Click()
    Print "0.06 * 14.8"
    Print 0.06 * 14.8
    Print "0.06 * 14.8 is"; 0.06 * 14.8
End Sub
```

The first **Print** statement in Event Procedure 3-2 contains a message, which is enclosed in double quotes. As the message consists of the characters 0.06 * 14.8, these characters will be displayed by the **Print** statement when it is executed. The second **Print** statement does not contain a message because no double quotes are used. Thus, the value of the expression 0.06 * 14.8, which is 0.888, is calculated and displayed when this statement is executed. Finally, the third **Print** statement contains both a message and an expression. When this statement is executed the message will be displayed first, and the value of the arithmetic expression will be calculated and displayed next. This produces the output:

```
0.06 * 14.8 is 0.888
```

Figure 3-2

Program 3-1's Interface

Program 3-1 illustrates using **Print** statements to display the results of simple arithmetic expressions within the context of a complete program. The interface for this project is shown on Figure 3-2. As illustrated the form contains a Command button and a Picture box. The Picture box icon is in the top row in the second column of the Toolbox.

A Picture box is very similar to a Text box, with one important difference: unlike a Text box, which can be used for both input and output, a Picture box can only be used for output.

Table 3-4 The Properties Table for Program 3-1

Object	Property	Setting
Form	Name	`frmMain`
	Caption	`Program 3-1`
Picture Box	Name	`picShow`
	Height	1455
	Width	2175
	TabStop	`False`
Command Button	Name	`cmdOps`
	Caption	`&ShowOps`

For this application the only procedure will be for the Command button's **Click** event. The required code is listed in Program 3-1's Event Code.

Program 3-1's Event Code

```
Private Sub cmdOps_Click()
   picShow.Print "OPERATION"
   picShow.Print "15.2 + 2 ="; 15.2 + 2
   picShow.Print "15.2 - 2 ="; 15.2 - 2
   picShow.Print "15.2 * 2 ="; 15.2 * 2
   picShow.Print "15.2 / 2 ="; 15.2 / 2
   picShow.Print "15.2 ^ 2 ="; 15.2 ^ 2
End Sub
```

↓ this separates.

The output displayed in the Picture box by Program 3-1's Event procedure when the Command button is clicked is shown in Figure 3-3.

Expression Types

A numeric expression that contains only integer values is called an *integer expression*. The result of an integer expression can be either an integer or a floating point value. For example, 8 / 4 is the integer 2, while 15 / 2 is the floating point value 7.5. Similarly, an expression containing only floating point operands (single and double precision) is called a *floating point expression*. The result of such an expression can also be either an integer or a floating point value. An expression containing both integer and floating point operands is called a *mixed-mode expression*.

Figure 3-3

The Output Displayed by Program 3-1

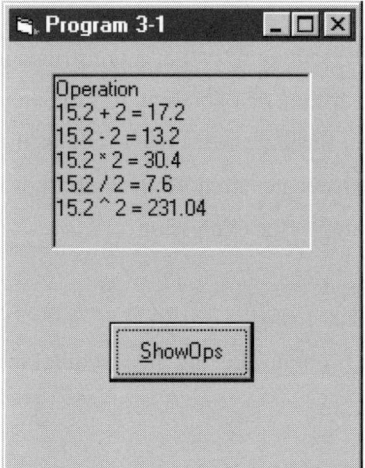

Integer Division

A special numeric operation supplied in Visual Basic is integer division, which is designated by the slash operator, (\). This operator divides two numbers and provides the result as an integer. When the result of the division is not an integer, the result is truncated (that is, the fractional part is dropped). Thus, 15 \ 2 is 7. This is calculated by first performing the normal division, 15 / 2 = 7.5, and then truncating the result to 7.

When an operand used in integer division is a floating point number, the floating point number is automatically rounded to the nearest integer before the division is performed. Thus,

> 14.6 \ 2 is calculated as 15 / 2 = 7.5, which is then truncated to 7.
> 14 \ 2.8 is calculated as 14 / 3 = 4.667, which is then truncated to 4.
> 14.6 \ 2.8 is calculated as 15 / 3 = 5, which is left as the integer 5.

The Mod Operator

There are times when we would like to retain the remainder of an integer division. To do this Visual Basic provides an arithmetic operator that captures the remainder when two integers are divided. This operator, called the modulus operator, uses the symbols Mod. For example,

```
9 Mod 4 is 1
17 Mod 3 is 2
14 Mod 2 is 0
```

Notice that in each case the result of the numeric expression is the remainder produced by the division of the second integer into the first. If any of the numbers used in the expression is a floating point number, the floating point number is automatically rounded to the nearest integer before calculating the remainder. Thus, 19 Mod 6.7 is 5, which is the same as 19 Mod 7, and 10.6 Mod 4.2 is 3, which is the same as 11 Mod 4.

A Unary Operator (Negation)

Besides the binary operators for addition, subtraction, multiplication, and division, Visual Basic also provides a few unary operators. One of these unary operators uses the same symbol that is used for binary subtraction (-). The minus sign used in front of a single numerical operand negates (reverses the sign of) the number. This operator can be used with all numeric types except the Byte type, because Bytes can only be positive values.

String Concatenation

String concatenation means the joining of two or more strings into a single string. Although string concatenation is not an arithmetic operation, it is the only operation that directly manipulates string data. Visual Basic provides two symbols, the ampersand (&) and the plus sign (+), for performing string concatenation. Both symbols produce the same effect when applied to string data. For example, the expression

```
"Hot" & " " & "Dog"
```

concatenates the three individual strings, "Hot ", " ", and "Dog" into the single string "Hot Dog". The same result is obtained using the + symbol in place of the & symbol.

Operator Precedence and Associativity

Besides such simple numeric expressions as 5 + 12 and .08 * 26.2, we frequently need to create more complex expressions. Visual Basic, like most other programming languages, requires that certain rules be followed when writing expressions containing more than one operator. These rules are

1. Two binary operators must never be placed adjacent to one another. For example, 12 / Mod 6 is invalid because the two binary operators / and Mod are placed next to each other. The expression 12 / -6, however, is valid and does not violate this rule because the - here is recognized as a unary operator that simply makes the +6 a -6. Thus, the result of this expression is -2.

2. Parentheses may be used to form groupings, and all expressions enclosed within parentheses are evaluated first. For example, in the expression (6 + 4) / (2 + 3), the 6 + 4 and 2 + 3 are evaluated first to yield 10 / 5. The 10 / 5 is then evaluated to yield 2. Sets of parentheses may also be enclosed by other parentheses. For example, the expression (2 * (3 + 7)) / 5 is valid. When parentheses are used within parentheses, the expressions in the innermost parentheses are always evaluated first. The evaluation continues from innermost to outermost parentheses until the expressions of all parentheses have been evaluated. The number of right-facing parentheses (( ) must always equal the number of left-facing parentheses ( )) so that there are no unpaired sets.

3. Parentheses cannot be used to indicate multiplication. The multiplication operator must be used. For example, the expression (3 + 4) (5 + 1) is invalid. The correct expression is (3 + 4) * (5 + 1).

As a general rule, parentheses should be used to specify logical groupings of operands and to indicate clearly to both the computer and any programmer reading the expression the intended order of arithmetic operations. In the absence of parentheses, expressions containing multiple operators are evaluated by the priority, or precedence, of each operator. Table 3-5 lists both the precedence and associativity of the operators considered in this section.

The precedence of an operator establishes its priority relative to all other operators. Operators at the top of Table 3-5 have a higher priority than operators at the bottom of the table. In expressions with multiple operators, the operator with the higher precedence is used before an operator with a lower precedence. For example, in the expression 6 + 4 / 2 + 3, the

Table 3-5 Arithmetic Operator Precedence and Associativity

Operation	Operator	Associativity
Exponentiation	^	left to right
Negation (unary)	–	left to right
Multiplication and division	* /	left to right
Integer division	\	left to right
Modulo arithmetic	Mod	left to right
Addition and subtraction	+ –	left to right

division is done before the addition, yielding an intermediate result of 6 + 2 + 3. The additions are then performed to yield a final result of 11.

When the minus sign precedes an operand, as in the expression -A ^ B, the minus sign negates (reverses the sign of) the number with a higher priority level than all other operators except exponentiation. For example, the expression -6 ^ 2 is calculated as -(6^2), which equals -36.

Expressions containing operators with the same precedence are evaluated according to their associativity. This means that evaluation for addition and subtraction, as well as multiplication and division, is from left to right and successive exponents are evaluated from right to left as each operator is encountered. For example, in the expression 8 + 40 / 8 * 2 + 4, the multiplication and division operators are of higher precedence than the addition operator and are evaluated first. Both the multiplication and division operators, however, are of equal priority. Therefore, these operators are evaluated according to their left-to-right associativity, yielding

```
8 + 40 / 8 * 2 + 4 =
8 +     5 * 2 + 4 =
8 +        10 + 4 =
```

The addition operations are now performed, again from left to right, yielding

```
18 + 4 = 22
```

When two exponentiation operations occur sequentially the resulting expression is evaluated from left to right. Thus, the expression 2^2^4 is evaluated as 4^4, which equals 256.

Exercises 3.1

1. Determine data types appropriate for the following data:
   a. The average of four speeds
   b. The number of transistors in a radio
   c. The length of the Golden Gate Bridge
   d. The part numbers in a machine
   e. The distance from Brooklyn, NY to Newark, NJ
   f. The names of inventory items

2. Convert the following numbers into standard decimal form:
   6.34E5   1.95162E2   8.395E1   2.95E-3   4.623E-4

3. Write the following decimal numbers using exponential notation:
   126.   656.23   3426.95   4893.2   .321   .0123   .006789

4. Show how the name KINGSLEY would be stored inside a computer using the ANSI code. That is, draw a figure similar to Figure 3-1 for the letters KINGSLEY.

5. Repeat Exercise 4 using the letters of your own last name.

6. Listed below are correct algebraic expressions and incorrect Visual Basic expressions corresponding to them. Find the errors and write corrected Visual Basic expressions.

Algebra	Visual Basic Expression
a. $(2)(3) + (4)(5)$	`(2)(3) + (4)(5)`
b. $\dfrac{6 + 18}{2}$	`6 + 18 / 2`
c. $\dfrac{4.5}{12.2 - 3.1}$	`4.5 / 12.2 - 3.1` 5/12.2 - 3.1
d. $4.6(3.0 + 14.9)$	`4.6(3.0 + 14.9)`
e. $(12.1 + 18.9)(15.3 - 3.8)$	`(12.1 + 18.9)(15.3 - 3.8)`

BoDMAS

7. Determine the value of the following expressions:
   a. `3 + 4 * 6`   = 27
   b. `3 * 4 / 6 + 6`
   c. `2.0 * 3 / 12 * 8 / 4`
   d. `10 * (1 + 7.3 * 3)`
   e. `20 - 2 / 6 + 3`
   f. `20 - 2 / (6 + 3)`
   g. `(20 - 2) / 6 + 3`
   h.. `(20 - 2) / (6 + 3)`

8. Assuming that `DISTANCE` has an integer value of 1, `V` has the integer value 50, `N` has the integer value 10, and `T` has the integer value 5, evaluate the following expressions:

   a. `N / T + 3`
   b. `V / T + N - 10 * DISTANCE`
   c. `V - 3 * N + 4 * DISTANCE`
   d. `DISTANCE / 5`
   e. `18 / T`
   f. `-T * N`
   g. `-V / 20`
   h. `(V + N) / (T + DISTANCE)`
   i. `V + N / T + DISTANCE`

9. Enter and run Program 3-1 on your computer system.

10. Modify the **Click** event procedure used in Program 3-1 so that the Picture box is cleared immediately before any data is displayed in the box.

11. Rewrite Program 3-1 to remove the Picture box and display the results directly on the screen generated by the form. (**Hint**: Review Program 2-1 in Chapter 2).

12. Add a Double-click event to Program 3-1 that causes the contents of the Picture box to be cleared when the user double-clicks the box.

13. Since Visual Basic uses different representations for storing integer, real, and string values, discuss how a program might alert Visual Basic to the data types of the various values it will be using.

Note: For the following exercise the reader should have an understanding of basic computer storage concepts. Specifically, if you are unfamiliar with the concept of a byte, refer to Section 1.7 before doing the next exercise.

14. Although the total number of bytes varies from computer to computer, memory sizes of 65,536 to more than 1 million bytes are not uncommon. In computer language, the letter *K* is used to represent the number 1024, which is 2 raised to the 10th power and the letter *m* is used to represent the number 1,048,576, which is 2 raised to the 20th power. Thus, a memory size of 640K is really 640 times 1024, or 655,360 bytes, and a memory size of 4MB is really 4 times 1,048,576 or 4,194,304 bytes. Using this information, calculate the actual number of bytes in

    a. A memory containing 512K bytes
    b. A memory containing 2M bytes
    c. A memory containing 8M bytes
    d. A memory consisting 16M bytes
    e. A memory consisting of 4M words, where each word consists of 2 bytes
    f. A memory consisting of 4M words, where each word consists of 4 bytes
    g. A floppy diskette that can store 1.44M bytes

3.2 Variables and Declaration Statements

All data used in an application is stored and retrieved from the computer's memory unit. Conceptually, individual memory locations in the memory unit are arranged like the rooms in a large hotel. Like hotel rooms, each memory location has a unique address ("room number"). Before high-level languages such as Visual Basic existed, memory locations were referenced by their addresses. For example, storing the integer values 45 and 12 in memory locations 1652 and 2548 (See Figure 3-4), respectively, required instructions equivalent to

put a 45 in location 1652
put a 12 in location 2548

Adding the two numbers just stored and saving the result in another memory location, for example at location 3000, required a statement comparable to

add the contents of location 1652
to the contents of location 2548
and store the result into location 3000

Clearly this method of storage and retrieval is a cumbersome process. In high-level languages like Visual Basic, symbolic names are used in place of actual memory addresses. Symbolic names used in this manner are called variables. A *variable* is simply a name given

Figure 3-4

Enough Storage for Two Integers

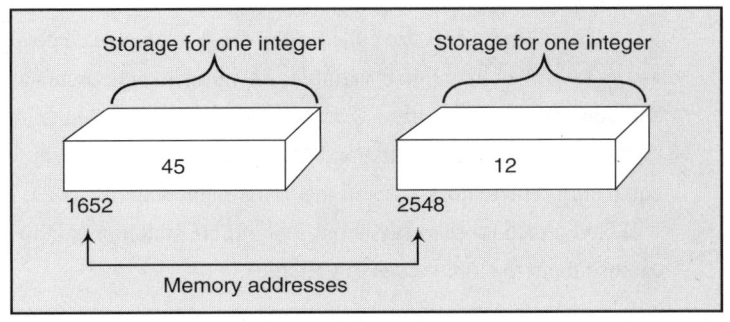

by the programmer to a memory storage location. The term variable is used because the value stored in the variable can change, or vary. For each name the program-

mer uses, the computer keeps track of the corresponding actual memory address. In our hotel room analogy, this is equivalent to putting a name on the door of a room and referring to the room by this name, such as the BLUE room, rather than using the actual room number.

In Visual Basic the selection of variable names is left to the programmer, as long as the following rules are observed:

1. The name must begin with a letter;
2. The name cannot contain arithmetic operators or any of the following symbols: . % & ! # @ $;
3. The name cannot exceed 255 characters;
4. The name cannot be a Visual Basic keyword, such as **Print**.

A variable name should also be a mnemonic. A *mnemonic* (pronounced NI-MONIC) is a memory aid. It should convey information about what the name represents. For example, a mnemonic name for a variable used to store a total value would be `sum` or `total`. Similarly, the variable name `width` is a good choice, if the value stored in the variable represents a width. Variable names that give no indication of the value stored, such as `r2d2`, `linda`, `bill`, and `dude` should not be selected.

Now, assume the first memory location illustrated in Figure 3-4, assigned address 1652, is given the name num1. Also assume that memory location 2548 is given the variable name `num2`, and memory location 3000 is given the variable name `total`, as illustrated in Figure 3-5.

Using these variable names, storing 45 in location 1652, 12 in location 2548, and adding the contents of these two locations is accomplished by the Visual Basic statements

```
num1 = 45
num2 = 12
total = num1 + num2
```

Figure 3-5

Naming Storage Locations

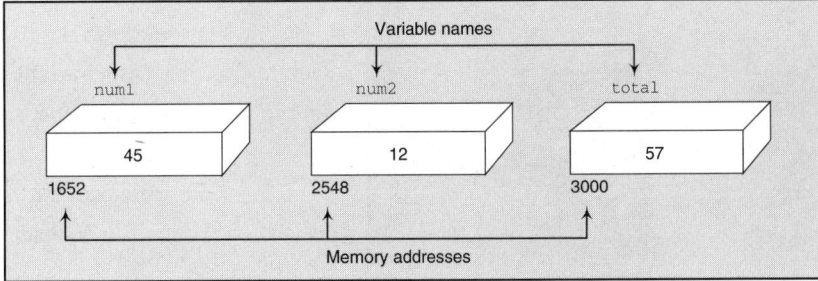

These statements are called *assignment statements* because they tell the computer to assign (store) a value into a variable. Assignment statements always have an equal (=) sign and one variable name immediately to the left of the equal sign. The value on the right of the equal sign is determined first and this value is assigned to the variable on the left of the equal sign. The blank spaces in the assignment statements are inserted for readability. We will have much more to say about assignment statements in the next section, but for now we can use them to store values in variables.

A variable name is useful because it frees the programmer from concern over where data is physically stored inside the computer. We simply use the variable name and let the computer worry about where in memory the data is actually stored. Before storing a value into a variable, however, we must clearly define the type of data that is to be stored in it. This requires telling the computer, in advance, the names of the variables that will be used for integers, the names that will be used for real numbers, and the names that will be used to store the other Visual Basic data types.

Declaration Statements

Naming a variable and specifying the data type that can be stored in it are accomplished using *declaration statements*. Declaration statements placed within a procedure are non-executable statements that have the general syntax

> **Dim** *variable-name* As *data-type*

where *data-type* designates any of the Visual Basic data types listed in Table 3-1, such as Integer, Single, Boolean, and String, and *variable-name* is a user-selected variable name. For example, the declaration statement

```
Dim total As Integer
```

declares total as the name of a variable capable of storing an integer value. Variables used to hold single-precision values are declared using the keyword **Single**, variables that will be used to hold double-precision values are declared using the keyword **Double**, variables that will be used to hold boolean values are declared using the keyword **Boolean**, and variables used to hold strings are declared using the keyword **String**. For example, the statement

```
Dim firstnum As Single
```

declares firstnum as a variable that can be used to store a single precision value (a number with a decimal point). Similarly, the statement

```
Dim secnum As Double
```

declares secnum as a variable that can be used to store a double precision value, and the declaration statements

```
Dim logical As Boolean
Dim message As String
```

declare logical as a boolean variable and message as a string variable.

Figure 3-6

Program 3-2's Interface

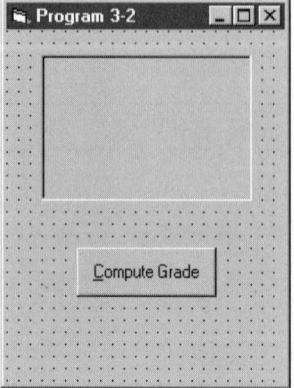

Table 3-6 The Properties Table for Program 3-2

Object	Property	Setting
Form	Name	frmMain
	Caption	Program 3-2
Picture Box	Name	picShow
	Height	1455
	Width	2175
	TabStop	False
Command Button	Name	cmdOps
	Caption	&Compute Grade

Although declaration statements may be placed anywhere within a procedure, most declarations are typically grouped together and placed immediately after the procedure's header line. In all cases, however, a variable should be declared before it can be used. If a variable is not declared, it is assigned the Variant type by default.

Figure 3-7

The Output Displayed by Program 3-2

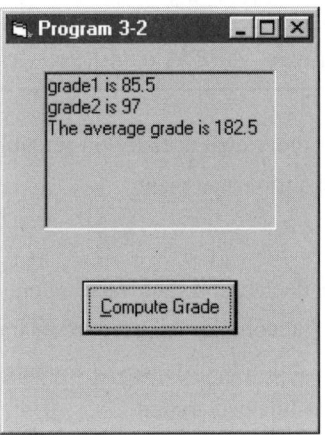

Program 3-2 illustrates using declaration statements within the context of a complete application. Except for the form and Command button captions, the application interface, shown in Figure 3-6, is essentially the same as we used in Program 3-1. As illustrated, the form contains a Command button and a Picture box.

For this application, the only procedure will be for the Command button's **Click** event. The required code is listed in Program 3-2's Event Code.

Program 3-2's Event Code

```
Private Sub cmdOps_Click()
    Dim grade1 As Single 'declare grade1 as a Single
    Dim grade2 As Single 'declare grade2 as a Single
    Dim total As Single 'declare total as a Single
    Dim average As Single 'declare average as a Single

    grade1 = 85.5
    grade2 = 97
    total = grade1 + grade2
    average = total / 2
    picShow.Print "grade1 is"; grade1
    picShow.Print "grade2 is"; grade2
    picShow.Print "The average grade is"; average
End Sub
```

blank line → (handwritten annotation)

Although the placement of the declaration statements in the event procedure is straightforward, notice the blank line after these statements. Placing a blank line after variable declarations is a common programming practice that improves both a procedure's appearance and readability: we will adopt this practice for all of our procedures. The output displayed by Program 3-2's event procedure when the Command button is clicked, is shown Figure 3-7.

```
                          Programmers' Notes

Atomic Data

The numeric and boolean variables we have declared have all been used to store atomic data values. An
atomic data value is a value that is considered a complete entity by itself and not decomposable into a
smaller data type supported by the language. For example, although an integer can be decomposed into
individual digits, Visual Basic does not have a numerical digit data type. Rather, each integer is regarded
as a complete value by itself and, as such, is considered atomic data. Similarly, since the integer data
type only supports atomic data values, it is said to be an atomic data type. As you might expect, boolean
and all floating point data types are atomic data types also. The string data type is not considered an
atomic data type because it is easily decomposable into individual characters and each string can be con-
structed by concatenation of individual characters.
```

Single-line Declarations

Visual Basic permits combining multiple declarations into one statement, using the syntax

> **Dim** *var-1* As *data-type*, *var-2* As *data-type*,...,*var-n* As *data-type*

Using this syntax, the four individual declaration statements used in Program 3-2 can be combined into the single declaration statement[2]

```
Dim grade1 As Single, grade2 As Single, total As Single, average As Single
```

Notice that in a single-line declaration each variable must still be declared, individually, with its own data type and that commas are used to separate declarations. Unfortunately, there is no way to declare multiple instances of a single data type using only one **As** keyword. For example, the single-line declaration

```
Dim grade1, grade2, total, average As Single
```

does not declare all four variables as single precision variables. Rather, when a specific data type is omitted, the variable is declared as the default **Variant** data type. Thus, this declaration is actually a shortened form of the declaration

```
Dim grade1 As Variant, grade2 As Variant, total As Variant, average as Single
```

At the end of this section we will describe the characteristics of the Variant data type. In certain situations, for example, when a data type is not known before hand, the **Variant** type becomes extremely useful. Unfortunately, however, it consumes four times as much memory space as a Single variable (16 as opposed to 4 bytes) and is less efficient in numeric expressions than pure numeric types. Thus, when the data type of a variable is known, it is more efficient to declare it with its actual data type.

---

[2]There are two schools of thought on using single-line declarations. Some programmers insist that variables of the same data type should be declared, space permitting, on the same line; others insist, with equal vehemence, that each variable should be declared on an individual line with an optional comment as to its purpose. This second approach also tends to reduce errors that inadvertently create Variant variables. We prefer a middle ground. Where a single-line declaration can be used to save space it is used. If a comment on an individual variable is advantageous, we will use separate declaration lines.

Introduction to Visual Basic

In the case of a String declaration, an optional length specifier can be applied to individual variables. For example, the declaration

```
Dim S2 As String*20
```

declares S2 to always be a fixed-length string variable consisting of 20 characters. If you try to place more than 20 characters in this string, the string will be truncated. If you use less than 20 characters, the string will automatically be padded with trailing spaces to total 20 characters. In the absence of a length specification, a declared string defaults to a variable-length that expands or contracts, as data is assigned to it. For example, consider the following section of code:

```
Dim S As String, S4 As String*4
S = "Algorithm"
S4 = "Algorithm"
Print "S = "; S
Print "S4 = "; S4
```

The output produced on the screen by this code is

```
S = Algorithm
S4 = Algo
```

This output is produced because S has been declared as a variable-length string. As such, S expands to include all of the characters assigned to it. S4, however, has been declared as a fixed-length string that can only accommodate 4 characters. Thus, when the string "Algorithm" is assigned to S4, only the first four characters are actually stored.

Initialization

The first time a value is stored in a variable, the variable is said to be *initialized*. In Visual Basic all declared numeric variables are initialized, by default, to zero. Thus, if you print the value of a declared numeric variable before you explicitly assign it a value, the displayed value will be 0. Similarly, all declared variable length strings are initialized to zero length strings containing no characters at all. Fixed length strings are not initialized and retain whatever characters ("garbage" values) happen to be in the string's allocated memory space.

The Option Explicit Statement

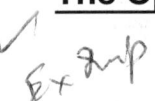

Specifying the data type of a variable, using a declaration statement, is referred to as *explicit data typing*. Programming languages that require all variables to be declared by declaration statements before they can be used, are called *strongly typed* languages. In this regard, Visual Basic is considered a weakly typed language because it does not require a declaration statement for every variable. In the absence of a declaration, Visual Basic permits identifying the data type of a variable by appending one of the type-declaration characters listed in Table 3-7 to the end of the variable's name.[3] If no type-declaration character is used, the variable defaults to the Variant type.

Table 3-7 Type Declaration Characters

Data Type	Type-Declaration Character	Example
Integer	%	count%
Long	&	longcount&
Single	!	grade!
Double	#	yield#
Currency	@	dollar@
String	$	message$
Variant	(None)	invalue

[3]There are no type-declaration characters for the other data types, such as Boolean and Date.

Figure 3-8

Entering the Option Explicit Statement

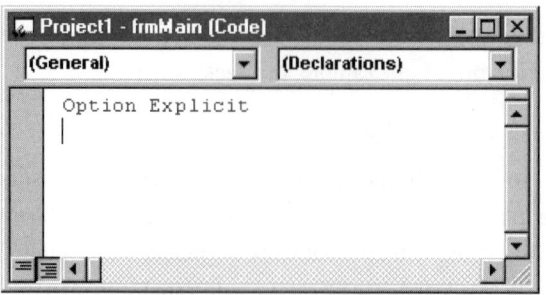

For example, if the variables ALPHA%, BETA&, GAMMA!, DELTA#, and SIGMA$ are used in an event procedure without first being explicitly declared, the data types for the variables would be an integer, a long, a single, a double, and a string, respectively.

The use of implied data declarations is a carry-over from very early versions of Basic. In Visual Basic this implied data typing can be changed using an **Option Explicit** statement, which provides a means of creating strongly typed programs. This is accomplished in the Code Window by placing this statement in the **(Declarations)** section of the **(General)** object, as shown in Figure 3-8.

When an **Option Explicit** statement is placed in the declarations section of the **General** object, it is applied to all procedures contained within the form module (that is, every procedure entered in the form's Code window). This statement informs Visual Basic that no implied declarations are to be accepted in any procedure. The effect of this statement is that Visual Basic will issue an error message for any undeclared variable, which eliminates an otherwise common and troublesome error caused by the misspelling of a variable's name within a program. For example, assume that a variable named distance is declared using the statement

```
Dim distance As Double
```

Now assume that this variable is assigned a value, but is later misspelled in the statement

```
mpg = distnce / gallons
```

Without the **Option Explicit** statement, Visual Basic would consider distnce as a new variable of type **Variant**. Variants are initialized with an empty value that is different from either a 0 or the zero-length string, "". When used in a numeric expression, the empty value is treated as a 0, and when used as a string, the empty value becomes a zero length string. Thus, in the previous numeric expression a value of zero would be assigned to

Figure 3-9

Setting the Option Explicit Default

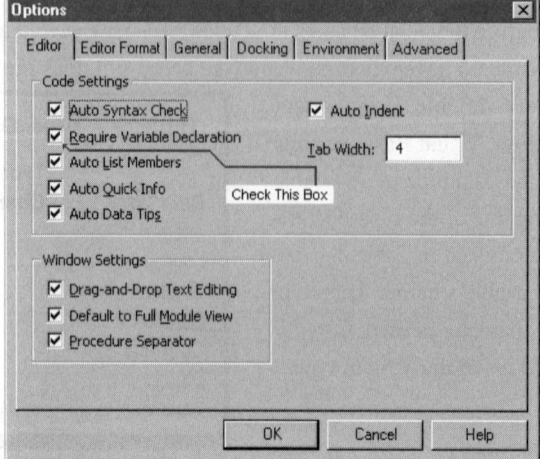

distnce, resulting in a calculated result of zero for mpg. Finding this error, or even knowing that an error occurred, could be extremely troublesome. Such errors are impossible when the **Option Explicit** statement is used, because the interpreter will highlight distnce in the Code window when the program is run and display the error message Variable

Programmers' Notes

The Option Explicit Statement

The **Option Explicit** statement can be placed in each event procedure separately, or it can be placed once in the (**Declarations**) section of the (**General**) form object. Placing the **Option Explicit** statement in the General declarations section activates it for every form module procedure, which is any procedure entered in the form's Code window. To automatically have this statement inserted into the (**Declarations**) section of each form module:

1. From the <u>T</u>ools menu select <u>O</u>ption.

2. Click on the Editor tab.

3. Click on the Require Variable Declaration box so that a check mark (✓) appears.

not defined. The interpreter cannot, of course, detect when one declared variable is typed in place of another variable.

All subsequent applications written in this text will include an **Option Explicit** statement within the (**General**) object's (**Declarations**) and explicitly declare all variable names in each procedure. The explicit declaration of variables is considered a good programming practice because it provides the programmer with an opportunity to carefully decide on variable names and their data types at the start of an application. It also provides a summary of all variables that have been used, which is extremely helpful if additional variables need to be named.

In order to have the **Option Explicit** statement automatically supplied by Visual Basic in every application that you create, without the need for you to type it in, do the following:

1. From the <u>T</u>ools menu select <u>O</u>ptions.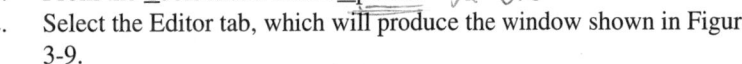

2. Select the Editor tab, which will produce the window shown in Figure 3-9.

 3. Click on the Require Variable Declaration box so that a check mark (✓) appears.

Specifying Storage Allocation

Declaration statements perform both a software and a hardware function. From a software perspective, declaration statements provide a convenient, up-front list of all variables and their data types. In addition to this software role, declaration statements also serve a distinct hardware task. Since each data type has its own storage requirements (see Table 3-1), the interpreter can only allocate sufficient storage for a variable after it knows the variable's data type. Because variable declarations provide this information, they also inform the interpreter of the physical memory storage that must be reserved for each variable. (In the hotel analogy introduced at the beginning of this section, this is equivalent to connecting adjoining rooms to form larger suites.)

Figure 3-10c

Defining the Double Variable Named secnum

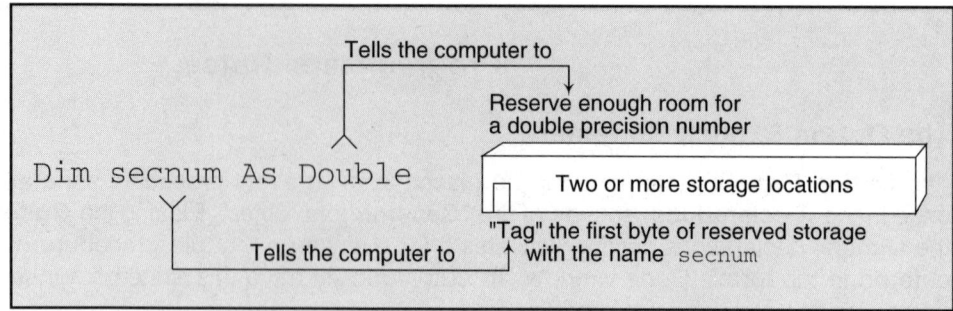

Figure 3-10d

Defining the Logical Variable Named key

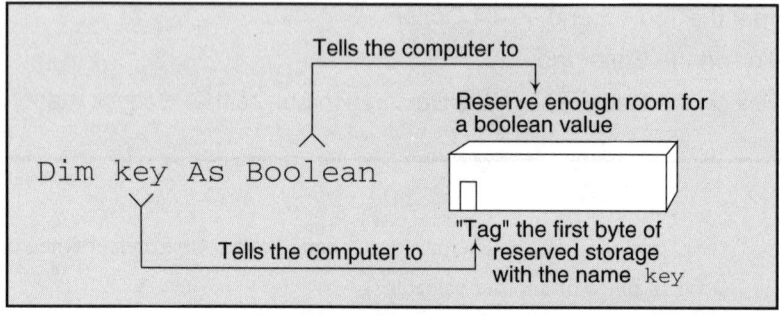

Figure 3-10a

Defining the Integer Variable Named total

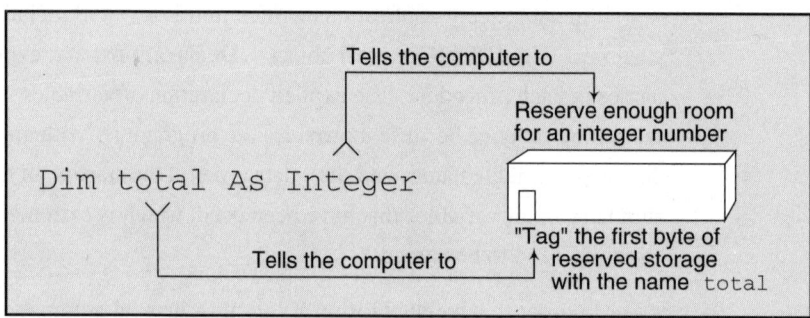

Figure 3-10b

Defining the Single Variable Named firstnum

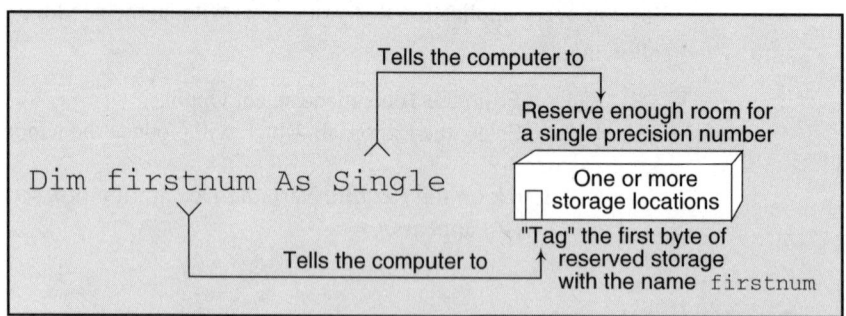

Figure 3-10 illustrates the series of operations set in motion by declaration statements in performing their memory allocation function. As illustrated, declaration statements cause both sufficient memory to be allocated for each data type and "tag" the reserved memory locations with a name. This name is, of course, the variable's name.

Within a program, the declared variable name is used by a programmer to reference the contents of the variable (that is, the variable's value). Where in memory this value is stored is generally of little concern to the programmer. Visual Basic, however, must be concerned with where each value is stored. In this task the interpreter uses the variable's name to locate the desired value. Knowing the variable's data type allows the interpreter to access the correct number of locations for each type of data.

The Variant Data Type[4]

The **Variant** data type in Visual Basic is capable of storing many kinds of data. Initially, a value stored in a **Variant** variable is stored as the data type requiring the least amount of storage. The stored value can then change, depending on the operation applied to it, or the stored value can remain the same but temporarily change data type within a computation.

For example, consider the following code:

```
Dim thisval   ' declare a Variant by default
thisval = "25" ' store the 2-character string "25"
Print "thisval - 5 ="; thisval - 5
Print "thisval & ""cents"" ="; thisval & "cents"
Print "thisval + ""cents"" ="; thisval + "cents
Print "thisval & ""5"" ="; thisval & "5"
Print "thisval + ""5"" ="; thisval + "5"
Print "thisval & 5 ="; thisval & 5
Print "thisval + 5 ="; thisval + 5
```

The display produced on the screen by this code is

```
thisval - 5 = 20
thisval & "cents" =25cents
thisval + "cents" =25cents
thisval & "5" =255
thisval + "5" =255
thisval & 5 =255
thisval + 5 = 30
```

In this particular example the value actually stored in thisval is always the string "25"; however, its usage changes from a string to a numeric within the various expressions. In the first **Print** statement the interpreter converts the string "25" into the number 25 and subtracts 5 from it, to produce a value of 20. In both the second and third **Print** statements

```
Print "thisval & ""cents"" ="; thisval & "cents"
Print "thisval + ""cents"" ="; thisval + "cents
```

the value in thisval is treated as a string in both expressions. Thus, both string concatenation operators (& and +) produce the same result, namely an output of 25cents. This same treatment of thisval as a string is retained when the string "5" is concatenated using the statements

```
Print "thisval & ""5"" = "; thisval & "5"
Print "thisval + ""5"" = "; thisval + "5"
```

The string value produced by both of these statements is 255. Now notice what happens when we use the numeric value 5 in the last two **Print** statements. The concatenation operator (&) in the statement

```
Print "thisval & 5 ="; thisval & 5
```

---

[4]This topic may be omitted on first reading with no loss of subject continuity.

clearly informs Visual Basic to perform a string concatenation, which again results in a string value of 255. But in the case of the expression `thisval + 5` used in the last **Print** statement

```
Print "thisval + 5 ="; thisval + 5
```

the interpreter assumes we mean arithmetic addition, and produces the value 30.

The importance of this example is to illustrate that **Variant** data can convert to various data types, depending on its usage. Many times this is an advantage, especially when data must be entered by a user. In such cases, it is very helpful to first store the entered data as a variant, and then determine its exact type. We shall see how to do this in Section 7.2.

In almost all other cases when we know the type of value being stored, it is much more efficient to avoid a **Variant** declaration by specifying the variable as the appropriate data type directly. Doing so saves memory storage space and avoids the requirement of the interpreter first determining the proper data representation, before evaluating an expression.

Exercises 3.2

1. State whether the following variable names are valid or not. If they are invalid, state the reason why.

prod_a	c1234	abcd	-c3	12345
newbal	Print	$total	new bal	a1b2c3d4
9ab6	sum.of	average	grade1	fin_grade

2. a. State whether the following variable names are valid or not. If they are invalid, state the reason why.

salestax	a243	r2d2	first_num	cc_a1
harry	sue	c3p0	average	sum
maximum	okay	a	awesome	go forit
3sum	for	tot.a1	c$five	newpay

   b. List which of the valid variable names found in Exercise 2a. should not be used because they clearly are not mnemonics.

3. a. Write a declaration statement to declare that the variable `count` will be used to store an integer. *Dim count As Integer*

   b. Write a declaration statement to declare that the variable `grade` will be used to store a single precision number. *Dim grade As Single*

   c. Write a declaration statement to declare that the variable `yield` will be used to store a double precision number. *Dim yield As Double*

4. For each of the following, write a single-line declaration statement:

   a. `num1`, `num2`, and `num3` used to store integer numbers

   b. `grade1`, `grade2`, `grade3`, and `grade4` used to store single precision numbers

   c. `tempa`, `tempb`, and `tempc` used to store double precision numbers

   d. `message1` and `message2` used to store strings *Dim message1 As String*

   e. `message1` and `message2` used to store fixed-length strings consisting of 15 characters each

5. For each of the following, write a single-line declaration statement:
    a. `firstnum` used to store an integer and `secnum` used to store a single precision number
    b. `speed` used to store a single precision number and `distance` used to store a double precision number
    c. `years` to store an integer, `yield` to store a single precision number, and `maturity` used to store a fixed-length string consisting of 8 characters

6. Rewrite each of these declaration statements as three individual declarations.
    a. `Dim month As Integer, day As Integer, year As Integer`
    b. `Dim hours As Single, rate As Single`
    c. `Dim price As Double, amount As Double, taxes As Double`
    d. `Dim inkey As String, choice As String * 5`

7. a. Enter and run Program 3-2 on your computer.
    b. Rewrite the event procedure in Program 3-2 so that it uses a single-line declaration statement.

8. a. Determine what event invokes the following procedure and the effect of each statement in the procedure.

    ```
    Private Sub cmdButton1_Click()
       Dim num1 As Integer, num2 As Integer, total As Integer

       picShow.Cls
       num1 = 25
       num2 = 30
       total = num1 + num2
       picShow.Print num1; " +"; num2; " ="; total
    End Sub
    ```

    b. What output will be printed when the event procedure listed in Exercise 8a. is run?

9. Write a Visual Basic program that stores the sum of the integer numbers 12 and 33 in a variable named sum. Have your program display the value stored in sum, along with an appropriate message telling the user what is being displayed. The display should appear in a Picture box when a Command button is pushed. There should also be a Command button to clear the Picture box display.

10. Write a Visual Basic program that stores the value 16 in the integer variable named `length` and the value 18 in the integer variable named `width`. Have your program calculate the value assigned to the variable perimeter, using the assignment statement

    ```
    perimeter = 2 * (length + width)
    ```

    and display the value stored in the variable perimeter. The display should appear in a Picture box when a Command button is clicked. There should also be a second Command button to clear the Picture box display. Make sure to declare all the variables as integers at the beginning of the event procedure.

11. Write a Visual Basic program that stores the integer value 16 in the variable num1 and the integer value 18 in the variable num2. Have your program calculate the total of these

numbers and their average. The total should be stored in an integer variable named total and the average in an integer variable named average. (Use the statement average = total/2 to calculate the average.) The display of the total and average should appear in a Picture box when a Command button is pushed. There should also be a second Command button to clear the Picture box display. Make sure to declare all the variables as integers at the beginning of the event procedure.

12. Repeat Exercise 11, but store the number 15 in num1 instead of 16. With a pencil, write down the average of num1 and num2. What do you think your program will store in the integer variable that you used for the average of these two numbers? What change must you make in the event procedure to ensure that the correct answer will be printed for the average?

13. Write a Visual Basic program that stores the number 105.62 in the variable firstnum, 89.352 in the variable secnum, and 98.67 in the variable thirdnum. Have your program calculate the total of the three numbers and their average. The total should be stored in the variable total and the average in the variable average. (Use the statement average = total/3 to calculate the average.) The display of the total and average should appear in a Picture box when a Command button is pushed. There should also be a second Command button to clear the Picture box display. Make sure to declare all the variables as either Single or Double at the beginning of the event procedure.

14. Every variable has at least two items associated with it. What are these two items?

Note: For Exercises 15 through 17: Use the storage allocations given in Table 3-1 and assume that variables are assigned storage in the order they are declared.

15. Using Figure 3-11, and assuming that the variable name miles is assigned to the byte at memory address 159, determine the addresses corresponding to each variable declared in the following statements:

```
Dim miles As Single
Dim count As Integer, num As Integer
Dim distance As Double, temp As Double
```

16. a. Using Figure 3-11, and assuming that the variable name rate is assigned to the byte having memory address 159, determine the addresses corresponding to each variable declared in the following statements. Also fill in the appropriate bytes with the data stored in each string variable (use letters for the characters, not the computer codes that would actually be stored).

```
Dim rate As Single
Dim message As String * 4
Dim taxes As Double
Dim num As Integer, count As Integer
message = "OKAY"
```

b. Repeat Exercise 16a, but substitute the actual byte patterns that a computer using the ANSI code would use to store the characters in the message variable. (**Hint**: Use Table 3-2.)

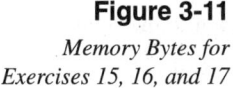

Figure 3-11

Memory Bytes for Exercises 15, 16, and 17

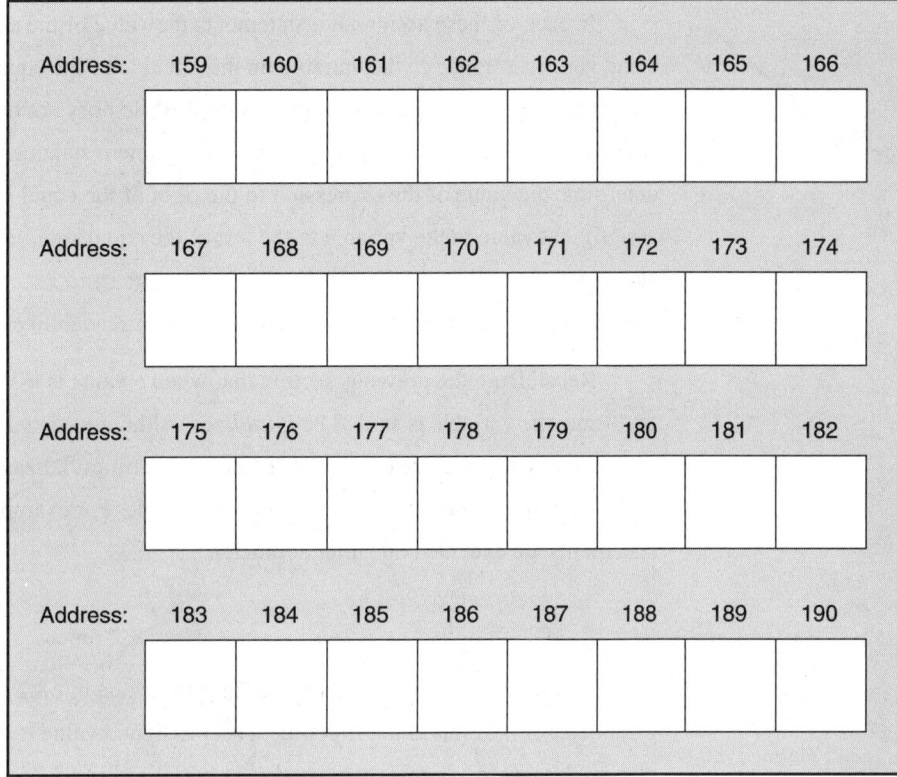

17. a. Using Figure 3-11, and assuming that the variable named `message` is assigned to the byte at memory address 159, determine the addresses corresponding to each variable declared in the following statements. Also, fill in the appropriate bytes with the data stored in the variables (use letters for the characters and not the computer codes that would actually be stored).

```
Dim message As String * 20
message = "HAVE A WONDERFUL DAY"
```

b. Repeat Exercise 17a. but substitute the actual byte patterns that a computer using the ANSI code would use to store the characters in each of the declared variables. (**Hint**: Use Table 3-2.)

3.3 Assignment Statements

We have already used simple assignment statements in the previous section. An assignment statement provides the most basic way to both assign a value to a variable and to perform calculations. This statement has the syntax

> variable = expression

The simplest expression in Visual Basic is a single constant, and in each of the following assignment statements, the expression to the right of the equal sign is a constant:

```
length = 25
width = 17.5
```

In each of these assignment statements the value of the constant to the right of the equal sign is assigned to the variable on the left side of the equal sign. It is extremely important to note that the equal sign in Visual Basic does not have the same meaning as an equal sign in algebra. The equal sign in an assignment statement tells the computer to first determine the value of the expression to the right of the equal sign and then to store (or assign) that value in the variable to the left of the equal sign. In this regard, the Visual Basic statement `length = 25` is read `"length is assigned the value 25."` The blank spaces in the assignment statement are inserted for readability only.

Recall from the previous section that when a value is assigned to a variable for the first time, the variable is said to be *initialized*. Although Visual Basic automatically initializes all explicitly declared variables to zero, the term initialization is frequently used to refer to the first time a user places a value into a variable. For example, assume the following statements are executed one after another:

```
temperature = 68.2
temperature = 70.6
```

The first assignment statement assigns the value of 68.2 to the variable named `temperature`. If this is the first time a user assigned value is stored in the variable, it is also acceptable to say that "temperature is initialized to 68.2." The next assignment statement causes the computer to assign a value of 70.6 to `temperature`. The 68.2 that was in `temperature` is overwritten with the new value of 70.6, because a variable can only store one value at a time. In this regard, it is sometimes useful to think of the variable to the left of the equal sign as a temporary parking spot in a huge parking lot. Just as an individual parking spot can only be used by one car at a time, each variable can only store one value at a time. The "parking" of a new value in a variable automatically causes the computer to remove any value previously parked there.

In its most common form, a Visual Basic expression is any combination of constants, variables, and operators that can be evaluated to yield a value[5]. Thus, the expression in an assignment statement can be used to perform calculations using the arithmetic operators introduced in Section 3.1 (see Table 3-3). Examples of assignment statements using expressions containing these operators are

```
sum = 3 + 7
difference = 15 - 6
taxes = 0.05 * 14.6
tally = count + 1
newtotal = 18.3 + total
price = 6.58 * quantity
totalweight = weight * factor
average = sum / items
newval = number ^ power
```

---

[5] Expressions can also include functions, which are presented in the next section.

Figure 3-12

Values Stored in the Variables

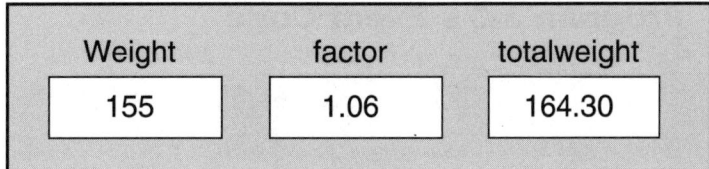

Weight	factor	totalweight
155	1.06	164.30

As always in an assignment statement, the equal sign directs the computer to first calculate the value of the expression to the right of the equal sign and then store this value in the variable to the left of the equal sign. For example, in the assignment statement `totalweight = weight * factor`, the expression `weight * factor` is first evaluated to yield a value. This value, which is a number, is then stored in the variable `totalweight`.

In writing assignment statements, you must be aware of two important considerations. Since the expression to the right of the equal sign is evaluated first, all variables used in the expression must be assigned values, if the result is to make sense. For example, the assignment statement `totalweight = weight * factor` will only cause a valid number to be stored in totalweight if the programmer first takes care to put valid numbers in weight and factor. Thus, the sequence of statements:

```
weight = 155.0
factor = 1.06
totalweight = weight * factor
```

ensures that we know the values being used to obtain the result that will be stored in the variable to the left of the equal sign. Figure 3-12 illustrates the values stored in the variables `weight`, `factor`, and `totalweight`.

The second consideration to keep in mind is that, since the value of an expression is stored in the variable to the left of the equal sign, there must only be one variable listed in this position. For example, the assignment statement

```
amount + extra = 1462 + 10 - 24
```

this is illegal . ✓

write .

is invalid. The right-side expression evaluates to the integer 1448, which can only be stored in a variable. Since `amount + extra` is not the valid name of a memory location (it is not a valid variable name), the interpreter does not know where to store the value 1448.

Figure 3-13

Determining the Volume of a Cylinder

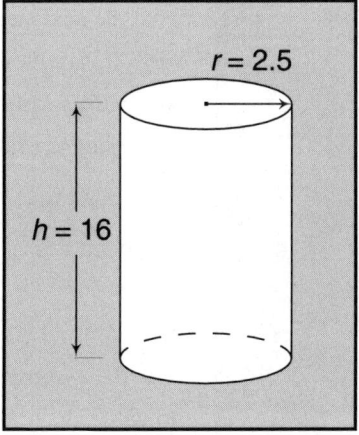

$r = 2.5$

$h = 16$

Program 3-3 illustrates the use of assignment statements to calculate the volume of a cylinder. As illustrated in Figure 3-13, the volume of a cylinder is determined by the formula, Volume = $\pi r^2 h$, where r is the radius of the cylinder, h is the height, and π is the constant 3.1416 (accurate to four decimal places).

The interface for Program 3-3 is shown on Figure 3-14. For this application, the only procedure will be for the Command button's **Click** event. The required code is listed in Program 3-1's Event Code.

Introduction to Visual Basic

Program 3-3's Event Code

```
Private Sub cmdVol_Click()
    Dim radius As Single, height As Single, volume As Single

    picShow.Cls
    radius = 2.5
    height = 16.0 ' Note: this will get changed to 16#
    volume = 3.1416 * radius ^ 2 * height
    picShow.Print "The volume of the cylinder is"; volume;
End Sub
```

Figure 3-14

Program 3-3's Interface

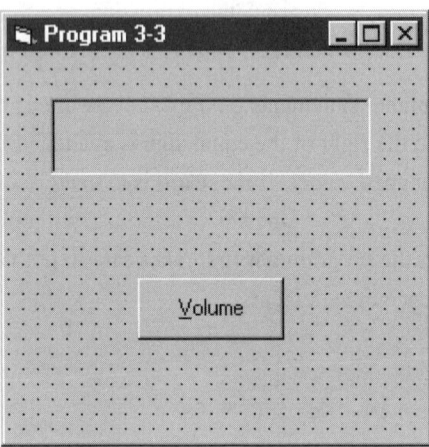

The output displayed in the Picture box by this event code, when the Command button is clicked, is shown Figure 3-15.

Notice the order in which statements are executed in the event procedure. The procedure begins with the header line and continues sequentially, statement by statement, until the **End Sub** statement is encountered. All procedures execute in this manner. The computer works on one statement at a time, executing that statement with no knowledge of

Table 3-8 The Properties Table for Program 3-3

Object	Property	Setting
Form	Name	frmMain
	Caption	Program 3-3
Picture Box	Name	picShow
	Height	615
	Width	2655
	TabStop	False
Command Button	Name	cmdVol
	Caption	&Volume

Figure 3-15

The Output Displayed by Program 3-3

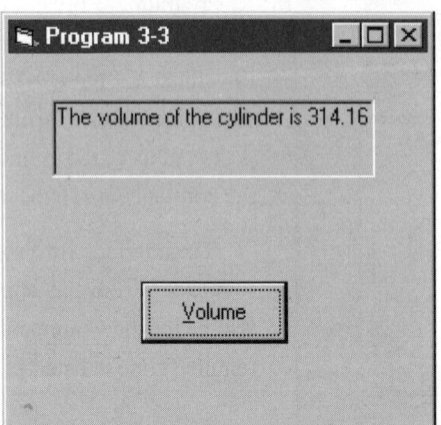

what the next statement will be. This explains why all variables used in an expression must have values assigned to them before the expression is evaluated.

When the computer executes the statement `volume = 3.1416 * radius ^ 2 * height`, it uses whatever value is stored in the variables `radius` and `height` at the time the assignment statement is executed. If no values have been specifically assigned to these variables before they are used in the assignment statement, the procedure uses whatever values happen to occupy these variables when they are referenced (in Visual Basic all numeric variables are automatically initialized to zero). The procedure does not look ahead to see that you might assign values to these variables later in the program.

Assignment Variations

Although only one variable is allowed immediately to the left of the equal sign in an assignment expression, the variable on the left of the equal sign can also be used on the right of the equal sign. For example, the assignment statement `total = total + 20` is valid. Clearly, in an algebraic equation total could never be equal to itself plus 20. But in Visual Basic, the statement `total = total + 20` is not an equation; it is a statement evaluated in two distinct steps. The first step is to calculate the value of `total + 20`. The second step is to store the computed value in `total`. See if you can determine the output of Event Procedure 3-3, when the form Click event is triggered

Event Procedure 3-3

```
Private Sub Form_Click()
  Dim total As Integer

  total = 15
  Print "The number stored in total is"; total
  total = total + 25
  Print "The number now stored in total is"; total
End Sub
```

Figure 3-16

The Integer 15 Is Stored in total

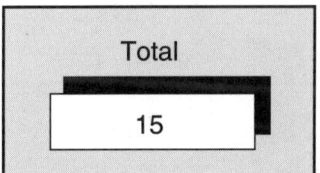

The assignment statement `total = 15` assigns the value in total to the number 15, as shown in Figure 3-16. The first **Print** statement then causes both a message and the value stored in total to be displayed on the form. The output produced by this statement for the form **Click** event is

```
The number stored in total is 15
```

The second assignment statement in the procedure, `total = total + 25` causes the computer to retrieve the 15 stored in `total` and add 25 to this number, yielding the number 40. The number 40 is then stored in the variable on the left side of the equal sign, which is the variable `total`. The 15 that was in `total` is simply erased and replaced, that is, overwritten, with the new value of 40, as shown in Figure 3-17.

Figure 3-17

`total = total + 25`
Causes a New Value to be Stored in `total`

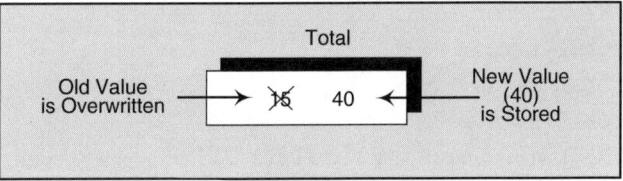

Accumulating

Assignment expressions like `total = total + 25` are very common in programming and are required in accumulating subtotals when data is entered one number at a time. For example, if we want to add the numbers 96, 70, 85, and 60 in calculator fashion, the following statements could be used.

Statement	Value in total
`total = 0`	0
`total = total + 96`	96
`total = total + 70`	166
`total = total + 85`	251
`total = total + 60`	311

The first statement initializes `total` to 0. This removes any number ("garbage" value) stored in the memory locations corresponding to `total` and ensures we start with 0 (this is equivalent to clearing a calculator before doing any computations). As each number is added, the value stored in `total` is increased accordingly. After completion of the last statement, `total` contains the total of all the added numbers.

The form **Click** procedure listed in Event Procedure 3-4 illustrates the effect of these statements by displaying `total`'s contents after each addition is made.

Event Procedure 3-4

```
Private Sub Form_Click()
  Dim total As Integer

  total = 0
  Print "The value of total is initially set to"; total
  total = total + 96
  Print " total is now"; total
  total = total + 70
  Print " total is now"; total
  total = total + 85
  Print " total is now"; total
  total = total + 60
  Print " The final value in total is"; total
End Sub
```

The output produced by the Form Click event in Event Procedure 3-4 is

```
The value of total is initially set to 0
 total is now 96
 total is now 166
 total is now 251
 The final value in total is 311
```

Although it is clearly easier to add the numbers by hand than to use the sequence of assignment statements listed, these statements do illustrate the subtotaling effect of repeated assignment statements having the form:

> variable = variable + *new value*

We will find many important uses for this type of statement when we become more familiar with the repetition statements introduced in Chapter 6.

Counting

A variation of the accumulating assignment statement is the counting statement. Counting statements have the form:

> variable = variable + *fixed number*

Examples of counting statements are

```
i = i + 1
totalStudents = totalStudents + 1
count = count + 1
j = j + 2
m = m + 2
kk = kk + 3
```

In each of these examples the same variable is used on both sides of the equal sign. After the statement is executed the value of the respective variable is increased by a fixed amount. In the first three examples the variables i, totalStudents, and count have all been increased by one. In the next two examples the respective variables have been increased by two, and in the final example the variable kk has been increased by three. Typically, integer variables with very simple names such as i, j, k, l, m, and n[6], or more mnemonic names, such as count, are used for counter variables. The following sequence of statements illustrates the use of a counter.

Statement	Value in COUNT
count = 0	0
count = count + 1	1
count = count + 1	2
count = count + 1	3
count = count + 1	4

The Form_Click procedure listed in Event Procedure 3-5 illustrates the effect of these statements within the context of a complete procedure.

---

[6]This is a carryover from the original version of the first high-level language, FORTRAN, in which any variable beginning in these letters was created as an integer variable.

Event Procedure 3-5

```
Private Sub Form_Click()
  Dim count As Integer

  count = 0
  Print "The initial value of count is"; count
  count = count + 1
  Print " count is now"; count
  count = count + 1
  Print " count is now"; count
  count = count + 1
  Print " count is now"; count
  count = count + 1
  Print " count is now"; count
End Sub
```

The output produced by the Form Click event in Event Procedure 3-5 is

```
The initial value of count is 0
 count is now 1
 count is now 2
 count is now 3
 count is now 4
```

Type Conversions

It is important to understand that data type conversions take place across the assignment statement. That is, the expression on the right side of the equal sign is converted to the data type of the variable to the left of the equal sign. For example, consider the evaluation of the expression

```
average = total / 2
```

where `total` is an integer variable having a stored value of 15 and `average` is also an integer variable. The result of the expression `total / 2` will be 7.5, the correct average value. Since, however, the left side of the assignment operator is an integer variable, the value of the expression `total / 2` is rounded to an integer value and stored in the variable `average`. Thus, at the completion of this assignment statement, the value stored in `average` is 8.

Automatic type conversions due to assignment take place whenever possible. For example, consider the following section of code

```
Dim s As String, number As Integer
s = "55"
number = s
```

Here, the value 55 is stored in `number`. If, however, the string `"AB"` is stored in s, the error `Type mismatch` will be displayed when the assignment statement `number = s` is executed.

To avoid unintentional conversions and type mismatch errors, the general rule is to always use the same data types on each side of the equal sign; that is, the integer types (byte, integer, and long) should be used with integer types, floating point types (single and double) with floating point types, strings with strings, and so on.

In addition to data type conversions made automatically across an equal sign, Visual Basic also provides for explicit user-specified type conversions. These conversion functions are presented in the next section.

Exercises 3.3

1. Write an assignment statement to calculate the circumference of a circle having a radius of 3.3 inches. The equation for determining the circumference, c, of a circle is $c = 2\pi r$, where r is the radius and π equals 3.1416.

2. Write an assignment statement to calculate the area of a circle. The equation for determining the area, a, of a circle is $a = \pi r2$, where r is the radius and $\pi = 3.1416$.

3. Write an assignment statement to convert temperature in degrees Fahrenheit to degrees Celsius. The equation for this conversion is *Celsius = 5/9 (Fahrenheit - 32)*.

4. Write an assignment statement to calculate the round trip distance, d, in feet, of a trip that is s miles long, one way.

5. Write an assignment statement to calculate the length, in inches, of a line that is measured in centimeters. Use the fact that there are 2.54 centimeters in one inch.

6. Write an assignment statement to calculate the value, in dollars, of an amount of money in francs. Assume that five francs are worth one dollar.

7. Determine the output of the following procedure:

```
Private Sub Form_Click()   ' a procedure illustrating integer truncation
    Dim num1 As Integer, num2 As Integer

    Cls
    num1 = 9/2
    num2 = 17/4
    Print "The first integer displayed is"; num1
    Print "The second integer displayed is"; num2
End Sub
```

8. Determine the output produced by the following procedure:

```
    Private Sub Form_Click()
    Dim average As Single

    Cls
    average = 26.27
    Print "The average is"; average
    average = 682.3
    Print "The average is"; average
    average = 1.968
    Print "The average is", average
    End Sub
```

9. Determine the output produced by the following procedure:

```
    Private Sub Form_Click()
    Dim sum As Single

    Cls
    sum = 0.0
    Print "The sum is"; sum
    sum = sum + 26.27
    Print "The sum is"; sum
    sum = sum + 1.968
    Print "The final sum is"; sum
    End Sub
```

Introduction to Visual Basic

10. a. Determine what each statement causes to happen in the following procedure.

```
Private Sub Form_Click()
Dim num1 As Integer, num2 As Integer
Dim num3 As Integer, total As Integer

Cls
num1 = 25
num2 = 30
total = num1 + num2
Print num1; " +"; num2; " ="; total
End Sub
```

b. What output will be produced when the event procedure listed in Exercise 10a. is triggered by clicking the mouse on the screen?

11. Determine and correct the errors in the following procedures.

a.
```
Private Sub Form_Click()
  width = 15
  area = length * width
  Print "The area is"; area
End Sub
```

b.
```
Private Sub Form_Click()
  Dim length As Integer, width As Integer, area As Integer
  area = length * width
  length = 20
  width = 15
  Print "The area is"; area
```

c.
```
Private Sub Form_Click()
  Dim length As Integer, width As Integer, area As Integer
  length = 20
  width = 15
  length * width = area
  Print "The area is; area
End Sub
```

12. Determine the output produced by the following event procedure.

```
Private Sub Form_Click()
Dim sum As Integer

sum = 0
sum = sum + 96
sum = sum + 70
sum = sum + 85
sum = sum + 60
Print "The value of sum is initially set to"; sum
Print " sum is now"; sum
Print " sum is now"; sum
Print " sum is now"; sum
Print " The final sum is"; sum
End Sub
```

13. Using Program 3-3, determine the volume of cylinders having the following radii and heights.

Radius (in.)	Height (in.)
1.62	6.23
2.86	7.52
4.26	8.95
8.52	10.86
12.29	15.35

3.4 Using Intrinsic Functions

As we have seen, assignment statements can be used to perform numeric computations. For example, the assignment statement

```
tax = rate * income
```

multiplies the value in `rate` times the value in `income` and then assigns the resulting value to `tax`. Although the common numeric operations, such as addition, subtraction, and so on, are easily accomplished using Visual Basic's numeric operators, no such operators exist for finding the square root of a number, the absolute value of a number, and other useful mathematical values. To facilitate the calculation of such quantities as well as the conversion between data types and other useful operations, Visual Basic provides a set of preprogrammed routines, referred to as *intrinsic functions,* that can be included in a procedure.

Before using one of Visual Basic's intrinsic functions, you must know:

- The name of the desired intrinsic function,
- What the intrinsic function does,
- The type of data required by the intrinsic function, and
- The data type of the result returned by the intrinsic function.

In practice, all functions operate in a manner similar to procedures, with one major difference. *A function always directly returns a single value.* This is an extremely important difference because it allows functions to be included within expressions.

Figure 3-18

Passing Data to the Sqr Function

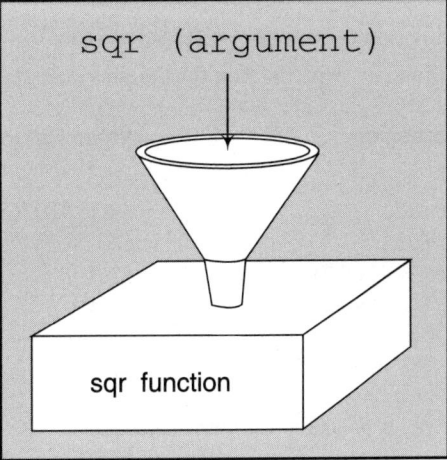

To illustrate the use of a Visual Basic intrinsic function, consider the intrinsic function named **Sqr**, which calculates the square root of a number. The square root of a number is computed using the expression

```
Sqr(number)
```

where the function's name, in this case **Sqr**, is followed by parentheses containing the number for which the square root is desired. The parentheses following the function name effectively provide a "funnel" through which data can be passed to the function (see Figure 3-18). The items passed to the function

Table 3-9 Visual Basic's Conversion Functions

Function Name and Argument(s)	Returned Value
`Asc(string)`	The character code corresponding to the first letter in the string.
`Chr$(string)`	Same as `Asc( )`.
`CBool(expression)`	If expression is zero, False is returned; otherwise, True is returned.
`CDbl(expression)`	The expression as a double-precision number. If expression lies outside the acceptable range for the Double data type, an error occurs.
`CInt(expression)`	The expression as an integer. If expression lies outside the acceptable range for the Integer data type, an error occurs.
`CSng(expression)`	The expression as a single precision integer. If expression lies outside the acceptable range for the Single data type, an error occurs.
`CStr(expression)`	The expression as a String. The expression argument must be a valid numeric or string expression.
`CVar(expression)`	The expression as a variant data type.
`Hex(n)`	The hexadecimal value of n, returned as a string (n is rounded to the nearest integer).
`Oct(n)`	The octal value of n, returned as a string (n is rounded to the nearest integer).
`Str(n)`	Same as `Cstr( )`.
`Val(string)`	The first number in the string (the function stops reading the string at the first nonnumeric character, except for a period, which is recognized as a decimal point)
`Var(variant)`	Returns 2 if integer, 3 if long, 4 if single, 5 if double, 6 if currency, 7 if date, 8 if string.

through the parentheses are called *arguments* of the function, and constitute its input data. For example, the following expressions are used to compute the square root of the arguments 4, 17, 25, 1043.29, and 6.4516:

```
Sqr(4)
Sqr(17)
Sqr(25)
Sqr(1043.29)
Sqr(6.4516)
```

The argument to the **Sqr** function can be any numeric expression that results in a positive value[7]. The **Sqr** function computes the square root of its argument and returns the result. The values returned by **Sqr** function for the previous expressions are

Expression	Value Returned
`Sqr(4)`	2
`Sqr(17)`	4.12310562561766
`Sqr(25)`	5
`Sqr(1043.29)`	32.3
`Sqr(6.4516)`	2.54

---

[7]A negative argument value results in the error message `Invalid procedure call` when the function is called.

Although we have used the square root function to illustrate how intrinsic functions are used, the most useful functions for commercial purposes are those that deal with formatting numbers, converting between data types, and operating on string data. Table 3-9 lists the commonly used conversion functions. The Format function and string manipulation functions are presented in Sections 4.5 and 7.3, respectively.

Exercises 3.4

1. List the four items you must know before using a Visual Basic intrinsic function.

2. How many values does a call to a single Visual Basic function return?   *one*

3. Write function calls to determine:
   a. The square root of 6.37.   *Sqr (6.37)*
   b. The square root of x - y.   *Sqr (x-y)*
   c. The square root of $a^2 - b^2$.   *Sqr (a2-b2)*

4. For a = 10.6, b = 13.9, c = -3.42, determine the value of
   a. CInt(a)   = *11*
   b. CInt(b)   = *14*
   c. CInt(c)   =
   d. CInt(a) + b   *= 11 + 13.9 = 24.9*
   e. CInt(a) + b + c   *= 11+ 13.9 +(-3.42)*
   f. CInt(a + b) + c   *= (10.6 +13.9) -3.42 = 25.0 -3.42 =21.58*
   g. CInt(a + b + c)   *= (10.6+13.9 -3.42 = 11 +14 -3.00 = 22*

5. Determine the returned value for the following function calls: *Ans—*
   a. Val("")   *= 0*
   b. Val("abc")   *= 0*
   c. Val("123abc")   *= 123*
   d. Val("123.4abc")   *= 123.4*
   e. Val("123.5.6abc")   *= 123.5*
   f. Val("123abc.456")   *= 123*

6. Write one Visual Basic Program that displays the value of each of the function calls listed in Exercise 5.

3.5 Common Programming Errors and Problems ▬▬▬▬▬

Part of learning any procedural programming language is making the elementary mistakes commonly encountered as you begin to use the language. These mistakes tend to be quite frustrating, since each language has its own set of common programming errors waiting for the unwary. Here is a list of the most common basic errors beginning Visual Basic programmers make:

1. Misspelling the name of a method; for example, typing `pint` instead of `Print`. A simple way to detect this is to type all entries in the Code window in lowercase. Keywords, such as **Print**, will then be automatically capitalized correctly and displayed in blue (or any other color selected under the Tools options). Any misspelled word will not be converted, making it easier to detect.

2. Forgetting to close messages to be displayed by the **Print** method within double quote symbols.

3. Incorrectly typing the letter O for the number zero (0), and vice versa.

4. Incorrectly typing the letter l, for the number 1, and vice versa.

5. Forgetting to declare all the variables used in a program. This error is detected by Visual Basic, and an error message is generated for all undeclared variables, if the **Option Explicit** statement is used.

6. Forgetting to use the **As** `data-type` clause in a single-line declaration, which causes the variable to be declared as **Variant** by default. For example, the declaration `Dim quantity, amount As Single` *does not* declare both `quantity` and `amount` as singles. Rather, `amount` is declared as a **Single** and `quantity` as a **Variant**. In this case, the correct declaration is `Dim quantity As Single, amount As Single`.

7. Storing an inappropriate data type value in a declared variable. This results in the assigned value being converted to the data type of the declared variable.

8. Using a variable in an expression before an explicit value has been assigned to the variable. Here, whatever value happens to be in the variable will be used when the expression is evaluated, and the result is usually incorrect.

9. Using an intrinsic function without providing the correct number of arguments of the proper data type.

10. Being unwilling to test an event procedure in depth. After all, since you wrote the procedure you assume it is correct, or you would have changed it before it was run. It can be very difficult to completely test your own software. As a programmer, you must constantly remind yourself that believing your program is correct does not make it so. Finding errors in your own program is a sobering experience, but one that will help you become a master programmer.

11. Saving an existing project using a new project name, without also saving all form modules using new form names so that both the original and new projects use the same form files. In this case, changing a form for the new project also changes the same form in the original project. Remember that the projects we have constructed are saved using two files—one for the project as a whole and one for the single form module it uses.

On a more fundamental level, it is worth repeating one of the errors mentioned in Chapter 1. A major programming error that almost all beginning programmers make is the rush to code and run a program before fully understanding what is required by each procedure. A symptom of this haste is the lack of either an outline of each proposed procedure or a written procedure itself. Many problems can be caught just by visually checking each procedure, either handwritten or listed from the computer, before it is ever run, and then testing it for a variety of inputs a user might enter.

3.6 Chapter Review

Key Terms

accumulating	integer number
ANSI	intrinsic function
assignment	long
associativity	mixed-mode
counting	mnemonic
declaration	precedence
Double	Print
double precision number	Single
expression	String
floating point number	type conversions
Integer	variable

Summary

1. Five types of data were introduced in this chapter: integer, floating point, boolean, string and variant. Each of these types of data is typically stored in a computer using different amounts of memory.

2. Every variable in a Visual Basic program should be declared as to the type of value it can store. Declarations within a procedure may be placed anywhere after the header line, but are usually placed together at the top of a procedure. Single variable declarations use the syntax

> **Dim** *var-1* As *data-type*

An example of using this syntax is

```
Dim quantity As Double
```

Multiple variable declarations may also be made on the same line using the syntax

> **Dim** *var-1* As *data-type*, *var-2* As *data-type*,...,*var-n* As *data-type*

An example using this syntax is

```
Dim amount As Single, price As Double, count As Integer
```

When the **As** data-type clause is omitted, the variable is declared as a **Variant** type by default.

3. Declaration statements always play a software role of defining a list of valid variable names. They also play a hardware role, because they cause memory storage locations to be set aside for each declared variable.

4. An *expression* is any combination of constants, variables, operators, and functions that can be evaluated to yield a value.

5. Expressions are evaluated according to the precedence and associativity of the operators used in them.

6. The **Print** method can be used to display both text and numerical results. Text should be enclosed in double quotes, and items to be printed should be separated by either a space or semicolon.

7. Assignment statements are used to store values into variables. The general syntax for an assignment statement is

$$\boxed{variable = expression}$$

8. Visual Basic provides intrinsic functions for calculating mathematical and string computations.

9. Data passed to a function are called *arguments* of the function. Arguments are passed to an intrinsic function by including each argument, separated by commas, within the parentheses following the function's name. Each function has its own requirements for the number and data types of the arguments that must be provided.

10. Every intrinsic function operates on its arguments to calculate a single value. To effectively use an intrinsic function you must know what the function does, the name of the function, the number and data types of the arguments expected by the function, and the data type of the returned value.

3.7 Looking Further: Basics of Forms Design

A form acts as the interface between the application and the user: its purpose is to permit the user to interact with the application in a convenient way. To achieve this purpose, Visual Basic provides two categories of objects that can be placed on the form: data controls and graphic controls. Data controls include Text boxes, Option buttons, Check boxes, and any other control used to get and display data. The graphic controls include Labels, Lines, Shapes, and Images, which are generally used to add visual interest to the form. In this section we present basic guidelines for using data and graphic controls to create attractive forms that are easy to use.

In designing a form it is useful to always remember that the form's main purpose is to control the flow of information to and from a user. It is also useful to understand that when a user views a screen, the user's eye typically starts at the left top corner of the screen and moves across and down the screen. And finally, users almost always judge an application based on how easy it is to use the screens and complete the tasks the application is meant to accomplish. With this in mind, the following guidelines should be observed:

1. General Design Considerations

- Place frequently read information towards the top left or top center of a screen.
- Keep at least 40 percent of a screen's overall area blank.
- When filling a line with a Label, Text box, or Picture box, make sure that each line is filled no more than 75 percent with controls.
- Make sure all controls are surrounded by blank spaces.

- Don't make a form larger than the screen's physical size. Although users can use scroll bars to access these areas, they are not accustomed to doing so.
- Create additional forms as needed with Command buttons that allow the user to switch between forms.

2. Label and Text Considerations

- Use Labels to describe the purpose of the form and what information is being asked for or displayed.
- Use only one or two fonts that are easy to read and use them for all text on the form. Generally, avoid script fonts as they are harder to read than non-script fonts.
- Use a point size of 10 or more, as smaller point sizes are difficult to read. To distinguish important data or make titles clearly identifiable, use larger point sizes.
- Don't use exotic fonts that may not be available on most of your users' computers.

3. Line and Shape Considerations

- Use lines and shapes to group related items on the form.
- Use lines and shapes to focus a user's eye on different sections of a form.

4. Color Considerations

- Use colors to create a soothing, rather than a dazzling, frenetic effect. Users quickly tire and become irritated when required to use a "glittery" or glaring form over an extended period of time. Blue colors tend to be soothing while "hot" colors, such as vivid pink or violet tend to be distracting.
- Use only two or three complimentary colors within a single form. Excessive colors tend to distract users.
- Use a darker color to emphasize headings or titles.
- Use color combinations between multiple forms to create a coding scheme for your application. For example, a blue and white color scheme might be used for an inventory receivables form and a red and gray scheme for an inventory disbursements form.
- Do not use red and green together. People with most common forms of color blindness cannot distinguish between these colors.

Multiple Forms—Creating a Splash Screen

Many applications use a *splash screen*, which is an initial informational screen displayed for a few seconds, before the main application screen comes up. Typically a splash screen is used to present a company's name and the name or purpose of the executing application, as for example, the screen

Figure 3-19

A Sample Splash Screen

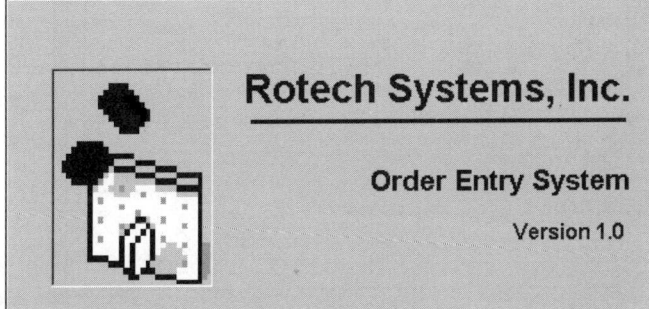

Introduction to Visual Basic

Figure 3-20

Adding a Second Form to a Project

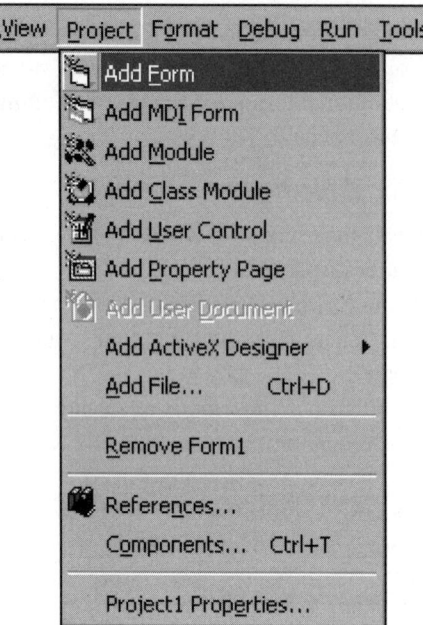

illustrated on Figure 3-19. Such screens are easily created, either using the Application Wizard (see Section 8-8) or manually.

In adding a splash screen, we also add a form to our application, so we will also use this to illustrate creating an application having multiple forms. To add a second form to an application, be it a splash screen or a second form for some other purpose, use the Add Form option of the Project menu, as shown in Figure 3-20. This will bring up the Add Form dialog box shown in Figure 3-21. As shown in this figure, you now have the opportunity to select a variety of form types, such as an About Dialog, Splash Screen, or simply a second generic form. For our particular purposed we will select the Splash Screen icon. This will add the form shown in Figure 3-22, which contains only images, labels, and lines, and can be modified to your own specifications.

At this stage, you will have two forms shown in the Project window, as illustrated in Figure 3-23. The trick now is to display this splash screen for a few seconds when the project is first executed, followed immediately by the frmMain screen, the first "working" screen in the application.

By default, a project's first form is designated as the startup form. When an application is run, this startup form is automatically displayed, and the first code to execute is the form's **Initialize** event procedure. There are times, however, when you might want a different form to be loaded and displayed first, as is the case with a splash screen. There are two solutions to this problem: either designate the splash screen as the first form to be loaded or designate

Figure 3-21

Selecting the Second Form as a Splash Screen

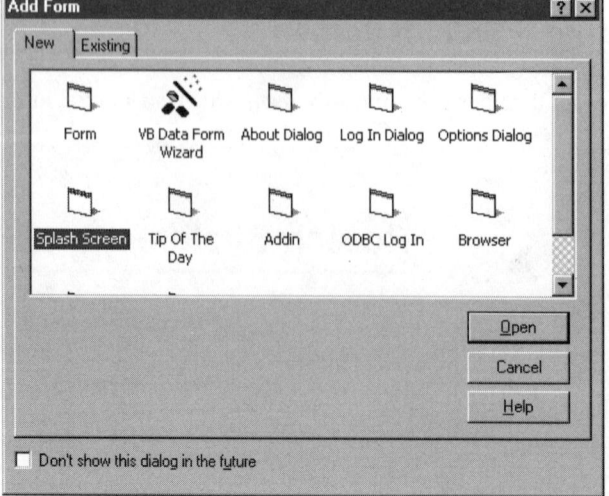

a separate procedure to begin processing before any form is loaded, and have that procedure load the appropriate forms in sequence. Although the second solution is the preferred one, for reasons which will become apparent, we consider each of these solutions, in turn, as they both yield insight into moving from one form to another within a single application.

Figure 3-22
The Default Splash Screen

To explicitly designate the `frmSplash` screen as the initial form to be loaded, select the last option from the Project menu (see Figure 3-24). When this option is selected, a dialog box similar to the one shown in Figure 3-25 is displayed. As illustrated, we have selected the `frmSplash` form

from the drop-down list as the Startup Object, rather than `frmMain` form. Although this will cause the splash screen to be displayed, we are still left with the problem of unloading this screen and loading the main form when we want the "working" part of the program to begin.

Switching from one form to another is typically accomplished using Command buttons. Assuming we have named the control `cmdContinue`, its **Click** event would be coded as listed in Event Procedure 3-6.

Event Procedure 3-6

```
Private Sub cmdContinue_Click()
  frmMain.Show
  frmMain.Refresh
  Unload frmSplash    form.
End Sub
```

This procedure uses the Show method to load and show the `frmMain`. It is followed by a **Refresh** method to ensure that all graphical elements are displayed. This is simply a safety to cover the case where the form's **AutoRefresh** property has been set to **False**. Finally, the `frmSplash` form is unloaded.

Providing a splash screen with a Command button is not the preferred method of determining when the screen will be unloaded, because it requires explicit action by the user to begin the working part of the program. However, the code used in Event Procedure 3-6 is extremely useful in showing how you can use a Command button to switch from one screen to another within a running application, and uses controls with which you are currently familiar. For specifically displaying splash screens, the more conventional method is to start an application with a procedure that contains a timing loop. Although we have not yet presented all of the elements required to achieve this, we will sketch out how this is done here, and more completely document the procedure in Section 8-8.

Figure 3-23
The Application's Project Window

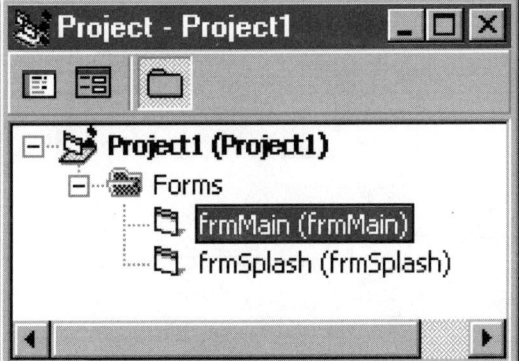

To start an application with a procedure rather than an initial form, the procedure must be named **Sub-Main** and be contained within a standard code (`.bas`) module. Suitable code for such a procedure is listed in Procedure Code 3-7.

Procedure Code 3-1

```
Sub Main()
Const DisplaySecs As Integer = 2
Dim start As Single

frmSplash.Show
frmSplash.Refresh
Start = Timer()  ' returns seconds from midnight
Do While Timer() < Start + DisplaySecs
Loop
Unload frmSplash
frmMain.Show
frmMain.Refresh
End Sub
```

[handwritten annotations: "Constant" pointing to Const line; "Shows the company's logo, symbol, graph element"; "Clear the splash."]

Figure 3-24

Changing a Project's Properties

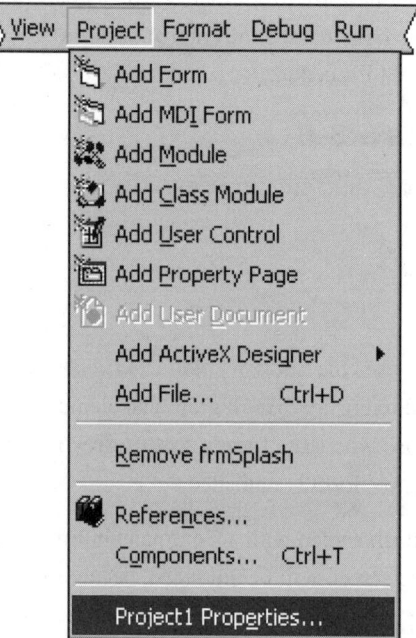

Notice that Procedure Code 3-1 contains statements which first show the frmSplash form and then refreshes it, in a similar manner to that used in Event Procedure 3-6 for the frmMain form. A simple loop (see Chapter 6) then causes the program to pause for two seconds, at which point the frmSplash screen is unloaded and the frmMain screen is displayed. All that remains to do is ensure that Procedure Code 3-1 is initially executed when the application is run. This is once again accomplished from within the Project menu by selecting this procedure as the Startup Object, rather than any of the two forms associated with the project. The complete procedure for accomplishing this is more fully explained in Section 8-8.

Figure 3-25

Selecting an Alternative Startup Object

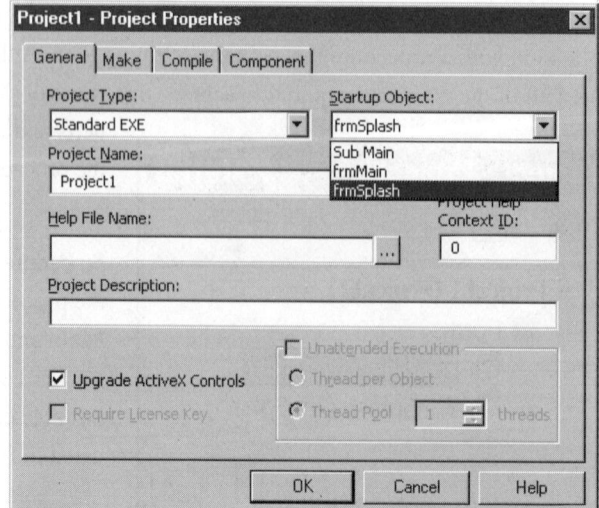

Introduction to Visual Basic

Controlling Input and Output

4.1 Interactive User Input

4.2 Formatted Output

4.3 Named Constants

4.4 Common Programming Errors and Problems

4.5 Chapter Review

4.6 Looking Further: Introduction to Version 5.0's Debugging Environment

In the previous chapters we explored how data is stored and processed using variables and assignment statements. In this chapter we complete this exploration by presenting additional input, output, and processing capabilities. On the input side we show how both the InputBox function and Text box control can be used to obtain data from a user while an application is executing. On the output side we show how numerical data can be formatted using the Format function and displayed in either a Text or Picture box.

4.1 Interactive User Input

Data for applications that only need to be executed once may be included directly in the appropriate procedure. For example, if we wanted to multiply the numbers 30.5 and 0.06, we could use Event Procedure 4-1.

Event Procedure 4-1

```
Private Sub Form_Click()
  Dim num1 As Single, num2 As Single, product As Single

  num1 = 30.5
  num2 = 0.06
  product = num1 * num2
  Print num1; " times"; num2; "  is"; product
End Sub
```

The output displayed by this procedure is

```
30.5 times 0.06 is 1.83
```

Event Procedure 4-1 can be shortened to the even simpler Event Procedure 4-2. Both procedures, however, suffer from the same basic problem: they must be rewritten in order to multiply other numbers. Neither procedure allows the user to substitute different values into the multiplication operation.

Event Procedure 4-2

```
Private Sub Form_Click()
    Print 30.5; " times"; 0.06; "  is"; 30.5 * 0.06
End Sub
```

Except for the programming practice they provide, event procedures that perform a single simple calculation are clearly not very useful. After all, it is easier to use a calculator to multiply two numbers than to enter and run either Event Procedure 4-1 or 4-2.

This section outlines two commonly used techniques for permitting a user to enter data into an executing Visual Basic application: the **InputBox** intrinsic function and the Text box control.

The InputBox Intrinsic Function

The **InputBox** intrinsic function provides a very simple way for users to enter a single input into a procedure while it is executing. A call to this function creates a dialog box (recall from Section 2.3 that a dialog is any box requiring the user to supply additional information to complete a task) that permits a user to enter a string at the terminal. The entered string, which frequently is converted to either an integer or a floating point number, is then stored directly in a variable. Figure 4-1 shows the relationship between an **InputBox** functionused for entering string data, and a **MsgBox** statement used for displaying string data.

The most commonly used syntax for calling the InputBox function is

InputBox(*prompt, title, default*)

where *prompt* is a required string and both *title* and *default*, which are also strings, are optional. If a title string is used, it is displayed in the title bar of the dialog box; otherwise, the application's name is placed in the title bar. If a default string is provided, it is placed within the input area of the dialog box. A *prompt* is a message telling a user that input is required. The prompt, which is always required, is displayed as a string within the input dialog box. For example, the statement

```
s = InputBox("Enter a value", "Input Dialog")
```

Figure 4-1

An InputBox Dialog Is Used to Enter and Display a String A MsgBox Dialog Is Used to Display a String

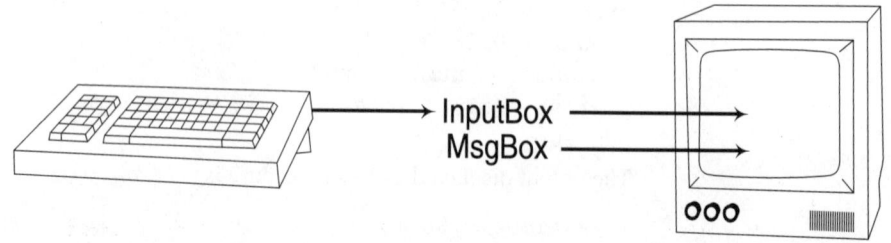

Figure 4-2

A Sample InputBox Dialog

calls the **InputBox** function with the arguments `"Enter a value"`, which is the prompt, `"Input Dialog"`, which is the title, and no default argument. When this statement is executed, the input dialog shown in Figure 4-2 is displayed.

Further examples of the InputBox function are

```
s = InputBox("Enter a Value")
s = InputBox("Enter a Value", "Sample", "5")
s = InputBox("Enter a Value",, "10")
```

↗ where is no title or name.

In all three examples, the prompt `Enter a Value` is displayed. In both the first and third examples the title bar is used to display the application's name, while in the second example, the title bar displays `Sample`. Finally, the last two examples provide default string values of 5 and 10 in the text input area. Notice that in the last example, where a default value is provided with no explicit title, the title argument is simply left blank but is separated from both the prompt and the default value by a comma.

Once an input box dialog box is displayed the keyboard is continuously scanned for data. As keys are pressed, the InputBox function displays them within the input area of the dialog. When either the [Enter] key is pressed or one of the two command buttons in the box

Figure 4-3

Program 4-1's Interface

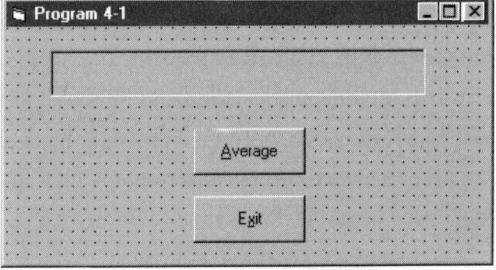

are clicked, input stops and the entered text is stored in the variable on the left side of the assignment statement. The procedure then continues execution with the next statement after the call to **InputBox**.

Program 4-1 illustrates using an **InputBox** function within the context of a complete application. The interface for this project is shown in Figure 4-3. As illustrated, the graphical user interface consists of two Command buttons and a Picture box.

Table 4-1 The Properties Table for Program 4-1

Object	Property	Setting
Form	Name	frmMain
	Caption	Program 4-1
Picture Box	Name	picShow
	Height	495
	Width	4095
	TabStop	False
Command Button	Name	cmdInput
	Caption	&Average

For this application the only procedure is the Command button **Click** event, which is listed in Program 4-1's event code.

Program 4-1's Event Code

```
Private Sub cmdInput_Click()
    Dim num1 As Single, num2 As Single
    Dim average As Single

    picShow.Cls
    num1 = InputBox("Enter a number", "Input Dialog", "0")
    num2 = InputBox("Great! Now enter another number", "Input Dialog", "0")
    average = (num1 + num2) / 2
    picShow.Print "The average of"; num1; " and"; num2; " is"; average
End Sub
```

(handwritten note: if the user doesn't type any value put zero or not)

The first input dialog displayed by Program 4-1's event procedure is shown in Figure 4-4. The 15 displayed in the input area of the dialog is the value that was entered from the keyboard. Before this value is entered the dialog displays a 0, which is the default provided in the **InputBox** function call. The default value is automatically removed as soon as the user presses any key.

Figure 4-4

The First InputBox Dialog after Data is Entered

Notice that the dialog prompt tells the user to enter a number. After this dialog is displayed, the **InputBox** function puts the application into a temporary paused state for as long as it takes the user to type in a value. The user signals the **InputBox** function that data entry is finished by clicking one of the Command buttons. If the user clicks the OK button (or presses the [Enter] key when this button is in focus), the entered value is stored in the variable on the left side of the assignment statement, which in this case is num1, and the application is taken out of its pause. Program execution then proceeds with the next statement, which in Program 4-1's Event procedure is another call to an **InputBox** function. The second **InputBox** dialog and the data entered in response to it, are shown in Figure 4-5.

Figure 4-5

The Second InputBox Dialog after Data is Entered

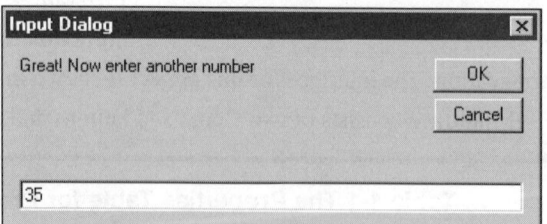

While the second dialog is displayed, the application is again put into a temporary waiting state while the user types a second value. This second number is stored in the variable num2. Based on these input values, the output produced by Program 4-1 is shown in Figure 4-6.

Figure 4-6

A Sample Output Produced by Program 4-1

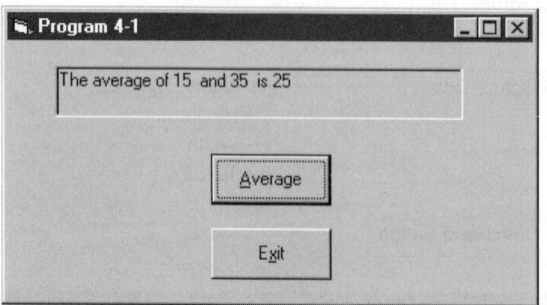

We now explain why a default value of 0 was used for each **InputBox** dialog. The reason touches on a much broader issue of constant concern to all good programmers.

A default value will handle the case where a user presses the OK command button accidentally, before any value is entered. Remember that the **InputBox** function actually accepts and returns a string, which allows a user to type in any text. Using a string as input provides a safety precaution because the programmer has no control over what a user might happen to enter. Accepting the input as a string ensures that whatever is typed will be accepted initially. After the data is entered, however, the programmer should validate the entered data. For example, if a number is required, the procedure should check that only digits, and possibly one decimal point, have been entered. Whenever invalid data is detected, an error message should be displayed and the user be given an opportunity to reenter valid data. Validating user input requires the selection statements presented in Chapter 5, so for now we can provide only minimal protection against invalid data entry. This is the reason for the default value.

If no default is provided and a user should accidentally click the OK button before any data is entered, the string returned from the dialog will contain no characters at all. This string is thus the zero-length empty string, `" "`. Now notice that in Program 4-1's event procedure the first assignment statement stores the entered and returned value in the variable `num1`, which is declared as a **Single**. In executing this assignment, Visual Basic will automatically convert the returned string, if possible, into a single precision number before storing it in `num1` (if this is unfamiliar to you, refer to the type conversions presented in Section 3.3). Thus, if the user enters only digits and possibly a single decimal point into the input dialog, the conversion can be made. If an entered string cannot be converted, the error message `Type mismatch` is displayed. Since an empty string has no valid numerical value, clicking on the OK button when no default or value has been entered would cause a `Type mismatch` error. Providing a zero default prevents this error from occurring.

Before leaving Program 4-1's event procedure, one last observation is worth making. Notice the parentheses in the statement

```
average = (num1 + num2) / 2
```

The parentheses here are required to produce a correct calculation. Without these parentheses, the only number that would be divided by two is the value in `num2` (since division has a higher precedence than addition).

The Text Box Control Reconsidered

By far, the most versatile and commonly used object for interactive input is the Text box control. This control permits the user to enter a string at the terminal. The string is then stored as the value for the Text box's **Text** property. A Text box control for input is almost always used in conjunction with a Label control, where the Label acts as a prompt and the Text box provides the actual means for the user to input data. For example, consider the interface shown in Figure 4-7. Here the Label is `Enter a Fahrenheit Temperature:` and the Text box

Figure 4-7

The Toolbox's Label and Text Box Icons

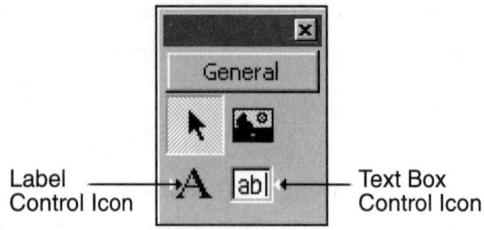

Label Control Icon

Text Box Control Icon

provides an input area. The Label and Text box icons, as they appear in the Toolbox, are illustrated on Figure 4-7.

Creating a Label is very simple; all that is required is selecting the Label from the Toolbox and setting its **Caption** property. By definition, a Label is a read-only control whose **Caption** property can only be changed at design-time or run-time under program control: it cannot be altered by the user while the program is executing.

Although it is the Label's **Caption** property that is displayed on an application's interface, two very useful properties in setting the caption are the AutoSize and WordWrap properties. If the **AutoSize** property is set to **False**, you must manually adjust the physical size of the Label at design time, using the sizing handles to fit the caption. It is generally easier to set the **AutoSize** property to **True**. Then, as you type in the caption, the Label will automatically expand its width to the right to fit the caption. If you prefer the label to expand downwards to fit a caption, you must also set the **WordWrap** property to **True**. This forces the left and right sides to remain fixed and the caption to word wrap down as it is entered. Note, however, that the **WordWrap** property, which essentially changes the direction of the automatic expansion from the right to the bottom of the Label, can only take effect if automatic expansion is activated by setting the **AutoSize** property to **True**.

The Text box provides the actual means for a user to enter data while a program is executing. All data entered in the Text box is assumed by Visual Basic to be string data. This means that if numbers are to be input, the entered string must be converted to numerical data, either explicitly or implicitly. It also means that some data validation is typically required to ensure that a user does not enter data that will cause the application to crash.

For example, consider again the interface for Program 4-2 shown in Figure 4-8, where the user is prompted to enter a temperature in degrees Fahrenheit. Once a user enters a Fahrenheit temperature, the program will compute the corresponding temperature in degrees Celsius and display the calculated value in the picture box. The properties for Program 4-2 are listed in Table 4-2.

Figure 4-8

Program 4-2's User Interface

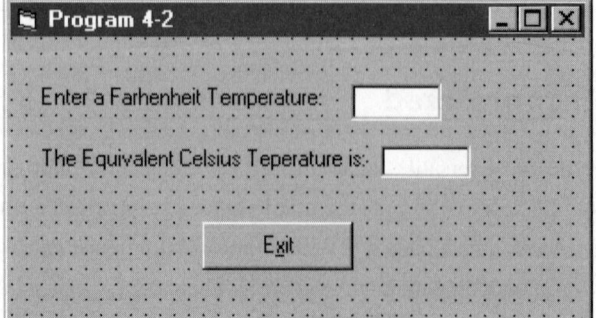

Now consider Program 4-2's event code, paying particular attention to the Text box **GotFocus** and **LostFocus** event procedures, as these are the two of the three procedures primarily used in processing Text box data.

Table 4-2 Program 4-2's Property Table

Object	Property	Setting
Form	Name	`frmMain`
	Caption	`Program 4-2`
Label	Name	`lblFahr`
	Caption	`Enter a Fahrenheit Temperature:`
	AutoSize	`True`
	WordWrap	`False`
Label	Name	`lblCelsius`
	Caption	`The Equivalent Celsius Temperature is:`
	AutoSize	`True`
	WordWrap	`False`
Text box	Name	`txtFahr`
	Text	`(Blank)`
Picture box	Name	`picCelsius`
	TabStop	`False`
Command button	Name	`cmdExit`
	Caption	`E&xit`

Program 4-2's Event Code

```
Private Sub txtFahr_GotFocus()
   picCelsius.Cls
End Sub

Private Sub txtFahr_LostFocus()
  Dim celsius As Single

  celsius = 5 / 9 * (Val(txtFahr.text) - 32)
  picCelsius.Print celsius
End Sub

Private Sub cmdExit_Click()
  Beep
  End
End Sub
```

The **GotFocus** event is triggered when an object receives focus and is used to perform any preprocessing associated with a user control. In Program 4-2 we use the Text box's **GotFocus** event to clear the Picture box of any data, prior to allowing a user to enter a new Fahrenheit temperature. This is done to ensure that a previously calculated Celsius temperature does not appear while the user is typing in new data.

The actual calculation and display of a Celsius temperature is performed by the Text box's **LostFocus** event. This event is triggered when the Text box loses focus, which occurs when the user signals completion of data entry either by pressing the Tab key or clicking on another control. The actual computation in the **LostFocus** event consists of the single calculation `celsius = (5 / 9) * (Val(txtFahr.Text) - 32)`, which converts a

Figure 4-9

*A Sample Run Using
Program 4-2*

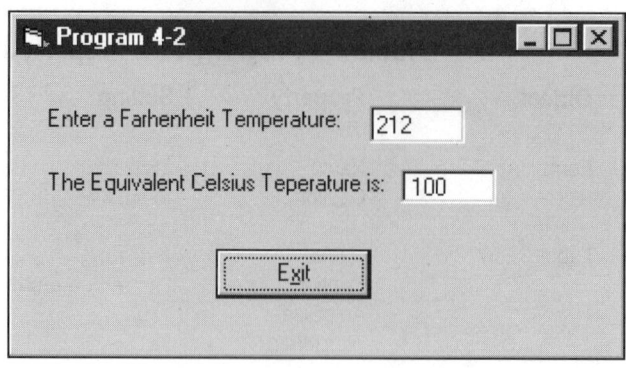

Fahrenheit temperature to its Celsius equivalent. This is followed by a call to the Picture box's **Print** method to display the calculated result. Figure 4-9 illustrates a completed run using Program 4-2. Notice that the focus in this figure is on the E̲xit Command button.

Before leaving Program 4-2, take a closer look at the assignment statement used to calculate a Celsius value. Specifically, notice the term `Val(txtFahr.Text)`. Here, the term `txtFahr.Text` accesses the data value entered in the Text box and stored in its **Text** property, which is a string value. Using this string as an argument to the **Val** function explicitly converts the string into a numerical value. Specifically, the **Val** function converts string data into numerical data for as many characters in the string as can be recognized as a number (see Table 3-9). Although the **Val** function will recognize a period as a decimal point, it stops the conversion at the first character that it cannot recognize as part of a number. For example, if the user entered the data `212abc`, the **Val** function would return the number 212. The function also returns a numerical value of zero if the string does not begin in either a digit or a decimal point.

The purpose of using the **Val** function is that it prevents the program from crashing if the user types in a non-numeric input such as the characters abc. For example, without the **Val** function the assignment statement would appear as

```
celsius = (5 / 9) * (txtFahr.Text - 32)
```

This statement operates correctly when a user enters any string that can be considered as a number, such as 212, because the string is automatically converted to a numeric value within the expression `(txtFahr.Text - 32)`. If a user inadvertently types in a string such as `212a`, however, the program stops and produces the message `Type mismatch error`, because the entered string cannot be converted into a numerical value. Using the **Val** function ensures that this error will not occur, because the string is always converted to a numerical value prior to being processed as part of the calculation.

A First Look at User-Input Validation

Validating user input and ensuring that a program does not crash due to unexpected input is a sign of a well-constructed program. Programs that respond effectively to unexpected user input are referred to as "bullet-proof" programs, and one of your jobs as a programmer is to produce this type of program.

Program 4-2 only touches on the topic of validating user input by employing one of the more commonly used techniques associated with Text box input; this is to explicitly convert string data to numerical data, using the **Val** function when a numerical value is expected. This conversion is done in the **LostFocus** event code, immediately after the user has completed using the Text box. Clearly, this is an ideal place to verify and validate data. This is one of the primary uses of the **LostFocus** event—to verify and validate data before any computation is made.

Another very important type of validation occurs directly as the user is entering data. Typically, this type of validation is made using the **KeyPress** and **KeyDown** events. Each of these events returns the key just pressed and permits action to be taken before the key's value is accepted into the input string. The difference between these two events is the amount of information returned. The **KeyPress** procedure receives only the ANSI value of a character keys as an argument, while the **KeyDown** event can detect and process the function, cursor, and shift keys in addition to the printable character keys. This type of validation, however, is based on selecting out desired characters and rejecting others from the entered string. The methods for performing such selections are described in the next chapter.

Exercises 4.1

1. Write assignment statements that store the returned value from an **InputBox** dialog in a variable named `test` for the following Input dialog specifications:

   a. prompt = Enter a grade
      title = Input dialog
      default = 0

   b. prompt = Enter a temperature
      title = Data Analysis
      default = 98.6

   c. prompt = Enter an interest rate
      title = Yield Analysis
      default = 0

   d. prompt = Enter a name
      title = Mail List Application
      no default value

   e. prompt = Enter a price
      title = Pricing Application
      default = 12.50

2. Determine what value is placed in the variable `num1` in Program 4-1's event procedure, if the Cancel button is clicked on the input dialog box.

3. a. Write, by hand, a Visual Basic event procedure named `cmdTax_Click` that can be used to display the following prompt in an Input dialog box:

   Enter the amount of the bill:

   After accepting a value for the amount of the bill, your procedure should calculate the sales tax, assuming a tax rate of 6 percent. The display of the sales tax, as a dollar amount, should appear in a Picture box named `picShow` when a Command button is clicked. A second Command button should be provided to terminate the application.

b. Include the event procedure written for Exercise 3b. in a working program. For testing purposes, verify your program using an initial amount of $36.00. After manually checking that the result produced by your program is correct, use your program to complete the following table:

Amount (dollars)	Sales Tax (dollars)
36.00	
40.00	
52.60	
87.95	
125.00	
182.93	

4. a. Write a Visual Basic program that can be used to convert Celsius temperatures to their equivalent Fahrenheit values. Use a Label to display the following prompt:

```
Enter the temperature in degrees Celsius:
```

After accepting a value entered from the keyboard into a Text box, the program should convert the entered temperature to degrees Fahrenheit, using the equation *Fahrenheit = (9.0 / 5.0) * Celsius + 32.0*. The program should then display the temperature in degrees Fahrenheit, in a clearly labeled Picture box named picShow. A Command button should be provided to terminate the application.

b. Verify your program, by first calculating the Fahrenheit equivalent of the following test data by hand, and then using your program to see it produces the correct results.

```
Test data set 1: 0 degrees Celsius.
Test data set 2: 50 degrees Celsius
Test data set 3: 100 degrees Celsius
```

c. When you are sure your procedure is working correctly, use it to complete the following table:

Celsius	Fahrenheit
45	
50	
55	
60	
65	
70	

5. Write and execute a Visual Basic program that displays the following prompts, using two Label controls:

```
Enter the length of the office:
Enter the width of the office:
```

Have your program accept the user input in two Text boxes. When a Command button is clicked your program should calculate the area of the office and display the area in a picture box. This display should be cleared whenever the input Text boxes receive the focus. A second Command button should be provided to terminate the application. Verify your procedure using the following test data:

```
Test data set 1: length = 12.5, width = 10
Test data set 2: length = 12.4, width = 0
Test data set 3: length = 0, width = 10
```

6. a. Write and execute a Visual Basic program that displays the following prompts and uses two Text boxes to receive the input data.

```
Enter the miles driven:
Enter the gallons of gas used:
```

The program should calculate and display the miles per gallon in a Picture box when a Command button is clicked. Use the equation *miles per gallon = miles / gallons used.* The display should be cleared whenever one of the Text boxes gets the focus. A second Command button should be provided to terminate the application. Verify your procedure using the following test data:

```
Test data set 1: Miles = 276, Gallons used = 10.
Test data set 2: Miles = 200, Gallons used = 15.5.
```

b. When you have completed your verification, use your procedure to complete the following table:

Miles Driven	Gallons Used	MPG
250	16.00	
275	18.00	
312	19.54	
296	17.39	

c. For the procedure written for Exercise 6a., determine how many verification runs are required to ensure the procedure is working correctly, and give a reason supporting your answer.

7. Write a Visual Basic Program that displays the following prompts:

```
Enter the length of the swimming pool:
Enter the width of the swimming pool:
Enter the average depth of the swimming pool:
```

Have your program accept the user input in three Text boxes. When a Command button is clicked your program should calculate the volume of the swimming pool and display the volume in a Picture box. This display should be cleared whenever the input Text boxes receive the focus. A second Command button should be provided to terminate the application. In calculating the volume use the equation

*volume = length * width * average depth*

8. a. Write and execute a Visual Basic program that provides three Text boxes for the input of three user input numbers. There should be a single Label prompt that tells the user to enter three numbers in the boxes. When the user clicks a Command button the program should calculate the average of the entered numbers and then display the average in a clearly labeled Picture box. The displayed value should be cleared whenever one of the Text boxes receives the focus. A second Command button

should be provided to terminate the application. Verify your procedure using the following test data:

```
Test data set 1: 100, 100, 100
Test data set 2: 100, 50, 0
```

When you have completed your verification, use your program to complete the following table:

Numbers	Average
92, 98, 79, 85	
86, 84, 75, 86	
63, 85, 74, 82	

9. Program 3-5's event procedure prompts the user to input two numbers, where the first value entered is stored in num1 and the second value is stored in num2. Using this procedure as a starting point, rewrite the procedure so that it swaps the values stored in the two variables.

10. Write a Visual Basic program that prompts the user to type in an integer number. Have your procedure accept the number as an integer and immediately display the integer. Run your procedure three times. The first time you run the procedure enter a valid integer number, the second time enter a floating point number, and the third time enter the string Help. Using the output display, see what numbers your procedure actually accepted from the data you entered.

11. Repeat Exercise 10, but have your procedure declare the variable used to store the number as a single precision floating point variable. Run the procedure four times. The first time enter an integer, the second time enter a decimal number with less than fourteen decimal places, the third time enter a number having more than fourteen decimal places, and the fourth time enter the string Oops. Using the output display, keep track of what number your procedure actually accepted from the data you typed in. What happened, if anything, and why?

12. a. Why do you think that most successful applications procedures contain extensive data input validity checks? (**Hint**: Review Exercises 10 and 11.)

    b. What do you think is the difference between a data type check and a data reasonableness check?

    c. Assume that a procedure asks the user to enter the speed and acceleration of a car . What are some checks that could be made on the data entered?

4.2 Formatted Output

Although it is essential that an application display correct results, it is also important that it present these results attractively. Most applications are judged, in fact, on the ease of data entry and the style and presentation of their output. For example, displaying a monetary result as 1.897256 is not in keeping with accepted report conventions. The display should be either $1.90 or $1.89, depending on whether rounding or truncation is used.

The format of displayed numeric values can be controlled by the intrinsic Format function. The general syntax of this function is

> **Format**(*expression, format string*)

The first argument supplied to the **Format** function is an expression to be formatted and the second argument is the desired format. The **Format** function formats the expression's value according to the given format string and returns the formatted expression as a string value. For numeric expressions the format string can be either one of the Visual Basic pre-defined format strings listed in Table 4-3[1], or a user defined format string. For example, the statement

```
Print Format(84675.03567, "Currency")
```

produces the printout

```
$84,675.04
```

Further examples illustrating the effect of the predefined formats listed in Table 4-3 are

Example	Returned String
Format(1234.567, "Currency")	$1,234.57
Format(1234.567, "Fixed")	1234.57
Format(1234.567, "General Number")	1234.567
Format(0.1234567, "Percent")	12.35%
Format(1234.567, "Scientific")	1.23E+03
Format(1234.567, "Standard")	1,234.57
Format(1234.567, "Yes/No")	Yes
Format(1234.567, "True/False")	True

[handwritten: If there is no number then say NO]

Table 4-3 Predefined Numeric Format Strings

String	Description
Currency	Displays a number with a leading dollar sign, thousands separator, if required, and two digits (rounded) to the right of the decimal point.
Fixed	Displays a number with at least one digit to the left of the decimal point and two digits (rounded) to the right of the decimal point.
General Number	Displays the number as is.
Percent	Displays the number multiplied by 100, with at least one digit to the left of the decimal point and two digits (rounded) to the right of the decimal point and a percent sign.
Scientific	Uses standard scientific notation.
Standard	Same as Fixed, except uses thousands separator as required by the magnitude of the number.
Yes/No	Displays No if the number is 0; otherwise displays Yes.
True/False	Displays False if the number is 0; otherwise displays True.

---

[1]These formats can be found under Formats, named, or Named Numeric Formats, using Visual Basic's Help facility.

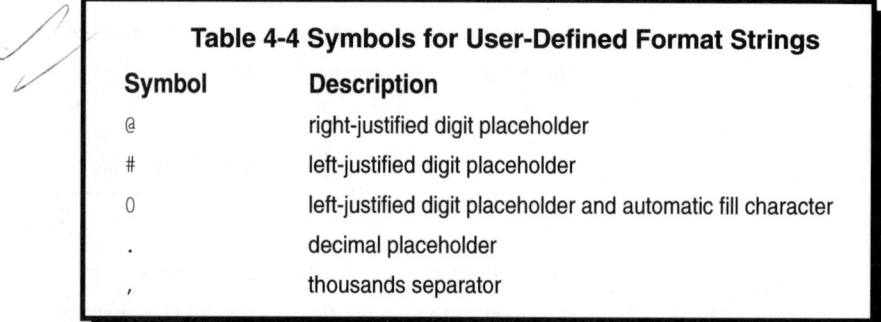

Table 4-4 Symbols for User-Defined Format Strings	
Symbol	**Description**
@	right-justified digit placeholder
#	left-justified digit placeholder
0	left-justified digit placeholder and automatic fill character
.	decimal placeholder
,	thousands separator

User-defined formats are useful for creating specialized output. Table 4-4 lists the acceptable symbols that can be included in a user-defined format string. For example, the format string in the statement

```
Print Format(12345.678,"#,###.##")
```

requires that the formatted number use a comma as a thousands separator and return two digits (rounded) to the right of the decimal place. In this case, the returned value is 12,345.68. Notice, however, that the statement

```
Print Format(345.60, "#,###.##")
```

produces the output 345.6. That is, if the # placeholder is used, and the number being formatted does not require all the places provided by the #'s in the format string, on either side of the decimal point, the extra #s are ignored. If the integer part of the number exceeds the number of #s to the left of the decimal point, however, additional space is allocated to accommodate the number.

These same rules apply to the 0 placeholder, with one important difference: if the number does not fill the space designated by the 0s, a 0 will fill each unused space. For example,

```
Print Format(12345.678,"0,000.00")
```

produces the output

```
12,234.68
```

but the statement

```
Print Format(345.6, "0,000.00")
```

produces the output

```
0,345.60
```

Since leading zeros are typically not required for numeric output, the # format symbol is frequently used to specify the integer part of a number, while the 0 format symbol is used to force a fixed number of decimal digits for the fractional part. For example, the statement

```
Print Format(345.6, "#,###.00")
```

produces the output

```
345.60
```

In addition to numeric placeholders, other symbols can be placed directly within a user specified format and are included in the string returned by the **Format** function. For example, the statement

```
mystr = Format(18005551212,"#(###)###-####")
```

assigns the string value 1(800)555-1212 to the string variable named mystr.

Using a bar symbol (|) to clearly mark the beginning and end of the returned string, Table 4-4 illustrates the effect of various user formats. Notice in Table 4-4 that the **Format** function ignores the specified integer format when the integer specification is too small, and always allocates enough space for the integer part of the number. The fractional part of a number is only displayed with the number of specified digits if the 0 placeholder is used. In this case, if the fractional part contains fewer digits than specified, the number is padded with trailing zeros. For both 0 and # placeholders, if the fractional part contains more digits than specified in the format, the number is rounded to the indicated number of decimal places.

Table 4-4 Examples of Numeric Formats

Format	Returned Number	String Value	Comments
"|##|"	3	|3|	Only one # position is used.
"|##|"	43	|43|	Both # positions are used.
"|##|"	143	|143|	# place holders ignored.
"|00|"	3	|03|	Leading 0 position is used.
"|00|"	43	|43|	Both 0 positions are used.
"|00|"	143	|143|	0 place holders ignored.
"|##.00|"	2.466	|2.47|	Fractional part rounded.
"|##.##|"	2.466	|2.47|	Fractional part rounded.
"|00.00|"	123.4	|123.40|	Leading place holders ignored. Fractional part forced to 2 decimal places.
"|00.##|"	123.4	|123.4|	Leading place holders ignored. Fractional part not forced to 2 decimal places.

Cursor Control Options

The real purpose of the semicolon in a **Print** statement is to control the cursor. When a semicolon is placed after an expression in a **Print** statement it causes the cursor to stop immediately after the last displayed character. For example, the sequence of statements

```
Print "Hello";
Print "There"
```

produces the output

```
HelloThere
```

This output occurs because the semicolon in the first statement forces the cursor to remain in position after displaying Hello. As we have seen, a semicolon performs in an identical

Figure 4-10

Print Zones

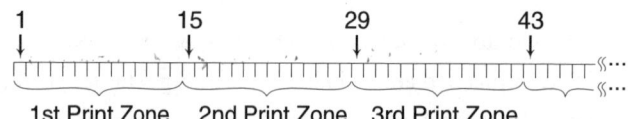

manner when separating items in a single **Print** statement. For example, the same output is produced by the statement

```
Print "Hello"; "There"
```

Here, the **Print** statement first displays the string `Hello`, the semicolon causes the cursor to remain in the position it finds itself after the display, and then the string `There` is displayed. Within a single **Print** statement, a space performs the same function as the semicolon.

In addition to the simple cursor control provided by the semicolon, Visual Basic provides a number of other cursor control options. To see how these controls work, however, you first need to understand how characters are positioned within a line of text.

Each displayed line within an object, such as a Picture box or window, consists of a fixed number of columns starting with column 1. For display purposes Visual Basic defines a print zone as 14 consecutive columns, with the first print zone beginning in column 1. Thus, as shown in Figure 4-10, print zone 1 occupies columns 1 through 14, print zone 2 occupies columns 15 through 28, and so on.

If a comma is encountered in a Print statement, the cursor automatically is moved to the first position in the next print zone. For example, assuming that the **Font** property is set to Courier, the statements

```
Print "12345678901234567890"
Print "Hello", "There"
```

produce the display

```
12345678901234567890
Hello         There
```

This display is produced because the comma in the print statement causes the cursor to move to the next print zone, which starts in column 15.

Print zones permit aligning data in fixed columns, assuming a fixed-size (or monospace) font, such as `Courier`, is used. In a Courier font each character moves the cursor by the same fixed amount, so that `w` and `i`, for example, both occupy the same amount of space on the display. This is not true for proportional fonts, such as Times, where w occupies more space than i. Thus, if you are trying to align data on output, make sure to set the font property to a fixed font, such as Courier. For proportional fonts, a print zone is defined as the width of 14 average character widths.

Space

The Tab and Spc Functions

The Tab function **Tab(n)** moves the cursor to the specified column number. For example, the statements

```
Print "12345678901234567890"
Print "Hello"; Tab(10); "There"
```

produce the display

```
12345678901234567890
Hello     There
```

Here the Tab function is used to tab over to column number 10. If the print position is beyond the column number in the **Tab** function call, the **Tab** function is ignored. A **Tab** by itself produces the same effect as a comma. Thus, the statement

```
Print "Hello"; Tab; "There"
```

produces the same output as the statement

```
Print "Hello", "There"
```

The space function, **Spc(n)**, moves the cursor over n spaces from its current position. As such, it effectively inserts n spaces into the output display. For example, the statements

```
Print "12345678901234567890"
Print "Hello"; Spc(6); "There"
```

produce the display

```
12345678901234567890
Hello     There
```

Centering Text

Every graphical object drawn on a form uses the coordinate system shown in Figure 4-11. The units of measurement for both the x and y axis are in *twips*, where there are 1,440 twips in an inch and 567 twips in a centimeter.

By default, the left and upper *x* and *y* positions of each object are defined as the coordinates (0,0) and printing always begins at these coordinates. To change the current starting coordinates, you can use the **CurrentX** and **CurrentY** properties. For example, the statements

```
CurrentX = 50
CurrentY = 100
```

Figure 4-11

A Form's Coordinate System

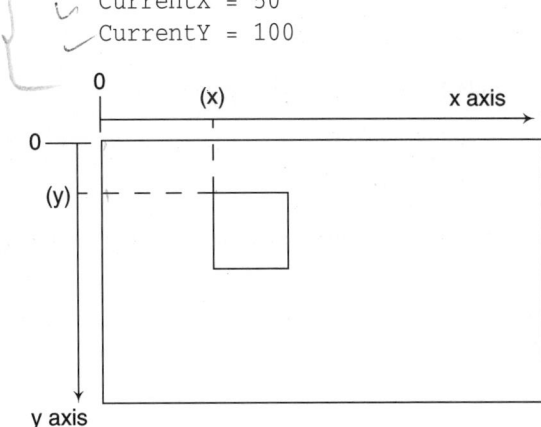

set the form's current *x* and *y* coordinates to 50 and 100 twips, while the statements

```
picBox1.CurrentX = 30
picBox1.CurrentY = 40
```

set the current *x* and *y* coordinates of the `picBox1` object to 30 and 40 twips, respectively. Setting the **CurrentX** and **CurrentY** properties permits text to be easily centered within an object. For example, the statements

```
CurrentX = (Width - TextWidth("Hello World")) / 2
CurrentY = (Height - TextHeight("Hello World")) /2
Print "Hello World"
```

center the text `Hello World` within a form. The **TextWidth** and **TextHeight** methods return a string's width and height, respectively, taking into account the object's font size and style. In a similar manner, you can set the current print position to the beginning of line number *n*, using the statement syntax

```
CurrentX = 0
CurrentY = object-name.TextHeight(string) * (n - 1)
```

For example, the statements

```
CurrentX = 0
CurrentY = TextHeight("Hello World") * 9
```

set the cursor to the beginning of line 10 in the current form.

Printer Output

Output can be sent to the printer in the same manner as output displayed on a screen object. This is because Visual Basic defines the printer as an object named **Printer**. Thus, the statement

```
Printer.Print "Hello World"
```

causes the text `Hello World` to be output on the printer. To force output onto a new page, the page-eject command

```
Printer.Newpage
```

can be used. Similarly, to ensure that all data is sent to the printer and not stored in an internal buffer area, the statement

```
Printer.EndDoc
```

should be issued as the last command to the printer after all output has been sent.

Exercises 4.2

1. Determine and write out the display produced by the following statements:

   ```
   Format(155.986, "Currency")
   Format(155.986, "Fixed")
   Format(155.986, "General Number")
   Format(0.155986, "Percent")
   Format(155.986, "Scientific")
   Format(155.986, "Standard")
   Format(155.986, "Yes/No")
   Format(155.986, "True/False")
   ```

   Round →

   155.99

   155.986

   15.60

   1.56E 02

   155.99

   Yes

   True

2. Determine and write out the display produced by the following statements:

   String val

   a. `Format(5, "##")` |5| only one # position is used

   b. `Format(5, "####")` |5| " " " " "

   c. `Format(56829, "####")` |56829| # place holder is ignored

   d. `Format(5.26, "###.##")` |5.26| only three # positions are used

   e. `Format(5.267, "###.##")` |5.27|

   f. `Format(53.264, "###.##")` |53.26|

   g. `Format(534.264, "###.##")` |534.26|

   h. `Format(534., "###.##")` |534|

3. Determine the errors in each of the following statements:

   a. `Format("##", 5)` ← (5, "##")

   b. `Format(56829, #####)` (56829, "#####")

   c. `Format("526.768", "###")` (526.768, "###")

   d. `Format("526.78", """".""")` (526.78,

   8.

4. Write out the display produced by the following statements:

   a. `Format(126.27, "###.##")` |126.27|
      `Format(82.3, "###.##")` |82.3|
      `Format(1.756, "###.##")` |1.76|

   b. `Format(26.27, "###.##")` |26.27|
      `Format(682.3, "###.##")` |682.3|
      `Format(1.968, "###.##")` |1.97|
      `Print "------"`
      `Format(26.27 + 682.3 + 1.968", "###.##")`

   c. `Format(26.27, "Currency")` $ 26.27
      `Format(682.3, "Currency")` $ 682.30
      `Format(1.968, "Currencly")` $ 1.97
      `Print "------"`
      `Format(26.27 + 682.3 + 1.968, "Currency")`

   d. `Format(34.164, "###.##")` |34.16|
      `Format(10.003, "###.##")` |10.00|
      `Print "------"`
      `Format(34.164 + 10.003, "###.##")`

4.3 Named Constants

Literal data is any data within a procedure that explicitly identifies itself. For example, the constants 2 and 3.1416 in the assignment statement

```
circumference = 2 * 3.1416 * radius
```

are also called literals because they are literally included directly in the statement. Additional examples of literals are contained in the following Visual Basic assignment statements. See if you can identify them.

```
perimeter = 2 * length * width
        y = (5 * p) / 7.2
salestax = 0.05 * purchase
```

The literals are the numbers 2, 5, and 7.2, and 0.05 in the first, second, and third statements, respectively.

Quite frequently, literal data used within a procedure have a more general meaning that is recognized outside the context of the procedure. Examples of these types of constants include the number 3.1416, which is the value of π accurate to four decimal places, 32.2 ft/sec^2, which is the gravitational constant, and the number 2.71828, which is Euler's number accurate to five decimal places.

The meaning of certain other constants appearing in a procedure are defined strictly within the context of the application being programmed. For example, in a procedure to determine bank interest charges, the value of the interest rate takes on a special meaning. Similarly, in determining the weight of various sized objects, the density of the material being used takes on a special significance. Constants such as these are sometimes referred to as both *manifest constants* and *magic numbers*. By themselves the constants are quite ordinary, but in the context of a particular application they have a special ("manifest" or "magical") meaning. Frequently, the same manifest constant appears repeatedly within the same procedure. This recurrence of the same constant throughout a procedure is a potential source of error, should the constant have to be changed. For example, if either the interest rate changes, or a new material is employed with a different density, the programmer has the cumbersome task of changing the value of the magic number everywhere it appears in the procedure. Multiple changes, however, are subject to error: if just one value is overlooked and not changed or if the same value used in different contexts is changed when only one of the values should have been, the result obtained when the procedure is run will be incorrect.

To avoid the problems of having such constants spread throughout a procedure, and to clearly permit identification of more universal constants, such as π, Visual Basic allows the programmer to give these constants their own symbolic names. Then, instead of using the constant throughout the procedure, the symbolic name is used instead. If the number ever has to be changed, the change need only be made once, at the point where the symbolic name is equated to the actual constant value. Equating numbers to symbolic names is accomplished using the **Const** statement. The syntax for this statement within a form's procedure is

> **Const** *name* As *data-type* = *expression*

For example, the number 3.1416 can be equated to the symbolic name `PI` using the **Const** statement $\pi = \frac{22}{7} \neq 3 \cdot 1416$

```
Const PI As Single = 3.1416
```

Constants used in this fashion are called both *named constants* and *symbolic constants*, and we shall use both terms interchangeably. The constant's name must be selected using the same rules as those for choosing a variable's name. Once a constant has been named, the name can be used in any Visual Basic statement in place of the number itself. For example, the assignment statement

```
circumference = 2 * PI * radius
```

makes use of the symbolic constant `PI`. This statement must, of course, appear after the declaration of the named constant is made. Within a form module, all **Const** statements must be placed

- In the **(Declaration)** section of the **(General)** object, either before or after the **Option Explicit** statement; or
- Anywhere within a procedure, though for clarity they are usually placed immediately after the procedure's header line.

In the first case, the constant can be used by all procedures connected to the form and its objects. In the second case, the constant can only be used within the procedure from its point of declaration to the end of the procedure. In this case, the constant is said to be local to the procedure declaring it.

Although we have typed the named constant `PI` in uppercase letters, lowercase letters could have been used. It is common in Visual Basic, however, to use uppercase letters for symbolic constants, at least for the initial letter of the name. Then, whenever a programmer sees an initial uppercase letter in a procedure, he or she will know the name is a symbolic constant defined in a **Const** statement, not a variable name declared in a declaration statement.

Program 4-3 illustrates the use of the **Const** statement declared within an event procedure. The interface for this project is shown on Figure 4-12. As illustrated, the graphical user interface consists of two Command buttons and a Picture box.

Figure 4-12

Program 4-3's Interface

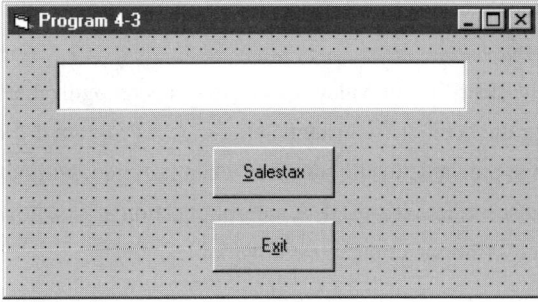

Table 4-5 The Properties Table for Program 4-3		
Object	**Property**	**Setting**
Form	Name	frmMain
	Caption	Program 4-3
Picture Box	Name	picShow
	Height	495
	Width	4095
	TabStop	False
Command Button	Name	cmdTax
	Caption	&Salestax
Command Button	Name	cmdExit
	Caption	E&xit

For this application the only procedures will be for the Command button **Click** events. The required procedures are listed in Program 4-3's Event Code.

Program 4-3's Event Code

always const (handwritten annotation)

```
Private Sub cmdOps_Click()
  Const TAXRATE As Single = 0.05
  Dim amount As Single, taxes As Single, total As Single

  picShow.Cls
  amount = InputBox("Enter the amount purchased", "Input Box", "0")
  taxes = TAXRATE * amount
  total = amount + taxes
  picShow.Print "The sales tax is "; Format(taxes, "Currency")
  picShow.Print "The total bill is "; Format(total, "Currency")
End Sub

Private Sub cmdExit_Click()
  Beep
  End
End Sub
```

Figure 4-13

A Sample Output Displayed by Program 4-3

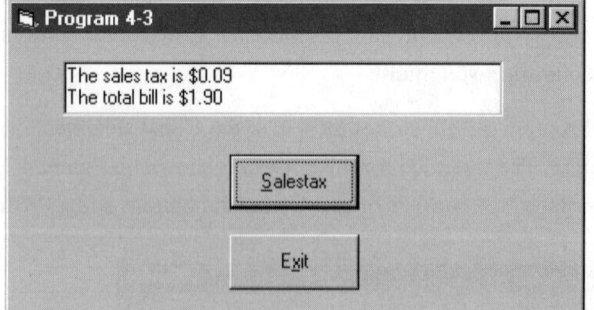

The output displayed in the Picture box, when the Command button is clicked and an input value of 36.60 is entered in the InputBox dialog, is shown Figure 4-13.

The advantage of using a symbolic constant such as PI is that it clearly identifies the value 3.1416 in terms recognizable to most people. The advantage of using the symbolic constant TAXRATE in Program 4-3 is that it permits a programmer to change the value of the salestax, when required, without having to search through the procedure to see where it's used. A natural question arises, however, as to the actual difference between symbolic constants and variables.

The value of a variable can be altered anywhere within a program. By its nature, a symbolic constant is a constant value that must not be altered after it is defined. Naming a constant, rather than assigning its value to a variable, ensures that the value in the constant cannot be subsequently altered. Whenever a symbolic constant appears in an instruction, it has the same effect as the constant it represents. Thus, TAXRATE in Program 4-3 is simply another way of representing the number 0.05. Since TAXRATE and the number 0.05 are equivalent, the value of TAXRATE may not be subsequently changed within the program. Once TAXRATE has been defined as a constant, an assignment statement such as

```
TAXRATE = 0.06
```

is meaningless and will result in an error message, because TAXRATE is not a variable. Since TAXRATE is only a stand-in for the value 0.05, this last statement is equivalent to writing the invalid statement 0.05 = 0.06.

In addition to using the **Const** statement to name constants, as in Program 4-3, this statement can also be used to equate the value of a constant expression to a symbolic name. A constant expression is an expression consisting of operators and constants only (no variables or intrinsic functions are allowed). For example, the statement

```
Const CONVERT As Single = 3.1416/180
```

equates the value of the constant expression 3.1416/180 to the symbolic name CONVERT. The symbolic name, as always, can be used in any statement following its definition. For example, since the expression 3.1416/180 is required for converting degrees to radians, the symbolic name selected for this conversion factor can be conveniently used whenever such a conversion is required.

A previously defined, symbolic constant can also be used in a subsequent **Const** statement. For example, the following sequence of statements is valid:

```
Const PI As Single = 3.1416
Const CONVERT As Single = PI/180
```

Since the constant 3.1416 has been equated to the symbolic name PI, it can be used legitimately in any subsequent definition, even within another **Const** statement.

An interesting modification to the **Const** statement is that **As** *data-type* clause may be omitted. When the data type is not explicitly declared, Visual Basic will select the data type that is most appropriate for the value. For example, if you use the statement

```
Const PI = 3.14159265358979
```

which has 14 digits of precision after the decimal point, Visual Basic will automatically make this a **Double** value.

Finally, you can place more than one constant declaration on a line, as long as each constant assignment is separated by a comma. For example, following **Const** statement is valid:

```
Const PI = 3.1415, CONVERT = 360/PI
```

Exercises 4.3

1. Rewrite the following event procedure using a **Const** statement for the constant 3.1416.

```
Private Sub Form_Click()
  Dim radius As Single, area As Single
  Dim circumference as Single
  Const PI AS Single = 3.1416
  radius = InputBox("Enter a radius:", "Input Dialog", "0")
  circumference = 2 * 3.1416 * radius
  area = 3.1416 * radius ^ 2
  Print "The circumference of the circle is "; circumference
  Print "The area of the circle is "; area
End Sub
```

2. Rewrite the following procedure so that the variable `prime` is changed to a symbolic constant.

```
Private Sub Form_Click()
  Dim prime As Single
  Dim amount As Single, interest As Single

  prime = 0.08        ' prime interest rate
  amount = InputBox("Enter the amount"; "Input Dialog", "0")
  interest = prime * amount
  Print "The interest earned is"; interest; " dollars"
End Sub
```

Const. prime As single = 0.08

3. Rewrite the following procedure to use the symbolic constant FACTOR in place of the expression (5/9) used in the procedure.

```
Private Sub Form_Click()
  Dim fahren As Single, celsius As Single

  fahren = InputBox("Enter a temperature in degrees Fahrenheit",,"0")
  celsius = (5/9) * (fahren - 32)
  Print "The equivalent Celsius temperature is "; celsius
End Sub
```

Const factor As single = 5/9

4.4 Common Programming Errors and Problems

The common programming errors and problems associated with the material presented in this chapter are:

1. Calling the **InputBox** function without assigning its return value to a variable. The **InputBox** function can only be used on the right hand side of an assignment statement.
2. Forgetting to clear the **Text** property of a Text box control that will be used for input purposes, unless an initial value is to be inserted in the Text box.
3. Mixing up the argument order used in the **Format** function. The first argument is the expression to be formatted, while the second argument is the desired format.
4. Forgetting to enclose the format argument in the **Format** function within double quotes.

4.5 Chapter Review

Key Terms

Format function	named constant
InputBox	print zones
Label	Text box
MsgBox	user-input validation

Summary

1. The **InputBox** function permits a user to enter a single value into an executing procedure. A commonly used syntax for this calling function is

    > **InputBox**(*prompt, title, default*)

    where *prompt* is a required string and both *title* and *default*, which are also strings, are optional. If a title string is used, it is displayed in the title bar of the dialog box; otherwise, the application's name is placed in the title bar. If a default string is provided, it is placed within the input area of the dialog box. A *prompt* is a message telling a user that input is required. The prompt, which is always required, is displayed as a string within the input dialog box. For example, the statement

    ```
    S = InputBox("Enter a value", "Input Dialog", "0")
    ```

    calls the **InputBox** function with the arguments `"Enter a value"`, which is the prompt, `"Input Dialog"`, which is the title, and a default string value of `0`. Here the returned value is assigned to the variable `S`.

2. A Label control is used to display text on a GUI. It is commonly used as a prompt for a Text box.

3. Text boxes are the most commonly used method of providing interactive user input. The data entered into a text box becomes the value of the Text box's **Text** property, and is always stored as a string. In addition to being set at run time by the user, the **Text** property can also be set at design time and at run time under program control. The **Text** property value is accessed using the standard object dot notation, in which the property name is separated from the object name using a dot. For example, the identifier `txtInput.Text` refers to the **Text** property of a Text box named `txtInput`.

4. A **Const** statement is used to equate a constant to a symbolic name. The syntax of this statement is

    > **Const** *name* As *data-type = constant expression*

    where a constant expression can only include constants and operators (no variables or intrinsic functions). For example, the number `3.1416` can be equated to the symbolic name `PI` using the **Const** statement

    ```
    Const PI As Single = 3.1416
    ```

    Once a symbolic name has been equated to a value, another value may not be assigned to the symbolic name.

4.6 Looking Further: Introduction to Version 5.0's Debugging Environment ▬▬

Debugging refers to the process of finding errors, or "bugs," in program code and correcting them. Visual Basic provides a number of debugging tools that can help in this process by analyzing program execution and permitting a look inside application code as it is running. This is accomplished by setting *breakpoints* in your code, which stop a program when they are reached; running your code in *single-step mode*, which executes one instruction at a time; or setting *watch expressions*, which permit you to monitor the values of selected variables and expressions while a program is executing. To accomplish this, and other useful debugging tasks, Version 5.0 provides three distinct debugging windows, which are shown in Figure 4-14, and two dialog boxes. Each of these debugging elements is described in Table 4-6.

Figure 4-14

The Three Debug Windows

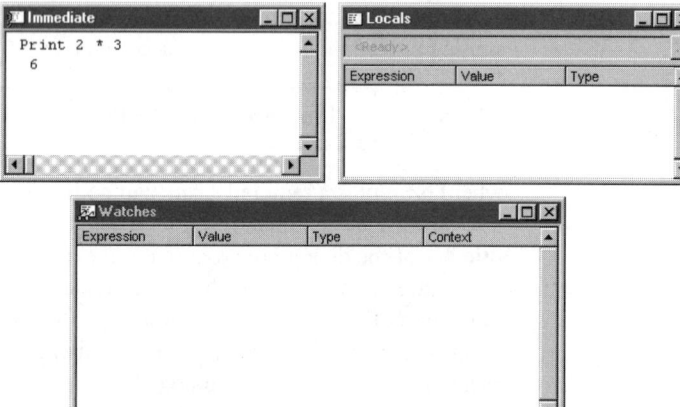

Table 4-6 The Debug Windows and Dialog Boxes

Name	Use
Immediate window (replaces prior versions' Immediate pane)	Displays information resulting from debugging statements in your code or from typed directly into this window. Useful for immediately determining the effect of a single-line statement (cannot accommodate multi-line statements). It is automatically opened in Break mode, but can also be used in Design mode. Code can be dragged, copied, and pasted between the Code and Immediate windows, but code cannot be saved in the Immediate window.
Watch window (replaces prior versions' Watch pane)	Used in Break mode to display the values of all current watch expressions. This window will automatically appear when watch expressions are defined in a project and selected variables can be dragged into the Watch window from the Code window. Can be viewed in Design mode.
Locals window (new feature)	Used in Break mode. This window automatically displays all of the declared variables in the current procedure and their values. The Locals window is automatically updated whenever there is a change from Run to Break mode or the Stack dialog box is accessed. Can be viewed in Design mode.
Quick Watch dialog (equivalent to prior versions' Instant Watch)	Only available in Break mode to display the current value of a single variable, property, or watch expression and the procedure in which it is currently being used.
Call Stack dialog (same as prior versions' Call Stack dialog)	Only available in Break mode to list the procedure calls in an application that have started but are not yet completed.

Figure 4-15

Activating the Debug Windows from the Menu Bar

Each of the three Debug windows can be activated in either Design or Break mode from within the View menu, as shown in Figure 4-15, while the dialog boxes can only be activated in Break mode. Additionally, the Debug windows and dialog boxes can be activated directly from the Debug toolbar, which is shown in Figure 4-16.

If the Debug toolbar is not visible, you can make it so using the Toolbars option from the View menu, as shown in Figure 4-17.

The Watch and Locals windows are most effective when used in Break mode. In this mode, a program's execution is temporarily suspended and the various Debug windows are used to gain a "snapshot" view of the values of variables and expressions at the point in your code where execution has been temporarily suspended. Once in a Debug window, during Break mode, you can change the value of variables and properties to see how the changes affect the application.

Figure 4-16

The Debug Toolbar's Buttons

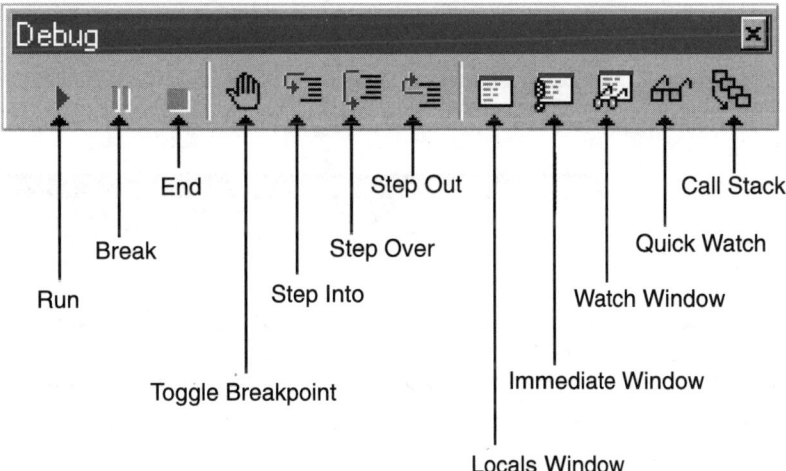

Break mode can only be reached from run-time mode. In Break mode program execution is suspended, which gives you an opportunity to both view and edit code. You can always determine the mode you are in by examining Visual Basic's title bar. Figure 4-18 shows how the title bar looks in each of the three modes: Design, Run, and Break.

Figure 4-17

Making the Debug Toolbar Visible

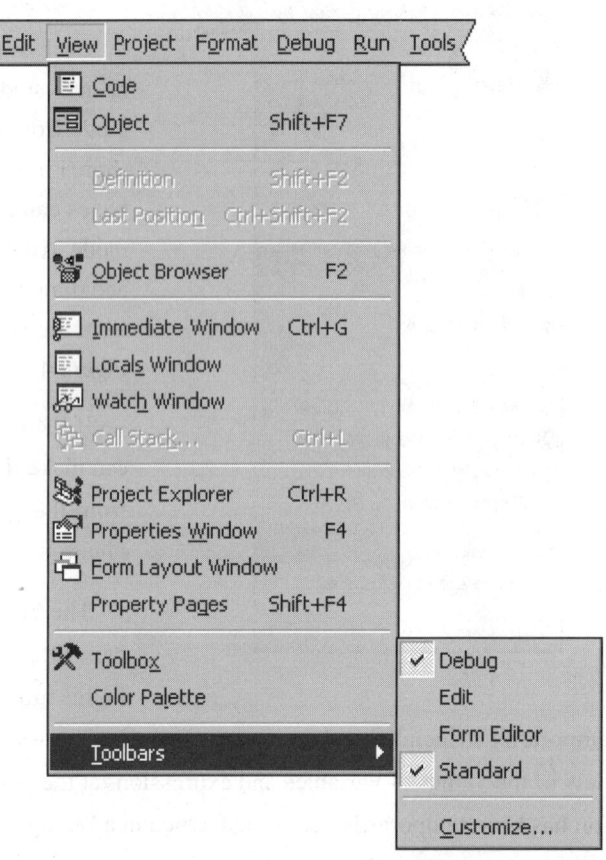

Figure 4-18

Identifying the Current Mode

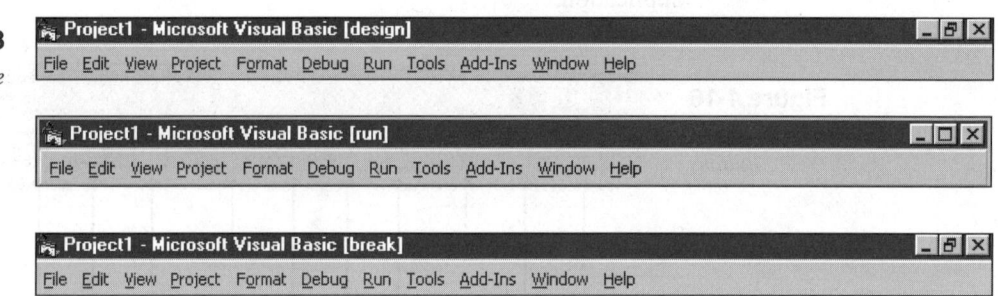

Table 4-7 Debug Window Facilities by Mode

Mode	Available Facility
Design Time	You can activate all three Debug windows, set breakpoints in the Code window, and create Watch expressions. You can only execute code from within the Immediate window.
Run Time	You can view code by running in either single-step mode or by having set a breakpoint. You cannot directly access any of the Debug windows.
Break	You can view and edit code in the Code window and you can examine and modify data in all of the Debug windows. You can restart the program, end execution, or continue execution from the suspended point.

The characteristics of each of Visual Basic's three operating modes, as they relate to Visual Basic's debugging facilities, are listed in Table 4-7

Figure 4-19

The Standard Toolbar's Start, Break, and End Buttons

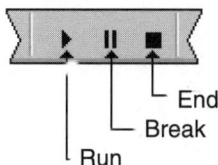

Switching from one mode to another can be accomplished using Menu options, Function keys, or Toolbar buttons. For example, you already know how to switch from Design mode to Run mode by using either the <u>R</u>un menu option or pressing the F5 function key. Additionally, you can use one of the three Standard Toolbar buttons illustrated in Figure 4-19 to switch between modes. Table 4-8 lists the buttons that are active in each mode. Notice that when in Break mode, the Start button becomes a Continue button.

With this as background, let's now write an application that uses the Immediate and Locals windows (in Section 7.8 we show how to use the Watch window). To do this, enter Event Procedure 4-3 in a new project.

Table 4-8 Toolbar Button Availability	
Mode	**Available Mode Buttons and Access Keys**
Design Time	Start (F5 key)
Run Time	Break (Ctrl + Break keys) and End
Break	Continue (F5 key) and End

Event Procedure 4-3

```
Private Sub Form_Click()
  Dim n As Single

  n = 5
  Cls
  Print n
  Debug.Print "Hello World!"
  Print n
End Sub
```

Once you have entered this event procedure, run the program but *do not* activate the form's **Click** event. Instead, press the Break toolbar button. At this point the Immediate window should appear (if it does not, activate it using the <u>V</u>iew menu options (see Figure 4-15). You can now use this window to examine the value of variables set in a program, change these values, or enter data to produce an immediate result. For example, type in the following lines in the Immediate window[2]:

```
a = 25
b = 2.5
c = a * b
? c
```

_____

[2]The Immediate window can also be activated and viewed from the <u>V</u>iew menu in both design or run modes. It can only be used to evaluate immediate commands, however, in break and design modes.

Programmers' Notes

Activating Break Mode

You can only move to Break mode while a program is executing. To switch to Break mode at run-time, do one of the following:

1. Press the Break Toolbar button.
2. Start the program in single-step mode.
3. Press the Ctrl and Break keys at the same time while the program is running.
4. Set a breakpoint in the program (see Section 7.8).

When you press the Enter key, the Immediate window should appear as shown in Figure 4-20. Notice that the question mark, which is a shorthand way of asking, "What is the value of?" and is equivalent to the keyword **Print**, causes the value of c to be displayed.

Figure 4-20

Using the Debug Immediate Window

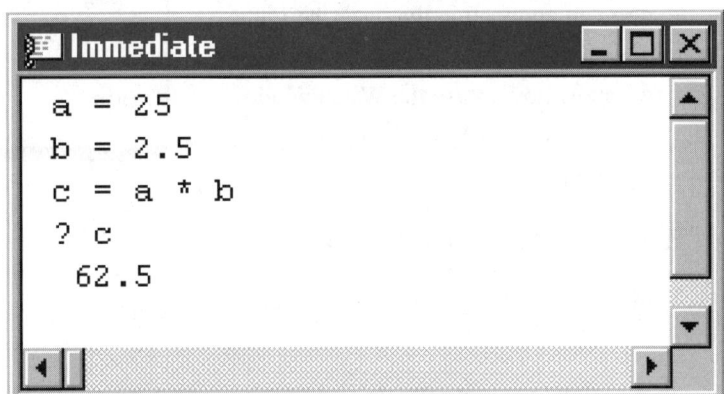

Single-Step Mode

Figure 4-21

The Initial Code Window

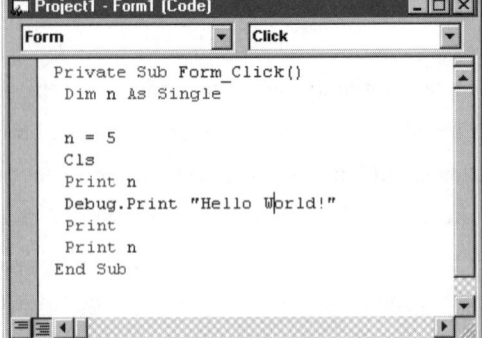

To illustrate how to use both the Locals and Immediate windows to view and change a variable's data, we will single step through Event Procedure 4-3. To begin this process make sure that the Code window illustrated in Figure 4-21 is showing on your design screen and then initiate single-step mode by using one of the following steps:

- Press the F8 key, or
- Select the Step Into option from the Debug menu, as shown on Figure 4-22, or
- Press the Step Into tool button on the Debug Toolbar (see Figure 4-16).

Figure 4-22

Activating Step Into Mode from the View Menu

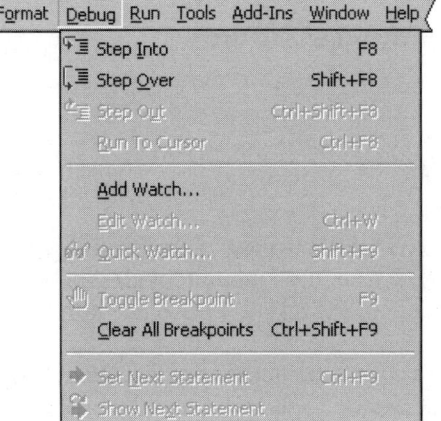

Once the program is running, click the mouse. This will activate the form's **Click** event and will result in the screen shown in Figure 4-23. The highlighting of the procedure's header line and the arrow pointing to it indicate that this is the next statement to be executed. Continue pressing either the [F8] key or the Step-Into toolbar button until your screen appears as shown in Figure 4-24.

Figure 4-23

The Click Event Procedure in Single-Step Mode

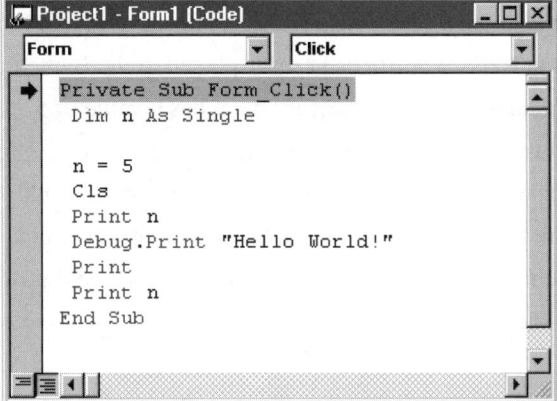

Notice in Figure 4-24 that the next statement to be executed is a **Print** statement, which will cause a blank line to be displayed on the form. At this point you are in Break mode. Activate both the Immediate and Locals windows using any of the following steps:

- Click on the partially hidden windows, or
- Select the windows from the <u>V</u>iew menu, or
- Select the windows from the Debug toolbar, or
- Press the [Ctrl]+[G] keys (this is the access key sequence) to select the Immediate window.

Figure 4-24

The Code Window after Five Single Steps

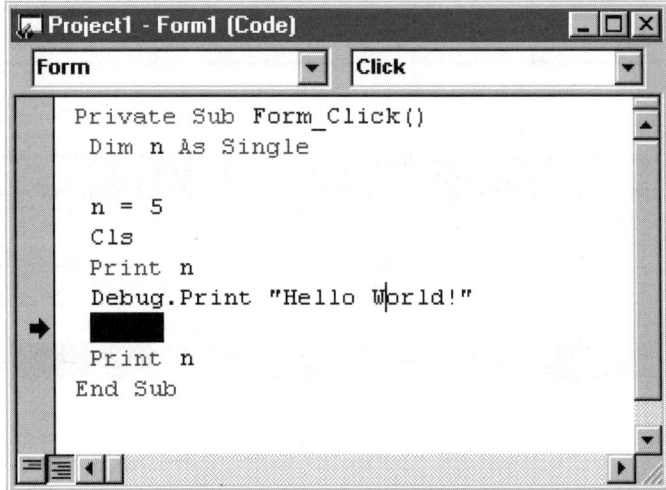

Programmers' Notes

Activating the Debug Windows

You can activate the various debug windows by doing one of the following:

1. Clicking on a partially hidden Debug window,
2. Selecting the desired window from the View menu (see Figure 4-15),
3. Selecting the desired window from the Debug toolbar (see Figure 4-16), or
4. Pressing the [Ctrl] and [G] keys at the same time to activate the Immediate window.[G]

The Immediate window can be used in both Design and Break modes. Although, both the Locals and Watch windows can be viewed in Design mode, they are only operationally only effective in Break mode.

At this point you should see the windows shown in Figures 4-25 and 4-26. Notice that the line Hello World! has been displayed in the Immediate window and that the Locals window shows that the variable n has a value of 5. The message in the Immediate window was printed by the statement `Debug.Print "Hello World!"` in the program code. The **Me** keyword listed in the Locals window is equivalent to an implicitly declared variable that refers to the current object, which in this case is the form object itself. If you click on this variable you will see the value of all properties associated with the form.

Figure 4-25

The Immediate Window After Five Single Steps

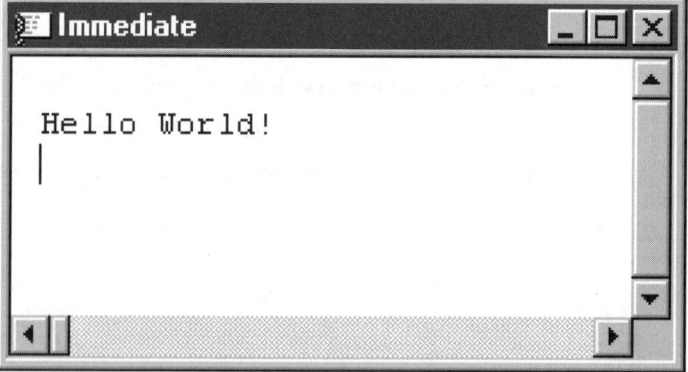

Figure 4-26

The Locals Window After Five Single Steps

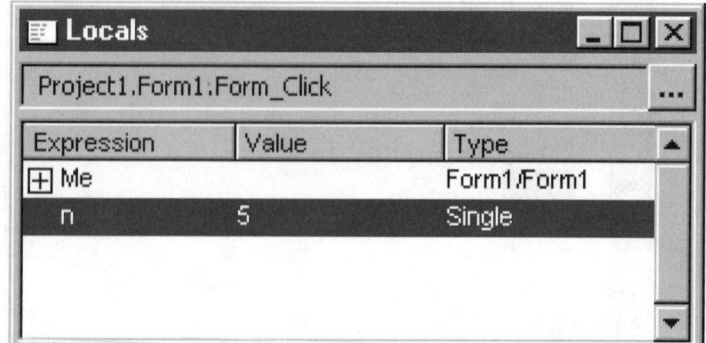

Once the Immediate and Locals windows are displayed we can use either of them
to both examine and alter the current state of each of the program's variables. For
example, enter the following two lines directly in the Immediate window:

```
? n
n = 10
```

The first line asks the value of the variable n, which was set to 5 by the program.
In response to this statement the value of 5 will be displayed in the Immediate
window. The second entered line changes the value of n to 10. Once these lines
have been entered, the Immediate and Locals windows will appear as shown in
Figure 4-27 and 4-28, respectively. Notice that once the statement n = 10 is
entered into the Immediate window and the ⌈Enter⌋ key is pressed, the value of n
changed from 5 to 10 in the Locals window. The value of this variable could just as
easily been changed directly in the Locals window. In practice, the Locals window
would be used, by itself, for examining and changing local variables, while the
Immediate window is used for entering a statement and immediately executing it to
determine its effect.

Figure 4-27

*Examining and Altering n's
Value From the
Immediate Window*

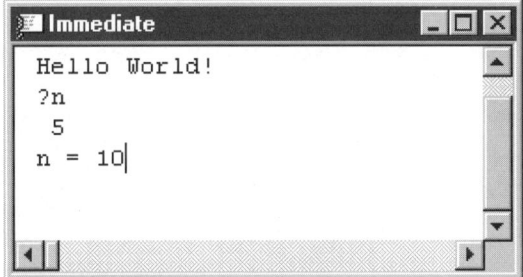

Figure 4-28

*Examining n's Value in the
Locals Window*

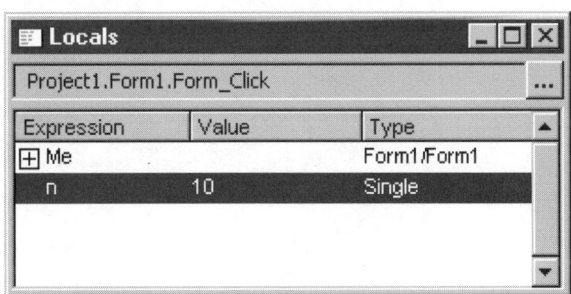

Now press the Run toolbar button to continue program execution. This will
take the program out of single-step mode and complete the event code's execution.
In Section 7.8 we will complete our introduction to the debugging environment by
showing you how to set breakpoints, create watch variables and use the Watch window.

Selection

5.1 Selection Controls

5.2 Relational Expressions

5.3 The If-Then-Else Structure

5.4 The If-Then-ElseIf Structure

5.5 The Select Case Structure

5.6 Common Programming Errors

5.7 Chapter Review

5.8 Looking Further: Errors, Testing, and Debugging

A decision requires making a choice between two or more alternatives. As you might expect, given the dual nature of Visual Basic, decisions can be implemented by both graphical and procedural means.

The graphical features consist of Toolbox control objects specifically designed to provide a selection of input choices. These controls are listed in Table 5-1. The first two, the Check box and Option button controls are presented in Section 5.1. The remaining controls are described in Chapters 11 and Appendix D.

On the procedural side, selection statements are used to make decisions on what action or computation should be performed based upon either an expression or property value. Examples of such basic decisions include setting a type in bold only if a Check box has been selected, performing a division only if the divisor is not zero, printing different messages depending upon the value of a grade received, and so on. In this way, selection statements determine the flow of control of procedural code execution based on tested conditions being True or False.

The term flow of control refers to the order in which a program's procedural code statements are executed. Unless directed otherwise, the normal flow of control for procedural statements within an event procedure is sequential. This means that once a procedure is invoked, statements within that procedure are executed in sequence, one after the other.

Selection statements, presented in this chapter starting with Section 5.2, permit this sequential flow of control to be altered in precisely defined ways. Specifically, selection statements determine the procedural code to be executed next, based on a comparison operation. Repetition statements, which are used to repeat a set of procedural code, can also alter a procedure's flow of control. They are presented in the next chapter.

Table 5-1 Selection Controls

Control	Use
Check Box	A Yes/No toggle selection.
Option Button	Select only one option from a group.
List Box	Select one or more options from a predefined list.
Combo Box	Select from a predefined list or type in a selection.
Horizontal and Vertical Scroll Bars	Select a number from a sequential range of numbers.

5.1 Selection Controls

Except for the Combo box control, which is a combination of a List box and a Text box control, all of the controls listed in Table 5-1 limit the user to selecting from a pre-defined set of choices. In this regard, both the Combo box and Text box controls are less restrictive. What this means in practice is that the procedural code used to decide what was entered in either a Text box or Combo box is generally more complex than that needed for the other controls listed in Table 5-1. We will see an example of this in Section 5-3, where the input from a Text box is processed to ensure that a user types in a legitimate value. The advantage of the controls listed in Table 5-1 (with the exception of the Combo box), is that they force a user to choose between programmer-defined choices. In this section we present the Check box and Option button input controls.

The Check box Control

The Check box control provides a user with a simple Yes-or-No option. For example, in the interface shown in Figure 5-1 there are two Check boxes. The Properties table for this interface is listed in Table 5.2.

As illustrated in Figure 5-1, both Check boxes are unchecked initially. These settings were set at design-time using the Check box's **Value** property and can be altered by the user at run-time, either by clicking on the box, pressing the Space Bar key when the box is in focus, or pushing the hot-key sequence defined for the box. It can also be changed at run-time using program code, where settings of 0, 1, or 2 correspond to unchecked, checked, and grayed (which represents unavailable), respectively.

Each Check box in an application is independent of any other Check box. This means that the choice made in one box has no effect on, and does not depend on, the choice made in another box. As such, Check boxes are useful for providing a set of one or more options

Figure 5-1

An Interface with Two Check boxes

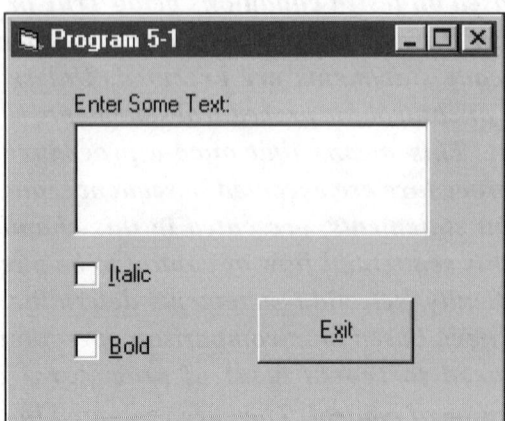

Introduction to Visual Basic

Table 5-2 The Properties Table for Figure 5-1

Object	Property	Setting
Form	Name	`frmMain`
	Caption	`Program 5-1`
Label	Name	`lblPrompt`
	Caption	`Enter Some Text`
Text box	Name	`txtBox1`
	Text	`(Blank)`
	Font	`Ms Sans Serif`
	FontBold	`False`
	FontItalic	`False`
	BackColor	`White (Palette tab)`
Check box 1	Name	`chkItalic`
	Caption	`&Italic`
	Value	`0-Unchecked`
Check box 2	Name	`chkBold`
	Caption	`&Bold`
	Value	`0-Unchecked`
Command button	Name	`cmdExit`
	Caption	`E&xit`

that can be in effect at the same time, provided that each option is individually of the Yes/ No, On/Off, or True/False type. For example, in the interface shown on Figure 5-1 the Check box options consist of a set of two Check boxes that permit independent selection of how the text is to be displayed. Selecting or deselecting Bold has no effect on the choice for Italic or nonItalic.

Because of their On/Off nature, Check boxes are also known as toggle selections, where a user can effectively toggle (switch back and forth) between a check mark and no check mark. If no check mark appears in a box, clicking on it changes its **Value** property to 1 and causes a check to appear; otherwise, if the box has a check, clicking on it changes its **Value** property to 0 and causes the check to be erased.

Although the Check boxes allow a user to make a selection easily, the programmer must still provide the code to activate that selection and then act appropriately on it. Doing so requires the **If-Else** selection statement described in the next section. In anticipation of this material, Program 5-1's event code is given below.

Program 5-1's Event Code

```
Private Sub chkItalic_Click()
  If chkItalic.Value = vbChecked Then
    txtBox1.FontItalic = True
  Else
    txtBox1.FontItalic = False
End Sub
```

(Continued)

```
Private Sub chkBold_Click()
  If chkBold.Value = vbChecked Then
    txtBox1.FontBold = True
  Else
    txtBox1.FontBold = False
End Sub

Private Sub cmdExit_Click()
  Beep
  End
End Sub
```

Notice in this event code that the **Click** events for both the Italic and Bold Check boxes use an **If** statement containing their respective **Value** properties. Based on the value, which will be either 1 or 0, the Text box **Font** property, **FontItalic** or **FontBold**, is set to either **True** or **False**. The term **vbChecked** is a system-defined named constant that has the value 1.

The Option button Control

The Option button control provides a user with a set of one or more choices, only one of which can be selected. Selecting one Option button immediately deselects and clears all the other buttons in the group. Thus, the choices in an Option button group are mutually exclusive. Because Option buttons operate in the same manner as the channel selector buttons provided on radios, where selecting one channel automatically deselects all other channels, Option buttons are also referred to as "radio buttons."

As an example, consider a form that requires information on the marital status of an employee. As the employee can be either Single, Married, Divorced, or Widowed, selecting one category automatically means the other categories are not selected. This type of choice is ideal for an Option button group, as shown in Figure 5-2, where the group consists of four individual Option buttons.

Each Option button placed on a form is automatically part of a group. To create separate groups of Option buttons you can place these controls on a form directly or inside both Picture boxes and Frames. All Option buttons placed directly on a form constitute a single option group. To create separate groups within either a Picture box or Frame you must draw these controls on the GUI *before* placing an Option button within them. Placing an Option button outside of a Picture box or Frame and then dragging them into the control, or drawing a Picture box or Frame around existing Option buttons, will not produce the same result. In either of these cases, the Option buttons will remain part of their original group.

Figure 5-2

An Option Button Group

For example, in the interface shown in Figure 5-3, we have added an Option button group to the interface previously used in Program 5-1. This option group consists of three individual Option buttons with the captions Courier, SansSerif, and

Seri£, respectively. We will use these buttons to select the style of print displayed in the text box. Since these styles are mutually exclusive, the choice of Option buttons for this selection is appropriate. The Properties table for this interface is listed in Table 5-3.

Figure 5-3

An Interface with an Option Button Group

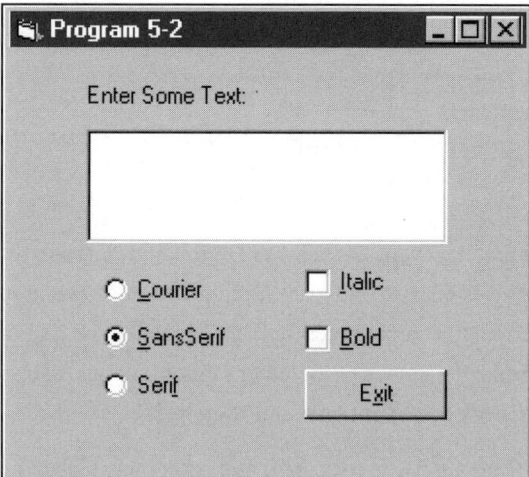

Notice in Properties Table 5-3 that only one of the Option button's **Value** properties has been set to **True**. Setting the second Option button **Value** to **True** automatically sets the remaining Option button's **Value** property to **False**. The event code for these Option buttons is listed below. The remaining event code for Program 5-2 is the same as listed for Program 5-1.

Table 5-3 Program 5-2's Properties Table

Object	Property	Setting
Form	Name	frmMain
	Caption	Program 5-1
Label	Name	lblPrompt
	Caption	Enter Some Text
Text box	Name	txtBox1
	Text	(Blank)
	Font	Ms Sans Serif
	FontBold	False
	FontItalic	False
	BackColor	White (Palette tab)
Check box 1	Name	chkItalic
	Caption	&Italic
	Value	0-Unchecked
Check box 2	Name	chkBold
	Caption	&Bold
	Value	0-Unchecked
Option Button 1	Name	optCourier
	Caption	&Courier
	Value	False
Option Button 2	Name	optSansSerif
	Caption	&SansSerif
	Value	True
Option Button 3	Name	optSerif
	Caption	Seri&f
	Value	False
Command Button	Name	cmdExit
	Caption	E&xit

Program 5-2's Option Button Event Code

```
Private Sub optCourier_Click()
  txtBox1.Font = "Courier"
End Sub

Private Sub optSansSerif_Click()
  txtBox1.Font = "Ms Sans Serif"
End Sub

Private Sub optSerif_Click()
  txtBox1.Font = "Ms Serif"
End Sub
```

Notice that the event code for an Option button group does not require any selection statements. This is because only one Option button can be in effect at a time. Thus, the **Click** event for each button can unilaterally change the text box's Font property, without the need to first determine the values of the other Option buttons, using a selection statement like that used for the Check box event code in Program 5-1.

When Program 5-2 is executed, and before any Check box or Option button is checked, the typeface of user entered text is determined by the Text box's **Font**, **FontBold**, and **FontItalic** Property values set at design-time (see Table 5-3). For these values the text This is a test would appear as shown in Figure 5-4.

The text illustrated in Figure 5-4 and any subsequently entered text can now be changed by the user using the Check boxes and Option buttons. An Option button is selected at run-time in one of four ways:

- Clicking the mouse on the desired button;
- Tabbing to the Option button group and using the arrow keys;
- Using the access (hot) keys; or
- Assigning its **Value** property to **True** under program control, as for example, optSansSerif.Value = True.

For example, if the user checks the Bold and Italic Check boxes and the Courier Option button, the text will appear as shown in Figure 5-5.

Before we leave Program 5-2, one further comment is in order. Notice that, unlike the Check box event code, no selection statement is required in the procedural code used to set the font. This is because a selected Check box can be in one of two states, checked or unchecked, but a selected Option button is automatically set to **True**. Thus, once an option box is selected, it can be acted upon immediately, with no further processing needed to determine the state of its **Value** property. As we will see in Chapter 7, however, there is an alternative

Figure 5-4

An Example of User-Entered Text

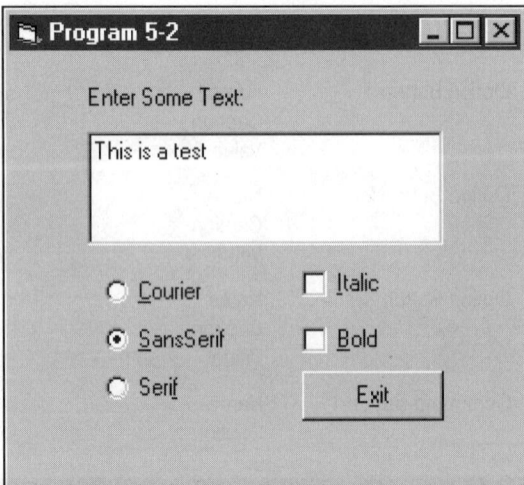

Figure 5-5

*The Text in Courier
Bold and Italic*

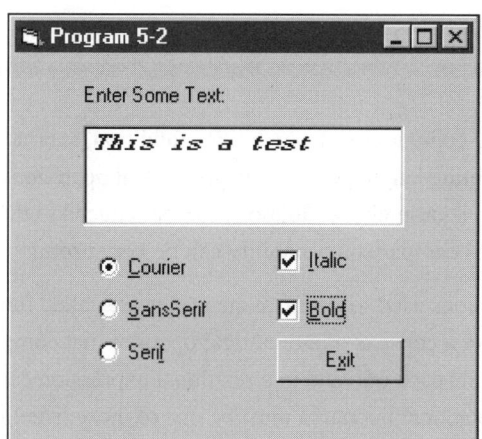

method of processing an Option button group that does use a selection statement. This method makes each button's **Click** event code call the same general procedure. This single general procedure then uses a selection statement to first determine which button's **Value** property is **True**, before setting the Text box's **Font** property.

Exercises 5.1

1. Determine whether the following choices should be presented on a GUI using either Check boxes or Option buttons:

   a. The choice of air conditioning or not on a new automobile order form.
   b. The choice of automatic or manual transmission on a new automobile order form.
   c. The choice of AM/FM, AM/FM Tape, or AM/FM CD radio on a new automobile order form.
   d. The choice of tape backup system or no tape backup system on a new computer order form.
   e. The choice of a 14-, 15-, or 17-inch color monitor on a new computer order form.
   f. The choice of CD-ROM drive or not on a new computer order form.
   g. The choice of a 4-, 6-, or 8-speed CD-ROM drive on a new computer order form.
   h. The choice of a 100-, 120-, or 200-MHZ Pentium processor on a new computer order form.

2. Enter and run Program 5-1 on your computer.

3. a. Modify Program 5-1 so that the choices presented by the Check boxes are replaced by Command buttons. (**Hint:** Each Check box can be replaced by two Command buttons.)
   b. Based on your experience with Exercise 3a., determine what type of input choice is best presented using a Check box rather than Command buttons.

4. a. Modify Program 5-1 so that the choices presented by the Check boxes are replaced by Option buttons.
   b. Based on your experience with Exercises 4a., determine what type of input choice is best presented using a Check box rather than an Option button.

5. Enter and run Program 5-2 on your computer.

6. Modify Program 5-2 so that the user can also specify the point size for the Text box. The default point size should be 10, with the user capable of choosing between 8, 10, and 12 points.

5.2 Relational Expressions

Besides providing computational capabilities (addition, subtraction, multiplication, division, etc.), all programming languages provide procedural operations for comparing quantities. Because many decision-making situations can be reduced to the level of choosing between two quantities, this comparison capability can be very useful.

The expressions used to compare quantities are called relational expressions. A *simple relational expression* consists of a relational operator that compares two operands as shown in Figure 5-6. While each operand in a relational expression can be any valid Visual Basic expression, the relational operators must be one of those listed in Table 5-4. These relational operators may be used with all of Visual Basic's data types, but must be typed exactly as given in Table 5-4. Thus, while the following examples are all valid:

```
age > 40        length <= 50       temp > 98.6
3 < 4           flag = done        id_num = 682
day <> 5        2.0 > 3.3          hours > 40
```

the following are invalid:

```
length =< 50     ' operator out of order
2.0 >> 3.3       ' invalid operator
```

Relational expressions are sometimes called *conditions,* and we will use both terms to refer to these expressions. Like all Visual Basic expressions, relational expressions are evaluated to yield a result. For relational expressions this result is one of the boolean values, **True** or **False**. For example, the expression 3 < 4 is always **True**, and the expression 2 > 3 is always **False**. Thus, the event code

```
Private Sub Form_Click()
    Print "The value of 3 < 4 is "; 3 < 4
    Print "The value of 2 > 3 is "; 2 > 3
End Sub
```

can be used to display the value of the expressions 3 < 4 and 2 > 3, respectively, and produce the display

```
The value of 3 < 4 is True
The value of 2.0 > 3.0 is False
```

The value of a relational expression such as hours > 40 depends on the value stored in the variable hours. In Visual Basic, a condition such as this is typically used as part of a selection statement. In these statements, which are presented in the next section, the selection of which statement is to be executed next is based on the value of the condition (**True** or **False**).

Figure 5-6

Structure of a Simple Relational Expression

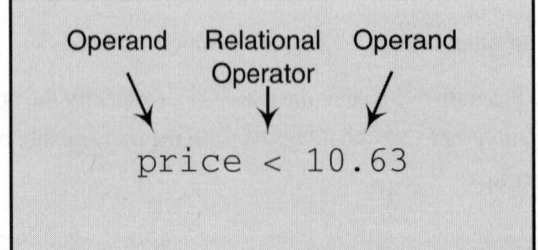

Table 5-4 Relational Operators

Operator	Meaning	Example
<	Less than	age < 30
>	Greater than	height > 6.2
<=	Less than or equal to	taxable <= 20000
>=	Greater than or equal to	temp >= 98.6
=	Equal to	grade = 100
<>	Not equal to	number <> 250

In addition to numerical operands, character data can also be compared using relational operators. For example, in ANSI code the letter 'A' is stored using code with a lower numerical value than that storing the letter 'B', the code for a 'B' is lower in value than the code for a 'C', and so on. For character sets coded in this manner, the following conditions are evaluated as listed:

Expression	Value
'A' > 'C'	False
'D' <= 'Z'	True
'E' = 'F'	False
'G' >= 'M'	False
'B' <> 'C'	True

Comparing letters is essential in alphabetizing names or using characters to select a particular option.

Finally, two string expressions may be compared using relational operators. Each character in a string is stored in binary using ANSI code. In this code, a blank precedes (is less than) all letters and numbers; the letters of the alphabet are stored in order from A to Z; and the digits are stored in order from 0 to 9. It is important to note that in ANSI the letters come before, or are less than, the digits.

When two strings are compared, their individual characters are compared one character pair at a time (both first characters, then both second characters, and so on). If no differences are found, the strings are equal; if a difference is found, the string with the first lower character is considered the smaller string. If all characters are the same but the end of the first string is reached before the end of the second string, the first string is considered less than the second string. Thus,

"JONES" is less than "SMITH" because the first 'J' in JONES is less than the first 'S' in SMITH.

"Hello" is less than "hello" because the first 'H' in Hello is less than the first 'h' in hello.

"Hello" is less than "Hello " because the second string is longer.

"Hello" is greater than "Good Bye" because the first 'H' in Hello is greater than the first 'G' in Good Bye.

"Behop" is greater than "Beehive" because the third character, the 'h', in Behop is greater than the third character, 'e', in Beehive.

"123" is greater than "1227" because the third character, '3', in 123 is greater than the third character, '2', in 1227.

"123" is less than "1237" because the first three characters are the same, but the first string is shorter.

Logical Operators

In addition to using simple relational expressions as conditions, more complex conditions can be created using the logical operators **And**, **Or**, and **Not**.

When the **And** operator is used with two simple expressions, the condition is **True** only if both individual expressions are **True** by themselves. Thus, the compound condition

```
(age > 40) And (term < 10)
```

is True only if age is greater than 40 and term is less than 10.

The logical **Or** operator is also applied between two expressions. When using the **Or** operator, the condition is satisfied if either one or both of the two expressions is **True**. Thus, the compound condition

```
(age > 40) Or (term < 10)
```

is **True** if either age is greater than 40, term is less than 10, or both conditions are True.

For the declarations

```
Dim i As Integer, j As Integer
Dim a As Single, b As Single
Dim complete as Boolean
```

the following represent valid conditions:

```
a > b
(i = j) Or (a < b) Or complete
(a/b > 5) And (i <= 20)
```

Before these conditions can be evaluated, the values of a, b, i, j, and complete must be known. Assuming

```
a = 12.0, b = 2.0, i = 15, j = 30, and complete = False
```

the previous expressions yield the following results:

Expression	Value
a > b	True
(i = j) Or (a < b) Or complete	False
(a/b > 5) And (i <= 20)	True

The **Not** operator is used to change an expression to its opposite state; that is, if the expression is **True**, then **Not** expression is **False**. Similarly, if an expression is **False** to begin with, then **Not** expression is **True**. For example, assuming the number 26 is stored in the variable age, the expression age > 40 is **False** and the expression Not(age > 40) is **True**. Since the **Not** operator is used with only one expression, it is a unary operator.

Relational and logical operators have a hierarchy of execution similar to the arithmetic operators. Table 5-5 lists the precedence of these operators, in relation to the other operators we have used. Since relational operators have a higher precedence then logical operators, the parentheses in an expression such as

```
(age > 40) And (term < 10)
```

Table 5-5 Precedence of Operators

Operation	Operator	Associativity
Exponentiation	^	Left to right
Negation	–	Left to right
Multiplication and Division	* /	Left to right
Integer Division	\	Left to right
Modulo arithmetic	Mod	Left to right
Addition and Subtraction	+ –	Left to right
String Concatenation	&	Left to right
Equality	=	Left to right
Inequality	<>	Left to right
Less than	<	Left to right
Greater than	>	Left to right
Less than or equal to	<=	Left to right
Greater than or equal to	>=	Left to right
Not	Not	Left to right
And	And	Left to right
Or	Or	Left to right

are not strictly needed. The evaluation of this expression is identical to the evaluation of the expression

```
age > 40 And term < 10
```

The following example illustrates the use of an operator's precedence and associativity to evaluate relational expressions, assuming the stated declarations and assignments:

```
Dim i As Integer, j As Integer, k As Integer
Dim x As Single
Dim key As String*1
i = 5
j = 7
k = 12;
x = 22.5;
key = "m"
```

Expression	Equivalent Expression	Value
`i + 2 = k - 1`	`(i + 2) = (k - 1)`	False
`3 * i - j < 22`	`(3 * i) - j < 22`	True
`i + 2 * j > k`	`(i + (2 * j)) > k`	True
`k + 3 <= -j + 3 * i`	`(k + 3) <= ((-j) + (3*i))`	False
`"a" <> "b"`	`"a" <> "b"`	True
`key < "p"`	`key < "p"`	True
`20.5 >= x + 10.2`	`25 >= (x + 10.2)`	False

As with arithmetic expressions, parentheses can be used both to alter the assigned operator priority and to improve the readability of relational and logical expressions. Since expressions within parentheses are evaluated first, the following complex condition is evaluated as

```
(6 * 3 = 36 / 2) Or (13 < 3 * 3 + 4) And Not (6 - 2 < 5) =
        (18 = 18) Or (13 < 9 + 4) And Not (4 < 5) =
            (True) Or (13 < 13)  And Not (True) =
            (True) Or  (False)  And (False) =
            (True) Or (False) =
                    True
```

A Numerical Accuracy Problem

A problem that can occur with Visual Basic's relational expressions is a subtle numerical accuracy problem relating to floating point and double precision numbers. Due to the way computers store these numbers, tests for equality of floating point and double precision values and variables using the relational operator = should be avoided.

The reason for this is that many decimal numbers, such as 0.1, for example, cannot be represented exactly in binary using a finite number of bits. Thus, testing for exact equality for such numbers can fail. When equality of non-integer values is desired, it is better to require that the absolute value of the difference between operands be less than some extremely small value. Thus, for non integer numerical operands, the general expression:

```
operand_1 = operand_2
```

should be replaced by the condition

```
Abs(operand_1 - operand_2) < 0.000001
```

where the value 0.000001 can be altered to any other acceptably small value. Thus, if the difference between the two operands is less than 0.000001 (or any other user selected amount), the two operands are considered essentially equal. For example if x and y are single precision variables, a condition such as

```
x/y = 0.35
```

should be programmed as

```
Abs(x/y - 0.35) < 0.000001
```

This latter condition ensures that slight inaccuracies in representing non-integer numbers in binary do not affect evaluation of the tested condition. Since all computers have an exact binary representation of zero, comparisons for exact equality to zero don't encounter this numerical accuracy problem.

Exercises 5.2

1. Determine whether the value of each of the following expressions is **True** or **False**. Assume a = 5, b = 2, c = 4, d = 6, and e = 3.

   a. `a > b`
   b. `a <> b`
   c. `d Mod b = c Mod b`
   d. `a * c <> d * b`
   e. `d * b = c * e`
   f. `Not(a = b)`
   g. `Not(a < b)`

2. Write relational expressions to express the following conditions (use variable names of your own choosing):

   a. A person's age is equal to 30.
   b. A person's temperature is greater than 98.6 degrees Fahrenheit.

    c. A person's height is less than 6 feet.

    d. The current month is 12 (December).

    e. The letter input is *m*.

    f. A person's age is equal to 30 and that person is taller than 6 feet.

    g. The current day is the fifteenth day of the first month.

    h. A person is older than 50 or has been employed at the company for at least 5 years.

    i. A person's identification number is less than 500 and that person is older than 55.

    j. A length is greater than 2 feet and less than 3 feet.

3. Determine the value of the following expressions, assuming a = 5, b = 2, c = 4, and d = 5.

```
a. a = 5
b. b * d = c * c
c. d Mod b * c > 5 Or c Mod b * d < 7
```

4. Using parentheses, rewrite the following expressions to correctly indicate their order of evaluation. Then evaluate each expression, assuming all variables are integers and that a = 5, b = 2, and c = 4.

```
a. a / b <> c And c / b <> a
b. a / b <> c Or c / b <> a
c. b Mod c = 1 And a Mod c = 1
d. b Mod c = 1 Or a Mod c = 1
```

5. Write a Visual Basic program to determine the value of the condition (2 > 1) >= (2 < 1). What does your result tell you about how Visual Basic orders a **True** value relative to a **False** value?

5.3 The If-Then-Else Structure

The **If-Then-Else** structure directs a procedure to perform a series of one or more instructions, based on the result of a comparison. For example, the state of New Jersey has a two–level state income tax structure. If a person's taxable income is less than $20,000, the applicable state tax rate is 2 percent. For incomes exceeding $20,000, a different rate is applied. The **If-Then-Else** structure can be used in this situation to determine the actual tax, based on whether the taxable income is less than or equal to $20,000. The general syntax of an **If-Then-Else** structure, which is referred to as the *block form*, is

```
If (condition) Then
    statement(s)
Else
    statement(s)
End If
```

This block structure is constructed using three, separate Visual Basic parts, each of which must reside on a line by itself: an **If** statement having the form **If** *condition* **Then**, an **Else**

Figure 5-7

The If-Then-Else Flowchart

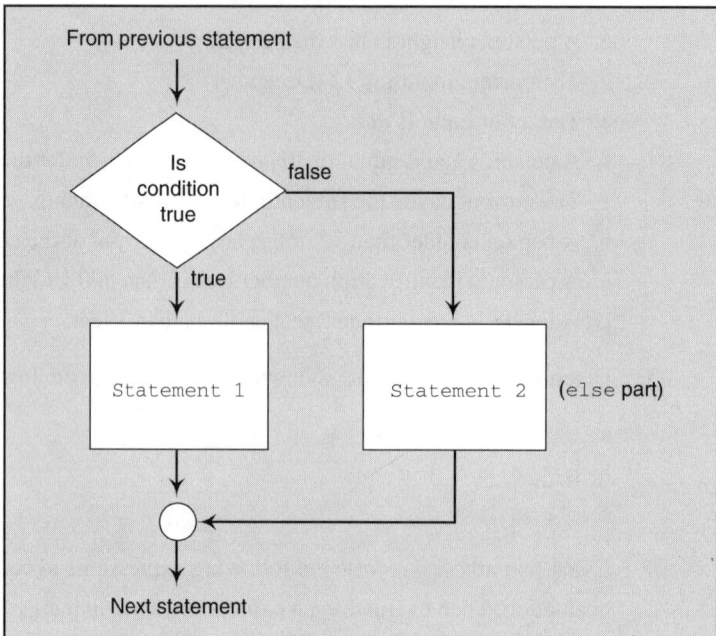

statement consisting of the keyword **Else**, and an **End If** statement consisting of the keywords **End** and **If**.

The condition in the **If** statement is evaluated first. If the condition is **True**, the first set of statements is executed. If the condition is **False**, the statements after the keyword **Else** are executed. Thus, one of the two sets of statements is always executed depending on the value of the condition. The flowchart for the **If-Then-Else** structure is shown in Figure 5-7.

As a specific example of an **If-Then-Else** statement, we will construct a Visual Basic application for determining New Jersey income taxes. As previously described, these taxes are assessed at 2 percent of taxable income for incomes less than or equal to $20,000. For taxable incomes greater than $20,000 state taxes are 2.5 percent of the income that exceeds $20,000 plus a fixed amount of $400. The expression to be tested is whether taxable income is less than or equal to $20,000. An appropriate **If-Then-Else** statement for this situation is

```
If (taxable <= 20000.00) Then
   taxes = 0.02 * taxable
Else
   taxes = 0.025 * (taxable - 20000.00) + 400.00
End If
```

Recall that the relational operator `<=` represents the relation "less than or equal to." If the value of `taxable` is less than or equal to `20000.00`, the condition is **True** and the statement `taxes = 0.02 * taxable` is executed. If the condition is **False**, the **Else** part of the statement is executed. Program 5-3 illustrates the use of this statement within the context of a complete application. The interface for this program is shown in Figure 5-8.

Figure 5-8

The Interface for Program 5-3

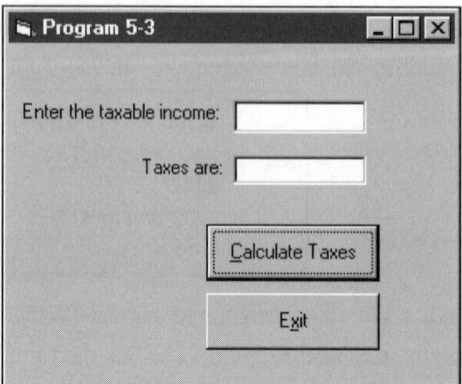

Introduction to Visual Basic

Table 5-6 Program 5-3's Properties Table

Object	Property	Setting
Form	Name	frmMain
	Caption	Program 5-3
Label	Name	lblIncome
	Caption	Enter the taxable income:
Label	Name	lblTaxes
	Caption	Taxes are:
Text box	Name	txtIncome
	Text	(Blank)
	BackColo	White (Palette tab)
Picture box	Name	chkItalic
	TabStop	False
	BackColor	White (Palette tab)
Command button	Name	cmdCalculate
	Caption	&Calculate Taxes
Command button	Name	cmdExit
	Caption	E&xit

The Properties table for Program 5-3 is given in Table 5-6. Notice that the **TabStop** property for the Picture box has been set to **False**. Thus, the user can only tab between the text box and the Exit Command button. Now look at Program 5-3's event code.

Program 5-3's Event Code

```
Private Sub txtIncome_GotFocus()
  pictaxes.Cls
End Sub

Private Sub cmdCalculate_Click()
  Const HIGHRATE As Single = 0.025
  Const LOWRATE As Single = 0.02
  Const FIXED As Single = 400.00
  Const CUTOFF As Single = 20000.00
  Dim taxable As Single, taxes As Single

  taxable = Val(txtIncome.Text)
  If (taxable <= CUTOFF) Then
    taxes = LOWRATE * taxable
  Else
    taxes = HIGHRATE * (taxable - CUTOFF) + FIXED
  End If

  pictaxes.Print Format(taxes, "Currency")
End Sub

Private Sub cmdExit_Click()
  Beep
  End
End Sub
```

Notice that the text box's **GotFocus** event is used to trigger the Picture box's **Cls** method. This ensures that whenever a user moves into the Text box to enter an income value, the Picture box will be cleared. Doing this prevents the situation of a previously calculated tax amount being visible for a newly entered income level before the user moves off the Text box. The actual calculation and display of the taxes due on the entered amount uses an **If-Then-Else** statement within the cmdCalculate_Click event.

Figures 5-9 and 5-10 illustrate the interface for two different values of taxable income. Observe that the taxable income shown in Figure 5-9 was less than $20,000 and the tax is correctly calculated as two percent of the number entered. In Figure 5-10 the taxable income is more than $20,000 and the **Else** part of the **If-Then-Else** statement yields a correct tax computation of

```
0.025 * ($30,000 - $20,000) + $400 = $650
```

Figure 5-9

Entering a Taxable Income Less Than $20,000

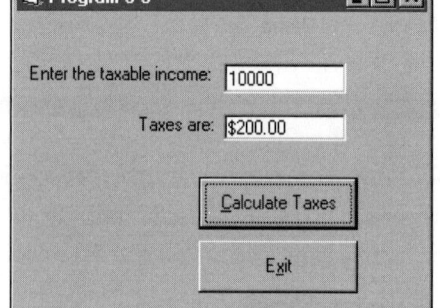

Figure 5-10

Entering a Taxable Income Greater Than $20,000

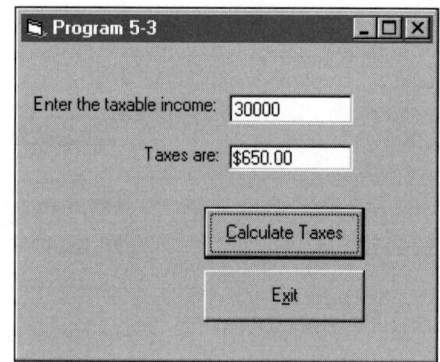

One-Way Selection and the Single-Line If-Then Statement

Figure 5-11

Flowchart for One-Way If Structure

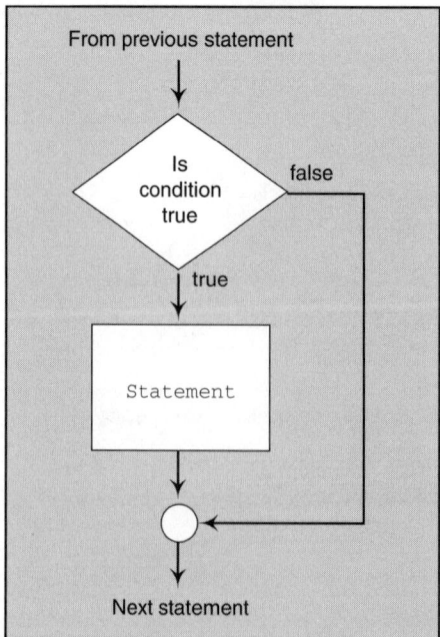

As we have seen, the **If-Then-Else** structure that we have been using consists of three separate Visual Basic parts: an **If-Then** part, an **Else** part, and an **End If** part. Any number of valid Visual Basic statements can be included with the **If** and **Else** parts of the structure. As a multiline statement it must, however, always be terminated with an **End If** statement. Use of the **Else** part, however, is optional. When the **Else** statement is not used, the **If** statement takes the shortened and frequently useful form:

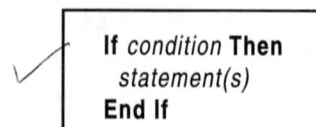

```
If condition Then
    statement(s)
End If
```

The statement or statements following the **If** condition are only executed if the condition is

---

Programmers' Notes

What is a Flag?

In current programming usage the term *flag* refers to an item, such as a variable or argument, that sets a condition usually considered as either active or nonactive. Flags are typically used in selecting actions based on the following pseudocode

> *If the flag is set*
>   *do the statements here*
> *Else*
>   *do the statements here*

where the flag being set means that the flag has a value that is **True**. Similarly, selection can also be based on the fact that the flag is not set, which corresponds to a **False** condition. Although the exact origin of the term *flag* in programming is not known, it probably originates from the use of real flags to signal a condition, such as the Stop, Go, Caution, and Winner flags commonly used at car races.

True. Figure 5-11 illustrates the flowchart for this combination of statements. This modified form of the **If** statement is called a *one-way If structure*. Program 5-3 uses this statement to selectively display a message in a Picture box for cars that have been driven more than 3000 miles. The program's interface is shown in Figure 5-12, and its Properties table is listed in Table 5-7. 6

Figure 5-12

Program 5-4's Interface

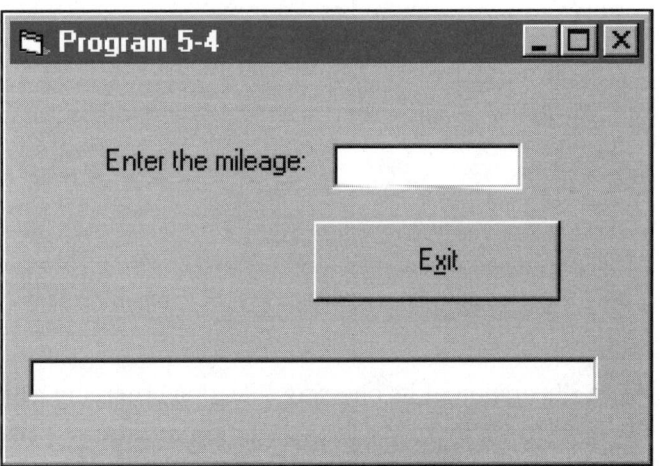

Notice in the event code for Program 5-4 that the Text box **GotFocus** event is used to clear the Picture box of any text. The actual calculation is contained in the Text box **LostFocus** event, which uses a one-way **If** statement to check the value in the Text box and display the message

```
This car is over the mileage limit
```

only if `mileage` is greater than `LIMIT`.

Introduction to Visual Basic   189

Table 5-6 The Properties Table for Program 5-4

Object	Property	Setting
Form	Name	frmMain
	Caption	Program 5-4
Label	Name	lblMiles
	Caption	Enter the mileage:
Text box	Name	txtMiles
	Text	(Blank)
	BackColor	White (Palette tab)
Picture box	Name	picError
	TabStop	False
	BackColor	White (Palette tab)
Command button	Name	cmdExit
	Caption	E&xit

Program 5-4's Event Code

```
Private Sub txtMiles_GotFocus()
  picError.Cls
End Sub

Private Sub txtMiles_LostFocus()
  Const LIMIT As Single = 3000.00
  Dim mileage As Single

  mileage = Val(txtMiles.Text)
  If mileage > LIMIT Then
    Beep
    picError.Print "This car is over the mileage limit"
  End If
End Sub

Private Sub cmdExit_Click()
  Beep
  End
End Sub
```

As an illustration of its one-way selection criteria in action, Program 5-4 was run twice, each time with different input data. Figure 5-13 illustrates the case where the input data causes the statements within the **If** to be executed, while in Figure 5-14 the input data is below the limit so that the message is not printed.

Figure 5-13

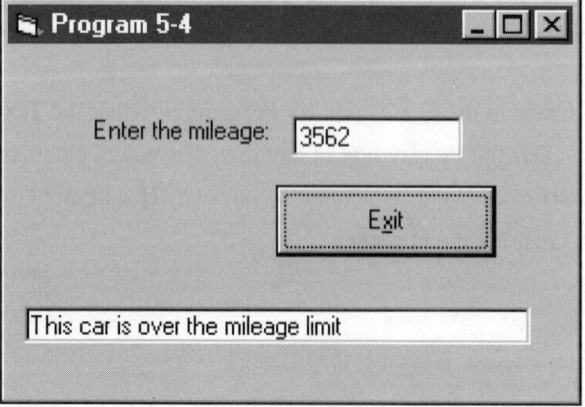

Figure 5-14

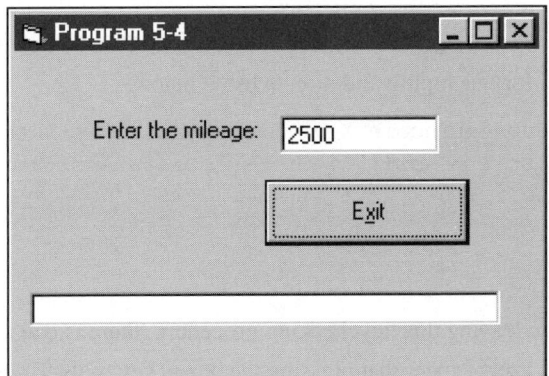

Input Data Validation

If statements can be used to select appropriate processing paths as in Programs 5-1, 5-2, and 5-3. These statements can also validate input data and prevent undesirable data from being processed at all. For example, a date such as 5/33/98 contains an obviously invalid day. Similarly, division of any number by zero within a program, such as 14/0, should not be allowed. Each of these examples illustrates the need for *defensive programming*, in which code is used to check for improper input data before attempting to process it further. The defensive programming technique of checking user input data for erroneous or unreasonable data is called *input data validation*. We now have the tools to supply input data validation to Program 5-3.

Clearly, Program 5-3 expects that the user will enter a number and not a text string into the Text box. To ensure that only numerical data is entered, we can validate each typed character and reject any keystrokes that do not result in one of the characters 0–9. This can be done using the a Text box's **KeyPress** event. The header line for this event is

```
Private Sub text-box-name_KeyPress(KeyAscii As Integer)
```

where the argument **KeyAscii** provides the ANSI value of the key that was pressed (Appendix C lists the ANSI values for each character.) Using a one-way **If** statement, this value can be compared to the ANSI values of the characters 0–9 using the following code:

```
If KeyAscii < Asc("0") Or KeyAscii > Asc("9") Then
   KeyAscii = 0
   Beep
End If
```

The **Asc** function in this code returns the ANSI value of its argument. For example, the value returned by ASC("0") is 48 and the value returned by ASC("9") is 57. Thus, the **If** statement checks whether the ANSI value of the typed character is outside the range 48 to 57, and is thus invalid. If the key is outside of this range the computer will beep and set the ANSI value to 0, which corresponds to the zero-length string (" "). This effectively intercepts each key and replaces any non-numeric key with no key. The complete event code that can be used for this input validation is listed below.

```
Private Sub txtIncome_KeyPress(KeyAscii As Integer)
  If KeyAscii < Asc("0") Or KeyAscii > Asc("9") Then
    KeyAscii = 0
    Beep
  End If
End Sub
```

Before leaving this keychecking procedure, there is one additional verification we can make. Most users expect that pressing the [Enter] key will terminate data input. Of course, this is not the case for Text boxes, where the user must either press the [Tab] key, click on another object, or use access ("hot") keys to move off the box. We can, however, check the value of the key just pressed, to determine if it was the [Enter] key. Since the ANSI value of the [Enter] key is 13, this check takes the form

```
Const ENTER As Integer = 13   ' the ANSI value of the Enter key
If KeyAscii = ENTER Then
  KeyAscii = 0
  cmdExit.SetFocus
End If
```

If the [Enter] key has been pressed, the key is reset to no key and the focus is set to the cmdExit object using the **SetFocus** method. Including this code with the prior check for a digit key results in the following event procedure:

```
Private Sub txtMiles_KeyPress(KeyAscii As Integer)
 Const ENTER As Integer = 13 ' the ANSI value of the Enter key

  If KeyAscii = ENTER Then
    KeyAscii = 0
    cmdExit.SetFocus
  ElseIf KeyAscii < Asc("0") Or KeyAscii > Asc("9") Then
    KeyAscii = 0
    Beep
  End If
End Sub
```

Single-Line If-Then Statement

An alternative to the one-way **If-Then** statement can be used when only a single statement needs to be executed if the tested condition is **True**. For this case, the single-line **If** statement, having the simplified syntax

> **If** condition **Then** statement

will suffice. For example, the statements:

```
If speed > 22896.0 Then a = b
If number < 0 Then sum = sum + number
If balance < reorder And Time > 5 Then newbal = balance
```

are all examples of single-line **If-Then** statements. In each case, the single statement following the condition is executed only if the tested condition is **True** and no **End If** statement is required.

It is possible to have more than one statement following the **Then** part of a single-line **If-Then** statement, provided that all statements are on the same line and are separated by colons. For example, the following single-line **If-Then** statement is valid:

```
If number > 0 Then sum = sum + number: count = count + 1
```

The only other restriction on the single-line **If-Then** statement is that another **If-Then** statement or the **For/Next** statement described in the next chapter may not follow the **Then** part.

Exercises 5.3

1. Write appropriate **If-Then-Else** statements for each of the following conditions:

    a. If `angle` is equal to 90 degrees, print the message `The angle is a right angle`, else print the message that `The angle is not a right angle`.

    b. If the `temperature` is above 100 degrees, display the message `above the boiling point of water`, else display the message `below the boiling point of water`.

    c. If the `number` is positive, add the number to `possum`, else add the number to `negsum`.

    d. If the `slope` is less than 0.5, set the variable `flag` to zero, else set `flag` to one.

    e. If the difference between `num1` and `num2` is less than 0.001, set the variable `approx` to zero, else calculate `approx` as the quantity `(num1 - num2) / 2.0`.

    f. If the difference between `temp1` and `temp2` exceeds 2.3 degrees, calculate `error` as `(temp1 - temp2) * factor`.

    g. If `x` is greater than `y` and `z` is less than 20, read in a value for `p`.

    h. If `distance` is greater than 20 and it is less than 35, read in a value for `time`.

2. Write **If-Then-Else** statements corresponding to the conditions illustrated by each of the following flowcharts.

a.
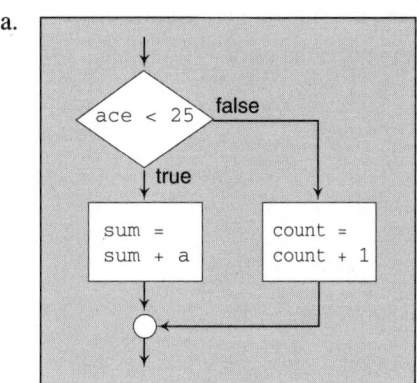

b.
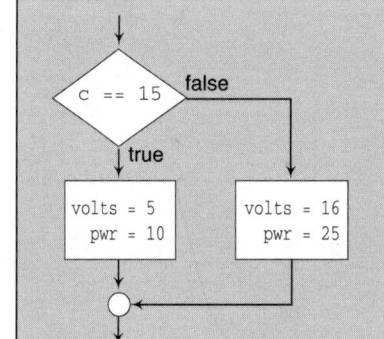

c.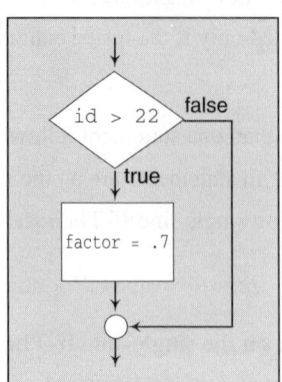

d.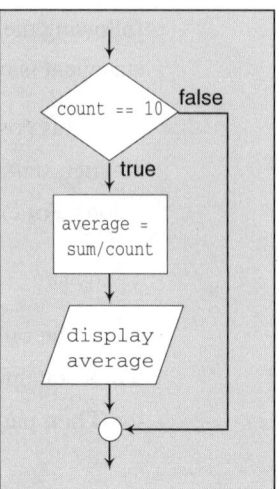

3. Write a Visual Basic program that lets the user input two numbers. If the first number entered is greater than the second number, the program should print the message `The first number is greater` in a Picture box, else it should print the message `The first number is smaller`. Test your program by entering the numbers 5 and 8 and then using the numbers 11 and 2. What do you think your program will display if the two numbers entered are equal? Test this case.

4. a. If money is left in a particular bank for more than two years, the interest rate given by the bank is 5.5 percent, else the interest rate is three percent. Write a Visual Basic program that uses a Text box to accept the number of years into the variable `nyrs` and display the appropriate interest rate in a Picture box, depending on the input value.

   b. How many runs should you make for the program written in Exercise 4a. to verify that it is operating correctly? What data should you input in each of the program runs?

5. a. In a pass/fail course, a student passes if the grade is greater than or equal to 70 and fails if the grade is lower. Write a Visual Basic program that accepts a grade and prints the message `A passing grade` or `A failing grade`, as appropriate.

   b. How many runs should you make for the program written in Exercise 5a. to verify that it is operating correctly? What data should you input in each of the program runs?

6. A student wrote the following code to both ensure that the input into a Text box was a number and to set the focus on the `cmdExit` button when the ⃞Enter key was pressed. When testing the code, the student noticed that the focus did not shift when the ⃞Enter key was pressed. Determine the error.

```
Private Sub txtMiles_KeyPress(KeyAscii As Integer)
  Const ENTER As Integer = 13 ' the ANSI value of the Enter key
  If KeyAscii < Asc("0") Or KeyAscii > Asc("9") Then
    KeyAscii = 0
    Beep
  ElseIf KeyAscii = ENTER Then
    KeyAscii = 0
    cmdExit.SetFocus
  End If
End Sub
```

5.4 The IF-Then-ElseIf Structure ▬▬▬▬▬▬

A modification to the **If-Then-Else** selection structure provided in Visual Basic uses an **ElseIf** part. When an **ElseIf** is included within an **If-Then-Else** statement, the complete syntax is

```
If condition-1 Then
    statement(s)
ElseIf condition-2 Then
    statement(s)
ElseIf condition-3 Then
    statement(s)
ElseIf condition-4 Then
        .
        .
        .
Else
    statement(s)
End If
```

only statement. *most popular*

Each condition is evaluated in the order it appears in this structure. For the first condition that is **True**, the corresponding statements between it and the next immediately following **ElseIf** or **Else** statement are executed; control is then transferred to the statement following the final **End If** statement. Thus, if condition-1 is **True**, only the first set of statements between condition-1 and conditon-2 are executed; otherwise, condition-2 is tested. If condition-2 is then **True**, only the second set of statements are executed; otherwise, condition-3 is tested. This process continues until a condition is satisfied or the **End If** statement is reached. The final **Else** statement, which is optional, is only executed if none of the previous conditions are satisfied. This serves as a default or "catch all" case that is frequently useful for detecting an error condition. Although only three **ElseIf** parts are illustrated, any number of **ElseIf** 's may be used in the structure, which must be terminated with an **End If** statement.

As a specific example, consider the following **If-Else-ElseIf** statement:

```
If Marcode = "M" Then
    picBox.Print "Individual is married."
ElseIf Marcode = "S" Then
    picBox.Print "Individual is single."
ElseIf Marcode = "D" Then
    picBox.Print "Individual is divorced."
ElseIf Marcode = "W" Then
    picBox.Print "Individual is widowed."
Else
    picBox.Print "An invalid code was entered."
End If
```

Execution through this **If** statement begins with the testing of the expression
`Marcode = M`. If the value in `Marcode` is an `M`, the message `Individual is mar-ried` is displayed, no further expressions in the chain are evaluated, and execution resumes
with the next statement immediately following the **End If** statement. If the value in
`Marcode` was not an `M`, the expression `Marcode = "S"` is tested, and so on, until a
True condition is found. If none of the conditions in the chain is **True**, the message `An invalid code` was entered is displayed. In all cases, execution resumes with whatever
statement immediately follows the **End If**. Program 5-5 uses this **If-Then-Else** statement
within a complete program. The interface and properties for Program 5-5 are illustrated in
Figure 5-15 and Table 5-7, respectively.

Figure 5-15

Program 5-5's Interface

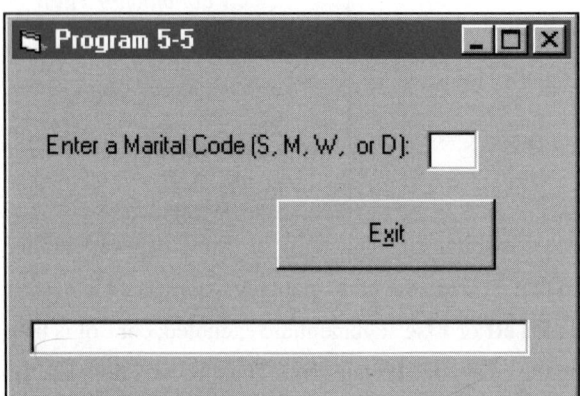

Since the message in the Picture box depends on the Text box input, we will use our
standard procedure of clearing the Picture box when the Text box gets the focus, and
calculate the message to be displayed based on the Text box's data when it loses the focus.
This is accomplished by the Text box **GotFocus** and **LostFocus** event code. Within the
LostFocus event code, the message that is displayed in the Picture box depends on the user
input value for `Marcode`.

Table 5-7 Program 5-5's Properties Table

Object	Property	Setting
Form	Name	frmMain
	Caption	Program 5-5
Label	Name	lblMcode
	Caption	Enter a Marriage Code (S, M, D, or W):
Text box	Name	txtMcode
	Text	(Blank)
	BackColor	White (Palette tab)
Picture box	Name	picBox
	TabStop	False
	BackColor	White (Palette tab)
Command button	Name	cmdExit
	Caption	E&xit

Program 5-5's Event Code

```
Private Sub txtMcode_GotFocus()
  picBox.Cls ' clear the picture box
End Sub

Private Sub txtMcode_LostFocus()
  Dim Marcode As String

  Marcode = txtMcode.Text

  If Marcode = "M" Then
    picBox.Print "Individual is married."
  ElseIf Marcode = "S" Then
    picBox.Print "Individual is single."
  ElseIf Marcode = "D" Then
    picBox.Print "Individual is divorced."
  ElseIf Marcode = "W" Then
    picBox.Print "Individual is widowed."
  Else
    picBox.Print "An invalid code was entered."
  End If
End Sub

Private Sub txtMcode_KeyPress(KeyAscii As Integer)
  Const ENTER As Integer = 13 ' the ANSI value of the Enter key

  If KeyAscii = ENTER Then
    KeyAscii = 0
    cmdExit.SetFocus
  End If
End Sub

Private Sub cmdExit_Click()
  Beep
  End
End Sub
```

As a final example illustrating the **If-Else** chain, let us calculate the monthly income of a computer salesperson using the following commission schedule:

Monthly Sales	Income
Greater than or equal to $50,000	$375 plus 16 percent of sales
Less than $50,000 but greater than or equal to $40,000	$350 plus 14 percent of sales
Less than $40,000 but greater than or equal to $30,000	$325 plus 12 percent of sales
Less than $30,000 but greater than or equal to $20,000	$300 plus 9 percent of sales
Less than $20,000 but greater than or equal to $10,000	$250 plus 5 percent of sales
Less than $10,000	$200 plus 3 percent of sales

The following **If-Then-Else** chain can be used to determine the correct monthly income, where the variable MonthlySales is used to store the salesperson's current monthly sales:

```
If MonthlySales >= 50000.00 Then
  income = 375.00 + 0.16 * MonthlySales
ElseIf MonthlySales >= 40000.00 Then
  income = 350.00 + 0.14 * MonthlySales
ElseIf MonthlySales >= 30000.00 Then
  income = 325.00 + 0.12 * MonthlySales
ElseIf MonthlySales >= 20000.00 Then
```

(continued)

```
        income = 300.00 + 0.09 * MonthlySales
ElseIf MonthlySales >= 10000.00 Then
   income = 250.00 + 0.05 * MonthlySales
Else
   income = 200.000 + 0.03 * MonthlySales
End If
```

Notice that this example makes use of the fact that the chain is stopped once a **True** condition is found. This is accomplished by checking for the highest monthly sales first. If the salesperson's monthly sales are less than $50,000, the **If-Then-ElseIf** chain continues checking for the next highest sales amount, until the correct category is obtained.

Program 5-6 uses this **If-Then-ElseIf** chain to calculate and display the income corresponding to the value of monthly sales input by the user in the Text box. The interface and properties for Program 5-6 are illustrated in Figure 5-16 and Table 5-8, respectively.

Figure 5-16

Program 5-6's Interface

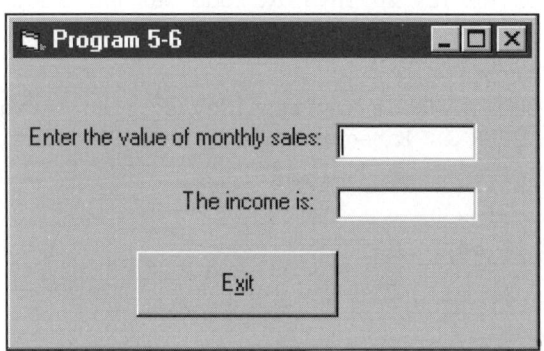

Table 5-8 Program 5-6's Properties Table

Object	Property	Setting
Form	Name	frmMain
	Caption	Program 5-6
Label	Name	lblSales
	Caption	Enter the value of monthly sales:
Label	Name	lblIncome
	Caption	The income is:
Text box	Name	txtSales
	Text	(Blank)
	BackColor	White (Palette tab)
Picture box	Name	picBox
	TabStop	False
	BackColor	White (Palette tab)
Command button	Name	cmdExit
	Caption	E&xit

Program 5-6's Event Code

```
Private Sub txtSales_GotFocus()
  picBox.Cls
End Sub

Private Sub txtSales_LostFocus()
  Dim MonthlySales As Single
  Dim income As Single

  MonthlySales = Val(txtSales.Text)
  If MonthlySales >= 50000.00 Then
    income = 375.00 + 0.16 * MonthlySales
  ElseIf MonthlySales >= 40000.00 Then
    income = 350.00 + 0.14 * MonthlySales
  ElseIf MonthlySales >= 30000.00 Then
    income = 325.00 + 0.12 * MonthlySales
  ElseIf MonthlySales >= 20000.00 Then
    income = 300.00 + 0.09 * MonthlySales
  ElseIf MonthlySales >= 10000.00 Then
    income = 250.00 + 0.05 * MonthlySales
  Else
    income = 200.00 + 0.03 * MonthlySales
  End If

  picBox.Print Format(income, "Currency")
End Sub

Private Sub txtSales_KeyPress(KeyAscii As Integer)
  Const ENTER As Integer = 13 ' the ANSI value of the Enter key
  Const DECPOINT As Integer = 46 ' the ANSI value of the decimal point

  If KeyAscii = ENTER Then
    KeyAscii = 0
    cmdExit.SetFocus
  ElseIf (KeyAscii < Asc("0") Or KeyAscii > Asc("9")) And KeyAscii <> DECPOINT Then
    KeyAscii = 0
    Beep
  End If
End Sub
Private Sub cmdExit_Click()
  Beep
  End
    End Sub
```

The selection code contained within the **LostFocus** event is simply the **If-Then-ElseIf** statement previously presented. A new feature of the event code, however, is contained within the **KeyPress** event procedure. Notice that we have included the ANSI code for the decimal point and have included the decimal point as one of the valid keys that may be pressed by a user when entering a number. Figure 5-17 illustrates a sample run using Program 5-6.

Figure 5-17

A Sample Run Using Program 5-6

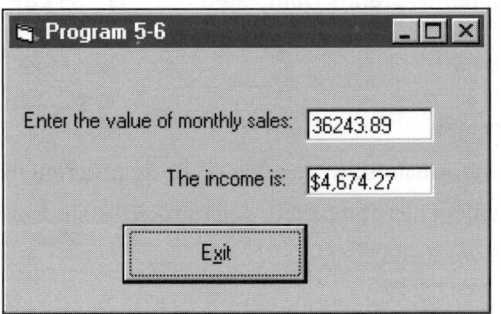

5.4 Exercises

1. Modify Program 5-5 to accept both lower- and uppercase letters as marriage codes. For example, if a user enters either an `m` or an `M`, the program should display the message `Individual is married.`

2. Write **If** statements corresponding to the conditions illustrated in each of the following flowcharts. (**Hint**: Use a logical operator.)

a.   b.

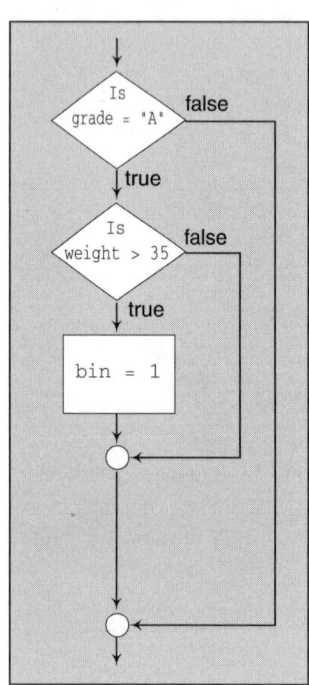   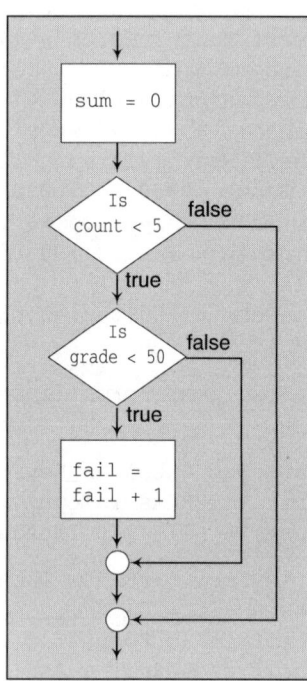

3. An angle is considered acute if it is less than 90 degrees, obtuse if it is greater than 90 degrees, and a right angle if it is equal to 90 degrees. Using this information, write a Visual Basic program that accepts an angle, in degrees, and displays the type of angle corresponding to the degrees entered.

4. The grade level of undergraduate college students is typically determined according to the following schedule:

Number of Credits Completed	Grade Level
Less than 32	Freshman
32 to 63	Sophomore
64 to 95	Junior
96 or more	Senior

Using this information, write a Visual Basic program that accepts the number of credits a student has completed, determines the student's grade level, and displays the grade level.

5. A student's letter grade is calculated according to the following schedule:

Numerical grade	Letter grade
Greater than or equal to 90	A
Less than 90 but greater than or equal to 80	B
Less than 80 but greater than or equal to 70	C
Less than 70 but greater than or equal to 60	D
Less than 60	F

Using this information, write a Visual Basic program that accepts a student's numerical grade, converts the numerical grade to an equivalent letter grade, and displays the letter grade.

6. The interest rate used on funds deposited in a bank is determined by the amount of time the money is left on deposit. For a particular bank, the following schedule is used:

Time on deposit	Interest rate
Greater than or equal to 5 years	7.5 percent
Less than 5 years but greater than or equal to 4 years	7.0 percent
Less than 4 years but greater than or equal to 3 years	6.5 percent
Less than 3 years but greater than or equal to 2 years	5.5 percent
Less than 2 years but greater than or equal to 1 year	4.65 percent
Less than 1 year	3.58 percent

With this information, write a Visual Basic program that accepts the time funds are left on deposit and displays the interest rate corresponding to the time entered.

7. Using the commission schedule from Program 5-6, a student coded the Text box's **LostFocus** event procedure as follows:

```
Private Sub txtSales_LostFocus()
  Dim MonthlySales As Single
  Dim income As Single

  MonthlySales = Val(txtSales.Text)
  If MonthlySales >= 50000.00 Then
    income = 375.00 +.16 * MonthlySales
  End If
  If MonthlySales >= 40000.00 && MonthlySales < 50000.00 Then
    income = 350.00 +.14 * MonthlySales
  End If
  If MonthlySales >= 30000.00 && MonthlySales < 40000.00 Then
    income = 325.00 +.12 * MonthlySales
  End If
  If MonthlySales >= 20000.00 && MonthlySales < 30000.00 Then
    income = 300.00 +.09 * MonthlySales
  End If
  If MonthlySales >= 10000.00 && MonthlySales < 20000.00 Then
    income = 250.00 +.05 * MonthlySales
  End If
  If MonthlySales < 10000.00 Then
    income = 200.00 +.03 * MonthlySales
  End If
  picBox.Print Format(income, "Currency")
End Sub
```

    a. Will this code produce the same output as Program 5-6?

    b. Which program is better and why?

8.   a. Will the following event code produce the same result as that used Program 5-6?

```
Private Sub txtSales_LostFocus()
  Dim MonthlySales As Single
  Dim income As Single

  MonthlySales = Val(txtSales.Text)
  If MonthlySales < 10000.00
     income = 200.00 +.03 * MonthlySales
  ElseIf MonthlySales >= 10000.00 Then
     income = 250.00 +.05 * MonthlySales
  ElseIf MonthlySales >= 20000.00 Then
     income = 300.00 +.09 * MonthlySales
  ElseIf MonthlySales >= 30000.00 Then
     income = 325.00 +.12 * MonthlySales
  ElseIf MonthlySales >= 40000.00 Then
     income = 350.00 +.14 * MonthlySales
  ElseIf MonthlySales >= 50000.00 Then
     income = 375.00 +.16 * MonthlySales
  End If
  picBox.Print Format(income, "Currency")
End Sub
```

    b. What does the event procedure do?

    c. For what values of monthly sales does this procedure calculate the correct income?

9.   a. Write a Visual Basic program that accepts two real numbers from a user, using individual Text boxes, and a `Select` code, using an Option box group. If the entered `Select` code is 1, have the program add the two previously entered numbers and display the result; if the `Select` code is 2, the second number should be subtracted from the first number; if the `Select` code is 3, the numbers should be multiplied; and if the `Select` code is 4, the first number should be divided by the second number.

    b. Determine what the program written in Exercise 9a. does when the entered numbers are 3 and 0, and the `Select` code is 3.

    c. Modify the program written in Exercise 9a. so that division by 0 is not allowed and so that an appropriate message is displayed when such a division is attempted.

10. a. Write a program that displays the following two Labels:

```
Enter a month (use a 1 for Jan, etc.):
Enter a day of the month:
```

    Have your program accept a user-input number in a Text box and store the number in a variable named `month`, in response to the first Label prompt. Similarly, accept and store a number entered in a second Text box in the variable `day` in response to the second Label prompt. If the month entered is not 1–12 (inclusive), print a message informing the user that an invalid month has been entered. If the day entered is not 1–31, print a message informing the user that an invalid day has been entered.

b. What will your program do if the user types a number with a decimal point for the month? How can you ensure that your **If** statements check for an integer number?

c. In a non-leap year, February has 28 days, the months January, March, May, July, August, October, and December have 31 days, and all other months have 30 days. Using this information, modify the program written in Exercise 10a. to display a message when an invalid day is entered for a user-entered month. For this program, ignore leap years.

11. All years that are evenly divisible by 400 or are evenly divisible by 4 and not evenly divisible by 100, are leap years. For example, since 1600 is evenly divisible by 400, the year 1600 was a leap year. Similarly, since 1988 is evenly divisible by 4 but not by 100, the year 1988 was also a leap year. Using this information, write a Visual Basic program that accepts the year as a user input, determines if the year is a leap year, and displays a message that tells the user if the entered year is or is not a leap year.

12. Based on an automobile's model year and weight, the state of New Jersey determines a car's weight class and registration fee using the following schedule:

Model Year	Weight	Weight Class	Registration Fee
1970 or earlier	Less than 2,700 lbs	1	$16.50
	2,700 to 3,800 lbs	2	$25.50
	More than 3,800 lbs	3	$46.50
1971 to 1979	Less than 2,700 lbs	4	$27.00
	2,700 to 3,800 lbs	5	$30.50
	More than 3,800 lbs	6	$52.50
1980 or later	Less than 3,500 lbs	7	$19.50
	3,500 or more lbs	8	$52.50

Using this information, write a Visual Basic program that accepts the year and weight of an automobile and determines and displays the weight class and registration fee for the car.

5.5 The Select Case Structure

An alternative to the **If-Then-ElseIf** structure presented in the previous section is the **Select-Case** structure. The syntax of the **Select-Case** construct is

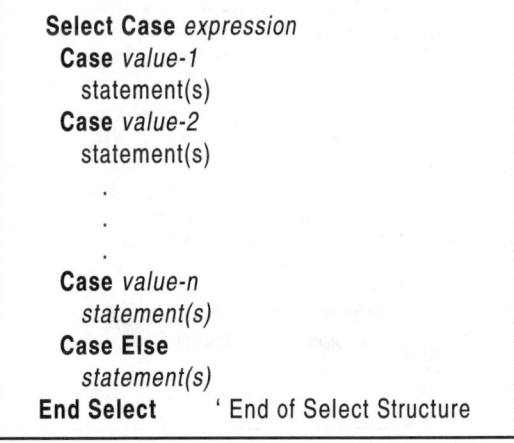

The **Select Case** structure uses three new Visual Basic statements, a single **Select Case** statement, one or more **Case** statements, and a required **End Select** statement. Let us see how these statements are used. The **Select Case** statement, which has the general form

> **Select Case** *expression*

identifies the start of the **Select Case** strucure. The expression in this statement is evaluated and the result of the expression compared to various alternative values contained within each **Case** statement.

Internal to the **Select Case** construct, the **Case** statement, which has the general syntax

> **Case** *list of values*

is used to identify individual values that are compared to the value of the **Select Case** expression. The expression's value is compared to each of these **Case** values, in the order that these values are listed, until a match is found. Execution then begins with the statement immediately following the matching **Case** and ends when either the next **Case** or **End Select** statement is encountered. The **Select Case** structure is then exited and program execution continues with the statement following the **End Select** statement. Thus, as illustrated in Figure 5-18, the value of the expression determines where in the **Case** construct execution actually begins.

Any number of **Case** labels may be contained within a **Select Case** structure, in any order; the only requirement is that the values in each **Case** statement must be of the same type as the expression in the **Select Case** statement. If the value of the expression does not match any of the case values, however, no statement within the structure is executed unless a **Case Else** statement is encountered. The keyword **Else** is optional in a **Select Case** structure and produces the same effect as the last **Else** in an **If-ElseIf** structure. If the value of the **Select Case** expression does not match any of the **Case** values, and the **Case Else** statement is present, execution begins with the statement following the word **Else**.

Once an entry point has been located by the **Select Case** structure, all further **Case** evaluations are ignored and execution continues until either a **Case** or **End Select** statement is encountered.

Figure 5-18

*The Expression Determines
an Entry Point*

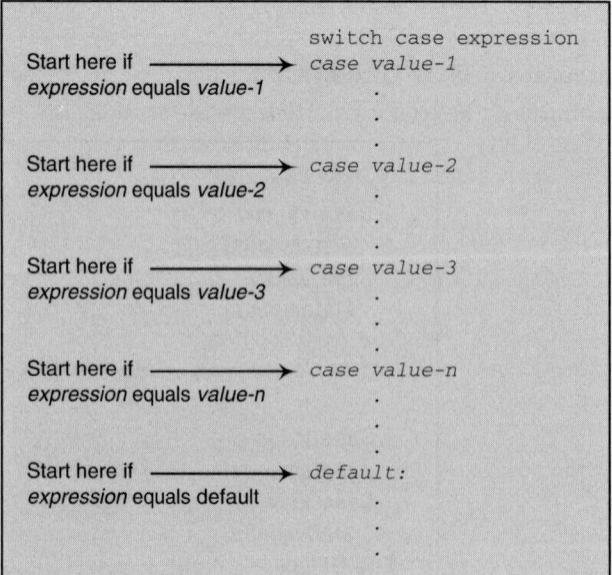

When writing a **Select Case** structure, you can use multiple case values to refer to the same set of statements; the default label is optional. For example, consider the following:

```
Select Case number
    Case 1
      Print "Have a Good Morning"
    Case 2
      Print "Have a Happy Day"
    Case 3, 4, 5
      Print "Have a Nice Evening"
End Select
```

If the value stored in the variable `number` is 1, the message `Have a Good Morning` is displayed. Similarly, if the value of `number` is 2, the second message is displayed. Finally, if the value of `number` is 3 or 4 or 5, the last message is displayed. Since the statement to be executed for these last three cases is the same, the cases for these values can be "stacked together," as shown in the example. Also, since there is no default, no message is printed if the value of `number` is not one of the listed case values. Although it is good programming practice to list case values in increasing order, this is not required by the **Select Case** statement. A **Select Case** statement may have any number of case values, in any order; only the values being tested for need be listed.

A **Select Case** structure can also be used to test the value of a string expression. For example, assuming that `letter` is a string variable, the following **Select Case** statement is valid:

```
Select Case letter
    Case "a", "e", "i", "o", "u", "A", "E", "I", "O", "U"
      Print "The character is a vowel"
    Case Else
      Print "The character is not a vowel"
End Select
```

2, 3, 4

Exercises 5.5

1. Rewrite the following **If-Else** chain using a **Select Case** structure:

```
If let_grad = "A"
  Print "The numerical grade is between 90 and 100"
ElseIf let_grad = "B"
  Print "The numerical grade is between 80 and 89.9"
ElseIf let_grad = "C"
  Print "The numerical grade is between 70 and 79.9"
ElseIf let_grad = "D"
  Print "How are you going to explain this one"
Else
  Print "Of course I had nothing to do with my grade."
  Print "It must have been the professor's fault."
End If
```

2. Rewrite the following **If-Else** chain using a **Select Case** structure:

```
If res_typ = 1
  a = b + c
ElseIf res_typ = 2
  a = b * c
ElseIf res_typ = 3
  a = b / c
ElseIf res_typ = 4
  a = 4
ElseIf res_typ = 5
  a = c/b
ElseIf res_typ = 6
  a = b + c/d
```

3. Each disk drive in a shipment of these devices is stamped with a code 1–4, which indicates a drive from among the following types:

Code	Disk	Drive Type
1	360 Kilobyte Drive	(5 1/2-inch)
2	1.2 Megabyte Drive	(5 1/2-inch)
3	722 Kilobyte Drive	(3 1/4-inch)
4	1.4 Megabyte Drive	(3 1/4-inch)

use Select Case

Write a Visual Basic program that accepts the code number as an input and, based on the value entered, displays the correct disk drive type.

5.6 Common Programming Errors and Problems

The common programming errors related to Visual Basic's selection statements include the following:

1. Omitting the keyword **Then** from an **If-Else** statement.
2. Writing the keyword **ElseIf** as the two words, **Else** and **If**.
3. Trying to use a logical operator without a relational expression or logical variable immediately following it. For example, the expression

   ```
   age >= 35 And < 40
   ```

   is invalid. The expression

   ```
   age >= 35 And age < 40
   ```

   which uses the **And** operator to connect the two relational expressions is valid.
4. This error presents a typical debugging problem. Here an **If** statement appears to select an incorrect choice and the programmer mistakenly concentrates on the tested condition as the source of the problem. For example, assume that the following **If-Else** statement is part of your program:

   ```
   If key = "F" Then
     temp = (5.0 / 9.0) * (temp - 32.0)
     txtBox.text = "Conversion to Celsius completed"
   Else
     temp = (9.0 / 5.0) * temp + 32.0
     txtBox.text = "Conversion to Fahrenheit completed"
   End If
   ```

This statement will always display `Conversion to Celsius completed` when the variable `key` contains an F. Therefore, if this message is displayed when you believe `key` does not contain F, investigation of `key`'s value is called for. As a general rule, whenever a selection statement does not act as you think it should, make sure to test your assumptions about the values assigned to the tested variables, by displaying these values. If an unanticipated value is displayed, you have at least isolated the source of the problem to the variables themselves, rather than the structure of the **If-Then** statement. From there you will have to determine where and how the incorrect value was obtained.

5.7 Chapter Review

Key Terms

Check box	nested **If**
condition	one-way selection
flag	Option button
If-Then-Else structure	**Select Case** structure
input data validation	simple relational expression
logical operators	

Summary

1. Relational expressions, which are also called *simple conditions*, are used to compare operands. The value of a relational expression is either **True** or **False**. Relational expressions are created using the following relational operators:

Relational Operator	Meaning	Example
<	Less than	`age < 30`
>	Greater than	`height > 6.2`
<=	Less than or equal to	`taxable <= 20000`
>=	Greater than or equal to	`temp >= 98.6`
=	Equal to	`grade = 100`
<>	Not equal to	`number <> 250`

2. More complex conditions can be constructed from relational expressions using Visual Basic's **And**, **Or**, and **Not** logical operators.
3. An **If** statement is used to select one or more statements for execution based on the value of a condition. The **If** statement has the syntax

```
If condition Then
```

and must always be used with an **End If** statement. Additionally, one **Else** statement and any number of **ElseIf** statements may be used with an **If** statement to provide multiple selection criteria. The common selection structures that can be created using an **If** statement include the following forms:

Form 1—Simple **If**:

```
If condition Then
    statement(s)
End If
```

Here, the statements between the **If** and **End If** statements are only executed if the condition being tested is **True**. The **If** and **End If** statements must be written on separate lines.

Form 2—Simple **If-Else**:

```
If condition Then
    statement(s)
Else
    statement(s)
End If
```

This is a two-way selection structure. Here the **Else** statement is used with the **If** to select between two alternative sets of statements based on the value of a condition. If the condition is **True**, the first set of statements is executed; otherwise, the set of statements following the keyword **Else** are executed. The **If**, **Else**, and **End If** statements must be written on separate lines.

Form 3—Simple **If-ElseIf-Else**:

```
If condition-1 Then
    statement(s)
ElseIf condition-2 Then
    statement(s)
Else
    statement(s)
End If
```

This is a three-way selection structure. Once a condition is satisfied, only the statements between that condition and the next **ElseIf** or **Else** are executed, and no further conditions are tested. The **Else** statement is optional, and the statements corresponding to the **Else** statement are only executed if neither condition-1 nor condition-2 is **True**. The **If**, **ElseIf**, **Else**, and **End If** statements must be written on separate lines.

Form 4—Multiple **Else-Ifs**:

```
If condition-1 Then
    statement(s)
ElseIf condition-2 Then
    statement(s)
        .
        .
        .
ElseIf condition-n Then
    statement(s)
Else
    statement(s)
End If
```

This is a multiway selection structure. Once a condition is satisfied, only the statements between that condition and the next **ElseIf** or **Else** are executed and no further conditions are tested. The **Else** statement is optional, and the statements corresponding to the **Else** statement are only executed if none of the conditions tested are **True**. The **If**, **Else**, and **End If** statements must be written on individual lines.

4. The **Then** keyword can be omitted if a one-way **If** statement fits on a single line:

```
If condition statement
```

5.8 Looking Further: Errors, Testing, and Debugging

The ideal in programming is to efficiently produce readable, error-free programs that work correctly and can be modified or changed with a minimum of testing required for reverification. In this regard, it is useful to know the different types of errors that can occur, when they are detected, and how to correct them.

Design-time and Run-time errors

A program error can be detected at a variety of times:

1. During design-time,
2. During run-time,
3. After the program has been executed and the output is being examined, or
4. Not at all.

Errors detected by the compiler are formally referred to as *design-time* errors and errors that occur while the program is being run are formally referred to as *run-time* errors.

Methods are available for detecting errors both before and after a program has been executed. The method for detecting errors after a program has been executed is called *program verification and testing*. The method for detecting errors before a program is run is called *desk checking* because the programmer sits at a desk or table and checks the program, by hand, for syntax and logic errors.

Syntax and Logic Errors

There are two primary types of errors, referred to as syntax and logic errors, respectively. A *syntax* error is an error in the structure or spelling of a statement. For example the statements

```
If a < b
  Print "There are four syntax errors here
  Pint " can you find tem"
End
```

contain four syntax errors. These errors are

1. The keyword **Then** is missing in the first line.
2. A closing double quote is missing in line two.
3. The keyword **Print** is misspelled in line three.
4. The **End** keyword in line four should be **End If**.

All of these errors will be detected by Visual Basic when the program is translated for execution. This is true of all syntax errors since they violate the basic rules of the language.[1] In some cases the error message is clear and the error is obvious; in other cases it takes a little detective work to understand the error message. Note that the misspelling of the word `tem` in the second Print statement is not a syntax error. Although this spelling error will result in an undesirable output line being displayed, it is not a violation of Visual Basic's syntactical rules. It is a simple case of a typographical error, commonly referred to as a "typo."

---

[1]They may not, however, all be detected at the same time. Frequently, one syntax error masks another error and the second error is only detected after the first error is corrected.

Logic errors result directly from some flaw in the program's logic. These errors, which are never caught during translation, may be detected by desk checking, by program testing, by accident when a user obtains an obviously erroneous output, while the program is executing, or not at all. If the error is detected while the program is executing, a run-time error occurs that results in an error message being generated and/or abnormal and premature program termination.

Since logic errors may not be detected during translation, they are always more difficult to detect than syntax errors. If not detected by desk checking, a logic error will reveal itself in several predominant ways.

No output: This is caused either by an omission of an output statement or by a sequence of statements that inadvertently bypasses an output statement.

Unappealing or misaligned output: This is caused by an error in an output statement.

Incorrect numerical results: This is caused either by incorrect values assigned to the variables used in an expression, the use of an incorrect arithmetic expression, an omission of a statement, a roundoff error, or the use of an improper sequence of statements.

Sometimes faulty or incomplete program logic will cause a run-time error. Examples of this type of logic error are attempts to divide by zero or to take the square root of a negative number.

Testing and Debugging

In theory, a comprehensive set of test runs would reveal all possible program errors and ensure that a program will work correctly for any and all combinations of input and computed data. In practice this requires checking all possible combinations of event activation and statement execution. Due to the time and effort required, this is an impossible goal except for extremely simple programs. Let us see why this is so. Consider the following event code that is activated on a Command button **Click** event:

```
Private Sub cmdTest_Click()
  Dim num As Integer

  num = val(txtBox.text)
  If num = 5 Then
    Print "Bingo!"
  Else
    Print "Bongo!"
  End If
End Sub
```

This event code has two paths that can be traversed when the event code is activated. The first path, which is executed when the input number is 5, consists of the statement:

```
        Print "Bingo!"
```

The second path, which is executed whenever any number except 5 is input, consists of the statement

```
Print "Bongo!"
```

To test each possible path through this event code requires two activations of the **Click** event, with a judicious selection of test input data to ensure that both paths of the **If** statement are exercised. The addition of one more **If-Else** statement in the program increases the number of possible execution paths by a factor of two and requires four (2^2) runs of the program for complete testing. Similarly, two additional **If-Else** statements increase the number of paths by a factor of four and requires eight (2^3) runs for complete testing, and three additional **If-Else** statements would produce a program that required sixteen (2^4) test runs.

Now consider a modestly sized application consisting of only ten event procedures, with each procedure containing five **If-Else** statements. Assuming the procedures are always activated in the same sequence, there are 32 possible paths through each module (2 raised to the fifth power) and more than 1,000,000,000,000,000 (2 raised to the fiftieth power) possible paths through the complete application (all modules executed in sequence). The time needed to create individual test data to exercise each path and the actual computer run-time required to check each path make the complete testing of such a program impossible to achieve.

The inability to fully test all combinations of statement execution sequences has led programmers to claim that there is no error-free program. It has also led to the realization that any testing should be well thought out to maximize the possibility of locating errors. At a minimum, test data should include appropriate values for input values, illegal input values that the program should reject, and limiting values that are checked by selection statements within the program.

Another important realization is that, although a single test can reveal the presence of an error, it cannot guarantee the absence of one. The fact that one error is revealed by a particular verification run does not indicate that another error is not lurking somewhere else in the program, and the fact that one test revealed no errors does not indicate that there are no errors.

Although there are no hard-and-fast rules for isolating the cause of an error, some useful techniques can be applied. The first of these is preventive. Many errors are simply introduced by the programmer in the rush to code and run a program, before fully understanding what is required and how the result is to be achieved. A symptom of this haste to get a program entered into the computer is the lack of an outline of the proposed program (pseudocode or flowcharts) or a handwritten program itself. Many errors can be eliminated simply by desk checking a copy of each procedure before it is ever entered or translated.

A second useful technique is to mimic the computer and execute each statement, by hand, as the computer would. This means writing down each variable as it is encountered in the program and listing the value that should be stored in the variable, as each input and assignment statement is encountered. Doing this also sharpens your programming skills, because it requires that you fully understand what each statement in your program causes to happen. Such a check is called program *tracing*.

A third debugging technique is to use one or more diagnostic **Print** statements to display the values of selected variables. In this same manner, another use of **Print** statements in debugging is to immediately display the values of all input data. This technique is referred to as *echo printing*, and is useful in establishing that the computer is correctly receiving and interpreting the input data.

The fourth and most powerful debugging technique is to use the debugger that comes with Visual Basic. The debugger was introduced in Chapter 4 and is discussed further in Chapter 7.

Finally, no discussion of program verification is complete without mentioning the primary ingredient needed for successful isolation and correction of errors. This is the attitude and spirit you bring to the task. Since you wrote the program, your natural assumption is that it is correct, or you would have changed it before it was executed. It is extremely difficult to back away and honestly test and find errors in your own software. As a programmer, you must constantly remind yourself that just because you *think* your program is correct does not make it so. Finding errors in your own programs is a sobering experience, but one that will help you become a master programmer. It can also be exciting and fun, if approached as a detection problem with you as the master detective.

Repetition Structures

The applications examined so far have illustrated the programming concepts involved in input, output, assignment, and selection capabilities. By this time you should have gained enough experience to be comfortable with these concepts and the mechanics of implementing them using Visual Basic. Many problems, however, require a repetition capability, in which the same calculation or sequence of instructions is repeated, over and over, using different sets of data. Examples of such repetition include continual checking of user data entries until an acceptable entry, such as a valid password, is entered; counting and accumulating running totals; and recurring acceptance of input data and recalculation of output values that only stops upon entry of a sentinel value.

This chapter explores the different methods that programmers use to construct repeating sections of code and how they can be implemented in Visual Basic. A repeated procedural section of code is commonly called a **loop** *because, after the last statement in the code is executed, the program branches or loops back to the first statement and starts another repetition. Each repetition is also referred to as an* **iteration** *or* **pass** *through the loop.*

6.1 Introduction

The real power of most computer programs resides in their ability to repeat the same calculation or sequence of instructions many times over, each time using different data, without the necessity of rerunning the program for each new set of data values. This ability is realized through repetitive sections of code. Such repetitive sections are written only once, but include a means of defining how many times the code should be executed.

Constructing repetitive sections of code requires four elements:

1. A *repetition statement* that both defines the boundaries containing the repeating section of code and controls whether or not that code will be executed. There are three different forms of repetition structures, all of which are provided in Visual Basic: **Do While** structures, **For** structures, and **Do / Loop Until** structures.
2. A *condition* that needs to be evaluated. Valid conditions are identical to those used in selection statements. If the condition is **True**, the code is executed; if it is **False**, the code is not executed.
3. A *statement* that initially *sets the condition*. This statement must always be placed before the condition is first evaluated to ensure correct loop execution the first time.
4. A *statement* within the repeating section of code that *allows the condition to become False*. This is necessary to ensure that, at some point, the repetitions stop.

Pretest and Posttest Loops

The condition being tested can be evaluated at either the beginning or the end of the repeating section of code. Figure 6-1 illustrates the case where the test occurs at the beginning of the loop. This type of loop is referred to as a *pretest loop*, because the condition is tested before any statements within the loop are executed. If the condition is **True**, the executable statements within the loop are executed. If the initial value of the condition is **False**, the executable statements within the loop are never executed at all, and control transfers to the first statement after the loop. To avoid infinite repetitions, the condition must be updated within the loop. Pretest loops are also referred to as *entrance-controlled loops*. Both the **Do While** and **For** loop structures are examples of such loops.

Figure 6-1

A Pretest Loop

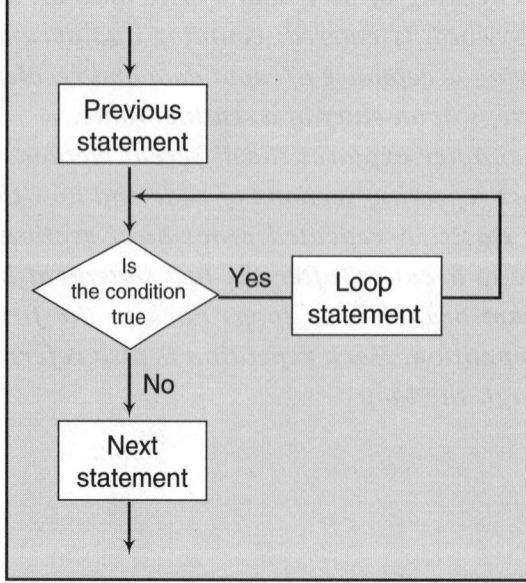

Figure 6-2

A Posttest Loop

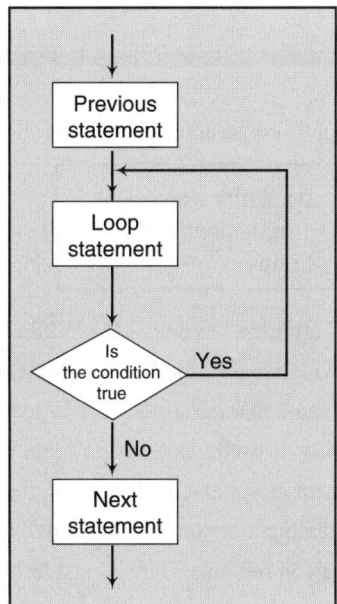

A loop that evaluates a condition at the end of the repeating section of code, as illustrated in Figure 6-2, is referred to as *posttest* or *exit-controlled loop*. Such loops always execute the loop statements at least once before the condition is tested. Since the executable statements within the loop are continually executed until the condition becomes **False**, there always must be a statement within the loop that updates the condition and permits it to become **False**. The **Do / Loop Until** structures is an example of a posttest loop.

Fixed Count Versus Variable-Condition Loops

In addition to where the condition is tested (pretest or posttest) , repeating sections of code are also classified as to the type of condition being tested. In a *fixed-count loop*, the condition is used to keep track of how many repetitions have occurred. For example, we might want to produce a very simple fixed design such as

In each of these cases, a fixed number of calculations is performed or a fixed number of lines is printed, at which point the repeating section of code is exited. All of Visual Basic's repetition statements can be used to produce fixed-count loops.

In many situations, the exact number of repetitions is not known in advance or the items are too numerous to count beforehand. For example, if we are working with a large amount of market research data, we might not want to take the time to count the number of actual data items that must be entered and so we would use a variable-condition loop. In a *variable-condition loop*, the tested condition does not depend on a count being achieved, but rather on a variable that can change interactively with each pass through the loop. When a specified value is encountered, regardless of how many iterations have occurred, repetitions stop. All of Visual Basic's repetition statements can also be used to create variable-condition loops.[1] In this chapter we will encounter examples of both fixed-count and variable-condition loops.

---

1 In this, Visual Basic differs from most other languages, such as BASIC, FORTRAN, and Pascal. In each of these languages the **For** structure (which is implemented using a DO statement in FORTRAN) can only be used to produce fixed-count loops. Visual Basic's **For** structure, as we will see shortly, is virtually interchangeable with its **While** structure.

6.2 Do While Loops

In Visual Basic, a **Do While** loop is constructed using the following syntax:

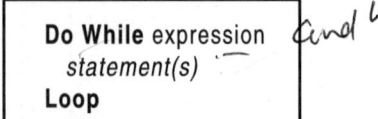

Do While expression   *and 4 .*
    statement(s)
Loop

The expression contained after the keywords **Do While** is the condition tested to determine if the statements provided before the **Loop** statement are executed. The expression is evaluated in exactly the same manner as that contained in an **If-Else** statement; the difference is in how the expression is used. As we have seen, when the expression is **True** in an **If-Else** statement, the statement or statements following the expression are executed once. In a **Do While** loop the statement or statements following the expression are executed repeatedly, as long as the expression remains **True**. Considering the expression and the statements following it, the process used by the computer in evaluating a **Do While** loops is

1. Test the expression, and
2. If the expression is **True**:
    a. Execute all statements following the expression up to the **Loop** statement, and
    b. Go back to Step 1.

    Else

    Exit the **Do While** statement and execute the next executable statement following the **Loop** statement.

Notice that Step 2b. forces program control to be transferred back to Step 1. This transfer of control back to the start of a **Do While** statement, in order to reevaluate the expression, is what forms the program loop. The **Do While** statement literally loops back on itself to recheck the expression until it becomes **False**. This naturally means that somewhere in the loop it must be possible to alter the value of the tested expression so that the loop ultimately terminates its execution.

The looping process produced by a **Do While** statement is illustrated in Figure 6-3. A diamond shape is used to show the two entry and two exit points required in the decision part of the **Do While** statement.

To make this a little more tangible, consider the relational expression `count <= 10` and the

Figure 6-3

Anatomy of a Do While Loop

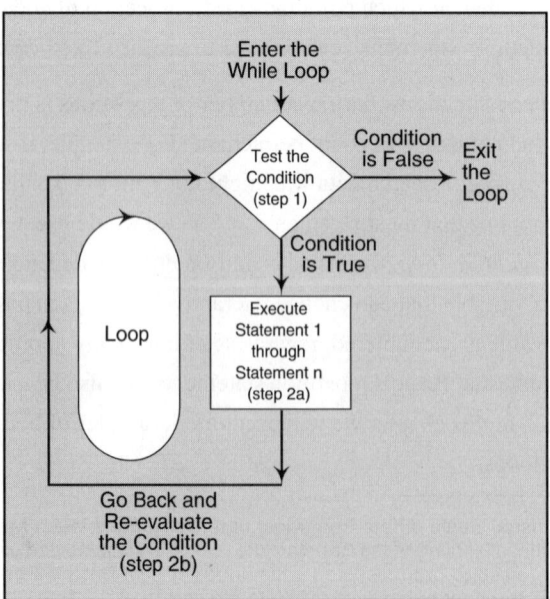

statement `Print count`. Using these, we can write the following valid **Do While** loop:

```
Do While count <= 10    -> exp
   Print count;     -> statement
Loop
```

Although the above loop structure is valid, the alert reader will realize that we have created a situation in which the **Print** statement either is called forever (or until we stop the program) or it is not called at all. Let us see why this happens.

If `count` has a value less than or equal to 10 when the expression is first evaluated, the **Print** statement is executed. When the **Loop** statement is encountered, the structure automatically loops back on itself and retests the expression. Since we have not changed the value stored in `count`, the expression is still **True** and another call to the **Print** method is made. This process continues forever, or until the program containing this statement is prematurely stopped by the user. However, if `count` starts with a value greater than 10, the expression is **False** to begin with and the **Print** method is never used.

How do we set an initial value in `count` to control what the **Do While** statement does the first time the expression is evaluated? The answer, of course, is to assign values to each variable in the tested expression before the **Do While** statement is encountered. For example, the following sequence of instructions is valid:

```
count = 1
Do While count <= 10
   Print count;
Loop
```

Using this sequence of instructions, we ensure that `count` starts with a value of 1. We could assign any value to `count` in the assignment statement—the important thing is to assign some value. In practice, the assigned value depends on the application.

We must still change the value of `count` so that we can finally exit the **Do While** loop. To do this requires an expression such as `count = count + 1` to increment the value of `count` each time the **Do While** statement is executed. All that we have to do is add a statement within the **Loop** structure that modifies `count`'s value so that the loop ultimately terminates. For example, consider the following expanded loop:

```
count = 1  ' initialize count
Do While count <= 10
   Print count;
   count = count + 1 ' increment count
Loop
```

Note that the **Do While** structure begins with the keywords **Do While** and ends with the keyword **Loop**. For this particular loop, we have included two statements within the loop structure:

```
Print count;
count = count + 1 ' increment count
```

Let us now analyze the complete section of loop code to understand how it operates. The first assignment statement sets `count` equal to 1. The **Do While** structure is then entered and the expression is evaluated for the first time. Since the value of `count` is less than or equal to 10, the expression is **True** and the two statements internal to the **Loop** structure are executed. The first statement within the loop is a **Print** statement that displays the value of `count`. The next statement adds 1 to the value currently stored in `count`, making this value equal to 2. The **Do While** statement now loops back to retest the expression. Since `count` is still less than or equal to 10, the loop statements are executed once again. This process continues until the value of `count` reaches 11. Event Procedure 6-1 illustrates these statements within the context of a complete **Form_Click** event procedure.

Event Procedure 6-1

```
Private Sub Form_Click
    Dim count As Integer

    count = 1  ' initialize count
    Do While count <= 10
        Print count;
        count = count + 1 ' increment count
    Loop
End Sub
```

The following output that will appear on the screen when Event Procedure 6-1 is activated:

1 2 3 4 5 6 7 8 9 10

There is nothing special about the name `count` used in Event Procedure 6-1. Any valid integer variable could have been used.

Before we consider other examples of the **Do While** statement, two comments concerning Event Procedure 6-1 are in order. First, the statement `count + 1` can be replaced with any statement that changes the value of `count`. The statement `count = count + 2`, for example, would cause every second integer to be displayed. Second, it is the programmer's responsibility to ensure that `count` is changed in a way that ultimately leads to a normal exit from the **Do While**. For example, if we replace the expression `count + 1` with the expression `count - 1`, the value of `count` will never exceed 10 and an infinite loop will be created. An infinite loop is a loop that never ends. The computer will not reach out, touch you, and say, "Excuse me, you have created an infinite loop." It just keeps displaying numbers, until you realize that the program is not working as you expected.

Now that you have some familiarity with the **Do While** structure, see if you can read and determine the output of Event Procedure 6-2.

Event Procedure 6-2

```
Private Sub Form_Click
    Dim I as integer

    I = 10  ' initialize I
    Do While I >= 1
        Print I ;
        I = I - 1     ' subtract 1 from i
    Loop
End Sub
```

The assignment statement in Event Procedure 6-2 initially sets the integer variable I to 10. The **Do While** statement then checks to see if the value of I is greater than or equal to 1. While the expression is **True**, the value of I is displayed by the **Print** method and the value of I is decremented by 1. When I finally reaches zero, the expression is **False** and the program exits the **Do While** statement. Thus, the following display is obtained when Event Procedure 6-2 is activated:

```
10 9 8 7 6 5 4 3 2 1
```

To illustrate the power of **Do While** loops, consider the task of printing a table of numbers from 1 to 10 with their squares and cubes. This can be done with a simple **Do While** loops structure, as illustrated by Event Procedure 6-3.

Event Procedure 6-3

```
Private Sub Form_Click()
  Dim num As Integer

  Cls ' clear the form
  Font = "Courier"
  Print "NUMBER", "SQUARE", "CUBE"
  Print "------", "------", "----"

  num = 1
  Do While num < 11
    Print num, num ^ 2, num ^ 3
    num = num + 1  ' increment num
  Loop
End Sub
```

When Event Procedure 6-3 is activated, the following display is produced on the form:

NUMBER	SQUARE	CUBE
------	------	----
1	1	1
2	4	8
3	9	27
4	16	64
5	25	125
6	36	216
7	49	343
8	64	512
9	81	729
10	100	1000

Note that the expression used in Event Procedure 6-3 is num < 11. For the integer variable num this expression is exactly equivalent to the expression num <= 10. The choice of which to use is entirely up to you.

If we want to use Event Procedure 6-3 to produce a table of 1000 numbers, all that needs to be done is to change the expression in the **Do While** statement from num < 11 to num < 1001. Changing the 11 to 1001 produces a table of 1000 lines—not bad for a simple five-line **Do While** structure.

All the program examples illustrating the **Do While** statement are examples of fixed-count loops, because the tested condition is a counter that checks for a fixed number of repetitions. A variation on the fixed-count loop can be made, where the counter is not incremented by one each time through the loop, but by some other value. For example, consider the task of producing a Celsius to Fahrenheit temperature conversion table. Assume that Fahrenheit temperatures corresponding to Celsius temperatures ranging from 5 to 50 degrees are to be displayed in increments of five degrees. The desired display can be obtained with the series of statements:

```
celsius = 5    ' starting Celsius value
Do While celsius <= 50
  fahren = 9.0/5.0 * celsius + 32.0
  Print celsius, fahren
  celsius = celsius + 5
Loop
```

As before, the **Do While** loop consists of everything from the words **Do While** through the **Loop** statement. Prior to entering the **Do While** loop, we have made sure to assign a value to the counter being evaluated, and there is a statement to alter the value of celsius within the loop (in increments of 5), to ensure an exit from the **Do While** loop. Event Procedure 6-4 illustrates the use of this code within the context of a complete Form_Click event.

Event Procedure 6-4

```
Rem - a procedure to convert Celsius to Fahrenheit
Private Sub Form_Click()
  Const MAX_CELSIUS As Integer = 50
  Const START_VAL As Integer = 5
  Const STEP_SIZE As Integer = 5
  Dim celsius As Integer
  Dim fahren As Single

  Cls ' clear the form
  Font = "Courier"

  Print "Degrees", " Degrees"
  Print "Celsius", "Fahrenheit"
  Print "-------", "----------"

  celsius = START_VAL
  Do While celsius <= MAX_CELSIUS
    fahren = (9.0/5.0) * celsius + 32.0
    Print celsius, fahren
    celsius = celsius + STEP_SIZE
  Loop
```

The following display is obtained on a form when Event Procedure 6-4 is activated:

Degrees Celsius	Degrees Fahrenheit
5	41
10	50
15	59
20	68
25	77
30	86
35	95
40	104
45	113
50	122

Exercises 6.2

1. *practice* Rewrite Event Procedure 6-1 to print the numbers 2 to 10 in increments of two. The output of your program should be

   2 4 6 8 10

2. Rewrite Event Procedure 6-4 to produce a table that starts at a Celsius value of -10 and ends with a Celsius value of 60, in increments of ten degrees.

3. a. For the following code, determine the total number of items displayed. Also determine the first and last numbers printed. *first no = 1, last no = 21*

   ```
   Dim num as integer
   Num = 0
    Do While Num <= 20
      Num = Num + 1
      Print Num;
   Loop
   ```

   b. Enter and run code from Exercise 3a. as a `Form_Click` event procedure to verify your answers to the exercise.

   c. *practice* How would the output be affected if the two statements within the loop were reversed, that is, if the **Print** statement were made before the Num = Num + 1 statement ? *first no = 0 last = 20 then Program will not calculate num = num +1*

4. Write a Visual Basic program that converts gallons to liters. The program should display gallons from 10 to 20 in one-gallon increments and the corresponding liter equivalents. Use the relationship that there are 3.785 liters to a gallon.

5. Write a Visual Basic program to produce the following display on a form.

```
0
 1
  2
   3
    4
     5
      6
       7
        8
         9
```

6. Write a Visual Basic program to produce the following displays on a form.

```
a.   ****              b.     ****
       ****                   ****
         ****                 ****
           ****               ****
```

7. Write a Visual Basic program that converts feet to meters. The program should display feet from 3 to 30 in three-foot increments and the corresponding meter equivalents. Use the relationship that there are 3.28 feet to a meter.

8. A machine purchased for $28,000 is depreciated at a rate of $4,000 a year for seven years. Write and run a Visual Basic program that computes and displays a depreciation table for seven years. The table should have the form:

Year	Depreciation	End-of-year value	Accumulated depreciation
----	------------	-----------	------------
1	4000	24000	4000
2	4000	20000	8000
3	4000	16000	12000
4	4000	12000	16000
5	4000	8000	20000
6	4000	4000	24000
7	4000	0	28000

9. An automobile travels at an average speed of 55 miles per hour for four hours. Write a Visual Basic program that displays the distance driven, in miles, that the car has traveled after 0.5, 1.0, 1.5, . . . hours, until the end of the trip.

10. An approximate conversion formula for converting Fahrenheit to Celsius temperatures is

$$Celsius = Fahrenheit - 30 / 2$$

a. Using this formula, and starting with a Fahrenheit temperature of zero degrees, write a Visual Basic program that determines when the approximate equivalent Celsius temperature differs from the exact equivalent value by more than four degrees. (**Hint:** use a **Do While** loop that terminates when the difference between approximate and exact Celsius equivalents exceeds four degrees.)

b. Using the approximate Celsius conversion formula given in Exercise 10a., write a Visual Basic program that produces a table of Fahrenheit temperatures, exact Celsius equivalent temperatures, approximate Celsius equivalent temperatures, and the difference between the correct and approximate equivalent Celsius values. The table should begin at zero degrees Fahrenheit, use two-degree Fahrenheit increments, and terminate when the difference between exact and approximate values differs by more than four degrees.

6.3 Interactive Do While Loops

Combining interactive data entry with the repetition capabilities of the **Do While** loop produces very adaptable and powerful programs. To understand the concept involved, consider Program 6-1, where a **Do While** statement is used to accept and then display four user-entered numbers, one at a time. Although it is simple, the program highlights the flow of control concepts needed to produce more useful programs.

Figure 6-4

Program 6-1's Interface

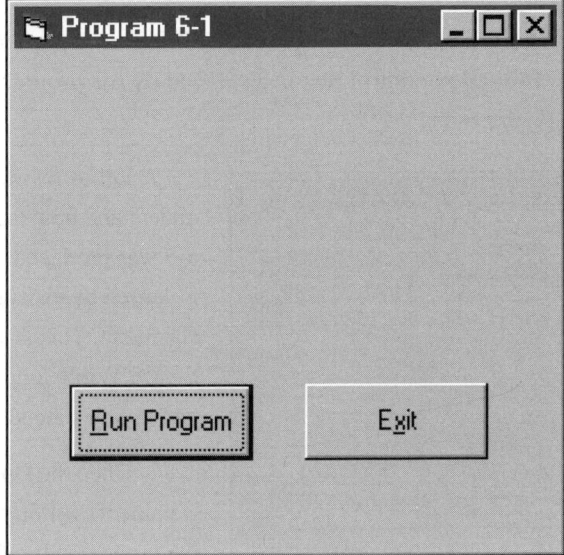

For this application, the only procedure code is the Command button's **Click** event, which is listed in Program 6-1's event code.

Program 6-1's Event Code

```
Private Sub cmdRun_Click()
  Const MAXNUMS As Integer = 4
  Dim count As Integer
  Dim num As Single

  Cls
  Print "This Program will ask you to enter"; MAXNUMS; "numbers"

  count = 1
  Do While count <= MAXNUMS
    num = Val(InputBox("Enter a number", "Input Dialog", 0))
    Print "The number entered is"; num
    count = count + 1
  Loop
End Sub

Private Sub cmdExit_Click()
  Beep
  End
End Sub
```

Table 6-1 The Properties Table for Program 6-1

Object	Property	Setting
Form	Name	frmMain
	Caption	Program 6-1
Command Button	Name	cmdRun
	Caption	&Run Program
Command Button	Name	cmdExit
	Caption	E&xit

Figure 6-5 illustrates a sample run of Program 6-1 after four numbers have been input. The **InputBox** control that is displayed by the program for the data entry is shown in Figure 6-6.

Figure 6-5

A Sample Run of Program 6-1

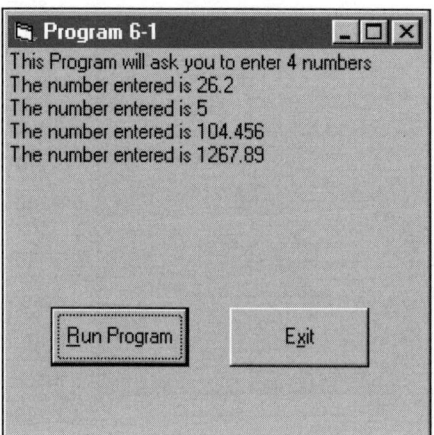

Let us review the program so we clearly understand how the output illustrated in Figure 6-5 was produced. The first message displayed is caused by execution of the first **Print** statement. This statement is outside and before the **Do While** loop, so it is executed once before any statement within the loop.

Once the **Do While** loop is entered, the statements within the loop are executed while the tested condition is **True**. The first time through the loop, the statement

```
num = InputBox("Enter a number", "Input Dialog", "0")
```

is executed. The call to the **InputBox** function displays the **InputBox** dialog shown in Figure 6-6, which forces the computer to wait for a number to be entered at the keyboard. Once a number is typed and the [Return] or [Enter] key is pressed, the **Print** statement within the loop displays that number. The variable count is then incremented by one. This process continues until four passes through the loop have been made and the value of count is 5. Each pass causes the **InputBox** and the message The number entered is to be displayed. Figure 6-7 illustrates this flow of control.

Program 6-1 can be modified to use the entered data rather than simply displaying it. For example, let us add the numbers entered and display the total. To do this we must be very careful about how we add the numbers since the same variable, num, is used for each number. Because of this, the entry of a new number in Program 6-1 automatically causes the previous number

Figure 6-6

The InputBox Displayed by Program 6-1

Figure 6-7

*Flow of Control Diagram
for the cmdRun_Click
Event Procedure*

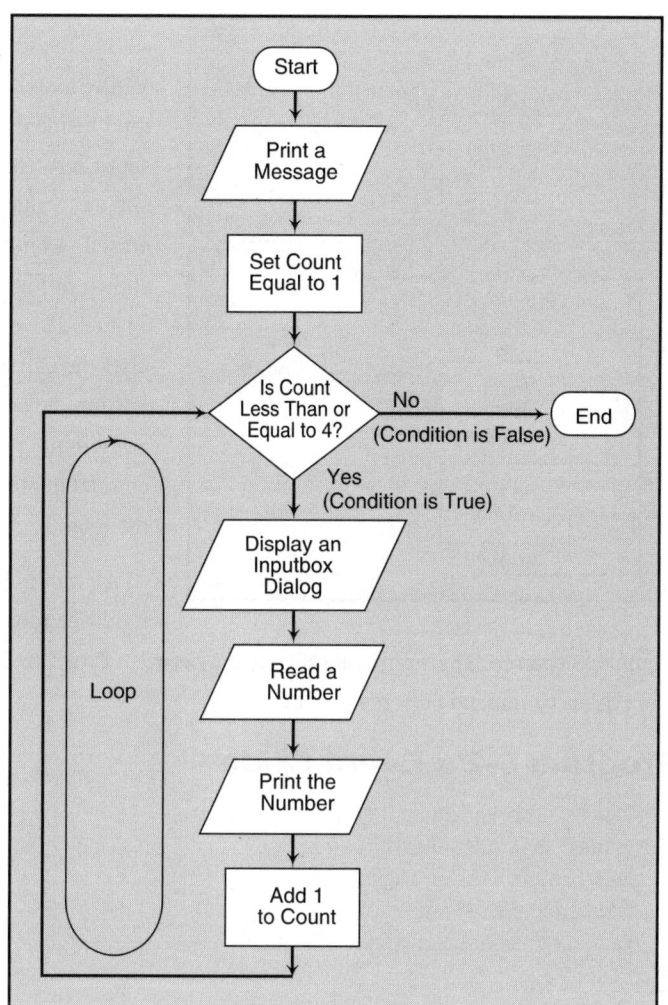

stored in num to be lost. Thus, each number entered must be added to the total, before another number is entered. The required sequence is

*Enter a number
Add the number to the total*

Figure 6-8

*Accepting and Adding a
Number to a Total*

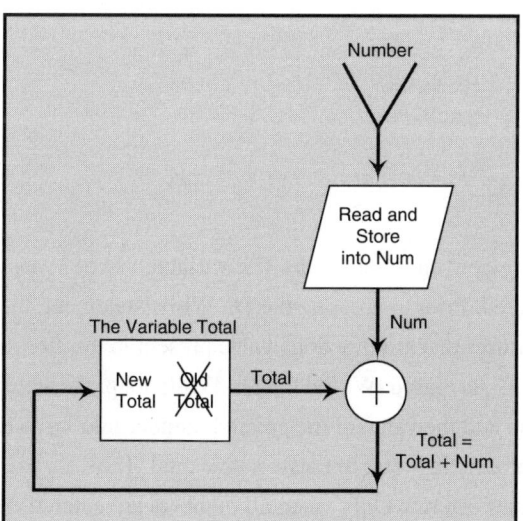

How do we add a single number to a total? A statement such as total = total + num does the job perfectly. This is the accumulating statement introduced in Section 3.3. After each number is entered, the accumulating statement adds the number into the total, as illustrated in Figure 6-8. The complete flow of control required for adding the numbers is illustrated in Figure 6-9.

Observe that in Figure 6-9 we have made a provision for initially

Figure 6-9

Accumulation Flow of Control

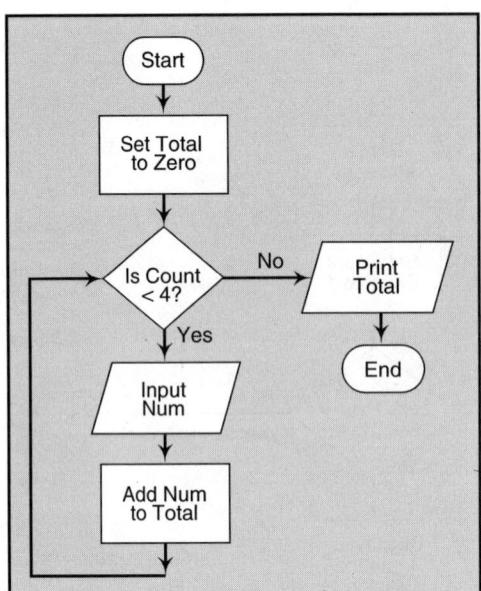

setting the total to zero before the **Do While** loop is entered. If we cleared the total inside the **Do While** loop, it would be set to zero each time the loop was executed and any value previously stored would be erased. As indicated in the flow diagram shown in Figure 6-9, the statement total = total + num is placed immediately after the call to the **InputBox** function. Putting the accumulating statement at this point in the program ensures that the entered number is immediately added to the total.

Program 6-2 incorporates the necessary modifications to Program 6-1 to total the numbers entered. The significant difference between Program 6-1 and 6-2 is the Run Program Command button's event code.

Program 6-2's Event Code

```
Private Sub cmdRun_Click()
  Const MAXNUMS As Integer = 4
  Dim count As Integer
  Dim num As Single
  Dim total As Single

  Cls
  Print "This Program will ask you to enter"; MAXNUMS; "numbers"

  count = 1
  total = 0
  Do While count <= MAXNUMS
    num = InputBox("Enter a number", "Input Dialog", "0")
    total = total + num
    Print "The number entered is"; num
    Print "The total is now"; total
    count = count + 1
  Loop
  Print "The final total is"; total
End Sub
```

Let us review this event code. The variable total was created to store the total of the numbers entered. Prior to entering the **Do While** statement, the value of total is set to zero. This ensures that any previous value present in the storage locations assigned to the variable total is erased. Within the **Do While** loop, the statement total = total + num is used to add the value of the entered number into total. As each value is entered, it is added into the existing total to create a new total. Thus, total becomes a running subtotal of all the values entered. Only when all numbers are entered does total contain the final

Figure 6-10

*A Sample Run of
Program 6-2*

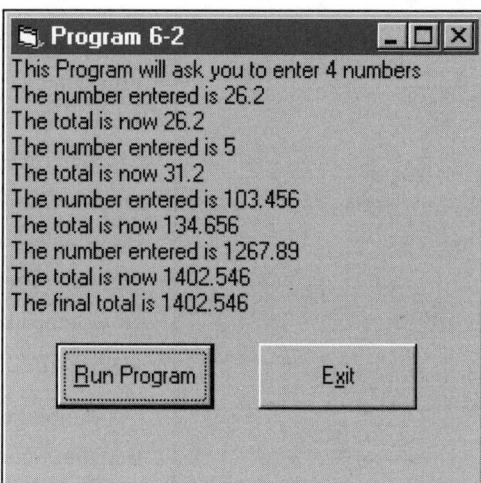

sum of all the numbers. After the **Do While** loop is finished, the last **Print** statement displays the final sum.

The results of a sample run of Program 6-2, using the same data we entered in the sample run for Program 6-1, are illustrated in Figure 6-10.

Having used an accumulating assignment statement to add the numbers entered, we can now go further and calculate the average of the numbers. Where do we calculate the average—within the **Do While** loop or outside of it?

In the case at hand, calculating an average requires that both a final sum and the number of items in that sum be available. The average is then computed by dividing the final sum by the number of items. At this point, we must ask, "At what point in the program is the correct sum available, and at what point is the number of items available?" In reviewing Program 6-2's event code, we see that the correct sum needed for calculating the average is available after the **Do While** loop is finished. In fact, the whole purpose of the **Do While** loop is to ensure that the numbers are entered and added correctly to produce a correct sum. With this as background, see if you can read and understand the event code used in Program 6-3.

Program 6-3's Event Code

```
Private Sub cmdRun_Click()
   Const MAXNUMS As Integer = 4
   Dim count As Integer
   Dim num As Single
   Dim total As Single
   Dim average As Single

   Cls
   Print "This Program will ask you to enter"; MAXNUMS; "numbers"

   count = 1
   total = 0
   Do While count <= MAXNUMS
      num = InputBox("Enter a number", "Input Dialog", "0")
      total = total + num
      Print "The number just entered is"; num
      count = count + 1
   Loop
   average = total / MAXNUMS
   Print "The average of these numbers is"; average
End Sub
```

*out side the loop
Calculate average*

Figure 6-11

A Sample Run of Program 6-3

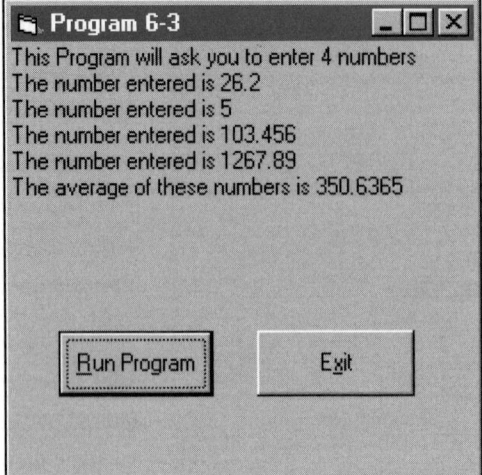

```
Program 6-3                              _ □ ✕
This Program will ask you to enter 4 numbers
The number entered is 26.2
The number entered is 5
The number entered is 103.456
The number entered is 1267.89
The average of these numbers is 350.6365




        Run Program              Exit
```

Program 6-3 is almost identical to Program 6-2, except for the calculation of the average. We have also removed the constant display of the total within and after the **Do While** loop. The loop in Program 6-3 is used to enter and add four numbers. Immediately after the loop is exited, the average is computed and displayed.

A sample run of Program 6-3 is illustrated in Figure 6-11.

The Do Until Loop Structure

In a **Do While** loop structure, the statements within the loop are executed as long as the condition is **True** (has a non-zero value). A variation of **Do While** loop is the **Do Until** loop, which executes the statements within the loop, as long as the condition is **False** (has a zero value). The syntax of a **Do Until** loop is

> **Do Until** *condition*
> *statement(s)*
> **Loop**

The **Do Until** loop, like its **Do While** counterpart, is an entrance-controlled loop. Unlike the **Do While** loop, which executes until the condition becomes **False**, a **Do Until** loop executes until the condition becomes **True**. If the condition tested in a **Do Until** loop is **True** to begin with, the statements within the loop will not execute at all. Generally, **Do Until** loops are not used extensively, for two reasons: first, most practical programming problems require performing a repetitive set of tasks while a condition is **True**. Next, if an entrance-controlled loop is required until a condition becomes **True**, it can always be restated as a loop that needs to be executed while the same condition remains False, using the syntax

> **Do While Not** *condition*
> *statement(s)*
> **Loop**

Sentinels

All of the loops we have created thus far have been examples of fixed-count loops, where a counter controls the number of loop iterations. By means of a **Do While** statement variable-condition loops may also be constructed. For example, when entering grades we may not want to count the number of grades that will be entered, but would prefer to enter the grades one after another and, at the end, type in a special data value to signal the end of data input.

In computer programming, data values used to signal either the start or end of a data series are called *sentinels*. The sentinel values must, of course, be selected so as not to conflict with legitimate data values. For example, if we were constructing a program to process a student's grades, and assuming that no extra credit is given that could produce a grade higher than 100, we could use any grade higher than 100 as a sentinel value. Program 6-4 illustrates this concept. In Program 6-4's event procedure, the grades are serially requested and accepted until a number larger than 100 is entered. Entry of a number higher than 100 alerts the program to exit the **Do While** loop and display the sum of the numbers entered.

Figure 6-12

Program 6-4's Interface

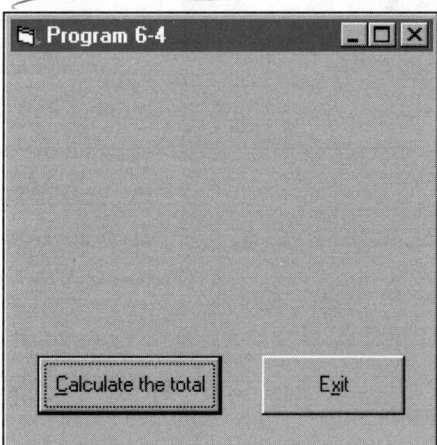

Table 6-2 The Properties Table for Program 6-4		
Object	**Property**	**Setting**
Form	Name	frmMain
	Caption	Program 6-2
Command Button	Name	cmdTotal
	Caption	&Calculate the total
Command Button	Name	cmdExit
	Caption	E&xit

Program 6-4's Event Code

```
Private Sub cmdTotal_Click()
   Const HIGHGRADE As Integer = 100
   Dim grade As Single, total As Single

   grade = 0
   total = 0
   Print "To stop entering grades, type in"
   Print "any number greater than 100."

   Do While grade <= HIGHGRADE
      grade = InputBox("Enter a grade", "Input Dialog", "0")
      Print "The grade just entered is"; grade
      total = total + grade
   Loop
   Print "The total of the valid grades is "; total - grade
End Sub

Private Sub cmdExit_Click()
   Beep
   End
End Sub
```

Figure 6-13

A Sample Run Using Program 6-4

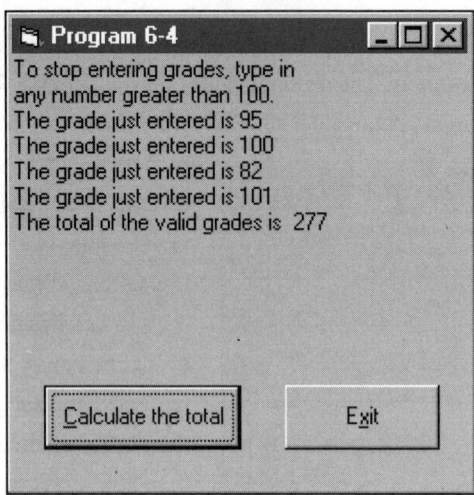

A sample run using Program 6-4 is illustrated in Figure 6-13. As long as grades less than or equal to 100 are entered, the program continues to request and accept additional data. When a number less than or equal to 100 is entered, the program adds this number to the total. When a number greater than 100 is entered, the program exits the loop and displays the sum of the grades.

Notice that the event procedure used in Program 6-4 differs from previous examples, in that termination of the loop is controlled by an externally supplied value, rather than a fixed-count condition. The loop in Program 6-4 will continue indefinitely until a sentinel value is encountered.

Breaking Out of a Loop

It is sometimes necessary to prematurely break out of a loop when an unusual error condition is detected. The means of doing this is provided by an **Exit Do** statement. For example, execution of the following **Do While** loop is immediately terminated if a number greater than 76 is entered.

```
Count = 1
Do While count <= 10
num = InputBox("Enter a number", "Input Dialog", "0")
If num > 76 Then
   Print "You lose!"
   Exit Do        ' break out of the loop
End If
Print "Keep on trucking!\n"
count = count + 1
Loop
   ' break jumps to here
```

The **Exit Do** statement violates pure structured programming principles because it provides a second, nonstandard exit from a loop. Nevertheless, this statement is extremely useful and valuable for breaking out of a **Do** loop.

[handwritten: early exit]

[handwritten: use = ATM when you type wrong password]

Exercises 6.3

1. Write a **Do While** loop to do the following:

    a. Display the multiples of 3 backward from 33 to 3, inclusive.

    b. Display the capital letters of the alphabet backward from Z to A.

2. Rewrite Program 6-2 to compute the average of eight numbers.

Introduction to Visual Basic

3. Rewrite Program 6-2 to display the following prompt in an **InputBox**:

   `Please type in the total number of data values to be added`

   In response to this prompt, the program should accept a user-entered number from the **InputBox** and then use this number to control the number of times the **Do While** loop is executed. Thus, if the user enters 5 in the **InputBox**, the program should request the input of five numbers, and display the total after five numbers have been entered.

4. a. Write a Visual Basic program to convert Celsius degrees to Fahrenheit. The program should request the starting Celsius value, the number of conversions to be made, and the increment between Celsius values. The display should have appropriate headings and list the Celsius value and the corresponding Fahrenheit value. Use the relationship Fahrenheit = 9.0 / 5.0 * Celsius + 32.0.

   b. Run the program written in Exercise 4a. on a computer. Verify that your program starts at the correct Celsius value and contains the exact number of conversions specified in your input data.

5. a. Modify the program written in Exercise 4 to request the starting Celsius value, the ending Celsius value, and the increment. Thus, instead of the condition checking for a fixed count, the condition will check for the ending Celsius value.

   b. Run the program written in Exercise 5a. on a computer. Verify that your output starts and ends on the correct values.

6. Rewrite Program 6-3 to compute the average of ten numbers.

7. Rewrite Program 6-3 to display the following prompt in an **InputBox**:

   `Please type in the total number of data values to be averaged`

   In response to this prompt, the program should accept a user-entered number from the InputBox, and then use this number to control the number of times the **Do While** loop is executed. Thus, if the user enters 6, the program should request the input of six numbers and display the average of the next six numbers entered.

8. By mistake, a programmer put the statement `average = total / count` within the **Do While** loop immediately after the statement `total = total + num` in Program 6-3. Thus, the **Do While** loop becomes

   ```
   count = 1
   total = 0
   Do While count <= MAXNUMS
     num = InputBox("Enter a number", "Input Dialog", "0")
     total = total + num
     Print "The number just entered is"; num
     average = total / count
     count = count + 1
   Loop
   Print "The average of these numbers is"; average
   ```

   Will the program yield the correct result with this **Do While** loop?

   From a programming perspective, which **Do While** loop is better to use, and why?

9. a. The following data was collected on a recent automobile trip.

	Mileage	**Gallons**
Start of trip:	22495	Full tank
	22841	12.2
	23185	11.3
	23400	10.5
	23772	11.0
	24055	12.2
	24434	14.7
	24804	14.3
	25276	15.2

Write a Visual Basic program that accepts a mileage and gallons value and calculates the miles per gallon (mpg) achieved for that segment of the trip. The mpg is obtained as the difference in mileage between fill-ups divided by the number of gallons of gasoline used in the fill-up.

   b. Modify the program written for Exercise 9a. to compute and display the cumulative mpg achieved after each fill-up. The cumulative mpg is calculated as the difference between each fill-up mileage and the mileage at the start of the trip divided by the sum of the gallons used to that point in the trip.

10. a. A bookstore summarizes its monthly transactions by keeping the following information for each book in stock:

   - International Standard Book Number (ISBN),
   - Inventory balance at the beginning of the month,
   - Number of copies received during the month, and
   - Number of copies sold during the month.

   Write a Visual Basic program that accepts this data for each book, and then displays the ISBN and an updated book inventory balance using the following relationship:

   New balance   = Inventory balance at the beginning of the month

                 + Number of copies received during the month

                 - Number of copies sold during the month

   Your program should use a **Do While** loop with a fixed-count condition, so that information on only three books is requested.

   b. Run the program written in Exercise 10a. on a computer. Review the display produced by your program and verify that the output produced is correct.

11. Modify the program you wrote for Exercise 11a. to keep requesting and displaying results until a sentinel identification value of 999 is entered. Run the program on a computer.

6.4 For/Next Loops

As we have seen, the condition used to control a **Do While** loop can either test the value of a counter or test for a sentinel value. Loops controlled by a counter are referred to as fixed-count loops, because the loop is executed a fixed number of times. The creation of fixed-count loops always requires initializing a counter variable, testing the counter variable, and modifying the counter variable. The general form we have used for these steps is

```
Initialize counter
Do While counter <= final value
    statement(s)
    counter = counter + increment
Loop
```

The need to initialize, test, and alter a counter to create a fixed-count loop is so common that Visual Basic provides a special structure, called the **For/Next** loop, that groups all of these operations together on a single line. The general syntax of a **For/Next** loop is

```
For variable = start To end Step increment
    statement(s)
Next variable
```

Although the **For/Next** loop looks a little complicated, it is really quite simple, if we consider each of its parts separately. A **For/Next** loop begins with a **For** statement. This statement, which begins with the keyword **For**, provides four items that control the loop: a variable name, a starting value for the variable, an ending value, and an increment value. Except for the increment, each of these items must be present in a **For** statement, including the equal sign and the keyword **To**, used to separate the starting and ending values. If an increment is included, the keyword **Step** must also be used, to separate the increment value from the ending value.

The variable name in the **For** statement can be any valid Visual Basic name and is referred to as the *loop counter* (typically the counter is chosen as an integer variable); *start* is the starting (initializing) value assigned to the counter; *end* is the maximum or minimum value the counter can have and determines when the loop is finished; and *increment* is the value that is added to or subtracted from the counter each time the loop is executed. If the increment is omitted, it is assumed to be one. Examples of valid **For** statements include:

```
For count = 1 To 7 Step 1
For I = 5 To 15 Step 2
For kk = 1 To 20
```

In the first **For** statement, the counter variable is named count, the initial value assigned to count is 1, the loop will be terminated when the value in count exceeds 7, and the increment value is 1. In the next **For** statement, the counter variable is named I, the initial value of I is 5, the loop will be terminated when the value in I exceeds 15, and the increment is 2. In the last **For** statement, the counter variable is named kk, the initial value of kk is equal to 1, the loop will be terminated when the value of *kk* exceeds 20, and a default value of one (1) is used for the increment.

For each **For** statement there must be a matching **Next** statement. The **Next** statement both defines where the loop ends and is used to increment the counter variable by the increment amount defined in the **For** statement. If no increment has been explicitly listed in the **For** statement, the counter is incremented by one.

The **Next** statement formally marks the end of the loop and causes the counter to be incremented. It then causes a transfer back to the beginning of the loop. When the loop is completed, program execution continues with the first statement after the **Next** statement.

Consider the loop contained within Event Procedure 6-5, as a specific example of a **For/Next** loop.

Event Procedure 6-5

```
Private Sub Form_Click()
   Dim count As Integer

   Cls
   Font = "Courier"
   Print "NUMBER", "SQUARE ROOT"
   Print "------", "-----------"
   For count = 1 To 5
      Print count, Format(Sqr(count), ".000000")
   Next count
End Sub
```

When Event Procedure 6-5 is executed, the following display is produced:

```
NUMBER      SQUARE ROOT
------      -----------
   1        1.000000
   2        1.414214
   3        1.732051
   4        2.000000
   5        2.236068
```

The first two lines displayed by the program are produced by the two **Print** statements placed before the **For** statement. The remaining output is produced by the statements within the **For/Next** loop. This loop begins with the **For** statement and ends with the **Next** statement.

The initial value assigned to the counter variable `count` is 1. Since the value in `count` does not exceed the final value of 5, the statements in the loop, including the **Next** statement, are executed. The execution of the **Print** statement within the loop produces the display:

```
1    1.0000000
```

The **Next** statement is then encountered, which increments the value in `count` to 2, and control is transferred back to the **For** statement. The **For** statement then tests if `count` is greater than 5, and repeats the loop, producing the display:

```
2    1.414214
```

This process continues until the value in `count` exceeds the final value of 5, producing the complete output table. For comparison purposes, an equivalent **Do While** loop to the **For/Next** loop contained in Event Procedure 6-5 is

```
count = 1
Do While count <= 5
  Print count, Format(Sqr(count), ".000000")
  count = count + 1
Loop
```

As seen in this example, the difference between the **For/Next** and **Do While** loops is the placement of the initialization, condition test, and incrementing items. The grouping together of these items together in a **For** statement is very convenient when fixed-count loops must be constructed. See if you can determine the output produced by Event Procedure 6-6.

Event Procedure 6-6

```
Private Sub Form_Click()
  Dim count As Integer

  Cls
  Font = "Courier"
  For count = 12 To 20 Step 2
    Print count
  Next count
End Sub
```

Did you figure it out? The loop starts with `count` initialized to 12, stops when `count` exceeds 20, and increments `count` in steps of two. The actual statements executed include all statements following the **For** statement, up to and including the **Next** statement. The output produced by Event Procedure 6-6 is

```
12
14
16
18
20
```

For/Next Loop Rules

Now that we have seen a few simple examples of **For/Next** loop structures, it is useful to summarize the rules that all **For/Next** loops must adhere to.

1. The first statement in a **For/Next** loop must be a **For** statement, and the last statement in a **For/Next** loop must be a **Next** statement.
2. The **For/Next** loop counter variable may be either a real or integer variable.
3. The initial, final, and increment values may all be replaced by variables or expressions, as long as each variable has a value previously assigned to it, and the expressions can be evaluated to yield a number. For example, the **For** statement

```
For count = begin To begin + 10 Step augment
```

   is valid and can be used as long as values have been assigned to the variables `begin` and `augment` before this **For** statement is encountered in a program.
4. The initial, final, and increment values may be positive or negative, but the loop will not be not executed at all, if either of the following is true:
   a. The initial value is greater than the final value and the increment is positive, or
   b. The initial value is less than the final value and the increment is negative.
5. An infinite loop is created if the increment is zero.
6. An **Exit For** statement may be embedded within a **For/Next** loop, to cause a transfer out of the loop.

Once a **For/Next** loop is correctly structured, it is executed as follows[2] :

Step 1. The initial value is assigned to the counter variable.

Step 2. The value in the counter is compared to the final value.
For positive increments, if the value is less than or equal to the final value:
- All **Loop** statements are executed; and
- The counter is incremented and Step 2 is repeated.

For negative increments if the value is greater than or equal to the final value:
- All **Loop** statements are executed; and
- The counter is decremented and Step 2 is repeated.

Else
- The loop is terminated.

It is extremely important to realize that no statement within the loop should ever alter the value in the counter because the increment or decrement of the loop counter is automatically done by the **Next** statement. The value in the counter may itself be displayed, as in Event Procedures 6-5 and 6-6, or used in an expression to calculate some other variable. It must, however, never be used either on the left-hand side of an assignment statement or altered within the loop. Also notice that when a **For/Next** loop is completed, the counter contains the last value that exceeds the final tested value.

---

[2] The number of times that a **For/Next** loop is executed is determined by the expression:
   Int((final value - initial value + increment)/increment)
If this expression results in a negative value, the loop is not executed.

Figure 6-14

For/Next Loop Flowchart for Positive Increments

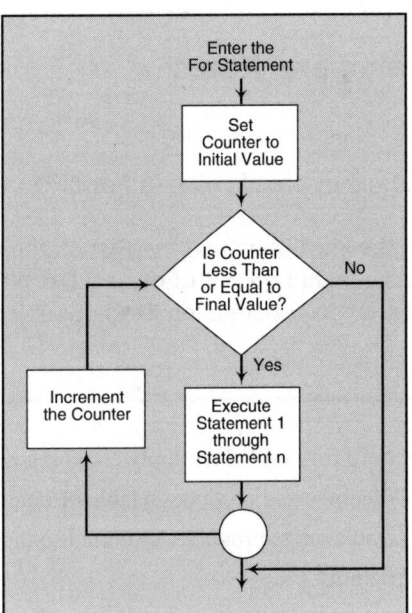

Figure 6-14 illustrates the internal workings of the **For/Next** loop for positive increments. To avoid the necessity of always illustrating these steps, a simplified flowchart symbol has been created. Using the following flowchart symbol to represent a **For/Next** statement

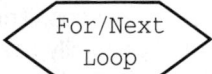

complete **For/Next** loops can be illustrated as shown on Figure 6-15.

To understand the enormous power of **For/Next** loops, consider the task of printing a table of numbers from 1 to 10, including their squares and cubes, using a **For/Next** statement. Such a table was previously produced, using a **Do While** loop in Event Procedure 6-3. You may wish to review Event Procedure 6-3 and compare it to Event Procedure 6-7 to get a further sense of the equivalence between **For/Next** and **Do While** loops. Both Event Procedures 6-3 and 6-7 produce the same output.

Event Procedure 6-7

```
Private Sub Form_Click()
  Dim num As Integer

  Cls ' clear the form
  Font = "Courier"
  Print "NUMBER", "SQUARE", "CUBE"
  Print "------", "------", "----"

  For num = 1 To 10
    Print num, num ^ 2, num ^ 3
  Next num
End Sub
```

Figure 6-15

Simplified For/Next Loop Flowchart

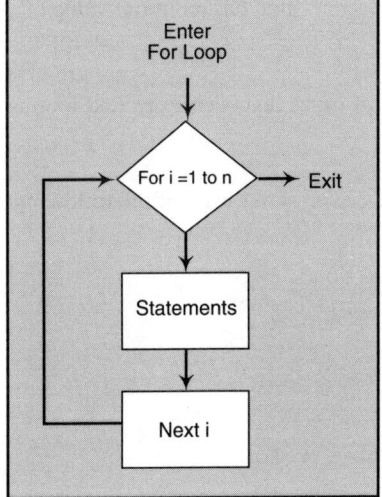

When Event Procedure 6-7 is activated, the following display is produced on the form:

NUMBER	SQUARE	CUBE
1	1	1
2	4	8
3	9	27
4	16	64
5	25	125
6	36	216
7	49	343
8	64	512
9	81	729
10	100	1000

Programmers' Notes

Which Loop Should You Use?

Beginning programmers often ask which structure they should use—a **For** or **Do While** loop?

In Visual Basic, the answer is relatively straightforward, because the **For** statement can only be used to construct fixed-count loops. Thus, in Visual Basic, although both **For** and **Do While** loops create pretest loops, you should generally use a **For/Next** loop when constructing fixed-count loops and **Do While** loops when constructing variable-condition loops.

In the **For/Next** statement of Program 6-11, simply changing the number 10 to 1000 creates a loop that is executed 1000 times and produces a table of numbers from 1 to 1000. As with the **Do While** loop, this small change produces an immense increase in the processing and output provided by the program.

Exercises 6.4

1. Write individual **For** statements for the following cases:

    a. Use a counter named `I` that has an initial value of 1, a final value of 20, and an increment of 1.

    b. Use a counter named `count` that has an initial value of 1, a final value of 20, and an increment of 2.

    c. Use a counter named `J` that has an initial value of 1, a final value of 100, and an increment of 5.

    d. Use a counter named `count` that has an initial value of 20, a final value of 1, and an increment of -1.

    e. Use a counter named `count` that has an initial value of 20, a final value of 1, and an increment of -2.

    f. Use a counter named `count` that has an initial value of 1.0, a final value of 16.2, and an increment of 0.2.

    g. Use a counter named `xcnt` that has an initial value of 20.0, a final value of 10.0, and an increment of -0.5.

2. Determine the number of times that each **For/Next** loop is executed for the statements written in Exercise 1.

3. Determine the value in `total`, after each of the following loops is executed.

    a.
    ```
    total = 0
    For I = 1 To 10
       total = total + I
    Next I
    ```

    b.
    ```
    total = 1
    For count = 1 To 10
       total = total * 2
    Next count
    ```

    c.
    ```
    total = 0
    For I = 10 To 15
       total = total + I
    Next I
    ```

    d.
    ```
    total = 50
    For I = 1 To 10
       total = total - I
    Next I
    ```

```
e. total = 1                 f. total = 1.0
   For icnt = 1 To 8            For J = 1 To 5
     total = total * icnt         total = total / 2.0
   Next icnt                   Next J
```

4. Determine the errors in the following **For/Next** statements:

   a. For I = 1,10

   b. For count 5,10

   c. For JJ = 1 To 10 Increment 2

   d. For kk = 1, 10, -1

   e. For kk = -1, -20

5. Determine the output of the following **For** loop:

   ```
   Dim I as Integer
   For I = 20 To 0 Step -4
     Print I
   Next I
   ```

   20
   16
   12
   8
   4
   0

6. Modify Event Procedure 6-7 to produce a table of the numbers 0 through 20 in increments of 2, with their squares and cubes.

7. Modify Event Procedure 6-7 to produce a table of numbers from 10 to 1, instead of 1 to 10 as it currently does.

8. Write a Visual Basic program that uses a **For/Next** loop to accumulate the sum $1 + 2 + 3 + ... + N$, where N is a user-entered integer. Then evaluate the expression $N * (N + 1) / 2$ to verify that this expression yields the same result as the loop.

9. a. An old Arabian legend has it that a fabulously wealthy but unthinking king agreed to give a beggar one cent the first day and double the previous day's amount for 64 days. Using this information write, run, and test a Visual Basic program that displays how much the king must pay the beggar on each day. The output of your program should appear as follows:

   ```
   Day        Amount Owed
   ---        -----------
    1            0.01
    2            0.02
    3            0.04
    .             .
    .             .
    .             .
   64             .
   ```

b. Modify the program you wrote for Exercise 9b. to determine on which day the king will have paid a total of one million dollars to the beggar.

10. Write and run a program that calculates and displays the amount of money available in a bank account that initially has $1000 deposited in it and that earns 8 percent interest a year. Your program should display the amount available at the end of each year for a period of ten years. Use the relationship that the money available at the end of each year equals the amount of money in the account at the start of the year plus 0.08 times the amount available at the start of the year.

11. A machine purchased for $28,000 is depreciated at a rate of $4000 a year for seven years. Write and run a Visual Basic program that uses a **For/Next** loop to compute and display a seven-year depreciation table. The table should have the form:

```
Depreciation Schedule
-----------  --------

Year           Depreciation   End-of-year      Accumulated
                                  value         depreciation

----           -----------    -----------      ------------
1              4000           24000            4000
2              4000           20000            8000
3              4000           16000            12000
4              4000           12000            16000
5              4000           8000             20000
6              4000           4000             24000
7              4000           0                28000
```

12. A well-regarded manufacturer of widgets has been losing 4 percent of its sales each year. The annual profit for the firm is 10 percent of sales. This year, the firm has had $10 million in sales and a profit of $1 million. Determine the expected sales and profit for the next 10 years. Your program should complete and produce a display similar to the following:

```
                    Sales and Profit Projection
                    ---------------------------
        Year        Expected sales   Projected profit
        ----        --------------   ----------------
        1           $10000000        $1000000
        2           $ 9600000        $ 960000
        3               .                .
        .               .                .
        .               .                .
        .               .                .
        10              .                .
        -----------------------------------------------------
        Totals:     $ .              $ .
```

13. According to legend, the island of Manhattan was purchased from the Native American population in 1626 for $24. Assuming that this money was invested in a Dutch bank paying 5 percent simple interest per year, construct a table showing how much money this would grow to at the end of each twenty-year period, starting in 1626 and ending in 2006.

6.5 Nested Loops

There are many situations in which it is very convenient to have a loop contained within another loop. Such loops are called *nested loops*. A simple example of a nested loop is

```
For I = 1 To 4    ' Start of Outer Loop
  Print "I is now"; I
  For J = 1 To 3  ' Start of Inner Loop
    Print " J = "; J
  Next J    ' End of Inner Loop
Next I      ' End of Outer Loop
```

Can hewritte I before J (handwritten note)

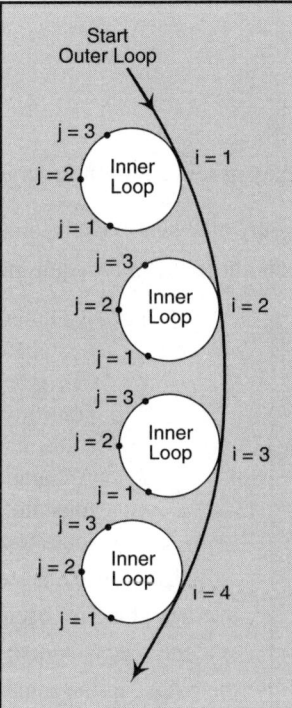

Figure 6-16

For Each I, J Makes a Complete Loop

Figure 6-17

Program 6-5's Interface

The first loop, controlled by the value of I, is called the *outer loop*. The second loop, controlled by the value of J, is called the *inner loop*. Notice that all statements in the inner loop are contained within the boundaries of the outer loop, and that we have used a different variable to control each loop. For each single trip through the outer loop, the inner loop runs through its entire sequence. Thus, each time the I counter increases by one, the inner **For/Next** loop executes completely. This situation is illustrated in Figure 6-16.

To understand the concept involved, consider Program 6-5, which uses a nested **For/Next** loop.

Table 6-3 The Properties Table for Program 6-5		
Object	**Property**	Setting
Form	Name	frmMain
	Caption	Program 6-5
Command Button	Name	cmdRun
	Caption	&Show Nested Loop
Command Button	Name	cmdExit
	Caption	E&xit

For this application, the procedure code for the Command button Click events is listed in Program 6-5's event code.

Program 6-5's Event Code

```
Private Sub cmdRun_Click()
  Dim I As Integer, J As Integer

  Cls
  For I = 1 To 4  '       <— Start of Outer Loop
    Print "I is now"; I
    For J = 1 To 3 '            <— Start of Inner Loop
      Print " J = "; J
    Next J    '       <— End of Inner Loop
  Next I      '       <— End of Outer Loop
End Sub

Private Sub cmdExit_Click()
  Beep
  End
End Sub
```

Figure 6-18 illustrates the display produced when Program 6-5 is executed.

In creating nested loops, using any of Visual Basic's loop structures (and the various structures can be nested within one another), the only requirements are

Figure 6-18

The Display Produced by Program 6-5

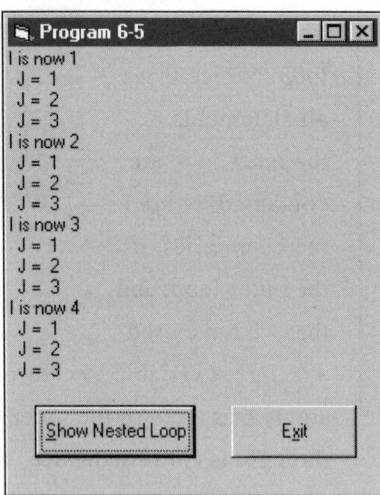

1. An inner loop must be fully contained within an outer loop,
2. The inner loop and outer loop control variables cannot be the same, and
3. An outer loop control variable must not be altered within an inner loop.

Let us use a nested loop to compute the average grade for each student in a class of 20 students. Each student has taken four exams during the course of the semester. The final grade for each student is calculated as the average of the four examination grades. The pseudocode for this example is

pseudo code

Do 20 times
  Set student total to zero
  Do 4 times
    Read in a grade
    Add the grade to the student total
  End inner Do
  Calculate student's average grade
  Print student's average grade
End outer Do

As described in the pseudocode, an outer loop consisting of 20 passes will be used to calculate the average for each student. The inner loop will consist of four passes, with one examination grade entered in each inner loop pass. As each grade is

Figure 6-19

Program 6-6's Interface

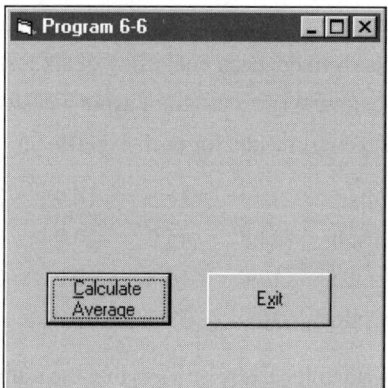

entered, it is added to the total for the student, and at the end of the loop, the average is calculated and displayed. Program 6-6 uses a nested loop to make the required calculations.

For this application, the procedure code for the Command button **Click** events is listed in Program 6-6's event code.

Table 6-4 The Properties Table for Program 6-6

Object	Property	Setting
Form	Name	frmMain
	Caption	Program 6-6
Command Button	Name	cmdRun
	Caption	&Calculate Average
Command Button	Name	cmdExit
	Caption	E&xit

Program 6-6's Event Code

```
Private Sub cmdRun_Click()
Rem: This program calculates the average grade for MAXSTUDENTS no. of students
    Const MAXSTUDENTS As Integer = 20
    Const NUMGRADES As Integer = 4

    Dim i As Integer, j As Integer
    Dim grade As Single, total As Single, average As Single

    Rem: This is the start of the outer loop
    For i = 1 To MAXSTUDENTS
      total = 0
      Rem: This is the start of the inner loop
      For j = 1 To NUMGRADES
         grade = InputBox("Enter an exam grade for this student", "Input Dialog", "0")
         total = total + grade
      Next j   ' End of inner loop
      average = total / NUMGRADES
      Print "The average for student"; i; "is ", average
    Next i   ' End of outer loop
End Sub

Private Sub cmdExit_Click()
    Beep
    End
End Sub
```

In reviewing Program 6-6, pay particular attention to the initialization of `total` within the outer loop before the inner loop is entered. `total` is initialized 20 times, once for each student. Also notice that the average is calculated and displayed immediately after the inner loop is finished. Since the statements that compute and print the average are also contained within the outer loop, 20 averages are calculated and displayed. The entry and addition of each grade within the inner loop use summation techniques we have seen before, which should now be familiar to you.

Exercises 6.5

1. Four experiments are performed, each consisting of six test results. The results for each experiment are given below. Write a program using a nested loop to compute and display the average of the test results for each experiment.

First experiment results:	23.2	31.5	16.9	27.5	25.4	28.6
Second experiment results:	34.8	45.2	27.9	36.8	33.4	39.4
Third experiment results:	19.4	16.8	10.2	20.8	18.9	13.4
Fourth experiment results:	36.9	39.5	49.2	45.1	42.7	50.6

2. Modify the program written for Exercise 1, so that the number of test results for each experiment is entered by the user. Write your program so that a different number of test results can be entered for each experiment.

3. a. A bowling team consists of five players. Each player bowls three games. Write a Visual Basic program that uses a nested loop to enter each player's individual scores and then computes and displays the average score for each bowler. Assume that each bowler has the following scores:

First bowler:	286	252	265
Second bowler:	212	186	215
Third bowler:	252	232	216
Fourth bowler:	192	201	235
Fifth bowler:	186	236	272

   b. Modify the program written for Exercise 3a., to calculate and display the average team score. (**Hint:** Use a second variable to store the total of all the players' scores.)

4. Rewrite the program written for Exercise 3a., to eliminate the inner loop. To do this, you will have to input three scores for each bowler rather than one at a time.

5. Write a program that calculates and displays values for Y when

   $$Y = XZ/(X-Z)$$

   Your program should calculate Y for values of X ranging between 1 and 5, and values of Z ranging between 2 and 10. X should control the outer loop and be incremented in steps of one, and Z should be incremented in steps of one. Your program should also display the message `Value Undefined` when the X and Z values are equal.

6. Write a program that calculates and displays the yearly amount available if $1000 is invested in a bank account for 10 years. Your program should display the amounts available for interest rates from 6 percent to 12 percent inclusively, in 1 percent increments. Use a nested loop, with the outer loop controlling the interest rate and the inner loop controlling the years. Use the relationship that the money available at the end of each year equals the amount of money in the account at the start of the year, plus the interest rate times the amount available at the start of the year.

Use For loop

7. In the Duchy of Penchuck, the fundamental unit of currency is the Penchuck Dollar, PD. Income tax deductions are base on Salary in units of 10,000 PD and on the number of dependents the employee has. The formula, designed to favor low-income families, is

*Deduction PD = Dependents * 500 + 0.05 * 50,000 - Salary*

Beyond five dependents and beyond 50,000 PD, the deduction does not change. There is no tax, hence no deduction, on incomes of less than 10,000 PD. Based on this information, create a table of Penchuck income tax deductions, with dependents 0 to 5 as the column headings and salaries of 10000, 20000, 30000, 40000, and 50000 as the rows.

6.6 Exit-Controlled Loops

The **Do While** and **For/Next** loops are both entrance-controlled loops, which means that they evaluate a condition at the start of the loop. A consequence of testing a condition at the top of the loop is that the statements within the loop may not be executed at all.

There are cases, however, where we always require a loop to execute at least once. For such cases, Visual Basic provides two exit-controlled loops, the **Do/Loop While** and **Do/ Loop Until** structures. Each of these loop structures tests a condition at the bottom of a loop, which ensures that the statements within the loop are executed at least one time. The syntax for the most commonly used exit-controlled loop is

```
Do
    statement(s)
Loop Until condition
```

The important concept to notice in the **Do/Loop Until** structure is that all statements within the loop are executed at least once before the condition is tested, and the loop is repeated until the condition becomes **True** (another way of viewing this is that the loop executes while the condition is **False**). A flowchart illustrating the operation of the **Do/Loop Until** structure is shown in Figure 6-20.

As illustrated in Figure 6-20, all statements within the **Do/Loop Until** loop are executed once before the condition is evaluated. Then, if the condition is **False**, the statements within the loop are executed again. This process continues until the condition becomes **True**.

Figure 6-20

The Do/Loop Until Structure's Flowchart

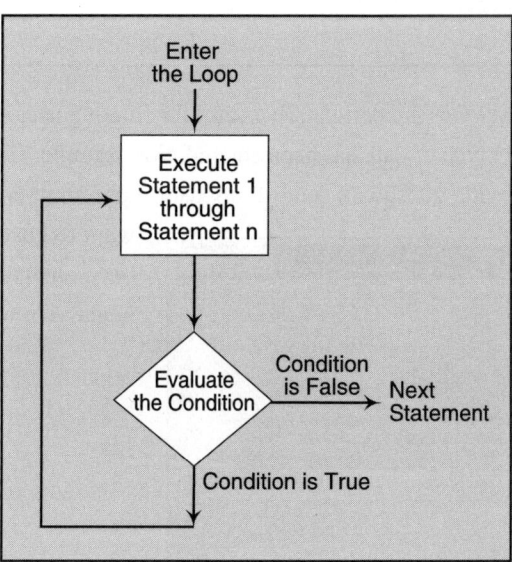

As an example of a **Do/Loop Until** structure consider the following loop:

```
i = 0
Do
   Print i;
   i = i + 5
Loop Until i > 20
```

[handwritten: post test - cond^n is not check before code.]

The output produced by this code is

```
0   5   10   15   20
```

The important point to notice here is that the condition is tested after the statements within the loop structure have been executed, rather than before. This ensures that the loop statements are always executed at least once. Also notice that exit-controlled loops require that you correctly initialize all variables used in the tested expression before the loop is entered, in a manner similar to that used in entrance-controlled loops. Similarly, within the loop itself, these same variables must be altered to ensure that the loop eventually terminates.

The Do/Loop While Structure

In a **Do/Loop Until** structure, the statements within the loop are executed as long as the condition is **False** (has a zero value). A variation of **Do/Loop Until** structure is the **Do/Loop While** structure, which executes the statements within the loop as long as the condition is **True** (has a non-zero value). The syntax of a **Do/Loop While** loop is

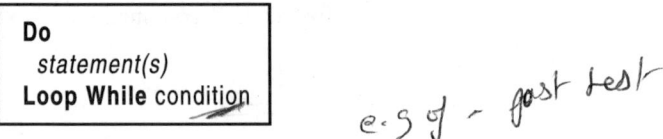

```
Do
   statement(s)
Loop While condition
```

[handwritten: e.g of - post test]

The **Do/Loop While** structure, like its **Do/Loop Until** counterpart, is an exit-controlled loop. Unlike the **Do/Loop Until** loop, which executes until the condition becomes **True**, a **Do/Loop While** structure executes until the condition becomes **False**. If the condition tested in a **Do/Loop While** loop is **False** to begin with, the statements within the loop will only execute once.

Validity Checks

Exit-controlled loops are particularly useful for filtering user-entered input and validating that the correct type of data has been entered. For example, assume that a program is being written to provide the square root of any user input number. For this application, we want to ensure that a valid number has been entered. Any invalid data, such as a negative number or a non-numeric input,

Figure 6-21
Program 6-7's Interface

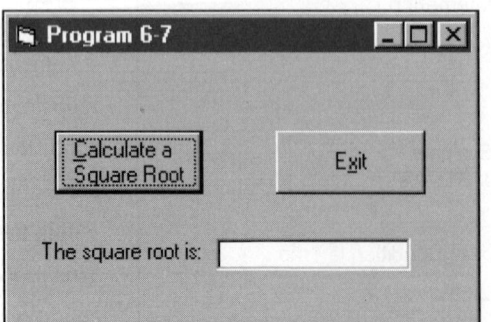

Introduction to Visual Basic

Table 6-5 The Properties Table for Program 6-7

Object	Property	Setting
Form	Name	frmMain
	Caption	Program 6-7
Picture Box	Name	picSquare
	Enabled	False
	BackColor	White (Palette tab)
Command Button	Name	cmdRun
	Caption	&Calculate a Square Root
Command Button	Name	cmdExit
	Caption	E&xit

should be rejected and a new request for input is to be made, until the user actually enters a valid number. Program 6-7 illustrates how this request can easily be accomplished using a **Do/Loop Until** structure.

Program 6-7's Event Code

```
Private Sub cmdRun_Click()
  Dim num As String

  Do
    picsquare.Cls
    num = InputBox("Enter a number", "Input Request", "0")
    If IsNumeric(num) And num >= 0 Then
      picsquare.Print Sqr(num)
    Else
      MsgBox "Invalid data was entered", vbInformation, "Error Message"
    End If
  Loop Until IsNumeric(num) And num >= 0

End Sub

Private Sub cmdExit_Click()
  Beep
  End
End Sub
```

Notice that, in the Run button **Click** code, a request for a number is repeated until a valid number is entered. This code is constructed so that a user cannot "crash" the program by entering either a non-numeric string or a negative number. This type of user-input validation is essential for programs that will be used extensively by other people and is a mark of professionally written programs.

Introduction to Visual Basic

Exercises 6.6

1. a. Using a **Do/Loop Until** structure, write a program to accept a grade. The program should continue to request a grade until a valid grade is entered. A valid grade is any grade greater than or equal to 0 and less than or equal to 101. After a valid grade has been entered, your program should display the value of that grade.

   b. Modify the program written for Exercise 1a. so that it allows the user to exit the program by entering the number 999.

   c. Modify the program written for Exercise 1b. so that it automatically terminates after five invalid grades are entered.

2. a. Modify the program written for Exercise 1a. as follows: if the grade is less than 0 or greater than 100, your program should print an appropriate message informing the user that an invalid grade has been entered; otherwise, the grade should be added to a total. When a grade of 999 is entered, the program should exit the repetition loop and compute and display the average of the valid grades entered.

   b. Run the program written in Exercise 2a. on a computer and verify the program, using appropriate test data.

3. a. Write a program to reverse the digits of a positive integer number. For example, if the number 8735 is entered, the number displayed should be 5378. (**Hint:** Use an exit-controlled loop, and continuously strip off and display the units digit of the number. If the variable num initially contains the number entered, the units digit is obtained as num Mod 10. After a units digit is displayed, dividing the number by 10 sets up the number for the next iteration. Thus, 8735 Mod 10 is 5 and 8735 / 10 is 873. The loop should repeat as long as the remaining number is not zero.

   b. Run the program written in Exercise 3a. on a computer and verify the program, using appropriate test data.

4. a. The outstanding balance on Rhona Karp's car loan is $8000. Each month, Rhona is required to make a payment of $300, which includes both interest and principal repayment of the car loan. The monthly interest is calculated as 0.10/12 of the outstanding balance. After the interest is deducted, the remaining part of the payment is used to pay off the loan. Using this information, write a Visual Basic program that produces a table indicating the beginning monthly balance, the interest payment, the principal payment, and the remaining loan balance after each payment is made. Your output should resemble and complete the entries in the following table until the outstanding loan balance is zero.

Beginning Balance	Interest Payment	Principal Payment	Ending Loan Balance
8000.00	66.67	233.33	7766.67
7766.67	64.73	235.28	7531.39
75531.39	.	.	.
.	.	.	.
.	.	.	0.00

amt = Input Box ("Enter", "Input Dialog")

b. Modify the program written in Exercise 4a. to display the total of the interest and principal paid at the end of the table produced by your program

5. Write, run, and test a Visual Basic program that prompts the user for the amount of a loan, the annual percentage rate, and the number of years of the loan, using **InputBox** functions that display the following prompts:

```
What is the amount of the loan?
What is the annual percentage rate?
How many years will you take to pay back the loan?
```

From the input data, produce a loan amortization table similar to the one shown below:

Testing values

into yearly payment accumulated loop

Amount	Annual % Interest	Years	Monthly Payment
1500	14	1	134.68

display, result.

Payment Number	Interest Paid	Principal Paid	Cumulative Interest	Total Paid to Date	New Balance Due
1	17.50	117.18	17.50	134.68	1382.82
2	16.13	118.55	33.63	269.36	1264.27
3	14.75	119.93	48.38	404.04	1144.34
4	13.35	121.33	61.73	538.72	1023.01
5	11.94	122.75	73.67	673.40	900.27
6	10.50	124.18	84.17	808.08	776.09
7	9.05	125.63	93.23	942.76	650.46
8	7.59	127.09	100.81	1077.45	523.37
9	6.11	128.57	106.92	1212.13	394.79
10	4.61	130.07	111.53	1346.81	264.72
11	3.09	131.59	114.61	1481.49	133.13
12	1.55	133.13	116.17	1616.17	0

In constructing the loop necessary to produce the body of the table, the following initializations must be made:

```
New balance due = Original loan amount
Cumulative interest = 0.0
Paid to date = 0.0
Payment number = 0
Monthly Interest Rate = Annual Percentage Rate / 1200
                 (Loan Amount) * (Monthly Interest Rate)
Monthly Payment = -----------------------------------------
                 1 - (1 + Monthly Interest Rate) -(Number of Months)
```

Within the loop, the following calculations and accumulations should be used:

Payment number = Payment number + 1
Interest paid = New balance due * Monthly interest rate
Principal paid = Monthly payment - Interest paid
Cumulative interest = Cumulative interest + Interest paid
Paid to date = Paid to date + Monthly payment
New balance due = New balance due - Principal paid

6. Modify the program written for Exercise 5 to prevent the user from entering an illegal value for the interest rate. That is, write a loop that asks the user repeatedly for the annual interest rate, until a value between 1.0 and 25.0 is entered.

6.7 Common Programming Errors and Problems

Three errors are commonly made by beginning Visual Basic programmers when using repetition statements.

1. Testing for equality in repetition loops when comparing floating-point or double-precision operands. For example, the condition num = 0.01 should be replaced by a test requiring that the absolute value of num = 0.01 be less than an acceptable amount. The reason for this is that all numbers are stored in binary form. Using a finite number of bits, decimal numbers such as .01 have no exact binary equivalent, so that tests requiring equality with such numbers can fail.

2. Failure to have a statement within a **Do** loop that alters the tested condition in a manner that terminates the loop.

3. Modifying a **For** loop's counter variable within the loop.

6.8 Chapter Review

Key Terms

counter loop	**For/Next** loop
Do/Loop Until loop	infinite loop
Do/Loop While loop	nested loop
Do Until loop	posttest loop
Do While loop	pretest loop
Exit Do	sentinel values
fixed-count loop	variable-condition loop

Summary

1. A section of repeating code is referred to as a *loop*. The loop is controlled by a repetition statement that tests a condition to determine whether the code will be executed. Each pass through the loop is referred to as a *repetition* or *iteration*. The tested condition must always be explicitly set, prior to its first evaluation by the repetition statement. Within the loop there must always be a statement that permits altering the condition so that the loop, once entered, can be exited.

2. There are three basic type of loops:
   a. **Do While**,
   b. **For/Next**, and
   c. **Do/Loop Until**.

   The **Do While** and **For/Next** loops are pretest or entrance-controlled loops. In this type of loop, the tested condition is evaluated at the beginning of the loop, which requires that the tested condition be explicitly set prior to loop entry. If the condition is **True**, loop repetitions begin; otherwise the loop is not entered. Iterations continue as long as the condition remains **True**.

The **Do/Loop Until** loop is a posttest or exit-controlled loop, where the tested condition is evaluated at the end of the loop. This type of loop is always executed at least once. **Do/Loop Until** loops continue to execute as long as the tested condition is **False**, and terminate when the condition becomes **True**.

3. Loops are also classified as to the type of tested condition. In a *fixed-count loop*, the condition is used to keep track of how many repetitions have occurred. In a *variable-condition loop* the tested condition is based on a variable that can change interactively with each pass through the loop.

4. In Visual Basic, the most commonly used form for a **While** loop is

```
Do While condition
    statement(s)
Loop
```

The condition is tested to determine if the statement or statements within the loop are executed. The condition is evaluated in exactly the same manner as a condition contained in an **If-Else** statement; the difference is how the condition is used. In a **Do While** statement, the statement(s) following the condition is (are) executed repeatedly, as long as the expression is **True**. An example of a **While** loop is

```
count = 1              ' initialize count
Do While count <= 10
   Print count;
   count = count + 1  ' increment count
Loop
```

The first assignment statement sets count equal to 1. The **Do While** loop is then entered and the condition is evaluated for the first time. Since the value of count is less than or equal to 10, the condition is **True** and the statements within the loop are executed. The first statement displays the value of count. The next statement adds 1 to the value currently stored in count, making this value equal to 2. The **Do While** structure now loops back to retest the condition. Since count is still less than or equal to 10, the two statements within the loop are again executed. This process continues until the value of count reaches 11.

The **Do While** loop always checks a condition at the top of the loop. This requires that any variables in the tested expression must have values assigned before the **Do While** is encountered. Within the **Do While** loop there must be a statement that alters the tested condition's value.

5. Sentinels are prearranged values used to signal either the start or end of a series of data items. Typically, sentinels are used to create **Do While** loop conditions that terminate the loop when the sentinel value is encountered.

6. The **For/Next** structure is extremely useful in creating loops that must be executed a fixed number of times. The initializing value, final value, and increment used by the loop are all included within the **For** statement. The general syntax of a **For/Next** loop is

```
For counter = start value To end value Step increment value
    statement(s)
Next counter
```

7. Both **Do While** and **For/Next** loops evaluate a condition at the start of the loop. The **Do/Loop Until** structure is used to create an exit-controlled loop, because it checks its expression at the end of the loop. This ensures that the body of the loop is executed at least once. The syntax for this loop structure is

```
Do
    statement(s)
Loop Until condition
```

The important concept to notice in the **Do/Loop Until** structure is that all statements within the loop are executed at least once before the condition is tested, and the loop is repeated until the condition becomes **True** (another way of viewing this is that the loop executes while the condition is **False**). Within the loop, there must be at least one statement that alters the tested expression's value.

6.9 Looking Further: Programming Costs

Any project that requires a computer incurs both hardware and software costs. The costs associated with hardware relate to the physical components of the system. These components include the computer itself, peripherals, and any other items, such as air conditioning, cabling, and associated equipment required by the project. The software costs include all costs associated with initial program development and subsequent program maintenance. As illustrated in Figure 6-22, software costs represent the greatest share of most computer projects.

The reason that software costs contribute so heavily to total project costs is that these costs are labor intensive; that is, they are closely related to human productivity, while hardware costs are more directly related to manufacturing technologies. For example, microchips that cost over $500 per chip 10 years ago can now be purchased for under $1 per chip.

It is far easier, however, to dramatically increase manufactur-

Figure 6-22

Software is the Major Cost of Most Engineering Projects

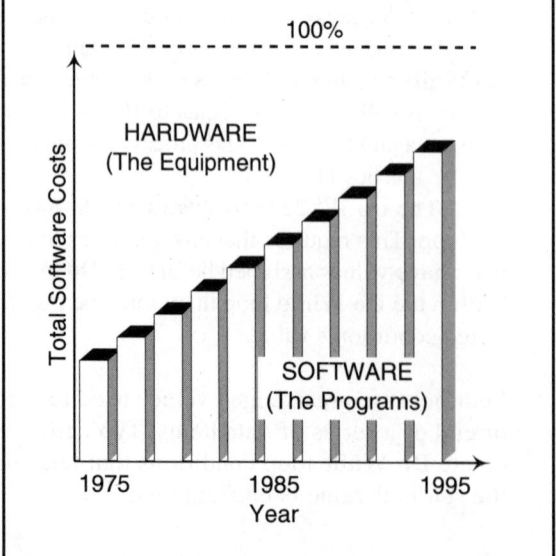

Introduction to Visual Basic

ing productivity by a thousand, with the consequent decrease in hardware costs, than it is for people to double either the quantity or the quality of their thought output. So, as hardware costs have plummeted, the ratio of software costs to total system costs (hardware plus software) has increased dramatically. As was previously noted in Section 1.2, (see Figure 1-11, repeated as Figure 6-23, for convenience) maintenance of existing programs accounts for the majority of software costs.

How easily a program can be maintained (debugged, modified, or enhanced) is related to the ease with which the program can be read and understood, which is directly related to the modularity with which the program was constructed. Modular programs are constructed using procedures, each of which performs a clearly defined and specific task. If each procedure is clearly structured internally and the relationship between procedures clearly specified, each procedure can be tested and modified with a minimum of disturbance or undesirable interaction with the other procedures in the program.

Just as hardware designers frequently locate the cause of a hardware problem by using test methods designed to isolate the offending hardware subsystem, modular software permits the software engineer to similarly isolate program errors to specific software units.

Once a bug has been isolated, or a potential new feature identified, the required changes can be confined to appropriate procedures, without radically affecting other procedures. Only if the procedure in question requires different input data or produces different outputs are its surrounding procedures affected. Even in this case the changes to the surrounding procedures are clear: they must either be modified to output the data needed by the changed procedure or be changed to accept the new output data. Procedures help the programmer determine where the changes must be made, while the internal structure of the procedure itself determines how easy it will be to make the change.

Although there are no hard-and-fast rules for well-written procedures, specific guidelines do exist. The total number of instructions in a procedure generally should not exceed 50 lines. This allows the complete procedure to fit on a standard 8-1/2-by-11-inch sheet of paper for ease of reading. Each procedure should have one entrance point and one exit point, and each control structure in the unit, such as a **Do** loop, should also contain a single entry and exit. This makes it easy to trace the flow of data when errors are detected. All the Visual Basic selection and repetition statements that alter the normal sequential program flow, conform to this single-input–single-output model.

Figure 6-23

Maintenance is the Predominant Software Cost

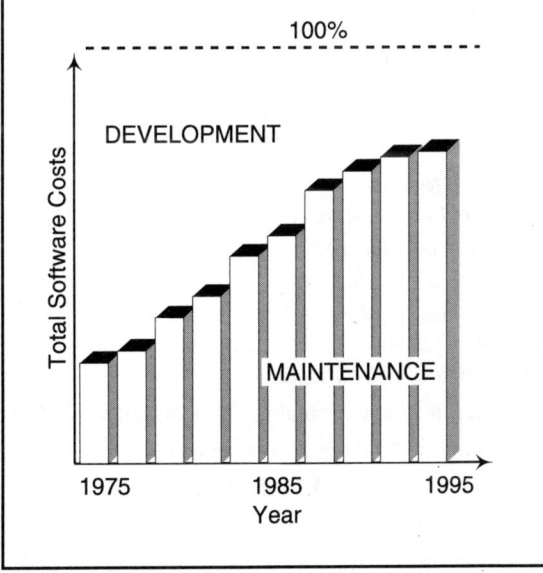

As we have stressed throughout the text, instructions contained within a procedure should use variable names that describe the data and are self-documenting.

This means that they tell what is happening without a lot of extra comments. For example, the statement

```
x = (a - b) / (c - d)
```

does not contain intelligent variable names. A more useful set of instructions, assuming that a slope is being calculated, is

```
slope = (y2 - y1) / (x2 - x1)
```

Here, the statement itself "tells" what the data represents, what is being calculated, and how the calculation is being performed. Always keep in mind that the goal is to produce programs that make sense to any programmer reading them, at any time. The use of mnemonic data names makes excessive comments unnecessary. The program should contain a sufficient number of comments explaining what a procedure does and any information that would be helpful to other programmers; excessive comments, however, are usually a sign of insufficient program design or poorly constructed coding.

Another sign of a good program is the use of indentation to alert a reader to nested statements and indicate where one statement ends and another begins. Consider the following pseudocode listing the algorithm for determining "What to Wear":

If it is below 60 degrees
If it is snowing
wear your lined raincoat
Else
wear a topcoat
If it is below 40 degrees
wear a sweater also
If it is below 30 degrees
wear a jacket also
ElseIf it is raining

wear an unlined raincoat

Because the **If** and **Else** statement matchings are not clearly indicated, the instructions in the module are difficult to read and interpret. For example, consider what you would wear if the temperature is 35 degrees and it is raining. Now consider the following version of "What to Wear":

If it is below 60 degrees
If it is snowing
wear your lined raincoat
Else
wear a topcoat
If it is below 40 degrees
wear a sweater also
If it is below 30 degrees
wear a jacket also
ElseIf it is raining
wear an unlined raincoat

The second version is indented, making it clear that we are dealing with one main **If-ElseIf** statement. If it is below 60 degrees, the set of instructions indented underneath the first **If** will be executed; otherwise the **ElseIf** condition will be checked. Although a Visual Basic program essentially ignores indention and will always pair an **ElseIf** with the closest matching **If**, indention is extremely useful in making the code accessible to the programmer.

Sub Procedures and Functions

7.1 Sub Procedures

7.2 Returning Values

7.3 Function Procedures

7.4 Variable Scope

7.5 Recursion

7.6 Common Programming Errors

7.7 Chapter Summary

7.8 Looking Further: Breakpoints, Watch Variables, and Step-Over Execution

As we have seen, the central element of a Visual Basic program is the form, which is stored in a form module. The basic processing units on a form consist of event-driven procedures, which are attached to the objects placed on the form. In addition to event procedures, Visual Basic programs may also contain any number of additional subprogram, function, and property procedures. To distinguish these procedure types from event procedures, these three new types of procedures are collectively referred to as **general** *procedures. By definition then, general procedures are not associated with specific events. Each Visual Basic general procedure is identified using one of three keywords:* **Sub, Function,** *or* **Property.** *In this chapter we learn how to write* **Sub** *and* **Function** *general procedures, how to pass data to these procedures, how to have the procedures process the passed data, and how they can be used to return a result.*

Professional programs are designed, coded, and tested very much like hardware, as a set of modules integrated to perform a completed whole. A good analogy of this is an automobile, where one major module is the engine, another is the transmission, a third the braking system, a fourth the body, and so on. Each of these modules is linked together and ultimately placed under the control of the driver, which can be compared to a supervisor or main program module. The whole now operates as a complete unit, able to do useful work,

---

Programmers' Note

What is a Subprogram?

User-defined, non-event procedures are generically referred to as subprograms. In Visual Basic, subprograms are constructed as both **Sub** and **Function** procedures. In Pascal, they are referred to as procedures and functions. Modula-2 names them PROCEDURES (even though some of them are actually functions). In C and C++, they are referred to as functions, while in JAVA they are called methods. COBOL refers to them as paragraphs, while FORTRAN refers to them as subroutines and functions.

---

such as driving to the store. During the assembly process, each module is individually constructed, tested, and freed of defects (bugs) before it is installed in the final product.

Now think of what you might do if you wanted to improve your car's performance. You might alter the existing engine or remove it altogether and bolt in a new engine. Similarly, you might change the transmission or tires or shock absorbers, making each modification individually, as your time and budget allows.

In this analogy, each of the major components of a car can be compared to a procedure designed to perform a specific task. For example, the driver calls on the engine when the gas pedal is pressed. The engine accepts inputs of fuel, air, and electricity to turn the driver's request into a useful product, power, and then sends this output to the transmission for further processing. The transmission receives the output of the engine and converts it to a form that can be used by the drive axle. An additional input to the transmission is the driver's selection of gears (reverse, neutral, first, second, etc.).

In each case, the engine, transmission, and other modules only "know" the universe bounded by their inputs and outputs. The driver need know nothing of the internal operation of the engine, transmission, drive axle, and other modules that are being controlled. The driver simply "calls" on a module, such as the engine, brakes, air conditioning, or steering, when that module's output is required. Communication between modules is restricted to passing needed inputs to each module as it is called upon to perform its task, and each module operates internally in a relatively independent manner. This same modular approach is used by programmers to create and maintain reliable Visual Basic applications, using general procedures in addition to event-specific procedures.

7.1 Sub Procedures

Each event procedure we have created is an example of a **Sub** procedure. The only restriction on these event procedures is that they are called into action by a specific event, such as clicking a button control. A second type of **Sub** procedure, which is referred to as a *general procedure*, has the same form as an event procedure but is called into action by the application code, rather than by a specific event. As their name indicates, such general procedures are meant to handle tasks broader in scope than a specific event. For example, as illustrated in Figure 7-1, an application might have three Text boxes, each of which is meant to receive

---

Figure 7-1

An Application that Requires the Input of Three Numbers

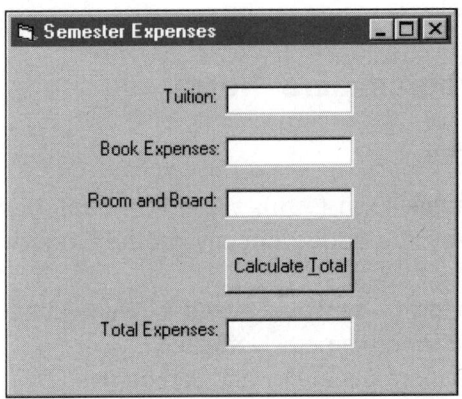

numeric input from a user. For each Text box's Lost_Focus event, we could include a check that a valid number was entered. Instead of repeating the same code, however, a more efficient strategy would be to create a general procedure that accepts a string and determines if the entered string represents a numeric value. Assuming such a general procedure was written, each Text box's `Lost_Focus` event could then activate this same general procedure. Figure 7-2 illustrates the connection between the general procedure and its three invoking event procedures. It is important to notice that when the called procedure has completed execution, control is returned to the calling procedure.

As illustrated in Figure 7-2, a **Sub** procedure is distinct in its own right, very similar to an event procedure. Its purpose is to receive data, operate on that data, and return as few or as many values as required. Although Figure 7-2 shows the **Sub** procedure being invoked by an event procedure, this is not a requirement. General procedures can be invoked by either event or other **Sub** procedures. They can also be written either as general procedures in a specific form, or in standard modules saved with a `.bas` extension.[1]

A general procedure is called into action (invoked) using a **Call** statement. For example, the statement

```
Call Message
```

initiates the execution of a general procedure named `Message`. This statement is used in Program 7-1 to call a general procedure that displays the message `Hello World`.

Figure 7-2

Using a Single General Procedure to Validate Numeric Input

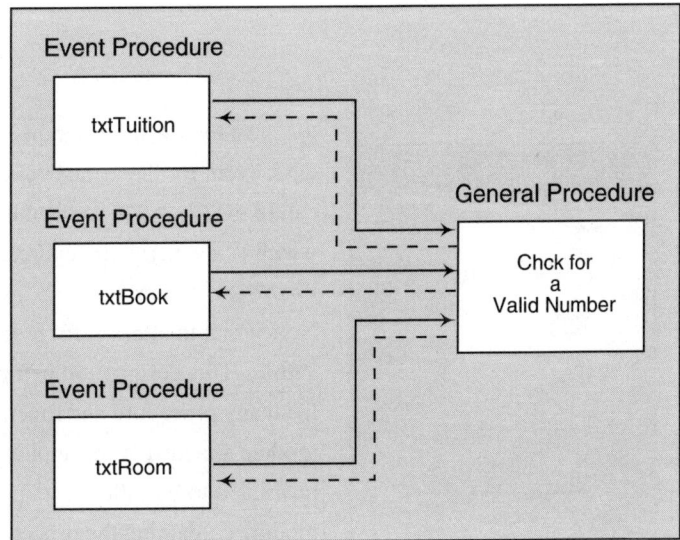

---

[1]Although the keyword **Call** is optional, we will always include it to explicitly indicate that a call to a general procedure is being made.

Program 7-1's Event and General Procedure Code

```
Private Sub cmdDisplay_Click()
   Call Message
End Sub


Public Sub Message()
   Print "Hello World"
End Sub


Private Sub cmdExit_Click()
   Beep
   End
End Sub
```

Figure 7-3
Program 7-1's Interface

In reviewing Program 7-1's code, notice that the click event for the `CmdDisplay` command button makes a call to the `Message` procedure. The `Message` procedure, which is a general procedure, simply displays the message `Hello World` on the form, as illustrated on Figure 7-4. Notice that the `Message` procedure has been declared as **Public**. This designation permits the procedure to be called from any procedure and function residing on any form or module attached to the application. A **Private** declaration restricts it to be called from procedures residing on the module containing the procedure. Also notice that since the general procedure code resides in the (**General**) section of the form's Code window, the **Print** method refers to the

Table 7-1 Program 7-1's Properties Table

Object	Property	Setting
Form	Name	frmMain
	Caption	Program 7-1
Command Button	Name	cmdDisplay
	Caption	&Display
Command Button	Name	cmdExit
	Caption	E&xit

Figure 7-4

The Output Created by Pressing Program 7-1's Display Button

current form, by default. If this general procedure was coded on a standard (.bas) form, the reference to this method would have to be explicitly written as

```
Public Sub Message()
    frmMain.Print "Hello World"
End Sub
```

As written, Program 7-1 makes no provision for passing data into the general procedure nor for transmitting data back from it. The program does, however, clearly illustrate the connection between one procedure making a call to another procedure. Before seeing how data can be exchanged between two procedures, let's see how to create the general procedure used in Program 7-1.

Creating a General Procedure

The steps necessary for creating a general procedure on a form module are as follows:

1. Make sure that the Code window is activated by

    *   Double-clicking on a form object, or
    *   Pressing the F7 function key, or
    *   Selecting the Code item from the View menu.

Once the Code window is active, type a procedure header line directly into the Code window. This line should have the form

> **Public Sub** *procedure-name*()

Visual Basic will complete the template for the new procedure when you have entered the header line (if you omit the **Public** keyword, the procedure will become **Public** by default). After Visual Basic has created the procedure's template, type in the required code in the same manner as you would for event procedures. Once you have created a general procedure you can always view or edit it by clicking on the (**General**) object and selecting the desired procedure in the Code window.

Programmers' Notes

Viewing and Editing a General Procedure

To view and edit an existing general procedure on a form:

1. Make sure that the Code window is activated by
   - Double-clicking on a form object, or
   - Pressing the F7 function key, or
   - Selecting the Code item from the View menu.

2. Select (General) from the Code window's object selection box.

3. Select the procedure's name from the Code window's procedure selection box.

Exchanging Data with a General Procedure

In exchanging data with a general procedure, we must be concerned with both the sending and receiving sides of the data exchange. Let us look at the sending of data into a general procedure first.

In its most general syntax, a general procedure is called into action using a **Call** statement having the form

> **Call** *procedure-name(argument list)*

Except for the addition of the parentheses and the argument list, this is identical to the **Call** statement used in Program 7-1. As always, the keyword **Call** tells the program to transfer control into a general procedure. The general procedure name, as illustrated in Figure 7-5, identifies which procedure is to be executed; the argument list is used to exchange data with the called general procedure[2]

Figure 7-5

Calling a General Procedure

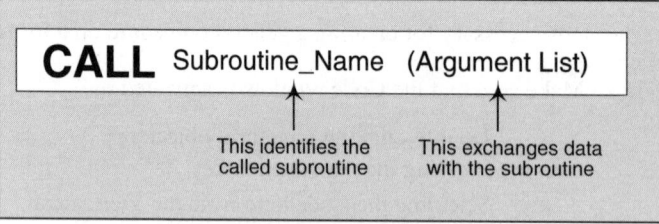

The arguments in a **Call** statement consist of constants, variables, or expressions that can be evaluated to yield a value at the time of the call. For example, the statement

```
Call Circumference(3.5)
```

both calls a general procedure named `Circumference` and make the number 3.5 available to it. Here the argument list consists of a single argument, the constant 3.5. Similarly, the statement

```
Call Display(2.67, 8)
```

---

[2]Again, the keyword **Call** is optional. If this keyword is not used, the arguments must not be enclosed in parentheses. Thus, for example, the calls `Call Display(2.78, 8)` and `Display 2.67, 8` are equivalent.

Introduction to Visual Basic

Figure 7-6

Program 7-2's Interface

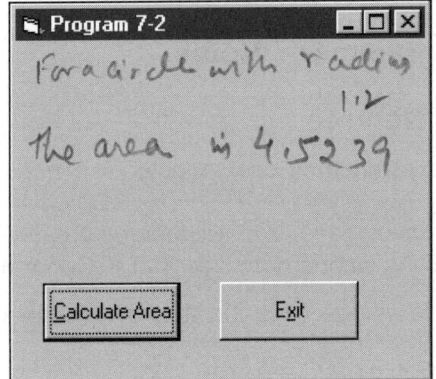

calls a general procedure named Display and makes two arguments, the real constant 2.67 and the integer constant 8, available to the called general procedure. In the following **Call** statement

```
Call Area(radius)
```

the general procedure Area is called using a variable named radius as an argument. To illustrate the use of this **Call** statement from within an event procedure, consider Program 7-2. Included within it is a general procedure named Area appropriate to receive the transmitted data.

<table>
<tr><td colspan="3" align="center">**Table 7-2 Program 7-2's Properties Table**</td></tr>
<tr><td>**Object**</td><td>**Property**</td><td>**Setting**</td></tr>
<tr><td>Form</td><td>Name
Caption</td><td>frmMain
Program 7-2</td></tr>
<tr><td>Command Button</td><td>Name
Caption</td><td>cmdRun
&Calculate Area</td></tr>
<tr><td>Command Button</td><td>Name
Caption</td><td>cmdExit
E&xit</td></tr>
</table>

Program 7-2's Event and General Procedure Code

```
Private Sub cmdCalculate_Click()
  Dim radius As Single

  radius = InputBox("Enter the radius", "Input Request", "0")
  Call Area(radius)   Procedure name
End Sub

Public Sub Area(r As Single)
  Const PI As Single = 3.1416

  Cls
  Print "For a circle with radius"; r          formula.
  Print "The area is "; Format(PI * r ^ 2, ".0000")
End Sub

Private Sub cmdExit_Click()
  Beep
  End
End Sub
```

1) a) passing by variable

Programmers' Notes

Creating and Using Standard (.bas) Modules

To create the first general procedure on a new standard (.bas) module:

1. Select the <u>A</u>dd Module option from the <u>P</u>roject menu. You will then be presented with a choice of activating a Code window in either a new or existing standard module with a (**General**) object.

2. Type a procedure header line into the Code window. This line should have the syntax

> Public Sub procedure-name()

Once a header line is entered, Visual Basic will complete the template for the new procedure. If the **Public** keyword is omitted, the procedure will still be **Public** by default. This permits the procedure to be called from within any form or module attached to the application.

3. Enter the desired code for the new general procedure.

In reviewing Program 7-2's code, notice that the **Call** statement in the `cmdCalculate Click()` procedure both calls the `Area` general procedure into action and makes one argument available to it. Let's now see how the general procedure `Area` has been constructed to correctly receive this argument.

Like all procedures, a general procedure begins with a header line and ends with an **End Sub** line, as illustrated in Figure 7-7. In addition to naming the general procedure, the procedure header is used to exchange data between the general procedure and its calling procedure. The purpose of the statements after the header line is to process the passed data and produce any values to be returned to the calling procedure.

Figure 7-7

The Structure of a General Sub Procedure

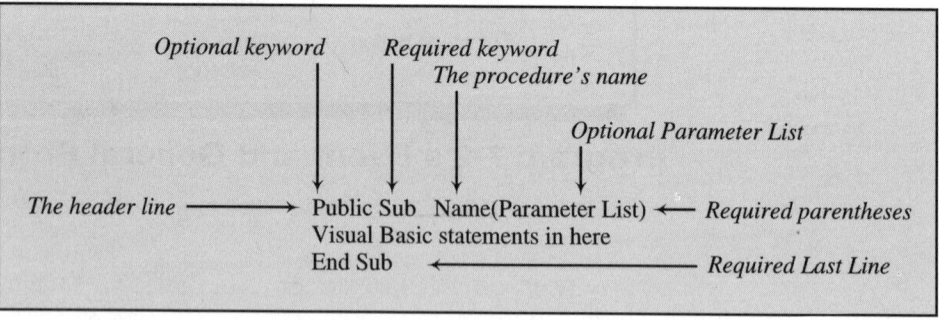

The general **Sub** procedure header line must include the keyword **Sub**, the name of the general procedure, and the names of any parameters that will be used by it. Here we have retained the convention that a *parameter* refers to the procedure's declaration of what data it will accept, while an *argument* refers to the data sent by the calling function (another name for a parameter is a *formal argument*, while the data sent by the calling procedure is sometimes referred to as *actual arguments*). For example, the header line of the general procedure in Program 7-2

```
Public Sub Area(r as Single)
```

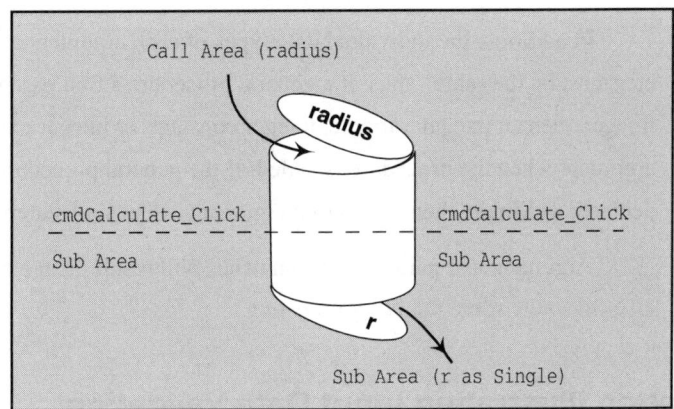

Figure 7-8

Exchanging Data with a Sub Procedure

contains a single parameter named r. The names of parameters are selected by the programmer according to the same rules used to select variable names. It should be noted that the names selected for parameters may, but need not be, the same as the argument names used in the **Call** statement.

The purpose of the parameters in a general procedure header is to provide names by which the general procedure can access values transmitted through the **Call** statement. Thus, the argument name r is used within the general procedure to refer to the value transmitted by the **Call** statement. In this regard, it is extremely useful to visualize arguments and parameters as containers or pipelines through which values can be transmitted between called and calling program units. As illustrated in Figure 7-8, the parameter named r effectively opens one side of the container through which values will be passed between the cmdCalculate_Click and Area procedures. Within the cmdCalculate_Click event procedure, the same container is known as the argument named radius, which is also a variable of this event procedure.

It is important to note that **Sub** procedures do not know where the values made available to them come from. As far as the Area general procedure is concerned, the parameter r can be treated as a variable that has been initialized externally. As such, however, parameters must still be declared in the procedure's header line. Once declared, a parameter can be used anywhere within the general procedure the same way a variable can be used. Also, as illustrated in Program 7-2, named constants used by the general procedure (in this case the constant PI) as well as variables internal to the procedure must also be declared.

Caution

Since an argument and its corresponding parameter both reference the same memory locations (see Figure 7-8), the rule concerning the correspondence between numbers and data types of arguments and parameters is simple: they must MATCH! If there are two arguments in a general procedure call, there must be two parameters in the general procedure's parameter list. The first argument becomes the first parameter and the second argument becomes the second parameter.

In addition, the individual data types of each argument and its corresponding parameter must be the same. Thus, if a general procedure's first parameter is declared as an integer, then an integer variable, integer constant, or integer expression must be used as an argument when the procedure is called. If the general procedure's second parameter has been declared as **Single**, then the second argument in the **Call** statement must also be a **Single**.

Argument and parameter mismatches will result in an `argument type mismatch` error message when the program is run.

A Practical Application Illustrating Input Data Validation

The examples presented so far have been useful in illustrating how to construct and call **Sub** procedures. Clearly, however, the **Sub** procedure calls were not necessary because the code in these general procedures could have been included directly in the event procedures making the calls. We now present an application that uses **Sub** procedures in a more useful and practical way.

Consider Figure 7-9, which illustrates the interface for a loan payment program. The program calculates the monthly payment due on a loan after the user enters the amount of the loan, the time in years, and the annual interest rate for the loan. The program uses the standard convention that payments must be made monthly and that the interest is calculated as a monthly compounded rate.

In addition to the three Text boxes shown on Figure 7-9 that will be used for data entry, the form contains two Picture boxes. The first Picture box, which is named `picPay`, will be used to display the calculated monthly payment for the loan. The second Picture box, at the bottom of the form, is named `picError`, and is used to display error messages. Table 7-3 lists the properties table for this interface.

As a practical matter, only positive numbers should be accepted for the user-entered data. Rather than including individual input validation code for each of the three Text boxes, a single data entry validation **Sub** procedure, named `CheckVal`, will be constructed. This procedure is called from each Text box when the user signals completion of data entry in the

Figure 7-9

Program 7-3's Interface

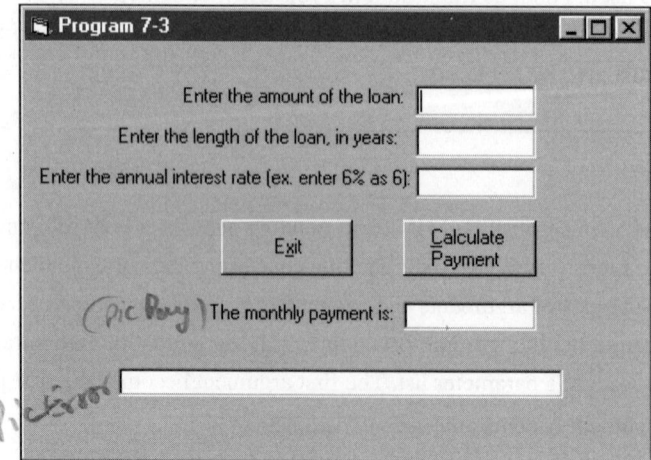

Table 7-3 Program 7-3's Properties Table

Object	Property	Setting
Form	Name	frmMain
	Caption	Program 7-3
Label	Name	lblAmt
	Caption	Enter the amount of the loan:
Label	Name	lblTime
	Caption	Enter the length of the loan, in years:
Label	Name	lblRate
	Caption	Enter the annual interest rate (ex. Enter 6% as 6):
Text Box	Name	txtAmt
	Text	(Blank)
	BackColor	White (Palette tab)
Text Box	Name	txtTime
	Text	(Blank)
	BackColor	White (Palette tab)
Text Box	Name	txtRate
	Text	(Blank)
	BackColor	White (Palette tab)
Picture Box	Name	picPay
	TabStop	False
	BackColor	White (Palette tab)
Picture Box	Name	picError
	TabStop	False
	BackColor	White (Palette tab)
Command Button	Name	cmdPay
	Caption	&Calculate Payment
Command Button	Name	cmdExit
	Caption	E&xit

box. This is done using the Text box's **KeyPress** event. For each Text box we "capture" the key press and determine when the [Enter] key was pressed (see Section 4.3 for a review of this). Once this key has been detected, the CheckVal data validation procedure is called. The algorithm used in CheckVal is

Clear all Picture boxes of text
If the entered text does not represent a valid number
   Print the message "Please enter a valid number"
   in the Error Picture box
Else if the entered text does not represent a positive number
   Print the message "The entered value must be positive"
   in the Error picture box
Else
   Set focus to the next control
Endif

Following is the complete event and general procedure code used in Program 7-3.

Program 7-3's Event and General Procedure Code

```
Rem: These named constants are entered in
Rem: the (General) object declarations section
Rem: As such, they can be used by any procedure on the form
Const ENTER As Integer = 13 ' the ANSI value of the Enter key
Const FromAmt As Integer = 1
Const FromTime As Integer = 2
Const FromRate As Integer = 3


Rem: These three event procedures clear the Picture boxes
Rem: whenever the Text boxes receive focus
Private Sub txtAmt_GotFocus()
  Call Clear
End Sub


Private Sub txtRate_GotFocus()
  Call Clear
End Sub


Private Sub txtTime_GotFocus()
  Call Clear
End Sub


Rem: These three event procedures accept data from
Rem: the Text boxes
Private Sub txtAmt_KeyPress(KeyAscii As Integer)
  If KeyAscii = ENTER Then
    Call CheckVal(txtAmt.Text, FromAmt)
  End If
End Sub


Private Sub txtTime_KeyPress(KeyAscii As Integer)
  If KeyAscii = ENTER Then
    Call CheckVal(txtTime.Text, FromTime)
  End If
End Sub


Private Sub txtRate_KeyPress(KeyAscii As Integer)
  If KeyAscii = ENTER Then
    Call CheckVal(txtRate.Text, FromRate)
  End If
End Sub


Rem: This is the event procedure that calculates the payment
Private Sub cmdPay_Click()
  Dim amt As Single, time As Single, rate As Single
  Dim payment As Single

  amt = Val(txtAmt.Text)
  time = Val(txtTime.Text) * 12 ' converted years to months
```

(continued on next page)

[handwritten: Xfer 139]

```
    rate = Val(txtRate.Text) / 1200 ' converted to monthly rate
    If amt * time * rate <> 0 Then
        payment = (amt * rate) / (1 - (1 + rate) ^ -time)
        picPay.Print Format(payment, "Currency")
    Else
        picError.Print "Please check all of the input data"
    End If
End Sub
```
[handwritten: new formulas. pic show print -]

```
Rem: This is the input data validation general Sub procedure
Private Sub CheckVal(s1 As String, fromwhere As Integer)
    Call Clear
    If Not (IsNumeric(s1)) Then
        picError.Print "Please enter a valid number"
    ElseIf Val(s1) <= 0 Then
    picError.Print "The entered value must be positive"
    Else ' a valid data was entered, so we shift the focus
        Select Case fromwhere
            Case FromAmt
                txtTime.SetFocus
            Case FromTime
                txtRate.SetFocus
            Case FromRate
                cmdPay.SetFocus
        End Select
    End If
End Sub
```
[handwritten left margin: Public]

```
Rem: This is a general Sub procedure used to clear all Picture boxes
Private Sub Clear()
    picPay.Cls
    picError.Cls
End Sub
```
[handwritten left margin: Public]

```
Private Sub cmdExit_Click()
    Beep
    End
End Sub
```

In reviewing Program 7-3's code, first notice that the **GotFocus** event procedures for each Text box call the `Clear` **Sub** procedure. This procedure simply clears both Picture boxes of text. The reason for this is that the Text boxes are used in this application for data entry. The rationale is that, once an input area receives the focus, all output messages and any calculations from prior data should be cleared.

Now concentrate on the three **KeyPress** event procedures and notice that each of these procedures calls the `CheckVal` **Sub** procedure when the Enter key has been pressed. The value for the Enter key has been set as a named constant in the declarations section of the (General) object; as such, this named constant can be used by any procedure on the form.

The `CheckVal` **Sub** procedure uses two parameters, a string and an integer. The string represents the text value from either the Amount, Time, or Rate Text boxes, while the integer is used to communicate which Text box event made the call. In addition, we have used three named constants for the integer arguments used in the **Call** statement. The named constants were entered in the (**General**) object of the Code window under the **Declarations** section. Like the ENTER named constant, each of these constants apply to the form module as a whole, and can be used by any procedure on the form.

The first task accomplished by the CheckVal procedure is to call the procedure Clear, which clears any prior text in the Picture boxes. Then, the procedure either produces an error message and keeps the focus in the current Text box, or moves the focus to the next control in the Tab sequence.

Finally, take a look at the cmdPay_Click procedure. This event procedure uses a common programming "trick" to determine when to make its calculation. If any of the text box values are zero, a valid payment cannot be calculated. Rather than checking each text box for a zero value, however, we can check all boxes at once by checking the expression Val(txtAmt.Text) * Val(txtTime.text) * Val(txtRate.Text). If any of the individual values are zero, the product of all three values will also be zero. Thus, we only make the payment calculation if all three boxes have a nonzero value. The calculation of the payment is made using the formula

$$\text{Monthly Payment} = \frac{(\text{Loan Amount}) * (\text{Time of Loan in Months})}{1 - (1 + \text{Monthly Interest Rate})^{-\text{Time of Loan in Months}}}$$

Since the input of interest rate is an annual percentage rate, and the time is in years, the entered rate is first divided by 1200 to convert it to a monthly decimal rate, and the number of years is multiplied by 12 to convert it to a time in months. Figure 7-10 illustrates a sample run using Program 7-3, once valid input data has been entered.

Figure 7-10

A Sample Run Using Program 7-3

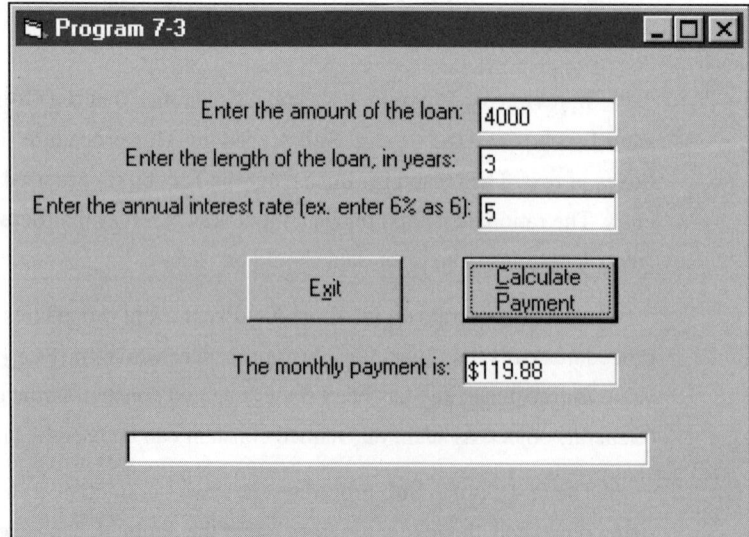

Exercises 7.1

[handwritten: order of arguments]

[handwritten: a. n]

[handwritten: b. type, yield, Maturity]

[handwritten: c. type, Price, maturity]

1. For the following general **Sub** procedure headers, determine the number, type, and order (sequence) of the arguments that must be passed to the procedure:

   a. ```Public Sub Factorial(n as Integer)```

   b. ```Public Sub Price(type as Integer, yield as Single, maturity as Single)```

   c. ```Public Sub Yield(type as Integer, price as Double, maturity as Double)```

   d. ```Public Sub Interest(flag as Boolean, price as Double, time as Double)```

   e. ```Public Sub Total(amount as Single, rate as Single)```

   f. ```Public Sub Roi(a as Integer, b as Integer, c as String, d as String, e as Single)```

   g. ```Public Sub Get_val(item as Integer, iter as Integer, decflag as Boolean, delim as Boolean)```

2. Write **Sub** procedure header lines and **Call** statements for the following:

   a. A procedure named ```Test``` having a single precision parameter named ```exper```. The corresponding argument used in calling ```Test``` is named ```value```.

   b. A procedure named ```Minute``` having an integer parameter named ```time```. The corresponding argument used in calling ```Minute``` is named ```second```.

   c. A procedure named ```Key``` having a boolean parameter named ```codeflag```. The corresponding argument used in calling ```Key``` is also named ```codeflag```.

   d. A procedure named ```Yield``` having a single precision parameter named ```rate``` and an integer parameter named ```n```. The arguments used in calling ```Yield``` are named ```coupon``` and ```years```.

   e. A procedure named ```Rand``` having two single precision parameters named ```seed``` and ```randno```, respectively. The arguments used in calling ```Rand``` are named ```Seed``` and ```Rval```.

3. a. Write a general **Sub** procedure named ```Check```, which has three parameters. The first parameter should accept an integer number, the second parameter a single precision number, and the third parameter a double precision number. The procedure should just display the values of the data passed to it when it is called. (**Note:** When tracing errors in general **Sub** procedures, it is very helpful to have the procedure display the values it has been passed. Quite frequently, the error is not in what the procedure does with the data, but in the data received and stored.)

   b. Include the general **Sub** procedure written in Exercise 3a. in a working program. Test the procedure by passing various data to it. For example, when the procedure is invoked by the statement ```Call Check(5, 6.27, -18.98765432)``` it should display the values ```5```, ```6.27```, and ```-18.98765432```.

4. a. Write a general **Sub** procedure named `Find_abs` that accepts a double-precision number passed to it, computes its absolute value, and displays the absolute value. The absolute value of a number is the number itself, if the number is positive, and the negative of the number, if the number is negative.

   b. Include the general **Sub** procedure written in Exercise 4a. in a working program. Test the procedure by passing various data to it.

5. a. Write a general **Sub** procedure named `Mult` that accepts two single-precision numbers as parameters, multiplies these two numbers, and displays the result.

   b. Include the general **Sub** procedure written in Exercise 5a. in a working program. Test the procedure by passing various data to it.

6. a. Write a general **Sub** procedure named `SquareIt` that computes the square of the value passed to it and displays the result. The procedure should be capable of squaring numbers with decimal points.

   b. Include the general **Sub** procedure written in Exercise 6a. in a working program. Test the procedure by passing various data to it.

7. a. Write a general **Sub** procedure named `RectangleArea` that accepts two parameters named `width` and `length` as **Single** data. The procedure should calculate the area of a rectangle by multiplying the passed data, and then display the calculated area.

   b. Include the `Area` general procedure written for Exercise 7a. in a working program. The calling procedure should correctly call and pass the values 4.4 and 2.0 to `Area`. Make sure to do a hand calculation to verify the result displayed by your program.

7.2 Returning Values

In addition to receiving inputs when it is called, every **Sub** procedure has the capability of returning one or more values to its calling routine. The mechanism for doing this relies on the correspondence between arguments used in the **Call** statement and the parameters used in the general procedure header. To illustrate how this correspondence can be used to return values from a general procedure, consider Procedure Code 7-1.

In the `Newval` **Sub** procedure within Procedure Code 7-1, it is extremely important to understand the connection between the arguments used in the **Call** statement and the parameters used in the general procedure header. *Both reference the same data items.* The significance of this is that the value in a calling argument can be altered by the general procedure, using the corresponding parameter name, and provides the basis for returning values from a general procedure. Thus, the parameters `xnum` and `ynum` do not store copies of the values in `firnum` and `secnum`, but directly access the locations in memory set aside for these two arguments. This type of general procedure call, where a general procedure's parameters reference the same memory locations as the arguments of the calling unit, is formally referred to as a *call by reference,* which in Visual Basic is named as a **ByRef** call.. The equivalence between argument and parameter names used in Procedure Code 7-1 is illustrated in Figure 7-11. As before, it is useful to consider both argument and parameter

Procedure Code 7-1

```
Rem: Here is the calling procedure
Private Sub Form_Click()
  Dim firnum As Single, secnum As Single

  firnum = Val(InputBox("Enter a number", "Input Request", "0"))
  secnum = Val(InputBox("Enter a number", "Input Request", "0"))
  Print "The value entered for firnum was:"; firnum
  Print "The value entered for secnum was:"; secnum

  Call Newval(firnum, secnum)

 Print
 Print "After the call to Newval:"
 Print "The value in firnum is now"; firnum
 Print "The value in secnum is now"; secnum
End Sub

Rem: Here is the called procedure
Public Sub Newval(xnum As Single, ynum As Single)
  xnum = 86.5
  ynum = 96.5
End Sub
```

names as different names referring to the same value. The calling procedure refers to the value, using an argument name, while the general procedure refers to the same value, using its parameter name.

A sample output produced by Procedure Code 7-1 is

```
The value entered for firnum was: 10
The value entered for secnum was: 20

After the call to Newval:
The value in firnum is now 86.5
The value in secnum is now 96.5
```

Figure 7-11

The Equivalence of Arguments and Parameters in Procedure Code 7-1

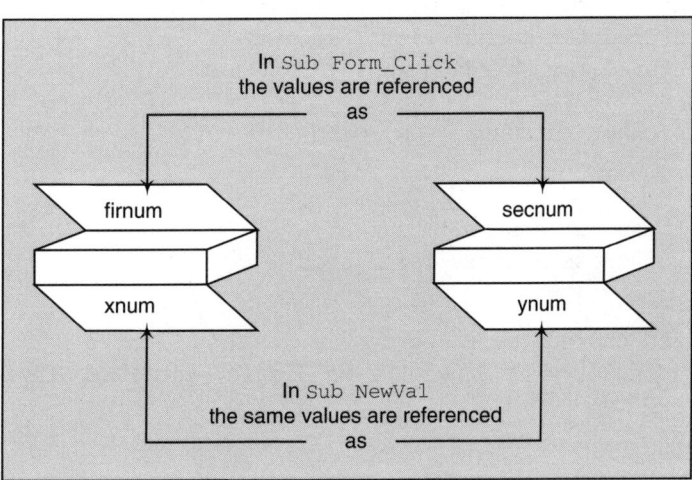

In reviewing this output, notice that the values displayed for the variables `firnum` and `secnum` have been changed immediately after the call to the `Newval` general procedure. This is because these two variables were used as arguments in the **Call** statement, which gives `Newval` access to them. Within `Newval`, these arguments are known as the parameters `xnum` and `ynum`, respectively. As illustrated by the final displayed values, the assignment of values to `xnum` and `ynum` within `Newval` is reflected in the calling procedure as the altering of `firnum`'s and `secnum`'s values.

The equivalence between calling arguments and a **Sub** procedure's parameters, illustrated in Procedure Code 7-1, provides the basis for returning any number of values from a **Sub** procedure. For example, assume that a **Sub** procedure is required to accept three values, compute these values' sum and product, and return these computed results to the calling routine. Naming the **Sub** procedure `Calc` and providing five parameters (three for the input data and two for the returned values), the following general procedure can be used:

```
Public Sub Calc(x as Single, y as Single, z as Single, total as Single, product as Single)
   total = x + y + z
   product = x * y * z
End Sub
```

This general procedure has five parameters, named `x`, `y`, `z`, `total`, and `product`, all declared as Single arguments. Within the general procedure, only the last two arguments are altered. The value of the fourth argument, `total`, is calculated as the sum of the first three arguments, and the last argument, `product`, is computed as the product of the arguments `x`, `y`, and `z`. Procedure Code 7-2 shows how this **Sub** procedure could be called from an event procedure.

Procedure Code 7-2

```
Rem: Here is the calling procedure
Private Sub Form_Click()
  Dim firnum As Single, secnum As Single, thirdnum as Single
  Dim sum As Single, prod As Single

  firnum = Val(InputBox("Enter a number", "Input Request", "0"))
  secnum = Val(InputBox("Enter a number", "Input Request", "0"))
  thirdnum = Val(InputBox("Enter a number", "Input Request", "0"))
  Print "The value entered for firnum was:"; firnum
  Print "The value entered for secnum was:"; secnum
  Print "The value entered for thirdnum was:"; thirdnum

  Call Calc(firnum, secnum, thirdnum, sum, prod)

  Print
  Print "The sum of these numbers is:"; sum
  Print "The product of these numbers is:"; prod
End Sub

Rem: Here is the called procedure
Public Sub Calc(x as Single, y as Single, z as Single, total as Single, product as Single)
   total = x + y + z
   product = x * y * z
End Sub
```

Figure 7-12

Relationship Between Arguments and Parameters for Procedure Code 7-2

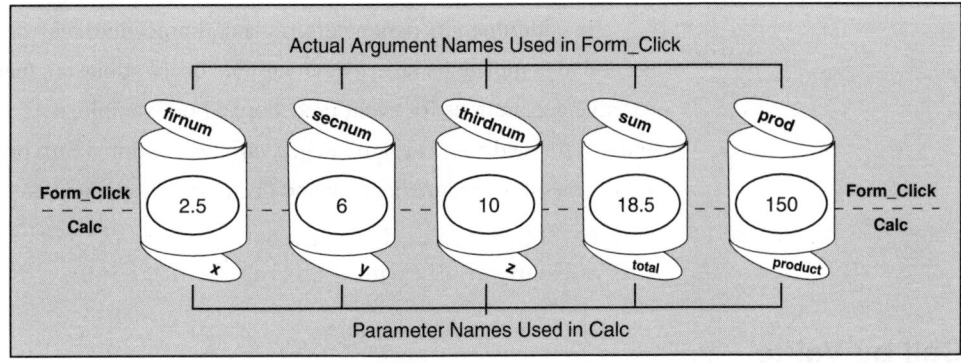

Within the calling event procedure, the `Calc` general procedure is called, using the five arguments `firnum`, `secnum`, `thirdnum`, `sum`, and `prod`. As required, these arguments agree in number and data type with the parameters declared by general procedure `Calc`. Of the five arguments passed, only `firnum`, `secnum`, and `thirdnum` are assigned values when the call to `Calc` is made. The remaining two arguments are not explicitly initialized and will be used to receive values back from `Calc` (these arguments will initially contain zero values). Figure 7-12 illustrates the relationship between argument and parameter names and the values they contain after the return from `Calc` for the following sample run using this procedure code:

```
The value entered for firnum was: 2.5
The value entered for secnum was: 6
The value entered for thirdnum was: 10

The sum of these numbers is: 18.5
The product of these numbers is: 150
```

Once Calc is called, it uses its first three parameters x, y, and z to calculate values for `total` and `product` and then returns control to the calling program. Because of the order of its calling arguments, the calling procedure knows the values calculated by `Calc` as `sum` and `prod`, which are then displayed.

Although all of the examples we have used have illustrated calling a general procedure from a event procedure, this is not required in Visual Basic. A general procedure can be called by any procedure, including another general procedure, including itself (as described in Section 7.5).

In general, the arguments used in calling a general procedure can be variables, as illustrated in Procedure Code 7-2, single constants, or more complex expressions yielding the correct argument data type. For example, one valid call to `Calc` is

```
Call Calc(2.0,3.0,6.2,sum,product)
```

When an argument is a constant value the corresponding parameter in the called general procedure must never be used on the left-hand side of an assignment statement. To do so would be an attempt to change the value of a constant within the called procedure.

In addition to its parameters, a general procedure may declare as many variables as needed to complete its task. These variable declarations are made in the same manner as variable declarations for event procedures. For example, if `i`, `j`, and `k` are integer parameters and `count` and `maxval` are integer variables within a **Sub** procedure named `Findmax`, a valid general procedure heading and declaration statement is

```
Public Sub Findmax(i as Integer, j as Integer, k as Integer)   parameters
    Dim count as Integer, maxval as Integer   variables
```

Call by Value

In a typical procedure call, the called procedure receives direct access to the variables of the calling procedure that were used as arguments. As we have seen, this forms the basis for returning values to the calling procedure and is referred to as a *call by reference*, or **ByRef** for short. In some cases you may not wish to provide the called procedure this access.

To prevent a called procedure from having access to the calling procedure's arguments, a *call by value* call can be made. In a call by value, the called procedure is provided numeric values that cannot be altered. We have already seen one method of doing this. For example, the statement

```
Call Calc (10, 20, 30, sum, prod)
```

calls the `Calc` procedure with three arguments that are values. Regardless of what the receiving parameter names are, changing these parameters' values will not alter the constants 10, 20, and 30 in the calling statement. In a similar manner, *the values of variables used as arguments can also be transmitted to a called procedure by enclosing the variable names within parentheses*. For example, the statement `Call Calc((firnum), (secnum), (thirdnum), sum, prod)` passes the first three arguments by value and the last two by reference. This is because the parentheses around each of the first three arguments causes Visual Basic to evaluate the expressions within the parentheses. The evaluation of an expression, even one consisting of a single variable, is a value. That value is then transmitted to the called procedure.

Finally, in writing a general procedure, you can ensure that only a value is received. This is accomplished by placing the keyword **ByVal** in front of the parameter's name when the parameter is declared. For example, the header line

```
Public Sub Calc(ByVal x As Single, ByVal y As Single, ByVal Z As Single, total As Single, product As Single)
```

ensures that the parameters x, y, and z are effectively named constants for the values being transmitted. As such, the values in x, y, and z cannot be altered from within `Calc`.

Exercises 7.2

1. a. Write a general **Sub** procedure, named `Find_abs`, that accepts a double-precision number passed to it, computes its absolute value, and returns the absolute value to the calling function. The absolute value of a number is the number itself if the number is positive, and the negative of the number if the number is negative.

   b. Include the function written in Exercise 1a. in a working program. Have the calling procedure display the returned value. Test the function by passing various data to it.

2. a. Write a general **Sub** procedure, named `Mult`, that accepts two double-precision numbers as parameters, multiplies these two numbers, and returns the result to the calling function.

   b. Include the function written in Exercise 2a. in a working program. Have the calling procedure display the returned value. Test the function by passing various data to it.

3. a. Write a general procedure, named `Findmax`, that accepts two parameters named `firnum` and `secnum` as single-precision values and returns the largest of these parameters in a third parameter named `max`.

   b. Include the `Findmax` general procedure written for Exercise 3a. in a working program.

4. a. Write a general procedure, named `RightTriangle`, that accepts the lengths of two sides of a right triangle and one of the angles as the parameters `a`, `b`, and `angle`, respectively. All of these parameters should be declared as Singles. The general procedure should determine and return the both the hypotenuse and the remaining angle of the triangle. (**Hint:** use the Pythagorean Theorem that $c^2 = a^2 + b^2$.)

   b. Include the `RightTriangle` procedure written for Exercise 4a. in a working program.

5. a. The time in hours, minutes, and seconds is to be passed to a general procedure named `Totsec`. Write `Totsec` to accept the input data, determine the total number of seconds in the passed data, and display the calculated value.

   b. Include the `Totsec` procedure written for Exercise 5a. in a working program. Use the following test data to verify your program's operation: hours = 10, minutes = 36, and seconds = 54. Make sure to do a hand calculation to verify the result displayed by your program.

6. a. Write a general procedure named `Time` that accepts an integer number of seconds in the parameter named `totsec` and returns the number of hours, minutes, and seconds corresponding to the total seconds in the three parameters named `hours`, `mins`, and `secs`.

   b. Include the `Time` procedure written for Exercise 6a. in a working program.

7. Write a general procedure named `Daycount` that accepts a month, day, and year as integer parameters, and estimates the total number of days from the turn of the century corresponding to the passed date, and returns the estimate, as a long integer, to the calling procedure. For this problem assume that each year has 365 days and each month has 30 days. Test your general procedure by verifying that the date 1/1/00 returns a day count of one.

8. Write a general **Sub** procedure named `Liquid` that is to be called using the statement Call Liquid(cups, gallons, quarts, pints). The procedure should determine the number of gallons, quarts, pints, and cups in the passed value named cups, and directly alter the respective arguments in the calling general procedure. Use the relationships of two cups to a pint, four cups to a quart, and 16 cups to a gallon.

9. a. A clever and simple method of preparing to sort dates into either ascending (increasing) or descending (decreasing) order is to first convert a date having the form month/day/yr into a long integer number using the formula date = year * 10000 + month * 100 + day. For example, using this formula the date 12/6/88 converts to the long integer 881206 and the date 2/28/90 converts to the long integer 900228. Sorting the resulting integer numbers automatically puts the dates into the correct order. Using this formula, write a general **Sub** procedure named `Convert` that accepts a month, day, and year; converts the passed data into a single integer; and returns the integer to the calling procedure.

   b. Include the `Convert` procedure written for Exercise 9a. in a working program. The main procedure should correctly call `Convert` and display the integer returned by the general procedure.

10. a. Write a general procedure named `Date` that accepts a long integer of the form described in Exercise 9a., determines the corresponding month, day, and year, and returns these three values to the calling procedure. For example, if `Date` is called using the statement

    ```
    Call Date(901116, month, day, year)
    ```

    the number 11 should be returned in `month`, the number 16 in `day`, and the number 90 in `year`.

    b. Include the `Date` procedure written for Exercise 10a. in a working program.

7.3 Function Procedures

Visual Basic provides two types of functions: intrinsic and subprogram. We are already familiar with intrinsic functions, such as **Abs, Sqr, Exp,** and so on (see Section 3.4),

Figure 7-13

A Function Directly Returns a Single Value

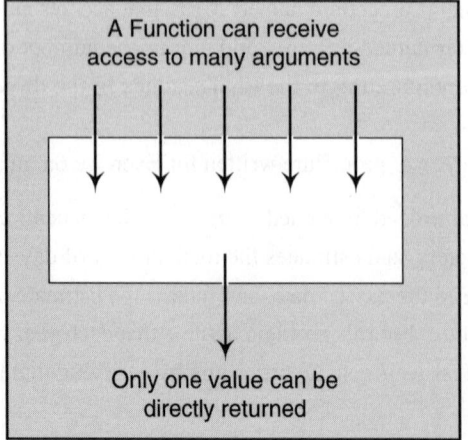

A Function can receive access to many arguments

Only one value can be directly returned

which are part of the Visual Basic language. Subprogram functions perform in a manner identical to intrinsic functions, except that they are user-written. A subprogram function, like a **Sub** procedure, is a distinct procedure containing multiple statements. The difference between **Sub** procedures and **Function** procedures, however, is that functions are intended to directly return a single value to its calling procedure (see Figure 7-13).

Figure 7-14 illustrates the general form of a function. As with **Sub** procedures, the purpose of the function header is to provide the function with a name and to specify the number and order of parameters expected by the function. In addition, the header identifies the data type of the value returned by the function. The statements after the header line are used to operate on the passed parameters and return a single value back to the calling function.

Figure 7-14

The Structure of a Function Procedure

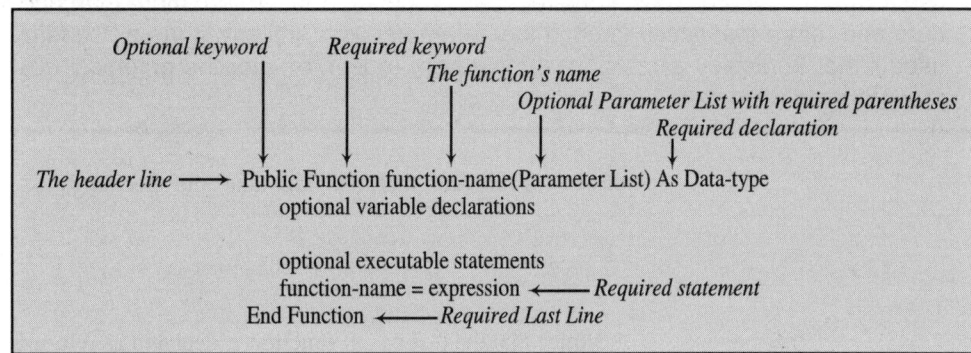

Notice that a function's header line includes a declaration of the data type of the value that will be returned by the function. This can be any of Visual Basic's data types. The parameters in the header line are intended for passing data into the function. For example, the following function header line can be used for a subprogram function named Fmax that receives two values and returns a single-precision value:

```
Public Function Fmax(x as Single, y as Single) As Single
```

The names of the arguments in the function header line, in this case x and y, are chosen by the programmer. Since the header declaration for Fmax includes two parameters, this function expects to receive two data items when it is called. Instead of the parameter names x and y, any two valid variable names could have been used to refer to the data passed to the function. Even if the function does not have any parameters, which is an extremely rare occurrence, the parentheses following the function name must always be included. As a specific application, consider the function Celsius that converts a Fahrenheit temperature into its equivalent Celsius value:

```
Public Function Celsius(fahrentemp As Single) As Single
    Celsius = 5 / 9 * (fahrentemp - 32)
End Function
```

The Celsius function illustrates a new feature found in function procedures; this is that the function must contain a statement that assigns a value to the function name. This is typically accomplished using an assignment statement of the form

```
function-name = expression
```

Programmers' Notes

Functions versus Sub Procedures

Students often ask, "When creating a general procedure, should I create a **Function** or a **Sub** procedure?" The answer to this question is rather straightforward. Since functions are designed to return a single value directly, use a function whenever the result of a processing operation is a single value; otherwise, use a **Sub** procedure. Thus, if the required procedure must return more than one value, use a **Sub** procedure and return the values through the parameter list. Similarly, if the procedure returns no values and is used either to display data, request input from a user, or alter the graphical user interface, construct the procedure as a function.

In our Celsius function, this statement takes the specific form

```
Celsius = 5 / 9 * (fahrentemp - 32)
```

Notice that the `Celsius` function is declared as returning a single-precision value and has one parameter, named `fahrentemp`. Within the function header line, `fahrentemp` is declared as a single-precision parameter. As written, `Celsius` expects to receive one single-precision argument. From a programming viewpoint, parameters can be considered as variables whose values are assigned outside of the function and passed to the function when it is called.

Within the `Celsius` function, the assignment statement both calculates an equivalent Celsius value and assigns the calculated value to `Celsius`, which is the name of the function. The function is then completed with the **End Function** statement.

Calling a Function Procedure

Having written a function named `Celsius`, we now turn our attention to how this function can be called by other procedures. User-written functions are called the same way intrinsic functions are called—by giving the function's name and passing any data to it in the parentheses following the function name (see Figure 7-15). At the same time the function is called, attention must be given to using its calculated value corectly.

To clarify the process of sending data to a function and using its returned value, consider Program 7-3, which calls the function `Celsius`.

Figure 7-15

Calling and Passing Data to a Function

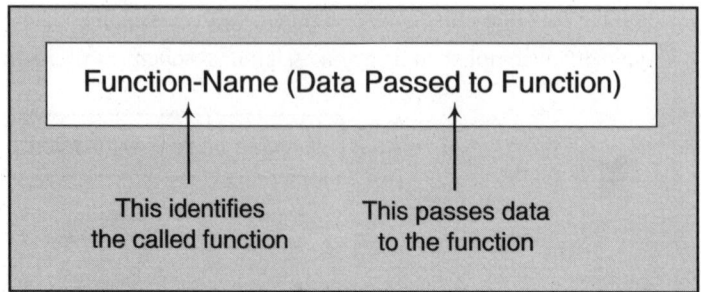

Figure 7-16

Program 7-4's Interface

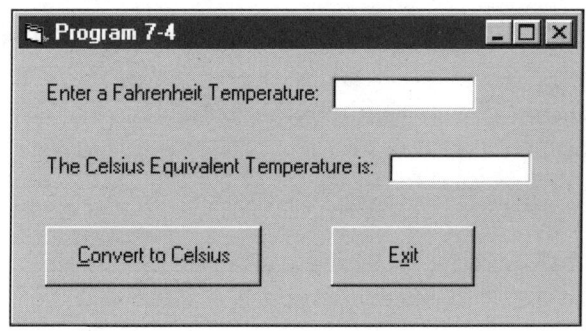

As illustrated in Program 7-4, calling a function is rather trivial. It requires only that the name of the function be used and that any data passed to the function be enclosed within the parentheses following the function name. The items enclosed within the parentheses are called *arguments* of the called function. As illustrated in Figure 7-17, the parameter `fahrentemp` within `Celsius` references the argument `fahrenheit` in the `cmdConvert_Click` event procedure[3]. The function itself does not know which procedure made the function call. The calling procedure must, however, provide arguments that match in number, order, and data type to the parameters declared by the function. As with general procedures, no data type conversions are made between argument and parameters.

Figure 7-17

Assigning Arguments to Parameters

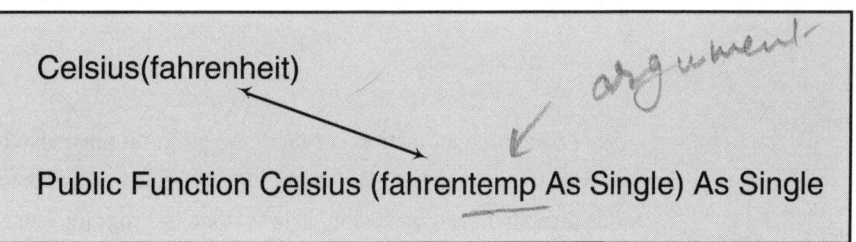

	Table 7-4 Program 7-4's Properties Table	
Object	**Property**	**Setting**
Form	Name	`frmMain`
	Caption	`Program 7-4`
Label	Name	`lblFahr`
	Caption	`Enter a Fahrenheit Temperature:`
Label	Name	`lblCelsius`
	Caption	`The Equivalent Celsius Temperature is:`
Text Box	Name	`txtFahr`
	Text	`(Blank)`
	BackColor	`White (Palette tab)`
Picture Box	Name	`picCelsius`
	TabStop	`False`
	BackColor	`White (Palette tab)`
Command Button	Name	`cmdConvert`
	Caption	`&Convert to Celsius`
Command Button	Name	`cmdExit`
	Caption	`E&xit`

Program 7-4's Event and General Procedure Code

```
Rem: This event procedure clears the picture box
Rem: whenever the text box gets focus
Private Sub txtFahr_GotFocus()
   picCelsius.Cls
End Sub

Rem: This event procedure calls the Function
Private Sub cmdConvert_Click()
   Dim fahrenheit as Single

   fahrenheit = Val(txtFahr.Text)
      picCelsius.Print Celsius(fahrenheit)
End Sub

Rem: This Function converts a Fahrenheit temperature to Celsius
Public Function Celsius(fahrentemp As Single) As Single
   Celsius = 5 / 9 * (fahrentemp - 32)
End Function

Rem: This is the Exit event procedure
Private Sub cmdExit_Click()
   Beep
   End
End Sub
```

[handwritten annotations: "f^n", "f(x) name", "arg.", "The result will go to the Celsius f^n", "this is for returned value which is in Celsius"]

At the time a function is called, the program must also have a way to use the value provided by the function. We must either provide a variable to store the value or use the value directly in an expression, as was done in Program 7-4. Storing the returned value in a variable is accomplished using a standard assignment statement. For example, the assignment statement

[handwritten annotation: "Variable name stores returned value."]

```
thistemp = Celsius(fahrenheit)
```

assigns Celsius' returned value in the variable named thistemp. This assignment statement does two things: the right-hand side calls Celsius and the result returned by the Celsius function is stored in the variable thistemp. Since the value returned by Celsius is single precision, the variable thistemp must also be declared as a **Single** data-typed variable within the calling function's variable declarations.

Caution

It is important to know that when a variable is used as an argument to a function, the function receives direct access to the variable. This is because the call is by reference in the same manner as a call to a **Sub** procedure. Thus, the function can inadvertently alter a calling procedure's variable by effectively returning a value through the parameter list. For example, the calling statement Celsius(fahrenheit) in Program 7-4 gives Celsius access to variable fahrenheit, even though this variable is "known" as fahrentemp

---

[3]The argument named fahrenheit was used here to illustrate the equivalence between arguments and parameters. Thus, the cmdConvert_Click() event could just have easily been written using the single statement picCelsius.Print Celsius(Val(txtFarh.text))

Figure 7-18

The Relationship between Argument and Parameters

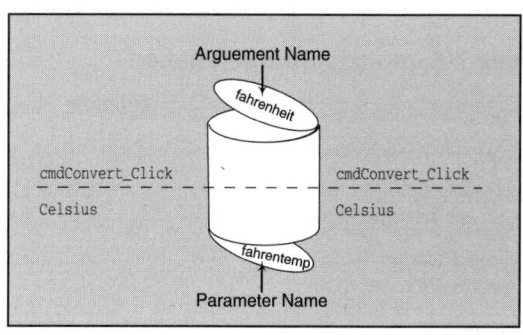

within `Celsius`. Thus, if the assignment statement `fahrentemp = 22.5` is contained in the function, both the value in `fahrentemp` and the value in `fahrenheit`, are changed within the calling procedure. The reason for this, as illustrated in Figure 7-18, is that both `fahrenheit` and `fahrentemp` *refer to the same storage location and are simply different names for the same variable.* Because of this equivalence, it is important that functions never assign values to their parameters.

As with **Sub** procedures, you can make the call to functions a call by value, either by placing parentheses around the arguments or by placing the keyword **ByVal** in front of the parameter's name when the parameter is declared. For example, the header line

```
Public Function Celsius(ByVal fahrentemp As Single)
```

ensures that the `fahrentemp` parameter is effectively a named constant for the values being transmitted. As such, the value in `fahrentemp` cannot be altered from within `Celsius`.

If a function must use an parameter in a way that will alter its value, the parameter should first be assigned to a new variable declared within the function. This variable name should then be used in subsequent expressions in place of the parameter name. Then, any change to the variable inside the function, even if the variable has the same name as a variable in another procedure, has no effect outside of the function.

String Functions

User-written functions that return a string value are written the same way as any other function procedures, except that the return data type must be declared as a string. For example, the header line

```
Public Function Addchar(s1 As String) As String
```

declares that the `Addchar` function accepts a string parameter named `s1` and returns a string. A commonly used default provided by Visual Basic is that the return **String** data declaration can be omitted if a dollar sign is appended to the end of the function's name. Thus, the declaration for `Addchar` can be written

```
Public Function Addchar$(s1 As String)
```

Here, the name of the function is `Addchar$`, and this complete name must be used whenever the function is being referred to. In general, functions that return strings are not

Table 7-5 Intrinsic String Functions

Name	Description	Example
Len(string)	Returns the number of characters in a string.	`Len("abcde") returns a 5`
Left(string, n)	Returns the leftmost n characters. If `n > Len(string)`, returns the complete string.	`s = Left("abcd",2) sets s = "ab"`
Right(string, n)	Returns the rightmost n characters. If `n > Len(string)` returns a zero-length string.	`s = Right("abc",2) sets s = "bc"`
Mid(string, m, n)	Returns n characters starting from position m. If `m > Len(string)` returns a zero-length string.	`s = Mid("abc",2,1) sets s = "b"`
InStr(n, string, str)	Returns the position of the first occurrence of str within string starting from position n.	`InStr(1,"abcd","b") returns a 2`
LTrim(string)	Trims leading blanks.	`s = LTrim(" abcd") sets s = "abcd"`
RTrimm(string)	Trims trailing blanks.	`s = RTrim("abcd ") sets s = "abcd"`
Trim(string)	Trims leading and trailing blanks.	`s = Trim(" abcd ") sets s = "abcd"`
StrConv(string, const)	Returns an uppercase string if `const = vbUppercase` or a lowercase string if `const = vbLowercase`.	`s = ("ab",vbUppercase) sets s = "AB"`
IsNumeric(string)	Returns a boolean value indicating whether the string can be evaluated as a number.	`s = IsNumeric("12.4") sets s to True`

often needed, because Visual Basic provides an extremely extensive set of intrinsic string functions. The more commonly used of these are listed in Table 7-5.

In addition to the string functions listed in Table 7-5, strings can be compared using Visual Basic's relational operators. Each character in a string is stored in binary, using the ANSI code. In the ANSI code, a blank precedes (is less than) all letters and numbers; the letters of the alphabet are stored in order from A to Z; and the digits are stored in order from 0 to 9. It is also important to note that, in ANSI, the digits come before, or are less than, the letters, and that uppercase letters come before lowercase letters.

Typically, Visual Basic's intrinsic string functions are used to create useful string manipulation **Sub** procedures. For example, consider Program 7-5, which processes a string to determine the number of vowels it contains.

Figure 7-19
Program 7-5's Interface

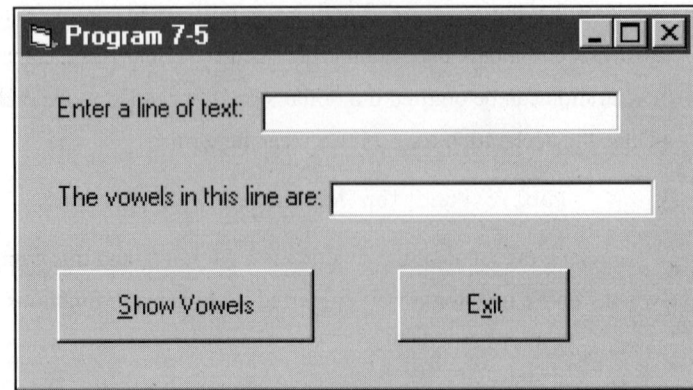

Introduction to Visual Basic

Table 7-6 The Properties Table for Program 7-5

Object	Property	Setting
Form	Name	frmMain
	Caption	Program 7-5
Label	Name	lblInput
	Caption	Enter a line of text:
Label	Name	lblVowels
	Caption	The vowels in this line are:
Text Box	Name	txtVowels
	Text	(Blank)
	BackColor	White (Palette tab)
Picture Box	Name	picVowels
	TabStop	False
	BackColor	White (Palette tab)
Command Button	Name	cmdShow
	Caption	&Show Vowels
Command Button	Name	cmdExit
	Caption	E&xit

Program 7-5's Event and General Procedure Code

```
Rem: This event procedure clears the picture box
Rem: whenever the text box gets focus
Private Sub txtVowels_GotFocus()
  picVowels.Cls
End Sub

Rem: This event procedure calls the Procedure
Private Sub cmdShow_Click()
  Call ShowVowels(txtVowels.Text)
End Sub

Rem: This Procedure displays the vowels
Public Sub ShowVowels(s1 As String)
  Dim n As Integer
  Dim i As Integer
  Dim c As String * 1, clower As String * 1
  Dim out As String

  out = ""
  n = Len(s1) ' find the string's length
  For i = 1 To n
    c = Mid(s1, i, 1) ' extract next character
    clower = StrConv(c, vbLowerCase)
    Select Case clower
      Case "a", "e", "i", "o", "u"
        out = out & c
    End Select
  Next i
  picVowels.Print out
End Sub

Rem: This is the Exit event procedure
Private Sub cmdExit_Click()
  Beep
  End
End Sub
```

In reviewing the `Showvowels` **Sub** procedure, notice that the length of the string is used to determine the terminating value of the **For** loop. In this loop, each character is "stripped off" using the **Mid** function and converted to its lowercase form. This is done so that both uppercase and lowercase vowels can be recognized by comparing all letters to the lowercase forms of the vowels. The converted character is then compared to the lowercase characters a, e, i, o, and u. If there is a match to one of these characters, the original character is appended to the output string. After each character in the string has been examined, the output string is displayed in the picture box. Figure 7-20 illustrates a sample output produced by Program 7-5.

Figure 7-20

A Sample Output Produced by Program 7-5

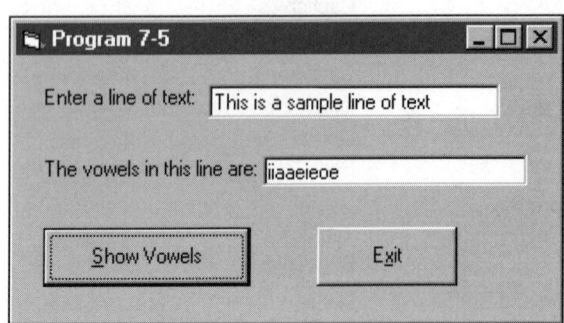

Exercises 7.3

1. For the following function header lines determine the number, type, and order (sequence) of the values that must be passed to the function and the type of value returned by the function:

   a. `Public Function IntToSingle(n As Integer) As Single`
   b. `Public Function Volts(res As Single, amp As Single) As Single`
   c. `Public Function Power(type As Boolean, cap As Single) As Double`
   d. `Public Function Flag(type As Boolean, time As Double) As Boolean`
   e. `Public Function Energy(pow As Double, time As Double) As Double`
   f. `Public Function Roi(a As Single, b As Single, c As Single, d As Integer) As Single`
   g. `Public Function Getval(item As Integer, delim As String) As Double`
   h. `Function Locase(c As String) As String`

2. a. Write a function named `Check` that has three parameters. The first parameter should accept an integer, the second parameter a single-precision number, and the third parameter a string. The function should display the values of the data passed to the function when it is called, and return a value of 1. (**Note:** When tracing errors in functions, it is very helpful to have the function display the values it has been passed. Quite frequently, the error is not in what the function does with the data, but in the data it receives and stores.)

   b. Include the function written in Exercise 2a. in a working program.

3. Write a function named `CelToFahr` that converts a Celsius temperature to a Fahrenheit temperature according to the formula *Fahrenheit = 9/5(Celsius) + 32*

4. Write a function named `Hyptns` that accepts the lengths of two sides of a right triangle and determines the triangle's hypotenuse. (The hypotenuse of a right triangle is equal to the square root of the sum of the squares of the other two sides.) Include `Hyptns` in a working program and verify that it works properly by passing various values to it, displaying the returned value, and checking that the displayed value is correct.

5. Write a function with the header line

   ```
   Public Function Absdif(x As Single, y As Single) As Single
   ```

   that returns the absolute value of the difference between two real numbers. For example, the function calls `Absdif(2,10)`, `Absdif(-1,-10)`, and `Absdif(-2,10)` should return the values, 8, 9, and 12, respectively. Include the function `Absdif` in a Visual Basic program and test the function, by passing various numbers to it, displaying the returned value, and checking that the displayed value is correct.

6. Write and execute a Visual Basic function that accepts an integer parameter and determines whether the passed integer is even or odd. (**Hint:** Use the **Mod** operator.)

7. a. Write a function named `Round` that rounds any single-precision value to two decimal places. Rounding to two decimal places is obtained using the following steps:
   Step 1: Multiply the passed number by 100.
   Step 2: Add 0.5 to the number obtained in Step 1.
   Step 3: Take the integer part of the number obtained in Step 2.
   Step 4: Divide the result of Step 3 by 100.

   b. Include the function written in Exercise 7a. in a working program. Test the function by passing various data to it and verifying the displayed values.

8. a. Modify the function written for Exercise 7a. to accept two values. The second passed value is the number of decimal places to which the first passed value should be rounded. For example, `Round(27.6485, 2)` should return the value 27.65 and `Round(27.6485, 3)` should return the value 27.649.

   b. Include the function written in Exercise 8a. in a working program. Test the function by passing various data to it and verifying the displayed values.

9. Modify the `Vowels` procedure in Program 7-5 to count and display the total number of vowels contained in the string passed to it.

10. Modify the `Vowels` procedure in Program 7-5 to count and display the numbers of each individual vowel contained in the string. That is, the function should display the total number of *a*s, *e*s, and so forth.

11. a. Write a Visual Basic function to count the total number of non-blank characters contained in a string. For example, the number of non-blank characters in the string `"     abc def "` is six.

    b. Include the function written for Exercise 11a. in a complete working program.

12. Write and test a procedure that reverses the characters in a string.

7.4 Variable Scope

By their very nature, Visual Basic procedures are constructed to be independent modules. This implies that variables declared in one procedure, be it an event or general procedure, cannot be accessed by another procedure, unless specific provisions are made to allow such access. As we have seen, one such access is provided through a procedure's parameter list. Given this fact, both event and general procedures may be compared to a closed box, with slots at the top through which values may be exchanged with the calling procedure.

The metaphor of a closed box is useful because it emphasizes the fact that what goes on inside the procedure, except for the altering of an parameter's value, is hidden from all other procedures. This includes any variables declared within the procedure. These internally declared variables, available only to the procedure itself, are said to be "local to the procedure," and are called *procedure-level* or *local variables*. This term refers to the *scope* of a variable, where scope is defined as the section of the program where the variable is valid, visible, or "known." A variable can have either a local, form-level, or global scope. A variable with a local scope is simply one that has had storage locations set aside for it by a declaration statement made within a procedure. Local variables are only meaningful when used in expressions or statements inside the procedure that declared them. This means that the same variable name can be declared and used in more than one procedure. For each procedure that declares the variable, a separate and distinct variable is created.

By definition, all Visual Basic variables that are declared within a procedure using the **Dim** keyword are local variables. Visual Basic does, however, provide two different means of extending the scope of a variable from one procedure into another. One way is to use a variable as an argument in a **Call** statement, which gives the called procedure access to the variable. The second method is to use module-level variables. *Module-level variables*, which are said to have *module-level scope*, are declared in the declarations section of the (**General**) object in a Code window. Such variables must be declared as either **Private** or **Public** (declaring a module-level variable with the **Dim** keyword is the same as making it **Private**). Module level variables that have been declared **Private** are accessible only to procedures in the module, and are referred to as *form-level* variables. **Public** module-level variables are available and shared between all modules and their procedures, and are referred to as *global* variables. Table 7-6 lists the scope of variables in Visual Basic. It should be noted that procedures share the same scope rules as module-level variables. That is, a **Public** procedure can be called from any module in an application, while a **Private** procedure can only be called by other procedures residing on the same module.

To illustrate the scope of both local and module-level variables, consider Procedure Code 7-3.

Figure 7-21

A Procedure Can be Considered a Closed Box

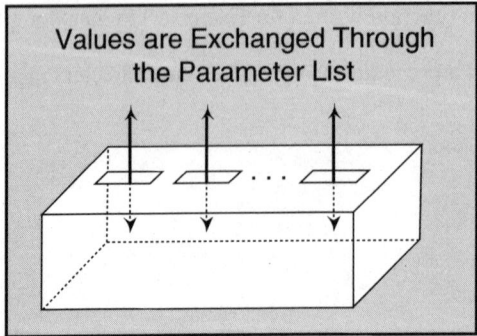

Values are Exchanged Through the Parameter List

Table 7-7 Variable Scope

Scope	Private or Dim	Public
Procedure-Level (Local Variables)	Variables are private to the procedure in which they are declared.	Not applicable. Local variables cannot be declared as Public.
Module-Level (Form-level and Global variables)	Variables are private within the module in which they are declared, and are referred to as form-level variables. They are shared and can be accessed by every procedure in the module.	Variables are available to all modules, and are referred to as global variables. They are shared and can be accessed by any procedure in the project, no matter where that procedure is located.

Procedure Code 7-3

```
Private firstnum As Integer ' create a module-level variable named
firstnum

Private Sub Form_Click()
   Call First
End Sub

Public Sub First()
   Dim secnum As Integer   'creates a local variable named secnum

   firstnum = 10 ' store a value into the module-level variable
   secnum = 20  ' store a value into the local variable
   Cls
   Print "From First: firstnum = "; firstnum
   Print "From First: secnum = "; secnum

  Call Second
   Print

   Print "From First again: firstnum = "; firstnum
   Print "From main again: secnum = "; secnum
End Sub

Private Sub Second()
   Dim secnum As Integer ' create a second local variable named secnum

  secnum = 30 ' this only affects this local variable's value

   Print
   Print "From Second: firstnum = "; firstnum
   Print "From Second: secnum = "; secnum

   firstnum = 40 ' this changes firstnum for both procedures
End Sub
```

Handwritten annotations:
- *applicable for all section*
- *General declare*
- *This is all the project (in general section)*
- *result 10* (next to Print "From First: firstnum")
- *20* (next to Print "From First: secnum")
- *= 10* (next to "From First again: firstnum")
- *= 30* (next to "From main again: secnum")
- *40 / 10* (circled, near firstnum = 40)

Figure 7-22

*The Three Storage Areas
Created by
Procedure Code 7-3*

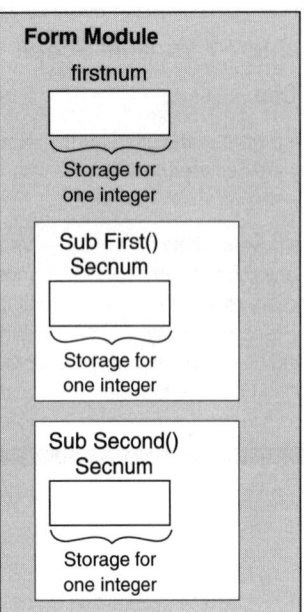

The variable `firstnum` in Procedure Code 7-3 is a module-level variable because its storage is created by a declaration statement located outside a procedure. Specifically, the declaration for this variable was entered in the declarations section of the (**General**) object in the Code window. Since both procedures, `First` and `Second`, are located on the form module in which `firstnum` is declared, both of these procedures can use this form-level variable with no further declaration needed. Procedure Code 7-3 also contains two separate local variables, both named `secnum`. Storage for the `secnum` variable named in First is created by the declaration statement located in `First`. A different storage area for the `secnum` variable in `Second` is created by the declaration statement located in the `Second` procedure. Figure 7-22 illustrates the three distinct storage areas reserved by the three declaration statements used in Procedure Code 7-3.

Each of the variables named `secnum` are local to the procedure in which their storage is created, and each of these variables can only be used from within the appropriate procedure. Thus, when `secnum` is used in `First`, the storage area reserved by `First` for its `secnum` variable is accessed, and when `secnum` is used in `Second`, the storage area reserved by `Second` for its `secnum` variable is accessed. The following output is produced when the `Form_Click` event in Procedure Code 7-3 is activated:

```
From First: firstnum = 10
From First: secnum = 20

From Second: firstnum = 10
From Second: secnum = 30

From First again: firstnum = 40
From First again: secnum = 20
```

Let us analyze the output produced by Procedure Code 7-3. Since `firstnum` is a form-level variable, both the `First` and `Second` procedures can use and change its value. Initially, both procedures print the value of 10 that `First` stored in `firstnum`. Before returning, `Second` changes the value of `firstnum` to 40, which is the value displayed when the variable `firstnum` is next displayed from within `First`.

Since each procedure only "knows" its own local variables, `First` can only display the value of its `secnum` and `Second` can only display the value of its `secnum` variable. Thus, whenever `secnum` is printed from `First`, the value of 20 is displayed, and whenever `secnum` is printed from `Second`, the value 30 is displayed.

Visual Basic does not confuse these two secnum, variables because only one procedure can execute at a given moment. While a procedure is executing, only those variables that are "in scope" for that procedure (module-level and local) can be accessed.

The scope of a variable in no way influences or restricts the data type of the variable. Local variables can be a character, integer, single, double, or any of the other data types (long, boolean, etc.) we have introduced, as can module-level variables. The scope of a variable is determined by a placement of the declaration statement that reserves storage for it. Finally, if both a form-level and local variable have the same name, the local variable will be accessed by the procedure in which that local variable is declared.

Using Module-Level Variables

Module-level variables are useful if a variable must be shared between many procedures. Rather than passing the same variable to each procedure, it is easier to define it once as module-level. Doing so also alerts anyone reading the program that many procedures use the variable. Most large programs make use of a few module-level variables and the majority of these variables should be named constants. Such named constants can then be shared by all procedures as "read-only" variables, which restricts any one procedure from altering the constant's value. Smaller programs containing a few procedures, however, should rarely contain global variables, though they may contain module-level constants. The reason for this is that module-level variables allow the programmer to "jump around' the normal safeguards provided by procedures. By indiscriminately making variables module-level you destroy the safeguards Visual Basic provides to make procedures independent and insulated from each other, including the necessity of carefully designating the type of parameters needed by a procedure, the variables used in the procedure, and the values returned.

By their very nature module-level variables provide all procedures with the ability to access and change their values. Since no single procedure has exclusive use of any variable, it is often difficult to determine which procedure actually accessed and changed a given variable's value. This makes debugging and maintaining code much more difficult.

Static Variables

The scope of a variable defines the location within a program where that variable can be used. Given any program, you could take a pencil and draw a box around the section of the program where each variable is valid. The space inside the box would represent the scope of each variable. From this viewpoint, the scope of a variable can be thought of as the space within the program where a variable is valid.

In addition to the space dimension represented by its scope, variables also have a time dimension. The time dimension refers to the length of time that storage locations are reserved for a variable. This time dimension is sometimes called the variable's "lifetime." For example, all local variable storage locations are released back to the computer when a procedure is finished running. Consider Procedure Code 7-4, where the **Sub** procedure Test is called four times when the Form_Click event is activated.

Procedure Code 7-4

```
Private Sub Form_Click()
  Dim count As Integer

  Cls
  count = 1
  For count = 1 To 4
    Call Test
  Next count
End Sub

Private Sub Test()
  Dim num As Integer

  Print "The value of num is "; num
  num = num + 1
End Sub
```

When the `Form_Click` procedure in this code is executed, the display produced is

```
The value of num is 0
The value of num is 0
The value of num is 0
The value of num is 0
```

This output is produced because each time `Test` is called, the local variable `num` is created and initialized to zero. When the **Sub** procedure returns control to the event procedure `Form_Click`, the variable `num` is destroyed along with any value stored in it. Thus, the effect of incrementing `num` in `Test` is lost.

The initialization used in `Test` is called a run-time initialization because it occurs each time the **Sub** procedure containing the variable is called. There are cases, however, where we would like a subroutine to preserve the value of its local variables between calls. This can be accomplished by declaring a variable inside a procedure using the **Static** keyword, rather than **Dim** keyword. For example, consider Procedure Code 7-5, which is identical to Procedure Code 7-4, except that local variable `num` in the **Sub** procedure `Test` has been declared as **Static**.

Procedure Code 7-5

```
Private Sub Form_Click()
  Dim count As Integer

  Cls
  count = 1
  For count = 1 To 4
    Call Test
  Next count
End Sub

Private Sub Test()
  Static num As Integer

  Print "The value of num is "; num
  num = num + 1
End Sub
```

The output produced by the activation of this code is

```
The value of num is 0
The value of num is 1
The value of num is 2
The value of num is 3
```

As illustrated by this output, the variable `num` is set to zero only once. The **Sub** procedure `Test` then increments this variable, just before relinquishing control back to its calling procedure. The value that `num` has when `Test` is finished executing is retained and displayed when `Test` is next called. The reason for this is that local **Static** variables are not created and destroyed each time the procedure declaring the static variable is called. Once created, they remain in existence for the life of the program.

Since local **Static** variables retain their values, they are not initialized in the same way as variables declared as **Dim**. Their initialization is done only once, when the program is translated into executable form. At translation time all **Static** numeric variables are created and initialized to zero.[4] Thereafter, the value in each variable is retained each time the function is called. To make all of the variables **Static** in a procedure, the procedure itself can be declared **Static**. This is done by placing the keyword **Static** immediately before the procedure's designation as either a **Sub** or **Function** procedure. For example, the heading

```
Private Static Sub Test()
```

makes all of `Test`'s variables `Static`. By definition, since all module level variables retain their values until an application is finished executing, the **Static** designation makes no sense for such variables.

Exercises 7.4

1. Describe what is meant by the word *scope*, as it is applied to variables.

2. What do you think is the scope of a procedure's parameters?

3. a. What is the scope of procedure-level variables that are declared as **Private**?
   b. What is the scope of procedure-level procedures that are declared as **Private**?

4. a. What is the scope of module-level variables that are declared as **Public**?
   b. What is the scope of module-level procedures that are declared as **Public**?

---

[4]**String** variables are initialized to zero-length strings.

5. a. The following procedures use the same variable and parameter names, n and sum, in both the calling and called procedures. Determine if this causes any problem for the program.

```
Private Sub Form_Click()
  Dim count As Integer
  Dim n As Single, sum As Single

 For count = 1 To 4
   n = InputBox("Enter a number", "Input Request", "0")
   Print "The number just entered is "; n
   sum = Accumulate(n)
 Next count
 Print "The sum of the numbers entered is"; sum
End Sub

Private Function Accumulate(n As Single) As Single
  Dim sum As Single

  sum = sum + n
  Accumulate = sum
End Function
```

   b. Assume that the numbers 10, 20, 30, and 40 were entered by a user, in response to the Event_Click procedure listed in Exercise 5a. Determine the output of the program for these inputs.

   c. What change in the function procedure will cause it to produce the correct sum?

7.5 Recursion[5]

Because Visual Basic allocates new memory locations for parameters and local variables each time a procedure is called, it is possible for all general procedures to call themselves. Procedure that do so, which can be both **Sub** and **Function** procedures, are referred to as *self-referential* or *recursive* procedures. When a procedure invokes itself, the process is called *direct recursion*. Similarly, a procedure can invoke a second procedure, which it turn invokes the first procedure. This type of recursion is referred to as *indirect* or *mutual recursion*.

Mathematical Recursion

Optional

The recursive concept is that a solution to a problem can be stated in terms of "simple" versions of itself. Some problems can be solved using an algebraic formula that shows recursion explicitly. For example, consider finding the factorial of a number *n*, denoted as n!, where *n* is a positive integer. This is defined as

$$1! = 1$$
$$2! = 2 * 1 = 2 * 1!$$
$$3! = 3 * 2 * 1 = 3 * 2!$$
$$4! = 4 * 3 * 2 * 1 = 4 * 3!$$

---

[5]This topic may be omitted on first reading with no loss of subject continuity.

and, so on. The definition for n! can be summarized by the following statements:

$$1! = 1$$

$$n! = n * (n\text{-}1)! \text{ for } n > 1$$

This definition illustrates the general specifications in constructong a recursive algorithm;

1. What is the first case?
2. How is the *n*th case related to the *(n-1)* case?

   Although the definition seems to define a factorial in terms of a factorial, the definition is valid, because it can always be computed. For example, using the definition, 3! is first computed as
   $$3! = 3 * 2!$$

   The value of 3! is determined from the definition as
   $$2! = 2 * 1!$$
   Substituting this expression for 2! in the determination of 3! yields
   $$3! = 3 * 2 * 1!$$
   1! is not defined in terms of the recursive formula, but is simply defined as being equal to 1. Substituting this value into the expression for 3! gives us
   $$3! = 3 * 2 * 1 = 6$$
   To see how a recursive procedure is defined in Visual Basic, we construct the function Factorial. In pseudocode, the processing required of this function is
   If n = 1
   Factorial = n
   Else
   *Factorial = n * Factorial(n - 1)*

Notice that this algorithm is simply a restatement of the recursive definition previously given. In Visual Basic, this can be written as

```
Public Function Factorial(n As Long) As Long
  If n = 1 Then
   Factorial = 1
  Else
   Factorial = n * Factorial(n - 1)
  End If
End Function
```

Notice that n has been declared as a long integer. The reason for this is that the factorial can easily exceed the bounds of an integer, which has a valid range from -32,768 to +32,767. (For example, the factorial of 8 is 40,320.) Program 7-5 illustrates the Factorial function within the context of a complete program.

Figure 7-23
Program 7-5's Interface

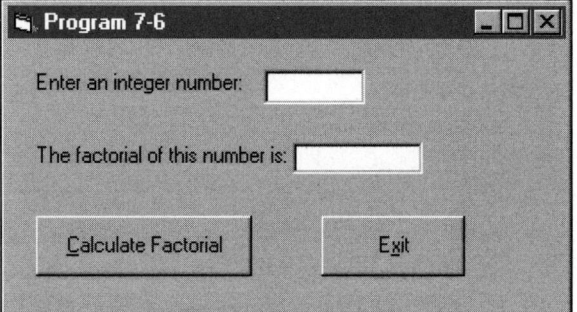

Table 7-8 The Properties Table for Program 7-5

Object	Property	Setting
Form	Name	frmMain
	Caption	Program 7-5
Label	Name	lblInput
	Caption	Enter an integer number:
Label	Name	lblFactorial
	Caption	The factorial of this number is:
Text Box	Name	txtInput
	Text	(Blank)
	BackColor	White (Palette tab)
Picture Box	Name	picFactorial
	TabStop	False
	BackColor	White (Palette tab)
Command Button	Name	cmdFactorial
	Caption	&Calculate Factorial
Command Button	Name	cmdExit
	Caption	E&xit

Program 7-5's Event and General Procedure Code

```
Rem: This event procedure clears the picture box
Rem: whenever the txtInput box gets focus
Private Sub txtInput_GotFocus()
  picFactorial.Cls
End Sub

Rem: This event procedure calls the Factorial Function
Private Sub cmdFactorial_Click()
  Dim n As Long
  Dim fact As Long

  n = Int(Val(txtInput.Text))
  fact = Factorial(n)
  picFactorial.Print fact
End Sub

Rem: This function calculates the factorial recursively
Public Function Factorial(n As Long) As Long
  If n = 1 Then
   Factorial = 1
  Else
   Factorial = n * Factorial(n - 1)
  End If
End Function

Rem: This is the Exit event procedure
Private Sub cmdExit_Click()
  Beep
  End
End Sub
```

Figure 7-24

A Sample Output of Program 7-5

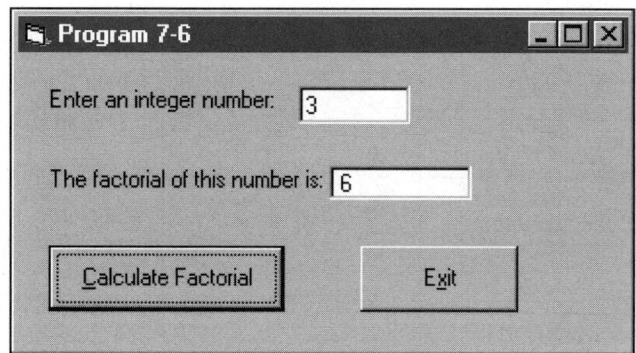

Figure 7-24 illustrates a sample run of Program 7-5.

How the Computation is Performed

The sample run of Program 7-5 initially invoked `Factorial` with a value of 3, using the call

```
fact = Factorial(n)
```

Let's see how the computer actually performs the computation. The mechanism that makes it possible for a Visual Basic procedure to call itself is that Visual Basic allocates new memory locations for all procedure parameters as each procedure is called. This allocation is made dynamically, as a program is executed, in a memory area referred to as the stack.

A *stack* is simply an area of memory used for rapidly storing and retrieving data. It is conceptually similar to a stack of trays in a cafeteria, where the last tray placed on top of the stack is the first tray removed. This last-in/first-out mechanism provides the means for storing information in order of occurrence. Each procedure call simply reserves memory locations on the stack for its parameters, its local variables, a return value, and the address where execution is to resume in the calling procedure when the called procedure has completed execution. Thus, when the procedure call `Factorial(n)` is made, the stack is initially used to store the address of the instruction being executed (`fact = Factorial(n)`); the parameter value for n, which is 3; and a space for the value to be returned by the `Factorial` procedure. At this stage, the stack can be envisioned as shown in Figure 7-25. From a program execution standpoint, the procedure that made the call to `Factorial`, in this case the `cmdFactorial` **Click** event, is suspended and the compiled code for the `Factorial` procedure starts executing.

Within the `Factorial` procedure itself, another procedure call is made. That this call is to `Factorial`, is irrelevant as far as Visual Basic is concerned. The call is simply another request for stack space. In this case, the stack stores the address of the instruction being executed in `Factorial`, the number 2, and a space for the value to be returned by the procedure. The stack can now be envisioned as shown in Figure 7-26. At this point, a second version of the

Figure 7-25

The Stack for the First Call to Factorial

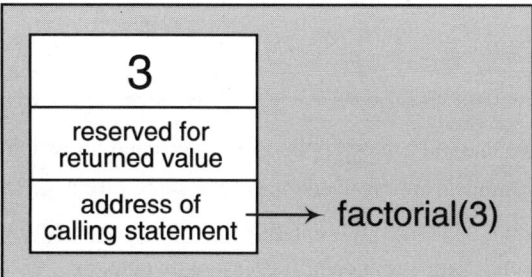

Figure 7-26

The Stack for the Second Call to Factorial

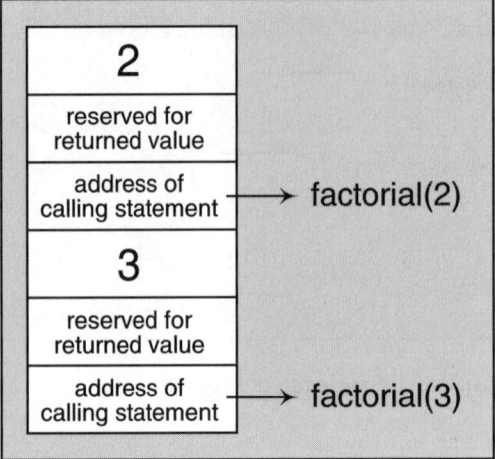

compiled code for Factorial begins execution, while the first version is temporarily suspended.

Once again, the currently executing code, which is the second invocation of Factorial, makes a procedure call. That this call is to itself, is irrelevant in Visual Basic. The call is once again handled in the same manner as any procedure invocation and begins with allocation of the stack's memory space. Here the stack stores the address of the instruction being executed in the calling procedure, which happens to be Factorial, the number 1, and a space for the value to be returned by the function. The stack can now be envisioned as shown in Figure 7-27. At this point the third and final version of the compiled code for Factorial begins execution, while the second version is temporarily suspended.

Figure 7-27

The Stack for the Third Call to Factorial

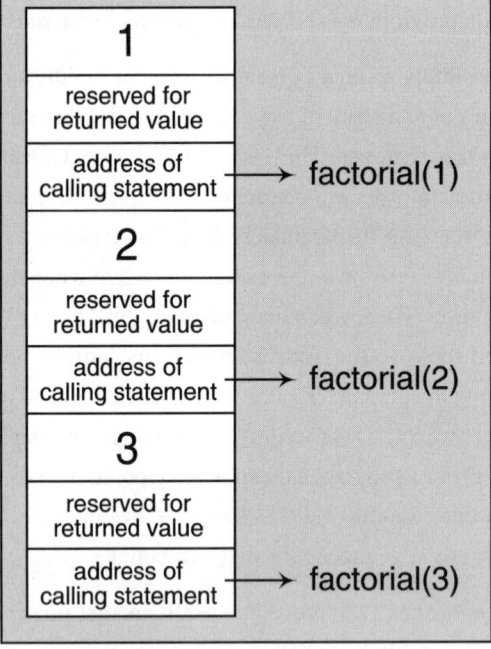

This third call to Factorial results in a returned value of 1 being placed on the stack. This completes the set of recursive calls and permits the suspended calling procedures to resume execution and be completed in reverse order. The value of 1 is used by the second invocation of Factorial to complete its operation and place a return value of 2 on the stack. This value is then used by the first invocation of Factorial to complete its operation and place a return value of 6 on the stack, with execution now returning to the cmdFactorial_Click event procedure. The original calling statement within this procedure stores the return value of its invocation of Factorial into the variable fact.

Recursion Versus Iteration

The recursive method can be applied to any problem in which the solution is represented in terms of solutions to simpler versions of the same problem. The most difficult tasks in implementing a recursive solution, however, are deciding how to create the process and visualizing what happens at each successive invocation.

Any recursive procedure can always be written in a nonrecursive manner using an iterative solution. For example, the factorial procedure can be written using an iteration algorithm as

```
Public Function Factorial(n As Long) As Long
  Dim fact As Long

  fact = 1
  Do
   fact = fact * n
   n = n - 1
  Loop While n > 0
  Factorial = fact
End Function
```

Since recursion is usually a difficult concept for beginning programmers, under what conditions would you use it in preference to a repetitive solution? The answer is rather simple.

If a problem solution can be expressed repetitively or recursively with equal ease, the repetitive solution is preferable because it executes faster (there are no additional procedure calls, which consume processing time) and uses less memory (the stack is not used for the multiple procedure calls needed in recursion). There are times, however, when recursive solutions are preferable.

First, some problems are simply easier to visualize using a recursive algorithm than a repetitive one. A second reason for using recursion is that it sometimes provides a much simpler solution. In these situations, obtaining the same result using repetition would require extremely complicated coding that can be avoided using recursion. An example of this is an advanced sorting algorithm known as the *Quicksort*.

Exercises 7.5

1. The Fibonacci sequence is 0, 1, 1, 2, 3, 5, 8, 13,... such that the first two terms are 0 and 1, and each term thereafter is defined recursively as the sum of the two preceding terms; that is,

$$\text{Fib}(n) = \text{Fib}(n-1) + \text{Fib}(n-2)$$

Write a recursive procedure that returns the nth number in a Fibonacci sequence, when n is passed to the procedure as a parameter. For example, when $n = 8$, the procedure should return the eighth number in the sequence, which is 13.

2. The sum of a series of consecutive numbers from 1 to n can be defined recursively as

$$\text{sum}(1) = 1;$$
$$\text{sum}(n) = n + \text{sum}(n - 1)$$

Write a recursive Visual Basic procedure that accepts n as a parameter and calculates the sum of the numbers from 1 to n.

3. a. The value of x^n can be defined recursively as

$$x^0 = 1$$
$$x^n = x * x^{n-1}$$

Write a recursive procedure that computes and returns the value of x^n.

b. Rewrite the procedure written for Exercise 3a. so that it uses a repetitive algorithm for calculating the value of x^n.

4. a. Write a procedure that recursively determines the value of the *n*th term in a geometric sequence defined by the terms

$$a, ar, ar^2, ar^3, ... ar^{n-1}$$

The parameters of the procedure should be the first term, *a*, the common ratio, *r*, and the value of *n*.

b. Modify the procedure written for Exercise 4a. so that the sum of the first n terms in the sequence is returned.

5. a. Write a procedure that recursively determines the value of the *n*th term of an arithmetic sequence defined by the terms

$$a, a+d, a+2d, a+3d, ... a+(n-1)d$$

The parameters of the procedure should be the first term, *a*, the common difference, *d*, and the value of *n*.

b. Modify the procedure written for Exercise 5a so that the sum of the first n terms of the sequence is returned. (**Hint:** This is a more general form of Exercise 2.)

7.6 Common Programming Errors

The common errors associated with general procedures are

1. Forgetting to use the word **Sub** or **Function** on the header line before the general procedure's name.
2. Using an argument list that does not match with the general procedure's parameter list. These errors fall into the following categories:
    a. The number of arguments is not the same as the number of parameters.
    b. The order of arguments and corresponding parameters do not match.
    c. The data types of arguments and corresponding parameters do not match.
3. Attempting to alter the value of a passed constant, expression, or function result. For example, assume that a general procedure named Area has the header line

```
Public Sub Area(radius As Single)
```

and is called using the statement

```
Call Area(Rad)
```

Here, the value in Rad is referenced within the general procedure as the parameter radius. If the general procedure subsequently alters the value of radius, the value of Rad is also changed. This is a consequence of the fact that both Rad and radius reference the exact same storage location area. Now assume that the general procedure is called using the following statement

```
Call Area(3.62)
```

Here the value in `radius` cannot be changed within `Area`. An attempt to do so is effectively an attempt to redefine the value of the constant 3.62, which usually causes a runtime error.

4. Inadvertently changing the value of a parameter inside a general procedure when the calling unit did not expect the change. This is an unwanted side effect that can be avoided by passing argument values by value, rather than by reference.

7.7 Chapter Review

Key Terms

actual argument	global variables
arguments	local scope
ByRef	local variables
ByVal	module-level variable
call by reference	parameters
call by value	recursive procedures
called procedure	scope
calling procedure	stack
form-level variables	**Static**
formal argument	static variables
general procedure	subprograms

Summary

1. The most commonly used syntax for a general **Sub** procedure is

```
Public Sub Name(Parameter List)
    Visual Basic statements in here
End Sub
```

Even if the **Sub** procedure has no parameter list, the parentheses must be present.

2. A general **Sub** procedure is called using a **Call** statement having the form

```
Call procedure-name(argument list)
```

The arguments in the **Call** statement may be constants, variables, or expressions using combinations of constants and variables. The data type, number, and order of the arguments used in the **Call** statement must agree with the data type, number, and order of the corresponding parameters in the general procedure's parameter list. In addition the parentheses surrounding the argument list can be omitted. If there are no arguments, the parentheses must be omitted.

3. Except for constants, arguments are passed by reference. This means that the called procedure can change the argument's value. To pass an argument by value, either enclose the argument in parentheses or declare the corresponding parameter using the **ByVal** keyword. For example, the declaration

```
Public Sub Test(ByVal radius As Single)
```

declares that the `radius` parameter references a value. Similarly, the **Call** statement

```
Call Message((Rad), (Angle))
```

passes values to the Message **Sub** procedure.

4. All functions (intrinsic and user-written) calculate and directly return a single value. The most commonly used syntax for a user-written function is

> **Public Function** *function-name(Parameter List) As Data-type*
>   optional variable declarations
>
>   optional executable statements
>   function-name = expression
> **End Function**

5. Functions that return a string can be declared as such by appending a dollar sign to the function's name. For example, the declarations

```
Public Function Test(s As String, n As Integer) As String
```
and
```
Public Function Test$( s As String, n As Integer)
```
are equivalent.

6. A function is called by using its name and passing any data to it in the parentheses following the name.

7. The arguments passed to a function must agree in type, order, and number with the function's parameters.

8. Every variable used in a procedure has a *scope*, which determines where in the program the variable can be used. The scope of a variable is either *local* or *global* and is determined by where the variable's definition statement is placed. A local variable is defined within a procedure and can only be used within its defining procedure. A global variable is defined outside a procedure. If the global variable is declared as **Private**, it can be used by any procedure located on the same module in which it is declared. Global variables declared as **Public** can be used by every procedure on any module in the application. Global variables are also referred to as *module-level* variables.

9. Global variables are in scope for the life of the application. Local variables are effectively destroyed when they go out of scope. To keep a local variable's value from being destroyed, the variable can be declared as **Static**. Additionally, placing the

Static keyword immediately in front of the keywords **Sub** and **Function** in a general procedure's header line makes all of the procedure's variables **Static**.

10. Procedures also have scope. **Private** procedures can only be called from procedures residing on the same module as the **Private** procedure, while **Public** procedures can be called by every procedure in the application, regardless of the module containing the calling procedure.

11. A recursive solution is one in which the solution can be expressed in terms of a "simpler" version of itself. A recursive algorithm must always specify:

    a. The first case or cases, and

    b. How the nth case is related to the $(n-1)$ case.

12. If a problem solution can be expressed repetitively or recursively with equal ease, the repetitive solution is preferable because it executes faster and uses less memory. In many advanced applications recursion is simpler to visualize and is the only practical means of implementing a solution.

7.8 Looking Further: Breakpoints, Watch Variables, and Step-Over Execution ▬▬

In Section 3.9 we introduced the three Debug windows (Immediate, Watch, and Local) and the single-step method of running a program. Single-step execution is extremely useful for analyzing both small programs and small sections of code contained within a larger program. For debugging larger programs a combination of breakpoints, single-step execution, step-over execution, and watch variables are typically used. In this section we introduce these new techniques and show how they are can be used together for debugging larger sections of code.

Breakpoints

A breakpoint statement, called a *breakpoint*, for short, is simply a designated statement at which program execution automatically stops and the mode switches from Run to Break. Once in Break mode the Immediate or Local Debug window can be activated and either window used to both examine and alter one or more variable's value. The program can then be continued in either single-step, step-over, or run mode.

Breakpoint statements are designated in either Design or Break mode in the Code window. This is accomplished by first placing the cursor on the designated line and

1. Pressing the F9 key, or
2. Selecting the Toggle Breakpoint option from the Debug menu, or
3. Pressing the Toggle Breakpoint (the hand) button on the Debug toolbar.

Once a statement has been designated as a breakpoint statement, it will be both highlighted in the Code window and bulleted in Code window's left-side margin. As an example of setting breakpoints, consider the event code illustrated in the Code window shown in Figure 7-28.

Figure 7-28

*Event Code with Two
Breakpoint Statements*

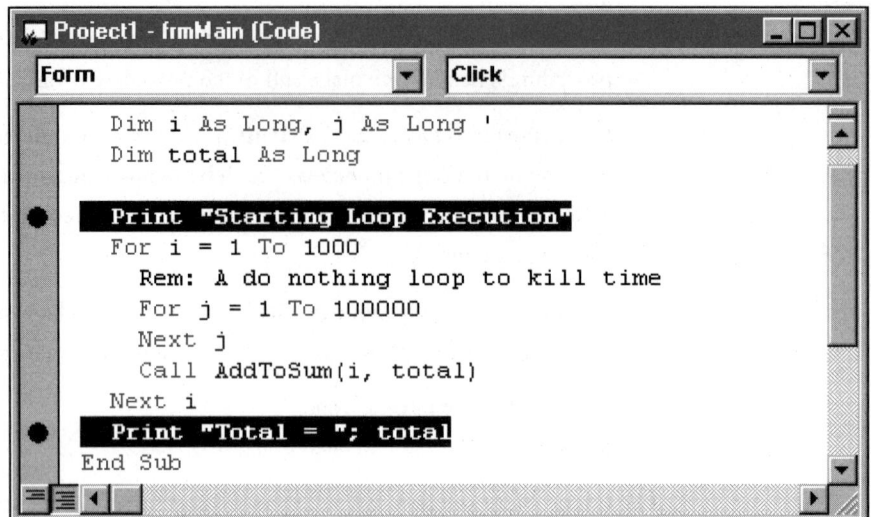

```
Dim i As Long, j As Long '
Dim total As Long

Print "Starting Loop Execution"
For i = 1 To 1000
    Rem: A do nothing loop to kill time
    For j = 1 To 100000
    Next j
    Call AddToSum(i, total)
Next i
Print "Total = "; total
End Sub
```

Notice in Figure 7-28 that two statements are highlighted and each of these statements
has a bullet mark in the Code window's left-side margin. The highlighting and bulleting
indicate that these two statements are breakpoint statements. This means that execution
during run-time will stop just prior to each statement being executed. When this occurs an
appropriate Debug window can be activated for examining and modifying all program
variables. Run-time mode can then be restarted by pressing either the Run toolbar button (or
the F5 key), the Step Into toolbar button (or the F8 key) for single-step execution, or the
Step Over toolbar button (or the Shift and F8 keys together) if execution was suspended
at a line that called either a **Sub** or **Function** procedure (the Debug toolbar is shown in
Figure 7-29).

To explicitly clear breakpoints you must also be in either Design or Break mode. For
specific breakpoints simply place the cursor on the desired statement in the Code window
and repeat one of the steps used to set the breakpoint. For example, if the breakpoint is on,
the F9 key will toggle it off. To explicitly clear all breakpoints in a program:

1. Press the Ctrl + Shift + F9 keys at the same time or
2. Select the Clear All Breakpoints option from the Debug menu.

In any case all breakpoints are implicitly cleared in a saved project. That is, breakpoints *are
not* saved when the file containing the code is saved.

Figure 7-29

The Debug Toolbar

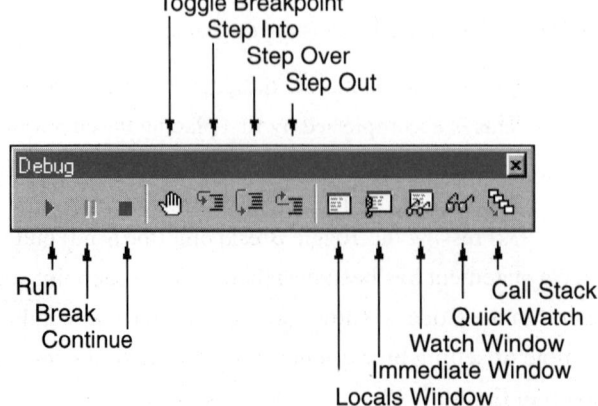

To illustrate how breakpoints work, create and execute the program containing the code previously shown in Figure 7-28. Notice that when the `Form_Click` event is activated the program suspends execution at the first breakpoint statement and opens up a Code window. For now, simply press the Continue toolbar button to restart program execution at the breakpoint statement. Notice that the code contains a nested **For** loop that uses the inner loop simply to waste time. This gives you sufficient time to experiment moving into Break mode by

1. Pressing the Break toolbar button or
2. Pressing the Ctrl and Break keys at the same time.

Try one or both of these methods to switch back to Break mode once the program has been restarted. Once in Break mode you activate the desired Debug window by

1. Clicking on the window, if it is visible,
2. Selecting the window from the View menu,
2. Selecting the window using a Debug toolbar icon, or
3. Pressing the Ctrl and G keys at the same time to activate the Immediate window

Figure 7-30a

The Locals Window

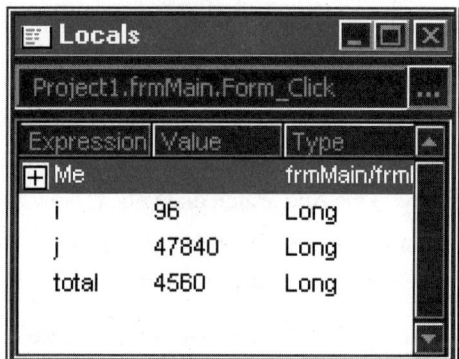

Figure 7-30 illustrates how the Locals and Immediate windows appeared for one such switch into Break mode. Clearly, the Locals window is easier to use because you don't have to enter either a question mark or a **Print** statement to display the a variable's value, as is required with the Immediate window. After you restart the program notice that the program automatically switches back to Break mode once again just prior to

Figure 7-30b

The Immediate Window

executing the **Print** statement located after the nested loop. This is because this statement is a breakpoint statement.

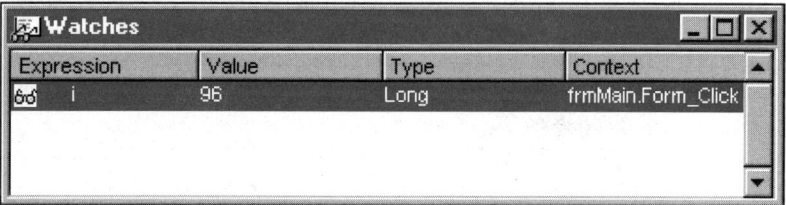

Watch Variables and Expressions

Frequently, while debugging a section of code, you will be interested in a selected group of variables or a selected expression. Instead of displaying all local variables in the Locals window, or printing out the value of the expression in the Immediate window, you can have selected variables and expressions automatically displayed in the Watch window. This is accomplished by designating one or more variables and expressions as *watched*. This allows you to observe theirs value in the Watch window, because such variables and expressions are automatically updated and displayed in that window whenever Break mode is entered. To

---

Programmers' Notes

Creating and Clearing Breakpoint Statements

Breakpoint statements are created and cleared using the same steps. In both cases you must either be in Design or Break mode. When you are on the desired line of code:

     1. Press the F9 key, or
     2. Select the Toggle Breakpoint option from the Debug menu, or
     3. Press the Toggle Breakpoint (the hand) button on the Debug toolbar.

Each of these steps is a toggle that both selects and deselects a statement as a breakpoint. To clear all breakpoints in either Design or Break mode do one of the following:

     1. Press the Ctrl+Shift+F9 keys at the same time or
     2. Select the Clear All Breakpoints option from the Debug menu.

Breakpoints are not saved when the code containing them is saved.

---

designate a variable or expression as watched, first highlight the selected variable or expression in the Code window and then select the Add Watch option from the Debug menu. This will bring up the Add Watch dialog box shown in Figure 7-31.

Pressing the OK command button on the Add Watch dialog box causes the selected variable to be added to a list of watched variables. Or, if you need to watch an expression that is not in your code, but consists of variables whose values can be watched, simply type in the expression directly in the Add Watch dialog box. Now, whenever you enter Break mode and display the Watch window the watched expression and its value will automatically be displayed in the Watch window, as illustrated in Figure 7-32.

If you simply need to determine the value of a variable or expression quickly, you can highlight the variable or expression and activate the Quick Watch toolbar button. This will both display the value of the variable or expression and also provide you with the opportunity of making the highlighted item a watched expression.

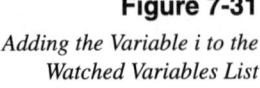

Figure 7-31

Adding the Variable i to the Watched Variables List

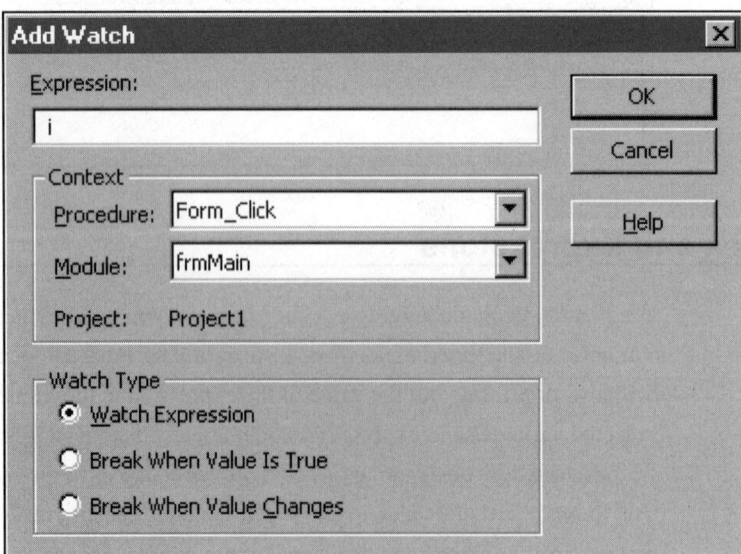

Figure 7-32

A Watch Window

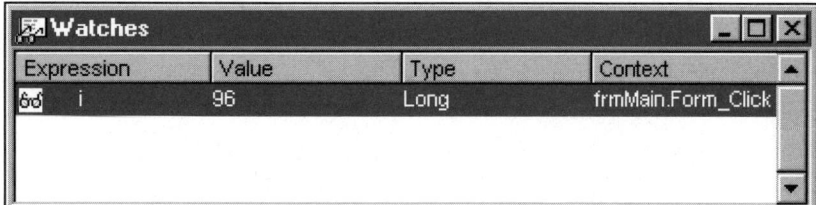

Step Over Execution

A very useful debugging procedure in conjunction with single-stepping through a section of code is to use the Step Over toolbar button whenever a call to a **Sub** procedure or function is encountered. The Step Over button causes the complete called procedure to execute but puts the program back into Break mode when the called procedure has completed execution. Thus, when you encounter a call to a general procedure and are interested in single-stepping through it use the Step Into toolbar button; otherwise use the Step Over toolbar button to complete the called procedure's execution and move to the next executable statement in the calling procedure's code.

Lab Exercises For Part I

Lab 1: Labels and Buttons

Topics: Label and Command controls

Reading: Chapter 2

Description: Create the run-time interface shown below. The application should display the message My first VB Program! when the first Command button is clicked, and the message Isn't this neat?!? when the second Command button is clicked.

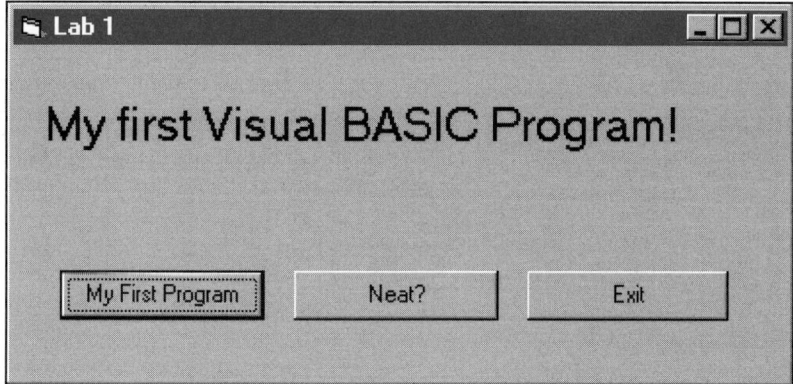

Extra Challenge:

If you finish early, try to make the label appear randomly somewhere on the form by using the intrinsic **rnd** function, the form's **Width** and **Height** properties and the Label's **Left** property.

Lab 2: Data Types and Variables

Topics: Integers and Strings

Reading: Chapter 3

Description: Construct a program that uses integer and string variables and the operations that can be performed on them. Follow the instructions below.

A. Integers

1. Open a new project called `lab2.vbp` and change the form's caption to `VB Data Types`.

2. Create an Exit Command control on your form named `cmdExit` that can be used to end the program.

3. Create a Picture box and Command control on your formed named `picDisplay1` and `cmdDisplay1`, respectively. Set the caption of the Command control to <u>D</u>isplay results.

4. Add the following commands to the Command control's **Click** event procedure, and run your program.

```
picDisplay1.Cls
picDisplay1.Print 1
picDisplay1.Print 3 + 4
picDisplay1.Print 3 + 4 - 5
picDisplay1.Print 3 + 4 * 5 - 10 / 2
picDisplay1.Print 3 / 4, 6 / 4, 8 / 4
picDisplay1.Print 6 ^ 2, 3 ^ 2 ^ 2
picDisplay1.Print 3;4;5;7-1
```

5. Now, add a Command button that causes the following code to be executed:

```
Dim a, b, c as Integer
picDisplay1.Cls
a = 5 : b = 2
picDisplay1.Print a + b, a - b
picDisplay1.Print a * b, a / b
picDisplay1.Print a ^ b; b ^ a;
picDisplay1.Print (a + b) / b * a - 13
picDisplay1.Print ((a - 3) * b) - 13 * 2
```

6. Now add a Command button to calculate and display the following:

- a * b where a = 10 and b = 7
- the average speed of a plane that traveled 600 miles in 2.5 hours
- the square root of 15

B. Strings

1. Create a new Picture box named `picDisplay2` and a Command button that activates the following code when it is clicked:

```
Dim today As String          'string variables
Dim fday As String
Dim tdate as String

picDisplay2.Cls
picDisplay2.Print "Hello";
picDisplay2.Print "There!"
today = "01/24/98"
picDisplay2.Print today
fday = "Friday"
picDisplay2.Print "Today is ";
picDisplay2.Print fday + ", " + today
tdate = fday + ", " + today
picDisplay2.Print tdate
picDisplay2.Print "400 + 125 = "; 400 + 125
```

Note: Adding two strings is called concatenation. The strings are simply "strung" together. Adding two integers adds up the numbers.

2. Add a new Command button that executes the following code:

```
Dim irate As Single
Dim net As Single
Dim principal As Single
Dim phrase As String

irate = 0.065
principal = 1000
phrase = "The balance after a year is "
net = (1 + irate) * principal
picDisplay2.Print "Using an interest rate of ";
picDisplay2.Print irate * 100; "%, ";phrase; net
```

3. Create one last Picture box named `picDisplay3`, and a Command control to activate the following code:

```
Dim n1 As Integer, n2 As Integer, n3 As Integer
Dim f1 As Single, f2 As Single, f3 As Single
Dim s1 As String, s2 As String, s3 As String

n1 = 3 : n2 = 4 : n3 = 5
f1 = 3 : f2 = 4 : f3 = 5
s1 = "3" : s2 = "4" : s3 = "5"
picDisplay3.Cls
picDisplay3.Print n1 * n2 * n3, n1 * Val(s2) * n3
n2 = n3 / n1
f2 = f3 / f1
picDisplay3.Print n2, f2
picDisplay3.Print n1+n2+n3, s1+s2+s3
picDisplay3.Print s1, n2, f2
picDisplay3.Print
picDisplay3.Print Val(s1) + n2 + f2, Val(s1)+ n2+ Int(f2)
```

Extra Challenge:

1. Use the Help facility to obtain information on the string functions **Left$**, **Right$**, **Mid$**, and **InStr**.

2. Create a Picture box and a Command control to activate the following code:

```
Dim S1 As String
Dim f1 As Single

s1 = "Hello There, World!"
picDisplay4.Print Left$(s1, 5)
picDisplay4.Print Mid$ (s1,7,5)
picDisplay4.Print Right$(s1,6)
picDisplay4.Print Instr(s1,"W")
f1 = 3.1415927
picDisplay4.Print "/";Str$(f1);"/",Mid$(Str$(f1),4,4)
picDisplay4.Print (s1) + Str(n1)
```

Use the results of this lab to answer the questions in Lab 3.

Lab 3: Data Types and Variables

Topics: Integers and Strings

Reading: Chapter 3

Description: Answer the following questions:

1. What happens when you divide two integers together and store the result into an integer variable?

2. What happens when you divide two integers together and store the result into a single precision variable?

3. What does the trailing semicolon do after a **Print** statement?

4. What does the trailing comma do after a **Print** statement?

5. What happens if a **Print** statement is called with nothing after it?

6. How do you clear (erase) a Picture box?

7. Is 3 ^ 2 ^ 2 equal to 81?

8. What is the value of the expression 3 + 4 * 5?

9. What is the value of the expression (3 + 4) * 5?

10. What is the value of the expression "3 + 4 * 5"?

11. What is the value of the expression "(3 + 4) * 5"?

12. What happens when two strings are added together?

13. What does an apostrophe do in Visual Basic?

14. What does a colon do in Visual Basic?

15. What does a comma do in a **Print** statement?

16. What does a semicolon do in a **Print** statement?

17. True or False: An assignment statement takes the value of the right-hand side of an equation and assigns it to the left-hand side.

18. Is the statement a + b = c + 5 a valid Visual Basic statement? Why or why not?

19. What type of data does the **Val** function expect to operate on and what data type does it return?

20. How do you ensure that each and every Visual Basic variable must be explicitly declared in a program?

Extra Challenge Questions:

21. What does the **Left$** function do?

22. What does the **Right$** function do?

23. What does the **Mid$** function do?

24. What is the exact value of the expression Str(3.1415)?

25. What does the **InStr** function return?

Lab 4 The Simple Calculator

Topics: Input and Output

Reading: Chapter 4

Description: Implement a simple calculator like the one pictured below. An executable example of the calculator can be found on the source diskette enclosed with the text. It is called lab4.exe.

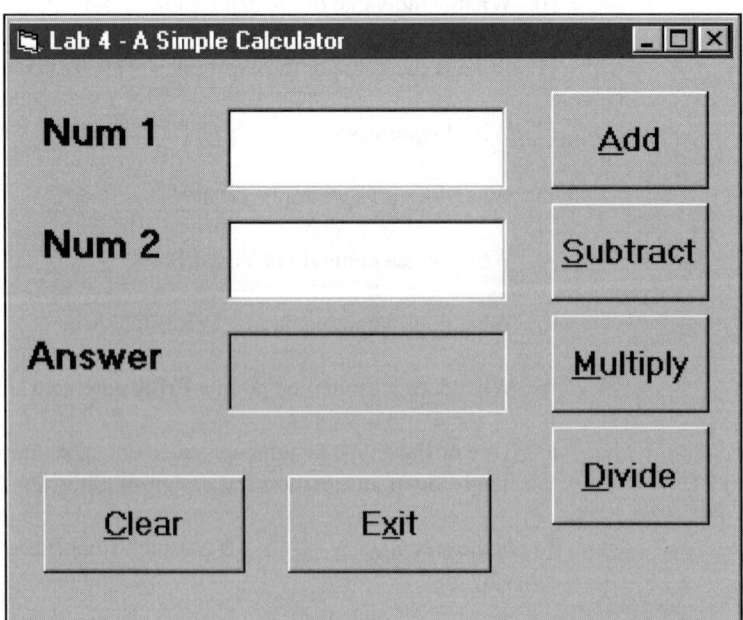

Features:

1. The buttons perform the indicated operation on the two text fields and display the answer in the Picture box to the right of the <u>A</u>nswer label.

2. When the calculator starts up, the first Text box field, to the right of the label Num 1, should have the focus.

3. The [TAB] key switches between the two Text box fields.

4. The <u>C</u>lear button clears the Text boxes, the answer, and sets the focus to the first Text box.

5. The <u>E</u>nd button ends the program.

The Solution (Hints):

1. Create a form having the following controls: 2 Text boxes, 1 Picture Box, 3 Labels, and 6 Command buttons.

2. Set the properties for all of the controls. Start with each control's name!

3. Deactivate the **TabStop** property for all but the two Text boxes, and set the **TabIndex** property of the Text boxes to 1 and 2, respectively.

4. Write the code for each Command button's **Click** event procedure. The <u>C</u>lear button should call the **SetFocus** method for the first Text box.

Extra Challenges:

If you finish early:

1. Add a <u>S</u>quare Root button that takes the square root of the answer.
2. Add a <u>N</u>egate button that negates (changes the sign of) the answer.

Lab 5: A Complete Calculator

Topics: Input and Output

Reading: Chapter 4 and Chapter 5

Description: Implement a calculator similar to the one pictured on the next page. An executable example of this calculator can be found on the source disk enclosed with the text as lab5.exe. Although you are free to design your calculator interface and functionality however you like, the button operation must be consistent with a typical calculator.

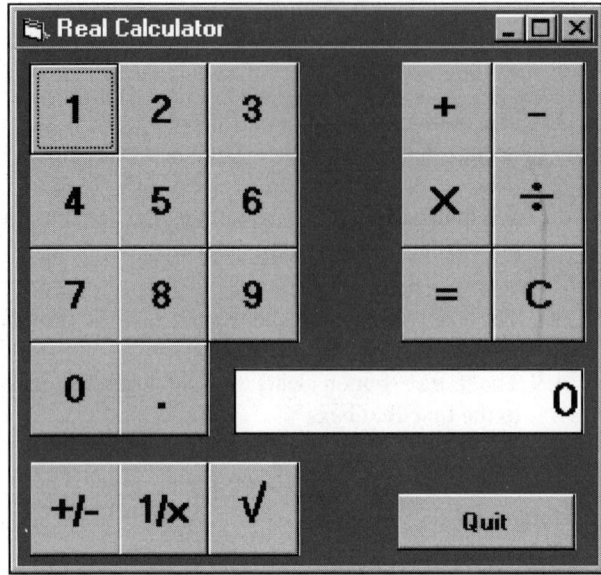

Requirements:

1. There can only be one number display (like a calculator).
2. Your calculator must have support for addition, subtraction, multiplication, and division.
3. Your calculator needs to have (at least) the following features:
   - A square root function,
   - An additive inverse function (+/- key to negate the display),
   - A multiplicative inverse function (1/x to get the reciprocal of the display), and
   - A clear key.
4. The Divide button needs to check for divide by zero using an **If-Then** statement.

Although you can start with the simple calculator completed for Lab 4, you will need to redesign it.

Lab 6: Option and Check Boxes

Topics: Option and Check Boxes

Reading: Chapter 5

Description: This lab deals with Option boxes, Check boxes, and text properties. After selecting the appropriate style for the text, clicking the Update button will update the text in a Text box. You will also need to use a Frame control, which is explained below.

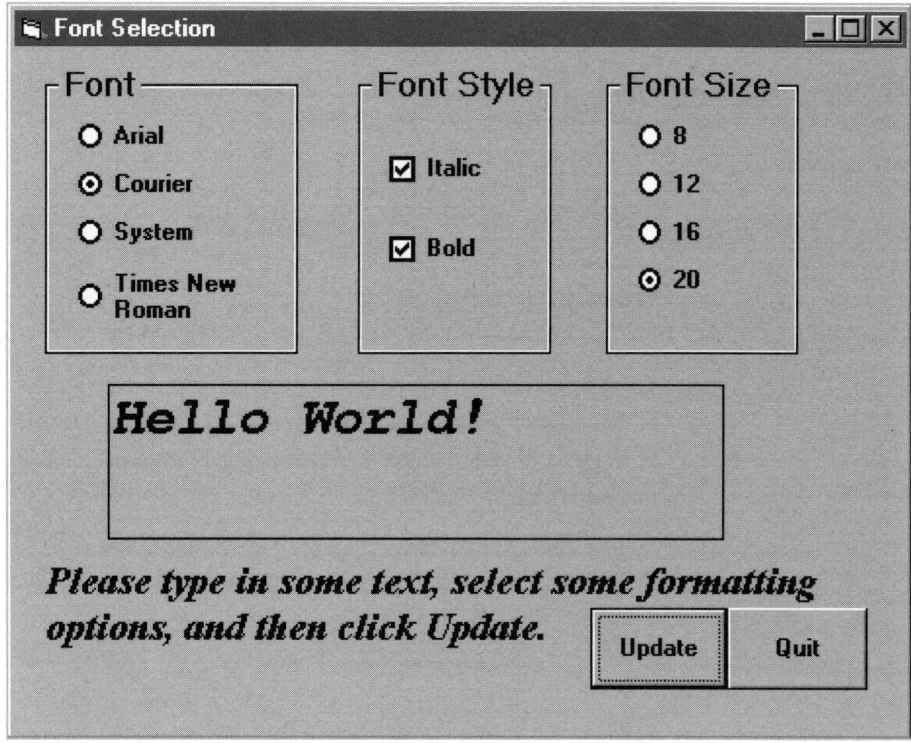

To Do This Lab:

1. Create the interface (the form and its controls).
2. Add Visual Basic Code to the Update button's **Click** event procedure. This code will consist of a series of **If-Then** type statements to set the properties of the Text box.
3. Set the **FontName** property before the **Size** and **Style** properties, or you may obtain inconsistent results.

A working version of this program, named lab6.exe, is contained on the disc enclosed within the text.

The Frame Control:

To use a Frame control, *first* put an object of this control type on your interface, *and then* place the desired set of Option boxes or Check boxes within the Frame control.

Lab 7: The Moving Dragster

Topics: Repetition Statements

Reading: Chapter 6

Description: The purpose of this lab is to create a moving car. An executable example of the required program can be found on the source disk enclosed with the text as `lab7.exe`. You don't have to reproduce the program exactly, but your program should work in a somewhat similar manner. To create your program you will need a loop for moving the car. You will also need to locate and use two icons that are provided with Visual Basic named `trffc16.ico` and `clould.ico`, which must be placed into either Picture or Image boxes at design time. A working version of this program, named `lab7.exe`, is contained on the disk enclosed with the text.

Hint: The basic idea for moving the car is to subtract a set increment form the top coordinate of the Image box using an algorithm such as

```
Do until "Car is off the screen"
    imgCar.top = imgCar.top - increment
Loop
```

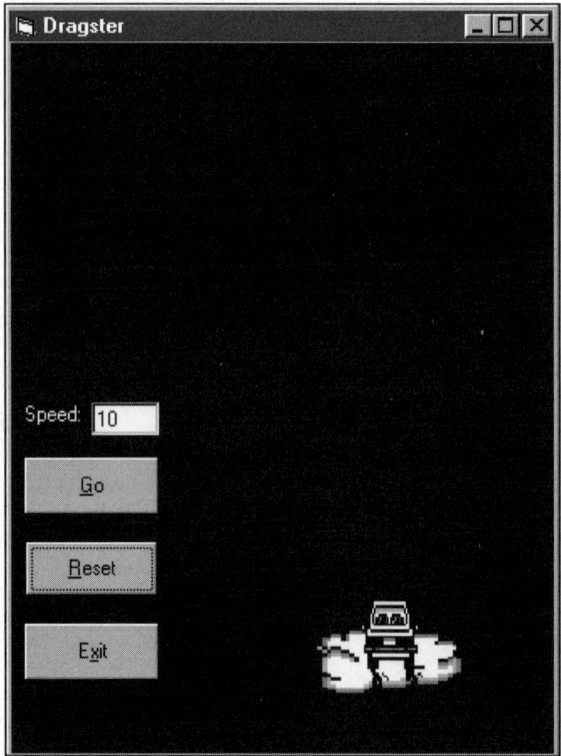

Extra Challenge:

If you finish early, put in clouds of smoke as the car moves. To do this, first create a control array of five Picture boxes, each containing a small cloud icon, all of whose **Visible** property is set to **False**. (See Section 8.3 for information on Control arrays.) Then, using a **For** loop, set each cloud image's **Visible** property to **True** when the bottom of the car image passes the top of the cloud image.

Part II
Data Structures and Storage

Structured Data

8.1 One-Dimensional Arrays

8.2 Additional Array Capabilities

8.3 Control Arrays

8.4 Structures

8.5 Searching and Sorting

8.6 Common Programming Errors

8.7 Chapter Review

8.8 Looking Further: Introduction to the Applications Wizard

The variables we have used so far have shared a common characteristic: each could store only one value at a time. For example, although the variables **key, count,** *and* **grade** *declared in the statements*

```
Dim key As String*1
Dim count As Integer
Dim grade As Single
```

are of different data types, each variable can store only one value of the declared data type. These types of variables are called **atomic variables.** *An atomic variable, which is also referred to as a scalar variable, has a value that cannot be further subdivided or separated into a legitimate data type.*

Another method of storing and retrieving data is to use a data structure. A data structure is a data type whose values can be decomposed into individual data elements, each of which is either atomic or another data structure and provides an access scheme for locating individual data elements within the structure. One of the

Table 8-1 Three Individual Lists		
Temperatures	Codes	Grades
95.75	Z	98
83.0	C	87
97.625	K	92
72.5	L	79
86.25		85
		72

simplest and most widely used **data structures,** *which is referred to as an* **array,** *consists of a set of logically related individual items, all of which have the same data type. For example, Table 8-1 illustrates three groups of items. The first group is a list of five single-precision temperatures, the second group is a list of four character codes, and the last group is a list of six integer grades.*

In this chapter we describe how arrays are declared, initialized, stored inside a computer, and used. We also introduce record structures. A record structure is a user-defined data type whose elements need not all be of the same data type. Both arrays and record structures require Visual Basic's built-in procedural operations for individual element access and manipulation. In Chapter 12 we present an advanced data structure, referred to as a Class, that requires the programmer to define both the type of data and the operations that can be used on individual elements in the data structure.

8.1 One-Dimensional Arrays

A *one-dimensional* array, which is also referred to as either a *single-dimensional* array or a vector, is a list of related values, with the same data type, stored using a single group name.[1] In Visual Basic, as in other computer languages, the group name is referred to as the array name. For example, consider the list of grades illustrated in Table 8-2.

Table 8-2 A List of Grades
98
87
92
79
85
72

All the grades in this list are integer numbers and must be declared as such. However, the individual items in the list do not have to be declared separately. The items in the list can be declared as a single unit and stored under a common variable name called the array name. For convenience, we will choose grades as the name for the list shown in Figure 8-2. The general syntax for declaring a one-dimensional array is

```
Dim arrayname(Lower-Index-Value To Upper-Index-Value) As data-type
```

For example, the declaration

```
Dim grades(1 To 6) As Single
```

specifies that grades is to store six individual integer values. Notice that this declaration statement gives the array (or list) name, the data type of items in the array, and the beginning and ending designations for items in the array. Figure 8-1 illustrates the grades array in memory with the correct designation for each array element.

Figure 8-1

The grades Array in Memory

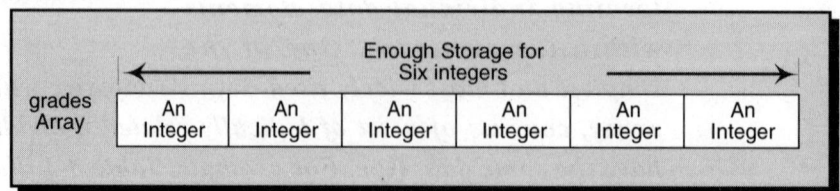

---

[1] Note that lists can be implemented in a variety of ways. An array is simply one implementation of a list in which all the list elements are of the same type and each element is stored consecutively in a set of contiguous memory locations.

Programmers' Notes

Structured Data Types

In contrast to atomic types, such as integer and single-precision data, there are structured types. A structured type, which is sometimes referred to as a data structure, is any type whose values can be decomposed and are related by some defined structure. Additionally, operations must be available for retrieving and updating individual values in the data structure.

Single-dimensional arrays are examples of a structured type. In a single-dimensional array, such as an array of integers, the array is composed of individual integer values, where integers are related by their position in the list. Indexed variables provide the means of accessing and modifying values in the array.

Each item in an array is called an *element* or *component* of that array. The individual elements stored in the array illustrated in Figure 8-1 are stored sequentially, with the first array element stored in the first reserved location, the second element stored in the second reserved location, and so on, until the last element is stored in the last reserved location. This contiguous storage allocation for the list is a key feature of arrays because it provides a simple mechanism for easily locating any single element in the list.

Since elements in the array are stored sequentially, any individual element can be accessed by giving the name of the array and the element's position. This position is called the element's *index* or *subscript* value (the two terms are synonymous). As declared, the first element of the `grades` array has an index of 1, the second element 1 has an index of 2, and so on, up to the number specified last in parentheses in the **Dim** statement used to declare the array. In Visual Basic, the array name and index of the desired element are combined by listing the index in parentheses after the array name. For example, given the declaration

```
Dim grades(1 To 6) As Integer:
```

- `grades(1)` refers to the first grade stored in the `grades` array,
- `grades(2)` refers to the second grade stored in the `grades` array,
- `grades(3)` refers to the third grade stored in the `grades` array,
- `grades(4)` refers to the fourth grade stored in the `grades` array,
- `grades(5)` refers to the fifth grade stored in the `grades` array, and
- `grades(6)` refers to the sixth grade stored in the `grades` array.

The indexed variable, `grades(1)`, is read as "grades sub one." This is a shortened way of saying "the grades array subscripted (that is, indexed) by one," and distinguishes the first element in an array from an atomic variable that could be declared as `grades1`. Similarly, `grades(2)` is read as "grades sub two," `grades(3)` as "grades sub three," and so on.

The Starting Index Number

In declaring an array, we have listed both the starting and ending index numbers. For example, in the following declarations

```
Dim temp(1 To 7) As Integer
Dim sample(3 To 6) As Single
Dim foo(0 To 5) As Double
```

Introduction to Visual Basic

the `temp` array has been declared with a starting index value of 1, the `sample` array with a starting index of 3, and the `foo` array with a starting index of 0.[2] Thus, the `temp` array consists of the seven elements from `temp(1)` to `temp(7)`, `sample` consists of the four elements from `sample(3)` to `sample(6)`, and `foo` consists of the six elements from `foo(0)` to `foo(5)`. A very useful option is to eliminate the starting index altogether, which forces the array to start with an index value of either 0 or 1, depending upon the default starting base value that is set using the **Option Base** statement. For example, the statement `Option Base 1` sets the default starting index value to 1, while the statement `Option Base 0` sets the default starting index value to 0. These are the only two forms of this statement, and if an explicit **Option Base** statement has not been set, the starting value will be 0 by default. For example, the declaration statement

```
Dim temp(5) As integer
```

creates an array of six integers consisting of elements `temp(0)` to `temp(5)`, except if the statement

```
Option Base 1
```

has been used. The **Option Base** statement is declared only once in the **Declarations** section of the (**General**) code window. Once this statement is used, all subsequently declared arrays, no matter where in the module they are declared, will begin at 1, not 0. For example, if you include this statement in the **Declarations** section and subsequently declare a `temp` array as `Dim temp(5) As Integer`, an array of exactly five locations will be created, with the first available location being `temp(1)` and the last available location being `temp(5)`. For all subsequent programs, we will use this form of the **Option Base** statement so that all of our arrays begin with the element having an index value of 1.[3]

Where To Declare Arrays

Arrays may be declared at either the procedure, module, or project level. An array declared within a procedure is local to the procedure and can only be accessed from within the procedure, unless it is passed as an argument to another procedure. An array declared in the **Declarations** section of a module's (**General**) code object will have either module or project scope, depending on the keyword used to declare the array. If the **Dim** keyword is used, the array will have module scope (that is, it can be accessed from any procedure in the module); otherwise, if the **Public** keyword is used, the array will have *project scope* (that is, it can be accessed from *any* procedure in any module attached to the project). Additionally, to create a local static array (one that will retain its elements' values between procedure calls) the array can be declared as **Static** within a procedure. Table 8-3 summarizes this information.

All of our programs will declare arrays at either the procedure or module level. Additionally, we will always use the `Option Base 1` statement to ensure that our arrays use a starting index value of 1. With this convention, good programming practice requires

---

2 Zero is the smallest permitted index value, as negative starting index values are not valid.

3 Another option is to simply ignore the fact that a zeroth element is available by not using it.

Table 8-3 Declaring Arrays

Placement	Declaration Keyword	Scope
Within a Procedure	Dim	Procedure Level
Within a Procedure	Static	Procedure Level but retains values between procedure calls.
Declaration section of the General code object	Dim	Module Level
Declaration section of the General code object	Public	Project Level

---

defining the upper index value (equivalent to the number of array items) as a constant before declaring the array. Thus, our array declarations will always use two statements such as

```
Const NUMGRADES As Integer = 6
Dim grades(NUMGRADES) As Integer
```

Further examples of this type of array declaration include:

```
Const NUMELS As Integer = 5
Dim temperature(NUMELS) As Integer

Const ARRAYSIZE As Integer = 4
Dim code(1 To ARRAYSIZE) As String*1
```
— *length of string*
```
Const SIZE As Integer = 100
Dim amount(1 To SIZE) As Single
```

In these declaration statements, each array is allocated sufficient memory to hold the number of data items declared. Thus, the array named `temperature` has storage reserved for five integer numbers, the array named `code` has storage reserved for four characters, and the array named `amount` has storage reserved for 100 single-precision numbers. The constant identifiers, NUMELS, ARRAYSIZE, and SIZE are programmer-selected names.

Using Indexed Variables

Indexed variables can be used anywhere that scalar variables are valid. Examples using the elements of the `grades` array are

```
grades(1) = 98
grades(2) = grades(1) - 11
grades(3) = grades(2)/2
grades(4) = 79
grades(4) = (grades(1) + grades(2) + grades(3)) / 2.2
sum = grades(1) + grades(2) + grades(3) + grades(4)
```

The index contained within parentheses need not be an integer constant; any expression that evaluates to an integer may be used as an index. In each case, of course, the value of the expression must be within the valid index range defined when the array is declared. For

---

Introduction to Visual Basic

example, assuming that i and j are integer variables, the following indexed variables are valid:

```
grades(i)
grades(2*i)
grades(j-i)
```

One extremely important advantage of using integer expressions as indices is that it allows sequencing through an array by using a loop. This makes statements like

```
sum = grades(1) + grades(2) + grades(3) + grades(4)
```

unnecessary. The index values in this statement can be replaced by a **For** loop counter to access each element in the array sequentially. For example, the code

```
sum = 0          ' initialize the sum to zero
For  i = 1 To 5
  sum = sum + grades(i)   ' add in a grade value
Next i
```

sequentially retrieves each array element and adds the element to sum. Here the variable i is used both as the counter in the **For** loop and as a index. As i increases by one each time through the loop, the next element in the array is referenced. The procedure for adding the array elements within the **For** loop is similar to the accumulation procedure we have used many times before.

The advantage of using a **For** loop to sequence through an array becomes apparent when working with larger arrays. For example, if the grades array contained 100 values rather than just five, simply changing the number 5 to 100 in the **For** statement is sufficient to sequence through the 100 elements and add each grades value to the sum.

As another example of using a **For** loop to sequence through an array, assume that we want to locate the maximum value in an array of 1000 elements named grades. The procedure we will use initially assumes that the first element in the array is the largest number. As we sequence through the array, the maximum is compared to each new element. When an element with a higher value is located, that element becomes the new maximum. The following code does the job.

```
Const NUMELS As Integer = 1000  ' This is declared in the General code
                                ' Declaration section

maximum = grades(1)                 ' set the maximum to element one
For  i = 2 To NUMELS                ' cycle through the rest of the array
  If grades(i) > maximum   Then     ' compare each element to the maximum
    maximum = grades(i)             ' capture the new high value
  End If
Next i
```

In this code, the **For** statement consists of one **If** statement. The search for a new maximum value starts with the second element of the array and continues through the last element. Each element is compared to the current maximum, and when a higher value is encountered, it becomes the new maximum.

Input and Output of Array Values

Individual array values can be assigned values and have their values displayed in the same manner used for scalar variables. Examples of individual data assignment statements include:

```
grades(1) = InputBox("Enter a value for grade 1", "Input request", "0")
grades(2) =  96.5
grades(3) = grade(2) * 1.2
```

In the first statement a single value will be read and stored in the indexed variable named grades(1). The second statement causes the value 96.5 to be in the indexed variable grades(2), while the last statement multiples grades(1) by 1.2 and assigns the value of this computation to grades(3).

Typically, for interactive data input, a loop is used to cycle through the array and each pass through the loop is used to assign a value to an array element. For example, the code

```
Const NUMELS As Integer = 5

message = "Enter a grade"
For i = 1 To NUMELS
    grades(i) = InputBox(message, "Input Dialog", "0")
Next i
```

prompts the user for five grades. The first value entered is stored in grades(1), the second value entered in grades(2), and so on until five grades have been input.

During output, individual array elements can be displayed using the **Print** method and complete sections of the array can be displayed by including a **Print** method within a loop. Examples of this include:

```
Print grades(2)
```
and
```
Print "The value of element "; i ;"  is"; grades(i)
```
and
```
Const NUMELS As Integer = 20

For  k = 5 To NUMELS
  Print k; amount(k)
Next k
```

The first statement displays the value of the indexed variable grades(2). The second statement displays the value of the index i and the value of grades(i). Before this statement can be executed, i would have to have an assigned value. Finally, the last example includes a **Print** method within a **For** loop. Both the value of the index and the value of the elements from 5 to 20 are displayed.

Program 8-1 illustrates these input and output techniques, using an array named grades that is defined to store six integer numbers. Included in the program are two **For** loops. The first **For** loop is used to cycle through each array element and allows the user to input individual array values. After six values have been entered, the second **For** loop is used to display the stored values.

Figure 8-2

Program 8-1's Interface

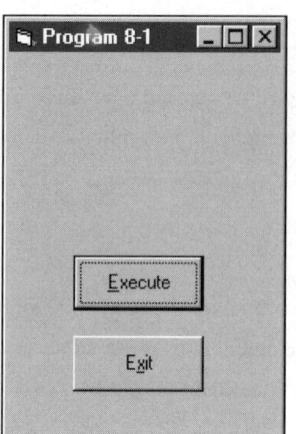

Table 8-4 Program 8-1's Properties Table		
Object	Property	Setting
Form	Name	frmMain
	Caption	Program 8-1
Command Button	Name	cmdExecute
	Caption	&Execute
Command Button	Name	cmdExit
	Caption	E&xit

Program 8-1's Event and General Object Code

```
Rem: General Object Declarations
Option Explicit
Option Base 1
Const MAXGRADES As Integer = 6
Dim grades(MAXGRADES)   ' create an array with 5 elements

Private Sub cmdShow_Click()
  Rem: preconditions - MAXGRADES and grades() set at the module level
  Dim i As Integer

  For i = 1 To MAXGRADES   ' Enter the grades
    grades(i) = InputBox("Enter a grade", "Input Dialog", "0")
  Next i

  For i = 1 To MAXGRADES       ' Print the grades
    Print "grades("; i; ") is "; grades(i)
  Next i
End Sub

Private Sub cmdExit_Click()
  Beep
  End
End Sub
```

(handwritten margin note: If we write them we Const them we can't change the value)

(handwritten annotations near code: 6 8)

Figure 8-3

A Sample Output Using Program 8-1

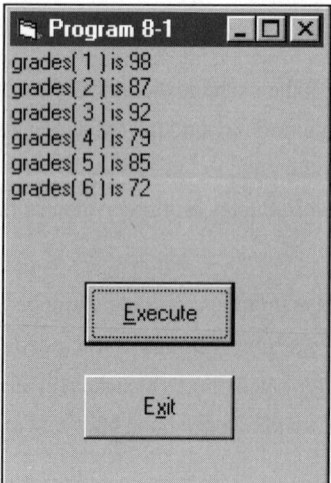

A sample run of Program 8-1 produced the output illustrated in Figure 8-3.

In reviewing the output produced by Program 8-1, pay particular attention to the difference between the index value displayed and the numerical value stored in the corresponding array element. The index value refers to the location of the element in the array, while the indexed variable refers to the value stored in the designated location. *(handwritten: of what is)*

In addition to simply displaying the values stored in each array element, the elements can also be processed by appropriately referencing the desired element. For example, assume that the `cmdShow_Click` event procedure in Program 8-1 is modified to Procedure Code 8-1.

Procedure Code 8-1

```
Private Sub cmdShow_Click()
   Rem: preconditions - MAXGRADES and grades() set at the module level
   Dim i As Integer
   Dim total As Integer
   Dim basestring As String
   Dim message As String

   basestring = "Enter grade "
   For i = 1 To MAXGRADES   ' Enter the grades
      message = basestring + Str(i)
      grades(i) = InputBox(message, "Input Dialog", "0")
   Next i

   Cls
   Print "The total of the grades"
   For i = 1 To MAXGRADES     ' Print the grades
      Print grades(i)
      total = total + grades(i)
   Next i
   Print "is"; total
End Sub
```

In this modified code the value of each element is accumulated in a total, which is displayed after the display of each array element. Also notice in this event code that we have included an "individualized" message within the **InputBox** function by concatenating the string version of the index i to the output message.

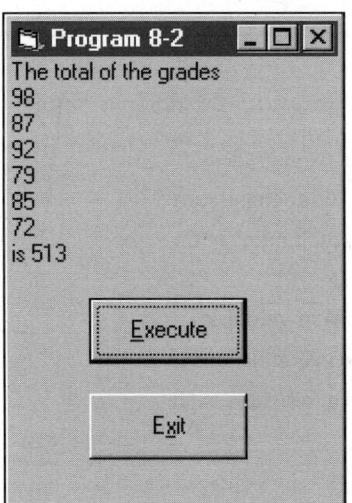

Figure 8-4

A Sample Output Using Program 8-2

Thus, the message displayed in first input box will be `Enter grade 1`, the message displayed in the second input request will be `Enter grade 2`, and so on. This event code is used in Program 8-2, which is identical in all respects to Program 8-1, except for the form's caption and the new `cmdShow_Click` event procedure. A sample output produced by executing this event code is shown in Figure 8-4.

Notice that in the output displayed in Figure 8-4, unlike that shown in Figure 8-3, only the values stored in each array element are displayed. Although the second **For** loop was used to accumulate the total of each element, the accumulation could also have been accomplished in the first loop by placing the statement `total = total + grades(i)` after the **InputBox** function was used to enter a value. Also notice that the **Print** used to display the total is made outside of the second **For** loop, so that the total is displayed only once, after all values have been added to the total. If this **Print** statement were placed inside of the **For** loop, six totals would be displayed, with only the last displayed total containing the sum of all of the array values.

The LBound and UBound Functions

Two useful Visual Basic functions that provide the smallest and largest available subscript value of an array, respectively, are the **LBound** and **UBound** functions. These function names are derived from the terms *Lower Bound* and *Upper Bound*. For example, if the array `test` is declared using the declaration statement

```
Dim test(10) As Integer
```

then `UBound(test)` will return a value of 10, and `LBound(test)` will return either a 0 or 1, depending on the setting or the **Option Base**. Similarly, for the declaration

```
Dim test(-5 to 7) As Integer
```

`UBound(test)` will return 7, and `LBound(test)` will return –5. These two functions are useful in processing array elements within **For** loops using the syntax

```
For i = LBound(array-name) To UBound(array-name)
    statement(s)
Next i
```

Exercises 8.1

1. Using the **Dim** keyword, write array declarations for the following:

   a. a list of 100 single precision grades
   b. a list of 50 single precision temperatures
   c. a list of 30 characters, each representing a code
   d. a list of 100 integer years
   e. a list of 32 single precision velocities
   f. a list of 1000 single precision distances
   g. a list of 6 integer code numbers

2. Write appropriate notation for the first, third, and seventh elements of the following arrays, assuming that the `Option Base 1` statement has been used.

    a. `Dim grade(20) As Integer`
    b. `Dim grade(10) As Single`
    c. `Dim amps(16) As Single`
    d. `Dim distance(15) As Integer`
    e. `Dim velocity(25) As Single`
    f. `Dim time(100) As Single`

3. a. Write individual **InputBox** function calls that can be used to enter values into the first, third, and seventh elements of each of the arrays declared in Exercises 2a. through 2f.
    b. Write a **For** loop that can be used to enter values for the complete array declared in Exercise 2a.

4. a. Write individual **Print** statements that can be used to print the values from the first, third, and seventh elements of each of the arrays declared in Exercises 2a. through 2f.
    b. Write a **For** loop that can be used to display values for the complete array declared in Exercise 2a.

5. List the elements that will be displayed by the following sections of code:

    ```
    a. For m = 1 To 5
           Print a(m)
       Next m
    ```

    ```
    b. For  k = 1 To 5 Step 2
           Print  a(k)
       Next k
    ```

    ```
    c. For j = 3 To 10 Step 1
           Print b(j)
       Next j
    ```

    ```
    d. For  k = 3 To 12  Step 3
           Print b(k)
       Next k
    ```

    ```
    e. For  i = 2 To  11 Step 2
           Print c(i )
       Next i
    ```

6. a. Write a program to input the following values into an array named `prices`: 10.95, 16.32, 12.15, 8.22, 15.98, 26.22, 13.54, 6.45, 17.59. After the data has been entered, have your program output the values.

b. Repeat Exercise 6a., but after the data has been entered, have your program display it in the following form:

```
10.95   16.32   12.15
 8.22   15.98   26.22
13.54    6.45   17.59
```

7. Write a program to input eight integer numbers into an array named `temp`. As each number is input, add the numbers into a total. After all numbers are input, display the numbers and their average.

8. a. Write a program to input 10 integer numbers into an array named `fmax` and determine the maximum value entered. Your program should contain only one loop and the maximum should be determined as array element values are being input. (**Hint:** Set the maximum equal to the first array element, which should be input before the loop used to input the remaining array values.)

   b. Repeat Exercise 8a., keeping track of both the maximum element in the array and the index number for the maximum. After displaying the numbers, print these two messages

```
The maximum value is: ___
This is element number ___ in the list of numbers
```

   Have your program display the correct values in place of the underlines in the messages.

   c. Repeat Exercise 8b., but have your program locate the minimum of the data entered.

9. a. Write a program to input the following integer numbers into an array named `grades`: 89, 95, 72, 83, 99. As each number is input, add the numbers to a total. After all numbers are input and the total is obtained, calculate the average of the numbers and use the average to determine the deviation of each value from the average. Store each deviation in an array named `deviation`. Each deviation is obtained as the element value less the average of all the data. Have your program display each deviation alongside its corresponding element from the `grades` array.

   b. Calculate the variance of the data used in Exercise 9a. The variance is obtained by squaring each individual deviation and dividing the sum of the squared deviations by the number of deviations.

10. Write a program that stores the following prices in an array named `prices`: 9.92, 6.32, 12.63, 5.95, 10.29. Your program should also create two arrays named `units` and `amounts`, each capable of storing five double-precision numbers. Using a **For** loop and an **InputBox** function call, have your program accept five user-input numbers into the `units` array when the program is run. Your program should store the product of the corresponding values in the `prices` and `units` arrays in the `amounts` array (for

example, `amounts(1)` = `prices(1)` * `units(1))` and display the following output (fill in the table appropriately).

```
Price   Units   Amount
-----   -----   ------
 9.92     .       .
 6.32     .       .
12.63     .       .
 5.95     .       .
10.29     .       .
                ------
Total:            .
```

11. Write a program that specifies three one-dimensional arrays named `prices`, `quantity`, and `amount`. Each array should be capable of holding 10 elements. Using a **For** loop, input values for the `prices` and `quantity` arrays. The entries in the `amount` array should be the product of the corresponding values in the `prices` and `quantity` arrays (thus, `amount(i)` = `price(i)` * `quantity(i))`. After all the data has been entered, display the following output:

```
Price   Quantity   Amount
-----   --------   ------
```

Under each column heading, display the appropriate value.

12. a. Write a program that inputs 10 float numbers into an array named `raw`. After 10 user-input numbers are entered into the array, your program should cycle through `raw` 10 times. During each pass through the array, your program should select the lowest value in `raw` and place the selected value in the next available slot in an array named `sorted`. Thus, when your program is complete, the `sorted` array should contain the numbers in `raw` in sorted order from lowest to highest. (**Hint:** Make sure to reset the lowest value selected during each pass to a very high number so that it is not selected again. You will need a second **For** loop within the first **For** loop to locate the minimum value for each pass.)

    b. The method used in Exercise 12a. to sort the values in the array is very inefficient. Can you determine why? What might be a better method of sorting the numbers in an array?

8.2 Additional Array Capabilities

All of the arrays we have considered have had modular scope. There are times, however, when you might want to declare an array within a procedure. Once such technique involves setting the array size during run-time based on user input, rather than at design-time. How this is done is described in this section. Also described is the method for passing local arrays into procedures as arguments. Finally, additional array processing techniques are presented, including the declaration and processing of multi-dimensional arrays.

Dynamic Arrays

There are times when you, as a designer, will not know how large an array must be. Fortunately, Visual Basic provides a means of changing an array's size at run-time. Such arrays are referred to as *dynamic arrays*. A dynamic array can be resized at any time during program execution. For example, you might need a very large array for a short period of time. Rather than allocate a fixed array size that will remain in effect throughout the program's execution, you can create a dynamic array. Then, when you no longer need the array, you can redimension it to a smaller size.

The method for creating a dynamic array is rather simple. First, in the **Declarations** section of the (**General**) code object, declare the array using either the **Public** or **Dim** keyword, to give the array either a project or module level scope, respectively. Alternatively, if you want the array to be local to a particular procedure, declare it using either the **Dim** or **Static** keyword within a procedure. The key, however, is to give the array an empty dimension value. For example, the declaration

```
Dim Dynar() As Integer
```

creates an integer dynamic array named `Dynar`. To actually set the size of the array you must use the **ReDim** statement, which can only appear within an procedure. The **ReDim** statement is an executable statement that redimensions the size of the array at run-time. For example, the statements:

```
n = InputBox("Enter the number of grades", "Input Dialog", "0")
ReDim Dynar(n)        how many slots the user wants
```

will cause the `Dynar` array to have the number of elements entered by the user in response to the Input dialog request. Similarly, the statement:

```
ReDim Dynar(10)
```

causes the `Dynar` array to be redimensioned to accommodate 10 integers.

Unless specific steps are taken to preserve the values in a dynamic array, these values will be lost when the array is redimensioned. If you want to resize an array without losing the existing element values, use the **Preserve** keyword. Thus, the statement

```
ReDim Preserve Dynar(UBound(Dynar) + 15)
```

enlarges the `Dynar` array by 15 elements, without losing the existing element values.

Arrays as Arguments

An individual array element can be passed to a general procedure (**Sub** and **Function**) in the same manner as any scalar variable. For a single array element this is done by including the element as an indexed variable in a **Call** statement's argument list. For example, the procedure call

```
Call Fmax(temp(2),temp(5))
```

makes the individual array elements `temp(2)` and `temp(5)` available to the `Fmax` procedure.

Passing a complete array to a procedure is, in many respects, an easier operation than passing individual elements. For example, if `temp` is an array, the statement `Call Fmax(temp)` makes the complete `temp` array available to the `Fmax` procedure.

On the receiving side, the called procedure must be alerted that an array is being made available. For example, assuming `temp` was declared as `Dim temp(5) As Integer`, a suitable procedure heading and parameter declaration for the `Fmax` procedure is

```
Public Sub Fmax(vals() As Integer)
```

In this procedure heading, the parameter name `vals` is local to the procedure. However, `vals` refers to the original array created outside the procedure. This is made clear in Procedure Code 8-2, where the `temp` array that is declared local to the `Form_Click` event procedure is passed to the `Fmax` procedure.

Procedure Code 8-2

```
Private Sub Form_Click()
Dim temp(5) As Integer

  temp(1) = 2
  temp(2) = 18
  temp(3) = 1
  temp(4) = 27
  temp(5) = 6
  Call Fmax(temp)
End Sub

Public Sub Fmax(vals() As Integer)
  Dim i As Integer

  max = vals(1)
  For i = 2 To 5
    If max < vals(i) Then max = vals(i)
  Next i
  Print "The maximum value is"; maximum
End Sub
```

Figure 8-5

Only One Array Is Created

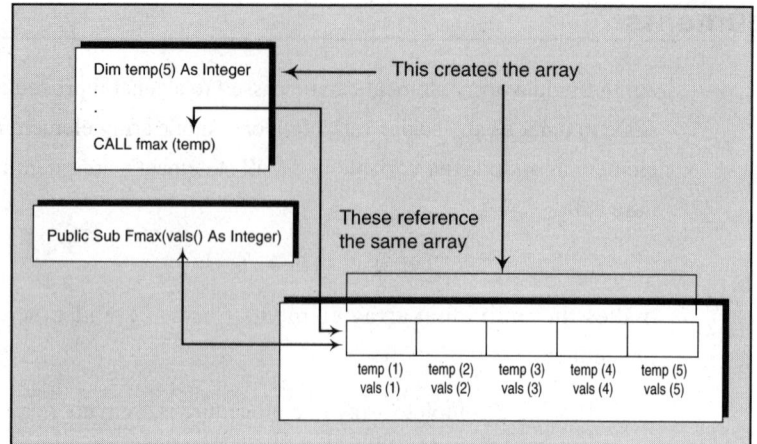

Only one array is created in Procedure Code 8-2. In the `Form_Click` procedure this array is known as `temp`, and in `Fmax`, the array is known as `vals`. As illustrated in Figure 8-5, both names refer to the same array. Thus, in Figure 8-5 `vals(3)` is the same element as `temp(3)`.

Figure 8-6

The Starting Location of the Array Is Passed

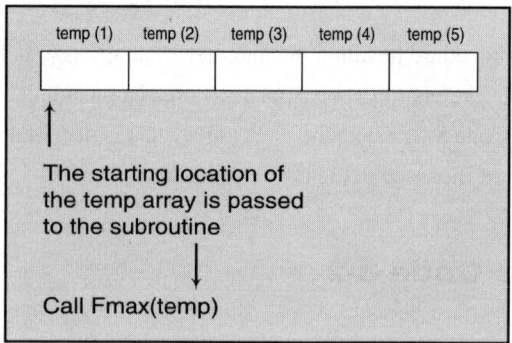

Notice that the parameter declaration for `vals` in `Fmax` does not contain the number of elements in the array. This makes sense when you realize that only one item is actually passed to `Fmax` when the procedure is called. As you might have suspected, the item passed is the starting location of the `temp` array. This is illustrated in Figure 8-6.

Now let us generalize `Fmax` to find and return the maximum value of an integer array of arbitrary size. Consider Procedure Code 8-3.

Procedure Code 8-3

```
Private Sub Form_Click()
  Const NUMELS As Integer = 5
  Dim temp(5) As Integer
  Dim maximum As Integer

  temp(1) = 2
  temp(2) = 18
  temp(3) = 1
  temp(4) = 27
  temp(5) = 6
  Call Fmax(temp, NUMELS, maximum)
  Print "The maximum value is"; maximum
End Sub
```

(continued)

```
Public Sub Fmax(vals() As Integer, final As Integer, max As Integer)
  Dim i As Integer

  max = vals(1)
  For i = 2 To final
    If max < vals(i) Then max = vals(i)
  Next i
End Sub
```

The more general form of `Fmax` listed in Procedure Code 8-3 returns the maximum value in any single-dimensioned integer array passed to it. The procedure expects that an integer array and the number of elements in the array will be passed into it as arguments. Then, using the number of elements as the boundary for its search, the procedure's **For** loop causes each array element to be examined in sequential order to locate the maximum value. This value is passed back to the calling routine through the third argument in the function call. The output displayed when the code is executed is

```
The maximum value is 27
```

Multi-Dimensional Arrays

In addition to one-dimensional arrays, Visual Basic provides the capability of defining and using larger array sizes. A *two-dimensional* array consists of both rows and columns of elements. For example, the array of numbers

$$
\begin{array}{cccc}
8 & 16 & 9 & 52 \\
3 & 15 & 27 & 6 \\
14 & 25 & 2 & 10
\end{array}
$$

is called a two-dimensional array of integers. This array consists of three rows and four columns. To reserve storage for this array, both the number of rows and the number of columns must be included in the array's declaration. For example, the declaration

```
Dim vals(3, 4) As Integer
```

specifies that `vals` is a two-dimensional array having 3 rows and 4 columns.[4]

Similarly, the declarations

```
Dim volts(10,5) As Single
Dim code (6,26) As String *4
```

specify that the array `volts` consists of 10 rows and 5 columns of single-precision numbers and that the array `code` consists of 6 rows and 26 columns, with each element capable of holding 4 characters.

---

[4] The more general declaration syntax is **Dim** array-name(n1 To n2, m1 To m2), where n1 and m1 represent the lower bounds, and n2 and m2 represent the upper bounds on the first and second index values, respectively.

Figure 8-7

*Each Array Element Is
Identified by Its Row and
Column Position*

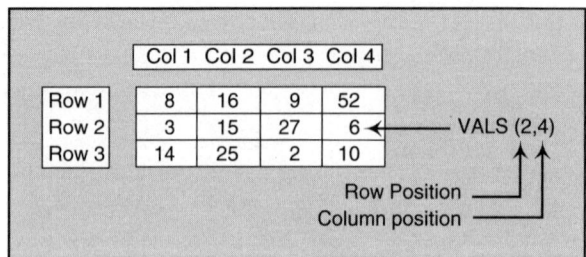

To make it possible to locate an element in a two-dimensional array, each element is identified by its position in the array. As illustrated in Figure 8-7, the term `vals(2,4)` uniquely identifies the element in row 2, column 4. As with one-dimensional array variables, two-dimensional array variables can be used anywhere that scalar variables are valid. Examples using elements of the `vals` array are

```
watts = vals(2,3)
vals(1,1) = 62
newnum = 4 * (vals(2,1) - 5)
sumrow1 = vals(1,1) + vals(1,2) + vals(1,3) + vals(1,4)
```

The last statement causes the values of the four elements in row 1 to be added and the sum to be stored in the scalar variable `sumrow1`.

As with one-dimensional arrays, two-dimensional arrays can be declared either at the project, module, or procedure level. Additionally, as with one-dimensional arrays, two-dimensional array elements are processed and displayed using individual element notation, as illustrated in Procedure Code 8-4.

Following is the display produced when Procedure Code 8-4 is executed:

```
Display of vals() by explicit element
10   20   30   40
15   25   35   45
50   60   70   89
Display of vals() using a nested loop
10   20   30   40
15   25   35   45
50   60   70   89
```

The first display of the `vals` array produced by Procedure Code 8-4 is constructed by explicitly designating each array element. The second display of array element values, which is identical to the first, is produced using a nested **For** loop. Nested loops are especially useful when dealing with two-dimensional arrays, because they allow the programmer to easily designate and cycle through each element. In Procedure Code 8-4, the variable `i` controls the outer loop and the variable `j` controls the inner loop. Each pass through the outer loop corresponds to a single row, with the inner loop supplying the appropriate column elements. After a complete column is printed, a new line is started for the next row. The effect is a display of the array in a row-by-row fashion.

Once two-dimensional array elements have been assigned to an array, processing can begin. Typically, **For** loops are used to process two-dimensional arrays because, as was previously noted, they allow the programmer to easily designate and cycle through each array element. For example, the nested **For** loop in the following code is used to multiply each element in the `vals` array by the scalar number 10.

Procedure Code 8-4

```
Rem: This code is in the [General] object's [declaration section]
Option Explicit
Option Base 1
Const ROWS As Integer = 3
Const COLS As Integer = 4
Dim vals(ROWS, COLS) As Integer

Rem: This is a [General] procedure used to initialize the array
Private Sub setvals()
  vals(1, 1) = 10
  vals(1, 2) = 20
  vals(1, 3) = 30
  vals(1, 4) = 40
  vals(2, 1) = 15
  vals(2, 2) = 25
  vals(2, 3) = 35
  vals(2, 4) = 54
  vals(3, 1) = 50
  vals(3, 2) = 60
  vals(3, 3) = 70
  vals(3, 4) = 80
End Sub

Private Sub Form_Click()
  Dim i As Integer, j As Integer      two subscripts
  Call setvals
  Cls
  Rem: display by explicit element
     Print "Display of vals() by explicit element"
     Print vals(1, 1); vals(1, 2); vals(1, 3); vals(1, 4)
     Print vals(2, 1); vals(2, 2); vals(2, 3); vals(2, 4)
     Print vals(3, 1); vals(3, 2); vals(3, 3); vals(3, 4)
  Rem: Display using a nested loop
     Print
     Print "Display of vals() using a nested loop"
     For i = 1 To ROWS
       For j = 1 To COLS
          Print vals(i, j);
       Next j
     Print
     Next i
End Sub
```

```
       For i = 1 To ROWS
         For j = 1 To COLS
            vals(i,j) = 10 * vals(i,j)
         Next j
       Next i
```

Although arrays with more than two dimensions are not commonly used, Visual Basic does allow larger arrays to be declared. This can be done by listing the maximum size of all indices for the array. For example, the declaration response(4, 10, 6) specifies a three-dimensional array. Assuming the **Option Base** has been set to 1, the first element in the array is designated as response(1,1,1) and the last element as response(4,10,6).[5]

Figure 8-8

Representation of a Three-Dimensional Array

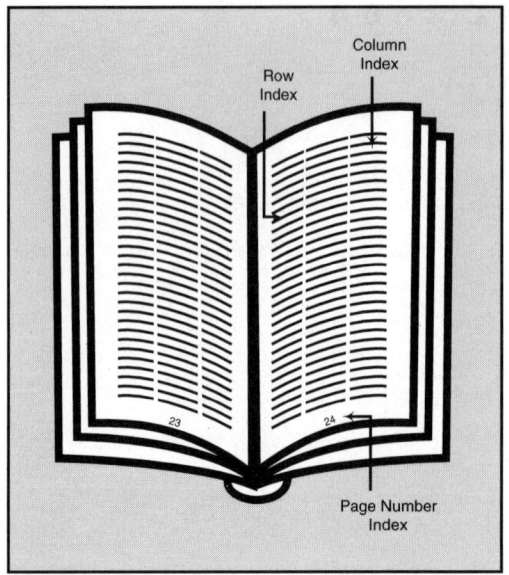

Conceptually, as illustrated in Figure 8-8, a three-dimensional array can be viewed as a book of data tables. Using this visualization, the first index can be thought of as the location of the desired row in a table, the second index value as the desired column, and the third index value as the page number of the selected table.

Similarly, arrays having at most sixty dimensions can be declared. Conceptually, a four-dimensional array can be represented as a shelf of books, where the fourth dimension is used to specify a desired book on the shelf, and a five-dimensional array can be viewed as a bookcase filled with books where the fifth dimension refers to a selected shelf in the bookcase. Using the same analogy, a six-dimensional array can be considered as a single row of bookcases where the sixth dimension references the desired bookcase in the row. Finally, a seven-dimensional array can be considered as multiple rows of bookcases where the seventh dimension references the desired row. Alternatively, three-, four-, five-, six-, and seven-dimensional arrays can be viewed as mathematical *n*-tuples of order three, four, five, six, and seven, respectively.

Passing Multi-dimensional Arrays

Multi-dimensional arrays are passed as arguments in a process identical to passing one-dimensional arrays. The called procedure receives access to the entire array. For example, consider Procedure Code 8-5.

Procedure Code 8-5

```
Private Sub Form_Click()
  Dim vals(2, 3) As Integer
  vals(1, 1) = 10
  vals(1, 2) = 20
  vals(2, 1) = 30
  vals(2, 2) = 40

  Call average(vals)
End Sub

Private Sub show(nums() As Integer)
  Dim i As Integer, j As Integer

  Print nums(1, 1)
  Print nums(1, 2)
  Print nums(2, 1)
  Print nums(2, 2)
End Sub
```

---

5 Again, as with single- and double-dimensioned arrays, both the lower and upper bounds of each index can be specified in the declaration statement for larger dimensioned arrays.

Only one array is created in Procedure Code 8-5. This array is known as `vals` in the calling procedure and as `nums` in the `show` procedure. Thus, `vals(1,2)` refers to the same element as `nums(1,2)`. The following display is produced when this procedure code is executed:

```
10
20
30
40
```

Arrays and Strings

Arrays and strings are frequently used together in many programming situations. For example, assume that we need to develop a function that returns the day of the week corresponding to its ordinal number. As a first attempt at solving this problem, consider Procedure Code 8-6.

Procedure Code 8-6

```
Private Sub Form_Click()
    Dim thisday As String
    Dim d As Integer

    d = InputBox("Enter a day (ex. 1 for Sunday)")
    thisday = Dayname(d)
    Print "This corresponds to "; thisday
End Sub

Public Function Dayname(dayint)
    Dim days(7) As String * 3

    days(1) = "Sun"
    days(2) = "Mon"
    days(3) = "Tue"
    days(4) = "Wed"
    days(5) = "Thu"
    days(6) = "Fri"
    days(7) = "Sat"
    Dayname = days(dayint)
End Function
```

The function `Dayname` listed in Procedure Code 8-6 uses an array of strings to store the seven day names, and selects the correct day, using each day's ordinal value as an index into the `days` array. While this solution works, we can actually do much better by considering the string data as a single array of characters. Using this conceptualization, the day name data is incorporated into a single `days` string as follows:

```
days ="SunMonTueWedThuFriSat"
```

In this string each group of three characters constitutes a day's name and the complete string is simply a convenient way of holding seven individual pieces of data. To extract any single name requires knowing the starting index position of the beginning letter and then extracting three characters from this position. For example, the expression Mid(days,4,3) extracts the characters `Mon`, starting from position 4 in the `days` string. Procedure Code 8-7 illustrates how this expression can be used within the `Dayname` function to locate and return the correct day.

Procedure Code 8-7

```
Private Sub Form_Click()
    Dim thisday As String
    Dim d As Integer

    d = InputBox("Enter a day (ex. 1 for Sunday)")
    thisday = Dayname(d)
    Print "This corresponds to "; thisday
End Sub

Public Function Dayname(dayint)
    Const DAYLENGTH As Integer = 3
    Dim days As String

    days = "SunMonTueWedThuFriSat"
    Dayname = Mid(days, DAYLENGTH * (dayint - 1) + 1, DAYLENGTH)
End Function
```

Notice that the starting index value into the string is determined by the expression `DAYLENGTH * (dayint - 1) + 1`, where `DAYLENGTH` is a named constant having a value of 3 and is the length of each day's name. Once the starting position is located, the next three characters are extracted. In using strings in this manner, the "trick" is always determining an expression that correctly locates the effective starting index value.

Arrays and Variants

Array elements can be of any type, including **Variants**, which we will consider shortly. First, however, we will create a **Variant** that contains an array. Although this is conceptually different from an array whose elements are of type **Variant**, the way that elements are accessed is the same. For example, consider the following code:

```
Dim A As Variant, B As Integer
A = Array(10, 20, 30, 40)
B = A(3)
A(4) = 50
```

Notice that A is a scalar variable of type **Variant**. The **Array** function is an intrinsic Visual Basic function that returns a **Variant** *containing* an array. Thus, the statement `A = Array(10, 20, 30, 40)` assigns an array of 4 integers to the variable A. At this point, A can be processed as a typical array. Thus, in the third statement we access an element from the `Variant` array and assign its value to the scalar variable B, while the last statement uses standard array notation to alter an element's value.

A very useful structure in connection with **Variant** variables is the **For Each** loop having the syntax

```
For Each element In variant-variable
    statement(s)
Next element
```

As an example using this repetition statement, consider Procedure Code 8-8.

Procedure Code 8-8

```
Private Sub Form_Click()
  Dim item As Variant
  Dim A As Variant
  Dim total As Single

  A = Array(10, 20, 30, 40)
  For Each item In A
    total = total + item
  Next item
  Print "The total is"; total
End Sub
```

The output produced by Procedure Code 8-8 is

```
The total is 100
```

The advantage of using a **For Each**, rather than a **For/Next** loop, is that the exact number of elements in the array need not be known. The disadvantage is that it requires an additional variable that must be a **Variant** data type. The loop itself, however, is not restricted to **Variant** arrays. For example, in Procedure Code 8-9 a **For Each** loop is used to cycle through an array of integers.

Procedure Code 8-9

```
Private Sub Form_Click()
  Const NUMELS As Integer = 4       name of array name
  Dim item As Variant
  Dim a(NUMELS) As Integer
  Dim total As Single

  a(1) = 10
  a(2) = 20
  a(3) = 30
  a(4) = 40
  For Each item In a               If we don't know the number
    total = total + item           for array. It must be variant.
  Next item
  Print "The total is"; total
End Sub
```

Having constructed a single **Variant** variable as an array using the **Array** function, as in Procedure Code 8-8, we can extend this concept by making each array element an array. For example, consider Procedure Code 8-10.

Procedure Code 8-10

```
Private Sub Form_Click()
  Const NUMELS As Integer = 3
  Dim unit As Variant
  Dim bowler(NUMELS) As Variant
  Dim total As Single
  Dim i As Integer, j As Integer
```

(continued)

```
Cls
bowler(1) = Array("Abrams, B.", 180, 219, 210)
bowler(2) = Array("Bohm, P.", 155, 250, 207)
bowler(3) = Array("Ernst, T.", 195, 245, 235)

For i = 1 To 3
  total = 0
  Print "Bowler: "; bowler(i)(1)
  For j = 2 To 4
    total = total + bowler(i)(j)
  Next j
  Print "  Average Score:"; total / 3
Next i
End Sub
```

In this code we have constructed an array of three **Variants**, each of which contains an array. The outer loop accesses each **Variant** element, while the inner loop accesses individual elements within each **Variant**. Notice, however, the unusual notation. For example, bowler(1) refers to the first **Variant** array. Within this array, the notation bowler(1)(1) refers to the first element, which is the name Abrams, B. Effectively, we have produced a one-dimensional array of one-dimensional arrays.

The **For** loop in Procedure Code 8-10 can be replaced by the following, which uses an **If** statement to determine the type of element being processed:

```
For i = 1 To 3
  total = 0
  For Each unit In bowler(i)
    If IsNumeric(unit) Then
      total = total + Val(unit)
    Else
      Print "Bowler: "; unit
    End If
  Next unit
  Print "  Average Score:"; total / 3
Next i
```

In using **Variant** variables, you should be aware of the following considerations:

1. A **Variant** variable has an **Empty** value before it is assigned a value. This is a special value, different from either the number 0 or the zero-length string "".
2. A **Variant** with an **Empty** value can still be used in an expression. Depending on the context, it will be treated either as a 0 or zero-length string.
3. The **Empty** value disappears as soon as a value is assigned to the **Variant**.
4. A **Variant** variable can be set back to an **Empty** value by assigning the keyword **Empty** to the variable.
5. A **Variant** variable can also be assigned the named constant **Null**.
6. The **IsNull** function can be used to test if a **Variant** variable contains the **Null** value

7. The **VarType** function can be used to test the type of value in a **Variant** or any variable, except for a user-defined type. This function is typically used within an **If** statement

> **If** VarType(*variable*) = *constant* **Then**
>   *statement(s)*
> **End If**

where **constant** is one of the named constants listed in Table 8-5.

Table 8-5 VarType Function Return Values

Constant	Value	Variable Argument's Data Type
vbEmpty	0	Empty (uninitialized)
vbNull	1	Null (no valid data)
vbInteger	2	Integer
vbLong	3	Long integer
vbSingle	4	Single-precision floating-point number
vbDouble	5	Double-precision floating-point number
vbCurrency	6	Currency
vbDate	7	Date
vbString	8	String
vbObject	9	Ole object
vbError	10	Error
vbBoolean	11	Boolean
vbVariant	12	Variant (used only with arrays of Variants)
vbDataObject	13	Non-OLE object
vbByte	17	Byte
vbAarray	8192	Array

The named constants listed in Table 8-5 are specified by Visual Basic and can be used in any procedure code.

Exercises 8.2

1. Modify the `Fmax` procedure in Procedure Code 8-3 to locate and return the minimum value of the passed array.

2. Write a program that stores the following numbers into a local array named `grades`: 65.3, 72.5, 75.0, 83.2, 86.5, 94.0, 96.0, 98.8, 100. There should be a procedure call to `show` that accepts the `grades` array as a parameter named `grades` and then displays the numbers in the array.

3. Write a program that declares three one-dimensional arrays named `price`, `quantity`, and `amount`. Each array should be capable of holding 5 single-precision numbers. The numbers that should be stored in `price` are 10.62, 14.89, 13.21, 16.55, 18.62. The numbers that should be stored in `quantity` are 4, 8.5, 6, 7.35, 9. Your program should pass these three arrays to a procedure called `extend`, which should calculate the elements in the `amount` array as the product of the equivalent elements in the `price` and `quantity` arrays (for example, `amount(1) = price(1) * quantity(1)`).

After `extend` has put values into the `amount` array, the values in the array should be displayed from within the procedure that called `extend`.

4. Write a program that includes two functions named `average` and `variance`. The average function should calculate and return the average of the values stored in an array named `testvals`. The `testvals` array should be declared as a local array and include the values 89, 95, 72, 83, 99, 86. The `variance` function should calculate and return the variance of the data. The variance is obtained by subtracting the average from each value in `testvals`, squaring the values obtained, adding them, and dividing by the number of elements in `testvals`. The values returned from `average` and `variance` should be displayed from within the procedure that called these functions.

5. Write appropriate declaration statements for

   a. an array of integers with 6 rows and 10 columns named `nums`
   b. an array of integers with 2 rows and 5 columns named `nums`
   c. an array of single characters with 7 rows and 12 columns named `codes`
   d. an array of single characters with 15 rows and 7 columns named `codes`
   e. an array of single precision numbers with 10 rows and 25 columns named `vals`
   f. an array of single precision numbers with 16 rows and 8 columns named `vals`

6. Write a Visual Basic function that can be used to add the values of all elements in the `nums` array used in Exercise 5a. and returns the total.

7. Write a Visual Basic program that adds equivalent elements of the two-dimensional arrays named `first` and `second`. Both arrays should have two rows and three columns. For example, element (1,2) of the resulting array should be the sum of `first(1,2)` and `second(1,2)`. The `first` and `second` arrays should be initialized as follows:

   ```
        first       second
   -------------------------
   16    18    23  24   52   77
   54    91    11  16   19   59
   ```

8. a. Write a Visual Basic program that finds and displays the maximum value in a two-dimensional array of integers. The array should be declared as a two-by-three array of integers and initialized with the following numbers: 16, 22, 99, 4, 18, -258.
   b. Modify the program written in Exercise 8a. so that it also displays the maximum value's row and column index values.

9. Write a procedure that multiplies each element of a three-row-by-four-column array by a scalar number. Both the array name and the number by which each element is to be multiplied are to be passed into the procedure as parameters.

10. Modify Procedure Code 8-7 so that the complete name of each day is returned. **Hint:** You will have to make `DAYLENGTH` equal to the length of the longest day.

11. Write a function named `Moname` that returns a month's name corresponding to the integer that represents the month. Use the string `months = "JanFebMarAprMayJunJulAugSepOctNovDec"` in your function.

12. a. Write a function named `Seasons` that return a season's name corresponding to the integer representing the season. Use the relationship that the numbers 1, 2, 3, and 4 correspond to the seasons Winter, Spring, Summer, and Autumn, respectively.

   b. Modify the function written for Exercise 12a. so that it returns the season corresponding to each month. Use the following assignments:

Months	Season
Dec, Jan, Feb	Winter
Mar, Apr, May	Spring
Jun, Jul, Aug	Summer
Sep, Oct, Nov	Autumn

Hint: Convert the month to an equivalent season using the expression (m Mod 12) / 3 + 1.

8.3 Control Arrays

Just as variables of the same data type can be grouped in an array, a set of controls having the same type can also be grouped as an array of controls. When this is done, a group of controls is referred to as a *control array*. Each control in the array shares the common group name, and individual controls are distinguished by an index number. Using control arrays can save coding because all the controls in the array share the same event procedures as well as the same group name. To see how this works in practice, consider the design-time interface shown in Figure 8-9.

If each Text box in Program 8-3's interface is given a unique name, then each control receives its own set of event codes. Let's assume that we want to clear both Picture boxes whenever a Text box receives the focus. Since there are three sets of **GotFocus** events (one for each Text box), we would have to code each event separately. Assuming the Picture boxes are named `picTotal` and `picError`, respectively, we would either have to include the two statements

```
picTotal.Cls
picError.Cls
```

in each Text box's **GotFocus** event procedure, or include these statements in a general procedure and place a call to this procedure in each Text box's **GotFocus** event procedure. Another solution is to give all three Text boxes the same name. When this is done the **Index** property of the first box gets automatically changed to 0, the second box gets an **Index** value of 1, and the third an

Figure 8-9

Program 8-3's Design-Time Interface

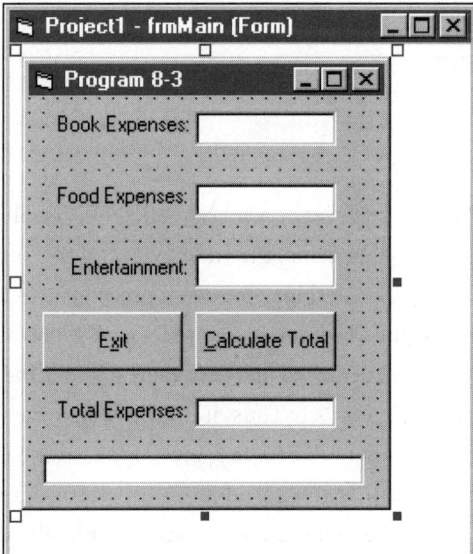

Index value of 2 (by default, each of these boxes has an initial **Index** property that is blank). Once a control has an **Index** value, it is accessed by giving both its **Name** and **Index** value (with the **Index** enclosed in parentheses). For example, assuming that the Text boxes in Figure 8-9 are all named `txtExpense`, then

```
txtExpense(0) refers to the Text box with Index value 0
txtExpense(1) refers to the Text box with Index value 1
txtExpense(2) refers to the Text box with Index value 2
```

All of these Text boxes now share the same name but have a unique **Index** property value used to distinguish one element of the control array from another. Each time one of the controls in the group activates an event, Visual Basic calls a common event procedure and passes the **Index** value as an argument. It is this **Index** value that identifies which control triggered the event. For example, the header line for the `txtExpense_GotFocus` event procedure is

```
Private Sub txtExpense_GotFocus(Index As Integer)
```

Thus, if the first Text box gets the focus, Visual Basic passes 0 as the **Index** parameter, if the second Text box gets the focus, a 1 is passed as the **Index** parameter, and so on. This **Index** parameter can then be used or not, as required, within the event procedure. In our application, for example, we will want to clear both Picture boxes, no matter which Text box receives the focus. So for this application the **GotFocus** event procedure will not need to distinguish between Text boxes. The code that we will use for this event is

```
Private Sub txtExpense_GotFocus(Index As Integer)
    picError.Cls
    picTotal.Cls
End Sub
```

The advantage here is that we have written one event code that is shared by three controls. In a similar manner, we will want to call an input validation procedure whenever the ⌷Enter⌷ key is pressed. Again, one event procedure will suffice for all three Text boxes in the control array. The code that we will use is

```
Private Sub txtExpense_KeyPress(Index As Integer, KeyAscii As Integer)
 If KeyAscii = ENTER Then
   Call CheckVal(txtExpense(Index).Text, Index)
 End If
End Sub
```

The header line for this event code is supplied by Visual Basic, and since we are using Text boxes that have the same name, the **Index** value of the Text box from which the **KeyPress** was activated is passed into the event procedure. In this case we first use the **Index** parameter within the event procedure to locate the correct Text value using the expression `txtExpense(Index)`. This **Text** value and the **Index** value are then used as arguments in the call to `CheckVal`. Thus, if the **KeyPress** event was activated from the first Text box, the arguments sent to `CheckVal` are `txtExpense(0).Text` and 0. Similarly, when the **KeyPress** event is triggered from the second Text box, the arguments `txtExpense(1).Text` and 1 are sent to `CheckVal`. Finally, when the **KeyPress** event is triggered from the third Text box, the arguments `txtExpense(2).Text` and 2 are sent to `CheckVal`. This event code is incorporated into Program 8-3. Table 8-6 provides the program's Properties table.

Program 8-3's Event and General Object Code

```
Rem: These are (General) declarations
Option Explicit
Const ENTER As Integer = 13 ' ANSI value of the ENTER key

Private Sub txtExpense_GotFocus(Index As Integer)
  picError.Cls
  picTotal.Cls
End Sub

Private Sub txtExpense_KeyPress(Index As Integer, KeyAscii As Integer)
 If KeyAscii = ENTER Then
   Call CheckVal(txtExpense(Index).Text, Index)
 End If

End Sub

Private Sub cmdTotal_Click()
  Dim i As Integer
  Dim total As Single

  For i = 0 To 2
   total = total + Val(txtExpense(i).Text)
  Next i
  picTotal.Print Format(total, "Currency")
End Sub

Private Sub CheckVal(s1 As String, fromwhere As Integer)
  If Not (IsNumeric(s1)) Then
    picError.Print "Please enter a valid number"
  Else  ' a valid data was entered, so we shift the focus
    Select Case fromwhere
      Case 0, 1
        txtExpense(fromwhere + 1).SetFocus
      Case 2
         cmdTotal.SetFocus
    End Select
  End If
End Sub
```

The two event codes listed for Program 8-3 are the common procedures relating to the Text box control array that have already been discussed. Notice in the `cmdTotal_Click` event procedure that the total of the values in the Text boxes are obtained by cycling through each Text box's **Text** property, using a **For** loop and indexed Text box names. Finally, in the `CheckVal` general procedure notice, that the `fromwhere` parameter is used within the `Select Case` statement as an index value in the statement `txtExpense(fromwhere + 1).SetFocus`. The index expression `fromwhere + 1`

Figure 8-10

*A Sample Output Using
Program 8-3*

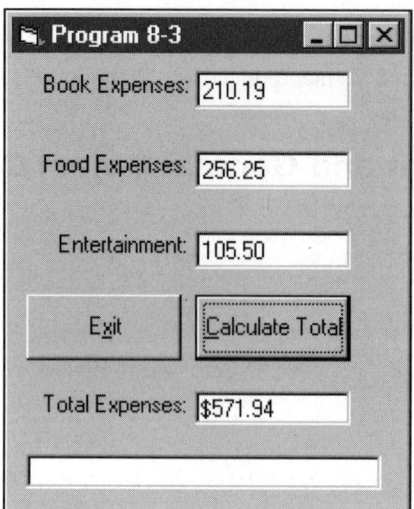

identifies the next Text box in the control array
from the Text box that activated the `CheckVal`
procedure. Thus, if the parameter `fromwhere` is
either 0 or 1, which identifies the current Text
box that activated the general procedure, the
focus will be set on the next Text box in the
control array at either **Index** value 1 or 2,
respectively. Figure 8-10 illustrates a sample run
using Program 8-3.

Table 8-6 Program 8-3's Properties Table

Object	Property	Setting
Form	Name	frmMain
	Caption	Program 8-3
Text Box	Name	txtExpense()
	Index	0 to 3
	Text	(blank)
	BackColor	White (Palette tab)
Command Button	Name	cmdTotal
	Caption	&Calculate Total
Command Button	Name	cmdExit
	Caption	E&xit
Picture Box	Name	picError
	TabStop	False
	BackColor	White (Palette tab)
Picture Box	Name	picTotal
	TabStop	False
	BackColor	White (Palette tab)
Label	Name	lblBooks
	Caption	Book Expenses:
Label	Name	lblFood
	Caption	Food Expenses:
Label	Name	lblEnt
	Caption	Entertainment:
Label	Name	lblTotal
	Caption	Total Expenses:

Constructing Control Arrays

Any set of the same type of control can be made into a control array. Thus, you can make control arrays from Option buttons, Check boxes, Text boxes, Picture boxes, Labels, etc. In addition, control arrays can be constructed at either design- or run-time. At design-time a control array can be created by

1. Assigning the same name to more than one control, or
2. Setting the **Index** property of a control to an integer value, or
3. Copying an existing control and then pasting in back onto a form.

The easiest method is the third one, which can be performed using the following steps:

1. Create one control of the desired type on the form.
2. Set the **Name** property and any other property value that you want reproduced for all controls in the array.
3. Press [Ctrl]+[C] to copy the control to the Clipboard.
4. Press [Ctrl]+[V] , to copy the control back onto the form—when the system displays a message box asking if you want to create a control array, answer Yes.
5. Repeat Step 4 to produce the desired number of control copies.

Using these steps, the first control will be assigned an **Index** property value of 0, and each new copy will have an **Index** property value that is incremented by 1.

Control arrays can also be added and removed at run-time. To do so, however, you must have created at least one control at design-time with its **Index** property set, usually to 0. New controls are added to the array, using the **Load** statement, which has the syntax

> **Load** *objectname(index number)*

where *objectname* is the name of the control object and *index number* is the value that you want to assign to its **Index** property. To make the newly added control visible, you must subsequently set its **Visible** property to **True**. You will also have to set its **Left** and **Top** properties to correctly position the box on the form.

An existing control within a control array can be deleted at run-time using the **UnLoad** statement, which has the syntax

> **UnLoad** *objectname(index number)*

Exercises 8.3

1. Create a user interface that has three Command buttons—all members of the same control array.

2. Create a user interface that has four Labels—all members of the same control array.

3. Modify Program 8-3 so that the four Label and two Picture controls are members of their respective control arrays.

Figure 8-11

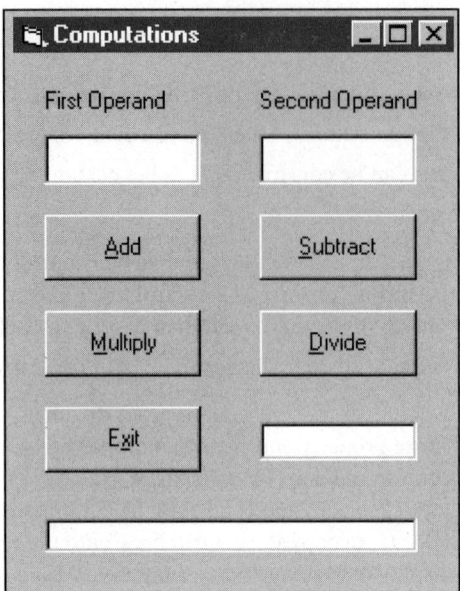

4.   a.   Create the user interface shown in Figure 8-11 so that the labels are in one control array, the Text boxes in a second control array, and the Command buttons in a third control array.

     b.   Write procedure code for the interface constructed in Exercise 4a., so that the program calculates a correct result based on the selected Command button.

Figure 8-12

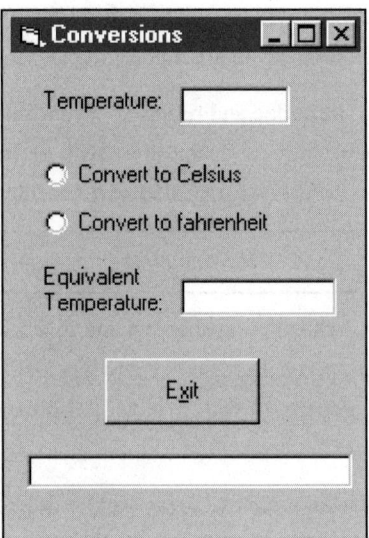

5.   a.   Create the user interface shown in Figure 8-12 so that the Option buttons are in one control array and the Text boxes in a second control array.

     b.   Write procedure code for the interface constructed in Exercise 4a. so that the program calculates the correct result based on the selected Option button.

8.4 Structures

An array allows access to a list or table of data of the same data type, using a single variable name. At times, however, we may want to store information of varying types—such as a string name, an integer part number, and a real price—together in one structure. A data structure that stores different types of data under a single variable name is called a *record*. [6]

    To make the discussion more tangible, consider data items that might be stored for a video game character, as illustrated in Figure 8-13.

---

[6] It should be noted that a single record can also be created using a **Variant** and the **Array** function, as described in Section 7.3. Similarly, an array of records can be created as an array of **Variants**.

Figure 8-13

Typical Components of a Video Game Character

```
Name:

Type:

Location in Dungeon:

Strength Factor:

Intelligence Factor:

Type of Armor:
```

Each of the individual data items listed in Figure 8-13 is an entity by itself, referred to as a *data field*. Taken together, all the data fields form a single unit, referred to as a *record*. In Visual Basic, a record is referred to as a *structure*.

Although there could be hundreds of characters in a video game, the form of each character's record is identical. In dealing with records, it is important to distinguish between a record's form and its contents.

A *record's form* consists of the symbolic names, data types, and arrangement of individual data fields in the record. The *record's contents* consists of the actual data stored in the symbolic names. Figure 8-14 shows acceptable contents for the record form illustrated in Figure 8-13.

Using a structure requires that the record must be created and variables declared to be of the new structure type. Then specific values can be assigned to individual variable elements. Creating a structure requires listing the data types, data names, and arrangement of data items. For example, the declaration

```
Type Birthdate
    int month
    int day
    int year
End Type
```

creates a structure named `Birthdate` that consists of three data items or fields, called *members* of the structure.

The term `Birthdate` is a structure type name: It creates a new data type that is a data structure of the declared form. By convention the first letter of a user-selected data type name is uppercase, as in the name `Birthdate`, which helps to identify it when it is used in subsequent declaration statements. Here, the declaration for the `Birthdate` structure creates a new data type and describes how individual data items are arranged within the structure. To use a structure, you must declare variables of that type. For example, the declaration statement

```
Dim mybirthday As Birthdate
```

Figure 8-14

The Form and Contents of a Record

```
Name: Golgar

Type: Monster

Location in Dungeon: G7

Strength Factor: 78

Intelligence Factor: 15

Type of Armor: Chain Mail
```

declares the variable `mybirthday` to be of type `Birthdate`. Assigning actual data values to the data items of a structure is called *populating* the structure, and is a relatively straightforward procedure. Each member of a structure is accessed by giving both the variable's name and individual data item name, separated by a period. Thus, `mybirthday.month` refers to the first member of the `mybirthday` structure, `mybirthday.day` refers to the second

---

┌───┐
│ **Programmers' Notes**   │
│   │
│ **Homogeneous and Heterogeneous Data Structures**   │
│   │
│ Both arrays and records are structured data types. The difference   │
│ between these two data structures is the types of elements they   │
│ contain. An array is a homogeneous data structure, which means that   │
│ each of its components must be of the same type. A record is a   │
│ heterogeneous data structure, which means that each of its components │
│ can be of different data types. Thus, an array of records would be a │
│ homogeneous data structure whose elements are of the same   │
│ heterogeneous type.   │
└───┘

member of the structure, and `mybirthday.year` refers to the third member. Table 8-7 lists where structures may be created and the scoping rules for their declaring variables of a structure type.

Table 8-7 Structure Creation and Declaration Scope		
Procedure/Module	**Creation of a Structure**	**Variable Declarations**
Procedure	Not Permitted	Local only
Form Module	Private only	Private only
Standard Module	Private or Public	Private or Public
Class Module	Private only	Private only

The individual members of a structure are not restricted to integer data types, as illustrated by the `Birthdate` structure. Any valid Visual Basic data type can be used. For example, consider an employee record consisting of the following data items:

Name:

Identification Number:

Regular Pay Rate:

Overtime Pay Rate:

A suitable structure for these data items is

```
Type Payrec
    name As String *20      width
    idnum As Long
    regrte As Single
    otrate(3) As Single    ' this is an array of three elements
End Type
```

(handwritten annotation: field — pointing to name As String line)

Before leaving single structures, it is worth noting that the individual members of a structure can be any valid Visual Basic data type, including both arrays and structures. For example, the `otrate` member of `Payrec` consists of an array. Accessing an element of a member array requires giving the structure's variable name, followed by a period, followed by the array designation. For example, if `employee` is of type `Payrec`, then `employee.otrate(2)` refers to the second value in the `employee.otrate` array.

Declaring an array of structures is the same as declaring an array of any other variable type. For example, an array of ten `Payrec` structures can be declared using the statement:

```
Dim employee(10) As Payrec
```

This declaration statement constructs an array named `employee` consisting of 10 elements (assuming **Option Base** is 1), each of which is a structure of the data type `Payrec`. Notice that the creation of an array of 10 structures has the same form as the creation of any other array. For example, creating an array of 10 integers named `employee` requires the declaration

```
Dim employee(10) As Integer
```

In this declaration the data type is integer, while in the former declaration for `employee` the data type is `Payrec`. Once an array of structures is declared, a particular data item is referenced by giving the position of the desired structure in the array followed by a period and the appropriate structure member. For example, the variable `employee(2).idnum` references the `idnum` member of the second employee structure in the `employee` array.

Exercises 8.4

1. Declare a structure data type named `Stemp` for each of the following records:

   a. a student record consisting of a student identification number, number of credits completed, and cumulative grade point average

   b. a student record consisting of a student's name, birth date, number of credits completed, and cumulative grade point average

   c. a mailing list consisting of a first name, last name, street address, city, state, and zip code

   d. a stock record consisting of the stock's name, the price of the stock, and the date of purchase

   e. an inventory record consisting of an integer part number, part description, number of parts in inventory, and an integer reorder number

2. For the individual data types declared in Exercise 1, define a suitable structure variable name, and initialize each structure with the appropriate following data:

   a. Identification Number: 4672
      Number of Credits Completed: 68
      Grade Point Average: 3.01

   b. Name: Rhona Karp
      Birth date: 8/4/60
      Number of Credits Completed: 96
      Grade Point Average: 3.89

    c. Name: Kay Kingsley

       Street Address: 614 Freeman Street

       City: Indianapolis

       State: IN

       Zip Code: 07030

    d. Stock: IBM

       Price Purchased: 134.5

       Date Purchased: 10/1/86

    e. Part Number: 16879

       Description: Battery

       Number in Stock: 10

       Reorder Number: 3

3. a. Write a Visual Basic program that prompts a user to input the current month, day, and year. Store the data entered in a suitably defined record and display the birthdate in an appropriate manner.

    b. Modify the program written in Exercise 3a. to use a record that accepts the current time in hours, minutes, and seconds.

4. Write a Visual Basic program that uses a structure for storing the name of a stock, its estimated earnings per share, and its estimated price-to-earnings ratio. Have the program prompt the user to enter these items for five different stocks, each time using the same structure to store the entered data. When the data has been entered for a particular stock, have the program compute and display the anticipated stock price based on the entered earnings and price-per-earnings values. For example, if a user entered the data XYZ 1.56 12, the anticipated price for a share of XYZ stock is $(1.56)*(12) = \$18.72$.

5. Write a Visual Basic program that accepts a user-entered time in hours and minutes. Have the program calculate and display the time one minute later.

6. a. Write a Visual Basic program that accepts a user-entered date. Have the program calculate and display the date of the next day. For purposes of this exercise, assume that all months consist of 30 days.

    b. Modify the program written in Exercise 6a. to account for the actual number of days in each month.

7. Define arrays of 100 structures for each of the data types described in Exercise 1 of this section.

8.5 Searching and Sorting

Most programmers encounter both the need to sort and search a list of data items at some time in their programming careers. For example, numerical data might have to be arranged in either increasing (ascending) or decreasing (descending) order for statistical analysis, lists of names may have to be sorted in alphabetical order, or a list of dates may have to be rearranged in ascending date order. Similarly, a list of names may have to be searched to find a particular name in the list, or a list of dates may have to be searched to locate a particular date. In this section we introduce the fundamentals of both sorting and searching lists. Although it is not necessary to sort a list before searching it, as we shall see, much faster searches are possible if the list is in sorted order.

Search Algorithms

A common requirement of many programs is to search a list for a given element. For example, in a list of names and telephone numbers, we might search for a specific name so that the corresponding telephone number can be printed, or we might wish to search the list simply to determine if a name is there. The two most common methods of performing such searches are the linear and binary search algorithms.

Linear Search

 *one slot at a time*

In a *linear search*, also known as a *sequential search*, each item in the list is examined in the order in which it occurs in the list until the desired item is found or the end of the list is reached. This is analogous to looking at every name in the phone directory, beginning with Aardvark, Aaron, until you find the one you want or until you reach Zzxgy, Zora. Obviously, this is not the most efficient way to search a long alphabetized list. However, a linear search has two advantages:

1. The algorithm is simple, and
2. The list need not be in any particular order.

In a linear search, the search begins at the first item in the list and continues sequentially, item by item, through the list. The pseudocode for a function performing a linear search is

> *Set the location to a -1*
> *For all the items in the list*
> > *Compare the item with the desired item*
> > *If the item was found*
> > > *Set the location to the index value of the current item*
> > > *Exit the For loop*
> > *Endif*
> *EndFor*
> *Return the location*

Notice that the return value indicates whether the item was found or not. If the return value is -1, the item was not in the list, otherwise, the return value within the **For** loop provides the index of where the item is located within the list. The function `linearSearch`, which is included in Program 8-4's procedure code, implements this linear search algorithm as a Visual Basic function. For testing purposes we have constructed the list as a **Variant** array (see Section 8.3).

Program 8-4's Event and General Object Code

```
Rem: This is the code contained in the [General] object section
Option Explicit
Option Base 1

Rem:  this function returns the location of key in the list
Rem: a -1 is returned if the value is not found
Public Function linearSearch(list As Variant, size As Integer, key As Integer) As Integer
    Dim i As Integer
    Dim location As Integer

  location = -1
  For i = 1 To size
    If list(i) = key Then
      location = i
        Exit For
    End If
  Next i
linearSearch = location
End Function

Private Sub cmdSearch_Click()
  Const NUMEL As Integer = 10
  Dim nums As Variant
  Dim item As Integer
  Dim location As Integer

  nums = Array(5, 10, 22, 32, 45, 67, 73, 98, 99, 101)

  item = Val(txtSearch.Text)
  location = linearSearch(nums, NUMEL, item)
  If location > -1 Then
    picSearch.Print "The item was found at index location "; location
  Else
    picSearch.Print "The item was not found in the list"
  End If

Private Sub txtSearch_GotFocus()
  picSearch.Cls
End Sub

Private Sub cmdExit_Click()
  Beep
  End
End Sub
```

Figure 8-15
The Desired Item is Found

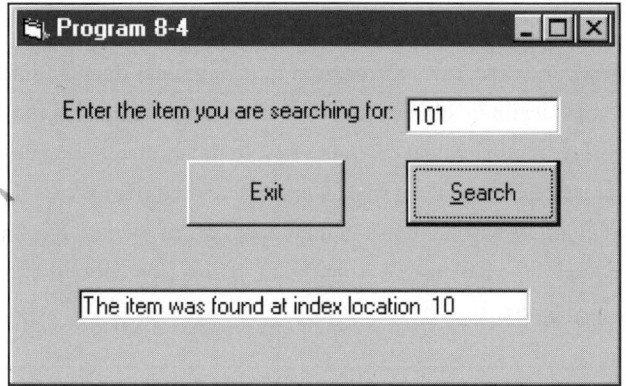

In reviewing the linearSearch function, notice that the **For** loop is simply used to access each element in the list, from first element to last, until a match is found with the desired item. If the desired item is located, the index value of the current item is returned, which causes the loop to terminate; otherwise, the search continues until the end of the list is encountered. Two sample runs of Program 8-4 are illustrated in Figures 8-15 and 8-16, respectively.

As has already been pointed out, an advantage of linear searches is that the list does not have to be in sorted order to perform the search. Another advantage is that if the desired item is toward the front of the list, only a small number of comparisons will be done. The worst case, of course, occurs when the desired item is at the end of the list. On average, however, and assuming that the desired item is equally likely to be anywhere within the list, the number of required comparisons will be N/2, where N is the list's size. Thus, for a 10-element list, the average number of comparisons needed for a linear search is 5, and for a 10,000-element list, the average number of comparisons needed is 5000. As we show next, this number can be significantly reduced using a binary search algorithm.

Figure 8-16
The Desired Item is Not in the List

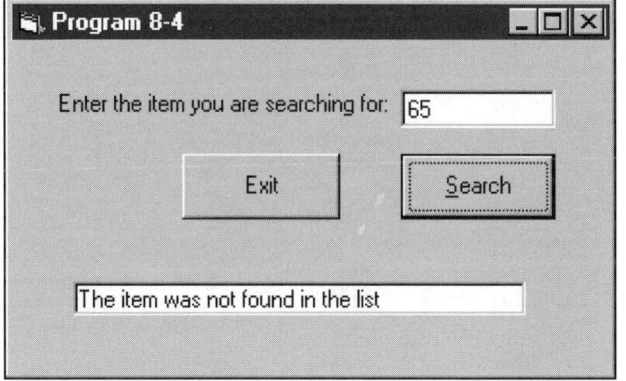

Binary Search

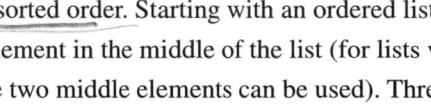

In a *binary search,* the list must be in sorted order. Starting with an ordered list, the desired item is first compared to the element in the middle of the list (for lists with an even number of elements, either of the two middle elements can be used). Three possibilities present themselves once the comparison is made: the desired item may be equal to the middle element, it may be greater than the middle element, or it may be less than the middle element.

In the first case, the search has been successful, and no further searches are required. In the second case, since the desired item is greater than the middle element, if it is found at all, it must be in the bottom part of the list. This means that the upper part of the list, consisting of all elements from the first to the midpoint element, can be discarded from any further search. In the third case, since the desired item is less than the middle element, if it is found at all, it must be found in the upper part of the list. For this case, the bottom part of the list, containing all elements from the midpoint element to the last element, can be discarded from any further search.

Figure 8-17

The Binary Search Algorithm

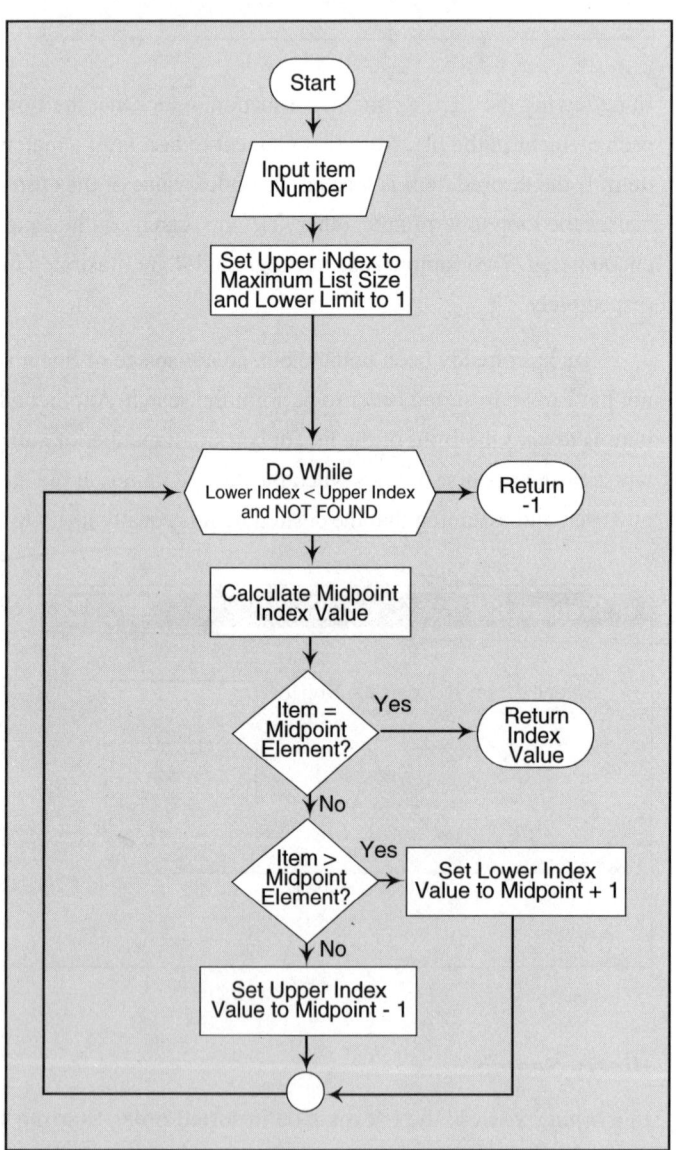

The algorithm for implementing this search strategy is illustrated in Figure 8-15 and defined by the following pseudocode:

Set the lower index to 1

Set the upper index to the size of the list

Begin with the first item in the list

Do While the lower index is less than or equal to the upper index

   Set the midpoint index to the integer average of the lower and upper index values

   Compare the desired item to the midpoint element

   If the desired element equals the midpoint element

      Return the index value of the current item

   Else If the desired element is greater than the midpoint element

      Set the lower index value to the midpoint value plus 1

   Else if the desired element is less than the midpoint element

      Set the upper index value to the midpoint value less 1

   Endif

End Do

Return -1 because the item was not found

As illustrated by both the pseudocode and the flowchart of Figure 8-17, a **Do While** loop is used to control the search. The initial list is defined by setting the lower Index value to 1 and the upper Index value to the number of elements in the list. The midpoint element is then taken as the integerized average of the lower and upper values. Once the comparison to the midpoint element is made, the search is subsequently restricted by moving either the lower Index to one integer value above the midpoint, or by moving the upper Index one integer value below the midpoint. This process is continued until the desired element is found or the lower and upper Index values become equal. The function `binarySearch` presents the Visual Basic version of this algorithm.

```
Rem: this function returns the location of key in the list
Rem: a -1 is returned if the value is not found
Public Function binarySearch(list As Variant, size As Integer, key As Integer) As Integer
   Dim left As Integer, right As Integer, midpt As Integer
   Dim location As Integer

  location = -1
  left = 1
  right = size
  Do While left <= right
    midpt = Int((left + right) / 2)
    If key = list(midpt) Then
      location = midpt
      Exit Do
    ElseIf key > list(midpt) Then
      left = midpt + 1
    Else
      right = midpt - 1
    End If
  Loop
    binarySearch = location
  End Function
```

Table 8-8

A Comparison of Do While Loop Passes for Linear and Binary Searches

Array Size	10	50	500	5,000	50,000	500,000	5,000,000
Average Linear Search Passes	5	25	250	2,500	25,000	250,000	2,500,000
Maximum Linear Search Passes	10	50	500	5,000	50,000	500,000	5,000,000
Maximum Binary Search Passes	4	6	9	13	16	19	23

The value of using a binary search algorithm is that the number of elements that must be searched is cut in half each time through the **Do While** loop. Thus, the first time through the loop, N elements must be searched, the second time through the loop, N/2 of the elements have been eliminated and only N/2 remain. The third time through the loop, another half of the remaining elements have been eliminated, and so on.

In general, after p passes through the loop, the number of values remaining to be searched is $N/(2^p)$. In the worst case, the search can continue until there is less than or equal to one element remaining to be searched. Mathematically, this can be expressed as $N/(2^p) \leq 1$. Alternatively, this may be rephrased as p is the smallest integer such that $2^p \geq N$. For example, for a 1000-element array, N is 1000 and the maximum number of passes, p, required for a binary search is 10. Table 8-8 compares the number of loop passes needed for a linear and binary search for various list sizes.

As illustrated, the maximum number of loop passes for a 50-item list is almost 10 times more for a linear search than for binary search, and is even more spectacular for larger lists. As a rule of thumb, 50 elements are usually taken as the switchover point: for lists smaller than 50 elements, linear searches are acceptable but for larger lists, a binary search algorithm should be used.

Big O Notation

On average, over a large number of linear searches with N items in a list, we would expect to examine half (N/2) of the items before locating the desired item. In a binary search the maximum number of passes, p, occurs when $(N/2)^p = 1$. This relationship can be algebraically manipulated to $2^p = N$, which yields $p = \log_2 N$, which approximately equals $3.33 \log_{10} N$.

For example, finding a particular name in an alphabetical directory with N = 1000 names would require an average of 500 (=N/2) comparisons using a linear search. With a binary search, only about 10 (= 3.33 * $\log_{10} 1000$) comparisons would be required.

A common way to express the number of comparisons required in any search algorithm using a list of N items is to give the order of magnitude of the number of comparisons required, on average, to locate a desired item. Thus, the linear search is said to be of order N and the binary search of order $\log_2 N$. Notationally, this is expressed as O(N) and O($\log_2 N$), where the O is read as "the order of."

Sort Algorithms

For sorting data, two major categories of sorting techniques exist, called internal and external sorts, respectively. *Internal sorts* are used when the data list is not too large and the complete list can be stored within the computer's memory, usually in an array. *External sorts* are used for much larger data sets that cannot be accommodated within the computer's memory as a complete unit.

Here we present two internal sort algorithms that are commonly used when sorting lists with less than approximately 50 elements. For larger lists, more sophisticated sorting algorithms are typically employed.

Selection Sort

One of the simplest sorting techniques is the selection sort. In a *selection sort*, the smallest value is initially selected from the complete list of data and exchanged with the first element in the list. After this first selection and exchange, the next smallest element in the revised list is selected and exchanged with the second element in the list. Since the smallest element is already in the first position in the list, this second pass need only consider the second through last elements. For a list consisting of *N* elements, this process is repeated *N-1* times, with each pass through the list requiring one less comparison than the previous pass.

For example, consider the list of numbers illustrated in Figure 8-18. The first pass through the initial list results in the number 32 being selected and exchanged with the first element in the list. The second pass, made on the reordered list, results in the number 155 being selected from the second through fifth elements. This value is then exchanged with the second element in the list. The third pass selects the number 307 from the third through fifth elements in the list and exchanges this value with the third element. Finally, the fourth and last pass through the list selects the remaining minimum value and exchanges it with the fourth list element. Although each pass in this example resulted in an exchange, no exchange would have been made in a pass if the smallest value were already in the correct location.

Figure 8-18

Sample Selection Sort

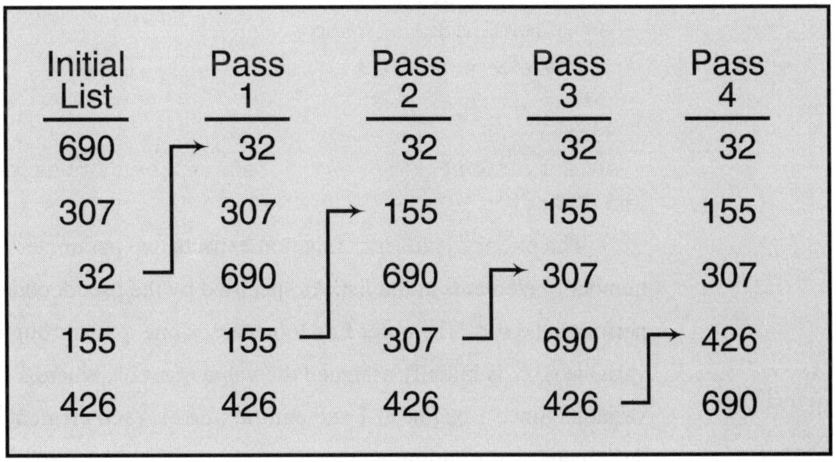

Initial List	Pass 1	Pass 2	Pass 3	Pass 4
690	32	32	32	32
307	307	155	155	155
32	690	690	307	307
155	155	307	690	426
426	426	426	426	690

In pseudocode, the selection sort is described as

Set interchange count to zero (not required, but done just to keep track of the interchanges)
For each element in the list from first to next-to-last
  Find the smallest element from the current element being referenced to the last element by:
    Setting the minimum value equal to the current element
    Saving (storing) the index of the current element
    For each element in the list from the current element + 1 to the last element in the list
      If element(inner loop index) < minimum value
        Set the minimum value = element(inner loop index)
        Save the index the new found minimum value
      Endif
    EndFor
    Swap the current value with the new minimum value
    Increment the interchange count
EndFor

Return the interchange count

The function `selectionSort` incorporates this algorithm into a Visual Basic function.

```
Public Function selectionSort(num As Variant, numel As Integer) As
Integer
    Dim i As Integer, j As Integer
    Dim min As Integer, minidx As Integer
    Dim temp As Integer, moves As Integer

    moves = 0
    For i = 1 To numel
      min = num(i)        ' assume minimum is the first array element
      minidx = i          ' index of minimum element
      For j = i + 1 To numel
        If num(j) < min Then   ' if we've located a lower value
          min = num(j)         ' capture it
          minidx = j
        End If
      Next j
      If min < num(i) Then    ' check if we have a new minimum
        temp = num(i)         ' and if we do, swap values
        num(i) = min
        num(minidx) = temp
        moves = moves + 1
      End If
    Next i
    selectionSort = moves   ' return the number of moves
End Function
```

The `selectionSort` function expects two parameters, the list to be sorted and the number of elements in the list. As specified by the pseudocode, a nested set of **For** loops performs the sort. The outer **For** loop causes one pass through the list. For each pass, the variable `min` is initially assigned the value `num(i)`, where `i` is the outer **For** loop's counter variable. Since `i` begins at 1 and ends at `numel`, each element in the list is successively designated as the current element.

The inner loop is used as the function cycles through the elements below the current element to select the next smallest value. Thus, this loop begins at the index value i+1 and continues through the end of the list. When a new minimum is found, its value and position in the list are stored in the variables named min and minidx, respectively. Upon completion of the inner loop, an exchange is made only if a value less than that in the current position was found.

Program 8-5 was constructed to test selectionSort. This program implements a selection sort for the same list of 10 numbers previously used to test our search algorithms. For later comparison to the other sorting algorithms, the number of actual moves made by the program to get the data into sorted order is counted and displayed. For convenience, only the event code contained within Program 8-5 that calls the selection sort function is listed.

Program 8-5's Event Procedure Code

```
Private Sub Form_Click()
 Const numel As Integer = 10
 Dim nums As Variant
 Dim i As Integer, moves As Integer

 nums = Array(22, 5, 67, 98, 45, 32, 101, 99, 73, 10)
 moves = selectionSort(nums, numel)
 Cls
 Print "The sorted list, in ascending order, is:"
 For i = 1 To numel
    Print "   "; nums(i);
 Next i
 Print
 Print moves; " moves were made to sort this list"
End Sub
```

The output produced by Program 8-5 is shown in Figure 8-19.

Figure 8-19

The Output Produced by Program 8-5

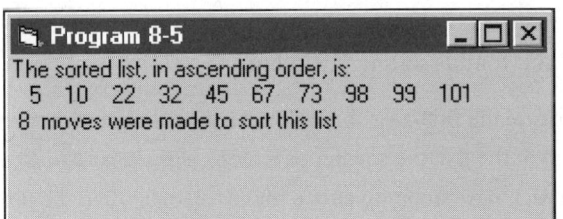

Clearly, the number of moves displayed depends on the initial order of the values in the list. An advantage of the selection sort is that the maximum number of moves that must be made is N-1, where *N* is the number of items in the list. Further, each move is a final move that results in an element residing in its final location in the sorted list.

A disadvantage of the selection sort is that N(N-1)/2 comparisons are always required, regardless of the initial arrangement of the data. This number of comparisons is obtained as follows: the last pass always requires one comparison, the next-to-last pass requires two comparisons, and so on, to the first pass, which requires N-1 comparisons. Thus, the total number of comparisons is

$$1 + 2 + 3 + .. + N\text{-}1 = N(N\text{-}1)/2 = N^2/2 - N/2.$$

For large values of *N*, the N^2 dominates, and the order of the selection sort is $O(N^2)$.

Exchange ("Bubble") Sort

In an *exchange sort,* elements of the list are exchanged with one another in such a manner that the list becomes sorted. One example of such a sequence of exchanges is provided by the bubble sort, where successive values in the list are compared, beginning with the first two elements. If the list is to be sorted in ascending (from smallest to largest) order, the smaller value of the two being compared is always placed before the larger value. For lists sorted in descending (from largest to smallest) order, the smaller of the two values being compared is always placed after the larger value.

For example, assuming that a list of values is to be sorted in ascending order, if the first element in the list is larger than the second, the two elements are interchanged. Then the second and third elements are compared. Again, if the second element is larger than the third, these two elements are interchanged. This process continues until the last two elements have been compared and exchanged, if necessary. If no exchanges were made during this initial pass through the data, the data is in the correct order and the process is finished; otherwise, a second pass is made through the data, starting from the first element and stopping at the next-to-last element. The reason for stopping at the next-to-last element on the second pass is that the first pass always results in the most positive value "sinking" to the bottom of the list.

As a specific example of this process, consider the list of numbers illustrated in Figure 8-20. The first comparison results in the interchange of the first two element values, 690 and 307. The next comparison, between elements two and three in the revised list, results in the interchange of values between the second and third elements, 690 and 32. This comparison and possible switching of adjacent values is continued until the last two elements have been compared and possibly switched. This process completes the first pass through the data and results in the largest number moving to the bottom of the list. As the largest value sinks to its resting place at the bottom of the list, the smaller elements slowly rise, or "bubble," to the top of the list. This bubbling effect of the smaller elements is what gave rise to the name "bubble" sort for this sorting algorithm.

Because the first pass through the list ensures that the largest value always moves to the bottom of the list, the second pass stops at the next-to-last element. This process continues, with each pass stopping at one higher element than the previous pass, until either N-1 passes through the list have been completed or no exchanges are necessary in any single pass. In both cases the resulting list is in sorted order. The pseudocode describing this sort is

Figure 8-20

The First Pass of an Exchange Sort

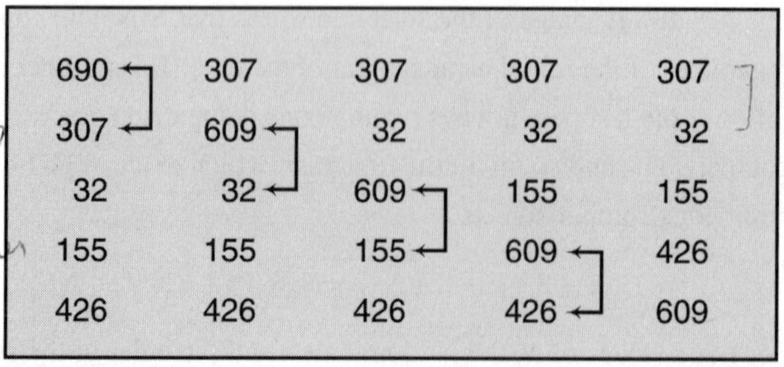

Set interchange count to zero (not required, but done just to keep track of the interchanges)
For the first element in the list to one less than the last element (i index)
For the second element in the list to the last element (j index)
If num(j) < num(j – 1)
Swap num(j) with num(j – 1)
Increment interchange count
End If
End For
End For
Return interchange count

This sort algorithm is coded in Visual Basic as the function bubbleSort, which is included within Program 8-6 for testing purposes. This program tests bubbleSort with the same list of 10 numbers used in Program 8-5. For comparison to the earlier selection sort, the number of adjacent moves (exchanges) made by bubbleSort is also counted and displayed.

Program 8-6's General and Event Object Code

```
Rem: This is the code contained in the [General] object section
Option Explicit
Option Base 1

Public Function bubbleSort(num As Variant, numel As Integer) As Integer
  Dim i As Integer, j As Integer
  Dim temp As Integer, moves As Integer

  moves = 0
  For i = 1 To (numel - 1)
    For j = 2 To numel
      If num(j) < num(j - 1) Then
        temp = num(j)
        num(j) = num(j - 1)
        num(j - 1) = temp
        moves = moves + 1
      End If
    Next j
  Next i
  bubbleSort = moves
End Function

Private Sub Form_Click()
 Const numel As Integer = 10
 Dim nums As Variant
 Dim i As Integer, moves As Integer

 nums = Array(22, 5, 67, 98, 45, 32, 101, 99, 73, 10)
 moves = bubbleSort(nums, numel)
 Cls
 Print "The sorted list, in ascending order, is:"
 For i = 1 To numel
    Print "  "; nums(i);
 Next i
 Print
 Print moves; " moves were made to sort this list"
End Sub
```

Figure 8-21 illustrates the output produced by Program 8-6.

As with the selection sort, the number of comparisons using a bubble sort is $O(N^2)$ and the number of required moves depends on the initial order of the values in the list. In the worst case, when the data is in reverse sorted order, the selection sort performs better than the bubble sort. Here both sorts require $N(N-1)/2$ comparisons, but the selection sort needs only N-1 moves, while the bubble sort needs $N(N-1)/2$ moves. The additional moves required by the bubble sort result from the intermediate exchanges between adjacent elements to "settle" each element into its final position. In this regard, the selection sort is superior, because no intermediate moves are necessary. For random data, such as that used in Programs 8-5 and 8-6, the selection sort generally performs equal to or better than the bubble sort. A modification to the bubble sort, which causes the sort to terminate when the list is in order, regardless of the number of passes made, can make the bubble sort operate as an $O(N)$ sort in specialized cases.

Figure 8-21

The Output Produced by Program 8-6

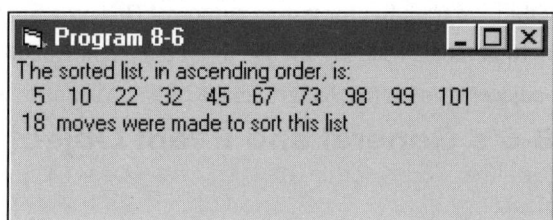

```
Program 8-6                          _ □ X
The sorted list, in ascending order, is:
  5   10   22   32   45   67   73   98   99   101
18  moves were made to sort this list
```

Exercise 8.5

1. a. Modify Program 8-5 to use a list of 100 randomly generated numbers and determine the number of moves required to put the list in order using a selection sort. Display both the initial list and the reordered list.
    b. Redo Exercise 1a. using a bubble sort.

2. For the functions `selectionSort` and `bubbleSort`, a simple modification can allow the sorting to be done in decreasing order. In each case, identify the required changes and then rewrite each function to accept a parameter indicating whether the sort should be in increasing or decreasing order. Modify each function to correctly receive and use this parameter .

3. The selection and bubble sort both use the same technique for swapping list elements. Replace the code in these two functions that performs the swap, by a call to a procedure named `swap`.

4. a. Modify Program 8-6 to use a larger test list consisting of 20 numbers.
    b. Modify Program 8-6 to use a list of 100 randomly selected numbers.

5. A company currently maintains two lists of part numbers, where each part number is an integer. Write a Visual Basic program that compares these lists of numbers and displays the numbers, if any, that are common to both. (**Hint**: Sort each list prior to making the comparison.)

6. Redo Exercise 5, but display a list of part numbers that are only on one list, but not both.

7. Rewrite the binary search algorithm to use recursion rather than iteration.

8.6 Common Programming Errors

Four common errors are associated with using arrays:

1. Forgetting to declare the array. This error results in a compiler error message equivalent to "Type mismatch" each time an indexed variable attempting to access the array is encountered.
2. Using a subscript that references a nonexistent array element. For example, declaring the array to be of size 20 and using a subscript value of 25. This error results in a run-time error and message that the "Subscript is out of range."
3. Not using a large enough conditional value in a **For** loop counter to cycle through all the array elements. This error usually occurs when an array is initially specified to be of size n and there is a **For** loop within the program of the form `For i = 1 To n`. The array size is then expanded but the programmer forgets to change the terminating value in the **For** loop. Declaring an array's size using a named constant and consistently using the named constant throughout the procedure eliminates this problem.
4. Forgetting to initialize the array. Although Visual Basic automatically sets all elements of numerical arrays to zero, all elements of string arrays to zero-length, and all elements of **Variants** to the **Empty** value,, it is up to the programmer to ensure that each array is correctly initialized before processing of array elements begins.

8.7 Chapter Review

Key Terms

big O notation	one-dimensional array
binary search	selection sort
bubble sort	single-dimensional array
Index	subscript
indexed variable	subscripted variable
linear (sequential) search	two-dimensional array

Summary

1. A single-dimensional array is a data structure that can store a list of values of the same data type. Such arrays must be declared by giving the data type of the values stored in the array and the array size. For example, the declaration

```
Dim num(100) As Integer
```

creates an array of 100 integers. It is preferable to first use a named constant to set the array size, and then use this constant in defining the array. For example:

```
Const int MAXSIZE As Integer = 100
```

and

```
Dim num(MAXSIZE) As Integer
```

2. Array elements are stored in contiguous locations in memory and referenced using the array name and a subscript, for example, num(22). Any integer valued expression can be used as an Index.

3. A two-dimensional array is declared by listing both a row and a column size with the data type and name of the array. For example, the statements

```
Const ROWS As Integer = 5
Const COLS As Integer = 7
Dim vals(ROWS, COLS) As Integer
```

creates a two-dimensional array consisting of five rows and seven columns of integer values.

4. Visual Basic permits the declaration of arrays with a maximum of sixty dimensions.

5. Arrays are passed to procedures by using the name of the array as an argument. Within the procedure, a parameter must be specified for the passed array name.

6. The linear search is an *O(N)* search. It examines each item in a list until the searched item is found or until it is determined that the item is not in the list.

7. The binary search is an $O(\log_2 N)$ search. It requires that a list be in sorted order before it can be applied.

8. The selection and exchange sort algorithms require an order of magnitude of N^2 comparisons for sorting a list of *N* items.

8.8 Looking Further: Introduction to the Application Wizard

A new feature introduced with Version 5.0 is the Application Wizard, or App Wizard, for short. The App Wizard can be used to create the foundation for an application, which can then be edited to fit your particular needs. In this section we will show you how to use the Application Wizard to create a remarkably functional application that includes a menu bar, toolbar, and status bar. Each of these bars will be created as dockable objects that can be detached and dragged across the screen. Additionally, we will let the App Wizard create a splash screen like the ones discussed in Section 3.7. We will then explore how this screen is called, so you can create your own splash screens independent of the App Wizard.

Figure 8-22

Specifying the Application Wizard

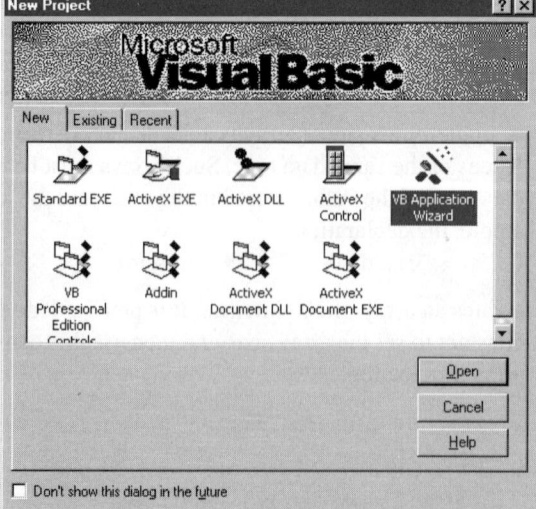

To create an application using the App Wizard, select the App Wizard icon when you start a new project, as shown in Figure 8-22. This selection will cause the App Wizard to display a series of dialog boxes, each of which elicits information about the basic structure of the application. Table 8-9 lists the information you specify in each dialog box and the sequence of dialog box presentation.

Table 8-9 Application Wizard Dialog Requests

Seq No.	Example	Name	Purpose
1	Fig. 8-23	Introduction	Instructional
2	Fig. 8-24	Interface type	Specify the type of application—SDI, MDI, or Explorer
3	Fig. 8-25	Menus	Specify the menu options—File, Edit, View, and Help
4	Fig. 8-26	Resources	Specify if a Resource file is required
5	Fig. 8-27	Internet Connectivity	Specify if you want the application to access the Internet
6	Fig. 8-28	Standard Forms	Specify if you want a Login Dialog, Splash Screen, About Box, or Options Dialog
7	Fig. 8-29	Data Access Forms	Specify if you want to connect to a Database (see Section 9.8)
8	Fig. 8-30	Finished!	Name the application, generate a summary report, and set Wizard defaults.
9	Fig. 8-31	Application Created	Informational—indicates a successful completion of the Wizard's process

Figure 8-23

The App Wizard's Introduction Dialog (Screen 1)

After selecting the Application Wizard from the New Project dialog box, the introductory screen shown in Figure 8-23 is displayed. Clicking the Next button on this dialog brings up the Interface Dialog shown in Figure 8-24.

The purpose of the Interface dialog is to inform the Wizard as to the type of application you desire. Here the acronym SDI refers to a Single Document Interface, where only one screen at a time can be displayed by an application. The acronym MDI refers to Multiple Document Interface, which consists of a single main window that can contain multiple "child" windows. For example, the Notepad application supplied with the Windows operating system is an SDI application, while Excel and Access are both MDI applications.

Figure 8-24

The Interface Dialog (Screen 2)

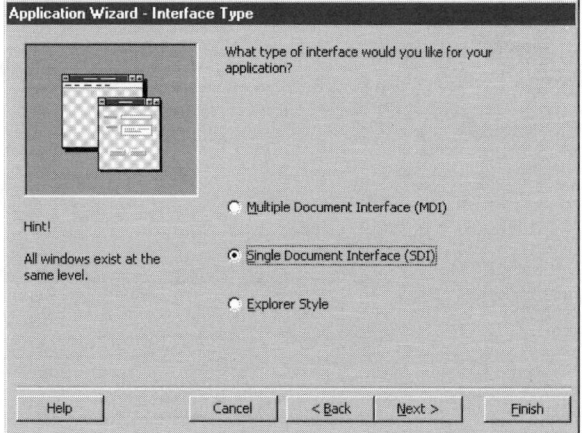

The selection of SDI does not mean that an application can have only one screen; rather, it means that only one screen at a time can be viewed by a user. In this type of application, when more than one screen is needed, a user effectively moves from one screen to another as necessary using Command buttons and/or hot keys. Thus, in a multi-screen application created as an SDI

Figure 8-25

The Menus Dialog
(Screen 3)

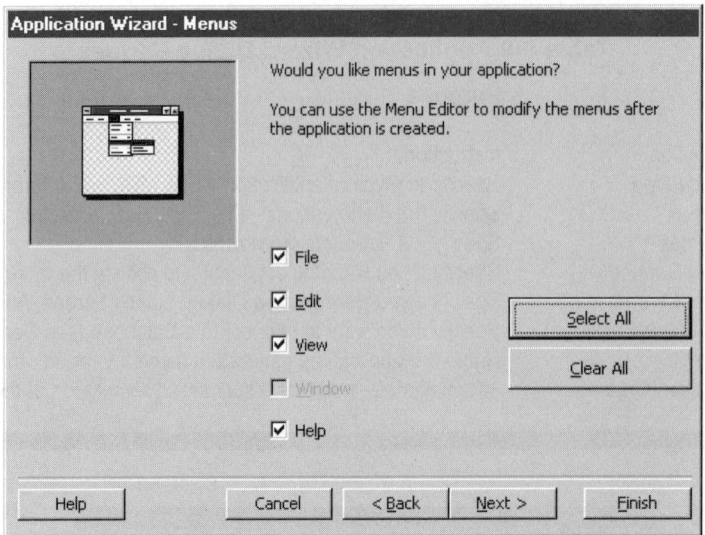

application, each screen is supplied with a Command button to load the next required screen, a Command button to go back one screen, and possibly a Command button to immediately jump back to the opening screen. This is, in fact, the exact type of operation that the Application Wizard uses to move from one screen to the next as it requests information from you. Frequently, in an SDI application, hot keys may also be provided for these tasks. In an MDI application all screens are contained within a single master screen and the user can jump and drag-and-drop data between screens using the mouse. For our application, we will select SDI as the interface type.

After specifying the interface type, the App Wizard presents the Menus dialog shown in Figure 8-25. This dialog permits you to specify what menu items you would like implemented in the final application. For our purposes we will select all of the menus.

The next two dialogs, shown in Figures 8-26 and 8-27, request information about multi-platform resource files and Internet connectivity. For both of these dialogs select the No Option button.

Figure 8-26

The Resources Dialog
(Screen 4)

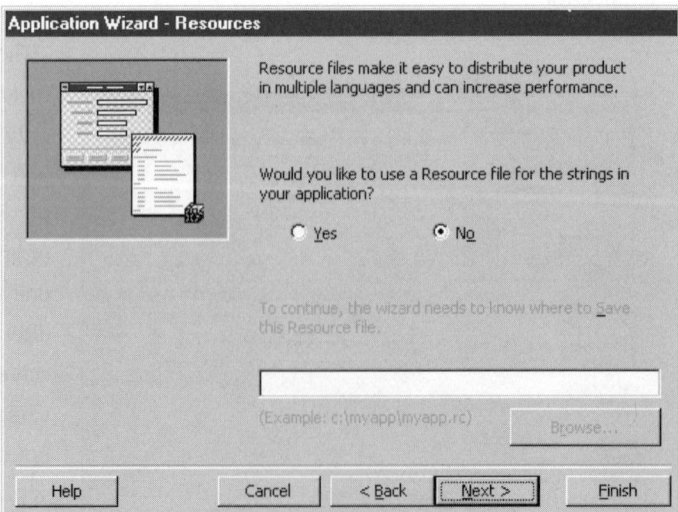

Introduction to Visual Basic

Figure 8-27

*The Internet
Connectivity Dialog
(Screen 5)*

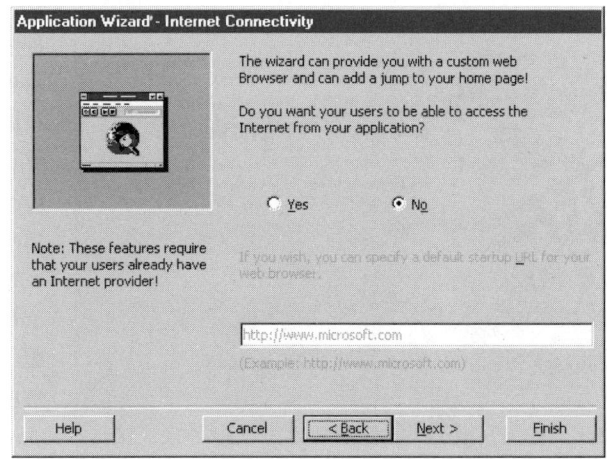

Figure 8-28

*The Standard Forms Dialog
(Screen 6)*

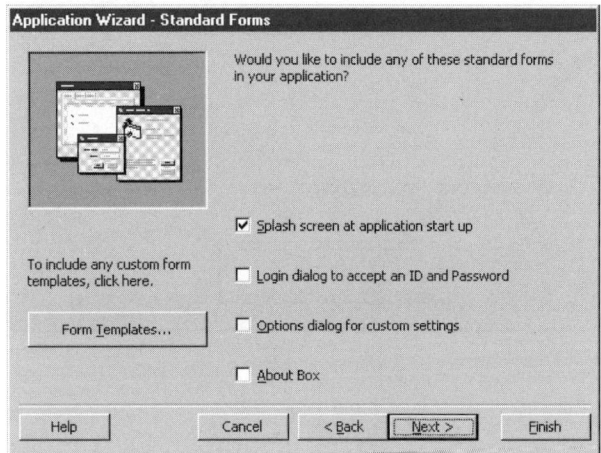

The sixth dialog box requests information about the additional forms that you want created for the application. For our purposes we will only select a splash screen, as indicated on Figure 8-28.

Figure 8-29

*The Data Access
Forms Dialog
(Screen 7)*

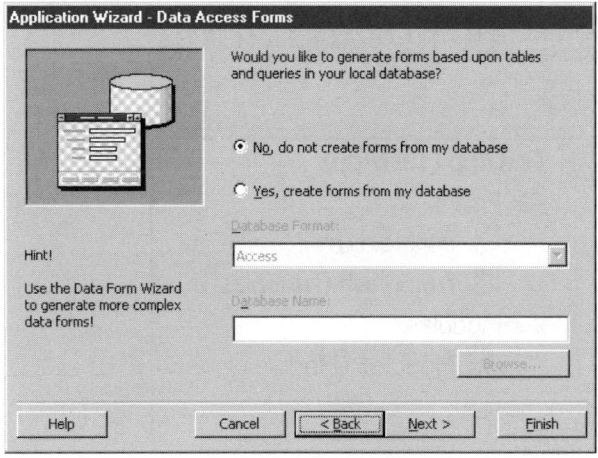

After you complete the Standard Forms dialog, the Data Access Forms dialog, illustrated in Figure 8-29, is displayed. For now we will check the No Option button, which means our current application will not access a database. (In section 9.8 we will show how this dialog is used to create a Visual Basic database application.)

Figure 8-30

The Finished! Dialog
(Screen 8)

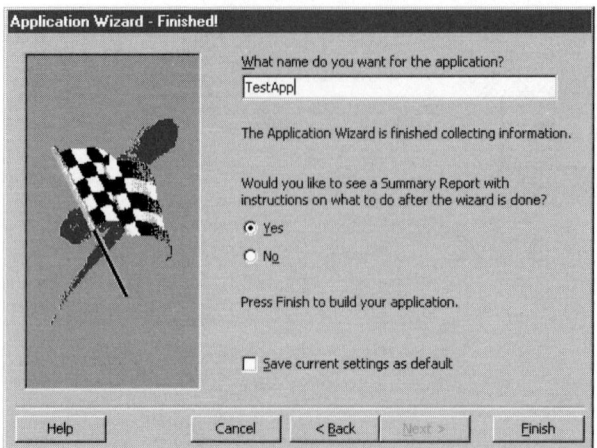

Pressing the <u>N</u>ext button on the Data Access Forms dialog brings up the Finished! dialog, which is shown in Figure 8-30. Press the <u>F</u>inish button to have the Wizard create an application that meets the specifications entered in prior dialogs. When the application is completed, the Wizard will display the screen shown in Figure 8-31.

Figure 8-31

The Application Created
Notification

The application created by the Wizard is a skeleton one that contains the essential elements you can use to "flesh out" your particular specifications. Nevertheless, the completed application has quite a bit of functionality built into it. Figure 8-32 shows the Project window for the created application—two forms and a code module.

Figure 8-32

The Application's
Project Window

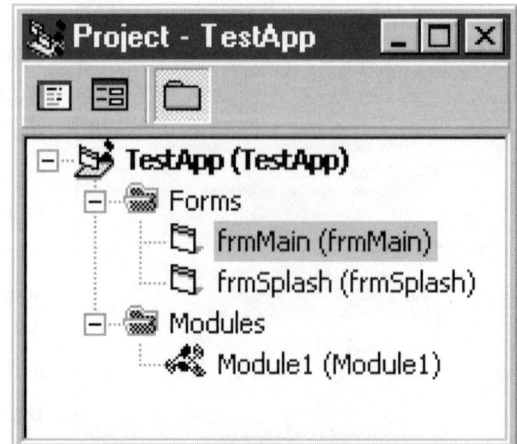

Figure 8-33a

The Initial Splash Screen

Figure 8-33b

A Modified Splash Screen

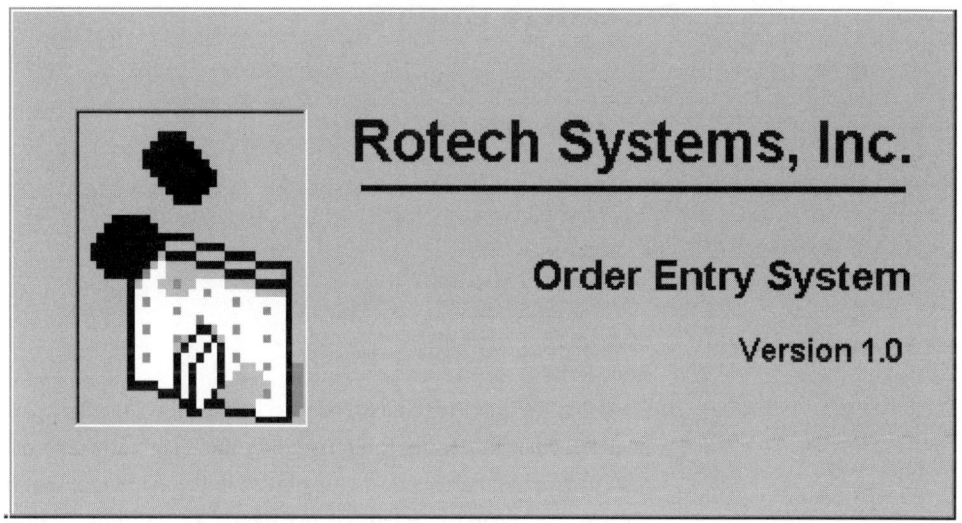

The `frmSplash` form contains the splash screen, which is shown in Figure 8-33a. This screen is easily modified to produce a custom splash screen by simply changing the labels the Wizard placed on the form. Figure 8-33b illustrates one such modified screen.

Figure 8-34

The frmMain Screen

Finally, Figure 8-34 shows the application's `frmMain` form with a Standard Toolbar, and a menu consisting of File, Edit, View, and Help options.

Calling Splash Screens

As previously described in Section 3.7, a splash screen is an initial informational screen that is displayed for a few seconds before the main application screen is presented. Typically it is used to present a company's name and the name or purpose of the executing application. Although we have used the Applications Wizard to create a splash screen, such screens are easily created manually, as was done in Section 3.7

By default, a project's first form is designated as the startup form. When an application is run, this startup form is automatically displayed, and the first code to execute is the form's **Initialize** event procedure. There are times, however, when you might want a different form to be loaded and displayed initially, or you might want your application to start with a code module. In the latter case, the code module must be a **Sub** procedure named `Main`, which is contained within a standard code (.bas) module. This is the approach we will take in displaying our splash screen. The code for a Sub Main procedure, which displays a splash screen for two seconds, and then displays the first "working" screen is listed as Procedure Code 8-11.

Procedure Code 8-11

```
Sub Main()
Const DisplaySecs As Integer = 2

frmSplash.Show
frmSplash.Refresh
Start = Timer()    ' Timer() returns seconds from Midnight
Do While Timer() < Start + DisplaySecs
Loop
Unload frmSplash
frmMain.Show
frmMain.Refresh
End Sub
```

Notice that Procedure Code 8-11 first shows the `frmSplash` form, which by default does a load of this form. It then invokes the form's **Refresh** method. This is done to ensure that all graphical elements are displayed in the event that that the form's **AutoRefresh** property has been set to False (see Chapter 11). A timing loop is then used to wait for two seconds, at which point the `frmSplash` screen is unloaded and the `frmMain` screen is displayed.

All that remains to do is ensure that Procedure Code 8-11 is initially executed when the application is run. This is accomplished from within the Project menu. When the project's Properties option in this menu item is selected, the dialog box shown in Figure 8-36 will be displayed. As illustrated, we have selected a Sub Main procedure to be the Startup Object, rather than any of the two forms associated with the project. Doing this explicitly selects the Sub Main procedure as the initial code to be executed when the application is run.

Figure 8-36

Changing a Project's Properties

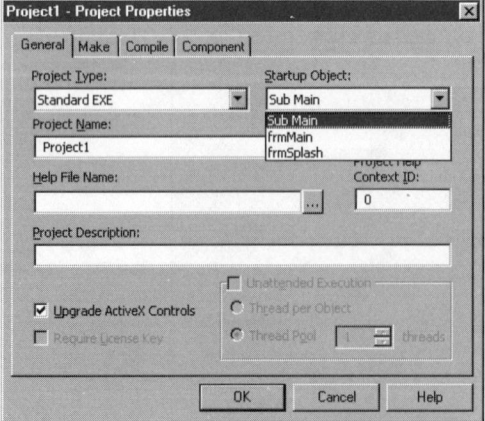

Introduction to Visual Basic

Accessing Databases

A growing area of importance for Visual Basic is the construction of database applications, which includes both the maintenance of existing data and the rapid retrieval and display of information stored in the database. In Section 9.1 we introduce the terminology and fundamental structures used in database design. The remaining sections then present the controls, methods, and events that permit construction of Visual Basic database applications.

9.1 Introduction to Databases

A *database* is defined as any collection of related data used by an organization. In this context *organization* is a generic term that refers to any self-contained social unit, such as a company, university, hospital, or family. Such organizations may wish to use:

- Student data,
- Patient data,
- Employee data,
- Customer data,
- Expense data,
- Product data, or
- Sales data.

The data in a database always consists of two types:

1. E*ntities* about which the organization needs to store information, such as employees, customers, suppliers, and products; and
2. R*elationships* that link the entities together and express the associations between them.

Introduction to Visual Basic   373

Table 9-1 Internal Employee Telephone Directory

(Table name is PhoneBook, the primary index is the ID field, and the table is also indexed on the Name field)

ID	Name	Ext	Office
1	Bronson, Bill	321	HM
2	Engle, Alan	234	HM
3	Dieter, Frank	289	F1
4	Dreskin, James	367	HM
5	Farrell, Mike	564	F1
7	Ford, Sue	641	F1
9	Gent, Hillary	325	HM
10	Grill, John	495	F1
11	Jones, Kay	464	F1
12	Jones, Mary	790	HM
14	Macleod, Jim	761	HM
15	Miller, Harriet	379	HM
21	O'Neil, Pat	856	F1
22	Schet, David	485	F1
23	Smith, Bill	251	F1
24	Smith, Dave	893	HM
26	Swan, Kurt	168	HM
27	Ward, Ann	726	F1
28	Williams, John	673	HM
30	Bass, Harriet	893	HM

As a specific example illustrating these concepts, consider that Rotech Systems, Inc. is a small corporation operating from two office locations. Assume that the company currently employs 20 people, each assigned to one of the two offices. In addition, the company employs ten salespeople working out of their homes and reporting to one of the two offices. The relevant data for these employees is listed in Tables 9-1 through 9-3.

Before examining the relationships among Tables 9-1 through 9-3, let's take a moment to concentrate on the tables themselves.

First, notice that the data stored in each table is relevant to a specific entity; for our example there are three tables corresponding to three entities: internal employee phone numbers, external sales force addresses, and office locations. Individually, each table is constructed to be a logical grouping of related information arranged in rows and columns. Mathematically, such a two-dimensional table is referred to as a *relation* if the following conditions hold:

Table 9-2 Sales Representatives Mailing Addresses

(Table name is SalesRep, the primary index is the ID field, and the table is also indexed on the LName field)

ID	Office	FName	MI	LName	Addr1	Addr2	City	State	Zip
1	HM	Mary	A	Gerardo	614 Tremont Ave.		Hoboken	NJ	07030
2	HM	Bill	J	Bottlecheck	892 Freeman St.		Orange	NJ	07050
3	HM	Jayne		Scott	Apt. 12	56 Lyons Ave.	Bloomfield	NJ	07060
4	HM	Melissa	V	Smyth	78 Barnstable Rd.		Summit	NJ	07045
5	HM	Brian		Russell	93 Fairmont Ter.		Mountainside	NJ	07036
6	HM	Sara		Blitnick	832 Addison Drive		Maplewood	NJ	07085
7	F1	Blake		DiLorenzo	642 Schuller Dr.		Cherry Hill	NJ	07961
8	F1	Helen		Thomas	745 SkyLine Dr.		Camden	NJ	07920
9	F1	Mark		Somers	Apt. 3B	17 Turney St.	Trenton	NJ	07936
10	F1	Scott		Edwards	Apt. 46	932 Coleridge Rd.	Atlantic City	NJ	07018

1. Each location in the table can contain a single value;
2. Each column in the table has a unique identifying name;
3. All values in a column have the same data type;
4. The data in each row is distinct (that is, no two rows have the same data);
5. No information is lost by reordering columns; and
6. No information is lost by reordering rows.

A *relational database* is defined as a collection of relations. As a practical matter, then, a relational database is simply any database that stores all of its data in table form. Since Visual Basic and most of the currently popular database programs, such as Access, Paradox, and dBase, deal with relational databases, this is the only type of database we will consider.

Each column in a table is designated by a heading, which is referred to as both a *field name* and an *attribute name* (the two terms are synonymous). For example, the four columns in Table 9-1 have the field names ID, Name, Ext, and Office, respectively. In a similar manner, each row in a table is referred to as a *record*. Thus, Table 9-1 has 20 records, Table 9-2 has 10 records, and Table 9-3 has two records.

In addition to storing information about each entity, a database must also provide information as to how the entities are related. Relationships between entities are typically signified by phrases such as "is related to," "is associated with," "consists of," "is employed by," "works for," and so forth. Such relationships between entities is conveniently expressed using an entity-relationship diagram (ERD), in which a straight line connects two or more

Table 9-3 Office Location List

(Table name is Offices and the Primary Index is the ID field)

ID	Office	Address	City	State	Zip
1	HM	33 Freeman St.	Orange	NJ	07050
2	F1	614 Tremont Ave.	Trenton	NJ	07936

Figure 9-1

ERD Symbols

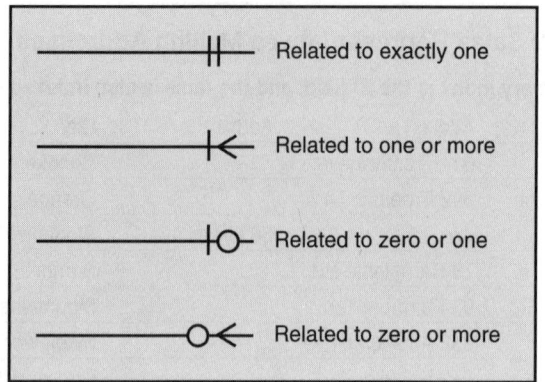

entities. The exact relationship between entities is then marked on the line using the symbols illustrated in Figure 9-1.

For example, Figure 9-2 illustrates the relationship between an employee and a company. ERD diagrams are always meant to be read from left-to-right and from right-to-left. When reading from one entity to another, the ERD symbol attached to the starting entry is ignored. Thus, reading Figure 9-1 from left to right, and ignoring the symbol closest to the company entity, we see that a company employs zero or more employees. Reading from the right entity to the left entity, and again ignoring the symbol closest to the starting entity, we see that an employee is "employed by" exactly one company. The designation "zero or more," or "exactly one" is termed the *cardinality* of the relationship and refers to the number of one entity that is related to another entity.

Figure 9-2

A Relationship Between Entities

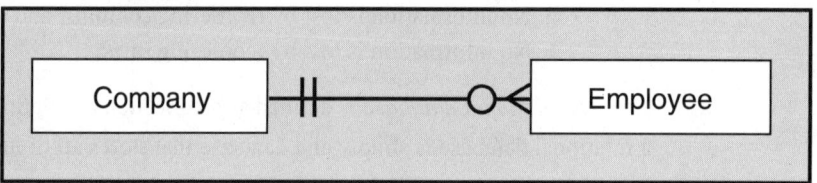

Figure 9-3 is the ERD diagram for our Rotech Company database. As illustrated in this diagram, the database consists of three entities. Reading from the Office entity to the Employees entity, we see that an office consists of one or more internal employees, and reading from the Office entity to the Sales Force entity, we see that an office consists of one or more sales representatives. Similarly, reading the ERD diagram from right-to-left, we see that an internal employee is related to exactly one office, as are the sales representatives.

The relationships illustrated in Figure 9-3 are both examples of *one-to-many* relationships. That is, one office may consist of many internal employees but each internal em-

Figure 9-3

The Rotech Company ERD Diagram

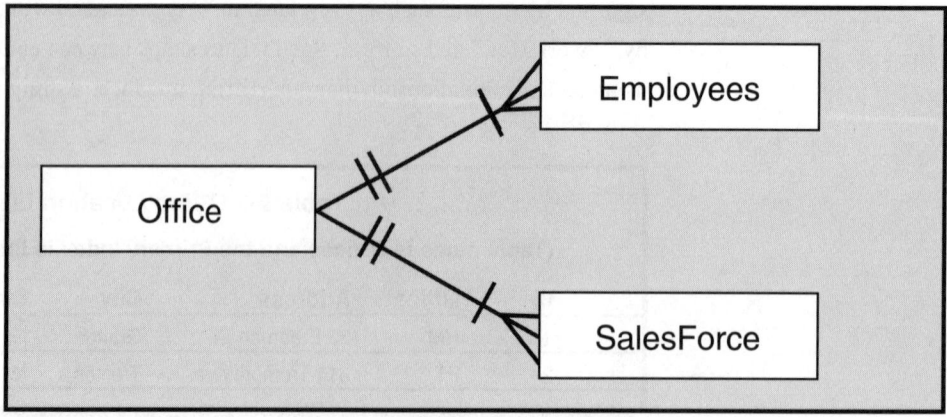

ployee can only be associated with one office. This same one-to-many relationship exists for the sales force.

In addition to a one-to-many relationship there is a many-to-many relationship. Such a relationship is illustrated in Figure 9-4, which relates authors to the books they write. As seen in this figure, an individual author can be associated with one or more titles, while an individual title can have more than one author.

Figure 9-4

A Many-to-Many Relationship

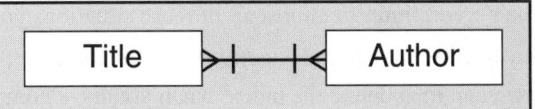

Stored and Index Ordering

As each record is added to a table it is typically appended to the end of the existing set of records. This ordering of records is referred to as the table's original, or *stored*, order. For example, notice the ordering of the telephone records illustrated in Table 9-1. These records are in stored order, the order in which records were added to the table.

Frequently, it is convenient to have a table's records ordered either alphabetically, numerically, or chronologically. Rather than resorting all of the records, which can be time consuming for large databases, indexes are used. An *index* is a separate table of record positions, called *pointers*, which list the positions of the table's records in the desired order. For example, if we frequently wanted to access Table 9-1 in alphabetical name order, we would create an index based on the Name field. The first entry in the Name index table would be record number 30, followed by record number 1, followed by record numbers 3 and 2, and so. Reading the telephone table in Name index order would then provide us with an alphabetical list of names and their respective extensions.

Each index created for a table relies on one or more fields. The field on which a table's records are ordered is referred to as a *key field*. Thus, if the records in Table 9-1 are ordered by the Name field, the key field for this ordering is the Name field. A *compound key* is one in which two or more fields are used to create the index. For example, you might wish a table of employees to be listed in departmental order and then in alphabetical last name order. Creating a compound key consisting of department name followed by last name, and then indexing the table based on this key, would produce the desired result.

In constructing a database table, it is advisable that each record have at least one key field that can be used to uniquely identify each record in a table. When a key field is used in this manner it is referred to as a primary key field, or *primary key*, for short. Typically, in the absence of any other key field, the record number is taken to be the primary key. The record number is assigned sequentially, starting from 1, to each new record added to a table. If a record is deleted from the table, the record number is also deleted and not used again. In all of our tables we will assume that the record number is the primary key. Thus, displaying a table in record number order is the same as displaying it in what we previously referred to as its stored order.

Structured Queries

In addition to ordering a table's records in either stored or index order, you will encounter situations that require either listing a single table's records in a manner that is different from an existing index order, combining records from one or more tables, or asking and answering specific question about the data. For example, you might need to determine how many customers have a balance outstanding over sixty days, or how many customers have exceeded their credit limit. In almost all of these situations you could construct a new index, based on outstanding days or outstanding amounts, for example, use the data in the new indexed order, and then delete the index when you have completed the task at hand. An alternative, however, is to use a structured query. A *structured query* is a statement, written according to the rules of a language called Structured Query Language (SQL — pronounced as both sequel or the letters S-Q-L), that uniquely identifies a set of records from one or more tables.[1] For example, a requirement such as

Select all of the internal employee names from the PhoneBook table (Table 9-1) who are assigned to the Office designated as HM

should result in all of the names being listed for those employees in Table 9-1 who are assigned to the home office. When this statement is written as an SQL structured statement, it becomes

```
Select Names From PhoneBook Where Office = "HM"
```

In Section 9.6 we present structured queries in detail, show how to construct such statements, and incorporate them within Visual Basic to create subsets of records from one or more tables.

The Jet Engine and RecordSets

A database management system (DBMS) is defined as a package of one or more computer programs designed to establish, maintain, and use a database The underlying DBMS provided with Visual Basic is Microsoft's *Jet* database engine, which is referred to as the Jet engine, for short.[2] The Jet engine is responsible for opening a database, locating records from among the tables, providing access to these records, maintaining the security of the records as defined for the database, and other such capabilities requisite to a DBMS.

When accessed by Visual Basic the Jet engine creates a workspace into which the engine writes a set of records that may be manipulated by Visual Basic controls and code. This set of records, referred to as a *RecordSet*, consists of one of the following:

1. All of the records in a single table, in stored order, or
2. All of the records in a single table, in an indexed order, or
3. A select group of records, from one or more tables, constructed using a structured query.

---

[1] The set of records can be empty; i.e., no records meet the selected criteria.

[2] The Jet engine is also the DBMS that underlies Microsoft's Access Database system.

Table 9-4 RecordSet Types

Type	Name	Usage
0	Table-Type	Construct a set of records that uses an index and can be updated, given the proper permissions.
1	Dynaset-Type	Construct a set of records that is either in stored order or is determined by a structured query, and can be updated, given the proper permissions.
2	Snapshot-Type	Construct a set of records that is either in stored order or is determined by a structured query, and that can only be examined but not updated.

To accommodate the different type of records that the Jet engine can create in a workspace, three different types of RecordSets can be constructed. Table 9-4 lists the three available types and their usage.

In the following sections we will explore how to use Visual Basic to create and use each of the RecordSet types listed in Table 9-4. This can be accomplished using code, using a Data control, or by a combination of these two techniques. Although both of these techniques, code and control, are presented in this chapter, we begin our exploration using the control technique.

Exercises 9.1

1. Define the following terms and identify how they are related:
   a. table
   b. record
   c. field

2. Define the following terms:
   a. ERD diagram
   b. cardinality
   c. index
   d. stored order
   e. key field
   f. primary key
   g. relational database

3. a. List the fifth record that will be printed if Table 9-1 were displayed in stored order.
   b. List the fifth record that will be printed if Table 9-1 were displayed in name index order.
   c. List the fifth record that would be printed if Table 9-1 were displayed in Extension index order.
   d. For your answers to Exercises 3b. and 3c., what specific order did you assume for the index?

4. a. List the sixth record that will be printed if Table 9-2 were displayed in stored order.

  b. List the sixth record that will be printed if Table 9-2 were displayed in last name index order.

  c. List the sixth record that would be printed if Table 9-2 were displayed in city index order.

  d. List the sixth record that would be printed if Table 9-2 were displayed in zip code order.

  e. For your answers to Exercises 4a., 4b., and 4c., what specific order did you assume for the index?

5. Microsoft provides a database named `Biblio` with Visual Basic that contains tables for authors, book titles, and publishers. The following figure illustrates the ERD diagram for these tables. Using this diagram, describe the relationships between the various entities.

The ERD Diagram for the Biblio Database

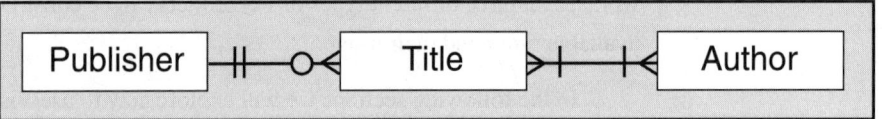

6. For the following queries, determine the record that will be displayed:

  a. Select all the internal employee names from the PhoneBook table (Table 9-1) whose extensions are between 100 and 200.

  b. Select all the internal employee named from the PhoneBook table (Table 9-1) whose last name begins with a B.

  c. Select all the sales representatives from the SalesForce table (Table 9-2) who are assigned to office HM.

  d. Select all the sales representatives from the SalesForce table (Table 9-2) who live in Orange, New Jersey.

  e. Select all the sales representatives from the SalesForce table (Table 9-2) who have a middle initial.

7. a. Assuming the ID field is a primary key whose value is the record number assigned by the Jet engine, determine how many records were deleted from Table 9-1.

  b. Assuming the ID field is a primary key whose value is the record number assigned by the Jet engine, determine how many records were deleted from Table 9-2.

8. a. Determine the type of RecordSet that should be used if you were using the Jet engine to construct a set of records created using an index.

  b. Determine the type of RecordSet that should be used if you were using the Jet engine to construct a set of records created using a structured query and needing to be updated.

  c. Determine the type of RecordSet that should be used if you were using the Jet engine to construct a set of records created using a structured query that is to be used for viewing only.

9.2 Using the Data Control

In accessing a database table, through either Visual Basic code or using a special control provided for this purpose, three items must always be specified. These are

1. The name and location of the database,
2. The name of the desired table, and
3. The type of RecordSet.

Each of these items can be specified using properties of the Data control. This control, as it appears in the Toolbox and on a form at design-time, is shown in Figures 9-5 and 9-6 respectively. The actions performed by the Data control's movement buttons are also listed in Figure 9-6.

Figure 9-5

The Toolbar's Data Control Icon

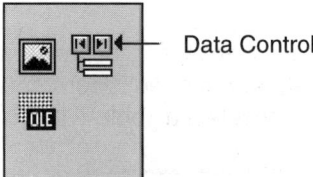

Data Control

Figure 9-6

The Data Control at Design-Time

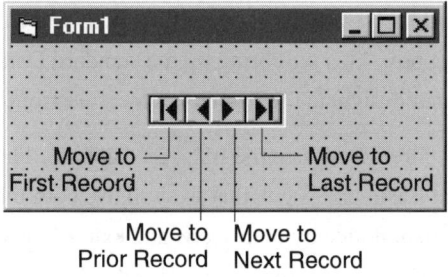

The Data control is placed on a form in the same manner as any other Visual Basic control. The standard prefix for a Data control is `dat`, and we will name our first control, using its **Name** property, `datPhone`. We will also clear the Data control's **Caption** property of all characters, as we have typically done with Text box controls. Table 9-5 lists the properties that must then be set for the database's location and name, desired table, and RecordSet type, respectively.

Each of the properties listed in Table 9-5, must be set for the Data control to be correctly attached to a specific table and to permit the Jet engine to produce a set of records that can be manipulated in Visual Basic. The general rule for Data controls is one control per table. At run-time the Data control calls upon the Jet engine to create a single workspace into which a single RecordSet is automatically written. Since our fist application will only use the PhoneBook table (Table 9-1), we will need only one Data control.

Table 9-5 Attaching a Data Control to a Table

To Set:	Use this Property:
Database location and name	DatabaseName
Table name	RecordSource
RecordSet Type	RecordsetType

Figure 9-7 shows how the database's location and name appear in the **DatabaseName** property setting box. The complete `Company` database, which includes Tables 9-1 through 9-3, is provided on the source code diskette that comes with this text book. On our computer, this database resides in the directory named `\Program Files\Microsoft Visual Basic`. Thus, the complete path name for the file, placed in the **DatabaseName** property, is

---

Programmers' Notes

Using a Data Control

For each set of records you wish to access, you can either set up a Data control or use Visual Basic code. If you use a control, the rule is one Data control per RecordSet. To set up and use a Data control, you must, at a minimum, set the following three properties:

1. DatabaseName, which names the desired database and defines where it is located,
2. RecordSource, which names the table or structured query from which a RecordSet is created, and
3. RecordSetType, which defines the type of RecordSet that the Jet engine will create.

The third property, RecordSetType, does not have to be explicitly set, because it uses a default Dynaset type. The Dynaset is fine for stored-order or structured-query defined record sets that can be updated. If you are going to use an index, however, you must explicitly select a Table-type RecordSet.

`C:\Program Files\Microsoft Visual Basic\Company.mdb`. If you don't want to type this path name into the DatabaseName setting box, you can click on the ellipses (...) to the right of the setting box. This will bring up the standard Database dialog, illustrated in Figure 9-8, and you can designate the database's location from within this dialog.

In reviewing Figure 9-8, notice the `Biblio` database. This database is provided by Microsoft with Visual Basic and is one that we will use both in the section exercises and later in this chapter. Also, notice by their icons and extensions (.mdb) that both the `Company` and `Biblio` databases are Access databases. This database type is the default used in Visual Basic. If you are working with a database created in another application, such as dBase or Paradox, you must change the database application name set for the **Connect** property.

Having set the location and database name using the **DatabaseName** property, we now continue to link the Data control to a specific database table. This is done, as indicated in Table 9-5, using the **RecordSource** property. As shown in Figure 9-9, once the **DatabaseName** has been set, Visual Basic will provide a drop-down list of available tables in the database, when the RecordSource property is accessed. In this case, we will select the PhoneBook table (Table 9-1).

The last property that must be set is the **RecordsetType**. Table 9-4, presented at the end of the previous section, provides the basis for the **RecordsetType** selection. As indicated in this table, if an index is to be used, the **RecordsetType** must be a Table-type; other-

Figure 9-7

Setting the DatabaseName Property

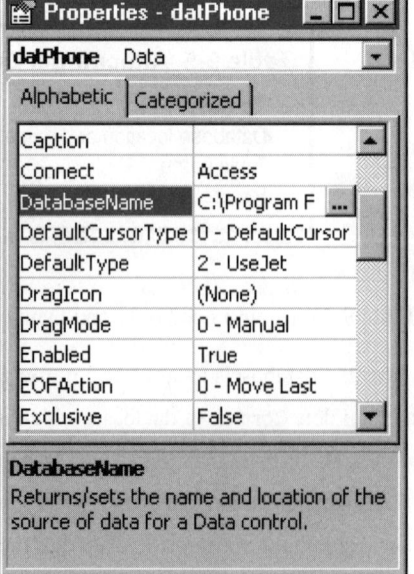

Figure 9-8

*Using the DatabaseName
Dialog Box*

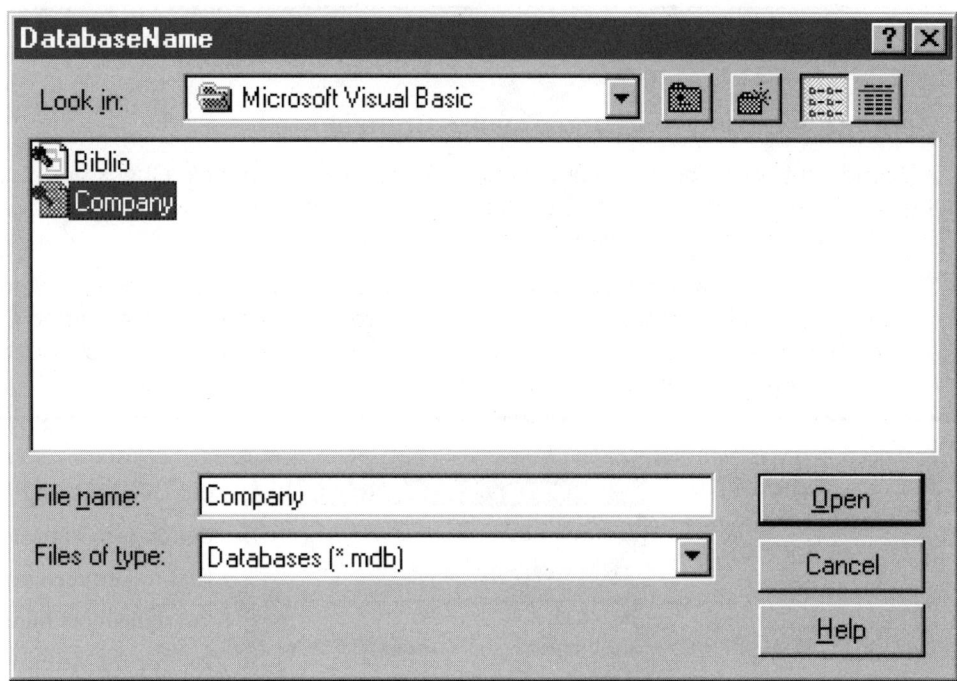

wise, either a Dynaset- or Snapshot-type can be used depending upon whether or not the records are to be updated.

For our first application we will simply use the Data control to display and update the PhoneBook's records in stored order. From Table 9-4 we see that the proper RecordSet for this usage is a Dynaset. Since this is the default value used for the **RecordsetType** property, no explicit setting need be made. Figure 9-10, however, shows the drop-down box provided for this property, and the three RecordSet types available for explicit selection.

The sole purpose of the Data control is to provide a connection between an application

Figure 9-9

*Setting the
RecordSource Property*

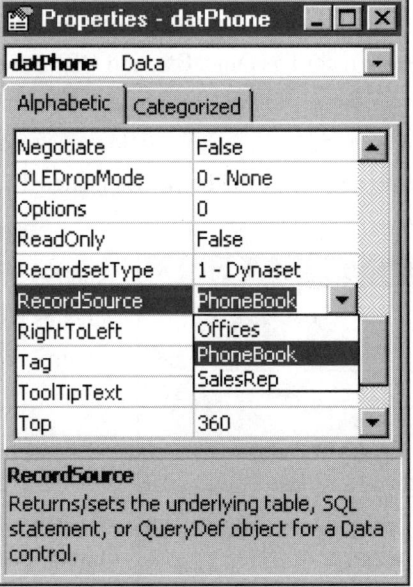

and an external database—when the application containing the control is executed, the table assigned to the Data control is opened, and a RecordSet created. In our specific case, since we have used a Dynaset type of RecordSet, all of the records in the PhoneBook table will be included in the RecordSet created by the Jet engine and made available to our Data control.

To move through the records in the RecordSet, which is referred to as *browsing* or *navigating* the table, we can use the buttons provided with the Data control. At any point in time, only one record is actually accessible, and this record is referred to as the *current record*. In

---

Programmers' Notes

Creating a Bound and Data–Aware Control

A Bound control can be a Text box, Label, Picture box, Image box, Check box, List box, Combo box, custom third-party controls, or OLE container control. The control becomes a Bound control by setting its **DataSource** property to the name of a Data control.

The control is then made data-aware by setting its **DataField** property to a field name. The field name must represent a field that is present in the Recordset accessed by the named Data control. Being *data-aware* means that the control has immediate access to the current record's data field value as identified by the control's **DataField** property setting.

Figure 9-10

Setting the RecordSet Type Property

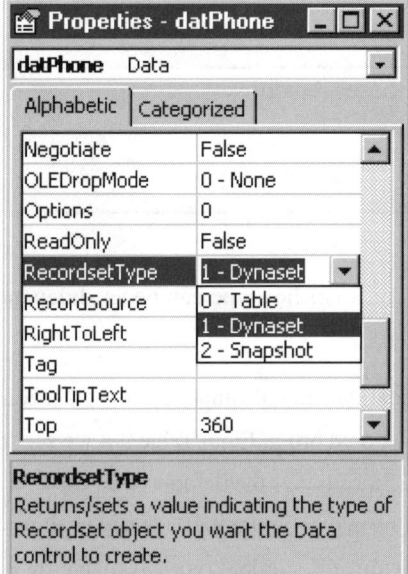

our case, clicking the Data control's left-most button (see Figure 9-6) makes PhoneBook's first record the current record, while clicking the right-most button makes the PhoneBook's last record the current record. Similarly, clicking the Previous Button and Next Button moves the record position forward and backward through the records contained in the RecordSet. There remains one significant problem, however, and this is that we have made no provision for actually seeing the data in the current record. This is accomplished using bound controls.

Bound Controls

Figure 9-11 illustrates Program 9-1's interface. As shown, three Text boxes are used to display the data in a current record's Name, Ext, and Office fields. To do this we will bind each of the three Text box controls to the Data control. Then, as we move through the RecordSet using the Data control's buttons, the field values from the current record will automatically be picked up and displayed in the designated Text boxes.

Figure 9-11

Program 9-1's Interface

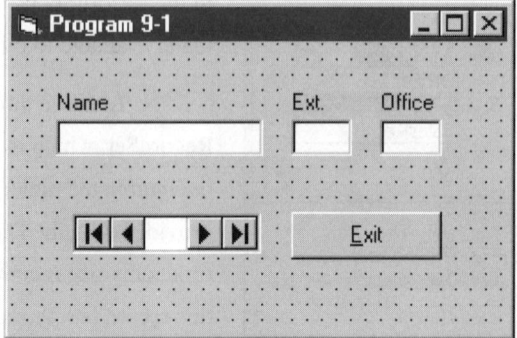

Binding an individual control, such as a Text box, to a Data control creates what is called a *data-aware* control. This means that the control has access to, or becomes aware of, the data field value in the current record identified by a Data control. Such controls, which can be a Text box, Label, Picture box, Image box, Check

---

Table 9-6 Program 9-1's Properties Table

Object	Property	Setting
Form	Name	frmMain
	Caption	Program 9-1
Label	Name	lblName
	Caption	Name
Label	Name	lblExt
	Caption	Ext.
Label	Name	lblOffice
	Caption	Office
Text Box	Name	txtName
	Text	(Blank)
	DataSource	datPhone
	DataField	Name
Text Box	Name	txtExt
	Text	(Blank)
	DataSource	datPhone
	DataField	Ext
Text Box	Name	txtOffice
	Text	(Blank)
	DataSource	datPhone
	DataField	Office
Data Control	Name	datPhone
	Caption	(Blank)
	DatabaseName	C:\Program Files\Microsoft Visual Basic\Company.mdb
	RecordSource	PhoneBook
	RecordsetType	Dynaset
Command Button	Name	cmdExit
	Caption	E&xit

Figure 9-12

Binding a Control to the datPhone Data Control

box, List box, Combo box, custom third-party controls, or OLE container controls, are then referred to as *bound controls*.

Binding a control, such as a Text box, to a Data control requires setting the control's **DataSource** and **DataField** properties. Setting the **DataSource** property binds the control to a specific Data control, while setting the **DataField** property makes the bound control aware of (that is, attached to) a specific field. For example, look at Figure 9-12, which shows the setting for the Text box that will be used to display the PhoneBook's **Name** field. Since all of the Text boxes used in Program 9-1

Figure 9-13

Setting the DataField Property

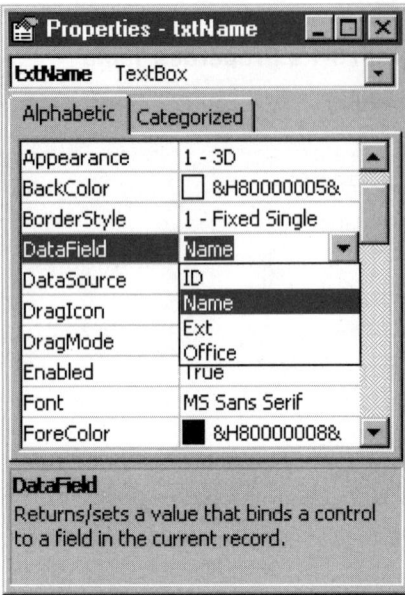

will be used for PhoneBook data, each of these control will be bound to the `datPhone` Data control using the setting shown in Figure 9-12.

Once a control is bound to a Data control, it is made data-aware by setting its **DataField** property. As illustrated in Figure 9-13, Visual Basic provides a dropdown list of all of the fields that can be assigned to the control. These fields are, of course, the fields for the RecordSet identified by the Data control. In our specific example, these include all of the PhoneBook table's fields.

Table 9-6 lists the relevant property settings for Program 9-1's controls (see Figure 9-11). As listed in this table, all of the Text boxes are bound to the `datPhone` Data control. The significant difference between each box is the field in the PhoneBook table that each box is made aware of. Label controls are provided as a means of clearly identifying the displayed fields.

If Program 9-1 is now run, without adding any code, the Text boxes will display the values of the current record determined by the Data control's push buttons. As we will see in Section 9-5, any changes made in the Text boxes will automatically be made to the underlying PhoneBook data, if appropriate access privileges are set.

Typically, applications that use a Data control do provide some code for the control. At a minimum, this code sets and maintains the Data control's **Caption** property to identify the currently displayed record. Doing this requires a single line of code, but first we must consider the Data control's event procedures to determine where this line of code should be placed.

Data Control Event Procedures

A number of event procedures and methods are particularly useful for applications that use a Data control. Some of these, like the `Form_Load` event, have much broader uses. Others, such as the **Refresh** method, have more limited use, but still have applicability beyond their connection to the Data control. Still others, such as the `Reposition` event, only have applicability to a Data control. We will examine each of these events and methods as they relate to the Data control.

The first method that we will examine is the **Refresh** method. As it relates to a Data control, this method is used to either open a database and build a new RecordSet, reopen a database and recreate a RecordSet with updated data, or reopen a database and rebuild a new RecordSet when one of the Data control properties listed in Table 9-7 has been changed at run-time.

Table 9-7 Effect of Using the Refresh Method

If this property is changed:	This is the effect of a Refresh operation:
Database Name	Database is reopened and the RecordSet rebuilt.
RecordSource	RecordSet is rebuilt.
Options	RecordSet is rebuilt.
Connect	Database is reopened and the RecordSet rebuilt.
Exclusive	Database is reopened and the RecordSet rebuilt.
ReadOnly	Database is reopened and the RecordSet rebuilt.

For our immediate purposes we will invoke the **Refresh** method from within a `Form_Load` event to explicitly open a Data-control specified database. Although the database would eventually be opened implicitly, by explicitly using the **Refresh** method at form-load time we ensure that a RecordSet is immediately available and can be directly manipulated using code as the need arises. This is a typical use for the `Form_Load` event—to include initialization code for a form, to specify initial control settings at run-time rather than at design-time, and to explicitly open all files used by an application. Thus, for our `datPhone` Data control the `Form_Load` event will initially appear as

```
Private Sub Form_Load()
  datPhone.Refresh
End Sub
```

In reviewing this code, pay particular attention to the dot notation used. Here, the **Refresh** method is applied to the Data control table named `datPhone`, and will cause the Jet engine to open and build a RecordSet when the form is loaded. Before leaving the `Form_Load` event, there is one other item that should be addressed—what to provide for the Data control's initial **Caption**. The three generally used options are

1. Provide the initial record's position in the RecordSet;
2. Provide a unique identification associated with initial record, such as its key value; and
3. Leave the **Caption** blank.

The first option is the one most commonly used and the one that we will use. This is accomplished by expanding the `Form_Load` event procedure to the following:

```
Private Sub Form_Load()
  datPhone.Refresh
  datPhone.Caption = 1
End Sub
```

Figure 9-14

The Opening Screen Presented by Program 9-1

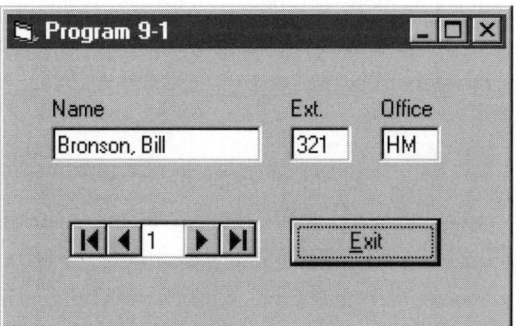

Figure 9-14 shows the effect of setting the **Caption** property to 1 in the `Form_Load` event by illustrating how the application looks when it is first executed.

Identifying the first record in a RecordSet with a caption of 1 is reasonable, because users generally expect to see the first record presented as record number 1, the second record as record number 2, and so on. However, this approach does have a drawback because a record's position in the RecordSet can vary, depending on the what is done to the records. For example, a record's position can change whenever a record is deleted or whenever a RecordSet is rebuilt. Thus, the record initially identified with a caption value of 2 may later become the first record in the set and be identified with a caption value of 1. Although this is usually not a problem, occasionally a user may either wonder about or complain that the same record appears to have two different record numbers.

The alternatives to assigning a possibly transient record position to the Data control's **Caption** value are either to provide no caption at all or to use a non-changing value, stored as a field value, that uniquely identifies each record. For the PhoneBook records, such a value is provided by the ID field. The following statement shows how this field's value is accessed and can be used to set the Data control's caption property:

```
datPhone.Caption = datPhone.Recordset("ID")
```

Notice a specific field is identified by enclosing the quoted field name within parentheses. The drawback to using a specific field's value, however, is that as a user sequentially moves through the RecordSet using the Data control's push buttons, the displayed caption value can appear to "jump." For example, if a user moves through the records from the first to the last in the RecordSet created by Program 9-1, the **Caption** value will change from 15 to 21 when the user moves from the twelfth record, corresponding to Harriet Miller, to the thirteenth record, corresponding to Pat O'Neil (see Table 9-1). For most users this type of jump is very disconcerting. A way around this problem is to attach a textual identification with the caption, as in the following statement:

```
datPhone.Caption = "ID No = " & datPhone.Recordset("ID")
```

Regardless of which approach you select, it is always important to try and anticipate how your decisions will affect a user. For small decisions, such as how a caption or label will appear, the program designer should make the decision, explain how it works, and be prepared to make modifications based on user feedback. For more important decisions, users should always be consulted beforehand. Be aware, however, that asking users for decisions on minor design criteria and especially on *how* an operation is performed, is typically construed as bothersome and an indication that the programmer is inexperienced. Similarly, not asking users for input on matters that directly affect them, such as *what* data they require as output from an application, is typically construed as an indication that the programmer is insensitive to their needs. Obtaining the proper balance is what distinguishes both very successful programmers from the not-so-successful, and very successful applications from annoying ones.

Having now selected the initial value displayed for the Data control's **Caption** (we will use the record number approach), it only remains to keep the caption current as the user moves through the RecordSet. To do this, we will use the Data control's `Reposition` event. This event is triggered *after* one of the control's push buttons has been activated and the current record has been changed. The required event procedure is

```
Private Sub datPhone_Reposition()
  datPhone.Caption = datPhone.Recordset.AbsolutePosition + 1
End Sub
```

The **AbsolutePosition** method, which is only applicable to Dynaset- and Snapshot-type RecordSets, returns the relative record position of the RecordSet's current record, with the first record identified as position 0. Adding 1 to the returned value alters the record position to begin with the number 1. The complete code provided for Program 9-1 is listed below.

Program 9-1's Event Code

```
Private Sub Form_Load()
  datPhone.Refresh
  datPhone.Caption = 1
End Sub

Private Sub datPhone_Reposition()
  datPhone.Caption = datPhone.Recordset.AbsolutePosition + 1
End Sub

Private Sub cmdExit_Click()
  Beep
  End
End Sub
```

The only change you might want to make in Program 9-1's event code is to replace the setting of the Data control's **Caption** to 1 in the `Form_Load` event with the setting method used in the `Reposition` event code. Both approaches to initializing the caption are equally valid.

Before leaving this event code, we make note of the fact that the `Form_Load` event procedure can also be used to set a Data control's **DatabaseName** and **RecordSource** properties at run-time. For example, the statements

```
datPhone.DatabaseName = App.Path & "\Company.mdb"
datPhone.RecordSource = "PhoneBook"
```

can be included in the `Form_Load` event procedure to set the respectively named property values. These statements would appear before the **Refresh** method is invoked. In setting the **DatabaseName** property, the keyword **App** is the name of a globally defined object that provides information about an application's title, path, and executable file name. When the **Path** method is applied to this object it specifies the path of the *project* file when the application is executed from the development environment, or the path of the *executable* file when the application is run as an executable file. Assuming that the `Company` database is located in the same directory, the expression `App.Path & "\Company.mdb"` correctly identifies the location and name of the desired database. An alternative is to provide the complete path name for the database, which is necessary if the database is located in a different directory than the application's form.

Index Ordering

When Program 9-1 is executed, the records built for the RecordSet will be in stored order. Typically, however, a user will expect the names to be accessed alphabetically, from A to Z. There are two approaches to creating this anticipated ordering. The first approach, which uses the **Name** index created for the PhoneBook table, is described next. The second approach, and a more powerful programming technique that uses structured queries, is presented in the next section.

To present the names provided by Program 9-1 in alphabetical order using an index requires minor changes to the program. The first modification, which is indicated by the information previously provided by Table 9-4, requires that the RecordSet type be a Table-type to accommodate a RecordSet built using an index. The final set of modifications is concerned with the code, which must set the active index to **Name** and update the Data control's **Caption** property correctly. To understand these changes, review Program 9-2's event code.

Program 9-2's Event Code

```
Private Sub Form_Load()
  datPhone.Refresh
  datPhone.Recordset.Index = "Name"
  datPhone.Caption = "ID = " & datPhone.Recordset("ID")
End Sub

Private Sub datPhone_Reposition()
  datPhone.Caption = "ID = " & datPhone.Recordset("ID")
End Sub

Private Sub cmdExit_Click()
  Beep
  End
End Sub
```

The first change to notice in the event code is the modification to the `Form_Load` event. Here we have used the **Index** method to explicitly set the index to **Name**. If this explicit setting was omitted, the RecordSet would be built using the table's primary index.

Next, notice that the Data control's **Caption** property is set and maintained using each record's ID value. Since the **AbsoluteProperty** method cannot be used with Table-type RecordSets, we must either keep track of record numbers by determining which push button was activated, or use the **Caption** property to display some other information, such as an ID value. We have chosen the latter approach both because of its simplicity and to reinforce use of the syntax required in directly accessing a record's field value.

Figure 9-15

The Opening Screen Presented by Program 9-2

Figure 9-15 shows how Program 9-2 appears when it is first executed. Notice that the first record displayed is, alphabetically, the first record in the PhoneBook table that was previously listed as Table 9-1. Also notice that the Data control **Caption** correctly identifies this as the record whose ID value is 30.

1. List the three Data control properties that must be set to correctly build a RecordSet.

2. a. Under what circumstances would you use a Table for a Data control's RecordSet property?

    b. Under what circumstances would you use a Dynaset for a Data control's RecordSet property?

    c. Under what circumstances would you use a Snapshot for a Data control's RecordSet property?

3. a. What is a bound control?

    b. List the controls that can be used as bound controls.

    c. List the properties that must be set to create a bound control.

4. Using the Code window, determine and list all event procedures associated with a Data control.

5. Using the Help facility, obtain documentation on the following terms:

    a. AbsolutePosition Property

    b. Dynaset-type Recordset

    c. Snapshot-type Recordset

    d. Table-type Recordset

    e. Path Property

    f. Refresh Method

    g. Validate Event

6. Enter and execute Program 9-1 on your computer.

7. a. Modify Program 9-1 so that the Data control's **Caption** displays the current record's ID field value.

    b. Modify Program 9-1 so that the Data control's **Caption** is always blank.

8. Enter and execute Program 9-2 on your computer.

9. Modify Program 9-2 so that the displayed names are presented in Extension value order. (**Hint:** The PhoneBook table has an index named *Ext*.)

10. a. Write a Visual Basic Program that uses a Data control to display the records in the Company database's SalesRep table (see Table 11-2.) The records should be displayed as they are stored in the table.

    b. Modify the program written for Exercise 10a. to display the records in last-name indexed order. (**Hint:** The SalesRep table has an index named *LName*.)

11. Write a Visual Basic Program that uses a Data control to display the records in the Company database's Office table (see Table 11-2.) The records should be displayed as they are stored in the table.

9.3 Creating RecordSets Using SQL

Using a table's name as a Data control's **RecordSource** property restricts us to viewing a single table's records in either stored or indexed order. There will be times, however, when you will need to either view records in an order for which no index exists, create a set of records that is constructed from more than one table, or view a subset of records that meets one or more criteria. For example, you might need to create a list of people whose outstanding balance is over sixty days old, or create a list of people who owe more than $500, or possibly cross check two tables to determine names that appear in both. For situations such as these, structured queries can be used as a **RecordSource** property value in place of a table's name.

For example, in Program 9-1, the **RecordSource** property was set to PhoneBook at design-time, which caused the Jet engine to create a RecordSet consisting of all this table's records in stored order. Instead of setting the **RecordSource** property to a table's name, a structured query can be used. For example, the same RecordSet created by Program 9-1 can be created by entering the following structured query into the **RecordSource** property:

```
Select * From PhoneBook
```

This statement is rather easy to read, once you understand that the * is a shortcut that means all fields are to be listed, in the order they appear in the table. Thus, this statement is read "*select* all fields *from the* PhoneBook table." Since no further constraints are placed on the table, the default is to select all of the table's records.

A structured query **Select** statement is quite different from Visual Basic's **Select Case** statement. As previously defined in Section 9.1, a *structured query* is a statement written according to the rules of a language called Structured Query Language (SQL—pronounced as both sequel or the letters S-Q-L), that uniquely identifies a set of records from one or more tables. Although obtaining all of the record's in a table is accomplished easier by using a table's name as the **RecordSource** property value, structured queries provide much more flexibility to create and order individualized sets of records. Structured queries can be entered as a **RecordSource** value either at design-time or set at run-time, and we show how to do both in this section. First, however, we must become familiar with the SQL **Select** statement.

SQL was developed by IBM in the 1970s, and became the foundation of its DB2 data management system. In 1986, an American National Standards Institute (ANSI) standard was approved for this language, and since that time many commercial DBMS products, including Microsoft's Jet engine, support it as an extremely powerful technique for extracting data from database tables.

The basic syntax of an SQL **Select** command, which is referred to as a structured query, is

Select *field-name(s)* **From** *table(s)* **Where** *condition(s)* **Order By** *field-name(s)*

Formally, this statement consists of four clauses; a **Select** clause, a **From** clause, a **Where** clause and an **Order By** clause. The words **Select, From, Where**, and **Order By**, are all SQL keywords.

At a minimum, a structured query must contain both a **Select** and **From** clause; the **Select** clause specifies the field values that will be returned by the query, while the **From** clause specifies the table or tables whose records will be searched. Additionally, if any restrictions are placed on the data to be selected, or if the selected information is to be presented in a specified order, the **Where** or **Order** clauses must be included, respectively. For example, in the statement

```
Select * From PhoneBook Order By Ext
```
→ *default in ascending*

the **Select** *clause specifies that all fields are to be obtained, the **From** clause specifies that the fields are to come from the PhoneBook table, and the **Order** clause specifies that the RecordSet is to be constructed in increasing (that is, ascending) order based on the values in the Ext field. If descending order is desired (that is, from highest to lowest extension values) the SQL keyword **Desc** must be placed after the field name in the **Order** clause. Thus, the SQL statement

```
Select * From PhoneBook Order By Ext Desc
```

performs the same function as the previous SQL statement, but returns the data in descending extension number order. If an index exists for the field name upon which the data is being ordered, the Jet engine will automatically use this index to sort the data; if no index exists, the Jet engine sorts the data in the specified order before creating the returned RecordSet. Because structured queries are so versatile and can be used to construct RecordSets that contain records constructed from more than one table, they are used extensively as the **RecordSource** property for many Visual Basic database applications. This, of course, implies that either a Dynaset- or Snapshot-type value is used for the **RecordsetType** property, because only these two types of RecordSets can be constructed using a structured query (see Table 9-4).

To illustrate the usefulness of creating RecordSets using structured queries, we present a number of examples using the SQL **Select** statement. In the first two examples we use the `Company` database, whose tables were previously listed as Tables 9-1 through 9-3. We then construct RecordSets with records derived from two tables. For these latter examples we will use the `Biblio` database provided by Microsoft with Visual Basic.

Example 1: Using the PhoneBook table, create a RecordSet consisting of all fields for employees in the home office.

The structured query for this example is

```
Select * From PhoneBook Where Office = 'HM'
```

Here we have used a **Where** clause, which creates a set of records where each record must meet the specified condition to be included in the final RecordSet. The resulting set of records is frequently referred to as a *filtered set*, and the **Where** clause itself is commonly

Table 9-8 Publishers

PubID	Name	Company Name	Address
1	ACM	Association for Computing Machinery	11 W. 42nd St., 3rd flr.
2	Addison-Wesley	Addison-Wesley Publishing Co Inc.	Rte 128
3	Bantam Books	Bantam Books Div of: Bantam Doubleday Dell	666 Fifth Ave
4	Benjamin/Cummings	Benjamin-Cummings Publishing Company Subs.	390 Bridge Pkwy.
5	Brady Pub.	Brady Books Div. of Prentice Hall Pr.	15 Columbus Cir.
6	Computer Science Press	Computer Science Press Inc Imprint	41 Madison Ave
7	ETN Corporation	ETN Corp.	RD 4, Box 659
8	Gale	Gale Research, Incorporated	835 Penobscot Bldg
9	IEEE	IEEE Computer Society Press	10662 Los Vaqueros
10	Intertext	Inntertext Publications/Multiscience	2633 E. 17th Ave.

referred to as a *filter*. In reviewing this clause, notice that the value being searched for (HM) is enclosed in single quotes. This is required in SQL when the field type of the desired item is a string type. If the field type were numeric, the value in the SQL **Where** clause would not be enclosed in single quotes. As always, the asterisk (*) in the query results in all fields in the selected records being included in the RecordSet, in the order that they exist in the underlying table. If you want to change this order, you can individually list the fields in the desired order. For example, the structured query

```
Select Office, Name, Ext, ID From PhoneBook Where Office = 'HM'
```

extracts the same data as the prior query, but creates a RecordSet in which each record has the field order listed in the **Select** statement. This ordering makes no difference to an application using a Data control, as long as the fields required by the data-aware controls are included in the query. Each data-aware control will subsequently extract its required field from the resulting RecordSet, no matter where the field is physically located within a record. If, however, a field is missing from the record required by a data-aware control, the error message `Item not found in this collection` is displayed.

Finally, notice that when explicit fields are listed within a **Select** clause, the individual field names are separated by commas. To cause this query to be the actual source of a RecordSet at design-time, it must be entered as a Data control's **RecordSource** property value.

Example 2: Using the SalesForce table, create a RecordSet consisting of all fields for employees living in Orange.

The structured query for this example is

```
Select * From SalesForce Where City = 'Orange'
```

In reviewing this query, notice that once again, since the City is a string field, we have enclosed the value being searched for within single quotes. As always, the query defines both the fields to be included in the RecordSet and the table from which these fields are to

Table 9-8 Publishers

City	State	Zip	Telephone	Fax	Comments
New York	NY	10036	212-869-7440		
Reading	MA	01867	617-944-3700	617-964-9460	
New York	NY	10103	800-223-6834	212-765-3869	GENERAL
Redwood City	CA	94065	800-950-2665	415-594-4409	
New York	NY	10023	212-373-8093	212-373-8292	
New York	NY	10010	212-576-9400	212-689-2383	Introductory
Montoursville	PA	17754-9433	717-435-2202	717-435-2802	Technical book
Detroit	MI	48226-4094	313-961-2242	313-961-6083	
Los Alamitos	CA	90720	800-272-6657	714-821-4010	PROFESSION
Anchorage	AK	99508			

be taken. Additionally, the **Where** clause creates a filtered record set, where each selected record meets the stated requirement.

Although both of the preceding two examples have used a simple relational expression in the **Where** clause, compound expressions using the **And** and **Or** keywords are valid. For example, the structured query

```
Select Name From PhoneBook Where  Ext < 300 And Ext > 900
```

produces a set of records consisting of the Name field only for those individuals having an extension number either less than 300 or greater than 900. Notice that since the Ext field is defined as a numeric field, the values within the relational expression have not been enclosed in single quotes.

Relationships Reconsidered

The `Company` database we have used consists of three tables that, in practice, would be used almost independently of each other. That is, we could easily construct three forms, each of which uses its own Data control to assess and display data from each of the three tables individually.

It is not unusual to encounter databases with tables that are related in a more significant manner. As an example of such a database, we will use the `Biblio` database provided by Microsoft with Visual Basic. This database consists of tables containing information about publishers, titles, and authors of current computer science text books. Tables 9-8 through 9-11 list the names and the first ten records of each of the four tables that comprise the `Biblio` database. The relationship between the Publishers, Titles, and Authors tables is shown by the ERD diagram illustrated in Figure 9-16.

As shown in Figure 9-16, and reading from left to right, a publisher can be associated with zero or more titles, and a title can have one or more authors. Similarly, reading from right to left, an author can be associated with one or more titles, while a title can only be

Table 9-9 Titles

Title	Year Published	ISBN	PubID	Description	Notes	Subject	Comments
Database management; developing application	1989	0-0131985-2-1	17	xx, 441 p. : il			
Select— SQL ; the relational database language	1992	0-0238669-4-2	12	xv, 446 p.			
dBase IV programming	1994	0-0280042-4-8	73				
Step-by-step dBase IV	1995	0-0280095-2-5	52				
Guide to ORACLE	1990	0-0702063-1-7	13	xii, 354 p. : ill	Includes I	ORACLE	
The database experts' guide to SQL	1988	0-0703900-6-1	10				
		00703					
Oracle/SQL; a professional programmer's guide	1992	0-0704077-5-4	13	xx, 543 p. : il			
SQL 400: A Professional Programmer's Guide	1994	0-0704079-9-1	52				
Database system concepts	1986	0-0704475-2-7	13				
Microsoft FoxPro 2.5 applications programming	1993	0-0705015-3-X	61	xiii, 412 p. : i			

associated with a single publisher. Using Tables 9-8 through 9-10 we can easily establish RecordSets for any of the one-to-many relationships shown in Figure 9-16. This is accomplished by matching a desired field value in the appropriate table. For example, if we needed to locate all titles associated with the publisher ETN, the following structured query could be entered as a **RecordSource** property value:

```
Select * From Titles Where PubID = 7
```

This type of query, which is a straightforward lookup in a single table, is typical of that used for a one-to-many relationship. The standard practice here is simply to locate all records in the table on the many side of the relationship that have a matching field value for the single entity on the one side of the relationship. Unfortunately, no such simple lookup generally exists for locating matching entries corresponding to a many-to-many relationship.

For example, assume that we need to locate all authors associated with a single title. Since the titles-to-authors relationship is a many-to-many relationship, each title can have one or more associated authors and each author can be associated with one or more titles. To handle such relationships, tables referred to as both *cross-reference, correlation,* and *intersection* tables (all three terms are synonymous) are used. An example of a correlation table is

Table 9-10 Authors

Au_ID	Author	Year Born
1	Adams, Pat	
2	Adrian, Merv	
3	Ageloff, Roy	1943
4	Andersen, Virginia	
5	Antonovich Michael P.	
6	Arnott, Steven E.	
7	Arntson, L. Joyce	
8	Ault, Michael R	
9	Avison, D. E.	
10	Bard, Dick	1941

illustrated by Table 9-11. Here, all authors associated with a particular ISBN number can be identified by locating all occurrences of the same ISBN number in the first column. Similarly, all books written by a single author can be identified by locating all occurrences of the author's ID number in the second column. Thus, if we needed to locate all the authors associated with the book entitled *Guide to ORACLE*, which has an ISBN number 0-0702063-1-7 (see the fifth record in Table 9-9), we could use the following structured query:

Table 9-11 TitleAuthor	
ISBN	**Au_ID**
0-0131985-2-1	13
0-0238669-4-2	113
0-0280042-4-8	11
0-0280042-4-8	120
0-0280095-2-5	171
0-0702063-1-7	26
0-0702063-1-7	65
0-0702063-1-7	104
0-0703900-6-1	96
0-0704077-5-4	59

```
Select * From TitleAuthor Where ISBN = '0-0702063-1-1'
```

Similarly, if we needed to identify all books associated with the author named Virginia Andersen (the fourth author listed in Table 9-10), who has the author identification number 4, we could use the following structured query:

```
Select * From TitleAuthor Where Au_ID = 4
```

Notice that in the first query the "looked for" value has been enclosed in single quotes, while in the second query no quotes are used. This is because the ISBN field is defined as a string field, while the Au_ID field is defined as a numeric field in the TitleAuthor table.

Figure 9-16

The ERD Diagram For The Biblio.mdb Database

Creating Multi-Table Recordsets

In addition to using structured queries to either filter or order data from a single table, they can be used to create sets of records derived from two or more tables. To illustrate this use of structured queries, we will again use the Biblio database (see Tables 9-8 through 9-11).

As a specific example, assume that we want to create a set of records that consist of a book's title and its publisher. Additionally, we want the final list of records to be in alphabetical order by publisher. To create this record set we would use the Titles table to locate all of the titles, and the Publishers table to locate all of the publishers. To connect a title with its publisher we use a **Where** clause with the condition that the PubID fields between the two tables match. Specifically, the following structured query locates the desired records and places them in the desired order:

```
Select Titles.Title, Publishers.Name
  From Titles, Publishers
  Where Titles.PubID = Publishers.PubID
  Order By Publishers.Name
```

For clarity we have written the query across four lines to easily identify each of the individual clauses. In practice, this single statement can be written as a single line in a Data control's **RecordSource** value.

In reviewing this query you should notice two items. The first is that the **From** clause identifies two tables. As with the **Select** clause where multiple fields can be identified, the **From** clause can include multiple table names. When this is done, individual table names must be separated by commas. The second item to note is the manner in which the field names have been identified throughout the query. Since we are dealing with two tables, both of which use the same field names, we must clearly establish which field is being referenced. This is accomplished using standard dot notation by listing the table name before the field name, and separating the two with a period. Thus the name `Titles.PubID` refers to the PubID field in the Titles table, and `Publishers.PubID` refers to the PubID in the Publishers table. This notation can be used wherever a field name is required, but if there is no ambiguity about which table is being used, the table name can always be omitted. Thus, the field name `Titles.Title` in the **Select** clause can be written simply as `Title`, because this field only exists in one of the tables referenced in the **From** clause.

Run-time Structured Queries

As we have already seen, a structured query can be entered as a Data control's **RecordSource** property value at design-time. For large queries, however, this can become error prone and provide queries that are cumbersome to debug. For example a query such as

```
Select Titles.Title, Publishers.Name
  From Titles, Publishers
  Where Titles.PubID = Publishers.PubID
  Order By Publishers.Name
```

is really too long to be conveniently entered as a **RecordSource** value. An alternative to entering such queries at design-time values is to set them at run-time. For example, consider Event Procedure 9-1, which uses the `Form_Load` event to set and refresh the RecordSet of a Data control named `datSQL`.

Figure 9-17

Program 9-3's Interface

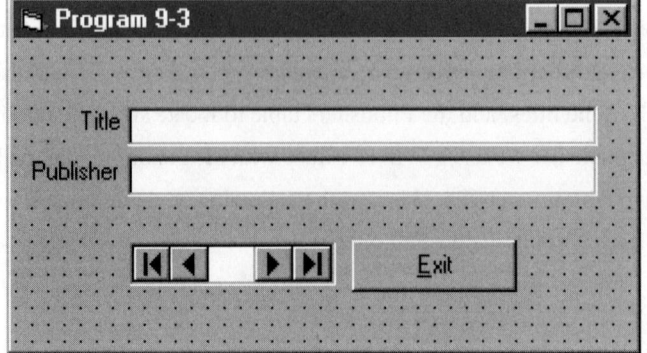

Table 9-12 Program 9-3's Properties Table

Object	Property	Setting
Form	Name	frmMain
	Caption	Program 9-3
Data Control	Name	datSQL
	Caption	(Blank)
	DatabaseName	C:\Program Files\Microsoft Visual Basic\Biblio.mdb
	RecordSource	(Blank)
	RecordsetType	Dynaset
Label	Name	lblTitle
	Caption	Title
Label	Name	lblPub
	Caption	Publisher
Text Box	Name	txtTitle
	Text	(Blank)
	DataSource	datSQL
	DataField	Title
Text Box	Name	txtPub
	Text	(Blank)
	DataSource	datSQL
	DataField	Name
Command Button	Name	cmdExit
	Caption	E&xit

Event Procedure 9-1

```
Private Sub Form_Load()
   Dim Sel As String, Frm As String
   Dim Whr As String, Ord As String
   Dim SQ As String

   Sel = "Select Titles.Title, Publishers.Name"
   Frm = " From Titles, Publishers"
   Whr = " Where Titles.PubID = Publishers.PubID"
   Ord = " Order By Publishers.Name"          ascending
   SQ = Sel & Frm & Whr & Ord

   datSQL.RecordSource = SQ
   datSQL.Refresh
   datSQL.Caption = 1
End Sub
```

The last two statements in this event procedure are the same as were previously used in Program 9-1. The new feature illustrated by this event procedure is the construction of a string named SQ and the assignment of this string to datSQL.RecordSource. Although we have constructed the SQ string from four strings, each of which highlights an individual SQL clause, this was done for the convenience of making each line a manageable size. The final setting of the **RecordSource** property could also have been made using the single statement

```
datSQL.RecordSource = "Select Titles.Title, Publishers.Name From Titles, Publishers Where
Titles.PubID = Publishers.PubID" Order By Publishers.Name"
```

Notice that the final **RecordSource** setting is identical to that which could have been entered as the RecordSource at design-time. Event Procedure 9-1 is used in Program 9-3, whose interface is shown in Figure 9-17.

Except for Event Procedure 9-1, the only other code used by Program 9-3 is the Exit procedure and Data control `Reposition` procedure previously used in Programs 9-1 and 9-2.

When Program 9-3 is executed the `Form_Load` event causes the Jet engine to create a RecordSet consisting of records constructed from both the Titles and Publishers tables. Each record in the set will consist of two fields, a Titles field, whose values come from the Titles table, and a Name field, whose values come from the Publishers table. Additionally, the records in the set will be in alphabetical order, by publisher's name. The screen that appears when this program is first run is shown in Figure 9-18.

Figure 9-18

*The Opening Screen
Presented by Program 9-3*

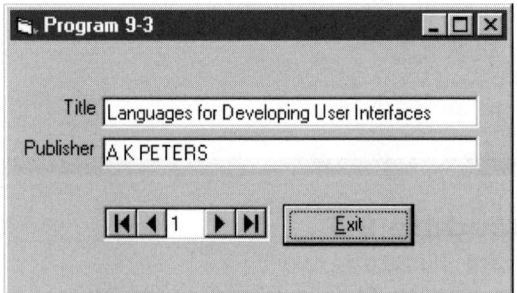

Exercises 9.3

1. a. List the four clauses that can be present in a structured query.

    b. What are the two clauses that must be present in a structured query.

2. Using the `Company` database (Tables 9-1 through 9-3) write a structured query to create a RecordSet consisting of all fields for the following criteria:

    a. All records from the SalesRep table (Table 9-2) whose representatives are assigned to office HM.

    b. All records from the SalesRep table (Table 9-2) whose representatives live in Orange, New Jersey.

    c. All records from the SalesRep table (Table 9-2) whose representatives have a middle initial.

    d. All records from the PhoneBook table (Table 9-1) of employees whose last name begins with a B.

    e. All records from the PhoneBook table (Table 9-1d) of employees who have an extension number between 100 and 200.

3. Using the Publishers Table (Table 9-8), write a structured query to create a RecordSet consisting of all fields for the following criteria:

   a. All records with a New York City field value.
   b. All records with a New York State field value.
   c. All records with both a New York City and State field value.
   d. All records with a Name field value beginning in the letter A.
   e. All records with a Zip code between 07000 and 07999.

4. Using the Authors Table (Table 9-10), write a structured query to create a RecordSet consisting of the indicated fields for the following criteria:

   a. All Author names for authors born before 1943.
   b. All Au_ID and Author fields for authors whose birth date field is blank.
   c. All Au_ID fields for authors whose name begins with the letter *C*.

5. Enter and run Program 9-3 on your computer.

6. a. Write a Visual Basic Program that can be used to display all Titles, ISBN numbers and Year Published from the Titles table (Table 9-9) in Year Published order.
   b. If you have access to the `Biblio` database, run the program you wrote for Exercise 6a.

7. a. Modify the program written for Exercise 6a. so that only texts published between 1989 and 1992 are accessed by your program.
   b. If you have access to the `Biblio` database, run the program that you wrote for Exercise 7a.

8. a. Write a Visual Basic Program that can be used to display all fields of the Author table (Table 9-10) for records that do not have any data in their Year Born field.
   b. If you have access to the `Biblio` database, run the program you wrote for Exercise 8a., and enter data into a Text box bound to the Year Born field. Describe what happens when you enter data, move to another record and then move back to the record in which you entered a date. Did the date remain with the record or was it erased?

9.4 Locating and Moving Through Records

The only means we currently have to locate a specific record is to move sequentially through a RecordSet using a Data control's push buttons. In this section we present alternative methods for directly locating a specific record and then moving through a RecordSet. We first introduce the **Find** methods, which can only be used with Dynaset- or Snapshot-type RecordSets, and then present the **Move** methods. Combining the **Move** methods with the **Find** methods permits us to construct a user interface that quickly locates a specific record and then cycles through any other records that match the search criteria. The last topic presented in the **Seek** method, which can only be used with indexes and Table-type RecordSets.

The Find Methods

The **Find** methods, which are listed in Table 9-13, can only be used with Dynaset- or Snapshot-type RecordSets. The syntax for each of the **Find** Methods is

> *table*.**Recordset**.Findmethod criteria

where

- *table* is the name of an existing Dynaset or Snapshot RecordSet;
- *Findmethod* is one of the **Find** methods listed in Table 9-13; and
- *criteria* is a string expression used to locate the desired record. It is constructed in the same manner as a structured query, but without the **Where** keyword.

For example, if we wanted to locate the first occurrence of extension number 464 in the PhoneBook table, the following statement can be used:

```
datPhone.Recordset.FindFirst "Ext = 464"
```

In a similar manner, to locate the first occurrence of the name John Grill, the following statement is valid:

```
datPhone.Recordset.FindFirst "Name = 'Grill, John' "
```

In reviewing these statements notice that the same convention is used for the **Find** criteria as that required in SQL: if the field value being searched for is a string, the value must be enclosed in single quotes. Also notice that the criteria itself, if it is a string literal, must be enclosed within double quotes.

When Visual Basic encounters a **Find** method, it searches through the RecordSet in the manner indicated in Table 9-13. If a record is found that matches the criteria, this record becomes the current record displayed by the Data control; otherwise the current record remains unchanged.

To indicate whether or not a search was successful, Visual Basic provides a **NoMatch** property. The value of this property is set either to **True** or **False** depending on whether the **Find** method was or was not successful in locating a record matching the given criteria. Typically, the **NoMatch** property is used in code such as the following:

```
datPhone.Recordset.FindFirst "Name = 'Grill, John' "
If datPhone.Recordset.NoMatch Then
  MsgBox "No match found"
Else
  Rem: include any desired processing of the located record in here
End If
```

Although all of the examples we have considered have tested for exact equality, this is not a requirement for the relational expression used within a search criteria. Any of Visual Basic's relational and logical operators can be used to construct a search criteria. For example, the statement

```
datPhone.Recordset.FindFirst "Ext >= 464"
```

Table 9-13 The Find Methods

Method Name	Search Begins At	Search Direction
FindFirst	Beginning of RecordSet	End of RecordSet
FindLast	End of RecordSet	Beginning of RecordSet
FindNext	Current Record Position	End of RecordSet
FindPrevious	Current Record Position	Beginning of RecordSet

can be used to find the first record whose extension field value is greater than or equal to 464. If a record exists that has this exact value, it becomes the current record; if not, the first record with an extension greater that 464 becomes the current record. If two or more records have the same value, the first record with this value becomes the current record.

In practice, a greater than or equal criteria, such as `"Name >= 'S' "` is typically used more often than a criteria that demands exact equality, such as `"Name = 'S' "`. The reason for this is that the searched for value is typically entered by a user, and the user may not know the exact name or value being searched for, may misspell an entered name, or transpose an entered number. Under these conditions a search for exact equality may fail, while a search using the >= relationship will move the current record close to the desired record. As a specific example of this, consider Program 9-4, which lets a user search the PhoneBook table for a desired name. The program's interface is presented in Figure 9-19. Except for the addition of the controls needed for finding a specific record, which include a Label, Text box, and the Find Command button, this interface is identical to that used in Programs 9-1 and 9-2. For this reason, Table 9-14 only lists the controls whose properties differ from these earlier programs.

In reviewing Table 9-14 notice that the `txtFind` box is not bound to a data control. The box's sole purpose is to provide a data entry area for a user to enter either a full or partial name. It is this entered string value that will be searched for when the Find control is pushed.

Next, pay attention to the fact that the Data control's **RecordSource** property is an SQL statement that orders the RecordSet in Name order. *Ordering records by the eventual search field or fields is essential if the Find methods are to operate in a manner expected by most users.* For example, if the PhoneBook RecordSet was constructed in its original order (see Table 9-1) and a search for a record having a name greater than or equal to 'D' was

Figure 9-19
Program 9-4's Interface

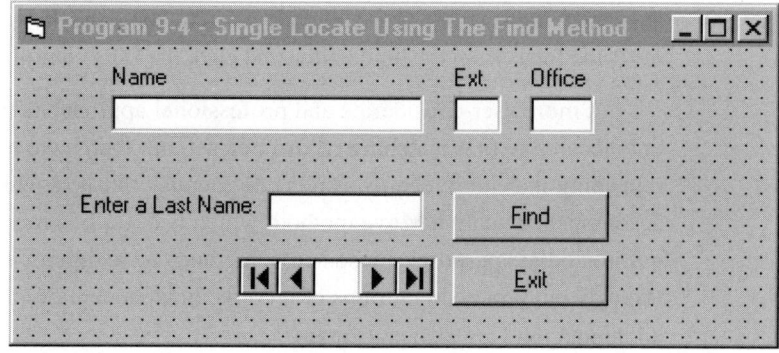

Table 9-14 Changed and Added Properties From Programs 9-1 and 9-2

Object	Property	Setting
Form	Name	`frmMain`
	Caption	`Program 9-4 Single Locate Using The Find Method`
Data control	Name	`datPhone`
	Caption	`(Blank)`
	DatabaseName	`C:\Program Files\Microsoft Visual Basic\Company.mdb`
	RecordSource	`Select * From datPhone Order By Name`
	RecordsetType	`Dynaset`
Label	Name	`lblFind`
	Caption	`Enter a Last Name:`
Text box	Name	`txtFind`
	Text	`(Blank)`
	DataSource	`(Blank)`
	DataField	`(Blank)`
Command button	Name	`cmdFind`
	Caption	`&Find`

undertaken, the located record would end up being for the name *Engle*. This occurs because, in unsorted order, the name *Engle* appears before any name beginning in the letter *D*. Thus, a search for a name greater than or equal to 'D,' starting from the beginning of the table, will stop at the name beginning in *E*, because 'E' is greater than or equal to 'D.'

Now consider Program 9-4's event code, which is identical to that used in Program 9-1 except for the addition of the `cmdFind_Click()` procedure. The first feature to notice is the construction of the search criteria as the string named `target`. This string is constructed in a manner that encloses the value entered in the `txtFind` Text box within single quotes; it is used as the search criteria by the **FindFirst** method contained in the very next statement. Finally, notice the use of the **NoMatch** property to alert the user when the **Find** method fails to find a record that matches the designated criteria.

Although Program 9-4 illustrates using the **FindFirst** method, it does have one drawback. As constructed, all the Find Command button can be used for is to locate the first record that matches a user entered name. In many cases, however, more than one record will satisfy a given criteria. For example, there are two *Smiths* in the PhoneBook table and four names that begin in the letter *S*. As written, Program 9-4 will correctly locate only the first occurrence of each of these criteria. Operationally, the Find button effectively "sticks" to the first matching record, no matter how many additional matching records exist. To examine any remaining matches, or even to know that another matching record exists, the user must move the focus from the Find button and click the Data control's **MoveNext** button.

A more user-considerate and professional approach is to have the **Find** button not only locate the first matching record in a set, but then have it cycle through all of the remaining matching records as it is continuously pushed. This type of operation is easily accomplished using a **Move** method, which is described next. Besides their value for our immediate purposes, these **Move** methods have greater applicability in cycling through and processing groups of records, independent of a Data control. Some of these additional uses are also presented.

Program 9-4's Event Code

```
Private Sub Form_Load()
  datPhone.Refresh
  datPhone.Caption = 1
End Sub

Private Sub datPhone_Reposition()
  datPhone.Caption = datPhone.Recordset.AbsolutePosition + 1
End Sub

Private Sub cmdExit_Click()
  Beep
  End
End Sub

Private Sub cmdFind_Click()
  Dim target As String

  target = "Name >=" & "'" & txtFind.Text & "'"

  datPhone.Recordset.FindFirst target
  If datPhone.Recordset.NoMatch Then
    MsgBox "No match found"
  Else
    datPhone.Caption = datPhone.Recordset.AbsolutePosition + 1
  End If
End Sub
```

The Move Methods

The current record , as we have seen, is the record in a RecordSet currently accessible and displayed by any controls bound to a Data control. Only one record can be the current record at any given time. This record can be changed by a Data control's push buttons or by using a **Find** or **Move** method in code. Moving around or changing the current record, as we have already noted, is referred to as *navigating* or *browsing* through a RecordSet.

Table 9-15 lists the **Move** methods that can be applied to a RecordSet to alter the current record. Each of these methods permits navigating through a RecordSet using code. For example, the statement:

```
datPhone.Recordset.MoveFirst
```

makes the first record in the RecordSet the current record. Similarly, the statement

```
datPhone.Recordset.MoveLast
```

makes the last record in the RecordSet the current record.

Table 9-15 The Move Methods

Name	Action	Example
MoveFirst	Make the first record in the RecordSet the current record.	`datPhone.RecordSet.MoveFirst`
MoveNext	Make the next record in the RecordSet the current record.	`datPhone.RecordSet.MoveNext`
MoveLast	Make the last record in the RecordSet the current record.	`datPhone.RecordSet.MoveLast`
MovePrevious	Make the prior record in the RecordSet the current record.	`datPhone.RecordSet.MovePrevious`

Each of the Data control push buttons performs one of the equivalent **Move** methods listed in Table 9-15, except that the Data control is programmed so that it will not move past either the first or last record in a RecordSet. When explicitly using a **Move** method, these same checks can be incorporated in your code using the RecordSet properties named **EOF** and **BOF**, which stand *for End of File* and *Beginning of File*.

The End of File (**EOF**) property is set to **True** only when the current record is positioned after the last record in a RecordSet. Similarly, the Beginning of File (**BOF**) is set to **True** only when the current record is positioned in front of the first record in a RecordSet. When either of these two property values is **True**, it means that the current record being pointed to is not valid. Table 9-16 lists the conditions indicated by various combinations of **EOF** and **BOF** property settings.

By checking either the **EOF** or **BOF** values, you can safely code loops that traverse a RecordSet from any direction. For example, the following code can be used as the basis for starting at the beginning of the PhoneBook table and correctly processing and cycling through each subsequent record.

```
datPhone.Recordset.MoveFirst
Do While datPhone.Recordset.EOF = False
   ' process the current record as needed
  datPhone.Recordset.MoveNext
Loop
```

Now that we have the **Move** methods to work with, we can modify the `cmdFind_Click()` event code used in Program 9-4, to not only locate the first occurrence of a name, but to correctly cycle through each subsequent name in the RecordSet that matches the entered criteria. When the last matching record is reached, we want the code to cycle back to the first match. Thus, for example, if a user enters the letter S, the Find button should locate the first name beginning in *S*, and then cycle through the remaining names beginning in *S* as the Find button is repeatedly pressed. When the last *S* name is located, the code should then relocate the current record to the first *S* name and begin the cycle again. This should work no matter how many letters the user enters. So, for example, if the user enters the letters Sm, the search should only locate names beginning in *Sm*, and so on. The required code algorithm is as follows:

Table 9-16 EOF/BOF Property Settings

Property Value	Meaning
EOF = True	The current record is positioned after the last record. Thus, the current record being pointed to is invalid.
BOF = True	The current record is positioned before the first record. Thus, the current record being pointed to is invalid.
EOF and BOF both True	There are no records in the RecordSet, and the current record being pointed to is invalid.
EOF and BOF both False	The current record is valid unless it has been deleted and no movement has occurred in the RecordSet.

Set the variable n equal to the length of the entered search string

If the first n characters of the current record do not match the entered search string

    Find and display the first record matching the search string

Else

    Move to the next record

    If the current record's position is past the last record

        Find and display the first record matching the search string

    Else if the first n characters of the current record do not match the search string

        Find and display the first record matching the search string

    End If

End If

If there is no match

    Display a message indicating that there is no match

Else

    Display the current record's position

End If

The first **If** statement in the algorithm checks whether the current record matches the entered criteria. If there is no match, the algorithm locates and displays the first matching record; otherwise, the current record matches the search criteria and we move to the next record. At that point, one of three things has happened: we have either moved to another match, moved past the last record, or moved to a record that does not match the criteria. In the latter two cases we have positioned the current record beyond the last record that

Figure 9-20

Program 9-5's Interface

matches the search criteria, and we then relocate back to the first matching occurrence; however, we must test for the first possibility by itself, for if we have positioned ourselves beyond the last record, any string test will result in an error since no valid current record exists. Finally, the last **If** statement informs the user if no record matches the given criteria.

The procedural code for this algorithm, which uses both **Find** and **Move** methods, is listed as Program 9-5's cmdFind_Click() event code. The interface for Program 9-5 is shown in Figure 9-20. Except for the form's caption and the revised cmdFind_Click() event code, Program 9-5 is identical to Program 9-4.

Program 9-5's cmdFind_Click() Event Code

```
Private Sub cmdFind_Click()
 Dim target As String
  Dim n As Integer

  n = Len(txtFind.Text)
  target = "Name >=" & "'" & txtFind.Text & "'"

  If Mid(datPhone.Recordset("Name"), 1, n) <> txtFind.Text Then
        datPhone.Recordset.FindFirst target
  Else ' current record matches the search criteria
    datPhone.Recordset.MoveNext
    If datPhone.Recordset.EOF = True Then
      datPhone.Recordset.FindFirst target
    ElseIf Mid(datPhone.Recordset("Name"), 1, n) <> txtFind.Text Then
      datPhone.Recordset.FindFirst target
    End If
  End If
  If datPhone.Recordset.NoMatch Then
    MsgBox "No match found"
  Else
    datPhone.Caption = datPhone.Recordset.AbsolutePosition + 1
  End If
End Sub
```

The Seek Method

Just as the **Find** methods can only be used with Dynaset- or Snapshot-type RecordSets, the **Seek** method is used to locate records in an indexed Table-type RecordSet. Specifically, the **Seek** method locates the first record in an indexed set that meets the specified criteria and makes that record the current record. The general syntax for the **Seek** method is

> *table*.**Recordset.Seek** *comparison value-1, value-2, ... value-n*

where

- *table* is the name of an existing Table-type RecordSet object;
- *comparison* is one of the string expressions "<", "<=", "=", ">=", or ">"; and
- *value-1, value-2, ...* are one or more values corresponding to the underlying table's index setting.

For example, the statement

```
datPhone.Recordset.Seek ">=", txtFind.Text
```

sets the current record to the first record that matches the string in the txtFind Text box and then sets the **NoMatch** property to **False**. If no record matches the criteria, the **NoMatch** property is set to **True**, and the current record is undefined. To use the **Seek** method a current index must be set. If the key value being searched for is not unique, the **Seek** method will locate the first record that matches the criteria.

Program 9-6, whose interface is shown in Figure 9-21, uses the **Seek** method to locate a user entered string value. The properties for this program are identical to those of Program 9-4 and 9-5, except for the form's caption and that the datPhone data control's **Recordset-Type** has been set to Table. The **Seek** method is used in the cmdFind_Click() event code listed within Program 9-6's event code.

Program 9-6's Event Code

```
Private Sub Form_Load()
  datPhone.Refresh
  datPhone.Recordset.Index = "Name"
  datPhone.Caption = "ID = " & datPhone.Recordset("ID")
End Sub

Private Sub datPhone_Reposition()
  datPhone.Caption = "ID = " & datPhone.Recordset("ID")
End Sub

Private Sub cmdExit_Click()
  Beep
  End
End Sub

Private Sub cmdFind_Click()
  Dim target As String

  datPhone.Recordset.Seek ">=", txtFind.Text
  If datPhone.Recordset.NoMatch Then
    MsgBox "No match found"
  Else
    datPhone.Caption = "ID = " & datPhone.Recordset("ID")
  End If
End Sub
```

Figure 9-21

Program 9-6's Interface

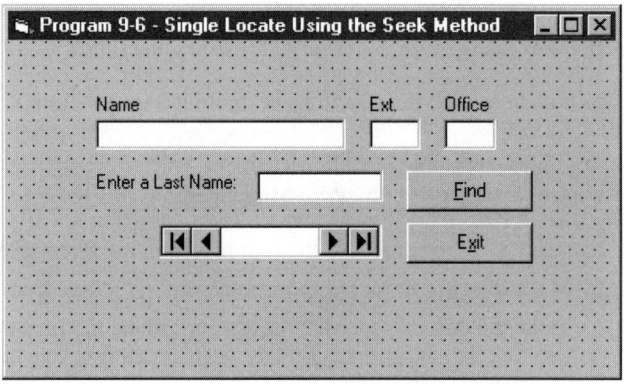

In reviewing Program 9-6's event code pay particular attention to the fact that the index for the table has been set in the `Form_Load()` event. Finally, notice the **Seek** method call in the `cmdFind_Click()` event. Here the method uses the value entered in the `txtFind` Text box as its search criteria. The comparison used (`">="`) means that the user does not have to enter an exact name for a match to occur. For example, if the user enters the letter S in the Text box, the search will locate the first record with a name beginning in the letter *S*. Finally, notice that a comma is used as a delimiter between the comparison expression and the value being searched for.

Exercises 9.4

1. Use Visual Basic's Help facility to an obtain documentation on the following:

   a. The **Find** Methods
   b. The **Move** Methods
   c. The **Seek** Methods
   d. **EOF** and **BOF**
   e. Positioning the Current Record Pointer (**Hint:** First search for "positioning current record.")

2. List and describe the functions of the four **Find** methods.

3. Assuming that the PhoneBook table (see Table 9-1) is the **RecordSource** for a Data control named `datPhone`, write **Find** method calls to locate records matching the following criteria:

   a. The first occurrence of the office value F1.
   b. The next occurrence of the office value F1.
   c. The last occurrence of the office value F1.
   d. The previous occurrence of the office value F1.

4. Assuming that the TitleAuthor table (see Table 9-11) is the **RecordSource** for a Data control named `datTAuth`, write **Find** method calls to locate records matching the following criteria:

   a. The first occurrence of an Au_ID equal to 59.
   b. The next occurrence of an Au_ID equal to 59.
   c. The last occurrence of an Au_ID equal to 96.
   d. The previous occurrence of an Au_ID equal to 96.

5. a. Define the term *current record*?
   b. How many current records can exist at one time?

6. List and describe the functions of the four **Move** methods.

7. Assuming that the Publishers table (see Table 9-8) is the **RecordSource** for a Data control named `datPub`, write **Move** method calls to

   a. Make the current record the first record in the RecordSet.
   b. Make the current record the next record in the RecordSet.
   c. Make the current record the last record in the RecordSet.
   d. Make the current record the previous record in the RecordSet.

8. Enter and run Program 9-4 on your computer.

9. Enter and run Program 9-5 on your computer.

10. Enter and run Program 9-6 on your computer.

11. Just as Program 9-5 modifies the cmdFind_Click() event to sequentially search for additional records that satisfy the search criteria, Program 9-6 can also be modified to do the same. Modify Program 9-6 in such a manner that repeated clicking of the cmdFind button causes the program to locate the next record that satisfies the entered criteria value. When the last match has been found, clicking the cmdFind button should revert to locating the first matching record.

12. If you have access to the Biblio database provided by Microsoft with Visual Basic, write a Visual Basic program that allows users to examine records in the Titles table (see Table 9-9). The specific fields that should be displayed are the title, year published, and ISBN number.

13. Modify the Program written for Exercise 12 so that records can be located by entering a title. The locate should work even if a partial title name is entered.

14. If you have access to the Biblio database provided by Microsoft with Visual Basic, write a Visual Basic program that allows users to examine records in the Publishers table (see Table 9-8). The specific fields that should be displayed are the company name, address, city, state, and zip code.

15. Modify the Program written for Exercise 14 so that records can be located by entering a company's name. The locate command should work even if a partial company name is entered.

9.5 Programming The Data Control

Programming a Data control means writing code to alter the control's current record. Effectively, we have already programmed a data control by using the **Find**, **Move**, and **Seek** methods, since each of these methods typically does change a data control's current record. In this section we complete this programming process by providing an interface that allows a user to update records using procedural code. In this context, the term *update* refers to either adding, deleting, or editing records in a RecordSet and its underlying database table. In addition, we will also show how edits and additions can be also be accomplished using a Data control without additional programming. The update methods provided by Visual Basic for programming a Data control are listed in Table 9-17.

To illustrate how the methods listed in Table 9-17 are used in practice, we will incorporate them into Program 9-7, whose interface is shown in Figure 9-22. Specifically, we will incorporate the **AddNew** and **Update** methods within the Add Command button's **Click** event and the **Delete** method within the Delete Command button's **Click** event. We

Table 9-17 Database Methods

Method Name	Description
AddNew	Creates a new record for both a Dynaset and Table type RecordSet. This method sets all fields to Nulls, or any predefined default values. After the new record has been created and the fields edited, either an Update method or movement to another record (using either a movement method or the data control's movement buttons) must be used to make the changes permanent.
Delete	Deletes the current record in both an open Dynaset and Table type RecordSet, and in the underlying database table.
Edit	Copies the current record from both a Dynaset and Table type RecordSet to a copy buffer for subsequent editing.
Update	Saves the contents of the copy buffer to the specified Dynaset or Table RecordSet and the underlying database table.

will then show how to edit and save all editing changes using the E̲xit Command button's **Click** event. Table 9-18 lists the relevant properties for these Command buttons, which have the captions A̲dd, D̲elete, and E̲x̲it, respectively. Except for the form's caption, the remaining form objects and their associated code are identical to that of Program 9-4.

Before you update (add, delete, or edit) a record, two items should be understood. The first is that the Jet database engine uses a special reserved location, called the *copy buffer*, to hold the contents of the record currently being updated. When the **AddNew** method is invoked, this copy buffer is cleared of its contents and any default values specified for the new record are set, while the **Edit** method causes the current record's contents to be copied into the buffer. Finally, the **Update** method causes all data in the copy buffer to be transferred and saved into both the RecordSet and the underlying database table.

Figure 9-22

Program 9-7's Interface

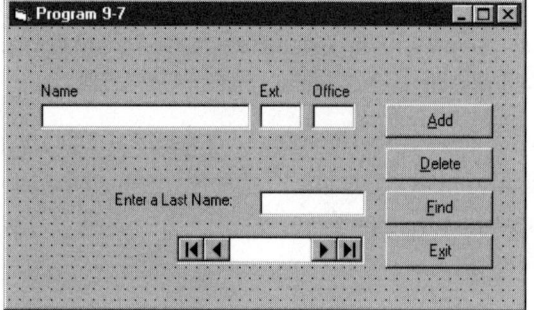

The second item concerns the permissions that must be set for updating to take place. Although the correct permissions are created by default, and we assume that the correct permissions have been set, the required permissions are explicitly presented at the end of this section.

Table 9-18 Program 9-7's Update Command Control Properties

Object	Property	Setting
Command Button	Name	cmdAdd
	Caption	&Add
Command Button	Name	cmdDel
	Caption	&Delete
Command Button	Name	cmdExit
	Caption	E&xit

Adding a Record

Records can be added to a RecordSet either by using the **AddNew** method in code, by setting a Data control's **EOFAction** property, or by using a combination of both techniques. We examine each of these techniques, in turn.

For example, to add a new PhoneBook record using the code in Program 9-7, the following statement is required:

```
datPhone.Recordset.AddNew
```

What this statement does is to clear the copy buffer and set any required default field values. Event Code 9-1 illustrates how this statement is used for Program 9-7's cmdAdd Command button's **Click** event.

Event Code 9-1

```
Private Sub cmdAdd_Click()
  datPhone.Recordset.AddNew  ' clear the copy buffer
  datPhone.Recordset("Name") = InputBox("Enter the Name")
  datPhone.Recordset("Ext") = InputBox("Enter an Extension")
  datPhone.Recordset("Office") = InputBox("Enter an Office code (HM or F1)")
  datPhone.Recordset.Update  ' write the copy buffer to the Recordset & database
  datPhone.Refresh
End Sub
```

When the cmdAdd Command button is clicked, the first statement in Event Code 9-1 causes the Jet engine to clear the copy buffer. The procedure then requests that a name, extension, and office location be entered. Upon completion of these requests, the **Update** method is invoked, which causes the entered data to be appended both to the PhoneBook table and the RecordSet. To correctly order the RecordSet in Name order, the **Refresh** method is invoked, which rebuilds the RecordSet according to the structured query defined for the Data control's **RecordSource** property. Since this query orders the records by Name (see Table 9-14), the added name will subsequently appear to the user in its correct alphabetical position.

The Data control's **EOFAction** property can also be used to add new records. The default setting for this property is 0, which corresponds to a system constant named **vbEOFActionMoveLast**. This default setting disables the Data control's MoveNext button when the current record is the last record in a RecordSet. By changing the **EOFAction** property to the named constant **vbEOFActionAddNew**, which has a numerical value of 2, the MoveNext button *is not* disabled at the last record; rather, the current record is positioned to a new record in the copy buffer. From an operational viewpoint, all bound controls will either be cleared, or set to the default values contained in the copy buffer. The user can then change any and all values in the new record using the bound controls (formally, the user is actually *editing* the new record at this point). By moving to a new record, using the **Move**, **Find**, or **Seek** methods, or by using any of the Data Control's Command buttons, the new record is automatically saved. Similarly, invoking the **Update** method also causes the new record to be saved.

Deleting a Record

To delete a record from a Data control's RecordSet and its underlying table, program code must be used. For example, to delete the current record displayed by Program 9-7's bound controls, the following statement is required:

```
datPhone.Recordset.Delete
```

In using this statement, however, we must provide for two contingencies. First, since all information in a deleted record is lost, we should build in a safety mechanism to protect against a user inadvertently activating the Delete button. The next item that we must take care of is to determine which record is to become the current record after a deletion has occurred. In relation to this second item, we will position the Data control according to the following algorithm:

If the last record in a RecordSet has been deleted

Position the Data control on the last record in the remaining set of records
Else if the first record in the RecordSet has been deleted

Position the Data control on the first record in the remaining set of records
Else

Position the Data control on the record immediately after the deleted record

Making use of the **EOF** and **BOF** properties, the procedural code for this algorithm becomes

```
datPhone.Recordset.Delete
If datPhone.Recordset.EOF = True Then
   datPhone.Recordset.MoveLast
ElseIf datPhone.Recordset.BOF = True Then
   datPhone.Recordset.MoveFirst
Else
   datPhone.Recordset.MoveNext
End If
```

Prior to invoking this code, however, we first want to ensure that the user really wants to proceed with the deletion. This "safety check" can be handled with a message box similar to the one shown in Figure 9-23. As illustrated, the message box consists of a critical icon and two Command buttons, with the default being the second, or Cancel button. Thus, if a user accidentally presses the Enter key, the deletion will not take place, and only a positive action on the part of the user will cause the deletion to occur. Using the message box constants listed in Appendix E, the appropriate message box can be created using the following code:

```
Dim MboxType As Integer

MboxType = vbCritical + vbOKCancel + vbDefaultButton2
goahead = MsgBox("Press OK to Delete", MboxType)
```

Figure 9-23

The Delete Warning Message Box

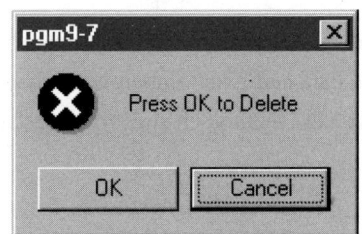

The combination of the "safety check" code and the positioning of the Data control after a deletion forms the basis for Program 9-7's `cmdDel` control's **Click** event, which is listed as Event Code 9-2.

Event Code 9-2

```
Private Sub cmdDel_Click()
  Dim MboxType As Integer
  Dim goahead As Integer

  MboxType = vbCritical + vbOKCancel + vbDefaultButton2
  goahead = MsgBox("Press OK to Delete", MboxType)
  If goahead = vbOK Then
    datPhone.Recordset.Delete
    If datPhone.Recordset.EOF = True Then
      datPhone.Recordset.MoveLast
    ElseIf datPhone.Recordset.BOF = True Then
      datPhone.Recordset.MoveFirst
    Else
      datPhone.Recordset.MoveNext
    End If
  End If
  datPhone.Caption = datPhone.Recordset.AbsolutePosition
End Sub
```

Notice that when a record is deleted using Event Code 9-2, the position of the remaining records in the RecordSet can change. For example, if the first record in the set is deleted, all subsequent records move up one position in the RecordSet. Thus, the record that was previously identified with a Data control **Caption** of 2 will now have a **Caption** of 1. This generally is no problem for most users, but you may either have to explain this operation or choose not to use the **Caption** property for displaying record positions. Also notice that since a record's position in a RecordSet can change, either due to deletions or a rebuild caused by a **Refresh**, the **AbsolutePosition** property should not be used to locate records. The recommended way of retaining and returning to a given position in a RecordSet is to use **Bookmarks**.

Finally, the **Delete** method can be used to delete a complete set of records using a loop. For example, the following code deletes every record in the PhoneBook table whose Office field is equal to 'F1'.

```
datphone.DatabaseName = "Company.mdb"
datPhone.RecordSource = "Select * From PhoneBook Where [Office] = 'F1' "
datPhone.Refresh

Do While datPhone.RecordSDet.EOF = False
  Print "Deleting "; datPhone.Recordset("Name")
  datPhone.Recordset.Delete
  datPhone.Recordset.MoveNext
Loop
```

In this code a **MoveNext** method is used after each deletion. This is necessary because a deleted record contains invalid data and if subsequently accessed as the current record, will cause an error. Using the **MoveNext** method ensures that the data control correctly points to a valid current record.

Editing a Record

An existing record's fields can be edited by modifying the desired field in the current record and then saved by using either the Data control's movement buttons or in code using either an **Update**, **Find**, **Move**, or **Seek** method. To edit a record without programming the Data control, do the following:

1. Make the desired record the current record (this can be done either by locating a record using one of the techniques described in the previous section or by using the Data control's movement buttons).
2. Assign new values to the desired fields.
3. Click one of the Data control's movement buttons, which causes the changes to be saved.

This procedure is generally the easiest for making changes to an existing record. The only pitfall occurs when a user makes a final editing change and immediately presses the Exit button. Since no movement button was pressed, this last change will not be saved. The solution is to either provide a Save command control, program the Exit command control to detect if a change was made to the current record and save this last change (possibly with user confirmation), or use both techniques. Generally, providing a Save button is not a good idea, because it tends to confuse most users: either they forget whether they pressed the button for one of their changes and become unsure whether a change was actually saved, or think that they can revert to the original record's contents by not pressing the Save button. Thus, it is typically easier simply to explain that any change is automatically made once the user moves to another record and not provide a separate Save button. To ensure that the last change is saved, however, it is a good idea to program the Exit button explicitly to save changes made to the last record. This can be accomplished using the following algorithm:

If the Exit button is pressed and the last record in a RecordSet has been modified
    Request confirmation to save the changes
   If confirmation is received
     Save the changes
   End If
End If
End the application

Notice that this algorithm asks for user confirmation to save any changes made to the last record. A case can be made that, since the user does not explicitly confirm changes made to any other records, the changes to the last record should also be automatically saved without explicit confirmation. Both approaches are used in practice. We continue with the approach that asks for confirmation to illustrate how to detect that a change has actually occurred.

To determine whether a bound control's value has been changed we use its **DataChanged** property. This property, which is only available at run-time, returns a boolean value of **True** only if the data in the bound control has been changed by a process other than that of retrieving data from the current record. Thus, to determine if any changes have been made to the current record, the following code segment can be used:

```
Dim DataChanged As Boolean

' Determine if any changes were made to the last record
DataChanged = txtName.DataChanged Or txtExt.DataChanged Or txtOffice.DataChanged
If DataChanged = True Then
   ' Statements to execute if the DataChanged is True
End If
```

Notice that the condition tested within the **If** statement is the value of the expression `DataChanged = True`. This tested expression can be replaced by a shorter expression that only uses the boolean variable's name. Thus, the statement

```
      If DataChanged = True Then
```

can be replaced by the shorter statement

```
      If DataChanged Then
```

Although this may appear confusing at first, the second statement is certainly more compact than the longer version. Here, if the value of the variable `DataChanged` is **True**, the expression itself is **True**. Since boolean variables are frequently tested by advanced Visual Basic programmers using just their name, as in the latter **If** statement, it is worthwhile being familiar with this convention. Event Code 9-3 incorporates this code segment, with the shorter **If** statement, within the final code used for Program 9-7's `cmdExit` control's Click event.

Event Code 9-3

```
Private Sub cmdExit_Click()
  Dim MboxType As Integer
  Dim MboxMessage As String
  Dim goahead As Integer
  Dim DataChanged As Boolean

  MboxType = vbCritical + vbYesNo
  MboxMessage = "Do you want to save the changes made to the last record?"
  ' Determine if any changes were made to the last record
  DataChanged = txtName.DataChanged Or txtExt.DataChanged Or txtOffice.DataChanged
  If DataChanged Then
    goahead = MsgBox(MboxMessage, MboxType)
    If goahead = vbYes Then
      datPhone.Recordset.Edit
      datPhone.Recordset.Update
    End If
  End If
  Beep
  End
End Sub
```

Figure 9-24

Program 9-7's Save Message Box

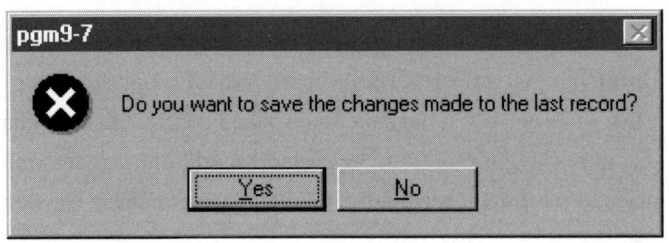

The only section of Event Code 9-3 that we have not discussed is the coding of the Message box. As coded, this box consists of a critical icon

consisting of Yes and No Command buttons (see Appendix E for a description of these constants) and produces the Message box shown in Figure 9-24. As is seen in this figure, the default Command button is the first, or Yes button. Thus, if the user inadvertently presses the Enter key, any changes to the last record are saved.

Finally, as with the other update methods, editing can be accomplished in code without using a bound control, as illustrated by the following code segment:

```
datphone.DatabaseName = "Company.mdb"
datPhone.RecordSouce = "PhoneBook"
datPhone.Refresh
datPhone.Recordset.Edit
datPhone.Recordset("Ext") = "711"
datPhone.Recordset.Update
```

This code sets the value of the Ext field to 711 for the current record, which in this case is the first record in the RecordSet.

Permissions

For changes to be made to a table's records using either code or the Data control directly, the following conditions must always be met:

1. The database itself must have permissions set that allow it to be updated, which is typically the default.
2. The desired field being edited must have been created to be updatable, which is typically the default.
3. The Data control's **ReadOnly** property has been set to **False**, which is the default value.
4. The RecordSet's **Updatable** property has been set to **True**, which is the default for Dynaset- and Table-types. Snapshot-type RecordSets are not updatable.

Each of these conditions can be checked using code. For example, assuming that the **RecordSource** for a Data control named datPhone has been set to PhoneBook, the following code can be used to check that the PhoneBook table can be updated (that is, either edited, added to, or deleted from):

```
If datPhone.Database.Updatable = False Or datPhone.ReadOnly = True _
Or datPhone.Recordset.Updatable = False Then
  MsgBox "This data cannot be altered"
End If
```

In a similar manner, the ability of a specific field to be updated can be tested by examining its **Attributes** property and its **dbUpdatableField** bit. For example, the following code can be used to determine if the PhoneBook table's Name field can be altered:

```
If datPhone.Recordset.Fields("Name").Attributes = True And dbUpdatableField = 0 Then
  MsgBox "This field cannot be altered"
End If
```

Exercises 9.5

1. a. Describe what the phrase *Programming a Data Control* means
    b. List and describe the four methods that can be used to update a Data control's records.

2. What update task cannot be accomplished without using program code.

3. List the ways in which changes to the current record become saved.

4. List and describe the four conditions that must be set for a record's fields to be updatable.

5. a. Enter and run Program 9-7.
    b. Modify Program 9-7 so that any change made to a record is automatically saved when the Exit button is pressed, whether or not it was updated using the Data control's movement buttons.

6. An interesting feature of Data controls is that they have an **Invisible** property. In this exercise you will be asked to set this property to **True**, which makes the control invisible at run-time. You will then be asked to replace the move functions provided by the Data control's movement buttons with programmed Command controls. To accomplish this, modify Program 9-7 as follows:

    - Set the Data control's **Invisible** property to **True**.
    - Add four Command buttons having the captions First, Next, Previous, and Last, respectively.

    Once you have made these changes, code each of the new Command controls, using appropriate **Move** methods, to move to the location in the RecordSet indicated by each control's caption.

9.6 Common Programming Errors and Problems

The common errors and problems encountered when using Visual Basic to access and update database tables are:

1. Forgetting to use either a Dynaset- or Snapshot-type RecordSet type when using a structured query as the **RecordSource**.

2. Forgetting to use a Table-type RecordSet when using an indexed table.

3. Using a **Find** method on a non-sorted RecordSet. Although the **Find** will locate a record, due to the possibly random ordering of records, the desired record can be missed.

4. Using a **Seek** method on a non-indexed RecordSet.

5. Forgetting to place a comma between the comparison expression and search criteria within a **Seek** method invocation.

6. Using the **AbsolutePosition** value to locate a record. Due to deletions and rebuilds, a record's position can change. A **Bookmark** should be used to retrieve a previously located record.

7. Not saving the last edit performed on a RecordSet. This occurs when the application is terminated before a movement button or movement method has been activated. When dealing with databases, an application's Exit button should always have a provision for saving the last edit.

9.7 Chapter Review

Key Terms

bound control	Jet engine
browsing	navigating
cardinality	organization
current record	record
data-aware control	relational database
Data control	relationships
database	Snapshot RecordSet
DBMS	SQL
Dynaset RecordSet	structured query
entities	Table RecordSet
field	update

Review

1. A *database* is defined as a collection of related data used by an organization, where an *organization* refers to any self-contained social unit, such as a company, university, hospital, or family.

2. A *relational database* is a database in which data is stored in tables.

3. Each row in a database table is referred to as a *record*, and each column is designated by a heading, referred to as a *field name*.

4. When records are ordered by the value of a particular field, the field is referred to as a *key field*.

5. An *index* is a special type of table that lists the position of another table's records in a key field order.

6. A structured query is a statement, written according to the rules of a language called Structured Query Language (SQL), that uniquely identifies a set of records from one or more tables. The set of records can be empty, if no records meet the selected criteria.

7. The basic syntax of an SQL Select command is

    Select *field-name(s)* **From** *table(s)* **Where** *condition(s)* **Order By** *field-name(s)*

    Formally, this statement consists of four clauses; a **Select** clause, a **From** clause, a **Where** clause and an **Order By** clause. The words **Select**, **From**, **Where**, and **Order By**, are all SQL keywords. At a minimum, a structured query must contain both a **Select** and **From** clause; the **Select** clause specifies the field values that will be returned by the query, while the **From** clause specifies the table or tables whose records will be searched. In addition, if any restrictions are placed on the data to be selected, or if the selected information is to be presented in a specified order, a **Where** or **Order By** clause must be included. For example, in the statement

    ```
    Select * From PhoneBook Order By Ext
    ```

    the **Select** clause specifies that all fields are to be obtained, the **From** clause specifies that the fields are to come from the PhoneBook table, and the **Order** clause specifies that the RecordSet is to be constructed in increasing (ascending) order based on the values in the Ext field.

8. A database management system (DBMS) is a package of one or more computer programs designed to establish, maintain, and access a database.

9. The Microsoft Jet engine is a DBMS that is used by Visual Basic to open, locate records from, update, and close a database. When accessed by Visual Basic, the Jet engine creates a set of records, which is referred to as a *RecordSet*, from one or more database tables. Three types of RecordSets can be created: a Table-type, which uses an index

for ordering the records, a Dynaset-type, which places records either in the order they are stored in their database table or are selected according to a structured query, or a Snapshot-type, which is identical to a Dynaset-type except that the records are read-only (cannot be updated).

10. RecordSets can be created and accessed using a Data control. To use a Data control, at a minimum, the following three properties must be specified:

- **DatabaseName**, which names the desired database and defines where it is located;
- **RecordSource**, which names the table or structured query from which a RecordSet is created; and
- **RecordsetType**, which defines the type of RecordSet that the Jet engine will create.

The third property, **RecordsetType**, does not have to be explicitly set, because it uses a default Dynaset type.

11. The *current record* is the record in a RecordSet that is currently accessible by a Data control. Only one record can be the current record at any given time. This record can be changed by a Data control's movement buttons or by using a **Move** method in code. Moving around or changing the current record is referred to as *navigating* or *browsing* through a RecordSet.

12. A *bound control* can be a Text box, Label, Picture Box, Image box, Check box, List box, Combo box, custom third-party controls, or OLE container control. The control becomes a bound control by setting its **DataSource** property to the name of a Data control. The control is then made *data-aware* by setting its **DataField** property to a field name. Being data-aware means that the control has access to a field value contained in the current record.

13. The **Find** methods, which are used to locate specific records in either a Dynaset- and Snapshot-type RecordSet are listed in Table 9-19. The syntax for each of the Find methods is

```
table.Recordset.Findmethod criteria
```

where
- *table* is the name of an existing Dynaset or Snapshot RecordSet;
- *Findmethod* is one of the **Find** methods listed in Table 9-19;
- *criteria* is a string expression used to locate the desired record. It is constructed in the same manner as a structured query, but without the **Where** keyword.

For a **Find** command to work correctly, the RecordSet must be ordered by the search criteria being applied.

Table 9-19 The Find Methods

Method Name	Search Begins at:	Search to:
FindFirst	Beginning of RecordSet	End of RecordSet
FindLast	End of RecordSet	Beginning of RecordSet
FindNext	Current Record Position	End of RecordSet
FindPrevious	Current Record Position	Beginning of RecordSet

14. The **Seek** method is used to locate records in an indexed Table-type RecordSet. Specifically, the **Seek** method locates the first record in an indexed set that meets the specified criteria and makes that record the current record. The general syntax for the Seek method is

table.**Seek** *comparison value-1, value-2, ... value-n*

where
- *table* is the name of an existing Table-type RecordSet object;
- *comparison* is one of the string expressions `"<"`, `"<="`, `"="`, `">="`, or `">"`; and
- *value-1, value-2, ...* are one or move values corresponding to the underlying table's index setting.

15. To indicate whether or not a **Find** or **Seek** method was successful in locating a record, Visual Basic provides a **NoMatch** property. The value of this property is set to either **True** or **False** depending, respectively, on whether or not the **Find** method was successful in locating a record matching the given criteria.

16. **Move** methods, which are listed in Table 9-20, can be applied to a RecordSet to alter the current record. Each of these methods permit navigating through a RecordSet using code.

    Each of a Data control's movement buttons perform one of the equivalent **Move** methods listed in Table 9-20.

Table 9-20 The Move Methods

Name	Action	Example
MoveFirst	Make the first record in the RecordSet the current record.	`datPhone.RecordSet.MoveFirst`
MoveNext	Make the next record in the RecordSet the current record.	`datPhone.RecordSet.MoveNext`
MoveLast	Make the last record in the RecordSet the current record.	`datPhone.RecordSet.MoveLast`
MovePrevious	Make the prior record in the RecordSet the current record.	`datPhone.RecordSet.MovePrevious`

Introduction to Visual Basic

Table 9-21 Update Methods

Method Name	Description
AddNew	Creates a new record for both a Dynaset and Table type RecordSet. This method sets all fields to Nulls, or any predefined default values. After the new record has been created and the fields edited, either an Update method or movement to another record (using either a movement method or the data control's movement buttons) must be used to make the changes permanent.
Delete	Deletes the current record in both an open Dynaset and Table type RecordSet, and in the underlying database table.
Edit	Copies the current record from both a Dynaset and Table type RecordSet to a copy buffer for subsequent editing.
Update	Saves the contents of the copy buffer to the specified Dynaset or Table RecordSet and the underlying database table.

17. A Data control is programmed so that it will not move past either the first or last record in a RecordSet. When explicitly using a **Move** method, these same checks can be incorporated using the RecordSet properties named **EOF** and **BOF**, which stand *for End of File* and *Beginning of File*. The End of File (**EOF**) property is set to **True** only when the current record is positioned after the last record in a RecordSet. Similarly, the Beginning of File (**BOF**) is set to **True** only when the current record is positioned in front of the first record in a RecordSet. When either or these two property values is **True**, it means that the current record being pointed to is not valid.

18. *Programming a Data control* means writing code to alter the control's current record. A Data control is programmed using the **Find**, **Move**, and **Seek** methods. Additionally, a Data control can be programmed to update records in a RecordSet, where the term *update* refers to either adding, deleting, or editing records in both a RecordSet and its underlying database table. The update methods provided by Visual Basic for programming a Data control are listed in Table 9-21.

9.8 Looking Further: Databases and the Application Wizard ▬▬▬▬

The Application Wizard, introduced in Section 8.8, is especially useful for developing database applications. [3] This is because it both creates forms with data-bound controls for each selected database table and provides code for refreshing and updating RecordSets. In this section, we show the additional steps required to use the Application Wizard for creating database applications. In addition, the DBGrid control, a data-bound grid control that presents record information in a spreadsheet format, is described.

---

[1] The Application Wizard cannot be used to modify existing projects.

Figure 9-25

*Using the Data Access
Forms Dialog to
Connect to a Database*

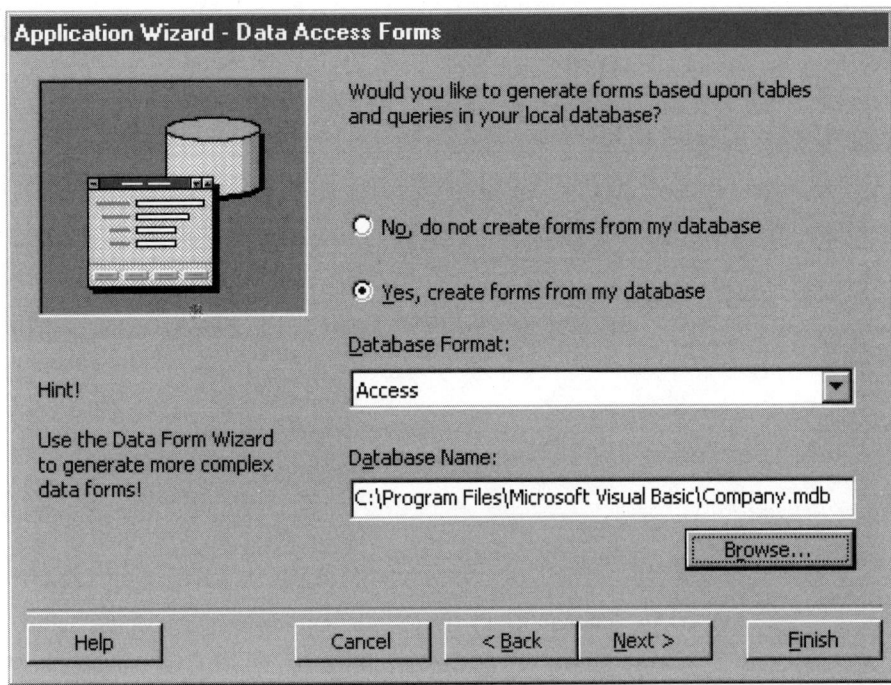

Recall from Section 8.8 that the basic Wizard dialogs used in creating an application are

- Introduction dialog;
- Interface Type dialog (SDI, MDI, or Explorer);
- Menu dialog (File, Edit, View, etc.);
- Resources dialog;
- Internet Connectivity dialog;
- Standard Forms dialog (Login, Splash Screen, etc.);
- Data Access Forms dialog; and
- Finished dialog.

For developing a database application, the only major change within this sequence is to use the Data Access Forms dialog to link to an existing database. As shown on Figure 9-25, this is accomplished by selecting the Yes Option button on this dialog, and then providing information as to the name and type of database being accessed. In the sample application, as is seen on Figure 9-25, we use the dialog to link the application to the Company database that we have been using throughout this chapter. Prior to using this dialog, we specified that this was to be an SDI application with only a View menu provided, and that no additional forms, such as Login or Splash screens, were to be included.

Once the connection to a database has been made, the App Wizard supplies an additional dialog box, named the Select Tables dialog, that requests information about the tables and queries in the selected database. Specifically, as shown in Figure 9-26, this new dialog permits selection of the tables and queries that we want included in the application.

When the Select Tables dialog is first displayed, the available tables and queries are listed in the List box labeled **Available**, which is located on the left side of the dialog. Either

Figure 9-26

The Select Tables Dialog

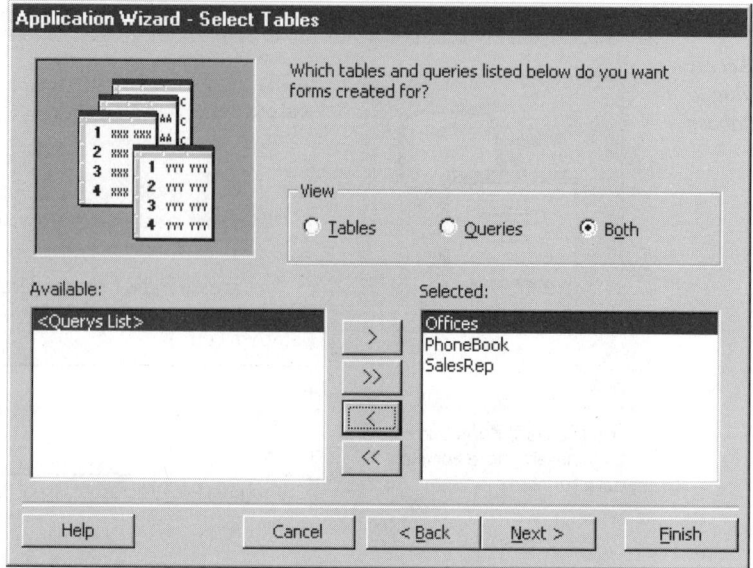

by double-clicking on desired items or using the single right-facing arrowhead between the List boxes, selected tables and queries are moved to the **Selected** List box (clicking on the double right-facing arrowheads moves the complete list over. In a similar manner, the left-facing arrowheads move items from the **Selected** list back into the **Available** list.) As is seen in Figure 9-26, we have selected the three tables contained in the Company database to be included in the final application created by the Wizard. What this means is that an individual form will be constructed for each selected table. As we will shortly see, the Wizard will also include a spreadsheet-like grid for viewing each table and Command buttons for adding records to, and deleting records from the RecordSet.

Figure 9-27 illustrates the menu window created by the Wizard for our application. As is seen in this figure, only a View menu (the option we selected from the Menus dialog) has been included. A Toolbar and Status bar are automatically added by the Wizard whenever a View menu is provided.

Figure 9-27

The Application's Menu Window

Introduction to Visual Basic

Figure 9-28

The Available Data Forms

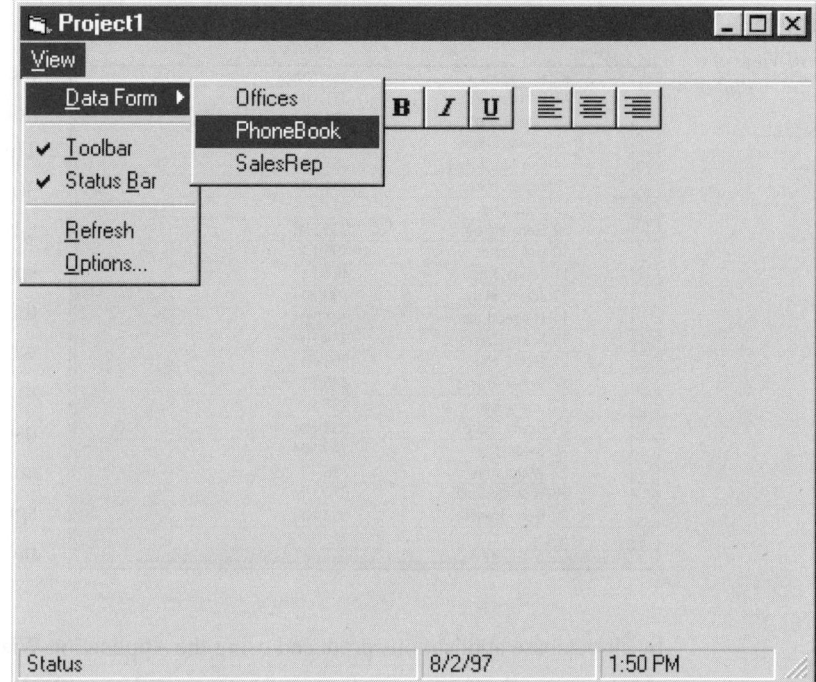

The reason for providing our application with a View menu is shown in Figure 9-28. The View menu provides the user with the ability to select from one of three data forms; one form for each table in the application. An interesting feature is that even if we had not checked the Menu dialog's View option, the Wizard would still have included a View menu. This is because the final application must provide a means for switching between selected tables.

Selecting a specific data form from the View menu shown in Figure 9-28 activates a menu **Click** event that displays the appropriate form. The details of how this menu operates and how menu options can be modified are explained in Section 11.6, and can also be examined by looking at the code contained in the application produced by the Wizard.

Figure 9-29 illustrates the data form created by the Wizard when the View menu's PhoneBook option is selected from an executing application. As expected, this form is similar to the ones that we have created throughout this chapter. Note, however, that the form also includes Command buttons for manipulating the table by adding, deleting, refreshing, and updating records. The application also includes a Grid Command button, which is a new feature.

Figure 9-29

The PhoneBook Table's Data Form

Figure 9-30

A DBGrid Control View of a Table

	ID	Name	Ext	Office
▶	1	Bronson, Bill	321	HM
	2	Engle, Alan	234	HM
	3	Dieter, Frank	289	F1
	4	Dreskin, James	367	HM
	5	Farrell, Mike	564	F1
	7	Ford, Sue	641	F1
	9	Gent, Hillary	325	HM
	10	Grill, John	495	F1
	11	Jones, Kay	464	F1
	12	Jones, Mary	790	HM
	14	Macleod, Jim	761	HM
	15	Miller, Harriet	379	HM
	21	O'Neil, Pat	856	F1
	22	Schet, David	485	F1
	23	Smith, Bill	251	F1
	24	Smith, Dave	893	HM
	26	Swan, Kurt	168	HM
	27	Ward, Ann	726	F1
	28	Williams, John	673	HM
	30	Bass, Harriet	893	HM
✱				

PhoneBook Grid — Refresh | Sort | Filter | Close

Selecting the Grid button causes the **DBGrid** (short for data-bound grid) control to appear. This control, shown in Figure 9-30, displays the records in a table within the context of a spreadsheet view. Each row in the grid corresponds to a record, while each column corresponds to a field. Using this control, a user can move between records and fields using standard spreadsheet navigational methods.

In addition to being supplied by all database applications produced using the Application Wizard, the **DBGrid** control can also be manually placed on a form at design-time. Figure 9-31 shows how the DBGrids icon appears within a Toolbox. The **DBGrid** control can be placed into a standard Toolbox by selecting it from the Controls tab of the Project menu's Components option, or it can be accessed using the extended object Toolbox.

Once a DBGrid control is added to a form, its **DataSource** property must be set to bind the control to an existing data control. When this is done and the application is run, the

Figure 9-31

The DBGrid Control Icon

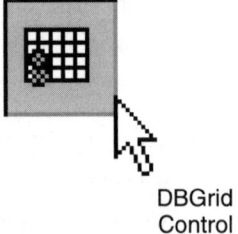

DBGrid
Control

specified table will be displayed in the DBGrid control. The control will appear with column headings taken from the data control's RecordSet and will add scroll bars, if necessary. Using the DBGrid control you can navigate through all of the table's fields and records and edit any field. Assuming that the underlying RecordSet can be updated and the control's **AllowUpdate** property is **True**, a field change is automatically made by moving to a different row. Also, if the control's **AllowDelete** property is set to **True**, any record can be deleted by selecting and deleting an entire row in the grid. Similarly, if the control's **AllowAddNew** is set to **True**, new records can be added to the table by entering them in the grid row that has an asterisk (*) in the left-hand column. In both cases, the deletions and additions will only be made if the underlying RecordSet is updatable.

Finally, in addition to being set at design-time, individual cells within the grid can be selected and manipulated at run-time. Specifically, each column has its own font, border, word-wrap, color, and other formatting attributes, and, at run-time only, each cell can be individually located using the grid's **Row** and **Col** properties.

10 Processing Visual Basic Data Files

*Any collection of data stored together under a common name on an external storage medium, such as a disk or tape, is referred to as a **file**. In the previous chapter we saw how to access database files that were under the control of a database management system. In this chapter we learn how to use files that are directly controlled by Visual Basic. The fundamentals of these files, and how they can be created and maintained by a Visual Basic application are presented. All files, no matter how they are maintained, permit an application to use data without the need for a user to enter it each time the application is executed. In addition, files provide the basis for sharing data between programs, so that the data output by one program can be input directly to another program*

10.1 Introduction to Visual Basic's File Types

A *file* is a collection of data that is stored together under a common name, usually on a disk, magnetic tape, or CD-ROM. For example, the Visual Basic project and form modules that you store on disk are examples of files. Each stored file is identified by file name, which is also referred to as the file's *external name*. This is the name of the file as it is known by the operating system, and as it is displayed when you open or save a file using the operating system.

Table 10-1 Maximum Allowable File Name Characters

Operating System	Maximum Length
DOS, VMX, and Windows 3.1	8 characters plus an optional period and 3 character extension
Windows 95	255 characters
UNIX	
Early Versions	14 characters
Current Versions	255 characters

Each computer operating system has its own specification as to the maximum number of characters permitted for an external file name. Table 10-1 lists these specifications for the most commonly used operating systems.

When using the Windows 95 operating system you should take advantage of the increased length specification to create descriptive file names within the context of a manageable length (generally considered to be no more that 12 to 14 characters). Very long file names should be avoided. Although such names can be extremely descriptive, they do take more time to type and are susceptible to typing errors.

Using the Windows 95 convention, the following are all valid file names:

balances.data	records	info.data
report.bond	prices.data	math.memo

File names should be chosen to indicate both the type of data in the file and the application for which it is used. Frequently, the initial characters are used to describe the data itself and an extension (the characters typed after a decimal point, which were limited to a maximum of three characters under DOS) are used to describe the application. For example, the Lotus 123 spreadsheet program automatically applies an extension .wk3 to all spreadsheet files, Microsoft's Word applies the extension .doc to its word processing files, while Corel's WordPerfect uses .wpx (where x is replaced by the version number). Visual Basic adds the extensions .frm and .vbp, respectively, to form and project files. When creating your own file names you should adhere to this practice. For example, the name prices.bond is appropriate in describing a file of prices used in a bond application.

On a fundamental level, the actual data stored in all files is nothing more than a series of related bytes. To access this data, a program must have some information as to what the bytes actually represent—characters, records, integers, etc. Depending on the type of data, various modes of access are appropriate. Specifically, Visual Basic directly provides three types of file access:

- Sequential,
- Random, and
- Binary.

The term *sequential access* refers to the fact that each item in the file must be accessed sequentially, one after another, starting from the beginning of the file. Thus, the fourth item in a file cannot be read or written until the previous three items have been read or written. Sequential access is appropriate for text files, where each stored character represents either a

Introduction to Visual Basic

text or control character, such as a carriage return, that is stored using the ANSI code. This type of storage permits such files to be read as ordinary text.

Random access, which is also referred to as *direct access*, is appropriate for files that consist of a set of identical-length records. Typically, in using such files, you must first create a user-defined type to define the various fields making up a single record. Then, since each record in the file is the same length, you can directly access any record in the file by skipping over the fixed number of bytes that correspond to all of the records prior to the desired one. This permits accessing any specific record within the file without the need to read sequentially through prior records. Random-access files are stored using binary codes, but since each record has a well-defined fixed-length size, individual records can be conveniently and individually accessed.

In binary-access, no assumptions are made about either record sizes or data types. The data is simply read and written as pure binary information. The advantage to this approach is that binary files typically use less space than text files. The disadvantages, however, are that the file can no longer be visually inspected using a text-editing program and that the programmer must know exactly how the data was written to the file in order to read it correctly.

Exercises 10.1

1. a. Define the term *file*.
    b. Describe the difference between a file that is maintained by a database management system and the files directly supported in Visual Basic.

2. Describe the difference between a text and binary file.

3. List the three types of file access provided in Visual Basic.

4. a. An easy method of constructing a text file is to use the DOS `Copy` command. Use these steps to create a text file named `testfile`.
    Step 1: In Windows 95, open up a DOS window.
    Step 2: In the DOS window, type the command `Copy Con: testfile`
    (**Note:** `testfile` is the file's name. Any legitimate file name can be used instead.)
    Step 3: Enter any text that you want stored in the file. For example, enter the following text, pressing the [Enter] key after each line is typed:
    ```
    Full many a gem of purest ray serene
        the dark unfathom'd oceans bear;
    Full many a flower is born to blush unseen,
        and waste its sweetness on the desert air.
    ```
    Step 4: Either press the [F6] function key or press the [Ctrl] and [Z] keys together. This will terminate data entry and close the `testfile` file.
    b. To view the contents of any text file, the DOS `Type` command can be used. For example, to view the file named `testfile` created in Exercise 4a., enter the command `Type testfile` directly into a DOS window. In response to this command, the file's contents will be displayed. Using this command display the contents of the `testfile` file.

5. List three differences between sequential and random-access files.

10.2 File System Controls

Before a file can be accessed for either reading or writing, that file must be identified by name and location. In this context, location means specifying a drive, such as A:, C:, or D:, and a directory path. Clearly, the simplest method of providing this information is to permit the user to enter a full path name into a Text box and then use code to verify that a valid path has been provided. In an actual application, however, a Text box is typically included within a dialog box, which permits the rapid location of drive, directory, and file using Visual Basic controls. This is accomplished in one of two ways, both of which are presented in this section.

In the first method, we will use Visual Basic's file controls to create a custom-built dialog form. The second method makes use of a built-in common dialog control.

Creating a Custom Dialog Form

Figure 10-1 illustrates the file-system controls provided by Visual Basic, which appear in the middle of the standard Toolbox. As shown, these consist of three controls that provide

Figure 10-1

*Visual Basic's
File-System Controls*

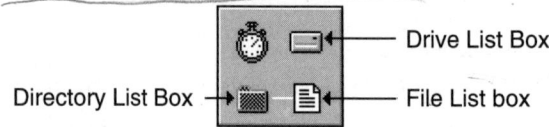

Drive List Box

Directory List Box

File List box

Figure 10-2 illustrates the interface for a custom dialog form that was created using the three file-system controls shown in Figure 10-1.

As is seen on Figure 10-2, the Drive list box is a drop-down box. What this means is that if the user clicks on the arrow provided in the box, a drop-down list of the drives connected to the system will be displayed. When a user clicks on a drive, it becomes the selected drive displayed in the Drive list box. The drive name itself is stored in the Drive box's **Drive** property. In a similar manner, the drive that appears when the box is first

Figure 10-2

A Custom-Designed Dialog

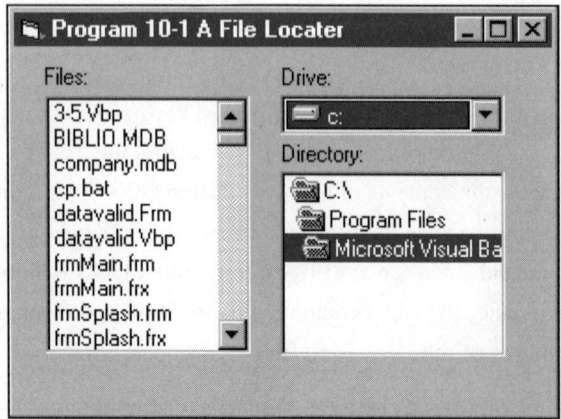

displayed can be set by assigning a suitable value to this property. For example, assuming the Drive box has been named `drvSelect`, the assignment statement

```
drvSelect.Drive = "a:\"
```

sets the initial displayed drive to `a:\`.

Once a drive has been selected, it can be used to set the directory tree that is displayed in the Directory list box. This directory tree displays a directory structure, starting with the topmost directory, with all subdirectories suitably indented and the current directory highlighted. Each item in the directory tree is subsequently highlighted as the user moves up or down the list, and a vertical scroll bar is automatically provided to accommodate tree structures that do not fit within the confines of the box. The currently highlighted directory is contained in the Directory box's **Path** property. By default, this directory has a **ListIndex** property value of –1. The directory immediately above the highlighted directory has a **ListIndex** value of –2, the one above that has a value of –3, and so on. Similarly, the directory immediately below the highlighted directory has a **ListIndex** value of 0, the one below that has a value of 1, and so on. To ensure that the directory tree displayed in the Directory list box always corresponds to the drive selected in the Drive list box requires assigning the Drive box's **Drive** property to the Directory box's **Path** property. Assuming that the Drive and Directory list boxes have been given the names `drvSelect` and `dirSelect`, respectively, the following assignment statement, which is included within the Drive list box's `Change()` event code, would be used:

```
dirSelect.Path = drvSelect.Drive
```

The last of the file-system controls, the File list box, displays a list of files for the path specified in the File list box's **Path** property. To ensure that this file list corresponds to the directory selected in the Directory list box requires assigning the Directory box's **Path** property to the File box's **Path** property. Assuming that the Directory and File list boxes have been given the names `dirSelect` and `filSelect`, respectively, the following assignment statement, which is included within the Directory list box's `Change()` event code, would be used:

```
filSelect.Path = drvSelect.Path
```

To display only a subset of files in the File list box, you can use its **Pattern** property. For example, and again assuming the File box has been named `filSelect`, the statement

```
filSelect.Pattern = "*.FRM; *.VBP"
```

causes only those files having an extension `.FRM` or `.VBP` to be displayed Finally, the highlighted file name is automatically assigned to the File box's **FileName** property.

The interface illustrated in Figure 10-2 is used within the context of a complete program to display the file names within the selected drive and directory.

For this application the only required code is to assign the Directory box's path from within the Drive box, and to assign the File box's path from within the Directory box. This is accomplished using the Drive and Directory boxes' `Change()` events, listed in Program 10-1's Event Code.

Programmers' Notes

Creating Valid Path Names

In creating a full path name for use in an **Open** statement, a file name entered in a Text box is typically appended to a path supplied by a Drive List box. The path name in the Drive box is always a complete path name, such as `C:\programs\vb5`, with no final backslash. Thus, adding a file name to this path name requires inserting a backslash between the Drive box's **Path** property and the file's name. For example, if the Drive box is named drvSelect and the file's name is entered in a Text box named txtFile, a statement such as

```
filename = drvSelect.Path + "\" + txtFile.Text
```

can be used to assign the complete path name into the string variable named `filename`, which would then be followed by an **Open** statement for the variable `filename`. This solution, however, will fail if the current directory happens to be a root directory, such as `c:\`. Here, adding a backslash between the Drive path and the file's name makes the full path name `c:\\file's name`, which contains an extra backslash. What is required is an **If** statement that first checks the last character of the Drive box's path name. If this right-most character is not a backslash, one should be added; otherwise, a backslash character should not be added between the path and file name, as is done in the following code:

```
If Right$(drvSelect.Path,1) = "\" Then
   filename = drvSelect.Path + txtFile.Text
Else
   filename = drvSelect.Path + "\" + txtFile.Text
End If
```

Table 10-2 The Properties Table for Program 10-1

Object	Property	Setting
Form	Name	frmMain
	Caption	Program 10-1 A File Locator
Drive List Box	Name	drvSelect
Directory List Box	Name	dirSelect
File List Box	Name	filSelect

Program 10-1's Event Code

```
Private Sub drvSelect_Change()
   dirSelect.Path = drvSelect.Drive
End Sub

Private Sub dirSelect_Change()
   filSelect.Path = dirSelect.Path
End Sub
```

Although the interface presented by Program 10-1 is useful for illustrating the relationship typically used for Drive, Directory, and File boxes, it limits the selection of file names to those already existing in a directory. In practice, we might need to open an entirely new file in which to store data or may find in easier simply to type in the name of an

---

Figure 10-3
Program 10-2's Interface

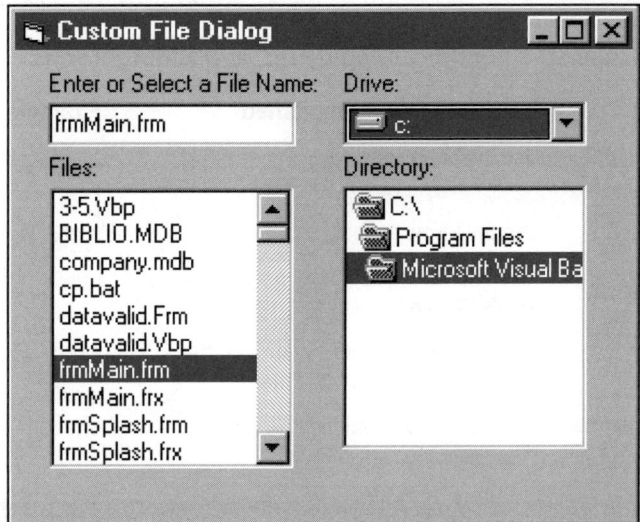

existing file without first going through each file-system list box. Both of these requirements are easily met by supplying a Text box in which the user can directly enter a file's name and location. The addition of a Text box to our custom-built file dialog is shown in Figure 10-3, the interface for Program 10-2.

In addition to making the assignments of drive and path that were made in Program 10-1, we have assigned the highlighted file name in the File list box as the Text box's **Text** property. Doing this permits the user either to select an existing file name from the file box or directly type in a file name into the Text box. The Text value is also cleared whenever the user changes either the Drive or Directory selections, as listed in Program 10-2's Event Code.

Table 10-3 The Properties Table for Program 10-2

Object	Property	Setting
Form	Name	frmMain
	Caption	Custom File Dialog
Drive List Box	Name	drvSelect
Directory List Box	Name	dirSelect
File List Box	Name	filSelect
Text Box	Name	txtSelect
	Text	(Blank)

Program 10-2's Event Code

```
Private Sub dirSelect_Change()
  filSelect.Path = dirSelect.Path
  txtSelect.Text = ""
 End Sub

Private Sub drvSelect_Change()
  dirSelect.Path = drvSelect.Drive
  txtSelect.Text = ""
End Sub

Private Sub filSelect_Click()
  txtSelect.Text = filSelect.filename
End Sub
```

Table 10-4 Loading, Displaying, and Hiding Forms

Task	How Task is Accomplished	Example
Load a form into memory but not display it.	Use the **Load** statement.	`Load frmDialog`
Load and display a form.	Use the **Show** method.	`Show frmDialog`
Display a loaded form.	Use the **Show** method or set the form's **Visible** property to **True.**	`Show frmCustom`
Hide a form from view.	Use the **Hide** method, or set the form's Visible property to **False.**	`Hide frmCustom`
Hide a form from view and unload it from memory.	Use the **Unload** statement.	`Unload frmDialog`

In practice, the custom file dialog used in Program 10-2 would be displayed by a `cmdClick()` event activated on an initial form, and the dialog itself would have an OK Command button to unload and hide itself and then return control to the calling form. Table 10-4 lists the various form-display tasks, the methods used to perform them, and examples for performing these function.

Using A Common Dialog Control

An alternative to creating your own dialog boxes for entering file location information is to use Visual Basic's Common Dialog control. This control provides a choice of the following built-in dialog boxes to be displayed:

- Open dialog,
- Save As dialog,
- Color Selection dialog,
- Font Selection dialog,
- Print Selection dialog, and
- Help Window dialog.

As each of these dialogs are the same ones used within Windows 95, they are generally familiar to most users. For example, Figures 10-5 and 10-6 illustrate the Open and Save As dialog boxes. To include a Common dialog box within a form, use the CommonDialog icon (see Figure 10-4) from the toolbox, as you would any other control. Note, however, that this control is not a built-in control contained in the standard toolbox; rather, it is provided as an external `.ocx` file; to access it you must open a new project using the VB Professional Edition controls.[1]

Figure 10-4

The CommonDialog Control Icon

 Common Dialog Control

---

[1] If the CommonDialog control icon is still not visible, make sure to select the `Microsoft Common Dialog Control 5.0` on the Control tab, from within the <u>P</u>roject menu's C<u>o</u>mponent option.

Figure 10-5

*The Open Common
Dialog Box*

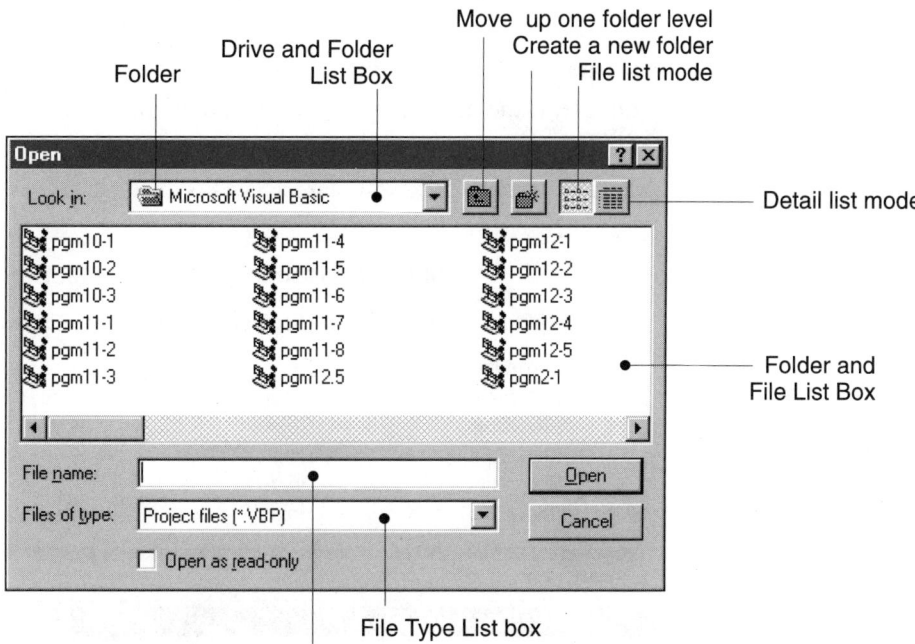

File Type List box

File Name Text box (Selected File)

Figure 10-6

*The Save As Common
Dialog Box*

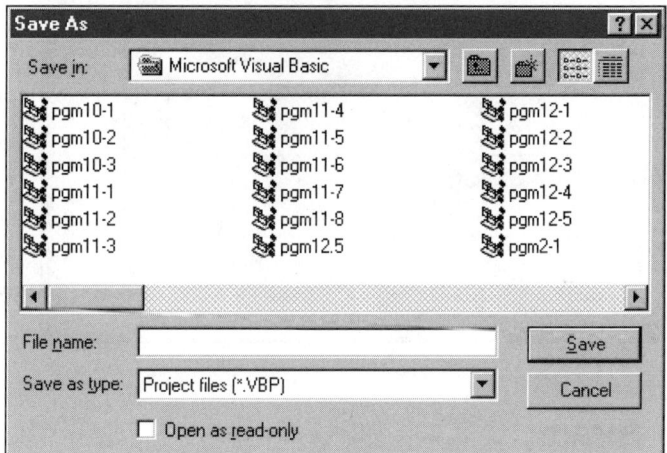

As is seen on Figures 10-5 and 10-6, the Open and Save As dialogs are very similar, in that both provide the following components:

- Drive and Folders drop-down List box, where the user can select a drive and parent directory;
- Folder and File List box, where the user can select a current folder and file;
- File Name Text box, where the name of the select file is displayed or where the user can enter a file name; and
- File Type List box, where the user can select the type of file to be displayed.

In addition, both dialogs provide a set of Command buttons for performing such functions as creating a new folder, moving up one folder level, switching between List and Detail modes, processing the selected file, or canceling the dialog. Each of these functions is labeled with its corresponding button on Figure 10-5.

Once a CommonDialog control is placed on a form, the choice as to which dialog to activate is made at run-time, using one of the methods listed in Table 10-5. For example, if the name of the CommonDialog control is `cdlSample`, the statement `cdlSample.ShowOpen` will cause an Open dialog to be displayed, while the statement `cdlSample.ShowSave` will cause a Save As dialog to appear.

Table 10-5 Common Dialog Selection Methods

Method	Displayed Dialog	Example
ShowOpen	Open	cdlSample.ShowOpen
ShowSave	Save As	cdlSample.ShowSave
ShowColor	Color	cdlSample.ShowColor
ShowFont	Font	cdlSample.ShowFont
ShowPrinter	Print	cldSample.ShowPrinter
ShowHelp	Help	cdlSample.ShowHelp

Figure 10-7

Program 10-3's Design-Time Interface

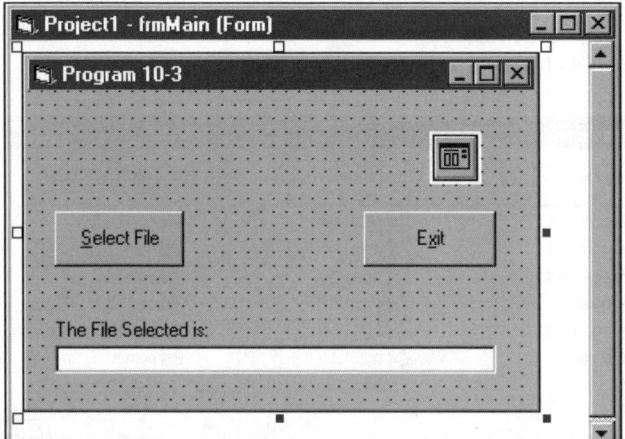

Figure 10-7 illustrates the design-time interface for Program 10-3, which uses a CommonDialog control to obtain a user-entered file name and location. When the CommonDialog control is placed on a form it will automatically resize itself, and like a timer control, it becomes invisible at run-time.

Program 10-3's Event Code

```
Private Sub cmdName_Click()
   picMessage.Cls
   cdlFile.Filter = "Project files (*.VBP)|*.VBP|All Files (*.*)|*.*"
   cdlFile.ShowOpen
   picMessage.Print cdlFile.filename
End Sub

Private Sub cmdExit_Click()
   Beep
   End
End Sub
```

In reviewing Program 10-3's event code, first notice the statement `cdlfile.ShowOpen`. This is the statement that causes the CommonDialog control to display an Open dialog box, similar to the one shown in Figure 10-4. In addition, the statement immediately above the call to show the Open dialog box, is a statement that sets the CommonDialog's **Filter** property. This property can be set either at design-time, using the Properties window, or at run-time, as is done here. The string assigned to the **Filter** property specifies a list of file filters displayed in the dialog's Files of type: List box. The general syntax for setting this property is

control-name.**Filter** = "description1|filter1|description2|filter2..."

For example, the statement

```
cdlFile.Filter = "Project files (*.VBP)|*.VBP|All Files (*.*)|*.*"
```

used in Program 10-3 sets two descriptions and two corresponding conditions, which can be selected by a user when the Open dialog is displayed. The first description displayed is

```
Project files (*.VBP)
```

and the second description, which is displayed when the user activates the Files of type: drop-down list is

```
All Files (*.*)
```

The actual filters used to select which file types are displayed are contained within the filter conditions. For the first description this corresponds to the filter *.VBP, and for the second description the actual filter is *.*. In setting a condition, it is important to note that you should *not* include any spaces either before or after the symbol (|) used to separate descriptions and filter conditions.

Figure 10-8 illustrates a sample run using Program 10-3, where the user entered the name test.dat into the Open dialog's Filename: Text box.

In reviewing the output displayed by Program 10-3, it is important to note that the selected file, test.dat, has not been opened and may not even exist within the indicated folder. By pressing the Open dialog's Open Command button the string entered into the Filename: Text box is stored into the CommonDialog control's **FileName** property. It is this value that is subsequently displayed in Figure 10-8.

Figure 10-8

A Sample Output Produced by Program 10-3

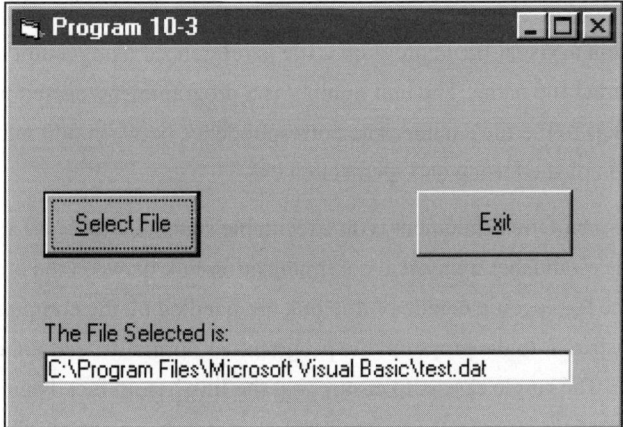

Table 10-6 The Properties Table for Program 10-3

Object	Property	Setting
Form	Name	`frmMain`
	Caption	`Program 10-3`
CommonDialog	Name	`cdlFile`
Command Button	Name	`cmdName`
	Caption	`&Select File`
Command Button	Name	`cmdExit`
	Caption	`E&xit`
Picture Box	Name	`picMessage`
	Text	`(Blank)`
	TabStop	`False`

Exercises 10.2

---

1. Enter and execute Program 10-1 on your computer.

2. Enter and execute Program 10-2 on your computer.

3. Write a Visual Basic program that uses an initial form to call the custom-designed dialog produced by the form used in Program 10-2. The call to the form containing the dialog should be invoked from a Command button on the initial form. In addition, the form containing the custom dialog box should contain a Command button with the caption OK that returns control to the calling form. The selected file name should then be displayed in a Picture box contained on the initial form. Note that your program will consist of two forms.

4. Enter and execute Program 10-3 on your computer.

5. Write a Visual Basic program that uses an initial form to call an Open Command dialog. The call to the dialog box should be invoked from a Command button on the initial form. The selected file name should then be displayed in a Picture box contained on the initial form.

10.3 Sequential-Access Files

Within a Visual Basic program a file is referenced using a unit number, rather than the file's external file name. The unit number is a programmer-selected positive integer that corresponds to the file's name. The correspondence between unit number and file name is accomplished using an **Open** statement.

An **Open** statement is an executable statement that performs two tasks. First, opening a file establishes a physical communication link between the application and the data file. Since the specific details of this link are handled by the computer's operating system and are transparent to the program, the programmer normally need not consider them, except in one case. The single case is to ensure that the link has, in fact, been established.

From a programming perspective, the second purpose of opening a file is more relevant. Besides establishing the actual physical connection between an application and file, the **Open** statement also equates the file's name to the integer unit number used by the application to reference the file. When a file is opened for sequential access, it is opened to perform one of the following operations:

- Output,
- Append, or
- Input.

To write to a file, it must be opened in either Output or Append modes. A file opened in Output mode creates a new file and makes it available for output by the procedure within which the file was opened. If a file exists with the same name as a file opened for output, the old file is erased. The general syntax of an **Open** statement that accomplishes this task is

> **Open** *filename* **For Output As** *#unit-number*

For example, the statement

```
Open "C:\programs\prices.data" For Output As #1
```

creates and opens a file named `prices.data` in the `programs` directory of the C drive. It is now possible to write to that file. Once the file has been opened, the application accesses the file using the unit number (#1) while the computer saves the file under the name `prices.data`. As is seen in this example, a full path name can be used to designate the file, but it is not required. If the drive and directory information is omitted, the file is created in the current directory.

A file opened for appending can have data appended to its end. The general syntax of an **Open** statement that accomplishes this task is

> **Open** *filename* **For Append As** *#unit-number*

The difference between a file opened in Output mode and one opened in Append mode is in how existing files are used and where the data is physically stored in the file. In Output mode, a new file is always created and the data is written starting at the beginning of the file, while in Append mode the data is written starting at the end of an existing file. If the file, however, does not exist to begin with, the two modes produce identical results. For files opened in either Output or Append modes, the statements used to write data to the file are similar to the used for printing data on a form, and are described shortly.

A file opened in Input mode retrieves an existing file and makes its data available as input to an application. The general syntax of an **Open** statement that accomplishes this task is

> **Open** *filename* **For Input As** *#unit-number*

For example, the **Open** statement

```
Open "C:\programs\prices.data" For Input As #1
```

Figure 10-9

*Program 10-4's
Design-Time Interface*

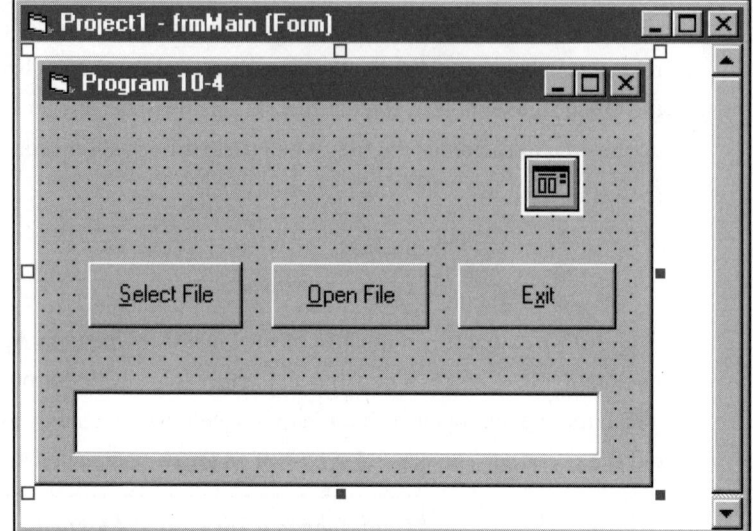

creates and opens a file named `prices.data` in the `programs` directory of the C drive and makes the data in the file available for input. Within the procedure opening the file, the file is read using the unit number (#1). Again, a full path name can be used to designate the file, but it is not required. If the drive and directory information is omitted, the file is assumed to exist in the current directory. The methods used to read data from a file are described shortly.

When opening a file for either input or output, good programming practice requires that you check that the connection has been established before attempting to use the file in any way. The check is made using an **On Error** statement. This statement tells the application what code to execute if an error occurs. Typically the **On Error** statement is used in code similar to the following, which attempts to open a file but reports an error message if the file was not successfully opened for input.

```
On Error GoTo FileError
Open cdlFile.filename For Input As #1
Rem:
Rem: Continue with normal file processing here
Rem:
Exit Sub
FileError: ' Control is only transferred here if there was an error
  MsgBox "The File was not successfully opened!", vbExclamation, "File Error Notification"
  Exit Sub
```

If an error occurs, control is transferred to the statement with the label `FileError`, which is a user-selected label that corresponds to Visual Basic's identifier rules. In this particular case a message box is displayed notifying the user of a file error, and the subsequent **Exit Sub** statement ends the procedure's execution. The first **Exit Sub** statement, immediately before the `FileError` label permits the procedure to avoid executing the error-handling statements if no error occurred. Throughout the remainder of this chapter, we will include this type of error checking whenever a file is opened.

Table 10-7 The Properties Table for Program 10-4

Object	Property	Setting
Form	Name	frmMain
	Caption	Program 10-4
Command Button	Name	cmdName
	Caption	&Name File
Command Button	Name	cmdOpen
	Caption	&Open File
Command Button	Name	cmdExit
	Caption	E&xit
Common Dialog	Name	cdlFile
Picture Box	Name	picMessage
	TabStop	False

Program 10-4 illustrates the statements required to open a file in Read mode and includes an error-checking routine to ensure that a successful open was obtained. Except for the addition of the cmdOpen control, the interface and event code for this program is essentially identical to that used in Program 10-3. The code presented in the cmdOpen_Click() event uses an **Open** statement and an **On Error** statement to verify that a successful open was established, with an appropriate message displayed in a Picture box.

Program 10-4's Event Code

```
Private Sub cmdName_Click()
 picMessage.Cls
 cdlFile.Filter = "Data Files(*.dat)|*.dat|All Files (*.*)|*.*"
 cdlFile.ShowOpen
 picMessage.Print cdlFile.filename
End Sub

Private Sub cmdOpen_Click()
  Dim CR As String

  picMessage.Cls
  On Error GoTo FileError
  CR = Chr(13) ' carriage return character
  Open cdlFile.filename For Input As #1
  picMessage.Print "The file "; cdlFile.filename; CR; "   has been successfully opened."
  Exit Sub
FileError:
  picMessage.Print "The file was not successfully opened"; CR;
  picMessage.Print "Please check that the file currently exists."
End Sub

Private Sub cmdExit_Click()
  Beep
  End
End Sub
```

Figure 10-10

A Sample Output Produced by Program 10-4

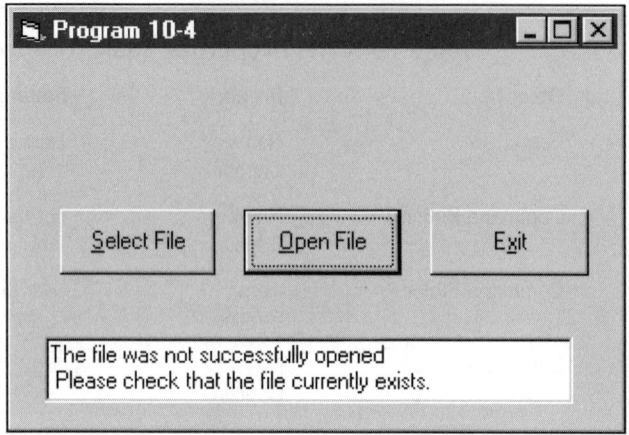

Figure 10-10 illustrates a sample run using Program 10-4 that attempted to open an nonexistent file for input. Although Program 10-4 can be used to open an existing file for input, it clearly lacks statements to either read the file's data or close the file. These topics are discussed next.

Formally, a **Close** statement is used to formally break the link established by the **Open** statement and releases the unit number, which can then be used for another file. The syntax for the **Close** statement is

> **Close** *unit-number list*

where the unit-number list consists of one or more unit numbers that were assigned to the files when they were opened. If more than one unit number is provided in the **Close** statement, the unit numbers must be separated by commas.

Since all operating systems have a limit on the maximum number of files that can be opened at one time, closing files that are no longer needed makes good sense. In the absence of a specific **Close** statement, all open files existing at the end of normal program execution are automatically closed by the operating system.

When a file is closed, a special end-of-file (**EOF**) marker is automatically placed by the operating system after the last character in the file. This **EOF** character has a unique numerical code that has no equivalent representation as a printable character. This special numerical value, which is system dependent, ensures that the **EOF** character can never be confused with a valid character contained within the file. As we will see shortly, this **EOF** character can be used as a sentinel when reading data from a file.

Writing to a Sequential File

After a file is opened in either Output or Append modes, it can be written to using either a **Print #** or **Write #** statement and correctly referencing the file's unit number. The general form of a **Print #** statement is

> **Print** #*unit-number, List of comma separated expressions*

For example, the statement *any price*

```
Print #1, price, txtAmt.Text, 36.25  user entered
```

causes the value of the variable named price, the contents of a Text box named txtAmt, and the number 36.25 to be written to a file previously opened as unit number 1. Notice

Programmers' Notes

Checking for a Successful Open and Error Trapping

It is important to check that the **Open** statement successfully established a connection between an application and an external program. This is because an **Open** is really a run-time request to the operating system that can fail for a variety of reasons. Chief among these reasons is a request to open an existing file for input that the operating system cannot locate. If the operating system cannot satisfy the open request, for whatever reason, you need to know about it and perform appropriate processing to avoid the inevitable abnormal program behavior or a subsequent program crash.

The most common method of checking for a successful connection is a fail code similar to the following:

```
On Error GoTo label          File error
Open filename For Input As #1
Rem:
Rem: Continue with normal file processing here
Rem:
Exit Sub ' if there is no error, skip the error-code and exit the procedure
FileError: ' Control is only transferred here if there was an error
MsgBox "The File was not successfully opened!", vbExclamation, "File Error Notification"
Exit Sub
```

Intercepting errors that occur at run-time, such as an **Open** error, is referred to as "trapping" an error. Trapping an error and then taking corrective action typically involves three steps—all visible in the above code:

1. Enabling an error trap by telling the application where to branch when an error occurs. In Visual Basic this is accomplished by the **On Error** statement.
2. Writing an error-handling routine that appropriately responds to anticipated errors. Typically, such routines provide a user message.
3. Exiting the error-handling routine in a manner that affords the user a subsequent opportunity to correct the problem while the application is still executing.

that the **Print** statement used to write to a file is the same as that used to display values on the form, with the addition of a unit number that directs output to a specific file instead of a form.

Program 10-5's design-time interface is shown in Figure 10-11. The program illustrates using a **Print #** statement for writing data to an opened file. The properties table for Program 10-5 is identical to Program 10-4's, except for the form caption, which is now `Program 10-5`, and the `cmdOpen` control caption, which is now `Write to File`. The significant difference between Programs 10-4 and 10-5 is in the `cmdOpen` control's event code, which is listed below for Program 10-5. When this event code is executed, the user-entered file name is created by the operating system. After the file is opened, a **Print #** statement is used to write a single line to the file, which appears as follows:

```
Batteries      59.95         23
```

Figure 10-11

*Program 10-5's
Design-Time Interface*

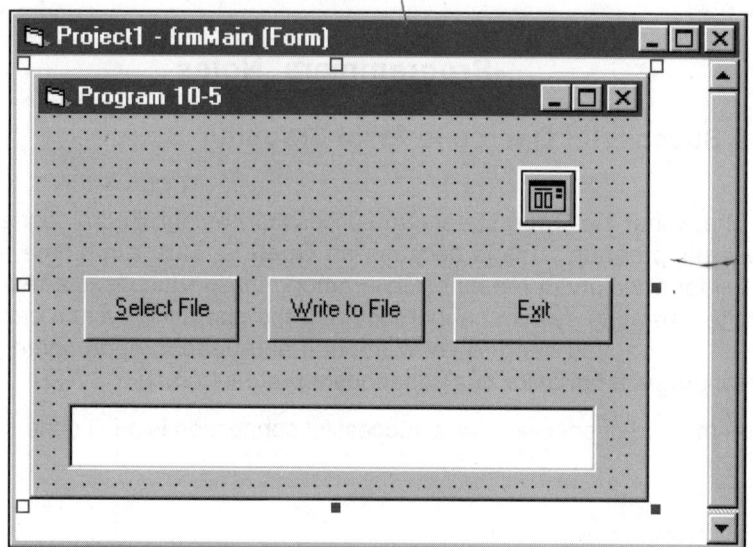

Program 10-5's cmdOpen_Click() Procedure

```
Private Sub cmdOpen_Click()
   Const description As String = "Batteries"
   Const price As Double = 59.95
   Const quantity As Double = 23
   Dim CR As String

   On Error GoTo FileError
   CR = Chr(13) ' carriage return character
   Open cdlFile.filename For Output As #1
   Print #1, description, price, quantity
   Close #1
   picMessage.Cls
   picMessage.Print "The file "; cdlFile.filename; CR; "   has been written."
   Exit Sub
FileError:
   picMessage.Print "The file was not successfully opened"; CR;
   picMessage.Print "Please check that the file currently exists."
End Sub
```

Figure 10-12

*A Sample Run Using
Program 10-5*

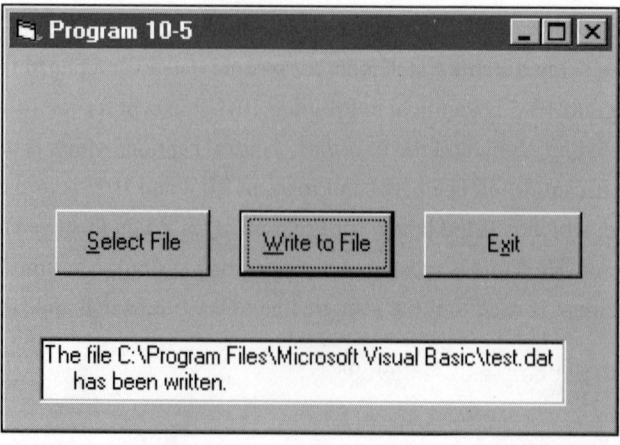

Figure 10-12 illustrates how Program 10-5's GUI looks upon completion of the output, assuming that the selected file was named test.dat. Now let's see how the actual data stored in this file looks.

Carpet care
network

650 965 2486
408 956 8091

For characters stored using the ANSI code, the file is physically stored as shown in Figure 10-13—as a sequence of 34 characters including blank spaces, a carriage return, and a line-feed character. For convenience, the character corresponding to each decimal code is listed below the code. A code of 32 represents the blank character, and the codes 13 and 10 represent a carriage return and line feed, respectively (see Appendix C). These are automatically placed at the end of each line produced by a **Print #** statement.

Figure 10-13

*The File Created by
Program 10-5*

66	97	116	116	101	114	105	101	115	32	32	32	32	32	32	53	57	46	57	53
B	a	t	t	e	r	I	e	s							5	9		9	5

32	32	32	32	32	32	32	32	32	50	51	32	13	10
									2	3		CR	LF

As illustrated in Program 10-5, writing to a file is essentially the same as writing to a form, except for the explicit designation of the file's unit number in the **Print #** statement. This means that all of the techniques that you have learned for creating output displays using a **Print** statement apply to file writes as well. For example, Event Procedure 10-1 illustrates storing data from an array into a file opened as unit number 3.

Event Procedure 10-1

```
Private Sub cmdOpen_Click()
  Dim result As Variant
  result = Array(16.25, 17.36, 15.75, 18.47, 19.51)
  Dim i As Integer

  Open cdlFile.filename For Output As #3
  For i = 0 To 4
    Print #3, i + 1, result(i)
  Next i
  Close #3
End Sub
```

When Event Procedure 10-1 is executed, the file name entered in the Common Dialog box named cdlFile is opened, and a **For** loop is used to invoke a **Print #** statement five times. Each time this statement is used, it prints one line to the file, which is automatically terminated with a carriage return and line-feed character. Thus, the written file consists of five lines, with each line containing two items. The file produced by this code, which we will assume has been written to a file named `exper.dat`, consists of the following data:

1   16.25
2   17.36
3   15.75
4   18.47
5   19.51

In addition to a **Print #** statement, Visual Basic also provides a **Write #** statement. This statement has the same syntax as the **Print #** statement, except that it puts quotation marks around each string expression that is written, and separates each written item with a comma.

Reading From a Sequential File

Once a sequential file has been created and written to, an **Input** statement can be used to read data from the file. The three types of **Input** statements available for reading data from a sequential file are

Statement	Description
`Input #, variable list`	Read data from a sequential file and assign the data to the variables in the variable list.
`Line Input #, string-variable`	Read a line from a sequential file and assign it to a string variable.
`Input(n, #)`	Read the next n characters from either a sequential or binary file.

For example, the statement:

```
Input #2, A, B, C
```

causes three values to be read from the sequential file opened as unit number 2 into the variables A, B, and C.

Reading data from a sequential file requires that the programmer knows how the data was originally written to the file. This is necessary for correct "stripping" of the data from the file into appropriate variables for storage. Program 10-6 illustrates this by using an **Input #** statement to read the data in the `exper.dat` file created using Event Procedure 10-1.

Figure 10-14

Program 10-6's Design-Time Interface

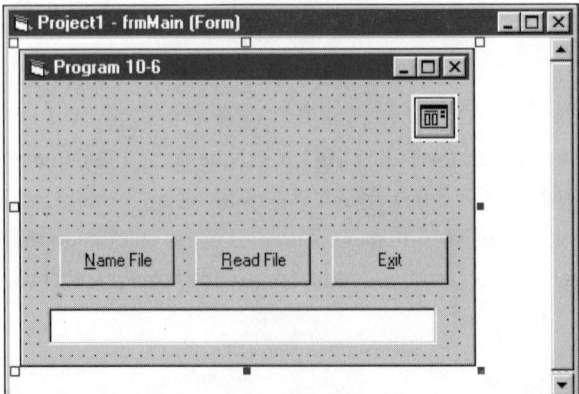

Table 10-8 Program 10-6's Properties Table

Object	Property	Setting
Form	Name	frmMain
	Caption	Program 10-6
Command Button	Name	cmdName
	Caption	&Name File
Command Button	Name	cmdOpen
	Caption	&Open File
Command Button	Name	cmdExit
	Caption	E&xit
Common Dialog	Name	cdlFile
Picture Box	Name	picMessage
	TabStop	False

Program 10-6's Event Code

```
Private Sub cmdName_Click()
  picMessage.Cls
  cdlFile.Filter = "Data Files(*.dat)|*.dat|All Files (*.*)|*.*"
  cdlFile.ShowOpen
  picMessage.Print cdlFile.filename
End Sub

Private Sub cmdOpen_Click()
  On Error GoTo FileError
  Dim i As Integer, n As Integer
  Dim value As Single
  Dim message As String

  Open cdlFile.filename For Input As #1
  For i = 1 To 5
    Input #1, n, value
    Print n, value
  Next i
  Close #1
  Exit Sub
FileError:
  message = "The file was not opened - please check that it exists."
  MsgBox message, vbExclamation, "File Error Notification"
End Sub

Private Sub cmdExit_Click()
  Beep
  End
End Sub
```

[handwritten annotation: "n° of record what we want to read."]

Program 10-6's cmdOpen_Click() event reads the data from the opened file. Each time the file is read, an integer and a single precision value are input to the program. Assuming Program 10-6 is used to read the exper.dat file created by Event Procedure 10-1, the display produced is illustrated on Figure 10-15.

Figure 10-15

The Output Produced by
Program 10-6

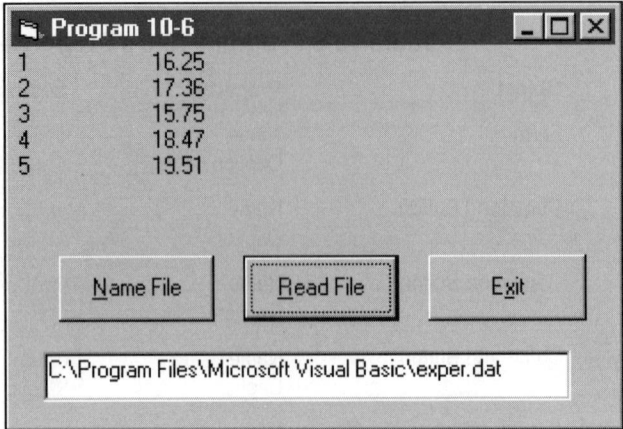

In addition to using a **For** loop to read a specific number of lines, as is done in Program 10-6, the **EOF** marker appended to each file can be used as a sentinel value. When the **EOF** marker is used in this manner, the following algorithm can be used to read and display each line of the file:

> ***Do Until the end-of-file has been reached***
> ***Read a line***
> ***Display a line***
> ***Loop***

For example, if this algorithm is incorporated into Program 10-6, the **For** loop in the `cmdOpen_Click` event would be replaced by the following **Do** loop:

```
Do Until EOF(1)
  Input #1, n, value
  Print n, value
Loop
```

Using this **Do** loop within Program 10-6 produces the same output as that produced by the **For** loop's output previously illustrated on Figure 10-15. Notice that Program 10-6, no matter which loop algorithm is used, is effectively a line-by-line copying program. If we are not interested in extracting individual values from each line in the file, we can use a **Line Input #** statement in place of the **Input #** statement. For example, if we declare the variable `lstring` as a string variable, the following loop can also be used in Program 10-6 to produce the same output shown in Figure 10-15.

```
Do Until EOF(1)
    Line Input #1, lstring
    Print lstring
Loop
```

The **Line Input #** statement reads a line at a time, but does not include any carriage return or new line characters it encounters within its returned string. It simply considers these characters as delimiters that terminates input for the current line.

An alternative to using either the **Input #** or **Line Input #** statements is to use the **Input()** function. This function, which can be used for both sequential and binary files, returns a string, but requires the number of bytes that are to be read and included in the returned string. Unlike the **Line Input #** statement, however, the **Input** function returns all of the characters it reads, which includes carriage returns and new line characters.

To determine the size of a file, which can then be used as an argument to the **Input()** function, Visual Basic provides the **LOF()** and **FileLen()** functions, both of which return the size of file, in bytes, as a long integer. The difference between these functions is that the **LOF()** function returns the size of an open file, while the **FileLen()** function returns the size of an unopened file. For example, assuming the exper.dat file has been opened as unit number 1, the statement n = LOF(1) returns the total number of bytes in the file and assigns this value to the variable n. Using the **LOF()** function as an argument to the **Input()** function, the entire contents of a file opened as unit number 1 can be read using the statement lstring = Input(LOF(1), #1), where the variable lstring can be replaced by any user-declared string variable. Thus, the **For** loop in Program 10-6 can also be replaced by the code:

```
lstring = Input(LOF(1), #1)
Print lstring
```

In this code, the *complete* contents of file number 1 are input into the string variable named lstring.

Exercises 10.3

1. a. Enter and execute Program 10-4 on your computer.
   b. Add a **Close** statement to Program 10-4 and then execute the program.

2. a. Enter and execute Program 10-5 on your computer and use it to create a file named test.dat.
   b. Substitute Event Procedure 10-1 into Program 10-5 and use it to create a file named exper.dat.

3. a. Enter and execute Program 10-6 on your computer.
   b. Substitute a **Do-Until** loop for the **For** loop used in Program 10-6 and use it to display the contents of the exper.dat file created in Exercise 2b. (or display the exper.dat file contained on the disk enclosed with this text).

4. Using the reference manuals provided with your computer's operating system, determine the maximum number of data files that can be open at the same time.

5. Would it be appropriate to call a saved Visual Basic form a file? Why or why not?

6. a. Write suitable **Open** statements to open each of the following files in Output mode: out_data, prices.dat, coupons, and file_1.
   b. Write suitable **Open** statements to open each of the following files in Input mode: in_date, rates.dat, distance, and file_2.

7. Write individual **Open** statements to link the following external data file names to the given unit numbers.

External Name	Unit Number	Mode
coba.memo	1	Output
book.letter	1	Output
coupons.bond	2	Append
yield.bond	2	Append
prices.data	3	Input
rates.data	4	Input

8. Write **Close** statements for each of the files opened in Exercise 7.

9. a. Write a Visual Basic program that stores the following numbers into a file named `results.dat`: 16.25, 18.96, 22.34, 18.94, 17.42, 22.63.

   b. Write a Visual Basic program to read the data in the `results.dat` file created in Exercise 9a. and display the data. In addition, the program should compute and display the sum and average of the data. Using a hand calculation, check the sum and average displayed by your program.

10. a. Write a Visual Basic program that prompts the user to enter five numbers, As each number is entered, the program should write the numbers into a file named `user.dat`.

    b. Write a Visual Basic program that reads the data in the `user.dat` file created in Exercise 10a. and displays each individual number.

11. a. Create a file containing the following car numbers, number of miles driven, and number of gallons of gas used by each car:

Car No.	Miles Driven	Gallons Used
54	250	19
62	525	38
71	123	6
85	1,322	86
97	235	14

    b. Write a Visual Basic program that reads the data in the file created in Exercise 11a. and displays the car number, miles driven, gallons used, and the miles per gallon for each car. The output should also contain the total miles driven, total gallons used, and average miles per gallon for all the cars. These totals should be displayed at the end of the output display.

12. a. Create a file with the following data containing the part number, opening balance, number of items sold, and minimum stock required:

Part Number	Initial Amount	Quantity Sold	Minimum Amount
QA310	95	47	50
CM145	320	162	200
MS514	34	20	25
EN212	163	150	160

    b. Write a Visual Basic program to create an inventory report based on the data in the file created in Exercise 12a. The display should consist of the part number, current balance, and the amount necessary to bring the inventory to the minimum level.

13. a. Create a file containing the following data:

Identification Number	Rate	Hours
10031	6.00	40
10067	5.00	48
10083	6.50	35
10095	8.00	50

e produce a reproduce

c. Write a Visual Basic program that uses the information contained in the file created in Exercise 13a to produce the following pay report for each employee:

ID No.	Rate	Hours	Regular Pay	Overtime Pay	Gross Pay

Any hours worked above 40 hours are paid at time and a half. At the end of the individual output for each employee, the program should display the totals of the regular, overtime, and gross pay columns.

add two records and for that open for Append

14. **a.** Store the following data into a file:

$$5 \quad 96 \quad 87 \quad 78 \quad 93 \quad 21 \quad 4 \quad 92 \quad 82 \quad 85 \quad 87 \quad 6 \quad 72 \quad 69 \quad 85 \quad 75 \quad 81 \quad 73$$

b. Write a Visual Basic program to calculate and display the average of each group of numbers in the file created in Exercise 14a. The data is arranged in the file so that each group of numbers is preceded by the number of data items in the group. Thus, the first number in the file (5) indicates that the next five numbers should be grouped together. The number 4 indicates that the following four numbers are a group, and the 6 indicates that the last six numbers are a group. (**Hint:** Use a nested loop. The outer loop should terminate when the **EOF** marker is encountered.)

10.4 Random-Access Files[2]

The manner in which records in a file are written and retrieved is called *file access*. All of the files created so far have used *sequential access*, which means that each item in the file is accessed sequentially, one after another. Thus, for example, the fourth item in a sequentially accessed file cannot be read without first reading the first three items in the file, the last item in the file cannot be read without first reading all of the previous items, and no item can be replaced without erasing all subsequent items. Due to this fact, updating a sequential-access file requires using a procedure in which a completely new file is created for each update. For those applications in which every record in a file must be updated, such as updating a monthly payroll file, sequential access conforms to the way the file must be updated and is not a restriction.

In some applications a direct access to each item in the file, where an individual item in the middle of the file can be retrieved, modified, and rewritten without reading or writing any other item, is preferable. *Random-access files*, which are also referred to as *direct-access files*, provide this capability. In this section we will see how to create and use such files. Note that the access method (sequential or random) refers to how data in the file are accessed and not to the codes used in storing the data. In point of fact, however, sequential files are stored by Visual Basic as text files, while random-access files are stored using the binary codes described in the next section.

In random-access files, the standard unit of storage is a record, where each record consists of one or more items. A record with only one field corresponds to any of Visual

---

[2] This topic may be omitted on first reading without loss of subject continuity.

<table>
<tr><td colspan="3">**Table 10-9 A Typical Bank Holiday Table**</td></tr>
<tr><td>**Holiday**</td><td>**Month**</td><td>**Day**</td></tr>
<tr><td>New Year' Day</td><td>1</td><td>1</td></tr>
<tr><td>President's Day</td><td>2</td><td>Depends on year</td></tr>
<tr><td>Memorial Day</td><td>5</td><td>Depends on year</td></tr>
<tr><td>Independence Day</td><td>7</td><td>4</td></tr>
<tr><td>Labor Day</td><td>9</td><td>Depends on year</td></tr>
<tr><td>Columbus Day</td><td>10</td><td>Depends on year</td></tr>
<tr><td>Veterans' Day</td><td>11</td><td>Depends on year</td></tr>
<tr><td>Christmas Day</td><td>12</td><td>25</td></tr>
</table>

Basic's built-in data types, while a record with more than one field must be a user-defined type. Due to the record structure required when using random-access files, such files are typically used only for small amounts of data and simple applications; for large amounts of data and more complicated applications, the record structure inherent in the database methods presented in Chapter 8 would be used instead.

To illustrate the use of random-access files, consider the following application. All banks and financial institutions keep a table of official bank holidays, like Table 10-9, which is referred to as a Holiday Table. As shown in the table, some holidays, such as New Year's Day are always celebrated on the same day date, while others, such as President's Day are celebrated on different days, depending on the year. The importance of a Holiday Table is in computing settlement and maturity dates for financial instruments, such as stocks and bonds. Most stock and bond transactions must be settled within five working days, which excludes Saturdays, Sundays, and all holidays. Since there are algorithms for determining which dates fall on a weekend (for example, Zeller's algorithm described in Section 12.1, Exercise10) the specific dates for each weekend need not be stored separately. This is not the case for holidays, and hence the need for a specific table listing all the holiday dates.

A suitable user-defined record type for each entry in Table 10-9 is

```
Private Type HolidayRecord
  Description As String * 20
  Hdate As Date
End Type
```

Using a user-defined record type within the context of a complete application requires opening a file for random access, writing to and reading from the file, and closing the file. Table 10-10 lists the four statements Visual Basic provides for performing these operations on random-access files.

The general syntax for an **Open** statement that opens a file for random access is

Open *filename* **For Random As** *#unit-number* **Len** = *recordlength*

For example, the statement:

```
Open "Holiday.dat" For Random As #1 Len = Len(HolidayRecord)
```

Table 10-10 Random-Access File Statements

Statement	Description	Example
Open	Open a File	`Open "Holiday.dat" For Random As #1 Len = Len(HolidayRecord)`
Close	Close a File	`Close #1`
Put #	Write a Record	`Put #1, LastRecord, Holiday`
Get #	Read a Record	`Get #1, LastRecord, Holiday`

will open a file named `Holiday.dat` as a random-access file as unit number 1. The **Len =** expression in the **Open** statement specifies the size (i.e., length) of each stored record. Since each record is required to be of the same type, the length specification applies to all records in the file. If the specified length is less than an actual record's length, a run-time error is generated; if the specified length is greater than necessary, the record is stored with additional spaces to fill out the specified length. To make the length specification agree exactly with a record's size, the **Len()** function can be used in the manner shown above.

The file name used in the **Open** statement can be either a full pathname as a string literal enclosed in double quotes or as a string variable. If the path is omitted, the file is assumed to exist on the current directory. Finally, the expression `For Random`, which is the default for this form of the **Open** statement, can be omitted.

Once a file has been opened for random access, a **Put #** statement is required to write a record to the file and a **Get #** statement is used to read a record from the file. Program 10-7 illustrates using a **Put #** statement to store the holiday data listed in Table 10-9. The design-time interface for this program is shown on Figure 10-16.

Figure 10-16
*Program 10-7's
Design-Time Interface*

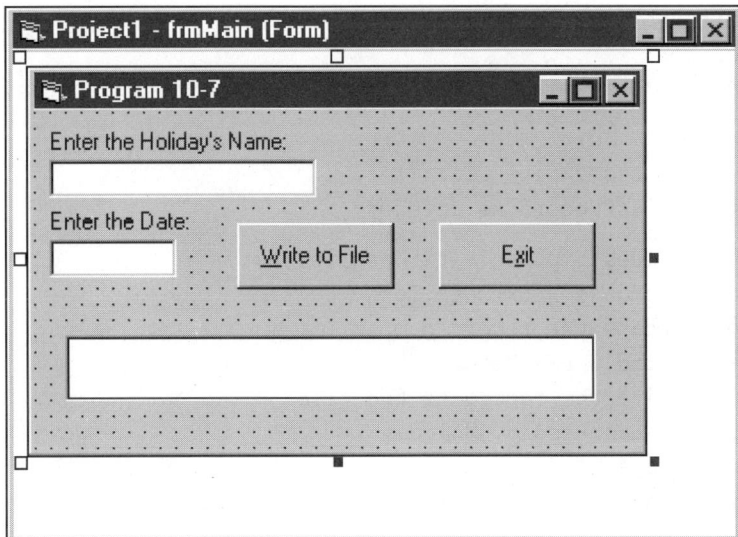

Table 10-11 Program 10-7's Properties Table

Object	Property	Setting
Form	Name	frmMain
	Caption	Program 10-7
Text Box	Name	txtDescrip
	Text	(Blank)
Text Box	Name	txtDate
	Text	(Blank)
Command Button	Name	cmdWrite
	Caption	&Write to File
Command Button	Name	cmdExit
	Caption	E&xit
Picture Box	Name	picMessage
	TabStop	False

Program 10-7's Event Code

```
General Declarations

Option Explicit
Rem: Define a Record Type
Private Type HolidayRecord
  Description As String * 20
  Hdate As Date
End Type

Rem: Declare a variable of the Record Type
Dim Holiday As HolidayRecord

Private Sub Form_Load()
  Const HolidayTable As String = "Holiday.dat"
  On Error GoTo FileError

  Open HolidayTable For Random As #1 Len = Len(Holiday)
  Exit Sub
FileError:
  MsgBox "The file " + HolidayTable + "was not opened.", vbExclamation
End Sub

Private Sub cmdWrite_Click()
  Static LastRecord As Integer

  Holiday.Description = txtDescrip.Text
  Holiday.Hdate = txtDate.Text
  Rem: Update the record number
  LastRecord = LastRecord + 1
  Rem: Write the record to the file
  Put #1, LastRecord, Holiday
  picMessage.Cls
  picMessage.Print "The record has been written."
End Sub
```

(continued)

```
Private Sub txtDate_Click()
  picMessage.Cls
End Sub

Private Sub txtDescrip_GotFocus()
  picMessage.Cls
End Sub

Private Sub cmdExit_Click()
  Close #1
  Beep
  End
End Sub
```

In reviewing Program 10-7's event code initially, take a look at the General Declaration section. It is here that we define the record type used by the program and declare a variable to be of this type (if you are unfamiliar with user-defined data types, review Section 8.4). Next, notice that the `Form_Load` event procedure is used to open the file. Finally, notice the **Put #** statement within the `cmdWrite_Click()` event procedure. Prior to executing this statement, the procedure assigns the fields within the `Holiday` variable to the data entered into the two Text boxes. This procedure also updates the record number for the next record that is to be written, and stores this record number in the variable named `LastRecord`, where it is used to write the record into a file. **Put #** statements have the general syntax

---

Put *#unit-number, record-position, variable-name*

The record number in the **Put #** statement can be any integer expression that evaluates to a positive number. Since records in a random-access file are accessed by record number, applications that use random-access files must contain a means of identifying each record's position in the file. If no record position is indicated, the record's contents will be written at the next available position; that is, the record is appended to the file. However, even if the record position is omitted, space must be indicated for it by separating the variable name from the unit number using two commas. In Program 10-7 the `LastRecord` variable is used to keep track of the current record position. Figure 10-17 illustrates how this program's run-time interface appears after a record has been entered and written.

Figure 10-17

Using Program 10-7 to Write a Record

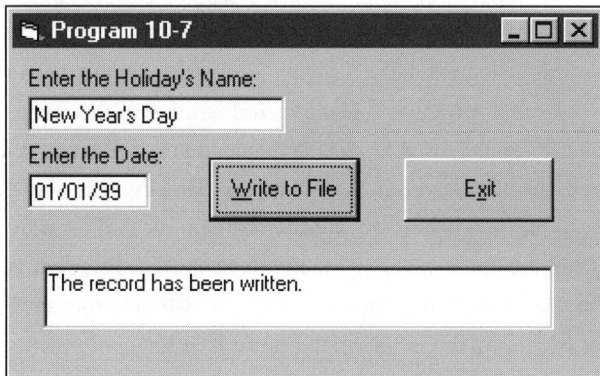

Programmers' Notes

A Way to Clearly Identify a File's Name and Location

During program development test files are usually placed in the same directory as the program. Therefore, an expression such as

```
Open "Holiday.dat" For Random As #1 Len = Len(HolidayRecord)
```

causes no problems to the operating system. In production systems, however, it is not uncommon for data files to reside in one directory while program files reside in another. For this reason it is always a good idea to include the full path name of any file opened. For example, if the `Holiday.dat` file resides in the directory `c:/test/files`, the **Open** statement should include the full path name:

```
Open "c:/test/files/Holiday.dat" For Random As #1 Len = Len(HolidayRecord)
```

Then, no matter where the program is run from, the operating system will know where to locate the file. Another important convention is to list all file names at the top of a program instead of embedding the names within the **Open** statement. This can easily be accomplished using a string variable to store each name, and placing this variable in the General Declarations section of the opening form. For example, if a declaration such as

```
Const Filename As String = "c:\test\files\Holiday.dat"
```

is placed within the General Declarations section, it clearly lists both the name of the desired file and its location. Then, if some other file is to be tested, all that is required is a simple one-line change at the top of the program. Within an **Open** statement this string variable would appear as follows:

```
Open Filename For Random As #1 Len = Len(HolidayRecord)
```

The counterpart to the **Put #** is the **Get #** statement, which is used to read a record from a random-access file. The general syntax of this statement is

> **Get** *#unit-number, record-position, variable-name*

In this statement the `unit-number` is the number used in the **Open** statement to open the file, `record-position` is the record number of the record to be read, and `variable-name` is the variable used to receive the contents of the record. If no record position is indicated, the next record in the file is read. However, as with the **Put #** statement, even if the record position is omitted, space must be indicated for it by separating the `variable-name` from the `unit-number` using two commas. Program 10-8 uses a **Get #** statement to read the records placed in the `Holiday.dat` file by Program 10-7. The design-time interface for Program 10-8 is shown in Figure 10-18.

Exercises 10-4

1. a. List the advantages of using a random-access file over a sequential file. What are the disadvantages?

    b. List two requirements in using a random-access file.

    c. Under what conditions would a database file be preferable to using a Visual Basic random-access file?

2. Enter and execute Program 10-7 on your computer.

3. Enter and execute Program 10-8 on your computer.

4. Modify Program 10-8 to include a Command button that can be used to read a previous record as well as the next record in the file.

5. A software distribution company is constantly opening and closing offices throughout the United States, Europe, and Asia. In its London office it maintains a file that contains an up-to-date listing of offices and their time zones. Currently the company's file contains the following data:

    ```
    Paris              +1
    London              0
    New York           -5
    Chicago            -6
    Dallas             -7
    San Francisco      -8
    Honolulu          -10
    Tokyo              +9
    ```

    The information in this file must be read each morning. It is then used by a program that automatically sends faxes to each office with the time adjusted to local time. For example, New York time is five hours behind London time and Tokyo is nine hours ahead of London time. Thus, when it is 12:00 noon in London, it is 7:00 a.m. in New York, and 9:00 p.m. in Tokyo. What management has asked you to do is write a Visual Basic program that can be used to create a random-access file for the current data.

6. Write a Visual Basic program that can be used to read and display the records created by the program written for Exercise 4a. Your program should include a Command button for reading the next record in the file and a Command button for reading the previous record.

10.5 Binary-Access Files[3]

The last type of file access supported in Visual Basic is binary access. Unlike a sequential file, where each digit in a number is stored using its text (ANSI) code, in a binary-access file all numerical values are stored using the computer's internal binary code. For example, assuming that the computer stores integer numbers internally using 16 bits in the two's complement format described in Section 1.7, the decimal number 8 is represented as the binary number 0000 0000 0000 1000, the decimal number 12 as 0000 0000 0000 1100, and the decimal number 497 as 0000 0001 111 1001. As hexadecimal numbers these numbers have the byte code 00 08, 00 0C, and 01 F1, respectively.

Since the external storage codes match the computer's internal storage representation, an advantage of using a binary format is that no intermediary conversions are required for storing or retrieving the data from the file. In addition, the resulting file usually requires less storage space that it would as a text file. For example, as text, the number 497 requires three bytes of storage consisting of the ANSI byte code sequence 34 39 37 (see Appendix C for these codes), while as a binary number it is stored using the two-byte sequence 01 F1. (For single-digit numbers, of course, the text format, which only requires one byte of storage, is smaller than the equivalent binary code.)

Like random-access files, the information in binary-access files is also accessed directly. The difference between the two file types, however, is that random-access files are organized as records, while binary-access files are organized by item. The same four statements used for opening, reading, writing , and closing random-access files are also used for binary-access files, with the main difference being that a byte position rather than a record position is used when reading and writing binary-access files. The general syntax for an **Open** statement, as it applies to a binary-access file is

> **Open** *filename* **For Binary** As *#unit-number*

For example, the statement

```
Open "bintest.dat" For Binary As #1
```

will open a file named `bintest.dat` as a binary-access file that is assigned unit number 1.

Notice that there is no **Len** = expression in the **Open** statement; if one is included it will be ignored. As always, the file name used in the **Open** statement can either be a full path name, as a string literal enclosed in double quotes, or a string variable. If the path is omitted, the file is assumed to exist on the current directory.

For writing data to a binary-access file, the **Put #** statement must be used. As it applies to binary files, this statement has the syntax:

> **Put** *#unit-number*, byte-*position*, *expression*

---

[3]This topic assumes that you are familiar with the computer storage concepts presented in Section 1.7.

Figure 10-20

*Program 10-9's Graphical
User Interface*

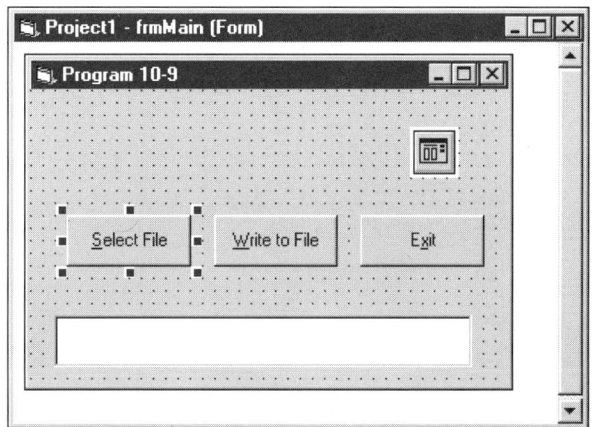

Table 10-13 Program 10-9's Properties Table

Object	Property	Setting
Form	Name	frmMain
	Caption	Program 10-9
Common Dialog	Name	cdlFile
Command Button	Name	cmdName
	Caption	&Select File
Command Button	Name	cmdWrite
	Caption	&Write to File
Command Button	Name	cmdExit
	Caption	E&xit
Picture Box	Name	picMessage
	TabStop	False

In this statement `unit-number` is the number used in the **Open** statement to open the file, and `byte-position` is any integer expression that evaluates to a positive number. If no byte position is specified, the next unused byte position in the file is used (that is, data is appended to the file). However, if a byte position is omitted, a space for it still must be indicated by separating the unit number from the variable name using two commas.

For reading data from a binary-access file either a **Get #** statement or **Input**() function can be used. The general syntax of the **Get #**, as it applies to binary-access files is

> **Get** *#unit-number,* byte-*position,* *variable-name*

Again, the `unit-number` is the number used in the **Open** statement to open the file, the `byte-position` is the position of the next item to be read, and the `variable-name` is the variable that is used to receive the contents of the item that will be read. If no byte position is specified, the next item in the file is read. As with the corresponding **Put #** statement, if a byte position is not included, space for it must still be indicated by separating the unit number from the variable name using two commas.

Program 10-9 illustrates creating a binary file and writing three items to the file. The design-time interface for this program is shown in Figure 10-20.

Introduction to Visual Basic   **463**

Program 10-9's Event Code

```
Private Sub cmdName_Click()
  picMessage.Cls
  cdlFile.Filter = "Data Files(*.dat)|*.dat|All Files (*.*)|*.*"
  cdlFile.ShowOpen
  picMessage.Print cdlFile.filename
End Sub

Private Sub cmdWrite_Click()
  On Error GoTo FileError

  CR = Chr(13) ' carriage return character
  Open cdlFile.filename For Binary As #1
    Put #1, , 8
    Put #1, , 12
    Put #1, , 497
    Put #1, , "abcdef"
  Close #1
  picMessage.Cls
  picMessage.Print "The file "; cdlFile.filename; CR; "   has been written."
  Exit Sub
FileError:
  picMessage.Print "The file was not successfully opened"; CR;
  picMessage.Print "Please check that the file currently exists."
End Sub

Private Sub cmdExit_Click()
  Beep
  End
End Sub
```

Of the three event procedures used in Program 10-9, the cmdName_Click() and cmdExit_Click() event codes are identical to those used in earlier programs. The only new features in this program are the **Open** and **Put #** statements in the cmdWrite_Click() event, as they relate to binary-access files. Notice that for each item written to the file, a separate **Put #** statement is required. Also notice that even though a specific byte position is not indicated in the **Put #** statements, a place for its position is reserved by placing two commas between the unit number and the expression value written to the file.

The binary file create by Program 10-9 is illustrated on Figure 10-21, which uses hexadecimal values to indicate the equivalent binary storage used for the file. As indicated in the figure, the file consists of twelve bytes, where the hexadecimal values correspond to the decimal values 8, 12, 497, and the characters a, b, c, d, e, and f.

Figure 10-21

The bintest.dat File as Stored by Program 10-9

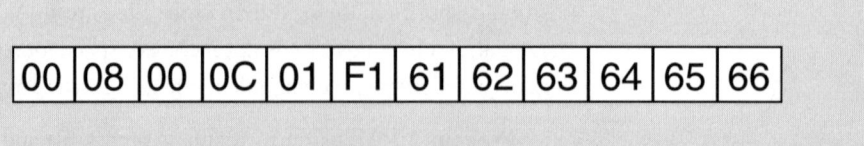

Exercises 10-5

1. List the similarities and differences between binary- and random-access files.

2. Enter and execute Program 10-9 on your computer.

3. Write and execute a Visual Basic program that reads and displays the binary file created by Program 10-9.

4. a. Write and execute a Visual Basic program that writes the numbers 92.65, 88.72, 77.46, and 89.93 to a binary-access file name `result.bin`.
    b. Using the data in the `result.bin` file created in Exercise 4a., write a Visual Basic program that reads the file's data, determines the average of the four numbers read, and displays that average. Verify the output produced by your program by manually calculating the average of the four numbers.

5. a. Write and execute a Visual Basic program that creates a binary-access file named `grades.dat` and writes the following numbers to the file:
    > 100, 100, 100, 100
    > 100, 0, 100, 0
    > 86, 83, 89, 94
    > 78, 59, 77, 85
    > 89, 92, 81, 88
    b. Using the data in the `grades.dat` file created in Exercise 5a., write a Visual Basic program that reads the file's data, computes the average of each group of four numbers read, and displays the average.

10.6 Common Programming Errors

Four programming errors are common when using files:

1. Incorrect format of the **Open** statement.

2. Failure to construct correct full path name when appending a file's name to its path for use in an **Open** statement.

3. Omitting the unit number when using the **Print**, **Put**, and **Get** statements. Programmers used to writing **Print** statements for output to a form, where a specific unit number is not required, sometimes forget to include a unit number when accessing data files.

4. Using the **Put** and **Get** statements without including a starting record or byte position for random-access and binary-access files. Even though such file accesses do not require a record or byte position, when the position is omitted, a double comma must be used as a placeholder for the starting position.

10.7 Chapter Review

Key Terms

binary-access file   file organization

Close   **Open**

data file   random-access file

direct-access file   sequential-access file

external file name   text file

file access

Summary

1. A *data file* is any collection of data stored together under a common name.

2. The manner in which records are written to and read from a file is called the file's *access method*.

    a. In a *sequential-access file*, each record must be accessed in a sequential manner. This means that the second item in the file cannot be read until the first item has been read, the third item cannot be read until the first and second items have been read, and so on. Similarly, an item cannot be written until all previous items have been written and a item cannot be replaced without destroying all following items.

    b. In a *random-access file*, storage is by record, where each record consists of the same number of items, and any record can be read, written, or replaced without affecting any other record in the file. Each record in a random-access file is uniquely located by its position in the file.

    c. In a *binary-access file*, storage is by individual item using the computer's internal binary code.

3. An **Open** statement is required to connect a file name to a unit number.

    a. For sequential files, the syntax for the **Open** statement is

    > **Open** *filename* **For Output As** *#unit-number*

    b. For random-access files, the syntax for the **Open** statement is

    > **Open** *filename* **For Random As** *#unit-number* Len = *recordlength*

    c. For binary-access files, the syntax for the **Open** statement is

    > **Open** *filename* **For Binary As** *#unit-number*

4. a. Data is written to a sequential file using either a **Print #** or **Write #** statement. The syntax for the **Print #** statement is

> **Print** *#unit-number, List of comma separated expressions*

Except for the keyword **Print**, a **Write #** statement uses the same syntax as the **Print #** statement. The **Write #** statement encloses each string in double quotes, and separates each written item with a comma.

b. Data is written to a random-access file using a **Put #** statement with the syntax

> **Put** *#unit-number, record-position, variable-name*

If a record position is not included, the record will be placed after the current record. If the record position is omitted, its place must still be indicated by including two commas between the unit number and variable name.

c. Data is written to a binary-access file using a **Put #** statement with the syntax

> **Put** *#unit-number, byte-position, variable-name*

If a byte position is not included, the record will be placed after the current record. if the byte position is omitted, its place must still be indicated by including two commas between the unit number and variable name.

5. a. Data is read from an existing sequential file using an **Input** statement. The three types of **Input** statements available for reading data from a sequential file are

Statement	Description
Input #, variable list	Read data from a sequential file and assign the data to the variables in the variable list.
Line Input #, string-variable	Read a line from a sequential file and assign it to a string variable.
Input(n, #)	Read the next n characters from either a sequential or binary file

b. Data is read from a random-access file using a **Get #** statement with the syntax

> **Get** *#unit-number, record-position, variable-name*

If a record position is not included, the record that is read is the next record after the current record. When omitting the record position, its place must still be indicated by including two commas between the unit number and variable name.

c. Data is read from a binary-access file using either an **Input()** function or a **Get #** statement, having the syntax

> **Get** #*unit-number*, byte-*position*, *variable-name*

If a byte position is not included, the record that is read is the next record after the current record. If the the byte position is ommitted, its place must still be indicated by including two commas between the unit number and variable name.

7. A **Close** statement is used to formally close a previously opened file and releases its unit number for further Program use. The general syntax of this statement is

> **Close** #*unit-number*

10.8 Looking Further: Creating ActiveX Controls Using the Interface Wizard

Constructing an ActiveX control is similar to constructing a Visual Basic application, except that in place of an initial form object upon which controls are placed, an initial UserControl object is used. For example, if you initiate a new project using the ActiveX icon rather than the Standard EXE icon, you will be presented with the UserControl object illustrated in Figure 10-22. The UserControl, which is the object upon which an ActiveX control is constructed, is similar in appearance to an initial form (see Figure 10-22).

Development Fundamentals

In developing an ActiveX control we will use almost the same techniques we have been using to create Visual Basic applications, except that we will be creating a component to be used in an application, rather than a complete application. Conveniently, at any point in the development of the ActiveX control, we can run it within the context of either a design-time or run-time application to see how it performs, similar to the way we can execute a Visual Basic application at any point in its development. A significant difference, as we will shortly see, is that the control can be executed directly on a design form, without running the form itself as a run-time application.

Figure 10-22

The UserControl Object

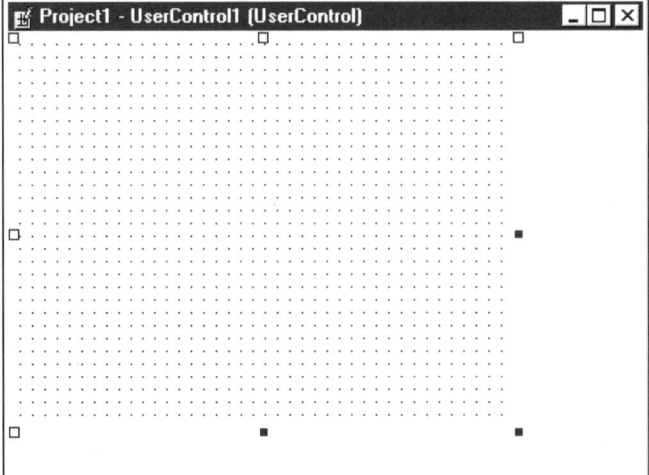

Like an initial form object onto which controls are placed, any standard Toolbox object, except the OLE container control (this object is described in Appendix F), and any other ActiveX control, can be placed onto a UserControl object. Controls placed on the UserControl object are referred to as *constituent controls*, and all of a constituent control's properties, events, and methods are available to us as developers of an ActiveX control. Once the control is developed, however, and placed in the Toolbox, a programmer using the control in a Visual Basic application will only have available the properties, events, and methods that we, as developers of the control, attach to it. Although there are a variety of events can be supplied with a control, two of the most important are the **Initialize** and **Resize** events. A programmer expects that any control placed on a form will be initialized correctly and can be resized using the standard sizing-handles.

With this as background, we are now ready to construct a working ActiveX control using the following steps:

Step 1. Initiate a project using the ActiveX icon.

Step 2. Place all desired constituent controls on the supplied UserControl object.

Step 3. Define an **Initialize** event that sets an initial state for each constituent control and a **Resize** event that resizes all constituent controls as the ActiveX control, as a whole, is resized.

Step 4. Invoke the Interface Wizard to add additional properties, events, and methods to the ActiveX control.

Step 5. Write any additional event code required by the ActiveX control.

At any stage in the development of an ActiveX control we can close the UserControl object, which automatically activates the control and places it in the current Toolbox. At that point we can add a standard EXE project to our ActiveX development project, place the ActiveX control on a design form, and test the current status and operation of the newly developed control. This design form, which is only created once, is added into the existing project following these steps:

Step A. Close the UserControl object's window (use the Close(X) button), which adds the object as an ActiveX control into the current Toolbox.

Step B. Add an EXE project that can be used to test the new ActiveX control. This is accomplished by using the Add Project option from the File menu, and *not* by closing the current project and opening a New or Existing project.

These steps can performed at any time after development Steps 1 and 2 have been completed. Then the new control is tested by placing it on the design form in the same manner as any other control is placed on a design-time form. Different results should be expected depending on at what stage in the development of the control it is tested. For example, if an ActiveX control is tested after Step 2, which is before a **Resize** event has been developed, the control itself can be resized when placed on the design-time form, but any constituent controls used in the control will remain the same size as they were when they were placed on the UserControl object. This is because we have not defined, in the **Resize** event, how these constituent controls should react to a resizing. We illustrate this effect next, as we develop a specific ActiveX control.

Constructing an ActiveX Control

To illustrate developing an ActiveX control, we will create and test a control that acts as a blinking strobe display. The constructed control consists of five rectangular bars that can be made to blink either from left to right or from right to left, depending on the state of a user-created property named **Direction**.

To begin constructing this specific control, use the Shape control and place a single rectangular shape onto the UserControl object previously shown in Figure 10-22. By definition, the Shape control is now a constituent control of the ActiveX control. Name this constituent Shape control `shpStrobe` and set the following properties: **Height =** 135 twips, **Width =** 495 twips, **FillStyle =** Solid, and **FillColor** set to Blue. Now copy and paste this shape four times, so that it appears as shown in Figure 10-23. When you are asked if you want to create a control array, answer Yes. Doing this will create five constituent controls named `shpStrobe(0)` to `shpStrobe(4)`. Also, as shown in the figure, add a Timer control named `tmrStrobe`.

At this stage let us test our control. To do so, first save and close the control. The control is closed by clicking on the **X** on the upper right-hand corner of the UserControl window. Notice that when the control is closed, its icon changes from grayed to active in the Toolbox.[4]

To test the control, we will need to create a design form onto which we can place our newly created (but , as yet, not completed) control. To do this,

- Save the UserControl object using either the <u>S</u>ave or Save <u>A</u>s option from the <u>F</u>ile menu;
- Close the UserControl object (see Step A, above);
- Add a standard EXE project using the A<u>d</u>d Project option from the <u>F</u>ile menu (see Step B, above); and
- Add the ActiveX component from the Toolbox onto the newly created form. (Since the ActiveX component is in the Toolbox, it can be placed on the form in the same manner as any standard Toolbox object.)

After placing the ActiveX component on the design screen, notice the component's resizing capabilities. Although the outside dimensions of the ActiveX component can be altered using its sizing handles, since we have not provided the control with a **Resize** event, the internal constituent control shapes will not be resized as the control itself is expanded or contracted. Thus, we will now shift back to developing the control and provide it with a

Figure 10-23

The Strobe Control's Interface

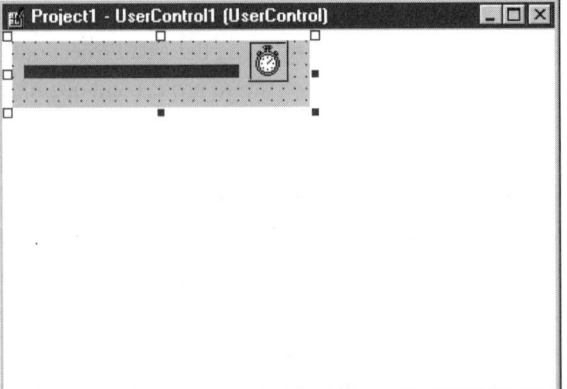

---

4   What is happening here is that the control itself changes from design mode to run mode. Note that you *do not* want to place the control in run mode by pressing either the [F5] key or clicking the Start button, because this would place the entire project into run mode, which precludes placing the control on a form.

Figure 10-24

Creating a Test Environment

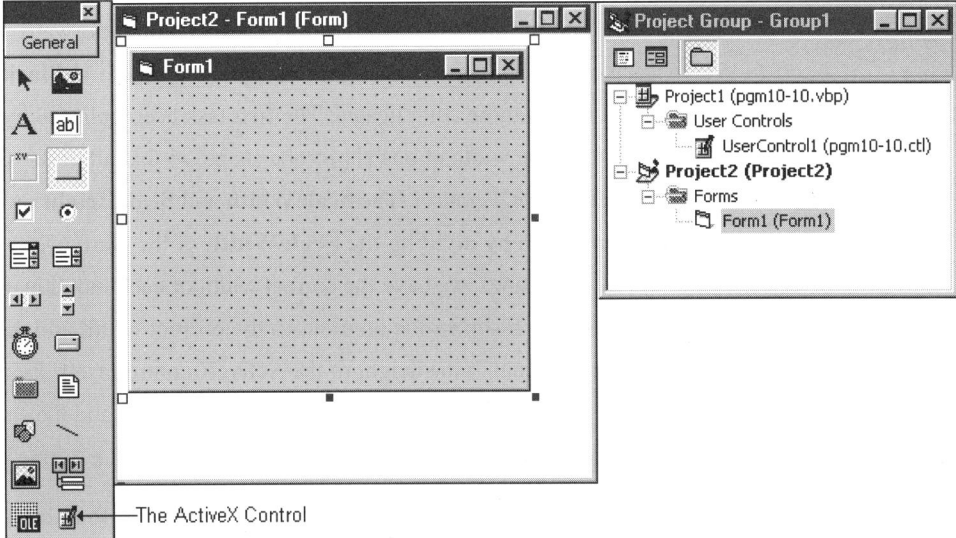

—The ActiveX Control

Resize event procedure that correctly modifies the shape of the control's internal shapes as the outer boundaries of the control are altered. We will also provide the control with an **Initialize** event procedure that causes the control to blink.

To create these event procedures, first click on the UserControl icon within the Project window shown in Figure 10-24. This will activate the UserControl design window. Once this window is active, double-click on the ActiveX control to bring up a Code window, and enter the code, including global declarations, listed in Event Procedure 10-2.

Event Procedure 10-2

```
Dim I As Integer
Const NumStrobes As Integer = 5

Private Sub UserControl_Initialize()
  Dim n As Integer
  For n = 0 To NumStrobes - 1
    shpStrobe(n).FillColor = vbBlue
  Next n
End Sub

Private Sub UserControl_Resize()
  Dim n As Integer
  Dim width As Integer

  Rem: determine the width of a single strobe
  width = Int(ScaleWidth / NumStrobes)
  Rem: Set the size and position of all the strobes
  For n = 0 To NumStrobes - 1
    shpStrobe(n).width = width
    shpStrobe(n).Height = ScaleHeight
    shpStrobe(n).Top = 0
    shpStrobe(n).Left = n * width
  Next n
End Sub
```

The **Initialize** event procedure is rather straightforward, in that it sets the fill color for each of the shpStrobe shapes to the symbolic constant **vbBlack**. The code for the **Resize** event is a bit more complicated. The first task accomplished by the **Resize** event code is to determine the width of one shpStrobe shape, so that all of the shpStrobe shapes will fit in the resized ActiveX control. The **ScaleWidth** and **ScaleHeight** properties refer to the ActiveX object. Thus, by dividing the **ScaleWidth** of the ActiveX control by the number of shpStrobe shapes, we have the correct width of each individual shpStrobe. The **For** loop then sets each shpStrobe element to the correct width and makes the height of each shpStrobe equal to the height of the ActiveX control itself. Finally, the top of each shpStrobe shape is aligned with the top of the ActiveX control, and the shapes are stacked, from left to right so that they align starting from the left side of the ActiveX control.

At this stage you can run the control and see that the internal shapes within it now resize correctly as the ActiveX control is resized. Do this by double-clicking on the Form icon shown in Figure 10-24, and resizing the control on the form. Notice that as the ActiveX control is resized, all of its constituent controls also change shape to conform to the new size.

Adding Properties and Events

At this stage we have an ActiveX component that has an initial color and can be resized but doesn't do very much. To complete its development we will need to add several custom properties and events. Specifically, we will add the three properties and single event listed in Table 10-14.

In reviewing Table 10-14 notice that the ActiveX's **Interval** property is designated as "Mapped to Timer Interval." This means that the constituent timer's **Interval** property will be assigned to the ActiveX's **Interval** property. In a similar manner the ActiveX control's **Tick** event will be assigned to the Timer's **Tick** event. To construct and correctly attach these properties and events to the ActiveX component we will use the Interface Wizard.

Table 10-14 Custom Properties and Events

Name	Type	Data Type	Initial Value
Blink	Property	Boolean	True
Direction	Property	Boolean	True
Interval	Property	Mapped to Timer Interval	1000
Tick	Event	Mapped to Timer Tick event	

Installing the Wizard

The Interface Wizard, which is new with Version 5.0, is invoked by selecting the ActiveX Control Interface Wizard option from the Add-Ins menu. If this is the first time you are constructing an ActiveX component, however, this option may not have been installed and available. If this is the case, select the Add-In Manager option from the Add-Ins menu, as shown in Figure 10-25. Selecting this option will bring up the Add-In Manager dialog shown in Figure 10-26. Simply checking the first box in this dialog, as illustrated on the figure, and clicking the OK button will add the Wizard to the Add-Ins menu.

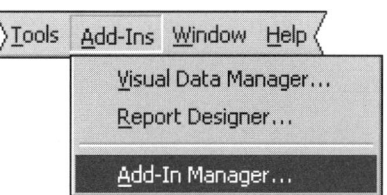

Figure 10-25
Invoking the Add-In Manger

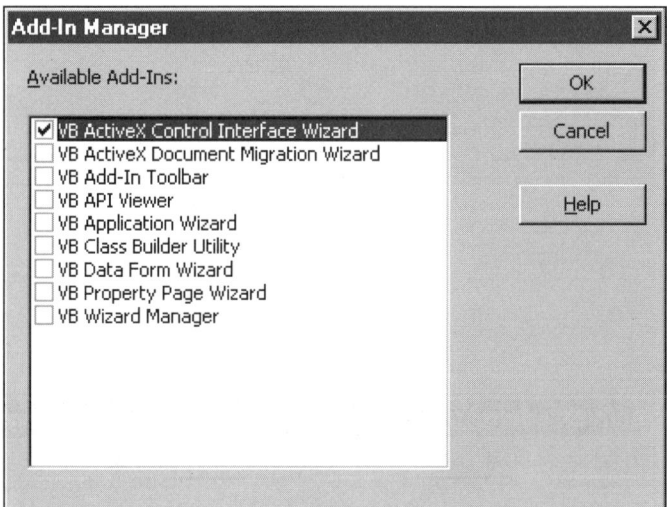

Figure 10-26
Activating the Interface Wizard

Using the Interface Wizard

Invoking the Interface Wizard is accomplished by selecting the ActiveX Control Interface Wizard option from the Add-Ins menu, as shown in Figure 10-27. This may be done to initially set an ActiveX component's initial properties, events, and methods, or to modify an existing ActiveX component currently on the UserControl .

Once the Wizard has been invoked, the initial Wizard dialog shown in Figure 10-28 is displayed. Click on the Next Command button to bring up the first "working" dialog, shown in Figure 10-29. This dialog is used to select from a set of predefined member properties, methods, and events. For our particular purpose we will only use custom-designed

Figure 10-27
Invoking the Interface Wizard

Figure 10-28

The Initial Interface Wizard Window

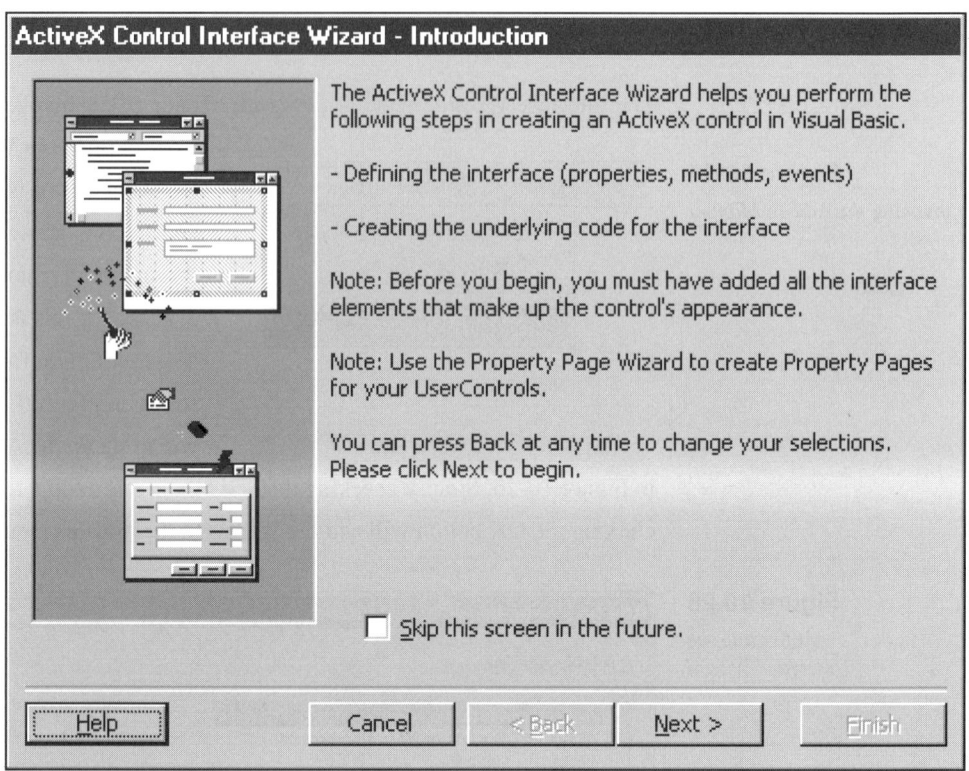

Figure 10-29

The First "Working" Interface Dialog

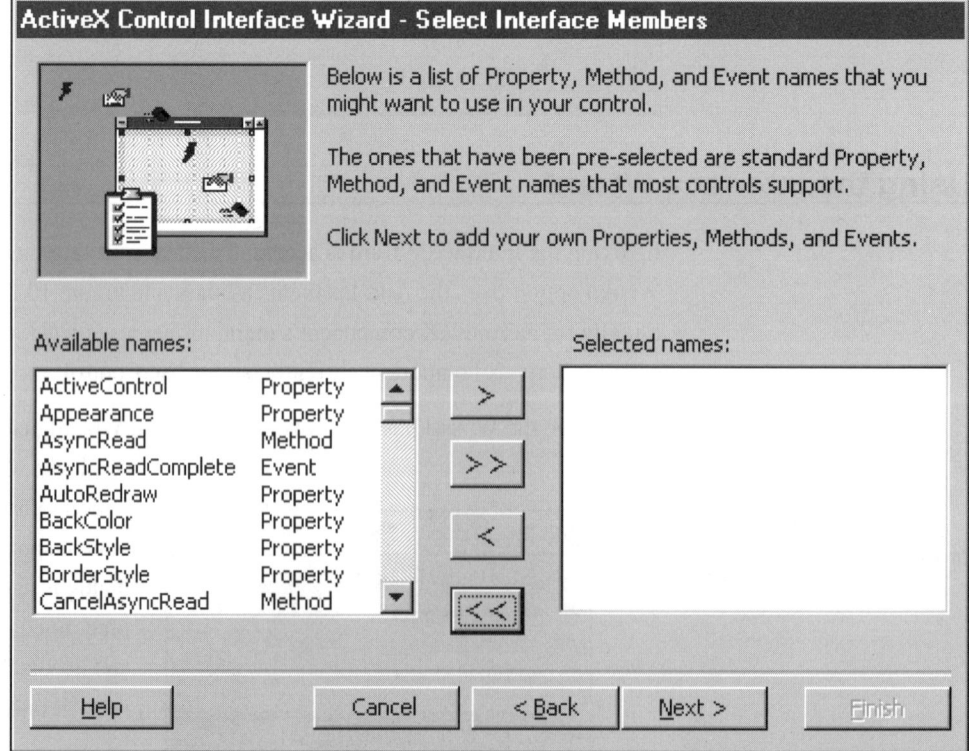

Figure 10-30

The Create Custom Interface Members Dialog

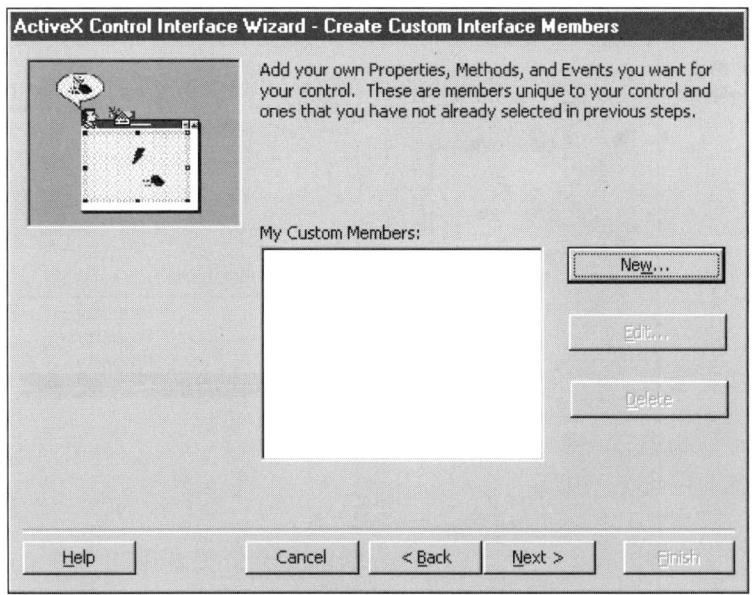

members, so for now, simply click on the <u>N</u>ext Command button, which brings up the dialog shown in Figure 10-30.

As we initially have no custom members for our ActiveX control, no members will be displayed in the List box area of this dialog. The procedure for adding new members is to click on the <u>N</u>ew button for each desired new member. Each time you click on this button, the `Add Custom Member` dialog, shown in Figure 10-31, is displayed. As illustrated on this figure, we have named a member `Interval` and have designated this member as a property by selecting this option from the Option buttons. Clicking the OK button will add this new member to the ActiveX control, and return you to the `Create Custom Interface Members` dialog previously shown in Figure 10-30.The process of creating new members should be done four times, once for each member previously listed in Table 10-14. When this is accomplished, the `Create Custom Interface Members` dialog will appear as shown in Figure 10-32.

Having defined all of our custom members, we are now ready either to map them to constituent members or to set their initial values. To do this, once the dialog shown in Figure 10-32 is present, press the <u>N</u>ext button. Doing this will bring up the `Set Mapping` dialog shown in Figure 10-33. Use this dialog to map the **Interval** property to the constituent `tmrStrobe` **Interval** property, as shown, and also to map the Tick event to the

Figure 10-31

Add Custom Member Dialog

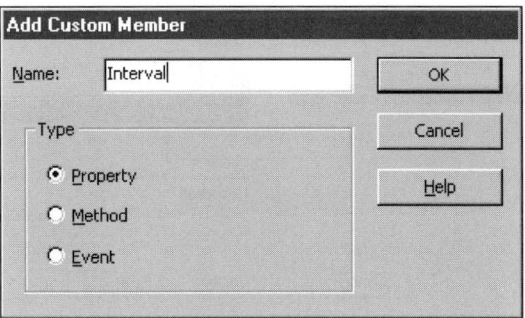

`tmrStobe`'s **Tick** event. Then press the <u>N</u>ext button, which will bring up the `Set Attributes` dialog shown in Figure 10-34.

The `Set Attributes` dialog illustrated on Figure 10-34 is used to define the attributes of any unmapped ActiveX control members. As shown

Figure 10-32

An ActiveX Control with Four Custom Members

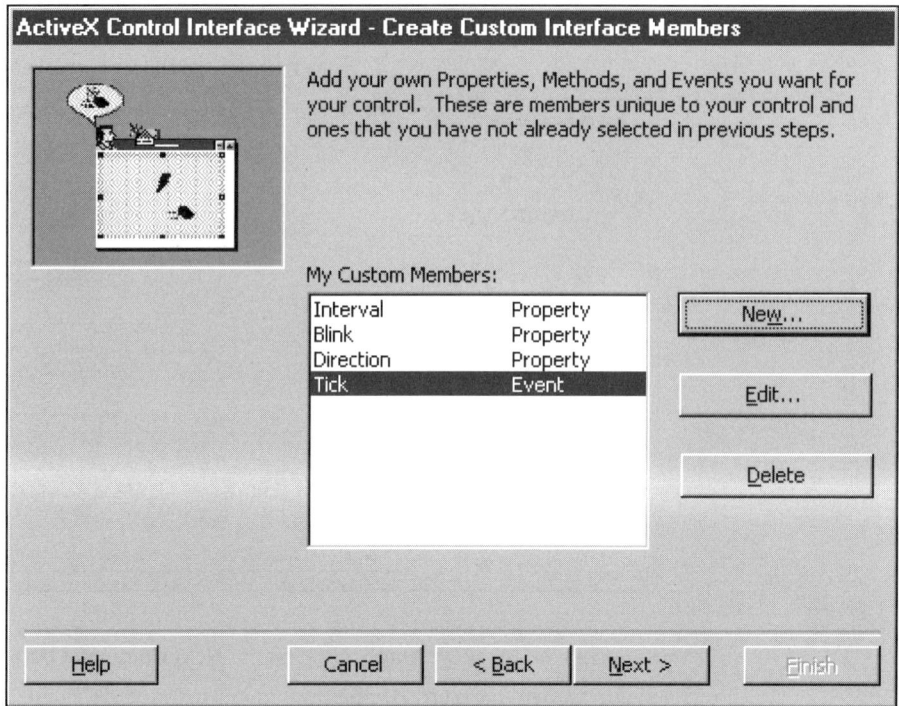

on this figure, the **Blink** and **Direction** property members are listed because they have not been mapped to any constituent controls. We will use this dialog to set the data types and initial values listed in Table 10-14. Once the attributes of both these properties have been defined, press the Next button, which will bring up the final Wizard dialog shown in Figure 10-35. When this last dialog is present, press the Finish button to complete the process.

Figure 10-33

Mapping ActiveX Members to Constituent Control Members

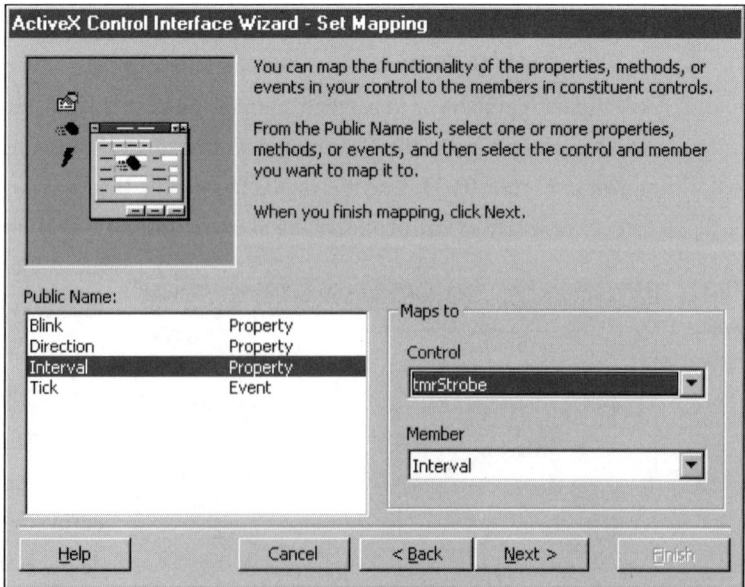

Figure 10-34

Defining UnMapped Members

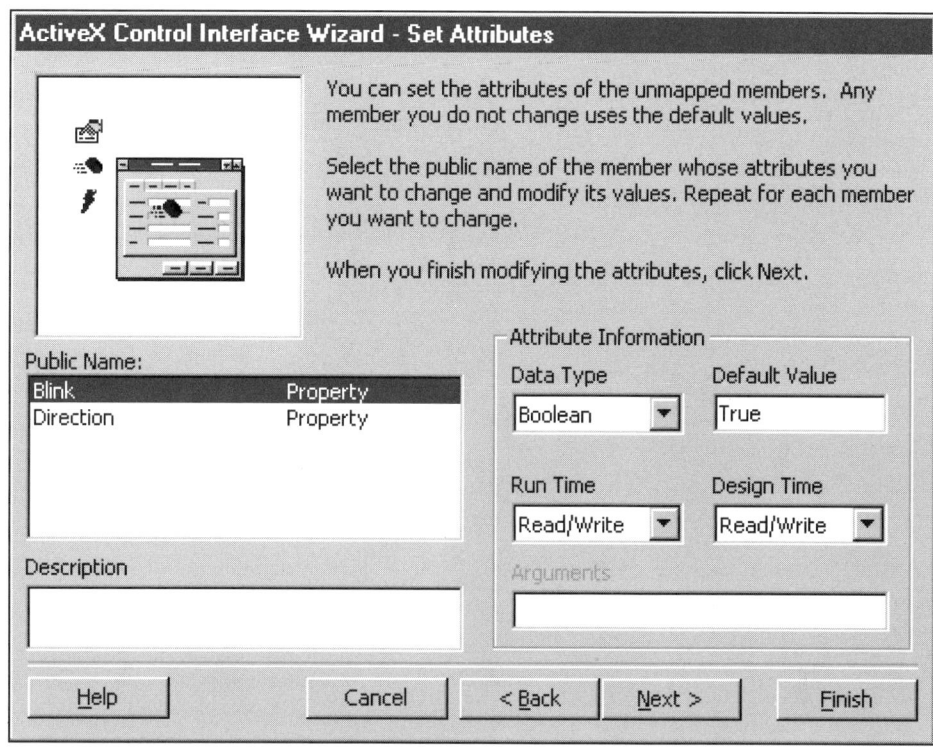

At this point you will have the same ActiveX control previously shown on Figure 10-23, which contains the properties and event listed in Table 10-14. It only remains to add code to the **Timer** event to cause the control to blink in the desired manner. The required code is listed as Event Procedure 10-3. Included in this procedure are two variables, named `m_Direction and m_Blink`, which were automatically defined by the Wizard when the **Direction** and **Blink** properties where created.

Figure 10-35

The Last Wizard Dialog

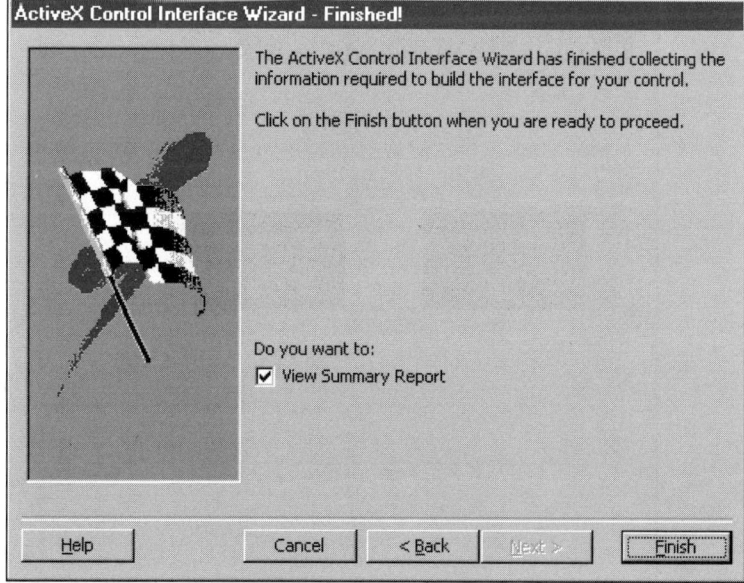

Event Procedure 10-3

```
Dim m_Direction As Boolean
Dim m_Blink As Boolean
m_Direction = True
m_Blink = True

Private Sub tmrStrobe_Timer()
  If m_Blink = False Then Exit Sub
  shpStrobe(I).FillColor = vbBlue
  If m_Direction Then ' blinking from left to right
   If I = NumStrobes - 1 Then
     I = 0
   Else
     I = I + 1
   End If
  Else ' blinking from right to left
   If I = 0 Then
     I = NumStrobes - 1
   Else
     I = I - 1
   End If
  End If
  shpStrobe(I).FillColor = vbWhite
  RaiseEvent Tick
End Sub
```

If you now test this ActiveX control by placing it on a design form, it will appear as
shown in Figure 10-36. Notice that the control begins blinking from left to right when it is
placed on the form. This is because the ActiveX control is active and we have set its initial
properties to activate blinking in this direction. It may seem odd that the component is
running at design-time, but the object we have created is, in fact, a completed and active
object once it is added to the Toolbox. By setting the control's **Blink** property to **False**, we
can deactivate its initial blinking, both at design- and run-time. Also notice that for
simplicity in describing how ActiveX controls are created, we have fixed the fill color of the constituent
`shpStrobe` elements to blink between **vbWhite** and **vbBlue**. A more robust control would add two more
properties to the ActiveX control that would permit the user to set the fill colors at design-time.

Figure 10-36

*An Executing
ActiveX Control*

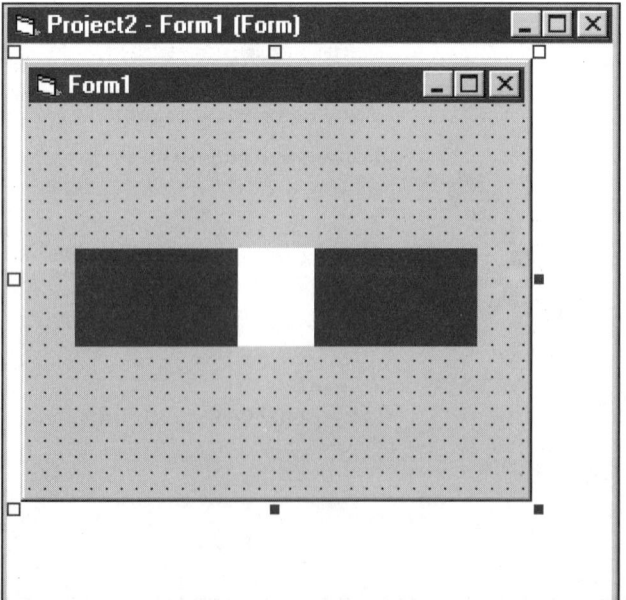

Lab Exercises For Part II

Lab 8: Introduction to Arrays

Topics: Arrays

Reading: Chapter 8

Description: Create three integer arrays. The elements in the third array will be obtained by multiplying corresponding elements in the first two arrays. Finally, the sum and average of each array's elements will be computed and displayed.

Write a Visual Basic program that stores the odd numbers from 1 to 19 in one array and the even numbers from 2 to 20 in another array. The program should then multiply the first element in the first array by the first element in the second array and store the product into a third array. The cross multiplication of corresponding elements in the first two arrays should continue until the product of the tenth element in each of the first two arrays is stored in the tenth element of the third array. Your program must then calculate and display the sum and average of the numbers in each of the three arrays.

First Array	Second Array	Third Array
1	2	2
3	4	12
5	6	30
.	.	.
.	.	.
19	20	3800

Notes: An array is like a super variable. Instead of storing a single value, it stores a set of values under the same name. The array index distinguishes one element from another. For example, where the declaration statement

```
Dim a As Integer
```

creates a single integer variable capable of storing a single integer value, a statement such as

```
Dim a(10) As Integer
```

creates an array capable of storing 11 integer values in the variables named a(0), a(1), a(2), . . ., a(10). If the statement Option Base 1 has been executed, the array will only store 10 integer values in the variables a(1) through a(10).

Lab 9 : A Multiplication Table

Topics: Arrays

Reading: Chapter 8

Description: Write a Visual Basic program that accepts two numbers from the user (in Text boxes) representing the rows and columns of a table. Using this input, display a multiplication table with the number of input rows and columns in a Picture box, such as that shown in the figure below. The maximum number of rows is 15 and the maximum number of columns is 10.

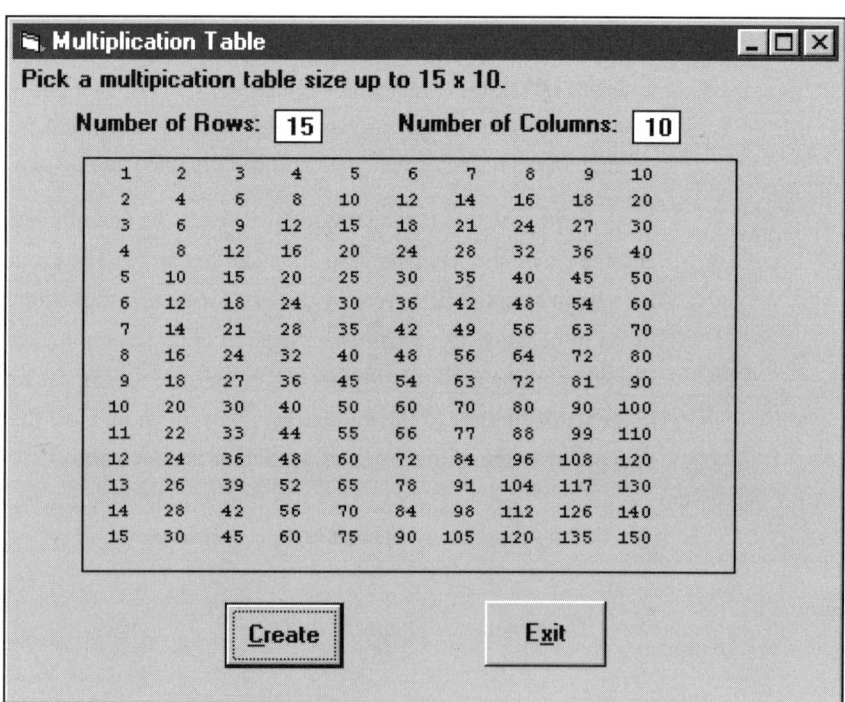

In constructing your program, be sure to

1. Comment your program;
2. Use proper formatting, indenting, etc.; and
3. Use Visual Basic constants (**Const**) where appropriate.

A working version of this program, named `lab9.exe`, is contained on the disk enclosed with the text.

Lab 10: The Unexceptional Race

Topics: Arrays

Reading: Chapter 8

Description: Write a Visual Basic program that implements four racing planes. The planes should move across the screen and the first one across a finish line is the winner. The planes' speed should be interactively controlled by a single Text box in which a user can enter a maximum speed for all of the planes.

For this project you are required to have a Command button with the caption S̲tart Race. When the race is over, the caption on this button should change to R̲eset, and the button should act as a reset button that positions each plane at its starting point. You will also need a Command button with the caption E̲xit that can be used to terminate the program.

At a high level, here's the algorithm you will need:

When the Start Race button is clicked:

    Using a For-Next loop move each plane

        Until one of them crosses the finish line (use a Do-Until loop)

For each movement, the planes should move from 1 to *maxspeed* units where *maxspeed* is the number entered in the Text box.

Hint: To generate a number between 1 and *maxspeed*, use the code

```
speed = Rnd * Val(txtSpeed.Text)
```

Rnd is an intrinsic Visual Basic function that generates a random number between 0 and 1.

Lab 11: A Phone Book—Part I

Topics: Files

Reading: Chapter 10

Description: Construct an application that uses a search form for input, and a message box to display the output. Using data from a sequential file consisting of names and phone extension numbers, search the file and locate the phone extension of a user-entered name. Your program should permit the user to select the name of the phone book file using either a custom-designed form or an Open Common Command dialog.

Requirements:

Using Open and Input commands, read the file named `phone.txt` provided on the disk enclosed with this text. Create a user-defined data type to accept the list of names and phone numbers. The data type has the format

```
Type person
  fname as string
  lname as string
  phone as string
End type
```

Provide an input form in which the user can enter the desired name and then search the list of names, which should be available as an array internal to the program. Then, display either the phone extension of the person whose name has been entered or an appropriate message if that person is not in the file.

Extra Challenges:

1. Make the program display all of the matching records, not just the first match.
2. Add addresses to the database.

Lab 12: A Phone Book

Topics: Files

Reading: Chapter 10

Description: Modify the phone book program written for Lab 11 to provide the capability of adding and deleting a record. To add a new record to the file you'll need to ask the user for a new name and phone number (use an Input box) and then add this information to the end of your internal array. Then, you'll need to rewrite the array out to a disk file. The delete capability should work in a similar fashion. Make sure your program permits the user to select the name of the phone book file using either a custom-designed form or an Open Common Command dialog.

Extra Challenges:

1. Make the program display all of the matching records, not just the first match.
2. Add addresses to the database.
3. Provide the capability to modify an existing record.

Part III
Additional Capabilities

11 Animation and Graphics

11.1 Animation

11.2 Colors and Coordinates

11.3 Graphical Controls and Methods

11.4 Common Programming Errors and Problems

11.5 Chapter Review

11.6 Looking Further: Creating a Menu System

Included within the Toolbox is a set of controls that make the inclusion of graphics within an application quite simple. In this chapter we introduce these controls and show how they can be used to create animation effects. In addition, we show how you can control both the color and position of objects placed on the GUI. Finally, we introduce the graphical methods that can be used to create run-time lines, rectangles, and circles.

11.1 Animation

Animation consists of creating a moving image from one or more fixed figures. This effect can be produced in two ways.

In the first way, a sequential set of figures is displayed, one after another, in the same position on the screen. Each succeeding figure is slightly different from the previous one, creating the illusion of progressive motion. The key to producing this type of image, therefore, is to provide *both* a set of figures *and* a means of switching them, such that only one figure is visible at a time. For a very simple illustration of how this can be accomplished, consider the graphical user interface shown in Figure 11-1.

Figure 11-1

Program 11-1's Graphical User Interface

The image shown on Figure 11-1 actually consists of the three individual images shown in Figure 11-2 layered over each other. Two of these images have their **Visible** property set to **False** so they will not appear on the form at run-time. The relevant properties for this interface are listed in Table 11-1.

In reviewing the properties listed in Table 11-1, pay particular attention to the three Image controls. An Image control, like the Picture box control, can be used to load a picture file. Specifically, Visual Basic supports display of three types of images listed in Table 11-2.

Table 11-1 Program 11-1's Properties Table

Object	Property	Setting
Form	Name	frmMain
	Caption	Program 11-1
Image	Name	imgGreen
	Visible	False
	Picture	Trffc10a.ico
Image	Name	imgYellow
	Visible	False
	Picture	Trffc10b.ico
Image	Name	imgRed
	Caption	True
	Picture	Trffc10c.ico
Command button	Name	cmdLight
	Caption	&Change Light
Command button	Name	cmdExit
	Caption	E&xit

The three images used in Program 11-1 are provided with Visual Basic and are typically found in the directory `/Program Files/Microsoft Visual Basic/Icons/Traffic` (as a DOS directory this path name is `/progra~1/micros~1/icons/traffic`). Notice that the **Visible** property of the first two images is set to **False** and only the third image's **Visible** property is set to **True**. This means that when the program is executed initially, only the Red-light image will be visible. Having provided a set of images, we

Figure 11-2

The Three Individual Images used in Program 11-1

still need a means of switching between each image to create an animation effect. This is provided by the `cmdLight_Click` event procedure listed in Program 11-1's procedure code.

Program 11-1's Procedure Code

```
Private Sub cmdLight_Click()
Rem: The light sequence is Red to Green to Yellow
  If imgRed.Visible = True Then
    imgRed.Visible = False
    imgGreen.Visible = True
  ElseIf imgGreen.Visible = True Then
    imgGreen.Visible = False
    imgYellow.Visible = True
  Else
    imgYellow.Visible = False
    imgRed.Visible = True
  End If
End Sub

Private Sub cmdExit_Click()
  Beep
  End
End Sub
```

Table 11-2 Acceptable Visual Basic Image Formats

Format	Description
Bitmap	An image defined as a pattern of dots (pixels). These images can be manipulated using the Paint program provided in Microsoft Windows 95's Accessories group of programs. These files are stored with either a .BMP or .DIB extension.
Icon	A special type of bitmap file confined to a maximum size of 32 pixels by 32 pixels. They require much less storage space than a standard bitmap image. Icon files are stored with an .ICO extension.
Metafile	An image defined by a series of coded lines and shapes. Metafiles are stored with either a .WMF or .EMF extension and are also referred to as "draw-type" images.

Each time that the `cmdLight` push button is pressed, the state of an image's **Visible** property is tested, starting with the Red-light image. If this image is visible, it is made invisible by setting its **Visible** property to **False** and the Green-light image is made visible; otherwise, the Green light's **Visible** property is tested. If the Green light is visible, it is made invisible by setting its **Visible** property to **False** and the Yellow-light image is made visible; otherwise, the Yellow light is made invisible and the Red light is activated. Thus, the sequence in the **If-Else** statement produces the rotating sequence of lights from Red to Green to Yellow, with the speed of animation controlled by the speed with which the `cmdLight` button is pressed.

Creating a Moving Image

Program 11-1 creates an image that appears to change within a fixed image area. We can also create an image that not only changes but moves across the screen. To create this more complicated type of animation, we will not only need a set of images, but a means of moving the area in which the image is displayed.[1] In addition, instead of controlling the switching of images with a control button, we will automate the procedure using a Timer control. The two images we will use are Microsoft's `BFLY1.BMP` and `BFLY2.BMP` bitmap images. As shown in Figure 11-3, these images represent a butterfly with its wings open and with its wings closed.

Program 11-2's form is illustrated in Figure 11-1. As shown, this form consists of three images, a timer, and two control buttons.

Figure 11-3
The BFLY1 and BFLY2 Bitmap Images

First concentrate on the three images shown on Figure 11-4. The two images at the top of the form will have their **Visible** properties set to **False**, so they will not be visible at run-time. The

---

[1] In this case, the set of figures can consist of a single figure since the movement is supplied by physically altering the position of the figure on the screen.

Introduction to Visual Basic

Figure 11-4

Program 11-2's Design-Time Form

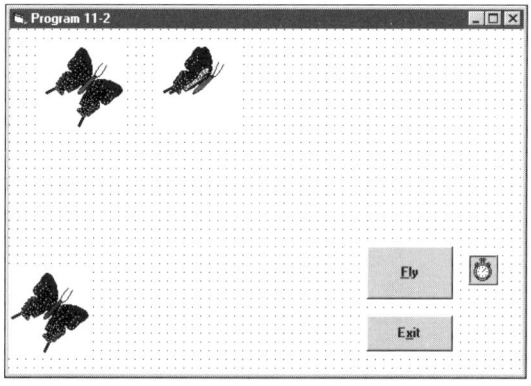

image at the bottom of the form will be visible and it is this image that we will move across the screen. Each time this image is moved, the displayed figure will be changed; this will be done by alternately loading the open- and closed-winged butterfly images into the moving Image control. The code that moves the image and loads it with one of the two fixed images is controlled by the Timer control.

A Timer control has only one event associated with it, which is called the Timer event. This event is automatically triggered by the Timer control at fixed intervals of time set by the timer's **Interval** property. For Program 11-2 we will set this property to 500, which means that the Timer event is activated every 500 milliseconds. Since there are 1000 milliseconds in one second, a setting of 500 means that the Timer event will trigger every half second. The timer is disabled by setting its **Enabled** property to **False**. By definition, timers are not visible at run-time, so this particular timer will be both invisible and inactive when the program is executed. The properties table for Program 11-2 is listed in Table 11-3.

From a user's point of view, Program 11-2 will appear as shown in Figure 11-5 when the program is first executed. The visible butterfly image's movement is initiated

Table 11-3 Program 11-2s Properties Table

Object	Property	Setting
Form	Name	frmMain
	Caption	Program 11-2
	WindowState	2-Maximized
	BackColor	White (Palette Tab)
Image	Name	imgOpen
	Visible	False
	Picture	BFLY1.BMP
Image	Name	imgClosed
	Visible	False
	Picture	BFLY2.BMP
Image	Name	imgMove
	Visible	True
	Picture	BFLY1.BMP
Timer	Name	tmrMove
	Interval	500
	Enabled	False
Command button	Name	cmdFly
	Caption	&Fly
Command button	Name	cmdExit
	Caption	E&xit

Introduction to Visual Basic

Figure 11-5

*Program 11-2's
Run-Time Interface*

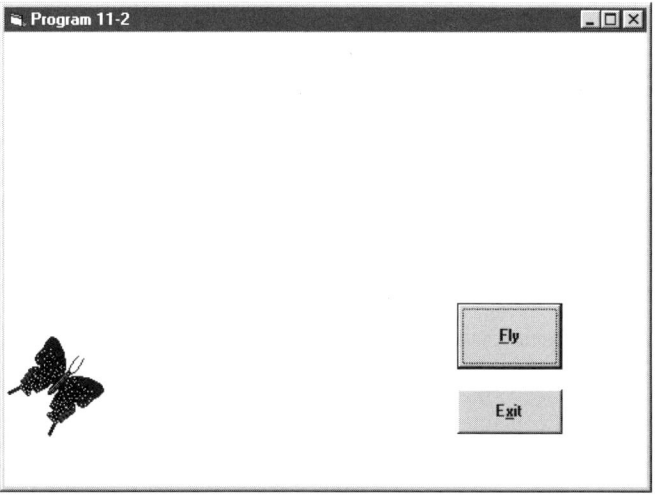

and stopped by the cmdFly Command button. When this button is first pushed the cmdFly_Click event procedure sets the **Enabled** property of the Timer control to **True**, which starts the animation.

Program 11-2's Procedure Code

```
Private Sub cmdFly_Click()
   If tmrMove.Enabled = True Then
      tmrMove.Enabled = False
      cmdFly.Caption = "&Fly"
   Else
      tmrMove.Enabled = True
      cmdFly.Caption = "&Stop"
   End If
End Sub
Private Sub cmdExit_Click()
   Beep
   End
End Sub
Private Sub tmrMove_Timer()
   Static picstate As Boolean

   Beep
   imgMove.Move imgMove.Left + 20, imgMove.Top - 10
   If picstate = True Then
     imgMove.Picture = imgOpen.Picture
   Else
     imgMove.Picture = imgClosed.Picture
   End If
   picstate = Not picstate
End Sub
```

Notice that the cmdFly_Click procedure toggles the timer's **Enabled** property between **True** and **False**. Also notice that each time that the cmdFly button is pushed, its **Caption** property is changed. Thus, the sole purpose of this control is to allow the user to start and stop the timer. When the timer is enabled, it controls the butterfly's movement across the screen. To see how this is done, consider the tmrMove_Timer event code.

Whenever the Timer event code is activated, a **Move** method is executed. The syntax of this method is

---

objectname.**Move** *horizontal-position, vertical-position, width, height*

---

where *objectname* is the name of the object that is to be moved, *horizontal-position* is the position to place the left-hand side of the object, *vertical-position* is the position to place the top of the object, *width* is the object's width, and *height* is the new object's height. The last two arguments, *width* and *height*, are optional and may be omitted. The unit of measurement for these four arguments is the *twip*, where there are 1440 twips to the inch. Thus, the statement contained in the `tmrMove_Timer` event code

```
imgMove.Move imgMove.Left + 20, imgMove.Top - 10
```

moves the imgMove object 20 twips to the right and 10 twips up from its current position. It also toggles the image loaded into the Moving Image control based on the state of the `picstate` flag. This flag variable is declared as **Static** so that it retains its state between procedure calls. Finally, the value of the flag is also toggled at the end of each Timer event by setting it to its **Not** state. Thus, when the flag has a **True** value the **Not** operation will set it to **False**, and when it is **False**, the **Not** operation sets it to **True**.

Exercises 11.1

1. Enter and execute Program 11-1 on your computer.

2. Enter and execute Program 11-2 on your computer.

3. Modify Program 11-1 so that the switching of the light is controlled by a timer that activates its Timer event every quarter of a second.

4. a. Experiment with the **Move** method used in Program 11-2 to alter the motion of the butterfly across the screen.
   b. Modify Program 11-2 so that the butterfly moves across the screen starting at the top left-hand corner, and moves down toward the bottom right-hand corner of the screen.

5. Modify Program 11-2 to add two additional moving butterfly images.

6. Modify Program 11-2 so that the image restarts at the left-hand side of the screen once it moves off the right-hand side.

7. Locate an icon or bitmap image, such as a plane or a rocket, that can be used to create an animated sequence. Include it in a working program.

11.2 Colors and Coordinates

Every object placed on a form has attributes of color and position. In this section, we describe how these fundamental attributes can be set at design-time and how they can be altered at run-time. We begin with the Color attribute.

Controlling Color

The two most obvious Color attributes of an object are its foreground and background colors. The foreground color determines the color of any displayed text or graphics, while the background color determines the color of the background. For example, the foreground color of this page is (mostly) black and its background color is white.

The vast majority of color monitors are of the RGB type, which means that they create their colors from combinations of Red, Green, and Blue. This color scheme is used in Visual Basic. Every color presented on the screen is defined by using three separate numbers, one for red, one for green, and one for blue.

Individually, the red, blue, and green components of a color are represented by a number between 0 and 255, which corresponds to a hexadecimal number between 0 and &HFF. The combined color is numerically represented as a long integer in the range 0 to 16,777,215. More conveniently, this is expressed as a hexadecimal number in the form &H00BB66RR, where RR, GG, and BB represent the color's red, green, and blue content. For example, since pure white is created using full red, full green, and full blue, its numerical representation is "255 255 255", which is represented in hexadecimal as &H00FFFFFF. Here, the last set of two hexadecimal digits (FF) represents the red content of the number, the next-to-last set the blue content, and the second set the green content. Notice that the color value effectively specifies the relative intensity of red, green, and blue in the final color. The actual color displayed will depend on the color monitor used to display it.

At design-time, the color code can be selected from the system's color palette or by typing in a numerical code in the designated property attribute, such as **ForeColor** and **BackColor**. At run-time, the color code can be selected in one of four ways:

- By using the RGB function;
- By using the QBColor function, which selects one of 16 Microsoft QuickBasic™ colors;
- By using a system intrinsic constant listed in the Object Browser; or
- By entering a color value directly.

To get a clear understanding of the color codes, we will use the *RGB function*. This function permits us to set the color code by individually specifying the red, blue, and green content of the desired final color. The format of this function, which returns a long integer representing the RGB color value, is

> RGB(*red, green, blue*)

Table 11-4 RGB Color Values

Color	Red Content	Green Content	Blue Content
Black	0	0	0
Blue	0	0	255
Cyan	0	255	255
Green	0	255	0
Magenta	255	0	255
Red	255	0	0
Yellow	255	255	0
White	255	255	255

where

- *Red* is a number in the range 0 to 255 that represents the color's red component,
- *Green* is a number in the range 0 to 255 that represents the color's green component, and
- *Blue* is a number in the range 0 to 255 that represents the color's blue component.

If a value greater that 255 is used for a color component, the number is assumed to be 255. Table 11-4 lists the red, green, and blue content of a few standard colors.

Program 11-3 can be used to determine the amount of red, green, and blue content in a color and the numerical value returned by the RGB function. This program uses horizontal scroll bars to select the individual intensity of each color component. The final color displayed in the Picture box is the color defined by the RGB function as the combination of all three components.

The advantage of using a Scroll Bar control is that the minimum and maximum values of the scroll can be set. In this case we will set the minimum and maximum values at 0 and 255, respectively, which represent the range of values accepted by the RGB function. Although we have used horizontal scroll bars, vertical scroll bars could have been used instead. As their names suggest, horizontal scroll bars scroll horizontally on the form, while vertical scroll bars scroll vertically. Figure 11-6 illustrates Program 11-3's design-time user interface.

Figure 11-6

Program 11-3's Design-Time User Interface

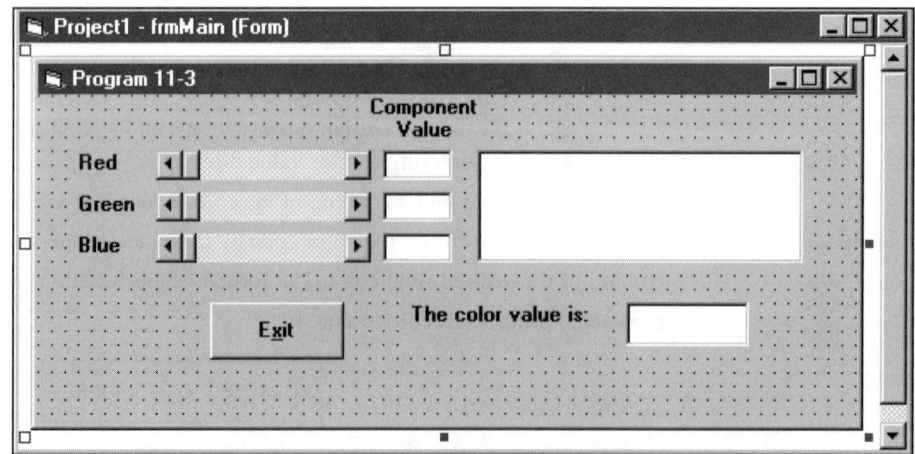

Introduction to Visual Basic

Table 11-5 Program 11-3's Properties Table

Object	Property	Setting
Form	Name	frmMain
	Caption	Program 11-3
Horizontal Scroll	Name	hsbRed
	Min	0
	Max	255
Horizontal Scroll	Name	hsbGreen
	Min	0
	Max	255
Horizontal Scroll	Name	hsbBlue
	Min	0
	max	255
Label	Name	lblRed
	Caption	Red
Label	Name	lblGreen
	Caption	Green
Label	Name	lblBlue
	Caption	Blue
Label	Name	lblValue
	Caption	Component Value
Label	Name	lblColor
	Caption	The color value is:
Picture box	Name	picRed
	TabStop	False
	BackColor	White (Palette tab)
Picture box	Name	picGreen
	TabStop	False
	BackColor	White (Palette tab)
Picture box	Name	picBlue
	TabStop	False
	BackColor	White (Palette tab)
Picture box	Name	picColor
	TabStop	False
	BackColor	White (Palette tab)
Picture box	Name	picValue
	TabStop	False
	BackColor	White (Palette tab)
Command button	Name	cmdExit
	Caption	E&xit

The central processing done by Program 11-3 is accomplished by the general procedure named `docolor`, which is listed within Program 11-3's procedural code. Notice that the `docolor` procedure clears all Picture boxes, calculates a new color value using the RGB function, and then displays all color values in their respective Picture boxes. This procedure is called by each horizontal scroll bar's **Scroll** and **Change** events. The reason for using two event procedures for each scroll bar is because the **Scroll** event is only activated as the thumb bar is moved, while the **Change** event is only activated by the arrow keys and the final placement of the thumb bar. Using both of these event procedures creates an output that is triggered, no matter how the user interacts with each scroll bar.

Program 11-3's Procedural Code

```
Rem: This is a [General] procedure
Private Sub docolor()
  Dim colorval As Long

  picRed.Cls
  picGreen.Cls
  picBlue.Cls
  picValue.Cls
  colorval = RGB(hsbRed.Value, hsbGreen.Value, hsbBlue.Value)
  picColor.BackColor = colorval
  picRed.Print hsbRed.Value
  picGreen.Print hsbGreen.Value
  picBlue.Print hsbBlue.Value
  picValue.Print colorval
End sub

Rem: Here are the event procedures
Private Sub hsbBlue_Change()
  docolor
End sub

Private Sub hsbBlue_Scroll()
  docolor
End sub

Private Sub hsbGreen_Change()
  docolor
End sub

Private Sub hsbGreen_Scroll()
  docolor
End sub

Private Sub hsbRed_Change()
  docolor
End sub

Private Sub hsbRed_Scroll()
 docolor
End sub

Private Sub cmdExit_Click()
  Beep
  End
End sub
```

Figure 11-7

A Sample Output using Program 11-3

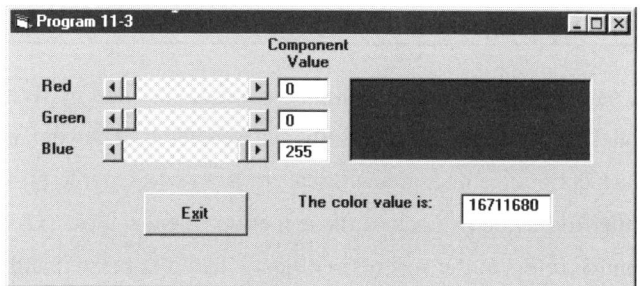

Figure 11-7 illustrates a sample output using Program 11-3. As listed in Table 11-4, the color yellow is achieved using the component values red = 0, green = 0, and blue = 255.

Controlling Position

The position of each object placed on a form is defined by the position of its left-hand, top-corner point, as shown in Figure 11-8.

As illustrated in Figure 11-8, a form's coordinate system consists of a two-dimensional grid, with the origin of the form located at its top, left-hand corner. The horizontal line along the top of the form is referred to as the x-coordinate axis (or x-axis, for short),while the vertical line drawn down the side of the form is referred to as the y-coordinate axis (or y-axis, for short).

By default, each axis is marked in fixed units of length, called a *twip*, where there are 1440 twips to an inch. This measurement scale defines the size of an object when it is printed, while the actual distances displayed on the screen can vary due to the monitor's size.

Whenever an object is placed inside another object, the outer object is referred to as a *container*. Within each container, the same coordinate system is used. Thus, the default coordinate system for every container, including the form, starts with the origin of the coordinate system at the container's upper-left corner. The usefulness of this coordinate system, which is referred to as a Cartesian system, is that any point in a container can be located from the container's top left-hand corner (the origin) using two numbers, the point's x and y coordinate values.

Figure 11-8

A Form's Coordinate System

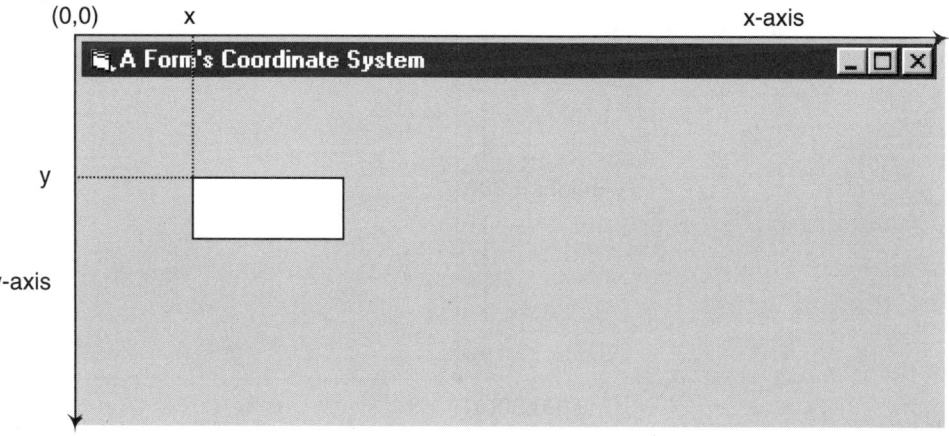

Altering the Coordinate System

A container's complete coordinate system is defined by five properties: **ScaleMode**, **ScaleLeft**, **ScaleTop**, **ScaleWidth**, and **ScaleHeight**. By default the **ScaleMode** is set to 1, which defines the measurement scale to be in twips. Table 11-6 provides a complete list of **ScaleMode** values. Each of these measurement scales, except for **ScaleMode** values of 0 and 3, refers to the size of an object when it is printed and not how it will appear on the screen.

The **ScaleTop** and **ScaleLeft** properties define the coordinate of the top left-hand corner of each container. By default, each of these values is set to 0, which defines the origin of a container as the point (0, 0). The **ScaleWidth** and **ScaleHeight** define the *internal* width and height of the container. These measurements do not include the border. All four of these property values can be either fractions or negative numbers. A negative setting for either the **ScaleWidth** or **ScaleHeight** properties simply reverses the respective coordinate axis orientation. Figure 11-9 illustrates the effects of the following property settings:

```
ScaleLeft = 100
ScaleTop = 200
ScaleWidth = 500
ScaleHeight = 300
```

In addition to setting individual scale property values, a custom scale can be designated using the **Scale** method. The syntax for this method is

$$\textit{objectname}.\textbf{Scale } (x1, y1)–(x2, y2)$$

where *x1* and *y1* designate the settings of the **ScaleLeft** and **ScaleTop** properties. The difference between *x*-coordinate values designates the ScaleWidth, and the difference between *y*-coordinate values designates the **ScaleHeight**. As such, (*x1*, *y1*) designates the top-left corner coordinates of the object and (*x2*, *y2*) designates the bottom-right corner coordinates. For example, the coordinate system shown in Figure 11-9 could have been

Figure 11-9

A Scale from (100, 200) to (600, 500)

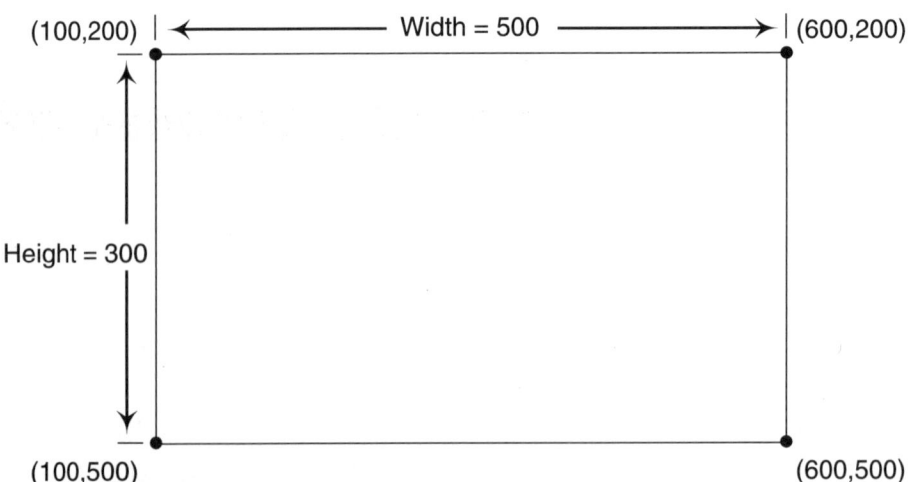

Table 11-6 Available ScaleMode Property Values

Value	Description
0	User defined. This value is automatically set to 0 if any of the four other properties are user set.
1	Twips. This is the default setting. There are 1,440 twips to an inch.
2	Points. There are 72 points to an inch.
3	Pixels. The number of pixels per inch is monitor dependent.
4	Characters.
5	Inches.
6	Millimeters
7	Centimeters.

created using the statement `Scale (100, 200) -(600,500)`. Assuming that imgTest is contained in a form that uses this scale, the following statement will cause the image to be moved one-fifth of the way across and one-third of the way down the form.

```
imgTest.Move  imgTest.Left + 100, img.Top + 100
```

Alternatively, the effect of this single statement can be produced by setting each corner independently, using the two statements

```
imgTest.Left = imgTest.Left + 100
imgTest.Top = imgTest.Top + 100
```

Clearly, if an object is to be moved in both a horizontal and vertical direction, the **Move** method is more efficient than individually altering its **Left** and **Top** property values. However, if an object is to be moved in only one direction, its appropriate **Left** or **Top** property can be changed without recourse to the **Move** method.

Exercises 11.2

1. Enter and execute Program 11-3

2. a. Modify Program 11-3 so that the `docolor` procedure is only called by a horizontal scroll bar **Scroll** event, and determine the effect of this change as seen by a user.

    b. Modify Program 11-3 so that the `docolor` procedure is only called by a horizontal scroll bar **Change** event, and determine the effect of this change as seen by a user.

3. Using the **ScaleLeft, ScaleTop, ScaleWidth,** and **ScaleHeight** properties, create a coordinate scale system for a form named `frmMain` that has the following characteristics (assume a default **ScaleMode** that uses twips):

    a. origin = (50, 50), width = 200, height = 200
    b. origin = (50, 100), width = 300, height = 600
    c. origin = (100, 200), width = 400, height = 500
    d. origin = (200, 200), width = 600, height = 600

4. Redo Exercise 3, using the **Scale** method to define each coordinate system.

5. Modify Program 11-2 by replacing the **Move** method used in the `tmrMove_Timer()` event procedure with two statements that individually adjust the imgMove's **Top** and **Left** properties.

Introduction to Visual Basic

11.3 Graphical Controls and Methods

Shapes, such as lines and circles, can be constructed using either Toolbox graphical controls or graphical methods. For simple lines and circles, the Toolbox's graphical controls shown in Figure 11-10 provide a fast and easy construction approach. For creating more complex visual effects, such as painting individual pixels or creating arcs, graphical methods must be used. In this section, we present both the controls and methods that Visual Basic provides for constructing graphical shapes.

Figure 11-10

The Line and Shape Controls

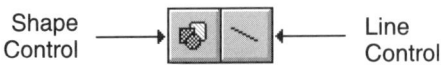

Shape Control → ← Line Control

The Line and Shape Controls

Lines and shapes, such as rectangles and squares, can be used to help users focus on specific areas of the screen and group related data within a well-defined screen area. The Line and Shape controls are available directly from the Toolbox. Both of these controls are quite easy to use and create predefined images that can be resized as necessary.

Figure 11-11

A Line Control

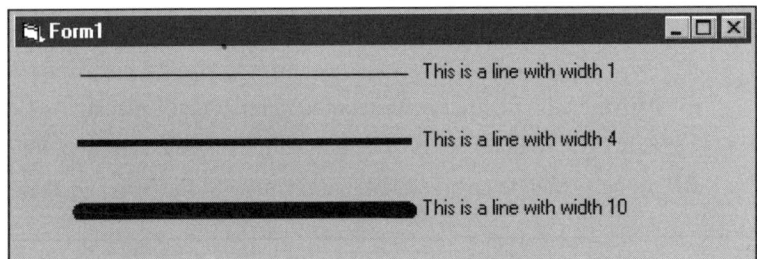

If you double-click on the Line tool, a default line will be placed on the form. Each end of this line can be dragged to resize the line and place it in the desired position. Alternatively, by single-clicking on the Line control and then clicking and holding the mouse within a form or object, you will set one end of the line. The second end of the line is established by dragging the mouse to the desired point. No matter how a line is established, it can always be resized by moving either or both end points. You can also alter the line's width, color, and style using the line's Property window. Figure 11-11 illustrates typical Line controls.

Shape controls that can be constructed using the Toolbox's Shape tool are shown in

Figure 11-12

Shape Controls

Figure 11-12. Each of these shapes is constructed in the same manner. If you double-click on the Shape tool, a default Shape control will be placed on the form. Each end of this control can be dragged to resize it and

Figure 11-13

Predefined Shape Options

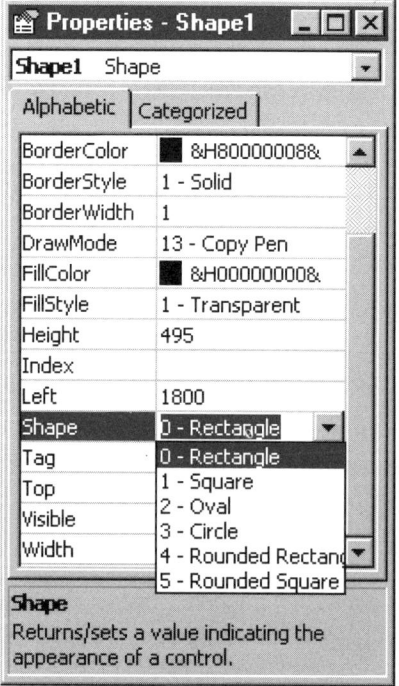

the complete control can be moved to place it in its desired position. Alternatively, by single-clicking on the Shape control, then clicking and holding the mouse within a form or object, you can establish an image's initial size.

The default Shape control is a rectangle. To alter this default to one of the other shapes shown in Figure 11-12, activate the shape's Properties window and select the shape you desire in the List box provided for the **Shape** property (see Figure 11-13).

Figure 11-14

Predefined FillStyle Options

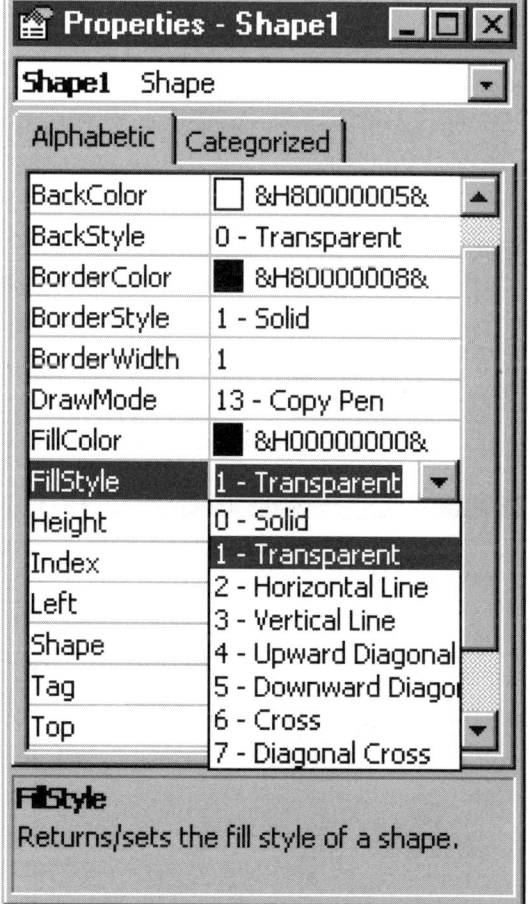

Two other very useful properties are provided for each Shape control: **FillStyle** and **FillColor**. The **FillStyle** provides a pattern that can be inserted into the shape, and ranges from a no-fill design (transparent), to a solid-fill design, to designs that consist of various combinations of lines and crosses. Figure 11-14 shows the List box options available for selecting a fill design for the **FillStyle** property. The color of the fill design is determined by the **FillColor** property. For any fill pattern except solid, the **BackColor** will show through the selected pattern.

Plotting Points

To locate a specific point in a object and set its color, Visual Basic provides the **PSet** method. The general syntax of this method is

$$objectname.\textbf{PSet Step}(x\ y),\ color$$

where *(x, y)* are required coordinate points, *color* is an optional argument, and **Step** is an optional keyword. If **Step** is omitted, the *x* and *y* coordinates represent absolute values, while if the **Step** keyword is present, *x* and *y* are increments added to the current point's coordinate values. As is standard, if the object name is omitted, the method locates and paints a point on the form that contains this statement. In addition, the *x* and *y* parameters are single-precision values that can be any numeric expression yielding a single-precision value. In the absence of a color value, the designated point will be set to the form's foreground color.

As an example, using the **PSet** method, consider Program 11-4, whose interface is shown on Figure 11-15. Program 11-4 uses a Timer control, which is always invisible at run-time and has only one event associated with it, the **Timer** event. This event is controlled by the timer's **Interval** and **Enabled** property settings. When the **Enabled** property is set to **True**, the interval setting, which is in units of milliseconds (there are 1000 milliseconds to a second), determines the time interval between **Timer** event activations. A timer is disabled when its **Enabled** property is set to **False**.

As indicated in Table 11-7, the Timer control is disabled initially. When it is enabled, it will have a timer interval of 100 milliseconds, which will activate its **Timer** event every one-tenth of a second. As indicated in Program 11-4's procedure code, the cmdShow_Click event is used to toggle the Timer control on and off. When activated, the **Timer** event calls the Confetti general procedure at 100 millisecond intervals. The Confetti procedure randomly sets both the red, green, and blue intensity values between 0 and 255 and the *x* and *y* coordinates of a point within the form's coordinate system. This action is provided by multiplying the returned value of the **Rnd** function , which is a value less than 1 but greater than or equal to 0, by appropriate scale factors. Finally, the Confetti function calls the **PSet** method to locate and paint the randomly selected point with the randomly selected color. Figure 11-16 shows how a sample run using Program 11-4 looks in black and white.

Figure 11-15

Program 11-4's Interface

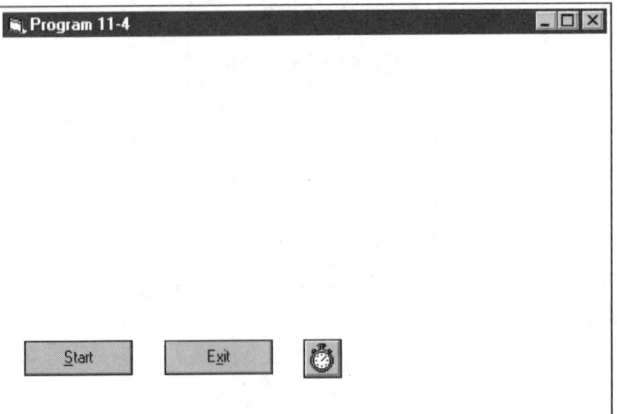

Introduction to Visual Basic

Table 11-7 Program 11-4's Properties Table

Object	Property	Setting
Form	Name	frmMain
	Caption	Program 11-4
	BackColor	White (Palette Tab)
Command button	Name	cmdShow
	Caption	&Start
Command button	Name	cmdExit
	Caption	E&xit
Timer	Name	tmrTime
	Enabled	False
	Interval	100

Program 11-4's Procedure Code

```
Private Sub cmdShow_Click()
  If cmdShow.Caption = "S&top" Then
    cmdShow.Caption = "&Start"
    tmrTime.Enabled = False
  Else
    cmdShow.Caption = "S&top"
    tmrTime.Enabled = True
  End If
End Sub

Private Sub cmdExit_Click()
  Beep
  End
End Sub

Private Sub tmrTime_Timer()
  Beep
  Call Confetti
End Sub

Rem: This is a [General] procedure
Public Sub Confetti()
  Dim red As Integer, green As Integer, blue As Integer
  Dim xcoord As Integer, ycoord As Integer

  red = 255 * Rnd
  green = 255 * Rnd
  blue = 255 * Rnd
  xcoord = ScaleWidth * Rnd
  ycoord = ScaleWidth * Rnd
  PSet (xcoord, ycoord), RGB(red, green, blue)
End Sub
```

Figure 11-16

A Sample Output Produced by Program 11-4

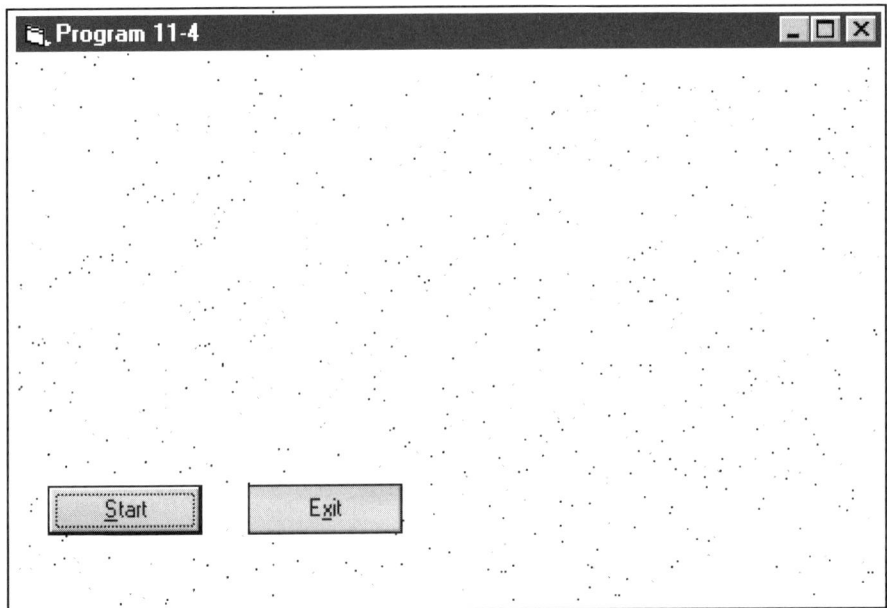

Drawing Lines

To locate and draw a line between two coordinates, Visual Basic provides a **Line** method. The simplest syntax for this method is

$$objectname.\textbf{Line}\ (x1,\ y1)-(x2,y2),\ color$$

where *(x1, y1)* and *(x2, y2)* represent the desired line's end points, and *color* represents the desired line color. If the object name is omitted, the method locates and draws the line on the current form. Both the first set of coordinates and the color argument are optional. In the absence of a color value, the designated line is drawn in the object's foreground color, while if the first set of coordinates is omitted, the object's current *x* and *y* values are used as the starting drawing point.

The line constructed by the **Line** method includes the first point but not the point defined by the second set of coordinates. This is done to facilitate creating figures or sequences of lines drawn end to end. The last point in the sequence can always be colored using the **PSet** method. Each set of coordinates can be preceded by the **Step** keyword, which

Figure 11-17

A Sample Output of Program 11-5

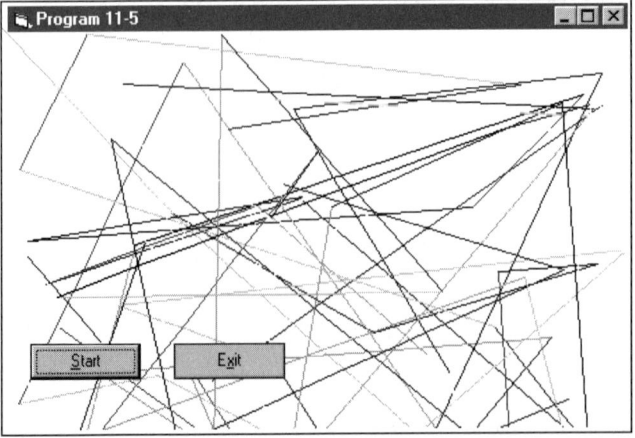

makes the individual coordinates incremental values that are relative to the current point. Finally, the *x* and *y* parameters are single-precision values that can be any numeric expression yielding a single-precision value.

As an example using the Line method, we will change the call to **PSet** in Program 11-4 from

```
PSet (xcoord, ycoord), RGB(red, green, blue)
```

to the Line call   *up to*   *when do you want to put the big slide*

```
Line -(xcoord, ycoord), RGB(red, green, blue)
```

This form of the **Line** method constructs a line that starts at the current point, which has coordinates (CurrentX, CurrentY), and ends at coordinates (xcoord, ycoord).[2] The output of this program, named Program 11-5, will appear as shown in Figure 11-17.

Drawing Boxes

Although a box can be constructed by suitable placement of the four lines that define it, a simpler way is to append a B after the **Line** method's color argument. When this is done, Visual Basic considers each set of coordinates to represent opposite corners of a rectangle. For example, the statement

```
Line (300, 400) - Step(500, 1000),  , B
```

produces a rectangle with opposite corners at the points (300, 400) and (800, 1400). Notice that when the color argument is omitted, two commas must be included before the B, which effectively creates a placeholder for the missing color argument. In this case the rectangle will be drawn in the current foreground color. In addition, the rectangle will be filled with the current **FillStyle**, which is typically transparent (that is, no fill). To create a solid fill, an F can be placed immediately after the B. For example, the statement

```
Line (300, 400) - Step(500, 1000),  , BF
```

produces the same rectangle as previously, but fills it with a solid foreground color. The F argument can only be used in conjunction with the B argument; it cannot be used alone.

✓ Drawing Circles

The **Circle** method is used to draw both circular and elliptical shapes. The required syntax for drawing circles is

> *objectname*.**Circle Step** *(x, y), radius, color*

where the arguments (x, y), radius, and color define the circle's center point, radius, and color, respectively. As always, the object name, **Step**, and color arguments are optional. If the **Step** keyword is included, the (x, y) coordinates become incremental values that are added to the current point's coordinate values. Similarly, if the object name is omitted, the circle is drawn on the current form and, lacking a color argument, the current foreground color is used to draw the circle. The unit of measurement for the *radius* argument is always that of the horizontal scale. As an example, using the **Circle** method, the statement

```
                x     Y     radius
Circle (3000, 4000), 2880
```

---

[2] The same effect can be obtained using the statement Line (XCurrent, YCurrent)-(xcoord, ycoord), RGB(red, green, yellow).

produces a circle with radius of 2880 twips (2 inches) whose center is the point (3000, 4000). Whether this circle will be visible on the form depends on the form's coordinate system. To ensure a visible circle, code such as the following should be used:

```
If ScaleLeft + ScaleWidth < ScaleTop + ScaleHeight then
  radius = (ScaleLeft + ScaleWidth) / 2
Else
  radius = (ScaleTop + ScaleHeight) / 2
Circle ((ScaleLeft + ScaleWidth) / 2, (ScaleTop + ScaleHeight) / 2), radius
```

In this code, the circle is centered on the form and its radius is set to one-half of the form's smaller length or width dimension. Program 11-6 incorporates the essentials of this code into a general procedure named Confetti and, except for the placement of the Exit Command button, uses the same interface as that provided for Program 11-4. Thus, the only procedural code difference between Programs 11-4 and 11-6 is the Confetti procedure. Figure 11-18 illustrates a sample output created by Program 11-6.

```
Public Sub Confetti()
  Dim red As Integer, green As Integer, blue As Integer
  Dim xval As Single, yval As Single
  Dim radius As Single

  red = 255 * Rnd
  green = 255 * Rnd
  blue = 255 * Rnd

  xval = (ScaleLeft + ScaleWidth) / 2
  yval = (ScaleTop + ScaleHeight) / 2
  If xval < yval Then
    radius = xval
  Else
    radius = yval
  End If
  radius = radius * Rnd
  Circle (xval, yval), radius, RGB(red, green, blue)
End Sub
```

Figure 11-18

A Sample Output Produced by Program 11-6

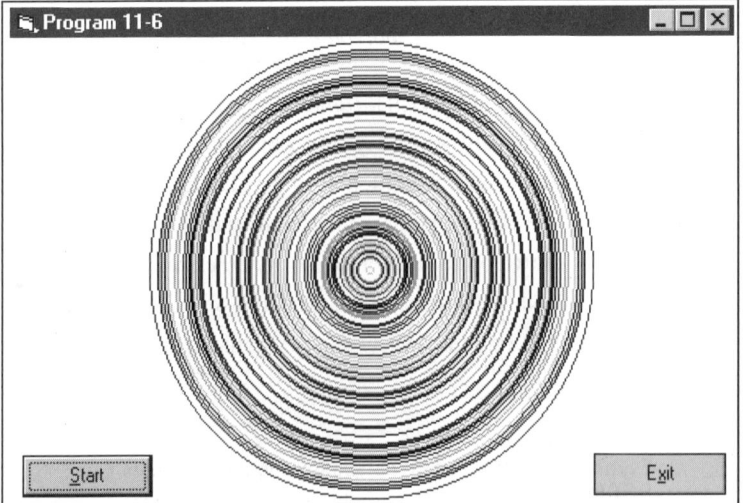

Drawing Ellipses and Arcs

An ellipse is defined by a major and minor axis, as shown in Figure 11-19. In Visual Basic, an ellipse is constructed using the **Circle** method and an aspect, where the aspect is the ratio of the ellipse's vertical to horizontal radii. Constructing an ellipse or arc requires using the following form of the **Circle** method's syntax:

*objectname.***Circle** (*x,y*), *radius, color, start, end, aspect*

The last four arguments are all optional and are set to the default values ForeColor, 0 radians, 2 Pi radians, and 1, respectively. Specifically, the *start* and *end* arguments specify the beginning and ending positions of an arc, and *aspect* represents an ellipse's aspect ratio as a single-precision positive number. For a perfect circle, this argument must be 1.

Figure 11-19

An Ellipse's Minor Radius a and Major Radius b

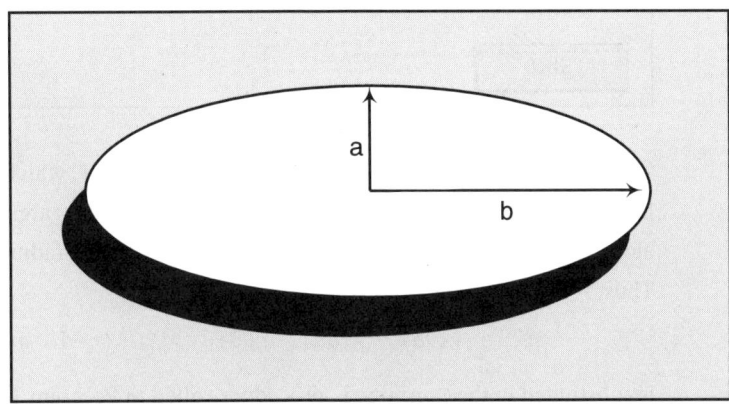

When using the **Circle** method to construct an ellipse, the *radius* argument is always used to specify the major axis and is always specified in terms of the horizontal scale. Thus, if *aspect* is greater than 1, which means the vertical radius is greater than the horizontal radius, the radius is the major axis along the *y*-axis. In this case the minor radius is calculated as the radius divided by the aspect ratio. As an example of constructing a set of ellipses, we can simply change the **Circle** call in Program 11-6 from

```
Circle (xval, yval), radius, RGB(red, green, blue)
```

to the following Circle call

```
Circle (xval, yval), radius, RGB(red, green, blue), , , 1.5
```

Notice that, even though we are omitting the *start* and *stop* arguments, we must include three successive arguments to act as placeholders for the omitted values. Assuming

Figure 11-20

A Sample Output Produced by Program 11-7

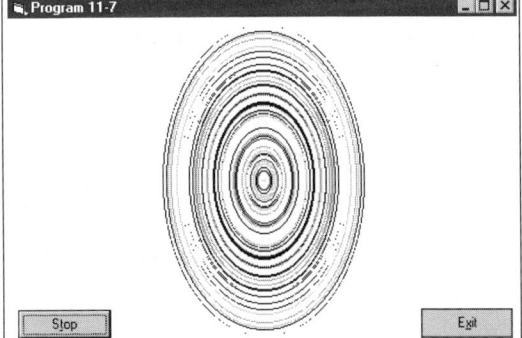

that we also change the form's caption to Program 11-7, a sample output produced by the new program will appear as shown on Figure 11-20. As indicated in this figure, each ellipse is drawn in a vertical position, which is a result of the aspect ratio being greater than 1.

Figure 11-21

A Sample Output Produced by Program 11-8

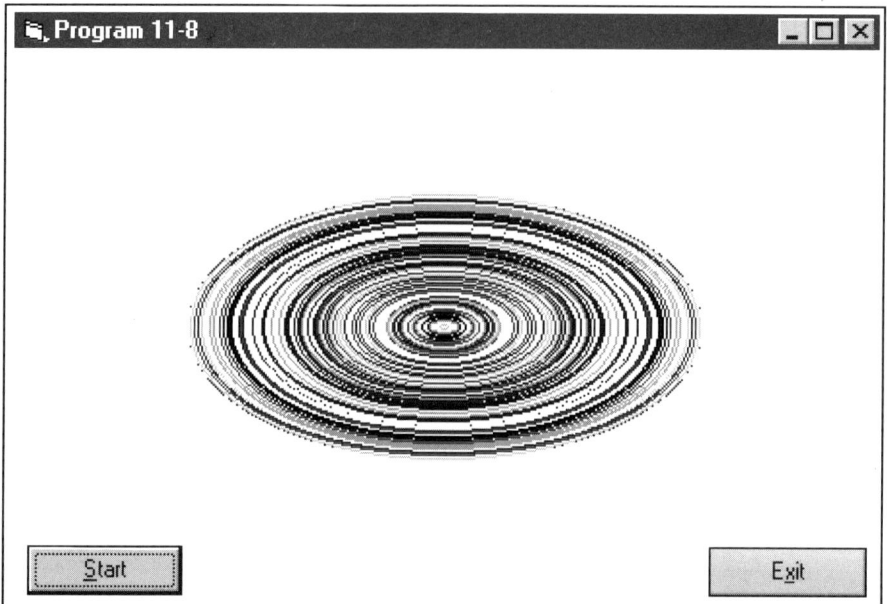

Finally, by using an aspect ratio that is less than 1, which means the vertical axis is less than the horizontal radius, the **Circle** method's radius argument will draw the major axis along the *x*-axis. The minor axis is then calculated as the radius length times the aspect ratio. Thus, if the statement

```
Circle (xval, yval), radius, RGB(red, green, blue), , , 0.5
```

is substituted in the `Confetti` procedure called in Program 11-6 and the form's caption is changed to `Program 11-8`, the display produced by the new program will appear as shown on Figure 11-21.

Exercises 11.3

1. Enter and execute Program 11-4 on your computer.

2. Enter and execute Program 11-5 on your computer.

3. Enter and execute Program 11-6 on your computer.

4. Using Program 11-4's interface, write a Visual Basic Program that constructs a triangle with vertices at the points (200, 400), (200, 1400), and (700, 1400). Use the **Line** method to construct the triangle.

5. a. Using Program 11-4's interface, write a Visual Basic Program that constructs a box with vertices at the points (200, 300), (1200, 300), and (1200, 700), and (200, 700). Use four calls to the **Line** method to construct each side of the box.

   b. Modify the program written for Exercise 5a. to use the B option with the **Line** method. Thus, your program should make only one call to the **Line** method.

6. Modify Program 11-5 so that it produces a random series of randomly colored boxes.

7. Write a Visual Basic program that uses the following code to create the image shown on Figure 11-22.

```
Public Sub Draw()
  Dim i As Single
  Dim pi As Double

  pi = 4 * Atn(1)   ' This calculates a value for pi

  Scale (-2 * pi, 1)-(2 * pi, -1)

  For i = -2 * pi To 2 * pi Step 0.05
      PSet (i, Sin(i)), RGB(255 * Rnd, 255 * Rnd, 255 * Rnd)
  Next i
End Sub
```

Figure 11-22

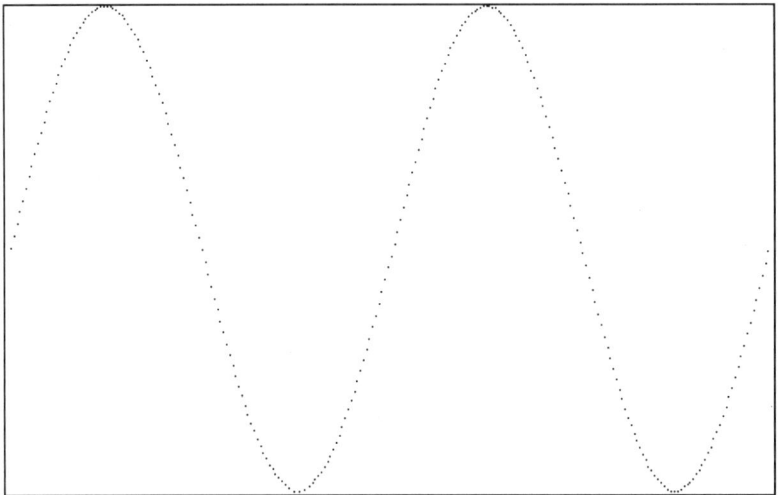

8. Modify the program written for Exercise 7 by changing the `Sin(i)` argument to `Cos(i)`.

9. Write a Visual Basic program that uses the following code to create the image shown on Figure 11-23.

Figure 11-23

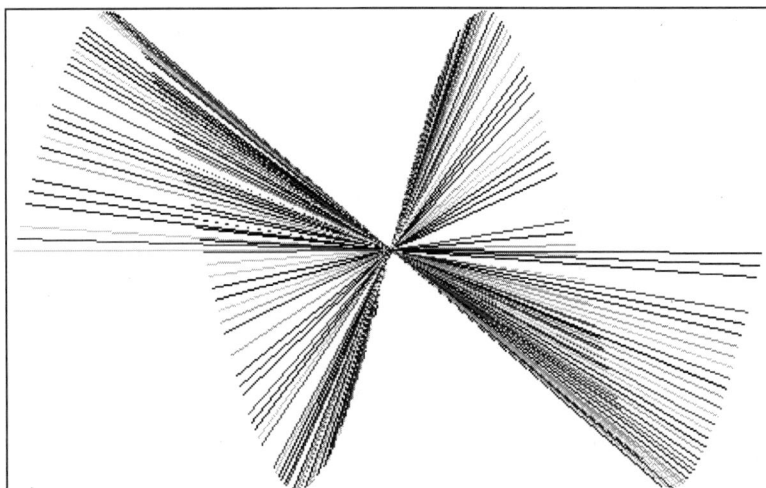

```
Public Sub Draw()
  Dim i As Single
  Dim pi As Double

  pi = 4 * Atn(1)   ' This calculates a value for pi

  Scale (-2 * pi, 1)-(2 * pi, -1)

  For i = -2 * pi To 2 * pi Step 0.05
    Line (0, 0)-(i, Sin(i)), RGB(255 * Rnd, 255 * Rnd, 255 * Rnd)
  Next i
End Sub
```

10. Modify the program written for Exercise 9 by changing the `Sin(i)` argument to `Cos(i)`.

11.4 Common Programming Errors and Problems ▬▬▬▬▬▬▬

In constructing images and using color, the following problems can occur:

1. Using combinations of colors that are glaring and annoying to a user.
2. Drawing images at run-time that do not fall within the boundaries of the desired container. Such images are invisible at run-time.
3. Not realizing that the measurement system is relative to how the image will appear on a printer. The image's screen appearance depends on the screen's size.
4. Not getting the syntax correct for the method being used. Images should always be tested to see how they actually appear at run-time. It is for this reason that the Line and Shape controls, which create their images at design-time, are preferable. If you use graphical methods for creating run-time images, as you must for constructing arcs and painting individual pixels, make sure they are both visible and correct by seeing how they look at run-time.

11.5 Chapter Review ▬▬▬▬▬▬▬

Key Terms

animation	**Line** method
BackColor	**Move** method
bitmap	**PSet** method
Circle method	RGB function
Container	**ScaleHeight**
FillColor	**ScaleLeft**
FillStyle	**ScaleMode**
ForeColor	**ScaleTop**
icon	**ScaleWidth**
	twip

Summary

1. Animation is produced by switching rapidly between two or more figures, each of which is slightly different, or by moving one or more images across the screen.
2. A bitmap image is defined as a pattern of dots (pixels).
3. An icon image is a special type of bitmap file that is confined to a maximum size of 32 pixels by 32 pixels.
4. RGB monitors produce colors by combining various intensities of red, green, and blue.
5. The RGB function returns a long integer in the range 0 to 16,777,215. The syntax of this function is

$$\textbf{RGB}(red,\ green,\ blue)$$

where each argument is a value between 0 and 255 that represents the intensity of the stated color.

6. Scroll bar controls can be either horizontal or vertical. Both types of scrolls include a thumb bar and arrow keys. When the thumb bar is placed at the left side of its scroll area for a horizontal scroll bar or at the bottom of its scroll area for a vertical scroll bar, the Scroll control's **Value** property is set to its **Minimum** property value. When positioned at the other end of the scroll area, the Scroll control's Value property is set to its **Maximum** property value.
7. A **Scroll** event is triggered by movement of the scroll's thumb bar.
8. A **Change** event is triggered by the final placement of the thumb bar or activation of the scroll's arrow keys.
9. A container is any object, including a form, onto which other objects are placed. A container's coordinate system is defined by its **ScaleMode**, **ScaleLeft**, **ScaleTop**, **ScaleWidth**, and **ScaleHeight** properties. The **ScaleMode** defines the measurement system, as listed in Table 11-5. By default, the measurement system is in twips, where there are 1440 twips to an inch, and refers to the size of an object when it is printed. The coordinate system's origin is defined as the point (**ScaleLeft**, **ScaleTop**), while the container's width and length are defined by its **ScaleWidth** and **ScaleHeight** properties.
10. An object's coordinate system can be set using the **Scale** method. The syntax for this method is

$$objectname.\textbf{Scale}\ (x1,\ y1)-(x2,\ y2)$$

where *x1* and *y1* designate the settings of the **ScaleLeft** and **ScaleTop** properties. The difference between *x*-coordinate values designates the **ScaleWidth**, and the difference between *y*-coordinate values designates the **ScaleHeight**.

11. Custom lines and predefined rectangles and ovals can be created at design-time using the toolbar's Line and Shape controls.
12. The **PSet** method can be used to locate a specific point and set its color. The general syntax of this method is

$$objectname.\textbf{PSet Step}(x\ y),\ color$$

where *(x, y)* are required coordinate points, *color* is an optional argument, and **Step** is an optional keyword. If **Step** is omitted, the *x* and *y* coordinates represent absolute values, while if the **Step** keyword is present, *x* and *y* are increments added to the current point's coordinate values.

13. The **Line** method can be used to locate and draw a line between two points. The simplest syntax for this method is

> *objectname.***Line** *(x1, y1)–(x2,y2), color*

where *(x1, y1)* and *(x2, y2)* represent the desired line's end points, and *color* represents the desired line color. If the first set of coordinates is omitted, the object's current *x* and *y* values are used as the starting drawing point.

In addition, each set of coordinates can be preceded by the **Step** keyword, which makes the individual coordinates incremental values relative to the current point. Each coordinate can be any numeric expression yielding a single-precision value.

14. A simple way to construct a rectangle is to append a B after the **Line** method's color argument. When this is done Visual Basic considers each set of coordinates to represent opposite corners of a rectangle.

15. The **Circle** method is used to draw both circular and elliptical shapes. The general syntax for this method is

> *objectname.***Circle** *(x,y), radius, color, start, end, aspect*

where the arguments *(x, y)*, *radius*, and *color* define the circle's center point, radius, and color, respectively, the *start* and *end* arguments specify the beginning and ending positions of an arc, and *aspect* represents an ellipse's aspect ratio as a single-precision positive number. For a perfect circle this argument must be 1. The last four arguments are all optional and are set to the default values **ForeColor**, 0 radians, 2 Pi radians, and 1, respectively.

11.6 Looking Further: Creating A Menu System

Many commercial applications are required to perform multiple tasks. In these situations, each task is typically assigned its own window. For example, in an inventory application one window might be dedicated to providing the user with the ability to update a master inventory list of products, while a second window is used to record all merchandise coming into inventory from suppliers, and a third window is used for recording shipments from inventory to customers.

Although, using the techniques presented in this text, each window can be added individually to a project, there is still the requirement for activating each window in a useful manner. This is accomplished by offering the user a menu of choices, typically on the application's opening window. These choices, each of which is effectively a call to unload the currently active window and display the window appropriate to the selected choice, can be created as either a set of Command buttons or as a menu bar. Each of these techniques is described in this section.

Command Button Menus

In a Command button menu each option is offered in a separate Command button. Typically, the first set of menu options is provided on an initial window that acts as both a splash and menu-selection window; that is, the window both furnishes information about the application and provides a current list of available choices as a sequence of Command buttons. As an example of this approach, consider Figure 11-24. The splash part of the window provides a graphic and informs the user that this is the Main Menu window of Rotech Systems' inventory control system, Version 1.0. In addition, this window provides four Command buttons. Pressing any of the buttons except E<u>x</u>it provides a call to the button's **Click** event to unload the current window and display the window connected to the selected menu choice; pressing the E<u>x</u>it button ends program execution.

In one common type of implementation, each Command button is programmed to call the same general procedure, with an argument that identifies which button was pressed. The

Figure 11-24

A Sample Command Button Menu System

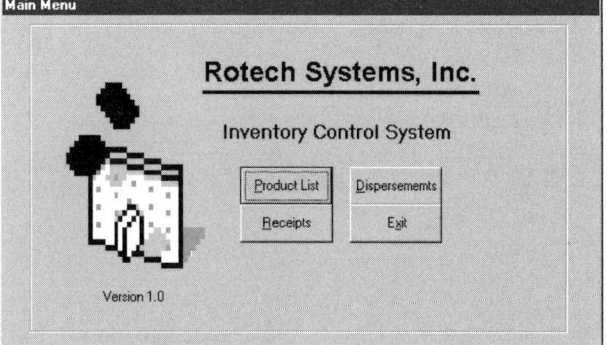

general procedure, which can be contained on the same form as the Command buttons, then uses this argument to select the appropriate window to display next. For example, Procedure Code 11-1 illustrates how this arrangement is constructed for the menu illustrated in Figure

11-24. It assumes that the figure's buttons have been given the names cmdProd, cmdRec, cmdDisp, and cmdExit.

Procedure Code 11-1

```
Rem:(General) Declarations Section Code
Option Explicit
Rem: These constants are used to identify which button was pressed
Const ProdButton As Integer = 1
Const RecButton As Integer = 2
Const DispButton As Integer = 3
Const ExitButton As Integer = 4

Private Sub cmdProd_Click()
 Call mainmenu(ProdButton)
End Sub

Private Sub cmdDisp_Click()
  Call mainmenu(DispButton)
End Sub

Private Sub cmdRec_Click()
  Call mainmenu(RecButton)
End Sub
```

```
Private Sub cmdExit_Click()
  Call mainmenu (ExitButton)
End Sub
```

Notice that each **Click** event in Procedure Code 11-1 is simply a call to a general procedure named `mainmenu`, with an argument that clearly identifies the clicked button. In developing an application with multiple windows, the `mainmenu` procedure would typically be coded as listed in Procedure Code 11-2.

Procedure Code 11-2

```
Public Sub mainmenu(frombutton As Integer)
  Unload frmMain
  Select Case frombutton
    Case ProdButton
      frmStub.Show
      frmStub.Refresh
    Case RecButton
      frmStub.Show
      frmStub.Refresh
    Case DispButton
      frmStub.Show
      frmStub.Refresh
    Case ExitButton
      Beep
      End
  End Select
End Sub
```

In reviewing the `mainmenu` **Sub** procedure, notice that the first task it accomplished is to unload the `frmMain` window, which is the name we used for the window shown in Figure 11-24.[3] A **Select Case** statement is then used to select the next form to be displayed depending on the value of the passed parameter. In each case, except when the E<u>x</u>it button is pressed, the same form, named `frmStub` is displayed. This form, which is illustrated in Figure 11-25, is used to test the operation of the menu and ensure that the call to the next window and return to the menu are working correctly. The reason for using both a **Show** and **Refresh** method in the `mainmenu` procedure is that, although the **Show** method automatically performs a load of the designated window, if the form's **AutoRefresh** property is set to **False**, all graphical elements on the form may not be displayed. Calling the **Refresh** method forces a redraw of all graphical elements on the form, which ensures a correct display.

Figure 11-25

A Sample Stub Window

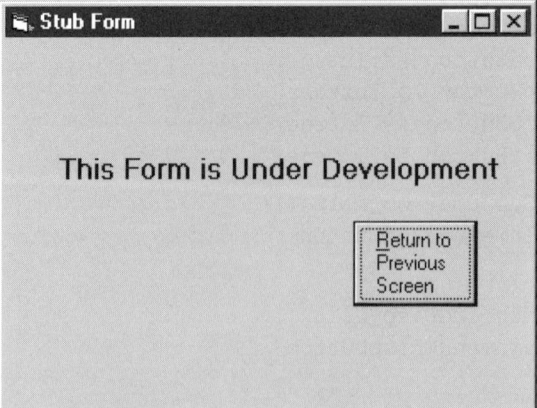

---

3 An alternative is to use the statement `Unload Me`, which causes the current window, whatever it is named, to be unloaded.

The code for the stub windows <u>R</u>eturn button's **Click** event is

```
Private Sub cmdReturn_Click()
   Unload Me
   frmMain.Show
   frmMain.Refresh
End Sub
```

That is, the <u>R</u>eturn button simply unloads the current stub form and displays the initial `frmMain` window. The advantage of using a stub window is that it permits us to run a complete application that does not yet meet all of its final requirements. As each successive window is developed, the call to the stub window can be replaced within the appropriate part of the **Select Case** statement. This incremental, or stepwise, refinement of the program is a standard development technique used by professional programmers.

Another advantage to this development approach is that, as new features are required, additional Command buttons can be added easily to the initial window and the **Select Case** statement within the `mainmenu` procedure easily expanded to include additional cases. Alternatively, some programmers prefer to unload the current form and display the appropriate new form directly from within each corresponding Command button's **Click** event. Although this approach eliminates the need for the procedure we have named `mainmenu`, it has the disadvantage of decentralizing and dispersing what is, in effect, a single task. Both approaches are used in practice and which one you adopt is really a matter of personal programming style.

Menu Bars

An alternative to a Command button menu is a Menu bar. This type of menu was initially popularized by the Lotus 123® spreadsheet program and is currently used in almost all commercially available PC software. It is the same type of menu provided in Visual Basic. Figure 11-26 shows how such a menu might look for our inventory application.

Constructing a Menu bar is accomplished using Visual Basic's Menu Editor, which is illustrated in Figure 11-27. This editor, which is used to create, edit, and delete Menu bars, is activated by choosing the <u>M</u>enu Editor from the <u>T</u>ools menu. Additionally, all menu properties of existing menus can be accessed using the Properties window.

Figure 11-26

An Application with a Menu Bar

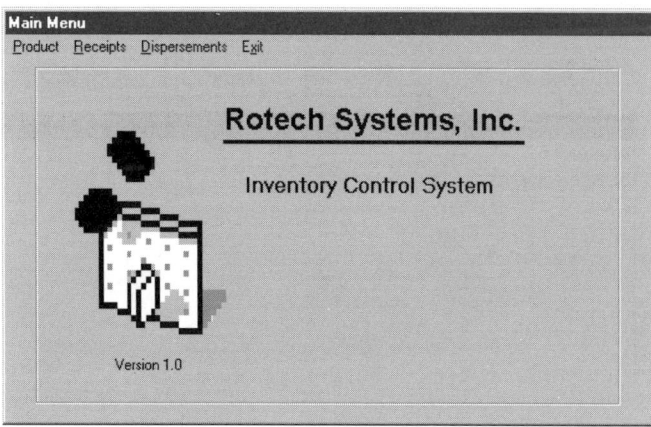

The Menu Editor shown in Figure 11-27 was used to create the Menu bar illustrated in Figure 11-26. Each entry in the List box corresponds to an option listed on the Menu bar. The ampersand (&) in front of a Menu option letter creates an access key, which permits the user to activate the menu option by pressing the [Alt] key and the designated letter.

In creating the Menu bar we named each item with the same name, `mnuMain`. What this does is to create a control array (see Section 8.3) in which each menu item shares common event procedures. It does require us, however, to assign index numbers to each item in the menu so that individual options can be uniquely identified. A requirement of assigning index numbers is that they be in increasing order for each option item added to the menu.

A distinct advantage of creating the menu options as a control array is that it simplifies our job of coding the menu, since we can use the menu control array's single **Click** event to determine which window to display next. The required code is listed as Procedure Code 11-3.

In reviewing Procedure Code 11-3 notice that the body of the `mnuMain_Click` procedure is identical to that of the `mainmenu` general procedure presented in Procedure Code 11-2. Both procedures unload the `frmMain` form, and then use the passed parameter value to determine the next displayed window. In this particular case, both procedures use a stub window (see Figure 11-25) as a placeholder until the final windows are developed.

Although the menu bar that we have created has only one set of options, this is not a restriction of Visual Basic. Submenu items can be created by clicking the right-facing arrow on the menu editor (see Figure 11-27). This will indent the submenu item in the Menu

Figure 11-27
The Menu Editor

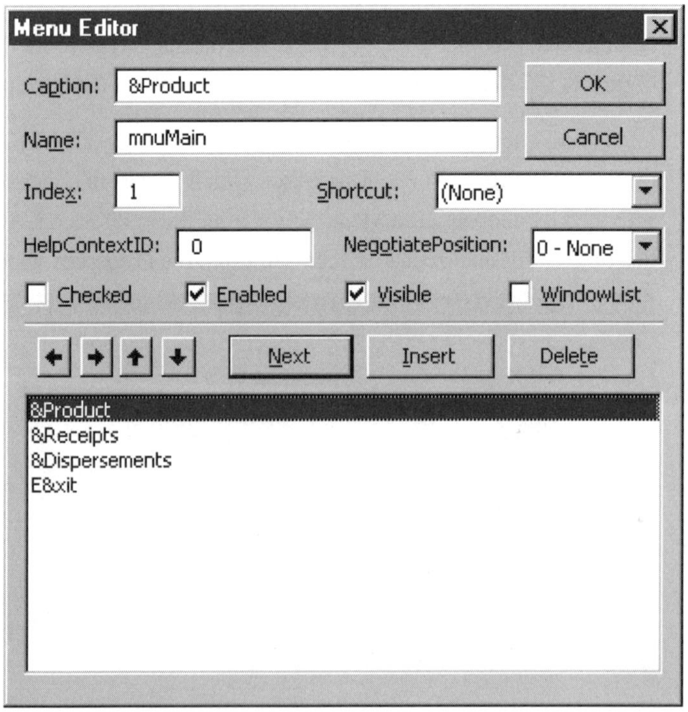

Editor. Each indent level displayed in the editor is preceded by four dots (....) and can be removed by highlighting the desired item and clicking the Menu Editor's left-facing arrow. In addition, access keys can be assigned to each submenu item by placing an ampersand (&) symbol in front of the desired letter. Shortcut keys, which cause a menu item to be run immediately, can also be assigned to all menu options using the Menu Editor. Finally, a menu option that uses a hyphen (-) for its **Caption** property creates a separator bar between items at the appropriate indented level.

Procedure Code 11-3

```
Rem:(General) Declarations Section Code
Option Explicit
Rem: These constants correspond to the Index values
Rem: assigned to each menu option in the menu editor
Const ProdButton As Integer = 1
Const RecButton As Integer = 2
Const DispButton As Integer = 3
Const ExitButton As Integer = 4

Private Sub mnuMain_Click(Index As Integer)
  Unload frmMain
  Select Case Index
    Case ProdButton
      frmStub.Show
      frmStub.Refresh
    Case RecButton
      frmStub.Show
      frmStub.Refresh
    Case DispButton
      frmStub.Show
      frmStub.Refresh
    Case ExitButton
      Beep
      End
  End Select
End Sub
```

12 Introduction to Classes

In contrast to procedural programming, where software is organized by what it does to the data (its function), object-oriented programming organizes software as a collection of discrete objects that include both data and functional behavior.

As such, procedural programs are constructed as a sequence of transformations that convert input data into output data. In a well-constructed procedural program, each transformation is captured within an individual procedure, which in Visual Basic is coded as either a procedure or a function. The method for converting inputs to outputs is described by an algorithm. Thus, procedural code is frequently defined as an algorithm written in a programming language.

In object-oriented programming, the packaging of data and processing is handled in a much different manner. Both the data and the processing that can be applied to it are combined and packaged in a new unit called an object. Once suitable objects are defined, object-oriented programming is concerned with the interactions between objects. Notice that this way of thinking about code does not remove the necessity of understanding data and their related operations and algorithms. It simply binds the data and procedures in a new package, an object, and then concerns itself with the interactions between objects. One advantage to this approach is that once objects are defined for one application, they can be used, without reprogramming, in other applications.

Visual Basic Versions 4.0 and 5.0 offer the ability to create user-defined objects. Central to this ability is the concept of an abstract, or programmer-defined, data type. In this chapter, we explore the implications of permitting programmers to define their own data types, and then present Visual Basic's mechanism for constructing abstract data types.

```
┌─────────────────────────────────────────────────────────────────────┐
│                        Programmers' Notes                             │
│                                                                       │
│  Program and Class Libraries                                          │
│                                                                       │
```

Programmers' Notes

Program and Class Libraries

The concept of a program library began with FORTRAN, which was the first commercial, high level language, introduced in 1954. The FORTRAN library consisted of a group of completely tested and debugged mathematical routines provided with the compiler. Since that time, every programming language has provided its own library of functions. In Visual Basic, this library is referred to as the *intrinsic program library*, and includes functions such as **Format, Str, Val, Asc**, and **Rnd**. The advantage of library functions and procedures is that they enhance program development and design by providing code known to work correctly, without the need for additional testing and debugging.

With the introduction of object-oriented languages, the concept of a program library has been extended to include class libraries. A *class library* is a library of tested and debugged classes. Generally, the class is provided as either an executable (EXE) or dynamic linked library (DLL) module (see Appendix F) that cannot be changed by a user, but can be accessed and incorporated into a user's application.

One of the key practical features of class libraries is that they help realize the goal of code reuse. By providing tested and debugged code, consisting of both data and function members, class libraries furnish large sections of prewritten and reusable code ready for incorporation within new applications. This shifts the focus of writing application programs from the creation of new code to understanding how to use predefined objects and stitching them together in a cohesive way. A prime example is the visual object class—consisting of Check boxes, List boxes, Dialogs, Command buttons, and Option buttons—provided in Visual Basic.

12.1 Classes and Class Modules

The programming environment has changed dramatically over the last few years with the emergence of mouse input, graphical-based color monitors, and the subsequent interest in Windows applications. Providing a graphical user interface (GUI), where a user can easily move around in even a single window, however, is a challenge using procedural code. Programming multiple and possibly overlapping windows on the same graphical screen increases the complexity enormously.

Unlike a pure procedural approach, however, an object-oriented approach fits well in graphical windowed environments, where each window can be specified as a self-contained rectangular object that can be moved and resized in relation to other objects on the screen. Within each window, other graphical objects, such as Check boxes, Option buttons, Labels, and Text boxes can easily be placed and moved.

Central to the creation of objects is the concept of abstraction and an abstract data type, which is simply a user-defined data type, as opposed to the built-in data types provided by all languages (such as integer and floating-point types), permitting a programmer to define new data types.

Table 12-1 Required Data Type Capabilities	
Capability	**Example**
Define one or more variables of the data type.	`Dim a As Integer`
Assign a value to a variable.	`a = 10`
Assign one variable's value to another variable.	`a = b`
Perform mathematical operations.	`a + b`
Perform relational operations.	`a > b`
Convert from one data type to another.	`a = 7.2`

Abstract Data Types

To gain a clear understanding of what an abstract data type is, consider the following three built-in data types supplied in Visual Basic: Integers, Singles, and Strings. In using these data types, we typically declare one or more variables of the desired type, use them in their accepted ways, and avoid using them in ways that are not specified. Thus, for example, we would not use the subtraction operator on two strings. Since this operation makes no sense for strings, it is never defined, in any programming language, for such data. Thus, although we typically don't consider it, each data type consists of *both* a type of data, such as integer or float, *and* specific operational capabilities provided for each type.

In computer terminology, the combination of data and its associated operations is defined as a *data type*. That is, a data type defines *both* the types of data and the types of operations that can be performed on the data. Seen in this light, the integer data type, the floating point data type, and the string data type provided in Visual Basic are all examples of *built-in* data types defined by a type of data and specific operational capabilities provided for initializing and manipulating the type. In a simplified form, this relationship can be described as

> Data Type = Allowable Data + Operational Capabilities

Thus, the operations we have been using in Visual Basic are an inherent part of each of the data types we have been using. For each of these data types the designers of Visual Basic had to carefully consider, and then implement, specific operations.

To understand the importance of the operational capabilities provided by a programming language, let's take a moment to list some of those supplied with Visual Basic's built-in data types. The minimum set of the capabilities provided by Visual Basic's built-in data types is listed in Table 12-1.

Now let's see how all this relates to abstract data types (ADTs). By definition an *abstract data type* is simply a user-defined type that describes both a type of data and the operations that can be performed on it. Such data types are required when we wish to create objects more complex than simple integers and characters. When we create our own data types we must consider both the type of data we are creating and the capabilities we will provide to initialize and manipulate it.

Programmers' Notes

Procedural, Hybrid, and Pure Object-Oriented Languages

Most high-level programming languages can be categorized into one of three main categories: *procedural, hybrid,* or *object-oriented.* FORTRAN, which was the first commercially available, high-level programming language, is procedural. This makes sense because FORTRAN was designed to perform mathematical calculations using standard algebraic formulas. Formally, these formulas were described as algorithms and then the algorithms were coded using function and subroutine procedures. Other procedural languages that followed FORTRAN included BASIC, COBOL, Pascal, and C.

Currently there are only two "pure" object-oriented languages; Smalltalk and Eiffel. The first requirement of such a language is that it contain three specific features: *classes, inheritance,* and *polymorphism* (each of these features is described in this chapter). In addition to providing these features, however, an object-oriented language must always use classes. In a pure object-oriented language, all data types are constructed as classes, all data values are objects, and every operation can only be executed using a class member procedure or function. *It is impossible in a pure language not to use object-oriented features* throughout a program. This is not the case in a hybrid language.

In a hybrid language, such as Visual Basic Version 5.0, *it is impossible not to use elements of a procedural program.* This is because the use of any built-in data type or operation effectively violates the pure object-oriented paradigm. In addition, hybrid languages need not even provide inheritance and polymorphic features but they *must* provide classes. Languages that use classes but do not provide inheritance and polymorphic features are referred to as *object-based* rather than *object-oriented* languages. Although, starting with Version 4.0, Visual Basic permitted the construction of classes, as well as their use, Visual Basic still does not provide true inheritance features. Thus, Visual Basic is classified as an object-based language.

As a specific example, assume we are programming an application that uses dates extensively and we wish to create our own Date data type independent of Visual Basic's built-in types. Clearly, from a data standpoint, a date must be capable of accessing and storing a month, day, and year designation. Although from an implementation standpoint there are a number of means of storing a date, from a user viewpoint the actual implementation is not relevant. For example, a date can be stored as three integers, one each for the month, day, and year. Alternatively, a single long integer in the form *yyyymmdd* can also be used. Using the long integer implementation the date 5/16/98 would be stored as the integer 19980516. For sorting dates, the long integer format is very attractive because the numerical sequence of the dates corresponds to their calendar sequence.

The method of internally structuring the date, unfortunately, supplies only a partial answer to our programming effort. We must still supply a set of operations that can be used with dates. Clearly, such operations could include assigning values to a date, subtracting two dates to determine the number of days between them, comparing two dates to determine which is earlier and which is later, and displaying a date in a form such as 6/3/96.

Notice that the details of how each operation works are dependent on how we choose to store a date (formally referred to as its data structure) and are only of interest to us as we develop each operation. For example, the implementation of comparing two dates will differ

---

Programmers' Notes

Abstraction

Abstraction is a concept central to object-oriented programming. In its most general usage, an abstraction is simply an idea or term that identifies general qualities or characteristics of a group of objects, independent of any one specific object in the group. For example, consider the term *car*. As a term, this is an abstraction: it refers to a group of objects, each containing the characteristics associated with a car, such as a motor, passenger compartment, wheels, steering capabilities, brakes, etc. A particular car, such as "my car" or "your car," is not an abstraction. All are real objects classified as "type car" because they have the attributes associated with a car.

Although we use abstract concepts all the time, we tend not to think about them as such. For example, the words *tree, dog, cat, table,* and *chair* are all abstractions, just as *car* is. Each of these terms refers to a set of qualities possessed by a group of particular things. For each of these abstractions there are many individual trees, dogs, and cats; each of which conforms to the general characteristics associated with the abstract term. In programming we are much more careful to label appropriate terms as abstractions than we are in everyday life. You have already encountered a programming abstraction with data types.

Just as "my car" is a particular object of the more abstract "type car," a particular integer, "5," for example, is a specific object or instance of the more abstract "type integer," where an integer is a signed or unsigned number having no decimal point. Thus, each type—integer, character, and floating-point—is considered an abstraction that defines a general type, of which specific examples can be observed. Such types, then, simply identify common qualities of each group and makes it reasonable to speak of integer types, character types, and floating-point types.

Having defined what we mean by a type, we can now create the definition of a data type. In programming terminology a *data type* consists of *both* an acceptable range of values of a particular type *and* a set of operations that can be applied to those values. Thus, the integer data type not only defines a range of acceptable integer values but also defines what operations can be applied to those values.

Although users of programming languages such as Visual Basic ordinarily assume that mathematical operations such as addition, subtraction, multiplication, and division will be supplied for integers, the designers of Visual Basic had to consider carefully what operations would be provided as part of the integer data type. For example, the designers of Visual Basic included an exponentiation operator, though this operation is not included in either the C or C++ languages (in which exponentiation is supplied as a library function).

The set of allowed values is more formally referred to as a data type's *domain*, and the following table lists the domain for Visual Basic's numeric data types.

Visual Basic's Numeric Data Types

Data Type	Domain
Byte	0 to 255
Integer	−32768 to +32767
Long	−2,147,483,648 to 2,147,483,647
Single	−3.402823E38 to −1.401298E-45
	.401298E-45 to 3.402823E38
Double	−1.79769313486231E308 to −4.94065645841247E-324
	+4.94065645841247E-324 to +1.79769313486231E308

All of the data types listed in this table are part of the Visual Basic language. As such, they are formally referred to as *built-in*, *intrinsic*, or *primitive* data types (the three terms are synonymous). In contrast to built-in data types, Visual Basic permits programmers to create their own data types; that is, define a type of value with an associated domain and operations that can be performed on the acceptable values. Such user-defined data types are formally referred to as *abstract data types*. In Visual Basic abstract data types are called *classes*, and the ability to create classes is provided in both Versions 4.0 and 5.0.

---

if we store a date using a single long integer as opposed to using separate integers for the month, day, and year.

The combination of the storage structure used for dates with a set of available operations appropriate to dates would then define an abstract Date data type. Once our Date type is developed, programmers who want to use it need never be concerned with *how* dates are stored or *how* the operations are performed. All they need to know is *what* each operation does and how to invoke it, which is as much as they know about Visual Basic's built-in operations. For example, we don't really care how the addition of two integers is performed but only that it is done correctly.

In Visual Basic an abstract data type is referred to as a *class*. Construction of a class is inherently easy and we already have all the necessary tools in variables and general procedures. What Visual Basic provides is a mechanism for packaging these two items together in a self-contained unit referred to as a *class module*. Let's see how this is done.

Class Construction

A class defines both data and procedures. This is usually accomplished by constructing a class in two parts, consisting of a data declaration section and a methods implementation section. As illustrated in Figure 12-1, the declaration section declares the data types of the class. The implementation section is then used to define the procedures and functions that will operate on this data.

First, notice that a class consists of code only. The variables, procedures, and functions provided in the declaration and implementation sections of the code are collectively referred to as *class members*. Individually, the variables are referred to as both *data members* and *instance variables* (the terms are synonymous), while the procedures and functions are referred to as *member methods*.

As a specific example of a class, consider the following definition we will construct and name `CLDate`.

Figure 12-1
Class Code Format

```
Rem: Data Declaration Section
        Declaration of all variables
Rem: Methods Implementation Section
        Procedures and Functions that
        can be used on the above
        declared variables
```

The CLDate Class Code—Version 1

```
Rem: Data Declaration Section
Private Month As Integer
Private Day As Integer
Private Year As Integer

Rem: Methods Implementation Section
Public Sub setdate(mm As Integer, dd As Integer, yy As Integer)
  Month = mm
  Day = dd
  Year = yy
End Sub
Public Function showdate() As String
  showdate = Format(Month, "00") + "/" + Format(Day, "00") + "/" + Format(Year, "00")
End Function
```

This class consists of both variable declarations and general procedure code. Notice that we have separated the declarations and remaining code into two sections—a declaration section and an implementation section. Both of these sections contain code you should be very familiar with.

The *declaration section* simply declares all variables that are to be members of the class. Although the initial capital letter is not required, it is conventionally used to designate a class data member. In this case the data members Month, Day, and Year are declared as integer variables. The keyword **Private** in each declaration defines the variable's access rights. The **Private** keyword specifies that the declared data member can only be accessed by using the procedures and functions defined in the *implementation section*. The purpose of the **Private** designation is specifically meant to enforce data security by requiring all access to private data members to go through member methods. This type of access, which restricts a user from seeing how the data is actually stored, is referred to as *data hiding*. Although a variable can be declared as **Public**, doing so permits any procedure or code that is not a part of the class module to access the variable.

The general procedures in the class have been declared as **Public**. This means that these class methods *can* be called from any code not in the class. In general, all class methods should be **Public**; as such, they furnish capabilities to manipulate the class variables from any code or form module outside of the class. For our class we have initially provided one procedure, named setdate, and one function, named showdate. These two methods have been written to permit assignment and display capabilities.

Specifically, the setdate procedure expects three integer parameters, mm, dd, and yy. The body of this procedure assigns the data members Month, Day, and Year with the values of its parameters. Finally, the last function header line in the implementation section defines a function named showdate. This function has no parameters and returns the values stored in Month, Day, and Year as a formatted string having the form mm/dd/yy. We will shortly see how our class can be used within the context of a complete program. But first, we will have to code this class using a class module.

Creating a Class Module

Figure 12-2

The Add Class Module Option

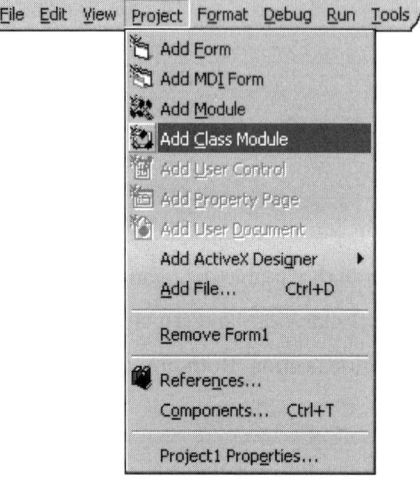

Creating a class requires inserting a class module into a project and then adding the class's code to that module. The steps used to insert a class module are almost identical to those for inserting a code module. They are

1. Open up either an existing or new project.

2. Choose the Add <u>C</u>lass Module option from the <u>P</u>roject menu (See Figure 12-2). Choosing this option will bring up the Add Class Module window shown in Figure 12-3.

Figure 12-3

The Add Class Module Window

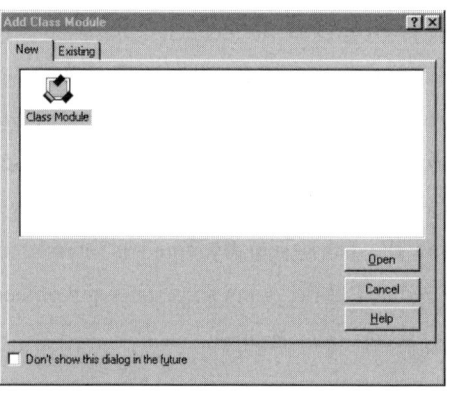

3. Select the Open Command button on the New tab (see Figure 12-3). Doing this will add a class module to the Project Explorer window, as shown in Figure 12-4.

4. If the Properties window is not visible, make it so by either choosing the Properties <u>W</u>indow option from the <u>V</u>iew menu or pressing the [F4] key.

5. Name the class in the Properties window.

Figure 12-4

The Project Window Containing a Class Module

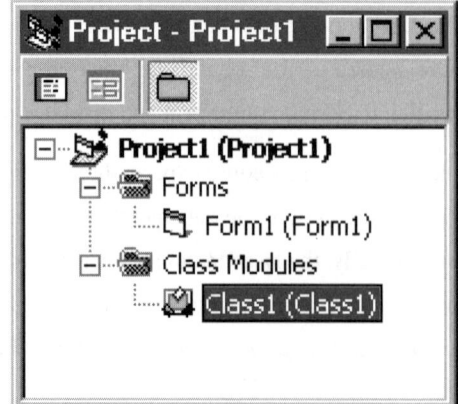

6. Click on the Class Code window and in the (**General**) object's (**Declarations**) section enter the class's data member declarations.

Figure 12-5

A Class Module Properties Window

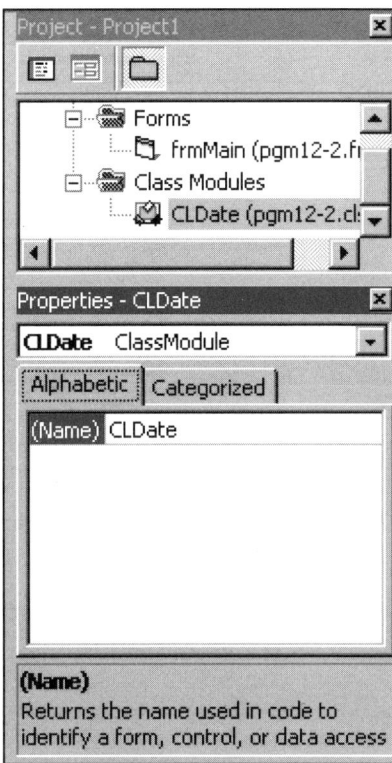

7. In the (**General**) object's (**Declarations**) section, type the header line for each class method and then complete the code in the template provided by Visual Basic.

Figure 12-5 shows the Project and Properties windows for a class that we have named CLDate (Step 5). By convention the first letter of a class name is capitalized. In this case we have chosen to capitalize the first three letters. You can always reactivate a class's Properties window at any time by pressing the F4 function key when the class module is active.

Figure 12-6

The Declaration Section for the CLDate Class

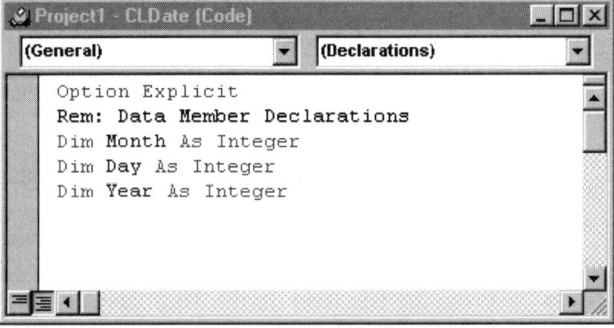

Figure 12-6 illustrates how the class's (**Declarations**) section will look, after you type in the data declarations. Notice that we have included the **Option Explicit** statement within this section so that all variables must be explicitly declared.

Figure 12-7

The setdate Procedure in the Code Window

```
Project1 - CLDate (Code)
(General)                              (Declarations)

Option Explicit
Rem: Data Member Declarations
Dim Month As Integer
Dim Day As Integer
Dim Year As Integer
Public Sub setdate(mm As Integer, dd As Integer, yy As Integer)
    Month = mm
    Day = dd
    Year = yy
End Sub
```

Figure 12-8

The showdate Procedure in the Code Window

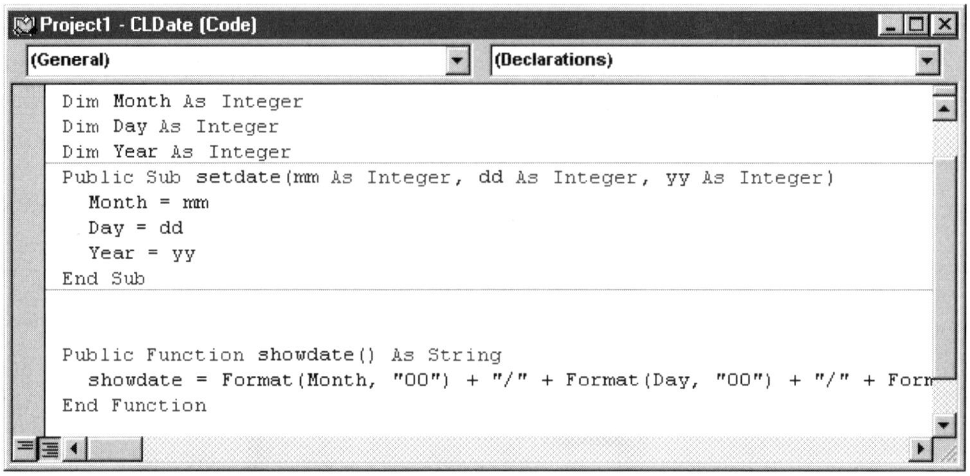

```
Project1 - CLDate (Code)                                          _ □ ×
(General)                        ▼    (Declarations)                    ▼
Dim Month As Integer                                                    ▲
Dim Day As Integer
Dim Year As Integer
Public Sub setdate(mm As Integer, dd As Integer, yy As Integer)
   Month = mm
   Day = dd
   Year = yy
End Sub


Public Function showdate() As String
   showdate = Format(Month, "00") + "/" + Format(Day, "00") + "/" + Form
End Function                                                            ▼
```

Figures 12-7 and 12-8 illustrate how the methods for the CLDate class will look when they have been entered in the class's Code window. Notice that, unlike a form module, which contains both a form and a Code window, a class module contains a Code window only.

Saving a Class Module

To save the module:

- Select the Save Option from the File's submenu, or

- Select the Save As option from the File's submenu, or

- Press the file icon on the Toolbar when the class module is active on the screen.

If you are using a class, your project will consist of at least two modules: a form module and a class module. To switch between modules you can double-click on the desired module within either the Project Explorer or Object Browser windows. The Project Explorer window is activated by

- Selecting Project Explorer from the View menu, or

- Pressing the Ctrl+R keys.

The Object Browser Window is activated by

- Selecting Object Browser from the View menu, or

- Pressing the F2 function key.

Whichever module is active is the one that will be saved if you choose the Save option from the File menu. That is, when a form module is active the File's submenu will appear as shown in Figure 12-9a. Similarly, if a class module is active, the File's submenu will appear as shown in Figure 12-9b. As shown in this figure, class modules are saved with a `.cls` extension.

Note that this procedure saves only the class module—it does not save any other modules associated with an application. Be aware that if you are using a class in a program, your project will consist of at least two modules: a form module and a class module. *Both modules should be saved*. To save a form module, make sure it is active on the screen and repeat the steps you used to save the class module. As always, the project definition as a whole, which includes all modules, can be saved at any time using either the Save Project or Save Project As options of the File menu, or by pressing the file icon on the toolbar.

Figure 12-9a

The File SubMenu When a Form Module is Active

Figure 12-9b

The File SubMenu When a Class Module is Active

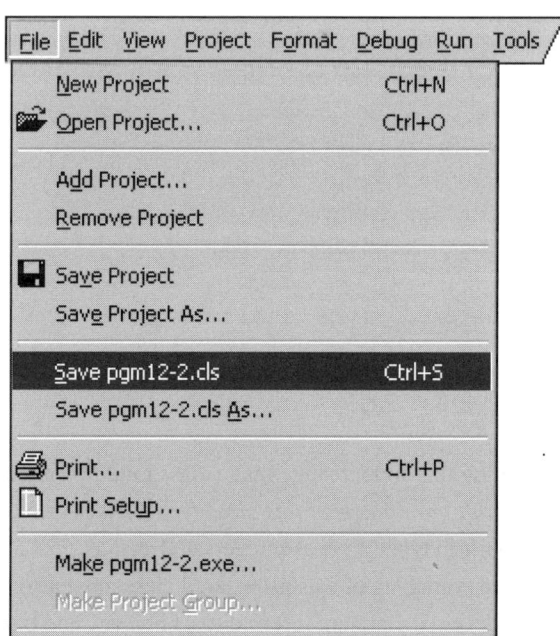

Using a Class

Once a class has been created, its public members can be used by any module within any project that includes the class module. For example, if we use the graphical interface shown in Figure 12-10 as Program 12-1's interface, enter the code listed as Program 12-1's procedure code, and insert the CLDate class into the project, we will have a completed application that uses the CLDate class.

Figure 12-10

*Program 12-1's
Graphical User Interface*

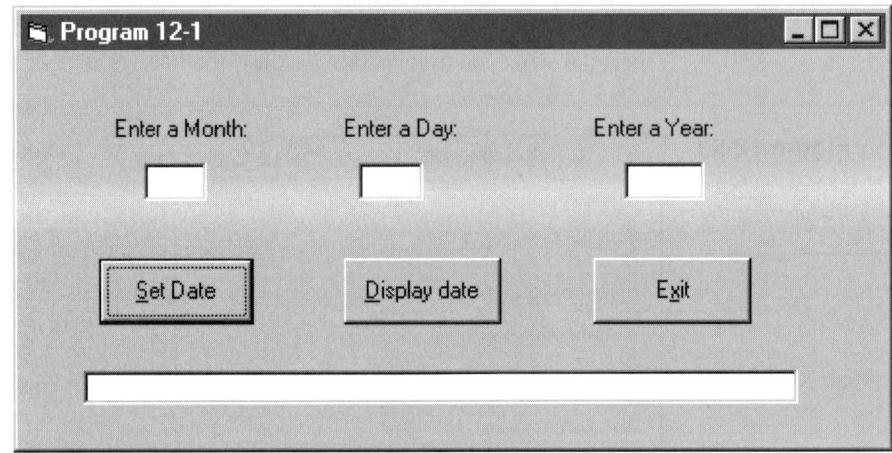

Program 12-1's Procedure Code

```
Rem: This is the code in the (Declarations) section
Option Explicit
Dim firstdate As New ClDate

Rem: This is the event code
Private Sub cmdDisplay_Click()
  picShow.Print "The date is "; firstdate.showdate()
End Sub

Private Sub cmdSet_Click()
  Dim mm As Integer, dd As Integer, yy As Integer

  picShow.Cls
  mm = Val(txtMonth.Text)
  dd = Val(txtDay.Text)
  yy = Val(txtYear.Text)
  Call firstdate.setdate(mm, dd, yy)
End Sub

Private Sub cmdExit_Click()
  Beep
  End
End Sub
```

In reviewing this code, realize that a class module only creates a data type, *it does not create any variables or objects of this class type*. This is true of all Visual Basic types, including the built-in types such as integers and strings. Just as a variable of an integer type must be declared, variables of a user-declared class must also be declared. Variables defined to be of a user-declared class are referred to as objects, and objects are declared using the

Table 12-2 Program 12-1's Properties Table

Object	Property	Setting
Form	Name	frmMain
	Caption	Program 12-1
Label	Name	lblMonth
	Caption	Enter a Month:
Label	Name	lblDay
	Caption	Enter a Day:
Label	Name	lblRate
	Caption	Enter a Year:
Text box	Name	txtMonth
	Text	(Blank)
	BackColor	White (Palette Tab)
Text box	Name	txtDay
	Text	(Blank)
	BackColor	White (Palette Tab)
Text box	Name	txtYear
	Text	(Blank)
	BackColor	White (Palette Tab)
Command button	Name	cmdSet
	Caption	&Set
Command button	Name	cmdDisplay
	Caption	&Display
Command button	Name	cmdExit
	Caption	E&xit
Picture box	Name	picShow
	TabStop	False
	BackColor	White (Palette Tab)

New keyword. Thus, the second statement in the (**Declarations**) section is a declaration statement that creates a new object of type CLDate class. Now notice the syntax for referring to an object's method. This syntax is

> *object-name.method-name(arguments)*

where *object-name* is the name of a specific object and *method-name* is the name of one of the methods defined for the object's class. Since we have defined all class methods as **Public**, a statement such as Call firstdate.setdate(mm,dd,yy) is valid inside an event procedure and is a call to the class's setdate procedure. This statement tells the setdate procedure to operate on the firstdate object with the arguments mm, dd, and yy. It is important to understand that, because all class data members were specified as **Private**, a statement such as firstdate.Month = mm is invalid from any procedure not on the class module. We are, therefore, forced to rely on member procedures to access data member values. For this same reason, a statement such as picShow.Print firstdate is invalid within the cmdDisplay_Click procedure, because the **Print** method does not know how to handle an object of class CLDate. Thus, we have supplied our class with a

---

Programmers' Notes

Interfaces, Implementations, and Information Hiding

The terms *interface*, *implementation*, and *information hiding* are used extensively in object-oriented programming literature. Each of these terms can be equated to specific parts of a class's declaration and implementation sections.

- An *interface* consists of the methods available to a programmer for using a class. Thus, a programmer should be provided with documentation as to the names and purpose of each class method, and how to correctly call and it. As such, the interface should be all that is required to tell a programmer how to use the class.

- The *implementation* consists of all the information contained in a class module. It is how the class is constructed. This information should not be needed by a user of the class.

- The implementation or class module is the essential means of providing information hiding. In its most general context, *information hiding* refers to the principle that the internal construction of a class is not relevant to any programmer who wishes to use that class. That is, the implementation can and should be hidden from all class users, precisely to ensure that the class is not altered or compromised in any way. All a programmer need know to correctly use a class should be given in the interface information.

---

procedure that can be used to access and display an object's internal values. Figure 12-11 illustrates a sample run using Program 12-1.

Figure 12-11

A Sample Output Using Program 12-1

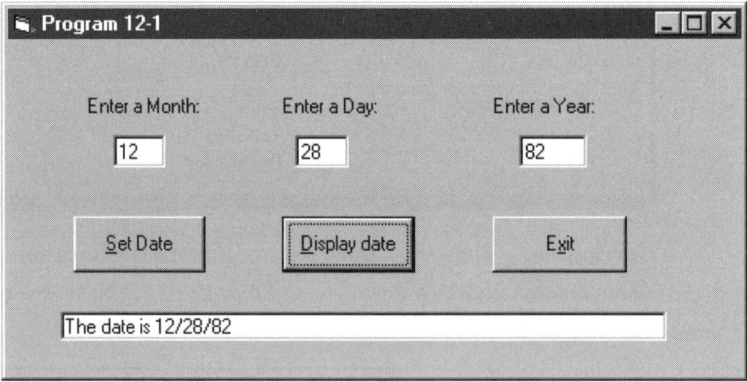

Terminology

As there is sometimes confusion about the terms *class*, *object*, and other terminology associated with object-oriented programming, we will take a moment to clarify and review the terminology.

A *class* is a programmer-defined data type out of which objects can be created. *Objects* are created from classes; they have the same relationship to classes as variables do to Visual Basic's built-in data types. For example, in the declaration

```
Dim firstdate as Integer
```

Programmers' Notes

Values and Identities

Apart from any behavior supplied to an object, a characteristic feature that objects share with variables is that they always have a unique identity. It is an object's identity that permits distinguishing one object from another. This is not true of a value, such as the number 5, because all occurrences of 5 are indistinguishable from one another. As such, values are not considered as objects in object-oriented programming languages such as Visual Basic.

Another distinguishing feature between an object and a value is that a value can never be container whose value can change, while an object clearly can. A value is simply an entity that stands for itself.

Now consider a string such as "Chicago". As a string, this is a value. However, since *Chicago* could also be a specific and identifiable object of type *City*, the context in which the name is used is important. Notice that when the string "Chicago" is assigned to an object's Name attribute, it reverts to being a value.

---

firstdate is said to be a variable, while in Program 12-1's declaration

```
Dim firstdate as New CLDate
```

firstdate is said to be an object. If it helps you to think of an object as a variable, do so.

Objects are also referred to as *instances* of a class and the process of creating a new object is frequently referred to as an *instantiation* of the object. Each time a new object is instantiated (created), a new set of data members belonging to the object is created.[1] The particular values contained in these data members determines the object's *state*.

Seen in this way, a class can be thought of as a blueprint out of which particular instances (objects) can be created. Each instance (object) of a class will have its own set of particular values for the set of data members specified in the class's (**Declarations**) section.

Notice that a class also defines the operations permitted to be performed on an object's data members. Users of the object need to know *what* these operations can do and how to activate them through function calls, but unless run-time or space implications are relevant, they do not need to know *how* the operation is done. The actual implementation details of an object's operations are contained in the implementation section, which can be hidden from the user. Other names for the operations defined in a class implementation section are *procedures, functions, services, methods*, and *behavior*. We will use these terms interchangeably throughout this chapter.

Exercises 12.1

1. Define the following terms:

   a. class
   b. object
   c. declaration section
   d. implementation section
   e. instance variable
   f. member method
   g. data member
   h. information hiding

2. Enter and execute Program 12-1 on your computer.

---

[1] Note that only one set of class methods is created. These methods are shared between objects.

Introduction to Visual Basic

3. a. Write a class definition for a class named `CLTime` that has integer data members named `Secs`, `Mins`, and `Hours`. The class should contain two methods named `settime` and `showtime` that can be used for setting and displaying a `CLTime` object.
   b. Include the class prepared for Exercises 3a. in a complete working program.

4. a. Write a class definition for a class named `Complex` that has floating-point members named `Real` and `Imaginary`. The class should contain two methods named `setcomplex` and `showcomplex` that can be used for setting and displaying a `Complex` object.
   b. Include the class prepared for Exercises 4a. in a complete working program.

5. Determine the errors in the following class declaration section:
```
Public Empnum As Integer
Public Name As String*20
```

6. a. Provide data input validation for Program 12-1 to ensure that only months between 1 and 12 are accepted.
   b. Provide data input validation for Program 12-1 to ensure that only days between 1 and 31 are accepted for the months 1, 3, 5, 7, 8,10, and 12; that only days between 1 and 30 are accepted for the months, 4, 6, 9, and 11; and that only days between 1 and 29 are accepted for month 2.
   c. Provide data input validation for Program 12-1 that converts years entered in the form 19*xx* to the number *xx*, and years entered in the form 20*yy* to the number *yy*.

7. a. Add another member method named `convrt` to the `CLDate` class in Program 12-1 that accesses the month, year, and day data members and then returns a long integer that is calculated as *year * 10000 + month * 100 + day*. For example, if the `CLDate` is 4/1/96, the returned value is 960401. (Dates in this form are useful when performing sorts, because placing the numbers in numerical order automatically places the corresponding `CLDates` in chronological order.)
   b. Include the modified `CLDate` class constructed for Exercise 7a. in a complete Visual Basic program.

8. a. Add an additional member method to Program 12-1's class definition named `leapyr` that returns a 1 when the year is a leap year and a 0 when it is not a leap year. A leap year is any year that is evenly divisible by 4 but not evenly divisible by 100, with the exception that all years evenly divisible by 400 are leap years. For example, the year 1996 is a leap year because it is evenly divisible by 4 and not evenly divisible by 100. The year 2000 will be a leap year because it is evenly divisible by 400.
   b. Include the class definition constructed for Exercise 8a. in a complete Visual Basic program. The program should display the message `"The year is a leap year"` or `"The year is not a leap year"` depending on the CLDate object's year value.

9. Modify the `CLDate` class in Program 12-1 to contain a method that compares two `CLDate` objects and returns the larger of the two. The method should be written according to the following algorithm:

> *Comparison method*
> *Accept two CLDate values as arguments*
> *Determine the later CLDate using the following procedure:*
> *Convert each CLDate into an integer value having the form yymmdd.*
> *Which can be accomplished using the algorithm described in Exercise 7.*
> *Compare the corresponding integers for each CLDate.*
> *The larger integer corresponds to the later CLDate.*
> *Return the later CLDate*

10. a. Add a member method to Program 12-1's class definition named `day_of_week` that determines the day of the week for any `CLDate` object. An algorithm for determining the day of the week, known as Zeller's algorithm, is the following:

> *If the month is greater than 2*
> *Set the variable mp = 0 and yp = year - 1*
> *Else*
> *set mp = Int(0.4 * month + 2.3) and yp = year*
> *Endif*
> *Set the variable t = Int(yp/4) - Int(yp/100) + Int(yp/400)*
> *Day-of-week = (365*year + 31*(month − 1) + day + t − mp) Mod 7*

Using this algorithm `Day-of-week` will have a value of 0 if the `CLDate` is a Sunday, 1 if a Monday, etc.

b. Include the class definition constructed for Exercise 10a. in a complete Visual Basic program. The program should display the name of the day (Sun, Mon, Tue, etc.) for the `CLDate` object being tested.

12.2 Initializing and Terminating Events

For each class, Visual Basic permits two event procedures: **Initialize** and **Terminate**. The first time a line of code that refers to a class object is executed, memory is allocated for the object and a class initialization event occurs. The header line for this event procedure is

```
Private Sub Class_Initialize()
```

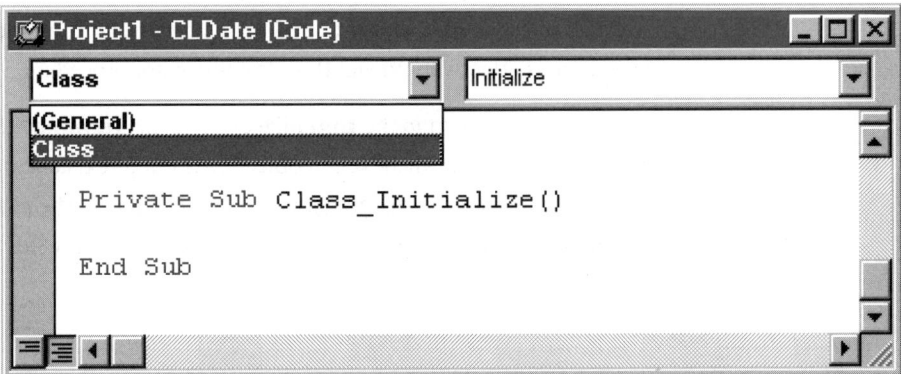

Any code that is placed in this event procedure is executed once, when the object is created, prior to the execution of any other method. As indicated by the event procedure's header line, it accepts no parameters. To access this procedure, select the **Initial** procedure in the class's Code window Class object, as shown in Figure 12-12. The Class object is always listed under the (**General**) object in the code window.

As an example, consider the following **Initialize** event code added to our CLDate class:

```
Private Sub Class_Initialize()
  Month = 1
  Day = 1
  Year = 97
  MsgBox ("*** A CLDate object has being initialized ***")
End Sub
```

When any CLDate object is created, this Initialize event code is automatically called. For example, if we create a CLDate object named firstdate, the data members of this object will be initialized to

```
firstdate.Month = 1
firstdate.Day = 1
firstdate.Year = 99
```

In addition, we have included a message box display within the **Initialize** event code so you can see when the event procedure is actually called. Program 12-2, which uses the same form module as Program 12-1, can be used to test this **Initialize** event. When Program 12-2 is run, the message box does not immediately appear. However, if the cmdDisplay button is the first button pushed, it will execute a line of code that refers to firstdate. As this is the first time this object is referenced, it is created and the Initialize event procedure is called, resulting in the display shown in Figure 12-13.

Figure 12-13

The Activation of the Initialize Event

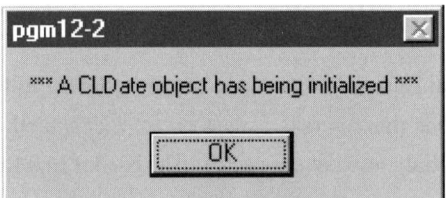

The intended purpose of the **Initialize** event procedure is to initialize a new object's data members. Although this event procedure can be used to perform other tasks when it is called, its use should generally be restricted to performing data member initialization. In other programming languages, the procedure used to initialize an object's member variables when an object is created, is referred to as a *constructor*. As such, the **Initialize** event procedure is effectively Visual Basic's constructor procedure.

The counterpart to the **Initialize** event is the **Terminate** event. This event procedure is automatically called whenever an object goes out of existence, and is meant to "clean up" any undesirable effects that might be left by the object. The header line for this event procedure, which can be found in the class's Code window for the Class object is

```
Private Sub Class_Terminate()
```

Figure 12-14

An Example of a Terminate Event Procedure

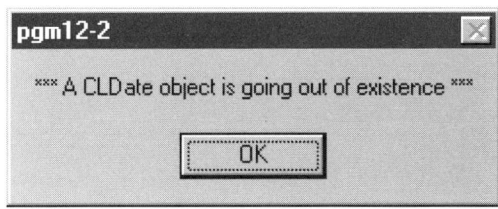

As this header indicates, the **Terminate** event procedure takes no parameters and returns no value. For purposes of illustrating when this event procedure is triggered, we have added the following Terminate event procedure to the `CLDate` class used by Program 12-2.

```
Private Sub Class_Terminate()
  MsgBox ("*** A CLDate object is going out of existence ***")
End Sub
```

When you close an executing version of Program 12-2, the message box shown in Figure 12-14 will appear.

Arrays of Object

Figure 12-15

The Interface for Program 12-3

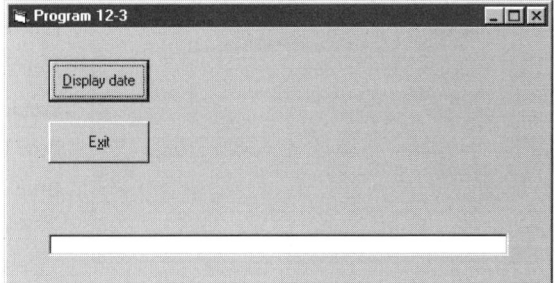

The importance of the **Initialize** event procedure becomes evident when arrays of objects are created. Since the Initialize event is called each time an object is created, this event provides an elegant way of initializing all objects to the same state.

Declaring an array of objects is the same as declaring an array of any built-in type. For example, the declaration

```
Option Base 1
Const NUMELS As Integer = 5
Dim adate(NUMELS) As New CLDate
```

can be used to create five objects, named `adate(1)` to `adate(5)`, respectively. Member methods for each of these objects are called by listing the object name followed by a dot (.) and the desired method. An example using an array of objects of type `CLDate` is provided by Program 12-3.

Table 12-3 The Properties Table for Program 12-3		
Object	**Property**	**Setting**
Form	Name	`frmMain`
	Caption	`Program 12-3`
Command button	Name	`cmdDisplay`
	Caption	`&Display`
Command button	Name	`cmdExit`
	Caption	`E&xit`
Picture box	Name	`picShow`
	TabStop	`False`
	BackColor	`White (Palette Tab)`

Program 12-3's Procedure Code

```
Rem: This is the code in the (declarations) section
Option Explicit
Option Base 1
Const NUMELS As Integer = 5
Dim adate(NUMELS) As New CLDate

Rem: This is the event code
Private Sub cmdDisplay_Click()
  Dim i As Integer
  For i = 1 To NUMELS
    picShow.Print "The date is "; adate(i).showdate()
  Next i
End Sub

Private Sub cmdExit_Click()
  Beep
  End
End Sub
```

Figure 12-16

A Sample Output using Program 12-3

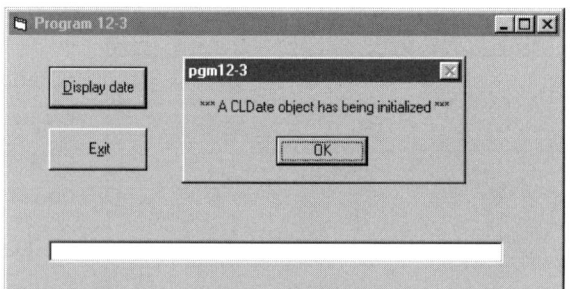

When the <u>D</u>isplay Command button is pushed for the first time, five `adate` objects will be created. Figure 12-16 illustrates how the interface will look at run-time as each object is created.

Exercises 12.2

1. Enter and execute Program 12-1 on your computer.

2. Enter and execute Program 12-2 on your computer.

3. a. Construct a class named `CLTime` that has integer data members named `Secs`, `Mins`, and `Hours`. The class should contain two methods named `settime` and `showtime` that can be used for setting and displaying a `CLTime` object and include an **Initialize** event that initializes all data members to 0.

    b. Include the class constructed in Exercise 3a. in a complete working program.

4. a. Write a class named `Complex` that has floating-point members named `Real` and `Imaginary`. The class should contain two methods named `setcomplex` and `showcomplex` that can be used for setting and displaying a `Complex` object and include an **Initialize** event that initializes all data members to 0.

    b. Include the class constructed in Exercises 4a. in a complete working program.

5. a. Construct a class named `CLCircle` that has integer data members named `Xcenter` and `Ycenter` and a floating-point data member named `Radius`. The class should contain two methods named `setradius` and `setcenter` to set the radius and center values, respectively, and two methods named `showradius` and `showcenter` to display these values. The class should also include an **Initialize** event that initializes all data members to 1.

   b. Include the class constructed in Exercises 5a. in a complete working program.

6. a. Construct a class named `System` that has string data members named `Computer`, `Printer`, and `Screen`, each capable of holding 30 characters, and floating-point data members named `Comp_price`, `Print_price`, and `Scrn_price`. The class should include an **Initialize** event procedure that initializes all strings to the NULL value and all numeric values to 0. Include methods that permit a programmer to both set and display member values.

   b. Include the class constructed in Exercise 6a. in a complete working program.

7. a. Construct a class named `Student` consisting of an integer student identification number, an array of five floating-point grades, and an integer representing the total number of grades entered. The **Initialize** event for this class should initialize all `Student` data members to zero. Included in the class should be member procedures to (1) enter a student ID number, (2) enter a single test grade and update the total number of grades entered, and (3) compute an average grade and display the student ID followed by the average grade.

   b. Include the class constructed in Exercise 7a. within the context of a complete program. Your program should declare two objects of type `Student` and accept and display data for the two objects to verify operation of the member procedures.

12.3 Access Procedures Let and Get

An *access procedure,* which is frequently referred to simply as an *accessor,* is any member method that accesses a class's private data members. For example, the procedure `showdate` in the `CLDate` class is an access procedure. Such procedures are extremely important because they provide the only public means of access to these data members.

When constructing a class, it is important to provide a complete set of access procedures. Each access procedure does not have to return a data member's exact value, but it should return a useful representation of the value. For example, assume that a date such as 12/25/98 is stored as a long integer member variable in the form 982512. Although an accessor procedure could display this value, a more useful representation would typically be either 12/25/98, or December 25, 1998.

Besides being used for output, accessors can also provide a means of data input. For example, the `setdate` procedure in the `CLDate` class is an example of an input access procedure. Although the **Initialize** and **Terminate** procedures also access a class's private data members, as event procedures these two are not formally classified as accessors.

Accessor procedures are considered so important that Visual Basic provides three procedures specifically designed for access purposes, referred to as **Property** procedures. The two most commonly used of these **Property** procedures are listed in Table 12-4.

Table 12-4 Visual Basic's Property Procedures

Name	Description	Usage
Property Get	Read a data member's value.	variable = objectname.procedure()
Property Let	Assign a data member's value.	objectname.procedure = expression

As an example of constructing property **Get** and **Let** procedures, consider the `CLDate` class that we have been using throughout this chapter. For convenience, this class's data member declaration section is repeated below:

```
Rem: The CLDate class data declaration section
Private Month As Integer
Private Day As Integer
Private Year As Integer
```

For this class we will construct three property **Let** and **Get** procedures, one pair for each data member. For the `Month` data member, a suitable pair of procedures is

```
Property Let accessMonth(mm As Integer)
 Month = mm
End Property

Property Get accessMonth() As Integer
 accessMonth = Month
End Property
```

The first item to notice about these two procedures is that they both share the same name, which is typical but not required. The second item to notice is that the **Get** procedure *always* take one less parameter than its related **Let** procedure. Here the **Let** procedure takes one parameter that is assigned to the `Month` data member and the related **Get** procedure returns the value of this data member. This brings up the third item required by a related pair of **Let** and **Get** procedures: the data type of the **Get** procedure *must be* the same as the data type of the last parameter in the related **Let** procedure. Our last version of the `CLDate` class, with **Property Let** and **Get** procedures for all data members, is listed as Version 3 below:

The CLDate Class—Version 3

```
Option Explicit
Private Month As Integer
Private Day As Integer
Private Year As Integer

Property Let accessMonth(mm As Integer)
   Month = mm
End Property

Property Get accessMonth() As Integer
   accessMonth = Month
End Property

Property Let accessDay(dd As Integer)
   Day = dd
End Property
```

(continued)

```
Property Get accessDay() As Integer
  accessDay = Day
End Property

Property Let accessYear(yy As Integer)
Rem: Make sure that Year is between 00 and 99
  If yy > 2000 Then
    Year = yy - 2000
  ElseIf yy > 1900 Then
    Year = yy - 1900
  Else
    Year = yy
  End If
End Property

Property Get accessYear() As Integer
  accessYear = Year
End Property

Private Sub Class_Initialize()
  Month = 1
  Day = 1
  Year = 97
End Sub
```

Except for the **Property Let** procedure for the `Year` data member, all of the **Let** and **Get** procedures are straightforward variations of the `accessMonth` procedures. The **Property Let** procedure for the `Year` data member includes additional processing to ensure that the final assigned value resides in the range 0 to 99.

Program 12-4 uses this version of the `CLDate` class within a complete application. The interface for this program is shown in Figure 12-17.

Figure 12-17
Program 12-4's Interface

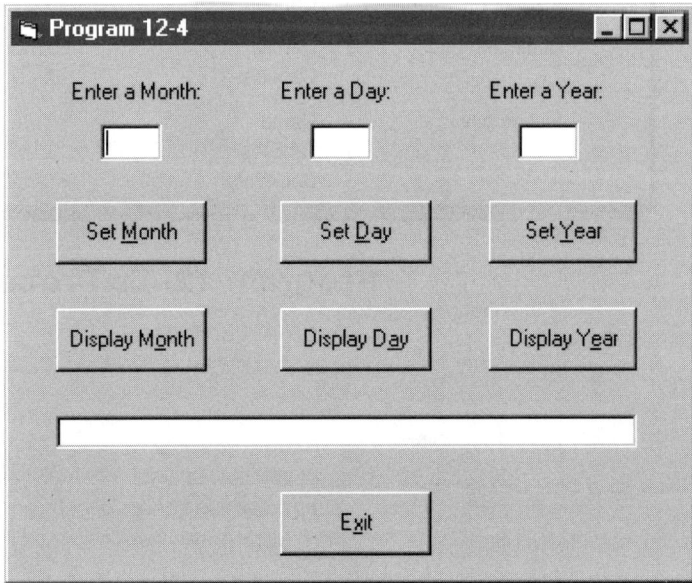

Table 12-5 Program 12-4's Properties Table

Object	Property	Setting
Form	Name	frmMain
	Caption	Program 12-4
Label	Name	lblMonth
	Caption	Enter a Month:
Label	Name	lblDay
	Caption	Enter a Day:
Label	Name	lblRate
	Caption	Enter a Year:
Text box	Name	txtMonth
	Text	(Blank)
	BackColor	White (Palette Tab)
Text box	Name	txtDay
	Text	(Blank)
	BackColor	White (Palette Tab)
Text box	Name	txtYear
	Text	(Blank)
	BackColor	White (Palette Tab)
Command button	Name	cmdSMonth
	Caption	Set &Month
Command button	Name	cmdSDay
	Caption	Set &Day
Command button	Name	cmdSYear
	Caption	Set &Year
Command button	Name	cmdDMonth
	Caption	Display M&onth
Command button	Name	cmdDDay
	Caption	Display D&ay
Command button	Name	cmdDYear
	Caption	Display Y&ear
Command button	Name	cmdExit
	Caption	E&xit
Picture box	Name	picShow
	TabStop	False
	BackColor	White (Palette Tab)

Program 12-4's Procedure Code

```
Option Explicit
Dim firstdate As New CLDate

Private Sub cmdDDay_Click()
  picShow.Cls
  picShow.Print "The Day has been set to";
firstdate.accessDay()
End Sub
```

(continued)

```
Private Sub cmdDMonth_Click()
  picShow.Cls
  picShow.Print "The Month has been set to"; firstdate.accessMonth()
End Sub

Private Sub cmdDYear_Click()
  picShow.Cls
  picShow.Print "The Year has been set to"; firstdate.accessYear()
End Sub

Private Sub cmdExit_Click()
  Beep
  End
End Sub

Private Sub cmdSDay_Click()
  firstdate.accessDay = Val(txtDay.Text)
End Sub

Private Sub cmdSMonth_Click()
  firstdate.accessMonth = Val(txtMonth.Text)
End Sub

Private Sub cmdSYear_Click()
  firstdate.accessYear = Val(txtYear.Text)
End Sub

Private Sub txtDay_GotFocus()
  picShow.Cls
End Sub

Private Sub txtMonth_GotFocus()
  picShow.Cls
End Sub

Private Sub txtYear_GotFocus()
  picShow.Cls
End Sub
```

It is worthwhile noting in Program 12-4's procedure code that the actual calls to both **Let** and **Get Property** procedures do not use a conventional **Call** statement. Rather, these procedures are used as variables following the syntax listed in Table 12-5.

Exercises 12.3

1. Enter and run Program 12-4 on your computer.

2. a. Modify the accessMonth **Let** procedure in Program 12-1 to ensure that only months between 1 and 12 are accepted. If an invalid month is entered, the modified procedure should display an error message using a **MsgBox** function.
    b. Modify the accessDay **Let** procedure in Program 12-1 to ensure that only days between 1 and 31 are accepted for the months 1, 3, 5, 7, 8, 10, and 12; that only days between 1 and 30 are accepted for the months, 4, 6, 9, and 11; and that only days between 1 and 29 are accepted for the month 2. If an invalid day is entered, the modified procedure should display an error message using a **MsgBox** function.
    c. Modify the accessDay **Let** procedure written for Exercise 2b. to account for leap years. (**Hint:** See Exercise 8a. in Section 12.1.)

Programmers' Notes

Encapsulation, Inheritance, and Polymorphism

An object-based language is one in which data and operations can be incorporated together in such a way that data values can be isolated and accessed through the specified class functions. The ability to bind the data members with operations in a single unit is referred to as *encapsulation*. In Visual Basic encapsulation is provided by its class capability.

For a language to be classified as object-oriented it must also provide inheritance and polymorphism. *Inheritance* is the capability to derive one class from another. A derived class is a completely new data type that incorporates all the data members and member functions of the original class with any new data and function members unique to itself. The class used as the basis for the derived type is referred to as the *base* or *parent* class and the derived data type is referred to as the *derived* or *child* class.

Polymorphism permits the same method name to invoke one operation in objects of a parent class and a different operation in objects of a derived class.

3. a. Construct a class named `CLTime` that has integer data members named `Secs`, `Mins`, and `Hours`. The class should contain three pairs of **Let** and **Get Property** procedures, one pair for each data member. Additionally, include an **Initialize** event that initializes all data members to 0.

   b. Include the class constructed in Exercises 3a. in a complete working program.

4. a. Write a class named `Complex` that has floating-point members named `Real` and `Imaginary`. The class should contain two pairs of **Let** and **Get Property** procedures, one pair for each data member. Additionally, include an **Initialize** event that initializes all data members to 0.

   b. Include the class constructed in Exercises 4a. in a complete working program.

5. a. Construct a class named `CLCircle` that has integer data members named `Xcenter` and `Ycenter` and a floating-point data member named `Radius`. The class should contain three pairs of **Let** and **Get Property** procedures, one pair for each data member. Additionally, the class should include an **Initialize** event that initializes all data members to 1.

   b. Include the class constructed in Exercises 5a. in a complete working program.

12.4 An Example: Constructing an Elevator Object

Now that we have an understanding of how classes are constructed and the terminology used in describing them, let us apply this knowledge to a particular application. In this application we simulate the operation of an elevator. We assume that the elevator can travel between the first and fifteenth floors of a building and that the location of the elevator must be known at all times.

For this application the location of the elevator corresponds to its current floor position and is represented by an integer variable ranging between 1 and 15. The value of this

---

variable, which we will name `Curfloor`, for current floor, effectively represents the current state of the elevator. An **Initialize** event procedure will set the initial floor position when a new elevator is put into service, and a `request` function will change the elevator's position (state) to a new floor. Putting an elevator in service is accomplished by declaring a single class instance (an object of type `Elevator`), while requesting a new floor position is equivalent to pushing an elevator button. To accomplish this, a suitable class definition is

```
Rem: Class Elevator

Rem: Data Declaration Section
Const MAXFLOOR As Integer = 15
Private Curfloor As Integer

Rem: Methods Implementation Section
Public Sub request(newfloor As Integer)
  If newfloor < 1 Or newfloor > MAXFLOOR Then
    frmMain.picError.Print "An invalid floor has been selected"
  ElseIf newfloor > Curfloor Then
    frmMain.picFloor.Print "Starting at floor"; Curfloor
    Do While newfloor > Curfloor
      Curfloor = Curfloor + 1
      frmMain.picFloor.Print "Going Up - now at floor"; Curfloor
    Loop
    frmMain.picFloor.Print "Stopping at floor"; Curfloor
  ElseIf newfloor < Curfloor Then
    frmMain.picFloor.Print "Starting at floor"; Curfloor
    Do While newfloor < Curfloor
      Curfloor = Curfloor - 1
      frmMain.picFloor.Print "Going Up - now at floor"; Curfloor
    Loop
    frmMain.picFloor.Print "Stopping at floor"; Curfloor
  End If
End Sub

Rem: Initialize Event Code
Private Sub Class_Initialize()
  Curfloor = 1
End Sub
```

Notice that we have declared one data member, `Curfloor`, and implemented one method and an initializing event procedure. The data member, `Curfloor` is used to store the current floor position of the elevator. As a private data member, it can only be accessed through member procedures and functions. The single member procedure named `request` defines the external services provided by each `Elevator` object and the **Initialize** procedure is used to initialize the starting floor position of each `Elevator` type object. The **Initialize** procedure is straightforward. Whenever an `Elevator` object is first accessed it is initialized to the first floor.

The `request` procedure defined in the implementation section is more complicated and provides the class's primary service; it is used to alter the position of the elevator. Essentially this procedure consists of an **If-Else** statement having three parts: (1) If an incorrect service is requested, an error message is displayed; (2) if a floor above the current

Table 12-6 Program 12-5's Properties Table

Object	Property	Setting
Form	Name	frmMain
	Caption	Program 12-5
Label	Name	lblFloor
	Caption	Enter a floor:
Text box	Name	txtFloor
	Text	(Blank)
	BackColor	White (Palette Tab)
Command button	Name	cmdFloor
	Caption	&Move Elevator
Command button	Name	cmdExit
	Caption	E&xit
Picture box	Name	picFloor
	TabStop	False
	BackColor	White (Palette Tab)
Picture box	Name	picError
	TabStop	False
	BackColor	White (Palette Tab)

position is selected, the elevator is moved up; and (3) if a floor below the current position is selected, the elevator is moved down. For movement up or down, the procedure uses a **Do/While** loop to increment the position one floor at a time, and reports the elevator's movement to a picFloor object located on frmMain. It is worth noting two points with respect to the notation used here.

First, since the picFloor control is not on the current class module (class modules cannot contain visual objects), the complete designation for where the object resides must be given. Hence the full name of the object, frmMain.picFloor, must precede the **Print** method name. This is the standard way of having code on one module access objects and methods defined on a different module. Next, the request method is over ambitious precisely because it references an object not contained within the class. Theoretically, a class should be self-contained and not require any object outside of the class for it to be executed correctly. In Exercise 4 we explore how to reconstruct this class to adhere to this requirement.

Figure 12-18

Program 12-5's Interface

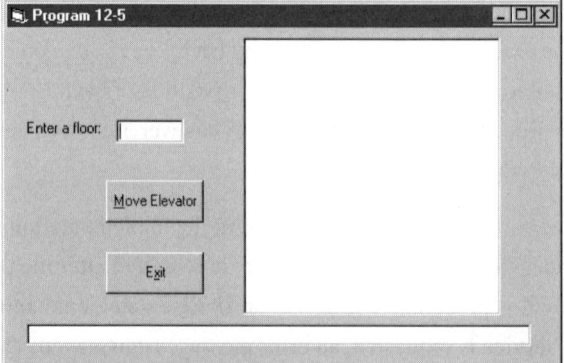

Program 12-5 includes this class in a working program. The interface for this program is shown in Figure 12-18.

Program 12-5's Procedure Code

```
Option Explicit
Private a As New Elevator

Private Sub txtFloor_GotFocus()
 picError.Cls
End Sub

Private Sub cmdFloor_Click()
 picFloor.Cls
 a.request (Val(txtFloor.Text))
End Sub

Private Sub cmdExit_Click()
 Beep
 End
End Sub
```

Program 12-5's procedure code is extremely simple, precisely because all the work in moving the elevator is contained within the class's `request` method. Notice that this method is called in the standard way by placing a period and an object's name before the method's name. A sample run using Program 12-5 is illustrated in Figure 12-19.

The basic requirements of object-oriented programming are evident in even as simple a program as Program 12-5. Before a form module can be written, a useful class must be constructed. This is typical of programs that use objects. For such programs, the design process is front-loaded with the requirement that careful consideration of the class—its declaration and implementation—be given. Code contained in the implementation section effectively removes code that would otherwise be part of a form's responsibility. Thus, any program that uses the object does not have to repeat the implementation details within its form's procedures. Rather, the form's procedures are only concerned with sending arguments to its objects to activate them appropriately. The details of how the object responds to the arguments and how the state of the object is retained are hidden within the class construction.

Figure 12-19

A Sample Run using Program 12-5

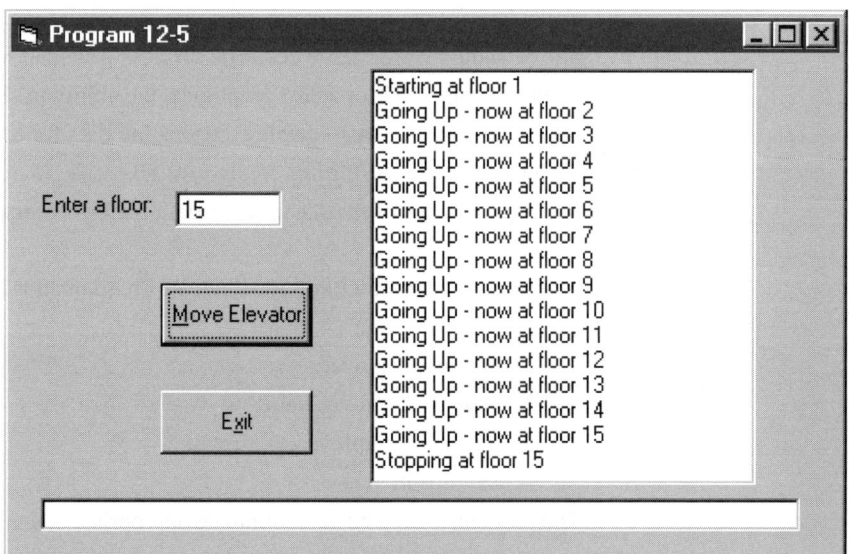

Exercises 12.4

1. Enter Program 12-5 in your computer and execute it.

2. Modify Program 12-5 to put a second elevator in service. Have this second elevator move to the twelfth floor and then move to the fifth floor.

3. Verify that the **Initialize** event procedure in Program 12-5 is called by adding a message within it that is displayed each time a new object is created. Run your program to ensure its operation.

4. The `Elevator` class violates pure class construction rules because one of its methods accesses an object that is not in the class. Modify the `Elevator` class to remove this violation. To do so, provide the class with a procedure named `oneup` and `onedown`, which add and subtract 1, to and from the current value of `Curfloor`. Then modify the `cmdMove_Click` procedure to incorporate an **If-Else** similar to the one used in `request`.

5. a. Modify the `CLDate` class used in Program 12-4 to include a `nextDay` procedure that increments a date by one day. Test your procedure to ensure that it correctly increments days into a new month and into a new year.

   b. Modify the `CLDate` class used in Program 12-4 to include a `priorDay` function that decrements a date by one day. Test your function to ensure that it correctly decrements days into a prior month and into a prior year.

6. a. In Exercise 3 of the previous section, you were asked to construct a `CLTime` class. For this class include a `tick` procedure that increments the time by one second. Test your procedure to ensure that it correctly increments into a new minute and a new hour.

   b. Modify the `Time` class written for Exercise 10a. to include a `detick` procedure that decrements the time by one second. Test your procedure to ensure that it correctly decrements time into a prior hour and into a prior minute.

7. a. Construct a class that can be used to represent an employee of a company. Each employee is defined by an integer ID number, a name consisting of no more than 30 characters, a floating-point pay rate, and the maximum number of hours the employee should work each week. The services provided by the class should be the ability to enter data for a new employee, the ability to change data for a new employee, and the ability to display the existing data for a new employee.

   b. Include the class definition created for Exercise 7a. in a working Visual Basic program that asks the user to enter data for three employees and displays the entered data.

   c. Modify the program written for Exercise 7b. to include a menu that offers the user the following choices:

   1. Add an Employee.
   2. Modify Employee data.
   3. Delete an Employee.
   4. Exit this menu.

   The program should be able to initiate appropriate action to implement a user's choice.

8. a. Construct a class that can be used to represent types of food. A type of food is classified as basic or prepared. Basic foods are further classified as either Dairy, Meat, Fruit, Vegetable, or Grain. The services provided by the class should be the ability to enter data for a new food, the ability to change data for a new food, and the ability to display the existing data for a new food.

   b. Include the class definition created for Exercise 8a. in a working Visual Basic program that asks the user to enter data for four food items and displays the entered data.

   c. Modify the program written for Exercise 8b. to include a menu that offers the user the following choices:

   1. Add a Food item.
   2. Modify a Food item.
   3. Delete a Food item.
   4. Exit this menu.

   In response to a choice, the program should initiate appropriate action to implement the choice.

12.5 Common Programming Errors

The more common programming errors initially associated with the construction and use of classes are

1. Failing to make data members **Private**.
2. Failing to make member methods **Public**.
3. Failing to include an appropriate **Initialize** event procedure.
4. Using a **Call** statement to access the **Let** and **Get Property** procedures.

12.6 Chapter Review

Key Terms

abstract data type	declaration section
class	implementation section
class library	inheritance
class members	instantiation
constructor	intrinsic program library
data members	member methods
data type	object
	polymorphism

Summary

1. A *class* is a programmer-defined data type. *Objects* of a class may be defined and have the same relationship to their class as variables do to Visual Basic's built-in data types.

2. A class definition consists of a declaration and implementation section. The most common form of a class definition is

```
Rem: Data Declaration Section
     Declaration of all variables
Rem: Methods Implementation Section
     Procedures and Functions that
     can be used on the above
     declared variables
```

The variables, procedures, and functions declared in the class declaration section are collectively referred to as *class members*. The variables are individually referred to as class *data members* and the procedures and functions as class *member methods*.

3. The keywords **Private** and **Public** are formally referred to as *access specifiers*, because they specify the access permitted to the class's variables and procedures. The **Private** keyword specifies that a class member is private to the class and can only be accessed by member methods. The **Public** keyword specifies that a class member may be accessed from outside the class. Generally, all data members should be specified as **Private** and all member methods as **Public**. This ensures that variables declared as **Private** within the Data Declaration section can only be accessed through member methods, and that the member methods are available and can be called from outside the class.

4. Objects are created using the **New** keyword. For example, if CLDate is the name of a class, the statement

```
Dim firstdate As New CLDate
```

declares firstdate as an object of type CLDate.

5. Visual Basic provides two event procedures for classes: **Initialize** and **Terminate**. The **Initialize** event procedure is automatically called when an object is first referenced. Its purpose is to initialize each created object. The **Terminate** event procedure is called when an object goes out of scope.

6. An *access procedure* is any member method that accesses a class's private data members. Two access procedures provided by Visual Basic are the **Let** and **Get Property** procedures. The purpose of the **Get** procedure is to read a data member's value, while the **Let** procedure is used to assign a value to a data member. Typically, **Let** and **Get** procedures are used in pairs that share a common property name. The **Get Property** procedure is called using the syntax

```
variable = objectname.procedure()
```

while the **Let** property procedure is called using the syntax:

```
objectname.procedure = expression
```

12.7 Looking Further: Insides and Outsides

Just as the concept of an algorithm is central to procedures, the concept of encapsulation is central to objects. In this section we present this encapsulation concept using an inside-outside analogy, which should help your understanding of what object-oriented programming is all about.

In programming terms, an object's attributes are described by data, such as the length and width of a rectangle, and the operations that can be applied to the attributes are described by procedures and functions.

As a practical example of this, assume that we will be writing a program that can deal a hand of cards. From an object-oriented approach, one of the objects we must model is clearly a deck of cards. For our purposes, the attribute of interest for the card deck is that it contains 52 cards, consisting of four suits (hearts, diamonds, spades, and clubs), with each suit consisting of thirteen pip values (ace to ten, Jack, Queen, and King).

Now consider the behavior of our deck of cards, which consists of the operations that can be applied to the deck. At a minimum we will want the ability to shuffle the deck and deal single cards. Let's now see how this simple example relates to encapsulation using an inside-outside concept.

A useful visualization of the inside-outside concept is to consider an object as a boiled egg, as shown in Figure 12-20. Notice that the egg consists of three parts: a very inside yolk, a less inside white surrounding the yolk, and an outside shell, which is the only part of the egg visible to the world.

In terms of our boiled egg model, the attributes and behavior of an object correspond to the yolk and white, respectively, which are inside the egg. The innermost protected area of an object, its data attributes, can be compared to the egg yolk. Surrounding the data attributes, as an egg's white surrounds its yolk, are the operations we choose to incorporate within an object. Finally, in this analogy, the interface to the outside world, the shell, represents how a user gets to invoke the object's internal procedures.

The egg model, with its eggshell interface separating the inside of the egg from the outside, is useful precisely because it so clearly depicts the separation between what should be contained inside an object and what should be seen from the outside. This separation forms an essential element in object-oriented programming. Let's see why this is so.

Figure 12-20

The Boiled Egg Object Model

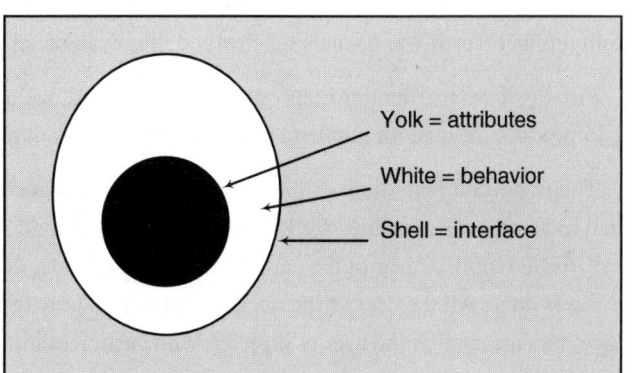

Yolk = attributes

White = behavior

Shell = interface

From an inside-outside perspective, an object's data attributes, the selected algorithms for controlling operations, and the ways these algorithms are actually implemented are always inside issues, hidden from the view of object users. On the other hand, the way a user or another object can actually activate an inside procedure, is an outside issue.

Now let's apply this concept to our card deck example. First, consider how we might represent cards in the deck. Any of the following attributes (and there are others) could be used to represent a card:

1. Two integer variables, one representing a suit (a number from 1 to 4) and one representing a value (a number from 1 to 13).
2. One character value and one integer value: the character represents a card's suit and the integer represents a card's value.
3. One integer variable having a value from 0 to 51: the expression **Int** (number / 13 + 1) provides a number from 1 to 4, which represents the suit, and the expression (number Mod 13 + 1) represents a card value from 1 to 13.

Whichever one we decide on, however, is not relevant to the outside. The specific way we choose to represent a card is an inside issue to be decided by the designer of the deck object. From the outside, all that is of concern is that we have access to a deck consisting of 52 cards having the necessary suits and pip values.

The same is true for the operations we decide to provide as part of our card deck object. Consider just the shuffling for now.

There are a number of algorithms for producing a shuffled deck. For example, we could use Visual Basic's random number function, **Rnd**, or create our own random number generator. Again, the selected algorithm is an inside issue to be determined by the designer of the deck. The specifics of which algorithm is selected and how it is applied to the attributes we have chosen for each card in the deck are not relevant from the object's outside. For purposes of illustration, assume that we decide to use Visual Basic's **Rnd** function to produce a randomly shuffled deck.

If we use the first attribute set previously given, each card in a shuffled deck is produced using **Rnd** at least twice; once to create a random number from 1 to 4 for the suit, and then again to create a random number from 1 to 13 for the card's pip value. This sequence must be done to construct 52 different attribute sets, with no duplicates allowed.

If, on the other hand, we use the second attribute set previously given, a shuffled deck can be produced in exactly the same fashion as above, with one modification: the first random number (from 1 to 4) must be changed into a character to represent the suit.

Finally, if we use the third representation for a card, we need to use **Rnd** once for each card, to produce 52 random numbers from 0 to 51, with no duplicates allowed.

The important point here is that the selection of an algorithm and how it will be applied to an object's attributes are implementation issues and *implementation issues are always inside issues*. A user of the card deck, who is outside, does not need to know how the shuffling is done. All the user of the deck must know is how to produce a shuffled deck. In practice, this means that the user is supplied with sufficient information to correctly invoke the shuffle function. This corresponds to the interface, or outer shell of the egg.

Abstraction and Encapsulation

The distinction between insides and outsides relates directly to the concepts of abstraction and encapsulation. Abstraction means concentrating on what an object is and does, before making any decisions about how the object will be implemented. Thus, abstractly, we define a deck and the operations we want to provide. (Clearly, if our abstraction is to be useful, it had better capture the attributes and operations of a real-world deck.) Once we have decided on the attributes and operations, we can actually implement them.

Encapsulation means separating and hiding the implementation details of the chosen abstract attributes and behavior from outside users of the object. The external side of an object should provide only the necessary interface to users of the object for activating internal procedures. Imposing a strict inside-outside discipline when creating objects is really another way of saying that the object successfully encapsulates all implementation details. In our deck-of-cards example, encapsulation means that users need never know how we have internally modeled the deck or how an operation, such as shuffling, is performed; they only need to know how to activate the given operations.

Code Reuse and Extensibility

A direct advantage of an inside-outside object approach is that it encourages both code reuse and extensibility. This is a result of having all interactions between objects centered on the outside interface and hiding all implementation details within the object's inside.

For example consider the object shown in Figure 12-21. Here, any of the two object's operations can be activated by correctly stimulating either the circle or square on the outside. In practice the stimulation is simply a method call. We have used a circle and square to emphasize that two different methods are provided for outside use. In our card deck example, activation of one method might produce a shuffled deck, while activation of the other method might result in a card suit and pip value being returned from the object.

Now assume that we want to alter the implementation of an existing operation or add more functionality to our object. *As long as the existing outside interface is maintained, the internal implementation of any and all operations can be changed without the user ever being aware that a change took place.* This is a result of encapsulating the attribute data and operations within an object.

Figure 12-21

Using an Object's Interface

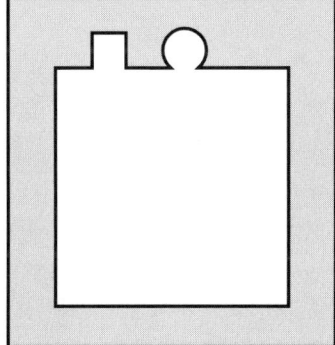

In addition, as long as the interface to existing operations is not changed, new operations can be added as they are needed. From the outside world, it looks like all that is being added is another function call accessing the inside attributes and modifying them in a new way.

Lab Exercises For Part III

Lab 13: Circles

Topics: Shapes

Reading: Chapters 5 and 11

Description: For this lab you will construct a set of circles of various colors, and keep track of some statistics on the circles drawn. The bulk of the code is attached to the Add Circle button shown in the figure below.

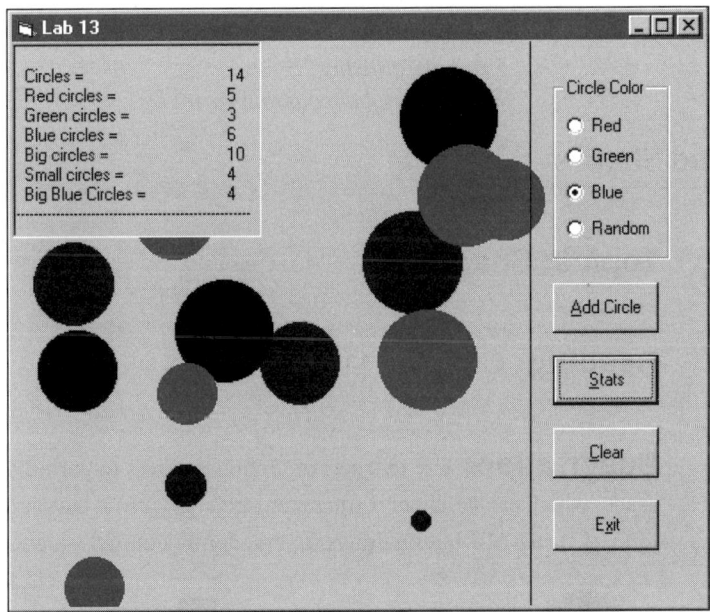

Requirements: You will need to understand the following things to do this lab:

1. The **If-Then-Else** statement;
2. The **Circle** method, including the **FillColor** and **FillStyle** properties;
3. Form Level variables (to keep track of the circles drawn) declared in the (**General**) **Declarations** section;
4. The **Cls** method; and
5. The **Rnd** function.

A working version of this program, named lab13.exe, is contained on the disc enclosed within the text.

Statistics: You are required to keep track of the seven statistical categories shown in the figure for this lab.. For this exercise, a big circle is defined as any circle having a radius greater than 300. All circles drawn on the form should have a randomly set radius assigned by the statement

```
radius = (Int(Rnd * 5) + 1) * 100
```

Hints:

1. The form level variable declarations should appear as follows:
   ```
   Dim totalcircles as Integer
   Dim numred as Integer
   Dim numbigblue as Integer
   ```

2. The algorithm for the <u>A</u>dd Circle button is
   Generate a random radius value
   Assign the circle's color
   Save the circle size and color into the global counting variables
   Generate a random position and draw the circle

3. The algorithm for the <u>C</u>lear button is
   Clear the form
   Reset the global counting variables

4. The algorithm for the <u>S</u>tats button is
   Clear the form
   Print the statistics
   Reset the global counting variables

Lab 14: Colors and Shapes

Topics: Shapes

Reading: Chapter 11

Description: Use two sets of Option controls to permit a user to select a color and a shape, which can be either a square or circle. A <u>D</u>raw button then draws the shape on the form. A Draw 10 button draws five randomly colored squares and five randomly colored

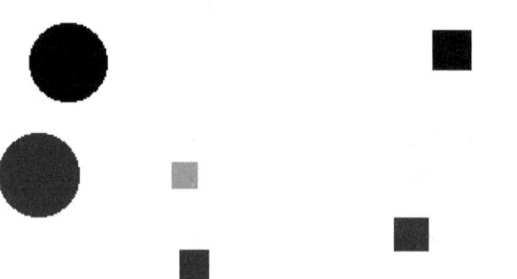

circles on the form. A working version of this program, named lab14.exe, is contained on the disc enclosed witin the text.

Extra Challenge:

Use a Combo box (described in Appendix D) to select a shape and a Combo box to select a color.

Appendix A: Keywords ▬▬▬▬▬▬▬▬▬▬▬▬▬▬▬▬

Abs	DoEvents	IsObject	Return
And	Double	Lbound	Rnd
Array	Else	Lcase	Second
Asc	End	Let	Seek
Atn	EOF	Like	Select Case
Beep	Eqv	Line Input #	Sin
Boolean	Erase	LOF	Single
Byte	Err	Log	Sqn
Call	Error	Long	Sqr
CBool	Exit	Loop	Static
Cbyte	Exp	Me	Static
Ccur	FileLen	Minute	Stop
Cdate	Fix	Month	Str
CDbl	For	New	String
Cdec	For Each	Next	Sub
Choose	Format	Not	Switch
Chr	Function	Now	Tab
Cint	Get	Object	Tan
Clear	GoSub	Oct	Then
Clng	GoTo	On	Time
Close	Hex	On Error	Timer
Const	Hour	Open	TimeSerial
Cos	If	Option Base	TimeValue
CSng	Imp	Option Explicit	TypeName
CStr	Input	Or	Ubound
Currency	Input #	Print	Ucase
CVErr	Int	Print #	Val
Date	Integer	Private	Variant
DateAdd	Is	Property Get	VarType
DateDiff	IsArray	Property Let	Weekday
DatePart	IsDate	Property Set	Wend
DateSerial	IsEmpty	Public	While
DateValue	IsError	Put	With
Day	IsError	Raise	Write #
Deftype	IsMissing	Randomize	Xor
Dim	IsNull	ReDim	Year
Do	IsNumeric	Reset	

Appendix B: Standard Control Object Prefixes

Control	Prefix	Example
Form	frm	frmMain
Check box	chk	chkOpenFile
Combo box	cbo	cboFileName
Data-bound combo box	dbc	dbcRecord
Command button	cmd	cmdAverage
Data	dat	datCompany
Directory list box	dir	dirSelect
Drive list box	drv	drvChoice
File list box	fil	filName
Frame	fra	fraCity
Grid	grd	grdSalary
Data-bound grid	dbg	dbgSalary
Horizontal scroll bar	hsb	hsbColor
Image	img	imgBfly
Label	lbl	lblGrade
Line	lin	linStraight
List box	lst	lstPhones
Data-bound list box	dbl	dblPhones
Menu	mnu	mnuChoices
Ole container	ole	oleObject
Option button	opt	optChannel
Picture box	pic	picBfly
Shape	shp	shpSquare
Test box	txt	txtGrade
Timer	tmr	tmrDelay
Vertical scroll bar	vsb	vsbColor

Appendix C: Supported ANSI Character Set

Value	Symbol	Value	Symbol	Value	Symbol	Value	Symbol
0	**	32	(space)	64	@	96	'
1	**	33	!	65	A	97	a
2	**	34	"	66	B	98	b
3	**	35	#	67	C	99	c
4	**	36	$	68	D	100	d
5	**	37	%	69	E	101	e
6	**	38	&	70	F	102	f
7	**	39	'	71	G	103	g
8	***	40	(	72	H	104	h
9	***	41	)	73	I	105	i
10	***	42	*	74	J	106	j
11	**	43	+	75	K	107	k
12	**	44	,	76	L	108	l
13	***	45	-	77	M	109	m
14	**	46	.	78	N	110	n
15	**	47	/	79	O	111	o
16	**	48	0	80	P	112	p
17	**	49	1	81	Q	113	q
18	**	50	2	82	R	114	r
19	**	51	3	83	S	115	s
20	**	52	4	84	T	116	t
21	**	53	5	85	U	117	u
22	**	54	6	86	V	118	v
23	**	55	7	87	W	119	w
24	**	56	8	88	X	120	x
25	**	57	9	89	Y	121	y
26	**	58	:	90	Z	122	z
27	**	59	;	91	[	123	{
28	**	60	<	92	\	124		
29	**	61	=	93	]	125	}
30	**	62	>	94	^	126	~
31	**	63	?	95	_	127	**

**   These characters are not supported by Microsoft Windows.

* *   Values 8, 9, 10, and 13 convert to a backspace, tab, linefeed, and carriage return character, respectively.

Value	Symbol	Value	Symbol	Value	Symbol	Value	Symbol
128	**	160	(space)	192	À	224	à
129	**	161	¡	193	Á	225	á
130	**	162	¢	194	Â	226	â
131	**	163	£	195	Ã	227	ã
132	**	164	¤	196	Ä	228	ä
133	**	165	¥	197	Å	229	å
134	**	166	¦	198	Æ	230	æ
135	**	167	§	199	Ç	231	ç
136	**	168	¨	200	È	232	è
137	**	169	©	201	É	233	é
138	**	170	ª	202	Ê	234	ê
139	**	171	«	203	Ë	235	ë
140	**	172	¬	204	Ì	236	ì
141	**	173	–	205	Í	237	í
142	**	174	®	206	Î	238	î
143	**	175	¯	207	Ï	239	ï
144	**	176	°	208	_	240	
145	'	177	±	209	Ñ	241	ñ
146	'	178	2	210	Ò	242	ò
147	**	179	3	211	Ó	243	ó
148	**	180	´	212	Ô	244	ô
149	**	181	µ	213	Õ	245	õ
150	**	182	¶	214	Ö	246	ö
151	**	183	·	215	x	247	÷
152	**	184	,	216	Ø	248	ø
153	**	185	1	217	Ù	249	ù
154	**	186	º	218	Ú	250	ú
155	**	187	»	219	Û	251	û
156	**	188	_	220	Ü	252	ü
157	**	189	_	221	Y	253	y
158	**	190	_	222	_	254	_
159	**	191	¿	223	ß	255	ÿ

**   These characters are not supported by Microsoft Windows.

Appendix D: Additional Controls ▬▬▬▬▬▬▬▬▬▬▬▬▬▬▬▬▬▬▬

In this appendix we present two of the remaining three controls provided in the standard Toolbox that have not been previously described: the List box and Combo box. The third control, which is the OLE container control, is presented in Appendix F.

If we categorize the standard Toolbox controls into two tiers, the controls presented in Part I (Command button, Text box, Label control, etc.) would be classified as tier one controls, because the vast majority of Visual Basic applications use them. Using this categorization, the remaining controls, including the List and Combo boxes, would be placed within the second tier of controls, in that they are extremely useful and important controls, but are not as widely or commonly used as the tier one controls.

The List Box Control

Figure D-1

The List Box Control

The List box control, whose Toolbox icon is shown in Figure D-1, is extremely useful for presenting a small list of items, such as might be obtained from a file, array, or user-input. At design time, the properties commonly set for a List box by programmers are those listed in Table D-1.

Table D-1

Property Name	Value(s)	Description
Columns	0 (default)	Single column with vertical scrolling.
	1	Single column with horizontal scrolling.
	>1	Multi-column with horizontal scrolling.
Sorted	True	Items are added in alphabetical order.
	False (default)	Items are not added in alphabetical order.
MultiSelect	0 (default)	Only a single item in the box can be highlighted.
	1	A Mouse click or Spacebar selects and deselects additional items in the box.
	2	The selection and deselection of items in the box can be made using a Shift+Click or Shift+arrow keys. In addition, a Ctrl+Click selects and deselects list items.

Table D-2 Commonly Used Run-Time List Box Properties

Property Name	Description
List	A string array in which each element is a list item.
ListIndex	The integer index value of the currently selected item.
ListCount	The number of items in the list.
Selected	The Boolean value (True or False) indicating if an item is selected.
Text	The value of the currently highlighted item.

At run-time, List boxes provide a number of additional properties that are not available at design-time. The most useful of these run-time properties are listed in Table D-2. For example, if we have a List box named lstItem, the value of the expression lstItem.ListCount is the number of items in the current list.

Within a List box, each item is uniquely identified by an integer index value ranging from 0, which corresponds to the first list item, to the value ListCount–1, which corresponds to the last list item. Thus, for a List box named lstItem, the value of the property

```
lstItem.List(lstItem.ListIndex)
```

is the item currently highlighted in the List box. As an alternative, this value can also be referenced as

```
lstItem.Text
```

Finally, a List box provides a number of methods, the most commonly used of which are listed in Table D-3.

Table D-3 Commonly Used List Box Methods

Method	Description
AddItem	Add an item to the list displayed in the List box.
RemoveItem	Remove an item from the list displayed in the List box.
Clear	Remove all items from the list displayed in the List box.
NewIndex	The index value of the most recently added item.

The general syntax for adding an item to a list is

> *ListBox-Name.***AddItem** *string*

For example, if we have a List box named lstItem and a Text box named txtItem, the statement

```
lstItem.AddItem txtItem.Text
```

causes the string contained in the Text box to be added to the list displayed in the List box. If the List box's **Sorted** property is **True**, the added item is inserted in alphabetical order within the existing list; otherwise, the item is appended to the end of the list. In a similar manner the general syntax for removing an item from the list is

> *ListBox-Name.***RemoveItem** *index-number*

For example, the statement

```
lstItem.RemoveItem lstItem.ListIndex
```

causes the currently highlighted value in the list to be removed. Finally, the general syntax required to clear the list of all items is

> *ListBox-Name.***Clear**

Figure D-2

Program D-1's
Design Time Interface

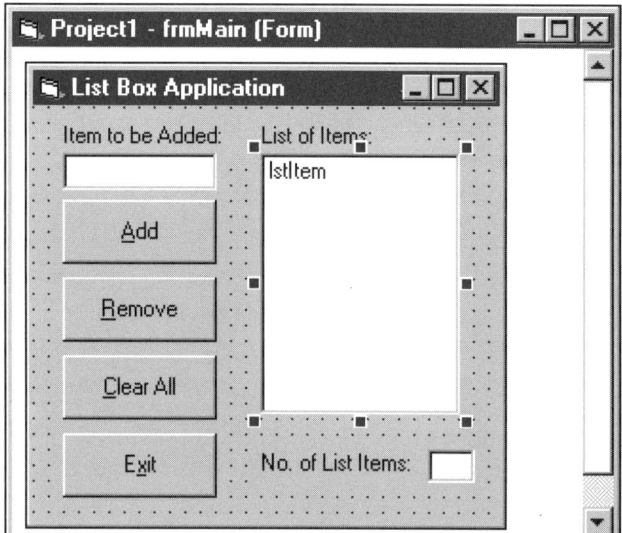

Thus, the statement `lstItem.Clear` would cause all items in the List box named `lstItem` to be removed, which would also set the value of `lstItem.ListCount` to 0.

Program D-1, whose design-time interface is shown in Figure D-2, illustrates a typical list handling application.

Table D-4 Program D_1's Properties Table

Object	Property	Setting
Form	Name	frmMain
	Caption	List Box Application
List Box	Name	lstIem
	Sorted	True
Text Box	Name	txtItem
	Text	(Blank)
Picture Box	Name	picItem
	TabStop	False
Command Button	Name	cmdAdd
	Caption	&Add
	TabStop	False
Command Button	Name	cmdRemove
	Caption	&Remove
	TabStop	False
Command Button	Name	cmdlear
	Caption	&Clear All
	TabStop	False
Command Button	Name	cmdExit
	Caption	E&xit
	TabStop	False

Program D-1's Event Code

```
Private Sub Form_Load()
  lstItem.AddItem "Zebra"
  lstItem.AddItem "Lion"
  lstItem.AddItem "Antelope"
  lstItem.AddItem "Monkey"
  lstItem.AddItem "Dog"
  lstItem.AddItem "Cat"
  picItem.Print lstItem.ListCount
  picItem.Refresh
End Sub

Private Sub cmdAdd_Click()
 If Len(txtItem.Text) > 0 Then
   lstItem.AddItem txtItem.Text
   txtItem.Text = ""    ' Clear text box
   txtItem.SetFocus
   picItem.Cls
   picItem.Print lstItem.ListCount
   picItem.Refresh
  Else
    Beep
  End If
End Sub

Private Sub cmdRemove_Click()
  Dim itemno As Integer

  itemno = lstItem.ListIndex
  If itemno >= 0 Then
    lstItem.RemoveItem itemno
    picItem.Cls
    picItem.Print lstItem.ListCount
    picItem.Refresh
  Else
    Beep
  End If
  txtItem.SetFocus
End Sub

Private Sub cmdClear_Click()
  lstItem.Clear
  txtItem.SetFocus
  picItem.Cls
  picItem.Print lstItem.ListCount
  picItem.Refresh
End Sub

Private Sub cmdExit_Click()
  Beep
  End
End Sub
```

Except for the `cmdExit_Click()` event, which we have used throughout the text, the remaining event procedures use methods and properties specifically applicable to List boxes. The first event procedure, which is the `Form_Load` event code, uses the **AddItem** method to

Figure D-3

Program D-1's Initial Run Time Interface

initialize the list. As a List box's contents cannot be set at design time, the `Form_Load` event is typically used to initialize a list, as is done in Program D-1. Since the List box's **Sorted** property was set to **True** at design time, the list will appear in the alphabetical order shown in Figure D-3. Notice also that the count displayed in the picture box is obtained using the **ListCount** property's value.

The `cmdAdd_Click` event procedure first determines that the Text box contains a string by checking for a string length greater than zero. If such a string is present in the Text box it is added to the list, and the new **ListCount** value is displayed. In a similar manner, the `cmdRemove_Click` event procedure first determines that an item has actually been selected from the list before the **RemoveItem** method is invoked. Finally, the `cmdClear_Click` event procedure invokes the **Clear** method to clear all items from the list. In each of these event codes the focus is reset back to the Text box in preparation for another item to be added to the list.

The Combo Box Control

A Combo box control can be considered as a List box control that includes a Text box.

Figure D-4

The Combo Box Control

Therefore, you should be familiar with the List box control as a prerequisite to reading this section. The difference in usage between the List box and Combo box is that a List box should be used when the list of choices presented to a user is to be limited, while a Combo box, with one exception, should be used to provide a list of *suggested* choices, to which the user can enter an item that is not on the list.

Additionally, since the list of choices presented in a Combo box is, with one exception, only displayed as a drop down list when the user clicks on the box's down-facing arrowhead, a Combo box can save a considerable amount of space on a form. Figure D-5 illustrates the three available types of Combo boxes, each of which is described in Table D-5.

Figure D-5

The Three Types of Comb Boxes as They Appear at Design Time

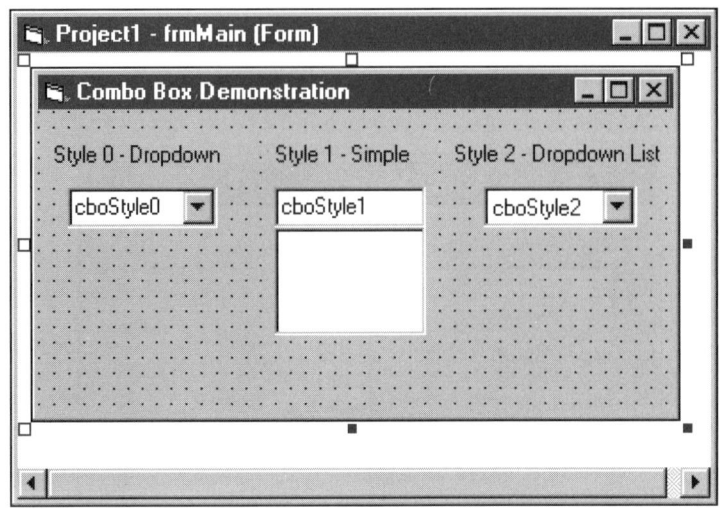

Table D-5 Available Combo Box Types

Type	Name	Description
Style 0	Drop-down Combo Box	By either clicking on the down-facing arrowhead of pressing the Alt + Down Arrow when the box has the focus, a Text box and a drop-down list is presented. A user can enter an item in the Text box by either selecting it from the list or by directly typing into the Text box. The entered item does not have to be in the list.
Style 1	Simple	The complete list is displayed at run-time only if the box has been made large enough at design-time; otherwise, a vertical scroll bar is automatically displayed. As with the Style 0 box, an item can be entered in the Text box by either selecting it from the list or by directly typing into the Text box. The entered item does not have to be in the list.
Style 2	Drop-down List Box	This is essentially a List box, whose items are displayed only when the down-facing arrow is clicked. As such, a user can not type into the Text box, but can only select an item in the list.

Like a List box, all three Combo box types have a **Sorted** property and **AddItem** and **RemoveItem** methods for adding and removing items from the list. Additionally, there is a **Style** property for setting the Combo box's type. For example, assuming the three Combo boxes shown in Figure D-5 are named cboStyle0, cboStyle1, and cboStyle2, respectively, the following Form_Load event code can be used to create the same list for each box.

Introduction to Visual Basic

```
Private Sub Form_Load()
  cboStyle0.Text = ""
  cboStyle0.AddItem "Zebra"
  cboStyle0.AddItem "Lion"
  cboStyle0.AddItem "Antelope"
  cboStyle1.Text = ""
  cboStyle1.AddItem "Zebra"
  cboStyle1.AddItem "Lion"
  cboStyle1.AddItem "Antelope"
  cboStyle2.AddItem "Zebra"
  cboStyle2.AddItem "Lion"
  cboStyle2.AddItem "Antelope"
End Sub
```

Assuming that the **Sorted** property for each box has been set to **True**, Figure D-6 shows how each Combo box appears at run-time. As is seen in this figure, the lists *do not* initially appear in either the Style 0 and Style 2 boxes; the lists will appear in these boxes when the down-facing arrows are clicked. Note, however, that the Style 1 box is the exception to this drop-down format. The list appears in a Style 1 Combo box as it would in a normal List box, and in this case is in alphabetical order because the **Sorted** property has been set to **True**.

Figure D-6

The Combo Boxes at Run-Time

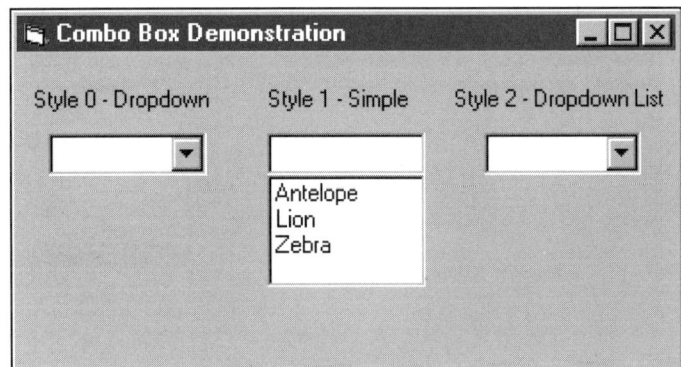

Figure D-7 shows how the list appears when the down arrow is clicked on the Style 0 Combo box. If a user clicks on any item in the list, the selected item will automatically appear in the Text box; alternatively, any item, whether it is in the list or not, can be directly typed into the Text box.

Figure D-7

Activation of the Style 0 Combo Box

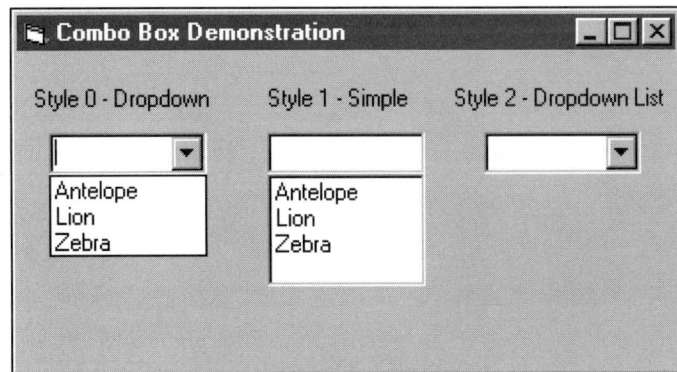

Figure D-8 shows what happens when an item in the Style 1 Combo box is selected. As shown, the selected item is automatically displayed in the Text box. As with the Style 0 box, a user can also enter any item, whether it is in the list or not, directly into the Text box.

Figure D-8

Selection of a Style 1 List Item

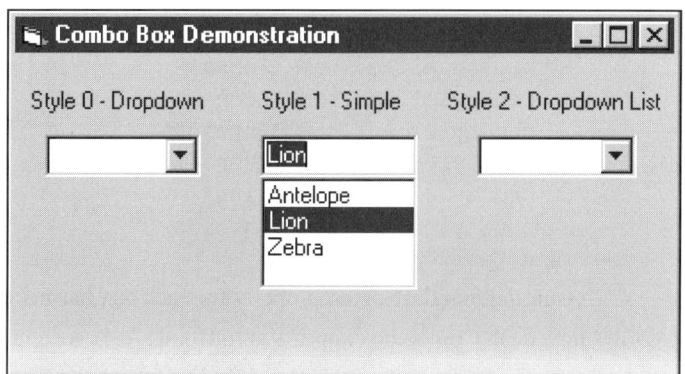

Finally, Figure D-9 shows the selection of an item from an activated Style 2 list. As with Style 0, this list is activated by clicking on the down-facing arrowhead. Unlike the Style 0 list, however, a user may not type into the Text box because only items in the list can be selected. Thus, a Style 2 Combo box is effectively a List box presented as a drop-down list.

Figure D-9

Selection of a Style 2 List Item

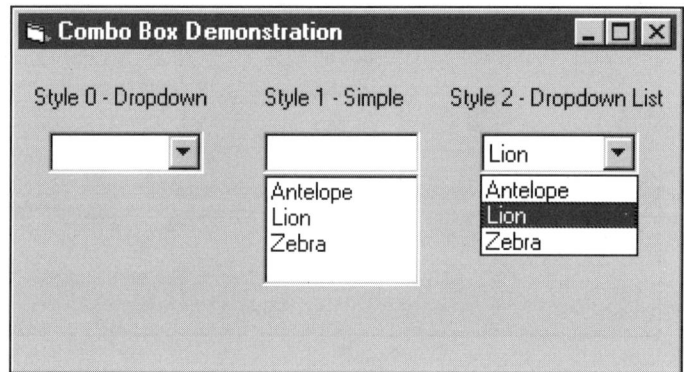

Introduction to Visual Basic

Appendix E: MsgBox Constants ▬▬▬▬▬▬▬▬▬▬▬

Table E.1 MsgBox Arguments

Constant	Value	Description
vbOKOnly	0	Display OK button only (default).
vbOKCancel	1	Display OK and Cancel buttons.
vbAbortRetryIgnore	2	Display Abort, Retry, and Ignore buttons.
vbYesNoCancel	3	Display Yes, No, and Cancel buttons.
vbYesNo	4	Display Yes and No buttons.
vbRetryCancel	5	Display Retry and Cancel buttons.
vbCritical	16	Display Critical image.
vbQuestion	32	Display query image.
vbExclamation	48	Display Exclamation image.
vbInformation	64	Display Information image.
vbDefaultButton1	0	The first button is the default (default).
vbDefaultButton2	256	The second button is the default.
vbDefaultButton3	512	The third button is the default.
vbApplicationModal	0	Present an application modal message box **(default).**
vbSystemModal	4096	Present a system modal message box.

Table E.2 MsgBox Return Values

Constant	Value	Description
vbOK	1	The OK button was pressed.
vbCancel	2	The Cancel button was pressed.
vbAbort	3	The Abort button was pressed.
vbRetry	4	The Retry button was pressed.
vbIgnore	5	The Ignore button was pressed.
vbYes	6	The Yes button was pressed.
vbNo	7	The No button was pressed.

Appendix F: OLE and ActiveX ▬▬▬▬▬▬▬▬▬▬

Prior to Version 5.0, the term OLE, which is an acronym for Object Linking and Embedding, was used in the following three related, but distinct contexts:

1. OLE Container Control - this is the control found on the standard Toolbox, which is sometimes simply referred to as the OLE Control. This control is used to either embed or link an object from another application, such as an Excel spreadsheet, into a Visual Basic application. A Visual Basic application that uses this control is referred to as a *container application*[1] . In Version 5.0 the term OLE retains this same meaning.

2. OLE Custom Controls - these are controls that are not part of the standard Toolbox's built-in controls, but are stored as separate files having either a .vbx or .ocx filename extension. A number of these controls come with Visual Basic and additional custom controls can either be purchased as third-party controls or created from within Visual Basic.[2] Custom controls can be added to the standard Toolbox using the procedure described later in this section. In Version 5.0 these custom controls have become, and are now known as, ActiveX controls.

3. OLE Automation - this defines a process in which an object is shared between client and server applications. Specifically, a Visual Basic application, which is known as the *client* application, is permitted to create objects from, and use methods that are part of another application's class. The class definition is contained within a second Visual Basic application known as the *server* application. The server application can either be an OLE DLL, which becomes dynamically linked to the client application, or an OLE EXE, which is a separate executable program. In Version 5.0 OLE DLLs are known as ActiveX DLLs and OLE EXEs are known as ActiveX EXEs.

Thus, in Version 5.0, the term ActiveX refers to a set of components that previously where referred to as OLE custom controls and OLE automation. Additionally, with Version 5.0, ActiveX components also include a new set of components, referred to as ActiveX documents. These documents are Visual Basic applications for the Internet, and exist in both DLL and EXE forms.

At its most fundamental level, an ActiveX component, be it a control, DLL, EXE, DLL document, or EXE document is simply a unit of executable code that can be created or purchased. All such components can be used and extended by any programming environment that supports the ActiveX specification. This means that an ActiveX component created in Visual Basic, for example, can be used and extended within a C++ environment that supports the ActiveX technology. In the remaining sections of this appendix we expand on the three types of OLE and ActiveX uses listed above.

---

[1] More formally, a container application is one that can display another application's objects.

[2] The Learning, Professional, and Enterprise editions provide eight, twenty, and twenty-one custom controls, respectively.

Using the OLE Container Control

The OLE container control, which is shown on Figure F-1, permits you to either link or embed an object into your current Visual Basic application. For example, suppose you have an existing Excel spreadsheet that you want to include within a Visual Basic application. If you link this spreadsheet into your application, both your application and Excel can access and modify the spreadsheet's data. What happens here is that *only one copy* of the spreadsheet is saved, and both applications can retrieve, modify, and save the file. From an operational viewpoint, the Visual Basic application contains a placeholder, or reference to

Figure F-1

The OLE Container Control

the spreadsheet. When you double click on the Visual Basic OLE control from within a running Visual Basic application, Excel is activated. In this context Excel becomes a server application running as an OLE EXE, while your Visual Basic application becomes the client application. Linking is extremely useful in maintaining one set of data that can be accessed from several applications.

In contrast to linking, you can tell the OLE container control to embed an object, such as a spreadsheet. In this case, an actual copy, or image, of the spreadsheet is stored as part of your application. Here, no other application has access to the data in the embedded object. As you might imagine, embedded objects can greatly increase the size of your Visual Basic files.

When you add an OLE control to your Visual Basic application, the OLE Dialog window shown in Figure F-2 will appear (you can always activate this dialog by clicking the right mouse button when the container control is active). As shown in Figure F-2, we have selected a Microsoft Excel Spreadsheet as the Object Type. By clicking the Create From File radio button, the dialog shown in Figure F-3 will appear.[3]

Figure F-2

The Initial OLE Container Dialog

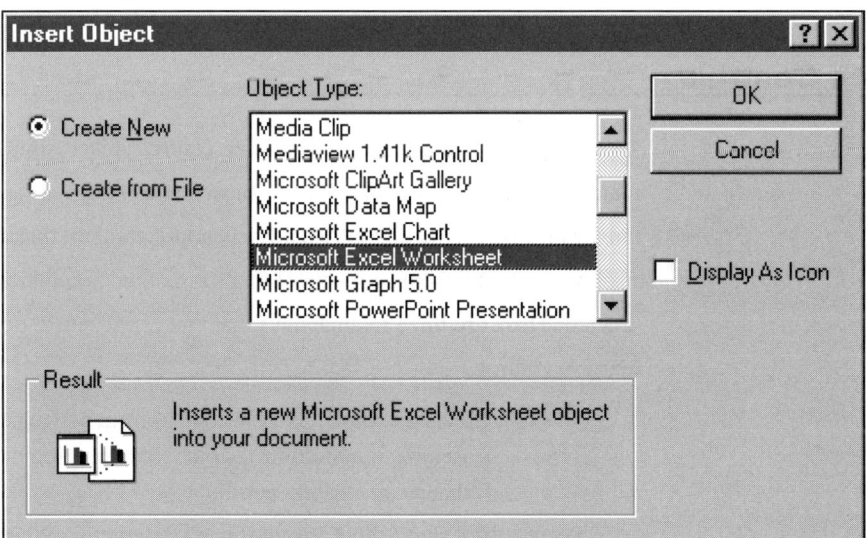

---

3 To have the application create a new spreadsheet, and not use an existing one, you would click the Create New Option Button. This creates an embedded file automatically.

Figure F-3

Selecting an Existing SpreadSheet

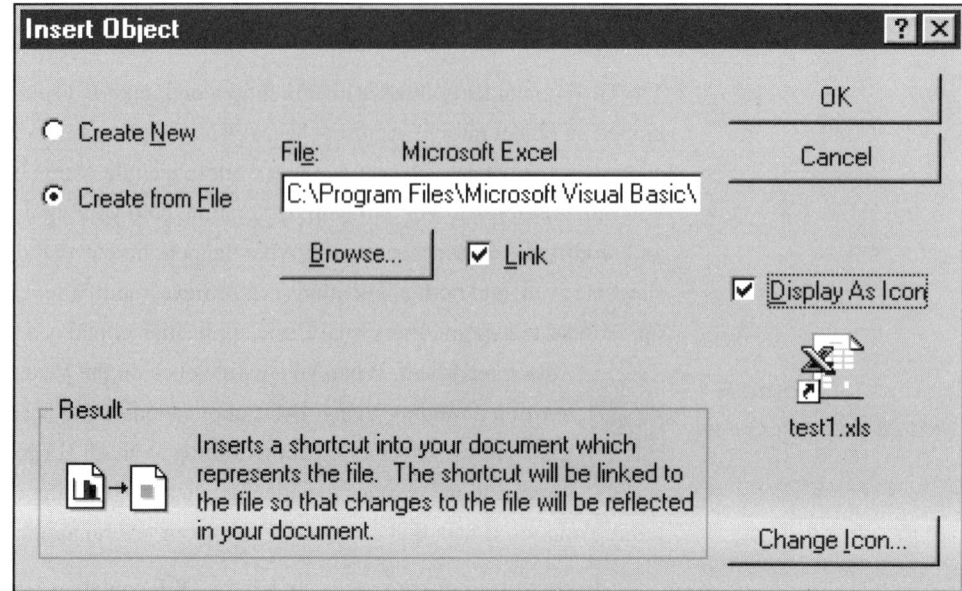

In Figure F-3 we have designated the spreadsheet with the full path name `C:\Program File\Microsoft Visual Basic\test1.xls` and also checked the <u>D</u>isplay As Icon Check box. Checking this box means that an icon of Excel will appear in the OLE container control rather than the spreadsheet. To activate the spreadsheet at run-time, the user simply double-clicks the icon rather than double-clicking a displayed portion of the spreadsheet. Finally, notice that <u>L</u>ink Check box has been checked. This creates the spreadsheet as a linked object; if this box is not checked the spreadsheet would be inserted as an embedded object.

ActiveX Controls

An ActiveX control is simply an external control object, similar in function to the built-in controls found in the standard Visual Basic Toolbox. Creating an ActiveX control involves a similar process as creating a Visual Basic application, in that a UserControl object is displayed, which is almost identical to a form object, on which the control is then constructed. There are three related ways that this UserControl object can be used to create an ActiveX control:

- Create a completely new control from scratch.
- Assemble a new control from a combination of existing controls.
- Enhance an existing control.

Section 10.8 shows how Visual Basic's Interactive Wizard can be used to assemble a new control from existing controls. When you want to use an existing ActiveX control in an application, you must first add the control to the Toolbox. This is accomplished by first

Figure F-4

The Components Dialog Box

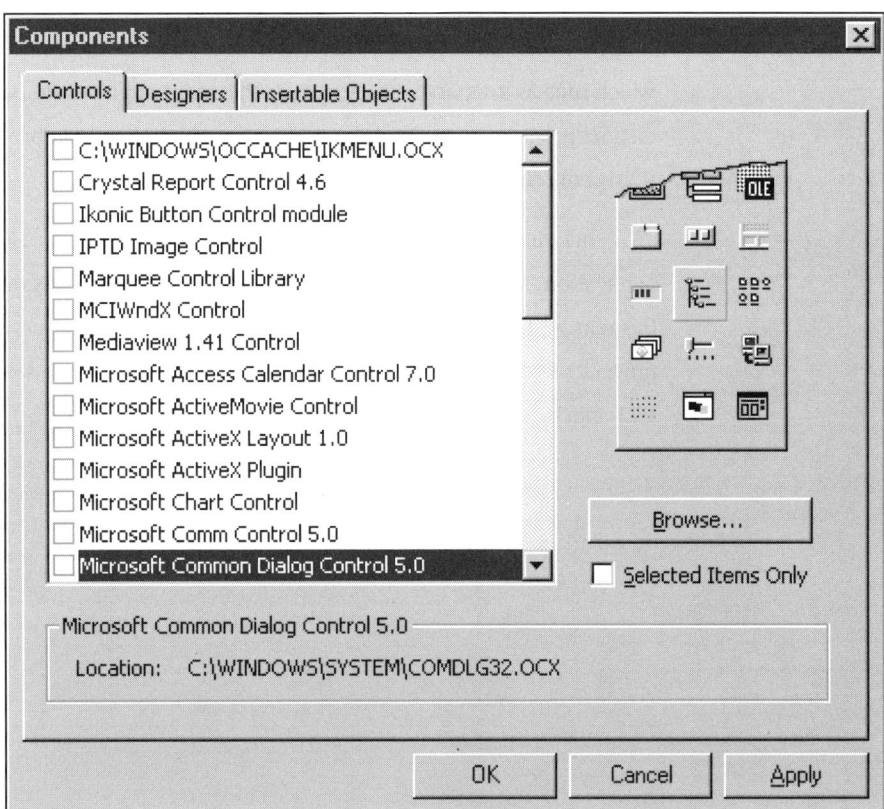

selecting the Components item from the Projects menu, which will bring up the Components dialog box shown in Figure F-4. To add an ActiveX control from the displayed list, select the Check box to the left of the desired control's name. When the OK Command button is subsequently clicked, all of the selected controls will appear in the Toolbox.

ActiveX DLLs and EXEs

Prior to Version 5.0, the term OLE automation was used to describe the process whereby one application, referred to as the *client application,* both accessed objects created from another application's class, and used methods and properties of the defining class. In Version 5.0 the term ActiveX has replaced the phrase OLE Automation; however, the underlying operation implied by both terms is identical.

The application that provides the objects, methods, and properties used by the client application is referred to as a *server application*, or server, for short. Servers come in two varieties, as dynamic linked libraries, which are referred to as DLLs, or as stand-alone executable programs, which are referred to as EXEs. The differences in these two types of programs is how they link with a client application.

An ActiveX EXE always runs as a separate process from the client application that uses it. For example, the spreadsheet program Excel is an ActiveX EXE. This means that another program, the client program, can effectively make a call to Excel to manipulate a linked spreadsheet object. When this is done, an executing version of Excel is initiated, which runs as a separate process from the client application. Because they execute as a distinct program, outside of the process in which the client program is executing, ActiveX EXEs are referred to as *out-of-process* servers.

In contrast to EXE servers, an ActiveX DLL becomes dynamically linked into a client application, so that the DLL runs within the same process as the client during run-time. For this reason, DLL's are frequently referred to as *in-process* servers. Since a call to an in-process server does not require the "firing up" of a separate server application, accessing a DLL can be considerably faster than accessing an EXE.

Appendix G: Creating an Executable Application

Once you have completed your program design and development, you can create an executable version of it, including an icon that can be used to launch the program, by selecting the Make Project.exe... submenu item from the File menu. Using this selection will provide you with the dialog shown in Figure G-1. The Save in: box shown in this figure is where you enter the directory folder in which the executable version of the program will be created and saved. As with all Save-In dialog boxes, you can use the arrow provided in the dialog to display a drop-down list, and select a storage folder by navigating through the list.

Figure G-1

Creating an Executable File

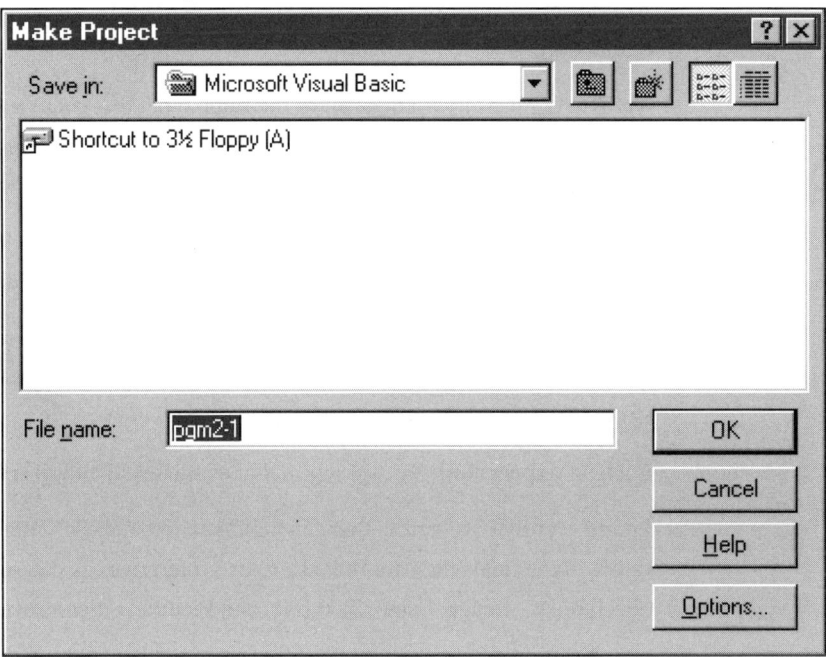

Appendix H: Glossary

Accelerator key: Any key sequence that initiates an action by pressing the [Alt] key and a designated letter. An accelerator key is created by preceding the designated letter with an ampersand (&) in an object's **Caption** property. Also referred to as a hot-key sequence.

Access key: Any key sequence that permits a user to open a menu or shift focus to a control by pressing the [Alt] key and a designated letter. The access key is always underlined.

Application: A collection of visual objects and procedural code that constitutes a complete program. Synonymous with the terms *program* and *project.*

Argument: A value or expression that is passed into a subprogram (subroutine, procedure, or function).

Array: A group of variables, all of the same type, that share a common name. Individual variables that comprise the array are referred to as array elements. Each array element is distinguished from another by its position in the array, which is designated by an integer value known as an index number.

Bitmap: A rectangular arrangement of dots, arranged to make a picture. Also referred to as a raster.

Bookmark: A system-generated string identifying the current record contained in a RecordSet object's Bookmark property.

Boolean expression: An expression that evaluates to either **True** or **False**.

Bound Controls: Controls that can be linked to database fields and are used to display the values in the fields they are linked to. Also referred to as data-aware controls, they include Check boxes, Image, Label, Text box, and Picture box controls.

Break Mode: Temporary suspension of program execution in the development environment. In Break mode, you can examine, debug, reset, step through, or continue program execution. You enter Break mode when you

- Encounter a break point during program execution;
- Press [Ctrl] + [Break] during program execution;
- Encounter a **Stop** statement or run-time error during program execution;
- Add a **Break When True** watch expression. Execution stops when the value of the watch changes and evaluates to **True**; or
- Add a **Break When Changed** watch expression. Execution stops when the value of the watch changes.

Breakpoint: A selected program line at which execution automatically stops. Breakpoints are not saved with your code.

Built-in: A data type, object type, function, or subroutine that comes with the Visual Basic language. Built-in data types are also referred to as primitive types.

Call: A request to execute a procedure. When the procedure is completed, control returns to the statement immediately following the statement making the call.

Call Stack Dialog: Lists the procedure calls in an application that have been started but are not yet completed. Available only in Break mode.

Check Box: A control that permits a user to make one or more selections by placing a check mark next to the desired item.

Code: Procedural instructions that are used to produce a result.

Code window: The window in which code is written and displayed.

Collection: An object that contains a set of related objects. An object's position in the collection can change whenever a change occurs in the collection; therefore, the position of any specific object in the collection may vary.

Combo box control: A control that is a combination of a List box and Text box control.

Command button: A control that is used to initiate an event procedure when it is clicked.

Comment: A remark used to document code. A comment is designated by the keyword **Rem** placed at the start of a line, or any text placed after an apostrophe. Remarks are non-executable code.

Compile time: The period during which source code is translated to executable code.

Control: An object that can be placed on a form with its own set of recognized properties, methods, and events. Controls are used to receive user input, display output, and trigger event procedures. Most controls can be manipulated using methods. In addition, some controls are interactive, which means that they are responsive to user actions, while other controls are static, which means that they are accessible only through code.

Control Array: A group of controls that share a common name, type, and common event procedures. Each control in the array has a unique index number that can be used to determine which control recognizes an event.

Copy Buffer: A location created by the Microsoft Jet database engine for the contents of a record that is open for editing. The Edit method copies the current record to the copy buffer; the AddNew method clears the buffer for a new record and sets all default values; and the Update method saves the data from the copy buffer to the database, replacing the current record or inserting the new record. Any statement that resets or moves the current record pointer, such as the MoveNext method, discards the copy buffer's contents.

Constant: A value that cannot change during program execution. It can be either a string constant, a number, or a symbolic constant.

Current record: The record in a RecordSet that is available for modification or examination. The Move methods can be used to reposition the current record in a RecordSet. In addition, for dynaset- or snapshot-type RecordSets, the Find methods may be used. For table-type Recordsets, the Seek method can be used.

Data Control: A control that incorporates the Microsoft Jet engine for accessing databases and is used to view database records in connection with bound controls.

Data Type: The characteristic of a variable that determines what kind of data it can hold. Data types include Byte, Boolean, Integer, Long, Currency, Single, Double, Date, String, Object, Variant (the default), and user-defined types, as well as specific types of objects.

Debug: To locate and eliminate errors in a program.

Declaration statement: A statement used to declare variables and constants.

Design-time: The time during which an application is constructed within the development environment by adding controls, setting control or form properties, and so on.

Development Environment: A set of software, presented as a unified environment, in which the software developer can efficiently work. Microsoft Visual Basic is an example of a development environment.

Dialog box: A box that requests user input. A modal dialog requires input before an application can continue, while a modeless box permits shifting the focus from the box and allows an application to continue without the box being closed.

Directory List box: A control that displays available directories on the current disk drive.

DLL: Dynamic Link Library; a file having the extension .DLL used to hold procedures that are dynamically linked into an application.

Drive List box: A control that displays available disk drives.

Drop-down: A list that is displayed in a drop-down fashion by either the clicking of a down-facing arrowhead or the action of an accelerator key.

Dynaset: A temporary set of data records selected from one or more database tables.

Embedded Object: An object created in one application and then embedded in a second application. All of the data associated with the embedded object is copied to and contained within the embedding application.

EOF: End-of-file. A condition that evaluates to **True** when the end of a sequential file or the end of a RecordSet object has been reached.

Error trapping: Detecting an error and invoking code when the designated error occurs.

Event: Any user or system action to which an object responds.

Event procedure: A **Sub** procedure that is attached to an object and initiated by an event.

Event Driven Program: A program that executes code based on user- and system-initiated events.

EXE: A stand-alone application that is executed as an individual process. Also refers to controls that are built in to Visual Basic and are displayed in the standard Toolbox.

Expression: A syntactically correct arrangement of constants, variables, operators, functions, and subroutines that evaluates to a single value.

Field: A single item that represents an attribute or entity of a database record.

File List box: A control that displays a list of file names that match the value set in the **Pattern** property.

Focus: The state that defines the currently active control. A control can receive focus by being tabbed to, clicked on, selected by access keys, or designated by program code.

Form: Forms are containers for controls. At run-time, a form becomes either a window or dialog box. Forms can be of two types, MDI or SDI.

Form-level: A variable, declared in the **(General) Declarations** section, that is accessible by all procedures on the form.

Format: The specification for how data will be displayed.

Frame: A control used to contain other controls. Typically used to provide containers for Option button controls in which each Option button group provides a separate set of options.

Function: A general procedure that directly returns a single value.

(General) Declarations section: The section of a code module that is used to declare module-level variables and symbolic constants.

General Procedure: A user-defined procedure that can be either a **Sub** or **Function** procedure.

Graphical User Interface: GUI. The graphical portion of a program that is visually presented to a user for interaction with the procedural code.

Grid control: A control having rows and columns that is used to display data in a similar manner to a spreadsheet.

Handle: A small square on a control that is visible at design-time and can be used to resize the control. Also referred to as a sizing handle.

Horizontal Scroll bar: A control that uses a horizontal scroll bar to set a numerical value. One end of the control corresponds to a minimum value, while the opposite end corresponds to a maximum value.

Image box control: A control used to hold a graphic, text, or other control. Although an Image box supports fewer properties than a Picture box control, it repaints faster and pictures can be stretched to fit the control's size.

Immediate window: A Debug window that is active during Break mode, and can be used to immediately evaluate an expression or determine the value of a variable.

Index: When used with a table-type RecordSet, the current index determines the order is which data records are returned to the RecordSet.

Instant Watch: A debug feature that permits determining the value of an expression or variable.

Key field: One or more combined fields on which records in a database are organized and searched.

Keyword: A word that has a special meaning in Visual Basic. Unrestricted keywords may be used as identifiers, but doing so precludes their use for the feature normally associated with them as keywords. Restricted keywords may only be used for their intended purpose.

Line control: A control that is used to produce a straight line on a Graphical User Interface.

Linked Object: An object created in one application that is linked to a second application. When an object is linked, a reference to the object is inserted into the second application, rather than the actual object. Unlike an embedded object, a linked object's data is stored in and managed by the application that created it.

List box: A control that displays a list of items from which one or more may be selected.

Local scope: The scope of a symbolic constant or variable in which visibility is limited to the declaring procedure.

Logic error: An error that causes an erroneous, unexpected, or unintentional result due to a flaw in the program's logic.

Logical operator: The **And**, **Or**, and **Not** operators used to construct compound relational expressions.

Message box: A dialog box that displays a message and one or more options that must be selected before an application can continue execution.

Method: A procedure that is connected to an object. The method is invoked by providing an object name, followed by a period, followed by the method's name.

Microsoft Jet database engine: A database management system that retrieves data from, and stores data into, user- and system-databases. The Jet engine can be thought of as a data manager component from which other data access systems, such as Visual Basic and Microsoft Access are built.

Modal dialog box: A dialog box that requires input from a user, and must be closed before an application can continue.

Modeless dialog box: A dialog box where focus can be shifted from the box, and one in which an application can continue without the box being closed.

Module: A set of declarations followed by procedures. May be a form module, a code module, or a class module. Each module is stored as a separate file.

Module level: Code and variables that are only available to procedures within the module.

Multiple Document Interface (MDI): An application that can support multiple windows from one application instance. An MDI application consists of a main window that contains internal windows referred to as child windows. The main window and its child windows can all be visible at the same time.

Numeric expression: Any expression that evaluates to a number. Elements of the expression can include keywords, variables, constants, operators, and subroutine calls.

OLE object: Object Linking and Embedding. An object that can be transferred and shared between applications, either by linking or embedding.

One-to-many relationship: An association between two tables in which the primary key value of each record in the primary table corresponds to the value in the matching field or fields of a number of records (or no record) in the related table.

Option button control: A control that permits selection of a single item from a group of items. If additional sets of options are required, a Frame control is used to contain the additional Option controls.

Parameter: A variable used by a procedure whose value is initialized outside of the procedure and transferred to the procedure when the procedure is called.

Pass by Reference: A transfer of data to a procedure in which the procedure has access to the memory location of the argument being passed. This permits the procedure to alter the value of the argument.

Pass by Value: A transfer of data to a procedure in which a copy of an argument's value is passed to the procedure.

Picture box control: A control used to hold a graphic, text, or other control. Although a Picture box supports more properties than an Image box control, it repaints slower and pictures cannot be stretched to fit the control's size.

Primary key: One or more fields whose value or values uniquely identify each record in a table. A table can have only one primary key.

Procedure: A named sequence of statements executed as a unit. **Function**, **Property**, and **Sub** are types of procedures. A procedure name is always defined at the module level. All executable code must be contained in a procedure. Procedures cannot be nested within other procedures.

Procedure template: An empty procedure that consists only of a header line and either an **End Sub** or **End Function** statement.

Project: The collection of elements that constitute an application.

Project window: A window that displays all of the forms, modules, and elements that comprise a project. Also referred to as the Project Resource window.

Property: A named attribute of an object. Properties define object characteristics, such as size, color, screen location, and the state of an object, such as **Enabled** or **Disabled**.

Public scope: The scope that permits a procedure or variable to be called from all project modules.

Quick Watch Dialog: Displays the current value of a variable, property, or watch expression. Only available in Break mode.

Random-access file: A file in which all records are fixed-length, and records may be read or written in any order.

Record: A group of related fields.

RecordCount: A method that returns the number of records accessed in a RecordSet.

RecordSet: The current set of records associated with a data control.

Run-time: The time during which a program is executing.

Scope: Defines the availability of a variable, procedure, or object, which is referred to as its visibility. For example, a variable declared as **Public** is available to all procedures in all modules in a project, unless the **Option Private** module is in effect. When the **Option Private** module is in effect, the module itself is private and, therefore, not visible to other projects. Variables declared in a procedure are visible only within the procedure and lose their value between calls unless they are declared as **Static**.

Single Document Interface (SDI): An application that supports a single visible document at a time. SDI applications can contain multiple windows, but only one can be visible at a time.

Sizing handle: A small square on a control that is visible at design-time and can be used to resize the control.

Snapshot: A RecordSet that is read-only and cannot be updated.

SQL statement: An expression that defines a Structured Query Language (SQL) command, such as **Select**, **Update**, or **Delete**, and includes clauses such as **Where** and **Order By**. SQL statements are typically used in queries.

Static variable: A variable whose value is retained between procedure calls.

String expression: Any expression that evaluates to a sequence of contiguous characters. Elements of the expression can include a function that returns a string, a string literal, a string constant, a string variable, a string variant, or a function that returns a string variant.

Sub procedure: A procedure that only returns values through its parameter list.

Symbolic constant: A constant that has been named using the **Const** keyword.

Syntax: The set of rules for formulating grammatically correct language statements.

Text box control: A control used for data entry and display.

Timer control: A control used to automatically execute an event at a specified interval of time.

Toolbar: A set of icons, referred to as buttons, that are used as shortcuts for menu options.

Toolbox: A window containing controls that can be placed on a form at design-time.

Transaction: A series of changes made to a database's data and structure. The beginning of a transaction starts with a **Begin Trans** statement, transaction are committed using a **Commit Trans** statement, and all changes made since the last **Begin Trans** statement can be undone using a **RollBack** statement.

Twip: A unit of measurement that is equivalent to 1/20 of a point and 1/1440 of an inch.

Variable: a named location containing data that can be modified during program execution. Each variable has a name that uniquely identifies it within its scope. Variable names must begin with an alphabetic character, must be unique within the same scope, cannot be longer than 255 characters, and cannot contain an embedded period or type-declaration character. Variables declared in a procedure are visible only within the procedure and lose their value between calls unless they are declared as **Static**.

Vertical Scroll Bar: A control that uses a vertical scroll bar to set a numerical value. One end of the control corresponds to a minimum value, while the opposite end corresponds to a maximum value.

Watch Expression: A user-defined expression that enables observation of a variable's or expression's behavior during program execution. Watch expressions appear in the Watch debug window and are automatically updated when Break mode is entered. The Watch window displays the value of an expression within a given context, and is not saved with a project's code.

Appendix I: Solutions and Source Code

The Solutions and Source Code disk that is packaged with this text contains three files:

```
solution.txt, which is a text file
srcode.zip, which is a compressed file
unzip.exe, which is an executable file
```

Solutions to selected odd-numbered problems are contained in the `solution.txt` text file included on the disk provided with this text. This file may be read, as is, using any of the currently available word-processing programs, such as Word® and WordPerfect®, or by using the DOS `Edit` command.

The source code to all of the programs contained in this text are stored in the file named `srcode.zip`, which is included on the disk provided with this text, and is a compressed file. To uncompress this file, first copy both the `srcode.zip` and `unzip.exe` files, both of which are one the diskette, to your hard disk. Then change directories to the directory where these two files have been copied, and issue the command `unzip srcode`.

For example, assuming that you want the final, uncompressed, source code files to reside in an existing directory named vbprogs on your C drive, and that the diskette is currently on the A drive, the following series of DOS commands can be used:

```
C:>cd  \vbprogs
C:\vbprogs>copy a:srcode.zip
C:\vbprogs> copy a:unzip.exe
C:\vbprogs> unzip srcode
C:\vbprogs> del srcode.exe
C:\vbprogs> del unzip.exe
```

INDEX

A

B

D

E

integer division, 101
integer expression, 101
integer values, 95
integrated development environment (IDE), 41
interactive Do While loops, 223
interactive user input, 139
interface, 530
interface wizard, 473-478
internal sort, 359
interpreted language, 4
interpreter, 4
intersection table, 395
intrinsic functions, 129
invocation, 16
iteration, 213

J

Jet Engine, 378

K

KeyAscii, 191
key field, 377
KeyPress, 191, 199, 265
keyword, 49

L

Label control, 37, 135
languages,
  high-level, 2
  low-level, 2
  object-based, 520
  object-oriented, 5, 520
  procedure-oriented, 4
language element, 28
LBound function, 326
less-than operator (<), 181
less-than-or-equal-to operator (<=), 181
Let procedure, 538
library functions, 518
LineInput function, 448
Line control, 498
Line method, 502
linear search, 358
List box control, 559
ListIndex property, 433
literal data, 158
local variables, 286
LOF function, 451
logic errors, 210

logical operators, 182
  And, 182
  Not, 182
  Or, 182
  precedence of, 183
long integer, 96
loops,
  breaking out of, 230
  Do Until, 228
  Do While, 217
  Do While Not, 228
  For Each, 338
  For/Next, 233
  infinite, 218
  inner, 241
  nested, 241
  outer, 241
  Do Loop Until, 245
  Do Loop While, 246
loop counter, 233
low-level languages, 2
Lower bound function (LBound), 326

M

machine language, 2
magnetic hard disk, 28
maintenance, 12
mathematical recursion, 292
Maximize button, 6
MDI, 36, 41, 367
member of structure, 349
memory unit, 27
Menu bar, 44, 513
menu systems, 510-515
metafile, 487
method(s), 39, 64
microprocessor, 29
Minimize button, 6
mixed-mode expressions, 101
mnemonic, 107
Mod operator, 102
modularity, 19
modules
  class 20
  code, 54
  form, 19
  module-level scope, 286
  module-level variables, 286, 289
  standard, 19
modulus operator(Mod), 102

programming,
object-oriented, 5, 520
procedural, 4
Programmers' Notes, 47, 50, 51, 54, 62, 64, 65, 72, 76, 86
110, 113, 168, 170, 189, 238, 256, 256, 260, 262, 278, 304,
319, 350, 382, 384, 434, 445, 458, 518, 520, 521, 530, 531, 542
project,
saving, 54
recalling, 54
Project window, 52
prompt, 140
properties, 37
Properties window, 48
activating, 76
PSet method, 500
pseudocode, 23
Public declaration, 258
Put# statement, 455, 457, 462

Q

quicksort, 297

R

radio button, 176
RAM (random access memory, 27
random access memory (RAM), 27
random file access, 431, 453
reading files, 448
read only memory (ROM), 27
ReadOnly property, 418
real numbers, 97
recalling a project, 54
record, 348
contents, 349
form, 349
RecordSet,378
RecordsetType property, 383
RecordSource property, 382, 392
record structure, 318
recursion, 292
versus iteration, 296
Redim statement, 330
refinement, 15
Refresh method, 137, 386
relation, 374
relational database, 375
relational expressions, 180
logical operators, 182
simple, 180
relational operators, 181

relationships, 373
remainder operator (Mod), 102
RemoveItem method, 560
repetition statement, 214
reserved word, 49
returning values, 270
RGB function, 497
ROM (read only memory), 27
Rnd function, 500
Row property, 428
run-time, 54
run-time errors, 209

S

saving a project, 54
scalar variables, 317
scientific method, 9
Scale method, 496
ScaleHeight property, 496
ScaleLeft property, 496
ScaleMode property, 496
ScaleTop property, 496
ScaleWidth property, 496
scope, 286, 320
Scroll bar control, 492
SDI, 36, 367
search, 353
algorithms, 353
binary, 355
linear, 353
sequential, 353
secondary storage, 28
Seek method, 408
Select Case structure, 203
Select (SQL) statement, 392
selection,
controls, 174
statements, 173
selection sort, 359
selection statements, 173
self-referential procedures, 292
sentinel values, 228
sequence, 16
sequential file access, 430, 440
sequential search, 353
SetFocus method, 192
Shape control, 498
simple numeric expression, 99
simple relational expression, 180
single-dimensional arrays, 318
single line declarations, 110
single line If-Then statement, 192
single precision numbers, 97

V

vacuum tubes, 29
Val function, 146
validation, 146
validity checks, 246
values (Vs identities) 531
variable condition loop, 215
variable scope, 186
variables, 106
   declared, 108
   form-level, 286
   global, 286
   names, 108
   private, 286
   public, 286
   scope, 286
   static, 289
 subscripted, 319
Variant, 115, 338
vbChecked property, 176
vbEOFActionAddNew property, 413
vbEOFActionMoveLast property, 413
very large scale integration (VLSI), 29
VLSI (very large scale integration), 29

W

watch, 303
While loop, 358
white space, 60
words, 31
writing files, 444
Write#, 444

What's New in This Edition

Welcome to the second edition of *Teach Yourself Windows Programming*! This book is designed to quickly get you up to speed on writing Windows 95 and Windows NT programs.

There are hundreds of pages of new, Windows 95–specific material in this edition. In particular, I show how to use nearly all the new elements of the Windows 95 interface. I also delve into lengthy descriptions of WIN32 techniques such as threading, consoles, memory-mapped files, and manipulating virtual memory.

Some of the important new Windows 95 common controls discussed in this book include treeviews, listviews, up/down controls (spinners), progress bars (sliders), property sheets, rich edits, toolbars, and status bars. I also include descriptions of other prominent, but less complex, interface issues such as long filenames, tooltips, floating menus, hotkey controls, and small icons.

These controls and techniques are used prominently in the Windows 95 interface. For instance, if you open Explorer, you will find that treeviews are used to present the hierarchical view of subdirectories shown in the program's lefthand window. On the righthand main window of the Explorer, you will find a listview tool that gives you four different views of the files and directories included in a particular subdirectory. A toolbar is used to hold the icons at the top of the Explorer, and a status bar is present at the bottom of the window. In other words, almost the entire interface of the Explorer consists of new Windows 95 controls that are described in this book.

Other tools that make heavy use of these and other new Windows 95 common controls include the new Control Panel, InBox, Briefcase, Network Neighborhood, and all the configuration dialogs such as the Display Properties dialog you access by right-clicking on the desktop. In short, much of the new Windows 95 interface consists of the common controls discussed in depth in the latter half of this book.

I should also make special mention of the tabbed dialogs and windows discussed in this book, as well as the rich edit control. You can use the rich edit control to edit very large documents that include text that is formatted with multiple fonts, colors, and attributes. For instance, this book shows how you can insert a rich edit control into one of your programs, then allow the reader to open a file that is much larger than 64KB in size. The user can then insert a title into the document, format it with a large Times Roman font, and then use other, smaller fonts for the main text. You can put as many different fonts and styles into your documents as you wish.

No discussion of Windows 95 would be complete without an examination of the huge 4GB address space owned by each program. This book discusses how Windows 95 and Windows NT manage memory, and how you can take advantage of the vast new resources available to your programs. You will also get a chance to read about memory mapped files, WIN32 heaps, and other advanced features including virtual memory.

The book provides four different sample programs that explore threads. I show how to create simple threads, how to manage multiple threads, and how to synchronize threads so that they can share access to your program's variables and resources. In particular, you will encounter discussions of key threading technologies such as mutexes and critical sections.

Windows 95 and Windows NT provide true preemptive multitasking for 32-bit programs, and this book explores this subject in a way that should make the material comprehensible to readers who come from a wide variety of backgrounds. Threads and multitasking are keys to some of the most powerful features in WIN32, and this book gives these subjects a thorough treatment in language that's as clear and straightforward as possible.

Portability is also a major theme throughout some sections of this book. Although many of the programs you will see run only on Windows 95 and Windows NT, there are some programs that deal strictly with core Windows API functions. Because many of these functions are backward compatible with Windows 3.1, I show how you can write a single program that will compile on Windows 3.1, Windows 95, and Windows NT. The transition between 16- and 32-bit code is likely to be slow in some areas of the industry, and so many programmers will be interested in writing portable code that compiles on a variety of Windows platforms. This book addresses that subject by introducing several powerful programming techniques that promote portability. I also provide information for creating makefiles and project files that are specific to each of these platforms.

Once again, this book is meant to be a general introduction to Windows programming. I work hard to introduce all the major topics in a clear and easy-to-understand manner. I start at the very beginning and carefully lay out everything you need to know to learn about Windows programming. By the time you are finished working through the book, you will understand how to write Windows programs, how to utilize the Windows architecture, and how to access the new features in Windows 95.

How to Use This Book

This book is about writing Windows 95 code. It has been designed from the bottom up to teach you this subject in the most lucid, enjoyable, and thorough manner possible.

An extremely wide range of material has been packed between the covers of this book. This book starts out with the basics by presenting you with a number of very easy-to-build Windows 95 programs that are approximately 10 lines in length. After you've had a chance to get a few of these short programs up and running, the book goes on to carefully introduce you to the proper method of constructing a classic Windows program. This second portion of the book was painstakingly designed and developed to show you the most flexible, up-to-date, and powerful methods for writing Windows code.

After that, the text proceeds to introduce you to all the classic elements in Windows 95 programming. Included in this middle, and largest, portion of the book are lively, in-depth discussions of many crucial topics, from dialogs and controls to callbacks and graphics.

After you've earned your wings and know how to fly from one end of the realm of Windows 95 programming to the other, the final portion of the book introduces you to such advanced topics as subclassing, dynamic link libraries, and multimedia.

Every page of this book was written with the conviction that Windows 95 programming can be not only challenging but also exciting and fun. These pages present you with all the basic knowledge you need to write good Windows 95 code, but they also give you a chance to have some fun designing and playing graphics-based games and writing multimedia programs that can play and record sounds, conversation, and music.

Special Features of This Book

This book contains some special features that will aid you in your quest to become a Windows 95 programmer. Syntax boxes show you how to use specific features of the Windows API. Each box provides concrete examples and a full explanation of the best way to use each feature. To get a feel for the style of the syntax boxes, look at the following example.

Syntax

SwapMouseButton

```
BOOL SwapMouseButton(BOOL)
```

   BOOL bSwap If TRUE then swap left and right mouse button messages.

SwapMouseButton returns TRUE if the mouse buttons are reversed; otherwise it returns FALSE.

This function swaps the functionality of the mouse buttons. You might want to give the user a chance to do this if they are left-handed, or if they have some other reason for wanting to change the way the mouse normally functions.

Here's an example:

```
SwapMouseButton(TRUE);
```

Other features of this book are do/don't boxes, notes, and cautions.

DO	DON'T

DO/DON'T Boxes: These give you specific guidance on what to do and what to avoid doing when you are programming in Windows 95.

Note: These provide essential background information so that you not only do things but also have a good understanding of what you're doing and why.

Caution: A caution alerts you to potential hazards regarding the topic currently being discussed.

Conventions Used in This Book

This book uses different typefaces to help you differentiate between code and regular English, and also to help you identify important concepts. Windows code is typeset in a special `monospace` font. New and important terms are typeset in *italic* type for emphasis.

Onward, Into the Breach

This book is designed to give you a very thorough knowledge of Windows programming. Ultimately, however, the responsibility for becoming a good Windows 95 programmer rests on your own shoulders. Specifically, if you want to become good at this challenging subject, you need to write lots of code. Nothing pays off like prolonged periods of serious hacking.

Teach
Yourself
Windows 95
Programming

in 21 Days,
Second Edition

Teach Yourself
Windows 95 Programming
in 21 Days,
Second Edition

Charles Calvert

SAMS
PUBLISHING

201 West 103rd Street
Indianapolis, Indiana 46290

Copyright © 1995 by Sams Publishing

SECOND EDITION

International Standard Book Number: 0-672-30531-3

Library of Congress Catalog Card Number: 94-66281

98 97 96 95   4   3   2   1

Interpretation of the printing code: The rightmost double-digit number is the year of the book's printing; the rightmost single-digit, the number of the book's printing. For example, a printing code of 95-1 shows that the first printing of the book occurred in 1995.

Composed in AGaramond and MCPdigital by Macmillan Computer Publishing

Printed in the United States of America

Publisher	*Richard K. Swadley*
Acquisitions Manager	*Greg Wiegand*
Development Manager	*Dean Miller*
Managing Editor	*Cindy Morrow*
Marketing Manager	*Gregg Bushyeager*

Acquisitions Editor
Christopher Denny

Development Editor
L. Angelique Brittingham

Production Editor
Kitty Wilson

Copy Editor
Marla Reece
Bart Reed
Joe Williams

Technical Reviewer
Bruneau Babet

Editorial Coordinator
Bill Whitmer

Technical Edit Coordinator
Lynette Quinn

Formatter
Frank Sinclair

Editorial Assistant
Sharon Cox

Cover Designer
Tim Amrhein

Book Designer
Alyssa Yesh

Production Team Supervisor
Brad Chinn

Production
Angela D. Bannan
Michael Brumitt
Terrie Deemer
Ayanna Lacey
Kevin Laseau
Paula Lowell
Nancy C. Price
Brian-Kent Proffitt
Bobbi Satterfield
SA Springer
Susan Van Ness
Mark Walchle

Overview

Contents

Day 16   Dialog Boxes and Mapping Modes   625

Day 17   Advanced Dialogs: Getting and Setting Data   669

Acknowledgments

For technical assistance, thanks to Bruneau Babet, Tommy Hui, and David Wilhelm. Bruneau was the tech editor for this book, and his comments and suggestions have helped to make the book not only more accurate, but also much more useful. The term may be a bit out of fashion these days, but I can't resist adding that Bruneau is one of the very rare souls from my generation who deserve to be called a gentleman. As always, whatever mistakes you find in the book crept in despite his efforts, and not because of them. Thanks also to Danny Thorpe, Steve Teixeira, and Jason Sprenger.

For their support, understanding, and patience, thanks to David Intersimone and Zack Urlocker. In particular, David has given me the encouragement, free reign, and opportunity to have one of the most interesting, exciting, and busy years of my life. Thank you, David! Thanks also to Karen Giles, Christine Sherman, Lisa Coenen, Scott Linman, Scott Clinton, Nancy Collins, Yolanda Davis, and Nan Borreson.

I also owe a big debt to my wife, Marjorie Calvert. It's hard to find happiness without a good spiritual life, interesting work, and a good spouse. Thanks, Margie, for helping me get all the good stuff!

Thanks to Angelique Brittingham and Dean Miller who helped to make this a much better book. Thank you, Angelique, for sticking with it when you knew you were right! Thanks also to Joe Williams and Kitty Wilson. There is no way I can ever sufficiently express my gratitude to folks like Angelique, Joe, and Kitty. These are the folks who got down in the trenches, went through the book sentence by sentence, correcting my mistakes and finding ways to improve the book. Every reader of this work owes you a debt of gratitude. I also want to send a special note of thanks to Chris Denny, whose patience, good manners, and consideration helped me get through the trauma of writing the book and turning it in to the editors. It's notoriously difficult to work with writers, and certainly I'm no exception to the rule.

Dedication

This book is dedicated to some good friends, some of whom I need to go way back down the years to remember: David McGrath, Michael Doar, Mark Hall, Michael Burroughs, Kemp Battle, Paul Alopena, Greg Thurman, John Crawford, Robin Hunt, Jason Kuschner, Laurie Campbell, Roberta Cohen, Bobbie Battle, Betsy Calvert, Mark and Heidi McFadden, Jim Allen from Madison, Robert Fitterman, Dave Barrett, George Rasmussen, Elmer Murphy, Dan from Elbe, Mark and Nancy Newey, Dan Richart, Bob Harris, Wayne Simila-Dickinson, Rick Riley Johnson, Xavier Pacheco, Jason Sprenger, Rich Jones, Lar Mader, Steve Teixeira, and especially Hallie Gay Bagley.

About the Author

Charles Calvert

Charles Calvert is the author of *Delphi Unleashed, Teach Yourself Windows Programming in 21 Days,* and *Turbo Pascal Programming 101* (all published by Sams). He has worked as a journalist for *The Morton Journal* and as an English teacher at an extension of Centralia College in Washington. For the last several years, Charlie has worked at Borland International, where he is now a manager in Developer Relations. He lives with his wife, Marjorie, in Santa Cruz, California.

1

This book is meant to be a guide for beginning- and intermediate-level Windows 95 and Windows NT programmers. In it I attempt to delineate the key concepts necessary to write Windows code. My goal is to paint all the major themes with broad strokes on a large canvas.

The first week eases you into the complexity of writing Windows code so that you can foresee climbing up to a height from which you can hope to attain mastery of the entire subject. There is a fair amount of detail to manage, but you will find that it's possible to isolate most of these specifics inside a broad, easy-to-comprehend framework.

Windows programs can be broken down into a handful of major pieces. To get started, you need to first understand how to handle the parameters passed to you at the program entry point. After that, there are four other key steps:

- ☐ Registering a window class
- ☐ Creating a window
- ☐ Setting up a message loop
- ☐ Responding to messages

The whole act of writing Windows code really boils down to an understanding of this sparse handful of concepts. Grasp them, and everything else will fall into place.

The goal of Week 1, then, is to get you to the point where your understanding of these concepts is intuitive and natural. I want to take you through the process in a simple, step-by-step manner that's enlivened with some interesting and thought-provoking examples. It's not enough just to learn the ideas—you also have to sense the excitement behind them. You need to understand not only how Windows programs are structured, but why that structure provides programmers with a powerful, flexible, and entertaining set of tools.

Structure is very important to Windows programmers. The Windows 95 and Windows NT operating systems are so complex that they can't be properly tamed without finding a way to organize their diversity. In particular, I have some specific ideas about how you can use the macros from WINDOWSX.H to produce code that is well structured, easy to read, and easy to maintain. There is no point in writing Windows code unless you have a predefined structure that makes program management and maintenance a reasonable and relatively painless task. This first week will get you off to the right start by showing you how to structure and organize a Windows program.

The broad themes outlined above run through the entirety of Week 1. However, there are some specific matters of interest that you will tackle on a day-to-day basis.

Days 1 and 2 show you how to compile and run a Windows program. They introduce you to the operating system, the compilers, and the basic tools you will use throughout the rest of the book.

Once you are familiar with the tools and concepts necessary to create very simple Windows programs, you will begin working on structure and theory. In particular, Day 3 shows you how to create a solid framework on which almost all your programs can rest. Day 3 is the pivotal chapter on which the entire book rests, and in it you will learn what Windows programming is really all about.

Days 4 and 5 familiarize you with the basic concepts behind an event-oriented, message-based operating system. WindowsX will play a big role in helping you organize this material. By the time you are through, you will have a good understanding of messages, events, and the basic flow behind a Windows program.

The final two chapters in Week 1 show off Windows resources that add color and power to a program. Resources can prove to be an unsuspected boon to programmers who come from the DOS or UNIX text-mode command prompt. With very little work on your part, you can use resources to add menus, bitmaps, icons, and string tables to your programs. These tools help give your program depth and power.

Taken as a whole, Windows programming is ornate enough to provide an engaging challenge for most people who seek to master it. It's an extremely fascinating subject that provides programmers with intriguing puzzles and seemingly limitless capabilities. This book aims to bring out the really fascinating aspects of Windows programming in a way that you will find not only instructive but also entertaining.

When you are done with Week 1, you will have attained a height from which the Windows programming horizon will be clearly delineated. You can then look forward to exploring the broad landscape provided by Windows 95 and Windows NT. By the time you are done with the book, will you will be master of everything you need to know to take advantage of the full breadth of advanced Windows programming.

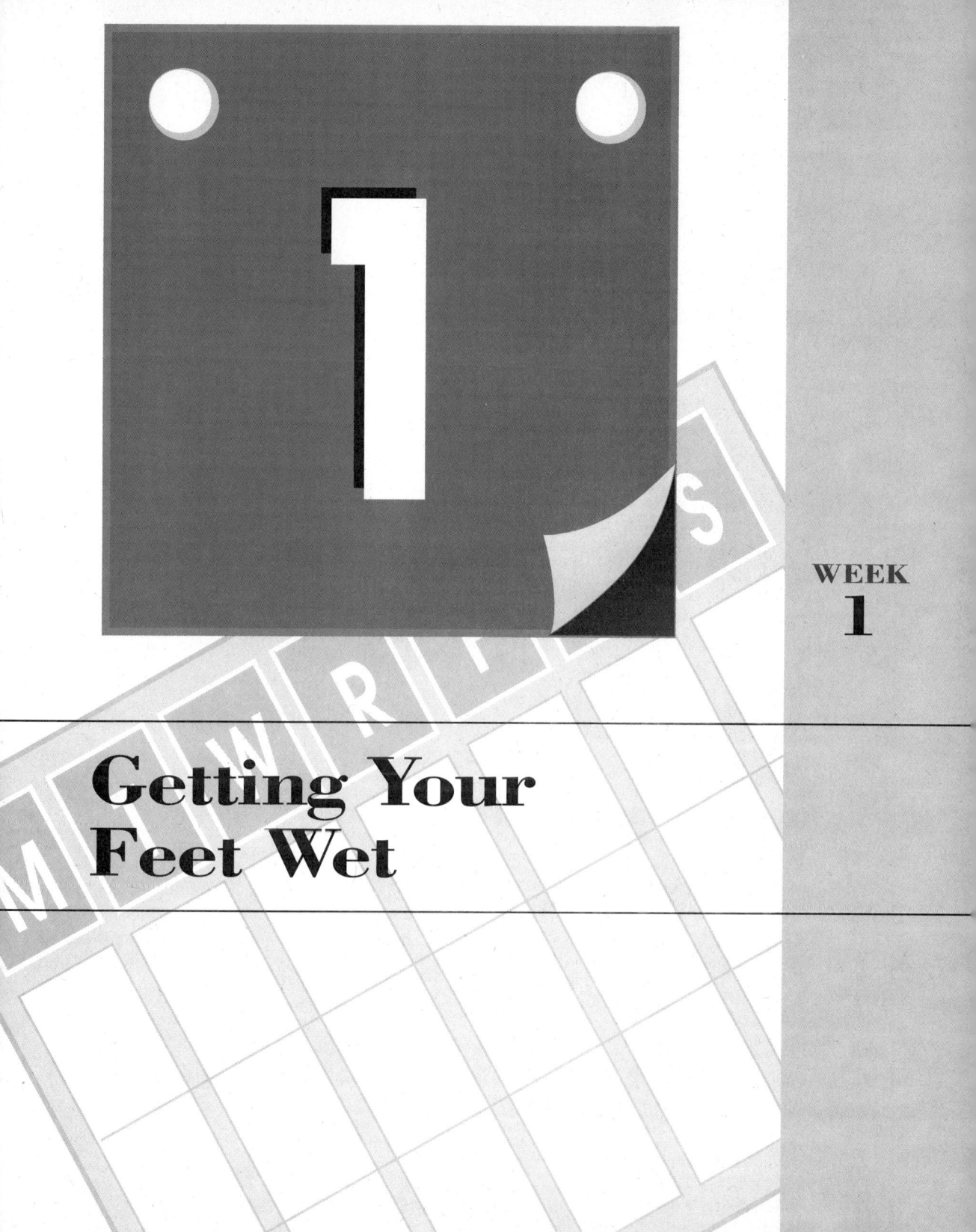

1

Getting Your Feet Wet

In this chapter, I provide a brief introduction to Windows programming, and then give two short sample programs that are designed to get you up and running quickly.

After you have had a chance to get some hands-on experience, I discuss more general topics. Specifically, the last half of this chapter covers

- ☐ Graphical user interfaces (GUIs)
- ☐ Recommended hardware
- ☐ Windows compilers
- ☐ Coding styles
- ☐ An overview of Windows
- ☐ An overview of upcoming chapters

In general, this chapter is an introduction to the art of Windows 95 programming. It lays the groundwork for the core task of this book, which is teaching 32-bit Windows programming from the ground up.

Windows 95 is not a perfect operating system, but it is a vast improvement over DOS and Windows 3.1. The big promise of Windows 95 is that it will bring us into the world of robust, large-scale, 32-bit computing. As you will see while reading this book, this claim is entirely valid.

Windows 95 and Windows NT change the meaning of the words *personal computer*. PCs that run these operating systems can no longer be considered toys. 32-bit Windows opens the door to some very powerful technology that can reside in small, very compact boxes. There is an enormous frontier opening in front of us, and this book provides some of the keys to that kingdom.

An Overview of This Book

The purpose of this book is to teach you how to write Windows programs using C or C++compilers. In particular, I show how you can use C/C++ to program Windows applications that exploit the full power of Windows 95 and Windows NT.

This book covers not only basic Windows programming issues, but also the new Windows 95 controls, Windows 95 console applications, and Windows 95 interfaces. It also covers multitasking and threads, as well as WIN32 flat address space programming issues such as creating multiple heaps and using memory-mapped files.

Despite the heavy coverage of Windows 95 and Windows NT–specific techniques, there are also many programs in this book that will run unchanged under Windows 95, Windows NT, and 16-bit Windows. This book starts from ground zero in terms of Windows programming. It covers many subjects that will be of general use to all Windows programmers. In covering those subjects, the book is careful to present them in a way that allows you to write

platform-independent code. In other words, if the technique is not specific to Windows 95 or Windows NT, I show how to use it so that it will compile on all Windows-based platforms, from Windows 3.1 on a 386 to Windows NT on a Pentium or P6 machine. (I have not tested on the MIPS or Alpha platforms, but the code from this book should also compile there without change.)

My intention is to talk to you about Windows programming using words that are friendly, easy to understand, and technically correct. I start at the very beginning, showing how to write basic Windows applications. Each chapter builds on its predecessors, so that by the time you are through, you will know all about writing code that calls the Windows API.

My goal is to present more than a simple primer on writing Windows code. I also want to give you a road map showing how to write advanced Windows code that exploits DLLs, threads, multimedia, and the full 4GB address space found on Windows 95 and Windows NT machines.

As mentioned previously, another primary goal of this book is to show you how to write code that is portable between Windows 95, Windows NT, and Windows 3.1. Furthermore, the techniques used to provide portability also help to simplify the act of writing Windows code. In other words, the techniques which provide portability also help you write programs that are simpler to write, read, and maintain than code that does not use these techniques. All of this portability comes without any hit in terms of system performance. If this were an object-oriented programming book covering OOP frameworks, such as OWL and MFC, you would also obtain this same portability, but you would pay a big price in terms of the size and speed of your application.

It's my belief that if you have a solid foundation, you will be able to climb to almost any height; but if you try to build on sand, every edifice you construct will eventually crumble. Therefore, I concentrate on the basics throughout many of the key early chapters. Much of this book is not particularly flashy or showy. Instead I have aimed to cover a very technical subject in clear, easy-to understand language.

The core of this book moves along at a slow, stately pace, always taking the time to outline all the major issues so you can see them clearly, even from a distance. To balance out this perhaps excessively conservative impulse, I've tried to keep the general mood of the text cheerful and high spirited.

Once again, let me emphasize the three major goals of this book:

- ☐ To teach the basics of writing Windows programs.
- ☐ To show you how to exploit the new features of the WIN32 platforms. In particular, you'll see how to use a flat 32-bit address space, and how to use the new Windows controls such as rich edits, treeviews, and toolbars.
- ☐ Whenever possible, I also show how to write portable code that runs unchanged on Windows 95, Windows NT, and Windows 3.1.

The techniques I use to give you portability come mostly from an industry standard file called WINDOWSX.H. WindowsX programming techniques have three great advantages:

☐ They are part of a Microsoft-created industry standard. WINDOWSX.H ships with all the major C/C++ compilers.

☐ Use of WindowsX allows you to simplify the act of writing Windows code.

☐ WindowsX provides portability between Windows 95, Windows NT, and Windows 3.1.

All this comes without having any effect on the runtime performance of your application.

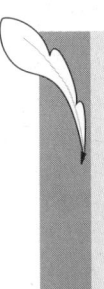

> **Note:** Updates for all the code in this book will be available from major online services and at various sites on the Internet. In particular, you can get the code from CompuServe, America Online, the Borland Web or ftp site, the Borland DLBBS, the Macmillan Web site, and several other places.
>
> On CompuServe, type GO SAMS, to enter the Macmillan Computer Publishing forum. Once there, enter the file library and search in library 7 (Sams-ProgLang+DataB) for the keyword CALVERT. The Borland Web site is www.borland.com, and the Macmillan site is www.mcp.com.

My task is considerably simplified by the Windows environment, which by its very nature is entertaining and exciting. In just a few lines of Windows code, you can implement tasks that DOS makes prohibitively complicated.

For instance, graphics, sound, and multitasking are three tasks that have challenged, frustrated, and often defeated a wide array of experienced DOS programmers. But these features are free for the asking when you're in the Windows environment. Graphics and sound capabilities have even evolved to the point that users can now show movies and write music on their PCs. Even more importantly, the new developments in Windows 95 and Windows NT enable program-mers to write multithreaded code that can use multiple processors at the same time. It also provides a simplified, 32-bit memory addressing scheme, as well as increased networking capabilities.

All these features are enormously intriguing. Windows programmers are standing with power at their fingertips—power that far outreaches even some of the wilder dreams of yesterday's science fiction writers. Ten years ago, it was hard to foresee that so much was going to happen so quickly, and that such technology was going to be available to almost everyone for relatively small sums of money.

I imagine you wouldn't have picked up this book if you weren't already convinced of the importance of Windows in today's and tomorrow's cultural and economic marketplace. As a result, you are probably eager to hear what this book covers and about how you can get started writing real Windows code.

How to Use This Book

One of the basic goals of this book is to give you a solid introduction to the fundamentals of Windows programming. To accomplish this end, I need two skills. The first is a solid knowledge of how Windows code is put together, and the second is a love of writing and teaching. When I sat down each evening to work on this book, I tried to be prepared. That is, I tried to have a thorough knowledge of the material to be covered, and a heartfelt willingness to share that information with you.

From your end, you need to come prepared with a desire to do some work and with a decent knowledge of programming. The scope of this book is such that there is no room to give a general introduction to the C/C++ language, or to the fundamentals of using a computer. I assume, for instance, that you know how to use the Windows Explorer, the Task Bar, the Program Manager, and the File Manager, and that you know how to work with the DOS directory structure.

Note: The list of Windows tools at the end of the last paragraph begs for an explanation. The Explorer and Task Bar are part of Windows 95, and also Windows NT 3.51, while the Program Manager and File Manager are part of Windows NT and Windows 3.1. Why do I mention all these tools in the same breath?

Well, one of the goals of this book is to show you how to write code that is portable between multiple environments. As a result, you will hear me frequently referencing features of both WIN32 (Windows NT, Windows 95) and WIN16 (Windows 3.1).

I am not a seer, and I have no sure idea of where the industry will head in the next few years. However, it appears that we are entering a world that will be dominated by 16- and 32-bit Windows platforms. Windows 95 is likely to have a huge impact on the market, but Windows 3.1 is unlikely to simply disappear over night. Instead, we are going to live in a world dominated by both operating systems, just as DOS and Windows 3.1 have dominated the PC world in the first half of this decade.

To survive in this world, we need to have a thorough knowledge of both environments. One of this book's goals is to show how it's possible to achieve that end.

I will, however, also take extensive forays into territory that is Windows 95 or Windows NT specific. In fact, I dedicate many hundreds of pages to those subjects. By the time you are done with the book, you should have a good understanding of not only general Windows programming topics but also the vast opportunities afforded by 32-bit platforms, such as Windows 95 and Windows NT.

I have made every attempt to make this material as approachable as possible. If you have had some experience programming, you should do fine with the material in this book as long as you study it in the order in which it's presented. In particular, you should come to the party with some knowledge of structured programming, variables, types, and computer memory. You should also know how to run a compiler and an editor. Although I will discuss the subject on Day 2, "Building Projects, Creating Windows," it will also be a big help if you know how to work with makefiles.

There is no need, however, for you to be an expert programmer. My goal in writing this book is to show you that you don't need to be a genius to become a first-rate Windows programmer. All you need is a lot of heart and a willingness to experiment and have some fun. Whenever technical material is particularly challenging, and I feel you absolutely need to understand it, I then slow down the pace and take the time to explain it to you as clearly as possible.

I picture my ideal reader as someone who has a modest knowledge of the basics of the C or C++ language. Starting from that point, I want to give you the tools you need to become an expert Windows programmer.

In order to accomplish this goal, I've tried to start out by making the first third of this book a kind of "quickstart" for Windows programming. That is, I try to give you the major tools you'll need to start producing standard Windows applications. In the second third of the book, I give you a more in-depth knowledge of how to use each of these fundamental Windows programming tools. The last third of the book covers advanced material.

I hope this approach makes this a dynamic and intuitive book. In particular, I try not to introduce a topic, and then force the reader to study it in such depth that they put the book down in frustration. Nor do I want readers to find themselves skipping back and forth in search of the "good stuff." Instead, I aim to give you the information you want when you want it. The details get covered, but only when you are ready to move past the basics.

Some programming books attempt to be comprehensive references, while others aim to present an organized method of study with a beginning, middle, and end. My goal is to find a middle ground between these two approaches, but when in doubt, I almost always forsake the reference model. Most compilers are equipped with good references; what's in short supply is plain talk about the core technical issues.

Before showing you your first program, I want to point out that this book has been designed and formatted so that you can make your way through its contents in just 21 days. (Plus some extra time for the 4 bonus days!) However, it should come as no surprise to you to learn that it wasn't written in 21 days, or even in 25 days. In fact, it took quite some time to put together. As a result, I won't mind at all if you spend longer than 21 days getting through it. In fact, you should feel free to take your time, if you have that luxury. To me, the key issue is not how fast you get through this book, but how much you can learn from it.

So, get ready for a spirited examination of the Windows programming environment. Be prepared to have some fun, to learn some new tricks, and to surprise yourself with how easily you can learn a new and exciting skill.

A Simplified C++ Windows Program

Whenever I start working with a new computer program, or a new language, I'm always anxious to get some hands-on experience as quickly as possible. Because you might feel exactly as I do, I've developed the short C++ Windows program shown in Listing 1.1. that you can get up and running in just a few minutes.

Figure 1.1 shows the output from Listing 1.1.

Listing 1.1. Your very first Windows program.

```
// Program LaoTzu.cpp
#include <windows.h>

// Some pragmas to surpress unneeded warnings
#pragma warning (disable: 4068)
#pragma argsused

int WINAPI WinMain(HINSTANCE hInst,
                   HINSTANCE hPrevInstance,
                   LPSTR lpszCmdParam, int nCmdShow)
{
  MessageBox(0,
             "He who is ruled by men lives in sorrow.",
             "He who rules men lives in confusion.",
             MB_OK|MB_ICONINFORMATION);
  return 0;
}
```

Figure 1.1.
*The LaoTzu program offers
a quote from an ancient
Chinese sage.*

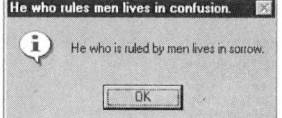

This is a totally legitimate C/C++ Windows application that follows the conventions and rules laid out for Windows programmers. The sole function of these simple lines is to display a message box with some words from a Taoist sage who lived about 2,500 years ago.

To run LAOTZU.CPP, all you need do is launch your development environment, type in the code in Listing 1.1, and compile it. So for now, just go ahead and follow the outlined plan—even if you don't really understand what the code means or why it works. The point of the LAOTZU.CPP isn't to teach you how Windows programs work, but to show you how simple they can be.

For instance, if you are using Borland C++, you can (at least in theory) type in the code, save the file as LAOTZU.CPP, and start it by pressing Alt+R to bring down the run menu; then press R to run the program. That's all there is to it. Now, who said Windows programming in C++ has to be difficult?

If you are using the Microsoft Visual C++ package, the process involved in getting the program up and running is equally simple. First, type in the previous program and save it as SHORT.CPP. Next, press Ctrl+F5 to compile the program. When the compilation is finished, press Ctrl+F5 again to run the program. Voilà! What could be simpler?

Well, at any rate, the process of compiling the program should theoretically be fairly simple. However, there is more to writing a Windows program than just typing in a few lines of code. In particular, you not only need to code your program, but you also need to program your compiler. You need to get the settings right in your compiler, or even the best written Windows code will be totally worthless to you.

Let's reiterate these points just so everything is out on the table right from the start. C/C++ Windows programmers have two jobs:

☐ Write the code for the program.
☐ Program the compiler.

This is what C/C++ programming is all about. These monolithic compilers give you control over everything so you can overturn the last stone on the darkest alley in the whole 80*x*86 architecture in order to create the best possible Windows program. (Yes, I know, Windows programs now run on non-Intel machines, such as the Alpha or MIPS, and indeed all the programs in this book should run fine on those platforms. However, the code in this book has only been tested on Intel machines.)

Getting the settings straight is a subject all by itself, and I cover the basics of this subject in the next chapter. I also provide you with makefiles, so that you can compile these programs from the command prompt without having to fiddle with the compiler settings. A second technique would be to open the project files that ship with your compiler and study the options shown there. You can also download the code for this book, which comes equipped with makefiles and project file for use with Borland and Microsoft compilers.

When working with the settings, you can get started by turning off anything having to do with OWL or MFC. This is not an object-oriented programming book. Also, make sure the paths to your INCLUDE and LIB directories are set up correctly. Borland users can set these from the Options|Project|Directories menu choice, and Microsoft users can set them with the DOS SET command that changes your environment. Microsoft users should also see the MSVCVARS.BAT or VCVARS32.BAT files in the \MSVC\BIN or \MSVC20\BIN subdirectories.

Listings 1.2 through 1.4 are three listings that should get you up and running with makefiles right away. The first listing is a makefile for the Borland compiler, using either 16- or 32-bit code. Listing 1.2 is a makefile for the Microsoft 32-bit compiler (MSVC20), and Listing 1.3 for the Microsoft 16-bit compiler (MSVC15). If you are still having trouble after viewing the makefiles and other information printed here, then you should download the programs from the disk you can purchase to accompany this book (see the disk offer at the end of the book) and load the code from there directly into the Borland or Microsoft IDE. If you have correctly installed the compiler, then the code samples should get you up and running right away. If it doesn't, try reinstalling the compiler.

Note: If you need to reach me for consultation, you can send e-mail to one of the following addresses:

Internet: ccalvert@wpo.borland.com

Compuserve: 76711,533

AOL: CHARLIECAL

The consultation is free, but it's apt to be rather hurried. The computer revolution waits for no one, least of all me.

The descriptions in the next few paragraphs are broken up into Microsoft and Borland sections. However, this will not be necessary throughout the vast majority of the book. It's just something I do once or twice in this chapter and on Day 2. I need to get you started working with the tools that ship with your compiler. Once you're past the basics, I'll just give you generic information and let you implement it as necessary on your own compiler.

LaoTzu, Borland Style

If you are using Borland C++ 4.5, you can load the copy of LAOTZU.IDE that's available online. To load the file, choose Project|Open from the main menu. LAOTZU.IDE contains all the settings you need to make sure that the program will compile without error. However, you should still check the Options|Project|Directories menu choice to be sure you have the right path to your INCLUDE and LIB subdirectories. (LAOTZU.IDE should also work with BC50, but it has not been tested against it, due to the discrepancy between the release dates of this book and the release dates of BC50.)

Borland users who downloaded the source code can also run the LAOTZU.MAK file, shown below, from the command prompt. This makefile will automatically build the program, passing all the correct settings to the command line compiler. I have provided a batch file called GO.BAT that will automatically call the Borland makefile and build the program. If you want to build a 16-bit version of the program, pass WIN16 to the batch file as a parameter:

```
GO WIN16
```

One final note for Borland users. If you want to speed up compilation under WIN32, you can add the following line at the top of the program:

```
#define WIN32_LEAN_AND_MEAN
```

This line doesn't change the final executable, but it makes the compilation go a lot faster.

Listing 1.2. The Borland makefile for the LaoTzu program.

```
# ------------------------
# Borland LaoTzu.mak
# ------------------------

!if !$d(BCROOT)
BCROOT  = $(MAKEDIR)
!endif

INCPATH = $(BCROOT)\INCLUDE
LIBPATH = $(BCROOT)\LIB

!if $d(WIN16)
COMPILER= BCC.EXE
FLAGS   = -W -ml -v -w4 -I$(INCPATH) -L$(LIBPATH)
!else
COMPILER= BCC32.EXE
FLAGS   = -W -v -w4 -I$(INCPATH) -L$(LIBPATH)
!endif

# link
LaoTzu.exe: LaoTzu.obj LaoTzu.def
  $(COMPILER) $(FLAGS) LaoTzu.obj

# compile
LaoTzu.obj: LaoTzu.cpp
  $(COMPILER) -c $(FLAGS) LaoTzu.cpp
```

To run this Borland makefile, first make sure the BIN subdirectory is on your path, and then type the following at the command prompt:

```
make -f laotzu.mak
```

This command compiles the program as a WIN32 executable. If you want to produce a 16-bit Windows 3.1 executable, then type

```
make -DWIN16 -f laotzu.mak
```

The Borland makefile shown above assumes that you have the system set up correctly, which means that BCROOT will be defined automatically. If you suspect that BCROOT is not correctly defined on your system, then type in the following at the command prompt and then try again:

```
set BCROOT=c:\bc45
```

Of course, you might specify a different path or directory name on your system, such as d:\bc50.

Here is a batch file called GO.BAT that automates the process of calling the above makefile:

```
@echo off
if %1==WIN16 goto WIN16

:WIN32
make -B -f laotzu.mak
goto end

:WIN16
make -B -DWIN16 -f laotzu.mak
goto end

:end
```

To run this batch file, type either GO, or GO WIN16. The former produces a Windows 95 executable, the latter a Windows 3.1 executable.

Rainy Day LaoTzu, Seattle Style

Microsoft users can download LAOTMS32.MAK from an online service, and then load it into the IDE by choosing File|Open. If you prefer, you can run the same program from the command prompt by using the NMAKE program that ships with MSVC20 and MSVC15. To help you get started, the source code available online comes with a batch file called MS.BAT. Run this batch file from the DOS prompt to automatically compile the program for WIN32. If you are using the 16-bit version of Microsoft's tools, then you should work with LAOTMS16.MAK or LAOTZUM.MAK. There are a number of different Microsoft makefiles provided with source code for this book. The same conventions for naming these files will be followed throughout the book. The makefiles for Visual C++ 2.0 IDE will always end in MS32, and the makefile for Visual C++ 1.5 IDE will always end in MS16. A more simplified command-line–oriented WIN32 makefile will end in MS, and a command-line–optimized 16-bit makefile will end in *M*:

☐ LAOTMS32.MAK—MSVC20 makefile for use inside the IDE.
☐ LAOTMS16.MAK—MSVC15 makefile for use inside the IDE.

☐ LAOTZUMS.MAK—MSVC20 makefile for use from the command prompt.

☐ LAOTZUM.MAK—MSVC15 makefile for use form the command prompt.

To run the makefiles from the DOS prompt, switch to the subdirectory where the program is stored and type either

```
nmake -f laotzums.mak
```

or

```
nmake -f laotzum.mak
```

Listing 1.3 shows the Microsoft makefile for the LaoTzu program.

Listing 1.3. The Microsoft makefile for the Windows 95 version of the LaoTzu program.

```
#-------------------------------------------------
# LAOTZUMS.MAK
# Microsoft makefile
#-------------------------------------------------

APPNAME=LAOTZU
TARGETOS=WIN95
APPVER=4.0
OBJS=$(APPNAME).OBJ

!include <win32.mak>

all: $(APPNAME).exe

# Update the object files if necessary

# compile
.cpp.obj:
  $(cc) $(cflags) $(cvars) $(cdebug) $<

# Update the executable file if necessary.

$(APPNAME).exe: $(OBJS)
  $(link) $(linkdebug) $(guiflags) -out:$(APPNAME).exe \
  $(OBJS) $(guilibs) comctl32.lib
```

To run this makefile from the command prompt, type

```
nmake -f laotzums.mak
```

If you have trouble, try running the VCVARS32.BAT or MSVCVARS.BAT files in your compiler's BIN subdirectory. Also, make sure that the BIN subdirectory is on your path.

Listing 1.4. A 16-bit–specific Microsoft makefile.

```
# -----------------------------
# Microsoft LaoTzuM.Mak
# -----------------------------

# linking
LaoTzu.exe: LaoTzu.obj LaoTzu.def
  link /CO LaoTzu, /align:16, NUL, /nod llibcew libw, LaoTzu

# compiling
LaoTzu.obj: LaoTzu.cpp
  cl -c -AL -GA -Ow -W3 -Zp -Zi LaoTzu.cpp
```

To run this file from the command prompt, type

```
nmake -f laotzum.mak
```

General Information on Compiling the LaoTzu Program

If you are not using either the Borland or the Microsoft compilers, you should still be able to compile the above program, but you may have to tweak the makefiles according to information supplied with your compiler. If you have trouble, you might want to just follow along through the ensuing discussion as best you can or use the code that comes with your compiler to find examples of how this chore is normally handled on your system.

On Day 2 you get a chance to see an in-depth discussion of running programs from the IDE, creating module definition files, and creating makefiles. After this chapter, all the programs in this book contain module definition files and makefiles that are referenced explicitly in the text of this book.

I've left module definition files out of this chapter because they can confuse people new to Windows programming. Furthermore, they are not absolutely necessary, especially for WIN32 programs. However, the lack of module definition files (.DEF) might cause warnings, particularly from 16-bit compilers, but this is not a reason for concern. The compiler will supply default settings that will work just fine on your system.

Note: I've been in the industry long enough to know that some readers will wonder why I focus on Microsoft's and Borland's compilers, and not, say, on Watcom's or Symantec's. The issue here is that I don't have the time or energy to install four different compilers, run the code against them all, and still find the means to write

a book that's going to be useful to the general reader. I had to make a decision on how to allocate my resources, and so I chose the two most popular compilers on the market.

Yes, I work for Borland, and of course I think we make the best compiler. But that wasn't the reason I didn't provide more help for other compilers. I do the most I can for the reader, given the resources at my command. That's all there is to it.

Having said that, I should add that the code I have written is tested thoroughly against several very rigorous standards. It should compile fine on any good Windows C/C++ programming tool. However, I have explicitly tested it only against Microsoft's and Borland's compilers.

For what it's worth, I should perhaps add that when I started programming in Windows, I used the IDE almost exclusively. It seemed the appropriate thing to do in a Windows based environment. However, over time I moved back to the command line and compiled my applications using makefiles. My tools of choice were the text-based Borland Brief editor and the Borland BC45 command line compiler. (I of course tested every program against both MSVC20 and, when appropriate, MSVC15.)

The Core of the LaoTzu Program

I've spent considerable time talking about the act of compiling the LaoTzu program. As it happens, the actual code that's part of the program is shorter than all but one of the makefiles. Nevertheless, the moment one starts looking beneath the surface of the program, one finds complexity. For instance, there's the `MessageBox` function, which seems simple enough on the surface. However, it offers a few twists and turns which you need to master.

The *MessageBox* Function

Syntax

```
int MessageBox(HWND, LPCSTR, LPCSTR, UINT);
```

The `MessageBox` function creates a window. It takes the following four parameters:

The first, an `HWND`, is a handle to the programs main window. In Listing 1.1, this is set to `0`, because the LaoTzu program has no main window.

The second parameter, a long pointer to a constant string, is the text you want to appear in the main portion of the message box, as shown in Figure 1.1.

The third parameter, also a far pointer to a string, is the title of the message box.

The fourth parameter includes one or more of the following flags:

```
// Buttons
//- - - - - - - - - - - - - - - - - - - - - - - - - -
#define MB_OK                 0x0000  Include okay button
#define MB_OKCANCEL           0x0001  Include cancel button
#define MB_ABORTRETRYIGNORE   0x0002  Abort, retry, ignore
#define MB_YESNOCANCEL        0x0003  Yes No Cancel buttons
#define MB_YESNO              0x0004  Yes No buttons
#define MB_RETRYCANCEL        0x0005  Retry, Cancel buttons


// Icons
#define MB_ICONHAND           0x0010  The stop icon
#define MB_ICONQUESTION       0x0020  The question mark icon
#define MB_ICONEXCLAMATION    0x0030  Exclamation mark icon
#define MB_ICONASTERISK       0x0040  Asterisk icon
#define MB_ICONINFORMATION    MB_ICONASTERISK
#define MB_ICONSTOP           MB_ICONHAND


// Scope and focus issues
#define MB_APPLMODAL          0x0000
#define MB_SYSTEMMODAL        0x1000
#define MB_TASKMODAL          0x2000


//  Default Button specification
MB_DEFBUTTON1                 0x0000
MB_DEFBUTTON1                 0x0100
MB_DEFBUTTON1                 0x0200


// WIN32
MB_SETFOREGROUND
MB_DEFAULT_DESKTOP_ONLY
```

If you want to use more than one of these flags at a time, you should OR them together, as shown in the following example. To see how this works, try replacing the MB_ICONEXCLAMATION with MB_ICONINFORMATION.

The MessageBox function returns an integer that specifies the button the user selected when the MessageBox was on-screen. For instance, if the user presses an OK button, the function will return IDOK. If the user presses a CANCEL button, the function will return IDCANCEL. The following are the possible return values:

IDABORT   User selected the Abort button.

IDCANCEL   User selected the Cancel button.

IDIGNORE   User selected the Ignore button.

IDNO   User selected the No button.

IDOK   User selected the OK button.

IDRETRY   User selected the Retry button.

IDYES   User selected the Yes button.

Here's an example:

```
MessageBox(0,
          "The astrolabe of the mysteries of God is love.",
          "Jalal-uddin Rumi said:",
          MB_OK¦MB_ICONEXCLAMATION);
```

Sound

Windows programs present the user with an elaborate user interface. Rather than simply showing line after line of written data, the goal of a Windows program is to present information conceptually through the use of pictures, graphs, and sounds.

On Bonus Day 3, "DLLs and Multimedia," you'll encounter a detailed look at the multimedia extensions to Windows. In those sections, you'll see how to add voices, music, and other audible or visual features to your programs.

If, however, you have a SoundBlaster or another sound card, or if you have access to Microsoft's SPEAKER.DRV file, you can start using multimedia sound right away. All you need to do is run the short program called CHIMES.EXE. It enables you to use SPEAKDER.DRV, or your sound card, to play .WAV (or "wave") files. Wave files reproduce the sound of musical instruments, the human voice, and other realistic sounds. If you don't have access to any of these tools, don't worry; I have another simple program, called BEEPER.EXE, that you can use to tell your computer to start making short sounds. (See Listing 1.5.)

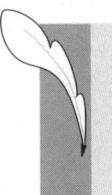

Note: The SPEAKER.DRV file is readily available. I got my copy by logging onto CompuServe, entering the Microsoft Library (GO MSL), and downloading the self-extracting file called SPEAK.EXE. This file also is available when you download or purchase the software that comes with this book.

To use SPEAKER.DRV in Windows: Copy speaker.drv into the WINDOWS directory. Modify the system.ini [drivers] section to include the line Wave=speaker.drv. Now restart the computer.

This book's software is available on the CompuServe Information Service. When you type GO SAMS, you enter the Macmillan Computer Publishing forum. Once there, enter the file library, and search in library 7 (Sams-ProgLang+DataB) for the keyword CALVERT. You can also look on www.mcp.com or www.borland.com.

Okay. Here are the two programs that show you how to start making sounds with your computer. The first version of this program (Listing 1.5) is the one you should use if you have SPEAKER.DRV or multimedia capabilities. The second version (Listing 1.6) runs on any

system that has the built-in speaker that comes with nearly all PCs. If you can, run both programs, because you should know about the MessageBeep procedure.

Listing 1.5. CHIMES.CPP enables you to tap into the new multimedia capabilities provided by Microsoft.

```
1: // Program CHIMES.CPP
2: #define STRICT
3: #include <windows.h>
4: #include <mmsystem.h>
5:
6: int WINAPI WinMain(HINSTANCE hInst,
7:                    HINSTANCE hPrevInstance,
8:                    LPSTR lpszCmdParam, int nCmdShow)
9: {
10:    sndPlaySound("BELL.WAV", SND_SYNC);
11:    return 0;
12: }
```

As shown in Listing 1.5, the Chimes program plays a file called CHIMES.WAV. This is a short musical file that, by default, the Windows 95 SETUP program places in your Windows subdirectory. On Windows 3.1 and Windows NT you can try CHIMES.WAV, or simply look on your hard drive for existing wave files. In short, if you want to hear other sounds, songs, or voices, you can enter the name of a different WAV file.

This program calls a single function named sndPlaySound. sndPlaySound is part of the Multimedia extensions to Windows. The purpose of the function is to play a .WAV file.

Notice the #define STRICT directive on line 2. Later in this chapter, and also in other portions of this book, you learn about using STRICT. On line 4, I include the MMSYSTEM.H file. The letters *mm* in this file name stand for *multi*media. Since the advent of Windows 3.1, the MMSYSTEM.H header file is a standard part of the Windows programming environment. It's discussed in more depth later in the book, but for now you should probably open it inside an editor and take a brief look at it.

The sndPlaySound function is part of the Multimedia extensions to Windows. As a result, you must include MMSYSTEM.H in your program in order to use this function. (MMSystem stands for multimedia system.) On some systems, if you have not defined WIN32_LEAN_AND_MEAN, then you should be able to omit a direct reference to MMSYSTEM.H. This is possible because the file is now usually referenced in WINDOWS.H.

sndPlaySound plays WAV files. These files usually have a .WAV extension and contain digital versions of analog sounds. As a result, they can hold nearly any kind of sound from voices to music.

Syntax

The *sndPlaySound* Function

sndPlaySound(*filename*, SND_*FORMAT*);

The sndPlaySound function is a high-level multimedia command that gives you a simple way to play WAV files. The first parameter, *filename*, is the name of the WAV file you want to play. The Chimes program in Listing 1.6 plays BELL.WAV, which is placed on your system by default when you install Windows. Other files you might want to try include CHORD.WAV, GUITAR.WAV, PIANO.WAV, and DING.WAV.

The second parameter, SND_*FORMAT*, contains one of the following constants, which relay simple commands to Windows:

SND_SYNC	0x0000	Play synchronously (default)
SND_ASYNC	0x0001	Play asynchronously
SND_NODEFAULT	0x0002	Don't use default sound
SND_MEMORY	0x0004	First param is a memory file
SND_LOOP	0x0008	Loop sound until next sndPlaySound
SND_NOSTOP	0x0010	Don't stop any currently playing sound

Here's an example:

```
sndPlaySound("Chord.Wav", SND_LOOP);
sndPlaySound("Guitar.Wav", SND_SYNC);
```

In Listing 1.6 you will find the Beeper program, which does not require multimedia capabilities. This program can, however, play multimedia files if your system supports that capability.

Listing 1.6. The BEEPER.CPP program will make a sound on any PC system.

```
1: // Program BEEPER.CPP
2: #define STRICT
3: #include <windows.h>
4:
5: int WINAPI WinMain(HINSTANCE hInst,
6:                    HINSTANCE hPrevInstance,
7:                    LPSTR lpszCmdParam, int nCmdShow)
8: {
9:    MessageBeep(-1);
10:    return 0;
11: }
```

The BEEPER.CPP file produces a short sound by using your system's built-in speaker.

This program uses the MessageBeep function to produce a beep or another sound, depending on how you set up your system. If you don't have multimedia sound available, you should always

pass a -1 to the MessageBeep function. If you have multimedia, try passing in MB_ICONEXCLAMATION as a parameter.

The *MessageBeep* Function

```
MessageBeep(0);
```

The MessageBeep function is one of the simplest calls in the entire Windows API. It takes a single parameter, which is usually set to -1.

By default, the MessageBeep function makes a simple beep noise, very similar to what you hear so often in DOS programs. Systems that have multimedia capabilities, or systems equipped with SPEAKER.DRV, can associate other sounds with the MessageBeep function. To do this, simply pass one of the following constants to MessageBeep:

```
MB_ICONASTERISK
MB_ICONEXCLAMATION
MB_ICONHAND
MB_ICONQUESTION
MB_OK
```

You also can change the sounds associated with the preceding constants—just open the Control Panel and select the Sound icon. Match the default sound from column A with the WAV file of your choice from column B (as shown in Figure 1.2). Now if you run the Beeper program, you'll hear an entirely new sound. (Remember, though, that these later capabilities are only available on systems equipped with multimedia sound.)

Here's an example:

```
MessageBeep(MB_OK);
```

Figure 1.2.

Associating a particular sound with the MessageBeep *function.*

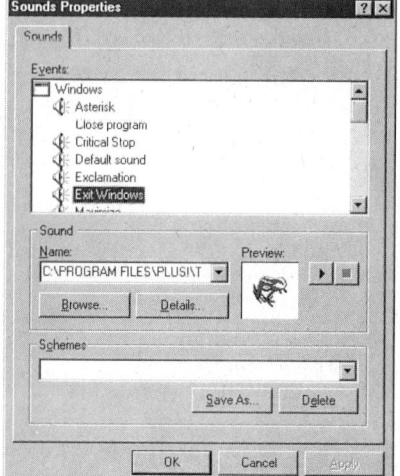

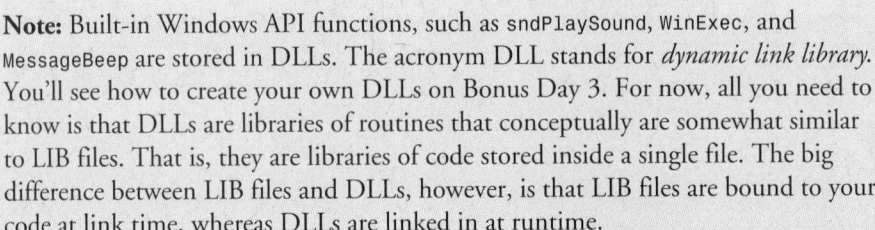

Note: Built-in Windows API functions, such as sndPlaySound, WinExec, and MessageBeep are stored in DLLs. The acronym DLL stands for *dynamic link library*. You'll see how to create your own DLLs on Bonus Day 3. For now, all you need to know is that DLLs are libraries of routines that conceptually are somewhat similar to LIB files. That is, they are libraries of code stored inside a single file. The big difference between LIB files and DLLs, however, is that LIB files are bound to your code at link time, whereas DLLs are linked in at runtime.

The major API calls, such as WinExec, sndPlaySound, and MessageBox, reside in DLLs and are linked dynamically at runtime. These DLLs have names such as GDI32.DLL, GDI.EXE, USER32.DLL, and USER.EXE. Also crucial are the "kernel" DLLs, called KERNEL32.DLL, KRNL386.EXE, and KRNL286.EXE.

Don't worry if DLLs don't make complete sense to you yet. The topic comes up again in the last half of the book. For now, all you need to know is that they're much like LIB files.

Define *STRICT* to Help Create More Robust Programs

Listings 1.5 and 1.6 contain only a few simple lines of code. In fact, their structure is identical to the LaoTzu program, except that they're defined as STRICT. Take a moment to think about the important STRICT preprocessor directive.

Preprocessor Directives

Syntax

```
#define CONSTANT value
```

Preprocessor directives are special messages written directly to the compiler. If you write

```
#define MYNUMBER 35
```

this tells the compiler to swap in 35 whenever it sees the word MYNUMBER. The STRICT directive does something similar. It's a message telling the compiler to perform a certain action. The next few paragraphs of this book describe that action.

STRICT type checking gives special Windows-based integer types, such as HINSTANCE, a whole new power, thereby helping programmers avoid careless errors. This is not the time or place to discuss STRICT type checking in-depth. Indeed, you should know that the code in this book will run even if STRICT is not turned on. However, from here on out, all the programs in this book will be defined as STRICT by default. I strongly recommend that you follow this convention. The key point to remember is that STRICT code brings *strict type checking* to your program.

If STRICT isn't defined, HINSTANCE is declared as an unsigned int; if a program uses STRICT, however, HINSTANCE is declared as a pointer. The compiler can perform careful type checking on pointers, whereas it quite naturally regards all integers as being the same type.

In this book, I often treat special Windows types, such as HINSTANCE, as simple variables (rather than pointers). This helps me present material in the clearest and simplest terms. In other words, even though I know that STRICT is turned on, I still speak of HINSTANCE as a simple integer value.

This brings us to a second important point: Most of the time you should be able to ignore the presence of the STRICT directive altogether. It is meant to exist transparently and to raise its head only when it can help you correct an error.

When the STRICT option is used, the compiler can make distinctions between types to which it would normally be blind. For instance, the compiler usually doesn't distinguish the handle to a window from the handle to a picture (or bitmap, as pictures are often called in Windows). However, when you use the STRICT directive, the compiler can warn you (at compile time) of bugs that might normally take hours or days to track down.

Remember that the STRICT directive gives your program strict type checking. This helps you avoid careless errors that can delay projects for hours, days, or even weeks.

What Is WINDOWS.H?

This is not the place to get bogged down in a discussion of too many technical details. You might find it helpful, however, to know something about the broad structure of the programs presented previously.

LAOTZU.CPP, CHIMES.CPP and BEEPER.CPP all begin by including a header file called WINDOWS.H:

```
#include <windows.h>
```

Every Windows program includes this file, because it defines a very wide range of constants, structures, macros, and functions, all of which make up the backbone of a typical Windows programs. (See Figure 1.3.)

All the programs in this book use WINDOWS.H. It's the key to the whole Windows programming experience. This book, and most other books that have been written on Windows programming, are really nothing more than commentaries on that essential document, and all the files that are related to it.

Figure 1.3.
WINDOWS.H provides the structure upon which most Windows programs are built.

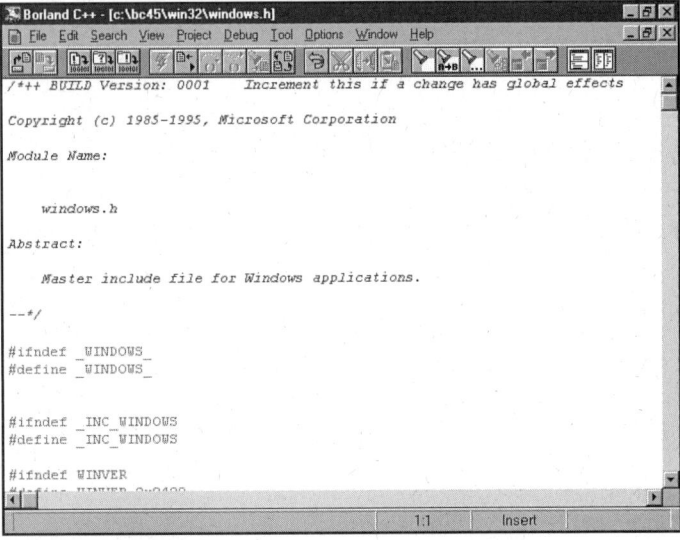

```
/*++ BUILD Version: 0001    Increment this if a change has global effects

Copyright (c) 1985-1995, Microsoft Corporation

Module Name:

    windows.h

Abstract:

    Master include file for Windows applications.

--*/

#ifndef _WINDOWS_
#define _WINDOWS_


#ifndef _INC_WINDOWS
#define _INC_WINDOWS

#ifndef WINVER
```

DO ████████████████████ **DON'T**

DO take the time to locate WINDOWS.H on your system. If you own Visual C++, the WINDOWS.H file was placed by default in the \msvc\include directory. If you own Borland C++, the file was placed by default in the \bc45\include directory.

WINDOWS.H used to consist of one single file. However, it is now broken up into a series of files, the contents of which will be discussed in more depth on Day 3, "A Standard Windows Program." If you work in the Borland IDE, you can use the mouse to expand the Project window so that it shows the various parts of WINDOWS.H.

Even though WINDOWS.H is now broken up into several files, I will still sometimes refer to it as simply WINDOWS.H. At other times I will talk about the WINDOWS.H complex of files, which refers to all the secondary header files referenced in WINDOWS.H.

DO ████████████████████ **DON'T**

DON'T start reading Day2 without first locating a copy of WINDOWS.H.

DO take the time to browse through the files that make up WINDOWS.H complex. Don't worry if they don't make any sense to you at this time. For now, all you need to do is get a sense for the vast scope of their content.

What Is *WinMain*?

Traditional C/C++ programs from the DOS or UNIX environment use the `main()` function as the program entry point. Windows programs, however, use `WinMain`. Functionally, the two routines have a great deal in common. That is, they both serve as the first function that gets called within a particular program.

The *WinMain* Function

The following declaration comes from Borland's copy of WINDOWS.H:

```
int WINAPI WinMain(HINSTANCE, HINSTANCE, LPSTR, int);
```

Here's the same Microsoft version of the declaration, which appears in WINBASE.H:

```
int
WINAPI
WinMain(
   HINSTANCE hInst,
   HINSTANCE hPrevInstance,
   LPSTR lpszCmdParam,
   int nCmdShow);
```

As I mentioned earlier, this referencing back and forth between the Microsoft and Borland versions of these files will abate considerably once you are through the first two chapters of this book. Furthermore, it's worth pointing out that the structure of these files is bound to change again when newer versions of these compilers hit the shelves. As a result, it's perhaps most important that you learn how to read these files, rather than just absorb everything I say as another item to be memorized. You should also learn how to use the Borland GREP.COM utility, and the Find program that ships with Windows 95. These tools can help you search through multiple files for particular references. For instance, you should take the time to learn how to scan through all the header files in the **\include directory that contain the letters `WinMain`.

The `WinMain` function takes four parameters:

1. The first parameter is a unique number, or handle, which is associated with the current program. For now, you can think of `HINSTANCE` as being an `int`; though later you'll see that there is a little more to this subject than first meets the eye.

2. The second parameter is important only in 16-bit Windows. It is a unique handle associated with another instance of this application, if it exists. For instance, if you start two copies of CLOCK.EXE, the second copy of the program receives the `HINSTANCE` of the first program in this parameter. If no previous instance of the program exists, this parameter is set to `NULL`. In Windows 95 and Windows NT this parameter is meaningless because each program runs in its own 4GB address space. In other words, each program runs in a kind of virtual world in which it believes itself to

be the sole inhabitant. Windows 95 programs are not aware of other programs running on the system, even if they happen to be a second instance of the same executable. As a result, the second parameter is always NULL in Windows 95 and Windows NT. Microsoft made it available on these platforms solely to provide compatibility with Windows 3.1.

3. The third parameter is a string containing any parameters passed to the program. The LPSTR type is Windows talk meaning a 32-bit pointer to a string.

4. The fourth parameter specifies whether the program should begin in a normal state, a maximized state, or a minimized state. A detailed example of how this is done is shown on Day 8, "Windows Animation: The Snake Game," and Day 13, "Subclassing Windows Controls."

WinMain returns an integer that Windows never actually examines. In other words, your application ends whenever WinMain ends; specific values returned are meant primarily to aid in debugging, or by making your code more readable. Therefore, it wouldn't really matter whether WinMain returns TRUE or FALSE at any particular point. I like to return FALSE when an error occurs, simply because it helps make the code readily comprehensible.

Here's an example:

```
int WINAPI WinMain(HINSTANCE hInst, HINSTANCE hPrevInstance,
                LPSTR lpszCmdParam, int nCmdShow)
```

Okay, that's enough for now. I'm sure you are interested in knowing more about the technical details that make up the programs shown in this chapter, but I'd rather leave that kind of discussion for Day 2. For now, you might want to just play around with your compiler and the Windows environment. Hands-on work is very important. Anyway, there will be plenty of time for technical discussions later in this book.

The rest of this chapter contains a few words about the kinds of compilers and hardware you'll need to write Windows code with the C++ language. I also mention a few stylistic issues, and from a theoretical standpoint, I give a general overview of the Windows environment. The chapter ends with a brief overview of the topics covered in the rest of this book.

The Sticky Matter of GUIs

Windows has a *graphical user interface* (GUI). This acronym is pronounced "gooey," as in a "gooey mass of cotton-candy-flavored bubble gum."

As a participant in the rapidly changing high-tech world of computers, you no doubt have heard people say that Windows is slow. Well, the reason for its reputed slowness is not that it's a protected-mode application, and not that it multitasks, but rather because it is a GUI.

GUIs were created primarily to make life simpler for the users of applications. They were most definitely not created to make life simpler for programmers.

In particular, GUIs enable users to begin to think in terms of colors, icons, and graphics. The mere idea of multiple resizable windows is not at all unique to a GUI. In fact, many DOS text-mode applications make excellent use of all these features. The bread and butter of a GUI are its graphical features. For instance, users like to see scrollbars that appear to exist in three dimensions and toolbars that are filled with intricate multicolored icons. When used properly, these aren't merely bells and whistles designed to make Windows appear slick and sophisticated. GUIs were created to make applications more usable, more functional, and more approachable.

People who live near the heart of the computer world can forget how utterly baffling these machines can be to outsiders. The average person, even the average very bright person, needs all the help he or she can get when sitting down at a computer. This is not just a minor point, not just a nicety addressed to humor weak-kneed technophobes. Rather, the whole idea of making computers user friendly has become a necessity—a hard-core art or science—which is being studied by the best minds in the world.

How Much Hardware Do You Need?

The GUI, which floats over the Windows core like a big dome, is a crucially important feature that every programmer who reads this book is going to have to come to terms with sooner or later. Specifically, you need to understand that GUIs are here to stay, and that they take up massive amounts of system resources.

You cannot dodge this issue. The whole idea of computing has changed because of the presence of GUIs, and because of the current move to 32-bit operating systems. As a result, you need to think seriously about the kind of hardware you are using when you program Windows.

There was a time when a 286 with a couple megs of RAM was considered a hot machine. Those days are over. If you want to program Windows, you want the fastest possible machine you can lay your hands on.

Most of the time, this doesn't mean that you should run down to the store and attempt to upgrade you current computer. Trying to assemble a modern computer out of bits and pieces of this and that, rarely works out right in the long run. If you can possibly afford it, you need a computer with some serious horsepower and with parts that work well together.

Let me just take a moment to underline this point. In my work, I have occasions to talk to people who are having trouble getting some very reliable programming tools up and running on their system. After the smoke clears, the discussions I have with these people usually focuses on one of two problems. The first, and more common, is that someone patched hardware together out of a hodgepodge of parts, some of which are four or five years old. The other problem represents the opposite extreme—namely, people who own some supposedly super-hot piece of hardware that exists on the bleeding edge of technology.

> **Note:** The figures shown below assume you want to program 32-bit code inside Windows 95.

A reasonable machine on which to program Windows is a reliable 486 or Pentium with at least 8MB of memory, a VGA or SuperVGA monitor, and at least a 500MB hard drive. A comfortable configuration, that treats you right, is a Pentium with at least 16MB of memory and a 1GB hard drive. Anything less than a 486 33MHz, with 8MB of memory, would probably be too big of a strain on your sanity—though the patient could probably get along somehow on a 386. (But I don't think I'd like to work too closely with the person who's using one!) Figure 1.4 uses the MSD.EXE program that comes with Windows to illustrate the features of a typical Windows development machine.

Figure 1.4.

The SYSINF95.EXE and SYSINFO.EXE programs display the features of a typical Windows develop-ment machine, circa summer 1995.

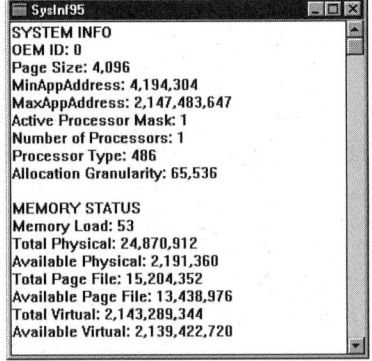

Notice that I don't mention my idea of an ideal machine. That's because every machine I've ever used in the last four or five years has been a little slower than I wanted it to be. Back in the old days, when all I had was an XT, I was satisfied. But ever since I got my hands on my first 286, I've had this inexplicable longing for a faster, more powerful machine. This appetite increased nearly tenfold when Windows came along. There's something about Windows that makes me dream about P6s, P7s, MIPS, Alphas, anything that promises to be just a little bit faster.

At any rate, I'm quite serious about recommending that you get the most powerful machine you can afford. You would definitely not be going overboard if you decide to buy a Pentium 90MHz machine with 16 to 24MB of RAM. No one who really understands Windows programming would claim that such a machine is overkill. In particular, if you want to use Windows NT, don't try to use less than 20MB of memory. In Windows 95 you can get along with 8MB, but the system is really a little starved if you have less than 12.

The Compiler

Just as important as your hardware, is the compiler you choose. All the code in this book is guaranteed to run on either Microsoft Visual C++ 2.0 or Borland C++ 4.53. In most cases, the only differences in the code are in the makefiles, and even those differences are minor.

Note: Your copy of Borland C++ 4.5x may need to be upgraded with the latest headers and libraries from Borland. At the time of this writing it appears that these files should be available for free, or at a nominal cost. However, Borland will be the final arbiter of these policies. Check CompuServe or the Borland Web site for further information or for copies of the actual files.

Either Microsoft's or Borland's compiler is more than adequate for the task. In fact, a number of other excellent compilers are on the market. I have not, however, had time to test this code on all those platforms. As a result, using this code on any other compiler could be problematic.

I want to stress again that I'm not promoting any one particular compiler. I simply want to write a good technical book that you'll find useful. I'm interested in programming, not PR.

I have, however, made every attempt to make the code in this book as up-to-date as possible. This means you'll be much better off if you own Borland C++ version 4.5 or later, or Microsoft Visual C++ version 2.0 or 1.5 or later. These are the compilers I used when writing this code. In particular, this book makes heavy use of a very important file called WINDOWSX.H. This file serves to extend and complement WINDOWS.H. It also helps make your code portable between WIN32 and 16-bit Windows. So before going further, you should check to be sure you have a copy of WINDOWSX.H.

Note: When I use the term WIN32, I am referring to the 32-bit Windows environments such as Windows NT and Windows 95. When I want to reference Windows 3.1, I sometimes call it WIN16, or 16-bit Windows. For the purposes of this book, Windows 3.0 is considered obsolete, and if you are still running this operating system, you should upgrade immediately. I know that there are some copies of Windows 3.0 still running out there, but I consider compatibility with Windows 3.0 to be an esoteric subject, and not valid material for a Windows programming book intended for general audiences.

It pains me to have to stress the need for powerful equipment and up-to-date compilers. Ordinarily, I'm not the type to be hip to all the latest trends. Windows, however, does exist very much on the cutting edge of existing computer technology, so you have to be prepared to make a considerable investment before you can sit down to play this particular game. (On the other hand, the rewards are high. If you master this material, you will almost surely be able to get or keep a good job programming Windows.)

Coding Styles and Other Nitty-Gritty Issues

Most of the code for this book was written using Borland C++ for Windows. As I was creating the programs, I developed project files, and only later converted those project files into makefiles. I think makefiles provide a convenient format that lets me share code with you easily. If you want to have access to my project files, however, the source code for these programs ships with this book, and I will distribute updates for the source code in this book on a wide array of BBSs.

Note: This book's software is available on the CompuServe Information Service. After you type GO SAMS, you enter the Macmillan Computer Publishing forum. Once there, enter the file library, and search in library 7 (Sams-ProgLang+DataB) for the keyword CALVERT. If you prefer you can check www.mcp.com or www.borland.com.

All the code in this book is written to conform with C++ standards. This doesn't necessarily mean the code *won't* compile on a standard C compiler—only that the code takes full advantage of the strong type checking that is inherent in the C++ language.

At all stages of code development, I make heavy use of debuggers such as CodeView and Turbo Debugger for Windows (there are other powerful tools, as well). I can't stress enough how vitally important debuggers can be to any successful coding project. Because this book is meant to appeal to you no matter which debugger you use, I don't concentrate on the techniques involved with using any particular debugging tool. Still, I believe it is of absolutely paramount importance that you learn to use the debugger that comes with your compiler—and that you lean on this friendly support as heavily as possible. The debugger is there to serve you. Learn to utilize its services. If you don't, you'll perish in a wasteland of lost messages, uninitialized pointers, and mind-boggling general protection faults.

What Is Windows?

Windows comes in several different flavors. For instance, there is Windows 3.1, which is an operating environment that runs on top of DOS. Many people feel that both DOS and Windows 3.1 are *not* true operating systems because they don't provide real preemptive multitasking or any robust form of protection against errors in ill-behaved programs. Windows NT provides all these things and much more. And to a large degree, so does Windows 95.

So how can I hope to tie all these different versions of Windows together into a single book that presents a coherent version of how to program? What's the glue that holds these tools together? Where's the common thread? It's something called the Windows API.

The Windows API

In the last section, I wrestled with the paradoxical fact that Windows both is and isn't an operating system. In short, the word Windows is quite generic and doesn't have any single specific referent.

This nasty Gordian knot can yield rather quickly to the sword when you understand that Windows NT, the operating system, Windows 95, the seeming operating system, and Windows 3.1, the operating environment, remain linked together by a common API, or *application programming interface.*

> **Note:** The phrase *Gordian knot* comes from a knot tied by King Gordius of Phrygia. This knot was meant to only be untied by the future ruler, but Alexander the Great cut the knot with his sword. Today, a Gordian knot represents an intricate problem—especially one insoluble in its own terms.

An API is a set of routines used to control either an entire computer, or a particular feature of a computer, such as a modem, video card, or mouse. Suppose, for instance, that you have a set of three routines designed to provide your program with a mouse interface. I'll call these routines `InitializeMouse`, `SetMousePosition`, and `GetMousePosition`.

These three routines could represent a simple API between your program and the mouse. They would let you start the mouse, set the mouse to a particular position, and get the current position of the mouse cursor. These simple capabilities are enough to form an *interface* between your *application* and a piece of hardware.

The Windows API is nothing more than a similar set of routines that form an interface between your application and the entire computer. For instance, the Windows API gives you the ability to both set and get the current position of the mouse cursor. But it doesn't stop there. It also gives you functions for creating windows on the screen, for moving and resizing those windows, for controlling modems, files, directories, and memory, and much, much more. Windows is really only an API, but at the same time, it's an incredibly powerful API.

By now it should be clear that because Windows 95, Windows 3.1, and Windows NT have a common API, they are tied together. For instance, many Windows 3.1 programs make use of a function called MoveWindow. Naturally enough, this function can cause a Window to move from one location to another. Well, it should come as no surprise to learn that Windows 95 and Windows NT also have a function called MoveWindow. It works exactly the same way the Windows 3.1 function works.

Of course, Windows 95, Windows 3.1, and Windows NT aren't exactly the same; they do have significant differences. Yet I am very much aware of the fact that many programmers want to program for all three environments. As a result, in this book I include some programs that work in all three environments without modification.

As stated previously, I frequently use a special header file called WINDOWSX.H that helps you write simple, clean code. It also provides a common interface between 16-bit Windows 3.1 code and WIN32 code. (WIN32 is the name for the type of 32-bit code that drives Windows 95 and Windows NT). As you learn to master WINDOWSX.H, you'll also learn how to write code that will run unchanged in Windows 95, Windows 3.1, and Windows NT.

What's This Stuff About 32 Bits?

One of my goals in this book is to avoid using excessively technical language. I'm not interested in writing a book that has an erudite aura of arcane technical knowledge that leaves you feeling intimidated, impressed, and not one whit the wiser.

Instead, I want to communicate things to you in the simplest possible terms. If you want to take that knowledge and make something complicated out of it, then believe me, programming Windows in C++ is going to give you every opportunity imaginable for doing just that.

Rather than push you toward the brink of unfathomable complexity, I want to find the big themes that run through Windows programming like super-highways. I want you to have a very solid grounding in the basics, knowing that from there you can reach any region covered by the API, no matter how remote.

Therefore, it is important for you to come to terms right from the start with this business about the 8-bit, 16-bit, and 32-bit operating systems, and also the 64KB, 640KB, and 4GB (GB stands for *gigabyte*, which is a billion bytes) limits. Like it or not, these relatively technical subjects lie very much at the heart of Windows development. It's quite possible that there wouldn't even be such a thing as Windows if it weren't for the 640KB limit.

I'll start at the beginning by talking about bits. As you probably know, everything in a computer boils down to a bunch of on/off switches. These switches are represented by a series of zeros and ones called *binary* numbers.

For instance, the numbers 0 and 1 each can be represented by a single binary digit. Here is the number 0 in binary notation:

0

And here is the number 1 in binary notation:

1

Not very impressive looking, are they? When you see these tiny numbers standing all alone on the stage, it doesn't seem as if they can have the power to do much of anything. But hold on a moment.

Here is the number 2 in binary notation:

10

And here is the number three:

11

Here, for your personal delectation, is the number 255:

11111111

And finally, here is the number 65,535 (also known as 64KB):

1111111111111111

This last number has dominated computing on PCs for approximately the last 15 years. The reason it's so important is because it's the largest number you can represent with 16 binary digits, that is, with a mere 16 *bits* of binary data.

Note: The word *bit* comes from extracting letters from the phrase "*bi*nary digi*t*."

If you try to go one higher, that is to 65,536, you end with a binary number that looks like this:

10000000000000000

This number is represented with 17 bits of information. Unfortunately, the famous 80286 Intel processor can only handle 16 bits of information at any time. That is why it is a 16-bit processor that has dominated the computer industry lo these many years.

Of course, it's possible to work with numbers much larger than 65,535 on a 286 computer. The problem is that you have to load up the coprocessor with several different bundles of information before you can count that high. That is fine when you are doing math, but it isn't fine when the computer is addressing memory. As a result, data structures on 8086 and 286 computers generally cannot be larger than 64KB—at least not without performing some fancy behind-the-scenes manipulations. Anyone who has used arrays before is almost certainly painfully aware of this problem.

The 64KB barrier is not the only limitation that DOS programmers have been wrestling with for some time now. The other problem involves the 640KB limitation that represents the space inside which DOS and its family of programs can run.

When Windows 3.0 and Windows 3.1 came along, they did much to break the limitations put in place during the years when DOS was king. However, both Windows 3.0 and Windows 3.1 are still fundamentally 16-bit operating environments. They help you escape the 640KB barrier by using protected mode, but they don't rid us of the constricting grasp of 64KB segments. It's up to Windows 95, Windows NT, and OS/2 to point beyond the claustrophobic 16-bit world in which we have lived since DOS first strapped us into the straight jacket.

At this late date, it's extremely easy to criticize the makers of DOS for limiting their operating system to such a relatively small memory space—and for not taking better advantage of the 1MB of memory available to them. Yet sometimes 20/20 hindsight is a bit too easy and too tempting. After all, DOS was the operating system that changed the face of the computing world and brought the wonders of the digital information age to over 100 million desktops. Given DOS's extraordinarily successful track record, it's really a bit much for all of us to suddenly stand up and say, "It was all a mistake."

The problem isn't so much that DOS was a mistake, but that programmers are now using computers to accomplish feats that the designers of the PC's memory architecture never imagined. On our desktops these days are 386s, 486s, Pentiums, P6s, and various RISC-based processors. A 286 computer can address 64KB of memory at one time, but a 386 is a 32-bit computer that can address 4GB of memory at one time.

Here are 16 bits and 32 bits lined up one on top of the other:

     16 bits: 1111111111111111
     32 bits: 11111111111111111111111111111111

Here are the decimal numbers addressed by that many bits of information:

     16 bits: 64,536
     32 bits: 4,294,967,296

Four billion, two hundred ninety-four million, nine hundred sixty-seven thousand, two hundred ninety-six is a number that starts to slide off my scale of comprehension. All that I really know is that it's real, real big.

Certainly, it's large enough to utterly dwarf the old familiar limitations we find on 16-bit machines. What is 64KB compared to 4GB? Nothing. It's irrelevant. It's simply ridiculous for owners of a 386 or better to sit around strapped in by the limitations imposed by DOS.

Once you begin to grasp these underlying facts, it becomes obvious that DOS, at least as we know it, is doomed. The computing world is moving inexorably towards 32-bit computing, and 32-bit operating environments, such as Windows 95, Windows NT, and OS/2, will carry us across the great divide.

There you have it. That's one of the major underlying themes of this book. We're studying a way of programming that's ready to address the future. Windows straddles the gap between 16-bit and 32-bit computing, and therefore, it's a very likely route into the future. That's why somebody has hired me to write this book. That's why you're sitting there hopefully totally prepared to do the work necessary to master Windows programming.

The issue is simply that Windows, and its close cousin OS/2, can lead the way into the future.

Even more remarkable is the fact that just as 16-bit computing has led to 32-bit computing, so will 32-bit computing inevitably lead to 64-bit computing, and even 128-bit computing. In other words, computing is going to go through a number of massive changes in the next 5, 10, and 25 years. The computers we will work on 10 years from now will make a 486 or a Pentium look like a child's toy. Without some understanding of these facts, you'll never really understand what Windows is about, or why it has taken on this particular shape.

Back Down from the Clouds

After this peek into the future, it's hard to come back down to reality. However, I want to concentrate for a moment on some specific traits of Windows 95. In particular, I want to compare it to Windows 3.1, that operating environment that is now beginning its slow descent into the happy hunting grounds where dead operating systems are laid to rest.

Windows 3.1 is not a 32-bit environment; it's a 16-bit environment that runs in *protected mode*. Windows 95 and Windows NT also both run in protected mode. Protected mode is part of the programming scheme that will dominate Intel based computers for as far into the future as we can currently see.

The past, however, in the form of 16-bit protected-mode programming, is still clinging to our shirttails, holding us back. Two major features of 16-bit protected-mode programming set it apart from both 32-bit programming and standard real-mode DOS programming.

Note: Real-mode programs are so named, because their addressing scheme refers to actual, or "real" addresses in memory. Protected-mode programs, on the other hand, use selectors rather than "real" addresses.

In the DOS world, every address is made up of two 16-bit numbers, a segment and an offset, which are combined by the operating system to form a 20-bit number. In 16-bit protected mode, however, the segment portion of an address is just an index into a table that holds 24-bit numbers. This index is called a *selector*.

Note: To convert two 16-bit numbers into a 20-bit number, use the following formula:

```
TwentyBitAddress = (Segment * 16) + Offset;
```

Multiplying by 16 is the same thing as shifting a number left 4 bits.

Right now, it's not necessary for you to get too bogged down in the details of how these addressing schemes work. Instead, concentrate on the fact that 16-bit protected mode enables programmers to use a 24-bit number, whereas in DOS real mode, they could only use a 16-bit number. As a result, even "lowly" 16-bit protected-mode programs can address up to a total of 16MB. In other words, 16-bit protected mode makes it possible for your programs to utilize more than 16 times the amount of memory that a DOS application can address.

This doesn't mean that the old 64KB limitation has disappeared for Windows 3.1 programmers. It's still a part of the 16-bit Windows 3.1 programming environment. You can, however, use WIN16 to combine a selector and an offset to break the 640KB limitation of real-mode DOS programs.

In addition to enabling you to address a larger portion of memory, 16-bit protected-mode programs also let you engage in a primitive form of multitasking. Selectors are the key to this process. They allow the operating system to move blocks of memory around without the program itself having to know what is happening. This makes it possible to swap programs or portions of programs to disk. It's also possible for the operating system to protect one program from the ill behaved behavior of a second program. These types of tricks makes a crude form of 16-bit protected-mode multitasking possible.

If you want to do real multitasking, you need to step up to Windows 95 and Windows NT. These environments allow you to truly multitask 32-bit programs. That is, the compiler gives each running program a slice of memory in which to work, and once it has used up that time,

the operating system moves on to the next program and gives it a tiny slice of time. As a result, the operating system keeps switching, at regular intervals, between programs. No one program hogs the processor. Under Windows 3.1, on the other hand, programs can easily steal the processor away from the operating system, thereby forcing the user to deal with an unpredictable system.

It's at the point when selectors come into play that you will finally begin to understand the meaning of protected mode. As I said earlier, selectors are only indexes into a table where real addresses are kept. As a result of this scheme, the operating system can monitor the use of every address so that it *protects* the user from careless or poorly written programs that try to write outside the program's memory space. In other words, protected-mode programs usually can't crash the system by writing to the wrong portions of memory. They are prohibited from doing so by the operating system itself, which monitors every address in the table where the selectors are kept.

At the same time, an efficient operating environment, such as Windows, can manipulate the memory addresses in this table so that different programs can share close quarters without crowding one another out. This task is much too complicated for individual programmers to have to take on every time they sit down to write an application. Because protected-mode programs use selectors instead of real addresses, the actual nitty-gritty of multitasking is turned over to the operating system.

To keep up with the core points outlined above, you just need to grasp two key concepts.

☐ 16-bit protected-mode applications can address not 640KB, but 16MB of memory. 32-bit protected-mode programs, on the other hand, can address 4GB of memory.

☐ Protected-mode programs can be multitasked because the memory they address is kept in a special table that can be manipulated by the operating system.

When 16-bit programs are multitasked under Windows 3.1 and Windows 95, they often share the same address space. That means that despite the advantages of protected mode, they can still step on each other's toes. That is, they can still accidentally write over memory that belongs to another program, or to the operating system itself.

When you are using a true 32-bit program under Windows 95 or Windows NT, it will run automatically in its own address space. Specifically, each Windows 95 program runs in Virtual Machine that is 4GB. Each program has its own 4GB address space that is not shared by other programs on the system. This provides for a very robust architecture.

Under Windows 95 and Windows NT, it is much, much harder to bring down the whole operating system simply by creating a general protection fault inside one 32-bit program. In other words, 32-bit programs running under Windows 95 and Windows NT are much more robust than programs that run under Windows 3.1 because each one runs in its own, separate, 4GB virtual machine.

I have been discussing the differences between 16-bit and 32-bit programs, and the difference between real-mode and protected-mode programs. But you don't actually need to know all these things to write Windows code.

I'm discussing these matters because I want you to understand what you are really doing when you write Windows code. If all I do is show you a set of rules to memorize, I can perhaps help you to become a fair Windows programmer of modest abilities. If, however, you learn the broad outlines of the underlying theory behind Windows, you'll be able to master any challenge. You will have not only knowledge, but also understanding.

A Look Ahead

Week 1, "Getting Started," is meant to be a general introduction to Windows programming. It acquaints you with the fundamentals without delving into too many details.

Week 2, "Getting Serious," includes an in-depth discussion of some important technical matters as well as a full-length Windows program and game. It also includes a chapter on working with WIN32 console applications, long filenames, and large address spaces. By the time you finish Week 3, "Advanced Topics," you should have a good feeling for how to write solid Windows programs that will appeal to a wide range of users.

The Bonus Days section covers Windows 95 controls and other advanced subjects. This section also examines threads, as well as Windows 95 memory management techniques.

The bonus days add important information about multimedia programming, DLLs, and advanced GDI programming. There is also a section on the multiple-document interface.

Between the three sections of the book you will find Week in Review sections that contain additional programs that demonstrate advanced features of Windows 95 and Windows 3.1. These extra programs will not necessarily run on all three platforms discussed in this book. Instead, they show off features particular to individual operating systems such as Windows 95 or Windows NT.

Summary

In this chapter, you read some general comments about Windows programming and then ran two simple Windows programs. Once the preliminaries were out of the way, you had a chance to step back and take a look at Windows from a theoretical standpoint. You have read a description of what Windows is, learned why it's important, and glimpsed its future.

You have also read about the tools needed to best pursue the goal of becoming a good Windows programmer. In particular, you know that I believe Windows programming requires up-to-date programming tools and powerful computers.

Now that the groundwork has been laid, the best thing you can do is to take some time to get set up. Load the compiler you want to work with and become familiar with its fundamentals. Take a look at the documentation you have available, and become familiar with it. Experiment with the editor you plan to use, and locate the compiler and debugger you'll depend on. Find the places in the manual that explain how to use these tools. To a good programmer, a debugger is nearly as essential as a compiler.

Take your time getting set up. I think programmers need to know how to putter. To me, programming isn't all just compulsive work, work, work, and more work. I need to enjoy playing with the tools I'm using when I'm on the job. If the whole thing doesn't seem at least a little bit like a large, very complicated, very elaborate game, I know something has gone wrong. As a rule, programmers work very, very hard. The thing that makes it possible is that some of that work is fun. So take the time to enjoy yourself, okay? If somebody's got you grinding away at some boring programming job from morning till night, then read this book through a few times. It will teach you things that will help you get a better job, or make you more respected in the job you have now.

Q&A

Q What is a program entry point?

A The program entry point is the place a program begins. When you click an icon and start a program, Windows loads that program into memory and then calls its `WinMain` function. This is the same process that goes on in DOS whenever a program is started. The big difference is that `WinMain` takes more parameters than does `main()`.

Q What is WINDOWS.H?

A WINDOWS.H is an include file, or a series of include files, that contain many of the most important constants, functions, structures, and macros used by Windows programs written in C++ or C. In some ways, it's the single most concise definition of the Windows programming environment available. As a commentary, however, it tends to be a bit too arcane, and so books such as this are written to explain the WINDOWS.H complex in language that is easy to understand.

Q Should I try to read the WINDOWS.H complex from beginning to end?

A I guess I would consider reading WINDOWS.H and its related files in their entirety to be a fairly extreme act. On the other hand, a lot of the best Windows programmers tend to be a bit extreme by nature. Certainly no harm would come to you if you read one or two modules. You might, however, want to start out by just dipping into WINDOWS.H (Borland) and WINBASE.H (Microsoft) for a few minutes from time to time in order to get a feeling for the way it looks. Even if it seems a bit boring at first, I promise it will become more interesting as you learn more about the Windows environment.

Q Will I be able to use my old 286 to program Windows?

A No way. If you are a professional, and the people in hardware want to know what kind of machine you need, tell them you *require* a Pentium 90MHz computer with 16MB of RAM and a 750MB hard drive. Tell 'em that's the minimum machine. If you are programming Windows NT, ask for 24MB. If you are a hobbyist, get at least a 486 75MHz with 8MB of RAM.

Workshop

The Workshop provides quiz questions to help you solidify your understanding of the material covered and exercises to provide you with experience in using what you've learned. Try to understand the quiz and exercise answers before continuing on to the next chapter. Answers are provided in Appendix A.

Quiz

1. What does the WinExec function do?
2. Name two differences between Windows and DOS.
3. What is a GUI?
4. Is Windows (that runs on top of DOS) a true operating system?
5. What is a PIF?
6. What is the name of the debugger that comes with your compiler?
7. Can two different Windows programs have the same HINSTANCE?
8. What is the name of the program entry point for a Windows program?
9. If only one copy of a program is running, what is the value of the second parameter passed to WinMain?
10. If two or more copies of a program are running, what is the value of the second parameter passed to WinMain?

Exercises

1. Write a program that WinExecs two other Windows programs.
2. Write a program that uses the third parameter of WinMain to specify, at runtime, which batch file you would like to run.
3. Write a batch file that runs a DOS batch file in a normal window, rather than in a minimized window.

Building Projects, Creating Windows

In this chapter, you get a chance to run another short program, one full-scale Windows program, and to see how to build Windows projects. If you've had trouble getting simple Windows programs to compile and run correctly, then this is the chapter that should set you straight.

In particular, you will see how to do the following:

- Create projects in both Borland C++ and Visual C++
- Use makefiles
- Use module-definition (DEF) files that work in both Windows 3.1 and Windows 95
- Pop up a traditional Window that can be resized, iconized, and maximized

The goal of this chapter is to get a lot of the configuration issues behind you so that you can concentrate on writing Windows code. In particular, you will learn how to enter the correct settings in a makefile, or in the Borland or Microsoft IDE. (When I say IDE, I am referring to the integrated development environment that you see when you launch BCW.EXE or MSVC.EXE.)

This chapter will have several discrete sections that address Microsoft or Borland developers specifically. As stated earlier, this process will continue to some extent into Day 3, "A Standard Windows Program," but it won't be necessary for most of the rest of the book. In other words, I will soon have the compiler-specific configuration issues out of the way, and we will be able to concentrate on writing code. None of the code shown in this book is compiler specific.

There are also a number of places in this chapter where I reference 16-bit Windows. If you have bought this book hoping to find out about Windows 95, don't worry. There is plenty of Windows 95 material present between the covers of this book. All of the Windows 95 controls will be discussed, as will threading, consoles, memory mapped files, and WIN32 memory management. However, as stated in the first chapter, I also want to address the subject of portability between operating systems. Since some of the code shown in this book is fully portable, it's necessary for me to address the subject of how to compile it in each environment. This chapter tackles that subject, and therefore introduces Windows 3.1–specific information in a few places. However, later in the book the subject of Windows 3.1 will rarely appear, and much of the book is dedicated entirely to Windows 95 and Windows NT–specific issues.

This book is chock full of many long sections on the latest, most cutting-edge issues in Windows 95 and Windows NT programming. However, it's also a cautious, carefully thought-out book, and so you will find me occasionally glancing over my shoulder at the 16-bit code that will be receding slowly into the distance over the next few years. In a book with this large a scope it's possible to expand the focus beyond a narrow area of the landscape. In the long run, I believe that this kind of broad knowledge makes for a more complete understanding of how Windows works, and of how to create powerful, well-designed Windows programs.

DEF Files and Makefiles

So far, all the programs you've run have consisted primarily of only one source file, although I have given a brief introduction to makefiles. Standard Windows programs, however, are usually made up of at least three files:

1. The program's main module or modules, extension .CPP
2. A module-definition file, extension .DEF
3. A project or makefile, extension .MAK

C/C++ Programmers also make heavy use of resource files, which in source form have an .RC extension. However, I do not broach that topic until Day 6, "Introduction to Resources," Of course, many programs also include header files (.H), but that familiar subject would only be a distraction at this stage of the game.

The *module-definition file* (DEF file) is of use to nearly all Windows programmers, particularly in Windows 3.1. It does more or less exactly what its name says it does; it defines the characteristics of the main module of a program. These characteristics include:

☐ The file's name

☐ A short description of its purpose or primary characteristics

☐ Its stack and heap size (Optional in WIN32)

☐ A few statements, such as PRELOAD, DISCARDABLE, or MOVEABLE, that define the way the program handles memory (not needed in WIN32)

It is possible to create Windows applications without first defining a module-definition file, and in fact this is becoming a fairly common practice in WIN32-based applications. Even if the compiler gives you a warning when you omit this file, this is usually not serious. After issuing the warning, the compiler will use default values in place of the ones which would have resided in your DEF file. In most cases, it will be fine if you let the compiler use these default values. However, it's arguably a good practice to define a DEF file under most circumstances, particularly if you are working with Borland's 4.x compilers, or any 16-bit application.

Makefiles are useful to all Microsoft developers and to those Borland developers who prefer to work from the command prompt. This book remains fairly neutral on the topic of whether it's best to work from the command prompt or from within a Windows IDE. I've included both Borland and Microsoft makefiles for all but one of the programs in the remainder of this book, and I have created project files for working within the IDE. If you want to get these project files, they are available online.

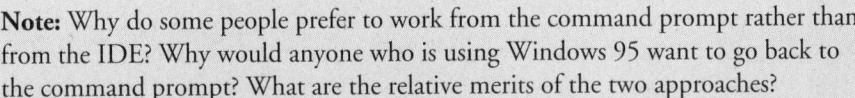

Note: Why do some people prefer to work from the command prompt rather than from the IDE? Why would anyone who is using Windows 95 want to go back to the command prompt? What are the relative merits of the two approaches?

These are all reasonable questions. There are, however, no firm answers to them. The perceived merits of the two environments are mostly matters of opinion, rather than of fact. However, in the next paragraphs I venture a few theories to help you begin thinking about this issue.

If you work inside the IDE it's easier to learn how to configure the compiler, particularly if you are a relatively inexperienced programmer. For instance, the IDE has dialogs that list and help explain the purpose of most of the settings used in a project. As a result, it's easier for some programmers to complete a correct compilation if they work inside the IDE.

Working from the command prompt can be a very reliable, automated way to produce an executable. All you have to do is create a relatively short makefile, and then allow it to tell the compiler what to do. In some cases this can be simpler than trying to flip through several pages of dialogs, making sure that all the settings are correct. (The major drawback to this system is the extreme obscurity of the makefile language. It's very terse, very cryptic, and poorly documented.)

If you work from the command prompt, compilation will be faster. The IDE, and particularly, the Microsoft IDE, tends to slow down compilation time. Also, if you work from the command prompt, you can easily use a whole slew of third-party editors, command-prompt extensions, and other tools, to customize and expedite the process of development. For instance, many programmers at Borland consider the DOS Brief editor and the 4DOS program from JP Software, to be absolute necessities when they are building applications.

Whatever decisions you make in regard to any of these matters ultimately have to be driven by your own personal preferences and your own sense of how you would prefer to work. These are personal matters of taste, and you should opt for the choices that make you feel the most comfortable.

A *makefile* helps you compile the disparate source files of a project into a single executable. Because the creation of these files is now automated by both the Borland and Microsoft IDEs, I do not delve into makefile syntax in this book. I did, however, discuss this subject in the first edition of this book, which was aimed at 16-bit Windows. I will include that discussion in the downloadable files that accompany this book, or with the diskette that you can order through the mail. Furthermore, you will find that several different sets of makefiles ship with the source, and I will discuss the use of some of those makefiles in this chapter.

> **Note:** In this book, and in the software you can purchase or download to accompany the book, I define makefiles for the Borland 32-bit compiler, the Microsoft 32-bit compiler, the Borland 16-bit compiler, and the Microsoft 16-bit compiler. (About a third of the programs included with the book won't compile in Windows 3.1, so I don't include 16-bit makefiles for those programs.)
>
> Although I include the makefiles, I should point out that for some readers it may be simplest to generate these makefiles automatically from inside the IDE. The act of creating these files will be discussed in this chapter. I will also clarify the techniques needed to use these files.
>
> To the hard-core programmers who disdain the use of an IDE, I offer the existing makefiles that ship with this book. If you use these makefiles, you do not need to open either the Microsoft or Borland IDEs if you do not so desire.

To give you a demonstration of how to use module-definition files and makefiles, I have put together the following little program. It is very similar to the LaoTzu program you saw on Day 1, "Getting Your Feet Wet," but it comes replete with a short DEF file. Before you run this program, you need to learn how to compile it using a project file or makefile. I'll explore that topic as soon as you type in Listings 2.1 through 2.4.

Listing 2.1. The BOX1.CPP program displays words from an ancient Chinese text.

```
 1: // Program BOX1.CPP
 2: #define STRICT
 3: #include <windows.h>
 4:
 5: #pragma argsused
 6: int pascal WinMain(HINSTANCE hInst,
 7:                    HINSTANCE hPrevInstance,
 8:                    LPSTR lpszCmdParam, int nCmdShow)
 9: {
10:    MessageBox(0,
11:               "He who knows does not speak",
12:               "He who speaks does not know",
13:               MB_OK | MB_ICONEXCLAMATION);
14:    return 0;
15: }
16:
17:
```

Listing 2.2. The Box1 definition file.

```
; BOX1.DEF
; The use of STACKSIZE can be omitted in most cases.
; The entire file may be ommitted in WIN32, but I like
; to preserve at least the NAME and DESCRIPTION fields.
NAME            BOX1
DESCRIPTION     'BOX1 Window'
CODE            PRELOAD MOVEABLE DISCARDABLE
DATA            PRELOAD MOVEABLE MULTIPLE
HEAPSIZE        10000
STACKSIZE       5120
```

Listing 2.3. The Borland makefile for the Box1 program.

```
#----------------------------------------------------------------
# The MakeFile: BOX1.MAK
#
# Type MAKE -B -DWIN16 -f BOX1.MAK to generate Windows 16 code.
# Type MAKE -B -f BOX1.MAK to generate WIN32 code.
#
# Install automatically creates file BCROOT.INC in BIN directory.
#----------------------------------------------------------------

!if !$d(BCROOT)
BCROOT  = $(MAKEDIR)
!endif

APPNAME = BOX1
INCPATH = $(BCROOT)\INCLUDE
LIBPATH = $(BCROOT)\LIB

!if $d(WIN16)
COMPILER= BCC.EXE
FLAGS   = -W -ml -v -w4 -I$(INCPATH) -L$(LIBPATH)
!else
COMPILER= BCC32.EXE
FLAGS   = -W -v -w4 -I$(INCPATH) -L$(LIBPATH)
!endif

# link
$(APPNAME).exe: $(APPNAME).obj $(APPNAME).def
  $(COMPILER) $(FLAGS) $(APPNAME).obj

# compile
$(APPNAME).obj: $(APPNAME).cpp
  $(COMPILER) -c $(FLAGS) $(APPNAME).cpp
```

Listing 2.4. The Microsoft makefile for the Box1 program.

```
#------------------------------------------------
# BOX1MS.MAK
# Microsoft makefile
#------------------------------------------------

APPNAME=BOX1
TARGETOS=WIN95
APPVER=4.0
OBJS=$(APPNAME).OBJ

!include <win32.mak>

all: $(APPNAME).exe

# Update the object files if necessary

# compile
.cpp.obj:
  $(cc) $(cflags) $(cvars) $(cdebug) $<

# Update the executable file if necessary.

$(APPNAME).exe: $(OBJS)
  $(link) $(linkdebug) $(guiflags) -out:$(APPNAME).exe \
  $(OBJS) $(guilibs) comctl32.lib
```

This program pops up the small window visible in Figure 2.1. Don't let the code for creating a message box give you the idea that windows are always this easy to create. As you will see later in this chapter, it's hard to create real windows that are maximizable, minimizable, and resizable. However, the Messagebox function serves as a nice interlude while building up to the real thing.

Figure 2.1.
The output from the BOX1.CPP program.

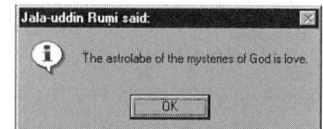

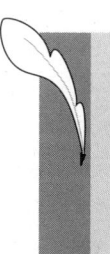

Note: Because the final updates for Borland's compilers were not available when this book went to print, it has not been possible for me to be absolutely certain about the setup for the INCLUDE macro in the Borland makefiles. As a result, you may need to slightly alter the INCLUDE macro in the Borland makefiles for this book. Here is one possible pattern that points at separate directories for WIN16 and WIN32 INCLUDE files:

```
!if $d(WIN16)
INCPATH = $(BCROOT)\INCLUDE\WIN16;$(BCROOT)\INCLUDE
```

49

```
COMPILER= BCC.EXE
FLAGS   = -W -ml -v -w4 -I$(INCPATH) -L$(LIBPATH)
!else
INCPATH = $(BCROOT)\INCLUDE\WIN32;$(BCROOT)\INCLUDE
COMPILER= BCC32.EXE
FLAGS   = -W -v -w4 -I$(INCPATH) -L$(LIBPATH)
!endif
```

Here is a second possible solution:

```
INCPATH = $(BCROOT)\INCLUDE\WIN32;$(BCROOT)\INCLUDE
!if $d(WIN16)
COMPILER= BCC.EXE
FLAGS   = -W -ml -v -w4 -I$(INCPATH) -L$(LIBPATH)
!else
COMPILER= BCC32.EXE
FLAGS   = -W -v -w4 -I$(INCPATH) -L$(LIBPATH)
!endif
```

The point here is that headers specific to Windows 95 may need to be added to your version of the compiler before you can work with the Windows 95 common controls. Those header files may be placed in the C:\BC45\INCLUDE subdirectory, or perhaps in a subdirectory called C:\BC45\INCLUDE\WIN32, or even in a directory called C:\BC45\WIN32. (In these examples I assume that you installed on the C drive, and I assumed you are using BC45. Of course, many readers of this book will have compilers where BCROOT resolves not to C:\BC45, but to C:\BC50.) The actual default location of these new header files is not clear at the time of this writing, so you may have to edit your makefiles accordingly.

The code that gets uploaded to the online sites will reflect the final default directories selected by the Borland developers. In other words, I will upload the code nearly a month after I turn in the final drafts of this book. By that time, the location of the files will be resolved. If necessary, I will update the online files further when BC50 ships, and at other times when they need to be tweaked.

I should add that my best guess is that the new Windows 95 header files will end up in the \BC45\INCLUDE subdirectory, but I can't be sure. Furthermore, it is unlikely to cause harm if the INCLUDE macro lists directories that do not exist, or that do not contain files important to your builds. In other words, it's okay if the INCLUDE macro lists the correct directory, and then some additional directories that do not exist, or that do not hold header files important to your build. (When reading this book, you may encounter variations on the INCLUDE macro in some of the makefiles you encounter. These variations are due to an assortment of temporary solutions that were developed either by myself, or by Borland developers, during the beta cycle.)

Overview of Compiling and Linking

In the Chimes, Beeper, and LaoTzu programs, the compiler automatically generated internal module-definition files that are very similar to the one accompanying the Box1 program. This was possible in part because module-definition files for most Windows programs look almost identical. (Alternatively, when you compiled those programs, you may have used the makefiles that come on the disk you can order for this book.)

Once you've written and understood one module-definition file, you can often copy it virtually unchanged from one program to the next! The same holds true for many of the makefiles included on disk. All you need do is copy the file, then use the search and replace mechanism from your editor to substitute all the references to the previous project name with references to the new project name. In particular, you need to change the one line from the above makefile that reads:

APPNAME=BOX1

so that is references another file, such as

APPNAME=MYNEWAPP

The point here is that you shouldn't feel overwhelmed by the presence of additional code. Most of the time, you can add makefiles and module-definition files to your program with a simple copy and paste process, augmented by a quick search and replace procedure.

In saying this, I need to point out that Microsoft's Visual C++ compiler uses makefiles from inside the IDE. You can, in fact, use these makefiles from the command prompt, but they are much more complex than the terse makefiles shown above. Because they are relatively easy to create from inside the IDE, and because they are very complex, it's perhaps best if you simply recreate the Visual C++ IDE makefiles from inside the IDE every time you start a new project.

If you keep these thoughts in mind, you should find that the ensuing description of makefiles and module-definition files are straightforward enough for most palates.

There are two quite different ways to compile the Box1 program. The first is from the command prompt, the second is from the IDE. If you are working with Microsoft's compilers, then you will use a makefile whether you are working from the IDE or from the DOS prompt. If you are working with Borland's tools, then you will use a project file inside the IDE and a makefile if you opt to work from the DOS prompt. Borland's project files use the letters ".IDE" as an extension. There is an option in the Borland menu that allows you to translate an IDE file to a makefile:

COMPILER	WINDOWS IDE	DOS PROMPT
Microsoft Users	makefile	makefile
Borland Users	IDE files	makefile

You are probably familiar with using makefiles from the command prompt, and this subject was broached in the last chapter. However, I will cover some of the key points a second time, just to be sure that they are understood. After all, the rest of this book will be meaningless to you if you can't get the programs to compile.

Makefiles are scripts run by a program called MAKE.EXE (Borland), or NMAKE.EXE (Microsoft). These scripts tell a compiler and linker how to build and link a program. The makefiles for the Box1 program can be run from the DOS prompt by typing one of the following commands:

```
make -fBox1        ( Borland )
```

or

```
nmake -fBox1.mak   ( Microsoft )
```

After typing and executing this command, you should have a working copy of BOX1.EXE on your hard disk. If this doesn't work, read the text in the following sections to learn how to set up the makefile for your particular system.

Note: The next two sections are a rarity in this book; the first describes features of Microsoft's makefiles, whereas the second describes features of Borland's makefiles. In general, I try to avoid mentioning compiler-specific information. Makefiles are so important, however, that I decided to make an exception.

Before closing this section, I should emphasize that you can create a either a Borland or Microsoft makefile from inside the IDE. You can also create makefiles by typing in a text editor. There are relatively simple ways to create short makefiles by hand for use with Borland's compiler. You can do the same thing for Microsoft makefiles, but this is an uncommon practice, and so I will expect that many readers will usually work only with IDE-generated Microsoft makefiles. However, I do include short versions of the Microsoft makefiles that can be typed in by hand and run from the command prompt.

Microsoft Projects and Makefiles

If you are using Borland's compiler, you can skip this section and move on to the next.

It is easiest for users of Microsoft tools to create their makefiles automatically from the IDE. However, the files generated in this fashion are very long and complex. As a result, I prefer to use a handcrafted makefile like the one shown in Listing 2.4. If you have the source code for the book, you can open up the text file called BOX1MS32.MAK to see what a Microsoft IDE-generated makefile looks like.

What are the steps necessary to create a makefile from inside the Microsoft IDE? Well, that depends on whether you are using MSVC15 or MSVC20. MSVC15 produces 16-bit applications, and MSVC20 produces 32-bit applications.

To get started with MSVC20, you should go to the Microsoft IDE and choose File|New. In the New dialog, select Project. In the New Project dialog, do the following:

1. Type in the Project Name as Box1.
2. Set the Project Type to Application.
3. Save the file in a directory called BOX1.

This process is illustrated in Figure 2.2.

Figure 2.2.
The New dialog from MSVC20, as it appears when you're creating the Box1 program.

You can then use the Project Files dialog to BOX1.CPP and BOX1.DEF to the project. If you have not previously created those files, you can close the Project Files dialog, then create the files in MSVC or in another text editor. Now right-click on the BOX1.MAK dialog, and select Files. Add the new files you have created to the project, so the result looks like the screen shot in Figure 2.3.

Figure 2.3.
The main project dialog for Box1.

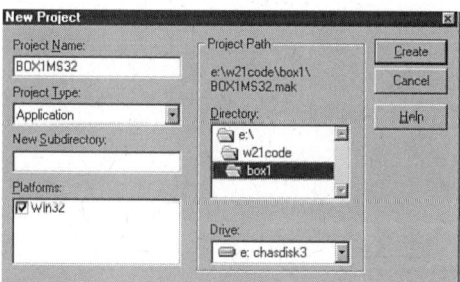

You can now select Project|Settings to fine-tune your application. You can create an application by selecting Build All from the Project menu. You can also compile the application from the command prompt.

If you are using MSVC 1.5, you can create a new project by first creating BOX1.CPP and BOX1.DEF as defined above and saving them in a subdirectory called BOX1.

1. Select Project|New from the menu.
2. Type in the Project Name as *drive*:\BOX1\BOX1.MAK, where the *drive* designates the drive in which you created the file. For instance, you might enter C:\BOX1\BOX1.MAK.
3. Set the Project type to Windows application (.EXE).
4. Make sure that Use Microsoft Foundation Classes is not selected.

The result should look something like the screen art shown in Figures 2.4 and 2.5.

Figure 2.4.

Creating a project with Microsoft Visual C++ 1.5.

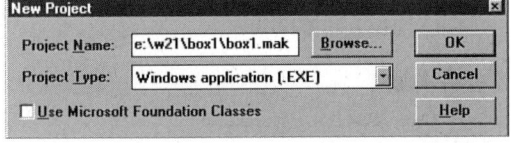

Figure 2.5.

Creating the Box1 project in MSVC15.

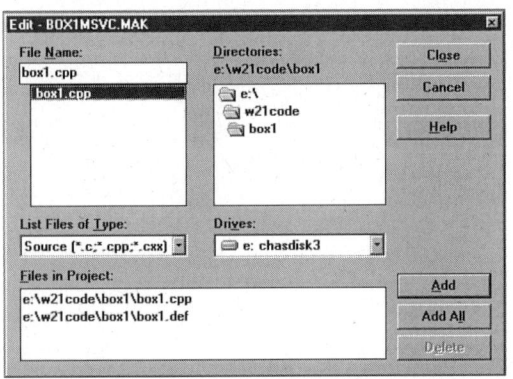

In the Edit dialog, use the Add button to add BOX1.CPP and BOX1.DEF to your project. Choose Close. You can compile the project by selecting Project|Build. You can also compile from the command prompt, but make sure the RESFLAGS settings in the makefile do not equal /nologo.

There are three different Microsoft makefiles that I have included on the disk you can order. These makefiles will always end with one of four options:

1. M, as in BOX1M.MAK. These files are for use with the old 16-bit Microsoft compilers and MSVC 1.5.

2. MS16, as in BOX1MS16.MAK. These files are for use with the 16-bit Microsoft Visual C++ compilers.

3. MS32, as in BOX1MS32.MAK. These files are for use with the 32-bit Microsoft Visual C++ 2.0 compiler.

4. MS, as in BOX1MS.MAK. These files are for use with the 32-bit Microsoft Visual C++ 2.*x* compiler. They are smaller and easier to read than the IDE-generated files that end in MS32. However, if you prefer to work from inside the IDE, then they won't be as useful to you, since the IDE can't glean quite as much information from them. This will not, however, affect the quality of the executables you produce; it just limits the amount of information visible to you in the project dialogs.

You can put these makefiles to work by entering one of the following lines at the DOS prompt:

```
nmake -f BOX1M.MAK
nmake -f BOX1MSVC.MAK
nmake -f BOX1MS32.MAK
nmake -f BOXMS.MAK
```

For additional information on the old style Microsoft makefiles, see the file called MSMAKE.WRI that is included on the disk you can order for this book.

Note that Microsoft ships a batch file called MSVCVARS.BAT or VCVARS32.BAT that will set up your environment correctly for compiling from the command prompt. If compilations don't proceed smoothly for you, try running this file first, and then entering one of the command lines shown above.

Before closing this section, let me remind you that two common errors in project construction are referencing MFC anywhere in the project or makefile, as well as using the wrong path to the INCLUDE and LIB directories.

The Borland Projects and Makefiles

If you are using the Microsoft compiler, you can skip this section and move on to the next.

To create a new project in the Borland IDE, choose the Project|New Project menu choice. In the Project Path and Name section, enter in the path and name of the file that you want to create. For instance, you might type in something like this:

```
c:\w21code\box1\box1.ide
```

When you type this in, the Target Name will automatically change to box1. This is the name of the executable you are going to create: BOX1.EXE. Here's how to fill in the rest of the settings for this dialog:

1. In the Target Type, you should choose Application [.exe].
2. For the Platform, you should choose WIN32 or Windows 3.x (16).
3. If you choose to build a 32-bit application, the Target Model should be GUI.
4. If you choose 16-bit Windows, the Target Model should be Large.
5. For the Standard Libraries, select only Runtime. The libraries can be either dynamic or static, though you should choose static if you are in doubt.

Figure 2.6 shows the Target Expert settings for a typical 32-bit application, and Figure 2.7 shows the Target Expert settings for a typical 16-bit application.

Figure 2.6.

Except for possible variations in your path, this is how the Target Expert should look when producing WIN32 applications.

In the Advanced section of the Target Expert, you should select the options to produce a CPP file and a DEF file. For now there is no need to produce RC files, though they will be common later in this book.

When you are done, you can press OK, and the expert will produce a project that produces BOX1.EXE and that contains BOX1.CPP and BOX1.DEF. If the files don't already exist, you can click either BOX1.CPP or BOX1.DEF and type in the code shown previously in the program listings for Box1.

Figure 2.7.

Except for possible variations in your path, this is how the Target Expert should look when producing 16-bit applications.

After creating a project, you can fine-tune it by selecting Options|Project. The Project Options dialog box will then open. You can iterate through its many pages of settings by clicking on the text in the Topics section. The standard settings for all the pages in this portion of the IDE are defined in the source code for this book. You can also look in the example files that ship with your compiler for additional models on which to base your programs.

Two common errors in project construction are referencing OWL somewhere in the project or makefile, and using the wrong path to the INCLUDE and LIB directories. (Of course, it isn't always an error to reference OWL, but it's not appropriate for this book!)

It is easy for users of the Borland IDE to automatically generate a makefile. To do so, you can create a normal project using the techniques described previously. When you are done, select the Project|Generate makefile menu option. The following code will be produced:

```
#
# Borland C++ IDE generated makefile
#
.AUTODEPEND


#
# Borland C++ tools
#
IMPLIB   = Implib
BCC32    = Bcc32 +BccW32.cfg
TLINK32  = TLink32
TLIB     = TLib
BRC32    = Brc32
TASM32   = Tasm32
```

```
#
# IDE macros
#


#
# Options
#
IDE_LFLAGS32 =  -LC:\BC45\LIB
IDE_RFLAGS32 =
LLATW32_box2dexe =  -Tpe -aa -c
RLATW32_box2dexe =  -w32
BLATW32_box2dexe =
CNIEAT_box2dexe = -IC:\BC45\INCLUDE -D
LNIEAT_box2dexe = -x
LEAT_box2dexe = $(LLATW32_box2dexe)
REAT_box2dexe = $(RLATW32_box2dexe)
BEAT_box2dexe = $(BLATW32_box2dexe)

#
# Dependency List
#
Dep_box2 = \
   box2.exe

box2 : BccW32.cfg $(Dep_box2)
  echo MakeNode

Dep_box2dexe = \
   box2.obj\
   box2.def

box2.exe : $(Dep_box2dexe)
  $(TLINK32) @&&¦
 /v $(IDE_LFLAGS32) $(LEAT_box2dexe) $(LNIEAT_box2dexe) +
C:\BC45\LIB\c0w32.obj+
box2.obj
$<,$*
C:\BC45\LIB\import32.lib+
C:\BC45\LIB\cw32.lib
box2.def
¦

box2.obj :  box2.cpp
  $(BCC32) -c @&&¦
 $(CEAT_box2dexe) $(CNIEAT_box2dexe) -o$@ box2.cpp
¦

# Compiler configuration file
BccW32.cfg :
   Copy &&¦
-R
-v
-vi
-H
-H=box2.csm
```

```
-W
¦ $@
```

I consider this code to be beyond the pale, even for a Windows programming book. If you are interested in the makefile language, you can order the BORMAKE.WRI file supplied on disk, or you can refer to the Borland manuals. Otherwise, the topic shall be considered beyond the scope of this book.

On disk, you will find that I have created Borland makefiles that are at least a little easier to read, as shown in Figure 2.3.

To use this file you can type either this:

```
MAKE -B -f BOX1.MAK
```

or this:

```
MAKE -B -DWIN16 -f BOX1.MAK
```

at the DOS prompt. The -B tells MAKE.EXE to build the project from scratch, which is the safest thing to do in some circumstances. If you want to save compilation time, you can omit this parameter and MAKE will try to use any existing parts of your project, such as existing OBJ files or EXE files. That's fine, if you know what you are doing, but it's safest just to choose Build. The -D part of the second command line shown above tells MAKE.EXE that you are defining WIN16. The makefile I have created above compiles 16-bit apps if WIN16 is defined, and otherwise compiles 32-bit applications.

When using the makefile shown above, it is important that the LIB and INCLUDE directories are correctly defined. When all is well, I get the following output from MAKE.EXE during WIN32 compilation:

```
BCC32.EXE -c -W -v -w4 -IC:\BC45\INCLUDE -LC:\BC45\LIB BOX1.cpp
```

Notice the section that reads:

```
-IC:\BC45\INCLUDE
```

This specifies the INCLUDE path which the compiler should use. If you have correctly installed BC45, and if the BC45 version of MAKE is the first one found on your path, then all should go well. In other words, you should edit the path in your AUTOEXEC.BAT (or wherever it is you set it) and make sure that \BC45\BIN is the first directory mentioned that contains tools for compiling applications.

To help simplify this process one step further, I have included a batch file called GO.BAT that activates MAKE automatically:

```
@echo off
if %1==WIN16 goto WIN16
```

```
:WIN32
make -B -f box1
goto end

:WIN16
make -B -DWIN16 -f box1
goto end
```

If you want to produce a 32-bit application, then just type GO at the command prompt. If you want to produce a 16-bit application, then type GO WIN16.

Before closing this section, let me repeat that you don't have to use makefiles to create Windows applications. If you want, you can do everything from inside the IDE. However, it's sometimes useful to have makefiles around, particularly if you have a favorite editor, such as Brief, MultiEdit, or CodeWright.

More on DEF Files

The next subject on the agenda is the module-definition file, or DEF file, as it is commonly called.

Before delving into the details, it's perhaps worth pondering the sonorous title of this particular syntactical conglomeration: The *module-definition file*, they call it. To hear this name, you might think you wandered into a lecture on Kant or Sartre. *The Critique of the Module-Definition File*, perhaps, or *Being, Nothingness, and the Module-Definition File*.

Before becoming too intimidated by the ominous ring of these words, you should know that one of the key aspects of Windows 3.1 is an undocumented area of memory called by the somewhat farcical name *BurgerMaster*. The BurgerMaster was named after a restaurant near Microsoft's headquarters, and I think that a name like that reveals more about the true spirit of Windows than a stuffy term like the "module-definition file." Like all truly interesting subjects, from Astronomy to Shakespeare, Windows isn't always inherently somber or frightening. Indeed, it's often stimulating and exciting. I would even posit that if it didn't have an aura of excitement and fun about it, it wouldn't be worth taking seriously.

At any rate, let's return to the subject of DEF files. These little charmers usually perform several functions associated with the act of linking the final executable together.

One such task is to give the module a name:

```
NAME        Box1
```

The DESCRIPTION portion of the file is interesting, because this text is actually inserted into the programs header:

```
DESCRIPTION   'Box1 example'
```

If you want a certain line of text to be buried in your executable at known offset, you can define it here.

The last two lines of the DEF file designate the heap size and stack size:

```
HEAPSIZE     4096
STACKSIZE    10240
```

The stack for this application has been set at the recommended minimum. As a general rule, never try to build a Windows application with less than 10,240 bytes of stack space. This area, of course, is used to store information when the program calls local functions.

Note: If you are using Microsoft's MSVC15 or MSVC10, you may get a warning by including the above STACKSIZE statement. The warnings come because the compiler usually automatically passes a stack size to the application on the command line. It won't do any harm to ignore this warning, but if you want to suppress it you can either delete the STACKSIZE line from the module-definition file, or you can go to Options|Project|Linker|Memory Image and delete everything from the Stack Size option. Don't put 0 in there; just leave the line totally blank. When you first opened the Linker page, you might have noticed that Microsoft sets the stack to 10240 by default.

The HEAPSIZE designates an initial size for the program's local heap in 16-bit Windows. If necessary, Windows can expand the local heap. Windows programs also can allocate memory from outside the local heap, if needed. In fact, Windows programs have access to heap spaces that frequently climb above 16MB in size. To find out how much heap is available on your machine, open the About box in the File Manager or Program Manager. Like a number of the options in the default DEF files defined here, this option is ignored under WIN32.

Note: HEAPSIZE is ignored under WIN32 because there is no local heap in 32-bit applications. Each 32-bit program is running in its own address space, which is defined by the operating system to be 4GB in size. Since there is no other program in the address space, it makes no sense to talk about local and global heaps. It's all just one huge, non-segmented chunk of memory.

You might ask how Windows can create a 4GB address space in a machine that has only 8, 16, 32, or at most (in our wildest dreams) 128MB of memory in it. Where does the 4GB come from? Well, the issue here is that WIN32 supports paged virtual memory, which means that any chunk of memory can be assigned, or mapped into, almost any "virtual" address. As a result, a program can access memory at the 2GB mark, even in a machine that has only 8MB of memory. In particular, there is an internal table called a descriptor table that holds references to real memory addresses. Therefore, you have a virtual address that your program manipulates and a real address that the operating systems tracks in the descriptor table. Every time you reference an actual area in memory, the operating system must take the virtual address used in your program and use the descriptor table to find out what part of real memory it references. Of course, there are occasions when the operating system can manipulate memory without having to translate a virtual address into a real address, but still, Windows memory management is by nature based on two layers of indirection.

This subject is explored further on Day 21, "Threads, Multitasking, and Memory Management."

The remaining two lines from the DEF file describe how portions of the program are handled in memory :

```
CODE        PRELOAD MOVEABLE DISCARDABLE
DATA        PRELOAD MOVEABLE
```

This is a somewhat more complicated subject, which is relevant primarily to 16-bit Windows. I had sections which covered this topic in this first edition of this book, but it's not germane to the topic of WIN32. I have included the deleted section on disk in the file WIN16DEF.TXT.

The CODE and DATA statements shown above are enough to get you by in either WIN32 or WIN16, though some of the statements are essentially ignored by 32-bit compilers. Note that these are the exact same statements that Borland uses by default if you omit a DEF file.

For further information, Borland users can see DEFAULT.DEF in the LIB subdirectory of the shipping version of BC45. Microsoft MSVC 1.0 and 1.5 users can refer to CL.DEF in the BIN subdirectory created by that product's install program. As stated above, this issue is not really germane to a pure 32-bit compiler such as MSVC20, or the upcoming BC50 compiler.

Creating Windows

So far, you've had a chance to look at several different Windows programs, but you haven't seen one real window! As it happens, there's a reason for this. And it's not that I'm being stingy. I want to talk to you about creating windows, and in fact, almost all the remaining programs in this book contain at least one window (whereas many of them will contain multiple windows).

The problem, however, is that the actual act of creating a real window is far from trivial. In fact, I've spent a considerable amount of time clearing the boards, so to speak, so you can concentrate all your attention on one key subject: creating windows.

Let's not make any bones about this. What you are going to see in the next few paragraphs, and what you'll see throughout the entirety of Day 3 is probably the most complicated single step you'll take in the beginning and intermediate stages of your Windows programming career. If you can master this one subject, everything else will fall into place.

At any rate, before you get too worried, you should know that, as with the previously shown DEF files and makefiles, the actual act of putting up a window is a three-step process that you can write once, then reuse, almost completely unchanged, in many different programs.

The vast majority of Windows programmers don't sit down and say to themselves: "Okay, now I'm calling CreateWindow. What's the first parameter, and what should I set it to this time? Fine. Now, what's the second parameter?" Instead, all they do is perform a quick cut and paste operation, make a few minor changes, and forget the whole process.

The act of creating a window is a process with a bark that's a lot worse than its byte!

What you're about to see is the shortest program (50 lines) I could come up with that creates a real window—one that acts the way you would expect a window to act.

At this stage, you don't have to understand anything but the broadest outlines of how this program works. In fact, this program is stripped of a number of important syntactical elements that I feel are essential for the creation of robust, easily maintainable programs. For a full-scale window of this type, you need only wait until Day 3.

Don't worry about any of the details. Just get the program (shown in Listings 2.5 through 2.7) up and running so you can see that this code does all the things you would expect a real Windows program to do. That is, you can maximize it, minimize it, or resize it, just as you would any professional Windows application.

When you are done, come back to the text and read a brief discussion of the main sections of the program. After that, you can call it quits for the day. Tomorrow, you'll have a chance to go after a full-fledged Windows program in all the excruciating detail you could ever want. But that's tomorrow, and this is today.

Listing 2.5. The MakeWin program creates a traditional window with a caption, border, and system menu.

```
// Program MakeWin.cpp
#define  STRICT
#include <windows.h>
#include <windowsx.h>
#include <string.h>

char Name[] = "MakeWin";
LRESULT CALLBACK WndProc(HWND, UINT, WPARAM, LPARAM);

#pragma warning (disable: 4068)
#pragma argsused
```

```
int WINAPI WinMain(HINSTANCE hInst,
                   HINSTANCE hPrevInstance,
                   LPSTR lpszCmdParam, int nCmdShow)
{
  HWND hwnd;
  MSG Msg;
  WNDCLASS W;

  memset(&W, 0, sizeof(WNDCLASS));
  W.style = CS_HREDRAW | CS_VREDRAW;
  W.lpfnWndProc = WndProc;
  W.hInstance = hInst;
  W.hbrBackground = (HBRUSH)(COLOR_WINDOW+1);
  W.lpszClassName = Name;
  RegisterClass(&W);

  hwnd = CreateWindow(Name, Name, WS_OVERLAPPEDWINDOW,
                      10, 10, 600, 400, NULL, NULL, hInst, NULL);

  ShowWindow(hwnd,nCmdShow);
  UpdateWindow(hwnd);

  while (GetMessage(&Msg, NULL, 0, 0))
  {
    TranslateMessage(&Msg);
    DispatchMessage(&Msg);
  }

  return Msg.wParam;
}

LRESULT CALLBACK WndProc(HWND hwnd, UINT Message,
                         WPARAM wParam, LPARAM lParam)
{
  if (Message == WM_DESTROY)
  {
    PostQuitMessage(0);
    return 0;
  }
  return DefWindowProc(hwnd, Message, wParam, lParam);
}
```

Listing 2.6. The Borland makefile for the MakeWin program.

```
# --------------------------
# Borland MakeWin.mak
# --------------------------

!if !$d(BCROOT)
BCROOT  = $(MAKEDIR)
!endif

INCPATH = $(BCROOT)\INCLUDE
LIBPATH = $(BCROOT)\LIB
```

continues

Listing 2.6. continued

```
!if $d(WIN16)
COMPILER= BCC.EXE
FLAGS    = -W -ml -v -w4 -I$(INCPATH) -L$(LIBPATH)
!else
COMPILER= BCC32.EXE
FLAGS    = -W -v -w4 -I$(INCPATH) -L$(LIBPATH)
!endif

# macros

# link
MakeWin.exe: MakeWin.obj MakeWin.def
  $(COMPILER) $(FLAGS) MakeWin.obj

# compile
MakeWin.obj: MakeWin.cpp
  $(COMPILER) -c $(FLAGS) MakeWin.cpp
```

Listing 2.7. The Microsoft makefile for the MakeWin program.

```
#-----------------------------------------------
# MAKEWIMS.MAK
# Microsoft Windows 95 makefile
#-----------------------------------------------

APPNAME=MAKEWIN
TARGETOS=WIN95
APPVER=4.0
OBJS=$(APPNAME).OBJ

!include <win32.mak>

all: $(APPNAME).exe

# Update the object files if necessary

# compile
.cpp.obj:
  $(cc) $(cflags) $(cvars) $(cdebug) $<

# Update the executable file if necessary.

$(APPNAME).exe: $(OBJS)
  $(link) $(linkdebug) $(guiflags) -out:$(APPNAME).exe \
  $(OBJS) $(guilibs) comctl32.lib
```

This program creates a simple empty window with a title bar, minimize and maximize buttons, and a system menu. (See Figure 2.8.)

Figure 2.8.

The MakeWin program creates a window that can be minimized, maximized, resized, and normalized.

The MakeWin program has two major parts:

1. The `WinMain` function
2. The `WndProc` function

The remainder of this chapter takes a brief look at each part.

The `WinMain` function can be divided into three sections:

☐ The first section (lines 18-24) is where the `window` is registered:

```
18:    memset(&W, 0, sizeof(WNDCLASS));
19:    W.style = CS_HREDRAW | CS_VREDRAW;
20:    W.lpfnWndProc = WndProc;
21:    W.hInstance = hInst;
22:    W.hbrBackground = (HBRUSH)(COLORWINDOW+1);
23:    W.lpszClassName = Name;
24:    RegisterClass(&W);
```

The `Register` procedure tells Windows about the characteristics of a `window` class. For now, there is no need to worry about why a window is registered or what this step means. You only need to note that this is the first thing that happens in a typical `WinMain` procedure. In later chapters, the complicated act of registering a Window will be isolated in its own procedure, as it should be according to the well-proven dictates of proper, structured design.

☐ The next step is to create the window (lines 26-30):

```
26: hwnd = CreateWindow(Name, Name, WS_OVERLAPPEDWINDOW, .
27: 10, 10, 600, 400, NULL, NULL, hInst, NULL);
28:
29: ShowWindow(hwnd,nCmdShow);
30: UpdateWindow(hwnd);
```

The act of creating a window involves two steps. The first is the call to `CreateWindow` (lines 26-27), and the second is the two calls to `ShowWindow` (line 29) and `UpdateWindow`

(line 30). As with the registration procedure, the act of creating a window is usually handled in its own separate procedure. This is done to isolate complexity, and to create a well-structured, robust program. For now though, I've just run the whole business together so you can get a feeling for how it fits into what politicians used to call "the big picture."

☐ The third portion of the WinMain procedure is called the message loop (lines 32–36):

```
32: while (GetMessage(&Msg, NULL, 0, 0))
33: {
34:   TranslateMessage(&Msg);
35:   DispatchMessage(&Msg);
36: }
```

When the user moves the mouse or strikes a key, messages are sent to the message loop. This is the *driver's seat* for a Windows program. This is command central, a loop that keeps repeating throughout much of the life of a program.

Don't worry if all of this doesn't make sense to you yet. It's not supposed to. The point of this last section of this chapter is simply to give you an overview of a typical Windows program. Tomorrow, you get all the detail you could ever hope for, and then some.

Right now, you need only think about the broadest issues, such as the three steps in a WinMain procedure:

1. Register the window

2. Create the window

3. Enter the message loop

There it is, just as simple as one, two, three!

The other key part of the program is the WndProc procedure, which responds to messages a program receives:

```
41: LRESULT CALLBACK _export WndProc(HWND hwnd, UINT Message,
42:                                  WPARAM wParam, LPARAM lParam)
43: {
44:   if (Message == WM_DESTROY)
45:   {
46:     PostQuitMessage(0);
47:     return 0;
48:   }
49:   return DefWindowProc(hwnd, Message, wParam, lParam);
50: }
```

The MakeWin program only responds explicitly to WM_DESTROY messages (line 44). All other messages get passed on to DefWindowProc (line 49). The DefWindowProc procedure, as you will see in the next chapter, does nothing more than handle the default behavior associated with a window. In other words, when you maximize a window, or minimize a window, the DefWindowProc procedure processes your message and knows what to do with it.

DefWindowProc doesn't, however, handle WM_DESTROY messages. That is your duty as a programmer. When the message comes down the pike, just call PostQuitMessage (line 46). When that's done, you can exit WndProc with a return value of 0 (line 47).

I know that some readers of this chapter will be confused about messages and the role they play in Windows programming. If you are new to this subject, don't worry. I will spend plenty of time talking about message-based operating systems. For now, just accept the fact that Windows programs respond to messages, rather than to interrupts. It's different from what many programmers are used to, but you will find that message-oriented operating systems have a very simple and elegant design.

In the next chapter, you'll see how to handle standard Windows messages with macros, so you can move the message response functions outside of the WndProc. The rationale is the same as for moving the Create and Register functions outside the WinMain procedure. That is, Windows programmers want to be able to create well-structured programs that are easy to maintain and debug. In this case, I have collapsed all these procedures back into the WinMain and WndProc functions, so you can see the overall structure of a typical Windows program.

For now, that's all you need to know about the MakeWin program. To summarize:

- [ ] There are two main parts in a program. The first is the WinMain procedure; the second is the WndProc procedure.
- [ ] The WinMain procedure has three parts. The first *registers* the Window, the second *creates* the window, and the third sends *messages* to the window through a loop.
- [ ] Any messages sent to a window pass through WndProc. This window procedure can explicitly handle the messages, or pass them on to DefWindowProc, which is the default message handler. In fact, some programs first handle the message, and then pass it on to DefWindowProc for further processing.

That's all you need to know about Windows programs at this stage. The point is just to grasp the overall flow of a typical windows program. Just get the broad issues clear in your mind, and then the details will become clear in the next chapter.

Summary

In this chapter you have learned about creating Windows projects and about the structure of a typical Windows program. Both of these subjects are sufficiently complicated to tax the minds of most readers. In fact, you won't fully understand either subject until you have been programming Windows for quite some time. For now, all that matters is that you can use your compiler to create executables, and that you understand something about the flow of a typical Windows program. To go beyond that starting point is the work of the rest of this book.

After having completed this chapter, you are ready to take an in-depth look at how to put together a full-fledged, totally functional Windows program. All the gory details that go into that process will be discussed in-depth in the next chapter. For now, you can just sit back and rest on your laurels, and prepare for the things that lie ahead.

Q&A

Q I've followed all your advice, and I still can't get these programs to compile. What should I do?

A Before giving up altogether, make sure that you have obtained the source by mail or online service and tried loading the MAK or IDE files in your IDE. If that doesn't help, then get online and ask questions. On CompuServe there are one or more Microsoft, Borland, and Sams forums that cover Windows programming. Go up there and ask questions. On the Internet, there are the COMP.LANG news groups, such as COMP.LANG.C and ALT.LANG.C, and many other areas dedicated to programming. AOL also has places where programming is discussed. Almost all serious programmers frequent these places. If you've tried some online services and still can't get any joy, then send me e-mail. These programs have been tested over time, and they all run fine. If you're having trouble with them, I'll get you up and running some how.

Q What is a module-definition file?

A A module-definition file specifies certain major characteristics of a particular application. For instance, DEF files give an application a name, add a description to the executable's header, and specify how the program treats memory. Most of the time, you can simply copy a DEF file from one project to the next, with only modest changes. These fellows seem complicated at first, but after a few days, you'll find that they tend to fade into the background and require only minimal thought. In WIN32, they really aren't very important, and I preserve them there primarily to provide portability between platforms and compilers.

Q If I'm working in WIN16, what memory model should I use?

A Most of the programs in this book are designed to run in the large memory model. Your choice of memory model is not so important in the earlier chapters of this book, but later on you will need to use the large memory model. WIN32 programmers don't need to think about this subject at all, since 32-bit Windows finally eliminates all this silliness about memory models.

Workshop

The Workshop provides quiz questions to help you solidify your understanding of the material covered and exercises to provide you with experience in using what you've learned. Try to understand the quiz and exercise answers before continuing on to Day 3. Answers are provided in Appendix A.

Quiz

1. What is the purpose of a Windows Stub file?

2. Name three things defined in a module-definition file.

3. What are the two main procedures in the MakeWin program?

4. What are the three main parts of every WinMain function?

5. Every main window in an application must respond to one message. What is it?

Exercises

1. If you have multimedia, create a program that uses the lpszCmdParam argument to snag the name of a WAV file off the command line. Once it has the name, have the program play the associated WAV file.

2. Create a program that pops up a MessageBox that contains your name.

A Standard
Windows Program

My goal in this chapter and the next is to analyze the underlying structure of a typical Windows program. Specifically, this chapter is where to turn for an overview of these topics:

- ☐ `WinMain`
- ☐ `RegisterClass`
- ☐ `CreateWindow`
- ☐ The `message` loop
- ☐ `WndProc`
- ☐ WINDOWS.H
- ☐ Hungarian notation

Some of this material will be expounded further on Day 4, "Messages, WindowsX, and Painting Text." I hit this material hard because it covers information you'll have to rely on again and again when doing serious Windows programming.

I would prefer to keep the early chapters of this book as clear and simple as possible. However, Windows presents programmers with a fairly formidable hurdle right in the first stages of development. This chapter addresses those challenges head on, and it's up to you to follow along and run the course.

In this chapter, I present several fairly lengthy digressions on subjects such as Hungarian notation and WINDOWS.H. When reading these sections, pay close attention, and don't fear—I will once again pick up the main thread as soon as I have laid some groundwork needed by all Windows programmers.

The First Functioning GUI

Windows has the reputation of being a very difficult environment to program. Whether or not this reputation is deserved is a matter of considerable debate.

Most programmers who try to master the art of coding in Windows come from the DOS environment. As a result, they are almost always startled, or even frightened, when they first see the brave new world of Windows code.

When reading this book, however, I hope you greet the new and the strange—not with a sense of fear and confusion, but with a sense of wonder and excitement. If Windows programming is sometimes difficult, it's only because it is ripe with possibilities. My hope is that you concentrate not on the difficulties, but on the opportunities Windows provides for an alert and adventuresome programmer. Where others see complexity, I want you to see opportunity.

Without further ado, I'll now show you a complete Windows program, designed to be both flexible and durable. (See Listing 3.1.) For the time being, just concentrate on getting the program up and running. Remember that it consists of several modules, each of which must be tied into the whole through the use of a makefile or project file. This means that the Window1

program is made up of all of the files listed here—though, of course, some or all of the makefiles will be optional, depending on your circumstances.

Listing 3.1. Window1 is a multimodule program that illustrates all the major components of a standard Windows program.

```
//////////////////////////////////// >
// Program Name: Window1
// Programmer: Charlie Calvert
// Description: Example Windows program.
////////////////////////////////////

#define STRICT
#define WIN32_LEAN_AND_MEAN
#include <windows.h>
#include <windowsx.h>
#pragma warning (disable: 4068)
#pragma warning (disable: 4100)

static char szAppName[] = "Window1";
static HWND MainWindow;

/*
  You do not need to use _export in WIN32. The
  EXPORT16 macro provides compatibility between
  WIN16 and WIN32.
*/

#if !defined(__WIN32__) && !defined(_WIN32)
#define EXPORT16 __export
#else
#define EXPORT16
#endif

LRESULT CALLBACK EXPORT16 WndProc(HWND hWindow, UINT Message,
                                  WPARAM wParam, LPARAM lParam); > BOOL
                                  Register(HINSTANCE hInst);
HWND Create(HINSTANCE hInst, int nCmdShow); >
// ==================================
// INITIALIZATION
// ==================================

////////////////////////////////////
// The WinMain function is the program entry point.
// Register the Window, Create it, enter the Message Loop.
// If either step fails, exit without creating the window
////////////////////////////////////
#pragma argsused
int WINAPI WinMain(HINSTANCE hInst, HINSTANCE hPrevInstance,
                   LPSTR lpszCmdParam, int nCmdShow)
{
  MSG  Msg;

  if (!hPrevInstance)
    if (!Register(hInst))
      return FALSE;
```

continues 73

Listing 3.1. continued

```
    MainWindow = Create(hInst, nCmdShow);
  if (!MainWindow)
    return FALSE;

  while (GetMessage(&Msg, NULL, 0, 0))
  {
     TranslateMessage(&Msg);
     DispatchMessage(&Msg);
  }

  return Msg.wParam;
 }

///////////////////////////////////////
// Register the window
///////////////////////////////////////
BOOL Register(HINSTANCE hInst)
 {
    /* You can use WNDCLASSEX and RegisterClassEx with WIN32 */ >
    WNDCLASS WndClass;

    WndClass.style       = CS_HREDRAW ¦ CS_VREDRAW;
    WndClass.lpfnWndProc = WndProc;
    WndClass.cbClsExtra  = 0;
    WndClass.cbWndExtra  = 0;
    WndClass.hInstance   = hInst;
    WndClass.hIcon        = LoadIcon(NULL, IDI_APPLICATION);
    WndClass.hCursor      = LoadCursor(NULL, IDC_ARROW);
    WndClass.hbrBackground  = (HBRUSH)(COLOR_WINDOW+1);
    WndClass.lpszMenuName    = NULL;
    WndClass.lpszClassName = szAppName;

    return (RegisterClass(&WndClass) != 0);
 }


///////////////////////////////////////·¦
// Create the window
///////////////////////////////////////
 HWND Create(HINSTANCE hInstance, int nCmdShow)
  {
    HWND hWindow = CreateWindowEx(0, szAppName, szAppName,
                     WS_OVERLAPPEDWINDOW,
                     CW_USEDEFAULT, CW_USEDEFAULT,
                     CW_USEDEFAULT, CW_USEDEFAULT,
                     NULL, NULL, hInstance, NULL);

    if (hWindow == NULL)
      return hWindow;

    ShowWindow(hWindow, nCmdShow);
    UpdateWindow(hWindow);

    return hWindow;
  }
```

```
// =====================================
// IMPLEMENTATION
// =====================================
#define Window1_DefProc     DefWindowProc
 void Window1_OnDestroy(HWND hwnd);


////////////////////////////////////////
// The window proc is where messages get processed
////////////////////////////////////////

    LRESULT CALLBACK EXPORT16 WndProc(HWND hWindow, UINT Message,
                                      WPARAM wParam, LPARAM lParam)
  {
    switch(Message)
    {
      HANDLE_MSG(hWindow, WM_DESTROY, Window1_OnDestroy);
      default:
        return Window1_DefProc(hWindow, Message, wParam, lParam);
    }
  }

////////////////////////////////////////
// Handle WM_DESTROY message
////////////////////////////////////////
 #pragma argsused
 void Window1_OnDestroy(HWND hwnd)
 {
   PostQuitMessage(0);
 }
```

Listing 3.2 shows the Window1 definition file.

Listing 3.2. WINDOW1.DEF.

```
1: ;  WINDOW1.DEF
2:
3: NAME           Window1
4: DESCRIPTION    'Window1 example'
5: CODE           PRELOAD MOVEABLE DISCARDABLE
6: DATA           PRELOAD MOVEABLE MULTIPLE
7:
8: HEAPSIZE       4096
9: STACKSIZE      5120
```

Listing 3.3 is the Window1 Borland makefile.

Listing 3.3. WINDOW.1MAK (Borland).

```
#---------------------------------------------------------------
# The MakeFile: WINDOW1.MAK
#
# Macros
#
# Install automatically creates file BCROOT.INC in BIN directory.
#---------------------------------------------------------------
```

Listing 3.3. continued

```
!if !$d(BCROOT)
BCROOT  = $(MAKEDIR)
!endif

INCPATH = $(BCROOT)\INCLUDE
LIBPATH = $(BCROOT)\LIB

!if $d(WIN16)
COMPILER= BCC.EXE
FLAGS    = -W -ml -v -w4 -I$(INCPATH) -L$(LIBPATH)
!else
COMPILER= BCC32.EXE
FLAGS    = -W -v -w4 -I$(INCPATH) -L$(LIBPATH)
!endif

# Link
WINDOW1.EXE: WINDOW1.OBJ WINDOW1.DEF
  $(COMPILER) $(FLAGS) WINDOW1.OBJ

# Compile
WINDOW1.OBJ: WINDOW1.CPP
  $(COMPILER) -c $(FLAGS) WINDOW1.CPP
```

Listing 3.4 is the Window1 Microsoft makefile.

Listing 3.4. WINDOW1.MAK (Microsoft).

```
# WINDOWMS.MAK
# Microsoft makefile

APPNAME=WINDOW1
TARGETOS=WIN95
APPVER=4.0
OBJS=$(APPNAME).OBJ

!include <win32.mak>

all: $(APPNAME).exe

# Update the object files if necessary

# compile
.cpp.obj:
  $(cc) $(cflags) $(cvars) $(cdebug) $<

# Update the executable file if necessary.

$(APPNAME).exe: $(OBJS)
  $(link) $(linkdebug) $(guiflags) -out:$(APPNAME).exe \
  $(OBJS) $(guilibs) comctl32.lib
```

The Windows1 program, which is produced by compiling all the preceding files, creates a simple example of the traditional window that is so familiar to all users of the Windows environment. An image of this window can be seen in Figure 3.1.

If you haven't done so already, you should set this book aside long enough to see Window1 in action. When compiling the program, remember that it consists of several different modules brought together to create a whole. Just as a gear shift, a steering wheel, and a transmission come together with other pieces of machinery to make up the sum total of a car, each module in a Windows program makes its own contribution toward creating a final executable.

Figure 3.1.

The output from running
WINDOW1.CPP.

If you are working with project files inside of Borland C++ or Microsoft C++, the process of getting the program up and running should be fairly simple. If you have ordered the source code disk that accompanies this book, Borland users can just load WINDOW1.IDE from the Project|Open Project menu item. Microsoft users can load WIN1MS32.MAK. You can also create WINDOW1.IDE or WIN1MS32.MAK from scratch. If you are having trouble creating these files, consult the material on this subject on Day 2, "Building Projects, Creating Windows."

If you aren't working from inside the Microsoft or Borland IDE, the first step is to run a makefile from the DOS prompt. Then you can either start the program dynamically from a run menu or add it as an icon to one of your program groups (and then start it from there).

Here is the command you should give if you want to use Borland C++ to compile Window1 from the DOS prompt:

```
make -f window1
```

Here is the command you should give if you want to use Microsoft Visual C++ to compile Window1 from the DOS prompt:

```
nmake -fwindow1.mak
```

Figure 3.2 shows a complete project as it appears when using the Borland C++ version.

The Microsoft equivalent is shown in Figure 3.3.

Copies of the appropriate project and makefiles for the Borland and Microsoft compilers are included with the disk and the online file that is available for this book.

Note: It's crucial that you compile the programs in this book. If you are having trouble getting over this initial hurdle, you might consider purchasing or downloading the disk that accompanies this book. It comes with working code, guaranteed to compile and run correctly with either the Borland or Microsoft compilers.

This book's software is available on CompuServe Information Service. When you type GO SAMS, you enter the Macmillan Publishing forum. Once there, enter the file library and search in library 7 (Sams-ProgLang+DataB) for the keyword CALVERT.

Figure 3.2.
The Borland IDE when creating the Window1 program.

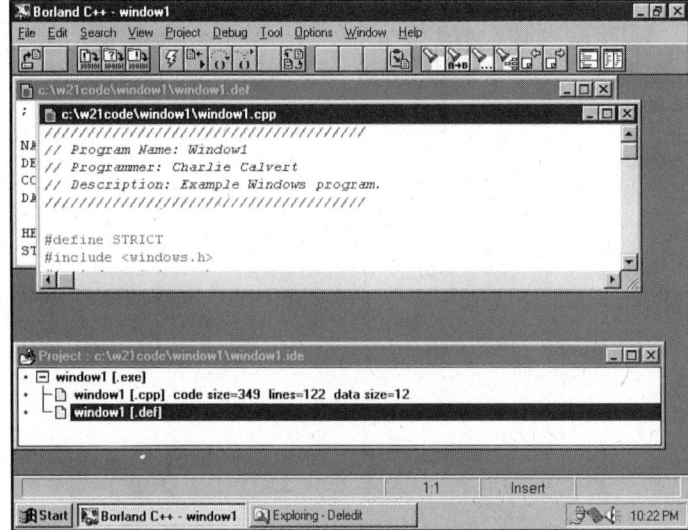

Figure 3.3.
The Microsoft project dialog when creating the Window1 program.

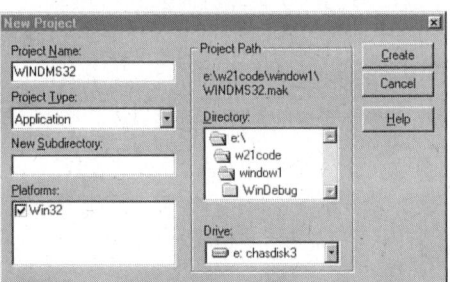

When you have the program up and running, take the time to play with it for a few minutes. Experiment with the program by maximizing it and minimizing it. Change its shape by pulling on its borders. Give yourself time to understand the functionality inherent in the lines of code you have typed in and compiled.

Of Apples, Oranges, Windows, and DOS

Some readers might feel a little overwhelmed by the size of the source code for the Window1 program. In fact, you might even feel yourself longing for the relative simplicity of the DOS world. If so, consider some of the ideas expounded in the next few paragraphs.

Certainly a lot has been written about the relative merits of the DOS and Windows programming environments. But is it fair to directly compare the rolling opacity of the source file WINDOW1.CPP with the sample code presented on the first few pages of a traditional DOS programming book? For instance:

```
#include <stdio.h>

main()
{
  printf("Hello, world");
}
```

A peek beneath the surface reveals that there are really only a few parallels between the rococo richness of the Windows application and the admirable simplicity of the DOS "Hello, world" program.

For instance, by changing only line 88 of the WINDOW1.CPP module, the program can be made to appear in its minimized state (as a small icon at the bottom of the screen). That same line of code can be changed again to maximize the window on startup. As shown in Figure 3.4, other very small changes can remove the caption, borders, and system menu, as well as the minimize and maximize icons in the top right of the window. (In various parts of this book, you'll learn how to make all these changes.)

To make equally radical changes to the "I Iello, world" program would require the addition of many lines of code—and days, if not weeks or months, of work. In the end, the code would have to be altered so radically that it wouldn't be recognizable as the same program.

Figure 3.4.

Minor changes to the code in WINDOWS1.CPP can radically change the appearance of the window it creates.

> **Note:** My point isn't that Windows is better than DOS, or that DOS is better than Windows. Rather, I believe that the two environments are radically different, and they can't always be readily compared.
>
> For instance, one can meaningfully compare the relative merits of a Mercedes and a VW Beetle. It's more difficult, however, to compare a Mercedes to a motorcycle or sailboat. The statement "A Mercedes is roomier than a VW," is relatively valid. The same can't be said of the statement "A Mercedes is roomier than a motorcycle," because each vehicle treats space in an entirely different manner. Likewise, the statement: "A Mercedes is faster than a sailboat," can seem a bit obtuse when you consider that they each operate in a different medium, and are usually intended to perform quite different functions.
>
> The same types of problems arise when people say "DOS is easier to program than Windows." Such statements aren't necessarily correct or incorrect, they're simply beside the point.

In the long run, the traditional "Hello, world" DOS program is probably not better or worse than a Windows program—only different. The computer world is very complex, and it's a mistake to always try to set one portion of it against another. The world isn't that simple. In this case, for instance, the one is an apple and the other an orange. As a result, the two can't be *fruitfully* compared.

Into the Code

Well, it's time to start talking about the juicy stuff that forms the core of interest for all real programmers.

The following is an extremely delicate part of the learning process. The things you'll learn about in the next few pages can appear a bit overwhelming, even to experienced Windows programmers. As a result, I want to be sure that you have some idea of what to expect.

☐ The next section presents a detailed conceptual overview of the `WinMain` and `WndProc` procedures. My goal is to give you a bird's-eye view of an entire Windows program without delving into too many specific lines of code. Once you have this image clear in your mind, you'll be prepared to see how the code is actually implemented. This section will appeal most to the theoretical or abstract portions of your intelligence.

☐ After the overview, the chapter swoops over the `WinMain` and `WndProc` code a second time. The purpose of this second pass is to take a careful look at the details of the `WinMain`, `Create`, and `Register` procedures. This section of the chapter features a line-by-line analysis of all three procedures and will appeal to your practical side.

☐ The final section focuses on the details of the WndProc procedure. The WndProc procedure controls the program while it's running. More specifically, the WinMain procedure launches the program, while the WndProc procedure helps run the program.

A Conceptual View of *WinMain* and *WndProc*

Following is the main function in the Window1 program:

```
#pragma argsused
int WINAPI WinMain(HINSTANCE hInst, HINSTANCE hPrevInstance,
                   LPSTR lpszCmdParam, int nCmdShow)
{
  MSG  Msg;

  if (!hPrevInstance)
    if (!Register(hInst))
      return FALSE;

  MainWindow = Create(hInst, nCmdShow);
  if (!MainWindow)
    return FALSE;

  while (GetMessage(&Msg, NULL, 0, 0))
  {
    TranslateMessage(&Msg);
    DispatchMessage(&Msg);
  }

  return Msg.wParam;
}
```

As stated earlier, the function WinMain (lines 32–51) takes the place of function main() in a standard DOS program. Windows applications, written in C or C++, almost always begin with a call to WinMain.

WinMain is divided into three parts. The first is the call to Register (line 38), the second is the call to Create (line 41), and the third is the while loop that handles the program's messages (lines 44–47). Before I explain matters in detail, it might be helpful if you repeat these three steps as if they were a litany: Register, Create, enter the message loop. One more time: Register, Create, enter the message loop.

Very good.

Now take a moment to consider the following extended metaphor:

The Register function is roughly parallel to doing the paperwork when buying a car. You talk with the dealer about the particular "class" of car you want to buy. You tell him you want a Volvo station wagon with stick shift, or you want a Mercedes with power steering. The Register function allows you to describe the kind of window you want to create, and to specify whether it has a particular color and icon, and so on.

The Create function, on the other hand, is similar to actually opening the door of a specific car, sitting down in the front seat, and turning the ignition. Now it's officially yours. You've bought this particular vehicle—not just a particular class of vehicle, but a specific vehicle. In other words, this is the moment when you create a specific instance of the window described in the Register function.

To complete this analogy, you can imagine that the message loop and WndProc are somewhat akin to the act of owning and maintaining a car. They are what you do after the cars is yours, and when you are taking care of it. In short, they manage the window while the program is running.

This analogy isn't without its flaws, but it serves as a concrete image you can utilize during the upcoming discussion.

The act of *registering* a window is totally foreign to many DOS programmers. Nothing in the DOS world is parallel to the act of a program turning to the Windows environment and saying, in effect, "Okay, before my main window appears on the scene, I want to register it with you so you know what class of window it is and what it's up to."

To return to the analogy of buying a car, one can say that the Register procedure is akin to when you haggle over what type of car you want to buy. You are saying, "I want to buy this class of car. I want to buy a Toyota with four-wheel drive, or I want to buy a Chevy with air conditioning." You are not talking about a particular instance of a car, but about a general type of car and the actual features you want. Of course, when you are creating a window, you don't need to establish whether you want power steering or a fancy stereo. Instead, you say what kind of icon you want, what kind of menu you want, what color window you want, and what name will be assigned to your window.

To summarize, the Register procedure enables you to register the class of window you want to use. The actual window you want to create is specified in the CreateWindow procedure.

Note: The existence of the Register procedure implies that a window is a separate entity with an existence of its own. It has a caretaker, which usually turns out to be the program itself. Furthermore, it can talk with Windows proper—that is, with the operating system.

After the window has been properly registered, the next step is to create it—to bring it into being. During this process, the shape, title, and style of the window are established. Then the window itself is brought into being, and the program takes over control of its existence.

This is roughly parallel to the act of actually buying a specific car. You sign the papers and become the owner of a particular vehicle. You can now sit behind the wheel; you can drive the car off the lot. At this stage, the program becomes the owner of the window and is responsible for its future. You are no longer talking about a general class of car; you are talking about a specific vehicle.

Notice that `WinMain` has a number of `if` clauses that must be navigated. If some of these clauses fail, the function will return `FALSE`, which means the window won't get created. In short, if the call to either `Register` or `Create` fails, the function `WinMain` is immediately aborted. It's as if your negotiations with the car dealer broke down and you left without a purchase. On the rare occasions when this happens, the application is summarily curtailed with little or no fanfare.

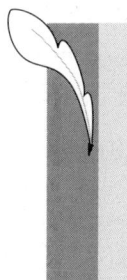

> **Note:** From the user's point of view, it would be nice if I added extra code that displayed message boxes explaining what went wrong when one of these calls fails. However, from the programmer's point of view, this only makes the syntax more complex, because it adds extra code to routines that are already fairly lengthy.
>
> In the end, I've traded simplicity of design for ease of use. In the current circumstances, I believe this is the best choice. However, if you try to run these programs, and they keep failing without giving any errors, you might consider the idea that one of these `if` statements has failed. Use the debugger to try to pinpoint the exact location of the error, and then compare the code you have typed in with the code I present here.

These `if` clauses also ensure that if a previous instance of the application already exists, the window class won't be registered a second time. In other words, if you go into the dealer to buy a second car of the same type, you won't need to haggle over the type of car you are interested in or the features you want to include. You go straight to the `Create` function, which is where you *buy* a specific window.

Don't worry too much about the exact way these `if` clauses work. I discuss these lines of code in-depth later in this chapter. Remember, I'm starting out with the 20,000-foot overview, and I will give you the details later.

The final step in `WinMain` is to enter the `message` loop. To continue the automotive analogy, one can think of the `message` loop as the windows of the car and the `WndProc` as the driver's seat and controls. From here, the driver can see any new messages coming in and can adjust the vehicle's course accordingly.

In order to fully understand the `message` loop and `WndProc`, you have to understand that Windows is, to some degree, object-oriented. That is, each window has an existence of its own, just as a car is an object that has an existence of its own.

Each window can be treated as a separate object with an autonomous existence. As such, they aren't manipulated directly by the main program or by the operating system. Instead, the operating system can send messages to the window, and the window itself will "decide" what to do with those messages. Or perhaps it would be closer to the mark to say that the programmer teaches the window how to respond to the messages it gets.

It might help if I give a concrete example with which most readers should be familiar. At the end of the day, we usually decide to close Program Manager, or some Program Manager substitute, thereby shutting down Windows for the night. When this happens, messages are sent to all the windows on the desktop asking them if they are ready to close.

More specifically, the message is sent to the message loop of each program. The message loop then passes the message on to the WndProc, and the WndProc decides what to do with the message.

Often, the WndProc replies: "Wait, I'm not ready! There's a file here that hasn't been saved." WndProc then pops up a window, like the one shown in Figure 3.5, asking whether you want to save the file in question, or whether you want to cancel the whole operation. If you select the Yes button, WndProc saves the file and tells the operating system that it can proceed with the shutdown. If you choose No, the file is not saved, but Windows is still closed. If you choose Cancel, the file is not saved, and your program tells Windows that it should remain open.

Figure 3.5.

A program turns to the user and asks a question.

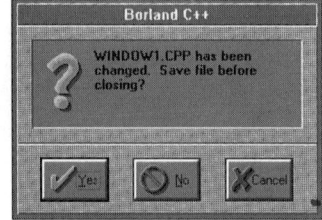

Note: The outline presented here is a bit of an oversimplification. For instance, there are times when the operating system might send a message directly to WndProc rather than sending it first to the message loop. For now, don't let this twist on the subject trip you up. You will hear more about the particulars of this process as you read through the chapters of this book. If it's not already clear to you, it will become so after a time.

During much of this process, a window acts as an autonomous object with a life of its own. It knows enough to tell the Program Manager something needs to be done. Even more remarkably, it knows how to communicate with the user and request that any loose ends be tied up before anything else happens. This is quintessential object-oriented behavior, even if the underlying code is not truly OOP-like in structure.

DO / DON'T

DO remember to register a window class the first time it appears on the screen. When a window is registered, the operating environment is informed of several traits specific to that class. For instance, it learns about

- [ ] the name of the window class
- [ ] the icon of the window
- [ ] the cursor associated with the window
- [ ] the background color of the window
- [ ] the name of the menu associated with the window

DON'T forget to create a window during early stages of the call to WinMain. While calling CreateWindow, you can define the window's title and dimensions, as well as perform other important initialization steps.

DON'T forget to set up the message loop properly. This is the engine which drives your program. A window without a message loop is like a car without any windows. The window won't know what's happening around it if it doesn't have a message loop. As a result, it will crash just as surely as a car will crash if a driver can't see!

3

So much for the overview of WinMain and WndProc in conceptual terms. Now it's time to change focus, to zoom in on the fine print. This is where you see the nitty-gritty details that concern most serious Windows programmers on a daily basis.

Calling *WinMain*

WinMain is the program entry point. When it is called, the program is launched. When this routine ends, the program is shut down.

Take another look at the header for the WinMain function:

```
int WINAPI WinMain(HINSTANCE hInst, HINSTANCE hPrevInstance,
          LPSTR lpszCmdParam, int nCmdShow)
```

Even though you were given a brief overview of them on Day 1, "Getting Your Feet Wet," a great deal remains to be said about the four parameters passed to WinMain. Before focusing in too closely on the details, here's a quick review:

- [ ] The first parameter, hInst, is a unique number that identifies the program. In WIN16, this number is unique across the entire machine. In WIN32, it is unique inside each address space. Because each WIN32 process gets its own address space, the uniqueness of this number is not particularly significant. However, in WIN32, this number will represent the base memory address at which the .EXE's code has been loaded. (More specifically, in Windows 95, the number is usually 4MB, or 0x00400000.)

☐ The second parameter, hPrevInstance, is a unique number associated with any previous instance of this program. If there is no other instance on the desktop, hPrevInstance is set to NULL. In WIN32, there can be no other instances of an application running in the current address space, so this value is always set to NULL. It is included only for the sake of helping you port your code from WIN16 to WIN32.

☐ The third parameter, lpszCmdParam, is a string containing any information passed from the command line. This is an ANSI string and not a Unicode string. If you want a Unicode string, then you must call one of the following functions:

```
LPTSTR GetCommandLine(void);
LPWSTR *CommandLineToArgvW(LPWSTR lpCmdLine, LPINT pArgc);
```

lpszCmdParam does not contain the name of the current executable as its first member. If you want that information, then you must call one of the two functions shown above, or else access __argz or __argv directly. If you want to work with environment variables, call GetEnvironmentVariable and SetEnvironmentVariable. However, it should be understood that environment variables are not the recommended way to communicate with an application under Windows.

☐ The fourth parameter, nCmdShow, tells whether the program should appear minimized, maximized, or simply assume a default size and shape.

The first and second parameters passed to WinMain are declared to be of type HINSTANCE. The type HINSTANCE is really nothing but a handle or unique number that Windows uses to identify a particular object on the desktop. (If you define STRICT, then HINSTANCE becomes a pointer that can be carefully type checked by the system. It's a 16-bit [near] pointer in WIN16, and a 32-bit pointer in WIN32. However, the pointer resolves to an int.)

Note: DOS gurus can draw a parallel between the way Windows assigns a unique handle for each window and the way DOS assigns a unique handle for each file. If it helps clarify matters somewhat, you can think of an HINSTANCE as the "file handle" for a window. (True DOS gurus might find an even closer parallel between window handles and the way DOS assigns a unique PSP to each application. The file handle analogy is a bit looser but might be familiar to a wider group of programmers. Use the analogy that is most helpful to you.)

The first parameter passed to an application identifies the *current instance* of an application. The second parameter identifies the *previous instance*, if it exists. In WIN16, each of these instances can be thought of as nothing more than a unique number assigned to a particular object for means of identification. In WIN32, the uniqueness of the first parameter is no longer an issue, and the second parameter is always set to NULL.

Each WIN32 application has its own address space. In other words, it has its own virtual 4GB computer in which it runs. Take a moment to grasp that fact. The application is launched, and the operating system sets up an artificial environment for it that looks and feels like a complete computer with 4GB of memory on it. Of course, it is very unlikely that a computer will really have 4GB of memory. The 4GB address space is a virtual memory area that is mapped into existing memory that might reside in RAM, or even on your hard disk. (Don't worry if this isn't all sinking in; just get what you can, and then keep reading. You don't have to understand the details yet, although it will help if you have some vague, general idea of how WIN32 memory is handled.)

There are no other applications running in the virtual 4GB address space given to each application. If another application is launched, it gets its own 4GB address space, even if the program is just a second instance of the first program. As a result, each application will believe that it is the only application running on that system.

Given this architecture, there will be (at least theoretically) only one HINSTANCE in a program's address space. There can be no hPrevInstance, because any potential second copy of that application will be running in an entirely different virtual 4GB address space. The two applications will not know about one another and cannot communicate directly without taking special measures. (These special measures include memory mapped files, OLE automation, and a few other specialized techniques.)

The 16-bit world of Windows 3.1 looks very different. The key issue is that 16-bit Windows is a quasi-multitasking operating system that launches all its programs into one address space. This is true even in Windows 95. That is, each 16-bit application launched under Windows 95 is put by default into the same address space as all other 16-bit applications running on the system.

Despite its limitations, 16-bit Windows can still fully support more than one copy of a program at a time. To help make this possible, it assigns a unique number to each program that runs. That number is passed to you in the first parameter of WinMain. Therefore, the first order of business in any WIN16 program is to establish the "number" (hInst) associated with the current instance of a program, and whether or not there is a previous instance (hPrevInstance) of the program.

If no previous instance of the program exists, hPrevInstance is set to NULL. Therefore, in 16-bit Windows it's possible to check whether or not a program has any siblings. This is done simply by typing

```
if(hPrevInstance)
  DoSomething();
```

87

 (in margin: 3)

87

where `DoSomething` will only be called if there is a previous instance. Sometimes a 16-bit programmer might decide that there should be only one copy of his or her program running at a time. As a result, a common use for this information is to preempt any attempt to create a second instance with something like the following code fragment:

```
if(hPrevInstance)
    return FALSE;
```

Of course, if you implement these two lines of code exactly as shown, your users would probably spend a lot of time clicking the icon for your application and wondering why nothing happens. In other words, it would probably be a good idea to pop up a message box explaining the situation before returning `NULL`:

```
if(hPrevInstance)
{
  MessageBox(0, "Only 1 copy allowed", " Notice", MB_OK);
    return FALSE;
}
```

Of course, this code would not be meaningful in a WIN32 application, since `hPrevInstance` is always set to `NULL`. One alternative means of finding out if another copy of your 32-bit application is running is to call `FindWindow`.

Earlier, I mentioned that Microsoft invented the `HINSTANCE` type to help you write easily readable, strongly typed code that helps you avoid careless errors. This is the primary reason for creating the `HINSTANCE` type. The compiler can check to make sure you are not just passing a parameter that expects an `int`, but one that specifically expects an `HINSTANCE` (`hInst` or `hPrevInstance`). However, on all platforms, the type resolves to an `int`.

Interlude: Hungarian Notation and WINDOWS.H

Before discussing `WinMain` any further, I want to digress into a discussion of Hungarian notation and the complex of files surrounding WINDOWS.H. (In particular, see WINDEF.H.) From an aesthetic perspective, this side trip is a bit of a nightmare, but you need this information if you want to understand the syntactical elements of `WinMain`.

Before going on, I ought to talk some about the quaint notion of Hungarian notation. This particular conceit involves the habit of prefixing a letter to a variable name. This is done to help identify this variable's type. In other words, the "h" in `hPrevInstance` is meant to indicate that `hPrevInstance` is of type `HINSTANCE` or of type `HANDLE`. Likewise, the "n" in `nCmdShow` designates that it's an integer.

This convention is a deep-rooted aspect of traditional Windows lore that also occasionally raises its head in the DOS world. Although Hungarian notation can sometimes confuse newcomers, and though its value has been somewhat mitigated by the advent of the STRICT option, it can still be a useful tool in the hands of wary veterans.

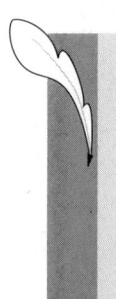

Note: One interesting note about Hungarian notation is the way it got its name. The technique was pioneered by an ace Microsoft programmer, Charles Simonyi, who was born in Hungary. The people who worked for him at Microsoft were taught to use this convention. To them it looked quite normal. However, outside observers of projects run by Simonyi would comment on the strange appearance of the code produced in his shop. The traditional reply was to assume a deadpan expression and say that the code was strange-looking because it was written in Hungarian. Hence the name: Hungarian notation.

I use Hungarian notation because it is now an established part of the Windows coding tradition. I'll leave it up to you to decide whether you find it appealing.

The following often-quoted chart (see Table 3.1) should help you navigate through the Hungarian landscape:

Table 3.1. Windows typedefs, from WINDOWS.H and/or WINDEF.H.

Prefix	Type	Windows Type
b (or f)	int	BOOL
by (or b)	unsigned char	BYTE
c	char	
dw	unsigned long	DWORD
fn	function	
h	unsigned int (UINT)	HANDLE
i	int	
l	long	LONG
lp	long pointer	
n	int or short	
s	string	
sz	null-terminated string	
w	unsigned short	WORD

Notice the third column. It introduces you to various new types that are frequently used in Windows programs. They exist for the same reasons that the HINSTANCE type exists. Don't let their appearance in Windows code confuse you. Nothing about them is tricky or difficult. In their simplest incarnation, they are just new names for the same old types that C programmers have been using for years. When STRICT is defined, however, they are often converted into pointers.

Note: You should always define your code as STRICT if you are concerned about porting back and forth between WIN16 and WIN32. STRICT enforces STRICT-type checking and helps you write clean code that avoids common, easy to make errors. When code is declared as STRICT, special types (such as HINSTANCE) become pointers rather than simple integers, as shown in these excerpts from the WINDOWS.H complex:

```
???Author: Preceding paragraph: #ifdef STRICT
typedef const void NEAR*        HANDLE;
#define DECLARE_HANDLE(name)    struct name##__ { int unused; }; \
                                typedef const struct name##__ NEAR* name
#define DECLARE_HANDLE32(name)  struct name##__ { int unused; }; \
                                typedef const struct name##__ FAR* name

#else   /* STRICT */
typedef UINT                    HANDLE;
#define DECLARE_HANDLE(name)    typedef UINT name
#define DECLARE_HANDLE32(name)  typedef DWORD name
#endif  /* !STRICT */


...


DECLARE_HANDLE(HINSTANCE);
```

The preceding code shows that HINSTANCE is declared as a DWORD if STRICT is not defined, and as a pointer to a structure if STRICT is defined. If STRICT is declared, the pointer HINSTANCE can be carefully type checked by the compiler, thereby helping you to write clean, portable code.

The mother of all reference manuals is WINDOWS.H and the files referenced inside it. WINDOWS.H is referenced at the top of every Windows program. The old Windows 3.1 version of WINDOWS.H was an almost entirely self-contained file that ran on for many pages. The newer versions of WINDOWS.H are shorter but contain references to many other header files. These referenced header files contain portions of the declarations and definitions that used

to be contained directly in WINDOWS.H, or which have recently been added to Windows. Because Microsoft and Borland have versions of these files that differ in many particulars, I will refer to them as the "WINDOWS.H complex of files" because this abstraction is general enough to cover the variations between the two versions.

The following are some of the files referenced in both Borland's and Microsoft's versions of WINDOWS.H:

```
WINDEF.H: Fundamental Type definitions. (Int, BOOL, UNIT, etc.)
WINBASE.H: 32 Windows Base APIs.
WINGDI.H: Graphics Device Interface (Drawing to screen, etc.)
WINUSER.H: Declarations from or associated with USER.EXE
WINNLS.H: National Language Support (Prepare for foreign countries).
WINCON.H: Console I/O instead of the GDI. That is, the process runs in a "DOS box".
```

Inside WINDOWS.H, or in one of the files referenced by WINDOWS.H, you'll find declarations and definitions for most of the functions and types native to the Windows environment. The following is a particularly important swatch of code that includes handy definitions:

```
/** Simple types & common helper macros **/

typedef int              BOOL;
#define FALSE            0
#define TRUE             1

typedef unsigned char    BYTE;
typedef unsigned short   WORD;
typedef unsigned long    DWORD;

typedef unsigned int     UINT;

#ifdef STRICT
typedef signed long      LONG;
#else
#define LONG long
#endif

#define LOBYTE(w)        ((BYTE)(w))
#define HIBYTE(w)        ((BYTE)((UINT)(w) >> 8))

#define LOWORD(l)        ((WORD)(l))
#define HIWORD(l)        ((WORD)((DWORD)(l) >> 16))
```

A few choice moments spent pondering this code should help to clarify a number of interesting aspects of Windows programming.

This is the end of the digression into the mysterious realms of Hungarian notation and WINDOWS.H. The complex of files surrounding WINDOWS.H is the place where many mysteries are explained. Hours dedicated to contemplating the contents of these files is time well spent.

3

Back to *WinMain*

After studying Hungarian notation and portions of the WINDOWS.H complex, you might find that it's possible to make sense out of the third parameter to `WinMain`:

```
32: int WINAPI WinMain(HINSTANCE hInst, HINSTANCE hPrevInstance,
33:                     LPSTR lpszCmdParam, int nCmdShow)
```

The strange prefix before the identifier `lpszCmdParam` is meant to identify the parameter as a long pointer to a null-terminated string. In particular, this string happens to contain the command line passed to the program at startup.

The final parameter to `WinMain` helps designate whether the program is to begin in a maximized, minimized, or normal state. You encountered this same constant when using `WinExec` on Day 1, "Getting Your Feet Wet."

When `nCmdShow` is set to `SW_SHOWMAXIMIZED`, the program's main window appears in its maximized state. Conversely, when `nCmdShow` is set to `SW_SHOWMINIMIZED`, the window starts out minimized. The default is `SW_SHOWNORMAL`. To see what different results these values produce, you can take the time to experiment with them.

There is one last important part of the `WinMain` header that I've not yet discussed. This is the use of the word `WINAPI`, which is defined as follows in WINDOWS.H:

```
#define WINAPI        far _pascal
#define WINAPI        stdcall
#define CALLBACK      far _pascal
```

I've included the definition for `CALLBACK`, because it is obviously related. Note also that `WINAPI` is redefined in various other places throughout the WINDOWS.H complex. In the old 16-bit days, Windows programs used the words `FAR PASCAL`, whereas programmers now use `WINAPI`. The new word was chosen to provide compatibility with operating systems, such as Windows NT, which has no use for the keyword `FAR`. (No use for the keyword `FAR`? What a wonderful, glorious, thought!)

All procedures labeled `CALLBACK` or `WINAPI` are automatically declared with the Pascal calling convention in WIN16, and with `__stdcall` in WIN32. (`__stdcall` follows neither the conventions of `cdecl` calling convention, nor the conventions of the Pascal calling convention). The standard 16-bit Pascal calling convention enforces the rule that when parameters are passed to this procedure, they are pushed onto the stack, starting with the parameter on the left, and ending with the parameter on the right. Traditional C programs take the opposite approach, but 16-bit Windows uses the Pascal calling convention because it is faster. `__stdcall` is an attempt to use the best features of both systems.

A number of new conventions raised their heads in the last few paragraphs. But underneath all this syntactical sugar you will find the same old types long familiar to C programmers. If you like, you can even think of the WIN16 header for `WinMain` as "really" looking something like this:

```
int WinMain(int Instance, int PrevInstance,
            char far* CmdParam, int CmdShow)
```

If it helps you get a "handle" on this stuff, you can think of `WinMain` as being declared in this simple manner. The rest is just part of the carnival. Baffle your friends! Confound your enemies! Come join in—it's fun!

Registration

Here's the formidable `Register` function:

```
56: BOOL Register(HINSTANCE hInst)
57: {
58:     WNDCLASS WndClass;
59:
60:     WndClass.style         = CS_HREDRAW | CS_VREDRAW;
61:     WndClass.lpfnWndProc   = WndProc;
62:     WndClass.cbClsExtra    = 0;
63:     WndClass.cbWndExtra    = 0;
64:     WndClass.hInstance     = hInst;
65:     WndClass.hIcon         = LoadIcon(NULL, IDI_APPLICATION);
66:     WndClass.hCursor       = LoadCursor(NULL, IDC_ARROW);
67:     WndClass.hbrBackground = GetStockBrush(WHITE_BRUSH);
68:     WndClass.lpszMenuName  = NULL;
69:     WndClass.lpszClassName = szAppName;
70:
71:     return (RegisterClass (&WndClass) != 0);
72: }
```

This code introduces you to one of the great Windows traditions—namely, the existence of structures and declarations so numerous and complex they send shivers down the spine of all but the most stout-hearted. Fortunately, these structures tend to lose their "byte" if you have either a good reference book handy or a good online help system.

Some day, you might want to memorize all the fields in the WNDCLASS structure. However, you don't need to do so immediately. Instead, you should probably dedicate your time to exploring the reference manuals or online help files in which these structures are listed.

For instance, Microsoft and Borland compilers come with information about the WNDCLASS structure. It looks like the image shown in Figure 3.6.

Alternatively, a few minutes spent perusing WINDOWS.H and its related files might help you find some additional information about the WNDCLASS structure:

```
typedef struct tagWNDCLASS
{
UINT        style;
WNDPROC     lpfnWndProc;
int         cbClsExtra;
int         cbWndExtra;
HINSTANCE   hInstance;
```

```
HICON       hIcon;
HCURSOR     hCursor;
HBRUSH      hbrBackground;
LPCSTR      lpszMenuName;
LPCSTR      lpszClassName;
} WNDCLASS;
```

The WNDCLASS structure lies at the heart of all Register procedures.

Figure 3.6.

An excerpt from the Borland C++ online help entry for the WNDCLASS structure.

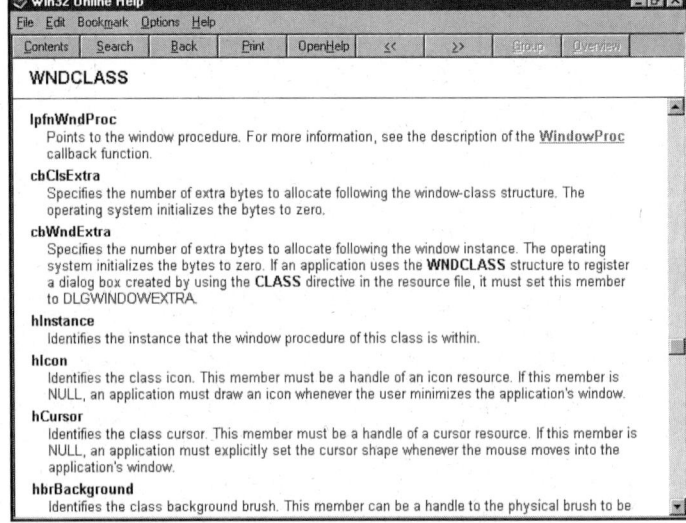

I've said that filling out the Register procedure is a bit like deciding what features you want to have on your new car. Now, you have a chance to see exactly what options are available whenever you register a new window:

☐ style field: What is the window's style? By changing the style field, you can radically change the behavior of a window. You can OR together more than one style, if you want, as shown above. The two styles usually passed in this parameter are CS_VREDRAW and CS_HREDRAW. Below is a list specifying the parameters that can be passed in this field (For additional information see the on line help.):

CS_BYTEALIGNCLIENT	Aligns a window's columns on the byte boundary for performance reasons.
CS_BYTEALIGNWINDOW	Aligns a window on a byte boundary (in the x direction) to enhance performance during operations that involve moving or sizing the window.

CS_CLASSDC	Makes all windows in a class share one device context (DC).
CS_DBLCLKS	Gets double-click messages.
CS_GLOBALCLASS	Allows an application to create a window of the class regardless of the value of the hInstance parameter passed to the CreateWindow or CreateWindowEx function. If you do not specify this style, the hInstance parameter passed to the CreateWindow (or CreateWindowEx) function must be the same as the hInstance parameter passed to the RegisterClass function.
CS_HREDRAW	Repaints an entire window if it's resized horizontally.
CS_NOCLOSE	Turns off Close command on the System menu.
CS_OWNDC	Gives each window of a class a unique device context.
CS_PARENTDC	Increases performance by having children use a parent window's device context.
CS_SAVEBITS	Saves a window as a bitmap for redrawing. Tends to slow things down.
CS_VREDRAW	Repaints an entire window if it's resized vertically.

- ☐ wndProc field: Use this field to specify the name and address of the window procedure.

- ☐ cbClsExtra, cbWndExtra: Is there any extra data to be associated with the window class or instance? For now, you shouldn't worry too much about these two fields. They are discussed in-depth on Day 14, "Stylish Windows."

- ☐ hInstance: Unique handle to an application.

- ☐ hIcon: The window's icon, if any.

- ☐ hCursor: The window's cursor, if any.

- ☐ hbrBackground: The color of the window.

- ☐ lpszMenuName: The menu for the window.

- ☐ lpszClassname: The name of the window class.

In WINDOW1.CPP, the style field is set to CS_HREDRAW and CS_VREDRAW (line 60). These two constants designate that the window is redrawn whenever the horizontal or vertical size of the window is changed. The presence of these two constants ensures that the contents of the window are always clearly visible to the user.

DO	**DON'T**

DO use the correct way to designate more than one Window style at a time by ORing them together with the ¦ symbol.

DON'T try to combine two window styles with an & or + operator.

The next step is to designate the window procedure. In some older code, WndProc is declared to return a long. If you define old code like that as STRICT, the resulting carefully monitored type checking would force you to perform a typecast:

```
WndClass.lpfnWndProc    = (WNDPROC)WndProc;
```

That extra bit of potentially confusing syntax can be avoided if WndProc is declared to return LRESULT:

```
WndClass.lpfnWndProc    = WndProc;
```

Of course, if you don't use STRICT, the latter syntax would probably compile on most standard C compilers (even if you did declare WndProc to return a long).

It goes without saying that typical Windows programs aren't going to get very far if you don't assign a window procedure to lpfnWndProc. So, no matter what path you take, all that really matters is that you somehow manage to assign a window procedure to lpfnWndProc. The actual technique you use is not nearly as important as the act itself.

The next two fields of the WndClass structure aren't important at this point. All cbClsExtra and cbWndExtra do is give you a chance to set aside some memory in which you can store information associated with your window. For now, there's no need to worry about such esoteric design issues.

The next step is to assign the hInstance field to the handle to your application. This is a simple, straightforward process:

```
WndClass.hInstance    = hInst;
```

The hIcon, hCursor, hbrBackground and lpszMenuName fields all describe common features of Windows. Later in the book, I describe how to tweak each of these features; for now, though, you might want to try a few simple experiments just to get a feel for what is going on. For instance, instead of assigning IDI_APPLICATION as your icon, try assigning IDI_EXCLAMATION or IDI_HAND:

```
WndClass.hIcon    = LoadIcon(NULL, IDI_HAND);
```

After you run your application, minimize it and you'll see that it has a different icon.

You can do the same sort of trick with the cursor simply by substituting IDC_WAIT, IDC_CROSS, or IDC_IBEAM for IDC_ARROW:

```
WndClass.hCursor        = LoadCursor(NULL, IDC_CROSS);
```

If you use the IDC_WAIT icon as your main cursor, you'll see the familiar hourglass symbol, as shown in Figure 3.7. Even when I'm the guy who makes this change, it seems to confuse me. Normally, the hourglass symbol only appears when Windows is telling the user to wait. As a result, I tend to hesitate when I see it on-screen, even if I know that I put it there only on a whim.

Figure 3.7.

A window using the famous hourglass cursor.

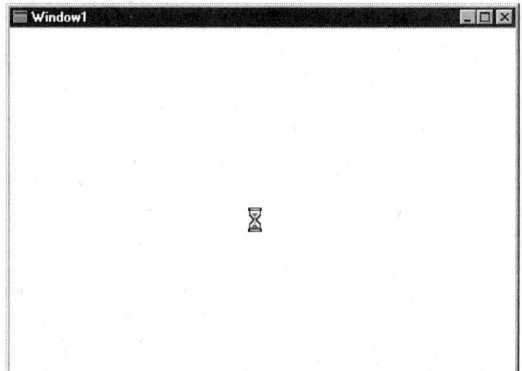

Seemingly trivial experiences such as this help show how powerful icons and other symbols can be. The human brain interacts very intimately with symbols of all types. Learn to take advantage of their power! Or, if you want, you can simply play with icons and cursors in order to see what peculiar effects you can create. Now *you* are the programmer, and you can get Windows to do any crazy thing you want it to do. If you're like me, you'll probably relish the opportunity to create a little good-natured mischief.

If you want to change the background color of your application, just substitute BLACK_BRUSH or GRAY_BRUSH for the constant WHITE_BRUSH. Remember that all these constants are defined in WINDOWS.H and are listed in detail in any good reference book.

Right now isn't the time to begin working with the menu, but the lpszClassName field needs a few brief words of explanation. This field gives you a chance to name your window. This is a very important act, because it's under this name that your window is registered. The class name is a bit like the key to an automobile. Without it, you can't sit down in the driver's seat and turn on the engine. In other words, a window must be registered under a particular name before it can be created. Whenever you want to create a window, you'll be helpless if you don't have the key—that is, if you don't know the class name.

At this point, further examination of the WNDCLASS structure isn't needed. The only thing left to do is to pass this information to Windows by calling RegisterClass and passing it the address of the WNDCLASS structure:

```
return (RegisterClass (&WndClass) != 0);
```

Note that I don't return the value of the RegisterClass procedure directly. Instead, I return a Boolean value specifying whether or not it is equal to 0. If it is equal to 0, then the call failed, and I return FALSE; otherwise, I return TRUE.

There are two key points I hope you remember from this section:

1. The Register procedure helps define the *class* of the window to appear on-screen. All windows are objects, and each object has a special set of traits. By filling out the WNDCLASS structure, a programmer tells Windows how he or she wants a particular object, or *class*, to be defined.

2. You often don't have to think about the Register method at all. Just copy and paste it into your program, and call it without even thinking about its contents. The default settings (previously shown) do fine in many cases. The Register function isn't something you have to fuss with every time you code; it is a series of opportunities available to you.

Creating the Window

Now it's time to consider the Create routine. Remember, this is the portion of the program where you define a specific window. The Register procedure defines a general class of window, and the Create procedure defines a specific instance of a window class:

```
77: HWND Create(HINSTANCE hInstance, int nCmdShow)
78: {
79:   HWND hWindow = CreateWindow(szAppName, szAppName,
80:                   WS_OVERLAPPEDWINDOW,
81:                   CW_USEDEFAULT, CW_USEDEFAULT,
82:                   CW_USEDEFAULT, CW_USEDEFAULT,
83:                   NULL, NULL, hInstance, NULL);
84:
85:   if (hWindow == NULL)
86:      return hWindow;
87:
88:   ShowWindow(hWindow, nCmdShow);
89:   UpdateWindow(hWindow);
90:
91:   return hWindow;
92: }
```

The core of this function is the call to CreateWindow, which takes a total of 11 glorious parameters, none of which you should take too seriously now:

`LPCSTR lpszClassName;`	Address of registered class name
`LPCSTR lpszWindowName;`	Address of window text—the caption
`DWORD dwStyle;`	Window style
`int x;`	Horizontal position of window
`int y;`	Vertical position of window
`int nWidth;`	Window width
`int nHeight;`	Window height
`HWND hwndParent;`	Handle of parent window
`HMENU hmenu;`	Handle of menu or child window ID
`HINSTANCE hinst;`	Handle of application instance
`void FAR* lpvParam;`	Address of window-creation data

Clearly, this function is equipped with enough arguments to keep the wolves awake.

Some of these arguments can be changed in order to implement simple, relatively obvious changes in your program. For instance, if you call `CreateWindow` with the following parameters, you'll get a window like the one depicted in Figure 3.8:

```
HWND hWindow = CreateWindow(szAppName,
"Tiny Window",
WS_OVERLAPPEDWINDOW,
1,
1,
100,
100,
NULL,
NULL,
hInstance,
                  NULL);
```

Figure 3.8.
*Window1 after making
some modifications to the
parameters passed to*
`CreateWindow.`

This example demonstrates how the second parameter passed to `CreateWindow` defines the window title, whereas the fourth through seventh parameters determine its initial size. The constant, `CW_USEDEFAULT`, tells Windows to choose the coordinates for a program.

The first parameter passed to `CreateWindow` is the *class name*. Remember that every window on the desktop is a separate entity, with some degree of autonomy. As a result, windows should have names by which they can be identified. Traditionally, the name of a program's main window is also the name of the application itself—but this doesn't have to be the case.

The other parameters passed to `CreateWindow` are discussed at the beginning of Week 2, when the subject of registering and creating windows is looked at in more detail. For now, use the previously listed defaults, unless there is some specific reason for doing otherwise.

> **Note:** Don't be confused by the seemingly cavalier way in which I put off discussing the other parameters passed to `CreateWindow`. Windows is not a difficult environment, but it *is* loaded with detail. I try to avoid bombarding you with too much material and cluttering the scene with a lot of information that isn't yet particularly relevant. Instead, I focus in on what is important at any particular stage.

Before moving on to a brief discussion of the window procedure and the `message` loop, take a glance at the two functions that make the window actually appear fully formed on the screen:

```
ShowWindow(hWindow, nCmdShow);
UpdateWindow(hWindow);
```

The `ShowWindow` function passes `nCmdShow` to Windows, thereby telling it to display the window in a particular state, such as:

`SW_SHOWMINIMIZED`	Minimized
`SW_SHOWMAXIMIZED`	Maximized
`SW_SHOW`	Normal

Refer to the online help for either `WinMain` or `ShowWindow` to find additional values that can be passed to `ShowWindow`.

The `UpDateWindow` call instructs Windows to send a `WM_PAINT` message to the newly created window. An in-depth explanation of how that process actually works is included on Day 4.

For now, you only need to know that both `ShowWindow` and `UpDateWindow` take an `HWND` as their first parameter. In this case, `HWND` is a handle to the application's main window. The issue is that many windows can open on the desktop at any one time, but the current goal is only to show the particular one just created. Therefore, it's necessary to pass the handle to that window, so Windows knows which object needs to be shown.

What Goes Around Comes Around

The last few lines of the `WinMain` procedure look like this:

```
44:     while (GetMessage(&Msg, NULL, 0, 0))
45:     {
```

```
46:      TranslateMessage(&Msg);
47:      DispatchMessage(&Msg);
48:   }
```

As I said earlier, this code is roughly equivalent to the windows in a new car. The message loop is the "eyes" of your application, and through it you can see what is happening around you. Specifically, you can use it tell if the user has pressed a key or mouse button, or if the operating system is trying to convey some other important event. All of these events or actions come to you in the form of messages.

Throughout the life of an application, Windows is sending it messages that report on actions taken by the user, or by other portions of the environment. These messages are placed in a queue, which the GetMessage function can dip into at will. As each message is retrieved, it's placed in a message structure that looks like this:

```
typedef struct tagMSG
{
HWND    hwnd;
UINT    message;
WPARAM  wParam;
LPARAM  lParam;
DWORD   time;
POINT   pt;
} MSG;
```

For now, you don't need to explore this structure in any depth. However, you can rest assured that I'll return to it again, on Day 4 and elsewhere.

After the message is retrieved from the message queue, it's passed to TranslateMessage, where processing helps make a message more comprehensible. For instance, if a function key is pressed, the message is originally placed in the queue in a very abstract form. The TranslateMessage function performs the processing that makes this message much easier for your application to understand.

The DispatchMessage function then proceeds to pass this message on to the specified window procedure, which, in this case, happens to be WndProc. After the message is dispatched, GetMessage is called to retrieve another message from the queue, if one is available.

It's important to understand that this loop, or one similar to it, is being executed over and over again throughout the entire life of an application. The process never stops. It lies very much at the heart of every Windows program. As such, it needs to be covered in-depth, so you'll find that the subject is broached repeatedly through this book.

The Window Procedure: An Overview

The message loop revolves around and around in circles. This process is repeated in an endless loop throughout much of the life of a typical Windows program. First, it gets messages from the operating environment; then, it passes the messages to the window procedure, or WndProc.

Here is the code from the Window1 program that is relevant to the WndProc:

```
LRESULT CALLBACK WndProc(HWND hWindow, UINT Message,
                         WPARAM wParam, LPARAM lParam);
#define Window1_DefProc      DefWindowProc
void Window1_OnDestroy(HWND hwnd);

// The window proc controls program flow
LRESULT CALLBACK WndProc(HWND hWindow,
                         UINT Message,
                         WPARAM wParam,
                         LPARAM lParam)
{
  switch(Message)
  {
    HANDLE_MSG(hWindow, WM_DESTROY, Window1_OnDestroy);
    default: return Window1_DefProc(hWindow, Message,
                                    wParam, lParam);
  }
}

// This routine is called when the window is destroyed.
#pragma argsused
void Window1_OnDestroy(HWND hwnd)
{
  PostQuitMessage(0);
}
```

The code shown here begins with a set of forward declarations and a definition:

```
LRESULT CALLBACK WndProc(HWND hWindow, UINT Message,
                         WPARAM wParam, LPARAM lParam);
void Window1_OnDestroy(HWND hwnd);
#define Window1_DefProc      DefWindowProc
```

WndProc and Window1_OnDestroy are routines that will be called during the run of the program. Nothing mysterious here. Window1_DefProc a is definition used to reference the standard windows API call known as DefWindowProc. More on this subject in just one moment.

The actual implementation of the window procedure looks like this:

```
LRESULT CALLBACK WndProc(HWND hWindow,
                         UINT Message,
                         WPARAM wParam,
                         LPARAM lParam)
{
  switch(Message)
  {
    HANDLE_MSG(hWindow, WM_DESTROY, Window1_OnDestroy);
    default: return Window1_DefProc(hWindow, Message,
                                    wParam, lParam);
  }
}
```

This code processes any messages sent to the program. These messages could come from the message loop or else be sent directly by the system. The HANDLE_MSG macro is from WINDOWSX.H, and will also be discussed later in this chapter and on Day 4.

Window procedures can be very long and complex, but this one is quite simple. Its simplicity stems from the fact that the Window1 program has no need to respond to most messages. It doesn't care if the user presses a key, and it doesn't care if the user moves the mouse. It has no menu and no controls. In short, it has no need to process any special messages other than the command to destroy itself. All other messages are handled by the default window procedure, referenced here by Window1_DefProc.

The final stage of the code shown above is the Window1_OnDestroy routine:

```
void Window1_OnDestroy(HWND hwnd)
{
    PostQuitMessage(0);
}
```

The call to PostQuitMessage tells Windows that an application or thread wants to terminate.

Comments on *WndProc*s

Most messages go directly to the window procedure where they can be handled individually. From there, they can be passed on to the default window procedure, DefWindowProc.

DefWindowProc knows how to handle nearly all the default behavior associated with a particular type of window. For instance, it knows how to handle mouse movements that minimize or maximize a window, as well as how to handle movements that expand or shrink a window.

Think about that last sentence for a moment. It states that one function handles all kinds of mouse movements and knows how to reshape a window. A great deal of functionality is packed into one simple call:

```
default:
    return Window1_DefProc(hWindow, Message, wParam, lParam);
```

Note that this call receives all the same parameters that WndProc receives. It behaves like an internal Windows version of the WndProc procedure you see here. Of course, this internal version of the procedure has a lot of complex default behavior associated with it.

If you look at the call to Window1_DefProc from one perspective, it seems a bit long and convoluted. However, if you remember how much functionality it brings to a program, it no longer seems so complicated. It would take me hundreds, even thousands of lines of code to pack this much functionality into a standard DOS program. Windows lets me do it with a single line of code. Windows programming is complex in part because it encapsulates so much functionality.

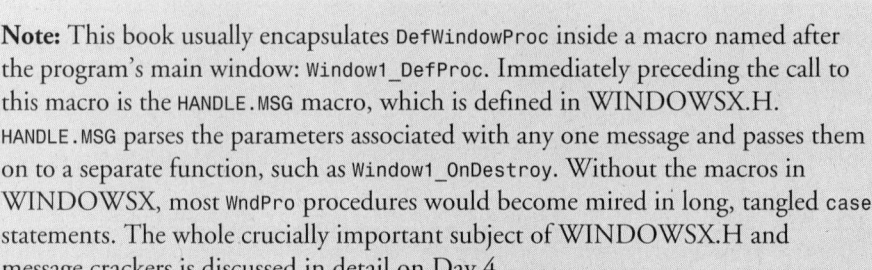

Note: This book usually encapsulates DefWindowProc inside a macro named after the program's main window: Window1_DefProc. Immediately preceding the call to this macro is the HANDLE.MSG macro, which is defined in WINDOWSX.H. HANDLE.MSG parses the parameters associated with any one message and passes them on to a separate function, such as Window1_OnDestroy. Without the macros in WINDOWSX, most WndPro procedures would become mired in long, tangled case statements. The whole crucially important subject of WINDOWSX.H and message crackers is discussed in detail on Day 4.

It's important that you don't confuse WINDOWS.H and WINDOWSX.H. WINDOWS.H is a primary reference file. It's your bible, the *sin qua non* of Windows programming. WINDOWSX.H, however, is a relatively recent addition to Windows programming. It includes numerous refinements and time-saving improvements, but it is not absolutely essential to most programming endeavors. However, WINDOWSX.H can be an extremely important file that might save you hours, days, and even weeks of work. Specifically, it makes it possible to write one application that runs under both 16-bit Windows and WIN32.

WINDOWSX.H is explained in more depth on Day 4 (and in succeeding chapters). Be sure to read about it. Both WINDOWS.H and WINDOWSX.H are essential to the structure of this book. I discuss both files again and reference them in nearly every chapter of this book.

Before the default window procedure is called, WndProc has a chance to respond to most messages it receives. WINDOW.CPP is a minimal Windows programming example. As a result, it is only necessary to respond to the message that tells the main window it is about to be destroyed. The HANDLE_MSG macro parses the parameters passed to WndProc and sends only relevant ones to the Window1_OnDestroy message function handler:

```
void Window1_OnDestroy(HWND hwnd)
{
  PostQuitMessage(0);
}
```

Many different messages can bombard a window at one time. The WM_PAINT message, for instance, tells a window that it's time for it to repaint itself. Others, such as WM_MOUSEMOVE, tell a window that the mouse is moving over it at a certain coordinate. Other messages tell a window that it's being minimized, maximized, resized, pulverized...well, there's not really a WM_PULVERIZE message, but there might as well be, because so many other messages float in and out of WndProc throughout the life of a typical window.

Throughout this book, I spend considerable time discussing WndProcs and the various ways they can be structured. For now, however, I only want you to have a general feeling for how a window procedure fits into the general flow of activity in a Windows program.

Summary

After reading this chapter, I hope you can visualize the main portions of a Windows program:

- ☐ First, the WinMain procedure contains Register, Create, and message loop sections.
- ☐ Beneath WinMain is the WindProc, which has a chance to handle any messages being sent to a window.

These two functions represent the main structure and the main flow of the program. If you can grasp the rudiments of how this system works, you can get some feel for how the Windows environment is put together.

In this chapter, you have taken a detailed look at the very heart of Windows programming. In particular, you have seen a sample application called WINDOW1.CPP that demonstrates how a Windows program is usually structured.

Specifically, this chapter shows how a Windows program is initialized by calling the RegisterWindow and CreateWindow functions and by showing the window to the user. In the process, you have read about many of the major types unique to Windows, such as an HINSTANCE and WORD. The chapter also covers the message loop and the WndProc procedure, both of which handle the stream of messages constantly being sent to an application.

Q&A

Q How can I find out about the special types used in a Windows application?

A There are several major sources of information. One is a book such as this. Other sources include reference books and online help systems. Perhaps the single most important reference is the WINDOWS.H file, which ships with your compiler and is included at the top of every Windows program. You can supplement the information found in WINDOWS.H by browsing through the important WINDOWSX.H file, which is covered in more detail on Day 4.

Q Windows is a *message-* or *event-oriented* environment. What does this mean?

A In the DOS environment, a user usually interacts directly with a program. But in Windows, the user's actions are first trapped by the operating system, and then passed to an application in the form of messages or events. This system gives Windows applications a kind of autonomy and independence (entirely lacking from the traditional DOS environment).

Workshop

The Workshop provides quiz questions to help you solidify your understanding of the material covered and exercises to provide you with experience in using what you've learned. Try to understand the quiz and exercise answers before continuing on to Day 4. Answers are provided in Appendix A.

Quiz

1. What is a WNDCLASS?
2. What is the purpose of the register function?
3. What is the purpose of the Create function?
4. What is the difference between ShowWindow and UpDateWindow?
5. What is the purpose of the WndProc?
6. What is the purpose of the message loop?
7. What is the purpose of the DefWindowProc?
8. What traditional C type is associated with a WORD?
9. What traditional C type is associated with a LONG?
10. What traditional C type is associated with a LPSTR?

Exercises

1. Create a program that appears in its maximized state.
2. Create a program that uses the hourglass cursor, which usually prompts the user to wait for a few moments.
3. Create a program that fails before even calling the function.
4. Create a program that has a light gray background.
5. Create a program that has your name visible in the title of its main window.

4

Messages, WindowsX, and Painting Text

Two major subjects are covered in this chapter:

1. How to write portable, easy-to-read, event-oriented code with the aid of WINDOWSX.H.
2. The most fundamental I/O issue: how to display text.

Many of the traits that give Windows its special flavor owe their character to the fact that Windows is an *event-oriented* (or message-based) system. If you don't understand messages, you won't understand Windows.

In this chapter, you get a chance to learn about event-oriented, message-based systems. You get an in-depth look at window procedures, messages, and message crackers. This is material that lies very much at the heart of Windows.

In particular, this chapter covers

- ☐ Messages
- ☐ WindowsX
- ☐ Message crackers
- ☐ Message handler functions
- ☐ Responses to `WM_PAINT` messages
- ☐ Device contexts
- ☐ Two ways to write text in a window

WindowsX and *STRICT*

This book uses two somewhat unusual techniques to help you write clean, portable code. WINDOWSX.H contains a series of macros that help you handle messages in a simple, easy-to-read manner, while at the same time creating code that is portable between WIN16 and WIN32.

Each message sent by the operating system is accompanied by two parameters of type `wParam` and `lParam`. In WIN16, `wParam` is declared as a 16-bit value, but in WIN32, it is declared as 32-bit value. `lParam` is declared as a 32-bit value under both operating systems. These changes mean that the information accompanying some messages is encoded differently in WIN32 than it was in 16-bit Windows. The message crackers in WindowsX hide these implementation details from you. More specifically, Microsoft and Borland compilers ship with two versions of WINDOWSX.H—one for 32-bit code, and one for 16-bit code.

WindowsX also helps you write clean code by providing macros that enable you to write simple, easy-to-read `WndProcs`. These macros give your code the simplicity and elegance usually obtained only through complex object-oriented systems such as OWL or MFC. Without WindowsX, even the best `WndProcs` can sprawl on for pages of unruly spaghetti code.

WINDOWSX.H helps you avoid having to typecast most of your calls to the Windows API. Normally Windows programming requires a huge number of type casts, all of which circumvent the normal type-checking procedures that help you write safe code. WINDOWSX.H lets you avoid typecasts and reasserts the primacy of type checking.

WINDOWSX.H contains a whole series of child-control macros that make it easy for you to write simple one-line procedures rather than use the complex `SendMessage` command. These one-line commands are portable between WIN16 and WIN32, while the equivalent `SendMessage` or `PostMessage` syntax is not necessarily portable. Passing parameters to `SendMessage` usually requires packing information into `lParam` or `wParam`, which is a complex and error-prone process. WindowsX avoids the whole mess and gives you a clean, easy-to-read interface to use instead of `SendMessage`.

Finally, WINDOWSX.H contains a series of API macros that make it simpler to use standard Windows functions such as `SelectObject` and `GetStockObject`. Every time you use these functions, you must make at least two messy-looking typecasts. WindowsX allows you to skip the typecasts and to write simple, clean functions that use macros such as `SelectFont` and `GetStockBrush`.

To reiterate, WindowsX provides three tools:

1. Message crackers
2. Child control macros
3. API macros

All three of these tools help you write clean, portable, easy-to-read code.

The `STRICT` directive helps you keep track of the type of parameters you are passing to a function. For instance, it's easy to accidentally write code that tries to use an `HWND` where Windows expects an `HDC`. If you define `STRICT`, then this will not happen to you. `STRICT` also enforces numerous rules that help you create programs that are portable and correct.

Not all Windows programmers use either `STRICT` or WINDOWSX.H. However, those who do use them are usually either very good programmers or else very well-informed programmers. If we can't always lay claim to the first category, we should at least strive to be part of the second. One step in the right direction is to use `STRICT` and WINDOWSX.H in all our non-OOP programs.

What Is a Message?

Day 3, "A Standard Windows Program," presented a bird's-eye view of a standard Windows program. It gave you a flyby over all the major portions of a Windows program, including the `WinMain`, `Register`, `Create`, and `WndProc` functions, as well as the `message` loop. The next step is to narrow the focus so that you get a closer look at the window procedure and the messages that are sent to it.

By now you should have a feeling for the difference between a message (or event-driven program) and a standard procedural program. In the former case, the operating system tells a program that an event has occurred. In the latter case, the program queries the system to find out what has happened.

Here's a more in-depth look at the differences between the traditional DOS and traditional Windows programming worlds:

☐ **Windows message-based model:** Once the program is launched, it simply waits for messages to be sent to it and then responds accordingly. Windows itself detects if a key has been pressed or if the mouse has been moved. When an event of this type occurs, Windows sends a predefined message to the program, telling it what has happened. The program usually has the option of either ignoring the message or responding to the message.

☐ **DOS procedural model:** C++ code usually executes linearly; that is, it starts at the beginning of a program and advances through to the end by *stepping* through code one line at a time or by branching or looping through various segments of code. The program discovers the user's commands by querying the system. That is, the program calls interrupt-based subroutines that are built into the operating system or the hardware. In return, these interrupts report whether a key has been pressed or the mouse has been moved.

It should come as no surprise to hear that messages are really just constants defined in the WINDOWS.H complex of files. Here, for instance, are the declarations for messages that handle keyboard and mouse movements:

```
/* Keyboard messages */
#define WM_KEYDOWN          0x0100 // Key was pressed
#define WM_KEYUP            0x0101 // Key was released
#define WM_CHAR             0x0102 // Processed keystroke
#define WM_DEADCHAR         0x0103 // Composite key
#define WM_SYSKEYDOWN       0x0104 // Alt key was pressed
#define WM_SYSKEYUP         0x0105 // Alt key was released
#define WM_SYSCHAR          0x0106 // Processed system keystroke
#define WM_SYSDEADCHAR      0x0107 // Composite system keystroke

/* Mouse input messages */
#define WM_MOUSEMOVE        0x0200 // Mouse was moved
#define WM_LBUTTONDOWN      0x0201 // Left button pressed
#define WM_LBUTTONUP        0x0202 // Left button released
#define WM_LBUTTONDBLCLK    0x0203 // Double click of left button
#define WM_RBUTTONDOWN      0x0204 // Right button down
#define WM_RBUTTONUP        0x0205 // Right button up
#define WM_RBUTTONDBLCLK    0x0206 // Double click, right button
#define WM_MBUTTONDOWN      0x0207 // Middle button down
```

```
#define WM_MBUTTONUP        0x0208 // Middle button up
#define WM_MBUTTONDBLCLK    0x0209 // Double click, middle button
```

Don't try to memorize these messages. Just look them over and become familiar with the way they look and the kinds of services they provide.

Clearly, nothing is very mysterious about the messages themselves. They are simply constants with useful names that inform a program about the current state of the system. When an event occurs, these messages are bundled with other useful bits of information and sent to one or more appropriate window procedures. Exactly what should then be done with those messages is the topic of this chapter.

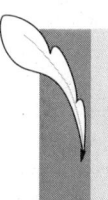

Note: You don't need to understand how Windows knows that the user moved the mouse or pressed a key. All you need do is trap messages and then decode them. For instance, whenever a message with the number hexadecimal 200 comes down the pike, it's an indication that the user moved the mouse.

Accompanying the message are additional codes that tell something about the location and state of the mouse. This information lies encoded in parameters called `wParam` and `lParam`.

Message-based systems give you a large degree of platform independence. Consider that the Intel architecture usually uses `Int 33h` to track mouse movements. Another platform may use an entirely different system. That won't matter, because in Windows all you need do is respond to predefined messages. Thus, Windows NT programmers can write one set of code that runs on Intel, MIPS, and Alpha platforms. This is true cross-platform portability, made possible by the presence of a single well-written operating system running on multiple types of CPUs.

Your Second Full-Scale Windows Program

The next few pages of this chapter focus on a three-part process that outlines exactly how messages are treated in a `WndProc`:

- [ ] Step one is to get a working example program up and running.
- [ ] Step two is to discuss WindowsX and message crackers. The discussion focuses primarily on two particular messages, `WM_DESTROY` and `WM_CREATE`.
- [ ] Step three takes a brief look at how WindowsX treats the default window procedure.

Note: Don't worry if you still are not totally clear on what WindowsX is all about. The WindowsX header file, and the macros it includes, represent a very broad topic that cannot be easily assimilated in just a few moments. Instead, you need to be prepared to allow for gradual increases in your knowledge of this complex and extremely important topic. For now you should feel content if you understand that the macros in WindowsX help to simplify Windows programming and help to ease the transition between 16-bit and 32-bit Windows code. The details will become clear in time as this book returns again and again to this intriguing topic.

Most of the code in the program I am about to show you is similar to the code you saw in Chapter 3. In fact, most Windows programs are based on a common template that changes little from program to program. As a result, you might want to copy the files used in making WINDOW1.EXE into a new subdirectory called EASYTEXT. Go through the files, changing the words Window1 to EasyText and renaming the files from WINDOW1.* to EASYTEXT.*. To perform this latter duty, enter the following command at the DOS prompt:

```
ren WINDOW1.* EASYTEXT.*
```

DO   **DON'T**

DO use pretested code as the basis of each program you write.

DON'T try to start each Windows program from scratch.

The steps previously outlined are very important. Almost every piece of Windows code you write will rest on the basic components created in Day 3. In other words, that code is very much reusable. In fact, you might want to keep it in a separate subdirectory where you can access it whenever you need to start a new program. As you probably know, the idea of reusing packets of code is very important in most modern programming endeavors.

DO   **DON'T**

DO copy as many files as possible from one project to the next one.

DON'T try to copy old project files or makefiles from directory to directory without carefully reviewing them. This is especially important if you work from inside the Microsoft or Borland IDE. Project files and makefiles generated by modern IDEs often contain the pathname of the files you add to a project. Don't make the mistake of moving your files to a new subdirectory and accidentally modifying

WINDOW1.CPP (or some other member of the original program), simply because it is still listed in your project file. Instead, IDE users should probably leave .PRJ, .IDE, and some .MAK files behind, and simply rebuild the project when you place it in a new subdirectory. In other words, IDE users should copy .H, .C, .CPP, and .def files over from the WINDOW1 directory but leave the other files behind.

It's now time to take a look at the code from the EasyText program, found in Listing 4.1. Take the time to get this program up and running. It will help you understand the rest of this chapter.

Listing 4.1. The CPP main source file.

```
/////////////////////////////////////
//  Program Name: EASYTEXT.CPP
//  Programmer: Charlie Calvert
//  Description: Demonstrate simple text I/O
//  Date: Feb 27, 1993
//  UpDate for WIN32: May 21, 1995
/////////////////////////////////////

#define STRICT
#include <windows.h>
#include <windowsx.h>
#include <string.h>
#pragma warning (disable: 4068)
#pragma warning (disable:4100)

// ----------------------------------------
// Interface
// ----------------------------------------

#if !defined(__WIN32__) && !defined(_WIN32)
#define EXPORT16 __export
#else
#define EXPORT16
#endif

// variables
static char szAppName[] = "EasyText";

// Class EasyText
#define EasyText_DefProc DefWindowProc
BOOL EasyText_OnCreate(HWND hwnd,
                       CREATESTRUCT FAR* lpCreateStruct);
void EasyText_OnDestroy(HWND hwnd);
void EasyText_OnPaint(HWND hwnd);

// variables
char Directions[100];
```

continues

Listing 4.1. continued

```
static HWND MainWindow;
static HINSTANCE hInst;

// functions

LRESULT CALLBACK EXPORT16 WndProc(HWND hwnd, UINT Message,
                                  wParam wParam, lParam lParam);
BOOL Register(HINSTANCE hInst);
HWND Create(HINSTANCE hInst, int nCmdShow);

// ----------------------------------------
// Initialization
// ----------------------------------------

//////////////////////////////////////////
// Program entry point
//////////////////////////////////////////
#pragma argsused
int WINAPI WinMain(HINSTANCE hInst, HINSTANCE hPrevInstance,
                   LPSTR  lpszCmdParam, int nCmdShow)
{
  MSG  Msg;

  if (!hPrevInstance)
    if (!Register(hInst))
      return FALSE;

  if (!Create(hInst, nCmdShow))
    return FALSE;

  while (GetMessage(&Msg, NULL, 0, 0))
  {
     TranslateMessage(&Msg);
     DispatchMessage(&Msg);
  }

  return Msg.wParam;
}

//////////////////////////////////////////
// Register the window
//////////////////////////////////////////
BOOL Register(HINSTANCE hInst)
{
  WNDCLASS WndClass;

  WndClass.style          = CS_HREDRAW | CS_VREDRAW;
  WndClass.lpfnWndProc    = WndProc;
  WndClass.cbClsExtra     = 0;
  WndClass.cbWndExtra     = 0;
  WndClass.hInstance      = hInst;
  WndClass.hIcon          = LoadIcon(NULL, IDI_APPLICATION);
  WndClass.hCursor        = LoadCursor(NULL, IDC_ARROW);
  WndClass.hbrBackground  = (HBRUSH)(COLOR_WINDOW+1);
```

```
    WndClass.lpszMenuName   = NULL;
    WndClass.lpszClassName  = szAppName;

    return (RegisterClass (&WndClass) != 0);
}

/////////////////////////////////////
// Create the window
/////////////////////////////////////
HWND Create(HINSTANCE hInstance, int nCmdShow)
{
    HWND hwnd = CreateWindow(szAppName, szAppName,
                             WS_OVERLAPPEDWINDOW,
                             CW_USEDEFAULT, CW_USEDEFAULT,
                             CW_USEDEFAULT, CW_USEDEFAULT,
                             NULL, NULL, hInstance, NULL);

    if (hwnd == NULL)
       return hwnd;

    ShowWindow(hwnd, nCmdShow);
    UpdateWindow(hwnd);

    return hwnd;
}

// -----------------------------------
// WndProc and Implementation
// -----------------------------------

/////////////////////////////////////
// The Window Procedure
/////////////////////////////////////
LRESULT CALLBACK EXPORT16 WndProc(HWND hwnd, UINT Message,
                                  wParam wParam, lParam lParam)
{
    switch(Message)
    {
      HANDLE_MSG(hwnd, WM_CREATE, EasyText_OnCreate);
      HANDLE_MSG(hwnd, WM_DESTROY, EasyText_OnDestroy);
      HANDLE_MSG(hwnd, WM_PAINT, EasyText_OnPaint);
      default:
        return EasyText_DefProc(hwnd, Message, wParam, lParam);
    }
}

/////////////////////////////////////
// The destructor handles WM_DESTROY
/////////////////////////////////////
#pragma argsused
BOOL EasyText_OnCreate(HWND hwnd, CREATESTRUCT FAR* lpCreateStruct)
{
    strcpy(Directions, "Try resizing this window.");
    return TRUE;
}
```

continues

Listing 4.1. continued

```
////////////////////////////////////
// The destructor handles WM_DESTROY
////////////////////////////////////
#pragma argsused
void EasyText_OnDestroy(HWND hwnd)
{
  PostQuitMessage(0);
}


////////////////////////////////////
// Handle WM_PAINT messages
// Show how to use TextOut and DrawText.
////////////////////////////////////
void EasyText_OnPaint(HWND hwnd)
{
  PAINTSTRUCT PaintStruct;
  RECT Rect;

  HDC PaintDC = BeginPaint(hwnd, &PaintStruct);

  SetBkMode(PaintDC, TRANSPARENT);

  TextOut(PaintDC, 10, 10, Directions, lstrlen(Directions));

  GetClientRect(hwnd, &Rect);

  DrawText(PaintDC, "The middle of the road", -1, &Rect,
           DT_SINGLELINE | DT_CENTER | DT_VCENTER);

  EndPaint(hwnd, &PaintStruct);
}

wParamlParamwParamlParam
```

Listing 4.2 is the EasyText definition file.

Listing 4.2. EASYTEXT.DEF.

```
1: ; EASYTEXT.DEF
2:
3: NAME          EasyText
4: DESCRIPTION   'EasyText Window'
5: HEAPSIZE      4096
6: STACKSIZE     5120
7: CODE          PRELOAD MOVEABLE DISCARDABLE
8: DATA          PRELOAD MOVEABLE MULTIPLE
```

Listing 4.3 shows the Borland EasyText makefile.

Listing 4.3. EASYTEXT.MAK.

```
# EASYTEXT.MAK

!if !$d(BCROOT)
BCROOT  = $(MAKEDIR)\..
!endif

# macros
APPNAME = EasyText
INCPATH = $(BCROOT)\INCLUDE
LIBPATH = $(BCROOT)\LIB

!if $d(WIN16)
COMPILER= BCC.EXE
FLAGS   = -W -ml -v -w4 -I$(INCPATH) -L$(LIBPATH)
!else
COMPILER= BCC32.EXE
FLAGS   = -W -v -w4 -I$(INCPATH) -L$(LIBPATH)
!endif

# link
$(APPNAME).exe: $(APPNAME).obj $(APPNAME).def
  $(COMPILER) $(FLAGS) $(APPNAME).obj

# compile
$(APPNAME).obj: $(APPNAME).cpp
  $(COMPILER) -c $(FLAGS) $(APPNAME).cpp
```

Listing 4.4 shows the Microsoft EasyText makefile.

Listing 4.4. EASYTEMS.MAK. is the Microsoft WIN32 makefile.

```
# EASYTEMS.MAK

APPNAME=EASYTEXT
TARGETOS=WIN95
APPVER=4.0
OBJS=$(APPNAME).OBJ

!include <win32.mak>

all: $(APPNAME).exe

# Update the object files if necessary

# compile
.cpp.obj:
  $(cc) $(cflags) $(cvars) $(cdebug) $<

# Update the executable file if necessary.

$(APPNAME).exe: $(OBJS)
  $(link) $(linkdebug) $(guiflags) -out:$(APPNAME).exe \
  $(OBJS) $(guilibs) comctl32.lib
```

Figure 4.1 shows the output from Listing 4.1.

The purpose of this program is to show you how to use message crackers and how to respond to WM_PAINT messages. The code pops up a standard window and prints two pieces of text on it. Notice that one piece of text always stays in the middle of the window, even when you resize it.

Figure 4.1.
EASYTEXT.EXE displays two pieces of text, one in the upper-left corner of the window, and one centered in the middle of the window.

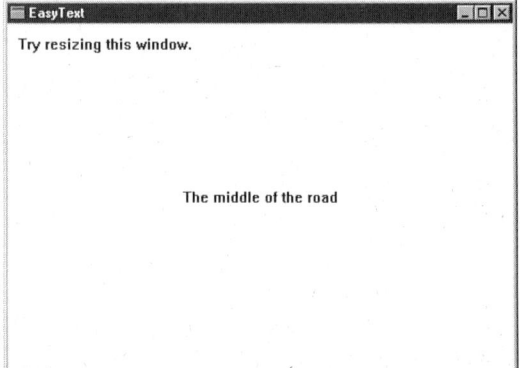

Note: You might notice that I add various pragmas to the code you see in this book. pragmas contain compiler-specific information. You can use them to tell a particular compiler to perform in a certain manner, while allowing other compilers to ignore the message altogether.

Throughout this book, I frequently include the following line of code in the listings:

```
#pragma argsused
```

This pragma tells the Borland compiler to suppress any error messages about unused arguments passed to a particular function. Another pragma you will see me use a lot is this:

```
#pragma warning (disable: 4068)
```

This pragma tells the Microsoft compiler to ignore any pragmas it doesn't understand. Ironically, Microsoft's compiler informs the user through a warning when it encounters an unknown pragma. Because I'd prefer not to see those warnings, I turn them off with the preceding line of code.

A third pragma you might see in my code looks like this:

```
#pragma hdrstop
```

This pragma tells the Borland compiler to terminate the list of files used in precompiled headers. For instance, in the following example, WINDOWS.H and

WINDOWSX.H are used in the precompiled header, but STRING.H and STDLIB.H are not:

```
#include <windows.h>
#include <windowsx.h>
#pragma hdrstop
#include <string.h>
#include <stdlib.h>
```

Overall, you should not be concerned about the pragmas included in this code. All the examples in this book will compile to the exact same binary code, whether or not you include any of my pragmas. Their only purpose is to optimize or smooth the actual course of compilation. They have absolutely no effect on the final code that is generated.

Switch Statements, WindowsX, and Message Crackers

4

The most obvious new feature of this program is the presence of text in the client area of the window. Before taking a look at how that text is painted on-screen, it's important to first understand the mechanisms at play in the WndProc function:

```
117: LRESULT CALLBACK _EXPORT16 WndProc(HWND hwnd, UINT Message,
118:                                   wParam wParam, lParam lParam)
119: {
120:    switch(Message)
121:    {
122:       HANDLE_MSG(hwnd, WM_CREATE, EasyText_OnCreate);
123:       HANDLE_MSG(hwnd, WM_DESTROY, EasyText_OnDestroy);
124:       HANDLE_MSG(hwnd, WM_PAINT, EasyText_OnPaint);
125:       default:
126:          return EasyText_DefProc(hwnd, Message, wParam, lParam);
127:    }
128: }
```

Notice first the use of the EXPORT16 macro, which is defined as follows:

```
#if !defined(__WIN32__) && !defined(_WIN32)
#define EXPORT16 __export
#else
#define EXPORT16
#endif
```

In Windows 95, there is no need to export your functions, primarily because they are running in one large address space, rather than in a segmented architecture. However, in Windows 3.1, you should export functions, although the compiler will rarely complain if you don't. To create code that would work properly in both environments, I created the EXPORT16 macro, which adds

an export statement to 16-bit programs, while leaving 32-bit programs unaffected. In other words, it's just a blank, empty macro in WIN32. This means you do not need to include the macro or the export statement in code that will be compiled only for 32-bit targets.

Note: Notice that I perform a little dance here with the words WIN32 and WIN16. You can, and of course often will, run 16-bit programs under Windows 95. In other words, you can target WIN16, and yet still plan to run under Windows 95. If you run 16-bit programs in Windows 95, then they are by default loaded into a single address space where all the other 16-bit programs run. They do not get the full benefit of Windows 95 memory protection, or multitasking. They are also more prone to run out of Windows resources than are true 32-bit applications. However, they will be backward compatible with Windows 3.1, which can be a benefit at times. Later in this book, you will see many programs that do not run under Windows 3.1. However, at this stage, we are talking about very general Windows programming concepts that apply to all platforms. It's only very occasionally that I am forced to add a conditional define in order to specify a difference between 16-bit code and Windows 95–specific code.

Back in the bad old days before WINDOWSX.H, the window procedure could become an extremely formidable foe that Windows programmers had to wrestle to the mat on a daily basis. The source of the trouble was the notorious switch statement found in window procedures. Even moderately complex programs contained WndProcs that tended to stretch on for page after page of mind-boggling code.

Now that WINDOWSX.H is here, the switch statement still exists, but it has been tamed by a series of message crackers that fairly effectively defang the serpent waiting within every window procedure. The message crackers do this by finding a simple way to move the body of your response to a message out of the WndProc and into functions that obey the basic rules of structured programming. Of course, using message crackers isn't an absolutely effortless process, but I believe you'll find them much easier to use than a lengthy switch statement.

Note: Because so much old code still exists, it's important for you to see how to handle window procedures that consist solely of long switch statements. To give you this opportunity, I will later show you some fairly interesting dialog procedures. Dialog procedures are to dialogs what window procedures are to windows. For various reasons, you don't often see WINDOWSX.H used in dialog procedures. As a result, dialog procedures provide an obvious method for examining some lengthy switch statements that aren't necessary in code that uses WindowsX.

The EasyText program explicitly handles three messages:

```
HANDLE_MSG(hwnd, WM_CREATE, EasyText_OnCreate);
HANDLE_MSG(hwnd, WM_DESTROY, EasyText_OnDestroy);
HANDLE_MSG(hwnd, WM_PAINT, EasyText_OnPaint);
```

As you can see, the messages are WM_CREATE, WM_DESTROY, and WM_PAINT. In the next few pages, you'll see how message crackers simplify the use of not only these messages, but all standard API messages.

When reading this discussion, remember that WindowsX helps shield you from complexity. Unfortunately, I have to delve right into the heart of that complexity in order to explain how message crackers work. But after you have a few basic ideas clear in your mind, you'll find that message crackers smooth the way for you over and over again.

Note: Message crackers help you use standard structured programming techniques throughout your WndProc. When I first learned structured programming, it seemed a bit complex. Over the years, however, it has saved me many, many frustrating days full of painful debugging. The same is true of message crackers—for many of the same reasons.

4

All right. It's time to gird your loins and focus your mind. The next few paragraphs contain a good deal of important information.

To begin, you need to know that WM_DESTROY messages are sent to a window whenever it's about to be closed. In the main window of an application, it's crucial that you remember to call PostQuitMessage in response to a WM_DESTROY message. If you don't do this, you'll immediately become involved in an inexplicable mass of bugs from which you'll never extract yourself until you finally figure out the nature of your error. If you forget to call PostQuitMessage, your application is toast!

Caution: PostQuitMessage sends a WM_QUIT message to Windows, which is the signal to break out of the message loop back in WinMain. In other words, the message loop would continue indefinitely were it not for the call to PostQuitMessage. Therefore, this call is absolutely essential for proper application termination.

In EasyText, the PostQuitMessage call is made in the EasyText_OnDestroy function:

```
144: void EasyText_OnDestroy(HWND hwnd)
145: {
```

```
146:    PostQuitMessage(0);
147: }
```

If WindowsX were not being used, this whole process would have been handled in the
WndProc:

```
switch (Message)
{
  case WM_DESTROY:
    PostQuitMessage(0);
    break;

  case WM_PAINT:
  etc..
}
```

With WindowsX, however, programmers have the option of handling WM_DESTROY messages in
a separate function. This helps promote good structured programming techniques.

In the source code for WINDOWSX.H, you can view the message cracker macros. These
nuggets of code "pick apart" the parameters to WndProc. The macros then pass on the important
finds to your message handler function. The issue is that every message sent to a window can
be accompanied by additional information—which usually comes in the form of the hwnd,
wParam, and lParam parameters.

Three problems occur as the result of sending messages in the hwnd, wParam, and lParam
parameters:

1. Not all messages use all three of these parameters. As a result, programmers always
   have to look in their reference books to see which of these parameters are utilized by a
   particular message.

2. Different pieces of information often are packed into a particular parameter. For
   instance, a programmer might have to look in the first word of lParam to get a piece of
   information, and look in the first and second bytes of wParam to get different pieces of
   information. After engaging in this trying process, the programmer often needs to
   typecast the information before it's usable.

3. The way information is packed into lParam and wParam sometimes differs depending
   on whether you are in 16-bit Windows or in WIN32.

You've learned that message crackers are really just a series of macros designed to pick apart the
various parameters passed to WndProc. They usually consist of two parts. The first part handles
the message itself; the second part can optionally pass the message on to DefWindowProc. For
instance, here are the macros for WM_DESTROY messages as they are listed in WindowsX:

```
/* void Cls_OnDestroy(HWND hwnd); */
#define HANDLE_WM_DESTROY(hwnd, wParam, lParam, fn) \
    ((fn)(hwnd), 0L)
#define FORWARD_WM_DESTROY(hwnd, fn) \
    (void)(fn)((hwnd), WM_DESTROY, 0, 0L)
```

Declaring Functions to Deal with Messages

ClassName_OnMessageName

The comment at the top of the WM_DESTROY excerpt from WindowsX shows you how to declare a function that responds to WM_DESTROY messages. In other words, you just copy the section in comments:

```
/* void Cls_OnDestroy(HWND hwnd); */
```

and then remove the comments and change the first word of the resultant code to the name of your "class":

```
void EasyText_OnDestroy(HWND hwnd);
```

The functions whose prototype you copy are called message handler functions, or sometimes, message response functions. The convention for naming a message handler function is to start by writing the class name. Follow the class name with an underscore, the word "On," and the name of the message.

Here's an example:

In EasyText, this results in a function name that looks like this:

```
EasyText_OnDestroy
```

You can think of this syntax as saying, "Class EasyText executes this function on receipt of a WM_DESTROY message." Of course, these aren't really "classes" in the sense that object-oriented code deals with classes. However, WindowsX provides some of the same syntactical benefits in terms of the clarity of the code you write.

Probably the most important part of the WM_DESTROY excerpt from WindowsX is the definition of the HANDLE_WM_DESTROY macro. This code fragment picks apart the parameters passed to WndProc, singling out only hwnd as being important in this particular case:

```
((fn)(hwnd), 0L)
```

This macro is the "cracker" that gives message crackers their name.

I'll restate the matter, just to make sure this very important concept is clear. The purpose of this macro is to zero in on the important parameters passed to WndProc. That's the job of a message cracker. In this particular case, neither the lParam nor the wParam arguments contain any useful information. As a result, the only important piece of associated information is the hwnd parameter, which is duly passed on by the WM_DESTROY message cracker:

```
#define HANDLE_WM_DESTROY(hwnd, wParam, lParam, fn) \
   ((fn)(hwnd), 0L)
```

4

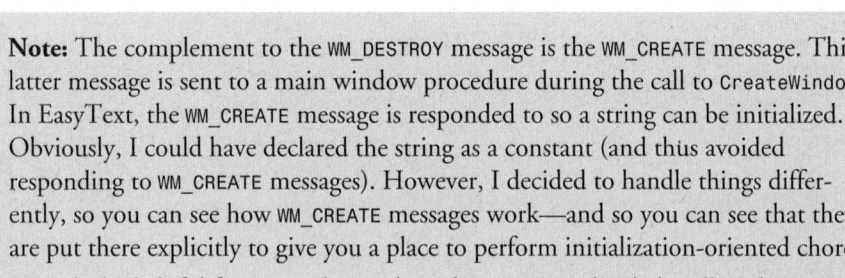
The second half of the message cracker is called FORWARD_WM_DESTROY:

```
#define FORWARD_WM_DESTROY(hwnd, fn) \
    (void)(fn)((hwnd), WM_DESTROY, 0, 0L)
```

The FORWARD_WM_DESTROY macro is used only if you want to pass the message to another function, such as the default window procedure after you have handled it. To make this part of the process work correctly, encapsulate the default window procedure in a macro containing the class name, as previously explained.

The WM_DESTROY message cracker is a good place to start exploring message crackers, because it's so simple. However, it also might help to take a look at a somewhat more complicated macro. Fortunately, the WM_CREATE message cracker provides a good illustration of how WindowsX can be used to pick apart more complex macros.

> **Note:** The complement to the WM_DESTROY message is the WM_CREATE message. This latter message is sent to a main window procedure during the call to CreateWindow. In EasyText, the WM_CREATE message is responded to so a string can be initialized. Obviously, I could have declared the string as a constant (and thus avoided responding to WM_CREATE messages). However, I decided to handle things differently, so you can see how WM_CREATE messages work—and so you can see that they are put there explicitly to give you a place to perform initialization-oriented chores.
>
> It might be helpful for you to know that whenever I explicitly handle either WM_CREATE or WM_DESTROY messages, I try to do it at the very beginning of a window procedure. That way, readers of my code can easily find the place where I handle the initialization (WM_CREATE) and the destruction (WM_DESTROY) of my window. Exactly why these two processes are so important becomes apparent in later examples. For now, you only need to remember that I like to handle these two chores first, and handle all other messages in alphabetical order.

Here is the WM_CREATE message cracker from WindowsX:

```
/* BOOL Cls_OnCreate(HWND hwnd,
                    CREATESTRUCT FAR* lpCreateStruct) */
#define HANDLE_WM_CREATE(hwnd, wParam, lParam, fn) \
    ((fn)((hwnd), (CREATESTRUCT FAR*)(lParam)) ? 0L :
    (LRESULT)-1L)
#define FORWARD_WM_CREATE(hwnd, lpCreateStruct, fn) \
    (BOOL)(DWORD)(fn)((hwnd), WM_CREATE, 0,
    (lParam)(CREATESTRUCT FAR*)(lpCreateStruct))
```

As you can see, HANDLE_WM_CREATE explicitly casts lParam as a pointer to a CREATSTRUCT and then ensures that this parameter, correctly typed, is passed on to the EasyText_OnCreate function:

```
BOOL EasyTxt_OnCreate(HWND hwnd,CREATESTRUCT FAR* lpCreateStruct)
```

At this point in the book, you don't need to ponder the many fields of a CREATSTRUCT, so I won't list them here. If you are interested, however, look them up in WINDOWSX.H.

If it weren't for the message cracker, you would have to handle the typecasting yourself, as follows:

```
lpCreateStruct = (CREATESTRUCT FAR*)lParam;
```

This is undesirable because it's an error-prone process that can prove especially tricky or confusing for people who are new to the Windows environment.

As you may notice, this macro returns either 0 or -1. If a program responds to a WM_CREATE message by returning 0, the program continues as usual. If it returns -1, however, the window will be summarily destroyed; that is, the CreateWindow function will return NULL.

These kinds of details can be confusing at times, so WindowsX clears up the whole matter in one clean stroke by declaring Cls_OnCreate a BOOL. As a result, all you need to do is return TRUE or FALSE, depending on whether or not you are able to initialize the areas in memory your program needed to access. If you return FALSE, the window is destroyed and your application ends.

The WM_COMMAND message cracker works with hwnd, wParam, and lParam. As a result, you might want to look it up in WINDOWSX.H to see what a really complex message cracker looks like. Note that the Borland 4.5 copy of WINDOWSX.H has two sections in it, one for 32-bit code and one for 16-bit Windows. As a result, WM_COMMAND, and all other macros, will be listed twice in the file. The MSVC20 compiler, of course, only has the 32-bit version of this file. You should at any rate be aware of versioning issues when you open WINDOWX.H. (Note, however, that you don't need to worry about versioning if all you need is to retrieve the prototype to your "class" declaration. A central feature of WindowsX is that the prototypes shown in the comment at the top of message crackers will be the same for WIN16 and WIN32. In fact, this feature is the main reason I'm using WindowsX in this book.)

The *HANDLE_MSG* Macro

I hope the previous paragraphs have shown you exactly what kind of complexity message crackers are designed to eliminate. However, the icing on the cake comes in the form of one last macro, which serves to simplify your program even further. This is the HANDLE_MSG macro, declared in WINDOWSX.H as follows:

```
#define HANDLE_MSG(hwnd, message, fn)    \
    case (message): return HANDLE_##message((hwnd), (wParam), (lParam), (fn))
```

The purpose of this macro is two-fold:

1. It eliminates the long case statement that plagues standard C WndProcs.
2. It relieves you of the responsibility of having to pass on the value returned by your message handler function (the function you declared using the Cls_OnXXXX template).

Returning the result of your function is an important responsibility. In fact, you *must* pass this value on, even if your message handler function is declared void. In such cases, the macro always returns 0L. At any rate, if you use the HANDLE_MSG macro, you don't have to worry about this return value at all.

If you don't use HANDLE_MSG, you must be sure your macro returns a value. More explicitly, in the case of the WM_CREATE message, you would have to write the following code in your WndProc every time you use a message handler function:

```
switch(Message)
{
case WM_CREATE:
return HANDLE_WM_CREATE(hwnd, wParam, EasyText_OnCreate);

etc...
}
```

HANDLE_MSG relieves you of this responsibility by letting you write the following:

```
switch(Message)
{
HANDLE_MSG(hwnd, WM_CREATE, Cls_OnCreate);
etc...
}
```

When coding, it seems that nearly every programmer has a different set of priorities. In my case, I put a very high premium on techniques that help me write clear, easy-to-read code. As a result, the HANDLE_MSG macro appeals to me. It helps me write code that is as simple and straightforward as possible.

WindowsX and the Default Window Procedure

As you might recall from Day 3, throughout the life of an application, the WndProc function is usually being bombarded by a vast array of messages. Indeed, there are times when these messages pour down in the same way that raindrops pour down on your head during a storm. In many applications, most of these messages are being handled by the default window procedure. The purpose of this section is to show how WindowsX handles DefWindowProc.

In applications that make use of WindowsX, standard operating procedure is to wrap a macro around the Windows API function called DefWindowProc:

```
#define EasyText_DefProc DefWindowProc
```

The primary reason for doing this is to prevent you from making careless errors.

In some cases, a window might not pass its messages on to `DefWindowProc`. For instance, some windows pass messages on to other functions, such as `DefDlgProc` or `DefMDIChildProc`. (For now, don't worry about when or why you might use these functions.)

The issue is that Windows programmers are always cutting and pasting their code from one program to another. As a result, it's easy to make a mistake, such as calling `DefMDIChildProc` when you mean to call `DefWindowProc`.

To prevent this, WindowsX programmers build the name of the class of the window right into the call to the `DefWindowProc` macro. This helps focus the programmer's mind on the primary issue: finding the correct default window procedure for this particular class. It also allows you to make a change in one place in your code that ripples throughout your source.

Another big benefit of the WindowsX programming style is that it gives the appearance of being object-oriented. OOP code is useful because it can be so easy to read. The call to the default window procedure, for instance, is explicitly marked as belonging to the EasyText window class:

```
return EasyText_DefProc(hwnd, Message, wParam, lParam);
```

This type of guide is invaluable when programmers are trying to write clean, readily comprehensible code. It fits in with an entire philosophy of modern programming practices—practices that have emerged at great cost and after much debate during the last 10 to 20 years.

DO	DON'T
DO declare a macro for handling the default window procedure in your window. **DON'T** forget to name the macro after the class of your window; also, don't forget to check to be sure you are calling the correct default window procedure for your class.	

Summing Up Message Crackers

Before moving on to discuss the all-important `WM_PAINT` message, it might be worth indulging in a short recap of the last few sections.

Message crackers help simplify Windows programs and eliminate careless errors. They do this by three means:

1. They break up the endless case statements typically found in `WndProcs` and help make your code conform to good structured programming practices.

2. They help pick apart or parse the `hwnd`, `lParam`, and `wParam` parameters by singling out the important ones and subjecting them to proper typecasting.

3. They unify all the functions related to a window class under a single title, by virtue of the `MyClass_OnXXX` naming convention.

Hopefully, all this has sunk in; I don't cover it again in any detail. From here on out, message crackers are going to be taken for granted and treated as if they were the only sane non-OOP way to handle messages in a window procedure. And indeed, I believe that to be the case.

It's possible to sum up most of the themes inherent in this discussion of WindowsX by showing you one tiny code fragment from EASYTEXT.CPP:

```
23: #define EasyText_DefProc DefWindowProc
24: BOOL EasyText_OnCreate(HWND hwnd,
25:                         CREATESTRUCT FAR* lpCreateStruct);
26: void EasyText_OnDestroy(HWND hwnd);
27: void EasyText_OnPaint(HWND hwnd);
```

These five lines give an overview of the entire functionality of the EasyText window class. When first viewing EASYTEXT.CPP, or some other program form this book, glance at the section of the program that contains lines that look like these. They show you immediately where in the program to focus your attention. If there were three or four different "classes" in this module, you could look at each of the definitions for these classes, know immediately what they're about, and see how they differ from one another.

This kind of concision can help you organize and clean up your code quickly. Let other programmers continue to flounder in the void; WindowsX is cool.

Note: If you want to learn more about message crackers, you can turn to some text files that come with your compiler. Microsoft users should look for a file called WINDOWSX.TXT, and Borland users should look for a file called WIN31.DOC. You can also look up the topic in the Microsoft Network Developer CD.

Painting Text

Every message sent to a window procedure is important. Yet somehow, the `WM_PAINT` message strikes me as being the central message around which most applications revolve. Certainly, nobody could deny that `WM_PAINT` messages perform a vital function in the life of nearly all windows applications.

`WM_PAINT` messages are sent to a window every time it needs to redraw the contents of its client area. When programmers speak of the client area of a window, they are usually referring to the

```
#pragma warning (disable: 4068)
#pragma warning (disable: 4100)

// ----------------------------------------------------------
// Interface
// ----------------------------------------------------------

// Some variables
static int XVal = 10;
static int YVal = 30;
static char szAppName[] = "KeyMouse";
static HWND MainWindow;

#if !defined(__WIN32__) && !defined(_WIN32)
#define EXPORT16 __export
#else
#define EXPORT16
#endif


// Some procs

LRESULT CALLBACK EXPORT16 WndProc(HWND hWindow, UINT Message,
                        wParam wParam, lParam lParam);
BOOL Register(HINSTANCE hInst);
HWND Create(HINSTANCE hInst, int nCmdShow);

#define KeyMouse_DefProc    DefWindowProc
void KeyMouse_OnDestroy(HWND hwnd);
void KeyMouse_OnChar(HWND hwnd, UINT ch, int cRepeat);
void KeyMouse_OnKey(HWND hwnd, UINT vk, BOOL fDown,
                    int cRepeat, UINT flags);
void KeyMouse_OnLButtonDown(HWND hwnd, BOOL fDoubleClick,
                            int x, int y, UINT keyFlags);
void KeyMouse_OnLButtonUp(HWND hwnd, int x, int y,
                          UINT keyFlags);
void KeyMouse_OnMouseMove(HWND hwnd, int x,
                          int y, UINT keyFlags);
void KeyMouse_OnPaint(HWND hwnd);
void KeyMouse_OnSysKey(HWND hwnd, UINT vk,
                       BOOL fDown, int cRepeat, UINT flags);


// ----------------------------------------------------------
// Initialization
// ----------------------------------------------------------

/////////////////////////////////////////
// Program entry point
/////////////////////////////////////////

#pragma argsused
int WINAPI WinMain(HINSTANCE hInst, HINSTANCE hPrevInstance,
LPSTR  lpszCmdParam, int nCmdShow)
{
  MSG  Msg;
```

continues

Listing 5.1. continued

```
    if (!hPrevInstance)
       if (!Register(hInst))
        return FALSE;

    MainWindow = Create(hInst, nCmdShow);
    if (!MainWindow)
      return FALSE;

    while (GetMessage(&Msg, NULL, 0, 0))
    {
       TranslateMessage(&Msg);
       DispatchMessage(&Msg);
    }

    return Msg.wParam;
}

//////////////////////////////////////
// Register the window
//////////////////////////////////////
BOOL Register(HINSTANCE hInst)
{
  WNDCLASS WndClass;

  WndClass.style           = CS_HREDRAW | CS_VREDRAW | CS_DBLCLKS;
  WndClass.lpfnWndProc     = WndProc;
  WndClass.cbClsExtra      = 0;
  WndClass.cbWndExtra      = 0;
  WndClass.hInstance       = hInst;
  WndClass.hIcon           = LoadIcon(NULL, IDI_APPLICATION);
  WndClass.hCursor         = LoadCursor(NULL, IDC_ARROW);
  WndClass.hbrBackground   = (HBRUSH)(COLOR_WINDOW+1);
  WndClass.lpszMenuName    = NULL;
  WndClass.lpszClassName   = szAppName;

  return RegisterClass (&WndClass);
}

//////////////////////////////////////
// Create the window
//////////////////////////////////////
HWND Create(HINSTANCE hInstance, int nCmdShow)
{

  HWND hwnd = CreateWindow(szAppName, szAppName,
          WS_OVERLAPPEDWINDOW,
          CW_USEDEFAULT, CW_USEDEFAULT,
          CW_USEDEFAULT, CW_USEDEFAULT,
            NULL, NULL, hInstance, NULL);

  if (hwnd == NULL)
    return hwnd;

  ShowWindow(hwnd, nCmdShow);
  UpdateWindow(hwnd);
```

```
    return hwnd;
}

// ---------------------------------------------------------
// WndProc and Implementation
// ---------------------------------------------------------

/////////////////////////////////////
// The Window Procedure
/////////////////////////////////////
LRESULT CALLBACK EXPORT16 WndProc(HWND hwnd, UINT Message,
                                 wParam wParam, lParam lParam)
{
  switch(Message)
  {
    HANDLE_MSG(hwnd, WM_DESTROY, KeyMouse_OnDestroy);
    HANDLE_MSG(hwnd, WM_CHAR, KeyMouse_OnChar);
    HANDLE_MSG(hwnd, WM_KEYDOWN, KeyMouse_OnKey);
    HANDLE_MSG(hwnd, WM_KEYUP, KeyMouse_OnKey);
    HANDLE_MSG(hwnd, WM_MOUSEMOVE, KeyMouse_OnMouseMove);
    HANDLE_MSG(hwnd, WM_LBUTTONDBLCLK,  KeyMouse_OnLButtonDown);
    HANDLE_MSG(hwnd, WM_LBUTTONDOWN, KeyMouse_OnLButtonDown);
    HANDLE_MSG(hwnd, WM_LBUTTONUP, KeyMouse_OnLButtonUp);
    HANDLE_MSG(hwnd, WM_PAINT, KeyMouse_OnPaint);
    HANDLE_MSG(hwnd, WM_SYSKEYUP, KeyMouse_OnSysKey);
    HANDLE_MSG(hwnd, WM_SYSKEYDOWN, KeyMouse_OnSysKey);
  default:
    return KeyMouse_DefProc(hwnd, Message, wParam, lParam);
  }
}

/////////////////////////////////////
// Handle WM_DESTROY
/////////////////////////////////////
#pragma argsused
void KeyMouse_OnDestroy(HWND hwnd)
{
  PostQuitMessage(0);
}

/////////////////////////////////////
// Handle regular keyboard hits
// Use if you want to trap the letter keys or number keys.
/////////////////////////////////////
#pragma argsused
void KeyMouse_OnChar(HWND hwnd, UINT ch, int cRepeat)
{
  char S[100];

  HDC DC = GetDC(hwnd);

  sprintf(S,
      "WM_CHAR ==> Ch = %c  cRepeat = %d    ", ch, cRepeat);

  SetBkColor(DC, GetSysColor(COLOR_WINDOW));
  TextOut(DC, XVal, YVal + 20, S, strlen(S));
```

Listing 5.1. continued

```c
    ReleaseDC(hwnd, DC);
}


/////////////////////////////////////
// Handle a key press
// Don't try to process letter or number keys here. Instead,
// use WM_CHAR messages.
/////////////////////////////////////
#pragma argsused
void KeyMouse_OnKey(HWND hwnd, UINT vk,
                    BOOL fDown, int cRepeat, UINT flags)
{
  char S[100];

  HDC DC = GetDC(hwnd);

  if (fDown)
    sprintf(S, "WM_KEYDOWN == > vk = %d  fDown = %d cRepeat = %d"
            " flags = %d           ", vk, fDown, cRepeat, flags);
  else
    sprintf(S, "WM_KEYUP == > vk = %d  fDown = %d cRepeat = %d "
            "flags = %d          ", vk, fDown, cRepeat, flags);

  SetBkColor(DC, GetSysColor(COLOR_WINDOW));

  TextOut(DC, XVal, YVal + 40, S, strlen(S));

  ReleaseDC(hwnd, DC);
}

/////////////////////////////////////
// This function is called when the left mouse button is
// click or when the user double-clicks the mouse
/////////////////////////////////////
void KeyMouse_OnLButtonDown(HWND hwnd, BOOL fDoubleClick, int x,
int y, UINT keyFlags)
{
  char S[100];

  HDC DC = GetDC(hwnd);

  if (fDoubleClick)
    sprintf(S,
      "WM_LBUTTONDBLCLK ==> Db = %d x = %d y = %d Flags = %d  ",
      fDoubleClick, x, y, keyFlags);
  else
    sprintf(S,
      "WM_LBUTTONDOWN ==> Db = %d x = %d y = %d Flags = %d  ",
      fDoubleClick, x, y, keyFlags);

  SetBkColor(DC, GetSysColor(COLOR_WINDOW));
  TextOut(DC, XVal, YVal + 100, S, strlen(S));

  ReleaseDC(hwnd, DC);
}
```

```
/////////////////////////////////////
// This function is called when the mouse button is released
/////////////////////////////////////
void KeyMouse_OnLButtonUp(HWND hwnd, int x, int y, UINT keyFlags)
{
  char S[100];
  HDC DC = GetDC(hwnd);

  sprintf(S, "WM_LBUTTONUP ==> x = %d y = %d F = %d    ",
          x, y, keyFlags);

  SetBkColor(DC, GetSysColor(COLOR_WINDOW));
  TextOut(DC, XVal, YVal + 120, S, strlen(S));

  ReleaseDC(hwnd, DC);
}


/////////////////////////////////////
// This function is called whenever the mouse moves
/////////////////////////////////////
void KeyMouse_OnMouseMove(HWND hwnd, int x, int y, UINT keyFlags)
{
  char S[100];
  HDC DC = GetDC(hwnd);

  sprintf(S, "WM_MOUSEMOVE ==> x = %d y = %d keyFlags = %d    ",
            x, y, keyFlags);
  if ((keyFlags & MK_CONTROL) == MK_CONTROL)
    SetTextColor(DC, RGB(0, 0, 255));
  if ((keyFlags & MK_LBUTTON) == MK_LBUTTON)
    SetTextColor(DC, RGB(0, 255, 0));
  if ((keyFlags & MK_RBUTTON) == MK_RBUTTON)
    SetTextColor(DC, RGB(255, 0, 0));
  if ((keyFlags & MK_SHIFT) == MK_SHIFT)
    SetTextColor(DC, RGB(255, 0, 255));

  SetBkColor(DC, GetSysColor(COLOR_WINDOW));
  TextOut(DC, XVal, YVal + 80, S, strlen(S));

  ReleaseDC(hwnd, DC);
}


/////////////////////////////////////
// Handle WM_PAINT messages.
/////////////////////////////////////
void KeyMouse_OnPaint(HWND hwnd)
{
  PAINTSTRUCT PaintStruct;
  RECT Rect;
  static char *Message[] =
  {
  "WM_CHAR",
  "WM_KEY",
  "WM_SYSKEY",
  "WM_MOUSEMOVE",
```

5

continues

Listing 5.1. continued

```
"WM_MOUSEDOWN",
"WM_MOUSEUP"
};

HDC PaintDC = BeginPaint(hwnd, &PaintStruct);

SetBkColor(PaintDC, GetSysColor(COLOR_WINDOW));

HFONT OldFont = SelectFont(PaintDC,
                GetStockObject(OEM_FIXED_FONT));

GetClientRect(hwnd, &Rect);
Rect.top = 5;
DrawText(PaintDC, "MOUSE AND KEYBOARD DEMONSTRATION", -1,
        &Rect, DT_CENTER);
Rect.top    = 20;
Rect.bottom = 40;
DrawText(PaintDC,
        "(Try experimenting with the mouse and keyboard)",
        -1, &Rect, DT_CENTER);

SelectFont(PaintDC, OldFont);

for (int i = 0; i < 6; i++)
  TextOut(PaintDC, XVal, YVal + (20 * (i + 1)),
          Message[i], strlen(Message[i]));

EndPaint(hwnd, &PaintStruct);
}

////////////////////////////////////////
// This function is called whenever the ALT key is pressed.
////////////////////////////////////////
void KeyMouse_OnSysKey(HWND hwnd, UINT vk, BOOL fDown,
                       int cRepeat, UINT flags)
{
  char S[100];

  HDC DC = GetDC(hwnd);
  SetBkColor(DC, GetSysColor(COLOR_WINDOW));

  if (fDown)
  {
    sprintf(S,"WM_SYSKEYDOWN == > "
            "vk = %d  fDown = %d cRepeat = %d flags = %d       ",
              vk, fDown, cRepeat, flags);
    TextOut(DC, XVal, YVal + 60, S, strlen(S));
    FORWARD_WM_SYSKEYDOWN(hwnd, vk, cRepeat, flags,
                          KeyMouse_DefProc);
  }
  else
  {
    sprintf(S, "WM_SYSKEYUP == > "
            " vk = %d  fDown = %d cRepeat = %d flags = %d       ",
              vk, fDown, cRepeat, flags);
```

```
        TextOut(DC, XVal, YVal + 60, S, strlen(S));
        FORWARD_WM_SYSKEYUP(hwnd, vk, cRepeat, flags,
                            KeyMouse_DefProc);
    } // end if

    ReleaseDC(hwnd, DC);
}


}
```

Listing 5.2 shows the KeyMouse definition file.

Listing 5.2. KEYMOUSE.DEF.

```
1: ;  KEYMOUSE.DEF
2:
3: NAME          KeyMouse
4: DESCRIPTION   'KeyMouse Window'
5: CODE          PRELOAD MOVEABLE DISCARDABLE
6: DATA          PRELOAD MOVEABLE MULTIPLE
7:
8: HEAPSIZE      4096
9: STACKSIZE     5120
```

Listing 5.3 shows the Borland makefile for KeyMouse.

Listing 5.3. KEYMOUSE.MAK (Borland).

```
# KEYMOUSE.MAK

!if !$d(BCROOT)
BCROOT  = $(MAKEDIR)
!endif

# macros
APPNAME = KeyMouse
INCPATH = $(BCROOT)\INCLUDE
LIBPATH = $(BCROOT)\LIB

!if $d(WIN16)
COMPILER= BCC.EXE
FLAGS   = -W -ml -v -w4 -I$(INCPATH) -L$(LIBPATH)
!else
COMPILER= BCC32.EXE
FLAGS   = -W -v -w4 -I$(INCPATH) -L$(LIBPATH)
!endif

# link
$(APPNAME).exe: $(APPNAME).obj $(APPNAME).def
  $(COMPILER) $(FLAGS) $(APPNAME).obj
```

continues

Listing 5.3. continued

```
# compile
$(APPNAME).obj: $(APPNAME).cpp
  $(COMPILER) -c $(FLAGS) $(APPNAME).cpp
```

Listing 5.4 shows the Microsoft makefile for KeyMouse.

Listing 5.4. KEYMOUSE.MAK (Microsoft).

```
#-----------------------------------------------
# KEYMOUMS.MAK
# Microsoft makefile
-----------------------------------------------

APPNAME=KEYMOUSE
TARGETOS=WIN95
APPVER=4.0
OBJS=$(APPNAME).OBJ

!include <win32.mak>

all: $(APPNAME).exe

# Update the object files if necessary

# compile
.cpp.obj:
  $(cc) $(cflags) $(cvars) $(cdebug) $<

# Update the executable file if necessary.

$(APPNAME).exe: $(OBJS)
  $(link) $(linkdebug) $(guiflags) -out:$(APPNAME).exe \
  $(OBJS) $(guilibs) comctl32.lib
```

When KEYMOUSE.CPP is run, it produces the output shown in Figure 5.1.

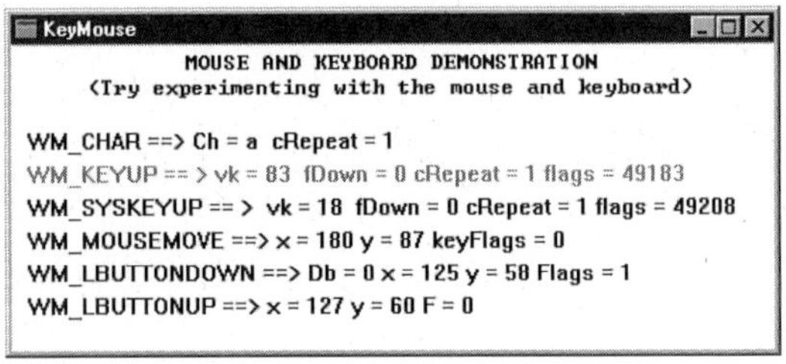

Figure 5.1.
KEYMOUSE.CPP shows the information conveyed by the most important mouse and keyboard messages.

146

The KeyMouse program provides two major services:

- [ ] It shows how to detect when a key has been pressed. In particular, it shows the value of the pressed key and a few pieces of related information.
- [ ] It shows how to detect when the mouse has been moved and if a mouse button has been pressed. In particular, it prints output to the screen showing the current location and status of the mouse.

Take a few moments to play with this program. Note the way it reacts when you move the mouse or press a key. Remember that whenever you press the Alt key, the system menu on the upper-left corner of the title bar is activated. Regular keyboard response won't resume until you press the Alt key again or take some other action that changes the focus. Detecting Alt key presses is discussed forthwith, in the section on WM_SYSKEY messages.

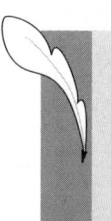

Note: The concept of *focus* is extremely important in Windows programming. Focused windows respond to keyboard and mouse input, whereas non-focused windows don't respond. For instance, if the File Manager or Program Manager has the focus, it responds to a press of the Alt+F key by popping open its File menu. However, if you bring the KeyMouse program to the foreground of the desktop, the Program Manager or File Manager no longer responds to the press of a keystroke. This occurs because the KeyMouse program now has the focus. You often can tell if a particular program has the focus by checking to see if its title bar is highlighted.

It's important to understand that only one window has the focus at a time. For instance, if you pop open the File menu, that newly opened menu has the focus, and the main window of the program is inactive. The same thing happens when you pop open the Options dialog from the View menu of the My Computer window. When the Options dialog has the focus, the rest of My Computer is inactive.

Windows Keyboard and Mouse Messages

KeyMouse is designed to show off nine Windows messages associated with the keyboard and mouse:

Message	Result
WM_CHAR	A number or letter key was pressed.
WM_KEYDOWN	A key was pressed.
WM_KEYUP	A key was released.
WM_LBUTTONDOWN	The left mouse button was pressed.
WM_LBUTTONUP	The left mouse button was released.
WM_LBUTTONDBLCLK	The left mouse button was double-clicked.
WM_MOUSEMOVE	The mouse was moved.
WM_SYSKEYDOWN	The Alt key was pressed.
WM_SYSKEYUP	The Alt key was released.

The majority of the rest of this chapter is dedicated to discussing these messages in one form or another. There will be a few side trips to discuss matters such as painting the screen, but the main focus will be on these very important messages.

Handling *WM_CHAR* Messages

WM_CHAR messages get sent whenever the user presses an alphanumeric key. That is, if you press one of the letters A–Z, or one of the numbers at the top of the keyboard, then you get a WM_CHAR message. WM_KEYDOWN messages are sent whenever any key is pressed, regardless of whether it's alphanumeric. For instance, pressing the Delete key produces a WM_KEYDOWN message but not a WM_CHAR message.

Here is the WM_CHAR handler for the KeyMouse program:

```
161: void KeyMouse_OnChar(HWND hwnd, UINT ch, int cRepeat)
162: {
163:   char S[100];
164:
165:   HDC DC = GetDC(hwnd);
166:
167:   sprintf(S,
168:     "WM_CHAR ==> Ch = %c   cRepeat = %d     ", ch, cRepeat);
169:   TextOut(DC, XVal, YVal + 20, S, strlen(S));
170:
171:   ReleaseDC(hwnd, DC);
172: }
```

In just a moment, I'll talk about the actual purpose of the KeyMouse_OnChar function and about how it handles WM_CHAR messages. Before I get to that subject, however, I want to make sure you understand the crucial difference between the way the KeyMouse_OnChar and the KeyMouse_OnPaint functions handle the device context. This is a point you have to get clear in your head, or you'll never get your programs to act correctly.

The first thing the KeyMouse_OnChar function does is get a device context. It does this not by calling BeginPaint and EndPaint but by snagging the device context with calls to GetDC (line 168) and ReleaseDC. The TextOut (line 172) method uses this device context to output information to the screen, just as the EasyText program did on Day 4.

To understand the difference between calling GetDC and calling BeginPaint, you only need to drag another program over the KeyMouse window. If, for instance, you were to temporarily obscure the right half of the KeyMouse window, the scene visible in Figure 5.2 would greet your eyes when the KeyMouse window is again brought to the fore.

Figure 5.2.
The KeyMouse program with some of its information blotted out after it was temporarily obscured by another program.

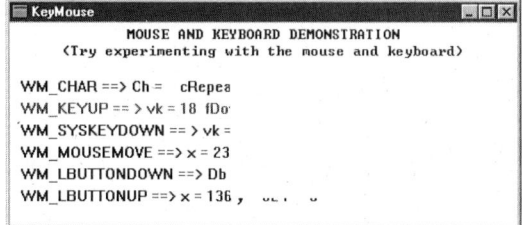

If you understand what has happened here, you are definitely getting a feel for the mechanisms employed by the Windows message system. A WM_PAINT message is sent to a window every time a portion obscured by another window is uncovered. Therefore, the title and the words on the far-left portion of the KeyMouse program are visible whenever the window is visible. However, any text painted in, say, the KeyMouse_OnChar function, won't be repainted. The reason for this, of course, is that only WM_CHAR messages are sent to the KeyMouse_OnChar method. It doesn't know, or care, if a WM_PAINT message is sent!

Note: In DOS programs, the contents of windows are frequently saved wholesale in a buffer and then restored whenever a window is brought back on top. This isn't the way Windows usually works. Instead, the contents of a window are restored by sending a WM_PAINT message. When it gets a WM_PAINT message, a window explicitly performs the acts necessary to repaint itself.

Nothing is terribly complicated about the mechanism I'm describing here. Here are the two sides to the story:

1. When responding to WM_PAINT messages, you should use BeginPaint and EndPaint.
2. At all other times, you should use GetDC and ReleaseDC.

The Mouse and the Keyboard

Now that you have a feeling for the difference between BeginPaint and GetDC, the next step is to tackle the WM_CHAR message. WM_CHAR messages are sent to a program whenever a user presses one of the standard keys. That is, if a user presses the A key or B key, a WM_CHAR message is sent. Notice that WM_CHAR messages are *not* sent when the user presses one of the function keys or the arrow keys on the numeric keyboard.

The value associated with a keypress is sent to the KeyMouse_OnChar function in the ch variable, which is declared to be an unsigned integer. In other words, if the user presses the A key, ch is set to ASCII value 97, which is the letter *a*. If the user holds down the Shift key while pressing A, the ASCII value 65 is sent in the ch variable. ASCII 65, of course, represents the letter *A*.

If a key is pressed repeatedly between calls to WM_CHAR, the number of key presses that occurred is sent in the cRepeat variable. Although this information is usually not very important, Windows still passes it on to you in case you have some use for it.

The KeyMouse_OnChar function serves as a set piece for the virtues of WindowsX. If KeyMouse didn't take advantage of WindowsX, it would have to parse the wParam and lParam variables sent to the program's WndProc in order to determine the correct value of the keypress and the repeat count. (See Figure 5.3.) The repeat count information, for instance, is stored in the low word of lParam. The high-order word holds several pieces of information that are generally not useful to applications. As a result, the high-order word is not passed on to KeyMouse_OnChar.

Figure 5.3.

A Borland Help Screen shows how information about keypresses is packed into lParam *and* wParam. *Thanks to WindowsX, detailed understanding of this information is no longer needed.*

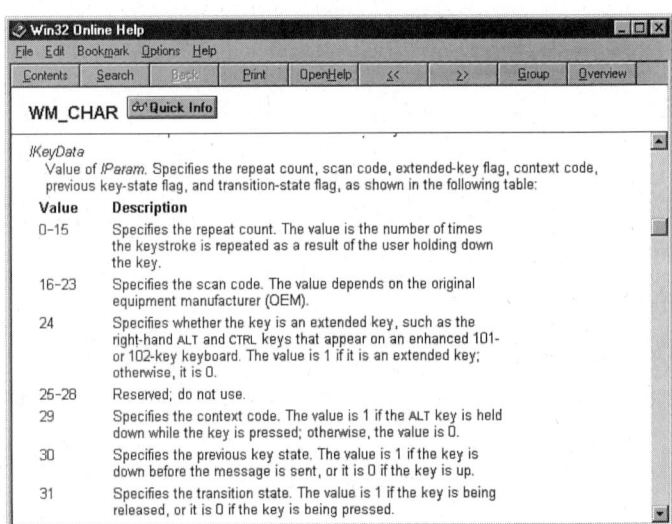

Before WindowsX came along, programmers ferreted out all this information on their own by reading the fine print in the reference manuals, and by studying the actual bits in wParam and lParam.

DO / DON'T

DO	DON'T

DO use WM_CHAR messages for reading the alphanumeric keys. These key presses are correctly translated by Windows before the WM_CHAR message is sent. Therefore, WM_CHAR messages are an ideal way to tell if a number or letter is selected by the user.

DON'T use WM_CHAR for trying to detect whether a function key or an arrow key has been pressed.

DO use WM_KEYDOWN messages to determine whether a function key or arrow key has been pressed.

DON'T use WM_KEYDOWN messages to read alphanumeric keys. Number keys and letter keys have not yet been properly translated (via the TranslateMessage function in the message loop) when WM_KEYDOWN messages are sent. Hence, you can easily misinterpret the value of the keystroke associated with a WM_KEYDOWN message. More information about WM_KEYDOWN messages is presented in the next section.

Detecting Key Presses with *WM_KEYDOWN*

As you saw earlier, the WM_CHAR message is, from the point of view of a DOS programmer, one of the simplest and most straightforward messages sent to the window procedure. The ch parameter, which is passed to the KeyMouse_OnChar message handler function, contains the value of the key pressed (as long as that key is a letter or number). The other parameters keep track of how many times that key was pressed since the last time a WM_CHAR message was sent.

To handle other key presses, such as presses of the left-arrow, right-arrow, or function keys, you should process the WM_KEYDOWN message:

```
180: void KeyMouse_OnKey(HWND hwnd, UINT vk,
181:                     BOOL fDown, int cRepeat, UINT flags)
182: {
183:    char S[100];
184:
185:    HDC DC = GetDC(hwnd);
186:
187:    if (fDown)
188:      sprintf(S, "WM_KEYDOWN == > vk = %d  fDown = %d cRepeat = %d"
189:             " flags = %d           ", vk, fDown, cRepeat, flags);
190:    else
191:      sprintf(S, "WM_KEYUP == > vk = %d  fDown = %d cRepeat = %d "
192:             "flags = %d          ", vk, fDown, cRepeat, flags);
193:    TextOut(DC, XVal, YVal + 40, S, strlen(S));
194:
195:    ReleaseDC(hwnd, DC);
196: }
```

5

Note: As you can see from the preceding code, the KeyMouse_OnKey routine is one of those rare cases in which a single WindowsX message handler function is sent more than one message. The fDown parameter tells whether the message being sent is a key press or key release, and the previous code shows that it's easy to perceive the distinction between the two simply by checking whether fDown is set to TRUE or FALSE.

Windows makes it very easy for programmers to discover when the right-arrow key, left-arrow key, or function key has been pressed. This information is packed into the message handler function's vk parameter in terms of one of a number of constants that are defined in WINDOWS.H. vk stands for *virtual key.*

The vk parameter is to the KeyMouse_OnKey function what the ch parameter is to the KeyMouse_OnChar function. In other words, if the user presses the A key, that value is passed to the KeyMouse_OnChar function in the ch variable. However, if the user presses, say, the left-arrow key, the VK_LEFT constant is passed to the KeyMouse_OnKey method via the vk parameter.

The VK_LEFT constant is one of several predefined constants declared in the WINDOWS.H complex. Here, for instance, is an excerpt from that list:

```
#define VK_END          0x23
#define VK_HOME         0x24
#define VK_LEFT         0x25
#define VK_UP           0x26
#define VK_RIGHT        0x27
#define VK_DOWN         0x28
#define VK_SELECT       0x29
#define VK_PRINT        0x2A
#define VK_EXECUTE      0x2B
#define VK_SNAPSHOT     0x2C
#define VK_INSERT       0x2D
#define VK_DELETE       0x2E
#define VK_HELP         0x2F
#define VK_NUMPAD0      0x60
#define VK_NUMPAD1      0x61
#define VK_NUMPAD2      0x62
#define VK_NUMPAD3      0x63
```

You can also find this information in various reference books, or in your online help files.

The following modified version of the KeyMouse_OnKey function shows how to detect a few of these keystrokes:

```
void KeyMouse_OnKey(HWND hwnd, UINT vk,
BOOL fDown, int cRepeat, UINT flags)
{
char S[100];
```

```
HDC DC = GetDC(hwnd);

switch (vk)
{
case VK_LEFT:
strcpy(S, "Left arrow pressed.          ");
break;
case VK_RIGHT:
strcpy(S, "Right arrow pressed.         ");
break;
case VK_F1:
strcpy(S, "F1 key pressed.              ");
break;
case VK_F12:
strcpy(S, "F12 key pressed.             ");
break;
case VK_CLEAR:
strcpy(S, "Numeric keypad 5, NumLock off");
break;
case VK_NUMPAD5:
strcpy(S, "Numeric keypad 5, NumLock on");
break;
default:
strcpy(S, "Out to lunch, back in five!  ");
}

TextOut(DC, XVal, YVal + 40, S, strlen(S));

ReleaseDC(hwnd, DC);
}
```

When examining this procedure, you might want to note the VK_CLEAR and VK_F12 constants. Capturing both of these keystrokes could be a bit complicated for DOS programmers working with certain compilers. But in Windows, this kind of information is readily available.

For now, that's all I'm going to say about the WM_KEYDOWN and WM_KEYUP messages. The subject is really very straightforward.

The System Key

In Windows, the system key is the Alt key. In other words, when you hold down the Alt key, you are holding down the system key.

Windows often gives more information than a user is ever likely to need. The KeyMouse program, for instance, traps WM_SYSKEYDOWN and WM_SYSKEYUP messages, which usually should be passed on directly to DefWndProc. The reason the messages need to be passed on is that the system keys handle a lot of default Windows keyboard behavior, such as the famous Alt+Tab keystroke that switches between applications. In cases like this, it is absolutely essential that you call the FORWARD_WM_XXX macros declared in WindowsX. This is shown in the following excerpt from KeyMouse_OnSysKey:

5

```
300:    if (fDown)
301:    {
302:      sprintf(S,"WM_SYSKEYDOWN == > "
303:             "vk = %d  fDown = %d cRepeat = %d flags = %d          ",
304:               vk, fDown, cRepeat, flags);
305:      TextOut(DC, XVal, YVal + 60, S, strlen(S));
306:      FORWARD_WM_SYSKEYDOWN(hwnd, vk, cRepeat, flags,
307:                          KeyMouse_DefProc);
308:    }
```

Even though I mentioned this issue on Day 4, it might be worthwhile to look explicitly at the message cracker for the WM_SYSKEYDOWN message as it's declared in WINDOWSX.H:

```
/* void Cls_OnSysKey(HWND hwnd, UINT vk, BOOL fDown,
                     int cRepeat, UINT flags); */
#define HANDLE_WM_SYSKEYDOWN(hwnd, wParam, lParam, fn) \
    ((fn)((hwnd), (UINT)(wParam), TRUE,
    (int)LOWORD(lParam), (UINT)HIWORD(lParam)), 0L)
#define FORWARD_WM_SYSKEYDOWN(hwnd, vk, cRepeat, flags, fn) \
    (void)(fn)((hwnd), WM_SYSKEYDOWN, (wParam)(UINT)(vk),
    MAKElParam((UINT)(cRepeat), (UINT)(flags)))
```

The key issue to focus on is the declaration of the FORWARD_WM_SYSKEYDOWN macro. This is the macro responsible for passing the WM_SYSKEYDOWN message to the default Window procedure.

I think it's inevitable that new Windows programmers occasionally will forget to pass on a message for further processing. To help remind you of the gravity of this error, you might want to try commenting out the FORWARD_WM_SYSKEYDOWN macro in KeyMouse_OnSysKey. Then recompile and run the program. Now try pressing Alt+Tab; notice that the default behavior associated with that key combination doesn't occur. Now, remove the comments, recompile, and note that the standard behavior returns.

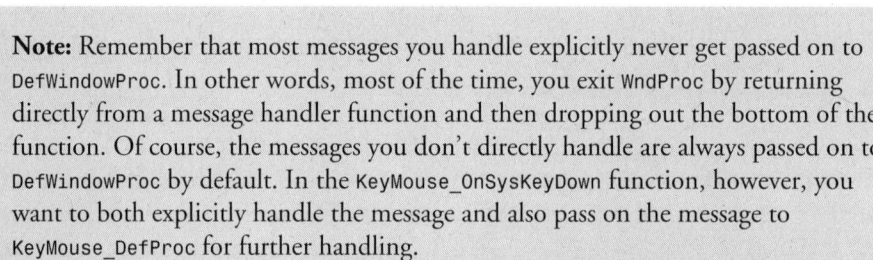

Note: Remember that most messages you handle explicitly never get passed on to DefWindowProc. In other words, most of the time, you exit WndProc by returning directly from a message handler function and then dropping out the bottom of the function. Of course, the messages you don't directly handle are always passed on to DefWindowProc by default. In the KeyMouse_OnSysKeyDown function, however, you want to both explicitly handle the message and also pass on the message to KeyMouse_DefProc for further handling.

This concept is a bit subtle, so you might want to take time to contemplate the WndProc function and to trace in your mind the usual path a message takes when it passes through:

```
LRESULT CALLBACK _ EXPORT16 WndProc(HWND hwnd, UINT Message, wParam
                               wParam, lParam lParam)
{
  switch(Message)
  {
```

```
          HANDLE_MSG(hwnd, WM_DESTROY, KeyMouse_OnDestroy);
          HANDLE_MSG(hwnd, WM_CHAR, KeyMouse_OnChar);
          HANDLE_MSG(hwnd, WM_KEYDOWN, KeyMouse_OnKey);
          HANDLE_MSG(hwnd, WM_KEYUP, KeyMouse_OnKey);
          HANDLE_MSG(hwnd, WM_MOUSEMOVE, KeyMouse_OnMouseMove);
          HANDLE_MSG(hwnd, WM_LBUTTONDBLCLK,     KeyMouse_OnLButtonDown);
          HANDLE_MSG(hwnd, WM_LBUTTONDOWN, KeyMouse_OnLButtonDown);
          HANDLE_MSG(hwnd, WM_LBUTTONUP, KeyMouse_OnLButtonUp);
          HANDLE_MSG(hwnd, WM_PAINT, KeyMouse_OnPaint);
          HANDLE_MSG(hwnd, WM_SYSKEYUP, KeyMouse_OnSysKey);
          HANDLE_MSG(hwnd, WM_SYSKEYDOWN, KeyMouse_OnSysKey);
          default:
          return KeyMouse_DefProc(hwnd, Message, wParam, lParam);
      }
  }
```

Remember that `KeyMouse_DefProc` does nothing more than call `DefWindowProc`!

In general, it's important to remember that erratic, inexplicable behavior in an application can sometimes be attributed to missing calls to the default window procedure. If one day you find yourself stuck in the midst of some lengthy, hair-pulling, patience-trying debugging session, you might want to consider the possibility that you've simply forgotten to pass on a message to the default window procedure for further processing.

The *WM_MOUSEMOVE* Message

5

There is something truly remarkable about the Windows message system. Even the simple act of moving a mouse across a window has a kind of fascination to it, especially when the coordinates being sent to the window are made visible, as they are in KeyMouse.

Stop for a moment and take a look at the WM_MOUSEMOVE message response function:

```
/////////////////////////////////////////////////////////////
// This function is called whenever the mouse moves
/////////////////////////////////////////////////////////////

239: void KeyMouse_OnMouseMove(HWND hwnd, int x, int y, UINT keyFlags)
240: {
241:    char S[100];
242:    HDC PaintDC = GetDC(hwnd);
243:
244:    sprintf(S, "WM_MOUSEMOVE ==> x = %d y = %d keyFlags = %d     ",
245:              x, y, keyFlags);
246:    TextOut(PaintDC, XVal, YVal + 80, S, strlen(S));
247:
248:    ReleaseDC(hwnd, PaintDC);
249: }
```

The first thing to notice is what a good job the WindowsX message cracker does of passing on relevant information to the KeyMouse_OnMouseMove function. If you look in a reference book, you'll see that when a window procedure gets a WM_MOUSEMOVE message, information is packed into the hwnd, wParam, and lParam parameters. The latter of these parameters carries information about the column the mouse is on in its low-order word, and it carries information about the row it's on in its high-order word. But thanks to the message crackers, this obscure information is translated into the x and y coordinates visible in the KeyMouse_OnMouseMoves header.

The KeyMouse_OnMouseMove function makes the x, y, and keyFlags parameters visible on-screen by first translating them into a string through the sprintf function and then by displaying them through the TextOut function. This is the same system you saw previously when studying the response to a key press.

Sometimes it seems to me that the WndProc function is weathering a storm of messages that come in at a rate that literally boggles the mind. You can get a feeling for how many WM_MOUSEMOVE messages are sent to the program by studying the KeyMouse_OnMouseMove function in action. Remember that every time a new set of mouse coordinates is shown on-screen, another message has been processed by the WndProc. It's as if the window procedure is walking through a blizzard of messages that descends on it in great flurries of activity.

Besides the x and y coordinates of the mouse, the other piece of information sent with every WM_MOUSEMOVE message is contained in the keyFlags argument. This parameter can have one of the following values:

Constant	Significance
MK_CONTROL	The control key is down.
MK_LBUTTON	The left mouse button is down.
MK_RBUTTON	The right mouse button is down.
MK_MBUTTON	The middle mouse button is down.
MK_SHIFT	The Shift key is down.

These constants are bit flags, which means that you have to use bitwise operators to test whether they are set. Doing this is really very simple. For instance, if you want to test to see if the Ctrl key is pressed while the mouse is moving, all you need to do is AND keyFlags with MK_CONTROL and then test the result:

```
if ((keyFlags & MK_CONTROL) == MK_CONTROL)
  DoSomething
```

To see exactly how this process works, you might want to take the time to modify the KeyMouse_OnMouseMove function so that the text output changes colors, depending on which keys are pressed:

```
void KeyMouse_OnMouseMove(HWND hwnd, int x, int y, UINT keyFlags)
{
char S[100];
HDC PaintDC = GetDC(hwnd);

sprintf(S, "WM_MOUSEMOVE ==> x = %d y = %d keyFlags = %d      ",
x, y, keyFlags);

if ((keyFlags & MK_CONTROL) == MK_CONTROL)
  SetTextColor(PaintDC, RGB(0, 0, 255));
if ((keyFlags & MK_LBUTTON) == MK_LBUTTON)
  SetTextColor(PaintDC, RGB(0, 255, 0));
if ((keyFlags & MK_RBUTTON) == MK_RBUTTON)
  SetTextColor(PaintDC, RGB(255, 0, 0));
if ((keyFlags & MK_SHIFT) == MK_SHIFT)
  SetTextColor(PaintDC, RGB(255, 0, 255));

TextOut(PaintDC, XVal, YVal + 80, S, strlen(S));

ReleaseDC(hwnd, PaintDC);
}
```

The modified KeyMouse_OnMouseMove function is capable of really showing off the powers inherent in the Windows message system. The line associated with the WM_MOUSEMOVE message smoothly changes colors as the mouse buttons and Ctrl and Shift keys are pressed.

Note: In the process of modifying the KeyMouse_OnMove function, I've introduced the SetTextColor and RGB API calls. These two calls are used over and over again in Windows programs. As a result, you might want to take a few moments to get a feeling for how they work.

The RGB macro returns a 4-byte value that designates a color. The color to be returned is defined by the three parameters passed to the macro, each of which can have a value from 0 to 255.

If the third parameter is set to 255 and the others are set to 0, the resulting color will be dark blue. If the first parameter is set to 255, and the others to 0, the resulting color will be red. The middle parameter controls the amount of green in the color returned by the RGB macro.

In the fourth example of the previous function, both the blue and the red are turned on all the way, resulting in a deep purple. If you wanted to produce a gray color, you could set all three values to 127. Setting them all to 0 produces a deep black, and setting them all to 255 produces white. If you turn on green and red simultaneously, you produce a bright yellow. With just a few minutes of experimentation, you should begin to get a feeling for all the interesting combinations that can be produced with this powerful macro.

5

The SetTextColor function is easier to understand than the RGB macro, because it does nothing more than its name implies. That is, it sets the text color output with the device context passed to it. In other words, it "copies" the result of the RGB function into the device context.

Processing Button Selections and Double-Clicks

The KeyMouse program uses the KeyMouse_OnLButtonDown and KeyMouse_OnLButtonUp functions to record button presses. These functions work very much like the other routines presented in this chapter, so you shouldn't have much trouble with them.

It's easier to understand what happens when a button is released than it is to understand what happens when a button is pressed. Therefore, let's start with the KeyMouse_OnLButtonUp function:

```
224: void KeyMouse_OnLButtonUp(HWND hwnd, int x, int y, UINT keyFlags)
225: {
226:    char S[100];
227:    HDC PaintDC = GetDC(hwnd);
228:
229:    sprintf(S, "WM_LBUTTONUP ==> x = %d y = %d F = %d    ",
230:            x, y, keyFlags);
231:    TextOut(PaintDC, XVal, YVal + 120, S, strlen(S));
232:
233:    ReleaseDC(hwnd, PaintDC);
234: }
```

All in all, nothing could be much simpler than this little fellow. Its purpose, of course, is simply to let the user know where the mouse was when the user released the left mouse button. This is accomplished through the tried-and-true method of snagging hold of the device context and then using it to print information to the screen.

Handling button presses is a bit more complex, however, because it is necessary to distinguish between ordinary button presses and button presses that are really double-clicks. Fortunately, Windows has a system that makes it relatively easy to distinguish between these two conditions.

Here comes a gotcha that can trip up many unsuspecting Windows programmers. If you want to process double-clicks on the left or right mouse button, you must begin by setting the window class style to CS_DBLCLKS. This is done in the Register method:

```
84: win.style = CS_HREDRAW | CS_VREDRAW | CS_DBLCLKS;
```

In this case, you can see that the style associated with the window class now contains three flags. I covered the first two in Day 3, "A Standard Windows Program." The `CS_DBLCLICKS` style informs Windows that this class needs to know when the user double-clicks the mouse in its client area. If you forget to do this, and if you don't figure out what's wrong, then you will begin pulling your hair out in about five minutes flat. I guarantee it.

The message sent when the user double-clicks the left mouse button is `WM_LBUTTONDBLCLK`, but the appropriate WindowsX message cracker forwards this information to the same message handler function that processes `WM_LBUTTONDOWN` messages.

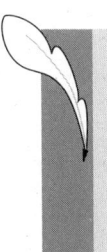

Note: As a rule, message crackers enable each individual message to have its own message handler function. But in a few cases, similar to the `WM_LBUTTONDBLCLK` message, WindowsX sends more than one message to a single function. This process is illustrated in several locations in the previous sample program. For instance, I've already mentioned that this happens with `WM_KEYDOWN` messages (lines 188 and 191). You should remember, however, that message handler functions that receive more than one message are the very rare exceptions to the rule. Most of the time, each message has its own message handler function.

Take the time to study exactly how the `KeyMouse_OnLButtonDown` function works:

```
202: void KeyMouse_OnLButtonDown(HWND hwnd, BOOL fDoubleClick, int x,
203:                             int y, UINT keyFlags)
204: {
205:   char S[100];
206:   HDC PaintDC = GetDC(hwnd);
207:
208:   if (fDoubleClick)
209:     sprintf(S,
210:       "WM_LBUTTONDBLCLK ==> Db = %d x = %d y = %d Flags = %d  ",
211:       fDoubleClick, x, y, keyFlags);
212:   else
213:     sprintf(S,
214:       "WM_LBUTTONDOWN ==> Db = %d x = %d y = %d Flags = %d  ",
215:       fDoubleClick, x, y, keyFlags);
216:   TextOut(PaintDC, XVal, YVal + 100, S, strlen(S));
217:
218:   ReleaseDC(hwnd, PaintDC);
219: }
```

After getting hold of the device context, the function checks to see whether this is a normal key press or a mouse double-click. In the latter case, the `fDoubleClick` parameter will be set to `TRUE`. In these cases, the function prints out a string stating that a `WM_LBUTTONDBLCLK` message has been sent; the function also informs the user about the current coordinates and flag settings.

5

Of course, if no double-click has occurred, the user is told that a WM_LBUTTONDOWN message has just come down the pike. The function then lays out the current state of all the parameters, including the *x* and *y* coordinates the mouse was at when the button press occurred.

As I suggested earlier, Windows programs respond to changes in their environment just as a good driver responds to highway signs, or to curves in the road. In other words, Windows makes sure that a program is sent plenty of information about its environment. The job of the programmer is to teach a program how to respond to these messages. You've seen that a Windows program can respond to a blizzard of keyboard and mouse messages yet still stay on the road.

Summary

In this chapter, you have dug beneath the surface of a Windows program to see how keyboard and mouse messages are handled.

In particular, you have taken a look at GetDC, ReleaseDC, RGB, and the SetTextColor functions. You have also been introduced to many Windows constants, such as VK_CLEAR, WM_LBUTTONDBLCLK, and MK_CONTROL. Obviously, most people are never going to be able to memorize all these identifiers, so you must learn how to use the reference books and online help services available to you. Don't try to memorize the constants; instead memorize the places where you can find them.

Of course, some messages are so important that you should always have them in mind. Messages that fit in this category include WM_PAINT, WM_KEYDOWN, WM_CHAR, WM_MOUSEMOVE, and WM_LBUTTONDOWN. These easy-to-comprehend messages prove their usefulness again and again when you are programming Windows applications.

It doesn't take a genius to see that the Windows message system works. It gives programmers the kind of control over the computer's hardware that DOS programmers often longed in vain to achieve. So, take the time to linger over the riches revealed in this chapter. But don't dally too long, because this stuff is nothing compared to the exciting graphics-specific code you'll see in Day 6, "Introduction to Resources."

Q&A

Q I'm still not clear about the differences between WM_KEYDOWN and WM_CHAR messages. Why does the latter event exist?

A The key point to remember is that WM_KEYDOWN messages occur whenever a key is pressed. However, when this message is sent to a window procedure, Windows has not yet translated the keystroke. As a result, it's easy to become confused about exactly which key has been pressed. WM_CHAR messages, however, are an ideal place to find out about which alphanumeric key the user has pressed.

Q **What is the difference between the `BeginPaint` and `GetDC` functions?**

A The `BeginPaint` and `EndPaint` functions are only used when responding to `WM_PAINT` messages. Because `WM_PAINT` messages are sent to a window whenever it needs to be updated, anything painted to the screen (with a DC retrieved by `BeginPaint`) is always visible when the window is visible. The `GetDC` function, however, can be called at virtually any time during the life of an application. As a result, it gives you considerably more flexibility than does the `BeginPaint` function. However, if you call `GetDC`, the screen won't be updated automatically after it was covered up by some other object (such as a window or dialog).

Q **In this program you use `SetBkColor` rather than `SetBkMode`, which you used in the last chapter. Why the change?**

A `SetBkColor` will cause `TextOut` to overwrite the text that underlies it, while `SetBkMode` leaves the old text exposed, unless it is directly overwritten by the characters themselves. Since the output from this program writes multiple lines of text at the same coordinates, it is necessary to ensure that the text which is being overwritten is entirely blanked out. `SetBkColor` does the job.

Workshop

The Workshop provides quiz questions to help you solidify your understanding of the material covered and exercises to provide you with experience in using what you've learned. Try to understand the quiz and exercise answers before continuing on to Day 6. Answers are provided in Appendix A.

5

Quiz

1. Name two messages that are sent to the `KeyMouse_OnLButtonDown` function.
2. What are the `VK` constants?
3. What is the `CS_DBLCLKS` style, and when and where do you use it?
4. What color is produced if all three parameters to `RGB` are set to zero?
5. How can you test to see if the `MK_CONTROL` bit has been set in a `keyFlags` parameter?
6. What is another name for the system key?
7. How can you pass a message from a message handler function to `DefWndProc`?
8. Where does the focus go when you press the system key when the `KeyMouse` programming is running?
9. On the whole, which function do you think gets called more often—`KeyMouse_OnKey` or `KeyMouse_OnChar`?
10. What would happen if you forgot to call `ReleaseDC` after calling `GetDC` in the `KeyMouse_OnMouseMove` function?

Exercises

1. Use `sprintf` to help you create a program that writes out the coordinates at which the user clicks the left and right mouse buttons—and which prints these coordinates at the location where the button-down event occurred.

2. Use the `SetTextColor` function and `RGB` macro to print out the word Red in red, the word Green in green, and the word Blue in blue.

6

Introduction
to Resources

This chapter presents an introduction to resources. Resources enable you to encapsulate visible and logical elements of your program, such as menus, string tables, and bitmaps, inside special files that can be linked into your program. The end result is a simple and flexible way to add powerful features to your code.

A number of specific techniques are discussed in this chapter, including

- ☐ Creating resource scripts
- ☐ Using the resource compiler
- ☐ Creating menus
- ☐ Creating icons
- ☐ Creating custom cursors
- ☐ Creating user-defined resources

By the end of the day, you should feel that you understand what resources are and how they can be used to enhance your programs. However, this chapter is really only part one in a two-part process. The second part, presented on Day 7, "Advanced Resources: Bitmaps and Dialogs," will greatly expand your knowledge of resources by showing you how to use bitmaps, dialogs, and string tables.

To ensure that you get plenty of hands-on experience, I have included a program called EMERSON.CPP that uses a menu, dialog, bitmap, string table, user-defined resource, custom icon, and custom cursor. This program is developed slowly through the course of this chapter and Day 7. My goals are to start with fairly simple resources in this chapter and to explore more complex, in-depth issues on Day 7.

By the end of this two-step process, you should begin to feel that you can create the kind of powerful and flexible programs for which Windows is renowned. In other words, these two chapters help you make the transition from beginner to intermediate status.

So What Are Resources Anyway?

Resources allow you to add features to your program, in much the same way you can add a clock, a stereo, or a pair of fuzzy dice to a new car. The point is that these are plug-and-play features that you can add without having to do a great deal of coding.

This is not to say that resources don't require any work on your part. If you add a new stereo to your car, you have to go through the process of installing the stereo. In the same way, if you add a bitmap or an icon to your program, you have to install the new feature. This requires some work, but it isn't as difficult as the process you would have to go through if you were starting from scratch. In other words, you don't need to build the stereo, you just have to install it.

There is no set limit to the number of different types of resources that can be added to a program. However, at this stage in the history of Windows, resources usually refer to menus, dialogs, bitmaps, icons, string tables, fonts, cursors, and perhaps one or two other tools.

Just so a common terminology is available, it might be worthwhile to take a moment to define each of the major resources being used in Windows programs:

- *Menus* usually appear along the top of a main window; they give the user verbal or iconic options for manipulating the features of a program. It is increasingly common to see programmers making use of pop-up menus that float freely on the desktop.

- *Dialog boxes* (or simply *dialogs*) are special windows that usually contain edit boxes, buttons, radio buttons, check boxes, and other controls that enable the user to enter data or select features.

- *Bitmaps* are graphical objects, such as photographs, pictures, or drawings, that can be painted onto a window or dialog. These files have a predefined format and usually end with a .BMP extension.

- *Icons* are very much like bitmaps, but they always have a predefined size. When a program is minimized, its icon is usually visible on the Windows 95 taskbar.

- A *string table* is a list of strings that is kept in an easy-to-use format. String tables have many uses; Windows programs frequently store lists of error messages in string tables.

- *Fonts* are the character sets that are used to draw text or symbols on-screen. The complex world of fonts is explored next week, on Day 9, "Font Basics," Day 10, "Window Controls," and Day 11, "Talking to Controls." Unlike all the resources listed here, fonts are usually not stored in a resource file that is part of your executable.

- *Cursors* show where the mouse is located on-screen. The arrow cursor, hourglass cursor, and I-beam cursor are frequently used in Windows, but you can create any type of cursor you want, and display it at any time during the life of your program. Figure 6.1 shows icon and menu resources in a Windows environment.

The previously listed items are only the most common types of resources. Many other types have been created, and others will surely be created in the future. In fact, some companies sell libraries of custom resources. The point is that Windows resources are designed to be extensible tools; they are limited only by the imagination of Windows programmers.

This book doesn't spend much time exploring custom resources, because that subject can become very involved. However, the Emerson program shows you how to create a very simple custom resource that consists solely of one long string. The string is displayed on-screen as a poem. Although this is an elementary example, it should serve to show you the possibilities waiting to be tapped by inventive programmers.

This overview of resources marks the beginning of a freewheeling exploration of the many special

Figure 6.1.

Icon and menu resources play a big part in the Windows environment.

features available to Windows programmers. A good deal of creative thought went into the design of the Windows environment and into the programming heritage from which it sprang. Be prepared to reap the harvest.

Resource Scripts

There are several different ways to create resources. Perhaps the simplest and most powerful methods are achieved through the use of Borland's Resource Workshop (WORKSHOP.EXE) and Microsoft's App Studio (APSTUDIO.EXE). Both are first-rate tools that enable you to create menus, dialogs, and bitmaps simply by drawing them on-screen with a mouse.

Although App Studio and the Resource Workshop are helpful and easy to use, this book works mostly with resource scripts. These scripts usually have the letters RC or DLG appended as an extension. I use these scripts in part because they adapt themselves well to a written medium such as a book.

After being created, these scripts can be run through a special compiler, made by either Microsoft or Borland, in order to produce binary resource files. These binary files all have .RES as an extension.

Both App Studio and the Resource Workshop can produce either .RES files or .RC files. As a result, I sometimes find myself switching back and forth between editing resources visually with the Resource Workshop, and editing them manually as text files. You might want to experiment so you can find which techniques work best for you. To compare the results of your visual

programming experiments with the samples presented here in the text, simply view the textual .RC or .DLG files you have created.

The Emerson Program, Part I

By now, I imagine you're ready to take a look at the Emerson program's source code. So, without further ado, I'll cut straight to the good stuff. When working with this program, don't forget to start by copying to a new subdirectory the files used in making WINDOW1.EXE. Go through the files, and change the word Window1 to Emerson and rename the files from WINDOW1.* to EMERSON.*.

Taking these steps will save you a good deal of time and will familiarize you with proper Windows coding technique. In other words, you aren't supposed to start each program from scratch. Instead, it's expected that you'll copy blocks of code from one program to the next. Don't think of this as cheating; think of it as proper Windows programming technique.

Listings 6.1 through 6.7 show the code for the first version of the Emerson program. You'll see a full implementation of the code on Day 7.

Listing 6.1. The Emerson program shows you how to utilize resources.

```
// ====================================================
// Program Name: EMERSON
// Project: Teach Yourself Windows Programming
// Copyright (c) 1995 by Charlie Calvert
// Description: Part 1 of 2 part exploration of resources
// Update for WIN32: 05/29/95
// ====================================================

#define STRICT
#define WIN32_LEAN_AND_MEAN
#include <windows.h>
#include <windowsx.h>
#pragma hdrstop
#include "Fmerson.h"
#pragma warning (disable : 4068)
#pragma warning (disable : 4100)

static char szAppName[] = "Emerson";
static HINSTANCE hInstance;
static HANDLE hResource;

int ScrollWidth;
int MaxLines  = 21;
int Start = 33;
int TextHeight;
int PageSize;
int nPosition = 0;
```

Listing 6.1. continued

```
// ===============================================
// INITIALIZATION
// ===============================================

//////////////////////////////////////
// The WinMain function is the program entry point.
// Register the Window, Create it, enter the Message Loop.
// If either of the first two steps fail, then quit
//////////////////////////////////////
#pragma argsused
int WINAPI WinMain(HINSTANCE hInst, HINSTANCE hPrevInstance,
                   LPSTR  lpszCmdParam, int nCmdShow)
{
  MSG  Msg;

  if (!hPrevInstance)
    if (!Register(hInst))
      return FALSE;

  if (!Create(hInst, nCmdShow))
    return FALSE;

  while (GetMessage(&Msg, NULL, 0, 0))
  {
    TranslateMessage(&Msg);
    DispatchMessage(&Msg);
  }

  return Msg.wParam;
}


//////////////////////////////////////
//Register Window
//////////////////////////////////////
BOOL Register(HINSTANCE hInst)
{
  WNDCLASS WndClass;

  WndClass.style          = CS_HREDRAW | CS_VREDRAW;
  WndClass.lpfnWndProc    = WndProc;
  WndClass.cbClsExtra     = 0;
  WndClass.cbWndExtra     = 0;
  WndClass.hInstance      = hInst;
  WndClass.hIcon          = LoadIcon(hInst, "Icon");
  WndClass.hCursor        = LoadCursor(hInst, "Cursor");
  WndClass.hbrBackground  = (HBRUSH)(COLOR_WINDOW+1);
  WndClass.lpszMenuName   = "Menu";
  WndClass.lpszClassName  = szAppName;

  return RegisterClass (&WndClass);
}
```

```
/////////////////////////////////////
// Create the window and show it.
/////////////////////////////////////
BOOL Create(HINSTANCE hInst, int nCmdShow)
{

    hInstance = hInst;

    HWND hwnd = CreateWindow(szAppName, szAppName,
                        WS_OVERLAPPEDWINDOW,
                        CW_USEDEFAULT, CW_USEDEFAULT,
                        CW_USEDEFAULT, CW_USEDEFAULT,
                        NULL, NULL, hInst, NULL);

    if (hwnd == NULL)
      return FALSE;

    ShowWindow(hwnd, nCmdShow);
    UpdateWindow(hwnd);

    return TRUE;
}


//=================================================
// IMPLEMENTATION
//=================================================


/////////////////////////////////////
// The window proc helps control the program at runtime
/////////////////////////////////////
LRESULT CALLBACK EXPORT16 WndProc(HWND hwnd, UINT Message,
                          WPARAM wParam, LPARAM lParam)
{
  switch(Message)
  {
    HANDLE_MSG(hwnd, WM_CREATE, Emerson_OnCreate);
    HANDLE_MSG(hwnd, WM_DESTROY, Emerson_OnDestroy);
    HANDLE_MSG(hwnd, WM_COMMAND, Emerson_OnCommand);
    HANDLE_MSG(hwnd, WM_PAINT, Emerson_OnPaint);
    default:
      return Emerson_DefProc(hwnd, Message, wParam, lParam);
  }
}


/////////////////////////////////////
// Create Window
// Load the Bitmap from resource
/////////////////////////////////////
#pragma argsused
BOOL Emerson_OnCreate(HWND hwnd, CREATESTRUCT FAR*
lpCreateStruct)
{
  hResource = LoadResource(hInstance,
              FindResource(hInstance, "Brahma", "CUSTOM"));
  return TRUE;
}
```

6

continues

Listing 6.1. continued

```
/////////////////////////////////////
// Destructor
// Delete Bitmap from memory
/////////////////////////////////////
#pragma argsused
void Emerson_OnDestroy(HWND hwnd)
{
  FreeResource(hResource);
  PostQuitMessage(0);
}


/////////////////////////////////////
//  The Emerson Dialog Procedure controls the dialog
/////////////////////////////////////
#pragma argsused
void Emerson_OnCommand(HWND hwnd, int id, HWND hwndCtl,
                       UINT codeNotify)
{
  switch(id)
  {
    case CM_ABOUT:
      NotYetAvailable(hwnd);
      break;

    case CM_BITMAP:
      NotYetAvailable(hwnd);
      break;

    case CM_BRAHMIN:
      NotYetAvailable(hwnd);
      break;

    case CM_WOODNOTES:
      NotYetAvailable(hwnd);
      break;

    case CM_SEASHORE:
      NotYetAvailable(hwnd);
      break;
  }
}

/////////////////////////////////////
// Handle WM_PAINT
// Paint a bunch of copies of TheBitmap
/////////////////////////////////////
void Emerson_OnPaint(HWND hwnd)
{
  PAINTSTRUCT PaintStruct;
  char far *Poem;
  RECT Rect;

  HDC PaintDC = BeginPaint(hwnd, &PaintStruct);

  SetBkMode(PaintDC, TRANSPARENT);
```

```
  Poem = (char far *)LockResource(hResource);
  GetClientRect(hwnd, &Rect);
  Rect.left += 10;
  Rect.top += 10;
  DrawText(PaintDC, Poem, -1, &Rect, DT_EXTERNALLEADING);
  GlobalUnlock(hResource);

  EndPaint(hwnd, &PaintStruct);
}


/////////////////////////////////////
// NotYetAvailable
/////////////////////////////////////
void NotYetAvailable(HWND hwnd)
{
  MessageBox(hwnd, "Not yet available",
             "Under Construction", MB_OK);
}
```

Listing 6.2. EMERSON.H.

```
// ================================================
// Name: EMERSON.H
// Programmer: Charlie Calvert
// Description: Header file for EMERSON.CPP
// ================================================

// macros
#define CM_ABOUT 101
#define CM_BITMAP 201
#define CM_BRAHMIN 202
#define CM_WOODNOTES 203
#define CM_SEASHORE 204

#if !defined(__WIN32__) && !defined(_WIN32)
#define EXPORT16 __export
#else
#define EXPORT16
#endif

// The Emerson Class
#define Emerson_DefProc    DefWindowProc
BOOL Emerson_OnCreate(HWND hwnd, CREATESTRUCT FAR* lpCreateStruct);
void Emerson_OnDestroy(HWND hwnd);
void Emerson_OnCommand(HWND hwnd, int id, HWND hwndCtl, UINT codeNotify);
void Emerson_OnPaint(HWND hwnd);

// Some procs
BOOL Register(HINSTANCE hInstance);
BOOL Create(HINSTANCE hInstance, int nCmdShow);
void NotYetAvailable(HWND hwnd);
LRESULT CALLBACK EXPORT16 WndProc(HWND hWindow, UINT Message,
                        WPARAM wParam, LPARAM lParam);
```

Listing 6.3. EMERSON.RC.

```
#define WIN32_LEAN_AND_MEAN
#include <windows.h>
#include "Emerson.h"

/*   The Emerson Menu      */
Menu MENU
BEGIN
  POPUP "Poems"
  BEGIN
    MENUITEM "Bitmap", CM_BITMAP
    MENUITEM "Brahmin", CM_BRAHMIN
    MENUITEM "Woodnotes", CM_WOODNOTES
    MENUITEM "SeaShore", CM_SEASHORE
  END
  MENUITEM "&About", CM_ABOUT
END


/*   The Emerson Icon      */
Icon ICON "Emerson.ico"

/*   The Emerson Cursor    */
Cursor CURSOR "emerson.cur"

/*   The Emerson Poem      */
Brahma CUSTOM Brahma.txt
```

EMERSON.ICO (32×32)   *EMERSON.CUR (32×32)*

Listing 6.4. A text file that contains the Emerson poem.

```
 1: Brahma
 2: by Ralph Waldo Emerson
 3:
 4: If the red slayer think he slays
 5:   Or if the slain think he is slain,
 6: They know not well the subtle ways
 7:   I keep and pass and turn again.
 8:
 9: Far or forget to me is near;
10:   Shadow and sunlight are the same;
11: The vanished gods to me appear;
12:   And one to me are shame and fame.
13:
14: They reckon ill who leave me out
15:   When me they fly, I am the wings;
```

```
16: I am the doubter and the doubt,
17:    And I the hymn the Brahmin sings.
18:
19: The strong gods pine for my abode,
20:    And pine in vain the sacred Seven;
21: But thou, meek lover of the good!
22:    Find me, and turn thy back on heaven.
```

Listing 6.5. EMERSON.DEF.

```
;   EMERSON.DEF
NAME            Emerson
DESCRIPTION     'Emerson example'
CODE            PRELOAD MOVEABLE DISCARDABLE
DATA            PRELOAD MOVEABLE MULTIPLE
HEAPSIZE        4096
STACKSIZE       8192
```

Listing 6.6. The Borland Emerson makefile: EMERSON.MAK.

```
# EMERSON.MAK
!if !$d(BCROOT)
BCROOT  = $(MAKEDIR)
!endif

APPNAME = EMERSON
INCPATH = $(BCROOT)\INCLUDE
LIBPATH = $(BCROOT)\LIB

!if $d(WIN16)
COMPILER= BCC.EXE
BRC= BRC.EXE
FLAGS   = -W -ml -v -w4 -I$(INCPATH) -L$(LIBPATH)
!else
COMPILER= BCC32.EXE
BRC= BRC32.EXE
FLAGS   = -W -v -w4 -I$(INCPATH) -L$(LIBPATH)
!endif

# linking
$(APPNAME).exe: $(APPNAME).Obj $(APPNAME).Def $(APPNAME).Res
  $(COMPILER) $(FLAGS) $(APPNAME).obj
  $(BRC)  -I$(INCPATH) $(APPNAME).res

# compiling
$(APPNAME).obj: $(APPNAME).cpp
  $(COMPILER) -c $(FLAGS) $(APPNAME).cpp

# resource
$(APPNAME).res: $(APPNAME).rc
  $(BRC) -R -I$(INCPATH) $(APPNAME).RC
```

6

Listing 6.7. The Microsoft Emerson makefile: EMERSON.MAK.

```
#-------------------------------------------------
# EMERSOMS.MAK
# Microsoft WIN32 makefile
#-------------------------------------------------
APPNAME=EMERSON
TARGETOS=WIN95
APPVER=4.0
OBJS=$(APPNAME).OBJ

!include <win32.mak>

all: $(APPNAME).exe

# Update the resource if necessary

$(APPNAME).res: $(APPNAME).rc $(APPNAME).h
  $(rc) $(rcflags) $(rcvars) $(APPNAME).rc

# Update the object files if necessary

# compile
.cpp.obj:
  $(cc) $(cflags) $(cvars) $(cdebug) $<

# Update the executable file if necessary.

$(APPNAME).exe: $(OBJS) $(APPNAME).res
  $(link) $(linkdebug) $(guiflags) -out:$(APPNAME).exe \
  $(OBJS) $(APPNAME).res $(guilibs) comctl32.lib
```

Here are some salient facts about the Emerson program:

☐ It has a custom cursor.

☐ It displays a poem, as shown in Figure 6.2.

☐ A simple menu is at the top of the program. If you select any of the Emerson menu options, you are informed that the program is not yet complete.

☐ When you minimize the program, it displays a custom icon.

Looking Ahead

The key to understanding resources is the RC file, which is listed in its entirety in the previous code listings. Most of the rest of this chapter is devoted to analyzing that file and to seeing how you can use its pieces in your program. In particular, I do the following:

☐ Describe the resource compilers

☐ Take a reasonably in-depth look at menus

☐ Devote a few paragraphs to the program's icon

☐ Devote a few more to its cursor

☐ Wind up the chapter by talking about displaying a custom resource

Figure 6.2.

The EMERSON.EXE program. The book in the upper-right corner of the main window is the program's cursor.

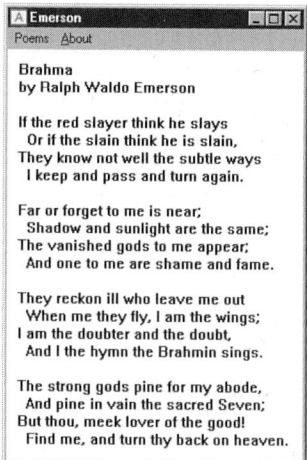

Day 7 includes an exploration of dialogs, bitmaps, and string resources.

The subject matter included in this chapter (and the next) is hardly an exhaustive exploration of resources, but it should be enough to get you started working with these useful tools. As this book progresses, other important facts about resources are explored in a natural way, when the subject arises.

Using the Resource Compiler

When learning about resources, the place to begin is with an overview of the resource compiler. You use the resource compiler to process RC scripts.

If you are using App Studio and the Resource Workshop, you don't normally have to go to the DOS prompt and explicitly run the resource compiler. Borland and Microsoft tools perform this chore for you. You should, however, understand that at some point something has to be compiled somewhere, even if you don't ever explicitly undertake the chore. In particular, you should know about the resource compiler if you like to create makefiles and work from the command prompt.

Here's the nub of the matter: After you've completed an RC file, you can compile it from the command line using Microsoft's Resource Compiler (RC.EXE) or the Borland Resource Compiler (BRC.EXE). The commands for using either compiler are essentially identical, but I've chosen to give examples of how to use Microsoft's tool. Borlanders can follow along by putting a *b* in front of the letters *rc*.

Here is the syntax to use when you want to compile an RC file into a RES file:

```
brc -r -ic:\bc\include emerson.rc
```

The result of executing this line should be a file called EMERSON.RES. If you get a bunch of error messages instead, you might want to compare your work again with the file listing shown previously.

While I'm on the subject, I'll list the most important options available to you while using the resource compiler. Suppose you have a precompiled executable file, called EMERSON.EXE, to which you want to add a resource. To do so, you need only type the following at the DOS prompt:

```
rc EMERSON.RC EMERSON.EXE
```

Or, if the RES file already exists, you can type

```
rc EMERSON.RES EMERSON.EXE
```

It turns out that in both of these examples it isn't necessary to enter the name of the executable file, because it shares the same name as the resource. As a result, you could type either

```
rc EMERSON.RC
```

or

```
rc EMERSON.RES
```

in lieu of the first two examples.

Of course, most of the time you'll probably not be using the resource compiler directly from the command line; you'll be calling it from the IDE, or from a project file or makefile (such as the Microsoft EMERSON.MAK text file used to generate EMERSON.EXE). A quick glance at this makefile reveals that it contains syntax not included in the makefile from Day 2, "Building Projects, Creating Windows," and Day 3, "A Standard Windows Program."

Most significant are the explicit rules for compiling the resource itself. Notice that at the bottom of the file, I've passed the -r parameter to the resource compiler, thereby instructing it to build a RES file without combining it with an executable file. The opposite approach is taken in the linking phase, which combines EMERSON.EXE with EMERSON.RC. In that case, you omit the -r parameter.

> **Note:** Borland users take a nearly identical approach to adding resource logic to their makefiles. In other words, a quick comparison of the Borland and Microsoft makefiles for the Emerson program reveals that both companies use the exact same syntax when adding resources to a project. Hurrah! The only curve ball you need to watch for is that Microsoft calls its resource compiler RC.EXE, while Borland opts for BRC.EXE.

Before plunging into a description of menus, I probably ought to make a brief reference to the `include` statements at the top of the RC file:

```
#include <windows.h>
#include "Emerson.h"
```

The EMERSON.H header file at the top of EMERSON.RC is brought in solely because it contains, among other things, the following constant:

```
#define CM_ABOUT    101
```

This constant is linked to the Emerson menu choice, and it's used to notify the program that the user wants to see the About dialog. The constant quite literally is sent to the program's main window procedure as part of a message whenever the Emerson menu item is chosen. Your job is to teach the Emerson program to respond properly when the number arrives at the `WndProc`.

You often need to include WINDOWS.H at the top of a resource script. This is done because various constants need to be accessed by the resource compiler. For instance, if you do not include WINDOWS.H in the RC file, Microsoft's compiler gives you the following message at compile time:

```
ABOUT.RC(18): error RW2001: undefined keyword: DS_MODALFRAME
```

BRC won't give you the error because Borland's tool already knows about the definitions in WINDOWS.H. As a result, Borland users don't need to include the file in their resources, or wait for it to be compiled during each build. However, it does no real harm to stick it in there, and it helps make your code compatible with the Microsoft way of doing things.

Creating a Simple Menu

In this section I'll explain how to create and name a menu. In the next section you'll see how to create the body of the menu.

Here is the code that creates the menu for the Emerson program:

```
5: Menu MENU
6: BEGIN
7:   POPUP "Poems"
8:   BEGIN
9:     MENUITEM "Bitmap", CM_BITMAP
10:     MENUITEM "Brahmin", CM_BRAHMIN
11:     MENUITEM "Woodnotes", CM_WOODNOTES
12:     MENUITEM "SeaShore", CM_SEASHORE
13:   END
14:   MENUITEM "&About", CM_ABOUT
15: END
```

EMERSON.RC obviously contains code that isn't going to be understood by a C compiler. Instead, it can be compiled by either RC.EXE or BRC.EXE.

Though written in a language you haven't seen before, the code for EMERSON.RC is simple enough that it shouldn't cause you any serious problems. The script begins by supplying both the name and the type of the resource to be used, as shown in line 5. This line says the resource is a menu, and its name is Menu. The menu can have almost any name. For instance, the following line also is valid:

```
ABOUT_MENU MENU
```

In the `Register` function, Emerson passes the menu name to the `WndClass` structure:

```
WndClass.lpszMenuName    = "Menu";
```

The name is your handle to this resource. It associates a menu with the program's main window. You don't need to do anything else to make the menu appear. All the dirty work is handled internally by Windows, without any assistance on your part.

Sometimes, programmers prefer to save memory by assigning a number, instead of a written name, to a menu:

```
125 MENU
BEGIN
  MENUITEM "Emerson", CM_ABOUT
END
```

Doing things this way forces you to take a slightly different approach to the `Register` function. For instance, if you had associated the number 125 with your menu, you could load it with the following line of code:

```
WndClass.lpszMenuName    = "#125";
```

Programmers sometimes accidentally associate a numeric identifier with a resource, even when they are trying to use a string as an identifier. In other words, they do something like this in their resource script:

```
#define MYMENU 125

MYMENU MENU
BEGIN
  MENUITEM "Emerson", CM_ABOUT
END
```

Then they accidentally try to associate the string MYMENU with the appropriate field in the WndClass structure:

```
WndClass.lpszMenuName    = "MYMENU";
```

This isn't going to work, because no such string is associated with a menu in the resource file. To correct the problem, you could write

```
WndClass.lpszMenuName = MAKEINTRESOURCE(MYMENU);
```

The MAKEINTRESOURCE macro converts numeric identifiers into something Windows' resources management facilities can understand. If you want to know more about MAKEINTRESOURCE, you can look it up in WINDOWS.H. For now, all you really need to know is that MAKEINTRESOURCE is an alternative to writing the "#125" syntax.

The act of naming a menu is one of those situations in which the number of options Windows gives you can make a relatively trivial operation appear difficult. But remember, to create a menu you need to do the following:

☐ Give a name to a menu resource.

☐ Assign that name to the appropriate field of the WndClass structure.

All this other stuff about numeric identifiers and MAKEINTRESOURCE is just icing on the cake. You don't have to use any of that unless you are desperate to save memory. My advice (even in those circumstances) is to think twice, or even three times, before abandoning the clarity of the string-based menu-naming technique. Get a working version of your program up and running first, then start worrying about optimization!

Designing Menus

So far, you have seen how to name a menu and how to make it appear on the screen. The next step is to see how to design the body of the menu. In other words, I want to talk some about what takes place within the BEGIN...END pair in the body of a menu definition.

The menu for the Emerson program consists of two separate parts, as shown in Figure 6.3.

Figure 6.3.
The first part of the Emerson menu is a pop-up; the second is a lone menu item.

```
MENU_1 MENU
BEGIN

    POPUP "Poems"
    BEGIN
      MENUITEM "Bitmap", CM_BITMAP
      MENUITEM "Brahmin", CM_BRAHMIN
      MENUITEM "Woodnotes", CM_WOODNOTES
      MENUITEM "SeaShore", CM_SEASHORE
    END

    MENUITEM "&About", CM_ABOUT

END
```

If the pop-up menu were removed from the Emerson program, the resource file for the menu would be very simple:

```
Menu MENU
BEGIN
  MENUITEM "About", CM_ABOUT
END
```

These few lines of code produce the menu shown in Figure 6.4.

Figure 6.4.

A close-up of a simplified version of the menu from the Emerson program.

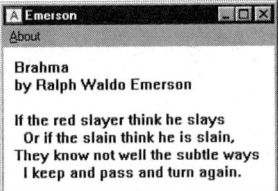

The following line of code defines the appearance of the very simple menu shown in Figure 6.4:

```
MENUITEM "About", CM_ABOUT
```

MENUITEM is a single entry in a menu, whereas POPUP is an entire window (such as the pop-up list that appears when you open the File menu in many major applications). After the MENUITEM declaration, the actual string to be shown in the menu is spelled out in quotes; finally, the constant to be associated with the menu item is declared.

This is a very simple language. For instance, if you want to add extra items to the menu, you can insert additional lines between the BEGIN...END pair and define constants to be associated with each new menu item:

```
/* EMERSON1.RC */
#define CM_DIALOG1 101;
#define CM_DIALOG2 102;
#define CM_DIALOG3 103;

MENU_1 MENU
BEGIN
  MENUITEM "Dialog1", CM_DIALOG1
  MENUITEM "Dialog2", CM_DIALOG2
  MENUITEM "Dialog3", CM_DIALOG3
END
```

This new resource file would create a menu like the one shown in Figure 6.5.

Figure 6.5.

The menu created by a modified version of EMERSON1.RC.

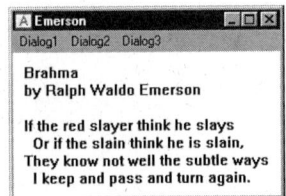

DO	DON'T

DO take a moment to notice the range of constants defined in the previous example file. The first item is defined as 101, but it could just as easily have been any positive unsigned integer. I chose 101 from force of habit.

DO choose integer values between 1 and 64KB for the constants used in your menus. Regardless of my predilections, some programmers think it best to avoid integers lower than 256 (0x100), because they may have a different significance in a Windows program.

DO associate an identifier with each menu item. For instance, I have associated `CM_DIALOG1`, `CM_DIALOG2`, and `CM_DIALOG3` with the menu items in the previous example. These names make your code easier to read and help you avoid dumb mistakes.

DON'T use the same number twice, unless you are absolutely sure you know what you are doing. If you try to use the same number for two different menu items, trouble is bound to ensue.

Working with Pop-up Menus

Pop-up menus are the standard drop-down menus you see at the top of most programs, such as the File menu at the top of your compiler.

The following bit of code produces the pop-up menu shown in Figure 6.6:

```
POPUP "Poems"
BEGIN
  MENUITEM "Bitmap", CM_BITMAP
  MENUITEM "Brahmin", CM_BRAHMIN
  MENUITEM "Woodnotes", CM_WOODNOTES
  MENUITEM "SeaShore", CM_SEASHORE
END
```

Figure 6.6.

A pop-up menu is activated when you click the menu bar. It's really just a window with text in it.

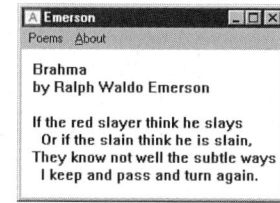

As you can see, a pop-up menu consists of a title line that is visible on the menu bar, and a set of menu items grouped together between a BEGIN...END pair. The menu items are what you see when the pop-up menu is activated. Note that each menu item is associated with a constant defined in EMERSON.H. These constants are sent to the program's WndProc when a menu selection is made by the user.

Responding to Menu Choices

When a particular menu item is selected by the user, the constant associated with that menu item is sent to the program's WndProc. Both the menu item and its associated constant arrive packaged in the form of a WM_COMMAND messages. As a result, they are handled by Emerson_OnCommand:

```
150: void Emerson_OnCommand(HWND hwnd, int id, HWND hwndCtl, UINT
                           codeNotify)
151: {
152:   switch(id)
153:   {
154:     case CM_ABOUT:
155:       NotYetAvailable(hwnd);
156:       break;
157:
158:     case CM_BITMAP:
159:       NotYetAvailable(hwnd);
160:       break;
161:
162:     case CM_BRAHMIN:
163:       NotYetAvailable(hwnd);
164:       break;
165:
166:     case CM_WOODNOTES:
167:       NotYetAvailable(hwnd);
168:       break;
169:
170:     case CM_SEASHORE:
171:       NotYetAvailable(hwnd);
172:       break;
173:   }
174: }
```

As you can see, a simple case statement enables the Emerson program to deal with each menu item. At this stage in the program's development, the response to menu selection is simply to pop up a MessageBox stating that the feature hasn't been implemented. The details of this implementation are filled in during the course of Day 7.

 **Note:** If you aren't using WindowsX, you can look in the LOWORD(wParam) argument sent to WndProc to determine the ID of the selected menu item. This is the same value passed on in the id field of Cls_OnCommand.

For now, I won't describe anything else about menus. If you want a more detailed description, you can skip ahead to Day 20, "Menus and Icons in Depth."

Adding an Icon and a Cursor to EMERSON.CPP

The only sensible way to create an icon is to use a tool such as App Studio or the Resource Workshop. While working with either product, the actual act of creating an icon is reduced to the enjoyable job of drawing a picture with the mouse.

> **Note:** Let's face it—drawing an icon doesn't demand the same kind of intellectual rigor that's inherent in even relatively simple programming chores. As a result, I'm not going to explain how to use the Resource Workshop or App Studio to perform this chore. Most readers will probably be able to figure that out with no more than a quick glance at the manual.
>
> This does not mean, however, that it's not important to take the time to create effective icons. The point is that even if you are the type of obsessive workaholic who insists on working yourself to the edge of utter distraction every single day of your life (that is, even if you are an ordinary programmer), you need to set aside time to enjoy yourself while you are engaged in the essential job of creating icons. If you don't, people won't respect your application. Users put incredible weight on seemingly trivial details—such as the appearance of icons.
>
> If the whole thing seems too much for you, or if you flunked Art 101, then you should probably hire someone who can do the work for you. What you are looking for is an artist, and artists are much less expensive to hire than programmers.

After you create your icon, you can add it to your project through a simple two-step process:

1. Add the following line to your RC file:

   ```
   Emerson ICON "Emerson.ico"
   ```

2. In your `Register` method, set the `WndClass.hIcon` field to your icon with this line of code:

   ```
   WndClass.hIcon = LoadIcon(hInst, "Emerson");
   ```

Take a moment to compare the preceding line from the `Register` method to the line used on Day 3, "A Standard Windows Program," Day 4, "Messages, WindowsX, and Painting Text," and Day 5, "The Mouse and the Keyboard":

```
WndClass.hIcon = LoadIcon(NULL, IDI_APPLICATION);
```

The differences here stem from the fact that the latter example loads a predefined Windows resource, and the former example loads a custom resource.

When loading a custom icon, set the first field of LoadIcon to the hInstance of the program that contains the icon resource; set the second field to the name of the icon. In most cases, the program that contains the icon you want to use is the current program, so all you need to do is pass in the global hInstance from your app.

When loading a predefined Windows resource, set the first field of LoadIcon to NULL and then specify the appropriate resource identifier in the second field. As mentioned earlier, predefined Windows resources are listed in WINDOWS.H:

```
#define IDI_APPLICATION      MAKEINTRESOURCE(32512)
#define IDI_HAND             MAKEINTRESOURCE(32513)
#define IDI_QUESTION         MAKEINTRESOURCE(32514)
#define IDI_EXCLAMATION      MAKEINTRESOURCE(32515)
#define IDI_ASTERISK         MAKEINTRESOURCE(32516)
```

If you think about it, the differences between these two approaches are not nearly as arbitrary as they might seem. Normally, you have to specify the HINSTANCE of the application where the icon resource resides. Built-in Windows resources, however, don't really belong to any application. They are just part of the system. As a result, you don't need to pass in an HINSTANCE; instead, you can pass in NULL.

After the previous explanation of creating icons, it's easy to move on to a discussion of cursors. Once again, you should start by carefully defining the cursor in the Resource Workshop or App Studio.

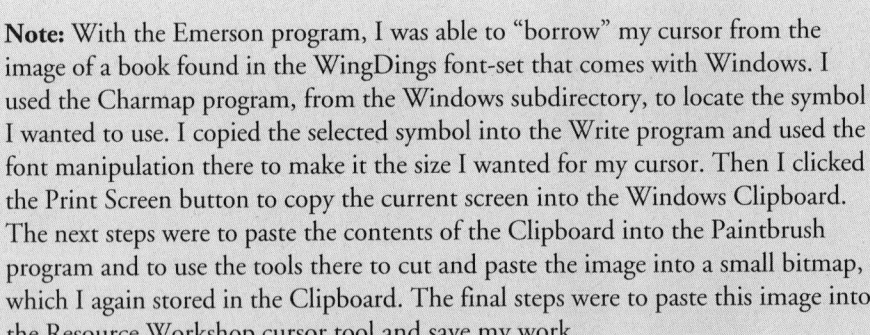

Note: With the Emerson program, I was able to "borrow" my cursor from the image of a book found in the WingDings font-set that comes with Windows. I used the Charmap program, from the Windows subdirectory, to locate the symbol I wanted to use. I copied the selected symbol into the Write program and used the font manipulation there to make it the size I wanted for my cursor. Then I clicked the Print Screen button to copy the current screen into the Windows Clipboard. The next steps were to paste the contents of the Clipboard into the Paintbrush program and to use the tools there to cut and paste the image into a small bitmap, which I again stored in the Clipboard. The final steps were to paste this image into the Resource Workshop cursor tool and save my work.

It sounds pretty complicated when I describe it like that. However, the whole process took only a few minutes—whereas it undoubtedly would have taken me several hours to create the image on my own.

One reason I tell you this story is that it shows the way Windows apps can work together to create a new kind of tool, with functionality that transcends the capabilities of any one application.

After you have created your cursor, you can link it into your application through the `Register` function. You can do this with the following line of code:

```
WndClass.hCursor = LoadCursor(hInst, "Cursor");
```

Once again, you should compare this line with the methods shown in earlier chapters:

```
WndClass.hCursor = LoadCursor(NULL, IDC_ARROW);
```

Clearly, the same rules that dictate the loading of an icon also dictate the loading of cursors.

DO	DON'T

DO pass the program's HINSTANCE as the first parameter to LoadCursor or LoadIcon if you are loading a custom cursor or custom icon.

DON'T pass the program's HINSTANCE to LoadCursor or LoadIcon if you are loading a system resource defined by one of the constants in WINDOWS.H.

That's all there is to it. From a technical standpoint, it's simple to add an icon or cursor to your program. However, icons and cursors can be used in ways that are a bit complex. These include drawing icons in a dialog, painting icons on a window, and switching cursors at runtime. Because these processes are more advanced, and less frequently used, I describe them on Day 20.

User-Defined Resources

I said earlier that you can create your own types of resources if you so desire. In the Emerson program, this technique is used to make a resource out of a text file.

The hot tip to grasp here is that Windows enables programmers to store raw data in a resource file. This data can assume any shape or format that you might find useful. To load this resource into your program, just retrieve a pointer to this data through the `LoadResource` function. After it turns over the pointer, Windows washes its hands of the whole episode and lets you do what you want with the binary data it gave you.

In effect, this means that anything you can store in memory can be placed in a resource file and retrieved through the `LoadResource` command. This obviously opens up an incredible range of possibilities for programmers who are willing to do a little creative work.

In this particular case, I don't want to get involved in anything very fancy, so Emerson uses a simple text resource, containing a poem that can easily be loaded from disk and displayed on-screen. By now, it should come as no surprise to hear that this process is started by defining the resource in an RC file.

6

To define the resource, simply type a text file and save it to disk. After creating the file, you can instruct Windows to store it in a RES file by entering the following line in EMERSON.RC:

```
Brahma CUSTOM Brahma.txt
```

This line follows the same format you saw when defining a cursor, bitmap, or icon in a resource file. In other words

- ☐ Give the resource a name, which in this case is Brahma.

- ☐ Give the resource a type. I have called this type CUSTOM, because it is a custom resource. In Windows 3.1, I could just as easily, however, have used the word POEM, the word TEXT, or the word FOOBAR. WIN32 is a little more fussy, however, so you should use the word CUSTOM.

- ☐ The final step is to list the name of the file I want to include in my program. Obviously, Windows treats this file as nothing more than an array of binary data. It doesn't care what is inside the file.

These steps ensure that after compiling the Emerson program, the resulting executable file contains a copy of the Brahma poem. The only chore left, then, is to load the poem from disk and into memory. This is done by calling FindResource and LoadResource in response to a WM_CREATE message:

```
hResource = LoadResource(hInstance,
            FindResource(hInstance, "Brahma", "TEXT"));
```

By now, the previous lines should be pretty much self-explanatory. The program simply passes in the HINSTANCE of the executable file that contains the resource, and then tells FindResource the name of the resource and its type. FindResource literally scans through the executable file to find the resource. After locating the resource, FindResource passes the resource's handle to LoadResource, which then physically moves the object into memory.

Note: In its literature, Microsoft states that LoadIcon and LoadCursor both call LoadResource and FindResource. In other words, the process described does little more than explicitly perform chores normally carried out by higher-level functions.

After you load the resource, you need to lock down the memory involved before you use it:

```
Poem = (char far *)LockResource(hResource);
```

As you can see, the Emerson program also typecasts the pointer returned by LoadResource. As a result of the typecast, the code now directly addresses the binary data returned by LockResource as if it were a string. Of course, this works out fine, because the data could indeed be thought of as nothing more than a long string saved into a text file. (The use of far obviously has no significance in WIN32, but it doesn't hurt to leave it in there if you want to preserve WIN16 compatibility.)

The Emerson program is now free to draw the string to the screen so that the user can view the poem. This is a two-step process that involves first obtaining the dimensions of the main window and then calling DrawText to fill the window with the poem.

After the text is displayed, the program is free to unlock the data and go about its business:

```
GlobalUnlock(hResource);
```

The act of unlocking the memory doesn't mean that the object has been destroyed. It only means that the memory is no longer locked down.

To completely free the resource, you need to explicitly call FreeResource, most likely in response to the WM_DESTROY message:

```
FreeResource(hResource)
```

It turns out, however, that this isn't absolutely necessary, because the memory will automatically be deallocated when the program ends.

Custom Resources: Additional Thoughts

I'm going to add a few more comments in this section, but you needn't get too bogged down in this material if it doesn't interest you. I present it mainly because some readers might be curious.

When a WIN16 program is first loaded into memory, its resources are not necessarily loaded along with it. This is possible because the format for executables has been completely redefined since the days when DOS was king. These files are now based on what is called the New Executable (NE) format. One of the features of this new type of file is the ability to coexist with, and to offer support for, resources.

If, for some reason, a WIN16 programmer didn't want the Brahma poem to remain on disk after the executable is loaded, you could specifically mark it PRELOAD:

```
Brahma TEXT PRELOAD FIXED Brahma.txt
```

As a result, it will be loaded into memory when the program is loaded into memory. That is, it will be *preloaded* before the call to LoadResource is made. Most of the time, however, memory considerations tempt programmers to keep resources on disk until they explicitly load them.

In WIN32, an entire executable file is loaded into a memory-mapped file, and then its threads are executed. This changes the dynamics of the situation described above, because the entire file can be paged in and out of memory as needed. In other words, the memory mapped file for the entire executable is set up, and the file is mapped in and out of memory as necessary. This means that terms such as PRELOAD and FIXED have no significance in WIN32. It doesn't do any harm to use them, and the compiler will accept them without complaint. However, they don't have any meaning inside the WIN32 environment, since the entire model on which they are based has disappeared. This is one of the points where you can see how radically different WIN32 is from WIN16. From many perspectives, 32-bit programs that run under Windows 95 and Windows NT are totally different beasts from programs that run in Windows 3.1. Windows 95 may feel a lot like Windows 3.1, but underneath the hood things are very different.

The Emerson program loads resources into memory by calling first FindResource and then LoadResource. This doesn't mean, however, that the resource is now permanently ensconced in memory. Windows regards resources as DISCARDABLE unless they are explicitly marked as FIXED, per the previous example.

DISCARDABLE objects can be shuffled off to the hard disk if Windows feels that other dynamic objects have more significance. If the Brahma resource is discarded, it must be laboriously reloaded back into memory when LockResource is called. The logic for doing this is built into LockResource, and the result of the function guarantees that the Brahma resource won't be moved or discarded until you call either UnlockResource or GlobalUnlock. In other words, if LoadResource is called, and it finds that the Brahma resource has been discarded, the program first reloads the Brahma resource from disk and then locks it in place. While locked, it can't be moved or shuffled back onto disk. This is a useful state of affairs, but not one that you want to prevail for a lengthy period of time. As a result, it's important to call GlobalUnlock as soon as possible after locking a resource and displaying it on-screen.

I hope this discussion clears up the difference between calling GlobalUnlock and calling FreeResource. The former call only gives Windows permission to move or discard the memory, whereas FreeResource explicitly tells Windows to deallocate the memory associated with the resource.

There is one final twist to this tale, which I might as well relate, now that I've gone this far. As you know, Windows can load multiple copies of a program into memory. It doesn't, however, normally load multiple copies of a program's resources into memory. In other words, if three

copies of the Emerson program are in memory, they all use the same copy of the Brahma custom resource. To accommodate this situation, Windows increments a flag when LoadResource is called and then decrements a flag when FreeResource is called. The memory for any particular resource is never really freed until a call to FreeResource decrements this flag back to zero. Therefore, the resource is available as long as a copy of the Emerson program is in memory.

As you can tell from the last few paragraphs, a good deal is going on behind the scenes that wasn't covered in my five-minute intro to custom resources. I want to stress, however, that you don't need to understand all of this in order to simply use a basic custom TEXT resource in your program. I've included this additional information for two related reasons:

1. Some people never really feel comfortable with a technique until they have not only a mechanical understanding of a subject but also a conceptual understanding.

2. If I'm going to give a real introduction to resources, I need to pull back the curtain a little bit so you can see the little man behind the scenes who tweaks the levers and pushes the buttons. Until you meet him, you haven't really had a thorough tour of the premises.

Summary

This chapter presents an introduction to resources. You have seen that resources are visual or logical elements that can be added to a program through a series of usually straightforward steps. You have also learned that resources are defined in an RC file, compiled into a RES file, and finally merged with the program's executable file.

Menus are among the resources specifically covered. You have learned how to assign a constant to a particular menu item, and you've seen that when a menu item is selected, these constants are sent to the WndProc in the form of a WM_COMMAND message. You have seen that inside the Emerson_OnCommand function each of these constants can be responded to in turn.

The discussion of icons and cursors shows the difference between resources that belong to the system and resources that are loaded from a disk. In the former case, you can specify NULL as the first parameter to LoadResource or LoadIcon. In the latter case, the program's HINSTANCE is required in the first parameter.

The last two sections in this chapter cover custom resources. That discussion ends with an overview of how Windows handles the memory associated with a resource.

Day 7 continues this discussion by examining bitmaps, dialogs, and string resources. See you there!

Q&A

Q **I'm confused by all these different compilers. What exactly are the differences between RC.EXE, BRC.EXE, WORKSHOP.EXE, APSTUDIO.EXE, and my compiler?**

A In the beginning, there was only one compiler, which was used "simply" to compile your C source code. When the idea of adding resources came along, Microsoft built RC.EXE, which can compile RC files and add them to a New Executable type file. BRC is simply Borland's clone of the Microsoft tool. After people had been working with resources for a while, it became clear that the creation of resources could be greatly simplified by enabling programmers to simply draw their elements on the screen. Hence, tools such as the Resource Workshop and App Studio were born. To make these tools more powerful, compiler makers gave them the capability to either call RC.EXE or to perform the same chores that RC.EXE performs. To bring things full circle, I should perhaps add that all of this activity regarding resources is separate from the chores performed by your basic C or C++ compiler.

Q **What's the difference between `UnlockResource` and `GlobalUnlock`?**

A `UnlockResource` is really just a macro that calls `GlobalUnlock` to do the real work. `GlobalUnlock` is most often used with the functions `GlobalAlloc`, `GlobalLock`, and `GlobalFree`. These functions are used for allocating memory, similar to the way that DOS C compilers use the `malloc` function to allocate memory. When using `GlobalAlloc`, it traditionally has been necessary to lock the memory before using it— just as you need to lock down a custom resource before using it.

Q **So who is this Emerson dude anyway?**

A Ralph Waldo Emerson, a native of New England, was born in 1803 and died in 1882. Early in his life, he was a minister in the Unitarian Church, but he later became one of the foremost proponents of Transcendentalism. He is remembered most often for his essays, but some people also have found value in his poetry. Walt Whitman regarded Emerson as a major influence.

Workshop

The Workshop provides quiz questions to help you solidify your understanding of the material covered and exercises to provide you with experience in using what you've learned. Try to understand the quiz and exercise answers before continuing on to Day 7. Answers are provided in Appendix A.

Quiz

1. How do you tell the resource compiler (RC.EXE) to convert the EMERSON.RC file into a RES file?

2. How do you tell the resource compiler to combine EMERSON.RES and EMERSON.EXE into one file?

3. In the following statement, what is the significance of the term CM_ABOUT?

   ```
   MENUITEM "About", CM_ABOUT
   ```

4. What is the difference between a pop-up menu and a menu item?

5. What is the first parameter passed to LoadIcon?

6. When a WM_COMMAND message is sent to a window, after a menu selection, which parameter of the WndProc holds the menu item ID?

7. What is the difference between FindResource and LoadResource?

8. What is the difference between GlobalUnlock and FreeResource?

9. What is a New Executable file?

10. Can resources be stored in a DLL?

Exercises

1. Using custom resources to store the text, write a program that displays its own WinMain procedure in its main window.

2. Write a program that can use custom resources to display two different pieces of text. Enable the user to switch back and forth between these two pieces of text by selecting different items from the menu.

6

Advanced Resources: Bitmaps and Dialogs

This chapter presents an overview of three sophisticated resources: dialogs, bitmaps, and string tables. String tables are fairly easy to use, but dialogs and bitmaps can be heady topics. In particular, dialogs and bitmaps involve some tricky allocation and deallocation of relatively complex system resources.

Here's a list of key topics covered in this chapter:

☐ Creating and using dialogs

☐ Creating and using bitmaps

☐ Creating and using string tables

☐ Creating and using scrollbars

I introduce scrollbars in this chapter primarily because the Emerson program needs them. You should note, however, that scrollbars are not resources, but controls. The whole subject of controls is discussed in-depth during Week 2.

The core of this chapter focuses on bitmaps and dialogs. Given sufficiently complex circumstances, both subjects could be expanded to fill several chapters' worth of material. My goal is to give you the basic knowledge you need to pop up dialogs and display bitmaps. During the next few chapters, you will get plenty of opportunity to practice these techniques. The early part of Week 3 contains tips about the more advanced aspects of both subjects.

Emerson2

The first order of business is to get the Emerson2 program on the table for all to see. This program is a more sophisticated version of the program you saw on Day 6, "Introduction to Resources."

See Listing 7.1 for the Emerson2 code. When you are viewing the code, you should note that one big difference between the two versions of this program is that Emerson2 uses string tables to store text, whereas the first Emerson program used custom resources.

Listing 7.1. A sample program with string table, dialog, and bitmap.

```
// ================================================
// Program Name: EMERSON2
// Copyright (c) 1995 by Charlie Calvert
// Project: Teach Yourself Windows Programming
// Description: Example program with string table,
//              dialog, and bitmap
// Update for WIN32: 05/28/95
// ================================================

#define STRICT
#define WIN32_LEAN_AND_MEAN
#include <windows.h>
```

```
#include <windowsx.h>
#pragma hdrstop
#include <string.h>
#include <stdlib.h>
#include "Emerson2.h"
#pragma warning (disable : 4100)
#pragma warning (disable : 4068)
static char szAppName[] = "Emerson2";
static HINSTANCE hInstance;

int MaxLines  = 21;
int Start = 0;
int TextHeight;
int PageSize = 3;
int nPosition = 0;
BOOL DrawBitmaps = TRUE;

// ================================================
// INITIALIZATION
// ================================================

///////////////////////////////////////
// The WinMain function is the program entry point.
///////////////////////////////////////
#pragma argsused
int WINAPI WinMain(HINSTANCE hInst, HINSTANCE hPrevInstance,
                   LPSTR  lpszCmdParam, int nCmdShow)
{
  MSG  Msg;

  if (!hPrevInstance)
    if (!Register(hInst))
      return FALSE;

  if (!Create(hInst, nCmdShow))
    return FALSE;

  while (GetMessage(&Msg, NULL, 0, 0))
  {
    TranslateMessage(&Msg);
    DispatchMessage(&Msg);
  }

  return Msg.wParam;
}


///////////////////////////////////////
// Register Window
///////////////////////////////////////
BOOL Register(HINSTANCE hInst)
{
  WNDCLASS WndClass;

  WndClass.style        = CS_HREDRAW | CS_VREDRAW;
```

continues

Listing 7.1. continued

```
    WndClass.lpfnWndProc    = WndProc;
    WndClass.cbClsExtra     = 0;
    WndClass.cbWndExtra     = 0;
    WndClass.hInstance      = hInst;
    WndClass.hIcon          = LoadIcon(hInst, "Emerson2");
    WndClass.hCursor        = LoadCursor(NULL, IDC_ARROW);
    WndClass.hbrBackground  = (HBRUSH)(COLOR_WINDOW+1);
    WndClass.lpszMenuName   = "MENU_1";
    WndClass.lpszClassName  = szAppName;

    return (RegisterClass (&WndClass) != 0);
}

///////////////////////////////////////
// Create the window and show it.
///////////////////////////////////////
BOOL Create(HINSTANCE hInst, int nCmdShow)
{

    hInstance = hInst;

    HWND hwnd = CreateWindow(szAppName, szAppName,
                            WS_VSCROLL ¦ WS_OVERLAPPEDWINDOW,
                            CW_USEDEFAULT, CW_USEDEFAULT,
                            CW_USEDEFAULT, CW_USEDEFAULT,
                            NULL, NULL, hInst, NULL);

    if (hwnd == NULL)
      return FALSE;

    ShowWindow(hwnd, nCmdShow);
    UpdateWindow(hwnd);

    return TRUE;
}

//================================================
// IMPLEMENTATION
//================================================

///////////////////////////////////////
// The window proc helps control the
// program while it is running
///////////////////////////////////////
LRESULT CALLBACK EXPORT16 WndProc(HWND hwnd, UINT Message,
                            WPARAM wParam, LPARAM lParam)
{
  switch(Message)
  {
    HANDLE_MSG(hwnd, WM_CREATE, Emerson_OnCreate);
    HANDLE_MSG(hwnd, WM_DESTROY, Emerson_OnDestroy);
    HANDLE_MSG(hwnd, WM_COMMAND, Emerson_OnCommand);
    HANDLE_MSG(hwnd, WM_KEYDOWN, Emerson_OnKey);
```

```
      HANDLE_MSG(hwnd, WM_PAINT, Emerson_OnPaint);
      HANDLE_MSG(hwnd, WM_VSCROLL, Emerson_OnVScroll);
      default:
        return Emerson_DefProc(hwnd, Message, wParam, lParam);
   }
}


/////////////////////////////////////
// Create Window
// Load the Bitmap from resource
/////////////////////////////////////
#pragma argsused
BOOL Emerson_OnCreate(HWND hwnd, CREATESTRUCT FAR*
lpCreateStruct)
{
  TEXTMETRIC TextMetrics;

  TheBitmap = LoadBitmap(hInstance, "Bitmap");
  if (!TheBitmap)
  {
    MessageBox(hwnd, "No Bitmap", "Fatal Error", MB_OK);
    return FALSE;
  }

  HDC PaintDC = GetDC(hwnd);
  GetTextMetrics(PaintDC, &TextMetrics);
  ReleaseDC(hwnd, PaintDC);
  TextHeight = TextMetrics.tmHeight +
               TextMetrics.tmExternalLeading;

  SetScrollRange(hwnd,  SB_VERT, 0,
                   -1, FALSE);

  return TRUE;
}


/////////////////////////////////////
// Destructor: Delete Bitmap from memory
/////////////////////////////////////
#pragma argsused
void Emerson_OnDestroy(HWND hwnd)
{
  DeleteBitmap(TheBitmap);
  PostQuitMessage(0);
}


/////////////////////////////////////
//  The Emerson2 Dialog Procedure controls the dialog
/////////////////////////////////////
#pragma argsused
void Emerson_OnCommand(HWND hwnd, int id,
                        HWND hwndCtl, UINT codeNotify)
{
  switch(id)
  {
```

7

continues

Listing 7.1. continued

```
    case CM_ABOUT:
    {
      FARPROC AboutBox =
        MakeProcInstance((FARPROC)AboutDlgProc, hInstance);
      DialogBox(hInstance, "About", hwnd, (DLGPROC)AboutBox);
      FreeProcInstance(AboutBox);
      break;
    }

    case CM_BRAHMIN:
      Start = 32;
      MaxLines = 22;
      SetScrollRange(hwnd,  SB_VERT, 0, MaxLines - 1, FALSE);
      InvalidateRect(hwnd, NULL, TRUE);
      DrawBitmaps = FALSE;
      break;

    case CM_WOODNOTES:
      Start = 0;
      MaxLines = 32;
      SetScrollRange(hwnd,  SB_VERT, 0, MaxLines - 1, FALSE);
      InvalidateRect(hwnd, NULL, TRUE);
      DrawBitmaps = FALSE;
      break;

    case CM_SEASHORE:
      Start = 64;
      MaxLines = 37;
      SetScrollRange(hwnd,  SB_VERT, 0, MaxLines - 1, FALSE);
      InvalidateRect(hwnd, NULL, TRUE);
      DrawBitmaps = FALSE;
      break;

    case CM_DRAWBITMAPS:
      DrawBitmaps = TRUE;
      // Negative value makes scrollbar disappear in WIN32
      SetScrollRange(hwnd,  SB_VERT, 0, -1, FALSE);
      InvalidateRect(hwnd, NULL, TRUE);
      break;   .
  }
}

/////////////////////////////////////
// Handle WM_KEYDOWN to aid in scrolling poems
/////////////////////////////////////
#pragma argsused
void Emerson_OnKey(HWND hwnd, UINT vk,
                   BOOL fDown, int cRepeat,
                   UINT flags)
{
  switch(vk)
  {
    case VK_HOME:
      SendMessage(hwnd, WM_VSCROLL, SB_TOP, 0L);
      break;
```

```
    case VK_DOWN:
      SendMessage(hwnd, WM_VSCROLL, SB_LINEDOWN, 0L);
      break;

    case VK_UP:
      SendMessage(hwnd, WM_VSCROLL, SB_LINEUP, 0L);
      break;

    case VK_PRIOR:
      SendMessage(hwnd, WM_VSCROLL, SB_PAGEUP, 0L);
      break;

    case VK_NEXT:
      SendMessage(hwnd, WM_VSCROLL, SB_PAGEDOWN, 0L);
      break;
  }
}

//////////////////////////////////////
// Handle WM_PAINT: Paint TheBitmap and poems
//////////////////////////////////////
void Emerson_OnPaint(HWND hwnd)
{
  PAINTSTRUCT PaintStruct;
  int NumImages = 15;
  char S[101];
  int Y = 0;

  HDC PaintDC = BeginPaint(hwnd, &PaintStruct);

  SetBkMode(PaintDC, TRANSPARENT);

  if (DrawBitmaps)
  {
    HDC BitmapDC = CreateCompatibleDC(PaintDC);
    HBITMAP OldBitmap = SelectBitmap(BitmapDC, TheBitmap);
    for (int i = 0; i < NumImages; i++)
      for (int j = 0; j < NumImages; j++)
        BitBlt(PaintDC, i * 66, j * 66, 64, 64,
               BitmapDC, 0, 0, SRCCOPY);
    SelectBitmap(BitmapDC, OldBitmap);
    DeleteDC(BitmapDC);
  }
  else
  {
    for (int i = nPosition; i < MaxLines; i++)
    {
      LoadString(hInstance, i + Start, S, 100);
      TextOut(PaintDC, 1, Y, S, strlen(S));
      Y += TextHeight;
    }
  }
```

7

continues

Listing 7.1. continued

```
    EndPaint(hwnd, &PaintStruct);
}

//////////////////////////////////////
// Handle WM_VSCROLL: Aid in scrolling poems
//////////////////////////////////////
#pragma argsused
void Emerson_OnVScroll(HWND hwnd, HWND hwndCtl,
                       UINT code, int pos)
{
  int ScrMove = 0, Temp, i;

  switch(code)
  {
    case SB_TOP:
      nPosition = 0;
      break;

    case SB_BOTTOM:
      nPosition = MaxLines;
      break ;

    case SB_LINEUP:
      if (nPosition > 0)
      {
        nPosition -= 1 ;
        ScrMove = TextHeight;
      }
      break ;

    case SB_LINEDOWN:
      if (nPosition < MaxLines)
      {
        nPosition += 1 ;
        ScrMove = -TextHeight;
      }
      break ;

    case SB_PAGEUP:
      if ((nPosition - PageSize) > 0)
      {
        for (i = 0; i < PageSize; i++)
          SendMessage(hwnd, WM_VSCROLL, SB_LINEUP, 0L);
      }
      break ;

    case SB_PAGEDOWN:
      if ((nPosition + PageSize) < MaxLines)
      {
        for (i = 0; i < PageSize; i++)
          SendMessage(hwnd, WM_VSCROLL, SB_LINEDOWN, 0L);
      }
      break ;
```

```
    case SB_THUMBTRACK:
      Temp = nPosition;
      nPosition = pos;
      ScrMove = (Temp - nPosition) * TextHeight;
      break;

    case SB_THUMBPOSITION:
      nPosition = pos;
      break;

  }
  nPosition = max(0, min (nPosition, MaxLines - 1)) ;
  SetScrollPos (hwnd, SB_VERT, nPosition, TRUE) ;
  ScrollWindow(hwnd, 0, ScrMove, NULL, NULL);
}

// ------------------------------------------
// Emerson Dialog
// ------------------------------------------

//////////////////////////////////////////////
//  The Emerson Dialog Procedure
//////////////////////////////////////////////
#pragma argsused
BOOL CALLBACK EXPORT16 AboutDlgProc(HWND hDlg, UINT Message,
                                WPARAM wParam, LPARAM lParam)
{
  switch(Message)
  {
    case WM_INITDIALOG:
      return TRUE;

    case WM_COMMAND:
      if (LOWORD(wParam) == IDOK ||
          LOWORD(wParam) == IDCANCEL)
      {
        EndDialog(hDlg, LOWORD(wParam));
        return TRUE;
      }
      break;
  }
  return FALSE;
}
```

Listing 7.2 shows the Emerson2 header file.

Listing 7.2. EMERSON2.H.

```
// ================================================
// Name: EMERSON2.H
// Programmer: Charlie Calvert
// Description: Header file for EMERSON2.CPP
// ================================================
```

7

continues

Listing 7.2. continued

```
#define CM_ABOUT 101
#define CM_DRAWBITMAPS 201
#define CM_BRAHMIN 202
#define CM_WOODNOTES 203
#define CM_SEASHORE 204

// Macros
#define max(a,b)     (((a) > (b)) ? (a) : (b))
#define min(a,b)     (((a) < (b)) ? (a) : (b))

#if !defined(__WIN32__) && !defined(_WIN32)
#define EXPORT16 __export
#else
#define EXPORT16
#endif

// The Emerson Class
#define Emerson_DefProc     DefWindowProc
BOOL Emerson_OnCreate(HWND hwnd,
                     CREATESTRUCT FAR* lpCreateStruct);
void Emerson_OnDestroy(HWND hwnd);
void Emerson_OnCommand(HWND hwnd, int id,
                     HWND hwndCtl, UINT codeNotify);
void Emerson_OnKey(HWND hwnd, UINT vk, BOOL fDown, int cRepeat, UINT flags);
void Emerson_OnPaint(HWND hwnd);
void Emerson_OnVScroll(HWND hwnd, HWND hwndCtl,
                     UINT code, int pos);

// Variables
HBITMAP TheBitmap;


// Some Procs
BOOL Register(HINSTANCE hInstance);
BOOL Create(HINSTANCE hInstance, int nCmdShow);
LRESULT CALLBACK EXPORT16 WndProc(HWND hWindow,
        UINT Message, WPARAM wParam, LPARAM lParam);
BOOL CALLBACK EXPORT16 AboutDlgProc(HWND hDlg, UINT Message,
                     WPARAM wParam, LPARAM lParam);
```

Listing 7.3 shows the Emerson2 resource file.

Listing 7.3. EMERSON2.RC.

```
1: /* The Emerson2 RC file */
2: #include <windows.h>
3: #include "Emerson2.h"
4:
5: /* The Bitmap reference */
6: Bitmap BITMAP "Bitmap.bmp"
7:
8: /*   The Emerson2 Menu     */
9: MENU_1 MENU
```

```
10: BEGIN
11:   POPUP "Poems"
12:     BEGIN
13:       MENUITEM "Bitmaps", CM_DRAWBITMAPS
14:       MENUITEM "Brahmin", CM_BRAHMIN
15:       MENUITEM "Woodnotes", CM_WOODNOTES
16:       MENUITEM "SeaShore", CM_SEASHORE
17:     END
18:
19:   MENUITEM "&About", CM_ABOUT
20: END
21:
22:
23: /*   The About Dialog   */
24: About DIALOG 18, 18, 141, 58
25: STYLE DS_MODALFRAME ¦ WS_POPUP ¦ WS_CAPTION ¦ WS_SYSMENU
26: CAPTION "About Dialog"
27: BEGIN
28:   PUSHBUTTON "Ok", IDOK, 5, 39, 132, 12,
29:             WS_CHILD ¦ WS_VISIBLE ¦ WS_TABSTOP
30:   CTEXT "Emerson Example", -1, 1, 9, 140, 8,
31:             WS_CHILD ¦ WS_VISIBLE ¦ WS_GROUP
32:   CTEXT "Copyright (c) World Community, Inc.",
33:         -1, 1, 23, 140, 10,
34:         WS_CHILD ¦ WS_VISIBLE ¦ WS_GROUP
35: END
36:
37: /*   The Emerson2 Icon   */
38: About ICON "Emerson2.ico"
39:
40: /*   The String Table   */
41: STRINGTABLE
42: BEGIN
43:     0, "Woodnotes (Part 1)"
44:     1, "by Ralph Waldo Emerson"
45:     2, ""
46:     3, "When the pine tosses its cones"
47:     4, "To the song of its waterfall tones,"
48:     5, "Who speeds to the woodland walks?"
49:     6, "To birds and trees who talks?"
50:     7, "Caesar of his leafy Rome,"
51:     8, "There the poet is at home."
52:     9, "He goes to the river-side,--"
53:     10, "Not hook nor line hath he;"
54:     11, "He stands in the meadows wide,--"
55:     12, "Nor gun nor scythe to see."
56:     13, "Sure some god his eye enchants:"
57:     14, "What he knows nobody wants,"
58:     15, "In the wood he travels glad,"
59:     16, "Without better fortune had,"
60:     17, "Melancholy without bad."
61:     18, "Knowledge this man prizes best"
62:     19, "Seems fantastic to the rest:"
63:     20, "Pondering shadows, colors, clouds,"
64:     21, "Grass-buds and caterpillar-shrouds,"
```

continues

Listing 7.3. continued

```
 65:        22, "Boughs on which the wild bees settle,"
 66:        23, "Tints that spot the violet's petal,"
 67:        24, "Why nature loves the number five,"
 68:        25, "And why the star-form she repeats:"
 69:        26, "Lover of all things alive,"
 70:        27, "Wonderer at all he meets,"
 71:        28, "Wonderer chiefly at himself,"
 72:        29, "Who can tell him what he is?"
 73:        30, "Or how meet in human elf"
 74:        31, "Coming and past eternities?"
 75:        32, "Brahma"
 76:        33, "by Ralph Waldo Emerson"
 77:        34, ""
 78:        35, "If the red slayer think he slays"
 79:        36, "  Or if the slain think he is slain,"
 80:        37, "They know not well the subtle ways"
 81:        38, "  I keep and pass and turn again."
 82:        39, ""
 83:        40, "Far or forget to me is near;"
 84:        41, "  Shadow and sunlight are the same;"
 85:        42, "The vanished gods to me appear;"
 86:        43, "  And one to me are shame and fame."
 87:        44, ""
 88:        45, "They reckon ill who leave me out"
 89:        46, "  When me they fly, I am the wings;"
 90:        47, "I am the doubter and the doubt,"
 91:        48, "  And I the hymn the Brahmin sings."
 92:        49, ""
 93:        50, "The strong gods pine for my abode,"
 94:        51, "  And pine in vain the sacred Seven;"
 95:        52, "But thou, meek lover of the good!"
 96:        53, "  Find me, and turn thy back on heaven."
 97:        64, "SeaShore"
 98:        65, " by Ralph Waldo Emerson"
 99:        66, ""
100:        67, "I heard or seemed to hear the chiding Sea"
101:        68, "Say, Pilgrim, why so late and slow to come?"
102:        69, "Am I not always here, thy summer home?"
103:        70, "Is not my voice thy music, morn and eve?"
104:        71, "My breath thy healthful climate in the heats,"
105:        72, "My trouch thy antidote, my bay thy bath?"
106:        73, "Was ever couch magnificent as mine?"
107:        74, "Lie on the warm rock-ledges, and there learn"
108:        75, "A little hut suffices like a town."
109:        76, "I make your sculptured architecture vain,"
110:        77, "Vain beside mine. I drive my wedges home,"
111:        78, "And carve the coastwise mountain into caves."
112:        79, "Lo! here is Rome and Nineveh and Thebes,"
113:        80, "Karnak and Pyramid and Giant's Stairs"
114:        81, "Half piled or prostrate; and my newest slab"
115:        82, "Older than all thy race."
116:        83, ""
117:        84, "Behold the Sea,"
118:        85, "The opaline, the plentiful and strong,"
119:        86, "Yet beautiful as is the rose in June,"
```

```
120:       87, "Fresh as the trickling rainbow of July;"
121:       88, "Sea full of food, the nourisher of kinds,"
122:       89, "Purger of earth, and medicine of men;"
123:       90, "Creating a sweet climate by my breath,"
124:       91, "Washing out harms and griefs from memory,"
125:       92, "And, in my mathematic ebb and flow,"
126:       93, "Giving a hint of that which changes not."
127:       94, "Rich are the sea-gods: -- who gives gifts but they?"
128:       95, "They grope the sea for pearls, but more than pearls:"
129:       96, "They pluck Force thence, and give it to the wise."
130:       97, "For every wave is wealth to Daedalus,"
131:       98, "Wealth to the cunning artist who can work"
132:       99, "This matchless strength. Where shall he find, O waves!"
133:      100, "A load your Atlas shoulders cannot lift?"
134: END
```

Listing 7.4 shows the Emerson2 module definition file.

Listing 7.4. EMERSON2.DEF.

```
;  EMERSON2.DEF
NAME           Emerson2
DESCRIPTION    'Emerson2 example'
CODE           PRELOAD MOVEABLE DISCARDABLE
DATA           PRELOAD MOVEABLE MULTIPLE
HEAPSIZE       4096
STACKSIZE      8192
```

Listing 7.5 shows the Borland makefile for Emerson2.

Listing 7.5. EMERSON2.MAK (Borland).

```
# EMERSON2.MAK

!if !$d(BCROOT)
BCROOT  = $(MAKEDIR)
!endif

APPNAME = EMERSON2
INCPATH = $(BCROOT)\INCLUDE
LIBPATH = $(BCROOT)\LIB

!if $d(WIN16)
COMPILER= BCC.EXE
BRC= BRC.EXE
FLAGS   = -W -ml -v -w4 -I$(INCPATH) -L$(LIBPATH)
!else
COMPILER= BCC32.EXE
BRC= BRC32.EXE
FLAGS   = -W -v -w4 -I$(INCPATH) -L$(LIBPATH)
!endif
```

continues

Listing 7.5. continued

```
# linking
$(APPNAME).exe: $(APPNAME).Obj $(APPNAME).Def $(APPNAME).Res
  $(COMPILER) $(FLAGS) $(APPNAME).obj
  $(BRC) -I$(INCPATH) $(APPNAME).res

# compiling
$(APPNAME).obj: $(APPNAME).cpp
  $(COMPILER) -c $(FLAGS) $(APPNAME).cpp

# resource
$(APPNAME).res: $(APPNAME).rc
  $(BRC) -R -I$(INCPATH) $(APPNAME).RC
```

Listing 7.6 shows the Microsoft makefile for Emerson2.

Listing 7.6. EMERSON2.MAK (Microsoft).

```
#-------------------------------------------------
# EMERS2MS.MAK
# Microsoft WIN32 makefile
#-------------------------------------------------

APPNAME=EMERSON2
TARGETOS=WIN95
APPVER=4.0
OBJS=$(APPNAME).OBJ

!include <win32.mak>

all: $(APPNAME).exe

# Update the resource if necessary

$(APPNAME).res: $(APPNAME).rc $(APPNAME).h
  $(rc) $(rcflags) $(rcvars) $(APPNAME).rc

# Update the object files if necessary

# compile
.cpp.obj:
  $(cc) $(cflags) $(cvars) $(cdebug) $<

# Update the executable file if necessary.

$(APPNAME).exe: $(OBJS) $(APPNAME).res
  $(link) $(linkdebug) $(guiflags) -out:$(APPNAME).exe \
  $(OBJS) $(APPNAME).res $(guilibs) comctl32.lib
```

At startup time, the background of the Emerson program consists of a single bitmap printed multiple times across the window, as shown in Figure 7.1. At the top of the program is a simple menu. If you select the About menu option, a dialog stating information about the program

appears on the screen. The Options menu enables you to display either the bitmap pattern or one of three different poems by Ralph Waldo Emerson. When you minimize the Emerson program, it displays a custom icon.

Figure 7.1.
EMERSON.EXE shown as it appears on-screen with its menu, dialog, and resource.

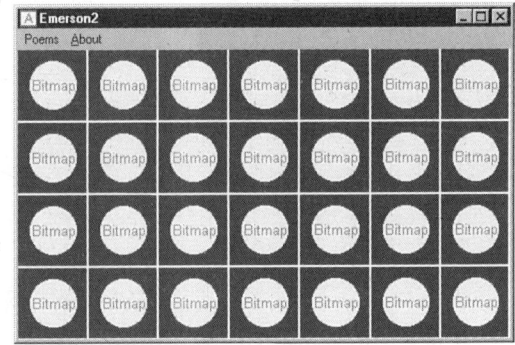

What Am I Supposed to Do with All These Files?

You've probably noticed that the source code for the Emerson project has grown to include eight different files: EMERSON.CPP, EMERSON.BMP, EMERSON.H, EMERSON.RC, EMERSON.DEF, EMERSON.ICO, EMERSON.CUR, and EMERSON.MAK. Whew!

The idea that so many different files belong to a single project takes a little getting used to. The thing to do is to relax and take things one step at a time.

There is nothing unusual about making use of such a wide variety of files in a single Windows program. To help you get a grasp on this ragtag menagerie, I've made up a copy of an often-shown schematic diagram depicting the various files that make up a typical Windows executable file. This diagram is shown in Figure 7.2.

This picture, in and of itself, doesn't really convey much new information. Use it to help organize your thoughts. If you want, you can take a look at this diagram now, and then refer back to it later when you have a better feeling for the way Windows programming works.

DO	DON'T

DO use abstractions to help organize your ideas. Think in terms of objects, structured programs, and modules. When you want to hold the whole ball of wax in your hand, think in terms of a project file or a makefile. The ability to handle abstract concepts is not a trivial gift. Take advantage of it!

Of course, you can switch back to the other mode when your boss, mother, husband, wife, or best friend comes by to see what you're doing. Then, you can lay all the pieces out in front of them and let them *ooh* and *ahh* over your work. You don't have to tell them that it's really not as complex as it seems!

DON'T become overwhelmed by the mere presence of so many files. Much of the complexity is merely numerical, not technical. In other words, taken one at a time, none of the previous files are difficult to understand. However, if you try to hold all the balls up in the air at once, the task begins to seem a bit daunting. The solution is to divide and conquer. This isn't just a cliché; it's a slogan to live by.

Figure 7.2.
A hierarchical diagram depicting the various portions of a Windows executable program.

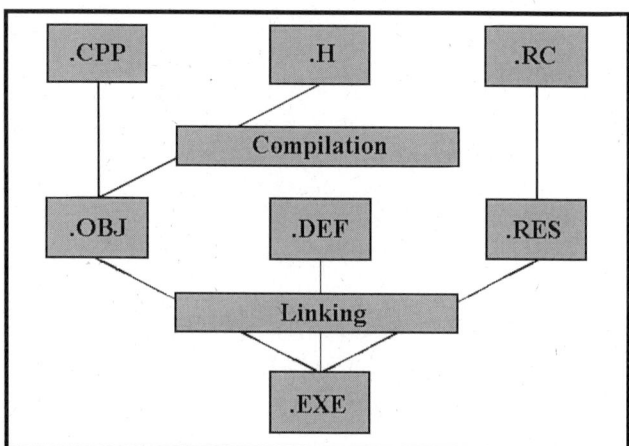

Creating the Dialog

In Chapter 6 you saw how to create the menu, icon, and cursor to be used with EMERSON2.CPP. The next step is to create the dialog, which is a considerably more complex operation. I'm going to spend several pages going over this material, because I feel that a good Windows programmer ought to have a thorough understanding of this process.

Using a dialog involves three steps:

1. Defining the dialog in a resource file.

2. Creating code to pop up the dialog on-screen.

3. Creating a dialog procedure to handle the user's input while the dialog is running. You can think of a dialog procedure as being a window procedure for dialogs, although, in fact, they are distinct entities. When added to EMERSON2.RC, the definition of the dialog looks like this:

```
23: /*   The About Dialog   */
24: About DIALOG 18, 18, 141, 58
25: STYLE DS_MODALFRAME ¦ WS_POPUP ¦ WS_CAPTION ¦ WS_SYSMENU
26: CAPTION "About Dialog"
27: BEGIN
28:   PUSHBUTTON "Ok", IDOK, 5, 39, 132, 12,
29:              WS_CHILD ¦ WS_VISIBLE ¦ WS_TABSTOP
30:   CTEXT "Emerson Example", -1, 1, 9, 140, 8,
31:              WS_CHILD ¦ WS_VISIBLE ¦ WS_GROUP
32:   CTEXT "Copyright (c) World Community, Inc.",
33:          -1, 1, 23, 140, 10,
34:          WS_CHILD ¦ WS_VISIBLE ¦ WS_GROUP
35: END
```

If you want to create the dialog using a visual tool, you should aim to create something that looks like the image shown in Figure 7.3. Remember that the About dialog is simply another resource added to EMERSON2.RC. You don't need to start another Resource Workshop project in order to create the dialog. It can be part of the original resource file. If at any time you have trouble re-creating the image using visual tools, edit the dialog as text and copy in the preceding code exactly as it appears. In other words, tools like the Resource Workshop let you edit resources either visually or as text. They are two-way tools.

When examining the source code for the About dialog, you should note that the first line includes a name for the dialog, followed by the declaration of its type and its dimensions. The next line ORs together four constants defined in WINDOWS.H:

DS_MODALFRAME	Creates a dialog box with a frame that works well with the WS_CAPTION and WS_SYSMENU styles.
WS_POPUP	Microsoft defines the WS_POPUP style by saying it creates a pop-up window. In addition, you should understand that windows with the WS_POPUP style can roam all over the desktop, and can be owned by a window other than the desktop. They are not confined within the bounds of their parent. Windows that can't move outside the bounds of their parent are child windows, and they use the WS_CHILD or WS_CHILDWINDOW style.
WS_CAPTION	Creates a dialog that has a title bar across the top.
WS_SYSMENU	Creates a dialog with the system menu icon in the upper-left corner of the caption bar.

Figure 7.3.
The About dialog consists of a push button with an ID of 1 (IDOK) and two static text items.

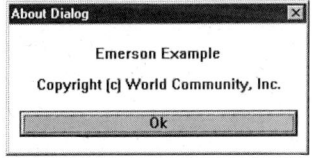

I discuss these constants in more depth on Day 14, "Stylish Windows." For now, you can experiment with them by omitting one or more from the Emerson program's dialog and by viewing the results on-screen.

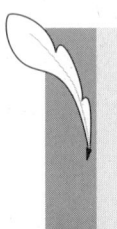

Note: The About dialog runs in the *modal state*. To understand what this means, simply run the Emerson2 program, pop up the dialog, and then try to select the main window (or one of the menu items from the main window). You'll find that you can't do this, because the dialog now has a lock on the program's focus. This is typical modal behavior. The dialog is, in effect, telling the user: "Deal with me before you try to do anything else with this program." In other words, you must close this dialog before you can continue using the program.

The opposite of a modal dialog is the less commonly used *modeless* dialog. When a modeless dialog is on-screen, you can access its features and the features of the main program. You'll get a chance to work with these dialogs during Week 2, when you look at the WinSize program.

Technically, the difference between the two types of dialogs has to do with the way their message loop is handled and whether or not they disable their parents by calling the EnableWindow function.

After the style of the About dialog is declared, the caption is defined:

```
CAPTION "About Dialog"
```

The caption appears in the title, or *caption bar*, at the top of the dialog. If you leave the caption statement out altogether, the bar will be blank. Of course, no text will appear if you don't use the WS_CAPTION style when defining the dialog.

The dialog definition ends with a few lines of code declared between a BEGIN…END pair. These lines define the dialog's push button and its two lines of text. You won't be able to make sense of these lines unless you understand that the push button and both text controls are also windows. In other words, the dialog box has three subwindows placed inside it—a push button and two static controls:

☐ The line that defines the push button takes seven parameters. The first is the text to be associated with the control, followed by the control's ID, bounding rectangle, and style. The bounding rectangle is defined by four numbers. The first is the *x* position, the second the *y* position, the third the control's *width*, and the fourth its *height*.

☐ Because the static controls containing the text are also windows, it should come as no surprise that they take the same parameters as the pushbutton. By default, static controls have no border.

Note: It can take a while to get comfortable with the idea that push buttons and static controls are windows. When I was first introduced to the Windows programming environment, I thought it got its name from the big on-screen windows in which programs ran. I was thinking of the Program Manager as one window and my compiler as a second window. It took me a while to grasp that any one program can be made of multiple windows.

For instance, complex visual tools, such as App Studio and the Resource Workshop, might have 20, 30, or more windows visible at one time. You shouldn't be afraid to add subwindows to your programs in order to make them easier to use. Creating a few windows on the desktop is not particularly expensive to the environment. If you need them, use them.

The menu in the EMERSON2.RC file uses a constant called CM_ABOUT, which is defined in EMERSON2.H. However, the IDOK identifier associated with the button in this dialog is defined in WINDOWS.H—which is included at the top of the RC file. The following excerpt from the WINDOWS.H complex shows where IDOK is declared and also features a series of related constants often associated with buttons in dialogs:

```
/* Standard dialog button IDs */
#define IDOK                1
#define IDCANCEL            2
#define IDABORT             3
#define IDRETRY             4
#define IDIGNORE            5
#define IDYES               6
#define IDNO                7
```

Note: Borland users should notice that both BRC and the Workshop already know about WINDOWS.H. As a result, they don't need to include WINDOWS.H at the top of the EMERSON.RC text file. If you are using other compilers, however, you may not be able to compile the resource unless you install WINDOWS.H.

The only thing I need to add is that static text items are often given an ID of -1 because static text items usually exist as inert objects on the desktop. Given the fact that there is rarely a need to communicate with them, there is also no need to have a unique ID that identifies them.

Popping Up a Dialog

Now that the dialog has been created, the next step is to pop it up on the desktop. This is another seemingly "magic" Windows programming process that involves a number of steps that might not be entirely intuitive to you at first.

I've divided this discussion of popping up a dialog into three sections:

1. The first is the one you are currently reading. It gives a brief overview of the code that makes the dialog resources visible to a user.
2. The second section is a meditation on the MakeProcInstance function.
3. The third section describes the DialogBox and AboutDialogProc functions. The latter is similar to a WndProc, except that it is associated with a dialog instead of a window.

As mentioned on Day 6, when the user selects the About menu item, it sends a WM_COMMAND message to the program's window procedure. After the message crackers are through parsing the WndProc's parameters, the ID associated with the chosen menu item is sent to About_OnCommand:

```
void About_OnCommand(HWND hwnd, int id, HWND hwndCtl, UINT codeNotify)
{
  switch(id)
  {
    case CM_ABOUT:
    {
      FARPROC AboutBox = MakeProcInstance((FARPROC)AboutDlgProc,
                                          hInstance);
      DialogBox(hInstance, "ABOUT", hwnd, (DLGPROC)AboutBox);
      FreeProcInstance(AboutBox);
      break;
    }

    case CM_DRAWBITMAPS:
    etc...

  }
}
```

All the menu selections in a program are associated with WM_COMMAND messages. As a result, Cls_OnCommand can become a quite lengthy and complex function governed by a long and very hairy switch statement. In the bad old days before WindowsX, programmers would embed this long switch statement in the midst of the even longer switch statement composing the body of a WndProc. What a mess!

By now, it should be clear that a CM_ABOUT identifier, attached to a WM_COMMAND message, comes cruising down the pike every time the user selects the About menu item. The program responds to this message by popping up the About dialog.

For WIN16 Users: All About *MakeProcInstance*

Take a look at the code that pops up the About dialog. As you can see, it begins by calling `MakeProcInstance`. As you learned earlier, you must call `MakeProcInstance` in WIN16, but WIN32 no longer requires its use. However, Microsoft allows you to continue using the call so that you can write portable code.

In the next few paragraphs I examine `MakeProcInstance` so that you will understand the call—if or when you need to use it. This subject is complex enough that I've decided to treat it in its own section.

In 16-bit Windows, `MakeProcInstance` needs to be called so the function passed to it can have access to the data in your application. It does this by creating a small chunk of code that binds the program's data segment to the dialog procedure.

This is simple enough to say, but a bit more difficult to understand. In fact, the whole subject of what `MakeProcInstance` does can be a bit confusing. As a result, it might be helpful to start by telling a little allegorical (and somewhat whimsical) science-fiction story.

I've mentioned before that Windows consists of a series of primitive objects. For just a moment, you might want to exercise your imagination by thinking of these objects as planetary systems in a faraway galaxy. In this case, one planet, called Windows, is the head of a very big and powerful empire. The other planet, called Emerson, is a smaller and less powerful colony of the Windows empire.

Sometimes it's necessary for Windows to send an emissary, or message carrier, to Emerson with an important message. When the message carrier gets to Emerson, he doesn't know anything about that planet's language or culture. As a result, there is a communication problem.

The solution is to call on the wise old hacker `MakeProcInstance`, known to his friends as Chief Handshake. Chief Handshake knows how to hack the Emerson `DataSegment`, which is a computerized library full of cultural information about the planet Emerson. Handshake gives the emissary links to the `DataSegment`. It turns out that once the message carrier is linked to the `DataSegment`, he can overcome the cultural differences between the Windows empire and the Emerson colony. As a result, he is able to deliver his message in a way that can be understood.

The point of this peculiar little tale is that Windows and the Emerson program exist in two different areas of memory that need to be reconciled. This job is done by `MakeProcInstance`, which in effect tells Windows where the Emerson program's data segment is located. When Windows calls the dialog procedure, it is possible for the dialog procedure to get access to the Emerson program's data segment, which in turn makes it possible for the two objects to communicate.

It might be helpful to take a look at this same issue from a slightly more technical perspective.

7

A dialog procedure is associated with the About dialog, just as a Windows procedure is associated with the main window. You know that window procedures are called by Windows itself. In other words, it isn't your program that calls WndProc; it's Windows. In the same way, the About dialog procedure is not called by your program; it's called by Windows.

The key fact to grasp is that the dialog procedure in effect "belongs" to Windows when being called by Windows. However, in WIN16, Windows and your program don't share the same data segment. Unless MakeProcInstance gives access to Emerson's data segment, the dialog procedure won't have access to the static and global variables associated with your program.

Because of the job it performs, you might want to think of MakeProcInstance as the Handshake procedure. The Handshake procedure creates a small snatch of prelude code for your program's dialog procedure. This prelude code acquaints Windows with your program's data segment. It introduces them, enabling them to shake hands and start talking.

> **Note:** Programmers who have worked with Interrupt Service Routines (ISRs) are familiar with the phenomenon previously described. DOS calls an ISR, but unless you take special precautions, the ISR won't have access to your program's data segment. To resolve this problem, programmers often hide the data segment of their program inside their program's code segment. Because the ISR also resides in your program's code segment, it's possible to retrieve the data segment and access your program's data. This isn't the same way Windows handles the problem, but the challenges involved are similar.

Every call to MakeProcInstance needs to be balanced with a call to FreeProcInstance. The FreeProcInstance function frees the dialog procedure from the data segment and deallocates resources expended by MakeProcInstance.

WIN32 doesn't have to wrestle with this problem because each program runs in its own 4GB address space. There is no separate data segment, and so there is no need to bind it to a function with MakeProcInstance.

DialogBox and *AboutDlgProc*

After the MakeProcInstance handshaking business is out of the way, the next step is to call DialogBox. This call is roughly parallel to the CreateWindow procedure in a program's initialization. In other words, when you create a dialog you aren't doing anything radically different from what you do when you create a window. In fact, at bottom, a dialog is nothing but a special window with certain distinguishing traits. It's not a different animal; it's just another window.

A quick glance at the Emerson2 program's dialog procedure helps underline the very close analogy between the WndProc function and AboutDlgProc:

```
327: BOOL CALLBACK _EXPORT16 AboutDlgProc(HWND hDlg, UINT Message,
328:                                       WPARAM wParam, LPARAM lParam)
329: {
330:   switch(Message)
331:   {
332:     case WM_INITDIALOG:
333:       return TRUE;
334:
335:     case WM_COMMAND:
336:       if (LOWORD(wParam) == IDOK ||
337:             LOWORD(wParam) == IDCANCEL)
338:       {
339:         EndDialog(hDlg, LOWORD(wParam));
340:         return TRUE;
341:       }
342:       break;
343:   }
344:   return FALSE;
345: }
```

Both WndProc and AboutDlgProc are never called directly by your program. Instead, they are both sent messages by the system, and they both use a switch statement to process these messages.

The message loop associated with your main window is superseded by another loop (internal to Windows) during the life of the AboutDlgProc. In effect, what happens is that the code associated with your main window is in limbo while the About dialog runs. You can imagine a sort of dead space between the call to DialogBox and the call to FreeProcInstance:

```
DialogBox(hInstance, "ABOUT", hwnd, (DLGPROC)AboutBox);
// Dead Space, a void while another message loop runs //
FreeProcInstance(AboutBox);
```

As I mentioned earlier, the dialog procedures in this book don't use message crackers. As a result, the AboutDlgProc closely resembles an old-fashioned, pre-WindowsX WndProc, replete with a potentially endless switch statement.

Fortunately, the switch statement in the Emerson AboutDlgProc is very close to a minimal dialog procedure. Most of it consists of a response to IDOK or IDCANCEL messages. The IDOK messages sent to the dialog originate in the OK button, defined in the EMERSON2.RC file. IDCANCEL messages are sent when the user double-clicks the system menu icon (located in the upper-left corner of the dialog).

What you've seen is a rough sketch of the way dialogs are handled in a Windows program. There is, of course, more to the story than I've told here. As usual, I introduce you to the big themes, and then come back later and show you how the details are put together. This way, each chapter won't overwhelm you with a mass of information too complicated to absorb in one reading.

7

I know that even in this simplified overview, dialogs can still be a bit tricky to grasp. As a result, it might be helpful to take another quick look at the main points:

☐ First, define the dialog in an RC file, either by editing it as text, or by using a tool like App Studio or the Resource Workshop.

☐ In 16-bit Windows, call `MakeProcInstance` in order to bind the program's data segment to the dialog procedure.

☐ Call `DialogBox` to create the dialog as a "physical entity" in the Windows environment.

☐ Respond to messages sent from Windows to the dialog's window procedure.

☐ Call `EndDialog` to shut down the dialog.

☐ Call `FreeProcInstance` in order to restore Windows to the state it was in before the call to `MakeProcInstance`.

This list can serve as a kind of guide, or recipe, for creating dialogs.

BMPs (An Aesthetic Interlude)

The next resource to be explored is the bitmap shown in Figure 7.4. You can create this bitmap using the Windows Paintbrush program or any other tool that produces BMP files. You don't need to imitate the BMP exactly, although you'll probably want to make your image the same size, which is 64 pixels wide by 64 pixels high. However, within those simple guidelines, you should feel free to either copy my resource as nearly as possible or improvise any sort of design that strikes your fancy.

Note: The upcoming discussion of bitmaps will also be a crash course in the Windows Graphics Device Interface (GDI). In the Windows world, the GDI is the gateway to graphics. Or, to state the matter somewhat more formally, the GDI is a subset of Windows designed to handle graphics programming.

The key letter in GDI is the *D*, which stands for *Device*. Device contexts (HDCs) are what the GDI is all about.

All the GDI functions are contained in special DLLs called either GDI.EXE or GDI32.DLL. When you want to show a bitmap on-screen, use GDI functions such as `BitBlt`. In fact, whenever you use a device context, you are using a GDI function. (Bonus Day 1, "GDI and Metafiles," gives an in-depth look at the GDI.)

If you are editing the RC file as text, you need to add only a single line to the top of the EMERSON.RC file:

```
Bitmap BITMAP "Bitmap.bmp"
```

That's all you need to do to create a bitmap. Like creating icons, this is a very simple step from a purely intellectual perspective. From an aesthetic perspective, however, creating bitmaps can be very challenging. Many programmers wisely decide to hire outside talent to produce the artwork for their programs.

At any rate, when you have some kind of a bitmap sketched, you need to take the steps to show it on-screen. Like the act of creating a dialog, this can prove to be a bit tricky. As a result, I've put the description of the whole process in its own section.

Figure 7.4.
A suggested bitmap for use in the Emerson program.

The Emerson Program Loads a Bitmap

The act of loading a bitmap into memory is very much like loading an icon, a cursor, or a custom resource. The following fragment of code from the Emerson_OnCreate function shows the whole process, including error checking:

```
      HBITMAP TheBitMap;
      ...
133:  TheBitmap = LoadBitmap(hInstance, "Bitmap");
134:  if (!TheBitmap)
135:  {
136:    MessageBox(hwnd, "No Bitmap", "Fatal Error", MB_OK);
137:    return FALSE;
138:  }
```

The LoadBitmap API function needs two parameters. The first is the instance of the executable file, or DLL, that contains the bitmap to be loaded. Remember that the hInstance variable is declared globally in the Emerson program. It's assigned a value during the program's Create function. The second parameter to LoadBitmap is the name of the bitmap.

Because LoadBitmap might fail, it's important to check to see that the bitmap handle, declared in the EMERSON.H file, hasn't been set to zero. If the resource's handle is zero, Emerson_OnCreate returns FALSE, which causes the program to fail. If you want to see how this works, you can intentionally misspell the second parameter to LoadBitmap so that it reads Batmap, or what have you. In such a case, the bitmap won't be loaded, and the program will fail.

DO	**DON'T**

DO remember to call LoadBitmap before you try to use a bitmap in your program. Just including it in your RC file is not enough.

DON'T forget to balance every call to LoadBitmap with a call to DeleteObject or DeleteBitmap. In the Emerson program, the call to DeleteBitmap occurs in response to the WM_DESTROY message. DeleteBitmap is a type-compatible WindowsX macro that encapsulates the functionality of DeleteObject. LoadBitmap, on the other hand, is a standard Windows API call.

Selecting a Bitmap into a Device Context

After loading the bitmap, EMERSON2.CPP displays it multiple times in response to a WM_PAINT message:

```
247:     HDC BitmapDC = CreateCompatibleDC(PaintDC);
248:     HBITMAP OldBitmap = SelectBitmap(BitmapDC, TheBitmap);
249:     for (int i = 0; i < NumImages; i++)
250:       for (int j = 0; j < NumImages; j++)
251:         BitBlt(PaintDC, i * 66, j * 66, 64, 64,
252:               BitmapDC, 0, 0, SRCCOPY);
253:     SelectBitmap(BitmapDC, OldBitmap);
254:     DeleteDC(BitmapDC);
```

Here's how the paint loop would look if the bitmap were displayed only one time:

```
HDC BitmapDC = CreateCompatibleDC(PaintDC);
HBITMAP OldBitmap = SelectBitmap(BitmapDC, TheBitmap);
BitBlt(PaintDC, 0, 0, 64, 64, BitmapDC, 0, 0, SRCCOPY);
SelectBitmap(BitmapDC, OldBitmap);
DeleteDC(BitmapDC);
```

This code creates a second device context compatible with the window's device context. The bitmap to be displayed must first be selected into this second device context before it can be shown, or *blitted* to the screen. The screen itself, of course, is represented by a device context called PaintDC.

SelectBitmap is a WindowsX macro that ends up calling SelectObject.

The SelectObject function "selects" an object into a given device context. SelectObject always returns the object that previously inhabited the device context. In this example, I copy TheBitmap into BitmapDC, and then carefully save OldBitmap in a variable created specifically for that purpose. After the bitmap has been displayed, I carefully copy OldBitmap back into the device context and then delete the entire DC.

DO	**DON'T**

DO remember to copy the bitmap into its own, specially created device context.

DO remember to save the old bitmap in a variable.

DON'T forget to copy this old bitmap back into the device context.

Internally, there is a structure in the device context that has fields for holding each of the resources available to the device context. For instance, there is one for the current pen and one for the current bitmap. If you want the device context to work with a second bitmap, you have to assign it to the field containing the current bitmap, and then you have to hold onto the old bitmap and replace it when you are through.

It might be helpful to take another view of device contexts, first introduced on Day 4, "Messages, WindowsX, and Painting Text." I sometimes think of a device context as a pool of water with various objects suspended in it. Every object in the pool takes on a special look, appropriate to the context and resulting from the refractory properties of the water. Think of plunging your hand into a mountain lake. Because your hand is now being seen in a new context, it becomes larger and somehow distorted by the process. (In other words, an object looks one way on 640×480 screen, another on an 800×600 screen, and yet a third way on a printer. It looks different depending on the device context, just as your hand looks different when it's submerged in a pool of water.)

Pretend there is only room for a certain number of objects in this pool. If you want to insert a new one, you must first remove an old one. When you are through, be sure to swap the old one back. (It's important to the pond's ecology.)

I'll be explicit about how this analogy works.

A bitmap copied into a device context for a standard VGA screen is seen in terms of a 640×480, 16-color VGA screen. This is different from the way it would look on a CGA screen. You see a bitmap in a new context when you copy it onto a VGA screen, just as your hand is seen in a new context when you plunge it into a pool of water.

When you call SelectObject, you are introducing a new element into the device context, that is, into the pool of water. Because there is only room for *x* number of items in the device context, one has to be removed before a new one can be copied in. When you are through with the new item, remove it, and then replace it with the original item.

7

> **Note:** The act of copying items in and out of a device context is accomplished by the `SelectObject` function. WindowsX supplies type-compatible alternatives to `SelectObject` with names like `SelectBitmap` and `SelectPen`. If you use them, you avoid having to perform annoying typecasts. You should, however, feel free to use either call, depending on your tastes.

Blasting Bits to the Screen

You are now ready to learn about the `BitBlt` function, which is pronounced "bit blit." `BitBlt` performs the chore of actually painting the bitmap on the screen.

I like to think of the name `BitBlt` as standing for "bit blast," because it quickly blasts the bitmap onto the screen. Authorities from Microsoft, however, state that it stands for *bit block transfer*. Regardless, the `BitBlt` function takes no less than nine parameters:

☐ The first parameter is a device context representing the screen.

☐ The next four parameters define the place in the client window where the bitmap appears.

☐ The next parameter is a compatible device context holding an in-memory copy of the bitmap. This device context is what gets blasted onto the screen, or rather, gets blasted into the device context that represents the screen.

☐ The next two parameters define the *x* and *y* positions inside the original bitmap. In other words, if the original bitmap were 128×128 pixels in size, and you wanted to show only a section 64×64 pixels in size, you would use these parameters to specify where that 64×64 block begins.

☐ The final parameter defines the logical operation to be performed when the bitmap is transferred to the screen.

It turns out that there are at least 15 different operations that can be selected using the last parameter to `BitBlt`. Most of the time, you simply use `SRCCOPY`, which paints the bitmap on the screen or on some other device context. On Day 8, "Windows Animation: The Snake Game," and in other places in this book, you'll see that other options are available:

BLACKNESS	Produces black output.
DSTINVERT	Inverts the destination bitmap.
MERGECOPY	Uses the AND operator to combine source and pattern.
MERGEPAINT	Uses OR to combine the inverted source and destination.

NOTSRCCOPY	Inverts source before copying it to its destination.
NOTSRCERASE	Inverts the result of combining destination and source.
PATCOPY	Copies the pattern to the destination bitmap.
PATINVERT	Uses the XOR operator to combine source and pattern.
PATPAINT	Uses OR to combine inverted source and pattern.
SRCAND	Uses the AND operator to combine source and pattern.
SRCCOPY	Copies the source bitmap to the destination bitmap.
SRCERASE	Inverts destination and combines with source using AND.
SRCINVERT	Uses XOR to combine source and destination.
SRCPAINT	Uses OR to combine the destination and source.
WHITENESS	Produces white output.

If these options don't make much sense to you, don't sweat it. I'm supplying them mostly so hot graphics jockeys from the DOS world will see what a rich set of alternatives is available to Windows programmers.

> **Note:** Windows provides a number of calls that allow you to increase the performance of graphics routines. Some of these routines will be discussed later in the book when I discuss DIBs and WinG. These functions allow you to work with two buffers, one on-screen, and the other off-screen. By swapping them back and forth you can get pretty good performance, even by DOS mode 13 standards.

Perhaps it will be helpful if I am frank here and state that the act of blitting bitmaps to the screen left me somewhat baffled when I first started writing Windows code. After all, the entire life cycle of a bitmap involves seven discrete steps:

1. Load the bitmap.
2. Create a compatible DC.
3. Select the bitmap into the DC.
4. BitBlt the compatible DC into the window's DC.
5. Select the old bitmap into the compatible DC.
6. Delete the compatible DC.
7. Delete the bitmap.

Now there's enough noise to keep the wolves awake!

These seven steps aren't merely a suggested course of action. In fact, a minor slip-up on even one of the seven steps can set in motion a slow but sure process that will inevitably deplete Windows of the resources it needs to run. In particular, it's absolutely essential that you do not forget to twice call SelectObject or to delete a DC.

If you fail to clean up after using a bitmap, the computer's *system resources* get depleted. When this happens, Windows starts to fall apart bit by bit, in a manner somewhat similar to the collapse of the computer HAL near the end of *2001: A Space Odyssey*. In particular, you might notice that bitmaps lose their colors, menus or text disappear, and eventually the whole machine freezes up. To keep track of available system resources, you can view the About box accessible from the Explorer.

A Limited General Solution for Painting Bitmaps

Because bitmaps are such a chore to work with, it's nice to have a routine that will take care of most of the dirty work for you. There is no simple way to write a single routine that will handle all the vagaries associated with a bitmap. However, if your needs are modest, the following routine will come in very handy:

```
void DrawBitmap(HDC PaintDC, int x, int y, HBITMAP TheBitmap)
{
  BITMAP BitData;

  HDC BitmapDC = CreateCompatibleDC(PaintDC);
  HBITMAP OldBitmap = SelectBitmap(BitmapDC, TheBitmap);
  GetObject(TheBitmap, sizeof(BITMAP), &BitData);
  BitBlt(PaintDC, x, y, BitData.bmWidth, BitData.bmHeight,
         BitmapDC, 0, 0, SRCCOPY);
  SelectBitmap(BitmapDC, OldBitmap);
  DeleteDC(BitmapDC);
}
```

This function takes an HDC, two coordinates, and a bitmap. In turn, it will paint the bitmap to the HDC at the coordinates you specify.

To accomplish its goal, DrawBitmap calls the GetObject function, which retrieves the width and height of a bitmap, along with some other related data. In particular, given a valid handle to a bitmap, GetObject fills in the following structure:

```
typedef struct tagBITMAP {  // bm
    LONG    bmType;
    LONG    bmWidth;
    LONG    bmHeight;
    LONG    bmWidthBytes;
    WORD    bmPlanes;
    WORD    bmBitsPixel;
    LPVOID  bmBits;
} BITMAP;
```

It turns out that GetObject can retrieve similar information about pens, brushes, fonts, and palettes. To find out more, see GetObject in the online help.

Once again, there are some limitations to the DrawBitmap function. For instance, it doesn't quite suit the needs of the Emerson2 program. However, in many situations, it can help to keep you sane. On a day-to-day basis, I couldn't imagine how any Windows programmer could get along without this function, or one similar to it.

String Tables

String tables are one of the simplest of all resources to use. They can also help you conserve memory. Here's how they work:

String resources are loaded into memory 16 items at a time. You can have a string resource containing hundreds of lines of text; but if you need access to only a subset of those items, the whole list of strings won't have to be loaded into memory at the same time. Once they are loaded into memory, you can blast them to the screen using TextOut or some other GDI function.

To create a string resource, you can simply add a few lines of text to your RC file. Following is a complete definition of a very small string resource:

```
STRINGTABLE
BEGIN
0, "Woodnotes (Part 1)"
1, "by Ralph Waldo Emerson"
END
```

Each executable file can contain only one string table, so you don't need to give the string table a name. Instead, you can simply declare its type, and then directly define the strings themselves. Give each string a unique number, and encase all of them inside a BEGIN...END pair.

Because strings are loaded into memory 16 items at a time, you should begin each block of strings on appropriate boundaries. For instance, the first set of strings might reside between 0 and 15, or 0 and 31. The next set would start at number 16, 32, or 48.

Loading strings into memory is simple. All you need do is call LoadString. LoadString takes four parameters:

1. The hInstance of the executable file or DLL that contains the string resource
2. The unique number associated with a string
3. A buffer to hold the contents of the string to be loaded
4. The length of the string buffer used in the third parameter

> **Note:** Two asides should be mentioned in conjunction with the second and third parameters to LoadString.
>
> 1. You can declare constant identifiers to be used with the second parameter. For instance, I could have declared a constant called CM_WOODNOTES_TITLE and set it equal to zero. Then I could have used this identifier instead of the numeral zero to retrieve the poem's title.
>
> 2. It's usually not a good idea to declare an array to hold an in-memory copy of the contents of a string table. The whole point of string tables is to keep the strings out of memory and on disk whenever possible. Therefore, Emerson holds all the strings in only one small buffer, being sure to write each of them to the screen as soon as they are retrieved.

The scheme for displaying the poems from the Emerson program is encapsulated primarily in the WM_COMMAND and WM_PAINT functions. In responding to the first message, the Emerson program learns which poem the user wants to view. In responding to the second message, the user actually displays the appropriate strings on-screen.

Here is an excerpt from the Emerson_OnCommand function:

```
case CM_BRAHMIN:
   Start = 32;
   MaxLines = 22;
   SetScrollRange(hwnd,  SB_VERT, 0, MaxLines - 1, FALSE);
   InvalidateRect(hwnd, NULL, TRUE);
   DrawBitmaps = FALSE;
   break;
```

If the user wants to see the Brahma poem, he or she clicks on the appropriate menu item. Windows then sends your WndProc a CM_BRAHMIN identifier in conjunction with a WM_COMMAND message. In response, the Emerson program sets two integer variables:

```
Start = 32;
MaxLines = 22;
```

The first is the offset of the first line of the poem in the string resource, and the second is the length of the poem in lines.

The next step is to force Windows to send a WM_PAINT message to the Emerson program. This is done by calling the highly valuable InvalidateRect function.

The essence of handling the WM_PAINT message is simply to call LoadString to get hold of each string that needs to be displayed, and then to paint that string to the screen with TextOut. To do this, all Emerson needs to do is enter a FOR loop that iterates from Start to *Start* + *Maxlines*:

```
for (int i = nPosition; i < MaxLines; i++)
{
  LoadString(hInstance, i + Start, S, 100);
  TextOut(PaintDC, 1, Y, S, strlen(S));
  Y += TextHeight;
}
```

The actual implementation, however, is complicated by the presence of scrollbars, as explained in the next section. In particular, the scrollbars determine the value of nPosition.

To summarize, a string table is a very simple, very powerful device that enables you to display huge chunks of text with only minimal costs in terms of memory usage. Many programmers use string tables to store lists of error strings to be displayed by their programs.

Scrollbars

The Emerson program's scrollbars enable the user to scroll through a long poem that can't be shown completely in a single window.

To understand how Emerson's scrollbars work, you need to concentrate on the variable called nPosition. nPosition tells Emerson what line in a poem is currently at the top of the screen. For instance, if a poem is 50 lines long, and the user has scrolled the first 20 lines above the top of the screen, nPosition would be set to 20. If the first line of the poem is at the top of the screen, nPosition would be set to 0.

The value of nPosition changes whenever the user presses an arrow key or clicks the scrollbar.

Adding scrollbars to a program is an easy, three-step process:

1. Create the scrollbar by using the WS_VSCROLL style in the program's Create function:

   ```
   HWND hwnd = CreateWindow(szAppName, szAppName,
                       WS_OVERLAPPEDWINDOW | WS_VSCROLL,
                       CW_USEDEFAULT, CW_USEDEFAULT,
                       CW_USEDEFAULT, CW_USEDEFAULT,
                       NULL, NULL, hInst, NULL);
   ```

2. Call SetScrollRange with the SB_VERT flag. The third and fourth parameters to this function designate the range over which the program will need to be able to scroll:

   ```
   SetScrollRange(hwnd, SB_VERT, 0,
             MaxLines, FALSE);
   ```

   In WIN32, you can make the scrollbar disappear by setting the fourth parameter (MaxLines) to a negative number.

3. The final step is to respond to WM_VSCROLL messages, which are sent whenever the user clicks the scrollbar.

Here is a greatly simplified `Emerson_OnVScroll` function:

```
void Emerson_OnVScroll(HWND hwnd, HWND hwndCtl, UINT code, int pos)
{
  int ScrMove = 0, Temp, i;
  HDC PaintDC;

  switch(code)
  {

    ...

    case SB_LINEUP:
     if (nPosition > 0)
     {
       nPosition -= 1 ;
       ScrMove = TextHeight;
     }
     break ;

    case SB_LINEDOWN:
      if (nPosition < MaxLines)
      {
        nPosition += 1 ;
        ScrMove = -TextHeight;
      }
      break ;

    ...

    case SB_THUMBTRACK:
      Temp = nPosition;
      nPosition = pos;
      ScrMove = (Temp - nPosition) * TextHeight;
      break;

    case SB_THUMBPOSITION:
      nPosition = pos;
      break;

  }
  nPosition = max(0, min (nPosition, MaxLines - 1));
  SetScrollPos (hwnd, SB_VERT, nPosition, TRUE);
  ScrollWindow(hwnd, 0, ScrMove, NULL, NULL);
}
```

If the user clicks the arrow at the top of the scrollbar, an `SB_LINEUP` flag is sent along with a `WM_VSCROLL` message. In response, Emerson decrements `nPosition` by one, then sets the scroll box with a call to `SetScrollPos`. The scroll box is the little square "thumb" shown in Figure 7.5. The final step is to call `ScrollWindow` so the poem on-screen is repositioned to reflect the user's request.

Figure 7.5.

The thumb on a scrollbar should reflect the screen's location.

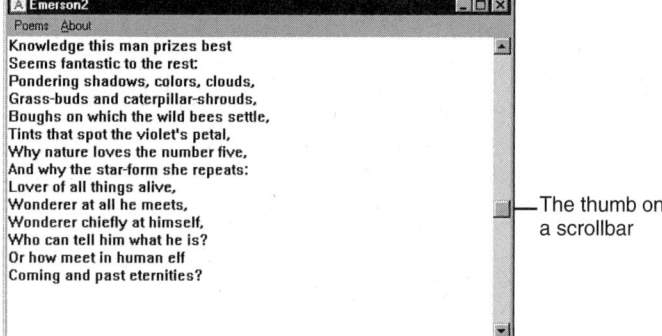

The thumb on a scrollbar

The tricky part is determining how much the window should scroll. The third parameter to `ScrollWindow` defines how many device units the window will be scrolled. The programmer's job is to determine the ratio between a device unit and the height of a line from the poem. In other words, if the poem needs to be scrolled five lines, you need to figure out how many device units are in five lines.

Note: For now, you can think of their being a one-to-one correspondence between device units and pixels. You will, however, find out much more about this complex subject on Day 16, "Dialog Boxes and Mapping Modes."

To translate device units to lines of text, you need to know the height of a line of text. That value is calculated way back at startup time, in the `WM_CREATE` message handler:

```
140:    HDC PaintDC = GetDC(hwnd);
141:    GetTextMetrics(PaintDC, &TextMetrics);
142:    ReleaseDC(hwnd, PaintDC);
143:    TextHeight = TextMetrics.tmHeight +
144:                 TextMetrics.tmExternalLeading;
```

This code begins by calling `GetDC` to get the device context to the main window. The HDC is needed in the call to `GetTextMetrics`, which retrieves a struct of type `TEXTMETRIC` containing information about the main window's default font. Two fields of the `TEXTMETRIC` struct are used to calculate the height of the font used to display the poem. This height is used both in the `WM_VSCROLL` handler and in the `WM_PAINT` method.

Once you know the ratio between the system's device units and the height of a line of text, you can then easily figure out what values to pass to `ScrollWindow`. The rest is just simple mechanics, plus a bit of fussing and optimizing. (Frankly, perfectionists can do a little more of both to improve the algorithms I've shown you here, but this should be enough for the needs of a relatively modest application.)

7

227

These same basic steps outlined above are repeated, with some minor variations, if the user clicks the arrow at the bottom of the scrollbar (SB_LINEDOWN), or if the user drags the thumb with the mouse (SB_THUMBPOSITION). The result is that the scrollbar enables you to give the user some control over a program's output.

Whenever the user clicks the scrollbar, a WM_VSCROLL message gets sent to the main window. But what happens when the user presses the up arrow or down arrow?

The Emerson program responds easily enough to this kind of input simply by handling WM_KEYDOWN messages. A press of the down arrow, for instance, results in a WM_KEYDOWN message with the VK_DOWN flag set. Emerson responds to this key press by creating its own WM_VSCROLL message:

```
221:    case VK_DOWN:
222:        SendMessage(hwnd, WM_VSCROLL, SB_LINEDOWN, 0L);
223:        break;
```

The SendMessage function recalls the WndProc, this time with a WM_VSCROLL message accompanied by the SB_LINEDOWN flag. Now the program can handle this message exactly as it would handle a mouse click on the down arrow portion of the scrollbar!

This wraps up the discussion of scrollbars and brings you to the end of this chapter. This is also the end of the discussion of the Emerson program. We've dwelt on it throughout most of the last two chapters, and I hope you've found it's been worth the effort.

Summary

Chapter 7 has introduced you to dialogs, bitmaps, string tables, and scrollbars. In particular, you have learned about

- ☐ Creating dialogs with resource scripts
- ☐ Using the MakeProcInstance function to bind the program's data segment to a dialog procedure
- ☐ Calling DialogBox to create a dialog
- ☐ Calling FreeProcInstance to detach a program's data segment from a dialog procedure
- ☐ Creating bitmaps
- ☐ Copying bitmaps into a compatible device context
- ☐ Blasting the bitmap from one device context onto another so it can be seen on-screen
- ☐ Preserving the original state of a device context and freeing bitmaps from memory
- ☐ Creating string tables
- ☐ Loading and reading string tables
- ☐ Managing string table resources

☐ Creating scrollbars with the WS_VSCROLL style

☐ Responding to WM_VSCROLL messages

Remember that this chapter contains only an introduction to dialogs and bitmaps. Both subjects are covered again in several different places throughout this book. In particular, on Day 17, "Advanced Dialogs: Getting and Setting Data," there is an in-depth discussion of dialog boxes.

Though you've had a fairly complete introduction to resources, I discuss this subject again on Day 20, "Menus and Icons in Depth." There, you'll get a chance to review certain advanced aspects of this large subject.

Once again, my goal is to introduce you to the basics of a topic and then to explore it again during a second pass. If I hit you with everything at once, you might be overwhelmed. For instance, it would not be good idea to introduce a student to James Joyce's *Ulysses* and a *Dick and Jane* book on the same day. Nor would most people want to learn geometry and calculus at the same time. My goal is to take one step at a time, building on the knowledge you gained in previous chapters.

Q&A

Q I still don't understand the relationship between the GDI and bitmaps. Can you go over that again?

A The people who created Windows tried to think in terms of discrete modules, or "objects." Eventually, it became clear that almost everything related to graphics needed to be treated in its own discrete category—which programmers called the Graphics Device Interface (GDI). More specifically, all calls that use a device context are by definition part of the GDI. If you look in your \Windows\System subdirectory, you'll find a file called GDI.EXE. This DLL contains all the calls that are part of the Graphics Device Interface.

Q Tell me more about dialogs.

A Dialogs are used either to display information, as in the About dialog box in this program, or to get information from the user. Many programs contain dialog boxes that pop up just long enough to get the user's name, or to ask the user to select one of several different choices. Most of these latter kinds of dialogs are modal, because the program often needs the user's input before it can continue. For instance, when you save a piece of source code, a dialog box is displayed to enable you to enter the name of the file where your source will be saved. This is usually a modal dialog box, because the program can't proceed until you specify a name or cancel the procedure. *Modal* dialogs are created by calls to DialogBox, whereas *modeless* dialogs are created by calls to CreateDialog.

Workshop

The Workshop provides quiz questions to help you solidify your understanding of the material covered and exercises to provide you with experience in using what you've learned. Try to understand the quiz and exercise answers before continuing on to Day 8. Answers are provided in Appendix A.

Quiz

1. What function is used to launch a modal dialog?

2. Trick question: What messages are sent to the program's main window when the About dialog box is on-screen?

3. What message is sent to the WndProc when a menu item is chosen?

4. Every call to MakeProcInstance must be balanced by a call to _____?

5. Every call to LoadBitmap must be balanced by a call to _____?

6. If you have strings stored in a string table, how do you retrieve them so the program can display them on-screen?

7. What message gets sent when a user clicks the scrollbar?

8. What is the TEXTMETRIC structure and where is it defined?

9. When you click the OK button in the About dialog, what message is generated and where is it sent?

10. What does the Emerson program do to call MakeProcInstance?

Exercises

1. The Emerson program creates a default background by repainting a single bitmap 15 times in the x and y directions. Optimize the program so that it only paints the minimum number of bitmaps needed to fill the main window, regardless of how large or small the user makes the program.

2. Add to the Emerson program a scrollbar that handles horizontal scrolling.

1

Consoles and Long Filenames

This week in review covers console applications, which look and feel like DOS applications but which have full access to the 4GB address space found in WIN32. You will also see how to work with long filenames and will get some exposure to WIN32 fileI/O issues.

All the programs in this week in review are Windows NT or Windows 95 specific. They will not run in 16-bit mode, and they will not run under Windows 3.1.

Topics covered in this chapter include:

- ☐ An overview of event-oriented programming from start to finish. Specifically, you will get a chance to create your own event loop.
- ☐ Mouse input in console applications.
- ☐ Raw console I/O routines.
- ☐ Calling GUI routines from a console application. (This is useful if you need to get a filename or perform some other operation that the Windows interface handles with ease.)
- ☐ Getting and using long filenames in both GUI and console applications.
- ☐ Iterating through the long filenames in a directory with `FindFirstFile` and `FindNextFile`.
- ☐ Creating a console window from a GUI application. (Useful for debugging.)

The pace at which you are being introduced to this material may seem a little relentless, but there is a great deal of territory to cover, and relatively little space to do it in. Onward, always onward—that is the watchword for this endeavor!

Console Applications

When most people think of Windows 95, one of the first things that comes to mind is GUIs. Windows 95 is supposed to be more graphically oriented than Windows 3.1, with more fancy graphical elements and more dependence on the way the user interacts with this material.

As a result, it came as something of a surprise to learn that Windows 95 fully supports text mode. You can build 32-bit Windows 95 applications that have full access to the WIN32 API but which run in text mode. You can start them from the command prompt, and they don't ever have to leave the command prompt. In other words, they don't have to pop up a traditional window. I say they don't *have* to, because actually they can pop up Windows if they need them. In fact, one of the examples in this chapter will show how to pop up a common dialog from a console application. (This is not necessarily a recommended course of action, but it's possible.)

From this perspective, it's a little hard to say just what role console applications will play in Windows 95. Will they be a big part of the show, or will they always be a sidelight? My opinion is that they are useful mostly to programmers who want to try out ideas. Traditional users aren't going to be attracted to console applications because such applications don't have the slick features of the Windows GUI. But that's just an opinion, and not a particularly strong one at that. Right now, it's just not clear what the future holds for console applications. This is a matter that will be decided over time, and it is programmers like yourself who will make the final judgment.

It's time now to get down to cases. Listings R1.1 through R1.4 show the Emily program, which is the first of several console applications to be introduced in this chapter.

Listing R1.1. The Emily application is a Windows 32 console application.

```
//////////////////////////////////////////////////////
// EMILY.CPP
// Copyright (c) 1995 Charlie Calvert.
// Demonstrate simple console application
//////////////////////////////////////////////////////

#define STRICT
#include <windows.h>
#include <stdio.h>


//////////////////////////////////////////////////////
// Program entry point
//////////////////////////////////////////////////////
int main(void)
{
  printf("\n\nThe soul selects her own society,\n");
  printf("Then shuts the door;\n");
  printf("On her devine majority\n");
  printf("Obtrude no more.\n\n");
  printf("Unmoved, she notes the chariot's pausing\n");
  printf("At her low gate;\n");
  printf("Unmoved, an emperor is kneeling\n");
  printf("Upon her mat.\n\n");
  printf("I've known her from an ample nation\n");
  printf("Choose one;\n");
  printf("Then close the valves of her attention\n");
  printf("Like stone\n");
  printf("\n-Emily Dickinson\n");

  printf("\n\n\nPress ENTER to close\n");
  getchar();

  return 0;
}
```

Listing R1.2. The DEF file for the Emily application.

```
; EMILY.DEF

NAME         EMILY
DESCRIPTION  'Simple console application'
```

233

Listing R1.3. The Borland makefile for the Emily application.

```
#----------------------------------------------------------------
# The MakeFile: EMILY.MAK
# Copyright (c) 1995 Charlie Calvert.
# Install automatically creates file BCROOT.INC in BIN directory.
#----------------------------------------------------------------

!if !$d(BCROOT)
BCROOT  = $(MAKEDIR)\..
!endif

APPNAME = EMILY

INCPATH = $(BCROOT)\INCLUDE\WIN32;$(BCROOT)\INCLUDE;$(BCROOT)\WIN32
LIBPATH = $(BCROOT)\LIB

COMPILER= BCC32.EXE
FLAGS   = -v -w4 -I$(INCPATH) -L$(LIBPATH)

# Link
$(APPNAME).EXE: $(APPNAME).OBJ $(APPNAME).DEF
  $(COMPILER) $(FLAGS) $(APPNAME).OBJ

# Compile
$(APPNAME).OBJ: $(APPNAME).CPP
  $(COMPILER) -c $(FLAGS) $(APPNAME).CPP
```

Listing R1.4. The Microsoft makefile for the Emily application.

```
#
# EMILY.MAK
#

!include <win32.mak>

APPNAME = EMILY

all: $(APPNAME).exe

$(APPNAME).obj: $(APPNAME).cpp
    $(cc) /Ox $(cflags) $(cvarsmtdll) $(APPNAME).cpp

$(APPNAME).exe: $(APPNAME).obj
    $(link) $(conflags) -out:$(APPNAME).exe \
    $(APPNAME).obj $(conlibsdll) $(guilibs)
```

When run, this program prints out the following poem in text mode:

```
The soul selects her own society,
Then shuts the door;
On her devine majority
Obtrude no more.
```

```
Unmoved, she notes the chariot's pausing
At her low gate;
Unmoved, an emperor is kneeling
Upon her mat.

I've known her from an ample nation
Choose one;
Then close the valves of her attention
Like stone

-Emily Dickinson
```

You can run this program from either the command prompt or from the Explorer. You could even create an icon for this application, if you wanted, and launch it on the task bar. However it is that you run it, the output, shown in Figure R1.1, is fairly bland by today's standards. (On the other hand, there are times when this is all you need. As I implied earlier, a big plus for console apps is that they're handy tools for programmers who want to test something out quickly. They can also provide the power for utilities that are used in house to accomplish mundane system-maintenance tasks.)

Figure R1.1.

The output from the Emily application.

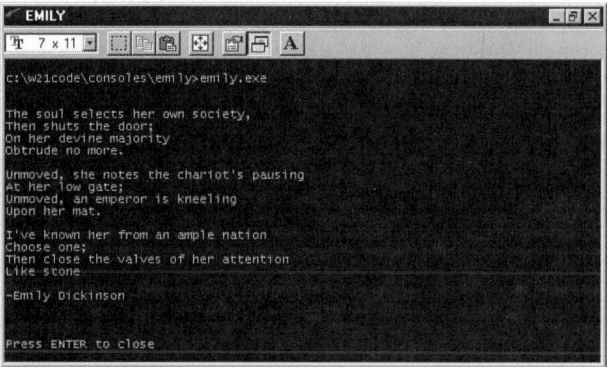

Note: You can compile and run these programs from either the command prompt or from inside the Borland or Microsoft IDE. If you do decide to compile from inside the IDE, you won't find any major challenges.

Borland users should create a standard WIN32 application, except that it is targeting the console and not a GUI. When you are in the Target Expert, choose Application Type EXE, Platform WIN32, Target Model Console, Standard Libraries Runtime and Static. You can use the Propeller Head advanced section to select just CPP and DEF files, because that's all you need when working with the Emily application. The key point is that you choose to target a console application instead of a GUI application. The compiler will

> know what to do from there. (If you have Borland 4.53, don't forget to choose the compiler option that compensates for the Pentium floating-point bug.)
>
> Microsoft users should choose New Project, then set the Project Name to Emily. Set the Project Type to Console Application. In the Project Files dialog, just add EMILY.CPP and EMILY.DEF to the project. That's all there is to it. The key move, of course, is setting Project Type to Console.

Despite the ease with which you can work on these programs from inside the Microsoft or Borland IDE, it still seems more sensible when working with a console app to both compile and run it from the command prompt. As always, I have provided batch files that will automate the act of compiling the applications. If you are a Borland user, just go to the appropriate subdirectory and run GO.BAT. Microsoft users should run MS.BAT. If your compiler is set up correctly, compilation will then be automatic. (Microsoft users may have to first run the MSVCVARS.BAT file in the \MSVC20\BIN subdirectory.)

If you stripped all the fancy hullabaloo away from the Emily program, this is what she would look like:

```
#include <stdio.h>

int main(void)
{
  printf("\n\nThe soul selects her own society,\n");
  return 0;
}
```

This is a programmer's dream, no? It's also a bonanza for technical writers. All I have to do is point out that this is just a traditional DOS application with WINDOWS.H thrown in for good measure. This is what the writing life is all about: just show some code, and if the readers don't understand, simply refer them to a book on basic C programming issues.

The point here is that console apps can be coded exactly like DOS applications, only you have to add WINDOWS.H to the list of included files. If you really don't understand how this kind of programming works, get a copy of *The Waite Group's New C Primer Plus*, by Mitchell Waite and Stephen Prata, published by Sams.

Constructing 4GB Arrays

If you've been programming for a while, you have probably come up against the 64KB limitation. This brick wall is endemic to 16-bit applications because you can't express a number larger than 64KB with only 16-bits. Even in Windows 3.1, the infamous 64KB limitation still held sway. That environment freed us at least in part from the 640KB

limitation, but we still had claustrophobic DGROUPs that had the data segment, stack and the heap all huddled together like Steve McQueen and his friends in the underground tunnel scenes from *The Great Escape.*

At any rate, console applications are not restricted by 64KB boundaries. You can allocate huge chunks of memory, if you wish. Of course, no one has the full 4GB of memory on their machine that a 32-bit system can address. And even if they did, they couldn't really create a 4GB array, because nearly half of that 4GB belongs to the system. Nevertheless, WIN32 programs feel very free and open compared to the old 16-bit world from which we've escaped.

Perhaps the people who will benefit the most from this new freedom are mathematicians and graphics programmers. (Programmers who needed to construct large arrays had the most to lose from the 64KB limitation.) However, everyone will benefit to some degree. If nothing else, it means large chunks of data can now reside in the data segment rather than having to go up on the heap.

Well, enough talk. It's time to see what it feels like to construct large arrays that aren't built on some kind of sleight-of-hand. This is the real thing—big arrays that stretch out across flat memory spaces. In WIN32, you can allocate the whole state of Kansas if you want! Just take a look at the big array program in Listings R1.5 through R1.8.

Listing R1.5. The main module for the BigArray program.

```
////////////////////////////////////////////////////////
// BIGARRAY.CPP
// Copyright (c) 1995 Charlie Calvert.
// Demonstrate simple console application
////////////////////////////////////////////////////////
#include <stdio.h>
#include <windows.h>


#define MAXX 20
#define MAXY 2000

////////////////////////////////////////////////////////
// Program entry point
////////////////////////////////////////////////////////
int main(void)
{
  int i, j;
  int BigOne[MAXX][MAXY];

  printf("\n\nThe size of the array is %d bytes.", sizeof(BigOne));

  printf("\n\n\nPress ENTER to continue\n");
  getchar();

  for (j = 0; j < MAXY; j++)
    for (i = 0; i < MAXX; i++)
```

continues

Listing R1.5. continued

```
      BigOne[i][j] = i;

  for (j = 0; j < MAXY; j++)
  {
    printf("Row:%d Data => ", j);
    for (i = 0; i < MAXX; i++)
      printf("%d ", BigOne[i][j]);
    printf("\n");
  }

  printf("\n\n\nPress ENTER to close\n");
  getchar();

  return 0;
}
```

Listing R1.6. The module definition file for the BigArray program.

```
; BIGARRAY.DEF

NAME        BIGARRAY
DESCRIPTION 'Simple console application'
```

Listing R1.7. The Borland makefile for the BigArray program.

```
#-------------------------------------------------------------
# The MakeFile: BIGARRAY.MAK
# Copyright (c) 1995 Charlie Calvert.
# Install automatically creates file BCROOT.INC in BIN directory.
#-------------------------------------------------------------

!if !$d(BCROOT)
BCROOT  = $(MAKEDIR)\..
!endif

APPNAME = BIGARRAY

INCPATH = $(BCROOT)\INCLUDE\WIN32;$(BCROOT)\INCLUDE;$(BCROOT)\WIN32LIBPATH =
$(BCROOT)\LIB

COMPILER= BCC32.EXE
FLAGS   = -v -w4 -I$(INCPATH) -L$(LIBPATH)

# Link
$(APPNAME).EXE: $(APPNAME).OBJ $(APPNAME).DEF
  $(COMPILER) $(FLAGS) $(APPNAME).OBJ

# Compile
$(APPNAME).OBJ: $(APPNAME).CPP
  $(COMPILER) -c $(FLAGS) $(APPNAME).CPP
```

Listing R1.8. The Microsoft makefile for the BigArray program.

```
#
# BIGARYMS.MAK
#

!include <win32.mak>

APPNAME = BIGARRAY

all: $(APPNAME).exe

$(APPNAME).obj: $(APPNAME).cpp
    $(cc) /Ox $(cflags) $(cvarsmtdll) $(APPNAME).cpp

$(APPNAME).exe: $(APPNAME).obj
    $(link) $(conflags) -out:$(APPNAME).exe \
    $(APPNAME).obj $(conlibsdll) $(guilibs)
```

The BigArray program declares an array that takes up 160,000 bytes. If you took out the reference to WINDOWS.H and tried to compile this application at the DOS prompt, you would get the following error at the point in the source where the array declaration is made:

```
Array size too large in function main().
```

The same thing would happen if you tried to compile the program in 16-bit Windows program using EasyWin or any other format.

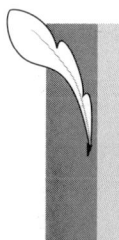

> **Note:** It's true that there is a HUGE type that would allow you to compile this type of code in 16-bit mode. However, the HUGE type didn't really allow you access to flat memory, but only to a set of routines that emulated it.
>
> Windows 95 is not by any means the first operating system to run in 32-bit memory areas. In fact, some special 32-bit protected-mode DOS programs were able to achieve this affect through some very fancy sleight-of-hand. But all of these systems exacted a price from the developer and from the user. Windows 95 and Windows NT are the real thing. They are true 32-bit operating systems.
>
> And yes, it is true that Windows 95 has many heavily used 16-bit subsystems. Nevertheless, when you compile a program in 32-bit mode, and when you run it under Windows 95, then you are getting access to a real 4GB address space. This isn't a kluge—it's the real thing. It also offers isolated address spaces that make it very difficult for 32-bit programs to step on one another.

When you run the BigArray program, you first get a report on the size of the array. Specifically, the text on the screen states that the array is 160,000 bytes in size.

Week 1 in Review

After you hit Enter, the program scrolls out a portrait of the entire array for your delectation. Obviously, this visual confirmation of what is happening serves no practical purpose; it just helps to make the whole 32-bit address space come to life in a concrete manner.

Needless to say, you can create arrays much larger than 160,000 bytes in size. I kept this one relatively small because I wanted to print the whole thing out to screen. Pentiums and 486s can manipulate arrays of this size in a blink of an eye, but screen I/O is still very slow on most computers.

Note: When working with these programs, you don't really have to add in a DEF file. I'm throwing it in here mostly because it helps emphasize that these are Windows programs. Also, it can serve to suppress some warnings on versions of some compilers.

My job as a writer isn't very complicated here. This book isn't about the kind of fundamental programming issues that are demonstrated in this program. However, my conscience drives me to point out that I use the `sizeof` operator to get the size of the array, as follows:

```
printf("\n\nThe size of the array is %d bytes.", sizeof(BigOne));
```

Note also that I declare macros defining the size of the array itself:

```
#define MAXX 20
#define MAXY 2000

int BigOne[MAXX][MAXY];
```

This allows me to make changes in one place of the code and then have it trickle down throughout the program:

```
for (j = 0; j < MAXY; j++)
  for (i = 0; i < MAXX; i++)
    BigOne[i][j] = i;
```

This type of technique is especially important with two-dimensional arrays. It's easy to get mixed up about which is the x axis and which is the y axis, and letting the preprocessor set up manifest constants helps keep your logic bug free.

In this section you have seen that Windows 95 breaks through the old 64KB limitation that used to restrict most Intel-based programmers. The new world has much broader horizons. However, the Windows 95 memory model is not as simple as it sounds at first.

I was surprised when I learned that my programs are usually loaded into memory at the 4MB mark, which is `0x00400000` in hex notation. To put it mildly, this is not what you would expect when you first consider these matters. However, the location at which your program is loaded

240

is recorded as the value of HINSTANCE in your application. Go ahead and run a program, and load HINSTANCE in the watch window of the debugger. The number you see is the address in virtual memory at which your program is loaded.

What does it mean to say that a program is loaded in at the 4MB mark? What about the memory below 4MB? Does your program have access to that memory? The short answer to that question is yes, it does. The longer answer involves an analysis of the virtual memory paging schemes used by Windows. My goal here is not to explain virtual memory in depth, but only to make it clear that things are not as simple as they might at first appear. For additional information, see the discussions of memory on Day 21, "Threads, Multitasking, and Memory Management." See also the explanation of the Snako program, on Bonus Day 4, "Snako for Windows."

Formatting Console Applications

As you have seen, many of the basic elements of screen I/O work just fine in console mode. In other words, you can use printf, gets, getchar, getch, and so on, just by including STDIO.H and/or CONIO.H. These routines should give you most of the control you need to output data to the screen. However, there are several built-in WIN32 console functions that you ought to know about.

In particular, you can get a handle to both standard in and standard out, and you can then use native WIN32 commands to write to the screen in a particular location and in a particular set of foreground and background colors.

Furthermore, as you will see in the upcoming Mouse program, you can also get access to the mouse, and to user input on a keystroke-by-keystroke basis. Once again, some of this is available from the C runtime libraries, but I want to show you the native Windows calls so you will understand what's actually happening inside of consoles.

I don't give them any real exposure in this book, but console applications also provide a very rich set of routines for manipulating screen buffers. In other words, you can define a text-mode window on the console screen and then move data in and out of that space. This is the basis of a windowing system, such as in TurboVision, and in other text-mode windowing schemes. Consoles also allow you to support using multiple screens at the same time, so you can be writing to an off-screen buffer, then swap it into memory with a single command.

All of this business about screen buffers is well outside the scope of this book. It's relatively complicated and would require several chapters to explore in depth. Right now there are bigger fish swimming inside the pond near which this book has set up camp. However, if you want to explore this matter further, you should open up WINCON.H, which ships with your compiler. Here are a couple of the goodies described therein:

```
typedef struct _CONSOLE_SCREEN_BUFFER_INFO {
    COORD dwSize;
    COORD dwCursorPosition;
    WORD  wAttributes;
    SMALL_RECT srWindow;
    COORD dwMaximumWindowSize;
} CONSOLE_SCREEN_BUFFER_INFO, *PCONSOLE_SCREEN_BUFFER_INFO;

typedef struct _CONSOLE_CURSOR_INFO {
    DWORD  dwSize;
    BOOL   bVisible;
} CONSOLE_CURSOR_INFO, *PCONSOLE_CURSOR_INFO;

WINBASEAPI BOOL WINAPI GetConsoleScreenBufferInfo(
    HANDLE hConsoleOutput,
    PCONSOLE_SCREEN_BUFFER_INFO lpConsoleScreenBufferInfo);

WINBASEAPI COORD WINAPI GetLargestConsoleWindowSize(
                        HANDLE hConsoleOutput);

WINBASEAPI BOOL WINAPI SetConsoleCursorInfo(
    HANDLE hConsoleOutput,
    CONST CONSOLE_CURSOR_INFO *lpConsoleCursorInfo);

WINBASEAPI BOOL WINAPI ScrollConsoleScreenBufferA(
    HANDLE hConsoleOutput, CONST SMALL_RECT *lpScrollRectangle,
    CONST SMALL_RECT *lpClipRectangle,
    COORD dwDestinationOrigin, CONST CHAR_INFO *lpFill);
```

The point is not that you assimilate all of this code instantly, but only that you have some sense of what is available.

To get back to the basic material that you ought to have some kind of grip on, I will show you the Faith program. Other than the little getchar routine right at the end, this code makes no use of the standard C library. Instead it does all the work using native WIN32 calls.

> **Note:** I throw a call to getchar in at the end of these programs just because they might be run from the Explorer rather than from the command prompt. The getch is there to keep the window from closing before you have a chance to view the output. At the very end of the chapter I show how to do this using native WIN32 calls.
>
> I would recommend running most of these programs from the command prompt, with the command window maximized via the Alt+Enter command. I find it easier to read the output if I set things up this way. Note, however, that WINCON.H has some functions in it designed to facilitate manipulating text in a scrolling window that comprises only a portion of the Windows desktop.

Below you will find the Faith program, which prints out a short poem by Emily Dickinson. It demonstrates basic console operations.

Listing R1.9. The main module for the Faith program shows how to use native WIN32 calls to write to the screen.

```
/////////////////////////////////////////////////////
// FAITH.CPP
// Copyright (c) 1995 Charlie Calvert.
// Demonstrate native windows console functions
/////////////////////////////////////////////////////

#include <windows.h>
#include <stdio.h>

#define ALT1 FOREGROUND_BLUE | FOREGROUND_GREEN

void ClrScr();
void WriteXY(int x, int y, LPSTR S, WORD Attr);

HANDLE hOut;

/////////////////////////////////////////////////////
// Program entry point.
/////////////////////////////////////////////////////
int main(void)
{
  int i;

  SetConsoleTitle("Emily Dickinson Console");

  hOut = GetStdHandle(STD_OUTPUT_HANDLE);

  ClrScr();

  WriteXY(0, 1, "Faith is a fine invention.", ALT1);
  WriteXY(0, 2, "For gentlemen who see;", ALT1);
  WriteXY(0, 3, "But microscopes are prudent", ALT1);
  WriteXY(0, 4, "In an emergency!", ALT1);

  getchar();

  return 0;
}

/////////////////////////////////////////////////////
// Blank the screen
/////////////////////////////////////////////////////
void ClrScr()
{
  DWORD NumWritten;
  COORD c;

  c.X = 0;
  c.Y = 0;
```

continues

Listing R1.9. continued

```
    FillConsoleOutputCharacter(hOut, ' ', 80 * 25, c, &NumWritten);
}

///////////////////////////////////////////////////////
// Write text at particular position
///////////////////////////////////////////////////////
void WriteXY(int x, int y, LPSTR S, WORD Attr)
{
  COORD c;
  DWORD result;

  c.X = x;
  c.Y = y;

  SetConsoleTextAttribute(hOut, Attr);
  SetConsoleCursorPosition(hOut, c);
  WriteConsole(hOut, S, strlen(S), &result, NULL);
}
```

Listing R1.10. The module definition file for the Faith program.

```
; FAITH.DEF

NAME        FAITH
DESCRIPTION 'Console basic IO example'
```

Listing R1.11. The Borland makefile for the Faith program.

```
#-----------------------------------------------------------------
# FAITH.MAK
# Copyright (c) 1995 Charlie Calvert.
# Install automatically creates file BCROOT.INC in BIN directory.
#-----------------------------------------------------------------

!if !$d(BCROOT)
BCROOT = $(MAKEDIR)\..
!endif

APPNAME = FAITH

INCPATH = $(BCROOT)\INCLUDE\WIN32;$(BCROOT)\INCLUDE;$(BCROOT)\WIN32
LIBPATH = $(BCROOT)\LIB

COMPILER= BCC32.EXE
FLAGS   = -v -w4 -I$(INCPATH) -L$(LIBPATH)

# Link
$(APPNAME).EXE: $(APPNAME).OBJ $(APPNAME).DEF
  $(COMPILER) $(FLAGS) $(APPNAME).OBJ
```

```
# Compile
$(APPNAME).OBJ: $(APPNAME).CPP
  $(COMPILER) -c $(FLAGS) $(APPNAME).CPP
```

Listing R1.12. The Microsoft makefile for the Faith program.

```
#
# FAITHMS.MAK
#

!include <win32.mak>

APPNAME = FAITH

all: $(APPNAME).exe

$(APPNAME).obj: $(APPNAME).cpp
    $(cc) /Ox $(cflags) $(cvarsmtdll) $(APPNAME).cpp

$(APPNAME).exe: $(APPNAME).obj
    $(link) $(conflags) -out:$(APPNAME).exe \
    $(APPNAME).obj $(conlibsdll) $(guilibs)
```

When you run this program, the following short poem is written to the screen in a light blue color with a black background:

```
Faith is a fine invention.
For gentlemen who see;
But microscopes are prudent
In an emergency!
```

This is one of Emily Dickinson's humorous but deceptively simple poems. When I read it, I hear several levels of irony in it. Over time I've come to hear the second line as resounding somewhat louder than last, though it's hard to hear through the irony my own prejudices—to what Emily actually meant.

I don't do it here, but you could start out this program by having it allocate its own console, as follows:

```
FreeConsole();
AllocConsole();
```

The first call will free the program from the current console, which is the command session. It will then allocate a new console, that is, it will start up its own window. In most cases, this is overkill, and will serve only to confuse the user. Calls to AllocConsole are useful mostly if you want to start a console window from inside a standard Windows program, which is demonstrated later in this chapter.

To set the title of a console, the Faith program uses the following API:

```
SetConsoleTitle("Emily Dickinson Console");
```

This is the title that appears if the program is run as a subwindow of the Windows desktop. It doesn't appear anywhere on the console itself, but only on the caption bar provided by the Windows GUI.

The next step is to get the input handle to which the program writes:

```
hOut = GetStdHandle(STD_OUTPUT_HANDLE);
```

hOut is declared to be of type handle. If you wanted to get the input handle, you would write:

```
hIn = GetStdHandle(STD_INPUT_HANDLE);
```

The Faith program expects to have control over the whole screen. That is, it's going to move the cursor around, and so it needs to know that the entire screen is blank. The following routine will blank the screen:

```
void ClrScr()
{
  DWORD NumWritten;
  COORD c;

  c.X = 0;
  c.Y = 0;

  FillConsoleOutputCharacter(hOut, ' ', 80 * 25, c, &NumWritten);
}
```

This routine has the same effect as the ClrScr command seen in numerous C runtime libraries.

FillConsoleOutputCharacter

The FillConsoleOutputCharacter function:

```
BOOL FillConsoleOutputCharacter(
    HANDLE  hConsoleOutput,     // standard output
    TCHAR   cCharacter,         // character to write
    DWORD   nLength,            // number cells to write
    COORD   dwWriteCoord,       // x and y of first cell
    LPDWORD lpNumberOfCharsWritten
                                // number of cells written to
    );
```

FillConsoleOutputCharacter takes the handle to standard out in the first parameter, a character to write in the second parameter, and the number of times you want to write it in the third parameter. The function returns the number of bytes written in the last parameter.

If the number of characters you are writing extends beyond the end of the line, then the output just wraps around to the next line. If you try to write past the end of the buffer, nothing

happens. The extra calls are never carried out. This makes it safe to hard code 80×25 into the program. If you wanted to calculate the exact number of characters to write to clear the entire screen, you could use GetConsoleScreenBufferInfo.

You should note that there is also a FillConsoleOutputAttribute routine, which is shown later in this chapter. It enables you to set the areas of the screen to one foreground and background color, just as FillConsoleOutputCharacter enables you to set the characters shown in a particular area of the screen.

Here's an example:

```
FillConsoleOutputCharacter(hOut, ' ', 80, c, &NumWritten);
```

If you want to write text to the screen, you can use the WriteConsole, SetConsoleTextAttribute, and SetConsoleCursorPosition functions:

```
void WriteXY(int x, int y, LPSTR S, WORD Attr)
{
  COORD c;
  DWORD result;

  c.X = x;
  c.Y = y;

  SetConsoleTextAttribute(hOut, Attr);
  SetConsoleCursorPosition(hOut, c);
  WriteConsole(hOut, S, strlen(S), &result, NULL);
}
```

By combining all three functions into one routine, I am able to write the text to the screen in a particular position, in a particular set of colors. Of course, you can also use WriteConsole all by itself.

SetConsoleTextAttribute takes the handle to standard out in the first parameter and an attribute in the second parameter. An attribute can be made up of one or more of the following: FOREGROUND_BLUE, FOREGROUND_GREEN, FOREGROUND_RED, FOREGROUND_INTENSITY, BACKGROUND_BLUE, BACKGROUND_GREEN, BACKGROUND_RED, and BACKGROUND_INTENSITY.

By combining them, you can create various effects. For instance, the following combination paints gold text on a blue background:

```
#define GOLDBLUE FOREGROUND_GREEN | FOREGROUND_RED | \
                 FOREGROUND_INTENSITY | BACKGROUND_BLUE
```

The SetConsoleCursorPosition depends on the following structure:

```
typedef struct _COORD { // coord.
    SHORT X;        // horizontal coordinate
    SHORT Y;        // vertical coordinate
} COORD;
```

Needless to say, this is just a variation on the POINT structure, which is used heavily in standard Windows GUI applications. You can pass this structure as the second parameter to SetConsoleCursorPosition and pass in a handle to the console screen buffer in the first parameter.

> **Note:** As a writer, I'm all in favor of using whole words to create meaningful identifiers. There is, however, a limit. My personal tolerance level is tested by such long names as SetConsoleCursorPosition. On the other hand, they are very easy to understand.

Below you will find a description of the WriteConsole routine. It's a native WIN32 routine to use in place of puts.

WriteConsole

This is the WriteConsole function:

```
BOOL WriteConsole(
    HANDLE  hConsoleOutput,     // handle of a console screen buffer
    CONST VOID  *lpvBuffer,     // address of buffer to write from
    DWORD  cchToWrite,          // number of characters to write
    LPDWORD  lpcchWritten,      // address of number of characters written
    LPVOID  lpvReserved         // reserved
    );
```

The WriteConsole function writes a string to the screen. Pass in the handle of the console screen buffer in the first parameter, a string in the second, and the number of characters to write in the third. The address of the number of characters written is returned in the next-to-last parameter, and the final parameter is reserved for Windows, or for future use.

Here's an example:

```
WriteConsole(hOut, "Hello", 5, &result, NULL);
```

Once again, I want to point out that I am just giving you an introduction to this topic. If you want to pursue it further, you should open up WINCON.H and start browsing around.

Handling the Mouse and Keyboard

The Mouse program gives you a feeling for how you can handle input from the mouse and the keyboard in console applications. This is a simple application that reports on the current position of the mouse, the current state of the mouse buttons, and any alphanumeric keys pressed by the user.

I want to stress that most of the standard C library I/O operations work just fine in command-prompt-based console applications. For instance, you can use `gets` to handle text input from the user. However, if you want to track the mouse, you will almost certainly want to use the built-in console routines. Furthermore, the actions of some standard library I/O routines are problematic if you launch a console window from inside a GUI application. If you want to run a console from inside a GUI application you should probably use the raw WIN32 routines shown here.

As with all the code in this chapter, the routines I show you here are fairly simple. However, this program is important because it creates its own event loop. I discussed event-oriented programming earlier in this book, but here is an example of how to create an event-oriented program from scratch. In other words, this code shows something of how the internal event-oriented Windows routines must actually work. If you have never seen this type of code before, it will be an invaluable aid because it gives some hints as to how a message-oriented operating system is structured.

Well, it's time to get the Mouse program up and running. You will find the source code in Listings R1.13 through R1.16. Go ahead and give it a spin, and then I will spend a few brief paragraphs discussing the high points of this simple application.

Listing R1.13. The Mouse program shows how to use the mouse in a console application.

```
////////////////////////////////////////////////////////
// MOUSE.CPP
// Copyright (c) 1995 Charlie Calvert.
// Demonstrate simple console application
////////////////////////////////////////////////////////

#define STRICT
#include <windows.h>
#include <stdio.h>

void HandleKey(KEY_EVENT_RECORD Key);
void HandleMouse(MOUSE_EVENT_RECORD Mouse);
void SayGoodBye(void);
void ClrScr(void);
void GotoXY(SHORT x, SHORT y);
void Write(LPSTR S);

HANDLE hOut, hIn;

////////////////////////////////////////////////////////
// Program entry point.
////////////////////////////////////////////////////////
int main(void)
{
  DWORD Result;
  INPUT_RECORD Buffer;
```

continues

Listing R1.13. continued

```
    hOut = GetStdHandle(STD_OUTPUT_HANDLE);
    hIn  = GetStdHandle(STD_INPUT_HANDLE);

    ClrScr();

    GotoXY(0, 24);
    Write("Move mouse, press keys, double click to Exit...");

    do
    {
      ReadConsoleInput(hIn, &Buffer, 1, &Result);

      if (Buffer.EventType==MOUSE_EVENT)
        HandleMouse(Buffer.Event.MouseEvent);

      if (Buffer.EventType==KEY_EVENT)
        HandleKey(Buffer.Event.KeyEvent);

    } while (!(Buffer.EventType == MOUSE_EVENT &&
              Buffer.Event.MouseEvent.dwEventFlags == DOUBLE_CLICK));

    SayGoodBye();

    return 0;
}

//////////////////////////////////////////////////////
// GOTOXY Move cursor to Col, Row
//////////////////////////////////////////////////////
void GotoXY(SHORT x, SHORT y)
{
  COORD c;
  c.X = x;
  c.Y = y;
  SetConsoleCursorPosition(hOut, c);
}

//////////////////////////////////////////////////////
// Blank a line of text at position Y
//////////////////////////////////////////////////////
void BlankLine(SHORT Y)
{
  DWORD NumWritten;
  COORD c;

  c.X = 0;
  c.Y = Y;

  FillConsoleOutputCharacter(hOut, ' ', 80, c, &NumWritten);
}

//////////////////////////////////////////////////////
// Clear the screen
//////////////////////////////////////////////////////
```

```
void ClrScr(void)
{
  SHORT i;

  for (i = 0; i < 25; i++)
    BlankLine(i);

  GotoXY(0,0);
}

//////////////////////////////////////////////////////
// Write a line of text
//////////////////////////////////////////////////////
void Write(LPSTR S)
{
  DWORD NumWritten;

  WriteConsole(hOut, S, strlen(S), &NumWritten, NULL);
}

//////////////////////////////////////////////////////
// Report on position of mouse
//////////////////////////////////////////////////////
void HandleMouse(MOUSE_EVENT_RECORD Mouse)
{
  char S[150];

  sprintf(S, "Buttons: %lu, X:%2lu Y:%2lu\n",
          Mouse.dwButtonState,
          Mouse.dwMousePosition.X,
          Mouse.dwMousePosition.Y);

  GotoXY(0, 0);
  Write(S);
}

//////////////////////////////////////////////////////
// Report on key strokes entered
//////////////////////////////////////////////////////
void HandleKey(KEY_EVENT_RECORD Key)
{
  char S[100];

  sprintf(S, "You pressed: %c", Key.uChar);
  GotoXY(0, 1);
  Write(S);
  sprintf(S, "Virtual key: %3d", Key.wVirtualKeyCode);
  GotoXY(0, 2);
  Write(S);
}

//////////////////////////////////////////////////////
// Input a string, process it, spit it back out.
//////////////////////////////////////////////////////
void SayGoodBye(void)
{
```

continues

Week 1 in Review

Listing R1.13. continued

```
    char S[100];

    ClrScr();
    printf("Enter your name: ");
    gets(S);
    printf("\nGoodbye %s!\n", S);
}
```

Listing R1.14. The module definition file for the Mouse program.

```
; MOUSE.DEF

NAME          MOUSE
DESCRIPTION 'Simple console application'
```

Listing R1.15. The Borland makefile for the Mouse program.

```
#-----------------------------------------------------------
# The MakeFile: MOUSE.MAK
# Copyright (c) 1995 Charlie Calvert.
# Install automatically creates file BCROOT.INC in BIN directory.
#-----------------------------------------------------------

!if !$d(BCROOT)\..
BCROOT  = $(MAKEDIR)
!endif

APPNAME = MOUSE

INCPATH = $(BCROOT)\INCLUDE\WIN32;$(BCROOT)\INCLUDE;$(BCROOT)\WIN32
LIBPATH = $(BCROOT)\LIB

COMPILER= BCC32.EXE
FLAGS   = -v -w4 -I$(INCPATH) -L$(LIBPATH)

# Link
$(APPNAME).EXE: $(APPNAME).OBJ $(APPNAME).DEF
  $(COMPILER) $(FLAGS) $(APPNAME).OBJ

# Compile
$(APPNAME).OBJ: $(APPNAME).CPP
  $(COMPILER) -c $(FLAGS) $(APPNAME).CPP
```

Listing R1.16. The Microsoft makefile for the Mouse program.

```
#
# MOUSEMS.MAK
#

!include <win32.mak>

APPNAME = MOUSE

all: $(APPNAME).exe

$(APPNAME).obj: $(APPNAME).cpp
    $(cc) /Ox $(cflags) $(cvarsmtdll) $(APPNAME).cpp

$(APPNAME).exe: $(APPNAME).obj
    $(link) $(conflags) -out:$(APPNAME).exe \
    $(APPNAME).obj $(conlibsdll) $(guilibs)
```

As I said previously, this program does little more than track the current position of the mouse and report back to you whenever the user presses a key. You should use Alt+Enter to make the command prompt take up the whole screen when you are running this application. This is an educational program, and not a real-world tool. As a result, I take the liberty of insisting that you run it in a maximized window, and preferably one that takes up the whole screen.

You can see the output from the main body of the program in Figure R1.2.

Figure R1.2.
The output from the text-mode Mouse program.

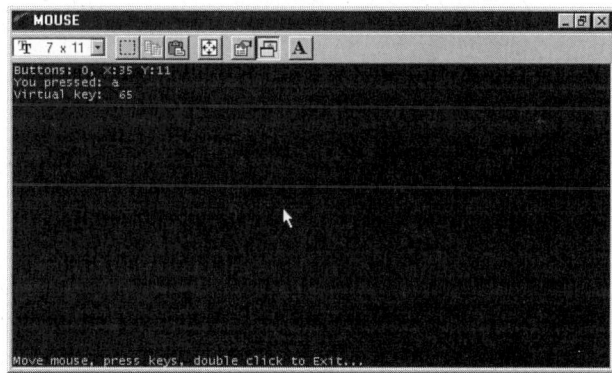

Here is the event loop that lies at the core of this program:

```
do
  {
    ReadConsoleInput(hIn, &Buffer, 1, &Result);

    if (Buffer.EventType==MOUSE_EVENT)
      HandleMouse(Buffer.Event.MouseEvent);
```

```
    if (Buffer.EventType==KEY_EVENT)
        HandleKey(Buffer.Event.KeyEvent);

    } while (!(Buffer.EventType == MOUSE_EVENT &&
```

This code loops around and around until the user double-clicks on the screen. Each iteration of the loop begins by checking for user input with the ReadConsoleInput routine.

ReadConsoleInput

```
BOOL ReadConsoleInput(
    HANDLE  hConsoleInput,         // handle of a console input buffer
    PINPUT_RECORD  pirBuffer,      // address of the buffer for read data
    DWORD   cInRecords,            // number of records to read
    LPDWORD  lpcRead               // address of number of records read
    );
```

These routines take many of the same parameters used in routines discussed earlier in this chapter. As a result, I won't repeat a description of them here.

The key new piece of information in the ReadConsole routine is the buffer of type INPUT_RECORD:

```
typedef struct _INPUT_RECORD { // ir
    WORD EventType;
    union {
        KEY_EVENT_RECORD KeyEvent;
        MOUSE_EVENT_RECORD MouseEvent;
        WINDOW_BUFFER_SIZE_RECORD WindowBufferSizeEvent;
        MENU_EVENT_RECORD MenuEvent;
        FOCUS_EVENT_RECORD FocusEvent;
    } Event;
} INPUT_RECORD;
```

This record tracks keyboard events, mouse events, buffer size changes, menu events, and events regarding the current focus. In particular, if the user moves the mouse or inputs something with the keyboard, the results of that action are recorded in the above structure. I will discuss the MOUSE_EVENT_RECORD and KEY_EVENT_RECORD below. If you are interested in the other structures, you should refer to the online help. The EventType field is also discussed later.

The fundamental idea you need to grasp about the ReadConsoleInput routine is that it allows the system to fill in the INPUT_RECORD with information about the current state of the program. The routine does not wait for the user to input information. Instead, it simply goes off and finds out what is happening right now. If there is nothing going on, then it comes back and tells you as much.

Here's an example:

```
ReadConsoleInput(hIn, &Buffer, 1, &Result);
```

Check out this loop very carefully, and take the time to understand how the ReadConsoleInput function fits into its cycles. It's crucial that you understand that somewhere deep in the bowels of Windows, a loop similar to this has to be executing. This is the way all event-oriented programs are structured.

Once you've called ReadConsoleInput, the next step is to check if something important has happened. Specifically, you want to know if a mouse event has occurred or if any of the keys on the keyboard have been pressed. The way to check for these events is to look at the EventType field of the INPUT_RECORD:

```
if (Buffer.EventType==MOUSE_EVENT)
   HandleMouse(Buffer.Event.MouseEvent);

if (Buffer.EventType==KEY_EVENT)
   HandleKey(Buffer.Event.KeyEvent);
```

If a mouse event occurs, the following routine is called:

```
void HandleMouse(MOUSE_EVENT_RECORD Mouse)
{
  char S[150];

  sprintf(S, "Buttons: %lu, X:%2lu Y:%2lu\n",
          Mouse.dwButtonState,
          Mouse.dwMousePosition.X,
          Mouse.dwMousePosition.Y);

  GotoXY(0, 0);
  Write(S);
}
```

A mouse event record looks like this:

```
typedef struct _MOUSE_EVENT_RECORD { // mer
    COORD dwMousePosition;   // Coordinates of mouse
    DWORD dwButtonState;     // Which button is pressed
    DWORD dwControlKeyState; // Alt key, control key, numlock etc.
    DWORD dwEventFlags;      // double click? Mouse moved?
} MOUSE_EVENT_RECORD;
```

The key fields here are the first two. The current mouse position is recorded in the first field, and the button that was pressed is recorded in the second field. For most purposes, you can just assume a press on the left button sets the button state to 1, and a press on the second button sets the button state to 2. However, to get an exact reading on what is happening, you need to perform bitwise operations, as explained in the online help. In other words, each mouse button is assigned to a bit in the 32-bit value involved in this field. This means the routine can handle fancy input devices with more than two, or even three, buttons.

The dwControlKeyState tells you what special keys are pressed. For instance, it tracks the Ctrl key, the Alt key, the Shift key, and so on.

The final parameter reports on whether a double click occurred or if the mouse was simply moved. To aid in reading input, the following values are defined:

```
DOUBLE_CLICK
MOUSE_MOVED
```

A value of 0 means a button was clicked.

After taking a look at this record, it's easy to see how the HandleMouse event works. It simply reports on the status of the first two fields of the record by writing their values to the top of the screen.

> **Note:** Throughout this chapter, I'm assuming you understand printf and other standard I/O routines from books on DOS programming. If you don't have this knowledge, then you should refer to an appropriate book, and then come back here after you have had some experience with the basic C library and its syntax.

The code that surrounds the HandleMouse routine is part and parcel of the essence of an event-oriented program. During execution of the majority of the Mouse program, a loop is whirring around over and over, at blinding speeds. Every time an event happens, certain routines are called. In this specific case, the routines will output data about the event to the screen. Inside Windows itself, nothing is sent to a window. Instead, messages are packaged and sent off. Your program responds to these messages by capturing WM_MOUSEMOVE, WM_KEYDOWN, WM_LBUTTONDOWN, and other messages. It's really very simple, once you get the feel for it.

The event that handles keyboard input is even simpler than the one for handling mouse input:

```
void HandleKey(KEY_EVENT_RECORD Key)
{
  char S[100];

  sprintf(S, "You pressed: %c", Key.uChar);
  GotoXY(0, 1);
  Write(S);
  sprintf(S, "Virtual key: %3d", Key.wVirtualKeyCode);
  GotoXY(0, 2);
  Write(S);
}
```

Here's what a KEY_EVENT_RECORD looks like:

```
typedef struct _KEY_EVENT_RECORD { // ker
    BOOL bKeyDown;              // True = press, false = release
    WORD wRepeatCount;         // how many time was it pressed?
    WORD wVirtualKeyCode;      // Virtual key codes from Day 3
    WORD wVirtualScanCode;     // Scan code
    union {
```

```
    WCHAR UnicodeChar;    // Windows NT only
    CHAR  AsciiChar;      // What alphanumeric key was pressed
  } uChar;
  DWORD dwControlKeyState; // Press on caps lock, shift, etc.
} KEY_EVENT_RECORD;
```

The important fields here are the wVirtualKeyCode and uChar fields. The virtual key codes were discussed on Day 3, "A Standard Windows Program," and are listed in the online help under the topic Virtual Key Codes. They help you track events involving special keys, such as the Enter key, the function keys (F1, F2), and the numeric keypad.

The uChar field translates these special key codes into standard ASCII characters, whenever possible. That is, if the key is an alphanumeric value or one of the low ASCII characters, it gets passed on in the uChar field. For instance, the wVirtualKeyCode for a press on the A key would be 65, while the uChar character would report either A or a, depending on the state of the shift key.

That's all I'm going to say about the Mouse program. You will find that it contains several other routines of interest to console programmers but nothing else that needs explanation here.

Long Filenames

Earlier in this chapter I showed how to allocate memory in chunks larger than 64KB. Many programmers have been waiting years for this ability to come to the PC. Now that it's finally here, you'd almost expect your first access of this capability to cause the computer to react by flashing lights and playing songs. Unfortunately, nothing quite that exciting happens, and instead you quite silently and unobtrusively enter a whole new age in PC programming.

The same thing is true of long filenames. Despite the extended delay in implementation, it turns out you don't have to do anything special to get access to this much-desired feature. Long filenames just appear automatically when you start using the relevant functions, many of which you have been using for years. You don't even have to include a special flag or define some special value.

Here are some of the particulars. If you've loaded Windows 95 and you have a 32-bit compiler, then without any fanfare, and without any warning, you will suddenly find that fopen can take a long filename in its first parameter. Say good-bye to this kind of code:

```
fp = fopen("LL071595.txt", "w+");
```

Say hello to code that looks like this:

```
fp = fopen("Love Letter to Margie dated 07-15-95.txt", "w+");
```

Week 1 in Review

This is a wonderful improvement, and certainly we should all be happy to see this day arrive. After all, it was hard to feel very romantic about a document called LL071595.TXT. This is a major breakthrough for a lot of lonely programmers.

Despite the greener pastures opening up before us, you should be aware that there are some limitations in the details of how this system is implemented. For instance, I could not have written:

```
fp = fopen("Letter to Dad dated 07/15/95.txt", "w+");
```

This particular limitation should come as no surprise, because the slash character has a more primary significance when used in pathnames, and therefore it can't also be used as a separator in a date. Nevertheless, there are some real limitations on what you can and cannot do with a long filename. This means you still might find yourself writing routines that parse pathnames for invalid characters. (Some help comes from the File Open and File Same common dialogs, shown later in this chapter, which should be used whenever possible. They are not a panacea, but they help you get valid input from the user.)

The new long-filename system lets you use the following:

- [ ] The standard letters
- [ ] The standard digits
- [ ] The standard three-letter extension
- [ ] ASCII codes greater than 127 (not recommended)
- [ ] The space character (ASCII 20h)

You can also use these special characters:

```
$ % ' - _ @   ~ ` ! ( ) { } ^ # &" + , ; = [ ]
```

The filename may be up to 256 characters in length. The path before the filename may be up to 246 characters in length. (This is 256 minus the length of a DOS 8.3 name.) This means you might want to put a damper on your desire to create very long directory names, especially if you are creating nested subdirectories.

Long filenames also recognize the case of the letters you use. In other words, they know the difference between a lowercase a and a capital A. However, this is not used to distinguish one file from the other. For instance, if you have a file called My File.txt and you then try to create a file called My file.txt in the same directory, the latter may overwrite the former but will preserve the name of the first file. In other words, the contents will change, but the name will remain as My File.txt.

If you go to the command prompt after creating a long filename, you will see some monstrosities that look like this:

```
acreat~1.txt      33    7-15-95   13:23
anfope~1.txt     721    7-15-95   13:05
anfope~2.txt     721    7-15-95   13:23
longname.cpp    3077    7-15-95   13:23
longname.def      78    7-14-95   12:28
longname.exe   46340    7-15-95   13:23
longname.mak     622    7-14-95   12:27
```

The bottom four names look sensible enough, but what's going on in the first three names? These are aliases created so that the old DOS file system can still work with long filenames!

Sigh.

Here's what the preceding names are supposed to look like:

```
A CreateFile long name.txt
An fopen long name 05-23-95.txt
An fopen long name 07-17-95.txt
```

Once you accept the basic premise of the endeavor, it's clear enough how Windows got from a name that looks like this:

```
A CreateFile long name.txt
```

to a name that looks like this:

```
acreat~1.txt
```

Note, however, that the next two long filenames are identical up to, and beyond, the eighth character. This means that Windows can't simply truncate the names and let the devil take the hindmost. It simply won't work.

The system created to avoid this crisis is to simply append a number on the end of the truncated name so that the first file is numbered 1, the second is numbered 2, and so on. Study the following examples to see more about how this works. Here's the long name:

```
An fopen long name 05-23-95.txt
An fopen long name 07-17-95.txt
```

Here are the truncated names:

```
anfope~1.txt     721    7-15-95   13:05
anfope~2.txt     721    7-15-95   13:23
```

Notice that the spaces have been removed. A space is a legal character in both file systems, but the DOS file systems don't handle it very well. (That last phrase is a bit of an understatement.)

What it all boils down to is that you cannot guess what short filename the system will use in place of a long filename. I'm sure people will develop systems that appear to be right most of the time, but you just can't be sure what name the boys and girls from Redmond might generate next. It's not documented, and it might change in future systems. It's undefined.

However, if you are really desperate to get into this one in depth, you should note that the following characters are valid in long filenames and not valid in the short aliases generated for the DOS prompt: the plus character (+), the comma (,), the semicolon (;), the equal sign (=), and the open and close brackets ([ ])

I don't recommend going down this road, but there they are if you need them!

It's time now to see an actual example of long filenames at work. As I suggested previously, there really isn't much to this particular subject. Long filenames come for free, and the code I have here is really meant just to prove that fact to you. See Listings R1.17 through R1.20 to get started.

Listing R1.17. The LongName program shows how to use the new long filenames used in Windows applications.

```
/////////////////////////////////////////////////////////
// LONGNAME.CPP
// Copyright (c) 1995 Charlie Calvert.
// How to create long file names, plus some file IO
// 07/14/95
/////////////////////////////////////////////////////////

#include <windows.h>
#include <stdio.h>

// Macros
#define MAXSIZE       100

#define OPEN_ERROR    1000
#define WRITE_ERROR   1001
#define CLOSE_ERROR   1002
#define FILE_SUCCESS  1003

// Funcs
void Report(int OutCome, LPSTR S);
int FOpenMethod(void);
BOOL CreateFileMethod(void);
void ShowFiles(void);

/////////////////////////////////////////////////////////
// Program entry point
/////////////////////////////////////////////////////////
int main(void)
{
  Report(FOpenMethod(), "File 1");

  Report(CreateFileMethod(), "File 2");

  ShowFiles();

  printf("\nPress ENTER to terminate.");
  getchar();

  return 0;
}
```

```
//////////////////////////////////////////////////////
// Report out come of file operation
//////////////////////////////////////////////////////
void Report(int OutCome, LPSTR S)
{
  switch(OutCome)
  {
    case OPEN_ERROR:
      printf("Error opening %s\n", S);
      break;

    case WRITE_ERROR:
      printf("Error writing %s\n", S);
      break;

    case CLOSE_ERROR:
      printf("Error closing %s\n", S);
      break;

    case FILE_SUCCESS:
      printf("Success: %s\n", S);
      break;
  }
}


//////////////////////////////////////////////////////
// Use fopen, etc, to open files
//////////////////////////////////////////////////////
int FOpenMethod(void)
{
  FILE *fp;
  int Num;

  fp = fopen("An fopen long name.txt", "w+");
  if (fp == NULL)
    return OPEN_ERROR;

  for (Num = 0; Num < 43; Num++)
    fprintf(fp, "Information: %d\n", Num);

  if (fclose(fp) != 0)
    return CLOSE_ERROR;

  return FILE_SUCCESS;
}


//////////////////////////////////////////////////////
// Use CreateFile, etc, to open files
//////////////////////////////////////////////////////
BOOL CreateFileMethod(void)
{
  DWORD NumWritten;
  char *S = "A little data for the second file";

  HANDLE hFile = CreateFile("A CreateFile long name.txt",
                   GENERIC_WRITE, 0, NULL, CREATE_ALWAYS,
```

continues

Listing R1.17. continued

```
                      FILE_ATTRIBUTE_NORMAL, NULL);

  if (hFile == INVALID_HANDLE_VALUE)
    return OPEN_ERROR;


  if (!WriteFile(hFile, S, strlen(S), &NumWritten, NULL))
    return WRITE_ERROR;

  if (!CloseHandle(hFile))
    return CLOSE_ERROR;

  return FILE_SUCCESS;
}

/////////////////////////////////////////////////////
// Show all the files in the current directory
/////////////////////////////////////////////////////
void ShowFiles(void)
{
  WIN32_FIND_DATA FindData;
  HANDLE Data;

  printf("\nDirectory Output:\n");

  Data = FindFirstFile("*.*", &FindData);
  while (Data != INVALID_HANDLE_VALUE)
  {
    printf("%s\n", FindData.cFileName);
    if (!FindNextFile(Data, &FindData))
      break;
  }

  FindClose(Data);
}
```

Listing R1.18. The module definition file for the LongName program.

```
; LONGNAME.DEF

NAME         LONGNAME
DESCRIPTION 'Use long file names';
```

Listing R1.19. The Borland makefile for the LongName program.

```
#-----------------------------------------------------------------
# The MakeFile: LONGNAME.MAK
#
```

```
# Macros
#
# Install automatically creates file BCROOT.INC in BIN directory.
#-------------------------------------------------------------

!if !$d(BCROOT)
BCROOT  = $(MAKEDIR)\..
!endif

APPNAME = LONGNAME

INCPATH = $(BCROOT)\INCLUDE\WIN32;$(BCROOT)\INCLUDE;$(BCROOT)\WIN32
LIBPATH = $(BCROOT)\LIB

COMPILER= BCC32.EXE
FLAGS   = -v -w4 -I$(INCPATH) -L$(LIBPATH)

# Link
$(APPNAME).EXE: $(APPNAME).OBJ $(APPNAME).DEF
  $(COMPILER) $(FLAGS) $(APPNAME).OBJ

# Compile
$(APPNAME).OBJ: $(APPNAME).CPP
  $(COMPILER) -c $(FLAGS) $(APPNAME).CPP
```

Listing R1.20. The Microsoft makefile for the LongName program.

```
#
# LONGNAMS.MAK
#

!include <win32.mak>

APPNAME = LONGNAME

all: $(APPNAME).exe

$(APPNAME).obj: $(APPNAME).cpp
    $(cc) /Ox $(cflags) $(cvarsmtdll) $(APPNAME).cpp

$(APPNAME).exe: $(APPNAME).obj
    $(link) $(conflags) -out:$(APPNAME).exe \
    $(APPNAME).obj $(conlibsdll) $(guilibs)
```

The output from this program looks something like this, depending a little on the details of the directory structure on your system:

```
Success: File 1
Success: File 2

Directory Output:
.
..
LONGNAME.MAK
```

```
LONGNAMS.MAK
GO.BAT
LONGNAME.DEF
LONGNAME.CPP
MS.BAT
LONGNAME.obj
LONGNAME.exe
A CreateFile long name.txt
An fopen long name 07-17-95.txt

Press ENTER to terminate.
```

The first two lines report whether the file operations for this program were successful:

```
Success: File 1
Success: File 2
```

If something went wrong, you would see an error message in place of these two success notifications. The error message will probably be generated by the LongName program itself. See the Report routine in LONGNAME.CPP for further details.

The core of the program creates the following two files:

```
A CreateFile long name.txt
An fopen long name 07-17-95.txt
```

It uses the native WIN32 CreateFile API to create the first file, and it uses the standard C library fopen routine to create the second file. Obviously the main feature here is that these are long filenames.

> **Note:** As explained previously, you won't be able to properly see these filenames if you type DIR from the command prompt. If you want to get a peek at them, use the LongName program itself, or else open up the Explorer.

Except for the two local routines called CreateFileMethod and ShowFiles, all of the code in this program is straight out of C Programming 101. You might want to refer to a reference book to see the order of parameters for fopen, but the basic concepts behind the procedure should be clear to the intended audience for this book. (However, if you are desperate for some additional information, I do cover the routine in a little more depth in Bonus Day 4.)

For now, the key subject of interest is the CreateFileMethod routine:

```
BOOL CreateFileMethod(void)
{
```

```
DWORD NumWritten;
char *S = "A little data for the second file";

HANDLE hFile = CreateFile("A CreateFile long name.txt",
                GENERIC_WRITE, 0, NULL, CREATE_ALWAYS,
                FILE_ATTRIBUTE_NORMAL, NULL);

if (hFile == INVALID_HANDLE_VALUE)
  return OPEN_ERROR;


if (!WriteFile(hFile, S, strlen(S), &NumWritten, NULL))
  return WRITE_ERROR;

if (!CloseHandle(hFile))
  return CLOSE_ERROR;

return FILE_SUCCESS;
}
```

This routine uses the WIN32 API functions called CreateFile, WriteFile, and CloseHandle. These routines are the primary file I/O routines for Windows 95, and should be used in place of outdated Windows APIs such as _lopen, _lclose, and so forth.

You will find that it is worthwhile to get a "handle" on the CreateFile routine because it is used not only for opening standard disk files, but also for opening named pipes, communications resources, and disk devices, and it can also be applied to consoles. Of course, it is fine to use the standard C library routines in its place, and many of them might map through to this call. However, this is the native Windows 95 way to perform file I/O.

CreateFile

```
HANDLE CreateFile(
    LPCTSTR  lpFileName,                          // File name
    DWORD    dwDesiredAccess,                     // read-write access
    DWORD    dwShareMode,                         // Can other apps read it?
    LPSECURITY_ATTRIBUTES lpSecurityAttributes,  // Security
    DWORD    dwCreationDistribution,             // overwrite, truncate, etc
    DWORD    dwFlagsAndAttributes,               // hidden, system, etc.
    HANDLE   hTemplateFile                        // file with attributes to copy
    );
```

This is the standard Windows routine for opening and closing files. You don't just use it to create a file. You can also use it to open an existing file. As already mentioned, it can also be used with named pipes, communications tools, storage devices, and consoles.

This is one of the most complex calls in the whole Windows API. In saying this, I don't mean that the function is necessarily hard to use, but rather that it has many, many flags that can be passed into it. If you want a full explanation of the routine, then see the online help. Here I'll only give you enough information so you can use the routine to open and close standard disk files.

The first parameter is simple in that it takes a pointer to a filename. The second parameter can have the following values:

0	Queries device without actually accessing the device.
GENERIC_READ	You can read the file, and move the file pointer.
GENERIC_WRITE	You can write to the file and move the file pointer.

The dwShareMode parameter can have one of the following values:

0	Prevents the file from being shared.
FILE_SHARE_READ	Others can open the file for read access.
FILE_SHARE_WRITE	Others can open the file for write access.

Security issues are generally relevant only to Windows NT, and so Windows 95 programmers can set the lpSecurityAttributes parameter to NULL.

The dwCreationDistribution field can have the following values:

CREATE_NEW	Fails if the specified file already exists.
CREATE_ALWAYS	Overwrites the file if it exists.
OPEN_EXISTING	The function fails if the file does not exist.
OPEN_ALWAYS	If the file does not exist, it is created.
TRUNCATE_EXISTING	File truncated to 0 bytes. (Use with GENERIC_WRITE.)

The dwFlagsAndAttributes field can have the following values:

FILE_ATTRIBUTE_ARCHIVE	Archive file. (It's been changed.)
FILE_ATTRIBUTE_COMPRESSED	The file or directory is compressed.
FILE_ATTRIBUTE_NORMAL	No attributes. Valid only if used alone.
FILE_ATTRIBUTE_HIDDEN	Hidden file.
FILE_ATTRIBUTE_READONLY	File is read-only.
FILE_ATTRIBUTE_SYSTEM	Used exclusively by the operating system.

It happens that there are many other possible attributes that can be used with CreateFile. However, the list shown here should be all you need for standard file operations.

Before moving on, I should point out that it is usually okay to use standard C library routines instead of CreateFile. C library file I/O calls will generally map through to CreateFile or other acceptable routines, but they are much easier to use. I would, however, feel remiss if I wrote a long book on Windows programming without ever mentioning the standard routines used by the operating system. You ought to know what these routines are and how to use them, even if they are not part of your day-to-day programming practice.

Here's an example:

```
HANDLE hFile = CreateFile("A CreateFile long name.txt",
                    GENERIC_WRITE ¦ GENERIC_READ,
                    0, NULL, CREATE_ALWAYS,
                    FILE_ATTRIBUTE_NORMAL, NULL);
```

After working with the console routines, you should not have any trouble with WriteFile. It is used, of course, to write data to a file, as follows:

```
BOOL WriteFile(
    HANDLE  hFile,     // handle of file to write to
    LPCVOID lpBuffer,      // data to write to the file
    DWORD  nNumberOfBytesToWrite,    // number of bytes to write
    LPDWORD lpNumberOfBytesWritten,// Number of bytes written
    LPOVERLAPPED lpOverlapped       // structyure for overlapped IO
    );
```

The code from the LongName program just writes a simple string to the file:

```
WriteFile(hFile, S, strlen(S), &NumWritten, NULL)
```

The first parameter is the handle returned from CreateFile, the second is the string you want to write, the third is the length of the string, and fourth is the number of bytes written. The fifth parameter has to do with asynchronous I/O when working with named pipes, sockets, mail slots, and so on.

When you want to close a file, all you have to do is pass its handle to the CloseHandle routine:

```
CloseHandle(hFile);
```

Like the WriteFile function, this is a Boolean routine that returns TRUE when successful.

If you want to read a long filename from disk, the best approach is to use one of the standard common dialogs. However, if you need to do it programmatically from inside the core of your application, you can use FindFirstFile, FindNextFile, and FindClose:

```
void ShowFiles(void)
{
  WIN32_FIND_DATA FindData;
  HANDLE Data;

  printf("\nDirectory Output:\n");

  Data = FindFirstFile("*.*", &FindData);
  while (Data != INVALID_HANDLE_VALUE)
  {
    printf("%s\n", FindData.cFileName);
    if (!FindNextFile(Data, &FindData))
      break;
  }

  FindClose(Data);
}
```

FindFirstFile takes two parameters. The first is a mask describing the type of file you want to find. For instance, you might pass in "*.c" or "ab*.txt" in this parameter. Assuming that a file of this description is found, the second parameter will then contain a filled out FindData structure:

```
typedef struct _WIN32_FIND_DATA { // wfd
    DWORD    dwFileAttributes;     // Attributes
    FILETIME ftCreationTime;       // Creation time
    FILETIME ftLastAccessTime;     // Last opened/accessed
    FILETIME ftLastWriteTime;      // Time file was last changed
    DWORD    nFileSizeHigh;        // Zero, unless very big
    DWORD    nFileSizeLow;         // The size of the file
    DWORD    dwReserved0;          // Reserved for future use
    DWORD    dwReserved1;          // Reseved for future use
    TCHAR    cFileName[ MAX_PATH ];     // Long File Name
    TCHAR    cAlternateFileName[ 14 ]; // The 8.3 alias
} WIN32_FIND_DATA;
```

This is truly more than you ever wanted to know about a file. Clearly we are into deep paranoia here! However, if you really want to know not only when the file was last changed, but also when it was created and when it was last accessed, then the information is available. Some future "Trial of the Century" will no doubt hinge on the information in one of these structures. For instance, some devious but unsuspecting person might try to cover up an action by just inserting a new file in place of an old file. However, because its creation date doesn't jive....

At any rate, once you get passed the implications of the WIN32_FIND_DATA structure, you will see that it can also be used to retrieve long filenames from a directory in the cFileName field. The size of the file is recorded in nFileSizeLow. If the file got to be very large, the digits representing its size could overflow into the nFileSizeHigh field.

You can use this function to find directories, hidden files, and other arcana. Just check the attributes in the first field to tell what kind of filename is being returned. The attributes used here are the same ones listed previously in the description of the CreateFile function.

If a call to FindFirstFile succeeds, then the handle returned by the function is not equal to INVALID_HANDLE_VALUE. Assuming that you successfully found one file, you might want to check to see if there are any others that are described by the mask you entered. To find these other files, use the FindNextFile routine:

```
FindNextFile(Data, &FindData);
```

FindNextFile takes the handle returned by FindFirstFile in the first parameter, and a WIN32_FIND_DATA structure in the second parameter. It returns TRUE if it succeeds, and FALSE if it fails.

Notice that the while loop used in the LongName program won't break until FindNextFile returns FALSE. (The while loop part of the structure is really a bit of red herring, used only

as a gateway for entering the loop.) Certainly there are other ways to construct these `"find first"` loops, but this one works just fine.

When you are done iterating through all the files in a directory, you should call `FindClose` to wrap up the procedure. This will close the handle to the operation. The issue here, of course, is that this is a multitasking operating system, and so more than one program could be calling `FindFirstFile` at the same time. That means the operating system could be running two simultaneous `FindFirstFile` loops. The logistics of this kind of process are expedited through the use of handles.

That's all I'm going to say about the LongName program. However, I'm not quite through with the subject of long filenames. In the next section I will talk about accessing long filenames from inside a GUI application.

Consoles and GUIs: More on Long Filenames

The following program shows two things:

☐ How to access long filenames from the GUI part of Windows.

☐ How to add a GUI dialog to a console application.

This sounds like a complicated topic, but it turns out to be very easy. The only really difficult thing is the act of popping up a common dialog. That subject will get short shrift in this chapter because it is discussed in more depth in Bonus Day 1, "GDI and Metafiles," and Bonus Day 3, "DLLs and Multimedia." Nevertheless, I will give you some idea of the basic principles involved in popping up a common dialog.

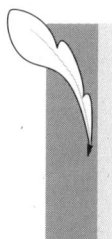

Note: Common dialogs were added to Windows in version 3.1. They are a series of dialogs that can be used by multiple programs for use in frequently performed tasks. For instance, no matter what program you are using, you often see the same dialog when you want to open a file, close a file, print, or select a color. These dialogs look alike because they are all common dialogs that ship with the operating system. Each program is only accessing these dialogs from inside COMMDLG32.DLL, which is the place where they are stored.

The goal of the ConDlg program, shown below, is simply to pop up a Windows common dialog of the type you see when you choose File|Open from BCW, MSVC, NotePad, WordPad, or any of a myriad other applications. The interesting thing about this process is that it will be done not from a standard Windows application, but from a console application.

Certainly it all sounds very exotic, but it turns out that there is no difference in creating a common dialog in a console app or in a GUI app. In fact, the code shown here can be cut and pasted into a standard Windows application. It will work exactly as is, even when transplanted to foreign soil.

In Listings R1.21 through R1.24, you will find the code to the ConDlg program. ConDlg stands for Console Dialog, and it got its name because it shows how to pop up a *dialog* from a *console* application.

Listing R1.21. There are only two routines in CONDLG.CPP.

```cpp
/////////////////////////////////////////////////////
// CONDLG.CPP
// Copyright (c) 1995 Charlie Calvert.
// How to pop up a GUI dialog from inside a console
/////////////////////////////////////////////////////

#include <windows.h>
#include <stdio.h>
#include <commdlg.h>
#pragma warning (disable : 4068)

/////////////////////////////////////////////////////
// GetFileName
/////////////////////////////////////////////////////
LPSTR GetFileName(HWND hwnd, LPSTR szFile, int StringSize)
{
  OPENFILENAME ofn;
  char szFileTitle[256];
  char szFilter[256];

  strcpy(szFilter, "All Files");
  strcpy(&szFilter[strlen(szFilter) + 1], "*.*");
  strcpy(szFileTitle, "Long File Name Search");
  szFile[0] = 0;

  memset(&ofn, 0, sizeof(OPENFILENAME));

  ofn.lStructSize    = sizeof(OPENFILENAME);
  ofn.hwndOwner      = hwnd;
  ofn.lpstrFilter    = szFilter;
  ofn.nFilterIndex   = 1;
  ofn.lpstrFile      = szFile;
  ofn.nMaxFile       = StringSize;
  ofn.lpstrTitle     = szFileTitle;
  ofn.Flags = OFN_FILEMUSTEXIST;

  if (GetOpenFileName(&ofn) != TRUE)
  {
     DWORD Errval;
     char Errstr[50]="Common Dialog Error: ";
     char buf[5];
```

```
      Errval=CommDlgExtendedError();
      if (Errval != 0)
      {
        wsprintf(buf, "%ld", Errval);
        strcat(Errstr, buf);
        MessageBox(NULL,Errstr,"WARNING",MB_OK¦MB_ICONSTOP);
      }
  }

  return szFile;
}

//////////////////////////////////////////////////////////
// Program Entry Point
//////////////////////////////////////////////////////////
void main(void)
{
  char FileName[MAX_PATH*2];
  HWND hwnd;

  printf("Press ENTER to see dialog");
  getchar();

  hwnd = GetForegroundWindow();

  GetFileName(hwnd, FileName, MAX_PATH*2);

  printf("\n\nYou choose: %s", FileName);

  getchar();
}
```

Listing R1.22. The module definition file for the Console program.

```
; CONDLG.DEF

NAME          CONDLG
DESCRIPTION 'Long file name console calls a dialog demo'
```

Listing R1.23. The Borland makefile for the Console program.

```
#-----------------------------------------------------------------
# The MakeFile: CONDLG.MAK
# Copyright (c) 1995 Charlie Calvert.
# BC Install creates file BCROOT.INC in BIN directory.
#-----------------------------------------------------------------

!if !$d(BCROOT)
BCROOT  = $(MAKEDIR)
!endif
```

continues

Week 1 in Review

Listing R1.23. continued

```
INCPATH = $(BCROOT)\INCLUDE\WIN32;$(BCROOT)\INCLUDE;$(BCROOT)\WIN32
LIBPATH = $(BCROOT)\LIB

APPNAME = CONDLG
COMPILER= BCC32.EXE
#RCCOMPILER= BRC32.EXE
// FLAGS   = -DWINVER=0x4000 -v -w4 -I$(INCPATH) -L$(LIBPATH)
FLAGS    = -v -w4 -I$(INCPATH) -L$(LIBPATH)

# Link
$(APPNAME).EXE: $(APPNAME).OBJ $(APPNAME).DEF
  $(COMPILER) $(FLAGS) $(APPNAME).OBJ
#  $(RCCOMPILER) $(APPNAME).res

# Compile
$(APPNAME).OBJ: $(APPNAME).CPP
  $(COMPILER) -c $(FLAGS) $(APPNAME).CPP

# Resource
#$(APPNAME).res : $(APPNAME).rc
#  $(RCCOMPILER) -R -I$(INCPATH) $(APPNAME).RC
```

Listing R1.24. The Microsoft makefile for the Console program.

```
#
# CONDLGMS.MAK
#

!include <win32.mak>

APPNAME = CONDLG

all: $(APPNAME).exe

$(APPNAME).obj: $(APPNAME).cpp
  $(cc) /Ox $(cflags) $(cvarsmtdll) $(APPNAME).cpp

$(APPNAME).exe: $(APPNAME).obj
  $(link) $(conflags) -out:$(APPNAME).exe \
  $(APPNAME).obj $(conlibsdll) $(guilibs)
```

When you run the Console Dialog program, you are first presented with a console window. In the window is a brief note telling you to press Enter if you want to see the dialog. This part of the program serves no function other than to orient the user. I want you to know that you are in a console application, and that you are about to see it launch a Windows common dialog. Without this message, the connection between the two windows might not be clear.

After you press Enter, the dialog appears, and you can browse with it through the directories on your hard drive. Note that it allows you to see long filenames. For instance, it will pick up on the long filenames created by the LongName program. If you are having trouble finding other long filenames to view, see if the operating system has created a subdirectory called Program Files on the root of your C drive, or in whatever drive hosts your Windows files.

When you are done viewing files, select one, and press the OK button. You will be returned to the console window, and the name you choose will be displayed as a standard text mode string.

The key point here is that the common dialogs give you automatic access to long filenames. You don't have to do anything special to get at them. Just fire one up, and it will automatically let you view and retrieve long filenames.

The heart of this program revolves around the following line:

```
hwnd = GetForegroundWindow();
```

This line of code returns the HWND for the console. If you wanted, you could also use the GetFocus routine to retrieve this handle.

Once you have the handle to the console window, there is nothing you can't accomplish. (Well, okay, maybe there are some things you can't do. For instance, I would stay away from the GDI. Nevertheless, your horizons have been considerably broadened.)

The actual act of popping up a common dialog is fairly complex, if only because there are a number of parameters to satisfy. As stated earlier, I'm going to put off an in-depth discussion of this function until later in the book. For now, I'll just hit you with the highlights.

One approach is to just treat the routine I've given you here as a black box. Just copy it to another program, pass in a valid HWND, a buffer to hold a filename, and the length of the buffer. Notice that this routine zeros out the filename. If you want to pass in a filename to be displayed when the dialog first appears, then remove the relevant line of code:

```
szFile[0] = 0;
```

The act of creating an Open File dialog has three parts:

- ☐ Zero out an OPENFILENAME structure.
- ☐ Fill in the fields of the structure you need to use.
- ☐ Pass the structure to GetOpenFileName.

Windows will then pop up the dialog and return the name the user chose, passing it on to you in the lpstrFile field. Note that there is an InitialDir field of the OPENFILENAME structure that can be used to choose the directory where the user starts browsing. For further information, look up OPENFILENAME and GetOpenFileName in the online help.

Week 1 in Review

That's all I'm going to say about this process at this time. However, on Day 21 I discuss popping up normal windows from inside a console application.

Debug Tip: Bringing Up a Console Window from a GUI

Now that you know how to get to the GUI interface from a console application, the next logical step is to reverse the process and pop up a console window from a standard graphics window. I put this subject last but not least. In fact, popping up console windows from a GUI is one of the big benefits of the Windows 95 interface. Certainly you wouldn't want to do this in a commercially released application, but it can be very helpful when you are deep in the coils of a some tumultuous debug session.

Without further ado, here is the code to the GUIText program (Listings R1.25 through R1.31).

Listing R1.25. The main module for the GUIText program.

```
///////////////////////////////////////////////////////////
//  Program Name: GuiText.cpp
//  Programmer: Charlie Calvert
//  Description: GuiText windows program
//  Date: 07/16/95
///////////////////////////////////////////////////////////

#define STRICT
#define WIN32_LEAN_AND_MEAN
#include <windows.h>
#include <windowsx.h>
#include <stdio.h>
#include "guitext.h"
#include "conbox.h"
#pragma warning (disable: 4068)


// -------------------------------------------------------
// Interface
// -------------------------------------------------------

static char szAppName[] = "GuiText";
static HWND MainWindow;
static HINSTANCE hInstance;


// -------------------------------------------------------
// Initialization
// -------------------------------------------------------


///////////////////////////////////////////////////////////
// Program entry point
///////////////////////////////////////////////////////////
```

274

```
#pragma argsused
int WINAPI WinMain(HINSTANCE hInst, HINSTANCE hPrevInstance, LPSTR lpszCmdParam,
int nCmdShow)
{
  MSG  Msg;

  if (!hPrevInstance)
    if (!Register(hInst))
      return FALSE;

  MainWindow = Create(hInst, nCmdShow);
  if (!MainWindow)
    return FALSE;

  while (GetMessage(&Msg, NULL, 0, 0))
  {
    TranslateMessage(&Msg);
    DispatchMessage(&Msg);
  }

  return Msg.wParam;
}

//////////////////////////////////////////////////////
// Register the window
//////////////////////////////////////////////////////
BOOL Register(HINSTANCE hInst)
{
  WNDCLASS WndClass;

  WndClass.style         = CS_HREDRAW | CS_VREDRAW;
  WndClass.lpfnWndProc   = WndProc;
  WndClass.cbClsExtra    = 0;
  WndClass.cbWndExtra    = 0;
  WndClass.hInstance     = hInst;
  WndClass.hIcon         = LoadIcon(NULL, IDI_APPLICATION);
  WndClass.hCursor       = LoadCursor(NULL, IDC_ARROW);
  WndClass.hbrBackground = (HBRUSH)(COLOR_WINDOW+1);
  WndClass.lpszMenuName   = "GuiTextMenu";
  WndClass.lpszClassName = szAppName;

  return RegisterClass (&WndClass);
}

//////////////////////////////////////////////////////
// Create the window
//////////////////////////////////////////////////////
HWND Create(HINSTANCE hInst, int nCmdShow)
{

  hInstance = hInst;

  HWND hwnd = CreateWindow(szAppName, szAppName,
                  WS_OVERLAPPEDWINDOW,
                  CW_USEDEFAULT, CW_USEDEFAULT,
                  CW_USEDEFAULT, CW_USEDEFAULT,
                  NULL, NULL, hInst, NULL);
```

continues

Listing R1.25. continued

```
    if (hwnd == NULL)
      return hwnd;

    ShowWindow(hwnd, nCmdShow);
    UpdateWindow(hwnd);

    return hwnd;
}

// --------------------------------------------------------
// WndProc and Implementation
// --------------------------------------------------------

////////////////////////////////////////////////////////
// The Window Procedure
////////////////////////////////////////////////////////
LRESULT CALLBACK WndProc(HWND hwnd, UINT Message, WPARAM wParam, LPARAM lParam)
{
  switch(Message)
  {
    HANDLE_MSG(hwnd, WM_DESTROY, GuiText_OnDestroy);
    HANDLE_MSG(hwnd, WM_COMMAND, GuiText_OnCommand);
    default: return GuiText_DefProc(hwnd, Message, wParam, lParam);
  }
}

////////////////////////////////////////////////////////
// Handle WM_DESTROY
////////////////////////////////////////////////////////
#pragma argsused
void GuiText_OnDestroy(HWND hwnd)
{
  PostQuitMessage(0);
}

////////////////////////////////////////////////////////
// WM_COMMAND: pop up a text mode console window
////////////////////////////////////////////////////////
#pragma argsused
void GuiText_OnCommand(HWND hwnd, int id, HWND hwndCtl, UINT codeNotify)
{
  char S[100];

  if (id == CM_CONSOLE)
  {
//    FreeConsole();
    AllocConsole();

    InitStdOut();

    ClrScr(GOLDBLUE);

    WriteXY(1, 1, "Console status report");
```

```
    sprintf(S, "HWND %x HINSTANCE %x ID %d", hwnd, hInstance, id);

    WriteXY(1, 2, S);

    WriteXY(1, 3, "Any key to close");

    WaitForKeypress();

    FreeConsole();
  }
}
```

Listing R1.26. The main header file for the GUIText program.

```
//////////////////////////////////////////////////////
// GUITEXT.H
// Copyright (c) 1995 Charlie Calvert.
//////////////////////////////////////////////////////

#define CM_CONSOLE 101

LRESULT CALLBACK WndProc(HWND hwnd, UINT Message, WPARAM wParam, LPARAM lParam);
BOOL Register(HINSTANCE hInst);
HWND Create(HINSTANCE hInst, int nCmdShow);

// Declarations for class GuiText
#define GuiText_DefProc     DefWindowProc
void GuiText_OnDestroy(HWND hwnd);
void GuiText_OnCommand(HWND hwnd, int id, HWND hwndCtl, UINT codeNotify);
```

Listing R1.27. Utility routines for accessing consoles.

```
//////////////////////////////////////////////////////
// CONBOX.CPP
// Copyright (c) 1995 Charlie Calvert.
// Routines for handling Screen IO from a console
//////////////////////////////////////////////////////

#include <windows.h>

static HANDLE hOut;
static HANDLE hIn;

//////////////////////////////////////////////////////
// Initialize handle: Call this routine before using others
//////////////////////////////////////////////////////
void InitStdOut(void)
{
  hOut = GetStdHandle(STD_OUTPUT_HANDLE);
  hIn = GetStdHandle(STD_INPUT_HANDLE);
}
```

continues

Listing R1.27. continued

```
///////////////////////////////////////////////////////
// GOTOXY Move cursor to Col, Row
///////////////////////////////////////////////////////
void GotoXY(int x, int y)
{
  COORD c;
  c.X = x;
  c.Y = y;
  SetConsoleCursorPosition(hOut, c);
}

///////////////////////////////////////////////////////
// WRITEXY
///////////////////////////////////////////////////////
void WriteXY(int x, int y, LPSTR S)
{
  DWORD result;

  GotoXY(x, y);
  WriteConsole(hOut, S, strlen(S), &result, NULL);
}

///////////////////////////////////////////////////////
// Blank out a line of text
///////////////////////////////////////////////////////
void BlankLine(int Y)
{
  DWORD NumWritten;
  COORD c;

  c.X = 0;
  c.Y = Y;

  FillConsoleOutputCharacter(hOut, ' ', 80, c, &NumWritten);
}

///////////////////////////////////////////////////////
// Clear the screen
///////////////////////////////////////////////////////
void ClrScr(WORD Attr)
{
  DWORD NumWritten;
  COORD c;
  int Space = 80 * 25;

  c.X = 0;
  c.Y = 0;

  FillConsoleOutputCharacter(hOut, ' ', Space, c, &NumWritten);
  FillConsoleOutputAttribute(hOut, Attr, Space, c, &NumWritten);

  GotoXY(0,0);
}
```

```
/////////////////////////////////////////////////////
// Write a line of text
/////////////////////////////////////////////////////
void Write(LPSTR S)
{
  DWORD NumWritten;

  WriteConsole(hOut, S, strlen(S), &NumWritten, NULL);
}

/////////////////////////////////////////////////////
// Write a line of text
/////////////////////////////////////////////////////
void WaitForKeypress(void)
{
  DWORD Result;
  INPUT_RECORD Buffer;

  do {

    ReadConsoleInput(hIn, &Buffer, 1, &Result);

  } while (Buffer.EventType != KEY_EVENT);
}
```

Listing R1.28. The header file for the utility routines used in CONDLG.CPP.

```
/////////////////////////////////////////////////////
// CONBOX.H
// Copyright (c) 1995 Charlie Calvert.
// Routines for handling Screen IO from a console
/////////////////////////////////////////////////////

#define BW FOREGROUND_RED ¦ FOREGROUND_GREEN ¦ FOREGROUND_BLUE
#define GOLDBLUE FOREGROUND_GREEN ¦ FOREGROUND_RED ¦ \
                 FOREGROUND_INTENSITY ¦ BACKGROUND_BLUE
#define PB FOREGROUND_RED ¦ FOREGROUND_BLUE
#define GB FOREGROUND_GREEN

void InitStdOut(void);
void GotoXY(int x, int y);
void WriteXY(int x, int y, LPSTR S);
void BlankLine(int Y);
void ClrScr(WORD Attr);
void Write(LPSTR S);
void WaitForKeypress();
```

Listing R1.29. The resource file for the GUIText program.

```
/////////////////////////////
// GUITEXT.RC
/////////////////////////////
#include "guitext.h"

GuiTextMenu MENU
BEGIN
  MENUITEM "Run Console" CM_CONSOLE
END
```

Listing R1.30. A quick module definition file for the GUIText program.

```
; GuiText.Def

NAME           GuiText
DESCRIPTION    'GuiText Window'
HEAPSIZE       4096
STACKSIZE      5120
CODE           PRELOAD MOVEABLE DISCARDABLE
DATA            PRELOAD MOVEABLE MULTIPLE
```

Listing R1.31. The Borland makefile for the GUIText program.

```
# GuiText.mak

# macros

!if !$d(BCROOT)
BCROOT = $(MAKEDIR)\..
!endif

APPNAME = GUITEXT
OBJS    = $(APPNAME).OBJ CONBOX.OBJ

INCPATH = $(BCROOT)\INCLUDE\WIN32;$(BCROOT)\INCLUDE;$(BCROOT)\WIN32
LIBPATH = $(BCROOT)\LIB

COMPILER= BCC32.EXE
BRC     = BRC32.EXE
FLAGS   = -W -v -w4 -I$(INCPATH) -L$(LIBPATH)


# link
$(APPNAME).exe: $(OBJS) $(APPNAME).def $(APPNAME).res
  $(COMPILER) $(FLAGS) $(OBJS)
  $(BRC) -I$(INCPATH) $(APPNAME).res

# compile
.cpp.obj:
```

```
  $(COMPILER) -c $(FLAGS) { $< }

# resource
$(APPNAME).res: $(APPNAME).rc
  $(BRC) -R -I$(INCPATH) $(APPNAME).RC
```

This program is a standard Windows application. It contains a main window with a single menu item in it. If you select that menu item, then a console window appears that displays some standard debug information. In particular, it shows the value of the program's HINSTANCE and the main window's HWND.

Here is the code that is called when a menu item is selected:

```
void GuiText_OnCommand(HWND hwnd, int id, HWND hwndCtl, UINT codeNotify)
{
  char S[100];

  if (id == CM_CONSOLE)
  {
    FreeConsole();
    AllocConsole();

    InitStdOut();
    ClrScr(GOLDBLUE);
    WriteXY(1, 1, "Console status report");
    sprintf(S, "HWND %x HINSTANCE %x ID %d", hwnd, hInstance, id);
    WriteXY(1, 2, S);
    WriteXY(1, 3, "Any key to close");
    WaitForKeypress();

    FreeConsole();
  }
}
```

The beauty of this system is that there is almost nothing for me to explain. The code simply allocates a console, then writes output to it which can be used for debugging purposes. In particular, it shows the current value of the HINSTANCE and HWND. You often need to check to make sure these values aren't set to 0, and here is one simple way to be sure.

All of the routines that I use for output are part of the WINCON.H portion of the WIN32 API. I have, however, wrapped most of these routines inside functions that have simpler names, such as WriteXY and ClrScr.

To help you reuse these routines later, I have stored them in a single file called CONBOX.H, which stands for *console toolbox*. As mentioned earlier, it's best to use these routines rather than standard C library routines when working with a console window created from inside a GUI application.

The routines in CONBOX.H should be readily comprehensible to you. For instance, here is one that can be used to clear the screen and set it to a particular color:

```
void ClrScr(WORD Attr)
{
  DWORD NumWritten;
  COORD c;
  int Space = 80 * 25;

  c.X = 0;
  c.Y = 0;

  FillConsoleOutputCharacter(hOut, ' ', Space, c, &NumWritten);
  FillConsoleOutputAttribute(hOut, Attr, Space, c, &NumWritten);

  GotoXY(0,0);
}
```

This routine assumes that you want to clear a full 80x25 text screen. As mentioned earlier, you can make more precise calculations as to the size of the current screen, if you so desire.

The ClrScr routine takes a single parameter, which designates a particular set of foreground and background colors. These colors are declared as follows:

```
#define BW FOREGROUND_RED ¦ FOREGROUND_GREEN ¦ FOREGROUND_BLUE
#define GOLDBLUE FOREGROUND_GREEN ¦ FOREGROUND_RED ¦ \
                 FOREGROUND_INTENSITY ¦ BACKGROUND_BLUE
#define PB FOREGROUND_RED ¦ FOREGROUND_BLUE
#define GB FOREGROUND_GREEN
```

BW is a standard black and white screen.

The only other routine I want to mention is called WaitForKeypress:

```
void WaitForKeypress(void)
{
  DWORD Result;
  INPUT_RECORD Buffer;

  do {

    ReadConsoleInput(hIn, &Buffer, 1, &Result);

  } while (Buffer.EventType != KEY_EVENT);
}
```

This function waits until the user presses a key. If you wanted, you could modify it so that it would also return a keypress. Note that the routine uses ReadConsoleInput to get the data from the user, then checks to see if it is a keyboard event of any type. If it is, the loop ends and your program resumes execution. If it is not a keyboard event, or if the user does not do anything, then the loop just keeps on spinning madly around in circles. For more details on this process, see the Mouse program described earlier in this chapter.

Summary

In this chapter you have had a look at console applications, event-oriented programming, long filenames, WIN32 file I/O, and the wide open spaces found in the data segment of a WIN32 application.

This is probably not the most important chapter in this book, but the information found here has a utilitarian value for your day-to-day programming chores. Console windows are an interesting part of Windows 95, especially for programmers. Whether they will play a big part in the lives of a typical user is not certain. However, they are very useful to programmers as well as for in-house projects involving network or system maintenance.

2

The major goal of the first week is to help you feel comfortable with writing standard Windows programs and to show you the power at your fingertips by exposing you to resources. Now that you have your sea legs, it's time to set sail and start exploring Windows in earnest.

Where You're Going

Week 2 focuses on windows controls, fonts, and windows classes. The programs you produce will become increasingly powerful—and increasingly complex.

The first additions to your toolkit are fonts. This turns out to be a surprisingly large subject. Fonts give you a thorough introduction to some of the impressive data structures, which are free for the asking in the windows operating environment. As you explore the LOGFONT and TEXTMETRIC structures, you'll learn that Windows is a storehouse of information about the capabilities of the system on which it is running.

Sometimes the information the operating system can send to a program comes in the form of a long list of complex data structures. To make this process manageable, Windows enables you to set up special functions, named *callbacks*, designed specifically to process lists of data. Callbacks are surrounded by an almost magical aura, and mastering them is one of the fine arts of Windows programming.

After you start learning how to mine the available resources, you can find some way to present them to the user. This is where window controls enter the scene.

Window controls form the interface between the user and a program's data. When the user needs to utilize a program's capabilities, he or she does so with window controls. When a programmer wants to display information to the user, the tool of choice is a window control.

Your exposure to window controls comes replete with an advanced course in the Windows messaging system. When programmers want to communicate with a control, such as a list box or a combobox, they do so by sending a message to the control. Conversely, when the user manipulates a control, a program finds out about this action by sampling the messages that are sent to its window procedures.

By the time you begin to master Windows' formidable array of data structures, callbacks, and controls, you'll be well into the fray. To help you manage the many available options, the designers of Windows have supplied you with a wide array of easy-to-use WindowsX macros. Present in WindowsX are a purity of logic and a nicety of design that can help you comprehend and deftly overcome the challenges you face.

The last chapter in Week 2 loops back to take a second look at the process of launching a window (as originally explained during Week 1). This second pass over the subject allows you to peer deep beneath the surface of a Windows program so that you can learn how to fine-turn its appearance and behavior. As you learn to manipulate the various elements of the WNDCLASS structure, you should feel that you're finally taking control of the environment in which you program.

Good programmers have an insatiable curiosity about the tools with which they work—and about the operating system in the midst of which they labor. People who have caught fire, who really want to learn, will find that Week 2 is loaded with valuable information and eye-opening tips. So gird you loins, tighten your suspenders, trim your sails, or do whatever it is you do when you are getting ready for some serious work. Week 2 is a cornucopia of knowledge—be prepared to have some fun (especially on Day 8, when you are introduced to the Snake game). When you're finished, you can move on to Week 3, where you will find the really good material about multimedia and graphics.

Windows Animation: The Snake Game

Now that you have made a few voyages across the deep space separating DOS from the world of Windows programming, you deserve to relax for a bit with the first cut of a Windows program called Snake. The Snake program is a graphics-oriented take on a famous game that's been available since before PCs existed.

The code shown here reappears in a different guise in Bonus Day 4, "Snako for Windows." There it is developed into something that might appeal to the rich palette of today's gamers.

This chapter is a review of Week 1 and a reward for all your hard work. I also introduce a few new concepts. In particular, you will learn about

- ☐ Creating and using timers
- ☐ Creating child windows
- ☐ Animation
- ☐ XORing bitmaps to the screen
- ☐ Dividing code into modules

This material can be approached in a more relaxed manner than some of the other material you've seen and will see in this book. However, many concepts, notably child windows and modularization, are very important. Getting some extra experience with bitmaps also should stand you in good stead. So, be prepared to have some fun, to review some old ideas, and to pick up a few new ones. Let's go!

The Promised Bonus Program

This first version of the Snake program, called Snake1, is designed to excite the imagination of people who enjoy games. My goal is to provide you with a functioning set of tools from which you can design your own game. At the same time, I want to give you a toy that is at least somewhat interesting in and of itself.

It is hoped that the potential of the Snake1 program will incite you to get involved in a little hands-on programming. Lots of improvements can be made to this program, and no one's better suited to implement them than yourself. If this code intrigues you, play around with it some. Add a few features; make a few optimizations. There is no better way to learn how to program than to get plenty of hands-on experience.

Note: The fact that games are entertaining doesn't make them trivial from a programmer's point of view. In fact, the best games are constructed by top-notch technicians whose techniques are studied by programmers at places such as NASA. Game programming includes a lot of cutting-edge technology and requires extremely refined skills.

I'll start by showing you the source so you can get the first version of Snake up and running. (See Listing 8.1.) Remember, the point of this exercise is not only to teach you something new, but also to enable you to flex your newly found muscle by retracing some already familiar portions of the Windows programming landscape.

Listing 8.1. The Snake1 program lets you have some fun while getting experience working with bitmaps and timers.

```
// ==========================================================
// Program Name: SNAKE1.CPP
// Copyright (c) 1993 by Charlie Calvert
// Description: Game with bitmaps, key handling and timer
// UpDate for WIN32: May 22, 1995
// ==========================================================

#define STRICT
#include <windows.h>
#include <windowsx.h>
#pragma hdrstop
#include <stdlib.h>
#pragma warning (disable : 4100)
#pragma warning (disable : 4068)
#include "snake1.h"
#include "grunt.h"

// statics
static char szAppName[] = "Snake";
static char szGameName[] = "GameWindow";
static HWND MainWindow;
static HWND hGameWindow;

// Shared variables
int Size = 32;
int StartCol;
int StartRow;
int MaxCols;
int MaxRows;
div_t NumXSects, NumYSects;

// Variables
HINSTANCE hInstance;
HBITMAP Head, Body, OneHundred;

//----------------------------------------------------------
// Setup
//----------------------------------------------------------

/////////////////////////////////////
// WinMain
/////////////////////////////////////
#pragma argsused
```

continues

Listing 8.1. continued

```
int WINAPI WinMain(HINSTANCE hInst, HINSTANCE hPrevInstance,
                   LPSTR  lpszCmdParam, int nCmdShow)
{
  MSG  Msg;

  if (!hPrevInstance)
    if (!Register(hInst))
      return FALSE;

  MainWindow = Create(hInst, nCmdShow);
  if (!MainWindow)
    return FALSE;

  while (GetMessage(&Msg, NULL, 0, 0))
  {
    TranslateMessage(&Msg);
    DispatchMessage(&Msg);
  }
  return Msg.wParam;
}

///////////////////////////////////////
// Save hInstance, Create window, Show window maximized
///////////////////////////////////////
HWND Create(HINSTANCE hInst, int nCmdShow)
{
  hInstance = hInst;

  HWND hWindow = CreateWindow(szAppName,
                              "A Snake and its Tail",
                              WS_OVERLAPPEDWINDOW,
                              CW_USEDEFAULT, CW_USEDEFAULT,
                              CW_USEDEFAULT, CW_USEDEFAULT,
                              NULL, NULL, hInst, NULL);

  if (hWindow == NULL)
    return hWindow;

  nCmdShow = SW_SHOWMAXIMIZED;

  ShowWindow(hWindow, nCmdShow);
  UpdateWindow(hWindow);

  return hWindow;
}

///////////////////////////////////////
// Register window
///////////////////////////////////////
BOOL Register(HINSTANCE hInst)
{
  WNDCLASS WndClass;
```

```
  WndClass.style          = CS_HREDRAW | CS_VREDRAW;
  WndClass.lpfnWndProc    = WndProc;
  WndClass.cbClsExtra     = 0;
  WndClass.cbWndExtra     = 0;
  WndClass.hInstance      = hInst;
  WndClass.hIcon          = LoadIcon(NULL, IDI_APPLICATION);
  WndClass.hCursor        = LoadCursor(NULL, IDC_ARROW);
  WndClass.hbrBackground  = GetStockBrush(GRAY_BRUSH);
  WndClass.lpszMenuName   = NULL;
  WndClass.lpszClassName  = szAppName;

  RegisterClass (&WndClass);

  WndClass.style          = CS_HREDRAW | CS_VREDRAW;
  WndClass.lpfnWndProc    = GameWndProc;
  WndClass.hIcon          = 0;
  WndClass.hCursor        = LoadCursor(NULL, IDC_ARROW);
  WndClass.hbrBackground  = GetStockBrush(WHITE_BRUSH);
  WndClass.lpszClassName  = szGameName;

  return (RegisterClass (&WndClass) != 0);
}

//---------------------------------------
// The Implementation
//---------------------------------------

/////////////////////////////////////////
// WndProc
/////////////////////////////////////////
LRESULT CALLBACK EXPORT16 WndProc(HWND hWindow, UINT Message,
                          WPARAM wParam, LPARAM lParam)
{
  switch(Message)
  {
    HANDLE_MSG(hWindow, WM_CREATE, Snake_OnCreate);
    HANDLE_MSG(hWindow, WM_DESTROY, Snake_OnDestroy);
    default:
      return Snake_DefProc(hWindow, Message, wParam,lParam);
  }
}

/////////////////////////////////////////
// WM_CREATE
/////////////////////////////////////////
#pragma argsused
BOOL Snake_OnCreate(HWND hwnd, CREATESTRUCT FAR*
lpCreateStruct)
{
  Head = LoadBitmap(hInstance, "Head");
  if (!Head)
  {
    MessageBox(hwnd, "No head", "Fatal Error", MB_OK);
    return FALSE;
  }
```

continues

Listing 8.1. continued

```
Body = LoadBitmap(hInstance, "Body");
if (!Body)
{
  MessageBox(hwnd, "No body", "Fatal Error", MB_OK);
  return FALSE;
}

OneHundred = LoadBitmap(hInstance, "Hundred");
if (!OneHundred)
{
  MessageBox(hwnd, "No OneHundred", "Fatal Error", MB_OK);
  return FALSE;
}

int CXFull = GetSystemMetrics(SM_CXSCREEN);
NumXSects = div(CXFull, Size);
MaxCols = (NumXSects.quot - 1) * Size;
int BordWidth = CXFull - MaxCols;
div_t StartC = div(BordWidth, 2);
StartCol = StartC.quot;

int CYFull = GetSystemMetrics(SM_CYFULLSCREEN);
NumYSects = div(CYFull, Size);
MaxRows = (NumYSects.quot - 1) * Size;
BordWidth = CYFull - MaxRows;
StartC = div(BordWidth, 2);
StartRow = StartC.quot;


hGameWindow = CreateWindow("GameWindow", "A",
                  WS_CHILD | WS_VISIBLE,
                  StartCol, BORDERSIZE, MaxCols, MaxRows,
                  hwnd, NULL, hInstance, NULL);

  return TRUE;
}

////////////////////////////////////////
// WM_DESTROY
////////////////////////////////////////
#pragma argsused
void Snake_OnDestroy(HWND hWindow)
{
  if (Head) DeleteObject(Head);
  if (Body) DeleteObject(Body);
  if (OneHundred) DeleteObject(OneHundred);
  PostQuitMessage(0);
}
```

Listing 8.2 shows the Snake1 header file.

Listing 8.2. SNAKE1.H.

```
//////////////////////////////////////
// Module Name: Snake1.h
// Programmer: Charlie Calvert
// Description: Header file with procs
//////////////////////////////////////

#if !defined(__WIN32__) && !defined(_WIN32)
#define EXPORT16 __export
#else
#define EXPORT16
#endif

// Class Snake
#define Snake_DefProc      DefWindowProc
BOOL Snake_OnCreate(HWND hWindow, CREATESTRUCT FAR*
lpCreateStruct);
void Snake_OnDestroy(HWND hWindow);


// Procs
HWND Create(HINSTANCE hInst, int nCmdShow);
BOOL Register(HINSTANCE hInst);
BOOL SetUpWindow(HWND hWindow);
LRESULT CALLBACK EXPORT16 WndProc(HWND, UINT, WPARAM, LPARAM);
```

Listing 8.3 shows the Grunt source code.

Listing 8.3. GRUNT.CPP.

```
// ==========================================================
// Module Name: GRUNT.CPP
// Programmer: Charlie Calvert
// Description: Do the grunt work of moving the snake
// ==========================================================

#define STRICT
#define WIN32_LEAN_AND_MEAN
#include <windowsx.h>
#define hdrstop
#include <string.h>
#include <stdlib.h>
#include "grunt.h"
#pragma warning (disable : 4100)
#pragma warning (disable : 4068)

// local variables
BOOL NewSect;
static int VK_p = 112;
static unsigned int SnakeTimer = 1;
static long TotalClicks = 0;
```

continues

Listing 8.3. continued

```
static int Sections;
static int NumPrizes;
static TPrize Prizes[MAXPRIZES];
static TSectInfo SectInfo[MAXSECTIONS];
TTurn TurnList[25];
int NumTurns;

// Global variables
extern div_t NumXSects;
extern div_t NumYSects;
extern int Size;
extern int MaxCols;
extern int MaxRows;
extern HBITMAP Head, Body, OneHundred;

/////////////////////////////////////
// GameWndProc
/////////////////////////////////////
LRESULT CALLBACK EXPORT16 GameWndProc(HWND hWindow,
          UINT Message, WPARAM wParam, LPARAM lParam)
{
  switch(Message)
  {
    HANDLE_MSG(hWindow, WM_CREATE, Game_OnCreate);
    HANDLE_MSG(hWindow, WM_CHAR, Game_OnChar);
    HANDLE_MSG(hWindow, WM_KEYDOWN, Game_OnKey);
    HANDLE_MSG(hWindow, WM_PAINT, Game_OnPaint);
    HANDLE_MSG(hWindow, WM_TIMER, Game_OnTimer);
    default:
      return Game_DefProc(hWindow, Message, wParam,lParam);
  }
}


/////////////////////////////////////
// WM_CREATE
/////////////////////////////////////
#pragma argsused
BOOL Game_OnCreate(HWND hwnd, CREATESTRUCT FAR* lpCreateStruct)
{
  if (!SetTimer(hwnd, SnakeTimer, 125, NULL))
  {
    MessageBox(hwnd, "No Timers Available", "Snake Info", MB_OK);
    return FALSE;
  }

  NumPrizes = 0;
  InitializeSections();

  return TRUE;
}


/////////////////////////////////////
// WM_DESTROY
/////////////////////////////////////
void Game_OnDestroy(HWND hWindow)
```

8

```
{
  KillTimer(hWindow, SnakeTimer);
}

//////////////////////////////////////
// WM_CHAR
//////////////////////////////////////
#pragma argsused
void Game_OnChar(HWND hWindow, UINT ch, int cRepeat)
{
  if (ch == UINT(VK_p))
    KillTimer(hWindow, SnakeTimer);
}

//////////////////////////////////////
// WM_KEYDOWN
//////////////////////////////////////
#pragma argsused
void Game_OnKey(HWND hWindow, UINT vk,
               BOOL fDown, int cRepeat, UINT flags)
{
  switch(vk)
  {
    case VK_DOWN: GetOldDir(Down); break;
    case VK_UP: GetOldDir(Up); break;
    case VK_LEFT: GetOldDir(Left); break;
    case VK_RIGHT: GetOldDir(Right); break;
  }
  MoveBitmap(hWindow);
}

//////////////////////////////////////
// WM_PAINT
//////////////////////////////////////
void Game_OnPaint(HWND hWindow)
{
  PAINTSTRUCT PaintStruct;

  HDC DC = BeginPaint(hWindow, &PaintStruct);

  HDC PicDC = CreateCompatibleDC(DC);

  // Draw Head
  HBITMAP OldBmp = SelectBitmap(PicDC, Head);
  BitBlt(DC, SectInfo[0].Col, SectInfo[0].Row,
         Size, Size, PicDC, 0, 0, SRCINVERT);
  SelectObject(PicDC, OldBmp);

  // Draw Body
  OldBmp = SelectBitmap(PicDC, Body);
  for (int i = 1; i <= Sections; i++)
    BitBlt(DC, SectInfo[i].Col, SectInfo[i].Row,
           Size, Size, PicDC, 0, 0, SRCINVERT);

  SelectObject(PicDC, OldBmp);
  DeleteDC(PicDC);
```

continues

295

Listing 8.3. continued

```
    EndPaint(hWindow, &PaintStruct);

    SectInfo[0].DirChange = FALSE;
}

///////////////////////////////////////
// WM_TIMER
///////////////////////////////////////
#pragma argsused
void Game_OnTimer(HWND hwnd, UINT id)
{
  HBITMAP SaveBmp;

  SetFocus(hwnd);

  if (id == SnakeTimer)
  {
    MoveBitmap(hwnd);
    TotalClicks++;

    if ((TotalClicks % 10) == 0)
    {
      SetSections();
      SetPrizes();

      HDC PaintDC = GetDC(hwnd);
      HDC PicDC = CreateCompatibleDC(PaintDC);

      NewSect = TRUE;

      // Paint new prize
      SaveBmp = SelectBitmap(PicDC, OneHundred);
      BitBlt(PaintDC, Prizes[NumPrizes].Col,
      Prizes[NumPrizes].Row, 32, 32, PicDC, 0, 0, SRCINVERT);
      SelectObject(PicDC, SaveBmp);

      DeleteDC(PicDC);
      ReleaseDC(hwnd, PaintDC);
    }
  }
}

//-------------------------------------
// The Implementation
//-------------------------------------

///////////////////////////////////////
// Called by MoveBitmap
// Keeps track of internal Col and Row
// for each section of snake
///////////////////////////////////////
void SetColRow(void)
{
  int i;
```

```
  for (i = 0; i <= Sections; i++)
   {
     SectInfo[i].OldCol = SectInfo[i].Col;
     SectInfo[i].OldRow = SectInfo[i].Row;

     switch(SectInfo[i].Dir)
     {
       case Up: SectInfo[i].Row -= Size; break;
       case Down: SectInfo[i].Row += Size; break;
       case Left: SectInfo[i].Col -= Size; break;
       case Right: SectInfo[i].Col += Size; break;
     }
   }

  for (i = Sections; i > 0; i—)
  {
    if (SectInfo[i - 1].DirChange)
    {
      SectInfo[i].DirChange = TRUE;
      SectInfo[i].Dir = SectInfo[i - 1].Dir;
      SectInfo[i - 1].DirChange = FALSE;
    }
  }
}


////////////////////////////////////
// Called by MoveBitmap
// Keeps track of which section of
// snake will turn next
////////////////////////////////////
void SetNewTurnSection(void)
{
  for (int i = 1; i <= Sections; i++)
  {
    if (TurnList[NumTurns].SectChangeDir[i] == TRUE)
    break;
  }
  TurnList[NumTurns].SectChangeDir[i] = FALSE;
  i++;
  TurnList[NumTurns].SectChangeDir[i] = TRUE;
}


////////////////////////////////////
// Make a noise and set constants
// when a collision occurs
////////////////////////////////////
void Boom(HWND hwnd)
{
  memset(SectInfo, 0, sizeof(SectInfo));
  Sections = 0;
  NumPrizes = 0;
  for (int i = 0; i < 10; i++)
    MessageBeep(-1);
  InitializeSections();
  InvalidateRect(hwnd, NULL, TRUE);
}
```

continues

Listing 8.3. continued

```c
//////////////////////////////////////
// Erase prizes
//////////////////////////////////////
void WhiteOut(HWND hwnd, int i)
{
  HDC PaintDC = GetDC(hwnd);
  HDC MemDC = CreateCompatibleDC(PaintDC);

  HBITMAP SaveBmp = SelectBitmap(MemDC, OneHundred);
  BitBlt(PaintDC, Prizes[i].Col,
          Prizes[i].Row, 32, 32, MemDC, 0, 0, SRCINVERT);
  SelectObject(MemDC, SaveBmp);

  DeleteDC(MemDC);
  ReleaseDC(hwnd, PaintDC);
}

//////////////////////////////////////
//
//////////////////////////////////////
void CheckForCollision(HWND hwnd)
{

  if (SectInfo[0].Col < 0) Boom(hwnd);
  if (SectInfo[0].Row < 0) Boom(hwnd);
  if (SectInfo[0].Col + Size > MaxCols) Boom(hwnd);
  if (SectInfo[0].Row + Size > MaxRows) Boom(hwnd);

  // See if Snake hit his own tail
  for (int i = 1; i <= Sections; i++)
    if (SectInfo[i].Col == SectInfo[0].Col &&
        SectInfo[i].Row == SectInfo[0].Row)
      Boom(hwnd);

  // Erase a prize when he hits it
  for (i = 0; i <= NumPrizes; i++)
  {
    if (Prizes[i].Exists)
    {
      if ( ((SectInfo[0].Row >= Prizes[i].Row) &&
            (SectInfo[0].Row <= Prizes[i].Row + (Size - 1))) &&
           ((SectInfo[0].Col >= Prizes[i].Col) &&
            (SectInfo[0].Col <= Prizes[i].Col + (Size - 1))) )
      {
        Prizes[i].Exists = FALSE;
        WhiteOut(hwnd, i);
      }
    }
  }
}

//////////////////////////////////////
// Init procedure at start of game
//////////////////////////////////////
void InitializeSections()
```

```
{
  int i, StartCol, StartRow;

  Sections = 5;
  StartCol = Size * 3;
  StartRow = Size * 3;

  for (i = 0; i <= Sections; i++)
  {
    SectInfo[i].Dir = Right;
    SectInfo[i].DirChange = FALSE;
    SectInfo[i].Col = StartCol - (Size * i);
    SectInfo[i].Row = StartRow;
    SectInfo[i].OldCol = SectInfo[i].Col;
    SectInfo[i].OldRow = SectInfo[i].Row;
  }
  NewSect = FALSE;
}

/////////////////////////////////////
//
/////////////////////////////////////
void GetOldDir(TDir NewDir)
{
  TurnList[NumTurns].Dir = NewDir;
  TurnList[NumTurns].SectChangeDir[1] = TRUE;

  SectInfo[0].OldDir = SectInfo[0].Dir;
  SectInfo[0].Dir = NewDir;
  SectInfo[0].DirChange = TRUE;
  TurnList[0].TurnCol = SectInfo[0].Col;
  TurnList[0].TurnRow = SectInfo[0].Row;
}

/////////////////////////////////////
// Draw the Snake
/////////////////////////////////////
void MoveBitmap(HWND hwnd)
{
  SetColRow();

  HDC DC = GetDC(hwnd);
  HDC PicDC = CreateCompatibleDC(DC);

  CheckForCollision(hwnd);

  // Paint head
  HBITMAP OldBmp = SelectBitmap(PicDC, Head);
  BitBlt(DC, SectInfo[0].OldCol, SectInfo[0].OldRow,
         Size, Size, PicDC, 0, 0, SRCINVERT);
  BitBlt(DC, SectInfo[0].Col, SectInfo[0].Row,
         Size, Size, PicDC, 0, 0, SRCINVERT);
  SelectObject(PicDC, OldBmp);

  // Paint body
  OldBmp = SelectBitmap(PicDC, Body);
  BitBlt(DC, SectInfo[1].Col, SectInfo[1].Row,
```

Listing 8.3. continued

```
            Size, Size, PicDC, 0, 0, SRCINVERT);
    BitBlt(DC, SectInfo[Sections].Col, SectInfo[Sections].Row,
            Size, Size, PicDC, 0, 0, SRCINVERT);

    // If he grew
    if (NewSect)
    {
      BitBlt(DC, SectInfo[Sections].Col, SectInfo[Sections].Row,
          Size, Size, PicDC, 0, 0, SRCINVERT);
      NewSect = FALSE;
    }

    SelectObject(PicDC, OldBmp);

    SectInfo[0].DirChange = FALSE;

    DeleteDC(PicDC);
    ReleaseDC(hwnd, DC);

    SetNewTurnSection();
}

/////////////////////////////////////
//
/////////////////////////////////////
void SetPrizes(void)
{
  NumPrizes++;

  Prizes[NumPrizes].Exists = TRUE;
  Prizes[NumPrizes].Row = (rand() % NumYSects.quot) * Size;
  Prizes[NumPrizes].Col = (rand() % NumXSects.quot) * Size;
}

/////////////////////////////////////
//
/////////////////////////////////////
void SetSections(void)
{
  Sections++;

  SectInfo[Sections].Dir = SectInfo[Sections - 1].Dir;
  SectInfo[Sections].DirChange = FALSE;

  switch (SectInfo[Sections].Dir)
  {
    case Left:
    {
      SectInfo[Sections].Col = SectInfo[Sections - 1].Col + Size;
      SectInfo[Sections].Row = SectInfo[Sections - 1].Row;
      break;
    }

    case Right:
```

```
    {
      SectInfo[Sections].Col = SectInfo[Sections - 1].Col - Size;
      SectInfo[Sections].Row = SectInfo[Sections - 1].Row;
      break;
    }

    case Up:
    {
      SectInfo[Sections].Col = SectInfo[Sections - 1].Col;
      SectInfo[Sections].Row = SectInfo[Sections - 1].Row + Size;
      break;
    }

    case Down:
    {
      SectInfo[Sections].Col = SectInfo[Sections - 1].Col;
      SectInfo[Sections].Row = SectInfo[Sections - 1].Row - Size;
      break;
    }
  } // end switch
  SectInfo[Sections].OldCol = SectInfo[Sections - 1].Col;
  SectInfo[Sections].OldRow = SectInfo[Sections - 1].Row;
}
```

Listing 8.4 shows the Grunt header file.

Listing 8.4. GRUNT.H.

```
//////////////////////////////////////
// Module Name: GRUNT.H
// Programmer: Charlie Calvert
// Description: Do the work of moving the snake
//////////////////////////////////////

#include <windows.h>
#include <windowsx.h>

#define BORDERSIZE 15
#define MAXSECTIONS 1024
#define MAXPRIZES 512

#if !defined(__WIN32__) && !defined(_WIN32)
#define EXPORT16 __export
#else
#define EXPORT16
#endif

// Type definitions
enum TDir {Left, Right, Up, Down};

struct TSectInfo
{
  BOOL DirChange;
  TDir Dir, OldDir;
  int SecNum;
```

Listing 8.4. continued

```
        int Row, Col;
        int OldRow, OldCol;
};

struct TTurn
{
  TDir Dir;
  BOOL SectChangeDir[256];
  int TurnCol, TurnRow;
};

struct TPrize
{
  BOOL Exists;
  int Value;
  int Col, Row;
};


// Class Game
#define Game_DefProc    DefWindowProc
BOOL Game_OnCreate(HWND hWindow,
                    CREATESTRUCT FAR* lpCreateStruct);
void Game_OnDestroy(HWND hWindow);
void Game_OnChar(HWND hWindow, UINT ch, int cRepeat);
void Game_OnKey(HWND hWindow, UINT vk,
                BOOL fDown, int cRepeat, UINT flags);
void Game_OnPaint(HWND hWindow);
void Game_OnTimer(HWND hWindow, UINT id);

// Procs
LRESULT CALLBACK EXPORT16 GameWndProc(HWND, UINT,
                             WPARAM, LPARAM);
void InitializeSections();
void GetOldDir(TDir NewDir);
void MoveBitmap(HWND hWindow);
void SetSections(void);
void SetPrizes(void);
```

Listing 8.5 lists the Snake1 resource file.

Listing 8.5. SNAKE1.RC.

```
1: // SNAKE1.RC
2: Body    BITMAP "body.bmp"
3: Head    BITMAP "head.bmp"
4: Hundred BITMAP "hundred.bmp"
```

Listing 8.6 shows the Snake1 definition file.

Listing 8.6. SNAKE1.DEF.

```
1: ; SNAKE1.DEF
2: NAME        SNAKE1
3: DESCRIPTION    'Snake1'
4: CODE        PRELOAD MOVEABLE DISCARDABLE
5: DATA        PRELOAD MOVEABLE MULTIPLE
6: HEAPSIZE  10240
7: STACKSIZE 10240
```

Listing 8.7 shows the Snake1 makefile for Borland compilers.

Listing 8.7. SNAKE1.MAK (Borland).

```
# Snake1.Mak

!if !$d(BCROOT)
BCROOT  = $(MAKEDIR)
!endif

APPNAME = Snake1
INCPATH = $(BCROOT)\INCLUDE
LIBPATH = $(BCROOT)\LIB

!if $d(WIN16)
COMPILER= BCC.EXE
BRC      = BRC.EXE
FLAGS   = -W -ml -v -w4 -I$(INCPATH) -L$(LIBPATH)
!else
COMPILER= BCC32.EXE
BRC      = BRC32.EXE
FLAGS   = -W -v -w4 -I$(INCPATH) -L$(LIBPATH)
!endif

# linking
$(APPNAME).exe: $(APPNAME).obj Grunt.obj $(APPNAME).def $(APPNAME).res
  $(COMPILER) $(FLAGS) $(APPNAME).obj Grunt.obj
  $(BRC) -I$(INCPATH) $(APPNAME).res

# compiling
$(APPNAME).obj: $(APPNAME).cpp
  $(COMPILER) -c $(FLAGS) $(APPNAME).cpp

# compiling
Grunt.obj: Grunt.cpp
  $(COMPILER) -c $(FLAGS) Grunt.cpp

# resource
$(APPNAME).res: $(APPNAME).rc
  $(BRC) -R -I$(INCPATH) $(APPNAME).RC
```

Listing 8.8 shows the Snake1 makefile for Microsoft compilers.

Listing 8.8. SNAKE1.MAK (Microsoft).

```
# SNAKEMS.MAK

APPNAME=SNAKE1
TARGETOS=WIN95
APPVER=4.0
OBJS=$(APPNAME).OBJ GRUNT.OBJ

!include <win32.mak>

all: $(APPNAME).exe

# Update the resource if necessary

$(APPNAME).res: $(APPNAME).rc $(APPNAME).h
  $(rc) $(rcflags) $(rcvars) $(APPNAME).rc

# Update the object files if necessary

# compile
.cpp.obj:
  $(cc) $(cflags) $(cvars) $(cdebug) $<

# Update the executable file if necessary.

$(APPNAME).exe: $(OBJS) $(APPNAME).res
  $(link) $(linkdebug) $(guiflags) -out:$(APPNAME).exe \
  $(OBJS) $(APPNAME).res $(guilibs) comctl32.lib
```

The game starts with a short snake moving slowly across the screen from left to right. (See Figure 8.1.) The direction the snake moves can be controlled with the arrow keys. The object of the game is to keep the snake from running into the sides of the playing field or into its ever-lengthening body. For variety, special little bonus bitmaps appear on screen from time to time. The snake is hungry and likes to eat these bonus bitmaps. You should steer the snake near them whenever possible.

To complete the code, you need to generate the three bitmaps shown below the source. All three bitmaps should be 32×32 pixels.

Figure 8.1.
The snake winds its way across the playing field.

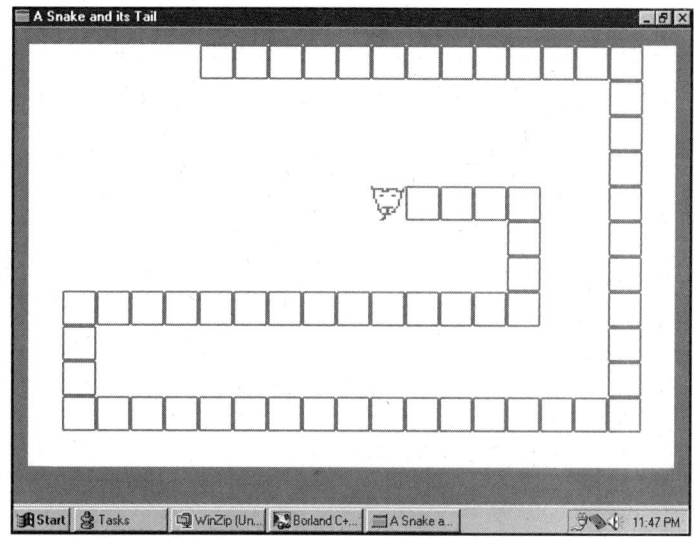

The Child Window

Snake1 has not one but *two* windows. The main window is visible only as a small gray border stretching around the outside of the playing field. The central playing field for the game is actually a child window called the GameWindow. The GameWindow exists primarily to simplify the mathematics in Snake1. The issue is that all three bitmaps used in the game are 32×32 pixels in size. As a result, it would be useful if the dimensions of the game board were a multiple of 32 and couldn't be resized. To achieve these goals, Snake1 maximizes its main window and then pops up a child window with *x* and *y* dimensions evenly divisible by 32. In other words, the dimensions of the main window for the program may not be evenly divisible by 32, but the smaller window fitted inside it will be a multiple of 32.

Maximizing a window on startup is very simple. All you need to do is set nCmdShow to the proper constant, as defined in WINDOWS.H:

```
nCmdShow = SW_SHOWMAXIMIZED;
ShowWindow(hWindow, nCmdShow);
```

After the main window is maximized, Snake1 creates the GameWindow in response to a WM_CREATE message. Creation is a three-step process:

1. Register the window.
2. Calculate the window's dimensions.
3. Call CreateWindow to make the window visible to the user.

In principle, creating a child window is no different from creating the main window of the program. The steps involved are identical. All you need to do is register the window and then create it.

You've seen these steps many times in this book. However, I'll walk through the process with you so there won't be any questions about what is happening. The idea of creating child windows is crucially important in Windows, and it's essential that you understand it. If the ideas come a little slowly to you, don't worry. This material is covered again and again in various guises throughout this book.

Snake1 registers the GameWindow in the same place that it registers its main window. If you look at the Register method, you'll see that it registers class Snake1 and then registers a second window called GameWindow:

```
19: static char szGameName[] = "GameWindow";

... /* Code to define the main window of Snake1 */

106:    RegisterClass (&WndClass);
/* Now register the game window */

109:    WndClass.lpfnWndProc     = GameWndProc;
110:    WndClass.hIcon           = 0;
111:    WndClass.hCursor         = LoadCursor(NULL, IDC_ARROW);
112:    WndClass.hbrBackground   = GetStockBrush(WHITE_BRUSH);
113:    WndClass.lpszClassName   = szGameName;
114:
115:    return RegisterClass (&WndClass);
```

It's not necessary to redefine all the fields of the WNDCLASS structure. Instead, many of them can be carried over unchanged from one class to the next. One field that has to be redefined, however, is the lpfnWndProc variable (line 109) designating the window procedure. The WndProc is the place where the behavior associated with a window is defined. Because the GameWindow is the program's playing field, it's obviously going to have a lot of specialized behavior associated with it. That behavior is defined in its own separate module, called Grunt. Grunt is explained in the next section. Figure 8.2 gives you some idea of how the GameWindow is placed. Notice the thick black border around the edge of the picture. That's not really a border. It's the background of the main window. The area shown in white is the game window.

Figure 8.2.
The GameWindow sits on top and in the center of the main window.

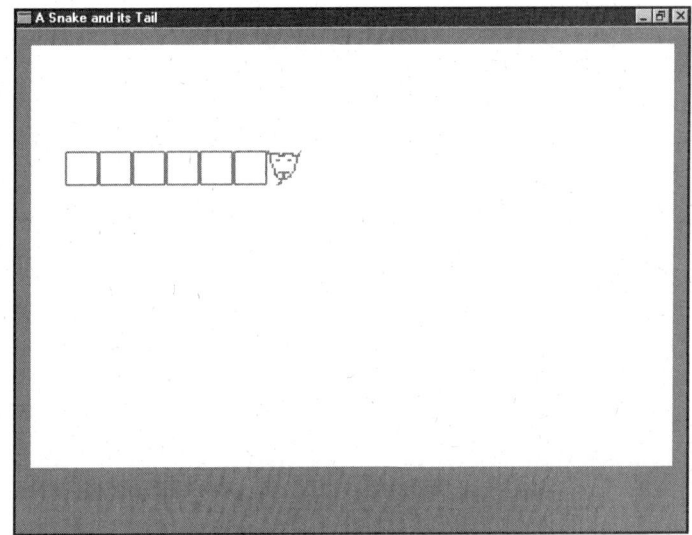

8

Okay. So far, you've seen the Snake1 program register the GameWindow. The next step is to create the window by calling `CreateWindow`. Snake1 performs this action in response to the `WM_CREATE` message.

Most of the previous programs in this book have passed `CW_USEDEFAULT` in the four parameters used to declare a window's dimensions. In this case, however, Snake1 specifically calculates the dimensions passed to `CreateWindow`.

The calculations are necessary because the program runs on a wide variety of platforms. Sometimes, the screen is 640×480; other times, it's 1024×768 or 800×600. (Right now, I'm not supporting any other dimensions, but this will cover 99 percent of the possible dimensions for a window.) Because there's no way to know the dimensions ahead of time, calculations must be made at runtime.

To find out about the current platform, Snake1 calls the `GetSystemMetrics` function. When passed `SM_CXSCREEN` and `SM_CYSCREEN` as arguments, `GetSystemMetrics` reports the dimensions (in pixels) of the current screen. Snake1 uses this information to calculate the largest comfortable playing field that can be created on the current screen. It saves the results in global variables called `MaxCols`, `MaxRows`, and `StartCol`. Following is the code that calculates `MaxCols`:

```
int CXFull = GetSystemMetrics(SM_CXSCREEN);
NumXSects = div(CXFull, Size);
MaxCols = (NumXSects.quot - 1) * Size;
  etc...
```

After Snake knows the GameWindow's optimum size, it is free to create it:

```
hGameWindow = CreateWindow("GameWindow", "A",
                           WS_CHILD | WS_VISIBLE,
                           StartCol, BORDERSIZE, MaxCols, MaxRows,
                           hwnd, NULL, hInstance, NULL);
```

You've seen code like this in the Create function of every full-scale Windows program shown in this book. It should be completely familiar, except for a few slight variations.

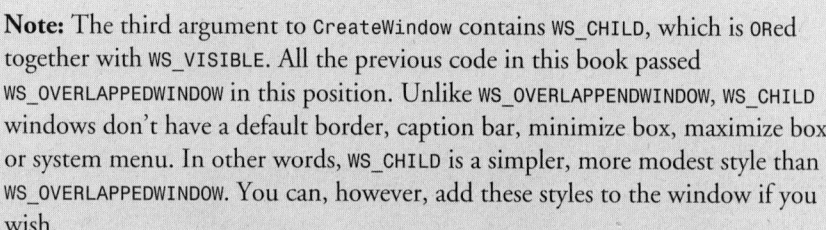

Note: The third argument to CreateWindow contains WS_CHILD, which is ORed together with WS_VISIBLE. All the previous code in this book passed WS_OVERLAPPEDWINDOW in this position. Unlike WS_OVERLAPPENDWINDOW, WS_CHILD windows don't have a default border, caption bar, minimize box, maximize box, or system menu. In other words, WS_CHILD is a simpler, more modest style than WS_OVERLAPPEDWINDOW. You can, however, add these styles to the window if you wish.

The addition of the WS_VISIBLE style enables you to create a window without explicitly calling ShowWindow or UpdateWindow. Programmers frequently use this style with ChildWindows but not with the main window of a program.

At this stage in the book, you shouldn't spend too much time worrying about window styles. You will, however, explore the subject in-depth on Day 14, "Stylish Windows."

The last few paragraphs outline the steps needed to create a child window. This is material that has already been covered in considerable depth in earlier chapters. I've gone through it again just to help orient you, to help you see the main points in the clearest possible terms.

Remember, all you need to do is

1. Register the window
2. Call CreateWindow to bring the window into existence

When you're done, the only step left is to maintain your creation by tending to its window procedure. Snake1 handles this process in the Grunt module.

The Grunt Module

The GameWindow gives three big benefits:

1. It provides a nice symmetrical board to play on, with dimensions evenly divisible by 32.
2. It isolates all the tricky calculations for running the snake in a single module.

3. It demonstrates how to create a stand-alone module that can be joined to a larger Windows program.

The first benefit was discussed in-depth in the last section. The second benefit helps simplify programming chores, eliminate bugs, and aid in program maintenance. In other words, it gives the benefits accrued whenever programmers use good structured programming techniques. The third benefit of GRUNT.CPP is that it shows you how to create a multimodule Windows program.

Snake1 isn't a particularly large program, but the techniques used in creating the Grunt module can serve as a guide showing you how to organize your own large Windows program. Figure 8.3 gives a conceptual picture demonstrating how modules can be linked to form a larger program.

Figure 8.3.
Two or more modules can be joined together to form a larger program.

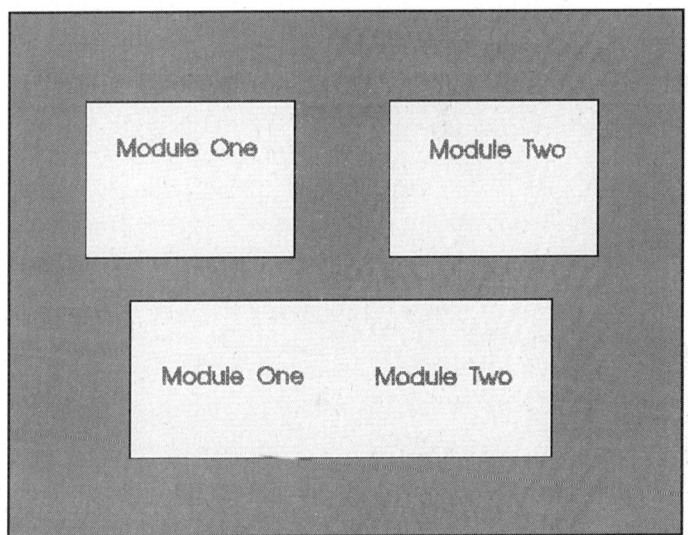

You can turn to this code to see how to declare external variables that can be shared between modules, and how to call a function located in a separate module. More importantly, you can see how to build a .CPP file around a single window, so that both the window and the module exist as parallel, easily identifiable entities. This is the central tenet of structured programming and the kernel idea from which object-oriented programming sprang.

The rules for splitting a program into modules aren't that different in Windows than they are in DOS. The basic themes are threefold:

1. Create header files for each of your modules.

2. Declare shared types and functions in those header files.

3. If you decide that you need to declare a global variable, you can use the extern keyword to make it available in more than one module, just as you would in DOS.

8

DO	**DON'T**

When you're creating modules to be linked into your main program:

DO create a header file for each module you want to share.

DON'T place anything except compiler directives, type declarations, and function declarations in the header file.

DO place global variables to be shared between the module and the main program inside the .CPP source files rather than in header files.

DO place the keyword `extern` in front of global variables that must be referenced outside of the module in which they are defined. For example, the variables `MaxCols` and `MaxRows` are referenced both in the main module and in the Grunt module. As a result, they are defined in the SNAKE1.CPP file, and then referenced with the `extern` keyword in the GRUNT.CPP file:

```
extern int MaxCols;
extern int MaxRows;
```

Considerably more can be said about creating large, multimodule programs. However, this material is covered in considerable depth in basic C and C++ programming books. Rather than repeat that material here, I'll try to stick to the subject at hand, which is Windows programming.

Did you notice that the code in the Grunt module can be divided into two main sections? At the top is the `GameWndProc`. Referenced in the window procedure and implemented directly beneath it are the `Game_OnCreate`, `Game_OnDestroy`, `Game_OnPaint`, `Game_OnChar`, `Game_OnKey`, and `Game_OnTimer` functions. Together, this code makes up the top half of the Grunt module.

Note: None of the code in the Grunt module is ever called directly from SNAKE1.CPP. Instead, SNAKE1.CPP creates the GameWindow in response to a `WM_CREATE` message (line 141). Then, `Game_OnXXX` functions are called by Windows, primarily in response to `WM_TIMER` messages (line 366) and `WM_KEYDOWN` messages (line 318). Whenever possible, it's good to implement code that works in this fashion. In other words, don't have code in one module be too tightly bound to the code in another module. Instead, make each module as independent as possible. If you must call one module directly from another module, it's often a good idea to have it do so through an interface routine that serves no other function than to provide a buffer between the two modules. This type of structure helps to promote code reuse.

The bottom half of the Grunt module contains the routines after which the module is named. This code does the dirty work of calculating where the snake should move next and testing to see whether it has collided with anything. These are not message handler functions, so their naming convention doesn't follow the Game_OnXXX format. Instead, they have simple utilitarian names such as MoveBitmap and CheckForCollisions.

The Timer

The engine that drives the Snake program depends on a Windows message called WM_TIMER.

Timers are devices that send WM_TIMER messages to a window at relatively even intervals. As you know, most of the messages sent to a window are generated by some action on the part of the user. However, timers keep chugging along without any input from the user or the programmer.

Note: I say that timers come at "relatively" even intervals. As it happens, the DOS/Windows message-based environment can't be counted on to send messages at absolutely regular intervals. Don't imagine that it can, and don't waste time wishing it were so. If you need to find more precise timers, you can look at the multimedia timers found in MMSYSTEM.H. (Although these timers aren't directly discussed in this book, you'll get a chance to explore other multimedia features in Bonus Day 3, "DLLS and Multimedia.") The timers you find in WIN32, however, are much more accurate. The true multitasking you find in Windows 95 and Windows NT makes it possible to receive timers at much more regular intervals. This is particularly true if you use timer callbacks.

The code in this book uses timer messages, but the SetTimer function, shown forthwith, also allows you to use timer callbacks. The callbacks are more efficient, and more reliable, in part because of the way Windows handles timer messages. (For more information on callbacks, see Chapter 11, "Talking to Controls.") The reason I use timer messages rather than timer callbacks is that timer messages are much easier to implement. Furthermore, timer messages work just fine for the majority of applications.

All messages in Windows are handled the same way, except for WM_PAINT messages and WM_TIMER messages. These two messages are sent to your application only when all the messages in the queue have already been processed. This is done so that Windows doesn't get bogged down with too many messages. Paint messages in particular can occur almost continuously under some circumstances, and so the only sensible thing to do is ignore them until the rest of the messages are processed.

Only then will the WM_PAINT or WM_TIMER messages be sent. Because WM_TIMER messages are only processed when the message queue is empty, it is obviously more efficient to use a Timer callback. However, the standard Windows timers are rarely, if ever, as accurate as the multimedia timers.

Handling timers is usually a relatively simple operation that has three parts:

1. Initialize the timer with a call to SetTimer
2. Respond to WM_TIMER messages in the Cls_OnTimer message handler function
3. Free the timer resources when you're through with the timer. This is accomplished by calling KillTimer

Snake1 performs the initialization of the timer in the Game_OnCreate function:

```
284:    if (!SetTimer(hwnd, SnakeTimer, 125, NULL))
285:    {
286:      MessageBox(hwnd, "No Timers Available", "Snake Info", MB_OK);
287:      return FALSE;
288:    }
```

The SetTimer function takes four parameters.

☐ The first parameter is the HWND of the window with which the timer is associated.

☐ The second parameter is a unique ID associated with the timer.

☐ The third parameter is the interval, in milliseconds, at which you want WM_TIMER messages to be sent to your window.

☐ The fourth parameter is the name of an optional callback procedure, which Windows can call in lieu of sending WM_TIMER messages to your window. As you can see, the Snake program opts to pass NULL in this fourth parameter. This tells Windows that the program wants to use messages rather than a callback. For more information, see the TimerProc function in the online help. (I never discuss Timer callbacks in this book, but I do discuss other callbacks in several places, including Day 11.)

After the timer is initialized, the Snake program simply responds to WM_TIMER messages:

```
void Snake_OnTimer(HWND hWindow, UINT id)
{
  MoveBitMap(hWindow);
  TotalClicks++;
  if ((TotalClicks % 10) == 0)
  {
    SetSections();
    SetPrizes();
    ...
    /* additional code for adding sections to snake etc... */
  }
}
```

In this program, WM_TIMER messages come cruising down the pike approximately every 150 milliseconds. If you want the snake to move faster, you can create a timer that sends a message every 75 milliseconds, 25 milliseconds, and so forth.

Timers are system resources, similar to bitmaps and icons. As a result, you must be careful to check that a call to SetTimer succeeds; you also must be sure to destroy timers when you are through with them. The proper way to destroy a timer is by calling KillTimer, passing it the HWND of the window to which the timer belongs, and passing it the ID of the timer itself:

```
KillTimer(hWindow, SnakeTimer);
```

If you forget to destroy a timer, the system might run out of timers. If there are no timers left, other applications on the system will be left high and dry, with no alternative but to pop up a series of embarrassing message boxes informing the user that the program can't run correctly because of a lack of resources. This is a question of etiquette, and Miss Manners said that we should be good citizens in such cases. Good citizens always destroy the timers they create, thereby ensuring that both their own programs and other programs will run smoothly.

DO	DON'T

DO balance every call to SetTimer with a call to KillTimer.

DON'T ever quit an application that uses a timer without first destroying that timer.

DON'T create any more timers than you absolutely have to use.

Now that you understand how timers work, I'm going to give only a very brief overview of the Snake_OnTimer function. If you want more details, start up the debugger, start setting breakpoints, and in general, be prepared to get your hands a bit dirty.

The main function of Snake_OnTimer is to call the MoveBitMap procedure, which paints the snake to the screen. However, as you can see, Snake_OnTimer includes extra logic for adding a new section to the snake once every 10 times the WM_TIMER message is sent. As a result, the snake keeps getting longer and longer, and the user finds it more and more difficult to steer the snake safely across the screen.

Some of the logic for painting the snake is duplicated in the Snake_OnPaint function. This is done only because it might be necessary to repaint the screen if it becomes covered up.

Painting the Snake

Whenever the code in Snake "blits" an image to the screen, it does so by using the SRCINVERT constant in the last parameter passed to BitBlt. As a result, these images are XORed to the screen.

This is an easy way to achieve a certain kind of animation that leaves the area beneath the blitted image intact.

When you XOR an image to the screen, you can erase it simply by XORing the same image a second time in the same place. In other words, the first time you XOR an image to the screen, you make it visible; the second time you make it invisible. This process doesn't disturb any images residing beneath the image blitted to the screen.

The key to animating an object is to blit it to the screen, erase it, move it forward a bit, blit it again, erase it, move it forward again, and so on (for as long as you want to create the illusion of movement).

At this point in the book, I don't want to burden you with additional information about XORing bitmaps or about the subtleties of the BitBlt function. I do, however, give some additional information about this subject in Bonus Day 1, "GDI and Metafiles."

You should note, however, that the use of SRCINVERT always reverses the colors of any bitmap you create. As a result, you might want to have two copies of the bitmaps used in this program. The first copy would be in the normal colors you want to use in the game; the second copy would be an inverted version for use with the RC file. When the inverted version is blitted to the screen with SRCINVERT, the bitmap will appear as you originally drew it. Most Windows paint programs include a feature for inverting bitmaps.

Snakes Alive!

The code that makes the snake move across the screen utilizes standard C/C++ coding practices and a review of subject matter that was covered earlier in this book. If you are having trouble picking up on the logic of this program, the key point to understand is that each section of the snake is a complete entity that knows its current and previous location and direction.

Whenever the head of the snake turns, a chain effect is set in motion, whereby the news that a move has been made is passed down the snake's body from section to section. In other words, when a WM_TIMER message is sent, each section takes on the state that the section preceding it in line had when the last WM_TIMER message was sent. The actual passing on of the information is done in the SetColRow function. The end result is that the "news" of a turn is passed down the line from the head to the tail. This algorithm is exercised religiously, even though only the first and last sections of the snake's body are painted in response to each WM_TIMER message.

I hope you'll find that the Snake program is an enjoyable and instructive experience. I've tried to make it intriguing enough so that you'll be drawn in by its charms—and in the process start to take to heart some of the lessons presented in the last few chapters.

Examples and explanations that illustrate fundamental programming principles can only take you so far. If you want to really learn how to program a particular language or environment, you have to start writing some code on your own. Adding additional features to the Snake program would be a good place to start.

Summary

The main purposes of this chapter are to let you have some fun and to give you some hands-on experience. Along the way, several new issues have been introduced. In particular, you have seen how to

- [ ] Create timers by calling SetTimer and destroy them by calling KillTimer
- [ ] Respond to WM_TIMER messages
- [ ] Create a child window
- [ ] Place a window in a separate module and call it from the main body of a program

Don't underestimate this knowledge just because it's given to you in the form of a game. If you take it to heart, it will help you make the transition from Windows programming neophyte to Windows programming guru.

Q&A

Q Why should you automatically maximize the main window of the Snake program? Doesn't this act negate the benefits of a multitasking environment?

A This is a philosophical or aesthetic question rather than a technical issue. My rationale for maximizing the window is simply that you can't properly multitask a game like this anyway, because the snake will run into a wall if it's left unattended for more than a few moments. Given those circumstances, a whole class of problems can be avoided by simply assuming that anyone playing Snake will want to give it their whole attention. If the user is going to be totally focused on one window, why not make the window as big as possible? Second, maximizing the window enables the Snake program to avoid the difficult (insane?) calculations that would be involved if the playing field were resized at runtime!

Q I thought Windows wasn't meant to be a gaming environment. Doesn't the Snake program violate the basic spirit of Windows?

A Every copy of Windows ships with at least two games built into it. The designers of this environment definitely did not mean to exclude gamers. However, there is some truth to the idea that DOS games perform better than Windows games. This is because DOS programmers have complete control over the machine. Yet the Snake program shows that reasonably fast graphics can be done in the Windows environment.

Other improvements can be bought by using WinG as well as the related DIB functions found in WIN32. More on that subject later.

Certainly, Windows gives game programmers a big leg up because of its powerful, built-in graphics support. In the long run, however, I think it's important to realize that no one programming environment has a monopoly on all the most sought after virtues. Right now, the best of all possible worlds probably would be one in which users and programmers had easy access to both DOS and Windows. Say what?

Workshop

The Workshop provides quiz questions to help you solidify your understanding of the material covered and exercises to provide you with experience in using what you've learned. Try to understand the quiz and exercise answers before continuing on to Day 9, "Font Basics." Answers are provided in Appendix A.

Quiz

1. What two steps are necessary to create a child window?
2. Why is `RegisterClass` called twice in the `Register` function of Snake1?
3. What is the name of the window procedure for the child window in Snake1?
4. Why doesn't the `Game_OnDestroy` function call `PostQuitMessage`?
5. How do you create a timer?
6. How can the Snake program be sure that `KillTimer` will be called before the program ends?
7. What constant do you use if you want to `XOR` a bitmap to the screen?
8. How can you find out how many pixels are needed to fill a single row on the screen of a computer?
9. Use your reference books or the online help to find 10 pieces of information that can be retrieved using the `GetSystemMetrics` function.
10. What's the purpose of the `Game_OnChar` message handler function?

Exercises

1. Have some fun, use your imagination, and add the features you feel are missing from the Snake program.
2. In the next few chapters, you'll learn a lot about dialogs and window controls. If you enjoy games, use some of these techniques to add spice to the Snake program. In other words, make the Snake program an ongoing project.

Font Basics

In this chapter you'll see how fonts are created in the Windows environment. In particular, the following subjects are covered:

- ☐ Creating fonts with the API calls `CreateFontIndirect`, `CreateFont`, and `GetStockObject`
- ☐ Getting information about the current font by calling `GetTextMetrics` and `GetTextFace`
- ☐ Using and analyzing the `LOGFONT` structure
- ☐ Using and analyzing the `TEXTMETRIC` structure
- ☐ Rotating a font
- ☐ Deleting fonts with `DeleteFont`

The point of this chapter is to give you a solid working knowledge of fonts that should hold you in good stead throughout most normal programming projects.

Day 10, "Window Controls," is dedicated primarily to an exploration of Window controls. However, it also continues the theme of this chapter by allowing you to enumerate the fonts on your system with a callback function.

Font Madness Arrives on the PC!

Not long after Windows 3.0 came out, I was freelancing, picking up various kinds of work—some of it programming and some of it just hell-for-leather consulting. One of the jobs I landed involved working for a graphics designer. He had a shop filled with expensive printers, scanners, Macs and—now that Windows was out—a few PCs.

I did technically straightforward tasks for him, such as cleaning up his WIN.INI file and cutting redundant calls out of his AUTOEXEC.BAT. A more technical part of my job involved satisfying his passionate interest in fonts.

People in the Mac world have, of course, been working with fonts for years. Because these resources were part of his business, all his Macs were loaded down with an incredible range of fonts. His goal was to match that diversity by arming his PCs with even more fonts. Not just 5 or 10 fonts—but 20, 30, maybe 40 or more fonts. He was very serious about his business, and people paid him good money for his trouble.

Unfortunately, Windows was new to him, and he didn't have the time to master all the details. What he needed was someone who could sort all those fonts for him, and more importantly, find out how he could get access to all of them from inside PageMaker, CorelDRAW!, and Word for Windows.

Unfortunately, the DOS world had done nothing to prepare me for this challenge. For years, I had stared at the same old DOS character set. When it came to fonts, I had the aesthetic sense of a duck-billed platypus. I didn't know Times from Courier, bold from italic, or WingDing from Symbol. I was utterly unaware of most of the aesthetic distinctions that lay very much at the heart of this guy's business.

Through hard work and good fortune, I eventually got most of the fonts straightened out. But it was a challenge. I just hadn't understood what a complicated and subtle subject I had stumbled across.

Over the years, I've always been grateful for that experience, not only because it taught me a lot, but because it showed me how passionately some people care about fonts. It's a subject that can arouse intense sentiments. My advice to new Windows programmers is to get a good grasp of this subject. If all else fails, you should simply give your users access to all the fonts on the system, letting them choose which ones they want in any particular situation. The point is, you never know when you will encounter someone who really cares about this subject.

Anyway, fonts are fun and can add flare to routine programs. As a result, I explore this subject in some depth over the next several chapters.

The Simple Font Program

You now should be ready to take a look at the first font example, SimpFont (see Listing 9.1). It shows you one very simple and straightforward way to create a font.

Listing 9.1. The SimpFont program explores methods for creating and manipulating fonts.

```
/////////////////////////////////////
//   Program Name: SIMPFONT.CPP
//   Copyright 1993 (c) by Charles Calvert
//   Description: SimpFont windows program
//   Date: 3/20/93
//   UpDate for WIN32: May 22, 1995
/////////////////////////////////////

#define STRICT
#include <windows.h>
#include <windowsx.h>
#pragma hdrstop
#include <stdio.h>
#include <stdlib.h>
#include <string.h>
#include "simpfont.h"
#include "fontstr.h"
#pragma warning (disable: 4068)

// variables
static char szAppName[] = "SimpFont";
static HWND MainWindow;
static HINSTANCE hInstance;
static LOGFONT LogFont;
static HFONT TheFont;
static char aFaceName[80];
TEXTMETRIC TextMets;
```

continues

Listing 9.1. continued

```
char * FontChoice[] = {"New Times Roman", "Arial",
                       "Symbol", "StockFont"};
enum TChoice {Roman, Swiss, Symbol, StockFont};
TChoice Choice;


// -----------------------------------
// Initialization
// -----------------------------------


///////////////////////////////////////
// Program entry point
///////////////////////////////////////
#pragma argsused
int WINAPI WinMain(HINSTANCE hInst, HINSTANCE hPrevInstance,
                   LPSTR  lpszCmdParam, int nCmdShow)
{

  MSG  Msg;

  if (!hPrevInstance)
    if (!Register(hInst))
      return FALSE;

  MainWindow = Create(hInst, nCmdShow);
  if (!MainWindow)
    return FALSE;

  while (GetMessage(&Msg, NULL, 0, 0))
  {
     TranslateMessage(&Msg);
     DispatchMessage(&Msg);
  }

  return Msg.wParam;
}


///////////////////////////////////////
// Register the window
///////////////////////////////////////
BOOL Register(HINSTANCE hInst)
{
  WNDCLASS WndClass;

  WndClass.style        = CS_HREDRAW | CS_VREDRAW;
  WndClass.lpfnWndProc  = WndProc;
  WndClass.cbClsExtra   = 0;
  WndClass.cbWndExtra   = 0;
  WndClass.hInstance    = hInst;
  WndClass.hIcon        = LoadIcon(NULL, IDI_APPLICATION);
  WndClass.hCursor      = LoadCursor(NULL, IDC_ARROW);
  WndClass.hbrBackground = GetStockBrush(WHITE_BRUSH);
  WndClass.lpszMenuName = "Menu";
  WndClass.lpszClassName = szAppName;

  return (RegisterClass (&WndClass) != 0);
}
```

```
/////////////////////////////////////
// Create the window
/////////////////////////////////////
HWND Create(HINSTANCE hInst, int nCmdShow)
{

  hInstance = hInst;

  HWND hWindow = CreateWindow(szAppName, szAppName,
                    WS_OVERLAPPEDWINDOW,
                    CW_USEDEFAULT, CW_USEDEFAULT,
                    CW_USEDEFAULT, CW_USEDEFAULT,
                    NULL, NULL, hInstance, NULL);

  if (hWindow == NULL)
    return hWindow;

  ShowWindow(hWindow, nCmdShow);
  UpdateWindow(hWindow);

  return hWindow;
}

// -------------------------------------
// WndProc and Implementation
// -------------------------------------

/////////////////////////////////////
// The Window Procedure
/////////////////////////////////////

LRESULT CALLBACK  EXPORT16 WndProc(HWND hWindow, UINT Message,
                        WPARAM wParam, LPARAM lParam)
{
  switch(Message)
  {
    HANDLE_MSG(hWindow, WM_DESTROY, SimpFont_OnDestroy);
    HANDLE_MSG(hWindow, WM_CREATE, SimpFont_OnCreate);
    HANDLE_MSG(hWindow, WM_COMMAND, SimpFont_OnCommand);
    HANDLE_MSG(hWindow, WM_PAINT, SimpFont_OnPaint);
    default:
      return SimpFont_DefProc(hWindow, Message, wParam, lParam);
  }
}

/////////////////////////////////////
// Get a new font, specify Escapement
/////////////////////////////////////
HFONT GetFont(int Escapement, char * Name)
{
  memset(&LogFont, 0, sizeof(LOGFONT));

  LogFont.lfHeight      = 37;
  LogFont.lfWeight      = 400;
  LogFont.lfEscapement  = Escapement;
  LogFont.lfItalic      = 1;
```

continues

Listing 9.1. continued

```
    LogFont.lfUnderline     = 1;
    LogFont.lfOutPrecision  = OUT_STROKE_PRECIS;
    LogFont.lfClipPrecision = CLIP_STROKE_PRECIS;
    LogFont.lfQuality       = DEFAULT_QUALITY;
    strcpy(LogFont.lfFaceName, Name);

    if (TheFont != 0) DeleteFont(TheFont);

    TheFont = CreateFontIndirect(&LogFont);

    return TheFont;
}

//////////////////////////////////////
// Handle WM_DESTROY
//////////////////////////////////////
#pragma argsused
void SimpFont_OnDestroy(HWND hwnd)
{
    if (TheFont != 0) DeleteFont(TheFont);
    PostQuitMessage(0);
}

//////////////////////////////////////
// Handle WM_CREATE
//////////////////////////////////////
#pragma argsused
BOOL SimpFont_OnCreate(HWND hwnd, CREATESTRUCT FAR*
lpCreateStruct)
{
    GetFont(0, "New Times Roman");
    return TRUE;
}

//////////////////////////////////////
// Handle WM_COMMAND
//////////////////////////////////////
#pragma argsused
void SimpFont_OnCommand(HWND hwnd, int id, HWND hwndCtl, UINT
codeNotify)
{
    char S[500];

    switch (id)
    {
        case CM_INFO:
            GetFontString(S, TextMets, aFaceName);
            MessageBox(hwnd, S, "Font Info", MB_OK);
            break;

        case CM_ROMAN:
            Choice = Roman;
            InvalidateRect(hwnd, NULL, TRUE);
            break;
```

```
  case CM_SWISS:
    Choice = Swiss;
    InvalidateRect(hwnd, NULL, TRUE);
    break;

  case CM_SYMBOL:
    Choice = Symbol;
    InvalidateRect(hwnd, NULL, TRUE);
    break;

  case CM_ANSI_FIXED_FONT:
    if (TheFont != 0) DeleteFont(TheFont);
    TheFont = GetStockFont(ANSI_FIXED_FONT);
    Choice = StockFont;
    InvalidateRect(hwnd, NULL, TRUE);
    break;

  case CM_ANSI_VAR_FONT:
    if (TheFont != 0) DeleteFont(TheFont);
    TheFont = GetStockFont(ANSI_VAR_FONT);
    Choice = StockFont;
    InvalidateRect(hwnd, NULL, TRUE);
    break;

  case CM_DEVICE_DEFAULT_FONT:
    if (TheFont != 0) DeleteFont(TheFont);
    TheFont = GetStockFont(DEVICE_DEFAULT_FONT);
    Choice = StockFont;
    InvalidateRect(hwnd, NULL, TRUE);
    break;

  case CM_OEM_FIXED_FONT:
    if (TheFont != 0) DeleteFont(TheFont);
    TheFont = GetStockFont(OEM_FIXED_FONT);
    Choice = StockFont;
    InvalidateRect(hwnd, NULL, TRUE);
    break;

  case CM_SYSTEM_FONT:
    if (TheFont != 0) DeleteFont(TheFont);
    TheFont = GetStockFont(SYSTEM_FONT);
    Choice = StockFont;
    InvalidateRect(hwnd, NULL, TRUE);
    break;

  case CM_SYSTEM_FIXED_FONT:
    if (TheFont != 0) DeleteFont(TheFont);
    TheFont = GetStockFont(SYSTEM_FIXED_FONT);
    Choice = StockFont;
    InvalidateRect(hwnd, NULL, TRUE);
    break;
  }
}
```

continues

Font Basics

Listing 9.1. continued

```
/////////////////////////////////////
// Handle WM_PAINT changing the color, and rotating the font
/////////////////////////////////////
void SimpFont_OnPaint(HWND hwnd)
{
  PAINTSTRUCT PaintStruct;
  HFONT OldFont;

  HDC PaintDC = BeginPaint(hwnd, &PaintStruct);

  if (Choice == StockFont)
  {
    OldFont = SelectFont(PaintDC, TheFont);
    GetTextFace(PaintDC, sizeof(aFaceName),
                (LPSTR) aFaceName);
    GetTextMetrics(PaintDC, &TextMets);
    SetTextColor(PaintDC, RGB(rand() % 255,
                rand() % 255, rand() % 255));
    TextOut(PaintDC, 10, 10, aFaceName, strlen(aFaceName));
    TextOut(PaintDC, 10, 30, "Stock Fonts", 11);
    TextOut(PaintDC, 10, 50, "Ten Letters", 11);
    SelectFont(PaintDC, OldFont);
  }
  else
  {
    for (int i = 0; i <= 3; i++)
    {
      TheFont = GetFont(900 * i, FontChoice[Choice]);
      OldFont = SelectFont(PaintDC, TheFont);
      SetTextColor(PaintDC, RGB(rand() % 255,
                  rand() % 255, rand() % 255));
      TextOut(PaintDC, 200, 200, "Ahoy!" , 5);
      GetTextFace(PaintDC, sizeof(aFaceName),
                  (LPSTR) aFaceName);
      GetTextMetrics(PaintDC, &TextMets);
      SelectFont(PaintDC, OldFont);
    }
    TextOut(PaintDC, 10, 10, aFaceName, strlen(aFaceName));
  }

  EndPaint(hwnd, &PaintStruct);
}
```

Listing 9.2 shows the SimpFont header file.

Listing 9.2. SIMPFONT.H.

```
/////////////////////////////////////
//   Program Name: SIMPFONT.H
//   Programmer: Charlie Calvert
//   Description: SimpFont windows program
/////////////////////////////////////
```

```
#define CM_INFO 100
#define CM_ROMAN 101
#define CM_SWISS 102
#define CM_SYMBOL 103

#define CM_ANSI_FIXED_FONT     201
#define CM_ANSI_VAR_FONT 202
#define CM_DEVICE_DEFAULT_FONT     203
#define CM_OEM_FIXED_FONT 204
#define CM_SYSTEM_FONT    205
#define CM_SYSTEM_FIXED_FONT 206

#if !defined(__WIN32__) && !defined(_WIN32)
#define EXPORT16 __export
#else
#define EXPORT16
#endif

// Declarations for class SimpFont
#define SimpFont_DefProc     DefWindowProc
BOOL SimpFont_OnCreate(HWND hwnd, CREATESTRUCT FAR*
lpCreateStruct);
void SimpFont_OnDestroy(HWND hwnd);
void SimpFont_OnCommand(HWND hwnd, int id, HWND hwndCtl,
UINT codeNotify);
void SimpFont_OnPaint(HWND hwnd);

// Procs
LRESULT CALLBACK EXPORT16 WndProc(HWND hWindow, UINT Message,
                       WPARAM wParam, LPARAM lParam);
BOOL Register(HINSTANCE hInst);
HWND Create(HINSTANCE hInst, int nCmdShow);
BOOL CALLBACK InfoDlgProc(HWND hDlg, WORD Message,
                       WPARAM wParam, LPARAM lParam);
```

Listing 9.3 shows the Fontstr source file.

Listing 9.3. FONTSTR.CPP.

```
1: /////////////////////////////////////////
2: //   Module Name: FONTSTR.CPP
3: //   Programmer: Charlie Calvert
4: //   Description: Simpfont program font analysis
6: /////////////////////////////////////////
7:
8: #define STRICT
9: #include <windows.h>
10: #include <windowsx.h>
11: #include <string.h>
12: #include <stdio.h>
13:
14: // variables
15: TEXTMETRIC TextMetrics;
16: static char TheFaceName[80];
```

Listing 9.3. continued

```
17:
18: // procs
19: char * GetType(char * S);
20: char * GetFamily(char * S);
21: char * GetCharSet(char * S);
22:
23: char * GetFontString(char * S, TEXTMETRIC TextMetric, char * FaceName)
24: {
25:    char szType[99], szFamily[99], szCharSet[99];
26:
27:    TextMetrics = TextMetric;
28:    strcpy(TheFaceName, FaceName);
29:
30:    GetType(szType);
31:    GetFamily(szFamily);
32:    GetCharSet(szCharSet);
33:
34:    sprintf(S, "Font: %s \n Height: %d \n "
35:               "Ascent: %d \n Descent: %d \n "
36:               "AveCharW: %d \n MaxCharW: %d \n "
37:               "Weight: %d \n Italic: %hd \n "
38:               "Underlined: %d \n"
39:               "%s \n %s \n %s ",
40:    TheFaceName,
41:    TextMetrics.tmHeight,
42:    TextMetrics.tmAscent,
43:    TextMetrics.tmDescent,
44:    TextMetrics.tmAveCharWidth,
45:    TextMetrics.tmMaxCharWidth,
46:    TextMetrics.tmWeight,
47:    TextMetrics.tmItalic,
48:    TextMetrics.tmUnderlined,
49:    szType, szFamily, szCharSet);
50:
51:    return S;
52: }
53:
54: char * GetType(char * S)
55: {
56:    strcpy(S, "Font Type: ");
57:    if ((TextMetrics.tmPitchAndFamily & TMPF_FIXED_PITCH) == 0)
58:    strcat(S, "Default <> ");
59:    if ((TextMetrics.tmPitchAndFamily & TMPF_FIXED_PITCH) ==
60:        TMPF_FIXED_PITCH)
61:    strcat(S, "Fixed <> ");
62:    if ((TextMetrics.tmPitchAndFamily & TMPF_VECTOR) ==
63:        TMPF_VECTOR)
64:    strcat(S, "Vector <> ");
65:    if ((TextMetrics.tmPitchAndFamily & TMPF_TRUETYPE) ==
66:        TMPF_TRUETYPE)
67:    strcat(S, "TrueType <> ");
68:    if ((TextMetrics.tmPitchAndFamily & TMPF_DEVICE) ==
69:        TMPF_DEVICE)
70:    strcat(S, "Device <> ");
```

```
71:
72:    if (strlen(S) > 11)
73:       S[strlen(S) - 3] = '\0';
74:
75:    return S;
76: }
77:
78: char * GetFamily(char * S)
79: {
80:    int R = TextMetrics.tmPitchAndFamily & 0XF0;
81:    strcpy(S, "Family: ");
82:    if (R == FF_DONTCARE) strcat(S, "Don't Care or don't know");
83:    if (R == FF_ROMAN)  strcat(S, "Roman");
84:    if (R == FF_SWISS)  strcat(S, "Swiss");
85:    if (R == FF_MODERN) strcat(S, "Modern");
86:    if (R == FF_SCRIPT) strcat(S, "Script");
87:    if (R == FF_DECORATIVE) strcat(S, "Decorative");
88:
89:    return S;
90: }
91:
92: char * GetCharSet(char * S)
93: {
94:    strcpy(S, "Char Set: ");
95:
96:    if (TextMetrics.tmCharSet == ANSI_CHARSET)
97:      strcat(S, "Ansi");
98:
99:    if (TextMetrics.tmCharSet == DEFAULT_CHARSET)
100:       strcat(S, "Default");
101:
102:    if (TextMetrics.tmCharSet == SYMBOL_CHARSET)
103:       strcat(S, "Symbol");
104:
105:    if (TextMetrics.tmCharSet == OEM_CHARSET)
106:       strcat(S, "OEM");
107:
108:    return S;
109: }
```

Listing 9.4 shows the Fontstr header file.

Listing 9.4. FONTSTR.H.

```
1: //////////////////////////////////////////
2: //  Module Name: FONTSTR.H
3: //  Programmer: Charlie Calvert
4: //  Description: Simpfont program font analysis
5: //  Date: 6/12/93
6: //////////////////////////////////////////
7:
8: char * GetFontString(char * S, TEXTMETRIC TextMetric,
9:                      char * FaceName);
```

Listing 9.5 shows the definition file for SimpFont.

Listing 9.5. SIMPFONT.DEF.

```
1: ; SIMPFONT.DEF
2:
3: NAME            SimpFont
4: DESCRIPTION     'SimpFont Window'
5: HEAPSIZE        10240
6: STACKSIZE       10240
7: CODE            PRELOAD MOVEABLE DISCARDABLE
8: DATA            PRELOAD MOVEABLE MULTIPLE
```

Listing 9.6 shows the SimpFont makefile for Borland compilers.

Listing 9.6. SIMPFONT.MAK (Borland).

```
# - - - - - - - - - - - - - - - - - - - - - - - - - - - - - - -
# SIMPFONT.MAK
# - - - - - - - - - - - - - - - - - - - - - - - - - - - - - - -

# macros
!if !$d(BCROOT)
BCROOT  = $(MAKEDIR)
!endif

APPNAME = SimpFont
INCPATH = $(BCROOT)\INCLUDE
LIBPATH = $(BCROOT)\LIB

!if $d(WIN16)
COMPILER= BCC.EXE
BRC     = BRC.EXE
FLAGS   = -W -ml -v -w4 -I$(INCPATH) -L$(LIBPATH)
!else
COMPILER= BCC32.EXE
BRC     = BRC32.EXE
FLAGS   = -W -v -w4 -I$(INCPATH) -L$(LIBPATH)
!endif

# link
$(APPNAME).exe: $(APPNAME).obj $(APPNAME).def \
                $(APPNAME).res FONTSTR.OBJ
  $(COMPILER) $(FLAGS) $(APPNAME).obj FONTSTR.OBJ
  $(BRC) $(APPNAME).res

# compile
$(APPNAME).obj: $(APPNAME).cpp
  $(COMPILER) -c $(FLAGS) $(APPNAME).cpp

# compile
FONTSTR.OBJ: FONTSTR.CPP
  $(COMPILER) -c $(FLAGS) FONTSTR.CPP
```

```
# compile
$(APPNAME).res: $(APPNAME).rc
  $(BRC) -R -I$(INCPATH) $(APPNAME).RC
```

Listing 9.7 shows the SimpFont makefile for Microsoft compilers.

Listing 9.7. SIMPFONT.MAK (Microsoft).

```
# SIMPFOMS.MAK

APPNAME=SIMPFONT
TARGETOS=WIN95
APPVER=4.0
OBJS=$(APPNAME).OBJ FONTSTR.OBJ

!include <win32.mak>

all: $(APPNAME).exe

# Update the resource if necessary

$(APPNAME).res: $(APPNAME).rc $(APPNAME).h
  $(rc) $(rcflags) $(rcvars) $(APPNAME).rc

# Update the object files if necessary

# compile
.cpp.obj:
  $(cc) $(cflags) $(cvars) $(cdebug) $<

# Update the executable file if necessary.

$(APPNAME).exe: $(OBJS) $(APPNAME).res
  $(link) $(linkdebug) $(guiflags) -out:$(APPNAME).exe $(OBJS) $(APPNAME).res
$(guilibs) comctl32.lib
```

When it starts up, this program prints out a single word four times in four randomly chosen colors. Each time the word is printed, it's aligned along another one of the major axes of a circle—that is, at the 90-degree mark, the 0-degree mark, the 270-degree mark, and the 180-degree mark. The output from this program is shown in Figure 9.1.

A menu at the top of the program enables you to select different fonts, including three TrueType fonts and all of the stock fonts on the system. The display of the stock fonts is less interesting than the TrueType display because it can't be rotated.

Because the SimpFont program outputs randomly chosen colors, there is always the chance that it will draw white text to the screen. White text, of course, is invisible on a white background. This is a flaw in the program, but one that will not show up very often, at least on 256-color systems.

Figure 9.1.

The output from the SIMPFONT.CPP program shows how text can be rotated around a 360-degree arc.

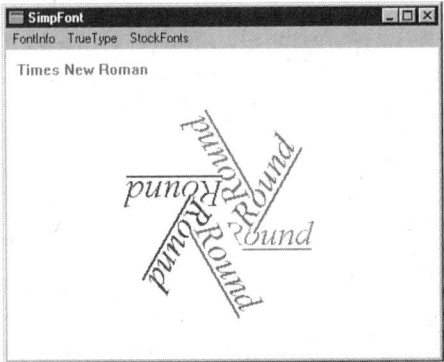

The SimpFont program is important, because it shows you how to create stock fonts, normal fonts, and TrueType fonts. This is knowledge that no Windows programmer can afford to do without.

Note: TrueType fonts appeared for the first time in Windows 3.1. They give the user high-quality letters, both on-screen and on a printer. In addition, they enable the programmer to port a font from one location to another. That is, TrueType fonts can be moved from the screen to the printer with a minimal loss of quality. Furthermore, they can be moved with a document from one system to another, through a technique called embedding (not discussed in this book).

Getting Started with Fonts

Fonts tend to have complicated lives. In general, they move through six phases:

1. They're designed by filling out a big structure called a LOGFONT.
2. They're created by calling CreateFontIndirect.
3. They're copied into a device context with SelectFont or SelectObject.
4. They're shown to the screen with TextOut or DrawText.
5. They're copied back out of the device context.
6. They're deleted from the system with a call to DeleteFont.

Clearly, this is no piece of cake. My goal is to make it palatable to you by explaining it in the simplest possible terms. Furthermore, I'll let the SimpFont program illustrate this process in considerable depth. By the end of the chapter, this whole subject should be old hat. You'll know what Windows fonts are and how to create them.

The key function in the SimpFont program is called GetFont. This is where the TrueType fonts used by this program are created:

```
130: HFONT GetFont(int Escapement, char * Name)
131: {
132:    memset(&LogFont, 0, sizeof(LOGFONT));
133:
134:    LogFont.lfHeight        = 37;
135:    LogFont.lfWeight        = 400;
136:    LogFont.lfEscapement    = Escapement;
137:    LogFont.lfItalic        = 1;
138:    LogFont.lfUnderline     = 1;
139:    LogFont.lfOutPrecision  = OUT_STROKE_PRECIS;
140:    LogFont.lfClipPrecision = CLIP_STROKE_PRECIS;
141:    LogFont.lfQuality       = DEFAULT_QUALITY;
142:    strcpy(LogFont.lfFaceName, Name);
143:
144:    if (TheFont != 0) DeleteFont(TheFont);
145:
146:    TheFont = CreateFontIndirect(&LogFont);
147:
148:    return TheFont;
149: }
```

The GetFont procedure has four parts:

1. The procedure first uses the memset function to zero out the LOGFONT structure.

2. Then, it fills out various fields of the LOGFONT structure.

3. Next, it checks to see if a variable called TheFont already holds the handle to a valid font. If it does, that font is deleted.

4. Finally, GetFont gives birth to the font by calling CreateFontIndirect.

This process, or one very much like it, is what you'll usually go through when you want to create a font. One exception to this rule is when you want a stock font. Stock fonts are easy to obtain, as you will see a bit later in this chapter.

For now, though, I want to concentrate on the GetFont function. The key, obviously enough, to the whole function is the traumatic LOGFONT structure, which has enough fields in it to host an entire football league. It's complex enough to warrant its own section here.

The Logical Fonts Section

By default, when you write text to the screen in Windows, you use the *system font*. This is a nice reliable tool that meets most day-to-day needs. However, there are times when you want to add more spice to a program and use fonts that can make your code more versatile, attractive, and appealing.

The key to this whole topic is the following, somewhat-daunting logical font structure, or LOGFONT (as it is called in WINDOWS.H):

```
typedef struct tagLOGFONT {
int    lfHeight;
int    lfWidth;
int    lfEscapement;
int    lfOrientation;
int    lfWeight;
BYTE   lfItalic;
BYTE   lfUnderline;
BYTE   lfStrikeOut;
BYTE   lfCharSet;
BYTE   lfOutPrecision;
BYTE   lfClipPrecision;
BYTE   lfQuality;
BYTE   lfPitchAndFamily;
BYTE   lfFaceName[LF_FACESIZE];
} LOGFONT;
```

If you want to create a font in Windows, you need to fill out a few fields in the preceding record and pass the record to a function called CreateFontIndirect.

> **Note:** You can pass this same list of fields to a function called CreateFont. It takes 14 parameters, all with the same names and the same import as the fields in the CreateFontIndirect function. Because they each have their advantages, it's really a toss-up as to which of the two functions you use.

The existence of CreateFont and CreateFontIndirect makes creating fonts very simple—at least in principle. The problem, of course, is knowing how to fill out the fields in the LOGFONT structure. The good news is that if you want, you can simply pass zero to all but the first and last fields and then let Windows choose default values for the rest. The following call to CreateFont shows how this can be done:

```
hfont = CreateFont(25, 0, 0, 0, 0, 0, 0, 0,
                   0, 0, 0, 0, 0, "Arial");
```

If you are using CreateFontIndirect, you can simply use memset to zero out the fields (as shown in the GetFont procedure).

The problem with this system, however, is that Windows frequently fails to fill out the missing fields with values that you would think appropriate. As a result, you can ask for an Arial font and end up with a Script font, and vice versa.

So, the best way to create a particular font is often to fill out at least four or five of the LOGFONT fields with specific values. To help you get an idea of how to proceed, I've provided the following list, which should give at least a minimal introduction to all the LOGFONT fields. For now, you'll

probably just want to glance through it. You can study this subject in more detail after you have the first example up and running. Once again, the point is not to memorize all these fields, but to know of their existences and purposes, and to know where you can look them up:

lfHeight	The height of the font. If the number is negative, the internal leading is ignored.
lfWidth	The width of the font. You can set this to 0 if you want Windows to calculate an appropriate width for you.
lfEscapement	The angle at which the font is printed. 0 is normal, 900 is straight up, 1800 is upside-down and backwards, and 2700 is straight down. TrueType fonts can hit all these positions and the positions in between. (See Figures 9.1 and 9.2.)
lfOrientation	Not implemented at this time, but someday it should affect the angle at which individual characters are printed.
lfWeight	The weight of the font, in increments of 100, starting at 0 and ending at 900. Entering 0 enables Windows to pick a default weight. 700 is usually the number associated with bold print.
lfItalic	Set to 0 for normal and 1 (nonzero) for italic.
lfUnderline	Set to 0 for normal and 1 (nonzero) for underlined.
lfStrikeOut	Set to 0 for normal and 1 (nonzero) if you want a line drawn through the center of the font—as if it were crossed out.
lfCharSet	The characters used by the font:

ANSI_CHARSET　　　　0
DEFAULT_CHARSET　　1
SYMBOL_CHARSET　　　2
SHIFTJIS_CHARSET　 128
OEM_CHARSET　　　　 255

The most common value for lfCharSet is 0. Although DEFAULT_CHARSET might seem like a safe and intuitive option, it's best to avoid it on most occasions:

lfOutPrecision	Specifies how precisely the font mapper tries to match your request. You can force the system to always use a TrueType font by choosing OUT_TT_ONLY_PRECIS.
lfClipPrecision	Dictates how Windows clips a font that runs off the edge of the window or that's partially covered by another window. CLIP_STROKE_PRECIS usually works fine.
lfQuality	Dictates how closely the font matches your request for height, width, underline, and so forth. If you choose DEFAULT_QUALITY, Windows tries to synthesize a font to meet your request. If you

choose PROOF_QUALITY, Windows might ignore your request in favor of a more aesthetically pleasing, precise, and well-formed font. DRAFT_QUALITY is somewhere in between the other two.

lfPitchAndFamily   Helps guide Windows toward a choice if the exact typeface requested isn't available. For instance, if you want New Times Roman, but the font isn't available on the system, choosing FF_ROMAN helps Windows find a good substitute. You can OR the family value with VARIABLE_PITCH, DEFAULT_PITCH, or FIXED_PITCH, depending on your needs.

lfFaceName   The name of the font you want to use.

As you can see, the people who put Windows together take the subject of fonts extremely seriously—as indeed they should. Typesetting is a long, time-honored tradition, and now this art form is being moved from the printed page to the computer screen.

DO	DON'T

DO take the time to experiment with some of the values used in the LOGFONT structure from the GetFont function. For instance, if you increase the value of the lfWeight field, you get a thicker, heavier font. If you increase the lfHeight field, the font gets bigger. If you set the lfItalic field to zero, the font is no longer italicized.

DON'T, however, squander time figuring out ways to create all the fonts available on your system. On Day 10 and Day 11, "Talking to Controls," I show you how to easily generate a wide range of fonts. After you have a means of automatically producing fonts, you can use the debugger or the code I provide to find out what values Windows has assigned to a particular LOGFONT structure. You can then copy those values to your own code and outfit your program with any fonts you might need.

Rotating a Font

In SimpFont, I've filled out the LOGFONT fields with sample values, choosing nice, hefty values for the height and weight and turning on the italic and underline features by setting them to nonzero values.

The field that SimpFont takes special control over is called lfEscapement. As mentioned in the previous list, this field dictates the angle at which the text appears on-screen. For instance, a value of zero prints the text in standard fashion from left to right, whereas 900, 1800, and 2700 move the text around the arcs of a circle in a counter-clockwise procession (as shown in Figure 9.2).

By the way, Microsoft really outdid themselves by finding such an esoteric name for this field. An escapement is part of a mechanical device, such as a watch or typewriter. The escapement enables a wheel or notched bar to move forward one step at a time, and only when instructed.

Figure 9.3 shows the escapement circle broken into ninths.

Figure 9.2.
This version of the SimpFont program illustrates the effect of passing specific numeric values in the lfEscapement *field.*

Figure 9.3.
It's possible to take the SimpFont example somewhat further by breaking the escapement circle into ninths.

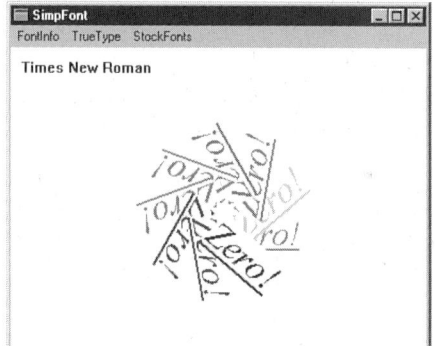

Creating a Font

After you fill out the fields of the LOGFONT structure, you're nearly ready to call CreateFontIndirect. Before making the call, however, be sure to check whether an old font needs to be deleted:

```
if (TheFont != 0) DeleteFont(TheFont);
```

Note: There's no way to overemphasize the importance of the call to `DeleteFont`. It's crucially important not to accidentally leave a resource, such as a font or a bitmap, in memory. Doing so will slowly but surely deplete the system resources and eventually bring Windows to its knees.

In the end, nearly any dedicated programmer can start creating fonts, bitmaps, and other resources. The hard part is cleaning up after yourself. I'm not simply being compulsive here. It's actually very difficult to be sure that all the system resources are cleaned up at the end of a program's run.

Remember that if you have the SDK, you can use the Debug version of Windows to help you track this sort of thing down. If you have the necessary tools, for heaven's sake get the Debug kernel up and running. It's a great educational tool.

While I'm on the subject, I'll point out the `WM_DESTROY` message handler function, which deletes the font before the program closes:

```
DeleteFont(TheFont);
```

Whatever you do, don't forget to delete your resources. I may sound a bit like a broken record when I'm emphasizing this point, but at least I'm stuck on an important, nay highly significant, groove.

Tip: By the way, `DeleteFont` is a WindowsX API macro that maps to `DeleteObject`. In this particular case, it wouldn't much matter whether you called `DeleteFont` or `DeleteObject`, but it is still good to get in the habit of using WindowsX whenever possible. In the long run it will help you create cleaner, more portable code.

After all the excitement leading up to it, the actual call to `CreateFontIndirect` comes as something of a letdown:

```
TheFont = CreateFontIndirect(&LogFont);
```

That's all there is to it. You just pass one parameter in and get the font back out on the other end.

So, creating fonts is simple, no? Okay, so it's not really so simple. In the next two chapters I show you ways to make this process a bit easier, or at least more manageable.

Stock Fonts

Now that you know how to make fonts with `CreateFont` and `CreateFontIndirect`, I'll take a moment to show you how to create a font with a call to `GetStockObject`, or its WindowsX type-specific macro, `GetStockFont`:

```
201:        case CM_ANSI_FIXED_FONT:
202:            if (TheFont != 0) DeleteFont(TheFont);
203:            TheFont = GetStockFont(ANSI_FIXED_FONT);
204:            Choice = StockFont;
205:            InvalidateRect(hwnd, NULL, TRUE);
206:            break;
207:
```

This code is an excerpt from the SimpFont_OnCommand function. It gets called when the user selects a menu item indicating his or her desire to see the ANSI_FIXED_FONT.

As you can see, SimpFont first checks to see if the TheFont variable already addresses a valid font. If it does, the font is deleted. The next step is the call to GetStockFont.

To obtain a stock font, pass in a constant that is defined in the WINDOWS.H complex, such as ANSI_FIXED_FONT or OEM_FIXED_FONT. All the available stock fonts are used in the SimpFont program. In fact, one of the program's goals is to give you a good look at the stock fonts on your system.

After SimpFont has a handle to a stock font, it sets a global enumerated variable called Choice to the value StockFont. These variables and types are specific to this program and are not part of Windows. As shown in the next section, the SimpFont_OnPaint function checks the Choice variable to see what information needs to be painted to the screen. The final step (in the previous code) is the call to InvalidateRect, which asks Windows to send a WM_PAINT message to the main window.

As you can see, creating stock fonts is very simple. It's so simple, in fact, that they seem a bit mysterious to programmers. At times, it's as if stock fonts come out of nowhere—as if they were created by magic. But, of course, this is not the case.

Stock fonts are predefined resources that are yours simply for the asking. In other words, you can create these same fonts by calling CreateFontIndirect with the appropriately filled out LOGFONT structure. The great virtue of stock fonts, however, is that they are easy to obtain because the LOGFONT structure has already been filled out for you. The drawback, of course, is that you don't have much control over what the system gives you.

Note: When running SimpFont, notice that each stock font has a particular face name that reveals the raw material from which Windows created the font. For instance, the ANSI_FIXED_FONT is a just a particular version of the standard Courier font. (See Figure 9.4.)

If this font is close to what you need, but not quite on target, use the SimpFont program to find out how to fill a LOGFONT with the appropriate values. Then create the font and begin to experiment with it. Change fields in the LOGFONT structure until you have exactly what you need.

You'll hear more on this subject in the upcoming section on the FONTSTR module. The FONTSTR module creates the long, skinny window shown in the middle of Figure 9.4.

Figure 9.4.

The SimpFont program can tell you what formula Windows used to create a stock font.

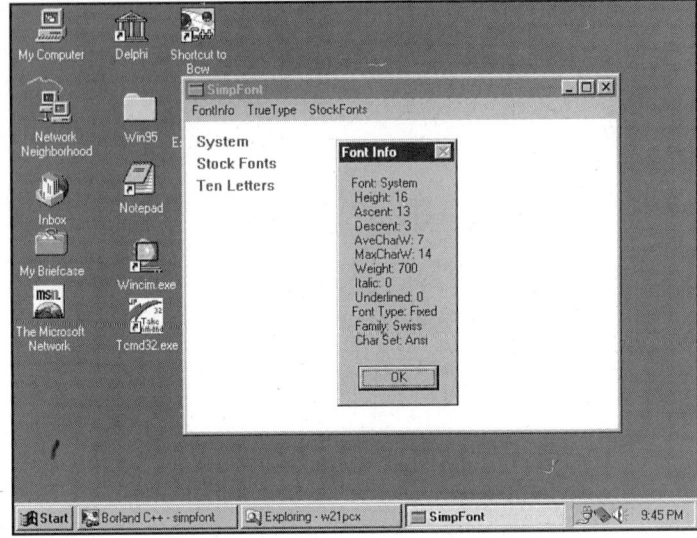

WM_PAINT Messages Call the Tune

When the user selects a new stock font or normal font from the SimpFont menu, the program calls InvalidateRect to coax Windows into sending a WM_PAINT message to the program. The response to these messages forms a crucial portion of the program's logic.

Step back a moment and think about what has happened. In the previous sections, you learned how to create a font. This section shows you how to paint a font on-screen. This is a three-step process:

1. Select the font into the device context and save a copy of the old font.

2. Call a procedure, such as TextOut or DrawText, that actually paints the font on-screen.

3. Preserve system resources by copying the old font back into the device context.

Now that you have an overview of what goes on, take a look at a specific example, as illustrated by the SimpFont program.

SimpFont_OnPaint features the traditional calls to BeginPaint and EndPaint. In between is code for painting both TrueType fonts and stock fonts. I treat each of these subjects separately, acting as if each were encapsulated in its own WM_PAINT message handler. The SimpFont program actually combines both sets of code into one function and examines the Choice variable to decide which part to call at any one moment.

Here is a stripped-down version of how SimpFont paints TrueType fonts:

```
void SimpFont_OnPaint(HWND hwnd)
{
```

```
PAINTSTRUCT PaintStruct;
HFONT OldFont;

HDC PaintDC = BeginPaint(hwnd, &PaintStruct);

for (int i = 0; i <= 3; i++)
{
  TheFont = GetFont(900 * i, FontChoice[Choice]);
  OldFont = SelectFont(PaintDC, TheFont);
  SetTextColor(PaintDC, RGB(rand() % 255,
            rand() % 255, rand() % 255));
  TextOut(PaintDC, 200, 200, "Ahoy!" , 5);
  SelectFont(PaintDC, OldFont);
}

TextOut(PaintDC, 10, 10, aFaceName, strlen(aFaceName));

EndPaint(hwnd, &PaintStruct);
}
```

SimpFont_OnPaint starts by creating the font with a call to GetFont. When making this call, SimpFont need only pass in a font name, along with the value associated with the lfEscapement field. This latter argument ensures that the font is printed at each of the points of the compass.

Note the vitally important calls to SelectFont, which is a WindowsX macro that calls SelectObject. At the beginning of the function, SelectFont copies the font to the device context. At the end, it copies it back out again. In this case, the device context happens to be the screen, but the process is similar when you're sending fonts to the printer.

The call to SetTextColor is straightforward enough for most purposes. I've complicated it here by throwing in the Rand function, which generates random numbers. If you strip that out, however, the call is reduced to something like the following compound statement:

```
SetTextColor(PaintDC, RGB(0, 0, 255));
```

The big difference, of course, is that in the SimpFont version, each of the fields of the RGB macro contain numbers generated by the Rand function. These randomly chosen numbers define the colors of the font.

> **Note:** As an experiment, try covering and uncovering the window numerous times in succession. Doing so forces a series of calls to the WM_PAINT message handler function. Each call produces a new random set of values to be passed to the SetTextColor API routine. If you only cover a small part of the window at a time, you can see exactly how the BeginPaint and EndPaint functions conspire to handle updating only the portions of the screen that have been hidden. This is the type of feature you might not want in a shipping product, but it's an ideal teaching tool. If you want to eliminate it, simply remove the calls to Rand.

The call to TextOut remains static through all four iterations of SimpFont_OnPaint's loop:

```
TextOut(PaintDC, 200, 200, "Ahoy!" , 5);
```

The font rotation and hue changes occur because of the variables passed to CreateFontIndirect and SetTextColor.

DO   **DON'T**

DO use CreateFontIndirect and SetTextColor to change the qualities of the font.

DON'T worry about how Windows actually paints the font.

DON'T try to optimize code by writing directly to video memory or by tweaking the algorithm used to draw shapes on-screen. These techniques belong to the DOS world. Instead…

DO things the Windows way. Windows programmers aren't dealing with hardware; they're dealing with abstract concepts, such as fonts or device contexts. To change the appearance of a font, change the objects associated with it. After you design the font, it will, in effect, display itself on-screen without your help (and in a manner beyond your control).

The SimpFont_OnPaint function also handles painting stock fonts to the screen. Here's an abbreviated version of the code:

```
OldFont = SelectFont(PaintDC, TheFont);
GetTextFace(PaintDC, sizeof(aFaceName), (LPSTR) aFaceName);
GetTextMetrics(PaintDC, &TextMets);
TextOut(PaintDC, 10, 10, aFaceName, strlen(aFaceName));
SelectFont(PaintDC, OldFont);
```

As you can see, stock fonts are painted to the screen in the same way as the other fonts. That's because they are really normal fonts, with their LOGFONT structure predefined by Windows.

Besides the calls to TextOut and the standard SelectFont two-step dance, the portions of the previous code that stand out most clearly are the calls to GetTextMetrics and GetTextFace. GetTextFace snags the name of the current font installed in a device context. The SimpFont program paints this font name to the screen, so you can see whether or not your system is actually capable of producing the font you requested.

The call to GetTextMetrics can't be explained so easily. In fact, I'll treat this call in its own section.

GetTextMetrics and the *FONTSTR* Module

When you create a font, you usually fill out a LOGFONT (or its equivalent fields) in a CreateFontIndirect call. You need to perform this operation in reverse when getting this information back from the system.

To reverse the process, call GetObject and pass the handle to a font in the first parameter, the size of a logfont structure in the second parameter, and a pointer to a logfont structure in the third parameter. This will enable you to retrieve a logfont structure when all you have to start with is the handle to the font.

Windows also provides detailed information about the current font through the GetTextMetrics call and the TEXTMETRIC structure that it retrieves. The TEXTMETRIC structure tells you how big the font is, whether it's underlined or italicized, what pitch and family it has, and so on.

Not to be outdone by the LOGFONT structure, the TEXTMETRIC structure includes no fewer than 20 fields! This proliferation of minutia enables you to learn more than you most likely ever wanted to know about the current font:

```
typedef struct tagTEXTMETRIC
{  /* tm */
  int   tmHeight;
  int   tmAscent;
  int   tmDescent;
  int   tmInternalLeading;
  int   tmExternalLeading;
  int   tmAveCharWidth;
  int   tmMaxCharWidth;
  int   tmWeight;
  BYTE  tmItalic;
  BYTE  tmUnderlined;
  BYTE  tmStruckOut;
  BYTE  tmFirstChar;
  BYTE  tmLastChar;
  BYTE  tmDefaultChar;
  BYTE  tmBreakChar;
  BYTE  tmPitchAndFamily;
  BYTE  tmCharSet;
  int   tmOverhang;
  int   tmDigitizedAspectX;
  int   tmDigitizedAspectY;
} TEXTMETRIC;
```

SimpFont wrestles with the TEXTMETRIC structure in an isolated module called FontStr. FontStr returns most of the TEXTMETRIC fields in a single string. This module is designed so it can be easily linked to another program, as you'll see on Day 10. (Always strive for reuse. Reuse is even better than optimization. Reuse is way cool.)

The core of FontStr is the GetFontString function. It contains the following straightforward, but lengthy, call to sprintf:

```
sprintf(S, "Font: %s \n Height: %d \n "
  "Ascent: %d \n Descent: %d \n "
  "AveCharW: %d \n MaxCharW: %d \n "
  "Weight: %d \n Italic: %hd \n "
  "Underlined: %d \n"
  "%s \n %s \n %s ",
  TheFaceName,
  TextMetrics.tmHeight,
  TextMetrics.tmAscent,
  TextMetrics.tmDescent,
  TextMetrics.tmAveCharWidth,
  TextMetrics.tmMaxCharWidth,
  TextMetrics.tmWeight,
  TextMetrics.tmItalic,
  TextMetrics.tmUnderlined,
  szType, szFamily, szCharSet);
```

As you can see from Figure 9.5, most of the information from the TEXTMETRIC structure is transferred into a single string. This string is returned to the WM_COMMAND handler function in the program's main module and displayed through a call to the MessageBox function:

```
// user selects FontInfo menu item.
case CM_INFO:
  GetFontString(S, TextMets, aFaceName);
  MessageBox(hwnd, S, "Font Info", MB_OK);
  break;
```

Figure 9.5.

The SimpFont program pops up a message box relating important information about the currently selected font.

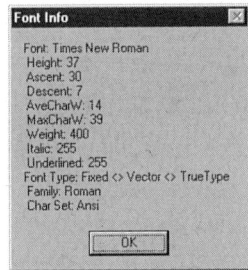

GetFontString is the only function in the FONTSTR module that is made global so it can be accessed from other modules.

The parts of the FONTSTR module described so far are fairly straightforward. The tricky sections involve deciphering the contents of the tmPitchAndFamily and the tmCharSet fields:

☐ The four low-order bits of `tmPitchAndFamily` describe the type of font, which can be one of the following values:

`TMPF_FIXED_PITCH`	A fixed-pitch font
`TMPF_VECTOR`	A vector font
`TMPF_TRUETYPE`	A TrueType font
`TMPF_DEVICE`	A device font

Many times, a font combines one or more of these values.

☐ The four high-order bits can be ANDed together with the hexadecimal value `0xF0` and then used to determine the current font family. Common font families include Roman, Swiss, Script, and Modern.

☐ The `tmCharSet` field is set to one of the following values:

`ANSI_CHARSET`	0
`DEFAULT_CHARSET`	1
`SYMBOL_CHARSET`	2
`SHIFTJIS_CHARSET`	128
`OEM_CHARSET`	255

Extracting this information from a `TEXTMETRIC` structure is the job of the following functions, all found in the `FONTSTR` module:

```
char * GetType(char * S);
char * GetFamily(char * S);
char * GetCharSet(char * S);
```

The `GetType` function uses `BitWise` operations to find the current font type. The `GetFamily` function uses the hex value `F0` to determine the font family, and the `GetCharSet` functions retrieves the current `CharSet`. If you want to understand these functions in-depth, you should crank up the debugger and start stepping through them one line at a time.

Note: Although SimpFont doesn't use it, I should probably also mention the `GetDeviceCaps` routine. It enables you to ask Windows what capabilities are associated with a particular device, such as a video screen or printer. You can use this function to discover whether the device can, for instance, print very large fonts, clip fonts, or stroked fonts.

You should keep both the `GetDeviceCaps` and `GetTextMetrics` functions in mind, because no serious work with fonts can be conducted without them. The subject of printing fonts will be addressed during Week 3.

Summary

Day 9 has been dedicated to a discussion of fonts. This is a big topic, so I have made no attempt to be exhaustive. Instead, I've tried to introduce the main ideas in a relatively simple and straightforward manner.

In particular, you have seen that the life of a typical font can have six parts:

1. Design it by filling out the LOGFONT structure.
2. Create it with CreateFontIndirect.
3. Copy it into a device context with a call to SelectFont or SelectObject.
4. Display the font by calling TextOut or DrawText.
5. Select the old font back into the device context with SelectFont or SelectObject.
6. Destroy the font by calling DeleteFont.

Here's an example:

```
if (theFont != 0) DeleteFont(TheFont);
memset(&LogFont, 0, sizeof(LOGFONT));
LogFont.ifHeight          = 45;
strcpy(LogFont.lfFaceName, "Arial");
TheFont = CreateFontIndirect(&LogFont);
OldFont = SelectFont(PaintDC, TheFont);
TextOut(PaintDC, 10, 10, 'hello', 50;
SelectFont(PaintDC, OldFont);
See the FontEasy example on the sample disk for further guidance.
```

If, at any time, you want to get information about the current font, you can do so by calling GetTextMetrics and by examining the TEXTMETRIC structure.

Although neither of the next two chapters focuses exclusively on fonts, they do include useful information about them. Day 10, for instance, focuses on retrieving all the currently available fonts from the system through a callback function. In Bonus Day 1, "GDI and Metafiles," you'll see how to use common dialogs to view and retrieve any font currently available on the system.

Q&A

Q What is a font family?

A Windows usually works with one of five different font families: Decorative, Modern, Roman, Script, or Swiss. Each family has its own traits. The Swiss family, for instance, has no serifs. (Serifs are the little strokes at the bottom of an F, an R, and a T, or the strokes that you see on the ends of an S and a Z.) The Roman family, on the other hand, has serifs. Typefaces in the Modern family have constant stroke widths.

It's as if they were made from a pipe that never varies in width. The Swiss and Roman families, on the other hand, have varying stroke widths. That's all I can say on this subject in this context, but if you want more information, many books about fonts are available—the best of which might not even mention the subject of computers.

Q I still don't understand TrueType fonts and stock fonts. Please explain.

A A stock font is simply a predefined font. Nothing at all is unusual about it except for the fact that Windows declared its dimensions ahead of time. TrueType fonts, on the other hand, are Microsoft's answer to PostScript fonts. As a rule, they have a higher quality and a greater degree of flexibility than the other fonts that come with Windows.

Workshop

The Workshop provides quiz questions to help you solidify your understanding of the material covered and exercises to provide you with experience in using what you've learned. Try to understand the quiz and exercise answers before continuing on to Day 10. Answers are provided in Appendix A.

Quiz

1. What functions can produce TrueType fonts?
2. What functions produce stock fonts?
3. What is a TrueType font?
4. What is a stock font?
5. How can you find out the name of the current font?
6. How can you find out the size of the current font?
7. What is the face name of the DEVICE_DEFAULT_FONT on your system?
8. What is the face name of the SYSTEM_FONT on your system?
9. How do you copy a font into a device context?
10. What is contained in the four low-order bits of the tmPitchAndFamily field?

Exercises

1. Round out the GetFontString function so that it reports on all of the fields from a TEXTMETRIC structure.
2. Try creating a Script font. Hint: On most systems, the key to this process is setting the LOGFONT lfCharSet field to OEM_CHARSET. See if this works on your system.

Window Controls

Window Controls

This chapter explores the FontsExp program, which displays all the fonts on the system. FontsExp uses a number of small subwindows called controls. These controls form an interface that enables the user to interact with the program.

Controls are another key aspect of Windows programming. To help bring this subject to light, I append three short programs to the end of this chapter and Day 11, "Talking to Controls." At the end of this chapter you will find short sample programs showing how to use:

- List boxes
- Combo boxes
- Edit controls

At the end of Day 11, I add three short sample programs showing how to use:

- Buttons
- Check boxes
- Radio buttons

The examination of FontsExp is divided into two sections. The first section, included in this chapter, studies the various window controls introduced in the FontsExp program. In particular, it includes an examination of

- Static controls, used primarily to display text that the user can't edit.
- List boxes, used to display lists of one line strings that can be scrolled by the user.
- Edit controls, which enable the user to edit a string.
- Check boxes, which are like the tiny boxes on a ballot or school quiz—if an × is in the box, the item is selected. Otherwise, it's either gray or blank.

The second section, included in Day 11, presents an explanation of how to communicate with controls and how to use a callback function to retrieve the fonts available on the system. In particular, that section shows

- How to use `SendMessage` and `PostMessage`
- How to communicate with list boxes and check boxes
- How to create user-defined messages
- How to call `EnumFontFamilies`

Controls form a key part of the Windows operating environment. In fact, controls are so important, I address the subject again in Day 12, "Window Controls and the Control Message API," and Day 13, "Subclassing Windows Controls."

Understanding Controls and Messages

Controls are interface elements (or interface tools) that help present information to the user in a clear and easily comprehensible manner.

It's possible to imagine a parallel between a window (or a series of windows) and the control panel for a stereo, tape recorder, or radio. When seen this way, visual tools, such as buttons, radio buttons, and check boxes, are like knobs or buttons on a stereo. Just as a button turns a stereo on and off and a knob adjusts its volume, controls manage the flow of events inside a computer.

Interface elements, such as controls, become very important when you are wrestling with large quantities of information. For instance, my friend at the graphics design shop had a large number of fonts on his machine. A simple written list of these fonts got to be as overwhelming as the list of fields in a big Windows structure. What people need is some sort of visual interface that can present these fonts to them in a readily comprehensible fashion. In your programs, you shouldn't just list the names of fonts, you should show users what the fonts look like. Let your users explore any particular font in detail. The FontsExp program shows one way to go about doing this.

10

Readers, writers, and users—all of us—need a way to grasp the vast amount of information that comes streaming at us in this confusing and fascinating information age. Windows controls are about presenting information to people. They're about interface design. Overall, they're one of the most important elements of the inspired vision that drives GUI environments such as Windows.

The Font Display

You can get started with controls by taking a look at an actual example showing how to manipulate the elements of a Windows interface. The window FontsExp creates is shown in Figure 10.1.

Figure 10.1.
The FontsExp program enables you to iterate through all the fonts on the system.

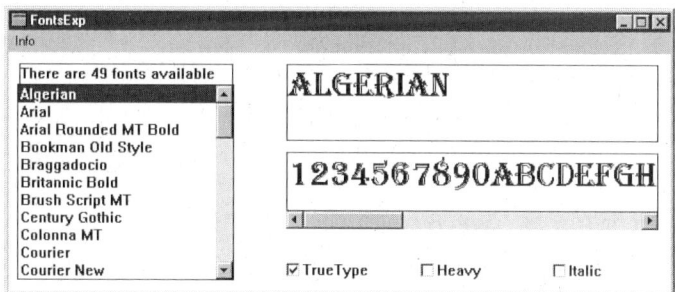

The visual front end of the FontsExp program bears a slight resemblance to the view you see when you pop up a Fonts common dialog. (Common dialogs are explored in Bonus Day 1, "GDI and Metafiles.") From a programmer's perspective, however, FontsExp is a very different type of program. It takes you inside the world of Windows fonts, letting you control how, where, and with what degree of detail fonts are presented to the user.

You can build on the knowledge presented in the next few pages to expand the FontsExp program into a world-class tool that many Windows users would love to have at their disposal. As always in the world of programming, there are plenty of opportunities. Let's start with a look at the code shown in Listing 10.1.

Listing 10.1. The FontsExp program demonstrates techniques for using fonts and controls.

```
////////////////////////////////////////
//   Program Name: FONTSEXP.CPP
//   Copyright (c) 1995 by Charlie Calvert
//   Description: FontsExp windows program
//   UpDate for WIN32: 05/22/95
////////////////////////////////////////

#define STRICT
#define WIN32_LEAN_AND_MEAN
#include <windows.h>
#include <windowsx.h>
#pragma hdrstop
#include <string.h>
#include "FontsExp.h"
#include "fontstr.h"
#pragma warning (disable: 4068)
#pragma warning (disable: 4100)


// ----------------------------------------------------------
// Interface
// ----------------------------------------------------------

static char szAppName[] = "FontsExp";
static HWND MainWindow;
static HINSTANCE hInstance;
static TEXTMETRIC TextMetrics;
char aTextFace[80];


// ----------------------------------------------------------
// Initialization
// ----------------------------------------------------------

////////////////////////////////////////
// Program entry point
////////////////////////////////////////
#pragma argsused
int PASCAL WinMain(HINSTANCE hInst, HINSTANCE hPrevInstance,
                   LPSTR  lpszCmdParam, int nCmdShow)
{
```

```
   MSG  Msg;

   if (!hPrevInstance)
     if (!Register(hInst))
       return FALSE;

   MainWindow = Create(hInst, nCmdShow);
   if (!MainWindow)
     return FALSE;

   while (GetMessage(&Msg, NULL, 0, 0))
   {
      TranslateMessage(&Msg);
      DispatchMessage(&Msg);
   }

   return Msg.wParam;
}

////////////////////////////////////
// Register the window
////////////////////////////////////
BOOL Register(HINSTANCE hInst)
{
  WNDCLASS WndClass;

  WndClass.style         = CS_HREDRAW | CS_VREDRAW;
  WndClass.lpfnWndProc   = WndProc;
  WndClass.cbClsExtra    = 0;
  WndClass.cbWndExtra    = 0;
  WndClass.hInstance     = hInst;
  WndClass.hIcon         = LoadIcon(NULL, IDI_APPLICATION);
  WndClass.hCursor       = LoadCursor(NULL, IDC_ARROW);
  WndClass.hbrBackground = (HBRUSH)(COLOR_WINDOW+1);
  WndClass.lpszMenuName  = "TheMenu";
  WndClass.lpszClassName = szAppName;

  return (RegisterClass (&WndClass) != 0);
}

////////////////////////////////////
// Create the window
////////////////////////////////////
HWND Create(HINSTANCE hInst, int nCmdShow)
{

  hInstance = hInst;

  HWND hwnd = CreateWindow(szAppName, szAppName,
                  WS_OVERLAPPEDWINDOW,
                  CW_USEDEFAULT, CW_USEDEFAULT,
                  CW_USEDEFAULT, CW_USEDEFAULT,
                    NULL, NULL, hInst, NULL);

  if (hwnd == NULL)
    return hwnd;
```

continues

Listing 10.1. continued

```
    ShowWindow(hwnd, nCmdShow);
    UpdateWindow(hwnd);

    return hwnd;
}

// ------------------------------------------------------
// WndProc and Implementation
// ------------------------------------------------------

//////////////////////////////////////
// The Window Procedure
//    The calls to MakeProcInstance and FreeProcInstance
//    are not necessay in WIN32.
//////////////////////////////////////
LRESULT CALLBACK EXPORT16 WndProc(HWND hwnd, UINT Message,
                        WPARAM wParam, LPARAM lParam)
{
  FONTENUMPROC lpfnEnumProc;
  ENUMSTRUCT EnumStruct;
  char S[100];

  switch(Message)
  {
    case WM_STARTFONTS:
    {
      HDC DC = GetDC(hwnd);
      lpfnEnumProc = (FONTENUMPROC)MakeProcInstance((FARPROC)FontCallBack,
                      hInstance);

      EnumStruct.Count = 0;
      EnumStruct.hWindow = hFontList;
      EnumFontFamilies(DC, NULL, lpfnEnumProc, (LONG)&EnumStruct);
      FreeProcInstance((FARPROC)lpfnEnumProc);

      ReleaseDC(hwnd, DC);

      wsprintf(S, "There are %d fonts available", EnumStruct.Count);
      SetWindowText(hNumFonts, S);

      SetFocus(hFontList);
      SendMessage(hFontList, LB_SETCURSEL, 0, 0);
      ShowTheFont(hwnd);
      return 1;
    }

    case WM_NEWFONT:
    {
      if (TheFont != 0)
        DeleteObject(TheFont);
      TheLogFont = (LPLOGFONT)lParam;
      TheFont = CreateFontIndirect(TheLogFont);
      return 1;
    }
```

```
      HANDLE_MSG(hwnd, WM_COMMAND, FontsExp_OnCommand);
      HANDLE_MSG(hwnd, WM_CREATE, FontsExp_OnCreate);
      HANDLE_MSG(hwnd, WM_DESTROY, FontsExp_OnDestroy);
      default:
        return FontsExp_DefProc(hwnd, Message, wParam, lParam);
   }
}

//////////////////////////////////////
// Handle WM_CREATE
//////////////////////////////////////
#pragma argsused
BOOL FontsExp_OnCreate(HWND hwnd, CREATESTRUCT FAR* lpCreateStruct)
{
  static char *Titles[] = { "TrueType" , "Heavy", "Italic" };

  hFontList = CreateWindow("listbox", NULL,
                       WS_CHILD | WS_VISIBLE | LBS_STANDARD,
                       9, 30, 201, 180, hwnd, HMENU(ID_LISTBOX),
                        hInstance, NULL);

  hNumFonts = CreateWindow("static", NULL,
                          WS_CHILD | WS_VISIBLE | WS_BORDER,
                          10, 10, 200, 20, hwnd, HMENU(-1),
                          hInstance, NULL);

  hFontName = CreateWindow("edit", NULL, WS_CHILD | ES_LEFT |
                     WS_VISIBLE | WS_BORDER | ES_READONLY,
                     260, 10, 350, 70, hwnd, HMENU(-1),
                     hInstance, NULL);

  hAlphaEdit = CreateWindow("edit", NULL, WS_CHILD |
                     WS_VISIBLE | WS_BORDER | WS_HSCROLL |
                     ES_LEFT | ES_AUTOHSCROLL | ES_MULTILINE,
                     260, 90, 350, 70, hwnd, HMENU(-1),
                     hInstance, NULL);

  for (int i = 0; i < 3; i++)
    ButtonWindows[i] = CreateWindow("button", Titles[i],
                          WS_CHILD | WS_VISIBLE | BS_CHECKBOX,
                          260  + (i * 125), 180, 100, 35, hwnd,
                          HMENU(-1), hInstance, NULL);

  TheFont = 0;

  PostMessage(hwnd, WM_STARTFONTS, 0, 0);

  return TRUE;
}

//////////////////////////////////////
// Handle WM_DESTROY
//////////////////////////////////////
#pragma argsused
void FontsExp_OnDestroy(HWND hwnd)
{
```

continues

Listing 10.1. continued

```
    if (TheFont != 0)
      DeleteObject(TheFont);
    PostQuitMessage(0);
}

/////////////////////////////////////
// Handle WM_COMMAND
/////////////////////////////////////
#pragma argsused
void FontsExp_OnCommand(HWND hwnd, int id, HWND hwndCtl, UINT codeNotify)
{
  char S[500];

  switch (id)
  {
    case ID_LISTBOX:
      if (codeNotify == LBN_SELCHANGE)
        ShowTheFont(hwnd);
      break;

    case CM_INFO:
      GetFontString(S, TextMetrics, aTextFace);
      MessageBox(hwnd, S, "Info", MB_OK);
      break;
  }
}

/////////////////////////////////////
// ShowTheFont
/////////////////////////////////////
void ShowTheFont(HWND hwnd)
{
  FONTENUMPROC lpfnEnumProc;
  char lpszBuffer[150];
  ENUMSTRUCT EnumStruct;
  HFONT SaveIt;

  char Alpha[] = {"1234567890abcdefghijklmnopqrstuvwxyz"
                  "ABCDEFGHIJKLMNOPQRSTUVWXYZ"};

  HDC DC = GetDC(hwnd);

  LRESULT Index = SendMessage(hFontList, LB_GETCURSEL, 0, 0);
  SendMessage(hFontList, LB_GETTEXT, WPARAM(Index), LPARAM(lpszBuffer));
  lpfnEnumProc = (FONTENUMPROC)MakeProcInstance(
                 (FARPROC)DescribeFontCallBack, hInstance);
  EnumStruct.Count = 0;
  EnumStruct.hWindow = hwnd;
  EnumFontFamilies(DC, lpszBuffer, lpfnEnumProc, (LONG)&EnumStruct);
  FreeProcInstance((FARPROC)lpfnEnumProc);

  if (TheFont != 0)
    SaveIt = SelectFont(DC, TheFont);
  GetTextMetrics(DC, &TextMetrics);
  HandleMetrics(TextMetrics);
  GetTextFace(DC, 150, aTextFace);
```

```
  if (TheFont != 0)
    SelectFont(DC, SaveIt);

  ReleaseDC(hwnd, DC);

  SendMessage(hFontName, WM_SETTEXT, 0, LPARAM(&lpszBuffer));
  SendMessage(hFontName, WM_SETFONT, WPARAM(TheFont), 0);

  SendMessage(hAlphaEdit, WM_SETTEXT, 0, LPARAM(&Alpha));
  SendMessage(hAlphaEdit, WM_SETFONT, WPARAM(TheFont), 0);
}

//////////////////////////////////////
// HandleMetrics
//////////////////////////////////////
void HandleMetrics(TEXTMETRIC TextMetrics)
{
  if ((TextMetrics.tmPitchAndFamily & TMPF_TRUETYPE) == TMPF_TRUETYPE)
    SendMessage(ButtonWindows[0], BM_SETCHECK, 1, 0L);
  else
    SendMessage(ButtonWindows[0], BM_SETCHECK, 0, 0L);

  if ((TextMetrics.tmWeight) > 600)
    SendMessage(ButtonWindows[1], BM_SETCHECK, 1, 0L);
  else
    SendMessage(ButtonWindows[1], BM_SETCHECK, 0, 0L);

  if (TextMetrics.tmItalic)
    SendMessage(ButtonWindows[2], BM_SETCHECK, 1, 0L);
  else
    SendMessage(ButtonWindows[2], BM_SETCHECK, 0, 0L);

}


//////////////////////////////////////
// FontCallback
//////////////////////////////////////
#pragma argsused
int CALLBACK EXPORT16 FontCallBack(LPENUMLOGFONT lpnlf,
                                   LPNEWTEXTMETRIC lpntm,
                                   int FontType,
                                   ENUMSTRUCT FAR * lpData)
{
  SendMessage(lpData->hWindow, LB_ADDSTRING, 0,
              LPARAM(lpnlf->elfLogFont.lfFaceName));
  lpData->Count++;
  return 1;
}

//////////////////////////////////////
// DescribeFontCallback
//////////////////////////////////////
#pragma argsused
```

continues

355

Listing 10.1. continued

```
int CALLBACK EXPORT16 DescribeFontCallBack(LPENUMLOGFONT lpnlf,
                                   LPNEWTEXTMETRIC lpntm,
                                   int FontType, ENUMSTRUCT FAR * lpData)
{
  SendMessage(lpData->hWindow, WM_NEWFONT, 0, LPARAM(&lpnlf->elfLogFont));
  return 1;
}
```

Listing 10.2 shows the header file for FontsExp.

Listing 10.2. FONTSEXP.H.

```
///////////////////////////////////////
//   Program Name: FONTSEXP.H
//   Programmer: Charlie Calvert
//   Description: FontsExp windows program
//   UpDate for WIN32: 05/22/95
///////////////////////////////////////

// constants
#define WM_STARTFONTS (WM_USER + 0)
#define WM_NEWFONT (WM_USER + 1)

#define ID_LISTBOX 1
#define CM_INFO 101

#if !defined(__WIN32__) && !defined(_WIN32)
#define EXPORT16 __export
#else
#define EXPORT16
#endif

// Types
typedef struct
{
  int Count;
  HWND hWindow;
}ENUMSTRUCT;

// Declarations for class FontsExp
#define FontsExp_DefProc    DefWindowProc
BOOL FontsExp_OnCreate(HWND hwnd, CREATESTRUCT FAR* lpCreateStruct);
void FontsExp_OnDestroy(HWND hwnd);
void FontsExp_OnCommand(HWND hwnd, int id, HWND hwndCtl, UINT codeNotify);

// Variables
HWND hFontList;
HWND hAlphaEdit;
HWND hTrueType;
HWND hNumFonts;
HWND hFontName;
static HFONT TheFont;
static LPLOGFONT TheLogFont;
HWND ButtonWindows[3];
```

```
// Procs
BOOL Register(HINSTANCE hInst);
HWND Create(HINSTANCE hInst, int nCmdShow);
void HandleMetrics(TEXTMETRIC TextMetrics);
void ShowTheFont(HWND hwnd);

LRESULT CALLBACK EXPORT16 WndProc(HWND hwnd, UINT Message,
                          WPARAM wParam, LPARAM lParam);
BOOL CALLBACK EXPORT16 FontCallBack(LPENUMLOGFONT lpnlf,
                          LPNEWTEXTMETRIC lpntm,
                          int FontType,
                          ENUMSTRUCT FAR * lpData);
int CALLBACK EXPORT16 DescribeFontCallBack(LPENUMLOGFONT lpnlf,
                          LPNEWTEXTMETRIC lpntm,
                          int FontType, ENUMSTRUCT FAR * lpData);
```

Listing 10.3 shows the source file for FontStr.

Listing 10.3. FONTSTR.CPP.

```
1: //////////////////////////////////////////////////
2: //   Program Name: FONTSTR.CPP
3: //   Programmer: Charlie Calvert
4: //   Description: Create description of a font
5: //   Date: 06/20/93
6: //////////////////////////////////////////////////
7:
8: #define STRICT
9: #include <windows.h>
10: #include <windowsx.h>
11: #include <string.h>
12: #include <stdio.h>
13:
14:
15: // variables
16: TEXTMETRIC TextMetrics;
17: static char TheFaceName[80];
18:
19: // procs
20: char * GetType(char * S);
21: char * GetFamily(char * S);
22: char * GetCharSet(char * S);
23:
24: char * GetFontString(char * S, TEXTMETRIC TextMetric,
                             char * FaceName)
25: {
26:    char szType[99], szFamily[99], szCharSet[99];
27:
28:    TextMetrics = TextMetric;
29:    strcpy(TheFaceName, FaceName);
30:
31:    GetType(szType);
32:    GetFamily(szFamily);
33:    GetCharSet(szCharSet);
```

continues

Listing 10.3. continued

```
34:
35:    sprintf(S, "Font: %s \n Height: %d \n "
36:                "Ascent: %d \n Descent: %d \n "
37:                "AveCharW: %d \n MaxCharW: %d \n "
38:                "Weight: %d \n Italic: %hd \n "
39:                "Underlined: %d \n"
40:                "%s \n %s \n %s ",
41:    TheFaceName,
42:    TextMetrics.tmHeight,
43:    TextMetrics.tmAscent,
44:    TextMetrics.tmDescent,
45:    TextMetrics.tmAveCharWidth,
46:    TextMetrics.tmMaxCharWidth,
47:    TextMetrics.tmWeight,
48:    TextMetrics.tmItalic,
49:    TextMetrics.tmUnderlined,
50:    szType, szFamily, szCharSet);
51:
52:    return S;
53: }
54:
55: char * GetType(char * S)
56: {
57:    strcpy(S, "Font Type: ");
58:
59:    if ((TextMetrics.tmPitchAndFamily & TMPF_FIXED_PITCH) ==
60:        TMPF_FIXED_PITCH)
61:    strcat(S, "Fixed <> ");
62:    if ((TextMetrics.tmPitchAndFamily & TMPF_VECTOR) == TMPF_VECTOR)
63:    strcat(S, "Vector <> ");
64:    if ((TextMetrics.tmPitchAndFamily & TMPF_TRUETYPE) ==
            TMPF_TRUETYPE)
65:    strcat(S, "TrueType <> ");
66:    if ((TextMetrics.tmPitchAndFamily & TMPF_DEVICE) == TMPF_DEVICE)
67:    strcat(S, "Device <> ");
68:
69:    if (strlen(S) > 11)
70:      S[strlen(S) - 3] = '\0';
71:
72:    return S;
73: }
74:
75: char * GetFamily(char * S)
76: {
77:    int R = TextMetrics.tmPitchAndFamily & 0XF0;
78:    strcpy(S, "Family: ");
79:    if (R == FF_DONTCARE)
80:      strcat(S, "Don't Care or don't know");
81:    if (R == FF_ROMAN)
82:      strcat(S, "Roman");
83:    if (R == FF_SWISS)
```

```
84:      strcat(S, "Swiss");
85:   if (R == FF_MODERN)
86:      strcat(S, "Modern");
87:   if (R == FF_SCRIPT)
88:      strcat(S, "Script");
89:   if (R == FF_DECORATIVE)
90:      strcat(S, "Decorative");
91:
92:   return S;
93: }
94:
95: char * GetCharSet(char * S)
96: {
97:   strcpy(S, "Char Set: ");
98:
99:   if (TextMetrics.tmCharSet == ANSI_CHARSET)
100:      strcat(S, "Ansi");
101:   if (TextMetrics.tmCharSet == DEFAULT_CHARSET)
102:      strcat(S, "Default");
103:   if (TextMetrics.tmCharSet == SYMBOL_CHARSET)
104:      strcat(S, "Symbol");
105:   if (TextMetrics.tmCharSet == OEM_CHARSET)
106:      strcat(S, "OEM");
107:
108:   return S;
109: }
```

Listing 10.4 shows the header file for FontStr.

Listing 10.4. FONTSTR.H.

```
1: ////////////////////////////////////////////////
2: //   Program Name: FontStr.h
3: //   Programmer: Charlie Calvert
4: //   Description: FontsExp windows program header
5: //   Date: 06/20/93
6: ////////////////////////////////////////////////
7: char * GetFontString(char * S, TEXTMETRIC TextMetric,
8:                      char * FaceName);
```

Listing 10.5 shows the resource file for FontsExp.

Listing 10.5. FONTSEXP.RC.

```
1: #include "fontsexp.h"
2: menu MENU
3: BEGIN
4:   MENUITEM "Info", CM_INFO
5: END
```

Listing 10.6 shows the definition file for FontsExp.

Listing 10.6. FONTSEXP.DEF.

```
1: ; FONTSEXP.DEF
2:
3: NAME            FontsExp
4: DESCRIPTION     'FontsExp Window'
5 CODE            PRELOAD MOVEABLE DISCARDABLE
6 DATA            PRELOAD MOVEABLE MULTIPLE
7
8:HEAPSIZE        10240
9:STACKSIZE       10240
```

Listing 10.7 shows the Borland makefile for FontsExp.

Listing 10.7. FONTSEXP.MAK (Borland).

```
# FontsExp.mak

!if !$d(BCROOT)
BCROOT  = $(MAKEDIR)
!endif

# macros
APPNAME = FontsExp
INCPATH = $(BCROOT)\INCLUDE
LIBPATH = $(BCROOT)\LIB

!if $d(WIN16)
COMPILER= BCC.EXE
RCCOMPIER=BRC.EXE
FLAGS   = -W -ml -v -w4 -I$(INCPATH) -L$(LIBPATH)
!else
COMPILER= BCC32.EXE
RCCOMPILER=BRC32.EXE
FLAGS   = -W -v -w4 -I$(INCPATH) -L$(LIBPATH)
!endif

# link
$(APPNAME).exe: $(APPNAME).obj $(APPNAME).def FontStr.obj $(APPNAME).res
  $(COMPILER) $(FLAGS) $(APPNAME).obj FontStr.obj
  $(RCCOMPILER) $(APPNAME).res

# compile
$(APPNAME).obj: $(APPNAME).cpp
  $(COMPILER) -c $(FLAGS) $(APPNAME).cpp

# compile
FontStr.obj: FontStr.cpp
  $(COMPILER) -c $(FLAGS) FontStr.cpp

# compile
$(APPNAME).res: $(APPNAME).rc
  $(RCCOMPILER) -R -I$(INCPATH) $(APPNAME).RC
```

Listing 10.8 shows the Microsoft makefile for FONTSEXP.

Listing 10.8. FONTSEXP.MAK (Microsoft).

```
# FONTEXMS.MAK

APPNAME=FONTSEXP
TARGETOS=WIN95
APPVER=4.0
OBJS=$(APPNAME).OBJ FONTSTR.OBJ

!include <win32.mak>

all: $(APPNAME).exe

# Update the resource if necessary

$(APPNAME).res: $(APPNAME).rc $(APPNAME).h
  $(rc) $(rcflags) $(rcvars) $(APPNAME).rc

# Update the object files if necessary

# compile
.cpp.obj:
  $(cc) $(cflags) $(cvars) $(cdebug) $<

# Update the executable file if necessary.

$(APPNAME).exe: $(OBJS) $(APPNAME).res
  $(link) $(linkdebug) $(guiflags) -out:$(APPNAME).exe \
  $(OBJS) $(APPNAME).res $(guilibs) comctl32.lib
```

The FontsExp program creates a window and populates it with static controls, edit controls, check boxes, and list boxes. It uses these controls to enable the user to display a series of fonts. As shown in Figure 10.2, the FontInfo menu choice lets the user view information about the current font.

Figure 10.2.

The FontExp program, displaying the system font in its list box and the Script font in an edit and static control.

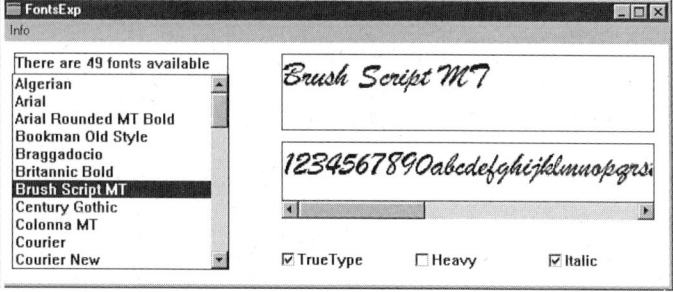

Now that you've seen the code, it's time to rev up your engines and pay special attention to the rest of this chapter. Most Windows programmers work with controls on a daily basis. Understand them thoroughly, and you'll be well on your way to creating powerful, robust programs that users love.

Static Controls

Users never interact with static controls—they're meant only to display text. Static controls are the easiest controls to utilize. Here are the minimum steps involved:

- ☐ Call `CreateWindow`.
- ☐ Fill in the first field of `CreateWindow`, called `lpszClassname`, with the word *static*.
- ☐ Fill in the third field, called `dwStyle`, with the `WS_CHILD` and `WS_VISIBLE` styles and any others you might need to add, such as `SS_LEFT` or `SS_SIMPLE`.
- ☐ Specify the control's dimensions.
- ☐ Fill in the program's `hwndParent` field with the `HWND` from the main window.
- ☐ Give the control a unique ID by filling in the `hMenu` field with a predefined constant. (Or, on occasion, you might calculate the number in a loop or some other code fragment. The point is that you should be able to predict what the ID will be so that you can reference it from other parts of your code.)
- ☐ Either specify the caption at creation or use `SetWindowText` to fill the control with a string.

As you'll see, there are a few other factors to keep in mind, but these steps form the core ideas used when creating static controls. In fact, you can use these steps as a template for creating all window controls. In other words, all controls are brought kicking and screaming into the world by calls to `CreateWindow`. Figure 10.3 shows the FontsExp program.

Figure 10.3.
A static control displays the number of fonts and a read-only edit control, which displays the font name.

Following is the call that creates the static control in the FontsExp program:

```
172:
173:    hFontName = CreateWindow("static", NULL,
174:                    WS_CHILD ¦ WS_VISIBLE ¦ WS_BORDER,
175:                    260, 10, 350, 70, hwnd, HMENU(-1), hInstance, NULL);
```

As you can see, this code looks like the routines used to create a main window, except that there's no need to first register a class. The reason for this omission is simply that the static class has been preregistered for you. That's what controls are all about. They are preregistered classes.

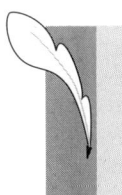

Note: The fact that a static control is just a preregistered window is such an important point that I want to take a moment to emphasize it.

In this book, you have learned how to create a number of different windows that behave in a particular way. You did this by filling out their WNDCLASS structure with values of your own choosing, and then writing message response functions called from a window procedure. In the process, you created several classes of potentially reusable windows that behave in various, predefined ways.

This is exactly what has already been done for you with the static, listbox, combobox, button, and scrollbar classes. Microsoft has already registered these classes and defined how they will respond to certain messages. The GameWindow class from the Snake1 program, for instance, has a certain defined behavior stemming from the structure of its WNDCLASS and WndProc. The same is true of the static class. Later in the book you will be introduced to a whole series of Windows 95–and Windows NT–specific classes such as toolbars, rich edits, progress bars, property sheets, and up/down controls.

You have been calling CreateWindow regularly since Day 2, "Building Projects, Creating Windows." When creating child window controls, however, you need to take special note of a few key points. The next few paragraphs outline those points for you while showing you how to create a static control.

The dwStyle field (line 169) of CreateWindow ORs together WS_CHILD, WS_VISIBLE, and WS_BORDER. The first and last styles simply tell Windows that this is a child window with a border. The WS_VISIBLE style is a nifty little flag that requests Windows to call the ShowWindow function. In past chapters, most calls to CreateWindow have been followed by calls to ShowWindow and UpdateWindow:

```
ShowWindow(hwnd, nCmdShow);
UpdateWindow(hwnd);
```

If you use the WS_VISIBLE style, this isn't necessary, because Windows does the dirty work for you.

The next set of fields you need be concerned with are those that define the size of the border surrounding the static control. When CreateWindow is being called for a main window, these fields are usually filled with CW_USEDEFAULT constants. With list boxes, however, you should explicitly fill in these fields with the actual dimensions you want associated with your list box.

The next step is to fill out the hwndParent parameter to CreateWindow. Controls are child windows, and children need parents. In this case, of course, the parent is the main window.

Another field you need to be aware of is the ninth, called hMenu (line 165). This is where you normally designate the menu to be associated with a window. Because objects such as static controls and child windows don't have menus, this field can be available as a place to specify an ID number to be associated with a window.

The ID number you pick can prove important later when you set up a line of communication between a control and its parent window. As a result, if you decide to specify a value in this field, you should pick a unique ID number for each control. This is especially true for controls that are embedded in dialogs. In those cases, the ID number is the only link between a dialog and a control.

Because programmers develop a lot of these ID constants in their programs, they've fallen into the habit of using #defines to act as mnemonics:

```
#define MYLISTBOX 101
#define MYBUTTON 102
#define MYWHATHAVEYOU 103
```

Notice that you need to typecast the ID number to an HMENU value before the program will compile.

Note: The FontsExp program usually communicates with a control through its HWND, which is carefully saved after every call to CreateWindow. This technique is easy to use when working with controls embedded in windows. Inside of dialogs, however, it's simpler to use an ID.

To make static controls useful objects, all you need to do is place a bit of text in them with the SetWindowText call:

```
SetWindowText(hNumFonts, S);
```

`hNumFonts` is the handle to a static or edit control, and `s` is the string that appears in the control's window.

Static controls are the simplest controls you're likely to use in a Windows program. Of course, nothing in Windows is ever devoid of syntactical verbosity. For instance, there are a number of changes you can run on static texts. You can change their borders and colors, or use them to seat icons or bitmaps.

Following are some of the valid styles that can be ORed into the `dwStyle` field of a static control:

```
SS_BLACKRECT  SS_BLACKFRAME
SS_GRAYRECT   SS_GRAYFRAME
SS_WHITERECT  SS_WHITEFRAME
SS_LEFTSS_RIGHT
SS_CENTERSS_ICON
```

Feel free to experiment with these styles. Take special note, however, of the simple examples I've included in the FontsExp program. They can remain as an image of what lies at the heart of every control: an ordinary window with something painted inside it.

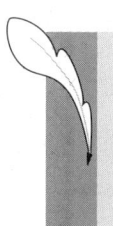

Note: In this sample program, a great deal goes on in the WM_CREATE message function handler. It's the place in which all the controls used in the program are created. This, of course, only makes sense. In fact, the idea of creating controls in response to a WM_CREATE message really defines what the message is all about. A WM_CREATE message is sent to a window specifically to say: "Hey, wake up there! It's time for you to create all your child windows and to do any other initialization you deem necessary!"

List Boxes

Of particular interest in the context of the current chapter is the code for creating list box controls:

```
163:    hFontList = CreateWindow("listbox", NULL,
164:                    WS_CHILD | WS_VISIBLE | LBS_STANDARD,
165:                    9, 30, 201, 180, hwnd, HMENU(ID_LISTBOX),
166:                    hInstance, NULL);
```

List boxes are rectangular windows that present the user with an array of items to select. A list box and a static control are shown in Figure 10.4.

Figure 10.4.

*A static control with a string
in it. Immediately beneath
it is a list box filled with
font names.*

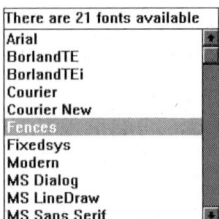

In the list box, the most important field is the third, in which you can define the style of the class:

```
WS_CHILD ¦ WS_VISIBLE ¦ LBS_STANDARD
```

By this time, I'm sure it won't come as a surprise to you that the LBS_STANDARD flag is part of another lengthy array of options. This is the Windows way of doing things. Good Windows programmers eventually develop a kind of love/hate relationship with these tables full of options and possibilities. After all, each list may be a bit confusing, but it also contains numerous tidbits that can be used to spice up your program.

Because Borland and Microsoft have already provided you with several copies of this list, I'll show you only the ones programmers are likely to use on a regular basis:

LBS_MULTIPLESEL	User can select more than one item at a time.
LBS_EXTENDEDSEL	Enables multiple items to be selected by using the Shift key and the mouse or special key combinations.
LBS_NOTIFY	When turned off, the parent window doesn't know whether the user has clicked or double-clicked a string.
LBS_STANDARD	The standard list box with a border and with LBS_NOTIFY turned on.
LBS_OWNERDRAW	The style you need if you want to display bitmaps or other nonstandard items in a list box.
LBS_USETABSTOPS	To simulate multiple columns in a single list box.
LBS_WANTKEYBOARDINPUT	Enables the programmer to pick up on keyboard input when the list box has the focus.

Of these items, the two most important are LBS_STANDARD and LBS_MULTIPLESEL. Multiple selection list boxes work like the windows in the File Manager: They let you select multiple items at one time. Of course, they don't have all the capabilities of the windows in the File Manager, but they do enable multiple selections.

In your day-to-day programming life, creating a list box will prove to be a trivial task that you can accomplish in just a few moments. Simply cut and paste the call from another program, or copy the CreateWindow call from your main window. There's really nothing to it.

The subject of communicating with a list box can become fairly involved. Therefore, I'll postpone any in-depth discussion of the topic until Day 11.

For now, a few simple examples should suffice. If you want to add a string to a list box, you can do so by sending it an LB_ADDSTRING message:

```
char * MyString[] = "Sambo";
SendMessage(hListBox, LB_ADDSTRING, 0, LPARAM(MyString));
```

Conversely, you can retrieve a string from a list box by first getting the index of the currently selected item with an LB_GETCURSEL message:

```
int Index = SendMessage(hFontList, LB_GETCURSEL, 0, 0);
```

Use the index to retrieve the string by using an LB_GETTEXT message:

```
SendMessage(hFontList, LB_GETTEXT, Index, LONG(lpszBuffer));
```

This material is being presented here mostly as a reference tool. For now, don't spend too much time worrying about the actual process involved in communicating with list boxes. The topic is reintroduced and explained in-depth on Day 11. In fact, you will find that WindowsX provides a few shortcuts that makes this process much simpler than the code shown here.

Check Boxes

Following are the calls that create all three of the check boxes used in this program:

```
static char *Titles[] = {"TrueType" , "Heavy", "Italic"};

for (int i = 0; i < 3; i++)
ButtonWindows[i] = CreateWindow("button", Titles[i],
                        WS_CHILD | WS_VISIBLE | BS_CHECKBOX,
                        260  + (i * 125), 180, 100, 35,
                        hwnd, HMENU(-1), hInstance, NULL);
```

To create a check box, you should specify the "button" class name and use the BS_CHECKBOX style. The preceding example also shows how to use constant arrays and for loops to create a series of three controls. This is a technique you'll probably use on many occasions.

Note: *Check boxes* are little square bordered windows with a name attached to them, as shown in Figure 10.5. If the bordered window has an × in it, that item is selected; otherwise, it's not selected. In most cases, users click a check box with a mouse to select or deselect an option. FontsExp, however, sends messages to select or deselect a check box, and the user never interacts with the box directly.

Window Controls

Figure 10.5 shows check boxes in the list box of the FontsExp program. If you use the arrow keys to move the highlight bar up and down the list, the check boxes blink on and off like Christmas lights.

Figure 10.5.

A selected check box has an × in it, whereas unselected check boxes are blank.

☒ TrueType ☐ Heavy ☒ Italic

I'm sure you've already guessed that the BS_CHECKBOX style is only one of many different possible styles that can be associated with a button control. This versatile class is one that Windows programmers rely on time and time again. Take a careful look at the following button styles:

BS_CHECKBOX	Creates a check box.
BS_DEFPUSHBUTTON	Has a heavy black border and is chosen by default when the user presses the Enter key in a dialog.
BS_GROUPBOX	Brings a group of controls together into a group.
BS_3STATE	Can be grayed as well as checked and unchecked.
BS_AUTO3STATE	Responds automatically to being selected.
BS_AUTOCHECKBOX	Responds when the user selects it.
BS_AUTORADIOBUTTON	Responds when the user selects it.
BS_LEFTTEXT	Text on the left (not the right) side of a check box or radio button.
BS_OWNERDRAW	Lets the programmer define the appearance of a button.
BS_PUSHBUTTON	Standard button.
BS_RADIOBUTTON	A small round button that can appear to be either selected or not selected. When placed in a group, the user usually only can select one of these at a time.

This list shows that buttons are very versatile tools. At first, you might not even make the connections between standard OK buttons, check boxes, and radio buttons. However, all these tools belong to the same class, and you should learn to think of them as being closely related.

Communicating with check boxes can be a fairly delicate matter. For now, I'll only state that you can use the BM_SETCHECK messages to perform the most important aspects of the job. The key point to remember is that passing 1 in the WM_PARAM field sets the check, whereas passing 0 clears the check mark:

```
SendMessage(ButtonWindows[0], BM_SETCHECK, 1, 0L);
```

If you want to query a check box as to the state of its button, use BM_GETCHECK:

```
SendMessage(ButtonWindows[0], BM_GETCHECK, 0, 0L);
```

Buttons with the BS_3STATE or BS_AUTO3STATE have a third grayed state selected by sending the value 2 to them.

Because I don't want to overwhelm you with too much material in one day, I'll delay any in-depth discussion of this topic until Day 11. There you'll see how FontsExp uses messages to control and query check boxes. I will show you later how to use WindowsX to expedite these chores.

Edit Controls

The FontsExp program also makes use of two edit controls, one of which is shown in Figure 10.6 and the other in Figure 10.3. Edit controls are used for getting input from a user through the keyboard, as in a text editor. In fact, edit controls can be used to create small text editors that can handle a few pages of text at a time.

You can also create read-only edit controls by giving them the ES_READONLY style. The ES_READONLY style makes an edit control behave as if it were a souped-up static control. Compared to static controls, you have better control over fonts and highlighting in an edit control even if it has the ES_READONLY style.

The following code creates a read-only edit control:

```
168:    hNumFonts = CreateWindow("edit", NULL, ES_LEFT | ES_READONLY |
169:                      WS_CHILD | WS_VISIBLE | WS_BORDER,
170:                      10, 10, 200, 20, hwnd, HMENU(-1),
171:                      hInstance, NULL);
```

Figure 10.6.

An edit control, with its scrollbar, displays the ever-useful WingDings font.

In this particular program, you might never type in either edit control; you might prefer to simply scroll the text back and forth. However, it's easy to see how a user might want to look at a particular combination of letters, so I've designed the program to respond to that contingency. Notice, however, that this is the only part of the program that requires any typing skills. Windows is a long way from the DOS prompt! The call to initialize the second edit control uses six different styles ORed together to form the third parameter:

```
177:    hAlphaEdit = CreateWindow("edit", NULL,
178:                 WS_CHILD | WS_VISIBLE | WS_BORDER | WS_HSCROLL |
179:                 ES_LEFT | ES_AUTOHSCROLL | ES_MULTILINE,
180:                 260, 90, 350, 70, hwnd, HMENU(-1),
181:                 hInstance, NULL);
```

| **DO** | **DON'T** |

DO add the WS_BORDER style if you want the control to be outlined in black. Scrollbars are handled automatically by list boxes. You can add this feature to your edit controls simply by using the WS_HSCROLL style.

DON'T confuse this style with either the ES_AUTOHSCROLL or ES_AUTOVSCROLL styles. These two styles let the user scroll text into view if it is hidden behind the right or bottom edge of a control.

I'm sure the astute reader has already prepared himself or herself for another long list of identifiers. So, without further delay, here are the edit control styles:

ES_AUTOHSCROLL	Automatically scrolls horizontally.
ES_AUTOVSCROLL	Automatically scrolls vertically.
ES_CENTER	Centers the text.
ES_LEFT	Aligns text on the left margin.
ES_LOWERCASE	Converts text to lowercase.
ES_MULTILINE	Uses multiple lines.
ES_NOHIDESEL	Forces Windows to keep the text highlighted, even if you set the focus to another control. (If you highlight a text fragment, Windows will normally not preserve the selection after the control loses focus.)
ES_OEMCONVERT	Helps preserve characters outside the range of normal letters and numbers.
ES_PASSWORD	Helps prevent other users from seeing what is being typed into an edit control.
ES_READONLY	Uses the edit control only for viewing text.
ES_RIGHT	Aligns text on the right margin.
ES_UPPERCASE	Sets all input to uppercase.
ES_WANTRETURN	Treats carriage returns normally, rather than sending them on to the default button.

This list is invaluable. Countless Windows programmers have spent hours trapping WM_KEYDOWN messages to handle carriage returns or to create edit controls appropriate for handling passwords. Don't become one of these poor, overworked programmers. Instead, take a careful look at these styles so you don't have to reinvent the proverbial wheel.

Communicating with edit controls is a fairly simple process. To insert text into an edit control, call SetWindowText, just as you do with a static control:

```
SetWindowText(hAlphaEdit, S);
```

To retrieve text from an edit control, call GetWindowText:

```
GetWindowText(hAlphaEdit, S, sizeof(S));
```

With GetWindowText, the first parameter is the HWND of the edit control; the second is a buffer to hold the string displayed in the control; the third is the maximum number of bytes the string can hold.

In Day 11 you'll see that the SendMessage function provides an alternative to this technique. For instance, the following call passes the string Alpha to an edit control:

```
SendMessage(hAlphaEdit, WM_SETTEXT, 0, LPARAM(&Alpha));
```

Don't worry if this last call still looks a bit obscure to you. It is explored in-depth on Day 11.

Besides WM_SETTEXT, edit controls also respond to a series of messages that enable you to directly manipulate their text. Most of these messages involve relatively advanced Windows programming issues, but you should at least be aware of their existence. Here is a small sample:

EM_CANUNDO	Checks whether an operation can be undone.
EM_GETMODIFY	Checks whether contents have changed.
EM_GETRECT	Gets a control's coordinates.
EM_GETSEL	Gets the position of the current selection.
EM_LIMITTEXT	Limits text in an edit control.
EM_REPLACESEL	Replaces current selection.
EM_SETPASSWORDCHAR	Sets password character.
EM_SETREADONLY	Sets the read-only state.
EM_SETSEL	Selects text.
EM_UNDO	Undoes the preceding operation.

Quick Examples

The code in the last sections of this chapter and the last sections of Day 11 show stripped-down, simple examples of how to use some of the major controls. Each program shows the minimum amount of code you need to write to get each of these types up and running in a standard window. A demonstration of how to write code that allows users to tab from one control to another is provided in the radio button example at the end of Day 11.

The code presented here might also be useful to programmers who want a quick and dirty reference or who want to find a convenient place from which to cut and paste code that runs each of the major controls. Note also that unlike the code shown previously, these examples make heavy use of WindowsX control macros.

Notes on Running the Control Samples

I do not provide examples of how to write the makefiles or module definition files for any of these examples, although I do provide these modules on the sample disk you can purchase (see the ad at the end of the book). The reason I omit this code is that I feel it will distract and confuse the reader. I want to keep these examples as simple as possible. Note that I store all the quick example programs in a separate subdirectory called CONTROLS.

If you want to add your own makefiles or DEF files for these examples, simply take the relevant modules from the WINDOW1 program in Day 3, "A Standard Windows Program," and change each instance of the term *WINDOW1* to the name of the example you want to run.

Combo Boxes

Combo boxes work almost exactly the same way that list boxes work. Specifically, you create a combo box by assigning a window the combobox class, and then passing in one of the combo box styles, such as CBS_SIMPLE or CBS_DROPDOWN:

```
CreateWindow("combobox", NULL,
            WS_CHILD ¦ WS_VISIBLE ¦ CBS_DROPDOWN,
            12, 50, 201, 180, hwnd, HMENU(ID_COMBOBOX),
            hInstance, NULL);
```

To fill up a list box with strings, use the WindowsX ComboBox_AddString macro, passing the HWND of the combo box in the first parameter and a string in the second. You can use the handy GetDlgItem API function to retrieve the HWND of the control:

```
for (int i = 0; i < 7; i++)
    ComboBox_AddString(GetDlgItem(hwnd, ID_COMBOBOX), List[i]);
```

When the user selects a new item in the combo box, you can determine that the change occurred by keeping watch on WM_COMMAND messages. Specifically, a WM_COMMAND message will appear with the ID of the combo box in WPARAM and CBN_SELCHANGE flag set in LPARAM. WindowsX, of course, passes this information to you in the ID parameter and in the codeNotify parameter:

```
void Combo1_OnCommand(HWND hwnd, int id,
                      HWND hwndCtl, UINT codeNotify)
{
  switch (ID)
  {
    ...
```

```
  case ID_COMBOBOX:
    if (codeNotify == CBN_SELCHANGE)
  ...
  }
}
```

Once you know the change has occurred, you can find the index of the item that the user highlighted by using the WindowsX `ComboBox_GetCurSel` macro. The next step is to pass this index back to Windows via the `ComboBox_GetLBText` macro. In return for your efforts, Windows will cough up the contents of the newly highlighted string. The code provided here displays this string via the good graces of the `MessageBox` function:

```
  case ID_COMBOBOX:
    if (codeNotify == LBN_SELCHANGE)
    {
      HWND ListWnd = GetDlgItem(hwnd, ID_LISTBOX);
      int index = ComboBox_GetCurSel(ListWnd);
      ComboBox_GetLBText(ListWnd, index, S);
      MessageBox(hwnd, S, "You selected",
                 MB_OK | MB_ICONINFORMATION);
    }
```

The following code demonstrates how to create and utilize a combo box.

Remember that you can create a module definition file and a makefile for this program simply by borrowing the relevant code from the WINDOW1 example in Day 3 and changing any instance of the term *Window1* to *Combo1*. The code for the program is shown in Listing 10.9.

Listing 10.9. A simple combo box example.

```
////////////////////////////////////////////////////////
// Program Name: Combo1.cpp
// Copyright (c) 1993 by Charles Calvert
// Description: Dropdown ComboBox windows Example
// Date: 12/19/93
// UpDate for WIN32: 05/22/95
////////////////////////////////////////////////////////

#define STRICT
#define WIN32_LEAN_AND_MEAN
#include <windows.h>
#include <windowsx.h>
#pragma warning (disable: 4068)
// -------------------------------------------------------
// Interface
// -------------------------------------------------------

#if !defined(__WIN32__) && !defined(_WIN32)
#define EXPORT16 __export
#else
#define EXPORT16
#endif
```

continues

Listing 10.9. continued

```
LRESULT CALLBACK EXPORT16 WndProc(HWND hwnd, UINT Message, WPARAM wParam, LPARAM
lParam);
BOOL Register(HINSTANCE hInst);
HWND Create(HINSTANCE hInst, int nCmdShow);

// Controls IDs
#define ID_COMBOBOX 101
#define ID_FILLBTN 102

// Declarations for class Combo1
#define Combo1_DefProc     DefWindowProc
BOOL Combo1_OnCreate(HWND hwnd, CREATESTRUCT FAR* lpCreateStruct);
void Combo1_OnDestroy(HWND hwnd);
void Combo1_OnCommand(HWND hwnd, int id, HWND hwndCtl, UINT codeNotify);
static char szAppName[] = "Combo1";
static HWND MainWindow;
static HINSTANCE hInstance;


// -------------------------------------------------------
// Initialization
// -------------------------------------------------------

////////////////////////////////////////
// Program entry point
////////////////////////////////////////
#pragma argsused
int WINAPI WinMain(HINSTANCE hInst, HINSTANCE hPrevInstance, LPSTR lpszCmdParam,
int nCmdShow)
{
  MSG  Msg;

  if (!hPrevInstance)
    if (!Register(hInst))
      return FALSE;

  MainWindow = Create(hInst, nCmdShow);
  if (!MainWindow)
    return FALSE;

  while (GetMessage(&Msg, NULL, 0, 0))
  {
    TranslateMessage(&Msg);
    DispatchMessage(&Msg);
  }

  return Msg.wParam;
}


////////////////////////////////////////
// Register the window
////////////////////////////////////////
BOOL Register(HINSTANCE hInst)
{
  WNDCLASS WndClass;
```

```
    WndClass.style          = CS_HREDRAW ¦ CS_VREDRAW;
    WndClass.lpfnWndProc    = WndProc;
    WndClass.cbClsExtra     = 0;
    WndClass.cbWndExtra     = 0;
    WndClass.hInstance      = hInst;
    WndClass.hIcon          = LoadIcon(NULL, IDI_APPLICATION);
    WndClass.hCursor        = LoadCursor(NULL, IDC_ARROW);
    WndClass.hbrBackground  = (HBRUSH)(COLOR_WINDOW+1);
    WndClass.lpszMenuName   = NULL;
    WndClass.lpszClassName  = szAppName;

    return (RegisterClass (&WndClass) != 0);
}


////////////////////////////////////
// Create the window
////////////////////////////////////
HWND Create(HINSTANCE hInst, int nCmdShow)
{

  hInstance = hInst;

  HWND hwnd = CreateWindow(szAppName, szAppName,
                    WS_OVERLAPPEDWINDOW,
                    CW_USEDEFAULT, CW_USEDEFAULT,
                    CW_USEDEFAULT, CW_USEDEFAULT,
                    NULL, NULL, hInst, NULL);

  if (hwnd == NULL)
    return hwnd;

  ShowWindow(hwnd, nCmdShow);
  UpdateWindow(hwnd);

  return hwnd;
}

// ---------------------------------------------------------
// WndProc and Implementation
// ---------------------------------------------------------

////////////////////////////////////
// The Window Procedure
////////////////////////////////////
LRESULT CALLBACK EXPORT16 WndProc(HWND hwnd, UINT Message, WPARAM wParam, LPARAM
lParam)
{
  switch(Message)
  {
    HANDLE_MSG(hwnd, WM_CREATE, Combo1_OnCreate);
    HANDLE_MSG(hwnd, WM_DESTROY, Combo1_OnDestroy);
    HANDLE_MSG(hwnd, WM_COMMAND, Combo1_OnCommand);
    default: return Combo1_DefProc(hwnd, Message, wParam, lParam);
  }
}
```

continues

Listing 10.9. continued

```c
/////////////////////////////////////
// Handle WM_CREATE
/////////////////////////////////////
#pragma argsused
BOOL Combo1_OnCreate(HWND hwnd, CREATESTRUCT FAR* lpCreateStruct)
{
  CreateWindow("button", "Fill ComboBox",
               WS_CHILD | WS_VISIBLE | BS_DEFPUSHBUTTON,
               10, 7, 203, 38, hwnd, HMENU(ID_FILLBTN),
               hInstance, NULL);

  CreateWindow("combobox", NULL,
               WS_CHILD | WS_VISIBLE | CBS_DROPDOWN,
               12, 50, 201, 180, hwnd, HMENU(ID_LISTBOX),
               hInstance, NULL);

  return TRUE;
}

/////////////////////////////////////
// Handle WM_DESTROY
/////////////////////////////////////
#pragma argsused
void Combo1_OnDestroy(HWND hwnd)
{
  PostQuitMessage(0);
}

/////////////////////////////////////
// Handle WM_COMMAND
/////////////////////////////////////
#pragma argsused
void Combo1_OnCommand(HWND hwnd, int id, HWND hwndCtl, UINT codeNotify)
{
  static char *List[7] = {"Sam", "Mike", "Anne", "Mary",
                          "David", "LouAnne", "Lisa"};

  char S[100];

  switch (id)
  {
    case ID_FILLBTN:
    {
      for (int i = 0; i < 7; i++)
        ComboBox_AddString(GetDlgItem(hwnd, ID_COMBOBOX), List[i]);
    }
    break;

    case ID_LISTBOX:
      if (codeNotify == CBN_SELCHANGE)
      {
        HWND ListWnd = GetDlgItem(hwnd, ID_LISTBOX);
        int index = ComboBox_GetCurSel(ListWnd);
        ComboBox_GetLBText(ListWnd, index, S);
```

```
            MessageBox(hwnd, S, "You selected", MB_OK ¦ MB_ICONINFORMATION);
        }
    break;
    }
}
```

Edits

Edit controls are instantiated by creating a window of the edit class and by passing in various other styles, such as ES_LEFT or ES_MULTILINE:

```
CreateWindow("edit", "Original Text",
            WS_CHILD ¦ WS_VISIBLE ¦ WS_BORDER ¦
            ES_LEFT ¦ ES_AUTOHSCROLL,
            10, 50, 410, 30, hwnd, HMENU(ID_EDIT),
            hInstance, NULL);
```

Communicating with edit controls is extremely simple. One commonly used method involves the Windows API calls SetWindowText and GetWindowText. The method shown here utilizes the WindowsX macros called Edit_SetText and Edit_GetText:

```
Edit_SetText(GetDlgItem(hwnd, ID_EDIT), "New Text");
Edit_GetText(GetDlgItem(hwnd, ID_EDIT), S, 100);
```

Needless to say, the Edit_SetText macro sets the text in a control, while the Edit_GetText macro retrieves the text. The second parameter passed to Edit_GetText is a string and the third parameter is the maximum length of the string. The example provided here borrows the functionality of the GetDlgItem API call when snagging the HWND of the edit control. It would, of course, be possible to simple save the HWND in a global variable at the time you create the control.

The code in Listing 10.10 demonstrates how to use an edit control in a window. Remember that you can create a module definition file and a makefile for this program simply by borrowing the relevant code from the WINDOW1 example in Day 3 and replaces all instances of the term *Window1* with *Edit1*.

Listing 10.10. A simple edit example.

```
/////////////////////////////////////////////////////////////
//   Program Name: Edit1.cpp
//   Copyright (c) 1993 by Charles Calvert
//   Description: Simple Edit Example
//   Date: 12/19/93
//   UpDate for WIN32: 05/22/95
/////////////////////////////////////////////////////////////

#define STRICT
#define WIN32_LEAN_AND_MEAN
#include <windows.h>
```

continues

Listing 10.10. continued

```c
#include <windowsx.h>
#pragma warning (disable: 4068)
// -------------------------------------------------------
// Interface
// -------------------------------------------------------

#if !defined(__WIN32__) && !defined(_WIN32)
#define EXPORT16 __export
#else
#define EXPORT16
#endif

LRESULT CALLBACK EXPORT16 WndProc(HWND hwnd, UINT Message, WPARAM wParam, LPARAM
lParam);
BOOL Register(HINSTANCE hInst);
HWND Create(HINSTANCE hInst, int nCmdShow);

// Controls IDs
#define ID_EDIT 101
#define ID_GETTEXT 102
#define ID_SETTEXT 103

// Declarations for class Edit1
#define Edit1_DefProc      DefWindowProc
BOOL Edit1_OnCreate(HWND hwnd, CREATESTRUCT FAR* lpCreateStruct);
void Edit1_OnDestroy(HWND hwnd);
void Edit1_OnCommand(HWND hwnd, int id, HWND hwndCtl, UINT codeNotify);
static char szAppName[] = "Edit1";
static HWND MainWindow;
static HINSTANCE hInstance;


// -------------------------------------------------------
// Initialization
// -------------------------------------------------------

/////////////////////////////////////
// Program entry point
/////////////////////////////////////
#pragma argsused
int WINAPI WinMain(HINSTANCE hInst, HINSTANCE hPrevInstance, LPSTR lpszCmdParam,
int nCmdShow)
{
  MSG  Msg;

  if (!hPrevInstance)
    if (!Register(hInst))
      return FALSE;

  MainWindow = Create(hInst, nCmdShow);
  if (!MainWindow)
    return FALSE;

  while (GetMessage(&Msg, NULL, 0, 0))
```

```
    {
      TranslateMessage(&Msg);
      DispatchMessage(&Msg);
    }

    return Msg.wParam;
}


/////////////////////////////////////
// Register the window
/////////////////////////////////////
BOOL Register(HINSTANCE hInst)
{
    WNDCLASS WndClass;

    WndClass.style          = CS_HREDRAW | CS_VREDRAW;
    WndClass.lpfnWndProc    = WndProc;
    WndClass.cbClsExtra     = 0;
    WndClass.cbWndExtra     = 0;
    WndClass.hInstance      = hInst;
    WndClass.hIcon          = LoadIcon(NULL, IDI_APPLICATION);
    WndClass.hCursor        = LoadCursor(NULL, IDC_ARROW);
    WndClass.hbrBackground  = GetStockBrush(WHITE_BRUSH);
    WndClass.lpszMenuName   = NULL;
    WndClass.lpszClassName  = szAppName;

    return (RegisterClass (&WndClass) != 0);
}


/////////////////////////////////////
// Create the window
/////////////////////////////////////
HWND Create(HINSTANCE hInst, int nCmdShow)
{

    hInstance = hInst;

    HWND hwnd = CreateWindow(szAppName, szAppName,
                    WS_OVERLAPPEDWINDOW,
                    CW_USEDEFAULT, CW_USEDEFAULT,
                    CW_USEDEFAULT, CW_USEDEFAULT,
                    NULL, NULL, hInst, NULL);

    if (hwnd == NULL)
        return hwnd;

    ShowWindow(hwnd, nCmdShow);
    UpdateWindow(hwnd);

    return hwnd;
}

// --------------------------------------------------------
// WndProc and Implementation
// --------------------------------------------------------
```

10

Listing 10.10. continued

```
/////////////////////////////////////
// The Window Procedure
/////////////////////////////////////
LRESULT CALLBACK EXPORT16 WndProc(HWND hwnd, UINT Message, WPARAM wParam, LPARAM
lParam)
{
  switch(Message)
  {
    HANDLE_MSG(hwnd, WM_CREATE, Edit1_OnCreate);
    HANDLE_MSG(hwnd, WM_DESTROY, Edit1_OnDestroy);
    HANDLE_MSG(hwnd, WM_COMMAND, Edit1_OnCommand);
    default: return Edit1_DefProc(hwnd, Message, wParam, lParam);
  }
}


/////////////////////////////////////
// Handle WM_CREATE
/////////////////////////////////////
#pragma argsused
BOOL Edit1_OnCreate(HWND hwnd, CREATESTRUCT FAR* lpCreateStruct)
{
  CreateWindow("button", "Get Text",
               WS_CHILD | WS_VISIBLE | BS_DEFPUSHBUTTON,
               10, 7, 200, 30, hwnd, HMENU(ID_GETTEXT),
               hInstance, NULL);

  CreateWindow("button", "Set Text",
               WS_CHILD | WS_VISIBLE | BS_DEFPUSHBUTTON,
               220, 7, 200, 30, hwnd, HMENU(ID_SETTEXT),
               hInstance, NULL);

  CreateWindow("edit", "Original Text",
               WS_CHILD | WS_VISIBLE | WS_BORDER |
               ES_LEFT | ES_AUTOHSCROLL,
               10, 50, 410, 30, hwnd, HMENU(ID_EDIT),
               hInstance, NULL);

  return TRUE;
}

/////////////////////////////////////
// Handle WM_DESTROY
/////////////////////////////////////
#pragma argsused
void Edit1_OnDestroy(HWND hwnd)
{
  PostQuitMessage(0);
}

/////////////////////////////////////
// Handle WM_COMMAND
/////////////////////////////////////
#pragma argsused
```

```
void Edit1_OnCommand(HWND hwnd, int id, HWND hwndCtl, UINT codeNotify)
{
  char S[100];

  switch (id)
  {
    case ID_SETTEXT:
      Edit_SetText(GetDlgItem(hwnd, ID_EDIT), "New Text");
      break;

    case ID_GETTEXT:
      Edit_GetText(GetDlgItem(hwnd, ID_EDIT), S, 100);
      MessageBox(hwnd, S, "You Entered", MB_OK | MB_ICONEXCLAMATION);
      break;
  }
}
```

10

List Boxes

You can instantiate a list box control by creating a window of class listbox. In most cases you will want to give it the LBS_STANDARD style, though there are a number of other styles such as LBS_SORT or LBS_MULTIPLESEL that you might find useful on occasion:

```
CreateWindow("listbox", NULL,
             WS_CHILD | WS_VISIBLE | LBS_STANDARD,
             12, 50, 201, 180, hwnd, HMENU(ID_LISTBOX),
             hInstance, NULL);
```

Communicating with a list box is very much like communicating with a combo box. For instance, you can use the WindowsX ListBox_AddString macro to place one or more strings inside a list box:

```
for (int i = 0; i < 7; i++)
  ListBox_AddString(GetDlgItem(hwnd, ID_LISTBOX), List[i]);
```

The example shown here simply iterates through an array of seven strings, placing each in turn into the list box. To obtain the HWND of the list box control the sample uses the GetDlgItem function. It passes the HWND returned from GetDlgItem directly to the ListBox_AddString macro.

To find out when the user has double-clicked on a selection in the list box you can use the following code, which pops up the new selection in the list box:

```
case ID_LISTBOX:
  if (codeNotify == LBN_DBLCLK)
  {
    HWND ListWnd = GetDlgItem(hwnd, ID_LISTBOX);
    int index = ListBox_GetCurSel(ListWnd);
    ListBox_GetText(ListWnd, index, S);
    MessageBox(hwnd, S, "You selected",
MB_OK | MB_ICONEXCLAMATION);
```

This code is part of a case statement that is called whenever a WM_COMMAND message is a sent to the program. If an event that involves the list box has occurred, the ID_LISTBOX portion of the case statement is executed. The first part of the code uses GetDlgItem to find the HWND of the list box. This information is passed to the WindowsX macro called ListBox_GetCurSel, which returns the index of the currently selected string. By passing this index and an empty string buffer to the ListBox_GetText WindowsX macro, you can retrieve the actual contents of the selected string. To sum up, you need to do three things to find the currently selected string in a list box:

- ☐ Procure the HWND of the list box control.
- ☐ Pass the HWND to ListBox_GetCurSel to retrieve the index of the currently selected item.
- ☐ Pass the index and an empty string buffer to ListBox_GetText in order to retrieve the selected string.

The following code demonstrates in a working example how to use a list box control in a window. Remember that you can create a module definition file and a makefile for this program simply by borrowing the relevant code from the WINDOW1 example in Day 3, and substituting the term *ListBox1* for each instance of the term *Window1*. (See Listing 10.11.)

Listing 10.11. A simple list box example.

```cpp
//////////////////////////////////////////////////////////////
//   Program Name: ListBox1.cpp
//   Programmer: Charlie Calvert
//   Description: ListBox1 windows program
//   Date: 12/19/93
//   UpDate for WIN32: 05/22/95
//////////////////////////////////////////////////////////////

#define STRICT
#define WIN32_LEAN_AND_MEAN
#include <windows.h>
#include <windowsx.h>
#pragma warning (disable: 4068)
// -------------------------------------------------------
// Interface
// -------------------------------------------------------

#if !defined(__WIN32__) && !defined(_WIN32)
#define EXPORT16 __export
#else
#define EXPORT16
#endif

LRESULT CALLBACK EXPORT16 WndProc(HWND hwnd, UINT Message,
                                  WPARAM wParam, LPARAM lParam);
BOOL Register(HINSTANCE hInst);
HWND Create(HINSTANCE hInst, int nCmdShow);
```

```
// Controls IDs
#define ID_LISTBOX 101
#define ID_FILLBTN 102


// Declarations for class ListBox1
#define ListBox1_DefProc    DefWindowProc
BOOL ListBox1_OnCreate(HWND hwnd, CREATESTRUCT FAR* lpCreateStruct);
void ListBox1_OnDestroy(HWND hwnd);
void ListBox1_OnCommand(HWND hwnd, int id, HWND hwndCtl, UINT codeNotify);
static char szAppName[] = "ListBox1";
static HWND MainWindow;
static HINSTANCE hInstance;


// -------------------------------------------------------
// Initialization
// -------------------------------------------------------

/////////////////////////////////////
// Program entry point
/////////////////////////////////////
#pragma argsused
int WINAPI WinMain(HINSTANCE hInst, HINSTANCE hPrevInstance, LPSTR lpszCmdParam,
int nCmdShow)
{
  MSG  Msg;

  if (!hPrevInstance)
    if (!Register(hInst))
      return FALSE;

  MainWindow = Create(hInst, nCmdShow);
  if (!MainWindow)
    return FALSE;

  while (GetMessage(&Msg, NULL, 0, 0))
  {
    TranslateMessage(&Msg);
    DispatchMessage(&Msg);
  }

  return Msg.wParam;
}


/////////////////////////////////////
// Register the window
/////////////////////////////////////
BOOL Register(HINSTANCE hInst)
{
  WNDCLASS WndClass;

  WndClass.style          = CS_HREDRAW | CS_VREDRAW;
  WndClass.lpfnWndProc    = WndProc;
```

10

continues

Listing 10.11. continued

```
        WndClass.cbClsExtra    = 0;
        WndClass.cbWndExtra    = 0;
        WndClass.hInstance     = hInst;
        WndClass.hIcon         = LoadIcon(NULL, IDI_APPLICATION);
        WndClass.hCursor       = LoadCursor(NULL, IDC_ARROW);
        WndClass.hbrBackground = (HBRUSH)(COLOR_WINDOW+1);
        WndClass.lpszMenuName  = NULL;
        WndClass.lpszClassName = szAppName;

        return (RegisterClass (&WndClass) != 0);
    }


    ////////////////////////////////////////
    // Create the window
    ////////////////////////////////////////
    HWND Create(HINSTANCE hInst, int nCmdShow)
    {

      hInstance = hInst;

      HWND hwnd = CreateWindow(szAppName, szAppName,
                      WS_OVERLAPPEDWINDOW,
                      CW_USEDEFAULT, CW_USEDEFAULT,
                      CW_USEDEFAULT, CW_USEDEFAULT,
                      NULL, NULL, hInst, NULL);

      if (hwnd == NULL)
        return hwnd;

      ShowWindow(hwnd, nCmdShow);
      UpdateWindow(hwnd);

      return hwnd;
    }


    // ---------------------------------------------------------
    // WndProc and Implementation
    // ---------------------------------------------------------


    ////////////////////////////////////////
    // The Window Procedure
    ////////////////////////////////////////
    LRESULT CALLBACK EXPORT16 WndProc(HWND hwnd, UINT Message, WPARAM wParam, LPARAM
    lParam)
    {
      switch(Message)
      {
        HANDLE_MSG(hwnd, WM_CREATE, ListBox1_OnCreate);
        HANDLE_MSG(hwnd, WM_DESTROY, ListBox1_OnDestroy);
        HANDLE_MSG(hwnd, WM_COMMAND, ListBox1_OnCommand);
        default: return ListBox1_DefProc(hwnd, Message, wParam, lParam);
      }
    }
```

```
/////////////////////////////////////
// Handle WM_CREATE
/////////////////////////////////////
#pragma argsused
BOOL ListBox1_OnCreate(HWND hwnd, CREATESTRUCT FAR* lpCreateStruct)
{
  CreateWindow("button", "Fill ListBox",
               WS_CHILD | WS_VISIBLE | BS_DEFPUSHBUTTON,
               10, 7, 203, 38, hwnd, HMENU(ID_FILLBTN),
               hInstance, NULL);

  CreateWindow("listbox", NULL,
               WS_CHILD | WS_VISIBLE | LBS_STANDARD,
               12, 50, 201, 180, hwnd, HMENU(ID_LISTBOX),
               hInstance, NULL);

  return TRUE;
}

/////////////////////////////////////
// Handle WM_DESTROY
/////////////////////////////////////
#pragma argsused
void ListBox1_OnDestroy(HWND hwnd)
{
  PostQuitMessage(0);
}

/////////////////////////////////////
// Handle WM_COMMAND
/////////////////////////////////////
#pragma argsused
void ListBox1_OnCommand(HWND hwnd, int id, HWND hwndCtl, UINT codeNotify)
{
  static char *List[7] = {"Sam", "Mike", "Anne", "Mary", "David", "LouAnne",
                          "Yo, Double click on a name!"};
  char S[100];

  switch (id)
  {
    case ID_FILLBTN:
    {
      for (int i = 0; i < 7; i++)
        ListBox_AddString(GetDlgItem(hwnd, ID_LISTBOX), List[i]);
    }
    break;

    case ID_LISTBOX:
      if (codeNotify == LBN_DBLCLK)
      {
        HWND ListWnd = GetDlgItem(hwnd, ID_LISTBOX);
        int index = ListBox_GetCurSel(ListWnd);
        ListBox_GetText(ListWnd, index, S);
        MessageBox(hwnd, S, "You selected", MB_OK | MB_ICONEXCLAMATION);
      }
    break;
  }
}
```

More Quick Examples at the End of Day 11

I provide three more quick examples at the end of Day 11. The point of these examples is to provide you with a handy reference for using controls. By dint of repetition, if nothing else, the basic techniques involved with Windows controls should now be becoming clear to you.

Summary

In this chapter you've had a chance to become acquainted with Windows controls. You have seen that these tools can be used to form an interactive interface between your program and a user.

This chapter covers the creation of five controls:

- Static controls
- List boxes
- Combo boxes
- Check boxes
- Edit controls

Because you've also looked at scrollbars, you now have knowledge of six different controls.

When creating window controls, the most important step is to fill in the first field of CreateWindow, called lpszClassName, with the class name of a control. For instance, if you want to create an edit control, copy the word edit into lpszClassName. Other controls are created by copying in one of the following words: static, scrollbar, listbox, or button.

This chapter also presents an in-depth discussion of the various styles used to define the behavior of a control. For instance, you have seen that the ES_CENTER style centers text in an edit control and the BS_CHECKBOX style converts an ordinary button into a check box.

Q&A

Q You showed us so many different window styles in this chapter. How are we ever supposed to keep up with all this information?

A Don't bother memorizing all the styles shown in this chapter. Instead, just absorb the fact that every control has a set of styles that can be used to fine tune, or even radically change, its appearance and behavior. Another helpful point is that the styles associated with each of the controls begin with a particular set of letters. For instance, edit-control styles all begin with ES. To help you understand how this works, here is a list of letters associated with each of the major control types:

Button	BS
Combo box	CBS
Edit	ES
List box	LBS
Static	SS

Q **I still don't understand this business of communicating with a style through an ID or an HWND. What gives?**

A Windows is monolithic in size, but it's also extremely flexible. Controls are designed so you can communicate with them either through their HWND or ID. When a control is embedded in a window, it's simplest to communicate with it through an HWND. Dialogs have a slightly different relationship with their controls, so it's easiest to communicate with a dialog's controls through their ID. Whether you use an HWND or an ID, the key point is that you have a unique handle associated with a control.

Workshop

The Workshop provides quiz questions to help you solidify your understanding of the material covered and exercises to provide you with experience in using what you've learned. Try to understand the quiz and exercise answers before continuing on to Day 11. Answers are provided in Appendix A.

Quiz

1. What single function can be used to create all the controls listed in this chapter?
2. Why don't you need to register the class of a static control?
3. How do you designate the parent of a control?
4. You can communicate with a control through its HWND or its _____?
5. How do you specify the ID of a control?
6. What logical operation is used to specify the style of a control?
7. Other than SendMessage, what two commands can be used to place or retrieve a string in an edit control or static control?
8. Why are list boxes and check boxes called controls?
9. What control is the EM_SETSEL message associated with, and what is its function?
10. How can you tell if a check box is selected?

Exercises

1. Write a small program with a single static control. Every time the user clicks the left mouse button, have the text in the edit control change.

2. Create a program with a single list box and a single edit control. Design the program so that the text in the edit control will be transferred to the list box when the user clicks the left mouse button.

Talking to Controls

This chapter has four main themes, most of which involve communication between controls and the main body of a program. In particular, this chapter seeks to do these things:

☐ Use the FontsExp program to continue the exploration of controls begun on Day 10, "Window Controls." In particular, you will learn more about list boxes, radio buttons, check boxes, and push buttons.

☐ Expand the study of fonts that you began on Day 9, "Font Basics," and show how to use callbacks to access the fonts on your system. In particular, you'll see the `EnumFontFamilies` function and the `EnumFontFamilies` callback. Because of the presence of a callback, this chapter also includes another brief look at `MakeProcInstance`, which is important in 16-bit Windows.

☐ Demonstrate the use of the debugger to see how Windows communicates with list boxes, edit controls, static controls, and buttons.

☐ Explain the `SendMessage` and `PostMessage` functions. `SendMessage` passes messages directly to the window procedure, while `PostMessage` places messages in the message queue.

When you are reading this chapter, try to pay particular attention to the material on the debugger. It's almost impossible for most people to do any serious programming without having an in-depth knowledge of their debugger.

At the end of the chapter you will have three more "quick control examples" like those that ended Day 10. These three short programs will help round out your understanding of control basics. The topics covered in the quick control examples are check boxes, push buttons, and radio buttons.

A Brief History of *WM_STARTFONTS*

From a purely conceptual point of view, this chapter covers fairly complex material. The theme for the day is communication—specifically the way Windows communicates with messages and callbacks.

The agenda is as follows:

☐ Learn about a user-defined message called `WM_STARTFONTS`.

☐ Trace `WM_STARTFONTS` from the moment of its conception until it sets off two calls to `EnumFontFamilies`, thereby causing messages to be sent that fill up the list box and other visual elements of the FontsExp program.

Each step on the agenda is explained methodically, starting from point one and working to the end. The narrative flow is provided by the life history of WM_STARTFONTS. In other words, the chapter starts by describing the declaration of WM_STARTFONTS, and then follows through by describing how the message is sent and processed. My theory is that if you watch a message from the moment it's defined, until it's finally delivered and processed, you'll get a complete overview of the subject—without any major gaps or omissions.

Delivering the Mail

WM_STARTFONTS is a user-defined message. It is not defined in WINDOWS.H; it is defined by the FontsExp program.

To begin the discussion of WM_STARTFONTS, it might be helpful to take just a moment to pick up the thread from Day 10. On Day10, you had a detailed look at the WM_CREATE method response function for the FontsExp program. In the process, you learned how to create edit controls, static controls, list boxes, and check boxes in the CreateWindow procedure.

I didn't mention one command in FontsExp_OnCreate—the call to PostMessage:

```
PostMessage(hwnd, WM_STARTFONTS, 0, 0);
```

To understand how PostMessage works, it's best to start out by defining messages from a new, and hopefully elucidating, perspective. WM_STARTFONTS is a user-defined message sent to tell the main window that it's time to fill up the list box and other controls with the names and descriptions of all the fonts on the system. There are two differences between user-defined messages and other messages:

☐ User-defined messages are declared by the programmer, whereas normal Windows messages are declared in WINDOWS.H, or in other header files that come with the system.

☐ User-defined messages normally have only local scope. This means that they can be defined for one class only.

More specifically, user-defined messages are calculated in terms of a constant called WM_USER, which is defined in WINDOWS.H.

```
/* NOTE: All messages below 0x0400 are RESERVED by Windows */
#define WM_USER         0x0400
```

As you can see, the comment in WINDOWS.H specifies that messages below 1024 (0X400) are reserved for internal use by Windows.

The WM_STARTFONTS message is defined in FONTSEXP.H:

```
#define WM_STARTFONTS (WM_USER + 0)
```

The preceding line of code simply states that WM_STARTFONTS should be assigned a number which will enable Windows to recognize it as a message of local import. By definition, it is intended specifically for the FontsExp class. To define additional messages, simply add 1 to the value of WM_STARTFONTS:

```
#define WM_STARTFONTS          (WM_USER + 0)
#define WM_NEWFONT             (WM_USER + 1)
```

and so on.

Of course, the WM_STARTFONTS message isn't the only message on the system that is assigned to hex value 400. In fact, the following messages from WINDOWS.H each have the same offset:

```
#define BM_GETCHECK            (WM_USER+0)
#define EM_GETSEL              (WM_USER+0)
#define CB_GETEDITSEL          (WM_USER+0)
#define DM_GETDEFID            (WM_USER+0)
#define STM_SETICON            (WM_USER+0)
```

If you are reasonably careful, this duplication of constants does not lead to confusion. The trick here is that all these messages are designed to be sent to a particular window. The window in question is designated by the HWND in the first parameter to PostMessage or SendMessage:

```
HWND hMainWindow, hCheckBox;  // Handles to windows
...
// Code to initialize the program and
// initialize hMainWindow and hCheckbox.
...
PostMessage(hMainWindow, WM_STARTFONTS, 0, 0L);
SendMessage(hCheckBox, BM_GETCHECK, 0, 0L);
...
```

This call states explicitly that WM_STARTFONTS is being sent to the program's main window. If it were accidentally sent to a check box, Windows would cheerfully ignore all the fonts on your system and return the state of the check box. The point here is that all will be on the up and up so long as you send the message to the correct window!

Note: One thing you can do when specifying the range of numbers employed by user-defined messages is to take WM_USER + 0x0100 as the offset for the first message you declare. This is probably overkill, but it will safely raise you above the level of constants declared in WINDOWS.H.

There are times when you need to create a message that is sent across the desktop to more than one application. To do so, call RegisterWindowMessage. This call returns a unique message, defined at runtime, to be used by your applications.

DO	DON'T

DO use WM_USER as an offset for messages that are going to be sent only to one class.

DON'T try to send these messages between applications.

DO use the RegisterWindowMessage function to assign numbers to messages that will be sent between applications.

SendMessage and *PostMessage*

Now that you know how WM_STARTFONTS is declared, you're ready to take a look at PostMessage and SendMessage. These are two of the more interesting API calls. They perform functions that appear to be similar but are actually quite different. As a result, they should occupy separate, but adjacent, living quarters in your imagination.

The basic purpose of both SendMessage and PostMessage is to tell a particular window to perform a task. The SendMessage function does this by explicitly calling the window procedure associated with the HWND in its parameter list. SendMessage doesn't return from that window procedure until the window has processed the message in question.

The PostMessage function, however, doesn't explicitly call a window procedure. Instead, it posts a message to the application's message queue and immediately returns.

Every 16-bit Windows application has a message queue that will, by default, handle up to eight messages at a time. WIN32 applications can automatically resize the queue. Messages are retrieved from the queue by the GetMessage function. If you glance at FontsExp's WinMain function, you can see that after GetMessage is called, a message is passed on to the window procedure with the DispatchMessage function.

What it all boils down to is that SendMessage delivers a message directly to a window procedure, whereas PostMessage just plops a message into a queue. In other words, SendMessage is the express route, and PostMessage is the slower, more laid-back way to deliver the mail. (See Figure 11.1.) SendMessage lets you deliver a message immediately, while PostMessage lets you immediately continue processing the code in the current routine.

Figure 11.1.

SendMessage *delivers a message directly to a window procedure, whereas* PostMessage *takes a more roundabout route.*

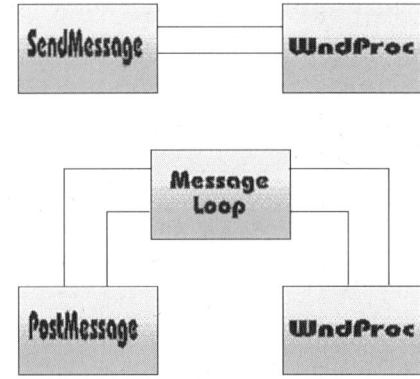

DO	DON'T

DO use SendMessage when time is of the essence, that is, when you want to be sure a message is processed before the SendMessage call ends.

DON'T use SendMessage if you can possibly put off processing the message.

DO remember that SendMessage won't return until its message has been processed.

DON'T forget that PostMessage returns immediately, enabling your program to continue on the next line of code.

In this particular case, FontsExp uses PostMessage for two reasons. The first reason is that there is no immediate need to process the message; the second reason is that the creation of the window should end before the WM_STARTFONTS message is processed.

How can FontsExp be sure that the creation of the window will be completed before the message is processed? To understand the reasoning, simply trace through the steps involved in starting a Windows application.

Start the debugger and place a breakpoint at the first call to CreateWindow. Next, start stepping through the program from the beginning, after WinMain is called. The first step is the call to RegisterWindow. Then, there are the calls to CreateWindow, ShowWindow, UpdateWindow, and GetMessage.

The WM_STARTFONTS message is posted at the end of a WM_CREATE message handler function. WM_CREATE messages are sent during the call to CreateWindow. This means that a window will finish creation, be shown, and be updated before GetMessage ever has a chance to pull the WM_STARTFONTS message out of the application queue.

Note: Because you might be using any one of a number of different compilers, I can't describe exactly how to use your debugger. If you are not yet familiar with your debugger, you should take the time to learn about it by reading your compiler's documentation.

For most programmers, there is nothing more important than a thorough knowledge of their debugger. You should take the time to get to know that tool, especially because most of the them are now built right into the IDE you are using. Specifically, be sure you know how to set break points, how to watch a variable, and how to step through your code one line at a time. Believe me, it will be well worth it.

Here's a step-by-step view of the process that occurs when you first start the FontsExp program:

1. Register the window.

2. Call `CreateWindow`. This is the stage at which a window handles `WM_CREATE` messages. This is also when the `WM_STARTFONTS` message is posted.

3. Show and update the window.

4. Start the `message` loop. It's during this stage that the `WM_STARTFONTS` message is actually passed on to `WndProc`.

That's the end of my introduction to Windows messages. I've discussed this topic in-depth because the whole idea of sending and posting messages is a crucial part of the life of a Windows application. Furthermore, you won't really understand what's being said in the rest of this chapter unless you first understand, at least in general terms, how `SendMessage` and `PostMessage` work.

Enumerating the System Fonts

In the last section, you saw the mail being delivered. You saw the posting of the `WM_STARTFONTS` message and then saw it through to its address in the `WndProc` procedure. After the post office has done its job, the next step is to process the message in the body of the `WndProc`. To follow this with your debugger, place a breakpoint on the line that begins with `lpfnEnumProc`. Now run the FontsExp program again from the beginning, and continue until you reach the breakpoint in `WM.STARTFONTS`:

```
case WM_STARTFONTS:
{
  HDC DC = GetDC(hwnd);
  lpfnEnumProc = (FONTENUMPROC)MakeProcInstance(
                 (FARPROC)FontCallBack, hInstance);
```

```
EnumStruct.Count = 0;
EnumStruct.hWindow = hFontList;
EnumFontFamilies(DC, NULL, lpfnEnumProc, (LONG)&EnumStruct);
FreeProcInstance((FARPROC)lpfnEnumProc);

ReleaseDC(hwnd, DC);

wsprintf(S, "There are %d fonts available", EnumStruct.Count);
SetWindowText(hNumFonts, S);

SetFocus(hFontList);
SendMessage(hFontList, LB_SETCURSEL, 0, 0);
ShowTheFont(hwnd);
return 1;
}
```

The goal of this code is to enumerate through the system fonts. It asks the system "What fonts do you have available?" The system answers "Arial, New Times Roman, Script (and so on)." This process becomes somewhat complex, primarily because it is Windows (not the FontsExp program) that knows which fonts are available. Therefore, the FontsExp program has to find a way to ask Windows which fonts are available on the system.

The solution is to set up an address for Windows to mail the information to and then to simply wait at that address while Windows iterates through all the available fonts. Each time a font is found, Windows sends a letter to the proper address in FontsExp. It's just like ordering something from the Land's End catalog. You send something in the mail and wait for the goodies to arrive. Anybody can do it. (See Figure 11.2.)

Figure 11.2.
FontsExp asks Windows what fonts are available, and Windows sends back information.

The first step is to set up the mailing address, which in this case happens to be a function called FontCallBack. Right now, don't worry about how this function works; just concentrate on the fact that it exists. It's a little post office box with its own address.

When working in 16-bit Windows, here's how to tell Windows the address of the `FontCallBack` function:

```
lpfnEnumProc = (FONTENUMPROC)MakeProcInstance(
               (FARPROC)FontCallBack, hInstance);
```

This is a fairly nasty piece of work. But don't worry; it's not that hard to sort the syntactical wheat from the syntactical chaff in a case like this. Furthermore, if you are working with WIN32, you don't need to understand `MakeProcInstance` and can therefore afford to skim through the next few paragraphs.

If you are working with WIN16, then you must call `MakeProcInstance`. This is the function that sets up an address for the `FontCallBack` procedure. More specifically, what actually happens is that Windows attaches a bit of prolog code to `FontCallBack`. This prolog code binds the FontsExp's data segment to the `FontCallBack` function. In WIN32, there is no need to call `MakeProcInstance`, since the data segment is mapped into the application's flat address space.

> **Note:** Here's some additional information for those who are working with 16-bit Windows.
>
> Setting up the `FontCallBack` procedure involves a similar process to the one you went through when you were learning how to set up a `DialogBox` procedure. All the issues are the same. The `FontCallBack` function is part of FontsExp, but it's going to be called by Windows. This means that `FontCallBack` is really a part of Windows (and not part of your application) when it is being called. As a result, the `FontCallBack` function would not normally have access to the FontsExp's data segment. One of the purposes of the call to `MakeProcInstance` is to resolve this problem through the auspices of the bit of prolog code (mentioned previously).
>
> If, by some chance, the last few paragraphs don't make a great deal of sense to you, you should turn back to the discussion of the `DialogBox` procedure, fall back to the mailing address analogy, use the debugger to set breakpoints on the `FontCallBack` function, and keep running or stepping through the program until this process begins to make sense. The point is that Windows and your program need to agree on the mailing address to which the list of fonts will be delivered. The `MakeProcInstance` function registers the address with the postal service and makes sure a clean path of communication is available.

In order to call `MakeProcInstance` successfully, you should typecast the value it returns as a `FONTENUMPROC`. This is necessary because the `EnumFontFamilies` procedure, which you will read about in a moment, expects to be passed an address of type `FONTENUMPROC`. You should also typecast the `FontCallBack` procedure as a simple `FARPROC`. A `FARPROC` is really only a generic procedure type, without any specific arguments or return value. Of course, it goes without saying that all FARPROCs are assumed to be declared FAR.

> **Note:** If you're not familiar with making typecasts, you can think of the specific one shown here like this: A Ford Mustang is a specific type of car, just as the FontCallBack function is a specific type of function; but a FARPROC is just a generic term for a procedure, just as the word *vehicle* or *car* can be substituted as a generic term for a Mustang. MakeProcInstance returns a generic term, and FontsExp performs a typecast so it can treat the return value as a specific type of address. It's saying: "As far as you are concerned, you're just delivering a car, but I know that this particular car is a Mustang, so I'm going to treat it that way." It's as if the guy who does the trucking just thinks: "Okay, I'm delivering a load of cars. I don't know what make they are, and I don't care." However, the dealer he's delivering to knows exactly what kinds of cars are being shipped; so, he can tell his workers "Go down to the shipping bay and pick up that Mustang that's coming in."

The next few lines look like this:

```
EnumStruct.Count = 0;
EnumStruct.hWindow = hFontList;
EnumFontFamilies(DC, NULL, lpfnEnumProc, (LONG)&EnumStruct);
```

The center of focus is the EnumFontFamilies call, which takes a device context as its first parameter. The second parameter is the name of a font family, which in this case is set to NULL. The third parameter is the address of the callback function, which is the post office box to which information will be sent. The final parameter is the address of some data that you can pass to the FontCallBack function. In many cases, you can set this last parameter to 0. However, I have filled it in here, primarily so you can see how to use it.

Feel free to pass in the address of any structure or type in this last parameter to the EnumFontFamilies function. In this specific case, I'm passing in a record that contains two fields: the first an integer and the second an HWND. The integer is used to keep track of how many fonts are available on the system, and the HWND belongs to the list box where the fonts will be displayed. I want to stress that I've customized this structure for my own purposes. If you prefer, you can pass a structure containing four strings and a float, the address of another procedure, or just plain old NULL. Any valid pointer address is fine.

When you are through calling EnumFontFamilies, you need to call FreeProcInstance, which frees up the FontCallBack function from the data segment bound to it during the call to MakeProcInstance:

```
FreeProcInstance((FARPROC)lpfnEnumProc);
```

You should also remember to free the device context used during the call to EnumFontFamilies:

```
ReleaseDC(hwnd, DC);
```

When you are working in WIN32, you don't need to call either MakeProcInstance or FreeProcInstance. However, it does no harm to call these procedures. They don't *do* anything in WIN32, but it's not harmful to call them.

If you are not concerned with writing portable code that will run in both WIN32 and WIN16, then you can change the opening lines of the above procedure so they look like this:

```
HDC DC = GetDC(hwnd);
EnumStruct.Count = 0;
EnumStruct.hWindow = hFontList;
EnumFontFamilies(DC, NULL, (FONTENUMPROC)FontCallBack,
                 (LONG)&EnumStruct);
ReleaseDC(hwnd, DC);
```

The only tricky part of this code is the typecast on the third parameter to EnumFontFamilies. Otherwise, the code is very simple. Obviously, this is one thing that works out much better in WIN32 than it does in WIN16.

The Callback Function

During the call to EnumFontFamilies, Windows sends the mail to the FontCallBack function. To see the connection here, use the debugger to set a break in FontCallBack, and then step into the EnumFontFamilies call in the WndProc. You should see the focus switch from EnumFontFamilies directly to FontCallBack.

The parameters to FontCallBack are defined by the EnumFontFamProc API function. In actual practice, you might never name a routine EnumFontFamProc. Instead, this function serves as a placeholder for a name defined inside of a particular program. Obviously, in the preceding code, I substituted the name FontCallBack for EnumFontFamProc. However, when you need to look up the parameters passed to this function, you should search for EnumFontFamProc in your documentation.

The *FontCallBack* Function

```
int CALLBACK FontCallBack(LPENUMLOGFONT, LPNEWTEXTMETRIC,
                          int, ENUMSTRUCT FAR*)
```

The parameters passed to FontCallBack tell almost everything any programmer could ever want to know about a font:

- ☐ The first parameter is the LOGFONT of the font.
- ☐ The second parameter is the TEXTMETRIC structure.

☐ The third parameter can be used to determine if the font is a TrueType font, or if it is meant to be displayed on a screen, a printer, neither, or both.

☐ The last parameter is the user-defined data passed in when EnumFontFamilies was called.

Between them, the first two parameters hold structures containing some 30 different fields that detail the characteristics of the font. (Use your debugger to examine these fields.)

Here's what the FontCallBack function looks like:

```
int CALLBACK FontCallBack(LPENUMLOGFONT lpnlf,
                          LPNEWTEXTMETRIC lpntm,
                          int FontType, ENUMSTRUCT FAR * lpData)
{
  SendMessage(lpData->hWindow, LB_ADDSTRING, 0,
              LONG(lpnlf->elfLogFont.lfFaceName));
  return 1;
}
```

As you can see, 90 percent of the data passed to FontCallBack is simply ignored. The only real area of interest is the lfFaceName field of the LOGFONT structure. This data is promptly sent off to the list box where it is displayed for the user's perusal. The process of sending the message to a list box is described in the next section.

Immediately after being sent off, the next piece of mail comes flying in (by airmail, as it were), courtesy of Windows itself. Once again, FontCallBack bundles up the font name and sends it off to the list box to be displayed. This whole process is continued until there are no more fonts left to iterate or the callback returns zero.

Well, there you have it. You've just seen a rough outline of how to enumerate the fonts on the system through a callback. There were seven steps involved (If you are working in WIN32, you can skip steps 3 and 6.):

1. Write a callback procedure.
2. Get a device context.
3. Call MakeProcInstance to create a link between your program and Windows proper.
4. Call EnumFontFamilies and wait for Windows to send the font information to your callback.
5. Process the information sent to your callback.
6. Use FreeProcInstance to free the prolog code allocated by MakeProcInstance.
7. Release the DC.

These outlined steps are all well and good in and of themselves. However, nothing described so far does anything to fill the user in on what has taken place. In order to give the call a visual element, FontsExp must first communicate directly with visual controls such as list boxes, check boxes, and edit and static controls.

Talking to a List Box

One of the most important parts of the FontCallBack function is the call to SendMessage:

```
SendMessage(lpData->hWindow, LB_ADDSTRING, 0,
            LONG(lpnlf->elfLogFont.lfFaceName));
```

This function actually sends the names of the enumerated fonts to the list box so the user can peruse them at his or her leisure.

You already know that SendMessage delivers a notice directly to a particular WndProc, which in this case happens to be the window procedure of the list box. Remember that the HWND of the list box was passed in via the custom user-defined date passed to EnumFontFamilies.

What's new here, of course, is the LB_ADDSTRING message. LB_ADDSTRING is one of nearly 40 predefined messages that can be sent to a list box. It tells Windows that the list box in question needs to have a new string added to it. When you use LB_ADDSTRING, the third and fourth parameters of SendMessage or PostMessage should be filled in as follows:

☐ The third parameter (WPARAM) should be set to 0.

☐ The fourth parameter is set to the address of the string that's going to be added to the list box. Because the fourth parameter of the SendMessage function is an LPARAM, it's necessary to typecast the string before sending it.

Following is a list of some of the more commonly used messages sent to a list box:

LB_ADDSTRING	Adds a string.
LB_DELETESTRING	Deletes a string.
LB_DIR	Adds a list of filenames.
LB_GETCOUNT	Gets the number of items.
LB_GETCURSEL	Gets the index of a selected item.
LB_GETSEL	Gets the selection state of an item.
LB_GETSELCOUNT	Gets the number of selected items.
LB_GETTEXT	Gets a string.
LB_GETTEXTLEN	Gets the length of a string.
LB_RESETCONTENT	Removes all items.

11

LB_SELECTSTRING	Selects a matching string in a list box.
LB_SELITEMRANGE	Selects consecutive items in a list box.
LB_SETCOLUMNWIDTH	Sets the width of columns in a list box.
LB_SETCURSEL	Selects an indexed string in a list box.
LB_SETSEL	Selects a string in a multiple-selection list box.
LB_SETTOPINDEX	Ensures that an item is visible.
LB_SETTABSTOPS	Sets tab stops.

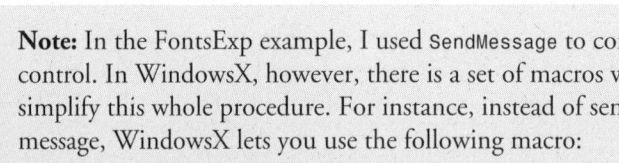

Note: In the FontsExp example, I used SendMessage to communicate with a control. In WindowsX, however, there is a set of macros which can somewhat simplify this whole procedure. For instance, instead of sending an LB_ADDSTRING message, WindowsX lets you use the following macro:

```
#define ListBox_AddString(hwndCtl, lpsz)
```

which is defined as follows:

```
((int)(DWORD)SendMessage((hwndCtl), LB_ADDSTRING,
                    0, (LPARAM)(LPCSTR)(lpsz)))
```

For many people, WindowsX macros are easier to use than the SendMessage function. However, in this book, I occasionally use SendMessage for two different reasons:

1. I feel it's important that you understand how the WindowsX macros actually work. WindowsX is fine, but you shouldn't use it unless you understand the foundation on which it rests.

2. You really should be thoroughly familiar with how to use SendMessage. You will encounter a great deal of code that's dependent on it.

I frequently use the WindowsX macros rather than SendMessage. I prefer WindowsX because it is elegant and readily portable to WIN32.

After the FontCallBack function has been sent the name of all the fonts on the system, the program needs to fill the static control above the list box (line 128 of FONTEXP.CPP):

```
wsprintf(S, "There are %d fonts available", EnumStruct.Count);
SetWindowText(hNumFonts, S);
```

These lines use the Count field, which was incremented every time FontCallBack was sent a new piece of mail. (See Figure 11.3.)

Figure 11.3.
The list box and its static text after they have been filled with information about the fonts on the system.

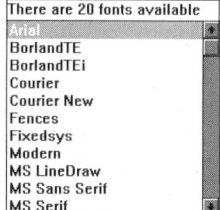

The next step in the program is to set the focus on the list box; then, highlight the first item in the box. (Use the debugger to step through lines 132 and 133, which, by the way, are *still* part of the response to WM_STARTFONT:

```
SetFocus(hFontList);
SendMessage(hFontList, LB_SETCURSEL, 0, 0);
```

This call to SetFocus makes it easy for the user to scroll through the fonts in the list box. A list box can respond when a user manipulates the arrow keys. However, the list box must first have the focus. To select a list box, call SetFocus with the HWND of the control as the sole parameter. This has the same effect as actually clicking the control with the mouse.

Selecting an item in a list box is a straightforward process. All you need to do is send the list box an LB_SETCURSEL message and the index of the item to highlight. The message itself instructs the list box to highlight a particular item. The index of the item to highlight is specified in WPARAM. Because the index is zero-based, a value of 0 in WPARAM instructs the list box to highlight the first item in the list. Check WINDOWSX.H for alternative means of selecting an item in a list box.

Showing the Font

At this point, you've had a look at all but one of the calls initiated by the WM_STARTFONTS message. The holdout is ShowTheFont.

The ShowTheFont function takes care of all the controls except the list box and static control immediately above it. More specifically, it displays the name of the currently selected font in a big static control, shows a selection of characters from that font in the scrollable edit control, and sets the check boxes to their appropriate values. (See Figure 11.4.)

Note: The ShowTheFont function is called twice. It is called once at the beginning of the program in response to WM_STARTFONTS message. Thereafter it is called every time the user selects a different font in the list box. In other words, the list box gets filled only one time—at program creation. ShowTheFont, however, gets called every time the user asks that another font be displayed.

Figure 11.4.

These controls are handled by the ShowTheFont *function.*

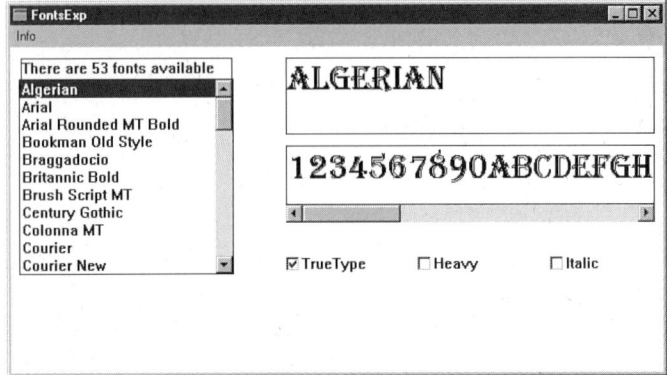

Following is the code for ShowTheFont. Take the time to step through the code with your debugger while you follow the discussion:

```
void ShowTheFont(HWND hwnd)
{
  FONTENUMPROC lpfnEnumProc;
  char lpszBuffer[150];
  ENUMSTRUCT EnumStruct;
  HFONT SaveIt;
  char Alpha[] = {"1234567890abcdefghijklmnopqrstuvwxyz"
                  "ABCDEFGHIJKLMNOPQRSTUVWXYZ"};

  HDC DC = GetDC(hwnd);

  int Index = SendMessage(hFontList, LB_GETCURSEL, 0, 0);
  SendMessage(hFontList, LB_GETTEXT, Index, LONG(lpszBuffer));
  lpfnEnumProc = (FONTENUMPROC)MakeProcInstance(
                    (FARPROC)DescribeFontCallBack, hInstance);
  EnumStruct.Count = 0;
  EnumStruct.hWindow = hwnd;
  EnumFontFamilies(DC, lpszBuffer, lpfnEnumProc, (LONG)&EnumStruct);
  FreeProcInstance((FARPROC)lpfnEnumProc);

  if (TheFont != 0)
    SaveIt = SelectFont(DC, TheFont);
  GetTextMetrics(DC, &TextMetrics);
  HandleMetrics(TextMetrics);
  GetTextFace(DC, 150, aTextFace);
  if (TheFont != 0)
    SelectFont(DC, SaveIt);

  ReleaseDC(hwnd, DC);

  SendMessage(hFontName, WM_SETTEXT, 0, LONG(&lpszBuffer));
  SendMessage(hFontName, WM_SETFONT, WPARAM(TheFont), 0);

  SendMessage(hAlphaEdit, WM_SETTEXT, 0, LONG(&Alpha));
  SendMessage(hAlphaEdit, WM_SETFONT, WPARAM(TheFont), 0);
}
```

The function starts by getting the name of the currently selected font from the list box. To do this, it must first find the index of the selected item, and then ask for the string associated with that item number.

> **Note:** When retrieving an item from a list box, you usually first find out which item the user has selected by sending a LB_GETCURSEL message. Then, use the LB_GETTEXT message to retrieve the string:
>
> ```
> int Index = SendMessage(hFontList, LB_GETCURSEL, 0, 0);
> SendMessage(hFontList, LB_GETTEXT, Index,
>             LONG(lpszBuffer));
> ```
>
> The LB_GETCURSEL message should have both the WPARAM and the LPARAM of the SendMessage function set to 0. The LB_GETTEXT message, on the other hand, expects the index of the string to be in the WPARAM argument, and a buffer to hold the string in LPARAM. The buffer in LPARAM must be long enough to hold the string and the NULL terminator. If you need to get the length of a particular string, send an LB_GETTEXTLEN message.
>
> Of course, the first time these messages are sent, the selected item will be the first item in the list box. However, this function gets called over and over again throughout the life of a program as shown in the next section. On later occasions, the user will most likely select a different item than the one set by default at the beginning of the program.

The next step in the ShowTheFont function is a second call to EnumFontFamilies. This time, the name of a font is passed in the second parameter. The mailing address, or callback, is the DescribeFontCallback:

```
#pragma argsused
int CALLBACK DescribeFontCallBack(LPENUMLOGFONT lpnlf,
                                  LPNEWTEXTMETRIC lpntm,
                                  int FontType,
                                  ENUMSTRUCT FAR * lpData)
{
  SendMessage(lpData->hWindow, WM_NEWFONT, 0,
              LONG(&lpnlf->elfLogFont));
  return 1;
}
```

During the previous call to EnumFontFamilies, the callback procedure was called once for every font on the system. This time, however, DescribeFontCallBack is called only once. The purpose of the first set of calls is to get the name of all the fonts on the system. The purpose of the second call is to get detailed information about a specific font, specified in the second parameter of EnumFontFamilies.

> **Note:** Obviously, it would have been possible to only call `EnumFontFamilies` once
> in this program. That is, I could have iterated through the fonts once and main-
> tained a linked list or dynamic array containing all the information about each font
> on the system. I opted not to take this route for the following reasons:
>
> ☐ I want to give you working examples demonstrating two different ways to call
>   `EnumFontFamiles`.
>
> ☐ I want to avoid complicating the code and wasting memory by introducing
>   an extraneous data structure, such as a linked list or dynamic array.
>
> ☐ I want to avoid duplicating available resources. If the information is directly
>   available from Windows, why should a programmer bother to keep a separate
>   list for his or her own program?
>
> Considerations such as these are typical of the kinds of factors Windows program-
> mers need to keep in mind when designing their programs.

The `DescribeFontCallBack` function, invoked by `EnumFontFamilies`, uses the `SendMessage`
procedure to inform the main program about the information it has received. This time, the
message sent is called `WM_NEWFONT`, and it is sent back directly to the main window, rather than
to a list box.

The information packaged along with the `WM_NEWFONT` message is a `LOGFONT`. You should note that
the dimensions of the font are chosen by Windows, and that this program makes no attempt
to change them.

Back in the `WndProc`, the response to the `WM_NEWFONT` message is simply to use the packaged
`LOGFONT` to create a new font for the main window:

```
case WM_NEWFONT:
{
  if (TheFont != 0)
    DeleteObject(TheFont);
  TheLogFont = (LPLOGFONT)lParam;
  TheFont = CreateFontIndirect(TheLogFont);
  return 1;
}
```

The code first deletes any existing font. Then, it typecasts `lParam` to get hold of the `LOGFONT` and
calls `CreateFontIndirect` to create a new font. The font itself is stored in a global variable. After
the `SendMessage` function is processed, the code returns to the `ShowTheFont` function.

Tip: Set debugger breakpoints on both the `DescribeFontCallBack` and the `WM_NEWFONT` case statements and then step through the program several times until you understand the relationship between the two code fragments. This is quintessential Windows programming—take the time to understand how it works.

Working with Check Boxes

Now that you have a copy of the new font available, show it to the user and display some information about the font.

The program first calls `GetTextMetric`, which provides all kinds of information about the font, including whether or not it is a TrueType font, whether it's italicized, and what its current weight is. This structure is shunted off to `HandleMetrics`, which sets the check boxes to reflect the state of this information:

```
void HandleMetrics(TEXTMETRIC TextMetrics)
{

if ((TextMetrics.tmPitchAndFamily &
     TMPF_TRUETYPE) == TMPF_TRUETYPE)
  SendMessage(ButtonWindows[0], BM_SETCHECK, 1, 0L);
else
  SendMessage(ButtonWindows[0], BM_SETCHECK, 0, 0L);

if ((TextMetrics.tmWeight) > 600)
  SendMessage(ButtonWindows[1], BM_SETCHECK, 1, 0L);
else
  SendMessage(ButtonWindows[1], BM_SETCHECK, 0, 0L);

if (TextMetrics.tmItalic)
  SendMessage(ButtonWindows[2], BM_SETCHECK, 1, 0L);
else
  SendMessage(ButtonWindows[2], BM_SETCHECK, 0, 0L);
}
```

Notice that the `BM_SETCHECK` message always takes 0 as its last parameter. You should set `WPARAM` to 1 to set the check, and 0 to erase the check. Once again, no one expects you to remember how to use the `BM_SETCHECK` message. All that's important is that you know it exists and that you know how to look up the information. If remembering all these bits of information comes to you easily, that's fine. But don't waste time struggling to remember all these details. Just know how to look them up when you need them.

The last few calls in `ShowTheFont` send the information to the two edit controls with the `WM_SETTEXT` message, which wants a string buffer sent in the last parameter. After sending the font to the control, set the font with the `WM_SETFONT` message. You'll probably want to take a close

11

look at those two `SendMessage` calls because they perform an important task that you might want to utilize in your own programs. Anyway, the FontsExp program wouldn't be nearly as useful, or as much fun if the text on-screen weren't written in the current font.

> **Note:** WindowsX provides alternatives to the calls to `SendMessage` shown previously. In particular, notice the following calls from WINDOWSX.H:
>
> ```
> #define Button_GetCheck(hwndCtl)
> #define Button_SetCheck(hwndCtl, check)
> ```
>
> Assuming you understand how `SendMessage` and `PostMessage` work, you should probably use these WindowsX macros in their stead when working with check boxes.

Hit Me with the Highlights!

Take a moment to review the steps of the `ShowTheFont` function (and if possible, follow along with your debugger):

1. Query the list box to find the currently selected font name.
2. Send the font name to Windows via a call to `EnumFontFamilies`.
3. Wait for Windows to send a `LOGFONT` structure to the `DescribeFontCallBack` function.
4. Use the `LOGFONT` supplied by Windows to create a global font.
5. Use the font's `TEXTMETRIC` to retrieve a few bits of detailed information for the user's perusal.

None of these steps are particularly difficult to perform. You just need to remember what has to be done, and then go about doing it in a logical, straightforward manner.

> **Note:** Focus for a moment on just one segment of this process:
>
> ☐ FontsExp calls `EnumFontFamilies`.
> ☐ `EnumFontFamilies` calls Windows.
> ☐ Windows sends information to the callback procedure.
> ☐ The callback function sends a message to the main window.
> ☐ The main window creates a copy of the font.

As you've seen by using the debugger, the logic outlined here is radically different from the sequential programming that goes on in most DOS programs. Messages are flying all over the place, in 16-bit Windows data segments are being patched up with prolog code, and the instruction pointer is flying from one part of your program to the next.

This is a classic example of what event-oriented programming is all about. Grasp these concepts, cup them in the palms of your hands, and examine them one by one. See how they all fit together and admire their complexity.

Don't waste time trying to decide whether this system is better or worse than the one that is familiar from command-line environments. That's an interesting topic in and of itself, but it's not the theme of this book. For now, concentrate on how Windows does things. It's a fascinating process, and it's not over yet, as you'll see in the next section.

The Return of *ShowTheFont*

Before I close the main body of this chapter, I want to turn your attention to the WM_COMMAND message function handler, which receives a message every time the user selects another item from the list box. To follow along with the debugger, set a breakpoint on the ShowTheFont function (line 219) of FontExpOnCommand:

```
void FontsExp_OnCommand(HWND hwnd, int id, HWND hwndCtl, UINT codeNotify)
{
  char S[500];

  switch (id)
  {
    case ID_LISTBOX:
    if (codeNotify == LBN_SELCHANGE)
    ShowTheFont(hwnd);
    break;

    case CM_INFO:
    GetFontString(S, TextMetrics, aTextFace);
    MessageBox(hwnd, S, "Info", MB_OK);
    break;
  }
}
```

The code checks to see whether the id parameter is set to ID_LISTBOX and whether the message being sent signifies that the selection in the list box has changed. If both statements are true, ShowTheFont is called. As mentioned, ShowTheFont knows how to set the controls in the window to exhibit an example and a description of the current font.

It's quite typical of Windows to make it so very easy to find out whether a selection has changed in a list box. Information about things the user has done almost always comes to you free of charge, courtesy of the people at Microsoft. However, it's also typical of Windows to make it fairly difficult for you to send information back to the user. Windows is such an ornate and powerful tool that creating an effective interface can sometimes be a little bit tricky.

Finally, you should notice that this program calls the GetFontString function (which was developed back on Day 9). This function displays additional information about the current font. I include it here for two reasons:

☐ It's useful to the user.

☐ It illustrates how simple it is to share a module between two different Windows programs. Code reuse is the most valuable skill in a Windows programmer's repertoire. Windows forces you to perform the same lengthy procedures over and over. Whenever possible, write reusable routines that automate the act of filling in the details.

More Quick Examples

Once again, I will wind up this chapter with three short examples that demonstrate how to use some of the standard Windows controls. The point of this section is to provide you with a handy reference, and to hammer home some the main themes of Day 9 and Day 10.

When compiling this code, you can create, make, and definition files simply by copying the relevant code from the WINDOW1 example on Day 3, "A Standard Windows Program." Then search through the MAK and DEF files you copied over and replace each instance of the term *WINDOW1* with the name of the new program you are trying to compile.

Push Buttons

Push buttons are created by assigning the word button to the first field of CreateWindow, and giving the button the BS_PUSHBUTTON or BS_DEFPUSHBUTTON style. A default push button has a dark border around it and will be automatically selected when the user presses the Enter button in a dialog.

```
CreateWindow("button", "Click on this Big Button",
            WS_CHILD ¦ WS_VISIBLE ¦ BS_DEFPUSHBUTTON,
            10, 7, 403, 238, hwnd, HMENU(ID_BUTTON),
            hInstance, NULL);
```

If a push button is selected by the user, a message is sent to the program's WM_COMMAND handler. The example program puts up a message box in response to this event:

```
    case ID_BUTTON:
      MessageBox(hwnd, "You pressed the button",
                 "Button Selection!",
                 MB_OK | MB_ICONEXCLAMATION);
```

Listing 11.1 is the example in its entirety. Remember that you can create a module definition file and a makefile for this program simply by borrowing the relevant code from the WINDOW1 example in Day 3.

Listing 11.1. A simple push button example.

```
//////////////////////////////////////////////////////////
//  Program Name: Button1.cpp
//  Programmer: Charlie Calvert
//  Description: Simple Button Example
//  Date: 12/19/93
//////////////////////////////////////////////////////////

#define STRICT
#define WIN32_LEAN_AND_MEAN
#include <windows.h>
#include <windowsx.h>
#pragma warning (disable: 4068)
// ---------------------------------------------------------
// Interface
// ---------------------------------------------------------

LRESULT CALLBACK WndProc(HWND hwnd, UINT Message, WPARAM wParam, LPARAM lParam);
BOOL Register(HINSTANCE hInst);
HWND Create(HINSTANCE hInst, int nCmdShow);

// Controls IDs
#define ID_BUTTON 101

// Declarations for class Button1
#define Button1_DefProc     DefWindowProc
BOOL Button1_OnCreate(HWND hwnd, CREATESTRUCT FAR* lpCreateStruct);
void Button1_OnDestroy(HWND hwnd);
void Button1_OnCommand(HWND hwnd, int id, HWND hwndCtl, UINT codeNotify);
static char szAppName[] = "Button1";
static HWND MainWindow;
static HINSTANCE hInstance;


// ---------------------------------------------------------
// Initialization
// ---------------------------------------------------------

////////////////////////////////////////
// Program entry point
////////////////////////////////////////
#pragma argsused
int WINAPI WinMain(HINSTANCE hInst, HINSTANCE hPrevInstance, LPSTR lpszCmdParam,
int nCmdShow)
{
```

continues

Listing 11.1. continued

```c
MSG  Msg;

if (!hPrevInstance)
  if (!Register(hInst))
    return FALSE;

MainWindow = Create(hInst, nCmdShow);
if (!MainWindow)
  return FALSE;

while (GetMessage(&Msg, NULL, 0, 0))
{
  TranslateMessage(&Msg);
  DispatchMessage(&Msg);
}

return Msg.wParam;
}


////////////////////////////////////
// Register the window
////////////////////////////////////
BOOL Register(HINSTANCE hInst)
{
  WNDCLASS WndClass;

  WndClass.style          = CS_HREDRAW | CS_VREDRAW;
  WndClass.lpfnWndProc    = WndProc;
  WndClass.cbClsExtra     = 0;
  WndClass.cbWndExtra     = 0;
  WndClass.hInstance      = hInst;
  WndClass.hIcon          = LoadIcon(NULL, IDI_APPLICATION);
  WndClass.hCursor        = LoadCursor(NULL, IDC_ARROW);
  WndClass.hbrBackground  = (HBRUSH)(COLOR_WINDOW+1);
  WndClass.lpszMenuName    = NULL;
  WndClass.lpszClassName = szAppName;

  return (RegisterClass (&WndClass) != 0);
}


////////////////////////////////////
// Create the window
////////////////////////////////////
HWND Create(HINSTANCE hInst, int nCmdShow)
{

  hInstance = hInst;

  HWND hwnd = CreateWindow(szAppName, szAppName,
                  WS_OVERLAPPEDWINDOW,
                  CW_USEDEFAULT, CW_USEDEFAULT,
                  CW_USEDEFAULT, CW_USEDEFAULT,
                  NULL, NULL, hInst, NULL);
```

```
    if (hwnd == NULL)
      return hwnd;

    ShowWindow(hwnd, nCmdShow);
    UpdateWindow(hwnd);

    return hwnd;
}

// --------------------------------------------------------
// WndProc and Implementation
// --------------------------------------------------------

/////////////////////////////////////
// The Window Procedure
/////////////////////////////////////
LRESULT CALLBACK WndProc(HWND hwnd, UINT Message, WPARAM wParam, LPARAM lParam)
{
  switch(Message)
  {
    HANDLE_MSG(hwnd, WM_CREATE, Button1_OnCreate);
    HANDLE_MSG(hwnd, WM_DESTROY, Button1_OnDestroy);
    HANDLE_MSG(hwnd, WM_COMMAND, Button1_OnCommand);
    default: return Button1_DefProc(hwnd, Message, wParam, lParam);
  }
}


/////////////////////////////////////
// Handle WM_CREATE
/////////////////////////////////////
#pragma argsused
BOOL Button1_OnCreate(HWND hwnd, CREATESTRUCT FAR* lpCreateStruct)
{
  CreateWindow("button", "Click on this Big Button",
               WS_CHILD | WS_VISIBLE | BS_DEFPUSHBUTTON,
               10, 7, 403, 238, hwnd, HMENU(ID_BUTTON),
               hInstance, NULL);

  return TRUE;
}

/////////////////////////////////////
// Handle WM_DESTROY
/////////////////////////////////////
#pragma argsused
void Button1_OnDestroy(HWND hwnd)
{
  PostQuitMessage(0);
}

/////////////////////////////////////
// Handle WM_COMMAND
/////////////////////////////////////
#pragma argsused
void Button1_OnCommand(HWND hwnd, int id, HWND hwndCtl, UINT codeNotify)
```

11

continues

Listing 11.1. continued

```
{
  switch (id)
  {
    case ID_BUTTON:
      MessageBox(hwnd, "You pressed the button",
                 "Button Selection!", MB_OK | MB_ICONEXCLAMATION);
      break;
  }
}
```

In the previous code, you should note that codeNotify will be set to 1 if the message is from an accelerator, and to 0 if it is from a menu.

Check Boxes

Check boxes are part of the button class and use the BS_AUTOCHECKBOX or BS_CHECKBOX style:

```
CreateWindow("button", "Generic CheckBox",
             WS_CHILD | WS_VISIBLE | BS_AUTOCHECKBOX,
             10, 50, 410, 30, hwnd, HMENU(ID_CHECKBOX),
             hInstance, NULL);
```

You can set a check box by passing the value 1 in the last parameter of the WindowsX Button_SetCheck macro. The first parameter is the HWND of the check box. A good way to get the HWND is via the GetDlgItem API function:

```
Button_SetCheck(GetDlgItem(hwnd, ID_CHECKBOX), 1);
```

To clear a check box, simply pass 0 in the last parameter of the WindsowsX Button_SetCheck macro:

```
Button_SetCheck(GetDlgItem(hwnd, ID_CHECKBOX), 0);
```

Use the WindowsX Button_GetCheck macro to determine if a button is checked or not. If the macro returns 0, then the button is not checked, a value of 1 means the button is checked:

```
int Result = Button_GetCheck(GetDlgItem(hwnd,
                             ID_CHECKBOX));
if (Result == 0)
  strcpy(S, "Button not Checked");
else
  strcpy(S, "Button Checked");
```

Listing 11.2 shows the code to the check box example. Remember that you can create a module definition file and a makefile for this program simply by borrowing the relevant code from the WINDOW1 example on Day 3.

Listing 11.2. A simple check box example.

```cpp
//////////////////////////////////////////////////////////
//   Program Name: ChkBox1.cpp
//   Copyright  1993 by Charlie Calvert
//   Description: Simple Edit Example
//   Date: 12/19/93
//   UpDate: 05/24/95
//////////////////////////////////////////////////////////

#define STRICT
#define WIN32_LEAN_AND_MEAN
#include <windows.h>
#include <windowsx.h>
#include <string.h>
#pragma warning (disable: 4068)
// --------------------------------------------------------
// Interface
// --------------------------------------------------------

LRESULT CALLBACK WndProc(HWND hwnd, UINT Message, WPARAM wParam, LPARAM lParam);
BOOL Register(HINSTANCE hInst);
HWND Create(HINSTANCE hInst, int nCmdShow);

// Controls IDs
#define ID_CHECKBOX 101
#define ID_CLEARBUTTON 102
#define ID_SETBUTTON 103
#define ID_GETBUTTON 104

// Declarations for class ChkBox1
#define ChkBox1_DefProc    DefWindowProc
BOOL ChkBox1_OnCreate(HWND hwnd, CREATESTRUCT FAR* lpCreateStruct);
void ChkBox1_OnDestroy(HWND hwnd);
void ChkBox1_OnCommand(HWND hwnd, int id, HWND hwndCtl, UINT codeNotify);
static char szAppName[] = "ChkBox1";
static HWND MainWindow;
static HINSTANCE hInstance;

// --------------------------------------------------------
// Initialization
// --------------------------------------------------------

///////////////////////////////////////
// Program entry point
///////////////////////////////////////
#pragma argsused
int WINAPI WinMain(HINSTANCE hInst, HINSTANCE hPrevInstance, LPSTR lpszCmdParam,
int nCmdShow)
{
  MSG  Msg;

  if (!hPrevInstance)
    if (!Register(hInst))
      return FALSE;
```

11

continues

Listing 11.2. continued

```
    MainWindow = Create(hInst, nCmdShow);
    if (!MainWindow)
      return FALSE;

    while (GetMessage(&Msg, NULL, 0, 0))
    {
      TranslateMessage(&Msg);
      DispatchMessage(&Msg);
    }

    return Msg.wParam;
}


///////////////////////////////////////
// Register the window
///////////////////////////////////////
BOOL Register(HINSTANCE hInst)
{
  WNDCLASS WndClass;

  WndClass.style          - CS_HREDRAW | CS_VREDRAW;
  WndClass.lpfnWndProc    = WndProc;
  WndClass.cbClsExtra     = 0;
  WndClass.cbWndExtra     = 0;
  WndClass.hInstance      = hInst;
  WndClass.hIcon          = LoadIcon(NULL, IDI_APPLICATION);
  WndClass.hCursor        = LoadCursor(NULL, IDC_ARROW);
  WndClass.hbrBackground  = (HBRUSH)(COLOR_WINDOW+1);
  WndClass.lpszMenuName    = NULL;
  WndClass.lpszClassName  = szAppName;

  return (RegisterClass (&WndClass) != 0);
}


///////////////////////////////////////
// Create the window
///////////////////////////////////////
HWND Create(HINSTANCE hInst, int nCmdShow)
{

  hInstance = hInst;

  HWND hwnd = CreateWindow(szAppName, szAppName,
                  WS_OVERLAPPEDWINDOW,
                  CW_USEDEFAULT, CW_USEDEFAULT,
                  CW_USEDEFAULT, CW_USEDEFAULT,
                  NULL, NULL, hInst, NULL);

  if (hwnd == NULL)
    return hwnd;

  ShowWindow(hwnd, nCmdShow);
  UpdateWindow(hwnd);
```

```
    return hwnd;
}

// -------------------------------------------------------
// WndProc and Implementation
// -------------------------------------------------------

/////////////////////////////////////
// The Window Procedure
/////////////////////////////////////
LRESULT CALLBACK WndProc(HWND hwnd, UINT Message, WPARAM wParam, LPARAM lParam)
{
  switch(Message)
  {
    HANDLE_MSG(hwnd, WM_CREATE, ChkBox1_OnCreate);
    HANDLE_MSG(hwnd, WM_DESTROY, ChkBox1_OnDestroy);
    HANDLE_MSG(hwnd, WM_COMMAND, ChkBox1_OnCommand);
    default: return ChkBox1_DefProc(hwnd, Message, wParam, lParam);
  }
}


/////////////////////////////////////
// Handle WM_CREATE
/////////////////////////////////////
#pragma argsused
BOOL ChkBox1_OnCreate(HWND hwnd, CREATESTRUCT FAR* lpCreateStruct)
{
  CreateWindow("button", "Clear Button",
               WS_CHILD | WS_VISIBLE | BS_PUSHBUTTON,
               10, 7, 120, 30, hwnd, HMENU(ID_CLEARBUTTON),
               hInstance, NULL);

  CreateWindow("button", "Set Button",
               WS_CHILD | WS_VISIBLE | BS_PUSHBUTTON,
               140, 7, 120, 30, hwnd, HMENU(ID_SETBUTTON),
               hInstance, NULL);

  CreateWindow("button", "Button Status",
               WS_CHILD | WS_VISIBLE | BS_PUSHBUTTON,
               270, 7, 120,30, hwnd, HMENU(ID_GETBUTTON),
               hInstance, NULL);

  CreateWindow("button", "Generic CheckBox",
               WS_CHILD | WS_VISIBLE | BS_AUTOCHECKBOX,
               10, 50, 410, 30, hwnd, HMENU(ID_CHECKBOX),
               hInstance, NULL);

  return TRUE;
}

/////////////////////////////////////
// Handle WM_DESTROY
/////////////////////////////////////
#pragma argsused
void ChkBox1_OnDestroy(HWND hwnd)
```

11

continues

Listing 11.2. continued

```
{
  PostQuitMessage(0);
}

//////////////////////////////////////
// Handle WM_COMMAND
//////////////////////////////////////
#pragma argsused
void ChkBox1_OnCommand(HWND hwnd, int id, HWND hwndCtl, UINT codeNotify)
{
  char S[100];

  switch (id)
  {
    case ID_SETBUTTON:
      Button_SetCheck(GetDlgItem(hwnd, ID_CHECKBOX), 1);
      break;

    case ID_CLEARBUTTON:
      Button_SetCheck(GetDlgItem(hwnd, ID_CHECKBOX), 0);
      break;

    case ID_GETBUTTON:
      int Result = Button_GetCheck(GetDlgItem(hwnd, ID_CHECKBOX));
      if (Result == 0)
        strcpy(S, "Button not Checked");
      else
        strcpy(S, "Button Checked");
      MessageBox(hwnd, S, "Button Status", MB_OK | MB_ICONINFORMATION);
      break;
  }
}
```

Radio Buttons

Radio buttons usually appear in groups of two or more, and as a result, they should be placed inside a group box so that the user will know which buttons work together as a unit. The buttons should always be arranged so that no more than one button in a group can be selected at a time.

The start of each group is designated by giving the first control in the group the WS_GROUP style. For instance, in the included example program the first control in the window and the first radio button control are each assigned the WS_GROUP style. If the program added a second group of radio buttons, or if it added any other control beneath the last radio button, then the next radio button or other control added should also have the WS_GROUP style. Specifically, if there were three groups of radio buttons, each containing three radio buttons, then the first member of each group should have the WS_GROUP style. Furthermore, if a button were placed beneath the last group of radio buttons, then that button also should be given the WS_GROUP style.

To create a radio button, first create a group box, and then create the radio button itself. To create a group box, create a window of class `button` and then assign it the `BS_GROUPBOX` style. To create a radio button, create a window of class `"button"` and assign it the `BS_RADIOBUTTON` or `BS_AUTORADIOBUTTON` style:

```
CreateWindow("button", "GroupBox with Auto-Tabbing",
             WS_CHILD | WS_VISIBLE | BS_GROUPBOX,
             10, 50, 320, 90, hwnd, NULL,
             hInstance, NULL);

HWND GWnd = CreateWindow("button", "Generic CheckBox1",
             WS_CHILD | WS_VISIBLE | WS_GROUP |
             WS_TABSTOP | BS_AUTORADIOBUTTON,
             20, 70, 200, 30, hwnd, HMENU(ID_RADBTN1),
             hInstance, NULL);
```

Group boxes have no real functionality in your program. They are there simply to help the user understand how your code works.

Use the `CheckRadioButton` API function to switch on a radio button. This function will automatically clear the settings of any other radio button in a group. The `CheckRadioButton` function takes four parameters. The first is the `HWND` of the window where the button resides. The second is the ID of the first radio button in a group, and the third parameter is the ID of the last radio button in a group. The fourth parameter is the ID of the button you want to set:

```
CheckRadioButton(hwnd, ID_RADBTN1, ID_RADBTN2, ID_RADBTN1);
```

If you want to tweak the settings of a particular radio button without changing any other buttons in a group, then you can use the WindowsX `Button_SetCheck` macro. This macro takes the `HWND` of the radio button in its first parameter. The second parameter is set to 0 if you want to turn the button off, and to 1 if you want to set the button. You can retrieve the `HWND` of the button via the handy `GetDlgItem` function, which works equally well in windows or in dialogs:

```
GWnd := GetDlgItem(hwnd, ID_RadioBtn);
Button_SetCheck(GWnd, 1);
```

You can use the WindowsX `Button_GetCheck` macro to query a radio button as to its current state:

```
int Result = Button_GetCheck(GetDlgItem(hwnd, ID_RADBTN1));
```

The return value is set to 0 if the button is cleared, and to 1 if it is set.

The last thing you need to know about radio buttons is how to tab through a series of them when they are placed in a window. The key to this process is to introduce the `IsDialogMessage` function into the program's `message` loop:

```
while (GetMessage(&Msg, NULL, 0, 0))
{
  if (!IsDialogMessage(MainWindow, &Msg))
  {
```

```
      TranslateMessage(&Msg);
      DispatchMessage(&Msg);
   }
 }
```

IsDialogMessage sends a `WM_GETDLGCODE` message to each control in the window. Unless one of the controls replies by saying that it wants to handle its own tabbing messages, `IsDialogMessage` will take over those chores. The end result is that the user will be able to tab to any control that has the `WS_TABSTOP` style. Needless to say, you should always set the `WS_TABSTOP` style in the first radio button in a group, and also in any other control that you want to be part of the programs tabbing loop.

The code in Listing 11.3 demonstrates how to use two or more radio button controls in a window. Remember that you can create a module definition file and a makefile for this program simply by borrowing the relevant code from the WINDOW1 example on Day 3, and then changing each instance of the term WINDOW1 to RADBTN1.

Listing 11.3. A simple radio button example.

```
/////////////////////////////////////////////////////////////
// Program Name: RadBtn1.cpp
// Copyright  1993 by Charlie Calvert
// Description: RadioButtons and Tabbing Example
//              Tabbing comes from IsDialogMessage
// Date: 12/19/93
// Update for WIN32 05/24/95
/////////////////////////////////////////////////////////////

#define STRICT
#define WIN32_LEAN_AND_MEAN
#include <windows.h>
#include <windowsx.h>
#include <string.h>
#pragma warning (disable: 4068)
// -------------------------------------------------------
// Interface
// -------------------------------------------------------

LRESULT CALLBACK WndProc(HWND hwnd, UINT Message, WPARAM wParam, LPARAM lParam);
BOOL Register(HINSTANCE hInst);
HWND Create(HINSTANCE hInst, int nCmdShow);

// Controls IDs
#define ID_RADBTN1 101
#define ID_RADBTN2 102
#define ID_SETBUTTON1 103
#define ID_SETBUTTON2 104
#define ID_GETBUTTON 105

// Declarations for class RadBtn1
#define RadBtn1_DefProc     DefWindowProc
BOOL RadBtn1_OnCreate(HWND hwnd, CREATESTRUCT FAR* lpCreateStruct);
```

```
void RadBtn1_OnDestroy(HWND hwnd);
void RadBtn1_OnCommand(HWND hwnd, int id, HWND hwndCtl, UINT codeNotify);
static char szAppName[] = "RadBtn1";
static HWND MainWindow;
static HINSTANCE hInstance;


// ------------------------------------------------------
// Initialization
// ------------------------------------------------------

/////////////////////////////////////
// Program entry point
/////////////////////////////////////
#pragma argsused
int WINAPI WinMain(HINSTANCE hInst, HINSTANCE hPrevInstance, LPSTR lpszCmdParam,
int nCmdShow)
{
  MSG  Msg;

  if (!hPrevInstance)
    if (!Register(hInst))
      return FALSE;

  MainWindow = Create(hInst, nCmdShow);
  if (!MainWindow)
    return FALSE;

  while (GetMessage(&Msg, NULL, 0, 0))
  {
    if (!IsDialogMessage(MainWindow, &Msg))
    {
      TranslateMessage(&Msg);
      DispatchMessage(&Msg);
    }
  }

  return Msg.wParam;
}


/////////////////////////////////////
// Register the window
/////////////////////////////////////
BOOL Register(HINSTANCE hInst)
{
  WNDCLASS WndClass;

  WndClass.style          = CS_HREDRAW | CS_VREDRAW;
  WndClass.lpfnWndProc    = WndProc;
  WndClass.cbClsExtra     = 0;
  WndClass.cbWndExtra     = 0;
  WndClass.hInstance      = hInst;
  WndClass.hIcon          = LoadIcon(NULL, IDI_APPLICATION);
  WndClass.hCursor        = LoadCursor(NULL, IDC_ARROW);
  WndClass.hbrBackground  = (HBRUSH)(COLOR_WINDOW+1);
```

11

continues

Listing 11.3. continued

```
  WndClass.lpszMenuName   = NULL;
  WndClass.lpszClassName = szAppName;

  return (RegisterClass (&WndClass) != 0);
}


////////////////////////////////////
// Create the window
////////////////////////////////////
HWND Create(HINSTANCE hInst, int nCmdShow)
{

  hInstance = hInst;

  HWND hwnd = CreateWindow(szAppName, "RadioButtons and Tabbing",
                  WS_OVERLAPPEDWINDOW,
                  CW_USEDEFAULT, CW_USEDEFAULT,
                  CW_USEDEFAULT, CW_USEDEFAULT,
                  NULL, NULL, hInst, NULL);

  if (hwnd == NULL)
    return hwnd;

  ShowWindow(hwnd, nCmdShow);
  UpdateWindow(hwnd);

  return hwnd;
}

// ---------------------------------------------------------
// WndProc and Implementation
// ---------------------------------------------------------


////////////////////////////////////
// The Window Procedure
////////////////////////////////////
LRESULT CALLBACK WndProc(HWND hwnd, UINT Message, WPARAM wParam, LPARAM lParam)
{
  switch(Message)
  {
    HANDLE_MSG(hwnd, WM_CREATE, RadBtn1_OnCreate);
    HANDLE_MSG(hwnd, WM_DESTROY, RadBtn1_OnDestroy);
    HANDLE_MSG(hwnd, WM_COMMAND, RadBtn1_OnCommand);
    default: return RadBtn1_DefProc(hwnd, Message, wParam, lParam);
  }
}


////////////////////////////////////
// Handle WM_CREATE
////////////////////////////////////
#pragma argsused
BOOL RadBtn1_OnCreate(HWND hwnd, CREATESTRUCT FAR* lpCreateStruct)
{
```

```
    CreateWindow("button", "Set Button 1",
            WS_CHILD | WS_VISIBLE | WS_GROUP |
                WS_TABSTOP | BS_PUSHBUTTON,
                10, 7, 120, 30, hwnd, HMENU(ID_SETBUTTON1),
                hInstance, NULL);

    CreateWindow("button", "Set Button 2",
                WS_CHILD | WS_VISIBLE |
                WS_TABSTOP | BS_PUSHBUTTON,
                140, 7, 120, 30, hwnd, HMENU(ID_SETBUTTON2),
                hInstance, NULL);

    CreateWindow("button", "Button Status",
                WS_CHILD | WS_VISIBLE |
                WS_TABSTOP | BS_DEFPUSHBUTTON,
                270, 7, 120,30, hwnd, HMENU(ID_GETBUTTON),
                hInstance, NULL);

    CreateWindow("button", "GroupBox with Auto-Tabbing",
                WS_CHILD | WS_VISIBLE | BS_GROUPBOX,
                10, 50, 320, 90, hwnd, NULL,
                hInstance, NULL);

    HWND GWnd = CreateWindow("button", "Generic CheckBox1",
            WS_CHILD | WS_VISIBLE | WS_GROUP |
            WS_TABSTOP | BS_AUTORADIOBUTTON,
                20, 70, 200, 30, hwnd, HMENU(ID_RADBTN1),
                hInstance, NULL);

    CreateWindow("button", "Generic CheckBox2",
                WS_CHILD | WS_VISIBLE | BS_AUTORADIOBUTTON,
                20, 100, 200, 30, hwnd, HMENU(ID_RADBTN2),
                hInstance, NULL);

    Button_SetCheck(GWnd, 1);

    return TRUE;
}

/////////////////////////////////////
// Handle WM_DESTROY
/////////////////////////////////////
#pragma argsused
void RadBtn1_OnDestroy(HWND hwnd)
{
    PostQuitMessage(0);
}

/////////////////////////////////////
// Handle WM_COMMAND
/////////////////////////////////////
#pragma argsused
void RadBtn1_OnCommand(HWND hwnd, int id, HWND hwndCtl, UINT codeNotify)
{
    char S[100];
```

continues

Talking to Controls

```
switch (id)
{
  case ID_SETBUTTON1:
    CheckRadioButton(hwnd, ID_RADBTN1, ID_RADBTN2, ID_RADBTN1);
    break;

  case ID_SETBUTTON2:
    CheckRadioButton(hwnd, ID_RADBTN1, ID_RADBTN2, ID_RADBTN2);
    break;

  case ID_GETBUTTON:
    int Result = Button_GetCheck(GetDlgItem(hwnd, ID_RADBTN1));
    if (Result == 0)
      strcpy(S, "First Button not Checked");
    else
      strcpy(S, "First Button Checked");
    MessageBox(hwnd, S, "Button Status", MB_OK | MB_ICONINFORMATION);
    break;
}
}
```

Summary

This chapter covers a lot of ground. You've learned about communicating with static controls, list boxes, check boxes, and edit controls. You've had another look at fonts and learned how to put them at your absolute beck and call with the EnumFontFamilies and GetTextMetrics calls.

By now you should be getting the sense that you have the ability to completely control your presentation of textual materials. You know all about LOGFONTs, TEXTMETRICs, and the EnumFontFamilies callbacks. This knowledge should help you convey written information to users with all the punch and flash you could ever desire.

I'm aware that some of the information about controls has come at you fairly fast and furious. Don't worry; rather than racing on to another topic, I'm going to slow the pace here a bit. On Day 12, "Window Controls and the Control Message API," you'll get a second look at Windows controls, and you'll get a chance to see how they can be used to manipulate directory information.

Q&A

Q I still really don't understand the EnumFontFamProc. Please say something to help clear the fog.

A When you work with callbacks, one of the key things you need to know is how to set up the mailbox to which information will be mailed. Not just any mailbox will do.

There has to be one with a particular set of characteristics. More specifically, Windows expects the function to which it sends information to have a certain number of arguments of a particular type. The EnumFontFamProc function defines what those types are, so you'll know how to set up the mailbox. The actual name, EnumFontFamProc, is just a placeholder reserving space for the name you want to give to the function. You can call it virtually anything you want.

Q You've given me two long lists of constants associated with list boxes. I can't make sense of them all. What gives?

A In the last chapter, I listed the *styles* you can apply to list boxes. You can pass list box styles (LBS), such as LBS_STANDARD or LBS_MULTIPLESEL, to CreateWindow when you want to design a particular type of list box. However, when you want to communicate with a list box, use the list box messages (LB) that are listed in this chapter: LB_GETSEL, LB_GETTEXT, and LB_SETSEL. Obviously, there's not much of an advantage in trying to memorize all the different messages that can be sent to a control. Instead, you should remember that there are two types of constants associated with each control. One type helps define its style and appearance. These types are used with CreateWindow. The second type helps you communicate with a control. These constants are used with SendMessage or PostMessage. For me, the best way to keep track of these messages is either through the online help, or by browsing through the WINDOWS.H complex.

Q Why is the second parameter to EnumFontFamilies empty the first time you call it, and filled the second?

A This question lies very much at the heart of this chapter. When you call EnumFontFamilies with the second parameter blank, the function enumerates all the fonts on the system, taking care to create a sample LOGFONT for each type. When you fill in the lpszFamily parameter, Windows retrieves information about a particular font. In both cases, the sample fonts retrieved are designed by Windows. If you want, you can study the actual LOGFONT structure that Windows creates either inside a debugger, or inside the FontsExp program.

Workshop

The Workshop provides quiz questions to help you solidify your understanding of the material covered and exercises to provide you with experience in using what you've learned. Try to understand the quiz and exercise answers before continuing on to Day 12. Answers are provided in Appendix A.

Quiz

1. How can you tell Windows to give a particular control the focus?

2. What is the difference between PostMessage and SendMessage?

3. What do you think the letters BM, in BM_SETCHECK, stand for?

4. How can you find out what to do with the WPARAM and LPARAM portions of an LB_GETTEXT message?

5. What is a callback?

6. What's the purpose of the prolog code created by MakeProcInstance?

7. Every call to MakeProcInstance must be matched by a call to _____?

8. How do you create a message with a unique identifier?

9. If a particular window class has only one user-defined message, what numerical value normally is associated with it?

10. What happens if you send a BM_GETCHECK message to the main window of the FontsExp program?

Exercises

1. Use the information retrieved by FontsExp to create a program that writes two strings to the screen, one using the New Times Roman font, and the second using WingDings. Hard code valid LOGFONTs for these fonts into your program.

2. Add additional static controls to the FontsExp program that displays the currently selected text's height and weight.

WEEK
2

Window Controls and the Control Message API

My primary purpose in this chapter is to give you additional exposure to window controls. In particular, you will get

- More information on radio buttons and an introduction to group boxes
- More information on how to use the WindowsX control message APIs in lieu of the SendMessage function
- Code demonstrating how to tab back and forth between window controls
- Code showing how to group controls together
- Code showing how to use ExitWindows to create a program that can log the user off from the current Windows session
- A brief introduction to the WM_PARENTNOTIFY message

The example program for this chapter, FileBox, enables the user to examine the contents of a subdirectory, change subdirectories, and launch another program. In 16-bit Windows, it can be used as a rudimentary substitute for the Program Manager.

Once again, the discussion of this program will be spread over two chapters. Chapter 13, "Subclassing Windows Controls," is devoted to four primary topics:

- Subclassing, a technique for changing the default behavior of a control
- An introduction to push buttons
- Using special properties of list boxes to aid in file management
- Controlling the size of a window with WM_GETMINMAXINFO messages

Creating a Windows Shell

When designing the FileBox program, my primary goal was to produce a program that demonstrates how to use window controls. In particular, I wanted to show how to subclass a window control and how to use push buttons, radio buttons, and some advanced features of list boxes.

Of course, it's always nice to spice up these example programs by giving them some additional functionality. One interesting trait of the FileBox program is that it can be used as a clumsy temporary substitute for the 16-bit Windows Program Manager or for the whole complex of files surrounding the Windows 95 Start button and Explorer.

It's helpful for programmers to understand exactly what function is served by the Program Manager and Explorer. It's a programmer's job to peer beneath the surface of the operating environment to see how things actually work.

I remember the surprise I felt the first time I started using my own program in lieu of the 16 Program Manager. It was a bit of a seminal event for me, marking one of the moments when I felt I was starting to get some real control over the operating system.

My surprise was even greater when I saw what happened when I changed the shell statement under Windows 95. It's amazing to see that the whole complex interface to Windows 95 is only a thin shell that we can replace with our own programs. Ah…to see beneath the surface! That's one of the great joys of programming. As a special bonus, when I run FileBox as the Windows shell, I finally get the kind of behavior I expect and want when I minimize applications. The program itself is shown in Figure 12.1.

Figure 12.1.
The FileBox program functioning as a Windows shell.

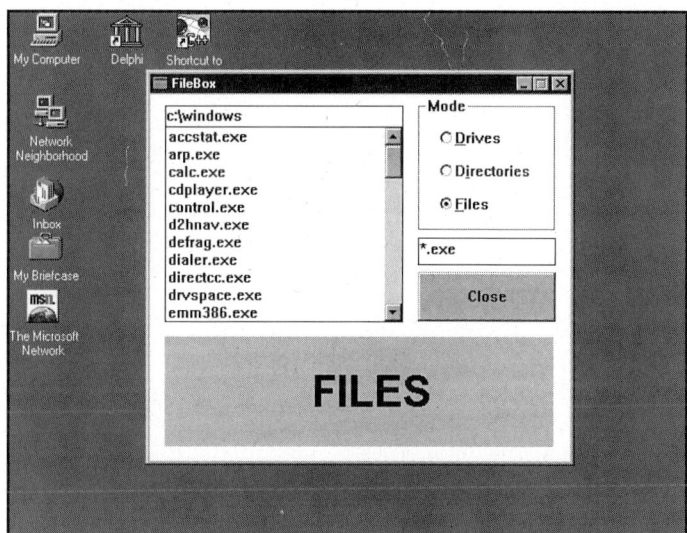

To use the FileBox program as a Windows shell, open the SYSTEM.INI file, in the Windows subdirectory, and change the line

```
shell=progman.exe  ; 16 bit windows
```

or

```
shell=explorer.exe ; Windows 95
```

so that it reads like this:

```
shell=c:\w21code\filebox\filebox.exe
```

where *c:\w21code\filebox* is the path to your copy of the FileBox program.

The next time you start Windows, the FileBox program will pop up instead of the Start menu or instead of the Program Manager. Now all you need to do is iterate through the subdirectories on the hard drive until you find an executable file that you want to run. Double-click the filename, and it will start up just as a file starts up when you double-click its icon in the Program Manager. Note that FileBox has three modes: one that lets you view directories, one that lets you view drives, and one that lets you view files. When viewing files, you can use a mask to specify the types of files you want to view.

Note: Because spelunking expeditions of this type can get you in trouble, Windows 95 programmers should remember that you can press F8 during system boot-up, and then start the system in DOS mode, and reset SYSTEM.INI so that it brings up the Explorer complex of programs.

In this discussion, I'm assuming that you are running Windows 95, Win3.1, or Win3.0 for DOS. If you are running Windows NT, the FileBox program may not work for you as a Program Manager substitute. You can, however, still run it as an ordinary Windows program.

You've probably noticed that when you choose Shut Down from the Start menu, or when you close the Program Manager, messages are sent out asking all the other applications to close. In the listing for the FileBox program, I don't include code that will reproduce this feature. I omit it because I don't want you to be accidentally shutting down the whole system every time you experiment with the FileBox program. In other words, the primary purpose of this program is to teach you about Windows controls. FileBox's second life as a Windows shell is only a sideshow. You can however, still run the program as a shell, then shut down the system by pressing Ctrl+Alt+Delete.

At any rate, if you want to imitate the Start Menu's or the Program Manager's behavior at closing time, make a few minor changes to FileBox's WM_CLOSE message handler function:

```
void FileBox_OnClose(HWND hwnd)
{
  if (MessageBox(hwnd, "Exit Windows?", "FileBox",
                 MB_ICONQUESTION | MB_OKCANCEL) == IDOK)
  {
    if (ExitWindows(0, 0))
      DestroyWindow(hwnd);
  }
}
```

All the magic is in the call to ExitWindows, which works under 16-bit Windows or under Windows 95. Note, however, that there is a similar function called ExitWindowsEx. This latter routine gives you access to some of the advanced features of Windows 95.

The *ExitWindows* and *ExitWindowsEx* Functions

Syntax

```
BOOL ExitWindows(DWORD, UNIT)
```

The ExitWindows function is used to log the current user off the system. It takes two parameters:

```
DWORD reserved;        /* reserved  */
UINT reserved;         /* reserved  */
```

You should set both of these parameters to 0 when using this function. Note that it does not shut down the whole system, but simply logs you off. It's like the "Close all windows and log on as a different user" option that you can get from the Shut Down dialog on the Windows 95 Start menu.

Here is a related function that gives you access to some of the powerful features of Windows 95 and Windows NT:

```
BOOL ExitWindowsEx(
    UINT   fuOptions,      // shutdown operation
    DWORD  dwReserved      // reserved
    );
```

ExitWindowsEx can be used to shut down or restart Windows. This routine will appeal to programmers who want to build a truly useful Windows 95 shell.

The first parameter to ExitWindowsEx can take one of the following values, as explained in this excerpt from the online help:

EWX_FORCE	Forces processes to terminate. Instead of bringing up the "application not responding" dialog box for the user, this value forces an application to terminate if it does not respond.
EWX_LOGOFF	Shuts down all processes running in the security context of the process that called the ExitWindowsEx function. Then it logs the user off.
EWX_POWEROFF	Shuts down the system and turns off the power. The application must have the SE_SHUTDOWN_NAME privilege, and the system must support the power-off feature.
EWX_REBOOT	Shuts down the system and then restarts the system. The application must have the SE_SHUTDOWN_NAME privilege.
EWX_SHUTDOWN	Shuts down the system to a point at which it is safe to turn off the power. All file buffers have been flushed to disk, and all running processes have stopped. The application must have the SE_SHUTDOWN_NAME privilege.

For more information on SE_SHUTDOWN_NAME, see the online help for both WindowsEx and AdjustTokenPrivileges.

Here is a practical example of how to use `ExitWindows`:

```
if (ExitWindows(0, 0))
  DestroyWindow(hwnd);
```

Before showing you the code for FileBox, I'll mention that it's a bit like the first version of the Snake program. It's designed to pique your interest, to titillate. Only the most rudimentary functionality is built into the FileBox program. If you want to create a Windows shell that's tailor-made to your own needs, FileBox can show you how to get started. There is no better way to learn how to program Windows than to actually sit down and design and implement your own programs.

The Code

Now that the preliminaries are out of the way, you can have some fun with a little bit of code that actually does something potentially useful. Listings 12.1 through 12.6 provide the source code for this example.

Listing 12.1. The FileBox program can be used as a Windows shell.

```
/////////////////////////////////////////
//   Program Name: FILEBOX.CPP
//   Copyright (c) 1995 by Charlie Calvert
//   Description: FileBox windows program
//   Last Modified: 07/29/95
/////////////////////////////////////////

#define STRICT
#define WIN32_LEAN_AND_MEAN
#include <windows.h>
#include <windowsx.h>
#pragma warning (disable: 4068)
#pragma hdrstop
#include <direct.h>
#include <string.h>
#include "filebox.h"

// --------------------------------------------
// Interface
// --------------------------------------------

// Variables
static char szAppName[] = "FileBox";
static HWND MainWindow;
static HINSTANCE hInstance;

char *ButtonText[] = {"&Drives", "D&irectories", "&Files"};
char *BmpName[] = {"DRIVES", "DIRS", "FILES"};
WORD DirShowVal[] = {DDL_DRIVES | DDL_EXCLUSIVE, DDL_DIRECTORY
                     | DDL_EXCLUSIVE, DDL_ARCHIVE};
HWND hControl[8];
```

```
HBITMAP Bmp[3];
HWND PathWin;
FARPROC lpfnNewEditProc;
char FilesWildCard[100];
HBRUSH BtnBrush;

// ----------------------------------------------------------
// Initialization
// ----------------------------------------------------------


////////////////////////////////////////
// Program entry point
////////////////////////////////////////
#pragma argsused
int WINAPI WinMain(HINSTANCE hInst, HINSTANCE hPrevInstance,
                   LPSTR   lpszCmdParam, int nCmdShow)
{
  MSG   Msg;


  if (!hPrevInstance)
    if (!Register(hInst))
      return FALSE;

  SetMessageQueue(20);

  MainWindow = Create(hInst, nCmdShow);
  if (!MainWindow)
    return FALSE;

  while (GetMessage(&Msg, NULL, 0, 0))
  {
    if (!IsDialogMessage(MainWindow, &Msg))
    {
      TranslateMessage(&Msg);
      DispatchMessage(&Msg);
    }
  }
  return Msg.wParam;
}


////////////////////////////////////////
// Register the window
////////////////////////////////////////
BOOL Register(HINSTANCE hInst)
{
  WNDCLASS WndClass;

  WndClass.style          = CS_HREDRAW | CS_VREDRAW;
  WndClass.lpfnWndProc    = WndProc;
  WndClass.cbClsExtra     = 0;
  WndClass.cbWndExtra     = 0;
  WndClass.hInstance      = hInst;
  WndClass.hIcon          = LoadIcon(NULL, IDI_APPLICATION);
  WndClass.hCursor        = LoadCursor(NULL, IDC_ARROW);
  WndClass.hbrBackground  = HBRUSH(COLOR_BTNFACE+1);
```

continues

Listing 12.1. continued

```
    WndClass.lpszMenuName  = NULL;
    WndClass.lpszClassName = szAppName;

    return (RegisterClass (&WndClass) != 0);
}

/////////////////////////////////////
// Create the window
/////////////////////////////////////
HWND Create(HINSTANCE hInst, int nCmdShow)
{

    hInstance = hInst;

    HWND hwnd = CreateWindow(szAppName, szAppName,
                        WS_OVERLAPPED ¦ WS_CAPTION ¦ WS_SYSMENU ¦
                        WS_MINIMIZEBOX ¦ WS_THICKFRAME,
                        CW_USEDEFAULT, CW_USEDEFAULT,
                        CW_USEDEFAULT, CW_USEDEFAULT,
                          NULL, NULL, hInst, NULL);

    if (hwnd == NULL)
      return hwnd;

    ShowWindow(hwnd, nCmdShow);
    UpdateWindow(hwnd);

    return hwnd;
}

// ----------------------------------------------------------
// WndProc and Implementation
// ----------------------------------------------------------

/////////////////////////////////////
// The Window Procedure
/////////////////////////////////////
LRESULT CALLBACK WndProc(HWND hwnd, UINT Message,
                         WPARAM wParam, LPARAM lParam)
{
  switch(Message)
  {
    HANDLE_MSG(hwnd, WM_CREATE, CopyAll_OnCreate);
    HANDLE_MSG(hwnd, WM_DESTROY, FileBox_OnDestroy);
    HANDLE_MSG(hwnd, WM_CLOSE, FileBox_OnClose);
    HANDLE_MSG(hwnd, WM_COMMAND, FileBox_OnCommand);
    HANDLE_MSG(hwnd, WM_GETMINMAXINFO, FileBox_OnGetMinMaxInfo);
    HANDLE_MSG(hwnd, WM_PAINT, FileBox_OnPaint);
    HANDLE_MSG(hwnd, WM_PARENTNOTIFY, FileBox_OnParentNotify);
    HANDLE_MSG(hwnd, WM_RBUTTONDOWN, FileBox_OnRButtonDown);
    #ifdef WIN32
    HANDLE_MSG(hwnd, WM_CTLCOLORBTN, FileBox_OnCtlColor);
    HANDLE_MSG(hwnd, WM_CTLCOLORSTATIC, FileBox_OnCtlColor);
    #else
```

```
      HANDLE_MSG(hwnd, WM_CTLCOLOR, FileBox_OnCtlColor);
    #endif
    default:
      return FileBox_DefProc(hwnd, Message, wParam, lParam);
  }
}

/////////////////////////////////////
// Create the Callback procedures
/////////////////////////////////////
void MakeCallBackProcs()
{
  #ifdef WIN32
  OldEditProc = (WNDPROC)SetWindowLong(hControl[ID_EDIT],
                       GWL_WNDPROC, LONG(NewEditProc));
  #else
  lpfnNewEditProc = MakeProcInstance((FARPROC)NewEditProc, hInstance);
  OldEditProc = (WNDPROC)SetWindowLong(hControl[ID_EDIT],
                       GWL_WNDPROC, LONG(lpfnNewEditProc));
  #endif
}

/////////////////////////////////////
// Handle WM_Create
/////////////////////////////////////
#pragma argsused
BOOL CopyAll_OnCreate(HWND hwnd, CREATESTRUCT FAR* lpCreateStruct)
{

  BtnBrush = CreateSolidBrush(GetSysColor(COLOR_BTNFACE));

  for (int i = 0; i < 3; i++)
  {
    Bmp[i] = LoadBitmap(hInstance, BmpName[i]);
    if (!Bmp[i])
    {
      MessageBox(hwnd, "No Bitmap", "Fatal Error", MB_OK);
      return FALSE;
    }
  }

  hControl[ID_FILELIST] = CreateWindow("listbox", NULL,
                    WS_CHILD | WS_VISIBLE |
                    LBS_STANDARD | WS_TABSTOP,
                    15, 30, 220, 180, hwnd, HMENU(ID_FILELIST),
                    hInstance, NULL);

  hControl[ID_GROUP] = CreateWindow("button", "Mode",
                    WS_CHILD | WS_VISIBLE | BS_GROUPBOX,
                    250, 2, 131, 122, hwnd, HMENU(ID_GROUP),
                    hInstance, NULL);


  for (i = 0; i < 3; i++)
    hControl[i] = CreateWindow("button", ButtonText[i],
                    WS_CHILD | WS_VISIBLE | BS_AUTORADIOBUTTON,
```

12

continues

Listing 12.1. continued

```
                        270, 25 + (i * 30), 95, 30, hwnd,
                        HMENU(i + 100), hInstance, NULL);

  hControl[ID_EDIT]  = CreateWindow("edit", "*.exe",
                        WS_CHILD ¦ WS_VISIBLE ¦ WS_BORDER¦
                        WS_TABSTOP ¦ WS_GROUP,
                        250, 130, 131, 25, hwnd, HMENU(ID_EDIT),
                        hInstance, NULL);

  hControl[ID_CLOSE] = CreateWindow("button", "Close",
                        WS_CHILD ¦ WS_VISIBLE ¦ BS_PUSHBUTTON ¦
                        WS_TABSTOP ¦ WS_GROUP,
                        250, 161, 131, 45, hwnd, HMENU(ID_CLOSE),
                        hInstance, NULL);

  PathWin  = CreateWindow("static", NULL,
                        WS_CHILD ¦ WS_VISIBLE ¦ WS_BORDER,
                        14, 10, 222, 20, hwnd,
                        HMENU(ID_PATHS),  hInstance, NULL);

  DlgDirList(hwnd, "*.*", ID_FILELIST,
            ID_PATHS, DirShowVal[DirShowType]);

  MakeCallBackProcs();

  Button_SetCheck(hControl[0], TRUE);
  SetFocus(hControl[ID_FILELIST]);

  strcpy(FilesWildCard, "*.exe");

  return TRUE;
}

/////////////////////////////////////
// Handle WM_DESTROY
/////////////////////////////////////
#pragma argsused
void FileBox_OnDestroy(HWND hwnd)
{
  for (int i = 0; i < 3; i++)
    DeleteBitmap(Bmp[i]);

  DeleteBrush(BtnBrush);

  SetWindowLong(hControl[ID_EDIT], GWL_WNDPROC,
              LONG(OldEditProc));
  #ifndef WIN32
  FreeProcInstance(lpfnNewEditProc);
  #endif
  PostQuitMessage(0);
}

/////////////////////////////////////
// Handle WM_CLOSE
/////////////////////////////////////
```

```
void FileBox_OnClose(HWND hwnd)
{
  if (MessageBox(hwnd, "Do you want to exit?", "FileBox",
        MB_ICONQUESTION | MB_OKCANCEL) == IDOK)
  {
      DestroyWindow(hwnd);
  }
}

////////////////////////////////////
// SetListbox
////////////////////////////////////
#pragma argsused
void SetListbox(HWND hwnd)
{
  RECT R;
  char WildCard[150];

  if (DirShowType == FILEMODE)
    strcpy(WildCard, FilesWildCard);
  else
    strcpy(WildCard, "*.*");

  ListBox_ResetContent(hControl[ID_FILELIST]);
  ListBox_Dir(hControl[ID_FILELIST], DirShowVal[DirShowType],
              WildCard);

  R.left = 14;
  R.top = 220;
  R.right = 14 + BMPX;
  R.bottom = 220 + BMPY;
  InvalidateRect(hwnd, &R, FALSE);
}


////////////////////////////////////
// Handle MouseClick on listbox for DIR or DRIVE change
////////////////////////////////////

#pragma argsused
void HandleMouseClick(HWND hwnd, int id, HWND hwndCtl, UINT codeNotify)
{
  char Buffer[MAXSTR];

  DlgDirSelectEx(hwnd, Buffer, MAXSTR, ID_FILELIST);
  DlgDirList(hwnd, Buffer, ID_FILELIST, ID_PATHS,
             DirShowVal[DirShowType]);
}


////////////////////////////////////
// Handle WM_COMMAND
////////////////////////////////////
#pragma argsused
void FileBox_OnCommand(HWND hwnd, int id, HWND hwndCtl, UINT codeNotify)
```

12

continues

Listing 12.1. continued

```c
{
  char S[MAXSTR], lpszBuffer[MAXSTR];

  switch(id)
  {
    case ID_DRIVES + 100:
      DirShowType = DRIVEMODE;
      SetListbox(hwnd);
      break;

    case ID_DIRS + 100:
      DirShowType = DIRMODE;
      SetListbox(hwnd);
      break;

    case ID_FILES + 100:
      DirShowType = FILEMODE;
      SetListbox(hwnd);
      break;

    case ID_FILELIST:
      if (codeNotify == LBN_DBLCLK)
      {
        if (DirShowType != FILEMODE)
          HandleMouseClick(hwnd, id, hwndCtl, codeNotify);
        else
        {
          int index = ListBox_GetCurSel(hControl[ID_FILELIST]);
          _getdcwd(0, S, 125);
          ListBox_GetText(hControl[ID_FILELIST], index,
                          lpszBuffer);
          strcat(S, "\\");
          strcat(S, lpszBuffer);
          WinExec(S, SW_SHOWNORMAL);
        }
      }
      break;

    case ID_CLOSE:
      SendMessage(hwnd, WM_CLOSE, 0, 0);
      break;
  }
}

///////////////////////////////////////////////////////
// WM_CTLCOLOR
///////////////////////////////////////////////////////
#pragma argsused
HBRUSH FileBox_OnCtlColor(HWND hwnd, HDC hdc, HWND hwndChild, int type)
{
  switch (type)
  {
    case CTLCOLOR_STATIC:
    case CTLCOLOR_BTN:
```

```
      SetBkMode(hdc, TRANSPARENT);
      return BtnBrush;
  }
  return NULL;
}


///////////////////////////////////
// Handle WM_GetMinMaxInfo
///////////////////////////////////
#pragma argsused
void FileBox_OnGetMinMaxInfo(HWND hwnd, MINMAXINFO FAR* lpMinMaxInfo)
{
  lpMinMaxInfo->ptMaxSize.x = XSIZE;
  lpMinMaxInfo->ptMaxSize.y = YSIZE;
  lpMinMaxInfo->ptMaxPosition.x = 100;
  lpMinMaxInfo->ptMaxPosition.y = 100;
  lpMinMaxInfo->ptMinTrackSize.x = XSIZE;
  lpMinMaxInfo->ptMinTrackSize.y = YSIZE;
  lpMinMaxInfo->ptMaxTrackSize.x = XSIZE;
  lpMinMaxInfo->ptMaxTrackSize.y = YSIZE;
}

void HandleRightButton(HWND hwnd)
{
  switch(DirShowType)
  {
    case DRIVEMODE:
      Button_SetCheck(hControl[1], TRUE);
      Button_SetCheck(hControl[0], FALSE);
      Button_SetCheck(hControl[2], FALSE);
      DirShowType = DIRMODE;
      break;

    case DIRMODE:
      Button_SetCheck(hControl[2], TRUE);
      Button_SetCheck(hControl[0], FAL3E);
      Button_SetCheck(hControl[1], FALSE);
      DirShowType = FILEMODE;
      break;

    default:
      Button_SetCheck(hControl[0], TRUE);
      Button_SetCheck(hControl[1], FALSE);
      Button_SetCheck(hControl[2], FALSE);
      DirShowType = DRIVEMODE;
  }
  SetListbox(hwnd);
}

void HandleRightButton2(HWND hwnd)
{
  switch(DirShowType)
  {
    case DRIVEMODE:
      CheckRadioButton(hwnd, 100, 102, 100);
      DirShowType = DIRMODE;
```

continues

12

Listing 12.1. continued

```
        break;

    case DIRMODE:
      CheckRadioButton(hwnd, 100, 102, 101);
      DirShowType = FILEMODE;
      break;

    default:
      CheckRadioButton(hwnd, 100, 102, 102);
      DirShowType = DRIVEMODE;
      break;
  }
  SetListbox(hwnd);
}

////////////////////////////////////
// Handle WM_PAINT
////////////////////////////////////
void FileBox_OnPaint(HWND hwnd)
{
  PAINTSTRUCT PaintStruct;
  HBITMAP OldBmp;

  HDC PaintDC = BeginPaint(hwnd, &PaintStruct);
  HDC BltDC = CreateCompatibleDC(PaintDC);

  OldBmp = SelectBitmap(BltDC, Bmp[DirShowType]);
  BitBlt(PaintDC, 14, 220, BMPX, BMPY, BltDC, 0, 0, SRCCOPY);

  SelectBitmap(BltDC, OldBmp);
  DeleteDC(BltDC);
  EndPaint(hwnd, &PaintStruct);
};

////////////////////////////////////
// Handle WM_PARENTNOTIFY
////////////////////////////////////
#pragma argsused
void FileBox_OnParentNotify(HWND hwnd, UINT msg,
                            HWND hwndChild, int idChild)
{
  if (msg == WM_RBUTTONDOWN)
    HandleRightButton(hwnd);
}

////////////////////////////////////
// Handle WM_RBUTTONDOWN
////////////////////////////////////
#pragma argsused
void FileBox_OnRButtonDown(HWND hwnd, BOOL fDoubleClick,
                           int x, int y, UINT keyFlags)
{
  HandleRightButton(hwnd);
}
```

```
// ---------------------------------------------------------
// The SubClassed WNDPROCS
// ---------------------------------------------------------

void SetNewWildCard(HWND hwnd)
{
  char Buffer[150];

  GetWindowText(hwnd, Buffer, sizeof(Buffer));
  strcpy(FilesWildCard, Buffer);
  if (DirShowType == FILEMODE)
    SetListbox(MainWindow);
}

/////////////////////////////////////
// SubClassing for RadioButtons
/////////////////////////////////////
LRESULT CALLBACK NewEditProc(HWND hwnd, UINT Message,
                             WPARAM wParam, LPARAM lParam)
{
  switch(Message)
  {
    case WM_GETDLGCODE:
      return DLGC_WANTALLKEYS;

    case WM_CHAR:
      if (wParam == VK_TAB)
        return 0;
      break;

    case WM_KEYDOWN:
      switch (wParam)
      {
        case VK_RETURN:
          SetNewWildCard(hwnd);
          SetFocus(hControl[ID_CLOSE]);
          break;

        case VK_TAB:
          int State = GetKeyState(VK_SHIFT);
          if (State & 0x8000)
            SetFocus(hControl[DirShowType]);
          else
            SetFocus(hControl[ID_CLOSE]);
          break;
      }

      break;

    case WM_KILLFOCUS:
      SetNewWildCard(hwnd);
      break;

    case WM_SETFOCUS:
      Edit_SetSel(hwnd, 0, -1);
      break;
```

continues

Listing 12.1. continued

```
        }

    return
        CallWindowProc(OldEditProc, hwnd, Message, wParam, lParam);
}
```

Listing 12.2. FILEBOX.H.

```
/////////////////////////////////////
// Module: FileBox.h
// Copyright (c) 1995 by Charlie Calvert
// Last Modified: 07/29/95
/////////////////////////////////////

// Constants
#define ID_DRIVES 0
#define ID_DIRS 1
#define ID_FILES 2
#define ID_CLOSE 3
#define ID_FILELIST 4
#define ID_GROUP 5
#define ID_EDIT 6
#define ID_PATHS 7

#define BMPX 365
#define BMPY 100

#define XSIZE 403
#define YSIZE 360

#define MAXSTR 150

// Types
enum TCurMode {DRIVEMODE, DIRMODE, FILEMODE};

// Declarations for class FileBox
#define FileBox_DefProc     DefWindowProc
BOOL CopyAll_OnCreate(HWND hwnd,
                      CREATESTRUCT FAR* lpCreateStruct);
void FileBox_OnDestroy(HWND hwnd);
void FileBox_OnClose(HWND hwnd);
void FileBox_OnCommand(HWND hwnd, int id,
                      HWND hwndCtl, UINT codeNotify);
void FileBox_OnGetMinMaxInfo(HWND hwnd,
                      MINMAXINFO FAR* lpMinMaxInfo);
void FileBox_OnPaint(HWND hwnd);
void FileBox_OnParentNotify(HWND hwnd, UINT msg,
                      HWND hwndChild, int idChild);
void FileBox_OnRButtonDown(HWND hwnd, BOOL fDoubleClick,
                      int x, int y, UINT keyFlags);
HBRUSH FileBox_OnCtlColor(HWND hwnd, HDC hdc, HWND hwndChild, int type);
```

```
// Funcs
#ifdef WIN32
LRESULT CALLBACK WndProc(HWND hWindow, UINT Message,
                         WPARAM wParam, LPARAM lParam);
LRESULT CALLBACK NewEditProc(HWND hWindow, UINT Message,
                             WPARAM wParam, LPARAM lParam);
#else
LRESULT CALLBACK _export WndProc(HWND hWindow, UINT Message,
                                 WPARAM wParam, LPARAM lParam);
LRESULT CALLBACK _export NewEditProc(HWND hWindow, UINT Message,
                                     WPARAM wParam, LPARAM lParam);
#endif
void HandleRightButton(HWND hwnd);
BOOL Register(HINSTANCE hInst);
HWND Create(HINSTANCE hInst, int nCmdShow);
TCurMode DirShowType;
WNDPROC OldEditProc;
```

Listing 12.3. FILEBOX.RC.

```
1: DRIVES BITMAP "DRIVE.BMP"
2: FILES BITMAP "FILES.BMP"
3: DIRS BITMAP "DIRS.BMP"
```

Listing 12.4. FILEBOX.DEF.

```
1: ; FILEBOX.DEF
2:
3: NAME            FileBox
4: DESCRIPTION     'FileBox Window'
5: HEAPSIZE        10240
6: STACKSIZE       10240
7: CODE            PRELOAD MOVEABLE DISCARDABLE
8: DATA            PRELOAD MOVEABLE MULTIPLE
```

Listing 12.5. FILEBOX.MAK (Borland).

```
# FILEBOX makefile

APPNAME = FILEBOX
OBJS = $(APPNAME).obj
LIBS  =
BCROOT = $(MAKEDIR)\..
INCPATH= $(BCROOT)\INCLUDE
LIBPATH= $(BCROOT)\LIB


!if !$d(WIN16)
COMPILER = BCC32.EXE
RCCOMPLR = BRC32.EXE -w32
```

12

continues

Listing 12.5. continued

```
CFLAGS   = -H -W -v -w4
!else
COMPILER = BCC.EXE
RCCOMPLR = BRC.EXE
CFLAGS   = -H -W -ml -v -w4
!endif

# Link
$(APPNAME).exe: $(OBJS) $(APPNAME).def $(APPNAME).res
  $(COMPILER) -L$(LIBPATH) $(CFLAGS) $(OBJS) $(LIBS)
  $(RCCOMPLR) $(APPNAME).res

# Compile
.cpp.obj:
  $(COMPILER) -c $(CFLAGS) -I$(INCPATH) { $< }

# Resource
$(APPNAME).res : $(APPNAME).rc
  $(RCCOMPLR) -R -I$(INCPATH) $(APPNAME).RC
```

Listing 12.6. FILEBOX.MAK (Microsoft).

```
# FILEBOMS.MAK

APPNAME=FILEBOX
TARGETOS=WIN95
APPVER=4.0
OBJS=$(APPNAME).OBJ

!include <win32.mak>

all: $(APPNAME).exe

# Update the resource if necessary

$(APPNAME).res: $(APPNAME).rc $(APPNAME).h
  $(rc) $(rcflags) $(rcvars) $(APPNAME).rc

# Update the object files if necessary

# compile
.cpp.obj:
  $(cc) $(cflags) $(cvars) $(cdebug) $<

# Update the executable file if necessary.

$(APPNAME).exe: $(OBJS) $(APPNAME).res
  $(link) $(linkdebug) $(guiflags) -out:$(APPNAME).exe \
  $(OBJS) $(APPNAME).res $(guilibs) comctl32.lib
```

The following are the bitmaps used in FileBox:

DRIVES

DRIVES.BMP (365×100)

FILES

FILES.BMP (365×100)

DIRECTORIES

DIRECTORIES.BMP (365×100)

12

When you run this program, you see an image like that shown in Figure 12.2. In the upper-right corner of the window is a set of three radio buttons inside a group box. Click one of these radio buttons, and the display changes to show the currently available directories, drives, or files. You can also switch between these three settings (or modes) by clicking the right mouse button on any portion of the program. When the Files option isn't selected, you can iterate through the currently available drives and directories with the left mouse button. When Files is selected, you can double-click to start an executable file. At all times, the currently selected mode is displayed at the bottom of the program's window in large letters. An edit control at the right-middle of the screen enables you to specify a new file mask. If you are in File mode, enter any value, and then press Enter or Tab in order to see the new file listing.

Figure 12.2.

The FileBox program displays information about the contents of a subdirectory.

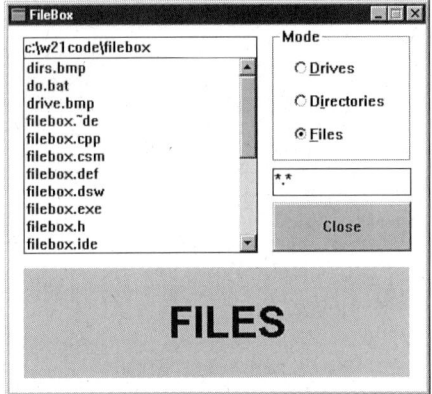

Creating Radio Buttons

A good place to get started with the FileBox program is in the WM_CREATE message handler. This is where the program creates the controls it uses, and this is where you can begin to see the underlying structure of the code that drives the program.

The WM_CREATE message handler function in FileBox looks a lot like its counterpoint in the FontExp program. Its fundamental task is to create a series of controls that interface with the user throughout the life of the program.

Four of the most important of those controls are a set of three radio buttons surrounded by a group box. The next few paragraphs describe how they work. Here are the main points you need to master:

☐ Both radio buttons and group boxes belong to the button class. The key to creating them is to assign them the right style, such as BS_RADIOBUTTON or BS_GROUPBOX.

☐ The BS_AUTORADIOBUTTON style enables radio buttons to automatically handle mouse clicks.

☐ Radio buttons should be arranged under the aegis of a single group box. You should use the WS_GROUP style to ensure that only one item inside a group box can be selected at a time.

☐ Group boxes are primarily visual tools. The functionality associated with the controls inside a group box is the result of using the WS_GROUP and WS_TABSTOP styles and has nothing to do with whether or not a group box is present.

☐ Users want to be able to tab between controls in a window. The IsDialogMessage function automatically gives you this behavior with only minimal work on your part.

Radio buttons (shown in Figure 12.3) enable the user to select one of several different, mutually exclusive options. For instance, the FileBox program makes it possible to select drives, directories, or files. You can't, however, select two options simultaneously, such as drives and directories, nor can you select all three at once.

Figure 12.3.

The radio buttons in the FileBox program are mutually exclusive: You can select only one at a time.

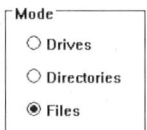

Throughout this chapter, and Chapter 13, I refer to each of these mutually exclusive options as different *modes*. In other words, the user can be in File mode, Directory mode, or Drive mode. When you're in File mode, you can view and manipulate the currently available files. When you're in Drive mode, you can view and manipulate the currently available drives, and so on. (This technique is a bit clumsy from the user's perspective, but it is very useful for people who are trying to understand how to program Windows.)

The group box, which encloses a set of radio buttons, shows the user which sets of radio buttons are meant to work together as a unit. In some programs, you might find the need to have several group boxes on one screen, each containing a set of mutually exclusive options. The message to the user is that he or she can choose one option from each group box.

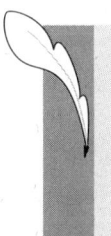

> **Note:** When you are coding dialogs, Windows supplies built-in behavior that helps to enforce the preceding rules. Inside a window, however, you need to call IsDialogMessage to ensure that radio buttons and other controls respond to key presses as the user expects. The built-in mouse behavior, however, remains intact whether you are in a window or in a dialog.
>
> I've decided to tackle IsDialogMessage, WS_TABSTOP, and the whole subject of tabbing through controls in the next section. My goal is to allow you to view the subject of tabbing in isolation so you can better grasp its importance.

Here is the code that creates the radio buttons and their encompassing group box:

```
hControl[ID_GROUP] = CreateWindow("button", "Mode",
                        WS_CHILD | WS_VISIBLE | BS_GROUPBOX,
                        250, 2, 131, 122, hwnd, HMENU(ID_GROUP),
                        hInstance, NULL);
```

```
hControl[ID_DRIVES] = CreateWindow("button",
                                   ButtonText[ID_DRIVES],
                                   WS_CHILD | WS_VISIBLE | BS_AUTORADIOBUTTON |
                                   WS_TABSTOP | WS_GROUP,
                                   270, 25 + (0 * 30), 95, 30, hwnd,
                                   HMENU(ID_DRIVES), hInstance, NULL);

for (i = 1; i < 3; i++)
  hControl[i] = CreateWindow("button", ButtonText[i],
                             WS_CHILD | WS_VISIBLE | BS_AUTORADIOBUTTON,
                             270, 25 + (i * 30), 95, 30, hwnd, HMENU(i),
                             hInstance, NULL);
```

You can see that the radio buttons belong to the button class. To differentiate one type of button from another, FileBox ORs an appropriate constant, such as BS_AUTORADIOBUTTON or BS_RADIOBUTTON, into CreateWindow's style field.

The distinction between the BS_RADIOBUTTON and BS_AUTORADIOBUTTON styles is that buttons with the latter style automatically respond when the user clicks them. This response includes displaying a *selected* radio button, as well as deselecting any other radio buttons in the current group.

If you look at the main listings for the FileBox program, you see that both the first of the radio buttons and the Close push button make use of the WS_GROUP style. When you turn this style on, it informs Windows that this and any following controls should be treated as a group. The end of the group is marked by the appearance of the next control that uses the WS_GROUP style. In particular, the three radio buttons are treated as one group, and the next group begins with the push button labeled Close. This behavior occurs because the first radio button and the push button are both assigned the WS_GROUP style.

The behavior associated with a particular group is twofold:

1. Only one member of a group of radio buttons can be selected at a time.
2. You can tab from this group to the next group in a single step without having to tab through each of the intervening radio buttons.

Note that the group box, which encloses the radio buttons, is also a member of the button class. This fact is somewhat counterintuitive, because group boxes don't look like buttons.

The function of group boxes is simply to enclose a set of controls in order to *group* them together logically by giving the user a visual hint as to their purpose. Group boxes lack the underlying complexity inherent in most features of the Windows programming environment. One keeps poking at them, expecting them to yield some hitherto unknown secret. It's a bit frustrating to have them remain so spare and immutable. The explanation for this atypical simplicity is that a group box's primary purpose is visual! It's not meant to do anything; it just informs the user about which controls are meant to be treated as a unit.

It's now time to move on to a description of IsDialogMessage and its relationship to the WS_TABSTOP and WS_GROUP styles.

IsDialogMessage **and Tabbing**

The theme of the previous few paragraphs is the importance of treating a set of radio buttons as a single group of controls. This simple act makes life considerably easier for the user. If he or she wants to select a particular option, there is no need to first turn one radio button on, and then go back and turn another off. Instead, the buttons work together in a logical and intuitive manner.

So far so good. The catch here is that I've been talking totally in terms of mouse clicks. The user also expects to be able to navigate through the program with the keyboard. All the careful grouping of controls discussed in the previous few paragraphs only applies to users armed with a mouse. Taming the keyboard is an entirely different issue.

When you are designing a modal dialog, Windows provides excellent support for the basic functionality associated with keyboards. In other words, you can automatically tab between controls, shift-tab backwards through controls, and select different radio buttons with the arrow keys. Inside a dialog, you don't have to do anything special to get this behavior. But all this functionality is turned off inside a window. It's gone. Vanished.

To bring it back, you need to change the message loop for your entire program. Specifically, you need to add a call to IsDialogMessage:

```
while (GetMessage(&Msg, NULL, 0, 0))
{
  if (!IsDialogMessage(MainWindow, &Msg))
  {
    TranslateMessage(&Msg);
    DispatchMessage(&Msg);
  }
}
```

Compare the preceding code with the standard message loop from the previous programs in this book:

```
while (GetMessage(&Msg, NULL, 0, 0))
{
  TranslateMessage(&Msg);
  DispatchMessage(&Msg);
}
```

The logic added to the FileBox program simply states that any dialog messages sent to FileBox should be handled separately and shouldn't be passed on to TranslateMessage and DispatchMessage.

The phrase "dialog messages" is really just a euphemism for "keyboard messages." IsDialogMessage grabs hold of any key presses the user makes and processes them separately. As a result, FileBox enables you to tab through controls and to use the arrow keys to select radio buttons.

The last piece in this puzzle is the WS_TABSTOP style, which is ORed into certain key controls in the FileBox program. Giving a control this style informs Windows that the user needs to be capable of tabbing to this control. It's equally important to know when to omit this style, because there are some controls you don't want the user to have to tab through every time he or she is trying to move the focus. In particular, you should only apply the WS_TABSTOP style to the first control in a group of radio buttons.

DO	**DON'T**

DO remember that the IsDialogMessage is useless to you if you forget to use the proper styles with your controls. IsDialogMessage, WS_TABSTOP, and WS_GROUP all need to work together to give the user access to your program's interface.

DON'T underestimate the importance of the IsDialogMessage function. This one call adds a great deal of functionality to your program at the price of only a minimal amount of work. It may not seem so important now, but a time will come when you'll absolutely need this function. Don't forget it!

Any control you want to tab to should have the WS_TABSTOP style. The first control in any set of controls should be assigned the WS_GROUP style. The end of the set is marked by assigning the first control of the next set the WS_GROUP style.

Using Radio Buttons to Switch Modes

Now that you've got a feeling for the subject of grouping controls and of tabbing between controls, it's time to dig a little deeper into the FileBox program. In particular, you'll learn how the program responds when the user clicks a radio button or selects it with the keyboard.

The FileBox program uses two different techniques for switching between the File, Directory, and Drive modes.

- ☐ The first technique involves responding to radio button selections with the mouse or arrow keys.
- ☐ The second technique involves responding to clicks to the right mouse button.

The next few paragraphs concentrate on the first technique. The second technique is discussed partially in this chapter and partially in the next.

IsDialogMessage and the BS_AUTORADIOBUTTON style conspire to make radio buttons extremely easy to use. All you really have to do is set up some code in the WM_COMMAND message handler function and then wait around for the user to select a radio button. In the FileBox program, the code looks like this:

```
case ID_DRIVES:
  DirShowType = DRIVEMODE;
  SetListbox(hwnd);
  break;

case ID_DIRS:
  DirShowType = DIRMODE;
  SetListbox(hwnd);
  break;

case ID_FILES:
  DirShowType = FILEMODE;
  SetListbox(hwnd);
  break;
```

If the user selects the Drive radio button, an enumerated variable called DirShowType is set to DRIVEMODE, and the SetListBox function is called. A discussion of the SetListBox function and the various global variables used in this program is included in the next chapter. For now, you need only note that this same process is repeated when the File or Directory radio buttons are selected.

Clearly, it's a cinch to write the code that handles mouse clicks on the radio buttons. The only time this code is likely to cause you any trouble is if you forget to set the WS_GROUP style at the beginning of each group, or if you forget that radio buttons keep you informed of their state (with WM_COMMAND messages). Keep these two ideas in mind, and you can spice your programs up with these nifty little controls any time you want.

In the last few paragraphs, you've learned about radio buttons and group boxes and about how they are created. Here are the key points to remember:

- Radio buttons and group boxes are buttons created with the BS_RADIOBUTTON or BS_GROUPBOX style.
- The BS_AUTORADIOBUTTON style enables radio buttons to automatically handle mouse clicks.
- Use the WS_GROUP style to arrange radio buttons under the aegis of a single group box.
- Group boxes are primarily visual tools.
- The IsDialogMessage function provides built-in tabbing between controls.

WindowsX: The Key to Portability

Before taking a closer look at radio buttons and group boxes, I need to first take a quick trip into some of the theory behind WindowsX. Take this short excursion with me, and when you come back, you will be better prepared to understand the material that lies ahead.

The control message API is a set of WindowsX macros that can be used instead of calls to SendMessage. These macros are spread throughout the program and help make the code easier to understand and maintain.

You have already seen something of the control message API, but still the major emphasis so far has been on SendMessage and PostMessage. The problem with the SendMessage and PostMessage interfaces for controls that you saw in the last two chapters is that they aren't particularly self-explanatory. They're visually cumbersome and force the programmer to perform a number of awkward typecasts. WINDOWSX.H supplies you with macros that cut through this complexity.

> **Note:** Other alternatives to the SendMessage interface include object-oriented frameworks, such as Borland's Object Windows Library (OWL) and Microsoft's Foundation Classes (MFC). These extensive code bases are quite elegant, and they rightfully attract many adherents.
>
> As someone who has made extensive use of OWL, I've come to believe that it's only semi-useful unless you first have a thorough understanding of the underlying API. In other words, good OWL programmers, by definition, must have an in-depth knowledge of the material presented in this book. MFC and OWL are useful tools, but you can't truly understand them unless you thoroughly comprehend the Windows API code base on which they stand.
>
> If you meet an OOP adherent who doesn't understand the kind of code in this book, then he or she doesn't really know much about programming Windows. You can study OWL and MFC for months, but unless you first know the material in this book, the exercise will be hollow and relatively fruitless.

You've already seen how WindowsX can be used to create order out of the rambling case statements in window procedures. An equally neat trick is performed by the control message APIs.

For instance, this line of code

```
SendMessage(hwndCtl, LB_ADDSTRING, 0, (LPARAM)lpszBuffer);
```

can be considerably simplified by using the control message API:

```
ListBox_AddString(hwndCtl, lpszBuffer);
```

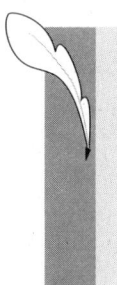

Note: Right now, the control message API is not listed in the Borland or Microsoft online help files. Three possible solutions involve

- ☐ Printing WINDOWSX.H and keeping the list by your desk.
- ☐ Using the Annotate feature of the online help system to add these listings to your help system. (See Figure 12.4.) This alternative would be especially attractive in big shops.
- ☐ Creating your own WindowsX help file.

Figure 12.4 shows the Annotate feature of the help system.

Figure 12.4.

Using the Annotate feature of the help system to document WindowsX features.

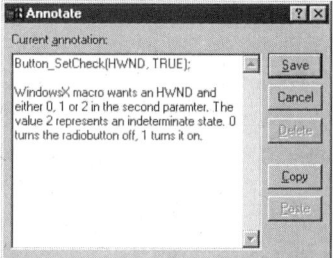

Overall, the control message API provides an excellent alternative to the SendMessage interface. It's not only considerably simpler to use, but it also can work with the STRICT compiler directive to harness the power of type-checking. This helps you create good, clean code the first time around.

Unlike the SendMessage interface, the control message API is fully portable between 16-bit Windows and WIN32. This means that using it can be a big help when you need to tweak your code so that it runs under Windows 95, Windows NT, and Windows 3.1. In this day and age, most experienced programmers are very anxious to adopt any coding methods that can make their programs more portable.

Put Your Right-Button Down

For years, the right mouse button was neglected in Windows programming. For some reason no one saw its power, and the remarkable potential therein remained entirely untapped. Borland applications, such as Quattro Pro and Paradox, and then later Microsoft Windows 95, have done much to change this state of affairs. However, many programmers still don't take full advantage of this useful tool.

Working with the right mouse button is easy. In Windows 95 or Windows NT, you can respond to WM_CONTEXTMENU messages or, if you want to create code portable to 16 bits, you can handle WM_RBUTTONDOWN messages. In other words, the WM_CONTEXTMENU message handles the right mouse button, but it isn't backwards compatible with WIN16. In an attempt to show what can be done with the right mouse button, I've thrown in the following code:

```
void HandleRightButton(HWND hwnd)
{
  switch(DirShowType)
  {
    case DRIVEMODE:
      Button_SetCheck(hControl[1], TRUE);
      Button_SetCheck(hControl[0], FALSE);
      Button_SetCheck(hControl[2], FALSE);
      DirShowType = DIRMODE;
      break;

    case DIRMODE:
      Button_SetCheck(hControl[2], TRUE);
      Button_SetCheck(hControl[0], FALSE);
      Button_SetCheck(hControl[1], FALSE);
      DirShowType = FILEMODE;
      break;

    default:
      Button_SetCheck(hControl[0], TRUE);
      Button_SetCheck(hControl[1], FALSE);
      Button_SetCheck(hControl[2], FALSE);
      DirShowType = DRIVEMODE;
  }
  SetListbox(hwnd);
}


///////////////////////////////////////
// Handle WM_RBUTTONDOWN
///////////////////////////////////////
#pragma argsused
void FileBox_OnRButtonDown(HWND hwnd, BOOL fDoubleClick,
                           int x, int y, UINT keyFlags)
{
  HandleRightButton(hwnd);
}
```

The preceding code iterates through the program's possible modes when the user clicks the right mouse button. Complications arise because it's necessary to keep the radio buttons in sync with the changes that are taking place.

Handling radio buttons this way is considerably more complicated than just responding to clicks directly on a button. The big difference is that the work performed as a result of the BS_AUTORADIOBUTTON style is no longer kicking in automatically. Instead, the FileBox program has to explicitly change the settings of the radio buttons.

If the user clicks the right mouse button while the program is in DRIVEMODE, the Drive radio button is turned off by a call to the Button_SetCheck macro. Then, the Directory radio button is turned on, and DirShowType is set to DIRMODE. Just to be sure all goes smoothly, the program sends a probably redundant call to ensure that the Drive radio button is turned off. A similar process occurs when the program is in DIRMODE or FILEMODE.

The syntax involved in this process is considerably simplified by the use of the message control API. These WindowsX macros are so intuitive that there is little need for me to explain how they work. However, it can't hurt to go through the process one time, just to be sure you've got your message control ducks all lined up in a neat, comprehensible row.

The Button_SetCheck macro fronts for the BM_SETCHECK message. If you were calling SendMessage directly, your code would look like this:

```
SendMessage(RadioBtns[0], BM_SETCHECK, WPARAM(TRUE), 0L);
SendMessage(RadioBtns[1], BM_SETCHECK, WPARAM(FALSE), 0L);
SendMessage(RadioBtns[2], BM_SETCHECK, WPARAM(FALSE), 0L);
```

WindowsX simplifies these calls by enabling you to write the following:

```
Button_SetCheck(RadioBtns[0], TRUE);
Button_SetCheck(RadioBtns[1], FALSE);
Button_SetCheck(RadioBtns[2], FALSE);
```

The actual macro definition in WINDOWSX.H for Button_SetCheck looks like this:

```
#define Button_SetCheck(hwndCtl, check)
 ((void)SendMessage((hwndCtl), BM_SETCHECK, (WPARAM)(int)(check), 0L))
```

The macro simply calls SendMessage, being careful to properly typecast the user's request to turn the button on or off. Needless to say, a value of 0 in WPARAM turns the radio button off, whereas a value of 1 turns it on.

It's unfortunate that the message control API isn't listed in the online help by either Microsoft or Borland. Nevertheless, it's worthwhile going through a little extra effort to use it in your program. Remember, the message control API has several advantages:

- [ ] It has an intuitive, easy-to-use syntax.
- [ ] It provides strong type-checking, at the same time alleviating the need to make potentially error-prone typecasts.
- [ ] It provides compatibility with WIN32 code that isn't necessarily available when you use SendMessage directly.

You will read more about WindowsX in the next chapter.

DAY
12

Note: There is a second way to get the functionality described in this section. If you are using the BS_AUTOREADIOBUTTON style, then you can call CheckRadioButton:

```
void HandleRightButton2(HWND hwnd)
{
  switch(DirShowType)
  {
    case DRIVEMODE:
      CheckRadioButton(hwnd, 100, 102, 100);
      DirShowType = DIRMODE;
      break;

    case DIRMODE:
      CheckRadioButton(hwnd, 100, 102, 101);
      DirShowType = FILEMODE;
      break;

    default:
      CheckRadioButton(hwnd, 100, 102, 102);
      DirShowType = DRIVEMODE;
      break;
  }
  SetListbox(hwnd);
}
```

The code shown here has the same effect as the first version of the HandleRightButton function.

CheckRadioButton takes the HWND of the current dialog or window in its first parameter. The second and third parameters take the id of the first and last radio buttons in the group, and the last parameter is the ID of the radio button you want to select. This code is more elegant and terse than the first technique, but it is specific to radio buttons and doesn't teach you general principles of Windows programming.

WM_PARENTNOTIFY Messages

There is one last important point to be made about the way FileBox handles right mouse clicks. A problem arises when the user clicks the right mouse button on one of the buttons or on the list box. The trouble occurs because the WM_RBUTTONDOWN message generated by Windows is absorbed by the control. Fortunately, the folks at Microsoft anticipated situations like this and they created the WM_PARENTNOTIFY message, which is sent to a control's parent in the event a control receives one of the following messages:

WM_CREATE
WM_DESTROY

```
WM_LBUTTONDOWN
WM_MBUTTONDOWN
WM_RBUTTONDOWN
```

The result is that the controls can become "semi-transparent" when the user clicks them with the right mouse button. Messages that would have been lost are piggy-backed on WM_PARENTNOTIFY messages, thereby informing the main window of what has happened.

It's easy to respond to a WM_PARENTNOTIFY message:

```
void FileBox_OnParentNotify(HWND hwnd, UINT msg,
                            HWND hwndChild, int idChild)
{
  if (msg == WM_RBUTTONDOWN)
  HandleRightButton(hwnd);
}
```

This technique works fine except if you are running Windows 95 and click on the program's edit control. As it happens, Windows 95 has its own way of handling right clicks on edit controls, and that takes precedence over the WM_ONPARENTNOTIFY message.

Summary

The primary focuses of this chapter have been radio buttons and the control message API. In particular, you have learned about

- [ ] How to create a Windows shell
- [ ] How to create radio buttons
- [ ] How to communicate with radio buttons through the Button_SetCheck macro and the CheckRadioButton API
- [ ] How to arrange radio buttons in groups with the WS_GROUP and WS_TABSTOP styles
- [ ] How to use the control message API to talk to list boxes or radio buttons
- [ ] How to use IsDialogMessage to handle keystrokes in a window

So far, you've heard only part of the tale to be told about the FileBox program. The second half of the story involves push buttons, list boxes, and window subclassing. You can read all about those subjects in the next chapter.

Q&A

Q I still don't understand IsDialogMessage. What's it all about?

A The act of tabbing between controls or selecting radio buttons with the arrow keys seems so intuitive to a user that it's easy to start to take it for granted. The process itself, however, must be handled manually, by literally setting the focus from one control to the next at the appropriate time. Fortunately, Windows has

internal logic that knows how to handle this type of situation. To take advantage of this logic, all you need to do is call `IsDialogMessage`. From that point on, Windows handles everything for you by actually tracking the keyboard messages and setting the focus accordingly.

Q You respond to `WM_CTLCOLOR` messages in this program. What do they do?

A You can use these messages to set the colors of controls, message boxes, and dialogs. For more information about the technical details involved, see Chapter 17, "Advanced Dialogs: Getting and Setting Data." In general, the subject of colors is more important in Windows 95 than it was in Windows 3.1. As a result, I have added code here that will respond to the system settings for colors. This can cause some fairly severe clashes between the bitmap colors I have chosen and the possible background colors selected by the user. Aesthetic issues of this sort or somewhat outside the scope of this book, so I have decided not to wrestle this one to the mat. Later in book, however, you will learn how to insert bitmaps that have "transparent" colors that blend in better with the background.

Workshop

The Workshop provides quiz questions to help you solidify your understanding of the material covered and exercises to provide you with experience in using what you've learned. Try to understand the quiz and exercise answers before continuing on to the next chapter. Answers are provided in Appendix A.

Quiz

1. What command can be used to automatically reboot the system and restart Windows?
2. What does the `IsDialogMessage` function do, and where in your program should you place it?
3. Group boxes belong to what class? How about radio buttons?
4. Where can you find a list of the control message API calls?
5. What standard `WM_xxx` message corresponds to the `Button_SetCheck` macro?
6. How can you get a radio button to automatically respond to button clicks?
7. What is the purpose of a group box?
8. How do you mark the beginning and end of a group of controls?
9. What is the difference between the `WS_GROUP` and `WS_TABSTOP` styles?
10. How can you check to see if a call to `WinExec` has succeeded, and what should you do if it fails?

Exercises

1. Create a program that uses two sets of radio buttons. Set them up so you can tab between groups and select one radio button from each group.

2. Add a menu to the top of the FileBox Windows shell with the following items listed in it:

   ```
   Calendar
   Control Panel
   Command Prompt
   Explorer
   Notepad
   WritePad
   ```

   When the user selects any of these items, launch the appropriate program. Remember that the best way to launch a DOS box is to start DOSPRMPT.PIF.

3. Pop up a message box that will report when a call to WinExec fails. Use the return code from WinExec to post an informative message for the user.

12

Subclassing
Window Controls

After covering some fairly straightforward material on push buttons, the WM_GETMINMAXINFO message, and list boxes, this chapter launches into an in-depth discussion of subclassing. This important technique represents the crucial last brick in the edifice of knowledge you are constructing around the subject of window controls.

Subclassing enables you to alter the behavior of a control by temporarily taking over its window procedure. As you will see, the end result is that you can modify a list box, push button, or other control so that it does exactly what you want.

As a special bonus, the end of this chapter contains a relatively short program that demonstrates how Windows 16 programmers can subclass a window that belongs to an entirely different program. This admittedly rather esoteric technique enables you to reach into other programs, or into the inner workings of Windows itself, and change the behavior of another programmer's code. Note that the separate address spaces for WIN32 programs means that this technique will not work under Windows 95 or Windows NT.

Here's a sketch of the major subjects covered in this chapter:

- [ ] An overview of push buttons
- [ ] WM_CLOSE messages and the DestroyWindow function
- [ ] A look at the WM_GETMINMAXINFO message
- [ ] A second look at list boxes, concentrating on their capability to display directory information with DlgDirList and DlgDirSelectEx
- [ ] An explanation about how a program iterates through the available drives or directories when the list box is clicked
- [ ] Extensive examples of how to subclass a window
- [ ] A discussion about how to read from and write to initialization (.INI) files
- [ ] An explanation about how to create menus on the fly

Working with Push Buttons

It's time to pick up the narrative thread where it was set down at the end of the last chapter. Specifically, the focus was on the new controls found in the FileBox program. The next tool up for discussion is the gray shaded push button, which users can select with the mouse.

Even the most inexperienced users can figure out how to shut down the FileBox program; all they have to do is click the big Close button (shown in Figure 13.1).

Here's the code from the FileBox_OnCreate function (from Listing 12.1 on Day 12, "Window Controls and the Control Message API") that creates the Close button:

```
199: hControl[ID_CLOSE] = CreateWindow("button", "Close",
```

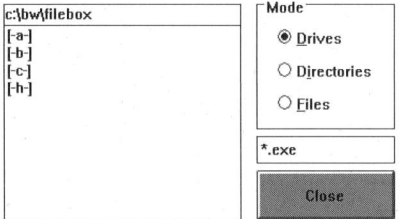

```
200:                    WS_CHILD | WS_VISIBLE | BS_PUSHBUTTON |
201:                    WS_TABSTOP | WS_GROUP,
202:                    250, 138, 131, 70, hwnd, HMENU(ID_CLOSE),
203:                    hInstance, NULL);
```

The effort involved in creating push buttons is almost non-existent compared to the functionality and elegance they bring to your program. To create the same visual effect in a typical DOS program would take many more lines of code and considerable planning.

Figure 13.1.

The FileBox's push button is nestled into the lower-right corner of this group of controls.

Note: The key points in the previous call to CreateWindow are simple:

☐ Designate the button class in the lpszClassName parameter of CreateWindow (line 199).

☐ Add BS_PUSHBUTTON style to the dwStyle field (line 200).

☐ Designate the button's coordinates (line 202).

☐ Typecast the HMENU field to assign the button an ID (line 203).

By now, this should be a very familiar process, requiring only minimal thought and effort.

It's just as simple to respond to a push button as it is to create one. The actual process is very similar to responding to a menu selection. That is, you set up camp in the Cls_OnCommand function and wait for Windows to send a WM_COMMAND message with the ID of your button attached. For instance, here is a very simple response to the selection of a push button:

```
case ID_CLOSE:
  MessageBox(hwnd, "Close Button pushed", "Beep", MB_OK);
  break;
```

This code pops up a MessageBox informing the user that he or she has pushed the Close button. It's not very practical, but certainly nothing could be simpler.

The actual code from FileBox_OnCommand function looks like this:

```
331: case ID_CLOSE:
332:   SendMessage(hwnd, WM_CLOSE, 0, 0);
333:   break;
```

13

The FileBox program relays the user's choice to a separate portion of the program by sending it a WM_CLOSE message (line 332). A WM_CLOSE message will shut down an application.

The FileBox program sends a WM_CLOSE message to itself because of a complication that pops up in many Windows programs. The complication occurs because there are two different ways to close the FileBox application:

1. Click the Close button.
2. Use the system icon in the upper-left corner of the program.

The system menu, of course, doesn't send ID_CLOSE messages to FileBox_OnCommand. Instead, it results in a WM_CLOSE message being sent to the main window.

Because the system menu's behavior is built into Windows, the FileBox program opts to go along with this prearranged scheme. It sends its own WM_CLOSE message, and then responds to both the system menu's and the Close button's messages with the following code:

```
void FileBox_OnClose(HWND hwnd)
{
  if (MessageBox(hwnd, "Do you want to exit?", "FileBox",
                 MB_ICONQUESTION | MB_OKCANCEL) == IDOK)
    DestroyWindow(hwnd);
}
```

Calling DestroyWindow on an application's main window is all that needs to be done to shut down a program. This one call deactivates a window, disposes of its menu and its child windows, flushes its queue, destroys its timers, disconnects it from the rest of the system, and sets the focus elsewhere. It goes without saying that DestroyWindow also sends a WM_DESTROY message to your main window.

If you don't override a window's default response to a WM_CLOSE message, it automatically calls DestroyWindow. FileBox doesn't really change the main window's response to a WM_CLOSE message—the end result is still a call to DestroyWindow. What the FileBox program does differently is prompt the user to confirm the action before carrying it through.

DO **DON'T**

When you want to shut down an application:

DO close an application by sending a WM_CLOSE message or by calling DestroyWindow directly.

DON'T ever try to call Cls_OnDestroy directly, and don't ever try to close a Window by sending it a WM_DESTROY message.

Restricting the Size of a Window

Unlike all the other examples you have seen in this book, the FileBox program can't be resized by a user pulling on its borders. Also, this program doesn't change size, even when you maximize it. This behavior, which is somewhat reminiscent of a dialog, is achieved by responding to the WM_GETMINMAXINFO message:

```
341:void FileBox_OnGetMinMaxInfo(HWND hwnd,
342:                             MINMAXINFO FAR* lpMinMaxInfo)
343: {
344:    lpMinMaxInfo->ptMaxSize.x = XSIZE;
345:    lpMinMaxInfo->ptMaxSize.y = YSIZE;
346:    lpMinMaxInfo->ptMaxPosition.x = 100
347:    lpMinMaxInfo->ptMaxPosition.y = 100
348:    lpMinMaxInfo->ptMinTrackSize.x = XSIZE;
349:    lpMinMaxInfo->ptMinTrackSize.y = YSIZE;
350:    lpMinMaxInfo->ptMaxTrackSize.x = XSIZE;
351:    lpMinMaxInfo->ptMaxTrackSize.y = YSIZE;
352: }
```

This message handler function receives two parameters:

☐ A copy of the HWND with which it's associated (line 341)

☐ A MINMAXINFO structure (line 342)

MINMAXINFO has six fields, each declared to be of type POINT. A POINT structure usually is used to designate a location on-screen. It has two fields of type integer: the first called x, and the second called y. See Table 13.1 for the MINMAXINFO structure fields.

Table 13.1. The fields of the MINMAXINFO structure.

ptReserved	Not used
ptMaxSize	How big the window will be when it's maximized
ptMaxPosition	Where the upper-left corner of the window should be positioned when the window is maximized
ptMinTrackSize	The smallest size the window can be when the user tries to resize it by pulling on its borders
ptMaxTrackSize	The largest size the window can be when the user tries to resize it by pulling on its borders

The WM_GETMINMAXINFO message comes cruising down the pike when the window is being created (or at the approximate time the WM_CREATE message gets sent).

13

> **Note**: If you don't use WINDOWSX.H, you need to typecast the `WndProc`'s `LPARAM` to type `MINMAXINFO` when responding to the `WM_MINMAXINFO` message. From that point on, your approach could be very similar to that of the code in FILEBOX.CPP.

When trying to control the size of a main window, programmers often mistakenly try to manipulate the `x`, `y`, `nWidth`, and `nHeight` fields passed to `CreateWindow`. As a rule, that's a mistake. It's best to pass `CW_USEDEFAULT` in those parameters. The real way to control the size and shape of a main window is by handling `WM_GETMINMAXINFO` messages. This isn't a hard and fast rule, but certainly, rather than directly modifying the coordinates passed to `CreateWindow`, you should consider responding to `WM_GETMINMAXINFO` messages.

Well, that's all there is to say about the `WM_GETMINMAXINFO` message. Technically, it's not very challenging, but in it's proper place, it can prove to be invaluable.

Directory Magic

FILEBOX.EXE fills the program's list box with the names of files, directories, or drives. This seemingly complicated task is greatly simplified by a few simple Window's API functions called `DlgDirList` and `DlgDirSelectEx`.

In and of themselves, neither of these functions are particularly hard to use. However, the FileBox program interacts with these functions through the use of global constants called `DirShowType` and `DirShowVal`. Both constants help make the program considerably easier to read and maintain. In the next few pages, you'll read about the new API calls and about the techniques for using them. The goal is to see how to avoid creating hopelessly confusing spaghetti code that even you won't be able to understand three months from now.

To get started, take a look at a fragment that appears just before the end of the `WM_CREATE` message handler function:

```
DlgDirList(hwnd, "*.*", ID_FILELIST,
          ID_PATHS, DirShowVal[DirShowType]);
```

The `DlgDirList` API call fills a list box with information about a particular drive or subdirectory. For instance, it can fill a list box with a list of the currently available files, drives, and subdirectories. See Table 13.2 for the parameters passed to `DlgDirList`.

Table 13.2. The parameters passed to `DlgDirList`.

`HWND hwndDlg`	Handle of the window or dialog containing the list box
`LPSTR lpszPath`	Wildcards designating the files to be shown
`int idListBox`	ID of the list box
`int idStaticPath`	ID of the static control for currently selected files(s)
`UINT uFileType`	Identifier designating the types of files to show

When calling `DlgDirList`, start by placing the ID of the appropriate list box in `DlgDirList`'s third parameter. Then, fill in the other parameters with information about the files or directories you want to display. Don't forget that `DlgDirList` automatically fills in a static control with the name of the currently selected file. All you need to do is hand over the ID of the control in `DlgDirList`'s fourth parameter. See Table 13.3 for `DlgDirLists`'s fifth parameter constants.

Table 13.3. The fifth parameter to `DlgDirList` consists of one or more constants that specify exactly what should be shown in the list box.

Constant	What It Means
`DDL_READWRITE`	Read-write data files
`DDL_READONLY`	Read-only files
`DDL_HIDDEN`	Hidden files
`DDL_SYSTEM`	System files
`DDL_DIRECTORY`	Directories
`DDL_ARCHIVE`	Archives
`DDL_POSTMSGS`	Posts messages to the application, not the dialog
`DDL_DRIVES`	Drives
`DDL_EXCLUSIVE`	Excludes normal files and lists only files of the specified type

If you pass in `DDL_READWRITE` in the fifth parameter of a call to `DlgDirList`, it fills up the designated list box with a list of files that have their read and write attributes set. If you send in the `DDL_DRIVES` identifier, you'll see all the normal files, and a list of drives. If you want to see only drives, pass in `DDL_DRIVES` ORed together with `DDL_EXCLUSIVE`.

In the FileBox program, a constant array is set up to designate each of three types of displays generated by the application:

```
WORD DirShowVal[] = {DDL_DRIVES | DDL_EXCLUSIVE,
                     DDL_DIRECTORY | DDL_EXCLUSIVE,
                     DDL_ARCHIVE};
```

13

DirShowVal is always set to one of the three modes displayed in its declaration. For instance, if the user selects the Files radio button, DirShowVal is set to DDL_ARCHIVE, which ensures that all the normal files in the current directory are shown. If the user chooses Directories, DirShowVal is set to DDL_DIRECTORY ¦ DDL_EXCLUSIVE, which shows only a list of the currently available subdirectories. (If you want to see both files and directories, use DDL_DIRECTORY.)

To index into DirShowVal, FileBox relies on the locally declared DirShowType variable, which is of type TCurMode:

```
enum TCurMode {DRIVEMODE, DIRMODE, FILEMODE};
TCurMode DirShowType;
```

The interaction of these different variables ensures that the call to DlgDirList always generates either a list of normal files, a list of directories, or a list of drives, depending on the current value of DirShowType.

One portion of the program can set the current value of DirShowType to either DRIVEMODE, DIRMODE, or FILEMODE:

```
DirShowType = FILEMODE;
```

Now, whenever you need to call DlgDirList, you can pass in the correct constants by indexing into the DirShowVal array:

```
DirShowVal[DirShowType]
```

The final call looks like this:

```
DlgDirList(hwnd,"*.*", ID_FILELIST,
           ID_PATHS, DirShowVal[DirShowType]);
```

There are, of course, other ways to handle this type of situation. I've shown you this one because it helps to simplify a type of coding chore that comes up frequently in Windows programming.

Note: Some people are confused by the constants that are spread throughout Windows code like confetti. In the case of DlgDirList, this confusion is compounded because only recent documents use the standard Windows declared constants rather than raw numbers.

The basic principle behind the constants is simply to declare a set of flags that have a certain meaning. This is really a very simple idea, no more complex than a child's game. Kids, for instance, love to set up codes that govern behavior. "If I say the number one, you turn to the left; if I say the number two, you turn to the right." That kind of thing—very simple, very straightforward.

The actual constants used with the DlgDirList function are defined in WINDOWS.H:

```
/* DlgDirList, DlgDirListComboBox flags values */
#define DDL_READWRITE      0x0000
#define DDL_READONLY       0x0001
#define DDL_HIDDEN         0x0002
#define DDL_SYSTEM         0x0004
#define DDL_DIRECTORY      0x0010
#define DDL_ARCHIVE        0x0020
#define DDL_POSTMSGS       0x2000
#define DDL_DRIVES         0x4000
#define DDL_EXCLUSIVE      0x8000
```

These can be translated into kid-talk like this: "If I say value one, you show me read-only files; if I say two, you show me the hidden files." It's an extremely simple system, complicated only slightly by the addition of logical operators.

In the declaration for the DirShowVal array, the DDL_DIRECTORY and the DDL_EXCLUSIVE values are ORed together. This is done by writing:

```
DDL_DIRECTORY | DDL_EXCLUSIVE
```

which is exactly the same thing as writing this:

```
0x0010 | 0x8000
```

There is no significant difference between the statements. For that matter, I could just as easily have written 0x8010, which is what the two values ORed together look like.

The problem, of course, is that writing 0x8010 isn't very intelligible to people who are trying to decipher the code several months or years later. So, Windows uses predeclared constants. It's not always the world's most aesthetically pleasing system, but it is very practical.

13

Before moving on, it might be helpful for me to sum up this section of the chapter:

☐ The DlgDirList function fills a list box with a list of files, directories, drives, and so forth.

☐ DlgDirList takes five parameters, all of which are fairly easy to handle under normal circumstances.

☐ FileBox's mode is specified by one of three sets of identifiers passed in DlgDirList uFileType parameter.

☐ To track these identifiers, the FileBox program sets up two global variables called DirShowType and DirShowVal.

Changing Drives and Directories

The next (and final) step is to see how FileBox responds when the user starts clicking the list box. In other words, you need to see how the FileBox program iterates through subdirectories and enables the user to run a particular program.

If a user clicks a directory or drive name in the list box, a message is sent to the WM_COMMAND message handler function. Inside FileBox_OnCommand, the following code is activated:

```
case ID_FILELIST:
if (codeNotify == LBN_DBLCLK)
{
  if (DirShowType != FILEMODE)
    HandleMouseClick(hwnd, id, hwndCtl, codeNotify);
  else
  {
    int index = ListBox_GetCurSel(hControl[ID_FILELIST]);
    _getdcwd(0, S, 125);
    ListBox_GetText(hControl[ID_FILELIST], index,
                    lpszBuffer);
    strcat(S, "\\");
    strcat(S, lpszBuffer);
    WinExec(S, SW_SHOWNORMAL);
  }
}
break;
```

FileBox checks to see if the user has double-clicked the list box. If the user has, the program does one of two things—depending on whether the user is in file mode. If the user is viewing a list of files, the program tries to call WinExec to launch the selected filename. If the user is in drive mode or directory mode, the HandleMouseClick function is called:

```
void HandleMouseClick(HWND hwnd, int id, HWND hwndCtl, UINT codeNotify)
{
  char Buffer[MAXSTR];

  DlgDirSelectEx(hwnd, Buffer, MAXSTR, ID_FILELIST);
  DlgDirList(hwnd, Buffer, ID_FILELIST, ID_PATHS,
             DirShowVal[DirShowType]);
}
```

The DlgDirSelectEx function retrieves the file the user clicked. If a directory or drive is selected, DlgDirSelectEx strips off the encasing brackets and/or hyphens and returns a valid directory or drive listing. Pass this value to DlgDirList, and Windows automatically changes to the specified drive or directory.

If you use DlgDirSelectEx, Windows does the dirty work of parsing filenames and changing directories. It also protects both the programmer and the user from the ugly stuff that used to take place at the DOS prompt. The goal is to try to produce a more intuitively obvious interface to the dark and obscure hardware that is always lurking just below the surface. People tend to love their machines, but they don't necessarily want to have to open up the hood and get their hands dirty. DlgDirList helps smooth the way; it makes computers more intelligible to humans.

Of course, some people want to open up the hood and have a peek at what is going on underneath. For those intrepid souls, I've stuck in the following function:

```
void SetListbox(HWND hwnd)
{
  RECT R;

  ListBox_ResetContent(BoxWin);
  ListBox_Dir(BoxWin, DirShowVal[DirShowType], "*.*");

  R.left = 14;
  R.top = 220;
  R.right = 14 + BMPX;
  R.bottom = 220 + BMPY;
  InvalidateRect(hwnd, &R, FALSE);
}
```

These first two lines of code, which utilize the control message API, perform pretty much the same task as DlgDirList. The ListBox_ResetContent function clears the list box, and the ListBox_Dir macro fills it with the appropriate information from the current subdirectory.

Unlike DlgDirSelectEx, these WindowsX macros don't change the directory. As it turns out, that's not a problem. It just happens that the SetListbox function doesn't need to change directories. It's called only when the user switches from file mode to directory mode, or from directory mode to drive mode (and so forth). As a result, at this point in the program, you don't have to change directories or drives.

Take a moment to consider the two WindowsX macros shown above. The ListBox_ResetContent macro fronts for the LB_RESETCONTENT message. Before the advent of WindowsX, list boxes were always cleared with the following line of code:

```
SendMessage(BoxWin, LB_RESETCONTENT, 0, 0L);
```

By now, you probably are catching on to the way these control message macros get their names. As a result, it should come as no surprise that the ListBox_Dir function fronts for the LB_DIR message. For instance, here is a typical SendMessage call that utilizes LB_DIR:

```
SendMessage(BoxWin, LB_DIR, DDL_DRIVES | DDL_EXCLUSIVE,
LPARAM(lpszBuffer));
```

In this example, the lpszBuffer might hold a string, such as *.* or *.EXE. FileBox uses the WindowsX macros and a few other tricks to simplify the call so that it looks like this:

```
ListBox_Dir(BoxWin, DirShowVal[DirShowType], "*.*");
```

It's still not a paradigm of syntactical clarity, but it's much easier to read.

13

Note: You might also want to pick up on the call to InvalidateRect, which lies at the bottom of the SetListbox function. InvalidateRect, you'll remember, causes a WM_PAINT message to be sent to a window. This is one of the rare cases in which you might want to use the second parameter of this API call. Passing a RECT in this parameter forces Windows to redraw only a defined portion of your window. The two reasons for passing a RECT are as follows:

☐ It saves clock cycles.

☐ It prevents unsightly blinking when the program is redrawn.

Introduction to Subclassing Window Controls

In the last few chapters you've had a look at many of the most commonly used controls:

check boxes	edits
group boxes	list boxes
push buttons	radio buttons
scrollbars	statics

By now, you should have a feeling for how crucial these tools are to the construction of any useful Windows program. Use them well, and you can create programs that are easy to use and easy to understand.

Note: Starting with Day 15, "Basic Windows 95 Controls," you will learn about another set of "common controls" available in Windows 95 and in Windows NT 3.51 and higher. Much of what you have learned so far about controls will apply to the Windows 95 common controls, but they tend to be a little more flexible, and a little more difficult to master.

However, there is one fairly serious catch. The problem is that controls remain black boxes to programmers. We can't know how they work internally, because Microsoft has never published their source code. Furthermore, there are times when we need to slightly alter their behavior so that they will fit seamlessly into our programs.

Obviously, I wouldn't introduce this topic unless Microsoft had provided a solution to the problem. That solution is called *subclassing*.

Just the sound of the word used to send a little shiver down my spine. It sounded so complicated, so technical, so incomprehensible. For some reason, it was a word that for me encompassed everything about Windows programming that was intimidating, mysterious, and somehow vaguely alluring.

As it turns, out, subclassing a window control isn't all that technically difficult. Despite my initial fears, it was mostly smoke and mirrors, with only a few simple ideas that needed to be mastered. Nevertheless, this technique will elude you unless you get your hands firmly around a few important new concepts.

Here's what you need to know:

- ☐ Just like a dialog or window, every control has a window procedure that dictates its behavior.
- ☐ The address of a control's window procedure is stored in memory, and it can be retrieved and/or replaced.
- ☐ If you replace the address of a window procedure for a control with the address of one of your own functions, you can get first crack at any messages sent to a control.
- ☐ After you've seen a particular message, you can either pass it on to the control's original window procedure or swallow it so that it disappears without a trace. In either case, you can respond to the message in a manner of your own choosing, thereby changing the predefined behavior of a control.

That's all there is to it. Overall, this is a fairly simple procedure, somewhat akin to the process you go through when creating dialogs or callbacks. In other words, the key steps involve setting up a "mailing address" to which Windows can send messages. (This means that 16-bit Windows programmers are going to have to drag out that tired war horse called `MakeProcInstance`.)

13

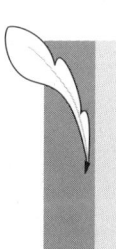

Note: In a book such as this, there is little need for discussion about subclassing a control. My goals are to show you the tools at hand and to give you examples of how they are supposed to work under normal, or even ideal, circumstances. In the real world, however, programmers tend to encounter "exceptions" to the rules almost as often as they encounter "normal" circumstances. As a result, subclassing controls is something programmers tend to do on a regular basis. In other words, this is another important topic, and you probably should take the time necessary to properly master this material.

Subclassing Controls: The Particulars

Now that you understand what subclassing is all about, it's time to start talking about a specific example. The FileBox program subclasses its edit control. It needs to do this for five partially interrelated reasons:

- ☐ It needs to handle WM_KILLFOCUS messages so it can check to see if the edit control needs to tell the list box that the user has changed the file mask. (See Figure 13.2.)
- ☐ It needs to handle WM_GETDLGCODE messages.
- ☐ It needs to handle the Enter key in a particular manner.
- ☐ It needs to restore the normal tabbing behavior it lost when it responded to WM_GETDLGCODE.
- ☐ It needs to highlight the text in the edit control every time it receives the focus, that is, when it receives a WM_SETFOCUS message.

Figure 13.2.

Residing just above the program's push button, FileBox's edit control contains a file mask.

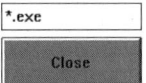

The previous list represents a fairly tangled web of ideas that quite accurately reflect the kind of challenge you should expect from a real-world Windows programming project. The only way out of this particular weave of problems is to start subclassing like mad.

To begin researching this problem, you might want to look at the WM_GETDLGCODE message, which interacts in some interesting ways with IsDialogMessage. As explained in the last chapter, IsDialogMessage grabs certain key presses and handles them for you, thereby providing your program with important built-in functionality, such as automatic tabbing between controls. The trade-off here is that IsDialogMessage forces you to relinquish control over those key presses that are being handled by Windows. In particular, unless the edit control specifically designates otherwise, IsDialogMessage decides that edit controls don't really need to see the Enter key.

But what if you want to respond to presses of the Enter key? Can't Windows give us a break here? Do we have to give up one kind of functionality in order to gain another?

Well, the answer is that Windows will let you do almost anything you want, so long as you know how to meet it face to face on its own home ground. Specifically, in this case you have to handle WM_GETDLGCODE messages by returning DLGC_WANTALLKEYS:

```
case WM_GETDLGCODE:
  return DLGC_WANTALLKEYS;
```

Now Windows will sheepishly turn over those presses on the Enter key.

However, Windows is not quite so easy to outwit. As it turns out, the saga isn't quite over, because the `DLGC_WANTALLKEYS` message effectively eliminates the built-in `IsDialogMessage` tabbing behavior for the program's edit control. In other words, we have once again traded away one benefit in order to gain another.

To keep marching toward its goal, the FileBox program needs to explicitly restore proper tabbing for edit controls. The best way it can do that is through subclassing.

If all this seems a bit confusing and complicated, that's because it *is* confusing and complicated. You're not looking at the type of prime real estate that the designers of Windows would want to show off to just anyone. Instead, you're examining the territory where the best Windows programmers earn their stripes.

What's been established so far is that the edit control in the FileBox program needs to be subclassed so that it can handle certain messages in a particular manner. In other words, the default behavior for edit controls just isn't good enough in these circumstances. As a result, you have to dig deep to learn how to alter that behavior. Here's how it works:

When you create a `WNDCLASS` structure in a register function, or when you pass information in with the `CreateWindow` call, under Windows 16 the operating system saves your work in the local heap of a dynamic link library called USER.EXE. In WIN32 the relevant file is called USER32.DLL. By making calls to a series of functions with names like `SetWindowLong` and `SetClassLong`, you can retrieve or replace most of this information.

Because controls are really just windows with their own `WNDCLASS` structures and their own internal data, there is no reason why you can't turn to Windows and ask for the address of their window procedure. When you have it, you can replace it with one of your own.

When you want to subclass a window control, start with the following two-step process:

1. In 16-bit Windows, create memory for a window procedure by calling `MakeProcInstance`.

2. Swap that window procedure into the place formerly occupied by Microsoft's window procedure.

Here's how the whole thing looks when you write code to subclass an edit control:

```
FARPROC lpfnNewEdit;
WNDPROC OldListProc;
HWND hEdit;

...

#ifdef WIN32
OldEditProc = (WNDPROC)SetWindowLong(hControl[ID_EDIT],
                     GWL_WNDPROC, LONG(NewEditProc));
```

```
#else
lpfnNewEditProc = MakeProcInstance(FARPROC(NewEditProc), hInstance);
OldEditProc = (WNDPROC)SetWindowLong(hControl[ID_EDIT],
                    GWL_WNDPROC, LONG(lpfnNewEditProc));
#endif
```

This code uses conditional directives to allow you to compile it one way under 16-bit Windows, and a second way under WIN32. In fact, the WIN16 method would work in both cases, but I want to make it clear how the call would look if you didn't have to dance with MakeProcInstance.

lpfnNewEdit is a pointer variable designed to point at the new window procedure supplied by FileBox. The OldEditProc variable, on the other hand, can be used to store the address of the old window procedure designed by Microsoft.

In WIN16, FileBox allocates prolog code for the new procedure by calling MakeProcInstance. It passes the address of the new procedure to Windows and saves the address of the old window procedure. This is done by calling SetWindowLong.

The next step is to design the new window procedure, which looks like this:

```
LRESULT CALLBACK NewEditProc(HWND hwnd, UINT Message,
WPARAM wParam, LPARAM lParam)
{
  switch(Message)
  {
    case WM_GETDLGCODE:
      return DLGC_WANTALLKEYS;

    case WM_KEYDOWN:
      ...                    // Code to handle tabbing
      break;

    case WM_KILLFOCUS:
      SetNewWildCard(hwnd);
      break;

    case WM_SETFOCUS:
      Edit_SetSel(hwnd, 0, -1);
      break;
  }
  return
    CallWindowProc(OldEditProc, hwnd, Message, wParam, lParam);
}
```

The declaration for NewEditProc looks exactly like the declaration for any other window procedure. It takes all the same parameters and returns exactly the same values. It's just like the FileBox's main window procedure, only it's used for an edit control.

The switch statement that forms the body for the window procedure, is exactly like the switch statement you might see in the main window's WNDPROC, or in a dialog box procedure.

In fact, the only difference between this window procedure and a normal window procedure is that it ends by referencing the CallWindowProc function, rather than DefWndowProc:

```
return CallWindowProc(OldEditProc,hwnd,Message,wParam,lParam);
```

Needless to say, the mission of `CallWindowProc` is to pass a message to the original window procedure. It's able to do this because you specifically pass the address of the original window procedure in the first parameter.

DO	DON'T

DO remember to pass messages to the original window procedure if you want them to be processed normally.

You **DON'T** have to pass on any messages that you don't want the control to process. For instance, many programmers subclass edit controls, and then simply neglect to pass on any non-numeric input. The result is an edit control that forces the user to type numbers and refuses to acknowledge any attempts to type letters. If you need an edit control to act like this, you can get one by subclassing.

As usual, the last step in this process is to clean up. In FileBox, this takes place in response to the `WM_DESTROY` message:

```
SetWindowLong(hEdit, GWL_WNDPROC, LONG(OldEditProc));
#ifndef WIN32
FreeProcInstance(lpfnNewEdit);
#endif
```

The call to `SetWindowLong` takes three parameters. The first is the handle to the window you want to change; the second is a constant designating an offset into the data associated with USER.EXE or USER32.DLL; and the third is the function you want to insert into memory.

After FileBox replaces the window procedure it so unceremoniously borrowed, the final step is to destroy the one it created. There—now everything is back the way its was before FileBox came on the scene. (Of course, you don't have to call `FreeProcInstance` if you are working in WIN32.)

You might want to take a moment to consider what has happened here. The key points to absorb are as follows:

- [ ] The FileBox program needed to change the default behavior of its edit control.
- [ ] In order to do this, it had to swap the address of its own custom-made window procedure, and get back the address of the old window procedure.
- [ ] It handled certain messages as it saw fit, and passed the others directly to the old window procedure.
- [ ] When finished, the FileBox program carefully cleaned up after itself by putting the old window procedure back where it found it. In 16-bit Windows, FileBox then called `FreeProcInstance` on the address of its own custom-made window procedure.

13

I hope you can see why subclassing has a little aura of magic around it. It's exciting territory that you can really have some fun with (if you are so inclined).

I also should mention that the subclassing shown here is specific to a particular window. It's possible to subclass an entire class of controls so that all the versions of the control (which appear in any program) exhibit a behavior that you define. For obvious reasons, this is something you wouldn't normally want to do, and as a result I don't cover it in this book.

Bonus Program: Subclassing the Windows Desktop

To round out this chapter, I've prepared a short example program called MenuAid that shows how to subclass a window that isn't part of your current program. The subclassing code in this program is specific only to 16-bit Windows, but I've put it in here because it's a light-hearted program that has some fun with the system created by the folks at Microsoft.

Note: If you want, you can add two lines of code to your applications to detect WIN32 and terminate gracefully. In particular, you can use `GetVersion()`, `GetVersionEx()`, or `GetWinFlags()` to find out which version you are running under.

WIN32 programmers should still find this program interesting. The code shows how to manipulate free floating pop-up menus, how to create menus on the fly, and how to work with INI files. (It won't do any harm to run a 32-bit version of this program under Windows 95, but don't run a 16-bit version. When running under WIN32, you can try out all the code except the bit that subclasses the Windows desktop. To bring up the free-floating pop-up menu under WIN32, just right-click on the list box in the center of the program.)

MenuAid hooks into the desktop window, which forms the backdrop on which the Windows 3.1 shell appears when you first boot the computer. MenuAid's sole task, when subclassing the desktop window, is to respond to right mouse clicks by sending a message back to its own main window procedure. When the main window receives this message, it pops up a menu of available programs. If the user selects an item from this menu, MenuAid runs the selected program. The end result is that the user can access a list of available programs by clicking the right mouse button on the desktop. (See Figure 13.3.)

Figure 13.3.
The iconized MenuAid program responds to right-clicks on the Windows desktop by popping up a menu.

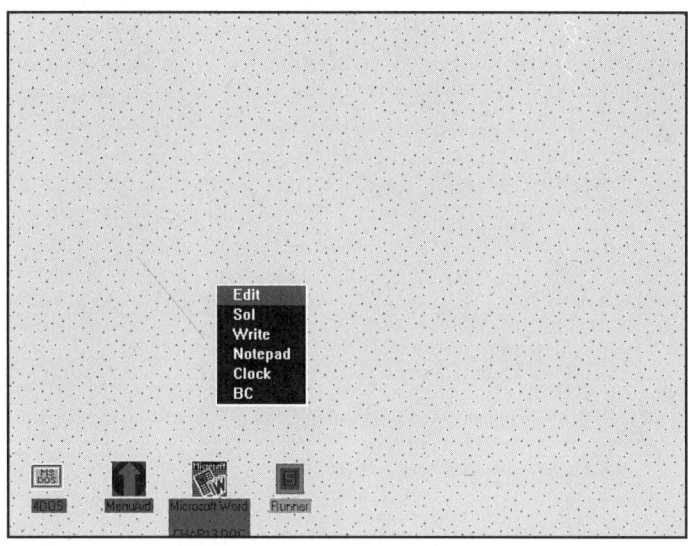

The idea for this program was suggested by Dave Wilhelm, a veteran C and Pascal programmer who works in Borland R&D. I decided to hack my own version for this book because it's an interesting program that serves a useful purpose. My thanks, and hats off, to Dave Wilhelm. He's an excellent programmer, and it's very generous of him to share his idea with us.

Listing 13.1 shows the code to the MenuAid program. Have fun with it!

Listing 13.1. The MenuAid program shows how to subclass the Windows desktop.

```
//////////////////////////////////////
// Program Name: MENUAID.CPP
// Programmer: Charlie Calvert
// Description: MenuAid windows program
// The subclassing part won't work under WIN32
// the code will still run fine, however.
//////////////////////////////////////

#define STRICT
#define WIN32_LEAN_AND_MEAN
#include <windows.h>
#include <windowsx.h>
#include <string.h>
#pragma warning (disable: 4068)


// -------------------------------------------------------
// Interface
// -------------------------------------------------------
```

continues

Listing 13.1. continued

```
#define CM_EDIT 1
#define WM_SPECIAL (WM_USER + 0x100)
#define ID_LISTBOX 102
#define CM_UPDATE 103
#define XSIZE 223
#define YSIZE 253

LRESULT CALLBACK WndProc(HWND hwnd, UINT Message, WPARAM wParam,
                                    LPARAM  lParam);
LRESULT CALLBACK NewDesktopProc(HWND hWindow, UINT Message,
                                    WPARAM wParam, LPARAM lParam);
BOOL Register(HINSTANCE hInst);
HWND Create(HINSTANCE hInst, int nCmdShow);
HMENU NewMenu(void);

// Declarations for class MenuAid
#define MenuAid_DefProc     DefWindowProc
BOOL MenuAid_OnCreate(HWND hwnd,
                    CREATESTRUCT FAR* lpCreateStruct);
void MenuAid_OnDestroy(HWND hwnd);
void MenuAid_OnCommand(HWND hwnd, int id,
                    HWND hwndCtl, UINT codeNotify);
void MenuAid_OnGetMinMaxInfo(HWND hwnd,
                    MINMAXINFO FAR* lpMinMaxInfo);

static char szAppName[] = "MenuAid";
static char IniName[] = "MenuAid.Ini";
static HWND MainWindow, DeskWnd, hListBox;
static HINSTANCE hInstance;
WNDPROC OldDesk;
FARPROC lpfnNewProc;
HMENU FloatingMenu;
static int ItemsInMenu = 1;

// ----------------------------
// Initialization
// ----------------------------

/////////////////////////////////////
// Program entry point
/////////////////////////////////////
#pragma argsused
int PASCAL WinMain(HINSTANCE hInst, HINSTANCE hPrevInstance, LPSTR
                    lpszCmdParam, int nCmdShow)
{
  MSG  Msg;

  if (!hPrevInstance)
    if (!Register(hInst))
      return FALSE;

  MainWindow = Create(hInst, nCmdShow);
  if (!MainWindow)
    return FALSE;
```

```
    while (GetMessage(&Msg, NULL, 0, 0))
    {
        TranslateMessage(&Msg);
        DispatchMessage(&Msg);
    }

    return Msg.wParam;
}

/////////////////////////////////////
// Register the window
/////////////////////////////////////
BOOL Register(HINSTANCE hInst)
{
    WNDCLASS WndClass;

    WndClass.style          = CS_HREDRAW | CS_VREDRAW;
    WndClass.lpfnWndProc    = WndProc;
    WndClass.cbClsExtra     = 0;
    WndClass.cbWndExtra     = 0;
    WndClass.hInstance      = hInst;
    WndClass.hIcon          = LoadIcon(hInst, "MenuAid");
    WndClass.hCursor        = LoadCursor(NULL, IDC_ARROW);
    WndClass.hbrBackground  = GetStockBrush(LTGRAY_BRUSH);
    WndClass.lpszMenuName   = NULL;
    WndClass.lpszClassName  = szAppName;

    return (RegisterClass (&WndClass) != 0);
}

/////////////////////////////////////
// Create the window
/////////////////////////////////////
HWND Create(HINSTANCE hInst, int nCmdShow)
{
    hInstance = hInst;
    DWORD Style = WS_OVERLAPPEDWINDOW & ~WS_MAXIMIZEBOX;

    HWND hwnd = CreateWindow(szAppName, szAppName,
                Style & ~WS_THICKFRAME,
                CW_USEDEFAULT, CW_USEDEFAULT,
                CW_USEDEFAULT, CW_USEDEFAULT,
                NULL, NULL, hInst, NULL);

    if (hwnd == NULL)
        return hwnd;

    nCmdShow = SW_SHOWMINIMIZED;

    ShowWindow(hwnd, nCmdShow);
    UpdateWindow(hwnd);

    return hwnd;
}
```

13

continues

Listing 13.1. continued

```c
// --------------------------------------------------------
// WndProc and Implementation
// --------------------------------------------------------

/////////////////////////////////////////
// The Window Procedure
/////////////////////////////////////////
LRESULT CALLBACK WndProc(HWND hwnd, UINT Message,
                         WPARAM wParam, LPARAM lParam)
{
  switch(Message)
  {
    case WM_SPECIAL:
    {
      #ifdef WIN32
      POINTS P = MAKEPOINTS(lParam);
      #else
      POINT P = MAKEPOINT(lParam);
      #endif
      FloatingMenu = NewMenu();
      TrackPopupMenu(FloatingMenu, TPM_LEFTALIGN,
                     P.x, P.y, 0, hwnd, NULL);
      return 0;
    }

    case WM_PARENTNOTIFY:
      if (LOWORD(wParam) == WM_RBUTTONDOWN)
        SendMessage(hwnd, WM_SPECIAL, 0, 0);
      return 0;

    HANDLE_MSG(hwnd, WM_CREATE, MenuAid_OnCreate);
    HANDLE_MSG(hwnd, WM_DESTROY, MenuAid_OnDestroy);
    HANDLE_MSG(hwnd, WM_COMMAND, MenuAid_OnCommand);
    HANDLE_MSG(hwnd, WM_GETMINMAXINFO, MenuAid_OnGetMinMaxInfo);
    default:
      return MenuAid_DefProc(hwnd, Message, wParam, lParam);
  }
}

void FillListBox(HWND hwnd)
{
  int Temp, Total = 0;
  const int Size = 1024;
  char Buffer[Size];

  ListBox_ResetContent(hwnd);
  ListBox_AddString(hwnd, "Edit");

  int Len = GetPrivateProfileString("Files", NULL, "",
                                    Buffer, Size, IniName);
  while(Len > Total)
  {
    ListBox_AddString(hwnd, Buffer);
    Temp = strlen(Buffer) + 1;
```

```
    Total += Temp;
    memmove(Buffer, &Buffer[Temp], Size - Total);
  }
}

/////////////////////////////////////
// Handle WM_DESTROY
/////////////////////////////////////
#pragma argsused
BOOL MenuAid_OnCreate(HWND hwnd, CREATESTRUCT FAR* lpCreateStruct)
{
  FloatingMenu = NULL;

  #ifndef WIN32
  DeskWnd = GetDesktopWindow();
  lpfnNewProc =
    MakeProcInstance(FARPROC(NewDesktopProc), hInstance);
  OldDesk = (WNDPROC)SetWindowLong(DeskWnd,
                      GWL_WNDPROC, LONG(lpfnNewProc));
  if (!OldDesk)
    MessageBox(hwnd, "Could not subclass!", "WM_CREATE Failue!", MB_OK);
  #endif
  hListBox = CreateWindow("ListBox", NULL,
              WS_CHILD | WS_VISIBLE | LBS_NOTIFY | WS_BORDER,
              10, 10, 200, 200, hwnd,
              HMENU(ID_LISTBOX), hInstance, NULL);

  FillListBox(hListBox);

  HMENU TheMenu = CreateMenu();
  HMENU AMenu = CreatePopupMenu();
  AppendMenu(AMenu, MF_STRING, CM_EDIT, "Edit");
  AppendMenu(AMenu, MF_STRING, CM_UPDATE, "Update");
  AppendMenu(TheMenu, MF_ENABLED | MF_POPUP,
            (UINT) AMenu, "&File");
  SetMenu(hwnd, TheMenu);

  FloatingMenu = NewMenu();

  return TRUE;
}

/////////////////////////////////////
// Handle WM_DESTROY
/////////////////////////////////////
#pragma argsused
void MenuAid_OnDestroy(HWND hwnd)
{
  SetWindowLong(DeskWnd, GWL_WNDPROC, LONG(OldDesk));
  FreeProcInstance(lpfnNewProc);
  DestroyMenu(FloatingMenu);
  PostQuitMessage(0);
}

/////////////////////////////////////
// Launch
/////////////////////////////////////
```

continues

Listing 13.1. continued

```c
void FAR Launch(int id)
{
  char FileName[50];
  char Buffer[200];

  if (GetMenuString(FloatingMenu, id, FileName,
                    sizeof(FileName), MF_BYCOMMAND) > 0)
    if (GetPrivateProfileString("Files", FileName, "",
                    Buffer, sizeof(Buffer), IniName) > 0)
      WinExec(Buffer, SW_SHOWNORMAL);
}

//////////////////////////////////////
// Handle WM_COMMAND
//////////////////////////////////////
#pragma argsused
void MenuAid_OnCommand(HWND hwnd, int id, HWND hwndCtl, UINT codeNotify)
{
  const int Size = 250;
  char Buffer[Size];
  char Buffer2[Size];

  if((id > CM_EDIT) && (id <= ItemsInMenu))
    Launch(id);
  else
    switch(id)
    {
      case CM_EDIT:
        GetWindowsDirectory(Buffer, Size);
        strcpy(Buffer2, Buffer);
        strcat(Buffer2, "\\notepad.exe ");
        strcat(Buffer2, Buffer);
        strcat(Buffer2, "\\MenuAid.Ini");
        WinExec(Buffer2, SW_SHOWNORMAL);
        break;

      case ID_LISTBOX:
        if(codeNotify == LBN_DBLCLK)
        {
          int Index = ListBox_GetCurSel(hListBox);
          SendMessage(hwnd, WM_COMMAND, Index + 1, 0L);
        }
        break;

      case CM_UPDATE:
        FillListBox(hListBox);
        FloatingMenu = NewMenu();
        break;
    }
}

//////////////////////////////////////
// Handle WM_GetMinMaxInfo
//////////////////////////////////////
```

```
#pragma argsused
void MenuAid_OnGetMinMaxInfo(HWND hwnd,
                             MINMAXINFO FAR* lpMinMaxInfo)
{
  lpMinMaxInfo->ptMaxSize.x = XSIZE;
  lpMinMaxInfo->ptMaxSize.y = YSIZE;
  lpMinMaxInfo->ptMaxPosition.x = 100;
  lpMinMaxInfo->ptMaxPosition.y = 100;
  lpMinMaxInfo->ptMinTrackSize.x = XSIZE;
  lpMinMaxInfo->ptMinTrackSize.y = YSIZE;
  lpMinMaxInfo->ptMaxTrackSize.x = XSIZE;
  lpMinMaxInfo->ptMaxTrackSize.y = YSIZE;
}

///////////////////////////////////
// NewMenu
///////////////////////////////////
HMENU NewMenu(void)
{
  int Temp, Total = 0;
  const int Size = 1024;
  char Buffer[Size];
  ItemsInMenu = 2;

  if (FloatingMenu) DestroyMenu(FloatingMenu);
  int Len = GetPrivateProfileString("Files", NULL, "",
                                    Buffer, Size, IniName);

  FloatingMenu = CreatePopupMenu();
  AppendMenu(FloatingMenu, MF_STRING, 1, "Edit");

  while(Len > Total)
  {
    AppendMenu(FloatingMenu, MF_ENABLED ¦ MF_STRING,
               ItemsInMenu, Buffer);
    Temp = strlen(Buffer) + 1;
    Total += Temp;
    memmove(Buffer, &Buffer[Temp], Size - Total);
    ItemsInMenu++;
  }

  return FloatingMenu;
}

///////////////////////////////////
// NewDesktopProc
///////////////////////////////////
LRESULT CALLBACK NewDesktopProc(HWND hwnd, UINT Message, WPARAM wParam,
                                LPARAM lParam)
{
  if (Message == WM_RBUTTONDOWN)
    PostMessage(MainWindow, WM_SPECIAL, 0, lParam);

  return CallWindowProc(OldDesk, hwnd, Message, wParam, lParam);
}
```

13

Listing 13.2 shows the definition file for MenuAid.

Listing 13.2. MENUAID.DEF.

```
 1: ; MENUAID.DEF
 2:
 3: NAME            MenuAid
 4: DESCRIPTION     'MenuAid Window'
 7: CODE            PRELOAD MOVEABLE
 8: DATA            PRELOAD MOVEABLE MULTIPLE
 9:
10: HEAPSIZE    10240
11: STACKSIZE   25120
```

Listing 13.3 shows the resource file for MenuAid.

Listing 13.3. MENUAID.RC.

```
1: // MENUAID.RC
2: MenuAid ICON "MENUAID.ICO"
```

Listing 13.4 shows the Borland makefile for MenuAid.

MENUAID.ICO (32×32)

Listing 13.4. MENUAID.MAK (Borland).

```
# MENUAID makefile

APPNAME = MENUAID
OBJS = $(APPNAME).obj
LIBS    =
BCROOT = $(MAKEDIR)\..
INCPATH= $(BCROOT)\INCLUDE
LIBPATH= $(BCROOT)\LIB


!if !$d(WIN16)
COMPILER = BCC32.EXE
RCCOMPLR = BRC32.EXE -w32
CFLAGS   = -H -W -v -w4
```

```
!else
COMPILER = BCC.EXE
RCCOMPLR = BRC.EXE
CFLAGS   = -H -W -ml -v -w4
!endif

# Link
$(APPNAME).exe: $(OBJS) $(APPNAME).def $(APPNAME).res
  $(COMPILER) -L$(LIBPATH) $(CFLAGS) $(OBJS) $(LIBS)
  $(RCCOMPLR) $(APPNAME).res

# Compile
.cpp.obj:
  $(COMPILER) -c $(CFLAGS) -I$(INCPATH) { $< }

# Resource
$(APPNAME).res : $(APPNAME).rc
  $(RCCOMPLR) -R -I$(INCPATH) $(APPNAME).RC
```

Listing 13.5 shows the Microsoft makefile for MenuAid.

Listing 13.5. MENUAID.MAK (Microsoft).

```
#-----------------------------------------------
# MENUAIMS.MAK
#-----------------------------------------------

# Some Macros
APPNAME=MENUAID
TARGETOS=WIN95
APPVER=4.0
OBJS=$(APPNAME).OBJ

!include <win32.mak>

all: $(APPNAME).exe

# Update the resource if necessary

$(APPNAME).res: $(APPNAME).rc
  $(rc) $(rcflags) $(rcvars) $(APPNAME).rc

# Update the object files if necessary

# compile
.cpp.obj:
  $(cc) $(cflags) $(cvars) $(cdebug) $<

# Update the executable file if necessary.

$(APPNAME).exe: $(OBJS) $(APPNAME).res
  $(link) $(linkdebug) $(guiflags) -out:$(APPNAME).exe \
  $(OBJS) $(APPNAME).res $(guilibs) comctl32.lib
```

13

This program enables you to launch applications either by clicking files in a list box or by selecting items from a floating menu. Under Windows 16, the menu can be reached by clicking the right mouse button anywhere on the desktop window.

MenuAid first appears in a minimized state. You can leave it that way if you want, or you can pop it open to reveal a list box containing the same list of files displayed in the program's floating menu. (See Figure 13.4.) The list of programs you can run is kept in a file called MENUAID.INI, which should be stored in the Windows subdirectory. The Edit option, in the program's menu, enables you to modify this file at any time in order to change the available files.

Figure 13.4.
By default, MenuAid appears on the desktop in iconized form; it looks like this if you open the icon.

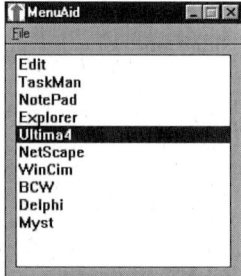

MenuAid in Brief

The code for the MenuAid program has been carefully tested and should run without a hitch under Windows 3.1. However, before you proceed, I'll warn you that subclassing the Windows desktop can be a rather delicate operation. As a result, you should be sure to save your work before you try it.

I'm not going to spend a lot of time discussing this program. In particular, I'm going to leave it up to you to discover how this program subclasses the desktop. This is secret bonus territory here, and you have to do your own spelunking. (Hint: Check out the first three calls in MenuAid_OnCreate, starting on line 179.)

There are, however, two important techniques used in this program that everyone should know about:

☐ MenuAid shows how to create menus dynamically at runtime.

☐ It also shows you how to read the contents of an initialization file, which in this case is called MENUAID.INI.

In the next two sections, I'll discuss both of these issues.

Working with Initialization Files

Windows programs store information in initialization files, all of which have an .INI extension. These files come in two flavors. The first is a small (but important) set of one called WIN.INI. You can access the contents of this file with the following functions:

GetProfileString	Retrieves a string from WIN.INI
GetProfileInt	Retrieves an integer value from WIN.INI
WriteProfileString	Writes a string to WIN.INI

Here are two excerpts from the WIN.INI file on my computer:

```
[SoundBlaster]
Port=220
Int=7
DMA=1

[PDOXWIN]
WORKDIR=C:\PDOXWIN\WORKING
PRIVDIR=C:\PDOXWIN\PRIVATE
```

If one of the drivers for my Sound Blaster card wants to know which port to use, it can access the information with GetProfileInt. If Paradox for Windows wants to know my current working directory, it can access the information by calling GetProfileString. Either piece of information can be changed by calling WriteProfileString.

The problem with this scheme is that any one Windows machine can have hundreds of programs, all of which might want to store initialization data. Before long, the WIN.INI file becomes even more unmanageable than it was when you first loaded Windows. The remedy for this situation is the following set of calls, which can be used to read or write information from a "private" initialization file bearing any name you choose:

GetPrivateProfileString	Retrieves a string from an INI file
GetPrivateProfileInt	Retrieves an integer from an INI file
WritePrivateProfileString	Writes a string to an INI file

The MenuAid program uses GetPrivateProfileString to read information from MENUAID.INI, which is stored in the Windows subdirectory. The format for MENUAID.INI looks like this:

```
[Files]
<FileName>=<PathToFile>
```

The key parts of this file can be described as follows:

- The word *Files* represents the title of the only section in the initialization file.
- The word *FileName* represents an entry that appears in the program's menu.
- The string *PathToFile* informs MenuAid where to find the program the user wants to run.

To help you understand how this simple format works in practice, take a look at Figure 13.5.

Given the previously shown initialization file, the first entry in the program's menu starts up the famous Windows Solitaire game. Specifically, if the user selects Sol from the program's floating menu, MenuAid can retrieve the location of the solitaire program by making the following call:

```
if (GetPrivateProfileString("Files", FileName, "",
    Buffer, sizeof(Buffer), IniName) > 0)
```

Figure 13.5.

Selecting Edit from the floating menu pops up the Notepad with an editable copy of MENUAID.INI.

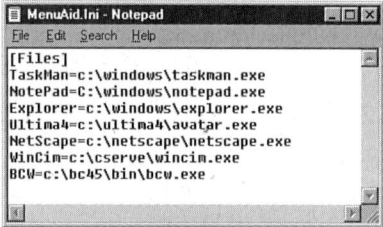

After MenuAid retrieves the path to the program that the user wants to run, it passes the information to WinExec, which launches the program. If you would like to study this process in more depth, take a look at the Launch procedure in the program's source code.

Syntax

GetPrivateProfileString

```
int GetPrivateProfileString(LPCSTR, LPCSTR, LPCSTR,
                            LPSTR, INT, LPCSTR)
```

GetPrivateProfileString takes six parameters:

LPCSTR lpszSection	The address of a section in the file
LPCSTR lpszEntry	The address of an entry, such as Sol
LPCSTR lpszDefault	A default string to return on failure
LPSTR lpszReturnBuffer	A buffer to hold a reply
int cbReturnBuffer	Size of the buffer that holds the reply
LPCSTR lpszFilename	Initialization file, such as MENUAID.INI

Use the `GetPrivateProfileString` function to return information from an initialization file other than WIN.INI. Just pass in the name of the file, the name of the section in the file, and the name of the entry you want to read. In return, `GetPrivateProfileString` retrieves your entry. If the function can't find your entry, it returns the default string you specify in the fourth parameter.

Here's an example:

```
GetPrivateProfileString("Files", FileName,"",
                        Buffer, sizeof(Buffer), IniName)
```

You should know that the MenuAid program also uses `GetPrivateProfileString` to return a list of all the entries in the MENUAID.INI file:

```
int Len = GetPrivateProfileString("Files", NULL, "",
Buffer, Size, IniName);
```

Called this way, `GetPrivateProfileString` returns a list of all the entries in the Files section of MENUAID.INI. Each entry is null terminated. The MenuAid program contains a function called `NewMenu` that demonstrates one possible technique for parsing this kind of buffer.

Dynamic Menus

The second technique that you can study in the MenuAid program involves the creation of dynamic menus. This process enables you to create menus on the fly. This is something that the MenuAid program has to do, because it never knows what might be in the MENUAID.INI file.

Strictly for teaching purposes, I also build the program's main menu from scratch at runtime. This is a technique you might need to use in your own programs, although it's less likely you'll need to build a floating menu from scratch at runtime.

Here's how it works:

```
HMENU TheMenu = CreateMenu();
HMENU AMenu = CreatePopupMenu();
AppendMenu(AMenu, MF_STRING, CM_EDIT, "Edit");
AppendMenu(AMenu, MF_STRING, CM_UPDATE, "Update");
AppendMenu(TheMenu, MF_ENABLED | MF_POPUP,
           (UINT) AMenu, "&File");
SetMenu(hwnd, TheMenu);
```

The program first creates a basic menu by calling `CreateMenu`. Next it builds a stand-alone pop-up menu by calling `CreatePopUpMenu`. These calls each return an `HMENU`, which is a handle to a menu.

After FileBox creates the menu, it fills in its contents by calling `AppendMenu`. Notice that `AppendMenu` is also used to add the pop-up menu to the main menu.

AppendMenu

Syntax

```
BOOL AppendMenu(HMENU, UINT, UINT, LPCSTR)
```

AppendMenu takes four parameters:

HMENU hmenu	Menu to which items are appended
UINT fuFlags	Flags, such as MF_STRING or MF_DISABLED
UINT idNewItem	An ID that is sent with WM_COMMAND
LPCSTR lpNewItem	The string or data to be shown

Use the AppendMenu function to add a new item to the bottom of an existing menu. The state of the item can be specified in the second parameter.

Here's an example:

```
AppendMenu(AMenu, MF_STRING, CM_EDIT, "Edit")
```

After you've created the menu for your program, you can display it to the user by calling SetMenu and DrawMenuBar.

One of the more interesting aspects of the MenuAid program is the call to TrackPopupMenu. This function creates a floating menu that responds to mouse clicks by sending WM_COMMAND messages to a window specified in its first parameter. In MenuAid, this menu is displayed outside the client area. However, you can program a floating menu to pop up when the user clicks the right mouse button on any window.

TrackPopupMenu has seven arguments:

HMENU hmenu	Pops up menu to be displayed
UINT fuFlags	Flags, such as TPM_RIGHTALIGN
int x	x, or column coordinate
int y	y, or row coordinate
int nReserved	Reserved
HWND hwnd	Window in which to send WM_COMMAND messages (owner)
const RECT FAR *lprc	Rectangle the user can click without dismissing the menu

As a general rule, nothing is tricky about working with menus. Windows covers this territory very thoroughly; by and large, they've done an excellent job providing tools that are easy to use from both the programmer's and the user's point of view.

If you want to place bitmaps inside a menu, however, the subject does get a bit more complicated. You'll see how to do this in Bonus Day 1, "GDI and Metafiles." In that chapter, you can look at a number of issues involving advanced menu programming.

Summary

This chapter has given you a fairly thorough introduction to subclassing.

You have also had a look at

- [ ] The WM_GETMINMAXINFO message
- [ ] Creating menus on the fly
- [ ] Creating push buttons
- [ ] Reading and manipulating initialization files
- [ ] The DlgDirList and DlgDirSelectEx functions

You should sit back and congratulate yourself on getting through the material about controls. Like Bob Dylan, you probably feel you need a dump truck to unload your head (though I doubt he was thinking about computers when he wrote that line). At any rate, why don't you kick back for a while and celebrate by just taking it easy? However, if you're a true, compulsive programmer, you'll want to sit down and write a little program that displays all the controls you've learned about in the last four chapters. Right?

Not!

Q&A

Q   **I still don't understand the relationship between IsDialogMessage and WM_GETDLGCODE. Please explain.**

A   The crux of the matter is that IsDialogMessage translates certain key strokes, such as Tab and Shift+Tab, so that they result in the next control, or group of controls, being selected. However, IsDialogMessage sends out WM_GETDLGCODE messages to all the controls in its purview. If any of them respond with DLGC_WANTALLKEYS, all keystrokes can get through to that specific control. FileBox needs to find a middle ground between these two extremes. To get that kind of control, you need to subclass.

Q   **Tell me more about when I should and shouldn't pass messages to CallWindowProc.**

A   The NewEditProc function changes the behavior of edit controls primarily by responding in a particular way to certain messages. For instance, when selected, it receives a WM_FOCUS message and responds by highlighting the contents of the edit control. An equally powerful technique is to simply swallow any messages that come into a control. For instance, if you don't want the user to delete anything typed in an edit control, you can refuse to pass on any Backspace or arrow key messages. This is a place where passive aggression can pay off in a big way!

13

Workshop

The Workshop provides quiz questions to help you solidify your understanding of the material covered and exercises to provide you with experience in using what you've learned. Try to understand the quiz and exercise answers before continuing on to the next chapter. Answers are provided in Appendix A.

Quiz

1. When calling CreateWindow, what styles are used to distinguish a push button from a radio button?

2. What WindowsX macro can you use in place of the LB_DIR message?

3. Name 10 macros from the control message API that can be used to manipulate list boxes.

4. What field of a WNDPROC function contains the MINMAXINFO structure when a WM_GETMINMAXINFO message is sent?

5. If you want a window to be a certain shape and size, why is it sometimes better to respond to WM_GETMINMAXINFO messages rather than change the coordinates in the arguments to CreateWindow?

6. What API call is used to replace the window function of a control with one of your own functions?

7. Find the WindowsX macro used in the FileBox program to highlight the text in the edit control.

8. How can you create a floating menu?

9. What's the difference between GetPrivateProfileString and GetProfileString?

10. What message gets sent every time InvalidateRect is called? What does the second parameter of InvalidateRect do?

Exercises

1. In FileBox, comment out the reference to CallWindowProc from the NewEditProc function and then run the program. What happens?

2. Modify the edit control so the user can't type in any illegal file characters (such as a space).

Stylish Windows

It's time to take a more in-depth look at the process of creating and registering windows. In particular, this chapter explores the following:

☐ How to change the style of a window

☐ How to create child windows and pop-up windows

☐ How to use `GetClassLong` and `SetClassLong` to change the style of a WIN32 window and how to use `GetClassWord` and `SetClassWord` to change a window's style in 16-bit Windows

☐ How to use `GetWindowLong` and `SetWindowLong` to take advantage of the `cbWndExtra` field of the `WNDCLASS` structure

Throughout this chapter, the text focuses on the WinStyle program, which displays 10 different child windows, each with a different combination of window styles.

Putting on the Style

You may have already surmised that it wasn't merely coincidental that Microsoft named its new operating environment Windows. Almost every programming technique discussed so far has revolved in one way or another around the creation, destruction, or maintenance of windows. I'm sure one day we will look back on all this and consider it very quaint, but for the time being, it is the ruling interface technique and philosophy.

Up to this point in the book, you've had little chance to learn about applications that create several different pop-up or child windows. To create additional space for displaying information or to get input from the user, these handy little tools can be spawned by the main window of a program. Like the program's main window, each of these children can be given a particular window style so that its appearance and functionality can be adopted to the purposes at hand. Figure 14.1 illustrates how changing the style field can affect the appearance of a child window.

Tip: If you click with the mouse on any of the child windows in the WinStyle program, a message box will appear. Inside the message box you will find a list of the window styles that were used to create that particular child window.

Figure 14.1.

The WinStyle program displays 10 child windows.

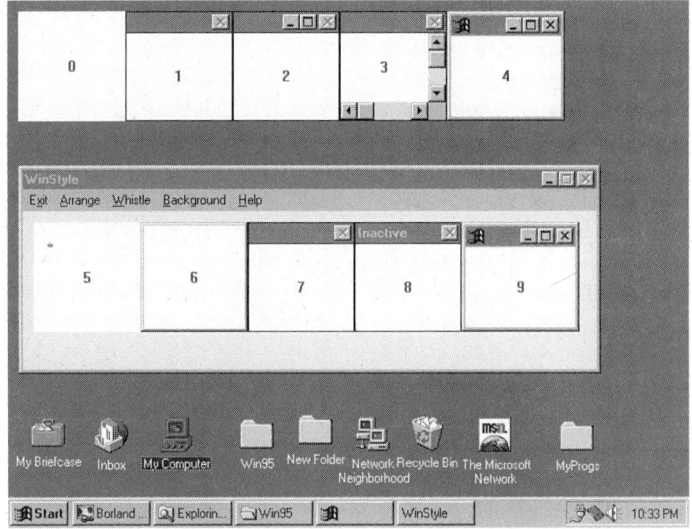

The 10 children of the WinStyle program stand in two groups. The first of these groups exists outside the physical bounds of the main window, whereas the second group lines up in a row in the window's client area. The first set of windows all have the WS_POPUP style associated with them, whereas the second set uses the WS_CHILD style. The lesson to be learned here is simple:

- ☐ WS_CHILD windows can't be moved outside the bounds of their parent window.
- ☐ WS_POPUP windows, on the other hand, can be moved anywhere on the desktop.

The style field of a CreateWindow call can be manipulated to request windows that differ radically from one another in appearance. For instance, some of the child windows in the WinStyle program have borders; others don't. Some have title bars, and some have scroll bars. Some windows with title bars don't have minimize boxes or maximize boxes; others do. In fact, the WinStyle program produces a wide range of windows, each with its own unique traits.

One of the key capabilities of the child windows in the WinStyle program is that they all can display their window styles as text shown inside of MessageBoxes. If you want to know how to make a child window show on-screen, all you have to do is click it once. It tells you what combination of styles were used in its creation.

Before you read any more about the WinStyle program, you should get the program up and running (see Listings 14.1 through 14.6) on your own machine so you can take it through its paces.

14

Listing 14.1. The WinStyle program demonstrates window styles and combinations of styles.

```
/////////////////////////////////////
//   Program Name: WINSTYLE.CPP
//   Copyright (c) 1993 by Charlie Calvert
//   Description: WinStyle windows program
//   Last Update: 08/02/95
/////////////////////////////////////

#define STRICT
#define WIN32_LEAN_AND_MEAN
#include <windows.h>
#include <windowsx.h>
#pragma warning (disable: 4068)
#pragma hdrstop
#include <string.h>
#include <stdlib.h>
#include "winstyle.h"
// ----------------------------------------------------
// Interface
// ----------------------------------------------------

static char szAppName[] = "WinStyle";
static char szChildName[] = "StyleChild";
static HWND MainWindow;
static HINSTANCE hInstance;
HWND ChildWindows[10];
HBRUSH hPurpleHaze;
HBITMAP Pattern1, Pattern2, Pattern3;

DWORD Styles[] = { WS_POPUP | WS_VISIBLE,
                   WS_POPUP | WS_VISIBLE | WS_CAPTION,
                   WS_POPUP | WS_VISIBLE | WS_CAPTION | \
                   WS_MINIMIZEBOX | WS_MAXIMIZEBOX,
                   WS_POPUP | WS_VISIBLE | WS_CAPTION | \
                   WS_HSCROLL | WS_VSCROLL,
                   WS_OVERLAPPEDWINDOW | WS_VISIBLE,
                   WS_CHILDWINDOW | WS_VISIBLE,
                   WS_CHILDWINDOW | WS_VISIBLE | WS_THICKFRAME,
                   WS_CHILDWINDOW | WS_VISIBLE | WS_BORDER | \
                   WS_CAPTION,
                   WS_CHILDWINDOW | WS_VISIBLE | WS_CAPTION | \
                   WS_DISABLED,
                   WS_OVERLAPPEDWINDOW | WS_VISIBLE
                 };

char *szStyles[] = { "WS_POPUP | WS_VISIBLE",
                     "WS_POPUP | WS_VISIBLE | WS_CAPTION",
                     "WS_POPUP | WS_VISIBLE | WS_CAPTION | \
                     WS_MINIMIZEBOX | WS_MAXIMIZEBOX",
                     "WS_POPUP | WS_VISIBLE | WS_CAPTION | \
                     WS_HSCROLL | WS_VSCROLL",
                     "WS_OVERLAPPEDWINDOW | WS_VISIBLE",
                     "WS_CHILDWINDOW | WS_VISIBLE",
                     "WS_CHILDWINDOW | WS_VISIBLE | \
```

```
                          WS_THICKFRAME",
                          "WS_CHILDWINDOW ¦ WS_VISIBLE ¦ WS_BORDER ¦ \
                          WS_CAPTION",
                          "WS_CHILDWINDOW ¦ WS_VISIBLE ¦ WS_CAPTION ¦ \
                          WS_DISABLED",
                          "WS_OVERLAPPEDWINDOW ¦ WS_VISIBLE"
                          };

// --------------------------------------------------------
// Initialization
// --------------------------------------------------------


/////////////////////////////////////
// Program entry point
/////////////////////////////////////
#pragma argsused
int WINAPI WinMain(HINSTANCE hInst, HINSTANCE hPrevInstance,
                   LPSTR lpszCmdParam, int nCmdShow)
{
  MSG  Msg;

  if (!hPrevInstance)
    if (!Register(hInst))
      return FALSE;

  MainWindow = Create(hInst, nCmdShow);
  if (!MainWindow)
    return FALSE;

  while (GetMessage(&Msg, NULL, 0, 0))
  {
    TranslateMessage(&Msg);
    DispatchMessage(&Msg);
  }

  return Msg.wParam;
}


/////////////////////////////////////
// Register the window
/////////////////////////////////////
BOOL Register(HINSTANCE hInst)
{
  WNDCLASS WndClass;

  WndClass.style          = CS_HREDRAW ¦ CS_VREDRAW;
  WndClass.lpfnWndProc    = WndProc;
  WndClass.cbClsExtra     = 0;
  WndClass.cbWndExtra     = 0;
  WndClass.hInstance      = hInst;
  WndClass.hIcon          = LoadIcon(NULL, IDI_APPLICATION);
  WndClass.hCursor        = LoadCursor(NULL, IDC_ARROW);
  WndClass.hbrBackground  = NULL;
  WndClass.lpszMenuName   = "MENU_1";
  WndClass.lpszClassName  = szAppName;
```

continues

Listing 14.1. continued

```
  BOOL Result = (RegisterClass(&WndClass) != 0);

  if (!Result)
    return FALSE;

  WndClass.lpfnWndProc    = ChildWndProc;
  WndClass.cbWndExtra     = sizeof(LONG);
  WndClass.hIcon          = NULL;
  WndClass.hCursor        = LoadCursor(NULL, IDC_IBEAM);
  WndClass.lpszMenuName   = NULL;
  WndClass.lpszClassName  = szChildName;

  return (RegisterClass (&WndClass) != 0);
}

//////////////////////////////////////
// Create the window
//////////////////////////////////////
HWND Create(HINSTANCE hInst, int nCmdShow)
{

  hInstance = hInst;

  HWND hWindow = CreateWindow(szAppName, szAppName,
                  WS_CAPTION ¦ WS_MINIMIZEBOX ¦ WS_THICKFRAME,
                  10, 150, CW_USEDEFAULT, CW_USEDEFAULT,
                  NULL, NULL, hInst, NULL);

  if (hWindow == NULL)
    return hWindow;

  ShowWindow(hWindow, nCmdShow);
  UpdateWindow(hWindow);

  return hWindow;
}

// -------------------------------------------------------
// WndProc and Implementation
// -------------------------------------------------------

//////////////////////////////////////
// The Window Procedure
//////////////////////////////////////
LRESULT CALLBACK WndProc(HWND hwnd, UINT Message,
                         WPARAM wParam, LPARAM lParam)
{
  switch(Message)
  {
    HANDLE_MSG(hwnd, WM_CREATE, WinStyle_OnCreate);
    HANDLE_MSG(hwnd, WM_DESTROY, WinStyle_OnDestroy);
    HANDLE_MSG(hwnd, WM_COMMAND, WinStyle_OnCommand);
    default:
      return WinStyle_DefProc(hwnd, Message, wParam, lParam);
```

```
  }
}


//////////////////////////////////
// ArrangeWinds
//////////////////////////////////
void ArrangeWinds(HWND hwnd)
{
  RECT R;
  int i;
  int j = 0;

  for (i = 0; i < 9; i++)
  {
    MoveWindow(ChildWindows[i], 10 + (j * 100),
               10, 100, 100, TRUE);
    if (i == 4)
      j = 0;
    else
      j++;
  }

  GetWindowRect(hwnd, &R);

  MoveWindow(ChildWindows[i],
             R.left + 10 +
             GetSystemMetrics(SM_CXFRAME) + (j * 100),
             R.top + GetSystemMetrics(SM_CYCAPTION) +
             GetSystemMetrics(SM_CYFRAME) +
             GetSystemMetrics(SM_CYMENU) +
             10, 100, 100, TRUE);
}

//////////////////////////////////
// Handle WM_Create
//////////////////////////////////
#pragma argsused
BOOL WinStyle_OnCreate(HWND hwnd, CREATESTRUCT FAR* lpCreateStruct)
{

  WORD i;

  Pattern1 = LoadBitmap(hInstance, "PATTERN1");
  if (!Pattern1)
    MessageBox(hwnd, "No Pattern", "Error", MB_OK);

  Pattern2 = LoadBitmap(hInstance, "PATTERN2");
  if (!Pattern2)
    MessageBox(hwnd, "No Pattern", "Error", MB_OK);

  Pattern3 = LoadBitmap(hInstance, "PATTERN3");
  if (!Pattern2)
    MessageBox(hwnd, "No Pattern", "Error", MB_OK);

  hPurpleHaze = CreateSolidBrush(RGB(127, 255, 255));
```

continues

Listing 14.1. continued

```
#ifdef WIN32
    SetClassLong(hwnd, GCL_HBRBACKGROUND, (WORD)hPurpleHaze);
#else
    SetClassWord(hwnd, GCW_HBRBACKGROUND, (WORD)hPurpleHaze);
#endif


  for (i = 0; i < 9; i ++)
  {
    ChildWindows[i] = CreateWindow(szChildName, NULL, Styles[i],
                        0,0,0,0, hwnd, NULL, hInstance, NULL);
  }

  ChildWindows[i] = CreateWindow(szChildName, NULL, Styles[i],
                     0, 0, 0, 0, NULL, NULL, hInstance, NULL);


  hPurpleHaze = CreateSolidBrush(RGB(255, 255, 127));

#ifdef WIN32
  SetClassLong(ChildWindows[0], GCL_HBRBACKGROUND,
               (WORD)hPurpleHaze);
#else
  SetClassWord(ChildWindows[0], GCW_HBRBACKGROUND,
               (WORD)hPurpleHaze);
#endif

  for (i = 0; i < 10; i++)
    SetWindowLong(ChildWindows[i], 0, i);

  ArrangeWinds(hwnd);

  SetWindowText(ChildWindows[8], "Inactive");
  return TRUE;
}

//////////////////////////////////////
// Handle WM_DESTROY
//////////////////////////////////////
#pragma argsused
void WinStyle_OnDestroy(HWND hwnd)
{
  HBRUSH OldBrush;

  DeleteObject(Pattern1);
  DeleteObject(Pattern2);
  DeleteObject(Pattern3);

#ifdef WIN32
  OldBrush = (HBRUSH)GetClassLong(hwnd, GCL_HBRBACKGROUND);
  SetClassLong(hwnd, GCL_HBRBACKGROUND,
               (WORD)GetStockObject(WHITE_BRUSH));
#else
```

```
  OldBrush = (HBRUSH)GetClassWord(hwnd, GCW_HBRBACKGROUND);
  SetClassWord(hwnd, GCW_HBRBACKGROUND,
              (WORD)GetStockObject(WHITE_BRUSH));
#endif
  DeleteBrush(OldBrush);

  PostQuitMessage(0);
}

///////////////////////////////////
// Set the brush
///////////////////////////////////
void HandleBrush(HWND hwnd, int id)
{
  HBRUSH OldBrush;

  #ifdef WIN32
  OldBrush = (HBRUSH)GetClassLong(hwnd, GCL_HBRBACKGROUND);
  #else
  OldBrush = (HBRUSH)GetClassWord(hwnd, GCW_HBRBACKGROUND);
  #endif

  switch (id)
  {
    case CM_RED:
      hPurpleHaze = CreateSolidBrush(RGB(255, 127, 127));
      break;
    case CM_GREEN:
      hPurpleHaze = CreateSolidBrush(RGB(127, 255, 127));
      break;
    case CM_BLUE:
      hPurpleHaze = CreateSolidBrush(RGB(127, 127, 255));
      break;
    case CM_SPECIAL1:
      hPurpleHaze = CreatePatternBrush(Pattern1);
      break;
    case CM_SPECIAL2:
      hPurpleHaze = CreatePatternBrush(Pattern2);
      break;
    case CM_SPECIAL3:
      hPurpleHaze = CreatePatternBrush(Pattern3);
      break;
  }
  #ifdef WIN32
  SetClassLong(hwnd, GCL_HBRBACKGROUND, (WORD)hPurpleHaze);
  #else
  SetClassWord(hwnd, GCW_HBRBACKGROUND, (WORD)hPurpleHaze);
  #endif
  DeleteBrush(OldBrush);
  InvalidateRect(hwnd, NULL, TRUE);
}

///////////////////////////////////
// Handle WM_COMMAND
///////////////////////////////////
#pragma argsused;
```

14

continues

Listing 14.1. continued

```c
void WinStyle_OnCommand(HWND hwnd, int id,
                        HWND hwndCtl, UINT codeNotify)
{
  HBRUSH OldBrush;

  switch (id)
  {
    case CM_ARRANGE:
      ArrangeWinds(hwnd);

    case CM_WHISTLE:
      SetFocus(ChildWindows[9]);
      break;

    case CM_RED:
    case CM_GREEN:
    case CM_BLUE:
    case CM_SPECIAL1:
    case CM_SPECIAL2:
    case CM_SPECIAL3:
      HandleBrush(hwnd, id);
      break;

    case CM_EXIT:
      SendMessage(ChildWindows[9], WM_CLOSE, 0, 0);
      #ifdef WIN32
      OldBrush = (HBRUSH)GetClassLong(ChildWindows[0],
                                      GCL_HBRBACKGROUND);
      SetClassLong(ChildWindows[0], GCL_HBRBACKGROUND,
                   (WORD)GetStockObject(WHITE_BRUSH));
      #else
      OldBrush = (HBRUSH)GetClassWord(ChildWindows[0],
                                      GCW_HBRBACKGROUND);
      SetClassWord(ChildWindows[0], GCW_HBRBACKGROUND,
                   (WORD)GetStockObject(WHITE_BRUSH));
      #endif
      DeleteBrush(OldBrush);

      DestroyWindow(hwnd);
      break;

    case CM_HELP:
      MessageBox(hwnd,
                 "Click on child windows to see their style",
                 "Help", MB_OK | MB_ICONASTERISK);
      break;
  }
}


// --------------------------------------------------------
// The StyleChild
// --------------------------------------------------------
```

```
/////////////////////////////////
// The Window Procedure
/////////////////////////////////
LRESULT CALLBACK ChildWndProc(HWND hwnd, UINT Message,
                                    WPARAM wParam, LPARAM lParam)
{
  switch(Message)
  {
    HANDLE_MSG(hwnd, WM_LBUTTONDOWN, StyleChild_OnLButtonDown);
    HANDLE_MSG(hwnd, WM_PAINT, StyleChild_OnPaint);
    default:
      return StyleChild_DefProc(hwnd, Message, wParam, lParam);
  }
}

/////////////////////////////////
// Handle WM_LBUTTONDOWN
/////////////////////////////////
#pragma argsused
void StyleChild_OnLButtonDown(HWND hwnd, BOOL fDoubleClick,
                                    int x, int y, UINT keyFlags)
{
  char szNum[100];

  LONG i = GetWindowLong(hwnd, 0);
  wsprintf(szNum, "Number: %ld", i);
  MessageBox(hwnd, szStyles[i], szNum,
            MB_OK | MB_ICONINFORMATION);
}

/////////////////////////////////
// Respond WM_PAINT
/////////////////////////////////
void StyleChild_OnPaint(HWND hwnd)
{
  PAINTSTRUCT PaintStruct;
  HDC PaintDC;
  char lpszBuffer[100];
  RECT R;

  LONG i = GetWindowLong(hwnd, 0);
  wsprintf(lpszBuffer, "%ld", i);

  PaintDC = BeginPaint(hwnd, &PaintStruct);

  SetTextColor(PaintDC, RGB(0, 0, 255));
  SetBkMode(PaintDC, TRANSPARENT);
  GetClientRect(hwnd, &R);
  DrawText(PaintDC, lpszBuffer, -1, &R,
            DT_SINGLELINE | DT_CENTER | DT_VCENTER);

  EndPaint(hwnd, &PaintStruct);
}
```

14

Listing 14.2. WINSTYLE.H: The header file for WinStyle.

```
/////////////////////////////////////
//   Program Name: WINSTYLE.H
//   Copyright (c) 1995 by Charlie Calvert
//   Description: WinStyle windows program
//   Last Update: 08/01/93
/////////////////////////////////////

// Const
#define CM_ARRANGE  1
#define CM_WHISTLE  2
#define CM_EXIT 3
#define CM_HELP 4
#define CM_BLUE     101
#define CM_RED 102
#define CM_GREEN 103
#define CM_SPECIAL1 104
#define CM_SPECIAL2 105
#define CM_SPECIAL3 106

// Declarations for class WinStyle
#define WinStyle_DefProc    DefWindowProc
BOOL WinStyle_OnCreate(HWND hwnd, CREATESTRUCT FAR* lpCreateStruct);
void WinStyle_OnDestroy(HWND hwnd);
void WinStyle_OnCommand(HWND hwnd, int id, HWND hwndCtl,
                        UINT codeNotify);

#define StyleChild_DefProc    DefWindowProc
void StyleChild_OnPaint(HWND hwnd);
void StyleChild_OnLButtonDown(HWND hwnd, BOOL fDoubleClick,
                              int x, int y, UINT keyFlags);

// Parent Procs
LRESULT CALLBACK WndProc(HWND hWindow, UINT Message,
                         WPARAM wParam, LPARAM lParam);
BOOL Register(HINSTANCE hInst);
HWND Create(HINSTANCE hInst, int nCmdShow);

// Child Procs
LRESULT CALLBACK ChildWndProc(HWND hwnd, UINT Message,
                              WPARAM wParam, LPARAM lParam);
```

Listing 14.3. WINSTYLE.RC.

```
 1: #include "winstyle.h"
 2:
 3: MENU_1 MENU
 4: BEGIN
 5:     MENUITEM "E&xit", CM_EXIT
 6:     MENUITEM "&Arrange", CM_ARRANGE
 7:     MENUITEM "&Whistle", CM_WHISTLE
 8:     POPUP "&Background"
 9:     BEGIN
10:       MENUITEM "&Blue", CM_BLUE
```

```
11:        MENUITEM "&Red", CM_RED
12:        MENUITEM "&Green", CM_GREEN
13:        MENUITEM "&Special_1", CM_SPECIAL1
14:        MENUITEM "&Special_2", CM_SPECIAL2
15:        MENUITEM "&Special_3", CM_SPECIAL3
16:     END
17:     MENUITEM "&Help", CM_HELP
18: END
19:
20: PATTERN1 BITMAP "PATTERN1.BMP"
21: PATTERN2 BITMAP "PATTERN2.BMP"
22: PATTERN3 BITMAP "PATTERN3.BMP"
```

Listing 14.4. The definition file for the WinStyle program.

```
; WinStyle.Def

NAME          WinStyle
DESCRIPTION   'WinStyle Window'
CODE          PRELOAD MOVEABLE DISCARDABLE
DATA          PRELOAD MOVEABLE MULTIPLE

HEAPSIZE      4096
STACKSIZE     5120
```

Listing 14.5. WINSTYLE.MAK (Borland).

```
# WINSTYLE.MAK

!if !$d(BCROOT)
BCROOT  = $(MAKEDIR)
!endif

APPNAME = WINSTYLE
INCPATH = $(BCROOT)\INCLUDE
LIBPATH = $(BCROOT)\LIB

!if $d(WIN16)
COMPILER= BCC.EXE
BRC= BRC.EXE
FLAGS   = -W -ml -v -w4 -I$(INCPATH) -L$(LIBPATH)
!else
COMPILER= BCC32.EXE
BRC= BRC32.EXE
FLAGS   = -W -v -w4 -I$(INCPATH) -L$(LIBPATH)
!endif

# link
$(APPNAME).exe: $(APPNAME).obj $(APPNAME).def $(APPNAME).res
  $(COMPILER) $(FLAGS) $(APPNAME).obj
  $(BRC) $(APPNAME).res
```

continues

Listing 14.5. continued

```
# compile
$(APPNAME).obj: $(APPNAME).cpp
  $(COMPILER) -c $(FLAGS) $(APPNAME).cpp

# resource
$(APPNAME).res: $(APPNAME).rc
  $(BRC) -R -I$(INCPATH) $(APPNAME).RC
```

Listing 14.6. WINSTYLE.MAK (Microsoft).

```
#------------------------------------------------
# WINSTYMS.MAK
#------------------------------------------------

# Some Macros
APPNAME=WINSTYLE
TARGETOS=WIN95
APPVER=4.0
OBJS=$(APPNAME).OBJ

!include <win32.mak>

all: $(APPNAME).exe

# Update the resource if necessary

$(APPNAME).res: $(APPNAME).rc $(APPNAME).h
  $(rc) $(rcflags) $(rcvars) $(APPNAME).rc

# Update the object files if necessary

# compile
.cpp.obj:
  $(cc) $(cflags) $(cvars) $(cdebug) $<

# Update the executable file if necessary.

$(APPNAME).exe: $(OBJS) $(APPNAME).res
  $(link) $(linkdebug) $(guiflags) -out:$(APPNAME).exe \
  $(OBJS) $(APPNAME).res $(guilibs) comctl32.lib
```

This program creates a series of child and pop-up windows that illustrate how the style field of CreateWindow can be used to control the appearance of a window. Notice that half the descendants of the main window have the WS_POPUP style and can roam freely on the desktop. The other half have the WS_CHILD style and are restricted to the main window's client area.

The goal of the program is to teach you about window styles. To help give you the picture in the clearest possible terms, I've made the program interactive. To see exactly what style is associated with a particular window, click it with the mouse. Up will pop a little dialog showing you the styles associated with the current window. Don't try this with the window called Inactive, because it won't respond.

The menu for the program demonstrates that all of the descendants created in this program can be controlled by the main window. That is, the main window is the parent; the others are the children and must do its bidding.

Creating the Child Windows

As has been the case in the last couple chapters, you need to focus on the WM_CREATE message handler function if you want to get a feeling for how this program works. The code to concentrate on looks like this:

```
static char szChildName[] = "StyleChild";

...
WORD i;

for ( i = 0; i < 9; i ++)
{
  ChildWindows[i] = CreateWindow(szChildName,NULL,
                          Styles[i], 0, 0, 0, 0,
                          hwnd, NULL, hInstance, NULL);
}

ChildWindows[i] = CreateWindow(szChildName,
                      NULL, Styles[i], 0, 0, 0, 0,
                      NULL, NULL, hInstance, NULL);
```

I'm sure this is just what you wanted to see—a few more calls to the CreateWindow function! Clearly, this is one of the key functions in Windows programming.

In this case, you can see that the window class is set to a name of my own choosing, called StyleChild, rather than to one of the predefined windows classes, such as button or list box. Because this class wasn't preregistered by Windows, the WinClass program is forced to register it.

There are no hard and fast rules as to where the best place might be for registering a window class. A rule of thumb is to register any big class in a separate module, and to register small classes in the same register function as the main window. In other words, if you have a big class with a long complicated WndProc, you might move it into its own module so you can get a good clear look at exactly what kind of beast you're wrestling with. This is purely a matter of taste, however, and programmers should feel free to develop or adopt any style that suits them (or their bosses).

14

> **Note:** A bit of confusion can stem from the fact that programmers tend to refer to any descendant of a window as a "child" window. In other words, there is the technical term WS_CHILD, and there are the more colloquial terms, such as child or children. Most of the time you have to use the context of a sentence to find out exactly what is going on.

At any rate, the StyleChild class is just a little fellow that would probably end up looking a bit out of place if it were isolated in a separate module. So I've hidden the registration code away in the Register function:

```
BOOL Register(HINSTANCE hInst)
{
  WNDCLASS WndClass;

  WndClass.style          = CS_HREDRAW | CS_VREDRAW;
  WndClass.lpfnWndProc    = WndProc;
  WndClass.cbClsExtra     = 0;
  WndClass.cbWndExtra     = 0;
  WndClass.hInstance      = hInst;
  WndClass.hIcon          = LoadIcon(NULL, IDI_APPLICATION);
  WndClass.hCursor        = LoadCursor(NULL, IDC_ARROW);
  WndClass.hbrBackground  = NULL;
  WndClass.lpszMenuName   = "MENU_1";
  WndClass.lpszClassName  = szAppName;

  BOOL Result = (RegisterClass (&WndClass) != 0);

  if (!Result)
    return FALSE;

  WndClass.lpfnWndProc    = ChildWndProc;
  WndClass.cbWndExtra     = sizeof(WORD);
  WndClass.hIcon          = NULL;
  WndClass.hCursor        = LoadCursor(NULL, IDC_IBEAM);
  WndClass.lpszMenuName   = NULL;
  WndClass.lpszClassName  = szChildName;

  return (RegisterClass (&WndClass) != 0);
}
```

The first half of this code is just like every other Register function you have seen so far, except that the hbrBackground field is set to NULL. This enables WinStyle to utilize a custom-made background, generated in the WinStyle_OnCreate function.

The real center of attraction in the Register function is the registration of the StyleChild class. There, four of the fields from the WinStyle class are reused, whereas the other six are redefined.

In particular, you might notice that StyleChild has its own WndProc and its own cursor. To see the cursor in action, load the program and move the mouse over one of the active child windows (such as window five). You'll see the cursor change from the arrow shape to the I-beam shape.

Alert readers have probably also noticed that the cbWndExtra field is allocated two bytes, which is the size of a WORD in the DOS Windows environment. All that's going on here is that Windows is being told to set aside two bytes of memory every time a new window of the StyleChild class is created. This memory is reserved for any purpose that might cross a programmer's mind. Windows will never touch that space. It is reserved for the programmer.

In this particular case, all WinStyle does with this extra memory is fill it with the number associated with each window. In other words, the first window has a 0 in this field, the second a 1, the third a 2, and so on. Then, during the child window's paint procedure, WinStyle gets the number back out of memory and paints it on-screen.

I'm getting ahead of myself here. For now, it's probably best to stay focused on the WM_CREATE message handler.

All the windows, except one, are created in a single loop. What sets the last window apart from the others is that it has no parent. Because of this, it can be hidden completely behind the main window—the user might entirely forget its existence. Since there might be a need to call the window to the fore, I've set things up so that all the user needs to do is "whistle," and the window will pop up from wherever it might be hiding. This is done via the good graces of the SetFocus function. If you haven't done so already, make a note of this one, as SetFocus is a procedure you are likely to want to call fairly often:

```
case CM_WHISTLE:
  SetFocus(ChildWindows[9]);
  break;
```

The *SetFocus* Function

Syntax

```
HWND SetFocus(HWND)
HWND hwnd: The handle of the window that is to receive the focus.
```

On success, SetFocus returns the HWND of the window that last had the focus. The function returns NULL on failure.

SetFocus is very easy to use; pass the handle of the window you want to focus in its sole parameter. The referenced window is brought to the fore, and further input from the keyboard is directed to it. This is especially easy to do in the WinStyle program, because it carefully saves the handles to all the child windows in an array. If you don't happen to have the HWND of a window or control available, you can usually retrieve it with a call to GetWindow or GetDlgItem.

Here's an example:

```
SetFocus(MyWindow);
```

During the call to CreateWindow, WinStyle sets all the coordinates of its children to 0. Specifically, it assigns 0 to the x, y, nwidth, and nheight fields. This is done, in part, because the calculations for their correct locations is somewhat convoluted. As a result, I store these long

14

lines of code in a separate function where they can be clearly seen. More importantly, this code can be called more than once. Every time the user chooses Arrange from the main menu, all the windows hurry back to the place they started. The key point is that the code for arranging the windows needs to be called both during program creation and when the Arrange menu item is selected. Therefore, it finds a home in its own function:

```
void ArrangeWinds(HWND hwnd)
{
  RECT R;
  int i;
  int j = 0;

  for ( i = 0; i < 9; i++)
  {
    MoveWindow(ChildWindows[i], 10 + (j * 100),
            10, 100, 100, TRUE);
    if (i == 4)
      j = 0;
    else
      j++;
  }

  GetWindowRect(hwnd, &R);

  MoveWindow(ChildWindows[i],  R.left + 10 +
          GetSystemMetrics(SM_CXFRAME) + (j * 100),
          R.top + GetSystemMetrics(SM_CYCAPTION) +
          GetSystemMetrics(SM_CYFRAME) +
          GetSystemMetrics(SM_CYMENU) +
          10, 100, 100, TRUE);
}
```

This code serves as an introduction to the nifty MoveWindow routine that will probably prove useful for you on numerous occasions.

The *MoveWindow* Function

Syntax

```
BOOL MoveWindow(HWND, int, int, int, int, BOOL)

HWND hwnd; /* Window handle */
int nLeft; /* x coordinate */
int nTop;        /* y coordinate */
int nWidth; /* width of window  */
int nHeight;     /* height of window  */
BOOL fRepaint;   /* repaint flag  */
```

The MoveWindow call is very straightforward. Place the HWND of the window you want to move in its first parameter, and place the rectangle you want the window to occupy in the last four parameters. In other words, MoveWindow not only changes the location of the upper-left corner of the window in question, it also changes the location of the lower-right corner. As a result, both the location and the size of a window can be changed at the same time. Don't let that last one slip by undigested; when you need to change the location, size, or shape of a dialog or window, you can do so with MoveWindow. (If MoveWindow doesn't quite suit your needs, additional control is given by a function called SetWindowPos.)

Here's an example:

```
MoveWindow(hMyWindow, 0, 0, 100, 100, TRUE)
```

What you must watch out for with the MoveWindow call is the fact that the position of a child window is defined by the coordinates of its owner, whereas the position of a pop-up window is defined by its position on-screen. In each case, the position 0,0 is regarded as the upper-left corner of the coordinate system. However, in the client coordinate system, 0,0 is usually the upper-left corner of a window; in the screen system, it's usually the upper-left corner of the screen.

In the WinStyle program, windows zero and five have the exact same coordinates, but they are located in entirely different places on the screen. The same is true for windows one and six, two and seven, and three and eight. The difference between each set of windows is that pop-up windows use screen coordinates, and child windows use client coordinates.

This distinction keeps reappearing throughout many different fragments of Windows code. For instance, the GetClientRect and GetWindowRect calls differ; the first retrieves the coordinates of a window relative to its own dimensions, whereas the latter returns a window's coordinates relative to its position on-screen. In other words, GetClientRect always returns 0,0 as the upper-left corner of a window.

Note: It happens that the location 0,0 is not—in actual point of fact—always defined as the upper-left corner of a screen or window. Yes, even this seemingly sacrosanct screen coordinate can be changed when a programmer decides to set the window or viewport origin by calling the Windows API functions SetViewportOrg and SetWindowOrg. Bonus Day 1, "GDI and Metafiles," discusses these powerful calls.

To test whether you really understand some of the basics of the Windows coordinate system, take a look at the call that defines the location of the last of the child windows, which is called window number nine, in memory of John Lennon. This window, as you recall, doesn't have a parent, and it isn't a child window. As a result, its dimensions are defined in screen coordinates.

However, I wanted to place it with the group of child windows so you could see that it can be hidden behind the main window. This is a trait unique to parentless windows. Its siblings always reside in front of their parent.

14

Take a good close look at the call that sets the dimensions of window number nine:

```
RECT R;

...

GetWindowRect(hwnd, &R);

MoveWindow(ChildWindows[i],
          R.left + 10 + (j * 100) +
          GetSystemMetrics(SM_CXFRAME),
          R.top + GetSystemMetrics(SM_CYCAPTION) +
          GetSystemMetrics(SM_CYFRAME) +
          GetSystemMetrics(SM_CYMENU) +
          10, 100, 100, TRUE);
```

The code starts by getting the screen-based coordinates of the program's main window. Both window number nine and its parent are defined in terms of their location on-screen. Ten is added to this location, and the presence of the four child windows is taken into account by multiplying *j* times the width of each of those windows.

However, that's not the end of the story. Before the preferred location of the parentless window can be calculated, the width of the WindowFrame must also be taken into account. To get the width of the window frame, the WinStyle program makes a call to GetSystemMetrics, and passes in the constant SM_CXFRAME. In short, the program asks Windows to return the width of this, and every other window's, left-hand border.

This same type of calculation must be performed before the location of the top of window number nine can be calculated correctly. In particular, WinStyle calls GetSystemMetrics to retrieve the height of the frame at the top of the window, the height of the caption, and the height of the menu bar. All this data is added to the screen coordinate for the top of its parent, and then it's incremented by 10.

Note: All the normal child windows don't need to take into account the height of the menu bar or the caption. This is because the menu bar, caption, and frame are never considered to be part of the client area of a window.

It has taken me quite a while to explain this funny business about screen coordinates and client coordinates, GetWindowRect and GetClientRect. However, I think it's worth pointing out that no portion of this coordinate system, in and of itself, is particularly complicated. If the accumulated weight of all these bits of information becomes a bit overwhelming at times, slow down and take things one step at a time. Just go slowly, take the time to reason things out. Microsoft tried to make each part of Windows programming as simple as possible. What's complicated is the accumulated weight of so many individual pieces of knowledge.

What Windows programming takes is dedication, not raw intelligence. You have to want to do this. If you don't want it, for heaven's sake just put this book down and go outside and enjoy yourself. Or go out and buy Delphi, which gives similar results with much less work. The big secret is that good Windows API code is written by programming wonks. You have to be at least 50 percent propeller-head to avoid experiencing untold miseries. However, if you like this kind of stuff, then this is paradise. If you like to dig into the core of complicated systems, Windows programming is Shangri-La.

You Need a Lot of Class if You Want to Do It with Style

This is probably as good a time as any to finally do some serious talking about the actual window styles. Here are the styles of the 10 child windows:

1. `WS_POPUP | WS_VISIBLE`
2. `WS_POPUP | WS_VISIBLE | WS_CAPTION`
3. `WS_POPUP | WS_VISIBLE | WS_CAPTION | WS_MINIMIZEBOX |WS_MAXIMIZEBOX`
4. `WS_POPUP | WS_VISIBLE | WS_CAPTION | WS_HSCROLL | WS_VSCROLL`
5. `WS_OVERLAPPEDWINDOW | WS_VISIBLE`
6. `WS_CHILDWINDOW | WS_VISIBLE`
7. `WS_CHILDWINDOW | WS_VISIBLE | WS_THICKFRAME`
8. `WS_CHILDWINDOW | WS_VISIBLE | WS_BORDER | WS_CAPTION`
9. `WS_CHILDWINDOW | WS_VISIBLE | WS_CAPTION | WS_DISABLED`
10. `WS_OVERLAPPEDWINDOW | WS_VISIBLE`

The first four windows all have the `WS_POPUP` style. (See Figures 14.2 through 14.4.) As a result, they use screen coordinates instead of client coordinates. Also, they can move outside their parents' boundaries, whereas the child windows aren't allowed to stray too far from the nest.

Figure 14.2.

Pop-up window number one uses the `WS_VISIBLE` *and the* `WS_CAPTION` *styles.*

14

Figure 14.3.
The third pop-up window uses the WS_VISIBLE, WS_CAPTION, WS_HSCROLL, *and* WS_VSCROLL *styles.*

Figure 14.4.
The fourth pop-up window uses the classic WS_OVERLAPPEDWINDOW *style in conjunction with* WS_VISIBLE.

Notice also that the fifth and the tenth windows have exactly the same style. The difference between them is that one has a parent window and the other does not. In other words, the eighth field of the fifth window contains the HWND of WinStyle's main window, and the eighth field of the tenth child window is set to NULL.

The WS_OVERLAPPEDWINDOW constant is really a combination of the following six styles:

```
WS_OVERLAPPED
WS_CAPTION
WS_SYSMENU
WS_THICKFRAME
WS_MINIMIZEBOX
WS_MAXIMIZEBOX
```

The makers of Windows created the WS_OVERLAPPEDWINDOW style because the six constants are frequently grouped together. They just figured everyone would get tired of writing the same six words over and over again; so they developed a shorthand. (Let's give the developers a hand—they did good!)

Most of the styles are fairly self-explanatory. An exception is child window nine, which has the WS_DISABLED style attached to it. Disabled windows are totally inert. You can't manipulate them with the mouse or the keyboard.

Note: Besides using the WS_DISABLED style, a common method of creating disabled windows is to call EnableWindow. This API function takes two parameters: the HWND of the window you want to disable and a BOOL set to FALSE. Calling this function with the second parameter set to TRUE re-enables the window.

Anyway, the whole purpose of the WinStyle program is to define the styles visually, through a program. You can see for yourself that some of them have borders, some have minimize boxes, and so on. To see exactly how a particular visual effect was created, just click the window.

This is the way the world's headed. Our textbooks are going to become increasingly interactive. Writers won't have to explain everything anymore; they can just show you by saying "Hey, why don't you just pop up the program and take a look? Just click one of the child windows and you'll see what I mean."

> **Note:** The styles for this program are stored in an array, similar to the way the file attributes for DlgDirList were stored in an array for the code on Day 13, "Subclassing Windows Controls." As I explain in some depth on Day 15, "Introduction to Windows 95 Controls," this technique of storing lists of identifiers or constants in arrays can help simplify your code. It's a technique all Windows programmers should master.

A Little Bit of Background

By now, you've had a look at the main elements of the WinStyle program. You know the difference between child and pop-up windows (illustrated by their opposite coordinate systems), and you know how to change the appearance of a window by altering its style. With these ideas under your belt, you're free to move on to an examination of how to change the background of a window. While studying this technique, you get a chance to master the SetWindowLong API function (which was introduced in the last chapter).

The following two lines of code alter the background of the WinStyle class:

```
hPurpleHaze = CreateSolidBrush(RGB(127, 255, 255));
SetClassWord(hwnd, GCW_HBRBACKGROUND, (WORD)hPurpleHaze);
```

Or, if you are working in WIN32, then you write

```
hPurpleHaze = CreateSolidBrush(RGB(127, 255, 255));
SetClassLong(hwnd, GCL_HBRBACKGROUND, (WORD)hPurpleHaze);
```

To get a good feeling for what is going on here, start by taking a look at the following excerpt from the Register function:

```
WndClass.hIcon        = LoadIcon(NULL, IDI_APPLICATION);
WndClass.hCursor      = LoadCursor(NULL, IDC_ARROW);
WndClass.hbrBackground = NULL;
WndClass.lpszMenuName = "MENU_1";
```

14

This, of course, is the place where some of the primary traits of this program's main window are defined. In particular, you might notice that this program has an `hbrBackground` field that's set to `NULL`.

In order to fill this field, the WinStyle program calls `SetClassLong` or `SetClassWord`, passes it an `HWND`, a constant, and the handle to a brush. In the past, many of the brushes used in this book were obtained through calls to `GetStockObject`. The `PurpleHaze` brush, however, was created through a call to `CreateSolidBrush`.

The *CreateSolidBrush* Function

Syntax

`CreateSolidBrush` takes a single parameter that defines the color of the brush you want to create. In this particular case, WinStyle defines a light cyan as the color for the brush. Of course, this choice makes it appear that this brush isn't very aptly named. However, during its youth, the WinStyle program was considerably more flamboyant than it is now. If you want to restore some of its youthful vigor, try passing RGB the following parameters:

```
hPurpleHaze = CreateSolidBrush(RGB(255, 100, 255));
```

Whew! That brings back some memories, doesn't it?

Besides passing `SetClassWord` an `HWND` and a brush, the WinStyle program also passes in the `GCW_HBRBACKGROUND` constant. If you look up this constant in your reference manuals, you'll see that it has a value of `-10`.

It's important for you to remember that the `CreateSolidBrush` function uses up some of the GDI resources available from the Windows environment. When the program shuts down, it must give these resources back (or bite the very hand that feeds it). As a result, the `WinStyle_OnDestroy` function includes the following code:

```
#ifdef WIN32
OldBrush = (HBRUSH)GetClassLong(hwnd, GCL_HBRBACKGROUND);
SetClassLong(hwnd, GCL_HBRBACKGROUND,
  (WORD)GetStockObject(WHITE_BRUSH));
#else
OldBrush = (HBRUSH)GetClassWord(hwnd, GCW_HBRBACKGROUND);
SetClassWord(hwnd, GCW_HBRBACKGROUND,
  (WORD)GetStockObject(WHITE_BRUSH));
#endif
DeleteBrush(OldBrush);
```

The `GetClassWord` or `GetClassLong` functions are the `SetClassWord` and `SetClassLong` functions in reverse. WinStyle uses `GetClassWord` or `GetClassLong` to retrieve the brush from the User heap where the `WNDCLASS` structure is stored. After WinStyle has the brush again, you would think it could proceed to delete it. However, this isn't the case. The problem is that after the brush is first retrieved, it still belongs to the system—the Windows operating environment.

To free the brush from the system, WinStyle gives Windows another brush in its stead. This brush is just a stock object, which means it belongs to the system anyway. Now that Windows is happy, WinStyle can proceed to delete the brush it created earlier. I know you've seen this kind of logic before in this book, but I reiterate it here because it's so important—and so very easy to forget. This is a place programmers can carelessly introduce bugs into their program that can take hours, or even days, to track down.

Remember that you should use `SetClassLong` with WIN32 and `SetClassWord` in 16-bit Windows. The way to keep this straight is to remember that WIN32 wants a 32-bit value, while WIN16 wants a 16-bit value. One wants a `LONG` and the other a `WORD`.

Changing Brushes in Midstream

If you choose the Background option from the program's main menu, you see the menu box shown in Figure 14.5.

Figure 14.5.
When selected, the Background menu option reveals six different choices.

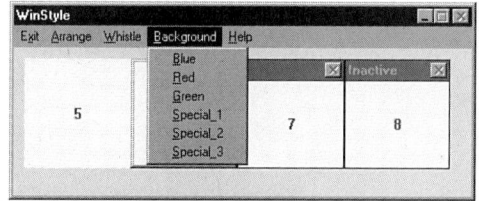

To create the Background menu box, you need to include the following code in WINSTYLE.RC:

```
POPUP "&Background"
BEGIN
  MENUITEM "&Blue", CM_BLUE
  MENUITEM "&Red", CM_RED
  MENUITEM "&Green", CM_GREEN
  MENUITEM "&Special_1", CM_SPECIAL1
  MENUITEM "&Special_2", CM_SPECIAL2
  MENUITEM "&Special_3", CM_SPECIAL3
END
```

This pop-up menu box contains six different menu items. When the user selects any of these items, a `WM_COMMAND` message is sent to the `WndProc`.

If the user chooses a new color from the menu, the system calls the following code from the `WinStyle_OnCommand` function:

```
#ifdef WIN32
OldBrush = (HBRUSH)GetClassLong(hwnd, GCL_HBRBACKGROUND);
#else
OldBrush = (HBRUSH)GetClassWord(hwnd, GCW_HBRBACKGROUND);
#endif
```

14

```
switch (id)
{
  case CM_RED:
    hPurpleHaze = CreateSolidBrush(RGB(255, 127, 127));
    break;
  case CM_GREEN:
    hPurpleHaze = CreateSolidBrush(RGB(127, 255, 127));
    break;
  case CM_BLUE:
    hPurpleHaze = CreateSolidBrush(RGB(127, 127, 255));
    break;
  case CM_SPECIAL1:
    hPurpleHaze = CreatePatternBrush(Pattern1);
    break;
  case CM_SPECIAL2:
    hPurpleHaze = CreatePatternBrush(Pattern2);
    break;
  case CM_SPECIAL3:
    hPurpleHaze = CreatePatternBrush(Pattern3);
    break;
}
#ifdef WIN32
SetClassLong(hwnd, GCL_HBRBACKGROUND, (WORD)hPurpleHaze);
#else
SetClassWord(hwnd, GCW_HBRBACKGROUND, (WORD)hPurpleHaze);
#endif
DeleteBrush(OldBrush);
InvalidateRect(hwnd, NULL, TRUE);
```

This code is closely related to what you saw earlier in the WM_DESTROY message handler function. Specifically, WinStyle first gloms onto the old brush from the User heap. Then, it creates a new brush and feeds the hungry maw of Windows with it via the SetClassWord or SetClassLong function. The next step is to delete the recently liberated brush; then, coerce Windows into showing the resulting change by forcing a repaint with the InvalidateRect function.

A slight variation on this theme is played out when the user chooses the Special_2 menu option. In this case, one of the program's three bitmaps is turned into a brush—thanks to the good graces of the CreatePatternBrush API function. Here's the whole process shown in a condensed 32-bit version:

```
278:    case CM_SPECIAL2:
279:        OldBrush = (HBRUSH)GetClassLong(hwnd, GCL_HBRBACKGROUND);
280:        hPurpleHaze = CreatePatternBrush(Pattern2);
281:        SetClassLong(hwnd, GCL_HBRBACKGROUND, (WORD)hPurpleHaze);
282:        DeleteBrush(OldBrush);
283:        InvalidateRect(hwnd, NULL, TRUE);
284:        break;
```

Take a moment to be sure you are absorbing this information. The key fact to remember is that Windows can convert a bitmap into a brush. The brush, at least in 16-bit Windows, should be exactly 8×8 pixels in size, as shown in Figure 14.6.

Figure 14.6.
A close-up of the three 8×8 pixel patterns used to create the WinStyle "Special" backgrounds.

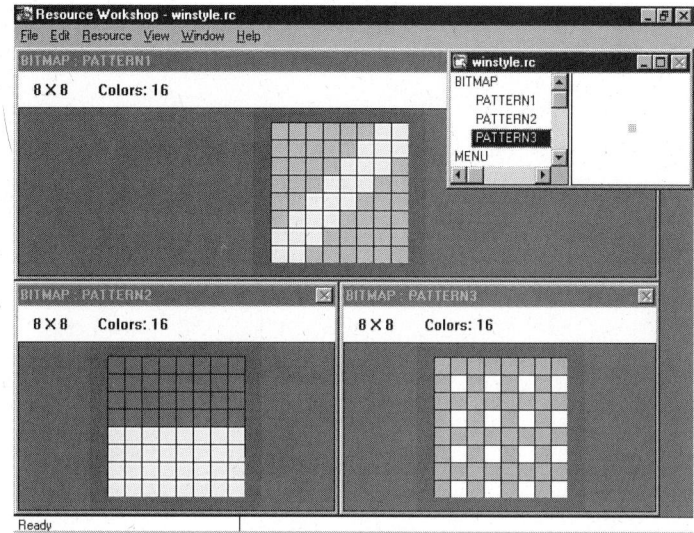

After you create a brush through this mechanism, Windows paints it repeatedly so that it fills in the entire background of a window. The second background, shown in Figure 14.6, for example, could be used to punish users who refuse to follow your carefully laid-down rules. You should, however, promise to replace it with a more copacetic background if they'll agree to be good. You might also notice that the background used in Special_3 should be familiar to all users of Borland's solemn (and now late-lamented) "chiseled steel" dialog boxes.

Using the *cbWndExtra* Bytes

The last little trick performed by the WinStyle program involves those two bytes it sets aside in the cbWndExtra field during the Register function. As mentioned, the WinStyle_OnCreate function fills those bytes with the number which is to be associated with each of the child windows:

```
200:   for (i = 0; i < 10; i++)
201:     SetWindowLong(ChildWindows[i], 0, i);
```

WinStyle uses the SetWindowLong function rather than the SetClassWord or SetClassLong function. The difference is that SetClassLong focuses on the cbWndExtra bytes rather than the cbClassExtra bytes.

The numbers stored in the cbWndExtra bytes are retrieved during the response to a WM_PAINT message:

```
352: void StyleChild_OnPaint(HWND hwnd)
353: {
354:   PAINTSTRUCT PaintStruct;
355:   HDC PaintDC;
356:   char lpszBuffer[100];
357:   RECT R;
358:
359:   LONG i = GetWindowLong(hwnd, 0);
360:   wsprintf(lpszBuffer, "%ld", i);
361:
362:   PaintDC = BeginPaint(hwnd, &PaintStruct);
363:
364:   SetTextColor(PaintDC, RGB(0, 0, 255));
365:   SetBkMode(PaintDC, TRANSPARENT);
366:   GetClientRect(hwnd, &R);
367:   DrawText(PaintDC, lpszBuffer, -1, &R,
368:           DT_SINGLELINE | DT_CENTER | DT_VCENTER);
369:
370:   EndPaint(hwnd, &PaintStruct);
371:
```

As you can see, WinStyle snatches the cbWndExtra bytes with the GetWindowLong function, translates them into a string, and pastes them up on the child windows for all to see.

Note that every instance of the StyleChild class shares this same paint method. As a result, they all paint their number in the middle of their screen.

The StyleChild_OnPaint method calls the DrawText method rather than the TextOut method to display its little message on-screen. The DT_SINGLELINE, DT_CENTER, and DT_VCENTER constants, discussed earlier in this book, are defined in your reference materials. The key point to remember is that the DT_VCENTER constant, which positions text in the vertical center of the screen, won't work unless used in conjunction with DT_SINGLELINE. Once again, don't try to memorize all these facts right away. Instead, just look 'em up when you need to use 'em.

Note: The online help states that WIN32 programmers should use `GetWindowLong` rather than `GetWindowWord`. Specifically, it says: "The `GWW_` values are obsolete in Win32. You must use the `GetWindowLong` function to retrieve information about the window." You will find that there are times when the function will work in 32-bit Windows, but that's only because you are lucky. Specifically, the high 16 bits you pass through are being lost. If there is no important data in those 16 bits, all will go well; otherwise, there could be trouble. The only safe thing to do is use `GetWindowLong`.

Summary

This whole chapter has been a meditation on window styles and the uses of the `WNDCLASS` structure. In particular, you have learned about `GetClassWord`, `GetClassLong`, `GetWindowWord`, and `GetWindowLong` functions, and about their cousins `SetClassWord`, `SetClassLong`, `SetWindowLong`, and `SetWindowWord`. You have also had a good look at child and pop-up windows and a little tour of the ever-useful `MoveWindow` function. All this information should come in handy many times throughout your Windows programming career.

Q&A

Q When I call `SetClassWord` or `SetClassLong`, what exactly is being changed?

A When you call `RegisterClass`, Windows allocates memory for your `WNDCLASS` structure and copies it into that memory. It also zeros out the `cbClassExtra` and `cbWndExtra` fields. This means that after the call to `RegisterWindow`, an actual copy of the `WNDCLASS` structure is in memory. `SetClassWord` and `GetClassWord` enable you to reach into memory and change the attributes of that structure. Note that this is only going to automatically affect windows created after the change was made.

Q I still don't understand the difference between `cbClassExtra` and `cbWndExtra`. Please explain this.

A Each window has its own `cbWndExtra` bytes, whereas there's only one copy of the `cbClassExtra` bytes—regardless of how many windows of this class currently are on the desktop. When WinStyle is executed, it registers the WinStyle and the `StyleChild` window classes. The first is the program's main window; the second is the class used when creating all the child windows. The `StyleChild` class is registered once, but there are nine instances of this class created by the program. Each of these nine instances has its own style fields and its own `cbWndExtra` field. In other words, Windows sets aside memory for one copy of the `StyleChild` `WNDCLASS`, but it sets additional memory aside

14

for each instance of the class that is created through a call to `CreateWindow`. That means the WinStyle program has one copy of the `cbClassExtra` field and at least nine copies of the `cbWndExtra` field. It's important to note, however, that some of the fields from the `WNDCLASS` structure are copied into each of the memory structures allocated when each instance of the child window is created.

Workshop

The Workshop provides quiz questions to help you solidify your understanding of the material covered and exercises to provide you with experience in using what you've learned. Try to understand the quiz and exercise answers before continuing on to the next chapter. Answers are provided in Appendix A.

Quiz

1. What is the difference between a child window and a pop-up window?
2. What is the difference between `GetClientRect` and `GetWindowRect`?
3. What is the purpose of the `WS_OVERLAPPEDWINDOW` style, and what other styles are associated with it?
4. What two calls can you use to make a window shrink to one-half its current size?
5. How can you find the width of the border on a window that has the `WS_THICKFRAME` style?
6. How can you disable a window?
7. Every single time, without exception, that you successfully call `CreateSolidBrush`, you also have to make another call. What is that call?
8. What is the difference between `GetClassLong` and `GetWindowLong`?
9. What is the purpose of `GCW_HBRBACKGROUND`?
10. Who decides how many extra bytes a window has, and what general types of purposes can they have?

Exercises

1. Use the `ShowWindow` function to create a child window without using the `WS_VISIBLE` style.
2. Use the `cbWndExtra` field of `WNDCLASS` to store a string that names each of the child windows (in this program) that has a caption. When the user clicks one of those windows, have the string appear in the caption.

2

8

9

10

11

12

13

14

Window Controls

Now that you've finished Week 2, you have reason to feel proud. By this time, you've covered many of the major topics involved in Windows programming. You should feel as though some of the significant projects you might want to undertake are within your grasp.

Week 3 is the part of the book where you are going to start to see a lot of Windows 95–specific issues. You've covered consoles already, which is one important aspect of Windows 95 and Windows NT programming. However, you will find that from here on out the subject matter will become increasingly WIN32 oriented—and also increasingly technical.

To mark this watershed in the book, I present you with two programs that help you explore your system. If you've gotten this far, you are no longer a beginning Windows programmer. You have veteran credentials now, and so it's time to sit back and review what you've learned and think about some of theories behind Windows programming.

This chapter features two programs: one that runs only in WIN32, and one that runs only in WIN16. Don't misunderstand me. Both programs run fine on Windows 95. However, one is exclusively a 16-bit application, and one is exclusively 32 bit.

Both programs explore the memory on your system and some of your system's capabilities. What's interesting about these programs is that the first explores the purely WIN32 aspects of Windows 95, while the second looks backward toward the 16-bit heritage that is still part of some portions of Windows 95. The second program will not run on Windows NT. It is the unique privilege of Windows 95 to incorporate the best of Windows 3.1 while still providing access to most of the important features of Windows NT. This chapter helps you see how Windows 95 preserves the heritage of the past, so you can still run Windows 3.1 application, while simultaneously embracing the future as represented by WIN32 and Windows NT.

What's best about Windows 95 is intimately related to some of its most glaring drawbacks. The operating system is not exclusively 32 bit. It has vestigial elements of the old 16-bit world inside it. This is both its greatest strength and its greatest weakness. In this chapter you get a chance to explore both sides of the operating system. Regardless of the hybrid nature of its structure, there is no question that it is an extraordinary technological marvel. This chapter lets you raise the curtain and get a look at what goes on behind the scenes. In the process, you will get a chance to review much of the material you have seen so far in the book.

A Windows 95 Memory Explorer

The SysInf95 program, which follows, gives you a reading on the available resources on your computer. It concentrates heavily on memory-related issues and delves into several complicated aspects of the Windows 95 memory-management system.

Don't get me wrong. The program itself is not complicated. In fact, it's one of the simplest programs you have seen since the first chapters of the book. However, you are likely to find the Windows 95 memory-management scheme very different from anything you have seen in DOS or in Windows 3.1. Under the hood, Windows 95 and Windows NT are very different from Windows 3.1. Few things could make this clearer than the SysInf 95 program.

The code for the program is in Listing R2.1.

Listing R2.1. The main body of the SysInfo program retrieves information about the current WIN32 operating environment.

```cpp
//////////////////////////////////////////////////////////
//   Program Name: SysInf95.cpp
//   Copyright (c) 1995 Charlie Calvert.
//   Description: Get System Information - WIN32 only
//   Date: 07/16/95
//////////////////////////////////////////////////////////

#define STRICT
#define WIN32_LEAN_AND_MEAN
#include <windows.h>
#include <windowsx.h>
#include <stdio.h>
#pragma warning (disable: 4068)


// -------------------------------------------------------
// Interface
// -------------------------------------------------------

LRESULT CALLBACK WndProc(HWND hwnd, UINT Message,
                         WPARAM wParam, LPARAM lParam);
BOOL Register(HINSTANCE hInst);
HWND Create(HINSTANCE hInst, int nCmdShow);

// Declarations for class SysInf95
#define SysInf95_DefProc    DefWindowProc
BOOL SysInf95_OnCreate(HWND hwnd, LPCREATESTRUCT lpCreateStruct);
void SysInf95_OnDestroy(HWND hwnd);
void SysInf95_OnSize(HWND hwnd, UINT state, int cx, int cy);

static char szAppName[] = "SysInf95";
static HWND MainWindow;
static HINSTANCE hInstance;
static HWND EditWin;

// -------------------------------------------------------
// Initialization
// -------------------------------------------------------

//////////////////////////////////////////////////////////
// Program entry point
//////////////////////////////////////////////////////////
#pragma argsused
int WINAPI WinMain(HINSTANCE hInst, HINSTANCE hPrevInstance,
                   LPSTR lpszCmdParam, int nCmdShow)
{
  MSG   Msg;

  if (!hPrevInstance)
    if (!Register(hInst))
      return FALSE;
```

continues

Listing R2.1. continued

```
    MainWindow = Create(hInst, nCmdShow);
    if (!MainWindow)
      return FALSE;

    while (GetMessage(&Msg, NULL, 0, 0))
    {
      TranslateMessage(&Msg);
      DispatchMessage(&Msg);
    }

    return Msg.wParam;
}


//////////////////////////////////////////////////////
// Register the window
//////////////////////////////////////////////////////
BOOL Register(HINSTANCE hInst)
{
  WNDCLASS WndClass;

  WndClass.style         = CS_HREDRAW | CS_VREDRAW;
  WndClass.lpfnWndProc   = WndProc;
  WndClass.cbClsExtra    = 0;
  WndClass.cbWndExtra    = 0;
  WndClass.hInstance     = hInst;
  WndClass.hIcon         = LoadIcon(NULL, IDI_APPLICATION);
  WndClass.hCursor       = LoadCursor(NULL, IDC_ARROW);
  WndClass.hbrBackground = (HBRUSH)(COLOR_WINDOW+1);
  WndClass.lpszMenuName  = NULL;
  WndClass.lpszClassName = szAppName;

  return RegisterClass (&WndClass);
}


//////////////////////////////////////////////////////
// Create the window
//////////////////////////////////////////////////////
HWND Create(HINSTANCE hInst, int nCmdShow)
{

  hInstance = hInst;

  HWND hwnd = CreateWindow(szAppName, szAppName,
                WS_OVERLAPPEDWINDOW,
                CW_USEDEFAULT, CW_USEDEFAULT,
                CW_USEDEFAULT, CW_USEDEFAULT,
                NULL, NULL, hInst, NULL);

  if (hwnd == NULL)
    return hwnd;

  ShowWindow(hwnd, nCmdShow);
  UpdateWindow(hwnd);

  return hwnd;
}
```

```
// ------------------------------------------------------
// WndProc and Implementation
// ------------------------------------------------------

//////////////////////////////////////////////////////////
// Retrieve information about the WIN32 system.
//////////////////////////////////////////////////////////
LPSTR GetSysInfo(LPSTR S)
{
  SYSTEM_INFO SystemInfo;
  MEMORYSTATUS MStatus;
  char Temp1[500];
  char Temp2[500];
  char CR[3];
  CR[0] = 13;
  CR[1] = 10;
  CR[2] = 0;

  GetSystemInfo(&SystemInfo);

  sprintf(Temp1, "%sOEM ID: %ld %sPage Size: %ld %s"
          "MinAppAddress: %ld %sMaxAppAddress: %ld %s"
          "Active Processor Mask: %lx %s"
          "Number of Processors: %ld %s"
          "Processor Type: %ld %s"
          "Allocation Granularity: %ld %s %s",
          CR, SystemInfo.dwOemId, CR,
          SystemInfo.dwPageSize, CR,
          SystemInfo.lpMinimumApplicationAddress, CR,
          SystemInfo.lpMaximumApplicationAddress, CR,
          SystemInfo.dwActiveProcessorMask, CR,
          SystemInfo.dwNumberOfProcessors, CR,
          SystemInfo.dwProcessorType, CR,
          SystemInfo.dwAllocationGranularity, CR, CR);


  MStatus.dwLength = sizeof(MEMORYSTATUS);
  GlobalMemoryStatus(&MStatus);

  sprintf(Temp2, "%sMemory Load: %ld %s"
          "Total Physical: %ld %s"
          "Available Physical: %ld %s"
          "Total Page File: %ld %s"
          "Available Page File: %ld %s"
          "Total Virtual: %ld %s"
          "Available Virtual: %ld",
          CR, MStatus.dwMemoryLoad, CR,
          MStatus.dwTotalPhys, CR,
          MStatus.dwAvailPhys, CR,
          MStatus.dwTotalPageFile, CR,
          MStatus.dwAvailPageFile, CR,
          MStatus.dwTotalVirtual, CR,
          MStatus.dwAvailVirtual);

  strcpy(S, "SYSTEM INFO");
```

continues

Listing R2.1. continued

```
      strcat(S, Temp1);
      strcat(S, "MEMORY STATUS");
      strcat(S, Temp2);

   return S;
}


//////////////////////////////////////////////////////
// The Window Procedure
//////////////////////////////////////////////////////
LRESULT CALLBACK WndProc(HWND hwnd, UINT Message,
                         WPARAM wParam, LPARAM lParam)
{
  switch(Message)
  {
    HANDLE_MSG(hwnd, WM_CREATE, SysInf95_OnCreate);
    HANDLE_MSG(hwnd, WM_DESTROY, SysInf95_OnDestroy);
    HANDLE_MSG(hwnd, WM_SIZE, SysInf95_OnSize);
    default: return SysInf95_DefProc(hwnd, Message, wParam, lParam);
  }
}


//////////////////////////////////////////////////////
// Create the edit control where the info is displayed
//////////////////////////////////////////////////////
BOOL SysInf95_OnCreate(HWND hwnd, LPCREATESTRUCT lpCreateStruct)
{
  char S[1000];

  EditWin = CreateWindow("edit", "Original Text",
            WS_CHILD | WS_VISIBLE | WS_BORDER |
            WS_VSCROLL | ES_READONLY |
            ES_LEFT | ES_AUTOVSCROLL | ES_MULTILINE,
            0, 0, 0, 0, hwnd, (HMENU)0,
            lpCreateStruct->hInstance, NULL);

  GetSysInfo(S);
  SetWindowText(EditWin, S);

  return TRUE;
}


//////////////////////////////////////////////////////
// Handle WM_DESTROY
//////////////////////////////////////////////////////
#pragma argsused
void SysInf95_OnDestroy(HWND hwnd)
{
  PostQuitMessage(0);
}


//////////////////////////////////////////////////////
// Size the edit control so if fills the whole window
//////////////////////////////////////////////////////
```

```
#pragma argsused
void SysInf95_OnSize(HWND hwnd, UINT state, int cx, int cy)
{
  if (EditWin)
    SetWindowPos(EditWin, NULL, 0, 0, cx, cy, SWP_NOZORDER);
}
```

Listing R2.2. The module definition file for the SysInf95 program.

```
; SysInf95.Def

NAME          SysInf95
DESCRIPTION   'SysInf95 Window'
```

Listing R2.3. The Borland makefile for the SysInf95 program.

```
# SysInf95.mak

# macros

!if !$d(BCROOT)
BCROOT  = $(MAKEDIR)\..
!endif

APPNAME = SysInf95
INCPATH = $(BCROOT)\WIN32;$(BCROOT);$(BCROOT)\INCLUDE
LIBPATH = $(BCROOT)\LIB

!if $d(WIN16)
COMPILER= BCC.EXE
BRC     = BRC.EXE
FLAGS   = -W -ml -v -w4 -I$(INCPATH) -L$(LIBPATH)
!else
COMPILER= BCC32.EXE
BRC     = BRC32.EXE
FLAGS   = -W -v -w4 -I$(INCPATH) -L$(LIBPATH)
!endif

# link
$(APPNAME).exe: $(APPNAME).obj $(APPNAME).def
  $(COMPILER) $(FLAGS) $(APPNAME).obj
#  $(BRC) -I$(INCPATH) $(APPNAME).res

# compile
$(APPNAME).obj: $(APPNAME).cpp
  $(COMPILER) -c $(FLAGS) $(APPNAME).cpp

# resource
$(APPNAME).res: $(APPNAME).rc
  $(BRC) -R -I$(INCPATH) $(APPNAME).RC
```

Listing R2.4. The Microsoft makefile for the SysInf95 program.

```
#//////////////////////////////////////
# SYSINFMS.MAK - Microsoft make file
# NMAKE -f SYSINF95.MAK
# Copyright (c) 1995 Charlie Calvert.
#//////////////////////////////////////

APPNAME=SYSINF95
TARGETOS=WIN95
APPVER=4.0
OBJS=$(APPNAME).OBJ

!include <win32.mak>

all: $(APPNAME).exe

# compile
.cpp.obj:
  $(cc) $(cflags) $(cvars) $(cdebug) $<

# Update the executable file if necessary.

$(APPNAME).exe: $(OBJS)
  $(link) $(linkdebug) $(guiflags) -out:$(APPNAME).exe\
  $(OBJS) $(guilibs) comctl32.lib
```

When this program is launched, you see the window shown in Figure R2.1. In the top half of this window is a report on the current system information available from Windows 95 or Windows NT. The bottom half of the program reports on the memory status. I will explain more about what all this means in a moment.

Figure R2.1.

A window that shows the current system informa-tion available and the memory status in Windows 95 or Windows NT.

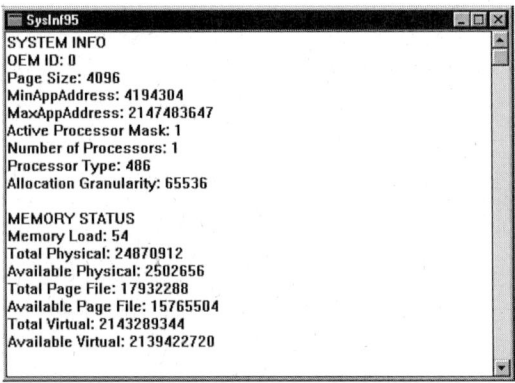

The basic structure of the program is very simple. The code responds only to WM_CREATE, WM_DESTROY, and WM_SIZE messages. In the WM_CREATE handler, an edit control is created and is filled with a large string. I will talk about the string momentarily. For now, you should concentrate on the statement that creates the edit control:

```
EditWin = CreateWindow("edit", "Original Text",
            WS_CHILD | WS_VISIBLE | WS_BORDER |
            WS_VSCROLL | ES_READONLY |
            ES_LEFT | ES_AUTOVSCROLL | ES_MULTILINE,
            0, 0, 0, 0, hwnd, (HMENU)0,
            lpCreateStruct->hInstance, NULL);
```

The basic format for this code was copied directly from the EDITS.CPP module that you saw earlier. I just copied the CreateWindow statement from it and made a few minor changes. In particular, I added the following:

- [ ] The ES_MULTILINE style so the control could handle multiple lines of text.

- [ ] The WS_VSCROLL style so the edit control would have a vertical scrollbar.

- [ ] The ES_AUTOVSCROLL style so it would scroll up and down automatically.

- [ ] The ES_READONLY style so the user would not be able to edit its contents.

After creating the control, I also responded to WM_SIZE messages so I could expand the edit control to take up the entire client area of the window. This way, the actual window will be hidden behind the edit control at all times, regardless of how the user sizes the window.

When it finally comes time to send the text to the window, I do it with the SetWindowText function, mostly because this is an easy and convenient way to get the job done. The first parameter of this routine takes the handle of the window where you want to insert the text. The second parameter takes the address of the string you want to send.

There are many different ways to paint text onto the surface of Window. The technique shown here has the advantage of providing a simple way to get a scrollbar in there that works. I showed you earlier how to get specific control over a scrollbar when you need it. In this case, just using the built-in scrollbar from the edit control is all that's needed.

Querying the System: *MEMORYSTATUS*

The information displayed in the SysInf95 program is just a line-by-line reading of two structures that the system has filled out. To get the information from the system, you pass the system a record of type SYSTEM_INFO and a record of type MEMORYSTATUS. The SYSTEM_INFO structure is passed in via a call to GetSystemInfo, and the MEMORYSTATUS structure via GlobalMemoryStatus.

By calling `GetSystemInfo` and `GlobalMemoryStatus`, the SysInf95 program is able to find out a lot about the memory on the current machine. Neither call is difficult to make. Each routine takes the address of a single parameter that contains a structure:

```
GetSystemInfo(&SystemInfo);
MStatus.dwLength = sizeof(MEMORYSTATUS);
GlobalMemoryStatus(&MStatus);
```

In the case of the `GlobalMemoryStatus` routine, you must pass in the size of the structure in the first field of the record.

In some future version of Windows, Microsoft might change the size of this record by adding new fields. It could then simply check the value in the `dwLength` field of the record to tell whether this is the old version of the `MEMORYSTATUS` record or the new version.

Here is the complete `MEMORYSTATUS` record:

```
typedef struct _MEMORYSTATUS { // mst
    DWORD dwLength;          // sizeof(MEMORYSTATUS)
    DWORD dwMemoryLoad;      // percent of memory in use
    DWORD dwTotalPhys;       // bytes of physical memory
    DWORD dwAvailPhys;       // free physical memory bytes
    DWORD dwTotalPageFile;   // bytes of paging file
    DWORD dwAvailPageFile;   // free bytes of paging file
    DWORD dwTotalVirtual;    // user bytes of address space
    DWORD dwAvailVirtual;    // free user bytes
} MEMORYSTATUS, *LPMEMORYSTATUS;
```

The first field of this record tells what percentage of the memory on the system is being used. I have two computers right now with Windows 95 loaded on them. One has 8MB of RAM on it and the other has 24MB. The 8MB machine reports that 100 percent of the memory is being used, and the 24MB machine reports that 50 percent of the memory is being used. Some veteran programmers regard these figures with a certain skepticism, but I'll take them at face value for the time being. Certainly the general tenor of these figures rings true in this particular case.

The `dwTotalPhys` field tells you how much physical memory is available. Some of the memory on your system may be reserved for the system BIOS, screen memory, and so on. As a result, it is not ever available for allocation and is subtracted out of the figure you see here. Therefore, you may find a slight difference between the number reported and the number of actual megabytes of memory you know to be installed on your machine. `dwAvailPhys` reports on how much memory is actually available for allocation on your system at this time.

`dwTotalPageFile` tells how many bytes of memory can be stored in the file on your disk where Windows swaps out its virtual memory. In other words, Windows can treat portions of your hard drive as if it were a special type of memory. This portion of your hard drive is called a paging file. Figure R2.1 shows how much memory can be stored in this file. It does not report the current size of the file. The `dwAvailPageFile` reports on how many bytes are currently available in the paging file.

The `dwTotalVirtual` and `dwTotalAvail` fields of the record report on the total size of the memory space dedicated to your program, as well as the amount of that space that is still available. In most cases, this figure will be approximately 2GB in size under Windows 95.

At this stage of the game, it's not important that you fully understand the figures being reported here. Most of this information will be explained in more depth on Day 21, "Threads, Multitasking, and Memory Management." For now, it's just interesting to see that you can keep track of these figures.

In particular, it's interesting to see the reserves of memory available on your hard disk. Even more interesting is the mysterious 2GB address space owned by your program. This is a huge reserve of memory, and it is the source of much of the power inherent in Windows 95. Over the remaining chapters of this book, you will learn more about this power and more about how you can access it.

Querying the System: *SYSTEM_INFO*

This is what the `SYSTEM_INFO` structure looks like:

```
typedef struct _SYSTEM_INFO { // sinf
    union {
        DWORD   dwOemId;
        struct {
            WORD wProcessorArchitecture;
            WORD wReserved;
        };
    };
    DWORD   dwPageSize;
    LPVOID  lpMinimumApplicationAddress;
    LPVOID  lpMaximumApplicationAddress;
    DWORD   dwActiveProcessorMask;
    DWORD   dwNumberOfProcessors;
    DWORD   dwProcessorType;
    DWORD   dwAllocationGranularity;
    WORD    wProcessorLevel;
    WORD    wProcessorRevision;
} SYSTEM_INFO;
```

Under Windows 95, the first field of this record will always be set to 0, which is the value assigned to the Intel architecture. On Windows NT, this value will probably be zero, but it could be one of the following:

```
PROCESSOR_ARCHITECTURE_INTEL
PROCESSOR_ARCHITECTURE_MIPS
PROCESSOR_ARCHITECTURE_ALPHA
PROCESSOR_ARCHITECTURE_PPC
```

In other words, this field lets you know if you are running on an 80X86 machine, a MIPS machine, an ALPHA machine, or a PowerPC.

The `dwPageSize` field lets you know the size of a page of memory on your system. In most cases this will be 4KB, or 4,096 bytes.

The `lpMinimumApplicationAddress` and `lpMaximumApplicationAddress` fields report on the lowest address in memory that is available to your system, as well as the highest address. On Windows 95, the low address will usually be around 4MB and the high address will be around 2GB. On Windows NT, the low value will be around 64KB and the high will be around 2GB. Both of these numbers help to define the scope of the `dwTotalVirtual` field from the `MEMORYSTATUS` record.

> **Note:** Once again, it would not be unusual if you do not totally understand these windows at this time. The goal is only that you get a sense for the vastness, and also the strangeness, of the WIN32 memory architecture. It's totally different from anything seen in DOS or Windows. For now, you can just gawk at these numbers; later in the book, many of them will come into focus as you learn more about Windows programming.

The `dwActiveProcessor` flag is a bitwise number that reports on the first 31 processors on your system. The first processor is assigned to bit 0, the second to bit 1, and so on up to 31. Since most of us only have one processor on our system, this number is usually going to be 1. But once again, it's interesting to see that WIN32 is set up and ready to work with multiprocessor systems. This is a whole new ball game.

The `dwNumberOfProcessors` field reports on the actual number of processors on the system. The `dwProcessorType` field tells whether you have a 386, 486, Pentium, MIPS_R4000, and so on. The `dwAllocationGranularity` field describes how the system reserves address space under WIN32. In all cases, this will be on 64KB boundaries. The final field in this structure reports on the current version of the processor. This is extremely esoteric information in most cases.

That's all I'm going to say about the SysInf95 program. The key point to get from this venture is that people coming from DOS or Windows 3.1 will necessarily regard Windows 95 as a whole new beast with an exotic new memory architecture. We are definitely not in Kansas anymore!

For further information on this topic, refer to Day 21. It will help to unwind many of the mysteries introduced by this program. For an in-depth explanation of the whole subject, see Jeffrey Richter's book *Advanced Windows,* published by the Microsoft Press. It's a great book and should be on the shelf of everyone who is serious about exploring the depths of Windows NT and Windows 95.

The WIN16 System
Information Program

Now that you've seen something about Windows 95, it's time to turn around and take a look back toward Windows 3.1. Just as the SysInf 95 program will compile only in 32-bit mode, so will the SysInfo program compile only in 16-bit mode. You can run the SysInfo program under Windows 3.1 and Windows 95, but not under Windows NT.

The WIN16 specific SysInfo program (see Listing R2.5) makes extensive use of dialogs to offer an in-depth look at the current state of a 16-bit Windows machine. This new version gives an in-depth, interrelated look at the classes, modules, and tasks available on your system. It also adds the capability to list all the objects on the GDI local heap, thereby giving you a specific look at how system resources are handled.

Listing R2.5. The final version of the SysInfo program.

```
 1: ///////////////////////////////////////////////
 2: //   Program Name: SYSINFO.CPP
 3: //   Programmer: Charlie Calvert
 4: //   Description: What I did on my system's vacation
 5: //   Date: 08/09/93
 6: ///////////////////////////////////////////////
 7:
 8: #define STRICT
 9: #include <windows.h>
10: #include <windowsx.h>
11: #include <toolhelp.h>
12: #include <stdio.h>
13: #include <string.h>
14: #include "SysInfo.h"
15:
16: #pragma warning (disable: 4068)
17: #pragma warning (disable: 4100)
18:
19: // -------------------------------------
20: // Interface
21: // -------------------------------------
22:
23: static char szAppName[] = "SysInfo";
24: static HWND MainWindow;
25: static HINSTANCE hInstance;
26: HBRUSH BlueBrush;
27:
28: // -------------------------------------
29: // Initialization
30: // -------------------------------------
31:
32: ///////////////////////////////////////////////
33: // Program entry point
34: ///////////////////////////////////////////////
35: #pragma argsused
```

Listing R2.5. continued

```
36: int PASCAL WinMain(HINSTANCE hInst, HINSTANCE hPrevInstance,
37:                     LPSTR  lpszCmdParam, int nCmdShow)
38: {
39:   MSG  Msg;
40:
41:   if (!hPrevInstance)
42:     if (!Register(hInst))
43:       return FALSE;
44:
45:   (MainWindow = Create(hInst, nCmdShow);
46:   if (MainWindow)
47:     return FALSE;
48:   while (GetMessage(&Msg, NULL, 0, 0))
49:   {
50:       TranslateMessage(&Msg);
51:       DispatchMessage(&Msg);
52:   }
53:
54:   return Msg.wParam;
55: }
56:
57: /////////////////////////////////////////
58: // Register the window
59: /////////////////////////////////////////
60: BOOL Register(HINSTANCE hInst)
61: {
62:   WNDCLASS WndClass;
63:
64:   WndClass.style            = CS_HREDRAW | CS_VREDRAW;
65:   WndClass.lpfnWndProc      = WndProc;
66:   WndClass.cbClsExtra       = 0;
67:   WndClass.cbWndExtra       = 0;
68:   WndClass.hInstance        = hInst;
69:   WndClass.hIcon            = LoadIcon(NULL, IDI_APPLICATION);
70:   WndClass.hCursor          = LoadCursor(NULL, IDC_ARROW);
71:   WndClass.hbrBackground    = GetStockBrush(LTGRAY_BRUSH);
72:   WndClass.lpszMenuName     = "MENU_1";
73:   WndClass.lpszClassName    = szAppName;
74:
75:   return RegisterClass (&WndClass);
76: }
77:
78: /////////////////////////////////////////
79: // Create the window
80: /////////////////////////////////////////
81: #pragma argsused
82: HWND Create(HINSTANCE hInst, int nCmdShow)
83: {
84:   hInstance = hInst;
85:
86:   HWND hWindow = CreateWindow(szAppName, szAppName,
87:                     WS_OVERLAPPEDWINDOW,
88:                     CW_USEDEFAULT, CW_USEDEFAULT,
89:                     CW_USEDEFAULT, CW_USEDEFAULT,
```

```
90:                        NULL, NULL, hInstance, NULL);
91:
92:    if (hWindow == NULL)
93:      return hWindow;
94:
95:    ShowWindow(hWindow, nCmdShow);
96:    UpdateWindow(hWindow);
97:
98:    return hWindow;
99: }
100:
101: // --------------------------------------
102: // WndProc and Implementation
103: // --------------------------------------
104:
105: ////////////////////////////////////////
106: // The Window Procedure
107: ////////////////////////////////////////
108: LRESULT CALLBACK _export WndProc(HWND hWindow, UINT Message,
109:                                  WPARAM wParam, LPARAM lParam)
110: {
111:    switch(Message)
112:    {
113:      HANDLE_MSG(hWindow, WM_CREATE, SysInfo_OnCreate);
114:      HANDLE_MSG(hWindow, WM_DESTROY, SysInfo_OnDestroy);
115:      HANDLE_MSG(hWindow, WM_COMMAND, SysInfo_OnCommand);
116:      HANDLE_MSG(hWindow, WM_PAINT, SysInfo_OnPaint);
117:      default: return SysInfo_DefProc(hWindow, Message,
118:                                      wParam, lParam);
118:    }
119: }
120:
121: ////////////////////////////////////////
122: // Handle WM_CREATE
123: ////////////////////////////////////////
124: #pragma argsused
125: BOOL SysInfo_OnCreate(HWND hwnd, CREATESTRUCT FAR*
                           lpCreateStruct)
126: {
127:    BlueBrush = CreateSolidBrush(RGB(0, 0, 255));
128:    return TRUE;
129: }
130:
131: ////////////////////////////////////////
132: // Handle WM_DESTROY
133: ////////////////////////////////////////
134: #pragma argsused
135: void SysInfo_OnDestroy(HWND hwnd)
136: {
137:    DeleteBrush(BlueBrush);
138:    PostQuitMessage(0);
139: }
140:
141: #pragma argsused
142: void SysInfo_OnCommand(HWND hwnd, int id,
143:                        HWND hwndCtl, UINT codeNotify)
```

continues

Listing R2.5. continued

```
144: {
145:   switch(id)
146:   {
147:     case CM_ABOUT:
148:     {
149:       FARPROC AboutBox =
                     MakeProcInstance((FARPROC)AboutDlgProc, hInstance);
150:       DialogBox(hInstance, "About", hwnd, (DLGPROC)AboutBox);
151:       FreeProcInstance(AboutBox);
152:       break;
153:     }
154:
155:     case CM_CLASS:
156:     {
157:       FARPROC ClassBox =
                     MakeProcInstance((FARPROC)ClassDlgProc, hInstance);
158:       DialogBox(hInstance, "ClassList", hwnd,
                                        (DLGPROC)ClassBox);
159:       FreeProcInstance(ClassBox);
160:       break;
161:     }
162:
163:     case CM_GDIWALK:
164:     {
165:       FARPROC LocalWalk =
                     MakeProcInstance((FARPROC)LocalDlgProc, hInstance);
166:       DialogBox(hInstance, "LocalWalk", hwnd,
                                        (DLGPROC)LocalWalk);
167:       FreeProcInstance(LocalWalk);
168:       break;
169:     }
170:
171:     case CM_MODULE:
172:     {
173:       FARPROC ModuleBox =
                     MakeProcInstance((FARPROC)ModuleDlgProc, hInstance);
174:       DialogBox(hInstance, "ModuleList", hwnd,
                                        (DLGPROC)ModuleBox);
175:       FreeProcInstance(ModuleBox);
176:       break;
177:     }
178:
179:     case CM_TASK:
180:     {
181:       FARPROC TaskBox = MakeProcInstance((FARPROC)TaskDlgProc,
182:                                              hInstance);
183:       DialogBox(hInstance, "TaskList", hwnd,
                                        (DLGPROC)TaskBox);
184:       FreeProcInstance(TaskBox);
185:       break;
186:     }
187:   }
188: }
189:
```

```
190: void SystemOutLine(HDC PaintDC, int Y)
191: {
192:   int len;
193:   int YInc = 25;
194:   char S[100];
195:   DWORD dwFlags;
196:
197:   dwFlags = GetWinFlags();
198:
199:   len = sprintf(S, "This is an %s system.",
200:      (dwFlags & WF_CPU286) ? "80286" :
201:      (dwFlags & WF_CPU386) ? "80386" :
202:      (dwFlags & WF_CPU486) ? "80486" : "unknown");
203:   TextOut(PaintDC, 10, Y + YInc, S, len);
204:
205:   len = sprintf(S, "A coprocessor is %s ",
206:      (dwFlags & WF_80x87) ? "present" : "not present");
207:   TextOut(PaintDC, 10, Y + 2 * YInc, S, len);
208:
209:   len = sprintf(S, "Mode: %s",
210:      (dwFlags & WF_ENHANCED) ? "Enhanced" : "Standard");
211:   TextOut(PaintDC, 10, Y + 3 * YInc, S, len);
212:
213:   len = sprintf(S, "Paging is %s",
214:       (dwFlags & WF_PAGING) ? "available" : "unavailable");
215:   TextOut(PaintDC, 10, Y +  4 * YInc, S, len);
216: }
217:
218: /////////////////////////////////////
219: // Handle WM_PAINT
220: /////////////////////////////////////
221: void SysInfo_OnPaint(HWND hwnd)
222: {
223:   HDC PaintDC;
224:   PAINTSTRUCT PaintStruct;
225:   SYSHEAPINFO Info;
226:   char S[100];
227:
228:   Info.dwSize = sizeof(SYSHEAPINFO);
229:   SystemHeapInfo(&Info);
230:   DWORD FreeSpace = GetFreeSpace(0) / 1024;
231:
232:   PaintDC = BeginPaint(hwnd, &PaintStruct);
233:   SetBkMode(PaintDC, TRANSPARENT);
234:   sprintf(S, "Percent free in the USER heap: %d",
235:           Info.wUserFreePercent);
236:   TextOut(PaintDC, 10, 10, S, strlen(S));
237:   sprintf(S, "Percent free in the GDI heap: %d",
238:           Info.wGDIFreePercent);
239:   TextOut(PaintDC, 10, 35, S, strlen(S));
240:   sprintf(S, "Kilobytes free on Global heap: %ld", FreeSpace);
241:   TextOut(PaintDC, 10, 60, S, strlen(S));
242:
243:   SystemOutLine(PaintDC, 60);
244:
245:   EndPaint(hwnd, &PaintStruct);
```

continues

Listing R2.5. continued

```
246: }
247:
248: // ---------------------------------------------
249: // SysInfo Dialog
250: // ---------------------------------------------
251:
252: //////////////////////////////////////////////////
253: // The SysInfo Dialog Procedure
254: //////////////////////////////////////////////////
255: #pragma argsused
256: BOOL CALLBACK AboutDlgProc(HWND hDlg, WORD Message,
257:                            WPARAM wParam, LPARAM lParam)
258: {
259:   switch(Message)
260:   {
261:     case WM_INITDIALOG:
262:       return TRUE;
263:
264:     case WM_COMMAND:
265:       if (wParam == IDOK || wParam == IDCANCEL)
266:       {
267:         EndDialog(hDlg, TRUE);
268:         return TRUE;
269:       }
270:       break;
271:   }
272:   return FALSE;
273: }
```

Listing R2.6 shows the header file for SysInfo.

Listing R2.6. SYSINFO.H.

```
 1: //////////////////////////////////////////////////
 2: //   Program Name: SYSINFO.H
 3: //   Programmer: Charlie Calvert
 4: //   Description: What I did on my system's vacation version 2
 5: //   Date: 08/09/93
 6: //////////////////////////////////////////////////
 7:
 8: #define CM_GDIWALK 105
 9: #define CM_ABOUT 101
10: #define CM_CLASS 102
11: #define CM_TASK 103
12: #define CM_MODULE 104
13:
14: #define ID_MODULELISTBOX 120
15: #define ID_MODULEEDIT 121
16:
17: #define ID_TASKLISTBOX 160
18: #define ID_TASKEDIT 161
19: #define ID_TASKCLASSLIST 162
```

```
20:
21: #define ID_CLASSLISTBOX 110
22: #define ID_CLASSSTYLE 111
23: #define ID_CLASSWINSTYLE 112
24:
25: #define ID_LOCALLIST 140
26:
27: typedef struct {
28:   UINT Style;
29:   LPSTR StyleStr;
30: }TCLASSSTYLE;
31:
32: // Declarations for class SysInfo
33: #define SysInfo_DefProc     DefWindowProc
34: BOOL SysInfo_OnCreate(HWND hwnd,
35:                       CREATESTRUCT FAR* lpCreateStruct);
36: void SysInfo_OnDestroy(HWND hwnd);
37: void SysInfo_OnCommand(HWND hwnd, int id,
38:                        HWND hwndCtl, UINT codeNotify);
39: void SysInfo_OnPaint(HWND hwnd);
40:
41: // Funcs
42: BOOL Register(HINSTANCE hInst);
43: HWND Create(HINSTANCE hInst, int nCmdShow);
44: LRESULT CALLBACK _export WndProc(HWND hWindow, UINT Message,
45:                                  WPARAM wParam, LPARAM
                                                          lParam);
46: BOOL CALLBACK AboutDlgProc(HWND hDlg, WORD Message,
47:                            WPARAM wParam, LPARAM lParam);
48: BOOL CALLBACK ClassDlgProc(HWND hDlg, WORD Message,
49:                            WPARAM wParam, LPARAM lParam);
50: BOOL CALLBACK ModuleDlgProc(HWND hDlg, WORD Message,
51:                             WPARAM wParam, LPARAM lParam);
52: BOOL CALLBACK TaskDlgProc(HWND hDlg, WORD Message,
53:                           WPARAM wParam, LPARAM lParam);
54: BOOL CALLBACK LocalDlgProc(HWND hDlg, WORD Message,
55:                            WPARAM wParam, LPARAM lParam);
56: BOOL HandleSysColor(WPARAM wParam, LPARAM lParam);
```

Listing R2.7 shows the source file for SysClass.

Listing R2.7. SYSCLASS.CPP.

```
1: ////////////////////////////////////////////
2: //   Module Name: SYSCLASS.CPP
3: //   Programmer: Charlie Calvert
4: //   Description: Part of SysInfo Application
5: //   Date: 08/09/93
6: ////////////////////////////////////////////
7:
8: #define STRICT
9: #include <windows.h>
10: #include <windowsx.h>
11: #include <toolhelp.h>
```

continues

Listing R2.7. continued

```
12: #include <stdio.h>
13: #include <string.h>
14: #include "sysinfo.h"
15: #pragma warning (disable: 4068)
16:
17: static int TotalStyles = 13;
18:
19: TCLASSSTYLE ClassStyle[] =
20: {
21:   CS_VREDRAW, "CS_VREDRAW",
22:   CS_HREDRAW, "CS_HREDRAW",
23:   CS_OWNDC, "CS_OWNDC",
24:   CS_CLASSDC, "CS_CLASSDC",
25:   CS_PARENTDC, "CS_PARENTDC",
26:   CS_SAVEBITS, "CS_SAVEBITS",
27:   CS_DBLCLKS, "CS_DBLCLKS",
28:   CS_BYTEALIGNCLIENT, "CS_BYTEALIGNCLIENT",
29:   CS_BYTEALIGNWINDOW, "CS_BYTEALIGNWINDOW",
30:   CS_NOCLOSE, "CS_NOCLOSE",
31:   CS_KEYCVTWINDOW, "CS_KEYCVTWINDOW",
32:   CS_NOKEYCVT, "CS_NOKEYCVT",
33:   CS_GLOBALCLASS, "CS_GLOBALCLASS",
34: };
35:
36: /////////////////////////////////////////
37: // SetClassContents
38: /////////////////////////////////////////
39: BOOL SetClassContents(void)
40: {
41:   CLASSENTRY Class;
42:   BOOL Result;
43:
44:   ListBox_ResetContent(hListBox);
45:   Class.dwSize = sizeof(CLASSENTRY);
46:   Result = ClassFirst(&Class);
47:   while (Result)
48:   {
49:     ListBox_AddString(hListBox, Class.szClassName);
50:     Result = ClassNext(&Class);
51:   }
52:   return TRUE;
53: }
54:
55:
56:
57:
58: /////////////////////////////////////////
59: // GetClass Instance
60: /////////////////////////////////////////
61: HINSTANCE GetClassInstance(LPSTR S)
62: {
63:   CLASSENTRY Class;
64:   BOOL Result = TRUE;
65:
```

```
66:    Class.dwSize = sizeof(CLASSENTRY);
67:    Result = ClassFirst(&Class);
68:    while (Result)
69:    {
70:      if (!strcmp(S, Class.szClassName))
71:        return Class.hInst;
72:      Result = ClassNext(&Class);
73:    }
74:    return NULL;
75: }
76:
77: /////////////////////////////////////////
78: // SetClassStyles
79: /////////////////////////////////////////
80: void SetClassStyles(HWND hDlg, UINT style)
81: {
82:    HWND hLBWnd = GetDlgItem(hDlg, ID_CLASSSTYLE);
83:    ListBox_ResetContent(hLBWnd);
84:
85:    for (int i = 0; i < TotalStyles; i++)
86:      if((style & ClassStyle[i].Style) == ClassStyle[i].Style)
87:        ListBox_AddString(hLBWnd, ClassStyle[i].StyleStr);
88: }
89:
90: /////////////////////////////////////////
91: // SpecifyAppsUsingClass
92: /////////////////////////////////////////
93: BOOL SpecifyAppsUsingClass(HWND hDlg, HINSTANCE hTempInst)
94: {
95:    TASKENTRY Task;
96:    BOOL Result = TRUE;
97:
98:    HWND hLBWnd = GetDlgItem(hDlg, ID_CLASSWINSTYLE);
99:    ListBox_ResetContent(hLBWnd);
100:   Task.dwSize = sizeof(TASKENTRY);
101:   Result = TaskFirst(&Task);
102:   while (Result)
103:   {
104:     if (hTempInst == Task.hModule)
105:       ListBox_AddString(hLBWnd, Task.szModule);
106:     Result = TaskNext(&Task);
107:   }
108:   return TRUE;
109: }
110:
111: /////////////////////////////////////////
112: // FillClassBox
113: /////////////////////////////////////////
114: BOOL FillClassBox(HWND hDlg, LPSTR S)
115: {
116:   WNDCLASS WndClass;
117:   HINSTANCE hTempInst;
118:   hTempInst = GetClassInstance(S);
119:   GetClassInfo(hTempInst, S, &WndClass);
120:   SetClassStyles(hDlg, WndClass.style);
121:   SpecifyAppsUsingClass(hDlg, hTempInst);
```

continues

545

Listing R2.7. continued

```
122:    return TRUE;
123:  }
124:
125:  ///////////////////////////////////////////
126:  // The SysInfo Class Dialog Procedure
127:  ///////////////////////////////////////////
128:  #pragma argsused
129:  BOOL CALLBACK ClassDlgProc(HWND hDlg, WORD Message,
130:                             WPARAM wParam, LPARAM lParam)
131:  {
132:    int Index;
133:    char S[100];
134:
135:
136:    switch(Message)
137:    {
138:      case WM_INITDIALOG:
139:      {
140:        SetClassContents(hDlg);
141:        ListBox_SetCurSel(GetDlgItem(hDlg, ID_CLASSLISTBOX), 0);
142:        HWND hLBWnd = GetDlgItem(hDlg, ID_CLASSWINSTYLE);
143:        SetWindowFont(hLBWnd, GetStockFont(ANSI_FIXED_FONT), 0);
144:        hLBWnd = GetDlgItem(hDlg, ID_CLASSSTYLE);
145:        SetWindowFont(hLBWnd, GetStockFont(ANSI_FIXED_FONT), 0);
146:        return TRUE;
147:      }
148:
149:      case WM_CTLCOLOR:
150:        return HandleSysColor(wParam, lParam);
151:
152:      case WM_COMMAND:
153:        switch (wParam)
154:        {
155:          case IDOK:
156:          case IDCANCEL:
157:            EndDialog(hDlg, TRUE);
158:            return TRUE;
159:
160:          case
161:            ID_CLASSLISTBOX:
162:            {
163:              if (HIWORD(lParam) == LBN_SELCHANGE)
164:              {
165:                HWND hListBox = (HWND)LOWORD(lParam);
166:                Index = ListBox_GetCurSel(hListBox);
167:
168:                strcpy(S, "Trouble");
169:                if (Index != LB_ERR)
170:                {
171:                  ListBox_GetText(hListBox, Index, S);
172:                  FillClassBox(hDlg, S);
173:                }
174:              }
175:              return TRUE;
```

```
176:            }
177:        }
178:
179:        break;
180:    }
181:    return FALSE;
182: }
```

Listing R2.8 shows the SysMod source file.

Listing R2.8. SYSMOD.CPP.

```
1: /////////////////////////////////////////////////
2: //  Module Name: SYSMOD.CPP
3: //  Programmer: Charlie Calvert
4: //  Description: Part of SysInfo Application
5: //  Date: 08/09/93
6: /////////////////////////////////////////////////
7:
8: #define STRICT
9: #include <windows.h>
10: #include <windowsx.h>
11: #include <toolhelp.h>
12: #include <stdio.h>
13: #include <string.h>
14: #include "sysinfo.h"
15: #pragma warning (disable: 4068)
16:
17: extern HBRUSH BlueBrush;
18:
19: /////////////////////////////////////////
20: // SetModuleContents
21: /////////////////////////////////////////
22: #pragma argsused
23: BOOL SetModuleContents(void)
24: {
25:    MODULEENTRY Module;
26:    BOOL Result;
27:
28:    ListBox_ResetContent(hListBox);
29:    Module.dwSize = sizeof(MODULEENTRY);
30:    ModuleFirst(&Module);
31:    while (Result)
32:    {
33:      ListBox_AddString(hListBox, Module.szModule);
34:      Result = ModuleNext(&Module);
35:    }
36:    return TRUE;
37: }
38:
39: /////////////////////////////////////////
40: // FillModuleBox
41: /////////////////////////////////////////
42: FillModuleBox(HWND hDlg, LPSTR S)
```

continues

Listing R2.8. continued

```
43: {
44:   MODULEENTRY Module;
45:   BOOL Result = TRUE;
46:
47:   HWND hEdWnd = GetDlgItem(hDlg, ID_MODULEEDIT);
48:   SetWindowFont(hEdWnd, GetStockObject(ANSI_FIXED_FONT), 0);
49:   Module.dwSize = sizeof(MODULEENTRY);
50:   ModuleFirst(&Module);
51:   if (!strcmp(Module.szModule, S))
52:     SetWindowText(hEdWnd, Module.szExePath);
53:
54:   while (Result)
55:   {
56:     Result = ModuleNext(&Module);
57:     if (!strcmp(Module.szModule, S))
58:       SetWindowText(hEdWnd, Module.szExePath);
59:   }
60:   return TRUE;
61: }
62:
63: /////////////////////////////////////////
64: // HandleSysColor
65: /////////////////////////////////////////
66: BOOL HandleSysColor(WPARAM wParam, LPARAM lParam)
67: {
68:   if (GetDlgCtrlID((HWND)LOWORD(lParam)) == -1)
69:   {
70:     SetTextColor((HDC)wParam, RGB(0, 0, 255));
71:     SetBkMode((HDC)wParam, TRANSPARENT);
72:     return (BOOL) GetStockBrush(GRAY_BRUSH);
73:   }
74:
75:   switch(HIWORD(lParam))
76:   {
77:     case CTLCOLOR_STATIC:
78:     case CTLCOLOR_LISTBOX:
79:       SetTextColor((HDC)wParam, RGB(255, 255, 0));
80:       SetBkMode((HDC)wParam, TRANSPARENT);
81:       return (BOOL) BlueBrush;
82:
83:     case CTLCOLOR_DLG:
84:       return (BOOL) GetStockBrush(GRAY_BRUSH);
85:   }
86:   return FALSE;
87: }
88: /////////////////////////////////////////
89: // The SysInfo Module Dialog Procedure
90: /////////////////////////////////////////
91: #pragma argsused
92: BOOL CALLBACK ModuleDlgProc(HWND hDlg, WORD Message,
93:                                 WPARAM wParam, LPARAM lParam)
94: {
95:   int Index;
96:   char S[100];
```

```
97:
98:    switch(Message)
99:    {
100:     case WM_INITDIALOG:
101:        SetModuleContents(hDlg);
102:        return TRUE;
103:
104:     case WM_CTLCOLOR:
105:        return HandleSysColor(wParam, lParam);
106:
107:     case WM_COMMAND:
108:       switch (wParam)
109:       {
110:        case IDOK:
111:        case IDCANCEL:
112:          EndDialog(hDlg, TRUE);
113:          return TRUE;
114:
115:        case ID_MODULELISTBOX:
116:          if (HIWORD(lParam) == LBN_SELCHANGE)
117:          {
118:            HWND hListBox = (HWND)LOWORD(lParam);
119:            Index = ListBox_GetCurSel(hListBox);
120:
121:            strcpy(S, "Trouble");
122:            if (Index != LB_ERR)
123:            {
124:              ListBox_GetText(hListBox, Index, S);
125:              FillModuleBox(hDlg, S);
126:            }
127:          }
128:        return TRUE;
129:       }
130:     }
131:     return FALSE;
132: }
```

Listing R2.9 shows the source file for SysTask.

Listing R2.9. SYSTASK.CPP.

```
1: //////////////////////////////////////////////
2: //   Module Name: SYSTASK.CPP
3: //   Programmer: Charlie Calvert
4: //   Description: Part of SysInfo Application
5: //   Date: 08/09/93
6: //////////////////////////////////////////////
7:
8: #define STRICT
9: #include <windows.h>
10: #include <windowsx.h>
11: #include <toolhelp.h>
12: #include <stdio.h>
13: #include <string.h>
```

continues

Listing R2.9. continued

```
14: #include "sysinfo.h"
15: #pragma warning (disable: 4068)
16: #pragma warning (disable: 4100)
17:
18: static HWND hTaskWnd, hLBWnd, hEdWnd;
19:
20: /////////////////////////////////////
21: // SetTaskContents
22: /////////////////////////////////////
23: BOOL SetTaskContents(void)
24: {
25:   TASKENTRY Task;
26:   BOOL Result;
27:
28:   ListBox_ResetContent(hListBox);
29:   Task.dwSize = sizeof(TASKENTRY);
30:   Result = TaskFirst(&Task);
31:   while(Result)
32:   {
33:     ListBox_AddString(hListBox, Task.szModule);
34:     Result = TaskNext(&Task);
35:   }
36:   return TRUE;
37: }
38: /////////////////////////////////////
39: // GetModule
40: /////////////////////////////////////
41: HMODULE GetModule(LPSTR S)
42: {
43:   MODULEENTRY Module;
44:   BOOL Result = TRUE;
45:
46:   Module.dwSize = sizeof(MODULEENTRY);
47:   ModuleFirst(&Module);
48:   if (!strcmp(Module.szModule, S))
49:   {
50:     SetWindowText(hEdWnd, Module.szExePath);
51:     return Module.hModule;
52:   }
53:
54:   while (Result)
55:   {
56:     Result = ModuleNext(&Module);
57:     if (!strcmp(Module.szModule, S))
58:     {
59:       SetWindowText(hEdWnd, Module.szExePath);
60:       return Module.hModule;
61:     }
62:   }
63:   return NULL;
64: }
65:
66: /////////////////////////////////////
67: // ShowWindowClasses
```

```
68: ////////////////////////////////////////
69: BOOL ShowWindowClasses(HMODULE hModule)
70: {
71:   CLASSENTRY Class;
72:   BOOL Result = TRUE;
73:
74:   ListBox_ResetContent(hLBWnd);
75:
76:   Class.dwSize = sizeof(CLASSENTRY);
77:   Result = ClassFirst(&Class);
78:   if (hModule == Class.hInst)
79:     ListBox_AddString(hLBWnd, Class.szClassName);
80:
81:   while (Result)
82:   {
83:     Result = ClassNext(&Class);
84:     if (hModule == Class.hInst)
85:       ListBox_AddString(hLBWnd, Class.szClassName);
86:   }
87:   return NULL;
88: }
89:
90: ////////////////////////////////////////
91: // The FillTaskBox
92: ////////////////////////////////////////
93: #pragma argsused
94: BOOL FillTaskBox(HWND hDlg, LPSTR S)
95: {
96:   HMODULE hModule = GetModule(S);
97:   ShowWindowClasses(hModule);
98:   return TRUE;
99: }
100:
101: ////////////////////////////////////////
102: // The SysInfo Task Dialog Procedure
103: ////////////////////////////////////////
104: #pragma argsused
105: BOOL CALLBACK TaskDlgProc(HWND hDlg, WORD Message,
106:                           WPARAM wParam, LPARAM lParam)
107: {
108:   char S[100];
109:   int Index;
110:
111:   switch(Message)
112:   {
113:     case WM_INITDIALOG:
114:       hTaskWnd = GetDlgItem(hDlg, ID_TASKLISTBOX);
115:       hLBWnd = GetDlgItem(hDlg, ID_TASKCLASSLIST);
116:       hEdWnd = GetDlgItem(hDlg, ID_TASKEDIT);
117:       SetWindowFont(hTaskWnd,
118:                     GetStockObject(ANSI_FIXED_FONT), 0);
119:       SetWindowFont(hLBWnd,
                        GetStockObject(ANSI_FIXED_FONT), 0);
119:       SetWindowFont(hEdWnd,
                        GetStockObject(ANSI_FIXED_FONT), 0);
120:       SetTaskContents();
```

continues

551

Listing R2.9. continued

```
121:        ListBox_SetCurSel(GetDlgItem(hDlg, ID_TASKLISTBOX), 0);
122:        return TRUE;
123:
124:    case WM_CTLCOLOR:
125:        return HandleSysColor(wParam, lParam);
126:
127:    case WM_COMMAND:
128:        switch (wParam)
129:        {
130:          case IDOK:
131:          case IDCANCEL:
132:            EndDialog(hDlg, TRUE);
133:            return TRUE;
134:
135:          case
136:            ID_TASKLISTBOX:
137:              if (HIWORD(lParam) == LBN_SELCHANGE)
138:              {
139:                HWND hListBox = (HWND)LOWORD(lParam);
140:                Index = ListBox_GetCurSel(hListBox);
141:
142:                strcpy(S, "Trouble");
143:                if (Index != LB_ERR)
144:                {
145:                  ListBox_GetText(hListBox, Index, S);
146:                  FillTaskBox(hDlg, S);
147:                }
148:              }
149:              return TRUE;
150:        }
151:    }
152:    return FALSE;
153: }
```

Listing R2.10 shows the source file for SysWalk.

Listing R2.10. SYSWALK.CPP.

```
 1: //////////////////////////////////////////////////
 2: //   Program Name: SYSWALK.CPP
 3: //   Programmer: Charlie Calvert
 4: //   Description: What I did on my system's vacation
 5: //   Date: 08/09/93
 6: //////////////////////////////////////////////////
 7:
 8: #define STRICT
 9: #include <windows.h>
10: #include <windowsx.h>
11: #include <toolhelp.h>
12: #include <stdio.h>
13: #include <string.h>
14: #include "SysInfo.h"
```

```
15:
16: char *GDITypes[] = {"Normal",
17:     "Pen", "Brush", "Font",
18:     "Palette", "Bitmap", "RGN",
19:     "DC", "Disabled_DC",
20:     "MetaDC", "Metafile", "Free"};
21:
22: char *WFlags[] = {"-", "Fixed",
23:                     "Free", "-",
24:                     "Moveable"};
25:
26: void FillLocalDlg(HWND hDlg)
27: {
28:   SYSHEAPINFO Info;
29:   LOCALENTRY LocalEntry;
30:   int Result = TRUE;
31:   char S[150];
32:   char *T = "Type: ";
33:   char *R = "Size: ";
34:   char *F = "Flags: ";
35:
36:   HWND hLocalList = GetDlgItem(hDlg, ID_LOCALLIST);
37:   SetWindowFont(hLocalList,
38:                   GetStockObject(ANSI_FIXED_FONT), 0);
38:   Info.dwSize = sizeof(SYSHEAPINFO);
39:   if (!SystemHeapInfo(&Info)) return;
40:   LocalEntry.dwSize = sizeof(LocalEntry);
41:   Result = LocalFirst(&LocalEntry, Info.hGDISegment);
42:   while (Result)
43:   {
44:     if (LocalEntry.wType < 12)
45:       sprintf(S, "%5s%-8s  %s%-6u %s%s", T,
46:               GDITypes[LocalEntry.wType],
47:               R, LocalEntry.wSize, F,
48:               WFlags[LocalEntry.wFlags]);
49:     else
50:       sprintf(S, "%5s%-8s  %s%-6u %s%s", T,
51:               GDITypes[11],
52:               R, LocalEntry.wSize, F,
53:               WFlags[LocalEntry.wFlags]);
54:     ListBox_AddString(hLocalList, S);
55:     Result = LocalNext(&LocalEntry);
56:   }
57: }
58: /////////////////////////////////////////////////
59: // The SysInfo Dialog Procedure
60: /////////////////////////////////////////////////
61: #pragma argsused
62: BOOL CALLBACK LocalDlgProc(HWND hDlg, WORD Message,
63:                             WPARAM wParam, LPARAM lParam)
64: {
65:   switch(Message)
66:   {
67:     case WM_INITDIALOG:
68:       FillLocalDlg(hDlg);
69:       return TRUE;
```

continues

Listing R2.10. continued

```
70:
71:    case WM_CTLCOLOR:
72:      return HandleSysColor(wParam, lParam);
73:
74:    case WM_COMMAND:
75:      switch(wParam)
76:      {
77:        case IDOK:
78:        case IDCANCEL:
79:          EndDialog(hDlg, TRUE);
80:          return TRUE;
81:      }
82:      break;
83:  }
84:  return FALSE;
85: }
```

Listing R2.11 shows the resource file for SysInfo.

Listing R2.11. SYSINFO.RC.

```
1: //////////////////////////////////////////////////
2: //   Module Name: SYSINFO.RC
3: //   Programmer: Charlie Calvert
4: //   Description: Resource File
5: //   Date: 08/09/93
6: //////////////////////////////////////////////////
7:
8: #include <windows.h>
9: #include "SysInfo.h"
10:
11: MENU_1 MENU
12: BEGIN
13:     POPUP "Local Walks"
14:     BEGIN
15:         MENUITEM "GDI Walk", CM_GDIWALK
16:         MENUITEM "E&xit", 3003
17:     END
18:     MENUITEM "Classes", CM_CLASS
19:     MENUITEM "Tasks", CM_TASK
20:     MENUITEM "Modules", CM_MODULE
21:     MENUITEM "About", CM_ABOUT
22: END
23:
24: About DIALOG 18, 24, 141, 58
25: STYLE DS_MODALFRAME | WS_POPUP | WS_CAPTION | WS_SYSMENU
26: CAPTION "About Dialog"
27: BEGIN
28:     CTEXT "What I Did on My System's Vacation",
29:       -1, 1, 9, 140, 8, WS_CHILD | WS_VISIBLE | WS_GROUP
30:     CTEXT "Copyright (c) 1993 Charlie Calvert",
31:       -1, 1, 23, 140, 10, WS_CHILD | WS_VISIBLE | WS_GROUP
```

```
32:        PUSHBUTTON "Ok", IDOK,
33:          5, 39, 132, 12, WS_CHILD ¦ WS_VISIBLE ¦ WS_TABSTOP
34: END
35:
36:
37: ClassList DIALOG 18, 16, 212, 181
38: STYLE DS_MODALFRAME ¦ WS_POPUP ¦ WS_CAPTION ¦ WS_SYSMENU
39: CAPTION "Classes"
40: BEGIN
41:        CONTROL "", ID_CLASSLISTBOX, "LISTBOX",
42:          LBS_STANDARD ¦ WS_CHILD ¦ WS_VISIBLE ¦ WS_TABSTOP,
43:          11, 9, 189, 90
44:        PUSHBUTTON "Ok", IDOK, 5, 162, 201, 14,
45:          WS_CHILD ¦ WS_VISIBLE ¦ WS_TABSTOP
46:        LISTBOX ID_CLASSSTYLE, 11, 114, 70, 41
47:        LISTBOX ID_CLASSWINSTYLE, 130, 114, 70, 41
48:        LTEXT "Styles", -1, 14, 104, 27, 8
49:        LTEXT "Modules", -1, 131, 104, 32, 8
50: END
51:
52: TaskList DIALOG 18, 18, 214, 149
53: STYLE DS_MODALFRAME ¦ WS_POPUP ¦ WS_CAPTION ¦ WS_SYSMENU
54: CAPTION "Tasks"
55: BEGIN
56:        CONTROL "", ID_TASKLISTBOX, "LISTBOX",
57:          LBS_STANDARD ¦ WS_CHILD ¦ WS_VISIBLE ¦ WS_TABSTOP,
58:          7, 15, 90, 90
59:        PUSHBUTTON "Ok", IDOK, 6, 130, 202, 14,
60:          WS_CHILD ¦ WS_VISIBLE ¦ WS_TABSTOP
61:        LTEXT "", ID_TASKEDIT, 7, 114, 200, 8
62:        LISTBOX ID_TASKCLASSLIST, 117, 15, 90, 90,
63:          LBS_NOTIFY ¦ WS_CHILD ¦ WS_VISIBLE ¦ WS_BORDER ¦
                           WS_VSCROLL
64:        LTEXT "Tasks", -1, 7, 4, 62, 8,
65:          WS_CHILD ¦ WS_VISIBLE ¦ WS_GROUP
66:        LTEXT "Classes in Task", -1, 117, 4, 80, 8,
67:          WS_CHILD ¦ WS_VISIBLE ¦ WS_GROUP
68: END
69:
70: ModuleList DIALOG 18, 18, 180, 159
71: STYLE DS_MODALFRAME ¦ WS_POPUP ¦ WS_CAPTION ¦ WS_SYSMENU
72: CAPTION "Modules"
73: BEGIN
74:        CONTROL "", ID_MODULELISTBOX, "LISTBOX",
75:          LBS_STANDARD ¦ WS_TABSTOP ¦ WS_CHILD ¦ WS_VISIBLE,
76:          23, 11, 133, 107
77:        PUSHBUTTON "Ok", IDOK, 10, 140, 160, 14,
78:          WS_CHILD ¦ WS_VISIBLE ¦ WS_TABSTOP
79:        LTEXT "", ID_MODULEEDIT, 23, 123, 134, 10,
80:          SS_LEFT ¦ WS_CHILD ¦ WS_VISIBLE ¦ WS_BORDER ¦ WS_GROUP
81: END
82:
83: LocalWalk DIALOG 31, 16, 248, 214
84: STYLE DS_MODALFRAME ¦ WS_POPUP ¦ WS_CAPTION ¦ WS_SYSMENU
85: CAPTION "Local Walk"
86: BEGIN
```

continues

Listing R2.11. continued

```
87:      CONTROL "", ID_LOCALLIST, "LISTBOX",
88:        LBS_NOTIFY ¦ WS_CHILD ¦ WS_VISIBLE ¦ WS_BORDER ¦
89:        WS_VSCROLL ¦ WS_TABSTOP, 18, 12, 213, 171
90:      PUSHBUTTON "Close", IDOK, 10, 194, 231, 14
91: END
```

Listing R2.12 shows the definition file for SysInfo.

Listing R2.12. SYSINFO.DEF.

```
 1: ; SYSINFO.DEF
 2:
 3: NAME          SysInfo
 4: DESCRIPTION   'SysInfo Vacation (c) 1993
                   by Charles Spence Calvert'
 5: EXETYPE       WINDOWS
 6: STUB          'WINSTUB.EXE'
 7: CODE          PRELOAD MOVEABLE DISCARDABLE
 8: DATA          PRELOAD MOVEABLE MULTIPLE
 9:
10: HEAPSIZE      4096
11: STACKSIZE     5120
```

Listing R2.13 shows the Borland makefile for SysInfo.

Listing R2.13. SYSINFO.MAK (Borland).

```
 1: # SYSINFO.MAK
 2:
 3: # macros
 4: APPNAME = SysInfo
 5: INCPATH = C:\BC\INCLUDE
 6: LIBPATH = C:\BC\LIB
 7: OBJS = $(APPNAME).obj SysMod.obj SysClass.obj SysTask.obj
    SysWalk.obj
 8: FLAGS = -ml -W -v -w4 -I$(INCPATH) -L$(LIBPATH)
 9:
10: # link
11: $(APPNAME).exe: $(OBJS) $(APPNAME).def $(APPNAME).res
12:   bcc $(FLAGS) $(OBJS)
13:   brc $(APPNAME).res
14:
15: # compile
16: .cpp.obj:
17:   bcc -c $(FLAGS) { $< }
18:
19: $(APPNAME).res: $(APPNAME).rc
20:   brc -r -I$(INCPATH) $(APPNAME).rc
```

Listing R2.14 shows the Microsoft makefile for SysInfo.

Listing R2.14. SYSINFO.MAK (Microsoft).

```
1: # SYSINFO.MAK for Microsoft
2:
3: APPNAME = SysInfo
4: LIBS = llibcew libw toolhelp
5: OBJS = $(APPNAME).obj SysMod.obj SysClass.obj SysTask.obj
    SysWalk.obj
6:
7: # linking
8: $(APPNAME).exe : $(OBJS) $(APPNAME).def $(APPNAME).res
9:   link $(OBJS), /align:16, NUL, /nod $(LIBS), $(APPNAME)
10:   rc $(APPNAME).res
11:
12: # compile
13: .cpp.obj:
14:   cl -AL -c -GA -Ow -W4 -Zp  { $< }
15:
16: # Compile
17: $(APPNAME).res: $(APPNAME).rc
18:   rc -r $(APPNAME).rc
```

By now, you should be aware that Windows stores a great deal of information in memory. This information usually can be made available to a program simply by calling a function or setting up a callback. In this particular case, SysInfo obtains information about classes, modules, and tasks with a set of ToolHelp functions called ClassFirst, TaskFirst, ModuleFirst, ClassNext, TaskNext, and ModuleNext. Anyone who has used the popular RTL functions FindFirst and FindNext should be familiar with the way these functions work.

SysInfo also reports on the current processor—that is, whether the machine is in standard or enhanced mode, whether a coprocessor is present, and whether or not paging is enabled. These last set of facts are retrieved from the system by calling a single function called GetWinFlags.

To display the information it obtains, the SysInfo program uses TextOut, listboxes, dialogs, push buttons, and other tools. TextOut is used to display information retrieved with GetWinFlags, whereas the push buttons and listboxes are enlisted to encapsulate the data from the ToolHelp functions.

The real work of retrieving information about classes, tasks, and modules can be illustrated by looking at the SetClassContents function:

```
39: BOOL SetClassContents(void)
40: {
41:   CLASSENTRY Class;
42:   BOOL Result;
43:
44:   ListBox_ResetContent(hListBox);
45:   Class.dwSize = sizeof(CLASSENTRY);
46:   Result = ClassFirst(&Class);
```

557

```
47:   while (Result)
48:   {
49:     ListBox_AddString(hListBox, Class.szClassName);
50:     Result = ClassNext(&Class);
51:   }
52:   return TRUE;
53: }
```

The first thing SysInfo does after the user selects the Class button is ensure that the program's list box is empty and ready for input. This is accomplished with a call to the WindowsX macro called ListBox_ResetContent. This macro takes a single parameter designating the list box's HWND.

SysInfo then calls ClassFirst, passing it a single parameter of type CLASSENTRY. Here's the way the CLASSENTRY struct is defined in TOOLHELP.H:

```
typedef struct tagCLASSENTRY
{
  DWORD dwSize;
  HMODULE hInst; /* This is really an hModule, which are WIN16 only*/
  char szClassName[MAX_CLASSNAME + 1];
  WORD wNext;
} CLASSENTRY;
```

The first field in the CLASSENTRY struct needs to be set to the size of the structure itself before it's passed to ClassFirst. This is done, in part, to keep your code compatible with any future releases of Windows that might change some portion of this structure.

In return for filling out the first field of the CLASSENTRY struct and passing it in with ClassFirst, Windows returns the name of the first class in its list of classes. SysInfo gloms onto this information, which is kept in the szClassName variable, and passes it to the list box with the aid of another WindowsX macro called ListBox_AddString.

After the first string is in place, SysInfo goes to the well a second time with a call to ClassNext. In return for these efforts, Windows returns the name of the next class on its internal lists. The process is repeated until all the classes in the system have been enumerated; this is signaled by ClassNext returning zero.

That's all you need to do to retrieve information about the available classes on the system. The process for retrieving modules and tasks is nearly identical. However, there are slight changes in naming conventions and some fairly major changes in the shape of the structure passed into Windows. Once you understand how the classes on the system are retrieved, you should have no trouble grasping the nearly identical code for retrieving tasks and modules.

Obtaining information from Windows with the GetWinFlags function is also a fairly straightforward process. GetWinFlags requires no parameters. It returns a 32-bit value that contains a series of flags specifying information about the current system. The flags are demonstrated in the SysInfo program and listed separately in your documentation or in the online help. To use these flags, simply test to see which ones are set with the bitwise logical AND operator:

```
len = sprintf(S, "This is an %s system.",
  (dwFlags & WF_CPU286) ? "80286" :
  (dwFlags & WF_CPU386) ? "80386" :
  (dwFlags & WF_CPU486) ? "80486" : "unknown");
TextOut(PaintDC, 10, Y + YInc, S, len);
```

Here you can see that SysInfo (using code taken nearly verbatim from the online help) checks to see if the current system is a 286, 386, or 486. After it finds the answer, SysInfo paints the answer to the screen for the user's benefit.

This program also contains a menu item that enables you to walk the GDI heap. Stripped down to its essentials, psuedocode for the function that walks the local heap looks like this:

```
void FillLocalDlg(HWND hDlg)
{
  SYSHEAPINFO Info;
  LOCALENTRY LocalEntry;
  int Result = TRUE;
  char S[150];

  ... // Code to set the font
  Info.dwSize = sizeof(SYSHEAPINFO);
  if (!SystemHeapInfo(&Info)) return;
  LocalEntry.dwSize = sizeof(LocalEntry);
  LocalFirst(&LocalEntry, Info.hGDISegment);
  while (Result)
  {
    ... // Code to make the string "S"
    ListBox_AddString(hLocalList, S);
    Result = LocalNext(&LocalEntry);
  }
}
```

The core of this function is represented by the calls to SystemHeapInfo, LocalFirst, and LocalNext.

The SystemHeapInfo function can be used to retrieve the current free space in the GDI and User heaps. This time, SysInfo enlists the function to retrieve a handle to the GDI heap. This handle is one of the pieces of information required by LocalFirst function.

By now, the act of calling LocalFirst and LocalNext should be familiar, because this same pattern was followed when calling similar TOOLHELP functions, such as ClassFirst and ClassNext. The difference here, of course, is that LocalFirst and LocalNext retrieve information about the actual objects stored on the GDI or User heap. This enables you to see the device contexts, brushes, pens, and so forth, that your program allocates. If you want, you can extend this program to compare the state of the GDI heap before and after you run a program or perform a particular function. (See Figure R2.2.) The information you obtain can help you be sure that your program properly cleans up after itself and can help you see exactly what memory your program is allocating (in terms of GDI resources).

Figure R2.2.
The GDI Walk dialog
displays information
about the GDI heap.

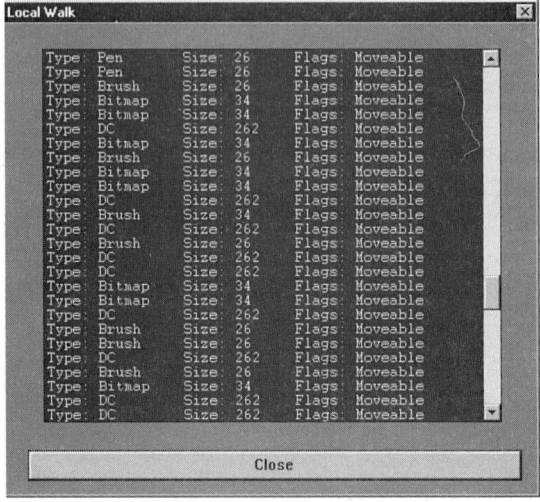

The GDI Walk dialog, shown in Figure R2.2, is used to display all the objects on the GDI local heap. In the left-hand column is the type of object itself, which might be a system resource, such as a brush, pen, or device context. Of course, it could also be nothing more than a free space on the heap, made available when some other resource was destroyed. The next column of information informs the user about the size of the object in question. The final column states whether the memory is fixed, moveable, or free. As you can see, most objects on the heap are moveable, which means Windows can change the address to which their selectors points. This latter technique enables the system to use virtual memory or to employ other tricks that maximize the power and functionality of the current system.

The Classes dialog box, shown in Figure R2.3, displays all the classes currently in memory. The two list boxes, shown at the bottom of the dialog, display information about the styles defined for the current class as well as the module with which the class is associated.

Figure R2.3.
The Classes dialog
displays information
about the classes currently
in use on the user's
system.

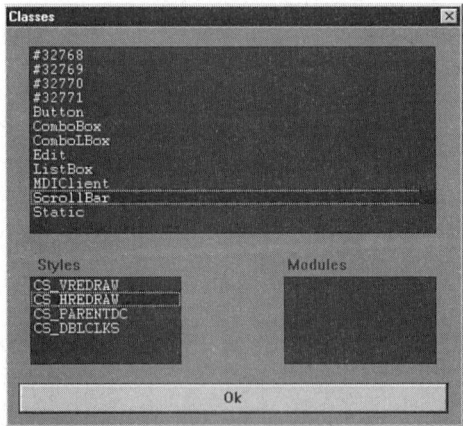

The Tasks dialog box, shown in Figure R2.4, presents the user with a list of the currently available tasks. It also shows the classes used in that task as well as the path to the actual executable in question.

Figure R2.4.

The Tasks dialog displays information about the Tasks currently running on the user's system.

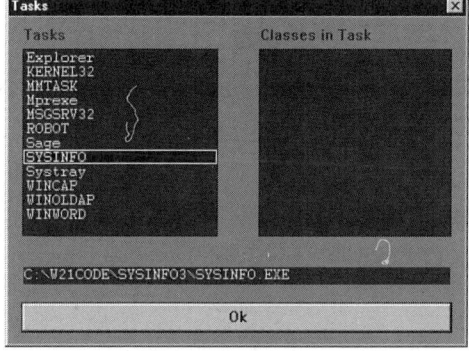

The Modules dialog (see Figure R2.5) shows the modules that have been loaded into memory as well as the path to the module. This information can be particularly useful, because it enables you to see which copy of a DLL, font, or what-have-you is actually being used.

Figure R2.5.

The Modules dialog displays information about the modules currently in memory on the user's system.

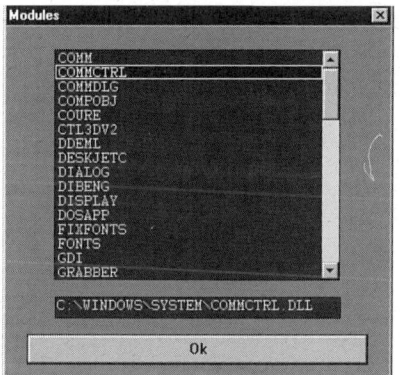

The Modules dialog also shows the remarkable number of tools that must be loaded into memory before Windows is ready to run. I think it helps to remember that a DLL is really just a special form of the standard Windows new executable format. Furthermore, the FON files and DRV files are just DLLs with special extensions. As a result, all the various DLLs, FON files, DRV files, and so forth that are loaded into memory are really separate executables; they need to be running before Windows can operate properly.

The Modules dialog is a reminder that even Windows 3.1 was a vast, complex, and intricately interrelated operating environment.

Summary

In this chapter you have had two peeks into the inner workings of Windows. Both of these programs are doors opening onto vast horizons with innumerable possibilities. By this point in the book, you are ready to move into the really exciting material that's available after you have mastered the basics and some of the important intermediate skills.

Congratulations on what you have accomplished so far. Now gird your loins, because the best is yet to come.

Most of Week 3 is dedicated to the new Windows 95 common controls. These are the tools that are used to create the operating system's interface. When you use the taskbar, Explorer, and Control Panel you are constantly manipulating Windows 95 common controls.

Nearly all the major parts of the Windows 95 interface are encapsulated in controls. For instance, the Windows 95 interface hosts property sheets, toolbars, status bars, treeview controls, listview controls, and exotic items such as spinners and progress bars. All of these subjects are covered in the upcoming chapters. (The only big one I leave out is the richedit control, and that's only because I save it for a goodbye present at the very end of the book!)

Week 3 also features a solid introduction to threads. Threads allow you to "multitask" various parts of your program. The end result is to give the appearance that your program is doing several things at once. This can be particularly useful if you want to set up a background task that's carried out while the user is engaged with some particular chore such as filing a form or selecting options from a dialog. Threading is an interesting and entertaining subject, and I suspect most of you will enjoy the sections that explore techniques that allow you to synchronize multiple threads so they work together in harmony.

Another key aspect of WIN32 that's covered in Week 3 is memory management. 32-bit Windows programs are now running in huge 4GB address spaces and have access to multiple heaps, memory-mapped files, and virtual memory. In the upcoming chapters you will see how to tap into these resources. In the process, you will begin to understand what Windows 95 and Windows NT are really all about, and exactly how you can give your users access to their power and flexibility.

Anyone familiar with the Windows environment realizes what an important role dialogs play in many of the best-designed programs. To further your knowledge of this subject, the second and third chapters in Week 3 focus on placing controls inside dialogs, as well as the art of setting and getting data from these controls. Other important dialog-related subjects involve changing the color of dialogs, delineating the differences between modal and modeless dialogs, working with common dialogs, and exploring dynamic changes in the appearance of dialogs at runtime. When you're finished with these chapters, you'll be able to use dialogs to communicate with users in a natural, intuitive manner.

Menus have been featured in most of the programs presented in this book. However, a number of advanced menuing techniques still need to be covered before you can take full advantage of these powerful and flexible resources. On Day 20, you'll learn about the system menu, nesting menus, and creating user draw menus. In addition, you'll learn how to make the interface to your program more intuitive through the creative use of cursors, icons, and accelerators. Accelerators enable you to add to your program hotkeys that give users immediate access to important features.

By the time you are done with Week 3 you will be pushing hard at the boundary that separates intermediate programmers from advanced programmers. There's lots of good material in the upcoming chapters, and plenty of chances to have fun with the Windows operating system. So put on your walking shoes, and get ready to advance on some very exciting Windows real estate.

Introduction to Windows 95 Controls

In this chapter you will get a look at trackbars, toolbars, progress bars, status bars, tooltips, floating menus, and a few other elements of the Windows 95 interface such as small icons and the WNDCLASSEX structure. There is nothing very challenging about this material, and most of it should consist simply of a romp through a series of new toys that make programs more colorful and versatile.

Most of the new controls mentioned in the first paragraph are called common controls. They are fundamentally very similar to the standard controls such as buttons, list boxes, radio buttons, and edits. The point is that these are prewritten window classes that you can utilize to spice up and simplify the interface to your programs.

Version Issues: Windows 95 Specific

The code that appears in this chapter is Windows 95 specific. Most of it will also execute on Windows NT 3.51, but I have not considered compatibility with this older 32-bit environment to be important. Because this is Windows 95 code, it will not run on Windows 3.11, although it can be compiled in 16-bit mode. Furthermore, you should be sure you have the most recent updates from your compiler maker before working with this code. For instance, the original versions of Borland C++ 4.5 and Microsoft Visual C++ 2.0 did not have all the header files necessary for running this code. In particular, they did not come with the correct version of COMMCTRL.H.

Note: Because the final updates for Borland's compilers were not available when this book went to print, it has not been possible for me to be absolutely certain about the setup for the INCLUDE macro in the Borland makefiles. As a result, you may need to slightly alter the INCLUDE macro in the Borland makefiles for this book. Here is one possible pattern that points at separate directories for WIN16 and WIN32 INCLUDE files:

```
!if $d(WIN16)
INCPATH = $(BCROOT)\INCLUDE\WIN16;$(BCROOT)\INCLUDE
COMPILER= BCC.EXE
FLAGS   = -W -ml -v -w4 -I$(INCPATH) -L$(LIBPATH)
!else
INCPATH = $(BCROOT)\INCLUDE\WIN32;$(BCROOT)\INCLUDE
COMPILER= BCC32.EXE
FLAGS   = -W -v -w4 -I$(INCPATH) -L$(LIBPATH)
!endif
```

Here is a second possible solution:

```
INCPATH = $(BCROOT)\INCLUDE\WIN32;$(BCROOT)\INCLUDE
!if $d(WIN16)
COMPILER= BCC.EXE
FLAGS   = -W -ml -v -w4 -I$(INCPATH) -L$(LIBPATH)
```

```
!else
COMPILER= BCC32.EXE
FLAGS   = -W -v -w4 -I$(INCPATH) -L$(LIBPATH)
!endif
```

The point here is that headers specific to Windows 95 may need to be added to your version of the compiler before you can work with the Windows 95 common controls. Those header files may be placed in the C:\BC45\INCLUDE subdirectory, or perhaps in a subdirectory called C:\BC45\INCLUDE\WIN32, or even in a directory called C:\BC45\WIN32. (In these examples, I assume that you installed on the C drive, and I assume you are using BC45. Of course, many readers of this book will have compilers where BCROOT resolves not to C:\BC45, but to C:\BC50.) The actual default location of these new header files is not clear at the time of this writing, so you may have to edit your makefiles accordingly.

The code that gets uploaded to the online sites will reflect the final default directories selected by the Borland developers. In other words, I will upload the code nearly a month after I turn in the final drafts of this book. By that time, the location of the files will be resolved. If necessary, I will update the online files further when BC50 ships, and at other times when they need to be tweaked.

I should add that my best guess is that the new Windows 95 header files will end up in the \BC45\INCLUDE subdirectory, but I can't be sure. Furthermore, it is unlikely to cause harm if the INCLUDE macro lists directories that do not exist, or that do not contain files important to your builds. In other words, it's okay if the INCLUDE macro lists the correct directory, and then some additional directories that do not exist, or that do not hold header files important to your build. (When reading this book, you may encounter variations on the INCLUDE macro in some of the makefiles. These variations are due to an assortment of temporary solutions that were developed either by myself, or by Borland developers, during the beta cycle.)

If you are able to acquire the proper header files, but do not have the proper LIB files, you can usually create the files you need with the tools provided by your compiler. For instance, Borland users can create COMCTL32.LIB by switching to the \WINDOWS\SYSTEM directory and typing the following at the DOS prompt:

```
implib comctl32.lib comctl32.dll
```

When you are done, you can copy or move COMCTL32.LIB into the \BC45\LIB (or \BC50\LIB) subdirectory.

It seems almost certain that both Microsoft and Borland will make it as easy as possible for you to upgrade your versions of their 32-bit compilers so that they work with the new controls. In particular, you should check to see if it is possible to acquire the necessary header files for some nominal cost. Of course, at the time of this writing I don't know how this matter will be handled, but you should check with your compiler vendor and browse through their online sites.

The core of Windows 95 is its memory management, multitasking, and multithreading tools. These are the big improvements that make Windows 95 so powerful and so important. The new Windows controls are merely a sprinkling of glitter on top of the real power inherent in the core of the operating system. Nevertheless, it's hard not to get at least a little excited about them. Each control is a little bit like a Christmas present. It will give your applications new functionality and new appeal without you having to do a great deal of work.

Common Controls

In this section, I will give you an overview of the common controls from a programmer's point of view. My goal is to give you some general pieces of information that will prove useful when you actually start writing common control code. I'm sure you are anxious to get the new controls up and running, but that process will go much more smoothly for you if you first get an overview of the subject.

The rest of this section of the chapter is dedicated to relatively abstract, general issues. When it's finished, I will plunge directly into the "hard stuff."

Throughout this chapter and the next, the key document is COMMCTRL.H. It contains almost all the declarations for the new Windows common controls that are stored in COMCTL32.DLL. At the time of this writing, property sheets are still being defined in a separate file called PRSHT.H, but it is possible that the two files will be folded together by the time of the general Windows 95 release. A third file of importance to this subject is RICHEDIT.H, and its companion file, RICHED32.DLL. These latter files provide access to the RTF control that will be discussed in the next chapter.

Though the online help is a great way to get information about the common controls, you should definitely take the time to open COMMCTRL.H and begin browsing through it. Here is one key section from near the top of my version of this file:

```
//
// Users of this header may define any number of these constants to avoid
// the definitions of each functional group.
//
//    NOTOOLBAR     Customizable bitmap-button toolbar control.
//    NOUPDOWN      Up and Down arrow increment/decrement control.
//    NOSTATUSBAR   Status bar control.
//    NOMENUHELP    APIs to help manage menus, especially with a status bar.
//    NOTRACKBAR    Customizable column-width tracking control.
//    NODRAGLIST    APIs to make a listbox source and sink drag&drop actions.
```

```
//    NOPROGRESS    Progress gas gauge.
//    NOHOTKEY      HotKey control
//    NOHEADER      Header bar control.
//    NOIMAGEAPIS   ImageList apis.
//    NOLISTVIEW    ListView control.
//    NOTREEVIEW    TreeView control.
//    NOTABCONTROL  Tab control.
//    NOANIMATE     Animate control.
//
```

Though it may not have been the intention of the programmers to do so, nevertheless this little swatch of code provides something of an overview of several of the major common controls. Take away the NO in front of each of these words, and you can find the names of the controls defined in this file. Most, but not all, of these controls will be covered somewhere in the next two chapters.

COMMCTRL.H is divided up into sections, with each section dedicated to a different control. For instance, the section on the header control begins like this:

```
//====== HEADER CONTROL =========================================
#ifndef NOHEADER

#ifdef _WIN32
#define WC_HEADERA            "SysHeader32"
#define WC_HEADERW            L"SysHeader32"
```

A little further down you will find the section dedicated to the toolbar control. It starts out like this:

```
#endif

//====== TOOLBAR CONTROL ========================================
#ifndef NOTOOLBAR

#ifdef _WIN32
#define TOOLBARCLASSNAMEW     L"ToolbarWindow32"
#define TOOLBARCLASSNAMEA     "ToolbarWindow32"
```

The pattern here is that each chunk of code is declared within a big block of code that can be ignored if you define NOHEADER, NOTOOLBAR, and so on. The code then declares the class names, one for regular code, and one for Unicode. The Unicode name ends in W, which stands for Wide. Under Windows 95, you can ignore the Unicode names since you will be working strictly with the regular 8-bit character sets that we have been using for lo these many years. (For now, Unicode is still strictly a Windows NT affair.)

In some cases, the definition for a class is relatively short. For instance, here is the complete set of declarations associated with the progress bar class:

```
//====== PROGRESS CONTROL ===============================
#ifndef NOPROGRESS
```

```
#ifdef _WIN32

#define PROGRESS_CLASSA          "msctls_progress32"
#define PROGRESS_CLASSW          L"msctls_progress32"

#ifdef UNICODE
#define  PROGRESS_CLASS          PROGRESS_CLASSW
#else
#define  PROGRESS_CLASS          PROGRESS_CLASSA
#endif

#else
#define PROGRESS_CLASS           "msctls_progress"
#endif


#define PBM_SETRANGE             (WM_USER+1)
#define PBM_SETPOS               (WM_USER+2)
#define PBM_DELTAPOS             (WM_USER+3)
#define PBM_SETSTEP              (WM_USER+4)
#define PBM_STEPIT               (WM_USER+5)

#endif
```

Most of the code shown here is just silliness regarding platform issues such as WIN32, WIN16 and Unicode. The core of the code is the name of the class:

```
#define PROGRESS_CLASSA          "msctls_progress32"
```

and the messages you can send to the class:

```
#define PBM_SETRANGE             (WM_USER+1)
#define PBM_SETPOS               (WM_USER+2)
#define PBM_DELTAPOS             (WM_USER+3)
#define PBM_SETSTEP              (WM_USER+4)
#define PBM_STEPIT               (WM_USER+5)
```

In particular, you can create the class by passing the class name to CreateWindow. The window handle you get back allows you to manipulate the class by sending it messages such as PBM_SETRANGE and PBM_SETPOS. You can safely read the PBM bit as "progress bar message." The rest of the name is purely descriptive. You still need the online help to find out what to pass in the WPARAM and LPARAM fields of the SendMessage call, but the majority of information is available for you just by glancing at COMMCTRL.H.

Note: The declarations I am showing you in this chapter are not meant to be definitive and should be checked against the final docs. However, it is unlikely that the information shown here will be incorrect. For instance, I doubt that any of the messages will disappear, or that they will be renamed. However, there may be new messages added late in the Windows 95 beta process.

The progress bar class is very simple compared to some of the more elaborate new tools such as imagelists and treeviews. Nevertheless, the same architectural principles embodied in it apply to the larger classes, even if there are a few more variations to learn.

In particular, you will find that many of the tricks used in WINDOWSX.H have now been incorporated directly into the core source files. For instance, the following declarations appear in the imagelist section of COMMCTRL.H:

```
#define LVM_SETIMAGELIST        (LVM_FIRST + 3)
#define ListView_SetImageList(hwnd, himl, iImageList) \
    (HIMAGELIST)(UINT)SendMessage((hwnd), LVM_SETIMAGELIST, (WPARAM)(iImageList), \
                        (LPARAM)(UINT)(HIMAGELIST)(himl))

#define LVM_GETITEMCOUNT        (LVM_FIRST + 4)
#define ListView_GetItemCount(hwnd) \
    (int)SendMessage((hwnd), LVM_GETITEMCOUNT, 0, 0L)
```

These declarations are almost identical in structure to the child control macros found in WindowsX.H:

```
#define ListBox_GetCount(hwndCtl) \
  ((int)(DWORD)SendMessage((hwndCtl), LB_GETCOUNT, 0L, 0L))

#define ListBox_ResetContent(hwndCtl) \
  ((BOOL)(DWORD)SendMessage((hwndCtl), LB_RESETCONTENT, 0L, 0L))
```

All of these macros wrap up Windows messages so that you can replace calls to SendMessage with a cleaner, easier to use API. For instance, instead of writing:

```
SendMessage((hwnd), LVM_GETITEMCOUNT, 0, 0L)
```

you can write:

```
ListView_GetItemCount(hwnd)
```

Instead of referencing WindowsX to find these kinds of macros, you should now turn to COMMCTRL.H. I can't emphasize the point too strongly: COMMCTRL is where to turn if you want WindowsX macros for use with the common controls.

You will also find that message crackers have been folded into COMMCTRL.H:

```
//====== WM_NOTIFY Macros ========================================

#define HANDLE_WM_NOTIFY(hwnd, wParam, lParam, fn) \
    (fn)((hwnd), (int)(wParam), (NMHDR FAR*)(lParam))
#define FORWARD_WM_NOTIFY(hwnd, idFrom, pnmhdr, fn) \
    (LRESULT)(fn)((hwnd), WM_NOTIFY, (WPARAM)(int)(idFrom), \
    (LPARAM)(NMHDR FAR*)(pnmhdr))
```

Right now it's hard to tell whether Microsoft will always be folding the WindowsX-like macros into the new header files they create, or whether WINDOWSX.H will continue to grow in the future. Whichever path is taken, it's clear that the WindowsX way of life continues to live on in the latest code coming out of Microsoft.

One final point should be made about COMMCTRL.H. Like all the other controls you saw earlier in this book, you can create common controls by calling `CreateWindow`. However, you will also find a series of functions or macros that can be used in lieu of `CreateWindow`. For instance, here is a declaration that can be used to create a toolbar:

```
WINCOMMCTRLAPI HWND WINAPI CreateToolbarEx(HWND hwnd,
    DWORD ws, UINT wID, int nBitmaps,
    HINSTANCE hBMInst, UINT wBMID, LPCTBBUTTON lpButtons,
    int iNumButtons, int dxButton, int dyButton,
    int dxBitmap, int dyBitmap, UINT uStructSize);
```

Code like this can help you create and configure a class all in one simple step. Without it, you would have to first call `CreateWindow`, and then send messages to the control to configure it. This is still a pattern you will follow on several occasions when working with common controls, but the `Create` commands, like the one shown above, can help to simplify your code. (Well, no command that takes 13 parameters can qualify as simple, but the code might still be considered useful!)

Enough of this mucking around in COMMCTRL.H. By now you should have a general feeling for the way you are going to handle common controls. The next step is to climb out of the muck and instead gets your hands dirty with a few hands-on examples. I'll start out with the simple stuff, and then build up to the complex controls such as treeviews and richedits.

A Windows 95 Application with a Progress Bar

You can use a progress bar to depict visually some internal process that is taking a long time to execute. The classic use of a progress bar would be during a program installation, or perhaps during a file copy. A screen shot from a program that uses a progress bar is shown in Figure 15.1.

Figure 15.1.
The progress bar that appears in the Progress program.

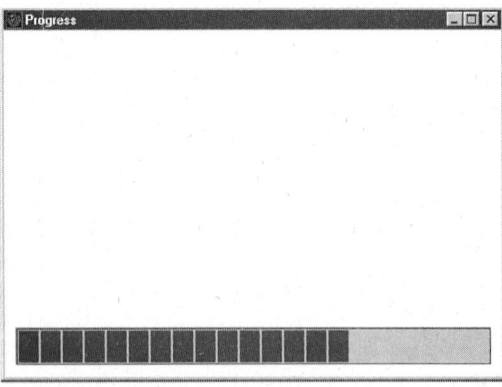

You saw a few things about progress bars in the last section, when I showed you the excerpts about it from COMMCTRL.H. Here is how to create a progress bar:

```
hProgress = CreateWindow(PROGRESS_CLASS, "Progress",
                    WS_CHILD | WS_VISIBLE | WS_BORDER,
                    10, 10, 200, 35, hwnd, NULL,
                    lpCreateStruct->hInstance, NULL);
```

This call creates a progress bar and stores a handle to it in the hProgress variable, which is of type HWND. CreateWindow should be old hat to you by now, so I will not discuss this call further at this time. If you need help with it, turn to the online help, or to Day 3, "A Standard Windows Program."

After you create the window, you can change its attributes by sending messages to it:

```
SendMessage(hProgress, PBM_SETRANGE, 0, MAKELONG(0, MAXPOS));
```

The code shown here sets the range of numbers used in the control. The starting range is 0, and the top range is MAXPOS, which in the example shown below happens to be 2500.

Speaking of the sample program, you are probably anxious to see it by this time, so I shall display it now in Listing 15.1 through Listing 15.5.

Before you compile this listing, you ought to be sure that COMCTL32.LIB is being linked into your program. You can do this in MSVC20 by bringing up the Project | Settings dialog and turning to the Link page. Check the Object/Library Modules settings and be sure this library is included. If it's not there, then simply append its name onto the end of the list. Now switch the Category to Output, and set the Version to 4.0 (Windows 95), or to some later version that may have shipped after this book was printed. (This is the Windows version number, not the version number of your compiler.)

Borland compilers add COMCTL32 to their projects by right clicking on the Project window and selecting Add Node. You can then simply append COMCTL32.LIB on to the list of files seen in this window. Remember that if the file does not ship with your version of the compiler, you can create it by running IMPLIB.EXE on COMCTL32.DLL. There is no way to create COMMCTRL.H by hand, but you may be able to obtain it from Borland if it did not ship with your version of the compiler, or if you have an outdated version of this file.

Listing 15.1. The main module from the Progress program.

```
//////////////////////////////////////////////////////////
//   Program Name: Progress.cpp
//   Copyright (c) 1995 Charlie Calvert
//   Description: Demonstrates PROGRESS BAR class
//   Comment: Windows 95 specific, maybe Windows NT 3.51
//   Date: 06/27/95
//////////////////////////////////////////////////////////

#define STRICT
```

continues

Listing 15.1. continued

```c
#define WIN32_LEAN_AND_MEAN
#include <windows.h>
#include <windowsx.h>
#include <commctrl.h>
#pragma warning (disable: 4068)


// --------------------------------------------------------
// Interface
// --------------------------------------------------------

#define MAXPOS 2500
#define STEPSIZE 20

enum DIRECTION {UP, DOWN};

LRESULT CALLBACK WndProc(HWND hwnd, UINT Message,
                         WPARAM wParam, LPARAM lParam);
BOOL Register(HINSTANCE hInst);
HWND Create(HINSTANCE hInst, int nCmdShow);

// Declarations for class Progress
#define Progress_DefProc     DefWindowProc
void Progress_OnDestroy(HWND hwnd);
BOOL Progress_OnCreate(HWND hwnd, LPCREATESTRUCT lpCreateStruct);
void Progress_OnTimer(HWND hwnd, UINT id);

static char szAppName[] = "Progress";
static HWND MainWindow;
static HWND hProgress;
static HINSTANCE hInstance;
static int ProgressTimer = 1;

// --------------------------------------------------------
// Initialization
// --------------------------------------------------------

////////////////////////////////////////////////////////////
// Program entry point
////////////////////////////////////////////////////////////
#pragma argsused
int WINAPI WinMain(HINSTANCE hInst, HINSTANCE hPrevInstance,
                   LPSTR lpszCmdParam, int nCmdShow)
{
  MSG  Msg;

  if (!hPrevInstance)
    if (!Register(hInst))
      return FALSE;

  MainWindow = Create(hInst, nCmdShow);
  if (!MainWindow)
    return FALSE;
```

```
  while (GetMessage(&Msg, NULL, 0, 0))
  {
    TranslateMessage(&Msg);
    DispatchMessage(&Msg);
  }

  return Msg.wParam;
}

/////////////////////////////////////////////////////
// Register the window
/////////////////////////////////////////////////////
BOOL Register(HINSTANCE hInst)
{
  WNDCLASSEX WndClassEx;

  WndClassEx.cbSize        = sizeof(WNDCLASSEX);
  WndClassEx.style         = CS_HREDRAW | CS_VREDRAW;
  WndClassEx.lpfnWndProc   = WndProc;
  WndClassEx.cbClsExtra    = 0;
  WndClassEx.cbWndExtra    = 0;
  WndClassEx.hInstance     = hInst;
  WndClassEx.hIcon         = LoadIcon(hInst, "ProgressIcon");
  WndClassEx.hCursor       = LoadCursor(NULL, IDC_ARROW);
  WndClassEx.hbrBackground = (HBRUSH)(COLOR_WINDOW+1);
  WndClassEx.lpszMenuName  = NULL;
  WndClassEx.lpszClassName = szAppName;
  WndClassEx.hIconSm       = LoadIcon(hInst, "ProgressIcon16");

  return (RegisterClassEx(&WndClassEx) != 0);
}

/////////////////////////////////////////////////////
// Create the window
/////////////////////////////////////////////////////
HWND Create(HINSTANCE hInst, int nCmdShow)
{

  hInstance = hInst;

  HWND hwnd = CreateWindow(szAppName, szAppName,
                    WS_OVERLAPPEDWINDOW,
                    CW_USEDEFAULT, CW_USEDEFAULT,
                    CW_USEDEFAULT, CW_USEDEFAULT,
                    NULL, NULL, hInst, NULL);

  if (hwnd == NULL)
    return hwnd;

  ShowWindow(hwnd, nCmdShow);
  UpdateWindow(hwnd);

  return hwnd;
}
```

continues

Listing 15.1. continued

```
// ------------------------------------------------------
// WndProc and Implementation
// ------------------------------------------------------

//////////////////////////////////////////////////////////
// The Window Procedure
//////////////////////////////////////////////////////////
LRESULT CALLBACK WndProc(HWND hwnd, UINT Message, WPARAM wParam, LPARAM lParam)
{
  switch(Message)
  {
    HANDLE_MSG(hwnd, WM_CREATE, Progress_OnCreate);
    HANDLE_MSG(hwnd, WM_DESTROY, Progress_OnDestroy);
    HANDLE_MSG(hwnd, WM_TIMER, Progress_OnTimer);
    default: return Progress_DefProc(hwnd, Message, wParam, lParam);
  }
}

//////////////////////////////////////////////////////////
// Handle WM_CREATE
//////////////////////////////////////////////////////////
BOOL Progress_OnCreate(HWND hwnd, LPCREATESTRUCT lpCreateStruct)
{
  InitCommonControls();

  RECT Rect;

  GetClientRect(hwnd, &Rect);

  hProgress = CreateWindow(PROGRESS_CLASS, "Progress",
                           WS_CHILD | WS_VISIBLE | WS_BORDER,
                           10, Rect.bottom - 45, Rect.right - 20,
                           35, hwnd, NULL,
                           lpCreateStruct->hInstance, NULL);

  SendMessage(hProgress, PBM_SETRANGE, 0, MAKELONG(0, MAXPOS));
  SendMessage(hProgress, PBM_SETSTEP, WPARAM(STEPSIZE), 0);

  SetTimer(hwnd, ProgressTimer, 100, NULL);

  return TRUE;
}

//////////////////////////////////////////////////////////
// Handle WM_DESTROY
//////////////////////////////////////////////////////////
#pragma argsused
void Progress_OnDestroy(HWND hwnd)
{
  KillTimer(hwnd, ProgressTimer);
  PostQuitMessage(0);
}
```

```
/////////////////////////////////////////////////////////
// Handle WM_TIMER
/////////////////////////////////////////////////////////
#pragma argsused;
void Progress_OnTimer(HWND hwnd, UINT id)
{
  SendMessage(hProgress, PBM_STEPIT, 0, 0);
}
```

Listing 15.2. The DEF file for PROGRESS.CPP.

```
; Progress.Def

NAME          Progress
DESCRIPTION   'Progress Window'
```

Listing 15.3. The resource file for PROGRESS.CPP.

```
////////////////////////////////////
// PROGRESS.RC
////////////////////////////////////

ProgressIcon ICON "PROGRESS.ICO"
ProgressIcon16 ICON "PROG16.ICO"
```

Listing 15.4. The Borland makefile for PROGRESS.CPP.

```
#///////////////////////////////////
# PROGRESS.MAK
#///////////////////////////////////

# macros

!if !$d(BCROOT)
BCROOT  = $(MAKEDIR)\..
!endif

APPNAME = Progress
INCPATH = $(BCROOT)\WIN32;$(BCROOT);$(BCROOT)\INCLUDE
LIBPATH = $(BCROOT)\LIB

COMPILER= BCC32.EXE
BRC     = BRC32.EXE
FLAGS   = -W -v -w4 -I$(INCPATH) -L$(LIBPATH)

# link
$(APPNAME).exe: $(APPNAME).obj $(APPNAME).def $(APPNAME).res
  $(COMPILER) $(FLAGS) $(APPNAME).obj
  $(BRC) -I$(INCPATH) $(APPNAME).res

# compile
```

continues

Listing 15.4. continued

```
$(APPNAME).obj: $(APPNAME).cpp
  $(COMPILER) -c $(FLAGS) $(APPNAME).cpp

# resource
$(APPNAME).res: $(APPNAME).rc
  $(BRC) -R -I$(INCPATH) $(APPNAME).RC
```

Listing 15.5. The Microsoft makefile for the Progress program.

```
#///////////////////////////////////////
# PROGRESS.MAK - Microsoft make file
# nmake -f skyvewms.mak
#  Copyright (c) 1995 Charlie Calvert.
#///////////////////////////////////////

APPNAME=PROGRESS
TARGETOS=WIN95
APPVER=4.0
OBJS=$(APPNAME).OBJ

!include <win32.mak>

all: $(APPNAME).exe

# Update the resource if necessary

$(APPNAME).res: $(APPNAME).rc
  $(rc) $(rcflags) $(rcvars) $(APPNAME).rc

# Update the object files if necessary

# compile
.cpp.obj:
  $(cc) $(cflags) $(cvars) $(cdebug) $<

# Update the executable file if necessary.

$(APPNAME).exe: $(OBJS) $(APPNAME).res
  $(link) $(linkdebug) $(guiflags) -out:$(APPNAME).exe \
  $(OBJS) $(APPNAME).res $(guilibs) comctl32.lib
```

Figures 15.2 and 15.3 show two icons you can use with the Progess program. It's not important that you duplicate the look of the icons, but you should use the Resource Workshop or similar tools to create one large icon that is 32×32, and a second small icon that is 16×16. The 16-pixel icon can be a plain BMP file rather than a real icon file. It's usually best to make icons with only 16 colors, since not all machines will be able to show 256 colors.

Figure 15.2.
*The suggested big icon for
the Progress program is 32×
32 pixels square and uses
16-color mode.*

Figure 15.3.
*The suggested little icon for
the Progress program is
16×16 pixels square and
uses 16-color mode.*

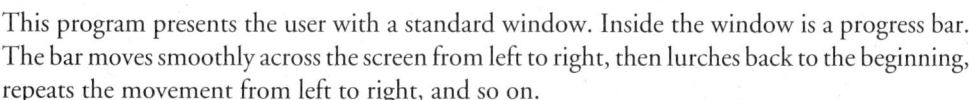

This program presents the user with a standard window. Inside the window is a progress bar. The bar moves smoothly across the screen from left to right, then lurches back to the beginning, repeats the movement from left to right, and so on.

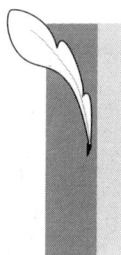

> **Note:** I have included a copy of the Borland makefile. This makefile no longer has any references to 16-bit code. PROGRESS.CPP is a Windows 95-specific program and will not compile under Windows 3.1.
>
> Also included are two suggested icons for the program. The actual icons you use are not important, and I've included my suggested samples merely for the sake of completeness.

Clearly, the introduction of Windows 95–specific code has not radically changed the shape of the programs you will write. Most of your old friends are still here. There are all the WindowsX macros, and the standard messages such as WM_CREATE, WM_COMMAND, and WM_TIMER.

However, some things have changed.

Take a look at the Register function:

```
BOOL Register(HINSTANCE hInst)
{
  WNDCLASSEX WndClassEx;

  WndClassEx.cbSize        = sizeof(WNDCLASSEX);
  WndClassEx.style         = CS_HREDRAW | CS_VREDRAW;
  WndClassEx.lpfnWndProc   = WndProc;
  WndClassEx.cbClsExtra    = 0;
  WndClassEx.cbWndExtra    = 0;
  WndClassEx.hInstance     = hInst;
  WndClassEx.hIcon         = LoadIcon(hInst, "ProgressIcon");
  WndClassEx.hCursor       = LoadCursor(NULL, IDC_ARROW);
```

```
WndClassEx.hbrBackground = (HBRUSH)(COLOR_WINDOW+1);
WndClassEx.lpszMenuName  = NULL;
WndClassEx.lpszClassName = szAppName;
WndClassEx.hIconSm       = LoadIcon(hInst, "ProgressIcon16");

    return (RegisterClassEx(&WndClassEx) != 0);
}
```

You've seen so many `Register` functions by this time that your eyes may glaze over when they drift into your ken. A second glance, however, reveals that the familiar `WNDCLASS` structure is now gone, and in its place is `WNDCLASSEX`.

`WNDCLASSEX` is clearly a kissing cousin of `WNDCLASS`, but note that it also has two new fields bracketing it like a pair of andirons:

```
WndClassEx.cbSize        = sizeof(WNDCLASSEX);
...
WndClassEx.hIconSm       = LoadIcon(hInst, "ProgressIcon16");
```

The `cbSize` field provides version information to Windows by reporting on the size of the structure itself. The `hIconSm` field holds a 16×16 icon that will appear in the upper-left corner of the main window, on the taskbar at the bottom of the screen, and inside the Explorer. If you use `WNDCLASS` instead of `WNDCLASSEX`, or if you put `NULL` in the `hIconSm` field, then you will still end up with tiny icons in these positions. These miniature portraits are the offspring of the program's main icon and the `StretchBlt` function and will sometimes look a bit the worse for their parentage.

Note: Throughout most of the Windows 95 specific programs in this book I will mark my miniature icons in some way so that you can easily distinguish them from the big 32×32 icons that you see when you Alt+Tab from application to application. For instance, the main icon for this program has a white background, while the small icon has a black background. Please forgive any aesthetic blunders that result from this conceit. I'm not an artist but aim instead to illustrate programming techniques.

When you want to create small icons, you can just launch the Resource Workshop, or the equivalent Microsoft tool, and create an icon that is 16×16 in size. There is nothing else special about these resources; they just happen to be small. When creating icons, you should usually make them with 16 colors rather than 256, since many target machines won't support super VGA features.

After you fill out the `WNDCLASSEX` structure, the next step is to pass it on to Windows by calling `RegisterClassEx`. This function works exactly like `RegisterClass`, except that it takes a `WNDCLASSEX` structure as a parameter.

Working with Progress Bars

To insert a progress bar in your application you must include COMMCTRL.H at the top of your program, and you must call InitCommonControls. I call InitCommonControls as the first step in the WM_CREATE handler:

```
BOOL Progress_OnCreate(HWND hwnd, LPCREATESTRUCT lpCreateStruct)
{
  InitCommonControls();

  RECT Rect;

  GetClientRect(hwnd, &Rect);

  hProgress = CreateWindow(PROGRESS_CLASS, "Progress",
                           WS_CHILD | WS_VISIBLE | WS_BORDER,
                           10, Rect.bottom - 45, Rect.right - 20,
                           35, hwnd, NULL,
                           lpCreateStruct->hInstance, NULL);

  SendMessage(hProgress, PBM_SETRANGE, 0, MAKELONG(0, MAXPOS));
  SendMessage(hProgress, PBM_SETSTEP, WPARAM(STEPSIZE), 0);

  SetTimer(hwnd, ProgressTimer, 100, NULL);

  return TRUE;
}
```

If you aren't going to include a WM_CREATE handler in your application, you might want to move this call up into the Create function itself. However you handle it, you need to be sure the call is made early on in the execution timeline for your application.

The next step for the Progress program features the actual creation of the progress bar:

```
hProgress = CreateWindow(PROGRESS_CLASS, "Progress",
                         WS_CHILD | WS_VISIBLE | WS_BORDER,
                         10, Rect.bottom - 45, Rect.right - 20,
                         35, hwnd, NULL,
                         lpCreateStruct->hInstance, NULL);
```

This function depends on GetClientRect to supply the basis for dimensions used by the progress bar. Specifically, I've inserted the progress bar down at the center of the bottom part of the window, as shown in Figure 15.1.

The progress bar moves across the screen from left to right in predefined increments. Here's the code that defines the size and range of those increments:

```
SendMessage(hProgress, PBM_SETRANGE, 0, MAKELONG(0, MAXPOS));
SendMessage(hProgress, PBM_SETSTEP, WPARAM(STEPSIZE), 0);
```

PBM_SETRANGE messages take a starting range in the low word of LPARAM and a maximum range in the high word. PBM_SETSTEP specifies a default value for incrementing the bar when it needs to be updated. In other words, you can simply ask the bar to "step" forward by sending a PBM_STEPIT message. After getting the message, it will automatically increment itself by the amount you specified when you sent it a PBM_SETSTEP message.

The Progress program sends PBM_STEPIT messages in response to reminders from WM_TIMER. The act of creating the timer is performed in the WM_CREATE handler:

```
SetTimer(hwnd, ProgressTimer, 100, NULL);
```

The function specifies that WM_TIMER messages should be sent once every 100 milliseconds, or once every tenth of a second. The handler for WM_TIMER is trivial:

```
#pragma argsused;
void Progress_OnTimer(HWND hwnd, UINT id)
{
  SendMessage(hProgress, PBM_STEPIT, 0, 0);
}
```

PBM_STEPIT messages don't utilize either WPARAM or LPARAM. This simple code increments the progress bar STEPSIZE ticks. Here's the declaration for the local STEPSIZE macro:

```
#define STEPSIZE 20
```

Besides the technique shown here, there are two other ways to change the position of a progress bar. The first is to send a PBM_SETPOS message, with the new position in WPARAM. The other is to utilize PBM_DELTAPOS, which increments the bar by the amount specified in WPARAM. The difference between PBM_SETPOS and PBM_DELTAPOS is that the first moves you directly to a particular location, while the second increments or decrements the current position by a specific value.

There is nothing to prevent you from moving the progress bar backwards, from right to left. For instance, you could use PBM_SETPOS to start the bar out at 2000, and then use PBM_DELTAPOS to move it backwards -20 places at a time. You will find, however, that Windows botches its drawing assignment when you try this technique. Clearly, the folks at Microsoft know how to write code that can a handle a task of this limited complexity. However, they did not do so in this case because they mean the progress bar to have a very specific scope. It's meant to move a line across the screen from left to right. That's all. It's not designed to have the relatively sophisticated functionality you might associate with a standard Delphi or VBX gauge control.

To help you get an overview of the progress bar, a quick review of its messages is presented in Table 15.1.

Table 15.1. Progress bar messages.

Message	wparam	lparam	Purpose
PBM_SETRANGE	0	Start range in low word, end range in high word	Sets the range
PBM_SETPOS	New position	0	Sets the position

Message	wparam	lparam	Purpose
PBM_DELTAPOS	Amount of increment	0 / 0	Moves the progress bar
PBM_SETSTEP	New increment	0	The amount of increment
PBM_STEPIT	0	0	Moves the progress bar

The Progress DEF, RC, and MAK Files

I have included a DEF, RC, and MAK file for the Progress program. You can see that the DEF file is so stripped down as to be almost unnecessary:

```
NAME        Progress
DESCRIPTION 'Progress Window'
```

New compiler defaults and the simplified 32-bit programming model have rendered all the other features of module definition files superfluous. In fact, you could leave out the DEF file without harm while working with either the Microsoft or Borland compiler.

The RC file is also very simple:

```
ProgressIcon ICON "PROGRESS.ICO"
ProgressIcon16 ICON "PROG16.ICO"
```

All that goes on here is that a couple of icons are linked in with the executable so that they can be snagged when needed at runtime. More specifically, both icons are used by the WNDCLASSEX structure described previously.

Getting back to the WNDCLASSEX structures brings us full circle. As it turns out, that's also about all there is to say about the progress bar and Progress program. A progress bar is the simplest, or one of the simplest, of all the new controls. Its simplicity reveals that there is nothing inherently complex about the Windows 95 common controls. The basic building blocks for these components are familiar and quite logically structured. However, you will see later on that some of the controls grow to be quite complex.

Using Toolbars and Tooltips

Toolbars have become popular over the years, in part because they are flashy, and in part because they provide a useful function. Both MSVC.EXE and BCW.EXE make heavy use of toolbars (or speedbars, as they are often called). Users have simply grown accustomed to having rows of brightly colored icons at the top of their programs, each of which serve as a shortcut to some feature listed in the menus.

Tooltips have become part of the toolbar mystique. These tiny windows of text are a natural companion to toolbars because they allow the user to run the mouse over a speed button and see a description defining the button's purpose. As a rule, you must hold the mouse over the button for a few moments before the tooltip will appear. (In other incarnations, tooltips have been called "fly-by help," and "mouse droppings.")

Note: By this time, popular controls such as toolbars, progress bars, tooltips, tabbed dialogs, and status bars have been implemented by thousands of different companies and vendors across the computer industry. With Windows 95, Microsoft is taking the most ubiquitous of these controls, and incorporating them directly into the operating system. It will be interesting to see if everyone now standardizes on Microsoft's tools, or whether there is a continued proliferation of third-party solutions to these interface needs.

At this stage, it's probably best if you go ahead and get the ToolBars program, shown in Listing 2.5, up and running. When you compile the program, don't forget that this is Windows 95-specific 32-bit code, and that you will need to include COMCTL32.LIB when you link. (On some occasions, it is also necessary to ensure that WINVER is defined as being larger or greater than 0x0400, where WINVER stands for the version of Windows.) (See Listings 15.6 through 15.9.)

Listing 15.6. The ToolBars program loads a toolbar and supports it with tooltips.

```
/////////////////////////////////////////////////////////
//   Program Name: Toolbars.cpp
//   Programmer: Charlie Calvert
//   Description: Toolbars windows program
//   Date: 06/24/95
//   Comment: For Windows 95 only
/////////////////////////////////////////////////////////

#define STRICT
#define WIN32_LEAN_AND_MEAN
#include <windows.h>
#include <windowsx.h>
#include <commctrl.h>
#include "toolbars.h"
#pragma warning (disable: 4068)

// -------------------------------------------------------
```

```
// Interface
// -------------------------------------------------------

static char szAppName[] = "Toolbars";
static HWND MainWindow;
static HINSTANCE hInstance;
static COLORREF ScreenColor = RGB(127, 127, 127);
static HWND hToolbar;

TBBUTTON ToolAry[NUMBUTTONS];

// -------------------------------------------------------
// Initialization
// -------------------------------------------------------

/////////////////////////////////////////////////////////
// Program entry point
/////////////////////////////////////////////////////////
#pragma argsused
int WINAPI WinMain(HINSTANCE hInst, HINSTANCE hPrevInstance,
                   LPSTR lpszCmdParam, int nCmdShow)
{
  MSG  Msg;

  hInstance = hInst;

  if (!hPrevInstance)
    if (!Register(hInst))
      return FALSE;

  MainWindow = Create(hInst, nCmdShow);
  if (!MainWindow)
    return FALSE;

  while (GetMessage(&Msg, NULL, 0, 0))
  {
    TranslateMessage(&Msg);
    DispatchMessage(&Msg);
  }

  return Msg.wParam;
}

/////////////////////////////////////////////////////////
// Register the window
/////////////////////////////////////////////////////////
BOOL Register(HINSTANCE hInst)
{
  WNDCLASSEX WndClassEx;

  WndClassEx.cbSize        = sizeof(WNDCLASSEX);
  WndClassEx.style         = CS_HREDRAW | CS_VREDRAW;
  WndClassEx.lpfnWndProc   = WndProc;
  WndClassEx.cbClsExtra    = 0;
  WndClassEx.cbWndExtra    = 0;
  WndClassEx.hInstance     = hInst;
```

continues

585

Listing 15.6. continued

```c
    WndClassEx.hIcon          = LoadIcon(hInst, "ToolbarIcon");
    WndClassEx.hCursor        = LoadCursor(NULL, IDC_ARROW);
    WndClassEx.hbrBackground  = (HBRUSH)(COLOR_WINDOW+1);
    WndClassEx.lpszMenuName   = NULL;
    WndClassEx.lpszClassName  = szAppName;
    WndClassEx.hIconSm        = LoadIcon(hInst, "ToolbarIcon16");

    return (RegisterClassEx(&WndClassEx) != 0);
}


/////////////////////////////////////////////////////////
// Create the window
/////////////////////////////////////////////////////////
HWND Create(HINSTANCE hInst, int nCmdShow)
{

    HWND hwnd = CreateWindow(szAppName, szAppName,
                    WS_OVERLAPPEDWINDOW,
                    CW_USEDEFAULT, CW_USEDEFAULT,
                    CW_USEDEFAULT, CW_USEDEFAULT,
                    NULL, NULL, hInst, NULL);

    if (hwnd == NULL)
        return hwnd;

    ShowWindow(hwnd, nCmdShow);
    UpdateWindow(hwnd);

    return hwnd;
}


// ------------------------------------------------------
// WndProc and Implementation
// ------------------------------------------------------

/////////////////////////////////////////////////////////
// The Window Procedure
/////////////////////////////////////////////////////////
LRESULT CALLBACK WndProc(HWND hwnd, UINT Message, WPARAM wParam, LPARAM lParam)
{
    switch(Message)
    {
        HANDLE_MSG(hwnd, WM_CREATE, Toolbars_OnCreate);
        HANDLE_MSG(hwnd, WM_DESTROY, Toolbars_OnDestroy);
        HANDLE_MSG(hwnd, WM_COMMAND, Toolbars_OnCommand);
        HANDLE_MSG(hwnd, WM_NOTIFY, Toolbars_OnNotify);
        HANDLE_MSG(hwnd, WM_PAINT, Toolbars_OnPaint);
        HANDLE_MSG(hwnd, WM_SIZE, Toolbars_OnSize);
        default: return Toolbars_DefProc(hwnd, Message, wParam, lParam);
    }
}
```

```
/////////////////////////////////////////////////////////////
// WM_CREATE: Create the toolbars
/////////////////////////////////////////////////////////////
#pragma argsused
BOOL Toolbars_OnCreate(HWND hwnd, LPCREATESTRUCT lpCreateStruct)
{
  InitCommonControls();

  for (int i = 0; i < 3; i++)
  {
    ToolAry[i].iBitmap   = i;
    ToolAry[i].idCommand = (INT)ID_RED + i;
    ToolAry[i].fsState   = TBSTATE_ENABLED;
    ToolAry[i].fsStyle   = TBSTYLE_BUTTON;
    ToolAry[i].dwData    = 0L;
    ToolAry[i].iString   = 0;
  }

  hToolbar = CreateToolbarEx(hwnd,
                WS_CHILD | WS_VISIBLE |
                TBSTYLE_TOOLTIPS | WS_BORDER,
                ID_TOOLBAR, NUMBITMAPS,
                lpCreateStruct->hInstance,
                TOOLBARBMP, ToolAry, NUMBUTTONS,
                BTNWIDTH, BTNHEIGHT, BMPWIDTH, BMPHEIGHT,
                sizeof(TBBUTTON)));

  return hToolbar != NULL;
}


/////////////////////////////////////////////////////////////
// Handle WM_DESTROY
/////////////////////////////////////////////////////////////
#pragma argsused
void Toolbars_OnDestroy(HWND hwnd)
{
  PostQuitMessage(0);
}


/////////////////////////////////////////////////////////////
// WM_COMMAND: Handle clicks on the toolbar
/////////////////////////////////////////////////////////////
#pragma argsused
void Toolbars_OnCommand(HWND hwnd, int id, HWND hwndCtl, UINT codeNotify)
{
  switch(id)
  {
    case ID_RED:
      ScreenColor = RGB(255, 0, 0);
      InvalidateRect(hwnd, NULL, FALSE);
      break;

    case ID_GREEN:
      ScreenColor = RGB(0, 255, 0);
      InvalidateRect(hwnd, NULL, FALSE);
      break;

    case ID_BLUE:
```

continues

Listing 15.6. continued

```
         ScreenColor = RGB(0, 0, 255);
         InvalidateRect(hwnd, NULL, FALSE);
         break;
   }
}

////////////////////////////////////////////////////////////
// WM_NOTIFY: Handle the tooltips
////////////////////////////////////////////////////////////
#pragma argsused
LRESULT Toolbars_OnNotify(HWND hwnd, int idFrom, NMHDR FAR * pnmhdr)
{
  switch(pnmhdr->code)
  {
    case TTN_NEEDTEXT:
      LPTOOLTIPTEXT ToolTip = LPTOOLTIPTEXT(pnmhdr);
      switch(idFrom)
    {
      case ID_RED:
        ToolTip->lpszText = "Red";
        break;
      case ID_GREEN:
        ToolTip->lpszText = "Green";
        break;
      case ID_BLUE:
        ToolTip->lpszText = "Blue";
        break;
    }
  }
  return 1;
}

////////////////////////////////////////////////////////////
// WM_PAINT: Paint the background of the main window
////////////////////////////////////////////////////////////
void Toolbars_OnPaint(HWND hwnd)
{
  PAINTSTRUCT PaintStruct;
  RECT Rect;

  HDC PaintDC = BeginPaint(hwnd, &PaintStruct);
  GetClientRect(hwnd, &Rect);
  HBRUSH NewBrush = CreateSolidBrush(ScreenColor);
  HBRUSH OldBrush = SelectBrush(PaintDC, NewBrush);
  Rectangle(PaintDC, 0, 0, Rect.right, Rect.bottom);
  SelectBrush(PaintDC, OldBrush);
  DeleteBrush(NewBrush);
  EndPaint(hwnd, &PaintStruct);
}

////////////////////////////////////////////////////////////
// WM_SIZE: Size toolbar when necessary
////////////////////////////////////////////////////////////
#pragma argsused
```

```
void Toolbars_OnSize(HWND hwnd, UINT state, int cx, int cy)
{
    SendMessage(hToolbar, WM_SIZE, state, MAKELONG(cx, cy));
}
```

Listing 15.7. The header file for the ToolBars program.

```
/////////////////////////////////////////////////////////
// Name: TOOLBARS.H
// Copyright (c) 1995 Charlie Calvert.
// From Teach Yourself Windows 95 Programming
/////////////////////////////////////////////////////////

#define ID_TOOLBAR    1
#define NUMBITMAPS    3
#define NUMBUTTONS    3
#define BTNWIDTH      0
#define BTNHEIGHT     0
#define BMPWIDTH      16
#define BMPHEIGHT     16
#define ID_RED        100
#define ID_GREEN      101
#define ID_BLUE       102
#define TOOLBARBMP    200

LRESULT CALLBACK WndProc(HWND hwnd, UINT Message, WPARAM wParam, LPARAM lParam);
BOOL Register(HINSTANCE hInst);
HWND Create(HINSTANCE hInst, int nCmdShow);

// Declarations for class Toolbars
#define Toolbars_DefProc    DefWindowProc
BOOL Toolbars_OnCreate(HWND hwnd, LPCREATESTRUCT lpCreateStruct);
void Toolbars_OnDestroy(HWND hwnd);
void Toolbars_OnCommand(HWND hwnd, int id, HWND hwndCtl, UINT codeNotify);
LRESULT Toolbars_OnNotify(HWND hwnd, int idFrom, NMHDR FAR * pnmhdr);
void Toolbars_OnPaint(HWND hwnd);
void Toolbars_OnSize(HWND hwnd, UINT state, int cx, int cy);

// WM_NOTIFY not in WINDOWSX.H but in COMMCTRL.H!!!
```

Listing 15.8. The resource file for the ToolBars program loads a BMP and some icons.

```
//////////////////////////////////////
// Module name: TOOLBARS.RC
//   Copyright (c) 1995 Charlie Calvert.
//////////////////////////////////////
#include "toolbars.h"

TOOLBARBMP BITMAP "TOOLBARS.BMP"
ToolbarIcon ICON "TOOLBAR.ICO"
ToolbarIcon16 ICON "TOOL16.ICO"
```

Listing 15.9. The very simple module definition file for the ToolBars program.

```
; Toolbars.Def

NAME          Toolbars
DESCRIPTION   'Toolbars Example Program'
STACKSIZE     10240
```

Figure 15.4 shows the bitmap for the ToolBars program.

Figure 15.4.

The bitmap for the ToolBars program consists of three colored squares, each 16×16 in size.

The ToolBars example, shown in Figure 15.5, displays a normal window with a simple toolbar at the top. There are three buttons on the toolbar: one colored red, the next green, and the last blue. If you click the red button, the background for the main window will turn red. If you click the blue button, it turns blue, and so on. The screen starts out with a gray background.

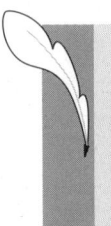

Note: I have not listed the icons for this program, though they are included on the disk you can order using the form at the end of the book. You can use the icons from the last program, or make up two of your own. All that matters is that the big icon is 32×32 and the small icon is 16×16. I would suggest creating them in 16 colors (4 bit), unless you are sure they will be running on machines with 256-color cards. Extra icons often ship with your compiler, and you will find a collection of them in the MORICONS.DLL found in your Windows subdirectory.

With very little modification, you can use the makefiles from the Progress program to compile the ToolBars program.

The ToolAry used in the loop at the beginning of the WM_CREATE handler is defined at the top of the program:

```
TBBUTTON ToolAry[NUMBUTTONS];
```

NUMBUTTONS, logically enough, is defined as 3.

Here is the TBBUTTON structure from COMMCTRL.H:

```
typedef struct _TBBUTTON {
    int iBitmap;
    int idCommand;
    BYTE fsState;
    BYTE fsStyle;
#ifdef _WIN32
    BYTE bReserved[2];
#endif
    DWORD dwData;
    int iString;
} TBBUTTON, NEAR* PTBBUTTON, FAR* LPTBBUTTON;
typedef const TBBUTTON FAR* LPCTBBUTTON;
```

Table 15.2. gives you an overview of the fields in this structure.

Table 15.2. The TBBUTTON structure.

Structure	Description
iBitmap	The ID of the bitmap in the button
idCommand	Message sent to WM_COMMAND when the button is pressed
fsState	One of several constants defined below
fsStyle	One of several styles defined below
dwData	Optional user defined data
iString	Optional number indexing into a stringlist

The iBitmap and idCommand fields are self-explanatory. The dwData and iString fields are also self-explanatory, but rarely used. (Remember that if you want to associate a string with a button, then you can use tooltips.) Here are the possible values for the fsState field, just as they appear in COMMCTRL.H:

```
#define TBSTATE_CHECKED         0x01
#define TBSTATE_PRESSED         0x02
#define TBSTATE_ENABLED         0x04
#define TBSTATE_HIDDEN          0x08
#define TBSTATE_INDETERMINATE   0x10
#define TBSTATE_WRAP            0x20
```

Figure 15.5.
The main window of the ToolBars program.

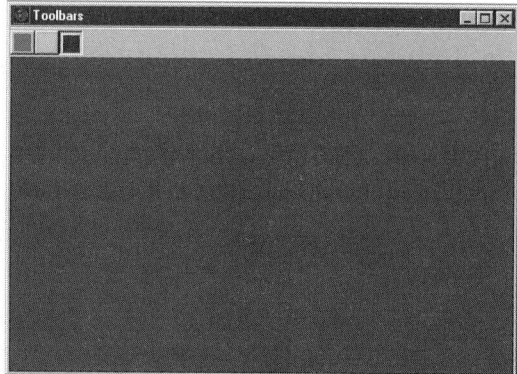

Creating Toolbars

The core functionality of the ToolBars program comes in the WM_CREATE handler:

```
BOOL Toolbars_OnCreate(HWND hwnd, LPCREATESTRUCT lpCreateStruct)
{
  InitCommonControls();

  for (int i = 0; i < 3; i++)
  {
    ToolAry[i].iBitmap   = i;
    ToolAry[i].idCommand = (INT)ID_RED + i;
    ToolAry[i].fsState   = TBSTATE_ENABLED;
    ToolAry[i].fsStyle   = TBSTYLE_BUTTON;
    ToolAry[i].dwData    = 0L;
    ToolAry[i].iString   = 0;
  }

  hToolbar = CreateToolbarEx(hwnd,
             WS_CHILD ¦ WS_VISIBLE ¦
             TBSTYLE_TOOLTIPS ¦ WS_BORDER,
             ID_TOOLBAR, NUMBITMAPS,
             lpCreateStruct->hInstance,
             TOOLBARBMP, ToolAry, NUMBUTTONS,
             BTNWIDTH, BTNHEIGHT, BMPWIDTH, BMPHEIGHT,
             sizeof(TBBUTTON));

  return hToolbar != NULL;
}
```

This function has three parts:

1. The call to `InitCommonControls` that belongs in all programs that use the new Windows 95 controls.

2. The loop that fills in three copies of a `TBBUTTON` structure used to define the bitmaps on the toolbar.

3. The call to `CreateToolbarEx`, which instantiates an instance of the toolbar.

591

The first four of these states are relatively self-explanatory. You need to understand, however, that a checked button is shown in the depressed state. TBSTATE_INDETERMINATE means the button should appear gray and inactive. TBSTATE_WRAP means the buttons following this one should appear on a new line.

Here are styles that can be associated with the controls that appear on the toolbar, and which are used when filling out a TBBUTTON structure:

TBSTYLE_BUTTON	Regular push button
TBSTYLE_SEP	A separator, as in Figure 15.6
TBSTYLE_CHECK	Alternates between being checked and being plain
TBSTYLE_GROUP	Is part of a group
TBSTYLE_CHECKGROUP	Combines TBSTYLE_CHECK and TBSTYLE_GROUP

Figure 15.6.
The TOOLBAR2.CPP code uses bitmaps supplied by the operating system and the TBSTYLE_SEP to break buttons into groups.

If you want a regular button that will not stick in the down position, then choose TBSTYLE_BUTTON. If you want a button that alternates between the down and up position each time you choose it, then choose TBSTYLE_CHECK. If you want a button that can be part of a mutually exclusive set of options, such that only one button in the group can be selected at a time, then choose TBSTYLE_CHECKGROUP.

The *CreateToolbarEx* Function

Syntax

```
WINCOMMCTRLAPI HWND WINAPI CreateToolbarEx(
    HWND hwnd,                  // Handle to parent window
    DWORD ws,                   // Styles such as WS_CHILD
    UINT wID,                   // The controls ID
    int nBitmaps,               // Number of bitmaps in control
    HINSTANCE hBMInst,          // Instance of exe containing bitmap resource
    UINT wBMID,                 // ID of the bitmap in the resource
    LPCTBBUTTON lpButtons,      // TBBUTTON array described above
    int iNumButtons,            // Number of buttons in control
    int dxButton,               // Button width, usually 0
    int dyButton,               // Button height, usually 0
    int dxBitmap,               // Width of each little bitmap
    int dyBitmap,               // Height of each little bitmap
    UINT uStructSize);          // sizeof(TBBUTTON)
```

Here are the styles that can be associated with the entire toolbar, and which are used in the ws field during a call to CreateToolbarEx:

```
TBSTYLE_TOOLTIPS   // Uses tooltips
TBSTYLE_WRAPABLE   // Will wrap to the next line if necessary
TBSTYLE_ALTDRAG    // Press the alt key and drag the button with the mouse!
```

The main thing you need to grasp about calling CreateToolbarEx is that each Toolbar has one large bitmap associated with it. Inside that bitmap are a bunch of smaller bitmaps, all lined up in a row, like a strip of film. To create this bitmap in the Windows Paint program you should use the Image | Attributes menu choice to create a bitmap that is nBitmaps×dxBitmap pixels wide and dyBitmap pixels high. (For some reason Paint refers to pixels as "pels.") Inside this larger canvas, create a bunch of smaller bitmaps that are each dxBitmap pixels in width. (If this sounds confusing to you, then just glance up at Figure 15.4, or open TOOLBAR.BMP inside of the Paint program that comes with Windows. The concept involved is simple enough, even if it takes a moment to describe.)

Here's an example:

```
hToolbar = CreateToolbarEx(hwnd,
            WS_CHILD | WS_VISIBLE |
            TBSTYLE_TOOLTIPS | WS_BORDER,
            ID_TOOLBAR, NUMBITMAPS,
            lpCreateStruct->hInstance,
            TOOLBARBMP, ToolAry, NUMBUTTONS,
            BTNWIDTH, BTNHEIGHT, BMPWIDTH, BMPHEIGHT,
            sizeof(TBBUTTON));
```

After you have created a toolbar, you can use the following messages to manipulate it:

```
#define TB_ENABLEBUTTON          (WM_USER + 1)
#define TB_CHECKBUTTON           (WM_USER + 2)
#define TB_PRESSBUTTON           (WM_USER + 3)
#define TB_HIDEBUTTON            (WM_USER + 4)
#define TB_INDETERMINATE         (WM_USER + 5)
#define TB_ISBUTTONENABLED       (WM_USER + 9)
#define TB_ISBUTTONCHECKED       (WM_USER + 10)
#define TB_ISBUTTONPRESSED       (WM_USER + 11)
#define TB_ISBUTTONHIDDEN        (WM_USER + 12)
#define TB_ISBUTTONINDETERMINATE (WM_USER + 13)
#define TB_SETSTATE              (WM_USER + 17)
#define TB_GETSTATE              (WM_USER + 18)
```

All of these messages pass the ID of the button in WPARAM, and many of them pass additional information in LPARAM. For instance, when you are sending TB_CHECKBUTTON messages, you pass the ID of the button in WPARAM, and set LPARAM to 0 if you want to clear the button and to non-zero if you want to check it. Of course, if you use TBSTYLE_GROUP, you won't have to worry about clearing and checking buttons manually. TB_ENABLEBUTTON and TB_HIDEBUTTON follow the same pattern, with the ID in WPARAM and the clear or set flag being designated by a 0 or non-zero value in LPARAM.

Another message called TB_ADDBITMAP has a slightly different structure than the messages shown above. Coverage of how it works is beyond the scope of this book.

Using the Bitmaps Supplied by Windows

Before going on to explain the rest of the ToolBars program, I should point out that many of the standard bitmaps used in Microsoft applications are defined in COMMCTRL.H:

```
#define STD_CUT          0
#define STD_COPY         1
#define STD_PASTE        2
#define STD_UNDO         3
#define STD_REDOW        4
#define STD_DELETE       5
#define STD_FILENEW      6
#define STD_FILEOPEN     7
#define STD_FILESAVE     8
#define STD_PRINTPRE     9
#define STD_PROPERTIES   10
#define STD_HELP         11
#define STD_FIND         12
#define STD_REPLACE      13
#define STD_PRINT        14
```

Each of these bitmaps is on display in the ToolBar2 program shown in Figure 15.6, and included on the disk you can order.

Here is how the WM_CREATE handler for the ToolBar2 program looks:

```
BOOL Toolbar2_OnCreate(HWND hwnd, LPCREATESTRUCT lpCreateStruct)
{
  int i;
  int BitMapAry[NUMBUTTONS] = {STD_CUT, STD_COPY, STD_PASTE,
                    -1, STD_UNDO, STD_REDOW, STD_DELETE,
                    -1, STD_FILENEW, STD_FILESAVE, STD_FILEOPEN,
                    -1, STD_PRINTPRE, STD_PROPERTIES, STD_HELP,
                    -1, STD_FIND, STD_REPLACE, STD_PRINT};

  InitCommonControls();

  for (i = 0; i < NUMBUTTONS; i++)
  {
    ToolAry[i].iBitmap   = BitMapAry[i];
    ToolAry[i].idCommand = ID_CUT + i;
    ToolAry[i].fsState = TBSTATE_ENABLED;
    ToolAry[i].fsStyle = TBSTYLE_BUTTON;
    if (BitMapAry[i] == -1)
      ToolAry[i].fsStyle = TBSTYLE_SEP;
    ToolAry[i].dwData    = 0L;
    ToolAry[i].iString   = 0;
  }
```

```
hToolbar = CreateToolbarEx(hwnd,
            WS_CHILD | WS_VISIBLE | TBSTYLE_TOOLTIPS | WS_BORDER,
            ID_TOOLBAR, NUMBITMAPS,
            HINST_COMMCTRL, IDB_STD_SMALL_COLOR,
            ToolAry, NUMBUTTONS,
            BTNWIDTH, BTNHEIGHT, BMPWIDTH, BMPHEIGHT,
            sizeof(TBBUTTON));

    return hToolbar != NULL;
}
```

In this case, NUMBUTTONS is defined as 19, and NUMBITMAPS is defined as 15. Four of the buttons on the toolbar are separators, and therefore have no bitmap associated with them.

The trick to using these pre-made bitmaps is revealed in this excerpt from COMMCTRL.H:

```
#define HINST_COMMCTRL          ((HINSTANCE)-1)
#define IDB_STD_SMALL_COLOR     0
#define IDB_STD_LARGE_COLOR     1
#define IDB_VIEW_SMALL_COLOR    4
#define IDB_VIEW_LARGE_COLOR    5
```

These values can be used to fill in the hBMInst and wBMID fields of CreateToolbarEx. Specifically, HINST_COMMCTRL is the HINSTANCE of COMCTL32.DLL, which is where the bitmaps are stored. The IDB constants refer to the IDs of the bitmaps in the DLL's resource. (If you want to see these resources, then launch Resource Workshop or AppStudio, load COMCTL32.DLL, and look at the bitmaps inside it.)

The actual code for TOOLBAR2.CPP's WM_CREATE handler is nearly identical to the code in TOOLBARS.CPP. As a result, I won't bother to discuss it further, other than to point out its use of the HINST_COMMCTRL and IDB_STD_SMALL_COLOR constants.

Working with Tooltips

To add tooltips to your toolbars you need to first add TBSTYLE_TOOLTIPS to the WS field of CreateToolbarEx:

```
hToolbar = CreateToolbarEx(hwnd,
            WS_CHILD | WS_VISIBLE | TBSTYLE_TOOLTIPS,
            ...}
```

You fill in the tooltip strings by responding to WM_NOTIFY messages. WM_NOTIFY is a new Windows message that is defined in COMMCTRL.H. As mentioned earlier, the WindowsX-style message cracker for this message is right there in the heart of COMMCTRL:

```
#define HANDLE_WM_NOTIFY(hwnd, wParam, lParam, fn) \
    (fn)((hwnd), (int)(wParam), (NMHDR FAR*)(lParam))
#define FORWARD_WM_NOTIFY(hwnd, idFrom, pnmhdr, fn) \
    (LRESULT)(fn)((hwnd), WM_NOTIFY, (WPARAM)(int)(idFrom),
    (LPARAM)(NMHDR FAR*)(pnmhdr))
```

I'm reiterating this fact because it's both fairly important and somewhat confusing. When you are working with components defined in COMMCTRL, you are going to make heavy use of WM_NOTIFY message. It's crucial that you remember where its message crackers are defined!

> **Note:** It's not important to WindowsX-style programmers, but you should still note that the NMHDR field passes idFrom in WPARAM and pnmhdr in LPARAM.

Here's what the NMHDR field looks like:

```
typedef struct tagNMHDR
{
  HWND hwndFrom; // Handle of the control send the message
  UNIT idFrom;   // Control ID
  UINT code;     // notification code describing
                 // the type of record being sent.
} NMHDR;
```

This record appears simple enough at first glance. But you will find out that there are some changes rung on it that makes it a bit of a sticking point for careless programmers.

To show you what I mean, take a look at the WM_NOTIFY handler from the ToolBars program:

```
#pragma argsused
LRESULT Toolbars_OnNotify(HWND hwnd, int idFrom, NMHDR FAR * pnmhdr)
{
  switch(pnmhdr->code)
  {
    case TTN_NEEDTEXT:
      LPTOOLTIPTEXT ToolTip = LPTOOLTIPTEXT(pnmhdr);
      switch(idFrom)
    {
      case ID_RED:
        ToolTip->lpszText = "Red";
        break;
      case ID_GREEN:
        ToolTip->lpszText = "Green";
        break;
      case ID_BLUE:
        ToolTip->lpszText = "Blue";
        break;
    }
  }
  return 1;
}
```

What's this lpszText field? I just showed you the NMHDR structure, and clearly it had no text fields in it at all. So what's going on? How can I get away with typecasting a NMHDR to a TOOLTIPTEXT structure? Where did this TOOLTIPTEXT structure come from, anyway?

As it turns out, in this case the `WM_NOTIFY` message doesn't really send an `NMHDR` structure, or rather, it sends it but cloaks it inside a second structure. What you are really sent is a `TOOLTIPTEXT` structure, which looks like this:

```
typedef struct tagTOOLTIPTEXTA {
    NMHDR hdr;              // Regular WM_NOTIFY header
    LPSTR lpszText;        // Method one: assign a pointer to this field
    char szText[80];       // Method two: use this string buffer
    HINSTANCE hinst;       // Method three: Set to NULL unless lpszText
                           // refers to a stringlist index
    UINT uFlags;
} TOOLTIPTEXTA, FAR *LPTOOLTIPTEXTA;
```

This little puppy takes some getting used to.

I've already stated that a `pnmhdr` parameter points to a standard record called `NMHDR`. Only, in this case, the header has been extended with several additional fields that are specific to the tooltips message.

> **Note:** Some programmers may not be aware of how structures reside in memory, and as a result they might appreciate a word or two about what's going on inside a `TOOLTIPTEXT` record. This discussion gets a bit abstract at times and covers a good deal of relatively fundamental material. Still, if you add it all up, it should help you see what is happening in this case.
>
> Suppose you have the following declarations:
>
> ```
> typedef struct tagFOO
> {
>   int A;
>   int B;
> }FOO;
>
> typedef struct tagFOO1
> {
>   int C;
>   int D;
> }FOO1;
>
> typedef struct tagFOOBAR
> {
>   FOO Foo;
>   FOO1 Foo1;
>   int E;
> }FOOBAR;
> ```
>
> Given the above declarations, `FOOBAR` has the same structure as a record declared like this:
>
> ```
> typedef struct tagFOOMAX
> ```

```
{
  int A;
  int B;
  int C;
  int D;
  int E;
}FOOMAX;
```

The fact that FOOBAR consists of a simple type and two structures and FOOMAX consists solely of simple types has no impact on the way the two types look when they reside in memory. They are identical in structure, it's just that you can use a different syntax for accessing the data of one than for accessing the data of the other.

Take this information, and apply it to the NMHDR structure shown above. A TOOLTIPTEXT structure is like the FOOBAR structure shown above. It's one struct with another struct folded inside it. You could also think of that structure as looking like the structure shown in the FOOMAX example. Embed one record inside the other, or list all the fields separately; in terms of memory imprint, it's all the same.

Since pnmhdr is a pointer to a struct, it doesn't matter exactly what fields are actually encapsulated in the struct. All it has to do is point at a struct. The actual structure of the record isn't important, so long as its initial fields are identical to a standard NMHDR. Furthermore, you can take the NMHDR structure and expand it simply by adding fields on to it.

Consider this declaration:

```
typedef struct tagFURBALL
{
  FOOMAX FooMax;
  int F;
}FURBALL;
```

Though you might reference its fields differently, this structure leaves the exact same memory imprint as the following structure:

```
typedef struct tagFUMAROLE
{
  int A;
  int B;
  int C;
  int D;
  int E;
  int F;
}FUMAROLE;
```

Because the initial fields of the FUMAROLE, FURBALL, and FOOMAX structs are identical, you can safely typecast them all to be of type FOOBAR. Apply the same logic to a WM_NOTIFY message, and you can see why it's okay to pass a TOOLTIPTEXT structure and cast it as a NMHDR.

> The creators of Windows may not be showing much respect for our sanity when they play these kinds of syntactical games, but if you give it a little thought, it's clear that this kind of fancy footwork keeps them well within the bounds of legal coding practices. In other words, we might emit a barely detectable sigh at the sight of this syntax, but the compiler happily gobbles it all up as perfectly legitimate practice.
>
> It's the programmatic equivalent of writing a legal brief, only it does no harm; it's more entertaining, and everyone is allowed to play.

I'm spending so much time dwelling on the practice of transforming an NMHDR into a TOOLTIPTEXT because it is a technique used over and over again in COMMCTRL.H. Consider the following declarations:

```
typedef struct _HD_NOTIFY
{
    NMHDR    hdr;
    int      iItem;
    int      iButton;
    HD_ITEMA FAR* pitem;
} HD_NOTIFYA;

typedef struct _NM_UPDOWN
{
    NMHDR hdr;
    int iPos;
    int iDelta;
} NM_UPDOWN, FAR *LPNM_UPDOWN;

typedef struct _NM_LISTVIEW
{
    NMHDR    hdr;
    int      iItem;
    int      iSubItem;
    UINT     uNewState;
    UINT     uOldState;
    UINT     uChanged;
    POINT    ptAction;
    LPARAM   lParam;
} NM_LISTVIEW, FAR *LPNM_LISTVIEW;

typedef struct _NM_TREEVIEWA {
    NMHDR        hdr;
    UINT         action;
    TV_ITEMA     itemOld;
    TV_ITEMA     itemNew;
    POINT        ptDrag;
} NM_TREEVIEWA, FAR *LPNM_TREEVIEWA;

typedef struct _TC_KEYDOWN
```

```
{
    NMHDR hdr;
    WORD wVKey;
    UINT flags;
} TC_KEYDOWN;
```

These are all variations on the same theme shown in the TOOLTIPTEXT record, only they apply to other controls such as headers, updowns, listviews, treeviews and tab controls. (By the way, this is not an inclusive list. There are other records of this type scattered throughout COMMCTRL.H. You can find them by searching on NMHDR.) I won't belabor this point any further, but if you don't understand how this system works, you should probably review the material shown above. You won't get far with the common controls unless you understand the sly tricks you can play with a NMHDR.

Now that you have the fundamentals down, it's easy to see what's actually happening in the WM_NOTIFY event handler:

```
switch(pnmhdr->code)
  {
    case TTN_NEEDTEXT:
      LPTOOLTIPTEXT ToolTip = LPTOOLTIPTEXT(pnmhdr);
      switch(idFrom)
    {
    case ID_RED:
      ToolTip->lpszText = "Red";
      break;
    case ID_GREEN:
      ToolTip->lpszText = "Green";
      break;
    case ID_BLUE:
      ToolTip->lpszText = "Blue";
      break;
    }
```

The code first checks to see if the message is of type TTN_NEEDTEXT. The TTN_NEEDTEXT message specifies that the tooltip needs more text. More specifically, TTN_NEEDTEXT lets you know that the pnmhdr parameter is really of type LPTOOLTIPTEXT. Therefore, the following typecast is legitimate:

```
LPTOOLTIPTEXT ToolTip = LPTOOLTIPTEXT(pnmhdr);
```

Once you have the ToolTip structure in your hand, then everything is clear sailing. Right?

Don't believe it for a second! This is Windows programming you're involved in here, and there is always another level of complexity residing just beneath the surface.

To hop onto this next bronco, you need to go all the way back up to the initial definition of the TOOLTIPTEXT structure shown above:

```
typedef struct tagTOOLTIPTEXTA {
    NMHDR hdr;          // Regular WM_NOTIFY header
    LPSTR lpszText;     // Method one: assign a pointer to this field
    char szText[80];    // Method two: use this string buffer
```

```
   HINSTANCE hinst;      // Method three: Set to NULL unless lpszText
                         // refers to a stringlist index
   UINT uFlags;
} TOOLTIPTEXTA, FAR *LPTOOLTIPTEXTA;
```

The notes I've added here make it clear that there are three different methods you can use to interpret this structure!

As it happens, none of the methods are particularly complex:

☐ The first involves treating lpszText as a pointer to a string, which is what I have done in the ToolBars program. I can do this because I use a string constant, which has memory preallocated for it by the compiler.

☐ The second method involves using the szText field, which has memory preallocated for it by Windows. More specifically, it has 80 bytes of memory, and you can use that buffer for doing something like this:

```
wsprintf(ToolTip->szText, "%d bottles of beer on the wall", x);
```

☐ The final technique allows you to use stringtables, which were covered back on Day 7, "Advanced Resources: Bitmaps and Dialogs." In this technique, you put the index of the stringtable in the lpszText field, and the HINSTANCE of the application holding the stringtable in the hInst field:

```
ToolTip->lpszText = MAKEINTRESOURCE(12);
ToolTip->hinst = hInstance;
```

The signal that you want to use this third technique is triggered when you set hinst to a non-NULL value.

The third technique shown above is useful, since it allows you to use stringtables. I illustrate this method in the TOOLBAR2.CPP module.

In TOOLBAR2.RC, I create the following string table:

```
#include "toolbar2.h"

STRINGTABLE
BEGIN
  ID_CUT, "Cut"
  ID_COPY, "Copy"
  ID_PASTE, "Paste"
  ID_UNDO, "Undo"
  ID_REDO, "Redo"
  ID_DELETE, "Delete"
  ID_FILENEW, "New File"
  ID_FILESAVE, "Save File"
  ID_FILEOPEN, "File Open"
  ID_PRINTPRE, "Print Preview"
  ID_PROPERTY, "Properties"
  ID_HELP, "Help"
  ID_FIND, "Find"
  ID_REPLACE, "Replace"
  ID_PRINT, "Print"
END
```

The definition for the IDs shown here are all declared in TOOLBAR2.H. I then use the following code to show the tooltips to the user.

```
LRESULT Toolbar2_OnNotify(HWND hwnd, int idFrom, NMHDR FAR * pnmhdr)
{
  switch(pnmhdr->code)
  {
  case TTN_NEEDTEXT:
    LPTOOLTIPTEXT ToolTip = LPTOOLTIPTEXT(pnmhdr);
    switch(idFrom)
    {
    case ID_CUT:
      ToolTip->lpszText = MAKEINTRESOURCE(idFrom);
      ToolTip->hinst = hInstance;
      break;
    case ID_COPY:
      ToolTip->lpszText = MAKEINTRESOURCE(idFrom);
      ToolTip->hinst = hInstance;
      break;
      ...
    }
  }
}
```

Responding to Commands, Resizing the Window

Whenever the user clicks on a speed button, the ID of the button is sent to the WM_COMMAND handler:

```
void Toolbars_OnCommand(HWND hwnd, int id, HWND hwndCtl, UINT codeNotify)
{
  switch(id)
  {
    case ID_RED:
      ScreenColor = RGB(255, 0, 0);
      InvalidateRect(hwnd, NULL, FALSE);
      break;

    case ID_GREEN:
      ScreenColor = RGB(0, 255, 0);
      InvalidateRect(hwnd, NULL, FALSE);
      break;

    case ID_BLUE:
      ScreenColor = RGB(0, 0, 255);
      InvalidateRect(hwnd, NULL, FALSE);
      break;
  }
}
```

This code resets a variable called ScreenColor, and then calls the WM_PAINT handler, which splashes an appropriately colored rectangle up on the screen:

```
HDC PaintDC = BeginPaint(hwnd, &PaintStruct);
GetClientRect(hwnd, &Rect);
HBRUSH NewBrush = CreateSolidBrush(ScreenColor);
HBRUSH OldBrush = SelectBrush(PaintDC, NewBrush);
Rectangle(PaintDC, 0, 0, Rect.right, Rect.bottom);
SelectBrush(PaintDC, OldBrush);
DeleteBrush(NewBrush);
EndPaint(hwnd, &PaintStruct);
```

Note the call to GetClientRect. That guarantees that the rectangle can be made the same size as the client area of the main window. The rest of the paint handler is just the standard system resource two step, with care being taken with the objects that are stored on the GDI heap.

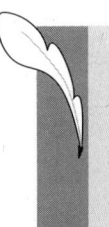

> **Note:** The GDI heap! Is it still necessary to be concerned about running out of resources on the GDI heap? Well, this is not a big issue for 32-bit programs, but the 16-bit programs that run under Windows 95 still have to wrestle with a 64KB limit on the size of the User and GDI local heaps. It happens that if you close all the 16-bit programs running on the system, then Windows will clean up any left-over objects in the 16-bit GDI heap, but that does not get us completely out of danger. The heap for GDI32.DLL is fairly large (640KB), and it will be cleaned up every time a 32-bit app closes. (In fact, it will even be cleaned up on a thread by thread basis in multithreaded applications.) Furthermore, it will hold 32,767 objects, while the 16-bit heap will hold only 200 objects. Clearly, the resource allocation issue is improved in Windows 95. However, you should still take care with system resources, as some mission critical apps run for days and weeks at a time. Anyone who is wasting resources will eventually bring the system down, covering themselves with shame. The great programming gods in the sky would not approve.

The final piece of information in the ToolBars program involves resizing the toolbar when the user changes the shape of the main window. You will be glad to hear that this is a trivial process:

```
void Toolbars_OnSize(HWND hwnd, UINT state, int cx, int cy)
{
  SendMessage(hToolbar, WM_SIZE, state, MAKELONG(cx, cy));
}
```

The step to take here, obviously enough, is to merely send a WM_SIZE message to the toolbar itself. A somewhat humorous touch is provided by the fact that I have to repack the WindowsX message cracker before sending the message off. To avoid this, you can handle the WM_SIZE message directly inside the WndProc.

That's all I'm going to say about toolbars and tooltips. I've gone at this subject in considerable detail since it can serve as a template for work with other common controls that ship with Windows 95 and Windows NT.

Working with the Trackbar and Status Bar

Trackbars are controls that are associated with multimedia tools, but you can use them in a wide variety of applications. They allow the user to select a value, such as the volume for a MIDI file, or the location to seek to in an AVI file. The Microsoft implementation is fairly complete, and provides most of the flexibility you might hope to get from this kind of tool.

Status bars rest on the bottoms of the main window of many of the most famous Windows applications. They provide a place where you can display information about the state of your program. For instance, Word uses them to track the current page number, section, total number of pages, position on the page, and the time. Whenever I save a file inside of Word, the status bar briefly hosts a progress bar that shows the status of a file save operation. When I switch over to DOS to do some coding, I find another, more primitive, status bar at the bottom of my copy of Brief.

By now you have had considerable experience with Windows 95 common controls, so you probably have a fair idea of what to expect. In fact, you might even want to close your eyes and see if you can guess some of the key architectural structures:

☐ Will status controls be created by a custom function, or by CreateWindow? What about trackbars?

☐ Will you configure the range of a trackbar with a style in the create function, or will it be with a message?

☐ How about those little sunken boxes on a status control? Are they defined with styles or by sending messages?

There are a definable set of options associated with any control, and if you have had some experience with them, you can begin to imagine how you might go about creating them. It's fun sometimes to see if your guesses correspond to the techniques dreamed up by the boys and girls in Redmond.

At any rate, Listing 15.10 holds TRACKBAR.CPP, and the rest of the program is shown in Listings 15.11 through 15.13. Take a few moments to study the code and to get the application up and running. Once you have seen how it works, you can read about the application in the remainder of this chapter.

Listing 15.10. TRACKBAR.CPP launches three trackbars and a status control.

```cpp
/////////////////////////////////////////////////////////////
//   Program Name: Trackbar.cpp
//   Programmer: Charlie Calvert
//   Description: Trackbar windows example with status bar
//   Comments: Win32 only. NT must be 3.51 or greater.
//   Date: 06/30/96
/////////////////////////////////////////////////////////////

#define STRICT
#define WIN32_LEAN_AND_MEAN
#include <windows.h>
#include <windowsx.h>
#include <commctrl.h>
#include <stdio.h>
#include "trackbar.h"
#pragma warning (disable: 4068)

// -------------------------------------------------------
// Interface
// -------------------------------------------------------

static char szAppName[] = "Trackbar";
static HWND MainWindow;
static HINSTANCE hInstance;
static HWND hTrackbar[COLORCOUNT];
static HWND hStatusWindow;
static COLORREF ShapeColor = RGB(127, 127, 127);
SHAPES Shapes = sEllipse;

// -------------------------------------------------------
// Initialization
// -------------------------------------------------------

/////////////////////////////////////////////////////////////
// Program entry point
/////////////////////////////////////////////////////////////
#pragma argsused
int WINAPI WinMain(HINSTANCE hInst, HINSTANCE hPrevInstance, LPSTR lpszCmdParam,
int nCmdShow)
{
  MSG  Msg;

  if (!hPrevInstance)
    if (!Register(hInst))
      return FALSE;

  MainWindow = Create(hInst, nCmdShow);
  if (!MainWindow)
    return FALSE;

  while (GetMessage(&Msg, NULL, 0, 0))
    if (!IsDialogMessage(MainWindow, &Msg))
    {
```

```
        TranslateMessage(&Msg);
        DispatchMessage(&Msg);
    }

    return Msg.wParam;
}


////////////////////////////////////////////////////
// Register the window
////////////////////////////////////////////////////
BOOL Register(HINSTANCE hInst)
{
    WNDCLASSEX WndClass;

    WndClass.cbSize          = sizeof(WNDCLASSEX);
    WndClass.style           = CS_HREDRAW | CS_VREDRAW;
    WndClass.lpfnWndProc     = WndProc;
    WndClass.cbClsExtra      = 0;
    WndClass.cbWndExtra      = 0;
    WndClass.hInstance       = hInst;
    WndClass.hIcon           = LoadIcon(hInst, "TrackIcon");
    WndClass.hCursor         = LoadCursor(NULL, IDC_ARROW);
    WndClass.hbrBackground   = (HBRUSH)(COLOR_WINDOW+1);
    WndClass.lpszMenuName    = NULL;
    WndClass.lpszClassName   = szAppName;
    WndClass.hIconSm         = LoadIcon(hInst, "TrackIcon16");

    return (RegisterClassEx (&WndClass) != 0);
}


////////////////////////////////////////////////////
// Create the window
////////////////////////////////////////////////////
HWND Create(HINSTANCE hInst, int nCmdShow)
{

    hInstance = hInst;

    HWND hwnd = CreateWindow(szAppName, szAppName,
                    WS_OVERLAPPEDWINDOW,
                    CW_USEDEFAULT, CW_USEDEFAULT,
                    CW_USEDEFAULT, CW_USEDEFAULT,
                    NULL, NULL, hInst, NULL);

    if (hwnd == NULL)
        return hwnd;

    ShowWindow(hwnd, nCmdShow);
    UpdateWindow(hwnd);

    return hwnd;
}

// -------------------------------------------------------
// WndProc and Implementation
// -------------------------------------------------------
```

continues

Listing 15.10. continued

```c
///////////////////////////////////////////////////////
// The Window Procedure
///////////////////////////////////////////////////////
LRESULT CALLBACK WndProc(HWND hwnd, UINT Message, WPARAM wParam, LPARAM lParam)
{
  switch(Message)
  {
    HANDLE_MSG(hwnd, WM_CREATE, Trackbar_OnCreate);
    HANDLE_MSG(hwnd, WM_DESTROY, Trackbar_OnDestroy);
    HANDLE_MSG(hwnd, WM_COMMAND, Trackbar_OnCommand);
    HANDLE_MSG(hwnd, WM_PAINT, Trackbar_OnPaint);
    HANDLE_MSG(hwnd, WM_HSCROLL, Trackbar_OnHScroll);
    HANDLE_MSG(hwnd, WM_RBUTTONDOWN, Trackbar_OnRButtonDown);
    HANDLE_MSG(hwnd, WM_SIZE, Trackbar_OnSize);
    default: return Trackbar_DefProc(hwnd, Message, wParam, lParam);
  }
}

///////////////////////////////////////////////////////
// Fill the text fields in the status bar
///////////////////////////////////////////////////////
void FillStatus(int Red, int Green, int Blue)
{
  char S[50];

  sprintf(S, "Red: %d", Red);
  SendMessage(hStatusWindow, SB_SETTEXT, 0, (LPARAM)S);
  sprintf(S, "Green: %d", Green);
  SendMessage(hStatusWindow, SB_SETTEXT, 1, (LPARAM)S);
  sprintf(S, "Blue: %d", Blue);
  SendMessage(hStatusWindow, SB_SETTEXT, 2, (LPARAM)S);
}

///////////////////////////////////////////////////////
// Calc dimensions of the sections in the status bar
///////////////////////////////////////////////////////
void SizeStatusSections(HWND hwnd)
{
  int Sections[COLORCOUNT], i;
  RECT Rect;

  GetClientRect(hwnd, &Rect);

  for (i = 1; i <= COLORCOUNT; i++)
    Sections[i-1] = Rect.right / COLORCOUNT * i;

  SendMessage(hStatusWindow, SB_SETPARTS, (WPARAM)COLORCOUNT, (LPARAM)Sections);
}

///////////////////////////////////////////////////////
// WM_CREATE: Create three trackbars
///////////////////////////////////////////////////////
BOOL Trackbar_OnCreate(HWND hwnd, LPCREATESTRUCT lpCreateStruct)
```

15

```
{
  int i;

  InitCommonControls();

  hStatusWindow = CreateStatusWindow(WS_CHILD | WS_VISIBLE,
                                     "StatusWindow", hwnd, 0);

  for (i = 0; i < COLORCOUNT; i++)
  {
    hTrackbar[i] = CreateWindow(TRACKBAR_CLASS, "Trackbar",
                      WS_CHILD | WS_BORDER | WS_VISIBLE | WS_TABSTOP,
                      0, 0, 400, TBHEIGHT, hwnd, (HMENU)ID_TRACKBAR,
                      lpCreateStruct->hInstance, NULL);

    SendMessage(hTrackbar[i], TBM_SETRANGE, (WPARAM)1, (LPARAM)MAKELONG(0, 255));
    SendMessage(hTrackbar[i], TBM_SETPOS, (WPARAM)1, (LPARAM)127);
  }

  if (hTrackbar[0] == NULL)
    MessageBox(hwnd, "no trackbar", NULL, MB_OK);

  return hTrackbar[0] != NULL;
}

/////////////////////////////////////////////////////
// Handle WM_DESTROY
/////////////////////////////////////////////////////
#pragma argsused
void Trackbar_OnDestroy(HWND hwnd)
{
  PostQuitMessage(0);
}

/////////////////////////////////////////////////////
// Redraw: Force a redraw of the colored shape
/////////////////////////////////////////////////////
void Redraw(HWND hwnd)
{
  RECT Rect, StatusRect;

  GetClientRect(hwnd, &Rect);
  GetClientRect(hStatusWindow, &StatusRect);
  Rect.top = (TBHEIGHT * 4);
  Rect.bottom -= StatusRect.bottom;
  InvalidateRect(hwnd, &Rect, TRUE);
}

/////////////////////////////////////////////////////
// WM_COMMAND: Popup menu changes the shape we draw
/////////////////////////////////////////////////////
#pragma argsused
void Trackbar_OnCommand(HWND hwnd, int id, HWND hwndCtl, UINT codeNotify)
{
  switch(id)
```

continues

609

Listing 15.10. continued

```
    {
      case ID_ELLIPSE:
        Shapes = sEllipse;
        Redraw(hwnd);
        break;
      case ID_RECTANGLE:
        Shapes = sRectangle;
        Redraw(hwnd);
        break;
      case ID_ROUNDRECT:
        Shapes = sRoundRect;
        Redraw(hwnd);
        break;
    }
}

//////////////////////////////////////////////////////////
// WM_PAINT: draw a colored ellipse
//////////////////////////////////////////////////////////
void Trackbar_OnPaint(HWND hwnd)
{
  PAINTSTRUCT PaintStruct;
  RECT Rect;

  int xPos = (TBHEIGHT * 4);
  GetClientRect(hwnd, &Rect);

  HDC PaintDC = BeginPaint(hwnd, &PaintStruct);
  HBRUSH NewBrush = CreateSolidBrush(ShapeColor);
  HBRUSH OldBrush = SelectBrush(PaintDC, NewBrush);
  switch (Shapes)
  {
    case sEllipse:
      Ellipse(PaintDC, 10, xPos, Rect.right - 20, Rect.bottom - 25);
      break;
    case sRectangle:
      Rectangle(PaintDC, 10, xPos, Rect.right - 20, Rect.bottom - 25);
      break;
    case sRoundRect:
      RoundRect(PaintDC, 10, xPos, Rect.right - 20,
                Rect.bottom - 25, 75, 75);
      break;
  }
  SelectBrush(PaintDC, OldBrush);
  DeleteBrush(NewBrush);
  EndPaint(hwnd, &PaintStruct);
}

//////////////////////////////////////////////////////////
// WM_HSCROLL: Respond to clicks on the trackbars.
//////////////////////////////////////////////////////////
```

```
#pragma argsused
void Trackbar_OnHScroll(HWND hwnd, HWND hwndCtl, UINT code, int pos)
{
  int RedColor, GreenColor, BlueColor, i;

  // Hit on one of our trackbars?
  for (i = 0; i < COLORCOUNT; i++)
    if (hTrackbar[i] == hwndCtl)
    {
      RedColor = SendMessage(hTrackbar[0], TBM_GETPOS, 0, 0);
      GreenColor = SendMessage(hTrackbar[1], TBM_GETPOS, 0, 0);
      BlueColor  = SendMessage(hTrackbar[2], TBM_GETPOS, 0, 0);
      ShapeColor = RGB(RedColor, GreenColor, BlueColor);
      FillStatus(RedColor, GreenColor, BlueColor);
      Redraw(hwnd);
    }
}

/////////////////////////////////////////////////////////
// WM_RBUTTONDOWN: change the shape, ellipse, rect, etc
/////////////////////////////////////////////////////////
#pragma argsused
void Trackbar_OnRButtonDown(HWND hwnd, BOOL fDoubleClick,
                            int x, int y, UINT keyFlags)
{
  HMENU Floater = CreatePopupMenu();
  AppendMenu(Floater, MF_STRING, ID_ELLIPSE, "Ellipse");
  AppendMenu(Floater, MF_STRING, ID_RECTANGLE, "Rectangle");
  AppendMenu(Floater, MF_STRING, ID_ROUNDRECT, "RoundRect");
  TrackPopupMenu(Floater, TPM_LEFTALIGN, x, y, 0, hwnd, NULL);
}

/////////////////////////////////////////////////////////
// WM_SIZE: Resize trackbar and status window
/////////////////////////////////////////////////////////
#pragma argsused
void Trackbar_OnSize(HWND hwnd, UINT state, int cx, int cy)
{
  int i;
  RECT Rect, RectClient;

  GetClientRect(hwnd, &RectClient);
  for (i = 0; i < COLORCOUNT; i++)
  {
    GetWindowRect(hTrackbar[i], &Rect);
    MoveWindow(hTrackbar[i], 10, (10 * (i+1)) + (TBHEIGHT * i),
               RectClient.right - 20, TBHEIGHT, TRUE);
  }

  SendMessage(hStatusWindow, WM_SIZE, state, MAKELONG(cx, cy));
  SizeStatusSections(hwnd);
}
```

Listing 15.11. The TRACKBAR.H file looks like it could belong to many of the programs in this book.

```
/////////////////////////////////////////////////////////
// TRACKBAR.H
// Copyright (c) 1995 Charlie Calvert.
// Date: 06/30/95
/////////////////////////////////////////////////////////

// Constants
#define ID_TRACKBAR 100
#define COLORCOUNT 3
#define TBHEIGHT 35
#define ID_ELLIPSE 101
#define ID_RECTANGLE 102
#define ID_ROUNDRECT 103

// Types
enum SHAPES {sEllipse, sRectangle, sRoundRect};

// Funcs
LRESULT CALLBACK WndProc(HWND hwnd, UINT Message, WPARAM wParam, LPARAM lParam);
BOOL Register(HINSTANCE hInst);
HWND Create(HINSTANCE hInst, int nCmdShow);

// Declarations for class Trackbar
#define Trackbar_DefProc      DefWindowProc
BOOL Trackbar_OnCreate(HWND hwnd, LPCREATESTRUCT lpCreateStruct);
void Trackbar_OnDestroy(HWND hwnd);
void Trackbar_OnCommand(HWND hwnd, int id, HWND hwndCtl, UINT codeNotify);
void Trackbar_OnPaint(HWND hwnd);
void Trackbar_OnHScroll(HWND hwnd, HWND hwndCtl, UINT code, int pos);
void Trackbar_OnSize(HWND hwnd, UINT state, int cx, int cy);
void Trackbar_OnRButtonDown(HWND hwnd, BOOL fDoubleClick,
                            int x, int y, UINT keyFlags);
```

Listing 15.12. The TRACKBAR.RC file references two icons.

```
/////////////////////////////////////////////////////////
// TRACKBAR.RC
// Copyright (c) 1995 Charlie Calvert.
// Teach Yourself Windows 95 Programming
/////////////////////////////////////////////////////////

/*   Trackbar big icon     */
TrackIcon ICON "trackbar.ico"

/*   Trackbar little icon    */
TrackIcon16 ICON "track16.ico"
```

Listing 15.13. TRACKBAR.DEF is stripped down to a few sparsely applied, rudimentary syntaxes.

```
; Trackbar.Def

NAME           Trackbar
DESCRIPTION    'Trackbar Window'
```

As always, you can feel free to do what you want with the icons for this program. However, I have included some default icons in Figures 15.7 and 15.8 that you can use if you wish. Remember that you can use the Resource Workshop or the App Studio to snap up icons from MORICONS.DLL, or other executables. MORICONS ships with Windows, and I can't foresee any copyright issues when using its files. However, you need to be careful when raiding other executables in a rapacious search for icons.

Figure 15.7.
The large icon for this program is a variation of one of the icons that ships with the MORICONS.DLL from the Windows directory.

Figure 15.8.
The small icon for the Trackbar application.

The Trackbar application shows three trackbars, a status bar and a large ellipse. If you move the trackbars, you can change the color of the ellipse. Each trackbar has a range from 0 to 255, and you can see the value of the currently selected position in the status bar at the bottom of the main window. You can also right-click on the main window and bring up a floating pop-up menu. The pop-up menu allows you to change the properties of the shape you want to draw. Specifically, you can change from an Ellipse, to a Rectangle, to a RoundRect.

The Trackbar program, shown in Figure 15.9, follows a classic pattern for this type of app that has been duplicated in numerous utilities and in several other programming books. It's interesting primarily because you can see how to mix colors to achieve different shades. On a 256-color system you will find interesting colors by setting the sliding bars to 0, 63, 127, 191, or 255. For instance, try setting two of the bars to 63, the third to 191, and so on.

Figure 15.9.

The Trackbar program, switching into RoundRect mode. Use right-clicks to set the mode.

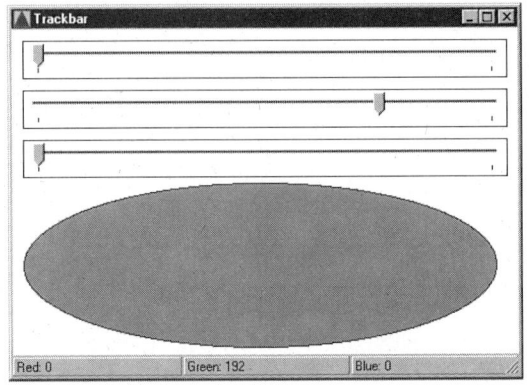

To help you navigate through the program, I have called `IsDialogMessage` in the message loop, as explained on Day 12, "Window Controls and the Control Message API." After adding this call, and giving the controls the `WS_TABSTOP` style, you can tab back and forth between the trackbars, and use the keyboard to slide the thumb back and forth. This gives you the kind of precise control you need to mix fine shades of color. (Try focusing a trackbar control and selecting the Home, End, PgUp, and PgDown keys. Check out the arrow keys.)

Trackbar Basics

Whenever you want to work with the Windows 95 common controls, you should start by calling `InitCommonControls`. Also, don't forget to include COMMCTRL.H at the top of the file, and to link with COMCTL32.LIB.

To create a trackbar, you can call `CreateWindow`, passing in all the standard parameters:

```
hTrackbar[i] = CreateWindow(TRACKBAR_CLASS, "Trackbar",
            WS_CHILD | WS_BORDER | WS_VISIBLE | WS_TABSTOP,
            0, 0, 400, TBHEIGHT, hwnd, (HMENU)ID_TRACKBAR,
            lpCreateStruct->hInstance, NULL);
```

As you can see, the class name for a trackbar is represented by the `TRACKBAR_CLASS` macro, which is defined like this in COMMCTRL.H:

```
#ifdef _WIN32

#define TRACKBAR_CLASSA         "msctls_trackbar32"
#define TRACKBAR_CLASSW         L"msctls_trackbar32"

#ifdef UNICODE
#define  TRACKBAR_CLASS         TRACKBAR_CLASSW
#else
#define  TRACKBAR_CLASS         TRACKBAR_CLASSA
#endif
```

```
#else
#define TRACKBAR_CLASS          "msctls_trackbar"
#endif
```

This is a definition only a mother could love, no? At any rate, the call resolves to `"msctls_trackbar32"`. Remember that `TRACKBAR_CLASSW` is the "wide" Unicode definition, which is not part of Windows 95. The non-32-bit version of this definition does not apply since this turned out to be Windows 95 and Windows NT specific code. (At this stage, it does not seem likely that most of the common controls will ever appear in Windows 3.1-specific versions. However, I am not a prophet and have no idea what direction Microsoft might take on this matter.)

In the call to `CreateWindow` shown above, there are a number of styles you can pass in with the third parameter:

TBS_AUTOTICKS	Tick marks used to delineate ranges
TBS_VERT	Has a vertical orientation
TBS_HORZ	Has a horizontal orientation (default)
TBS_TOP	Tick marks appear on top
TBS_BOTTOM	Tick marks appear on bottom
TBS_LEFT	Tick marks on left of vertical bar
TBS_RIGHT	Tick marks on right of vertical bar
TBS_BOTH	Tick marks on both sides of a bar
TBS_NOTICKS	No tick marks
TBS_ENABLESELRANGE	A selected range on the bar is highlighted
TBS_FIXEDLENGTH	Uses the fixed length style
TBS_NOTHUMB	The bar has no thumb for you to drag

To use any of these styles, simply OR them into the third parameter:

```
WS_CHILD | TBS_VERT
```

After creating the window, I send two messages to it that help to define the way it behaves:

```
SendMessage(hTrackbar[i], TBM_SETRANGE, (WPARAM)1, (LPARAM)MAKELONG(0, 255));
SendMessage(hTrackbar[i], TBM_SETPOS, (WPARAM)1, (LPARAM)127);
```

The `TBM_SETRANGE` message defines starting and ending values for the top and bottom of the trackbar. If `WPARAM` is 0, the trackbar will not be redrawn. `LPARAM` has the minimum value for the control in the low word and the maximum value in the high word.

`TBM_SETPOS` again uses a non-zero value in `WPARAM` to force a redraw of the control. The final parameter specifies the position where you want to move the thumb.

Table 15.3 gives you a few of the commonly used messages associated with a trackbar. The name of each message is sufficiently descriptive to preclude the need for a comment field in the table.

Table 15.3. Some commonly used trackbar messages.

Message	WPARAM	LPARAM
TBM_GETPOS	0	0
TBM_GETRANGEMAX	0	0
TBM_GETRANGEMIN	0	0
TBM_SETRANGEMAX	Non-zero to redraw	Max Range
TBM_SETRANGEMIN	Non-zero to redraw	Min Range

Here are a few additional messages found in COMMCTRL.H. You can use the online help to find out more about these messages:

```
TBM_GETTIC TBM_SETTIC TBM_CLEARTICS TBM_SETSEL
TBM_SETSELSTART TBM_SETSELEND TBM_GETPTICS TBM_GETTICPOS
TBM_GETNUMTICS TBM_GETSELSTART TBM_GETSELEND TBM_CLEARSEL
TBM_SETTICFREQ TBM_SETPAGESIZE TBM_GETPAGESIZE TBM_SETLINESIZE
TBM_GETLINESIZE TBM_GETTHUMBRECT TBM_GETCHANNELRECT TBM_SETTHUMBLENGTH
TBM_GETTHUMBLENGTH
```

Responding to Trackbars

A trackbar sends WM_HSCROLL or WM_VSCROLL messages when its thumb is moved. Here is how the Trackbar app responds to these messages:

```
void Trackbar_OnHScroll(HWND hwnd, HWND hwndCtl, UINT code, int pos)
{
  int RedColor, GreenColor, BlueColor, i;
  RECT Rect;

  // Hit on one of our trackbars?
  for (i = 0; i < COLORCOUNT; i++)
    if (hTrackbar[i] == hwndCtl)
    {
      RedColor   = SendMessage(hTrackbar[0], TBM_GETPOS, 0, 0);
      GreenColor = SendMessage(hTrackbar[1], TBM_GETPOS, 0, 0);
      BlueColor  = SendMessage(hTrackbar[2], TBM_GETPOS, 0, 0);
      ShapeColor = RGB(RedColor, GreenColor, BlueColor);
      FillStatus(RedColor, GreenColor, BlueColor);

      Redraw(hwnd);
    }
}
```

The code shown here first checks whether the control that sent this message is one of the three trackbars used in this application. In the Trackbar app, the answer to this question is always going to be yes. However, you could create an app that would send you WM_HSCROLL messages in response to some other action by the user. (To learn more about WM_XSCROLL messages, see Day 7.)

Assuming that it was one of the trackbars that sent the message, the next job is to find the current position of the thumb on each control:

```
RedColor   = SendMessage(hTrackbar[0], TBM_GETPOS, 0, 0);
GreenColor = SendMessage(hTrackbar[1], TBM_GETPOS, 0, 0);
BlueColor  = SendMessage(hTrackbar[2], TBM_GETPOS, 0, 0);
```

In this case, RedColor, GreenColor, and BlueColor are all declared as integers. This is the simplest possible kind of SendMessage call and needs no explanation on my part.

To help increase readability, you can translate "TBM" as "Track Bar Message." At the time of this writing, Microsoft has not wrapped this call in a macro. However, if you want to make the code even more readable, you could write a simple macro that would let you make this kind of call:

```
RedColor := Trackbar_GetPos(hTrackbar[0]);
```

The macro in question would look like this:

```
#define Trackbar_GetPos(hwnd) \
    (int)SendMessage((hwnd), TBM_GETPOS, 0, 0L)
```

For the moment, I won't discuss the call to FillStatus, as that properly belongs in the discussion of status bars. The purpose of the call, of course, is to display, in numerical form, the currently selected RGB values in the status bar at the bottom of the window.

Before leaving this section, I should perhaps quickly mention the call to Redraw. This function forces the shape displayed in the window to redraw itself:

```
void Redraw(HWND hwnd)
{
  RECT Rect, StatusRect;

  GetClientRect(hwnd, &Rect);
  GetClientRect(hStatusWindow, &StatusRect);
  Rect.top = (TBHEIGHT * 4);
  Rect.bottom -= StatusRect.bottom;
  InvalidateRect(hwnd, &Rect, TRUE);
}
```

Ninety percent of the time, when you call InvalidateRect, you pass NULL in the second parameter. This tells Windows to be concerned about redrawing the entire client area, depending, of course, on the value of the third parameter. In this case, however, I don't want everything redrawn, only the area containing the ellipse, rectangle or roundrect. As a result, I

make a quick and dirty calculation of the area in the window where the shape appears, and then pass that rectangle on to Windows in the second parameter of InvalidateRect. The result is that the screen doesn't blink too badly when you move the thumbs on the trackbars, or when you change the type of shape you want to view.

Trackbars are a very nice contribution to the Windows interface, and they contain most of the key features you want in this type of control. Remember that if you want to get an overview of their capabilities, you should just open up COMMCTRL.H, wander down to the section on trackbars, and see what's available. Given the wholesome naming conventions Microsoft has adopted, this kind of overview of the subject is thorough and concise enough for most tastes. When you need additional information, you can turn to books like this one, or to the online help.

Creating a Status Bar

For religious reasons, I don't spend a lot of time in this book stressing all the new user guidelines that have been dreamed up in Redmond during the last few years. Still, it's interesting to note that Microsoft strongly recommends creating a consistent user interface that specifically makes use of tooltips, status bars, right clicks, property sheets, and some of the other controls used in this book. In particular, Microsoft defines "consistent" to mean that you make your application follow the look, feel and conventions used in Explorer and in the other parts of the shell, such as the desktop.

As a rule, I consider most of the guidelines that Microsoft recommends to be no-brainers. It's nice to have toolbars, tooltips, status bars, and right-click support in your application. However, I'm not the kind of guy who's likely to dwell on these matters at great length. In other words, I'll show you how to do these kinds of things, but I won't launch into a lecture about how you "ought" to do them.

Enough about the new user guidelines. If you want to find out more about them, you should refer to the *Windows 95 User Guidelines*, published by Microsoft.

The call to create a status bar looks like this:

```
hStatusWindow = CreateStatusWindow(WS_CHILD | WS_VISIBLE,
                                   "StatusWindow", hwnd, 0);
```

Here is an annotated declaration for the command:

```
WINCOMMCTRLAPI HWND WINAPI CreateStatusWindowA(
                        LONG style,        // The window style
                        LPCSTR lpszText,   // Optional text
                        HWND hwndParent,   // The parent window
                        UINT wID);         // Optional ID
```

The text you specify in the `lpszText` parameter will show up in the first of the panes inside the status bar. In this case, it's probably best to declare the text as blank, or to set it to 127, but I put `StatusWindow` in there so you will see clearly what this parameter does when you first launch the program. (127 is appropriate because I start the first trackbar off in the middle of its range, which is 127.)

You could, of course, call `CreateWindow` rather than `CreateStatusWindow`, but in most cases that would simply cause you additional work without additional benefit.

Managing the Panes in a Status Bar

After creating the status bar, the next step is to manage the panes which appear on it. Take another look at Figure 15.9 if you aren't sure what the panes in the status bar look like. In this case I am printing a separate RGB number in each of the panes.

To create the panes, you send an `SB_SETPARTS` message. This message takes the number of panes in `WPARAM`, and an array of points defining the coordinate for the right side of the pane in `LPARAM`. If you set the last value in this array to `-1`, then it will automatically take up all the remaining room on the right side of the control.

Here's an example of how to create the panes for a status bar:

```
void SizeStatusSections(HWND hwnd)
{
  int Sections[COLORCOUNT], i;
  RECT Rect;

  GetClientRect(hwnd, &Rect);

  for (i = 1; i <= COLORCOUNT; i++)
    Sections[i-1] = Rect.right / COLORCOUNT * i;

  SendMessage(hStatusWindow, SB_SETPARTS, (WPARAM)COLORCOUNT, (LPARAM)Sections);
}
```

This code calls our old friend `GetClientRect`, and thereby snags the width of the control. Using this information, it's easy to divide the status bar up into thirds, and to store that information in an array of integers. This data is then passed on to Windows via an `SB_SETPARTS` message. `COLORCOUNT`, of course, is a constant defining the number of colors to track.

So far so good. As it happens, you can define some of the panes to spring back and forth depending on the size of the text inside them. If you choose this style, called `SBT_SPRING`, then the array mentioned in the last paragraph will define the minimum size for each of the panes that get this style. You can also make the panes pop in or out (like the various kinds of bellybuttons that concerned us so fervently when we were children). The style that controls this feature is called `SBT_POPOUT`, and both modes are used in a typical configuration of the taskbar.

So how exactly do you define the style for a pane? Well, that's part and parcel of the technique you use for setting the text in each pane. Specifically, you set text in a pane by sending the control an SB_SETTEXT message. The WPARAM of this message tells Windows which pane you are referring to, and the LPARAM contains the text. If you want to change the style of the pane, then you OR that value into the pane number held in WPARAM.

Here is one way to set the text for the status window panes:

```
void FillStatus(int Red, int Green, int Blue)
{
  char S[50];

  sprintf(S, "Red: %d", Red);
  SendMessage(hStatusWindow, SB_SETTEXT, 0, (LPARAM)S);
  sprintf(S, "Green: %d", Green);
  SendMessage(hStatusWindow, SB_SETTEXT, 1, (LPARAM)S);
  sprintf(S, "Blue: %d", Blue);
  SendMessage(hStatusWindow, SB_SETTEXT, 2, (LPARAM)S);
}
```

This code passes the pane number in WPARAM, and the string in LPARAM. Very straightforward.

If you want to tweak the styles for a status window, you can refine the code shown above like this:

```
void FillStatus(int Red, int Green, int Blue)
{
  char S[50];

  sprintf(S, "Red: %d", Red);
  SendMessage(hStatusWindow, SB_SETTEXT, 0 | SBT_POPOUT, (LPARAM)S);
  sprintf(S, "Green: %d", Green);
  SendMessage(hStatusWindow, SB_SETTEXT, 1 | SBT_POPOUT, (LPARAM)S);
  sprintf(S, "Blue: %d", Blue);
  SendMessage(hStatusWindow, SB_SETTEXT, 2 | SBT_POPOUT, (LPARAM)S);
}
```

Note that I OR the pane number with the SBT_POPOUT style. The result is that each pane appears to be raised, rather than sunken. (Note that Windows 95 always shows the light coming from the top left of the screen when it draws three dimensional controls. This is, incredibly enough, part of the guidelines for the Windows 95 user interface!)

Creating Pop-up Menus

It's easy to create pop-up menus:

```
void Trackbar_OnRButtonDown(HWND hwnd, BOOL fDoubleClick,
                            int x, int y, UINT keyFlags)
{
  HMENU Floater = CreatePopupMenu();
  AppendMenu(Floater, MF_STRING, ID_ELLIPSE, "Ellipse");
```

```
AppendMenu(Floater, MF_STRING, ID_RECTANGLE, "Rectangle");
AppendMenu(Floater, MF_STRING, ID_ROUNDRECT, "RoundRect");
TrackPopupMenu(Floater, TPM_LEFTALIGN, x, y, 0, hwnd, NULL);
}
```

This code is called every time the user right-clicks on the main window. In response to the click, the Trackbar program creates a pop-up menu by calling the `CreatePopupMenu` API. In other words, I've opted to create the menu dynamically, rather than defining it ahead of time in a resource. This is arguably the best course to take with floating menus, since there will be times when you might need to change them dynamically.

To add items to the menu, you can call `AppendMenu`. Both this call and the `TrackPopupMenu` call were described in the section on dynamic menus on Day 13, "Subclassing Window Controls." With `AppendMenu`, the key points to remember are that:

☐ The first parameter contains a handle to a menu

☐ The second parameter contains a set of predefined flags

☐ The third parameter is the ID that's used in the `WM_COMMAND` handler

☐ The fourth parameter contains the string to show in the menu

`TrackPopupMenu` is the call that actually shows the menu to the user. Recall that the fifth parameter is reserved and should be set to `0`. The final parameter represents an optional rectangle the user can click without dismissing the menu. The rest of the parameters are self-explanatory.

After the user has selected an option from the menu, his choice is forwarded on to the `WM_COMMAND` handler:

```
void Trackbar_OnCommand(HWND hwnd, int id, HWND hwndCtl, UINT codeNotify)
{
  switch(id)
  {
    case ID_ELLIPSE:
      Shapes = sEllipse;
      Redraw(hwnd);
      break;
    case ID_RECTANGLE:
      Shapes = sRectangle;
      Redraw(hwnd);
      break;
    case ID_ROUNDRECT:
      Shapes = sRoundRect;
      Redraw(hwnd);
      break;
  }
}
```

This code sorts the data, and then forces a repaint of the shape shown at the bottom of the main window. The local `Redraw` function is explained above.

That's it for the discussion of the trackbar program. In it you learned how to create trackbars, status bars and reviewed pop-up menus. Trackbars are fun but will be of use in only a limited set of circumstances. Status bars and floating menus could well end up being included in most of the Windows 95 programs you create.

Summary

This chapter has hit pretty hard at the subject of Windows 95 controls. Overall, this has not been a particularly difficult chapter, and it has the virtue of showing you several nifty controls that help make your program sparkle in the eyes of your users.

Remember that you need to include COMMCTRL.H in all your common control programs, and that you should link with COMCTL32.DLL. You also need to include the InitCommonControls API call in all of your programs that use these components.

Q&A

Q Just how important are the new common controls? Are they an essential part of Windows 95, or are they merely window dressing?

A The common controls have nothing to do with the key features of Windows 95, which are 32-bit code, real multitasking, and threads. However, Microsoft is fairly serious about trying to present the user with a predefined interface that is consistent from application to application. The whole point of this effort is to make Windows more appealing to the average non-power user who may be a little bit intimidated by computers. This is a serious goal, worthy of respect. As such, there is a very serious, well-thought-out side to the creation and definition of Windows 95 common controls. Ultimately, I think many programmers will use these controls because they are fun, and because they fill a need. We all want people to buy and use our applications, and these controls help make our code more appealing. However, you should also be aware that there is a philosophical underpinning to all these flashy tools, and that Microsoft is promoting this philosophy with considerable fervor.

Q Are there other available implementations of any of the controls mentioned in this chapter?

A Yes. Both Microsoft and Borland have some alternatives to these controls included with OWL and MFC. Other components are available from third parties. Over time, Microsoft will probably meld its MFC components in with the rest of the common controls so that they share a common code base. However, third parties will no doubt continue to create alternatives to the components that ship in COMCTL32.DLL. Most programmers will want to choose implementations that most closely match the needs and styles of their programs.

Q Can you use any of these controls with Windows NT?

A Yes. Windows NT 3.51 ships with a version of the Windows 95 user interface. As a result, many of the common controls are now available in Windows NT.

Workshop

The Workshop provides quiz questions to help you solidify your understanding of the material covered and exercises to provide you with experience in using what you've learned. Try to understand the quiz and exercise answers before continuing on to the next chapter. Answers are provided in Appendix A.

Quiz

1. What DLL holds the common controls listed in this chapter?
2. What header file contains the declarations of the controls used in this chapter?
3. What library should be linked in with your program when using the controls from this chapter?
4. Can you use the common controls with Windows 3.1?
5. Have macros for the common controls been merged into WINDOWSX.H?
6. Name three Windows API calls used to dynamically create a floating menu.
7. Name two messages used to define the number and size of the panes in a status bar.
8. Other than `CreateWindow`, name a call that can be used to create a status bar. How about a toolbar?
9. What does the `W` in `TRACKBAR_CLASSW` stand for? Why is it there?
10. If you want to pass a string in the last parameter of a call to `SendMessage`, how should you typecast it?

Exercises

1. Link up a trackbar and progress bar so that changes to the position of the trackbar change the state of the blue blocks that show the state of the progress bar.
2. Add a toolbar to the WinStyle program shown on Day 14. Have the toolbar duplicate all the functions shown in the menu, including the changes to the background color or pattern.

WEEK
3

Dialog Boxes and
Mapping Modes

In this lesson you'll learn about dialog boxes and the variations you can run on the Windows coordinate system.

In particular, you will learn about

- Modal dialog boxes
- Modeless dialog boxes
- Mapping modes
- Logical coordinates
- Setting the viewport origin

This chapter introduces two programs, one called ShowCord and one called WinSize. Both programs help you learn about the Windows coordinate system. ShowCord is a fairly simple utility which illustrates the basic facts about mapping modes and the viewport origin.

WinSize demonstrates both how to create and run dialogs, and also how to manipulate six of the coordinate systems available to Windows programmers. Creating modal and modeless dialogs is also covered in this chapter. Controlling the color of a dialog and manipulating its data displayed are subjects covered on Day 21, "Threads, Multitasking, and Memory Management."

This chapter is arranged so that most of the material on mapping modes occurs in its first half, and most of the material on dialogs occurs in the second half.

Coordinating the Coordinates

As shown in Figure 16.1, the WinSize program has two dialogs for displaying data; it also has a main window in which geometric figures can be drawn. The Size dialog shows the coordinates of the main window when the program is using any of six different mapping modes.

Note: There are eight possible Windows mapping modes: MM_TEXT, MM_HIENGLISH, MM_LOENGLISH, MM_LOMETRIC, MM_HIMETRIC, MM_TWIPS, MM_ISOTROPIC, and MM_ANISOTROPIC. This chapter covers the first six and leaves the last two for Bonus Day 2, "MDI: The Multiple-Document Interface."

Use the Make Shape dialog to change the shape's origin. Watch the Size dialog when you change the origin into the center of the window. Notice that the coordinates shown in the Size Dialog will change dynamically if you resize the main the window. (You won't be able to resize the window when the Make Shape dialog is open, so you should close it, and then try resizing the window.)

The first thing you need to know about mapping modes is that they are an attribute of the GDI and their associated device contexts. You have to be using a device context before mapping modes are relevant to the work you are doing. If you use the `GetClientRect` function, then mapping modes won't impact your work. They are irrelevant because `GetClientRect` does not use a device context. If you use the `Rectangle` or `Ellipse` function, then mapping modes are relevant to your work. Both `Rectangle` and `Ellipse` take an `HDC` as their first parameter, and therefore they are going to be influenced by the current mapping mode.

The point here is that there are two Windows coordinate systems. One is a logical mapping system associated with the GDI, and the other is a physical coordinate system associated with all non-GDI functions. This subject will be brought up again later in the chapter under the heading "So What's all this Business about the GDI?"

Mapping modes are ways of describing the units of measurement used to define a window's coordinates. By default, a program uses the `MM_TEXT` mapping mode, which depends on the convention that each unit of measurement in a window is equivalent to one pixel. If you use the `MM_TEXT` mapping mode, then the size of a unit will be the same in the physical and logical coordinate systems, but the origin of the coordinate system will not necessarily be the same. That is, the point labeled as 0,0 might still be different.

Note: A pixel is the smallest visible unit that can be manipulated on a screen. For instance, if a program takes over the entire screen and renders it completely black except for the smallest possible point in the upper-left corner of the screen, that single point would be a pixel. Though they are not demonstrated in the WinSize program, Windows provides routines, called `SetPixel` and `GetPixel`, for manipulating the screen on this level.

The standard VGA screen has 640 pixels running from left to right, and 480 pixels running from top to bottom. SuperVGA modes are typically either 800×600 pixels or 1024×768 pixels.

Figure 16.1.

The WinSize program uses two dialogs to display basic information about the Windows coordinate system.

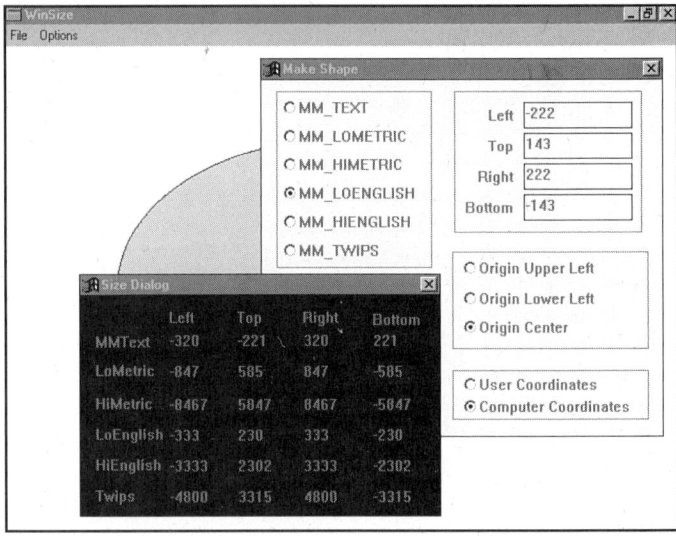

Because screens can have a variable number of pixels on them, programmers sometimes want to abandon the MM_TEXT coordinate system and use a more stable unit of measurement in its place. In an attempt to give the programmer what he or she seeks, the Windows environment provides several logical coordinate systems.

Note: The physical coordinate system on a monitor is always measured in pixels. These are units which have an actual, physical presence on-screen. The monitor and computer think of the coordinate system on-screen as being a reflection of the number of pixels in any particular area. As humans, though, we might think, "OK, look down about three inches from the top of the screen." Or maybe, "About 20 millimeters from the left of the screen, there's a small red line." When people map these human measurement systems on top of the screen's physical system, it's called creating a *logical* mapping mode. The real bottom line, however, is always the physical pixels on the screen. The MM_TEXT mapping mode is measured in pixels, so it appears to be a physical, rather than logical, coordinate system. However, the GDI coordinate system is always a logical coordinate system. For instance, you can move the 0,0 point in the MM_TEXT coordinate system from the upper-left part of a window to the center of a window. The physical coordinate system always regards the 0,0 point as either the upper left-hand corner of the screen, or the upper-left corner of a window.

Rather than working in pixels, the Windows logical coordinate systems measure the screen in inches, millimeters, and twips. Or at least it attempts to measure things that way. The reality is that Windows currently has no way to make sure of the distance from point to point on most computer screens.

Note: Twips are units used when measuring typefaces. More specifically, a twip is $1/20$ point, and a point is about $1/72$ inch. Therefore, a twip is $1/20 \times 1/72$, or $1/1440$ inch.

It turns out that Windows is never entirely accurate in describing anything other than the MM_TEXT mapping mode. Windows always knows exactly how many pixels are on-screen or inside of a particular area, but it can't always determine exactly how large an inch or a millimeter might be on a particular system. Part of the reason for this is that a hardware device, such as a monitor, will usually not reveal its size to the software running on a system. That is, Windows can't tell the difference between a 14-inch and a 15-inch monitor.

Changing the Mapping Mode

If you want to start working with the Windows GDI, it's obviously key that you get a grip on what mapping mode you are currently using, and on how you can change mapping modes. By default, you will always be in the MM_TEXT mapping mode. However, you can change mapping modes at any time.

If you want to change from the MM_TEXT system to the MM_HIMETRIC system, then you need some tools to help you achieve your goal. Here are the functions you normally employy when you want to change from any one mode into another:

- ☐ SetMapMode
- ☐ GetMapeMode

The two syntax boxes shown below lay out the key facts about these routines.

The *SetMapMode* Function

Syntax

```
int SetMapMode(HDC, int)
```

The SetMapMode function takes two parameters. The first is the current device context, and the second is one of the fnMapMode constants, such as MM_TEXT or MM_TWIPS. The function returns the previous mapping mode. (See lines 188, 205, and 301 in WINSIZE.CPP.)

Here's an example:

```
SetMapMode(PaintDC, MM_TEXT);
```

The *GetMapMode* Function

```
int GetMapMode(HDC);
```

The easy-to-use `GetMapMode` function retrieves the current mapping mode from a device context. The device context you want to know about serves as the sole argument to this function. `GetMapMode` returns one of the `fnMapMode` constants listed in Table 16.1.

Here's an example:

```
int CurrentMappingMode = GetMapMode(PaintDC);
```

where the returned value is once again one of the `fnMapMode` constants.

The size of a unit of measurement will almost always change when you change mapping modes. In the `MM_TEXT` mapping mode, a unit of measurement is the size of a pixel. In the `MM_TWIPS` mapping mode, a unit of measurement is 1/1440 inch, which is usually much smaller than a pixel. Table 16.1 helps you see the relative size of units of measurement in six of Windows mapping modes.

Table 16.1. A table outlining the six major mapping systems.

Mapping Mode	Logical Units	Physical Unit	X++	Y++
MM_TEXT	1	Device pixel	Right	Down
MM_HIENGLISH	1000	1 inch	Right	Up
MM_HIMETRIC	100	1 millimeter	Right	Up
MM_LOENGLISH	100	1 inch	Right	Up
MM_LOMETRIC	10	1 millimeter	Right	Up
MM_TWIPS	1440	1 inch	Right	Up

This table shows that each unit in the `MM_HIENGLISH` mapping system is .001 inches in size, whereas each unit in the `MM_HIMETRIC` system is .01 mm in size. In all cases except the `MM_TEXT` mapping mode, the x values by default get larger as you move to the right, and the y values by default get larger as you move up the screen.

One way to get a handle on these ideas is to think of the `MM_TEXT` coordinate system as being arranged like the words on a page. That is, you start reading in the upper left-hand corner, move to the right, and then move down. The other mapping modes are more like the standard Cartesian grid, with the 0,0 point being located in the upper-left corner of the screen, and the screen itself being a portion of the bottom-right quadrant of the grid. These concepts are demonstrated in Figure 16.2.

Figure 16.2.

The MM_HIENGLISH *mapping mode treats the screen as if it were part of the bottom right-hand quadrant of a Cartesian grid.*

16

In this chapter I have opted not to discuss the MM_ISOTROPIC and MM_ANISOTROPIC mapping modes. These modes are useful when you want to make shapes conform to the size of your window. For instance, if you are using the MM_ISOTROPIC mapping mode, then you can draw a square with one set of unchanging coordinates that will always remain whole and will always remain square, regardless of how you reshape a window. The size of the square may change as you make the window larger or smaller, but it will always appear to be square. If you use the MM_ANISOTROPIC mapping mode, then you can draw a rectangle with one set of unchanging coordinates. If you make the rectangle about the same size as the window, then it will stretch to fill up the entire window, no matter how you stretch the window. More on this confusing subject in Bonus Day 2.

GDI and Device Coordinates

After you get a feeling for the various mapping modes, the next thing to grasp is that the origin from which the Windows coordinates are calculated can be moved around the screen to any location you choose. The easiest way to do this is with the SetViewportOrgEx command. The following code fragment moves the viewpoint origin to its default position in the upper-left corner of a window:

```
SetViewportOrgEx(PaintDC, 0, 0, NULL);
```

The next set of commands moves the origin to the center of the screen, as shown in Figure 16.3:

```
GetClientRect(hwnd, &Rect);
SetViewportOrgEx(PaintDC, Rect.right / 2, Rect.bottom / 2, NULL);
```

Figure 16.3.
The Windows coordinates look like this when you use the MM_HIENGLISH *mapping mode and move the origin to the center of the screen.*

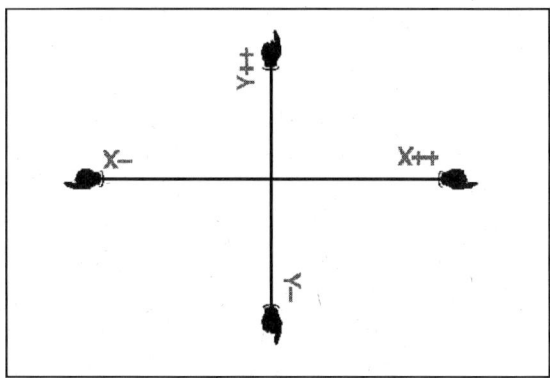

So What's All This Business About the GDI?

Lying just beneath the surface of this subject is one of the most important ideas in Windows programming. The entire field of creating graphics output in Windows is subsumed under a single heading called the Graphics Device Interface (GDI). As a rule, GDI commands work with an HDC, that is, with a device context. And finally (here's the kicker), device contexts always work with some particular type of mapping mode. (The GDI is discussed further on Bonus Day 1, "GDI and Metafiles.")

Just to make sure this idea is clear in your mind, let's turn the coin over and look at it from the opposite side. Logical coordinates are always associated with GDI objects, that is, with device contexts. This means that non-GDI commands, such as GetClientRect or GetWindowRect, never return logical coordinates. These commands don't utilize an HDC, and they aren't GDI commands. Therefore, they don't retrieve information in logical coordinates. They always deal in pixels.

This same detachment from the GDI coordinate system is demonstrated by the Windows messaging system. For instance, WM_SIZE, WM_MOVE, and WM_LBUTTONDOWN messages always send device coordinates rather than logical coordinates, because they are not part of the GDI.

Because of this disparity between logical and device coordinates, the Windows environment provides two functions, called LPtoDP and DPtoLP, which quickly translate logical points to device points and device points to logical points. The latter of these two functions is demonstrated in the WinSize program.

The *DPtoLP* Function

```
BOOL DPtoLP(HDC, POINT FAR *, int)
```

This function converts a point or series of points on the device coordinate system to a point or series of points on the logical coordinate system. The first parameter is a device context, the second an array of points to be translated, and the third the number of points in the array.

Here's an example:

```
RECT SizeData;
DPtoLP(PaintDC, (LPPOINT)&SizeData, 2);
```

This code follows a pattern mirrored throughout the WinSize program, because it uses a RECT structure rather than a POINT structure. This is done because DPtoLP is often used to translate values returned from GetClientRect or GetWindowRect. RECT structures, of course, are really just two contiguous POINT structures. (See lines 189 and 301 in WINSIZE.CPP.)

An Interactive Program That Demonstrates Mapping Modes

The ShowCord program gives you an interactive way to get hold of the basic facts about the mapping modes and the coordinates associated with them. In a sense, the ShowCord is just an interactive, dynamic version of the Figures 16.2 and 16.3. The code for the program is shown in Listings 16.1 through 16.3.

Listing 16.1. The ShowCord program shows mapping modes.

```
/////////////////////////////////////////////////////////
//   Program Name: ShowCord.cpp
//   Copyright © 1995 by Charlie Calvert
//   Description: ShowCord windows program
//   Date: 06/07/95
/////////////////////////////////////////////////////////

#define STRICT
#define WIN32_LEAN_AND_MEAN
#include <windows.h>
#include <windowsx.h>
#include <stdio.h>
#include "showcord.h"
#pragma warning (disable: 4068)


// -----------------------------------------------------
// Interface
// -----------------------------------------------------
```

continues

Listing 16.1. continued

```
// Variables
BOOL CenterOrigin;
int CurMode;
int YPos = 2;
int XPos = 2;
int XPosStart = 2;
int XPosEnd = 12;
int YPosStart = 2;
int YPosEnd = 12;

// --------------------------------------------------------
// Initialization
// --------------------------------------------------------


////////////////////////////////////////////////////////
// Program entry point
////////////////////////////////////////////////////////
#pragma argsused
int WINAPI WinMain(HINSTANCE hInst, HINSTANCE hPrevInstance, LPSTR lpszCmdParam,
int nCmdShow)
{
MSG  Msg;
if (!hPrevInstance)
if (!Register(hInst))
return FALSE;

MainWindow = Create(hInst, nCmdShow);
if (!MainWindow)
return FALSE;
while (GetMessage(&Msg, NULL, 0, 0))
  {
TranslateMessage(&Msg);
DispatchMessage(&Msg);
  }

return Msg.wParam;
}


////////////////////////////////////////////////////////
// Register the window
////////////////////////////////////////////////////////
BOOL Register(HINSTANCE hInst)
{
WNDCLASS WndClass;
  WndClass.style         = CS_HREDRAW | CS_VREDRAW;
  WndClass.lpfnWndProc   = WndProc;
  WndClass.cbClsExtra    = 0;
  WndClass.cbWndExtra    = 0;
  WndClass.hInstance     = hInst;
  WndClass.hIcon         = LoadIcon(NULL, IDI_APPLICATION);
  WndClass.hCursor       = LoadCursor(NULL, IDC_ARROW);
WndClass.hbrBackground = (HBRUSH)(COLOR_WINDOW+1);
```

```
WndClass.lpszMenuName  = "SHOWMENU";
WndClass.lpszClassName = szAppName;
return RegisterClass (&WndClass) !=0;
}


/////////////////////////////////////////////////////////
// Create the window
/////////////////////////////////////////////////////////
HWND Create(HINSTANCE hInst, int nCmdShow)
{

hInstance = hInst;
HWND hwnd = CreateWindow(szAppName, szAppName,
WS_OVERLAPPEDWINDOW,
CW_USEDEFAULT, CW_USEDEFAULT,
CW_USEDEFAULT, CW_USEDEFAULT,
NULL, NULL, hInst, NULL);
if (hwnd == NULL)
return hwnd;
ShowWindow(hwnd, nCmdShow);
UpdateWindow(hwnd);
return hwnd;
}


// --------------------------------------------------------
// WndProc and Implementation
// --------------------------------------------------------


/////////////////////////////////////////////////////////
// The Window Procedure
/////////////////////////////////////////////////////////
LRESULT CALLBACK WndProc(HWND hwnd, UINT Message, WPARAM wParam, LPARAM lParam)
{
switch(Message)
   {
HANDLE_MSG(hwnd, WM_CREATE, ShowCord_OnCreate);
HANDLE_MSG(hwnd, WM_DESTROY, ShowCord_OnDestroy);
HANDLE_MSG(hwnd, WM_COMMAND, ShowCord_OnCommand);
HANDLE_MSG(hwnd, WM_PAINT, ShowCord_OnPaint);
HANDLE_MSG(hwnd, WM_TIMER, ShowCord_OnTimer);
default: return ShowCord_DefProc(hwnd, Message, wParam, lParam);
   }
}


/////////////////////////////////////////////////////////
// Handle WM_Create
/////////////////////////////////////////////////////////
#pragma argsused
BOOL ShowCord_OnCreate(HWND hwnd, CREATESTRUCT FAR* lpCreateStruct)
{
if (SetTimer(hwnd, SHOWTIMER, 25, NULL) == 0)
  {
MessageBox(hwnd, "Out of Timers!", NULL, MB_OK);
return FALSE;
  }
```

continues

Listing 16.1. continued

```
CurMode = MM_TEXT;
return TRUE;
}

////////////////////////////////////////////////////////
// Handle WM_DESTROY
////////////////////////////////////////////////////////
#pragma argsused
void ShowCord_OnDestroy(HWND hwnd)
{
KillTimer(hwnd, SHOWTIMER);
PostQuitMessage(0);
}


////////////////////////////////////////////////////////
// ClearModes
////////////////////////////////////////////////////////
void ClearModes(HWND hwnd)
{
XPos = 2; YPos = 2;
InvalidateRect(hwnd, NULL, TRUE);
}

////////////////////////////////////////////////////////
// Handle WM_COMMAND
////////////////////////////////////////////////////////
#pragma argsused
void ShowCord_OnCommand(HWND hwnd, int id, HWND hwndCtl, UINT codeNotify)
{
switch(id)
   {
case CM_RTEXT:
CurMode = MM_TEXT;
ClearModes(hwnd);
break;
case CM_RHIMETRIC:
CurMode = MM_HIMETRIC;
ClearModes(hwnd);
break;
case CM_RLOMETRIC:
CurMode = MM_LOMETRIC;
ClearModes(hwnd);
break;
case CM_RHIENGLISH:
CurMode = MM_HIENGLISH;
ClearModes(hwnd);
break;
case CM_RLOENGLISH:
CurMode = MM_LOENGLISH;
ClearModes(hwnd);
break;
```

```
case CM_RTWIPS:
CurMode = MM_TWIPS;
ClearModes(hwnd);
break;
case CM_LEFTORIGIN:
CenterOrigin = FALSE;
ClearModes(hwnd);
break;
case CM_CENTERORIGIN:
CenterOrigin = TRUE;
ClearModes(hwnd);
break;
case CM_ABOUT:
DialogBox(hInstance, MAKEINTRESOURCE(ID_HELPDIALOG), hwnd, AboutBoxProc);
break;
    }
}

/////////////////////////////////////////////////////////
// Set the origin and mapping mode
/////////////////////////////////////////////////////////
void SetWindowCoords(HWND hwnd, HDC DC)
{
RECT Rect;
GetClientRect(hwnd, &Rect);
SetMapMode(DC, CurMode);
if (CenterOrigin == TRUE)
SetViewportOrgEx(DC, Rect.right / 2, Rect.bottom / 2, NULL);
else
    {
if (CurMode != MM_TEXT)
SetViewportOrgEx(DC, 1, Rect.bottom - 1, NULL);
else
SetViewportOrgEx(DC, 1, 1, NULL);
    }
}

/////////////////////////////////////////////////////////
// Do the real work of painting
/////////////////////////////////////////////////////////
void DoPaint(HWND hwnd, HDC PaintDC)
{
HBRUSH ABrush, OldBrush;
HPEN APen, OldPen;

SetWindowCoords(hwnd, PaintDC);
ABrush = CreateSolidBrush(RGB(0, 255, 0));
OldBrush = SelectBrush(PaintDC, ABrush);
APen = CreatePen(PS_SOLID, 1, RGB(0, 255, 0));
OldPen = SelectPen(PaintDC, APen);
Rectangle(PaintDC, XPosStart, YPosStart, XPosEnd, YPos);
Rectangle(PaintDC, XPosEnd-1, YPosStart, XPos, YPosEnd);
```

continues

Listing 16.1. continued

```
SelectPen(PaintDC, OldPen);
DeletePen(APen);
SelectBrush(PaintDC, OldBrush);
DeleteBrush(ABrush);
}

//////////////////////////////////////////////////////////
// Handle WM_PAINT
//////////////////////////////////////////////////////////
#pragma argsused
void ShowCord_OnPaint(HWND hwnd)
{
PAINTSTRUCT PaintStruct;
HDC PaintDC;
RECT Rect;
HBRUSH ABrush, OldBrush;
PaintDC = BeginPaint(hwnd, &PaintStruct);
GetClientRect(hwnd, &Rect);
ABrush = CreateSolidBrush(RGB(255, 0, 0));
OldBrush = SelectBrush(PaintDC, ABrush);
Rectangle(PaintDC, 0, 0, Rect.right, Rect.bottom);
SelectBrush(PaintDC, OldBrush);
DeleteBrush(ABrush);
DoPaint(hwnd, PaintDC);
EndPaint(hwnd, &PaintStruct);
}

//////////////////////////////////////////////////////////
// Handle WM_DESTROY
//////////////////////////////////////////////////////////
#pragma argsused
void ShowCord_OnTimer(HWND hwnd, UINT id)
{
RECT Rect;
int Y;
char S[100];

GetClientRect(hwnd, &Rect);
HDC DC = GetDC(hwnd);
SetMapMode(DC, CurMode);
DPtoLP(DC, (LPPOINT)&Rect, 2);
if (CurMode == MM_TEXT)
Y = Rect.bottom;
else
Y = -Rect.bottom;
if ((YPos + 12) < Y)
YPos += 12;
if ((XPos + 12) < Rect.right)
XPos += 12;
if (((YPos + 12) < Y) || ((XPos + 12) < Rect.right))
  {
```

```
sprintf(S, "ShowCoords: %d %d Cur: %d %d", Rect.right, Rect.bottom, XPos, YPos);
SetWindowText(hwnd, S);
DoPaint(hwnd, DC);
   }

ReleaseDC(hwnd, DC);
}

//////////////////////////////////////////////
//   The ShowCord Dialog Procedure
//////////////////////////////////////////////
#pragma argsused
BOOL CALLBACK AboutBoxProc(HWND hDlg, UINT Message,
WPARAM wParam, LPARAM lParam)
{
char *S = "This program demonstrates the windows coordinate "\
"system. It draws two lines in the positive X and Y "\
"coordinates. You can set the viewpoint origin to the"\
"center of the screen or the left of the screen. "\
"If the origin is on the left, then "\
"if the mapping mode is MM_TEXT "\
"the viewpoint origin is in the topleft of the "\
"window, otherwise it is at the bottom left.";

switch(Message)
   {
case WM_INITDIALOG:
Static_SetText(GetDlgItem(hDlg, ID_EXPLAIN), S);
return TRUE;
case WM_COMMAND:
if (LOWORD(wParam) == IDOK || LOWORD(wParam) == IDCANCEL)
      {
EndDialog(hDlg, IDOK);
return TRUE;
      }
break;
   }
return FALSE;
}
```

Listing 16.2. The header file for the ShowCord program.

```
#define ID_EXPLAIN 100
#define ID_HELPDIALOG 101

#define CM_RTEXT 201
#define CM_RLOMETRIC 202
#define CM_RHIMETRIC 3203
#define CM_RLOENGLISH 3204
#define CM_RHIENGLISH 3205
#define CM_RTWIPS 3206
#define CM_ABOUT 3207
#define CM_LEFTORIGIN 3208
#define CM_CENTERORIGIN 3209
```

continues

Listing 16.2. continued

```
#define SHOWTIMER 1
// Declarations for class ShowCord
#define ShowCord_DefProc    DefWindowProc
BOOL ShowCord_OnCreate(HWND hwnd, CREATESTRUCT FAR* lpCreateStruct);
void ShowCord_OnCommand(HWND hwnd, int id, HWND hwndCtl, UINT codeNotify);
void ShowCord_OnDestroy(HWND hwnd);
void ShowCord_OnPaint(HWND hwnd);
void ShowCord_OnTimer(HWND hwnd, UINT id);
static char szAppName[] = "ShowCord";
static HWND MainWindow;
static HINSTANCE hInstance;

// functions
LRESULT CALLBACK WndProc(HWND hwnd, UINT Message,
WPARAM wParam, LPARAM lParam);
BOOL CALLBACK AboutBoxProc(HWND hDlg, UINT Message,
WPARAM wParam, LPARAM lParam);
BOOL Register(HINSTANCE hInst);
HWND Create(HINSTANCE hInst, int nCmdShow);
```

When you run the ShowCord program it will slowly and interactively draw one of four different shapes. The exact type of shape to be created is defined by the various choices in the program's menu. However, all the shapes in the program have one thing in common: They are drawn by making two lines, one that moves outward in the positive x direction and one that moves outward in the positive y direction. By watching these two lines being drawn, you can see how the x and y coordinates differ depending on which mapping mode you choose.

Here are the two different forces that define the four basic shapes drawn:

- In the MM_TEXT mode, if you add one to y, you move down the screen. In all other modes, if you add one to y, you move up the screen. Here's another way to say the same thing: In MM_TEXT mode the positive y direction is down, while in all the other modes increasing the value of y will move you further up the screen.

- The ShowCord program lets you set the 0, 0 origin to either the left part of the screen, or the center of the screen. If you set the origin on the left, then ShowCord will choose the top left of the screen as the origin if you are in MM_TEXT mode. Otherwise, it chooses the bottom left of the screen as the origin. These three origins mirror the three most likely places for orienting a computer screen. The top left is a good origin in the MM_TEXT mode, while the bottom left is a good origin spot for all other modes. Sometimes it makes more sense to abandon both of these "left-handed" schemes and instead move the origin into the center of the screen.

I've written the ShowCord program because it is hard for most people to understand how the Windows coordinate system works. You need to not only hear a description of the coordinate system, but you also need to see it in action. The ShowCord program gives you the kind of hands-on experience you need to fully understand the intricacies of the Windows coordinate system. Get it up and running. Play with it. Then, if necessary, come back and reread the preceding paragraphs a few times. Read the words, run the program. Between the two media you should be able to nail this stuff cold.

In particular, you should run the program and choose each of the six possible mapping modes from the program's main menu. Notice what kind of shape is drawn to the screen. Notice the relative size of the shapes drawn to the screen. Mapping modes with large units of measurement draw large shapes, mapping modes with small units of measurement draw tiny shapes. Now use the menu to switch the origin from the left part of the screen to the center of screen. Once again run through all the possible mapping modes and view the results.

I'm not going to spend much time discussing the code for the ShowCord program. Most of what you see in it is review of topics already covered. However, it's worth pointing out what happens when you change the program's mapping mode or viewport origin by choosing the appropriate option from the menu. First a WM_COMMAND message is sent to the program's WndProc. The window procedure then sorts out the individual commands in a case statement:

```
// change mapping mode
case CM_RTEXT:
CurMode = MM_TEXT;
ClearModes(hwnd);
break;
case CM_RHIMETRIC:
CurMode = MM_HIMETRIC;
ClearModes(hwnd);
break;

// Change origin
case CM_LEFTORIGIN:
CenterOrigin = FALSE;
ClearModes(hwnd);
break;
case CM_CENTERORIGIN:
CenterOrigin = TRUE;
ClearModes(hwnd);
break;
```

The excerpts shown here show that a global variable called CurMode is set to the mapping mode chosen by the user, and a global variable called CenterOrigin reflects whether or not the user wants the viewport origin to be in the center of the window. Then a function called ClearModes is called:

```
void ClearModes(HWND hwnd)
{
XPos = 2; YPos = 2;
InvalidateRect(hwnd, NULL, TRUE);
}
```

ClearModes is a very simple function that resets the current value of the x and y coordinates to their starting position, and then asks the window to redraw itself. In other words, it ensures that the program starts redrawing the shape again from the beginning, with the properties of the shape now reflecting the new settings.

Each time the window is redrawn, the SetWindowCoords function is called:

```
void SetWindowCoords(HWND hwnd, HDC DC)
{
RECT Rect;
GetClientRect(hwnd, &Rect);
SetMapMode(DC, CurMode);
if (CenterOrigin == TRUE)
SetViewportOrgEx(DC, Rect.right / 2, Rect.bottom / 2, NULL);
else
   {
if (CurMode != MM_TEXT)
SetViewportOrgEx(DC, 1, Rect.bottom - 1, NULL);
else
SetViewportOrgEx(DC, 1, 1, NULL);
   }
 }
```

This function copies the current mapping mode into the window's device context. It then sets the viewport origin to the center of the window, or to the left of the window, depending on the user's request. Note that if the user chooses to set the origin on the left, then the y value of the origin is moved to the top or bottom of the screen depending on whether the user selected the MM_TEXT mapping mode.

The rest of the code in the program concerns itself primarily with copying various brushes and pens in and out of the device context. That code is not unimportant, but it is covered elsewhere in the book and has only tangential relevance to the current topic.

Advanced Mapping Concepts

When studying the ShowCord program you need to make a distinction between viewport coordinates and window coordinates. The device or viewport coordinates are always measured in pixels. Window coordinates, however, are measured in terms of whatever logical units are associated with the current mapping mode, such as inches, millimeters, or twips.

When you want to set the origin of the coordinate system, you almost always use the SetViewportOrgEx function, that is, you change the origin in terms of the windows physical coordinates. However, you can do the same thing with the SetWindowOrgEx function, though this option is used less often. The SetViewportOrgEx function is more popular because you usually first call GetClientRect to calculate the parameters passed to SetViewportOrgEx. Because GetClientRect returns device coordinates, it makes sense to pass them to a function like SetViewportOrgEx that also uses device coordinates. You could, however, call GetClientRect, then translate those results using DPtoLP, and then pass the translated coordinates to SetWindowOrgEx. A process similar to this is performed in the ShowCord_OnTimer method.

Syntax

SetViewportOrgEx and *SetWindowOrgEx*

```
DWORD SetWindowOrgEx(HDC, int, int, LPPOINT);
DWORD SetViewportOrgEx(DC, int, int, LPPOINT);
```

`SetViewportOrgEx` sets the origin for the device coordinate system.

`SetWindowOrg` sets the origin for the logical coordinate system.

Both functions take three parameters:

- [ ] The first is a device context: `HDC`.
- [ ] The second is a signed integer specifying the x origin for the coordinate system.
- [ ] The third is a signed integer specifying the y origin for the coordinate system.
- [ ] The fourth parameter can be used to capture the previous origin. The function returns the coordinates of the previous origin, with the column value in the x field of a `POINT` structure and the row value in the y field of a `POINT` structure.
- [ ] The function returns true of it succeeds, false if it fails.

Here are two examples:

```
SetViewportOrgEx(PaintDC, 100, 100, NULL);
SetWindowOrgEx(PaintDC, 100, 100, NULL);
```

You should refer to the source to see more practical examples of how to call these functions. (See lines 211, 215, and 219 of WINSIZE.CPP.)

Passing the same coordinates to `SetViewportOrgEx` and `SetWindowOrgEx` often yields radically different results, depending on the current mapping mode. Because the window origin is calculated in terms of the viewport origin, the following calls will move the viewport origin to the center of the screen, and then move the window origin to the right and down, relative to the new viewport origin:

```
GetClientRect(hwnd, &Rect);
SetViewportOrgEx(PaintDC, Rect.right / 2, Rect.bottom / 2, NULL);
SetWindowOrgEx(PaintDC, -Rect.right / 2, -Rect.bottom / 2, NULL);
```

DO	DON'T

DO use `SetViewportOrgEx` rather than `SetWindowOrgEx` under most circumstances.

DON'T ever use the `SetWindowExtEx` or `SetViewPortExtEx` functions with any of the mapping modes discussed in this chapter. These two functions are not mentioned in this chapter outside of this one paragraph, but you are still likely to come across them while exploring this territory. Don't be fooled by their seeming similarity to `SetViewPortOrgX` and `SetWindowOrgEX`. They are reserved solely for use with the `MM_ISOTROPIC` and `MM_ANISOTROPIC` modes.

> **DON'T** change window and viewport coordinates at the same time, unless you are absolutely certain you can see your way through to some very clearly defined "logical" destination. The one notable exception involves the MM_ISOTROPIC and MM_ANISOTROPIC mapping modes. These two mapping modes are discussed in Bonus Day 2.

Before You Move On

I'm well aware that the stuff I've been talking about in the last few pages can lead to a serious meltdown of certain essential neural centers. So instead of turning up the juice, I'll just leave you with a taste of the possibilities inherent in this system and let the young at heart and adventuresome of spirit pursue these matters to whatever extremes they deem necessary. This is not to imply that I don't find this subject both important and intriguing—only that this book isn't the right place to pursue it in detail. Anyway, the WinSize program gives you another crack at these same concepts in the hope that it will help clarify the issues involved.

Speaking of the WinSize program (see Listings 16.3 through 16.8), it's time for you to get it up and running. Pay close attention, because this program contains tricks that you'll use over and over again when hacking Windows.

Listing 16.3. WINSIZE.CPP is the main module in the WinSize program.

```
///////////////////////////////////////
// WINSIZE.CPP — What Size is the Window?
// Copyright (c) 1995 Charlie Calvert
// Demonstrate dialogs and the Windows coordinate system
///////////////////////////////////////

#define STRICT
#define WIN32_LEAN_AND_MEAN
#include <windows.h>
#include <windowsx.h>
#pragma hdrstop
#include <stdio.h>
#include <stdlib.h>
#include <string.h>
#include "winsize.h"
#pragma warning (disable: 4068)

// ----------------------------------------------------
// Setup
// ----------------------------------------------------

// Variables
static char szAppName[] = "WinSize";
```

```
static HWND MainWindow;
static HINSTANCE hInstance;
FARPROC lpfnSizeBox;
FARPROC lpfnMakeShape;
HBRUSH BlueBrush, GreenBrush;
HWND hSizeBox;
TModeCase ModeCase = TEXT;
TOriginMode OriginMode = ORG_UPLEFT;
int RLeft = 10;
int RTop = 10;
int RRight = 100;
int RBottom = 100;
TShape Shape;
BOOL UseCompCords = TRUE;
int Modes[] = {MM_TEXT, MM_LOMETRIC, MM_HIMETRIC,
               MM_LOENGLISH, MM_HIENGLISH, MM_TWIPS,
               MM_ISOTROPIC, MM_ANISOTROPIC};

/////////////////////////////////////
// Program entry point
/////////////////////////////////////
#pragma argsused
int WINAPI WinMain(HINSTANCE hInst, HINSTANCE hPrevInstance,
                   LPSTR  lpszCmdParam, int nCmdShow)
{
  MSG  Msg;

  hInstance = hInst;

  if (!hPrevInstance)
    if (!Register(hInst))
      return FALSE;

  MainWindow = Create(hInst, nCmdShow);
  if (!MainWindow)
    return FALSE;

  while (GetMessage(&Msg, NULL, 0, 0))
  {
    TranslateMessage(&Msg);
    DispatchMessage(&Msg);
  }

  return Msg.wParam;
}

/////////////////////////////////////
// Register the window
/////////////////////////////////////
BOOL Register(HINSTANCE hInst)
{
  WNDCLASS WndClass;

  WndClass.style          = CS_HREDRAW | CS_VREDRAW;
  WndClass.lpfnWndProc    = WndProc;
  WndClass.cbClsExtra     = 0;
```

continues

16

Listing 16.3. continued

```
    WndClass.cbWndExtra    = 0;
    WndClass.hInstance     = hInst;
    WndClass.hIcon         = LoadIcon(NULL, IDI_APPLICATION);
    WndClass.hCursor       = LoadCursor(NULL, IDC_ARROW);
    WndClass.hbrBackground = (HBRUSH)(COLOR_WINDOW + 1);
    WndClass.lpszMenuName  = "MENU";
    WndClass.lpszClassName = szAppName;

    return RegisterClass (&WndClass);
}


/////////////////////////////////////
// Create the window
/////////////////////////////////////
HWND Create(HINSTANCE hInst, int nCmdShow)
{
    HWND hWindow = CreateWindow(szAppName, szAppName,
                    WS_OVERLAPPEDWINDOW,
                    CW_USEDEFAULT, CW_USEDEFAULT,
                    CW_USEDEFAULT, CW_USEDEFAULT,
                    NULL, NULL, hInst, NULL);

    if (hWindow == NULL)
        return hWindow;

    ShowWindow(hWindow, nCmdShow);
    UpdateWindow(hWindow);

    return hWindow;
}


//-----------------------------------------------------------
// The Implementation
//-----------------------------------------------------------


//-----------------------------------------------------------
// The WndProc
//-----------------------------------------------------------

LRESULT CALLBACK WndProc(HWND hwnd, UINT Message,
                        WPARAM wParam, LPARAM lParam)
{
    switch (Message)
    {
        HANDLE_MSG(hwnd, WM_COMMAND, WinSize_OnCommand);
        HANDLE_MSG(hwnd, WM_CREATE, WinSize_OnCreate);
        HANDLE_MSG(hwnd, WM_PAINT, WinSize_OnPaint);
        HANDLE_MSG(hwnd, WM_SIZE, WinSize_OnSize);
        HANDLE_MSG(hwnd, WM_DESTROY, WinSize_OnDestroy);
        default:
            return WinSize_DefProc(hwnd, Message, wParam, lParam);
    }
}
```

```
///////////////////////////////////
// Handle WM_CREATE
///////////////////////////////////
#pragma argsused
BOOL WinSize_OnCreate(HWND hwnd, CREATESTRUCT FAR*
lpCreateStruct)
{
  lpfnSizeBox =
    MakeProcInstance((FARPROC)SizeBoxProc,
                     lpCreateStruct->hInstance);

  BlueBrush = CreateSolidBrush(RGB(0, 255, 255));
  GreenBrush = CreateSolidBrush(RGB(255, 255, 127));

  return TRUE;
}


///////////////////////////////////
// Handle WM_DESTROY
///////////////////////////////////
#pragma argsused
void WinSize_OnDestroy(HWND hwnd)
{
  DeleteObject(BlueBrush);
  DeleteObject(GreenBrush);
  FreeProcInstance(lpfnSizeBox);
  PostQuitMessage(0);
}


///////////////////////////////////
// WM_COMMAND
///////////////////////////////////
#pragma argsused
void WinSize_OnCommand(HWND hwnd, int id, HWND hwndCtl, UINT
codeNotify)
{
  switch(id)
  {
    case CM_SIZEBOX:
      if (hSizeBox == 0)
      {
        hSizeBox = CreateDialog(hInstance, "SizeDialog",
                                hwnd,(DLGPROC)lpfnSizeBox);
        InvalidateRect(hwnd, NULL, FALSE);
      }
      break;

    case CM_MAKESHAPE:
      lpfnMakeShape = MakeProcInstance((FARPROC)MakeShapeProc,
                                       hInstance);
      DialogBox(hInstance, "MakeShape",
                hwnd,(DLGPROC)lpfnMakeShape);
      FreeProcInstance(lpfnMakeShape);
      InvalidateRect(hwnd, NULL, FALSE);
      break;
```

continues

Listing 16.3. continued

```
      case CM_EXIT:
        DestroyWindow(hwnd);
        break;
  }
}


//////////////////////////////////////
//  If the Size Dialog is open, this will fill it in with
//  the size of the window as expressed in each of the
//  different mapping modes
//////////////////////////////////////
void FillSizeBox(HWND hwnd, HDC PaintDC)
{
  TSIZEDATA    SizeData;
  for (int i = 0; i < 6; i++)
  {
    SetMapMode(PaintDC, Modes[i]);
    GetClientRect(hwnd, &SizeData[i]);
    DPtoLP(PaintDC, (LPPOINT)&SizeData[i], 2);
  }
  SendMessage(hSizeBox, WM_SETDATA, 0, (long)&SizeData);
}


//////////////////////////////////////
// WM_PAINT
//////////////////////////////////////
void WinSize_OnPaint(HWND hwnd)
{
  RECT         Rect;
  HDC          PaintDC ;
  PAINTSTRUCT  ps ;

  PaintDC = BeginPaint (hwnd, &ps) ;
  SetMapMode (PaintDC, Modes[ModeCase]);
  GetClientRect(hwnd, &Rect);

  switch (OriginMode)
  {
    case ORG_UPLEFT :
      SetViewportOrgEx(PaintDC, 0, 0, NULL);
      break;

    case ORG_LOWLEFT:
      SetViewportOrgEx(PaintDC, 0, Rect.bottom, NULL);
      break;

    case ORG_CENTER:
      SetViewportOrgEx(PaintDC,Rect.right/2,Rect.bottom / 2, NULL);
      break;
  }

  HBRUSH OldBrush = SelectBrush(PaintDC, BlueBrush);

  switch (Shape)
```

```
  {
    case RECTANGLE:
      Rectangle(PaintDC, RLeft, RTop, RRight, RBottom);
      break;

    case CIRCLE:
      Ellipse(PaintDC, RLeft, RTop, RRight, RBottom);
      break;
  }
  SelectObject(PaintDC, OldBrush);

  if (hSizeBox != 0)
    FillSizeBox(hwnd, PaintDC);

  EndPaint (hwnd, &ps) ;
}

//////////////////////////////////////
// WM_SIZE
//////////////////////////////////////
#pragma argsused
void WinSize_OnSize(HWND hwnd, UINT state, int cx, int cy)
{
  HDC PaintDC = GetDC(hwnd);
  if (hSizeBox != 0)
    FillSizeBox(hwnd, PaintDC);
  ReleaseDC(hwnd, PaintDC);
}

//////////////////////////////////////
// MakeShape Dialog
//////////////////////////////////////
void SetRectText(HWND hwnd)
{
  char S[45];
  HWND ParentWindow;

  ParentWindow = GetWindow(hwnd, GW_OWNER);
  InvalidateRect(ParentWindow, NULL, TRUE);
  sprintf(S, "%d", RLeft);
  Edit_SetText(GetDlgItem(hwnd, ID_RLEFT), S);
  sprintf(S, "%d", RRight);
  Edit_SetText(GetDlgItem(hwnd, ID_RRIGHT), S);
  sprintf(S, "%d", RTop);
  Edit_SetText(GetDlgItem(hwnd, ID_RTOP), S);
  sprintf(S, "%d", RBottom);
  Edit_SetText(GetDlgItem(hwnd, ID_RBOTTOM), S);
}

//////////////////////////////////////
// GetUserCords
//////////////////////////////////////
void GetUserCords(HWND hwnd)
{
  char S[100];
```

continues

Listing 16.3. continued

```
        Edit_GetText(GetDlgItem(hwnd, ID_RLEFT), S, 100);
        RLeft = atoi(S);
        Edit_GetText(GetDlgItem(hwnd, ID_RTOP), S, 100);
        RTop = atoi(S);
        Edit_GetText(GetDlgItem(hwnd, ID_RRIGHT), S, 100);
        RRight = atoi(S);
        Edit_GetText(GetDlgItem(hwnd, ID_RBOTTOM), S, 100);
        RBottom = atoi(S);
}

//////////////////////////////////////
// MakeShape
//////////////////////////////////////
void MakeShape(HWND hDlg)
{
  RECT R;

  GetClientRect(GetParent(hDlg), &R);
  HDC DC = GetDC(GetParent(hDlg));
  SetMapMode(DC, Modes[ModeCase]);
  DPtoLP(DC,(LPPOINT)&R, 2);
  ReleaseDC(GetParent(hDlg), DC);

  switch (OriginMode)
  {
    case ORG_CENTER:
      RLeft = -(R.right / 3);
      RTop = -(R.bottom / 3);
      RRight = (R.right / 3);
      RBottom = (R.bottom / 3);
      break;

    case ORG_LOWLEFT:
      RBottom = -(R.bottom / 3);
      RLeft = R.left / 3;
      RTop = R.top / 3;
      RRight = R.right / 3;
      break;

    case ORG_UPLEFT:
      RLeft = R.left / 3;
      RTop = R.top / 3;
      RRight = R.right / 3;
      RBottom = R.bottom / 3;
      break;
  }
}


//////////////////////////////////////
// DoDraw
//////////////////////////////////////
void DoDraw(HWND hwnd)
{
```

```
    if (UseCompCords)
      MakeShape(hwnd);
    SetRectText(hwnd);
}

///////////////////////////////////////
// DoRectCommand
///////////////////////////////////////
BOOL DoRectCommand(HWND hwnd, WORD wParam)
{
  switch(wParam)
  {
    case ID_DRAW:
      GetUserCords(hwnd);
      InvalidateRect(GetParent(hwnd), NULL, TRUE);
      return TRUE;

    case ID_RTEXT:
      ModeCase = TEXT;
      DoDraw(hwnd);
      return TRUE;

    case ID_RLOMETRIC:
      ModeCase = LOMETRIC;
      DoDraw(hwnd);
      return TRUE;

    case ID_RHIMETRIC:
      ModeCase = HIMETRIC;
      DoDraw(hwnd);
      return TRUE;

    case ID_RLOENGLISH:
      ModeCase = LOENGLISH;
      DoDraw(hwnd);
      return TRUE;

    case ID_RHIENGLISH:
      ModeCase = HIENGLISH;
      DoDraw(hwnd);
      return TRUE;

    case ID_RTWIPS:
      ModeCase = TWIPS;
      DoDraw(hwnd);
      return TRUE;

    case ID_ORGUPLEFT:
      GetUserCords(hwnd);
      OriginMode = ORG_UPLEFT;
      DoDraw(hwnd);
      return TRUE;

    case ID_ORGLOWLEFT:
      GetUserCords(hwnd);
      OriginMode = ORG_LOWLEFT;
```

continues

Listing 16.3. continued

```
          DoDraw(hwnd);
          return TRUE;

      case ID_ORGCENTER:
        GetUserCords(hwnd);
        OriginMode = ORG_CENTER;
        DoDraw(hwnd);
        return TRUE;

      case ID_USERCORDS:
        GetUserCords(hwnd);
        UseCompCords = FALSE;
        return TRUE;

      case ID_COMPCORDS:
        UseCompCords = TRUE;
        return FALSE;

      case ID_RECT:
        Shape = RECTANGLE;
        DoDraw(hwnd);
        return TRUE;

      case ID_CIRCLE:
        Shape = CIRCLE;
        DoDraw(hwnd);
        return TRUE;

      case IDOK:
      case IDCANCEL:
      {
        EndDialog(hwnd, wParam);
        return TRUE;
      }
    }
  }
  return FALSE;
}

///////////////////////////////////////////////////
// WM_CTLCOLOR
///////////////////////////////////////////////////
#pragma argsused
HBRUSH Shape_OnCtlColor(HWND hwnd, HDC hdc, HWND hwndChild, int type)
{
  switch(type)
  {
    case CTLCOLOR_STATIC:
    case CTLCOLOR_EDIT:
    case CTLCOLOR_BTN:
      /* Set text to white and background to green */
      SetTextColor(hdc, RGB(0, 127, 0));
      SetBkMode(hdc, TRANSPARENT);
      return GreenBrush;
```

```
      case CTLCOLOR_DLG:
        return GreenBrush;
  }
  return NULL;
}


///////////////////////////////////
// MakeShapeProc
///////////////////////////////////
#pragma argsused
BOOL CALLBACK MakeShapeProc(HWND hDlg, WORD Msg,
                                  WORD wParam, LONG lParam)
{
  switch(Msg)
  {
    case WM_INITDIALOG:
      Button_SetCheck(GetDlgItem(hDlg, ID_RTEXT), 1);
      Button_SetCheck(GetDlgItem(hDlg, ID_RECT), 1);
      Button_SetCheck(GetDlgItem(hDlg, ID_ORGUPLEFT), 1);
      Button_SetCheck(GetDlgItem(hDlg, ID_COMPCORDS), 1);
      return TRUE;

    case WM_COMMAND:
      return (!DoRectCommand(hDlg, wParam));

    #ifdef WIN32
    case WM_CTLCOLORSTATIC:
    case WM_CTLCOLORBTN:
    case WM_CTLCOLOREDIT:
      return HANDLE_WM_CTLCOLORSTATIC(hDlg, wParam, lParam, Shape_OnCtlColor);
    case WM_CTLCOLORDLG:
      return HANDLE_WM_CTLCOLORDLG(hDlg, wParam, lParam, Shape_OnCtlColor);
    #else
    case WM_CTLCOLOR:
      return HANDLE_WM_CTLCOLOR(hDlg, wParam, lParam, Shape_OnCtlColor);
    #endif
  }
  return FALSE;
}


/////////////////////////////////////////////////////
// WM_CTLCOLOR
/////////////////////////////////////////////////////
#pragma argsused
HBRUSH Size_OnCtlColor(HWND hwnd, HDC hdc, HWND hwndChild, int type)
{
  switch (type)
  {
    case CTLCOLOR_STATIC:
      SetTextColor(hdc, RGB(255, 0, 0));
      SetBkMode(hdc, TRANSPARENT);
      return GetStockBrush(BLACK_BRUSH);

    case CTLCOLOR_DLG:
      return GetStockBrush(BLACK_BRUSH);
  }
```

continues

Listing 16.3. continued

```
      return NULL;
    }

    //----------------------------------------------
    // SizeBoxProc Dialog
    //----------------------------------------------
    #pragma argsused
    BOOL CALLBACK SizeBoxProc(HWND hDlg, WORD Msg,
                                 WORD wParam, LONG lParam)
    {
      TSIZEDATA SizeData;
      void *lpSizeData;
      char S[20];
      int i;

      int Indexs[] = {2100, 2200, 2300, 2400, 2500, 2600};

      switch(Msg)
      {
        case WM_CLOSE:
          DestroyWindow(hDlg);
          hSizeBox = 0;
          return TRUE;

        #ifdef WIN32
        case WM_CTLCOLORSTATIC:
          return HANDLE_WM_CTLCOLORSTATIC(hDlg, wParam, lParam, Size_OnCtlColor);
        case WM_CTLCOLORDLG:
          return HANDLE_WM_CTLCOLORDLG(hDlg, wParam, lParam, Size_OnCtlColor);
        #else
        case WM_CTLCOLOR:
          return HANDLE_WM_CTLCOLOR(hDlg, wParam, lParam, Size_OnCtlColor);
        #endif

        case WM_SETDATA:
          lpSizeData = (void *)lParam;
          memcpy(SizeData, lpSizeData, sizeof(TSIZEDATA));
          for (i = 0; i < 6; i++)
            {
            sprintf(S, "%d", SizeData[i].left);
            Edit_SetText(GetDlgItem(hDlg, Indexs[i] + 1), S);
            sprintf(S, "%d", SizeData[i].right);
            Edit_SetText(GetDlgItem(hDlg, Indexs[i] + 2), S);
            sprintf(S, "%d", SizeData[i].top);
            Edit_SetText(GetDlgItem(hDlg, Indexs[i] + 3), S);
            sprintf(S, "%d", SizeData[i].bottom);
            Edit_SetText(GetDlgItem(hDlg, Indexs[i] + 4), S);
            }
          return TRUE;
      }
      return FALSE;
    }
```

Listing 16.4 WINSIZE.H is the header file for the WinSize program.

```
/////////////////////////////////////
// WINSIZE.H
// Programmer: Charlie Calvert
/////////////////////////////////////

// Constants
#define WM_SETDATA      (WM_USER + 1)
#define CM_EXIT         101
#define CM_SIZEBOX      1000
#define CM_MAKESHAPE    1001
#define RECTSIZE        2000
#define ID_MMLEFT       2101
#define ID_MMRIGHT      2102
#define ID_MMTOP        2103
#define ID_MMBOTTOM     2104
#define ID_LMLEFT       2201
#define ID_LMRIGHT      2202
#define ID_LMTOP        2203
#define ID_LMBOTTOM     2204
#define ID_HMLEFT       2301
#define ID_HMRIGHT      2302
#define ID_HMTOP        2303
#define ID_HMBOTTOM     2304
#define ID_LELEFT       2401
#define ID_LERIGHT      2402
#define ID_LETOP        2403
#define ID_LEBOTTOM     2404
#define ID_HELEFT       2501
#define ID_HERIGHT      2502
#define ID_HETOP        2503
#define ID_HEBOTTOM     2504
#define ID_TLEFT        2601
#define ID_TRIGHT       2602
#define ID_TTOP         2603
#define ID_TBOTTOM      2604
#define ID_RTEXT        3101
#define ID_RLOMETRIC    3102
#define ID_RHIMETRIC    3103
#define ID_RLOENGLISH   3104
#define ID_RHIENGLISH   3105
#define ID_RTWIPS       3106
#define ID_RISOTROPIC   3107
#define ID_RANSITROPIC  3108
#define ID_RLEFT        3110
#define ID_RRIGHT       3111
#define ID_RTOP         3112
#define ID_RBOTTOM      3113
#define ID_DRAW         3115
#define ID_COMPCORDS    3117
#define ID_USERCORDS    3118
#define ID_ORGUPLEFT    3120
#define ID_ORGLOWLEFT   3121
#define ID_ORGCENTER    3122
#define ID_RECT         4001
```

continues

Listing 16.4 continued

```
#define ID_CIRCLE         4002

// Types
typedef RECT TSIZEDATA[6];
typedef enum TModeCase {TEXT, LOMETRIC, HIMETRIC, LOENGLISH,
                HIENGLISH, TWIPS, ISOTROPIC, ANSITROPIC};
typedef enum TOriginMode {ORG_UPLEFT, ORG_LOWLEFT, ORG_CENTER};
typedef enum TShape {RECTANGLE, CIRCLE};

// Declarations for class Generic
#define WinSize_DefProc     DefWindowProc
BOOL WinSize_OnCreate(HWND hwnd,
                    CREATESTRUCT FAR* lpCreateStruct);
void WinSize_OnDestroy(HWND hwnd);
void WinSize_OnCommand(HWND hwnd, int id,
                    HWND hwndCtl, UINT codeNotify);
void WinSize_OnPaint(HWND hwnd);
void WinSize_OnSize(HWND hwnd, UINT state, int cx, int cy);

// procs
LRESULT CALLBACK WndProc(HWND hwnd, UINT Message,
                            WPARAM wParam, LPARAM lParam);
BOOL Register(HINSTANCE hInst);
HWND Create(HINSTANCE hInst, int nCmdShow);
BOOL CALLBACK MakeShapeProc(HWND hWindow, WORD Msg,
                            WORD wParam, LONG lParam);
BOOL CALLBACK SizeBoxProc(HWND hWindow, WORD Msg,
                            WORD wParam, LONG lParam);
```

Listing 16.5. WINSIZE.RC is the resource file for the WinSize program.

```
/////////////////////////////////////
// WINSIZE.RC -- What Size is the Window?
// programmer: Charlie Calvert
/////////////////////////////////////

#include "WinSize.h"
#include "Windows.h"

/////////////////////////////////////
// I've defined the following styles in order to make the
// code that follows at least somewhat more readable.
// This is not necessarily a programming technique, but rather
// something I've done to make the book more legible.
/////////////////////////////////////
#define STY_STANDARD WS_CHILD ¦ WS_VISIBLE ¦ WS_GROUP
#define STY_GRPCHILD BS_GROUPBOX ¦ WS_CHILD ¦ WS_VISIBLE
#define STY_RTEXT SS_RIGHT ¦ WS_CHILD ¦ WS_VISIBLE ¦ WS_GROUP
#define STY_AUTRAD \
        BS_AUTORADIOBUTTON ¦ WS_CHILD ¦ WS_VISIBLE ¦ WS_TABSTOP
#define STY_STATLEFT \
```

```
            ES_LEFT ¦ WS_CHILD ¦ WS_VISIBLE ¦ WS_BORDER ¦ WS_TABSTOP
#define STY_AUTRADGRP \
          BS_AUTORADIOBUTTON ¦ WS_CHILD ¦ WS_VISIBLE ¦ \
          WS_GROUP ¦ WS_TABSTOP

Menu MENU
BEGIN
  POPUP "File"
  BEGIN
     MENUITEM "E&xit", CM_EXIT
  END
  POPUP "Options"
  BEGIN
     MENUITEM "Size Dialog", CM_SIZEBOX
     MENUITEM "Make Shape", CM_MAKESHAPE
  END
END

SizeDialog DIALOG 16, 18, 170, 100
STYLE WS_POPUP ¦ WS_CAPTION ¦ WS_SYSMENU ¦ WS_VISIBLE ¦ DS_MODALFRAME
CAPTION "Size Dialog"
BEGIN
  LTEXT "MMText", -1, 7, 17, 40, 9, STY_STANDARD
  LTEXT "LoMetric", -1, 7, 30, 40, 9, STY_STANDARD
  LTEXT "HiMetric", -1, 7, 45, 40, 9, STY_STANDARD
  LTEXT "LoEnglish", -1, 7, 59, 40, 9, STY_STANDARD
  LTEXT "HiEnglish", -1, 7, 73, 40, 9, STY_STANDARD
  LTEXT "Twips", -1, 7, 87, 40, 9, STY_STANDARD
  CONTROL "", ID_MMLEFT, "STATIC", STY_STATLEFT, 42, 16, 27, 11
  CONTROL "", ID_MMRIGHT, "STATIC", STY_STATLEFT, 105, 16, 27, 11
  CONTROL "", ID_MMTOP, "STATIC", STY_STATLEFT, 74, 16, 27, 11
  CONTROL "", ID_MMBOTTOM, "STATIC", STY_STATLEFT, 138,16, 27, 11
  CONTROL "", ID_LMLEFT, "STATIC", STY_STATLEFT, 42, 30, 27, 11
  CONTROL "", ID_LMRIGHT, "STATIC", STY_STATLEFT, 105, 30, 27, 11
  CONTROL "", ID_LMTOP, "STATIC", STY_STATLEFT, 74, 30, 27, 11
  CONTROL "", ID_LMBOTTOM, "STATIC", STY_STATLEFT, 138,30, 27, 11
  CONTROL "", ID_HMLEFT, "STATIC", STY_STATLEFT, 42, 45, 27, 11
  CONTROL "", ID_HMRIGHT, "STATIC", STY_STATLEFT, 105, 45, 27, 11
  CONTROL "", ID_HMTOP, "STATIC", STY_STATLEFT, 74, 45, 27, 11
  CONTROL "", ID_HMBOTTOM, "STATIC", STY_STATLEFT, 138,45, 27, 11
  CONTROL "", ID_LELEFT, "STATIC", STY_STATLEFT, 42, 59, 27, 11
  CONTROL "", ID_LERIGHT, "STATIC", STY_STATLEFT, 105, 59, 27, 11
  CONTROL "", ID_LETOP, "STATIC", STY_STATLEFT, 74, 59, 27, 11
  CONTROL "", ID_LEBOTTOM, "STATIC", STY_STATLEFT, 138,59, 27, 11
  CONTROL "", ID_HELEFT, "STATIC", STY_STATLEFT, 42, 73, 27, 11
  CONTROL "", ID_HERIGHT, "STATIC", STY_STATLEFT, 105, 73, 27, 11
  CONTROL "", ID_HETOP, "STATIC", STY_STATLEFT, 74, 73, 27, 11
  CONTROL "", ID_HEBOTTOM, "STATIC", STY_STATLEFT, 138,73, 27, 11
  CONTROL "", ID_TLEFT, "STATIC", STY_STATLEFT, 42, 87, 27, 11
  CONTROL "", ID_TRIGHT, "STATIC", STY_STATLEFT, 105, 87, 27, 11
  CONTROL "", ID_TTOP, "STATIC", STY_STATLEFT, 74, 87, 27, 11
  CONTROL "", ID_TBOTTOM, "STATIC", STY_STATLEFT, 138, 87, 27, 11
  LTEXT "Left", -1, 42, 6, 16, 8, STY_STANDARD
  LTEXT "Top", -1, 74, 6, 16, 8, STY_STANDARD
  LTEXT "Right", -1, 105, 6, 25, 8, STY_STANDARD
  LTEXT "Bottom", -1, 138, 7, 25, 7, STY_STANDARD
```

continues

Listing 16.5. continued

```
END

MakeShape DIALOG 18, 18, 190, 162
STYLE WS_POPUP ¦ WS_CAPTION ¦ WS_SYSMENU ¦ WS_VISIBLE ¦ DS_MODALFRAME
CAPTION "Make Shape"
BEGIN
  CONTROL "MM_TEXT",ID_RTEXT,"BUTTON",STY_AUTRADGRP,10,8,66,10
  CONTROL "MM_LOMETRIC", ID_RLOMETRIC, "BUTTON", STY_AUTRAD,
          10, 21, 66, 10
  CONTROL "MM_HIMETRIC", ID_RHIMETRIC, "BUTTON", STY_AUTRAD,
          10, 34, 66, 10
  CONTROL "MM_LOENGLISH", ID_RLOENGLISH, "BUTTON", STY_AUTRAD,
          10, 47, 66, 10
  CONTROL "MM_HIENGLISH", ID_RHIENGLISH, "BUTTON", STY_AUTRAD,
          10, 60, 66, 10
  CONTROL "MM_TWIPS", ID_RTWIPS, "BUTTON", STY_AUTRAD,
          10, 73, 66, 10
  EDITTEXT ID_RLEFT, 124, 10, 52, 12, STY_STATLEFT
  EDITTEXT ID_RTOP, 124, 24, 52, 12, STY_STATLEFT
  EDITTEXT ID_RRIGHT, 124, 38, 52, 12, STY_STATLEFT
  EDITTEXT ID_RBOTTOM, 124, 52, 52, 12, STY_STATLEFT
  CONTROL "Origin Upper Left",
          ID_ORGUPLEFT, "BUTTON", STY_AUTRADGRP, 95, 81, 84, 10
  CONTROL "Origin Lower Left",
          ID_ORGLOWLEFT, "BUTTON", STY_AUTRAD, 95, 95, 84, 10
  CONTROL "Origin Center",
          ID_ORGCENTER, "BUTTON", STY_AUTRAD, 95, 108, 84, 10
  CONTROL "User Coordinates",
          ID_USERCORDS, "BUTTON", STY_AUTRADGRP, 95, 133, 84, 12
  CONTROL "Computer Coordinates",
          ID_COMPCORDS, "BUTTON", STY_AUTRAD, 95, 144, 84, 10
  PUSHBUTTON "Close", IDOK, 5, 134, 33, 21,
          WS_CHILD ¦ WS_VISIBLE ¦ WS_TABSTOP
  PUSHBUTTON "Draw", ID_DRAW, 48, 134, 33, 21
  RTEXT "Left", -1, 94, 12, 25, 8, STY_RTEXT
  RTEXT "Right", -1, 94, 40, 25, 8, STY_RTEXT
  RTEXT "Top", -1, 94, 26, 25, 8, STY_RTEXT
  RTEXT "Bottom", -1, 94, 54, 25, 8, STY_RTEXT
  CONTROL "", 3116, "button", STY_GRPCHILD, 90, 128, 94, 27
  CONTROL "", 3119, "button", STY_GRPCHILD, 90, 74, 94, 49
  CONTROL "", 3107, "button", STY_GRPCHILD, 5, 88, 77, 35
  CONTROL "Rectangle",ID_RECT,"BUTTON",STY_AUTRADGRP,11,95,66,10
  CONTROL "Ellipse",ID_CIRCLE,"BUTTON",STY_AUTRAD,11,109,66,10
  CONTROL "", 3108, "button", STY_GRPCHILD, 91, 1, 90, 69
  CONTROL "", 3109, "button", STY_GRPCHILD, 7, 1, 74, 85
END
```

Listing 16.6 shows the WinSize definition file.

Listing 16.6. WINSIZE.DEF.

```
; WinSize.def
NAME          WinSize
DESCRIPTION   'Mapping Modes Info'
CODE          PRELOAD MOVEABLE DISCARDABLE
DATA          PRELOAD MOVEABLE MULTIPLE
HEAPSIZE      4096
STACKSIZE     8192
```

Listing 16.7 shows the Borland makefile for WinSize.

Listing 16.7. WINSIZE.MAK (Borland).

```
# ----------------------
# WINSIZE.MAK
# ----------------------
#
# macros
#

!if !$d(BCROOT)
BCROOT  = $(MAKEDIR)
!endif

APPNAME = WinSize
INCPATH = $(BCROOT)\INCLUDE
LIBPATH = $(BCROOT)\LIB

!if $d(WIN16)
COMPILER= BCC.EXE
BRC= BRC.EXE
FLAGS   = -W -ml -v -w4 -I$(INCPATH) -L$(LIBPATH)
!else
COMPILER= BCC32.EXE
BRC= BRC32.EXE
FLAGS   = -W -v -w4 -I$(INCPATH) -L$(LIBPATH)
!endif

# link
$(APPNAME).exe: $(APPNAME).obj $(APPNAME).def $(APPNAME).res
  $(COMPILER) $(FLAGS) $(APPNAME).obj
  $(BRC) -I$(INCPATH) $(APPNAME).res

# compile
$(APPNAME).obj: $(APPNAME).cpp
  $(COMPILER) -c $(FLAGS) $(APPNAME).cpp

# resource
$(APPNAME).res: $(APPNAME).rc
  $(BRC) -R -I$(INCPATH) $(APPNAME).RC
```

Listing 16.8 shows the Microsoft makefile for WinSize.

Listing 16.8. WINSIZE.MAK (Microsoft).

```
# WINSIZE.MAK

APPNAME=WINSIZE
TARGETOS=WIN95
APPVER=4.0
OBJS=$(APPNAME).OBJ

!include <win32.mak>

all: $(APPNAME).exe

# Update the resource if necessary

$(APPNAME).res: $(APPNAME).rc $(APPNAME).h
  $(rc) $(rcflags) $(rcvars) $(APPNAME).rc

# Update the object files if necessary

# compile
.cpp.obj:
  $(cc) $(cflags) $(cvars) $(cdebug) $<

# Update the executable file if necessary.

$(APPNAME).exe: $(OBJS) $(APPNAME).res
  $(link) $(linkdebug) $(guiflags) -out:$(APPNAME).exe \
  $(OBJS) $(APPNAME).res $(guilibs) comctl32.lib
```

Figure 16.4 shows the WinSize program and its dialogs.

Figure 16.4.

Output you might see during a typical run of the WinSize program.

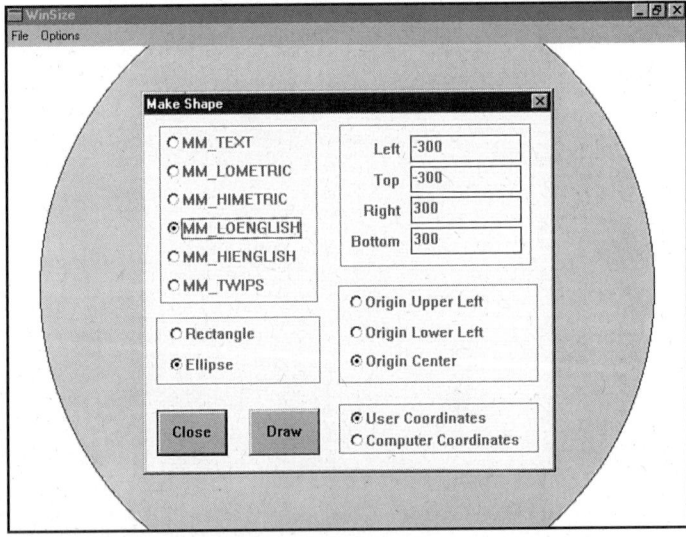

The WinSize program draws a rectangle or an ellipse in a window. It also lets you open two dialogs: the Make Shape dialog (Figure 16.5) and the Size dialog (Figure 16.6). The Size dialog reports on the size of the entire window when measured in any of the following mapping modes: MM_TEXT, MM_HIENGLISH, MM_LOENGLISH, MM_HIMETRIC, MM_LOMETRIC, or MM_TWIPS. The Make Shape dialog enables you to change the type of shape being shown and its dimensions. It also enables you to change the mapping mode and the viewpoint origin.

If you use the Make Shape dialog to change the dimensions of a shape, select user coordinates from the dialog; then, enter the new values in the edit controls at the upper-right corner of the dialog. Click the Draw button to see the result.

It's possible to enter coordinates that will move the shape entirely off the screen. The primary purpose of the Computer Coordinates option is to force the computer to automatically calculate coordinates that will place the shape so it will be visible to the user.

Dialogs Overview and Review

Before discussing the inner workings of the WinSize program, there are a few key points about dialogs that need to be emphasized:

- [ ] Dialogs are just a special form of a window.

- [ ] All dialogs have a dialog procedure associated with them. This dialog procedure is really just a minor variation on the standard window procedures you've seen so often in this book.

- [ ] As a rule, dialogs are populated with controls that are defined in RC files, just as menus are defined in RC files.

- [ ] The controls that reside inside dialogs are identical to the window controls discussed in detail during Week 2.

- [ ] It's usually easier to draw the first draft of a dialog (such as the ones shown in Figures 16.5 and 16.6) with the Resource Workshop, App Studio, or similar visual tool, than it is to design it strictly with code. When you've got something close to what you want, use the method that seems simplest.

Figure 16.5.

The Make Shape dialog.
The simplest way to create
a dialog like this is with
a visual tool.

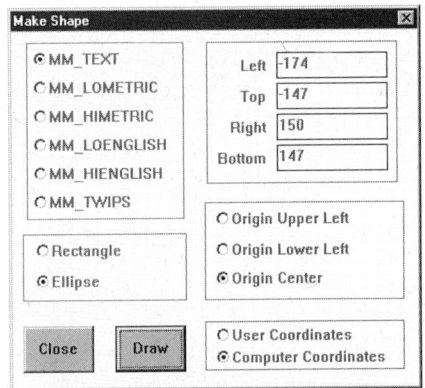

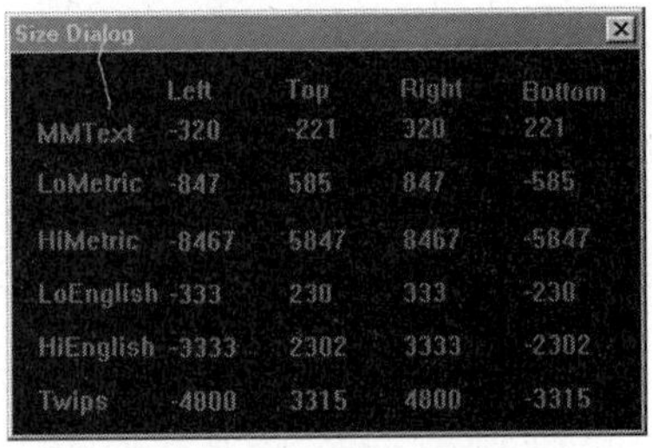

Figure 16.6.

When the modeless Size
dialog is on-screen, you
can still use the main
window's menu.

At this stage in the game, it might be easiest for you to think of dialogs as existing primarily so programmers can have an easy way to manipulate window controls when carrying on a "dialog" with the user.

You can pop into the Resource Workshop or App Studio and design the interface for a dialog in just a few minutes. Popping up the newly created dialog on-screen involves just a few simple calls. When you're done, you have an easy way of carrying on a conversation, or "dialog," with a user. Trying to do the same thing by laboriously calling CreateWindow on each control is much more effort. Window controls are easier to use when they appear in dialogs.

On Day 12, "Window Controls and the Control Message API," and Day 13, "Subclassing Window Controls," you learned about setting the WS_GROUP style for the first radio button inside a group. This same process must be implemented inside of dialogs, as shown in these excerpts from WINSIZE.RC:

```
15: #define STY_STANDARD WS_CHILD | WS_VISIBLE | WS_GROUP
```

Also, the WS_TABSTOP style is set for all the controls in the Make Shape dialog that a user might want to reach with the Tab key:

```
108:    PUSHBUTTON "Close", IDOK, 5, 134, 33, 21,
109:            WS_CHILD | WS_VISIBLE | WS_TABSTOP
```

Understanding Modal and Modeless Dialogs

The remainder of this chapter is dedicated to showing you the differences between creating modal dialogs, such as the Make Shape dialog, and modeless dialogs, such as the Size dialog. These are the two main categories of dialogs, and as a result, all Windows programmers need to understand what these terms mean.

The key points to grasp about modal and modeless dialogs are as follows:

- Modal dialogs "disable" the rest of a program so that the users can't do anything else until they make a selection from the current dialog and close it.

- Modeless dialogs are a lot like windows created with the WS_CHILD style. They float on top of the main window and let the user access the other features of the program.

- Under 16-bit Windows, both kinds of dialogs are created by calling MakeProcInstance to allocate a stub for the dialog procedure. Then, either CreateDialog (modeless) or DialogBox (modal) is called to launch the dialog.

- Under WIN16, when you are all done, call FreeProcInstance to clean up the allocated memory. This is not necessary under WIN32.

All four of these points are clarified in the next few paragraphs. In particular, you'll see that although modal and modeless dialogs are created through similar calls, some specific differences in implementation occur.

If you haven't done so already, pop up the WinSize program and start experimenting with the two dialogs. You'll probably notice that you have access to the program's main menu when the Size dialog is up, but you can't access it when the Make Shape dialog is on-screen. This is because the Make Shape dialog is a modal dialog, and the Size dialog is a modeless dialog.

Modal dialog boxes usually don't prevent you from changing from one application to another. In other words, if you are using the Make Shape dialog, you can switch to the File Manager or Explorer, but you can't use the main menu of the WinSize program. The only exception to this rule is on the rare occasion you might use a system modal dialog box. System modal dialogs only enable the user to work inside of one dialog and don't let the user switch to any other program.

In this particular case, the Size dialog is modeless because the user needs to be able to watch the figures in the dialog change when he or she tugs at the borders surrounding the WinSize program. The issue here is that the Size dialog shows the dimensions of the main window as measured in several different mapping modes. When someone changes the size of the main window, the numbers in the Size dialog change. If the Size dialog were modal, it wouldn't be possible to bear witness to this effect.

Coding Modal and Modeless Dialogs

Although the actual implementations of modal and modeless dialogs are quite similar in principle, there are a number of specific differences in the ways they are created. The next few paragraphs explore some of those differences.

Those who are interested in 16-bit Windows need to first turn to the `WinSize_OnCreate` function. The WinSize program takes a relatively straightforward approach to the initialization of its main window. Instead, most of the real work is done in the `WinSize_OnCommand` function. At any rate, here's what WinSize does with `WM_CREATE` messages:

```
BOOL WinSize_OnCreate(HWND hwnd,
CREATESTRUCT FAR* lpCreateStruct)
{
HINSTANCE hIn;
hIn = lpCreateStruct->hInstance;
lpfnSizeBox = MakeProcInstance((FARPROC)SizeBoxProc, hIn);
BlueBrush = CreateSolidBrush(RGB(0, 255, 255));
GreenBrush = CreateSolidBrush(RGB(255, 255, 127));
return TRUE;
}
```

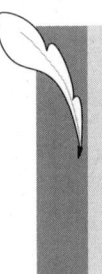

Note: It happens that the `CREATSTRUCT`, piggybacking on top of the `WM_CREATE` message, contains a copy of the program's `HINSTANCE`. In previous chapters, the code in this book generally used a globally declared `HINSTANCE` variable. The code fragment preceding this note shows an alternative method of accessing the program's `HINSTANCE`. It's particularly useful if you want to move a `Cls_OnCreate` function outside the scope of your main module without engaging in the dubious practice of declaring variables global to more than one module.

The call to `MakeProcInstance` results in the initialization of the `lpfnSizeBox` variable, which is needed in 16-bit Windows when it's time to create the Size dialog. The issues involved here are nearly the same as those encountered on Day 11, "Talking to Controls," when you saw that `MakeProcInstance` was called prior to `EnumFontFamilies`. That is, you need to bind the data segment of the WinSize program to the window procedure for the Size dialog. As a result, even though Size dialog's window procedure is called by Windows, it still has access to the program's variables.

I'm not going to go any further than to point out that the stub for the Size dialog's window procedure is allocated in response to the `WM_CREATE` message, but calling `MakeProcInstance` on the Make Shape's dialog procedure is delayed until later in the program's history. The exact reason for these divergent courses of action will become clear in the next few paragraphs.

Now it's time to take a look at the portion of the WM_COMMAND message handler function where the two dialog boxes are actually launched. Needless to say, either of the following code fragments are called only after the user has made a selection from the program's menu:

```
case CM_SIZEBOX:
if (hSizeBox == 0)
  {
hSizeBox = CreateDialog(hInstance, "Options", hwnd,
(DLGPROC)lpfnSizeBox);
InvalidateRect(hwnd, NULL, FALSE);
  }
break;
case CM_MAKESHAPE:
lpfnMakeShape = MakeProcInstance((FARPROC)MakeShapeProc, hInstance);
DialogBox(hInstance, "MakeShape", hwnd, (DLGPROC)lpfnMakeShape);
FreeProcInstance(lpfnMakeShape);
InvalidateRect(hwnd, NULL, FALSE);
break;
```

This code starts on line 154 of WINSIZE.CPP. CM_SIZEBOX messages get sent to the program whenever the Size dialog option is selected from the menu, and CM_MAKESHAPE messages get sent whenever the user selects the Make Shape option from the menu.

As you can see, the WinSize program reacts differently to CM_SIZEBOX messages than it does to CM_MAKESHAPE messages. This is because modal dialog boxes are created by calls to the DialogBox function, whereas modeless dialogs are created by calls to the CreateDialog function. Furthermore, the call to the DialogBox procedure doesn't end until the user has closed the Make Shape dialog. This is why it's possible to call MakeProcInstance, DialogBox, and FreeProcInstance in quick succession:

```
lpfnMakeShape = MakeProcInstance((FARPROC)MakeShapeProc,
hInstance);
DialogBox(hInstance, "MakeShape", hwnd,
(DLGPROC)lpfnMakeShape);
FreeProcInstance(lpfnMakeShape);
```

It's okay for FreeProcInstance to deallocate the memory for the dialog box procedure, because the Make Shape dialog has already been closed by the time FreeProcInstance is called. (Of course, under WIN32, it's not necessary to call either MakeProcInstance or FreeProcInstance.)

The CreateDialog procedure operates under a different set of rules because it creates a modeless dialog procedure. This is why the WinSize program calls MakeProcInstance for the Size dialog in response to a WM_CREATE message, and why it destroys the allocated thunk while processing the WM_DESTROY message. The point here is that there is no way to know when the user is likely to close the Size dialog, so the lpfnSizeBox variable can only be safely destroyed after the user has closed the main window.

Furthermore, it's necessary to check the value of the hSizeBox variable before making any calls to CreateDialog:

```
if (hSizeBox == 0)
{
hSizeBox = CreateDialog(hInstance, "Options", hwnd,
(DLGPROC)lpfnSizeBox);
InvalidateRect(hwnd, NULL, FALSE);
}
```

This is done to ensure that the user doesn't end up crowding the screen with a whole series of instances of the Size dialog. The same thing isn't necessary with the Make Shape dialog, because the user can't get at the menu while a modal dialog is on-screen. Without access to the menu, the user won't be able to send more CM_MAKESHAPE messages to the WndProc.

As you know, both of these dialog procedures are really just special types of window procedures, which in their most simplified form look like this:

```
BOOL CALLBACK GenericDialogProc(HWND hDlg, WORD Message,
WPARAM wParam, LPARAM lParam)
{
switch(Message)
  {
case WM_INITDIALOG:
return TRUE;
case WM_COMMAND:
if (wParam == IDOK || wParam == IDCANCEL)
    {
EndDialog(hDlg,  wParam);
return TRUE;
    }
break;
  }
return FALSE;
}
```

As you can see, dialogs can be closed by calls to EndDialog.

Note: Dialog box procedures aren't identical to window procedures. For instance, they return a BOOL rather than an LRESULT. That is, dialog box procedures don't include calls to DefWindowProc. Instead, they simply return TRUE or FALSE. Another significant difference is that dialog box procedures process WM_INITDIALOG messages rather than WM_CREATE messages.

A glance at the source code for WinSize reveals that both the MakeShapeProc and the SizeBoxProc are considerably more complicated than the code fragment (previously listed). The extra code inside these functions is used primarily to change their color, and to set and retrieve data from their controls. The actual details of that process will be discussed on Day 17, "Advanced Dialogs: Getting and Setting Data."

Summary

In this chapter you have learned about the Windows coordinate system, and about creating modal and modeless dialogs. Specifically, you have learned that

☐ There are eight logical mapping modes. Only the one called MM_TEXT has at least a quasi-direct relationship to the physical device coordinates, which are pixels.

☐ The strictly logical coordinate systems, such as MM_LOENGLISH, are useful to programmers but are still not entirely precise.

☐ You can change the origin of a coordinate system by calling SetViewportOrgEx.

☐ There are two different types of dialogs—modal and modeless.

☐ Modal dialogs take over the focus of a program until the user closes them.

☐ Modeless dialogs give the user the freedom to return at any time to the program's main menu, or to any other available features.

On Day 17, you'll see how to communicate with both modal and modeless dialog boxes. In particular, you'll see how to transfer data into a dialog and how to get the data back out again to see if the user has changed it.

Day 18, "Windows 95 Dialogs and Controls," also includes a utility to be used when designing the playing board for the Snako program. The utility fits into the theme of Day 17, because it makes heavy use of dialog boxes.

Q&A

Q I still don't understand why anyone would ever want to change the mapping mode of a window. What gives?

A There are several different reasons for changing mapping modes, but one of the most important is the fact that device coordinates change radically from system to system. People running one of your programs in high-resolution super VGA modes might have 1024 pixels on the x axis, whereas the next person might have only 640 pixels on the x axis. If you define your main window to be 400×300 pixels, it will be nearly half the size on the second system as on the first. One way to reconcile these differences is to switch to the MM_LOENGLISH mapping mode and define your main window as being 4 inches wide and 3 inches tall. Now your window will be approximately the same size, regardless of what type of system your users own.

Q Why does WinSize call MakeProcInstance in response to WM_CREATE, and FreeProcInstance in response to WM_DESTROY?

A It's important to understand that the decision to do things this way is not in any sense arbitrary. Each call to MakeProcInstance must be matched by one (and only one) call to FreeProcInstance; it's crucial that FreeProcInstance is not called while the dialog is on-screen. The only way to guarantee that things will work out this way is to call MakeProcInstance on the SizeBoxProc right at the very beginning of the program's life, and to free this memory only after the user has decided to destroy the main window. Other plans might accidentally enable calls to FreeProcInstance while the dialog is on-screen, or even worse, try to launch the dialog without calling MakeProcInstance. Once again, you don't need to call MakeProcInstance or FreeProcInstance if you are working strictly in WIN32.

Workshop

The Workshop provides quiz questions to help you solidify your understanding of the material covered and exercises to provide you with experience in using what you've learned. Try to understand the quiz and exercise answers before continuing on to the next chapter. Answers are provided in Appendix A.

Quiz

1. What is a mapping mode?
2. What is a pixel?
3. On a 14-inch monitor in standard VGA mode, is the fundamental unit of the MM_LOMETRIC mapping mode larger or smaller than a pixel?
4. What is a Viewpoint origin?
5. What is the difference between logical coordinates and device coordinates?
6. What is the difference between SetWindowOrg and SetViewportOrg?
7. What is the primary difference between modal and modeless dialogs?
8. What function is used to create a modal dialog?
9. What function is used to create a modeless dialog?
10. What are two differences between dialog procedures and window procedures?

Exercises

1. Before calling CreateDialog, the WinSize program checks to see if hSizeBox is set to NULL. Try removing this line of code and then recompile. What happens if you choose Size dialog in the menu three times in succession?
2. Convert the Size dialog into a modal dialog. What are the advantages and disadvantages of this new arrangement?

17

Advanced Dialogs: Getting and Setting Data

Today you'll learn how to adjust the color of dialogs and how to set and retrieve data from a dialog's controls. Also included in this chapter is an example of how to stretch and shrink bitmaps before you "blit" them to the screen.

Specifically, this chapter contains information about

☐ `SendDlgItemMessage` and `GetDlgItem`

☐ `WM_CTLCOLOR` messages

☐ Using `StretchBlt` to shrink or expand a bitmap before painting it on-screen

Much of this chapter focuses on the WinSize program, which was introduced on Day 16, "Dialog Boxes and Mapping Modes." A new program, called Mapper, is presented near the end of this chapter. Mapper is part of the Snake project (which was introduced on Day 8, "Windows Animation: The Snake Game," and which will be completed in Bonus Day 4, "Snako for Windows"). The Mapper program is presented in this chapter because its two dialogs fit in well with the current theme of dialogs and their controls.

Setting Data in the Size Dialog

When the Size dialog (see Figure 17.1) from the WinSize program appears on-screen, it lists the current coordinates of the main window when measured in the `MM_TEXT`, `MM_LOMETRIC`, `MM_HIMETRIC`, `MM_LOENGLISH`, `MM_HIENGLISH`, and `MM_TWIPS` mapping systems. This section contains a description of how the WinSize program calculates this information and how it displays it inside the dialog.

Figure 17.1.

The Size dialog lists the coordinates of the current window.

Size Dialog				
	Left	Top	Right	Bottom
MMText	-124	-59	125	59
LoMetric	-328	156	331	-156
HiMetric	-3281	1561	3307	-1561
LoEnglish	-129	61	130	-61
HiEnglish	-1292	615	1302	-615
Twips	-1860	885	1875	-885

In brief outline form, the steps are as follows:

☐ The actual calculations are performed in a tight loop that calls `SetMapMode`, `GetClientRect`, and `DPtoLP` in quick succession.

☐ The results of the calculations are placed in an array and then sent in the form of a message to the Size dialog.

☐ The Size dialog places this information in its static controls with a series of calls to `SendDlgItemMessage`.

The next few paragraphs review each of these steps, detailing exactly how they work.

In response to the user-defined CM_SIZEBOX message, the modeless Size dialog is created by a call to CreateDialog. Immediately after this call, WinSize executes an InvalidateRect function call, which ensures that a WM_PAINT message is sent to the main window. (The WinSize_OnPaint function is listed on lines 197-240 of WINSIZE.CPP.)

There are four major steps to using the WinSize_OnPaint function:

1. Copy the user-selected mapping mode into the current device context.
2. Copy the user-selected viewport origin into the current device context.
3. Draw the user-selected shape (whether it's a square or an ellipse).
4. If the Size dialog is on-screen, fill it with the appropriate data.

You have already had a look at how the mapping mode and the viewport origin are set in a Window with calls to SetMapMode and SetViewPortOrgEx. Drawing a rectangle or an ellipse is, for the most part, a simple matter of defining a RECT that encompasses the particular shape. This subject is covered in-depth in Bonus Day 1, "GDI and Metafiles."

This leaves only the fourth part of the WinSize_OnPaint function, which is not executed unless the Size dialog has been created and is made visible on-screen:

```
if (hSizeBox != 0)
  FillSizeBox(hwnd, PaintDC);
```

hSizeBox is the HWND of the Size Dialog. If hSizeBox is not 0, the non-API FillSizeBox procedure is called, and the Size dialog is filled with the window's coordinates (see Figure 17.1.)

The FillSizeBox procedure (line 182) gets passed the main window's HWINDOW and a handle to the current device context:

```
void FillSizeBox(HWND hwnd, HDC PaintDC)
{
  TSizeData SizeData;
  for (int i = 0; i < 6; i++)
  {
    SetMapMode(PaintDC, Modes[i]);
    GetClientRect(hwnd, &SizeData[i]);
    DPtoLP(PaintDC, (LPPOINT)&SizeData[i], 2);
  }
  SendMessage(hSizeBox, WM_SETDATA, 0, (long)&SizeData);
}
```

This code fragment shows how WinSize iterates through the six mapping modes discussed on Day 16. It does so by referencing the following enumerated type, which contains a list of the relevant constants.

```
int Modes[] = {MM_TEXT, MM_LOMETRIC, MM_HIMETRIC,
               MM_LOENGLISH, MM_HIENGLISH, MM_TWIPS};
```

17

The first of the six times `SetMapMode` is called, the `MM_TEXT` constant is used; the second time, the `MM_LOMETRIC` is brought on stage, followed by `MM_HIMETRIC`, and so on.

After the mapping mode is set, the window's current location, expressed in *device coordinates*, is copied into a structure of type `TSizeData`:

```
typedef RECT TSizeData[6];
```

`TSizeData` is an array of our old friend `RECT`, which is just a structure used to define the coordinates of a rectangle by specifying the points comprising its upper-left and lower-right corners.

The purpose of the Size dialog is to give the window's dimensions, not in device coordinates, but in logical coordinates. As a result, a call is made to the `DPtoLP` function, which translates device points to logical points.

Making the Data Visible

At this stage of the game, the WinSize program has the numbers it wants to display. Now it needs to get the numbers out where the viewer can see them.

This is accomplished by first sending the numbers to the Size dialog's window procedure:

```
SendMessage(hSizeBox, WM_SETDATA, 0, (long)&SizeData);
```

Sending information to a dialog is exactly like sending information to a control. There are no new techniques to learn and no new concepts to grasp. The only portion of this code that might be confusing is the typecast in the last parameter. There, WinSize opts to treat the address of the `SizeData` array as a 4-byte `long`.

Of course, the `WM_SETDATA` message is a user-defined message, so it's up to the WinSize program to respond to it (line 501):

```
case WM_SETDATA:
  lpSizeData = (void *)lParam;
  memcpy(SizeData, lpSizeData, sizeof(TSizeData));
  for (i = 0; i < 6; i++)
  {
    sprintf(S, "%d", SizeData[i].left);
    SendDlgItemMessage(hDlg, Indexs[i] + 1,
                       WM_SETTEXT, 0, long(S));
    sprintf(S, "%d", SizeData[i].right);
    SendDlgItemMessage(hDlg, Indexs[i] + 2,
                       WM_SETTEXT, 0, long(S));
    sprintf(S, "%d", SizeData[i].top);
    SendDlgItemMessage(hDlg, Indexs[i] + 3,
                       WM_SETTEXT, 0, long(S));
    sprintf(S, "%d", SizeData[i].bottom);
    SendDlgItemMessage(hDlg, Indexs[i] + 4,
                       WM_SETTEXT, 0, long(S));
```

```
    }
    return TRUE;
```

WinSize battles with the Windows messaging system without the protecting armor of the WindowsX macros. As a result, it's necessary to perform the aesthetically embarrassing task of converting the data referenced by LPARAM into something that can be readily utilized:

```
TSIZEDATA lpSizeData = (void *)lParam;
memcpy(SizeData, lpSizeData, sizeof(TSizeData));
```

The code casts LPARAM as a pointer and then copies the data addressed by the pointer into a variable of type TSizeData.

Now that WinSize has the data in usable form, it converts it into a string and sends it to the static controls on the dialog's surface:

```
sprintf(S, "%d", SizeData[i].left);
SendDlgItemMessage(hDlg, Indexs[i] + 1, WM_SETTEXT, 0, long(S));
```

This code introduces the SendDlgItemMessage function, which acts as a convenient alternative to the SendMessage function. The problem with SendMessage is that it requires an HWND before it can send a message to a control. Obviously, it would be very complicated to keep track of the HWND for each control in a dialog. SendDlgItemMessage lightens the programmer's burden by enabling him or her to use a control's ID in lieu of its HWND.

The *SendDlgItemMessage*

Syntax

```
SendDlgItemMessage(HWND, int, UINT, WPARAM, LPARAM);
```

Here are the parameters to SendDlgItemMessage:

HWND hwndDlg;	HWND of dialog box containing the control
int idDlgItem;	ID of the control
UINT uMsg;	Message sent to the control
WPARAM wParam;	2-byte parameter
LPARAM lParam;	4-byte parameter

Use the SendDlgItemMessage function to send a message to a control located inside a dialog. This function requires the HWND of the dialog and the ID of the control in its first two parameters. After that, everything is exactly the same as with SendMessage. In other words, the next three parameters are the message itself, and then the standard WPARAM and LPARAM fields. There's nothing tricky about SendDlgItemMessage—it's simply a convenient way to call SendMessage when you are working with the controls of a dialog.

Here's an example:

```
SendDlgItemMessage(hDlg, ID_CONTROL, WM_SETTEXT, 0, long(S));
```

17

It's important to understand the close relationship between the `SendMessage` and `SendDlgItemMessage` calls. For instance, the following two calls are entirely equivalent:

```
SendMessage(GetDlgItem(hDlg,Indexs[i] + 1),WM_SETTEXT,0,long(S));
SendDlgItemMessage(hDlg, Indexs[i] + 1, WM_SETTEXT, 0, long(S));
```

`SendDlgItemMessage` lets you sidestep the call to `GetDlgItem` (see the following explanation). Otherwise, it's exactly the same as `SendMessage`.

The *GetDlgItem* Function

Syntax

```
GetDlgItem(HWND, int);
```

`GetDlgItem` can be used to snag the `HWINDOW` of any control that happens to catch your fancy. It's a function that programmers often overlook until the crucial moment in which it becomes absolutely vital to their program; then, they simply have to have it.

Here are the parameters to `GetDlgItem`:

`HWND hwndDlg;`	HWND of the dialog which owns the control
`int idControl;`	The ID of the control

The return value, of course, is the `HWND` of the control.

Here's an example:

```
GetDlgItem(hDlg, ID_CONTROL);
```

There are other ways to set text in the control of a dialog. For instance, you might want to look up the `SetWindowText` API function, as well as the `Static_SetText` and `Edit_SetText` WindowsX macros. Here's how the code would look if you used WindowsX:

```
case WM_SETDATA:
      lpSizeData = (void *)lParam;
      memcpy(SizeData, lpSizeData, sizeof(TSIZEDATA));
      for (i = 0; i < 6; i++)
        {
        sprintf(S, "%d", SizeData[i].left);
        Edit_SetText(GetDlgItem(hDlg, Indexs[i] + 1), S);
        sprintf(S, "%d", SizeData[i].right);
        Edit_SetText(GetDlgItem(hDlg, Indexs[i] + 2), S);
        sprintf(S, "%d", SizeData[i].top);
        Edit_SetText(GetDlgItem(hDlg, Indexs[i] + 3), S);
        sprintf(S, "%d", SizeData[i].bottom);
        Edit_SetText(GetDlgItem(hDlg, Indexs[i] + 4), S);
        }
      return TRUE;
```

For setting text in a dialog, that's the end of the story. It's been such a short story primarily because the idea of sending a message has been one of the primary themes of this book. By now, the `SendMessage`, `PostMessage`, and `SendDlgItemMessage` functions should be old hat to you. `Edit_SetText` runs a slight variation on this theme, but the WindowsX syntax is always so clean

and precise that it rarely needs much explanation. (As a rule, I prefer to use WINDOWSX.H whenever possible. It's safe, more portable, and easier to read.)

To make the code in this section work, WinSize had to do the following:

- ☐ Create a dialog by calling `MakeProcInstance` and `CreateDialog` (16-bit Windows only)
- ☐ Fill out an array with calls to `GetMapMode`, `GetClientRect`, and `DPtoLP`
- ☐ Send the array to a dialog with `SendMessage`
- ☐ Unpackage the array with a typecast
- ☐ Send the individual portions of the array to the appropriate control through `SendDlgItemMessage`

Master this process and digest it so thoroughly that it becomes second nature to you. In doing so, you are laying a foundation that will enable you to advance from an intermediate level to the beginnings of real work on advanced issues.

Of course, setting the text of controls in a dialog is only half the story. The second portion of the tale is getting the text back out. Because there is no need to get the text from the Size dialog, a discussion of this process is included in the next section, where the Make Shape dialog is the focus.

Theory: A Modal Dialog Talks to Its Parent

The Make Shape dialog is a modal dialog that does something a bit unusual: It interacts quite frequently with the program's main window. Specifically, you can change the shape of the figures on the main window by pushing buttons on the modal Make Shape dialog. This demonstrates that a modal dialog isn't isolated from its parent window or from any other part of a program.

This is an important point, and I want to repeat it in a slightly different way. Modal dialogs prevent users from manipulating the main body of a program. For instance, users can't get at the main menu of a program while a modal dialog is on-screen. This same restriction doesn't hold true for programmers. Nothing prevents programmers from sending messages from a dialog to the main body of a program. In other words, from the programmer's point of view, the lines of communication are still wide open—at least in one direction.

Using the linear paradigm, programmers got used to the idea that instruction A would be executed before instruction B, and that C would be executed before instruction D. This orderly progression made it possible for DOS programmers to step through their programs from beginning to end with the debugger. As you've probably noticed by now, the same thing isn't possible in a Windows program. Instead, you must place breakpoints on sections of code you want to examine and then wait until the relevant line is executed and the breakpoint takes effect.

675

In the WinSize program, the `DialogBox` procedure is called; while it's executing, the `WinSize_OnPaint` and `FillSizeBox` routines may be executed. As you'll see in a few moments, this is accomplished by sending a message from the dialog box procedure to the main window. The end effect is that WinSize has access to most of the functionality associated with its main window, even while the "modal" `DialogBox` procedure is executing.

Note: To the uninitiated, a process such as this appears to be Windows magic. You're at point D in your program, the `DialogBox` procedure. Suddenly, you skip to point B, the `WinSize_OnPaint` procedure, and then to the `FillSizeBox` procedure, and then back to point D again. (Use the debugger to see how this works.) Whether this newly found freedom is a blessing or a curse is a question that must be answered by each individual user. Some people enjoy it, some don't. It's up to you.

Practice Getting Data from the Make Shape Dialog

The Make Shape dialog enables the user to take control of the WinSize program. It's a pilot seat from which the user can "steer" the program in whatever direction seems appropriate.

The first order of business in the Make Shape dialog procedure is to initialize the radio buttons on the dialog's surface:

```
case WM_INITDIALOG:
  Button_SetCheck(GetDlgItem(hwnd, ID_RTEXT), 1);
  Button_SetCheck(GetDlgItem(hwnd, ID_RECT), 1);
  Button_SetCheck(GetDlgItem(hwnd, ID_ORGUPLEFT), 1);
  Button_SetCheck(GetDlgItem(hwnd, ID_COMPCORDS), 1);
  return TRUE;
```

Here you can see the usual clarity that you find associated with WindowsX-based code. Prefacing the macros with the word `Button` makes it clear what we are talking to, and the rest of the code is equally easy to read. However, some readers may prefer not to use WindowsX. If such is the case, you can accomplish the same ends by writing:

```
case WM_INITDIALOG:
  SendDlgItemMessage(hwnd, ID_RTEXT, BM_SETCHECK, 1, 0L);
  SendDlgItemMessage(hwnd, ID_RECT, BM_SETCHECK, 1, 0L);
  SendDlgItemMessage(hwnd, ID_ORGUPLEFT, BM_SETCHECK, 1, 0L);
  SendDlgItemMessage(hwnd, ID_COMPCORDS, BM_SETCHECK, 1, 0L);
  return TRUE;
```

By now, this type of code should be quite familiar. The goal is simply to set the default button for each of the major groups on-screen. This is accomplished by sending BM_SETCHECK messages to each of the appropriate controls. Nothing could be simpler.

The heart of the Make Shape dialog procedure is its response to WM_COMMAND messages. Because this is a long and involved process, WinSize handles it in a separate function called DoRectCommand.

The DoRectCommand function (line 343) features a lengthy case statement that executes whenever the user selects one of the push buttons or radio buttons on the dialog's surface. For instance, if the user selects the Draw button, the following code is executed:

```
case ID_DRAW:
  GetUserCords(hwnd);
  InvalidateRect(GetParent(hwnd), NULL, TRUE);
  return TRUE;
```

As you might recall, the edit controls in the Make Shape dialog can be manipulated by the user whenever he or she wants to specify a new set of coordinates for the shape shown on the main window. The purpose of these lines of code is to get the coordinates from the dialog's edit controls and to use these coordinates to describe the size of a shape drawn in the main window's client area.

The GetUserCords function demonstrates the WindowsX way to retrieve data from edit controls in a dialog (line 277):

```
void GetUserCords(HWND hwnd)
{
  char S[100];

  Edit_GetText(GetDlgItem(hwnd, ID_RLEFT), S, 100);
  RLeft = atoi(S);
  Edit_GetText(GetDlgItem(hwnd, ID_RTOP), S, 100);
  RTop = atoi(S);
  Edit_GetText(GetDlgItem(hwnd, ID_RRIGHT), S, 100);
  RRight = atoi(S);
  Edit_GetText(GetDlgItem(hwnd, ID_RBOTTOM), S, 100);
  RBottom = atoi(S);
}
```

Here's an alternate method that does not use WindowsX:

```
void GetUserCords(HWND hwnd)
{
  char S[100];

  GetWindowText(GetDlgItem(hwnd, ID_RLEFT), S, 100);
  RLeft = atoi(S);
  GetWindowText(GetDlgItem(hwnd, ID_RTOP), S, 100);
  RTop = atoi(S);
  GetWindowText(GetDlgItem(hwnd, ID_gRIGHT), S, 100);
  RRight = atoi(S);
  GetWindowText(GetDlgItem(hwnd, ID_RBOTTOM), S, 100);
  RBottom = atoi(S);
}
```

17

In this particular case, WinSize uses `GetWindowText` rather than `Edit_GetText` or a `SendDlgItemMessage` call accompanied by a `WM_GETTEXT` message. I'm showing you this choice so you'll have a wide range of options.

The *GetWindowText* Function

Syntax

```
int GetWindowText(HWND, LPSTR, int)
```

The actual call to `GetWindowText` is very simple. The function requires only three parameters:

☐ The first parameter is the `HWND` of the control containing the text.

☐ The second parameter is a string to hold the information in the control.

☐ The last parameter is the longest possible length of the string.

Here's an example:

```
GetWindowText(hControl, MyStr, 100);
```

After the text has been retrieved from the control, it's translated into numeric form and used in `WinSize_OnPaint` to describe the `RECT`. A rectangle or ellipse is drawn inside the `RECT`.

Once again, the experience you've had in this book allows me to outline this relatively complex process in a few short paragraphs. Naturally, this doesn't mean that getting data from dialogs is not an extremely important part of windows programming. The issue is that you've already seen an in-depth description of how to transfer data in and out of an edit control, static text, push button, radio button, or other control. None of the principles involve change in any significant way because you're working with a dialog instead of a window.

What it all boils down to is that working with dialogs is simply a matter of common sense. For instance, if you want to display a street address from a database in a dialog, here are the steps you would follow:

1. Read the address out of a text or binary file and place it inside a structure.
2. Send this structure to a dialog, just as you sent an array to the dialog in the last section.
3. Use `SetWindowText`, `Edit_SetText`, or `SendDlgItemMessage` to set each individual field of the structure in a separate edit control.
4. Wait until the user presses a button signaling that he or she is finished editing or viewing the address.
5. Retrieve the text from the edit controls with `GetWindowText`, `Edit_GetText`, or `SendDlgItemMessage`.
6. Send the structure back to the main body of the program with a call to `SendMessage`.
7. If the structure has changed, have the main body of the program write the new data to a disk file.

Responding to Changes in Mapping Mode

Before closing this portion of the chapter, it might be worthwhile to take a brief glance at the code that gets executed whenever the user changes mapping modes by selecting a radio button (line 352):

```
case ID_RTEXT:
  ModeCase = TEXT;
  DoDraw(hwnd);
  return TRUE;
```

The ModeCase variable is one of several enumerated types declared in WINSIZE.H. It's used to keep track of the user's current selections:

```
enum TModeCase {TEXT, LOMETRIC, HIMETRIC, LOENGLISH,
                HIENGLISH, TWIPS, ISOTROPIC, ANSITROPIC};
enum TOriginMode {ORG_UPLEFT, ORG_LOWLEFT, ORG_CENTER};
enum TShape {RECTANGLE, CIRCLE};
```

All the radio buttons on the dialog's surface are reflected in the values encompassed by these enumerated types. Therefore, the first order of business after a user selects a button is to set the values of the associated enumerated type. The code performs this function by setting the enumerated variable ModeCase to TEXT.

The next thing to check is whether the user or the WinSize program will select the coordinates (line 333):

```
void DoDraw(HWND hwnd)
{
  if (UseCompCords)
    MakeShape(hwnd);
  SetRectText(hwnd);
}
```

If the chore is left to WinSize, the MakeShape procedure is called and the current device coordinates are translated into Window coordinates with calls to GetClientRect and LPtoDP. This is the same process used in the FillSizeBox procedure.

While still inside MakeShape (line 294), the WinSize program calculates the dimensions of the shape to be drawn:

```
case ORG_CENTER:
  RLeft = -(R.right / 3);
  RTop = -(R.bottom / 3);
  RRight = (R.right / 3);
  RBottom = (R.bottom / 3);
  break;
```

The actual size of the shape isn't important. Instead, the preceding code is designed to assure that the shape is always visible and always covers the same percentage of area in proportion to

the window's total size. Also, the WinSize program makes sure that the shape covers the same area in terms of device coordinates, as long as any one particular viewpoint origin is selected. The logical coordinates, of course, change radically every time the user selects a new mapping mode. This enables the user to see the effects of the various mapping modes on the logical coordinate system.

Controlling the Color of a Dialog

It's almost time to bring the discussion of the WinSize program to a close. The only thing left to do is see how the colors for the dialog are changed.

As it turns out, this moderately complex subject brings us to one of the very few places where you simply have to use #IFDEFs to write portable code. The issue here is that the original 16-bit WM_CTLCOLOR message took three parameters, two of which became 32-bit parameters in WIN32. As a result, this one single message had to be broken into multiple messages under WIN32. (The issue here is that there are only two available parameters, wParam and lParam, and each one can have only 32 bits. Therefore, two 32-bit parameters took up all the available space and left no room for a third parameter.)

Because of this change in structure, the simplest way to write portable code is to use #IFDEFs to separate the control color code that appears in WIN32 and the code that appears in 16-bit Windows. Note, however, that WindowsX can still be used to greatly simplify the code you must write.

When the Size dialog is being initialized, WinSize carefully sets up the appropriate colors for the dialog. If I weren't using WINDOWSX.H, here is how the 16-bit Windows code would look:

```
case WM_CTLCOLOR:
  switch(HIWORD(lParam))
  {
    case CTLCOLOR_STATIC:
    SetTextColor((HDC)wParam, RGB(255, 0, 0));
    SetBkMode((HDC)wParam, TRANSPARENT);
    return (BOOL) GetStockBrush(BLACK_BRUSH);

    case CTLCOLOR_DLG:
    return (BOOL) GetStockBrush(BLACK_BRUSH);
  }
  return (BOOL) NULL;
```

WM_CTLCOLOR messages get sent to a dialog in great flurries—one message for each of the possible controls. In the preceding case, WinSize sets static controls so they have red text on a black background. Notice the use of the SetBkMode call, which makes the background of a static text transparently reflect the color lying beneath it. In this case, the background is simply the surface of the dialog set to the color designated by the standard BLACK_BRUSH.

Here's the way to do the same thing in WIN32:

```
case WM_CTLCOLORSTATIC:
  SetTextColor((HDC)wParam, RGB(255, 0, 0));
  SetBkMode((HDC)wParam, TRANSPARENT);
  return (BOOL) GetStockBrush(BLACK_BRUSH);

case WM_CTLCOLORDLG:
  return (BOOL) GetStockBrush(BLACK_BRUSH);
```

As you can see, WIN32 breaks each type of control color response out into a separate message.

Note: The previous code fragments respond to the CTLCOLOR_STATIC and CTLCOLOR_DLG identifiers. Following is a complete list of these constants as used in WIN16; they're sent to a dialog whenever one of the relevant controls needs to be updated:

CTLCOLOR_BTN	Changes the color of buttons (obsolete)
CTLCOLOR_DLG	Changes the color of dialog boxes
CTLCOLOR_EDIT	Changes the color of edit controls
CTLCOLOR_LISTBOX	Changes the color of list boxes
CTLCOLOR_MSGBOX	Changes the color of message boxes
CTLCOLOR_SCROLLBAR	Changes the color of scrollbars
CTLCOLOR_STATIC	Changes the color of static controls

Here is the corresponding list of messages used in WIN32:

WM_CTLCOLORBTN	The color of a button
WM_CTLCOLORDLG	The color of a dialog
WM_CTLCOLOREDIT	The color of an edit
WM_CTLCOLORLISTBOX	The color of a list box
WM_CTLCOLORMSGBOX	The color of a message box
WM_CTLCOLORSCROLLBAR	The color of a scrollbar
WM_CTLCOLORSTATIC	The color of a static control

In 16-bit windows, the parameters listed in the preceding note are passed in the high word of the LPARAM that accompanies every CTL_COLOR message. The low word of the LPARAM contains the HWND of the control, which is currently being painted. This means that you can distinguish between individual controls, even when they are in the same class, thereby painting one static control red and the next green. Finally, the HDC of the control is passed in the WPARAM parameter, as shown in the previous code fragment.

In 32-bit Windows, the device context is in the WPARAM, and the window handle is in the LPARAM.

If you didn't have WINDOWSX.H, you would have to write the two versions of the code shown above, and ifdef them so one was a 16-bit block and the next a 32-bit block. If you use WindowsX, you can simplify the matter by using message crackers:

```
HBRUSH Shape_OnCtlColor(HWND hwnd, HDC hdc, HWND hwndChild, int type)
{
  switch(type)
  {
    case CTLCOLOR_STATIC:
    case CTLCOLOR_EDIT:
    case CTLCOLOR_BTN:
      /* Set text to white and background to green */
      SetTextColor(hdc, RGB(0, 127, 0));
      SetBkMode(hdc, TRANSPARENT);
      return GreenBrush;

    case CTLCOLOR_DLG:
      return GreenBrush;
  }
  return NULL;
}

#pragma argsused
BOOL CALLBACK MakeShapeProc(HWND hDlg, WORD Msg,
                            WORD wParam, LONG lParam)
{
  switch(Msg)
    #ifdef WIN32
    case WM_CTLCOLORSTATIC:
    case WM_CTLCOLORBTN:
    case WM_CTLCOLOREDIT:
      return HANDLE_WM_CTLCOLORSTATIC(hDlg, wParam,
                                      lParam, Shape_OnCtlColor);
    case WM_CTLCOLORDLG:
      return HANDLE_WM_CTLCOLORDLG(hDlg, wParam,
                                   lParam, Shape_OnCtlColor);
    #else
    case WM_CTLCOLOR:
      return HANDLE_WM_CTLCOLOR(hDlg, wParam, lParam, Shape_OnCtlColor);
    #endif
  }
}
```

The Shape_OnColor function handles both 16- and 32-bit code without forcing the programmer to use conditional defines. The dialog procedure does use conditional defines, but the WindowsX macros make the code easy to read.

Notice that I use the HANDLE_WM_XXX macros rather than HANDLE_MSG. As a rule, HANDLE_MSG was meant to be used in window procedures, and not in dialog procedures.

The Make Shape dialog also responds to `WM_CTLCOLOR` messages. You might want to glance at that code, because it makes use of brushes which aren't just stock objects. When examining the code, notice that the brushes being used are created in the `WM_CREATE` message handler function for the main window and destroyed in the `WM_DESTROY` message handler.

DO	DON'T

DO change the color of dialogs by responding to a `WM_CTLCOLOR` message.

DON'T try to change the color of a dialog in the same way you change the color of a window.

DON'T expect Win32 to handle `WM_CTLCOLOR` the same way as the 16-bit code. This is one of the few places where 16- and 32-bit codes diverge.

DO use the WindowsX message crackers to help sort out the various brands of control color messages sent to your 16- and 32-bit Windows applications.

17

The Mapper Program

After all the hard work you've been doing, it's time to relax with another excerpt from the Snake game (see Listing 17.1). This is a visual programming tool designed to enable programmers to quickly and easily sketch the background of a two-dimensional game board.

Listing 17.1. A program that enables you to design custom playing boards for the Snako program.

```
////////////////////////////////////
//   Program Name: MAPPER.CPP
//   Copyright (c) 1993 by Charlie Calvert
//   Description: Mapper windows program
//   Date: 7/18/93
//   Update for WIN32: 06/10/95
////////////////////////////////////

#define STRICT
#define WIN32_LEAN_AND_MEAN
#include <windows.h>
#include <windowsx.h>
#pragma hdrstop
#include <string.h>
#include <stdio.h>
#include <stdlib.h>
```

continues

Listing 17.1. continued

```c
#include "mapper.h"
#pragma warning (disable: 4068)
#pragma warning (disable: 4100)

// -----------------------------------
// Interface
// -----------------------------------

// Variables
static char szAppName[] = "Mapper";
static HWND MainWindow;
static HINSTANCE hInstance;
static FARPROC lpfnNewBitProc, lpfnArrowBox;
char Map[MaxY][MaxX];
WNDPROC StatProc1, StatProc2;
HBITMAP Grass, Road;
TDAT Dat;

// -----------------------------------
// Initialization
// -----------------------------------

///////////////////////////////////////
// Program entry point
///////////////////////////////////////
#pragma argsused
int WINAPI WinMain(HINSTANCE hInst, HINSTANCE hPrevInstance,
                   LPSTR  lpszCmdParam, int nCmdShow)
{
  MSG  Msg;

  if (!hPrevInstance)
    if (!Register(hInst))
      return FALSE;

  MainWindow = Create(hInst, nCmdShow);
  if (!MainWindow)
    return FALSE;

  while (GetMessage(&Msg, NULL, 0, 0))
  {
     TranslateMessage(&Msg);
     DispatchMessage(&Msg);
  }

  return Msg.wParam;
}

///////////////////////////////////////
// Register the window
///////////////////////////////////////
BOOL Register(HINSTANCE hInst)
{
  WNDCLASS WndClass;
```

```
  WndClass.style          = CS_HREDRAW ¦ CS_VREDRAW;
  WndClass.lpfnWndProc    = WndProc;
  WndClass.cbClsExtra     = 0;
  WndClass.cbWndExtra     = 0;
  WndClass.hInstance      = hInst;
  WndClass.hIcon          = LoadIcon(NULL, IDI_APPLICATION);
  WndClass.hCursor        = LoadCursor(NULL, IDC_ARROW);
  WndClass.hbrBackground  = GetStockBrush(WHITE_BRUSH);
  WndClass.lpszMenuName   = NULL;
  WndClass.lpszClassName  = szAppName;

  return (RegisterClass (&WndClass) != 0);
}


//////////////////////////////////////
// Create the window
//////////////////////////////////////
HWND Create(HINSTANCE hInst, int nCmdShow)
{

  nCmdShow = SW_MAXIMIZE;
  hInstance = hInst;

  HWND hWindow = CreateWindow(szAppName, szAppName,
                              WS_POPUP,
                              CW_USEDEFAULT, CW_USEDEFAULT,
                              CW_USEDEFAULT, CW_USEDEFAULT,
                              NULL, NULL, hInstance, NULL);

  if (hWindow == NULL)
    return hWindow;

  ShowWindow(hWindow, nCmdShow);
  UpdateWindow(hWindow);

  return hWindow;
}

// ----------------------------------------
// WndProc and Implementation
// ----------------------------------------


//////////////////////////////////////
// The Window Procedure
//////////////////////////////////////
LRESULT CALLBACK WndProc(HWND hwnd, UINT Message,
                         WPARAM wParam, LPARAM lParam)
{
  switch(Message)
  {
    case WM_DIALOG: {
      FARPROC OptionsBox =
        MakeProcInstance((FARPROC)OptionsDlgProc, hInstance);
        DialogBox(hInstance, "Options", hwnd, (DLGPROC)OptionsBox);
```

continues

Listing 17.1. continued

```c
          FreeProcInstance(OptionsBox);
        return FALSE;
      }

    case WM_CUSTOMHELP:
      {
      char *S = "MAPPER\n\n"
          "Use this program to design screens for SNAKO\n\n"
          "RSCREEN takes you one screen to the right\n"
          "LSCREEN takes you one screen to the left\n"
          "LEFT takes you one column to the left\n"
          "RIGHT takes you one column to the right\n"
          "To save a screen open the options DIALOG";
        MessageBox(hwnd, S, "Info",
                  MB_OK | MB_ICONINFORMATION);
        return FALSE;
      }
      HANDLE_MSG(hwnd, WM_CREATE, Mapper_OnCreate);
      HANDLE_MSG(hwnd, WM_DESTROY, Mapper_OnDestroy);
      HANDLE_MSG(hwnd, WM_LBUTTONDOWN, Mapper_OnLButtonDown);
      HANDLE_MSG(hwnd, WM_RBUTTONDOWN, Mapper_OnRButtonDown);
      HANDLE_MSG(hwnd, WM_PAINT, Mapper_OnPaint);
      default: return Mapper_DefProc(hwnd, Message, wParam, lParam);
    }
}

int ReadArray(HWND hwnd)
{
  FILE * fp;

  if ((fp = fopen("Screen.Dta", "r")) == NULL)
  {
    MessageBox(hwnd, "Can't find SCREEN.DTA" , NULL, MB_OK);
    return 0;
  }

  fread(&Map, sizeof(Map), 1, fp);
  fclose(fp);

  for (int i = 0; i < MaxY; i++)
    for (int j = 0; j < MaxX; j++)
      if (Map[i][j] != 1)
        Map[i][j] = 2;

  return 1;
}

//////////////////////////////////////
// Handle WM_CREATE
//////////////////////////////////////
#pragma argsused
BOOL Mapper_OnCreate(HWND hwnd, CREATESTRUCT FAR* lpCreateStruct)
{
  Grass = LoadBitmap(hInstance, "Grass");
  Road = LoadBitmap(hInstance, "Road");
```

```
        if ((!Grass) ¦¦ (!Road))
        {
          MessageBox(hwnd, "Bitmaps missing!",
                     "Fatal", MB_OK ¦ MB_ICONSTOP);
          return FALSE;
        }

        int X = GetSystemMetrics(SM_CXSCREEN);

        if (X == 1024)
        {
          Dat.GrassX = Dat.GrassY = 32;
          Dat.SizeX = Dat.SizeY = 32;
        }

        if (X == 800)
        {
          Dat.GrassX = Dat.GrassY = 25;
          Dat.SizeX = Dat.SizeY = 25;
        }

        if (X == 640)
        {
          Dat.GrassX = Dat.GrassY = 20;
          Dat.SizeX = Dat.SizeY = 20;
        }

      Dat.SPos = 0;
      Dat.MenuSpace = 3;

      lpfnArrowBox =
          MakeProcInstance((FARPROC)ArrowDlgProc, hInstance);
          CreateDialog(hInstance, "Arrows", hwnd, (DLGPROC)lpfnArrowBox);
          ReadArray(hwnd);

      return TRUE;
}

//////////////////////////////////////
// Handle WM_DESTROY
//////////////////////////////////////
#pragma argsused
void Mapper_OnDestroy(HWND hwnd)
{
  DeleteObject(Road);
  DeleteObject(Grass);
  FreeProcInstance(lpfnArrowBox);
  PostQuitMessage(0);
}

//////////////////////////////////////
// OnRButtonDown
//////////////////////////////////////
#pragma argsused
```

continues

687

Listing 17.1. continued

```c
void Mapper_OnRButtonDown(HWND hwnd, BOOL fDoubleClick,
                          int x, int y, UINT keyFlags)
{
  char BoxX = (x / Dat.GrassX) + Dat.SPos;
  char BoxY = (y / Dat.GrassY) - Dat.MenuSpace;
  Map[BoxY][BoxX] = 2;
  InvalidateRect(hwnd, NULL, FALSE);
}


//////////////////////////////////////
// OnLButtonDown
//////////////////////////////////////
#pragma argsused
void Mapper_OnLButtonDown(HWND hwnd, BOOL fDoubleClick,
                          int x, int y, UINT keyFlags)
{
  char BoxX = (x / Dat.GrassX) + Dat.SPos;
  char BoxY = (y / Dat.GrassY) - Dat.MenuSpace;
  Map[BoxY][BoxX] = 1;
  InvalidateRect(hwnd, NULL, FALSE);
}


//////////////////////////////////////
// PAINT Bitmaps
// The GrassX * MenuSpace leaves room for menu
//////////////////////////////////////
void PaintBitmaps(HDC PaintDC, HDC GrassDC, HDC RoadDC)
{
  for (int i = 0; i < MaxY; i++)
    for (int j = Dat.SPos; j < MaxX; j++)
    {
      if (Map[i][j] == 1)
        BitBlt(PaintDC, (j - Dat.SPos) * Dat.GrassX,
               (i * Dat.GrassY) + (Dat.GrassX * Dat.MenuSpace),
               Dat.GrassX, Dat.GrassY, GrassDC, 0, 0, SRCCOPY);
      else
        BitBlt(PaintDC, (j - Dat.SPos) * Dat.GrassX,
               (i * Dat.GrassY) + (Dat.GrassX * Dat.MenuSpace),
               Dat.GrassX, Dat.GrassY, RoadDC, 0, 0, SRCCOPY);
    }
}


//////////////////////////////////////
// WM_PAINT
//////////////////////////////////////
void Mapper_OnPaint(HWND hwnd)
{
  PAINTSTRUCT PaintStruct;
  HBITMAP OldGrass, OldRoad, OldGrass1, OldRoad1;

  HDC PaintDC = BeginPaint(hwnd, &PaintStruct);

  HDC TGrassDC = CreateCompatibleDC(PaintDC);
  HDC TRoadDC = CreateCompatibleDC(PaintDC);
```

```
  HDC GrassDC = CreateCompatibleDC(PaintDC);
  HDC RoadDC = CreateCompatibleDC(PaintDC);
  HBITMAP TGrass =
    CreateCompatibleBitmap(PaintDC, Dat.GrassX, Dat.GrassY);
  HBITMAP TRoad =
    CreateCompatibleBitmap(PaintDC, Dat.GrassX, Dat.GrassY);

  OldGrass = SelectBitmap(TGrassDC, Grass);
  OldRoad = SelectBitmap(TRoadDC, Road);
  OldGrass1 = SelectBitmap(GrassDC, TGrass);
  OldRoad1 = SelectBitmap(RoadDC, TRoad);

  StretchBlt(GrassDC, 0, 0, Dat.GrassX, Dat.GrassY,
             TGrassDC, 0, 0, BITWIDTH, BITHEIGHT, SRCCOPY);
  StretchBlt(RoadDC, 0, 0, Dat.GrassX, Dat.GrassY,
             TRoadDC, 0, 0, BITWIDTH, BITHEIGHT, SRCCOPY);

  PaintBitmaps(PaintDC, GrassDC, RoadDC);

  SelectBitmap(TGrassDC, OldGrass);
  SelectBitmap(TRoadDC, OldRoad);
  SelectBitmap(GrassDC, OldGrass1);
  SelectBitmap(RoadDC, OldRoad1);
  DeleteObject(TRoad);
  DeleteObject(TGrass);

  DeleteDC(GrassDC);
  DeleteDC(RoadDC);
  DeleteDC(TGrassDC);
  DeleteDC(TRoadDC);

  EndPaint(hwnd, &PaintStruct);
}

// ------------------------------------
// The Dialog procs
// ------------------------------------

/////////////////////////////////////
// Save Array
/////////////////////////////////////
int SaveArray(HWND hwnd)
{
  FILE * fp;

  if ((fp = fopen("screen.dta", "w+")) == NULL)
  {
    MessageBox(hwnd, "Can't save SCREEN.DTA", NULL, MB_OK);
    return 0;
  }

  fwrite(&Map, sizeof(Map), 1, fp);
  fclose(fp);

  MessageBox(hwnd, "SCREEN.DTA saved", "Success", MB_OK);
```

continues

Listing 17.1. continued

```
    return 1;
}

///////////////////////////////////////
//  The Options Dialog Procedure
///////////////////////////////////////
#pragma argsused
BOOL CALLBACK OptionsDlgProc(HWND hDlg, WORD Message,
                            WPARAM wParam, LPARAM lParam)
{
  char S[100];
  HWND hwnd1, hwnd2;

  switch(Message)
  {
    case WM_DESTROY:
      hwnd1 = GetDlgItem(hDlg, ID_BITMAP1);
      hwnd2 = GetDlgItem(hDlg, ID_BITMAP2);
      SubclassWindow(hwnd1, StatProc1);
      SubclassWindow(hwnd2, StatProc2);
      FreeProcInstance(lpfnNewBitProc);
      return TRUE;

    case WM_INITDIALOG:
      itoa(Dat.GrassX, S, 10);
      SetWindowText(GetDlgItem(hDlg, ID_XSIZE), S);
      itoa(Dat.GrassY, S, 10);
      SetWindowText(GetDlgItem(hDlg, ID_YSIZE), S);

      itoa(MaxX, S, 10);
      SetWindowText(GetDlgItem(hDlg, ID_NUMX), S);
      itoa(MaxY, S, 10);
      SetWindowText(GetDlgItem(hDlg, ID_NUMY), S);

      lpfnNewBitProc =
      MakeProcInstance(FARPROC(BitmapProc), hInstance);
      hwnd1 = GetDlgItem(hDlg, ID_BITMAP1);
      StatProc1 = SubclassWindow(hwnd1, lpfnNewBitProc);
      hwnd2 = GetDlgItem(hDlg, ID_BITMAP2);
      StatProc2 = SubclassWindow(hwnd2, lpfnNewBitProc);
      return TRUE;

    case WM_COMMAND:
      switch(wParam)
      {
        case IDOK:
        case IDCANCEL:
          EndDialog(hDlg, TRUE);
          return TRUE;

        case ID_SAVE:
          SaveArray(hDlg);
          return TRUE;
```

```
        case ID_HELP:
          PostMessage(GetParent(hDlg), WM_CUSTOMHELP, 0, 0);
          return TRUE;
      }
  }
  return FALSE;
}


BOOL ExitMapper(HWND hDlg)
{
  int Result = MessageBox(hDlg, "Are you sure you want to quit?",
                "Are we thinking?", MB_YESNO | MB_ICONQUESTION);
  if (Result == IDYES)
  {
    SendMessage(GetParent(hDlg), WM_CLOSE, 0, 0);
    return TRUE;
  }
  else
    return FALSE;
}

//////////////////////////////////////
// HandleCommand
//////////////////////////////////////
BOOL HandleCommand(HWND hDlg, WPARAM wParam)
{
  switch(wParam)
  {
    case IDOK:
    case IDCANCEL:
      PostMessage(hDlg, WM_CLOSE, 0, 0);
      return TRUE;

    case ID_RIGHT:
      Dat.SPos++;
      InvalidateRect(GetParent(hDlg), NULL, TRUE);
      return TRUE;

    case ID_LEFT:
      Dat.SPos—;
      if (Dat.SPos < 0)
        Dat.SPos = 0;
      InvalidateRect(GetParent(hDlg), NULL, TRUE);
      return TRUE;

    case ID_RSCREEN:
      if (Dat.SPos < JUMPSPACE)
        Dat.SPos = JUMPSPACE;
      else
        if (Dat.SPos < JUMPSPACE * 2)
          Dat.SPos = JUMPSPACE * 2;
```

continues

Listing 17.1. continued

```
            else
               if (Dat.SPos < JUMPSPACE * 3)
                 Dat.SPos = JUMPSPACE * 3;
               else
                 Dat.SPos = JUMPSPACE * 3;
          InvalidateRect(GetParent(hDlg), NULL, TRUE);
          return TRUE;

      case ID_LSCREEN:
        if (Dat.SPos <= JUMPSPACE)
          Dat.SPos = 0;
        else
          if (Dat.SPos <= JUMPSPACE * 2)
            Dat.SPos = JUMPSPACE;
          else
            if (Dat.SPos <= JUMPSPACE * 3)
              Dat.SPos = JUMPSPACE * 2;
            else
              Dat.SPos = JUMPSPACE * 3;
        InvalidateRect(GetParent(hDlg), NULL, TRUE);
        return TRUE;

      case ID_DIALOG:
        PostMessage(GetParent(hDlg), WM_DIALOG, 0, 0);
        break;

      case ID_HELP:
        PostMessage(GetParent(hDlg), WM_CUSTOMHELP, 0, 0);
        break;

      case ID_QUIT:
        ExitMapper(hDlg);
        return TRUE;
  }

  return FALSE;
}

///////////////////////////////////////
//  The Bitmap Dialog Procedure
///////////////////////////////////////
LRESULT CALLBACK BitmapProc(HWND hwnd, UINT Message,
                                WPARAM wParam, LPARAM lParam)
{
  LRESULT lResult = 0;
  BOOL CallOrig = TRUE;
  HDC PaintDC, MemDC;
  HBITMAP OldBitmap;
  PAINTSTRUCT PaintStruct;

  #ifdef WIN32
  LONG id = GetWindowLong(hwnd, GWL_ID);
  #else
  WORD id = GetWindowWord(hwnd, GWW_ID);
  #endif
```

```
switch(Message)
{
   BITMAP Bits;

   case WM_PAINT:
     PaintDC = BeginPaint(hwnd, &PaintStruct);

     MemDC = CreateCompatibleDC(PaintDC);
     switch(id)
     {
       case ID_BITMAP1:
         OldBitmap = SelectBitmap(MemDC, Road);
         break;
       case ID_BITMAP2:
         OldBitmap = SelectBitmap(MemDC, Grass);
         break;
       case ID_BITMAP3:
         break;
       case ID_BITMAP4:
         break;
     }
     GetObject(Grass, sizeof(BITMAP), &Bits);
     BitBlt(PaintDC, 1, 1, Bits.bmWidth, Bits.bmHeight,
            MemDC, 0, 0, SRCCOPY);
     SelectBitmap(MemDC, OldBitmap);
     DeleteDC(MemDC);

     EndPaint(hwnd, &PaintStruct);
     CallOrig = FALSE;
     break;
   }

   if (CallOrig)
    if (id == ID_BITMAP1)
      lResult = CallWindowProc(StatProc1, hwnd,
                               Message, wParam, lParam);
    else
      lResult = CallWindowProc(StatProc2, hwnd,
                               Message, wParam, lParam);

   return lResult;
}

/////////////////////////////////////
//  The Arrow Dialog Procedure
/////////////////////////////////////
#pragma argsused
BOOL CALLBACK ArrowDlgProc(HWND hDlg, WORD Message,
                           WPARAM wParam, LPARAM lParam)
{
  switch(Message)
  {
    case WM_COMMAND:
      return HandleCommand(hDlg, wParam);
```

continues

Listing 17.1. continued

```
        case WM_CLOSE:
          ExitMapper(hDlg);
          return TRUE;
    }
    return FALSE;
}
```

Listing 17.2 shows the header file for Mapper.

Listing 17.2. MAPPER.H.

```
//////////////////////////////////////
//   Program Name: MAPPER.H
//   Copyright (c) 1993 by Charlie Calvert
//   Description: Mapper windows program
//   Date: 07/18/93
//   Update for WIN32: 06/10/95
//////////////////////////////////////

// Const
#define WM_DIALOG (WM_USER + 0x100)
#define WM_CUSTOMHELP (WM_USER + 0x101)

// Arrows Dialog
#define ID_LEFT      150
#define ID_RIGHT     251
#define ID_DIALOG    252
#define ID_QUIT      253
#define ID_START     254
#define ID_END       255
#define ID_RSCREEN   256
#define ID_LSCREEN   257
#define ID_HELP      1001

// Options dialog constnants
#define ID_XSIZE    101
#define ID_YSIZE    102
#define ID_NUMX     103
#define ID_NUMY     104
#define ID_SAVE     105
#define ID_BITMAP1 120
#define ID_BITMAP2 121
#define ID_BITMAP3 122
#define ID_BITMAP4 123

#define MaxY 21
#define MaxX 4 * 32

#define BITHEIGHT 32
#define BITWIDTH 25

#define JUMPSPACE 32
```

```
// Types
struct TDAT
{
  int MenuSpace;
  int SizeX, SizeY;
  int SPos;
  int GrassX;
  int GrassY;
};

// Declarations for class Mapper
#define Mapper_DefProc      DefWindowProc
BOOL Mapper_OnCreate(HWND hwnd,
                     CREATESTRUCT FAR* lpCreateStruct);
void Mapper_OnDestroy(HWND hwnd);
void Mapper_OnMouseMove(HWND hwnd, int x, int y, UINT keyFlags);
void Mapper_OnLButtonDown(HWND hwnd, BOOL fDoubleClick,
                          int x, int y, UINT keyFlags);
void Mapper_OnRButtonDown(HWND hwnd, BOOL fDoubleClick,
                          int x, int y, UINT keyFlags);
void Mapper_OnPaint(HWND hwnd);

// Procs
LRESULT CALLBACK WndProc(HWND hwnd, UINT Message,
                         WPARAM wParam, LPARAM lParam);
LRESULT CALLBACK BitmapProc(HWND hwnd, UINT Message,
                            WPARAM wParam, LPARAM lParam);
BOOL Register(HINSTANCE hInst);
HWND Create(HINSTANCE hInst, int nCmdShow);
BOOL CALLBACK OptionsDlgProc(HWND hDlg, WORD Message,
                             WPARAM wParam, LPARAM lParam);
BOOL CALLBACK ArrowDlgProc(HWND hDlg, WORD Message,
                           WPARAM wParam, LPARAM lParam);
```

Listing 17.3 shows the resource file for Mapper.

Listing 17.3. MAPPER.RC.

```
1: //////////////////////////////////////////////////////////
2: //   Program Name: MAPPER.RC
3: //   Programmer: Charlie Calvert
4: //   Description: Resource file for Mapper Windows program
5: //   Date: 9/08/93
6: //////////////////////////////////////////////////////////
7:
8: #include "windows.h"
9: #include "mapper.h"
10:
11: ROAD BITMAP "road2.bmp"
12: GRASS BITMAP "grass.bmp"
13:
14: #define STY_PUSH WS_CHILD ¦ WS_VISIBLE ¦ WS_TABSTOP
15: #define STY_TEXT SS_BLACKFRAME ¦ WS_CHILD ¦ WS_VISIBLE ¦ WS_GROUP
```

continues

695

Listing 17.3. continued

```
16: #define STY_TEXT2 SS_LEFT ¦ WS_CHILD ¦ WS_VISIBLE ¦ WS_GROUP
17:
18: Options DIALOG 37, 35, 184, 118
19: STYLE DS_MODALFRAME ¦ WS_POPUP ¦ WS_CAPTION ¦ WS_SYSMENU
20: CAPTION "Options"
21: BEGIN
22:     PUSHBUTTON "Close", IDOK, 3, 98, 52, 14, STY_PUSH
23:     PUSHBUTTON "Save", ID_SAVE, 66, 98, 52, 14, STY_PUSH
24:     LTEXT "XSize:", -1, 7, 9, 22, 8, STY_TEXT2
25:     LTEXT "YSize:", -1, 6, 32, 23, 8, STY_TEXT2
26:     LTEXT "", ID_XSIZE, 30, 9, 25, 12
27:     LTEXT "", ID_YSIZE, 30, 32, 25, 12
28:     LTEXT "NumX:", -1, 7, 58, 22, 8, STY_TEXT2
29:     LTEXT "NumY:", -1, 6, 80, 23, 8, STY_TEXT2
30:     LTEXT "", ID_NUMX, 30, 58, 25, 12
31:     LTEXT "", ID_NUMY, 30, 80, 25, 12
32:     PUSHBUTTON "Help", ID_HELP, 129, 98, 52, 14, STY_PUSH
33:     CONTROL "Text", ID_BITMAP1, "STATIC", STY_TEXT, 75,15,32,32
34:     CONTROL "Text", ID_BITMAP2, "STATIC", STY_TEXT, 129,15,32,32
35:     CONTROL "Text", ID_BITMAP3, "STATIC", STY_TEXT, 129,51,32,32
36:     CONTROL "Text", ID_BITMAP4, "STATIC", STY_TEXT, 75,51,32,32
37:     CONTROL "", 104, "button",
38:     BS_GROUPBOX ¦ WS_CHILD ¦ WS_VISIBLE, 63, 3, 108, 88
39: END
40:
41: Arrows DIALOG 92, 38, 102, 75
42: STYLE WS_POPUP ¦ WS_VISIBLE ¦ WS_CAPTION
43: CAPTION "Directions"
44: BEGIN
45:   PUSHBUTTON "Start", ID_START, 0, 0, 34, 25, STY_PUSH
46:   PUSHBUTTON "Left", ID_LEFT, 0, 25, 34, 25, STY_PUSH
47:   PUSHBUTTON "LScreen", ID_LSCREEN, 0, 50, 34, 25, STY_PUSH
48:   PUSHBUTTON "Dialog", ID_DIALOG, 34, 0, 34, 25, STY_PUSH
49:   PUSHBUTTON "QUIT", ID_QUIT, 34, 25, 34, 25, STY_PUSH
50:   PUSHBUTTON "Help", ID_HELP, 34, 50, 34, 25, STY_PUSH
51:   PUSHBUTTON "End", ID_END, 68, 0, 34, 25, STY_PUSH
52:   PUSHBUTTON "Right", ID_RIGHT, 68, 25, 34, 25, STY_PUSH
53:   PUSHBUTTON "RScreen", ID_RSCREEN, 68, 50, 34, 25, STY_PUSH
54: END
```

ROAD2.BMP (25×32)

GRASS.BMP (25×32)

Listing 17.4 shows the definition file for Mapper.

Listing 17.4. MAPPER.DEF.

```
; MAPPER.DEF

NAME          Mapper
DESCRIPTION   'Mapper Window'
CODE          PRELOAD MOVEABLE DISCARDABLE
DATA          PRELOAD MOVEABLE MULTIPLE
HEAPSIZE      4096
STACKSIZE     5120
```

Listing 17.5 shows the Borland makefile for Mapper.

Listing 17.5. MAPPER.MAK (Borland).

```
# Mapper.mak

BCROOT = $(MAKEDIR)\..
INCPATH= $(BCROOT)\INCLUDE
LIBPATH= $(BCROOT)\LIB

!if !$d(WIN16)
COMPILER = BCC32.EXE
RCCOMPILER = BRC32.EXE -w32
FLAGS    = -WE -v -w4
!else
COMPILER = BCC.EXE
RCCOMPILER = BRC.EXE
FLAGS    = -WE -ml -v -w4
!endif

APPNAME = Mapper

# link
$(APPNAME).exe: $(APPNAME).obj $(APPNAME).def $(APPNAME).res
  $(COMPILER) $(FLAGS) $(APPNAME).obj
  $(RCCOMPILER) $(APPNAME).res

# compile
$(APPNAME).obj: $(APPNAME).cpp
  $(COMPILER) -c $(FLAGS) $(APPNAME).cpp

# resource
$(APPNAME).res: $(APPNAME).rc
  $(RCCOMPILER) -R -I$(INCPATH) $(APPNAME).RC
```

Listing 17.6 shows the Microsoft makefile for Mapper.

Listing 17.6. MAPPER.MAK (Microsoft).

```
# MAPPER.MAK

APPNAME=MAPPER
TARGETOS=WIN95
APPVER=4.0
OBJS=$(APPNAME).OBJ

!include <win32.mak>

all: $(APPNAME).exe

# Update the resource if necessary

$(APPNAME).res: $(APPNAME).rc $(APPNAME).h
  $(rc) $(rcflags) $(rcvars) $(APPNAME).rc

# Update the object files if necessary

# compile
.cpp.obj:
  $(cc) $(cflags) $(cvars) $(cdebug) $<

# Update the executable file if necessary.

$(APPNAME).exe: $(OBJS) $(APPNAME).res
  $(link) $(linkdebug) $(guiflags) -out:$(APPNAME).exe \
  $(OBJS) $(APPNAME).res $(guilibs) comctl32.lib
```

Figure 17.2 shows the Mapper program, which contains two dialogs. One dialog is on-screen whenever the program is in memory.

The Mapper program is a utility you can use to design the playing board for the Snake program. Snake, as you might recall, is an arcade game (started Day 8). Bonus Day 4 completes the discussion of this game.

The original version of the Snake program had an entirely blank playing field on which the Snake roved at will. The more advanced version, to be presented on Bonus Day 4, has a background consisting of a road weaving back and forth on a grassy plane, as shown in Figure 17.3. The rules of the game declare that the snake must stay on the road, and that it will die if it's accidentally steered onto the grass.

Figure 17.2.

The Mapper program.

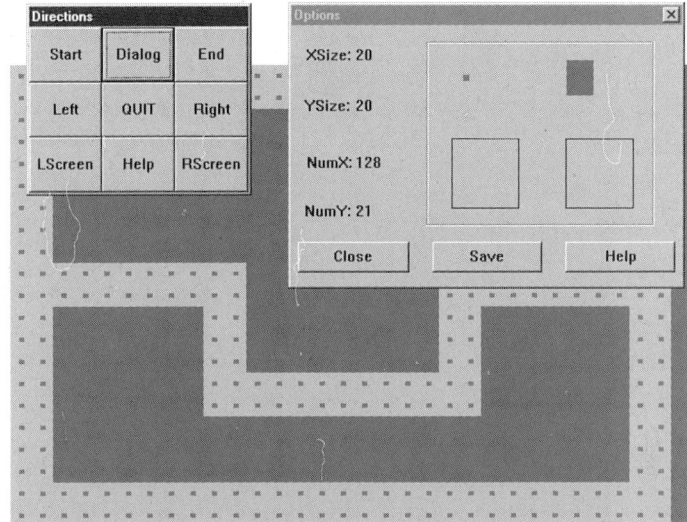

Figure 17.3.

A screen shot from the complete Snako program.

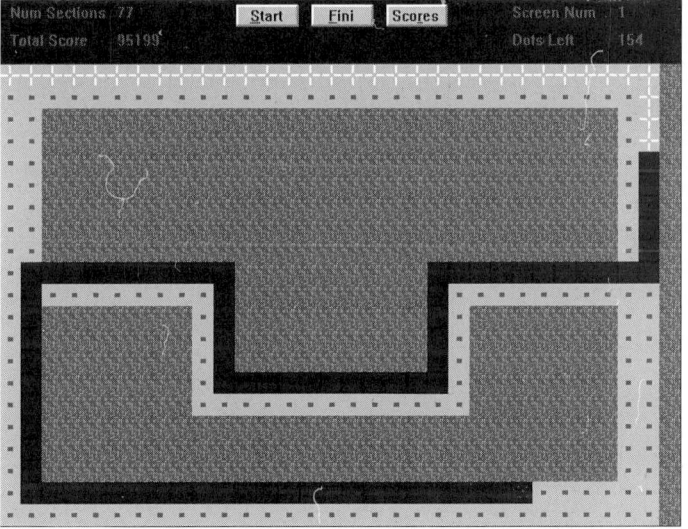

The game consists of a series of levels, where each level has a more complex pattern than the last. Furthermore, each level consists of four screens. Each time the snake erases all the dots on one screen, it is given a bridge to the next screen. When it has completed all four screens on one level, it starts again on the next level. The screens are arranged from left to right, as shown in Figure 17.4. When the snake completes the first screen in a series, it moves to the screen on its right, and so on, until a level is completed.

Figure 17.4.

Four screens form each level of the Snako program.

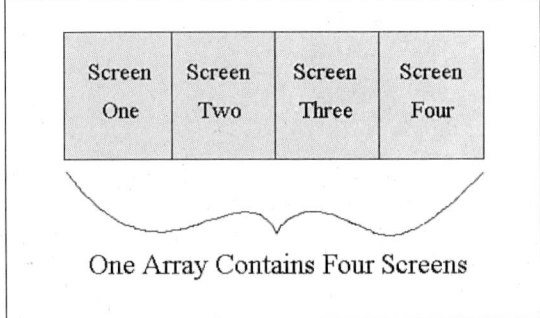

Each level is represented internally by an array of bitmaps 15 squares high and 100 squares wide. Here, for instance, is an excerpt from that array, showing the data necessary to represent one quarter of a level, or one screen:

```
int AnArry[15][25]   = {
{2,2,2,2,2,2,1,1,1,1,1,1,1,1,1,1,1,1,1,1,1,1,1,1,1},
{2,2,2,2,2,2,1,1,1,1,1,1,1,1,1,1,1,1,1,1,1,1,1,1,1},
{1,1,1,1,2,2,1,1,1,1,1,1,1,1,1,1,1,1,1,1,2,2,2,2,2},
{1,1,1,1,2,2,2,2,2,2,2,2,2,2,1,1,1,1,1,2,2,2,2,2,2},
{1,1,1,1,2,2,2,2,2,2,2,2,2,2,1,1,1,1,1,2,2,1,1,1,1},
{1,1,1,1,2,2,1,1,1,1,1,1,1,2,2,1,1,1,1,1,2,2,1,1,1},
{1,1,1,1,2,2,1,1,1,1,1,1,1,2,2,1,1,1,1,1,2,2,1,1,1},
{1,1,1,1,2,2,1,1,1,1,1,1,1,2,2,1,1,1,1,1,2,2,1,1,1},
{1,1,1,1,2,2,1,1,1,1,1,1,1,2,2,2,2,2,2,2,2,2,1,1,1},
{1,1,1,1,2,2,1,1,1,1,1,1,1,2,2,2,2,2,2,2,2,2,1,1,1},
{1,1,1,1,2,2,1,1,1,1,1,1,1,1,2,2,1,1,1,1,1,1,1,1,1},
{1,1,1,1,2,2,1,1,1,1,1,1,1,1,2,2,1,1,1,1,1,1,1,1,1},
{1,1,1,1,2,2,1,1,1,1,1,1,1,1,2,2,1,1,1,1,1,1,1,1,1},
{1,1,1,1,2,2,2,2,2,2,2,2,2,1,1,2,2,1,1,1,1,1,1,1,1},
{1,1,1,1,2,2,2,2,2,2,2,2,2,1,1,2,2,1,1,1,1,1,1,1,1}
};
```

Any spot with a 1 contains a bitmap depicting a square of grass, whereas any section with a 2 contains a section of road.

If programmers work directly with arrays of numerical values, designing the screens for each playing level would be an extremely tedious, time-consuming, and error-prone process. The whole purpose of the Mapper program is to simplify this chore to the point that you can concentrate on design issues when you are constructing an array. More specifically, the Mapper program is a visual programming tool that enables you to design screens by clicking them with the mouse. For instance, a left-click of the mouse turns a square into a grass patch, and a right-click turns it into a section of road.

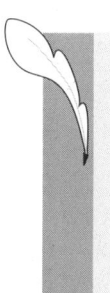

> **Note:** When you work with the Mapper program, you'll find that certain features are hard coded into this implementation. For instance, there is only support for two different bitmaps, and for only one particular size of map array. As it turns out, this program represents an early implementation of a more flexible tool that can be used to design the background for any game or application that has a two-dimensional background made from two or more bitmaps. For the purposes of this chapter, the simple version shown here is probably more appropriate than the complex code used to create a more flexible tool.

17

Mapper from the Programmer's Perspective

The main purpose of the Mapper program is utilitarian. That is, it's meant primarily to be a tool for designing two-dimensional screens. However, it does contain one important new programming trick, as well as a review of several important programming techniques. Because of space considerations, I only have time to briefly mention the review issues; then, I'll go into a short description of the important new technique presented in this program.

This book has been very code-heavy. I've presented a new program in all but one chapter, and most of these programs have been fairly long. I do this because I believe examples are one of the best possible learning tools. The Mapper program gives several additional coding examples from which to learn:

☐ Mapper shows how to subclass a static control so that it can be used as a setting for displaying a bitmap on a dialog. This is an important technique utilized by many programmers. The subclassed static control resides on the Options dialog. The actual subclassed window procedure, `BitmapProc`, begins on line 475. Notice that instead of calling `SetWindowLong`, the Mapper program subclasses the window with a call to the WindowsX macro named `SubClassWindow`.

☐ Mapper also contains two dialogs—one modal and the other modeless. The modeless dialog, called the Arrow dialog (Figure 17.4), appears when the program is first launched. It's destroyed only when the rest of the program is closed. The Arrow dialog is interesting primarily because it serves as an alternative form of a menu. The Mapper program needs this kind of tool because I wanted to leave open the possibility that the program would be used to design a screen that takes up the entire available display, with no room for a menu at the top.

Something New: *StretchBlt*

Like the Snake1 program presented on Day 8, the Mapper program has to be smart enough to be shown in multiple resolutions. Specifically, it "knows" about 640×480 displays, 800×600 displays, and 1024×768 displays. The resolution to this problem in Chapter 8 was fairly simple, but matters are more complex in this case. The problem is that the bitmaps depicting the grass and the road are both 25×32 pixels. Mapper (and Snako) must be able to have 32 of these bitmaps per column, with the left-most bitmap touching the left edge of the screen and the right-most touching the right edge of the screen. This has to be done regardless of the current screen resolution.

Of course, one solution would have been to have three different sets of bitmaps, one for each size screen. This is a reasonable solution to the problem. However, I decided against it, because it puts additional weight on the artist.

The solution Mapper utilizes involves the StretchBlt function, which enables you to shrink or expand a given bitmap to fit a particular set of dimensions.

The *StretchBlt* Function

```
BOOL StretchBlt(HDC, int, int, int, int,
                HDC, int, int, int, int, DWORD)
```

The StretchBlt function "blits" a bitmap from one device context to another, while automatically stretching or shrinking the bitmap to fit the designated destination rectangle. Here is an in-depth look at the parameters:

HDC hdcDest;	The destination device context
int nXOriginDest;	The x coordinate of the destination
int nYOriginDest;	The y coordinate of the destination
int nWidthDest;	The width of the destination
int nHeightDest;	The height of the destination
HDC hdcSrc;	The source device context
int nXOriginSrc;	The x coordinate of the source rectangle

int nYOriginSrc;	The y coordinate of the source rectangle
int nWidthSrc;	The width of the source rectangle
int nHeightSrc;	The height of the source rectangle
DWORD fdwRop;	Logical raster operation (as SRCCOPY)

Here's an example:

```
StretchBlt(PaintDC, 0, 0, 25, 25,
MemryDC, 0, 0, 32, 32, SRCCOPY);
```

A brief examination of the StretchBlt call shows that it's very similar to BitBlt. When used in the Mapper program, however, a few curves are thrown at the programmer; these curves require a little special attention.

The big complication stems from the fact that StretchBlt is a relatively time-consuming call. The Mapper program, on the other hand, has to blit not one, but 32×21, or 672 bitmaps to the screen. StretchBlt, however, requires too many clock cycles for a function that needs to be called 672 times in a row.

The solution is to stretch each of the program's two bitmaps one time, and then to blit the resulting device contexts to the screen. In other words, Mapper stretches the bitmaps into shape, and then works with these newly created bitmaps rather than the originals.

The following excerpts from lines 270-297 of MAPPER.CPP show how the Mapper OnPaint function would look if the program handled only one bitmap at a time:

```
HDC TGrassDC = CreateCompatibleDC(PaintDC);
HDC GrassDC = CreateCompatibleDC(PaintDC);

HBITMAP TGrass =
CreateCompatibleBitmap(PaintDC, Dat.GrassX, Dat.GrassY);

OldGrass = SelectBitmap(TGrassDC, Grass);
OldGrass1 = SelectBitmap(GrassDC, TGrass);

StretchBlt(GrassDC, 0, 0, Dat.GrassX, Dat.GrassY,
TGrassDC, 0, 0, 32, 32, SRCCOPY);

... // Code to BitBlt GrassDC to the screen 200 or so times

SelectBitmap(TGrassDC, OldGrass);
SelectBitmap(GrassDC, OldGrass1);
DeleteObject(TGrass);

DeleteDC(GrassDC);
DeleteDC(TGrassDC);
```

As you can see, Mapper starts by creating two valid device contexts with calls to CreateCompatibleDC. It then creates a compatible bitmap which can be selected into one of the device contexts. The other device context is used to hold the original bitmap.

17

When you are done with this stage, you have two device contexts:

☐ The first holds a blank bitmap, which has the appropriate dimensions for the current screen resolution.

☐ The second holds the original bitmap, with its predefined 25×32 dimensions still intact.

Mapper now uses StretchBlt to copy the original bitmap into the blank bitmap. The result is a properly sized bitmap, residing in a compatible device context. Now, Mapper is free to use this bitmap with the speedy BitBlt function.

Of course, when you're done, you have to go through the tedious, error-prone process of carefully deleting all the bitmaps and DCs you've created. To be sure you have done this properly, run the Debug version of Windows to verify the validity of your efforts.

Summary

The first half of this chapter focuses on the techniques used to create and communicate with dialogs. In particular, you have learned about the CTLCOLOR messages. Additional code demonstrates how to respond to button clicks and how to handle the associated messages when they're sent to a dialog procedure. The last half of the chapter introduces the Mapper program and the powerful StretchBlt function.

Q&A

Q The Mapper program blits a bitmap into a static control on the Options dialog. How else can you display a bitmap on a dialog?

A By responding to WM_PAINT messages, you can paint the bitmap directly on the dialog's surface. This isn't always appropriate, however, because the dimensions of dialogs are calculated in a rather peculiar fashion. As a result, using static controls is often the answer. A third alternative is posed by push buttons, which can be given the BS_OWNERDRAW style and used in a similar fashion. Borland's Resource Workshop provides a shortcut method for using BWCC owner draw push buttons. However, there is a specific button style called BS_BITMAP, used to create bitmap buttons. This is demonstrated in the TabDemo program, found on Day 18, "Windows 95 Dialogs and Controls."

Q In the last answer, you mentioned that dialogs use a peculiar coordinate system. What's that all about?

A Rather than base their dimensions on pixels, dialog boxes use a coordinate system based on a unit that is one-quarter the size of a character in the system font. This is done to guarantee that dialogs will keep their relative proportions, regardless of the resolution of the current system. If, based on dialog dimensions, you want to make calculations at runtime, use the `GetDialogBaseUnits` function to retrieve the size of the units and the `MapDialogRect` function to convert them to pixels. For additional accuracy, use TrueType fonts in your dialogs. Windows can more accurately size TrueType fonts, and so they usually scale better when you are moving back and forth between different resolutions.

Workshop

The Workshop provides quiz questions to help you solidify your understanding of the material covered and exercises to provide you with experience in using what you've learned. Try to understand the quiz and exercise answers before continuing on to the next chapter. Answers are provided in Appendix A.

Quiz

1. What is the difference between `SendDlgItemMessage` and `SendMessage`?
2. If all you know is the ID of a control that resides in a dialog, how can you get its `HWND`?
3. How do you convert the coordinates retrieved by `GetClientRect` into logical coordinates using the `MM_TWIPS` mapping mode?
4. If you have access to nothing but the `HWND` of the current dialog, how can you find the `HWND` of its owner?
5. Is it possible to set up lines of communication between a modal dialog and its parent? If not, why? If so, how?
6. Using a debugger, you can't step through a program in a linear fashion until it reaches a portion of the dialog procedure you want to examine. How do you get around this limitation so that you can debug a dialog proc?
7. Why does the Mapper program subclass a static control?
8. Why doesn't the Options dialog draw bitmaps directly on its own surface?
9. What is the difference between `StretchBlt` and `BitBlt`?
10. Why does Mapper have to call `CreateCompatibleBitmap`?

Exercises

1. Respond to a `WM_CTLCOLOR` message by giving the background of a dialog the Borland "chiseled steel" look (shown in the last chapter).
2. In a note at the end of the section entitled "Getting Data from the Make Shape Dialog," I describe how to use dialogs as the interface for a database of names and addresses. Create your own personal address book by implementing your own version of this database.

Windows 95 Dialogs and Controls

In this chapter you will learn about several new controls found in Windows 95. In particular, the focus is on the following:

- ☐ tab controls
- ☐ property sheets
- ☐ spinners
- ☐ hotkeys
- ☐ bitmap buttons

You will also hear a good deal about the relationship between window and dialog coordinate systems, CreateWindowEx, and using WindowsX message crackers in dialogs.

There are two major programs covered in this chapter. The first explores tab controls and ends up raising a number of interesting and fairly challenging questions about sizing modeless child dialogs. This program also contains a modal dialog that shows some new common controls and gives you some general tips on using Windows 95 components in dialogs. The second program, called PSheet, is considerably easier to construct. However, it covers property sheets, which are perhaps the single most important new element in the Windows 95 interface.

Tab and Property Sheet Theory

If you flip through the Windows 95 interface, you will find that one of the major features of Windows 3.1 is totally missing. At first its absence is not so obvious, but when you stop to think about it, you will notice that the multiple-document interface (MDI), has been banished to the outer Mongolian hinterlands.

The absence of MDI stems in part from the fact that Microsoft sees programs becoming more modularized, more object-oriented. The new holy grail is allowing users to take discreet objects and plug them into various different programs, much the way we now plug controls and common dialogs into our own code. The MDI interface does little to support this metaphor. Instead of homogenous Windows all designed with the same look and feel, this new world view points to a series of separate windows, each floating in their own space on the desktop.

Furthermore, tests at Microsoft revealed that many users were confused by the MDI interface. Something simpler was needed, and the Windows 95 taskbar, Explorer, and desktop icons may be part of the answer.

To support this new vision, there needs to be a revamped way of bringing various windows together into one application. The idea of tabbed controls is one possible solution. It may, in fact, be that tabbed controls prove to be one of the key metaphors for presenting information to computer users living on the waning cusp of the Twentieth Century.

The success of this new style interface is probably measured only in the subjective reactions of each individual user. However, there is no question that this is the direction that Microsoft expects us to take over the next few years. Test the following TabDemo and PSheet programs and decide for yourself whether you believe in this new vision.

Tab Control Basics

I first noticed tabs showing up in games such as Sierra's "The Dagger of Amon Ra," although I'm sure there must have been earlier incarnations. Shortly thereafter I saw them in Borland's version of Quattro Pro and in parts of the OS/2 interface. After that there was a seeming landslide of tabbed controls appearing virtually everywhere, from Microsoft Office products to Delphi.

Windows 95 gives you two different types of tabbed controls to work with. One is the standard tab control featured in the next example program, called TabDemo, and shown in Figure 18.1. The other common tab style is the property sheet. Property sheets usually appear in dialogs such as the one which appears when you right click on the Windows 95 desktop. (Actually, in their internal implementation, property sheets use tab controls. However, the two controls have separate interfaces with their own particular rules and styles. Therefore, some users tend to regard property sheets and tab controls as entirely separate tools.)

From a programmer's point of view, property sheets are relatively easy to work with, while tab controls can be a bit tricky. However, neither control poses any major problems, especially after you've learned a few tricks for taming the gnarly gremlins who lurk around the dark edges of our code.

The TabDemo program has a number of different features in it, including hotkey controls,

Figure 18.1.
The TabDemo program features tab controls and two large bitmap buttons, one of which is visible in this figure.

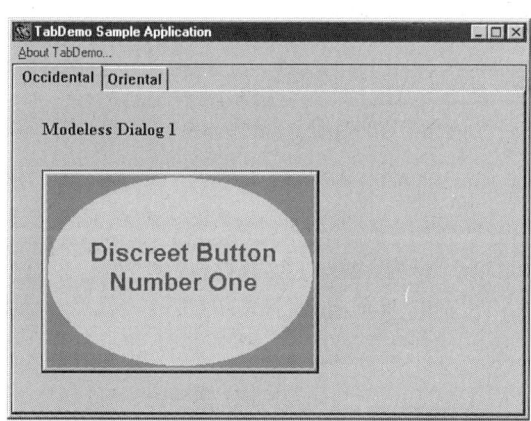

spinners, a trackbar, and a status control. However, the key feature of the program is the tab controls in the main window and, of course, the colorful BS_BITMAP-style buttons.

This is a fairly long program with at least one subtle piece of machinery in it, so it's probably best if you go ahead and get it running so that you can begin to see beneath the hood and find out what makes its engine purr. So fire up your computer and compile the program, which is found in Listings 18.1 through 18.8.

Listing 18.1. The TabDemo program shows how to size dialogs and the controls that reside on their surface.

```cpp
/////////////////////////////////////////////////////////////
// TABDEMO.CPP
// Copyright (c) 1995 Charlie Calvert.
// From: Teach Yourself Windows 95
// Demonstrate tabs, spinners, hotkeys
// WIN32 only. Will not run under Windows 3.1
/////////////////////////////////////////////////////////////

#include <windows.h>
#include <windowsx.h>
#include <commctrl.h>              // Common controls
#include "tabdemo.h"               // specific to this program
#pragma warning (disable : 4068)   // unknown pragma

static HINSTANCE   hInstance;
static HWND hTab;
static HWND hEastWestDlg;
char szAppName[] = "TabDemo";
char szTitle[]   = "TabDemo Sample Application";
static char PageStr[100];
static int ASpace = 125;

/////////////////////////////////////////////////////////////
// WinMain: Program entry point
/////////////////////////////////////////////////////////////
#pragma argsused
int APIENTRY WinMain(HINSTANCE hInst, HINSTANCE hPrevInstance,
                     LPSTR lpCmdLine, int nCmdShow)
{
    MSG msg;

    hInstance = hInst;

    if (!hPrevInstance)
        if (!Register(hInst))
            return (FALSE);

    if (!Create(hInst, nCmdShow))
        return (FALSE);

    while (GetMessage(&msg, NULL, 0, 0))
    {
```

```
      TranslateMessage(&msg);
      DispatchMessage(&msg);
    }

    return (msg.wParam);
}

///////////////////////////////////////////////////////
// Register
///////////////////////////////////////////////////////
BOOL Register(HINSTANCE hInstance)
{
  WNDCLASSEX  wc;

  wc.cbSize         = sizeof(WNDCLASSEX);
  wc.style          = CS_HREDRAW | CS_VREDRAW;
  wc.lpfnWndProc    = (WNDPROC)WndProc;
  wc.cbClsExtra     = 0;
  wc.cbWndExtra     = 0;
  wc.hInstance      = hInstance;
  wc.hIcon          = LoadIcon (hInstance, "TabDemoIcon");
  wc.hCursor        = LoadCursor(NULL, IDC_ARROW);
  wc.hbrBackground  = GetStockBrush(LTGRAY_BRUSH);
  wc.lpszMenuName   = szAppName;
  wc.lpszClassName  = szAppName;
  wc.hIconSm        = LoadIcon(hInstance, "TabDemoIcon16");

  return RegisterClassEx(&wc) != 0;
}

///////////////////////////////////////////////////////
// Create
///////////////////////////////////////////////////////
BOOL Create(HINSTANCE hInstance, int nCmdShow)
{
    HWND    hWnd; // Main window handle.

    hWnd = CreateWindowEx(
        WS_EX_TOPMOST,          // Use an extended style, just for fun.
        szAppName,              // See RegisterClass() call.
        szTitle,                // Text for window title bar.
        WS_OVERLAPPEDWINDOW,    // Window style.
        CW_USEDEFAULT, 250, CW_USEDEFAULT, 175, // positioning
        NULL,                   // Overlapped windows have no parent.
        NULL,                   // Use the window class menu.
        hInstance,              // This instance owns this window.
        NULL                    // We don't use any data
        );

    if (!hWnd)
        return (FALSE);

    ShowWindow(hWnd, nCmdShow); // Show the window
    UpdateWindow(hWnd);         // Sends WM_PAINT message

    return (TRUE);              // We succeeded...
```

continues

Listing 18.1. continued

```
  }

//////////////////////////////////////////////////////////
// Window Procedure
//////////////////////////////////////////////////////////
LRESULT CALLBACK WndProc(HWND hwnd, UINT Message,
                         WPARAM wParam, LPARAM lParam)
{
  switch (Message)
  {
    HANDLE_MSG(hwnd, WM_CREATE, TabDemo_OnCreate);
    HANDLE_MSG(hwnd, WM_DESTROY, TabDemo_OnDestroy);
    HANDLE_MSG(hwnd, WM_COMMAND, TabDemo_OnCommand);
    HANDLE_MSG(hwnd, WM_NOTIFY, TabDemo_OnNotify);
    HANDLE_MSG(hwnd, WM_SIZE, TabDemo_OnSize);
    default:
      return TabDemo_DefProc(hwnd, Message, wParam, lParam);
  }
}

//////////////////////////////////////////////////////////
// Size the child dialogs in the main window
//////////////////////////////////////////////////////////
void SizeDialog(HWND hwnd)
{
  RECT Rect;

  GetClientRect(hwnd, &Rect);
  MoveWindow(hTab, 0, 0, Rect.right, Rect.bottom, TRUE);

  TabCtrl_AdjustRect(hTab, FALSE, &Rect);
  MoveWindow(hEastWestDlg, Rect.left, Rect.top,
             Rect.right - Rect.left, Rect.bottom - Rect.top, TRUE);

  ShowWindow(hEastWestDlg, SW_SHOWNORMAL);
}

//////////////////////////////////////////////////////////
// WM_CREATE
//////////////////////////////////////////////////////////
BOOL TabDemo_OnCreate(HWND hwnd, LPCREATESTRUCT lpCreateStruct)
{
  TC_ITEM Item;
  RECT Rect;

  InitCommonControls();

  GetClientRect(hwnd, &Rect);
  hTab = CreateWindow(WC_TABCONTROL, "",
                  WS_CHILD | WS_VISIBLE | WS_BORDER | ES_LEFT,
                  0, 0, Rect.right, Rect.bottom, hwnd, HMENU(ID_EDIT),
                  lpCreateStruct->hInstance, NULL);

  Item.mask = TCIF_TEXT;

  Item.iImage = -1;
```

```
   Item.pszText = "Occidental";
   TabCtrl_InsertItem(hTab, 0, &Item);
   Item.pszText = "Oriental";
   TabCtrl_InsertItem(hTab, 1, &Item);

   hEastWestDlg = CreateDialog(hInstance, "OccidentalDlg",
                              hTab, (DLGPROC)OccidentalProc);

   PostMessage(hwnd, WM_SIZE, 0, MAKELONG(Rect.right, Rect.bottom));

   return hTab != 0;
}

///////////////////////////////////////////////////////
// WM_DESTROY
///////////////////////////////////////////////////////
#pragma argsused
void TabDemo_OnDestroy(HWND hwnd)
{
  if (hEastWestDlg)
    DestroyWindow(hEastWestDlg);
  PostQuitMessage(0);
}

///////////////////////////////////////////////////////
// WM_COMMAND
///////////////////////////////////////////////////////
#pragma argsused
void TabDemo_OnCommand(HWND hwnd, int id, HWND hwndCtl, UINT codeNotify)
{
  switch (id)
  {
    case IDM_ABOUT:
        DialogBox(hInstance, "AboutBox", hwnd, (DLGPROC)About);
      break;
  }
}

///////////////////////////////////////////////////////
// WM_NOTIFY: The pages change.
///////////////////////////////////////////////////////
#pragma argsused
LRESULT TabDemo_OnNotify(HWND hwnd, int idFrom, NMHDR FAR * pnmhdr)
{
  if (pnmhdr->code == TCN_SELCHANGE)
  {
    if (hEastWestDlg) DestroyWindow(hEastWestDlg);
    int Num = TabCtrl_GetCurSel(pnmhdr->hwndFrom);
    switch(Num)
    {
      case 0:
        hEastWestDlg = CreateDialog(hInstance, "OccidentalDlg",
                                   hTab, (DLGPROC)OccidentalProc);
        SizeDialog(hwnd);
        break;
```

continues

18

Listing 18.1. continued

```
        case 1:
          hEastWestDlg = CreateDialog(hInstance, "OrientalDlg",
                                hTab, (DLGPROC)OrientalProc);
          SizeDialog(hwnd);
          break;
      }
    }
    return 0;
}


/////////////////////////////////////////////////////////
// WM_SIZE
/////////////////////////////////////////////////////////
#pragma argsused
void TabDemo_OnSize(HWND hwnd, UINT state, int cx, int cy)
{
  if (hEastWestDlg)
    SizeDialog(hwnd);
}
```

Listing 18.2. The header for the TabDemo program.

```
/////////////////////////////////////////////////////////
// TABDEMO.H
// Copyright (c) 1995 Charlie Calvert.
// 07/02/95
/////////////////////////////////////////////////////////

#define ID_EDIT           100
#define ID_UPDOWN         101
#define ID_PROG           110
#define ID_STAT           111
#define ID_FIRSTBTN       120
#define ID_SECONDBTN      121
#define ID_FIRSTTXT       122
#define ID_SECONDTXT      123
#define IDM_ABOUT         303

#define ID_HOTKEY1        500
#define ID_HOTKEY2        501
#define ID_HOTKEY3        502
#define ID_SPINBUDDY      503
#define ID_SPINNER        504

#define TEXTWIDTH         60
#define TEXTHEIGHT        8

BOOL Register(HANDLE);
BOOL Create(HANDLE, int);
LRESULT CALLBACK WndProc(HWND, UINT, WPARAM, LPARAM);
BOOL CALLBACK About(HWND, UINT, WPARAM, LPARAM);
BOOL CALLBACK OccidentalProc(HWND, UINT, WPARAM, LPARAM);
```

```
BOOL CALLBACK OrientalProc(HWND, UINT, WPARAM, LPARAM);

#define TabDemo_DefProc     DefWindowProc
BOOL TabDemo_OnCreate(HWND hwnd, LPCREATESTRUCT lpCreateStruct);
void TabDemo_OnDestroy(HWND hwnd);
void TabDemo_OnCommand(HWND hwnd, int id, HWND hwndCtl, UINT codeNotify);
void TabDemo_OnSize(HWND hwnd, UINT state, int cx, int cy);
LRESULT TabDemo_OnNotify(HWND hwnd, int idFrom, NMHDR FAR * pnmhdr);
```

Listing 18.3. The first page of the two tab controls is in its own module, which contains one WindowsX-style dialog procedure.

```
///////////////////////////////////////////////////////
// DLGWEST.CPP
// Project: TABDEMO
// Copyright (c) 1995 Charlie Calvert.
///////////////////////////////////////////////////////

#include <windows.h>
#include <windowsx.h>
#include <commctrl.h>
#include "tabdemo.h"
#pragma warning (disable : 4068) // unknown pragma

static HBITMAP Bitmap;

///////////////////////////////////////////////////////
// WM_INITDIALOG: Put the bitmap in the button
///////////////////////////////////////////////////////
#pragma argsused
BOOL DlgOccidental_OnInitDialog(HWND hwnd, HWND hwndFocus, LPARAM lParam)
{
  HINSTANCE hInstance;

  hInstance = (HINSTANCE)GetWindowLong(hwnd, GWL_HINSTANCE);
  Bitmap = LoadBitmap(hInstance, "TabDemoBMP1");
  if (!Bitmap) MessageBox(hwnd, "!Bitmap", NULL, MB_OK);
  SendMessage(GetDlgItem(hwnd, ID_FIRSTBTN), BM_SETIMAGE,
              IMAGE_BITMAP, LPARAM(Bitmap));
  return TRUE;
}

///////////////////////////////////////////////////////
// WM_COMMAND: Respond to button, close dialog
///////////////////////////////////////////////////////
#pragma argsused
void DlgOccidental_OnCommand(HWND hwnd, int id, HWND hwndCtl, UINT codeNotify)
{
  switch (id)
  {
    case ID_FIRSTBTN:
      MessageBox(hwnd, "Cease from anger and forget wrath!",
```

continues

Listing 18.3. continued

```
            "Wisdom is better than strength!", MB_OK | MB_ICONEXCLAMATION);
        break;

    case IDOK:
    case IDCANCEL:
      if (Bitmap) DeleteBitmap(Bitmap);
      PostQuitMessage(0); // See DestroyWindow in OnNotify
      break;
    }
}


//////////////////////////////////////////////////////////////
// WM_SIZE: Get the dialog units and calc button coords
//////////////////////////////////////////////////////////////
#pragma argsused
void DlgOccidental_OnSize(HWND hwnd, UINT state, int cx, int cy)
{
    SetWindowPos(GetDlgItem(hwnd, ID_FIRSTBTN), 0,
                0, 0, 260, 185, SWP_NOZORDER | SWP_NOMOVE);
}


//////////////////////////////////////////////////////////////
// Dialog1Proc: Modeless dialog in main window
//////////////////////////////////////////////////////////////
#pragma argsused
BOOL CALLBACK OccidentalProc(HWND hDlg, UINT Message,
                        WPARAM wParam, LPARAM lParam)
{
  switch(Message)
  {
    case WM_INITDIALOG:
        return HANDLE_WM_INITDIALOG(hDlg, wParam,
                lParam, DlgOccidental_OnInitDialog);

    case WM_CTLCOLORSTATIC:
        SetBkMode((HDC)wParam, TRANSPARENT);
        return (BOOL)GetStockBrush(LTGRAY_BRUSH);

    case WM_CTLCOLORDLG:
        return (BOOL) GetStockBrush(LTGRAY_BRUSH);

    case WM_SIZE:
        HANDLE_WM_SIZE(hDlg, wParam, lParam, DlgOccidental_OnSize);
        break;

    case WM_COMMAND:
        HANDLE_WM_COMMAND(hDlg, wParam, lParam, DlgOccidental_OnCommand);
        return TRUE;
    }
    return (FALSE); // Didn't process the message
}
```

Listing 18.4. Compare the `WM_SIZE` handler in this dialog with the one from DLGPROC1.CPP.

```cpp
////////////////////////////////////////////////////
// DLGEAST.CPP
// Project: TABDEMO
// Copyright (c) 1995 Charlie Calvert.
////////////////////////////////////////////////////

#include <windows.h>
#include <windowsx.h>
#include <commctrl.h>
#include "tabdemo.h"
#pragma warning (disable : 4068) // unknown pragma

static HBITMAP Bitmap;


////////////////////////////////////////////////////
// WM_INITDIALOG: Put the bitmap in the button
////////////////////////////////////////////////////
#pragma argsused
BOOL DlgOriental_OnInitDialog(HWND hwnd, HWND hwndFocus, LPARAM lParam)
{
  HINSTANCE hInstance;

  hInstance = (HINSTANCE)GetWindowLong(hwnd, GWL_HINSTANCE);
  Bitmap = LoadBitmap(hInstance, "TabDemoBMP2");
  if (!Bitmap) MessageBox(hwnd, "!Bitmap", NULL, MB_OK);
  SendMessage(GetDlgItem(hwnd, ID_SECONDBTN), BM_SETIMAGE,
              IMAGE_BITMAP, LPARAM(Bitmap));
  return TRUE;
}


////////////////////////////////////////////////////
// WM_COMMAND
////////////////////////////////////////////////////
#pragma argsused
void DlgOriental_OnCommand(HWND hwnd, int id, HWND hwndCtl, UINT codeNotify)
{
  switch (id)
  {
    case ID_SECONDBTN:
      MessageBox(hwnd,
        "Trying to dominate events goes against the current of the Tao.",
        "Accomplish the great task by a series of small acts.",
        MB_OK | MB_ICONEXCLAMATION);
      break;

    case IDOK:
    case IDCANCEL:
      if (Bitmap) DeleteBitmap(Bitmap);
      PostQuitMessage(0);  // See DestroyWindow in OnNotify
      break;
```

continues

Listing 18.4. continued

```
    }
}

//////////////////////////////////////////////////////////
// WM_SIZE
//////////////////////////////////////////////////////////
#pragma argsused
void DlgOriental_OnSize(HWND hwnd, UINT state, int cx, int cy)
{
  int Width, Height;
  RECT Rect2;

  Width = (cx / 2) - 130;
  Height = (cy / 2) - 92;
  MoveWindow(GetDlgItem(hwnd, ID_SECONDBTN),
            Width, Height, 260, 184, TRUE);
  GetClientRect(GetDlgItem(hwnd, ID_SECONDTXT), &Rect2);
  Rect2.left = (cx / 2) - (Rect2.right / 2);
  MoveWindow(GetDlgItem(hwnd, ID_SECONDTXT),
            Rect2.left, Rect2.top, Rect2.right, Rect2.bottom, TRUE);
}

//////////////////////////////////////////////////////////
// Dialog2Proc: Modeless dialog in main window
//////////////////////////////////////////////////////////
#pragma argsused
BOOL CALLBACK OrientalProc(HWND hDlg, UINT Message,
                    WPARAM wParam, LPARAM lParam)
{
  switch(Message)
  {
    case WM_INITDIALOG:
      return HANDLE_WM_INITDIALOG(hDlg, wParam,
                lParam, DlgOriental_OnInitDialog);

    case WM_CTLCOLORSTATIC:
      SetBkMode((HDC)wParam, TRANSPARENT);
      return (BOOL)GetStockBrush(LTGRAY_BRUSH);

    case WM_CTLCOLORDLG:
      return (BOOL) GetStockBrush(LTGRAY_BRUSH);

    case WM_SIZE:
      HANDLE_WM_SIZE(hDlg, wParam, lParam, DlgOriental_OnSize);
      return TRUE;

    case WM_COMMAND:
      HANDLE_WM_COMMAND(hDlg, wParam, lParam, DlgOriental_OnCommand);
      return TRUE;
  }
  return (FALSE); // Didn't process the message
}
```

Listing 18.5. The About box contains four different Windows 95 common controls.

```cpp
///////////////////////////////////////////////////////
// DLGABOUT.CPP
// PROJECT: TABDEMO
// Copyright (c) 1995 Charlie Calvert.
///////////////////////////////////////////////////////

#include <windows.h>
#include <windowsx.h>
#include <commctrl.h>
#include <stdio.h>
#include "tabdemo.h"

///////////////////////////////////////////////////////
// Deal with the hotkeys in the dialog
///////////////////////////////////////////////////////
void SetupHotKeys(HWND hwnd)
{
  // Use only control key,
  SendDlgItemMessage (hwnd, IDD_HOTKEY2, HKM_SETRULES,
                       (WPARAM)(HKCOMB_SA | HKCOMB_S | HKCOMB_A),
                       (LPARAM)HOTKEYF_CONTROL);

  SendDlgItemMessage(hwnd, IDD_HOTKEY3, HKM_SETRULES,
                      (WPARAM)(HKCOMB_A | HKCOMB_SA | HKCOMB_CA),
                      (LPARAM)HOTKEYF_CONTROL);

  // Set the Spinner #1 range from -10 to 10
  SendDlgItemMessage(hwnd, IDD_SPINNER1, UDM_SETRANGE,
                      (WPARAM)0, MAKELPARAM(-10,10));
}

///////////////////////////////////////////////////////
// Deal with the trackbar in the dialog
///////////////////////////////////////////////////////
void SetupTrackbar(HWND hDlg)
{
  HWND hwnd = GetDlgItem(hDlg, ID_PROG);
  SendMessage(hwnd, TBM_SETRANGE, (WPARAM)1, (LPARAM)MAKELONG(0, 10));
  SendMessage(hwnd, TBM_SETPOS, (WPARAM)1, (LPARAM)5);
}

///////////////////////////////////////////////////////
// The modal About dialog procedure
///////////////////////////////////////////////////////
#pragma argsused
BOOL CALLBACK About(HWND hDlg, UINT Message,
                    WPARAM wParam, LPARAM lParam)
{
  LRESULT TrackPos, UpDownPos;
  char S[100];
```

18

continues

Listing 18.5. continued

```
switch(Message)
{
  case WM_INITDIALOG:
  {
    SetupHotKeys(hDlg);
    SetupTrackbar(hDlg);
    return (TRUE);
  }

  case WM_CTLCOLORSTATIC:
    SetBkMode((HDC)wParam, TRANSPARENT);
    return (BOOL)GetStockBrush(LTGRAY_BRUSH);

  case WM_CTLCOLORDLG:
    return (BOOL) GetStockBrush(LTGRAY_BRUSH);

  case WM_HSCROLL:
    // Handle Trackbar;
    TrackPos = SendMessage(GetDlgItem(hDlg, ID_PROG),
                           TBM_GETPOS, 0, 0);
    SendMessage(GetDlgItem(hDlg, IDD_SPINNER1),
                UDM_SETPOS, (WPARAM)1, (LPARAM)TrackPos);
    break;

  case WM_VSCROLL:
    // UPDOWN Controls
    UpDownPos = SendMessage(GetDlgItem(hDlg, IDD_SPINNER1), UDM_GETPOS, 0, 0);
    sprintf(S, "UpDown Position: %d", UpDownPos);
    SetWindowText(GetDlgItem(hDlg, ID_STAT), S);
    break;

  case WM_COMMAND:
    if (LOWORD(wParam) == IDOK ||
        LOWORD(wParam) == IDCANCEL)
    {
      EndDialog(hDlg, LOWWORD(wParam));
      return (TRUE);
    }
    break;
  }
  return (FALSE); // Didn't process the message
}
```

Listing 18.6. The resource file features bitmaps, icons, and numerous Windows 95 controls.

```
///////////////////////////////////////////////////////
// Name: TABDEMO.RC
// Copyright (c) 1995 Charlie Calvert.
// Project: TABDEMO
// Date: 06/01/95
///////////////////////////////////////////////////////
```

```
#include "windows.h"
#include "tabdemo.h"
#include "commctrl.h"

#define WS_TABDEMO WS_CHILD ¦ WS_BORDER ¦ WS_TABSTOP


TabDemoIcon ICON "tabdemo.ico"
TabDemoIcon16 ICON "tabdem16.ico"
TabDemoBMP1 BITMAP "tabdemo1.bmp"
TabDemoBMP2 BITMAP "tabdemo2.bmp"


TabDemo MENU
BEGIN
   MENUITEM "&About TabDemo...",          IDM_ABOUT
END

ABOUTBOX DIALOG 22, 17, 167, 120
STYLE DS_MODALFRAME ¦ WS_CAPTION ¦ WS_SYSMENU
CAPTION "About TabDemo"
BEGIN
   CONTROL "&All", -1, "static",
     WS_CHILD ¦ SS_RIGHT, 5, 6, 45, 8
   CONTROL "", ID_HOTKEY1, HOTKEY_CLASS,
     WS_TABDEMO,  50, 5,  80, 12

   CONTROL "&Only Ctrl", -1, "static",
     WS_CHILD ¦ SS_RIGHT, 5, 21, 45, 8
   CONTROL "", ID_HOTKEY2,
     HOTKEY_CLASS, WS_TABDEMO, 50, 20, 80, 12

   CONTROL "&Not Alt", -1, "static",
     WS_CHILD ¦ SS_RIGHT, 5, 36, 45, 8
   CONTROL "", ID_HOTKEY3, HOTKEY_CLASS,
     WS_TABDEMO, 50, 35, 80, 12

   CONTROL "1", ID_SPINBUDDY, "Edit",
     WS_TABDEMO, 30, 50, 30, 12
   CONTROL "", ID_SPINNER, UPDOWN_CLASS,
     UDS_AUTOBUDDY ¦ WS_CHILD ¦ UDS_SETBUDDYINT, 60, 50, 10, 12

   CONTROL "", ID_PROG, TRACKBAR_CLASS,
     WS_TABDEMO ¦ TBS_AUTOTICKS, 30, 75, 100, 16
   CONTROL "Crate", ID_STAT, STATUSCLASSNAME,
     WS_CHILD ¦ WS_BORDER, 0, 0, 0, 0

   DEFPUSHBUTTON    "OK", IDOK, 70, 95, 32, 14, WS_GROUP
END


OccidentalDlg DIALOG 0, 0, 200, 100
STYLE WS_CHILD
BEGIN
 CTEXT "Modeless Dialog 1", ID_FIRSTTXT, 10, 10, 60, 8
 CONTROL "Data", ID_FIRSTBTN, "BUTTON",
    BS_BITMAP, 10, 30, 65, 80
END
```

18

continues

Listing 18.6. continued

```
OrientalDlg DIALOG 0, 0, 200, 100
STYLE WS_CHILD
BEGIN
  CTEXT "Modeless Dialog 2", ID_SECONDTXT, 66, 25, 60, 8
  CONTROL "Data", ID_SECONDBTN, "BUTTON",
    BS_BITMAP, 64, 40, 65, 80
END
```

Listing 18.7. The very simple module definition file for TabDemo.

```
; TABDEMO.DEF

NAME TabDemo
DESCRIPTION 'Tab Control example'
```

Listing 18.8. A makefile for users of the Borland compiler.

```
# TabDemo.mak

# macros

!if !$d(BCROOT)
BCROOT  = $(MAKEDIR)\..

!endif

APPNAME = TabDemo
INCPATH = $(BCROOT)\WIN32;$(BCROOT);$(BCROOT)\INCLUDE
LIBPATH = $(BCROOT)\LIB

COMPILER= BCC32.EXE
BRC     = BRC32.EXE
FLAGS   = -W -v -w4 -H -I$(INCPATH) -L$(LIBPATH)
OBJS    = $(APPNAME).obj DlgEast.obj DlgWest.obj DlgAbout.obj

# link
$(APPNAME).exe: $(OBJS) $(APPNAME).def $(APPNAME).res
  $(COMPILER) $(FLAGS) $(OBJS)
  $(BRC) -I$(INCPATH) $(APPNAME).res

# compile
.cpp.obj:
  $(COMPILER) -c $(FLAGS) { $< }

# resource
$(APPNAME).res: $(APPNAME).rc
  $(BRC) -R -I$(INCPATH) $(APPNAME).RC
```

The bitmaps shown in Figures 18.2 and 18.3 are merely suggested images. It doesn't matter exactly what your bitmaps look like. To create them, you should use the Paint program that ships with Windows. You can change the size of the bitmap in the Paint program by choosing Image | Attributes and then setting Units to Pels.

Figure 18.2.
The bitmap for the Occidental button is 250×175 pixels. Call it TABDEMO1.BMP.

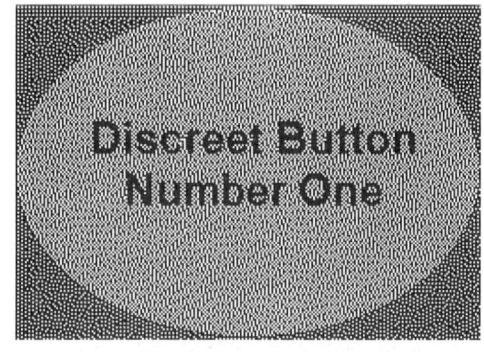

Figure 18.3.
You need not recreate this TABDEMO2.BMP exactly, but you should be sure your version is 250×175 pixels in size.

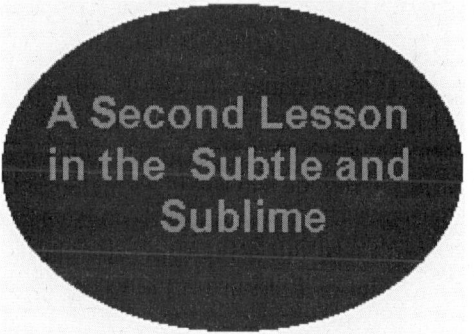

When you run the TabDemo program, you are first presented with two pages: one called Occidental and the other Oriental. In the middle of each page is a large, colorful button. Click on the Western button and you can read some occidental wisdom from the Bible, click on the Eastern button and you can read some oriental wisdom from the *Tao Te Ching*.

Each page of the TabDemo program is made up of a separate dialog. In other words, you don't usually draw directly on the tab control, but instead you let it serve as the background on which you can place windows or dialogs. The trickiest code in the program sizes the dialogs and arranges the controls that reside on their surface.

There is also a simple menu in the program. If you click on this menu, an About dialog box appears, as shown in Figure 18.4. This dialog has several controls on it, including hotkeys, a spinner, a trackbar, and a status bar. I show you these controls mostly so you can see how to create common controls from within a dialog.

Both the spinner (up/down) control and hotkey control are new with this chapter. The spinner control is fairly popular with users and gets heavy use in many programs. The hotkey control has a very specialized and obscure purpose, but I thought I'd throw it in on the off chance that you ever needed to have the user-defined hotkeys at runtime! What?

Figure 18.4.

The About TabDemo dialog features a trackbar, spinner, status bar, and hotkey common control.

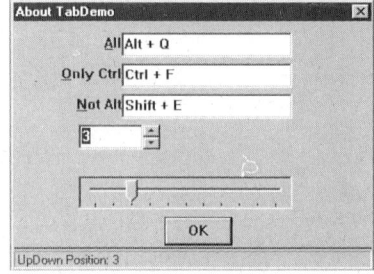

If you look at the TABDEMO.MAK file, you can get an overview of all the modules used in the program. As you can see, there are four main source files, plus a header, a resource, and a DEF file.

I opted to break this program up into so many modules in part because it gives you a simple way to deal with the pages found on the main window. When one page has the focus, it is, in a sense, its own discreet object. It has the focus, as if it were the main window of a standalone project. As a result, it deserves its own file, and so I give it one. If I build an app with six or seven complex pages, I find it helps me think clearly if I keep each page in its own module. However, this is just an opinion, and it need not be taken as gospel. Many good programmers prefer to work with one large file rather than a series of small files. Choose the option that best suits your development style or the needs of your current project.

Using *CreateWindowEx*

If you look at the Create function for this application, you can see that it has one small change in it when compared to the cookie cutter sameness found in earlier chapters:

```
hWnd = CreateWindowEx(
    WS_EX_TOPMOST,              // Use an extended style, just for fun.
    szAppName,                  // See RegisterClass() call.
    szTitle,                    // Text for window title bar.
    WS_OVERLAPPEDWINDOW,        // Window style.
    CW_USEDEFAULT, 250, CW_USEDEFAULT, 175, // positioning
    NULL,                       // Overlapped windows have no parent.
    NULL,                       // Use the window class menu.
    hInstance,                  // This instance owns this window.
    NULL                        // We don't use any data
    );
```

Instead of calling CreateWindow, TabDemo calls CreateWindowEx. This function is identical to CreateWindow, except it adds an additional field at the top of the record that can be assigned various styles. For instance, the TabDemo program uses the WS_EX_TOPMOST style, which ensures that the window will be the top window on the desktop. You can add or remove this style dynamically at runtime by calling SetWindowPos. The SetWindowPos function is discussed later in this chapter and in a slightly different context.

> **Note:** It's generally not considered polite to use the WS_EX_TOPMOST style. I'm sticking it in here because it's fun and easy to use, not because I think it's something you should add to most of your applications. Of course, if you really need it—well, now you know how to use it. But I would recommend avoiding it whenever possible. In real-world programs you should use SetWindowsPos so the user has the option to set or remove the flag.

Another trick you can play with CreateWindowEx is to pass in the WS_EX_TRANSPARENT style, which you can use to create an entirely transparent window. These can be useful when you need to trap mouse input on a particular area of your main window. For instance, you can draw some pattern directly on your window and then place a transparent window over it. By responding to WM_LBUTTONDOWN clicks on the transparent window, you can perform hit tests for the area on your main window where you have drawn a particular pattern. More specifically, you could draw a clown's face on the screen, and then put a tiny window over the clown's nose. When the user clicks on the tiny window, you could respond with some appropriate comment such as this: Go ahead, it's all right—squeeze the wheeze!

At any rate, CreateWindowEx is important in Windows 95 because it contains so many new styles for creating windows that have a special look and feel and convey a message to the user. These styles are well explained in the online help, so there is no reason for me to repeat them here in depth. However, the following table should give you a brief overview:

`WS_EX_ABSPOSITION`	Window won't move with the working area
`WS_EX_ACCEPTFILES`	Accepts drag-drop files
`WS_EX_APPWINDOW`	Win 95: top-level window seen in taskbar
`WS_EX_CLIENTEDGE`	Border has a sunken edge
`WS_EX_CONTEXTHELP`	A question mark appears in the title bar
`WS_EX_CONTROLPARENT`	Win 95: tab navigates among child windows
`WS_EX_DLGMODALFRAME`	Window has a double border
`WS_EX_LEFT`	Win 95: has left-aligned properties
`WS_EX_LEFTSCROLLBAR`	Win 95: vertical scrollbar to the left of client area
`WS_EX_LTRREADING`	Win 95: has left-to-right reading order
`WS_EX_MDICHILD`	Creates an MDI child window
`WS_EX_NOPARENTNOTIFY`	Don't send `WM_PARENTNOTIFY` messages
`WS_EX_OVERLAPPEDWINDOW`	Win 95: `WS_EX_CLIENTEDGE`¦`WS_EX_WINDOWEDGE`
`WS_EX_PALETTEWINDOW`	Win 95: combines the `WS_EX_WINDOWEDGE`, `WS_EX_TOOLWINDOW`, and `WS_EX_TOPMOST` styles
`WS_EX_RIGHT`	Win 95: has right-aligned properties
`WS_EX_RIGHTSCROLLBAR`	Win 95: vertical scrollbar on right
`WS_EX_RTLREADING`	Win 95: text arranged right-to-left
`WS_EX_STATICEDGE`	Win 95: a 3D border style
`WS_EX_TOOLWINDOW`	Win 95: creates a toolbar window
`WS_EX_TOPMOST`	Window placed above other windows
`WS_EX_TRANSPARENT`	Window is transparent
`WS_EX_WINDOWEDGE`	Win 95: raised edge on window border

Notice that a number of these styles are marked "Win 95." This means that they are Windows 95 only. They won't have any effect under Windows 3.1. Once again, this onslaught of new styles is part of the effort to make Windows easier to use, especially for newcomers.

If you already understand `CreateWindow`, it's easy to upgrade to `CreateWindowEx`. However, just reading about these styles isn't enough to get you up and running. If you want to know more about this subject, you really need to experiment. One way to get started would be to take the Window1 or the generic sample that ships with this book and have it call `CreateWindowEx` rather than `CreateWindow`. Then just start passing in styles in the first parameter. If you want, try ORing several styles together to create complex effects.

Creating Tab Controls

It's time to start digging into the nitty-gritty of tab controls. When you get down to cases, this really isn't that difficult a subject. There are a few messages you need to master, and you need to think about responding to WM_SIZE messages, but overall it isn't too bad, especially considering the nice interfaces you can create with this new component. So enough of the preliminaries, it's time to dig into the fun stuff.

Here is the WM_CREATE handler from TABDEMO.CPP:

```
BOOL TabDemo_OnCreate(HWND hwnd, LPCREATESTRUCT lpCreateStruct)
{
  TC_ITEM Item;
  RECT Rect;

  InitCommonControls();

  GetClientRect(hwnd, &Rect);
  hTab = CreateWindow(WC_TABCONTROL, "",
                  WS_CHILD ¦ WS_VISIBLE ¦ WS_BORDER ¦ ES_LEFT,
                  0, 0, Rect.right, Rect.bottom, hwnd, HMENU(ID_EDIT),
                  lpCreateStruct->hInstance, NULL);

  Item.mask = TCIF_TEXT;

  Item.iImage = -1;
  Item.pszText = "Occidental";
  TabCtrl_InsertItem(hTab, 0, &Item);
  Item.pszText = "Oriental";
  TabCtrl_InsertItem(hTab, 1, &Item);

  hEastWestDlg = CreateDialog(hInstance, "OccidentalDlg",
                             hTab, (DLGPROC)OccidentalProc);

  PostMessage(hwnd, WM_SIZE, 0, MAKELONG(Rect.right, Rect.bottom));

  return hTab != 0;
}
```

The code starts out by calling InitCommonControls, which is mandatory when you are dealing with these new components. It's also necessary for you to include COMMCRTL.H and to link with COMCTL32.LIB. With some compilers, it may also be important to define the Windows version number as 4.0 or higher.

In most cases, you want the tab to cover the entire page, so you should call GetClientRect to retrieve the dimensions of the main window. You are also going to need to resize the tabs and their accompanying dialogs in response to WM_SIZE messages. However, I don't want to open that can of worms quite yet.

18

Once you have the dimensions of the tabs you want to create, the actual call to CreateWindow contains no surprises. Pass in WC_TABCONTROL as the class name, don't bother to pass in the window name, and fill everything else out as expected. Note that I use the lpCreateStruct parameter to grab the HINSTANCE of the application. Throughout most of the application, I use this technique or GetWindowLong in order to snag HINSTANCE. This approach is useful in multiple-module applications where you don't want to use EXTERN to publish a global variable.

It's not enough, however, just to create the tab control. You need to also insert the actual tab pages by using a TC_ITEM structure:

```
typedef struct _TC_ITEM {
    UINT mask;          // Flags - TCIF_TEXT, TCIF_IMAGE
    UINT lpReserved1;   // Reserved; do not use
    UINT lpReserved2;   // Reserved; do not use
    LPSTR pszText;      // Text to show in the tab
    int cchTextMax;     // size of pszText buffer
    int iImage;         // index in a tab control's imagelist
    LPARAM lParam;      // application-defined data
} TC_ITEM;
```

You can think of the *TC* in TC_ITEM as standing for *tab control.* There are four possible styles associated with this structure, and you should select one or more of them for use in the mask field:

TCIF_TEXT	Use text.
TCIF_IMAGE	Use an image.
TCIF_PARAM	lParam has data in it.
TCIF_RTLREADING	Win 95: pszText room uses right-to-left reading order.

In general, you will use the pszText field to specify the text you want to show in the tab. That means you should set the mask field to TCIF_TEXT. If you are not going to use the iImage field, then you should set it to -1. The TextMax field specifies the size of the text buffer for the pszText field. lParam can contain optional data that you might want to associate with the tab. For instance, you could store a handle to a bitmap or dialog here.

Once you have filled out the TC_ITEM structure, you then send it to Windows with a TCM_INSERTITEM message (TCM = tab control message). In particular, here is the WindowsX-type macro you can use to send the message:

```
#define TabCtrl_InsertItem(hwnd, iItem, pitem)   \
    (int)SendMessage((hwnd), TCM_INSERTITEM, \
      (WPARAM)(int)iItem, (LPARAM)(const TC_ITEM FAR*)(pitem))
```

Here is a typical call to TabCtrl_InsertItem:

```
TabCtrl_InsertItem(hTab, 0, &Item);
```

The first parameter is the handle to the tab control; the second is the position of the tab, and the third is the TC_ITEM structure. (Other messages used with TC_ITEM include TCM_SETITEM and TCM_GETITEM.)

If you did nothing else but call CreateWindow and send a TCM_INSERTITEM message, then you would end up with two very nice-looking tabs on your page. However, if you look up at the WM_CREATE handler, you will see that I take two other steps before closing out the procedure. I'm going to ask you to push those guys on the stack for a moment, because I can better explain them after talking about WM_NOTIFY messages for a moment.

What Happens When the User Clicks on a Tab?

To respond to clicks on the tab by the user, you can set up a WM_NOTIFY handler and look for TCN_SELCHANGE messages:

```
LRESULT TabDemo_OnNotify(HWND hwnd, int idFrom, NMHDR FAR * pnmhdr)
{
  if (pnmhdr->code == TCN_SELCHANGE)
  {
    int Num = TabCtrl_GetCurSel(pnmhdr->hwndFrom);
    switch(Num)
    {
      case 0:
        MessageBox(hwnd, "Choose Page One", "Info", MB_OK);
        break;

      case 1:
        MessageBox(hwnd, "Choose Page Two", "Info", MB_OK);
        break;
    }
  }
  return 0;
}
```

This code is a simplified version of the TabDemo_OnNotify code that appears in the sample code you can download or order to go with this book. This code merely pops up a message box when the user changes tabs. In the real program, a dialog is displayed. However, I wanted to show you a simplified version of the program before discussing dialog creation inside this particular context.

In case you need a reminder, here is what the NMHDR looks like:

```
typedef struct tagNMHDR {
    HWND hwndFrom; // HWND that send the message
    UINT idFrom;   // ID of control that sent the message
    UINT code;     // A code such as NM_CLICK or NM_DBLCLICK
} NMHDR;
```

If you look up NMHDR in the online help, you will get a nice list of the possible values for the code field. They include NM_CLICK, NM_DBLCLK, NM_KILLFOCUS, NM_OUTOFMEMORY, NM_RCLICK, NM_RDBLCLK, NM_RETURN, and NM_SETFOCUS. In this case, however, the program needs to know when nmhdr.code is equal to TCN_SELCHANGE, which means that the user has selected a new tab.

If a new page has been requested by the user, then the program calls `TabCtrl_GetCurSel`. `TabCtrl_GetCurSel` is another WindowsX-like macro. It takes the handle of the tab control as a parameter and returns the number of the currently selected tab (1) or -1 if there is a failure. In other words, the user has clicked on a new tab, thereby selecting it. In response, the program needs to bring up a new dialog page.

Once you have the number of the newly selected tab, you can respond by painting the screen as you see fit. As a rule, it's best to paint the screen by creating a dialog. Specifically, here's the complete version of the code, showing how TabDemo creates dialogs:

```
if (pnmhdr->code == TCN_SELCHANGE)
{
  if (hEastWestDlg) DestroyWindow(hEastWestDlg);

  int Num = TabCtrl_GetCurSel(pnmhdr->hwndFrom);

  switch(Num)
  {
    case 0:
      hEastWestDlg = CreateDialog(hInstance, "OccidentalDlg",
                            hTab, (DLGPROC)OccidentalProc);
      SizeDialog(hwnd);
      break;

    case 1:
      hEastWestDlg = CreateDialog(hInstance, "OrientalDlg",
                             hTab, (DLGPROC)OrientalProc);
      SizeDialog(hwnd);
      break;
  }
}
```

The key point you need to focus on here is that `CreateDialog` produces modeless dialogs rather than the modal dialogs you get from calling `DialogBox`. In this example, I am creating and destroying the dialog each time the user asks to see it. As a result, I call `DestroyWindow` at the start to make sure that I don't squander system resources.

> **Note:** If you remember back to the `TC_ITEM` structure, you may recall that there is an `lParam` field included in it. Rather than creating and destroying the dialog each time, you could instead leave a pointer to it in the `lParam` field. When you close the application, you could then call `DestroyWindow` on the data in the `lParam` field. In cases like this, there is no definitive "correct" way to handle the situation. You should choose the method that seems most appropriate for your code.

Here is the definition of one of the dialogs as it appears in the RC file:

```
OccidentalDlg DIALOG 0, 0, 200, 100
STYLE WS_CHILD
BEGIN
 CTEXT "Modeless Dialog 1", ID_FIRSTTXT, 10, 10, 60, 8
 CONTROL "Data", ID_FIRSTBTN, "BUTTON",
   BS_BITMAP, 10, 30, 65, 80
END
```

Notice that the dialog has no caption and no border and that it is declared as having the WS_CHILD rather than the WS_POPUP style. This is exactly what you want. If you used WS_POPUP, then the dialog would get left behind when you moved the parent around the screen. WS_CHILD, on the other hand, ensures that the dialog will follow its parent as it moves. Furthermore, the main window of the application already has a caption and border, so a second, internal caption and border would not look right to the user.

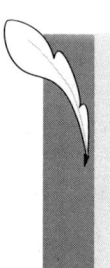

Note: Borland 4.5 users should know that if you OR the numeral 4 onto the dialog style, then you will end up with real Windows 95 dialogs. The Microsoft tools should do this for you automatically, but you may not get this with the Borland tools unless you explicitly OR in 0x4. Your dialogs will be fine either way, but you should probably go for the Windows 95 look whenever possible. Note, however, that true Windows 95 dialogs usually don't use the system font, which can have various implications, most of which will become clear later in this chapter.

18

After you create your dialog, you need to size it:

```
void SizeDialog(HWND hwnd)
{
  RECT Rect, ARect;

  GetClientRect(hwnd, &Rect);
  MoveWindow(hTab, 0, 0, Rect.right, Rect.bottom, TRUE);

  TabCtrl_AdjustRect(hTab, FALSE, &Rect);
  MoveWindow(hEastWestDlg, Rect.left, Rect.top,
          Rect.right - Rect.left, Rect.bottom - Rect.top, TRUE);

  ShowWindow(hEastWestDlg, SW_SHOWNORMAL);
}
```

The first part of this code shows how to adjust the size of the whole tab so that it fits properly into the window. Having done that, you then have to fit the dialog into the tab. That's a more complicated process because you need to take into account the space at the top of the window where the tabs display. In other words, if the dialog was the same size as the entire tab control, then it would cover the tabs themselves. Needless to say, this is not the effect you want to create.

To get information about the size of the little tab windows, you need the TCM_ADJUSTRECT message. It can help you find the display area within the tab. In other words, it finds that smaller rectangle within the tab that excludes the tiny tab windows. (TCM_GETITEMRECT has the opposite effect—that is, it gets the size of the tiny tab windows at the top of the tab control.)

Here is the TabCtrl_AdjustRect macro which wraps the TCM_ADJUSTRECT message:

```
#define TCM_ADJUSTRECT          (TCM_FIRST + 40)
#define TabCtrl_AdjustRect(hwnd, bLarger, prc) \
    (int)SendMessage(hwnd, TCM_ADJUSTRECT,
    (WPARAM)(BOOL)bLarger, (LPARAM)(RECT FAR *)prc)
```

This macro can be used to get coordinates so you can change the size of the tab to fit the dialog or change the size of the dialog to fit the tab. Here is the lowdown on the parameters:

- [ ] The first parameter is the HWND of the tab control.

- [ ] If you want to change the tab so it fits the dialog, then you pass TRUE in the second parameter. If you want to fit the dialog into the tab, you pass in FALSE. In this case, its the second option which is relevant.

- [ ] The last parameter is the rectangle that you want to adjust. Remember, you can't just pass in any old rectangle with random or zeroed-out coordinates. You must pass in a particular rectangle. In this case it must be the rectangle that represents the size of the whole tab control in client coordinates. In TabDemo, that rectangle happens to be available because you called GetClientRect on the whole window and then adjusted the tab control with a call to MoveWindow.

After you send the TCM_ADJUSTRECT message, you can call MoveWindow to fit your dialog into the tab. When calling MoveWindow, you need to subtract the top-left coordinates from the bottom-right coordinates so that the dialog doesn't stick out over the edges on the bottom. Once you've done this, however, the fit will be exact, to the pixel, and will take into account the borders of the tab.

If you recall, a while back I said that there were two calls from the WM_CREATE method that I wanted to push onto the old mental stack for a bit. Now that you have seen the whole process of creating the tabs and sizing them, you can pop those last two commands off your internal mental stack and take a look at them:

```
hEastWestDlg = CreateDialog(hInstance, "OccidentalDlg",
                    hTab, (DLGPROC)OccidentalProc);

PostMessage(hwnd, WM_SIZE, 0, MAKELONG(Rect.right, Rect.bottom));
```

This code ensures that there is a dialog in place right at the start, before there have been any WM_NOTIFY messages sent to your main window. For good measure, I then send an extra WM_SIZE message to make sure that everything fits in correctly when the user starts the application.

In this section I've shown you how to fit a dialog into a tab. The calculations are somewhat more complex if you want to go the other way around, but you now have all the pieces so you can proceed apace.

Showing a Bitmap in a Button

The new WIN32 commands make it easy to fit a bitmap into a button. First, you need to declare the button so that it has the BS_BITMAP style:

```
CONTROL "Data", ID_FIRSTBTN, "BUTTON",
  BS_BITMAP, 10, 30, 65, 80
```

In this case, I'm creating the button in a resource file, but you would pass in the same style if you were using CreateWindow. The code to insert the bitmap into the button looks like this:

```
hInstance = (HINSTANCE)GetWindowLong(hwnd, GWL_HINSTANCE);
Bitmap = LoadBitmap(hInstance, "TabDemoBMP2");
if (!Bitmap)
  MessageBox(hwnd, "!Bitmap", NULL, MB_OK);
else
  SendMessage(GetDlgItem(hwnd, ID_SECONDBTN), BM_SETIMAGE,
          IMAGE_BITMAP, LPARAM(Bitmap));
```

This is an excerpt from DLGEAST.CPP, and it gets called in response to a WM_INITDIALOG message. Here's a blow by blow:

- [ ] The code starts by retrieving the HINSTANCE of the application.
- [ ] It uses the HINSTANCE to pick up the bitmap from the resource via a call to LoadBitmap. The string "TabDemo2BMP" is defined in the RC file.
- [ ] The final step is to send a BM_SETIMAGE message to the button in order to place the bitmap in the button. When sending a BM_SETIMAGE message, you pass the IMAGE_BITMAP constant in wParam and the bitmap in lParam. You can use GetDlgItem to retrieve the HWND of the button.

Well, Windows 95 has certainly made it easy enough to put a bitmap in a button!

However, in this particular case, your work is not quite done yet. Before your dialog is going to look right, you have to size the button so that it fits the bitmap. In particular, this bitmap is 250 pixels wide times 175 pixels high. You want to make sure the button is slightly larger than the bitmap so that you can see not only the entire bitmap but also the fancy 3D border of the button.

Sizing the button is trickier than it seems at first because the button resides in a dialog. A dialog does not use pixels as a standard unit of measurement regardless of which mapping mode you are in. Instead it uses separate units of measurement based on the size of the current font. This means you are going to have to take some special measures.

18

> **Note:** None of the "special measures" that I use to size the button in a dialog are
> needed if you put the bitmap button in a regular window. In that case, you can size
> the button at creation time during the call to CreateWindow. The issue here is that
> CreateWindow thinks in terms of pixels and that the bitmap itself is measured in
> pixels. Everyone is thinking in pixels, so the operation is simple.
>
> I stated this previously, but it's worth repeating: Dialog units are not measured in
> pixels, but rather in a special set of measurements that are dependent upon the
> current font. More about this subject in just one moment.

When working with a bitmap button in a dialog, you will have to size the window yourself at
runtime, calling the SetWindowPos function to do the work:

```
void DlgOccidental_OnSize(HWND hwnd, UINT state, int cx, int cy)
{
    SetWindowPos(GetDlgItem(hwnd, ID_FIRSTBTN), 0,
                 0, 0, 260, 185, SWP_NOZORDER ¦ SWP_NOMOVE);
}
```

It's best to use SetWindowPos rather than MoveWindow because the former call provides support
for the SWP_NOMOVE flag.

The *SetWindowPos* Function

Syntax

```
BOOL SetWindowPos(
    HWND  hwnd,              // handle of window
    HWND  hwndInsertAfter,   // specify z-order
    int   x,                 // left
    int   y,                 // top
    int   cx,                // width
    int   cy,                // height
    UINT  fuFlags            // window-positioning flags
    );
```

This function is a close kin to the MoveWindow function, except that it has a number of extra
capabilities.

The first, third, fourth, fifth, and sixth parameters of the SetWindowPos function perform exactly
as expected. That is, you pass the handle of the window you want to move in the first parameter
and set the position you want the window to move to in the third, fourth, fifth, and sixth
parameters.

You can use the second parameter of the function to set the z-order of the window on the
desktop. Remember that in coordinate systems, x handles the horizontal location, y the vertical
location, and z the third dimension of depth. Of course, there is no real third dimension on the
standard Windows desktop, but some windows do appear in front of other windows. This is a
kind of poor man's third dimension, and it is what z-order is all about.

The following flags are passed in with the second parameter to control the z-order:

HWND_BOTTOM	Puts the window at the bottom of the z-order
HWND_NOTOPMOST	Puts the window above all non-topmost windows
HWND_TOP	Puts the window at the top of the z-order
HWND_TOPMOST	Puts the window above all topmost windows

The last parameter is used for a number of special purposes. Here are the flags that are passed in the last parameter:

SWP_DRAWFRAME	Draws a frame around the window
SWP_FRAMECHANGED	Sends a WM_NCCALCSIZE message to the window
SWP_HIDEWINDOW	Hides the window
SWP_NOACTIVATE	Does not activate the window
SWP_NOCOPYBITS	Doesn't copy the contents of the client area
SWP_NOMOVE	Ignores x and y parameters
SWP_NOSIZE	Ignores cx and cy parameters
SWP_NOREDRAW	Does not redraw changes
SWP_NOZORDER	Retains z-order, and ignores the hwndInsertAfter
SWP_SHOWWINDOW	Displays the window

You can read more about these flags by turning to online help.

Here's an example:

```
SetWindowPos(GetDlgItem(hwnd, ID_FIRSTBTN), 0,
             0, 0, 260, 185, SWP_NOZORDER | SWP_NOMOVE);
```

When using the SetWindowPos function, the TabDemo program takes advantage of the SWP_NOZORDER flag because there is no need, and no desire, to change the z-order. The SWP_NOMOVE flag ensures that the top-left corner of the window is not moved. That would be a serious mistake because it's difficult to recalculate the location of a window that appears in a dialog. The issue, of course, is that dialog units are not the same as pixels. As a result, it's okay to change the location of the bottom-right corner, but you should leave the top-left one where it is. In short, I use SetWindowPos instead of MoveWindow because it has the capability to move one portion of a window at a time.

Note: Previously, I stated that it is not a good idea to move a window in a dialog. But suppose you do need to move the window? What can you do?

The following function demonstrates how you can calculate the relationship between the pixels on the desktop and the dialog units you use in an RC file:

```
void DlgOccidental_OnSize(HWND hwnd, UINT state, int cx, int cy)
{
  int BaseUnit, BaseUnitX, BaseUnitY;
  int X, Y;

  BaseUnit = GetDialogBaseUnits();
  BaseUnitX = LOWORD(BaseUnit);
  BaseUnitY = HIWORD(BaseUnit);
  X = (10 * BaseUnitX) / 4;
  Y = (30 * BaseUnitY) / 8;
  MoveWindow(GetDlgItem(hwnd, ID_FIRSTBTN), X, Y, 260, 185, TRUE);
}
```

The call to `GetDialogBaseUnits` retrieves a constant you can use to translate back and forth between dialog units and pixels. Use the `LOWORD` and `HIWORD` macros to retrieve the *X* and *Y* base units. Now plug them into the following formulas:

```
PixelX = (DlgUnitX * BaseUnitX) / 4;
PixelY = (DlgUnitY * BaseUnitY) / 8;
```

In the Occidental dialog, I get the numbers 10 and 30 from the actual declaration of the button in the RC file. In other words, these are the particular x and y dimensions that I want to calculate.

The `GetDialogBaseUnits` function only works if you are using the system font. The problem here is that the dialog's units are calculated in terms of the current font. If you choose a larger font or if Windows 95 selects one for you, then the dialog units become larger and your whole dialog grows. As a result, if you are not using the system font in your dialog, then you need to use the following formulas:

```
PixelsX = (DlgUnitX * average width  of font) / 4
PixelsY = (DlgUnitY * average height of font) / 8
```

For further information, see the Microsoft SDK Knowledge Base article titled "How to Calculate Dialog Base Units with Non-System-Based Fonts." Remember that calling `GetSystemMetrics` to get information on the current font in a dialog is not always a straightforward operation!

In this context, I should also mention the `MapDialogRect` function, which perhaps provides a cleaner solution than the ones I have outlined previously. If you want to incorporate this kind of code into your shipping products, be sure to look over the `MapDialogRect` function in the online help.

In the examples discussed previously, the goal was to keep the controls in the dialog at the same positions they were in when they were defined in your RC file. However, there are times when

you might not want to keep the exact same position in terms of dialog units but rather the same relative position in terms of the whole window. In other words, if you put a control in the center of the dialog, you would want it to stay there even if you moved the dialog.

Here is how the OrientalDialog keeps the button in the center of the dialog, and keeps the static control on the top row, and in the horizontal center, of the dialog:

```
void DlgOriental_OnSize(HWND hwnd, UINT state, int cx, int cy)
{
  int Width, Height;
  RECT Rect2;

  Width = (cx / 2) - 130;
  Height = (cy / 2) - 92;
  MoveWindow(GetDlgItem(hwnd, ID_SECONDBTN),
          Width, Height, 260, 184, TRUE);
  GetClientRect(GetDlgItem(hwnd, ID_SECONDTXT), &Rect2);
  Rect2.left = (cx / 2) - (Rect2.right / 2);
  MoveWindow(GetDlgItem(hwnd, ID_SECONDTXT),
          Rect2.left, Rect2.top, Rect2.right, Rect2.bottom, TRUE);
}
```

To understand this function, you need to remember that the bitmap is 250×175 pixels in size. Furthermore, you want the button's three-dimensional edges to be on display and not hidden behind the button. To achieve that effect, you need to find the center of the window and then count back half the width of the button and half its height. Using that point as the button's upper-left corner does the trick. The code performs similar manipulations to move the static text into the top center of the window.

That's it for the discussion of tab controls and dialogs. This has been a relatively complex discussion, but I've been able to cover a number of useful topics that should help you create your own programs that follow this powerful model.

Dialogs and WINDOWSX.H

Prior to this chapter, I have used message crackers in the main WndProc for a program, but not in a dialog. If you look at the main body of the OrientalProc, you will see that it makes use of some WindowsX message crackers. For instance, the WM_INITDIALOG, WM_SIZE, and WM_COMMAND messages all feature the WindowsX style.

Dialog procedures return BOOL, while WndProcs return LRESULT. The message crackers, of course, were designed to work explicitly with WndProcs. As a result, you need to push them a bit to work with dialogs. In particular, the HANDLE_MSG macro does not work with dialogs. Instead, you need to work directly with the HANDLE_WM_xxx macros, which are hidden from your sight when you use WindowsX in a WndProc.

Here's how WindowsX message crackers look in a dialog procedure:

```
BOOL CALLBACK OrientalProc(HWND hDlg, UINT Message,
                     WPARAM wParam, LPARAM lParam)
{
  switch(Message)
  {
    case WM_INITDIALOG:
      return HANDLE_WM_INITDIALOG(hDlg, wParam,
               lParam, DlgOriental_OnInitDialog);

    case WM_CTLCOLORSTATIC:
      SetBkMode((HDC)wParam, TRANSPARENT);
      return (BOOL)GetStockBrush(LTGRAY_BRUSH);

    case WM_CTLCOLORDLG:
      return (BOOL) GetStockBrush(LTGRAY_BRUSH);

    case WM_SIZE:
      HANDLE_WM_SIZE(hDlg, wParam, lParam, DlgOriental_OnSize);
      return TRUE;

    case WM_COMMAND:
      HANDLE_WM_COMMAND(hDlg, wParam, lParam, DlgOriental_OnCommand);
      return TRUE;
  }
  return (FALSE); // Didn't process the message
}
```

If you look at this dialog procedure, you can see that I have moved all the long code blocks that require message cracking out of the main body of the procedure via the HANDLE_WM_*XXX* macros. The short easy commands, such as WM_CTLCOLOR, have been handled directly in the main body of the function.

Some WindowsX message handlers return values:

```
BOOL DlgOccidental_OnInitDialog(HWND hwnd, HWND hwndFocus, LPARAM lParam)
```

while others don't:

```
void DlgOccidental_OnCommand(HWND hwnd, int id, HWND hwndCtl, UINT codeNotify)
```

If the function does return a value, then you can handle it like this:

```
case WM_INITDIALOG:
    return HANDLE_WM_INITDIALOG(hDlg, wParam,
      lParam, DlgOriental_OnInitDialog);
```

If it doesn't return a value, then you need to take two lines to process the message:

```
case WM_SIZE:
      HANDLE_WM_SIZE(hDlg, wParam, lParam, DlgOriental_OnSize);
      return TRUE;
```

Overall, I think that WindowsX is a good way to handle complex dialog functions. It's not worth it if your dialog procedure is only a few lines long. But if you build a whole application around

the shell of the TabDemo program, then you will probably need to create some fairly complex dialogs. One good way to give those big dialog procedures some structure is to break them up with WindowsX.

Note: When working with WindowsX day in and day out, you can greatly simplify your life by using an editor that lets you write macros. That way you can place all the message cracker function definitions inside of macros and call them up when needed. Here are a couple simple macros to be used with Borland's Brief editor:

```
void Command()
{
  insert("void Cls_OnCommand(HWND hwnd, int id, HWND hwndCtl, UINT
codeNotify)\n");
}

void Size()
{
  insert("void Cls_OnSize(HWND hwnd, UINT state, int cx, int cy)\n");
}

void InitDialog()
{
  insert("BOOL Cls_OnInitDialog(HWND hwnd, HWND hwndFocus, LPARAM
lParam)\n");
}
```

After creating and compiling these macros, I can automatically insert the WM_COMMAND, WM_SIZE, and WM_INITDIALOG function headers into my application simply by selecting an option and typing the word Command, Size, or InitDialog. Additional Brief macros of this type are included with the online code.

The TabDemo Dialog

The TabDemo program sports a dialog that allows you to see how common controls look inside of resources. It features a slew of different controls and allows you to interact with them all so that you can see how they work. The dialog aims to be educational and does not attempt to perform any other more mundane task. In other words, it doesn't really do anything sensible, it just gives some common controls a good workout.

Note: Unlike DLGWEST.CPP and DLGEAST.CPP, the DLGABOUT.CPP module does not use the WindowsX message crackers. I took this course because it allows you to see a variety of coding styles and because the dialog itself is simple enough not to call for any complex parsing of wParam and lParam.

The dialog gets its start in life in the WM_COMMAND handler for the main window:

```
case IDM_ABOUT:
  DialogBox(hInstance, "AboutBox", hwnd, (DLGPROC)About);
  break;
```

Because this is WIN32, we can skip the MakeProcInstance and FreeProcInstance business. The end result is an admirable simplicity of syntax. Though nonprogrammers may not appreciate the fact, large address spaces aren't the only benefits of WIN32!

Here is the definition for the About dialog:

```
ABOUTBOX DIALOG 22, 17, 167, 120
STYLE DS_MODALFRAME | WS_CAPTION | WS_SYSMENU
CAPTION "About TabDemo"
BEGIN
  CONTROL "&All", -1, "static",
    WS_CHILD | SS_RIGHT, 5, 6, 45, 8
  CONTROL "", ID_HOTKEY1, HOTKEY_CLASS,
    WS_TABDEMO, 50, 5, 80, 12

  CONTROL "&Only Ctrl", -1, "static",
    WS_CHILD | SS_RIGHT, 5, 21, 45, 8
  CONTROL "", ID_HOTKEY2,
    HOTKEY_CLASS, WS_TABDEMO, 50, 20, 80, 12

  CONTROL "&Not Alt", -1, "static",
    WS_CHILD | SS_RIGHT, 5, 36, 45, 8
  CONTROL "", ID_HOTKEY3, HOTKEY_CLASS,
    WS_TABDEMO, 50, 35, 80, 12

  CONTROL "1", ID_SPINBUDDY, "Edit",
    WS_TABDEMO, 30, 50, 30, 12
  CONTROL "", ID_SPINNER, UPDOWN_CLASS,
    UDS_AUTOBUDDY | WS_CHILD | UDS_SETBUDDYINT, 60, 50, 10, 12

  CONTROL "", ID_PROG, TRACKBAR_CLASS,
    WS_TABDEMO | TBS_AUTOTICKS, 30, 75, 100, 16
  CONTROL "Crate", ID_STAT, STATUSCLASSNAME,
    WS_CHILD | WS_BORDER, 0, 0, 0, 0

  DEFPUSHBUTTON   "OK", IDOK, 70, 95, 32, 14, WS_GROUP
END
```

When creating this dialog I used the following custom style:

```
#define WS_TABDEMO WS_CHILD | WS_BORDER | WS_TABSTOP
```

Warning: The WS_TABDEMO style is just a shorthand way of writing WS_CHILD | WS_BORDER | WS_TABSTOP. I use it because it helps to make the RC file shorter, less intimidating, and somewhat more readable.

If you look carefully at the definition of the RC file you will see that I have included four special Windows 95 controls. Here is the code that brings in a trackbar:

```
CONTROL "", ID_PROG, TRACKBAR_CLASS,
    WS_TABDEMO | TBS_AUTOTICKS, 30, 75, 100, 16
```

After creating the trackbar, you still need to set its range and starting position in response to a `WM_INITDIALOG` message:

```
void SetupTrackbar(HWND hDlg)
{
  HWND hwnd = GetDlgItem(hDlg, ID_PROG);
  SendMessage(hwnd, TBM_SETRANGE, (WPARAM)1, (LPARAM)MAKELONG(0, 10));
  SendMessage(hwnd, TBM_SETPOS, (WPARAM)1, (LPARAM)5);
}
```

This code was explained on Day 15, "Introduction to Windows Controls," so I won't reference it further here.

Here's code for creating the status bar:

```
CONTROL "Crate", ID_STAT, STATUSCLASSNAME,
    WS_CHILD | WS_BORDER, 0, 0, 0, 0
```

For now, I'll put off a description of how to fill in the status bar, though the basic theory should be clear to you from Day 15.

18

> **Note:** As always, it's easier to instantiate an instance of a control inside a dialog than it is to call `CreateWindow` in the main body of your program. This held true for standard controls such as listboxes and buttons, and it's also true for the new common controls.
>
> You can create not only premade Windows classes this way, but also your own custom classes. Just define and call the `Register` procedure for your class in the main body of your code and then pass the class name in to an `RC CONTROL` statement like those shown here.

There are two new WIN32 common control classes used in the About dialog. One is called the hotkey class and the other is the spinner class. I discuss them in the next two sections.

Hotkey Controls

Here is code for creating an instance of the hotkey class:

```
CONTROL "", ID_HOTKEY3, HOTKEY_CLASS,
    WS_TABDEMO, 50, 35, 80, 12
```

At runtime, these fellows look like edit controls, as shown in Figure 18.4. The hotkey control is meant to allow the user to select hotkeys at runtime. For instance, if you want the user to assign a hotkey of his or her own choice to a particular action, then you might ask the user to type the key combination in a hotkey control, and then you would record it. The hotkey control echoes back the users' input so that users can get visual confirmation of their actions. For instance, if they press the Shift and A keys, then they will see Shift+A written out in the hotkey control.

As I mentioned earlier, this is not exactly an earth-shattering feature. For instance, it's hard to imagine someone saying, "Well, I used to be a dyed-in-the-wool UNIX hacker, but after I heard about the hotkey control I figured I had to switch to Windows!"

No, this is definitely not what you'd call a "revolutionary" feature. But it does provide a way for users to define hotkeys, which is a nice touch if you want to provide a more usable, customizable interface to your programs. Actually, I kind of like the idea of letting the user decide which hotkeys do what, rather than always having the programmer follow some semi-arbitrary standard.

At any rate, after you have created the hotkey control, you might want to pass some messages to it at runtime so that it follows a particular set of rules:

```
void SetupHotKeys(HWND hwnd)
{
  // Use only control key,
  SendDlgItemMessage(hwnd, ID_HOTKEY2, HKM_SETRULES,
                     (HKCOMB_SA | HKCOMB_S | HKCOMB_A),
                     HOTKEYF_CONTROL);

  SendDlgItemMessage(hwnd, ID_HOTKEY3, HKM_SETRULES,
                     (HKCOMB_A | HKCOMB_SA | HKCOMB_CA),
                     HOTKEYF_CONTROL);
}
```

The HKM_SETRULES message tells the hotkey what key combinations are not valid. For instance, the HKCOMB_S message tells the hotkey not to accept the Shift key. Here is an unexpurgated entry from the online help that shows other possible combinations of rules:

```
HKCOMB_A      ALT
HKCOMB_C      CTRL
HKCOMB_CA     CTRL+ALT
HKCOMB_NONE   Unmodified keys
HKCOMB_S      SHIFT
HKCOMB_SA     SHIFT+ALT
HKCOMB_SC     SHIFT+CTRL
HKCOMB_SCA    SHIFT+CTRL+ALT
```

After specifying the rules in wParam, you then use lParam to tell Windows what to do if the user types in the wrong key. For instance, the previous code tells Windows to automatically insert the control key if the user hits one of the illegal keys. Here's a list of the possible values to put in lParam:

```
HOTKEYF_ALT        ALT key
HOTKEYF_CONTROL    CTRL key
```

```
HOTKEYF_EXT          Extended key
HOTKEYF_SHIFT        SHIFT key
```

The same values can be used when you want to retrieve or insert hotkey information using the HKM_GETHOTKEY or HKM_SETHOTKEY message.

The Up/Down Control

The final control that appears in the About dialog is the useful spinner control. Spinner controls consist of two back-to-back arrows that can be selected by the user. Press one arrow, and the value associated with the control is incremented. Press the other, and it is decremented.

Microsoft likes to come up with new, or at least uncommon, names for some of these Windows 95 controls. For instance, it calls the slider control a trackbar. In this case, Microsoft calls these fellas up/down controls instead of spinner controls.

Be that as it may, the up/down control ends up getting heavy use throughout the Windows 95 interface, and it's likely that you will also find a role for it in some of your programs. For an example of how Microsoft uses these controls, just double-click on the clock at the bottom right of the taskbar. This brings up the Date/Time Properties box shown in Figure 18.5.

Figure 18.5.

The Date/Time Properties box is a standard part of the Windows 95 interface.

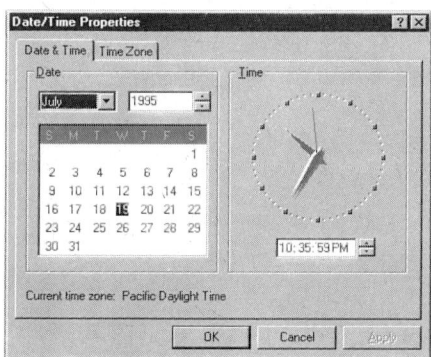

You can create an up/down control by calling CreateUpDownControl or by using a resource file. The About box, naturally enough, uses the RC file method:

```
CONTROL "1", ID_SPINBUDDY, "Edit",
  WS_TABDEMO, 30, 50, 30, 12
CONTROL "", ID_SPINNER, UPDOWN_CLASS,
  UDS_AUTOBUDDY | WS_CHILD | UDS_SETBUDDYINT, 60, 50, 10, 12
```

Up/down controls are usually paired with a "buddy" control that displays the output from the user's selection. In this case, an edit control does the honors. You do not have to do anything to an edit control to make it a buddy to the spinner. Instead, you give the spinner a UDS_AUTOBUDDY style. This means that the control that appears previous to the spinner in the z-order will be its buddy. In this case, the order of declaration in the RC files define the z-order

in the dialog. Note the use of the `UDS_SETBUDDYINT` style. This ensures that the control uses the `WM_SETTEXT` message to place a value in the edit control.

> **Note:** If you don't want to use the `UDS_AUTOBUDDY` style, another way to pair controls is with the `UDM_SETBUDDY` message. Pass the handle of the window in `wParam` and set the `lParam` to zero.
>
> To retrieve the handle of the current buddy window, use the `UDM_GETBUDDY` message. `UDM_GETBUDDY` sets both `wParam` and `lParam` to zero.
>
> Here are other possible messages used with up/down controls: `UDM_GETACCEL`, `UDM_GETBASE`, `UDM_GETPOS`, `UDM_GETRANGE`, `UDM_SETACCEL`, `UDM_SETBASE`, and `UDM_SETPOS`. They are well documented in the online help.

The `UDM_SETRANGE` message can be used to set the range of a spinner control. Here is an example from the TabDemo program:

```
// Set the Spinner #1 range from -10 to 10
SendDlgItemMessage(hwnd, ID_SPINNER, UDM_SETRANGE,
                    (WPARAM)0, MAKELPARAM(-10,10));
```

Like a scrollbar, a spinner control can be either horizontal or vertical, depending on whether you give it the `UDS_HORZ` style.

When the user increments or decrements a spinner, two things happen. First `UDN_DELTAPOS` notification is sent via a `WM_NOTIFY` message. This notification gives you a chance to respond to the user's action before any changes appear on-screen. You could, for instance, use this message to refuse the user the right to make the change.

Assuming the user's action gets passed the `UDN_DELTAPOS` notification, the change is then sent on in the form of a `WM_VSCROLL` message. In TabDemo, only spinners are sending `WM_VSCROLL` messages:

```
case WM_VSCROLL:
    // UPDOWN Controls
    UpDownPos = SendMessage(GetDlgItem(hDlg, ID_SPINNER), UDM_GETPOS, 0, 0);
    sprintf(S, "UpDown Position: %d", UpDownPos);
    SetWindowText(GetDlgItem(hDlg, ID_STAT), S);
    break;
```

The code shown here uses the `UDM_GETPOS` message to retrieve the new position. This value is then sent on to the status bar via a call to `SetWindowText`. (On Day 15 I showed you other, more official ways to update a status bar.)

The About dialog responds to not only WM_VSCROLL messages but also to WM_HSCROLL messages. These latter messages come from the trackbar and are handled as follows:

```
case WM_HSCROLL:
      // Handle Trackbar;
      TrackPos = SendMessage(GetDlgItem(hDlg, ID_PROG),
                             TBM_GETPOS, 0, 0);
      SendMessage(GetDlgItem(hDlg, ID_SPINNER),
               UDM_SETPOS, (WPARAM)1, (LPARAM)TrackPos);
      break;
```

The TBM_GETPOS message retrieves the current value in the trackbar, and the UDM_SETPOS message inserts the same value in the up/down control. As stated above, it's not very practical from any but the purely pedagogical point of view.

That's all I'm going to say about the TabDemo program. It has proven to be an unusually rich source of information that has sparked descriptions of tab controls, dialog coordinates, WM_NOTIFY messages, bitmap buttons, spinners, hotkeys, and various other features of the Windows API. After all this fervent huffing and puffing, you will find the following description of property sheets to be considerably more straightforward.

Using Property Sheets

For some reason I am rather partial to the flexibility offered by tab controls. However, if you want a much simpler way to achieve the same end, you can just pop up a property sheet. These tools appear everywhere on the Windows 95 interface, particularly in response to right-clicks with the mouse. You saw one property sheet previously in Figure 18.5. You can see the one from the next sample program in Figure 18.6.

Figure 18.6.

The property sheet in the PSheet demo allows you to change the color and features of the shape drawn in the main window.

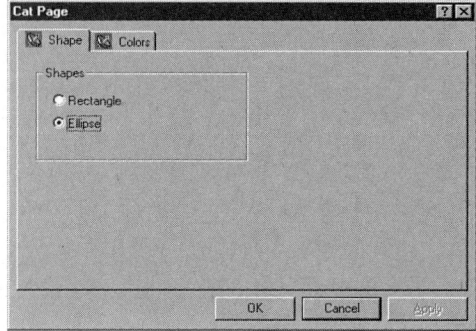

At this stage, it would probably be simplest if you get the PSheet program up and running, and then I will discuss some of its main features. The code for the program appears in Listings 18.9 through 18.16.

Listing 18.9. The main module from the PSheet sample program.

```
//////////////////////////////////////////////////////////
//   Program Name: PSheet.cpp
//   Programmer: Charlie Calvert
//   Description: PSheet windows program
//   Date: 06/27/95
//////////////////////////////////////////////////////////

#define STRICT
#define WIN32_LEAN_AND_MEAN
#include <windows.h>
#include <windowsx.h>
#include <prsht.h>
#include "psheet.h"
#pragma warning (disable: 4068)


// ----------------------------------------------------------
// Interface
// ----------------------------------------------------------

static char szAppName[] = "PSheet";
static HWND MainWindow;
static HINSTANCE hInstance;
TDLGDATA DlgData;
static BOOL UseWizard;


// ----------------------------------------------------------
// Initialization
// ----------------------------------------------------------


//////////////////////////////////////////////////////////
// Program entry point
//////////////////////////////////////////////////////////
```

```
#pragma argsused
int WINAPI WinMain(HINSTANCE hInst, HINSTANCE hPrevInstance, LPSTR lpszCmdParam,
int nCmdShow)
{
  MSG  Msg;

  hInstance = hInst;

  if (!hPrevInstance)
    if (!Register(hInst))
      return FALSE;

  MainWindow = Create(hInst, nCmdShow);
  if (!MainWindow)
    return FALSE;

  while (GetMessage(&Msg, NULL, 0, 0))
  {
    TranslateMessage(&Msg);
    DispatchMessage(&Msg);
  }

  return Msg.wParam;
}

//////////////////////////////////////////////////////
// Register the window
//////////////////////////////////////////////////////
BOOL Register(HINSTANCE hInst)
{
  WNDCLASSEX WndClass;

  WndClass.cbSize        = sizeof(WNDCLASSEX);
  WndClass.style         = CS_HREDRAW | CS_VREDRAW;
  WndClass.lpfnWndProc   = WndProc;
  WndClass.cbClsExtra    = 0;
  WndClass.cbWndExtra    = 0;
  WndClass.hInstance     = hInst;
  WndClass.hIcon         = LoadIcon(hInst, "PSheetIcon");
  WndClass.hCursor       = LoadCursor(NULL, IDC_ARROW);
  WndClass.hbrBackground = (HBRUSH)(COLOR_WINDOW+1);
  WndClass.lpszMenuName  = "PSheetMenu";
  WndClass.lpszClassName = szAppName;
  WndClass.hIconSm       = LoadIcon(hInst, "PSheetIcon16");

  return (RegisterClassEx (&WndClass) != 0);
}

//////////////////////////////////////////////////////
// Create the window
//////////////////////////////////////////////////////
HWND Create(HINSTANCE hInst, int nCmdShow)
{
```

18

continues

Listing 18.9. continued

```
          HWND hwnd = CreateWindowEx(0, szAppName, szAppName,
                        WS_OVERLAPPEDWINDOW,
                        CW_USEDEFAULT, CW_USEDEFAULT,
                        CW_USEDEFAULT, CW_USEDEFAULT,
                        NULL, NULL, hInst, NULL);

    if (hwnd == NULL)
      return hwnd;

    ShowWindow(hwnd, nCmdShow);
    UpdateWindow(hwnd);

    return hwnd;
}

// ------------------------------------------------------
// WndProc and Implementation
// ------------------------------------------------------

///////////////////////////////////////////////////////////
// The Window Procedure
///////////////////////////////////////////////////////////
LRESULT CALLBACK WndProc(HWND hwnd, UINT Message,
                         WPARAM wParam, LPARAM lParam)
{
  switch(Message)
  {
    HANDLE_MSG(hwnd, WM_CREATE, PSheet_OnCreate);
    HANDLE_MSG(hwnd, WM_DESTROY, PSheet_OnDestroy);
    HANDLE_MSG(hwnd, WM_COMMAND, PSheet_OnCommand);
    HANDLE_MSG(hwnd, WM_PAINT, PSheet_OnPaint);
    default: return PSheet_DefProc(hwnd, Message, wParam, lParam);
  }
}

///////////////////////////////////////////////////////////
// WM_CREATE: Set UseWizard, and check menu option
///////////////////////////////////////////////////////////
#pragma argsused
BOOL PSheet_OnCreate(HWND hwnd, LPCREATESTRUCT lpCreateStruct)
{

  HMENU hMenu = GetMenu(hwnd);

  UseWizard = FALSE;

  CheckMenuItem (hMenu, CM_TABS,
                 MF_BYCOMMAND ¦ UseWizard==FALSE ?
                 MF_CHECKED : MF_UNCHECKED );

  return TRUE;
}

///////////////////////////////////////////////////////////
// WM_DESTROY: Clean up
///////////////////////////////////////////////////////////
```

```
#pragma argsused
void PSheet_OnDestroy(HWND hwnd)
{
  PostQuitMessage(0);
}


///////////////////////////////////////////////////////
// CHECKMENUS: Did the user choose Wizards or Tabs?
///////////////////////////////////////////////////////
void CheckMenus(HWND hwnd)
{

  HMENU hMenu = GetMenu(hwnd);

  CheckMenuItem (hMenu, CM_TABS,
                 MF_BYCOMMAND | UseWizard==FALSE ?
                 MF_CHECKED : MF_UNCHECKED );
  CheckMenuItem (hMenu, CM_WIZARD,
                 MF_BYCOMMAND | UseWizard==TRUE ?
                 MF_CHECKED : MF_UNCHECKED );

}


///////////////////////////////////////////////////////
// WM_ONCOMMAND: What menu item was chosen?
///////////////////////////////////////////////////////
#pragma argsused
void PSheet_OnCommand(HWND hwnd, int id, HWND hwndCtl, UINT codeNotify)
{
  int SheetRun;
  TDLGDATA Temp;

  switch(id)
  {
    case CM_SHOWTABS:
      Temp = DlgData;
      SheetRun = CreatePropertySheet(hwnd, hInstance);
      if (SheetRun != IDOK)
        DlgData = Temp;
      else
        InvalidateRect(hwnd, NULL, FALSE);
      break;

    case CM_WIZARD:
      UseWizard = TRUE;
      CheckMenus(hwnd);
      break;

    case CM_TABS:
      UseWizard = FALSE;
      CheckMenus(hwnd);
      break;
  }
}


///////////////////////////////////////////////////////
// WM_PAINT: Draw the shapes
///////////////////////////////////////////////////////
```

Listing 18.9. continued

```c
void PSheet_OnPaint(HWND hwnd)
{
  PAINTSTRUCT PaintStruct;
  RECT Rect;
  COLORREF Color;

  GetClientRect(hwnd, &Rect);

  HDC PaintDC = BeginPaint(hwnd, &PaintStruct);

  switch(DlgData.Color)
  {
    case ddRed:
      Color = RGB(255, 0, 0);
      break;
    case ddGreen:
      Color = RGB(0, 255, 0);
      break;
    case ddBlue:
      Color = RGB(0, 0, 255);
      break;
  }

  HBRUSH NewBrush = CreateSolidBrush(Color);
  HBRUSH OldBrush = SelectBrush(PaintDC, NewBrush);

  if (DlgData.Shape == ddRectangle)
    Rectangle(PaintDC, 10, 10, Rect.right - 20, Rect.bottom - 20);
  else
    Ellipse(PaintDC, 10, 10, Rect.right - 20, Rect.bottom - 20);

  SelectBrush(PaintDC, OldBrush);
  DeleteBrush(NewBrush);

  EndPaint(hwnd, &PaintStruct);
}

///////////////////////////////////////////////////////
// Define the dialogs shown in the tabs dialog
///////////////////////////////////////////////////////
void DefinePropertyPage(PROPSHEETPAGE* psp, int idDlg,
                        LPSTR pszProc, DLGPROC pfnDlgProc)
{
  psp->dwSize = sizeof(PROPSHEETPAGE);
  psp->dwFlags = PSP_USETITLE | PSP_USEICONID;
  psp->hInstance = hInstance;
  psp->pszTemplate = MAKEINTRESOURCE(idDlg);
  psp->pszIcon = "PSheetIcon16";
  psp->pfnDlgProc = pfnDlgProc;
  psp->pszTitle = pszProc;
  psp->lParam = 0;
}
```

```
/////////////////////////////////////////////////////
// CreatePropertySheet
/////////////////////////////////////////////////////
#pragma argsused // MS stack bug?
int CreatePropertySheet(HWND hwnd, HINSTANCE hInst)
{
  PROPSHEETPAGE psp[NUMPROPPAGES];
  PROPSHEETHEADER psh;

  DefinePropertyPage(&psp[0], ID_DIALOG1, TEXT("Shape"), ShapeDialog);
  DefinePropertyPage(&psp[1], ID_DIALOG2, TEXT("Colors"), ColorDialog);

  psh.dwSize = sizeof(PROPSHEETHEADER);
  if (UseWizard == TRUE)
    psh.dwFlags = PSH_PROPSHEETPAGE ¦ PSH_WIZARD ¦ PSH_NOAPPLYNOW;
  else
    psh.dwFlags = PSH_PROPSHEETPAGE;
  psh.hwndParent = hwnd;
  psh.pszCaption = "Rupert the Cat Sheet";
  psh.nPages = NUMPROPPAGES;
  psh.ppsp = (LPCPROPSHEETPAGE) &psp;

  return (PropertySheet(&psh));
}
```

18

Listing 18.10. The header file for the property sheet example.

```
///////////////////////////////////////
// PSHEET.H
// Copyright (c) 1995 Charlie Calvert.
// 07/03/95
///////////////////////////////////////

// Constants
#define ID_DIALOG1     200
#define ID_DIALOG2     201
#define CM_SHOWTABS    101
#define CM_TABS        102
#define CM_WIZARD      103
#define ID_ELLIPSE     104
#define ID_RECTANGLE   105
#define ID_GROUPBOX1   106
#define ID_RED         107
#define ID_GREEN       108
#define ID_BLUE        109
#define ID_GROUPBOX2   110

#define NUMPROPPAGES   2

// Types
enum DLGDATASHAPES  {ddRectangle, ddEllipse};
enum DLGDATACOLORS  {ddRed, ddGreen, ddBlue};
```

continues

751

Listing 18.10. continued

```
typedef struct tagShape
{
  DLGDATASHAPES Shape;
  DLGDATACOLORS Color;
} TDLGDATA;

// Funcs
BOOL Register(HINSTANCE hInst);
HWND Create(HINSTANCE hInst, int nCmdShow);
LRESULT CALLBACK WndProc(HWND hwnd, UINT Message,
                        WPARAM wParam, LPARAM lParam);

// Declarations for class PSheet
#define PSheet_DefProc    DefWindowProc
BOOL PSheet_OnCreate(HWND hwnd, LPCREATESTRUCT lpCreateStruct);
void PSheet_OnDestroy(HWND hwnd);
void PSheet_OnCommand(HWND hwnd, int id, HWND hwndCtl, UINT codeNotify);
void PSheet_OnPaint(HWND hwnd);

int CreatePropertySheet(HWND hwnd, HINSTANCE hInst);
BOOL APIENTRY ShapeDialog(HWND hDlg, UINT message,
                        WPARAM wParam, LPARAM lParam);
BOOL APIENTRY ColorDialog(HWND hDlg, UINT message,
                        WPARAM wParam, LPARAM lParam);
```

Listing 18.11. The dialog in the property sheet that governs the selection of shapes.

```
/////////////////////////////////////////////////////////
// DLGSHAPE.CPP
// PROJECT: PSHEET
// Copyright (c) 1995 Charlie Calvert.
// DescriptionL: Handle the shape page of property sheet
/////////////////////////////////////////////////////////

#define STRICT
#include <windows.h>
#include <windowsx.h>
#include <commctrl.h>
#include "psheet.h"

extern TDLGDATA DlgData;

/////////////////////////////////////////////////////////
// Respond to user request to change shapes
/////////////////////////////////////////////////////////
#pragma argsused
void DlgShape_OnCommand(HWND hwnd, int id, HWND hwndCtl, UINT codeNotify)
{
  switch(id)
  {
```

```
      case ID_RECTANGLE:
        DlgData.Shape = ddRectangle;
        break;

      case ID_ELLIPSE:
        DlgData.Shape = ddEllipse;
        break;
    }
  }

  ////////////////////////////////////////////////////////
  // Property sheet messages comming in...
  ////////////////////////////////////////////////////////
  #pragma argsused
  LRESULT DlgShape_OnNotify(HWND hwnd, int idFrom, NMHDR FAR * pnmhdr)
  {
    switch (pnmhdr->code)
    {
      case PSN_KILLACTIVE:
        SetWindowLong(hwnd, DWL_MSGRESULT, FALSE);
        break;

      case PSN_RESET:
        SetWindowLong(hwnd, DWL_MSGRESULT, FALSE);
        break;

      case PSN_SETACTIVE:
        PropSheet_SetWizButtons(GetParent(hwnd), PSWIZB_NEXT);
        break;

      case PSN_WIZBACK:
        break;

      case PSN_WIZNEXT:
        break;

      default:
        return FALSE;
    }
    return TRUE;
  }

  ////////////////////////////////////////////////////////
  // Dialog governing the shape
  ////////////////////////////////////////////////////////
  #pragma argsused
  BOOL APIENTRY ShapeDialog(HWND hDlg, UINT message,
                            WPARAM wParam, LPARAM lParam)
  {
    switch (message)
    {
      case WM_INITDIALOG:
        DlgData.Shape = ddRectangle;
        return TRUE;
```

18

continues

Listing 18.11. continued

```
        case WM_COMMAND:
          HANDLE_WM_COMMAND(hDlg, wParam, lParam, DlgShape_OnCommand);
          return TRUE;

        case WM_NOTIFY:
          return HANDLE_WM_NOTIFY(hDlg, wParam, lParam, DlgShape_OnNotify);

        default:
          return FALSE;
   }
}
```

Listing 18.12. The dialog in the property sheet that governs the selection of colors.

```
/////////////////////////////////////////////////////////
// DLGSHAPE.CPP
// PROJECT: PSHEET
// Copyright (c) 1995 Charlie Calvert.
// DescriptionL: Handle the shape page of property sheet
/////////////////////////////////////////////////////////
#define STRICT
#include <windows.h>
#include <windowsx.h>
#include <commctrl.h>
#include "psheet.h"

extern TDLGDATA DlgData;

/////////////////////////////////////////////////////////
// WM_COMMAND: Handle color choices in the property sheet
/////////////////////////////////////////////////////////
#pragma argsused
void DlgColor_OnCommand(HWND hwnd, int id, HWND hwndCtl, UINT codeNotify)
{
  switch(id)
  {
    case ID_RED:
      DlgData.Color = ddRed;
      break;

    case ID_GREEN:
      DlgData.Color = ddGreen;
      break;

    case ID_BLUE:
      DlgData.Color = ddBlue;
      break;
  }
}
```

```
//////////////////////////////////////////////////////
// WM_NOTIFY: Setup the buttons for the wizard style
//////////////////////////////////////////////////////
#pragma argsused
LRESULT DlgColor_OnNotify(HWND hwnd, int idFrom, NMHDR FAR * pnmhdr)
{
  switch (pnmhdr->code)
  {
    case PSN_KILLACTIVE:
      SetWindowLong(hwnd, DWL_MSGRESULT, FALSE);
      break;

    case PSN_RESET:
      // rest to the original values
      SetWindowLong(hwnd, DWL_MSGRESULT, FALSE);
      break;

    case PSN_SETACTIVE:
      PropSheet_SetWizButtons(GetParent(hwnd), PSWIZB_BACK | PSWIZB_FINISH);
      break;

    case PSN_WIZBACK:
      break;

    case PSN_WIZNEXT:
      break;

    default:
      return FALSE;
  }
  return TRUE;
}


//////////////////////////////////////////////////////
// The dialog governing the color of the shape
//////////////////////////////////////////////////////
BOOL APIENTRY ColorDialog(HWND hDlg, UINT message,
                          WPARAM wParam, LPARAM lParam)
{
  switch (message)
  {
    case WM_INITDIALOG:
      DlgData.Color = ddRed;
      break;

    case WM_COMMAND:
      HANDLE_WM_COMMAND(hDlg, wParam, lParam, DlgColor_OnCommand);
      break;

    case WM_NOTIFY:
      return HANDLE_WM_NOTIFY(hDlg, wParam, lParam, DlgColor_OnNotify);

    default:
      return FALSE;
```

18

continues

Listing 18.12. continued

```
    }
    return TRUE;
}
```

Listing 18.13. The RC file for the PSheet program.

```
#include "windows.h"
#include "psheet.h"

PSheetIcon ICON "psheet.ico"
PSheetIcon16 ICON "psheet16.ico"

ID_DIALOG1 DIALOG 6, 15, 148, 86
STYLE DS_MODALFRAME ¦ WS_POPUP ¦ WS_VISIBLE ¦ WS_CAPTION ¦ WS_SYSMENU
CAPTION "Shape"
FONT 10 "ARIAL"
{
 CONTROL "Rectangle", ID_RECTANGLE, "BUTTON", BS_AUTORADIOBUTTON, 19, 23, 60, 12
 CONTROL "Ellipse", ID_ELLIPSE, "BUTTON", BS_AUTORADIOBUTTON, 19, 36, 60, 12
 GROUPBOX "Shapes", ID_GROUPBOX1, 9, 8, 132, 57, BS_GROUPBOX
}

ID_DIALOG2 DIALOG 6, 15, 148, 86
STYLE DS_MODALFRAME ¦ WS_POPUP ¦ WS_VISIBLE ¦ WS_CAPTION ¦ WS_SYSMENU
CAPTION "Colors"
FONT 10, "Arial"
{
 CONTROL "Red", ID_RED, "BUTTON", BS_AUTORADIOBUTTON, 23, 19, 60, 12
 CONTROL "Green", ID_GREEN, "BUTTON", BS_AUTORADIOBUTTON, 23, 32, 60, 12
 CONTROL "Blue", ID_BLUE, "BUTTON", BS_AUTORADIOBUTTON, 23, 45, 60, 12
 GROUPBOX "Colors", ID_GROUPBOX2, 6, 8, 128, 55, BS_GROUPBOX
}

PSheetMenu MENU
{
 POPUP "Options"
 {
  MENUITEM "Tabs", CM_TABS
  MENUITEM "Wizard", CM_WIZARD
 }

 MENUITEM "Show Tabs", CM_SHOWTABS
}
```

Listing 18.14. The module definition file.

```
; PSheet.Def

NAME          PSheet
DESCRIPTION   'PSheet Window'
```

Listing 18.15. The Borland makefile for the PSheet program.

```
# PSheet.mak

# macros

!if !$d(BCROOT)\..
BCROOT  = $(MAKEDIR)
!endif

APPNAME = PSheet
INCPATH = $(BCROOT)\WIN32;$(BCROOT);$(BCROOT)\INCLUDE
LIBPATH = $(BCROOT)\LIB

COMPILER= BCC32.EXE
BRC     = BRC32.EXE
FLAGS   = -W -v -w4 -I$(INCPATH) -L$(LIBPATH)
OBJS    = $(APPNAME).obj DlgColor.obj DlgShape.obj

# link
$(APPNAME).exe: $(OBJS) $(APPNAME).def $(APPNAME).res
  $(COMPILER) $(FLAGS) $(OBJS) comctl32.lib
  $(BRC) -I$(INCPATH) $(APPNAME).res


# compiling
.cpp.obj:
  $(COMPILER) -c $(FLAGS) { $< }

# resource
$(APPNAME).res: $(APPNAME).rc
  $(BRC) -R -I$(INCPATH) $(APPNAME).RC
```

Listing 18.16. The Microsoft makefile for the PSheet program.

```
# -------------------------------
# PSHEETMS.MAK
# -------------------------------

TARGETOS=WIN95
APPVER=4.0
OBJS=PSHEET.OBJ DLGCOLOR.OBJ DLGSHAPE.OBJ

!include <win32.mak>

all: psheet.exe

# Update the resource if necessary

psheet.res: psheet.rc psheet.h
    $(rc) $(rcflags) $(rcvars) psheet.rc

# Update the object file if necessary
```

continues

Listing 18.16. continued

```
psheet.obj: psheet.cpp psheet.h
    $(cc) $(cflags) $(cvars) $(cdebug) psheet.cpp

dlgcolor.obj: dlgcolor.cpp psheet.h
    $(cc) $(cflags) $(cvars) $(cdebug) dlgcolor.cpp

dlgshape.obj: dlgshape.cpp psheet.h
    $(cc) $(cflags) $(cvars) $(cdebug) dlgshape.cpp

# Update the executable file if necessary,

psheet.exe: $(OBJS) psheet.res
    $(link) $(linkdebug) $(guiflags) -out:psheet.exe \
    $(OBJS) psheet.res $(guilibs) comctl32.lib
```

When working with the PSheet program, you should create two icons called PSHEET.ICO and PSHEET16.ICO. The first should be 32×32 pixels, and the second 16×16. They should both use 16 colors. I provide sample icons on disk, or you can just create your own. (I promise the code will work exactly the same no matter how you color the icons.)

The PSheet program has a main window in which I draw a colored shape. The menu allows you to bring up a property sheet that has two dialogs in it. The first dialog allows you to choose the shape of the GDI object in the main window. The second dialog allows you to choose the color of the object drawn in the main window.

A pop-up menu on the main window allows you to select whether the property sheet will appear as a tabbed control (see Figure 18.7) or as a wizard (see Figure 18.8). If the wizard option is chosen, Next and Previous buttons appear in the dialog. Wizards are called experts by Borland and have various other names when created by other companies. Microsoft uses a wizard when you create a new project inside of MSVC.EXE.

Figure 18.7.

Standard property sheets have tabs to allow the user to switch pages.

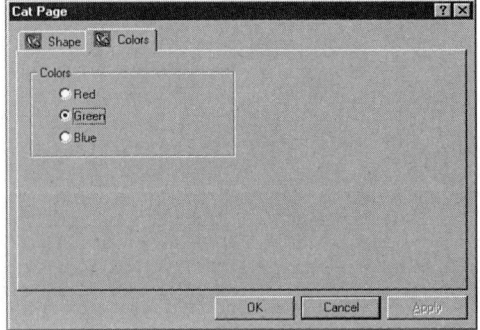

Figure 18.8.
Wizard property sheets allow the user to move between pages by using the Next, Back, and Finish buttons.

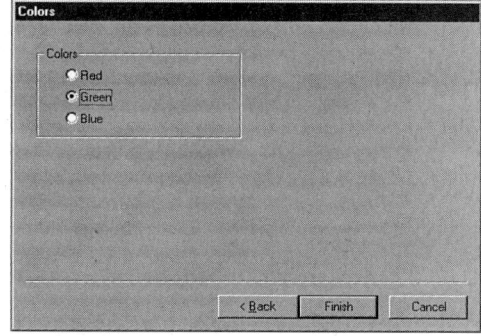

Working Property Sheets

The PSheet program is divided up into three main modules, following a pattern very similar to the one used in the TabDemo program. Specifically, I split out the two dialogs shown in the property sheet into the DLGCOLOR.CPP and DLGSHAPE.CPP modules. The main body of the program is responsible for creating the property sheets, but the code that handles the active dialogs is split off into separate units.

Like some of the other common controls you have seen, creating a property sheet is a multi-step process:

First, you need to fill out the structures that define the dialogs in the property sheet, being sure to hang each structure in an application defined array. The structures are of type PROPSHEETPAGE, and you need to declare an array of them:

```
PROPSHEETPAGE psp[NUMPROPPAGES];
```

I explain the PROPSHEETPAGE structure below.

After filling out the array, you assign it as a field in a larger structure called a PROPSHEETHEADER. Now send the whole kit and caboodle off to Windows via the PropertySheet function. It's this latter routine that actually creates the property sheet.

PropertySheet

```
int PropertySheet(LPCPROPSHEETHEADER lppsph);
```

Unless you define the PSH_MODELESS style, a call to PropertySheet will create a modal dialog.

The key to the PropertySheet function is PROPSHEETHEADER:

```
typedef struct _PROPSHEETHEADER { // psh
    DWORD       dwSize;     // Size in bytes of structure
    DWORD       dwFlags;    // Which fields of structure will be used?
    HWND        hwndParent; // Owner
    HINSTANCE   hInstance;  // Instance of file holding resources
    union {
```

```
      HICON   hIcon;       // Icon handle
      LPCTSTR pszIcon;     // or Icon resource string
  };
  LPCTSTR    pszCaption;// Title of Property sheet
  UINT       nPages      // Number of pages in array
  union {
      UINT  nStartPage   // Initial page, zero based
      LPCTSTR pStartPage;// Name of page that's shown first.
  };
  union {
      LPCPROPSHEETPAGE   ppsp;      // The array of PROPSHEETPAGEs
      HPROPSHEETPAGE FAR *phpage;   // Handles to an array of pages
  };
  PFNPROPSHEETCALLBACK pfnCallback; // Callback function if PSP_CALLBACK
} PROPSHEETHEADER, FAR *LPPROPSHEETHEADER;
typedef const PROPSHEETHEADER FAR *LPCPROPSHEETHEADER;
```

Now this is a lovely little number, by all accounts. The key point is that the structure is designed to give you considerable flexibility regarding the choices you make when filling it out. For instance, you can designate the first page to show by either giving its zero-based index in nStartPage or by specifying its name in pStartPage. This is an either/or proposition. Furthermore, you can use an index in a stringlist to specify the name in the pStartPage parameter. So, you have two mutually exclusive options, plus two different ways to fill out one of the possible options.

A moment's contemplation of this bouquet of options and I begin to feel overwhelmed, as author, if not as programmer. To help simplify the whole bundle, I am going to propose a recommended way to fill out the structure, and then let you dig around in the online help if you want to try some of the other options.

If you want to create a standard property sheet, then fill out the record as follows:

```
PROPSHEETHEADER psh;

psh.dwSize = sizeof(PROPSHEETHEADER);
psh.dwFlags = PSH_PROPSHEETPAGE;
psh.hwndParent = hwnd;
psh.pszCaption = (LPSTR)TEXT("Rupert the Cat Page");
psh.nPages = NUMPROPPAGES;
psh.ppsp = (LPCPROPSHEETPAGE) &psp;
```

If you want to create a wizard, then change the flags in the second field so they look like this:

```
psh.dwFlags = PSH_PROPSHEETPAGE | PSH_WIZARD | PSH_NOAPPLYNOW;
```

The PSH_PROPSHEETPAGE flag tells Windows to use the ppsp field rather than the phpage field of the last union in the record. The PSH_WIZARD flag creates a wizard-like property sheet. The PSH_NOAPPLYNOW button removes the Apply Now button. See the online help for a list of the many possible flags to use in this position.

The dwSize field gets filled out in the traditional manner that Microsoft uses when it wants to track versioning issues. The hwndParent gets the HWND of the main window, and the pszCaption field gets typecast and mangled into utter oblivion. (If you want, most compilers will accept:

psh.pszCaption = "Rupert the Cat Page".) When you fill out the nPages field, you can enter the number explicitly as I do above, or you can calculate the pages dynamically by entering the following:

```
sizeof(psp) / sizeof(PROPSHEETPAGE)
```

The final field is a pointer to an array of PROPSHEETPAGE structures which needs to be filled out separately. This syntax box already has enough in it, however, so I am going to cover the PROPSHEETPAGE structure below.

Here's an example:

```
ProateverySheet(&psh);
```

Here is a PROPSHEETPAGE structure:

```
typedef struct _PROPSHEETPAGE {    // psp
    DWORD       dwSize;            // Size of structure
    DWORD       dwFlags;          // What fields to use and ignore, etc.
    HINSTANCE hInstance;         // Where to find the resources
    union {
        LPCTSTR         pszTemplate; // The dialog to load from resource
        LPCDLGTEMPLATE pResource; // Dialog template in memory
    };
    union {
        HICON   hIcon;            // Handle of icon to use as small icon
        LPCTSTR pszIcon;          // Icon resource to use as small icon
    };
    LPCTSTR pszTitle;             // Title or string resource index to title
    DLGPROC pfnDlgProc;           // DialogProc
    LPARAM  lParam;               // Optional custom data added by programmer
    LPFNPSPCALLBACK pfnCallback;  // Optional call back
    UINT FAR * pcRefParent;       // Reference count
} PROPSHEETPAGE, FAR *LPPROPSHEETPAGE;
typedef const PROPSHEETPAGE FAR *LPCPROPSHEETPAGE;
```

Here's the way I fill out this structure in the PSheet program:

```
psp->dwSize = sizeof(PROPSHEETPAGE);
psp->dwFlags = PSP_USETITLE | PSP_USEICONID;
psp->hInstance = hInstance;
psp->pszTemplate = MAKEINTRESOURCE(ID_DIALOG1);
psp->pszIcon = "PSheetIcon16";
psp->pfnDlgProc = ShapeDialog;
psp->pszTitle = "Shape";
psp->lParam = 0;
```

In the first field, I pass in PSP_USETITLE and PSP_USEICONID. The former flag tells the compiler to use the title I specify in the PROPSHEETPAGE structure rather than the dialog title hard coded into the RC file. PSP_USEICONID specifies that the PROPSHEETPAGE structure I pass in will use the pszIcon field of the record.

Given the flags specified in the last paragraph, everything else falls together fairly easily: The HINSTANCE where the resources are stored is passed in, and then the information to grab the dialog and its icon from the resource stored in the current EXE. Next, the dialog procedure is filled in as well as the new title of the dialog. Finally, there is no custom data to be associated with this record, so I zero out that field.

You now have all the knowledge you need to get a property sheet up and running. More specifically, here is the way the chore is handled in the PSheet program:

```
void FillOutPropPage(PROPSHEETPAGE* psp, int DialogID,
                     LPSTR pszTitle, LPSTR pszIcon,
                     DLGPROC pfnDialogProc)
{
  psp->dwSize = sizeof(PROPSHEETPAGE);
  psp->dwFlags = PSP_USETITLE | PSP_USEICONID;
  psp->hInstance = hInstance;
  psp->pszTemplate = MAKEINTRESOURCE(DialogID);
  psp->pszIcon = pszIcon;
  psp->pfnDlgProc = pfnDialogProc;
  psp->pszTitle = pszTitle;
  psp->lParam = 0;
}

int CreatePropertySheet(HWND hwnd, HINSTANCE hInst)
{
  PROPSHEETPAGE psp[NUMPROPPAGES];
  PROPSHEETHEADER psh;

  FillOutPropPage(&psp[0], ID_DIALOG1, "Shape",
                  "PSheetIcon16", ShapeDialog);
  FillOutPropPage(&psp[1], ID_DIALOG2, "Colors",
                  "PSheetIcon16", ColorDialog);

  psh.dwSize = sizeof(PROPSHEETHEADER);
  if (UseWizard == TRUE)
    psh.dwFlags = PSH_PROPSHEETPAGE | PSH_WIZARD | PSH_NOAPPLYNOW;
  else
    psh.dwFlags = PSH_PROPSHEETPAGE;
  psh.hwndParent = hwnd;
  psh.pszCaption = (LPSTR) TEXT("Valentine the Cat Page");
  psh.nPages =  sizeof(psp) / sizeof(PROPSHEETPAGE);
  psh.ppsp = (LPCPROPSHEETPAGE) &psp;

  return (PropertySheet(&psh));
}
```

The FillOutPropPage function simplifies the act of filling out the PROPSHEETPAGE structure. If you plug it in to your programs, then you can make this task fairly routine. Notice that I call the function twice—once for each dialog that appears in the property sheet.

The PROPSHEETHEADER is filled out the same way as explained above, except that I use the PSH_WIZARD style only if the user states that he wants to create a wizard. More specifically, this is how the code reacts to the user's wishes regarding whether he or she wants tabbed dialogs or a wizard-style set of dialogs.

Most programmers don't offer their users an option to choose between these styles but instead force one or the other. The idea of providing an option is merely an expediency created by someone who wants to show the reader a wide variety of styles in a relatively confined space.

If you glance up at the RC file, you will see that the actual dialogs used in a property sheet are completely standard. There is nothing at all unusual about them. All the magic is performed by the PropertySheet function; as a programmer, you don't have to do anything but fill out the records and then pass them to PropertySheet. You need not worry about any of the complex sizing issues faced in the tab control demo.

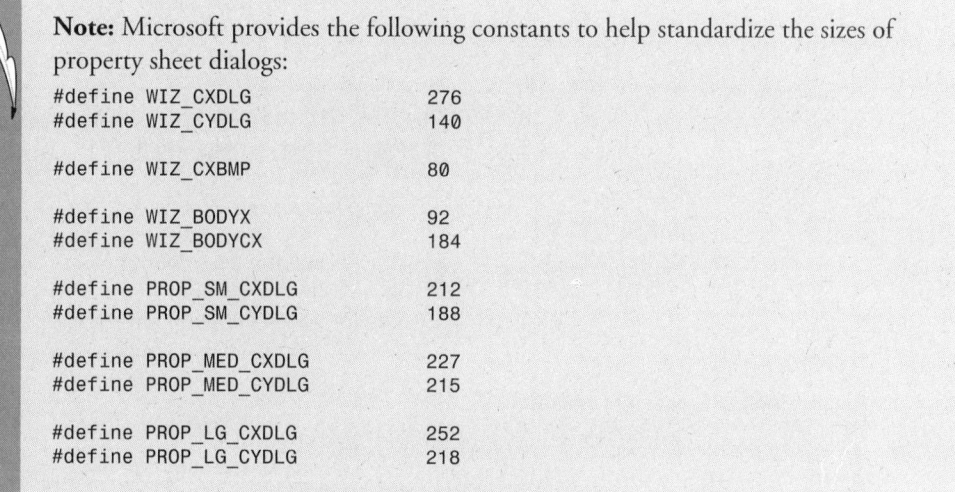

Note: Microsoft provides the following constants to help standardize the sizes of property sheet dialogs:

```
#define WIZ_CXDLG          276
#define WIZ_CYDLG          140

#define WIZ_CXBMP          80

#define WIZ_BODYX          92
#define WIZ_BODYCX         184

#define PROP_SM_CXDLG      212
#define PROP_SM_CYDLG      188

#define PROP_MED_CXDLG     227
#define PROP_MED_CYDLG     215

#define PROP_LG_CXDLG      252
#define PROP_LG_CYDLG      218
```

You don't have to perform any cleanup of the property sheets, since this is a modal dialog that is being created. However, if you used the PSH_MODELESS flag, then you would need to call DestroyWindow when you were through with the dialog. For more details on this latter process, see the online help.

That's all I'm going to say about creating property sheets. The records involved in this process seem fairly complex at first glance, mostly because they are designed to be very flexible. To help make them more manageable, just pick a particular strategy for using them and then stick with it. That way you can build functions like those shown above that will help simplify the act of creating property sheets.

Handling Property Sheets at Runtime

If you look in DLGCOLOR.CPP and DLGSHAPE.CPP you will see that the dialogs used in property sheets are pretty standard. I do, however, use WindowsX inside them, since it makes the code cleaner and easier to read.

The only code in the dialog procedure that's worth discussing at this point in the book is the response to WM_NOTIFY messages:

```
LRESULT DlgColor_OnNotify(HWND hwnd, int idFrom, NMHDR FAR * pnmhdr)
{
  switch (pnmhdr->code)
  {
    case PSN_KILLACTIVE:
      SetWindowLong(hwnd, DWL_MSGRESULT, FALSE);
      break;

    case PSN_RESET:
      // rest to the original values
      SetWindowLong(hwnd, DWL_MSGRESULT, FALSE);
      break;

    case PSN_SETACTIVE:
      PropSheet_SetWizButtons(GetParent(hwnd), PSWIZB_BACK | PSWIZB_FINISH);
      break;

    case PSN_WIZBACK:
      break;

    case PSN_WIZNEXT:
      break;

    default:
      return FALSE;
  }
  return TRUE;
}
```

I've written this code to be more educational than practical. As you can see, I don't respond to all the messages blocked out, but they are included so you can see some of the options open to you. This should also help you find the right structure for your WM_NOTIFY response methods.

You can think of *PSN* as standing for *property sheet notification*. Here is a list of all the possible notification messages sent in the NMHDR.code field sent with WM_NOTIFY messages:

PSN_APPLY	User chose the OK or Apply button.
PSN_HELP	User chose the Help button.
PSN_KILLACTIVE	User chose OK or switched to another page.
PSN_QUERYCANCEL	Chance to verify the user's selection of the Cancel button.
PSN_RESET	User chose the Cancel button—revert to last good values.
PSN_SETACTIVE	The page is about to be activated—initialize data.
PSN_WIZBACK	User chose the Back button in a wizard.
PSN_WIZFINISH	User chose the Finish button in a wizard.
PSN_WIZNEXT	User chose the Next button in a wizard.

When responding to PSN_KILLACTIVE messages, you should verify the user's input to see if it is valid. If it is valid, then use SetWindowLong to tell Windows that everything is okay:

```
SetWindowLong(hwnd, DWL_MSGRESULT, FALSE);
```

If something is wrong, you pass TRUE in the last parameter of SetWindowLong. You should then also use MessageBox or some other function to let the user know that there is a problem.

The code included in the PSheet program takes advantage of the PropSheet_SetWizButtons macro:

```
PropSheet_SetWizButtons(GetParent(hwnd), PSWIZB_BACK | PSWIZB_FINISH);
```

This macro wraps the PSM_SETWIZBUTTONS message and allows you to identify the buttons you want to include with the wizard. In this case, I specify the Back and Finish buttons. That information is passed in lParam of SendMessage, and wParam is set to zero. The other possible value to include is PSWIZB_NEXT, which sets the next button. Obviously, this code only takes effect if you are using the PSH_WIZARD style.

That's all I'm going to say about property sheets. All in all, this is not a particularly difficult subject. Property sheets are, however, very powerful tools that will play a role in many applications.

Declaring Global Data for Use in Dialogs

18

Though I haven't dwelled on the matter, this application shows a nice technique for tracking data that is going to be manipulated by the user in a dialog. In particular, the TDLGDATA structure is externed so that it can be used in all the modules of the application:

```
typedef struct Shape
{
  DLGDATASHAPES Shape;
  DLGDATACOLORS Color;
} TDLGDATA;
```

When a dialog is active, it can change the fields of this structure. For instance, here is how the ShapeDialog handles WM_COMMAND:

```
void DlgShape_OnCommand(HWND hwnd, int id, HWND hwndCtl, UINT codeNotify)
{
  switch(id)
  {
    case ID_RECTANGLE:
      DlgData.Shape = ddRectangle;
      break;

    case ID_ELLIPSE:
      DlgData.Shape = ddEllipse;
      break;
  }
}
```

The changes made while this dialog is active will be available to the rest of the program, without you needing to pass data back and forth. The key, of course, is the global DlgData structure.

It's generally not an ideal solution to declare global data that spans multiple modules of your application. However, it's considered acceptable if there is some good reason for it.

The key point to remember is that it's sloppy to declare global data that could easily be localized within one or two functions. Only if you have a compelling reason should you indulge yourself in declaring cross-module global data. In my opinion, moving data easily in and out of dialogs might, in some cases, be one of those "compelling reasons."

Summary

In this chapter you have looked at tabbed controls and property sheets. You've had a chance to learn a lot about the way these controls operate and how they can be used to create better programs.

Much of the focus of the chapter has been on dialogs. You've seen how to create child dialogs that change shape as the window to which they belong is reshaped by the user. You've seen how to work with some of the differences between dialog and window coordinates. You've also seen how to put common controls in dialogs and how to manipulate them.

Q&A

Q You keep talking about the Windows 95 User Interface guidelines. What's the story with all these various strictures, recommendations, and proposals?

A The key point to grasp about the Windows 95 interface is that it is attempting to move us towards an object-oriented world. The MDI interface wedded disparate windows under one stylistic and thematic canopy. The goal was to homogenize all the pieces of an app so that they seemed to be part of one global whole. Windows 95 is attempting to break that juggernaut up into smaller discreet chunks that can be plugged in and out of custom-designed applications. The goal has not yet been achieved, but you can sense it lurking in the background, waiting for a future version of Windows to capture this elusive Holy Grail. There is some talk that Cairo, the next version of Windows NT, might actually attempt to make this theory a reality.

A related concept is the idea that documents should be the center of a user's world rather than applications. The idea behind this theory is that the document would be primary, while various helper objects would just be used to bring the document to its completed state. This is an interesting theory, but to me its scope seems limited, in part because the operating system itself and many applications don't use documents in any form. Key applications, such as compilers, use documents (source code), but it's hard to imagine a general purpose document-centric programming model. In fact, many new programming models are becoming more visual and less document centered. Games also seem to exist outside the scope of a document-centered operating system.

Nevertheless, I find myself attracted to the idea of breaking up certain big applications, such as Word, into smaller modules that can be chosen individually by the user. Document-centric? Well, maybe, within some limited experimental scope. Object oriented? Yeah, probably.

Q **I sometimes hear people use the term *object-oriented* in two very different ways. What's the scoop?**

A There are two completely different types of object orientation. One is a programmatic issue having to do with inheritance, polymorphism, and encapsulation. OWL, MFC, Delphi, and SmallTalk are all object oriented in this "pure," or technical sense of the term. You will also hear about treating controls as objects, or treating dialogs as objects, or "right-clicking" on objects to learn about their properties. This is a much more abstract vision of object orientation, which is really about interface design issues rather than technical programming issues. To some degree, Delphi and SmallTalk already combine both of these theories. A Delphi form is an object in both senses of the word. It's an interface element that you can treat as a discreet object with its own properties. At the same time, a Delphi form also supports inheritance, polymorphism, and encapsulation. In the near future, it's possible that OLE 2.0 custom controls will also wed these two concepts on a significantly large scale in terms of popular acceptance. For the nonce, however, you need to think about two discreet issues: one having to do with interfaces and the other having to do with technical programming techniques. Windows 95 is object oriented in the sense that its interface supports discreet objects. It is not object oriented in the sense that it directly supports inheritance, polymorphism, or encapsulation. When you hear people talk about objects, you need to get which sense of the word they are using. Watch out for companies that claim to be object oriented in the technical sense, when all they really have is an object-oriented approach to their interface!

Q **You treat Windows 95 common controls as being 32 bit only, yet I see some references to 16-bit code in the headers. What's up?**

A You can use some of the Windows common controls in 16-bit applications, but only under Windows 95. In other words, you can't use the controls under Windows 3.1. To me, there is not much sense in creating 16-bit apps that are meant to run only under Windows 95. The only value of 16-bit applications is that they are compatible with Windows 3.1. If you are going to have to run under Windows 95 or Windows NT, then you might as well build a 32-bit application and thereby get the full benefit of the operating system. Therefore, I feel that these controls are basically only of value under Windows 95 or Windows NT, and I did not bother creating code that will work with a 16-bit compiler. However, I realize that my needs may not match up with some of yours, so I've added this note to set the record straight on this matter.

18

Workshop

The Workshop provides quiz questions to help you solidify your understanding of the material covered and exercises to provide you with experience in using what you've learned. Try to understand the quiz and exercise answers before continuing on to the next chapter. Answers are provided in Appendix A.

Quiz

1. What style can you give to a Windows 95 button if you want to put a bitmap in it?
2. What is the difference between CreateWindowEx and CreateWindow? Name the position and the specific parameter that differentiates them.
3. What is the constant lpszClassName field of CreateWindow so that you can create a tab control?
4. What function can you use to retrieve the HINSTANCE of an application?
5. What function is used to launch property sheets and what parameter do you pass to it?
6. When working with tab controls, what does a TC_ITEM structure do?
7. TabCtrl_InsertItem is a macro that wraps what message?
8. What do the MoveWindow and SetWindowPos functions have in common?
9. What style can you use in a PROPSHEETHEADER structure if you want to create a wizard?
10. What function can you use to create an up/down control?

Exercises

1. Rewrite the WinSize program from Day 16, "Dialog Boxes and Mapping Modes," so that its dialogs appear in a property sheet instead of in two separate dialogs.
2. If you are feeling particularly ambitious, you might want to try and create a program that uses tab controls to present the user with a series of multiline edit controls, each of which can be used to write and edit small text files. The goal would be to allow the user to edit multiple documents at the same time, with each document on its own page in the tab control. The tabbed pages for each document would need to be created and destroyed at runtime. That way, if the user were editing only one document, there would be one tab, but if he or she were editing multiple documents, there would be multiple tabs. At the very end of this book is an explanation of richedit controls. If you inherited richedit controls instead of edit controls in this program, then it might come close to being a commercially viable application. It would, however, be unlikely to be the only tool of its kind on the market.

Advanced
Windows 95
Controls

Today you will learn about some of the more advanced Windows 95 controls. I will begin by talking about imagelists, which are relatively straightforward. From there the focus will switch to listviews, which usually include imagelists as a sub-component.

Listviews are more complicated than most of the controls you've seen so far in this book. However, they are not prohibitively difficult to grok, and you will soon find it relatively easy to include them in your own programs.

Due to space considerations, I haven't included treeviews and RTF controls in this chapter. However, the former subject is covered in "Week 3 in Review" and the latter in "Bonus Days in Review." *Treeviews* are very closely related to listviews; it would benefit you to read about them in conjunction with the material presented in this chapter. *Richedit controls* enable you to enter very large blocks of text into a control while controlling the color and fonts of individual portions of the text. In a sense, the richedit control is the most useful of all of the new Windows 95 controls; you should be sure to read about it and run the included sample program featured in "Bonus Days in Review."

This chapter covers a good deal of territory, and you should find at least some of the material moderately challenging. However, you should take the time to master the material since these new controls are very powerful and will give you the capability to create robust, easy-to-use programs.

Is It Easier to Draw Than to Blit?

Imagelists provide a simple means for you to manipulate a list of images. In fact, it's simpler to draw even a single image to the screen with an imagelist than it is to `BitBlt` a bitmap to the screen. If you want to work with multiple images of the same size, imagelists are very convenient when compared to standard methods of blitting.

Although imagelists are useful as standalone components, they are meant primarily to be used as an adjunct to other, more complicated controls such as listviews and treeviews. Later in this chapter, and in "Week 3 in Review," you will get a chance to see them in this context, but for now it's important to focus only on the bare object, which is useful in its own right.

An important advantage of imagelists is that they enable you to save system resources. If you load 10 bitmaps into memory, you need to keep handles to them and to create device contexts for them. You can avoid most of this overhead if you use imagelists. Specifically, imagelists enable you to consume only one handle and one DC while working with multiple images.

Without further ado, I'll show you the code to the SkyView program, which uses an imagelist. The program discusses the basic facts about loading a bitmap into an imagelist, and it shows you how to drag-and-drop that image across the screen. As a bonus, the code shows how to animate the image so that it appears to "fly" across the main window of the program. The source code for the program is found in Listings 19.1 through 19.7.

Note: Despite their ease of use, imagelists do have several fairly complicated aspects that I will not pursue in this book. As always, my goal is to give you the information you need to use imagelists the way they are implemented 95 percent of the time. If the scope of this book weren't so large, I could also dedicate a section to that remaining 5 percent. However, that kind of detailed examination would be inappropriate in a book that covers such a wide range of important technical material.

Listing 19.1. The main module for the SkyView program shows how to create and manipulate imagelists.

```
/////////////////////////////////////////////////////////
// SKYVIEW.CPP
// Copyright  1995 Charlie Calvert.
// Description: Demonstrate the IMAGELIST class
/////////////////////////////////////////////////////////

#define STRICT
#define WIN32_LEAN_AND_MEAN
#include <windows.h>
#include <windowsx.h>
#pragma hdrstop                 // End Precompiled header section
#include <prsht.h>
#include <commctrl.h>
#include "SkyView.h"            // specific to this program
#pragma warning (disable : 4068)


HINSTANCE          hInstance;
HWND               hWndClient;
TSKYDATA           SkyData;
HIMAGELIST         hImageList;       // Image list handle
static  HBITMAP    hSky;
char szAppName[]   = "SkyView";
char szTitle[]     = "SkyView Sample Application";

/////////////////////////////////////////////////////////
// WinMain: The program entry point
/////////////////////////////////////////////////////////
#pragma argsused
int APIENTRY WinMain(HINSTANCE hInstance, HINSTANCE hPrevInstance,
                     LPSTR lpCmdLine, int nCmdShow)
{
   MSG msg;

   if (!hPrevInstance)
      if (!Register(hInstance))
         return (FALSE);
```

continues

Listing 19.1. continued

```
    if (!Create(hInstance, nCmdShow))
        return (FALSE);

    while (GetMessage(&msg, NULL, 0, 0))
    {
        TranslateMessage(&msg);// Translates virtual key codes
        DispatchMessage(&msg); // Dispatches message to window
    }
    return (msg.wParam);
}

/////////////////////////////////////
// Register the window
/////////////////////////////////////
BOOL Register(HINSTANCE hInst)
{
    WNDCLASSEX WndClass;

    hInstance = hInst;

    WndClass.cbSize        = sizeof(WNDCLASSEX);
    WndClass.style         = CS_HREDRAW | CS_VREDRAW;
    WndClass.lpfnWndProc   = WndProc;
    WndClass.cbClsExtra    = 0;
    WndClass.cbWndExtra    = 0;
    WndClass.hInstance     = hInst;
    WndClass.hIcon         = LoadIcon(hInst, "ImageListIcon");
    WndClass.hCursor       = LoadCursor(NULL, IDC_ARROW);
    WndClass.hbrBackground = (HBRUSH)(COLOR_WINDOW+1);
    WndClass.lpszMenuName  = "Menu";
    WndClass.lpszClassName = szAppName;
    WndClass.hIconSm       = LoadIcon(hInst, "ImageListIcon16");

    return (RegisterClassEx(&WndClass)) != 0;
}

/////////////////////////////////////
// Create the window
/////////////////////////////////////
HWND Create(HINSTANCE hInstance, int nCmdShow)
{
    HWND hWindow = CreateWindowEx(0, szAppName, szAppName,
                     WS_OVERLAPPEDWINDOW,
                     CW_USEDEFAULT, CW_USEDEFAULT,
                     400, 300,
                     NULL, NULL, hInstance, NULL);

    if (hWindow == NULL)
        return hWindow;

    ShowWindow(hWindow, nCmdShow);
    UpdateWindow(hWindow);

    return hWindow;
```

```
}

///////////////////////////////////////
// WINPROC
///////////////////////////////////////
#pragma argsused
LRESULT CALLBACK WndProc(HWND hwnd, UINT message,
                         WPARAM wParam, LPARAM lParam)
{
  switch (message)
  {
   HANDLE_MSG(hwnd, WM_CREATE, SkyView_OnCreate);
   HANDLE_MSG(hwnd, WM_DESTROY, SkyView_OnDestroy);
   HANDLE_MSG(hwnd, WM_COMMAND, SkyView_OnCommand);
   HANDLE_MSG(hwnd, WM_LBUTTONDOWN, SkyView_OnLButtonDown);
   HANDLE_MSG(hwnd, WM_LBUTTONUP, SkyView_OnLButtonUp);
   HANDLE_MSG(hwnd, WM_MOUSEMOVE, SkyView_OnMouseMove);
   HANDLE_MSG(hwnd, WM_PAINT, SkyView_OnPaint);
   default:
      return DefWindowProc(hwnd, message, wParam, lParam);
  }
}

///////////////////////////////////////
// WM_DESTROY
///////////////////////////////////////
#pragma argsused
BOOL SkyView_OnCreate(HWND hwnd, LPCREATESTRUCT lpCreateStruct)
{
  InitCommonControls();

  hImageList = ImageList_LoadBitmap(hInstance, "Bird", IMGWIDTH,
                                    1, RGB (255,0,0));
  if (hImageList == NULL)
    return FALSE;

  hSky = LoadBitmap(hInstance, "Sky");

  SkyData.CurImage = 0;

  return TRUE;
}

///////////////////////////////////////
// WM_DESTROY
///////////////////////////////////////
#pragma argsused
void SkyView_OnDestroy(HWND hwnd)
{
   if (hImageList)
   {
     ImageList_Destroy(hImageList);
     hImageList = NULL;
   }

   PostQuitMessage (0);
```

continues

Listing 19.1. continued

```c
}

//////////////////////////////////////////////////////////
// Start Flying
//////////////////////////////////////////////////////////
#pragma argsused
void SkyView_OnCommand(HWND hwnd, int id, HWND hwndCtl, UINT codeNotify)
{
  switch (id)
  {
    case CM_FLY:
      SkyData.XPos = 0;
      SkyData.YPos = 250;

      SkyData.Dragging = TRUE;
      InvalidateRect(hwnd, NULL, TRUE);
      UpdateWindow(hwnd);
      SkyView_OnFly(hwnd);
      break;

    case CM_IMAGE1:
      SkyData.CurImage = 0;
      InvalidateRect(hwnd, NULL, TRUE);
      break;

    case CM_IMAGE2:
      SkyData.CurImage = 1;
      InvalidateRect(hwnd, NULL, TRUE);
      break;

    case CM_IMAGE3:
      SkyData.CurImage = 2;
      InvalidateRect(hwnd, NULL, TRUE);
      break;
  }
}

//////////////////////////////////////////
// WM_LBUTTONUP
//////////////////////////////////////////
#pragma argsused
void SkyView_OnLButtonUp(HWND hwnd, int x, int y, UINT keyFlags)
{
  if (SkyData.Dragging)
    Util_EndDrag(hwnd, x ,y);
}

//////////////////////////////////////////
// WM_LBUTTONDOWN
//////////////////////////////////////////
#pragma argsused
void SkyView_OnLButtonDown(HWND hwnd, BOOL fDoubleClick, int x, int y, UINT
keyFlags)
```

```
{
  BOOL Hit = Util_IsSelected(x, y);

  if (hImageList && Hit)
    Util_StartDrag(hwnd);
}


/////////////////////////////////////
//  WM_MOUSEMOVE
/////////////////////////////////////
#pragma argsused
void SkyView_OnMouseMove(HWND hwnd, int x, int y, UINT keyFlags)
{
  if(SkyData.Dragging)
    ImageList_DragMove(x, y);
}


/////////////////////////////////////
//  WM_PAINT
/////////////////////////////////////
void SkyView_OnPaint(HWND hwnd)
{
  PAINTSTRUCT PaintStruct;
  HDC PaintDC = BeginPaint(hwnd, &PaintStruct);

  Util_DrawBitmap(PaintDC, hSky, 0, 0);

  if ((hImageList) && (!SkyData.Dragging))
    ImageList_Draw(hImageList, SkyData.CurImage, PaintDC,
                   SkyData.XPos, SkyData.YPos, ILD_NORMAL);

  EndPaint (hwnd, &PaintStruct);
}


////////////////////////////////////////////////////////
//  Fly the image
////////////////////////////////////////////////////////
#pragma argsused;
void SkyView_OnFly(HWND hwnd)
{
  int x, y, i, j;

  Util_StartDrag(hwnd);
  x = SkyData.XPos;
  y = SkyData.YPos;
  for (i = 0; i < 215; i++)
  {
    x += 1;
    y -= 1;
    for (j = 0; j < 200000; j++);
    ImageList_DragMove(x, y);
  }
  Util_EndDrag(hwnd, x, y);
}
```

19

Listing 19.2. The header file for the SkyView program.

```
///////////////////////////////////////////////////////
// SKYDATA.H
// Copyright  1995 Charlie Calvert.
///////////////////////////////////////////////////////

// Custom Macros
#define NUMIMAGES    3
#define IMGWIDTH     80
#define IMGHEIGHT    50
#define CM_FLY       100
#define CM_IMAGE1    101
#define CM_IMAGE2    102
#define CM_IMAGE3    103

// Types
typedef struct tagSkyData
{
  BOOL Dragging;  // If the user is dragging the image
  int  XPos;      // X Location of image
  int  YPos;      // Y Location of image
  int  CurImage;  // Which image to draw
} TSKYDATA;

// ImageList Funcs
BOOL SkyView_OnCreate(HWND hwnd, LPCREATESTRUCT lpCreateStruct);
void SkyView_OnDestroy(HWND hwnd);
void SkyView_OnCommand(HWND hwnd, int id, HWND hwndCtl, UINT codeNotify);
void SkyView_OnLButtonDown(HWND hwnd, BOOL fDoubleClick, int x, int y, UINT
keyFlags);
void SkyView_OnLButtonUp(HWND hwnd, int x, int y, UINT keyFlags);
void SkyView_OnMouseMove(HWND hwnd, int x, int y, UINT keyFlags);
void SkyView_OnPaint(HWND hwnd);
void SkyView_OnFly(HWND hwnd);

// Core Funcs
BOOL Register(HINSTANCE hInst);
HWND Create(HINSTANCE hInstance, int nCmdShow);
LRESULT CALLBACK WndProc(HWND, UINT, WPARAM, LPARAM);

// Util Funcs
void Util_DrawBitmap(HDC PaintDC, HBITMAP Bitmap, int XVal, int YVal);
BOOL Util_IsSelected(int x, int y);
void Util_StartDrag(HWND hwnd);
void Util_EndDrag(HWND hwnd, int x, int y);
void Util_YieldToOthers();
```

Listing 19.3. SKYUTIL.CPP contains several utility routines that support the functionality of the SkyView program.

```
///////////////////////////////////////////////////////
// SKYUTIL.CPP
// Copyright  1995 Charlie Calvert.
// Project: SKYVIEW
///////////////////////////////////////////////////////
```

```
#define STRICT
#include <windows.h>
#include <windowsx.h>
#include <commctrl.h>
#include "skyview.h"

extern TSKYDATA SkyData;
extern HIMAGELIST hImageList;

int XSkip(void)
{
  return GetSystemMetrics(SM_CXFIXEDFRAME);
}

int YSkip(void)
{
  return GetSystemMetrics(SM_CYFIXEDFRAME) +\
            GetSystemMetrics(SM_CYCAPTION) +\
            GetSystemMetrics(SM_CYMENU);
}

////////////////////////////////////
// Draw Bitmap in menu
////////////////////////////////////
void Util_DrawBitmap(HDC PaintDC, HBITMAP Bitmap, int XVal, int YVal)
{
  HDC MemDC;
  HBITMAP OldBitmap;
  BITMAP BStruct;

  MemDC = CreateCompatibleDC(PaintDC);
  OldBitmap = SelectBitmap(MemDC, Bitmap);
  GetObject(Bitmap, sizeof(BITMAP), &BStruct);
  BitBlt(PaintDC, XVal, YVal, BStruct.bmWidth,
        BStruct.bmHeight, MemDC, 0, 0, SRCCOPY);
  SelectBitmap(MemDC, OldBitmap);
  DeleteObject(MemDC);
}

////////////////////////////////////////////////////////
// ISSELECTED: Hit on the target
////////////////////////////////////////////////////////
BOOL Util_IsSelected(int x, int y)
{
  RECT   Rect;    // Rect of image (for hit testing)
  POINT  APoint;  // Cursor pos

  APoint.x = x;
  APoint.y = y;

  // Figure the hit test region of the image
  SetRect(&Rect, SkyData.XPos, SkyData.YPos,
```

continues

Listing 19.3. continued

```
                SkyData.XPos + IMGWIDTH, SkyData.YPos + IMGHEIGHT);

  return  PtInRect(&Rect, APoint);
}

/////////////////////////////////////////////////////////////
// STARTDRAG: Start Dragging
/////////////////////////////////////////////////////////////
void Util_StartDrag(HWND hwnd)
{
  SkyData.Dragging = TRUE;
  ShowCursor(FALSE);
  SetCapture(hwnd);

  ImageList_SetDragCursorImage(hImageList, SkyData.CurImage, 0, 0);
  ImageList_BeginDrag(hImageList, SkyData.CurImage, 0, 0);
  ImageList_DragEnter(hwnd, SkyData.XPos + XSkip(), SkyData.YPos + YSkip());
}

/////////////////////////////////////////////////////////////
// ENDDRAG: End the drag process
/////////////////////////////////////////////////////////////
void Util_EndDrag(HWND hwnd, int x, int y)
{
  SkyData.XPos = x - XSkip();
  SkyData.YPos = y - YSkip();

  ImageList_DragLeave(hwnd);
  ImageList_EndDrag();
  ReleaseCapture();
  ShowCursor(TRUE);

  InvalidateRect(hwnd, NULL, FALSE);
  SkyData.Dragging = FALSE;
}

/////////////////////////////////////////////////////////////
// Spin your wheels while something else is happening
/////////////////////////////////////////////////////////////
void Util_YieldToOthers()
{
  MSG Msg;

  while (PeekMessage(&Msg,NULL,0,0,PM_REMOVE))
  {
    if (Msg.message == WM_QUIT) break;
    TranslateMessage(&Msg);
    DispatchMessage(&Msg);
  }
}
```

Listing 19.4. The resource file for the SkyView program.

```
///////////////////////////////////////////////////
// SKYVIEW.RC
// Copyright  1995 Charlie Calvert.
///////////////////////////////////////////////////

#include "skyview.h"

ImageListIcon ICON skyview.ico
ImageListIcon16 ICON sky16.ICO

Bird BITMAP bird1.bmp
Sky  BITMAP sky.bmp

Menu MENU
BEGIN
  MENUITEM "Fly", CM_FLY
  POPUP "Images"
  BEGIN
    MENUITEM "Bird" CM_IMAGE1
    MENUITEM "Turtle" CM_IMAGE2
    MENUITEM "Piggy" CM_IMAGE3
  END
END
```

Listing 19.5. The module definition file for the SkyView program.

```
; SKYVIEW.DEF

NAME        SkyView
DESCRIPTION 'Image List Example Program'
```

Listing 19.6. The Borland makefile for the SkyView program.

```
# SKYVIEW.MAK

# macros

!if !$d(BCROOT)
BCROOT  = $(MAKEDIR)\..
APPNAME = SkyView
INCPATH = $(BCROOT)\WIN32;$(BCROOT);$(BCROOT)\INCLUDE
LIBPATH = $(BCROOT)\LIB

COMPILER= BCC32.EXE
BRC     = BRC32.EXE
FLAGS   = -W -v -w4 -I$(INCPATH) -L$(LIBPATH)
OBJS    = $(APPNAME).obj SkyUtil.obj
```

continues

Listing 19.6. continued

```
# link
$(APPNAME).exe: $(OBJS) $(APPNAME).def $(APPNAME).res
  $(COMPILER) $(FLAGS) $(OBJS) comctl32.lib
  $(BRC) -I$(INCPATH) $(APPNAME).res

# compiling
.cpp.obj:
  $(COMPILER) -c $(FLAGS) { $< }

# resource
$(APPNAME).res: $(APPNAME).rc
  $(BRC) -R -I$(INCPATH) $(APPNAME).RC
```

Listing 19.7. The Microsoft makefile for the SkyView program.

```
# SKVEWMS.MAK

APPNAME=SKYVIEW
TARGETOS=WIN95
APPVER=4.0
OBJS=SKYVIEW.OBJ SKYUTIL.OBJ

!include <win32.mak>

all: $(APPNAME).exe

# Update the resource if necessary

$(APPNAME).res: $(APPNAME).rc $(APPNAME).h
  $(rc) $(rcflags) $(rcvars) $(APPNAME).rc

# Update the object files if necessary

# compile
.cpp.obj:
  $(cc) $(cflags) $(cvars) $(cdebug) $<

# Update the executable file if necessary.

$(APPNAME).exe: $(OBJS) $(APPNAME).res
  $(link) $(linkdebug) $(guiflags) -out:$(APPNAME).exe\
    $(OBJS) $(APPNAME).res $(guilibs) comctl32.lib
```

Figures 19.1 through 19.4 show the bitmaps and icons used in the SkyView program. Once again, there is no need for you to duplicate these bitmaps or icons exactly, though you should try to re-create their dimensions.

Figure 19.1.
The background bitmap called SKY.BMP measures 400×300.

Figure 19.2.
The bird that moves across the screen is 80×40 and has a bright red background: RGB(255, 0, 0).

Figure 19.3.
The 32×32 icon.

19

Figure 19.4.
The 16×16 icon.

When you first open the SkyView program, you see a blue sky with a few picturesque cumulus clouds suspended in the atmosphere of a warm summer day. In the upper-left corner is a bird hovering above the clouds. Click on the bird and you will be able to drag him to a new position. A screen shot of the program appears in Figure 19.5.

There is a menu at the top of the program. The first menu item is labeled Fly. Select this item and the bird will appear to fly from the bottom left of the screen up toward the top right. A pop-up menu labeled Images enables you to change the image of the bird to that of a turtle or a pig.

Figure 19.5.
The SkyView program shows the user two bitmaps and a menu.

The interesting thing about the program is that it enables you to drag an image across a complex, multicolored background. The idea of animating the same image is also rife with possibilities. In general, the imagelist control offers some interesting tools for programmers while at the same time simplifying the act of drawing a bitmap to the screen.

Imagelist Basics

In its simplest, most stripped-down form, there are only three key facts you have to know about an imagelist:

- How to load an image with `ImageList_LoadBitmap`
- How to display an image with `ImageList_Draw`
- How to delete an imagelist with `ImageList_Destroy`

The idea here is that you can load a picture into an imagelist with `ImageList_LoadBitmap` and can then display the picture with `ImageList_Draw`. You can load multiple bitmaps or icons into an imagelist but can destroy the whole imagelist at one fell swoop with `ImageList_Destroy`. With these three functions you can program like a beribboned GDI guru, while actually having to master only the simplest types of calls.

When working with an imagelist, the core concept to grasp is that it bears a close resemblance to a strip of film. Frame 1 of the film contains one image; Frame 2 contains a second image of the same size, as does Frame 3, and so on. In other words, an imagelist is a list of pictures arranged exactly as the pictures in a strip of film are arranged. It's like a series of rectangles placed end-to-end in a horizontal direction.

The name *imagelist* implies the use of multiple images, and indeed its greatest benefits come when you load it up with several different bitmaps or icons. However, you do not have to load more than one image into an imagelist. If you stick with a single image, you will have the equivalent of a single frame of film. If you add a second image to the imagelist, you will have

two frames of film. You can add images to imagelists dynamically at runtime. In other words, an imagelist that contains three images can be expanded to hold four, five, six, or more images.

Here is the core of a simplified version of the SkyView program, called ImagList, that does nothing more than load a single bitmap and display it. The bitmap in question is the sky bitmap that forms the background for the SkyView program. I show you this code because it isolates the most basic functions involved with manipulating an imagelist.

```cpp
/////////////////////////////////////////
// WM_CREATE
/////////////////////////////////////////
BOOL ImagList_OnCreate(HWND hwnd, LPCREATESTRUCT lpCreateStruct)
{
  InitCommonControls();

  hImageList = ImageList_LoadBitmap(hInstance, "Sky", 400,
                                    1, RGB (255,0,0));

  if (hImageList == NULL)
    return FALSE;

    return TRUE;
}


/////////////////////////////////////////
// WM_DESTROY
/////////////////////////////////////////
void ImagList_OnDestroy(HWND hwnd)
{
    if (hImageList)
    {
      ImageList_Destroy(hImageList);
      hImageList = NULL;
    }

    PostQuitMessage (0);
}


/////////////////////////////////////////
// WM_PAINT
/////////////////////////////////////////
void ImagList_OnPaint(HWND hwnd)
{
  PAINTSTRUCT PaintStruct;
  HDC PaintDC = BeginPaint(hwnd, &PaintStruct);

  if (hImageList)
    ImageList_Draw(hImageList, 0, PaintDC, 0, 0, ILD_NORMAL);

  EndPaint (hwnd, &PaintStruct);
}
```

This entire program is available with the online code as IMAGLIST.CPP. These listings are found on the various BBSs and Web sites listed on Day 1, "Getting Your Feet Wet." After downloading the code, you will find the program stored in its own subdirectory. It comes with

19

accompanying resource, DEF, and makefiles. I assume that most readers who have made it this far in the book can also re-create the program by cutting and pasting into a copy of the Window1 program presented on Day 3, "A Standard Windows Program." First create a new subdirectory, then copy the Window1 project into it. Now simply add the methods shown above to the copy of the Window1 program, tweak a few other details, and you should be up and running. Here is the RC file for the program:

```
/////////////////////////////////////////////////////////
// IMAGLIST.RC
// Copyright  1995 Charlie Calvert.
/////////////////////////////////////////////////////////

ImageListIcon ICON ImagList.ico
ImageListIcon16 ICON Image16.ICO

Sky  BITMAP sky.bmp
```

The code starts out by loading the bitmap using the ImageList_LoadBitmap call.

Syntax

```
HIMAGELIST WINAPI ImageList_LoadBitmap(
    HINSTANCE  hi,    // EXE or DLL that holds bitmap resource
    LPCSTR  lpbmp,    // Name of the resource
    int  cx,          // Width of each image in resource
    int  cGrow,       // How much you can grow the list by.
    COLORREF  crMask  // A bitmask for a transparent color
    );
```

This call is somewhat more complicated than LoadBitmap, but after you have the imagelist loaded, it's easier to work with imagelists than it is to work with raw bitmaps.

You need to know several things about ImageList_LoadBitmap. First, it's a macro that wraps around a somewhat more complicated call named ImageList_LoadImage. In a sense, ImageList_LoadImage is the more primary call; that is, it's the base on which LoadBitmap is built. However, ImageList_LoadBitmap is useful because it enables you to simplify the task of loading an imagelist. In particular, it enables you to load a single, large bitmap that has several small bitmaps inside it. (The ImageList program loads only one bitmap, but the SkyView program uses multiple bitmaps stored as *frames* inside a larger bitmap.)

The first two parameters of the call are the same parameters you would pass to LoadBitmap; that is, they are the HINSTANCE of the new executable where the bitmap is found and the resource name for that bitmap.

Because each bitmap can contain more than one image, you must state the size of the smaller images found inside the larger image. Windows can then automatically break the bigger bitmap into smaller ones for you. Each of the smaller images must be identical in size; that is, they must all have the same width and height. The bitmaps are always spread out horizontally from left to right and never appear in multiple rows. Use the cx parameter to specify the width of each smaller bitmap residing inside the larger bitmap.

The cGrow parameter specifies how much you can grow the list if you need to expand it at runtime. This value is typically set to 1, but you can grow a list multiple times during the run of a program.

The final parameter specifies the color, which will be transparent. To designate the color, you can use the RGB macro, explained on Day 5, "The Mouse and the Keyboard."

Some readers are probably unclear as to what is meant by a *transparent* color. If you run the SkyView program, you will see that the bitmaps set against its background each appear to be irregular in shape. In other words, they don't appear to be rectangular but instead appear to be the shape of an animal. You and I both know that bitmaps aren't really irregular in shape—they are always rectangular. What's going on here is that one color is selected to be transparent. Whenever that color appears in the bitmap, you can see through it to the window behind it. This trait is not always associated with bitmaps, but you are used to seeing icons that have this functionality. (You can more laboriously obtain this same functionality outside of imagelists by using fancy bitwise operations on two images, one of which is a mask. However, the use of a transparent color automates this process and provides a much simpler way to achieve the same end.)

Transparent colors have a number of uses. For instance, you could create a bitmap that has words printed on it in some custom font of your own design. If you made the background of the bitmap a transparent color, you could lay it over another background and only the words would appear.

Here's an example:

```
hImageList = ImageList_LoadBitmap(hInstance, "Sky", 400,
                                  1, RGB (255,0,0));
```

It turns out that there are several different APIs for creating imagelists, some of which are used later in this book. If it's not convenient to create one pre-made bitmap with a series of smaller images arranged inside it, you can explore the whole range of functions for creating imagelists and adding and removing images:

☐ Creating image lists

```
ImageList_Create
ImageList_Destroy
ImageList_LoadBitmap
ImageList_LoadImage
```

☐ Adding and removing images

```
ImageList_Add
ImageList_AddIcon
ImageList_AddMasked
ImageList_Remove
```

☐ Replacing and merging images

```
ImageList_Replace
ImageList_ReplaceIcon
ImageList_Merge
```

19

As you can see, there is quite a bit of complex functionality associated with imagelists.

Note that imagelist controls can be used to work with icons rather than bitmaps. For an example of how to work with icons and imagelists and how to use some of the calls shown in the list, see the PoemList program shown later in this chapter and the PoemTree program explained in "Week 3 in Review."

After you have created an imagelist, the next step is to draw it:

Syntax

```
BOOL WINAPI ImageList_Draw(
    HIMAGELIST  himl, // Handle to imagelist
    int  i,           // index of picture to draw
    HDC  hdcDst,      // HDC
    int  x,           // x coordinate
    int  y,           // y coordinate
    UINT  fStyle      // one of four drawing styles
    );
```

Needless to say, the purpose of the ImageList draw function is to paint one of the smaller pictures inside an imagelist to the screen. The first parameter is the handle you got when you called ImageList_LoadBitmap; the second is the zero-based index of the picture you want to draw. In other words, the second parameter specifies the single frame in the roll of pictures that make up an imagelist.

The third, fourth, and fifth parameters are the HDC to which you will draw and the coordinates inside the HDC where you want the drawing to begin. These are the same kinds of parameters you would pass to a function like TextOut.

The final parameter is a set of flags that can have one of the following values:

ILD_BLEND25	Blends 25 percent with the system highlight color
ILD_BLEND50	Blends 50 percent with the system highlight color
ILD_FOCUS	Same as ILD_BLEND25
ILD_MASK	Draws the mask
ILD_NORMAL	Draws the image using the background color
ILD_TRANSPARENT	Draws the image transparently using the mask

Most of the time it's simplest to draw to the screen using the ILD_NORMAL or ILD_TRANSPARENT flags, each of which has the same results when used in the SkyView program. The remaining flags create various effects that shade the image you are drawing. For instance, the two blend flags make the seagull appear to be grayish blue, whereas the mask field turns it into a blackbird.

As stated earlier, imagelists are used in other controls such as the treeview and listview controls from the Explorer. If you open the Explorer and select one of the items in its list of folders, you will see what the ILD_FOCUS flag is all about. In other words, a normal folder in the Explorer is probably drawn with ILD_NORMAL flag, whereas a focused folder is obviously drawn with the

ILD_FOCUS flag. The same effect can be seen in the PoemList and PoemTree programs presented later in this book. (If you want, you can run the ImageList or SkyView program and start experimenting with these values. Just plug one in and see what results you get. Two minutes of hands-on work will clear all of this up for you, as this is the kind of thing that's easier to show with pictures than to explain with words.)

Here's an example:

```
ImageList_Draw(hImageList, 0, SomeDC, 0, 0, ILD_FOCUS);
```

In addition to the ImageList_Draw function, there are several other techniques you can use if you want work with imagelists and their drawing capabilities:

```
ImageList_Draw
ImageList_DrawEx
ImageList_ExtractIcon
ImageList_GetBkColor
ImageList_GetIcon
ImageList_SetBkColor
INDEXTOOVERLAYMASK
```

I'm not going to discuss most of these functions in this book, although some of them are used in the PoemList and TreeList sample programs.

Before leaving this section of the chapter, you should go back and look at the ImageList_OnCreate, ImageList_OnDestroy, and ImageList_OnPaint methods. (Remember, these functions are from the tiny sample program included with the online code and not from the ImageList_XXX API found in COMMCTRL.H.) These three functions summarize the material presented in this section and show you a very simple way to use a bitmap in one of your programs. If you then go back and look at the SkyView program, you will find the same functions in the midst of a somewhat more complex example.

Dragging Images

Clearly there is nothing very complicated about the basics of showing a frame from an imagelist on the screen. As I said earlier, this is such a simple mechanism that many programmers will undoubtedly use it in place of LoadBitmap and BitBlt.

The most exciting aspect of the raw imagelist control, however, is its capability to enable you to drag an image across the screen. To understand how this is done, you first need to grasp a few specifics of the SkyView program.

Here is the local TSKYDATA type, declared in SKYVIEW.H and used to track the current image, its state, and its position:

```
typedef struct tagSkyData
{
```

```
   BOOL Dragging;   // If the user is dragging the image
   int  XPos;       // X Location of image
   int  YPos;       // Y Location of image
   int  CurImage;   // Which image to draw
} TSKYDATA;
```

If Dragging is set to TRUE, the image is currently in the process of being dragged by the mouse. The XPos and YPos parameters show the current position of the image, except during the time that it is actually being dragged. During dragging, the only way to track the image is to get the current position of the mouse.

The final parameter, CurImage, describes which of the images in the bitmap currently has the focus. In other words, the current image can be a bird, a turtle, or a pig, depending on choices the user makes with the menu. The bird is in Frame 0 of the imagelist, the turtle is at the first offset, and the pig is in the last frame.

Here is the WM_PAINT handler for the SkyView program:

```
//////////////////////////////////////////
// WM_PAINT
//////////////////////////////////////////
void SkyView_OnPaint(HWND hwnd)
{
  PAINTSTRUCT PaintStruct;
  HDC PaintDC = BeginPaint(hwnd, &PaintStruct);

  Util_DrawBitmap(PaintDC, hSky, 0, 0);

  if ((hImageList) && (!SkyData.Dragging))
    ImageList_Draw(hImageList, SkyData.CurImage, PaintDC,
                   SkyData.XPos, SkyData.YPos, ILD_NORMAL);

  EndPaint (hwnd, &PaintStruct);
}
```

As you can see, the ImageList_Draw function uses SkyData.CurImage to specify which image is to be drawn to the screen. If the user uses the menu to choose the turtle image, the program sets CurImage to 1 and employs InvalidateRect to send a WM_PAINT message to the main screen. Here's the relevant excerpt from the WM_COMMAND handler:

```
    case CM_IMAGE2:
      SkyData.CurImage = 1;
      InvalidateRect(hwnd, NULL, TRUE);
      break;
```

Now when the WM_PAINT method is called, the turtle image will be blitted to the screen by the ImageList_Draw function.

Note: Looking at the WM_PAINT handler, you are bound to notice the call to Util_DrawBitmap, which is similar to another function presented elsewhere in this book. This is not an API call, but instead calls into the local SkyUtil unit, where this code appears:

```
void Util_DrawBitmap(HDC PaintDC, HBITMAP Bitmap, int XVal, int YVal)
{
  HDC MemDC;
  HBITMAP OldBitmap;
  BITMAP BStruct;

  MemDC = CreateCompatibleDC(PaintDC);
  OldBitmap = SelectBitmap(MemDC, Bitmap);
  GetObject(Bitmap, sizeof(BITMAP), &BStruct);
  BitBlt(PaintDC, XVal, YVal, BStruct.bmWidth,
        BStruct.bmHeight, MemDC, 0, 0, SRCCOPY);
  SelectBitmap(MemDC, OldBitmap);
  DeleteObject(MemDC);
}
```

I use this function to blit the background bitmap to the screen. This bitmap cannot be part of the imagelist because it is much larger than the other images that appear in the list. I also found it is simpler not to create two imagelists when you want to engage in dragging operations. Finally, I include the DrawBitmap function simply because it is a useful utility that you can use in many of your own programs.

Util_DrawBitmap does the standard resource-preservation two-step that you can avoid when using imagelists. (Create the DC, select things into it, preserve them, delete them, and so on.) It's a lot of trouble to go to when all you want is to show an image on the screen. However, you get the widest possible degree of flexibility if you have access to each of the low-level steps involved in the process. In other words, this system lets you decide if you want to create and destroy resources at draw time, as the function shown here does, or if you want to perform these functions inside some broader scope, such as WM_CREATE and WM_DESTROY handlers.

To call the Util_DrawBitmap function, just pass in an HDC, the bitmap returned by the LoadBitmap function, and an x and y coordinate. In the SkyView program I always pass in 0,0 in the x and y coordinates, but I provide the parameters in case you need them in another context.

As you've seen, the SkyView program includes two modules called SKYVIEW.CPP and SKYUTIL.CPP. The first module contains the main body of the program; the second contains a series of utility functions. The utility functions are linked into the main program automatically

19

by the linker. All you need to do is place their headers in SKYVIEW.H and then pass the SKYUTIL.OBJ module to the linker. For instance, here's how the chore is handled in the Borland makefile:

```
APPNAME=SKYVIEW
OBJS    = $(APPNAME).obj SkyUtil.obj

# link
$(APPNAME).exe: $(OBJS) $(APPNAME).def $(APPNAME).res
  $(COMPILER) $(FLAGS) $(OBJS) comctl32.lib
  $(BRC) -I$(INCPATH) $(APPNAME).res
```

Notice that the OBJS macro is explicitly listed in the parameters passed to the compiler at link time.

The most important of the utility functions found in SKYUTIL.CPP are those that are called when you click the left mouse button and carry out a drag procedure.

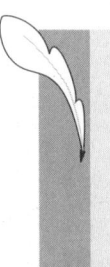

> **Note:** The actual act of handling the mouse occurs in the WM_LBUTTONDOWN, WM_LBUTTONUP, and WM_MOUSEMOVE move handlers. I won't discuss these here, as this material has been painstakingly laid out in several other places in this book. (For more details, see Day 5 and especially Bonus Day 1, "GDI and Metafiles.")
>
> The key point is that you respond to WM_LBUTTONDOWN messages to start the drag procedure, being sure to set SkyData.Dragging to TRUE in the process, WM_MOUSEMOVE helps you track the mouse's position during the drag, and WM_LBUTTONUP gives you the mouse coordinates when the procedure is complete. Be sure to set SkyData.Dragging to FALSE in response to WM_LBUTTONUP messages.

Here's the Util_StartDrag function:

```
void Util_StartDrag(HWND hwnd)
{
  SkyData.Dragging = TRUE;
  ShowCursor(FALSE);
  SetCapture(hwnd);

  ImageList_SetDragCursorImage(hImageList, SkyData.CurImage, 0, 0);
  ImageList_BeginDrag(hImageList, SkyData.CurImage, 0, 0);
  ImageList_DragEnter(hwnd, SkyData.XPos + XSkip(), SkyData.YPos + YSkip());
}
```

The code shown here sets SkyData.Dragging to TRUE, then hides the cursor and captures its output so that Windows won't let you down if you happen to drag the mouse off the edge of the window. (If you want a more detailed examination of the subject of dragging, see Bonus Day 1.)

With the preliminaries out of the way, the next step is to tell Windows what image to show when you are dragging the mouse. The `ImageList_SetDragCursorImage` function enables you to do this by providing the handle to the imagelist, the frame of the imagelist to use, and two coordinates specifying hotspots within the image. (Hotspots are essentially ignored in this sample program.)

Take a moment to review what has happened so far. The original mouse cursor was hidden and the mouse was captured so that it belonged to the current window during the drag procedure. Now I will use a new image to replace the old mouse cursor. This image is obtained from the imagelist and put in place by the `ImageList_SetDragCursorImage` function.

`ImageList_BeginDrag` initiates the dragging procedure and `ImageList_DragEnter` shows the new cursor on the screen.

Syntax

```
BOOL WINAPI ImageList_BeginDrag(
    HIMAGELIST  himlTrack,    // Imagelist that holds the image
    int  iTrack,              // The frame number of the image
    int  dxHotspot,           // XHotspot
    int  dyHotspot            // YHotspot
);
```

This function initiates the drag process. The first parameter specifies the imagelist that contains the image to be dragged, and the second parameter specifies the offset of the image in the imagelist. The last two parameters reference the location of the drag position relative to the upper-left corner of the image.

As a rule, this function, paired with the `ImageList_DragEnd` and `ImageList_DragMove` functions, will enable you to move an image from one location on the window to another. However, you usually won't see the image during the actual drag process. To bring the image onto the screen so that it follows the cursor, you have to call the `ImageList_DragEnter` function. In other words, you will usually want to call `ImageList_DragEnter` in conjunction with `ImageList_DragBegin` and vice versa.

Here's an example:

```
ImageList_BeginDrag(hImageList, 0, 0, 0);
```

The `ImageList_DragEnter` function takes the handle of the window that owns the imagelist in its first parameter. The second and third parameters are the standard x and y coordinates that you'd expect to pass to this function, but they are measured from the upper-left corner of the window, not the client area. Unfortunately, `SkyData.XPos` and `SkyData.YPos` are measured in client coordinates. As a result, you need to perform some hand-waving in order to call the functions:

```
ImageList_DragEnter(hwnd, SkyData.XPos + XSkip(), SkyData.YPos + YSkip());
```

This `XSkip` and `YSkip` business looks like this:

19

```
int XSkip(void)
{
  return GetSystemMetrics(SM_CXFIXEDFRAME);
}

int YSkip(void)
{
  return GetSystemMetrics(SM_CYFIXEDFRAME) +\
            GetSystemMetrics(SM_CYCAPTION) +\
            GetSystemMetrics(SM_CYMENU);
}
```

XSkip gets the width of the frame around the window, which is usually four pixels or so. YSkip needs to take into account not only the frame, but also the menu and caption. All in all it's a bit fussy, but not very difficult, and when you finally begin the dragging process you will find that you're right on top of the spot where the image began.

The actual act of dragging the image across the screen is the proverbial no-brainer:

```
void SkyView_OnMouseMove(HWND hwnd, int x, int y, UINT keyFlags)
{
  if(SkyData.Dragging)
    ImageList_DragMove(x, y);
}
```

It's hard to think of anything very interesting to say about this function. The code simply moves the new "mouse cursor" around the screen by following the coordinates passed to the program by Windows.

When you are done, SkyView gets an WM_LBUTTONUP message, and you can respond by calling the Util_EndDrag procedure:

```
void Util_EndDrag(HWND hwnd, int x, int y)
{
  SkyData.XPos = x - XSkip();
  SkyData.YPos = y - YSkip();

  ImageList_DragLeave(hwnd);
  ImageList_EndDrag();
  ReleaseCapture();
  ShowCursor(TRUE);

  InvalidateRect(hwnd, NULL, FALSE);
  SkyData.Dragging = FALSE;
}
```

The code calculates the current position of the mouse in window coordinates and then leaves the dragging process, ends the drag functionality, releases the mouse, shows the cursor, and tells the WM_PAINT handler to redraw the screen. It's all very simple; you just need to be sure you actually do drop the image in the location specified by the user. In other words, you have to make sure the image doesn't jump around the screen after the user lifts up the left mouse button. The code shown here should do the job.

The SkyView program lets you tap into the same technology when you "fly" the image from the bottom left of the screen toward the top right. The code for actually making the flight is as follows:

```
void SkyView_OnFly(HWND hwnd)
{
  int x, y, i, j;

  Util_StartDrag(hwnd);
  x = SkyData.XPos;
  y = SkyData.YPos;
  for (i = 0; i < 215; i++)
  {
    x += 1;
    y -= 1;
    for (j = 0; j < 200000; j++);
    ImageList_DragMove(x, y);
  }
  Util_EndDrag(hwnd, x, y);
}
```

This code calls the `Util_StartDrag` function described previously, then mechanically moves the image across the screen with `ImageList_DragMove`, and finally cleans up the process with `Util_EndDrag`. I also call an empty loop in the middle of the process to slow things down enough so the flight is interesting to watch.

Note: To put it mildly, the formula I use to calculate the image's flight path is a bit hokey by the standards of DOOM and Descent. If you want to engage in some slightly more interesting geometry, you might want to make the bird fly around the screen in a circle. However, the code I've shown here has the virtue of being easy to implement and easy to understand.

19

Here's the code in the `WM_COMMAND` handler that calls the `SkyView_OnFly` method:

```
case CM_FLY:
  SkyData.XPos = 0;
  SkyData.YPos = 250;

  SkyData.Dragging = TRUE;
  InvalidateRect(hwnd, NULL, TRUE);
  UpdateWindow(hwnd);
  SkyView_OnFly(hwnd);
  break;
```

You might have noticed that this code includes a call to `UpdateWindow`. I use this API because I want to have time to repaint the screen between the moment the user chooses the Fly menu and the moment when the flight begins. The repainting is necessary because I want to erase the old position of the image and redraw it in the bottom-left corner of the screen.

Here's the scoop. The standard call to repaint the screen is `InvalidateRect`. This sends a `WM_PAINT` message to your window. However, SkyView won't have a chance to process `WM_PAINT` messages if you keep it busy moving the bird across the screen. In other words, you need to relinquish control from the processor for a few clock cycles so that Windows can process messages.

In addition to using threads, there are two obvious ways to go about giving Windows a few cycles of the clock: call `PeekMessage` or call `UpdateWindow`. I've opted for the latter because `PeekMessage` can cause troubles under certain, rather unlikely circumstances. (None of these circumstances is particularly applicable in the current program, however, so it would almost surely be safe to call `PeekMessage` here.)

This code first moves the image coordinates to the bottom left of the screen and then calls `InvalidateRect`. In order to give Windows a chance to process the `WM_PAINT` messages, I next call `UpdateWindow`. That way, when the `SkyView_OnFly` function is at last called, the screen has been repainted and the user doesn't have to look at two images of the bird, mouse, or turtle.

Note: The `SkyView_OnFly` function is not a message handler. I still put the SkyView name in front of it, however, partly on a whim and partly because this technique can be a helpful way of identifying what are local functions and what functions are part of the Windows API. At any rate, here's one example of technique for organizing your code, and you can decide if it will be useful to you in your own programs.

If you don't want to use `UpdateWindow`, or if you are just interested in learning more about how Windows works, here's an alternative technique:

```
case CM_FLY:
  SkyData.XPos = 0;
  SkyData.YPos = 250;

  SkyData.Dragging = TRUE;

  InvalidateRect(hwnd, NULL, TRUE);
  Util_YieldToOthers();
  SkyView_OnTimer(hwnd, ATimer);
  break;
```

This code calls `InvalidateRect` and then puts the code in a `PeekMessage` loop just long enough to process the `WM_PAINT` messages:

```
void Util_YieldToOthers()
{
  MSG Msg;

  while (PeekMessage(&Msg,NULL,0,0,PM_REMOVE))
```

```
  {
    if (Msg.message == WM_QUIT) break;
    TranslateMessage(&Msg);
    DispatchMessage(&Msg);
  }
}
```

As you can see, a PeekMessage loop looks much like the GetMessage loop found in WinMain. It snags messages from the queue and passes them on to TranslateMessage and DispatchMessage, which in turn pass them to the WndProc for your application. (Some notes from Microsoft state that PeekMessage isn't always very good at grabbing WM_PAINT messages. However, the previous code does work in this context. Nevertheless, you might consider this warning from Microsoft to be yet another reason to use UpdateWindow rather than PeekMessage.)

After calling YieldToOthers, the code then calls the SkyView_OnFly function. Because the PeekMessage loop was set up, the screen should be redrawn by the time you enter SkyView_OnFly.

I want to stress that some programmers feel there are some reasons why you should not set up PeekMessage loops in some circumstances. Most of the time it will do no harm, but it can cause trouble, particularly if you have a modal dialog box on the screen. In particular, modal dialog boxes have their own PeekMessage loops, which means calls to YieldToOthers can place your program in a space where it has multiple PeekMessage loops running. Thinking about all of those message loops whirring around inside my computer is too much for my brain to handle, so I tend to avoid that solution. Besides, YieldToOthers does not include calls to TranslateAccelerator and IsDialogMessage, both of which might be important in some programs. I should add, however, that even if your program has more than one message loop, it will by default still have only one message queue. Furthermore, there is not anything necessarily wrong in having multiple PeekMessage loops in a single program that includes active modal dialogs. I am simply pointing out that this is an area that deserves special thought in your programs.

> **Note:** During this rather lengthy discussion of processing messages, some readers are undoubtedly anxious to emphasize a third solution to this problem: threads. Yes, you could start a thread that would be responsible for repainting the screen. This is a clean solution, although quite a bit of work for such a small gain. You will learn more about threads on Day 21, "Threads, Multitasking, and Memory Management."

To sum up, one simple way to process a message in the midst of some other task is simply to call UpdateWindow. It's not a very sexy solution, but it's clean and simple to use. If you are in a place in your program where you are processing things in a loop and you need to display information to the user, techniques to consider are setting up timers, calling PeekMessage, calling UpdateWindow, or posting a series of messages to yourself with PostMessage.

I've spent a considerable amount of time talking about dragging things around on the screen. Before leaving this subject, I should perhaps list the following set of functions, all of which relate to the subject. Some of them have been discussed in this chapter; others might warrant a brief trip to the online help on your part:

```
ImageList_BeginDrag
ImageList_DragEnter
ImageList_DragLeave
ImageList_DragMove
ImageList_DragShowNolock
ImageList_EndDrag
ImageList_GetDragImage
ImageList_SetDragCursorImage
ImageList_SetOverlayImage
```

Here are two more functions you might find interesting if you want to write imagelists to disk:

```
ImageList_Read
ImageList_Write
```

I don't discuss either of these streaming functions in the book, but I wanted to point them out in case you need them.

That's it for the discussion of imagelists. All in all, this is a nice contribution to the Windows API, and it should end up playing an important role in a number of programs. I should point out, however, that the imagelist drawing functions described in this chapter are separate from the fancy, optimized, multimedia drawing capabilities you find in WinG, OpenGL, and elsewhere. I have some fun with imagelists in this chapter, but I don't want to leave you with an overblown idea of their importance. If you want to build an application that makes heavy use of animation, look around a bit before choosing your tools. However, if you need a quick fix for a modest task, imagelists might be just what you need.

Listview Basics

Listviews play a big part in Windows 95. You will find them in the right-hand side of the Explorer, My Computer, My Briefcase, Network Neighborhood, Control Panel, and elsewhere. If you are not familiar with them, open the Control Panel and choose View|Large Icons, View|Small Icons, View|List, or View|Details. The last option is shown in Figure 19.6.

When you are thinking about listviews, you need to multitask your brain so you can give some time slices to the idea of treeviews. Treeviews appear on the left side of the Explorer. (Treeviews on the left, listviews on the right, onward into the valley of death...) Both listviews and treeviews are the flower children of a stodgy wedding between list boxes and combo boxes. They make their parents seem a bit square, but programmers have to pay a price if they want to flirt with youngsters who have such rococo tastes in apparel.

Figure 19.6.
*The Windows 95 Control
Panel in Details mode.*

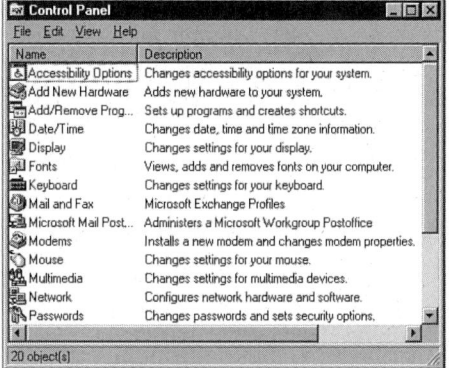

Note: I had originally planned to include a discussion of treeviews in this chapter, but it would have pushed the page count out beyond the bounds of reason. Thus, you can find them in "Week 3 in Review." Hopefully when you read about treeviews you won't have forgotten that they are close siblings to listviews, raised in the same hothouse atmosphere.

At this stage it's time to start focusing your attention on a specific program—in particular, the sample program for the latter half of this chapter. It is called PoemList, and it gives you a chance to see what can be done with listviews.

Before running the PoemList program you must make sure the applications you are producing are being marked as Windows 95 apps. If they are correctly marked, the dialog boxes in your applications will have the Windows 95 look and feel. More importantly, you won't be able to flip back and forth between the different types of lists in listview if you don't have you application properly marked. If you are running Microsoft's compiler, you can simply check the option on the Linker page of the Project|Setup dialog box that ensures that the 4.0 versioning information is hard coded into your application. If you are not running Microsoft's compiler, and specifically if you are running Borland C++ 4.5, this information might not be coded properly in your executables. However, do not despair. I have included an application written by Eric Bergman-Terrell that will imprint your executables with the proper information. You can find the application in the CHI_INS subdirectory with the online code for this book. You can also download the file from the MSWIN32 forum on CompuServe. The name of the file is CHI_LNF.ZIP.

19

Note: You should also examine the DS_3DLOOK style that gets short shrift in this book. In fact, it's probably worth your while to look it up in the online help and experiment with it sufficiently to understand what it does. I've discussed this style briefly on Day 18, "Windows 95 Dialogs and Controls," mentioning that it resolves to the number 4. If your headers don't define DS_3DLOOK, then you can use the number 4 directly rather than referencing the style. You can OR this value into the STYLE section in the declarations for your dialog boxes to give them the Windows 95 look without marking the application as a Windows 95 app. The issue here is that if you mark the application as Windows 95, it won't run on Windows 3.1. Using this style gives you the Windows 95 look without marking the application as being Version 4.0. I should add, however, that you need to physically mark the application as Version 4.0 to get the listview to work correctly. Borland C++ 5.0 and the new Microsoft compilers allow you to automatically mark your applications as Windows 95 apps. However, if you are using Borland C++ 4.5, then you will probably want to download the CHI_LNF file referenced above.

When working with listviews, you should also be sure to call InitCommonControls in the beginning of your program. This ensures that COMCTL32.DLL is loaded into memory. Of course, you should also be sure COMCTL32.LIB is included at link time.

Without further ado, see Listings 19.8 through 19.13 for the code for the PoemList program.

Listing 19.8. The module for the PoemList program.

```
//////////////////////////////////////////////////////////
// POEMLIST.CPP
// Copyright  1995 Charlie Calvert.
// Demonstrates the new Windows 95  ListView control
//////////////////////////////////////////////////////////

#define STRICT
#include <windows.h>
#include <windowsx.h>
#include <commctrl.h>
#include <string.h>
#include "poemlist.h"
#pragma warning (disable : 4068) // unknown pragma

HINSTANCE   hInst;          // current instance
HWND        hPoemList;
HWND        hWndHeader;    // Header control
HWND        WndMain;

HIMAGELIST  hSmallImage;
HIMAGELIST  hLargeImage;
```

```
// Header labels
const static LPSTR Headers[NUMHEADERS] =
  { "Poet", "First", "Born", "First Line" };

const static LPSTR FirstLines[] =
{
  {"To sing of Wars, of Captains, and of Kings..."},
  {"Give all to love; Obey thy heart..."},
  {"Out of the cradle endlessly rocking..."},
  {"Something there is that doesn't love a wall..."},
  {"The pure products of America go crazy..."}
};

// Last one in the list is the icon name
POETLIST PoetList[NUMITEMS] =
{
  {0, 0, "Bradstreet", {"Ann",   "1612", FirstLines[0], "rcBradstreet"}},
  {1, 1, "Emerson", {"Waldo",  "1803", FirstLines[1], "rcEmerson"}},
  {2, 2, "Whitman", {"Walt", "1819", FirstLines[2],  "rcWhitman"}},
  {3, 3, "Frost", {"Robert", "1875", FirstLines[3],  "rcFrost"}},
  {4, 4, "Williams", {"Carlos", "1883", FirstLines[4],  "rcWilliams"}}
};

char szAppName[] = "PoemList";
char szTitle[]   = "PoemList Example"; // The title bar text

////////////////////////////////////////////////////////
// Program entry point, hPrevInstance a WIN16 artifact
////////////////////////////////////////////////////////
#pragma argsused
int APIENTRY WinMain(HINSTANCE hInstance, HINSTANCE hPrevInstance,
                     LPSTR lpCmdLine, int nCmdShow)
{
  MSG msg;

  // hPrevInstance not relevant in WIN32
  if (!Register(hInstance))
    return (FALSE);

  if (!Create(hInstance, nCmdShow))
    return (FALSE);

  while (GetMessage(&msg, NULL, 0, 0))
  {
    TranslateMessage(&msg);// Translates virtual key codes
    DispatchMessage(&msg); // Dispatches message to window
  }

  // Returns the value from PostQuitMessage
  return (msg.wParam);
}

////////////////////////////////////////////////////////
// Register the main window class
////////////////////////////////////////////////////////
```

continues

Listing 19.8. continued

```
BOOL Register(HINSTANCE hInstance)
{
    WNDCLASSEX  WndClassEx;

    WndClassEx.cbSize         = sizeof(WNDCLASSEX);
    WndClassEx.style          = CS_HREDRAW | CS_VREDRAW;
    WndClassEx.lpfnWndProc    = (WNDPROC)WndProc;
    WndClassEx.cbClsExtra     = 0;
    WndClassEx.cbWndExtra     = 0;
    WndClassEx.hInstance      = hInstance;
    WndClassEx.hIcon          = LoadIcon (hInstance, "PoemListIcon");
    WndClassEx.hCursor        = LoadCursor(NULL, IDC_ARROW);
    WndClassEx.hbrBackground  = (HBRUSH)(COLOR_WINDOW+1);
    WndClassEx.lpszMenuName   = szAppName;
    WndClassEx.lpszClassName  = szAppName;
    WndClassEx.hIconSm        = LoadIcon(hInstance, "PoemList16");

    return (RegisterClassEx(&WndClassEx) != 0);
}


////////////////////////////////////////////////////////////
// Create the main window
////////////////////////////////////////////////////////////
BOOL Create(HINSTANCE hInstance, int nCmdShow)
{
  hInst = hInstance;

  WndMain = CreateWindow(
      szAppName,            // See RegisterClass() call.
      szTitle,             // Text for window title bar.
      WS_OVERLAPPEDWINDOW, // Window style.
      CW_USEDEFAULT, 0, CW_USEDEFAULT, 0,// Use default positioning
      NULL,                // Overlapped windows have no parent.
      NULL,                // Use the window class menu.
      hInstance,           // This instance owns this window.
      NULL                 // We don't use any data in our WM_CREATE
      );

    if (!WndMain)
      return (FALSE);

    ShowWindow(WndMain, nCmdShow); // Show the window
    UpdateWindow(WndMain);         // Sends WM_PAINT message

    return (TRUE);                 // We succeeded...
}


////////////////////////////////////////////////////////////
// WndProc
////////////////////////////////////////////////////////////
LRESULT CALLBACK WndProc(HWND hwnd, UINT message,
                         WPARAM wParam, LPARAM lParam)
{
```

```
  switch (message)
  {
    HANDLE_MSG(hwnd, WM_CREATE, PoemList_OnCreate);
    HANDLE_MSG(hwnd, WM_DESTROY, PoemList_OnDestroy);
    HANDLE_MSG(hwnd, WM_COMMAND, PoemList_OnCommand);
    HANDLE_MSG(hwnd, WM_NOTIFY, PoemList_OnNotify);
    HANDLE_MSG(hwnd, WM_SIZE, PoemList_OnSize);
    default:
      return (DefWindowProc(hwnd, message, wParam, lParam));
  }
}

/////////////////////////////////////////////////////////////
// WM_CREATE
/////////////////////////////////////////////////////////////
BOOL PoemList_OnCreate(HWND hwnd, LPCREATESTRUCT lpCreateStruct)
{
  InitCommonControls();

  CreateImageLists(&hSmallImage, &hLargeImage);

  hPoemList = CreateWindowEx(0L, WC_LISTVIEW, "",
                WS_VISIBLE ¦ WS_CHILD ¦ LVS_ICON ¦
                LVS_SINGLESEL ¦ LVS_AUTOARRANGE,
                0, 0, 0, 0, hwnd,(HMENU)ID_LIST,
                lpCreateStruct->hInstance, NULL);

  ListView_SetImageList(hPoemList, hSmallImage, LVSIL_SMALL);
  ListView_SetImageList(hPoemList, hLargeImage, LVSIL_NORMAL);

  if (hPoemList)
  {
    SetHeader(hPoemList);
    SetPoemData(hPoemList);
  }

  return (hPoemList != NULL);
}

/////////////////////////////////////////////////////////////
// WM_DESTROY
/////////////////////////////////////////////////////////////
#pragma argsused
void PoemList_OnDestroy(HWND hwnd)
{
  if (hSmallImage)
    ImageList_Destroy(hSmallImage);
  if (hLargeImage)
    ImageList_Destroy(hLargeImage);
  PostQuitMessage(0);
}

/////////////////////////////////////////////////////////////
// WM_COMMAND
/////////////////////////////////////////////////////////////
```

19

continues

Listing 19.8. continued

```c
#pragma argsused
void PoemList_OnCommand(HWND hwnd, int id, HWND hwndCtl, UINT codeNotify)
{
  int dwStyle;

  switch (id)
  {
    case IDM_EXIT:
      DestroyWindow (hwnd);
      break;

    case IDM_ICONFORMAT:
      dwStyle = GetWindowLong(hPoemList, GWL_STYLE);
      dwStyle &= ~(LVS_TYPEMASK);
      dwStyle |= LVS_ICON;
      SetWindowLong(hPoemList, GWL_STYLE, dwStyle);
      break;

    case IDM_SMALLICONFORMAT:
      dwStyle = GetWindowLong(hPoemList, GWL_STYLE);
      dwStyle &= ~(LVS_TYPEMASK);
      dwStyle |= LVS_SMALLICON;
      SetWindowLong(hPoemList, GWL_STYLE, dwStyle);
      break;

    case IDM_LISTFORMAT:
      dwStyle = GetWindowLong(hPoemList, GWL_STYLE);
      dwStyle &= ~(LVS_TYPEMASK);
      dwStyle |= LVS_LIST;
      SetWindowLong(hPoemList, GWL_STYLE, dwStyle);
      break;

    case IDM_REPORTFORMAT:
      dwStyle = GetWindowLong(hPoemList, GWL_STYLE);
      dwStyle &= ~(LVS_TYPEMASK);
      dwStyle |= LVS_REPORT;
      SetWindowLong(hPoemList, GWL_STYLE, dwStyle);
      break;
  }
}

/////////////////////////////////////////////////////////
// Utility function to grab selected listview item
/////////////////////////////////////////////////////////
LPSTR GetSelectedItem(LPSTR S)
{
  LV_ITEM lvi;
  int ItemData;

  ItemData = ListView_GetNextItem(hPoemList, -1, LVNI_SELECTED);
  if (ItemData < 0)
  {
    strcpy(S, "None Selected");
```

```
     return S;
  }
  lvi.mask = LVIF_TEXT;
  lvi.pszText = S;            // preallocated string!
  lvi.cchTextMax = MAXSTR;   // Size of string buffer!
  lvi.iItem = ItemData;
  lvi.iSubItem = 0;
  ListView_GetItem(hPoemList, &lvi);

  return lvi.pszText;
}

////////////////////////////////////////////////////////
// WM_NOTIFY
////////////////////////////////////////////////////////
#pragma argsused
LRESULT PoemList_OnNotify(HWND hwnd, int idFrom, NMHDR FAR * pnmhdr)
{
  char S[MAXSTR], Buffer[MAXSTR];
  LV_KEYDOWN * Keys;

  switch (pnmhdr->code)
  {
    case LVN_GETDISPINFO:
      GetDisplayInfo((LV_DISPINFO *)pnmhdr);
      return 1;

    case LVN_ITEMCHANGED:
      strcpy(S, szTitle);
      strcat(S, " => ");
      strcat(S, GetSelectedItem(Buffer));
      SetWindowText(hwnd, S);
      break;

    case NM_DBLCLK:
      if (pnmhdr->hwndFrom == hPoemList)
      {
        strcpy(S, GetSelectedItem(Buffer));
        MessageBox(hwnd, S, "You Selected", MB_OK);
        SetFocus(hPoemList);
      }
      break;

    case LVN_KEYDOWN:
      LV_KEYDOWN * Keys = (LV_KEYDOWN *)pnmhdr;
      if (Keys->wVKey == VK_RETURN)
      {
        strcpy(S, GetSelectedItem(Buffer));
        MessageBox(hwnd, S, "You Selected", MB_OK);
        SetFocus(hPoemList);
      }
      break;
  }
  return FORWARD_WM_NOTIFY(hwnd, idFrom, pnmhdr, DefWindowProc);
}
```

19

continues

Listing 19.8. continued

```c
/////////////////////////////////////////////////////
// WM_SIZE
/////////////////////////////////////////////////////
#pragma argsused
void PoemList_OnSize(HWND hwnd, UINT state, int cx, int cy)
{
  if (hPoemList)
  {
    MoveWindow(hPoemList, 0, 0, cx, cy, FALSE);
    InvalidateRect(hPoemList, NULL, FALSE);
  }
}

/////////////////////////////////////////////////////
// Check functions that return -1 as an error code
/////////////////////////////////////////////////////
BOOL CheckIt(int i)
{
  if (i == -1)
  {
    MessageBox(WndMain, "List Error", NULL, MB_OK);
    return FALSE;
  }
  return TRUE;
}

/////////////////////////////////////////////////////
// Set the header text for a ListView
/////////////////////////////////////////////////////
BOOL SetHeader(HWND hPoemList)
{
  LV_COLUMN lvc;
  int       i;

  lvc.mask  = LVCF_FMT ¦ LVCF_WIDTH ¦ LVCF_TEXT ¦ LVCF_SUBITEM;
  lvc.fmt   = LVCFMT_LEFT;
  lvc.cx    = 75;

  // Add the columns.
  for (i = 0; i < NUMHEADERS; i++)
  {
    lvc.iSubItem = i;
    lvc.pszText  = Headers[i];
    if (i == 3)
      lvc.cx = 300;
    if (!CheckIt(ListView_InsertColumn(hPoemList, i, &lvc)))
      return FALSE;
  }
  return TRUE;
}

/////////////////////////////////////////////////////
// Fill the ListView control with data.
/////////////////////////////////////////////////////
BOOL SetPoemData(HWND hPoemList)
```

```
{
  LV_ITEM lvi;
  int i;

  lvi.mask  = LVIF_TEXT | LVIF_IMAGE | LVIF_STATE;
  lvi.state = lvi.stateMask = 0;

  for (i = 0; i < NUMITEMS; i++)
  {
    lvi.iItem      = i;
    lvi.iSubItem   = 0;
    lvi.pszText    = LPSTR_TEXTCALLBACK;
    lvi.cchTextMax = 0;
    lvi.iImage     = i;

    if (!CheckIt(ListView_InsertItem(hPoemList, &lvi)))
      return FALSE;
  }
  return TRUE;
}

//////////////////////////////////////////////////////
// DisplayInfo
//////////////////////////////////////////////////////
void GetDisplayInfo(LV_DISPINFO * DisplayInfo)
{
  char *S;
  int i = DisplayInfo->item.iItem;
  int j = DisplayInfo->item.iSubItem;

  if (j == 0)
    S = PoetList[i].Poet;
  else
    S = PoetList[i].SubLabel[j - 1];

  DisplayInfo->item.pszText = S;
}


//////////////////////////////////////////////////////
// Put the Images in the ImageList
//////////////////////////////////////////////////////
BOOL FillInImages(HIMAGELIST *SmallImageList,
                  HIMAGELIST *LargeImageList)
{
  HBITMAP Bmp;
  HICON Ico;
  int i;
  char SBmp[60];

  for (i = 0; i < NUMITEMS; i ++)
  {
    strcpy(SBmp, PoetList[i].SubLabel[3]);
    strcat(SBmp, "Bmp");
    Bmp = LoadBitmap(hInst, SBmp);
    if (!CheckIt(ImageList_AddMasked(*SmallImageList, Bmp, TRANCOLOR)))
```

continues

19

Listing 19.8. continued

```
      return FALSE;

    Ico = LoadIcon(hInst, PoetList[i].SubLabel[3]);
    if (!CheckIt(ImageList_AddIcon(*LargeImageList, Ico)))
      return FALSE;
  }

  return TRUE;
}

/////////////////////////////////////////////////////////
// Create the large and small image lists
/////////////////////////////////////////////////////////
BOOL CreateImageLists(HIMAGELIST *SmallImageList,
                      HIMAGELIST *LargeImageList)
{
  *SmallImageList = ImageList_Create(16,16, ILC_MASK, NUMITEMS, 1);
  if (!*SmallImageList)
    return FALSE;

  *LargeImageList = ImageList_Create(32,32, ILC_MASK, NUMITEMS, 1);
  if (!*LargeImageList)
  {
    ImageList_Destroy(*SmallImageList);
    return FALSE;
  }

  return FillInImages(SmallImageList, LargeImageList);
}
```

Listing 19.9. The header file for the PoemList listview example.

```
/////////////////////////////////////////////////////////
// PoemList.h
// Copyright  1995 Charlie Calvert.
/////////////////////////////////////////////////////////

// Macros
#define MAXSTR              250
#define TRANCOLOR           RGB(0, 128, 0)
#define NUMITEMS            5
#define SUBITEMS            3
#define NUMHEADERS          (SUBITEMS+1)

#define ID_LIST             100
#define IDM_EXIT            106
#define IDM_LINK            204
#define IDM_LINKS           205

#define IDM_ICONFORMAT      206
#define IDM_SMALLICONFORMAT 207
#define IDM_LISTFORMAT      208
```

```
#define IDM_REPORTFORMAT       209

#define IDM_HELPCONTENTS       300
#define IDM_HELPSEARCH         301
#define IDM_HELPHELP           302
#define IDM_ABOUT              303

#define DLG_VERFIRST           400
#define DLG_VERLAST            404

// Types
typedef struct tagPOETLIST
   {
   int     iImageBig;
   int     iImageSmall;
   LPSTR   Poet;
   LPSTR   SubLabel[SUBITEMS+1];
   }
POETLIST, FAR * LPPOETLIST;

// Funcs
BOOL Register(HINSTANCE);
BOOL Create(HINSTANCE, int);
LRESULT CALLBACK WndProc(HWND, UINT, WPARAM, LPARAM);
LRESULT CALLBACK About  (HWND, UINT, WPARAM, LPARAM);

BOOL PoemList_OnCreate(HWND hwnd, LPCREATESTRUCT lpCreateStruct);
void PoemList_OnDestroy(HWND hwnd);
void PoemList_OnCommand(HWND hwnd, int id,
                        HWND hwndCtl, UINT codeNotify);
LRESULT PoemList_OnNotify(HWND hwnd, int idFrom, NMHDR FAR * pnmhdr);
void PoemList_OnSize(HWND hwnd, UINT state, int cx, int cy);

BOOL SetHeader(HWND hWndListView);
BOOL SetPoemData(HWND hPoemList);
void GetDisplayInfo(LV_DISPINFO * lpLVDispInfo);
BOOL CreateImageLists(HIMAGELIST *SmallImageList,
                      HIMAGELIST *LargeImageList);
```

19

Listing 19.10. The resource file for the PoemList program.

```
//////////////////////////////////////////////////////
// POEMLIST.RC
//   Copyright  1995 Charlie Calvert.
//////////////////////////////////////////////////////

#include "poemlist.h"

PoemListIcon      ICON      poemlist.ICO
PoemList16        BMP       poemls16.ICO

rcBradStreet      ICON      brad.ico
rcEmerson         ICON      emerson.ico
rcWhitman         ICON      whitman.ico
```

continues

Listing 19.10. continued

```
rcFrost          ICON      frost.ico
rcWilliams       ICON      williams.ico

rcWilliamsBmp    BITMAP    colors.bmp
rcEmersonBmp     BITMAP    firecrak.bmp
rcBradstreetBmp  BITMAP    lock.bmp
rcWhitmanBmp     BITMAP    tao.bmp
rcFrostBmp       BITMAP    world.bmp

PoemList MENU
BEGIN
  POPUP "&File"
  BEGIN
    MENUITEM "E&xit",    IDM_EXIT
  END
  POPUP "&Mode"
  BEGIN
    MENUITEM "Icon Format",        IDM_ICONFORMAT
    MENUITEM "Small Icon Format",  IDM_SMALLICONFORMAT
    MENUITEM "List Format",        IDM_LISTFORMAT
    MENUITEM "Report Format",      IDM_REPORTFORMAT
  END
END
```

Listing 19.11. The complex and labyrinthine module definition file for the PoemList program.

```
; POEMLIST.DEF

NAME          POEMLIST
DESCRIPTION 'PoemList Sample'
```

Listing 19.12. The Borland makefile for the PoemList program.

```
#////////////////////////////////////////////////
# POEMLIST.MAK
# Copyright  1995 Charlie Calvert.
#////////////////////////////////////////////////

# macros

!if !$d(BCROOT)
BCROOT  = $(MAKEDIR)\..
!endif

APPNAME = PoemList
INCPATH = $(BCROOT)\WIN32;$(BCROOT);$(BCROOT)\INCLUDE
LIBPATH = $(BCROOT)\LIB

COMPILER= BCC32.EXE
```

```
BRC     = BRC32.EXE
FLAGS   = -W -v -w4 -I$(INCPATH) -L$(LIBPATH)
OBJS    = $(APPNAME).obj

# link
$(APPNAME).exe: $(OBJS) $(APPNAME).def $(APPNAME).res
  $(COMPILER) $(FLAGS) $(OBJS) comctl32.lib
  $(BRC) -I$(INCPATH) $(APPNAME).res

# compiling
.cpp.obj:
  $(COMPILER) -c $(FLAGS) { $< }

# resource
$(APPNAME).res: $(APPNAME).rc
  $(BRC) -R -I$(INCPATH) $(APPNAME).RC
```

Listing 19.13. The Microsoft makefile for the PoemList program.

```
# POEMLIMS.MAK
# Microsoft make file

APPNAME=POEMLIST
TARGETOS=WIN95
APPVER=4.0
OBJS=$(APPNAME).obj

!include <win32.mak>

all: $(APPNAME).exe

# Update the resource if necessary

$(APPNAME).res: $(APPNAME).rc $(APPNAME).h
  $(rc) $(rcflags) $(rcvars) $(APPNAME).rc

# Update the object files if necessary

# compile
.cpp.obj:
  $(cc) $(cflags) $(cvars) $(cdebug) $<

# Update the executable file if necessary.

$(APPNAME).exe: $(OBJS) $(APPNAME).res
  $(link) $(linkdebug) $(guiflags) -out:$(APPNAME).exe\
          $(OBJS) $(APPNAME).res $(guilibs) comctl32.lib
```

When working with this program, remember that the icons and bitmaps shown in Table 19.1 are only part of a recommended interface for your program. It doesn't matter how the icons you use actually look. The only relevant factor is that the icons all be 32×32 pixels in size, whereas the BMPs should be 16×16.

Table 19.1. Icons and bitmaps you can use with your program.

	brad.ico
	emerson.ico
	frost.ico
	poemlist.ico
	poemls16.ico
	whitman.ico
	williams.ico
	colors.bmp
	firecrak.bmp
	lock.bmp
	tao.bmp
	world.bmp

The PoemList program presents you with a view of five poets. If you select one of the poets with the mouse or keyboard, his or her name appears appended to the caption at the top of the program. If you select one of the poets by double-clicking, the poet's name appears in a message box. If you select one of the poets and press Enter, the poet's name again appears in a message box.

From the menu at the top of the program, you can choose one of the following four possible modes for a listview:

☐ LVS_ICON: The items in the list appear as five large icons, much like the view in the old Program Manager that was so popular back when the Earth's crust was still cooling.

☐ LVS_SMALLICON: The items in the list appear next to small icons, like the default views in the Explorer.

☐ LVS_LIST: Like the small icon format, but always arranged vertically down the screen.

☐ LVS_REPORT: Like the list format, but with additional columns of information visible. This is like the Details view in the right-hand side of the Explorer.

The LVS appended to these names can be thought of as standing for List View Style.

By far the best way to get a good feeling for these four views is to actually fire up the computer and see how they look in practice. In the meantime, take a look at Figures 19.7 and 19.8 to see how the LVS_ICON and LVS_REPORT views of the PoemList program appear to the user.

Figure 19.7.

The PoemList program in icon view.

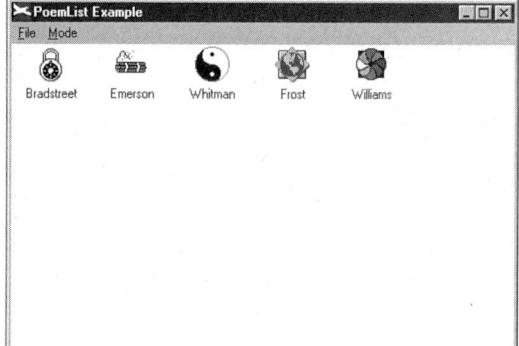

Figure 19.8.

The PoemList program in report view.

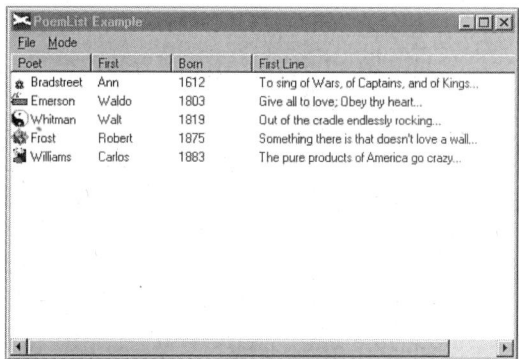

PoemList first appears in icon view. The initial mode is set in the call to CreateWindowEx; it is changed thereafter by calling SetWindowLong and GetWindowLong. But I'm getting ahead of myself. Here is the call to CreateWindowEx that gets the ball rolling:

```
hPoemList = CreateWindowEx(0L, WC_LISTVIEW, "",
            WS_VISIBLE ¦ WS_CHILD ¦ LVS_ICON ¦
            LVS_SINGLESEL ¦ LVS_AUTOARRANGE,
            0, 0, 0, 0, hwnd,(HMENU)ID_LIST,
            lpCreateStruct->hInstance, NULL);
```

There's nothing unusual here other than the listview styles. LVS_ICON you already know about. LVS_SINGLESEL ensures that only one item can be selected at a time, and LVS_AUTOARRANGE lets Windows take care of arranging the icons on the screen.

Following are some other possible options with very abbreviated descriptions (for more detailed information, see the online help):

LVS_ALIGNLEFT	Left-aligned in icon and small icon views.
LVS_ALIGNTOP	Align with top in icon and small icon views.
LVS_AUTOARRANGE	Auto-arrange in icon and small icon views.
LVS_BUTTON	Icons look like buttons in icon view.
LVS_EDITLABELS	Text to be edited in place.
LVS_ICON	Icon view.
LVS_LIST	List view.
LVS_NOCOLUMNHEADER	No column header.
LVS_NOLABELWRAP	Text on a single line in icon view.
LVS_NOSCROLL	Disables scrolling.
LVS_NOSORTHEADER	Column headers do not work like buttons.
LVS_OWNERDRAWFIXED	Owner window paints items in report view.
LVS_REPORT	Report view.
LVS_SHAREIMAGELISTS	Don't dispose of image list when done.
LVS_SHOWSELALWAYS	Show selection even when the control is not focused.
LVS_SINGLESEL	One item selected at a time, please.
LVS_SMALLICON	Small icon view.
LVS_SORTASCENDING	Sorts item text in ascending order.
LVS_SORTDESCENDING	Sorts item text in descending order.

After you have created the listview, the next step is to create the imagelists that hold the icons shown in the control. This turns out to take a few lines of code, so I have created a wrapper function called CreateImageLists that performs the actual grunt work:

```
CreateImageLists(&hSmallImage, &hLargeImage);
```

Here's the local function that is actually called:

```
BOOL CreateImageLists(HIMAGELIST *SmallImageList,
                      HIMAGELIST *LargeImageList)
{
  *SmallImageList = ImageList_Create(16,16, ILC_MASK, NUMITEMS, 1);
  if (!*SmallImageList)
    return FALSE;

  *LargeImageList = ImageList_Create(32,32, ILC_MASK, NUMITEMS, 1);
  if (!*LargeImageList)
  {
    ImageList_Destroy(*SmallImageList);
```

```
    return FALSE;
  }

  return FillInImages(SmallImageList, LargeImageList);
}
```

The SkyView program called `ImageList_LoadBitmap` to create an imagelist. As I said when discussing that function, it provides a convenient shortcut that helps you get an imagelist up and running quickly. The PoemList program is more complicated and has a greater need for control over how the list is constructed. As a result, it calls `ImageList_Create` rather than `ImageList_LoadBitmap`.

Syntax

```
HIMAGELIST WINAPI ImageList_Create(
    int   cx,        // Width of each frame in pixels
    int   cy,        // Height of each frame
    UINT  flags,     // Flag
    int   cInitial,  // number of initial frames
    int   cGrow      // How much can it grow by at one time
);
```

The first two parameters are the width and height of the frames in the imagelist. The third parameter can be a combination of the following flags:

ILC_COLOR4	4-bit DIB
ILC_COLOR8	8-bit DIB
ILC_COLOR16	16-bit DIB
ILC_COLOR24	24-bit DIB
ILC_COLOR32	32-bit DIB
ILC_COLORDDB	Device-dependent bitmaps
ILC_MASK	Uses a mask
ILC_PALETTE	A color palette is used with the imagelist

The fourth parameter is set to the number of images in the initial version of the list. In the PoemList program this number is hard coded as 5 and never changes through the run of the program. The last parameter specifies how much the list can grow, and it is set to 1 although this list will not change in size.

Here's an example:

```
List = ImageList_Create(32,32, ILC_MASK | ILC_COLOR, 12, 1);
```

Inserting Bitmaps into Listviews

After creating the lists, your next step is to fill them with bitmaps. Once again, in the SkyView program, this was all part of the single call to `ImageList_LoadBitmap`. Now the chore is broken out into small chunks, for the reasons stated previously and also because doing things this way helps build character—Not!

19

Here is the function that loads the bitmaps and icons:

```
BOOL FillInImages(HIMAGELIST *SmallImageList,
                  HIMAGELIST *LargeImageList)
{
  HBITMAP Bmp;
  HICON Ico;
  int i;
  char SBmp[60];

  for (i = 0; i < NUMITEMS; i ++)
  {
    strcpy(SBmp, PoetList[i].SubLabel[3]);
    strcat(SBmp, "Bmp");
    Bmp = LoadBitmap(hInst, SBmp);
    if (!CheckIt(ImageList_AddMasked(*SmallImageList, Bmp, TRANCOLOR)))
      return FALSE;

    Ico = LoadIcon(hInst, PoetList[i].SubLabel[3]);
    if (!CheckIt(ImageList_AddIcon(*LargeImageList, Ico)))
      return FALSE;
  }

  return TRUE;
}
```

The PoetList structure contains a set of strings that identify the various icon and bitmap resources. Here is the relevant declaration:

```
typedef struct tagPOETLIST
  {
  int    iImageBig;
  int    iImageSmall;
  LPSTR  Poet;
  LPSTR  SubLabel[SUBITEMS+1];
  }
POETLIST, FAR * LPPOETLIST;
```

The members of this structure are hard coded into the application, but that might not be an ideal approach in most circumstances. The issue here is that you might want to change the lines dynamically at runtime, and therefore should not hard code them into the application itself. This subject is discussed in more depth later in this chapter as well as in "Week 3 in Review":

```
POETLIST PoetList[NUMITEMS] =
{
  {0, 0, "Bradstreet", {"Ann",   "1612", FirstLines[0], "rcBradstreet"}},
  {1, 1, "Emerson",    {"Waldo", "1803", FirstLines[1], "rcEmerson"}},
  {2, 2, "Whitman",    {"Walt",  "1819", FirstLines[2], "rcWhitman"}},
  {3, 3, "Frost",      {"Robert","1875", FirstLines[3], "rcFrost"}},
  {4, 4, "Williams",   {"Carlos","1883", FirstLines[4], "rcWilliams"}}
};
```

For now, what's important in this declaration is the third field of the subarray, which contains the names of resources from POEMLIST.RC:

```
rcBradStreet      ICON      brad.ico
rcEmerson         ICON      emerson.ico
rcWhitman         ICON      whitman.ico
rcFrost           ICON      frost.ico
rcWilliams        ICON      williams.ico

rcWilliamsBmp     BITMAP    colors.bmp
rcEmersonBmp      BITMAP    firecrak.bmp
rcBradstreetBmp   BITMAP    lock.bmp
rcWhitmanBmp      BITMAP    tao.bmp
rcFrostBmp        BITMAP    world.bmp
```

Notice that I have set things up so that you can simply append the letters *bmp* onto the icon names in order to get the names of the resources. This arrangement makes it easy to get at the bitmaps and icons stored in the executable.

After you've loaded the resources into memory, you still have to get them into the imagelist. This is accomplished through a call to `ImageList_AddMasked` and `ImageList_AddIcon`. Both of these functions are very easy to use, although perhaps a word is in order about the last parameter of the `ImageList_AddMasked` function:

```
int WINAPI ImageList_AddMasked(
  HIMAGELIST himl,      // handle to the image list
  HBITMAP    hbmImage,  // handle to the bitmap
  COLORREF   crMask     // color used to generate mask
);
```

The concept behind the `crMask` field should be familiar to you from the SkyView program. This is the color that will become "transparent." In the PoemList program it's a kind of sickly green that was used nowhere else in the bitmaps. Notice that you don't have to worry about the transparent color with icons because it is built into them from the proverbial get-go.

When you are calling `ImageList_AddIcon` or `ImageList_AddMasked`, you might want to check the operation to see if it proceeds correctly. Both of these functions return -1 on error, so you can test their outcome with the following local function:

```
BOOL CheckIt(int i)
{
  if (i == -1)
  {
    MessageBox(WndMain, "List Error", NULL, MB_OK);
    return FALSE;
  }
  return TRUE;
}
```

The code shown here automatically pops up a messagebox if something goes wrong.

> **Tip:** I probably don't put enough emphasis on the importance of checking error codes returned by functions. It's a very valuable addition to your code that can often save you hours of debugging time. Functions such as `CheckIt` make it easy for you to test the results of functions. If you are working on a big project, it is well worth your time to write and employ similar routines.

All in all, it's not that difficult to create the imagelists and load them into memory. When they're present, you can stick them into the listview with the following simple call:

```
ListView_SetImageList(hPoemList, hSmallImage, LVSIL_SMALL);
ListView_SetImageList(hPoemList, hLargeImage, LVSIL_NORMAL);
```

Rather than clutter up the page with an in-depth description of this simple and intuitive call, I'll just say that it takes a handle to the listview in the first parameter, a handle to the imagelist in the second call, and one of the following flags in the third parameter:

LVSIL_NORMAL	Image list with large icons
LVSIL_SMALL	Image list with small icons
LVSIL_STATE	Image list with state images

It should come as no surprise to hear that `ListView_SetImageList` is a macro that wraps the `LVM_SETIMAGELIST` message.

> **Note:** If you need to test the images in your imagelist to make sure they are being created correctly, you can write this code in your `WndProc`:
>
> ```
>     int i;
> case WM_PAINT:
>     PaintDC = BeginPaint(hwnd, &PaintStruct);
>     for (i = 0; i < NUMIMAGES; i++)
>     {
>       ImageList_Draw(hLargeImage, i, PaintDC, 50 * i, 100, ILD_NORMAL);
>       ImageList_Draw(hSmallImage, i, PaintDC, 50 * i, 200, ILD_NORMAL);
>     }
>     EndPaint(hwnd, &PaintStruct);
>     break;
> ```
>
> When you are running this code, make sure that you comment out the lines that create the listview. Listviews cover up the window in which they paint, so you might not be able to see the output from a paint procedure or the output might be only a brief flash on the screen.

Inserting Text into Listviews

It probably seems like you have been reading about the creation of this listview object for most of your natural life. However, there is still more to come. Specifically, if you run your mind back over the process you will notice that the actual text associated with each item has not yet been defined. That is, the bitmaps and icons are now in place, but not the text associated with them.

Here's the code in the WM_CREATE handler that calls the functions that add the strings to the listview:

```
if (hPoemList)
{
  SetHeader(hPoemList);
  SetPoemData(hPoemList);
}
```

When the program is in report mode, there are a set of headers along the top of the listview control. *Headers* are a separate Windows 95 control just like trackbars, status bars, and so on. Here is how to fill one out from inside a listview:

```
BOOL SetHeader(HWND hPoemList)
{
  LV_COLUMN lvc;
  int       i;

  lvc.mask    = LVCF_FMT | LVCF_WIDTH | LVCF_TEXT | LVCF_SUBITEM;
  lvc.fmt     = LVCFMT_LEFT;
  lvc.cx      = 75;

  // Add the columns.
  for (i = 0; i < NUMHEADERS; i++)
  {
    lvc.iSubItem = i;
    lvc.pszText  = Headers[i];
    if (i == 3)
      lvc.cx = 300;
    if (!CheckIt(ListView_InsertColumn(hPoemList, i, &lvc)))
      return FALSE;
  }
  return TRUE;
}
```

The key line of code here is the call to the ListView_InsertColumn macro, which is a WindowsX-like wrapper around the LVM_INSERTCOLUMN message. Pass the column number in the first parameter (wParam) and an LV_COLUMN structure in the second parameter (lParam).

Here's a quick look at the LV_COLUMN structure:

```
typedef struct _LV_COLUMN {
    UINT mask;        // mask
    int fmt;          // format
    int cx;           // width of the column
    LPTSTR pszText;   // string to show in column
```

```
      int cchTextMax;   // size of pszText buffer
      int iSubItem;     // Index of subitem link
} LV_COLUMN;
```

Here are the possible values for the mask field:

LVCF_FMT	The fmt member is valid.
LVCF_SUBITEM	The iSubItem member is valid.
LVCF_TEXT	The pszText member is valid.
LVCF_WIDTH	The cx member is valid.

Once again, I have hard coded the header labels into the program:

```
const static LPSTR Headers[NUMHEADERLABELS] =
  { "Poet", "First", "Born", "First Line" };
```

These strings are passed in with the pszText field of the LV_COLUMN structure.

Notice that I set the width of all of the columns but the last to 75. The final column needs to be wider because it will contain a relatively long string consisting of a quote from a poem:

```
const static LPSTR FirstLines[] =
{
  {"To sing of Wars, of Captains, and of Kings..."},
  {"Give all to love; Obey thy heart..."},
  {"Out of the cradle endlessly rocking..."},
  {"Something there is that doesn't love a wall..."},
  {"The pure products of America go crazy..."}
};
```

I don't actually insert the text from the poem in this function. I'm just showing you the quotes so you'll understand why the column needs to be so wide.

Now that the headers are inserted, it is at long last time to begin the process of adding the actual text displayed in the list. It turns out that there are two different methods for doing this. You can either

☐ Add the strings directly, or

☐ Add the strings via a callback that comes in the form of a WM_NOTIFY message.

I will show you how to use both techniques, but the actual version of PoemList that's shown here uses the callback technique.

Here's the relevant code from the PoemList program:

```
BOOL SetPoemData(HWND hPoemList)
{
  LV_ITEM lvi;
  int i;

  lvi.mask  = LVIF_TEXT | LVIF_IMAGE | LVIF_STATE;
  lvi.state = lvi.stateMask = 0;

  for (i = 0; i < NUMITEMS; i++)
```

```
  {
    lvi.iItem      = i;
    lvi.iSubItem   = 0;
    lvi.pszText    = LPSTR_TEXTCALLBACK;
    lvi.cchTextMax = 0;
    lvi.iImage     = i;

    if (!CheckIt(ListView_InsertItem(hPoemList, &lvi)))
      return FALSE;
  }
  return TRUE;
}
```

This code tells Windows that the text will be supplied in a WM_NOTIFY-based callback. In other words, the code doesn't actually supply the strings; it just tells Windows that the strings will be provided later.

The key structure here is of type LV_ITEM:

```
typedef struct _LV_ITEM {
    UINT    mask;         // mask
    int     iItem;        // index of item in list
    int     iSubItem;     // zero if there is no subitem
    UINT    state;        // Current state of the item
    UINT    stateMask;    // Current state mask
    LPTSTR  pszText;      // Text or LPSTR_TEXTCALLBACK
    int     cchTextMax;   // Length of text buffer
    int     iImage;       // index of the list view item's icon
    LPARAM  lParam;       // 32-bit value to associate with item
} LV_ITEM;
```

You will use this structure repeatedly when working with listviews, so it's worth looking at carefully.

Here are some of the currently available masks (more might appear by the time Windows 95 actually ships):

LVIF_TEXT	pszText is valid.
LVIF_IMAGE	iImage is valid.
LVIF_PARAM	lParam is valid.
LVIF_STATE	State member is valid.

In the code for this program the pszText field is set to LPSTR_CALLBACK, which tells other programmers that the data will be supplied later in the WM_NOTIFY handler.

When everything is all set, the LV_ITEM structure is inserted into the list via a call to ListView_InsertItem. This function takes the handle of the window in the first parameter and a pointer to the LV_ITEM structure in the second parameter.

To sum up, the SetPoemData function encapsulates two steps:

☐ Fill out the fields in the LV_ITEM structure.

☐ Pass the lot onto the listview via a call to ListView_InsertItem.

19

Note: Before talking about the `WM_NOTIFY`-based callback, I should perhaps mention how to supply the data directly. In that case, you would fill in the `pszText` field of `LV_ITEM` structure with the names of each item; that is, with Bradstreet, Emerson, Whitman, Frost, and Williams.

If you also wanted to use the `LVM_GETITEMTEXT` message, you would fill in the `cchTextMax` field. To utilize the field, set the `cchTextMax` field to a reasonable size, such as 100:

```
for (i = 0; i < iNumItems; i++)
{
  lvi.iItem      = i;
  lvi.iSubItem   = 0;
  lvi.pszText    = lpPoetList[i].Poet;
  lvi.cchTextMax = 100;
  lvi.iImage     = i;
  lvi.lParam     = 0;
}
```

After filling out the structure, you could then insert it into the listview as described.

Each of the subitems seen in the report view could be filled in by a call to `ListView_SetItemText` macro, which is a wrapper around the `LVM_SETITEMTEXT` message:

```
int iSubItem;

for (iSubItem = 1; iSubItem < SUBITEMS; iSubItem++)
  ListView_SetItemText(hPoemList, iItem, iSubItem, NULL);
```

Here are the actual fields of the macro:

```
VOID WINAPI ListView_SetItemText(
    HWND hwnd,         // Handle to the listview
    int i,             // Item to work with
    int iSubItem,      // Want to change a subitem?
    LPCSTR pszText);   // Text to insert.
```

You can use this macro to change the main item of the text. If that is your goal, set the `iSubItem` field to zero. If `iSubItem` is nonzero, you are filling in the text for one of the columns seen in report mode. Note that you can call this function at any time, and that it can be used in place of the callback I am about to describe.

The key point to grasp here is that there are two methods of filling in the text. One is shown here in this note, and the other will be explained in the following text. Obviously I feel it's helpful for you to know both methods. That leaves you with the option to choose the method you feel is most useful. Note, however, that the PoemList program uses the callback method.

The callback comes in the form of a WM_NOTIFY message. (Frankly, I usually think of a callback as involving a specific function address rather than a message, but I suppose the two concepts are closely related.) At any rate, the key point here is simply that you are getting a chance to fill in the text for the list dynamically in response to a WM_NOTIFY message rather than only during the creation of the list, as shown in the previous note.

Here's the key line in the WM_NOTIFY handler:

```
case LVN_GETDISPINFO:
  GetDisplayInfo((LV_DISPINFO *)pnmhdr);
  return 1;
```

The LVN that proceeds this name can be thought of as standing for List View Notification. The message, then, is a request for you to supply the display information, where *display information* means text or icon.

Here's how to obtain the information from the hard coded PoetList structure shown previously:

```
void GetDisplayInfo(LV_DISPINFO * DisplayInfo)
{
  char *S;
  int i = DisplayInfo->item.iItem;
  int j = DisplayInfo->item.iSubItem;

  if (j == 0)
    S = PoetList[i].Poet;
  else
    S = PoetList[i].SubLabel[j - 1];

  DisplayInfo->item.pszText = S;
}
```

The LV_DISPINFO structure is like the TOOLTIPTEXT structure you learned about on Day 15, "Introduction to Windows 95 Controls." That is, it's simply the NMHDR structure with a few fields added onto it:

```
typedef struct tagLV_DISPINFO {
    NMHDR   hdr;
    LV_ITEM item;
} LV_DISPINFO;
```

In particular, you are now getting a second crack at the LV_ITEM structure you filled out in the SetPoemData function. But this time you are actually going to put text in the pszText field.

If the iSubItem field of the LV_ITEM structure is zero, you have a main text item to fill in; if it is nonzero, you have a subitem to fill in. At this stage I pass in the hard coded data from the top of the program. But you could pass in anything at this point, and Windows will happily display it for you. This means you could change the text any time you get an LVN_GETDISPINFO message.

19

At long last you are through! All of the icons and bitmaps have been supplied to the listview, and all of the text has been filled in. Clearly this whole process is rather involved, particular if you consider all the choices available to you. Remember that I have shown you several different ways to insert the text into the listview, and that the whole process is somewhat simpler if you focus on one method.

Changing the Mode of a Listview

Well, at long last you have a complete description of how to get the PoemList program initialized. It's taken quite a while to get this new control up and running, but from here on things are much simpler.

When you need to change from icon mode to small icon mode, or in and out of any of the other modes, you can use `GetWindowLong` and `SetWindowLong`:

```
case IDM_ICONFORMAT:
    dwStyle = GetWindowLong(hPoemList, GWL_STYLE);
    dwStyle &= ~(LVS_TYPEMASK);
    dwStyle |= LVS_ICON;
    SetWindowLong(hPoemList, GWL_STYLE, dwStyle);
    break;
```

This code

☐ retrieves the current style, then

☐ zeroes out its type mask, and finally

☐ ORs in the new style and sends it back to Windows.

The same process is repeated when you need to move in and out of any of the other modes:

```
case IDM_SMALLICONFORMAT:
    dwStyle = GetWindowLong(hPoemList, GWL_STYLE);
    dwStyle &= ~(LVS_TYPEMASK);
    dwStyle |= LVS_SMALLICON;
    SetWindowLong(hPoemList, GWL_STYLE, dwStyle);
    break;
```

Each of these changes occurs, of course, in response to clicks on the menu. The menu selection causes a `WM_COMMAND` message to be sent to your program, and then the code shown here is executed.

Remember that this process will not work correctly unless you have explicitly marked your application as a Windows 4.*x* application. This is fairly easy in Microsoft's compilers, and it will be easy in Borland C++ 5.0. However, if you are using Borland C++ 4.5, you might want to run the utility program in the CHI_INS subdirectory that accompanies the online listings for this book. Once again, you can get the code by signing on to CompuServe and typing `GO SAMS`, or by attaching to `www.borland.com` or `www.mcp.com`.

Which Item Did the User Pick?

If you have the PoemList program up and running correctly, the user can select items from the list and the program will give you feedback on the user's selection. Note that the act of selecting items in the list won't work properly unless you forward the WM_NOTIFY messages on to the DefWindowProc:

```
return FORWARD_WM_NOTIFY(hwnd, idFrom, pnmhdr, DefWindowProc);
```

If you forget to do this, you will end up clicking madly on each of the items in the list, but none of them will ever get the focus.

To find out which item the user has selected, you can call ListView_GetItemNext and ListView_GetItem:

```
LPSTR GetSelectedItem(LPSTR S)
{
  LV_ITEM lvi;
  int ItemData;

  ItemData = ListView_GetNextItem(hPoemList, -1, LVNI_SELECTED);
  if (ItemData < 0)
  {
    strcpy(S, "None Selected");
    return S;
  }
  lvi.mask = LVIF_TEXT;
  lvi.pszText = S;            // preallocated string!
  lvi.cchTextMax = MAXSTR;    // Size of string buffer!
  lvi.iItem = ItemData;
  lvi.iSubItem = 0;
  ListView_GetItem(hPoemList, &lvi);

  return lvi.pszText;
}
```

ListView_GetNextItem is another WindowsX-like macro, this time fronting for the LVM_GETNEXTITEM message. If you pass in the LVNI_SELECTED flag in lParam and set wParam to -1, you can retrieve the index of the currently selected item. If no item is selected, the function returns -1.

When you have the selected item, you can find out about it by calling ListView_GetItem. This macro retrieves the LV_ITEM structure, whose acquaintance you made on several occasions earlier in this chapter. As you know, the LV_ITEM structure has a field that holds the text for the item in question.

So that's that. Now you have a function called GetSelectedItem that shows how to find the currently focused item and how to retrieve its text.

Following are three notifications that are part of a WM_NOTIFY message:

```
    case LVN_ITEMCHANGED:
```

19

```
      strcpy(S, szTitle);
      strcat(S, " => ");
      strcat(S, GetSelectedItem(Buffer));
      SetWindowText(hwnd, S);
      break;

  case NM_DBLCLK:
    if (pnmhdr->hwndFrom == hPoemList)
    {
      strcpy(S, GetSelectedItem(Buffer));
      MessageBox(hwnd, S, "You Selected", MB_OK);
      SetFocus(hPoemList);
    }
    break;

  case LVN_KEYDOWN:
    LV_KEYDOWN * Keys = (LV_KEYDOWN *)pnmhdr;
    if (Keys->wVKey == VK_RETURN)
    {
      strcpy(S, GetSelectedItem(Buffer));
      MessageBox(hwnd, S, "You Selected", MB_OK);
      SetFocus(hPoemList);
    }
    break;
}
```

I use the first one to track when the user has highlighted a new item. To provide feedback, I change the caption of the program. In other words, the currently focused item is always displayed in the program's caption because PoemList responds to LVN_ITEMCHANGED messages.

If the user double-clicks on the listview, I retrieve the text for the currently selected item and show it in a list box.

The same thing occurs when the user presses the Enter key. Here is what an LV_KEYDOWN structure looks like:

```
typedef struct tagLV_KEYDOWN {
    NMHDR hdr;
    WORD wVKey;
    UINT flags;
} LV_KEYDOWN;
```

This is another structure that's like the TOOLTIPTEXT record shown on Day 15. Of particular interest is the wVKey field, which holds the virtual key that's been pressed. Virtual keys are discussed on Day 5. (A second method for trapping hits on the Enter key involves using NM_RETURN.)

In short, responding to LVN_ITEMCHANGED, LVN_KEYDOWN, and NM_DBLCLK messages is trivial when you have a way of retrieving the currently selected item. Note that the first two messages referenced in this paragraph are specific to listviews, whereas the third is just a general WM_NOTIFY code. If you haven't done so already, you should bring up the online help and search on NM_*, or look at the information on NMHDR. Both techniques will get the following list of messages associated with WM_NOTIFY:

NM_CLICK	Left mouse button click.
NM_DBLCLK	Double-click.
NM_KILLFOCUS	Control lost the input focus.
NM_OUTOFMEMORY	Out of memory.
NM_RCLICK	Right mouse button click.
NM_RDBLCLK	Right mouse button double-click.
NM_RETURN	Control has focus and the user pressed Enter.
NM_SETFOCUS	Control received the input focus.

That's all I'm going to say about listviews. This has been a fairly long discussion, but you should come out of it with a good feel for how to take advantage of these useful tools. In this section you've seen that listviews are fairly easy to work with after you have them up and running.

Summary

This chapter starts with a discussion of imagelists. They are useful and fun in their own right, but you will find that they are a near-essential component of other controls such as listviews and treeviews.

The second half of this chapter discusses listviews. Remember, this is one of the most visible and heavily used items in the entire Windows 95 interface. Microsoft clearly thinks a lot of this little fellow, and perhaps sees it as the successor to the list boxes that were so popular in Windows 3.1.

To find out more about Windows 95 controls, you should read "Week 3 in Review," which concentrates on treeviews, and "Bonus Days in Review," which concentrates on RTF controls.

19

Q&A

Q You use imagelists and listviews together. Is this absolutely necessary?

A You can bring up both listviews and treeviews without supplying any icons or bitmaps. When working with treeviews, this probably even makes a certain amount of sense under some circumstances. However, I feel that both treeviews and listviews make much better use of icons than did the Windows 3.1 Program Manager. For instance, when I open up the Explorer, I sometimes move into subdirectories that have 50 or 60 files in them, only two of which are executables. If I'm looking for the executables, I can find them easily because they are marked with a special icon. To me, this system makes sense; it's not just cluttering up my screen with meaningless pictures the way the Program Manager did. Furthermore, the listview large icon and small icon views don't really make much sense unless you are using bitmaps and icons. So yes, you can use these controls without adding imagelists, but it probably won't win you many accolades among users. Windows 95 is serious about icons!

Workshop

The Workshop provides quiz questions to help you solidify your understanding of the material covered and exercises to provide you with experience in using what you've learned. Try to understand the quiz and exercise answers before continuing on to the next chapter. Answers are provided in Appendix A.

Quiz

1. Name two methods for creating imagelists that are used in this chapter.

2. Name a method that enables you to draw an image from an imagelist to the screen.

3. The `ImageList_LoadBitmap` functions takes a parameter called `crMask`. What is its purpose?

4. Name a function used to load an icon into an imagelist.

5. If you want to give the screen a change to update itself during the middle of a loop or another patch of code, how can you do it?

6. When you want to start dragging a frame from an imagelist across the screen, what three functions should you call?

7. How can you install an imagelist in a listserv?

8. If you want to use a callback to fill in the text in a listview, what message and what notification submessage should you use?

9. What macro can you use to find the index of the currently selected item in a listview?

10. What two Windows API functions can you use to change the current mode of a listview from, say, `LVS_SMALLICON` to `LVS_ICON`?

Exercises

1. Because of its complexity, I have not tackled the subject of dragging and dropping items in an imagelist. However, this functionality is supported, and if you want a challenge, you can try to implement it in listviews and in the treeview example presented in "Week 3 in Review."

2. Listviews support in-place editing of names. If you want an advanced challenge, see if you can master that API. Use the online help and COMMCTRL.H as references.

20

Menus and Icons
in Depth

Today, you'll learn some fancy things you can do with menus, icons, cursors, and bitmaps. In particular, you'll learn

- ☐ How to create nested pop-up menus
- ☐ How to modify the system menu
- ☐ How to create owner draw menus and simple bitmap menus
- ☐ How to create and display your own cursors
- ☐ How to work with icons
- ☐ How to add accelerators to your programs that enable users to activate menu items through hotkeys (such as Alt+1 or Ctrl+F1)

With the possible exception of owner draw menus, nothing in this chapter poses any serious challenge to the programmer. In fact, most of the new coding techniques you're about to see are really nothing more than fancy tricks that can add a maximum amount of pizzazz to your program with a minimal amount of effort on your part.

In order to put these techniques on display, I've thrown together a sample application that puts menus through their paces in ways that you'll hopefully find educational and at least somewhat entertaining. The program's name is MENUTEST.CPP.

Overall, you should find this chapter a bit of a respite from the intense pace of the last few chapters. Take advantage of this relatively simple material while it lasts, because tricky code is waiting in the next few chapters.

What's on the Menu?

By this time, you've probably found out two things:

- ☐ Most menus aren't very difficult to construct or display.
- ☐ Both Microsoft and Borland strip whatever latent difficulty there might be from menus by supplying you with powerful interactive tools such as the Resource Workshop. These tools churn menus out in a few relatively effortless moments.

Menus are so easy to use, however, that instead of popping up the Resource Workshop or App Studio, you might find it simpler to construct or modify menus with an editor. As a result, it's probably worthwhile to take a quick look at the naked beast itself—the code for the menu in the MenuTest program:

```
MENU_1 MENU
BEGIN

  POPUP "&File"
  BEGIN
    MENUITEM "&New", CM_NEW
```

```
    MENUITEM "&Open...", CM_OPEN
    MENUITEM "&Save", CM_SAVE
    MENUITEM "Save &as...", CM_SAVEAS
    MENUITEM SEPARATOR

    POPUP "&Print..."
    BEGIN
      MENUITEM "Print To Disk", CM_PRNDISK
      MENUITEM "Print LPT1", CM_PRNLPT1
    END

    MENUITEM "Page se&tup...", CM_PAGESETUP
    MENUITEM "P&rinter setup...", CM_PRINTERSETUP
    MENUITEM SEPARATOR
    MENUITEM "E&xit", CM_EXIT
  END

  POPUP "&Cursors"
  BEGIN
    MENUITEM "&Round Cursor\tAlt+F1", CM_ROUNDCURSOR
    MENUITEM "&Diamond Cursor\tCtrl+F2", CM_DIAMONDCURSOR
    MENUITEM "&Draw Icon\tShift+F3", CM_ICONCURSOR
  END

  POPUP "BitCursors"
  BEGIN
    MENUITEM "Item", CM_BITMENU1
    MENUITEM "Item", CM_BITMENU2
    MENUITEM "Item", CM_BITMENU3
  END

  MENUITEM "&Help", CM_HELP
END
```

Figure 20.1 shows the menu for the MenuTest program.

Figure 20.1.

The close-up view of the menu for the MenuTest program, with the BitCursors pop-up exposed.

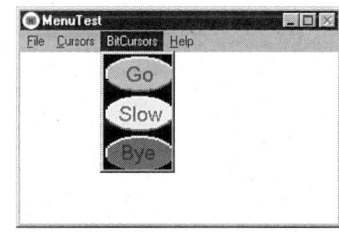

Although I briefly discussed menus earlier in this book, my basic approach to them is to let you, at your own pace and to what degree you deem necessary, pick up on their syntax. (The big exception was the quick introduction to creating dynamic menus in Day 13, "Subclassing Window Controls.") The decision to treat menu creation as essentially intuitive has been predicated on the fact that the Resource Workshop and App Studio make it at least theoretically possible for you to become an excellent Windows resource programmer without having to write a single line of code for an RC script.

Nevertheless, it's nice to know that the syntactical backbone of menus consists primarily of the simple statements BEGIN, END, MENUITEM, and POPUP. The BEGIN and END statements are nothing but bookends that wrap around the body of an entire menu and around the body of any particular pop-up menu. (You can substitute curly brackets for the BEGIN...END pair on most compilers, but I prefer the clarity of BEGIN...END statements.)

Pop-up menus, of course, are really windows that drop down to display a list of choices when they are selected. It's possible to nest two pop-up menus to appear simultaneously on-screen (see Figure 20.2).

A menu item, on the other hand, is a single item in a pop-up menu. It can also be a stand-alone item on a menu bar. These types of stand-alone menu items don't cause a pop-up menu to appear on-screen but instead lead directly to a particular action. In Figure 20.2, the words New, Open, Save, and so forth are all menu items that are part of a pop-up, while the Help menu item stands alone with no associated pop-up.

Figure 20.2.

The File menu from the MenuTest program contains nested pop-up menus and a bitmap menu item to emphasize the exit option.

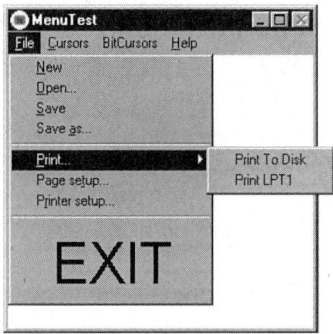

The correct way to create nested pop-up menus is simply to insert a second pop-up menu directly within the primary pop-up:

```
POPUP "&File"
BEGIN
  MENUITEM "&New", CM_NEW
  ...
  MENUITEM SEPARATOR

  POPUP "&Print..."
  BEGIN
    MENUITEM "Print To Disk", CM_PRNDISK
    MENUITEM "Print LPT1", CM_PRNLPT1
  END

  ...
```

This code creates a nested menu called Print. When selected, the options Print To Disk and Print LPT1 are made available to the user, as shown in Figure 20.2.

In the preceding code, you can see the statement MENUITEM SEPARATOR. These words insert a black horizontal line in the middle of a menu. SEPARATORs are menu items and can be treated exactly like any other item in a menu; that is, they can be deleted, inserted, or modified dynamically at runtime. However, they do not lead to any particular option in the program. They are purely cosmetic.

Checked Menu Items, Grayed Menu Items

Before getting into the fancy stuff, I should perhaps spend a moment more talking about some of the options that can be appended onto the code for creating a menu item or pop-up menu. These optional statements enable you to perform actions such as putting a check mark in front of a menu item or graying a menu item. For instance, the following line of RC code produces a menu item with a check before it, as shown in Figure 20.3:

```
MENUITEM "&Round Cursor\tAlt+F1", CM_ROUNDCURSOR, CHECKED
```

The following line of code produces a checked and grayed menu item:

```
MENUITEM "&Round Cursor\tAlt+F1", CM_ROUNDCURSOR, CHECKED, GRAYED
```

Later in this chapter, during the discussion of the MenuTest program, I'll show you how you can manipulate checked menu items at runtime.

 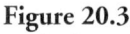

Note: The \t notation inserts a Tab character into a menu. The result, shown in Figure 20.3, gives the user a very legible notification of any accelerator keys associated with a menu option. Accelerators are discussed later in this chapter.

20

Figure 20.3.
A check mark in front of a menu item informs the reader that a particular option has been selected.

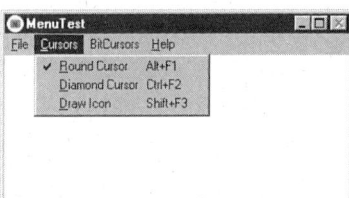

Besides the checked and grayed options, you also can make use of the MENUBREAK and MENUBARBREAK statements, which place a particular menu item in a pop-up menu on a new line (see Figure 20.4). The MENUBARBREAK statement places a black line between each column, whereas MENUBREAK leaves only white space between each column.

20

Menus and Icons in Depth

Figure 20.4.

The MENUBARBREAK *statement creates multiple columns inside a single pop-up.*

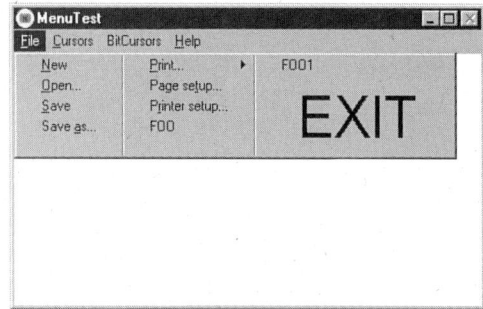

Following is the code for the menu shown in Figure 20.4. You'll probably notice that I've placed two bogus items, named Foo and Foo1, into the menu in order to give it more symmetry. I've done this simply so you can get a feeling for how you can use the MENUBARBREAK statement to present lengthy columns of options in an orderly arrangement. Users can manipulate these columns with relative ease.

```
MENU_1 MENU
BEGIN
  POPUP "&File"
  BEGIN
    MENUITEM "&New", CM_NEW
    MENUITEM "&Open...", CM_OPEN
    MENUITEM "&Save", CM_SAVE
    MENUITEM "Save &as...", CM_SAVEAS,

    POPUP "&Print...", MENUBARBREAK
    BEGIN
      MENUITEM "Print To Disk", CM_PRNDISK
      MENUITEM "Print LPT1", CM_PRNLPT1
    END

    MENUITEM "Page se&tup...", CM_PAGESETUP
    MENUITEM "P&rinter setup...", CM_PRINTERSETUP
    MENUITEM "FOO", 65000
    MENUITEM "FOO1", 65001, MENUBARBREAK
    MENUITEM "E&xit", CM_EXIT
  END
```

The MenuTest Program

Now that you've had a look at the basic techniques for creating menus, it's time to explore some ways you can manipulate menus at runtime to create various effects that can make your program easier (or more fun) to use. Before going further, you should look at the code and take a few minutes to get it up and running (see Listings 20.1 through 20.6).

Listing 20.1. The MenuTest program demonstrates how to use menus to create an attractive, easy-to-use interface.

```cpp
//////////////////////////////////////
//   Program Name: MENUTEST.CPP
//   Copyright (c) 1995 by Charlie Calvert
//   Description: MenuTest windows program
//   Last Update 07/30/95
//////////////////////////////////////

#define STRICT
#define WIN32_LEAN_AND_MEAN
#include <windows.h>
#include <windowsx.h>
#pragma hdrstop
#include "menutest.h"
#pragma warning (disable: 4068)
#pragma warning (disable: 4100)
// -------------------------------------------------------
// Interface
// -------------------------------------------------------

static char szAppName[] = "MenuTest";
static HWND MainWindow;
static HINSTANCE hInstance;
static HACCEL hAccel;

// Constant
const char FAR *HelpStr="Choose ROUND CURSOR or DIAMOND CURSOR to "
                " see new cursors. Choose DRAW ICON to draw on the"
                " screen. Choose GO or SLOW to set background, "
                " choose BYE to reset screen. The close option "
                " has been removed from the system menu, so exit "
                " using the File menu";

// variables
HICON Icon1;
HBRUSH EditBrush;
HCURSOR Cursor1, Cursor2, Cursor3;
HBITMAP Bitmap1, Bitmap1a, Bitmap2, Bitmap2a;
HBITMAP Bitmap3, Bitmap3a, BMPExit;
BITMAP BStruct;
BOOL PaintIcon, PaintGo, PaintSlow, PaintStop;

// -------------------------------------------------------
// Initialization
// -------------------------------------------------------

//////////////////////////////////////
// Program entry point
//////////////////////////////////////
#pragma argsused
int WINAPI WinMain(HINSTANCE hInst, HINSTANCE hPrevInstance,
                   LPSTR lpszCmdParam, int nCmdShow)
{
  MSG  Msg;
```

continues

Listing 20.1. continued

```
    if (!hPrevInstance)
      if (!Register(hInst))
        return FALSE;

    MainWindow = Create(hInst, nCmdShow);
    if (!MainWindow)
      return FALSE;

    while (GetMessage(&Msg, NULL, 0, 0))
    {
      if (!hAccel ¦¦ !TranslateAccelerator(MainWindow, hAccel, &Msg))
      {
        TranslateMessage(&Msg);
        DispatchMessage(&Msg);
      }
    }

    return Msg.wParam;
}

/////////////////////////////////////
// Register the window
/////////////////////////////////////
BOOL Register(HINSTANCE hInst)
{
  WNDCLASS WndClass;

  WndClass.style         = CS_HREDRAW ¦ CS_VREDRAW;
  WndClass.lpfnWndProc   = WndProc;
  WndClass.cbClsExtra    = 0;
  WndClass.cbWndExtra    = 0;
  WndClass.hInstance     = hInst;
  WndClass.hIcon         = LoadIcon(hInst, "ICON_1");
  WndClass.hCursor       = LoadCursor(NULL, IDC_ARROW);
  WndClass.hbrBackground = GetStockBrush(WHITE_BRUSH);
  WndClass.lpszMenuName  = "MENU_1";
  WndClass.lpszClassName = szAppName;

  return (RegisterClass (&WndClass) != 0);
}

/////////////////////////////////////
// Create the window
/////////////////////////////////////
HWND Create(HINSTANCE hInst, int nCmdShow)
{

  hInstance = hInst;

  HWND hWindow = CreateWindow(szAppName, szAppName,
                    WS_OVERLAPPEDWINDOW,
                    CW_USEDEFAULT, CW_USEDEFAULT,
                    CW_USEDEFAULT, CW_USEDEFAULT,
                      NULL, NULL, hInst, NULL);
```

```
    if (hWindow == NULL)
      return hWindow;

    ShowWindow(hWindow, nCmdShow);
    UpdateWindow(hWindow);

    return hWindow;
}


// -------------------------------------------------------
// WndProc and Implementation
// -------------------------------------------------------


/////////////////////////////////////
// The Window Procedure
/////////////////////////////////////
LRESULT CALLBACK WndProc(HWND hwnd, UINT Message,
                          WPARAM wParam, LPARAM lParam)
{
  switch(Message)
  {
    HANDLE_MSG(hwnd, WM_CREATE, MenuTest_OnCreate);
    HANDLE_MSG(hwnd, WM_DESTROY, MenuTest_OnDestroy);
    HANDLE_MSG(hwnd, WM_COMMAND, MenuTest_OnCommand);
    HANDLE_MSG(hwnd, WM_DRAWITEM, MenuTest_OnDrawItem);
    HANDLE_MSG(hwnd, WM_LBUTTONDOWN, MenuTest_OnLButtonDown);
    HANDLE_MSG(hwnd, WM_MOUSEMOVE, MenuTest_OnMouseMove);
    HANDLE_MSG(hwnd, WM_MEASUREITEM, MenuTest_OnMeasureItem);
    HANDLE_MSG(hwnd, WM_PAINT, MenuTest_OnPaint);
    default:
      return MenuTest_DefProc(hwnd, Message, wParam, lParam);
  }
}


/////////////////////////////////////
// Handle WM_CREATE
/////////////////////////////////////
#pragma argsused
BOOL MenuTest_OnCreate(HWND hwnd,
                        CREATESTRUCT FAR* lpCreateStruct)
{
  Cursor1 = LoadCursor(hInstance, "CURSOR_1");
  Cursor2 = LoadCursor(hInstance, "CURSOR_2");
  Cursor3 = LoadCursor(hInstance, "CURSOR_3");

  Icon1 = LoadIcon(hInstance, "ICON_1");

  Bitmap1 = LoadBitmap(hInstance, "BITMAP_1");
  Bitmap1a = LoadBitmap(hInstance, "BITMAP1A");
  Bitmap2 = LoadBitmap(hInstance, "BITMAP_2");
  Bitmap2a = LoadBitmap(hInstance, "BITMAP2A");
  Bitmap3 = LoadBitmap(hInstance, "BITMAP_3");
  Bitmap3a = LoadBitmap(hInstance, "BITMAP3A");
  BMPExit = LoadBitmap(hInstance, "BMPEXIT");

  GetObject(Bitmap1, sizeof(BITMAP), &BStruct);
```

continues

Listing 20.1. continued

```
    ModifyMenu(GetMenu(hwnd),
            CM_BITMENU1, MF_BYCOMMAND | MF_OWNERDRAW,
            CM_BITMENU1, (LPCSTR)LONG(Bitmap1));
    ModifyMenu(GetMenu(hwnd), CM_BITMENU2,
            MF_BYCOMMAND | MF_OWNERDRAW,
            CM_BITMENU2, (LPCSTR)LONG(Bitmap2));
    ModifyMenu(GetMenu(hwnd), CM_BITMENU3,
            MF_BYCOMMAND | MF_OWNERDRAW,
            CM_BITMENU3, (LPCSTR)LONG(Bitmap3));
    ModifyMenu(GetMenu(hwnd), CM_EXIT,
            MF_BYCOMMAND | MF_BITMAP,
            CM_EXIT, (LPCSTR)LONG(BMPExit));

    HMENU SysMenu = GetSystemMenu(hwnd, FALSE);

    DeleteMenu(SysMenu, 5, MF_BYPOSITION);
    DeleteMenu(SysMenu, 5, MF_BYPOSITION);

    EditBrush = CreateSolidBrush(RGB(255, 127, 255));
    PaintIcon = FALSE;
    PaintGo = FALSE;
    PaintSlow = FALSE;
    PaintStop = TRUE;

    hAccel = LoadAccelerators(hInstance, "MYKEYS");

    if (hAccel == NULL)
      MessageBox(MainWindow, "No Accelerators", "Warning", MB_OK);

    return TRUE;
}

////////////////////////////////////
// Handle WM_DESTROY
////////////////////////////////////
#pragma argsused
void MenuTest_OnDestroy(HWND hwnd)
{
  DeleteBrush(EditBrush);
  DeleteBitmap(Bitmap1);
  DeleteBitmap(Bitmap1a);
  DeleteBitmap(Bitmap2);
  DeleteBitmap(Bitmap2a);
  DeleteBitmap(Bitmap3);
  DeleteBitmap(Bitmap3a);
  DeleteBitmap(BMPExit);
  DestroyCursor(Cursor1);
  DestroyCursor(Cursor2);
  DestroyCursor(Cursor3);
  DestroyIcon(Icon1);
  PostQuitMessage(0);
}
```

```
//////////////////////////////////
// Check menu if user selects a cursor
//////////////////////////////////
void CheckItem(HWND hwnd, int ID)
{
  HMENU Menu = GetMenu(hwnd);
  CheckMenuItem(Menu,
                CM_ROUNDCURSOR, MF_BYCOMMAND ¦ MF_UNCHECKED);
  CheckMenuItem(Menu,
                CM_DIAMONDCURSOR, MF_BYCOMMAND ¦ MF_UNCHECKED);
  CheckMenuItem(Menu,
                CM_ICONCURSOR, MF_BYCOMMAND ¦ MF_UNCHECKED);
  if (ID)
    CheckMenuItem(Menu, ID, MF_BYCOMMAND ¦ MF_CHECKED);
}

//////////////////////////////////
// EnableCursor utility function
//////////////////////////////////
HCURSOR EnableCursor(HWND hwnd, HCURSOR Cursor)
{
  #ifdef WIN32
  SetClassLong(hwnd, GCL_HCURSOR, (LONG)Cursor);
  #else
  SetClassWord(hwnd, GCW_HCURSOR, (WORD)Cursor);
  #endif
  return SetCursor(Cursor);
};

//////////////////////////////////
// Handle WM_COMMAND
//////////////////////////////////
#pragma argsused
void MenuTest_OnCommand(HWND hwnd, int id, HWND hwndCtl, UINT
codeNotify)
{
  FARPROC lpfnHelpBox;

  switch(id)
  {
    case CM_NEW:
    case CM_OPEN:
    case CM_SAVE:
    case CM_SAVEAS:
    case CM_PRNDISK:
    case CM_PRNLPT1:
    case CM_PAGESETUP:
    case CM_PRINTERSETUP:
      MessageBox(hwnd, "Not yet implemented", "Info",
                MB_OK ¦ MB_ICONINFORMATION);
      break;

    case CM_EXIT:
      DestroyWindow(hwnd);
      break;
```

continues

Listing 20.1. continued

```
    case CM_ROUNDCURSOR:
      EnableCursor(hwnd, Cursor1);
      PaintIcon = FALSE;
      CheckItem(hwnd, CM_ROUNDCURSOR);
      break;

    case CM_DIAMONDCURSOR:
      EnableCursor(hwnd, Cursor2);
      PaintIcon = FALSE;
      CheckItem(hwnd, CM_DIAMONDCURSOR);
      break;

    case CM_ICONCURSOR:
      EnableCursor(hwnd, Cursor3);
      PaintIcon = TRUE;
      CheckItem(hwnd, CM_ICONCURSOR);
      break;

    case CM_BITMENU1:
      PaintGo = TRUE;
      PaintSlow = FALSE;
      PaintStop = FALSE;
      InvalidateRect(hwnd, NULL, TRUE);
      break;

    case CM_BITMENU2:
      PaintGo = FALSE;
      PaintSlow = TRUE;
      PaintStop = FALSE;
      InvalidateRect(hwnd, NULL, TRUE);
      break;

    case CM_BITMENU3:
      PaintGo = FALSE;
      PaintSlow = FALSE;
      PaintStop = TRUE;
      InvalidateRect(hwnd, NULL, TRUE);
      EnableCursor(hwnd, LoadCursor(NULL, IDC_ARROW));
      CheckItem(hwnd, 0);
      PaintIcon = FALSE;
      break;

    case CM_HELP:
      lpfnHelpBox =
        MakeProcInstance((FARPROC)HelpBoxProc, hInstance);
      DialogBox(hInstance, "HELPBOX", hwnd,
               (DLGPROC)lpfnHelpBox);
      FreeProcInstance(lpfnHelpBox);
      break;
  }
}

///////////////////////////////////////
// Draw Bitmap in menu
///////////////////////////////////////
```

```
void DrawBitmap(HDC PaintDC, HBITMAP Bitmap, int YVal)
{
  HDC MemDC;
  HBITMAP OldBitmap;

  MemDC = CreateCompatibleDC(PaintDC);
  OldBitmap = SelectBitmap(MemDC, Bitmap);
  BitBlt(PaintDC, 0, YVal * BStruct.bmHeight, BStruct.bmWidth,
          BStruct.bmHeight, MemDC, 0, 0, SRCCOPY);
  SelectBitmap(MemDC, OldBitmap);
  DeleteObject(MemDC);
}

/////////////////////////////////////
// Handle WM_DRAWITEM
/////////////////////////////////////
#pragma argsused
void MenuTest_OnDrawItem(HWND hwnd,
                         const DRAWITEMSTRUCT FAR* lpDrawItem)
{
  switch(lpDrawItem->itemID)
  {
    case CM_BITMENU1:
      if (lpDrawItem->itemState & ODS_SELECTED)
        DrawBitmap(lpDrawItem->hDC, Bitmap1a, 0);
      else
        DrawBitmap(lpDrawItem->hDC, Bitmap1, 0);
      break;

    case CM_BITMENU2:
      if (lpDrawItem->itemState & ODS_SELECTED)
        DrawBitmap(lpDrawItem->hDC, Bitmap2a, 1);
      else
        DrawBitmap(lpDrawItem->hDC, Bitmap2, 1);
      break;

    case CM_BITMENU3:
      if (lpDrawItem->itemState & ODS_SELECTED)
        DrawBitmap(lpDrawItem->hDC, Bitmap3a, 2);
      else
        DrawBitmap(lpDrawItem->hDC, Bitmap3, 2);
      break;
  }
}

/////////////////////////////////////
// Handle WM_LBUTTONDOWN
/////////////////////////////////////
#pragma argsused
void MenuTest_OnLButtonDown(HWND hwnd, BOOL fDoubleClick, int x,
                            int y, UINT keyFlags)
{
  if (PaintIcon)
  {
    HDC PaintDC = GetDC(hwnd);
    DrawIcon(PaintDC, x, y, Icon1);
```

20

continues

Listing 20.1. continued

```
      ReleaseDC(hwnd, PaintDC);
  }
}

/////////////////////////////////////
// Handle WM_MEASUREITEM
/////////////////////////////////////
#pragma argsused
void MenuTest_OnMeasureItem(HWND hwnd, MEASUREITEMSTRUCT
                                FAR* lpMeasureItem)

{
  WORD CheckWidth;

  CheckWidth = LOWORD (GetMenuCheckMarkDimensions());
  switch ( lpMeasureItem->itemID )
  {
    case CM_BITMENU1:
    case CM_BITMENU2:
    case CM_BITMENU3:
     lpMeasureItem->itemWidth = BStruct.bmWidth - CheckWidth - 3;
     lpMeasureItem->itemHeight = BStruct.bmHeight - 1;
     break;
  }
}

/////////////////////////////////////
// Handle WM_MOUSEMOVE
/////////////////////////////////////
void MenuTest_OnMouseMove(HWND hwnd, int x, int y, UINT keyFlags)
{
  if (((keyFlags & MK_LBUTTON) == MK_LBUTTON) && (PaintIcon))
  {
    HDC PaintDC = GetDC(hwnd);
    DrawIcon(PaintDC, x, y, Icon1);
    ReleaseDC(hwnd, PaintDC);
  }
}

/////////////////////////////////////
// Handle WM_PAINT
/////////////////////////////////////
void MenuTest_OnPaint(HWND hwnd)
{
  PAINTSTRUCT PaintStruct;
  HDC PaintDC, MemDC;
  RECT R;
  HBITMAP OldBitmap;

  PaintDC = BeginPaint(hwnd, &PaintStruct);

  if (!PaintStop)
  {
    GetClientRect(hwnd, &R);
    int i = R.right / BStruct.bmWidth;
    int j = R.bottom / BStruct.bmHeight;
```

```
    MemDC = CreateCompatibleDC(PaintDC);

    if (PaintSlow)
      OldBitmap = SelectBitmap(MemDC, Bitmap2);
    else
      OldBitmap = SelectBitmap(MemDC, Bitmap1);

    for (int x = 0; x <= i; x++)
      for (int y = 0; y <= j; y++)
        BitBlt(PaintDC, BStruct.bmWidth * x, BStruct.bmHeight * y,
          BStruct.bmWidth, BStruct.bmHeight, MemDC, 0, 0, SRCCOPY);

    SelectBitmap(MemDC, OldBitmap);
    DeleteDC(MemDC);
  }

  EndPaint(hwnd, &PaintStruct);
}

////////////////////////////////////////////////////////
// You can't always use HANDLE_MSG with dialogs
////////////////////////////////////////////////////////
#pragma argsused
HBRUSH Help_OnCtlColor(HWND hwnd, HDC hdc, HWND hwndChild, int type)
{
  switch (type)
  {
    case CTLCOLOR_STATIC:
      return EditBrush;

    case CTLCOLOR_EDIT:
      SetTextColor(hdc, RGB(0,0,255));
      SetBkColor(hdc, RGB(255, 127, 255));
      return GetStockBrush(LTGRAY_BRUSH);

    case CTLCOLOR_DLG:
      return EditBrush;
  }
  return NULL;
}

// --------------------------------------------
// AboutBox: You can't handle all DLG messages as I do CtlColor
// --------------------------------------------
#pragma argsused
BOOL CALLBACK HelpBoxProc(HWND hDlg, WORD Message,
                          WPARAM wParam, LPARAM lParam)
{
  switch(Message)
  {
    case WM_INITDIALOG:
      SendDlgItemMessage(hDlg, ID_HELPEDIT,
                         WM_SETTEXT, 0, LPARAM(HelpStr));
      return TRUE;
```

Listing 20.1. continued

```
#ifdef WIN32
HANDLE_MSG(hDlg, WM_CTLCOLORSTATIC, Help_OnCtlColor);
HANDLE_MSG(hDlg, WM_CTLCOLOREDIT, Help_OnCtlColor);
HANDLE_MSG(hDlg, WM_CTLCOLORDLG, Help_OnCtlColor);
#else
case WM_CTLCOLOR:
  return (BOOL)HANDLE_WM_CTLCOLOR(hDlg, wParam, lParam, Help_OnCtlColor);
#endif

case WM_COMMAND:
  if (wParam == IDOK ¦¦ wParam == IDCANCEL)
  {
    EndDialog(hDlg, wParam);
    return TRUE;
  }
  break;
}
return FALSE;
}
```

Listing 20.2. MENUTEST.H. shows the header file for MenuTest.

```
///////////////////////////////////
//   Program Name: MENUTEST.H
//   Copyright (c) 1995 by Charlie Calvert
//   Description: MenuTest windows program
//   Last Update: 07/30/95
///////////////////////////////////

#define CM_NEW 101
#define CM_OPEN 102
#define CM_SAVE 103
#define CM_SAVEAS 104
#define CM_PRNDISK 151
#define CM_PRNLPT1 152
#define CM_PAGESETUP 105
#define CM_PRINTERSETUP 106
#define CM_EXIT 107

#define CM_ROUNDCURSOR 201
#define CM_DIAMONDCURSOR 202
#define CM_ICONCURSOR 203

#define CM_BITMENU1 301
#define CM_BITMENU2 302
#define CM_BITMENU3 303

#define CM_HELP     401
#define ID_HELPEDIT 402

// Declarations for class MenuTest
#define MenuTest_DefProc    DefWindowProc
```

```
BOOL MenuTest_OnCreate(HWND hwnd,
                       CREATESTRUCT FAR* lpCreateStruct);
void MenuTest_OnDestroy(HWND hwnd);
void MenuTest_OnCommand(HWND hwnd, int id,
                        HWND hwndCtl, UINT codeNotify);
void MenuTest_OnDrawItem(HWND hwnd,
                       const DRAWITEMSTRUCT FAR* lpDrawItem);
void MenuTest_OnLButtonDown(HWND hwnd, BOOL fDoubleClick,
                            int x, int y, UINT keyFlags);
void MenuTest_OnMeasureItem(HWND hwnd,
                       MEASUREITEMSTRUCT FAR* lpMeasureItem);
void MenuTest_OnMouseMove(HWND hwnd, int x,
                          int y, UINT keyFlags);
void MenuTest_OnPaint(HWND hwnd);

// function
LRESULT CALLBACK WndProc(HWND hWindow, UINT Message,
                         WPARAM wParam, LPARAM lParam);
BOOL Register(HINSTANCE hInst);
HWND Create(HINSTANCE hInst, int nCmdShow);
BOOL CALLBACK HelpBoxProc(HWND hDlg, WORD Message,
                          WPARAM wParam, LPARAM lParam);
```

Listing 20.3. MENUTEST.RC.

```
1: ////////////////////////////////////////////////////////
2: //   Program Name: MENUTEST.RC
3: //   Programmer: Charlie Calvert
4: //   Description: MenuTest windows program resource script
5: //   Date: 04/28/93
6: ////////////////////////////////////////////////////////
8: #include <windows.h>
9: #include "menutest.h"
10: MYKEYS ACCELERATORS
11: BEGIN
12:     VK_F1, CM_ROUNDCURSOR, VIRTKEY, ALT
13:     VK_F2, CM_DIAMONDCURSOR, VIRTKEY, CONTROL
14:     VK_F3, CM_ICONCURSOR, VIRTKEY, SHIFT
15:    "1", CM_ROUNDCURSOR, VIRTKEY, ALT
16:    "2", CM_DIAMONDCURSOR, VIRTKEY, ALT
17:    "3", CM_ICONCURSOR, VIRTKEY, ALT
18: END
19:
20: CURSOR_1 CURSOR "cursor1.cur"
21: CURSOR_2 CURSOR "cursor2.cur"
22: CURSOR_3 CURSOR "cursor3.cur"
23:
24: ICON_1 ICON "icon1.ico"
25:
26: BITMAP_1 BITMAP "iconbmp.bmp"
27: BITMAP1A BITMAP "bitmap1a.bmp"
28: BITMAP_2 BITMAP "bitmap2.bmp"
29: BITMAP2A BITMAP "bitmap2a.bmp"
30: BITMAP_3 BITMAP "bitmap3.bmp"
```

continues

843

Listing 20.3. continued

```
31: BITMAP3A BITMAP "bitmap3a.bmp"
32: BMPEXIT BITMAP "exit.bmp"
33:
34: MENU_1 MENU
35: BEGIN
36:     POPUP "&File"
37:     BEGIN
38:         MENUITEM "&New", CM_NEW
39:         MENUITEM "&Open...", CM_OPEN
40:         MENUITEM "&Save", CM_SAVE
41:         MENUITEM "Save &as...", CM_SAVEAS,
42:         MENUITEM SEPARATOR
43:         POPUP "&Print..."
44:         BEGIN
45:             MENUITEM "Print To Disk", CM_PRNDISK
46:             MENUITEM "Print LPT1", CM_PRNLPT1
47:         END
48:         MENUITEM "Page se&tup...", CM_PAGESETUP
49:         MENUITEM "P&rinter setup...", CM_PRINTERSETUP
50:       MENUITEM SEPARATOR
51:         MENUITEM "E&xit", CM_EXIT
52:     END
53:     POPUP "&Cursors"
54:     BEGIN
55:         MENUITEM "&Round Cursor\tAlt+F1", CM_ROUNDCURSOR
56:         MENUITEM "&Diamond Cursor\tCtrl+F2", CM_DIAMONDCURSOR
57:         MENUITEM "&Draw Icon\tShift+F3", CM_ICONCURSOR
58:     END
59:     POPUP "BitCursors"
60:     BEGIN
61:         MENUITEM "Item", CM_BITMENU1
62:         MENUITEM "Item", CM_BITMENU2
63:         MENUITEM "Item", CM_BITMENU3
64:     END
65:     MENUITEM "&Help", CM_HELP
66: END
67:
68: HELPBOX DIALOG 18, 18, 166, 119
69: STYLE DS_MODALFRAME | WS_POPUP | WS_CAPTION | WS_SYSMENU
70: CAPTION "Help Dialog"
71: BEGIN
72:     PUSHBUTTON "Close", IDOK, 11, 97, 144, 14
73:     CONTROL "Icon_1", -1,  "STATIC", SS_ICON | WS_CHILD |
74:             WS_VISIBLE | WS_GROUP, 137, 9, 16, 16
75:     CONTROL "Icon_1", -1, "STATIC", SS_ICON | WS_CHILD |
76:             WS_VISIBLE | WS_GROUP, 13, 9, 16, 16
77:     CONTROL "", ID_HELPEDIT, "EDIT", ES_CENTER | ES_MULTILINE |
78:             ES_READONLY | WS_CHILD | WS_VISIBLE | WS_BORDER |
79:             WS_VSCROLL | WS_TABSTOP, 6, 34, 154, 56
80: END
```

ICON1.ICO (32×32)

CURSOR1.CUR (68×36)

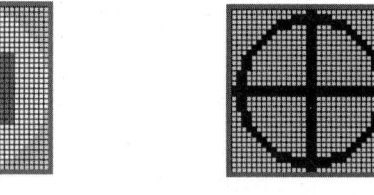

CURSOR2.CUR (68×36)

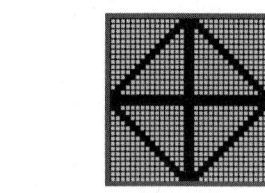

CURSOR3.CUR(32×32)

ICONBMP.BMP(68×36)

BITMAAP1A.BMP (68×36)

BITMAP2.BMP (68×36)

BITMAP2A.BMP (68×36)

Slow

BITMAP3.BMP (68×36)

BITMAP3A.BMP (68×36)

EXIT.BMP (128×64)

EXIT

Listing 20.4 shows the definition file for MenuTest.

Listing 20.4. MENUTEST.DEF.

```
1: ; MENUTEST.DEF
2: NAME          MenuTest
3: DESCRIPTION   'MenuTest Window'
4: HEAPSIZE      4096
5: STACKSIZE     5120
6: CODE          PRELOAD MOVEABLE DISCARDABLE
7: DATA          PRELOAD MOVEABLE MULTIPLE
```

Listing 20.5 shows the Borland makefile for MenuTest.

Listing 20.5. MENUTEST.MAK (Borland).

```
# MENUTEST.MAK

# macros
APPNAME = MenuTest

BCROOT = $(MAKEDIR)\..
INCPATH= $(BCROOT)\INCLUDE
LIBPATH= $(BCROOT)\LIB


!if !$d(WIN16)
COMPILER = BCC32.EXE
RCCOMPILER = BRC32.EXE -w32
FLAGS    = -WE -v -w4
!else
COMPILER = BCC.EXE
RCCOMPILER = BRC.EXE
FLAGS    = -WE -ml -v -w4
!endif

# link
$(APPNAME).exe: $(APPNAME).obj $(APPNAME).def $(APPNAME).res
  $(COMPILER) $(FLAGS) $(APPNAME).obj
  $(RCCOMPILER) $(APPNAME).res

# compile
$(APPNAME).obj: $(APPNAME).cpp
  $(COMPILER) -c $(FLAGS) $(APPNAME).cpp

#compile
MenuTest.res: $(APPNAME).rc
  $(RCCOMPILER) -R -I$(INCPATH) MENUTEST.RC
```

Listing 20.6 shows the Microsoft makefile for MenuTest.

Listing 20.6. MENUTEST.MAK (Microsoft).

```
#------------------------------------------------
# MENUTEMS.MAK
#------------------------------------------------

# Some Macros
APPNAME=MENUTEST
TARGETOS=WIN95
APPVER=4.0
OBJS=$(APPNAME).OBJ

!include <win32.mak>

all: $(APPNAME).exe
```

```
# Update the resource if necessary

$(APPNAME).res: $(APPNAME).rc $(APPNAME).h
  $(rc) $(rcflags) $(rcvars) $(APPNAME).rc

# Update the object files if necessary

# compile
.cpp.obj:
  $(cc) $(cflags) $(cvars) $(cdebug) $<

# Update the executable file if necessary.

$(APPNAME).exe: $(OBJS) $(APPNAME).res
  $(link) $(linkdebug) $(guiflags) -out:$(APPNAME).exe \
  $(OBJS) $(APPNAME).res $(guilibs) comctl32.lib
```

Figure 20.5 shows the MenuTest program.

Figure 20.5.
The MenuTest program enables you to place bitmaps in menus and to paint patterns on-screen with an icon.

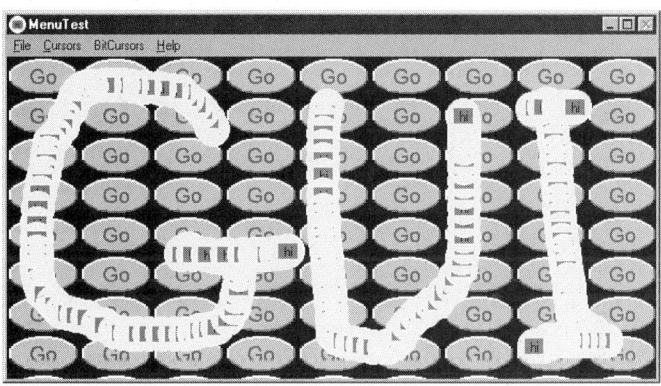

Outside of its usefulness as a learning tool, the MenuTest program has little practical functionality. When creating it, my goal was to show some of the important variations that can be run on menus, including using bitmaps and owner draw menus. MenuTest also demonstrates how to change a cursor dynamically at runtime and how to place an icon in a dialog. As a little bonus, MenuTest enables you to paint patterns in its main window with the program's icon.

To take it through its paces, select each of the menu items from the Cursors and BitCursors pop-up menus. The options from the Cursors menu change the shape of the program's cursor. The DrawCursor menu item lets you draw on the main window by pressing the left mouse button.

20

More on Menus

The first portion of this chapter gave an in-depth description of how to create a menu inside of an RC file. The next stage is to see what you can do with menus dynamically at runtime. Specifically, the text covers

- ☐ Placing a bitmap in a menu, as shown in the EXIT choice on the file menu
- ☐ Placing or removing a check mark in front of a menu item
- ☐ Creating owner draw menus that change shape and texture as the user selects individual menu items
- ☐ Deleting items from the system menu

Placing a Bitmap in a Menu

The key to placing a bitmap in a menu is the ModifyMenu command. This command enables you to modify the contents of an existing menu item. More specifically, it lets you change the string displayed in a menu item or entirely replace that string with a bitmap (as MenuTest does when it places the EXIT bitmap in the File menu).

Syntax

The *ModifyMenu* Function

```
BOOL ModifyMenu(HMENU, UINT, UINT, UINT, LPCSTR)
```

HMENU hmenu;	Handle of the menu to modify
UINT idItem;	ID or the position of the menu item or pop-up
UINT fuFlags;	Multipurpose flag (see following explanation)
UINT idNewItem;	New ID of menu item
LPCSTR lpNewItem;	The new menu item, usually a string or bitmap

Most of the time, you just need to change the string or ID associated with a menu item. To do that, you need to pay special attention to the second and third fields of this function. If you pass MF_BYCOMMAND in the fuFlags field, you're telling Windows that the idItem field will be an ID. If you pass in MF_BYPOSITION, you're telling Windows that the second field is a zero-based offset from the beginning of the menu.

The third field also can be used to designate whether the lpNewItem argument is a string or bitmap. For instance, the following command designates the second field as an ID (rather than a position) and the last field as a string:

```
ModifyMenu(GetMenu(hwnd), CM_MYID,
        MF_BYCOMMAND | MF_STRING,
        CM_MYID, (LPCSTR)"My New MenuItem");
```

The MenuTest program uses the `ModifyMenu` command to change the Exit option on the file menu to a bitmap:

```
ModifyMenu(GetMenu(hwnd), CM_EXIT,
           MF_BYCOMMAND | MF_BITMAP,
           CM_EXIT, (LPCSTR)LONG(BMPExit));
```

The key portions of this call are in the third parameter, where the `MF_BITMAP` flag is placed, and the fifth parameter, where the handle to a bitmap is translated into a pointer and passed on to Windows. `BMPExit`, of course, is just a regular bitmap, designed with a paint program and loaded with a call to `LoadBitmap`.

To summarize, here's what I think about the `ModifyMenu` command: Sometimes programmers want to delete a menu with the `DeleteMenu` command or append a menu with the `AppendMenu` command. A third alternative is to modify an existing menu with the `ModifyMenu` command. In other words, when you want to change the contents of an existing menu, use the `ModifyMenu` command.

ModifyMenu and *MF_OWNERDRAW*

The real power of the `ModifyMenu` command becomes apparent in the BitCursors pop-up menu, which features three owner draw menus, as shown in Figure 20.1. To be utterly frank, I find that after all these years, the standard Windows menu system sometimes becomes a bit of a bore, and I'm willing to do just about anything to spice it up. This is when an owner draw menu comes to the rescue. This little tool can be used to create stunning menus that can make your program stand out.

Following are the steps you take to create an owner draw menu:

1. Call `ModifyMenu` and set the `MF_OWNERDRAW` flag.
2. Tell Windows how large to make the pop-up menu window by responding to `WM_MEASUREITEM` messages.
3. Respond to `WM_DRAWITEM` messages by drawing either a selected or non-selected menu item, depending on the state of the `ODS_SELECTED` flag.

The rest of this section explains these concepts in depth.

To get started with owner draw menus, just make a `ModifyMenu` call that looks something like this:

```
ModifyMenu(GetMenu(hwnd),
           CM_BITMENU1, MF_BYCOMMAND | MF_OWNERDRAW,
           CM_BITMENU1, (LPCSTR)LONG(Bitmap1));
```

As you can see, this call is similar to the call to place a bitmap in a menu, except that the `MF_OWNERDRAW` flag is used in lieu of the `MF_BITMAP` flag.

20

Turning on the MF_OWNERDRAW flag means that the program's main window needs to start responding to WM_MEASUREITEM and WM_DRAWITEM messages. The first of these messages comes down the pike when the menu is first displayed, and it gives MenuTest a chance to designate the size of the pop-up window that will hold your menu bitmaps. The second message gives MenuTest a chance to actually display the bitmap in question, a chore that must be handled explicitly by the program. (That's why they call it *owner draw*: the drawing is handled by the program, not by Windows.)

At first, it would seem that responding to WM_MEASUREITEM messages would be simple. The gotcha on this one is that Windows sets aside a space before each menu in which a check mark can appear. (Refer to Figure 20.3 for an example of how a check mark appears in a normal menu.)

When working with owner draw menus, however, the MenuTest program ignores the whole idea of inserting check marks. Therefore, it has to query Windows to find out how much space is set aside for check marks; it then subtracts that from the total width of the bitmap. This whole process is carried out through the auspices of the aptly named GetMenuCheckMarkDimensions function:

```
void MenuTest_OnMeasureItem(HWND hwnd,
                            MEASUREITEMSTRUCT FAR* lpMeasureItem)
{
  WORD CheckWidth;

  CheckWidth = LOWORD (GetMenuCheckMarkDimensions());
  switch ( lpMeasureItem->itemID )
  {
    case CM_BITMENU1:
    case CM_BITMENU2:
    case CM_BITMENU3:
    lpMeasureItem->itemWidth = BStruct.bmWidth - CheckWidth - 3;
    lpMeasureItem->itemHeight = BStruct.bmHeight - 1;
    break;
  }
}
```

This code, from line 350 of MENUTEST.CPP, shows how the program handles WM_MEASUREITEM messages. First get the width of the area set aside for check marks, then subtract that from the width of the bitmap. Windows uses this information to set the size of the window enclosing the menu items.

BStruct (see following explanation) is a BITMAP struct containing the dimensions of the current bitmap. MenuTest obtains these dimensions with a call to GetObject.

The *GetObject* Function

```
int GetObject(HGDIOBJ, int, void FAR *)
```

HGDIOBJ hgdiobj;	Handle of the bitmap, font, brush, or pen
int cbBuffer;	Size of the buffer in the third argument
void FAR* lpvObject;	Buffer to hold information retrieved by call to GetObject

When retrieving information about bitmaps, the structure used in the third parameter looks like this:

```
typedef struct tagBITMAP {   /* bm */
  int     bmType;
  int     bmWidth;
  int     bmHeight;
  int     bmWidthBytes;
  BYTE    bmPlanes;
  BYTE    bmBitsPixel;
  void FAR* bmBits;
} BITMAP;
```

Here's an example call to GetObject:

```
GetObject(Bitmap1, sizeof(BITMAP), &BStruct);
```

After MenuTest responds to WM_MEASUREITEM, the bitmap is drawn in response to WM_DRAWITEM messages. This excerpt from the MenuTest_OnDrawItem function (line 318) shows how this is done:

```
void MenuTest_OnDrawItem(HWND hwnd,
                         const DRAWITEMSTRUCT FAR *lpDrawItem)
{
  switch(lpDrawItem->itemID)
  {
    case CM_BITMENU1:
      if (lpDrawItem->itemState & ODS_SELECTED)
      DrawBitmap(lpDrawItem->hDC, Bitmap1a, 0);
      else
      DrawBitmap(lpDrawItem->hDC, Bitmap1, 0);
      break;
    ...  // Code to handle other menu items
  }
}
```

The central issue is that the menu items in question can be in one of two states, either selected or not selected. Each of these states needs to be depicted differently, as shown in Figure 20.6. (The next Van Gogh I'm not, but these ought to be sufficient to give you an idea of what's needed.)

20

Figure 20.6.

On the left is a normal menu; on the right is a selected menu.

Whenever the user selects a menu item, Windows politely informs MenuTest by setting the ODS_SELECTED flag. MenuTest responds by sending the appropriate bitmap to the DrawBitmap function (line 299 in MENUTEST.CPP):

```
void DrawBitmap(HDC PaintDC, HBITMAP Bitmap, int YVal)
{
  HDC MemDC;
  HBITMAP OldBitmap;

  MemDC = CreateCompatibleDC(PaintDC);
  OldBitmap = SelectBitmap(MemDC, Bitmap);
  BitBlt(PaintDC, 0, YVal * BStruct.bmHeight, BStruct.bmWidth,
         BStruct.bmHeight, MemDC, 0, 0, SRCCOPY);
  SelectBitmap(MemDC, OldBitmap);
  DeleteObject(MemDC);
}
```

This function is similar to a standard paint function, except that the device context is supplied directly by Windows without the user having to call either BeginPaint or GetDC. (Notice the calls to the WindowsX SelectBitmap macro rather than to SelectObject. Use these calls to get improved type checking.)

That's all there is to it. After MenuTest has blitted the bitmap to the screen, it can forget all about its owner draw menus—at least until the next WM_DRAWITEM message comes down the pike.

Following is a quick review of the steps needed to create owner draw menus:

1. Set the MF_OWNERDRAW flag in the fuFlags argument to ModifyMenu.

2. Respond to WM_MEASUREITEM messages so Windows will know how large to make the pop-up menu.

3. Respond to WM_DRAWITEM messages by blitting a bitmap to the screen; pay special attention to the ODS_SELECTED flag.

Despite the presence of a few slippery spots, working with owner draw menus isn't too complex. Hopefully, this is a feature that will be included in more programs in the near future. Certainly, I think any programmer designing a program aimed at a young audience should use owner draw menus. These menus can give a program a playful, friendly interface. (On the other hand, I suppose they could just as easily be used to create very professional-looking custom menus that give your app a sophisticated feel.)

Note: Owner draw menus are a classic example of how Windows puts a special burden on the programmer in order to make a program easier to use and more attractive to the user.

Modifying the System Menu

The MenuTest program removes the Close option from the system menu. (See Figures 20.7 and 20.8.)

Figure 20.7.
A standard system menu.

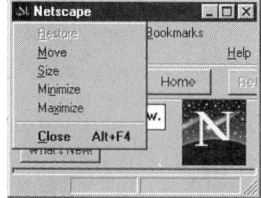

Figure 20.8.
The system menu from the MenuTest program.

The end result of this action is to force the user to use the Exit option from the File menu, rather than exiting the program through the system menu. You should notice, for instance, that it's no longer possible to exit the program by double-clicking the system menu icon.

This code shows how to retrieve the handle to a system with a call to GetSystemMenu. You can then pass this handle to DeleteMenu. The DeleteMenu function removes entries from a menu, as explained in the following syntax box. The end result is that lines 159-162 modify the system menu in such a way that it can no longer be used to exit a program.

```
159; HMENU SysMenu = GetSystemMenu(hwnd, FALSE);
160:
161: DeleteMenu(SysMenu, 5, MF_BYPOSITION);
162: DeleteMenu(SysMenu, 5, MF_BYPOSITION);
```

20

This code from `MenuTest_OnCreate` (lines 159 –162), shows how to retrieve the system menu with a call to `GetSystemMenu` and then delete the menu with a call to `DeleteMenu`.

The *DeleteMenu* Function

```
BOOL DeleteMenu(HMENU, UINT, UINT)
```

`HMENU hmenu;`	Handle of the menu containing item to delete
`UINT idItem;`	ID or position of the item to delete
`UINT fuFlags;`	Flag specifying `MF_BYPOSITION` or `MF_BYCOMMAND`

The `DeleteMenu` call is very straightforward. The only thing you need to watch out for is that after you delete an item by position, the next item in the menu assumes the number of the item you just deleted. That's why the code shown deletes Items 5 and 6 from the menu by deleting Item 5 twice. In the previous example, the two items being deleted are the `Close` string and the menu item Separator.

Here's an example:

```
DeleteMenu(hMenu, ID_MYMENUITEM, MF_BYCOMMAND);
```

Placing a Check Before a Menu Item

Whenever the user chooses a new cursor for the MenuTest program, a check appears in front of the newly selected option from the Cursors pop-up menu. The following code performs this action:

```
HMENU Menu = GetMenu(hwnd);
CheckMenuItem(Menu, CM_ROUNDCURSOR, MF_BYCOMMAND ¦ MF_CHECKED);
```

As you can see, MenuTest retrieves the handle to the program's menu with a call to `GetMenu`, and then sends a message asking that a particular menu item be checked. By now, the details of how this type of command works should be obvious to you without any detailed explanation. However, the following flags can be sent in the third parameter of `CheckMenuItem`:

`MF_BYCOMMAND`	The second parameter is an ID.
`MF_BYPOSITION`	The second parameter is a zero-based position.
`MF_CHECKED`	Place a check mark before a menu item.
`MF_UNCHECKED`	Remove a check mark from a menu item.

Selecting a New Cursor

Every on-screen window has a cursor associated with it. For instance, the main window of the NotePad program uses the I-beam cursor, whereas the menu of the NotePad program uses the arrow cursor. If you open up the File | Open dialog from the NotePad program, you can watch the cursor change when you move it over the edit control in its upper-left corner.

The seemingly rather insignificant chore of setting a new cursor for a window sends a very clear message to the user about the current state or purpose of a window. Unlike icons, cursors usually convey a great deal of very useful information to the user—often without ever quite forcing a particular thought to appear on the conscious level. That is, people instinctively seem to know to point with the arrow cursor, write with the I-beam cursor, and wait when the hourglass cursor appears. No one has to tell users the meaning of these cursors, nor do users have to consciously think about their meaning.

Note: Some people get confused about the difference between a cursor and a caret. A *cursor* is always associated with the mouse. It moves around the screen as the mouse moves. A *caret* is usually associated with a window, such as an edit control. It enables you to find your place when type in and edit information. There are a whole series of commands for controlling the caret. They include: CreateCaret, DestroyCaret, SetCaretBlinkTime, HideCaret, and ShowCaret. Here's a translation for DOS users: A cursor is what DOS users generally call a mouse cursor, and a caret is what DOS users generally call a cursor.

There are two common ways to change the cursor in a window. The first method is to go all the way into the internals of Windows and change the structure of a window's class with SetClassWord:

```
#ifdef WIN32
SetClassLong(hwnd, GCL_HCURSOR, (LONG)Cursor1);
#else
SetClassWord(hwnd, GCW_HCURSOR, (WORD)Cursor1);
#endif
SetCursor(Cursor1);
```

This code uses SetClassWord to reach GCW_HCURSOR or GCL_HCURSOR bytes into the internal Windows-owned data structure that defines the attributes of MenuTest's main window. At that location, Windows finds the old cursor for the program's main window and replaces it with a user-defined cursor. The code then makes the new cursor visible by calling SetCursor. It's important to understand that this is a two-step process: change the cursor for the class and then make the new cursor visible.

20

> **Note:** Because you will so often call `SetClassLong` and `SetCursor` in conjunction with one another, the MenuTest program provides a single utility function which encapsulates both chores in a single function:
>
> ```
> HCURSOR EnableCursor(HWND hwnd, HCURSOR Cursor)
> {
>   #ifdef WIN32
>   SetClassLong(hwnd, GCL_HCURSOR, (LONG)Cursor);
>   #else
>   SetClassWord(hwnd, GCW_HCURSOR, (WORD)Cursor);
>   #endif
>   return SetCursor(Cursor);
> };
> ```
>
> If you use this function, you can change the cursor by making one simple call, regardless of whether you are in WIN32 or WIN16:
>
> ```
> EnableCursor(hwnd, Cursor1);
> ```
>
> When you find handy functions such as `EnableCursor`, you might want to copy them into a separate file for reuse in other programs.

Before discussing the second way of changing a cursor, I should mention that it's possible to change the cursor for a window by calling `SetCursor` alone, without reference to `SetClassWord`. However, the change is fleeting unless you have first set the cursor for the class to zero. Even then, the change only lasts until the cursor leaves the current window. Therefore, you should call `SetCursor` in conjunction with `SetClassWord`, except when they are used together in a single complex statement. (See the following description.)

The second technique for changing a cursor is the one used when a programmer wants to pop up the hourglass cursor while a particular process is taking place. For instance, when a complex search is being conducted in a database, programmers usually pop up an hourglass cursor and close off all other options. This way, the user is forced to wait until the search is completed.

If you want to change the cursor to an hourglass and leave it that way until an operation is completed, call `SetCursor` and `SetCapture` in immediate succession. (See the following code.) When you are done, reset the cursor to its old value and call `ReleaseCapture`:

```
SetCapture(hwnd);
hCursor OldCursor = SetCursor(LoadCursor(0, IDC_HOURGLASS);
... // Perform code and/or time-intensive operation
SetCursor(OldCursor);
ReleaseCapture();
```

Typically, programmers call SetCapture on an inert window, such as a static text, or on a push button with an ID, such as IDABORT or IDCANCEL. If used with an inert window, the user can't do anything until ReleaseCapture is called. If used with an Abort or Cancel button, the user is capable only of aborting or canceling the current operation.

The *SetCapture* Function

```
HWND SetCapture(HWND)
```

The SetCapture function takes one parameter. This parameter is the window to which you should direct all mouse input until ReleaseCapture is called. SetCapture returns the HWND of the window that previously had the focus, or returns NULL if there is no such window. ReleaseCapture takes a void argument and returns a void.

Here's an example:

```
SetCapture(IDCANCEL);
ReleaseCapture();
```

Following is a list of the standard cursors that come with the system:

IDC_ARROW	Arrow cursor
IDC_CROSS	Similar to the x- and y-axes on a Cartesian grid
IDC_IBEAM	I-beam cursor
IDC_ICON	Empty icon
IDC_SIZE	Similar to IDC_CROSS with arrows at the end of each axis
IDC_SIZENESW	Arrows pointing northeast and southwest
IDC_SIZENS	Arrows pointing north and south
IDC_SIZENWSE	Arrows pointing northwest and southeast
IDC_SIZEWE	Arrows pointing west and east
IDC_UPARROW	Big arrow pointing north
IDC_WAIT	The classic hourglass cursor

You can load any of these cursors by calling LoadCursor, with the first parameter set to zero:

```
LoadCursor(NULL, IDC_WAIT);
```

The opposite of a system-defined cursor is a user-defined cursor. The MenuTest program displays a number of user-defined cursors. These cursors can be designed in either the Resource Workshop or the App Studio. All you need to do is make the appropriate menu selections and then start drawing with the mouse.

Given a set of predefined cursors, MenuTest loads them in response to a WM_CREATE message (Lines 130–132):

20

```
Cursor1 = LoadCursor(hInstance, "CURSOR_1");
Cursor2 = LoadCursor(hInstance, "CURSOR_2");
Cursor3 = LoadCursor(hInstance, "CURSOR_3");
```

Unlike system cursors, the Microsoft documentation states that you should call `DestroyCursor` on any custom cursors you load into a program (see lines 192–194 of MENUTEST.CPP). The debug version of Windows doesn't complain if you don't do this, but I suggest you play it safe and follow the Microsoft documentation.

That wraps up this discussion of cursors. In this section you've learned two main points:

☐ To associate a cursor permanently with a window, call both `SetClassWord` and `SetCursor`.

☐ During the course of an operation that can't be interrupted, you can set a temporary cursor by calling `SetCursor`; follow that with a call to `SetCapture`. When you finish, be sure to restore the original cursor and call `ReleaseCapture`.

Advanced Icons

If you pop up the Help dialog for the MenuTest program, you'll see that it contains two icons (as shown in Figure 20.9).

Figure 20.9.
The Help dialog has two embedded icons.

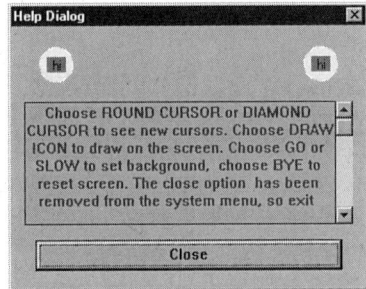

While you create the RC file for this dialog, you can give a static control the capability to house an icon. Simply assign the static control the `SS_ICON` style and supply it with the name of an icon:

```
ICON_1 ICON "icon1.ico"

CONTROL "Icon_1", -1, "STATIC",
        SS_ICON ¦ WS_CHILD ¦ WS_VISIBLE ¦ WS_GROUP,
        137, 9, 16, 16
```

Notice that this code refers to the icon by its assigned name, not by its filename. Also, the last two parameters, designating the width and height of the static text, are ignored. They're ignored because the static text box is automatically sized to fit the icon.

MenuTest's second trick with icons enables you to repeatedly paint the surface of the main window with the image of the program's icon (as shown in Figure 20.10).

Figure 20.10.

MenuTest uses DrawIcon *and* WM_MOUSEMOVE *messages to paint patterns on its main window.*

The following code is used to paint the icon on-screen:

```
void MenuTest_OnMouseMove(HWND hwnd, int x, int y, UINT keyFlags)
{
  if (((keyFlags & MK_LBUTTON) == MK_LBUTTON) && (PaintIcon))
  {
    HDC PaintDC = GetDC(hwnd);
    DrawIcon(PaintDC, x, y, Icon1);
    ReleaseDC(hwnd, PaintDC);
  }
}
```

Whenever the mouse is moved over the main window, the program checks to see whether the left mouse button is down and whether the Boolean PaintIcon variable is set to TRUE. If both conditions are met, MenuTest retrieves the device context of the main window and paints (with the DrawIcon function) an icon on-screen at the current mouse location.

20

DO	DON'T

DO load icons into memory with the LoadIcon call, passing zero in the first parameter if the icon is a system icon, such as IDI_APPLICATION.

DON'T forget to dispose of the memory associated with an icon by calling DestroyIcon.

Accelerators—Briefly

Finally, the issue of accelerators is up for discussion. Accelerators, or *hotkeys*, enable you to define custom key combinations so a user can gain quick access to certain features of your program. For instance, the MenuTest program lets you switch cursors by pressing Alt+1, Alt+2, and Alt+3. Because you might be interested in defining more complex hotkey combinations, MenuTest also accesses these same icons with Alt+F1, Ctrl+F2, and Shift+F3. Each of these latter combinations are shown to the user in the menu. (Obviously these later set of hotkeys are not intended to be user friendly, but only to show you how to work with the Alt, Ctrl, and Shift keys. If I'd wanted to make a more friendly app, then the key combinations would have used the same special key, yielding something like this: Alt+F1, Alt+F2, Alt+F3.)

Note: I use the word *hotkey* above in a loose, generic sense. I'm not referring to the hotkey common control examined on Day 18, "Windows 95 Dialogs and Controls." I'm using the term here merely to convey a concept to the reader, and I don't mean to draw a direct parallel between accelerators and the common controls. It's true that accelerators and hotkey controls are related, but they are not identical.

Accelerators are easy to use. To define them, just pop up the Resource Workshop or App Studio and use the custom tools they include for defining accelerators. It's also very easy to design accelerators with a word processor:

```
MYKEYS ACCELERATORS
BEGIN
  VK_F1, CM_ROUNDCURSOR, VIRTKEY, ALT
  VK_F2, CM_DIAMONDCURSOR, VIRTKEY, CONTROL
  VK_F3, CM_ICONCURSOR, VIRTKEY, SHIFT
  "1", CM_ROUNDCURSOR, VIRTKEY, ALT
  "2", CM_DIAMONDCURSOR, VIRTKEY, ALT
  "3", CM_ICONCURSOR, VIRTKEY, ALT
END
```

Note: I assign some options to the Alt key, and others to the Shift or Ctrl key. Typically, hotkeys are defined with the Alt+key and any other number or letter key. However, for your personal edification, the MenuTest program also provides examples of how to use the Alt, Control, and Shift keys in combination with one of the function keys.

After you've defined an accelerator table, you need to load it into memory:

```
static HACCEL  hAccel
hAccel = LoadAccelerators(hInstance, "MYKEYS");
if (hAccel == NULL)
  MessageBox(MainWindow, "No Accelerators", "Warning", MB_OK);
```

The MenuTest program performs this simple operation in response to WM_CREATE messages. However, there is an argument for moving the whole process into WinMain, because the hAccel value returned from LoadAccelerators is used in the program's message loop (see following explanation). Either course is fine. I chose to load the accelerators in MenuTest_OnCreate because I performed all program initialization there, and I wanted to remain consistent. (A benefit of doing all your initialization in response to WM_CREATE is that it leaves the WinMain, Create, and Register functions almost completely static from one program to the next, thereby letting you ignore them—except for a quick check of the WNDCLASS structure and the message loop.)

The final step in using accelerators is simply to add a TranslateAccelerator line to the message loop, just as you did when calling IsDialogMessage in the FileBox program:

```
while (GetMessage(&Msg, NULL, 0, 0))
{
  if (!hAccel ¦¦ !TranslateAccelerator(MainWindow, hAccel, &Msg))
  {
    TranslateMessage(&Msg);
    DispatchMessage(&Msg);
  }
}
```

The obvious purpose of TranslateAccelerator is to handle any of the hotkeys defined in your program before they are passed on to the destination window procedure with DispatchMessage. In other words, Windows checks to see if the user has pressed a hotkey; if so, Windows translates the key press into a message. Otherwise, it just passes the message on directly to your main window procedure.

DO   DON'T

DO call LoadAccelerators to load accelerators into memory.

DON'T worry about disposing of accelerators. Windows handles that task internally.

Summary

This chapter contains few surprises. Most of the code has been useful, but not particularly difficult to understand. Following is a quick review of the high points:

☐ You can add variety and/or flexibility to menus by nesting pop-up menus, or by using the statements SEPARATOR, MENUBARBREAK, GRAYED, CHECKED, or UNCHECKED.

☐ To really spice up a menu, modify it with either the MF_BITMAP or MF_OWNERDRAW styles.

☐ You can change the cursor associated with a window in order to clue the user to its purpose or current status.

☐ Icons can be placed in dialogs or painted directly on-screen.

☐ The keyboard interface to a program can be enhanced by using accelerators.

All this material is useful, even vital, but the only really fancy code shown in this chapter involved creating owner draw menus. Like the right mouse button before Windows 95, menus are a relatively wide-open field in Windows programming. Anyone willing to do a little creative work could easily come up with some very interesting innovations in this area.

Q&A

Q I still don't really understand the relationship between MF_OWNERDRAW, WM_MEASUREITEM, and WM_DRAWITEM. What's the scoop?

A When you set the MF_OWNERDRAW flag, you are in effect telling Windows that you want to handle the drawing of the menu item in question. Windows responds: "Fine, that's okay with me. Just tell me how big you want the pop-up window that's going to hold your bitmaps." You answer this question by responding to WM_MEASUREITEM messages. Now that all the preparations are complete, Windows politely sends you a WM_DRAWITEM message every time a menu item needs to be drawn or updated. (I should add that owner draw menus don't have to deal with bitmaps. You can draw anything here, or simply print your own text. I use bitmaps because they are familiar, and easily understood.)

Q One more time, just so I'm sure, when I'm setting a cursor, when should I call SetCapture, and when should I call SetClassWord or SetClassLong?

A Call the SetClass functions when you want to permanently change the cursor for a window without affecting its performance in any other way. This change will stay in effect until you call SetClassLong again, or until the window in question is closed. Call SetCapture when you want to temporarily funnel all mouse input to one particular window, while simultaneously assuring that the cursor doesn't change—regardless of which window it is over. Typically, this kind of thing is done when you want to change the cursor to an hourglass while a lengthy processor intensive operation is taking place.

Workshop

The Workshop provides quiz questions to help you solidify your understanding of the material covered and exercises to provide you with experience in using what you've learned. Try to understand the quiz and exercise answers before continuing on to the next chapter. Answers are provided in Appendix A.

Quiz

1. The MenuTest program specifies hotkeys in the menu items that are part of the Cursors pop-up menu (Figure 20.3). How does it separate these hotkey assignments from the regular menu text?

2. How do you place an underline beneath a letter in a menu? What effect does this have?

3. What call needs to be inserted into a program's message loop if the program is making use of accelerators?

4. How can you tell whether a menu item is selected or not selected when you get the WM_DRAWITEM message?

5. Use your reference materials to specify at least seven different flags used in the third field (fuFlags) of the ModifyMenu function.

6. What's the difference between MF_BYPOSITION and MF_BYCOMMAND?

7. If you are using the MF_BYPOSITION flag, is the first menu item listed a zero or a one?

8. What purpose does the SS_ICON style serve?

9. What function must a programmer call every time he or she calls SetCapture? (Hint: the answer isn't SetCursor!)

10. How can you obtain the dimensions of a bitmap at runtime?

Exercises

1. Create a user draw menu that beeps and/or changes the background color of the main window every time the user focuses it with the arrow keys. (Extra credit: Animate an owner draw menu!)

2. Demonstrate how to use the SetCursor and SetCapture functions to globally change the cursor to an hourglass. Keep the change in effect until the user clicks the left mouse button on the program's main window.

20

Threads, Multitasking, and Memory Management

This chapter is about advanced Windows 95 and Windows NT programming. It is a gateway to the upper echelons of Windows programming and will introduce you to some of the most powerful capabilities of WIN32.

In particular, this chapter covers:

- [ ] Processes
- [ ] Threads
- [ ] WIN32 memory management
- [ ] Heaps
- [ ] Memory mapped files
- [ ] Virtual memory

All of these are advanced subjects that are entirely Windows 95 and Windows NT specific. The programs included in this chapter will not run under Windows 3.1.

My goal is to isolate some of the most important aspects of advanced Windows programming and to introduce you to them in clear language so you can use them in your applications. I present five different programs in this chapter, each designed to show off a key feature related to advanced Windows programming.

I've used the word "advanced" in this overview several times, but you will find that most of the code in this chapter is easy to use. I've sought to show you simple ways to get at some of the most powerful new features in Windows 95. I would need another five or six hundred pages to cover these subjects in depth, but the material you find here will get you started with these invaluable technologies. In fact, there is plenty of information in this lengthy chapter to allow you to incorporate threading and advanced memory management techniques in your own programs.

Processes and Memory

A *process* is the hip WIN32 term for a program that is currently loaded. An executable file on disk is just a file. If it's been started, then it's a process.

If you want to create a process, call CreateProcess. This function does what the WinExec function did in Windows 3.1. WinExec is now obsolete, and you should use CreateProcess in its stead.

Processes don't do anything. They just exist. The thing that does something inside a program is called a *thread*. Each program has at least one thread, and indeed most programs that currently run on Windows have only one thread. All Windows 3.1 programs by definition have only one thread. The idea that a program can have multiple threads is specific to fancy operating systems like UNIX, OS/2, Windows NT, and Windows 95.

When Windows loads a process, it just opens up a memory-mapped file and sucks the contents of an executable file or DLL into memory. Processes are inert. They don't do anything. Threads *do* things. Processes merely exist.

All processes have an HINSTANCE associated with them. This is the first parameter passed to WinMain. You have been working with this value since Day 1, "Getting Your Feet Wet," and have used it explicitly since the end of Day 2, "Building Projects, Creating Windows."

The HINSTANCE of an application is the base memory address where it is loaded. In Windows 95, this value is typically 0×00400000, or 4,194,304. In other words, the program is usually loaded in at the 4MB mark. It then ranges from that point up to the 2GB mark. This means a Windows 95 program has 2GB minus 4MB worth of room in which to stretch out.

> **Note:** I've mentioned this before, but people who are relatively new to this subject may need a reminder. A kilobyte (KB) is approximately one thousand (1,000) bytes. A megabyte (MB) is approximately one million (1,000,000) bytes. A gigabyte (GB), is approximately one billion (1,000,000,000) bytes. Therefore, there are 1,000 megabytes in 1 gigabyte. (Here are the precise figures: 1024KB, 1,048,576MB, 1,073,741,824GB. If you are interested, here's 4GB: 4,294,967,296.)

Both the program's code and its data are loaded into this 2GB address space. This means the operating system gives you virtually unlimited resources in which to run your program. (Your hardware may not, however, share the operating system's largesse.)

What does it mean to say that a program is loaded into a 4GB address space? If we only have a few megabytes of memory on our machines, what sense does it make to talk about such huge amounts of memory?

The answer is that each program is assigned, not an actual area in physical RAM, but only a virtual address space. That is, it's assigned a range of addresses. When you need to access that memory, physical addresses are assigned to it. The act of assigning physical addresses to virtual memory is called "mapping."

Windows is constantly mapping virtual memory into physical address spaces. That is, it's assigning physical addresses to virtual memory. Because of this system, people with only 8MB of memory on their system can have variables, or even entire processes, that have addresses in the 3 to 4GB range. Every program thinks it's running in its own, private 4GB address space, and that it can use 2GB of this space as it pleases. What's really happening is that pages of that virtual 4GB space are being mapped into the actual 8MB of memory available on your system.

21

Note: Because each process runs in its own 4GB address space, the `hPrevInstance` parameter passed to `WinMain` is meaningless in WIN32. There can't be a previous instance of a program because each program is running in its own virtual world, and there is only one virtual world in all the universe. (Actually, there is more than one world inside of a computer. But each process is convinced that it is alone—the only virtual world in existence. Its world is 4GB in size, guaranteed, and the inhabitants of that world are prepared to prove it to you. And it's the only one there is. Any science-fiction writers want to pick up this ball and run with it?)

A page of memory is typically 4KB in size, which is 4,096 bytes. Windows 95 is always mapping pages of virtual memory into physical address spaces. When this happens, the address your program sees does not change. There is another table that Windows maintains that translates these virtual addresses into physical addresses. This is called indirection, or perhaps, more accurately, double indirection. (The pointer itself is one level of indirection, the virtual address is a second level.) The addresses that you see in your program are never direct references to real memory. Instead they are indirect references. You see one address in your program, and then Windows maintains a table that allows the virtual addresses you see to be mapped into physical memory that resides in RAM. RAM is physical memory; the addresses you see are virtual memory. Virtual memory is not real memory any more than virtual reality is "real" reality.

Why does Windows maintain this elaborate fiction of having virtual addresses? The main reason is to protect one process from another. Each process is running in its own 4GB address space. It thinks it owns the whole computer. It has no idea that there are other processes on the computer.

Because each process is totally separated from the other processes on the computer, there is much less chance that they will overwrite one another. This means it is unlikely that an invalid memory access by one program will overwrite another program, or overwrite some part of the operating system. Each process is boxed away in a safe virtual world where it can't get at any other programs. This makes inter-process communication very different than it was in Windows 3.1. However, it also makes it much less likely that your computer will crash.

Furthermore, when you close down a WIN32 program, all the resources allocated to it are automatically closed out. By definition they can only reside inside that program's one virtual world. When the virtual world is closed out, all the resources associated with that process are also closed out. If you forget to deallocate memory, or if you forget to deallocate resources, all your mistakes will be covered up the moment you close your program. (This is not, however, a theory on which to base program memory management. You should at least *try* to handle memory correctly. But if you make a mistake, you are not permanently sullying the operating systems environment the way you did in Windows 3.1.)

Note: 16-bit Windows programs that run on Windows 95 all share the same address space. It's as if they are all running on their own miniature version of Windows 3.1. That means errors made by one 16-bit process can affect other 16-bit processes. However, when you close out all the 16-bit applications, then their virtual world will disappear, and all the resources dedicated to it will be reclaimed. If one 16-bit program is giving you trouble, then don't just close it. Close all the 16-bit programs in your Windows 95 session, then reopen the ones that you feel are running properly. That one program dirtied the water that all the other 16-bit programs used. The only thing to do in that case is to close all the 16-bit programs, then create a new, pristine virtual 16-bit world by reopening one of them. Remember, this is Windows 95 I'm talking about here, not Windows NT.

That's all I'm going to say about processes. The key point is that a process is a loaded program. It's not running; it's not executing. Processes don't run; they don't execute. They just exist in a vast 4GB virtual address space. They have direct access to about 2GB of that space, and the operating system owns the rest. Threads run. Threads execute. Threads are the doers.

Threads and Multitasking

Each process has one or more threads assigned to it. Threads are the part of a program that executes.

Windows 95 is a true multitasking operating system. At any one time, it has x number of threads running. It assigns a time slice to each of these threads. The technical name for a time slice is a quantum, but don't worry, I'm not going to call them that.

Each thread on the system has something called a CONTEXT. A CONTEXT is a data structure that contains information about the state of a thread. More specifically, it contains information about the state of the registers in the CPU when that thread is running. If you want to see one of these structures, look in the WINNT.H file that ships with your compiler.

For the moment, think of all the threads in a computer as if they were placed on a big wheel, like the wheels that spin round at a gambling casino. As the wheel spins, there is a time when each of the threads will be near the top of the wheel. Starting a few degrees before it reaches the top of the wheel, and extending a few degrees after, is the period of time when a thread is actually executing. The moment the thread comes into that range, its context is loaded. That is, the CPU register values that it stores in its CONTEXT record are loaded into the physical CPU found on the computer. Then that thread begins executing at the point where its instruction pointer is currently located. It executes for a few cycles, until the wheel that owns it spins out of range. Just before it goes out of range, its CONTEXT is updated with the current state of the CPU.

This is one way to think of how multitasking works under Windows 95. The key point is that each thread is given a time slice. It executes during the duration of its time slice, and then another thread gets a chance. While it is running, the thread has its own unique set of register values. When its time slice is over, the values are stored in a record, and the next thread's CPU values are loaded into memory.

No two threads are ever running at the same time. However, it seems to us as if they are all running at the same time. That's because computers are fast. Like most sleight-of-hand tricks, a computer's multitasking ability is based on speed and dexterity. Computers don't really do the impossible; they just *seem* to be doing the impossible.

> **Note:** It's important to understand that threads can be assigned priorities. A thread with a high priority will get called more frequently than a thread with a low priority. This means you can (at least theoretically) start a thread that will perform some task entirely in the background. It will never take up any of the system's time unless all the other threads are idle.

There's a lot of loose talk going on about Windows 95 right now. Some of it is valid. However, don't let anyone convince you that Windows 95 is not a real multitasking operating system. This book teaches you how to write 32-bit programs. 32-bit programs that run on Windows 95 are really multitasked. (The 16-bit programs in their single address space are not really multitasked, but you don't have to run them if you don't want. And even they can't steal the show entirely from other 32-bit apps, but only from each other. Therefore, you are not so badly off if you run only one 16-bit process at a time.)

Windows 95 has what is called *preemptive multitasking*. Preemptive multitasking is the process that I described above. When a task's time slice is up, it is preempted. It's cut off, and it can't do any more damage until it gets another time slice. This means that no one program can hog the CPU.

Windows 3.1 had what is called *non-preemptive multitasking*. Non-preemptive multitasking allows a program to take control of the CPU and return it only when it is good and ready. In truth, most good Windows 3.1 programmers tried hard not to hog the CPU. They used timers, PeekMessage loops, PostMessage, and other tools to ensure that the system could get the CPU back if it needed it. However, there were times when a program would not give the CPU back to the system. For instance, it might get stuck in an infinite loop. When the program started looping, it would not give you a chance to preempt it. Therefore, you could not even switch to another program long enough to save your data before the system crashed. You just sat their helplessly, while everything went to hell.

Preemptive multitasking puts an end to this nightmare. If a program is stuck in an infinite loop, or if it is just busy doing something that takes a long time, then it won't affect the user. The user can always switch away to another program. That new program will keep getting time slices, regular as clock work, right on schedule, despite what might be going on in the first program.

This new system is better from two different perspectives. First, it means that users don't have to face disaster if something goes wrong. Second, programmers don't have to work so hard to make sure that their programs are polite and well behaved.

That's enough theory for now. I will, however, discuss WIN32 memory-related issues more carefully after you get some hands-on experience with threads. Remember, the stuff I'm talking about here regards advanced 32 programming issues. Intermediate programmers don't have to know about this stuff. However, you will be a better programmer if you do learn how processes, threads, multitasking, and memory work.

Threads: A Simple Example

There is something about the topic of threads that is innately intimidating. Somehow it sounds as if it must be part of the guru's guru's bag of tricks.

As it turns out, simple thread programs are almost embarrassingly easy to write. In fact, all the issues surrounding threads that will be discussed in this chapter are fairly easy to understand. In some cases, threads might become complicated in the sense that programming a console application can be complicated. The basic EMILY.CPP console application I showed you earlier is trivial in the extreme. However, it's possible to write console applications that are complex. The same is true of threads. Just starting a single thread is simple. Not quite as simple as writing a basic console application, but still simple.

It's only when you get multiple threads running at the same time, and only when they are concurrently trying to access the same data, that things can get a bit more complex. Thread synchronization, thread local storage, and related topics do have their complex side. However, I think you will be surprised at how easy it is to add threads to your programs. Even some of the more advanced thread synchronization related topics, such as critical sections and mutexes, are both fairly simple, at least in principle.

As usual, it's hard to get specific without having an example program to examine. Listings 21.1 through 21.6 show how to create a simple thread. Go ahead and run the program, then come back and read about how it works.

21

Remember: Don't worry about this one. Basic thread theory is simple.

Listing 21.1. The main module of the Thread1 program.

```cpp
////////////////////////////////////////////////////////////
//   Program Name: Thread1.cpp
//   Programmer: Charlie Calvert
//   Description: Threads windows program
//   Date: 07/16/95
////////////////////////////////////////////////////////////

#define STRICT
#define WIN32_LEAN_AND_MEAN
#include <windows.h>
#include <windowsx.h>
#include <stdlib.h>
#include "thread1.h"
#pragma warning (disable: 4068)


// --------------------------------------------------------
// Interface
// --------------------------------------------------------

LRESULT CALLBACK WndProc(HWND hwnd, UINT Message,
                         WPARAM wParam, LPARAM lParam);
BOOL Register(HINSTANCE hInst);
HWND Create(HINSTANCE hInst, int nCmdShow);

// Declarations for class Threads
#define Thread1_DefProc     DefWindowProc
void Thread1_OnDestroy(HWND hwnd);
void Thread1_OnCommand(HWND hwnd, int id,
                       HWND hwndCtl, UINT codeNotify);


static char szAppName[] = "Threads";
static HWND MainWindow;
static HINSTANCE hInstance;


// --------------------------------------------------------
// Initialization
// --------------------------------------------------------

////////////////////////////////////////////////////////////
// Program entry point
////////////////////////////////////////////////////////////
#pragma argsused
int WINAPI WinMain(HINSTANCE hInst, HINSTANCE hPrevInstance,
                   LPSTR lpszCmdParam, int nCmdShow)
{
  MSG  Msg;

  if (!hPrevInstance)
    if (!Register(hInst))
      return FALSE;

  MainWindow = Create(hInst, nCmdShow);
  if (!MainWindow)
    return FALSE;
```

```
  while (GetMessage(&Msg, NULL, 0, 0))
  {
    TranslateMessage(&Msg);
    DispatchMessage(&Msg);
  }

  return Msg.wParam;
}

/////////////////////////////////////////////////////
// Register the window
/////////////////////////////////////////////////////
BOOL Register(HINSTANCE hInst)
{
  WNDCLASS WndClass;

  WndClass.style          = CS_HREDRAW | CS_VREDRAW;
  WndClass.lpfnWndProc    = WndProc;
  WndClass.cbClsExtra     = 0;
  WndClass.cbWndExtra     = 0;
  WndClass.hInstance      = hInst;
  WndClass.hIcon          = LoadIcon(hInst, "ThreadsIcon");
  WndClass.hCursor        = LoadCursor(NULL, IDC_ARROW);
  WndClass.hbrBackground  = (HBRUSH)(COLOR_WINDOW+1);
  WndClass.lpszMenuName     = "ThreadMenu";
  WndClass.lpszClassName  = szAppName;

  return (RegisterClass (&WndClass) != 0);
}

/////////////////////////////////////////////////////
// Create the window
/////////////////////////////////////////////////////
HWND Create(HINSTANCE hInst, int nCmdShow)
{

  hInstance = hInst;

  HWND hwnd = CreateWindow(szAppName, szAppName,
                    WS_OVERLAPPEDWINDOW,
                    CW_USEDEFAULT, CW_USEDEFAULT,
                    CW_USEDEFAULT, CW_USEDEFAULT,
                    NULL, NULL, hInst, NULL);

  if (hwnd == NULL)
    return hwnd;

  ShowWindow(hwnd, nCmdShow);
  UpdateWindow(hwnd);

  return hwnd;
}

// ----------------------------------------------------
// WndProc and Implementation
// ----------------------------------------------------
```

continues

Listing 21.1. continued

```
///////////////////////////////////////////////////////
// The Window Procedure
///////////////////////////////////////////////////////
LRESULT CALLBACK WndProc(HWND hwnd, UINT Message, WPARAM wParam, LPARAM lParam)
{
  switch(Message)
  {
    HANDLE_MSG(hwnd, WM_DESTROY, Thread1_OnDestroy);
    HANDLE_MSG(hwnd, WM_COMMAND, Thread1_OnCommand);
    default: return Thread1_DefProc(hwnd, Message, wParam, lParam);
  }
}

///////////////////////////////////////////////////////
// Handle WM_DESTROY
///////////////////////////////////////////////////////
#pragma argsused
void Thread1_OnDestroy(HWND hwnd)
{
  PostQuitMessage(0);
}

///////////////////////////////////////////////////////
// This is the thread created by this application
///////////////////////////////////////////////////////
unsigned long _stdcall ThreadFunc(void *)
{
  int i;
  char S[100];

  HDC DC = GetDC(MainWindow);

  for (i = 0; i < 10000; i++)
  {
    itoa(i, S, 10);
    TextOut(DC, 10, 10, S, strlen(S));
  }

  ReleaseDC(MainWindow, DC);
  return 0;
}

///////////////////////////////////////////////////////
// WM_COMMAND: Create the thread
///////////////////////////////////////////////////////
#pragma argsused
void Thread1_OnCommand(HWND hwnd, int id, HWND hwndCtl, UINT codeNotify)
{
  DWORD ThreadID;

  switch(id)
  {
```

```
        case ID_GOTHREAD:
          HANDLE hthread = CreateThread(
                              NULL,         //Security attribute
                              0,            //Initial Stack
                              ThreadFunc,   //Starting address of thread
                              NULL,         // argument of thread
                              0,            // Create flags
                              &ThreadID);   // thread ID

          if (!hthread)
            MessageBox(hwnd, "No Thread", NULL, MB_OK);

          break;
      }
    }
```

Listing 21.2. The labyrinthine header file for the Thread1 program.

```
/////////////////////////////////////////////////////////
// THREAD1.H
// Copyright (c) 1995 Charlie Calvert.
/////////////////////////////////////////////////////////

#define ID_GOTHREAD    100
```

Listing 21.3. The resource file for the Thread1 program.

```
/////////////////////////////////////////////////////////
// THREAD1.RC
// Copyright (c) 1995 Charlie Calvert.
/////////////////////////////////////////////////////////

#include "thread1.h"

ThreadsIcon ICON "thread1.ico"

ThreadMenu MENU
BEGIN
  MENUITEM "Run Thread" ID_GOTHREAD
END
```

21

Listing 21.4. The module definition file for the Thread1 program.

```
; Thread1.Def

NAME          Thread1
DESCRIPTION   'Thread1 Window'
```

Listing 21.5. The Borland makefile for the Thread1 program.

```
# Thread1.mak

# macros

!if !$d(BCROOT)
BCROOT  = $(MAKEDIR)\..
!endif

APPNAME = THREAD1
INCPATH = $(BCROOT)\WIN32;$(BCROOT);$(BCROOT)\INCLUDE
LIBPATH = $(BCROOT)\LIB

COMPILER= BCC32.EXE
BRC     = BRC32.EXE
FLAGS   = -W -v -w4 -I$(INCPATH) -L$(LIBPATH)

# link
$(APPNAME).exe: $(APPNAME).obj $(APPNAME).def $(APPNAME).res
  $(COMPILER) $(FLAGS) $(APPNAME).obj
  $(BRC) -I$(INCPATH) $(APPNAME).res

# compile
$(APPNAME).obj: $(APPNAME).cpp
  $(COMPILER) -c $(FLAGS) $(APPNAME).cpp

# resource
$(APPNAME).res: $(APPNAME).rc
  $(BRC) -R -I$(INCPATH) $(APPNAME).RC
```

Listing 21.6. The Microsoft makefile for the Thread1 program.

```
# Nmake macros for building Windows 32-Bit apps

APPNAME=THREAD1
TARGETOS=WIN95
APPVER=4.0
OBJS=$(APPNAME).obj

!include <win32.mak>

all: $(APPNAME).exe

# Update the resource if necessary

$(APPNAME).res: $(APPNAME).rc $(APPNAME).h
  $(rc) $(rcflags) $(rcvars) $(APPNAME).rc

# Update the object files if necessary

# compile
.cpp.obj:
  $(cc) $(cflags) $(cvars) $(cdebug) $<
```

```
# Update the executable file if necessary.

$(APPNAME).exe: $(OBJS) $(APPNAME).res
  $(link) $(linkdebug) $(guiflags) -out:$(APPNAME).exe\
  $(OBJS) $(APPNAME).res $(guilibs)
```

When this program begins, it displays the simple window shown in Figure 21.1. If you select the Run Thread menu item, then it displays a number on the screen. As you watch, this number is incremented from 0 to 9999.

Figure 21.1.

The Thread1 program counts from zero to 9999 when the user selects its sole menu item.

The structure of the Thread1 program is very simple. It has all the normal elements of a Windows program, plus one menu item. If you select the menu item, a thread is created. This thread does nothing more than count from 0 to 9999. As it counts, it displays each number in the program's main window.

When working with threads, you have two main tasks:

1. Create the thread
2. Create a function that serves as the "thread entry point."

As you learned above, each program has one thread by default. In a sense, this thread is started during the call to WinMain. (Actually the thread is created earlier, by the system. However, you first see it when WinMain is called.) Just as WinMain is the entry point for a program, so is the thread function you create, the entry point for a thread. Unlike WinMain, the thread function can be assigned any name that catches your fancy.

The call to create a thread is known (naturally enough) as CreateThread. As you just learned, the thread function itself can have any name. However, it always takes one 32-bit pointer or variable as a parameter. It always returns a 32-bit value. The parameter of the function is of type LPVOID. That is, it's just a generic pointer. As such, you can pass in a pointer to almost any structure in this variable. More on this later.

21

Here is the portion of the WM_COMMAND handler that creates the thread:

```
DWORD ThreadID;

HANDLE hthread = CreateThread(
            NULL,         //Security attribute
            0,            //Initial Stack
            ThreadFunc,   //Starting address of thread
            NULL,         // argument of thread
            0,            // Create flags
            &ThreadID);   // thread ID

    if (!hthread)
      MessageBox(hwnd, "No Thread", NULL, MB_OK);
```

This code does nothing more than attempt to create a thread. If something goes wrong, it pops up a message box informing the user that there has been an error.

CreateThread

This is the CreateThread syntax:

```
HANDLE CreateThread(
    // address of thread security attributes
    LPSECURITY_ATTRIBUTES  lpThreadAttributes,
    DWORD  dwStackSize,     // size of stack for thread
    // address of thread function
    LPTHREAD_START_ROUTINE  lpStartAddress,
    LPVOID  lpParameter,    // argument for new thread
    DWORD  dwCreationFlags,    // creation flags
    LPDWORD  lpThreadId     // Returned thread identifier
    );
```

The first parameter takes a series of security attributes. If this parameter is NULL, then the default security attributes are used. On Windows 95 it is standard to set this parameter to NULL. The only time you might want to vary from this pattern is if you want child processes to inherit the thread.

If the second parameter for the thread is 0, then the stack size for the thread will be the same as the stack size for the application. In other words, the primary thread and the thread you are starting will both have stacks that are the same size. The stack will automatically grow, if necessary. In short, you can usually set this parameter to 0.

The lpStartAddress parameter is the most important portion of the function call. It is where you specify the name of the thread function that is called when the thread begins execution. Just enter the name of the function in this field.

If you want to pass a parameter to your function, then specify it in lpParameter. Typically, you will create a structure, and pass in its address in this parameter. The variable you use does not have to be a structure, and could be a string or some other type of variable.

dwCreationFlags allows you to pass in certain flags that are associated with your thread. The Microsoft documentation I've seen so far only specifies one possible flag for this field. That flag is called CREATE_SUSPENDED. If you create a suspended thread, then the thread itself is created, its stack is created, its CONTEXT structure is filled with CPU values, but the thread is never assigned any CPU time. It's all set to go, but it won't execute until you call ResumeThread. If you want, you can then suspend the thread again by calling SuspendThread. This whole subject of suspended threads is really an advanced topic relating to thread synchronization. For now, you should just pass in 0 in this parameter.

The final parameter, lpThreadID, holds a pointer to a variable that is assigned a unique ID by the system. On Windows 95 this parameter can be NULL, and indeed most of the time you won't use the thread ID, so you might have an inclination to set it to NULL. On Windows NT, however, this parameter cannot be NULL. If you are interested in portability between Windows 95 and Windows NT, then you better not set this value to NULL. In other words, if your application will go into general release, then you should pass in the address of a DWORD and should not set this value to NULL.

Here's an example:

```
HANDLE hthread = CreateThread(NULL, 0, ThreadFunc, NULL, 0, &ThreadID);
```

After you've created a non-suspended thread, the function you passed to it will automatically be called. In other words, after you create a thread, the function representing the entry point for that thread will be called almost immediately. Here is the thread for the Thread1 program:

```
unsigned long _stdcall ThreadFunc(void *)
{
  int i;
  char S[100];

  HDC DC = GetDC(MainWindow);

  for (i = 0; i < 10000; i++)
  {
    itoa(i, S, 10);
    TextOut(DC, 10, 10, S, strlen(S));
  }

  ReleaseDC(MainWindow, DC);
  return 0;
}
```

There isn't much for me to say about this function; it's just "C Programming 101" material.

As you can see, there isn't anything very complicated about threads when you are looking at them from the most elemental level. What's complicated is when you have multiple threads trying to access the same data at the same time. When that happens, you need to find a way to get the threads to synchronize with one another, so that they are working together, and not working at cross purposes.

21

One Program, Multiple Threads

Now that you know the basics about threads, the next step is to see how to run multiple threads from inside the same program. This is a bit like multitasking inside a single program, though of course the operating system doesn't necessarily treat two threads inside one program any differently than it would treat two threads from separate programs.

The code in Listings 21.7 through 21.12 shows how a program can have four separate threads running at the same time. Three of the threads will be painting a graphic to the screen. The fourth thread is the main thread for the program. It will continue functioning normally even when the other threads are active.

Listing 21.7. The main code for the Thread2 program.

```
/////////////////////////////////////////////////////////
//   Program Name: Thread2.cpp
//   Programmer: Charlie Calvert
//   Description: Threads windows program
//   Date: 07/12/95
/////////////////////////////////////////////////////////

#define STRICT
#define WIN32_LEAN_AND_MEAN
#include <windows.h>
#include <windowsx.h>
#include <stdlib.h>
#include <stdio.h>
#include <math.h>
#include "thread2.h"
#pragma warning (disable: 4068)


// -------------------------------------------------------
// Interface
// -------------------------------------------------------

LRESULT CALLBACK WndProc(HWND hwnd, UINT Message,
                         WPARAM wParam, LPARAM lParam);
BOOL Register(HINSTANCE hInst);
HWND Create(HINSTANCE hInst, int nCmdShow);

// Declarations for class Threads
#define Thread2_DefProc    DefWindowProc
BOOL Thread2_OnCreate(HWND hwnd, LPCREATESTRUCT lpCreateStruct);
void Thread2_OnDestroy(HWND hwnd);
void Thread2_OnCommand(HWND hwnd, int id,
                       HWND hwndCtl, UINT codeNotify);
void Thread2_OnPaint(HWND hwnd);

typedef struct tagData
{
  int xPos;
  int yPos;
}TDATA, *LPDATA;
```

```
static char szAppName[] = "Threads";
static HWND MainWindow;
static HINSTANCE hInstance;
HBITMAP EarthMap;
int AHeight;
int AWidth;


// --------------------------------------------------------
// Initialization
// --------------------------------------------------------


//////////////////////////////////////////////////////////
// Program entry point
//////////////////////////////////////////////////////////
#pragma argsused
int WINAPI WinMain(HINSTANCE hInst, HINSTANCE hPrevInstance,
                   LPSTR lpszCmdParam, int nCmdShow)
{
  MSG   Msg;

  if (!hPrevInstance)
    if (!Register(hInst))
      return FALSE;

  MainWindow = Create(hInst, nCmdShow);
  if (!MainWindow)
    return FALSE;

  while (GetMessage(&Msg, NULL, 0, 0))
  {
    TranslateMessage(&Msg);
    DispatchMessage(&Msg);
  }

  return Msg.wParam;
}


//////////////////////////////////////////////////////////
// Register the window
//////////////////////////////////////////////////////////
BOOL Register(HINSTANCE hInst)
{
  WNDCLASS WndClass;

  WndClass.style          = CS_HREDRAW | CS_VREDRAW;
  WndClass.lpfnWndProc    = WndProc;
  WndClass.cbClsExtra     = 0;
  WndClass.cbWndExtra     = 0;
  WndClass.hInstance      = hInst;
  WndClass.hIcon          = LoadIcon(hInst, "ThreadsIcon");
  WndClass.hCursor        = LoadCursor(NULL, IDC_ARROW);
  WndClass.hbrBackground  = (HBRUSH)(COLOR_WINDOW+1);
  WndClass.lpszMenuName    = "ThreadMenu";
  WndClass.lpszClassName  = szAppName;
```

continues

21

Listing 21.7. continued

```
    return (RegisterClass (&WndClass) != 0);
}

////////////////////////////////////////////////////////
// Create the window
////////////////////////////////////////////////////////
HWND Create(HINSTANCE hInst, int nCmdShow)
{

  hInstance = hInst;

  HWND hwnd = CreateWindow(szAppName, szAppName,
                   WS_OVERLAPPEDWINDOW,
                   CW_USEDEFAULT, CW_USEDEFAULT,
                   CW_USEDEFAULT, CW_USEDEFAULT,
                   NULL, NULL, hInst, NULL);

  if (hwnd == NULL)
    return hwnd;

  nCmdShow = SW_SHOWMAXIMIZED;

  ShowWindow(hwnd, nCmdShow);
  UpdateWindow(hwnd);

  return hwnd;
}

// ------------------------------------------------------
// WndProc and Implementation
// ------------------------------------------------------

////////////////////////////////////////////////////////
// The Window Procedure
////////////////////////////////////////////////////////
LRESULT CALLBACK WndProc(HWND hwnd, UINT Message,
                         WPARAM wParam, LPARAM lParam)
{
  switch(Message)
  {
    HANDLE_MSG(hwnd, WM_CREATE, Thread2_OnCreate);
    HANDLE_MSG(hwnd, WM_DESTROY, Thread2_OnDestroy);
    HANDLE_MSG(hwnd, WM_COMMAND, Thread2_OnCommand);
    HANDLE_MSG(hwnd, WM_PAINT, Thread2_OnPaint);
    default: return Thread2_DefProc(hwnd, Message, wParam, lParam);
  }
}

#pragma argsused
BOOL Thread2_OnCreate(HWND hwnd, LPCREATESTRUCT lpCreateStruct)
{
  BITMAP BStruct;

  EarthMap = LoadBitmap(lpCreateStruct->hInstance, "Earth");
  GetObject(EarthMap, sizeof(BITMAP), &BStruct);
```

```
    AWidth = BStruct.bmWidth;
    AHeight = BStruct.bmHeight;

    CreateWindow("edit", "4294967296",
                 WS_CHILD | WS_VISIBLE | WS_BORDER |
                 ES_LEFT | ES_AUTOHSCROLL,
                 (AWidth * 2) + 20, 10, 75, 30, hwnd, HMENU(ID_EDIT),
                 hInstance, NULL);

    CreateWindow("button", "Sqrt",
                 WS_CHILD | WS_VISIBLE | BS_DEFPUSHBUTTON,
                 (AWidth * 2) + 20, 75, 75, 30, hwnd, HMENU(ID_BUTTON),
                 hInstance, NULL);

    return TRUE;
}

/////////////////////////////////////////////////////////
// Handle WM_DESTROY
/////////////////////////////////////////////////////////
#pragma argsused
void Thread2_OnDestroy(HWND hwnd)
{
    DeleteObject(EarthMap);
    PostQuitMessage(0);
}

/////////////////////////////////////////////////////////
// The thread routine
/////////////////////////////////////////////////////////
unsigned long _stdcall ThreadFunc(LPVOID D)
{
    int i, j;
//  TDATA  Data = *(TDATA *)D;
    LPDATA Data = (LPDATA)D;
    COLORREF P;

    HDC DC = GetDC(MainWindow);
    for (j = 0; j < AHeight; j++)
      for (i = 0; i < AWidth; i++)
      {
        P = GetPixel(DC, i, j);
        SetPixel(DC, i + Data->xPos, j + Data->yPos, P);
      }

    ReleaseDC(MainWindow, DC);
    free(Data);

    return 0;
}

/////////////////////////////////////////////////////////
// The entry point for the threads
/////////////////////////////////////////////////////////
void RunThread(HWND hwnd)
{
```

21

continues

Listing 21.7. continued

```c
    LPDATA Data;
    DWORD ThreadID;


    Data = (LPDATA)malloc(sizeof(TDATA));
    Data->xPos = AWidth;
    Data->yPos = 0;
    HANDLE hThread1 = CreateThread(NULL, 0, ThreadFunc,
                        Data, 0, &ThreadID);

    Data = (LPDATA)malloc(sizeof(TDATA));
    Data->xPos = 0;
    Data->yPos = AHeight;
    HANDLE hThread2 = CreateThread(NULL, 0, ThreadFunc,
                        Data, 0, &ThreadID);

    Data = (LPDATA)malloc(sizeof(TDATA));
    Data->xPos = AWidth;
    Data->yPos = AHeight;
    HANDLE hThread3 = CreateThread(NULL, 0, ThreadFunc,
                        Data, 0, &ThreadID);


  if (!hThread1 || !hThread2 || !hThread3)
     MessageBox(hwnd, "No Thread", NULL, MB_OK);
}

//////////////////////////////////////////////////////////
// WM_COMMAND
//////////////////////////////////////////////////////////
#pragma argsused
void Thread2_OnCommand(HWND hwnd, int id, HWND hwndCtl, UINT codeNotify)
{
  char S[60];
  double R1, R2;

  switch(id)
  {
    case ID_GOTHREAD:
      RunThread(hwnd);
      break;

    case ID_BUTTON:
      GetWindowText(GetDlgItem(hwnd, ID_EDIT), S, 60);
      R1 = atof(S);
      R2 = sqrt(R1);
      sprintf(S, "%f", R2);
      SetWindowText(GetDlgItem(hwnd, ID_EDIT), S);
      break;

  }
}

/////////////////////////////////////////
// Draw Bitmap in menu
/////////////////////////////////////////
```

```
void DrawBitmap(HDC PaintDC, HBITMAP Bitmap, int XVal, int YVal)
{
  HDC MemDC;
  HBITMAP OldBitmap;

  MemDC = CreateCompatibleDC(PaintDC);
  OldBitmap = SelectBitmap(MemDC, Bitmap);
  BitBlt(PaintDC, XVal, YVal, AWidth,
         AHeight, MemDC, 0, 0, SRCCOPY);
  SelectBitmap(MemDC, OldBitmap);
  DeleteObject(MemDC);
}

//////////////////////////////////////////////////////
// WM_PAINT
//////////////////////////////////////////////////////
void Thread2_OnPaint(HWND hwnd)
{
  PAINTSTRUCT PaintStruct;

  HDC PaintDC = BeginPaint(hwnd, &PaintStruct);
  DrawBitmap(PaintDC, EarthMap, 0, 0);
  EndPaint(hwnd, &PaintStruct);
}
```

Listing 21.8. The header file for the Thread2 program.

```
//////////////////////////////////////////////////////
// THREAD2.H
// Copyright (c) 1995 Charlie Calvert.
//////////////////////////////////////////////////////

#define ID_GOTHREAD    100
#define ID_EDIT        101
#define ID_BUTTON      102
```

Listing 21.9. The resource file for the Thread2 program.

```
//////////////////////////////////////////////////////
// THREADS.RC
// Copyright (c) 1995 Charlie Calvert.
//////////////////////////////////////////////////////

#include "thread2.h"

ThreadsIcon ICON "thread2.ico"
Earth BITMAP "earth.bmp"

ThreadMenu MENU
BEGIN
  MENUITEM "Run Thread" ID_GOTHREAD
END
```

Listing 21.10. The module definition file for the Thread2 project.

```
; Thread2.Def

NAME          Thread2
DESCRIPTION   'Thread2 Window
```

Listing 21.11. The Borland makefile for the Thread2 program.

```
# Thread2.mak

# macros

!if !$d(BCROOT)
BCROOT  = $(MAKEDIR)\..
!endif

APPNAME = THREAD2
INCPATH = $(BCROOT)\WIN32;$(BCROOT);$(BCROOT)\INCLUDE
LIBPATH = $(BCROOT)\LIB

COMPILER= BCC32.EXE
BRC     = BRC32.EXE
FLAGS   = -W -v -w4 -I$(INCPATH) -L$(LIBPATH)

# link
$(APPNAME).exe: $(APPNAME).obj $(APPNAME).def $(APPNAME).res
  $(COMPILER) $(FLAGS) $(APPNAME).obj
  $(BRC) -I$(INCPATH) $(APPNAME).res

# compile
$(APPNAME).obj: $(APPNAME).cpp
  $(COMPILER) -c $(FLAGS) $(APPNAME).cpp

# resource
$(APPNAME).res: $(APPNAME).rc
  $(BRC) -R -I$(INCPATH) $(APPNAME).RC
```

Listing 21.12. The Microsoft makefile for the Thread2 program.

```
# Nmake macros for building Windows 32-Bit apps

APPNAME=THREAD2
TARGETOS=WIN95
APPVER=4.0
OBJS=$(APPNAME).obj

!include <win32.mak>

all: $(APPNAME).exe

# Update the resource if necessary
```

```
$(APPNAME).res: $(APPNAME).rc $(APPNAME).h
  $(rc) $(rcflags) $(rcvars) $(APPNAME).rc

# Update the object files if necessary

# compile
.cpp.obj:
  $(cc) $(cflags) $(cvars) $(cdebug) $<

# Update the executable file if necessary.

$(APPNAME).exe: $(OBJS) $(APPNAME).res
  $(link) $(linkdebug) $(guiflags) -out:\
  $(APPNAME).exe $(OBJS) $(APPNAME).res $(guilibs) comctl32.lib
```

When you first run this program, a bitmap appears in the upper-left corner of the screen. If you click on the program's sole menu item, three other copies of this bitmap will slowly be painted in, as shown in Figure 21.2.

Figure 21.2.

The Thread2 program after three copies of the original bitmap were made by three separate threads.

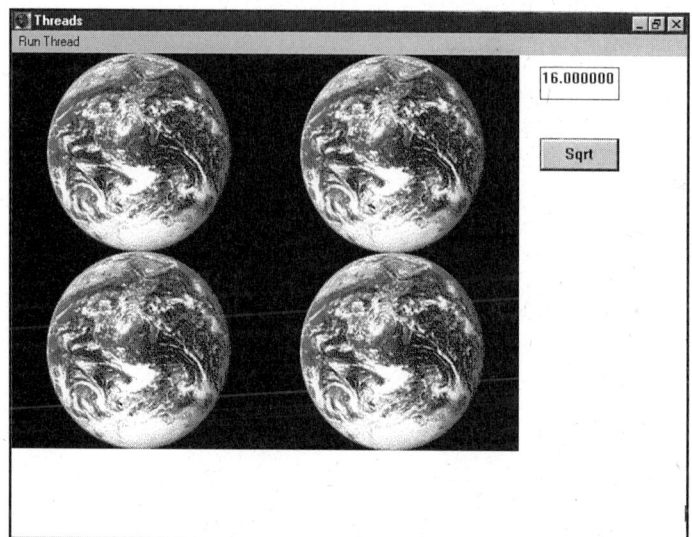

When the program starts, it loads a bitmap from its resource file via a call to LoadBitmap in the WM_CREATE handler. This original bitmap is shown in the upper-left corner of the screen. It is placed there by a call to BitBlt from the WM_PAINT handler:

```
MemDC = CreateCompatibleDC(PaintDC);
OldBitmap = SelectBitmap(MemDC, Bitmap);
BitBlt(PaintDC, XVal, YVal, AWidth,
       AHeight, MemDC, 0, 0, SRCCOPY);
SelectBitmap(MemDC, OldBitmap);
DeleteObject(MemDC);
```

This is the traditional method of painting a bitmap, and it is relatively fast.

887

I could have made additional copies of the bitmap by blitting it to the screen multiple times in different locations. However, in this case I didn't want to do things the fast way. Instead, I wanted things to go slowly so you can watch a thread at work. In other words, I didn't want the thread to be over before it had seemingly begun, which is what would have happened if I had called BitBlt from inside each of the three secondary threads in the program.

So instead of BitBlt, I had each of the secondary threads read the original bitmap, one pixel at a time, and then copy it, again one pixel at a time, to another portion of the screen:

```
for (j = 0; j < AHeight; j++)
  for (i = 0; i < AWidth; i++)
  {
    P = GetPixel(DC, i, j);
    SetPixel(DC, i + Data->xPos, j + Data->yPos, P);
  }
```

This time-consuming process has the side benefit of being fun to watch.

So now you understand the core of the Thread2 program. A bitmap is blitted to the screen. Three threads are started. Each of the threads laboriously copies the original bitmap to the screen, one pixel at a time.

You probably noticed that the Thread2 program also created a button and an edit control. If you enter a number in the edit control, you will find that a press on the program's button will give you its square root. In fact, the program starts out with an outrageously high number in the edit control. If you press the button several times, this number will have its square root taken several times, until you start approaching the number 1.

What's interesting about the Thread2 program is not that it knows how to get a square root. (It's a given that a computer can do that for you.) What's amazing is that you can be asking it to calculate square roots at the same time that all three threads are busy copying the original bitmap.

The point here is that there is no apparent degradation in the ways the button and edit control respond. The computer is obviously very busy copying pixels, yet it always lets you type in numbers and calculate square roots almost exactly as it would if you had the entire CPU to yourself. This is what preemptive multitasking is all about. When the time slices for the secondary threads are up, then the processor is given over to the other threads on the system. There is no delay or degradation of performance that is apparent to the user. The computer appears to be doing at least four things at the same time. In fact, for all practical purposes, it *is* doing four things at the same time!

The Thread2 program takes advantage of the lpParameter parameter of CreateThread, as shown by the Data parameter in the following code sample:

```
HANDLE hThread1 = CreateThread(NULL, 0, ThreadFunc,
                   Data, 0, &ThreadID);
```

The thread function is called `ThreadFunc`, and the parameter passed to it is of type `DATA`:

```
typedef struct tagData
{
  int xPos;
  int yPos;
}TDATA, *LPDATA;
```

The x and y fields of this structure are used to designate the point at which each thread should start its copy of the picture.

Now here's the interesting part. Suppose you declared `Data` to be a global variable. Then suppose you assigned this global variable a starting x and y location for a picture, and passed it to a thread. Then suppose you assigned this same variable a new value and started a new thread. When you assigned the global variable a new value, it automatically changed the value passed to the first thread. This means that the first thread would now start painting at the place where the second picture should be, and not in the place you originally asked it to paint. (One way around this type of problem is to use something called *thread local storage*, but that is beyond the scope of this book.)

As you saw in the last paragraph, simply declaring a global variable is not a solution to the problem presented by these three threads. A second possible idea would be to declare the `Data` variable as local to the `WM_COMMAND` handler. However, if you did this you would get into even deeper trouble. Specifically, you would assign the variable a value, then pass it to the thread. At that point the `WM_COMMAND` handler would go out of scope, and the value that the thread was trying to use would suddenly disappear from underneath it. So this alternative won't work either.

A third alternative, and the one used in this program, involves using pointers. First allocate memory for a variable, then pass it to the first thread. Next allocate memory for a second variable, and pass it to the second thread. Finally, you could allocate memory for a third variable, and pass it in to the third thread. Each variable would of course contain a different set of coordinates:

```
LPDATA Data;

Data = (LPDATA)malloc(sizeof(TDATA));
Data->xPos = AWidth;
Data->yPos = 0;
HANDLE hThread1 = CreateThread(NULL, 0, ThreadFunc,
                    Data, 0, &ThreadID);

Data = (LPDATA)malloc(sizeof(TDATA));
Data->xPos = 0;
Data->yPos = AHeight;
HANDLE hThread2 = CreateThread(NULL, 0, ThreadFunc,
                    Data, 0, &ThreadID);

Data = (LPDATA)malloc(sizeof(TDATA));
Data->xPos = AWidth;
Data->yPos = AHeight;
HANDLE hThread3 = CreateThread(NULL, 0, ThreadFunc,
                    Data, 0, &ThreadID);
```

 21

The preceeding code calls `malloc` three times, once for each copy of the TDATA structure. It assigns values to the structure's fields, and then passes them in to the appropriate thread.

Given the scenario outlined above, each thread is then responsible for deallocating the structure passed in to it:

```
HDC DC = GetDC(MainWindow);
for (j = 0; j < AHeight; j++)
  for (i = 0; i < AWidth; i++)
  {
    P = GetPixel(DC, i, j);
    SetPixel(DC, i + Data->xPos, j + Data->yPos, P);
  }

ReleaseDC(MainWindow, DC);
free(Data);
```

The relevant call in this case is the last one, where the `Data` variable is freed.

The process described here shows one way of handling data that is passed in to a thread. The issue here is that you have one thread but create three instances of it. This means you have to create three separate instances of the data you pass in to it.

As it turns out, the basic problem of how a thread handles data is one that has many implications. As a rule, the issues surrounding this subject are categorized under a topic called thread synchronization. The reason they are given this name will become clear in just a moment.

Critical Sections: Getting Threads to Work Together

The classic problem encountered when using threads involves a piece of global data that is being accessed by more than one thread. Variations on this theme involve a series of threads, all of which have to access the same file, the same DLL, the same communications resource, or any of a number of different objects.

To take a classic database-related problem, imagine what would happen if two threads were accessing the same database. Suppose one of them opened a record, and made some changes to the record's data. Then suppose a second program came along and made some changes to a different part of the same record and wrote them to the database. Now the first program writes its changes to the database, and in the process effectively undoes the changes made by the second program.

This scenario described in the last paragraph is a classic, and very familiar, problem as it would apply to thread synchronization. There are many different variations on this type of problem and many different solutions to them. The programs you are about to see use critical sections and mutexes to resolve this problem.

Critical sections solve the problem described above by effectively blocking the second thread from accessing the sensitive data when it is being used by the first thread. In particular, it stops the second thread from executing by ensuring that it doesn't get any time slices.

The mechanisms involved in this process are not hard to understand. Critical Sections are a simple solution to what sounds like a fairly complex problem. Go ahead and get the CritSect program (see Listings 21.13 through 21.18) up and running. After you read the description of how it works, you'll see that this whole issue is easy to resolve.

Listing 21.13. The main module of the CritSect program.

```
///////////////////////////////////////////////////////////
//   Program Name: CRITSECT.CPP
//   Programmer: Charlie Calvert
//   Description: Threads and Critical Sections, WIN32 only!
//   Date: 07/12/95
///////////////////////////////////////////////////////////

#define STRICT
#define WIN32_LEAN_AND_MEAN
#include <windows.h>
#include <windowsx.h>
#include <stdlib.h>
#include <stdio.h>
#include <math.h>
#include "CritSect.h"
#pragma warning (disable: 4068)


// -------------------------------------------------------
// Interface
// -------------------------------------------------------

LRESULT CALLBACK WndProc(HWND hwnd, UINT Message,
                         WPARAM wParam, LPARAM lParam);
BOOL Register(HINSTANCE hInst);
HWND Create(HINSTANCE hInst, int nCmdShow);

// Declarations for class Threads
#define CritSect_DefProc    DefWindowProc
BOOL CritSect_OnCreate(HWND hwnd, LPCREATESTRUCT lpCreateStruct);
void CritSect_OnDestroy(HWND hwnd);
void CritSect_OnCommand(HWND hwnd, int id,
                        HWND hwndCtl, UINT codeNotify);
void CritSect_OnPaint(HWND hwnd);

static char szAppName[] = "CritSect";
static HWND MainWindow;
static HINSTANCE hInstance;
static int GlobalData;
CRITICAL_SECTION Sect1;
static BOOL CritSects;
```

continues

21

891

Listing 21.13. continued

```c
// -----------------------------------------------------
// Initialization
// -----------------------------------------------------


///////////////////////////////////////////////////////////
// Program entry point
///////////////////////////////////////////////////////////
#pragma argsused
int WINAPI WinMain(HINSTANCE hInst, HINSTANCE hPrevInstance,
                   LPSTR lpszCmdParam, int nCmdShow)
{
  MSG   Msg;

  if (!hPrevInstance)
    if (!Register(hInst))
      return FALSE;

  MainWindow = Create(hInst, nCmdShow);
  if (!MainWindow)
    return FALSE;

  while (GetMessage(&Msg, NULL, 0, 0))
  {
    TranslateMessage(&Msg);
    DispatchMessage(&Msg);
  }

  return Msg.wParam;
}


///////////////////////////////////////////////////////////
// Register the window
///////////////////////////////////////////////////////////
BOOL Register(HINSTANCE hInst)
{
  WNDCLASS WndClass;

  WndClass.style          = CS_HREDRAW | CS_VREDRAW;
  WndClass.lpfnWndProc    = WndProc;
  WndClass.cbClsExtra     = 0;
  WndClass.cbWndExtra     = 0;
  WndClass.hInstance      = hInst;
  WndClass.hIcon          = LoadIcon(hInst, "ThreadsIcon");
  WndClass.hCursor        = LoadCursor(NULL, IDC_ARROW);
  WndClass.hbrBackground  = (HBRUSH)(COLOR_WINDOW+1);
  WndClass.lpszMenuName    = "ThreadMenu";
  WndClass.lpszClassName = szAppName;

  return (RegisterClass (&WndClass) != 0);
}


///////////////////////////////////////////////////////////
// Create the window
///////////////////////////////////////////////////////////
```

```
HWND Create(HINSTANCE hInst, int nCmdShow)
{

  hInstance = hInst;

  HWND hwnd = CreateWindow(szAppName, szAppName,
                    WS_OVERLAPPEDWINDOW,
                    CW_USEDEFAULT, CW_USEDEFAULT,
                    CW_USEDEFAULT, CW_USEDEFAULT,
                    NULL, NULL, hInst, NULL);

  if (hwnd == NULL)
    return hwnd;

  nCmdShow = SW_SHOWMAXIMIZED;

  ShowWindow(hwnd, nCmdShow);
  UpdateWindow(hwnd);

  return hwnd;
}

// ------------------------------------------------------
// WndProc and Implementation
// ------------------------------------------------------

//////////////////////////////////////////////////////////
// The Window Procedure
//////////////////////////////////////////////////////////
LRESULT CALLBACK WndProc(HWND hwnd, UINT Message, WPARAM wParam, LPARAM lParam)
{
  switch(Message)
  {
    HANDLE_MSG(hwnd, WM_CREATE, CritSect_OnCreate);
    HANDLE_MSG(hwnd, WM_DESTROY, CritSect_OnDestroy);
    HANDLE_MSG(hwnd, WM_COMMAND, CritSect_OnCommand);
    HANDLE_MSG(hwnd, WM_PAINT, CritSect_OnPaint);
    default: return CritSect_DefProc(hwnd, Message, wParam, lParam);
  }
}

#pragma argsused
BOOL CritSect_OnCreate(HWND hwnd, LPCREATESTRUCT lpCreateStruct)
{
  CreateWindow("listbox", NULL,
               WS_CHILD | WS_VISIBLE | WS_BORDER,
               12, 50, 200, 180, hwnd, HMENU(ID_LISTBOX1),
               hInstance, NULL);

  CreateWindow("listbox", NULL,
               WS_CHILD | WS_VISIBLE | WS_BORDER,
               215, 50, 200, 180, hwnd, HMENU(ID_LISTBOX2),
               hInstance, NULL);

  InitializeCriticalSection(&Sect1);
```

continues

21

Listing 21.13. continued

```c
    CritSects = FALSE;

    return TRUE;
}

/////////////////////////////////////////////////////////
// Handle WM_DESTROY
/////////////////////////////////////////////////////////
#pragma argsused
void CritSect_OnDestroy(HWND hwnd)
{
  DeleteCriticalSection(&Sect1);

  PostQuitMessage(0);
}

/////////////////////////////////////////////////////////
// The thread routine
/////////////////////////////////////////////////////////
unsigned long _stdcall ThreadFunc1(LPVOID)
{
  int i, j;
  char S[100];

  ListBox_ResetContent(GetDlgItem(MainWindow, ID_LISTBOX1));

  for (j = 0; j < 10; j++)
  {
    if (CritSects) EnterCriticalSection(&Sect1);
    Sleep(0);
    GlobalData += 3;
    i = GlobalData - 3;
    sprintf(S, "Information: %d", i);
    ListBox_AddString(GetDlgItem(MainWindow, ID_LISTBOX1), S);
    GlobalData -= 3;
    if (CritSects) LeaveCriticalSection(&Sect1);
  }
  return 0;
}

/////////////////////////////////////////////////////////
// The thread routine
/////////////////////////////////////////////////////////
unsigned long _stdcall ThreadFunc2(LPVOID)
{
  int i, j;
  char S[100];

  ListBox_ResetContent(GetDlgItem(MainWindow, ID_LISTBOX2));

  for (j = 0; j < 10; j++)
  {
    if (CritSects) EnterCriticalSection(&Sect1);
    Sleep(3);
```

```
    GlobalData -= 3;
    i = GlobalData + 3;
    sprintf(S, "Information: %d", i);
    ListBox_AddString(GetDlgItem(MainWindow, ID_LISTBOX2), S);
    GlobalData += 3;
    if (CritSects) LeaveCriticalSection(&Sect1);
  }

  return 0;
}

/////////////////////////////////////////////////////////
//
/////////////////////////////////////////////////////////
void RunThread(HWND hwnd)
{
  DWORD ThreadID1;
  DWORD ThreadID2;
  HANDLE ThreadHandles[2];

  GlobalData = 100;

  ThreadHandles[0] = CreateThread(NULL, 0, ThreadFunc1,
                         NULL, 0, &ThreadID1);
  ThreadHandles[1] = CreateThread(NULL, 0, ThreadFunc2,
                         NULL, 0, &ThreadID2);

  if (!ThreadHandles[0] || !ThreadHandles[1])
    MessageBox(hwnd, "No Thread", NULL, MB_OK);

}

/////////////////////////////////////////////////////////
// WM_COMMAND
/////////////////////////////////////////////////////////
#pragma argsused
void CritSect_OnCommand(HWND hwnd, int id, HWND hwndCtl, UINT codeNotify)
{
  switch(id)
  {
    case ID_GOTHREAD:
      RunThread(hwnd);
      break;

    case ID_CRITSECTS:
      CritSects = !CritSects;
      break;
  }
}

/////////////////////////////////////////////////////////
// WM_PAINT
/////////////////////////////////////////////////////////
void CritSect_OnPaint(HWND hwnd)
{
  PAINTSTRUCT PaintStruct;
```

21

continues

Listing 21.13. continued

```
    HDC PaintDC = BeginPaint(hwnd, &PaintStruct);
    TextOut(PaintDC, 1, 1, "Test", 4);
    EndPaint(hwnd, &PaintStruct);
}
```

Listing 21.14. The header file for the CritSect program.

```
//////////////////////////////////////////////////////
// CRITSECT.H
// Copyright (c) 1995 Charlie Calvert.
//////////////////////////////////////////////////////

#define ID_GOTHREAD     100
#define ID_LISTBOX1     101
#define ID_LISTBOX2     102
#define ID_CRITSECTS    103
```

Listing 21.15. The CritSect resource file.

```
//////////////////////////////////////////////////////
// CRITSECT.RC
// Copyright (c) 1995 Charlie Calvert.
//////////////////////////////////////////////////////

#include "CritSect.h"

ThreadsIcon ICON "CritSect.ico"

ThreadMenu MENU
BEGIN
  MENUITEM "Run Thread" ID_GOTHREAD
  MENUITEM "Toggle CritSections" ID_CRITSECTS
END
```

Listing 21.16. The module definition file for the CritSect program.

```
; CritSect.Def

NAME        CritSect
DESCRIPTION 'CritSect Window'
```

Listing 21.17. The Borland makefile for the CritSect program.

```
#------------------------------------------
# CRITSECT.MAK
#------------------------------------------

# macros
```

```
!if !$d(BCROOT)
BCROOT  = $(MAKEDIR)\..
!endif

APPNAME = CRITSECT
INCPATH = $(BCROOT)\WIN32;$(BCROOT);$(BCROOT)\INCLUDE
LIBPATH = $(BCROOT)\LIB

COMPILER= BCC32.EXE
BRC     = BRC32.EXE
FLAGS   = -W -v -w4 -I$(INCPATH) -L$(LIBPATH)

# link
$(APPNAME).exe: $(APPNAME).obj $(APPNAME).def $(APPNAME).res
  $(COMPILER) $(FLAGS) $(APPNAME).obj
  $(BRC) -I$(INCPATH) $(APPNAME).res

# compile
$(APPNAME).obj: $(APPNAME).cpp
  $(COMPILER) -c $(FLAGS) $(APPNAME).cpp

# resource
$(APPNAME).res: $(APPNAME).rc
  $(BRC) -R -I$(INCPATH) $(APPNAME).RC
```

Listing 21.18. The Microsoft makefile for the CritSect program.

```
#----------------------------------------
# CRITSEMS.MAK
#----------------------------------------

APPNAME=CRITSECT
TARGETOS=WIN95
APPVER=4.0
OBJS=$(APPNAME).obj

!include <win32.mak>

all: $(APPNAME).exe

# Update the resource if necessary

$(APPNAME).res: $(APPNAME).rc $(APPNAME).h
  $(rc) $(rcflags) $(rcvars) $(APPNAME).rc

# Update the object files if necessary

# compile
.cpp.obj:
  $(cc) $(cflags) $(cvars) $(cdebug) $<

# Update the executable file if necessary.

$(APPNAME).exe: $(OBJS) $(APPNAME).res
```

21

continues

Listing 21.18. continued

```
$(link) $(linkdebug) $(guiflags) -out:$(APPNAME).exe \
$(OBJS) $(APPNAME).res $(guilibs) comctl32.lib
```

The CritSect program has a single window with two list boxes and a menu. If you select the Run Thread menu item, then the list boxes are filled with numbers, as shown in Figure 21.3.

Figure 21.3.

The CritSect program as it appears when its threads are not synchronized.

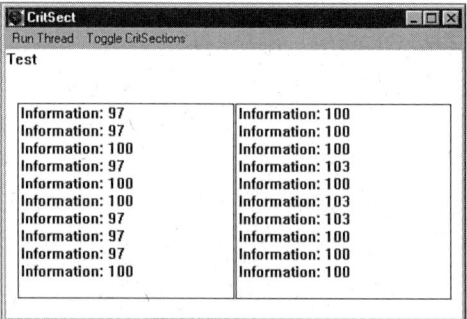

As you can see, the two columns of numbers are not identical. For reasons that will be explained in just a moment, this is the way the program appears when its threads are not synchronized. If you select the Toggle CritSections menu, and then choose Run Thread a second time, you will see that the two columns are now identical in appearance, as shown in Figure 21.4. For reasons that will be explained in just a moment, this is the way program looks when its threads are synchronized.

Figure 21.4.

The CritSect program as it appears when its threads are synchronized.

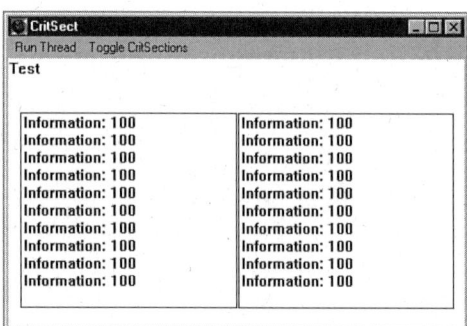

The CritSect program has a single global variable called GlobalData, which is of type int. Each of the threads in the program manipulates this global data and then restores it to its original value. For instance, the first thread adds 3 to this number, then sets a second variable called i to the new value GlobalData - 3, and then shows the number in the first list box:

```
GlobalData += 3;
i = GlobalData - 3;
sprintf(S, "Information: %d", i);
ListBox_AddString(GetDlgItem(MainWindow, ID_LISTBOX1), S);
GlobalData -= 3;
```

If you add 3 to a number, and then subtract 3 from that same number, then it should be restored to its original value. In fact, one would have to be living in a very non-euclidean, non-linear world if adding 3 to a number and then subtracting it out did not take you back to the original number. 100 plus 3 equals 103, and 103 minus 3 equals 100. That's all there is to it, and there's no point in talking about the matter any further—except for the fact that when the CritSect program tries to do this, sometimes it gets 100, and sometimes it gets 97. The other thread in the program, the one that writes to the second list box, does the exact opposite. It subtracts 3 from 100, and then adds 3 back to the new number. Obviously this process would have to yield 100 as a result each and every time. That's the way the universe is put together, and that's the way things have to be.

Only it doesn't turn out that way. Instead of getting the result you'd expect, there are times when you do not get 100, but 103. Clearly there is something very wrong here.

What's going on is not some metaphysical curiosity, but only the kind of complication that ensues when two threads are accessing and manipulating the same data. Specifically, one thread will add three to the global data, thereby setting it equal to 103. Then the second thread will access the data, and subtract 3 from it, thereby setting it equal to 100. When the second thread then adds back the 3 that it took away, the result is not 100, but 103. Or conversely, when the first thread subtracts 3 back out, it gets not 100, but 97. It's all a matter of timing.

As you can see, what's happening here is the same type of problem I described when I was talking about two threads simultaneously accessing the same record. The problem is one of synchronization. One thread needs to be able to tell the other that the global data is in a sensitive or critical state and that it shouldn't be touched!

Clearly, this is what critical sections are all about. They are a way of designating that a particular piece of data is currently off-limits, and can't be touched.

21

The implementation of the solution to this problem is extremely literal minded. What you do is mark the blocks of code that manipulate the data as "critical sections." Before the code in these sections can be executed, the computer has to check a global record that records whether or not some other thread is currently in the middle of a critical section. (Furthermore, it checks to see if this critical section is related to the first critical section. That is, you could have different sets of critical sections in the same program.)

Here's how it works. In the WM_CREATE handler, the CritSects program initializes a variable of type CRITICAL_SECTION:

```
CRITICAL_SECTION Sect1;
InitializeCriticalSection(&Sect1);
```

> **Note:** The operating system defines CRITICAL_SECTION to be of type RTL_CRITICAL_SECTION. It's not really important what CRITICAL_SECTION looks like, but you can in fact find the structure defining its type in WINNT.H:
>
> ```
> typedef struct _RTL_CRITICAL_SECTION {
>     PRTL_CRITICAL_SECTION_DEBUG DebugInfo;
>
>     //
>     //  The following three fields control entering and exiting the critical
>     //  section for the resource
>     //
>
>     LONG LockCount;
>     LONG RecursionCount;
>     HANDLE OwningThread;        // from the thread's ClientId->UniqueThread
>     HANDLE LockSemaphore;
>     DWORD Reserved;
> } RTL_CRITICAL_SECTION, *PRTL_CRITICAL_SECTION;
> ```

Here is how you mark a section of code as a critical section:

```
if (CritSects) EnterCriticalSection(&Sect1);
...
// First swatch of Critical code appears here ...
...
if (CritSects) LeaveCriticalSection(&Sect1);
```

The moment EnterCriticalSection is passed Sect1, it sets one or more of its fields to reflect the fact that a critical section is active. Now, if a second critical section is called by another thread, then EnterCriticalSection can see that a critical section is active, and so it will put the second thread to sleep:

```
if (CritSects) EnterCriticalSection(&Sect1);
...
// Second swatch of Critical code appears here ...
...
if (CritSects) LeaveCriticalSection(&Sect1);
```

While the second thread is asleep, it will not get any time slices. It's marked as inactive, and the CPU will waste no time trying to call it. This is an extremely efficient system, and very few clock cycles are wasted by a process that has been put to sleep.

When the first critical section exits, then `LeaveCriticalSection` is called. The variables in `Sect1` are then changed, and the second thread is free to execute. The second thread, will, of course, immediately enter its own critical section, thereby preventing the first thread from executing the offending code.

By using the process described above, you can mark the areas where a thread accesses the `GlobalData` variable as critical. Therefore, only one thread will be able to access the data at a time. This effectively solves the problem. When the critical sections are active, the program always produces the results you'd expect, as shown in Figure 21.4.

When you are through using a variable of type `CRITICAL_SECTION`, you should always delete it:

```
DeleteCriticalSection(&Sect1);
```

This is an important step because it frees up system resources. However, you want to be sure that you do not call `EnterCriticalSection` or `LeaveCriticalSection` with an invalid variable. To do so will cause an exception.

I've spent a fair amount of time on critical sections only because they are probably going to be a new concept to most readers. At any rate, they were to me when I first saw them in Windows 95. As a result, I've tried to explain them in some depth, even though the concepts behind them are quite simple. As I said before, the whole issue of synchronization at least *seems* like a fairly complex problem. However, the solution to the problem is very simple. Critical sections are easy to use.

Working with Mutexes

Mutexes are very similar to critical sections, except they will work not only in one process but they can also be used in multiple processes at the same time. In other words, they can help to synchronize not only two or more threads in a single application, but also two or more threads which may reside in separate applications.

Mutexes get their name from the words "mutually exclusive." Only one thread can own a mutex at a time. If a thread owns that mutex, then the mutex is said to be *signaled*. If no thread owns the mutex, then the mutex is said to be *non-signaled*. (This is confusing terminology for a very simple concept. If you want, you can just think of the mutex as being owned or free.)

To create a mutex, you call `CreateMutex`.

CreateMutex

This is the `CreateMutex` syntax:

```
HANDLE CreateMutex(
   // address of security attributes
   LPSECURITY_ATTRIBUTES  lpMutexAttributes,
   BOOL  bInitialOwner, // flag for initial ownership
   LPCTSTR  lpName      // address of mutex-object name
   );
```

The first parameter is a structure that defines the security attributes for the mutex. If you set this field to NULL, the mutex will be assigned a default set of security attributes. For more information on this field, see the online help.

The second parameter specifies whether or not the mutex is owned by the calling thread. An owned mutex is signaled, and an unowned mutex is non-signaled. You can use these parameters to specify whether the mutex should go immediately into the signaled state.

The final parameter is used to give the mutex a name. If one process creates a mutex and gives it a name, and then if a second process attempts to create or open a mutex of the same name, it will get the same mutex back in return. The two processes can then use the mutex to synchronize their actions. You can pass in NULL in this parameter if you like. This produces an unnamed mutex.

Here's an example:

```
hMutex = CreateMutex(NULL, FALSE, NULL);
```

In Listings 21.19 through 21.24 you will find the Mutex program. It is nearly identical to the CritSect program. The only difference is that the Mutex program uses mutexes rather than critical sections.

Listing 21.19. The main module for the Mutex program.

```
//////////////////////////////////////////////////////////////
//   Program Name: MUTEX1.CPP
//   Programmer: Charlie Calvert
//   Description: Threads windows program
//   Date: 07/12/95
//////////////////////////////////////////////////////////////

#define STRICT
#define WIN32_LEAN_AND_MEAN
#include <windows.h>
#include <windowsx.h>
#include <stdlib.h>
#include <stdio.h>
#include <math.h>
#include "Mutex.h"
#pragma warning (disable: 4068)
```

```
// --------------------------------------------------------
// Interface
// --------------------------------------------------------

LRESULT CALLBACK WndProc(HWND hwnd, UINT Message,
                         WPARAM wParam, LPARAM lParam);
BOOL Register(HINSTANCE hInst);
HWND Create(HINSTANCE hInst, int nCmdShow);

// Declarations for class Threads
#define Mutex1_DefProc     DefWindowProc
BOOL Mutex1_OnCreate(HWND hwnd, LPCREATESTRUCT lpCreateStruct);
void Mutex1_OnDestroy(HWND hwnd);
void Mutex1_OnCommand(HWND hwnd, int id,
                      HWND hwndCtl, UINT codeNotify);
void Mutex1_OnPaint(HWND hwnd);

static char szAppName[] = "Threads";
static HWND MainWindow;
static HINSTANCE hInstance;
static int GlobalData;
static HANDLE hMutex;
static BOOL CritSects;


// --------------------------------------------------------
// Initialization
// --------------------------------------------------------

//////////////////////////////////////////////////////////
// Program entry point
//////////////////////////////////////////////////////////
#pragma argsused
int WINAPI WinMain(HINSTANCE hInst, HINSTANCE hPrevInstance,
                   LPSTR lpszCmdParam, int nCmdShow)
{
  MSG  Msg;

  if (!hPrevInstance)
    if (!Register(hInst))
      return FALSE;

  MainWindow = Create(hInst, nCmdShow);
  if (!MainWindow)
    return FALSE;

  while (GetMessage(&Msg, NULL, 0, 0))
  {
    TranslateMessage(&Msg);
    DispatchMessage(&Msg);
  }

  return Msg.wParam;
}
```

continues

Listing 21.19. continued

```
//////////////////////////////////////////////////////
// Register the window
//////////////////////////////////////////////////////
BOOL Register(HINSTANCE hInst)
{
  WNDCLASS WndClass;

  WndClass.style         = CS_HREDRAW | CS_VREDRAW;
  WndClass.lpfnWndProc   = WndProc;
  WndClass.cbClsExtra    = 0;
  WndClass.cbWndExtra    = 0;
  WndClass.hInstance     = hInst;
  WndClass.hIcon         = LoadIcon(hInst, "ThreadsIcon");
  WndClass.hCursor       = LoadCursor(NULL, IDC_ARROW);
  WndClass.hbrBackground = (HBRUSH)(COLOR_WINDOW+1);
  WndClass.lpszMenuName    = "ThreadMenu";
  WndClass.lpszClassName = szAppName;

  return (RegisterClass (&WndClass) != 0);
}

//////////////////////////////////////////////////////
// Create the window
//////////////////////////////////////////////////////
HWND Create(HINSTANCE hInst, int nCmdShow)
{

  hInstance = hInst;

  HWND hwnd = CreateWindow(szAppName, szAppName,
                    WS_OVERLAPPEDWINDOW,
                    CW_USEDEFAULT, CW_USEDEFAULT,
                    CW_USEDEFAULT, CW_USEDEFAULT,
                    NULL, NULL, hInst, NULL);

  if (hwnd == NULL)
    return hwnd;

  nCmdShow = SW_SHOWMAXIMIZED;

  ShowWindow(hwnd, nCmdShow);
  UpdateWindow(hwnd);

  return hwnd;
}

// --------------------------------------------------------
// WndProc and Implementation
// --------------------------------------------------------

//////////////////////////////////////////////////////
// The Window Procedure
//////////////////////////////////////////////////////
LRESULT CALLBACK WndProc(HWND hwnd, UINT Message, WPARAM wParam, LPARAM lParam)
{
```

```
    switch(Message)
    {
      HANDLE_MSG(hwnd, WM_CREATE, Mutex1_OnCreate);
      HANDLE_MSG(hwnd, WM_DESTROY, Mutex1_OnDestroy);
      HANDLE_MSG(hwnd, WM_COMMAND, Mutex1_OnCommand);
      HANDLE_MSG(hwnd, WM_PAINT, Mutex1_OnPaint);
      default: return Mutex1_DefProc(hwnd, Message, wParam, lParam);
    }
}

#pragma argsused
BOOL Mutex1_OnCreate(HWND hwnd, LPCREATESTRUCT lpCreateStruct)
{
  CreateWindow("listbox", NULL,
               WS_CHILD | WS_VISIBLE | WS_BORDER,
               12, 50, 200, 180, hwnd, HMENU(ID_LISTBOX1),
               hInstance, NULL);

  CreateWindow("listbox", NULL,
               WS_CHILD | WS_VISIBLE | WS_BORDER,
               215, 50, 200, 180, hwnd, HMENU(ID_LISTBOX2),
               hInstance, NULL);

  hMutex = CreateMutex(NULL, FALSE, NULL);

  CritSects = FALSE;

  return TRUE;
}

/////////////////////////////////////////////////////////
// Handle WM_DESTROY
/////////////////////////////////////////////////////////
#pragma argsused
void Mutex1_OnDestroy(HWND hwnd)
{
  CloseHandle(hMutex);

  PostQuitMessage(0);
}

/////////////////////////////////////////////////////////
// The thread routine
/////////////////////////////////////////////////////////
unsigned long _stdcall ThreadFunc1(LPVOID)
{
  int i, j;
  char S[100];

  ListBox_ResetContent(GetDlgItem(MainWindow, ID_LISTBOX1));

  for (j = 0; j < 10; j++)
  {
    if (CritSects) WaitForSingleObject(hMutex, INFINITE);
    Sleep(0);
    GlobalData += 3;
```

continues

Listing 21.19. continued

```
    i = GlobalData - 3;
    sprintf(S, "Information: %d", i);
    ListBox_AddString(GetDlgItem(MainWindow, ID_LISTBOX1), S);
    GlobalData -= 3;
    if (CritSects) ReleaseMutex(hMutex);
  }
  return 0;
}


/////////////////////////////////////////////////////////
// The thread routine
/////////////////////////////////////////////////////////
unsigned long _stdcall ThreadFunc2(LPVOID)
{
  int i, j;
  char S[100];

  ListBox_ResetContent(GetDlgItem(MainWindow, ID_LISTBOX2));

  for (j = 0; j < 10; j++)
  {
    if (CritSects) WaitForSingleObject(hMutex, INFINITE);
    Sleep(3);
    GlobalData -= 3;
    i = GlobalData + 3;
    sprintf(S, "Information: %d", i);
    ListBox_AddString(GetDlgItem(MainWindow, ID_LISTBOX2), S);
    GlobalData += 3;
    if (CritSects) ReleaseMutex(hMutex);
  }

  return 0;
}


/////////////////////////////////////////////////////////
// Thread
/////////////////////////////////////////////////////////
void RunThread(HWND hwnd)
{
  DWORD ThreadID1;
  DWORD ThreadID2;
  HANDLE ThreadHandles[2];

  GlobalData = 100;

  ThreadHandles[0] = CreateThread(NULL, 0, ThreadFunc1,
                        NULL, 0, &ThreadID1);
  ThreadHandles[1] = CreateThread(NULL, 0, ThreadFunc2,
                        NULL, 0, &ThreadID2);

  if (!ThreadHandles[0] ¦¦ !ThreadHandles[1])
    MessageBox(hwnd, "No Thread", NULL, MB_OK);

}
```

```
/////////////////////////////////////////////////////
// WM_COMMAND
/////////////////////////////////////////////////////
#pragma argsused
void Mutex1_OnCommand(HWND hwnd, int id, HWND hwndCtl, UINT codeNotify)
{
  switch(id)
  {
    case ID_GOTHREAD:
      RunThread(hwnd);
      break;

    case ID_CRITSECTS:
      CritSects = !CritSects;
      break;
  }
}


/////////////////////////////////////////////////////
// WM_PAINT
/////////////////////////////////////////////////////
void Mutex1_OnPaint(HWND hwnd)
{

  PAINTSTRUCT PaintStruct;

  HDC PaintDC = BeginPaint(hwnd, &PaintStruct);
  TextOut(PaintDC, 1, 1, "Test", 4);
  EndPaint(hwnd, &PaintStruct);
}
```

Listing 21.20. The header file for the Mutex program.

```
#define ID_GOTHREAD      100
#define ID_LISTBOX1      101
#define ID_LISTBOX2      102
#define ID_CRITSECTS     103
```

Listing 21.21. The resource file for the Mutex program.

```
/////////////////////////////////////////////////////
// MUTEX.RC
// Copyright (c) 1995 Charlie Calvert.
/////////////////////////////////////////////////////

#include "mutex.h"

ThreadsIcon ICON "mutex.ico"

ThreadMenu MENU
BEGIN
  MENUITEM "Run Thread" ID_GOTHREAD
  MENUITEM "Toggle Mutex" ID_CRITSECTS
END
```

Listing 21.22. The module definition file for the Mutex program.

```
; Mutex.Def

NAME          Mutex
DESCRIPTION   'Mutex Window'
```

Listing 21.23. The Borland makefile for the Mutex program.

```
# Mutex.mak

# macros

!if !$d(BCROOT)
BCROOT  = $(MAKEDIR)
!endif

APPNAME = MUTEX
INCPATH = $(BCROOT)\WIN32;$(BCROOT);$(BCROOT)\INCLUDE
LIBPATH = $(BCROOT)\LIB

COMPILER= BCC32.EXE
BRC     = BRC32.EXE
FLAGS   = -W -v -w4 -I$(INCPATH) -L$(LIBPATH)

# link
$(APPNAME).exe: $(APPNAME).obj $(APPNAME).def $(APPNAME).res
  $(COMPILER) $(FLAGS) $(APPNAME).obj
  $(BRC) -I$(INCPATH) $(APPNAME).res

# compile
$(APPNAME).obj: $(APPNAME).cpp
  $(COMPILER) -c $(FLAGS) $(APPNAME).cpp

# resource
$(APPNAME).res: $(APPNAME).rc
  $(BRC) -R -I$(INCPATH) $(APPNAME).RC
```

Listing 21.24. The Microsoft makefile for the Mutex program.

```
#----------------------------------------
# MUTEX.MAK
#----------------------------------------

APPNAME=MUTEX
TARGETOS=WIN95
APPVER=4.0
OBJS=$(APPNAME).obj

!include <win32.mak>

all: $(APPNAME).exe
```

```
# Update the resource if necessary

$(APPNAME).res: $(APPNAME).rc $(APPNAME).h
  $(rc) $(rcflags) $(rcvars) $(APPNAME).rc

# Update the object files if necessary

# compile
.cpp.obj:
  $(cc) $(cflags) $(cvars) $(cdebug) $<

# Update the executable file if necessary.

$(APPNAME).exe: $(OBJS) $(APPNAME).res
  $(link) $(linkdebug) $(guiflags) -out:$(APPNAME).exe\
  $(OBJS) $(APPNAME).res $(guilibs) comctl32.lib
```

As I stated earlier, the Mutex and CritSect programs are nearly identical. In fact, from the user's point of view, their behavior is indistinguishable.

Mutex calls `CreateMutex` in the part of the `WM_CREATE` handler where CritSect called `InitializeCriticalSection`. Instead of calling `EnterCriticalSection`, the Mutex program calls `WaitForSingleObject`. Instead of calling `LeaveCriticalSection`, the Mutex program calls `ReleaseMutex`:

```
    if (CritSects) WaitForSingleObject(hMutex, INFINITE);
    Sleep(0);
    GlobalData += 3;
    i = GlobalData - 3;
    sprintf(S, "Information: %d", i);
    ListBox_AddString(GetDlgItem(MainWindow, ID_LISTBOX1), S);
    GlobalData -= 3;
    if (CritSects) ReleaseMutex(hMutex);
```

`WaitForSingleObject` takes two parameters. The first is the handle to a mutex, and the second is the number of milliseconds the function should wait before returning. `WaitForSingleObject` only returns if the mutex becomes signaled, or if the time specified has elapsed. That is, it will return when it owns the mutex, or when the time interval specified in the second parameter elapses. If you pass in the `INFINITE` flag in this parameter, then the routine will return only when the mutex is signaled, that is, only when the thread owns the mutex. (There is a function called `WaitForMultipleObjects`. The name says it all, though you can look up the particulars in the online help.)

When a thread is finished with a mutex it should call `ReleaseMutex`, which takes a handle to a mutex as a parameter. When you are completely done with a mutex and don't need it any more, you should close it:

```
CloseHandle(hMutex);
```

21

Note: Both the Mutex and the CritSect program call the Sleep function. Sleep suspends the execution of a thread for a specified number of milliseconds. A value of INIFINITE causes the thread to sleep for an indefinite period of time.

I call Sleep in the Mutex and CritSect program because I want to exaggerate the two thread's innate lack of synchronicity. In other words, I use this call to force the two threads out of sync so that it is almost certain that they will not both normally print out 100 each time. Because I use the function, the chance of coincidental synchronicity between the two threads is low. This means I have to use critical sections or mutexs to get them in line.

You've seen that even fairly sophisticated manipulation of threads is not difficult. Using the information presented in this book, you can add a great deal of powerful thread technology to your programs. However, I would be careful not to make your whole program nothing but a series of threads. If you get too carried away, you are likely to get into some very complicated design problems. Use threads when you need them and when you can see how they will fit into your program from beginning to end. Try to avoid creating programs that become a mangled tangle of threads. This could become a new form of spaghetti code called mangled tangled code. Avoid it.

That's all I'm going to say about mutexes, and indeed, this is the end of the section on threads. Clearly, this is a revolutionary subject that is going to change the way we write code. In particular, on multiprocessor systems, different threads can end up in effect executing on different processors, which is an enormously powerful concept. The information presented here is complete in itself, and it can serve as a reliable basis for using threads in an application. However, it is not the whole story, and you should pursue the matter further if you are interested in the subject and its possibilities.

Windows 95 Memory Management

It's time now to turn away from the subject of threads, and to look instead at memory management issues.

This book teaches you how to program Windows. Once you understand how to write Windows applications, the next step is to learn the theory behind Windows so that you can improve the scope and design of your applications. The remainder of this chapter has valuable information in it, but it is also a pointer towards those more advanced realms that would be a natural next step in your exploration of WIN32.

WIN32 memory management is as different from WIN16 memory management as a lion is from a house cat. They are two different beasts, and it is totally wrong to assume that knowledge of 16-bit protected mode memory applies to Windows 95 or Windows NT.

Let me say this again, just for the sake of clarity. The WIN32 memory management scheme is totally different from the memory management scheme in 16-bit Windows. It uses different calls, it has a different structure, it uses different ranges of memory, and it has several major new features that are different from anything you had in the old 16-bit world. For instance, in WIN32:

☐ Each 32-bit process has a 4GB flat memory-model address space. (A non-segmented architecture.) Contrast this with Windows 3.1, where all processes share a single address space. Remember that you can think of a process as an executable or DLL loaded into memory, as explained in the beginning of this chapter.

☐ Each program has only one type of heap, but it can have multiple copies of these heaps and can create them on the fly. This allows you to isolate one set of objects from another. For instance, you can place a linked list in its own heap, where it can endanger only itself, and not any other parts of your program. Contrast this with Windows 3.1 where each program has two heaps: the local heap and the global heap.

☐ Each WIN32 heap belongs to one and only one process. There is no such thing as a global, shared heap in a 32-bit Windows 95 process. Contrast this with Windows 3.1, where each application has a local heap and then shares a single global heap with every other application on the system. The single Windows 3.1 global heap contained memory allocations from not only the current task, but also from all the tasks on the system. It was a huge stew of different kinds of allocations from different kinds of programs, all mixed together in one potentially dangerous concoction. (Note also that the lack of WIN32 local heaps means that DLLs can no longer be used to share memory between processes—at least not by using the same techniques exploited in Windows 3.1.)

☐ There is a very powerful set of routines for manipulating virtual memory. Virtual memory is treated just like normal memory, but it can be kept either in RAM or in a "paging file" that is stored on disk. This kind of virtual memory is not discussed in this book. However, you can call the VirtualAlloc function to allocate memory in that paging file. You can then read and write to this memory. Reserving virtual memory and writing to it is called committing physical storage. Use VirtualAlloc to reserve or commit physical storage, and VirtualFree to decommit physical storage.

☐ WIN32 supports memory mapped files, which can help you share memory between applications and also access files on disk. It is used by the system to load executables and DLLs. As its name implies, memory mapped files allow you to map a file on disk into the address space of your program. It is then possible to manipulate the file using standard library routines such as memcpy and even strcpy.

21

The bulleted points make it clear that WIN32 has not one but three different ways of handling memory. The first is through virtual memory, the second is through memory mapped files, and the third is through heaps. Large arrays of data can usually be best stored in virtual memory. If you need to share memory between processes, or if you need to work with large streams of data (files), then you can use memory mapped files. If you want to create a linked list, or some similar structure that requires lots of small memory allocations, then you should probably use the heap.

As you can see, there is more to Windows 95 memory management than just the bare presence of a 4GB address space. Furthermore, you will see that your program doesn't just get loaded into the bottom of this 4GB space. Nor does it then proceed to use the remaining 3.9GB for its personal playground. Instead, in Windows 95, it usually gets loaded in at the 4MB mark, and it finds that at least half of the rest of the address space is reserved for the system. In Windows NT, programs usually get loaded in at the 64KB mark and can range up to within 64KB of the 2GB mark. The two 64KB blocks are used to trap errant pointers.

Windows 3.*x* had three possible modes of operation: real mode, standard mode, and enhanced mode. Windows 95 does not support either real mode or standard mode when running Windows applications. (It does support DOS real-mode programs running in a virtual DOS box.) This limitation should be seen as part and parcel of your vision of Windows 95 as a true 32-bit operating system. Real mode and standard mode are ways of handling 16-bit applications. By their definition they are tied to applications that have very limited address spaces. Windows 95 is about wide open address spaces.

You will be glad to hear that most of the key 16-bit Windows memory management routines port over to Windows 95 applications. However, they are available just for compatibility and are inefficient when compared to the new memory calls. In particular, the old `GlobalAlloc` call has been replaced with `HeapAlloc`, `VirtualAlloc`, and memory mapped files. For compatibility reasons `GlobalAlloc` still works. However, it is not as efficient as `HeapAlloc` or `VirtualAlloc`. Furthermore, there is no longer any distinction between `GlobalAlloc` and `LocalAlloc`. Both calls end up allocating memory from the process's primary heap. But I'm getting ahead of myself.

Note: People who argue that Windows 95 is just a thin veneer over a bunch of 16-bit DOS calls are ignoring some very important aspects of this new operating system. Yes, there are still portions of Windows 95 that are 16-bit. However, the memory model for Windows 95 is totally different from Windows 3.1. What computer programs do is manipulate memory. Every significant API or C library call made on a computer ends up manipulating memory in one way or another. You can't even make the call without manipulating memory. If the memory model has changed radically, then everything has changed radically.

It's interesting to study the similarities between Windows 95 and Windows 3.1, but it's a gross misunderstanding of the facts to claim that they are just two versions of the same operating system. I can be as cynical about Windows 95 as the next guy. But look again at the list of new WIN32 memory features just shown. Say what you will, Windows is in the big league now. Windows 95 is a real operating system, and it's a very powerful one at that. The mere presence of some 16-bit code does not cancel out the extraordinary developments in multithreading, multi-tasking, and memory management.

This section has given you a very general overview of some of the key points about WIN32 memory management. Further information is available in advanced books on Windows programming or on the Microsoft Developers CD.

Why You Don't Need to Understand This Stuff

Memory management is an extremely important topic. However, Windows 95 has such a huge address space that it's often not important for intermediate-level Windows programmers to master the subject. In 16-bit Windows, everyone had to know at least something about memory management. If you didn't understand the DGROUP and 64KB segments, you were going to get in trouble.

Why is Windows 95 different? Part of the reason is that each process has its own 4GB address space. A gigabyte is one billion bytes, or a thousand megabytes. A megabyte is a million bytes. DOS programs used to run in 1MB of memory. In other words, you can fit 4,000 DOS machines inside one 4GB address space. Back in the 1980s, you could have powered several hundred medium-sized companies with 4,000 DOS machines.

A program's data and code are both loaded into a 2GB virtual address space. This means you are not going to run out of code and data space in your programs. The whole subject of code segments and data segments is essentially moot for intermediate-level Windows programmers. You just don't have to worry about it. (OK, you have to worry about whether the machines you are running on have enough physical RAM to give your programs reasonable performance. However, there is usually no practical reason to be concerned that you will exceed the limits of the operating system. Yes, it's possible to exceed this limit, but not likely.)

Furthermore, each process, and each thread in that process, by default gets its own 1MB stack. (It's exactly 1MB in Windows NT, and 1MB plus 128KB in Windows 95.) In the past, you always had to be thinking about the size of the stack in your application. Now by default you

get a stack that is one megabyte in size. Most of the time a 1MB stack is going to give you all the memory you need, and then some. Managing stacks in Windows 3.1 could be a subtle and difficult process that nearly every programmer needed to consider to some degree. Now most programmers can simply ignore the subject, and the system will take care of it automatically.

> **Note:** The only reason there is a 1MB limit on the size of the stack is to catch runaway recursive processes before they get totally out of control.
>
> Recursive functions call themselves. Every time they call themselves, information is pushed on the stack. A recursive process should end automatically after it reaches some predefined goal. However, sometimes something goes wrong and the recursive process keeps calling itself over and over again, pushing more data on the stack with each call. Because the stack has a 1MB limit, the operating system has a chance to automatically stop this process before it consumes all the memory on the system.

The key point to understand is that most Windows 95 programmers don't have to worry a great deal about memory management under most circumstances. Advanced programmers need to understand this subject, and indeed, an in-depth understanding of this subject is what defines advanced Windows programmers. If you want to be really good, then you should know this stuff cold.

So yes, it's always good to know about memory. However, if you don't, you are not nearly as likely to get bit by Windows 95 or Windows NT as you were by Windows 3.1. When compared to Windows 3.1, WIN32 gives you more power, more freedom, with less work and less anxiety.

Allocating Memory, Creating Heaps

The next example program, called HeapMem, shows how to allocate memory from a program's default heap. It also shows how to create new heaps when you need them.

Here's a brief overview of the key points covered in this section: You can get the current WIN32 heap by calling GetProcessHeap. You can create a new heap by calling CreateHeap and can destroy it by calling HeapDestroy. You can manipulate memory in a heap by calling HeapAlloc, HeapReAlloc, HeapSize, and HeapFree. (HeapFree deallocates a single memory allocation, DestroyHeap destroys the entire heap. Don't get them confused.)

As I explained earlier, heaps don't necessarily play the same role in Windows 95 as they did in Windows 3.1 or DOS. For one thing, you are not nearly as likely to run out of room in your program's address space for data or code. If there is plenty of RAM on your machine, then there

is plenty of room for even very large amounts of code and data in your program's address space. Even if there is a shortage of RAM, Windows can usually swap memory to disk to make room for the core parts of your program. Your code will run much slower in that case, but it will still run.

If you do need additional room, there is always the virtual memory in your paging file, or you could use memory mapped files, as described below. However, if you want to make a series of relatively small allocations, then your program's heap would be a good place to make them.

Your program can have more than one heap. As mentioned above, you can create and destroy new heaps by calling CreateHeap and DestroyHeap. There are two primary reasons to create a heap:

☐ You might want to isolate a sensitive memory operation from the rest of the program so that it cannot corrupt the core routines in your code. For example, you could put a linked list in its own heap.

☐ You might want to optimize routines by placing allocations of a similar size in their own unique heap. This helps prevent heap fragmentation, and increases the access time when you need to get at the memory.

Despite the seemingly esoteric nature of this subject, the actual calls to HeapAlloc, HeapFree, CreateHeap, and HeapDestroy are simple enough to master. In Listings 21.25 through 21.30 you will find a program that exercises each of these calls.

Listing 21.25. The main module for the HeapMem program.

```
/////////////////////////////////////////////////////////
//   Program Name: HeapMem.cpp
//   Programmer: Charlie Calvert
//   Description: HeapMem windows program
//   Date: 07/17/95
/////////////////////////////////////////////////////////

#define STRICT
#define WIN32_LEAN_AND_MEAN
#include <windows.h>
#include <windowsx.h>
#include <stdio.h>
#include "heapmem.h"
#pragma warning (disable: 4068)
// ----------------------------------------------------
// Interface
// ----------------------------------------------------

LRESULT CALLBACK WndProc(HWND hwnd, UINT Message,
                         WPARAM wParam, LPARAM lParam);
BOOL Register(HINSTANCE hInst);
HWND Create(HINSTANCE hInst, int nCmdShow);
```

continues

Listing 21.25. continued

```c
// Declarations for class HeapMem
#define HeapMem_DefProc      DefWindowProc
BOOL HeapMem_OnCreate(HWND hwnd, LPCREATESTRUCT lpCreateStruct);
void HeapMem_OnDestroy(HWND hwnd);
void HeapMem_OnCommand(HWND hwnd, int id, HWND hwndCtl, UINT codeNotify);
void HeapMem_OnSize(HWND hwnd, UINT state, int cx, int cy);

static char szAppName[] = "HeapMem";
static HWND MainWindow, hEdit;
static HINSTANCE hInstance;


// --------------------------------------------------------
// Initialization
// --------------------------------------------------------

/////////////////////////////////////////////////////////
// Program entry point
/////////////////////////////////////////////////////////
#pragma argsused
int WINAPI WinMain(HINSTANCE hInst, HINSTANCE hPrevInstance,
                   LPSTR lpszCmdParam, int nCmdShow)
{
  MSG  Msg;

  if (!hPrevInstance)
    if (!Register(hInst))
      return FALSE;

  MainWindow = Create(hInst, nCmdShow);
  if (!MainWindow)
    return FALSE;

  while (GetMessage(&Msg, NULL, 0, 0))
  {
    TranslateMessage(&Msg);
    DispatchMessage(&Msg);
  }

  return Msg.wParam;
}

/////////////////////////////////////////////////////////
// Register the window
/////////////////////////////////////////////////////////
BOOL Register(HINSTANCE hInst)
{
  WNDCLASS WndClass;

  WndClass.style          = CS_HREDRAW | CS_VREDRAW;
  WndClass.lpfnWndProc    = WndProc;
  WndClass.cbClsExtra     = 0;
  WndClass.cbWndExtra     = 0;
  WndClass.hInstance      = hInst;
```

```
    WndClass.hIcon        = LoadIcon(NULL, IDI_APPLICATION);
    WndClass.hCursor      = LoadCursor(NULL, IDC_ARROW);
    WndClass.hbrBackground = (HBRUSH)(COLOR_WINDOW+1);
    WndClass.lpszMenuName   = "HeapMemMenu";
    WndClass.lpszClassName = szAppName;

    return (RegisterClass (&WndClass) != 0);
}

//////////////////////////////////////////////////////
// Create the window
//////////////////////////////////////////////////////
HWND Create(HINSTANCE hInst, int nCmdShow)
{

    hInstance = hInst;

    HWND hwnd = CreateWindow(szAppName, szAppName,
                    WS_OVERLAPPEDWINDOW,
                    CW_USEDEFAULT, CW_USEDEFAULT,
                    CW_USEDEFAULT, CW_USEDEFAULT,
                    NULL, NULL, hInst, NULL);

    if (hwnd == NULL)
      return hwnd;

    ShowWindow(hwnd, nCmdShow);
    UpdateWindow(hwnd);

    return hwnd;
}

// ------------------------------------------------------
// WndProc and Implementation
// ------------------------------------------------------

//////////////////////////////////////////////////////
// The Window Procedure
//////////////////////////////////////////////////////
LRESULT CALLBACK WndProc(HWND hwnd, UINT Message,
                         WPARAM wParam, LPARAM lParam)
{
    switch(Message)
    {
      HANDLE_MSG(hwnd, WM_DESTROY, HeapMem_OnDestroy);
      HANDLE_MSG(hwnd, WM_COMMAND, HeapMem_OnCommand);
      default: return HeapMem_DefProc(hwnd, Message, wParam, lParam);
    }
}

//////////////////////////////////////////////////////
// Handle WM_DESTROY
//////////////////////////////////////////////////////
#pragma argsused
void HeapMem_OnDestroy(HWND hwnd)
{
```

21

continues

Listing 21.25. continued

```
      PostQuitMessage(0);
  }

  void DoAlloc(HWND hwnd, HANDLE AHeap, LPSTR S)
  {
    DWORD ASize;
    HDC DC;
    char AllocStr[30];

    LPSTR MemStr = (LPSTR)HeapAlloc(AHeap, HEAP_ZERO_MEMORY, MAXSIZE);

    strcpy(MemStr, S);
    ASize = HeapSize(AHeap, 0, MemStr);
    sprintf(AllocStr, "Alloc Size: %d", ASize);

    DC = GetDC(hwnd);
    TextOut(DC, 10, 10, MemStr, strlen(MemStr));
    TextOut(DC, 10, 40, AllocStr, strlen(AllocStr));
    ReleaseDC(hwnd, DC);

    HeapFree(AHeap, 0, S);
  }

  void DoNewHeap(HWND hwnd)
  {
    HANDLE NewHeap;

    NewHeap = HeapCreate(0, 0x4000, 0);

    DoAlloc(hwnd, NewHeap, "Using the new heap!");

    HeapDestroy(NewHeap);
  }

  ///////////////////////////////////////////////////////
  // WM_COMMAND
  ///////////////////////////////////////////////////////
  #pragma argsused
  void HeapMem_OnCommand(HWND hwnd, int id,
                         HWND hwndCtl, UINT codeNotify)
  {
    switch (id)
    {
      case ID_ALLOC:
        DoAlloc(hwnd, GetProcessHeap(), "Using process heap.");
        break;

      case ID_NEWHEAP:
        DoNewHeap(hwnd);
        break;
    }
  }
```

Listing 21.26. The header file for the HeapMem program.

```
//////////////////////////////////////////////////
// HEAPMEM.H
// Copyright (c) 1995 Charlie Calvert.
//////////////////////////////////////////////////

#define MAXSIZE 500

#define ID_ALLOC 100
#define ID_NEWHEAP 101
```

Listing 21.27. The resource file for the HeapMem program.

```
//////////////////////////////////////////////////
// HEAPMEM.RC
// Copyright (c) 1995 Charlie Calvert.
//////////////////////////////////////////////////

#include "heapmem.h"

HeapMemMenu MENU
BEGIN
  POPUP "Options"
  BEGIN
    MENUITEM "Allocate Memory" ID_ALLOC
    MENUITEM "Create New Heap" ID_NEWHEAP
  END
END
```

Listing 21.28. The module definition file for the HeapMem program.

```
; HeapMem.Def

NAME          HeapMem
DESCRIPTION   'HeapMem Window'
```

Listing 21.29. The Borland makefile for the HeapMem program.

```
# HeapMem.mak

# macros

!if !$d(BCROOT)
BCROOT  = $(MAKEDIR)\..
!endif

APPNAME = HeapMem
INCPATH = $(BCROOT)\WIN32;$(BCROOT);$(BCROOT)\INCLUDE
LIBPATH = $(BCROOT)\LIB
```

21

continues

Listing 21.29. continued

```
!if $d(WIN16)
COMPILER= BCC.EXE
BRC      = BRC.EXE
FLAGS    = -W -ml -v -w4 -I$(INCPATH) -L$(LIBPATH)
!else
COMPILER= BCC32.EXE
BRC      = BRC32.EXE
FLAGS    = -W -v -w4 -I$(INCPATH) -L$(LIBPATH)
!endif

# link
$(APPNAME).exe: $(APPNAME).obj $(APPNAME).def $(APPNAME).res
   $(COMPILER) $(FLAGS) $(APPNAME).obj
   $(BRC) -I$(INCPATH) $(APPNAME).res

# compile
$(APPNAME).obj: $(APPNAME).cpp
   $(COMPILER) -c $(FLAGS) $(APPNAME).cpp

# resource
$(APPNAME).res: $(APPNAME).rc
   $(BRC) -R -I$(INCPATH) $(APPNAME).RC
```

Listing 21.30. The Microsoft makefile for the HeapMem program.

```
#----------------------------------------
# HEAPMEM.MAK
#----------------------------------------

APPNAME=HEAPMEM
TARGETOS=WIN95
APPVER=4.0
OBJS=$(APPNAME).obj

!include <win32.mak>

all: $(APPNAME).exe

# Update the resource if necessary

$(APPNAME).res: $(APPNAME).rc $(APPNAME).h
   $(rc) $(rcflags) $(rcvars) $(APPNAME).rc

# Update the object files if necessary

# compile
.cpp.obj:
   $(cc) $(cflags) $(cvars) $(cdebug) $<

# Update the executable file if necessary.

$(APPNAME).exe: $(OBJS) $(APPNAME).res
   $(link) $(linkdebug) $(guiflags) -out:$(APPNAME).exe\
   $(OBJS) $(APPNAME).res $(guilibs) comctl32.lib
```

This program allows you to print two simple strings to the screen, as shown in Figure 21.5. When you select one of the program's menu options, the memory for the strings is allocated from the default process heap. When you choose the other option, the memory for the strings is allocated from a new, custom heap.

Figure 21.5.

The HeapMem program shows how to allocate memory using native WIN32 routines.

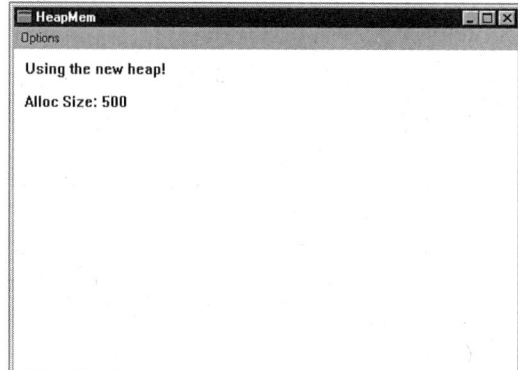

The following code shows how to allocate memory for a string, how to check the size of the allocation, and how to free the memory:

```
void DoAlloc(HWND hwnd, HANDLE AHeap, LPSTR S)
{
  DWORD ASize;
  HDC DC;
  char AllocStr[30];

  LPSTR MemStr = (LPSTR)HeapAlloc(AHeap, HEAP_ZERO_MEMORY, MAXSIZE);

  strcpy(MemStr, S);
  ASize = HeapSize(AHeap, 0, MemStr);
  sprintf(AllocStr, "Alloc Size: %d", ASize);

  DC = GetDC(hwnd);
  TextOut(DC, 10, 10, MemStr, strlen(MemStr));
  TextOut(DC, 10, 40, AllocStr, strlen(AllocStr));
  ReleaseDC(hwnd, DC);

  HeapFree(AHeap, 0, S);
}
```

This routine calls HeapAlloc to allocate memory, HeapSize to check the size of the allocation, and HeapFree to free the memory.

HeapAlloc

```
LPVOID HeapAlloc(
    HANDLE  hHeap,      // The handle of the heap you want to use.
    DWORD   dwFlags,    // Flags such as HEAP_ZERO_MEMORY
    DWORD   dwBytes     // The amount of memory you need
    );
```

Use `HeapAlloc` to allocate memory, just as you use `malloc` from the C library, or `GlobalAlloc` from Windows 3.1. The memory allocated may be larger than the amount you request, in which case you can use the entire amount returned. Use the `HeapSize` function to find how much memory was actually allocated. You do not need to lock down this memory as you did in Windows 3.1. However, this memory is non-moveable.

The first parameter is the handle to the heap you want to use. To use the default heap for your program, just call `GetProcessHeap`. If you want to create a new heap, call `CreateHeap`, as shown below.

There are three flags you can pass to this routine in its second parameter. One is `HEAP_GENERATE_EXCEPTION`, which means that on failure the operating system will generate an error rather than returning `NULL`. The `HEAP_ZERO_MEMORY` flag causes the system to fill the block of memory with zeros. You can also pass in `HEAP_NO_SERIALIZE`, but this latter option is beyond the scope of this book.

The last parameter is the size of the block of memory you want to create. In principle, this number can be as large as you want. However, if you want to request large chunks of memory, then you should consider calling `VirtualAlloc` rather than `HeapAlloc`. Furthermore, requests for large chunks of memory are usually satisfied by the system calling `VirtualAlloc` automatically, even though you made the request with `HeapAlloc`. The only concrete limitation on this number occurs if you explicitly called `CreateHeap`, and you explicitly made the heap you created non-growable. In that case, this number should not exceed 0×7FFF8, which is 524,280.

Here's an example:

```
LPVOID Buffer = HeapAlloc(GetProcessHeap(),
                 HEAP_ZERO_MEMORY, 4096);
```

The `HeapSize` routine returns the size of the current heap allocation. In other words, if you allocate 500 bytes with `HeapAlloc`, then call `HeapSize`, the value returned will be `500`. Remember that Windows sometimes returns more memory than you requested, in which case `HeapSize` will return a value larger than the amount you requested. It's the value returned by `HeapSize` that is correct, not the value you requested.

Here is the declaration:

```
DWORD HeapSize(
    HANDLE  hHeap,      // handle to the heap
    DWORD dwFlags,      // heap size control flags
    LPCVOID lpMem       // pointer to memory to return size for
    );
```

This is a very simple function to use. Just pass in a heap in the first parameter, `0` in the second parameter, and the pointer you want to know about in the third parameter. (The second parameter can be set to `HEAP_NO_SERIALIZE`, but that's an advanced topic not covered in this book.)

Syntax

HeapFree

Here's the declaration for the `HeapFree` function:

```
BOOL HeapFree(
    HANDLE  hHeap,   // Value returned by CreateHeap
                     // or GetProcessHeap
    DWORD  dwFlags, // usually zero, can be HEAP_NO_SERIALIZE
    LPVOID  lpMem    // pointer to the memory to free
   );
```

This function frees memory allocated with `HeapAlloc`. The first parameter is the handle to the heap. The second is usually set to `0`. The third parameter is a pointer to the memory you want to free.

The function returns `TRUE` when successful.

Here's an example:

```
HeapFree(AHeap, 0, S);
```

The following code fragment shows how to create a new heap:

```
HANDLE NewHeap;

NewHeap = HeapCreate(0, 0x4000, 0);
DoAlloc(hwnd, NewHeap, "Using the new heap!");
HeapDestroy(NewHeap);
```

The declaration for `HeapCreate` looks like this:

```
HANDLE HeapCreate(
    DWORD  flOptions,          // heap allocation flag
    DWORD  dwInitialSize,     // initial heap size
    DWORD  dwMaximumSize)      // maximum heap size
```

You can pass in `0` in the first parameter, or one of the following flags: `HEAP_GENERATE_EXCEPTIONS`, `HEAP_NO_SERIALIZE`. Use `HEAP_GENERATE_EXCEPTIONS` if you want the operating system to report errors, rather than simply returning `NULL`.

The second parameter is the amount of memory you want to allocate for the heap. If you pass in `0` in the third parameter, then the heap will grow automatically if you request more than `dwInitialSize` bytes of memory via calls to `HeapAlloc`. If you do not pass in `0` in `dwMaximumSize`, then the heap will not grow, and requests for memory beyond the limits of the heap will fail.

When you want to destroy a heap, call DestroyHeap, and pass in the handle to the heap as the sole parameter:

```
DestroyHeap(AHeap);
```

This section of the chapter telegraphed to you the information you need to manipulate native WIN32 heaps. You now know how to allocate memory, how to free it, and how to create and destroy your own heaps.

Remember that this is not the only way to manipulate memory. Windows 95 and Windows NT also provide memory mapped files and virtual memory. If you want to allocate very large chunks of memory, then see the description of the VirtualAlloc function in the online help. To get started with memory mapped files, see the next (and last) section of this lengthy chapter.

Mapping a File into Memory

Memory-mapped files are one of the more interesting, and powerful, features of the WIN32 landscape. They allow you to map the memory on your hard disk into the address space of your program. This means you can manipulate the bytes in a file as if they resided in memory. Instead of using one set of routines to manipulate files, and another set of routines for manipulating memory, you can now use the same set of routines in both places. Furthermore, two processes can map the same file simultaneously, thus giving them a relatively simple way to share memory.

Use CreateFile to create or open a memory-mapped file. Use CloseHandle to close a memory-mapped file. Other important APIs include MapViewOfFile, UnmapViewOfFile, and CreateFileMapping. You will also need to use the CreateFile function, explained in "Week 1 in Review."

An example of memory-mapped files is shown in Listings 21.31 through 21.36. I have to confess that this example does not represent a very complete examination of this subject. Instead, my goal is to introduce you to the topic so you will understand what memory-mapped files are all about. After all, seeing is believing, and in this case I think most programmers will be intrigued by what they see. If you are interested in exploring this subject in depth, you should get a book on advanced Windows programming, or else study the online help.

Listing 21.31. The main module for the MemFile program.

```
///////////////////////////////////////////////////////////
//   Program Name: MemFile.cpp
//   Programmer: Charlie Calvert
//   Description: MemFile windows program
//   Date: 07/17/95
///////////////////////////////////////////////////////////

#define STRICT
#define WIN32_LEAN_AND_MEAN
```

```
#include <windows.h>
#include <windowsx.h>
#include <stdio.h>
#include <stdlib.h>
#include <commdlg.h>
#include "memfile.h"
#pragma warning (disable: 4068)


// --------------------------------------------------------
// Interface
// --------------------------------------------------------

#define STRSIZE 350

LRESULT CALLBACK WndProc(HWND hwnd, UINT Message,
                           WPARAM wParam, LPARAM lParam);
BOOL Register(HINSTANCE hInst);
HWND Create(HINSTANCE hInst, int nCmdShow);

// Declarations for class MemFile
#define MemFile_DefProc      DefWindowProc
void MemFile_OnDestroy(HWND hwnd);
void MemFile_OnCommand(HWND hwnd, int id,
                       HWND hwndCtl, UINT codeNotify);
BOOL MemFile_OnCreate(HWND hwnd, LPCREATESTRUCT lpCreateStruct);
void MemFile_OnSize(HWND hwnd, UINT state, int cx, int cy);

static char szAppName[] = "MemFile";
static HWND MainWindow;
static HINSTANCE hInstance;
static HWND hEdit;
static HANDLE hMapping;
static LPVOID Data;

// --------------------------------------------------------
// Initialization
// --------------------------------------------------------


/////////////////////////////////////////////////////////
// Program entry point
/////////////////////////////////////////////////////////
#pragma argsused
int WINAPI WinMain(HINSTANCE hInst, HINSTANCE hPrevInstance,
                   LPSTR lpszCmdParam, int nCmdShow)
{
  MSG  Msg;

  if (!hPrevInstance)
    if (!Register(hInst))
      return FALSE;

  MainWindow = Create(hInst, nCmdShow);
  if (!MainWindow)
    return FALSE;
```

continues

Listing 21.31. continued

```
    while (GetMessage(&Msg, NULL, 0, 0))
    {
      TranslateMessage(&Msg);
      DispatchMessage(&Msg);
    }

    return Msg.wParam;
}

////////////////////////////////////////////////////////
// Register the window
////////////////////////////////////////////////////////
BOOL Register(HINSTANCE hInst)
{
  WNDCLASS WndClass;

  WndClass.style         = CS_HREDRAW | CS_VREDRAW;
  WndClass.lpfnWndProc   = WndProc;
  WndClass.cbClsExtra    = 0;
  WndClass.cbWndExtra    = 0;
  WndClass.hInstance     = hInst;
  WndClass.hIcon         = LoadIcon(NULL, IDI_APPLICATION);
  WndClass.hCursor       = LoadCursor(NULL, IDC_ARROW);
  WndClass.hbrBackground = (HBRUSH)(COLOR_WINDOW+1);
  WndClass.lpszMenuName    = "MemFileMenu";
  WndClass.lpszClassName = szAppName;

  return (RegisterClass (&WndClass) != 0);
}

////////////////////////////////////////////////////////
// Create the window
////////////////////////////////////////////////////////
HWND Create(HINSTANCE hInst, int nCmdShow)
{

  hInstance = hInst;

  HWND hwnd = CreateWindow(szAppName, szAppName,
                 WS_OVERLAPPEDWINDOW,
                 CW_USEDEFAULT, CW_USEDEFAULT,
                 CW_USEDEFAULT, CW_USEDEFAULT,
                 NULL, NULL, hInst, NULL);

  if (hwnd == NULL)
    return hwnd;

  ShowWindow(hwnd, nCmdShow);
  UpdateWindow(hwnd);

  return hwnd;
}

// ------------------------------------------------------
// WndProc and Implementation
// ------------------------------------------------------
```

```
//////////////////////////////////////////////////////
// The Window Procedure
//////////////////////////////////////////////////////
LRESULT CALLBACK WndProc(HWND hwnd, UINT Message,
                         WPARAM wParam, LPARAM lParam)
{
  switch(Message)
  {
    HANDLE_MSG(hwnd, WM_CREATE, MemFile_OnCreate);
    HANDLE_MSG(hwnd, WM_DESTROY, MemFile_OnDestroy);
    HANDLE_MSG(hwnd, WM_COMMAND, MemFile_OnCommand);
    HANDLE_MSG(hwnd, WM_SIZE, MemFile_OnSize);
    default: return MemFile_DefProc(hwnd, Message, wParam, lParam);
  }
}

BOOL MemFile_OnCreate(HWND hwnd, LPCREATESTRUCT lpCreateStruct)
{
  hEdit = CreateWindow("edit", "Original Text",
              WS_CHILD | WS_VISIBLE | WS_BORDER |
              WS_VSCROLL | ES_LEFT | ES_AUTOVSCROLL |
              ES_MULTILINE | ES_READONLY,
              0, 0, 0, 0, hwnd, (HMENU)0,
              lpCreateStruct->hInstance, NULL);

  return TRUE;
}

//////////////////////////////////////////////////////
// Handle WM_DESTROY
//////////////////////////////////////////////////////
#pragma argsused
void MemFile_OnDestroy(HWND hwnd)
{
  PostQuitMessage(0);
}

//////////////////////////////////////////////////////
// GetFileName
//////////////////////////////////////////////////////
LPSTR GetFileName(HWND hwnd, LPSTR szFile, int StringSize)
{
  OPENFILENAME ofn;
  char szFileTitle[256];
  char szFilter[256];

  strcpy(szFilter, "Text Files");
  strcpy(&szFilter[strlen(szFilter) + 1], "*.txt");
  strcpy(szFileTitle, "Long File Name Search");
  szFile[0] = 0;

  memset(&ofn, 0, sizeof(OPENFILENAME));

  ofn.lStructSize    = sizeof(OPENFILENAME);
  ofn.hwndOwner      = hwnd;
  ofn.lpstrFilter    = szFilter;
```

continues

Listing 21.31. continued

```
ofn.nFilterIndex   = 1;
ofn.lpstrFile      = szFile;
ofn.nMaxFile       = StringSize;
ofn.lpstrTitle     = szFileTitle;
ofn.Flags = OFN_FILEMUSTEXIST;

if (GetOpenFileName(&ofn) != TRUE)
{
    DWORD Errval;
    char Errstr[50]="Common Dialog Error: ";
    char buf[5];

    Errval=CommDlgExtendedError();
    if (Errval != 0)
    {
      wsprintf(buf, "%ld", Errval);
      strcat(Errstr, buf);
      MessageBox(NULL,Errstr,"WARNING",MB_OK¦MB_ICONSTOP);
    }
}

    return szFile;
}

/////////////////////////////////////////////////////////
// Open a map file and prepare to access it
/////////////////////////////////////////////////////////
int OpenMappedFile(LPSTR FileName, LPDWORD FileSize)
{
  HANDLE hFile;
  DWORD HighSize;
  LPSTR S1;

  if (strlen(FileName) == 0)
    return FILE_SUCCESS;

  hFile = CreateFile(FileName, GENERIC_READ,
            FILE_SHARE_READ, NULL, OPEN_EXISTING,
            FILE_FLAG_SEQUENTIAL_SCAN, NULL);

  if (hFile == NULL)
    return OPEN_ERROR;

  *FileSize = GetFileSize(hFile, &HighSize);

  hMapping = CreateFileMapping(hFile, NULL, PAGE_READONLY,
                          0, 0, NULL);

  if (hMapping == NULL)
  {
    CloseHandle(hFile);
    return MAPPING_ERROR;
  }

  CloseHandle(hFile);
```

```
    Data = MapViewOfFile(hMapping, FILE_MAP_READ, 0, 0, 0);

    if (Data == NULL)
      return MAPPING_ERROR;
    else
      return FILE_SUCCESS;
}

/////////////////////////////////////////////////////////
// WM_COMMAND
/////////////////////////////////////////////////////////
#pragma argsused
void MemFile_OnCommand(HWND hwnd, int id, HWND hwndCtl, UINT codeNotify)
{
  char FileName[STRSIZE];
  DWORD FileSize;
  LPSTR S1;

  switch(id)
  {
    case ID_READFILE:
      GetFileName(hwnd, FileName, STRSIZE);
      OpenMappedFile(FileName, &FileSize);

      S1 = LPSTR(malloc(FileSize));
      memcpy(S1, Data, FileSize);
      S1[FileSize - 1] = 0;
      SetWindowText(hEdit, S1);
      free(S1);

      UnmapViewOfFile(Data);
      CloseHandle(hMapping);
      break;
  }
}

/////////////////////////////////////////////////////////
// Make sure edit fills entire window
/////////////////////////////////////////////////////////
#pragma argsused
void MemFile_OnSize(HWND hwnd, UINT state, int cx, int cy)
{
  if (hEdit)
    SetWindowPos(hEdit, NULL, 0, 0, cx, cy, SWP_NOZORDER);
}
```

21

Listing 21.32. The MemFile program.

```
/////////////////////////////////////////////////////////
// MEMFILE.H
// Copyright (c) 1995 Charlie Calvert.
/////////////////////////////////////////////////////////

#define ID_READFILE 101
```

continues

Listing 21.32. continued

```
#define OPEN_ERROR    1000
#define WRITE_ERROR   1001
#define CLOSE_ERROR   1002
#define FILE_SUCCESS  1003
#define MAPPING_ERROR 1004
```

Listing 21.33. The resource file for the MemFile program.

```
/////////////////////////////////////////////////////
// MEMFILE.RC
/////////////////////////////////////////////////////
#include "memfile.h"

MemFileMenu MENU
BEGIN
  MENUITEM "ReadFile" ID_READFILE
END
```

Listing 21.34. The module definition file for the MemFile program.

```
; MemFile.Def

NAME          MemFile
DESCRIPTION   'MemFile Window'
```

Listing 21.35. The Borland makefile for the MemFile program.

```
# MemFile.mak

# macros

!if !$d(BCROOT)
BCROOT  = $(MAKEDIR)\..
!endif

APPNAME = MemFile
INCPATH = $(BCROOT)\WIN32;$(BCROOT);$(BCROOT)\INCLUDE
LIBPATH = $(BCROOT)\LIB

COMPILER= BCC32.EXE
BRC     = BRC32.EXE
FLAGS   = -W -v -w4 -I$(INCPATH) -L$(LIBPATH)

# link
$(APPNAME).exe: $(APPNAME).obj $(APPNAME).def $(APPNAME).res
  $(COMPILER) $(FLAGS) $(APPNAME).obj
  $(BRC) -I$(INCPATH) $(APPNAME).res
```

```
# compile
$(APPNAME).obj: $(APPNAME).cpp
  $(COMPILER) -c $(FLAGS) $(APPNAME).cpp

# resource
$(APPNAME).res: $(APPNAME).rc
  $(BRC) -R -I$(INCPATH) $(APPNAME).RC
```

Listing 21.36. The Microsoft makefile for the MemFile program.

```
#------------------------------------------------
# MEMFILE.MAK
#------------------------------------------------

APPNAME=MEMFILE
TARGETOS=WIN95
APPVER=4.0
OBJS=$(APPNAME).obj

!include <win32.mak>

all: $(APPNAME).exe

# Update the resource if necessary

$(APPNAME).res: $(APPNAME).rc $(APPNAME).h
  $(rc) $(rcflags) $(rcvars) $(APPNAME).rc

# Update the object files if necessary

# compile
.cpp.obj:
  $(cc) $(cflags) $(cvars) $(cdebug) $<

# Update the executable file if necessary.

$(APPNAME).exe: $(OBJS) $(APPNAME).res
  $(link) $(linkdebug) $(guiflags) -out:$(APPNAME).exe\
  $(OBJS) $(APPNAME).res $(guilibs) comctl32.lib
```

The MemFile program has a standard window and one menu item. If you select the menu item, the program will open a file in read-only mode, read it into memory, use memcpy to copy its contents into a string variable, and will then send the file to an edit control with SetWindowText.

I should point out that one of the advantages of memory-mapped files is that you can use them to work with huge blocks of memory. In other words, you can open up a file that is several gigabytes in size and manipulate it with the same routines shown in the MemFile program.

21

Figure 21.6.

The MemFile program maps a file from your hard drive into memory.

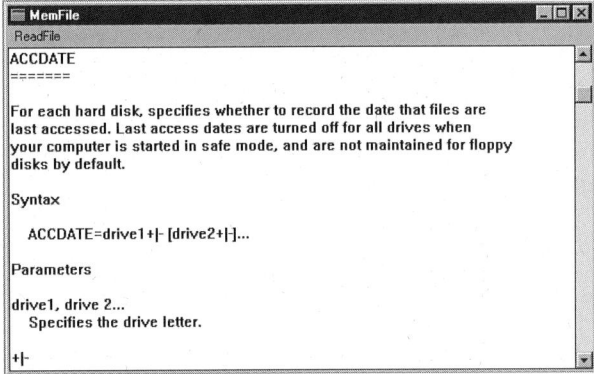

Note: Memory-mapped files are powerful enough to work with huge files. However, I display the contents of the file you choose in an edit control, which means this particular program will not be able to work with huge files. If you want to use these routines with really big files, combine this program with the RTF control example used in the chapter "Bonus Days in Review."

I should note, however, that it usually doesn't make any sense to map a really big file into memory all at once. Instead, you want to read in sections of the file and then work with these sections one at time. You will find the routines I show you in the HeapMem example have provisions for this kind of process, though I do not exploit them. In particular, you can specify the offset where you want to begin mapping a file. You can use this offset to map in chunks of a file at a time. Note, however, the provisions mentioned below regarding the granularity of memory allocations.

There are two important routines in the MemFile program. The first prepares the memory-mapped file, and the second reads it into memory and manipulates it. The first routine is called `OpenMappedFile`, and the second is the `WM_COMMAND` handler.

Here is the routine that maps the file into memory:

```
int OpenMappedFile(LPSTR FileName, LPDWORD FileSize)
{
  HANDLE hFile;
  DWORD HighSize;
  LPSTR S1;

  if (strlen(FileName) == 0)
    return FILE_SUCCESS;
```

```
hFile = CreateFile(FileName, GENERIC_READ,
            FILE_SHARE_READ, NULL, OPEN_EXISTING,
            FILE_FLAG_SEQUENTIAL_SCAN, NULL);

if (hFile == NULL)
  return OPEN_ERROR;

*FileSize = GetFileSize(hFile, &HighSize);

hMapping = CreateFileMapping(hFile, NULL, PAGE_READONLY,
                            0, 0, NULL);

if (hMapping == NULL)
{
  CloseHandle(hFile);
  return MAPPING_ERROR;
}

CloseHandle(hFile);

Data = MapViewOfFile(hMapping, FILE_MAP_READ, 0, 0, 0);

if (Data == NULL)
  return MAPPING_ERROR;
else
  return FILE_SUCCESS;
}
```

The routine shown here uses the CreateFile routine to open the file. This function was discussed during "Week 1 in Review." Because this program displays its output in an edit control, there is a limit on the size of the file you can read.

The file handle returned by CreateFile is used to determine the file's size, and to create a file mapping object. The CreateFileMapping function is discussed below.

CreateFileMapping

This is the CreateFileMapping function:

```
HANDLE CreateFileMapping(
    HANDLE  hFile,     // handle of file to map
    // optional security attributes
    LPSECURITY_ATTRIBUTES  lpFileMappingAttributes,
    DWORD  flProtect,     // protection for mapping object
    DWORD  dwMaximumSizeHigh,     // high-order 32-bits of object size
    DWORD  dwMaximumSizeLow,     // low-order 32-bits of object size
    LPCTSTR  lpName     // name of file-mapping object
    );
```

21

The first parameter of this function contains the handle of the file you want to map. You get this handle by calling CreateFile.

You can pass in NULL in the second parameter to use the default security attributes.

The `flProtect` parameter can have one of the following values, plus some additional values specified in the online help:

`PAGE_READONLY`	Committed part of the file has read-only access.
`PAGE_READWRITE`	`CreateFile` must use `GENERIC_READ` and `GENERIC_WRITE`.
`PAGE_WRITECOPY`	`CreateFile` must use `GENERIC_READ` and `GENERIC_WRITE`.

If you set the `dwMaximumSizeHigh` and `dwMaximumSizeLow` parameters to 0, then the system will automatically fill them in with the size of the file associated with the handle passed to this function.

The last parameter contains the name of the file-mapping object. This parameter allows different processes to enter the same name when calling this function, thereby gaining access to the same file. This allows you to share memory between two applications. You can pass `NULL` in this parameter if you don't need to specify a name.

Here's an example:

```
hMapping = CreateFileMapping(hFile, NULL, PAGE_READONLY,
                             0, 0, NULL);
```

After successfully calling and using `CreateFile` and `CreateFileMapping`, you should call `CloseHandle` to close out the files.

A call to `CreateFileMapping` does not actually allow you to use mapped files. In other words, it opens up a file-mapping object, but it does not return a pointer to the "memory" in that file. To get at the actual contents of that file, call `MapViewOfFile` or `MapViewOfFileEx`.

Here is the declaration for a call to `MapViewOfFile`:

```
LPVOID MapViewOfFile(
    HANDLE  hFileMappingObject, // Object returned
                                // by CreateFileMapping
    DWORD  dwDesiredAccess,     // access mode (FILE_MAP_READ)
    DWORD  dwFileOffsetHigh,    // high-order 32-bits of file offset
    DWORD  dwFileOffsetLow,     // low-order 32-bits of file offset
    DWORD  dwNumberOfBytesToMap // number of bytes to map
  );
```

The first parameter is the mapping object you want to work with. This value is obtained by calling `CreateFileMapping`. The next parameter specifies the kind of access you want. It can contain the following values:

`FILE_MAP_WRITE`	Read-write access.
`FILE_MAP_READ`	Read-only access.
`FILE_MAP_ALL_ACCESS`	Same as `FILE_MAP_WRITE`.
`FILE_MAP_COPY`	Copy on write access.

You should see the online help for additional information.

The dwFileOffsetHigh and dwFileOffsetLow are the high and low DWORDS of the value specifying the offset into the file at which you want to read. The file has to be very large before you need to use the dwFileOffsetHigh parameter. The dwFileOffsetLow parameter must be a multiple of the system's memory allocation granularity. You obtain this number via a call to GetSystemInfo. (This latter call is discussed in "Week 2 in Review.") If you want to start reading from the beginning of the file, set both dwFileOffsetHigh and dwFileOffsetLow to 0.

The final parameter is the number of bytes to map. If you want to read the whole file, just set this value to 0. Otherwise it should be either the granularity value returned by GetSystemInfo, or else some amount smaller than the granularity.

Once you have the pointer to the data in a file, then you can use it to access the contents of the file. To help illustrate this point, I use memcpy to copy the contents of the file into a string. I then set the last byte in the string to 0, and send it off to the edit control so you can look at it:

```
S1 = LPSTR(malloc(FileSize));
memcpy(S1, Data, FileSize);
S1[FileSize - 1] = 0;
SetWindowText(hEdit, S1);
free(S1);
```

The point here is that file mapping allows you to treat the contents of a file as if it were memory. (You're calling memcpy on the contents of a file.) If the last bytes in two files were both 0, then you could append them by using strcpy or strcat, or you could compare them with strcmp. If you had a routine that reversed the bytes in a block of memory, or that scanned memory for data, then you could use them with memory mapped files. Furthermore, you can allow two programs to share memory by giving them both access to the same file.

When you are through using a file you should close out the variables you have been using:

```
UnmapViewOfFile(Data);
CloseHandle(hMapping);
```

Once again, the purpose of this discussion of memory mapped files is not to give you an encyclopedic overview of the entire, rather complex, subject. Instead, I just want to give you a feeling for what memory mapped files can do for you. This is a taste of something very powerful that's meant to inspire you to pursue the subject further. You should also consider looking into to VirtualAlloc and its associated routines.

Summary

This chapter has introduced you to some of the advanced features of Windows 95. You have had a look at processes, threads, and WIN32 memory management.

When working with threads, you've seen how to create single threads. You've also seen how to allocate memory so that you can pass in data to a single thread that has multiple copies of itself running at one time. You've also seen the reverse of this process: how to synchronize multiple

21

threads so that they can all share access to a single block of data. In particular, you have studied critical sections and mutexes.

In the second half of the chapter you looked at memory management issues such as allocation, and creating multiple heaps. You also saw how to create memory-mapped files.

Besides providing specific coding examples, I tried to give you an overview of Windows 95 multitasking and memory management. These are complex subjects that are introduced here in broad, general terms. However, this material should make you aware of some of the major theories behind Windows 95 and Windows NT. Hopefully it has pointed you in the right direction so you can see where to concentrate your future studies.

Q&A

Q **You don't provide an example of using VirtualAlloc in this chapter. Is there a reason for that?**

A An example of using VirtualAlloc was omitted simply because of space reasons, although perhaps I should have found a way to work it in. VirtualAlloc is a very important call in Windows 95, and one that anyone who is serious about Windows 95 programming should take the time to explore. It allows you to allocate memory from the virtual address space of your program. This memory can be paged from disk as necessary. Programmers often use this function when they need to allocate large blocks of memory. Here are the parameters to the call:

```
LPVOID VirtualAlloc(

    LPVOID  lpvAddress,          // address of region to reserve or commit
    DWORD   cbSize,              // size of region
    DWORD   fdwAllocationType,   // type of allocation
    DWORD   fdwProtect           // type of access protection
    );
```

When you are through with the memory claimed by VirtualAlloc, you can dispose of it by calling VirtualFree.

Please take the time to look up both of these calls in the online help. If you have Jeffrey Richter's book, *Advanced Windows*, published by Microsoft Press, you should read about the calls in that volume. Richter's book has also traditionally been included on the Microsoft Developer's CD. Also, use online services to pursue additional information about these calls.

Once again, VirtualAlloc is a very important call in WIN32, and one that you should use in a wide variety of circumstances. The omission of an in-depth discussion of this routine is not meant to imply that it is less important than memory mapped files or the HeapAlloc family of calls. Windows memory management is a complex topic, and

this chapter is meant to serve as an introduction to the topic. Let your pursuit of the `VirtualAlloc` function serve as a bridge between this book and more advanced works on WIN32.

Workshop

The Workshop provides quiz questions to help you solidify your understanding of the material covered and exercises to provide you with experience in using what you've learned. Try to understand the quiz and exercise answers before continuing on to Bonus Day 1, "GDI and Metafiles." Answers are provided in Appendix A.

Quiz

1. How large is the address space for a WIN32 program?
2. In a typical Windows 95 program, what is the value of the first parameter to `WinMain`?
3. By default, does each 16-bit program running under Windows 95 get its own address space?
4. How can a computer that has only 8MB of memory host a program that runs in a 4GB address space?
5. What are CONTEXT structures?
6. There are two types of multitasking described in this chapter. What are their names? Which belongs to theWindows 3.1, and which to WIN32?
7. What is the flaw in the Windows 3.1 multitasking scheme?
8. What does the `Sleep` function do?
9. What is a memory-mapped file?
10. What does the `VirtualAlloc` function do, and how important is it?

Exercise

The chapter on MDI applications has a module called Fern that draws fractal images to the screen. Either now, or after you have read the MDI chapter, attempt to use the Fern module, or the code included therein, in a threaded application. In particular, the drawing of the fractal takes a few seconds. Use threads to relegate this activity to a background task, so that the user can work in the foreground while the Fern is drawing. Don't use PeekMessage loops or some other Windows 3.1-specific technique for allowing code to process in the background. Use threads!

21

3

Treeview Controls

This chapter covers treeviews, which are some of the most important and useful of the new Windows 95 controls. This will be a fairly challenging chapter, but it contains lots of interesting material.

Although I had originally hoped to cover treeviews on Day 19, "Advanced Windows 95 Controls," it turns out they form an excellent topic for a week in review. While exploring them, you will get a chance to go over many of the concepts you've discovered in Week 3. If you can master treeviews, then you can rest assured that you understand how the new Windows 95 common controls are put together.

Working with Hierarchies

One of the things that computers do best is keep track of lists of data. This concept is so central to the art of computing that whole computer languages, such as Lisp and Prologue, have been built around this one principle.

Computers also demand that we arrange data in some orderly manner. Everyone has made the mistake of just throwing data into a computer in a haphazard fashion. When you do that, you risk discovering later that it is nearly impossible to retrieve unorganized data.

The facts in this matter are fairly simple. Computers like lists, and they like order—preferably hierarchical order. Certainly it is possible that some very interesting computer breakthroughs will come out of the study of chaos; nonetheless, computers are nicer to you if you approach things from a systematic, hierarchical point of view.

Treeviews are interesting because they give programmers a friendly, easily comprehensible way to arrange data in hierarchies. It's the nature of computers to store data in hierarchies, so it's only natural that a tool which depicts hierarchies is going to be useful to programmers.

Now that the tool is available, I think we will see treeviews used in many programs and in many creative ways. This Microsoft implementation of treeviews is robust and flexible enough to find its way into a number of programs. This brief chapter will show you how they work.

Treeviews Are Like Listviews— Only Different

In order to introduce you to treeviews, I have created a program called PoemTree. This program uses data that is very similar to the data used in the PoemList program from Day 19. As you will see, the PoemTree program itself is very similar to the PoemList program. Both sets of code demonstrate means of displaying symmetrical sets of data to the user. In a listview, however, the data is arranged sequentially in rows and columns, while in a treeview you get a hierarchical view.

Perhaps the classic use of the treeview control is in the left side of the Explorer program that ships with Windows 95. (On the right side, you find a listview, but I don't want to exhume that subject just now, not after it's been at least temporarily laid to rest.)

If you click on the icons on the left side of the Explorer, you find that some of them open up to reveal subdirectories hidden under the main node. These directories have other directories, and so on. On some machines, subdirectories can be nested six, seven, or more levels deep. Treeviews can easily depict these complex relationships. Take a look at Figure R3.1 to get a sense of what I mean.

Figure R3.1.
*The hierarchical
structure of subdirectories
as depicted on the left
pane of the Explorer.*

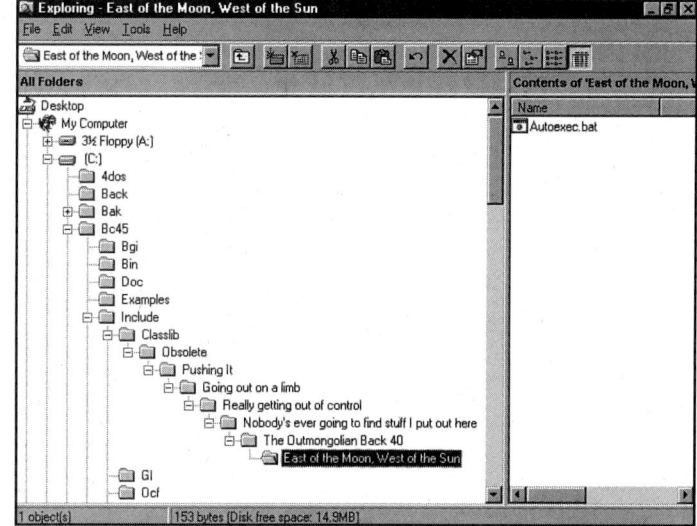

The best way to proceed from here is to dig into a practical example of treeviews. Listings R3.1
through R3.6 give the complete code for the PoemTree program. Take a look at it and then
turn to the CD so you can get the code up and running.

Listing R3.1. The main module for the PoemTree program.

```
//////////////////////////////////////////////////////
// POEMTREE.CPP
// Copyright (c) 1995 Charlie Calvert.
// COMMENT: A treeview sample program for Windows 95
// DATE: 07/07/95
//////////////////////////////////////////////////////

#define STRICT
#include <windows.h>
#include <windowsx.h>
#include <commctrl.h>
#include "poemtree.h"
#pragma warning (disable : 4068) // unknown pragma

HINSTANCE    hInst;                   // current instance
HWND         hWndMain;
HWND         hWndTreeView;
HIMAGELIST   hPoetImageList;
TIMAGES      Img;

char szAppName[] = "PoemTree";        // The name of this application
char szTitle[]   = "Poet's corner";   // The title bar text
```

continues

Listing R3.1. continued

```
//////////////////////////////////////////////////////
// Program entry point
//////////////////////////////////////////////////////
#pragma argsused
int APIENTRY WinMain(HINSTANCE hInstance, HINSTANCE hPrevInstance,
                     LPSTR lpCmdLine, int nCmdShow)
{
   MSG msg;

   if (!Register(hInstance))
     return (FALSE);

   if (!Create(hInstance, nCmdShow))
     return (FALSE);

   while (GetMessage(&msg, NULL, 0, 0))
   {
     TranslateMessage(&msg);// Translates virtual key codes
     DispatchMessage(&msg); // Dispatches message to window
   }

   return (msg.wParam);
}


//////////////////////////////////////////////////////
// Register
//////////////////////////////////////////////////////
BOOL Register(HINSTANCE hInstance)
{
   WNDCLASSEX  WndClassEx;
   WndClassEx.cbSize        = sizeof(WNDCLASSEX);
   WndClassEx.style         = CS_HREDRAW ¦ CS_VREDRAW;
   WndClassEx.lpfnWndProc   = (WNDPROC)WndProc;
   WndClassEx.cbClsExtra    = 0;
   WndClassEx.cbWndExtra    = 0;
   WndClassEx.hInstance     = hInstance;
   WndClassEx.hIcon         = LoadIcon (hInstance, "PoemIcon");
   WndClassEx.hCursor       = LoadCursor(NULL, IDC_ARROW);
   WndClassEx.hbrBackground = (HBRUSH)(COLOR_WINDOW+1);
   WndClassEx.lpszMenuName  = szAppName;
   WndClassEx.lpszClassName = szAppName;
   WndClassEx.hIconSm       = LoadIcon(hInstance, "PoemIcon16");

   return (RegisterClassEx(&WndClassEx));
}


//////////////////////////////////////////////////////
// Create
//////////////////////////////////////////////////////
BOOL Create(HINSTANCE hInstance, int nCmdShow)
{
   hInst = hInstance;
```

```
    hWndMain = CreateWindow(szAppName, szTitle,
            WS_OVERLAPPEDWINDOW, CW_USEDEFAULT, 0,
            CW_USEDEFAULT, 0, NULL, NULL, hInstance, NULL);

    if (!hWndMain)
      return (FALSE);

    ShowWindow(hWndMain, nCmdShow);
    UpdateWindow(hWndMain);              // Send WM_PAINT

    return (TRUE);
}

//////////////////////////////////////////////////////////
// Window Procedure
//////////////////////////////////////////////////////////
#pragma argsused
LRESULT CALLBACK WndProc(HWND hwnd, UINT message,
                          WPARAM wParam, LPARAM lParam)
{
  switch (message)
  {
    HANDLE_MSG(hwnd, WM_CREATE, PoemTree_OnCreate);
    HANDLE_MSG(hwnd, WM_DESTROY, PoemTree_OnDestroy);
    HANDLE_MSG(hwnd, WM_COMMAND, PoemTree_OnCommand);
    HANDLE_MSG(hwnd, WM_NOTIFY, PoemTree_OnNotify);
    HANDLE_MSG(hwnd, WM_SIZE, PoemTree_OnSize);
    default:
      return DefWindowProc(hwnd, message, wParam, lParam);
  }
}

//////////////////////////////////////////////////////////
// Get an icon from the resource in this exe
//////////////////////////////////////////////////////////
int GetIcon(LPSTR S)
{
  return
    ImageList_AddIcon(hPoetImageList, LoadIcon(hInst, S));
}

//////////////////////////////////////////////////////////
// A utility function for reading in the icons
//////////////////////////////////////////////////////////
void SetupIcons(void)
{
    Img.Emerson      = GetIcon("Emerson");
    Img.Emerson0     = GetIcon("Emerson0");
    Img.Bradstreet   = GetIcon("Bradstreet");
    Img.Bradstreet0  = GetIcon("Bradstreet0");
    Img.Whitman      = GetIcon("Whitman");
    Img.Whitman0     = GetIcon("Whitman0");
    Img.Frost        = GetIcon("Frost");
    Img.Frost0       = GetIcon("Frost0");
    Img.Williams     = GetIcon("Williams");
    Img.Williams0    = GetIcon("Williams0");
```

continues

Listing R3.1. continued

```
        Img.Poem        = GetIcon("Poem");
        Img.SelPoem     = GetIcon("SelPoem");
        Img.FirstLine   = GetIcon("FirstLine");
}


/////////////////////////////////////////////////////
// Creates the imagelist and treeview, fills in tree
/////////////////////////////////////////////////////
#pragma argsused
BOOL PoemTree_OnCreate(HWND hwnd, LPCREATESTRUCT lpCreateStruct)
{
    RECT Rect;

    InitCommonControls(); // This MUST be called
    GetClientRect(hwnd, &Rect);
    hWndTreeView = CreateWindow (WC_TREEVIEW, "",
                    WS_VISIBLE ¦ WS_CHILD ¦ WS_BORDER ¦
                    TVS_HASLINES ¦ TVS_EDITLABELS,
                    0, 0, Rect.right, Rect.bottom,
                    hwnd, (HMENU)NULL, hInst, NULL);

    if (hWndTreeView)
    {
        hPoetImageList = ImageList_Create(32, 32, TRUE, 5, 1);
        SetupIcons();
        TreeView_SetImageList(hWndTreeView, hPoetImageList, TVSIL_NORMAL);
        FillTree (hWndTreeView);
    }
    return TRUE;
}


/////////////////////////////////////////////////////
// WM_DESTROY
/////////////////////////////////////////////////////
#pragma argsused
void PoemTree_OnDestroy(HWND hwnd)
{
    if (hPoetImageList)
        ImageList_Destroy(hPoetImageList);
    PostQuitMessage(0);
}


/////////////////////////////////////////////////////
// WM_COMMAND
/////////////////////////////////////////////////////
#pragma argsused
void PoemTree_OnCommand(HWND hwnd, int id,
                        HWND hwndCtl, UINT codeNotify)
{
    switch (id)
    {
        case IDM_EXIT:
            DestroyWindow (hwnd);
            break;
    }
}
```

```
/////////////////////////////////////////////////////
// Fit treeview within window
/////////////////////////////////////////////////////
#pragma argsused
void PoemTree_OnSize(HWND hwnd, UINT state, int cx, int cy)
{
  if (hWndTreeView)
    SetWindowPos(hWndTreeView, NULL, 0, 0, cx, cy, SWP_NOZORDER);
}

/////////////////////////////////////////////////////
// WM_NOTIFY
/////////////////////////////////////////////////////
#pragma argsused
LRESULT PoemTree_OnNotify(HWND hwnd, int idFrom, NMHDR FAR * pnmhdr)
{
 TV_DISPINFO* DisplayInfo;

 switch (pnmhdr->code)
 {
  case TVN_GETDISPINFO:
    DisplayInfo = (TV_DISPINFO *)pnmhdr;
    if (DisplayInfo->item.state & TVIS_EXPANDED)
    {
      switch (DisplayInfo->item.lParam)
      {
        case STBRADSTREET:
          DisplayInfo->item.iImage =
          DisplayInfo->item.iSelectedImage = Img.Bradstreet;
          break;

        case STEMERSON:
          DisplayInfo->item.iImage =
          DisplayInfo->item.iSelectedImage = Img.Emerson;
          break;

        case STWHITMAN:
          DisplayInfo->item.iImage =
          DisplayInfo->item.iSelectedImage = Img.Whitman;
          break;

        case STFROST:
          DisplayInfo->item.iImage =
          DisplayInfo->item.iSelectedImage = Img.Frost;
          break;

        case STWILLIAMS:
          DisplayInfo->item.iImage =
          DisplayInfo->item.iSelectedImage = Img.Williams;
          break;
      }
    }
    else  // Collapsed item
      {
      switch (DisplayInfo->item.lParam)
        {
```

continues

Listing R3.1. continued

```
          case STBRADSTREET:
            DisplayInfo->item.iImage =
            DisplayInfo->item.iSelectedImage = Img.Bradstreet0;
            break;

          case STEMERSON:
            DisplayInfo->item.iImage =
            DisplayInfo->item.iSelectedImage = Img.Emerson0;
            break;

          case STWHITMAN:
            DisplayInfo->item.iImage =
            DisplayInfo->item.iSelectedImage = Img.Whitman0;
            break;

          case STFROST:
            DisplayInfo->item.iImage =
            DisplayInfo->item.iSelectedImage = Img.Frost0;
            break;

          case STWILLIAMS:
            DisplayInfo->item.iImage =
            DisplayInfo->item.iSelectedImage = Img.Williams0;
            break;
        }
      }
    return TRUE;
  }
  return FORWARD_WM_NOTIFY(hwnd, idFrom, pnmhdr, DefWindowProc);
}

//////////////////////////////////////////////////////////
// Add an item to the tree
//////////////////////////////////////////////////////////
HTREEITEM AddItem(HWND hWndTV, HTREEITEM hParent,
                  int iImage, int iSelectedImage,
                  LPSTR szText, LPARAM lParam)
{
  TV_ITEM            tvItem;
  TV_INSERTSTRUCT    tvIns;

  tvItem.mask = TVIF_TEXT | TVIF_IMAGE | TVIF_SELECTEDIMAGE | TVIF_PARAM;

  // Set the attribytes
  tvItem.pszText       = szText;
  tvItem.iImage        = iImage;
  tvItem.iSelectedImage = iSelectedImage;
  tvItem.lParam        = lParam;
```

```
  // Fill out the TV_INSERTSTRUCT
  tvIns.hParent         = hParent;
  tvIns.hInsertAfter    = TVI_LAST;
  tvIns.item            = tvItem;

  return TreeView_InsertItem (hWndTV, &tvIns);
}

//////////////////////////////////////////////////////////
// Get the data from the string list
//////////////////////////////////////////////////////////
LPSTR GetData(int Offset, LPSTR Data)
{
  LoadString(hInst, Offset, Data, MAXSTR);
  return Data;
}

//////////////////////////////////////////////////////////
// Fill in the data and images for the poet tree
//////////////////////////////////////////////////////////
void FillPoetTree(HWND hTree, int Offset)
{
  HTREEITEM  hRoot, hParent;    // Parent node to add to.
  char Data[MAXSTR];


  hRoot = AddItem(hTree, TVGN_ROOT,
            I_IMAGECALLBACK, I_IMAGECALLBACK,
            GetData(Offset, Data), Offset);

  hParent = AddItem(hTree, hRoot, Img.Poem, Img.SelPoem,
            GetData(Offset + 1, Data), 0);

  AddItem(hTree, hParent, Img.FirstLine, Img.FirstLine,
            GetData(Offset + 2, Data), 0);

  hParent = AddItem(hTree, hRoot, Img.Poem, Img.SelPoem,
            GetData(Offset + 3, Data), 0);

  AddItem(hTree, hParent, Img.FirstLine, Img.FirstLine,
            GetData(Offset + 4, Data), 0);
}

//////////////////////////////////////////////////////////
// Fill out the tree
//////////////////////////////////////////////////////////
void FillTree(HWND hTree)
{
  int i;

  for (i = 1000; i < 6000; i += 1000)
    FillPoetTree(hTree, i);
}
```

Listing R3.2. The header file for the PoemTree program lists macros, types, and functions.

```
//////////////////////////////////////////////////////
// POEMTREE.H
// Copyright (c) 1995 Charlie Calvert.
//////////////////////////////////////////////////////

// Macros
#define STBRADSTREET    1000
#define STEMERSON       2000
#define STWHITMAN       3000
#define STFROST         4000
#define STWILLIAMS      5000

#define MAXSTR          200
#define IDM_EXIT        101

// Types
typedef struct tagIMAGES {
  int Bradstreet;
  int Emerson;
  int Whitman;
  int Frost;
  int Williams;
  int Bradstreet0;
  int Emerson0;
  int Whitman0;
  int Frost0;
  int Williams0;
  int Poem;
  int SelPoem;
  int FirstLine;
} TIMAGES;

// Funcs
BOOL Register(HINSTANCE);
BOOL Create(HINSTANCE, int);
LRESULT CALLBACK WndProc(HWND, UINT, WPARAM, LPARAM);
LRESULT CALLBACK About(HWND, UINT, WPARAM, LPARAM);

// The PoemTree class
BOOL PoemTree_OnCreate(HWND hwnd, LPCREATESTRUCT lpCreateStruct);
void PoemTree_OnDestroy(HWND hwnd);
void PoemTree_OnCommand(HWND hwnd, int id, HWND hwndCtl, UINT codeNotify);
void PoemTree_OnLButtonUp(HWND hwnd, int x, int y, UINT keyFlags);
void PoemTree_OnMouseMove(HWND hwnd, int x, int y, UINT keyFlags);
LRESULT PoemTree_OnNotify(HWND hwnd, int idFrom, NMHDR FAR * pnmhdr);
void PoemTree_OnSize(HWND hwnd, UINT state, int cx, int cy);

// Utils
void FillTree(HWND hWndTV);
```

Listing R3.3. The resource file for PoemTree program holds the strings and icons that are shown in the treeview.

```
//////////////////////////////////////////////////////
// POEMTREE.RC
// Copyright (c) 1995 Charlie Calvert.
// Some icons, a menu and string table
//////////////////////////////////////////////////////

#include "poemtree.h"

PoemIcon ICON POEMTREE.ICO
PoemIcon16 ICON POEM16.ICO

BRADSTREET  ICON brad.ico
EMERSON     ICON emerson.ico
WHITMAN     ICON whitman.ico
FROST       ICON frost.ico
WILLIAMS    ICON williams.ico

BRADSTREET0 ICON brad0.ico
EMERSON0    ICON emersn0.ico
WHITMAN0    ICON whitman0.ico
FROST0      ICON frost0.ico
WILLIAMS0   ICON william0.ico

POEM        ICON rider1.ico
SELPOEM     ICON rider2.ico
FIRSTLINE   ICON frstline.ico

PoemTree MENU
BEGIN
  POPUP "&File"
  {
    MENUITEM "E&xit",          IDM_EXIT
  }
END

STRINGTABLE
BEGIN
  STBRADSTREET, "Anne BradStreet"
  STBRADSTREET + 1, "The Prologue"
  STBRADSTREET + 2, "To sing of Wars, of Captains, and of Kings..."
  STBRADSTREET + 3, "The Author to her Book"
  STBRADSTREET + 4, "Thou ill-form'd offspring of my feeble brain..."

  STEMERSON, "Ralph Waldo Emerson"
  STEMERSON + 1, "Brahma"
  STEMERSON + 2, "If the red slayer thinks he slays..."
  STEMERSON + 3, "The Sphinx"
  STEMERSON + 4, "The sphinx is drowsy, Her wings are furled..."
```

continues

Listing R3.3. continued

```
      STWHITMAN, "Walt Whitman"
      STWHITMAN + 1, "Out of the Cradle Endlessly Rocking"
      STWHITMAN + 2, "Out of the mockingbirds throat..."
      STWHITMAN + 3, "Song of Myself"
      STWHITMAN + 4, "I celebrate myself, and sing myself..."

      STFROST, "Robert Frost"
      STFROST + 1, "Mending Wall"
      STFROST + 2, "Something there is that doesn't love a wall..."
      STFROST + 3, "The Gift Outright"
      STFROST + 4, "The land was ours before we were the land's..."

      STWILLIAMS, "William Carlos Williams"
      STWILLIAMS + 1, "By the road to the contagious hospital"
      STWILLIAMS + 2, "under the surge of the blue..."
      STWILLIAMS + 3, "The Dance"
      STWILLIAMS + 4, "In Breughal's great picture, The Kermess..."
END
```

Listing R3.4. The PoemTree module definition file is lean and short.

```
; POEMTREE.DEF

NAME        POEMTREE
DESCRIPTION 'POEMTREE Example'
```

Listing R3.5. The PoemTree makefile for Borland developers.

```
# POEMTREE.MAK

# macros

!if !$d(BCROOT)
BCROOT  = $(MAKEDIR)\..
!endif

APPNAME = PoemTree
INCPATH = $(BCROOT)\WIN32;$(BCROOT);$(BCROOT)\INCLUDE
LIBPATH = $(BCROOT)\LIB

COMPILER= BCC32.EXE
BRC     = BRC32.EXE
FLAGS   = -W -v -w4 -I$(INCPATH) -L$(LIBPATH)
OBJS    = $(APPNAME).obj

# link
$(APPNAME).exe: $(OBJS) $(APPNAME).def $(APPNAME).res
  $(COMPILER) $(FLAGS) $(OBJS) comctl32.lib
  $(BRC) -I$(INCPATH) $(APPNAME).res
```

```
# compiling
.cpp.obj:
  $(COMPILER) -c $(FLAGS) { $< }

# resource
$(APPNAME).res: $(APPNAME).rc
  $(BRC) -R -I$(INCPATH) $(APPNAME).RC
```

Listing R3.6. The PoemTree makefile for Microsoft developers.

```
#////////////////////////////////////
# SKYVEWMS.MAK - Microsoft make file
# nmake -f skyvewms.mak
#  Copyright (c) 1995 Charlie Calvert.
#////////////////////////////////////

APPNAME=POEMTREE
TARGETOS=WIN95
APPVER=4.0
OBJS=$(APPNAME).OBJ

!include <win32.mak>

all: $(APPNAME).exe

# Update the resource if necessary

$(APPNAME).res: $(APPNAME).rc $(APPNAME).h
  $(rc) $(rcflags) $(rcvars) $(APPNAME).rc

# Update the object files if necessary

# compile
.cpp.obj:
  $(cc) $(cflags) $(cvars) $(cdebug) $<

# Update the executable file if necessary.

$(APPNAME).exe: $(OBJS) $(APPNAME).res
  $(link) $(linkdebug) $(guiflags) -out:$(APPNAME).exe\
  $(OBJS) $(APPNAME).res $(guilibs) comctl32.lib
```

The items shown in Table R3.1 are used primarily in the imagelist shown in the body of the treeview control. The actual images shown are not important; the point is simply that you have a set of icons with the names shown in Table R3.1.

Table R3.1. Icons you can use in the imagelist.

Icon	Name
	poemtree.ico
	poem16.ico
	brad.ico
	emerson.ico
	whitman.ico
	frost.ico
	williams.ico
	brad0.ico
	emersn0.ico
	whitman0.ico
	frost0.ico
	william0.ico
	rider1.ico
	rider2.ico
	frstline.ico

When you first open the PoemTree program, you see a list of five poets. If you click on one of the poet's names, a node in a tree will open and you will see the titles of two poems written by that particular poet. To get more information, you can click on the icons representing either of the two poems. After you do so, a third node will appear. This node provides the first line from one of the poems listed in the second node. If the title of the poem is also the first line of the poem, then I quote the second line in the third node.

All this confusing talk about the "umpteenth line of the uttermost node" points out the key issue when working with trees: If you are not careful, they can get a bit out of control. The point of the upcoming discussion is to help you manage all this logic in simple, discrete chunks.

Despite the rather austere and rigid structure of the treeview component, it nonetheless serves as a handy rack for hanging up a wide range of apparel. For instance, poets and their poetry feel just as snug when stretched on this tool as do the directories from a hard drive. The point is that this is a colorful tool meant to create a pleasing—and intuitive—interface for the user.

A PoemTree Grows in the Garden

It's simple enough to start the process of adding a treeview to one of your own programs. To get started, be sure to call InitCommonControls, so that COMCTL32 is loaded into memory:

```
InitCommonControls(); // This MUST be called
```

After that, you can call CreateWindow or CreateWindowEx so that your treeview can take root:

```
GetClientRect(hwnd, &Rect);
hWndTreeView = CreateWindow (WC_TREEVIEW, "",
                WS_VISIBLE | WS_CHILD | WS_BORDER |
                TVS_HASLINES | TVS_EDITLABELS,
                0, 0, Rect.right, Rect.bottom,
                hwnd, (HMENU)NULL, hInst, NULL);
```

Notice that I also call GetClientRect so I can assure that the treeview will fit properly in its parent window. The PoemTree program also responds to WM_SIZE messages and, in so doing, keeps the two windows in sync:

```
void PoemTree_OnSize(HWND hwnd, UINT state, int cx, int cy)
{
  if (hWndTreeView)
    SetWindowPos(hWndTreeView, NULL, 0, 0, cx, cy, SWP_NOZORDER);
}
```

Once you've created the treeview, the next step is to populate the imageview associated with it and to fill in the branches with these images and their accompanying strings. You don't have to associate an imagelist with a treeview, but most users will appreciate the extra effort and might even think a bit ill of you if you can't find time for it.

Here is the code from the WM_CREATE method that causes the imagelist to be created and the treeview to be filled out with its leaves:

```
if (hWndTreeView)
{
  hPoetImageList = ImageList_Create(32, 32, TRUE, 5, 1);
  SetupIcons();
  TreeView_SetImageList(hWndTreeView, hPoetImageList, TVSIL_NORMAL);
  FillTree (hWndTreeView);
}
```

I first introduced ImageList_Create on Day 19, so I won't go through that one again.

The SetupIcons method is long but very simple:

```
void SetupIcons(void)
{
   Img.Emerson     = GetIcon("Emerson");
   Img.Emerson0    = GetIcon("Emerson0");
   Img.Bradstreet  = GetIcon("Bradstreet");
   Img.Bradstreet0 = GetIcon("Bradstreet0");
   Img.Whitman     = GetIcon("Whitman");
   Img.Whitman0    = GetIcon("Whitman0");
   Img.Frost       = GetIcon("Frost");
   Img.Frost0      = GetIcon("Frost0");
   Img.Williams    = GetIcon("Williams");
   Img.Williams0   = GetIcon("Williams0");
   Img.Poem        = GetIcon("Poem");
   Img.SelPoem     = GetIcon("SelPoem");
   Img.FirstLine   = GetIcon("FirstLine");
}
```

GetIcon is just a little utility function I created to help make my code more readable. Note that it calls both LoadIcon and ImageList_AddIcon. In other words, it first loads the icon from the resource, and then adds it to the imagelist:

```
int GetIcon(LPSTR S)
{
  return
    ImageList_AddIcon(hPoetImageList, LoadIcon(hInst, S));
}
```

Together, the GetIcon and SetupIcons functions prepare the imagelist for use with the treeview. Here are the actual resources declared in the RC file:

```
BRADSTREET  ICON brad.ico
EMERSON     ICON emerson.ico
WHITMAN     ICON whitman.ico
FROST       ICON frost.ico
WILLIAMS    ICON williams.ico

BRADSTREET0 ICON brad0.ico
EMERSON0    ICON emersn0.ico
WHITMAN0    ICON whitman0.ico
FROST0      ICON frost0.ico
WILLIAMS0   ICON william0.ico

POEM        ICON rider1.ico
SELPOEM     ICON rider2.ico
FIRSTLINE   ICON frstline.ico
```

Many of these icons are divided up into pairs. For instance, EMERSON.ICO is shown when a branch of the tree is open, and EMERSN0.ICO is shown when the branch is closed. RIDER2.ICO is shown when a node of the tree is selected, and RIDER1.ICO is shown when it is closed.

This section of the code is very straightforward. The only aspect of it that deserves comment here is the call to GetIcon. As I said earlier, I've wrapped the ImageList_AddIcon call in another function because I wanted to write cleaner, easier-to-read code. But is this worth the overhead of a function call? Well, that would depend on your circumstances. My primary goal is to write lucid code that's useful for readers. The overhead of a function call is almost imperceptible on a 486 or Pentium, so it's simple for me to opt for the clean syntax offered by a call like GetIcon. You, on the other hand, may be writing an app that needs to be as small and as fast as possible. In that case, the overhead, though very small, might still be suspect. The balance you need to strike is between "readability and maintainability" on the one hand, and "speed and size" on the other.

Once the imagelist is prepared, it needs to be added to the treeview:

```
TreeView_SetImageList(hWndTreeView, hPoetImageList, TVSIL_NORMAL);
```

This is another WindowsX-like macro that wraps a message. By now, you might be able to guess that the message's name is TVM_SETIMAGELIST. The first parameter is the HWND of the treeview, the second a handle to the imagelist, and the third a flag saying that this is a normal imagelist with no special attributes. The alternative flag is called TVSIL_STATE. This second flag specifies that it is a "state" imagelist of the type used when the treeview is in a particular user-defined mode.

> **Note:** TreeView_SetImageList doesn't say anything about where the individual frames of the imagelist will be shown on the tree. All it does is say that the imagelist is to be associated with the tree. No specific actions are taken regarding the placement of the images. This is a little like a family member who sets a box full of ornaments next to a Christmas tree. Everyone knows that the images from the imagelist will eventually be hung on the tree, but for now each image is simply left sitting in a box next to the tree. That's the sole purpose of the TreeView_SetImageList function. It just brings the imagelist into the room and sets it next to the tree. The actual hanging of the Christmas ornaments comes later.

The final call in the WM_CREATE handler is to the FillTree function:

```
FillTree(hWndTreeView);
```

FillTree is a deceptively simple call that is really a gateway into the functions that add the strings and icons on specific nodes of the treeview.

In this particular case, I think it's easiest to work from the inside out. In other words, I will start by describing the code that actually adds a string to the tree, and then I will work outward to describe how I decide what parameters to pass to this function.

It's relatively easy to actually add a string to a node in the list. What's a bit trickier is telling Windows where that node fits into the hierarchy of the tree.

Suppose you had a Christmas tree that needed to have ornaments hung on it. The act of hanging the ornaments is relatively simple. However, it might be complex to describe which branch of the tree to assign to which ornament. To make the analogy more specific, think how hard it would be to describe which branch to use if you couldn't just point at the branch. That is, if instead of pointing, you had to describe the branch to someone else. That's the task you have when you are constructing a treeview.

So, it's easy to hang the text on a node of the tree, and it's somewhat more difficult to describe the node that you want to decorate. Given these facts, how can you begin? Well, perhaps it's best to just jump right into the middle of the code and see how things shake out:

```
HTREEITEM AddItem(HWND hWndTV, HTREEITEM hParent,
                  int iImage, int iSelectedImage,
                  LPSTR szText, LPARAM lParam)
{
  TV_ITEM              tvItem;
  TV_INSERTSTRUCT      tvIns;

  tvItem.mask = TVIF_TEXT | TVIF_IMAGE | TVIF_SELECTEDIMAGE | TVIF_PARAM;

  // Set the attributes
  tvItem.pszText       = szText;
  tvItem.iImage        = iImage;
  tvItem.iSelectedImage = iSelectedImage;
  tvItem.lParam        = lParam;

  // Fill out the TV_INSERTSTRUCT
  tvIns.hParent        = hParent;
  tvIns.hInsertAfter   = TVI_LAST;
  tvIns.item           = tvItem;

  return TreeView_InsertItem (hWndTV, &tvIns);
}
```

You should be familiar with the general theory behind TV_ITEM structure since it is similar to the LV_ITEM structure associated with the listviews on Day 19:

```
typedef struct _TV_ITEM {  tvi
    UINT       mask;
    HTREEITEM  hItem;
    UINT       state;
    UINT       stateMask;
    LPSTR      pszText;
    int        cchTextMax;
    int        iImage;
```

```
      MessageBox(hwnd, ErrString,  NULL, MB_OK ¦ MB_ICONHAND);
      return(FALSE);
   }

   return TRUE;
}

//////////////////////////////////////
// Allocate memory for meta bits
//////////////////////////////////////
HANDLE AllocMetaMemory(HWND hwnd, METAHEADER *mfHeader)
{
   char *ErrString1 = "Memory allocation error";
   HANDLE   hMem;

   hMem = GlobalAlloc(GHND, (mfHeader->mtSize * 2L));
   if (!hMem)
   {
     MessageBox(hwnd, ErrString1, NULL, MB_OK ¦ MB_ICONHAND);
     return hMem = 0;
   }
   return hMem;
}

BOOL ReadMetafileBits(HWND hwnd, HFILE fh, METAHEADER mfHeader,
                      LPSTR lpMem, HANDLE * hMem)
{
   DWORD BytesRead;
   char *ErrString = "Unable to read metafile bits";

   if (mfHeader.mtSize > 10000)
     return FALSE;


   _llseek(fh, sizeof(ALDUSMFHEADER), 0);
   BytesRead = _lread(fh, lpMem, (mfHeader.mtSize * 2L));

   if(BytesRead <= 0)
   {
     MessageBox(hwnd, ErrString, NULL, MB_OK ¦ MB_ICONHAND);
     GlobalUnlock(*hMem);
     GlobalFree(*hMem);
     return FALSE;
   }
   return TRUE;
}

//////////////////////////////////////
// RenderMeta
//////////////////////////////////////
BOOL RenderPlaceableMeta(HWND hwnd, HFILE fh)
{
   BYTE * lpMem;
   HANDLE   hMem;
```

continues

Listing BD1.4. continued

```
      if ((bMetaInRam) && (hmf))
        DeleteMetaFile(hmf);
    _llseek(fh, 0, 0);

      if (!ReadPlaceableHeader(hwnd, fh)) return FALSE;
      if (!ReadHeader(&mfHeader, hwnd, fh)) return FALSE;
      hMem = AllocMetaMemory(hwnd, &mfHeader);
      if (!hMem) return FALSE;
      lpMem = (BYTE *)GlobalLock(hMem);
      if(!ReadMetafileBits(hwnd, fh, mfHeader, (LPSTR)lpMem, &hMem))
      {
        GlobalUnlock(hMem);
        return FALSE;
      }

      #ifdef WIN32
      hmf = SetMetaFileBitsEx(mfHeader.mtSize * 2, lpMem);
      #else
      hmf = SetMetaFileBits(hMem);
      #endif

      if (!hmf)
      {
        GlobalUnlock(hMem);
        return(FALSE);
      }
      GlobalUnlock(hMem);
      return(TRUE);
    }

    /////////////////////////////////////
    // OpenMetaFile
    /////////////////////////////////////
    BOOL OpenMetaFile(HWND hwnd, char * lpFileName)
    {
        HFILE fh;
        int wBytesRead;
        LONG dwIsAldus;

        fh = _lopen(lpFileName, OF_READ);

        if (fh != -1)
        {
          // See if it is a placeable wmf
          wBytesRead =
            _lread(fh,(LPSTR)&dwIsAldus, sizeof(dwIsAldus));
          if (wBytesRead == HFILE_ERROR || wBytesRead < sizeof(dwIsAldus))
          {
            _lclose(fh);
            MessageBox(hwnd, "unable to read file", NULL,
                        MB_OK | MB_ICONEXCLAMATION);
            return (FALSE);
          }
```

```
        if (dwIsAldus != ALDUSKEY)
        {
          IsAldus = FALSE;
          hmf = GetMetaFile(lpFileName);
        }
        else
        {
          IsAldus = TRUE;
          RenderPlaceableMeta(hwnd, fh);
        }
        _lclose(fh);
    }
    return TRUE;
}

//////////////////////////////////////
// GetFileName
//////////////////////////////////////
LPSTR GetFileName(HWND hwnd, char * szFile, int StringSize)
{
  OPENFILENAME ofn;
  char szDirName[256];
  char szFileTitle[256];

  szFile[0] = 0;
  memset(&ofn, 0, sizeof(OPENFILENAME));

  ofn.lStructSize = sizeof(OPENFILENAME);
  ofn.hwndOwner = hwnd;
  ofn.lpstrFilter = "Metafiles (*.WMF)\0*.wmf\0";
  ofn.nFilterIndex = 1;
  ofn.lpstrFile= szFile;
  ofn.nMaxFile = StringSize;
  ofn.lpstrFileTitle = szFileTitle;
  ofn.nMaxFileTitle = sizeof(szFileTitle);
  ofn.lpstrInitialDir = szDirName;
  ofn.Flags = OFN_FILEMUSTEXIST;

  GetOpenFileName(&ofn);

  return szFile;
}

//////////////////////////////////////
// LoadFile
//////////////////////////////////////
void LoadFile(HWND hwnd)
{
  char S[100];
  bMetaInRam = TRUE;
  memset(&S, 0, 100);

  GetFileName(hwnd, S, 100);

  OpenMetaFile(hwnd, S);
```

continues

Listing BD1.4. continued

```c
    if (!hmf)
      MessageBox(hwnd, "The Metafile was not created!", "Error in MetaUtil!", MB_OK);

    InvalidateRect(hwnd, NULL, TRUE);

}

////////////////////////////////////////
// GetSaveName;
////////////////////////////////////////
char *GetSaveName(HWND hwnd, char * SaveName)
{
    OPENFILENAME ofn;
    char szDirName[256];
    char szFile[256], szFileTitle[256];
    UINT  i;
    char  chReplace;
    char  szFilter[256];

    _getdcwd(0, szDirName, 255);

    strcpy(szFilter,
            "Metafiles(*.wmf)¦*.wmf¦Bitmap Files(*.bmp)¦*.bmp¦");
    chReplace = szFilter[strlen(szFilter) - 1];
    for (i = 0; szFilter[i] != '\0'; i++)
    {
        if (szFilter[i] == chReplace)
            szFilter[i] = '\0';
    }

    /* Set all structure members to zero. */

    memset(&ofn, 0, sizeof(OPENFILENAME));

    /* Initialize the OPENFILENAME members. */

    szFile[0] = '\0';

    ofn.lStructSize = sizeof(OPENFILENAME);
    ofn.hwndOwner = hwnd;
    ofn.lpstrFilter = szFilter;
    ofn.lpstrFile= szFile;
    ofn.nMaxFile = sizeof(szFile);
    ofn.lpstrFileTitle = szFileTitle;
    ofn.nMaxFileTitle = sizeof(szFileTitle);
    ofn.lpstrInitialDir = szDirName;

    ofn.Flags = OFN_OVERWRITEPROMPT;

    if (GetSaveFileName(&ofn))
      strcpy(SaveName, ofn.lpstrFile);
    else
      strcpy(SaveName, "");

    return SaveName;
}
```

```
int FileExists(const char *path)
{
  FILE *f = fopen(path, "r");
  if (!f)
    return FALSE;
  else
  {
    fclose(f);
    return TRUE;
  }
}

void SaveFile(HWND hwnd, char * OldName)
{
  char Name[256];
  int i;

  GetSaveName(hwnd, Name);

  if (strlen(Name) == 0) return;

  if (FileExists(Name))
  {
    i = remove(Name);
    if (i != 0)
      MessageBox(hwnd, "Error deleting", "No", MB_OK);
  }

  i = rename(OldName, Name);
  if (i != 0)
    MessageBox(hwnd, "Error renaming", "No", MB_OK);

  OpenMetaFile(hwnd, Name);
}

void TurnOffSave(HWND hwnd)
{
  HMENU hMenu = GetMenu(hwnd);
  EnableMenuItem(hMenu, CM_ENDMETA, MF_BYCOMMAND | MF_GRAYED);
}
```

Listing BD1.5. The header file for METAUTIL.H.

```
/////////////////////////////////////
// Module: METAUTIL.H
// Copyright (c) 1993 by Charlie Calvert
// Description: Part of Meta project
// Update for WIN32: 06/13/95
/////////////////////////////////////
#define  ALDUSKEY        0x9AC6CDD7L


// types
```

continues

Listing BD1.5. continued

```
/* I need types that will be the same size in WIN16
   and WIN32. I never really work with an ALDUSMFHEADER
   so I just define its size, which is 22 bytes. If
   you need the fields, I've left them for your
   delectation */

typedef struct {
/*DWORD  key;
  WORD   hmf;
  RECT bbox;
  WORD    inch;
  DWORD   reserved;
  WORD    checksum;*/
  BYTE Data[22];
} ALDUSMFHEADER;

// Procs
void CreateMeta(HWND hwnd);
void LoadFile(HWND hwnd);
BOOL IsAldusFile(void);
void SaveFile(HWND hwnd, char * OldName);
void TurnOffSave(HWND hwnd);
```

Listing BD1.6. METAENUM.CPP.

```
1: /////////////////////////////////////////////////////////
2: //   Program Name: METAENUM.CPP
3: //   Programmer: Charlie Calvert
4: //   Description: Part of Metaphor Windows project
5: //   Date: 7/23/93
6: /////////////////////////////////////////////////////////
7:
8: #define STRICT
9: #include <windows.h>
10: #include <windowsx.h>
11: #pragma warning (disable: 4068)
12: int CALLBACK EnumMetaFileProc(HDC hdc, HANDLETABLE FAR* lpHTable,
13:    METARECORD FAR* lpMFR, int cObj, BYTE FAR* lpClientData);
14:
15: /////////////////////////////////////
16: // EnumTheMeta
17: /////////////////////////////////////
18: void EnumTheMeta(HWND hwnd, HMETAFILE AMeta)
19: {
20:   MFENUMPROC lpEnumMetaProc;
21:   HDC PaintDC;
22:   HINSTANCE hInst;
23:
24:   PaintDC = GetDC(hwnd);
25:   hInst = (HINSTANCE)GetClassWord(hwnd, GCW_HMODULE);
26:   lpEnumMetaProc = (MFENUMPROC) MakeProcInstance(
27:     (FARPROC) EnumMetaFileProc, hInst);
28:   EnumMetaFile(PaintDC, AMeta, lpEnumMetaProc, NULL);
```

```
29:   FreeProcInstance((FARPROC) lpEnumMetaProc);
30:
31:   ReleaseDC(hwnd, PaintDC);
32: }
33:
34: // --------------------------
35: // Callbacks, etc
36: // --------------------------
37:
38: /////////////////////////////////
39: // EnumMetaFileProc
40: /////////////////////////////////
41: #pragma argsused
42: int CALLBACK EnumMetaFileProc(HDC hdc, HANDLETABLE FAR* lpHTable,
43:     METARECORD FAR* lpMFR, int cObj, BYTE FAR* lpClientData)
44: {
45:     PlayMetaFileRecord(hdc, lpHTable, lpMFR, cObj);
46:     return 1;
47: }
```

Listing BD1.7. METAENUM.H.

```
1: //////////////////////////////////////////////////////////////
2: //   Program Name: METAENUM.H
3: //   Programmer: Charlie Calvert
4: //   Description: Part of Metaphor windows project
5: //   Date: 7/23/93
6: //////////////////////////////////////////////////////////////
7:
8: void EnumTheMeta(HWND hwnd, HMETAFILE AMeta);
```

Listing BD1.8. METAPHOR.RC.

```
1: /////////////////////////////////////
2: // File: METAPHOR.RC
3: // Description: Resource file for Metaphor project
4: /////////////////////////////////////
5: #include "metaphor.h"
6:
7: Head2 METAFILE "head2.wmf"
8:
9: MetaMenu MENU
10: BEGIN
11:   POPUP "&File"
12:   BEGIN
13:     MENUITEM "Load", CM_LOAD;
14:     MENUITEM SEPARATOR;
15:     MENUITEM "Save_Meta", CM_ENDMETA;
16:     MENUITEM SEPARATOR;
17:     MENUITEM "Quick_Meta", CM_NEWMETA;
18:     MENUITEM SEPARATOR;
```

continues

Listing BD1.8. continued

```
19:      MENUITEM "Exit", CM_EXIT;
20:   END
21:
22:   POPUP "&Shape"
23:   BEGIN
24:     MENUITEM "Line", CM_LINE;
25:     MENUITEM "Ellipse", CM_ELLIPSE;
26:     MENUITEM "Rectangle", CM_RECTANGLE;
27:     MENUITEM "Empty Rectangle", CM_ERECTANGLE;
28:   END
29:
30:   POPUP "&Pen_Color"
31:   BEGIN
32:     MENUITEM "Red", CM_RED;
33:     MENUITEM "Green", CM_GREEN;
34:     MENUITEM "Blue", CM_BLUE;
35:   END
36:
37:   POPUP "&Fill_Color"
38:   BEGIN
39:     MENUITEM "Red", CM_FRED;
40:     MENUITEM "Green", CM_FGREEN;
41:     MENUITEM "Blue", CM_FBLUE;
42:   END
43:
44:   POPUP "Pen_&Size"
45:   BEGIN
46:     MENUITEM "1", CM_ONE;
47:     MENUITEM "5", CM_FIVE;
48:     MENUITEM "10", CM_TEN;
49:     MENUITEM "20", CM_TWENTY;
50:     MENUITEM "40", CM_FORTY;
51:     MENUITEM "80", CM_EIGHTY;
52:   END
53: END
```

Listing BD1.9. METAPHOR.DEF.

```
1: ; METAPHOR.DEF
2:
3: NAME          Metaphor
4: DESCRIPTION   'Metaphor Window'
5: HEAPSIZE      4096
6: STACKSIZE     5120
7: CODE          PRELOAD MOVEABLE DISCARDABLE
8: DATA          PRELOAD MOVEABLE MULTIPLE
```

Listing BD1.10. METAPHOR.MAK (Borland).

```
# METAPHOR.MAK

# macros
APPNAME = Metaphor
OBJS = MetaUtil.obj MetaEnum.obj

BCROOT = $(MAKEDIR)\..
INCPATH= $(BCROOT)\INCLUDE
LIBPATH= $(BCROOT)\LIB

!if !$d(WIN16)
COMPILER = BCC32.EXE
RCCOMPILER = BRC32.EXE -w32
FLAGS    = -WE -v -w4
!else
COMPILER = BCC.EXE
RCCOMPILER = BRC.EXE
FLAGS    = -WE -ml -v -w4
!endif

# link
$(APPNAME).exe: $(APPNAME).obj $(OBJS) $(APPNAME).def $(APPNAME).res
  $(COMPILER) $(FLAGS) $(APPNAME).obj $(OBJS)
  $(RCCOMPILER) $(APPNAME)

# compile
.cpp.obj:
  $(COMPILER) -c $(FLAGS) { $< }

#resource
$(APPNAME).res: $(APPNAME).rc
  $(RCCOMPILER) -R -I$(INCPATH) $(APPNAME).RC
```

Listing BD1.11. METAPHOR.MAK (Microsoft).

```
#-----------------------------------------------
# METAPHMS.MAK
#-----------------------------------------------

# Some Macros
APPNAME=METAPHOR
TARGETOS=WIN95
APPVER=4.0
OBJS=$(APPNAME).OBJ METAUTIL.OBJ METAENUM.OBJ

!include <win32.mak>

all: $(APPNAME).exe

# Update the resource if necessary

$(APPNAME).res: $(APPNAME).rc $(APPNAME).h
  $(rc) $(rcflags) $(rcvars) $(APPNAME).rc
```

continues

989

Listing BD1.11. continued

```
# Update the object files if necessary

# compile
.cpp.obj:
  $(cc) $(cflags) $(cvars) $(cdebug) $<

# Update the executable file if necessary.

$(APPNAME).exe: $(OBJS) $(APPNAME).res
  $(link) $(linkdebug) $(guiflags) -out:$(APPNAME).exe \
  $(OBJS) $(APPNAME).res $(guilibs) comctl32.lib
```

Figure BD1.3 shows the Metaphor program.

The Metaphor program lets you use the mouse to draw lines, rectangles, and ellipses on the main

Figure BD1.3.

The Metaphor program can be used to draw simple geometric shapes.

window. By using the menu, you can change the color and thickness of the pen that outlines each shape, and also change the color of the solid fill pattern that forms the body of each shape.

The Metaphor program enables you to save the images you have created and reload them later. In order to simplify the design of the program, Metaphor only allows you to create one shape per session, and you must create the shape before loading any other files. You can't edit any of the designs you create, but the program could be expanded to include this feature.

Besides letting you draw metafiles, the Metaphor program supports loading and displaying these graphical images. The program is fully capable of reading and displaying the so-called "Aldus" metafiles that have a slightly different header than the one found in standard Windows metafiles. Metaphor examines any metafile you choose to read and then automatically chooses the correct method for loading and displaying it.

The Shape of Things to Come

The rest of this chapter is divided into three sections:

1. An examination of *rubber banding*—the technique used for drawing shapes dynamically on the screen with the mouse

2. An examination of creating, reading, and saving metafiles

3. A brief introduction to the common dialogs—a theme that's carried through to the next chapter

Rubber Banding

Before reading this section, fire up the Metaphor program and practice drawing ellipses and rectangles on-screen so you can see how the rubber-band technique works. If for some reason you can't run the Metaphor program, open up Windows Paintbrush and draw some squares or circles with the appropriate tools from the Tools menu on the left edge of the screen. Watch the way these programs create an elastic square or circle that you can drag around the desktop. Play with these shapes as you decide what dimensions and location you want for your geometric figure.

Such tools appear to be difficult for a programmer to create, but thanks to the Windows API, the code is relatively trivial. Following are the main steps involved, each of which will be explained in depth later in this section:

1. When the user clicks the left mouse button, Metaphor "memorizes" the x,y coordinates of the WM_LBUTTONDOWN event.

2. As the user drags the mouse across the screen, with the left button still down, Metaphor draws a square or circle each time it gets a WM_MOUSEMOVE message. Just before painting each new shape, the program blanks out the previous square or circle. The dimensions of the new shape are calculated by combining the coordinates of the original WM_LBUTTONDOWN message with the current coordinates passed in the WM_MOUSEMOVE message.

3. When the user generates a WM_LBUTTONUP message, Metaphor paints the final shape in the colors and pen size specified by the user.

Although this description obviously omits some important details, the outlines of the algorithm should take shape in your mind in the form of only a few, relatively simple, logical strokes. Things get a bit more complicated when the details are mulled over one by one, but the fundamental steps should be relatively clear.

Zooming in on the details, here's a look at the response to a WM_LBUTTONDOWN message (lines 370–379):

```
void Meta_OnLButtonDown(HWND hwnd, BOOL fDoubleClick,
                        int x, int y, UINT keyFlags)
{
  Dat.ButtonDown = TRUE;
  Dat.Drawing = FALSE;
  OldRect.left = -32000;
  Dat.DownX = x;
  Dat.DownY = y;
  SetCapture(hwnd);
}
```

After initializing some variables, the final steps in Meta_OnLButtonDown involve "memorizing" the location of the event and "capturing" the mouse. The call to SetCapture is necessary because the user might drag the mouse off the window in the process of drawing a shape. If this happens, the user doesn't want the focus to drift off to some other window or program.

After the left mouse button is pressed, the program picks up all WM_MOUSEMOVE messages that come flying into Metaphor's ken (lines 346–364):

```
void Meta_OnMouseMove(HWND hwnd, int x,
                      int y, UINT keyFlags)
{
  if (Dat.ButtonDown)
  {
    Dat.Drawing = TRUE;

    HDC PaintDC = GetDC(hwnd);

    SetROP2(PaintDC, R2_NOTXORPEN);
    if (OldRect.left != -32000)
    DrawShape(hwnd, PaintDC, OldRect);
    OldRect.left = Dat.DownX;
    OldRect.top = Dat.DownY;
    OldRect.right = x;
    OldRect.bottom = y;
    DrawShape(hwnd, PaintDC, OldRect);
    ReleaseDC(hwnd, PaintDC);
  }
}
```

The first line of the function uses one of several possible techniques for checking to see if the left mouse button is down. If the button isn't down, the function ignores the message. If it is down, the function gets the device context, sets the drawing mode to R2_NOTXORPEN, memorizes the current dimensions of the figure, draws it, and releases the device context.

The SetROP2 function sets the current drawing mode in a manner similar to the way the last parameter in BitBlt sets the current painting mode. In this case, Metaphor uses the logical XOR and NOT operations to blit the elastic image to the screen. This logical operation is chosen because it paints the old shape directly on top of the original image, thereby effectively erasing each shape:

☐ If you XOR a square to the screen, the square will show up clearly.

☐ If you XOR that same image again in the same location, the image will disappear.

Such are the virtues of simple logical operations in graphics mode.

> **Note**: Aficionados of graphics logic will note that the logical operation employed by Metaphor (R2_NOTXORPEN) is a variation on the exclusive OR (XOR) operation. This variation ensures that the fill in the center of the shape to be drawn won't blot out what's beneath it. The Microsoft documentation explains the difference like this:
>
> ```
> R2_XOR          final pixel = pen ^ screen pixel
> R2_NOTXORPEN    final pixel = ~(pen ^ screen pixel)
> ```
>
> This code tests to see whether the pixels to be XORed belong to a pen.

Don't waste too much time worrying about logical operations and how they work. If they interest you, fine; if they don't, that's okay. The subject matter of this book is programming, not logic.

The *SetROP2* Function

```
int SetROP2(HDC, int)
```

HDC hdc;	Device context
int fnDrawMode;	Drawing mode

SetROP2 determines the features of the current drawing mode. More specifically, it defines how the pen and the interior of an object are to be combined with the current contents of the screen.

The second parameter can contain a wide range of possible operations, all of which are listed in WINDOWS.H and in your online help files. A small sample includes the following options:

R2_BLACK	Draws shape in black pixels.
R2_WHITE	Draws shape in white pixels.
R2_NOP	Doesn't change the pixels.
R2_NOT	Makes the current pixel the inverse of the screen color.
R2_COPYPEN	Makes the pixel the color of the current pen.

Here's an example:

```
SetROP2(PaintDC, R2_NOT);
```

GDI and Metafiles

Notice that `Meta_OnMouseMove` calls `DrawShape` twice. The first time, it passes in the dimensions of the old figure that needs to be erased. That means it XORs the same image directly on top of the original image, thereby erasing it. Then `Meta_OnMouseMove` records the location of the latest `WM_MOUSEMOVE` message and passes this new information to `DrawShape`, which paints the new image to the screen. This whole process is repeated over and over again (at incredible speeds) until the user lifts the left mouse button.

In the `DrawImage` function (line 265), Metaphor first checks to see which shape the user has selected and then proceeds to draw that shape to the screen using the default pen and fill color.

The final step in the whole operation occurs when the user lifts his or her finger off the mouse:

```
void Meta_OnLButtonUp(HWND hwnd, int x,
                      int y, UINT keyFlags)
{
  if ((Dat.ButtonDown) && (Dat.Drawing))
  {
    Dat.Drawing = FALSE;
    HDC PaintDC = GetDC(hwnd);
    DrawFinalShape(hwnd, PaintDC, OldRect);
    ReleaseDC(hwnd, PaintDC);
    ReleaseCapture();
  }
  Dat.ButtonDown = FALSE;
}
```

This code checks to see that the mouse is down and that the user is drawing a shape. If so, the following occurs:

- ☐ A flag is set stating that the user has decided to stop drawing.
- ☐ The final image is painted to the screen.
- ☐ The "captured" mouse is released.

The code that paints the final shape takes into account the colors and the pen thickness that the user selected with the menus. This excerpt from `DrawFinalShape` (line 290), shows what happens:

```
HPEN Pen = CreatePen(PS_INSIDEFRAME, Dat.Thickness, Dat.Color);
HPEN OldPen = SelectPen(PaintDC, Pen);

switch(Dat.Shape)
{
  case ELLIPSE:
    OldBrush = SelectBrush(PaintDC, FBrush);
    Ellipse(PaintDC, R.left, R.top, R.right, R.bottom);
    SelectObject(PaintDC, OldBrush);
    break;
  ... // code for drawing rectangles, lines, etc
```

Metaphor creates a pen in the user-selected color and thickness, and then copies the user-selected brush into the device context. The call to draw the shape follows, and then the program carefully cleans up after itself. This code is in contrast to the code that is called to draw the "elastic shape."

BD1

When drawing the "rubber band," Metaphor relies on the default brush and pen, but it employs the same `switch` statement and the same calls to `Ellipse`, `Rectangle`, and so forth.

Well, there you have it. That's how you draw shapes to the screen using the rubber-band technique. Overall, if you take one thing at a time, the process isn't complicated. Just so you can keep those steps clear in your mind, here they are again:

☐ Remember where the `WM_LBUTTONDOWN` took place.

☐ Draw the shape each time you get a `WM_MOUSEMOVE` message.

☐ Draw the final shape when you get a `WM_LBUTTONUP` message.

That's all there is to it.

What Are Metafiles?

When writing code for a book such as this, I make design decisions based on the needs of students rather than the needs of users. For instance, the Metaphor program contains a very short function that creates, designs, and writes a very simple metafile called QUICKMET.WMF to disk. This code serves no functional role in the program. It's just there for educational purposes.

Following is the code, which starts on line 30 of METAUTIL.CPP:

```
void CreateMeta(HWND hwnd)
{
  HDC MetaDC;
  HPEN OldPen;
  char FName[256];

  _getdcwd(0, FName, MAXSIZE);
  strcat(FName, "\\quickmet.wmf");
  MetaDC = CreateMetaFile(FName);
  if (MetaDC != NULL)
  {
    HPEN Pen = CreatePen(PS_SOLID, 10, RGB(0, 255, 127));
    OldPen = SelectPen(MetaDC, Pen);
    Ellipse(MetaDC, 200, 200, 100, 100);
    SelectObject(MetaDC, OldPen);
    DeleteObject(Pen);
    Pen = CreatePen(PS_SOLID, 10, RGB(255, 0, 0));
    OldPen = SelectPen(MetaDC, Pen);
    Rectangle(MetaDC, 20, 20, 100, 100);
    SelectObject(MetaDC, OldPen);
    DeleteObject(Pen);
    hmf = CloseMetaFile(MetaDC);
  }
}
```

If you haven't done so already, run Metaphor, choose Quick_Meta from the menu, and load the QUICKMET.WMF file into the main window. The resulting image is shown in Figure BD1.4.

995

Figure BD1.4.

*The metafile produced by
the* CreateMeta *function
consists of two simple
geometric shapes.*

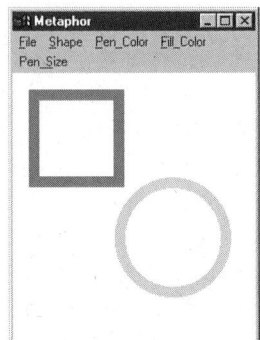

Though it may look a bit intimidating at first, the preceding code contains only one or two new ideas. The code starts by doing some handwaving to create a valid filename and then calls CreateMetaFile.

The *CreateMetaFile* Function

HDC CreateMetaFile(LPCSTR)

      LPCSTR lpszFile;   String specifying the metafile's name

The CreateMetaFile function returns a valid device context for a metafile.

Here's an example:

MyMetaDC = CreateMetaFile("c:\\Metafile.wmf");

After you've retrieved the DC for a metafile, all you need to do is copy shapes, pens, and brushes into it—just as you would with the device context for the screen. When you are done, call CloseMetafile, passing it the device context in its sole parameter. In return, it writes the file to disk and returns a handle to an in-memory copy of the file—which is of type HMETAFILE. An HMETAFILE is just like an HINSTANCE, HBITMAP, or HPEN. However, it's the handle to a metafile.

The final step is to display the metafile for the user with the easy-to-use PlayMetaFile function.

The *PlayMetaFile* Function

BOOL PlayMetaFile(hdc, hmf)

      HDC hdc;   The device context for the screen or printer

      HMETAFILE hmf;   The handle to a metafile

The PlayMetaFile function displays a metafile to the screen or the printer. Notice that the device context in its first parameter isn't the device context from the metafile; it's the DC of the device on which the file will be displayed.

Here's an example:

```
PlayMetaFile(PaintDC, hmf);
```

In short, a metafile is nothing but a list of structures, each of which contains information about a basic GDI call, such as `Rectangle`, `SelectObject`, or `Ellipse`. The `PlayMetaFile` command simply iterates through this list, displaying each shape in turn and as defined.

Best of all, metafiles are extremely compact. A full 800×600 SuperVGA bitmap might use over 200,000 bytes when saved to disk as a BMP. An equivalent metafile might be as small as 200 or 300 bytes. Even a complex metafile, such as the one shown in Figure BD1.5, is less than 15KB in size.

Figure BD1.5.
An image that ships with CorelDRAW! can be transformed into a metafile that is 12,492 bytes in size.

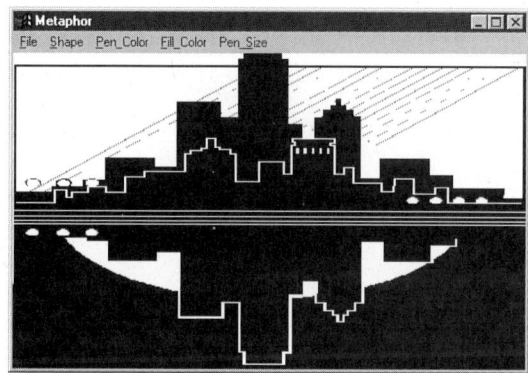

Because of the big savings in size, you should always check whether it is possible to use a metafile instead of a bitmap. This is particularly true if you want to work with a bitmap larger than 64×64 pixels in size.

To review, here is the simplest possible set of steps involved in creating a metafile:

1. Call `CreateMetaFile` and hang on to the device context it returns.
2. Copy the pens, brushes, and figures you want to use into the device context.
3. Call `CloseMetaFile` to write the image to disk and to retrieve a handle to the metafile.
4. Show the metafile to the user by calling `PlayMetaFile`.

Creating Metafiles Interactively

It's easy to make the jump from `CreateMetaFile` to an interactive system that enables the user to design his or her own metafiles. In fact, this is the purpose of the code that lies at the heart of the Metaphor program.

At startup, Metaphor calls `CreateMetaFile` in response to the user-defined `CM_STARTMETA` message:

```
case CM_STARTMETA:
  GooberDC = CreateMetaFile(TempName);
  break;
```

The device context retrieved from the call to `CreateMetaFile` is global to the program's main module; all the user-specified shapes and colors will be copied into it.

The actual figures to be placed in the file are defined by the user with the rubber-band code. When the user-selected shape is drawn to the screen in its final form, its type, color, and dimensions are also copied into the device context for the metafile. To see how this works, just take a moment to revisit the `DrawFinalShape` function (line 290, METAPHOR.CPP):

```
void DrawFinalShape(HWND hwnd, HDC PaintDC, RECT R)
{
  HBRUSH B, OldBrush, OldGBrush;

  HPEN Pen = CreatePen(PS_INSIDEFRAME, Dat.Thickness, Dat.Color);
  HPEN OldPen = SelectPen(PaintDC, Pen);
  HPEN OldGPen = SelectPen(GooberDC, Pen);

  switch(Dat.Shape)
  {
    case ELLIPSE:
      OldBrush = SelectBrush(PaintDC, FBrush);
      OldGBrush = SelectBrush(GooberDC, FBrush);
      Ellipse(PaintDC, R.left, R.top, R.right, R.bottom);
      Ellipse(GooberDC, R.left, R.top, R.right, R.bottom);
      SelectObject(PaintDC, OldBrush);
      SelectBrush(GooberDC, OldGBrush);
      break;
```

Here, Metaphor copies the geometric figure directly into both the screen's device context and the device context for the metafile. This same operation is repeated each time the user blocks out a new shape on-screen with the rubber-band technique.

When the user is done, he or she can select Save from the File menu, and the device context can be passed to `CloseMetaFile`. This writes the final file to disk and returns an `HMETAFILE`, which can be displayed on-screen whenever a `WM_PAINT` message comes down the pike.

The actual act of saving and loading a file is discussed in the section about common dialogs.

Turning a Metaphor into *Das Ding an Sich*

If you want to turn the metaphor program into a real paint program, that is, into the "thing itself," you obviously need to find some way to start iterating through the contents of an

HMETAFILE. This functionality is not included in the Metaphor program, but the program does drop hints as to one possible course to pursue.

The technique that comes to the rescue is an old friend: the callback function. In this case, there happens to be a native Windows callback that iterates through the contents of a metafile. Appropriately enough, it's called EnumMetaFile.

Before I describe the details of the function, take a moment to consider how it works. As you recall, the EnumFontFamilies function sent copies of all the fonts on the system to a callback function (see Day 11, "Talking to Controls"). The callback function can pass descriptions of the fonts back to the main program. The same thing happens in this case. That is, when you pass EnumMetaFile a handle to a metafile, it will iterate through the records in the metafile, passing each in turn to your user-defined function—the address of which is passed in the third argument to EnumMetaFile. These records define the GDI function that will be called and the parameters to be passed to it.

The *EnumMetaFile* Function

Syntax

```
BOOL EnumMetaFile(HDC, HLOCAL, MFENUMPROC, LPARAM)
```

HDC hdc;	Device context for the screen
HLOCAL hmf;	Handle of the metafile
MFENUMPROC mfenmprc;	The callback function
LPARAM lParam;	User-defined data to pass to the callback function

This function iterates through a series of structures containing information on all the calls used in the metafile. The key field in EnumMetaFile is the third, which contains the address of the callback function. The last parameter can be set to NULL, or it can contain any data the user wants to pass on to the EnumMetaFileProc.

Here's an example:

```
EnumMetaFile(PaintDC, MyMetaFile, lpMyMetaProc, MyData);
```

Here's the actual callback, as defined in the Metaphor program:

```
int CALLBACK EnumMetaFileProc(HDC hdc,
                              HANDLETABLE FAR* lpHTable,
                              METARECORD FAR* lpMFR,
                              int cObj,
                              BYTE FAR* lpClientData)
{
  PlayMetaFileRecord(hdc, lpHTable, lpMFR, cObj);
  return 1;
}
```

As you can see, this particular callback does nothing with the records it receives except pass them to PlayMetaFileRecord, which displays them on-screen.

The parameters to the `EnumMetaFileProc` are listed in Table BD1.2.

Table BD1.2. `EnumMetaFileProc` takes five parameters.

`HDC hdc;`	Device context on which to paint
`HANDLETABLE FAR* lpht;`	Address of table the object handles
`METARECORD FAR* lpmr;`	Address of metafile record
`int cObj;`	Number of objects in handle table
`LPARAM lParam;`	Data defined by the user

The key parameter in Table BD1.2 is the `METARECORD`, which is a pointer to a structure containing three fields:

```
struct {
  DWORD rdSize;
  WORD rdFunction;
  WORD rdParm[];
}
```

`rdSize` defines the size of the entire record, which can vary depending on the length of the last field. `rdFunction` specifies the GDI function—such as `Ellipse`, `Rectangle`, or `SelectObject`— packaged in the structure. The last argument lists the parameters passed to the function.

Consider the following call to `Rectangle`:

```
Rectangle(PaintDC, 0, 0, 96, 46);
```

The record designating this call would look like this:

```
rdSize: 7
rdFunction: 041B // Code for Rectangle function
rdParm 0046, 0096, 0000, 0000 // Parameters in reverse order
```

The codes designated in the second field are listed in the *Microsoft Windows 3.1 Programmers Reference, Volume 4: Resources*. For instance, `BitBlit` has a function number of `0x0922` or `0x0940`. `TextOut` is associated with function number `0x0521`.

Metaphor uses the `EnumMetaFileProc` solely to paint images to the screen quickly and efficiently. However, I've discussed the `METARECORDS`, because they reveal how metafiles are put together— and exactly how easy it is to begin manipulating them.

Reading Metafiles from Disk

As mentioned, there are two different kinds of metafiles in use. One is the standard Windows metafile created by the Metaphor program. The other is the Aldus, or placeable metafile, which is produced by programs commonly used throughout the industry.

When you are dealing with standard metafiles, all you need to do is call `GetMetaFile`, and it will suck the data up off the disk and pass it back in the form of an `HMETAFILE` handle. This is much simpler than the task you confront when you encounter a placeable metafile.

To identify an Aldus metafile, simply read the first `DWORD` size block from the file and compare it with the following constant: `0x9AC6CDD7L`. If you have a match, this is a placeable metafile. You should handle this file as follows:

- ☐ Strip off the 22-byte header which starts the file.
- ☐ Use the `SetMetaFileBits` function to transform what is left into a conventional metafile.

If you want to study this process in more depth, view the relevant code in the METAUTIL.CPP file, lines 66 through 243. In particular, you should note that the `OpenMetaFile` function determines whether or not the file is an Aldus metafile. If that is indeed the case, `RenderPlaceableMeta` is called. If the file isn't an Aldus metafile, the program relies on the `GetMetaFile` API function. The real grunt work of reading a placeable metafile is performed by `RenderPlaceableMeta`, which begins on line 138.

If you like, you can treat this whole process as a black box. In other words, the simplest way to proceed is to first link the `MetaUtil` modules into your own programs. Then, call `LoadFile` and be sure to pass in the `HWND` of the active window in your program. `LoadFile` pops up a common dialog enabling you to choose a file. When you do, it initializes a global variable called `hmf`, which is a handle to the metafile you selected.

Common Dialogs

Starting with Version 3.1, Windows includes a set of common dialogs meant to ease certain frequently performed tasks. For example, the Metaphor program uses the `GetOpenFileName` common dialog (see Figure BD1.6) and the `GetSaveFileName` common dialog (see Figure BD1.7) to aid in the loading and saving of files. The actual act of reading and writing files from disk still needs to be coded by the programmer. These dialogs are designed solely to handle the interface with the user.

Figure BD1.6.

The `GetOpenFileName` dialog enables you to choose files to be loaded into a program or window.

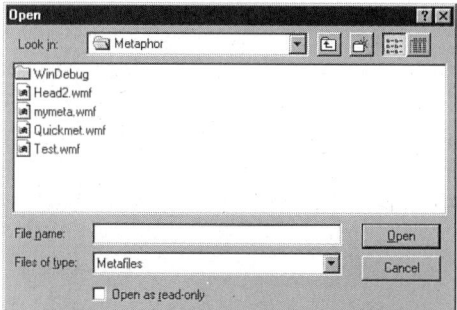

Figure BD1.7.

The `GetSaveFileName` *dialog is visually almost identical to the* `GetOpenFileName` *dialog.*

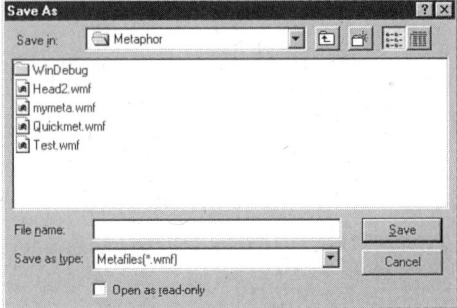

The difference between these two dialogs is not in the way they look, but in the way they behave. The `GetSaveFileName` dialog, for instance, has the capability of prompting the user before it overwrites a file.

Both of these functions involve working with a single large structure of type OPENFILENAME, which is described in the online help, or in COMMDLG.H. COMMDLG.H is to common dialogs as WINDOWS.H is to the rest of Windows. That is, it's the bible and main source of information. Here's a look at the OPENFILENAME structure as it appears in COMMDLG.H. I've included a few sparse comments to define each field. For a more in-depth description, see the online documentation:

```
typedef struct tagOFN
{
  DWORD     lStructSize;        // Size of OPENFILENAME
  HWND      hwndOwner;          // Owner of dialog
  HINSTANCE hInstance;          // Program that owns dialog
  LPCSTR    lpstrFilter;        // Types of files to view
  LPSTR     lpstrCustomFilter;  // Custom filters
  DWORD     nMaxCustFilter;     // Length of custom filter
  DWORD     nFilterIndex;       // Index for use with filters
  LPSTR     lpstrFile;          // Holds filename on success
  DWORD     nMaxFile;           // Size of lpstrFile
  LPSTR     lpstrFileTitle;     // Path & filename on success
  DWORD     nMaxFileTitle;      // Length of lpstrFileTitle
  LPCSTR    lpstrInitialDir;    // Initial file directory
  LPCSTR    lpstrTitle;         // String for caption bar
  DWORD     Flags;              // Initialization flags
  UINT      nFileOffset;        // Offset into lpstrFile
  UINT      nFileExtension;     // Offset into lpstrFile
  LPCSTR    lpstrDefExt;        // Default extension
  LPARAM    lCustData;          // Used with callbacks
  UINT      (CALLBACK *lpfnHook)(HWND, UINT, WPARAM, LPARAM);
  LPCSTR    lpTemplateName;     // Substitute resource for dlg
}   OPENFILENAME;

typedef OPENFILENAME FAR* LPOPENFILENAME;
```

Whenever you are working with a common dialog, there are three steps you must follow:

1. Zero out the record associated with the common dialog and fill in its first field with the size of the structure itself:

```
OPENFILENAME ofn;
 memset(&ofn, 0, sizeof(OPENFILENAME));
ofn.lStructSize = sizeof(OPENFILENAME);
```

2. Fill in any of the other fields in the structure that are either required or of special interest to your program. Of particular importance is the Flag field. This turns certain features of the dialog on and off, such as whether it will contain a Help button and whether it will prompt the user before overwriting an existing file.

3. Pass the structure to the API function that runs the dialog and handles input from the user. For instance, if you want to load a file from disk, make this call:

```
GetOpenFileName(&ofn);
```

In the lower-left corner of the common dialogs example is a drop-down combo box listing the types of files commonly used by a particular dialog. For instance, the GetSaveFileName dialog has both .WMF and .BMP files listed, as shown in Figure BD1.8. As you can see, this list box includes both the file extension and a brief description.

Figure BD1.8.

The combo box that displays the files that can be handled by a particular dialog.

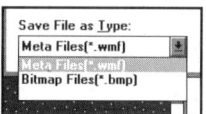

The text to be placed in the combo box is passed in with the lpstrFilter field of the OPENFILENAME struct. There are two ways to fill out this field. The first is relatively straightforward conceptually but a bit clumsy to implement. The second is easy to implement but a bit confusing at first glance.

The goal of this procedure is to fill the lpstrFilter field with pairs of null-terminated strings. The first null-terminated string contains the description of the file type, and the second contains the extension itself. The end of the list should contain two contiguous null characters. Here's an example:

```
memset(&ofn, 0, sizeof(OPENFILENAME));
ofn.lpstrFilter = "Metafiles (*.WMF)\0*.wmf\0";
```

The second technique works with a string that contains placeholders designating where the null characters should be inserted. To make the following code work, the last character in this string should be an example of the placeholder. The for loop in the code replaces each of the placeholders with a null character.

```
strcpy(szFilter,
"Metafiles(*.wmf)¦*.wmf¦Bitmap Files(*.bmp)¦*.bmp¦");
chReplace = szFilter[strlen(szFilter) - 1];
```

```
for (i = 0; szFilter[i] != '\0'; i++)
{
  if (szFilter[i] == chReplace)
  szFilter[i] = '\0';
}
```

If you want a more in-depth discussion of common dialogs, turn to the next chapter, which examines the ChooseFont common dialog. For now, you should be able to get your own programs up and running by using the GetFileName and GetSaveName functions (listed on lines 200 and 250 of METAUTIL.CPP).

Summary

A good deal of ground has been covered in this chapter. The highlights include descriptions of how to do the following:

☐ Draw basic geometric shapes, such as ellipses and rectangles

☐ Keep a record of these shapes in a metafile

☐ Display a metafile (using two methods)

☐ Read placeable metafiles

☐ Work with the GetSaveFileName and GetOpenFileName common dialogs

Though not as important as bitmaps, metafiles can still play a prominent role in many applications because they are so small and fast. They also can be a convenient way of passing graphical or textual information (don't forget that TextOut is a GDI function) between two applications or windows.

Q&A

Q The makefile for this program looks different. What's up?

A The Metaphor program contains three separate CPP files that need to be linked. Writing out explicit rules for compiling each of those files becomes a monotonous task that cries out for some form of automation. The solution provided by the creators of Make is to write something called an *implicit* rule, that says, in effect, "every time you need to perform a particular type of task, here's how to do it." For instance, the following code says: "Every time you see a file with an .OBJ extension, you can create it by running a CPP file through the Borland command-line compiler."

```
.cpp.obj:
  {$COMPILER} -c $(FLAGS) { $< }
```

Here's the same line applied to the Microsoft compiler:

```
.cpp.obj:
  $(cc) $(cflags) $(cvars) $(cdebug) $<
```

The $< syntax appended to the end of these statements is a built-in macro that automatically supplies the name of the file in question, along with its extension.

Q How do you gray the Save menu item in the File menu?

A Sometimes, a programmer wants to prevent a user from selecting a particular menu item. To do this, simply call EnableMenuItem as follows:

```
HMENU hMenu = GetMenu(hwnd);
EnableMenuItem(hMenu, CM_ENDMETA, MF_BYCOMMAND | MF_GRAYED);
```

The EnableMenuItem function takes three parameters. The first is the handle to a menu; the second is the ID or position of the menu item in question. The third parameter is a set of flags specifying whether the second parameter is a position or command value, and whether or not you want the menu item grayed and disabled (MF_GRAYED), disabled but not grayed (MF_DISABLED), or enabled (MF_ENABLE).

Q What are NULL brushes used for?

A NULL brushes make a particular set of pixels transparent. For instance, if you paint the interior of a rectangle with a NULL brush, you'll be able to see through it to what lies beneath.

Workshop

The Workshop provides quiz questions to help you solidify your understanding of the material covered and exercises to provide you with experience in using what you've learned. Try to understand the quiz and exercise answers before continuing on to the next chapter. Answers are provided in Appendix A.

Quiz

1. What non-numerical field is common to every GDI function?
2. Name six GDI functions for creating geometric figures.
3. How do you change the color of the interior of an ellipse?
4. How do you change the color of the outline of a rectangle?
5. What's the difference between a placeable Windows metafile, and a standard Windows metafile?
6. Identify two ways to display a metafile.
7. What is returned by CreateMetaFile and what do you do with it?
8. What is returned by CloseMetaFile and what can you do with it?
9. What is the second field in a METARECORD, how can you find the values listed in it, and how can you get hold of a METARECORD in the first place?

10. What is the first field in an OPENFILENAME struct, and what are you supposed to do with it?

Exercises

1. Write a program displaying a polygon with six sides.

2. (Optional) Create a metafile containing three ellipses and three rectangles. Modify the EnumMetaFileProc function so that every time it encounters one of the ellipses, it changes its color to green. (HINT: The function number for an ellipse is 0x0422. Its parameters are stored the same way as the parameters in the Rectangle function, as shown in the previous example.)

3. (Optional) The function numbers for LineTo and MoveTo are 0x0213 and 0x0214. Create some metafiles with about 10 geometric figures in them, and then pop up a message box that lists the order of the figures and their type. Obtain this information solely from an examination of the metafile itself. Sample output:

```
Figure 1: Rectangle
Figure 3: Ellipse
Figure 5: LineTo
...etc.
```

Bonus Day

2+

MDI: The Multiple-Document Interface

In this chapter you'll learn how to code applications that feature a multiple-document interface (MDI). MDI programs enable you to have more than one document open inside an application at a time. Both the Borland 4.5 and Microsoft IDEs are MDI applications, as well as such popular applications as Quattro Pro for Windows and Word for Windows.

Following is an overview of the main points covered in this chapter:

- ☐ An explanation of MDI and its purposes
- ☐ Registering and creating MDI Windows
- ☐ Working with MDI menus
- ☐ Using the WNDCLASS extra bytes to store data
- ☐ Using the WM_QUERYENDSESSION message
- ☐ Using MDI specific messages
- ☐ Sharing CPU time with other windows or applications
- ☐ The difference between MM_ANISOTROPIC and MM_ISOTROPIC

To demonstrate these ideas to you, I've included a sample program called MDIPaint that displays four different types of child windows. This application has been divided into six different modules: one for the main program, one for a set of common routines, and one for each of the children. This approach enables a simple, clean design, with each module comprising a relatively self-contained and easy-to-understand piece of the whole.

It's worth noting that Microsoft is no longer pushing the MDI as intently as it did in the past. Instead of using child windows inside a parent's frame, the new metaphor is the single-document interface, or SDI. (Other names for SDI applications include project model and workbook.) Delphi, Visual Basic, and the Explorer are all examples of SDI applications. MDI is not dead, and even flagship Microsoft products such as MSVC20 still use it. However, it points toward the past, while the SDI points towards the future. Think tabs, think property sheets, think pop-up windows—these are key aspects of the new interface. Though it's not wrong to use MDI, you should think twice before building a WIN32-based application with an MDI.

Overall, I find that the MDI presents a more complicated challenge than some of the other subjects approached in this book. However, it's not prohibitively difficult. You just need to take your time and think ahead.

What Is the MDI?

The first thing to understand about the MDI is that it is a standard, and more specifically, a 16-bit Windows standard. Way back in ancient computer history, when the earth's crust was still cooling—that is, in 1989—IBM wrote a specification for something called the multiple-document interface.

This standard is explained in a book called *Systems Application Architecture Common User Access Advanced Interface Design Guide*, or more commonly, *SAA CUA Interface Design Guide*, published by IBM in June 1989. The Windows MDI conforms to the standard laid out in this book. An example MDI application is shown in Figure BD2.1.

Figure BD2.1.

The File Manager is the MDI application.

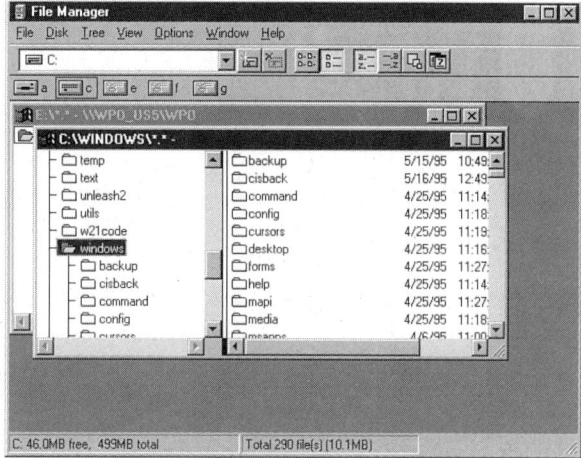

BD2

This standard is not only a programmer's standard but also a user's standard. MDI isn't just a technical specification for hackers, but an interface that Windows 3.1 users know, understand, and count on. More specifically, users count on the fact that each MDI program will behave in a similar fashion. In that way, users can catch on fairly quickly to the best methods for using the application. All Windows MDI applications automatically exhibit the following behavior:

- ☐ The application consists of a main window and a series of child windows. All the child windows stay within the parent's boundaries.

- ☐ The application, and each child window, can be maximized and minimized. Minimized child windows stay within the frame of the main window.

- ☐ A list of all the child windows is maintained in a pop-up menu usually named either File or Window. (The actual specification prefers the latter choice, but many programmers believe a list of files belongs in the File menu.)

- ☐ Alt+F4 closes an application, whereas Ctrl+F4 closes a child. Use Ctrl+F6 to switch between documents.

If you implement a Windows MDI application correctly, all these options are executed automatically. With some additional work, you can also teach your MDI app to do the following:

☐ Tile and cascade its child windows.

☐ Arrange the icons resting in the main window.

☐ Prompt the user before closing a child window. Even if the whole application is being shut down in one step (through the system menu or another mechanism), you should be able to prompt the user before closing a window.

The previous points specify the main features of any Windows MDI application. Of course, these ideas might be familiar to you from general experience, or from the use of the Borland or Microsoft IDEs.

Creating the Client Window

From a technical point of view, you should remember these two key ideas:

1. Instead of using CreateWindow, send a WM_MDICREATE message when you want to create the MDI child window.

2. The "main window" really consists of two windows: the frame window and the client window.

WM_MDICREATE is discussed in-depth after the code is listed. However, it's important that you first come to terms with the frame and client windows.

Every MDI application creates a main window exactly the same way a normal main window is created. In addition, MDI applications should create a client window while responding to the WM_CREATE message. This child window uses the preregistered MDICLIENT class.

The client window is the key to all MDI applications. It manages all the chores listed above, while remaining hidden to the user (and also, to a more limited degree, to the programmer).

Note: On most machines, if you give the client and the frame windows different colors, you can actually see the client covering up the main window. The MDIPaint program creates a brush for its main window using the COLOR_APPWORKSPACE constant (line 87), which is the same constant used by the MDICLIENT class. If you use a stock BLACK_BRUSH or WHITE_BRUSH for the frame, you might see both windows for a moment when the application first appears on-screen:

```
wndclass.hbrBackground = GetStockBrush(BLACK_BRUSH)
```

The actual call to create a client window is fairly straightforward. You need to remember, however, to pass a CLIENTCREATESTRUCT in the last parameter of CreateWindow. The following excerpts from MDIPAINT.CPP show the code for creating a client window (starting at line 175):

```
175:    hMenuInit = LoadMenu(hInstance, "MdiMenuInit");
176:    hMenuMultiple = LoadMenu(hInstance, "MDIMultiple");
177:    SetMenu(hwnd, hMenuInit);
178:
179:    // Load accelerator table
180:    hWndClient = GetWindow (hwnd, GW_CHILD);
181:    hAccel = LoadAccelerators (hInstance, "MdiAccel");
182:
183:    hMenuFileInit = GetSubMenu(hMenuInit, 0);
184:    hMenuFileInit = GetSubMenu(hMenuInit, 0);
185:
186:    clientcreate.hWindowMenu = hMenuFileInit;
187:    clientcreate.idFirstChild = IDM_FIRSTCHILD;
188:
189:    hWndClient = CreateWindow ("MDICLIENT", NULL,
190:                    WS_CHILD ¦ WS_CLIPCHILDREN ¦ WS_VISIBLE,
191:                    0, 0, 0, 0, hwnd, HMENU(1), hInstance,
192:                    (LPSTR) &clientcreate);
```

Figure BD2.2.

The menu from the MDIPaint program can hold a numbered list of the current children.

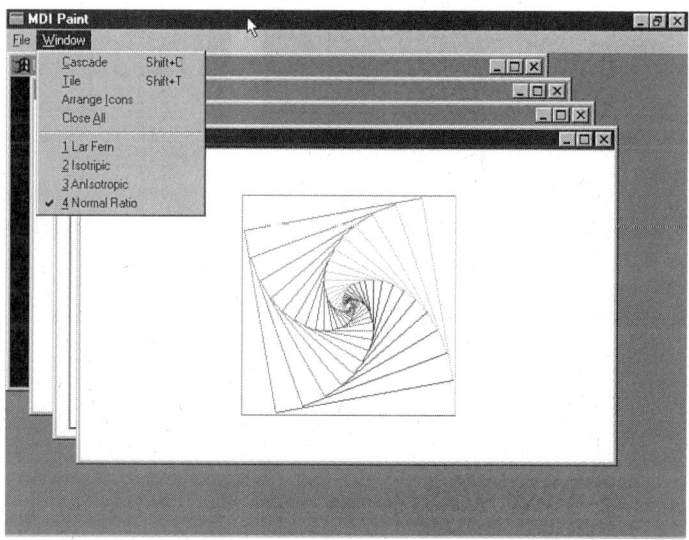

As you can see, a CLIENTCREATESTRUCT has two fields:

☐ The first field holds a menu. This is the menu that contains a list of the current child windows. (I discuss MDI menus later in this chapter, after the code.)

☐ The second field, called idFirstChild, holds the ID of the first MDI child window the application creates. To make this work, pass in an ID that is higher than any other ID used in your application. When you create MDI children, Windows automatically assigns them IDs based on idFirstChild. It uses these IDs to determine the number to be associated with each child window. These numbers are listed in the menu supplied by the first field of the CLIENTCREATESTRUCT. (See Figure BD2.2.)

Note that the call to CreateWindow uses MDICLIENT in the szClass field. As mentioned, MDICLIENT is a preregistered class that responds to many of the key messages sent to the MDI application. In other words, that one field of CreateWindow looks small compared to the code in the rest of the program, but its significance is very large indeed.

The MDIPaint Program

Now that you understand some of the principles behind creating an MDI application, it's time to actually get one up and running.

Listings BD2.1 through BD2.12 show the source for MDIPaint. This program draws geometric shapes and a simple fractal inside of four separate classes of an MDI window.

Listing BD2.1. MDIPAINT.CPP.

```
/////////////////////////////////////////
// Program Name: MDIPAINT.CPP
// Programmer: Charlie Calvert
// Description: MDI sample program
// Note: Use Smart Callbacks or Explicit Exports
// Date: 07/13/95
/////////////////////////////////////////

#define STRICT
#include <windows.h>
#include <windowsx.h>
#include "mdipaint.h"
#pragma warning(disable : 4068)

#if !defined(__WIN32__) && !defined(_WIN32)
#define EXPORT16 __export
#else
#define EXPORT16
#endif

// global variables
static HWND hWndFrame, hWndClient;
static char szFrameClass[] = "MDI_Frame";
static char szIsotropic[] = "MDI_AnIsotropic";
```

```
static char szAnIsotropic[] = "MDI_Isotropic";
static char szNormal[] = "MDI_Normal";
static char szFern[] = "MDI_Fern";
static HINSTANCE hInstance;
HMENU   hMenuInit, hMenuMultiple;
HMENU   hMenuFileInit, hMenuFileMultiple;
HACCEL hAccel;

//#define Frame_DefProc DefFrameProc
BOOL Frame_OnCreate(HWND hwnd, CREATESTRUCT FAR* lpCreateStruct);
void Frame_OnDestroy(HWND hwnd);
void Frame_OnClose(HWND hwnd);
void Frame_OnCommand(HWND hwnd, int id, HWND hwndCtl, UINT
                     codeNotify);
BOOL Frame_OnQueryEndSession(HWND hwnd);

/////////////////////////////////////
// DefProc for the Frame window.
/////////////////////////////////////
LRESULT Frame_DefProc (HWND hwnd, UINT uMsg, WPARAM wParam,
LPARAM lParam)
{
   return(DefFrameProc(hwnd, hWndClient, uMsg, wParam, lParam));
}

/////////////////////////////////////
// Program entry point
/////////////////////////////////////
#pragma argsused
int PASCAL WinMain (HINSTANCE hInst, HINSTANCE hPrevInstance,
                    LPSTR lpszCmdLine, int nCmdShow)
{
  MSG      msg;

  if (!hPrevInstance)
    if (!Register(hInst))
      return FALSE;

  hWndFrame = Create(hInst, nCmdShow);
  if (!hWndFrame)
    return FALSE;

  while (GetMessage (&msg, NULL, 0, 0))
  {
    if (!TranslateMDISysAccel (hWndClient, &msg) &&
        !TranslateAccelerator (hWndFrame, hAccel, &msg))
      {
        TranslateMessage (&msg);
        DispatchMessage (&msg);
      }
  }
  return msg.wParam;
}

/////////////////////////////////////
// Register classes with the OS
/////////////////////////////////////
```

Listing BD2.1. continued

```
BOOL Register(HINSTANCE hInst)
{
  WNDCLASS wndclass;

  // Register the frame window class
  wndclass.style         = CS_HREDRAW | CS_VREDRAW;
  wndclass.lpfnWndProc   = FrameWndProc;
  wndclass.cbClsExtra    = 0;
  wndclass.cbWndExtra    = 0;
  wndclass.hInstance     = hInst;
  wndclass.hIcon         = LoadIcon (NULL, IDI_APPLICATION);
  wndclass.hCursor       = LoadCursor (NULL, IDC_ARROW);
  wndclass.hbrBackground =
          CreateSolidBrush(GetSysColor(COLOR_APPWORKSPACE));
  wndclass.lpszMenuName  = NULL;
  wndclass.lpszClassName = szFrameClass;

  if(!RegisterClass (&wndclass))
    return FALSE;

  // Register the Isotropic window class
  wndclass.lpfnWndProc   = IsotropicWndProc;
  wndclass.hIcon         = LoadIcon (NULL, IDI_APPLICATION);
  wndclass.hbrBackground = GetStockBrush(WHITE_BRUSH);
  wndclass.lpszMenuName  = NULL;
  wndclass.lpszClassName = szIsotropic;

  if(!RegisterClass (&wndclass))
    return FALSE;

  // Register the AnIsotropic window class
  wndclass.lpfnWndProc   = AnIsotropicWndProc;
  wndclass.hIcon         = NULL;
  wndclass.lpszClassName = szAnIsotropic;

  if(!RegisterClass (&wndclass))
    return FALSE;

  // Register the Normal window class
  wndclass.lpfnWndProc   = NormalWndProc;
  wndclass.lpszClassName = szNormal;

  if(!RegisterClass (&wndclass))
    return FALSE;

  // Register the Normal window class
  wndclass.lpfnWndProc   = FernWndProc;
  wndclass.hbrBackground = GetStockBrush(BLACK_BRUSH);
  wndclass.lpszClassName = szFern;

  return RegisterClass(&wndclass);
}

//////////////////////////////////////
// Create the main window
//////////////////////////////////////
```

BD2

```
HWND Create(HINSTANCE hInst, int nCmdShow)
{
  hInstance = hInst;

  HWND hwnd = CreateWindow (szFrameClass, "MDI Paint",
                            WS_OVERLAPPEDWINDOW | WS_CLIPCHILDREN,
                            CW_USEDEFAULT, CW_USEDEFAULT,
                            CW_USEDEFAULT, CW_USEDEFAULT,
                            NULL, hMenuInit, hInstance, NULL);

  if (hwnd == NULL)
    return hwnd;

  ShowWindow (hwnd, nCmdShow);
  UpdateWindow (hwnd);

  return hwnd;
}

LRESULT CALLBACK EXPORT16 FrameWndProc(HWND hwnd, UINT message,
                                    WPARAM wParam, LPARAM lParam)
{
  switch (message)
  {
      HANDLE_MSG(hwnd, WM_CREATE, Frame_OnCreate);
      HANDLE_MSG(hwnd, WM_DESTROY, Frame_OnDestroy);
      HANDLE_MSG(hwnd, WM_CLOSE, Frame_OnClose);
      HANDLE_MSG(hwnd, WM_COMMAND, Frame_OnCommand);
      HANDLE_MSG(hwnd, WM_QUERYENDSESSION,
                 Frame_OnQueryEndSession);
      default:
        return(DefFrameProc(hwnd, hWndClient, message, wParam,
lParam));
  }
}

/////////////////////////////////////
// WM_CREATE   Create the client window
/////////////////////////////////////
#pragma argsused
BOOL Frame_OnCreate(HWND hwnd, CREATESTRUCT FAR* lpCreateStruct)
{
  CLIENTCREATESTRUCT clientcreate;

  hMenuInit = LoadMenu(hInstance, "MdiMenuInit");
  hMenuMultiple = LoadMenu(hInstance, "MDIMultiple");
  SetMenu(hwnd, hMenuInit);

  // Load accelerator table
  hWndClient = GetWindow (hwnd, GW_CHILD);
  hAccel = LoadAccelerators (hInstance, "MdiAccel");

  hMenuFileInit = GetSubMenu(hMenuInit, 0);
  hMenuFileMultiple = GetSubMenu(hMenuMultiple, 0);

  clientcreate.hWindowMenu  = hMenuFileInit;
  clientcreate.idFirstChild = IDM_FIRSTCHILD;
```

continues

Listing BD2.1. continued

```
     hWndClient = CreateWindow ("MDICLIENT", NULL,
                    WS_CHILD ¦ WS_CLIPCHILDREN ¦ WS_VISIBLE,
                    0, 0, 0, 0, hwnd, HMENU(1), hInstance,
                    (LPSTR) &clientcreate);
  if (hWndClient == NULL)
    return FALSE;

  return TRUE;
}

/////////////////////////////////////
// Handle WM_DESTROY
/////////////////////////////////////
#pragma argsused
void Frame_OnDestroy(HWND hwnd)
{
  DestroyMenu(hMenuMultiple);
  SetMenu(hwnd, NULL);
  DestroyMenu(hMenuInit);
  PostQuitMessage(0);
}

/////////////////////////////////////
// Handle WM_CLOSE
/////////////////////////////////////
void Frame_OnClose(HWND hwnd)
{
  if (NULL != GetWindow (hWndClient, GW_CHILD))
    SendMessage (hwnd, WM_COMMAND, CM_CLOSEALL, 0L);

  if (NULL != GetWindow (hWndClient, GW_CHILD))
    return;

  DestroyWindow(hwnd);
}

/////////////////////////////////////
// Create an MDI child, HANDLE WM_MDICREATE
/////////////////////////////////////
HWND CreateMDIChild(LPCSTR szClass, LPCSTR szTitle)
{
  MDICREATESTRUCT    MCS;

  MCS.szClass = szClass;
  MCS.szTitle = szTitle;
  MCS.hOwner  = hInstance;
  MCS.x       = CW_USEDEFAULT;
  MCS.y       = CW_USEDEFAULT;
  MCS.cx      = CW_USEDEFAULT;
  MCS.cy      = CW_USEDEFAULT;
  MCS.style   = 0;
  MCS.lParam  = NULL;
  return FORWARD_WM_MDICREATE(hWndClient, &MCS, SendMessage);
}
```

```
/////////////////////////////////
// Handle WM_COMMAND
/////////////////////////////////
#pragma argsused
void Frame_OnCommand(HWND hwnd, int id, HWND hwndCtl, UINT
codeNotify)
{
  WNDENUMPROC         lpfnEnum;
  HWND                hwndChild;

  // Do default processing for any system commands (SC_*).
  if ((unsigned) id >= 0xF000u) goto DWP; // thanks to J. Richter

  switch (id)
  {
    case CM_ISOTROP:
      CreateMDIChild(szIsotropic, "Isotropic");
break;

    case CM_ANISOTROP:
      CreateMDIChild(szAnIsotropic, "AnIsotropic");
      break;

    case CM_NORMAL:
      CreateMDIChild(szNormal, "Normal Ratio");
      break;

    case CM_FERN:

      CreateMDIChild(szFern, "Lar Fern");
      break;

    case CM_CLOSE:          // Close the active window
      hwndChild = (HWND)LOWORD(SendMessage(hWndClient,
                        WM_MDIGETACTIVE, 0, 0L));
      if (SendMessage(hwndChild, WM_QUERYENDSESSION, 0, 0L))
        SendMessage(hWndClient, WM_MDIDESTROY,
                (WPARAM)hwndChild, 0L);
      break;

    case CM_EXIT:           // Exit the program
      SendMessage (hwnd, WM_CLOSE, 0, 0L);
      break;

    case CM_TILE:
      SendMessage (hWndClient, WM_MDITILE, 0, 0L);
      break;

    case CM_CASCADE:
      SendMessage (hWndClient, WM_MDICASCADE, 0, 0L);
      break;

    case CM_ARRANGE:
      SendMessage (hWndClient, WM_MDIICONARRANGE, 0, 0L);
      break;
```

continues

Listing BD2.1. continued

```
        case CM_CLOSEALL:        // Attempt to close all children
          lpfnEnum = (WNDENUMPROC)MakeProcInstance(
                            (FARPROC)EnumChildWnds, hInstance);
          EnumChildWindows (hWndClient, lpfnEnum, 0L);
          FreeProcInstance ((FARPROC)lpfnEnum);
          break;

        default:                 // Pass to active child
          hwndChild = (HWND)LOWORD(SendMessage(hWndClient,
                      WM_MDIGETACTIVE, 0, 0L));
          if (IsWindow (hwndChild))
            SendMessage (hwndChild, WM_COMMAND, id, codeNotify);
          break;           // and then to DefFrameProc
      }
    DWP:
      FORWARD_WM_COMMAND(hwnd, id, hwndCtl,
                        codeNotify, Frame_DefProc);
  }

  ////////////////////////////////////////
  // Handle WM_QUERYENDSESSION
  ////////////////////////////////////////
  #pragma argsused
  BOOL Frame_OnQueryEndSession(HWND hwnd)
  {
    if (NULL != GetWindow (hWndClient, GW_CHILD))
      SendMessage (hwnd, WM_COMMAND, CM_CLOSEALL, 0L);

    if (NULL != GetWindow (hWndClient, GW_CHILD))
      return FALSE;
    else
      return TRUE;
  }

  // -------------------------------------
  // Callbacks
  // -------------------------------------

  ////////////////////////////////////////
  // Callbacks
  ////////////////////////////////////////
  #pragma argsused
  BOOL CALLBACK EnumChildWnds(HWND hwnd, LONG lParam)
  {
    if (GetWindow(hwnd, GW_OWNER)) // Icon Title?
      return TRUE;

    SendMessage (GetParent(hwnd), WM_MDIRESTORE, (WPARAM)hwnd, 0L);
    if (!SendMessage (hwnd, WM_QUERYENDSESSION, 0, 0L))
      return TRUE;

    SendMessage (GetParent(hwnd), WM_MDIDESTROY, (WPARAM)hwnd, 0L);
      return TRUE;
  }
```

Listing BD2.2. MDIPAINT.H.

```
/////////////////////////////////////
// Program Name: MDIPAINT.H
// Programmer: Charlie Calvert
// Description: MDI windows sample program
// Date: 07/13/95
/////////////////////////////////////

#if !defined(__WIN32__) && !defined(_WIN32)
#define EXPORT16 __export
#else
#define EXPORT16
#endif

#define CM_ISOTROP      100
#define CM_ANISOTROP    101
#define CM_NORMAL       112
#define CM_FERN         113
#define CM_CLOSE        114
#define CM_EXIT         115

#define CM_TILE         130
#define CM_CASCADE      131
#define CM_ARRANGE      132
#define CM_CLOSEALL     133

#define IDM_FIRSTCHILD  150

// funcs
LRESULT CALLBACK EXPORT16 AnIsotropicWndProc(HWND, UINT,
                                             WPARAM, LPARAM);
LRESULT CALLBACK EXPORT16 IsotropicWndProc(HWND, UINT,
                                           WPARAM, LPARAM);
LRESULT CALLBACK EXPORT16 NormalWndProc(HWND, UINT,
                                        WPARAM, LPARAM);
LRESULT CALLBACK EXPORT16 FernWndProc(HWND, UINT, WPARAM, LPARAM);
LRESULT CALLBACK EXPORT16 FrameWndProc(HWND, UINT,
                                       WPARAM, LPARAM);
BOOL CALLBACK EXPORT16 EnumChildWnds(HWND, LONG);
BOOL Register(HINSTANCE hInst);
HWND Create(HINSTANCE hInst, int nCmdShow);
void Frame_SetMenu(HMENU hMenu, int winMenuIndex);
```

Listing BD2.3. ANISOTROP.CPP.

```
/////////////////////////////////////
// Program Name: ANISOTRP.CPP
// Programmer: Charlie Calvert
// Description: MDI sample program
// Date: 07/13/95
/////////////////////////////////////

#define STRICT
#include <windows.h>
```

continues

Listing BD2.3. continued

```c
#include <windowsx.h>
#pragma hdrstop
#include <stdlib.h>
#include "draw.h"
#include "mdipaint.h"
#pragma warning(disable : 4068)

extern HMENU hMenuMultiple, hMenuInit;
extern HMENU hMenuFileMultiple, hMenuFileInit;
static HWND hWndClient, hWndFrame ;

// AnIsotrop_Play Object
#define AnIsotrop_DefProc DefMDIChildProc
BOOL AnIsotrop_OnCreate(HWND hwnd,
                            CREATESTRUCT FAR* lpCreateStruct);
void AnIsotrop_MDIActivate(HWND hwnd, BOOL fActive,
                            HWND hwndActivate, HWND hwndDeactivate);
void AnIsotrop_OnPaint(HWND hwnd);

//////////////////////////////////////
// The WndProc
//////////////////////////////////////
LRESULT CALLBACK AnIsotropicWndProc (HWND hwnd, UINT message,
                                        WPARAM wParam, LPARAM lParam)
{
  switch (message)
  {
    HANDLE_MSG(hwnd, WM_CREATE, AnIsotrop_OnCreate);
    HANDLE_MSG(hwnd, WM_MDIACTIVATE, AnIsotrop_MDIActivate);
    HANDLE_MSG(hwnd, WM_PAINT, AnIsotrop_OnPaint);
  default:
    return AnIsotrop_DefProc(hwnd, message, wParam, lParam) ;
  }
}

//////////////////////////////////////
// Handle WM_CREATE
//////////////////////////////////////
#pragma argsused
BOOL AnIsotrop_OnCreate(HWND hwnd, CREATESTRUCT FAR* lpCreateStruct)
{
  hWndClient = GetParent (hwnd) ;
  hWndFrame  = GetParent (hWndClient) ;
  return TRUE;
}

//////////////////////////////////////
// Handle WM_ACTIVATE
//////////////////////////////////////
#pragma argsused
void AnIsotrop_MDIActivate(HWND hwnd, BOOL fActive,
                            HWND hwndActivate,
                            HWND hwndDeactivate)
{
```

```
#if defined(WIN32)
  BOOL Refresh = TRUE;
#else
  BOOL Refresh = FALSE;
#endif

  if (fActive)
    FORWARD_WM_MDISETMENU(hWndClient, Refresh,
                          hMenuMultiple,
                          GetSubMenu(hMenuMultiple, 1),
                          SendMessage);
  DrawMenuBar(hWndFrame);
  if (!fActive)
    FORWARD_WM_MDISETMENU(hWndClient, Refresh,
                          hMenuInit,
                          GetSubMenu(hMenuInit, 1),
                          SendMessage);
  DrawMenuBar(hWndFrame);
}

/////////////////////////////////////
// Handle WM_PAINT
/////////////////////////////////////
void AnIsotrop_OnPaint(HWND hwnd)
{
  HDC PaintDC;
  PAINTSTRUCT PaintStruct;
  RECT R;

  PaintDC = BeginPaint (hwnd, &PaintStruct);

  SetMapMode(PaintDC, MM_ANISOTROPIC);
  GetClientRect(hwnd, &R);
  #ifdef WIN32
  SetWindowExtEx(PaintDC, 210, 210, NULL);
  SetViewportExtEx(PaintDC, R.right, R.bottom, NULL);
  SetViewportOrgEx(PaintDC, R.right / 2, R.bottom / 2, NULL);
  #else
  SetWindowExt(PaintDC, 210, 210);
  SetViewportExt(PaintDC, R.right, R.bottom);
  SetViewportOrg(PaintDC, R.right / 2, R.bottom / 2);
  #endif
  DoDraw(PaintDC);

  EndPaint (hwnd, &PaintStruct);
}
```

Listing BD2.4. FERN.CPP.

```
/////////////////////////////////////
// Program Name: FERN.CPP
// Programmer: Charlie Calvert
// Description: MDI sample program
// Date: 07/13/95
/////////////////////////////////////
```

Listing BD2.4. continued

```c
#define STRICT
#include <windows.h>
#include <windowsx.h>
#include <stdlib.h>
#include "draw.h"
#include "mdipaint.h"
#pragma warning(disable : 4068)

int FernTimer = 1;

// constants
double a[4] = {0, 0.85, 0.2, -0.15};
double b[4] = {0, 0.04, -0.26, 0.28};
double c[4] = {0, -0.04, 0.23, 0.26};
double d[4] = {0.16, 0.85, 0.22, 0.24};
double e[4] = {0, 0, 0, 0};
double f[4] = {0, 1.6, 1.6, 0.44};
double x = 0;
double y = 0;

// variables
static double TempX, TempY;
static int MaxX, MaxY, k;
static long MaxIterations, Count;
static HWND hWndClient, hWndFrame;

// externs
extern HMENU hMenuMultiple, hMenuInit;
extern HMENU hMenuFileMultiple, hMenuFileInit;
extern HACCEL hAccel;

#define FernPlay_DefProc DefMDIChildProc
BOOL FernPlay_OnCreate(HWND hwnd,
                       CREATESTRUCT FAR* lpCreateStruct);
void FernPlay_OnClose(HWND hwnd);
void FernPlay_OnTimer(HWND hwnd, UINT id);
void FernPlay_MDIActivate(HWND hwnd, BOOL fActive,
                          HWND hwndActivate,
                          HWND hwndDeactivate);
BOOL FernPlay_OnQueryEndSession(HWND hwnd);
void FernPlay_OnPaint(HWND hwnd);
void FernPlay_OnSize(HWND hwnd, UINT state, int cx, int cy);

/////////////////////////////////////////
// The Window Procedure
/////////////////////////////////////////
LRESULT CALLBACK FernWndProc(HWND hwnd, UINT message, WPARAM wParam,
                             LPARAM lParam)
{
  switch (message)
  {
    HANDLE_MSG(hwnd, WM_CREATE, FernPlay_OnCreate);
    HANDLE_MSG(hwnd, WM_CLOSE, FernPlay_OnClose);
```

```
      HANDLE_MSG(hwnd, WM_TIMER, FernPlay_OnTimer);
      HANDLE_MSG(hwnd, WM_MDIACTIVATE, FernPlay_MDIActivate);
      HANDLE_MSG(hwnd, WM_PAINT, FernPlay_OnPaint);
      HANDLE_MSG(hwnd, WM_QUERYENDSESSION,
                        FernPlay_OnQueryEndSession);
      HANDLE_MSG(hwnd, WM_SIZE, FernPlay_OnSize);
    default:
      return FernPlay_DefProc(hwnd, message, wParam, lParam);
    }
}


///////////////////////////////////
// Handle WM_CREATE
///////////////////////////////////
#pragma argsused
BOOL FernPlay_OnCreate(HWND hwnd, CREATESTRUCT FAR* lpCreateStruct)
{
  hWndClient = GetParent (hwnd);
  hWndFrame  = GetParent (hWndClient);
  Count = 0;
  SetTimer(hwnd, FernTimer, 0, NULL);
  return TRUE;
}


///////////////////////////////////
// Handle WM_MDIACTIVATE
///////////////////////////////////
#pragma argsused
void FernPlay_MDIActivate(HWND hwnd, BOOL fActive, HWND hwndActivate,
                          HWND hwndDeactivate)
{
  #if defined(WIN32)
    BOOL Refresh = TRUE;
  #else
    BOOL Refresh = FALSE;
  #endif

  if (fActive)
    FORWARD_WM_MDISETMENU(hWndClient, Refresh,
                          hMenuMultiple,
                          GetSubMenu(hMenuMultiple, 1),
                          SendMessage);

  if (!fActive)
    FORWARD_WM_MDISETMENU(hWndClient, Refresh,
                          hMenuInit,
                          GetSubMenu(hMenuInit, 1),
                          SendMessage);

  DrawMenuBar(hWndFrame);
}


///////////////////////////////////
// Handle WM_CLOSE
///////////////////////////////////
void FernPlay_OnClose(HWND hwnd)
```

continues

Listing BD2.4. continued

```
{
  Count = MaxIterations;
  if (IDOK != MessageBox (hwnd, "OK to close window?",
                "Fern", MB_ICONQUESTION | MB_OKCANCEL))
    return;
  else
    FORWARD_WM_CLOSE(hwnd, FernPlay_DefProc);
}


///////////////////////////////////
// Handle WM_QUERYENDSESSION
///////////////////////////////////
BOOL FernPlay_OnQueryEndSession(HWND hwnd)
{
  Count = MaxIterations;
  if (IDOK != MessageBox (hwnd, "OK to close window?",
                "Fern", MB_ICONQUESTION | MB_OKCANCEL))
    return FALSE;
  else
    return TRUE;
}


///////////////////////////////////
// Handle WM_SIZE
///////////////////////////////////
#pragma argsused
void FernPlay_OnSize(HWND hwnd, UINT state, int cx, int cy)
{
  RECT R;
  GetClientRect(hwnd, &R);
  MaxX = R.right;
  MaxY = R.bottom;
  MaxIterations = long(MaxY) * 50;
  if (state == SIZE_MINIMIZED)
    MaxIterations = 175;

  // MUST forward WM_SIZE messages
  FORWARD_WM_SIZE(hwnd, state, cx, cy, FernPlay_DefProc);
}


///////////////////////////////////
// Handle WM_PAINT
///////////////////////////////////
void FernPlay_OnPaint(HWND hwnd)
{
  Count = 0;
  KillTimer(hwnd, FernTimer);
  SetTimer(hwnd, FernTimer, 0, NULL);
  FORWARD_WM_PAINT(hwnd, FernPlay_DefProc);
}


///////////////////////////////////
// Paint the fern
///////////////////////////////////
```

```
void DoPaint(HWND hwnd)
{
  HDC PaintDC;
  k = rand() % 100;
  if ((k > 0 ) && (k <= 85))
    k = 1;
  if ((k > 85) && (k <= 92))
    k = 2;
  if (k > 92) k = 3;
  TempX = a[k] * x + b[k] * y + e[k];
  TempY = c[k] * x + d[k] * y + f[k];
  x = TempX;
  y = TempY;
  if ((Count >= MaxIterations) || (Count != 0))
  {
    PaintDC = GetDC(hwnd);
    SetPixel(PaintDC, (x * MaxY / 11 + MaxX / 2),
          (y * -MaxY / 11 + MaxY), RGB(0, 0XFF, 0));
    ReleaseDC(hwnd, PaintDC);
  }
  Count++;
}


//////////////////////////////////////
// Handle WM_TIMER
//////////////////////////////////////
#pragma argsused
void FernPlay_OnTimer(HWND hwnd, UINT id)
{
  if (Count >= MaxIterations)
    KillTimer(hwnd, FernTimer);

  for (int i = 0; i < 200; i++)
  {
    if (Count >= MaxIterations)
      return;
    DoPaint(hwnd);
  }
}
```

Listing BD2.5. ISOTROP.CPP.

```
//////////////////////////////////////
// Program Name: ISOTROP.CPP
// Programmer: Charlie Calvert
// Description: MDI sample program
// Date: 07/13/95
//////////////////////////////////////

#define STRICT
#include <windows.h>
#include <windowsx.h>
#include "draw.h"
#include "mdipaint.h"
```

continues

Listing BD2.5. continued

```
#pragma warning(disable : 4068)

extern HMENU hMenuMultiple, hMenuInit;
extern HMENU hMenuFileMultiple, hMenuFileInit;
static HWND hWndClient, hWndFrame;

#define Isotrop_DefProc DefMDIChildProc
BOOL Isotrop_OnCreate(HWND hwnd,
                      CREATESTRUCT FAR* lpCreateStruct);
void Isotrop_MDIActivate(HWND hwnd, BOOL fActive, HWND hwndActivate,
                         HWND hwndDeactivate);
void Isotrop_OnPaint(HWND hwnd);
BOOL Isotrop_OnQueryEndSession(HWND hwnd);

///////////////////////////////////////
// The Windows Procedure
///////////////////////////////////////
LRESULT CALLBACK IsotropicWndProc(HWND hwnd, UINT message,
                                  WPARAM wParam, LPARAM lParam)
{
  switch (message)
  {
    HANDLE_MSG(hwnd, WM_CREATE, Isotrop_OnCreate);

    HANDLE_MSG(hwnd, WM_MDIACTIVATE, Isotrop_MDIActivate);
    HANDLE_MSG(hwnd, WM_PAINT, Isotrop_OnPaint);
    HANDLE_MSG(hwnd, WM_QUERYENDSESSION,
               Isotrop_OnQueryEndSession);
    default:
      return Isotrop_DefProc(hwnd, message, wParam, lParam);
  }
}

///////////////////////////////////////
// HANDLE WM_QUERYENDSESSION
///////////////////////////////////////
BOOL Isotrop_OnQueryEndSession(HWND hwnd)
{
  if (IDOK != MessageBox (hwnd, "OK to close window?",
                "Isotropic", MB_ICONQUESTION | MB_OKCANCEL))
    return FALSE;
  else
    return TRUE;
}

///////////////////////////////////////
// HANDLE WM_CREATE
///////////////////////////////////////
#pragma argsused
BOOL Isotrop_OnCreate(HWND hwnd,
                      CREATESTRUCT FAR* lpCreateStruct)
{
  hWndClient = GetParent(hwnd);
  hWndFrame = GetParent(hWndClient);
  return TRUE;
}
```

BD2

```
//////////////////////////////////
// HANDLE WM_MDIACTIVATE
//////////////////////////////////
#pragma argsused
void Isotrop_MDIActivate(HWND hwnd, BOOL fActive,
                            HWND hwndActivate, HWND hwndDeactivate)
{
  #if defined(WIN32)
    BOOL Refresh = TRUE;
  #else
    BOOL Refresh = FALSE;
  #endif

  if (fActive)
    FORWARD_WM_MDISETMENU(hWndClient, Refresh,
                          hMenuMultiple,
                          GetSubMenu(hMenuMultiple, 1),
                          SendMessage);

  if (!fActive)
    FORWARD_WM_MDISETMENU(hWndClient, Refresh,
                          hMenuInit,
                          GetSubMenu(hMenuInit, 1),
                          SendMessage);

  DrawMenuBar(hWndFrame);
}

//////////////////////////////////
// HANDLE WM_PAINT
//////////////////////////////////
void Isotrop_OnPaint(HWND hwnd)
{
  HDC PaintDC;
  PAINTSTRUCT PaintStruct;
  RECT R;

  PaintDC = BeginPaint (hwnd, &PaintStruct);

  SetMapMode(PaintDC, MM_ISOTROPIC);
  GetClientRect(hwnd, &R);
  #ifdef WIN32
  SetWindowExtEx(PaintDC, 210, 210, NULL);
  SetViewportExtEx(PaintDC, R.right, R.bottom, NULL);
  SetViewportOrgEx(PaintDC, R.right / 2, R.bottom / 2, NULL);
  #else
  SetWindowExt(PaintDC, 210, 210);
  SetViewportExt(PaintDC, R.right, R.bottom);
  SetViewportOrg(PaintDC, R.right / 2, R.bottom / 2);
  #endif
  DoDraw(PaintDC);

  EndPaint (hwnd, &PaintStruct);
}
```

Listing BD2.6. NORMAL.CPP.

```cpp
////////////////////////////////////
// Program Name: NORMAL.CPP
// Programmer: Charlie Calvert
// Description: MDI sample program
// Date: 07/13/95
////////////////////////////////////
#define STRICT
#include <windows.h>
#include <windowsx.h>
#include "draw.h"
#include "mdipaint.h"
#pragma warning(disable : 4068)

extern HMENU hMenuMultiple, hMenuInit;
extern HMENU hMenuFileMultiple, hMenuFileInit;
static HWND hWndClient, hWndFrame;

#define NormalPlay_DefProc DefMDIChildProc
BOOL NormalPlay_OnCreate(HWND hwnd,
                         CREATESTRUCT FAR* lpCreateStruct);
void NormalPlay_MDIActivate(HWND hwnd, BOOL fActive,
                            HWND hwndActivate,
                            HWND hwndDeactivate);
void NormalPlay_OnPaint(HWND hwnd);

////////////////////////////////////
// The Window Procedure
////////////////////////////////////
LRESULT CALLBACK NormalWndProc(HWND hwnd, UINT message,
                               WPARAM wParam, LPARAM lParam)
{
  switch (message)
  {
    HANDLE_MSG(hwnd, WM_CREATE, NormalPlay_OnCreate);
    HANDLE_MSG(hwnd, WM_MDIACTIVATE, NormalPlay_MDIActivate);
    HANDLE_MSG(hwnd, WM_PAINT, NormalPlay_OnPaint);
  default:
    return NormalPlay_DefProc(hwnd, message, wParam, lParam);
  }
}

////////////////////////////////////
// HANDLE WM_CREATE
////////////////////////////////////
#pragma argsused
BOOL NormalPlay_OnCreate(HWND hwnd,
                         CREATESTRUCT FAR* lpCreateStruct)
{
  hWndClient = GetParent (hwnd);
  hWndFrame = GetParent (hWndClient);
  return TRUE;
}

////////////////////////////////////
// HANDLE WM_MDIACTIVATE
////////////////////////////////////
```

BD2

```
#pragma argsused
void NormalPlay_MDIActivate(HWND hwnd, BOOL fActive,
                            HWND hwndActivate,
                            HWND hwndDeactivate)
{
  #if defined(WIN32)
    BOOL Refresh = TRUE;
  #else
    BOOL Refresh = FALSE;
  #endif

  if (fActive)
    FORWARD_WM_MDISETMENU(hWndClient, Refresh,
                          hMenuMultiple,
                          GetSubMenu(hMenuMultiple, 1),
                          SendMessage);
  if (!fActive)
    FORWARD_WM_MDISETMENU(hWndClient, Refresh,
                          hMenuInit,
                          GetSubMenu(hMenuInit, 1),
                          SendMessage);
  DrawMenuBar(hWndFrame);
}

///////////////////////////////////
// HANDLE WM_NORMAL
///////////////////////////////////
void NormalPlay_OnPaint(HWND hwnd)
{
  HDC PaintDC;
  PAINTSTRUCT PaintStruct;
  RECT R;

  PaintDC = BeginPaint (hwnd, &PaintStruct);
  GetClientRect(hwnd, &R);
  #ifdef WIN32
  SetViewportOrgEx(PaintDC, R.right / 2, R.bottom / 2, NULL);
  #else
  SetViewportOrg(PaintDC, R.right / 2, R.bottom / 2);
  #endif

  DoDraw(PaintDC);
  EndPaint (hwnd, &PaintStruct);
}
```

Listing BD2.7. DRAW.CPP.

```
///////////////////////////////////
// Program Name: DRAW.CPP
// Programmer: Charlie Calvert
// Description: Multimedia MDI windows sample program
// Date: 07/13/95
///////////////////////////////////
```

continues

Listing BD2.7. continued

```c
#define STRICT
#include <windows.h>
#include <windowsx.h>
#include <math.h>
#include "draw.h"

#define PI 3.14159265358979323846

/////////////////////////////////////
// Draw the shape
/////////////////////////////////////
void DrawSquare(HDC PaintDC, double Scale, int Theta)
{
  int x1,y1;
  int xt,yt;
  int i;
  HPEN Pens[5], OldPen;
  TCDS CDS;

  Pens[1] = CreatePen(PS_SOLID, 1, RGB(255, 0, 0));
  Pens[2] = CreatePen(PS_SOLID, 1, RGB(0, 255, 0));
  Pens[3] = CreatePen(PS_SOLID, 1, RGB(0, 0, 255));
  Pens[4] = CreatePen(PS_SOLID, 1, RGB(255, 0, 255));

  CDS[0].x = -100;
  CDS[0].y = -100;
  CDS[1].x = 100;
  CDS[1].y = -100;
  CDS[2].x = 100;
  CDS[2].y = 100;
  CDS[3].x = -100;
  CDS[3].y = 100;
  CDS[4].x = -100;
  CDS[4].y = -100;

  for (i = 0; i < 5; i++)
  {
    x1 = CDS[i].x;
    y1 = CDS[i].y;
    xt = Scale * (x1 * cos(Theta * PI / 180) + y1 *
                  sin(Theta * PI/180));
    yt = Scale * (y1 * cos(Theta * PI / 180) - x1 *
                  sin(Theta * PI/180));
    if (i == 0)
      #ifdef WIN32
      MoveToEx(PaintDC, xt, yt, NULL);
      #else
      MoveTo(PaintDC, xt, yt);
      #endif
    else
    {
      OldPen = SelectPen(PaintDC, Pens[i]);
      LineTo(PaintDC, xt, yt);
```

```
      SelectPen(PaintDC, OldPen);
    }
  }
  for (i = 1; i < 5; i++)
    DeleteObject(Pens[i]);
}

////////////////////////////////////
// Loop through the draw
////////////////////////////////////
void DoDraw(HDC PaintDC)
{
  double Scale;
  int Theta;
  int Square;

  Scale = 1.0;
  Theta = 0;

  for (Square = 1; Square < 25; Square++)
  {
    DrawSquare(PaintDC, Scale, Theta);
    Theta = Theta + 10;
    Scale = Scale * 0.85;
  }
}
```

Listing BD2.8. DRAW.H.

```
////////////////////////////////////
// Program Name: DRAW.CPP
// Programmer: Charlie Calvert
// Description: Multimedia MDI windows sample program
// Date: 07/13/95
////////////////////////////////////

#define STRICT
#include <windows.h>
#include <windowsx.h>
#include <math.h>
#include "draw.h"

#define PI 3.14159265358979323846

////////////////////////////////////
// Draw the shape
////////////////////////////////////
void DrawSquare(HDC PaintDC, double Scale, int Theta)
{
  int x1,y1;
  int xt,yt;
  int i;
  HPEN Pens[5], OldPen;
  TCDS CDS;
```

Listing BD2.8. continued

```
      Pens[1] = CreatePen(PS_SOLID, 1, RGB(255, 0, 0));
      Pens[2] = CreatePen(PS_SOLID, 1, RGB(0, 255, 0));
      Pens[3] = CreatePen(PS_SOLID, 1, RGB(0, 0, 255));
      Pens[4] = CreatePen(PS_SOLID, 1, RGB(255, 0, 255));

      CDS[0].x = -100;
      CDS[0].y = -100;
      CDS[1].x = 100;
      CDS[1].y = -100;
      CDS[2].x = 100;
      CDS[2].y = 100;
      CDS[3].x = -100;
      CDS[3].y = 100;
      CDS[4].x = -100;
      CDS[4].y = -100;

      for (i = 0; i < 5; i++)
      {
        x1 = CDS[i].x;
        y1 = CDS[i].y;
        xt = Scale * (x1 * cos(Theta * PI / 180) + y1 *
                    sin(Theta * PI/180));
        yt = Scale * (y1 * cos(Theta * PI / 180) - x1 *
                    sin(Theta * PI/180));
        if (i == 0)
          #ifdef WIN32
          MoveToEx(PaintDC, xt, yt, NULL);
          #else
          MoveTo(PaintDC, xt, yt);
          #endif
        else
        {
          OldPen = SelectPen(PaintDC, Pens[i]);
          LineTo(PaintDC, xt, yt);
          SelectPen(PaintDC, OldPen);
        }
      }
      for (i = 1; i < 5; i++)
        DeleteObject(Pens[i]);
    }

    /////////////////////////////////////
    // Loop through the draw
    /////////////////////////////////////
    void DoDraw(HDC PaintDC)
    {
      double Scale;
      int Theta;
      int Square;

      Scale = 1.0;
      Theta = 0;

      for (Square = 1; Square < 25; Square++)
```

```
  {
    DrawSquare(PaintDC, Scale, Theta);
    Theta = Theta + 10;
    Scale = Scale * 0.85;
  }
}
```

Listing BD2.9. MDIPAINT.RC.

```
///////////////////////////////////
// Program Name: MDIPAINT.RC
// Programmer: Charlie Calvert
// Description: MDI sample program
// Date: 07/13/95
///////////////////////////////////

#include <windows.h>
#include "MDIPaint.h"

MdiMenuInit MENU
BEGIN
  POPUP "&File"
  BEGIN
    MENUITEM "&Isotropic\tAlt+I", CM_ISOTROP
    MENUITEM "&AnIsotropic\tAlt+A", CM_ANISOTROP
    MENUITEM "&Normal\tAlt+N", CM_NORMAL
    MENUITEM "&Fern\tAlt+R", CM_FERN
    MENUITEM SEPARATOR
    MENUITEM "E&xit", CM_EXIT
  END
END

MDIMultiple MENU
BEGIN
  POPUP "&File"
  BEGIN
    MENUITEM "&Isotropic\tAlt|I", CM_ISOTROP
    MENUITEM "&AnIsotropic\tAlt+A", CM_ANISOTROP
    MENUITEM "&Normal\tAlt+N", CM_NORMAL
    MENUITEM SEPARATOR
    MENUITEM "E&xit", CM_EXIT
  END
  POPUP "&Window"
  BEGIN
    MENUITEM "&Cascade\tShift+C", CM_CASCADE
    MENUITEM "&Tile\tShift+T", CM_TILE
    MENUITEM "Arrange &Icons", CM_ARRANGE
    MENUITEM "Close &All", CM_CLOSEALL
  END
END

MdiAccel ACCELERATORS
BEGIN
  "C", CM_CASCADE, VIRTKEY, SHIFT
```

continues

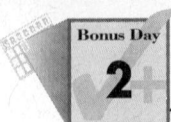

Listing BD2.9. continued

```
    "T", CM_TILE, VIRTKEY, SHIFT
    "I", CM_ISOTROP, VIRTKEY, ALT
    "A", CM_ANISOTROP, VIRTKEY, ALT
    "N", CM_NORMAL, VIRTKEY, ALT
    "R", CM_FERN, VIRTKEY, ALT
END
```

Listing BD2.10. MDIPAINT.DEF.

```
NAME           MDIPaint
DESCRIPTION    'MDIPaint program (c) Charlie Calvert'
CODE           PRELOAD MOVEABLE DISCARDABLE
DATA           PRELOAD MOVEABLE MULTIPLE
```

Listing BD2.11. MDIPAINT.MAK (Borland).

```
# MDIPaint makefile
# Use /WE switch

MAIN = MDIPaint
OBJS = $(MAIN).obj Isotrop.obj AnIsotrp.obj Normal.obj \
       Fern.obj Draw.obj
LIBS =
BCROOT = $(MAKEDIR)\..
INCPATH= $(BCROOT)\INCLUDE
LIBPATH= $(BCROOT)\LIB


!if !$d(WIN16)
COMPILER = BCC32.EXE
RCCOMPLR = BRC32.EXE -w32
CFLAGS   = -WE -v -w4
!else
COMPILER = BCC.EXE
RCCOMPLR = BRC.EXE
CFLAGS   = -WE -ml -v -w4
!endif

# Link
$(MAIN).exe: $(OBJS) $(MAIN).def $(MAIN).res
  $(COMPILER) -L$(LIBPATH) $(CFLAGS) $(OBJS) $(LIBS)
  $(RCCOMPLR) $(MAIN).res

# Compile
.cpp.obj:
  $(COMPILER) -c $(CFLAGS) -I$(INCPATH) { $< }

# Resource
$(MAIN).res : $(MAIN).rc
  $(RCCOMPLR) -R -I$(INCPATH) $(MAIN).RC
```

Listing BD2.12. MDIPAINT.MAK (Microsoft).

```
# Nmake macros for building Windows 32-Bit apps

APPNAME=MDIPAINT
TARGETOS=WIN95
APPVER=4.0
OBJS=$(APPNAME).OBJ FERN.OBJ ISOTROP.OBJ \
     ANISOTRP.OBJ NORMAL.OBJ DRAW.OBJ

!include <win32.mak>

all: $(APPNAME).exe

# Update the resource if necessary

$(APPNAME).res: $(APPNAME).rc $(APPNAME).h
  $(rc) $(rcflags) $(rcvars) $(APPNAME).rc

# Update the object files if necessary

# compile
.cpp.obj:
  $(cc) $(cflags) $(cvars) $(cdebug) $<

# Update the executable file if necessary.

$(APPNAME).exe: $(OBJS) $(APPNAME).res
  $(link) $(linkdebug) $(guiflags) -out:$(APPNAME).exe \
  $(OBJS) $(APPNAME).res $(guilibs) comctl32.lib
```

Figure BD2.3 shows the output of this program.

Figure BD2.3.
*MDIPaint comes with
different types of child
windows.*

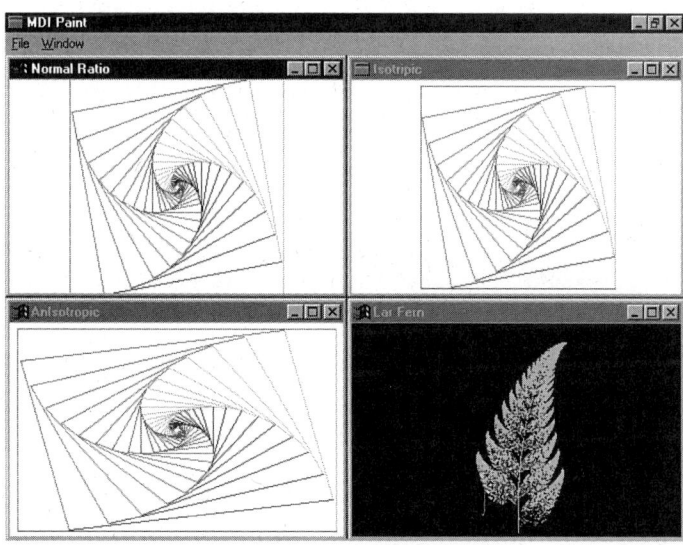

The MDIPaint program has four different MDI child windows, three of which show the same figure painted with different mapping modes. Specifically, the Normal window uses the default MM_TEXT mapping mode; the Isotropic window uses the MM_ISOTROPIC mapping mode, and the AnIsotropic windows uses the MM_ANISOTROPIC mapping mode. I've included all three of these windows in order to graphically illustrate the differences between these commonly used mapping modes. The fourth window shows an image of a fern, which is painted with standard fractal techniques.

MDIPaint has two different menus: The first appears at startup, and the second appears after the user opens a child window. If all the child windows are closed, the first menu reappears.

The differences between the two menus are twofold:

☐ The first menu has one pop-up, called File, which enables the user to open any of the four child windows or to exit the application.

☐ The second menu has two pop-ups. The first, called File, enables the user to start the Normal, Isotropic, and AnIsotropic windows. The second, called Window, lets the user arrange the icons or tile, cascade, and close all the child windows.

MDIPaint enables only one copy of the Fern window on the desktop at a time. To enforce this rule, the program places the option to open the Fern window only in the File menu, which appears at startup, or when all other windows are closed. This means that you must display the Fern window first or lose the option to open it.

Before the Fern window is closed (or when it's open and the entire application is being closed), it prompts the user. The Isotropic window prompts the user when the whole application is being closed (see Figure BD2.4). Normally, such a prompt asks the user whether he or she wants to save a file. In this particular case, however, the prompt is inserted merely to show you how to iterate through all the child windows and how to respond to WM_QUERYENDSESSION messages.

Some children in the MDIPaint program set their WNDClass.hIcon field to NULL. As a result, under Windows 3.1, the image seen in their main window gets duplicated in their icon when they are minimized.

Note: Once again, the makefile for this program uses an implicit rule to automatically compile all the CPP files into OBJ files. Under Windows 3.1, it's also very important that you use the /WE (Borland) or /GA (Microsoft) switches to the compiler to ensure that the window procedures for this application get properly exported. To do this in the Borland IDE, choose Options|Compiler|Entry/Exit Code—Windows Explicit Functions Exported. In the MSVC IDE, choose Options | Project | Compiler | Windows Prolog/Epilog—Protected Mode

Application Functions. The point of all this is to ensure that functions explicitly labeled _export do get exported. If you don't take these steps, the program might still run okay, but the debug version of Windows will complain of the omission. None of this information is important under Windows 95 or Windows NT.

Figure BD2.4.
The Isotropic window prompts the user before closing.

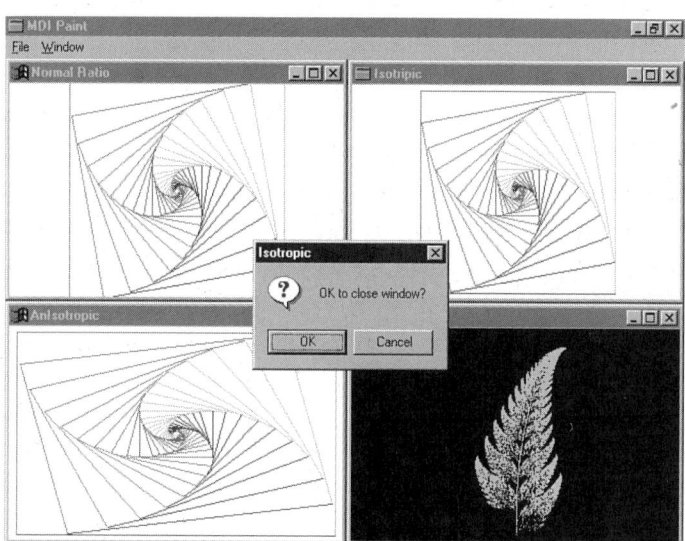

Creating Child Windows

Each of the child windows can be started either through a menu or through an accelerator key (Alt+A for AnIsotropic, Alt+I for Isotropic, and so forth). In either case, a message is sent along with WM_COMMAND and is responded to in the following manner (line 260, MDIPAINT.CPP):

```
case CM_ANISOTROP:
  CreateMDIChild(szAnIsotropic, "AnIsotropic");
  break;
```

CreateMDIChild is user-defined and hides a fair degree of complexity. The mechanism for creating MDI children involves using SendMessage to post a WM_MDICREATE message along with a structure called MDICREATESTRUCT, which holds most of the fields seen in a call to CreateWindow.

The *MDICREATESTRUCT* Structure

Following is an MDICREATESTRUCT:

```
typedef struct tagMDICREATESTRUCT {
LPCSTR     szClass;      // Class name
LPCSTR     szTitle;      // A title for caption bar
HINSTANCE  hOwner;       // The Instance of the app
int        x;            // X dimension of upper left corner
int        y;            // Y dimension of upper left corner
int        cx;           // X dimension of lower right corner
int        cy;           // Y dimension of lower right corner
DWORD      style;        // Is app minimized, maximized, etc
LPARAM     lParam;       // User defined data, usually NULL
} MDICREATESTRUCT;
```

From an intellectual point of view, filling out the structure is no big challenge. You just need a little patience and a reference, such as this book or the online help.

The style field can host a combination of the following styles:

WS_MINIMIZE   Creates window in a minimized state

WS_MAXIMIZE   Creates window in a maximized state

WS_HSCROLL   Creates window with a horizontal scroll bar

WS_VSCROLL   Creates window with a vertical scroll bar

The following code shows how a typical call to create a window might look:

```
MDICREATESTRUCT MDICreate;

MDICreate.szClass = szMyMDIClass ;
MDICreate.szTitle = "MyMDIClass" ;
MDICreate.hOwner  = hInstance ;
MDICreate.x       = CW_USEDEFAULT ;
MDICreate.y       = CW_USEDEFAULT ;
MDICreate.cx      = CW_USEDEFAULT ;
MDICreate.cy      = CW_USEDEFAULT ;
MDICreate.style   = 0;
MDICreate.lParam  = NULL ;

hwndChild = SendMessage(hWndClient, WM_MDICREATE, 0,
(LPARAM)(LPMDICREATESTRUCT)&MDICreate);
```

Note that the WPARAM field of SendMessage must be set to zero.

The preceding syntax box tells you the basic facts about creating MDI children. However, the actual code you need to use can be simplified considerably with just a little work. MDIPaint, for instance, includes the following function, which can be used whenever you need to create a child window:

```
HWND CreateMDIChild(LPCSTR szClass, LPCSTR szTitle)
{
  MDICREATESTRUCT    MCS;
```

```
    MCS.szClass = szClass;
    MCS.szTitle = szTitle;
    MCS.hOwner  = hInstance;
    MCS.x       = CW_USEDEFAULT;
    MCS.y       = CW_USEDEFAULT;
    MCS.cx      = CW_USEDEFAULT;
    MCS.cy      = CW_USEDEFAULT;
    MCS.style   = 0;
    MCS.lParam  = NULL;
    return FORWARD_WM_MDICREATE(hWndClient, &MCS, SendMessage);
}
```

The CreateMDIChild call makes use of one of the WindowsX FORWARD_WM_X macros. This is a programmer's trick really, not part of the standard usage of WindowsX as defined by Microsoft in their documentation. I added it simply because it shows how to avoid getting hung up in a lot of unsightly typecasts, such as the one shown in the SendMessage statement from the last Syntax box.

Using the above function involves simply passing in two string parameters. For instance, you might write:

```
CreateMDIChild(szFern, "Lar Fern");
```

in which the first parameter is the class name and the second is the title for the caption bar. You can copy CreateMDIChild into your own programs, but if you keep it in a separate module, you'll probably want to pass in the HINSTANCE as a third parameter.

Special MDI Messages That Must Be Forwarded

There are two sets of messages that you must pay special attention to when working with MDI applications. The first set involves messages that must be passed back to Windows from the window procedure of an MDI child:

WM_CHILDACTIVATE	Handles sizing, showing, and moving of children
WM_GETMINMAXINFO	Calculates the size of maximized window
WM_MENUCHAR	Passes keystrokes on to the main window
WM_MOVE	Needed for the scrollbars (if present)
WM_SETFOCUS	Activates child windows when they get the focus
WM_SIZE	Essential when maximizing or restoring child windows
WM_SYSCOMMAND	Handles various default hot keys and commands

You've seen most of these messages before. In fact, the descriptions I've added for each message do little to explain the message itself. Rather, my notes are meant to point out why it is necessary to forward each of these messages on to Windows if you want your MDIChild to act as the user expects.

A key point to remember is that MDI child windows have a special default function, called `DefMDIChildProc`, which they must use in lieu of `DefWindowProc`. To find which messages need to be passed on, look up `DefMDIChildProc` in the online help, and you'll find a copy of the list previously displayed.

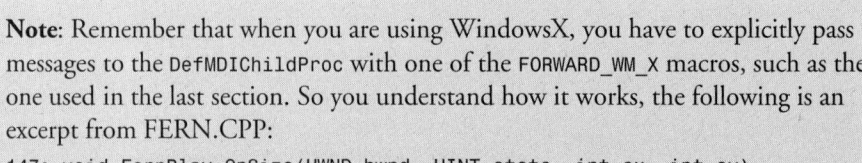

> **Note:** Remember that when you are using WindowsX, you have to explicitly pass messages to the `DefMDIChildProc` with one of the `FORWARD_WM_X` macros, such as the one used in the last section. So you understand how it works, the following is an excerpt from FERN.CPP:
>
> ```
> 147: void FernPlay_OnSize(HWND hwnd, UINT state, int cx, int cy)
> 148: {
> 149:   RECT R;
> 150:   GetClientRect(hwnd, &R);
> 151:   MaxX = R.right;
> 152:   MaxY = R.bottom;
> 153:   MaxIterations = long(MaxY) * 50;
> 154:   if (state == SIZE_MINIMIZED)
> 155:     MaxIterations = 175;
> 156:
> 157:   // MUST forward WM_SIZE messages
> 158:   FORWARD_WM_SIZE(hwnd, state, cx, cy, FernPlay_DefProc);
> 159: }
> ```
>
> The `FernPlay_DefProc`, referenced in the call to `FORWARD_WM_SIZE`, is declared like this:
>
> ```
> #define FernPlay_DefProc DefMDIChildProc
> ```
>
> All the other parameters sent to `FORWARD_WM_SIZE` are copied verbatim from the argument list to `FernPlay_OnSize`. This same pattern is followed in all the `FORWARD_WM_XXX` macros. As a result, the macros are virtually effortless to use.

Messages Specific to MDI Applications

Now that you know some basics about MDI child windows, you're ready to turn your attention to the following messages. These messages define most of the behavior specific to MDI children. I've grouped them into four separate categories.

The first category includes the messages used to create and destroy MDI children:

`WM_MDICREATE`	Creates an MDI window
`WM_MDIDESTROY`	Used to close an MDI child window

I've explained the `WM_MDICREATE` message in detail. `WM_MDIDESTROY` messages are easy to use because they require nothing more than the handle of the window to be closed in `wParam`.

The following messages can be used to find out which window has the focus. They can also be used to change the focus:

WM_MDIACTIVATE	Activates the window specified in WPARAM
WM_MDINEXT	Focuses the next window in the child list
WM_MDIGETACTIVE	Finds the active window

The WM_MDIACTIVATE message plays a dual role in Windows programming. The application first sends this message to the client window. At this point in its career, WM_MDIACTIVATE carries the handle of the window to be activated in WPARAM. After the client receives the message, it forwards it to both the child being activated and the one being deactivated.

Programmers rarely have to explicitly send WM_MDIACTIVATE messages, but they frequently must respond to these messages:

WM_MDIMAXIMIZE	Maximizes a window
WM_MDIRESTORE	Restores a window

In the MDIPaint application, responding to these messages is important, because they tell the application when to change the menu.

The next message, WM_MDINEXT, is sent to the client window. This message activates the MDI child that is behind the currently active window. The window that was active is placed behind the other child windows. The list of child windows manipulated by this message is maintained by Windows and displayed in the program's menu.

The final message in this category, WM_MDIGETACTIVE, is an extremely useful message that every programmer absolutely requires sooner or later. When using this message, set both WPARAM and LPARAM to 0 and expect the handle of the focused child in the return value. You should send this message to the client window.

> **Note:** WM_MDIGETACTIVE works differently in Windows 3.1 than in WIN32. In Windows 3.1, the low order word of the return value is set to the handle of the window, and the high order word is set to 1 if the window in question is maximized. In WIN32, the return value says nothing about the state of the Windows. Instead, you can track this value in lParam.

The following four messages need little explanation, though their importance is obvious:

WM_MDITILE	Tiles the children.
WM_MDICASCADE	Cascades the children.

WM_MDIICONARRANGE   Arranges iconized children.

When you are tiling windows, you can arrange them horizontally or vertically, depending on the value of a flag passed in WPARAM. For instance, the MDITILE_HORIZONTAL flag creates the image shown in Figure BD2.5, whereas the MDITILE_VERTICAL creates the image shown in Figure BD2.6.

The final message specific to MDI children is WM_MDISETMENU. This is used in conjunction with WM_MDIACTIVATE messages, as shown in the next section.

WM_MDISETMENU   Changes the pop-up menu containing the list of children, the main MDI menu, or both the pop-up menu and the main menu.

Figure BD2.5.
Horizontal tiling with the
MDITILE_HORIZONTAL flag.

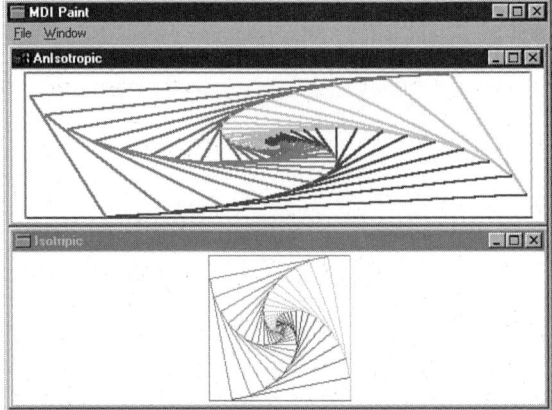

Figure BD2.6.
Vertical tiling with the
MDITILE_VERTICAL flag.

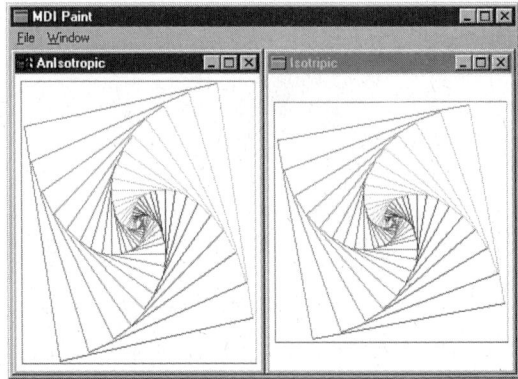

Handling MDI Menus

The MDIPaint program only has two menus, but some MDI programs have five or ten different menus. An example of such a program is Borland's Resource Workshop.

The key point to remember is that the menu shown to a user should reflect the options available at the time. In normal applications, this isn't an issue, because these applications only perform one function. However, MDI applications can perform several different functions, depending on which MDI child the user has focused at any one time. For instance, when working with a resource development tool, users don't need the same set of menus when creating a string table as they do when creating an icon or bitmap.

BD2

The next obvious question is How do you find out when a user activates a particular window? After reading the last section, astute readers will guess that the solution to this problem is the WM_MDIACTIVATE message, which gets sent down the pike whenever a window is about to get or lose the focus. As you recall, the WM_MDIACTIVATE message plays two roles in Windows programming. The first is to discover the currently focused child. In its second incarnation, it gets sent to a child window whenever the window is about to get or lose the focus.

The *WM_MDIACTIVATE* Message

Syntax

When receiving WM_MDIACTIVATE under WIN32, WPARAM contains the handle of the child being deactivated and LPARAM contains the handle of the child being activated.

Therefore, LPARAM and hwnd are identical when the window is being activated.

When receiving WM_MDIACTIVATE under Windows 3.1, you can process the following parameters:

WPARAM   If this is set to something other than zero, the window is being activated.

LPARAM   The low word of LPARAM contains the handle of the child being activated; the high word contains the handle of the child being deactivated.

When sending WM_MDIACTIVATE, WPARAM contains the handle of the window to activate and LPARAM must be set to zero.

When this message is sent to a child window, WINDOWSX.H breaks it down as follows:

WIN32   The fActive variable is determined by comparing lParam and the hwnd sent with the message. The handles to the activated and deactivated windows are culled from wParam and lParam and are called hwndActivate and hwndDeactivate.

WIN16   wParam is contained in a boolean variable called fActive, and the handles to the activated and deactivated windows are called hwndActivate and hwndDeactivate and are derived from lParam.

Here's an example:

```
SendMessage(hwnd, WM_MDIACTIVATE, hMyMDIChild, 0);
```

The following code shows how the Fern window handles the WM_MDIACTIVATE message:

```
void FernPlay_MDIActivate(HWND hwnd, BOOL fActive, HWND hwndActivate,
                          HWND hwndDeactivate)
{
  #if defined(WIN32)
    BOOL Refresh = TRUE;
  #else
    BOOL Refresh = FALSE;
  #endif

  if (fActive)
    FORWARD_WM_MDISETMENU(hWndClient, Refresh,
                          hMenuMultiple,
                          GetSubMenu(hMenuMultiple, 1),
                          SendMessage);

  if (!fActive)
    FORWARD_WM_MDISETMENU(hWndClient, Refresh,
                          hMenuInit,
                          GetSubMenu(hMenuInit, 1),
                          SendMessage);

  DrawMenuBar(hWndFrame);
}
```

As you can see, the center of attention is the fActive parameter. This parameter is set to TRUE whenever a window is receiving the focus and to FALSE whenever it's losing the focus. This enables the Fern menu to set its own menu whenever the window is coming into focus and to restore the main menu whenever it's losing the focus.

MDIPaint uses the WM_MDISETMENU message to manipulate its menus.

The *WM_MDISETMENU* Message

When receiving WM_MDISETMENU under WIN32, WPARAM contains the new frame window. If set to 0, the frame window menu is not changed and LPARAM contains the new window menu.

When receiving WM_MDISETMENU under Windows 3.1, WPARAM specifies whether to refresh the current menus or whether LPARAM specifies new menus. Refreshing the menus includes the act of updating the current list of children. LPARAM works like this: The low-order word specifies a new main menu (or a new menu for the frame window). The high-order word specifies a new menu to hold the list of child windows shown to the user.

Use WM_MDISETMENU to manipulate the menus of an MDI application and to specify which menu should hold the list of available child windows.

MDIPaint uses this message to swap the main set of menus with the menus used whenever a child is open. It does this by keeping both sets of menus in memory as global variables, and then swapping them with WM_MDISETMENU whenever a WM_MDIACTIVATE message comes down the pike.

Instead of using `SendMessage` directly (which entails typecasting), you can use the WindowsX macros:

```
#define
FORWARD_WM_MDISETMENU(HWND hwnd,          // handle to window
                      BOOL fRefresh,       // new menu or refresh
                      HMENU hmenuFrame,    // New menu
                      HMENU hmenuWindow,   // Where window lists?
                      fn)                  // Function to use
```

You need to be careful with the `fRefresh` parameter. This parameter has no real use in the standard WIN32 version of the message, and it may not behave as you expect under WindowsX.

Here's an example of how to use the macro:

```
FORWARD_WM_MDISETMENU(hWndClient, Refresh,
                      hMenuInit,
                      GetSubMenu(hMenuInit, 1),
                      SendMessage);
```

Every typecast a programmer makes is another platform-specific opportunity to make a careless error. As a result, the WindowsX macros are definitely worth careful consideration whenever you need to use `SendMessage`. Remember that these macros can help ensure that your code will run both on 16-bit and 32-bit platforms.

If you compare what `wParam` and `lParam` do in 16-bit Windows and in WIN32, you can see that WindowsX has an especially big role to play in this particular case. However, even with the help of WindowsX, you still won't get through this trial without some `ifdefing` of your code. Specifically, the Refresh option causes the menus to refresh under WIN16, but it causes the menus to switch to a new menu under WIN32. What a mess!

Here's an example:

```
FORWARD_WM_MDISETMENU(hWndClient, TRUE, hMenuMultiple,
                      GetSubMenu(hMenuInit, 1), SendMessage);
```

Setting menus is not my favorite part of writing an MDI application. Nevertheless, the code shown here compiles and runs cleanly under both 16- and 32-bit Windows with both Microsoft and Borland compilers.

Closing Up Shop

The next thing you need to know about MDI applications involves the proper way of closing them. This section makes the following points:

☐ When closing an MDI application, you can use the `WM_QUERYENDSESSION` and `WM_CLOSE` messages to ensure that the program gives the user a chance to save any work in progress.

☐ If a child window needs to prompt the user to save work, it responds to the WM_CLOSE message whenever it's shut down by the user.

☐ Each child window can respond to WM_QUERYENDSESSION messages. These are sent out to each child by MDIPaint when the user wants to shut down the whole application.

☐ MDIPaint can iterate through all the child windows on its desktop, sending each a WM_QUERYENDSESSION message. To do this, it uses the EnumChildWindows callback function.

The next few paragraphs go through each of these points in detail, so you can get a balanced view of the issues involved in shutting down an MDI child or MDI application.

When it's time to shut down an application or window, you need to keep track of two different messages. The first message is WM_QUERYENDSESSION, and the second is WM_CLOSE. You need to respond to these messages so the user has a chance to save any work that might be in progress. (MDIPaint doesn't need to respond to these messages, because there isn't any work to save in any of its windows. However, I do so anyway, just so you can see how the process works.)

WM_QUERYENDSESSION messages are typically sent by the Explorer or another Windows shell whenever it's time to shut down. If an application returns TRUE in response to this message, shutdown proceeds; if it returns FALSE, the session continues.

It's traditional, or at least common, for an MDI application to send this WM_QUERYENDSESSION message to its children to see if they're ready to close. In other words, if the user wants to close the whole application, MDIPaint sends this message to each of its children. If they all return TRUE, the MDI application shuts down; otherwise the session continues.

By now, you should be able to take a good guess at how a window might respond to this message. For instance, here's how the Isotrop window reacts whenever it gets a WM_QUERYENDSESSION message:

```
BOOL Isotrop_OnQueryEndSession(HWND hwnd)
{
  if (IDOK != MessageBox (hwnd, "OK to close window?",
                "Isotropic", MB_ICONQUESTION ¦ MB_OKCANCEL))
    return FALSE;
  else
    return TRUE;
}
```

If the user clicks the system icon of a child window, that window receives a WM_CLOSE message. Therefore, you should respond to WM_CLOSE messages in the same way you respond to WM_QUERYENDSESSION messages. For an example, take a look at the Fern_OnClose function (line 101 of FERN.CPP).

At first, you might be confused by the differences between the WM_CLOSE and WM_QUERYENDSESSION messages as they apply to MDI applications. To graphically illustrate the issues involved, I've supplied the Fern window with responses to both messages (whereas the Isotrop window

responds only to WM_QUERYENDSESSION messages). Try closing both windows by clicking the child's system icon, by closing the MDIPaint application, and by shutting down Windows altogether. The different responses you see should help clarify exactly how the two messages work. Specifically:

- ☐ The Fern window responds to all three methods of closing down a child window because it handles both WM_CLOSE and WM_QUERYENDSESSION.

- ☐ The Isotrop window closes without complaint if you shut it down with its system icon. However, it pops up a message box if you close down the whole application or if you shut down Windows. This occurs because it responds to WM_QUERYENDSESSION, not to WM_CLOSE.

When the user asks to close MDIPaint, the program can iterate through all the child windows on its desktop by calling EnumChildWindows. For instance, if the user clicks the system icon for the MDIPaint frame window, WM_CLOSE is called. WM_CLOSE then sends out a custom message called CM_CLOSEALL, which causes MDIPaint to respond like this:

```
300:    case CM_CLOSEALL:  // Children ready to close?
301:      lpfnEnum = (WNDENUMPROC)MakeProcInstance(
302:                       (FARPROC)EnumChildWnds, hInstance);
303:      EnumChildWindows (hWndClient, lpfnEnum, 0L);
304:      FreeProcInstance ((FARPROC)lpfnEnum);
305:      break;
```

These lines of code set up a classic windows callback of the type you have seen several times in this book. In particular, EnumChildWindows iterates through all the child windows belonging to any particular parent, such as a dialog, a main window, or an MDI client.

In MDIPaint, the callback that is set up to respond to the EnumChildWindows function looks like this:

```
BOOL CALLBACK EnumChildWnds(HWND hwnd, LONG lParam)
{
  if (GetWindow(hwnd, GW_OWNER)) // Icon Title?
  return TRUE;

  SendMessage (GetParent(hwnd), WM_MDIRESTORE, (WPARAM)hwnd, 0L);
  if (!SendMessage (hwnd, WM_QUERYENDSESSION, 0, 0L))
    return TRUE;

  SendMessage (GetParent(hwnd), WM_MDIDESTROY, (WPARAM)hwnd, 0L);
  return TRUE;
}
```

This function gets called once for every child on the MDI desktop, and it receives the handle for that window in its first parameter.

The code first checks to see if the child window in question is the title for an icon. If so, it returns without doing anything. If the window is a real MDI child, the next step is to restore the window and send it a WM_QUERYENDSESSION message. If the child doesn't want to close, EnumChildWnds returns. If the window does want to close, EnumChildWnds shuts it down with a WM_MDIDESTROY message.

After the application has iterated through all the child windows, control returns to the original WM_CLOSE response function (line 212 of MDIPAINT.CPP). MDIPaint can then check to see if any child windows are still open. If so, the application knows that it shouldn't shut down; otherwise, it closes.

Obviously, there are a hundred variations that can be run on this theme, some of which are considerably more elegant than the relatively simplistic approach taken by MDIPaint. However, the code outlined in this section should be enough to show you how to go about shutting down an MDI application and how to make sure the user doesn't lose any information in the process.

Extra Bytes and Sharing the CPU

Before moving on to a discussion of MM_ISOTROPIC and MM_ANISOTROPIC, I want to pause for a moment to make two quick, totally unrelated points:

- ☐ If you need to save window-specific information, do so by using the cbWndExtra field of the WNDCLASS structure.
- ☐ The Fern window is interesting because it shows one way of sharing CPU time with other windows and applications during the duration of a lengthy computation.

The first point mentioned is really very important. The issue is that you may have multiple copies of a particular type of window open on the MDI desktop, and each one of these windows might have a certain amount of specific data associated with it. For instance, if you have three edit windows open at one time in an MDI program, each of them might have a different block of text associated with it.

To handle a situation like this, you should use the cbWndExtra bytes, as illustrated in the child window's program you saw on Day 14, "Stylish Windows." As you recall, the keys to this process are the SetWindowLong and GetWindowLong functions.

The next point to consider involves the loop that draws the fractal fern in the Fern window. This code is a translation of a Pascal program written by Lar Mader, ace Windows hacker.

The issue is that the Fern window can take a sizable period of time to complete its drawing. If it does so without ever yielding control back to Windows, the application could hog the available clock cycles—even if the user wants to do something else, such as switch applications or tile windows. Doing this is not only impolite and annoying, but it can be dangerous, because Windows users expect to be able to respond to a variety of different circumstances on relatively short notice.

On Day 19, "Advanced Windows 95 Controls," I showed one solution to this problem, which involves calling PeekMessage. Another solution, which is generally a bit easier to implement, involves sending WM_TIMER messages to a function. Each time the message comes zooming in, the function can perform a few iterations of its task and then yield control back to Windows. Because timers are fairly slow, the best course is to perform 200 or 300 iterations of a loop and then pass control back to windows. Doing just one iteration at a time can make the process unbearably lengthy.

MDIPaint uses the WM_TIMER message to draw its fern. However, when applications have more sophisticated demands, they should use threads. Regardless, the key point is that no first-rate Windows application should ever steal the CPU for a lengthy period of time, except in the most dire circumstances. Certainly drawing a fern on the screen isn't a dire circumstance.

BD2

The Old Isotropic Versus AnIsotropic Issue

The MDIPaint program gives me an opportunity to fulfill a promise I gave you in Bonus Day 1, "GDI and Metafiles." That chapter explains the MM_TEXT, MM_LOENGLISH, MM_HIENGLISH, MM_LOMETRIC, MM_HIMETRIC, and MM_TWIPS mapping modes. The two modes left out were MM_ISOTROPIC and MM_ANISOTROPIC. MDIPaint illustrates these latter two mapping modes by drawing the same image with the same dimensions—once in both of these mapping modes and once in the MM_TEXT mapping mode. (See Figure BD2.7.)

Figure BD2.7.
MDIPaint shows the results of changing the mapping mode while drawing the same figure with the same dimensions.

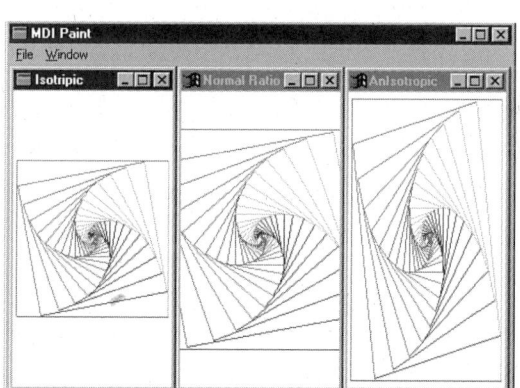

Both of these modes are used primarily when a programmer wants to draw as big an image as possible inside a window that's likely to be frequently resized. (Remember the old Clock application that came with Windows 3.1? It used this technique. And so did the old version of

Paintbrush.) Put as simply as possible, the following is the difference between MM_ISOTROPIC, MM_ANISOTROPIC, and standard mapping modes:

☐ Use MM_ISOTROPIC when you want your picture to maintain the ratio of its dimensions, just as the Clock program does.

☐ Use MM_ANISOTROPIC when you want your drawing to stretch to fill up all available space, as seen in the controls for the Windows 3.1 version of the Paintbrush program.

☐ Use any other mode when you want the drawing to maintain its same dimensions, regardless of how often the window is changed. This is the way the Program Manager works.

With the MDIPaint program, you should notice that the geometric shapes drawn in the AnIsotropic window distort themselves to fill the available space as completely as possible. (See Figure BD2.8.) This functionality has a great deal in common with the StretchBlt function.

Figure BD2.8.

No matter how you distort an MM_ANISOTROPIC *window, the image inside attempts to stretch to fill the available space.*

The shapes inside the MM_ISOTROPIC window, on the other hand, always maintain the ratio of their original dimensions. The concepts involved have a lot in common with those you encounter when calculating the proper aspect ratio in a typical DOS graphics program. (See Figure BD2.9.)

Finally, notice that the shape in the Normal window never changes, regardless of how you change the dimensions of the window in which it resides. The end result is that portions of the shape can be obscured when the window is shrunk.

The following code is used to set up the Isotrop window:

```
SetMapMode(PaintDC, MM_ISOTROPIC);
GetClientRect(hwnd, &R);
SetWindowExtEx(PaintDC, 210, 210, NULL);
SetViewportExtEx(PaintDC, R.right, R.bottom, NULL);
SetViewportOrgEx(PaintDC, R.right / 2, R.bottom / 2, NULL);
```

This code differs slightly in Windows 3.1; check the source for details. MDIPaint first sets the mapping mode; then, it sets the windows extent. Look at the DRAW.CPP module and you'll see that the largest rectangle drawn in the Isotrop window has a dimension of 200×200. Therefore, the Isotrop window sets itself up to always be just a little larger than 200×200 *logical* units in size.

Figure BD2.9.

The image inside an
`MM_ISOTROPIC` *window*
always maintains its
original shape.

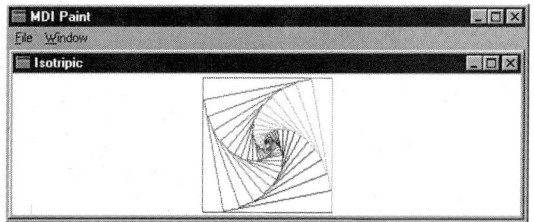

The calls to `SetWindowExtEx` and `SetViewportExtEx` are mandatory when working with `MM_ISOTROPIC` windows. The purpose of these two calls is to give Windows enough information so it can figure out how to translate physical device coordinates into logical coordinates (and vice versa).

Given the above code, an Isotropic window with dimensions of 420×420 will have two physical pixels for every logical pixel specified by its user. The key is that the Isotrop window will always have 210×210 logical pixels, regardless of how the user reshapes it. Therefore, if the user sizes a window so that its device (physical) coordinates are 420×420, Windows must paint two physical pixels for every one logical pixel—or the shape won't properly fill its bounding window.

The final step is to move the origin to the center of the screen by calling `SetViewportOrg`. This call isn't mandatory, but MDIPaint makes the call to simplify the drawing of the rotated squares that it displays.

The code for setting up the AnIsotropic window looks exactly like the code shown previously, except the mapping mode is set to `MM_ANISOTROPIC` instead of `MM_ISOTROPIC`. If you want to compare the samples, see line 77 in the ANISOTRP.CPP file.

Summary

In this chapter, you've learned about MDI windows and about the `MM_ISOTROPIC` and `MM_ANISOTROPIC` mapping modes. Specifically, the main points covered in this chapter are the following:

☐ MDI windows follow a standard called CUA, which was set up by IBM.

☐ You can create an MDI window by sending `WM_MDICREATE` messages.

☐ You need to respond to `WM_MDIACTIVATE` messages in order to set up an MDI child's menu.

☐ Use the extra bytes found in the `WNDCLASS` structure to store data specific to a window.

☐ Respond to `WM_QUERYENDSESSION` and `WM_CLOSE` messages to prompt a user before a child window closes.

☐ There are a number of messages that MDI applications must pass on to
DefMDIChildProc.

☐ Use MM_ANISOTROPIC and MM_ISOTROPIC when you want an image to automatically
expand or shrink with the window it occupies.

All in all, the MDI specification is a fairly tricky bit of work, but it is one that almost all Windows
programmer's have to master sooner or later. Although working with this kind of application
isn't prohibitively difficult, you must pay attention while coding. The reward is an interface
that's both powerful and easy to use—though not necessarily in accord with the latest thinking
about Windows 95 interface guidelines. It is not, however, obsolete, as evidenced by the fact that
Microsoft still uses it in several of its major applications.

Q&A

**Q I still don't understand the difference between a frame window and a client
window. What's up?**

A The frame window is the standard main window for an MDI application. It has a
child called a client window. The MDIClient class is predefined by Windows and
contains most of the functionality associated with MDI applications. It is literally
painted over the top of the frame window, and it knows how to respond to most of
the MDI specific messages. The user needs to set up a window procedure for frame
windows, but not for client windows. Rather than calling DefWindowProc, MDI frame
windows should call DefFrameProc. Be sure to pass WM_COMMAND messages to
DefFrameProc.

**Q Can you explain more about why I would want to use a FORWARD_WM_XXX macro
rather than SendMessage?**

A The issue here is that you often have to typecast the parameters sent in the lParam and
wParam fields of a SendMessage or PostMessage call. The WindowsX message crackers
perform this typecasting for you. Rather than having to try to stuff information into
lParam and wParam, you can use a FORWARD_WM_XXX macro. When doing so, you will
find that lParam and wParam have disappeared, and in their place are properly typed
parameters with meaningful names. This is easier and safer than trying to use
SendMessage.

Workshop

The Workshop provides quiz questions to help you solidify your understanding of the material
covered and exercises to provide you with experience in using what you've learned. Try to
understand the quiz and exercise answers before continuing on to the next chapter. Answers are
provided in Appendix A.

Quiz

1. What class do you use when creating client windows?
2. What function is used to iterate through the child windows on an MDI desktop?
3. What message can you send to find out which MDI child has the focus?
4. What message is sent when a particular MDI child is getting or losing the focus?
5. What is the purpose of the LPARAM field accompanying a WM_MDISETMENU message?
6. How can you tell that the Clock program that comes with Windows uses the MM_ISOTROPIC style?
7. What structure do you have to fill out every time you create an MDI child?
8. What message does a Windows shell send out when the user wants to close the entire environment?
9. When iterating through the windows on the desktop, how can you tell if the window you have is a real window or just the title of an icon?
10. If you have multiple copies of a specific class of an MDI child on the desktop, how can you store data associated with each instance of that class?

Exercises

1. Change calls to CreateWindow and MDICreateChild so that the MDIPaint program creates children that have no border and can't be minimized.
2. Add an option to the MDIPaint menu that will enable the user to tile windows either horizontally or vertically.

Bonus Day

3+

DLLs and Multimedia

This chapter has two significant topics:

1. Dynamic link libraries
2. The multimedia extensions to Windows

The core of this chapter is a program called Harmony, which uses dynamic link libraries (DLLs) to demonstrate easy-to-use techniques for playing CD-ROMs, MIDI files, and WAV files. Along the way, you'll also learn about creating something called a *dialog window,* which is really just a standard dialog that is used as the main window for a program.

A list of specific topics to be covered in this chapter includes:

☐ The media control interface (MCI), which forms one of the key nexus in the multimedia extensions to Windows

☐ The mciSendCommand function, which plays a central role in the MCI

☐ The ImpLib utility, which can simplify the task of using DLLs

☐ The _export and declspec keywords

☐ The use of CreateDialog in lieu of CreateWindow, when you want a dialog to form the center of attention in a Windows program

When you roll the phrase "dynamic link library" or "the multimedia extensions to Windows" around on your tongue, it's hard not to get the feeling that these must be terribly difficult subjects that will immerse programmers in a sea of technical details. It turns out, however, that both subjects are surprisingly easy to master. In fact, even the technique of using a dialog as a main window turns out to be so simple it needs no more than a few paragraphs of explanation.

Better yet, the code in this chapter is easily reusable. DLLs are meant to be used over and over again by a variety of different programs. Harmony features two DLLs, one for playing CDs, and one for playing WAV and MIDI files. You can reuse this code, completely unchanged, in many different programs. In other words, this chapter teaches you not only how to play WAV, MIDI, and CD-ROM files, but also how to quickly and easily use DLLs to add multimedia to a wide variety of your programs.

So sit back and be prepared to have a little fun. All of the material in this chapter is relatively easy to master. This is payoff time. You've done the hard work, and now (in this chapter and the next) you can sit back and reap the harvest.

Groping for a Definition of Multimedia

Multimedia tools are so new that it would be helpful to spend a few moments clarifying exactly what this subject encompasses.

The first term to come to grips with is MPC, or Multimedia PC. This is a hardware standard meant to define the minimum configuration of any personal computer that can play multimedia programs. The key elements in the MPC1 standard are a 386 or better computer with a VGA video system, a mouse, a sound board, and a CD-ROM.

Here is a brief overview of level-two requirements:

- CPU: Minimum requirement—25MHz 486SX (or compatible) microprocessor
- RAM: Minimum requirement—4MB of RAM (8MB recommended)
- Magnetic storage: Requirement—3.5" high density (1.44MB) floppy disk drive; Minimum requirement—160MB hard drive
- Optical storage: Requirement—CD-ROM drive capable of sustained 300KB/second transfer rate

BD3

And finally, here are the level-three requirements as specified in the document called MPCSPECS.RTF, available from the Microsoft Network, and most likely other services as well:

- Processor: 75MHz Pentium.
- RAM: 8MB.
- Hard drive: 540MB minimum, 15ms access time, 1.5MB/second sustained throughput.
- CD-ROM drive: Sustained 600KB/second transfer rate, average access time of 250ms (in 4x mode); CD-ROM drive with CD-DA (Red Book) outputs and volume control; CD-ROM drive must have on-board buffers and implement read-ahead buffering.
- Sequential access time: An application via the standard operating system access methods must have the ability to read sequential, error-free, 16KB blocks every 33.3ms with each read taking no more than 13.3ms.
- Background CPU utilization: The driver must not use CPU cycles except in response to a host system request.
- Audio: 6-bit digital-to-analog converter. (DAC) with linear PCM sampling; DMA or FIFO buffered transfer capability with interrupt on buffer empty; 44.1, 22.05, and 11.025KHz sample rate mandatory; stereo channels; no more than 10 percent of the CPU bandwidth required to output 22.05 and 11.025KHz; it is recommended that no more than 15 percent of the CPU bandwidth be required to output 44.1KHz. 16-bit analog-to-digital converter (ADC) with Linear PCM sampling; 44.1, 22.05, and 11.025KHz sample rate mandatory; DMA or FIFO buffered transfer capability with interrupt on buffer full; microphone input. Wavetable capability required. CPU utilization for 16-bit stereo sound and wavetable cannot exceed 10 percent.
- Speakers: Must be at least a two-piece system, frequency response from 120Hz to 17.5KHz.

☐ Subwoofer requirements: Frequency response must be at least 40Hz to 250Hz (+/- 3dB).

☐ Graphics performance: Color space conversion and scaling capability are required. Direct access to frame buffer for video-enabled graphics subsystem required with a resolution of 352×240 at 30fps (or 352×288 at 25fps) at 15 bits/pixel, unscaled, without cropping. Test suite will test for acceptable graphics performance.

☐ System software: Multimedia PC system software must offer binary compatibility with Windows 3.11. System must offer binary compatibility with DOS version 6.0 or higher.

☐ Minimum full system configuration: CPU, RAM, hard drive, floppy drive, CD-ROM drive, audio, graphics performance, video playback, user input, I/O, system software.

The program in this chapter was tested on a variety of 486s. Some of the machines had Creative Labs' Sound Blaster Pro card; others had cards from MediaVision and a variety of other companies. Most of the CD-ROMs I've tested this code on were made be either Creative Labs or NEC. A sound card is a requirement for playing MIDI and WAV files with the code presented in this book. And of course, you won't be able to play compact disks unless you have a CD-ROM drive or comparable hardware.

Note: If you don't have any of the previously listed tools, you won't be able to run any of the code in this chapter. It's important to understand that the widely distributed SPEAKER.DRV file won't be enough to enable you to run the included code, and it may not be available for Windows 95. The reason for this is that the calls used in this chapter are too low level for the limited WAV-file support available with SPEAKER.DRV.

Now that you've read about the hardware requirements, it's time to move on to a discussion of the various devices referenced in this chapter. It is probably safe to assume that everyone now knows what a CD-ROM is, but there may be some lingering confusion about WAV and MIDI files.

A WAV file is a Microsoft standard file format generally used for recording non-musical sounds, such as the human voice or a car horn. The key fact to know about a WAV file is that it can store about 1 second of sound in 11KB of disk space, or one minute of sound in 1MB of disk space. As a result, this medium tends to be extremely disk-intensive and is used mostly for adding short sound effects to a program or to the entire Windows environment.

The word MIDI stands for Musical Instrument Digital Interface. Put in the simplest possible terms, MIDI files can be thought of as containing a series of notes, such as C sharp or A flat. These

notes are sent to a synthesizer with instructions to play the note using the sounds associated with a particular instrument such as a piano, horn, or guitar.

The synthesizer I used when writing the Harmony program came as a standard part of the Sound Blaster Pro card. Most sound cards and MIDI files can play between 6 and 16 notes at once, and they can imitate between 3 and 9 instruments. MIDI files can store one minute of fairly high quality musical sound in about 5KB of disk space. Because they take up about one-twentieth the space, MIDI files are much more useful than WAV files for many purposes.

Narrowing the Focus

Now that you know something about the media involved, it's time to focus on the programming techniques used to make computer-generated sounds. As it happens, Microsoft provides three separate interfaces that can enable you to access multimedia devices. Two of these are part of MCI; the third is a low-level API, which is very rigorous and demanding. Windows 95 also includes an interface called MCIWnd. It is available in the VFW.H header file.

Note: In an ideal world, I would have found time to also explore the MCIWnd class. This is a powerful set of macros that wrap the MCI interface described below. Here is a sample patch of MCI code, taken from VFW.H:

```
hwnd = MCIWndCreate(hwndParent, hInstance, 0, "chimes.wav");
MCIWndPlay(hwnd);
MCIWndStop(hwnd);
MCIWndPause(hwnd);
MCIWndDestroy(hwnd);
```

This will create a window with a play/pause, stop, and a playbar and start playing the WAV file.

The low-level API is not appropriate for this book, and so that leaves only three remaining programming techniques. The first is a string-based interface meant primarily to provide support for very high-level languages, such as Visual Basic. MCIWND is also a powerful option, and one that should be explored by all multimedia programmers. Because this is a C programming book, it is possible to use the third technique—a powerful message-based interface.

The MCI command-message interface relies very heavily on a single routine called mciSendCommand, which takes four parameters. Though this might sound limiting at first, in practice it turns out to be a flexible system.

Syntax

The *mciSendCommand* Function

```
DWORD mciSendCommand(UINT, UINT, DWORD, DWORD);
```

UINT	wDeviceID	ID used to identify the current device
UINT	wMessage	Message specifying requested action
DWORD	dwParam1	Flags qualifying the wMessage field
DWORD	dwParam2	Pointer to structure containing additional data

mciSendCommand returns 0 if the function was successful. Otherwise, it returns error information that can be passed to mciGetErrorString. The function itself sends a command to the MCI, which automatically carries out the requested action. See the following text for further details.

Here's an example:

```
MCI_STATUS_PARMS Info;
DWORD ErrorNum, Flags;

memset(&Info, 0, sizeof(MCI_STATUS_PARMS));
Info.dwItem = MCI_STATUS_LENGTH;
Flags = MCI_STATUS_ITEM;
mciSendCommand(wDeviceID, MCI_STATUS, Flags, DWORD(&Info));
```

The first parameter passed to MciSendCommand is a handle or ID number used to identify the particular device in question. When Harmony first opens up a CD drive, it passes 0 in this parameter since it doesn't yet have an ID for the device. Thereafter, however, it passes in the ID that was returned by Windows.

Key to this interface is the second parameter, which is a message conveying a particular command. Following is a list of the twelve most common of these messages and their meanings:

MCI_GETDEVCAPS	Queries the devices capabilities
MCI_CLOSE	Closes a device
MCI_INFO	Queries type of hardware being used
MCI_OPEN	Opens a device
MCI_PLAY	Plays a song or piece on a device
MCI_RECORD	Records to a device
MCI_RESUME	Resumes playing or recording
MCI_SEEK	Moves media forward or backward
MCI_SET	Changes the settings on a device
MCI_STATUS	Is device paused, playing, and so on
MCI_STOP	Stops playing or recording

Complementing these commands are a set of flags and records giving programmers the kind of fine-tuned control they need to do the job right. For instance, the MCI_PLAY message has four important flags that can be ORed together to form its third parameter:

MCI_NOTIFY   Posts MM_MCINOTIFY message on completion

MCI_WAIT   Completes operation before returning

MCI_FROM   Specifies starting position

MCI_TO   Specifies finishing position

The last two flags presented can be ORed together like this:

MCI_FROM ¦ MCI_TO

This way, they inform MCI that a starting and finishing position will be specified in the last parameter.

The fourth parameter is a pointer to a structure that varies in composition, depending on which message is being sent. The structure accompanying MCI_PLAY looks like this:

```
typedef struct {
  DWORD dwCallback;
  DWORD dwFrom;
  DWORD dwTo;
} MCI_PLAY_PARMS;
```

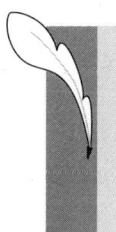

Note: This naming convention is followed over and over again, so that MCI_STATUS works with MCI_STATUS_PARMS, and MCI_OPEN works with MCI_OPEN_PARMS.

All the multimedia structures or constants discussed in this book are listed in the online help, and in MMSYSTEM.H. You should definitely take the time to become familiar with these files.

Sometimes it's necessary to fill out all three fields of this structure; at other times, some, or none of them can be filled out. For instance, if you set the MCI_NOTIFY flag in the second parameter of mciSendCommand, you'll probably want to set dwCallback equal to the HWND of the Window you want MCI to notify. Specifically, if you are inside a dialog when you start playing a WAV file, you should pass the dialog's HWND in dwCallback, so that the dialog would be informed with an MM_NOTIFY message when the WAV file stops playing.

Of course, if you set both the MCI_FROM and MCI_TO flags, you should fill out both the dwFrom and the dwTo fields of the MCI_PLAY_PARMS record (and so on).

The only major aspect of the mciSendCommand function that I've not discussed is its return value, which happens to be an error number kept in the low-order word of a LongInt. Microsoft comes through with a nice touch at this point by adding the mciGetErrorString function, which provides you with a ready-made string that explains the error. mciGetErrorString will even send you back a pleasant little message that all has gone well, if that is the case.

The *mciGetErrorString* Function

Syntax

UINT mciGetErrorString(DWORD, LPSTR, UINT)

DWORD	dwError	Error code returned from mciSendCommand
LPSTR	lpstrBuffer	Buffer to hold error message
UINT	wLength	Length of the buffer in lpstrBuffer

mciGetErrorString returns TRUE if successful.

mciSendCommand returns a number listing the error that has occurred. The mciGetErrorString function returns a string, which describes an error, as shown in Figure BD3.1.

Here's an example:

```
char S[MsgLen];

if (!mciGetErrorString(RC, S, MsgLen))
strcpy(S, "No message available");
```

Figure BD3.1.
The strings retrieved from
mciGetErrorString
are well-written and
informative.

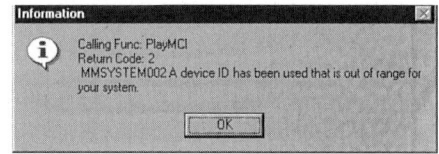

Coming to Terms with MCI

If you have never dealt with code similar to the MCI interface, a few words of explanation are in order. Over time, I've found that some programmers are a little intimidated by the opaque surface of message-based APIs such as mciSendCommand and SendMessage. In particular, mciSendCommand features a rather mean and nasty-looking bunch of constants and structures such as MCI_STATUS and MCI_STATUS_PARMS. If all this bristling syntax puts you off a bit at first, just have patience. mciSendCommand is really a very simple command which presents the programmer with a very easy-to-use interface. Newcomers often find it strange, but after a little experience with it you are bound to have a satisfying epiphany or two, and then you will feel right at home. I promise. Go at it with a will, and you will find it easy enough.

MCI encapsulates the multimedia API inside a message-based system that isolates multimedia programmers from the details of the code base's actual implementation. In other words, when using this mid-level interface, there is no point at which you or I would actually call a true multimedia API function.

The reason for this is that hardware and operating systems change over time. As a result, APIs are forced to change with them. When APIs change, existing code bases are rendered obsolete, and last year's work has to be done all over again.

The MCI command-message interface protects the programmer from any fluctuations in the API. For all practical purposes, all you are doing is sending messages into a dark hole. What goes on inside of that hole is of little concern. (To get some ideas, run Harmony with the debug version of Windows!) Five years from now, CDs may have six times their current capacity and have cut their access time down to a fifth of the current snail-like pace. But none of that is going to affect the code now. All we do is say that we want a particular track to be played. How it's played is of no concern to us.

Another crucial advantage of this style of programming is that it gives the user a common interface to a series of radically different pieces of hardware. For instance, the MCI command interface works with the following different types of devices, which are listed here opposite their MCI name:

animation	Animation device
cdaudio	CD audio
datDigital	audio tape device
digitalvideo	Digital video device
scanner	Image scanner
sequencer	MIDI
vcr	Videotape Harmony
videodisc	Videodisc device
waveaudio	A device that plays WAV files

What MCI has tried to do is find the things that all these devices have in common, and use those similarities to bind them together. In particular, it makes sense to ask all of these devices to play something, to stop playing, to pause, to seek to a particular location in its medium, and so on. In other words, they all respond to the set of commands as the primary MCI messages.

Talk about device independence! The Windows multimedia extensions not only protect you from the details of how a particular device might work, but they also frequently enable you to treat one device exactly the same way you treat another. For instance, Harmony uses the same code to play a WAV file as a MIDI file. The only difference is that in one case you tell MCI that you want to work with a "waveaudio" device, and the next time you say you want to work with a "sequencer."

The Harmony Program

Listing BD3.1 shows the code for the Harmony program.

Listing BD3.1. HARMONY.CPP.

```
/////////////////////////////////////
//   Program Name: HARMONY.CPP
//   Programmer: Charlie Calvert
//   Description: Harmony windows program
//   Date: 08/07/93
/////////////////////////////////////

#define STRICT
#include <windows.h>
#include <windowsx.h>
#include <mmsystem.h>
#include <stdio.h>
#include <string.h>
#include "harmony.h"
#include "playinfo.h"
#include "cdinfo.h"
#include "cdutil.h"
#include "wavemidi.h"
#pragma warning (disable: 4068)
// -------------------------------------
// Interface
// -------------------------------------

static char szAppName[] = "Harmony";
static HWND MainWindow;
static HINSTANCE hInstance;

BYTE State;
BYTE PlayType;
char DirStr[DIRSTRSIZE];
char DeviceString[DEVICESTRSIZE];
static char NoCDOnSystem;

// -----------------------------------------------------
// Initialization
// -----------------------------------------------------

/////////////////////////////////////
// Program entry point
/////////////////////////////////////
#pragma argsused
int PASCAL WinMain(HINSTANCE hInst, HINSTANCE hPrevInstance,
                   LPSTR lpszCmdParam, int nCmdShow)
{
  MSG  Msg;

  if (!hPrevInstance)
    if (!Register(hInst))
      return FALSE;
```

```
  MainWindow = Create(hInst, nCmdShow);
  if (!MainWindow)
    return FALSE;

  while (GetMessage(&Msg, NULL, 0, 0))
  {
     TranslateMessage(&Msg);
     DispatchMessage(&Msg);
  }

  return Msg.wParam;
}

/////////////////////////////////////
// Register the window
/////////////////////////////////////
BOOL Register(HINSTANCE hInst)
{
  WNDCLASS WndClass;

  WndClass.style         = CS_HREDRAW | CS_VREDRAW;
  WndClass.lpfnWndProc   = WndProc;
  WndClass.cbClsExtra    = 0;
  WndClass.cbWndExtra    = DLGWINDOWEXTRA;
  WndClass.hInstance     = hInst;
  WndClass.hIcon         = LoadIcon(NULL, IDI_APPLICATION);
  WndClass.hCursor       = LoadCursor(NULL, IDC_ARROW);
  WndClass.hbrBackground = GetStockBrush(WHITE_BRUSH);
  WndClass.lpszMenuName  = NULL;
  WndClass.lpszClassName = szAppName;

  return (RegisterClass (&WndClass)  != 0);
}

/////////////////////////////////////
// Create the window
/////////////////////////////////////
HWND Create(HINSTANCE hInst, int nCmdShow)
{

  hInstance = hInst;

  HWND hwnd = CreateDialog(hInst, szAppName, 0, NULL);

  if (hwnd == NULL)
    return hwnd;

  if (NoCDOnSystem)
    EnableWindow(GetDlgItem(hwnd, CM_COMPACT), FALSE);

  ShowWindow(hwnd, nCmdShow);

  return hwnd;
}
```

continues

Listing BD3.1. continued

```
// -------------------------------------------------------
// WndProc and Implementation
// -------------------------------------------------------


//////////////////////////////////////
// The Window Procedure
//////////////////////////////////////
LRESULT CALLBACK WndProc(HWND hwnd, UINT Message,
                         WPARAM wParam, LPARAM lParam)
{
  switch(Message)
  {
    HANDLE_MSG(hwnd, WM_CREATE, Harmony_OnCreate);
    HANDLE_MSG(hwnd, WM_DESTROY, Harmony_OnDestroy);
    HANDLE_MSG(hwnd, WM_FILLLISTBOX, Harmony_OnFillListBox);
    HANDLE_MSG(hwnd, WM_COMMAND, Harmony_OnCommand);
    HANDLE_MSG(hwnd, MM_MCINOTIFY, Harmony_OnMCINotify);
    HANDLE_MSG(hwnd, WM_TIMER, Harmony_OnTimer);
    default: return Harmony_DefProc(hwnd, Message, wParam, lParam);
  }
}

#pragma argsused
BOOL Harmony_OnCreate(HWND hwnd, CREATESTRUCT FAR* lpCreateStruct)
{
  PlayType = WAVE;
  State = CLOSED;
  strcpy(DeviceString, "waveaudio");
  GetWindowsDirectory(DirStr, 200);
  FORWARD_WM_FILLLISTBOX(hwnd, PostMessage);
  if (!DoesDeviceExistOnSystem("cdaudio"))
    NoCDOnSystem = TRUE;
  else
    NoCDOnSystem = FALSE;
  return TRUE;
}


//////////////////////////////////////
// Handle WM_DESTROY
//////////////////////////////////////
#pragma argsused
void Harmony_OnDestroy(HWND hwnd)
{
  PostQuitMessage(0);
}


//////////////////////////////////////
// Handle WM_COMMAND
//////////////////////////////////////
#pragma argsused
void Harmony_OnCommand(HWND hwnd, int id, HWND hwndCtl, UINT
codeNotify)
{
  char S[100];
```

```
switch (id)
{
  case CM_MIDI:
    CheckForClose();
    strcpy(DeviceString, "sequencer");
    PlayType = MIDI;
    FORWARD_WM_FILLLISTBOX(hwnd, PostMessage);
    break;

  case CM_WAVE:
    CheckForClose();
    strcpy(DeviceString, "waveaudio");
    PlayType = WAVE;
    FORWARD_WM_FILLLISTBOX(hwnd, PostMessage);
    break;

  case CM_COMPACT:
    if (PlayType != COMPACT)
    {
      CheckForClose();
      PlayType = COMPACT;
      strcpy(DeviceString, "cdaudio");
      FORWARD_WM_FILLLISTBOX(hwnd, PostMessage);
    }
    break;

  case CM_DIRECTORY:
    LoadFile(hwnd);
    FORWARD_WM_FILLLISTBOX(hwnd, PostMessage);
    break;

  case IDOK:
    CheckForClose();
    FORWARD_WM_CLOSE(hwnd, Harmony_DefProc);
    break;

  case CM_PAUSE:
  case CM_STOP:
    switch (PlayType)
    {
      case MIDI: HandleMIDIPAndS(hwnd, id); break;
      case WAVE: HandleWAVEPAndS(hwnd, id); break;
      case COMPACT: HandleCDPAndS(hwnd, id); break;
    }
    break;

  case CM_WAVEPLAY:
    if (State == PLAYING)
      return;

    if (PlayType == COMPACT)
    {
      PlayCD(hwnd);
      return;
    }
```

continues

Listing BD3.1. continued

```
          if (FileOpen(hwnd))
          {
            State = PLAYING;
            SetWindowText(GetDlgItem(hwnd, ID_MODE), "Playing");
            SetTimeFormatMs();
            DWORD Result = GetLen();
            sprintf(S, "%ld ms", Result);
            SetWindowText(GetDlgItem(hwnd, ID_LENGTH), S);
            SetWindowText(GetDlgItem(hwnd, ID_NUMTRACKS),
                          GetInfo(S));
            if (PlayMCI())
              SetTimer(hwnd, HARMONY_TIMER, 10, NULL);
            else
            {
              CloseMCI();
              State = CLOSED;
              SetWindowText(GetDlgItem(hwnd, ID_MODE), "CLOSED");
            }
          }
          break;

        case ID_FILELIST:
          if (codeNotify == LBN_DBLCLK)
            MessageBox(hwnd, "They're talking to me!", NULL, MB_OK);
          break;

        case CM_RECORD:
          if ((PlayType == MIDI) || (PlayType == COMPACT))
            return;
          if (OpenMCI(hwnd, "", DeviceString))
          {
            DoRecord(10000);
            State = RECORDING;
            SetTimer(hwnd, HARMONY_TIMER, 10, NULL);
          }
          break;
      }
}

//////////////////////////////////////
// Handle WM_FILLLISTBOX
//////////////////////////////////////
#pragma argsused
void Harmony_OnFillListBox(HWND hwnd)
{
  if (PlayType == COMPACT)
  {
    FillCDTrackBox(hwnd);
    return;
  }

  char S[200];

  strcpy(S, DirStr);
  switch (PlayType)
```

```
  {
    case MIDI: strcat(S, "\\*.mid"); break;
    case WAVE: strcat(S, "\\*.wav"); break;
  }

  if(!DlgDirList(hwnd, S, ID_FILELIST, 0, DDL_ARCHIVE))
    MessageBox(hwnd, "No way", NULL, MB_OK);

  switch (PlayType)
  {
    case COMPACT:
      Button_SetCheck(GetDlgItem(hwnd, CM_COMPACT), TRUE); break;
    case MIDI:
      Button_SetCheck(GetDlgItem(hwnd, CM_MIDI), TRUE); break;
    case WAVE:
      Button_SetCheck(GetDlgItem(hwnd, CM_WAVE), TRUE); break;
  }
  SetWindowText(GetDlgItem(hwnd, ID_DIREDIT), DirStr);

  ListBox_SetCurSel(GetDlgItem(hwnd, ID_FILELIST), 0);
}

/////////////////////////////////////
// Handle MM_ONMCINOTIFY
/////////////////////////////////////
#pragma argsused
void Harmony_OnMCINotify(HWND hwnd, UINT status, int DeviceID)
{
  char S[100];

  if (State == ERROR_OCCURED)
    return;

  switch (status)
  {
    case MCI_NOTIFY_ABORTED:
      strcpy(S, "Aborted");
      break;

    case MCI_NOTIFY_SUCCESSFUL:
      if (State == RECORDING)
      {
        SaveFile("Albert.wav");
        DlgDirList(hwnd, S, ID_FILELIST, 0, DDL_ARCHIVE);
      }
      State = CLOSED;
      if (PlayType == COMPACT)
        CloseCDMCI();
      else
        CloseMCI();
      strcpy(S, "Success");
      break;

    case MCI_NOTIFY_SUPERSEDED:
      strcpy(S, "Superseded");
      break;
```

continues

Listing BD3.1. continued

```c
      case MCI_NOTIFY_FAILURE:
        State = CLOSED;
        if (PlayType == COMPACT)
        CloseCDMCI();
        else
          CloseMCI();
        strcpy(S, "Failure");
        break;
  }
  SetWindowText(GetDlgItem(hwnd, ID_MODE), S);
  SetWindowText(GetDlgItem(hwnd, ID_LENGTH), "...");
  SetWindowText(GetDlgItem(hwnd, ID_POSITION), "...");
  SetWindowText(GetDlgItem(hwnd, ID_NUMTRACKS), "...");
//  MessageBox(hwnd, S, "MCI_NOTIFY", MB_OK);
}

/////////////////////////////////////
// Handle WM_TIMER
/////////////////////////////////////
#pragma argsused
void Harmony_OnTimer(HWND hwnd, UINT id)
{
  char S[100];

  switch (State)
  {
    case PAUSED:
      KillTimer(hwnd, HARMONY_TIMER);
      break;

    case STOPPED:
    case CLOSED:
      KillTimer(hwnd, HARMONY_TIMER);
      break;

    case RECORDING:
    case PLAYING:
      if (PlayType == COMPACT)
      {
        HandleCDTimer(hwnd);
        return;
      }

      LONG Result = GetLocation();

      if (Result == -1)
      {
        KillTimer(hwnd, HARMONY_TIMER);
        State = ERROR_OCCURED;
        SetWindowText(GetDlgItem(hwnd, ID_MODE), "ERROR");
        return;
      }

      sprintf(S, "%ld ms", Result);
      SetWindowText(GetDlgItem(hwnd, ID_POSITION), S);
```

```
    case CM_PAUSE:
      State = PAUSED;
      SetWindowText(GetDlgItem(hwnd, ID_MODE), "Paused");
      PauseMCI();
      break;

    case CM_STOP:
      if (State != CLOSED)
      {
        State = CLOSED;
        SetWindowText(GetDlgItem(hwnd, ID_MODE), "Stopped");
        StopMCI();
        CloseMCI();
      }
      break;
  }
}

//////////////////////////////////////
// HandleWAVEPAndS
//////////////////////////////////////
void HandleWAVEPAndS(HWND hwnd, int id)
{
  switch(id)
  {
    case CM_PAUSE:
      State = PAUSED;
      SetWindowText(GetDlgItem(hwnd, ID_MODE), "Paused");
      PauseMCI();
      break;

    case CM_STOP:
      if (State != CLOSED)
      {
        State = CLOSED;
        SetWindowText(GetDlgItem(hwnd, ID_MODE), "Stopped");
        StopMCI();
        CloseMCI();
      }
      break;
  }
}
```

Listing BD3.7 shows the header file for WaveMidi.

Listing BD3.7. WAVEMIDI.H.

```
1: //////////////////////////////////////
2: //  Module Name: WAVEMIDI.H
3: //  Programmer: Charlie Calvert
4: //  Description: Harmony windows program
5: //  Date: 08/07/93
6: //////////////////////////////////////
7:
```

continues

Listing BD3.7. continued

```
8: BOOL FileOpen(HWND hwnd);
9: void PlayCD(HWND hwnd);
10: void HandleMIDIPAndS(HWND hwnd, int id);
11: void HandleWAVEPAndS(HWND hwnd, int id);
12: void LoadFile(HWND hwnd);
```

Listing BD3.8 shows the resource file for the Harmony program.

Listing BD3.8. HARMONY.RC.

```
1: /////////////////////////////////////////
2: //   Module Name: HARMONY.RC
3: //   Programmer: Charlie Calvert
4: //   Description: Harmony windows program
5: //   Date: 08/07/93
6: /////////////////////////////////////////
7: #include <windows.h>
8: #include "harmony.h"
9:
10: Harmony DIALOG 18, 23, 246, 208
11: STYLE DS_MODALFRAME ¦ WS_OVERLAPPED ¦ WS_CAPTION
            ¦ WS_SYSMENU ¦ WS_MINIMIZEBOX
12: CLASS "Harmony"
13: CAPTION "Harmony"
14: BEGIN
15:       CONTROL "", ID_GROUP, "BUTTON", BS_GROUPBOX ¦
16:         WS_CHILD ¦ WS_VISIBLE, 6, 5, 107, 93
17:       CONTROL "Mode", -1, "STATIC", SS_LEFT ¦ WS_CHILD ¦
18:         WS_VISIBLE, 17, 15, 39, 11
19:       CONTROL "...", ID_MODE, "STATIC", SS_LEFT ¦ WS_CHILD ¦
20:         WS_VISIBLE, 56, 15, 53, 11
21:       CONTROL "Track", -1, "STATIC", SS_LEFT ¦ WS_CHILD ¦
22:         WS_VISIBLE, 17, 37, 39, 11
23:       CONTROL "...", ID_NUMTRACKS, "STATIC", SS_LEFT ¦
24:         WS_CHILD ¦ WS_VISIBLE, 56, 37, 53, 11
25:       CONTROL "Position", -1, "STATIC", SS_LEFT ¦ WS_CHILD ¦
26:         WS_VISIBLE, 17, 59, 39, 11
27:       CONTROL "...", ID_POSITION, "STATIC", SS_LEFT ¦
28:         WS_CHILD ¦ WS_VISIBLE, 56, 59, 53, 11
29:       CONTROL "Length", -1, "STATIC", SS_LEFT ¦ WS_CHILD ¦
30:         WS_VISIBLE, 17, 81, 39, 11
31:       CONTROL "...", ID_LENGTH, "STATIC", SS_LEFT ¦
32:         WS_CHILD ¦ WS_VISIBLE, 56, 81, 53, 11
33:       CONTROL "", ID_FILELIST, "LISTBOX", LBS_NOTIFY ¦
34:         LBS_USETABSTOPS ¦ WS_CHILD ¦ WS_VISIBLE ¦
35:         WS_BORDER ¦ WS_VSCROLL, 132, 9, 107, 94
36:       CONTROL "", ID_PLAYLIST, "COMBOBOX", CBS_DROPDOWNLIST ¦
37:         WS_CHILD ¦ WS_VISIBLE ¦ WS_TABSTOP, 6, 115, 107, 33
38:       CONTROL "", ID_DIREDIT, "EDIT", ES_LEFT ¦ WS_CHILD ¦
39:         WS_VISIBLE ¦ WS_BORDER ¦ WS_TABSTOP, 132, 115, 107, 12
40:       CONTROL "", 102, "button", BS_GROUPBOX ¦ WS_CHILD ¦
41:         WS_VISIBLE, 7, 156, 71, 45
```

```
42:        CONTROL "Help", CM_HELP, "BUTTON", BS_PUSHBUTTON ¦
43:          WS_CHILD ¦ WS_VISIBLE ¦ WS_TABSTOP, 7, 135, 71, 17
44:        CONTROL "Compact Disk", CM_COMPACT, "BUTTON",
45:          BS_AUTORADIOBUTTON ¦ WS_CHILD ¦ WS_VISIBLE ¦
46:          WS_GROUP ¦ WS_TABSTOP, 13, 162, 58, 12
47:        CONTROL "WAVE", CM_WAVE, "BUTTON", BS_AUTORADIOBUTTON ¦
48:          WS_CHILD ¦ WS_VISIBLE ¦ WS_TABSTOP, 13, 174, 28, 12
49:        CONTROL "MIDI", CM_MIDI, "BUTTON", BS_AUTORADIOBUTTON ¦
50:          WS_CHILD ¦ WS_VISIBLE ¦ WS_TABSTOP, 13, 186, 28, 12
51:        CONTROL "Directory", CM_DIRECTORY, "BUTTON",
52:          BS_PUSHBUTTON ¦ WS_CHILD ¦ WS_VISIBLE ¦ WS_GROUP ¦
53:          WS_TABSTOP, 88, 135, 71, 17
54:        CONTROL "Play", CM_WAVEPLAY, "BUTTON", BS_PUSHBUTTON ¦
55:          WS_CHILD ¦ WS_VISIBLE ¦ WS_TABSTOP, 88, 160, 71, 17
56:        CONTROL "Close", IDOK, "BUTTON", BS_PUSHBUTTON ¦ WS_CHILD ¦
57:          WS_VISIBLE ¦ WS_TABSTOP, 88, 184, 71, 17
58:        CONTROL "Record", CM_RECORD, "BUTTON", BS_PUSHBUTTON ¦
59:          WS_CHILD ¦ WS_VISIBLE ¦ WS_TABSTOP, 169, 135, 71, 17
60:        CONTROL "Pause", CM_PAUSE, "BUTTON", BS_PUSHBUTTON ¦
61:          WS_CHILD ¦ WS_VISIBLE ¦ WS_TABSTOP, 169, 160, 71, 17
62:        CONTROL "Stop", CM_STOP, "BUTTON", BS_PUSHBUTTON ¦
63:          WS_CHILD ¦ WS_VISIBLE ¦ WS_TABSTOP, 169, 184, 71, 17
64:        CONTROL "Now Playing", -1, "STATIC", SS_LEFT ¦ WS_CHILD ¦
65:          WS_VISIBLE ¦ WS_GROUP, 6, 105, 57, 8
66:        CONTROL "Current Directory", -1, "STATIC", SS_LEFT ¦
67:          WS_CHILD ¦ WS_VISIBLE ¦ WS_GROUP, 132, 105, 99, 8
68: END
```

Listing BD3.9 shows the PlayInfo source file.

Listing BD3.9. PLAYINFO.CPP.

```
/////////////////////////////////////
// Program: PLAYINFO.CPP
// Copyright (c) 1995 by Charlie Calvert
// Date: August 6, 1993
// Update for WIN32: 06/17/95
// Description: DLL Module from Harmony program
/////////////////////////////////////

#define STRICT
#include <windows.h>
#include <windowsx.h>
#include <mmsystem.h>
#include <stdio.h>
#include <string.h>
#include "playinfo.h"
#pragma warning (disable : 4068)
#pragma argsused

static HWND PlayWindow;
static UINT wDeviceID;
```

continues

Listing BD3.9. continued

```
//////////////////////////////////
// LibMain in 16 bits,
// DLLEntryPoint for Borland in WIN32
// DLLMain for Microsoft in WIN32
// Try removing comments before MessageBox functions
// to see how LibMain, DLLMain and DLLEntryPoint are called.
// When MessageBox is called in WIN32, you may have to use
// ALT-TAB to close the MessageBox, especially
// when opening the common dialogs
//////////////////////////////////
#pragma argsused
#if !defined(WIN32)
int PASCAL LibMain(HINSTANCE hInstance, WORD wDataSeg,
                   WORD wHeapSize, LPSTR lpszCmdLine)
{
// MessageBox(0, "Play LibMain", NULL, MB_OK);
#else
  #if defined(__BORLANDC__)
  int WINAPI DllEntryPoint(HINSTANCE hInst, DWORD reason, LPVOID)
  #else
  int WINAPI DllMain(HINSTANCE hInst, DWORD reason, LPVOID)
  #endif
{
// MessageBox(0, "Play Entry point", NULL, MB_OK);
#endif

  #ifndef WIN32
  if (wHeapSize > 0)
      UnlockData(0);
  #endif
  return 1;
}

#ifndef WIN32
//////////////////////////////////
// WEP
//////////////////////////////////
#pragma argsused
int EXPORT WEP (int nParameter)
{
  return 1;
}
#endif


//////////////////////////////////
// GetDeviceID
//////////////////////////////////
UINT EXPORT GetDeviceID(void)
{
  return wDeviceID;
}


//////////////////////////////////
// GetErrorMessage
//////////////////////////////////
```

```
LPSTR GetErrorMessage(DWORD RC, LPSTR S)
{
  if (!mciGetErrorString(RC, S, MsgLen))
    strcpy(S, "No message available");
  return S;
}


///////////////////////////////////////
// ErrorMs
///////////////////////////////////////
BOOL EXPORT ErrorMsg(DWORD Error, LPSTR CallingFunc)
{
  char S[MsgLen + 50];
  char S1[MsgLen];

  GetErrorMessage(Error, S1);
  sprintf(S, "Calling Func: %s\nReturn Code: %ld\n %s",
          CallingFunc, Error, S1);
  if (Error)
  {
    MessageBox(0, S, "Information", MB_OK ¦ MB_ICONINFORMATION);
    return FALSE;
  }
  return TRUE;
}


///////////////////////////////////////
// CloseMCI
///////////////////////////////////////
BOOL EXPORT CloseMCI(void)
{
  DWORD ErrorNum;

  ErrorNum = mciSendCommand(wDeviceID, MCI_CLOSE, 0, 0);
  if (ErrorNum)
  {
    ErrorMsg(ErrorNum, "CloseMCI");
    return FALSE;
  }
  wDeviceID = 0;
  return TRUE;
}


///////////////////////////////////////
// GetInfo
///////////////////////////////////////
LPSTR EXPORT GetInfo(LPSTR S)
{
  MCI_INFO_PARMS Info;
  DWORD Flags, ErrorNum;

  Info.dwCallback = 0;
  Info.lpstrReturn = S;
  Info.dwRetSize = MsgLen;
```

continues

BD3

Listing BD3.9. continued

```
  Flags = MCI_INFO_PRODUCT;
  ErrorNum =
    mciSendCommand(wDeviceID, MCI_INFO, Flags, DWORD(&Info));
  if (ErrorNum)
  {
    ErrorMsg(ErrorNum, "GetInfo");
    return NULL;
  }
  return S;
}

////////////////////////////////////
// GetLen
////////////////////////////////////
LONG EXPORT GetLen(void)
{
  MCI_STATUS_PARMS Info;
  DWORD ErrorNum, Flags;

  memset(&Info, 0, sizeof(MCI_STATUS_PARMS));
  Info.dwItem = MCI_STATUS_LENGTH;
  Flags = MCI_STATUS_ITEM;
  ErrorNum =
    mciSendCommand(wDeviceID, MCI_STATUS, Flags, DWORD(&Info));
  if (ErrorNum)
  {
    ErrorMsg(ErrorNum, "GetLen");
    return -1;
  }
  return Info.dwReturn;
}

////////////////////////////////////
// GetLocation
////////////////////////////////////
LONG EXPORT GetLocation(void)
{
  MCI_STATUS_PARMS Info;
  DWORD Flags, ErrorNum;

  Info.dwItem = MCI_STATUS_POSITION;
  Flags = MCI_STATUS_ITEM;
  ErrorNum = mciSendCommand(wDeviceID, MCI_STATUS,
                            Flags, DWORD(&Info));
  if (ErrorNum)
  {
    ErrorMsg(ErrorNum, "GetLocation");
    return -1;
  }
  return Info.dwReturn;
}

////////////////////////////////////
// GetMode
////////////////////////////////////
```

```
LONG EXPORT GetMode(void)
{
  MCI_STATUS_PARMS Info;
  DWORD ErrorNum, Flags;

  memset(&Info, 0, sizeof(MCI_STATUS_PARMS));
  Info.dwItem = MCI_STATUS_MODE;
  Flags = MCI_STATUS_ITEM;
  ErrorNum = mciSendCommand(wDeviceID, MCI_STATUS,
                            Flags, DWORD(&Info));
  if (ErrorNum)
  {
    ErrorMsg(ErrorNum, "GetMode");
    return -1;
  }
  return Info.dwReturn;
}


///////////////////////////////////////
// OpenMCI
///////////////////////////////////////
BOOL EXPORT OpenMCI(HWND PWindow, LPSTR FileName,
                              LPSTR DeviceType)
{
  MCI_OPEN_PARMS OpenParms;
  DWORD Style, ErrorNum;

  PlayWindow = PWindow;
  OpenParms.lpstrDeviceType = DeviceType;
  OpenParms.lpstrElementName = FileName;
  Style = MCI_OPEN_TYPE | MCI_OPEN_ELEMENT;
  ErrorNum = mciSendCommand(0, MCI_OPEN,
                            Style, DWORD(&OpenParms));
  if ( ErrorNum)
  {
    ErrorMsg(ErrorNum, "OpenMCI");
    return FALSE;
  }
  wDeviceID = OpenParms.wDeviceID;
  return TRUE;
}


///////////////////////////////////////
// PauseMCI
///////////////////////////////////////
BOOL EXPORT PauseMCI(void)
{
  MCI_GENERIC_PARMS Info;
  DWORD ErrorNum;

  memset(&Info, 0, sizeof(MCI_GENERIC_PARMS));
  ErrorNum = mciSendCommand(wDeviceID, MCI_PAUSE,
                            0, DWORD(&Info));
  if (ErrorNum)
  {
    ErrorMsg(ErrorNum, "PauseMCI");
```

BD3

Listing BD3.9. continued

```
      return FALSE;
   }
   return TRUE;
}


/////////////////////////////////////
// PlayMCI
/////////////////////////////////////
BOOL EXPORT PlayMCI(void)
{
   DWORD ErrorNum;
   MCI_PLAY_PARMS Info;

   Info.dwCallback = DWORD(PlayWindow);
   ErrorNum = mciSendCommand(wDeviceID, MCI_PLAY,
                        MCI_NOTIFY, DWORD(&Info));
   if (ErrorNum)
   {
      ErrorMsg(ErrorNum, "PlayMCI");
      return FALSE;
   }
   return TRUE;
}


/////////////////////////////////////
// SetTimeFormatMS
/////////////////////////////////////
BOOL EXPORT SetTimeFormatMs(void)
{
   MCI_SET_PARMS Info;
   DWORD ErrorNum, Flags;

   Info.dwTimeFormat = MCI_FORMAT_MILLISECONDS;
   Flags = MCI_SET_TIME_FORMAT;
   ErrorNum = mciSendCommand(wDeviceID, MCI_SET,
                        Flags, DWORD(&Info));
   if (ErrorNum)
   {
      ErrorMsg(ErrorNum, "SetTimeFormatMS");
      return FALSE;
   }
   return TRUE;
}


/////////////////////////////////////
// StopMCI
/////////////////////////////////////
BOOL EXPORT StopMCI(void)
{
   DWORD ErrorNum;
   MCI_GENERIC_PARMS Info;

   Info.dwCallback = 0;
   ErrorNum = mciSendCommand(wDeviceID, MCI_STOP,
```

```
                           MCI_NOTIFY, DWORD(&Info));
  if (ErrorNum)
  {
    ErrorMsg(ErrorNum, "StopMCI");
    return FALSE;
  }
  return TRUE;
}


/////////////////////////////////////
// Can a device perform a function such
// as record, or pause, etc.
/////////////////////////////////////
BOOL EXPORT CanPerformFunction(DWORD Test)
{
  DWORD ErrorNum, Flags;
  MCI_GETDEVCAPS_PARMS Info;

  memset(&Info, 0, sizeof(MCI_GENERIC_PARMS));
  Info.dwItem = Test;
  Flags = MCI_GETDEVCAPS_ITEM;
  ErrorNum = mciSendCommand(wDeviceID, MCI_GETDEVCAPS,
                            Flags, DWORD(&Info));
  if (ErrorNum)
  {
    ErrorMsg(ErrorNum, "CanPerformFunction");
    return FALSE;
  }

  return Info.dwReturn > 0;
}


/////////////////////////////////////
// Can this system play "waveaudio", or
// "cdaudio" or "sequencer" etc.
/////////////////////////////////////
BOOL EXPORT DoesDeviceExistOnSystem(LPSTR DeviceType)
{
  DWORD ErrorNum, Flags;
  MCI_OPEN_PARMS Info;

  Info.lpstrDeviceType = DeviceType;
  Flags = MCI_OPEN_TYPE;
  ErrorNum = mciSendCommand(0, MCI_OPEN, Flags, DWORD(&Info));

  if (ErrorNum)
    return FALSE;
  else
  {
    wDeviceID = Info.wDeviceID;
    CloseMCI();
    return TRUE;
  }
}
```

BD3

continues

Listing BD3.9. continued

```
/////////////////////////////////////
// DoRecord
/////////////////////////////////////
DWORD EXPORT DoRecord(DWORD MMSecs)
{
  MCI_RECORD_PARMS Info;
  DWORD Result, Flags;

  Info.dwCallback = (DWORD)PlayWindow;
  Info.dwTo = MMSecs;
  Flags = MCI_TO | MCI_NOTIFY;
  Result = mciSendCommand(wDeviceID, MCI_RECORD,
                          Flags, DWORD(&Info));
  if (Result)
  {
    ErrorMsg(Result, "DoRecord");
    return FALSE;
  }
  return TRUE;
}


/////////////////////////////////////
// SaveFile
/////////////////////////////////////
BOOL EXPORT SaveFile(char *FileName)
{
  MCI_SAVE_PARMS MCISave;
  DWORD Result, Flags;

  MCISave.lpfilename = FileName;
  Flags = MCI_SAVE_FILE | MCI_WAIT;
  Result = mciSendCommand(wDeviceID, MCI_SAVE,
                          Flags, DWORD(&MCISave));
  if (Result)
  {
    ErrorMsg(Result, "SaveFile");
    return FALSE;
  }
  return TRUE;
}
```

Listing BD3.10 shows the PlayInfo header file.

Listing BD3.10. PLAYINFO.H.

```
/////////////////////////////////////
// Program: PLAYINFO.H
// Programmer: Charlie Calvert
// Date: August 6, 1993
// Description: DLL Module from Harmony program
/////////////////////////////////////

// This file shows how to use extern "C", which is needed to
// link a DLL into a Pascal or straight C programs.
```

```
#include <mmsystem.h>
#define MsgLen 200

#if defined(__BORLANDC__)
  #define EXPORT CALLBACK _export
#else
  #if !defined(_EXPORT_)
    #define EXPORT __declspec(dllimport)
  #else
    #define EXPORT __declspec(dllexport)
  #endif
#endif

extern "C" {
BOOL EXPORT CloseMCI(void);
BOOL EXPORT ErrorMsg(DWORD Error, LPSTR CallingFunc);
UINT EXPORT GetDeviceID(void);
LPSTR EXPORT GetInfo(LPSTR S);
LONG EXPORT GetLen(void);
LONG EXPORT GetLocation(void);
LONG EXPORT GetMode(void);
BOOL EXPORT OpenMCI(HWND Pwindow, LPSTR FileName, LPSTR DeviceType);
BOOL EXPORT PauseMCI(void);
BOOL EXPORT PlayMCI(void);
BOOL EXPORT SetTimeFormatMs(void);
BOOL EXPORT StopMCI(void);
BOOL EXPORT DoesDeviceExistOnSystem(LPSTR DeviceType);
DWORD EXPORT DoRecord(DWORD MMSecs);
BOOL EXPORT SaveFile(char *FileName);
}
```

Listing BD3.11 shows the PlayInfo definition file.

Listing BD3.11. PLAYINFO.DEF.

```
1: ; PLAYINFO.DEF
2:
3: LIBRARY        PlayInfo
4: DESCRIPTION    'PlayInfo (C) 1993 Charlie Calvert'
6: CODE           PRELOAD MOVEABLE DISCARDABLE
7: DATA           PRELOAD MOVEABLE SINGLE
8: HEAPSIZE  5200
```

Listing BD3.12 shows the CDInfo source file.

Listing BD3.12. CDINFO.CPP.

```
/////////////////////////////////////
// Program: CDINFO.CPP
// Copyright (c) 1995 by Charlie Calvert
// Date: August 6, 1993
// Description: DLL Module from Harmony program
/////////////////////////////////////
```

Listing BD3.12. continued

```
#define STRICT
#include <windows.h>
#include <windowsx.h>
#include <mmsystem.h>
#include <stdio.h>
#include <string.h>
#pragma warning (disable : 4068)
#include "cdinfo.h"

static UINT wDeviceID;
#define MsgLen 200

/////////////////////////////////////
// LibMain in 16 bits,
// DLLEntryPoint for Borland in WIN32
// DLLMain for Microsoft in WIN32
// Try removing comments before MessageBox functions
// to see how LibMain, DLLMain and DLLEntryPoint are called.
// When MessageBox is called in WIN32, you may have to use
// ALT-TAB to close the MessageBox, especially
// when opening the common dialogs
/////////////////////////////////////
#pragma argsused
#if !defined(WIN32)
int PASCAL LibMain(HINSTANCE hInstance, WORD wDataSeg,
                   WORD wHeapSize, LPSTR lpszCmdLine)
{
// MessageBox(0, "LibMain", NULL, MB_OK);
#else
  #if defined(__BORLANDC__)
  int WINAPI DllEntryPoint(HINSTANCE hInst, DWORD reason, LPVOID)
  #else
  int WINAPI DllMain(HINSTANCE hInst, DWORD reason, LPVOID)
  #endif
{
// MessageBox(0, "Entry point", NULL, MB_OK);
#endif
  #ifndef WIN32
  if (wHeapSize > 0)
      UnlockData(0);
  #endif

  return 1;
}

#ifdef WIN32
/////////////////////////////////////
// Wep
/////////////////////////////////////
#pragma argsused
int EXPORT WEP (int nParameter)
{
  return 1;
}
#endif
```

```
///////////////////////////////////
// GetErrorMessage
///////////////////////////////////
LPSTR GetErrorMessage(DWORD RC, LPSTR S)
{
  if (!mciGetErrorString(RC, S, MsgLen))
    strcpy(S, "No message available");
  return S;
}


///////////////////////////////////
// ErrorMsg
///////////////////////////////////
BOOL EXPORT ErrorMsg(DWORD Error, LPSTR CallingFunc)
{
  char S[MsgLen + 50];
  char S1[MsgLen];

  GetErrorMessage(Error, S1);
  sprintf(S, "Calling Func: %s\nReturn Code: %ld\n %s",
          CallingFunc, Error, S1);
  if (Error)
  {
    MessageBox(0, S, "Information",
               MB_OK | MB_ICONINFORMATION);
    return FALSE;
  }
  return TRUE;
}


///////////////////////////////////
// OpenCD
///////////////////////////////////
BOOL EXPORT OpenCD(HWND PWindow)
{
  MCI_OPEN_PARMS Info;
  DWORD Result, Flags;

  memset(&Info, 0, sizeof(MCI_OPEN_PARMS));
  Info.dwCallback = DWORD(PWindow);
  Info.lpstrDeviceType =
                  MAKEINTRESOURCE(MCI_DEVTYPE_CD_AUDIO);
  Flags = MCI_OPEN_TYPE | MCI_OPEN_TYPE_ID;
  Result = mciSendCommand(0, MCI_OPEN, Flags, DWORD(&Info));

  wDeviceID = Info.wDeviceID;

  if (Result)
  {
    ErrorMsg(Result, "OpenCD");
    return FALSE;
  }
  return TRUE;
}
```

continues

BD3

Listing BD3.12. continued

```
/////////////////////////////////////
// CloseCDMCI
/////////////////////////////////////
BOOL EXPORT CloseCDMCI(void)
{
  DWORD ErrorNum;
  MCI_GENERIC_PARMS Info;

  memset(&Info, 0, sizeof(MCI_GENERIC_PARMS));
  ErrorNum = mciSendCommand(wDeviceID, MCI_CLOSE,
                            MCI_NOTIFY, DWORD(&Info));
  if (ErrorNum)
  {
    ErrorMsg(ErrorNum, "CloseCDMCI");
    return FALSE;
  }
  return TRUE;
}


/////////////////////////////////////
// StopCDMCI
/////////////////////////////////////
BOOL EXPORT StopCDMCI(void)
{
  DWORD ErrorNum;
  MCI_GENERIC_PARMS Info;

  Info.dwCallback = 0;
  ErrorNum = mciSendCommand(wDeviceID, MCI_STOP,
                            MCI_NOTIFY, DWORD(&Info));
  if (ErrorNum)
  {
    ErrorMsg(ErrorNum, "StopCDMCI");
    return FALSE;
  }
  return TRUE;
}


/////////////////////////////////////
// PauseCDMCI
/////////////////////////////////////
BOOL EXPORT PauseCDMCI(void)
{
  MCI_GENERIC_PARMS Info;
  DWORD ErrorNum;

  memset(&Info, 0, sizeof(MCI_GENERIC_PARMS));
  ErrorNum = mciSendCommand(wDeviceID, MCI_PAUSE,
                            0, DWORD(&Info));
  if (ErrorNum)
  {
    ErrorMsg(ErrorNum, "PauseCDMCI");
    return FALSE;
  }
```

```
  return TRUE;
}

/////////////////////////////////
// SetTMSFasFormat
/////////////////////////////////
void EXPORT SetTMSFasFormat(void)
{
  MCI_SET_PARMS Info;
  DWORD Result;

  Info.dwCallback = 0;
  Info.dwTimeFormat = MCI_FORMAT_TMSF;
  Info.dwAudio = 0;

  Result = mciSendCommand(wDeviceID, MCI_SET,
                      MCI_SET_TIME_FORMAT, DWORD(&Info));

  if (Result)
    ErrorMsg(Result, "SetTMSFasFormat");
}

/////////////////////////////////
// PlayCDOneTrack
/////////////////////////////////
void EXPORT PlayCDOneTrack(BYTE StartTrack)
{
  MCI_PLAY_PARMS Info;
  DWORD Flags, Result;

  memset(&Info, 0, sizeof(MCI_PLAY_PARMS));
  Info.dwFrom = MCI_MAKE_TMSF(StartTrack,0,0,0);

  Flags = MCI_FROM | MCI_NOTIFY;
  Result = mciSendCommand(wDeviceID, MCI_PLAY,
                          Flags, DWORD(&Info));

  if (Result)
    ErrorMsg(Result, "PlayCDOneTrack");
}

/////////////////////////////////
// PlayMCICD
/////////////////////////////////
void EXPORT PlayMciCD(BYTE StartTrack, BYTE EndTrack)
{
  MCI_PLAY_PARMS Info;
  DWORD Flags, Result;

  memset(&Info, 0, sizeof(MCI_PLAY_PARMS));
  Info.dwFrom = MCI_MAKE_TMSF(StartTrack,0,0,0);
  Info.dwTo   = MCI_MAKE_TMSF(EndTrack, 0,0,0);

  Flags = MCI_FROM | MCI_TO | MCI_NOTIFY;
  Result = mciSendCommand(wDeviceID, MCI_PLAY,
                          Flags, DWORD(&Info));
```

BD3

continues

Listing BD3.12. continued

```
    if (Result) ErrorMsg(Result, "PlayCDMCI");
}

///////////////////////////////////////
// GetCDNumTracks
///////////////////////////////////////
LONG EXPORT GetCDNumTracks(void)
{
  MCI_STATUS_PARMS Info;
  DWORD Result;


  Info.dwCallback = 0;
  Info.dwReturn   = 0;
  Info.dwItem     = MCI_STATUS_NUMBER_OF_TRACKS;
  Info.dwTrack    = 0;
  Result = mciSendCommand(wDeviceID, MCI_STATUS,
                  MCI_STATUS_ITEM, DWORD(&Info));
  if (Result)
  {
    ErrorMsg(Result, "GetCDNumTracks");
    return -1;
  }

  return Info.dwReturn;
}

///////////////////////////////////////
// GetCDTrackLength
///////////////////////////////////////
void EXPORT GetCDTrackLength(DWORD TrackNum,
                    BYTE *Min, BYTE *Sec, BYTE *Frame)
{
  MCI_STATUS_PARMS Info;
  DWORD Result, MSF;

  memset(&Info, 0, sizeof(MCI_STATUS_PARMS));
  Info.dwTrack    = TrackNum;
  Info.dwItem     = MCI_STATUS_LENGTH;

  Result = mciSendCommand(wDeviceID, MCI_STATUS,
                  MCI_STATUS_ITEM | MCI_TRACK,
                  DWORD(&Info));

  if (Result)
  {
    ErrorMsg(Result, "GetCDTrackLength");
    return;
  }

  MSF =Info.dwReturn;

  *Min = MCI_MSF_MINUTE(MSF);
  *Sec = MCI_MSF_SECOND(MSF);
```

```
    *Frame = MCI_MSF_FRAME(MSF);
}

///////////////////////////////////////
// GetLengthofEachTrack
///////////////////////////////////////
void EXPORT GetLengthOfEachTrack(DWORD TrackNum, BYTE *Min,
                                      BYTE *Sec, BYTE *Frame)
{
  MCI_STATUS_PARMS Info;
  DWORD Result, Flags, MSF;

  memset(&Info, 0, sizeof(MCI_STATUS_PARMS));
  Info.dwTrack = TrackNum;
  Info.dwItem = MCI_STATUS_LENGTH;
  Flags = MCI_STATUS_ITEM | MCI_TRACK;
  Result = mciSendCommand(wDeviceID, MCI_STATUS,
                           Flags, DWORD(&Info));

  if (Result)
  {
    ErrorMsg(Result, "GetLengthOfEachTrack");
    return;
  }

  MSF = Info.dwReturn;
  *Min = MCI_MSF_MINUTE(MSF);
  *Sec = MCI_MSF_SECOND(MSF);
  *Frame = MCI_MSF_FRAME(MSF);
}

///////////////////////////////////////
// GetCurrentCDTrack
///////////////////////////////////////
DWORD EXPORT GetCurrentCDTrack(void)
{
  MCI_STATUS_PARMS Info;
  DWORD Result;

  memset(&Info, 0, sizeof(MCI_STATUS_PARMS));
  Info.dwItem    = MCI_STATUS_CURRENT_TRACK;

  Result = mciSendCommand(wDeviceID, MCI_STATUS,
                     MCI_STATUS_ITEM, DWORD(&Info));

  if (Result)
  {
    ErrorMsg(Result, "GetCurrentCDTrack");
    return FALSE;
  }
  return Info.dwReturn;
}

///////////////////////////////////////
// HasDiskInserted
///////////////////////////////////////
```

BD3

continues

Listing BD3.12. continued

```
BOOL EXPORT HasDiskInserted(void)
{
  MCI_STATUS_PARMS Info;
  DWORD Flags, Result;

  memset(&Info, 0, sizeof(MCI_STATUS_PARMS));
  Info.dwItem = MCI_STATUS_MEDIA_PRESENT;

  Flags = MCI_STATUS_ITEM;
  Result=mciSendCommand(wDeviceID, MCI_STATUS,
                        Flags, DWORD(&Info));

  if (Result)
  {
    ErrorMsg(Result, "HasDiskInserted");
    return FALSE;
  }

  return Info.dwReturn > 0;
}

/////////////////////////////////////
// EjectCD
/////////////////////////////////////
void EXPORT EjectCD(void)
{
  MCI_SET_PARMS Info;
  DWORD Flags, Result;

  memset(&Info, 0, sizeof(MCI_SET_PARMS));
  Flags = MCI_SET_DOOR_OPEN;
  Result = mciSendCommand( wDeviceID, MCI_SET,
                           Flags, DWORD(&Info));
  if (Result)
    ErrorMsg(Result, "EjectCD");
}

/////////////////////////////////////
// GetCDLocation
/////////////////////////////////////
LONG EXPORT GetCDLocation(void)
{
  MCI_STATUS_PARMS Info;
  DWORD Flags, ErrorNum;

  Info.dwItem = MCI_STATUS_POSITION;
  Flags = MCI_STATUS_ITEM;
  ErrorNum = mciSendCommand(wDeviceID, MCI_STATUS,
                            Flags, DWORD(&Info));
  if (ErrorNum)
  {
    ErrorMsg(ErrorNum, "GetLocation");
```

```
      return -1;
  }
  return Info.dwReturn;
}
```

Listing BD3.13 shows the CDInfo header file.

Listing **BD3.13. CDINFO.H.**

BD3

```
//////////////////////////////////////
// Program: CDINFO.H
// Copyright (c) 1995 by Charlie Calvert
// Date: August 6, 1993
// Update for WIN32: 06/17/95
// Description: DLL Module from Harmony program
//////////////////////////////////////

#include <mmsystem.h>

#if defined(__BORLANDC__)
  #define EXPORT CALLBACK _export
#else
  #if !defined(_EXPORT_)
    #define EXPORT __declspec(dllimport)
  #else
    #define EXPORT __declspec(dllexport)
  #endif
#endif

extern "C" {
BOOL EXPORT OpenCD(HWND PWindow);
BOOL EXPORT CloseCDMCI(void);
BOOL EXPORT PauseCDMCI(void);
void EXPORT PlayMciCD(BYTE StartTrack,
                                 BYTE EndTrack);
void EXPORT PlayCDOneTrack(BYTE StartTrack);
void EXPORT SetTMSFasFormat(void);
LONG EXPORT GetCDNumTracks(void);
void EXPORT GetCDTrackLength(DWORD TrackNum,
                  BYTE *Min, BYTE *Sec, BYTE *Frame);
DWORD EXPORT GetCurrentCDTrack(void);
BOOL EXPORT HasDiskInserted(void);
void EXPORT EjectCD(void);
BOOL EXPORT StopCDMCI(void);
LONG EXPORT GetCDLocation(void);
}
```

Listing BD3.14 shows the CDInfo definition file.

Listing BD3.14. CDINFO.DEF.

```
1: LIBRARY CDInfo
2:
3: DESCRIPTION 'CDInfo (C) 1993 Charlie Calvert'
4: CODE PRELOAD MOVEABLE DISCARDABLE
5: DATA PRELOAD MOVEABLE SINGLE
6: HEAPSIZE 5120
```

Listing BD3.15 shows the Borland makefile for the Harmony program.

Listing BD3.15. HARMONY.MAK (Borland).

```
# HARMONY.MAK

BCROOT = $(MAKEDIR)\..
INCPATH= $(BCROOT)\INCLUDE
LIBPATH= $(BCROOT)\LIB
PATHS  = -I$(INCPATH) -L$(LIBPATH)


!if !$d(WIN16)
COMPILER = BCC32.EXE
RCCOMPILER = BRC32.EXE -w32
# CFLAGS    = -WE -v -w4
FLAGS = -H -R -W -v -w4 -vi- -wpro -weas -wpre
DLLFLAGS = -R -WDE -v  -wpro -weas -wpre
!else
COMPILER = BCC.EXE
RCCOMPILER = BRC.EXE
FLAGS = -H -R -ml -2 -W -v -w4 -vi- -wpro -weas -wpre
DLLFLAGS = -ml -R -WDE -2 -v  -wpro -weas -wpre
# CFLAGS    = -WE -ml -v -w4
!endif

APPNAME = Harmony
LIBS = PlayInfo.lib CDInfo.lib
OBJS = Harmony.obj WaveMidi.obj CDUtil.obj

# goal
ALL: PlayInfo.dll CDInfo.dll $(APPNAME).exe

# link EXES
$(APPNAME).exe: $(OBJS) $(APPNAME).def $(LIBS) $(APPNAME).res
  $(COMPILER) $(FLAGS) $(OBJS) $(LIBS)
  $(RCCOMPILER) -I$(INCPATH) $(APPNAME).res

# link DLLS
playinfo.dll: playinfo.obj playinfo.def
  $(COMPILER) $(DLLFLAGS) $(PATHS) playinfo.obj

cdinfo.dll: cdinfo.obj cdinfo.def
  $(COMPILER) $(DLLFLAGS) $(PATHS) cdinfo.obj
```

```
# compile
$(APPNAME).obj: $(APPNAME).cpp
  $(COMPILER) -c $(FLAGS) $(PATHS) $(APPNAME).cpp

# compile
CDUtils.obj: CDUtils.cpp
  $(COMPILER) -c $(FLAGS) $(PATHS) CDUtils.cpp

# compile
WaveMidi.obj: WaveMidi.cpp
  $(COMPILER) -c $(FLAGS) $(PATHS) WaveMidi.cpp

# compile
.cpp.obj:
  $(COMPILER) -c $(DLLFLAGS) $(PATHS) { $< }

# resource
.rc.res:
  $(RCCOMPILER) -r -I$(INCPATH) { $< }

# libraries
.dll.lib:
  implib $&.lib $&.dll
```

BD3

Listing BD3.16 shows the Microsoft MSVC 1.5 16-bit makefile for Harmony. To create the 32-bit version, use the IDE. The makefiles for use in the 32-bit IDE are too long and complex to include here, but you can get them by downloading the code.

Listing BD3.16. HARMONY.MAK (Microsoft).

```
 1: # HARMONY.MAK
 2:
 3: APPNAME = Harmony
 4: DLLCOMPFLAGS = -c -ALw -Gsw -Ow -W2 -Zp
 5: DLLLINKFLAGS = /align:16, NUL, /nod ldllcew libw mmsystem
 6: COMPFLAGS = -c -Gsw -Ow -W3 -AL -Zp
 7: LINKFLAGS = /align:16, NUL, /nod llibcew libw
 8: OBJS = Harmony.obj WaveMidi.obj CDUtil.obj
 9: LIBS = PlayInfo.lib CDInfo.lib
10:
11: # goal
12: ALL: $(APPNAME).exe PlayInfo.dll CDInfo.dll
13:
14: # link EXES
15: $(APPNAME).exe: $(OBJS) $(APPNAME).def $(APPNAME).res $(LIBS)
16:    link $(OBJS), $(LINKFLAGS) $(LIBS) CommDlg, $(APPNAME)
17:    rc $(APPNAME).res
18:
19: # link DLLS
20: playinfo.dll: playinfo.obj playinfo.def
21:    link playinfo, playinfo.dll $(DLLLINKFLAGS), playinfo
22:
```

continues

Listing BD3.16. continued

```
23: cdinfo.dll: cdinfo.obj cdinfo.def
24:    link cdinfo, cdinfo.dll $(DLLLINKFLAGS), cdinfo
25:
26: # compile
27: $(APPNAME).obj: $(APPNAME).cpp
28:    cl $(COMPFLAGS) $(APPNAME).cpp
29:
30: # compile
31: CDUtils.obj: CDUtils.cpp
32:    cl $(COMPFLAGS) CDUtils.cpp
33:
34: # compile
35: WaveMidi.obj: WaveMidi.cpp
36:    cl $(COMPFLAGS) WaveMidi.cpp
37:
38: # compile
39: .cpp.obj:
40:    cl $(DLLCOMPFLAGS) $(PATHS) { $< }
41:
42: # resource
43: harmony.res: harmony.rc
44:    rc -r harmony.rc
45:
46: # libraries
47: playinfo.lib: playinfo.dll
48:    implib playinfo.lib playinfo.dll
49:
50: cdinfo.lib: cdinfo.dll
51:    implib cdinfo.lib cdinfo.dll
```

Figure BD3.2 shows the Harmony program.

Figure BD3.2.

The Harmony program enables the user to play MIDI files, WAV files, and CDs.

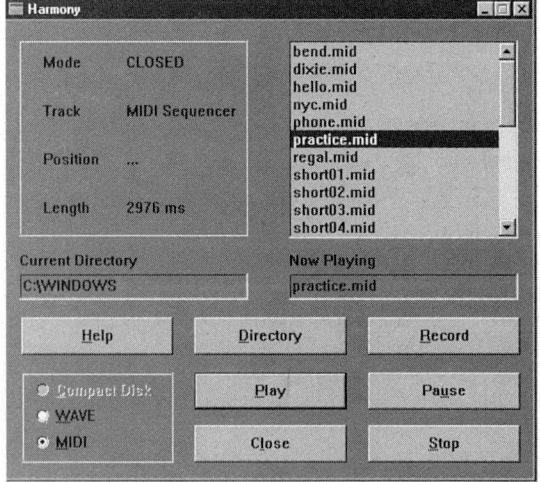

The Harmony program is divided into two major sections, a main file and a set of DLLs:

> Main section: HARMONY.EXE
>
> Supporting section (DLLs): PLAYINFO.DLL, CDINFO.DLL

Specifically, there are two DLLs, one containing the MCI code for playing WAV and MIDI files (PLAYINFO.DLL), and one containing the MCI code for playing CDs (CDINFO.DLL).

The part that is not a DLL pops up a main window with dialog, which enables the user to play files (see Figure BD3.2). General purpose code is kept in HARMONY.CPP, code specific to CD files is kept in CDUTIL.CPP, and code specific to WAV or MIDI files is kept in WAVEMIDI.CPP.

The big advantage of this structure is that it provides you with two ready-made multimedia DLLs that you can plug into any program you create. When it comes time to make music, or to play an audio track from a CD-ROM, the work is already done. All you have to do is call the DLLs included in this program.

On Startup

The first MCI-specific code used in Harmony checks to see if the current system supports CD files. If it doesn't, the radio button that switches the program into CD mode is disabled with a call to EnableWindow. The code that checks for CD capabilities is located in PLAYINFO.CPP:

```
BOOL CALLBACK _export DoesDeviceExistOnSystem(LPSTR DeviceType)
{
  DWORD ErrorNum, Flags;
  MCI_OPEN_PARMS Info;

  Info.lpstrDeviceType = DeviceType;
  Flags = MCI_OPEN_TYPE;
  ErrorNum = mciSendCommand(0, MCI_OPEN, Flags, DWORD(&Info));

  if (ErrorNum)
    return FALSE;
  else
  {
    wDeviceID = Info.wDeviceID;
    CloseMCI();
    return TRUE;
  }
}
```

As you can see, this code first checks to see if it can open a CD driver. If that code fails, the function returns FALSE. Otherwise, it calls CloseMCI so the device is not left open while the program runs. Notice that the DLL carefully saves the device ID in a global variable before calling CloseMCI.

The end result of these activities is that the user is informed immediately if CD capabilities are available. This same technique could be used to query Windows about WAV or MIDI files, or any other device.

Note: If you have trouble getting the MIDI services to work, you might try tweaking the Drivers and MIDI Mapper tools in the Control Panel (Figure BD3.3). In addition, it sometimes helps to literally rearrange the order in which the MIDI drivers are listed in the "drivers" and "mci" section of the SYSTEM.INI file. Furthermore, you can use the Media Player utility that comes with Windows to test whether its your code or the system setup that is causing trouble.

Figure BD3.3 shows the Drivers and MIDI Mapper tools in the Control Panel.

Figure BD3.3.

Using the Drivers utility from the Control Panel to initialize multimedia capabilities.

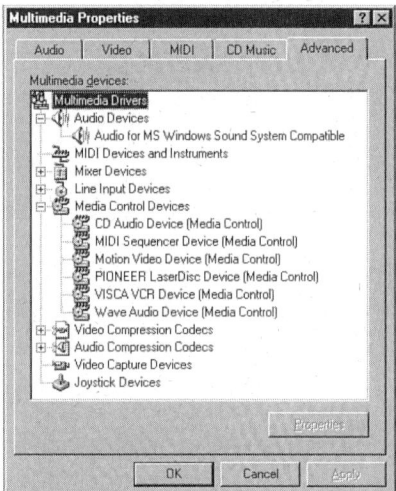

General MCI Strategies

The Harmony program checks to see if the user's attempts to open a device and/or file are successful. If either or both of these steps fail, the program exits as gracefully as possible. Because of the mciGetErrorString function, you can easily post an appropriate error message for the user.

After opening up the file, it's a good idea to report on its length and format before playing it. While the user is listening to the file, Harmony reports on the file's progress, which is particularly important when playing CD or MIDI files (that can last for several minutes or longer).

When the file stops playing, or when the user aborts the play, the program closes the device before exiting. At all times, Harmony checks the results of particular calls so that it responds appropriately if an error occurs. This process needs to be taken considerably further in programs that are aimed at the general public, rather than at a group of programmers.

Details

At this point, all that remains to be covered are a few details that might cause confusion to the reader. In particular, you should notice the function called SetTimeFormatMS:

```
BOOL CALLBACK _export SetTimeFormatMs(void)
{
  MCI_SET_PARMS Info;
  DWORD ErrorNum, Flags;

  Info.dwTimeFormat = MCI_FORMAT_MILLISECONDS;
  Flags = MCI_SET_TIME_FORMAT;
  ErrorNum = mciSendCommand(wDeviceID, MCI_SET,
  Flags, DWORD(&Info));
  if (ErrorNum)
  {
    ErrorMsg(ErrorNum, "SetTimeFormatMS");
    return FALSE;
  }
  return TRUE;
}
```

This code uses the MCI_SET_PARMS struct:

```
typedef struct  {
  DWORD dwCallback;
  DWORD dwTimeFormat;
  DWORD dwAudio;
} MCI_SET_PARMS;
```

The key member of this structure is dwTimeFormat, which is used to select a particular time format. The Harmony program uses milliseconds to measure the length of WAV and MIDI files, and minutes and seconds for CD files.

Notice that SetTimeFormatMS receives MCI_SET_TIME_FORMAT in the flag parameter. Other messages I could have passed in its stead include MCI_SET_DOOR_CLOSED and MCI_SET_DOOR_OPEN. This latter flag can be used to eject a CD from a CD player, as shown in CDINFO.CPP.

I was bit surprised to find that the MCI_SET message was the place to issue the command to eject a disc. This highlights one possible criticism of the MCI command interface. Specifically, it can lack the clarity of non-message–based APIs that feature commands such as EjectCD. In all fairness, I should perhaps add that the mciSendCommand interface can be clean enough under the right circumstances. For instance, MCI_PLAY causes a medium to play, MCI_STOP causes it stop. That's as neat and clean as a Miles Davis solo. The interface can, however, turn into an invitation to create a baroque Coltranesque syntax. For instance, you need to be on your toes to catch the subtle modulation that turns the MCI_SET command into a method for controlling the state of the CD-ROM's door.

One final point involves the posting of MM_NOTIFY messages to the dialog objects in the main program. These messages are routed to standard Windows message handler functions, such as this one quoted in part from HARMONY.CPP:

```
void Harmony_OnMCINotify(HWND hwnd, UINT status, int DeviceID)
{
  char S[100];

  if (State == ERROR_OCCURED)
    return;

  switch (status)
  {
    case MCI_NOTIFY_ABORTED:
    strcpy(S, "Aborted");
    break;

    ... // addition code

    case MCI_NOTIFY_SUPERSEDED:
      strcpy(S, "Superseded");
      break;

  }
  SetWindowText(GetDlgItem(hwnd, ID_MODE), S);
}
```

To fully understand the Harmony_OnMCINotify method, you have to understand that Harmony receives a message whenever anything important happens to the file being played. For instance, if the file ends, or if the user presses the Pause button, an MM_NOTIFY message is posted.

> **Note:** To fill in the gaps between MM_NOTIFY messages, Harmony uses a timer to check on the status of the device being played. For instance, if a MIDI file is being played, the timer enables you to check up on its progress at set intervals. In this particular program, the intervals are 10 milliseconds in duration. For an example of how Harmony deals with this kind of thing, see the HandleCDTimer method.

When the file currently being played finishes, or when the user asks to abort the play, the proper response is to close the device. Of course, this is not what you want to do if the user has simply paused the file. To distinguish between these two events, the harmony program maintains a variable called State, which can be set to one of the following values:

```
// States
#define PAUSED 1
#define PLAYING 2
#define STOPPED 3
#define CLOSED 4
#define OPENED 6
#define RECORDING 7
#define ERROR_OCCURED 8
```

By setting the State variable, the program can always know what is taking place, and it can respond appropriately. If you want, you can handle this same task with the MCI_STATUS message.

Introducing DLLs

The purpose of a DLL is to give programmers a place to store routines that can be called by one or more programs. DLLs are very similar in concept to DOS libraries, or even to a standard OBJ file. Unlike OBJ files and LIB files, the routines stored in a DLL are linked at runtime. During compilation and linking, a program is merely informed of the presence of a DLL that contains the routines the program needs. After the program is loaded, these routines are linked in dynamically.

What's the difference between linking at compile time and linking at runtime? If you link in routines at compile time, then the routines become part of the executable that you are creating. If you copy an EXE file from one machine to another, then the routines you wrote travel with that EXE file because they were linked into it at compile time. If you link at runtime, then the routines involved are linked while the programming is executing. The routines themselves reside in a separate file called a DLL, and they are linked into the program at runtime. If you copy your executable from one machine to another, you must be sure to also copy the DLL, or you must be sure that another copy of the DLL resides on that second machine. If the DLL is missing, then your program probably won't even load, and certainly won't work correctly.

After reading the above paragraph, it may seem that it's more sensible to always link your routines directly into an executable rather than using DLLs. However, there are some strong arguments in favor of using DLLs. In particular, DLLs can promote reuse, and can help you manage very large projects.

Let me say it again: DLLs are all about reuse! Every single program that runs in Windows uses routines from KERNEL32.DLL and USER32.DLL, and/or their 16-bit equivalents, KRNL386.EXE and USER.EXE. All four of these files are DLLs, and they are called every day by tens of thousands of different programs. That's reuse!

To get a feeling for the importance of DLLs, take a look at the \WINDOWS\SYSTEM directory on your computer. My main Windows 95 machine has about 36 MB of files in that directory, and most of them are DLLs. (It doesn't matter what extension you give to a DLL. For instance, many DLLs are given the .DRV extension to show that they are DLLs that serve as drivers for some device.)

The plethora of DLLs in the \Windows\System directory shows that Windows is in large part a DLL-driven operating system. This is the glue that holds the operating system together.

All of the Windows API calls that you make are to DLLs. CreateWindow, SendMessage, mciSendCommand, PostQuitMessage, all these commands live in DLLs. No matter what Windows API function you call, it resides inside a DLL. The operating system itself is literally DLL based!

So what are DLLs? Why is this format so popular?

DLLs are very similar to executables, except they consist not of a single program, but of a library of routines that can be called from programs or from other DLLs.

Whenever you have a routine that might be used by multiple programs, you should consider placing it in a DLL. That way it can easily be used by multiple programs. If you didn't place the call in a DLL, then each executable on the system would have to link in the code for that routine. The result would be that the same code would be taking up space in many executables. This is not an ideal model. Instead, it's better to have the routine stored in one DLL and have all the different executables making calls to that one file. This is a more intelligent use of system resources. It also helps you quickly introduce upgrades and bug fixes to key routines used by multiple programs.

Besides reuse, another potential reason for using DLLs is that they let you break large programs up into a series of small pieces. For instance, you can break a big program up into one small executable and a series of different DLLs. When the user is involved in one part of the program, you can load the appropriate DLL into memory. Then when the user moves onto a different part of the program, you can unload the first DLL and load a second into memory. This can make it possible for you to create huge programs that do not severely tax the system's resources.

Overall, DLLs are one of the most important features of Windows programming. As you will see, however, they are not particularly difficult to master. There are a few hurdles for you to surmount, but once you are over them, you will have a powerful new tool in your hands.

The Syntax of DLLs

DLLs are a lot like EXE files except that they use a function called LibMain, DLLMain, or DLLEntryPoint in lieu of the WinMain function. You can use this DLL entry point as a place to initialize variables or to allocate memory. (To deallocate the memory, use DLLMain or the WEP, as described next.)

All DLLs sport a function called LibMain, DLLEntryPoint (Borland), or DLLMain (Microsoft). These functions roughly correspond with the role WinMain plays in a standard executable. In 16-bit Windows, you can also include a function called the WEP, which has at least a remote relationship to a Cls_OnDestroy function. WIN32 has no direct parallel to the WEP, but instead calls DLLMain again when an application or process is detaching from a DLL.

In pure 32-bit Windows, you will probably always want to use DLLMain (Microsoft) or DLLEntryPoint (Borland). LibMain and WEP are valid WIN16 constructs, but they provide no compatibility with 32-bit code. As a result, I need to use conditional compilation to call them only in WIN16. In WIN32, I need to call DLLMain for Microsoft compilers, and DLLEntryPoint for Borland 4.5*x*. DLLMain and DLLEntryPoint are WIN32 only, and will not compile in WIN16.

The *LibMain* Function

Syntax

```
int FAR PASCAL LibMain (HINSTANCE, WORD, WORD, LPSTR);
```

HINSTANCE hInstance	Contains instance handle of the DLL
WORD wDataSeg	The data segment (DS) for the DLL
WORD cbHeapSize	The size of the local heap
LPSTR lpCmdLine	The command line passed to the DLL

LibMain is called automatically when a 16-bit DLL is loaded into memory. DLLMain and DLLEntryPoint are called automatically when a 32-bit DLL is loaded into memory, and when it is unloaded. You must supply either this routine or the DLLMain and DLLEntryPoint calls. If neither of them exist, your file will not compile. (Note that a DLL can be loaded or unloaded by multiple applications. As a result, the words attach and detach are more explicitly correct than load and unload. However, there is something abstract about attach and detach that can be confusing to readers who are new to this subject. As a result, I will sometimes use load and attach synonomously. The point here is that if one application has already loaded a DLL into memory, then the second application that accesses it will merely attach to it.)

You can see that there is a strong parallel between LibMain, DLLMain, DLLEntryPoint, and WinMain. The functions play very similar roles in the two types of projects, and you can think of LibMain, DLLMain, and DLLEntryPoint as a DLL's version of the WinMain function. However, you don't usually need to respond to LibMain or DLLMain functions by calling CreateWindowEx and RegisterClass. In other words, LibMain and DLLMain are usually much simpler to write than WinMain. (In this case I am using DLLMain to refer to both DLLEntryPoint and DLLMain. Syntactically and functionally the two routines are identical, only the names differ.)

Here's an example:

```
int CALLBACK LibMain(HINSTANCE hInstance, WORD wDataSeg,
                     WORD wHeapSize, LPSTR lpszCmdLine)
{
  return 1;
}
```

Just before a DLL is unloaded from memory, Windows calls either DLLMain (WIN32) or the WEP (WIN16) routine. As a result, these are good places to deallocate any memory allocated for the DLL. Borland automatically supplies a WEP for all DLLs, but users of the Microsoft compiler should be sure to explicitly include one if they are not using DLLMain.

`DLLMain` and `DLLEntryPoint` are two different names for the same function. Borland called their version something different than Microsoft did primarily because of a miscommunication between the two companies. There is no functional difference between the two calls. Everything that I say about `DLLMain` also applies to `DLLEntryPoint`.

Here is the declaration for `DLLMain`:

```
BOOL   WINAPI   DllMain (HANDLE hInst,
                         ULONG ul_reason_for_call,
                         LPVOID lpReserved)
```

The first parameter is the `HINSTANCE` for the DLL. This is similar to the `HINSTANCE` passed to a `WinMain` function.

Unlike the `LibMain` function, `DLLMain` can be called multiple times during the "life" of a DLL. For instance, it is called at load time, and when the DLL is unloaded. It is also called when a thread accesses the DLL, and when a thread detaches from a DLL. It will be called each time a new process accesses the DLL. Because of this architecture, the second parameter to `DLLMain` can have one of four different values, depending on when the function is being called:

`DLL_PROCESS_ATTACH`	An application (process) is loading the DLL.
`DLL_THREAD_ATTACH`	A thread from a process is accessing the DLL.
`DLL_PROCESS_DETACH`	A process is detaching from the DLL.
`DLL_THREAD_DETACH`	A thread is detaching from the DLL.

Remember that you would do the same thing in a `WEP` that you do when you get the reason parameter set to `DLL_THREAD_DETACH`. Remember also that all applications are processes. (Turn to Day 21, "Threads, Multitasking, and Memory Management," for further information on processes and threads.)

The third parameter to `DLLMain` is reserved, and so you can safely ignore it.

You don't have to declare and implement `DLLMain`. The compiler will generate a substitute for you that does nothing but return `TRUE`. However, most of the time you will want to implement this function, if for no other reason than for the sake of clarity. Its primary purpose, of course, is to give you a place to initialize any variables used by the DLL and also to allocate any memory used by the DLL. If you are not doing any of these things you need not supply the function, but I find it best to put it in anyway, just to be sure I know what is going on.

When writing this book, I have attempted to show you code that can work across multiple platforms and multiple compilers. This is one case where that goal becomes something of a mess:

```
#pragma argsused
#if !defined(WIN32)
int PASCAL LibMain(HINSTANCE hInstance, WORD wDataSeg, WORD wHeapSize, LPSTR
lpszCmdLine)
{
```

```
// MessageBox(0, "LibMain", NULL, MB_OK);
#else
  #if defined(__BORLANDC__)
  int WINAPI DllEntryPoint(HINSTANCE hInst, DWORD reason, LPVOID)
  #else
  int WINAPI DllMain(HINSTANCE hInst, DWORD reason, LPVOID)
  #endif
{
// MessageBox(0, "Entry point", NULL, MB_OK);
#endif
  #ifndef WIN32
  if (wHeapSize > 0)
      UnlockData(0);
  #endif

  return 1;
}
```

If you take away all the folderol, this is what you get in Borland's compiler:

```
int WINAPI DllEntryPoint(HINSTANCE hInst, DWORD reason, LPVOID)
{
  return 1;
}
```

Obviously there is nothing innately difficult about the call, but it seems complex due to the conditional defines that I have been forced to add in this case.

In the code fragments supplied with CDINFO.CPP and PLAYINFO.CPP I include calls to MessageBox that have been commented out. If you are feeling some confusion about what is going on with DLLMain or LibMain, then you should remove these comments, recompile the DLL, and run HARMONY.EXE. Each time the DLL is called the MessageBox function will pop up a window. If you are confused by this call, the actual site of the MessageBox statements can help to make the process more concrete. There's nothing all that complex happening here, but sometimes it comes clear if you see it, rather than just hear about it. (Be careful with these calls, however, because they can make your system appear to lock up. If you have trouble, try Alt+Tabbing around to see if the MessageBox is simply hidden behind another window, waiting for you to press its OK button!)

Here is a bit of code borrowed from the Microsoft docs that show how to respond to each of the possible values in the reason parameter:

```
BOOL APIENTRY DLLMain( HANDLE hModule,
                       DWORD ul_reason_for_call,
                       LPVOID lpReserved )
{
    switch( ul_reason_for_call ) {
    case DLL_PROCESS_ATTACH:
    ...
    case DLL_THREAD_ATTACH:
    ...
    case DLL_THREAD_DETACH:
    ...
```

```
case DLL_PROCESS_DETACH:
...
}
return TRUE;
}
```

For most DLLs, the sample shown here would be overkill. After all, you usually won't be concerned about threads accessing your DLL. However, if you are selling your DLL to the public, then you might want to study this code so you can be prepared for all possible contingencies.

If you just need to construct simple DLLs for your own use, then you shouldn't let this stuff confuse you. Neither LibMain, DLLMain, DLLEntryPoint nor the WEP play a very big role in most DLLs. In fact, for the types of DLLs shown in this book, you can just block copy this code from one DLL to another. Don't let it confuse you. For now, you can think of it as little more than some colorful syntactical sugar you can sprinkle on top of a DLL. However, if you want to dig deep and access the full power of DLLs, then I have supplied you with enough information to get you started.

Exporting and Importing Functions from a DLL

If you want to write a routine and place it in a DLL so that it can be used by multiple programs, then you must *export* the routine from the DLL. It's not enough just to put a routine in a DLL. You must explicitly tell Windows that you want to export it. At the same time, you must consider the time when the users of your DLL *import* your routine into their program at runtime.

Functions that are exported from DLLs are declared by Borland 4.5 users and all WIN16 users with the CALLBACK and export keywords:

```
BOOL CALLBACK _export CloseMCI(void);
```

Microsoft and Borland 5.0 users work with the __declspec keyword:

```
__declspec(dllexport) BOOL CloseMCI;
```

Furthermore, if you want to import a function from a DLL, then you need to turn the __declspec function around by writing:

```
__declspec(dllimport)
```

Because the syntax branches into such divergent paths, I was compelled to indulge in the aesthetic malapropism of macro making. Here is the sleight of hand that I came up with for writing code that will compile on both Microsoft and Borland systems, in both 16- and 32-bit modes:

```
#if defined(__BORLANDC__)
  #define EXPORT CALLBACK _export
#else
  #if !defined(_EXPORT_)
    #define EXPORT __declspec(dllimport)
  #else
    #define EXPORT __declspec(dllexport)
  #endif
#endif
```

This code lets you define functions in your DLL so that they look like this:

```
BOOL EXPORT ErrorMsg(DWORD Error, LPSTR CallingFunc);
UINT EXPORT GetDeviceID(void);
LPSTR EXPORT GetInfo(LPSTR S);
LONG EXPORT GetLen(void);
```

Furthermore, if __BORLAND__ is not defined automatically on your system by the compiler, then you should define the word _EXPORT_ when you are building a DLL. In particular, you should be sure the following code is passed on the command line:

```
/D"_EXPORT_"
```

In Microsoft Visual C++ 2.0, you can add this line in the IDE by finding the place in the C/C++ page of the Settings dialog where you can add Preprocessor Definitions. Or, if you want, you can hard code the definition into your files:

```
#define _EXPORT_
```

Although I don't like this latter alternative.

It's not directly relevant to the current discussion, but perhaps I should add that on Borland systems, you can do the same thing by writing the following on the command line:

```
/D_EXPORT_
```

or

```
-D_EXPORT_
```

If you are working in the IDE, go to Options|Project|Compiler|Defines and enter the words you want to define.

> **Note:** As a rule, I don't like to create my own macros, though I will do so at times. The problem with macros, especially in a book like this, is that they imply that the language has a certain capability which is in fact not supported on all systems.

> My job is to explain Windows programming. As a result, I need to work with the actual standards that exist. It's not helpful for me to create macros that conceal the actual nature of the tool I'm trying to explain. My macros may make my code look prettier, but when you move to a different system that doesn't have my macro files on it, you won't know what to do. In other words, macros can prevent me from performing my job as a writer. So as a rule, I don't write my own macros unless there is no good alternative.
>
> I will, however, make heavy use of macros that are defined as part of a universally accepted standard. WINDOWSX.H, for instance, is full of macros that I promote heavily in this book. I like WindowsX because it's a standard. All good Windows compilers ship with WINDOWSX.H, and it performs the invaluable task of helping you write clean, easy to read, portable code.

The EXPORT macro resolves differently under different systems. For instance, if you are on a Borland system, EXPORT resolves to CALLBACK _export. If you are on a Microsoft system, then you need to define the word _EXPORT_ so that the macro resolves into __declspec(dllexport). On Microsoft systems that are calling a DLL from a main program, the macro should automatically resolve into __declspec(dllimport).

Despite the seeming complexity of this confusing barrage of syntax, the end result is that the routines you declare in this manner can be exported or imported from DLLs. See past the syntax, and the principles involved can be easily grasped. In other words, just put my macro at the top of your DLL header files and then use the word EXPORT in the definition of all the routines you want to "export" from your DLL! If it's confusing, don't try to understand it. Just plug in the pieces and move on to something more interesting.

So now you know how to declare a function if you want to export it from a DLL. However, there are some additional steps you need to take if you want to create a useful DLL. In particular, you must perform the following steps:

1. Include a header file in your project containing the declarations of the files you want to link into your program.
2. Run a utility called ImpLib on the DLL containing the functions you want to call.

ImpLib is run from the DOS prompt. It expects two parameters. The first is the name of the library you want to create, and the second is the name of the DLL in question:

```
ImpLib MyFuncs.lib MyFuncs.dll
```

The end result is a file called MYFUNCS.LIB, which you can link into your program just as you would any other library. The difference here, however, is that this library file does not contain the actual code for the functions you want to use. Instead, it simply refers your program to the DLL, which will be linked in at runtime.

Another Borland file, called IMPLIPW, runs from inside of Windows. It is shown in Figure BD3.4.

 **Note:** It's important to understand that you need to compile a DLL with different settings than you use for the normal portions of your program. If you are using the Borland or Microsoft IDEs, you can simply use the supplied menus to automatically obtain these settings, as described in your documentation. If you are using a makefile, you should use the settings shown in HARMONY.MAK.

Figure BD3.4.
The IMPLIBW.EXE program is easier to use than IMPLIB.EXE, and you can use it from inside Windows.

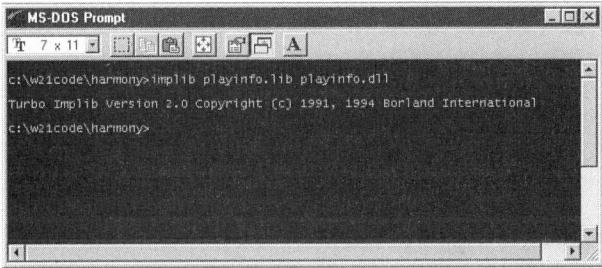

After running ImpLib, you have to remember to include the library file you have created in the projects you want to develop. You have to explicitly reference these libraries just as you have to explicitly add a new CPP file to your project if you want to call one of the routines in that project.

For instance, if you are in the Borland IDE, you have to go to the project window at the bottom of the screen, right click on HARMONY.EXE, and choose Add Node from the pop-up menu. Then you should search for the library file you have created and add it to your project.

Microsoft IDE users have to do the same thing, except they must be careful because MSVC20 sometimes makes two sets of files with the .LIB extension. You want the LIB files that are deposited in the WINDEBUG or WINREL subdirectories, not the ones placed in the main subdirectory where your source code is stored.

If you are working from the command line, you must also explicitly reference these libraries:

```
LIBS = PlayInfo.lib CDInfo.lib

# link EXES
$(APPNAME).exe: $(OBJS) $(APPNAME).def $(LIBS) $(APPNAME).res
```

```
bcc $(FLAGS) $(OBJS) $(LIBS)
rc $(APPNAME).res
```

As you can see, I first define LIBS, and then reference that definition when I am linking the executable. Remember these library files are just like standard DOS ".LIB" files, except they contain references to a DLL rather than the actual implementation of the functions you want to call.

Note also that it's not enough just to distribute a DLL by itself to other programmers. You also need to distribute your header file. In other words, if you want to use PLAYINFO.DLL in a second program, you must have both the DLL and the header file. There are means to find out what functions are exported from a DLL, but if you don't have the header, you have to use advanced debugging techniques, along with guesswork, to determine the proper parameters. If you want to call a DLL from another language, you usually must translate these header files into the other language before you can call routines in the DLL. Note, also, that this system of distributing DLLs and header files allows you to sell your libraries to other developers without having to give away the source code.

To sum up the steps involved in making a DLL:

1. First write the functions you want to call, making sure that you explicitly export these functions using the EXPORT macro shown above. If you are working with Microsoft's compiler, then you must also define the word _EXPORT_. As explained forthwith, you should also usually define all the export functions as extern "C".

2. Run ImpLib so that you create a LIB file.

3. Link the LIB file into your executable by explicitly adding it to your project. (If you are working inside the Borland IDE, you will probably be able to add a DLL directly to your project, and the IDE will run IMPLIB for you directly. However, if you are working from the command line, then you should explicitly create the LIB file by defining the appropriate commands in a makefile.)

You now know the basics of how to create DLLs. Just concentrate on the simple steps shown here and you will be able to produce industry standard DLLs that can be used by yourself and hundreds—or even thousands—of other programmers.

DLLs and Memory

If you compare the DEF file for the CDInfo DLL with the other DEF files used in this book you will see that it:

☐ Uses the LIBRARY statement instead of the NAME statement

☐ Declares its DATA as single rather than multiple

For ready comparison, here is the CDINFO.DEF file:

```
LIBRARY CDInfo

DESCRIPTION 'CDInfo (C) 1993 Charlie Calvert'
EXETYPE WINDOWS
CODE  PRELOAD MOVEABLE DISCARDABLE
DATA  PRELOAD MOVEABLE SINGLE
HEAPSIZE 5120
```

Under 16-bit Windows the DATA segment for a DLL is single, because only one copy of a DLL is loaded into memory at a time. Secondly, the DLL has no stack. This means that it uses the stack of the program that calls it! This is a factor you must consider when you call a DLL. Note also that you sometimes can devise methods of increasing the data space available to your program by moving variables out of your local DGROUP and into a DLL.

Under 32-bit Windows each DLL no longer shares a single data segment with all the applications that access it, and so the SINGLE directive listed above is ignored. Instead, the DLL gets mapped into the address space of the application that calls it. In 32-bit Windows, each process that accesses a DLL will have its own copy of the DLL's data, but in 16-bit Windows they can share data by accessing a single data segment associated with the DLL. (I'm oversimplifying here just a bit. In 32-bit Windows it is possible to share the data if you explicitly declare the DLL in a particular manner, though this is not a recommended course of action because it makes very poor use of memory.)

The disadvantage to the 16-bit system is that you are stuck working with 64KB segments, which can be very limiting. In particular, the DLLs local heap and the DLLs data segment are both competing for space in the same 6KB segment. Because each DLL has only one data segment, you can use this data segment to share information between applications. If you wanted, you could even create a DLL whose sole purpose was to allow two applications to talk to one another.

Under 32-bit Windows, you no longer have to worry about 6KB segments. This is an enormous freedom. However, this freedom comes with a price, because you can no longer share data easily through a single DLL that is shared by multiple applications. For information on using this trick, see Jeffrey Richter's book *Advanced Windows*, which is available on the Microsoft Developers Network. In that book he discusses using

```
#prgrma data_seg("shared")
```

to create a new section in your DLL. You can then use the -SECTION switch on the linkers command line:

```
SECTION:Shared,RWS.
```

The final point to make in this quick overview of DLLs is that it is possible to load a DLL into memory dynamically at runtime by calling LoadLibrary or LoadLibraryEx. Conversely, you can unload the library by calling FreeLibrary.

If you are using this technique, you shouldn't link an ImpLib-created LIB file into your program. Instead, you should count on `GetProcAddress` to create a pointer to the function. You also sometimes need to know the index of a function. You'll find out how to obtain that index in the next section.

The difference between using ImpLib and `LoadLibrary` is that the first technique loads the DLL into memory when your program is loaded, and unloads it when your program ends. If you use `LoadLibrary` and `FreeLibrary`, you can load and unload the DLL dynamically.

Pulling Back the Veil from DLLs

Not only will DLLs enable you to store reusable code outside of your main executable, they also reveal the technique used for storing all the Windows API routines. As mentioned above, functions, such as `CreateWindow` or `BitBlt`, are actually stored in DLLs called by names such as USER.EXE, GDI.EXE, and KRNL386.EXE. This means you have been using DLLs since (literally) Day 1. The only difference is that now you are writing some of your own.

DLLs are great, but sometimes they can appear as black boxes that stubbornly refuse to reveal their secrets. One way to find out about the contents of a DLL is to run a Borland program called ImpDef that ships with the Borland compiler. This will tell you what functions are in a DLL, and what index is associated with each function. The syntax of ImpDef is just like the syntax of ImpLib, except you specify a text file to hold the output in the second parameter.

```
impdef MyDLL.txt MyDLL.dll
```

If you are using a real copy of DOS, the following command line will echo the output to the console, as shown in Figure BD3.5.

```
impdef con MyDLL.dll
```

However, the line shown here will not work correctly in a Windows 95 command session. Instead, you must pipe the information into a text file, as shown above.

Note: When exporting functions from a DLL, you have to decide whether or not to use name mangling. Figure BD3.5 shows one function that uses name mangling, whereas the others are exported as they would be from a standard C or Pascal compiler. The name mangling, which C++ compilers use by default, will make it very difficult for you to link your DLL into a Pascal or straight C program. The header file for CDINFO.CPP leaves name mangling turned on; PLAYINFO.H shows how to turn it off by using `extern "C"`. One way to find out whether a DLL or other binary file uses name mangling is with TDump or ExeHdr.

For ready comparison, here is the CDINFO.DEF file:

```
LIBRARY CDInfo

DESCRIPTION 'CDInfo (C) 1993 Charlie Calvert'
EXETYPE WINDOWS
CODE  PRELOAD MOVEABLE DISCARDABLE
DATA  PRELOAD MOVEABLE SINGLE
HEAPSIZE 5120
```

Under 16-bit Windows the DATA segment for a DLL is single, because only one copy of a DLL is loaded into memory at a time. Secondly, the DLL has no stack. This means that it uses the stack of the program that calls it! This is a factor you must consider when you call a DLL. Note also that you sometimes can devise methods of increasing the data space available to your program by moving variables out of your local DGROUP and into a DLL.

Under 32-bit Windows each DLL no longer shares a single data segment with all the applications that access it, and so the SINGLE directive listed above is ignored. Instead, the DLL gets mapped into the address space of the application that calls it. In 32-bit Windows, each process that accesses a DLL will have its own copy of the DLL's data, but in 16-bit Windows they can share data by accessing a single data segment associated with the DLL. (I'm oversimplifying here just a bit. In 32-bit Windows it is possible to share the data if you explicitly declare the DLL in a particular manner, though this is not a recommended course of action because it makes very poor use of memory.)

The disadvantage to the 16-bit system is that you are stuck working with 64KB segments, which can be very limiting. In particular, the DLLs local heap and the DLLs data segment are both competing for space in the same 6KB segment. Because each DLL has only one data segment, you can use this data segment to share information between applications. If you wanted, you could even create a DLL whose sole purpose was to allow two applications to talk to one another.

Under 32-bit Windows, you no longer have to worry about 6KB segments. This is an enormous freedom. However, this freedom comes with a price, because you can no longer share data easily through a single DLL that is shared by multiple applications. For information on using this trick, see Jeffrey Richter's book *Advanced Windows*, which is available on the Microsoft Developers Network. In that book he discusses using

```
#prgrma data_seg("shared")
```

to create a new section in your DLL. You can then use the -SECTION switch on the linkers command line:

```
SECTION:Shared,RWS.
```

The final point to make in this quick overview of DLLs is that it is possible to load a DLL into memory dynamically at runtime by calling LoadLibrary or LoadLibraryEx. Conversely, you can unload the library by calling FreeLibrary.

If you are using this technique, you shouldn't link an ImpLib-created LIB file into your program. Instead, you should count on `GetProcAddress` to create a pointer to the function. You also sometimes need to know the index of a function. You'll find out how to obtain that index in the next section.

The difference between using ImpLib and `LoadLibrary` is that the first technique loads the DLL into memory when your program is loaded, and unloads it when your program ends. If you use `LoadLibrary` and `FreeLibrary`, you can load and unload the DLL dynamically.

Pulling Back the Veil from DLLs

Not only will DLLs enable you to store reusable code outside of your main executable, they also reveal the technique used for storing all the Windows API routines. As mentioned above, functions, such as `CreateWindow` or `BitBlt`, are actually stored in DLLs called by names such as USER.EXE, GDI.EXE, and KRNL386.EXE. This means you have been using DLLs since (literally) Day 1. The only difference is that now you are writing some of your own.

DLLs are great, but sometimes they can appear as black boxes that stubbornly refuse to reveal their secrets. One way to find out about the contents of a DLL is to run a Borland program called ImpDef that ships with the Borland compiler. This will tell you what functions are in a DLL, and what index is associated with each function. The syntax of ImpDef is just like the syntax of ImpLib, except you specify a text file to hold the output in the second parameter.

```
impdef MyDLL.txt MyDLL.dll
```

If you are using a real copy of DOS, the following command line will echo the output to the console, as shown in Figure BD3.5.

```
impdef con MyDLL.dll
```

However, the line shown here will not work correctly in a Windows 95 command session. Instead, you must pipe the information into a text file, as shown above.

Note: When exporting functions from a DLL, you have to decide whether or not to use name mangling. Figure BD3.5 shows one function that uses name mangling, whereas the others are exported as they would be from a standard C or Pascal compiler. The name mangling, which C++ compilers use by default, will make it very difficult for you to link your DLL into a Pascal or straight C program. The header file for CDINFO.CPP leaves name mangling turned on; PLAYINFO.H shows how to turn it off by using `extern "C"`. One way to find out whether a DLL or other binary file uses name mangling is with TDump or ExeHdr.

Over the years, most experienced C/C++ programmers have found that it is best to create DLLs that don't use name mangling. The problem is that different compilers use different techniques to perform name mangling. As a result, DLLs that don't use extern "C" are often not much use to anyone but the person who produced them. This is especially true if you want to call the DLL from some other language such Delphi, Pascal, Fortran, COBOL, or Visual Basic. I would therefore recommend always using extern "C" to prevent name mangling and to be sure your functions are exported in all uppercase.

Figure BD3.5.

The results of running ImpDef on PLAYINFO.DLL. In this example, CanPerformFunction *has name mangling, whereas the others use* extern "C".

BD3

```
MS-DOS Prompt                                              _ 8 X
T  7 x 11 ▾   □ 🗏 📋   ⊞   🗗 🗗   A

LIBRARY       PLAYINFO.DLL

EXPORTS
    @CanPerformFunction$qul          @18   ; CanPerformFunction(unsigned long)
    @LibMain$qp11HINSTANCE__ususpc   @16   ; LibMain(HINSTANCE__*,unsigned short,un
signed short,char*)
    @WEP$qi                          @17   ; WEP(int)
    CloseMCI                         @1
    DoRecord                         @14
    DoesDeviceExistOnSystem          @13
    ErrorMsg                         @2
    GetDeviceID                      @3
    GetInfo                          @4
    GetLen                           @5
    GetLocation                      @6
    GetMode                          @7
    OpenMCI                          @8
    PauseMCI                         @9
    PlayMCI                          @10
    SaveFile                         @15
    SetTimeFormatMs                  @11
    StopMCI                          @12

c:\w21code\harmony>
```

An excellent way to find out what is happening inside a DLL is to use the Microsoft ExeHdr utility or the TDump utility from Borland. If you run TDump on a DLL or executable, you can learn all about its structure, as well as which functions it exports or imports.

Sooner or later, all good Windows programmers spend an afternoon or evening running ExeHdr or TDump on KERNEL32.DLL, USER32.DLL, KRNL386.EXE, GDI.EXE, or USER.EXE. The output you see will be voluminous, but it will serve to lift back the veil on the inner workings of Windows. An added bonus is that this technique reveals the existence of numerous undocumented functions, as shown in this excerpt from the KRNL386.EXE that ships with 16-bit Windows:

```
Name: GETPROCADDRESS             Entry:    50
Name: _HWRITE                    Entry:   350
Name: __A000H                    Entry:   174
Name: LSTRLEN                    Entry:    90
Name: DIRECTRESALLOC             Entry:   168
Name: GETSYSTEMDIRECTORY         Entry:   135
Name: BUNNY_351                  Entry:   351
Name: GETTEMPFILENAME            Entry:    97
Name: GETWINFLAGS                Entry:   132
Name: __B000H                    Entry:   181
```

Here is some output from KERNEL32.DLL:

```
0266    FreeConsole
0267    FreeEnvironmentStringsA
0268    FreeEnvironmentStringsW
0269    FreeLSCallback
0270    FreeLibrary
0271    FreeLibraryAndExitThread
0272    FreeResource
```

Note that WIN32 doesn't export functions by an index number, but instead just uses a highly optimized alternative method that allows you to always reference functions directly by name.

That's all I'm going to say about DLLs in this book. The central point to remember is that if you stick with ImpLib, CALLBACK, and _export, DLLs can be very flexible and extremely easy to use.

Dialog Windows

The other technique you need to master before you can understand the Harmony program is the use of a dialog as the main window. This is a surprisingly simple little trick that has three key steps.

The first step is that you need to use CreateDialog, instead of CreateWindow, when launching the program's main window:

```
HWND hwnd = CreateDialog(hInst, szAppName, 0, NULL);
```

You've seen this routine before; the only difference is that this time you don't pass in the handle to a parent, because this dialog does not have a parent.

The second step involves setting the window extra bytes to a constant called DLGWINDOWEXTRA:

```
WndClass.cbWndExtra    = DLGWINDOWEXTRA;
```

This constant, when declared in WINDOWS.H, looks like this:

```
/* cbWndExtra needed by dialog manager for dialog classes */
#define DLGWINDOWEXTRA  30
```

The third and final step necessary to create a dialog is to use the CLASS statement in the dialog definition:

```
Harmony DIALOG 18, 23, 246, 208
STYLE DS_MODALFRAME ¦ WS_OVERLAPPED ¦ WS_CAPTION ¦ WS_SYSMENU
CLASS "Harmony"
CAPTION "Harmony"
BEGIN
CONTROL "", ID_GROUP, "BUTTON", BS_GROUPBOX ¦
WS_CHILD ¦ WS_VISIBLE, 6, 5, 107, 93

... // additional code
```

Note that the CLASS name Harmony matches up with the contents of the szAppName parameter passed to CreateDialog. If this string matching is not successful, your program may still run, but messages will not be properly passed on to your window procedure.

That's all there is to it. Dialog windows are really much easier to use than ordinary windows. As an extra bonus, you get to use the Resource Workshop or the App Studio to create all the controls in your windows. All of these controls will be initialized for you automatically at startup. This means you can create the visual side of your program in only a few minutes.

The rest of the Harmony program looks just like any ordinary Windows program. That is, there is a window procedure that receives all the same messages, and responds in the same way as any standard main window. The only major difference is the Cls_OnCreate function, which isn't supplied with a valid HWND. To make up for this, however, the Create function automatically creates all the child windows on your main window.

Summary

This chapter introduces DLLs and the multimedia extensions to Windows. In particular, you have learned:

- How to use mciSendCommand to control multimedia functions
- How to get error strings with mciGetErrorString
- How to find out about available multimedia capabilities on a system
- How to create a DLL and how to export functions from it
- How to use a dialog as the main window of your program

If you want to learn more about multimedia, the best thing you can do is study the included example and the MMSYSTEM.H interface unit, which ship with your compiler. Microsoft also ships additional documentation with the SDK, and separately in the form of two books: *The Microsoft Windows Multimedia Programmer's Reference* and *Microsoft Windows Multimedia Programmer's Workbook*. Both volumes are published by Microsoft Press.

Q&A

Q Are there any additional ways of finding out about the capabilities of the system on which a multimedia program is running?

A Yes, you can use the MCI_GETDEVCAPS message. When sending this message, fill in the MCI_GETDEVCAPS_PARMS.dwItem with constants that ask whether a particular device can Play, Pause, Record, and so forth. One way to use this message is to query to see if a particular device is available (as shown in the DoesDeviceExistOnSystem function). If the device is available, send an MCI_GETDEVCAPS message.

Q **Besides using ImpLib, is there another method for accessing functions exported from a DLL?**

A Yes. You can also list exported functions in the EXPORTS section of a DEF file:

```
EXPORTS    MyFunc1
           MyFunc2
```

This technique used to be fairly popular. However, it's not as easy to use as ImpLib because you have to explicitly import all the functions in the DEF file of your program:

```
IMPORTS
       MyDLL.MyFunc1
       MyDLL.MyFunc2
```

Workshop

The Workshop provides quiz questions to help you solidify your understanding of the material covered and exercises to provide you with experience in using what you've learned. Try to understand the quiz and exercise answers before continuing on to Bonus Day 4, "Snako for Windows." Answers are provided in Appendix A.

Quiz

1. What does MCI stand for?

2. In terms of disk space, what is the difference between MIDI files and WAV files?

3. What do you do with the device ID field when you are first opening a multimedia device?

4. What value does mciSendCommand return?

5. What does the MCI_NOTIFY flag do?

6. What two words are included in the declaration of functions exported from a DLL?

7. How can you inform the linker that certain functions used in your program reside inside a DLL?

8. Harmony uses the PLAYINFO.H and CDINFO.H file for learning about the declarations of routines in CDINFO.DLL and PLAYINFO.DLL. How does your program know about the declarations of the routines in GDI.EXE and USER.EXE?

9. What is the purpose of the CLASS statement in HARMONY.RC?

10. If you use TDump or ExeHdr on both HARMONY.EXE and PLAYINFO.DLL, you'll find that they have very similar structures and are both examples of something called the new executable format. Given this similarity, it follows that there should be an equivalent to WinMain inside a DLL. What is it?

Exercises

1. Use the empty combo box in the left-center of the Harmony main window to display a list of files queued up to play. The user should be able to double-click files in the program's list box, and then have them transferred to the combo box. When the user clicks the play button, the files should be selected one at a time for the combo box.

2. The Harmony program only enables the user to record a message in a WAV file that lasts for a preset period of time. Using Windows controls, such as radio buttons, edits, and scrollbars, create a dialog that will enable the user to designate how long he or she wants a recording to last. You could also extend the functionality of the record button by letting the user gracefully terminate a recording anytime.

Bonus Day

4

Snako for Windows

Today you'll see the final version of the Snako program. The main purpose of this chapter is to allow you to have some fun with the skills you have learned, and to discuss some of the principles behind creating and designing Windows programs.

A few new ideas do come up in this chapter. In particular, you will find a discussion of

☐ Memory issues: the DGROUP and its data, stack, and local heap

☐ Using pointers to move data out of the local heap

☐ Simple file I/O

☐ Centering dialogs

None of these subjects will tax your intellect to any great degree. They basically involve concepts that should already be very familiar to you from your experience in the DOS world.

Besides memory allocation, the main theme of this chapter is that it is important to get back to our roots as avid hackers. Presumably most programmers enter the profession because they love to code. Certainly, most of us got interested in this field simply because it is fascinating and entertaining. I believe that losing this initial sense of playfulness destroys many good programmers. It's good to take time out to have some fun with the tools of the trade. If I ever lose that sense of excitement about the technology, I hope I will have the sense to go find another job. This is too much work to do for any reason other than fun.

Snako

The Snako program shown in this chapter consists of eight screens arranged on two different levels. An ever-lengthening snake winds its way through these screens, eating all the red dots on one screen in order to open a door that leads to the next screen (see Figure BD4.1). At any time, the snake is free to go back and visit any previously visited screen on the current level.

The danger in the game springs from running into the sides of the screen, the "grass" through which the snake's path winds its way, or any part of the snake's tail. Once you are past the first screen, you can make as many attempts as you want at completing any one screen. Victory comes when the snake makes it all the way to the eighth screen and eats all the red dots there.

The nature of the game is such that the first few screens are only moderately challenging. It's only after the snake gets some 50 sections or more in length that the action begins to heat up. If you design sufficiently complex screens, the last levels can get to be extremely intense, so you need to combine physical coordination, logic, forethought, and a nimble mind in order to find your way to victory.

Figure BD4.1.
The Snako program and its snake.

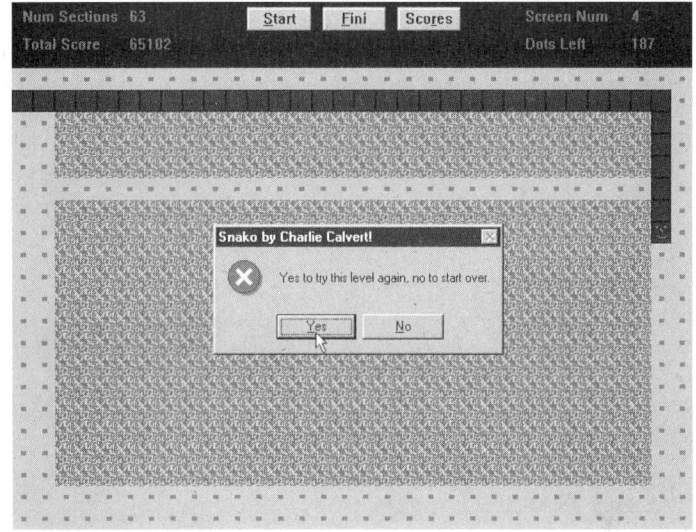

Though the Snako program is presented as a complete and original entertainment, this is a programming book and so I assume you'll want to modify the code to suit your needs. For instance, it would be interesting if the user could adjust the snake's speed and its growth rate. Other interesting improvements might be enabling the snake to climb through more than two levels and letting the user save a game in progress to disk.

At any rate, you should feel free to modify the game in any way you like (though the version that ships with this book, and any future versions of the game that I may design, are mine to do with as I like). As with all the code in this book, however, you are free to distribute copies of this game to anyone who wants it, as long as you don't actually charge a fee for the transaction. This is a learning tool, not an exercise in entrepreneurship.

The Code

The primary reason this chapter introduces so few new topics is simply that Snako is a relatively lengthy program. As such, it presents its own challenges and reveals much about the design issues faced by real-world Windows programmers.

The code that drives the program is presented in the following listings, but much of the challenge in the game comes from the appearance of individual screens. In other words, you could design screens that make it a cakewalk to move all the way to the end of the game, and in fact, I kept a set of those screens available for when I was debugging. On the other hand, creating overly complex screens can make it all but impossible to get off the first level. Figures BD4.2 and BD4.3

show suggested designs for the eight screens used in the program. These are just suggestions, and I more or less assume that anyone interested in this game will want to create screens of their own (or modify the ones shown here).

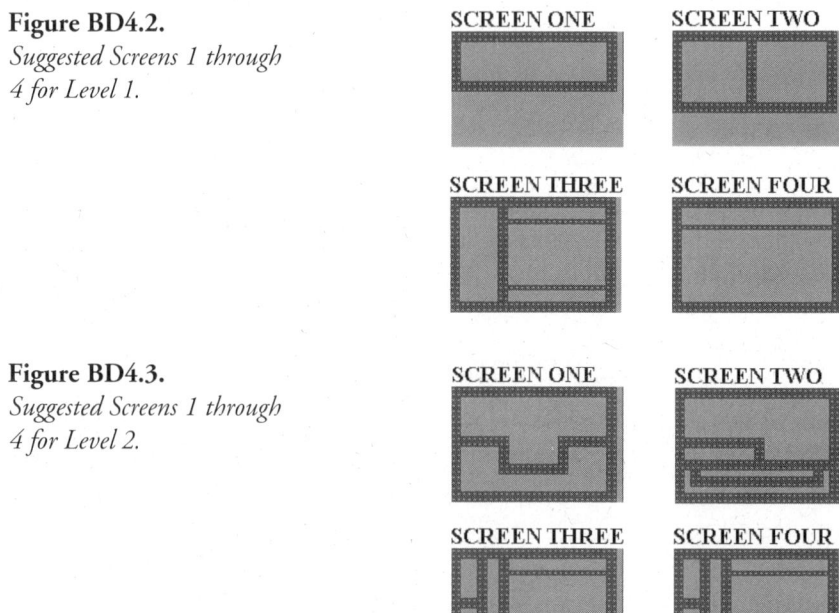

Figure BD4.2.
Suggested Screens 1 through 4 for Level 1.

SCREEN ONE SCREEN TWO

SCREEN THREE SCREEN FOUR

Figure BD4.3.
Suggested Screens 1 through 4 for Level 2.

SCREEN ONE SCREEN TWO

SCREEN THREE SCREEN FOUR

Listing BD4.1 shows the logic for the Snako program.

Listing BD4.1. The Snako program is an arcade type game for Windows.

```
////////////////////////////////////
//   Program Name: SNAKO.CPP
//   Programmer: Charlie Calvert
//   Description: A windows game
//   Date: 08/05/93
////////////////////////////////////

#define STRICT
#include <windows.h>
#include <windowsx.h>
#pragma hdrstop
#include <string.h>
#include <stdlib.h>
#include "snako.h"
#include "score.h"
```

```
#include "grunt.h"
#include "snakutil.h"
#pragma warning (disable : 4068)
#pragma warning (disable : 4100)

static char szAppName[] = "Snako";
static char szScoreClass[] = "ScoreKeeper";

HWND MainWindow;

// Varialbles
HINSTANCE hInstance;
HWND hScoreWindow;
TSNAKEMAP SMap;
PGAMEINFO G, SaveGame;
//--------------------------------------------------------
// Setup
//--------------------------------------------------------

#pragma argsused
int PASCAL WinMain(HINSTANCE hInst, HINSTANCE hPrevInstance,
                   LPSTR  lpszCmdParam, int nCmdShow)
{
  MSG  Msg;

  if (!hPrevInstance)
    if (!Register(hInst))
      return FALSE;

  MainWindow = Create(hInst, nCmdShow);
  if (!MainWindow)
    return FALSE;

  while (GetMessage(&Msg, NULL, 0, 0))
  {
    TranslateMessage(&Msg);
    DispatchMessage(&Msg);
  }
  return Msg.wParam;
}

/////////////////////////////////////
// Save hInstance, Create window,
//   Show window maximized
/////////////////////////////////////
HWND Create(HINSTANCE hInst, int nCmdShow)
{
  hInstance = hInst;

  HWND hWindow = CreateWindow(szAppName,
                    "A Snake and its Tail",
                    WS_POPUP, CW_USEDEFAULT, CW_USEDEFAULT,
                    CW_USEDEFAULT, CW_USEDEFAULT,
                    NULL, NULL, hInst, NULL);
```

continues

Listing BD4.1. continued

```
  if (hWindow == NULL)
    return hWindow;

  nCmdShow = SW_SHOWMAXIMIZED;

  ShowWindow(hWindow, nCmdShow);
  UpdateWindow(hWindow);

  return hWindow;
}

/////////////////////////////////////
// Register window
/////////////////////////////////////
BOOL Register(HINSTANCE hInst)
{
  WNDCLASS WndClass;

  WndClass.style          = CS_HREDRAW ¦ CS_VREDRAW;
  WndClass.lpfnWndProc    = WndProc;
  WndClass.cbClsExtra     = 0;
  WndClass.cbWndExtra     = 0;
  WndClass.hInstance      = hInst;
  WndClass.hIcon          = LoadIcon(NULL, IDI_APPLICATION);
  WndClass.hCursor        = LoadCursor(NULL, IDC_ARROW);
  WndClass.hbrBackground  = GetStockBrush(BLACK_BRUSH);
  WndClass.lpszMenuName   = NULL;
  WndClass.lpszClassName  = szAppName;

  if (!RegisterClass (&WndClass))
    return FALSE;

  WndClass.lpfnWndProc    = ScoreWndProc;
  WndClass.hIcon          = NULL;
  WndClass.hbrBackground  = NULL;
  WndClass.lpszClassName  = szScoreClass;

  return (RegisterClass (&WndClass) != 0);
}

// ------------------------------------------------
// The Implementation
// ------------------------------------------------


// ------------------------------------------------
// WndProc
// ------------------------------------------------
LRESULT CALLBACK EXPORT16 WndProc(HWND hwnd, UINT Message,
                          WPARAM wParam, LPARAM lParam)
{
  switch(Message)
  {
    HANDLE_MSG(hwnd, WM_CREATE, Snake_OnCreate);
```

```
      HANDLE_MSG(hwnd, WM_DESTROY, Snake_OnDestroy);
      HANDLE_MSG(hwnd, WM_CHAR, Snake_OnChar);
      HANDLE_MSG(hwnd, WM_KEYDOWN, Snake_OnKey);
      HANDLE_MSG(hwnd, WM_PAINT, Snake_OnPaint);
      HANDLE_MSG(hwnd, WM_TIMER, Snake_OnTimer);
      HANDLE_MSG(hwnd, WM_START, Snake_OnStart);
      HANDLE_MSG(hwnd, WM_SIZE, Snake_OnSize);
      default: return Snake_DefProc(hwnd, Message, wParam, lParam);
  }
}

///////////////////////////////////
// Handle WM_CREATE
///////////////////////////////////
#pragma argsused
BOOL Snake_OnCreate(HWND hwnd, CREATESTRUCT FAR* lpCreateStruct)
{
  if((G = (PGAMEINFO)malloc(sizeof(TGAMEINFO))) == NULL)
  {
     MessageBox(hwnd, "Memory is hosed!", "Closing Snako", MB_OK);
     return FALSE;
  }

  InitializeSections();

  G->Dat.Speed = 250;
  int XScreen = GetSystemMetrics(SM_CXSCREEN);

  if (XScreen == 1024)
  {
    G->Dat.GrassX = G->Dat.SizeX = 32;
    G->Dat.GrassY = G->Dat.SizeY = 32;
  }

  if (XScreen == 800)
  {
    G->Dat.GrassX = G->Dat.SizeX = 25;
    G->Dat.GrassY = G->Dat.SizeY = 25;
  }

  if (XScreen == 640)
  {
    G->Dat.GrassX = G->Dat.SizeX = 20;
        G->Dat.GrassY = G->Dat.SizeY = 20;
  }

  G->Dat.MaxScore = 3 * G->Dat.GrassX;
  G->Dat.MenuSpace = 3;
  G->Dat.TotalClicks = 0;

  SMap.Grass = LoadBitmap(hInstance, "Grass");
  SMap.Road = LoadBitmap(hInstance, "Road");
  SMap.Road2 = LoadBitmap(hInstance, "Road2");
  if ((!SMap.Grass) || (!SMap.Road) || (!SMap.Road2))
```

continues

Listing BD4.1. continued

```
  {
    MessageBox(hwnd, "No Grass! No Road! No Road2!",
               "Fatal Error", MB_OK | MB_ICONSTOP);
    return FALSE;
  }

  SMap.Head = LoadBitmap(hInstance, "Head");
  if (!SMap.Head)
  {
    MessageBox(hwnd, "No head", "Fatal Error", MB_OK);
    return FALSE;
  }

  SMap.Body = LoadBitmap(hInstance, "Body");
  if (!SMap.Body)
  {
    MessageBox(hwnd, "No body", "Fatal Error", MB_OK);
    return FALSE;
  }

  hScoreWindow = CreateWindow(szScoreClass, "Score",
                   WS_CHILD | WS_VISIBLE | WS_CLIPSIBLINGS,
                   10, 10, 100, 100, hwnd,
                   HMENU(50), hInstance, NULL);

  if(!hScoreWindow)
        return FALSE;

  G->ScoreRep.Level = 1;
  ReadArray(hwnd);
  SaveGame = NULL;

  return TRUE;
}

///////////////////////////////////////
// Handle WM_DESTROY
///////////////////////////////////////
#pragma argsused
void Snake_OnDestroy(HWND hwnd)
{
  if (SMap.Head) DeleteObject(SMap.Head);
  if (SMap.Body) DeleteObject(SMap.Body);
  if (SMap.Grass) DeleteObject(SMap.Grass);
  if (SMap.Road) DeleteObject(SMap.Road);
  if (SMap.Road2) DeleteObject(SMap.Road2);
  free(G);
  if (SaveGame)
    free(SaveGame);
  PostQuitMessage(0);
}

///////////////////////////////////////
// Handle WM_CHAR -- Stub code to implement
```

```
// a pause feature by pressing the p key
/////////////////////////////////////
#pragma argsused
void Snake_OnChar(HWND hwnd, UINT ch, int cRepeat)
{
  switch (ch)
  {
    case 'p':
      KillTimer(hwnd, SNAKETIMER);
      break;
    case 's':
      SendMessage(hwnd, WM_START, 0, 0L);
      break;
    case 'r':
      SendMessage(hScoreWindow, WM_COMMAND, ID_SCORE, 0);
      break;
    case 'f':
      SendMessage(hScoreWindow, WM_COMMAND, ID_FINI, 0);
      break;
  }
}

/////////////////////////////////////
// Handle WM_KEYDOWN
/////////////////////////////////////
#pragma argsused
void Snake_OnKey(HWND hwnd, UINT vk, BOOL fDown,
                int cRepeat, UINT flags)
{
  switch(vk)
  {
    case VK_DOWN:
      SetNewDir(DOWN);
      MoveBitMap(hwnd);
      break;
    case VK_UP:
      SetNewDir(UP);
      MoveBitMap(hwnd);
      break;
    case VK_LEFT:
      SetNewDir(LEFT);
      MoveBitMap(hwnd);
      break;
    case VK_RIGHT:
      SetNewDir(RIGHT);
      MoveBitMap(hwnd);
      break;
  }

  // In case you hit no accidentally
  if (G->Dat.NewScreenStarted == 2)
  {
    G->Dat.NewScreenStarted = FALSE;
    SetTimer(hwnd, SNAKETIMER, G->Dat.Speed, NULL);
```

continues

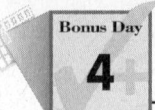
Listing BD4.1. continued

```c
    InvalidateRect(hwnd, NULL, TRUE);
  }
}

//////////////////////////////////////
// -- Snake_OnPaint --
// Repaint the playing board
//////////////////////////////////////
void Snake_OnPaint(HWND hwnd)
{
  PAINTSTRUCT PaintStruct;

  HDC PaintDC = BeginPaint(hwnd, &PaintStruct);
  PaintPlayingField(PaintDC);
  EndPaint(hwnd, &PaintStruct);

  G->SectInfo[0].DirChange = FALSE;
  InvalidateRect(hScoreWindow, NULL, FALSE);
}

//////////////////////////////////////
// Set the position of the score window
//////////////////////////////////////
void Snake_OnSize(HWND hwnd, UINT state, int cx, int cy)
{
  MoveWindow(hScoreWindow, 0, 0, cx, G->Dat.MaxScore - 1, FALSE);
  FORWARD_WM_SIZE(hwnd, state, cx, cy, Snake_DefProc);
}


//////////////////////////////////////
// Handle the user defined WM_START message
// when the start button is pressed
//////////////////////////////////////
void Snake_OnStart(HWND hwnd)
{
  HDC PaintDC;

  SetFocus(hwnd);
  InitializeSections();
  ReadArray(hwnd);
  PaintDC = GetDC(hwnd);
  PaintPlayingField(PaintDC);
  ReleaseDC(hwnd, PaintDC);
  SetUpWindow(hwnd);
  InvalidateRect(hScoreWindow, NULL, TRUE);
}

//////////////////////////////////////
// -- Snake_OnTimer --
// Gets called when the timer runs out.
// Call MoveBitMap to move the snake.
```

```
// If the Timer has been called 15 times in
// a row, then add a new section to the Snake
//////////////////////////////////////
#pragma argsused
void Snake_OnTimer(HWND hwnd, UINT id)
{
  MoveBitMap(hwnd);
  G->Dat.TotalClicks++;
  //  QuickScan(); // debug routine found in SnakUtil
  SendMessage(hScoreWindow, WM_SETNUMSEGS, 0, (LPARAM)&G->ScoreRep);

  if (G->ScoreRep.NumPrizes > 60000) G->ScoreRep.NumPrizes = 0;

  #ifdef _DEBUG
    if (G->ScoreRep.NumPrizes <= 20)
      if(G->Map[BRIDGEX1][G->Dat.MaxCols - 1] != ROADMAP)
        MakeGateWay(hwnd);
  #else
    if (G->ScoreRep.NumPrizes <= 0)
      if((G->Map[BRIDGEX1][G->Dat.MaxCols - 1] != ROADMAP) ¦¦
         (G->ScoreRep.ScreenNum == 4))
        MakeGateWay(hwnd);
  #endif

  if ((G->Dat.TotalClicks % 15) == 0)
    AddSection();

  G->ScoreRep.NumSects = G->Dat.Sections;

  if (G->Dat.NewScreenStarted == 2)
  {
    G->Dat.NewScreenStarted = FALSE;
    SetTimer(hwnd, SNAKETIMER, G->Dat.Speed, NULL);
    InvalidateRect(hwnd, NULL, TRUE);
  }
}
```

BD4

Listing BD4.2 is the Snako header file.

Listing BD4.2. SNAKO.H.

```
//////////////////////////////////////
// Program Name: SNAKO.H
// Programmer: Charlie Calvert
// Description: A Windows game
// Date: 08/05/93
//////////////////////////////////////

#if !defined _SNAKE_H
#define _SNAKE_H

#if !defined(__WIN32__) && !defined(_WIN32)
```

continues

Listing BD4.2. continued

```
#define EXPORT16 __export
#else
#define EXPORT16
#endif

// const
#define SNAKETIMER 1
#define GRASSMAP 1
#define PRIZEMAP 2
#define ROADMAP 3

#define MAXY 21      // Max rows for maze on one level
#define MAXX 32 * 4  // Max cols for maze on one level
#define JUMPSPACE 32 // Width of one screen in bitmaps
#define XWIDTH 25    // Bitmap width in pixels
#define YHEIGHT 25   // Bitmap height in pixels
#define MAXSECTS 512 // Max length of snake: very flexible

#define BRIDGEX1 0   // Row for bridge to next screen
#define BRIDGEX2 1   // Row for bridge to next screen

#define LEFT 0
#define RIGHT 1
#define UP 2
#define DOWN 3

// Type
struct TSCOREREP{
  int NumSects;
  WORD NumPrizes;
  LONG TotalScore;
  WORD ScreenNum;
  WORD Level;
};

// Types
typedef struct  {
    HDC CompDC;
    HDC TCompDC;
    HBITMAP CompBmp;
    HBITMAP OldBmp;
    HBITMAP OldTBmp;
} TSAVEBITMAP;
typedef TSAVEBITMAP TSAVEBITMAPARY[6];

typedef struct
{
  int MaxScore;
  int MaxCols;
  int MinCols;
  int GrassX;
  int GrassY;
  int XPos;
  int MenuSpace;
  int SizeX;
```

```
    int SizeY;
    long TotalClicks;
    BOOL NewScreenStarted;
    int Speed;
    int NumTurns, Sections;
} TDATA;

typedef struct TSNAKEMAP {
    HBITMAP Head, Body, Grass, Road, Road2;
}SNAKEMAP;

typedef struct TSECTINFO {
    BOOL DirChange;
    int Dir;
    int Col, Row;
    int OldCol, OldRow;
} SECTINFO;

typedef struct {
    TSCOREREP ScoreRep;
    char Map[MAXY][MAXX];
    TDATA Dat;
    TSECTINFO SectInfo[MAXSECTS];
} TGAMEINFO;
typedef TGAMEINFO *PGAMEINFO;

#endif

// Macros
#define HANDLE_WM_START(hwnd, wParam, lParam, fn) \
    ((fn)(hwnd), 0L)
#define FORWARD_WM_START(hwnd, fn) \
    (void)(fn)((hwnd), WM_START, 0, 0L)


// Class Snake
#define Snake_DefProc      DefWindowProc
BOOL Snake_OnCreate(HWND hWindow,
                    CREATESTRUCT FAR* lpCreateStruct);
void Snake_OnDestroy(HWND hWindow);
void Snake_OnChar(HWND hWindow, UINT ch, int cRepeat);
void Snake_OnKey(HWND hWindow, UINT vk, BOOL fDown,
                 int cRepeat, UINT flags);
void Snake_OnPaint(HWND hWindow);
void Snake_OnSize(HWND hwnd, UINT state, int cx, int cy);
void Snake_OnStart(HWND hwnd);
void Snake_OnTimer(HWND hWindow, UINT id);


// Procs
HWND Create(HINSTANCE hInst, int nCmdShow);
BOOL Register(HINSTANCE hInst);
BOOL SetUpWindow(HWND hWindow);
void PaintPlayingField(HDC PaintDC);
LRESULT CALLBACK EXPORT16 WndProc(HWND, UINT, WPARAM, LPARAM);
void InitializeSections(HWND hwnd);
int ReadArray(HWND hwnd);
```

BD4

Listing BD4.3 shows the Grunt source file.

Listing BD4.3. GRUNT.CPP.

```cpp
/////////////////////////////////////
// Module: GRUNT.CPP
// Project: Snake
// Programmer: Charlie Calvert
// Date: May 29, 1993
// Description: Do the real work of moving the snake.
/////////////////////////////////////

#define STRICT
#include <windows.h>
#include <windowsx.h>
#pragma hdrstop
#include <stdlib.h>
#include <string.h>
#include "grunt.h"
#include "snako.h"
#include "score.h"
#include "snakutil.h"
#include "snakopnt.h"
#pragma warning (disable : 4100)

extern TSNAKEMAP SMap;
extern HWND hScoreWindow;
extern PGAMEINFO G;

int FindSafe(HWND hwnd)
{
  int Result;

  KillTimer(hwnd, SNAKETIMER);
  if ((G->ScoreRep.Level != 1) ¦¦ (G->ScoreRep.ScreenNum != 1))
  {
     Result = MessageBox(hwnd,
        "Yes to try this level again, no to start over.",
        "Snako by Charlie Calvert!", MB_YESNO ¦ MB_ICONSTOP);
  }
  else
  {
     Result = MessageBox(hwnd, "Dead Snake!",
            "Snako by Charlie Calvert!", MB_OK ¦ MB_ICONSTOP);
  }
  if ((Result == IDOK) ¦¦ (Result == IDNO))
  SendMessage(hScoreWindow, WM_SCORE, 0,
               (LPARAM)G->ScoreRep.TotalScore);
  if (Result != IDYES)
  {
    DoSnakePainting(hwnd);
    memset(&G->SectInfo, '\0', sizeof(G->SectInfo));
    memset(&G->ScoreRep, '\0', sizeof(TSCOREREP));
    G->ScoreRep.Level = 1;
  }
```

```
      else
        G->Dat.NewScreenStarted = 2;
      return FALSE;
    }


    /////////////////////////////////////
    // Will the snake hit its own body if it
    // goes in the direction user asked for?
    /////////////////////////////////////
    BOOL DidSnakeHitSnake(HWND hwnd)
    {
      int C = G->SectInfo[0].Col;
      int R = G->SectInfo[0].Row;

      for (int i = 1; i <= G->Dat.Sections; i++)
        if ((C == G->SectInfo[i].Col) && (R == G->SectInfo[i].Row))
        {
          FindSafe(hwnd);
          return TRUE;
        }

      return FALSE;
    }


    /////////////////////////////////////
    // This only gets called for the head.
    // It tests if head is going to hit the
    // body of the snake or if it hits the grass
    // In either case it returns FALSE, else TRUE
    /////////////////////////////////////
    BOOL FindNextSpace(HWND hwnd)
    {
      int Test;

      switch(G->SectInfo[0].Dir)
      {
        case UP:
          if (G->SectInfo[0].Row <= 0)
            return FindSafe(hwnd);
          Test = G->Map[G->SectInfo[0].Row - 1][G->SectInfo[0].Col];
          if ((Test == GRASSMAP) || (G->SectInfo[0].Row <= 0))
            return FindSafe(hwnd);
          G->SectInfo[0].Row -= 1;
          break;

        case DOWN:
          Test = G->Map[G->SectInfo[0].Row + 1][G->SectInfo[0].Col];
          if ((Test == GRASSMAP) || (G->SectInfo[0].Row >= MAXY - 1))
            return FindSafe(hwnd);
          G->SectInfo[0].Row += 1;
          break;

        case LEFT:
          Test = G->Map[G->SectInfo[0].Row][G->SectInfo[0].Col - 1];
```

continues

1137

Listing BD4.3. continued

```c
      if ((Test == GRASSMAP) || (G->SectInfo[0].Col < 1))
        return FindSafe(hwnd);
      G->SectInfo[0].Col -= 1;
      break;

    case RIGHT:
      Test = G->Map[G->SectInfo[0].Row][G->SectInfo[0].Col + 1];
      if ((Test == GRASSMAP) || (G->SectInfo[0].Col > MAXX))
        return FindSafe(hwnd);
      G->SectInfo[0].Col += 1;
      break;
  }

  if (Test == PRIZEMAP)
  {
    G->ScoreRep.TotalScore += (LONG)100;
    G->ScoreRep.NumPrizes--;
  }

  G->Map[G->SectInfo[0].Row][G->SectInfo[0].Col] = ROADMAP;

  if(DidSnakeHitSnake(hwnd))
    return FALSE;
  else
    return TRUE;
}

//////////////////////////////////////
// This moves each section of the
// snake on one place. It never
// gets called for the head.
//////////////////////////////////////
void SetNextSection(int i)
{
  switch(G->SectInfo[i].Dir)
  {
    case UP: G->SectInfo[i].Row -= 1; break;
    case DOWN: G->SectInfo[i].Row += 1; break;
    case LEFT: G->SectInfo[i].Col -= 1; break;
    case RIGHT: G->SectInfo[i].Col += 1; break;
  }
}

//////////////////////////////////////
// When ever the snake moves back and forth
// across a screen, we need to know which
// number screen he is on so we can tell the user
//////////////////////////////////////
void SetScreenNum(void)
{
  switch (G->Dat.MaxCols)
  {
    case JUMPSPACE: G->ScoreRep.ScreenNum = 1; break;
    case JUMPSPACE * 2: G->ScoreRep.ScreenNum = 2; break;
```

```
      case JUMPSPACE * 3: G->ScoreRep.ScreenNum = 3; break;
      case JUMPSPACE * 4: G->ScoreRep.ScreenNum = 4; break;
  }
}

/////////////////////////////////////
// Move things left one screen or
// right one screen if we hit end of screen
/////////////////////////////////////
void CheckForEndScreen(HWND hwnd, int i)
{
  if ((i == 0) && (G->SectInfo[i].Col >= G->Dat.MaxCols))
  {
    if (G->Dat.XPos != (MAXX - JUMPSPACE))
    {
      G->Dat.XPos += JUMPSPACE;
      G->Dat.MaxCols += JUMPSPACE;
      G->Dat.MinCols += JUMPSPACE;
      G->ScoreRep.NumPrizes = 10000;
      InvalidateRect(hwnd, NULL, TRUE);
      SetScreenNum();
      G->Dat.NewScreenStarted = TRUE;
    }
  }

  if ((i == 0) && (G->SectInfo[i].Col < G->Dat.MinCols))
  {
    if (G->Dat.XPos != 0)
    {
      G->Dat.XPos -= JUMPSPACE;
      G->Dat.MaxCols -= JUMPSPACE;
      G->Dat.MinCols -= JUMPSPACE;
      G->ScoreRep.NumPrizes = 10000;
      InvalidateRect(hwnd, NULL, TRUE);
      SetScreenNum();
    }
  }
}

/////////////////////////////////////
// Move the whole snake forward. The calls to
// FindNextSpace move the head and test to see
// if move is legal. Once we know the move is legal,
// then move everything else by calling SetNextSection.
// CheckForEndScreen moves to next screen or back
/////////////////////////////////////
void SetColRow(HWND hwnd)
{
  int i;
  BOOL Result;

  for (i = 0; i <= G->Dat.Sections; i++)
  {
    G->SectInfo[i].OldCol = G->SectInfo[i].Col;
    G->SectInfo[i].OldRow = G->SectInfo[i].Row;
```

continues

Listing BD4.3. continued

```
          if (i == 0)
          {
            Result = FindNextSpace(hwnd);
            if(G->Dat.NewScreenStarted == 2)
              return;
          }
          else
            SetNextSection(i);

          if (Result)
            CheckForEndScreen(hwnd, i);
        }

      if (Result)
        for (i = G->Dat.Sections; i > 0; i--)
        {
          if (G->SectInfo[i - 1].DirChange)
          {
            G->SectInfo[i].DirChange = TRUE;
            G->SectInfo[i].Dir = G->SectInfo[i - 1].Dir;
            G->SectInfo[i - 1].DirChange = FALSE;
          }
        }
}

/////////////////////////////////////
// Set New Direction when we turn
/////////////////////////////////////
void SetNewDir(int NewDir)
{
  G->SectInfo[0].Dir = NewDir;
  G->SectInfo[0].DirChange = TRUE;
}

/////////////////////////////////////
// Make the snake a little longer
/////////////////////////////////////
void AddSection(void)
{
  G->Dat.Sections++;

  G->SectInfo[G->Dat.Sections].Dir =
     G->SectInfo[G->Dat.Sections - 1].Dir;
  G->SectInfo[G->Dat.Sections].DirChange = FALSE;

  switch (G->SectInfo[G->Dat.Sections].Dir)
  {
    case LEFT:
    {
      G->SectInfo[G->Dat.Sections].Col =
         G->SectInfo[G->Dat.Sections - 1].Col + 1;
```

```
      G->SectInfo[G->Dat.Sections].Row =
        G->SectInfo[G->Dat.Sections - 1].Row;
      break;
    }
    case RIGHT:
    {
      G->SectInfo[G->Dat.Sections].Col =
        G->SectInfo[G->Dat.Sections - 1].Col - 1;
      G->SectInfo[G->Dat.Sections].Row =
        G->SectInfo[G->Dat.Sections - 1].Row;
      break;
    }

    case UP:
    {
      G->SectInfo[G->Dat.Sections].Col =
        G->SectInfo[G->Dat.Sections - 1].Col;
      G->SectInfo[G->Dat.Sections].Row =
        G->SectInfo[G->Dat.Sections - 1].Row + 1;
      break;
    }

    case DOWN:
    {
      G->SectInfo[G->Dat.Sections].Col =
        G->SectInfo[G->Dat.Sections - 1].Col;
      G->SectInfo[G->Dat.Sections].Row =
        G->SectInfo[G->Dat.Sections - 1].Row - 1;
      break;
    }
  } // end switch

  G->SectInfo[G->Dat.Sections].OldCol =
    G->SectInfo[G->Dat.Sections - 1].Col;
  G->SectInfo[G->Dat.Sections].OldRow =
    G->SectInfo[G->Dat.Sections - 1].Row;
}


//////////////////////////////////
// Game is over
//////////////////////////////////
void YouWin(HWND hwnd)
{
  KillTimer(hwnd, SNAKETIMER);
  MessageBox(hwnd, "You Win!", "Victory!",
             MB_ICONEXCLAMATION | MB_OK);
  SendMessage(hScoreWindow, WM_SCORE, 0,
             (LPARAM)G->ScoreRep.TotalScore);
}

//////////////////////////////////
// Make a bridge to the next screen,
```

continues

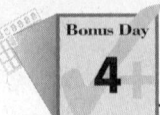

Listing BD4.3. continued

```
// start the next level or proclaim victory.
/////////////////////////////////////
void MakeGateWay(HWND hwnd)
{
  if (G->ScoreRep.ScreenNum == 4)
  {
    if (G->ScoreRep.Level == 2)
    {
      YouWin(hwnd);
      return;
    }
    G->ScoreRep.Level++;
    StartNewScreen(hwnd);
    KillTimer(hwnd, SNAKETIMER);
    MessageBox(hwnd, "Get Ready for a new Level", "Snako",
            MB_OK | MB_ICONEXCLAMATION);
    if (!SetTimer(hwnd, SNAKETIMER, G->Dat.Speed, NULL))
      MessageBox(hwnd,"No Timers Available","Snako",MB_OK);

    SaveGameToMemory(hwnd);
    return;
  }
  MakeAndPaintBridge(hwnd);
}


/////////////////////////////////////
// Command Central for the whole of Grunt
/////////////////////////////////////
void MoveBitMap(HWND hwnd)
{
  SetColRow(hwnd);
  if (G->Dat.NewScreenStarted == 2)
  {
    ReadGameFromMemory();
    G->Dat.NewScreenStarted = 2;
  }
  DoSnakePainting(hwnd);
  G->ScoreRep.TotalScore += 1;
  G->SectInfo[0].DirChange = FALSE;
  if (G->Dat.NewScreenStarted == 1)
  {
    G->Dat.NewScreenStarted = FALSE;
    SaveGameToMemory(hwnd);
  }
}
```

Listing BD4.4 shows the Grunt header file.

Listing BD4.4. GRUNT.H.

```
1: /////////////////////////////////////
2: // Module: GRUNT.H
3: // Project: Snake
```

```
4: // Programmer: Charlie Calvert
5: /////////////////////////////////
6:
7: #include "snako.h"
8:
9: // Procs
10: void AddSection(void);
11: void MoveBitMap(HWND hwnd);
12: void SetNewDir(int NewDir);
13: void MakeGateWay(HWND hwnd);
```

Listing BD4.5 shows the SnakoPnt source file.

Listing BD4.5. SNAKOPNT.CPP.

```
1: /////////////////////////////////////////////
2: //   Program Name: SNAKOPNT.CPP
3: //   Programmer: Charlie Calvert
4: //   Description: Draw playing field and the snake
5: //   Date: 08/05/93
6: /////////////////////////////////////////////
7:
8: #define STRICT
9: #include <windows.h>
10: #include <windowsx.h>
11: #include "snako.h"
12: #include "snakutil.h"
13:
14: extern PGAMEINFO G;
15: extern TSNAKEMAP SMap;
16: enum Bmps {EHead, EBody, EGrass, ERoad, ERoad2};
17:
18: // ----------------------------------------
19: //   The Paint Section
20: // ----------------------------------------
21:
22: /////////////////////////////////////////////
23: // The Drawing of the snake
24: /////////////////////////////////////////////
25: int PaintTheSnake(HDC PaintDC, HDC HeadDC, HDC BodyDC)
26: {
27:   BitBlt(PaintDC,
28:        (G->SectInfo[0].Col - G->Dat.XPos) * G->Dat.SizeX,
29:        (G->SectInfo[0].Row + G->Dat.MenuSpace) * G->Dat.SizeY,
30:         G->Dat.SizeX, G->Dat.SizeY, HeadDC, 0, 0, SRCCOPY);
31:
32:   for (int i = 1; i <= G->Dat.Sections; i++)
33:     BitBlt(PaintDC,
34:        (G->SectInfo[i].Col - G->Dat.XPos) * G->Dat.SizeX,
35:        (G->SectInfo[i].Row + G->Dat.MenuSpace) * G->Dat.SizeY,
36:         G->Dat.SizeX, G->Dat.SizeY, BodyDC, 0, 0, SRCCOPY);
```

BD4

continues

Listing BD4.5. continued

```
37:    return --i;
38: }
39:
40: /////////////////////////////////////////
41: // After snake has been somewhere, get rid of prize
42: // bitmap and just put in regular road.
43: /////////////////////////////////////////
44: void FillInWhereSnakeHasBeen(HDC PaintDC, int i)
45: {
46:    TSAVEBITMAPARY SaveBmp;
47:    HDC RoadDC;
48:
49:    RoadDC = GetScaledDC(PaintDC, SaveBmp, SMap.Road, ERoad);
50:
51:    BitBlt(PaintDC,
52:      (G->SectInfo[i].OldCol - G->Dat.XPos) * G->Dat.SizeX,
53:      (G->SectInfo[i].OldRow + G->Dat.MenuSpace) * G->Dat.SizeY,
54:       G->Dat.SizeX, G->Dat.SizeY, RoadDC, 0, 0, SRCCOPY);
55:
56:    DisposeScaledDC(SaveBmp, ERoad);
57: }
58:
59: /////////////////////////////////////////////////
60: // Command central for painting the snake
61: // GetScaledDC in SnakUtils
62: /////////////////////////////////////////////////
63: void DoSnakePainting(HWND hwnd)
64: {
65:    TSAVEBITMAPARY SB;
66:    HDC DC = GetDC(hwnd);
67:
68:    HDC HeadDC = GetScaledDC(DC, SB, SMap.Head, EHead);
69:    HDC BodyDC = GetScaledDC(DC, SB, SMap.Body, EBody);
70:
71:    int i = PaintTheSnake(DC, HeadDC, BodyDC);
72:
73:    DisposeScaledDC(SB, EHead);
74:    DisposeScaledDC(SB, EBody);
75:
76:    if ((G->SectInfo[i].OldRow > -1) &&
77:        (G->SectInfo[i].OldCol > -1))
78:      FillInWhereSnakeHasBeen(DC, i);
79:
80:    ReleaseDC(hwnd, DC);
81: }
82:
83: /////////////////////////////////////////////
84: // Used with PaintBitmaps below
85: /////////////////////////////////////////////
86: void BlitIt(HDC PaintDC, HDC BmpDC, int i, int j)
87: {
88:    BitBlt(PaintDC, (j - G->Dat.XPos) * G->Dat.GrassX,
```

```
89:         (i * G->Dat.GrassY) + (G->Dat.GrassY * G->Dat.MenuSpace),
90:          G->Dat.GrassX, G->Dat.GrassY, BmpDC, 0, 0, SRCCOPY);
91: }
92:
93: /////////////////////////////////////////////
94: // This is used to paint the background
95: // not to paint the snake.
96: /////////////////////////////////////////////
97: void PaintBitmaps(HDC PaintDC, HDC GrassDC,
98:                   HDC RoadDC, HDC Road2DC)
99: {
100:   G->ScoreRep.NumPrizes = 0;
101:   for (int i = 0; i < MAXY; i++)
102:     for (int j = G->Dat.MinCols; j < G->Dat.MaxCols; j++)
103:     {
104:       switch (G->Map[i][j])
105:       {
106:         case ROADMAP:
107:           BlitIt(PaintDC, RoadDC, i, j);
108:           break;
109:
110:         case GRASSMAP:
111:           BlitIt(PaintDC, GrassDC, i, j);
112:           break;
113:
114:         case PRIZEMAP:
115:           BlitIt(PaintDC, Road2DC, i, j);
116:           G->ScoreRep.NumPrizes++;
117:           break;
118:       }
119:     }
120: }
121:
122: /////////////////////////////////
123: // Paint The Field of Play
124: /////////////////////////////////
125: void PaintPlayingField(HDC PaintDC)
126: {
127:   TSAVEBITMAPARY SB;
128:
129:   HDC GrassDC = GetScaledDC(PaintDC, SB, SMap.Grass, EGrass);
130:   HDC RoadDC = GetScaledDC(PaintDC, SB, SMap.Road, ERoad);
131:   HDC Road2DC = GetScaledDC(PaintDC, SB, SMap.Road2, ERoad2);
132:
133:   PaintBitmaps(PaintDC, GrassDC, RoadDC, Road2DC);
134:
135:   DisposeScaledDC(SB, EGrass);
136:   DisposeScaledDC(SB, ERoad);
137:   DisposeScaledDC(SB, ERoad2);
138: }
139:
140: /////////////////////////////////////////////
141: // Draw the actual bridge to next screen
142: /////////////////////////////////////////////
```

continues

1145

Listing BD4.5. continued

```
143: void MakeAndPaintBridge(HWND hwnd)
144: {
145:    TSAVEBITMAPARY SB;
146:
147:    G->Map[BRIDGEX1][G->Dat.MaxCols - 1] = ROADMAP;
148:    G->Map[BRIDGEX2][G->Dat.MaxCols - 1] = ROADMAP;
149:
150:    HDC PaintDC = GetDC(hwnd);
151:    HDC RoadDC = GetScaledDC(PaintDC, SB, SMap.Road, ERoad);
152:
153:    BitBlt(PaintDC, (JUMPSPACE - 1) * G->Dat.GrassX,
154:        (BRIDGEX1 * G->Dat.GrassY) +
155:        (G->Dat.GrassY * G->Dat.MenuSpace),
156:         G->Dat.GrassX, G->Dat.GrassY, RoadDC, 0, 0, SRCCOPY);
157:    BitBlt(PaintDC, (JUMPSPACE - 1) * G->Dat.GrassX,
158:        (BRIDGEX2 * G->Dat.GrassY) +
159:        (G->Dat.GrassY * G->Dat.MenuSpace),
160:         G->Dat.GrassX, G->Dat.GrassY, RoadDC, 0, 0, SRCCOPY);
161:
162:    DisposeScaledDC(SB, ERoad);
163:    ReleaseDC(hwnd, PaintDC);
164: }
```

Listing BD4.6 shows the SnakoPnt header file.

Listing BD4.6. SNAKOPNT.H.

```
1: ////////////////////////////////////////////////
2: // Program Name: SNAKOPNT.H
3: // Programmer: Charlie Calvert
4: // Description: Draw playing field and the snake
5: // Date: 08/05/93
6: ////////////////////////////////////////////////
7:
8: void MakeAndPaintBridge(HWND hwnd);
9: void DoSnakePainting(HWND hwnd);
10: void PaintPlayingField(HDC PaintDC);
11: void PaintNewSection(HWND hwnd);
```

Listing BD4.7 shows the SnakUtil source file.

Listing BD4.7. SNAKUTIL.CPP.

```
1: ////////////////////////////////////////////////
2: // Program Name: SNAKUTIL.CPP
3: // Programmer: Charlie Calvert
4: // Description: Miscellaneous routines
5: // Date: 08/05/93
6: ////////////////////////////////////////////////
```

```
 7:
 8:  #define STRICT
 9:  #include <windows.h>
10:  #include <windowsx.h>
11:  #include <stdlib.h>
12:  #include <string.h>
13:  #include <stdio.h>
14:  #include "snako.h"
15:
16:  extern PGAMEINFO SaveGame;
17:  extern PGAMEINFO G;
18:
19:  ////////////////////////////////
20:  //   Save Game from Memory
21:  ////////////////////////////////
22:  BOOL ReadGameFromMemory(void)
23:  {
24:    memcpy(G, SaveGame, sizeof(TGAMEINFO));
25:    return TRUE;
26:  }
27:
28:  ////////////////////////////////
29:  //   Save Game to Memory
30:  ////////////////////////////////
31:  BOOL SaveGameToMemory(HWND hwnd)
32:  {
33:    if (!SaveGame)
34:    {
35:      free(SaveGame);
36:      SaveGame = NULL;
37:    }
38:
39:    if((SaveGame = (PGAMEINFO)malloc(sizeof(TGAMEINFO))) == NULL)
40:      MessageBox(hwnd,"Memory is hosed!","Closing Snako",MB_OK);
41:      return FALSE;
42:    }
43:    memcpy(SaveGame, G, sizeof(TGAMEINFO));
44:    return TRUE;
45:  }
46:
47:
48:  ////////////////////////////////////////
49  // Stretch the bitmaps to fit users
50:  // screen resolution
51:  ////////////////////////////////////////
52:  HDC GetScaledDC(HDC PaintDC, TSAVEBITMAPARY SB,
53:                  HBITMAP Bmp, int Num)
54:  {
55:    SB[Num].CompDC = CreateCompatibleDC(PaintDC);
56:    SB[Num].TCompDC = CreateCompatibleDC(PaintDC);
57:    SB[Num].CompBmp = CreateCompatibleBitmap(PaintDC,
58:                         G->Dat.GrassX, G->Dat.GrassY);
59:    SB[Num].OldBmp = SelectBitmap(SB[Num].CompDC, Bmp);
```

continues

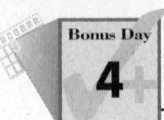

Listing BD4.7. continued

```
60:    SB[Num].OldTBmp = SelectBitmap(SB[Num].TCompDC,
61:                       SB[Num].CompBmp);
62:
63:    StretchBlt(SB[Num].TCompDC,
64:                 0, 0, G->Dat.GrassX, G->Dat.GrassY,
65:                   SB[Num].CompDC, 0, 0, XWIDTH, YHEIGHT, SRCCOPY);
66:
67:    return SB[Num].TCompDC;
68: }
69:
70: /////////////////////////////////////////
71: // Dispose resources created in GetScaledDC
72: /////////////////////////////////////////
73: BOOL DisposeScaledDC(TSAVEBITMAPARY SB, int Num)
74: {
75:    SelectBitmap(SB[Num].CompDC, SB[Num].OldBmp);
76:    SelectBitmap(SB[Num].TCompDC, SB[Num].OldTBmp);
77:    DeleteBitmap(SB[Num].CompBmp);
78:    DeleteDC(SB[Num].CompDC);
79:    DeleteDC(SB[Num].TCompDC);
80:    return TRUE;
81: }
82:
83: /////////////////////////////////////////
84: // Called whenever a new game is started
85: /////////////////////////////////////////
86: void InitializeSections(void)
87: {
88:    int i, StartCol, StartRow;
89:
90:    StartCol = -1;
91:    StartRow = 0;
92:    G->Dat.XPos = 0;
93:    G->Dat.Sections = 1;
94:    G->Dat.MaxCols = 32;
95:    G->Dat.MinCols = 0;
96:    G->Dat.NewScreenStarted = FALSE;
97:
98:    G->ScoreRep.ScreenNum = 1;
99:    G->ScoreRep.TotalScore = 0;
100:    G->ScoreRep.NumPrizes = 0;
101:    G->ScoreRep.Level = 1;
102:
103:    for (i = 0; i < 2; i++)
104:    {
105:      G->SectInfo[i].Dir = RIGHT;
106:      G->SectInfo[i].DirChange = FALSE;
107:      G->SectInfo[i].Col = StartCol - i;
108:      G->SectInfo[i].Row = StartRow;
109:      G->SectInfo[i].OldCol = G->SectInfo[i].Col;
110:      G->SectInfo[i].OldRow = G->SectInfo[i].Row;
111:    }
112: }
113:
```

```
114: ////////////////////////////////////////
115: // So you made it level two...
116: ////////////////////////////////////////
117: void InitializeNewLevel(void)
118: {
119:   int i, StartCol, StartRow;
120:
121:   StartCol = -1;
122:   StartRow = 0;
123:   G->Dat.XPos = 0;
124:   G->Dat.MaxCols = 32;
125:   G->Dat.MinCols = 0;
126:   G->ScoreRep.ScreenNum = 1;
127:
128:   // line 'em up off screen one behind next
129:   for (i = 0; i <= G->Dat.Sections; i++)
130:   {
131:     G->SectInfo[i].Dir = RIGHT;
132:     G->SectInfo[i].DirChange = FALSE;
133:     G->SectInfo[i].Col = StartCol - i;
134:     G->SectInfo[i].Row = StartRow;
135:     G->SectInfo[i].OldCol = G->SectInfo[i].Col;
136:     G->SectInfo[i].OldRow = G->SectInfo[i].Row;
137:   }
138: }
139:
140: ////////////////////////////////////////
141: // Crossing the border...
142: ////////////////////////////////////////
143: void StartNewScreen(HWND hwnd)
144: {
145:   InitializeNewLevel();
146:   ReadArray(hwnd);
147:   InvalidateRect(hwnd, NULL, FALSE);
148: }
149:
150: ////////////////////////////////////////
151: // Read screen arrays into memory
152: // Change case statement to add levels
153: ////////////////////////////////////////
154: int ReadArray(HWND hwnd)
155: {
156:   FILE * fp;
157:   char FileName[50];
158:
159:   switch (G->ScoreRep.Level)
160:   {
161:     case 1: strcpy(FileName, "Screen.Dta"); break;
162:     case 2: strcpy(FileName, "Screen1.Dta"); break;
163:   }
164:
165:   if ((fp = fopen(FileName, "r")) == NULL)
166:   {
167:     MessageBox(hwnd, "No Stream", "NULL", MB_OK);
168:     return FALSE;
169:   }
```

continues

Listing BD4.7. continued

```
170:
171:    if((fread(G->Map, sizeof(G->Map), 1, fp)) == 0)
172:    {
173:      MessageBox(hwnd, "No map", "Grunt", MB_OK);
174:      return FALSE;
175:    }
176:
177:    fclose(fp);
178:
179:    return TRUE;
180: }
181:
182: //////////////////////////////////////////
183: // If you ever get caught on a level
184: // and can't get out even though
185: // you've eaten all dots, call this
186: // from third line of Snako_OnTimer
187: //////////////////////////////////////////
188: void QuickScan(void)
189: {
190:    G->ScoreRep.NumPrizes = 0;
191:    int TotalX = G->Dat.MinCols + JUMPSPACE;
192:
193:    for (int i = 0; i < MAXY; i++)
194:      for (int j = G->Dat.MinCols; j < TotalX; j++)
195:        if(G->Map[i][j] == PRIZEMAP)
196:          G->ScoreRep.NumPrizes++;
197: }
198:
199: //////////////////////////////////////////
200: // Perform setup => initialize Timer
201: //////////////////////////////////////////
202: BOOL SetUpWindow(HWND hwnd)
203: {
204:    if (!SetTimer(hwnd, SNAKETIMER, 175, NULL))
205:    {
206:      MessageBox(hwnd, "No Timers Available", "Snako", MB_OK);
207:      return FALSE;
208:    }
209:      return TRUE;
210: }
```

Listing BD4.8 shows the SnakUtil header file.

Listing BD4.8. SNAKUTIL.H.

```
1: //////////////////////////////////////////////////
2: // Program Name: SNAKUTIL.H
3: // Programmer: Charlie Calvert
4: // Description: Miscellaneous routines
5: // Date: 08/05/93
6: //////////////////////////////////////////////////
```

```
 7:
 8: #include "snako.h"
 9:
10: BOOL ReadGameFromMemory(void);
11: BOOL SaveGameToMemory(HWND hwnd);
12: BOOL DisposeScaledDC(TSAVEBITMAPARY SB, int Num);
13: void StartNewScreen(HWND hwnd);
14: int ReadArray(HWND hwnd);
15: void InitializeSections(void);
16: void QuickScan(void);
17: BOOL SetUpWindow(HWND hwnd);
18: HDC GetScaledDC(HDC PaintDC, TSAVEBITMAPARY SB,
19:                 HBITMAP Bmp, int Num);
```

Listing BD4.9 shows the Score source file.

Listing BD4.9. SCORE.CPP.

```
/////////////////////////////////////
// Program Name: SCORE.CPP
// Programmer: Charlie Calvert
// Description: Score window and SaveScore dialog
// Date: 08/05/93
/////////////////////////////////////

#define STRICT
#include <windows.h>
#include <windowsx.h>
#pragma hdrstop
#include <stdLib.h>
#include <stdio.h>
#include <string.h>
#include "snako.h"
#include "score.h"
#pragma warning(disable: 4068)
#pragma warning(disable: 4100)
#define TOTALSCORES 16

struct TSCORESTRUCT {
  char Name[SCORESIZE];
  LONG Total;
} SCORESTRUCT;

// Variables
LONG NewScore;
HBRUSH Pattern;
TSCORESTRUCT Scores[TOTALSCORES];
HWND hStaticWind, hStaticScore;
HWND hStatScreen, hDotsLeftWin;
HINSTANCE hInst;
HBITMAP Patternmap;
BOOL ScoreRecorded = FALSE;
```

continues

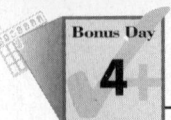

Listing BD4.9. continued

```
extern BOOL ChangeScore = FALSE;
FILE * fp;

///////////////////////////////////////
// ScoreDlgProc
///////////////////////////////////////
void DoScoreDlg(HWND hwnd, HINSTANCE hInst)
{
  FARPROC ScoreBox;

  ScoreBox = MakeProcInstance((FARPROC)ScoreDlgProc, hInst);
  DialogBox(hInst, "Scores", hwnd, (DLGPROC)ScoreBox);
  FreeProcInstance(ScoreBox);
  ChangeScore = FALSE;
}


///////////////////////////////////////
// The window procedure
///////////////////////////////////////
LRESULT CALLBACK EXPORT16 ScoreWndProc(HWND hwnd, UINT Message,
                                    WPARAM wParam, LPARAM lParam)
{
  TSCOREREP * ScoreRep;
  char S[10];

  switch(Message)
  {
    case WM_SETNUMSEGS:
      ScoreRep = (TSCOREREP *)lParam;
      SetWindowText(hStaticWind,itoa(ScoreRep->NumSects,S,10));
      SetWindowText(hDotsLeftWin,ltoa(ScoreRep->NumPrizes,S,10));
      SetWindowText(hStaticScore,ltoa(ScoreRep->TotalScore,S,10));
      SetWindowText(hStatScreen,itoa(ScoreRep->ScreenNum,S,10));
      return 0;

    case WM_SCORE:
      ChangeScore = TRUE;
      NewScore = lParam;
      DoScoreDlg(hwnd, hInst);
      return 0;

    HANDLE_MSG(hwnd, WM_CREATE, Score_OnCreate);
    HANDLE_MSG(hwnd, WM_DESTROY, Score_OnDestroy);
    HANDLE_MSG(hwnd, WM_COMMAND, Score_OnCommand);
    #if defined(WIN32)
    HANDLE_MSG(hwnd, WM_CTLCOLORSTATIC, Score_OnCtlColorStatic);
    HANDLE_MSG(hwnd, WM_CTLCOLORBTN, Score_OnCtlColorBtn);
    HANDLE_MSG(hwnd, WM_CTLCOLOREDIT, Score_OnCtlColorEdit);
    #else
    HANDLE_MSG(hwnd, WM_CTLCOLOR, Score_OnCtlColor);
```

```
    #endif
    default: return Score_DefProc(hwnd, Message, wParam, lParam);
  }
}

/////////////////////////////////////
// Handle WM_CREATE
/////////////////////////////////////
#pragma argsused
BOOL Score_OnCreate(HWND hwnd, CREATESTRUCT FAR* lpCreateStruct)
{
  int YTopRow = 5;    // Place where top row of statics appear
  int YSecRow = 30;   // Second row of statics start here
  int SHeight = 17;   // Height of statics
  int BHeight = 22;   // Height of Buttons

  hInst = lpCreateStruct->hInstance;

  Patternmap = LoadBitmap(hInst, "Pattern");
  if (!Patternmap)
  {
    MessageBox(hwnd, "No Pattern", "Fatal Error", MB_OK);
    return FALSE;
  }

  Pattern = CreatePatternBrush(Patternmap);
  #if defined(WIN32)
  SetClassLong(hwnd, GCL_HBRBACKGROUND, (WORD)Pattern);
  #else
  SetClassWord(hwnd, GCW_HBRBACKGROUND, (WORD)Pattern);
  #endif

  CreateWindow("static", "Num Sections",
               WS_CHILD | WS_VISIBLE | SS_LEFT,
               10, YTopRow, 95, SHeight, hwnd, NULL,
               hInst, NULL);

  hStaticWind = CreateWindow("static", "0",
               WS_CHILD | WS_VISIBLE | SS_LEFT,
               110, YTopRow, 50, SHeight, hwnd, NULL,
               hInst, NULL);

  CreateWindow("static", "Total Score ",
               WS_CHILD | WS_VISIBLE | SS_LEFT,
               10, YSecRow, 95, SHeight, hwnd, NULL,
               hInst, NULL);

  hStaticScore = CreateWindow("static", "0",
               WS_CHILD | WS_VISIBLE | SS_LEFT,
               110, YSecRow, 50, SHeight, hwnd, NULL,
               hInst, NULL);

  // Right Screen

  int XVal = GetSystemMetrics(SM_CXFULLSCREEN) - 160;
```

BD4

continues

Listing BD4.9. continued

```
        CreateWindow("static", "Screen Num",
                    WS_CHILD | WS_VISIBLE | SS_LEFT,
                    XVal, YTopRow, 95, SHeight, hwnd, NULL,
                    hInst, NULL);

        hStatScreen  = CreateWindow("static", "0",
                    WS_CHILD | WS_VISIBLE | SS_LEFT,
                    XVal + 100, YTopRow, 50, SHeight, hwnd, NULL,
                    hInst, NULL);

        CreateWindow("static", "Dots Left",
                    WS_CHILD | WS_VISIBLE | SS_LEFT,
                    XVal, YSecRow, 95, SHeight, hwnd, NULL,
                    hInst, NULL);

        hDotsLeftWin = CreateWindow("static", "0",
                    WS_CHILD | WS_VISIBLE | SS_LEFT,
                    XVal + 100, YSecRow, 50, SHeight, hwnd, NULL,
                    hInst, NULL);

        int Width = GetSystemMetrics(SM_CXSCREEN) / 2;

        CreateWindow("button", "&Start",
                    WS_CHILD | WS_VISIBLE | BS_PUSHBUTTON,
                    Width - 100, YTopRow, 60, BHeight, hwnd,
                    HMENU(ID_START), hInst, NULL);

        CreateWindow("button", "&Fini",
                    WS_CHILD | WS_VISIBLE | BS_PUSHBUTTON,
                    Width - 30, YTopRow, 60, BHeight, hwnd,
                    HMENU(ID_FINI), hInst, NULL);

        CreateWindow("button", "Sco&res",
                    WS_CHILD | WS_VISIBLE | BS_PUSHBUTTON,
                    Width + 40, YTopRow, 60, BHeight, hwnd,
                    HMENU(ID_SCORE), hInst, NULL);

        return TRUE;
}


/////////////////////////////////////
// Handle WM_DESTORY
/////////////////////////////////////
#pragma argsused
void Score_OnDestroy(HWND hwnd)
{
  #if defined WIN32
  SetClassLong(hwnd, GCL_HBRBACKGROUND, NULL);
  #else
  SetClassWord(hwnd, GCW_HBRBACKGROUND, NULL);
  #endif
  DeleteBrush(Pattern);
```

```
    DeleteBitmap(Patternmap);
    PostQuitMessage(0);
}


/////////////////////////////////////
// Handle WM_COMMAND
/////////////////////////////////////
#pragma argsused
void Score_OnCommand(HWND hwnd, int id,
                     HWND hwndCtl, UINT codeNotify)
{
  switch(id)
  {
   case ID_START:
     SendMessage(GetParent(hwnd), WM_START, 0, 0L);
     break;

   case ID_FINI:
     SendMessage(GetParent(hwnd), WM_CLOSE, 0, 0L);
     break;

   case ID_SCORE:
     DoScoreDlg(hwnd, hInst);
     break;
  }
}


/////////////////////////////////////
// Color of controls for ScoreWindow
/////////////////////////////////////
#ifdef WIN32
#pragma argsused
HBRUSH Score_OnCtlColorStatic(HWND hwnd, HDC hdc, HWND hwndChild, int type)
{
  SetTextColor(hdc, RGB(0, 127, 0));
  SetBkMode(hdc, TRANSPARENT);
  return GetStockBrush(BLACK_BRUSH);
}


#pragma argsused
HBRUSH Score_OnCtlColorBtn(HWND hwnd, HDC hdc, HWND hwndChild, int type)
{
  SetTextColor(hdc, RGB(0, 127, 0));
  SetBkMode(hdc, TRANSPARENT);
  return GetStockBrush(BLACK_BRUSH);
}


#pragma argsused
HBRUSH Score_OnCtlColorEdit(HWND hwnd, HDC hdc, HWND hwndChild, int type)
{
  SetTextColor(hdc, RGB(0, 127, 0));
  SetBkMode(hdc, TRANSPARENT);
  return GetStockBrush(BLACK_BRUSH);
}
```

BD4

continues

Listing BD4.9. continued

```
#else
HBRUSH Score_OnCtlColor(HWND hwnd, HDC hdc,
                        HWND hwndChild, int type)
{
  switch(type)
  {
    case CTLCOLOR_STATIC:
    case CTLCOLOR_BTN:
    case CTLCOLOR_EDIT:
      SetTextColor(hdc, RGB(0, 127, 0));
      SetBkMode(hdc, TRANSPARENT);
      return GetStockBrush(BLACK_BRUSH);
  }
  return FORWARD_WM_CTLCOLOR(hwnd, hdc, hwndChild,
                            type, Score_DefProc);
}
#endif

///////////////////////////////////////
// ScoreDlgProc
///////////////////////////////////////
int OpenScores(FILE * fp)
{
  if ((fp = fopen("Scores.Dta", "r+")) == NULL)
  {
    fp = fopen("Scores.Dta", "w+");
    memset(Scores, '\0', sizeof(Scores));
  }
  else
    fread(&Scores, sizeof(Scores), 1, fp);

  fclose(fp);
  return 1;
}

///////////////////////////////////////
// File io
///////////////////////////////////////
BOOL CloseScores(HWND hwnd, FILE * fp)
{
  int Result;

  if ((fp = fopen("Scores.Dta", "w+")) == NULL)
  {
    MessageBox(hwnd, "Error", "er", MB_OK);
    return 0;
  }

  Result = fwrite(&Scores, sizeof(Scores), 1, fp);
  if(!Result)
  {
    MessageBox(hwnd, "Error", "er", MB_OK);
```

```
    return 0;
  }

  fclose(fp);
  return 1;
}

/////////////////////////////////////
// FillListBox
/////////////////////////////////////
void FillListBox(HWND hDlg)
{
  char S[150];

  for (int i = 1; i < TOTALSCORES; i++)
  {
    if (strlen(Scores[i].Name) == 0)
      strcpy(Scores[i].Name, "Sammy");
    sprintf(S, "%2i) %-20s %10ld", i,
            Scores[i].Name, Scores[i].Total);
    SendDlgItemMessage(hDlg, ID_SCOREBOX,
                      LB_ADDSTRING, 0, (LPARAM)S);
  }
}

/////////////////////////////////////
// Swap routine
/////////////////////////////////////
void Swap(int i, int j)
{
  TSCORESTRUCT temp;
  temp = Scores[i];
  Scores[i] = Scores[j];
  Scores[j] = temp;
}

/////////////////////////////////////
// SortScores
/////////////////////////////////////
void SortScores(void)
{
  for (int i = TOTALSCORES; i >= 1; i--)
    for (int j = 2; j <= i; j++)
      if (Scores[j - 1].Total < Scores[j].Total)
        Swap(j-1, j);
}

/////////////////////////////////////
// RecordScore
/////////////////////////////////////
void RecordScore(HWND hDlg)
{
  SendDlgItemMessage(hDlg, ID_SCORENAME, WM_GETTEXT, SCORESIZE,
```

continues

Listing BD4.9. continued

```
                          (LPARAM)Scores[TOTALSCORES - 1].Name);
    Scores[TOTALSCORES-1].Total = NewScore;
    SortScores();
      SendDlgItemMessage(hDlg, ID_SCOREBOX, LB_RESETCONTENT,0,0);
    FillListBox(hDlg);
}


////////////////////////////////////////
// Automatically center a dialog
////////////////////////////////////////
void CenterDialog(HWND hDlg)
{
  RECT R;
  int i = GetSystemMetrics(SM_CXSCREEN);
  int j = GetSystemMetrics(SM_CYSCREEN);
  int Height = GetSystemMetrics(SM_CYCAPTION);
  Height += (GetSystemMetrics(SM_CYDLGFRAME) * 2);
  int Width = GetSystemMetrics(SM_CXDLGFRAME) * 2;
  GetClientRect(hDlg, &R);
  MoveWindow(hDlg, (i / 2)-(R.right / 2),  (j / 2)-R.bottom / 2,
             R.right + Width, R.bottom + Height, FALSE);
}


////////////////////////////////////////
// The Score Dialog Proc so user can
// see lists of scores and add his own
////////////////////////////////////////
#pragma argsused
BOOL CALLBACK ScoreDlgProc(HWND hDlg, WORD Message,
                          WPARAM wParam, LPARAM lParam)
{
  switch(Message)
  {
    case WM_INITDIALOG:
      SetWindowFont(GetDlgItem(hDlg, ID_SCOREBOX),
                  GetStockObject(SYSTEM_FIXED_FONT), FALSE);
      Edit_LimitText(GetDlgItem(hDlg, ID_SCORENAME), 20);
      OpenScores(fp);
      FillListBox(hDlg);
      if (ChangeScore)
        PostMessage(hDlg, WM_FOCUS, 0, 0);
      else
        {
          MoveWindow(GetDlgItem(hDlg, ID_SCOREBOX),
                    10, 6, 365, 225, FALSE);
          MoveWindow(GetDlgItem(hDlg, IDOK),
                    8, 240, 370, 25, FALSE);
          ShowWindow(GetDlgItem(hDlg, ID_SCORENAME), SW_HIDE);
          ShowWindow(GetDlgItem(hDlg, ID_SCORESTAT), SW_HIDE);
          ShowWindow(GetDlgItem(hDlg, ID_NEWNAME), SW_HIDE);
        }
      CenterDialog(hDlg);
      return TRUE;
```

```
      case WM_FOCUS:
        SetFocus(GetDlgItem(hDlg, ID_SCORENAME));
        break;

      case WM_COMMAND:
        switch(wParam)
        {
          case IDOK:
          case IDCANCEL:
            if (!ScoreRecorded)
              RecordScore(hDlg);
            if (ChangeScore)
              CloseScores(hDlg, fp);
            ScoreRecorded = FALSE;
            EndDialog(hDlg, TRUE);
            return TRUE;

          case ID_NEWNAME:
            RecordScore(hDlg);
            ScoreRecorded = TRUE;
            return TRUE;
        }
    }
    return FALSE;
}
```

BD4

Listing BD4.10. SCORE.H.

```
//////////////////////////////////////
// SCORE.H
// Used in SNAKE.CPP
// Programmer: Charlie Calvert
//////////////////////////////////////

#if !defined _SCORE_H
#define _SCORE_H

#if !defined(__WIN32__) && !defined(_WIN32)
#define EXPORT16 __export
#else
#define EXPORT16
#endif

// Const
#define SCORESIZE 75
#define WM_SETNUMSEGS (WM_USER + 0)
#define WM_START (WM_USER + 1)
#define WM_FINI (WM_USER + 2)
#define WM_SCORE (WM_USER + 3)
#define WM_FOCUS (WM_USER + 4)
#define ID_START 190
#define ID_FINI 191
#define ID_SCORE 192
```

continues

Listing BD4.10. continued

```
#define ID_SCOREBOX 175
#define ID_SCORENAME 176
#define ID_SCORESTAT 177
#define ID_NEWNAME 178

// Class Score
#define Score_DefProc    DefWindowProc
BOOL Score_OnCreate(HWND hwnd, CREATESTRUCT FAR* lpCreateStruct);
void Score_OnDestroy(HWND hwnd);
void Score_OnCommand(HWND hwnd, int id,
                     HWND hwndCtl, UINT codeNotify);
#if defined(WIN32)
HBRUSH Score_OnCtlColorStatic(HWND hwnd, HDC hdc, HWND hwndChild, int type);
HBRUSH Score_OnCtlColorBtn(HWND hwnd, HDC hdc, HWND hwndChild, int type);
HBRUSH Score_OnCtlColorEdit(HWND hwnd, HDC hdc, HWND hwndChild, int type);
#else
HBRUSH Score_OnCtlColor(HWND hwnd, HDC hdc,
                        HWND hwndChild, int type);
#endif

#endif

// Procs
LRESULT CALLBACK EXPORT16 ScoreWndProc(HWND, UINT,
                              WPARAM, LPARAM);
BOOL CALLBACK ScoreDlgProc(HWND hDlg, WORD Message,
                           WPARAM wParam, LPARAM lParam);
```

Listing BD4.11. SNAKO.RC.

```
 1: /////////////////////////////////////////////
 2: //   Program Name: SNAKO.RC
 3: //   Programmer: Charlie Calvert
 4: //   Description: A Windows game
 5: //   Date: 08/05/93
 6: /////////////////////////////////////////////
 7:
 8: #include <windows.h>
 9: #include "score.h"
10:
11: Body    BITMAP "body.bmp"
12: Head    BITMAP "head.bmp"
13: Pattern BITMAP "pattern.bmp"
14: Grass   BITMAP "grass.bmp"
15: Road    BITMAP "road.bmp"
16: Road2   BITMAP "road2.bmp"
17:
18: #define NORMALSTY WS_CHILD | WS_VISIBLE | WS_TABSTOP
19: #define LISTBOXSTY LBS_NOTIFY | WS_CHILD | WS_VISIBLE | \
20:                    WS_BORDER | WS_VSCROLL
21:
```

```
22: Scores DIALOG 18, 18, 193, 136
23: STYLE DS_MODALFRAME ¦ WS_POPUP ¦ WS_VISIBLE ¦
          WS_CAPTION ¦ WS_SYSMENU
24: CAPTION "Score Dialog"
25: BEGIN
26:       PUSHBUTTON "Close", IDOK, 8, 121, 176, 10, NORMALSTY
27:       LISTBOX ID_SCOREBOX, 10, 6, 172, 91, LISTBOXSTY
28:       LTEXT "Enter Name", ID_SCORESTAT, 13, 104, 41, 8
29:       EDITTEXT ID_SCORENAME, 56, 102, 124, 12
30: END
```

Listing BD4.12 shows the Snako definition file.

Listing BD4.12. SNAKO.DEF.

```
;SNAKO.DEF

NAME            SNAKO
DESCRIPTION     'Snako (c) 1995 Charlie Calvert'
CODE            PRELOAD MOVEABLE DISCARDABLE
DATA            PRELOAD MOVEABLE MULTIPLE
HEAPSIZE        20000
STACKSIZE       5120
```

Listing BD4.13 shows the Borland makefile for Snako.

Listing BD4.13. SNAKO.MAK (Borland).

```
# SNAKO.MAK

!if !$d(BCROOT)
BCROOT  = $(MAKEDIR)\..
!endif

INCPATH = $(BCROOT)\INCLUDE
LIBPATH = $(BCROOT)\LIB

!if $d(WIN16)
COMPILER= BCC.EXE
RCCOMPILER = BRC.EXE
FLAGS   = -WE -ml -v -w4 -I$(INCPATH) -L$(LIBPATH)
!else
COMPILER= BCC32.EXE
RCCOMPILER = BRC32.EXE -w32
FLAGS   = -WE -v -w4 -I$(INCPATH) -L$(LIBPATH)
!endif

APPNAME = Snako
OBJS = SNAKO.OBJ SCORE.OBJ GRUNT.OBJ SNAKUTIL.OBJ SNAKOPNT.OBJ
```

continues

BD4

Listing BD4.13. continued

```
# linking
$(APPNAME).exe: $(OBJS) $(APPNAME).def $(APPNAME).res
  $(COMPILER) $(FLAGS) $(OBJS)
  $(RCCOMPILER) $(APPNAME).res

# compiling
.cpp.obj:
  $(COMPILER) -c $(FLAGS) { $< }

# resource
$(APPNAME).res: $(APPNAME).rc
  $(RCCOMPILER) -R -I$(INCPATH) $(APPNAME).RC
```

Listing BD4.14 shows the Microsoft makefile for Snako.

Listing BD4.14. SNAKO.MAK (Microsoft).

```
# SNAKOMS.MAK

APPNAME=SNAKO
TARGETOS=WIN95
APPVER=4.0
OBJS=$(APPNAME).OBJ SCORE.OBJ GRUNT.OBJ \
     SNAKUTIL.OBJ SNAKOPNT.OBJ

!include <win32.mak>

all: $(APPNAME).exe

# Update the resource if necessary

$(APPNAME).res: $(APPNAME).rc $(APPNAME).h
  $(rc) $(rcflags) $(rcvars) $(APPNAME).rc

# Update the object files if necessary

# compile
.cpp.obj:
  $(cc) $(cflags) $(cvars) $(cdebug) $<

# Update the executable file if necessary.

$(APPNAME).exe: $(OBJS) $(APPNAME).res
  $(link) $(linkdebug) $(guiflags) -out:$(APPNAME).exe \
  $(OBJS) $(APPNAME).res $(guilibs) comctl32.lib
```

The following bitmaps are used when constructing the Snake program. These bitmaps are compiled into the programs resource file and loaded when the code processes WM_CREATE messages:

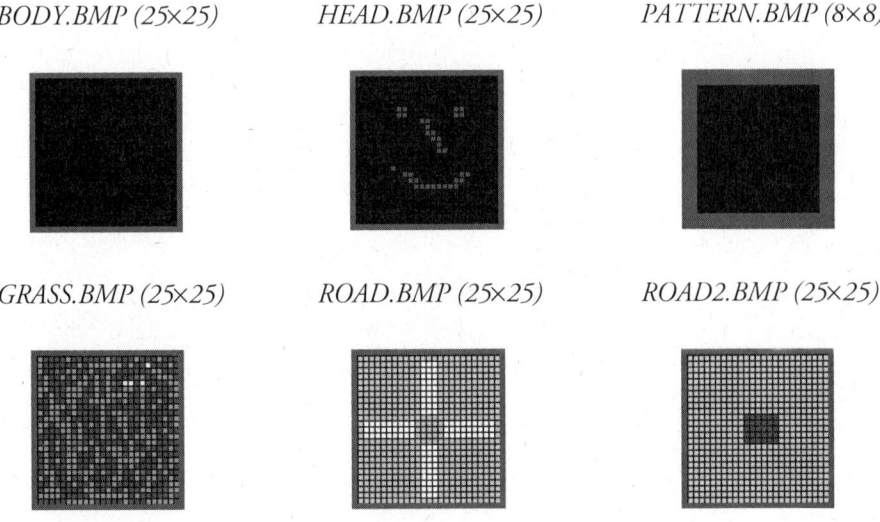

BODY.BMP (25×25)   *HEAD.BMP (25×25)*   *PATTERN.BMP (8×8)*

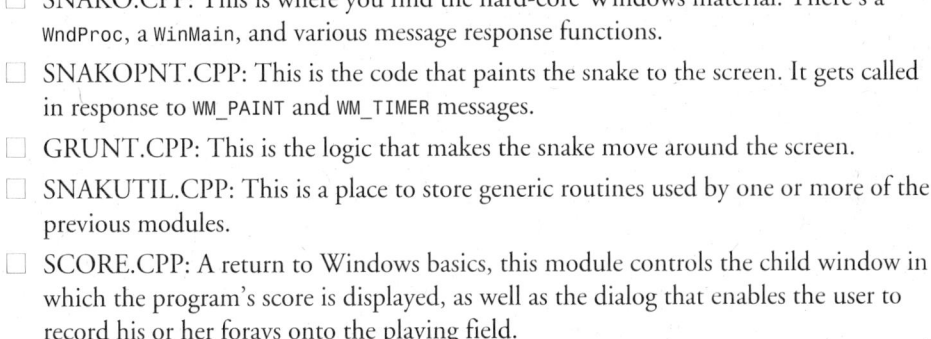

GRASS.BMP (25×25)   *ROAD.BMP (25×25)*   *ROAD2.BMP (25×25)*

Take the time to run the program a few times so that you get a sense of how it looks. A typical scene from the program is shown in Figure BD4.4.

To make things comprehensible and maintainable, I have divided the code into five modules:

- ☐ SNAKO.CPP: This is where you find the hard-core Windows material. There's a `WndProc`, a `WinMain`, and various message response functions.

- ☐ SNAKOPNT.CPP: This is the code that paints the snake to the screen. It gets called in response to `WM_PAINT` and `WM_TIMER` messages.

- ☐ GRUNT.CPP: This is the logic that makes the snake move around the screen.

- ☐ SNAKUTIL.CPP: This is a place to store generic routines used by one or more of the previous modules.

- ☐ SCORE.CPP: A return to Windows basics, this module controls the child window in which the program's score is displayed, as well as the dialog that enables the user to record his or her forays onto the playing field.

This outline should serve as your guide to finding your way around the Snako program. The key point to grasp is that each major function of the program takes place in its own module. Once you grasp the basic categories involved, you should know where to look for a particular routine.

Figure BD4.4.
The Snako program as it appears just after the user has made an error.

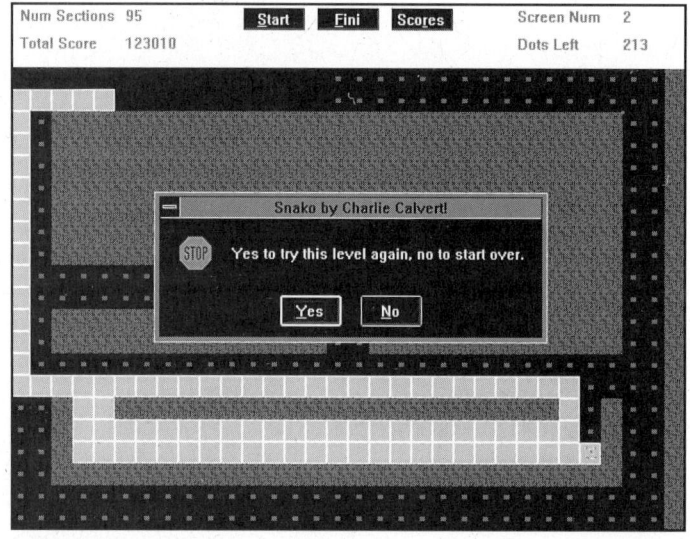

Note: If you want to try the program in 16-bit mode, note that the Snako program is designed to be compiled in the Large memory model. In general, this is probably the best model for all 16-bit Windows programs, but it is especially useful in this particular case because of the way the program uses pointers.

Remember that the Mapper program, presented on Day 17, "Advanced Dialogs: Getting and Setting Data," is used to design the screens for the Snako program. At some point, you should probably take the time to reread what is said there because it reveals much about the basic structure behind Snako.

Strategic Overview

In its simplest possible form, here's the logic that drives the program:

1. The entire state of the game is stored in a single variable called G, which is of type PGAMEINFO. PGAMEINFO is a pointer to a structure defined in SNAKO.H.

2. The game is driven by a single timer. Snake_OnTimer calls MoveBitMap, which is found in the GRUNT.CPP module.

3. MoveBitMap first calls SetColRow. This function is the guiding hand in the Grunt module. It calculates where the snake will go next and updates the program's data accordingly. If the snake is going to die, this is where the error is detected.

4. `MoveBitMap` then calls `DoSnakePainting`, which is located in SNAKOPNT.CPP. This is where all the painting takes place. Notice that the snake is painted separately from the background. If the snake and the background were painted in the same procedure, the whole background would have to be drawn whenever the snake moves. Such a solution proves to be too expensive in terms of clock cycles. (Of course, you could have only the subset of the background where the snake lies be repainted, but that is really just another way of saying that the snake needs to be repainted separately.) Ultimately, it's best to have the snake be one object and the background another. It's a cleaner implementation.

5. Whenever the user moves on to a new screen, the current state of the game is saved into a pointer of type `PGAMEINFO`. If the user makes a mistake, the game can be restored from the information kept in this pointer. The logic that decides when to store and restore the game is in GRUNT.CPP. The actual copying of the pointer is performed in SNAKUTIL.CPP. ·

6. Every time the user earns the right to move on to a new screen, the `MakeGateWay` function, found in GRUNT.CPP, gets called. This function detects a change in level and whether or not the user has won the game.

As I stated earlier, this chapter is included in this book so that you can have a little fun both playing and hacking the Snako game. As a result, I'm not going to spend a lot of time discussing technical issues. But I am going to take a few minutes to describe pointers, file I/O, and a method for centering a dialog. The first two of these subjects are relatively easy to master, but they are essential cornerstones in the construction of most Windows programs.

Using Pointers

The Snako program allocates memory for two pointers. In so doing, it reopens the topic of WIN32 memory management.

Over the next few sections I'm going to be talking about memory issues while using the Snako program as a starting point and concrete example. Day 21, "Threads, Multitasking, and Memory Management," deals with this same subject, primarily from the point of view of a Windows 95 program. This time the subject will be revisited, but from the point of view of a program that needs to run under both Windows 95 and Windows 3.1. Day 21 is about Windows 95-specific memory issues. This chapter is about Windows 95 portability issues, and they way they relate to memory.

The Way We Were...

In the old days, as exemplified by Windows 3.1, programmers used pointers primarily because the data segment was only 64KB in size, which was too confining a space for most program's needs. So instead of using the data segment, programmers branched out into the global heap, where more memory could be found. To understand why this was necessary, you have to understand something about the way a typical 16-bit Windows program treats memory.

Most 16-bit Windows programs are forced to keep their data, stack, and local heap in a single 64KB segment called the DGROUP. This means that there is usually very little room for a program's data. To make up for this lack of available real estate, most Windows 3.1 programs end up allocating memory from the global heap.

For instance, the snake in the Snako program could become very large. As a result, there is a potential need for a good deal of memory. Furthermore, when the user starts a new screen, all the program's data is copied into a variable where it can be retrieved if the user needs to take a second crack at a particular screen. In other words, the Snako program needs to keep track of two fairly large chunks of memory. Because of the way 16-bit Windows programs are structured, there is little room for the program's data. As a result, there is a need to create one or more additional segments in memory with an allocation from the system.

It's time now to become a little more specific and to mention some of the key data structures in the Snako program. In order to keep things simple, Snako initializes a single struct that holds the current state of the game. This structure is called G; its memory is allocated during the call to Snako_OnCreate and deallocated during the call to Snako_OnDestroy.

Struct G is of type PGAMEINFO and holds the current state and shape of the snake, the current appearance of the screen, the score, and the screen and level numbers. More specifically, it encapsulates three additional structs and an array, all of which are defined in SNAKO.H:

```
typedef struct {
  TSCOREREP ScoreRep;
  char Map[MAXY][MAXX];
  TDATA Dat;
  TSECTINFO SectInfo[MAXSECTS];
} TGAMEINFO;
```

If you want to understand Snako, you have to become familiar with TGAMEINFO. Remember that it contains all the variables that define the current state of the game. Following is a brief overview of the structure:

☐ TSCOREREP is a structure that keeps track of the current level, screen, score, and the number of sections in the snake's body. Most of this information is displayed to the user in the SCORE.CPP module.

☐ Map holds the two-dimensional array that defines the current appearance of the game board. Each item in the array is set to either 1, 2, or 3 (GRASSMAP, PRIZEMAP, or ROADMAP), depending on whether it designates the grass bitmap, prize bitmap, or road bitmap.

☐ TDATA contains information about the current screen dimensions as well as a number of other miscellaneous variables that need a home.

☐ TSECTINFO is used in an array in which each member defines the current state of a particular section of the snake.

Here's how Snako allocates the memory for G:

```
if((G = (PGAMEINFO)malloc(sizeof(TGAMEINFO))) == NULL)
{
  MessageBox(hwnd, "No Memory!", "Closing Snako", MB_OK);
  return FALSE;
}
```

As you can see, nothing unusual is going on here. This is just a simple call to malloc, exactly as it would be performed in DOS. The end result is an allocation of memory designated explicitly for Snako's data. In other words, in 16-bit Windows, it moves the program's data out of the cramped DGROUP and into the wide open spaces of the heap! In WIN32, it moves the memory into the program's sole heap. Is this necessary in Windows 95? No. The original address space the program was mapped into was plenty big enough for a structure of this size. You don't need to create a pointer, but it won't cause any significant harm either. The point is that this system allows you to write code that can be ported back and forth between Windows 95 and Windows 3.1. Portability can be a very important feature in the current market, so it's worth considering.

Note: Suppose you create a program that is of general interest to the public. If 50 percent of your users are on Windows 3.1 and 50 percent on Windows 95, then if you write Windows 95–specific code, you are losing half your potential audience. So you want to write code that can be recompiled for both platforms. That's why portability is important.

From a conceptual point of view, very different things are happening in WIN32 and WIN16. On Day 21 you saw just how different.

Notice that this program uses malloc rather than going directly to Windows API calls such as GlobalAlloc, HeapAlloc, or VirtualAlloc. If you use standard runtime calls such as malloc, then it's up to the compiler to map your code through to the best possible Windows API function. In general, it's a good idea to respect the knowledge of the compiler developers who choose these calls. Memory-management routines are generally coded by the best developers at places such as Borland, Microsoft, or Watcom. Unless you have a profound understanding of Windows memory management, it's usually not a bad idea to trust their judgment. In other words, they will probably map the 16-bit version of this call to `GlobalAlloc` and the 32-bit version of the call to `HeapAlloc` or `VirtualAlloc`. (In most cases, `VirtualAlloc` will be favored over `HeapAlloc`, but both calls are useful.) You could have done the same with conditional compilation, but it's easier, and perhaps wiser, to let the compiler makers do it for you. Furthermore, these calls provide instant portability between different environments. Portability is one of the main reasons to use the C programming language, and you should take advantage of it whenever possible.

The *malloc* Function

Syntax

```
void *malloc(size_t size);
```

The `malloc` function returns a block of memory from the heap. It takes one parameter that designates the desired size of the memory allocation. Programmers typically use the `sizeof` keyword in this parameter in order to let the compiler calculate the size of a variable. Most of the time it's necessary to typecast the result of `malloc` to the type of the variable for which you are allocating memory. Even in the wide open spaces of WIN32, programmers need to be aware that a call to `malloc` might fail due to a lack of memory. This is much less likely on most Windows machines, but it is still an issue that you can't afford to overlook. The example below shows how to check for out-of-memory errors.

Here's an example:

```
#define MAXSTRLEN 100
char * MyString;

if((MyString = (char *)malloc(MAXSTRLEN)) == NULL)
{
  MessageBox(hwnd, "No Memory!", "Error", MB_OK);
  return FALSE;
}
```

When it comes time to destroy the memory allocated by `malloc`, you need to do nothing more than make a simple call to `free`:

```
free(G);
```

I have chosen to concentrate on `malloc` because it should be familiar to the widest possible audience. However, you can use either the `new` and `delete` operators or native Windows functions such as `VirtualAlloc` and `VirtualFree`, or `HeapAlloc` and `HeapFree`. (None of these functions is better than the other. However, in order of preference, I would go with `new` or `malloc` first, then `VirtualAlloc`, then `HeapAlloc`. However, all the calls are very useful, and they are so similar that no one call should take precedence over the others in your mind.) The `GlobalAlloc` and `GlobalFree` functions are available for compatibility with Windows 16. However, it's both simpler and wiser to call either `new` or `malloc` rather than calling `GlobalAlloc` directly (see the note following the Syntax section). In other words, `GlobalAlloc` is out of date and should not be called unless you have no other choice.

The *GlobalAlloc* Function

`HGLOBAL GlobalAlloc(UINT fuAlloc, DWORDcbAlloc)`

`UINT fuAlloc`	A flag designating the traits of the memory to be allocated. Use this field to state whether you want the memory to be moveable, fixed, discardable, and so forth.
`DWORD cbAlloc`	A parameter that specifies how much memory you want to allocate.

Every time you call `GlobalAlloc`, you should also make a call to `GlobalLock` before you attempt to use the memory. To deallocate the memory, call `GlobalUnlock` and `GlobalFree`.

Remember, this is a Windows 3.1–specific call. It still works under Windows NT or Windows 95, but it's kept active only for compatibility reasons. It is not as efficient as calling the WIN32 `HeapAlloc` function directly.

BD4

Here's an example:

```
HGLOBAL hglb;
char FAR* MyString;

hglb = GlobalAlloc(GPTR, 1024);
MyString = (char *)GlobalLock(hglb);
strcpy(MyString, "Fine Tuna");
MessageBox(hwnd, MyString, "Info", MB_OK);
GlobalUnlock(hglb);
GlobalFree(hglb);
```

Note: Under Windows 3.1, smaller allocations of memory are often handled by a compiler's suballocator. Suballocators exist because no 16-bit protected mode program can ask the system for more than 8,192 memory allocations. In other words, on any one system, only 8,192 pointers can be requested from the operating environment at any one time. This means that if your program makes 8,000 allocations in a linked list, all other programs on the system only have 192 allocations available to them.

As a result, many compilers automatically allocate blocks of memory and then parcel chunks out to programs with a suballocator when needed. That is, the compiler allocates a chunk of some 4,000 bytes and then parcels this memory out to you in bits and pieces when you need it. As a result, only the initial 4,000-byte hit takes up one of the 8KB of available handles. Each suballocation comes to you free, at least in terms of the 8,192 available handles.

This Windows 3.1–specific process takes place transparently, without the programmer ever having to worry about how it works. Requests for relatively large blocks of memory, however, are passed directly to Windows with a call to GlobalAlloc. The results of this call are passed back to your program. The presence of these suballocator schemes is one of the major reasons for using malloc or new rather than calling GlobalAlloc directly. See your compiler documentation for details. Really. Go look at the docs.

Here's the portion of the SNAKUTIL.CPP file in which a backup copy of the game's data is copied to a second pointer of type PGAMEINFO:

```
31: BOOL SaveGameToMemory(HWND hwnd)
32: {
33:   if (!SaveGame)
34:   {
35:     free(SaveGame);
36:     SaveGame = NULL;
37:   }
38:
39:   if((SaveGame = (PGAMEINFO)malloc(sizeof(TGAMEINFO))) == 40 NULL)
40:   {
41:     MessageBox(hwnd, "No Memory!", "Closing Snako", MB_OK);
42:     return FALSE;
43:   }
44:   memcpy(SaveGame, G, sizeof(TGAMEINFO));
45:   return TRUE;
46: }
```

Once again, this code should look very familiar to anyone who has used pointers in DOS, UNIX, or elsewhere.

The basic plan is simply to allocate some memory, and then use memcpy to move the program's data from one place on the heap to another. When it's time to get it back, the process is carried out in reverse. Notice that Snako is careful to check to see whether it needs to dispose of the SaveGame pointer before allocating new memory and copying the program's data into it. The program can always tell whether memory has been allocated for SaveGame by checking if the pointer has been set to NULL. To make this system work, you must specifically assign NULL to a pointer at startup time.

When the game is done, both G and SaveGame are deallocated, if necessary, in response to a WM_DESTROY message. You have to be absolutely certain that you always destroy every pointer you allocate, because in Windows 3.1 allocations can remain intact even after your program has ended. This can muddy the waters so badly that the entire Windows system can come crashing down around the user's ears.

Under Windows 95, a 16-bit program that makes this kind of error won't necessarily bring down the whole system. It is more likely to simply damage the performance of other 16-bit programs running on the system. If you close all the 16-bit programs that are running, then you can clean up the mess without having to restart Windows.

Under Windows 95, each program has its own address space. Therefore, if it wastes resources, all you have to do to clean it up is to shut down the program. When the program closes, all the resources associated with it are also disposed.

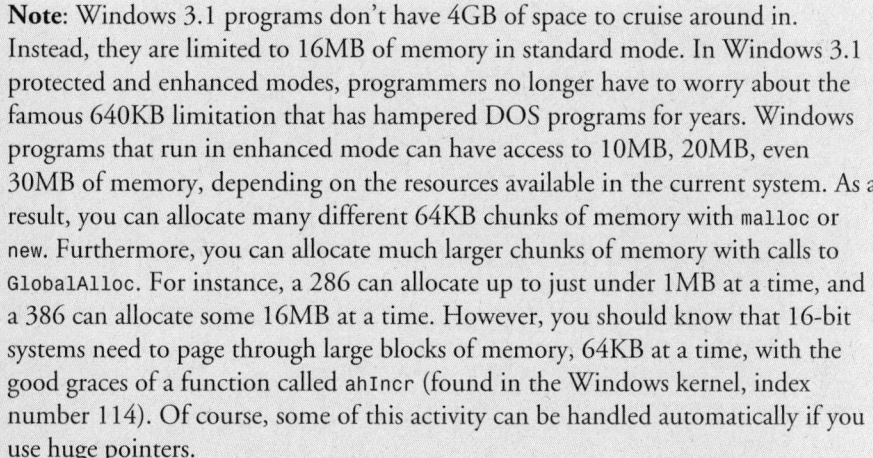

Note: Windows 3.1 programs don't have 4GB of space to cruise around in. Instead, they are limited to 16MB of memory in standard mode. In Windows 3.1 protected and enhanced modes, programmers no longer have to worry about the famous 640KB limitation that has hampered DOS programs for years. Windows programs that run in enhanced mode can have access to 10MB, 20MB, even 30MB of memory, depending on the resources available in the current system. As a result, you can allocate many different 64KB chunks of memory with malloc or new. Furthermore, you can allocate much larger chunks of memory with calls to GlobalAlloc. For instance, a 286 can allocate up to just under 1MB at a time, and a 386 can allocate some 16MB at a time. However, you should know that 16-bit systems need to page through large blocks of memory, 64KB at a time, with the good graces of a function called ahIncr (found in the Windows kernel, index number 114). Of course, some of this activity can be handled automatically if you use huge pointers.

None of these confusing limitations hamper WIN32 programs. In fact, Windows 95 programmers can forget all of this stuff and just assume that there is plenty of room in the immediate address space of their program. If they want to allocate memory, they can use the heap, or else use virtual memory to tap into the potentially vast resources of space that reside on their hard drives.

Because Windows 95 uses virtual memory so readily, it is usually a good idea not to fill your hard drive to the brim. Instead, you should always try to leave 30 or 40MB free for it to roam. (No, I can't find 40 free megabytes either, but this is what we *ought* to be doing.)

BD4

After reading this last section, it should be clear to you that memory is a radically different beast in Windows than in DOS, and even more radically different in Windows 95 and Windows NT. The presence of functions like `malloc` or operators like `new` can serve to make the strange familiar; but you should always be aware that there are many new ideas to master. However, if all you need to do is create additional data space for your program, your DOS- or UNIX-based knowledge of pointers will stand you in good stead.

To sum up:

☐ Always remember that under Windows 3.1 your stack, data, and local heap have to share 64KB data segments. This means many Windows programs have to use pointers to store their data. If you are willing to forego Windows 3.1 compatibility, then you can step out from under the shadow of this red rock and into the vast reaches of the 4GB frontier.

☐ It's often not a bad idea to use `malloc` or the `new` operator rather than `VirtualAlloc`, `HeapAlloc`, or `GlobalAlloc`. Parts of the standard C library such as `malloc` or `new` are useful because they will be ported back and forth between WIN16 and WIN32 by the compiler.

☐ Use `GlobalAlloc` (WIN16) or `HeapAlloc` (WIN32) to grab chunks of memory that are many megabytes in size. If you want safe access to really huge chunks of memory, WIN32 programmers can use `VirtualAlloc` or memory-mapped files (`CreateFile`).

A Little File I/O

The main theme of the last section was that you can handle pointers in Windows much the way they are handled in DOS or UNIX. The same is true of file I/O.

For instance, here is a function from SCORE.CPP that opens up the file containing a list of people's names and their scores. The information retrieved from disk in the `OpenScores` function is displayed in a dialog, as shown in Figure BD4.5.

Here is the code for the OpenScores function:

```
231: int OpenScores(FILE * fp)
232: {
233:   if ((fp = fopen("Scores.Dta", "r+")) == NULL)
234:   {
235:     fp = fopen("Scores.Dta", "w+");
236:     memset(Scores, '\0', sizeof(Scores));
237:   }
238:   else
239:     fread(&Scores, sizeof(Scores), 1, fp);
240:
241:   fclose(fp);
242:   return 1;
243: }
```

Figure BD4.5.
The Score *dialog.*

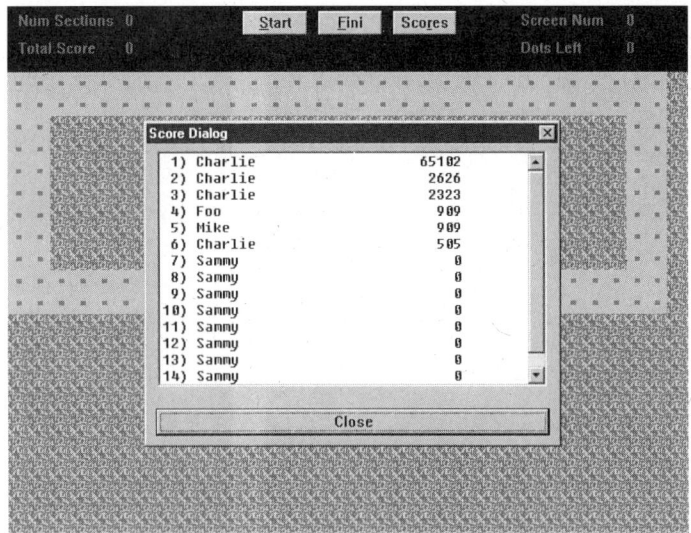

This is the same type of code you might see in a primer for the C language. The calls to fopen, fread, and fclose are all totally standard, though there is a dearth of error checking.

The point here is simply that you can perform file I/O in DOS-based Windows applications exactly as you do in UNIX or DOS. The only possible exception is when you need to copy a file from one location to another. In that case, you might want to call on the handy LZCopyFile API function.

The *LZCopy* Function

```
LONG LZCopy(hfSource, hfDest)
```

> HFILE hfSource;   Handle obtained from CreateFile, or any C library routine
> that opens a file in binary mode.
>
> HFILE hfDest;   Handle to a destination file obtained from the previously listed
> sources.

If the file in question were compressed with the COMPRESS.EXE program, which comes with the Borland and Microsoft compilers, this function would decompress and copy the file. Otherwise it would simply copy the file. Don't use OpenFile or _lopen with this procedure. These functions are now obsolete and are available only for compatibility reasons. Windows 95 and Windows NT programmers should use CreateFile or one of the C runtime library routines.

Here's an example:

```
HFILE Source, Dest;
LZCopy(Source, Dest);
```

BD4

1173

That's all I'm going to say about file I/O. The reason this subject is so easy to explain is simply that it's one part of the Windows 3.1 environment that is inherited almost entirely intact from the DOS world. If you want to learn more about file I/O in Windows, you should see Week 1 in Review or Day 21.

Dynamic Dialogs and Centering a Dialog

The Score dialog, shown in Figures BD4.5 and BD4.6, is interesting because it can be seen in one of two different states. In one case, all that appears at the bottom of the dialog is a single Close button, whereas at other times, there are a Close button, an edit control, and a static control.

Figure BD4.6.

Compare this image with Figure BD4.5 to see two different views of the Score dialog.

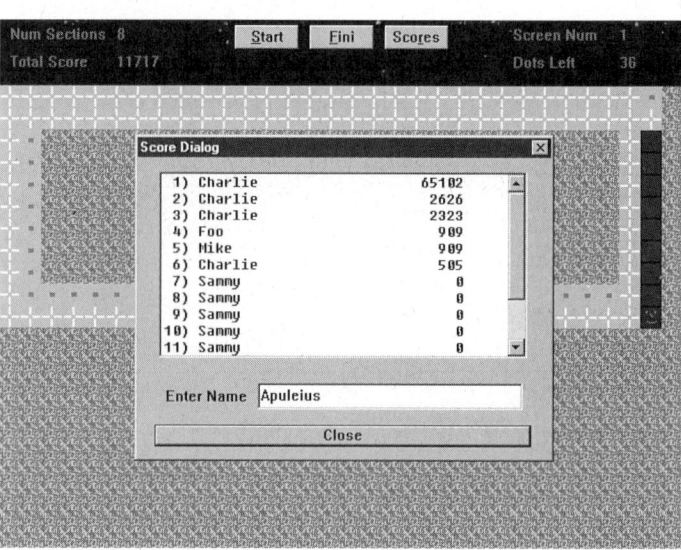

Rather than design two separate dialogs, Snako opts to change the appearance of ScoreDlg at runtime. It does so with the following code, drawn from SCORE.CPP:

```
MoveWindow(GetDlgItem(hDlg, ID_SCOREBOX), 10,6,365,225, FALSE);
MoveWindow(GetDlgItem(hDlg, IDOK), 8, 240, 370, 25, FALSE);
ShowWindow(GetDlgItem(hDlg, ID_SCORENAME), SW_HIDE);
ShowWindow(GetDlgItem(hDlg, ID_SCORESTAT), SW_HIDE);
```

This code first decreases the size of the listbox that holds the scores for the program. Then it adjusts the size of the Close button and hides both the static text and the edit control normally found at the bottom of the dialog. Notice that the HWND of the controls is obtained through calls to GetDlgItem, and that any window can be hidden by calling ShowWindow with the SW_HIDE identifier.

In addition to the handwaving that changes the appearance of the score dialog, SCORE.CPP also contains a useful little function that ensures that the dialog always appears in the middle of the screen (see Figure BD4.6). This function, called `CenterDialog`, can be used with any standard dialog that is declared with the `WS_CAPTION` and `DS_MODALFRAME` styles:

```
325: void CenterDialog(HWND hDlg)
326: {
327:   RECT R;
328:   int i = GetSystemMetrics(SM_CXSCREEN);
329:   int j = GetSystemMetrics(SM_CYSCREEN);
330:   int Height = GetSystemMetrics(SM_CYCAPTION);
331:   Height += (GetSystemMetrics(SM_CYDLGFRAME) * 2);
332:   int Width = GetSystemMetrics(SM_CXDLGFRAME) * 2;
333:   GetClientRect(hDlg, &R);
334:   MoveWindow(hDlg, (i / 2)-(R.right / 2),
335:             (j / 2)-R.bottom / 2,
336:                 R.right + Width, R.bottom + Height, FALSE);
337: }
```

`CenterDialog` uses `GetSystemMetrics` to query Windows for the resolution of the current screen and `GetClientRect` to obtain the size of the dialog. It then uses this information to calculate where the dialog should be placed to find the center of the screen. The additional code takes into account the thickness of the dialog's frame and caption. Notice that the frame's width and height have to be factored in twice because they are found on both the top and bottom as well as the left and right of every dialog.

Closing Thoughts: Is Snako Really a Windows Program?

In terms of design, Snako breaks every stricture laid down in the Windows interface guides. In so doing, it shows that Windows gives the programmer a very flexible set of tools that can produce a wide variety of results. Most of the time it's best to stick with the traditional elements of a Windows program. However, if you want to break out of that mold, there is no need to regard the elements of the Windows interface as a straight jacket.

Intellectual experimentation has always been at the heart of the computer world. Individual programmers, and not bureaucratic committees, will almost always be the ones who make the breakthroughs that point the way to how applications are constructed in the future.

On the other hand, I want to make it clear that the classic Windows interface, used in 90 percent of the programs in this book, is anything but trivial. Most of the time, it's best to write programs that everyone can readily understand. The best way to do that is to give your application an interface that's already familiar thanks to thousands of other well-crafted programs. The heritage of interface design, represented by the classic Windows program, is the fruit of many years of experience. Use it and enjoy it.

In particular, be sure to study the new interface guidelines that ship with Windows 95 compilers. Microsoft spent a lot of time testing the new interface. They brought people into rooms, turned cameras on them, and measured how they reacted to all kinds of different screen elements. When they were done, they had some fairly concrete data on how to construct at least one kind of interface.

Besides the recent research by Microsoft, you should also consider obtaining a copy of *Systems Application Architecture Common User Access Advanced Interface Design Guide (SAA CUA Interface Design Guide)*, published by IBM.

My main point, however, is that if you have an idea for a totally different type of program, you should try to bring it to fruition. Windows shouldn't become a straitjacket. All these silly committees can outlaw everything but your imagination!

Whatever happens, remember the following key rules:

☐ Good programmers write reams of code. Most of the programs in this book are meant to be starting points and clues for dedicated, hard-working hackers. Don't be content with these starting points. Push the code to the limit and go on to develop your own ideas.

☐ Windows can be difficult at times, but it's also extremely seductive. If you're not having fun and are not fascinated by what you are doing, it will become more and more difficult to write good code. Willpower and ambition are two important characteristics of a good programmer, but they don't tell the whole story. You need more than discipline—you need passion leavened with a lively sense of humor. The passion helps you write the best possible code; the humor helps you preserve your sanity.

Summary

This chapter contains an overview of the Snako program, some general discussion of Windows coding techniques, and coverage of the following issues:

☐ Using `malloc`, `new`, and `GlobalAlloc` to obtain memory from the heap

☐ Simple file I/O in Windows

☐ Centering dialogs

Q&A

Q **I want Windows 3.1 compatibility, but I'm having trouble working inside the limitations of the 64KB DGROUP. What else can I do to save data space?**

A If possible, you should save all your program's strings into a string resource, or a user-defined resource. Techniques for doing this were explored on Day 6, "Introduction to Resources," and Day 7, "Advanced Resources: Bitmaps and Dialogs." If you need to move things onto the heap, remember that arrays are the data structures that tend to take up the most space. If you can move an array onto the heap, you'll probably gain back a sizable chunk of your data segment. Remember also that you can change the structure of your heap by working with the HEAPSIZE and STACKSIZE variables in a project's DEF file.

Q **What is the difference between the Windows 3.1 local heap and the global heap?**

A A Windows 3.1 local heap resides inside the 64KB of the DGROUP, along with a program's stack and its data. The global heap is really just another name for any free-floating, unassigned memory available on a Windows 3.1 system. It is limited in size only by the amount of RAM and virtual RAM available on a particular machine. Windows has two sets of memory allocation routines: one for the local heap and one for the global heap. For instance, the local counterpart of GlobalAlloc is called LocalAlloc. LocalAlloc has an accompanying LocalFree function. In general, LocalAlloc is somewhat faster than GlobalAlloc and should be used for small, short-term memory needs. Neither function is very efficient under Windows 95. Furthermore, there is no distinction between the two functions in Windows 95, since there is no such thing as either a WIN32 local heap or global heap. These functions are outdated and should be replaced with the memory schemes shown on Day 21.

Q **Is there a relationship between a Windows 3.1 local heap and the resources that get expended when a program calls the GDI?**

A Good question. The reason you have to be so careful to free the resources obtained from Windows 3.1 GDI calls is that they are all stored on the GDI.EXE local heap. When you make calls to RegisterClass or CreateWindow, the information you supply is stored in the USER.EXE local heap. Because these areas are never larger than 64KB in size, you have to be very careful to free the memory back up again; if not, the GDI heap will be expended. If you want to see the contents of your own local heap, or any other local heap, you can do so by using the ToolHelp DLL and the LocalInfo, LocalFirst, and LocalNext functions. This limitation on the size of the GDI heap is mitigated considerably under Windows 95. However, 16-bit programs run on Windows 95 still have to contend with it, even though the situation is not as severe as before. 32–bit programs run under Windows 95 are relatively free of these types of restraints. However, they can be affected by an errant 16-bit application that is

BD4

wasting its resources. This type of problem makes it clear that we as programmers should do all we can to move everyone to WIN32 code as soon as possible. 16-bit programming is history; the future is Windows 95, Windows NT, and perhaps OS/2.

Workshop

The Workshop provides quiz questions to help you solidify your understanding of the material covered and exercises to provide you with experience in using what you've learned. Try to understand the quiz and exercise answers before continuing on to the next chapter. Answers are provided in Appendix A.

Quiz

1. What book defines the elements of the Windows interface and who publishes it?
2. The acronym CUA stands for what three words?
3. What does the `malloc` function return?
4. What three functions are normally called whenever you call `GlobalAlloc`?
5. What three types of memory appear in the `DGROUP`?
6. How many times can a single program call `GlobalAlloc`?
7. What is a suballocator, and why would you ever want to use one?
8. How can you hide a window so that the user does not know it is in memory?
9. What single native Windows function can be used to copy a file from one subdirectory to another?
10. Name at least one function used to change the location of a dialog.

Exercises

1. Change Snako so that it is possible to go through four different levels and a total of 16 screens.
2. Work out a way to enable users to save the state of a Snako game to disk and then reload it later.
3. Change the Snako program so it will not save the state of the game to memory if a user is entering a screen for the second time. In other words, save the state of the game only the first time the user enters a new screen.
4. Enable the user to select the speed at which the snake moves and the speed at which it grows.

4

Richedits: Creating Your Own Word Processor

BONUS DAYS

IN REVIEW

BD 1

BD 2

BD 3

BD 4

In this chapter you will get a look at the richedit control. This is another one of the Windows 95 common controls, so this program will only compile for WIN32.

I'm putting this control last in the book because I think it's one of the more useful and interesting controls in all of Windows 95. In particular, you can use richedit controls to format text with different fonts and different colors. Unlike using a standard edit control, you can also switch fonts as many times as you want throughout a single document. That is, you can have the first word in your document be in one particular font and in one particular color, and the next word can then have a different font and a different color. In fact, you can change fonts or colors at any time.

About RTF

The letters RTF stand for rich text format. This is a standard format created by Microsoft and used to port documents from one platform to another. It is particularly useful when people need to take a formatted document from a Macintosh and send it over to a PC, but it could also be used to port from one word processor to another.

The RTF format is used by the Windows help compiler. All the help files that you read while in Windows presumably pass through an RTF stage at one time or another. The help compiler chews on RTF files the same way a C compiler gobbles up text files.

Here is what a typical, very small RTF file looks like:

```
{\rtf1\ansi\deff0\deftab720
{\fonttbl{\f0\fnil MS Sans Serif;}
{\f1\fnil\fcharset2 Symbol;}
{\f2\fswiss\fprq2 System;}}
{\colortbl\red0\green0\blue0;}
\deflang1033\pard\plain\f2\fs20\b A little text to look at
\par }
```

When used in an RTF control, this code produces a single line of text in the system font, as shown in Figure RB.1.

It's not important that you understand how RTF code works. However, a quick glance at the lines above reveal that the code establishes the type of font to use and the color of the font, then lists the text. The \par symbol marks a new paragraph. If you want additional information, the entire RTF spec is available for downloading from Microsoft forums on CompuServe, the World Wide Web, MSN, and so on.

The RTF format is not particularly easy to read, and it is notoriously weak on structure. However, it's a powerful tool for formatting and porting text. Microsoft Word understands it, as does WordPerfect, and a number of other editors. Now that the control is available for general distribution by all Windows programmers, we can expect to see this format used with much greater frequency. In fact, I would assume that the days of the Windows NotePad application are numbered.

Figure RB.1.

The SimpRTF program displaying a single line of text.

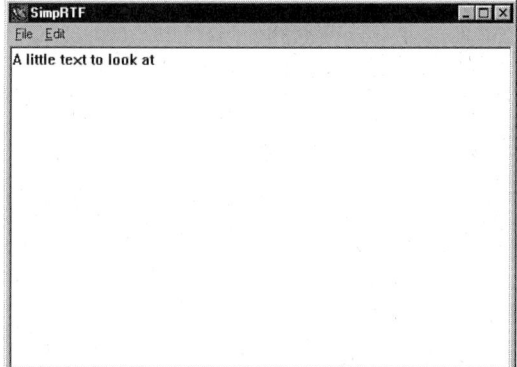

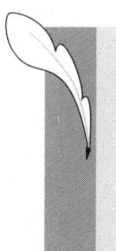

Note: The RTF control is not nearly as powerful as Microsoft Word, or as WordPad. However, it is much smaller.

The SimpRTF program included with this chapter loads about as quickly as the Windows NotePad, but it is much more powerful in terms of its formatting capabilities and in terms of the size of the file it can handle. The power of the RTF control raises the possibility that the RTF format eventually will become the *lingua franca* of the Windows world.

That's enough talk. It's time now to get the SimpRTF program up and running. This program does not exercise all of the capabilities of the RTF control, but it gives you enough code to get a feeling for what you can do with this tool. You will find the code for the SimpRTF program in Listings RB.1 through RB.8.

Listing RB.1. The main file for the SimpRTF program.

```
//////////////////////////////////////////////////////
// SIMPRTF.CPP
// Copyright (c) 1995 Charlie Calvert.
// COMMENT: Demonstrates the RTF control. WIN32 only.
// DATE: 07/18/95
//////////////////////////////////////////////////////

#define STRICT
#include <windows.h>
#include <windowsx.h>
#include <richedit.h>
#include <commctrl.h>
#pragma hdrstop
#include <stdio.h>
#include "rtffuncs.h"
```

continues

Listing RB.1. continued

```
#include "simprtf.h"
#pragma warning (disable : 4068)

HINSTANCE hInst;
char szAppName[] = "SimpRTF";
char szTitle[]   = "Simple RTF";
CHAR FileName[STRSIZE];
HINSTANCE hRichEditLib;
HWND hRichEdit;

///////////////////////////////////////////////////////////
// Program entry point
///////////////////////////////////////////////////////////
#pragma argsused
int APIENTRY WinMain(HINSTANCE hInstance, HINSTANCE hPrevInstance,
                     LPSTR lpCmdLine, int nCmdShow)
{
    MSG msg;

    if (!Register(hInstance))
        return (FALSE);

    if (!Create(hInstance, nCmdShow))
        return (FALSE);


    while (GetMessage(&msg, NULL, 0, 0))
    {
        TranslateMessage(&msg); // get virtual key codes
        DispatchMessage(&msg);
    }
    return (msg.wParam);
}


///////////////////////////////////////////////////////////
// Register
///////////////////////////////////////////////////////////
BOOL Register(HINSTANCE hInstance)
{
    WNDCLASSEX  WndClass;

    WndClass.cbSize        = sizeof(WNDCLASSEX);
    WndClass.style         = CS_HREDRAW | CS_VREDRAW;
    WndClass.lpfnWndProc   = (WNDPROC)WndProc;
    WndClass.cbClsExtra    = 0;
    WndClass.cbWndExtra    = 0;
    WndClass.hInstance     = hInstance;
    WndClass.hIcon         = LoadIcon(hInstance, "SimpRTFIcon");
    WndClass.hCursor       = LoadCursor(NULL, IDC_ARROW);
    WndClass.hbrBackground = (HBRUSH)(COLOR_WINDOW+1);
    WndClass.lpszMenuName  = szAppName;
    WndClass.lpszClassName = szAppName;
    WndClass.hIconSm       = LoadIcon(hInstance, "SimpRTFIcon16");

    return (RegisterClassEx(&WndClass) != 0);
}
```

```
//////////////////////////////////////////////////
// Create
//////////////////////////////////////////////////
BOOL Create(HINSTANCE hInstance, int nCmdShow)
{
  hInst = hInstance;

  HWND hWindow = CreateWindowEx(0, szAppName, szAppName,
                    WS_OVERLAPPEDWINDOW,
                    CW_USEDEFAULT, CW_USEDEFAULT,
                    CW_USEDEFAULT, CW_USEDEFAULT,
                    NULL, NULL, hInstance, NULL);

  if (!hWindow)
    return FALSE;

  ShowWindow(hWindow, nCmdShow);
  UpdateWindow(hWindow);

  return TRUE;
}


//////////////////////////////////////////////////
// Window Procedure
//////////////////////////////////////////////////
#pragma argsused
LRESULT CALLBACK WndProc(HWND hwnd, UINT message,
                         WPARAM wParam, LPARAM lParam)
{
  switch (message)
  {
    HANDLE_MSG(hwnd, WM_CREATE, SimpRTF_OnCreate);
    HANDLE_MSG(hwnd, WM_DESTROY, SimpRTF_OnDestroy);
    HANDLE_MSG(hwnd, WM_CLOSE, SimpRTF_OnClose);
    HANDLE_MSG(hwnd, WM_COMMAND, SimpRTF_OnCommand);
    HANDLE_MSG(hwnd, WM_SETFOCUS, SimpRTF_OnSetFocus);
    HANDLE_MSG(hwnd, WM_SIZE, SimpRTF_OnSize);
    default:
      return SimpRTF_DefProc(hwnd, message, wParam, lParam);
  }
}

//////////////////////////////////////////////////
// WM_CREATE: Create the RichEdit Control
//////////////////////////////////////////////////
BOOL SimpRTF_OnCreate(HWND hwnd, LPCREATESTRUCT lpCreateStruct)
{
  hRichEditLib = LoadLibraryEx("RICHED32.DLL", NULL, 0);
  if (!hRichEditLib)
  {
    MessageBox(hwnd, "Can't find RICHED32.DLL", NULL, MB_OK);
    return FALSE;
  }

  hRichEdit = CreateWindow("RICHEDIT", "",
```

continues

Listing RB.1. continued

```
            WS_CHILD | WS_VISIBLE | WS_BORDER |
            ES_MULTILINE | WS_VSCROLL | ES_AUTOVSCROLL |
            ES_NOHIDESEL, 0, 0, 0, 0, hwnd, NULL,
            lpCreateStruct->hInstance, NULL);

   SendMessage(hRichEdit, EM_SETEVENTMASK, 0, ENM_SELCHANGE);

   FileName [0] = 0;

   return TRUE;
}

///////////////////////////////////
// WM_DESTROY
///////////////////////////////////
#pragma argsused
void SimpRTF_OnDestroy(HWND hwnd)
{
  if (hRichEditLib)
  {
    FreeLibrary(hRichEditLib);
    hRichEditLib = NULL;
  }
  PostQuitMessage(0);
}

///////////////////////////////////////////////////////
// WM_CLOSE: File need to be saved?
///////////////////////////////////////////////////////
void SimpRTF_OnClose(HWND hwnd)
{
  if (WasFileChanged(hwnd, hRichEdit))
    DestroyWindow(hwnd);
}


///////////////////////////////////////////////////////
// Set Title to current file name
///////////////////////////////////////////////////////
void SetTitle(HWND hwnd)
{
  char S[STRSIZE];

  sprintf(S, "%s - %s", szTitle, FileName);
  SetWindowText(hwnd, S);
}

///////////////////////////////////////////////////////
// Save File, check to be sure it has a name
///////////////////////////////////////////////////////
void HandleSave(HWND hwnd)
{
  BOOL SaveAs = FALSE;
```

```
  if (FileName[0] == 0)
    SaveAs = TRUE;

  if (SaveFile(hwnd, hRichEdit, SaveAs))
  {
    SendMessage(hRichEdit, EM_SETMODIFY, FALSE, 0);
    SetTitle(hwnd);
  }
}

////////////////////////////////////
// WM_COMMAND
////////////////////////////////////
#pragma argsused
void SimpRTF_OnCommand(HWND hwnd, int id, HWND hwndCtl, UINT codeNotify)
{
  switch (id)
  {
    case ID_EXIT:
      SendMessage(hwnd, WM_CLOSE, 0, 0);
      break;

    case ID_BOLD:
      SetAttributes(hRichEdit, CFM_BOLD, CFE_BOLD);
      UpdateMenu(hRichEdit, hwnd);
      break;

    case ID_ITALIC:
      SetAttributes(hRichEdit, CFM_ITALIC, CFE_ITALIC);
      UpdateMenu(hRichEdit, hwnd);
      break;

    case ID_UNDERLINE:
      SetAttributes(hRichEdit, CFM_UNDERLINE, CFE_UNDERLINE);
      UpdateMenu(hRichEdit, hwnd);
      break;

    case ID_BIGGERFONT:
      SetFontSize(hRichEdit, 4);
      break;

    case ID_SMALLERFONT:
      SetFontSize(hRichEdit, -4);
      break;

    case ID_SETFONTDLG:
      ChangeFont(hwnd, hRichEdit);
      UpdateMenu(hRichEdit, hwnd);
      break;

    case ID_NEW:
      if (WasFileChanged(hwnd, hRichEdit))
      {
        CHARRANGE cr;

        FileName[0] = 0;
```

continues

Listing RB.1. continued

```
        cr.cpMin = 0;
        cr.cpMax = -1;

        SendMessage(hRichEdit, WM_SETREDRAW, FALSE, 0);
        SendMessage(hRichEdit, EM_EXSETSEL,   0, (LPARAM)&cr);
        SendMessage(hRichEdit, WM_SETREDRAW, TRUE, 0);
        SendMessage(hRichEdit, EM_REPLACESEL, 0, (LPARAM)"");
        SendMessage(hRichEdit, EM_SETMODIFY, FALSE, 0);
        SetTitle(hwnd);
        }
        break;

    case ID_OPEN:
      if (WasFileChanged(hwnd, hRichEdit))
      {
        OpenFile(hwnd, hRichEdit);
        SendMessage(hRichEdit, EM_SETMODIFY, FALSE, 0);
        SetTitle(hwnd);
      }
      break;

    case ID_SAVE:
      HandleSave(hwnd);
      break;

    case ID_SAVEAS:
      if (SaveFile(hwnd, hRichEdit, TRUE))
      {
        SendMessage(hRichEdit, EM_SETMODIFY, FALSE, 0);
        SetTitle(hwnd);
      }
      break;
  }
}

////////////////////////////////////////////////////////
// WM_NOTIFY
////////////////////////////////////////////////////////
LRESULT SimpRTF_OnNotify(HWND hwnd, int idFrom, NMHDR FAR * pnmhdr)
{
  switch (pnmhdr->code)
  {
    case EN_SELCHANGE:
      UpdateMenu(hRichEdit, hwnd);
      break;
  }
  return FORWARD_WM_NOTIFY(hwnd, idFrom, pnmhdr, DefWindowProc);
}

////////////////////////////////////////////////////////
// WM_SETFOCUS: Focus stays on edit control
////////////////////////////////////////////////////////
#pragma argsused
```

```
void SimpRTF_OnSetFocus(HWND hwnd, HWND hwndOldFocus)
{
  SetFocus(hRichEdit);
}

//////////////////////////////////////
// WM_SIZE
//////////////////////////////////////
#pragma argsused
void SimpRTF_OnSize(HWND hwnd, UINT state, int cx, int cy)
{
  if (hRichEdit)
    MoveWindow(hRichEdit, 0, 0, cx, cy, TRUE);
}

//////////////////////////////////////
// Set the menu to current text attributes
//////////////////////////////////////
#pragma argsused
void UpdateMenu(HWND hwndRTF, HWND hwnd)
{
  int CurStyle[3];
  int Style[3] = {ID_BOLD, ID_ITALIC, ID_UNDERLINE};
  int FMStyle[3] = {CFM_BOLD, CFM_ITALIC, CFM_UNDERLINE};
  int FEStyle[3] = {CFE_BOLD, CFE_ITALIC, CFE_UNDERLINE};
  HMENU hMenu;

  hMenu = GetMenu(hwnd);

  for (int i = 0; i < 3; i++)
    CurStyle[i] = GetAttributes(hRichEdit, FMStyle[i], FEStyle[i]);

  for (i = 0; i < 3; i++)
  {
    if (CurStyle[i] == ATTRIB_TRUE)
      CheckMenuItem(hMenu, Style[i], MF_BYCOMMAND | MF_CHECKED);
    else
      CheckMenuItem(hMenu, Style[i], MF_BYCOMMAND | MF_UNCHECKED);
  }
}
```

Listing RB.2. The header file for the main module.

```
//////////////////////////////////////////////////////
// SIMPRTF.H
// Copyright (c) 1995 Charlie Calvert.
//////////////////////////////////////////////////////

#define ID_SAVEAS       100
#define ID_EXIT         101
#define ID_BOLD         102
#define ID_NEW          103
#define ID_OPEN         104
#define ID_SAVE         105
```

continues

Listing RB.2. continued

```
#define ID_ITALIC          106
#define ID_UNDERLINE        107
#define ID_BIGGERFONT       108
#define ID_SMALLERFONT      109
#define ID_SETFONTDLG       110

// Funcs
#define SimpRTF_DefProc DefWindowProc
BOOL SimpRTF_OnCreate(HWND hwnd, LPCREATESTRUCT lpCreateStruct);
void SimpRTF_OnDestroy(HWND hwnd);
void SimpRTF_OnCommand(HWND hwnd, int id, HWND hwndCtl, UINT codeNotify);
void SimpRTF_OnClose(HWND hwnd);
LRESULT SimpRTF_OnNotify(HWND hwnd, int idFrom, NMHDR FAR * pnmhdr);
void SimpRTF_OnSetFocus(HWND hwnd, HWND hwndOldFocus);
void SimpRTF_OnSize(HWND hwnd, UINT state, int cx, int cy);

BOOL Register(HINSTANCE hInst);
BOOL Create(HINSTANCE hInstance, int);
LRESULT CALLBACK WndProc(HWND, UINT, WPARAM, LPARAM);
void UpdateMenu(HWND hwndRTF, HWND hwnd);
```

Listing RB.3. The RTFFUNCS module contains utility routines for use with the SimpRTF program.

```
/////////////////////////////////////////////////////
// RTFFUNCS.CPP
// RTF control routines
// DATE: 07/17/95
/////////////////////////////////////////////////////

#define STRICT
#include <windows.h>
#include <richedit.h>
#include <stdio.h>
#include "rtffuncs.h"

extern char FileName[STRSIZE];
static LOGFONT LogFont;
static COLORREF FontColor;

/////////////////////////////////////////////////////
// ChooseFont Common Dialog
/////////////////////////////////////////////////////
BOOL ChooseAFont(HWND hwnd)
{
  CHOOSEFONT cfn;

  memset(&cfn, 0, sizeof(CHOOSEFONT));
  HDC DC = GetDC(hwnd);

  cfn.lStructSize = sizeof(CHOOSEFONT);
  cfn.hwndOwner = hwnd;
```

```
  cfn.hDC = DC;
  cfn.lpLogFont = &LogFont;
  cfn.Flags = CF_EFFECTS | CF_SCREENFONTS | CF_INITTOLOGFONTSTRUCT;
  cfn.rgbColors = FontColor;
  cfn.nFontType = SCREEN_FONTTYPE;

  BOOL Result = ChooseFont(&cfn);

  if (Result)
    LogFont = *cfn.lpLogFont;

  FontColor = cfn.rgbColors;

  ReleaseDC(hwnd, DC);

  return Result;
}

//////////////////////////////////////////////////////////
// Make sure common dialog starts with current font
//////////////////////////////////////////////////////////
void SetUpFont(CHARFORMAT CharFormat)
{
  memset(&LogFont, 0, sizeof(LOGFONT));

  FontColor = CharFormat.crTextColor;
  LogFont.lfHeight = CharFormat.yHeight / -20;
  if(CharFormat.dwEffects & CFE_BOLD)
    LogFont.lfWeight = FW_BOLD;
  else
    LogFont.lfWeight = FW_NORMAL;
  LogFont.lfItalic =(BOOL)(CharFormat.dwEffects & CFE_ITALIC);
  LogFont.lfUnderline =(BOOL)(CharFormat.dwEffects & CFE_UNDERLINE);
  LogFont.lfCharSet = DEFAULT_CHARSET;
  LogFont.lfQuality = DEFAULT_QUALITY;
  LogFont.lfPitchAndFamily = CharFormat.bPitchAndFamily;
  strcpy(LogFont.lfFaceName, CharFormat.szFaceName);
}

///////////////////////////////////////////
// Change the font in the selected text.
///////////////////////////////////////////
void ChangeFont(HWND hwnd, HWND hRichEdit)
{
  CHARFORMAT CharFormat;

  CharFormat.cbSize = sizeof(CHARFORMAT);
  SendMessage(hRichEdit, EM_GETCHARFORMAT, TRUE, (LPARAM)&CharFormat);

  SetUpFont(CharFormat);

  if (ChooseAFont(hwnd))
  {
    CharFormat.dwMask = CFM_BOLD | CFM_FACE | CFM_ITALIC |
                        CFM_COLOR | CFM_OFFSET | CFM_SIZE |
                        CFM_UNDERLINE;
```

continues

Listing RB.3. continued

```
    CharFormat.yHeight = LogFont.lfHeight * -20;

    CharFormat.dwEffects = 0;
    if(FW_BOLD == LogFont.lfWeight)
      CharFormat.dwEffects |= CFE_BOLD;
    if(LogFont.lfItalic)
      CharFormat.dwEffects |= CFE_ITALIC;
    if(LogFont.lfUnderline)
      CharFormat.dwEffects |= CFE_UNDERLINE;
    CharFormat.crTextColor = FontColor;

    CharFormat.bPitchAndFamily = LogFont.lfPitchAndFamily;
    strcpy(CharFormat.szFaceName, LogFont.lfFaceName);
    SendMessage(hRichEdit, EM_SETCHARFORMAT,
                SCF_SELECTION, (LPARAM)&CharFormat);
  }
}


//////////////////////////////////////
// Change the size of the text
//////////////////////////////////////
void SetFontSize(HWND hRichEdit, int iPointChange)
{
  CHARFORMAT CharFormat;

  CharFormat.cbSize = sizeof(CHARFORMAT);

  SendMessage(hRichEdit, EM_GETCHARFORMAT, TRUE,(LPARAM)&CharFormat);

  CharFormat.dwMask      = CFM_SIZE;
  if(((CharFormat.yHeight + 20*iPointChange) <=(128*20)) &&
     ((CharFormat.yHeight + 20*iPointChange) >=(6*20)))
    CharFormat.yHeight += 20*iPointChange;

  SendMessage(hRichEdit, EM_SETCHARFORMAT,
              SCF_SELECTION, (LPARAM)&CharFormat);
}


////////////////////////////////////////////////////////
// Apply attributes to selected text
////////////////////////////////////////////////////////
void SetAttributes(HWND hRichEdit, DWORD dwMask, DWORD dwEffects)
{
  CHARFORMAT CharFormat; // From RICHEDIT.H

  CharFormat.cbSize = sizeof(CHARFORMAT);
  SendMessage(hRichEdit, EM_GETCHARFORMAT,
              TRUE, (LPARAM)&CharFormat);
  CharFormat.dwMask = dwMask;
  CharFormat.dwEffects ^= dwEffects;
  SendMessage(hRichEdit, EM_SETCHARFORMAT,
              SCF_SELECTION, (LPARAM)&CharFormat);
}
```

```
/////////////////////////////////////////////////////
// Get attributes of text
/////////////////////////////////////////////////////
int GetAttributes(HWND hRichEdit, DWORD dwMask, DWORD dwEffects)
{
  CHARFORMAT CharFormat;

  CharFormat.cbSize = sizeof(CHARFORMAT);
  SendMessage(hRichEdit, EM_GETCHARFORMAT,
              TRUE, (LPARAM)&CharFormat);

  if(CharFormat.dwMask & dwMask)
  {
    if(CharFormat.dwEffects & dwEffects)
      return ATTRIB_TRUE;
    else
      return ATTRIB_FALSE;
  }
  else
    return ATTRIB_BOTH;
}

///////////////////////////////////////
// Has file been changed?
///////////////////////////////////////
BOOL WasFileChanged(HWND hwnd, HWND hRichEdit)
{
  char S[350];
  int  id;

  if (SendMessage(hRichEdit, EM_GETMODIFY, 0, 0L))
  {
    if(strlen(FileName) != 0)
      sprintf(S, "Save current file %s?", FileName);
    else
      strcpy(S, "Save current file?");

    id = MessageBox(hwnd, S, "Information",
                    MB_YESNOCANCEL | MB_ICONQUESTION);

    switch(id)
    {
      case IDYES:
        SaveFile(hwnd, hRichEdit, TRUE);
        return TRUE;

      case IDNO:
        return TRUE;

      case IDCANCEL:
        return FALSE;
    }
  }
  return TRUE;
}
```

continues

Listing RB.3. continued

```
/////////////////////////////////////////////////////////
// GetFileName
/////////////////////////////////////////////////////////
BOOL GetFileName(HWND hwnd, LPSTR szFile,
                 int StringSize, BOOL SaveAs)
{
  OPENFILENAME ofn;
  char szFileTitle[256];
  char szFilter[256];
  BOOL Result;

  strcpy(szFilter, "RTF Files");
  strcpy(&szFilter[strlen(szFilter) + 1], "*.rtf");
  strcpy(szFileTitle, "Long File Name Search");
  szFile[0] = 0;

  memset(&ofn, 0, sizeof(OPENFILENAME));

  ofn.lStructSize     = sizeof(OPENFILENAME);
  ofn.hwndOwner       = hwnd;
  ofn.lpstrFilter     = szFilter;
  ofn.nFilterIndex    = 1;
  ofn.lpstrFile       = szFile;
  ofn.nMaxFile        = StringSize;
  ofn.lpstrTitle      = szFileTitle;
  ofn.Flags           = OFN_PATHMUSTEXIST;

  if(SaveAs)
    Result = GetSaveFileName(&ofn);
  else
    Result = GetOpenFileName(&ofn);


  if (!Result)
  {
    DWORD Errval;
    char Errstr[50]="Common Dialog Error: ";
    char buf[5];

    Errval=CommDlgExtendedError();
    if (Errval != 0)
    {
      wsprintf(buf, "%ld", Errval);
      strcat(Errstr, buf);
      MessageBox(NULL,Errstr,"WARNING",MB_OK¦MB_ICONSTOP);
    }
  }

  return Result;
}

/////////////////////////////////////////////////////////
// Callback for the RTF_Save function
/////////////////////////////////////////////////////////
DWORD CALLBACK SaveCallback(DWORD dwcookie, LPBYTE Buffer,
                    LONG BufSize, LONG *NumWritten)
```

```
{
  WriteFile((HANDLE)dwcookie, Buffer,
            BufSize, (LPDWORD)NumWritten, NULL);
  return 0;
}


////////////////////////////////////
// Save an RTF file.
////////////////////////////////////
BOOL SaveFile(HWND hwnd, HWND hRichEdit, BOOL SaveAs)
{
  HANDLE hFile;
  EDITSTREAM Stream;
  BOOL Result = TRUE;

  if (SaveAs)
    Result = GetFileName(hwnd, FileName, STRSIZE, SaveAs);

  if (Result)
  {
    hFile = CreateFile(FileName,
             GENERIC_WRITE, 0, NULL, CREATE_ALWAYS,
             FILE_ATTRIBUTE_NORMAL, NULL);

    Stream.dwCookie =(DWORD)hFile;
    Stream.dwError = 0;
    Stream.pfnCallback = SaveCallback;

    SendMessage(hRichEdit, EM_STREAMOUT, SF_RTF,(LPARAM)&Stream);

    CloseHandle(hFile);

    return TRUE;
  }

  return FALSE;
}


////////////////////////////////////
// This callback does the real work of reading the rtf file.
////////////////////////////////////
DWORD CALLBACK OpenCallback(DWORD Cookie, LPBYTE Buffer,
                            LONG BufSize, LONG * BytesRead)
{
  ReadFile((HANDLE)Cookie, Buffer, BufSize, (LPDWORD)BytesRead, NULL);
  return 0;
}


////////////////////////////////////
// Read a file. See OpenCallback function
////////////////////////////////////
BOOL OpenFile(HWND hwnd, HWND hRichEdit)
{
  HANDLE hFile;
  EDITSTREAM Stream;
```

continues

Listing RB.3. continued

```
if (GetFileName(hwnd, FileName, STRSIZE, FALSE))
{
  hFile = CreateFile(FileName,
            GENERIC_READ, 0, NULL, OPEN_EXISTING,
            FILE_ATTRIBUTE_ARCHIVE, NULL);

  if(hFile)
  {
    Stream.dwCookie = (DWORD)hFile;
    Stream.dwError = 0;
    Stream.pfnCallback = OpenCallback;

    SendMessage(hRichEdit, EM_STREAMIN, SF_RTF, (LPARAM)&Stream);

    CloseHandle(hFile);
  }
  return TRUE;
}
return FALSE;
}
```

Listing RB.4. The header file for the utility routines.

```
////////////////////////////////////////
// RTFFUNCS.H
// Fonts Printing Save and Opening Files
////////////////////////////////////////

// Text has attributes, does not have attribute, is a mixture.
#define ATTRIB_FALSE  0
#define ATTRIB_TRUE   1
#define ATTRIB_BOTH   2
#define STRSIZE      256


// Funcs
void SetAttributes(HWND hRichEdit, DWORD dwMask, DWORD dwEffects);
int GetAttributes(HWND hRichEdit, DWORD dwMask, DWORD dwEffects);
void SetFontSize(HWND hRichEdit, int iPointChange);
void ChangeFont(HWND hWnd, HWND hRichEdit);

// Save the file
BOOL OpenFile(HWND hwnd, HWND hRichEdit);
BOOL SaveFile(HWND hwnd, HWND hRichEdit, BOOL SaveAs);
BOOL WasFileChanged(HWND hwnd, HWND hRichEdit);
```

Listing RB.5. The resource file for the SimpRTF program.

```
///////////////////////////////////////////////////////
// SIMPRTF.RC
// Copyright (c) 1995 Charlie Calvert.
///////////////////////////////////////////////////////

#include "simprtf.h"

SimpRTFIcon   ICON SIMPRTF.ICO
SimpRTFIcon16 ICON SIMP16.ICO

SimpRTF MENU
BEGIN
  POPUP "&File"
  BEGIN
    MENUITEM "&New", ID_NEW
    MENUITEM "&Open...", ID_OPEN
    MENUITEM "&Save", ID_SAVE
    MENUITEM "Save &As...", ID_SAVEAS
    MENUITEM SEPARATOR
    MENUITEM "E&xit", ID_EXIT
  END
  POPUP "&Edit"
  BEGIN
    MENUITEM "&Bold", ID_BOLD
    MENUITEM "&Italic", ID_ITALIC
    MENUITEM "&Underline", ID_UNDERLINE
    MENUITEM SEPARATOR
    MENUITEM "I&ncrease Font Size", ID_BIGGERFONT
    MENUITEM "&Decrease Font Size", ID_SMALLERFONT
    MENUITEM SEPARATOR
    MENUITEM "Font...", ID_SETFONTDLG
  END
END
```

Listing RB.6. The DEF file for the SimpRTF program.

```
; SimpRTF.DEF

NAME        SimpRTF
DESCRIPTION 'SimpRTF Window'
```

Listing RB.7. The Borland makefile for the SimpRTF program.

```
# SIMPRTF.MAK

!if !$d(BCROOT)
BCROOT  = $(MAKEDIR)\..
!endif

APPNAME = SIMPRTF
INCPATH = $(BCROOT)\WIN32;$(BCROOT);$(BCROOT)\INCLUDE
LIBPATH = $(BCROOT)\LIB
```

continues   **1195**

Listing RB.7. continued

```
!if $d(WIN16)
COMPILER= BCC.EXE
BRC     = BRC.EXE
FLAGS   = -W -ml -v -w4 -I$(INCPATH) -L$(LIBPATH)
!else
COMPILER= BCC32.EXE
BRC     = BRC32.EXE
FLAGS   = -W -v -w4 -I$(INCPATH) -L$(LIBPATH)
!endif

# linking
$(APPNAME).exe: $(APPNAME).obj rtffuncs.obj $(APPNAME).res
  $(COMPILER) $(FLAGS) $(APPNAME).obj rtffuncs.obj
  $(BRC) $(APPNAME).res

# Compile any CPP files that need to be compiled
.cpp.obj:
  $(COMPILER) -c $(FLAGS) { $< }

# resource
$(APPNAME).res: $(APPNAME).rc
  $(BRC) -R -I$(INCPATH) $(APPNAME).RC
```

Listing RB.8. The Microsoft makefile for the SimpRTF program.

```
#////////////////////////////////////
# SIMPRTMS.MAK - Microsoft makefile
# nmake -f SIMPRTMS.MAK
# Copyright (c) 1995 Charlie Calvert.
#////////////////////////////////////

APPNAME=SIMPRTF
TARGETOS=WIN95
APPVER=4.0
OBJS=$(APPNAME).OBJ RTFFUNCS.OBJ

!include <win32.mak>

all: $(APPNAME).exe

# Update the resource if necessary

$(APPNAME).res: $(APPNAME).rc $(APPNAME).h
  $(rc) $(rcflags) $(rcvars) $(APPNAME).rc

# Update the object files if necessary

# compile
.cpp.obj:
  $(cc) $(cflags) $(cvars) $(cdebug) $<

# Update the executable file if necessary.
```

```
$(APPNAME).exe: $(OBJS) $(APPNAME).res
  $(link) $(linkdebug) $(guiflags) -out:$(APPNAME).exe \
  $(OBJS) $(APPNAME).res $(guilibs) comctl32.lib
```

When this program loads into memory, it looks like a modified version of the NotePad program. If you type in the main window, text appears, and you will find that you have full editing capabilities when working with that text. If you highlight a section of text and then choose the Edit menu, you can change the attributes of the selected characters. For instance, you can make the font larger or smaller, you can change its color, you can italicize it, and you can bring up a font dialog and change the font itself.

Working with RTF Controls

If you want to work with a richedit control, you must first load RICHEDIT.DLL:

```
HINSTANCE hRichEditLib;

...

hRichEditLib = LoadLibraryEx("RICHED32.DLL", NULL, 0);
if (!hRichEditLib)
{
  MessageBox(hwnd, "Can't find RICHED32.DLL", NULL, MB_OK);
  return FALSE;
}
```

By doing this you automatically register the richedit class and prepare to create an instance of the control. Whenever you call LoadLibrary or LoadLibraryEx, you should be sure to free the library's HINSTANCE either at the end of the program or when you no longer need the library:

```
void SimpRTF_OnDestroy(HWND hwnd)
{
  if (hRichEditLib)
  {
    FreeLibrary(hRichEditLib);
    hRichEditLib = NULL;
  }
  PostQuitMessage(0);
}
```

It's easy to create an RTF control. All you have to is call CreateWindow and pass in "RICHEDIT" as the class name:

```
hRichEdit = CreateWindow("RICHEDIT", "",
      WS_CHILD | WS_VISIBLE | WS_BORDER |
      ES_MULTILINE | WS_VSCROLL | ES_AUTOVSCROLL,
      0, 0, 0, 0, hwnd, NULL,
      lpCreateStruct->hInstance, NULL);
```

Note that you can use the same styles with a richedit control that you can use with an edit control. For instance, here I use the WS_VSCROLL and ES_AUTOVSCROLL styles to ensure that the text scrolls properly in the window.

```
WS_CHILD | WS_VISIBLE | WS_BORDER |
ES_MULTILINE | WS_VSCROLL | ES_AUTOVSCROLL |
ES_NOHIDESEL,
```

The ES_NOHIDESEL flag ensures that the user's selection won't disappear if he or she wants to pop up a dialog. For instance, if you pop up the font dialog, you want the selected text that you wish to change to remain highlighted.

At creation time, you also want to check which events you want to be notified about. For instance, the SimpRTF program asks to be notified when the user moves the cursor or changes the text that is selected:

```
SendMessage(hRichEdit, EM_SETEVENTMASK, 0, ENM_SELCHANGE);
```

The EM_SETEVENTMASK message takes zero in wParam, and it takes a flag, or a series of flags, in lParam. Because SimpRTF sets the ENM_SELCHANGE flag, WM_NOTIFY messages will be sent to the control whenever the insertion point moves or the selection changes.

Here are the possible values sent by a richedit control to your program via WM_NOTIFY:

```
EN_DROPFILES, EN_PROTECTED, EN_REQUESTRESIZE, EN_SELCHANGE, EN_MSGFILER,
EN_CORRECTTEXT
```

The following messages are sent to a program from a richedit control via the WM_COMMAND message:

```
EN_HSCROLL, EN_VSCROLL, EN_UPDATE
```

Remember that you won't get any of these messages unless you first request them via an ENM_SETEVENTMASK message. The flag to set for each message is simply the original message name with an M added to its prefix. For instance, the flag for EN_COORECTTEXT is ENM_CORRECTTEXT, and for EN_UPDATE, it's ENM_UPDATE, and so on.

The SimpRTF program responds to EN_SELCHANGE messages by setting the menu items to reflect the current state of the selected text. For instance, if the text is bold, then the Bold menu item is checked, and if the text is italicized, then the Italic menu item is checked.

Here's the WM_NOTIFY handler:

```
LRESULT SimpRTF_OnNotify(HWND hwnd, int idFrom, NMHDR FAR * pnmhdr)
{
  switch (pnmhdr->code)
  {
    case EN_SELCHANGE:
      UpdateMenu(hRichEdit, hwnd);
      break;
  }
  return FORWARD_WM_NOTIFY(hwnd, idFrom, pnmhdr, DefWindowProc);
}
```

As you can see, the EN_SELCHANGE message is passed in with the NMHDR parameter. This structure was discussed in Week 3, "Advanced Topics."

Before we look at getting and setting character attributes, notice that WM_NOTIFY forwards the messages it gets to DefWindowProc. It's important that these messages get passed on and that you don't just swallow them. If you don't let them through, the control will not respond properly to all the events sent to it.

Getting and Setting Attributes

One of the most important features of the richedit control is its ability to get and set the attributes of the characters it displays. For instance, the GetMenu routine queries the richedit control to find out about the currently selected text. The question, of course, is how does it get this information.

When you want to get and set text attributes, there are two things you need to do:

1. You need to send either an EM_SETCHARFORMAT message or an EM_GETCHARFORMAT message.

2. You need to process a CHARFORMAT structure.

The purpose of the EM_SETCHARFORMAT and EM_GETCHARFORMAT messages is clear from their names. You send the former message when you want to change the attributes of text, and you send the latter message when you want to learn about the attributes of a block of text.

I will explain EM_GETCHARFORMAT first.

If you set the wParam of an EM_GETCHARMESSAGE to TRUE, then you want to work with the currently selected text. If you set it to FALSE, then you want to work with the default text attributes for the entire control. If you set wParam to TRUE and no text is selected, then naturally enough you get back information about the current selection point—that is, the place where the text caret is currently located.

The lParam part of this message is set to the address of a CHARFORMAT structure. Most of the messages, structures, and routines associated with a richedit control are listed in RICHEDIT.H. If you look in that file, then you will find the CHARFORMAT structure:

```
typedef struct _charformat
{
  UINT     cbSize;     // Set to sizeof(CHARFORMAT)
  _WPAD    _wPad1;     //
  DWORD    dwMask;     // Attributes you want to change (CFM)
  DWORD    dwEffects;  // Actual state of attributes (CFE)
  LONG     yHeight;    // Size in twips
  LONG     yOffset;    // > 0 for superscript, < 0 for subscript
  COLORREF crTextColor; // Color unless dwEffects has CFE_AUTOCOLOR
  BYTE     bCharSet;   // The character set from LOGFONT structure
```

```
   BYTE      bPitchAndFamily; // From the LOGFONT
   TCHAR     szFaceName[LF_FACESIZE]; // Name of font, as in LOGFONT
   _WPAD     _wPad2;
} CHARFORMAT;
```

One glance at this fellow and you can tell you have found the gold mine. This number plays the same role with richedit controls that the LOGFONT structure does with the fonts in a standard device context.

Most of the fields are easy enough to understand. The first field is the standard versioning tool that you have seen often enough in this book. Just set it to the current size of the CHARFORMAT structure. crTextColor, yHeight, bCharSet, bPitchAndFamily, and szFaceName are all self-explanatory. (If you need a little help with the CharSet and PitchAndFamily fields, refer to the explanation of LOGFONTs from Day 9, "Font Basics.")

The key fields in this structure are dwMask and dwEffects. The dwEffects field records the current state of the text. If you want to read or set the current attributes of the text, this is the field you check. Here are the possible values for the field:

```
/* CHARFORMAT effects */
#define CFE_BOLD                        0x0001
#define CFE_ITALIC                      0x0002
#define CFE_UNDERLINE          0x0004
#define CFE_STRIKEOUT            0x0008
#define CFE_PROTECTED           0x0010
/* NOTE: CFE_AUTOCOLOR corresponds to CFM_COLOR, which controls it */
#define CFE_AUTOCOLOR           0x40000000
```

So far so good. This all sounds very simple. However, there is a catch.

If you are working with a block of text, then it is possible that this block of text will have some parts that are italicized and some parts that are not italicized. If the entire block is in italics, then the dwMask field will have the CFM_ITALIC flag. Here is a complete list of the possible values for this field:

```
#define CFM_BOLD                                0x00000001
#define CFM_ITALIC                              0x00000002
#define CFM_UNDERLINE              0x00000004
#define CFM_STRIKEOUT               0x00000008
#define CFM_PROTECTED              0x00000010
#define CFM_SIZE                                    0x80000000
#define CFM_COLOR                          0x40000000
#define CFM_FACE                              0x20000000
#define CFM_OFFSET                        0x10000000
#define CFM_CHARSET                    0x08000000
```

Look carefully at the two sets of flags shown above. The first set of flags is associated with the dwEffects field and the second with the dwMask field. The dwMask field tells you if a particular attribute is the same throughout a block of text. If they are, then you can check the dwEffects field to tell whether that attribute is turned on or off.

Once again, just for the sake of clarity: The dwMask field tells you whether an attribute is the same throughout a block of text. The dwEffects field tells you whether it is turned on or off. dwMask states whether it is consistent. dwEffects states whether it is on or off. That's simple enough once you get the hang of it.

To get information about a particular attribute, you first retrieve a CHARFORMAT structure, as follows:

```
SendMessage(hRichEdit, EM_GETCHARFORMAT, TRUE,
           (LPARAM)&CharFormat);
```

Then you check the structure to see if an attribute is the same throughout the selected text:

```
IsTheSame = CharFormat.dwMask & CFM_ITALIC;
```

The variable IsTheSame will be set to TRUE if the selected text is either italicized or not italicized from beginning to end. It will be set to FALSE if part of the text is one way and part of the text is another way.

Assuming that the text is the same all the way through, this is how you check to see if it is actually italicized:

```
IsItalic = CharFormat.dwEffects & CFE_ITALIC;
```

IsItalic will be TRUE if the text is italicized, and it will be FALSE if it is not italicized. There is no point in checking the value of an effect if its mask is not set to TRUE. How can the system tell you if the text is italicized or not italicized if it is half one way and half the other? All it can do is report back that it is not consistent through the current block. In that case, the dwEffects field is irrelevant as far as reading an attribute is concerned.

So now you have the key facts in hand. Given this information, you are ready to see a generic routine that gets the text attributes from a given block of text:

```
int GetAttributes(HWND hRichEdit, DWORD dwMask, DWORD dwEffects)
{
  CHARFORMAT CharFormat;

  CharFormat.cbSize = sizeof(CHARFORMAT);
  SendMessage(hRichEdit, EM_GETCHARFORMAT,
              TRUE, (LPARAM)&CharFormat);

  if(CharFormat.dwMask & dwMask)
  {
    if(CharFormat.dwEffects & dwEffects)
      return ATTRIB_TRUE;
    else
      return ATTRIB_FALSE;
  }
  else
    return ATTRIB_BOTH;
}
```

This is the routine you are looking for, the one you can use in your programs. To call this routine, pass in the handle of the richedit and then a synchronized masks-and-effects pair:

```
Result = GetAttributes(hRichEdit, CFM_ITALIC, CFE_ITALIC);
```

The function will return the current state of the text in regard to the attribute you choose. For instance, if the text is in italics, the function will return ATTRIB_TRUE. If it is not in italics, it will return ATTRIB_FALSE. If it is mixed, it will return ATTRIB_BOTH. (These are local constants declared in the program. They are not systemwide values.)

So there you have it. Now you know how to read attributes found in the text of a richedit control. The next step is to reverse the process—that is, to learn to set the attributes of a block of text.

When you want to set an attribute in a chunk of text, you first need to get the current state of the text by sending a WM_GETCHARFORMAT message:

```
CharFormat.cbSize = sizeof(CHARFORMAT);
SendMessage(hRichEdit, EM_GETCHARFORMAT,
            TRUE, (LPARAM)&CharFormat);
```

You then XOR the value you want to change into dwEffects:

```
CharFormat.dwEffects ^= CFE_ITALIC;
```

Now you are almost ready to send your request back to the system. All you need to do is tell Windows what attribute you want to work with:

```
CharFormat.dwMask = CFM_ITALIC;
```

And then you are ready to send off the message:

```
SendMessage(hRichEdit, EM_SETCHARFORMAT,
            SCF_SELECTION, &CharFormat);
```

When you pass in the EM_SETCHARFORMAT message, the wParam for this message can be set to one of the following:

☐ SCF_SELECTION: if you want to change a selection

☐ SCF_WORD: if you want to change a word or words

You can OR these two values together if you want to change both. The lParam for this message is set to a CHARFORMAT structure, just as it was for the EM_GETCHARFORMAT message.

Given this information, you are now ready to see a routine that provides a general solution to this kind of problem:

```
void SetAttributes(HWND hRichEdit, DWORD dwMask, DWORD dwEffects)
{
  CHARFORMAT CharFormat; // From RICHEDIT.H

  CharFormat.cbSize = sizeof(CHARFORMAT);
```

```
SendMessage(hRichEdit, EM_GETCHARFORMAT,
              TRUE, (LPARAM)&CharFormat);
CharFormat.dwMask = dwMask;
CharFormat.dwEffects ^= dwEffects;
SendMessage(hRichEdit, EM_SETCHARFORMAT,
              SCF_SELECTION, (LPARAM)&CharFormat);
}
```

This routine expects a mask-and-effects pair in its parameters and then sets the currently selected block of text to the values you pass in. For instance, if you pass CFM_ITALIC and CFE_ITALIC, the selected text will be italicized.

That's all I'm going to say about changing text attributes. The SimpRTF program does this in several different places. There is quite a bit of code involved, but all of the routines end up just performing variations on the two themes I have shown in this section. The point is that you now have a set of routines that will automate this process.

Streaming Text

The SimpRTF program knows how to read and write files. This sounds complicated at first, but it turns out that RTF controls provide built-in streaming mechanisms via the EM_STREAMIN and EM_STREAMOUT messages.

If you want to read a file, first open it with the CreateFile method, which was explained back in "Week 1 in Review":

```
hFile = CreateFile(FileName,
            GENERIC_READ, 0, NULL, OPEN_EXISTING,
            FILE_ATTRIBUTE_ARCHIVE, NULL);
```

Then fill out an EDITSTREAM record, which is declared in RICHEDIT.H:

```
typedef struct _editstream
{
  DWORD dwCookie;                              // First
parameter, typically a handle
  DWORD dwError;                               // last
error
  EDITSTREAMCALLBACK pfnCallback;       // The call back function
} EDITSTREAM;
```

This structure usually takes the handle of a file in the first parameter, then zeroes out the second, and specifies a callback in the third. The callback is defined like this in RICHEDIT.H:

```
typedef DWORD (CALLBACK *EDITSTREAMCALLBACK)
      (DWORD dwCookie, LPBYTE pbBuff, LONG cb, LONG *pcb);
```

However, I usually change the names of the parameters somewhat, just so I'll feel like the routine was written by someone who speaks English:

```
DWORD CALLBACK OpenCallback(DWORD Cookie, LPBYTE Buffer,
                          LONG BufSize, LONG * BytesRead)
```

Here is one way to fill out the EDITSTREAM record:

```
EDITSTREAM Stream;

Stream.dwCookie = (DWORD)hFile;
Stream.dwError = 0;
Stream.pfnCallback = OpenCallback;
```

After you have filled out the record, you send it with an EM_STREAMIN message:

```
SendMessage(hRichEdit, EM_STREAMIN, SF_RTF, (LPARAM)&Stream);
```

After you send the message, your callback will be queried continually. The purpose of the callback is to give you a chance to read in the file one block at a time. Therefore, each time your function is called, it's expected that you will read in some of the file in question. When you report back that there are no more bytes being read from the file, then the callback is finished and the file is assumed to be read in. You use the BytesRead parameter to signal that there are no more bytes to read. Here's an example of what the whole routine looks like in action:

```
DWORD CALLBACK OpenCallback(DWORD Cookie, LPBYTE Buffer,
                            LONG BufSize, LONG * BytesRead)
{
  ReadFile((HANDLE)Cookie, Buffer, BufSize, (LPDWORD)BytesRead, NULL);
  return 0;
}
```

After your message returns, you should close the handle of the file you opened:

```
CloseHandle(hFile);
```

And that's it! That's all you have to do when you want to stream in a file. To my eye, this is a very nice architecture, giving me precisely the tools I need to stream text in and out of a variety of locations.

You perform this exact same process in reverse when you want to stream a file out to disk:

```
////////////////////////////////////////////////////////
// Callback for the RTF_Save function
////////////////////////////////////////////////////////
DWORD CALLBACK SaveCallback(DWORD dwcookie, LPBYTE Buffer,
                            LONG BufSize, LONG *NumWritten)
{
  WriteFile((HANDLE)dwcookie, Buffer,
            BufSize, (LPDWORD)NumWritten, NULL);
  return 0;
}

/////////////////////////////////////////
// Save an RTF file.
/////////////////////////////////////////
BOOL SaveFile(HWND hwnd, HWND hRichEdit, BOOL SaveAs)
{
  HANDLE hFile;
  EDITSTREAM Stream;
  BOOL Result = TRUE;
```

SAMS
Sams
Learning
Center
SAMS
PUBLISHING

```
  if (SaveAs)
    Result = GetFileName(hwnd, FileName, STRSIZE, SaveAs);

  if (Result)
  {
    hFile = CreateFile(FileName,
              GENERIC_WRITE, 0, NULL, CREATE_ALWAYS,
              FILE_ATTRIBUTE_NORMAL, NULL);

    Stream.dwCookie =(DWORD)hFile;
    Stream.dwError = 0;
    Stream.pfnCallback = SaveCallback;

    SendMessage(hRichEdit, EM_STREAMOUT, SF_RTF,(LPARAM)&Stream);

    CloseHandle(hFile);

    return TRUE;
  }

  return FALSE;
}
```

Here you send an EM_STREAMOUT message instead of an EM_STREAMIN message. And instead of reading from the file in the callback, this time you use the function to write to the file:

```
DWORD CALLBACK SaveCallback(DWORD dwcookie, LPBYTE Buffer,
                            LONG BufSize, LONG *NumWritten)
{
  WriteFile((HANDLE)dwcookie, Buffer,
          BufSize, (LPDWORD)NumWritten, NULL);
  return 0;
}
```

That's all there is to it. RTF controls make this process very simple. Needless to say, you could run some variations on these routines if you wanted to save information to a paging file or if you wanted to send it over a communications device.

Choosing a Font

It seems to me that this has been a rather long book and that it's probably time to wrap things up. However, I suppose I should throw in one last goodie, just as a farewell:

```
BOOL ChooseAFont(HWND hwnd)
{
  CHOOSEFONT cfn;

  memset(&cfn, 0, sizeof(CHOOSEFONT));
  HDC DC = GetDC(hwnd);

  cfn.lStructSize = sizeof(CHOOSEFONT);
  cfn.hwndOwner = hwnd;
  cfn.hDC = DC;
```

```
cfn.lpLogFont = &LogFont;
cfn.Flags = CF_EFFECTS ¦ CF_SCREENFONTS ¦ CF_INITTOLOGFONTSTRUCT;
cfn.rgbColors = FontColor;
cfn.nFontType = SCREEN_FONTTYPE;

BOOL Result = ChooseFont(&cfn);

if (Result)
  LogFont = *cfn.lpLogFont;

FontColor = cfn.rgbColors;

ReleaseDC(hwnd, DC);

return Result;
}
```

This function fills in a CHOOSEFONT structure and then pops up a ChooseFont dialog, as shown in Figure RB.2.

Figure RB.2.

A ChooseFont common dialog, used for selecting fonts.

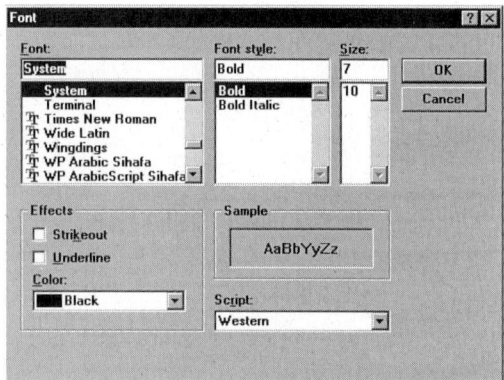

Just as with an Open File dialog, the first step is to zero out the record you will be sending to the system:

```
memset(&cfn, 0, sizeof(CHOOSEFONT));
```

This assures that there are no stray values in it. The code then sends in a handle to a window, a device context for a window, the LOGFONT structure you want to work with, some flags, a color, and the type of font you are using:

```
cfn.hwndOwner = hwnd;
cfn.hDC = DC;
cfn.lpLogFont = &LogFont;
cfn.Flags = CF_EFFECTS ¦ CF_SCREENFONTS ¦ CF_INITTOLOGFONTSTRUCT;
cfn.rgbColors = FontColor;
cfn.nFontType = SCREEN_FONTTYPE;
```

The CF_EFFECTS flag gives you access to the part of the dialog that involves selecting colors as well as striking out and underlining text. If you didn't pass this flag in, then those parts of the dialog would be blank. The CF_SCREENFONTS flag makes sure that the dialog lists only those fonts that are supported by the monitor, video card, and font files that you use. Two alternatives to this value would be CF_PRINTERFONTS or CF_SCALABLEONLY. The CF_INITTOLOGFONTSTRUCT flag tells the system to initialize the ChooseFont dialog to the current state of the LOGFONT and the colors you are passing in. In other words, the dialog will mirror back the current font and attributes that you pass to it. This is what users intuitively expect from this kind of dialog, and I know I have used them to just check the name and style of the current font.

Notice that you have to pass in the font color in a separate field. This is because the designers of the LOGFONT structure decided to omit a color field.

After you have filled out the record, you pop up the dialog by passing it to the ChooseFont function:

```
BOOL Result = ChooseFont(&cfn);

if (Result)
{
  LogFont = *cfn.lpLogFont;
  FontColor = cfn.rgbColors;
}
```

If the user pressed the OK button, then you gather in the new information culled from the dialog box, and you laboriously fill in a CHARFONT structure and send it off to the system with an EM_SETCHARFORMAT message.

I'd explain this latter process to you in depth, but as I mentioned above, this has been a long book, and anyway, I think I can see the sun creeping up over the trees. It must be time to go to bed.

Summary

In this chapter you have gotten a look at richedit controls. I decided to throw this common control in last because it's a useful tool you can have some fun with.

Ten years ago I felt lucky to have a routine that would reliably let a user edit a single line of text in black and white. Now I can create programs that have an edit control without a 64KB limit. Furthermore, this control supports a wide range of fonts, colors, and attributes. And this isn't even part of some expensive toolbox. It just comes for free with the system. Is this programming nirvana or what?

Happy trails!

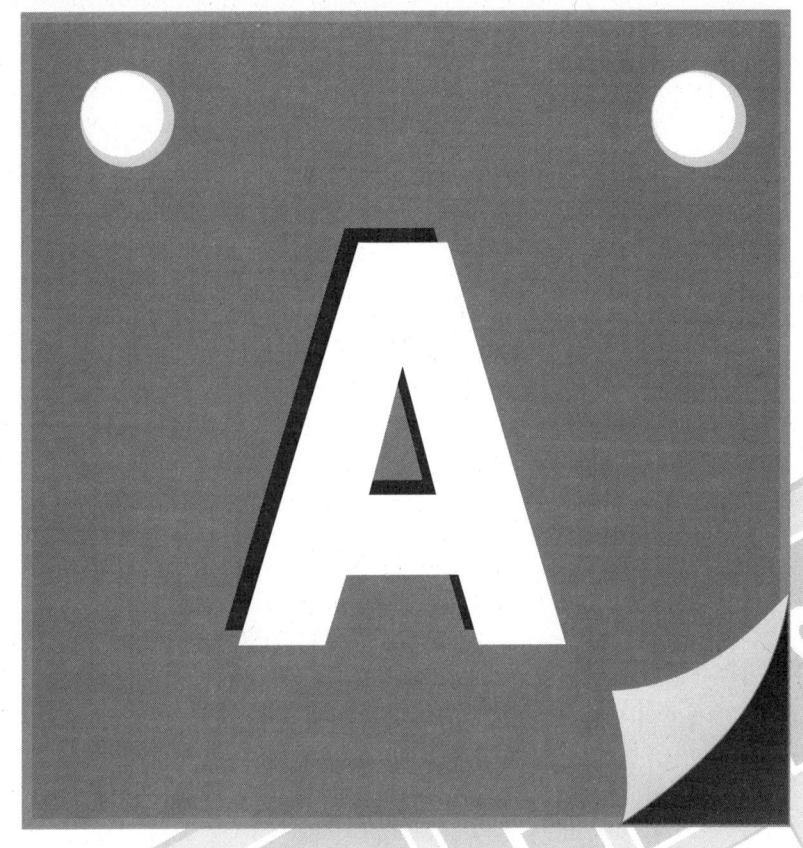

Answers

Day 1 Quiz

1. Use the WinExec function to launch a Windows or DOS application.

2. Windows is a multitasking environment with built-in mouse support that runs in graphics mode, whereas DOS was designed to run only one application at a time and by default runs in text mode. Programmers must design their own mouse interface if they want to use a mouse in a DOS program.

3. A GUI is a graphical user interface. Traditionally, these interfaces feature mouse support and familiar graphical features such as windows, scrollbars, buttons, and dialogs. Most GUIs are designed to present a relatively uniform interface to the user, regardless of which application is being run at the time.

4. No. Unlike Windows 3.1, Windows 95 is more than a DOS extention. It does take over many of the duties associated with an operating system but will farm out other tasks, such as file I/O, to DOS. It also lacks some of the more elaborate features, such as preemptive multitasking, that are often associated with true operating systems.

5. A PIF is a place for storing information that Windows can use when it runs a DOS session. For instance, users can utilize PIF files to specify whether a DOS session should be full screen or windowed, or to specify the amount of memory Windows should allocate for a DOS session.

6. The Borland debugger is called TD32, and the Microsoft debugger is called Codeview. A very popular third-party tool is called Bounds Checker for Windows.

7. No. Windows uses the HINSTANCE assigned to a program to distinguish that program from other executables currently running on the system.

8. From the programmer's point of view, the program entry point is the WinMain function. However, you should be aware that there is some startup code that executes before WinMain is called.

9. hPrevInstance is always 0 if there is no previous instance of a program available. This provides the clue you need in order to check to see whether a previous instance is running.

10. In 16-Bit Windows if more than one instance of a program is running, the hPrevInstance is set to the hInstance of the last copy of the program to be loaded into memory. In Windows 95 and Windows NT hinstance is always NULL.

Day 2 Quiz

1. In Windows 3.1 WinStub is the DOS program that is executed if a Windows 3.1 program is run from the DOS command line. It usually puts up a message that says something like, "This program requires Microsoft Windows." In Windows 95, you can runWindows programs directly from the DOS prompt, so Winstubs are no longer relevant.

2. The module definition file contains information about the size of the stack and heap, as well as the name of the WinStub, the module name, and a short description of the file.

3. WinMain and WndProc

4. Code to register the mainWindow, code to create the main window, and code to define the main message loop.

5. WM_DESTROY.

Day 3 Quiz

1. WNDCLASS is a structure used to define the major features of a window class such as its name, its icon, and its cursor.

2. Use the Register function to define the fields of the WNDCLASS structure and to register this structure with windows by calling RegisterClass.

3. Use the create function to realize and make visible a program's main windows. These functions are performed with calls to CreateWindow, ShowWindow, and UpDateWindow.

4. ShowWindow sets a windows visibility state. It is usually used to make a window either visible or hidden. The UpDateWindow function sends a WM_PAINT message to a window, thereby causing its interior to be redrawn.

5. WndProc enables you to define the behavior associated with a particular window. Specifically, it gives the programmer a chance to say how a window will handle any of the messages sent to it.

6. The message loop acts as a guardian at the gate of the window procedure. It can be used to filter, coordinate, or modify messages before they are sent to the window procedure.

7. DefWindowProc is used to pass a message on to Windows proper. In some cases, a programmer might want to swallow a message without sending it on. To do this, it is only necessary to exit the window procedure without ever passing the message to DefWindowProc.

The following answers apply to 32-bit Windows:

8. WORD: unsigned short (unsigned int in 16-bit Windows)

9. LONG: signed long

10. LPSTR char _far*. (That is, it's a pointer to null-terminated string.)

 **Answers**

Day 4 Quiz

1. `HANDLE_MSG` lets programmers avoid creating `case` statements such as this:

```
case WM_CREATE:
   return HANDLE_WM_CREATE(hwnd, wParam,
                           lParam, MyCls_OnCreate);
```

   In lieu of the code shown above, you can write easy-to-read code that looks like this:

```
HANDLE_MSG(hwnd, WM_CREATE, MyCls_OnCreate);
```

2. The second macro is called `FORWARD_WM_xxx`, and it can be used to pass a message back to the default window procedure.

3. `TextOut` and `DrawText`

4. `GetDC`. When you are done, don't forget to call `ReleaseDC`. It is not appropriate to call `GetDC` when responding to `WM_PAINT` messages.

5. Most information is kept in the `wParam` and `lParam` parameters, although the message itself is the `UINT` parameter, which is the second parameter.

6. The printer.

7. It either gets ignored altogether or passed on to the default window procedure.

8. Look it up in WINDOWS.H. Here's an example:

```
#define WM_CREATE          0x0001
```

9. Windows programs usually start with at least two files, one with a .CPP or .C extension, and one with a .DEF extension. Many projects also include a makefile and a resource file. One good way to start a new project is to copy a generic set of these files into a new subdirectory.

10. Traditional DOS programs run in text mode, one task at a time, and with no mouse support. Windows programs come with built-in mouse support, run in graphics mode, and can be multitasked. Another important difference is that Windows programs are event-oriented by default.

Day 5 Quiz

1. `WM_LBUTTONDBLCLK` and `WM_LBUTTONDOWN`

2. The `VK` constants specify virtual keys, such as `VK_DOWN` and `VK_UP`. For a complete list, see WINDOWS.H.

3. `CS_DBLCLK` is a class style. Use it with windows you want to respond to mouse double-clicks.

4. Black

5. The following code checks whether the `MK_CONTROL` flag is set:

```
if ((keyFlags & MK_CONTROL) == MK_CONTROL)
   DoSomething
```

6. The system key is also called the Alt key.

7. Use a `FORWARD_WM_xxx` macro.

8. To the system icon in the upper-left corner of the window.

9. `KeyMouse_OnKey`, because nearly all key presses get passed on to it. Some of these messages are then translated and passed on to `Cls_OnChar` function.

10. Failure to call `ReleaseDC` results in the slow depletion of system resources. The end result is a complete failure of the system.

Day 6 Quiz

1. For Microsoft products, type

   `rc -r emerson.rc`

   For Borland, type

   `brc -r emerson.rc`

2. For Microsoft products, type

   `rc emerson.res.`

   For Borland, type

   `brc emerson.res`

3. `CM_ABOUT` is the identifier associated with a menu item. When the user selects this item from a menu, the numeric value associated with `CM_ABOUT` is sent to the program's window procedure via a `WM_COMMAND` message.

4. A pop-up menu has a small window associated with it that drops down when the user selects that portion of the menu. A menu item is merely one of the words listed in a pop-up menu, or a single word listed along the menu bar at the top of the program.

5. `HINSTANCE`. `HINSTANCE` is the unique handle that identifies an application.

6. In WIN32 it's `LOWORD(wParam)`. This gets translated into the parameter `id` that is passed to the `Cls_OnCommand` function. In 16-Bit Windows you can use all of `inParam`.

7. `FindResource` searches through a file for a particular resource, such as an icon or user-defined text, while `LoadResource` actually moves the item into memory.

8. `GlobalUnlock` decrements an internal counter associated with a chunk of memory. If the counter reaches zero, that memory can be moved or discarded if `FreeResource` is called. `FreeResource` actually deallocates the memory associated with a resource if its counter is set to `0`.

9. A *new executable* is the format used by EXEs and DLLs. Windows 3.1 uses NE (new executables), OS/2 uses LE (linear executables), and Windows 95 and Windows NT use PE (portable executables).

10. Yes

Day 7 Quiz

1. `DialogBox`

2. None. The About dialog is a modal dialog, and so nearly all messages associated with a program are sent to it while it is on-screen. There are a few minor exceptions to this rule, but the main point is simply that a modal dialog takes over an application while it is on-screen, effectively rendering the application inert until the dialog box is closed.

3. `WM_COMMAND`

4. `FreeProcInstance` is used to free up a function that has been bound to a data segment with a call to `MakeProcInstance`.

5. Use `DeleteObject` to free the memory associated with a bitmap. Even better, if you have included WindowsX, use the `DeleteBitmap` macro, which includes type checking.

6. Use `LoadString` to retrieve text from a string resource.

7. `WM_VSCROLL` messages are sent whenever the user clicks a scrollbar. It carries information about the direction or manner in which the user wants to scroll, as well as the current position of the thumb on the scrollbar.

8. The `TEXTMETRIC` structure contains detailed information about a font. It is defined in WINDOWS.H and in Borland's and Microsoft's online help.

9. The OK button in a dialog generates an `IDOK` message, which is sent to the dialog procedure associated with a dialog.

10. `MakeProcInstance` binds a function to a chunk of prolog code. This prolog code gives a function access to a program's data segment (`mov ax, ds`), thereby ensuring that a function will have access to a program's variables and data.

Day 8 Quiz

1. First register its class (if necessary) and then call `CreateWindow`.

2. The first time it is called for the main window of the application, and the second time for the child window.

3. `GameWndProc`

4. Because this is not necessary for child windows. `PostQuitMessage` tells Windows that an application wants to close, and most of the time users don't want the entire application to close just because they've closed a child window. (In this program, the two occur at more or less the same time, but that is just coincidence. There is no reason the first window can't be closed while the application is still running.)

5. `SetTimer` is the API function to use when you want to create a timer. Be sure to check the result, because the timer is not always available.

6. Because it resides in the `WM_DESTROY` function for the child window, and Windows always calls this function automatically before the app is closed.

7. `SRCINVERT`

8. Call `GetSystemMetrics` to find out about many important facts regarding the hardware and software settings on the current system.

9. Answers will vary, but here is some possible selections:

   Width of a window frame
   Height of a window frame
   Width of a cursor
   Height of a cursor
   Width of an icon
   Height of an icon
   Width of the screen
   Height of the screen
   Whether or not a mouse is present
   Whether or not the current version of Windows is a debugging version

10. I threw `Game_OnChar` into the program to enable the user to pause the snake at a particular point on its path. You would need to call `SetTimer` to get things moving again.

Day 9 Quiz

1. `CreateFont` and `CreateFontIndirect`

2. `GetStockObject` or, if you are using WindowsX, `GetStockFont`.

3. TrueType fonts were developed by Microsoft for Windows 3.1. Their main virtue is that they are a high-quality, highly portable set of fonts that can be used for free by all Windows owners.

4. A stock font is just like any other font on the system, except it has been predefined. In other words, a stock font might be an ordinary Courier font that could be created with a call to `CreateFontIndirect`. However, the tedious part of the job has already been done for you, so all you need to do is call `GetStockObject` or `GetStockFont`.

5. `GetTextFace` retrieves the name of the currently selected font.

6. To find the size of the current font, call `GetTextMetrics` to retrieve a `TEXTMETRIC` structure. The `TEXTMETRIC` structure has the information you need.

7. Answer varies depending on your system.

8. Answer varies depending on your system.

Answers

9. Copy the font into a device context via a call to `SelectObject`, or, if you are using WindowsX, a call to `SelectFont`.

10. The type of the font. For instance, the font could be TrueType, Vector, or Fixed_Pitch.

Day 10 Quiz

1. To create a control, call `CreateWindow`.

2. It has been preregistered by Windows.

3. The eighth parameter to `CreateWindow` is called `hwndParent`, and it should hold the `HWND` of the owner of a control.

4. `ID`. To get the `HWND` of a control from its `ID`, call `GetDlgItem`.

5. By typecasting the `hmenu` field while calling `CreateWindow`.

6. You should `OR` together the various styles of a control.

7. `SetWindowText` and `GetWindowText`. Also the WindowsX macros `Edit_GetText`, `Edit_SetText`, `Static_GetText`, and `Static_SetText`.

8. List boxes and check boxes can be used to *control* the flow of a program (the same way the knob on a stereo can be used to *control* the volume of a piece of music).

9. An `EM_SETSEL` message is associated with edit controls. You know this because it begins with the letters `EM`. It enables you to select a particular range of letters in an edit control.

10. Call `SendMessage` with a `BM_GETCHECK` message, or call the WindowsX macro, `Button_GetCheck`.

Day 11 Quiz

1. Call `SetFocus` and pass it the handle to the control.

2. `SendMessage` will send a message directly to the appropriate window procedure, while `PostMessage` will place the message in the application message queue. As a result, `PostMessage` tends to be slower than `SendMessage`.

3. `ButtonMessage`

4. The best way is to look up the information in an online help file. Another good method is to look up the information in a reference book. The important thing is to find a simple way of obtaining this information. You should make the process as close to effortless as possible, because you will frequently need to look up this type of information.

1216

A

5. A callback is a function that is called directly by Windows, rather than by some other routine in your application. Typically, you pass the address of a callback to Windows and use the `MakeProcInstance` function to ensure that the function will have access to your program's data. Once you have this process down cold, you can sometimes "cheat" by using the "smart callbacks" option instead of `MakeProcInstance`.

6. `MakeProcInstance` links in some prolog code that gives the function access to your program's variables and other data.

7. `FreeProcInstance`

8. Pound (#) `define` an identifier and use `WM_USER` as the starting offset:

   `#define MyMessage (WM_USER + 0)`

9. `WM_USER`

10. Nothing. The `BM_GETCHECK` message is a button message, and the main window will simply ignore it.

Day 12 Quiz

1. `ExitWindows`, the first parameter of which can contain either `EW_REBOOTSYSTEM` or `EW_REBOOTWINDOWS`.

2. `IsDialogMessage` enforces normal tabbing among controls when you place them inside a window. This function automatically handles special key combinations such as Tab or Shift+Tab.

3. Both group boxes and radio buttons are part of the button class.

4. The macros are listed in WINDOWSX.H. Other places to look include the WINDOWSX.TXT file that ships with Microsoft's compiler, or the WIN31.DOC file that ships with Borland's compiler.

5. The `BM_SETCHECK` is sent every time you call the WindowsX `Button_SetCheck` macro.

6. Give it the `BS_AUTORADIOBUTTON` style.

7. Group boxes have no built-in functionality. Their primary purpose is merely visual. They give the user a clue as to how to think about certain controls, and about how the tabbing system for the controls works.

8. Give the first item in any group of controls the `WS_GROUP` style. The end of one group of controls is marked by the beginning of the next group.

9. The `WS_TABSTOP` style designates that the user can tab to a particular control, but it does not state that the user will always automatically tab to that control if it is next to the child window list. The `WS_GROUP` style marks the beginning of a group of controls. Sometimes a group of controls, such as a set of radio buttons, will handle tabs in a special way, even though the `WS_TABSTOP` style is set for every member of the group.

Answers

For instance, if you tab to a group of radio buttons, only the currently selected button will receive the focus, even though all of the buttons in the group have the WS_TABSTOP style. This is very convenient for the user, but a bit confusing to the programmer who is trying to understand how the WS_GROUP and WS_TABSTOP styles actually work.

10. Check to see if the return value from WinExec is less than 32. If it is, you should pop up a message box that displays one of the predefined errors shown below:

0   Out of memory, executable corrupt, or relocation error
2   File not found
3   Path not found
5   Attempt to dynamically link to task, or sharing error
6   Library required separate data segments for each task
8   Insufficient memory to start the application
10 Windows version incorrect
11 Executable file invalid
12 Application designed for a different operating system
13 Application designed for MS-DOS 4.0
14 Type of executable file unknown
15 Can't load real-mode apps from old Windows versions
16 Attempt to load a second instance of an executable file containing multiple data segments that were not marked read-only
19 Attempt to load a compressed executable file
20 DLL required to run this file is invalid
21 This app requires 32-bit extensions

Day 13 Quiz

1. BS_PUSHBUTTON and BS_RADIOBUTTON

2. ListBox_Dir

3. Here's a relatively complete list:

```
ListBox_Enable(hwnd, fEnable)
ListBox_GetCount(hwnd)
ListBox_ResetContent(hwnd)
ListBox_AddString(hwnd, lpsz)
ListBox_InsertString(hwnd, lpsz, index)
ListBox_AddItemData(hwnd, data)
ListBox_InsertItemData(hwnd, lpsz, index)
ListBox_DeleteString(hwnd, index)
ListBox_GetTextLen(hwnd, index)
ListBox_GetText(hwnd, index, lpszBuffer)
ListBox_GetItemData(hwnd, index)
ListBox_SetItemData(hwnd, index, data)
ListBox_FindString(hwnd, indexStart, lpszFind)
ListBox_FindItemData(hwnd, indexStart, data)
ListBox_SetSel(hwnd, fSelect, index)
```

```
ListBox_SelItemRange(hwnd, fSelect, first, last)
ListBox_GetCurSel(hwnd)
ListBox_SetCurSel(hwnd, index)
ListBox_SelectString(hwnd, indexStart, lpszFind)
ListBox_SelectItemData(hwnd, indexStart, data)
ListBox_GetSel(hwnd, index)
ListBox_GetSelCount(hwnd)
ListBox_GetTopIndex(hwnd)
ListBox_GetSelItems(hwnd, cItems, lpIndices)
ListBox_SetTopIndex(hwnd, indexTop)
ListBox_SetColumnWidth(hwnd, cxColumn)
ListBox_GetHorizontalExtent(hwnd)
ListBox_SetHorizontalExtent(hwnd, cxExtent)
ListBox_SetTabStops(hwnd, cTabs, lpTabs)
ListBox_GetItemRect(hwnd, index, lprc)
ListBox_SetCaretIndex(hwnd, index)
ListBox_GetCaretIndex(hwnd)
ListBox_SetAnchorIndex(hwnd, index)
ListBox_GetAnchorIndex(hwnd)
ListBox_Dir(hwnd, attrs, lpszFileSpec)
ListBox_AddFile(hwnd, lpszFilename)
ListBox_SetItemHeight(hwnd, index, cy) 3.1 only
ListBox_GetItemHeight(hwnd, index) 3.1 only
```

4. You'll need to typecast the LPARAM argument to get ahold of the MINMAXINFO structure if you are not using WindowsX.

5. The WM_GETMINMAXINFO message ensures that the user cannot change the shape of a window beyond certain limits defined by the programmer. CreateWindow starts a window out at a certain size, but will not prevent the user from resizing a framed window.

6. Use SetWindowLong (in combination with MakeProcInstance) whenever you want to subclass a control.

7. Edit_SetSel is the macro you want to use. It relies on the EM_SETSEL message.

8. Use the TrackPopupMenu function.

9. Use GetProfileString to retrieve information from the WIN.INI file, and use GetPrivateProfileString to retrieve information from any other INI file.

10. InvalidateRect generates WM_PAINT messages. The second parameter is the size of the rectangle that you want to update. If this is set to NULL, the whole window is updated. Compare to UpDateWindow.

Day 14 Quiz

1. The big difference is that a child window will always stay within the confines of its parent's client rectangle, whereas a pop-up window is free to rove anywhere on-screen.

2. GetClientRect gets the dimensions of a window with the upper-left coordinate, expressed as 0,0. GetWindowRect retrieves the dimensions of a window with the upper-left corner expressed in terms of that corner's location relative to the entire screen.

Answers

3. The `WS_OVERLAPPEDWINDOW` style is used to define a standard window with a frame, caption bar, system menu, and minimize and maximize box. It literally consists of the following styles ORed together into one style:

```
WS_OVERLAPPEDWINDOW = WS_OVERLAPPED | WS_CAPTION |
                      WS_SYSMENU | WS_THICKFRAME |
                      WS_MINIMIZEBOX | WS_MAXIMIZEBOX;
```

4. Either `MoveWindow` or `SetWindowPos`

5. Use `GetSystemMetrics` to retrieve information about the width of a window's frame. Pass in `SM_CXFRAME` and `SM_CYFRAME`.

6. Call `EnableWindow`, passing in the `HWND` of the window you want to disable in the first parameter. The second parameter is set to `FALSE` to disable the window, and `TRUE` to enable the window.

7. Balance all calls to `CreateSolidBrush` with calls to `DeleteObject`.

8. `GetClassLong` retrieves information about an entire class of windows, and `GetWindowWord` or `GetWindowLong` retrieves information about a specific instance of a window.

9. When you are calling `GetClassLong`, this identifier can be used to retrieve the handle of the background brush. It is actually an offset into a structure.

10. In most cases, this is up to the programmer. Use the extra bytes you associate with a window to store information specific to the window, such as variables owned by that window.

Day 15 Quiz

1. COMCTL32.DLL

2. COMMCTRL.H

3. COMCTL32.LIB

4. No

5. No

6. `CreatePopupMenu`, `AppendMenu`, and `TrackPopupMenu`

7. `SB_SETPARTS` and `SB_SETTEXT`

8. `CreateStatusWindow` and `CreateToolbarEx`

9. *W* stands for wide. It's included for use with Windows NT programs that take advantage of Unicode.

10. `(LPARAM)s`

Day 16 Quiz

1. Mapping modes define the relationship between device units and logical units, as well as the orientation of the x- and y-axes.

2. A pixel is the smallest single point of light that can be manipulated on the screen at one time by the programmer. There is a one-to-one correspondence between pixels and device units.

3. It is smaller. A logical unit in the MM_LOMETRIC is equal to .1 mm, which is considerably smaller than a pixel on virtually all VGA systems. To see this relationship, open the Size dialog in the WinSize program and compare the coordinates of the window in the MM_TEXT mode to those in the MM_LOMETRIC mode.

4. The viewport origin is the origin, or 0,0 point, of the device coordinate system as opposed to the logical coordinate system.

5. Device coordinates are based on the physical pixels seen on-screen, or the physical dots drawn on a printer. Logical coordinates ignore these device-dependent factors and attempt to base GDI coordinates on logical units such as inches or millimeters.

6. SetViewportOrg sets the origin for the device coordinate system, and SetWindowOrg sets the origin for the logical coordinate system.

7. Modeless dialogs give the user access to the rest of the program to which they belong. While modal dialogs are on-screen, they are the sole focus of user input for the program to which they belong.

8. You can create a modeless dialog by calling CreateDialog.

9. You can create a modal dialog by calling DialogBox.

10. Answers may vary. Dialog procedures receive WM_INITDIALOG messages rather than WM_CREATE messages. You should pass messages intended for default processing to DefDlgProc rather than DefWndProc. You might also be interested to know that dialogs have a standard window procedure (that looks just like any other window procedure) that actually calls your dialog procedure. When you return TRUE or FALSE from a dialog procedure, the result is handled by the dialog's window procedure.

Day 17 Quiz

1. You can use SendDlgItemMessage to handle communications between a dialog and its controls. SendMessage, on the other hand, can be used whenever you need to send messages between any two points in a program or on the desktop.

2. Use GetDlgItem to retrieve the handle of a control if all you know is its ID.

3. Use DPtoLP to convert device coordinates into logical coordinates.

4. Use GetParent to find the HWND of a window's parent.

Answers

5. Yes, a modal dialog can communicate freely with its parent with the SendMessage function. Communications in the other direction are more difficult, although by no means impossible. For instance, you could use a timer to send messages at specified intervals between a parent and a modal dialog.

6. Set breakpoints on the portion of the dialog procedure you want to examine. (I should perhaps qualify this point by saying that at the deepest level—that is, at the machine level—a Windows program running on an Intel processor is still very much a linear program. However, this is not at all the way things appear to a C++ programmer who writes standard Windows code. For all practical purposes, C++ Windows code is nonlinear, however, the processor still executes machine instructions in a linear fashion.)

7. The mapper program subclasses a static control in order to display a bitmap inside the control's boundaries.

8. There are a number of possible answers, but one important explanation is that it enables you to circumvent the unusual coordinate system in dialogs. That is, you can design the dialog and locate the static control using Resource Workshop or AppStudio, and then simply paint the bitmap at the 0,0 coordinates of the static control. This saves you the trouble of making a calculation at runtime that must be based on the size of the current font.

9. StretchBlt will, if necessary, compress or stretch a bitmap when it copies it from a source to a destination. BitBlt, on the other hand, simply copies a bitmap from one device context to the next.

10. The program calls StretchBlt so the original bitmaps can be stretched into a new shape. This means they must be copied from one bitmap to another. The call to CreateCompatibleBitmap creates the new bitmaps into which the old bitmaps will be copied.

Day 18 Quiz

1. The BS_BITMAP style

2. There is an extra parameter in the CreateWindowEx call. It's the first parameter, and it's called dwExStyle.

3. WC_TABCONTROL

4. GetWindowLong

5. PropertySheet and PROPSHEETHEADER

6. You can use it to define the tabs placed on the control.

7. TCM_INSERTITEM

A

8. They can both be used to resize a window, or to move a window.

9. `PSH_WIZARD`

10. `CreateUpDownControl`

Day 19 Quiz

1. `ImageList_LoadBitmap` and `ImageList_Create`

2. `ImageList_Draw`

3. Use the `crMask` field to designate a transparent color for the bitmap.

4. `ImageList_AddIcon`

5. Call `UpdateWindow`, or call `PeekMessage`.

6. `ImageList_BeginDrag`, `ImageList_DragEnter`, and `ImageList_SetDragCursorImage`

7. Call `ListView_SetImageList`.

8. `WM_NOTIFY` and `LVN_GETDISPINFO`

9. `ListView_GetNextItem` and `LVNI_SELECTED`

10. `GetWindowLong` and `SetWindowLong`

Day 20 Quiz

1. Hotkeys designated in menus are separated from the rest of the menu text with tab character. Specifically, they use the \t syntax: &Round Cursor\tAlt+F1.

2. To place an underline beneath a letter in a menu, use the ampersand symbol (&). The end result is that the user can select that item by pressing Alt and the specified key. If you are inside a pop-up menu, pressing the Alt key is optional (that is, you can select the option by pressing the letter alone).

3. Add to your message loop a call to `TranslateAccelarators` whenever you use accelerators.

4. See if the `itemState` field of `DRAWITEMSTRUCT` has the `ODS_SELECTED` flag set.

5. Answers will vary, but here's a complete list from WINDOWS.H that includes the associated constants:

```
#define MF_BYCOMMAND        0x0000
#define MF_BYPOSITION       0x0400
#define MF_SEPARATOR        0x0800
#define MF_ENABLED          0x0000
#define MF_GRAYED           0x0001
#define MF_DISABLED         0x0002
#define MF_UNCHECKED        0x0000
#define MF_CHECKED          0x0008
#define MF_USECHECKBITMAPS  0x0200
```

1223

```
#define MF_STRING        0x0000
#define MF_BITMAP        0x0004
#define MF_OWNERDRAW     0x0100
#define MF_POPUP         0x0010
#define MF_MENUBARBREAK  0x0020
#define MF_MENUBREAK     0x0040
#define MF_UNHILITE      0x0000
#define MF_HILITE        0x0080
#define MF_SYSMENU       0x2000
#define MF_HELP          0x4000
#define MF_MOUSESELECT   0x8000
```

6. The MF_BYPOSITION flag designates the position of the menu item in question in terms of the other menu items in the menu. For instance, it might be the fifth menu item or the sixth menu item. MF_BYCOMMAND identifies a menu item with its ID.

7. BY_POSITION is a zero-based offset.

8. The SS_ICON style can be used to designate that a particular static control has an icon associated with it.

9. A call to SetCapture must be matched with a call to ReleaseCapture.

10. Use the GetObject function to obtain the dimensions of bitmap at runtime.

Day 21 Quiz

1. 4GB

2. The first parameter to WinMain, hInst, is usually set to the virtual address at which the program is loaded into memory. This is usually 4MB.

3. No

4. The 4GB assigned to each program is virtual memory. The operating system maps the accessed portions of the 4GB address space into real memory.

5. A thread's CONTEXT structure contains information about the state of the CPU.

6. Preemptive multitasking is part of WIN32, and non-preemptive multitasking is part of Windows 3.1.

7. Non-preememptive multitasking systems don't schedule the time allocated to each task. As a result, a single program can monopolize the CPU, thereby potentially bringing the whole system to its knees.

8. The sleep function suspends the execution of a thread for a specified interval.

9. Memory-mapped file is a disk file that has been mapped into RAM so that it can be accessed as if it contained raw memory. It also provides a technique for sharing memory between programs.

10. VirtualAlloc allows you allocate memory in the virtual address space of the calling function. This memory will be automatically paged from disk as necessary. It's a very important memory-management technique.

Bonus Day 1 Quiz

1. The HDC field is part of every GDI function.

2. chord, ellipse, polygon, rectangle, pie, and roundrect are all GDI functions that draw geometric shapes.

3. To change the color that fills an ellipse, select a new brush into the current device context.

4. To change the color of the boundary of a rectangle, select a new pen into the current device context.

5. A placeable, or Aldus, metafile has a 22-byte header.

6. To display a metafile, use PlayMetaFile, or use the EnumMetaFile and EnumMetaFileProc callback along with the PlayMetaFileRecord function.

7. CreateMetaFile returns a device context. You can copy pens, brushes, and other GDI elements into this device context.

8. If you pass the HDC obtained from CreateMetaFile to CloseMetaFile, it will return an HMETAFILE object. An HMETAFILE can be shown to the screen simply by passing it to PlayMetaFile.

9. The second field in a METARECORD is a function number. Each GDI function has a function number associated with it. For instance, Polygon is assigned function number 0x0324. You can find this information in the *Microsoft Windows 3.1 Programmer's Reference Volume 4: Resources*, which is available from Microsoft Press.

10. The first field of OPENFILENAME is called lStructSize. You should set this field equal to the size of the OPENFILENAME struct before passing the struct to GetOpenFileName:

    ```
    OpenFileName.lStructSize = sizeof(OPENFILENAME);
    ```

Bonus Day 2 Quiz

1. When creating client windows, assign the szClass field to MDICLIENT.

2. Use EnumChildWnds and the EnumChildWindows function to iterate through all the windows on the desktop.

3. The WM_MDIGETACTIVE function finds the active window.

4. The client window sends a WM_MDIACTIVATE message to each child window about to gain or lose the focus.

5. The lParam field accompanying the WM_MDISETMENU message contains a new menu or pop-up menu.

6. The easiest way to tell is to make it very wide and very shallow. In other words, make the clock about ¹/₂ inch high and 4 or 5 inches wide. The actual image of the clock stays symmetrical, even though its frame has been distorted.

Answers

7. You need to fill out an MDICREATESTRUCT before creating an MDI child.

8. A WM_QUERYENDSESSION message is sent out whenever a properly constructed Windows shell is about to close down.

9. Call GetWindow and pass it the HWND of your window and the GW_OWNER constant. If it returns TRUE, you're dealing with the child of an icon:

    ```
    if (GetWindow(hwnd, GW_OWNER)) // Icon Title?
        return TRUE;
    ```

10. Use the cbWndExtra bytes to store information specific to each window.

Bonus Day 3 Quiz

1. MCI stands for the *Media Control Interface*.

2. WAV files can hold one second in 11KB, or one minute in 1MB. MIDI files can hold one minute in about 5KB of disk space.

3. When you first open a multimedia device, you should pass zero in this field. After opening a multimedia device, you should save the device ID so that you can use it in future calls relating to the device.

4. mciSendCommand returns zero if the call is a success. Otherwise, it returns an error code. You can pass the error codes to mciGetErrorString if you want to retrieve an error string to show your users.

5. If you pass in an HWND along with the MCI_NOTIFY flag, it will send MM_MCINOTIFY messages to the designated window. The WPARAM associated with the MM_MCINOTIFY message reveals information about the state of the current multimedia device. For instance, WPARAM can be set to MCI_NOTIFY_ABORTED or MCI_NOTIFY_SUCCESSFUL.

6. All the functions in the book that are exported from a DLL use the keywords _export and CALLBACK. _export ensures that the function is properly exported from the DLL (that is, that it is placed in an export table). It also creates prolog code that will properly set up the data segment after the function is linked. CALLBACK is shorthand for ensuring that a function is declared FAR PASCAL.

7. To inform your program about the routines in a DLL, use IMPLIB to create a LIB file that can be linked into your program.

8. The declarations for the standard Windows API routines are placed in WINDOWS.H.

9. When you are creating a dialog window to act as the main window of an application, you need to give it a unique class name so that Windows can send messages to the right location.

10. Inside a DLL, the function called LibMain plays a role very similar to the one usually played by WinMain in a standard Windows executable.

Bonus Day 4 Quiz

1. The elements of the Windows interface are described in the *SAA CUA Advanced Interface Design Guide*, published by IBM.

2. CUA stands for *common user interface.*

3. On success, the `malloc` function returns a pointer of type void; on failure, it returns `NULL`.

4. Calls to `GlobalAlloc` are usually accompanied by calls to `GlobalLock`, `GlobalUnlock`, and `GlobalFree`.

5. The program's data, stack, and local heap are all normally kept in the `DGROUP`.

6. `GlobalAlloc` only can be called 8,192 times on a protected-mode 16-bit system such as the one used by the version of Windows that runs on top of DOS.

7. Suballocators use `GlobalAlloc` to grab chunks of memory from the operating environment. They then parcel this memory out to a program in bits and pieces whenever the program allocates memory through calls to malloc or new. This system helps a program or suite of programs circumvent the 8KB limit on the number of global memory objects that can be allocated during the course of a single 16-bit Windows session.

8. To make a window invisible, pass `SW_HIDE` to `ShowWindow`.

9. Use `LZCopy` to copy a file from one directory to another.

10. Use either `MoveWindow` or `SetWindowPos` to move a window from one location to another.

Index

16-bit memory

controls

dialog boxes

fonts

functions

listings

TBBUTTON structure

X-Y-Z

PLUG YOURSELF INTO...

THE MACMILLAN INFORMATION SUPERLIBRARY™

Free information and vast computer resources from the world's leading computer book publisher-—online!

FIND THE BOOKS THAT ARE RIGHT FOR YOU!

A complete online catalog, plus sample chapters and tables of contents give you an in-depth look at *all* of our books, including hard-to-find titles. It's the best way to find the books you need!

● STAY INFORMED with the latest computer industry news through our online newsletter, press releases, and customized Information SuperLibrary Reports.

● GET FAST ANSWERS to your questions about MCP books and software.

● VISIT our online bookstore for the latest information and editions!

● COMMUNICATE with our expert authors through e-mail and conferences.

● DOWNLOAD SOFTWARE from the immense MCP library:
   - Source code and files from MCP books
   - The best shareware, freeware, and demos

● DISCOVER HOT SPOTS on other parts of the Internet.

● WIN BOOKS in ongoing contests and giveaways!

TO PLUG INTO MCP: ➔ WORLD WIDE WEB: **http://www.mcp.com**

GOPHER: gopher.mcp.com

FTP: ftp.mcp.com

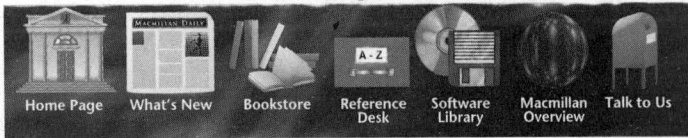

Add to Your Sams Library Today with the Best Books for Programming, Operating Systems, and New Technologies

The easiest way to order is to pick up the phone and call

1-800-428-5331

between 9:00 a.m. and 5:00 p.m. EST.
For faster service please have your credit card available.

ISBN	Quantity	Description of Item	Unit Cost	Total Cost
0-672-30602-6		Programming Windows 95 Unleashed (book/CD)	$49.99	
0-672-30474-0		Windows 95 Unleashed (book/CD)	$35.00	
0-672-30611-5		Your Windows 95 Consultant	$19.99	
0-672-30765-0		Navigating the Internet with Windows 95	$25.00	
0-672-30685-9		Windows NT 3.5 Unleashed	$39.99	
0-672-30568-2		Teach Yourself OLE Programming in 21 Days (book/CD)	$39.99	
0-672-30448-1		Teach Yourself C in 21 Days, Bestseller Edition	$24.95	
0-672-30594-1		Programming WinSock (book/disk)	$35.00	
0-672-30655-7		Developing Your Own 32-Bit Operating System (book/CD)	$49.99	
0-672-30620-4		Teach Yourself Visual Basic 4 in 21 Days, Third Edition	$35.00	
0-672-30667-0		Teach Yourself Web Publishing with HTML	$25.00	
0-672-30737-5		World Wide Web Unleashed, Second Edition	$35.00	
❏ 3 ½" Disk		Shipping and Handling: See information below.		
❏ 5 ¼" Disk		TOTAL		

Shipping and Handling: $4.00 for the first book, and $1.75 for each additional book. Floppy disk: add $1.75 for shipping and handling. If you need to have it NOW, we can ship product to you in 24 hours for an additional charge of approximately $18.00, and you will receive your item overnight or in two days. Overseas shipping and handling adds $2.00 per book and $8.00 for up to three disks. Prices subject to change. Call for availability and pricing information on latest editions.

201 W. 103rd Street, Indianapolis, Indiana 46290

1-800-428-5331 — Orders   1-800-835-3202 — FAX   1-800-858-7674 — Customer Service

Book ISBN 1-672-30531-3

**Organizational Policy
and Strategic Management:**

Text and Cases

Organizational Policy and Strategic Management:
Text and Cases

James M. Higgins
Auburn University at Montgomery

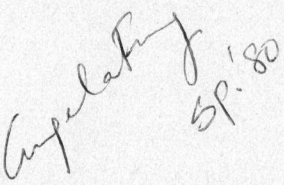

 The Dryden Press   Hinsdale, Illinois

Library of Congress Catalog Card Number: 78-56201
ISBN: 0-03-022186-2

Printed in the United States of America
9 074 98765432

To Ellen, Tracy, and Laura

Duncan
Essentials of Management, 2nd edition

Gellerman
Management of Human Relations

Gellerman
Management of Human Resources

Gellerman
Managers and Subordinates

Glueck
Management

Glueck
Management Essentials

Glueck and Jauch
The Managerial Experience: Cases, Exercises and Readings

Grad, Glans, Holstein, Meyers and Schmidt
Management Systems, 2nd edition

Higgins
Organizational Policy and Strategic Management: Text and Cases

McFarlan, Nolan and Norton
Information Systems Administration

Robinson
International Business Management, 2nd edition

Preface

This book is designed: 1. to provide the student with knowledge of the strategic management and organizational policy processes. 2. to provide the student with the opportunity to employ this knowledge and to practice strategic decision making and policy formation through the use of the case method. The commonly recognized objectives of a course in strategic management and organizational policy include the following:

1. To integrate the student's knowledge of the functional business disciplines (marketing, production, finance, accounting, management, personnel, information systems, and so forth), and to create an awareness of their interdependence.
2. To teach the student how to make decisions by forcing him to make decisions.
3. To acquaint the student with strategic management—its formulation and the resultant strategy content, policy, organization, implementation, and control.
4. To acquaint the student with the role of policy in the organization.
5. To relate to the student the purposes of functional activity and to cause the student to become objective oriented.
6. To acquaint the student with business's multiple roles within the society, especially those external constraints with which business is confronted.
7. To familiarize the student with the role of the general manager.

Text and cases are used to accomplish these objectives. The text summarizes the growing body of literature related to strategic management and organizational policy. Its length has been carefully kept to a minimum in order that the student will have time to examine as many cases as possible. The text focuses on the major views of how strategic management and organizational policy should be practiced and the manner in which the research evidence suggests that they actually are practiced. Key strategic management concepts such as contingency theory, the matrix technique of strategic assessment, and the organizational coalition are examined. A comprehensive organizational process model is used to integrate the textual material and relate it to the cases. The central focus of both the text and the cases is strategy formation. However, text material and cases are included for the subsequent phases of the organization process—intermediate planning, organization, implementation, and evaluation and control—so that the student may comprehend the relationships of organization and activity to strategy, policy, and objectives.

The case portion includes cases on large and small organizations in both profit and nonprofit sectors of the economy. The cases are comprehensive in nature, examining multiple issues in differing situations. Cases on well-known organizations and on industries and issues of interest to students are central (I have found that students learn more and more quickly when they are interested in the subject), and they emphasize the need for environmental awareness. In addition to normal environmental demands, business, society, and governmental interface issues are an integral part of several of the cases.

Both the text and case portions employ strategy and policy formation as the integrative mechanism as opposed to functional area reviews and cases, which have characterized many policy textbooks in the past. Subject content similar to what would be expected to be found in texts for other courses has been held to a minimum.

The author is indebted to many individuals who contributed both directly and indirectly to this book. I wish to express my appreciation to those who have researched strategic management and organizational policy, for they have dispelled many of the myths associated with these processes. Special thanks is due to the authors who so graciously contributed their cases and to those top managers who allowed their organizations to be examined and aided the case development process. Recognition is due to Lillian Avilla, Kay Raybill, Shirley Pritchett, and Betty Beville for their typing assistance. My special thanks goes to Betty Smith, who typed the final manuscript. I also owe my appreciation to the reviewers. I want to thank Bob Fulmer for his encouragement in the early phases. I also want to thank Daniel Tomcheff of The Dryden Press for his developmental and production assistance. Bill Glueck's guidance also proved valuable. And, finally, I want to thank John Trever for the clever cartoons, most of which he created especially for this book.

James M. Higgins
Montgomery, Alabama
June 1, 1978

Contents

Chapter 8

The Narrowing of Strategic Alternatives:
Business and Its Environment,
Now and in the Future   155

Cases   **Case Studies**

Strategy Formation

Contents   xi

Organizational Policy and Strategic Management:

Text and Cases

Chapter 1

Strategic Management and Organizational Policy:

A Conceptual Framework

If we could first know where we are tending, we could then better judge what to do and how to do it.

Abraham Lincoln

The subjects of this book are strategic management and organizational policy.

Strategic management is the process of managing the pursuit of the accomplishment of organizational mission coincident with managing the relationship of the organization to its environment.

The major concerns of strategic management are:

1. The formulation of a Master Strategy for accomplishing organizational mission and managing environmental relationships.
2. The creation of appropriate organizational policy which will insure that the Master Strategy is properly formulated and properly implemented throughout the organization.

Strategic management focuses on the formation of strategic objectives and the strategic plans and policies designed to accomplish those objectives. To that end, it is principally concerned with the executive actions of strategy formation, organization, control, motivation, integration, and policy formation as practiced and as they should be practiced. Strategic management stresses managing the organization's relationship with its environment as a means to mission accomplishment. Strategic management recognizes that most organizations operate in increasingly volatile and often hostile environments.

Organizational policy is comprised of broad forms of guidance established to aid managers in formulating and in implementing the Master Strategy.

Such guidance ranges from very broad statements to somewhat more specific constraints on allowable or intended courses of action. Policy guidance is necessary if the actions taken by organization members are to be consistent with the organization's missions. Policy provides a framework within which organization members may function.

In this chapter, a largely normative model of the organizational process is introduced for the purpose of examining strategic management in all types of organizations: business, government, and private sector nonprofit. Throughout Part I, empirical research as related to this model and the strategic management process is discussed. This evidence is presented to aid the student of strategic management in solving real world problems. These research findings may be used in solving the simulation of real world problems, e.g., cases, such as may be found in Part II. Cases 1 through 19 relate directly to strategic management situations. While all organizations are considered in this text, the business organization is used most often. Examples of nonprofit practices are utilized where these are perceived to differ substantially from business practices.

The Master Strategy

The term strategy derives from the Greek word for general, *strategos*. Its usage dates back to approximately 400 B.C. Until the 19th century, the term strategy related to the plans of action used by a military force in battle. More recently the term strategy has taken on new meanings and is most frequently used to refer to the endeavors of various organizations, primarily business organizations, to anticipate, respond to, and generally survive in their respective environments. While the term strategy is defined differently in the varying organizational contexts in which it may be encountered,[1] there is general agreement that a strategy consists of major organizational objectives and the plans of action to reach those objectives. Strategies have commonly been classified according to:

1. Scope—organization-wide, corporate, business, division, program, etc.
2. Basic actions—competition, growth, diversification, divestment, etc.
3. Organizational function—marketing, production, finance, personnel, etc.
4. Management function—planning, organizing, controlling, leading, motivating, etc.

The primary focus of the strategic management process is the formation of the Master Strategy—an organization-wide strategy comprised of several substrategies. An organization's Master Strategy is:

1. That group of major objectives which states what the organization wishes to become, and
2. The associated strategic plans which tell how it will accomplish these objectives as it manages its relationship with its environment.

Every organization's Master Strategy commences with its basic missions. These are the "whys" of the organization, the basic reasons for the organization's existence. Normally missions would be stated in rather broad terms. For example, most business organizations would have the socioeconomic

Figure 1.1 The Relationship of Mission to the Master Strategy

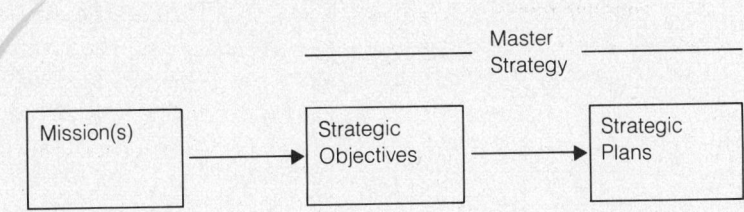

missions of producing certain goods or services at a profit while maintaining satisfactory relationships with major environmental constituents. Successful organizations express these missions in terms of achievable objectives. Plans are then established to accomplish these specific objectives. This relationship is portrayed in Figure 1.1. The exact objectives and plans of action comprising the Master Strategy differ among organizations as the consequence of many variables. Within any organization context, the Master Strategy has three main components. Table 1.1: Primary Mission Strategy, Mission Supportive Strategy, and Strategic Issues Strategies. Many, if not most, businesses define the Master Strategy as if it were an exercise in marketing. They view strategy in general as a competitive endeavor and thus define it in terms of the first component—the strategic objectives and strategic plans for competing in the marketplace. Other business organizations, in addition to concerns with competition, include elements of the second component—Mission Support—in their definition of the Master Strategy. Finally, some organizations also include any major objective and plan of action related to mission accomplishment and the management of environmental relationships. This last approach is most consistent with the definition of the Master Strategy presented earlier, but the less inclusive variations are still more common.

Typical of Master Strategy statements based on the Primary Mission Component (competitive strategy for business) is the following classic example. In 1965, Heublein's stated objectives were three in number:

1. To make Smirnoff the number one liquor brand in the world.
2. To continue a sales growth of 10 percent a year through internal growth, acquisition, or both.
3. To maintain a return on equity above 15 percent.

The essence of its plans of action to accomplish these objectives was as follows:

1. substantive advertising
2. certain types of distribution

Table 1.1   The Components of the Master Strategy

1. **Primary Mission Strategy** (For Business—The Mission Competitive Strategy)

   This is the strategy designed to accomplish the primary mission. For business, the contents of this strategy are normally related to:

   Basic Action Strategies
   a. Competition
   b. Growth
   c. Diversification
   d. Acquisition
   e. Divestment
   f. Retrenchment
   g. Stabilization

   Organization Function Strategies (Economic Functions)
   a. Marketing

2. **Mission Supportive Strategies**

   These strategies detail how the organization supports the primary mission. For business, the contents of this strategy are normally related to:

   Organization Function Strategies (Economic Functions)
   a. Production
   b. Finance
   c. Personnel
   d. Information Systems
   e. R&D, Market Research
   f. Other Significant Areas

   Management Function Strategies
   a. Planning
   b. Organizing
   c. Implementing
   d. Controlling
   e. Staffing
   f. Leading
   g. Motivating
   h. Communicating
   i. Decision Making
   j. Integrating

3. **Strategic Issues Strategies**

   These strategies are designed to cope with contingencies, known and unknown. The strategies employed may be any of the Basic Action, Organizational Functional, or Management Functional Strategies necessary to cope with the following:

   Known Contingencies
   a. Equal Employment Opportunity
   b. Environmental Protection, etc.

   Surprises
   a. Competitor Changes Strategy, etc.

3. careful selection of products and acquisitions with high cash flows (to allow substantive advertising)

Heublein, in these statements, quite succinctly captured what it wanted to be and how it was to accomplish these ends. Note again that Heublein did not embellish its Master Strategy with any considerations not associated directly with its competitive activity. In nonprofit organizations, similar definitions of the Master Strategy in terms of the primary mission may be found. For example, the Equal Employment Opportunity Commission (EEOC) has as its mission the enforcement of Title VII of the Civil Rights Act of 1964, as amended. To that end, the EEOC developed a strategy to solve the problem of discrimination in employment. As a major objective, it sought to ensure that as many jobs as possible were opened to equal employment opportunity. Pressure, conciliation, and legal suits were brought against the very largest, most visible employers such as American Telephone and Telegraph, the entire U.S. steel industry, General Motors, and numerous others. The EEOC's strategy recognized that given its limited manpower the visual evidence of its enforcement efforts might be used to scare the majority of employers into compliance. While this is a precise statement of strategy for the accomplishment of primary mission, this strategy fails to consider many other aspects of the organization's total environment.

In contrast to Heublein and the EEOC examples, IBM approaches its Master Strategy from the viewpoint of its more encompassing definition. IBM's Master Strategy contains two principal components: mission—which contains competitive and supportive statements—and strategic issues. Each year IBM reviews its Master Strategy as its operating businesses (products) and its support functions establish objectives and plans for the year. This process occurs within the policies established for strategy formation. Certain corporate Master Strategy considerations, such as diversification and divestment (when necessary), are treated as assumptions. Strategic issues are managed separately.

Currently, more organizations are reflecting statements in their overall strategy concerned with the total environment and the total organization, not just those aspects related to competition. For example, Union Carbide has a complex strategy for improving its environmental protection activity. Its Environmental Impact Analysis program (EIA) is headed by a high-ranking corporate official. Each company plant is rated on numerous aspects of products and processes on a scale of 0 to 4 as to how these impact on several environmental areas of concern—air quality, noise, water pollution, etc. Potential problem areas are immediately observable. Public opinion is also rated. Most of the rating system is computerized, as are the corporation's processes. Inputs and outputs are measured. Wastes and pollution are determined and controlled. Corrective actions are taken.

The Master Strategy is an umbrella beneath which specific primary, supportive, and strategic issue objectives and plans may be established. A Master

Strategy may include any number of strategies of varying scope, basic actions, organizational functions, or management functions.

Organizational Policy

The term *policy* is normally used to designate broad guidance created to insure the successful formulation and implementation of strategy. Most policies have a broad and major impact on the organization, but some have a more limited impact and are designed to guide decisions through the use of more specific constraints. Policies provide organization members, primarily managers, with a framework within which decisions may be made. Examples of policies include the following:

1. Only products with at least a 15 percent return on investment (ROI) will be considered as an addition to existing product lines.
2. Only products with high quality will be chosen for inclusion in our product line.

Because of these policies, business and division managers will not select products which do not provide at least this rate of return or which do not have high quality. These policies save time and effort because managers do not have to determine what level of ROI is appropriate or what level of product quality is sought for the accomplishment of organizational mission. This has already been considered and incorporated into policy.

As with the term strategy, the usage of the term policy varies greatly. The student of strategic management should recognize this but should not allow these semantic problems to interfere with organizational analysis. The term is often employed to describe what was earlier defined as strategy. Or the term may be used to describe very specific rules such as "No Smoking" or "Employees Retire at Age 65." Often policy is considered to be a component of strategy as opposed to objectives and plans. Regardless of the designation, an organization must have major objectives and plans of action in order to accomplish its mission. The organization must also have some form of broad guidance for formulating and implementing them. These components of effective organizations are labeled here as strategy and policy, respectively.

The Organization as a System

Figure 1.2 is a model of the organizational process, used throughout this text to integrate the various points of discussion. In using this model, the organization must be viewed as a system in two primary ways. First, it is composed

Figure 1.2 The Organization—An Organization Process Model

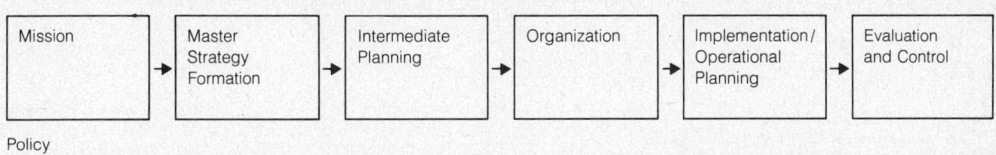

Policy

of subsystems, within and among which social systems develop. These social relationships will play a major role in strategy formation. Secondly, the organization itself is a system, but it is also a single subsystem within a pluralistic societal/economic system. As a result, the strategic manager must be concerned with the relationships which develop between the organization and other systems in its environment.

The Organization as a System Composed of Subsystems

Examining the organization internally from the systems perspective, it is apparent that it is composed of subsystems which correspond to functional disciplines.[2] One view of the organization as a system which has been adapted to the typical Weberian bureaucratic organizational model is depicted in Figure 1.3. For the purpose of the example the organization has four subsystems—reflecting those normally characterized as the most important line and staff functions: production, marketing, finance, and personnel. In viewing the organization in this manner, the stage is set for the examination of the top management role in strategy formation.

On a formal basis, strategic planning decisions are made by a group of top managers here referred to as the organization's strategists. Depending on size, ownership characteristics, and other variables, this top management group may consist of the owner(s), the board of directors, the president, the division chiefs, vice presidents, professional planners, and other key upper level management members representing the various organizational units—production, marketing, finance, personnel, and others.

Studies of the strategy formation process have revealed that a powerful informal group of top managers may emerge within this formal planning group. This informal group, referred to as the coalition, may, in fact, establish an organization's strategies dependent upon the entrepreneurial leadership characteristics of the organization's formal leader. When the coalition is stronger than the organization's formal leader, then bargaining will determine organization strategies and policy. Members of the coalition will negotiate strategic and policy matters among themselves, with powerful individuals, or with other coalitions which may develop internally or externally to the

Figure 1.3 Typical Weberian Bureaucratic Organizational Model

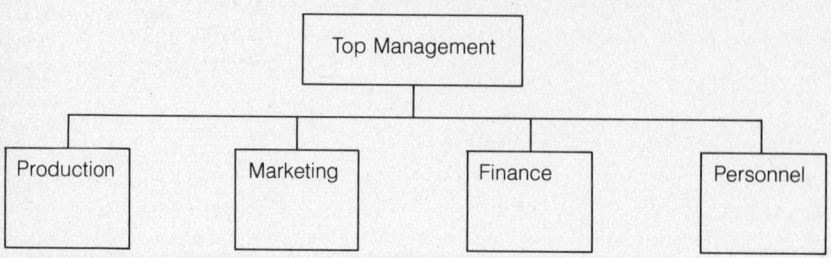

organization. At the center of this bargaining process is the conflict which exists between the manager's desire to accomplish his particular subunit's objectives and to protect his subunit's interests (and his own), and the requirement of the organization to accomplish organizational objectives. Because managers seek to improve subunit performance in organizations with scarce resources, they must compete with other managers. But total competition would be detrimental. Bargaining and tradeoffs of strategic or policy matters occur. The result is often suboptimization and failure to accomplish the mission. While much of this concept is in opposition to the traditional view of the all-powerful chief executive officer, significant empirical support substantiates this view and is reviewed in more detail in Chapter 4.

Business and Other Systems as Open Systems

As a system, business may be viewed as a processing unit. It receives inputs, processes these, and distributes resultant outputs as shown in Figure 1.4. Other organizations also process inputs and yield outputs. What makes business unique is that it sells its product and service outputs for more than the cost of the inputs and processing. This difference is called profit. Without profit, business cannot survive. But profit is not business's only consideration. The events of the 1960s taught business leaders an important lesson—business is an open system. That is, it has transactions across system boundaries with more than just customers, suppliers, and unions. It has interactions with society and government and with members of pressure groups such as environmentalists and minority interest organizations. Contrary to popular opinion and widespread antibusiness literature, business does not act solely in accordance with its own self-interests in search of profit. It does consider the demands of other systems. It must consider these if it is to accomplish its mission in the long run. Business today faces many severe problems as a result of these demands, but it is learning to cope with them. These challenges to the business system are discussed at length in Chapter 8.

Figure 1.4   The Input-Output Business Model

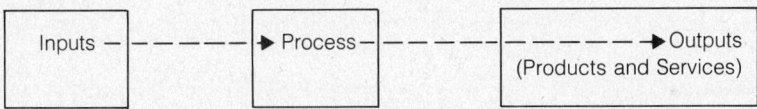

The very essence of understanding strategic management in all organizations is recognizing the interdependence of the organizational subsystems and recognizing an organization's role as a subsystem within other greater systems. For example, with regard to business as a system composed of subsystems, financial strategy results mainly from strategic decisions made in the functional areas of marketing and production. Marketing strategy is dependent upon the functioning within the production, finance, and personnel areas, and so forth. All of these decisions result partially from consideration of the external environment. Strategic management stresses managing the organization's environmental interface. In summary, the manager must view the organization in a systems perspective if objectives are to be efficiently and effectively accomplished. This requires that the manager determine the impact of his decisions upon other subsystems within the organization and that the impact of these decisions upon external systems be considered.

Strategic Management in the Organization: An Organization Process Model

The role of strategic management in the organization can be readily examined through the use of an organization process model such as that presented in Figure 1.2, and a master strategy formation model such as that presented in Figure 1.5. The organization's strategic managers are concerned primarily with the Master Strategy and with policy, but the effective strategic manager also concerns himself to a relevant degree with the remainder of the organization process. He thus formulates better strategies and better policies. Figure 1.5 may be used to describe how any strategy leads to organizational action, but the Master Strategy is the strategy of primary concern at this point. How this model is actually operationalized varies from organization to organization. The Organization Process Model contains the principal components of the effective organization:

1. Mission—organizations exist to accomplish a mission(s). Successful organizations know their mission(s).
2. Master Strategy—successful organizations establish objectives and plans to reach those objectives.

3. Intermediate Planning—the Master Strategy must be defined in more precise terms if it is to be operationalized.
4. Organization—the tasks required by the plans of action must be specifically defined and sufficient authority distributed in order to carry out those tasks. The organization's structure is dictated by its strategy.
5. Implementation—individuals take action and accomplish their tasks.
6. Evaluation and Control—was the Master Strategy successful? If not, why not? The organization's strategists must know if they are to successfully practice strategic management.

7. Policy—guidance must be available for the entire process.
In the following pages, each of these components is examined briefly. In the remainder of Part I, these components are examined in more detail.

Mission and Master Strategy Formation

In strategy formation, the organization's strategists assess internal and environmental factors for their impacts upon strategy in light of mission and policy. They determine organizational strengths, weaknesses, threats, and opportunities. They propose strategic alternatives, evaluate these, and formulate strategy as the result of decision making. Figure 1.5 examines this process in more detail. Strategy formation commences with the organization's mission—the why (or whys) of the organization. Any organization's strategy must be based on its missions. Missions determine what objectives are established and the major plans that are chosen for reaching these objectives. The policies to be considered in strategic formation are derived from these missions. These master policies are normally formulated by the board of directors and the organization's chief executive or by other organization strategists. Typically, such policies describe the types of businesses the firm will engage in, the social responsibility position of the organization, the organizational climate to be established, some statement of product quality, and so forth. In some firms, these policies become quite specific, almost comprising a Master Strategy.

The term **organizational strategists** is used in larger organizations to refer either to those top managers who plan and/or to the staff members of the planning units who may be delegated some of the chief executive officer's (CEO) planning duties. Top management planners usually include the board of directors, the CEO, his immediate staff, professional planners, and the division level managers. In smaller organizations planning, when performed, may be the result of a single individual's effort or the efforts of a committee of top managers. Often no planning unit exists in small organizations. In such cases, information related to strengths, weaknesses, threats, and opportunities may be unrefined inputs from organization members.

Internally, the major informational considerations are organization

Figure 1.5   Master Strategy Formation

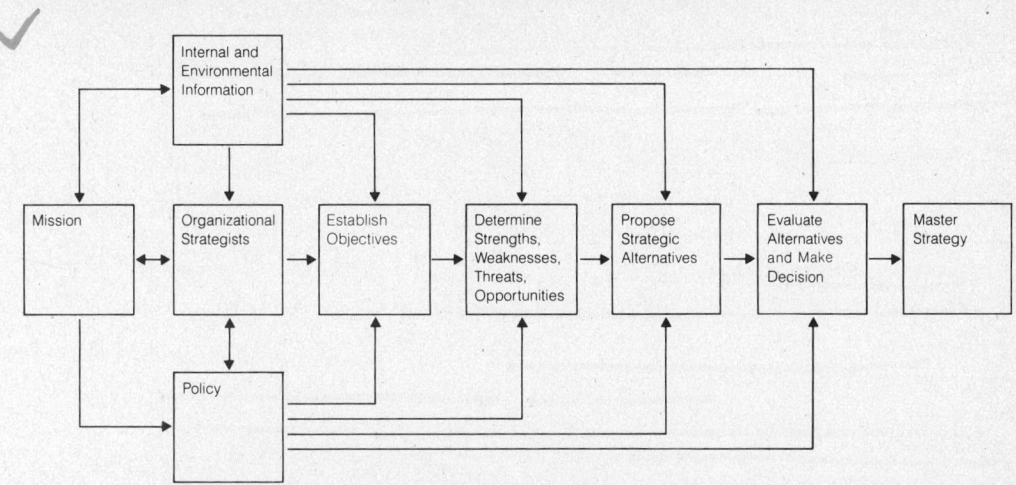

strengths and weaknesses relative to mission and relative to the organization's external environment. Typical concerns are human, capital, and financial resources; stockholder and management expectations. In the external environment, the major factors to be considered include: government,[3] technology (for many organizations), competition, society, the economy, labor, and natural resources (for many organizations). All of these factors help determine the organization's opportunities and associated threats.

While smaller organizations cannot commit resources which larger organizations are able to commit, it is believed that they should establish a formal planning function. This function can be performed by just one man who for one day a month develops and coordinates a master strategy with organizational managers. Larger organizations such as AT&T may have as many as 100 staff members in their planning units. Regardless of the configuration of the planning unit, and recognizing that planning is an ongoing process, every organization needs to participate in a periodic formal planning exercise— strategy assessment and reformation (if necessary)—preferably on at least an annual basis.[4]

Conceptually, top managers determine organizational strengths, weaknesses, threats, and opportunities; list alternatives; evaluate their impacts; and make strategic decisions based on these evaluations. To a large extent, this is the process followed, but it is not an entirely rational process. The organization is a system composed of subsystems. Top management representatives from the various subsystems confer to determine strategy with the CEO. Dependent on relative strengths, either the coalition, the CEO, or the professional planner will usually determine strategy. In the strategy formation stage, top management filters the information they receive regarding internal and environmental factors as related to mission in the light of their own personalities and social group relationships. They assess the situation (the organization, its mission, and its environment), propose alternatives, and choose among these based on social interactions, personal interests, and their perceptions of the information. Strategy formation is very often a social/political process, as opposed to being a strictly rational process. Regardless of how the information for planning is obtained and how decisions are determined, the CEO and/or the divisional level managers and the board of directors are responsible for formally approving planning decisions.

The Stages of Planning:
Strategy, Intermediate, and Operational Planning

The result of top management's considerations of information, mission, and policy is strategy, here the Master Strategy. It is the first of three major levels of plans: strategy, intermediate, and operational plans which integrate organization action with the mission. This is accomplished through successive levels of objectives and plans to reach those objectives.

The objectives toward which strategic plans are directed should be specific. Examples include a 15 percent return on investment, a 20 percent penetration of the product market, a 10 percent increase in sales per year, and so forth. The plans, however, at the strategic planning stage, need not be stated so specifically. In fact, at the strategy stage, these plans are usually very broad statements. But as planning progresses through the next two stages, intermediate and operational planning, the plans will become more specific regarding the how of objective accomplishment. Intermediate plans translate strategy into more specific courses of action for major organizational subsystems. Operational plans translate intermediate plans into very specific courses of action for lower level subsystems and for individuals. Usually the planning process includes a series of increasingly complex and detailed subobjectives, subplans, subpolicies, sub-subobjectives, sub-subplans, and sub-subpolicies, and so forth, until objectives and actions are parcelled to the individual worker. Again, as with most management terminology, there are no generally accepted definitions which describe the various levels of plans established to accomplish the Master Strategy. Although it should be recognized that these differences exist, they should be allowed for in the examination of strategy and in the practice of strategic management.

There are various dimensions of strategy which must be incorporated into any discussion of its stages. One of the major considerations is the time horizon—the length of time which a plan covers. The three primary stages of planning—strategy (*long-range planning*), intermediate planning, and operational planning—are classified primarily according to their time horizon dimension. Strategy is normally concerned with a time horizon of five to seven years. This means that firms formulate strategy five to seven years in advance of anticipated implementation. Intermediate planning has a time horizon of a few months to five years. Operational planning normally has a time horizon of a few weeks to one year. These time horizon planning phases are depicted in Figure 1.2 from left to right. These time horizons may vary according to several factors. During a period of a turbulent environment, time horizons are usually reduced. Another consideration when discussing plans is the amount of detail contained in each type of plan. In Figure 1.2, the plans become more detailed as they near the operational stage. Finally, strategies are much more comprehensive than are operational plans. Strategies have the potential to commit far more resources than do operational plans.

Intermediate planning is the next phase of planning once strategy is formulated. (See Cases 20 and 21.) Exactly where strategies end and these intermediate plans begin is difficult to determine in many organizations. Depending upon the organization which one encounters, this phase of planning may have as many as 50 to 100 different types of plans. The exact titles of these actions vary with numerous factors such as scope, the task which the organizational unit is attempting to accomplish, the type of organization, the technology involved, and so forth. Therefore, these plans may vary in the degree of detail, comprehensiveness, and time horizon. They may range from broad plans which are not very specific and cover hundreds or perhaps even thousands of workers to those which cover only a few workers and resources and are very specific, covering a relatively short time period. Most of what are often called *medium-range plans* are found within this section. From the perspective of the total organization these plans may be labeled as intermediate. A particular product division may consider these plans to comprise its Master Strategy.

Operational plans are those which translate intermediate plans into action. Normally, these are one-year plans which have a specific series of objectives and associated actions designed to carry out broader plans. One type of operational plan would be the budget. The term *short-range plan* is often used to describe these plans. Numerous operational plans exist in most organizations. As with intermediate plans, these plans have varying degrees of detail and comprehensiveness.

What are procedures? Procedures are very specific operational plans. They are the series of steps which are to be used by individuals in carrying out more comprehensive operational plans. Procedures are task oriented and are usually quite detailed. They are steps which are to be followed as long as a task is to be performed. These are usually found in the corporate policy manual. An individual would utilize these when performing his job. Examples would include procedures for budget preparation, affirmative action training, drilling a hole, and welding parts together.

What are tactics? Tactics and tactical planning are phrases often used and just as often misunderstood. The term *tactics* is often employed to describe what was defined earlier as strategy. But tactics are more properly classified as intermediate plans. They involve the deployment of resources to achieve the objectives of a strategy.

It should be noted that most organizations do not simply start with strategy and follow it through to implementation. A typical organization may have its Master Strategy in effect at the same time that it has begun to implement a change in this strategy. This means that it may have intermediate and operational plans, as well as implementation procedures and rules which relate to its Master Strategy. At the same time it may also be commencing a new Master Strategy and perhaps even intermediate plans for its new Master Strategy. A typical multinational, multidiversified organization may have several different major strategies in effect simultaneously. It may have 100 plans in various degrees of the intermediate stage, and perhaps hundreds of plans in various degrees of the operational stage. In addition, it may have virtually thousands of procedures to carry out the exact tasks which have been specified in the various planning processes. Similarly, it may have hundreds of policies which are being followed by employees at numerous stages of the process throughout the organization. In short, planning is a continuous, ongoing, iterative process. Because of the multiplicity of objectives and plans, control, which will be examined more thoroughly later, is an important determinant of a successful strategy.

Organization and Implementation

As the firm nears the point of implementation of the plans determined in the other phases, it must organize to carry out these plans and accomplish their objectives. The firm must determine functions, jobs, positions, and distributions of authority as commonly depicted on organization charts. Unless the firm is just commencing operations, it already has an existing organization structure. This organization process normally occurs as a form of reorganization. Organization requires close coordination with operational planning. (See Cases 22 and 23.)

The firm must next implement its plans. It must select individuals to perform the functions of the positions established in organization. Implementation involves the actual performance of these required tasks. Implementation is perceived to be best accomplished through the usage of the management functions by managers. The best results are obtained when managers plan, organize, control, motivate, coordinate, lead, and make decisions in an appropriate fashion. Through these processes the organization assures the accomplishments of objectives. (See Cases 24, 25, and 26.)

Evaluation and Control

The final stage in the process is control. The organization must determine if it has accomplished its predetermined objectives. Control involves the comparison of performance with objectives and the taking of corrective action if performance is less than the objectives. For example, if the strategy requires objectives of 10 percent return on investment (ROI) and a 10 percent increase in sales, management should compare actual performance measures to these objectives. If the organization has not reached its objectives, it should determine why. Sometimes the problems are managerial or technical; and sometimes the problems result from environmental circumstances over which the organization has little or no control. Feedback information regarding performance is given to the organization's strategists and to the individuals who carry out the functions. Typical control devices include: budgets, product quality control reports, and financial statement analyses. The control process often leads to the changing of actions and not infrequently to the modification of plans and objectives. (See Cases 27 and 28.)

A Brief Examination of the Model as Applied

Each January at IBM, the corporate staff develops targets (gross and net income by year) for each of its seven operating divisions. After review by top management these are forwarded to operating division managements. From March to June, the operating units respond with proposed goals including supporting documentation ranging from 6 to 20 pages and a formal presentation to corporate management required two to three weeks subsequent to objectives submission. The various corporate staffs review these objectives and are prepared to agree with or contest them. Support documentation for objectives does not consist of plans but rather statements of threats and opportunities. These objectives, once agreed to, become control points for operating unit performance.

IBM considers its primary mission strategy to result from business area (product) considerations. For each of 50-plus business areas, each of which reports to one of the seven operating units, an annual strategy statement is required. This strategy statement contains all of the elements described by the basic model: environmental analysis, statements of threats, objectives, plans of action, resource requirements, and so forth. These strategies must be updated annually and must be consistent with the implementation efforts of the operating units, the primary operational component of the organization. The operating units are charged with improving productivity, tracking the environment, and implementing the business area strategies. The business area strategies are the central vehicle for the operating unit to use in developing plans in support of the objectives to which it has previously agreed.

During the last three months of the year, the operating units submit plans to corporate management for approval. The time horizon of these plans varies according to perceived critical factors and lead times to implementation. Budgets are required for the first two years of the plans only. Various review procedures by staff and corporate management units occur until the operating unit head formally presents his plans to top management. Once approved, these plans form the basis for future objectives and control. Flexibility in response to contingencies is incorporated into the overall process. Strategic issues (as defined previously) are responded to and planned for, aside from the annual planning process.

This process is similar to what other organizations with formal planning processes do on a periodic basis to accomplish mission and achieve a satisfactory relationship with the environment. Inherent to all of these processes are basic questions: What are we now? What do we want to be? How do we get there? Do we have the resources? What do we do if something goes wrong?

What Organizations Practice Strategic Management?

One fact which we can be assured of is that corporations feel that strategic planning is worthwhile. Surveys of top corporations have continually shown an active and increasing program of strategic planning. Similar surveys of

"We've had to depend rather heavily on strategic management."

smaller companies have also shown considerable and increasing interest in strategic planning. Companies are extremely concerned about the planning process. Major revisions of techniques and the exploration of new methodologies are widespread. For example, Naylor and Schonland report that they personally are aware of over 2,000 corporations in the United States, Canada, and Europe that are using or planning to develop some form of corporate planning simulation model.

In addition, it is well known that the federal government practices strategic planning in many of its activities. In fact, it has been observed that many of the strategic management techniques that business utilizes were copied from government. The data on other nonprofit organizations is less extensive, but it is unlikely that they are not planning. This information suggests that probably all organizations of significant size practice strategic planning in some form.

Does Strategic Management Pay?

In 1916, Henri Fayol was one of the first proponents of planning and the first major proponent of long-range planning. He recommended one- and ten-year plans as a means for insuring accomplishment of organizational purpose. Since that time, the assumption has always been that planning produces greater profits than not planning. Planning has been viewed as essential. Yet, is it really? The premise of this book is that planning is profitable, but should you accept that on faith alone? Even though there is a certain common sense about the value of strategy, justification must be proven.

Thune and House reported the first evidence which strongly supported this benefit contention. They examined 36 firms, in matched pairs of formal planning versus nonformal planning firms in six industries for seven years. Firms were matched in terms of size, growth, etc., prior to the commencement of the study. They concluded first that planning firms outperformed nonplanning firms in terms of ROI, ROE, and growth in earnings per share, and generally equalled or surpassed nonplanners in sales growth. Secondly, planning firms outperformed themselves prior to the time they adopted formal planning systems. Another study was performed by Herold, who extended the study begun by Thune and House using similar measures but adding pretax profits. Given the changes that occur over time, i.e., mergers, acquisitions, etc., Herold's study involved only a limited number of the original firms (ten) for the additional four years of his study. However, the formal planners continued to outperform the nonplanners generally across all measures.

Another study, much more tentative than the two above, examined planning with respect to mergers and acquisitions. Ansoff, Avener, Brandenberg, Portener, and Radosevich observed the impact on planning of mergers and acquisitions in 93 firms for the period 1946–65. Both subjective and objective measures of performance were used. While the subjective measures proved of little assistance in supporting the planning benefit tenet, the objective measures supported planning as an important determinant of sales growth, earnings per share growth, earnings growth, etc. In addition, the planners were better able to predict the outcome of their decisions than were the nonplanners.

Three studies indicate that in certain situations planning may pay and in other situations it may not. These studies also show that various kinds of planning processes may lead to various types of success. In the first of these, additional but indecisive support for the proposition that planning pays was provided by Rue and Fulmer. In surveying planning practices in 432 firms, Rue and Fulmer found that "in service industries, the non-planners outperformed the planners; while in the durable industries, the planners outperformed the non-planners." They concluded that no across-the-board relationship could be stated between financial success of a firm and long range planning.

Stagner, in studying 217 top managers in 109 large American firms, found that strategic planning configurations using committees produced the largest profit as a percentage of capital. Where discussions among all top executives were used and decisions carefully weighed for cost benefit, these firms had the largest profit as a percent of sales.

Schoeffler, Buzzell, and Heany examined 57 large corporations, studying the effects of strategic planning on profit performance. The situation reported was one of information sharing among a group of participating firms. The results indicate that planning data is important to financial success but that success varies according to certain situational aspects.

Finally, Malik, by questionnaire, examined the relationship in 38 firms between formal and nonformal planning and measures of financial performance. For all but three of thirteen hypotheses, formal planners outperformed informal planners.

Studies using fewer quantitative performance objectives have been reported by Henry, Guynes, Najjar, and Eastlack and McDonald and were mixed with respect to supporting the benefit tenet. Henry, through the use of questionnaires and interviews, reported a favorable relationship between long range planning and corporate satisfaction with planning. Guynes, through a questionnaire, determined a statistical correlation between certain but not all aspects of 150 firms' planning and nonquantitatively measured results. Najjar questioned the CEOs of 94 small Ohio firms as to whether or not they felt planning made their firms more successful. Those who planned did not necessarily perceive themselves as more successful, but—note—Najjar did not examine actual performance. Eastlack and McDonald studied 211 companies. Their conclusion was that CEOs who were involved in the strategic management process headed the fastest growing companies. This is mild support for the benefit tenet.

In summary, the evidence is not conclusive but it is very supportive of the proposition that planning leads to greater profits. As research continues, it appears probable that the basic tenet will be supported.

The Plan of This Book

This chapter introduced the concept of strategic management and a basic, largely normative, comprehensive model that interrelates strategic, intermediate, and operational planning as well as organization, implementation, and control. This chapter also has shown there is growing evidence that strategic management is a worthwhile (profitable) endeavor.

The following chapters will examine the various parts of the basic model in greater detail, emphasizing variations in application and the reported research. In Chapters 2, 3, and 4 various aspects of strategy formation are discussed. Chapter 2 examines the four primary factors in strategy formation: mission, policy, strategic information, and the organizational strategists. Chapter 3 focuses on the technical aspects of strategy formation, including a contingency approach. In Chapter 4, the strategic management decision process is examined in detail. Chapter 5 reviews the content of the Master Strategy and the nature of intermediate planning. Chapter 6 is concerned with the organization and implementation of strategy. Appropriate strategy structure combinations as indicated by research are emphasized in the first portion of this chapter with systems for implementation being emphasized in the second part of the chapter. Chapter 7 focuses on evaluation and control of performance. Chapter 8 discusses the business, government, and society interface, now and in the future, with special emphasis on the resultant narrowing of strategic alternatives.

In Part II cases are presented. This part begins with a commentary on the case method in order to prepare for working with the cases. The cases in Part II are arranged in the same order as the basic model presented in this chapter. Most of the cases involve Master Strategy formation, but cases are contained in sections related to Intermediate Planning, Organization, Implementation, Control, and International Business. All cases were carefully chosen with respect to their content and with respect to their interest to the student.

Discussion Questions

1. What are the seven major elements in the organizational process model? What is the role of each element? Apply this model to a profit-oriented

organization with which you are familiar. How are the elements of the model operationalized in this firm?

2. Think of a nonprofit organization. Now apply the organizational process model to this organization. What differences are there between profit and nonprofit applications, for example, contents of the Master Strategy, policy statements, environmental interaction, and so forth.

Footnotes

1. A commonly agreed-upon definition for most management terms is elusive. The content and formative processes of the specific activities which are described by management terms frequently vary for two primary reasons. First, various authors' and practitioners' definitions reflect their individual perceptions of the differences in the events taking place. Second, management is a recent addition to the sciences. Until such time as an overall governing body or an author or authors provide commonly acceptable definitions, differences in definitions will be encountered. The student of management, here strategic management, must learn to recognize the commonality of activity regardless of the descriptive terminology. This text does attempt to maintain consistency, consistency among the terms used within the text and consistency with those terms as they are more commonly used in the literature related to strategic management. Obviously some compromise between these two objectives will be necessary. Definitions become, as Ackoff has observed, "relative."

2. These subsystems may also be business, divisional, or product depending upon the organizational structure.

3. When the organization of concern is a government subunit, it too can often face constraints—laws placed on it by other government subunits.

4. In addition, another planning resource is available. Consulting organizations can generate for their clients simulations of alternative strategies and otherwise assist their customers in developing strategies, policies, and the overall planning processes.

References

Ackoff, R. L. "General Systems Theory and Systems Research Contrasting Conceptions of Systems Science." *General Systems* 8 (1963): 117–121.

————. "The Meaning of Strategic Planning." In *Business Planning and Policy Formulation*, edited by Robert J. Mockler. New York: Appleton-Century-Crofts, 1972.

Ansoff, H. I. "The Concept of Strategic Management." *Journal of Business Policy*, Summer 1972.

Ansoff, H. I., et al. "Does Planning Pay? The Effect of Planning in Success of Acquisitions in American Firms." *Long Range Planning,* December 1970, pp. 2–7.

Benge, E. A. "The Common Sense of Long-Range Planning." In *Management in Perspective,* edited by W. G. Schlender, W. G. Scott, and A. C. Filley, pp. 203–204. Boston: Houghton Mifflin, 1965.

Carroll, A. "Strategic Planning for Boundary Spanning Relations." *Managerial Planning,* January/February 1976, p. 1.

"Corporate Planning: Piercing Corporate Fog in the Executive Suite." *Business Week,* April 28, 1975, p. 47.

Cyert, R. M., and J. G. March. *A Behavioral Theory of the Firm.* Englewood Cliffs, N.J.: Prentice-Hall, Inc., 1963.

Eastlack, J., Jr., and P. McDonald. "CEO's Role in Corporate Growth." *Harvard Business Review,* May/June 1970, pp. 150–163.

"EEOC Steps Up the Pressure." *Business Week,* February 23, 1974, pp. 87–88.

Fayol, H. *Industrial and General Administration.* New York: Pitman Publishing Corp., 1949.

Frankenhoff, W. P., and C. H. Granger. "Strategic Management: A New Managerial Concept for an Era of Rapid Change." *Long Range Planning,* April 1971, pp. 7–12.

General Electric Annual Report, 1975.

Guynes, C. S. "An Analysis of Planning in Large Texas Manufacturing Firms." Unpublished doctoral dissertation, Texas Technical University, 1969.

Henry, H. W. "Long-Range Planning in Industrial Corporations: An Analysis of Formalized Practices." Unpublished doctoral dissertation, the University of Michigan, 1965.

Herold, D. M. "Long Range Planning and Organizational Performance: A Cross Validation Study." *Academy of Management Journal,* March 1971, pp. 91–102.

Heublein, Inc., (A) George A. Smith, Jr., C. Roland Christensen, and Norman A. Berg, *Policy Formulation and Administration* (Homewood, Illinois: Irwin, 1968).

Hofer, C. W. "Research in Strategic Planning: A Survey of Past Studies and Suggestions for Future Efforts." *Journal of Economics and Business,* Spring/Summer 1976, p. 281.

"How Union Carbide Has Cleaned Up Its Image." *Business Week,* August 2, 1976, p. 46.

Irwin, P. H. "Towards Better Strategic Management." *Long Range Planning,* December 1974, pp. 64–67.

Kinnunen, R. M. "A Strategic Framework for Teaching and Researching Corporate Strategy." In *Proceedings: Academy of Management,* edited by A. G. Bedeian, A. A. Armenakin, W. H. Hadley, Jr., and H. S. Field, Jr., pp. 70–72. Academy of Management, 1975.

Malik, Z. A. "Formal Long Range Planning and Organizational Performance: A Study." Unpublished doctoral dissertation, Rensselaer Polytechnic Institute, 1974.

Mintzberg, H. "Policy as a Field of Management Theory." *Academy of Management Review,* January 1977, pp. 88–103.

Najjar, M. A. "Planning in Small Manufacturing Companies: An Empirical Study." Unpublished doctoral dissertation, Ohio State University, 1966.

Naylor, T. H., and H. Schonland. "A Survey of Users of Corporate Planning Models." *Management Science* 22 (May 1976): 927–937.

Newman, W. H. "Shaping the Master Strategy of Your Firm." *California Management Review,* 1967, no. 3, pp. 77–88.

Prudential Social Report, 1976.

Rue, L. W. "Theoretical and Operational Implications of Long Range Planning on Selected Measures of Financial Performance in U.S. Industry." Unpublished doctoral dissertation, Georgia State University, 1973.

Rue, L. W., and R. M. Fulmer. "Is Long Range Planning Profitable?" *Proceedings: Academy of Management Meetings,* 1973, pp. 66–73.

Schendel, D. E., and K. J. Hatten. "Business Policy or Strategic Management: A Broader View for an Emerging Discipline." *Proceedings: Academy of Management Meetings,* 1972, pp. 99–102.

Schoeffler, S.; R. D. Buzzell; and D. F. Heany. "Impact of Strategic Planning on Profit Performance." *Harvard Business Review,* March/April 1974, pp. 137–145.

Shuman, J. C. "Corporate Planning in Small Companies." *Long Range Planning,* October 1975, pp. 81–90.

Smalter, D. J., "The Influence of Department of Defense Practices on Corporate Planning." *Management Technology,* December 1964.

Stagner, R. "Corporate Decision Making." *Journal of Applied Psychology,* February 1969, pp. 1–13.

Steiner, G. A. *Top Management Planning.* New York: Collier Macmillan Ltd., 1969.

Thoroman, D. G. "Strategic Planning in IBM." *Long Range Planning,* January/February 1971, pp. 2–6.

Thune, S. S., and R. T. House. "Where Long Range Planning Pays Off." *Business Horizons,* August 1970, pp. 81–87.

Young, S. "Organization of the Total System." *California Management Review,* 1968, no. 3, pp. 21–32.

Chapter 2

Strategy and Policy Formation:

Four Primary Formative Factors

Most battles are won—or lost—before they are engaged, by men who take no part in them; by their strategists.

From *Vom Kriege*
K. von Clausewitz

Mission is the organization's "raison d'etre," the reason to be. Mission is the primary consideration upon which organization policy and strategy are based. Strategists in all organizations formulate strategies to accomplish missions. In formulating strategies, strategists depend on policies and information for guidance. This chapter will examine in more detail the four major strategy formation factors presented in the Master Strategy Formation model: 1. Mission, 2. Policy, 3. Strategic Information regarding internal strengths and weaknesses, environmental threats, and opportunities, and 4. the Organizational Strategists. This chapter will also examine some of the other aspects of strategic decision making. The subjects considered in this chapter are presented in Figures 2.1 and 2.2.

Strategy Formation: A Decision Perspective

Figure 2.2 indicates the major components of Master Strategy formation. Organization strategists formulate strategy to accomplish mission. They formulate strategy within the constraints provided by policy and based on the information they receive as related to internal strengths and weaknesses, external threats, and opportunities. Strategy formation is a decision process. Once informaion indicates that a problem or opportunity exists, then alter-

Figure 2.1   The Organization—An Organization Process Model

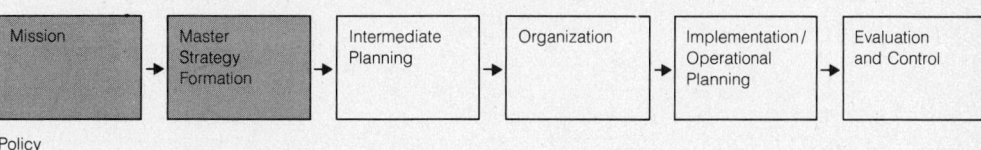

| Mission | Master Strategy Formation | Intermediate Planning | Organization | Implementation/ Operational Planning | Evaluation and Control |

Policy

Figure 2.2 Master Strategy Formation

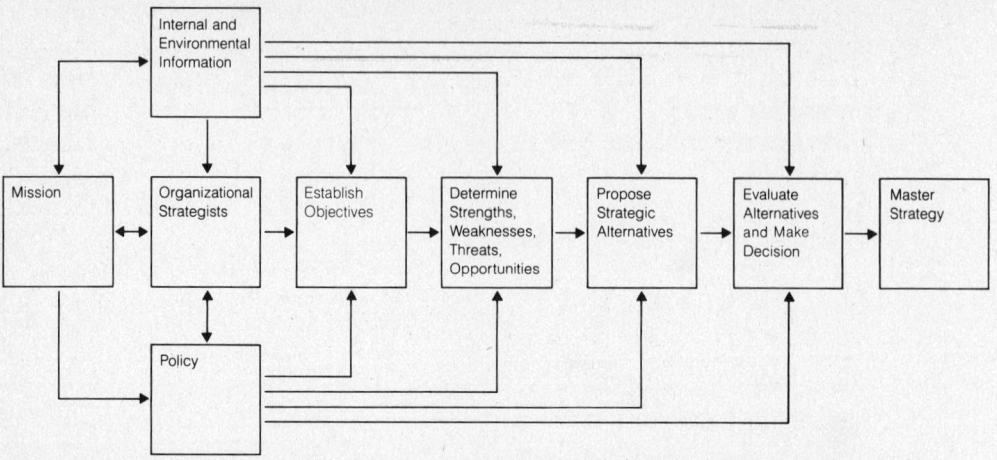

natives must be generated. These alternatives must be evaluated. And, finally, a decision must be made.

The strategy formation decision process parallels the classic conceptualization of decision making depicted in Figure 2.3. This model has five phases. In the recognition phase, decision makers become aware of a problem or an opportunity. A problem is defined as the difference between "what is" and "what should be." Problems result from many factors, but primarily problems result from internal weaknesses and/or external threats. Opportunities are defined as the difference between "what is" and "what could be." Opportunities result primarily from favorable environmental circumstances and from internal strengths. In the identification phase, problems and opportunities are better defined. In the recognition phase, problems and opportunities are not well understood. Rather there is an awareness that a problem or an opportunity exists. In the identification phase, these problems or opportunities are carefully defined. In the solution phase, alternative plans of action are generated either to solve problems or to take advantage of opportunities. These alternatives are evaluated by using information and the constraints of policy. Finally, a decision is made. Implementation of the decision occurs next. This decision will then be subject to control efforts in order to assure its effectiveness.

With respect to strategy formation, as seen in Figure 2.2, recognition oc-

Figure 2.3 Basic Decision Process Model

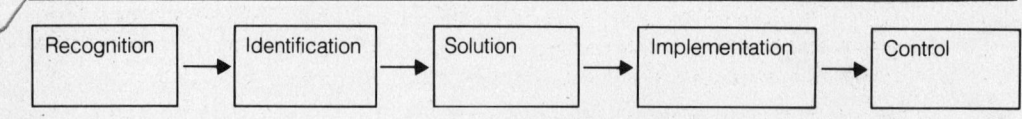

curs when information alerts organization strategists to the existence of a problem or an opportunity. Strategists then further identify problems and opportunities. These phases involve three of the primary formative factors—mission, organizational strategists, and information. Next, strategy formation enters the solution phase as strategists generate and evaluate alternatives to accomplish mission, using information and guided by policy. Finally, decisions are made. Once the strategy content is determined, intermediate planning and organization will follow. Next, implementation occurs. Finally, control measures indicate the success of the strategy. Implementation and control are portrayed relative to strategy in Figure 2.1.

Let us now examine in more detail the four primary formative factors—mission, policy, organizational strategists, and information—and the impact that these have on the formation of strategy.

4 Primary Formative factors:

(1) Mission or Purpose

Classifying organizations into various typologies is useful in understanding and predicting organizational strategy. Classification factors which might be expected to impact on strategy composition would include: organization size—small, medium, and large; geographic scope—local, national, multinational; and the number and diversity of products—single product, diversified, conglomerate. However, the most rudimentary of the factors which affect strategy composition is mission. The most obvious segmentation of organizations according to mission is into categories of profit and nonprofit. More definitively, Blau and Scott have identified four major types of organizations according to the group which receives the greatest amount of benefit from the organization's existence. This classification scheme is essentially one of mission or purpose. These classifications are not mutually exclusive. An organization may, in fact, be appropriately classified into more than one category. These typologies are:

1. The business concern which benefits the owners (and we might add, the employees and most of those who transact with it): for example, General Motors.
2. The mutual benefit association which benefits the members themselves: for example, a union or a club.
3. The service organization which benefits its clients: for example, United Way and the U.S. Department of Health, Education, and Welfare (HEW).
4. The commonweal organization which benefits society in general: for example, the U.S. Department of Defense or HEW.

One would anticipate that differing missions would result in varying strategies. With respect to specific objectives, it is quite clear that varying strategies result. Even organizations possessing the same mission have differing strategies to accomplish this mission. However, each Master Strategy possesses the same major components: primary mission, mission supportive, and strategic issues. (See Chapter 1 for earlier discussion.) Each and every organization must give consideration to these components if it is to successfully accomplish its mission. All organizations must take action to benefit their owners, their clients, their members, or the commonweal. They must support this effort, and they must manage strategic issues.

In summary, all organizations, regardless of mission, have similar major components of strategy, but the specific strategy compositions vary, not just as the result of mission, but as the result of numerous other factors. The private, profit oriented, product or service organization will be the principal organization example throughout this text. When appropriate, examples of the application of the principles of strategic management to organizations with other missions will be given.

Organizational Policy—At the Master Strategy Level

The Master Strategy derives from the organization's mission and from the policies which exist to provide guidance in formulating this strategy. These policies are usually created by the owners, the board of directors, or the chief executive officer (CEO). However, other organizational strategists may aid in their formulation. Some organizations refer to this guidance as their "basic assumptions." Other organizations designate this guidance as "primary objectives." Still others refer to these policies as their "master policies." But regardless of its designation, certain guidance must be available to the organization's strategists as they formulate the Master Strategy. In the business organization, this guidance normally relates to the following issues although exact policies vary from firm to firm:

1. The return on investment desired and other performance criteria
2. The scope of the strategy
3. The basic actions in which the organization may engage: competition, growth, diversification, etc.
4. The industries to be entered
5. The qualifications of products to be offered
6. Where a vital ingredient, the organization's climate
7. The geographic location of the basic action
8. The role of the corporation in the total society

Based on the above, and on consideration of mission and internal and environmental information, the organization's strategists formulate strategies. After considering information related to internal and environmental factors, the organization's strategists may, from time to time, redefine the basic policies which guide the formation of the Master Strategy and its component strategies. For example, examination of internal factors may reveal critical inabilities which preclude diversification. Or exploration of the external environment may reveal that new industry opportunities are available. These Master Policies must remain flexible if the organization is to be successful.

The Organization Strategists

Organizational strategists conceptually include the owners, the board of directors, the CEO, the top line and staff officers, and the professional planners. Research has shown that an organization's strategic decision processes are normally dominated either by an entrepreneurial chief executive, a coalition of high ranking corporate officers, or by the planning department.

Additional research reveals that the board of directors performs few of its classic functions, such as strategic decision making. While the board may passively approve of the organization's objectives and strategies, it normally has very little impact on their formulation. Furthermore, the evidence indicates that most board members are ill prepared to make such decisions. The actions of the board naturally vary from firm to firm. However, the coalitions which may develop on these boards are very important, since the board must finally approve of the chosen strategies. Research reveals that top management often controls the board rather than vice versa, as is normally conceptualized.

The strategic decision process is examined in detail in Chapter 4, with special attention being given to the coalition process. Since the role of the chief executive is a familiar one, the remainder of this discussion will focus on the role of the professional planner. In addition, organizational structure and corporate planning unit relationships, characteristics of the effective planner, and the apparent future of the professional organizational planner are examined.

Planning Units and Professional Planners. When the duties associated with strategy formation become too constraining for the CEO to accomplish alone, he will normally delegate these responsibilities to a planning committee of top managers and/or a professional planning unit. In those organizations which utilize a professional planning unit, the role of the unit and its personnel is largely one of data collection, data analysis, information provision, alternative generation, and alternative evaluation. Professional planners and planning units exist most commonly in the larger business organizations. However, as planning models become more widely computerized and as information sharing within an industry becomes more pronounced, planning units should become more common even in smaller business organizations. The size of planning units varies from the planner and his secretary to a staff of fifty or more in the largest corporations. A study by Greiner indicates that planners spend up to half of their time reading reports. In these reports, the areas which the planning unit is expected to investigate would include:

1. strategic issue surprises of all types

2. strategic issue known contingency actions
3. research into new product and new market opportunities
4. forecasting of all relevant data
5. competitor strategies
6. economic situations—especially change—and how these relate to the organization
7. technological changes
8. societal demands
9. government—legal and political trends
10. internal financial, production, marketing, and personnel information
11. other internal information, other external information

The planner should be the manager and the designer of the strategic information system. The planner influences top and lower levels of management in their planning efforts. He provides information, establishes planning rules, consults, and integrates the various plans submitted. The planner's role in many firms is not so much one of a chief planner but rather one of a planning coordinator. This means then that the planner becomes a monitor, a controller, and a critic of subsystem plans and planning.

Recently, another dimension has been added to the planning function, that of the futurist. While strategists might be concerned with five-year forecasts, futurists peer 20 years or more into the future attempting to define major economic, social, governmental, and technological trends. One of their primary functions appears to be that of asking discerning questions—"what if" questions about the results of traditional forecasting techniques. For example, population forecasts using traditional extrapolatory techniques overlook the impact of changes in birth control practices. The futurist's duty is to query, "What if the use of birth control devices increased or decreased by X%?" Even more dramatic questions may be asked by futurists: "What if the government of a certain country is overthrown, by leftists or rightists? How would this affect our business?" Or, "What if there is another Arab oil embargo?" Although a futurist's primary role is to question, he must also suggest some implications from these findings. Not all organizations would benefit from such predictions, but for many organizations, to ignore some of these areas would be folly.

Finally, from time to time, the planning unit may in fact decide future courses of action for the organization. The power to do so results from their knowledge of and skill in strategy formation and from their control of the information needed to make strategic decisions. This portion of their role will be discussed in Chapter 4.

Organization structure and corporate planning units. Every planning system is unique because it results from particular situational circumstances. Similarly, the position of the planning unit in the organization's structure varies both in terms of duties and responsibilities, and the authority it possesses to carry out these duties and responsibilities. Interest in these differences stems from the need to predict which arrangement would be most appropriate for a particular situation. Numerous variations exist and, frankly, the research on this subject is too limited to permit a refined prediction as to which is most appropriate. The limited research indicates the alternatives which are available and some of the causes and implications of the various structures.

The following are common organizational structure arrangements for planning units:

1. The Executive Group: in this arrangement, there is no professional planner but rather the top executive group performs the planning function.
2. The Functional Structure: the office of the corporate planner is subordinated to an organizational functional subsystem executive, e.g., finance.
3. The Corporate Planning Group: the corporate planner reports directly to the president.
4. The Corporate Planning Committee: a committee is formed to perform the planning function.
5. The Corporate Planning Group and Committee: both a planning committee and a professional planning unit are established.
6. The Corporate Planning Group and Divisional Committees: a divisional planning committee is added to the structure in No. 5.
7. Corporate and Divisional Planning Groups: a divisional planning group is added to the structure in No. 6.

With regard to the impacts that structural arrangements have on strategy formation, the following observations can be made. An executive group or committee would not be expected to be able to devote the time to planning or possess the planning expertise which a professional planning group would possess. Access to the president or CEO is an obvious consideration in the political influence aspect of corporate strategy formation. Furthermore, potential for conflict exists where corporate and divisional planning groups and/or committees exist.

Dobbie has shown that the types of goals resulting from the strategic process vary according to structure. Where the functional structure is employed, goals are routinely expressed in pro forma financial statement terms, reflecting the bias of the functional subsystem, usually the financial function. Dobbie also correlated CEO involvement in the planning process with the type of structure. He concluded that where the "corporate planner" reports to the president or where no planner exists, then strategic planning is more likely to occur at the president's level than where a committee or a functional area has the responsibility for planning. Lorange found that planners perceived their influence on strategy as high when direct reporting to the president occurred and low when reports were made to a functional subunit executive.

Normatively, it would seem appropriate to involve the chief executive in planning or at least to obtain top management support for strategic planning. It also seems appropriate to have the planning group reporting directly to the president. These recommendations have been supported by several empirical but admittedly largely descriptive examinations of corporate planning processes. Political bargaining often occurs in a planning committee of top executives. Such committees may interfere with the planning group. But since top management is involved, these committees can function partially to gain top management support for the resultant strategy.

As to the future position of the planning unit in the organization structure, Johnson, Kast, and Rosenzweig have suggested that a business is a series of flows of material, energy, and information flowing to and from major subsystems within the organization. The key variables in their model (Figure 2.4) are the Master Planning Council, which assumes a dominant role in their view of the organization, and the Resource Allocation and Operations

Figure 2.4   A Systems Model: Top Management

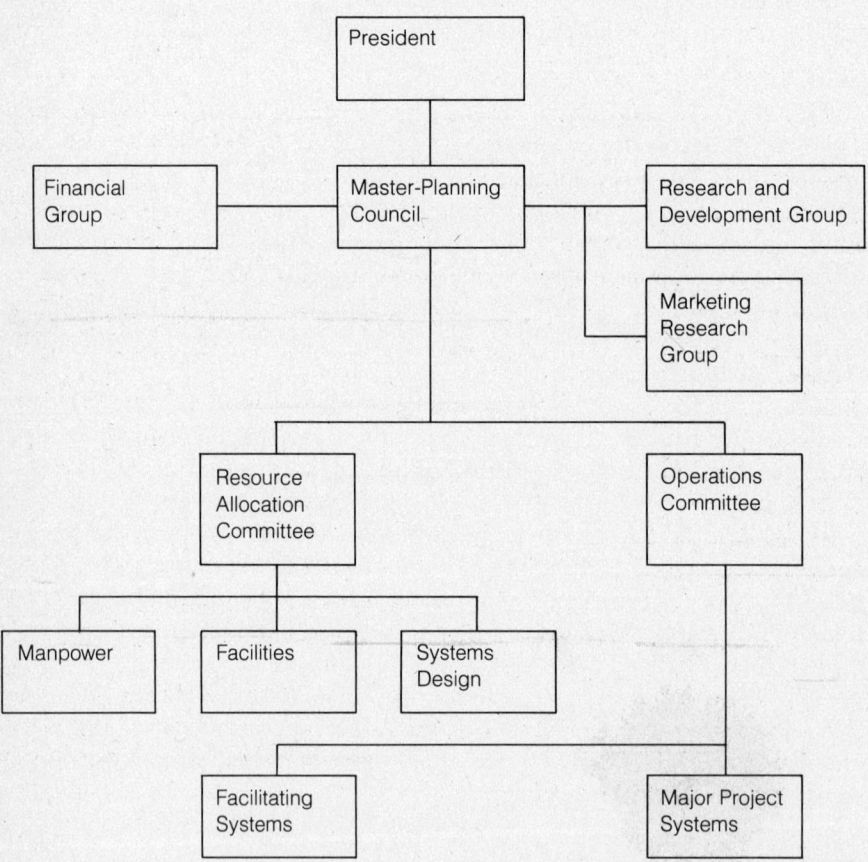

Source: Richard A. Johnson, Fremont E. Kast, and James E. Rosenzweig, "Designing Management Systems," *The Business Quarterly*, Summer 1964, Exhibit 1, pp. 59-63. Reprinted by permission.

Committees which coordinate activities, objectives, and resources. This model suggests a possible future role for strategic planning.

Characteristics of the effective corporate planner. Strategy formation, like much of management, has been described as an intuitive and as a rational endeavor. Planning and management require both skills. The collection and analysis of data is a rational process, one which would require the ability to process massive amounts of information. But the effective utilization of the resultant information, in terms of generating alternatives and forecasting the future, requires creativity. It may occasionally call for the employment of nonrational alternative generation techniques. In the capacity of reviewer of subsystem plans, the corporate planner must use both science and intuition. In addition to these skills, the planner must possess a keen ability in the politics of the organization.[1] The planner must possess social skills since much of his effort involves group activity. Since these subjects are discussed in detail in other books, they will not be pursued further. The effective planner needs a minimum of several skills: conceptual, creative, rational, political, and social.

The future of the professional planner. The evidence indicates that organizational environments are becoming more variable and more volatile with each passing year. The major business environmental factors—society, government, technology, competition, labor, the economy, and natural resource availabilities—are increasingly unpredictable. As a result, the organization will become more dependent upon professional strategists to interpret the meanings of these changes and to create strategies which will fulfill organizational mission. The time horizon of strategies which are developed may be compressed, but these plans of action must nonetheless be formulated. In fact, numerous alternative contingency strategies will be produced to cope with numerous possible situations. Several firms are currently generating multiple strategies, each of which is designed to be employed given a certain set of circumstances.

As the task of strategy formulation becomes more complex, the professional strategists will assume more of a strategic decision-making role. Computer simulations will become necessities because as the environment becomes more turbulent, the need to ask "what if" questions becomes even greater. Overall, the professional planner would seem to have a promising future and one which could lead to the chief executive's office. The individual or group helping the organization cope with its problems gains power. As the planning unit is required to respond to greater challenges, it and its chief administrator should become more powerful.

Strategic Information Systems

Information has two primary roles in strategy formation. First, information indicates the existence of problems and opportunities. Second, informa-

"Bob Faust here will be giving us an edge in forecasting—he's sold his soul to the devil."

tion on the strengths and weaknesses of the organization in relation to environmental threats and opportunities is used to formulate strategies. The strategist generates and evaluates alternatives based on information. Information systems will indicate the existence of many problems and many opportunities. Most of these will not require the reformulation of the Master Strategy. Most problems are solved and most opportunities are taken advantage of at lower levels of planning, control, and implementation. Occasionally strategic information systems may indicate the need to formulate or reformulate the Master Strategy and cause the strategic decision process to be pursued.

Certain informational inputs are required in the strategic decision process, and it is the function of the strategic information system (SIS) to provide these inputs. Any decision, and specifically the strategic decision, can be only as satisfactory as the information upon which it is based. An information system which provides accurate, timely, and relevant information for use in the strategic decision process is an important organizational resource because executives can be virtually overwhelmed by information. Various structural arrangements exist in organizations to provide strategic information. In larger organizations, sizable profesional planning units utilizing elaborate management information systems (MIS) provide this information. In smaller organizations, the CEO may occasionally scan the environment and assess his organization in an attempt to determine where the organization is and where it ought to be. Numerous variations exist between these two extremes. In addition to providing strategic information, major functions of the MIS include communication of objectives and plans and the provision of information related to the control of performance.

Strategic information systems may be either formal or informal. Both types of systems play a vital role in strategy formation. The formal SIS is a component of the formal MIS. Of special concern to strategic planning are demand forecasts for products and services balanced against the capacity and capabilities to produce them. Ultimately these balances are reflected in the operating plan and in the operating budget. Also appearing in the operating budget would be resource distribution actions and actual production commitments. Most organizations strategically plan on an annual, cyclical basis. For such purposes routinization of data storage and reporting may occur. Since strategic decision making may occasionally be crisis oriented (that is, strategic issue surprises must be reacted to), there are few predictable boundaries as to the types of information which might be needed. It is therefore necessary to store almost all conceivable types of information, often in a "raw" form, in order to meet the demands of the situation. As seen in Figure 2.5, a centralized formal data bank stores the data necessary for generating routine and nonroutine reports on internal and environmental phenomena. Internal information is presented in this figure as being reported on a functional basis. It could be readily sorted on a division/functional or other basis if necessary. Much of the strategic information routinely exists in reports and reporting formats already in use in the firm, especially the formal internal data. Examples would include financial statements, cost control reports, quality control reports, inventory level reports, division performance reports, absenteeism and turnover reports, etc. Much of this information is derived from control reports as depicted in Figure 2.6.

Recently, corporate "war rooms" with comprehensive computer-linked, visual data display systems have become a reality. While "war rooms" have existed for many years, in the past they used hand printed charts on limited subjects. Now any corporate information can appear instantaneously on large television screens. Gould Inc. possesses one of the most advanced of these systems. They have virtual real time information on every facet of corporate activity. This information can even be made available to interested but geographically dispersed managers via remote terminals. IBM marketed a similar system (software package) in 1976, the Trend Analysis 370, which even displays graphs in several colors.

To this point the discussion of the SIS has stressed the formal information system. But the importance of informal information should not be overlooked. Many times, personal contacts with individuals within the organization or external to the organization will produce significant information related to

Figure 2.5 Strategic Information System

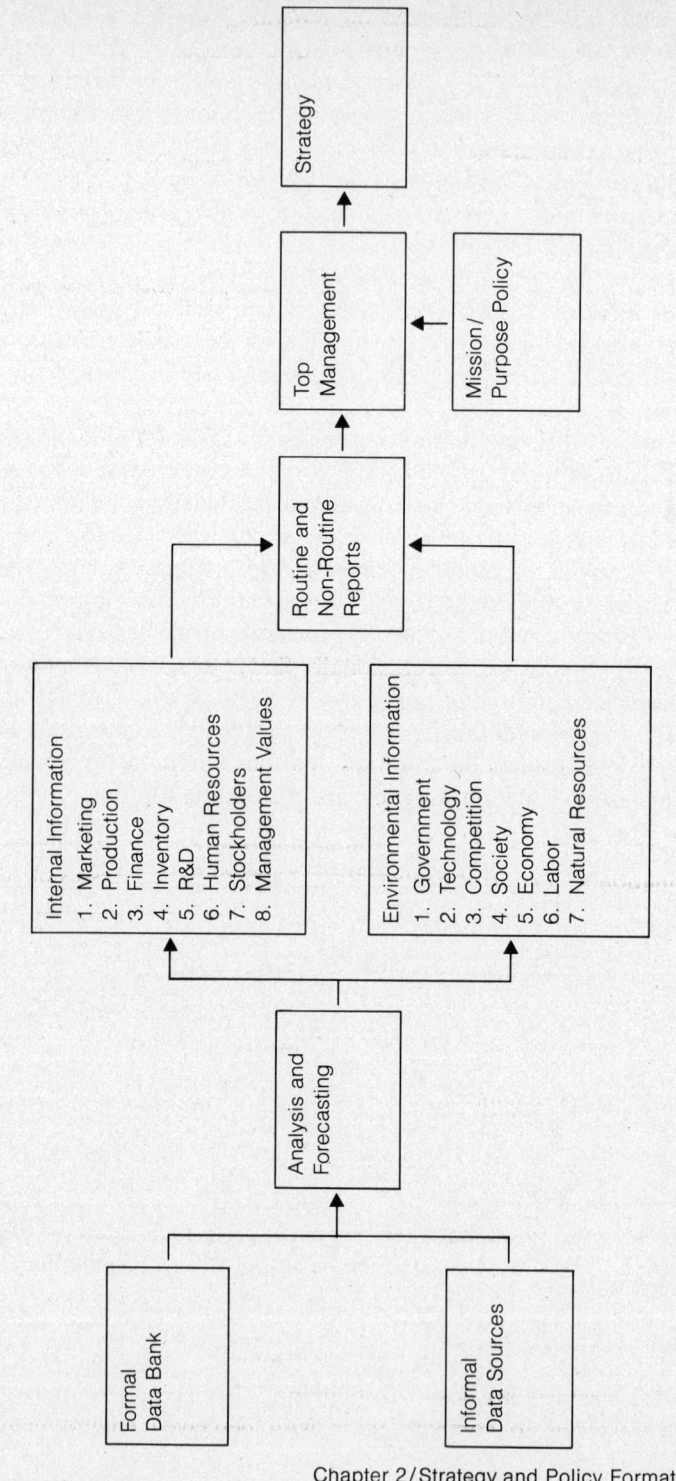

Chapter 2/Strategy and Policy Formation

the future. For example, tips on federal government legislation may prove extremely beneficial. Or rumors about a competitor's strategy may, when investigated, prove to be an important indicator of profitable strategic actions. The evidence strongly suggests that, while normatively the formal system may be proposed as the critical element, the informal system is the most consistently used basis for many top management decisions. Research indicates that 40 to 75 percent of the information used by top managers comes from informal sources.

Finally, a pragmatic note: in utilizing planning information, especially internal information, there is the need to maintain a transitionary perspective from historical data to future orientation. Normally, this necessity is understood with respect to environmental information, which often has already been changed in time horizon before it reaches top management. Strategists often overlook this transition when dealing with internal strengths and weaknesses. Even though the decisions must be made now, it is future as well as current strengths and weaknesses that are compared to future as well as current threats and opportunities in the strategic decision process.

In the ideal strategic decision situation, the processes described above would be accomplished in the formal information system, preferably under the direction of members of the professional planning group. At the opposite extreme, the CEO may occasionally find it necessary to either search for the information and/or perform analyses personally.

The following is a brief comment on information sources which are common to the business organization. Various analytical tools which can be used to analyze the raw information are then discussed.

Sources of Internal and Environmental Information. As suggested earlier, information related to the internal strengths and weaknesses of the organization should be available in the organization's MIS. This information may also be gathered through informal sources. Few problems should exist in obtaining relevant internal information if the MIS is properly designed and implemented. Caution must be observed, however, as to the nature of human resource information contained in most systems. Organizations are only beginning to recognize the need for and application of this type of information. While organizations usually collect absenteeism, tardiness, and turnover data, and so forth, seldom do they measure organizational climate, satisfaction, and leadership style—subordinate personality congruencies. These are important ingredients in explaining human resource productivity information.

In addition to standardized control reports (suggested by Figure 2.6), nonroutine control activities may be desirable. These include management audits, social audits, operational audits (of any subsystem), productivity audits, financial audits, and so forth. Both routine and nonroutine control activities are discussed at greater length in Chapter 7.

The strategic purpose of obtaining information on internal strengths and weaknesses is to compare them with perceived environmental threats and

Figure 2.6   Internal Information Subsystem

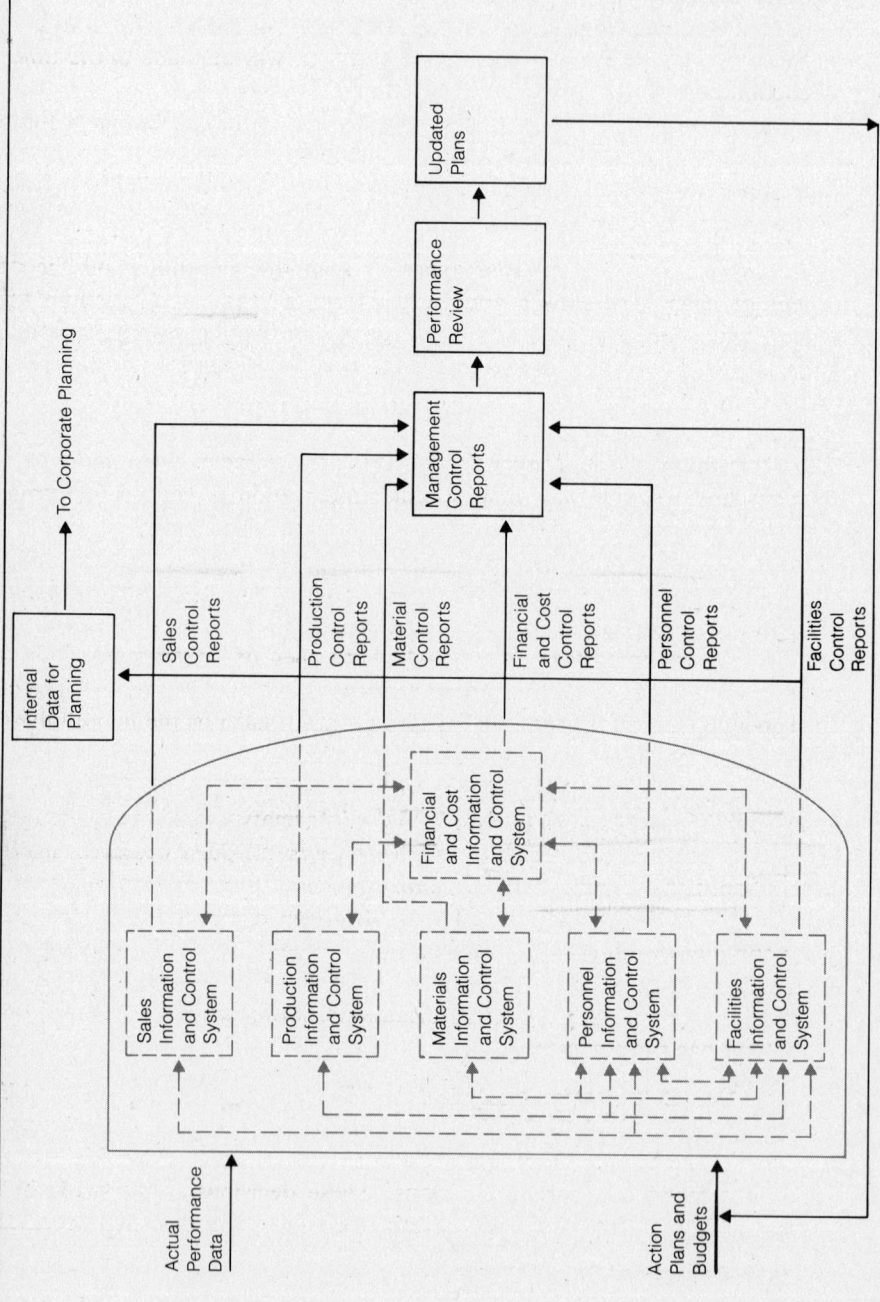

Source: From R. N. Kashyap, "Management Information System for Corporate Planning and Control," *Long Range Planning*, June 1972, Figure 4, p. 28. Reprinted by permission of Pergamon Press Ltd., Oxford, England.

opportunities and to make decisions based on these. With respect to obtaining these latter types of information, Aguilar has described four modes of environmental scanning:

1. Undirected viewing—general exposure to information with no purpose other than possibly exploration;
2. conditioned viewing—directed exposure to, but not active search for, specific kinds of data of which an assessment will be made at the time of encounter;
3. informal search—activity searching specific information but in a limited and relatively unstructured manner; and
4. formal search—active, deliberate, structured search for specific information with a purpose in mind.

Most organizations use all four types of scanning, depending on the cost benefit of each. These four approaches form a scanning continuum from general exposure to information to active and deliberate search for specific information. Every firm must remain alert to the general environment and to its own operations. As bits and pieces of information obtained in this scanning indicate changes in factors relevant to the formulation of strategy, then other, more directed types of scanning are desirable. These more formal searches are desirable any time specific information is needed for strategy formation.

Information on environmental factors may be obtained through various sources. For example, the *Wall Street Journal, Fortune, Business Week, Harvard Business Review;* numerous scholarly, popular, and trade journals; and newspapers are important sources. Any number of government, industry, news media, research, and reporting services provide additional information. In Appendix I to this chapter, a list of sources for each of the major environmental factors identified in Figure 2.5 is presented.

The various information sources vary in validity and reliability, as well as accessibility and frequency. Much of the information used is gathered from secondary sources, but primary data gathering through research may be undertaken if the organization can afford the cost. While internal information sources may allow the organization to approach a real-time, on-line MIS, due to the constraining nature of the environmental sources, a real time environmental MIS is unlikely. The informal information system may be used more than the formal system. Information sharing among organizations is useful and has proven successful.

Making Use of the Data: Analytical and Forecasting Techniques for Alternative Generation and Evaluation. Once strategic data have been accumulated, they must be transformed into information which will enable decision makers to make appropriate decisions. These decisions, while made in the present, relate to future events. Certain techniques are designed specifically to provide inferences about the future. These are called forecasting techniques. Other methodologies, labeled descriptive techniques, provide only information about current situations but obviously inferences about the future can be made after examining the information provided by these methodologies.[2] Simulation, one of the most important of these techniques, is reviewed below.

The role of forecasting in strategic management is to reduce uncertainty and aid decision making. In strategic decision situations, seldom if ever can the uncertainty be totally eliminated. Ultimately decision makers attempt to quantify the uncertainty that remains. This is usually referred to as risk analysis. Compounding the uncertainty reduction problem, there is evidence that the amount of uncertainty is increasing as the environment becomes more volatile and previously unknown strategic problems confront organizations. These events are made more pronounced because of the long time horizons present in most strategy formulation situations.

Three or more years frequently may transpire from conception to the actual marketing of a new product. During this time, the assumptions (premises) upon which the strategy was based may change significantly. But, since much of the uncertainty can be reduced, the strategic manager should become familiar with those uncertainty reduction techniques at his disposal. Put simply, forecasting is vital. While it is assumed as given in most planning models, forecasting is not an easy task.

Simulation Modeling and Other Uses of the Computer. The most significant of the recently developed analytical/forecasting techniques is simulation modeling. Simulation allows the strategist to ask "what if" questions. For example: "What if the price of raw material rose 1 percent? What if the union negotiated a 10 percent increase in benefits? What if our firm raises prices by 5 percent?" The answers to these and many other vital questions can be rendered quickly and accurately if the organization possesses a valid simulation model of its operations. Simulation models are expensive, so they are not within the financial capability of every organization. But for those who can afford these systems, they are becoming a necessity, not a luxury. To date, only simulations of internal operations are available. Environmental simulations, with the exception of models of the national economy, simply do not exist. These are in the development stages.

Simulations are computerized models which aid management in decision making. Simulation models abstract reality—normally an organization's internal flows—in terms of logically arranged, algebraic equations, expressed symbolically. These models are interactive; that is, they allow managers to "talk" with them. Simulations in business are usually accomplished on the basis of computer time sharing. The normal use of simulations is to assume a change in one or more inputs to the system and view the resulting changes in the system as portrayed by the model. Simulations have evolved over a period of years but have been important only since 1970, when appropriate systems oriented software packages were developed and time sharing became feasible. Boulden has summarized the requirements for an "on-line, real-time" shared computer system as follows:

Simplicity	Accessibility
Secrecy	Data Availability
Conversational	Flexibility
Fast Response	Economy

To date, the most advanced and widely used of these systems is the General Purpose Operating System II developed by Planmetrics, Inc., formerly On-Line Decisions, Inc., a management consulting group based in Chicago. In their general systems program approach, the corporate planner states his assumptions. These are utilized by the computer program in interactions with the Data Base and the Corporate Model Logic to perform data analysis and to generate reports and simulations of events. Almost any conceivable type of report might be generated.

Any simulation commences with an exhaustive analysis of the actual interrelationships of the organization, its subsystems, and subsystem components. Planmetrics's approach is a modular one. It develops models for each of the major structural divisions, functions or subsystems, combining these at an interface point into a total corporate model. Eventually, every quantifiable, internal resource event or flow is incorporated into a modular model. Modules are then combined and interrelationships interfaced in a similar manner.

The evidence indicates that the number of business firms employing simulations is large and growing. Numerous types of simulations are utilized, but few totally integrated corporate models exist. By this is meant that, while certain modules have been created, few firms have combined these and developed a total corporate model. Surveyed firms most frequently employ models in the areas of financial analysis and planning and evaluation of policy alternatives. The development costs of "tailor made" simulations have reached $1 million, but more recent Planmetrics prices commence at $75,000. Because of the initial cost, most simulation users must have annual sales over $250 million, although one rule of thumb is that annual sales of at least $10 million are necessary in order to justify the initial development costs. Packaged simulation software is available through software distributors and substantially reduces the cost but also, unfortunately for many, the comprehensiveness and accuracy of the resultant output.

There is limited simulation usage in state, city, and local governments, but frequent usage is found at the federal government level—although not on a total entity basis, except again for the model of the national economy. Little evidence of usage is found in the nonprofit, nonpublic sector, probably due to cost. Usage of simulations is almost nonexistent in firms with sales less than

$10 million. With the increased usage of mini-computers by small businesses and other small organizations, it would seem to be only a matter of time before relevant simulation software packages become available.

The future of simulations is exceptionally promising, as future generations of computers and software will provide significant advances on today's models. Numerous problems are involved in the implementation of any system. Hammond has outlined several approaches to proper implementation with which any probable user should become familiar. Any simulation will require some debugging and some adjustment to the particular circumstances of the organization, especially as the situation changes over time. One interesting nonbusiness use of simulations has occurred in the predicting of future scenarios for man's environment and the probabilities of the survival of mankind. The Club of Rome, building on the business oriented Industrial Dynamics, has made some very noteworthy predictions utilizing what has been termed *World Dynamics*.

In addition to simulation modeling, other uses of the computer in strategic management include the obvious task of providing timely information at lower levels which should eventually improve strategic decision making; the more common models for financial analysis, forecasting, descriptive statistical analysis, capital budgeting, etc.; and even the training of executives to ask the right questions in strategy formation.

In closing this section, it seems appropriate to remember that the computer only aids the strategist; it does not and cannot replace him. The strategist must utilize a certain amount of intuition as well as science in the strategic management process. It is this ability to meaningfully interpret and relate the scientifically derived information and to make appropriate strategic decisions that separates the strategist from the operational manager.

Analytical Techniques: A Comment. Numerous forecasting techniques exist. For example, virtually hundreds of methodologies have been suggested for societal and technological forecasting, but there just is not time to discuss all of these here. (See Footnote 2.) The important points to remember are these:

1. Numerous techniques exist, some better than others for a particular situation.
2. By using more than one technique, forecasting should be improved.
3. The output of a technique is no better than its inputs and its assumptions.
4. Cost benefit analysis should be performed before expensive techniques are undertaken.
5. Evaluation of the techniques should be accomplished.
6. Regardless of the amount of time and money invested, the environment is uncertain and undergoing an increasing amount of change. Forecasting failures will occur. Flexibility must be maintained.

Summary

The organization strategists formulate strategy to accomplish mission based on the comparison of organizational strengths and weaknesses, threats, and opportunities. Strategy varies not only as the result of mission and policy, but with information. As the organization scans its internal operation and its external environment, it observes certain problems and opportunities. Not every problem or opportunity encountered leads to strategy formulation or reformulation; some lead to problem solving of an intermediate or operational nature. But where information indicates that strategy should be changed and/or a new strategy created, rational strategic decision making must transpire. The organization's strategists must be able to generate alternatives, evaluate these, and arrive at a decision. Mission provides the direction, policy the guidance, and information the knowledge with which the organizational strategists may make appropriate strategic decisions.

The next chapter discusses some of the comparative and formulative methodologies which exist to aid in the alternative generation and evaluation processes. Since alternative generation is a basic process, that portion of strategic decision making will not be reviewed in detail in this book. One approach to alternative strategy formation, the contingency approach, is discussed in Chapter 3. Also, methodologies for evaluating alternatives and evaluating internal and external information in order to generate alternatives are discussed in the next chapter.

Discussion Questions

1. Of the four primary strategy formation factors, which do you view as most critical? Why? *Information*
2. Suppose you are the CEO of a business firm. What is your mission? What master policies would you have? Who are the organizational strategists? Where do you obtain strategic information?
3. Suppose you are the chief executive of a nonprofit organization. What are your "Master Policies"? Who are the organizational strategists? Where do the organizational strategists obtain internal and external information?
4. How are analytical and forecasting techniques used in strategic decision making? How could your organization employ simulations?

Footnotes

1. The political/power aspects of the organization and its impacts are discussed in more detail in Chapter 4.
2. See David A. Heenan and Robert B. Addleman, "Quantitative Techniques for Today's Decision Makers," *Harvard Business Review,* May/June 1976,

pp. 32–46, 62, for a discussion of multivariant analysis techniques which are especially useful in problems where many variables must be considered. Also see Spyros Makridakis and Steven Wheelwright, "Integrating Forecasting and Planning," *Long Range Planning,* September 1973, pp. 61–63, for considerations relevant to choosing various techniques; and Steven C. Wheelwright and Spyros Makridakis, *Forecasting Methods for Management* (New York: John Wiley & Sons, 1973), for a description of most commonly used techniques.

Appendix 1 to Chapter 2   Sources for Major Environmental Factors

1. Government
   a. *Code of Federal Regulations, Federal Register,* other federal publications
   b. Various publishing house services—Commerce Clearing House (CCH), Bureau of National Affairs (BNA), Prentice-Hall (PH), etc.
   c. Lobbyists
   d. *Kiplinger Washington Newsletter*
   e. *Monthly Catalog of United States Government Publications*
   f. Monthly checklist of state publications

2. Technology
   a. *Statistical Abstract of the United States*
   b. *Applied Science and Technology Index*
   c. Scientific and Technical Information Service
   d. Congressional hearings, university reports, "think tank" reports
   e. Department of Defense and military department publishers
   f. Industrial reports
   g. Computer assisted information search
   h. National Science Foundation, *Annual Report*
   i. *Research and Development Directory*
   j. Industry contacts, salesmen, professional meetings
   k. Patents

3. Market and Competition
   a. Annual reports of companies in question
   b. Securities and Exchange Commission (10-K Report)
   c. *Fortune 500 Directory, Forbes, Wall Street Transcript, Barrons*
   d. Investment services and directories: Dun & Bradstreet, Standard & Poor's Value Line, Moody's, Starch Marketing
   e. Trade association publications

f. Professional meetings, salesmen, industry contacts

g. Espionage

h. Surveys, for example, market research

i. *County and City Data Book*

j. *County Business Patterns*

4. Society

a. Pressure group publications and pronouncements

b. Books which might affect societal attitudes

c. Government (see No. 1, "Government")

d. Surveys

e. Judgment, opinion, scenario forecasting (Delphi)

f. The media, especially television and newspapers

g. Articles in sociological, psychological, and political journals

h. Various institute and foundation reports such as the Ford Foundation's and the Brookings Institute's

5. Economy

a. National Economy

i. U.S. Department of Commerce

(a) Bureau of Census, such as *Survey of Manufacturers, Statistical Abstract of the United States, Current Population Reports,* census reports on various industries, housing, population

(b) Office of Business Economics, such as *Survey of Current Business*

(c) Bureau of Economic Analysis, such as *Business Conditions Digest*

(d) Business and Defense Services Administration, such as *U.S. Industrial Outlook*

ii. Council of Economic Advisors
Economic Indicators, Annual Report

iii. Securities and Exchange Commission "Quarterly Financial Reports," "Quarterly Report of Plant and Equipment Expenditures of U.S. Corporations," "Quarterly Report of Working Capital of U.S. Corporations"

iv. St. Louis Federal Reserve Bank "Quarterly Report"

v. The Conference Board

vi. Trade Association Publications

vii. Federal Trade Commission

viii. U.S. Chamber of Commerce/American Manufacturers Association

ix. INSEAD—The European Institute of Business Administration; IMEDE—Management Development Institute Lausanne

x. University of Michigan Survey Research Center

xi. *Federal Reserve Bulletin*
b. International Economic Conditions
    i. U.S. Department of Commerce
      (a) Bureau of Census—"Guide to Foreign Trade Statistics"
      (b) Bureau of International Commerce—"Overseas Business Reports," "Foreign Economic Trends and Their Implications for the U.S."
    ii. O. E. C. D.
    Economic Outlook and Main Economic Indicators
    iii. United Nations
    Statistical Yearbook
    iv. O. I. T.
    International Labor Office—*Yearbook of Labor Statistics*
    v. Business International
    newsletters
    vi. St. Louis Federal Reserve Bank
    vii. National plans of European countries

6. Labor
a. *Labor Law Journal* and other related journals, including law school journals
b. Various publications house services such as CCH, BNA, PH
c. Various labor union publications
d. U.S. Department of Labor publications, *Monthly Labor Review*
e. U.S. Department of Commerce

7. Natural Resources
a. U.S. Department of the Interior
Bureau of Mines—*Minerals Yearbook, Geological Survey*
b. U.S. Department of Agriculture
Agricultural Abstract
c. Federal Power Commission
statistics of electric utilities/statistics of gas pipe companies
d. Publications of various institutions:
American Petroleum Institute, U.S. Atomic Energy Commission, Coal Mining Institute of America, American Steel Institute, Brookings Institute
8. General Information
a. Indexes and periodical directories
b. Bibliographies and special guides
c. Other basic sources

Sources: C. R. Goeldner and Laura M. Kirks, "Business Facts: Where to Find Them," *MSU Business Topics*, Summer 1976, pp. 23-76; Francois E. deCarbonnel and Roy G. Donance, "Information Sources for Planning Decisions," *California Management Review*, Summer 1973, pp. 42-53; and A. B. Nutt, R. C. Lenz, Jr., H. W. Lanford, and M. J. Cleary, "Data Sources for Trend Extrapolation in Technological Forecasting," *Long Range Planning*, February 1976, pp. 72-76.

References

Adams, C. R. "How Management Users View Information Systems." *Decision Sciences,* April 1975, pp. 337–345.

Aguilar, F. J. *Scanning the Business Environment.* New York: Macmillan, 1967.

Bearse, A. W., and G. J. King. "Social-Business Decision (SBO) Model." Paper presented to the Academy of Management, 1974, at Seattle, Washington.

Blau, P. M., and W. R. Scott. *Formal Organizations.* New York: Chandler, 1962.

Boulden, J. B., and E. S. Buffa. "Corporate Models: On-Line, Real-Time Systems." *Harvard Business Review,* July/August 1970, pp. 65–67.

"Breakthrough in Management Planning." Advertising brochure, Planmetrics, n.d.

"The Board: It's Obsolete Unless Overhauled." *Business Week,* May 22, 1971, pp. 50–58.

Chambers, J. C.; S. K. Mullick; and D. D. Smith. "How to Choose the Right Forecasting Technique." *Harvard Business Review,* July/August 1971, pp. 45–74.

Clendenin, W. D. "Company Presidents Look at the Board of Directors." *California Management Review,* Spring 1972, pp. 60–66.

Collings, R. "Scanning the Environment for Strategic Information." Unpublished doctoral dissertation, Harvard Business School, 1968.

"Corporate 'War Rooms' Plug into the Computer." *Business Week,* August 23, 1976, pp. 65–67.

Dearden, J. "MIS Is a Mirage." *Harvard Business Review,* January/February 1972, pp. 90–99.

deCarbonnel, F. E., and R. G. Donance. "Information Sources for Planning Decisions." *California Management Review,* Summer 1973, pp. 42–53.

Dobbie, J. W. "Guides to a Foundation for Strategic Planning in Large Firms." Paper presented at the Academy of Management Meetings, 1974, at Seattle, Washington.

Edwards, J. B. "The Corporate Planner and Creativity." *Managerial Planning,* March/April 1975, pp. 11–22.

Gallese, L. R. "The Soothsayers: More Companies Use 'Futurists' to Discern What Is Lying Ahead." *Wall Street Journal,* March 31, 1975, pp. 1, 8.

Gessford, J. E. "Management Information Systems Development." *Managerial Planning,* January/February 1973, pp. 15–20, 29.

Greiner, L. E. "Integrating Formal Planning into Organizations." In *Formal Planning Systems,* edited by F. J. Aguilar, R. A. Howell, and R. F. Vancil. Cambridge, Mass.: Graduate School of Business, Harvard University, 1970.

Grinyer, P. H., and J. Woller. "Computer Models for Corporate Planning." *Long Range Planning,* February 1975, p. 14.

Groobey, J. A. "Making the Board of Directors More Effective." *California Management Review,* Spring 1974, pp. 25–34.

Hall, R. H. *Organizations.* Englewood Cliffs, N.J.: Prentice-Hall, 1972.

Hall, W. K. "Forecasting Techniques for Use in the Corporate Planning Process." *Managerial Planning,* November/December 1972, pp. 5–10, 33.

————. "The Uncertainty of Uncertainty in Business Planning." *Managerial Planning,* September/October 1974, p. 8.

Hammond, J. S., III. "Do's and Don't's of Computer Models for Planning." *Harvard Business Review,* March/April 1974, pp. 110–123.

Heller, M. F., Jr. "The Board of Directors: Legalistic Anachronism or Vital Force." *California Management Review*, Spring 1972, pp. 24–29.

Hofer, C. W. "Research on Strategic Planning: A Survey of Past Studies and Suggestions for Future Efforts." *Journal of Economics and Business,* Spring/Summer 1976, pp. 261–272.

Keegan, W. "Scanning the International Business Environment." Unpublished doctoral dissertation, Harvard Business School, 1967.

Leavitt, H. J. "Beyond the Analytic Manager: Part II." *California Management Review,* Summer 1975, pp. 11–21.

Lebell, D., and O. J. Krasner. "Selecting Environmental Forecasting Techniques from Business Planning Requirements." *Academy of Management Review,* July 1977, pp. 373–383.

Linnemann, R. E., and J. D. Kennell. "Shirtsleeve Approach to Long-range Plans." *Harvard Business Review*, March/April 1977, pp. 141–150.

Lorange, P. "The Planner's Dual Role—A Survey of U.S. Companies." *Long Range Planning,* March 1973, pp. 12–16.

Mace, M. L. "The President and Corporate Planning." *Harvard Business Review*, January/February 1965, pp. 49–67.

Makridakis, S., and S. Wheelwright. "Integrating Forecasting and Planning." *Long Range Planning,* September 1973, pp. 53–63.

Mason, R. H. "Developing a Planning Organization." *Business Horizons* 12 (August 1969): 61–70.

Meadows, D. H., et al. *The Limits to Growth.* New York: Signet-Universe, 1972.

Mintzberg, H. *The Nature of Managerial Work.* New York: Harper & Row, 1973.

—————. "Planning on the Left Side and Managing on the Right." *Harvard Business Review,* July/August 1976, pp. 49–58.

—————. "Strategy Making in Three Modes." *California Management Review,* Winter 1973, pp. 45–46.

Murphy, R. C. "A Computer Model Approach to Budgeting." *Management Accounting,* June 1975, pp. 34–36.

Naumes, W. "Effects of Responsive Computer Interaction in the Strategic Planning Process." Unpublished doctoral dissertation, Stanford University, 1971.

Naylor, T. H., and H. Schauland. "A Survey of Users of Corporate Planning Models." *Management Science,* May 1976, p. 936.

Nolan, R. L. "Computer Data Bases: The Future Is Now." *Harvard Business Review,* September/October 1973, pp. 98–114.

Ringbaak, K. S. "Organized Corporate Planning Systems: An Empirical Study of Planning Practice and Experiences in American Big Business." Unpublished doctoral dissertation, University of Wisconsin, 1968.

Rue, L. W. "Tools and Techniques of Long Range Planners." *Long Range Planning,* October 1974, p. 65.

Schoeffler, S.; R. O. Buzzell; and D. F. Heany. "Impact of Strategic Planning on Profit Performance." *Harvard Business Review,* March/April 1974, pp. 137–145.

Small, F. T., and W. B. Lee. "In Search of an MIS." *MSU Business Topics*, August 1975, pp. 47–55.

Sprague, R. H., Jr., and H. J. Watson. "MIS Concepts: Part I." *Journal of Systems Management,* January 1975, p. 35.

Steiner, G. A. *Managerial Long Range Planning.* New York: McGraw-Hill, 1963.

————. *Pitfalls in Comprehensive Long-Range Planning.* Oxford, Ohio: The Planning Executives Institute, 1972.

————. "Rise of the Corporate Planner." *Harvard Business Review,* September/October 1970, pp. 133–139.

Steiner, G. A., and H. Schollhammer. "Pitfalls in Comprehensive Long-Range Planning: A Comparative Multinational Survey." *Proceedings of the Third International Conference of the International Affiliation of Planning Societies.* Brussels, Belgium, September 1973.

Taylor, R. N. "Psychological Aspects of Planning." *Long Range Planning,* April 1976, pp. 66–74.

Tipgos, M. A. "Structuring a Management Information System for Strategic Planning." *Managerial Planning,* January/February 1975, pp. 10–16.

Vancil, R. F. "The Accuracy of Long Range Planning." *Harvard Business Review,* September/October 1970, pp. 98–101.

Voich, D., Jr.; H. J. Mottice; and W. A. Schrode. *Information Systems for Operations and Management.* Cincinnati: South-Western Publishing, 1975.

Wall, J. "What the Competition Is Doing: Your Need to Know." *Harvard Business Review,* November/December 1974, pp. 22–38, 162–170.

Wheelwright, S. C. "Management by Model during Inflation." *Business Horizons,* June 1975, pp. 33–42.

Withington, F. G. "Five Generations of Computers." *Harvard Business Review,* July/August 1974, pp. 99–108.

Wrapp, H. E. "Organization for Long-Range Planning." *Harvard Business Review,* January/February 1957, pp. 37–47.

Chapter 3

Strategy Formation:

The Contingency Approach and Assessment Techniques

The wise leader considers the
days that are yet to come.

Persian Proverb

An examination of the contingency approach to strategy formation (alternative generation) is now presented. The contingency approach suggests that for a given set of circumstances a "best" strategy exists. The contingency approach is in its formative stages, but the related research is increasing rapidly. This approach has been currently applied only to profit-oriented organizations, but it may be extended to nonprofit organizations in the future.

Once alternatives have been generated, either in the periodic planning exercise or as the result of information uncovered in perpetual surveillance, the strategic decision maker(s) must determine the best strategy for achieving organizational mission. Critical to the strategy evaluation process are the assessment techniques employed. In this chapter, the assessment process and related factors of the strategy formation models (Figures 3.1 and 3.2) are reviewed.

Figure 3.1   The Organization—An Organization Process Model

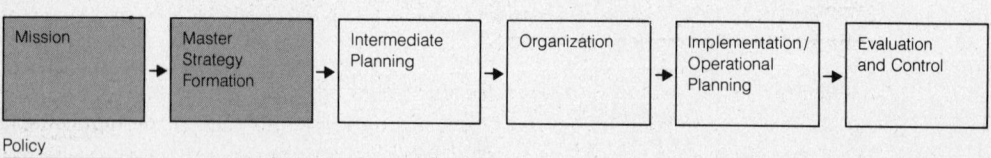

Policy

The Product Life Cycle Contingency Approach to Strategy Formation

The science of strategic management has not yet reached the degree of sophistication that will allow executives to know the exact strategy which should

Figure 3.2   Master Strategy Formation

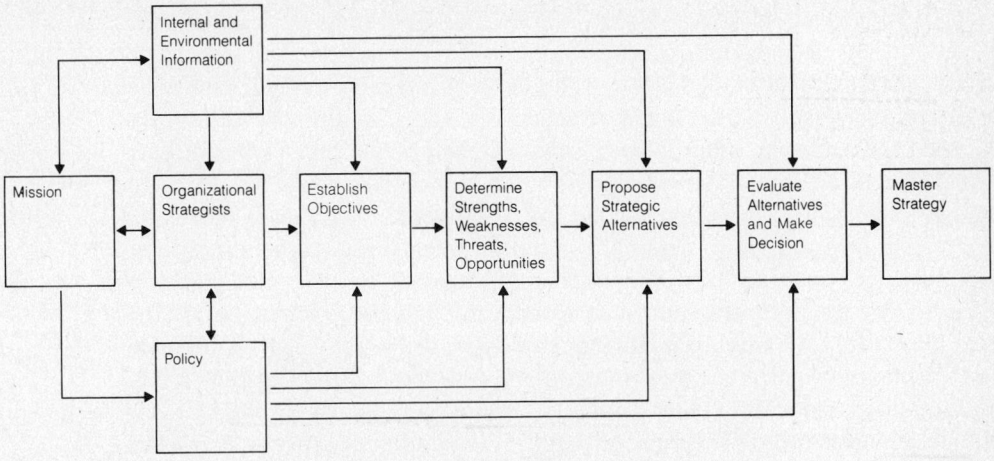

be followed for every situation. However, research supplemented by rationally derived normative propositions has now pointed towards a set of environmental and organizational variables which have significant impact on the content of strategy, at least with regard to one product. While strategic management may be largely situational, certain factors have been shown to be those upon which strategic decisions are contingent. Furthermore, for some specific situations appropriate strategies have been identified. Most of these admittedly are also for a single product. In the following pages, major strategic variables will be reviewed and the few variable strategy combinations which have been identified will be discussed.

Strategic Contingency Variables—Factors to Be Considered When One Product Is Involved

After reviewing the research and normative propositions mentioned previously, Hofer concluded that the most important single variable in the determination of strategy is the particular life cycle stage of the product for which the strategy is being formulated. Table 3.1 portrays the key variables which his review efforts have suggested as appropriate to each stage of the product life cycle. The table is arranged so that the first factor listed in each cell is the most important variable perceived.

The table would be utilized in this manner: When a firm has a product in a particular stage of the product life cycle, it would consult the table to determine what the key variables were which should be considered in the formulation of strategy. For example, suppose a firm has a product in the maturity stage of the product life cycle. The firm's strategic managers would review information related to each of the factors listed under the maturity life cycle for each of the types of variables listed in order to assure that a proper strategy is employed. Under Market and Consumer Behavioral Variables, market segmentation is considered to be the most influential factor. Buyer needs, purchase frequency, and buyer concentration also influence strategy significantly. The firm's strategic managers would gather information on these and the other factors listed for each of the other types of variables. Based on these factors, strengths and weaknesses would be obtained.

Note, no strategy is recommended in the table. Rather, that is left to the individual organization to determine based on these suggested factors. Classical strategies such as those presented in Table 5.2 or the postulations of Fox (Table 5.4), Glueck, and others cited in Chapter 5 (referenced in this chapter) might be employed. Research is available which suggests that certain actions are more successful than others, regardless of the situation. These will be discussed shortly. The conceptualization presented in Table 3.1 is extremely important and highly contributive. Actual strategic decisions as well as their simulations in the classroom, such as are required by case analyses, may be improved through the utilization of this table. Some caution is necessary, however. These factors have not been tested, as presented, in actual corporations. Furthermore, some very limited evidence suggests that product life cycle strategies are not appropriate to every product. Nonetheless, at this point, the stage of the product life cycle appears as the single most important factor in determining strategy.

The Contingency Theory Applied

Contingency theories of management are based on the assumption that for a given set of factors in a situation, a best series of management actions exists. If a situation is encountered where the given set of factors is predominant, then the manager—here the strategist—should act in a certain way. The advantages of establishing contingency actions for a given set of circumstances are obvious: corporate performance should improve. Hofer has suggested a limited number (seven) of normative contingency strategy propositions for the maturity stage of the product life cycle. After defining the situation in terms of the key contingency variables (Table 3.1), an appropriate strategy is suggested. Two of these propositions are as follows:

N² When the degree of product differentiation is low, the nature of buyer needs primarily non-economic, the degree of market segmentation slight, the degree of specialization within the industry low, the marketing intensity high, the manufacturing economies of scale medium, and the ratio of distribution costs to manufacturing value added high, businesses should:

1. use universal rather than specialized marketing appeals;

2. reduce their geographic scope or increase their marketing expenditures sufficiently so that their per capita marketing expenditures within their geographic service area are in excess of the industry average;
3. attempt to keep their degree of capacity utilization high and their fixed assets relatively modern; and
4. withdraw from the industry if their market share falls to less than 20% of that held by the industry leader within their geographic service area.

N[3] When the degree of product differentiation is high, the nature of the buyer's needs primarily non-economic, the degree of market segmentation moderate to high, the product complexity high, the purchase frequency low, and the barriers to entry in the distribution or technology areas, businesses should:

1. focus their R & D funds first on modifying and upgrading their existing product line, second on developing new products, and last on process innovations;
2. allocate substantial funds to the maintenance and enhancement of their distinctive competencies, especially those in the marketing area;
3. develop a strong service capability in their distribution systems; and
4. seek to expand the geographic scope of their operations, if possible.

Source: Charles W. Hofer, "Toward a Contingency Theory of Business Strategy," *Academy of Management Journal* 18 (December 1975): 803-805. Reprinted by permission of the *Academy of Management Journal*.

In observing these propositions, the difficulties in formulating contingency statements become increasingly clear. One of the major barriers to the formation of a usable contingency theory is the large number of variables to be considered. Hofer, in identifying the major strategic variables, suggests that some fifty-plus major variables exist which could affect strategy on a contingency basis. He admits that this list is probably incomplete in terms of other explanatory variables such as management techniques or a firm's social responsibility values. Just taking his variables into account, some 18,000,-000,000,000,000 different combinations of circumstances could be considered. This would mean that in order to have a true contingency variable theory, an almost infinite number of contingency statements would have to be formulated. However, as Hofer has observed, the number of situations can be reduced substantially by approaching the task from a life cycle stage basis.

As suggested in Table 3.1, certain factors have more impact on one stage of the product life cycle than on another. These are the factors to be considered. Even with these limitations, however, the number of possible situations which could exist is very high in some of the stages of the product life cycle and extremely high in others. The number of combinations of factors increases when the variables that have not been identified in this table are

Table 3.1   Environmental and Organizational Variables Which Are Strategically Significant at Different Stages of the Product Life Cycle

Types of Variables*	Life Cycle Stages Introduction	Growth
Market & Consumer Behavior Variables	buyer needs purchase frequency	buyer needs buyer concentration purchase frequency
Industry Structure Variables	uniqueness of the product rate of technological change in product design	type of product rate of technological change in product design number of equal products barriers to entry
Competitor Variables		degree of specialization within the industry
Supplier Variables		
Broader Environmental Variables	interest rates money supply	GNP trend money supply
Organizational Variables	quality of products	market share quality of products marketing intensity

*Within each category, the specific variables identified have been ranked in terms of their degree of significance for formulating viable business strategies. For instance, in the maturity stage of the life cycle, only two competitor variables are considered to be significant for the formulation of a business strategy; namely, the degree of specialization in the industry and the degree of capacity utilization,

considered. This suggests that the future of contingency theory probably lies in identifying the major factors which should be considered, as has been done in Table 3.1, and combining these with hypothesized strategies such as those of Fox (see Chapter 5).

There is an additional consideration which should be used in determining

Maturity	Saturation	Decline
market segmentation	market size	market size
buyer needs	market segmentation	buyer loyalty
purchase frequency	elasticity of demand	elasticity of demand
buyer concentration	buyer loyalty	
	seasonality	
	cyclicality	
type of product	degree of product	degree of product
rate of technological	differentiation	differentiation
change in process	price/cost structure	price/cost structure
design	experience curves	marginal plant size
degree of product	degree of integration	transportation &
differentiation	economics of scale	distribution costs
number of equal products		
transportation &		
distribution costs		
barriers to entry		
degree of specialization	degree of seller	degree of specialization
within the industry	concentration	within the industry
degree of capacity	aggressiveness of	degree of capacity
utilization	competition	utilization
	degree of specialization	
	in the industry	
degree of supplier	degree of supplier	major changes in
concentration	concentration	availability of raw
	major changes in	materials
	availability of raw	
	materials	
GNP trend	growth of population	interest rates
antitrust	age distribution of	age distribution of
regulations	population	population
	regional shifts of	
	population	
	life style changes	
market share	market share	market share
quality of products	quality of products	quality of products
value added	length of the	length of the pro-
degree of customer	production cycle	duction cycle
concentration	P/S newness	relative wage rate
marketing intensity	relative wage rate	degree of customer
discretionary cash	marketing intensity	concentration
flow/gross capital		
investment		

and of these, the degree of specialization is thought to be the more important.

Source: Charles W. Hofer, "Toward a Contingency Theory of Business Strategy," *Academy of Management Journal* 18 (December 1975): 800-801. Reprinted by permission of the *Academy of Management Journal*.

an appropriate strategy. The Behavioral Theory of Strategy Formulation, which has often been labeled as part of the contingency theory, identifies certain behaviors which have been employed by the more successful firms in most, if not all, circumstances. The following paragraphs discuss some of the postulates of this strategy formation theory.

The Behavioral Theory of Strategy Formation

In the past few years research studies utilizing regression analysis and other analytical techniques on various firms in different industries have demonstrated that successful firms engage in definite patterns of behavior in order to increase return on investment. While this research uncovered some surprises and some contradictions, most of the factors were factors which theory would have identified as appropriate. The following paragraphs review some of these studies to determine the factors which are of primary interest.

PIMS, Profit Impact on Market Strategies, was a project organized in 1972 by the Market Science Institute, a nonprofit research organization affiliated with the Harvard School of Business. This project was a strategic information-sharing experience among 57 major North American corporations. The project had two phases. In Phase One, only 36 corporations supplied information on some 350 businesses. In Phase Two, 57 companies provided information on 620 businesses. The original intent of the program was to determine the profit impact of market strategy. In addition the project sought a basis upon which to estimate ROI for organizations in varying situations. Such a basis could aid in the selection of businesses in which to diversify, projects in which to invest, projects of which to divest, and in general the balancing of the corporation's investment portfolio. Information relating to 37 major variables from these corporations was regressed against the ROI of these organizations. The intent was to determine which of these variables was the most explanatory. Some of the more significant contributory variables found included the following:

1. Market Share—the ratio of dollar sales by business in a given time period to total sales by all competitors in the same market;
2. Product (Service) Quality—quality of each participating company's offerings appraised in several terms;
3. Marketing Expenditures—total cost for sales force, advertising, sales promotion, market research, and marketing administration;
4. R & D Expenditures—total cost of prior development of process improvement;
5. Investment Intensity—ratio of total investment to sales (has a high negative impact on sales);
6. Corporate Diversity—ratios which affect the number of different industrial categories in which most corporations engage; and
7. Other Company Factors—characteristics of a company that owns a business; the primary concern here is one of organizational size.

As with any preliminary research, these findings are limited in their applicability until additional supporting research is reported. Furthermore, correlation/regression techniques such as were used in the PIMS Project are not truly explanatory but rather indicate the strengths of relationships. And the variables mentioned above have several exceptions. Some are more applicable in certain situations than in others. Other explanatory variables exist but either were not included in the PIMS Project or did not prove to be sufficiently explanatory in this particular study. However, this project has shown that for large, multifaceted business corporations, in varying industries and in differing situations, some common indicators of return on investment can be found.

Kirchoff felt that the interorganizational analysis used in the PIMS Project was subject to methodological problems caused primarily by the difficulty of equating measurements contained in the different accounting systems employed by the PIMS Project films. Therefore, he chose to analyze one organization by intraorganizational analysis. He analyzed two of four major divisions of a capital intensive manufacturing firm within a mature industry. The firm manufactured separate but technologically similar products. In total, some 50 geographically separate profit centers existed: 31 in division A, 13 in division B, 3 each in divisions C and D. Analysis applied only to divisions A and B, since divisions C and D were too small to allow regression to take appropriate effect.

Kirchoff chose 17 factors, several of which were not used in the PIMS Project, for example, personnel factors, which he felt would be important. These are displayed in Table 3.2 for Division A. Gross profit per unit and total profit per unit best explained ROI in Division A. These were surrogates for market price, therefore market price was isolated as a major determinant of ROI. Several labor attitude and productivity variables were also shown to be significant. Absenteeism and accident frequency decreased ROI, and labor/ machine productivity was shown to increase it. These are extremely important findings because these factors have been given little treatment in strategic literature, but these results clearly suggest that personnel factors have a great impact on ROI. Production also emerged as a significant variable, indicating that control over customer credit and bad debts is important. In general, those factors which were most important can be summarized as cost control factors or price factors.

Noticeably absent was the market share variable reported as most important by the PIMS Project. Kirchoff suggests that this was a result of a very high demand in the market for products of most organizations at the time of the study, including all businesses of the organization he examined. Market share had limited impact. Less favorable economic conditions would probably cause market share to be more important.

With respect to the total corporation, the number of variables indicated in Table 3.2 was reduced to eight because of the inability to find common measurements for these variables across all four divisions. The inventory to sales ratio exerted the greatest influence on ROI. The less inventory a profit center had, the higher its ROI. Collection period had the second greatest influence on ROI. The longer the collection time, the lower was the ROI.

Table 3.2 Independent Variables Included in the Analysis

No.	Description	Division A	All Combined*
1	Labor/machine productivity index	Included	NCM
2	Gross profit per unit	Included	NCM
3	Units produced per labor hour	Included	NCM
4	Factory cost per unit	Redundant with 5	NCM
5	Total cost per unit	Included	NCM
6	Units sold per salesman	Redundant with 7	NCM
7	Sales revenue per salesman	Included	Included
8	Marketing expense as percent of sales revenue	Included	Included
9	Marketing expense per unit	Redundant with 8	NCM
10	Output to capacity ratio	Included	Included
11	Collection period	Included	Included
12	Inventory to sales ratio (dollars)	Redundant with 13	Redundant with 13
13	Inventory to sales ratio (units)	Included	Included
14	Market share	Included	NCM
15	Labor absenteeism	Included	Included
16	Accident frequency	Included	Included
17	Labor turnover	Included	Included

*NCM indicates that no common measurement was found for the variable.

Source: Bruce A. Kirchoff, "Empirical Analysis of Strategic Factors Contributing to Return on Investment," paper presented in *Proceedings: Academy of Management*, 1975, p. 47. Reprinted by permission of the Academy of Management.

Sales revenue per salesman was the third major variable. This is a measure of salesman productivity. Absenteeism had a similar effect on the total organization as it did on Division A. One interesting finding—accident frequency correlated negatively with ROI. That is, as accidents increased so did ROI. Obviously, this should not occur, and some unforeseen moderator variable is influencing this data. The three variables which did not have a significant impact were capacity utilization, marketing expenses as a percent of sales revenue, and labor turnover. The major contribution of this study is in showing the importance of internal variables as opposed to the external variables approach of the PIMS Project. Also the notation of the limitation of the universality of the market share factor was important.

Hatten, employing multiple regression and other statistical techniques, as well as case study investigation, closely examined strategic variables in 13 major breweries for the 20-year period 1952–1971. Rather than specific behavior patterns for most firms, his results suggest that within a given industry certain strategies are successful for one group of firms, another set of strategies is successful for another group of firms, and so forth. For instance, he found that strategic success for large national brewers was not caused by the same factors as proved successful for regional brewers. His findings support the classical belief that size is an important factor in determining competitive strategy. More importantly, his findings point to the need to investigate claims that certain behaviors ultimately lead to success. They do apparently only in certain situations.

Some earlier studies provide limited corroborative evidence of appropriate behaviors. For example, the Boston Consulting Group's (BCG) findings in 24 technology oriented industries support market share as an important contributor to ROI. BCG also notes the importance of price and price/cost relationships in various product life cycle stages. Other early efforts support a more contingent point of view. Fruhan found that the BCG results are not universal. The strategies recommended by the BCG were not found to be applicable to the industries he examined. Government was observed as a major determinant of which competitive strategy would be acceptable. In summary, the view that certain behaviors are applicable to all firms is limited empirically. The choice of a strategy is at least partially a function of industry. Additional research should isolate commonly successful behaviors for certain industries and for groups of firms within those industries.

Other Contingency Theories

There is increasing evidence that human behavioral factors are extremely important in strategy formation. Some "contingency theories" view variations in strategy at least partially, if not primarily, as resulting from human factors. Three of these contingency theories are presented below. In the next chapter, many of these variables will be examined in greater detail.

As the result of the examination of cases using various statistical analyses, Miller found that successful firm scenarios could be differentiated from unsuccessful firm scenarios. He found that within each of these categories, successful and unsuccessful firms, quite different types of firms existed. The external environments of the more successful firms had not changed significantly over the previous five years, while the volatility of the environment of unsuccessful firms had increased. With respect to organizational traits, successful firms were characterized by more sophisticated controls, environmental scanning, delegation, and technocratization, and had more resources and lacked bureaucratic constraints. Their strategy making was characterized by adaptiveness, innovativeness, integration, multiplicity, and analytical emphasis. Within the successful firms, there seemed to be a progression from those which were successful largely because of the existing stable environment to those which were able to manage in more hostile conditions. Those in this

"So Much For Plan A. Now . . . ."

study which were successful in stable environments were similar to what have been deemed mechanistic organizations. Those which were successful in a more hostile environment resembled what have been called organic organizations. Mechanistic firms are more centralized, more bureaucratic, and less adaptive than are organic organizations.

Among the unsuccessful firms, a progression such as that found in the successful firms could not be detected. These firms were characterized individually by some particular type of pathology which resulted in maladaptive strategy. For example, one firm's scenario was characterized by a bold and reckless entrepreneur who was proactive and a high risk taker. In another instance, a very traditional firm was unable to adapt to change and thus had difficulty surviving.

This study suggests that environmental factors have a significant impact upon choices of appropriate strategy, especially the amount of change in the environment. This study indicates that it is the type of organizational structure—centralization versus decentralization—in relation to the amount of change which causes a firm to succeed or not to succeed. Top management variables such as conservatism or extremely arbitrary risk taking were suggested as significant in determining whether or not a firm is successful or un-

Figure 3.3 The Basic Contingency Model

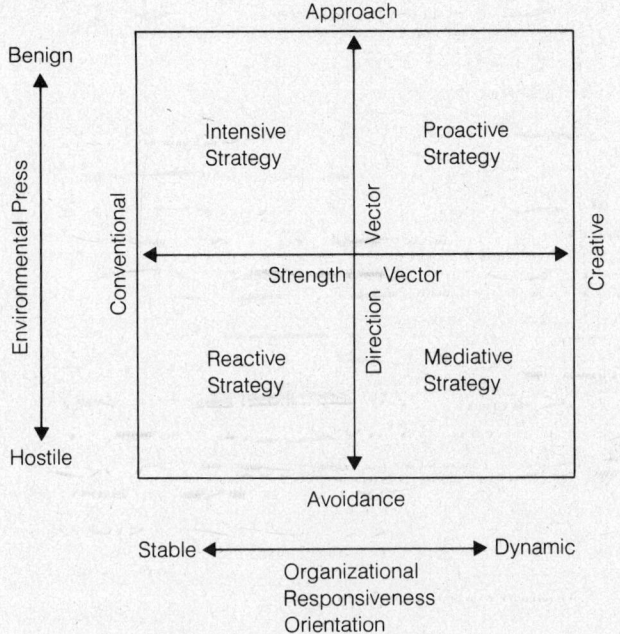

Source: Curtis W. Cook, "Corporate Strategy Change Contingencies," paper presented in *Proceedings: Academy of Management,* 1975, p. 52. Reprinted by permission of the *Academy of Management Journal.*

successful. Unsuccessful firms did not employ techniques such as environmental scanning, environmental analysis, or analysis of any kind in terms of strategic formulation as often as did successful firms. This study suggests that the human variable may be an important predictor of strategic success and that therefore strategy may be contingent upon this variable.

Cook reviewed the strategic and organizational behavioral literature and suggested that a combination of organizational responsiveness orientation and environmental press will cause strategy to be formulated in one of four primary ways: intensive strategy, proactive strategy, mediative strategy, or reactive strategy.[1] This contingency model is presented in Figure 3.3. This model is a basic four-cell matrix with any cell resulting from a combination of the factors on each of the axes. This model was used to hypothesize the following:

1. Stable organizations facing benign press tend to enact intensification strategy.

2. Dynamic organizations facing benign press tend to enact proactive strategy.

3. Stable organizations facing hostile press tend to enact reactive strategy.
4. Dynamic organizations facing hostile press tend to enact mediative strategy.

Cook's study examined data from 14 supermarket chains in the Los Angeles market area. After statistical analysis, strong support was found for Hypotheses 1 through 3. Hypothesis 4 was tentatively supported. This study suggests that organizations will react in a certain way regardless of what is a "best" strategy. It also indicates that perceptions may play a very important role in causing strategy to be formulated in a certain manner. Top management's perception of the environment, when combined with a predisposition to react in a certain manner, could cause strategy to be formulated in a very different pattern from what concept might predict.

This study sampled one industry in one geographical location, so its findings are not universally applicable. Nonetheless, it does suggest that a very important aspect of strategy formation is the human variable. This variable will be discussed in more detail in the next chapter, but it is increasingly apparent that strategy may be contingent upon human variables not previously subjected to examination.

In a related effort, Anderson and Paine hypothesized, again employing a four-cell matrix as shown in Figure 3.4, that the strategy formation process which will be employed depends upon managerial perceptions of two major factors—internal change and uncertainty. As a result of these interactions, four major types of strategy formation situations result. Each of the four cells is characterized in terms of five major factors indicated by the key. The hypotheses associated with this model have not been proved through substantial empirical research, rather the model is conceptual in nature. But, again, it is hypothesized that behavioral factors play an important part in the final formulation of strategy.

Anderson and Paine suggest that in their view each of these quadrants would seem to have a definite pattern of behavior associated with it. They suggest that organizations operating in Cell 1 would have a process planning mode orientation (see Chapter 4); they would not actually search the environment, and they are basically stability motivated. Firms in Cell 2 would probably have a planning or entrepreneurial orientation; would have less of an active search for environmental information; but would have a high motivation for change. These firms are characterized as seeking to take advantage of the environment by improving their strengths and reducing their weaknesses. Those firms operating in Cell 3 search the environment for information; are adaptively oriented; but stability motivated. Firms within this cell would be characterized as having to be dominated by a coalition. Those firms operating in Cell 4 would be actively searching for environmental information; would be quite adaptive or have an entrepreneurial orientation; and would be characterized by internal change motivation. These firms would have a divided coalition of influencer forces which might be overcome

Figure 3.4 The Perceptually Based Strategy Model

Perceived Need for Internal Change

	Low	High
Certain	**Cell 1** 1. Fixed and well defined 2. Optimization; maintenance; efficiency 3. Process planning; maintain competence 4. Closed/stable/mechanistic 5. Commitment to existing power structure; less active search for environmental information	**Cell 2** 1. Need for identification and readjustment 2. Optimization; improve economies of operation; planned change 3. Process planning; integration; improve distinctive competence 4. Closed/stable/mechanistic 5. Commitment to existing power structure; systematic; conservative; less active search for environmental information; "integrative," entrepreneur
Uncertain	**Cell 3** 1. Continually adjusted to feedback 2. Satisficing; maintain capacity to cope with uncertainty 3. Adaptive or contingency planning; search of advance information; penetration 4. Open/adaptive/organic 5. Adaptive planner; information gathering	**Cell 4** 1. Varied and flexible 2. Satisficing; survival; develop effective problem solving 3. Adaptive or contingency planning; divestiture; merger; diversification 4. Open/adaptive/organic 5. Search for external information; adaptive; "sharp departure" entrepreneur

Perceived Environmental Uncertainty (vertical axis label)

Key:
1. Mission or domain
2. Objectives
3. Strategies and policies
4. Organization form
5. Role performance of policy maker

Source: Carl R. Anderson and Frank T. Paine, "Managerial Perceptions and Strategic Behavior," *Academy of Management Journal*, December 1975, p. 817. Reprinted by permission of *Academy of Management Journal*.

by an enthusiastic entrepreneurial type. Each of these cells is subject to variation from the basic theme presented above and in Figure 3.4.

Assessing Internal and Environmental Factors

Once information is gathered and analyzed, alternatives are generated and expressed in terms of objectives. Courses of action are designed either to solve problems or to take advantage of opportunities. Current and anticipated future strengths and weaknesses and environmental threats and opportunities are assessed simultaneously with respect to each other and to mission and policy. Assessment occurs when generating and when evaluating alternatives. While there is no consensus, the list of internal factors to be surveyed usually commences with top management functioning, proceeds to product and/or functional area considerations, and concludes with the recognition that the human resource is of vital importance. Some firms review strengths and weaknesses, others just check for strengths. More specifically, the following are suggested as a few of the strengths which organizations might possess. Conversely, their absence would denote weakness.

Strengths

Top Management

1. experienced and knowledgeable executives
2. performance of appropriate functions

Master Strategy

1. objectives and plans of action—appropriate Primary Mission, Mission Supportive, and Strategic Issue strategies
2. a competitive advantage which is being exploited
3. a formal planning system

Marketing

1. superior market share
2. small (a niche) or large size
3. good distribution systems
4. favorable image
5. effective advertising program, promotion
6. sales force that produces results
7. integrated product line
8. location appropriate to market
9. a superior product
10. price advantage

Production

1. efficiency of labor and/or equipment
2. labor nonunionized, competitors unionized
3. vertical integration
4. integration of marketing and production—for example, scheduling
5. location (nearness to raw materials or customers)
6. superior technology

Finance

1. sound debt structure
2. adequate financial management/information systems
3. difficulty of entry into market
4. high cash flow

Personnel

1. high quality first-line employees and managers
2. effective motivation systems
3. appropriate organization climate
4. relatively low cost labor

Others

1. appropriate political, government relations
2. ethical managers
3. growth
4. proper organization structure
5. social responsibility

Similarly, a business would look for a product market situation characterized by the following:

Opportunities

Market

1. profit
2. growth potential
3. suitable potential ease of entry characteristics
4. absence of government/legal interference
5. suitable distribution channels

Competition

1. weak or nonexistent competition
2. the availability of a niche if competition is strong

Technology

1. dominance

2. favorable change rate
3. energy situation satisfactory

Finance

1. affordability of marketing/production strategies
2. capital requirements suitable

Societal

1. environmental protection requirements reasonable
2. other societal concerns favorable

Management

1. compatible with top management's values and needs

The actual process of matching strengths and weaknesses against threats and opportunities is not a precise science. Few heuristics and even fewer scientific methods exist for weighting the relative values of these factors because it is impossible to accurately quantify many of the critical elements examined in strategic assessment. Firms often assign nonparametric values—checks, pluses, minuses, and zeroes—to one of several possible scale descriptions. These descriptions might include strong plus, plus, neutral, minus, and strong minus to each line item in strategic factors checklists: strengths and weaknesses, threats and opportunities. Or ordinal values such as +2, +1, 0, −1, −2 may be assigned. Frequently no value is assigned. Various techniques are employed to interpret the meanings of these checklists. Simple scanning or mathematical summation of assigned values is normally employed. Some descriptive or mathematical cut-off point is usually established which will indicate the desirability of a strategic action, for example, investment. This is an extremely complex process and one which requires careful consideration. However, one technique which has proven helpful is the Strategy Matrix. General Electric employs this in what it designates its "Stoplight Strategy" (Figure 3.5).

General Electric's "Stoplight Strategy" for Planning

General Electric Co. thinks it has found at least a partial solution to an age-old corporate planning problem: how to put a value on those critical elements in planning it is impossible to attach a number to. In a decision on whether a product will live or die, for example, the value of a patent or the impact of social change cannot be quantified. By using its Strategic Business Planning Grid, or "stoplight strategy," GE can at least evaluate such factors with something more than just a gut reaction.

Figure 3.5 General Electric's "Stoplight Strategy" for Planning

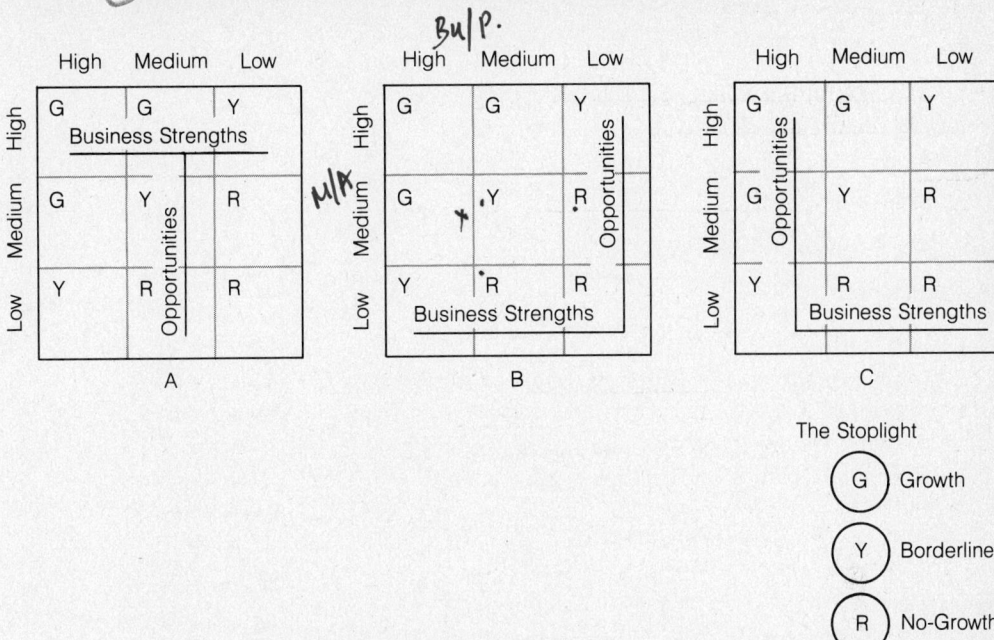

Source: From "General Electric's 'Stoplight Strategy' for Planning," p. 49. Reprinted from the April 28, 1975, issue of *Business Week* by special permission. © 1975 by McGraw-Hill, Inc.

"It's the best way we've found to sort disparate businesses," says GE planner Reuben Gutoff. "You eventually have to make a subjective decision, but you put into it all the hard information you can. It's one way to compare apples and oranges." GE, with 43 distinct businesses, has a lot of apples and oranges. In every annual planning review, each individual business is rated not only on numerical projections of sales, profit, and return on investment, but also on such hard-to-quantify factors as volatility of market share, technology needs, employee loyalty in the industry, competitive stance, and social need. The result is a high, medium, or low rating on both attractiveness of an industry and GE's strengths in the field.

How It Works

If industry attractiveness is seen as medium and GE's strengths as high (Chart A) [Figure 3.5], an "invest and grow"—or green light—decision would result, because the evaluation bars cross in a green square. Both industry attractiveness and business strength are low in Chart B, indicating a red light strategy, or a business which will continue to generate earnings but no longer warrants much additional investment by GE. Chart C represents a business with high industry attractiveness but low GE strength— a "yellow" business that might go either way.

A green business is expected to grow. A red operation's strategy, on the other hand, may involve consolidation of plants, limited technology infusion, reduced investment, and strong cash flow. A yellow business could be borderline, or the business—say, electronic components—could be diverse enough to have both red and green units.

"We don't give definitive weights to the non-numerical factors," says Gutoff, "but they do have weights. At the end of our discussion there is a good consensus on what's green, red, or yellow." The result, he says, is "semiquantitative." After three or four critiques at various levels, the final grids— and decisions—are made by the corporate policy committee—the chairman, three vice-chairmen, five senior vice-presidents, and the vice-president for finance.

The process is not just window dressing. It may prevent costly mistakes. "Interestingly," says one GE planner, "the financial projections are often best on businesses that turn up worst (in the red) on the grid."

Source: "General Electric's 'Stoplight Strategy' for Planning," p. 49. Reprinted from the April 28, 1975, issue of *Business Week* by special permission. Ⓟ 1975 by McGraw-Hill, Inc.

In using the stoplight technique, GE's top management assigns values to these strategic factors:

For Business Strengths	For Industry Attractiveness
Size	Size
Growth	Market Growth, Pricing
Share	Market Diversity
Position	Competitive Structure
Profitability	Industry Profitability
Margins	Technical Role
Technology Position	Social
Strengths/Weaknesses	Environment
Image	Legal
Pollution	Human
People	

Note that the factors considered include not only those competitive and supportive factors such as sales, profit, and loss, but more difficult to quantify items such as technology needs, social responsibility, and employee needs.

The grid is utilized primarily to manage the current or prospective businesses of the organization, especially in balancing the investment portfolio. GE uses the grid to determine the type of strategy it should employ based on the assessment of factors referenced previously. In Figure 3.6, the alternative related strategies are indicated. For those current or potential businesses of the organization rated by collective executive judgment as positioned in the green sectors of the matrix, a growth strategy will result. For those positioned in the yellow sectors of the matrix, a selective strategy based on earnings will be pursued. For those in the red sectors, a harvest/divest strategy will be employed.[2] The matrix may be used to reevaluate investments as the environment changes. This is accomplished simply by changing the criteria (the factors considered) and the weights given to the criteria relative to each other.

The matrix technique is commonly used by large organizations for the purpose of business project/product selection, although the color coding is perhaps unique to GE. For example, the PIMS[3] Project organizations, some 50 of them, employ this type of matrix for purposes of market share analysis and project selection.

With regard to how strategists define corporate strengths and opportunities, Stevenson found in studying 50 managers in six diverse business organizations that managers tend to treat strengths differently from weaknesses. While the steps for defining strengths and weaknesses are essentially the same, the specific factors examined and the criteria for use in judging these factors vary according to the operational requirements of the business and its history. He found that other factors served to modify the exact way in which the manager carries out the definition process. The primary moderating factors are the manager's position and responsibility in the organization. No single type of measurement or criteria exists for the measurement of all attributes of strengths and weaknesses. In explaining these results, Stevenson reports that personality, perceived role, and position influences were so strong as to cause serious doubt as to the value of a formal assessment process. Computational limitations and differing perceptions of requirements decreased the probability of a successful analysis. The differing criteria for strengths and weaknesses also result partially from the availability of historical data on weaknesses. Strengths are relatively well known and based on historical data. Potential weaknesses, however, represent a perceived gap between present attainments and normatively derived future objectives. Weakness evaluations depend on normative criteria.

The implications of this are important. Stevenson notes that with regard to continuing an internal evaluation, managers should: view the evaluation as an aid to task accomplishment; develop areas of examination tailored to

Figure 3.6   Alternative Related Strategies

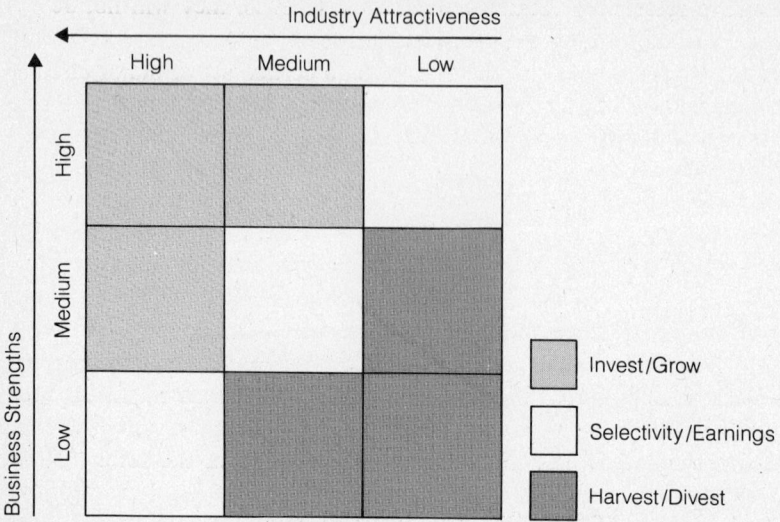

Industry Attractiveness

Source: "General Electric's 'Stoplight Strategy' for Planning," p. 49. Reprinted from the April 28, 1975, issue of *Business Week* by special permission. © 1975 by McGraw-Hill, Inc.

the responsibility and authority of each manager; make criteria explicit to provide a common framework; understand the differences in use of identified strengths and weaknesses; and recognize the strategic importance of defining these attributes. In addition, it also seems possible to have the evaluation accomplished by an external consultant. Such an action would alleviate most of the problems associated with the evaluation as it is now conducted.

On the basis of a single research study one can hardly discount all evaluations of strengths and weaknesses (or threats and opportunities). However, this study points out the need to be aware of the human variable in the strategic decision process. While this chapter has been devoted to the techniques involved in strategic decision making, the following chapter concentrates exclusively and extensively on the human variable. As shall be seen, the strategic decision process is extremely complex, much more so than the normative models which describe this process usually depict. In fact, much of the rationality desired and built into the decision system through techniques is negated by the human variable.

The Strategy Matrix is not employable in solving every strategic problem or in evaluating every opportunity. Other options which may be utilized include simulations (see Chapter 2), decision trees, goal programming, various mathematical models, the Kepner and Tregoe decision model, and simply following the basic decision model presented earlier without the use of sophisticated techniques. The latter method is the most commonly used. Since the above referenced techniques are familiar ones, they will not be described here in detail. Rather, the preceding pages have examined an approach to strategy formation which suggests that given a certain set of major circumstances in a situation, a best strategy is determinable. Wherever those circumstances are encountered, a specific strategy should be employed.

Summary

This chapter reviewed some techniques which might be used by the organizational strategist to assess the information which he receives, which might be used to formulate alternative strategies, and which might be used to evaluate these in light of mission and policy. It was proposed that it is possible to identify variables which must be considered in the formation of strategy. It was also noted that it is very difficult to determine what a strategy ought to be in any specific instance. It was then observed that not only should certain factors be considered in a given situation but also that there might exist certain behaviors which should be followed in most situations. Finally, regardless of the particular analytical techniques employed, strategy formation, and the resultant content of strategy may, in fact, be principally a function of certain human variables which are not normally included in the strategic literature. In the next chapter this latter aspect will be explored in more detail.

Discussion Questions

1. If the contingency theory and behavioral theory are limited in their applications, then what is the best approach to strategy formation?
2. In addition to the methods suggested in this chapter as aiding the alternative generation process, what are some other techniques which may be used to generate alternatives? What role do you think creativity plays in alternative generation?
3. Using the "Stoplight Strategy" Matrix, pick a firm and determine which strategy it would use with regard to a product. Explain why. (Some research may be necessary.)
4. How would you employ Table 3.1 in a case?

Footnotes

1. Proactive means actively seeking to make the environment favorable and

to create success. Mediative suggests bargaining, avoidance, and problems not confronted. Reactive suggests responding and adapting to the environment. Intensive means taking advantage of the environment. Organizational responsiveness orientation indicates the manner in which organizations tend to respond. Environmental press simply indicates type of environment in which an organization operates.

2. A selective strategy means that projects are carefully selected for potential. A harvest and divest strategy means that investment in businesses or projects in this category will be reduced. The emphasis is on recovery of cash and only very selective investments. Chapter 5 describes these strategies at greater length.

3. The Profit Impact of Market Strategies (PIMS) firms share market information and utilize regression analysis to determine the appropriate strategic contingency factors.

References

Allen, M. G. "Strategic Problems Facing Today's Corporate Planner." Paper presented to the Academy of Management, August 1976, at Kansas City.

Anderson, C. R., and F. T. Paine. "Managerial Perceptions and Strategic Behavior." *Academy of Management Journal,* December 1975, pp. 811–823.

Ansoff, H. I. *Corporate Strategy.* New York: McGraw-Hill, 1965.

Ansoff, H. I., and J. Stewart. "Strategies for a Technology-Based Business." *Harvard Business Review,* November/December 1967, pp. 71–83.

The Boston Consulting Group. *Perspectives on Experience.* Boston: The Boston Consulting Group, 1968.

————. *Perspectives on Experience.* Boston: The Boston Consulting Group, 1970.

Buchele, R. B. "How to Evaluate a Firm." *California Management Review,* Fall 1962, pp. 5–16.

Burns, T., and G. M. Stalker. *The Management of Innovation.* London: Tavistock, 1961.

Cook, C. W. "Corporate Strategy Change Contingencies." *Proceedings: Academy of Management,* August 1976, pp. 52–54.

"Corporate Planning: Piercing Future Fog." *Business Week,* April 28, 1975, pp. 46–54.

Dhalla, N. K., and S. Yuspeh. "Forget the Product Life Cycle Concept." *Harvard Business Review,* January/February 1976, pp. 102–112.

Fox, H. W. "A Framework for Functional Coordination." *Atlanta Economic Review,* November/December 1973, pp. 8–11.

Fruhan, W. E., Jr. *The Fight for Competitive Advantage: A Study of U.S. Domestic Trunk Air Carriers.* Boston: Division of Research, Harvard Business School, 1972.

————. "Pyrrhic Victories in Fights for Market Share." *Harvard Business Review,* September/October 1972, pp. 100–107.

Glueck, W. F. "Business Policy: Reality and Promise." *Proceedings: Academy of Management,* Minneapolis, 1972, pp. 108–111.

Greenwood, W. T. "An Annual Policy Audit of the Corporation." In *Management Perspectives on Organizational Effectiveness,* edited by D. F. Ray and T. B. Green. Southern Management Association, November 1975, p. 11.

Gutmann, P. M. "Strategies for Growth." *California Management Review,* Summer 1964, pp. 81–86.

Hatten, K. J. "Strategic Models in the Brewing Industry." Unpublished doctoral dissertation, Purdue University, 1974.

————. "Strategy, Profits, and Beer." Paper presented at the Academy of Management Meetings, August 1975, at New Orleans.

Henry, Harold W. "Appraising Company Strengths and Weaknesses." Paper presented at the Academy of Management Meeting, August 1977, at Kissimmee, Fla.

Hofer, C. W. "Toward a Contingency Theory of Business Strategy." *Academy of Management Journal,* December 1975, pp. 784–810.

Hursey, D. E. "The Corporate Appraisal: Assessing Company Strengths and Weaknesses." *Long Range Planning,* December 1968, pp. 19–25.

Katz, R. L. *Cases and Concepts in Corporate Strategy.* Englewood Cliffs, N.J.: Prentice-Hall, 1970.

Khandwalla, P. "The Techno-Economic Ecology of Corporate Strategy." Paper presented at the 1974 National Meeting of the Academy of Management, Business Policy and Planning Division sessions, August 20, 1974, at Seattle, Washington.

Kirchoff, B. A. "Empirical Analysis of Strategic Factors Contributing to Return on Investment." *Proceedings: Academy of Management,* 1975, pp. 46–48.

Kitching, J. "Why Do Mergers Miscarry?" *Harvard Business Review,* November/December 1967, pp. 84–101.

Kubicon, T. "Organizational Planning: What It Is and How to Do It: Part I—The Organizational Audit." *Cost and Management,* January/February 1972, pp. 33–41.

Levitt, T. "Exploit the Product Life Cycle." *Harvard Business Review,* November/December 1965, pp. 81–94.

Lorange, P. "Divisional Planning: Setting Effective Direction." *Sloan Management Review,* Fall 1975, pp. 77–91.

Metzner, H. E.; J. L. Wall; and W. F. Glueck. "Product Life Cycle and Stages of Growth: An Empirical Analysis." *Proceedings: Academy of Management,* 1975, pp. 61–63.

Michael, G. "Product Petrification: A New Stage in the Life Cycle." *California Management Review,* Fall 1971, pp. 88–91.

Miller, D. "Towards a Contingency Theory of Strategy Formulation." *Proceedings: Academy of Management,* 1975, pp. 64–66.

Rumelt, R. P. *Strategy, Structure, and Economic Performance in Large American Industrial Corporations.* Boston: Harvard University Press, 1974.

Schoeffler, S. "Profit Impact on Marketing Strategy." Internal memorandum, *Marketing Research Institute,* November 1972.

Schoeffler, S.; R. D. Buzzell; and D. F. Heany. "The Impact of Strategic Planning on Profit Performance." *Harvard Business Review,* March/April 1974, pp. 137–145.

Stevenson, H. H. "Defining Corporate Strengths and Weaknesses." *Sloan Management Review,* Spring 1976, pp. 51–66.

Tilles, S. "Strategies for Allocating Funds." *Harvard Business Review,* January/February 1966, pp. 72–80.

Udell, J. G. *Successful Marketing Strategies.* Madison, Wis.: Mimir Publishers, 1972.

Warren, E. K. "The Capability Inventory: Its Role in Long Range Planning." *Management of Personnel Quarterly*, Winter 1965, pp. 31–39.

Wasson, C. R. *Dynamic Competitive Strategy and Product Life Cycle.* St. Charles, Ill.: Challenge Books, 1974.

Chapter 4

Strategy Formation:

The Strategic Decision Process— A Behavioral View

The most common source of mistakes in management decisions is emphasis on finding the right answers rather than the right questions.

Peter Drucker

Should always balance out the past performance w/ goals + objectives in dealing w/ present performance

Decision making is the most important of all of the activities in which managers engage. It is through decision making that the other functions of management are accomplished. A decision is a choice from among alternatives, but decision making also involves problem or opportunity identification, recognition, implementation, and control. This chapter focuses on the actual decision process involved in the formation of strategy. Earlier, in Chapters 2 and 3, the strategic decision process was viewed as it is normally conceptualized and some of the techniques which may be employed in that process were noted. Reviewing the behavioral aspects of all types of decision making, this chapter focuses on the strategic decision process. This includes discussions of specific components of the strategic decision process, especially the solution component. This chapter is concerned with those portions of the planning models indicated in Figures 4.1 and 4.2.

Figure 4.1   The Organization—An Organization Process Model

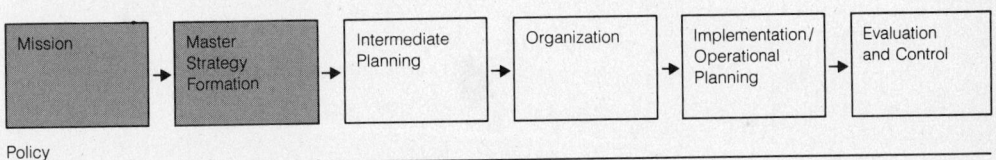

Policy

The Complexity of Organizational Decision Making

The five part decision process model presented in Chapter 2, while appealing because of its simplicity, understates the complexity of the organizational decision process. Decision making occurs within constraints. These include psychological, environmental, and decision related factors. Psychologically, the decision maker is constrained by his own personality, primarily his needs,

Figure 4.2 Master Strategy Formation

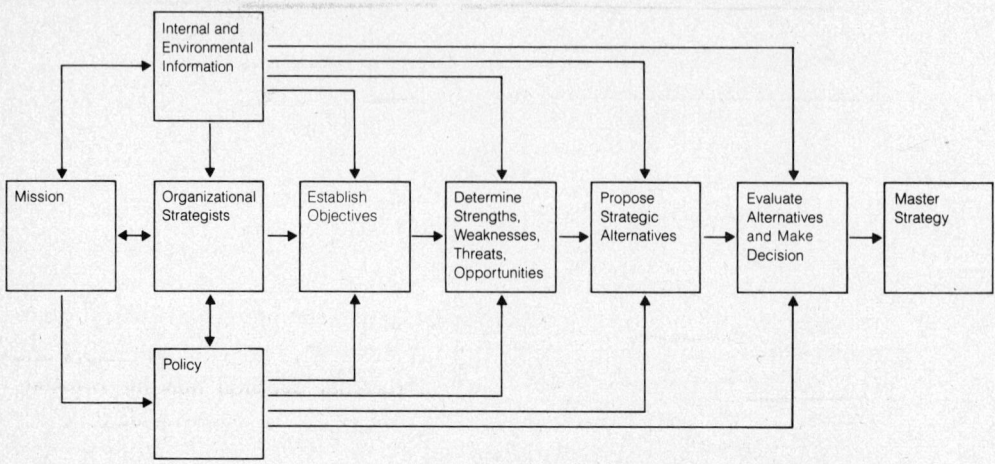

but also his knowledge, risk propensity, aspirations, values, skills, experience, perceptions, and limited cognitive ability. Decision related environmental constraints include organizational factors such as objectives and policy, organization environment and structure, reference groups and group dynamics, and roles. Decision related factors include the importance of the decision, the time with which to make the decision, the information available, and multiple decision makers. As a result of these and numerous other factors, the decision process is much more complex than classically conceptualized. The following statements provide a more realistic view of decision making in an organization.

1. Objectives are often vague, in conflict, and not agreed upon.
2. All too frequently managers are unaware that a problem or opportunity exists, that is, they do not recognize a problem or opportunity.
3. When problems are recognized, managers often react to symptoms and not causal factors. Mitroff has labeled this phenomenon an "error of the third kind"—solving the wrong problem.[1]
4. Since decisions are based on models, rationality, if applied, can be applied only to the perceived most important aspects of the situation. Omission of vital data, variables, and relationships is not an infrequent occurrence.
5. Since it is normally mentally and physically impossible to observe all or even most alternatives in complete detail, the search behavior is much less extensive than conceptualized; few impacts are considered. The decision maker's knowledge of the situation is limited.

6. Very few managers have a maximizing criterion in mind. Most will settle for an alternative which satisfies very minimal and very minimally considered objectives. These are known as "satisficing" criteria.
7. Managers make decisions based on rules of thumb and frequently do not evaluate alternatives even by the satisficing criteria. Managers apparently believe that whatever worked last time will work this time.
8. Social relationships greatly affect the decision maker's rationality.

The Strategic Decision Process

The normative role of top management in strategy formation is to review policy and the information which it possesses related to internal factors and the external environment, then, through rational decision making, translate mission into more specific objectives and subsequently establish major plans of action to reach those objectives. Often the information will indicate a need to reformulate strategy and trigger the strategic decision process. More often than not, this information will indicate the need to change only some element of strategy. The strategic decision process is complex.

The strategic decision is characterized by the five phases common to other decisions. Research related to the first four of these phases, especially the solution phase, will be explored in detail. The control phase parallels that in Figure 4.1 and is not discussed here in detail. Emphasis is placed on describing the actual strategic decision process as opposed to the classical conceptualization. Most discussions of decision making focus on problem solving. Note that in the strategic situation, decision making occurs not only as the result of problems—the difference between what should be and what is—but also as the result of opportunities—the difference between what could be and what is. The discussion in this chapter treats both opportunities and problems as initiators of the strategic decision process. While it is questionable whether or not smaller businesses engage in opportunity searches, larger businesses clearly treat strategy as an exercise in opportunity exploration routinely employing various portfolio management techniques.

A Strategic Decision Process Model

Examining the strategic decision process is important to actual organizational experiences because it leads to a better understanding of organizational objectives, organizational plans, organizational structure, and the resulting everyday operations of the organization. In studying the cases in Part II of this book, this examination of the actual decision process will lead to a better

Figure 4.3   Strategic Decision Process Model

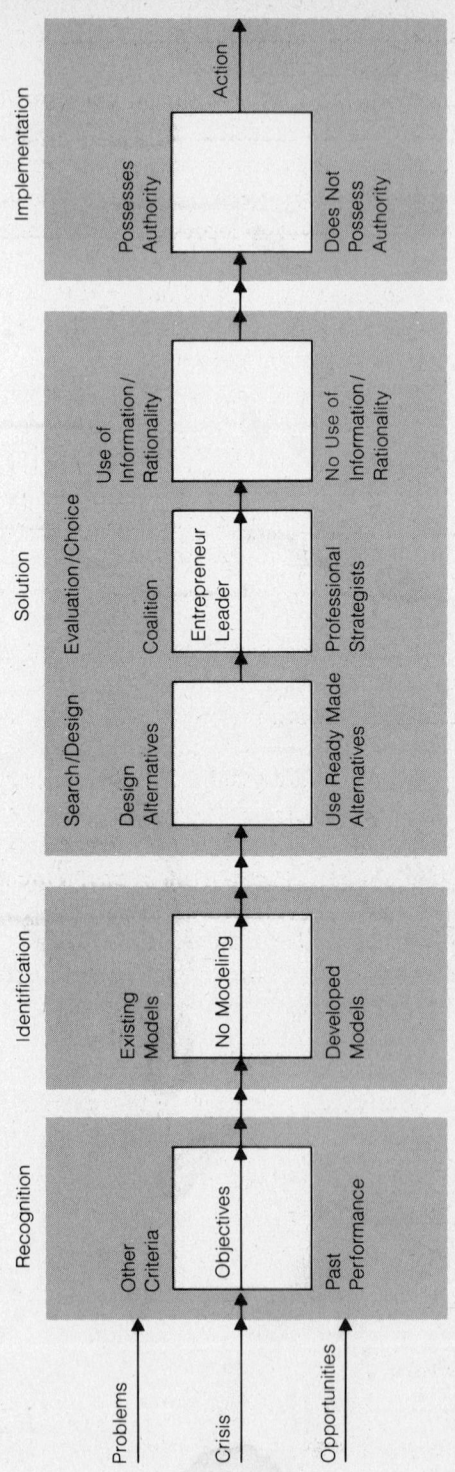

understanding of the objectives, plans, structure, and operations of the organizations involved in these cases.

The behavioral aspects of strategic decision making are somewhat complex, but they can be modeled. In Figure 4.3, a model which incorporates the available research evidence and the normative/descriptive literature is presented. To begin: problems, crises (severe problems),[2] or opportunities initiate the strategic decision process. Recognition occurs as a result of reference to objectives, past performance, or other perceived critical criteria. Such criteria might include potential objectives which would aid in the recognition of opportunities. Where recognition and identification are synonymous, the decision maker moves directly to searching for alternatives and no modeling occurs. However, where identification occurs, the decision maker identifies either in relation to existing problem/opportunity models or models developed for the specific problem or opportunity. Search occurs for ready-made alternatives, but search normally must be expanded to include the design of specifically related alternatives. Evaluation and choice normally involve either a single entrepreneurial leader, a coalition of top managers, and/or significant involvement in the decision process by professional planners.

Each of these decision makers may or may not utilize information and follow a rational choice process. Normally, the professional strategists would be expected to use information and rational decision processes, but the other two decision makers would not necessarily be expected to. Where the decision makers do not possess the needed approval authority, they must seek it if the decision is to be implemented. The model may be iterative to the extent that the process is repeated as an issue progresses upwards through the decision levels of the organization hierarchy. Often, however, the higher level decision process is abbreviated as decisions are based on lower level recommendations. Once authority is possessed, implementation action ensues. Various interruptions and delays to this process may occur (none portrayed in Figure 4.3) and may result in variances in the exact decision process in any particular situation.

The Component Phases of Decision Making: A Closer Examination

Let us now examine each of the first three component phases of the strategic decision process model in order to increase our understanding of them.

Recognition

In order to know if a problem exists, the term *problem* must be defined. A problem occurs when objective accomplishment differs negatively from the objectives established—when results are not as great as the objectives. (This implies that objectives have been established.) In theory, it is the function of information systems to alert the manager to this situation. Information systems should be designed to discover problems before they become serious. While it might be assumed that problems are here precisely defined, this stage involves more of a vague feeling that something is not right or a feeling that something is wrong. It is in the identification phase that more precise modeling transpires.

One of the weaknesses of the decision making/problem solving process is the fact that this first stage of the process is not well understood. Too few organizations and too few decision makers have seriously approached the question, "How do we know when we have a problem?" A study by Pounds, one of the few studies which has analyzed the problem recognition process, reveals that business managers do not utilize objectives to establish the existence of problems. Conceptually, a manager should know that he has a problem when performance does not equal objectives. Objectives should be the benchmark against which progress is measured. But this study revealed that managers most frequently use previous performances as a reference, as opposed to using this year's objectives. This approach to problem recognition results in problems not being recognized because the reference is to past performance rather than to current objectives. In addition to past performance, some managers may compare performance to the performances of external organizations doing similar tasks or to some external model to which they believe they can compare their own organization. Of these four possible performance comparisons—that is, objectives, previous performance, external similar organizations, and external models—the first is the most appropriate for determining whether or not organizational goals have been accomplished. Yet, objectives are apparently seldom used.

An opportunity exists when a firm determines that "what is" is less than "what could be." First, of course, a firm must establish what could be. With respect to opportunities, little research has examined how firms determine opportunities. Normatively, organizations must scan their environments as suggested in Chapter 2 in order to be able to recognize opportunities. Entrepreneurial ability plays an important role; although many might assess the same information, only one might see the opportunities revealed.

Identification

Once it is known that a problem or opportunity exists, that is, an information system indicates differences between stated objectives and progress towards those objectives or progress towards those objectives and some potential, more favorable position, and a manager perceives these differences, then the causal factors must be identified or the opportunity more clearly defined.

With the problem solving system that most managers employ, the real problem or opportunity is often overlooked. Managers often jump right in, assuming they know the problem or opportunity. As with recognition, identification is a decision making phase which has been little researched or considered. Information again plays an important role in this process.

Kepner and Tregoe, in one of the few discussions of problem solving identification, suggest that the process of specification is helpful. In specification, decision makers must determine for each problem exactly what the specific problem is, where and when it occurred, whom or what it affected, and the extent of its effect. The decision maker must distinguish what is different about the problem consequences from other events in similar situations. This occurs as a result of examining the situational data. Specification aims at factually separating what the problem is from what it is not. The underlying causal problem determination then becomes a matter of deduction from what should be to what is. This process is not simple, it is at least partly intuitive and it relies partially on experience. The decision maker must learn to ask himself a series of questions which aid in this process. For example, what is the urgency and severity of each problem? How are these problems related? Which problems result from other problems? What could uniquely produce these consequences? The end result of this phase will be a model of the problem. The model routinely summarizes and conceptualizes the situation under examination.

Solution

As related in Chapters 2 and 3, in the solution component of the decision making process, the decision maker(s) first of all searches for alternative solutions or courses of action to solve the problem or exploit the opportunity and then arrays these in some fashion which will facilitate a choice among these alternatives. The search for alternative processes can be extremely time-consuming and complicated. The information system problems have already been related. We will now examine in detail the social processes involved in the solution process in order to better understand how the content of strategy comes to be as it is.

The Top Management Coalition. Since the entrepreneurial/leader concept is familiar to most and the role of professional strategists was presented in Chapter 2, further detail is unnecessary. Suffice it to say that while the entrepreneur guides many, if not the majority, of organizations, not all such leaders are sufficiently strong to cope with all countervailing forces which they encounter. Where weaker chief executives head an organization, and/or especially strong power centers exist, the coalition is perceived as the dominant factor in strategy determination.

Cyert and March first noted the existence of the coalition. Organizational objectives are determined in the coalition process through a bargaining mechanism. This is essentially a trading process involving exchanges of what have been termed "policy side payments" for alliance with a certain coalition on some particular strategic objective or plan. These payments may take the form of money, policy, future objectives, personal treatment, authority, and so forth. Other features of the process include vague objectives varying over time and reflecting the aspiration levels of various coalition members. Conflict within the organization is never fully resolved (because of the bargaining, compromising, vague manner in which objectives are set). This latter characteristic Cyert and March referred to as the "quasi-resolution of conflict." As an example of this phenomenon, there exists a constant struggle between marketing, accounting, and production subunits regarding the amount of inventory that should be maintained. The marketing director seeks high inventories of all items in order to be able to satisfy customers. The comptroller seeks low inventories to reduce carrying costs. The production executive may align himself with either, depending on how his performance is judged and the rewards he will receive for his alliance. This problem is usually quasi-resolved. That is, no party receives a clear victory for its cause. As a result, the issue remains as a roadblock to organizational mission achievement. However, if the marketing manager finally wins and the company agrees to maintain a great number of products across a diversified number of product lines, then a policy side payment will be forthcoming. What emerges is a view of strategy formation as an exchange process, one that is based on power.

While much of the following discussion on coalitions focuses on internal coalitions; organizations, their subunits, and individual members may also form coalitions with major constituents, especially where they are dependent on these constituents. In the relationship of the customer to the supplier, for example, exchanges take place and bargaining occurs where one has "relative power" over the other. Each is somehow dependent on the other. Coalitions with unions, government, competition (restraints of trade), and various pressure groups may also exist. For example, many business organizations have attempted to work "with" environmentalists and minority interest groups rather than fight them. In so doing, they are forming coalitions, exchanging increased social responsibility commitments for decreased protest.

Surprisingly, there has been little research attempting to verify the coalition concept. Perhaps this is because most practitioners and researchers have experienced this phenomenon or because the concept seems so intuitively valid. The following are the major studies which have dealt with this process.

Thompson was the first to elaborate on the coalition phenomena in his discussion of organizations. He observed that the relationship of the organization to its environment was important in determining coalition functioning. He also expressed the view that the future of the organization's objectives was a function of the perceptions of the dominant coalition.

Carter empirically tested Cyert and March's behavorial theory of decision making. He examined six different but related major decisions for a small computer firm. Carter's results essentially verified the Cyert and March hypotheses. However, he suggested certain changes in their theory. One such change was that instead of a single large dominant coalition which resolved conflicts within itself, there existed a series of small groups engaged in bargaining at each level of the organization. As a decision passed through each level of the organization on its way to final executive approval, a new coalition might exert its influence on the eventual decision.

Saunders reported that in an 8-year study of the planning formation process (in a single firm), observed behaviors did not differ significantly from those described by Cyert and March. In reviewing the coalition process, he concluded that in complex organizations strategy formation was a highly diffuse and highly political process. He viewed environmental factors as important determinants of an organization member's efforts to influence the firm's activities. His research also supported the concept of a dominant coalition.

Mintzberg et al., over a 5-year period, closely scrutinized 25 strategic decisions: 9 in service firms, 5 in quasi-governmental agencies, 5 in government agencies, and 6 in manufacturing firms. The results of their study supported the coalition concept. Coalition bargaining behavior was reported in over half of the decisions which they observed.

With the exception of these four studies, much of what is known about the coalition results from studies of power relationships within the organization. The coalition is after all a power concept. In recent years, interest in power in the organization has increased as its significance has been recognized. Organizational politics results from the need for power.

Power and the Political Aspects of Strategic Decision Making. The use of power (politics) to further one's own interests is not new to the organization. Its use in planning is certainly not new, nor is the recognition of its importance. Anthony Jay addressed this aspect of corporate life in his book *Management and Machiavelli*. He observed that while controlling this problem is not too difficult at the lower levels of organization, it is quite difficult to control at the higher management levels. (Note: these are the strategic decision levels.) Stagner indicated that business executives reported key (strategic) decisions in their organizations were often settled by power rather than by rational man maximization criteria. Baldridge reported that the coalition model more nearly resembled decision making at New York University than did rational man or collegial models. What has become increasingly

"OK, Accounting agrees to bigger inventories, but we get to keep our offices
in the upwind wing. . . !"

clear is that while rationality may be a formally proclaimed method of making strategic decisions, power and personality play important roles in this process.

Much of the coalition phenomenon results from competition among organizational subsystems. Relative power among these subsystems is determined by such factors as the ability to cope with uncertainty (helping the organization to cope with uncertainty) and the essentiality of the subsystem to the organization. Apparently the composition of the dominant coalition and its power distribution result to a great extent from the effects of environmental change. The point is that the organization is composed of interdependent subsystems: a problem for one is a problem for another. The coalition or coalition member who is able to provide the means for coping with change, has lower substitutability, or is more central to the work flow gains power. The implication is obvious: the subunit manager is in a position to gain power. This coping is one obvious basis for the increasing power of planning units in larger organizations. This power can lead to dominance by the planner.

While research regarding the coalition is not abundant, that which exists is supportive of Cyert and March's postulations. Obviously, more research is necessary, especially that which would sample behavior across many firms of varying sizes in several industries and in nonprofit organizations. However, we must not overlook the abundant informal group research which is available. While this research mainly examines groups at lower levels of the organization, it should not be dismissed. In general, it also concludes that power is relative, is bargained for (exchanged), and that an informal group at lower levels can counteract the power of the formal managerial leader. This does not differ from the evidence provided above and is in fact quite supportive of the coalition concept. This then substantiates the view that the coalition is of vital concern to the student of strategic management.

The role of power (and politics) cannot be overemphasized. Remember that a subunit of General Electric or a similar sized organization may be larger than several entire companies against which it competes. Considerable resource allocations are involved in the coalition process. Additional evidence of the importance of power is as follows: The president of a large strategic planning consulting firm indicates that organizational politics plays an important role in preventing the adoption of his firm's recommended planning models. And the recognition of the correlation between political behavior and success in the organization has been increasingly discussed in the strategic management literature. For example, Gilmore has outlined a four-stage strategy for assisting the executive in his efforts to have his plans adopted by the organization. Brief and Filley have outlined a similar series of propositions for selling proposals for change before committees. Several books are also available which offer advice to the aspiring manager in the political organization.

Coalition activity, power, and politics in strategic decision making are interdependent. As coalition power centers develop, admission to these becomes partially a function of politics. As objectivity in decision making is reduced, power and politics become increasingly important to those who aspire and have a high need for achievement. Success becomes a function of power. As the old saying observes, "It's not so much what you know, but who you know that counts."

Incremental Decision Making. Examination of the strategic decision process reveals that, in many organizations, decisions are made in a series of small steps—hence the term *incrementalism*. As portrayed by Lindblom and Braybrooke, incrementalism is based on the beliefs that a rational approach does not account for man's limited problem solving capacity; his lack of information; the impact of values on decisions; the openness of systems; the high cost of total rationality; the need for sequencing of decisions; and the variations in policy problem situations. It is based on the concept that most governmental policy decisions involve small changes not guided by a high level of understanding. Political decisions indeed proceed by small steps—first attempted, performance measured, and correctively attempted again; and such an approach is best because it allows for the recognition of the problems associated with the rational approach to decision making. Related research supports the existence of incremental process (but not necessarily its assumptions).

Aharoni observed the foreign investment decision processes of 38 United States firms using structured and unstructured interviews. His research suggests that incremental decision making is at least partially a function of organization structure. However, his research is more important because it substantiates the incremental observations of Lindblom and Braybrooke as well as the coalition propositions of Cyert and March. He concluded that decision making in large complex organizations was a continuous social bargaining process composed of many small parts. He observed that different people were involved at divergent points in the organization and at different times. Personal interests were found to play a key role in these decisions.

Two additional studies supporting both bargaining and incremental decision making are those of Bower and Ackerman. Both studies were concerned with investment decisions. Bower examined one firm's decisions extensively. Subsequently, Ackerman, testing Bower's resultant decision model, observed four firms extensively. A third effort by Gilmour examined simultaneously the work of Cyert and March, Bower, and traditional capital budgeting theory. As the result of his study of divestiture in three large United States businesses in different industries, he postulated a revised theory which focused on the concept of individual commitment. He proposed that, as an individual would become committed to a self-generated solution to a perceived discrepancy between personal or organizational goals, he would implement the decision if he had the power. If not, he would attempt to persuade others to follow his recommended course of action. Finally, Trevelyan, in researching the strategic decision process in two large organizations, substantiated the concept of incremental decision making. Each successive commitment to a course of action was found to reinforce others of a similar nature. Eventually, a new course of action (strategy) might result.

The incremental decision process in business organizations appears to result from organization structure, that is, reviews of strategic decisions at every organizational level. In Figure 4.3, this is reflected under the Implementation Component. Where the individual does not possess the authority, he or she would refer the decision upward in the organization. Additional iterations of the strategic decision process would then be necessary. Incremental decision making for public policy (governmental) decisions, while resulting partially from structure, would appear to result primarily from the desire of the politician to "not rock the voter boat." Several iterations of the model would occur, but not necessarily because the decision maker did not possess the proper authority. In business, the initial impetus for strategic incrementalism (which, importantly, is not characteristic of all decisions) is the initiation of strategic commitments at lower levels, which, once approved by successively higher levels of management, leave little room for rejection at the highest level. But in government, incrementalism allows the politician who does not make waves to be reelected.

Three Common Strategic Planning Modes

With respect to the solution and implementation component of the process, Mintzberg suggests that three common modes of planning exist. These modes summarize most of the research presented in this chapter and reveal the most common paths through the model in Figure 4.3. The first of these he labels as the entrepreneurial mode. The traditional concept of strategy formation holds that it is the entrepreneurial leader who guides the organization to its destiny through strategic decision making. This view of the entrepreneurial leader resulted primarily from the classical economic literature, which saw the entrepreneur as the risk taker, the decision maker. When corporations became the dominant form of enterprise, the characteristics were transposed to the CEO, who normally does not start the enterprise but rather manages it. Certainly many organizations, especially smaller business organizations, are headed by chief executives who fit this model and who do indeed guide almost single-handedly their organizations' fortunes. Among the characteristics of this mode Mintzberg lists the following:

1. . . . strategy-making is dominated by the active search for new opportunities.
2. . . . power is centralized in the hands of the chief executive.
3. . . . Strategy-making . . . is characterized by dramatic leaps forward in the face of uncertainty.
4. . . . Growth is the dominant goal. . . .

This model is congruent with how most conceptualize strategic management, but, as the material presented earlier in this chapter has shown, other modes exist. Another mode which Mintzberg identifies is referred to as "the adaptive mode." This mode is characterized by the coalition and by incremental decision making. Mintzberg characterizes this adaptive planning mode as follows:

1. Clear goals do not exist . . . strategy-making reflects a division of power among members of a complex coalition.
2. . . . the strategy-making process is characterized by the "reactive" solution to existing problems rather than the "proactive"[3] search for new opportunities.
3. The adaptive organization makes its decision in incremental, serial steps.
4. Disjointed decisions are characteristic of the adaptive mode.

Mintzberg also suggests a third mode—the planning mode. At the center of this mode are rationality and the corporate planner, especially the analyst. He characterizes this mode as follows:

1. . . . the analyst plays a major role in strategy-making.
2. [It] focuses on systematic analysis, particularly in the assessment of the costs and benefits of competing proposals.
3. [It] is characterized above all by the integration of decisions and strategies.

Mintzberg summarizes the key characteristics and conditions of these modes in Table 4.1. In retrospect what appear to distinguish these three modes are:

1. the source of power; especially
2. single versus multiple decision makers;
3. the decision process utilized; especially
4. the use or absence of systematic planning and planning information; and
5. the number and types of decisions made.

These three modes represent the three most common paths through the model presented in Figure 4.3. Other variations exist, of course.

Table 4.1   Characteristics and Conditions of the Three Modes

Characteristic	Entrepreneurial Mode	Adaptive Mode	Planning Mode
Motive for Decisions	Proactive	Reactive	Proactive & Reactive
Goals of Organization	Growth	Indeterminate	Efficiency & Growth
Evaluation of Proposals	Judgmental	Judgmental	Analytical
Choices Made by	Entrepreneur	Bargaining	Management
Decision Horizon	Long Term	Short Term	Long Term
Preferred Environment	Uncertainty	Certainty	Risk
Decision Linkages	Loosely Coupled	Disjointed	Integrated
Flexibility of Mode	Flexible	Adaptive	Constrained
Size of Moves	Bold Decisions	Incremental Steps	Global Strategies
Vision of Direction	General	None	Specific
Conditions for Use			
Source of Power	Entrepreneur	Divided	Management
Objectives of Organization	Operational	Non-Operational	Operational
Organizational Environment	Yielding	Complex, Dynamic	Predictable, Stable
Status of Organization	Young, Small or Strong Leadership	Established	Large

Source: From Henry Mintzberg, "Strategy Making in Three Modes," *California Management Review,* Winter 1973. © 1973 by the Regents of the University of California. Reprinted from *California Management Review,* volume XVI, number 2, p. 49, by permission of the Regents.

Summary

Strategic decision making has been shown to be a multifactor process, but one which follows definite, if not predictable, patterns. Briefly, several different views of strategic planning have emerged. In some organizations, all of these may be found. Mintzberg has shown that three common strategic planning modes exist. The concept of "the" decision maker has been shown to be largely a myth. In many strategic decisions, more than one decision maker will play an important role. All phases of the process need to be examined more closely. From the research evidence available, it is clear that the process is much less rational and much more a function of psychological and sociological variables than classically conceptualized. For an individual involved in this process, one inference which can be drawn is the need to master power relationships since coalition bargaining characterizes many strategic decision situations. Insistence on well defined objectives can eliminate many of the problems associated with the coalition, but if the formal organizational leader is weak, who will demand such objectives? The diverse factions which exist can and should be integrated. It is precisely the coalition situation which Lawrence and Lorsch describe when they discuss the role of the integrator. When accomplished properly, integration goes beyond compromise. The integrator establishes and then moves the organization towards the common, but specifically stated, objectives. The business organizational constraints which are a partial cause of incremental decisions are designed to facilitate objective decision making through review processes. They should be used in this manner. Normatively, rationality should be embodied in the strategic decision process in each of the phases. Realistically, it is often difficult to obtain complete information and to truly be cognizant of the impacts of all decision variables.

Discussion Questions

1. How do the social relationships among organizational strategists play a role in determining strategy content?
2. Describe the coalition, incremental decision making, and the adaptive mode.
3. Think of an organization with which you are familiar. Imagine a strategic decision of this organization. Now follow this decision through the model in Figure 4.3.
4. Which of the three modes of strategic planning do you feel is the most common? Why?

Footnotes

1. Technically, Mitroff defines an error of the third kind as "the probability

of solving the wrong problem." The error of the third kind is an extension of the Type I and Type II errors associated with hypothesis testing.
2. Unfortunately, problems often become crises before they are reacted to by the organization. So this important initiator of the strategic decision process is identified separately.
3. This term is used by Abraham Zalesnik. It refers to the behavior of a manager who changes the environment in the organization's interest—as opposed to "reacting" to the environment.

References

Ackerman, R. W. "Influence of Integration and Diversity on the Investment Process." *Administrative Science Quarterly*, September 1970, pp. 341–352.
_____. "Organization and the Investment Process: A Comparative Study." Unpublished doctoral dissertation, Harvard Business School, 1968.
Aharoni, Y. *The Foreign Investment Decision Process*. Boston: Division of Research, Harvard Business School, 1966.
Alexis, M., and C. Z. Wilson, eds. *Organizational Decision Making*. Englewood Cliffs, N.J.: Prentice-Hall, 1967.
Baldridge, J. V. *Power and Conflict in the University*. New York: Wiley, 1971.
Bauer, R. A., and K. J. Gergan. *The Study of Policy Formation*. New York: Free Press, 1971.
Bower, J. L. *Managing the Resource Allocation Process*: *A Study of Corporate Planning and Investment*. Boston: Division of Research, Harvard Business School, 1970.
Brief, A. P., and A. C. Filley. "Selling Proposals for Change." *Business Horizons*, April 1976, pp. 22–25.
Carter, E. E. "A Behavioral Theory Approach to Firm Investment and Acquisition Decisions." Unpublished doctoral dissertation, Graduate School of Industrial Administration, Carnegie Mellon University, 1970.
_____. "The Behavioral Theory of the Firm and Top-Level Corporate Decision." *Administrative Science Quarterly,* December 1971, pp. 413–429.
Gilmore, F. F. "Overcoming the Perils of Advocacy in Corporate Planning." *California Management Review*, Spring 1973, pp. 127–137.
Gilmour, S. C. "The Divestment Decision Processes." Unpublished doctoral dissertation, Harvard Business School, 1973.
Hickson, D. I., et al. "A Strategic Contingencies Theory of Intraorganizational Power." *Administrative Science Quarterly*, June 1971, pp. 216–229.
Hill, W. "The Goal Formation Process in Complex Organizations." *Journal of Management Studies,* May 1969, pp. 198–208.
Hinings, C. R., et al. "Structural Conditions of Intraorganizational Power." *Administrative Science Quarterly,* March 1974, pp. 22–44.
Jacobs, D. "Dependency and Vulnerability: An Exchange Approach to the Control of Organizations." *Administrative Science Quarterly*, March 1974, p. 50.
Jay, A. *Management and Machiavelli,* New York: Holt, Rinehart and Winston, 1967.

Karda, M. *Power: How to Get It, How to Use It*. New York: Random House, 1973.

Lawrence, P. R., and J. W. Lorsch. *Organization and Environment*. Homewood, Ill.: Dorsey Press, 1967.

Lindblom, C. E. *The Intelligence of Democracy*. New York: Free Press, 1965.

————. *The Policy-Making Process*. Englewood Cliffs, N.J.: Prentice-Hall, 1968.

————. "The Science of 'Muddling Through.'" *Public Administration Review* 19 Spring (1959): 79–88.

Lindblom, C. E., and D. Braybrooke. *A Strategy of Decision*. New York: Free Press, 1963.

"Machiavellian Tactics for B School Students." *Business Week,* October 13, 1975, p. 86.

March, J. G., and H. A. Simon. *Organizations*. New York: Wiley, 1958.

Mason, R. O. "A Dialectical Approach to Strategic Planning." *Management Science,* April 1969, pp. B403–B414.

McMurry, R. N. "Power and the Ambitious Executive." *Harvard Business Review*, November/December 1973, p. 140.

Mintzberg, H. "Planning on the Left Side and Managing on the Right." *Harvard Business Review,* July/August 1976, pp. 49–58.

Mintzberg, H.; D. Raisinghani; and A. Theoret. "The Structure of Unstructured Decision Processes." *Administrative Science Quarterly*, June 1976, p. 258.

Mittroff, J. "On Helping a Large Governmental Organization to Do Research on Planning on Itself: A Case Study." Unpublished working paper, University of Pittsburgh.

Neale, G. *Proceedings: Second Annual National Planning Conference*, p. 143. Chicago: On-Line Decisions, 1973.

Rondinelli, D. A. "Public Planning and Political Strategy." *Long Range Planning*, April 1976, p. 76.

Saunders, C. B. "What Should We Know about Strategy Formulation." In *Proceedings: Academy of Management, 1973*, p. 32.

Simon, H. A. *Administrative Behavior*. New York: Free Press, 1957.

————. "Theories of Decision Making in Economics and Behavioral Science." *American Economic Review* 49 (June 1959): 253–283.

Soelberg, P. "Unprogrammed Decision Making." In *Research toward Development in Management Thought: Proceedings of the 1966 Annual Meeting of the Academy of Management,* edited by H. P. Hottenstein and R. W. Williams, 1976, pp. 3–16.

Sloan, A. P. *My Years at General Motors*. New York: Doubleday, 1963.

Stagner, R. "Corporate Decision Making: An Empirical Study." *Journal of Applied Psychology*, Vol. 53 (February 1969), pp. 1–13.

Thompson, J. D. *Organizations in Action*, pp. 127–128. New York: McGraw-Hill, 1967.

Trevelyan, E. W. "The Strategic Process in Large, Complex Organizations: A Pilot Study of New Business Development." Unpublished doctoral dissertation, Harvard Business School, 1974.

Wrapp, E. H. "Good Managers Don't Make Policy Decisions." *Harvard Business Review,* September/October 1967, pp. 91–99.

Zalesnik, A. "Power and Politics in Organizational Life." *Harvard Business Review,* May/June 1970, p. 47.

Chapter 5

Master Strategy Content and Intermediate Planning

All decision is compromise.
Herbert Simon

The result of the strategic decision process is the Master Strategy. The specific objectives and strategic plans which each organization would incorporate into its Master Strategy vary. However, firms include certain common components in their Master Strategies. Identifiable, common substrategies are employed by most firms. These common components and common substrategies are reviewed in this chapter. Appropriate characteristics for these strategies and other plans are also noted. In addition, the role and nature of intermediate planning are discussed. Finally, Management by Objectives, an important integrative technique, is reviewed. The components of the organization process model which are included in this chapter are portrayed in Figure 5.1.

Figure 5.1   The Organization—An Organization Process Model

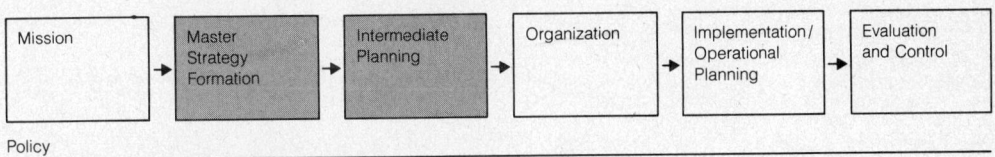

Policy

Master Strategy Content

Table 5.1 provides a brief summary of the major substrategies which are contained in the Master Strategy. Chapter 1 briefly mentioned the three primary components of the Master Strategy: mission competitive, mission supportive, and strategic issues. Table 5.1 suggests how the factors in Table 5.2 might be divided within these three components. Many variations exist and, as suggested in Chapter 1, each firm has its own definition of strategy and thus of differing component contents.

The component items in Table 5.2 are by no means mutually exclusive. For example, growth is a substrategy for which organization, finance, marketing, production, planning and control, personnel, and other substrategies will be

Primary Mission Strategy (For Business—The Mission Competitive Strategy)

This is the strategy designed to accomplish the primary mission. For business, the contents of this strategy are normally related to:

Basic Action Strategies

a. Competition
b. Growth
c. Diversification
d. Acquisition
e. Divestment
f. Retrenchment
g. Stabilization

Organization Function Strategies (Economic Functions)

a. Marketing

2. **Mission Supportive Strategies**

These strategies detail how the organization supports the primary mission. For business, the contents of this strategy are normally related to:

Organization Function Strategies (Economic Functions)

a. Production
b. Finance
c. Personnel
d. Information Systems
e. R&D, Market Research
f. Other Significant Areas

Management Function Strategies

a. Planning
b. Organizing
c. Implementing
d. Controlling
e. Staffing
f. Leading
g. Motivating
h. Communicating
i. Decision Making
j. Integrating

3. **Strategic Issues Strategies**

These strategies are designed to cope with contingencies, known and unknown. The strategies employed may be any of the Basic Action, Organizational Functional, or Management Functional strategies necessary to cope with the following:

Known Contingencies

a. Equal Employment Opportunity
b. Environmental Protection, etc.

Surprises

a. Competitor Changes in Strategy, etc.

Table 5.2   Major Strategic Considerations

1. **Competition**—firms must determine if they wish to compete or find a niche.

2. **Growth**—if a firm wishes to grow, it must plan for it.

3. **Diversification**—firms must protect themselves from market fluctuation.

4. **Acquisition, Divestment, Retrenchment, Stabilization**—firms must determine if these are appropriate basic actions.

5. **Marketing**—minimal considerations must be given to the target market, the product, promotion, price, distribution, and differential advantage. Whatever the product or service is, it must be sold if the firm is to continue in business.

6. **Production**—while many may assume that the production function is given, it remains a vexing problem to many firms. The appropriate location and arrangement of facilities and work must be matched with logistics management, ergonomics, product control, and quality assurance.

7. **Finance**—while most financial strategies are concerned with the issue of raising capital either internally or externally, taxes, depreciation, dividends, credit, liquidity, profitability, working capital, budgets, transfer pricing, uses of funds, and other issues must be considered if the firm is to be properly financed.

8. **Personnel/Staffing**—the organization must plan its work force, at all levels, to fill the needs resulting from its other strategies.

9. **Information Systems**—in recognition of the importance of information, the design of appropriate systems must be matched to the needs of the managers. The point here is that as the organization and its overall strategy evolve, the information needed changes. Fulfilling these changing needs is a function of planning.

10. **R&D and Market Research**—to some firms, R&D is the key to survival. To these firms and to those that similarly depend on market research, plans of action are necessities.

11. **Other**—varies from firm to firm.

12. **Planning and Control Systems**—Chapter 1 established the importance of planning. Planning, like any other major activity, must be planned. In addition, control systems must be developed which will insure that the objectives of the strategy are accomplished.

13. **Motivation and Leadership (Implementing)**—if those personnel employed are to achieve maximum productivity, then some thought must be given as to how to motivate and lead them. Obviously, situational variables dictate the appropriate style.

14. **Organization**—the matching of strategy and structure is essential if the firm is to achieve maximum profitability.

15. **Communicating**—what formal and informal channels will be used? Will the organization have open communication?

16. **Decision making**—what techniques will be used, and how much participation will be employed?

17. **Integration**—how will the firm integrate the various organizational subsystems (to achieve the common objectives)?

18. **Social Responsibility**—because of the ever increasing social responsibility demands made upon business, business must have plans for meeting these contingencies.

19. **Surprises**—how will the firm handle certain contingencies should they occur?

required. Or, perhaps, the decision as to whether to compete or to seek a niche will be the essential proposition in a firm's marketing strategy. If so, this will result in the need for a marketing strategy, financial strategy, and so forth. In practice, the formulation of the Master Strategy follows two common paths:

1. The strategy developed to accomplish organizational mission. This is the prime concern of the annual planning process and is comprised of two principal components: mission competitive and mission supportive.
2. Strategic issues. Peripheral or unforeseen threats and opportunities are normally managed and planned for outside the annual planning exercise. Strategic issues are usually managed on a response basis. But contingencies may be planned for periodically as issues which, while not vital to mission, must be considered as threatening to it.

In business, the emphasis in mission strategy is on the competitive component, especially marketing. While marketing is central to this component, the basic action strategies of growth and competition play important roles. Furthermore, elements of supportive strategy may be key ingredients in certain organizations' competitive strategies. As an example, high cash flows, a finance tactic, may be used to support substantive advertising. Or, some firms may place an emphasis on providing a satisfying organizational climate in order to insure high product quality, which is the major selling point of the product. Competitive strategies are formulated with deliberate focus on an opponent, more specifically, on beating that opponent in the market. Within the competitive component, several common strategies are employed.

Mission Competitive Strategies: A Common Scenario

There exist many competitive strategies which may be undertaken to fulfill the common business mission. These strategies usually consist of combinations of basic action, marketing, distribution, and selected supportive strategies. The complexities of the strategies employed increase as the organization grows in size and as it expands the number of products or services which it offers. Firms normally have either a single product or service or a series of multiple products or services which they offer to their customers. Each service or product, or service or product line, may be considered separately in terms of competitive/supportive strategy. This product strategy is the common element among all strategy considerations. However, for those firms which have multiple products, managing the service or product line requires a strategy, especially with respect to balancing the risks of the services or products offered. Despite the complexities, there exists a series of steps which firms commonly carry out. Each of these steps, whether for single product or multiple product firms, is an element of an overall growth strategy. Assuming that a firm wishes to grow (and not all do), the firm begins with single product strategies according to classical marketing theory. If these efforts are successful, stabilization usually follows. Next, diversification occurs for protection. Finally, divestiture may occur in order to maintain ROI. Retrenchment strategies may be employed in unfavorable situations. And, when organizations find themselves in difficulty, they may seek to "turn around" the organization's fortunes by employing turnaround strategies. There are several additional types of strategies, but only the above will be reviewed to any degree.

Single Product Strategy

Single product strategies are based on any number of variables (see Chapter 3). The phase of the product life cycle indicates the major factors which should be considered in formulating strategy. The life cycle stages include introduction, growth, maturity (saturation), and decline. The exact strategy which is appropriate varies with the particular stage of the cycle. Other factors, for example top management assumptions about how a mission should be accomplished, are important determinants of the final strategy. The traditional approach to the competitive strategies which should be employed in the product life cycle stages is presented in Table 5.3. In very brief terms, the actions taken include introduction, growth and investment, substantive profit extraction with continued investment, and profit taking without investment. Divestiture of the product is the final step.

The particular elements in any strategy must be predicated upon the overall market situation, with careful attention paid to the competition and the actions of the competition. Much of what passes as strategy in many firms is really nothing more than reaction to the market. Strategic management stresses anticipation of the market. There are no specific rules which dictate exactly the strategy which an organization should follow. These strategies are subject to certain limitations, as was observed in Chapter 3.

Multiple Product Strategies

When some degree of stability is reached with a single product, most organizations will seek to increase their overall economic viability by diversifying. This means seeking new products or services. Organizations may do so through direct acquisition, through internal technological innovation, or through mergers. Diversification is a process in which firms engage in order to protect themselves from the vagaries of the marketplace. Diversification normally requires that firms seek different types of product lines from those which they currently offer. Products in the same general industry may be selected for diversification purposes. Greater protection from market fluctuation is normally gained by seeking those products upon which the economy would have different effects. The rationale for remaining in similar product lines is that

Table 5.3 Strategies for the Product Life Cycle

Strategic Area	Phase I Introduction	Phase II Growth	Phase III Maturity	Phase IV Decline
Objective	Introducing the customer to the product; promoting initial adoption by trade, customers	Increasing trade channels; establishing brand, franchises	Maintaining trade support; leveling production; lowering costs; maintaining market share by competitive pricing	Monitor contribution to total product offering and profit
Characteristics	Learning and development in the market and the product	Demand exceeds supply; competition enters market	Sales saturation; low product differentiation	Competitors leave the market
Product	Limited line; adaption to initial adoptors	Addition of variations, improvements	Cost considerations; uniformity for mass production	Simplification of the line
Promotion	Personal selling; missionary selling; awareness, interest; advertising, if any, usually introductory offers	Awareness; interest; evaluations; brand stress; personal selling decreases; advertisement	Mass advertisements as reminder; trade promotion	Minimal
Distribution	Exclusive or direct	Selective	Extensive	Customer option
Price	Introductory, high discounts to facilitate initial adoption by trade, customers	High unit margins or competitive for high market share	Highly competitive	Profit maintenance
Profit Margin	Low	High initially to recover R&D, introductory cost, investment; lower as competition enters	Normal to low, as volume stabilizes	High to compensate for lower and declining sales

Source: Henry E. Metzner, Jerry L. Watt, and William F. Glueck, "Product Life Cycle and Stages of Growth, an Empirical Analysis," Table 1, in *Proceedings: Academy of Management*, 1975, pp. 61-63. Reprinted by permission of The Academy of Management.

Chapter 5/Master Strategy Content and Intermediate Planning

the corporation's expertise is in these areas. Diversification becomes an important consideration whenever an organization has "all of its eggs in one basket," and has the internally generated expertise and/or the extra cash flow with which it can expand to other products.

Often firms will acquire products or services which do not continue to provide sufficient ROI. When products fail to meet the goals which the organization has established in terms of accomplishing its mission, then these products or services should be eliminated. This may mean dropping them from the product line or selling them to others. This process is known as divesting. Occasionally, losses must be taken, but the calculation of possible greater long-term losses must be made and balanced against the current short-term losses. Routinely, firms will extract as much profit as possible while investing very little in products which they intend to divest.

Once the organization has several products or product lines, especially across different industry areas, the strategy of the total firm consists largely of an umbrella statement of goals and very general plans of how to reach those goals, such as the Heublein strategy mentioned in Chapter 1. In these situations, top management, corporate planning executives, and the corporate planning team serve as portfolio managers over divisional and/or functional business areas' proposed investment plans. The strategy becomes a matter of balancing product life cycles, risks, and potential ROIs. Firms must balance those projects in which investment is made for growth, which should be carefully selected for earnings potentials, against those which should be harvested and divested. In essence, the strategy formulation process consists of approving or rejecting lower level submissions. The Master Policies must be carefully formulated.

Retrenchment Strategies

Organizations may choose to retrench, that is, stop growth and move towards stability. This normally includes cost reductions and perhaps reductions in product lines and functional activity. This strategy is followed by firms in trouble or by firms operating in an unfavorable economy. Retrenchment is not characteristically practiced by the entrepreneurial leader but is often necessary to forestall disaster.

Turnaround Strategies

Schendel and Patton have studied various strategies that organizations may follow when they need to "turn around" corporate fortunes. Most of these strategies employ combinations of the above-mentioned strategies. They found that firms that turned around company performance had sound investments and stressed expansion in order to generate rapid sales growth. It appears that successful turnaround may be a function of several variables, for ex-

Table 5.4 Fox's Hypotheses about Appropriate Business Strategies over the Product Life Cycle

	Functional Focus	R & D	Production	Marketing	Physical Distribution
Precommercialization	Coordination of R&D and other functions	Reliability tests Release blueprints	Production design Process planning Purchasing department lines up vendors & subcontractors	Test marketing Detailed marketing plan	Plan shipping schedules, mixed carloads Rent warehouse space, trucks
Introduction	Engineering: debugging in R&D production and field	Technical corrections (engineering changes)	Subcontracting Centralize pilot plants; test various processes; develop standards.	Induce trial; fill pipelines; sales agents or commissioned salesmen; publicity	Plan a logistics system
Growth	Production	Start successor product	Centralize production Phase out subcontractors Expedite vendors' output; long runs	Channel commitment Brand emphasis Salaried sales force Reduce price if necessary	Expedite deliveries Shift to owned facilities
Maturity	Marketing and logistics	Develop minor variants Reduce costs through value analysis Originate major adaptations to start new cycle	Many short runs Decentralize Import parts, low-priced models Routinization Cost reduction	Short-term promotions Salaried salesmen Cooperative advertising Forward integration Routine marketing research: panels, audits	Reduce costs and raise customer service level Control finished goods inventory
Decline	Finance	Withdraw all R&D from initial version	Revert to subcontracting; simplify production line channel Careful inventory control; buy foreign or competitive goods; stock spare parts	Revert to commission basis; withdraw most promotional support Raise price Selective distribution Careful phase-out, considering entire	Reduce inventory and services

Source: Harold Fox, "A Framework for Functional Coordination," *Atlanta Economic Review*, November/December 1973, pp. 10-11. Reprinted by permission of *Atlanta Economic Review*.

ample, implementation. But it is difficult at this time to tell exactly why some organizations succeed and others do not. Success may or may not occur even when different firms use the same strategies. For example, Schendel and Patton note that one matched pair in their sample study, the Melvill Shoe Corporation and SCOA Industries Inc., had almost identical turnaround strategies. And yet SCOA suffered continuous decline in fortunes from the 1950s through 1970, while Melvill was much more successful. Exactly why this occurred is uncertain, although SCOA's implementation appeared to be faulty.

Other Strategies

Strategies for mergers and acquisitions are commonly encountered. To some firms, these are extremely important strategies. Contingency strategies are increasingly popular as the operating environment becomes more turbulent.

Personnel	Finance	Management Accounting	Other	Customers	Competition
Recruit for new activities Negotiate operational changes with unions	LC plan for cash flows, profits, invest-ments, subsidiaries	Payout planning: full costs/revenues Determine optimum lengths of LC stages thru present-value method	Final legal clearances (regulatory hurdles, patents) Appoint LC coordinator	Panels & other test respondents	Neglects opportunity or is working on similar idea
Staff and train middle management Stock options for executives	Accounting deficit; high net cash outflow Authorize large pro-duction facilities	Help develop produc-tion & distribution standards Prepare sales aids like sales management portfolio		Innovators and some early adopters	(Monopoly) Disparagement of innovation Legal & extralegal interference
Add suitable personnel for plant Many grievances Heavy overtime	Very high profits, net cash outflow still rising Sell equities	Short-term analyses based on return per scarce resource		Early adopters & early majority	(Oligopoly) A few imitate, improve, or cut prices
Transfers, advance-ments; incentives for efficiency, safety, and so on Suggestion system	Declining profit rate but increasing net cash inflow	Analyze differential costs/revenue Spearhead cost reduc-tion, value analysis, and efficiency drives	Pressure for resale price maintenance Price cuts bring price wars; possible price collusion	Early adopters, early & late majority, some laggards; first discon-tinued by late majority	(Monopoly competition) First shakeout; yet many rivals
Find new slots Encourage early retirement	Administer system, retrenchment Sell unneeded equipment Export the machinery	Analyze escapable costs Pinpoint remaining outlays	Accurate sales forecast very important	Mainly laggards	(Oligopoly) After second shakeout, only few rivals

Contingency strategies are multiple standby strategies which would be employed when the major contingencies upon which they were predicated come into being. Many large firms have several major strategies prepared. This trend towards multiple strategies should continue.

Mission Supportive Strategies

The exact content of supportive strategies is primarily dependent upon the content of the organization's mission competitive strategies. However, mission supportive strategy content has been the subject of several normative propositions such as those displayed in Table 5.4 and the contingency views of Hofer presented in Table 3.1. Table 5.4 portrays the importance of integrating supportive strategy efforts with competitive strategy. This table could be used in conjunction with Table 3.1 to suggest possible actions to be undertaken in the various stages of the product life cycle. These tables suggest that certain functional and organizational activities must be accomplished if the organization is to achieve its mission.

Strategic Issues Management

Strategic Issues Management (SIM) refers to the management of surprises and known contingencies:[1]

1. *Surprises*—despite the most complex organizational planning and control systems, surprises may occur. These may be either threats of major profit loss or the potential of a major opportunity. These may be either internal or external to the firm. To this end Ansoff has designed an SIM System which gradually increases response as information becomes available. Changes in technology, competitor strategy, and the economy are examples of these "surprises." The basic concept of the SIM is to scan the environment for weak signals of change. More directed scanning should occur where significant weak signals are detected.

2. *Known Contingencies*—the accomplishment of primary mission can be hampered by certain peripheral threats and opportunities, strengths and weaknesses. These may originate as surprises but inasmuch as they become known and planned for on a recurring basis, they will be designated as known contingencies.

In recent years, the corporate organization in pursuit of profit and service has encountered numerous strategic issues which, while not directly associated with the mission strategy, could cause it to remain unaccomplished. Most of the major contingencies have resulted from societal and/or government pressures. Equal employment opportunity, pollution control, consumerism, employee health, and safety are but a few of the issues. Clearly, each of these issues has added to the product cost which, in turn, has the potential to reduce sales. Businesses have had to develop strategies to contend with these issues. Some strategic issue strategies have, in fact, been incorporated into the annual mission strategy formulation process. However, many of these issues are confronted, albeit on an annual, cyclical basis, as peripheral contingent phenomena. In some cases the strategies utilized to cope with the problems raised by these issues are no less complex than the mission strategy. They do, however, usually receive less emphasis in most firms, dependent as always upon the situation. IBM has, for example, structured its strategic planning into two major divisions, one which compares formally to that of mission as depicted in this text, and one entitled Key Corporate Strategic Issues.

The importance of these strategic issues cannot be overemphasized. It is through SIM as Ansoff depicts it that the organization is able to survive the unforeseen. Certainly, each of the surprises and known contingencies mentioned above, as well as numerous others, has the potential for seriously endangering the accomplishment of the mission.

Some Important Characteristics of Plans

The contents of strategy also have another important dimension—their characteristics. It is relevant to note that all plans should have certain characteristics and that the contents of strategy, intermediate, and operational plans should reflect these. A few of these characteristics are listed below.

Flexibility

In today's volatile environment, organizations must remain flexible in their planning processes so that as changes arise and are indicated as necessary, organizations will be able to adapt. Some organizations have developed numerous contingency plans and multiple master strategies for the purpose of coping with the changing requirements of the environment. Given the occurrence of certain events, alternative strategies already developed can thus be implemented accordingly.

Contents

Any plan should include, to the appropriate degree, specification of:

Who will be involved—the organization level and individuals
What will be required—resources
Where action will occur—geographically, organization level
When action will occur—time horizon, implementation date
Why action will occur—the goal
How the why will be accomplished—what actions are necessary, which is indicated somewhat by who, what, and where, the means of implementation
Control—some provision for evaluation

Consistency

Plans developed within a strategy and among strategies should be consistent with one another. The objectives of the Master Strategy must be included in the development of intermediate and operational plans. These must also be consistent with structure. Such considerations are especially important to the functional area division plans. These objectives often suboptimize the total strategy because of the inherent inclusion of functional area or product division needs without the proper analysis of their impact on overall organizational objective accomplishment.

Timeliness

To be effective, a plan must be timely. Had the Edsel been introduced just two years sooner or later, it might have succeeded. Notwithstanding the fact that some felt it unattractive, it was a big car introduced when the consumer was looking for a small car.

Risk

This is a major element. To have a high probability of success, the strategy must have the proper level of risk. Richards has shown that risk, in fact, is the key factor in strategic failure. What is risk? Risk is the probability of return. It is extremely difficult to calculate and involves some highly subjective probability estimation, usually under conditions of uncertainty.

Society and Government Acceptance

Also relevant to the external factors section, business's social responsibility is so important that every plan must be specifically concerned with societal impact analysis. If society and government do not accept an organization's actions as appropriate, profit may suffer. In addition, sanctions can be levied against the firm so that the firm will eventually be forced to change.

Intermediate Planning

In the intermediate planning phase, the broader plans of strategy are more specifically delineated. In the large, diversified organization, these more refined plans are on a business/product division basis. For the few- or single-product firms or the business/product division, these plans are formulated on an organization functional (marketing, production, finance, personnel) basis. Some firms attempt to skip the intermediate phase entirely, going directly from strategy to operation. This usually results in ineffective operations, since strategies are so broad and operations so specific that additional intermediate planning is necessary for a smooth transition. As indicated in Chapter 1, intermediate plans vary greatly in their scope, time horizon, comprehensiveness, and degree of detail. Normally, several successive intermediate plans would be required to translate strategy into operations. For example, in a large multinational firm, the Master Strategy might consist of several business/product division strategies, which might consist of competitive, support-

"Chief, production has a question for the site selection committee . . . ."

ive, and strategic issues strategies. Any one of these components has several substrategies, each of which would require intermediate plans.

Examine the production substrategy. An intermediate plan would be required to translate the production strategy into requirements for the various countries involved. Another intermediate plan would be required to allocate objectives and actions to plants within those countries. Then within each plant another intermediate plan would be required to allocate objectives and actions to departments within that plant. Finally, operational planning would occur to allocate objectives and tasks to individuals. At each of these plan levels, coordinated policies would be generated to aid managers in decision making.

Planning, the setting of objectives and the determination of plans to reach those objectives, is that which connects mission with individual performance. Intermediate plans play an important role in this process. By establishing successive levels of objectives, plans to reach those objectives and coordinated policies to insure proper implementation of those plans, organizations greatly improve their chances of success. The individuals who must perform operational tasks can do so in a correct fashion only if they know precisely what it is that they are supposed to do. The intermediate planning process aids in forming proper individual role prescriptions by parcelling strategic objectives, plans, and policies into more manageable dimensions at each successive level of the firm. As these successive levels of planning occur, they involve primarily business/product organization function managers. The following section discusses the differences in perspectives between corporate and business/ product division general managers and between general managers and functional division managers.

Difference in Perspective:
Division versus Corporate Strategists

For the very large business organization with numerous businesses or products, divisions are usually established based on these businesses or products. Normally, these divisions develop their own objectives and plans; choosing among new products, new marketing strategies, and new R&D projects as points of investment. All are subject, however, to the approval of top corporate management. To the division, these plans constitute strategy, but to the corporation, these strategies are forms of intermediate planning. There exist certain differences in strategic perspective at the division level from those that occur at the corporate level. The most obvious difference is that the division is responding to corporate objectives and policies while the corporate top management is establishing these objectives and policies.

Because of this, the role of the division manager is usually one of great responsibility, but also one of less than commensurate authority. The division general manager must translate objectives into action and action into measurement. He must satisfy his superiors, compete and cooperate with his peers, and lead his subordinates—usually organization function managers, product managers, or geographic area managers. He operates in a highly political environment. He is, in fact, a man in the middle. The division general manager's position is most often filled by a former functional specialist. The transition to generalist is often too great, the viewpoint too different, for many who have been appointed to this position. The corporate general manager, in contrast to the division manager, acts primarily as a superior and as an objective and policy setter.

As a result of the lack of appreciation of the differences in these perspectives, Lorange suggests that perhaps the resulting divisional strategies are too conservative given the total corporate investment portfolio. He believes that for a very large organization, a risky venture could be "averaged out." Often the divisional manager feels he cannot accept a product with high risk because his performance is measured on return and his compensation is based on his performance. The result is often the loss of considerable gain. After viewing this problem, Lorange has proposed that the business strategy (attractive-

Figure 5.2 Matrix for Determination and Evaluation of Business Line Product Strategy

Business Attractiveness

Market Growth Rate
Purchase Frequency of Product
Degree of Customer Concentration
Barriers to New Competition
Structure of New Competition
Size of Market

Competitive Strength in Business

Market Share
Strategic Expenditure Level
Product Quality
Capacity Utilization

Consolidation Attractiveness

Shape of Cash Flow
Size of Cash Flow
Risk of Cash Flow
Covariance of Cash Flows
Production Synergy Effects
Marketing Synergy Effects
R&D Synergy Effects
Substitution Opportunity

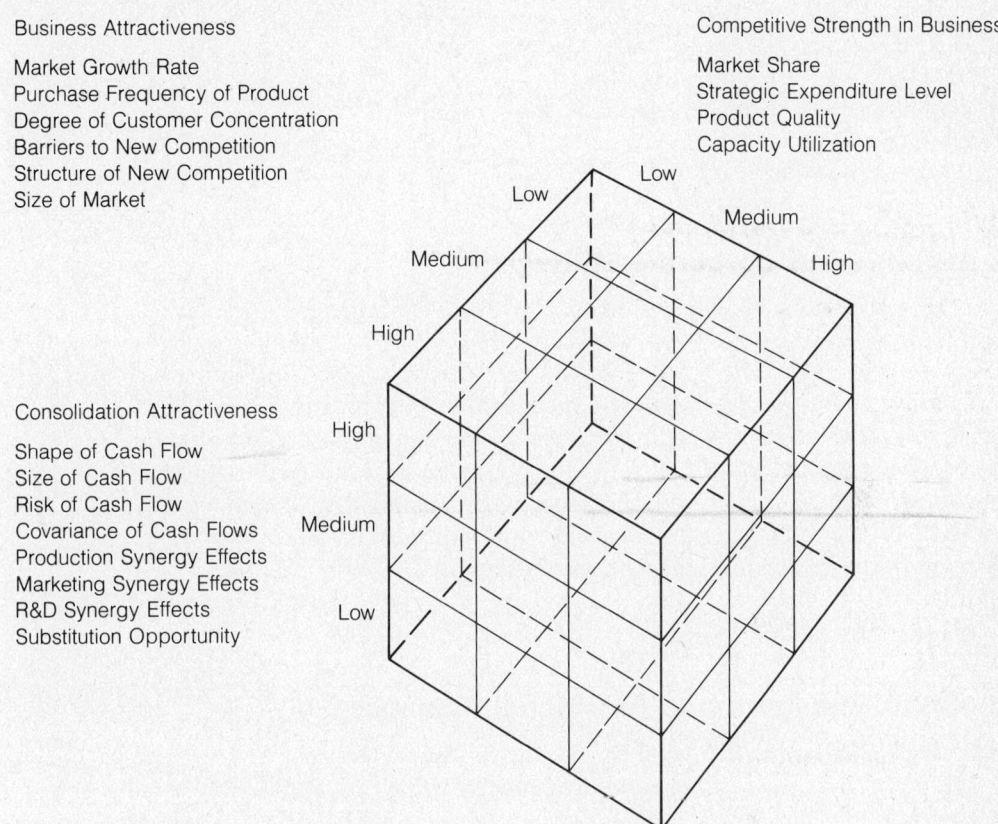

Source: Peter Lorange, "Divisional Planning: Setting Effective Direction," *Sloan Management Review*, Fall 1975, p. 87. Reprinted by permission of *Sloan Management Review*.

ness/competitive strength) matrix (the GE stoplight was an example of this) be made three-dimensional to allow firms to account for the attractiveness of investment opportunities on a consolidated corporate basis. Figure 5.2 portrays this three-dimensional approach.

The motivation scheme for divisional managers must be designed to incorporate the difficulty of the task and the need to manage in light of corporate as well as divisional interests. In one division manager's motivational scheme, General Electric incorporates in both its choice of managers for its various businesses (Figure 5.3) and the motivation scheme for these managers (Figure 5.4) key factors related to the type of business (product) in terms of its

Figure 5.3   Choice of Managers

Investment Category	Manager's Key Strengths
Invest/Grow	Entrepreneur-Leader
Selectivity/Earnings	Sophisticated/Critical
Harvest/Divest	Solid/Experienced

Source: Michael G. Allen, Vice President, General Electric Co., "Strategic Problems Facing Today's Corporate Planner," paper presented to the Academy of Management, August 1976, at Kansas City. Reprinted by permission of General Electric Company.

desirability and the resultant strategy. Such approaches are vital if the division level manager is to be of the utmost utility to the corporation. If the division or product manager is not motivated to support corporate efforts, then mission is not likely to be accomplished. Note how the approaches in these figures account for the differing environments confronting the organizations to be managed. Too few firms appreciate these differences.

General Managers and Functional Managers

The single greatest problem with the difference in perspectives between these two types of managers is the activity orientation which inevitably occurs on the part of functional managers. Functional managers are paid to manage the accomplishment of functional activities which contribute effectively and efficiently to the accomplishment of organizational mission. All too often, functional managers forget that their functions must contribute to organizational objectives. Functional managers are all too often concerned with their own functional area interests at the expense of corporate interests. Again, motivation and the defining of objectives play key roles in assuring that activity results in objective accomplishment and not just activity. The identification of contribution is more complex here than with business/product division since the components of profit, and not profit alone, are generated by functional areas: revenues and expenses. The responsibility for and the impact of actions must be identified. Objectives are more specific definitions of mission specifying what it is that is expected to be accomplished. Every strategy, every plan is created to accomplish objectives. Objectives serve to parcel mission requirements into manageable portions.

Figure 5.4 Bonus Matched to Business

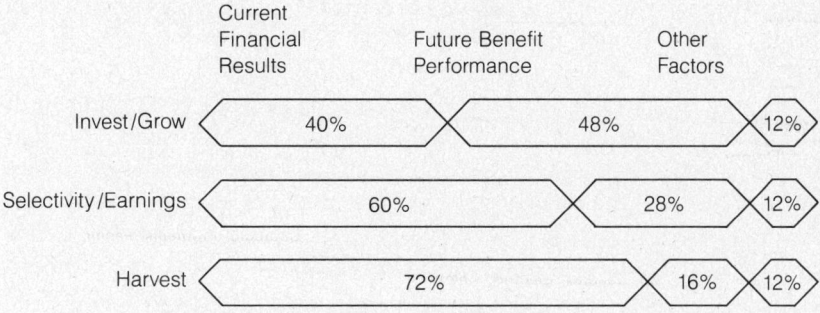

	Current Financial Results	Future Benefit Performance	Other Factors
Invest/Grow	40%	48%	12%
Selectivity/Earnings	60%	28%	12%
Harvest	72%	16%	12%

Source: Michael G. Allen, Vice President, General Electric Co., "Strategic Problems Facing Today's Corporate Planner," paper presented to the Academy of Management, August 1976, at Kansas City. Reprinted by permission of General Electric Company.

Integration Mechanisms—Organizational Objectives

Objectives are the results sought by the plans of action. The following paragraphs examine a program for establishing effective objectives—management by objectives (MBO)—and the types of objectives which organizations establish. Throughout this text the need for specific objectives has been emphasized. Vague objectives, at the very least, lead to misinterpretation and a lack of accountability for performance. It is precisely to end such events that MBO was established. MBO as used here embodies specific objective-setting programs and does not focus on the more behavioral concepts of subordinate development often associated with this program.

MBO: Concepts and Implications for Strategy

Management by objectives is a management planning, control, communication, and subordinate development system. It is probably the most frequently discussed management practice in the last 20 years. Few can agree on its specific contents, but there do appear to be three common dimensions upon which most would agree:

1. The establishment of objectives
2. Employee participation (even if the amount is zero)
3. Evaluation and control of performance

The normal MBO process involves the establishment of specific objectives by top management in all performance areas—strategic mission as well as strategic issues. These are then communicated to the next lower level of management, which may or may not have participated in their development. At each level, objectives may then be distributed to the appropriate managers for their acceptance or rejection. Or these managers may submit to their superiors' proposals which state their commitments to the accomplishment of these objectives. What evolves is a situation determined discussion–negotiation–agreement meeting between a manager and his superior manager. Once agreement is reached, the process shifts to the next lower level of management and continues until objective distribution reaches the supervisory level. The process usually terminates at this level because repetitive first-line positions cannot properly utilize this technique.

MBO was first introduced by Peter Drucker, who had observed its successful functioning at General Motors. Since that time countless studies and reviews of its effective and ineffective components have been reported, variations in its methodology have been suggested, and corrective actions for its weaknesses proposed. Below are listed just a few of the major findings regarding MBO.

Positive results:

1. Improved performance—quantity and quality
2. Communications and understanding improved
3. Improved job satisfaction
4. Individual growth
5. Clarifies role prescription

Negative results:

1. Managers may become more critical
2. Managers may use MBO objectives as a "whip"
3. Establishing objectives entails all sorts of problems: scale unit bias, too high or too low, acceptance, inflexibility, lack of objectives in nonquantifiable areas
4. Too short-run oriented
5. Seems to lose its effect over time
6. Monetary rewards are insufficient to maintain performance
7. Takes too much time
8. Leaves out the group
9. There are after all physical and mental limitations for the individual
10. Delimitation—goals established become maximums even where they could be exceeded

The negative results reported far outnumber the positive effects, especially when one realizes that at least 20 more could be listed. However, this is a relative matter. Most of the studies have been performed in different situations causing varying results. More importantly, many have reported that the technique was not the problem, but, rather, how it was implemented. It appears that when an appropriate implementation procedure is followed and top management is involved and concerned, MBO is more effective. The point here is this: MBO is based on specific objectives. MBO works if implemented properly. Specific objectives eliminate misinterpretation, a common problem in the organization dominated by a coalition.

Latham and Yukl, in reviewing published and unpublished field research related to specific objectives, report that in MBO programs and in non-MBO situations, specific objectives led to superior performance. MBO is a major component of successful strategy implementation and control because specific objectives increase performance. Some have suggested that specific objectives are not necessary in every situation, and indeed McCaskey's "directional planning" may be sufficient for certain limited situations. John Mee's "Principle of the Objective" is especially relevant: "Before initiating any course of action the objectives must be clearly determined, understood and stated." In summary, without specific objectives, the strategy is eventually performance-less.

The Objectives Established

Organizations establish many and varied types of objectives. Some objectives may be specific, some not. For many organizations, no objectives are specific. Some organizations establish only a limited number. Others establish objectives for many areas of operating performance. The following are two research studies which reveal the nature of business objectives.

Rue, reporting on a survey of 400 predominantly large firms in several major industries, found that most firms have multiple, quantitative, written objective statements as presented in Table 5.5. This table indicates that more firms established earnings and sales objectives than return objectives. Rue also examined financial analyses associated with objectives established. He found that profit (income statement) was of primary concern but that most firms were also concerned with balance sheet and cash flow analysis (Table 5.6).

Dobbie, in an examination of 50 large California-based firms (all over $100 million in annual sales), found the firms tended to express objectives according to the type of strategy which they were employing. His strategy classifications included: personal (the aims of the chief executive); opportunity; geographic expansion; financial growth; and business (experienced in planning or diversified firms). The types of objectives examined included: various return methods; growth in sales and/or earnings; pro-forma financial statements or resource control. His related findings are summarized in Table 5.7. Dobbie also observed that managerial style and the position of the planning unit within the organization structure impacted on the type of objectives chosen. While Dobbie's sample size limits generalization, his study at least

Table 5.5   Objectives Stipulated in Plans

Industry	Number of Firms	Sales	Earnings	Return of Investment	Capital Growth	Share of the Market	Sales/ Earnings Ratio	No Quantified Objectives
Mining	19	16	18	14	8	4	3	0
Food	26	26	26	21	17	15	18	0
Textiles and Paper	28	24	27	23	14	13	16	0
Chemical	46	42	46	35	22	24	22	0
Oil	17	9	16	13	8	5	4	1
Steel and Aluminum	18	17	18	15	9	9	7	0
Machinery	42	40	42	33	23	29	24	0
Electrical	49	47	47	38	23	29	26	1
Vehicles and Acc	29	27	28	27	15	19	14	0
Transport and Communication	12	9	10	8	8	7	4	0
Wholesale and Retail	34	33	33	26	22	8	21	0
Services	8	6	7	6	2	2	3	0
Total	328	296	318	259	171	164	162	2

Source: From Leslie W. Rue, "Tools and Techniques of Long-Range Planning," *Long Range Planning,* October 1974, p. 62. Reprinted by permission of Pergamon Press Ltd., Oxford, England.

suggests that as complexity of operations and experience in strategy formation increase, the number of objectives and diversity of these increase.

The multiplicity of objectives which organizations may employ in their strategies is not limited to economic (mission competitive-profit) objectives. Other types of objectives exist. These might include employee development and social responsibility. And while it is apparent that most business organizations are today primarily concerned with mission objectives, the latter issue is expected to become of increasing concern as society (and government) continually demand more of business.

The key to successful planning is the process of specific objective establishment at each succeeding level of the organization. Objectives "tie" the organization together. The number and composition of these objectives vary and are changing.

Summary

The content of strategy varies from organization to organization. Several common components and substrategies of the Master Strategy were found to be identifiable regardless of the business and its situation. Several common strategies were noted for the growth oriented business firm. Intermediate plans were viewed primarily as a function of perspectives. Finally, MBO was discussed as an important ingredient in the successful organization.

Table 5.6   Pro-Forma Statements Used in Planning

Industry	Number of Firms	Balance Sheet	Income Statement	Cash Flow	None
Mining	19	13	18	17	0
Food	26	20	24	23	0
Textile and Paper	28	22	26	24	2
Chemical	46	34	45	43	0
Oil	17	11	16	17	0
Steel and Aluminum	18	16	17	16	0
Machinery	42	33	41	37	1
Electrical	49	43	43	39	3
Vehicles and Acc	29	26	27	24	1
Transportation and Communication	12	6	11	8	1
Wholesale and Retail	34	30	33	31	1
Services	8	6	8	7	0
Total	328	245	294	287	9

Source: From Leslie W. Rue, "Tools and Techniques of Long-Range Planning," *Long Range Planning*, October 1974, p. 64. Reprinted by permission of Pergamon Press Ltd., Oxford, England.

Table 5.7   Primary Statement Form of Long-Range Goals versus Form of Strategy

Primary Form of
Long-Range Goals

	Business	Financial Growth	Geographic	Opportunity	Personal
Various Returns Methods	4		1		
Growth in Sales and/or Earnings	7	7	1	2	
Pro-Forma Financial Statements or Resource Control	14	9	3	1	6

Form of Strategic Plan
Basis: 55 Firms

Source: John W. Dobbie, "Guides to a Foundation for Strategic Planning in Large Firms," paper presented to the 34th Annual Meeting of the Academy of Management, Seattle, Washington, 1974, p. 14. Reprinted by permission of the Academy of Management.

Discussion Questions

1. Describe the contents of the Primary Mission, Mission Supportive, and Strategic Issue strategies for an organization.
2. If you had a new product, any product, to market, describe your Master Strategy for the next ten years.
3. Why are intermediate plans necessary?
4. How does MBO integrate the organization? What other techniques can be used to integrate the organization?

Footnote

1. Ansoff, H. I., "Managing Strategic Surprise by Response to Weak Signals," *California Management Review,* Winter 1975, pp. 21–33. Ansoff discusses only the first of these two types of strategic issues. While using his term, I have expanded its meaning to include the second of these.

References

Allen, M. G. "Strategic Problems Facing Today's Corporate Planner." Paper presented to the Academy of Management, August 1976, at Kansas City.

Ansoff, H. I. "Managing Strategic Surprise by Response to Weak Signals." *California Management Review,* Winter 1975, pp. 21–33.

Dobbie, J. W. "Guides to Foundations for Strategic Planning in Large Firms." Paper presented to the Academy of Management, August 1974, at Seattle.

Enis, B. M.; R. LaGarce; and A. E. Prell. "Extending the Product Life Cycle." *Business Horizons,* June 1977, pp. 46–60.

Fayol, H. *Industrial and General Administration,* pp. 43–52. New York: Pitman Publishing, 1949.

Fox, H. "A Framework for Functional Coordination." *Atlanta Economic Review,* November/December 1973, pp. 10–11.

Hamberg, D. "Invention in the Industrial Laboratory." *Journal of Political Economy,* April 1963, pp. 95–115.

Keusch, R. B. "Directional Planning: Some Further Consideration." In *Management Perspectives on Organizational Effectiveness*, edited by D. F. Ray and Thad B. Green, pp. 4–6. Southern Management Association, November 1975.

Latham, G. P., and G. A. Yukl. "A Review of Research on the Application of Goal Setting in Organizations." *Academy of Management Journal,* December 1975, pp. 827–832.

Lorange, P. "Divisional Planning: Setting Effective Direction." *Sloan Management Review,* Fall 1975, pp. 82–83.

McCaskey, M. B. "A Contingency Approach to Planning: Planning with Goals and Planning without Goals." *Academy of Management Journal,* June 1974, pp. 281–291.

Mee, J. "The Principle of the Objective." In "Management Philosophy for Professional Executives." *Business Horizons,* December 1956, pp. 5–11.

Odiorne, G. *Management by Objectives.* New York: Pitman Publishing, 1965.

Richards, M. "Risk and Strategic Failure." *Proceedings*: *Academy of Management,* August 1974, pp. 40–46.

Rue, L. W. "Tools and Techniques of Long-Range Planning." *Long Range Planning,* October 1974, pp. 61–65.

Schendel, D., and A. C. Cooper. "Strategic Responses to Technological Threats." *Business Horizons,* February 1976, pp. 61–69.

Thoroman, D. G. "Strategic Planning in IBM." *Long Range Planning,* September 1971, pp. 2–6.

Tosi, H. "Effective and Ineffective MBO." *Management by Objectives* 4 (1975): 7–14.

Uyterhoeven, H. E. R.; R. W. Ackerman; and J. W. Rosenblum. *Strategy and Organization.* Homewood, Ill.: Irwin, 1972.

Chapter 6

Organization and Implementation

[handwritten notes in margin:]

Structure based on:
- product division
- functional (more common)
- geographic

Matrix structure (together w/ pyramid)
Project or Product

[handwritten table sketch with M A B labels]

Whole product coordinated : Adv.
impose coordination ; Disadv.

A great many administrators and managers carry in their heads a pattern of the "ideal" organization. That pattern is the classic hierarchy, the family tree; one man at the top, with three below him, each of whom has three below him, and so on with fearful symmetry unto the seventh generation, by which stage there is a row of 729 junior managers and an urgent need for a very large triangular piece of paper.

Anthony Jay

In the organizational structuring process, the tasks and jobs required to achieve objectives are determined, and authority is delegated to perform these tasks. This structuring process has a significant impact upon mission accomplishment:

1. Because structure defines the specific actions to be taken in implementation, and
2. Because structure establishes the degree of autonomy each individual has in performing his implementation activities.

Implementation is equally critical to mission accomplishment because the actions taken by organizational members must be effective and efficient. In this text, implementation is viewed as the summation of activities in which organizational members engage in order to accomplish the objectives of the strategy. Successful implementation results primarily from appropriate managerial functioning at lower levels of management. Successful implementation also depends on integrated planning and control systems and on proper managerial functioning in other levels of management.

Organization and implementation are highly interdependent processes. For example, operational planning and procedures, two components of implementation, are used in defining the organization's structure. And, the amount of authority a manager has places limits on his ability to lead and to motivate —two critical managerial implementation processes. Organizations are normally ongoing. Therefore, most organizations are not concerned with organizing for the first time, but rather they are concerned with achieving an appropriate strategy/structure/implementation combination. The components of the organizational process model discussed in this chapter are indicated in Figure 6.1.

Figure 6.1 The Organization—An Organization Process Model

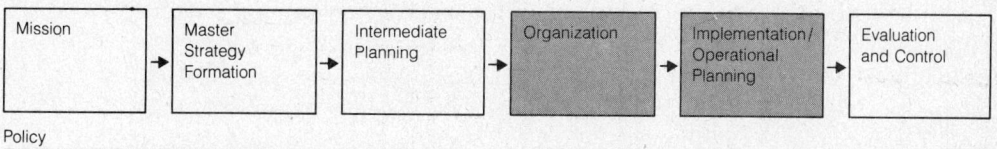

Policy

Organizational Structure

An organization's structure is viewed as the combination of its formal and informal structures. Most perceive the organization structure as those boxes and connecting lines depicted on the formal organization chart. But, if the actual concept and relationships portrayed are to be realistically envisioned, then the informal organization must be included in the discussion of organization structure. The primary *formal* structure dimensions include:

1. Roles as required by plans and successive divisions of labor.
2. The delegation of authority to the various roles and groupings of roles on a continuum from centralization to substantive decentralization.[1]

Other structural dimensions include:

1. The manager's span of control.
2. The grouping of roles and spans of control into departments on a functional, product, customer, project, or geographic division basis.
3. The formalization of processes as revealed in records and reports (both quantity and the nature thereof).
4. The existence of written policies, procedures and rules governing behavior.
5. Written communication.
6. The number of levels of authority in the organization.

The *informal organization* is defined as consisting of:

1. The individuals who fill the role prescriptions prescribed by the formal structure.
2. The informal groups which develop within the formal structure.

While much of what follows in this chapter is primarily related to formal structure, the individual and the group as determinants of structure will be discussed where relevant, but not in great detail. The following paragraphs examine factors which are considered to be the primary determinants of structure. Next, proper strategy/structure combinations will be discussed.

Formal Structure and Its Determinants

In organizing to implement strategy there are three basic organization structures from which to choose: the classical pyramid, the matrix, and the team. These choices are based primarily on the division of labor and the distribution of authority. The pyramidal form is that found in most organizations and is the product of classical organization theory. The exact shape of a particular organization's pyramid is primarily a function of the spans of control which exist. These can be related to any number of factors. Staff positions may be added throughout the pyramid but do not change its basic shape. Since it is the pyramidal organization structure which characterizes most organizations, most decisions which have to be made regarding structure are concerned with:

1. What division of labor is appropriate for a given situation?
2. Should the organization be centralized or decentralized, how and to what degree?

The determinants of structure have been examined extensively both in the normative and empirical literature. It is evident that no single unique factor exactly determines structure. Rather, multiple factors are responsible for the structures used by organizations. The primary determinants appear to vary from situation to situation. However, consideration of positive and normative information indicates that the following seven factors are the most important determinants of structure in most situations. Since these factors and related research should be familiar, they will not be reviewed in depth.

1. Size (Growth)—organizational size is a significantly explanatory structural variable. As organizations grow to certain sizes, they encounter various structural problems.
2. Technology—the types and complexity of the technology employed to accomplish an organization's tasks have been shown to be significantly related to structure. This complexity is not only an issue at lower organization levels, where much of the research has been performed, but also at upper levels where the complexity of tasks facing top management often requires structural solutions.
3. Environment—several environmental factors should be considered in the determination of structure but the amount of change in the environment appears to be the most important factor to consider.
4. Top Management Prerogative/Philosophy—top management may intentionally choose to structure the organization in a certain manner for reasons unrelated to technology, size, or environment. For example, in order to develop its managers' decision abilities, some firms may require large spans of control. Or, in order to cut overhead, middle management may be virtually eliminated.
5. Geographic Considerations—as organizations expand geographically, either within the same country or into different countries, certain divisions

of labor must obviously occur. Geographic decentralization, as it is normally referred to, does not necessarily require decision decentralization, but the latter often follows. However, with geographic decentralization, new divisions of labor must result.

6. The Informal Organization—the people who fill the positions may, in fact, demand a particular type of formal structure. For example, professionals —engineers, accountants, and scientists—will not tolerate a mechanistic, formalized work situation.

7. Strategy—Chandler, in his classic book *Strategy and Structure*, was the first to expound upon the relationship between these two concepts. In his examination of the histories of General Motors, Dupont, Standard Oil of New Jersey, and Sears Roebuck & Company, he found that the decentralized, multidivisional structure resulted largely from trial and error attempts to meet environmental conditions. He stressed that outside market opportunity was the primary causal variable for strategy structure, since structure followed strategy. Also, while supporting the view that size contributed to variations in structure, he observed that task complexity at top management levels also accounted for a significant amount of variation in organization structure. It is logical that what an organization wishes to become and how it will do so while managing its interactions with the environment would to a great extent determine most of the other structure determinants as well—technology, size, environment, and geographic dispersion. Strategy by definition, and as noted in the organizational process model, leads to structure. In addition to Chandler's efforts, little research has been performed strictly on the strategy/structure mix. However, both Parsons and Selznik have argued that there exists a very definite relationship between organizational charter (mission) and structure.

These seven factors are not mutually exclusive. Their interdependence has made scientific analysis difficult but not impossible. Clearly, strategy and top management prerogative are primary determinants. Once, however, these commitments are made, the other factors have varying impacts on the eventual structural pattern. Only in recent years, as multivariate techniques have been utilized, has the relative importance of these factors been better understood, and what has been apparent through extensive research is that the relative importance is situational. The following summary observations can be made:

1. All of the factors, plus some not mentioned, contribute to structure, but structure begins with strategy. As Chandler has noted, "Unless structure follows strategy, inefficiency results."
2. Management prerogatives play a critical role in some firms.
3. Size is a primary determinant of structure.
4. Within departments (whether based on product, function, customer, project, or geography), operational technology usually plays a significant role

in determining structure specifically impinged on by the work flow. Supportive (knowledge) technology may also play an important role in determining structure. Technology has more of an impact on smaller organizations than on large ones, on manufacturing organizations than on service organizations. Operational technology has little impact on administrative structures or decentralization.

5. Organizations vary substantially in the manner in which they are structured. Subsystems also vary substantially in the manner in which they are structured both within and among organizations. These differences result from the processes of differentiation and integration—coping with the environment while accomplishing mission.

6. It is not just size, but also task complexity, which determines structure. The more tasks and the more specialized these tasks are, the greater the need for structured arrangements of coordination and control; that is, formalization. Size and complexity of task are relevant to top management levels and result in the need for decentralization.

7. The routineness, predictability, or certainty of environment and/or tasks and problem solving orientation have all been depicted as the underlying factor which explains much of the variation in structure. These appear to describe the same phenomenon.

8. The Weberian structure model, while common and useful, is limited in its utility as a description of certain types of situations.

9. An organization is not independent of its environment. The degree of interaction and dependency varies, but no organization completely escapes bargaining or accountability. Structure changes as a result.

10. Size is a key determinant of decentralization—but only a partial determinant of complexity and hence formalization.

11. Structure is not and cannot be static in a changing environment.

12. Various dimensions of structure—formalization, specialization, and decentralization—may be caused by various factors such as technology or size.

13. It would seem reasonable to assume that the structure of staff as well as line components is governed by these factors but in relatively different degrees.

Designing organizations to meet the demands of the situation is not an easy task. There are few if any authoritative guidelines. The research is just now beginning to suggest what separates the effective from the ineffective organization. There has always been an implication that for a given environment or technology a certain structure was appropriate. Based on empirical evidence to date, this view is not supported. Rather, many factors result in the selection of structure and in the proper strategy/structure combination. The next few paragraphs review some of the more common problems associated with organization structure.

"No, this is Fawning & Groveling—you want Buttering-Up & Brown-Nosing, two doors down. . . ."

Strategy and Structure:
Size, Growth, and Environment—A Discussion

Given the results of research and the nature of the strategy formation process, the organization's primary concern with structure becomes one of matching strategy to structure and structure to size and environment. Size is invariably a direct result of growth. The importance of growth as a factor in structure determination is obvious since most organizations, especially businesses, grow and have growth strategies. Growth has, of course, been discussed at length, and several theories of resultant structural relationships have emerged. In examining these theories and other empirical and normative data, several commonly occurring problem areas related to the growth, size-structure relationship may be observed.

   In its most rudimentary form, a firm begins as an individual entrepreneur with an idea. As he starts his business, he soon realizes that he cannot perform all of the tasks related to his product or service himself. The first structural problem arises. To solve it he must pursue a division of labor and hire additional employees on a functional basis. Soon, however, a second structural problem arises. The entrepreneurial leader has not delegated any authority. The functional area personnel are not allowed to manage. They have no autonomy. Eventually the leader must delegate. The amount of authority delegated varies but usually increases as the firm continues to expand. As the organization grows, it arrives at a point where it wishes to expand geographically. The third structural problem arises. If the expansion is entirely within one country, geographic decentralization (division of labor) follows. Increased decision decentralization may or may not ensue. If the expansion is into other countries, then a somewhat different pattern of actions is employed. The fourth problem (or third, if diversification occurs before geographic expansion) is related to diversification. The organization may decide to offer additional product lines or services. The size and task complexity become too much for one leader to closely manage. A decision decentralized, product division structure normally emerges. A fifth structure problem—control—is associated with all acts of decentralization—for example, delegation to cure problem number two above and in response to decentralization for problems three and four above. When authority is delegated, results must be assured. Formalization is pursued, but the organization becomes mechanistic and unadaptive. Eventually, the organization must develop a means of control by specific objectives, with the division or functional area managers delegated authority to proceed within policy to accomplish those objectives. Other approaches, such as team management, have also been attempted, but their utilities have as yet to be fully substantiated. While this model is a simplification, it does point to the major problems normally encountered as organizations grow. Each of these problem situations will now be discussed in more detail.

Entrepreneurial Commencement—The Need for Functionalization. In practice, most firms commence with some type of functional structure. The problem at this stage of organizational growth is the determination of the exact division of labor among the employees. Smaller organizations have difficulty in fully utilizing the efficiencies associated with the division of labor because these firms are just not large enough to take full advantage of all of the possible task simplifications. The cost-benefit tradeoff of hiring additional personnel to perform more efficiently is often just not sufficiently positive to justify this action. The recruitment of a work force with multiple task skills is therefore required and unfortunately not easily accomplished.

A Crisis of Autonomy—A Solution of Delegation. Some entrepreneurs never can relinquish authority. One clothing manufacturer who had 250 employees and annual sales of $6 million could be found working at 10 P.M. on weekends on the accounts payable ledger, even though he had an accounting staff. Advised to better use his time, he was still continuing this activity six months later. In another case an Air Force missile wing commander personally inspected Montana State Highway bridges for tonnage requirements because a bridge had collapsed while supporting a truck carrying a missile. He also personally sanded the base gymnasium floor to make certain a good job was done. And, he personally approved every purchase order over $50. The syndrome is a common one. The question is: who will inform the leader of his faults? Just as importantly: how does one cause him to change his behavior? A change agent (consultant) may be requested, but often only after a catalyst, usually a serious downturn in organizational fortunes, has taken place. It is normally the catalyst which calls attention to the need for delegation. This pattern occurs in smaller organizations and the largest multidivisioned organizations as well. Managers have a natural propensity for holding on to power.

The Problem of Geographic Expansion—A Solution of Decentralization. When expansion occurs within the same country, the structural patterns routinely include some decision decentralization as well as geographic decentralization. The greater the physical distance, the more decision decentralization which would seem to naturally follow. When expansion occurs into new countries, a somewhat different but largely similar pattern of events normally transpires. Brooke and Remmers indicate that this sequence usually begins with the establishment of a base of operations. This is characterized by initial expansion and accumulation of resources. Second, a single executive is appointed to head foreign operations. Third, new organizational arrangements are developed to administer expansion and new products. A fourth stage of development is emerging, a type of structure in which functional departments service all divisions in all countries. And while decentralization is apparently effective in developed countries, research has suggested that decentralization may be dysfunctional in certain developing countries. The structures of multinationals develop in such a way as to reveal a cultural influence. The structures and succession of structures of multinational businesses may vary according to the country of origin.

Diversification—Decentralization: The Divisionalized Structure. When an organization, here the business firm, diversifies into additional products and services, the characteristic structure utilized is one known as the product division structure. In this structure, the product division is the first level of the corporate hierarchy below the CEO. These divisions usually have a functional structure internally. The transition from an organization operating on a functional basis to an organization operating primarily on a product basis is apparently required by the complexity of the top management process in highly diversified situations.

Walker and Lorsch have identified three classical criteria for choosing the product or function structure:

1. Which approach permits the maximum use of special technical knowledge?
2. Which provides the most efficient utilization of machinery and equipment?
3. Which provides the best hope of obtaining the required control and coordination?

Recognizing, however, the immensity of the problem, some of the behavioral consequences, and the significance of information obtained through research since the classical criteria were formulated, they offer the following as more relevant points for choice:

1. How will the choice affect differentiation among specialists? Will it allow the necessary differences in viewpoint to develop so that specialized tasks can be performed effectively?
2. How does the decision affect the prospects of accomplishing integration? Will it lead, for instance, to greater differentiation, which will increase the problems of achieving integration?
3. How will the decision affect the ability of organization members to communicate with each other, resolve conflicts, and reach the necessary joint decisions?

These are extremely helpful criteria because they focus on the central point of departure as indicated by the research. It is precisely because of differentiation and integration characteristics that the product division structure is normally chosen.

Wrigley found that among larger, diversified firms, the product division structure is quite common and is the dominant form (approximately 90 percent) in the Fortune 500 companies. A whole series of studies performed at the Harvard School of Business reveals that the divisional form has in the past 15 to 25 years become the dominant form in the largest firms in the United States, Europe, and Japan. Franko, in a separate survey, found similar results among European firms. However, he suggested that the divisional structure in Europe resulted primarily from competition and not product diversification strategies, as seems to be the common cause in the United States.

As observed previously, the product division structure may become tangled by mechanistic control systems which attempt to maintain activity congruent with overall objectives. Commonly, people refer to these as red tape. Red tape is found in business, in government, and in nonprofit private sector organizations. Various means of removing red tape have been suggested, but the best at this time appears to be autonomy for the decision decentralized divisions within very broad policy (but employing specific objectives), with the plans of actions to be formulated by the divisions themselves. In this process, the information and control systems play significant roles. It may very well be that there is a point of diminishing returns with regard to size.

Team management has been offered as a solution to these problems. If team management should prove to be the appropriate device for controlling large, multidivision organizations, then presumably another structure problem would result—based on past experience. Only time will tell what problems will result from team management.

In Summary. Organization structure, both formal and informal, has been reviewed. No one factor clearly causes a particular structure. Rather, several factors act as determinants. The relevance of each is situational, although strategy begins with structure and management prerogative—two considerations often neglected in current research. Organizations were found to pass through various stages of growth, each of which results in certain structural problems. Finally, it should be observed that the final problem associated with growth beyond the team managed organization is as yet undetermined.

Implementation

Implementation is the process of translating intermediate plans and policies into results. It is the summation of activities in which human resources engage in utilizing other resources to accomplish the objectives of the strategy. Proper implementation is the consequence of two primary factors. First, integrative planning and control systems must be utilized. These function to insure that implementation activities, for example decision making or actual physical labors, are in accordance with strategy. Vital to this end are objectives, plans, and policy. Operational planning is especially critical to successful implementation, since in this planning effort the exact actions to be taken by first-line employees are delineated. Second, once resources—human, financial, and capital—are committed to the tasks established in organizing, they must be properly managed. Appropriate human resource management is the essence of successful implementation.

Key Elements in Successful Implementation

Little has been written and probably less is understood about successful implementation per se than any other phase of strategic management. There is virtually no research on this subject as such, and therefore much of what follows is only conceptually normative. Importantly, however, much has been written and substantive research undertaken with regard to the topics perceived to be embodied in the process of implementation. As perceived, the topic of strategy implementation is expansive. Almost all of the management functions—planning, controlling, organizing, motivating, leading, directing, integrating, communicating and innovating—are in some degree applied in the implementation process. This text is not the appropriate medium with which to embark upon a long discourse as to the nature of successful implementation. The focus of the following is on those aspects of implementation which are viewed as the most essential and which would normally not have been covered extensively in other courses. Where the reader is expected to be familar with the topic, the discussion is brief and the emphasis is on relating how these more familiar topics relate to successful implementation.

Integrated Planning and Control Systems. Integrated planning and control commences with Master Strategy formation and is of concern in the formulation of all plans derived from the Master Strategy. Successful implementation requires that precise objectives be stipulated in strategies and in the intermediate and operational plans derived therefrom. This is accomplished through the use of MBO, as was discussed in Chapter 5. Precise objectives, by clarifying role prescription for executives, managers, and first-line employees:

1. assure that these individuals will know what is expected of them, and
2. provide built-in standards against which performance can be compared for control purposes.

Integration of the efforts of the organization's subsystems is assisted by these systems and by network planning models such as the now familiar Program Evaluation Review Technique (PERT), the Critical Path Method (CPM), and Gantt Charts. Since control is the subject of the next chapter, this chapter focuses on the planning aspects of these systems. The following sections discuss these planning and control systems: Functional Policy, Operational Planning, and Budgets.

Functional Policy: Guidance for Decision Making. Policies play an important role in assuring that operative activities are congruent with organizational strategy. Some of the most important policies which any organization can possess are those which define the constraints for the organization functional subdivisions. Proper implementation cannot occur if functional subsystems lack appropriate guidance. The precise content of functional policy depends on the firm. Large firms will have policies on almost any type of imaginable functional or divisional plan or potential problem. Small firms may not have any written policies and may have only implied policies for major functional areas. The basis of these policies is functional organization activities. At a minimum the firm will be expected to have policies concerning marketing, production, finance, and personnel—the making, selling, and financing of each product and the staffing of the organization to accomplish those tasks. Beyond these, any number of other functional areas may be included in functional policy. For example, policies may be established with regard to setting objectives, planning, and setting policies. Or policies may be created for information systems, research and development, market research, or the organization's structure. Finally, policies related to management philosophy, motivation, communications, social responsibility, and other factors may be created. Examples of questions these policies might answer include the following:

Production
1. How is location of facilities determined?
2. How does the firm determine when to purchase new facilities?
3. How much is to be invested in plant and equipment?
4. How is the work designed; that is, according to what factors?
5. What are acceptable rates of product rejection?

Marketing
1. What is the target market?
2. What is the promotional mix?
3. What is the price?
4. What differential advantage is to be exploited?

Finance
1. When are dividends issued?
2. What types of debt are to be used—internal or external, long term or short term?
3. What uses are made of excess cash?
4. What uses will be made of a budget?

Personnel
1. How are position openings determined?
2. What are the EEO requirements to be considered?
3. How is recruitment accomplished?
4. How is selection accomplished?
5. What are the bases for employee rewards?

Operational Planning. Operational planning is normally considered to be a component of implementation. Operational plans normally cover a period of one year, although their length varies with the particular organization. These plans are used to translate intermediate plans into definitive, result producing actions. The descriptions of these actions and their objectives are normally referred to as procedures, roles, or job descriptions. It is operational plans that give substance to strategy. They have the most specific objectives and the most specific activity requirements of any of the plans. They specify the exact resources needed and the precise manner in which they are to be obtained and utilized. Operational planning involves the middle and lower levels of management. It is the continuous iterative process of parceling strategic objectives into annually obtainable objectives that makes planning pragmatic as opposed to pie in the sky. General Electric and many other organizations label these one-year operating plans as their Profit Plans.

As observed by Anderson, operating plans emphasize automatic decision rules, procedures, and integrative activity. These plans are concerned with the adjustment of production, marketing, and financial capacity to the levels of operation. They aim to increase the efficiency of operating activities. They provide specific detail of short term operations. Operational planning focuses on the ways and means of accomplishing strategic objectives.

Budgets. The most common of the specific operational planning and control systems is the budget. The budget is usually referred to as a financial operating plan. The budget translates plans of action, usually operating plans, into dollar commitments. Through the budget, the organization determines whether or not an operating plan is acceptable on the bottom line (anticipated profit). There are normally two major types of budgets: the operating budget and the financial budget. The operating budget consists of various functional budgets. This budget begins with a revenue forecast. For business this is the sales forecast. For government this is the tax receipt estimate and the monetary manipulations forecast. For nonprofit private sector organizations this may be forecast contributions. In budgeting, estimated expenditures are matched against anticipated revenues and role expectations emerge. Usually some provisions are made for unforeseen variations in budgeted performance expectations. The operational budget's impacts upon the financial health of the firm are portrayed in the financial budget composed of various cash and capital budgets. These, in turn, are used to develop pro-forma financial statements. Figure 6.2 details the relationships of the major types of budgets.

Recently, the zero based budget, or zero based planning system as it is sometimes referred to, has been increasingly utilized in all types of organizations, profit and nonprofit. Originated by Texas Instruments to curb the funding of programs no longer needed, this system requires that each manager ascertain for each operating cycle what is required to accomplish his unit's portion of the mission. In so doing, the zero base eliminates the automatic inclusion of unnecessary people and programs. Each manager begins without any guaranteed funds and must justify all programs each year.

Resource Management

After operational planning has been accomplished, what remains is to insure that resources are appropriately utilized. It is the management of the human resource upon which the following paragraphs focus because if these resources are effective and efficient in fulfilling their roles, then the remaining resources will be effectively and efficiently managed.

Human Resource Management: Assuring Desired Organizational Behavior. An exhaustive treatment of organizational behavior would be inappropriate in this text. Organizational behavior is the subject of other texts and other courses. Yet, a brief review will relate its importance to strategy. Once the organization is committed to a course of action, it is motivation and leadership which assure successful implementation. Therefore a brief review of the major facets of these two important concepts is relevant. Moreover, the other functions of management should not be ignored. Lower level managers, those primarily responsible for implementation, must plan—to an appropriate degree, communicate, organize, control, integrate, and make decisions. Also critical to this process are the actions of the personnel division as it obtains human resources for the organization and as it provides organizational systems to aid the individual manager in his motivation and leadership efforts.

A Note on the Personnel Function. Once the organization structure has been

Figure 6.2   The Budget

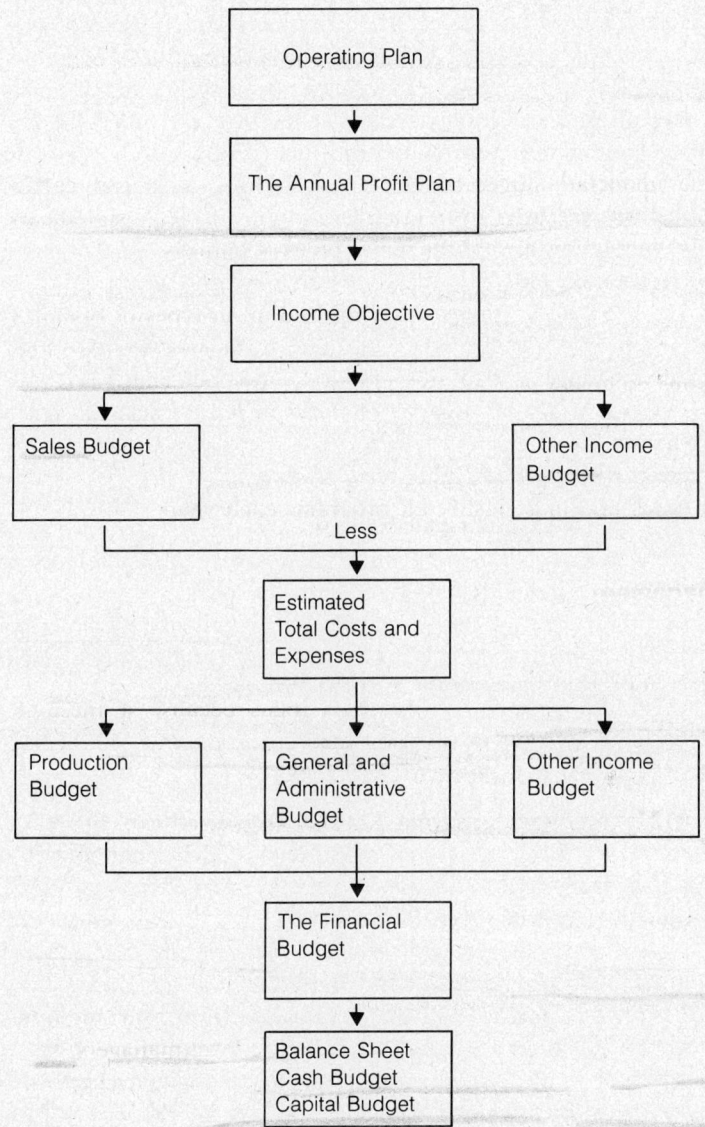

designed, individuals must be recruited, selected, oriented, trained and developed to fulfill the resultant role prescriptions. These tasks are commonly carried out in larger firms by the organization's personnel department, and in smaller firms by the owner/manager. Furthermore, the organization provides—either intentionally or unintentionally and again normally through the personnel department but also as the result of top management philosophy—motivation and leadership systems. These are expressed in organizational compensation, benefit, security, safety, discipline, evaluation, and termination programs as well as overall organizational climate (over which the personnel department has limited control). The thrust of this note is this—the individual manager operates within the organization. The organization provides systems of, and constraints upon, managerial motivation and leadership. Many of these systems and constraints emanate from the personnel department.

Motivation. Motivation, in an organizational context, is the managerial stimulation of subordinates to accomplish the objectives of the organization. This is accomplished by providing an environment in which the employee can satisfy his needs and in so doing accomplish organizational objectives. Motivation begins with an individual's perception of his needs. The organization may provide need satisfiers; so may the manager. Because of organizational motivation systems, managers often have limited latitude in providing need satisfiers. The manager's motivation dilemma may evolve into attempts to build satisfaction into a particular job and to provide rewards where no organizational opportunities exist. For example, to reward superior performance when no merit compensation is given by the organization, the manager may have to develop some enterprising recognition techniques.

Motivation theories may be conveniently categorized into two subdivisions: content and process theories. Content theories focus on the specific needs to be satisfied. The number of needs and hence need satisfiers is substantial. Typical needs include physiological, safety, social, esteem, self actualization, power, achievement, objective accomplishment, and role fulfillment. And while needs appear to be ordered in a hierarchy, it is proving to be a different hierarchy than that conveyed by Maslow. Needs may be classified as intrinsic or extrinsic with respect to a particular position, but are not factually stereotyped into motivators or hygienic factors as originally proposed by Herzberg. Motivation is further complicated by the fact that individual needs are multiple, change over time, and vary from situation to situation. Process theories observe that as need satisfiers are offered, certain moderator variables may impinge and prevent the need satisfiers from having the desired impact. Process theories attempt to explain why.

The individual manager's role in motivation is to correctly diagnose the situation; determine the appropriate need satisfier or need satisfiers; offer these or effective substitutes; and insure that motivation process consequences are congruent with expected results, all within organizational and nonorganizational constraints. This is obviously not an easy task, but it is essential if employees are to fulfill their tasks. If individuals work to only half of their capability, then the organization may fall short of mission accomplishment. It is motivation which causes the employee to work to his full potential.

Leadership. Management is situational; leadership, a major function in the total management process, could hardly be otherwise. The situational approach to leadership proposes that the manager identify the major factors in each situation and that he adjust his leadership techniques to match those factors. The difficulty lies in identifying the most critical factors. Having acknowledged the situational aspects of this function, it is important to note that it has been shown that where leaders follow certain behaviors, success, measured in terms of productivity and employee satisfaction, will occur. For example, Bowers and Seashore have proposed that four common behaviors have repeatedly been identified by research as leading to success. These four behaviors include: 1. supporting subordinates' egos; 2. interaction facilitation —working well with groups; 3. emphasizing objectives; and 4. work facilitation—practicing the functions of management and knowing subordinates' jobs to a relevant degree. Obviously, the same behaviors are not appropriate in all situations or for all managers. Finally, leadership style is to a great extent explained by organizational climate. The individual manager's propensity for authoritative versus democratic management style is tempered by how the organization prefers to be led. Organizational preferences are defined in policy and become a part of structure.

Summary

Organization structure has several major determinants with their importance varying with the situation. Common structural problems exist for most business organizations. Once structured, the organization must implement its plans. Successful implementation depends upon proper integrative planning and control techniques and upon appropriate managerial functioning— especially motivation and leadership. Obviously, the relationships between organization structure and implementation are of critical importance.

What can be said in complete certainty with regard to organization and implementation is that there is no one best way to organize or to implement. Various factors moderate the effects of actions taken. The primary factors affecting each individual situation should be determined and a course of action taken based on this analysis. Some actions are appropriate in most situations.

Discussion Questions

1. Describe an organization situation in which each of the seven major organization structure determinants plays the major role in determining structure.

2. What did Chandler mean when he said that "structure follows strategy"?
3. How are size (growth) and structure related?
4. What is the relationship of structure to implementation?
5. Why is policy so important to successful implementation?
6. Why is human resource management so critical to successful implementation? ⟹ *lower level mgt. involving a lot of use of human resource*
7. Why are structure and implementation so important to mission accomplishment? *Motiv leadership to ensure efficiency*

Footnote

1. Substantive decentralization is a term used by Waino Soujanen to distinguish complete decision decentralization from partial decentralization.

References

Ackoff, R. L. *A Concept of Corporate Planning.* New York: Wiley-Interscience, 1970.

Aldrich, H. E. "Technology and Organization Structure: A Reexamination of the Findings of the Aston Group." *Administrative Science Quarterly,* March 17, 1972, pp. 26–43.

Anderson, T. A. "Coordinating Strategic and Operational Planning." *Business Horizons,* Summer 1965, p. 51.

Barrow, J. C. "The Variables of Leadership: A Review and Conceptual Framework." *Academy of Management Review,* April 1977, pp. 231–245.

Blake, R. R.; W. E. Avis; and J. S. Mouton. *Corporate Darwinism.* Houston: Gulf, 1966.

Boulanger, D. G. "Program Evaluation and Review Technique." *Advanced Management Journal,* July/August 1961, pp. 8–12.

Bowers, D. G., and S. E. Seashore. "Predicting Organizational Effectiveness with a Four Factor Theory of Leadership." *Administrative Science Quarterly,* June 1966, pp. 238–249.

Brooke, M., and H. L. Remmers, editors. *The Multinational Company in Europe: Some Key Problems.* Ann Arbor: University of Michigan Press, 1972.

Brummet, R. L.; W. C. Pyle; and E. G. F. Flamholtz. "Accounting for Human Resources." *Michigan Business Review,* March 1968, pp. 20–25.

Campbell, J. P., et al. *Managerial Behavior, Performance, and Effectiveness.* New York: McGraw-Hill, 1970.

Chandler, A. D. *Strategy and Structure.* Cambridge, Mass.: MIT Press, 1962.

Chandler, A., Jr., and H. Daems. "The Rise of Managerial Capitalism and Its Impact on Investment Strategy in the Western World and Japan." Working paper, European Institute for Advanced Studies in Management, 1974.

Channon, D. F. "Strategy and Structure of British Enterprise." Unpublished doctoral dissertation, Harvard Business School, 1971.

Clark, W. *The Gantt Chart: A Working Tool of Management.* New York: Ronald Press, 1922.

Davis, K. *Human Behavior at Work.* New York: McGraw-Hill, 1972.

Fiedler, F. *A Theory of Leadership Effectiveness.* New York: McGraw-Hill, 1967.

Ford, J. D., and J. W. Slocum, Jr. "Size, Technology, Environment and the Structure of Organizations." *Academy of Management Review,* October 1977, pp. 561–575.

Fouraker, L. E., and J. M. Stopford. "Organizational Structure and the Multinational Strategy." *Administrative Science Quarterly,* March 1968, p. 62.

Franklin, J. L. "Relations among Four Social-Psychological Aspects of Organizations." *Administrative Science Quarterly,* September 1975, pp. 422–433.

Franko, L. G. "The Move toward a Multidivisional Structure in European Organizations." *Administrative Science Quarterly,* December 1974, pp. 493–506.

Gibson, J. L.; J. M. Ivancevich; and J. H. Donnelly, Jr. *Organizations: Behavior, Structure, Processes,* pp. 231–242. Dallas: BPI, 1976.

Grant, J. H. "Managing the Strategies of Systems-Oriented Business." *Proceedings: Academy of Management,* 1975, pp. 58–60.

Greiner, L. E. "Evolution and Revolution as Organizations Grow." *Harvard Business Review,* July/August 1972, pp. 37–46.

Herzberg, F. *Work and the Nature of Man.* New York: World Publishing, 1966.

Levy, F. K.; G. L. Thompson; and J. D. Wiest. "The ABC's of the Critical Path Method." *Harvard Business Review,* September/October 1963, pp. 98–108.

Miner, J. B., and H. P. Dachler. "Personnel Attitudes and Motivation." *Annual Review of Psychology,* 1973, pp. 379–402.

Minimer, G. S. *An Evaluation of the Zero Base Budgeting Systems in Government Institutions.* Atlanta: Georgia State University, School of Business, Publishing Services Division, 1975.

Montanari, J. R. "Operationalizing Strategic Choice." Paper presented at the Academy of Management Meeting, August 1977, at Kissimmee, Fla.

Neghandi, A. R., and B. C. Reimann. "A Contingency Theory of Organization Reexamined in the Context of a Developing Country." *Academy of Management Journal,* June 1972, pp. 137–147.

Parsons, T. "Suggestion for a Sociological Approach to the Theory of Organization: I and II." *Administrative Science Quarterly,* June 1956, pp. 63–85; September 1956, pp. 225–239.

Pavan, R. J. "Strategy and Structure of Italian Enterprise." Unpublished doctoral dissertation, Harvard School of Business, 1972.

————. "Strategy and Structure: The Italian Experience." *Journal of Economics and Business,* Spring/Summer 1976, pp. 254–260.

Pennings, J. M. "The Relevance of the Structural Contingency Model for Organizational Effectiveness." *Administrative Science Quarterly,* September 1975, p. 393.

Pitts, R. A. "Incentive Compensation and Organization Design." *Personnel Journal,* May 1974, p. 338.

Pooley, G. "Strategy and Structure of French Enterprise." Unpublished doctoral dissertation, Harvard School of Business, 1972.

Pugh, D. S., et al. "The Context of Organizational Structures." *Administrative Science Quarterly,* December 1969, p. 91.

Rumelt, R. P. *Strategy, Structure and Economic Performance of the Fortune "500."* Cambridge, Mass.: Division of Research, Harvard School of Business, 1974. (1969 data.)

Salter, M. "Stages of Corporate Development." *Journal of Business Policy,* Autumn 1970.

Schollhammer, H. "Organization Structures of Multinational Corporations." *Academy of Management Journal,* September 1971, pp. 345–365.

Scott, B. R. "The Industrial State: Old Myths and New Realities." *Harvard Business Review,* March/April 1973, pp. 133–149.

————. *Stages in Corporate Development: Part II.* Cambridge, Mass.: Harvard School of Business, 1971.

Selznik, P. *TVA and the Grass Roots.* Berkeley: University of California Press, 1949.

Simonetti, J. L., and F. L. Simonetti. "The Impact of Management Policy and Organization Structure on the Management Effectiveness of Firms Operating in Italy." *Journal of Business and Economics,* Spring/Summer 1976, pp. 249–252.

Soujanen, W. *The Dynamics of Management.* New York: Holt, Rinehart and Winston, 1966.

Stonich, P. J. "Zero Base Planning—A Management Tool." *Managerial Planning,* July/August 1976, pp. 1–4.

Thain, D. H. "Stages of Corporate Development." *Business Quarterly,* Winter 1969, pp. 32–45.

Thanheiser, H. "Strategy and Structure of German Enterprise." Unpublished doctoral dissertation, Harvard School of Business, 1972.

Walker, A. H., and J. W. Lorsh. "Organizational Choice: Product versus Function." *Harvard Business Review,* November/December 1968, pp. 131–132.

Wrigley, L. "Divisional Autonomy and Diversification." Unpublished doctoral dissertation, Harvard School of Business, 1970. (1967 data.)

Chapter 7

The Evaluation and Control of Organizational Strategy

The best laid schemes o' mice an' men gang aft agley.

Robert Burns

There are three primary types of organizational control: strategic control, management control, and operational control. Strategic control is the process of evaluating strategy. Strategic control is practiced both after strategy is formulated and subsequent to its implementation. The organization's strategists evaluate strategy once it is formulated to ascertain whether or not it is appropriate to mission accomplishment and again once it is implemented to determine if the strategy is accomplishing its objectives. Management control is the process of assuring that major subsystems' progress towards the accomplishment of strategic objectives is satisfactory. For example, is Division A's ROI performance acceptable? Or, is the Production Department meeting its quality control objectives? Operational control is the process of ascertaining whether or not individual and work group role behaviors (performance) are congruent with individual and work group role prescriptions.[1] For example, is Tom reaching his sales quota?

As with the phases of planning, the types of control are not distinct entities. Rather, in various organizations, one type of control may be almost indistinguishable from another. Furthermore, the devices used in one type of control may also be employed in another. For example, management control devices such as ROI may be used to measure not only the performance of organizational components but the total organization as well. Finally, while most operational and many management control systems may possess automatic correction activities, the evaluation of strategy requires executive judgment.

Figure 7.1   The Organization—An Organization Process Model

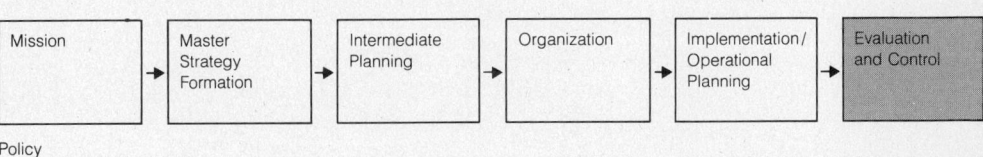

Mission → Master Strategy Formation → Intermediate Planning → Organization → Implementation/ Operational Planning → Evaluation and Control

Policy

This chapter is concerned with those parts of the comprehensive model indicated in Figure 7.1. This chapter begins with a discussion of control, followed by a review of some normative/qualitative observations of how to evaluate strategy. Next, some of the more common types of strategic/management control techniques are reviewed. Certain of the more relevant of these are discussed at length. Finally, the dysfunctional consequences of control are presented, followed by some concluding remarks on control.

Control and Strategy

Strategic, management, and operational control systems perform an important integrative function. The measurement of performance as related to objective accomplishment coordinates activity. Experience and research have revealed that any number of variables may cause performance to be incongruent with strategy. For example, the assumptions under which strategy was formulated may change. Or, adherence to strategy, plans, and policies may not occur. Deviations from either assumptions or guidance lead to unsatisfactory results. Therefore the successful strategy must have control as one of its dimensions. What is controlled varies from level to level in the organization. The organization's strategists are responsible for strategic control, as are the stockholders, theoretically. Management control is principally the function of top management, especially the CEO. Operational control is primarily the concern of lower level managers. Strategic control and management control are concerned with broader perspectives than the details dealt with in operational control. Note, however, that war rooms and strategic information systems allow top management to view the details of operations if necessary. While much of what follows is related to formal control systems, informal control systems may suffice in the smaller organization, especially for operational control where personal observation is possible.

Control may be depicted as a six-step feedback model as follows:

1. The establishment of standards of performance: standards are specific points on a criterion measure against which actual performance will be judged. As such they are more detailed expressions of strategic objectives and are the bases of role prescriptions. Establishing these for organizational subcomponents is the first step in management control, and establishing these for individuals is the first step in operational control.

2. The statement of acceptable tolerances: the standard is a single point on a criterion measure, but it is not usually necessary to perform exactly to that point. Normally, deviation from standards will be tolerated within certain control limits.

3. Measurement of actual performance: this is the third step in management or operational control, the identification of role behavior either for com-

ponents or individuals. Measurement techniques vary from situation to situation and are often imprecise.

4. Comparison of standards and performance: while this might appear to be a simple task, it is quite complex in the more qualitative performance areas because of the inability to quantify either or both—standards and performance.

5. Action: where performance is satisfactory—congruent with standards—no action is necessary. But where it is not, corrective action must be taken.

6. Preventive action: Greenwood has correctly observed that it is insufficient to just correct problems. Rather, action must be taken to assure that these problems do not occur again.

This model focuses on results (outputs). Most control systems—strategic, management, or operational—focus on results. Often the consequence of utilizing these feedback control systems is that the unsatisfactory performance continues until the malfunctioning is discovered. One technique for reducing the problems associated with "feedback" control systems is "feedforward control." First suggested by Koontz and Bradspies, feedforward control focuses on the inputs to the system attempting to anticipate potential problems with outputs. (See Figure 7.2.) With respect to strategy and planning, feedforward control has wide applicability. For example, the feedforward principle underlies the concept of simulation modeling. "What if" questions are, after all, examinations of hypothesized inputs to determine resultant effects on system outputs. Simulations of performance can be made in any number of strategic situations to test for changes in basic assumptions. In fact, any situation with identifiable inputs which can be modeled can and should utilize the feedforward approach.

Figure 7.2   The Organization as a Processing System

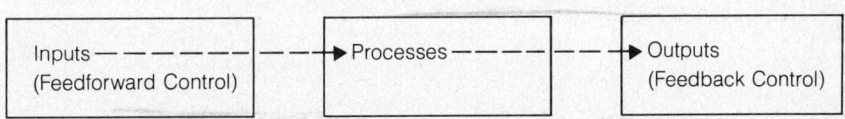

Strategic Control: The Evaluation of Corporate Strategy

Once strategy has been formulated, it should be evaluated. Several largely normative statements which constitute criteria (Step 1 of the six-step control model) have been suggested. The best known of these, the Tilles model, is summarized as follows:

1. Is the strategy internally consistent, for example, with mission and among its own plans?
2. Is it consistent with the environment?
3. Is it consistent with internal resources?
4. Does it have an appropriate amount of risk?
5. Does it have a proper time horizon?
6. Is it workable?

Learned, Christensen, Andrews, and Guth, building on the Tilles model, suggest that the following are also proper evaluative questions:

7. Is it identifiable? Has it been stated clearly and consistently and are people aware of it?
8. Is it appropriate to the personal values and aspirations of key managers?
9. Does it constitute a clear stimulus to organizational effort and commitment?
10. Is it socially responsible?
11. Are there early indications of the responsiveness of markets and market segments to the strategy?

Argenti also suggests asking:

12. Does it rely on weaknesses or do anything to reduce them?
13. Does it exploit major opportunities?
14. Does it avoid, reduce, or mitigate the major threats? If not, are there adequate contingency plans?

These questions are intuitively sound. More importantly, they relate directly to the Organizational Process Model constructed in Chapter 1. In fact, these questions, when considered in total, comprise a checklist to determine if the Organizational Process Model was properly followed. All of these questions can be applied as the strategy progresses through its various stages, including implementation. Progress and changes could thus be observed. Specific standards of performance are established by the objectives of the Master Strategy and its component strategies. Once implementation occurs, measurements will be taken to determine if these objectives were reached. The tolerances established (Step 2 of the model) vary from firm to firm. Tolerances are primarily judgmental—how much deviation from the standard can we live with? Corrective and preventive actions may require that strategy be changed.

Management Control

Management control becomes a distinct concern when decentralization occurs. Where management control is imposed, it functions within the framework established by the strategy. Management control focuses on the accomplishment of the objectives of the various substrategies comprising the Master Strategy and on the accomplishment of the objectives of the intermediate plans. Normally these objectives (standards) are established for major sub-systems within the organization, such as programs, projects, products, functions, and responsibility centers. Allowable tolerances vary from organization to organization. Typical management control measures include ROI, residual income, cost, product quality, efficiency measures, and so forth. These control measures are essentially summations of operational control measures. When corrective or preventive action is taken it may involve very minor or very major changes in the strategy. Often, top management strategists may be removed from their positions as the consequence of poor performance indicated by these control measures. One large firm has a policy for its European operating division managers: "Two consecutive quarters of declining ROI and you're fired!"

Operational Control

Operational control systems are designed to insure that day to day actions are consistent with established plans and objectives. Operational control is concerned with individual and group role performance as compared with the individual and group role prescriptions required by organizational plans. Operational control systems are normally concerned with the past (unless feedforward systems are being utilized). Operational control focuses on events in a recent period. Operational control systems are derived from the requirements of the management control system. Specific standards for performance are derived from the objectives of the operating plans, which are based on intermediate plans, which are based on strategy. Performance is compared against objectives at the individual and group levels. Corrective or preventive action is taken where performance does not meet the standards. This may require training, motivation, leadership, discipline, or termination.

Step 3 of the Control Model, which involves measures used to evaluate strategy once it has been implemented, will now be examined.

Strategic and Management Control Measures of Performance

For most firms, strategic and management control techniques subsequent to the implementation of strategy are identical. The most commonly used measures of strategic and management performance are financial statements and analyses of these. Included are considerations of profit, ROI, return on equity, ratio analyses, trends in the financial statement items, and several additional factors. Inspection of these may occur in routine reporting cycles, as the result of consulting efforts, or as the result of internal or external audits. Budgets, program planning budgeting systems, and zero based budgets and planning systems also serve as important financial indicators of strategic and management performance but most often only for a specific operating period. The objective of all of these endeavors is financial control. Financial control features include information on revenues, costs, profits, and funds flows within the control of responsibility centers and for the organization in total.

But financial control is only part of the total strategic or management control process. Why? Because much of the activity that affects financial performance is nonfinancial in nature. Recognizing this, firms have recently widely employed more comprehensive measures of strategic and managerial performance not normally found on traditional financial statements. These include considerations of labor efficiency and productivity; production quantity and quality; human resource factors such as absenteeism, turnover, and tardiness; as well as, on a very limited basis, human resources accounting and personnel satisfaction measures; and more commonly management by objectives systems; social performance measurements—social audits; cost benefit analysis; operational audits of any functional, divisional, or staff component; distribution cost and efficiency; network planning models; Gantt charts; market share analyses; inventory analyses; management audits; modeling; and so forth. The list is almost endless and there is not time here to discuss each of these. In most instances, these measures (or in some cases, measuring devices) stress short-run results. The obvious consequence is that managers place their emphasis on "looking good" in the short run, not the long run, as would be appropriate. One notable exception is at General Electric, which as part of its operational control standards for executives (and the company and its components) emphasizes a balance between long range and short range objectives and emphasizes personnel development as well.

Most of the above mentioned measures are familiar. However, in the following paragraphs a few of the more important or promising of these measures are reviewed in order to provide a common analytical base.

Ratio Analysis

Ratios of financial statement items (here balance sheets and income statements) are widely used to measure strategic and management performance. With the exception of the current and quick ratios, few generally acceptable and appropriate ratio values exist. The exact number of ratios to use, in what circumstances, their components, and their exact meanings are often not agreed upon. Every financial analyst seems to have his own preferred system. Fortunately, there is common support for several ratios. These are presented in Table 7.1. These ratios are divided into four main subdivisions, each of which tells the analyst about a specific facet of corporate performance. As is shown in Table 7.1, a firm's ratios are normally compared with the ratios of other firms in the same industry. A firm's ratios may also be compared with its own historical ratios. Trends or deviations are the primary con-

Table 7.1 Summary of Financial Ratio Analysis

Ratio	Formula for Calculation	Calculation	Industry Average	Evaluation
Liquidity				
Current	$\dfrac{\text{current assets}}{\text{current liabilities}}$	$\dfrac{\$\,700{,}000}{\$\,300{,}000}$ = 2.3 times	2.5 times	Satisfactory
Quick, or acid test	$\dfrac{\text{current assets} - \text{inventory}}{\text{current liabilities}}$	$\dfrac{\$\,400{,}000}{\$\,300{,}000}$ = 1.3 times	1.0 times	Good
Leverage				
Debt to total assets	$\dfrac{\text{total debt}}{\text{total assets}}$	$\dfrac{\$1{,}000{,}000}{\$2{,}000{,}000}$ = 50 percent	33 percent	Poor
Times interest earned	$\dfrac{\text{profit before taxes plus interest charges}}{\text{interest charges}}$	$\dfrac{\$\,245{,}000}{\$\,45{,}000}$ = 5.4 times	8.0 times	Fair
Fixed charge coverage	$\dfrac{\text{income available for meeting fixed charges}}{\text{fixed charges}}$	$\dfrac{\$\,273{,}000}{\$\,73{,}000}$ = 3.7 times	5.5 times	Poor
Activity				
Inventory turnover	$\dfrac{\text{sales}}{\text{inventory}}$	$\dfrac{\$3{,}000{,}000}{\$\,300{,}000}$ = 10 times	9 times	Satisfactory
Average collection period	$\dfrac{\text{receivables}}{\text{sales per day}}$	$\dfrac{\$\,200{,}000}{\$\,8{,}333}$ = 24 days	20 days	Satisfactory
Fixed assets turnover	$\dfrac{\text{sales}}{\text{fixed assets}}$	$\dfrac{\$3{,}000{,}000}{\$1{,}300{,}000}$ = 2.3 times	5.0 times	Poor
Total assets turnover	$\dfrac{\text{sales}}{\text{total assets}}$	$\dfrac{\$3{,}000{,}000}{\$2{,}000{,}000}$ = 1.5 times	2 times	Poor
Profitability				
Profit margin on sales	$\dfrac{\text{net profit after taxes}}{\text{sales}}$	$\dfrac{\$\,120{,}000}{\$3{,}000{,}000}$ = 4 percent	5 percent	Poor
Return on total assets	$\dfrac{\text{net profit after taxes}}{\text{total assets}}$	$\dfrac{\$\,120{,}000}{\$2{,}000{,}000}$ = 6.0 percent	10 percent	Poor
Return on net worth	$\dfrac{\text{net profit after taxes}}{\text{net worth}}$	$\dfrac{\$\,120{,}000}{\$1{,}000{,}000}$ = 12.0 percent	15 percent	Poor

Source: J. Fred Weston and Eugene F. Brigham, *Managerial Finance*, 5th ed. (Hinsdale, Ill.: Dryden Press, 1975), p. 32. Reprinted by permission of Dryden Press, a division of Holt, Rinehart and Winston.

sideration. Comparative industry figures are often difficult to obtain, although certain organizational figures are available through services provided by Dun & Bradstreet and Robert Morris Associates. In addition, *Dun's Review* publishes annually (usually in November) "Ratios of Manufacturing"; annually in May and June, *Fortune* publishes selected ratios and financial statement items and evaluations thereof for the Fortune 1000 and the Fortune 50s; annually in January, *Forbes,* in "The Annual Report on American Industry," provides evaluative commentary and analysis; *Business Week* reports selected large firms' financial information quarterly; finally, Compustat will provide financial information for most large corporations. The major problem with using these sources is finding the exact industry or group of firms against which to compare the subject firm. While large organization data is abundant, the multiplicity and diversity of products among firms makes comparisons suspect. Small firm data is available only from Robert Morris, and not all industries are available. Intermediate sized firm data is virtually nonexistent. Even where comparative ratios are available, they must be used with caution. Financial statement information is subject to varying accounting practices which hamper comparisons. Footnotes to these statements often make significant differences as to the true value of certain items.

Return on Investment (ROI)

As the result of the positive aspects associated with decentralization, it has become a popular organizational design technique. As indicated in the last chapter, the need arises to control the resulting subsystems. With respect to financial control of these decentralized units, two primary types of control systems exist: those that control projects and those that control responsibility centers. Anthony, Dearden, and Vancil describe five types of responsibility centers.

1. Standard cost centers are those for which standard costs can be computed. By multiplying this cost times units, an output measure is devised.
2. Revenue centers are those for which revenues can be determined.
3. Discretionary expense centers are organizational units, normally staff units, whose output is not commonly measured in financial terms.
4. Profit centers are subsystems for which both costs and revenues may be measured and responsibility for the difference—profit—has been assigned.
5. Investment centers are profit centers for which the assets employed in obtaining profit are identified.

ROI is the performance measure most frequently used for the last of these responsibility centers—the investment center. In this role, ROI has several advantages, but perhaps more importantly, it has several limitations.

ROI is expressed by the formula $\dfrac{\text{Net Income}}{\text{Total Assets}}$. As suggested in Chapter 5 in the discussion on motivation, ROI is a critical issue in large organizations. Inappropriate division control systems reduce executive motivation. This can and usually does result in reduced profits.

ROI Advantages:
1. It is a single comprehensive figure influenced by everything that happens.
2. It measures how well the division manager uses the property of the company to generate profits. It is a good way to also check on accuracy of capital investment proposals.
3. ROI is a common denominator which can be compared with many entities.
4. It provides an incentive to use existing assets efficiently.
5. It provides an incentive to acquire new assets only when this would increase the return.

ROI Limitations:
1. ROI is very sensitive to depreciation policy. Depreciation write-off variances between divisions affect ROI performance. Accelerated depreciation techniques reduce ROI, conflicting with capital budgeting discounted cash flow analysis.
2. ROI is sensitive to book value. Older plants with more depreciated assets have relatively lower investment bases than newer plants (note also effect of inflation), thus increasing ROI. Note that asset investment may be held down or assets disposed of in order to increase ROI performance.
3. In many firms that use ROI, one division sells to another. As a result, transfer pricing must occur. Expenses incurred affect profit. Since in theory the transfer price should be based on total impact on firm profit, some investment center managers are bound to suffer. Equitable transfer prices are difficult to determine.
4. If one division operates in an industry with favorable conditions and another in an industry with unfavorable conditions, one will automatically "look" better than the other.
5. The time span of concern here is short range. The performance of division managers should be measured in the long run. This is top management's time span capacity.
6. The business cycle strongly affects ROI performance, often despite managerial performance.

Despite these criticisms, ROI will likely continue as the leading index of management performance if for no other reason than its simplicity. Importantly, ROI must be supplemented with other decision information. (See Chapter 5.)

ROI is an important concept in terms of both total organizational control and subsystem control. It is the most widely used measure of a firm's operating efficiency.[2] While ROI represents the net income as a percentage of total assets, it is a function of many variables. (See Figure 7.3.) ROI results from the product of two key factors, profit margin on sales and assets turnover. The contributive aspects to these two ratios are outlined in the figure. Rather than discuss them here at length, readers unfamiliar with the Dupont System of Financial Analysis presented in this figure are urged to work through the numbers given in Figure 7.3, coordinating their efforts with the contributive factors surrounding the model.

Management Audits

One of the major questions confronting organizations today is how to evaluate the performance of the top management team. In order to achieve this end, several factors must be considered:

1. Did top management accomplish the objectives which they established?
2. How good were the objectives which they had established? How good were the strategies which they employed to accomplish these objectives?
3. What factors beyond the control of top management affected their performance?[3]
4. How well have they responded to and how well have they anticipated these factors?

These questions then are operational control criteria of top management. Note, it is strategy that is at issue.

Several systems have attempted to measure top management's performance. One of the more promising of these techniques is the management audit which examines all facets of organizational activity. One management audit which is familiar to many management practitioners is that developed by the American Institute of Management (AIM). This audit examines ten categories perceived by AIM's founder, Jackson Martindell, as contributing to strategic success. The AIM audit consists of a questionnaire containing about 300 questions, each related to organizational performance in one of these categories. The questionnaires are completed by a team of AIM auditors. Questions are answered and additional information provided through interviews with organizational managers, through analysis of reports, and through third party sources. At the end of the audit process, point values are assigned to the organization in each of the audit categories. An excellent rating is given if the indicated point values are achieved. The audit has been widely used in many of the largest corporations and smaller firms as well. Importantly, the audit can be adapted to organizations with other missions—commonweal, service, and mutual benefit organizations.

Several additional approaches to the management audit have been suggested, but management audit activity has seemed to decline in recent years. Of interest is Greenwood's management audit. He suggests that a management audit should examine: 1. strategy and strategy determinants, especially environmental factors; 2. the major functional activities of a firm—marketing,

Figure 7.3 Financial Analysis Using ROI

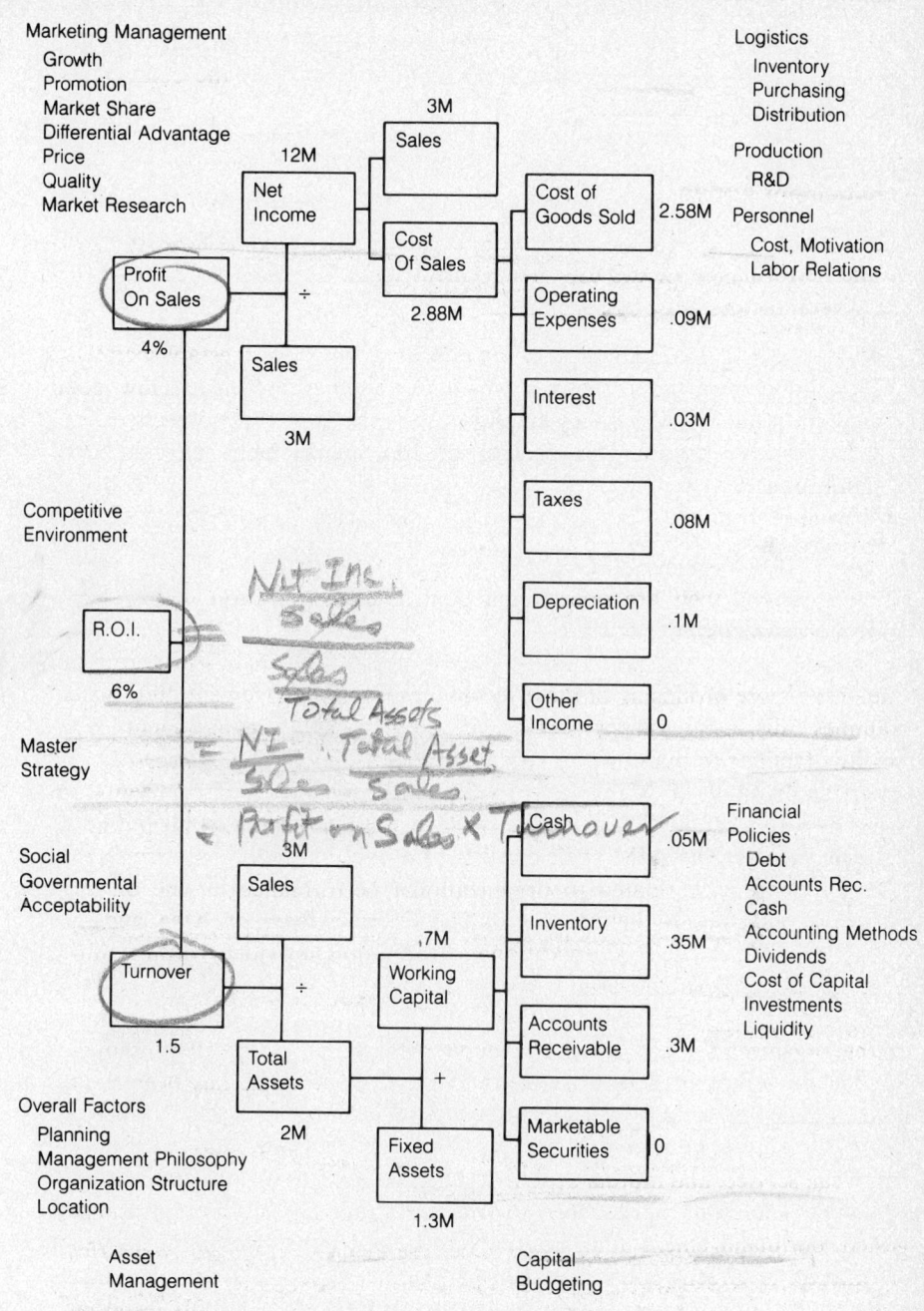

Marketing Management
  Growth
  Promotion
  Market Share
  Differential Advantage
  Price
  Quality
  Market Research

Competitive
Environment

Master
Strategy

Social
Governmental
Acceptability

Overall Factors
  Planning
  Management Philosophy
  Organization Structure
  Location

Asset
Management

Logistics
  Inventory
  Purchasing
  Distribution

Production
  R&D

Personnel
  Cost, Motivation
  Labor Relations

Financial
Policies
  Debt
  Accounts Rec.
  Cash
  Accounting Methods
  Dividends
  Cost of Capital
  Investments
  Liquidity

Capital
Budgeting

Source: Ray Bressler, adapted from unpublished working paper, 1977.

Chapter 7/The Evaluation and Control of Organizational Strategy   **143**

operations (production), personnel, and accounting and finance; and 3. whether or not managers are performing the major functions of management —planning, organizing, staffing, direction, and controlling. Finally, Greenwood recognizes the need for an annual organization policy audit. In this audit, Greenwood has followed a more traditional management theory approach than has Martindell.

Management audits may also be performed utilizing a format parallel to the content of the Master Strategy. (See Chapter 2, Table 2.1.) The analysis is divided into three major components: Primary Mission, Mission Supportive, and Strategic Issues. This approach includes recognition of product division structures (organization) but examines on the basis of functional activities within divisions if they exist. For those who prefer a management function approach, they may be investigated with respect to each functional activity.

In observing any technique it is important to note its weaknesses. While the strength of the management audit is that it has been able to successfully predict corporate performance, it is not always accurate. The system has predicted success for some companies that failed miserably. First, and probably the most important consideration at this time, the environment may change drastically. A management audit would probably have rated General Motors very high in 1973, and yet in 1974, GM had a disastrous year. Strategic issues management must be monitored for surprises. Secondly, in observing the manner in which ratings are assigned, it becomes obvious that the process is rather arbitrary. There is not a specific point value for a positive response to each question, and such strict values are probably not feasible. The auditors who audit a company and obtain responses to audit questions often disagree on the rating of the firm.

Regardless of which format is employed, the audit serves an important function in its comprehensive examination of the organization. While examination of the "bottom line" indicates problems, the auditing of other areas is vital in explaining the causes of these problems. The audit is primarily effective because it looks beyond financial information and systematically appraises the performance of top management.

Adaptive Techniques—The Project Planning Continuum

One of the more promising of the management control techniques, the Project Planning Continuum, is employed on a continuing basis once the strategy is implemented. Developed by Pekar and Burack, this technique is useful in predicting turning points in cost overruns for various projects and programs. The planning continuum consists of two primary components as seen in Figure 7.4. The first is the uncertainty and complexity model. Through the development and subsequent administration of the indicated questionnaires, uncertainty (U)—"predictability or likelihood that a particular event

or occurrence will happen"— and complexity (C)—"the processes, interrelationships, activities, and organizational units that have to interact to obtain specified results"—perception indexes are computed. Importantly, these indexes and differing contributive factors are computed for both the project planning group and the original top management planning and assessment team. The Uncertainty and Complexity Profile Questionnaire is administered using the Delphi Technique. Once the various inputs are complete, the U/C measures are computed. The second part of the model, the Resource Appraisal Models (RAM I and II), are types of forecasting techniques known as smoothing techniques.

As seen in Figure 7.4, these models analyze deviations from budget and planned work completion. The primary purpose of each iteration of the total model is the prediction of deviations from budget and work completion as planned. Cost overruns and the inability to fulfill contract commitments may be predicted in advance and warn top management of impending difficulties. At the center of this technique are the U/C measures. Where these are high and where early deviations occur, the need for project reappraisal is auto-

Figure 7.4 Graphic Portrayal of the Project Planning Continuum

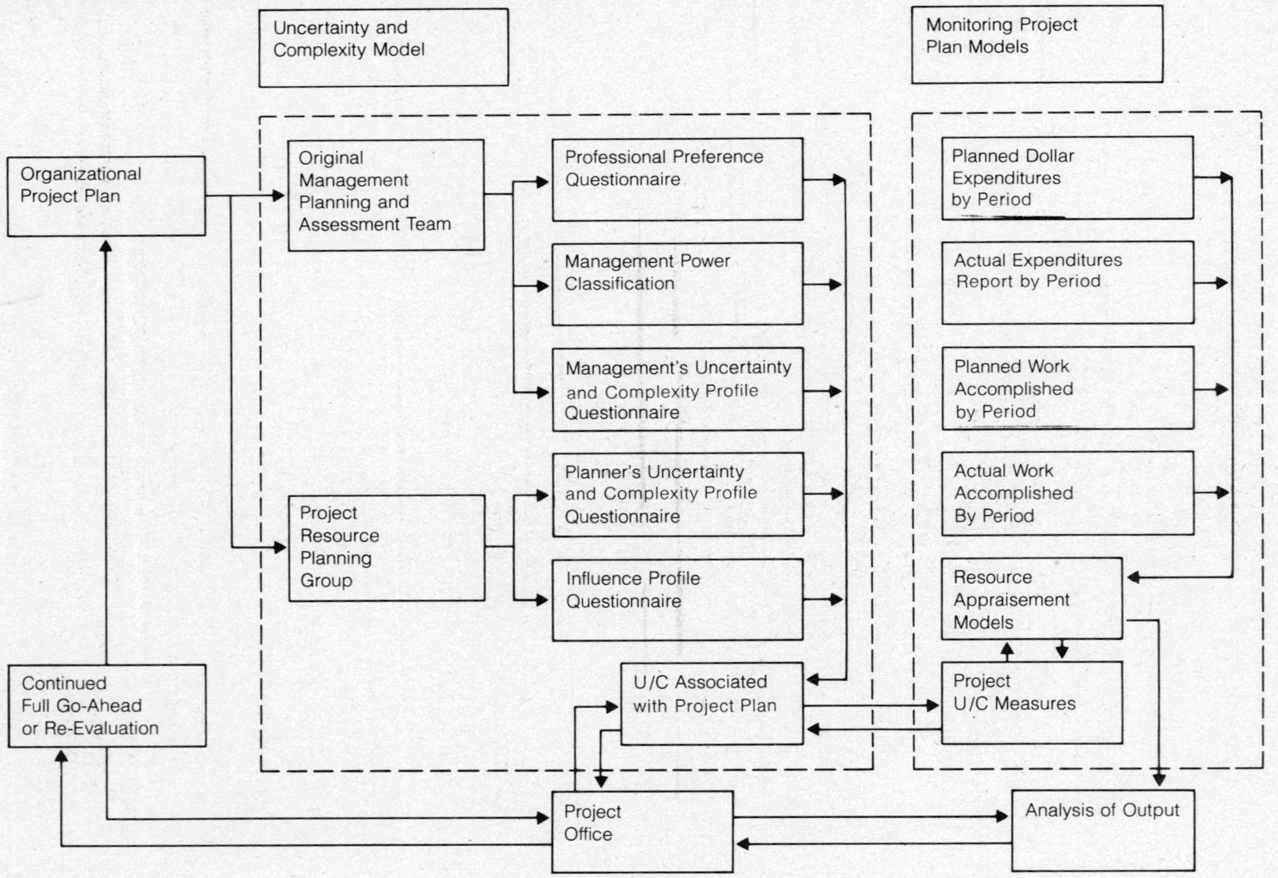

Source: Peter Paul Pekar and Elmer H. Burack, "Management Control of Strategic Plans through Adaptive Techniques," *Academy of Management Journal*, March 1976, p. 81. Reprinted by permission.

matically denoted by the planning continuum output. Lockheed, Convair, and countless others probably would have been able to save millions had this technique been utilized. This technique is also important because it analyzes the impact of behavioral variables on strategic management, a practice almost nonexistent. As this and other uses of behavioral approaches are successful, the recognition of their importance to strategic management should increase.

Human Resource Accounting (HRA)

The evaluation of human assets offers great promise, but to date this promise has been largely unfulfilled. The relevance of human resource accounting to strategic management is connected principally to evaluating the worth of abilities, skills, knowledge, aspirations, and so forth, of the strategic decision makers. But, in addition, the evaluation of corporate strengths and weaknesses requires an assessment of all employees and their potentials related to threats and opportunities. To date, much of the implementation of HRA has involved calculations of the historical cost of human "assets" to the organization. The best known of these efforts is the system employed by R. G. Barry Corporation, which observes the cost of recruiting and acquisition, formal training, orientation, development, familiarization, and related human resource expenses in making its personnel decisions. Other HRA cost models exist: opportunity cost—for example, lost revenues of uncharged time and replacement cost—based on historical cost with operation costs added. In addition to cost models of HRA, one other major model—the economic value approach—exists in aggregate or on an individual basis. Ultimately, this latter is the information sought, but the difficulties, and even impossibilities of estimation, in this author's opinion, severely limit the applicability of the approach. The main problem with the economic value approaches would be one of validity. These approaches require substantive estimation of the worth of individuals to the organization. The question is: How can one be sure that these estimations are meaningful? Nonetheless, the number of firms attempting HRA is growing and includes such firms as American Telephone and Telegraph, GTE in Michigan, and Texas Instruments.

The Social Audit

In recent years, business's critics have demanded that social audits of corporations be accomplished. The term social audit refers to any device which attempts to evaluate an organization's social performance. Areas which might be audited include: environmental protection, equal employment opportunity, consumer satisfaction, governmental relationships, energy usage, and employee job satisfaction.

Ultimately the aim is to determine the social impact of the firm on the communities it affects. While some social areas are readily definable, a quantitative measure of both requirements and performance is extremely difficult, if not impossible, to obtain for many of these areas. Furthermore, it is difficult to obtain agreement as to exactly what business should accomplish. Each pressure group seems to have its own set of demands. Obviously, business cannot respond to all of them. Many corporations have audited their activities in several of the social responsibility areas, and the scoring systems which have been used are becoming more quantitatively oriented.

Other Aspects of Control

Several additional factors need to be considered with respect to control. The following paragraphs examine these.

A Note on the Role of Information in Control

A decision can be only as good as the information upon which it is based. In strategic control, management control, and operational control situations, for both feedforward and feedback control systems, comparison and adjustment occur as the result of information received. The absence of information, such as is the rule in management-by-exception control systems, is also important. There are differences in the characteristics of the information required in strategic control, management control, and operational control. These are portrayed in Table 7.2. The mass of information at operational levels must be meaningfully reduced before top management reports are prepared.

Table 7.2 Information Requirements by Type of Control

Characteristics of Information	Operational Control	Management Control	Strategic Control
Source	Largely Internal	Internal, Partly Environmental	Internal and Environmental
Scope	Well Defined, Narrow	Moderately Broad	Broad in Scope
Level of Aggregation	Detailed	Aggregated	Aggregated
Time Horizon	Historical	Historical	Future and Historical
Frequency of Use	Very Frequent, Continuous	Periodic	Occasional, but with Increasing Frequency

Source: Adapted from G. Anthony Garry and Michael S. S. Morton, "A Framework for Management Information Systems," *Sloan Management Review,* Fall 1971, p. 59. Reprinted by permission.

Integrated Planning and Control Systems

In the last chapter, the importance of integrated planning and control was stressed from a planning perspective—objectives provide direction and motivation. Objectives are the anticipated results. As such, for control purposes, these objectives provide criteria, that is, standards, against which to compare performance. PERT, CPM, MBO, PPBS, budgets, and other planning and control systems can and should be applied to insure successful mission accomplishment. It is essential that implementation be controlled if implementation is to be effective.

Management Control in Nonprofit Organizations

To this point, this chapter has addressed the issues involved with control in the profit oriented organization. Normally, the techniques described for profit oriented organizations are appropriate for nonprofit organizations. However, management control measures, especially financial control measures—specifically profit and ROI—are not very relevant to the nonprofit organization. The problem of control is made more complex by the nature of the planning system employed by nonprofits. Nonprofit organizations generally have vague objectives, and ill-defined plans of action. Because of the inability to quantify objectives, and on many occasions the unwillingness to do so, nonprofits employ the budget as the principal control device. And, unlike the business firm, nonprofits have far too little linkage between objectives and the budget. This approach is unsound. The primary concern should be objective accomplishment—not expenditure. Activity is equated with achievement. The results are often inefficiency and waste. Anyone who has experienced military service or been employed by the federal government is familiar with the resulting "mad" rush to spend as much as possible at the end of each fiscal year (whether the items are needed or not) in order to assure a similar budget amount for the next fiscal year.

Planning Program Budgeting Systems (PPBS) are designed to eliminate some of these problems by requiring that programs be matched more closely to budgets and that the need for programs and budgeted amounts be verified each year. Several states have adopted the zero based budgeting programs normally associated with PPBS. But the inescapable truth remains—it is virtually impossible to delineate what it is that many of these organizations are supposed to accomplish. Therefore, it is rather difficult to control performance towards this nonentity. Responsibility, one of the keys to control, is rather difficult to affix in such situations.

While it is encouraging that public management is now being accepted and even taught in the major universities with some significant successes reported, the major problem—how to establish measurable objectives—remains. Until this problem can be solved, improvements will be limited. Furthermore, this problem is not one which many politicians in the public nonprofit sector would like to solve. Vague objectives and nonconsequential reactive decisions allow politicians to be reelected. Many government agencies have never established objectives before. The coalitions which form and the political promises to various power groups which must be kept often prohibit meaningful plans of actions and objective accomplishment as well as suitable administration. If performance measures were available and accountability became possible, performance would be more common.

With regard to private nonprofits, specifically charities, little is really known, but the evidence suggests little or no planning, control, or management in general. The nonprofits can use many of the control concepts suggested in this chapter: responsibility centers (cost centers); program management; flexible budgets; even "profit" centers for the purpose of transfer pricing; standard costs; and variance analyses. Unfortunately, they have been slow in doing so.

The Dysfunctional Consequences of Control Systems

Control systems are sometimes formulated without consideration of the human beings who will be controlled by them. The behavioral results are often dysfunctional. For example, in the Vietnam War, an Air Force general falsified control reports submitted to the Pentagon regarding missions flown over North Vietnam. At least 28 unauthorized missions were flown before the military hierarchy became aware of these deviations from established standards. The Boy Scouts of America initiated control reporting systems in an attempt to increase badly dwindling membership roles. As a result of the great pressure for new members, divisional level officials falsified the number of new memberships obtained.

More typically, in business, it is often observed that divisional managers may intentionally not invest in needed new plant and equipment in order to improve ROI results by reducing the size of the divisor in the ROI calculation of total assets. Or managers may not expend monies for the development of personnel, thereby increasing the dividend of the ROI calculation, net profit. Budgets have also been shown to result in undesirable consequences. For example, pressures associated with budgets may lead to resentment of managers. Inefficiency may result, or pressure from the staff agencies requiring budget preparations may lead to staff-line conflicts.

Some universities restrict the number of days of consulting that business school faculty may have each month. (Of course, nothing is said about the number of days that faculty may play tennis.) By insisting that faculty "get their forty hours in," university administrators fall victim to activity orientation. Professors do not necessarily contribute any more to the university by being there longer. It would seem to make more sense to require certain outputs than to legislate for inferior inputs. If faculty perform, let them have as many days consulting as they desire—as long as they do not miss classes or at least they do not miss an unreasonable number of classes. Other examples could be cited. The point here is this, if organizations have control systems, they must recognize that individuals can find ways to beat them. Furthermore, the implications are that control systems may often be so poorly designed that they are activity and not performance centered. Much of the behavioral literature addresses the identification and removal of such dysfunctional activities.

Summary

In order to place control in proper perspective, it is appropriate to review the events which have transpired prior to activation of control mechanisms. To begin, organizational mission is identified. Next, top management formulates a Master Strategy to accomplish this mission. This strategy usually consists of specific objectives, but less specific, general strategic plans of action to accomplish those objectives. In the ongoing, large organization, multiple strategies, objectives, plans of action, and policies are normally encountered. These may have varying time horizons, degrees of detail, and impacts on resource commitments. In the large, diversified organization, new product and other strategies are treated as capital investment projects. Once objectives and plans are established, an appropriate organization structure to accomplish these objectives must be constructed. Various contingency factors have been identified which affect the choice of structure. As the structure takes form, more specific objectives and plans of action to reach those objectives must be formulated for each of the subsystems in the structure. These include divisions—such as product divisions, projects, and programs; functional areas —such as marketing, production and finance; departments; work groups; and individuals. Once positions are created and authority is delegated, implementation commences. Individuals are hired and the processes of motivation and leadership become instrumental in the success of the organization. Successful implementation is also dependent upon the parcelling of objectives to the various structural subunits. It is these objectives and associated plans and policies which integrate organizational subsystem efforts to achieve strategic success. Budgets play an important role in translating operating plans into financial commitments. The planning process is essentially iterative and periodic but also responsive to strategic issues.

Control techniques are employed to ensure that the mission is accomplished. Three principal types of control systems are created to that end: strategic control, management control, and operational control. Strategic control is concerned with the appropriateness of strategy to mission accomplishment. Such control is an ongoing process. Management control and operational control systems control extensions of the strategy. That is, once the strategy is more specifically defined and implemented, it must be ascertained whether or not the planned results, objectives, were achieved both at the major component or total organizational level, via management control, and at the individual or group level, via operational control. Management and operational control systems are designed then to control the more articulated objectives and plans of action which emanate from strategy. These systems also provide indications of changes in the premises upon which the strategy was formulated, an important contribution.

Much of the organizational control system depends on financial information —information provided by the accounting system. The most sophisticated of the techniques are definitely financial and profit related. But, other types of control measures are being increasingly utilized and do offer some promise, especially the objective oriented techniques. The essence of the various control systems is accountability and responsibility.

Discussion Questions

1. What is controlled by each of the three types of control? Why are three different types of control necessary?
2. Describe each of the strategic/management control measures mentioned in the chapter. Why is each necessary?
3. Try to define in specific terms the objectives of the U.S. Department of Health, Education, and Welfare. Now, how would you measure performance for each of these objectives?
4. How can the dysfunctional consequences of control be overcome?

Footnotes

1. Other types of control exist in the organization. For example, individuals and informal groups may also establish control over operational behavior.
2. Stockholders usually prefer to utilize Return on Equity (ROE) instead of ROI. ROE indicates the extent to which financial leverage is used. Leverage improves stockholders' return on their investment.
3. Top management's performance is sometimes not related to objective accomplishment at all. The president of one major firm had a total compensation in 1974 of close to one million dollars including profit sharing. In 1975, his total compensation was only $250,000 including profit sharing. His adjustment to the financial stress was, of course, difficult, but the point is this, the slump in the economy caused the drop in his company's sales and the resultant slump in his profit sharing. There were no profits to share! The truth is there was very little, if anything, that the president of this organization or any of his executive staff could have done to have helped accomplish the objectives they had established. He and they probably

worked harder and "accomplished more" in that year of little profits than in more profitable years past. The assumptions under which the strategy is formulated sometimes change.

References

Anthony, R. N. *Planning and Control Systems: A Framework for Analysis,* pp. 24, 27, 29. Boston: Harvard University Graduate School of Business Administration, 1965.

Anthony, R. N.; J. Dearden; and R. F. Vancil. *Management Control Systems,* pp. 200–203. Homewood, Ill.: Irwin, 1972.

Argenti, J. *Systematic Corporate Planning.* New York: Wiley, 1974.

Argyris, C. "Human Problems with Budgets." *Harvard Business Review* 31 (January/February 1953): 97–110.

Baker, G. M. N. "The Feasibility and Utility of Human Resource Accounting." *California Management Review,* Summer 1974, pp. 17–23.

Bales. C. F. "Practice of Business Strategic Control: The President's Paradox." *Business Horizons,* June 1977, pp. 17–28.

Berkwitt, G. J. "Do Profit Centers Really Work?" *Management Review,* July/August 1969, pp. 15–20.

Cammann, C., and B. A. Nadler. "Fit Control Systems to Your Managerial Style." *Harvard Business Review,* January/February 1976, pp. 65–72.

Cunningham, J. B. "Approaches to the Evaluation of Organizational Effectiveness." *Academy of Management Review,* July 1977, pp. 463–474.

Dalton, G. W. "Motivation and Control in Organizations." In *Motivation and Control in Organizations,* edited by G. W. Dalton and P. R. Lawrence. Homewood, Ill.: Irwin, 1971.

Dearden, J. "Appraising Profit Center Managers." *Harvard Business Review,* May/June 1968, pp. 80–87.

————. "The Case against ROI Control." *Harvard Business Review,* May/June 1969, pp. 124–135.

Garry, G. A., and M. S. S. Morton. "A Framework for Management Information Systems." *Sloan Management Review,* Fall 1971, pp. 55–70.

Greenwood, W. T. *Business Policy: A Management Audit Approach.* New York: Macmillan, 1967.

————. *Decision Theory and Information Systems.* Cincinnati: South-Western Publishing, 1965.

————. *Management and Organizational Behavioral Theories.* Cincinnati: South-Western Publishing, 1965.

Higgins, J. M. "The Case Method: A More Structured Approach." Paper presented to Southern Management Association, November 1976, at Atlanta, Georgia. In *Expanding Dimensions of Management Thought and Action,* edited by Dennis F. Ray and Thad B. Green. November 1976, pp. 94–96.

Kirchoff, B. A. "Organization Effectiveness Measurement and Policy Research." *Academy of Management Review,* July 1977, pp. 347–354.

Koontz, H., and R. W. Bradspies. "Managing through Feedforward Control." *Business Horizons,* June 1972, pp. 25–36.

"Lavelle's Private War." *Time,* June 26, 1972, p. 14.

Learned, E. P., et al. *Business Policy: Text and Cases,* pp. 22–25. Homewood, Ill.: Irwin, 1969.

Lewis, R. W. *Planning, Managing, and Measuring the Business: A Case Study of Management Planning and Control at General Electric Company.* New York: Controllership Foundation, 1955.

Lindblom, C. E., and D. Braybrooke. *A Strategy of Decision.* New York: Free Press, 1963.

Martindell, J. *The Appraisal of Management.* New York: Harper & Bros., 1962.

Minimer, G. S. *An Evaluation of the Zero Base Budgeting Systems in Government Institutions.* Atlanta: Georgia State University, School of Business, Publishing Services Division, 1975.

Mirvis, P. H., and B. A. Macy. "Human Resources Accounting: A Measurement Perspective." *Academy of Management Review,* April 1976, pp. 74–83.

Mockler, R. J. "Developing the Science of Management Control." *Financial Executive,* December 1967, p. 84.

"The New Public Managers." *Business Week,* April 19, 1976, pp. 150–151.

Ogan, P., and S. Matulich. "Human Resource Accounting: Dead or Alive." *Atlanta Economic Review,* July/August 1976, pp. 13–16.

Pekar, P. P., Jr., and E. H. Burack. "Management Control of Strategic Plans through Adaptive Techniques." *Academy of Management Journal,* March 1976, pp. 79–97.

"A Record Year for Charities, but Where Does the Money Go?" *U.S. News & World Report,* October 18, 1976, pp. 61–64.

Smith, J. H. "An Investigation of the Concept of Management Auditing." Unpublished doctoral dissertation, University of Illinois, 1967.

Tanzola, F. J. "Performance Rating for Divisional Control." *Financial Executive,* March 1975, pp. 20–24.

Tilles, S. "How to Evaluate Corporate Strategy." *Harvard Business Review,* July/August 1963, pp. 111–121.

Voich, D., Jr.; H. J. Mottice; and W. J. Shrode. *Information Systems for Operations and Management.* Cincinnati: South-Western Publishing, 1975.

Chapter 8

The Narrowing of Strategic Alternatives:

Business and Its Environment, Now and in the Future

The thing to do with the future is not to forecast it, but to create it. The objective of planning should be to design a desirable future and to invent ways to bring it about.

Russell Ackoff

In 1946 the federal government's budget of $34.8 billion was 12.8 percent of GNP. A surplus of $3.4 billion existed. By fiscal year 1977, the federal government's budget of $365.6 billion constituted 23.6 percent of GNP. The deficit for fiscal year 1979 is projected to be $40 billion. One-third of the work force is now employed in the not-for-profit sector. In 1974, 1975, and 1976, the monetary policies of the Federal Reserve and the fiscal policies of the federal government directly dictated the level and composition of GNP and the level and composition of business activity. In 1948, in 1957, and in virtually every year since 1963, major federal laws have been passed which directly affect the manner in which businesses conduct their activities. These laws are related to labor relations, wages and prices, consumer protection, the pollution of the physical environment, equal employment opportunity, energy consumption, occupational health and safety, transportation, and numerous other laws written to define the operational limitations of the activities of selected individual industries. The pace of life, especially the change in technology, is accelerating.

In 1946, two countries dominated the world, both economically and militarily. Currently, several countries have substantial economic and/or military power. The United States has lost much of its relative power. While U.S. businesses once controlled their investments in emerging nations, these coun-

Figure 8.1 The Organization—An Organization Process Model

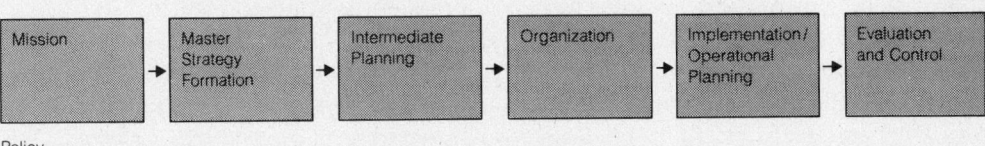

Policy

tries now often choose to expropriate all foreign industry. In 1973, the industrialized world suffered a severe energy crisis as OPEC (Organization of Petroleum Exporting Countries) withheld oil and raised prices substantially. The lack of energy has pointed towards shortages of several raw materials and consumer goods. Finally, in the 1960s and 1970s, considerable pressure was brought upon the strategy formulation processes of many major businesses by various interest groups as they marched and demonstrated in protest against businesses and their conduct of their activities. What do all of these and numerous other similar events have in common? The answer is that business is currently facing an environment which is more demanding, more changeful, and more constraining than any business has previously encountered. And, unfortunately, the future holds little promise of a more favorable situation. The result? The strategic alternatives available to business have been reduced. And if the past is any indicator of the future, business's strategies may become negotiated rather than formulated.

In this chapter selected major environmental factors confronting business are examined. The topics discussed include Technology and Natural Resources; Demographics; Labor; the Economy; International Events; and Society and Government. These factors were chosen for discussion because each has significantly narrowed the strategic alternatives available to business. Many of these issues, both present and future, are concerns of the businesses and other organizations in the cases in Part II of this book. Comments on current and recent events as well as a discussion of possible future scenarios are presented. For most firms, these issues pose problems. But for some businesses, the problems of others are opportunities to be rightfully pursued. Much of the second half of this chapter focuses on business's social responsibilities because social responsibility issues have posed serious problems for most of the firms operating in the United States, including several of the firms depicted in the cases in Part II of this text.

Technology and Natural Resources

Two of the primary concerns of most businesses are technology and natural resources. Many if not most businesses depend on technology for a competitive advantage or, at the very least, for products to sell. The American way of life has become one of consuming more and more of the latest and greatest. Since business is so dependent on technology, it must be ever mindful of technological strategic surprise. In addition, because of the secondary and tertiary impacts of technology, especially upon the natural physical environment, business must guard against future environmental catastrophes such as damage done by DDT. Finally, recent events have revealed that resources are indeed scarce and fixed on a finite planet. When whole industries depend on one resource, for example natural gas, they may disappear overnight if they have not prepared for the future. In summary, a reconstitution of the current economy based on technological innovation and insatiable consumption is occurring. Business must be mindful of its implications and ramifications.

Technology

There are few major industries in this country which do not depend on technology. Television, computers, calculators, airplanes, pacemakers, Corningware, lasers, and photocopy machines are just a few of the many examples of major industrial products which are technology-based. When a major technology comes into existence, an entire new industry may be created, such as occurred with the computer industry or the photocopying industry. Businesses must first of all concern themselves with new technology in their particular industry, that is, the technological developments of their competitors. This concern has often led to industrial espionage. Moreover, the rapid changes occurring in the business technological environment have resulted in an increase in business's efforts to forecast technology. This process involves using many of the judgmental forecasting techniques which are available. Technological forecasting is not easy, nor is it very accurate. With luck, the management of strategic issues surprises is a 50–50 proposition. Most competitors' technologies are unknown until the product is brought to the market.

In an interesting study of the responses to technological threats, Cooper and others found that traditional firms encounter great difficulty in responding successfully to major technological innovations introduced into their industry, especially during maturity or saturation stages of the product life cycle. While their sample was small, for those firms and those industries examined, virtually no well-established firm was able to launch a successful counterthreat to the introduction of a new technology into that industry. This suggests then that even when firms are cognizant of new technologies and respond, the response strategy may be ill-advised. Considering the product life cycle contingency theory, one can see that when new technology is introduced, the introducer gains a distinct competitive advantage over those who do not have this technology. If it is successfully able to capture a considerable share of the market, then the competitor who previously had the market has no advantage over any other firm coming into the market for this new product. Utterback and Abernathy found that firms in early stages of growth tended to introduce more technological innovations than did firms which were very large and complex in nature. This suggests that as firms mature, they may stagnate.

In sum, these studies suggest that technological innovation may be difficult to counteract where a firm is in the mature stage of the product life cycle. The available information also suggests that technology is the source of product innovation, and that new firms and new industries may be quite successful based on this innovation.

With respect to the secondary and tertiary impacts of technology on the physical environment, all organizations, not just business, must engage in technology assessment. DDT, nuclear waste (governmental and commercial), oil spills, and PCBs are all examples of technology out of control. Even less exotic and seemingly innocent wastes or products of industry and/or government can in mass destroy the environment. Such is the case with automobile exhaust fumes, nonbiodegradable detergents, and garbage. From a strategic viewpoint, industry must be responsive not just to the profit motive but also to the greater needs of the society and to the quality of life. This is not just a moral position, but rather hard reality; where business is not responsive to these needs, it has in the past often been forced by society and by government to respond in a manner that is ultimately more costly and less profitable. Technology assessment recognizes the concept that within the ecosystem, all systems are interrelated and that what affects one ultimately affects another. There is a balance to be maintained between concern for economics and concern for the quality of life. At present, concern for both is being expressed.

Business must chart a careful course of action. Such planning is required by the Environmental Protection Agency and other federal and state agency requirements in environmental impact statements for areas of obvious impact. But business and other organizations must be ever alert to the less obvious impacts of their actions. The federal government has already created an Office of Technology Assessment (OTA), and as soon as a major detrimental consequence of technology occurs, the OTA may be expected to grow into a formidable control agency.

Natural Resources

The winter of 1976–1977 strongly reinforced the belief that the United States, as great as it may be, is severely handicapped by the inadequate supply of natural resources, especially natural gas and other forms of energy. But energy is not the only resource in short supply in the United States. Government studies have revealed that several major metals and other primary manufacturing materials are in short supply. Living space in large cities, clean air, and clean water, as well as natural areas of beauty, are also in short supply. And, on a worldwide basis, food is in extremely short supply for most of the population. In short, the earth's inhabitants face an ever increasing population with a limited number of supplies with which to support this multitude. This creates great problems for businesses and for governments. The resource shortage problem will be further compounded in the future as developing nations seek to emulate industrialized nations. One study estimates that by the year 2000 the demand for seven key industrial materials will grow five times and that the United States' share of total consumption of these will decrease significantly. The United States depends upon many developing nations for the provision of these materials, a situation which has led and will continue to lead to a power position in bargaining for the providing nations.

While stockpiles of some of the metals and other materials which are needed may be created, stockpiling of some, for example energy, is a rather difficult task. And while the United States has made some effort to increase the amount of petroleum which can be stored in this country, the U.S. in 1978 is more dependent upon foreign petroleum than it was in 1973 when the first Arab oil embargo came about. And, unfortunately, a federal energy policy is virtually nonexistent some five years after the first embargo. Even with an energy policy, unless a significant technological breakthrough occurs, the energy problem will remain as a detriment to the United States economy and the economies of other industrialized countries for some time.

While energy appears to be the key resource problem of the United States, the inadequate supply of food is the most critical resource shortage for most nations. And while the United States is able to produce a great deal of food, its food technology is a highly energy-dependent technology which could collapse given its current energy situation. Therefore, the United States' model of food production is not widely applicable outside of its borders. It is clear

"We decided on a motto, Mr. Simon . . ."

Source: John Trever. Reprinted courtesy of Sentinel Newspapers (Denver, CO).

that the nations of the world must come to grips with the reality that the supply of materials is not inexhaustible, and that the number of people who are to live upon this planet must be kept to a minimum level if each of the individuals in the world is to enjoy a quality of life which is desirable. The impact upon business of these events will be discussed at length in the International Events section of this chapter, but briefly the consequences to business of overpopulation include: expropriation, bargaining, and political power demonstrations by the underdeveloped nations who possess natural resources.

Finally, there are several impacts which will result from the fact that an economy based on a growing population will end. For example, in the United States where birth control is a common practice, those companies specializing in baby-related products have found it necessary to diversify because of decreased demand in traditional markets. More positively speaking, the opportunity exists, at least for the agricultural portion of business, to make a significant profit while aiding the rest of the world. With regard to the scarcity of other materials, businesses can learn to produce the products which we all have come to depend upon without or with fewer of these materials.

Demographic Changes

Perhaps the most significant of the changes coming in the future which will affect business are the increases in population and the geographic shifts in population as well as in composition by age group. In the United States, for example, *U.S. News and World Report* estimates that by 1984 the population will reach approximately 231 million people from its current 215 million. Children under age 13 as a percentage of population will increase by 3.4 percent; teens ages 13 to 19 will decrease by 13.3 percent; adults ages 20 to 64 will increase by 13.2 percent; and most significantly the elderly age 65 and over will increase by 14.7 as a percentage of the population. It is also clear that many of the people who are currently living in the north, northeast, and midwest will move to the south and to the west, but primarily to the south and southwest and to what is known as the "sun belt." More white-collar jobs will be created in proportion to those in the blue-collar occupations. Incomes may be expected to rise, but it is difficult at this time to determine the impact which inflation will have upon this rise in income. The shifts in market areas, as well as the shifts in the composition of the market, provide growth opportunities and problems for the business community.

On an international basis, the most significant factor is the sheer increase in population, especially in the developing nations. With a current population of over 4 billion, some estimate that this population could double by the year 2000 and most certainly reach 7 billion. The consequences of this enormous population have not even begun to be imagined. One current major impact on the United States has been an increase in the entrance of illegal aliens into this country. These aliens place a significant strain on the taxpayer. On the other hand, the increasing population represents a huge potential market if the developing nations can achieve economic success.

Business and Labor

Organized labor made significant strides in the last few years in securing increased wages and benefits. Their efforts to organize both blue-collar and white-collar workers in the south can be expected to continue. However, significant changes in the attitude of all employees, whether they are organized or not, also occurred during the 1960s and 1970s. Such changes can be expected to continue in the future. These attitudes primarily relate to the nature of the work ethic and to the concept of codetermination in which lower level employees help the organization's management make its decisions, strategic as well as operational. Let us now examine organized labor and attitude change among all employees and how these have affected business and may affect it in the future.

Organized Labor

Organized labor is an extremely powerful determinant of the national economy and of the supportive strategies and policies of the businesses which operate within that economy. There is significant evidence to indicate that in the states in which organized labor is strong—those, for example, in the east, the northwest, midwest, and much of the far west—organized labor successfully elects its candidates to both the state and federal legislatures. And labor's impact upon the Presidential as well as gubernatorial and mayoral races is significant. Some major government decisions in recent years have favored the organized labor movement. As a result, the number of prerogatives which business retained with regard to its personnel practices and even with regard to many of its other decisions has been reduced by this increase in power of organized labor. For many employers, unions have increased the cost of business significantly. Thus a distinct and desirable competitive edge has been gained by those firms which have been able to prevent unions from unionizing their employees, either through provision of adequate satisfiers or by movement to the south. However, as unions organize both blue-collar and white-collar jobs in the south, this sanctuary of unionization will disappear. Several large unions dominate the work force. Among these are the AFL-CIO, the Teamsters, the United Auto Workers, the United Mine Workers, and the National Education Association. One distinct possibility which may emerge in the near future is the placement of union representatives on the corporation's board of directors. This practice is currently being employed in Europe and one might expect this movement to come to the United States eventually. The placement of union representatives on corporate boards can be expected to have a significant impact upon corporate strategic decisions.

Changing Employee Attitudes

One of the most significant factors in the decrease of productivity in the United States has been the changing of the worker's attitude towards work. Most of the surveys which have been made found that the "Protestant work ethic" is diminishing among American workers, especially younger workers. The concept of working hard is no longer acceptable to many. A changing of view from one of the equality of opportunity to the equality of reward regardless of effort is seen in the United States today. This egalitarian approach to society is contradictory to the precepts upon which the United States economy is based. In addition to the above, the expectations of workers in the United States at all levels of the organization have been increased through education. As a result, employees demand more from their jobs. But the reality is that not all jobs can be made exciting and worthwhile. These two key factors combined with the power of unions make the successful implementation of strategy very difficult because they make motivation a very difficult task. The manager today who must motivate employees is highly constrained by numerous conditions many of which he has no control over.

Business and the Economy

Clearly, the most significant changes in the economy are caused by the actions of the federal government, either through its fiscal policies or through the monetary policies of the Federal Reserve Board. In recent years, the deficits in federal spending have caused double digit inflation, and the monetary policies of the Federal Reserve have caused significant unemployment. These actions have dictated the level and composition of business activity. Even the nature of government purchases and expenditures, which has changed significantly within the last ten years, has an impact on business. The gigantic Health, Education and Welfare Department now consumes approximately 44 percent of the federal budget. Most of these expenditures do not go for goods or services but rather constitute transfer payments, taking from the working and giving to the nonworking. As a result, the government receives nothing in return for its money, and business receives no business (except for basic food and shelter businesses). Previously, for example, when Defense Department expenditures constituted 60 percent of the federal budget, much of this money went for procurement of weapons systems and hardware, and business was created. Now the Department of Defense's (DOD) share of the budget is approximately 30 percent. But even in the Defense Department the nature of the purchase is changing. Half of its budget now goes for wages or retirement benefits, neither of which can be compared to the provision of military hardware—weapons systems—such as the DOD used to buy.

The United States in all economic aspects—the consumer, the business, and government—is now an economy based on debt. The City of New York collapsed into financial ruin in 1975 when its debt maintenance, that is its interest, approximated 14 percent of its revenues. In 1976 the federal budget of 365.6 billion dollars contained 37.1 billion dollars for interest, approximately 10 percent of its budget. The burden upon business people as well as upon the other members of society to pay for the various government programs which have been already promised to millions of people, especially those related to social security, Medicare and Medicaid, and federal employee pension programs, is astronomical.

It is clear that government controls the economy and that business must react to its actions. Capital investments, for example, have decreased recently as business reacted to federal monetary policies. This naturally served, as it was intended, to decrease the number of jobs available, which was meant to reduce inflation, but this also increased unemployment and transfer payments. A clear-cut solution to the dilemma is not forthcoming in the immediate future, but it is clear that the future promises more governmental control of the economy. The alternatives available to business are reduced.

Business and International Events

There appears to be one major factor in the international situation which business must be cognizant of now and in the future, and that is the changing power structure, on an economic, political, and social level.

Immediately after World War II, the United States was clearly the most powerful nation in the world since it alone possessed the atomic bomb and it had the most successful economy. In recent years, the United States has witnessed not only a continued reduction of its military strength at home but the continued increase of the military strength of other nations. Furthermore, other economies are proving to be as viable as that of the United States. Japan, some of the European nations, the U.S.S.R., China, India, Brazil, Canada, and the OPEC nations all have significant economic or military power, which, while not equal to that of the United States, with the possible exception of the U.S.S.R., is significant enough to create major spheres of influence which counteract the efforts of the United States both economically and militarily.

With respect to this power structure, many nations are undergoing internal social change with redistributions of wealth being the primary end of this change. Frequently, this is done in a violent way under the banner of communism. Since 1946 literally hundreds of millions of people have become communists. While communism may be dealt with to some degree from an economic perspective, it constricts the ability of United States businesses to engage in trade in foreign countries. Why? Because most communist nations are not willing to trade with the United States on a large scale, especially the new emerging nations. This therefore restricts both the number of potential consumers and the sources of raw materials. Another factor to consider is that regardless of whether it is a communist or other form of dictatorship, dictatorships are the dominant form of government throughout the world. The democracies are limited in number and are on the verge of becoming extinct. Nationalism is everywhere increasing, and United States business usually suffers as the result. Other problems in doing business in foreign countries include cultural differences, lack of local management talent, double taxation, and monetary translations. As a result of the difficulties of coping with the environmental situations in foreign countries, many firms are reassessing the need to operate in many of these countries. These problems have also caused changes in United States foreign policy.

Business and Society, Business and Government: The Question of Social Responsibility

Until the 1960s, business apparently considered itself to be a closed system, that is, one which operated without having significant transactions with those outside the economic system. But the events of the 1960s and the 1970s—the marchers, the protests, the demonstrations, the riots, and the bombings—convinced business that society did not hold the same view. Those in society were concerned with the impact business had upon them. Government responded to society's concerns and created numerous laws which affected the operation of business. The perceived role of business was expanded to include much more than the mere production of goods and services. Business is now expected to contribute to the society in other ways, for example, through the employment of the economically and culturally disadvantaged. Business has learned that it must respond to the demands of the society, especially the demands of those groups which can bring significant pressure upon business.

But this responsiveness leads to a reduction of strategic alternatives. In fact, Murray has suggested that for many businesses, especially those regulated to a great extent by the federal government, or against whom significant action has been taken by large pressure groups, their decisions are more negotiated than they are formulated from within. When major environmental constituents demand certain responses and through the bargaining coalition process the organization essentially complies, then one must indeed question whether or not strategy was formulated or negotiated. In this regard, Murray has proposed the following propositions:

1. The less the effective power of the firm relative to other institutions in its environment with which it must interact, the more the change in strategy of the firm over time will be disjointed and incremental rather than integrated and comprehensive, irrespective of nature and environmental opportunities and threats facing the firm.
2. The greater the degree of fragmentation of decisions of strategic significance to the firm yet external to it, the more the change in the strategy of the firm over time will be disjointed and incremental rather than integrated and comprehensive, irrespective of nature and environmental opportunities and threats facing the firm.

His comments remind us of the concept of incremental decision making and coalition bargaining which was referred to as the adaptive planning mode in Chapter 4. While that chapter stressed internal coalitions, Murray's comments explore adaptive planning as the result of powerful external influences. Murray continues in his paper with an examination of a public utility and its frustration in attempting to comply with requirements of its environment— specifically environmentalists and the federal government. His examination of this utility and its problems supported both of the above hypotheses. He also raised the question as to the need for many organizations to often comply with what seem to be irrational and/or contradictory regulations and requirements of different groups, or more commonly, requirements levied upon them by different agencies of the federal government. Often even within the same agency of the federal government, differing requirements may be issued. Murray has raised an important issue here as to whether or not in fact strategy under these circumstances—circumstances which are increasingly common for more and more firms and industries—can be adequately described as formulated. Let us now explore the issue of social responsibility to better determine its content and impacts.

Business's Social Responsibilities

One of the major problems with which business has been confronted is the inability to define exactly what constitutes corporate social responsibility. Numerous pressure groups such as the NAACP, the Sierra Club, the state and federal government, and Ralph Nader have made varying demands on the organization. Many times these demands are contradictory. The organization is caught in a dilemma: To whom does it respond? Clearly, it must respond to the law and to those who can bring the most pressure upon the organization and/or who have been able to define their demands most explicitly. But business cannot react to all of the demands with which it is confronted, nor should it. Demands are made of some businesses that are not made of others. Importantly, society's major demands have been fairly well-defined, at least legally. Business has legally required social responsibilities for protecting the natural physical environment, providing equal employment opportunity, properly treating the consumer, maintaining satisfactory relations with government, and practicing business in an ethical manner. In addition, energy conservation has become an important and major responsibility of business as well as the nation as a whole and is likely to be further legislated during 1979 or 1980. Interestingly, many individuals are now concerned that business renew its efforts to produce goods and services at a profit, and more specifically to increase productivity and provide jobs. The demands seem to have come full circle.

Table 8.1 presents a list of the major federal laws which have been passed in each of several major areas, or whose provisions have been enforced more stringently in recent years. As can be seen by this table, in each of several major categories, business has had many of its strategic mission alternatives limited both in terms of competitive and supportive components. Further, these laws have served to increase business's strategic issues activity. Alternatives may be limited additionally through the process of enforcing these laws since enforcement varies from law to law and geographic area to geographic area. For example, with regard to the mission supportive element of production, almost all manufacturing organizations have been affected by the en-

Table 8.1   Laws Affecting Business

Recent Laws

Environment

Federal Insecticide, Fungicide, and Rodenticide Act of 1947
Federal Water Pollution Control Act of 1956
Clean Air Act of 1963
Solid Wastes Disposal Act of 1965, as amended
Water Quality Act of 1965
A federal court broadly interpreted the provisions of
    "The Refuse Act of 1899" in 1966
Air Quality Act of 1967
National Environmental Policy Act of 1970
Noise Abatement and Control Act of 1970
Resource Recovery Act of 1970
Clean Air Act Amendments of 1970

Equal Employment Opportunity

Equal Pay Act of 1963 as amended by the Education Amendments of 1972
Title VII of the Civil Rights Act of 1964 as amended by the Equal
    Employment Opportunity Act of 1972

Presidential Executive Orders 11246, 11375, 11478, 11758. (1967-75)
Age Discrimination in Employment Act of 1967
Sections 500 and 503 of the Rehabilitation Act Amendments of 1974
Veteran's Employment and Readjustment Act of 1972, as amended

Consumerism

Meat Inspection Act of 1906
Federal Food, Drug and Cosmetic Act 1938, as amended by presidential executive
  order: The Office of Consumer Affairs 1964
National Traffic and Motor Vehicle Safety Act of 1966 as amended
Fair Packaging and Labeling Act of 1966
Federal Cigarette Labeling and Advertising Act 1967
Consumer Credit Protection Act 1968
Toy Safety Act 1969
Truth in Lending Act of 1969
Consumer Product Safety Act of 1972
Fair Credit Billing Act of 1974
The Equal Credit Opportunity Act of 1974
Consumer Product Warranties Act of 1975
Consumer Goods Pricing Act of 1975
Fair Trade Laws repealed, 1977

Energy

Federal Energy Administration Act of 1974
Energy Reorganization Act of 1974 (established ERDA)
Energy Supply and Environmental Coordination Act of 1974
Energy Policy and Conservation Act of 1975

Economics

Economic Stabilization Act of 1970, as amended

Labor

Occupational Safety and Health Act of 1970
Employee Retirement Income Security Act 1974

Older Major Laws Still Affecting Business

Interstate Commerce Act of 1887
Sherman Act 1890
Pure Food and Drug Act 1906
Sixteenth Amendment 1913 (income tax)
Clayton Act 1914
Federal Trade Commission Act 1914
Federal Communications Act 1934
Social Security Act 1935
Wagner Act 1935
Robinson-Patman Act 1936
Fair Labor Standards Act 1938 (Wage and Hour Act)
Taft-Hartley Act 1947
Anti-Merger Act 1950
Automobile Information Disclosure Act of 1958
Landrum-Griffin Act 1959

vironmental protection requirements and have suffered significant additions to production costs. Also, virtually all organizations of any size have had to make comprehensive changes in their personnel practices as the result of equal opportunity laws. For many organizations, personnel practices have been dictated by federal government agencies as the result of these laws. The consumer issue has resulted in numerous recalls of automobiles to Detroit and other products to other manufacturers in other cities. And the energy problem and its laws have caused Detroit to completely redesign the automobile, making it lighter, smaller, and more fuel efficient.

But these laws are not the only government restraints on business. Table 8.2 indicates some of the regulatory agencies whose primary functions involve the control and observation of business. As can be seen, the number of agencies and individuals at the federal level whose function is to regulate business is extremely high. Not included are state regulatory agencies, which would, for example, control all public utilities; the state environmental protection agencies, which are the true enforcement mechanisms of the federal environmental law; the state consumer protection agencies; all of the various state agencies related to the building of houses for the housing industry; and all the various licensing and permit-granting—state, federal, and local—organizations. These agencies as well as the various pressure groups such as the NAACP, the Sierra Club, and Ralph Nader and his group have significant impact upon the strategy formulation of many businesses. As can be seen in some of the cases presented in Part II of this text, many times it is necessary to change the major plans of actions known as strategy in order to accommodate the demands of these organizations. Many times, companies have abandoned plans or strategies because of such demands. It should be noted that sometimes the demands of these organizations were appropriate, given the greater requirements of the society. Sometimes business had taken actions which were highly questionable with respect to overall benefit to society. Regardless of the moral perspective, these external forces act as constraints. With respect to constraints in the future, the move towards national planning is evident. The federal government at both legislative and executive levels has proposed that national planning be instituted. There is also evidence that some businesses would be receptive to such actions as a way of evening out the business cycle and as a way of forcing the federal government to better define its intentions with regard to certain industry actions. Some legislators have even suggested that business ought to be allowed to make only a certain percentage of profit. The ramifications of such a bill would be unbelievable.

Many legislators have called for business to do more than it is currently doing in solving the economic problems of the country. The tax burden related to social security can be expected to increase for both the employer and the employee. In fact, by the year 1987 each will be paying approximately $3,000 a year into social security. The tax burden to business can be expected to increase in general because of the continued transfer payment situation

Table 8.2   Number of Employees with Regulatory Functions as of June 30, 1975

Agriculture Department—animal, plant health inspection; Packers and Stockyards Administration	14,054
Environmental Protection Agency	9,203
Food and Drug Administration	6,405
Labor Department—employment standards, occupational safety	4,715
Treasury Department—Bureau of Alcohol, Tobacco and Firearms	3,760
Federal Energy Administration	3,125
Interior Department—mine safety	2,851
National Labor Relations Board	2,454
Equal Employment Opportunity Commission	2,189
Securities and Exchange Commission	2,086
Transportation Department—highway and rail safety	2,079
Interstate Commerce Commission	2,061
Federal Communication Commission	1,971
Federal Trade Commission	1,569
Federal Power Commission	1,320
Other Agencies	3,602
Total Federal Regulators	63,444

Source: "The Regulators: They Cost You $130 Billion a Year," reprinted from *U.S. News & World Report*, June 30, 1975, p. 24. Copyright 1975 U.S. News & World Report, Inc.

which indicates that by the year 2000, of the available people of a working age who are not nonworking wives or dependents, half of these will be supported by the other half. It is clear also that international trade and international business will be affected greatly by government legislation. In sum, the future holds little promise of less constraint. Business's future appears to be one of greater regulation and control by federal, state, and local governments, especially the federal government, and of an ever increasing insistence on this control by the society.

The Formulation of Appropriate Corporate Social Policy

Many corporate social policies are general and not as specific in content as they should be. While not all contingencies can be anticipated, social issues have usually given sufficient warning to allow for development of more than "do good" statements. Many firms have been noticeably deficient in planning to meet external societal pressures. Appropriate corporate social policy should result from the same sort of rigorous analysis required of other anticipated corporate interactions with internal and external factors affecting the accomplishment of organizational goals. Social pressures change but so do other elements in the corporate environment. Change must be accepted and adapted to. Otherwise, the costs to the firm will be high, both in terms of immediate measurable dollars and those nebulous factors such as image,

Source: John Trever, Albuquerque Journal. Reprinted courtesy of Albuquerque Journal.

morale, and productivity which eventually affect profits. With proper planning and control, corporate social problems can be realistically and satisfactorily solved. Corporate leadership must be appropriate to the challenge of social responsibility. This means that business's leaders must be appreciative of value orientations other than those economic values traditionally held. Societal responsiveness and ethical considerations must be emphasized. Most importantly, business must remember that the consequence of social power is social responsibility.

Summary

This chapter has outlined some of the major environmental challenges confronting business today and in the immediate future. While many more such challenges could have been discussed, for example, inflation, interest rates, and international competition, the trend is clear. The strategic alternatives available to business are narrowing. Strategy is no longer completely formulated by top management strategists. Rather strategies are often negotiated with those external to the firm—government and various pressure groups. Even when not negotiated, the strategy is formulated in a highly constrained environment. It is clear that the number of threats is increasing and the available alternatives are decreasing. The future apparently promises only more of the same for business. But business operates in an environment. It can change it or it can live with it.

Discussion Questions

1. What is meant by the statement that strategy is becoming more negotiated than it is formulated?
2. What are the major environmental threats to most businesses? In what sense are they threats?
3. What is U.S. business's future internationally? Within the U.S.?
4. What are business's social responsibilities?
5. If you were the president of General Motors, what would be your social responsibility policies?

References

Cooper, A. C., et al. "Strategic Responses to Technological Threats." *Proceedings*: *Academy of Management*, 1974.

Higgins, J. M. "A Social Audit of Equal Employment Opportunity Programs." *Human Resource Management*, Fall 1977, pp. 2–7.

"A Look at Trends Now Shaping the Future." *U.S. News & World Report*, November 29, 1976, pp. 50–51.

Murray, E. A., Jr. "Limitations on Strategic Alternatives." *Proceedings*: *Academy of Management*, 1976, pp. 140–144.

"U.S. Red Ink." *U.S. News & World Report*, January 24, 1977, p. 75.

Utterback, J. M., and M. J. Abernathy. "The Test of a Conceptual Model Linking States in Firms' Process and Product Innovation." Working Paper Number 74–23. Boston: Harvard School of Business, 1974.

Van Dam, A. "The Future of Global Business Forecasting." *Business Horizons*, August 1977, pp. 46–50.

"A Worldwide Hunger for Materials." *Business Week*, May 5, 1973, p. 56.

Case Studies

The cases are arranged according to
the model presented in the text.
Cases on strategy formation are
followed by cases on intermediate
planning, organization, implementation, evaluation, control, and
international business.

Introduction to the Case Method

We learn best by doing.
Anonymous

The content of a strategic management and organizational policy course may vary substantially given the diversity of the objectives of this course. (See the preface for a discussion of these objectives.) However, since this is a text and case book, it is obvious that I have chosen these two instruments as the most appropriate method for teaching these diversified subjects to the majority of students. Having reviewed strategic management and organizational policy through the use of text material, it is now time to apply this knowledge to the cases. But, first, an introduction to the case method is in order. In the following pages the case method is reviewed and some of its dimensions are explored. The intent is to acquaint you as a student with the case method in order that you will be able to better utilize the cases which follow.

The case method has become a popular tool in teaching strategic management and organizational policy because it brings realism to the classroom. The case method involves the examination of an actual organizational event or series of events. The depicted situations usually involve statements in which problems or opportunities are contained. These problems (internal weaknesses or external threats) or opportunities must be recognized, identified, and solved. In short, strategic decisions must be made. The events are described in textual material, usually 15 to 30 pages in length, commonly referred to as a case. Longer and shorter cases are frequently encountered. Cases are usually written by management consultants or by other individuals who were involved in the problem. Cases are almost always derived from real life occurrences, but occasionally cases may be hypothetical. Not infrequently, the identity of the firm involved will be disguised in order to protect the firm from unwanted publicity. The case method is especially useful because it adds realism to classroom discussions. Reading theories and concepts is the beginning of knowledge, but in order to complete the student's education, it is believed necessary that some practical experience be gained.

While attaining access to internal corporate information is difficult for the average student, it is relatively easy for the student to observe an organization through the use of the case method. The case method as a presentation of a real situation does have one weakness, and that is that the student is not allowed to interact with the data, that is, the student does not change the data nor does the data change. However, this is not a major problem, and some actions can be taken to reduce its effects—for example changing certain assumptions of the case. The case method is predicated on the belief that one learns by doing.

Cases are occasionally accompanied by notes which are usually industry data and survey information to be used with more than one case.

Objectives

The case method objectives are:

1. to add realism to the classroom.
2. to cause the student to integrate knowledge of the functional areas and to employ principles of strategic management.
3. to improve the decision making ability of the individual; this occurs primarily through having the individual practice making decisions.
4. to cause the individual to see the interrelationships of facts and what they mean in a practical as well as theoretical sense.
5. to cause individuals to be self-assertive. This occurs when the student is required to respond in class on the basis of attracting the professor's attention through both physical and mental assertion. That is, if the student does not "seize the floor," then he will probably never be heard from and will not do well in the course.
6. to improve an individual's communication skills.

Approaches

There are two general approaches to the case method based on the preclassroom preparation. In the first, the student has a format which he follows in analyzing a case. He reads the case and attempts to identify the principal problems and principal factors involved in these problems by utilizing a specific list of predetermined key factors which are believed relevant to proper management functioning. This is referred to as the "structured" approach. In the second approach, the individual is not provided with a particular format but is left to derive his own methodology. This is commonly referred to as an "unstructured" approach. Individual instructors will indicate which is to be utilized. Case analyses for class may be either written or oral, or a combination of these.

Types of Organizations Encountered

There tend to be two primary types of organizations, according to size, which are encountered in cases: the large national or multinational, and the entrepreneurship or small business. They tend to have differing types of problems and opportunities, and these require somewhat different types of resultant analyses. And there are two primary types of organizations encountered according to the mission: profit and nonprofit. Again, these often have differing types of problems and opportunities.

Planning Level of Problems, Opportunities Encountered

Most of the problems and opportunities which confront the case analyst occur at the strategy formation level. However, in this text, a limited number of cases are presented in the other stages of the planning cycle, so that their interrelationships may be interpreted. In fact most of the cases involve multiple stages since these stages are so highly interdependent. For example, control information points to the need to reformulate strategy, strategy leads to structure, and so forth. One case on international business is included.

Classroom Pedagogy

Group versus Individual Analyses. There are two ways in which individuals may engage in the preclass and class analysis of a case. The first is in a group. This method is appropriate where students are able to come together for lengthy periods of time in order to analyze the case. As with all group activities, there may be those who work on the group's project and those who do not. Appropriate peer group evaluations should be accomplished. Working in a group does not require conformity. Here too, strength of personality may be developed. Prior to the group analysis, the individual should go through the recommended steps of analysis which conclude this introduction. In the second method, the individual studies an entire case by himself and must cover all facets of the case individually.

Student Classroom Participation. In some classes, students must seize the floor in order to be heard. Here it becomes imperative that the individual become self-assertive. The student must also realize that he may make a mistake. He must be willing to learn to accept criticism and/or not make mistakes in judgment (a tough task for anyone). The student should anticipate that the instructor will attempt to find those who disagree with his position and analyses. The risks of nonassertion (failing grades) are, of course, somewhat motivating. Competition increases to some extent the amount of analysis which occurs. A student will be somewhat reluctant to expose himself with a quick analysis. The quality of work increases proportionately to the risks. Specific questions may be asked of a student on a nonvoluntary basis. Similar comments on the need to be prepared as were noted in the above discussion are appropriate. Or in a third approach, student preparation may be read and debated in class. Some combination of these three is common.

Instructor's Role. Normally the instructor leads the discussion; he may also participate in it. He is usually viewed as a resource person.

Preclassroom Analysis. There is never enough data in any real life situation and there is therefore never enough data in any case to make a perfect decision. One of the most important factors to remember is that decision making is a function of time and data availability. No one ever has enough time or enough data. Therefore the common criticism by students that the case may leave out data is not an acceptable one. Students must realize they have a certain amount of data and that is all the data they have. This is like the real world. Students are able and allowed to undertake extra research, the more the better. But for most cases the decision can and should be made based on the data presented. Furthermore, while research of timely information, especially industry information, is encouraged, students should not seek to find out what happened subsequent to the time of the case.

The Answers. There are no right answers to a case situation. There are, however, better answers. The only true test of the decision is in its implementation and, unfortunately, using the case method we do not have a chance to implement our decisions. The right answer is an unknown. Only the better answer can be determined. Students who make decisions based on insufficient analysis usually come up with worse answers and correspondingly worse grades. It is the facts upon which decisions are made that are important; several acceptable solutions may be derived.

Degree of Difficulty. Sometimes the point of the case will be obvious. At other times it will be necessary for the individual to read, reread, and reanalyze the case in order to determine what is the major problem or opportunity. Often cases will have a series of numerous technique problems which are not the major problem but which are only symptoms of a major problem.

Viewpoint. One factor to be considered is the viewpoint of the student. Should he envision himself as a consultant or should he view himself as a member of the organization? Various perspectives with respect to how easily solutions might be implemented are related to the choice of viewpoints.

Results. One important factor to consider is this: in many situations, no matter what the decision, the results may very well be ineffective. There are many factors, especially factors which may occur in the environment, which are, or which will be, completely out of the control of the organization and for which there are no correct decisions. There may be only decisions which allow an organization to minimize the loss which it might incur.

Strength of Analyses. Most students will not uncover all of the factors which will eventually be revealed in the classroom discussions. This constitutes one of the most important factors of learning which is gained from the case method—that there is always something which the individual will overlook. This is very much like real life.

Perspective. For both the student and the instructor, the case method is a difficult process. In traditional learning, students have been assigned the roles of listeners and nonparticipants. The case method requires thinking, action, and participation in order for it to be effective. In order for a student to receive a good grade in most classes, he must participate. He must think, he must analyze, he must conceptualize, he must relate facts. He must, in short, achieve the higher levels of learning as opposed to being merely a receptive and passive member of a lecturer's audience. The role of a strategic manager is one which would demand this kind of behavior.

Case Bias

One must be aware of the inherent bias in a case. The case is related as it is perceived by someone else, the case writer. The reader of a case does not have the benefit of knowing how the information was obtained or the factors which the individual considered in writing the case. While facts may appear to be facts, this is not always so. Their presence or absence is a critical factor as is their manner of presentation. Occasionally facts may be distorted, especially facts related to statements about the personalities of individuals. Often individuals' personalities are the key problems in a case, and yet the reader can never be sure that the statements about personalities of those in the case are exactly accurate.

Use of Knowledge

It is the considered opinion of this author that the strategic management theories and concepts which have been learned by the student should be used in analyzing cases.

A Suggested Course of Action

1. Read the case; become familiar with the situation. If possible, put it aside for a while, then—
2. Reread the case and:
   a. Summarize any pertinent information.
   b. Pay special attention to information in tables and figures, for example, financial statements, sales figures, etc.
   c. Read the questions at the end of each case. Do they give clues as to what to do next? What are these clues?
3. Establish a decision framework:
   a. What is the major area of concern—strategy formation, intermediate planning, organization, implementation, evaluation, or control?
   b. What are the organization's missions, objectives, policies, and strategies?
   c. What are the decision constraints?
4. If this is a strategy formation problem, normally you would:
   a. Determine current Master Strategy.
   b. Identify strengths, weaknesses, threats, and opportunities (SWTO).
   c. If certain substrategies require analyses, perform these.
5. Ask yourself—Do I really understand what's happening? If not, retrace your steps.
6. Search for and delineate alternatives. If the strategy must be reformulated, follow the strategic management process procedures discussed in

this text. Be especially careful to match strengths and weaknesses against threats and opportunities. The alternative generation process involves examining the basic action strategies which are available and choosing the most appropriate. Next, the marketing strategy should be generated. In both of these actions, the product life cycle should be observed for its impacts. Finally, supportive and strategic issues strategies should be formulated. Table 3.1 lists factors which should be considered in formulating strategy while Table 5.3 lists classical marketing strategies. Both of these tables provide information for each stage of the product life cycle. Table 5.4 suggests possible supportive strategies by product life cycle stage. Numerous additional possible strategies exist, but these tables are a good place to begin. If these tables fail to yield what you consider to be appropriate strategies, then use your creativity to formulate additional ones.

7. Choose the appropriate alternatives. The evaluation process involves examining proposed alternatives to determine how well they match SWTO, mission, objectives, policies, the dominant planning mode, and other relevant criteria. The GE Strategy Matrix or Stoplight is one approach which may be used in this endeavor where multiple alternatives are available. The evaluation process is partly rational, partly intuitive, and partly skill. In many situations, it will also be partly social. Once choices are made, the total Master Strategy should be viewed for compliance with the strategic control items noted in Chapter 7. Think through its consequences.

8. Set priorities for your solutions.

9. Be prepared to implement these decisions, i.e., consider if they would and could be implemented. Eliminate "pie in the sky" solutions and marshal sufficient evidence to defend your solutions. Do your solutions solve the problems or exploit the opportunities?

10. If written or class presentation is required, be professional. Use charts, handouts, slides, etc.

The above is a suggested series of general actions. Questions at the end of each case may direct that other actions be taken. The instructor may also choose other courses of action. Use what you have learned, for example:

1. Determine stage of product life cycle.
2. What are the contingency factors for this stage?
3. What actions are appropriate?
4. Use the strategy matrix where applicable (GE Stoplight).
5. Make certain you determine what it is that your decision is supposed to accomplish.
6. Review the strategic control checklists in Chapter 7.

The Cases*

The cases on strategy formation emphasize major strategic problems and opportunities encountered by both large and small organizations in a variety of industries and situations. These cases generally have several major issues to be considered and several problems or opportunities to be solved or taken advantage of.

The cases on intermediate planning deal with the problems encountered by subsystems within a larger organization as they attempt to comply with overall corporate strategy and policy.

In the organization section of cases, the problems encountered by two firms as they attempt to cope with success and its related growth-strategy-structure problems are presented.

The implementation cases deal with the efforts of three organizations to carry out the strategies and policies which guide them.

In the evaluation and control section, the two cases reveal just how catastrophic inappropriate and inadequate control can be.

The international business case poses an interesting and all too common problem faced by the multinational firm.

By arranging the cases in this order, the student may see just how strategy becomes results. The cases were carefully selected for their subject areas of interest and recognition. The following is a listing of the cases giving the order in which they appear.

Strategy Formation

1. Wall Drug
2. A Note on Alternative Energy Sources
3. Solar Enterprises Incorporated (SEI)—A Solar Energy Company
4. Sebring-Vanguard, Inc.: The CitiCar
5. Artisan Industries
6. Jones Foundry Company
7. Pamida Incorporated
8. Note on the Fast Food Industry
9. Wendy's International, Inc. "Old Fashioned Hamburgers"
10. A Strategic Problem (A Student Generated Case)
11. The U.S. Brewery Industry, 1974
12. Adolph Coors Company
13. Miller Brewing Company
14. Vail Associates at Beaver Creek

*All cases are designed to be used as a basis for class discussion rather than to illustrate either effective or ineffective handling of an administrative situation. Questions added to cases contributed by other authors are this author's and not those of the original contributors.

1/Wall Drug

James D. Taylor,
Robert L. Johnson,
and Gene B. Iverson

Ted and Bill Hustead, primary owners and managers of Wall Drug, in Wall, South Dakota, faced a serious decision in the winter of 1973. Should they invest heavily in stock for the tourist season of 1974, anticipating an increase in business, or should they buy conservatively? Should they continue to expand Wall Drug in the future or should they seek some other alternative? Although the Hustead's Wall Drug had experienced unprecedented growth for the last 27 years and had been written up in newspapers and magazines for several years, times seem to be more precarious now. Rising gasoline prices, periodic shortages, and gasoline stations closing, trouble with the American Indian Movement (AIM) at Wounded Knee, and the highway beautification laws threatening more of Wall Drug's famous roadside signs, seemed to threaten tourist travel and Wall Drug in particular.

The History of the Wall Drug—Free Ice Water.[1] In June of 1969 *America Illustrated*, the United States Information Agency publication in the Soviet Union and Poland, featured a story entitled "The Lure and Fascination of Seven Fabulous Stores," by Mal Oettinger. The seven stores were Macy's, Wall Drug Store, Rich's, L. L. Bean, Inc., Neiman-Marcus, Gump's, and Brentano's.

In the later summer of 1973, the *Wall Street Journal* carried a story about Wall Drug. These are but two of the many feature articles about Wall Drug that have appeared in newspapers and magazines all over North America. The *Wall Street Journal* article is typical of those appearing over the years and accurately describes much of the history and operation of this famous establishment that has become an institution of South Dakota.

Ted Hustead is a pharmacist who graduated from the University of Nebraska, class of 1929, at the age of 27. He and his wife Dorothy, a Colman, South Dakota girl, bought the drugstore in Wall in December, 1931. Dorothy and Ted and their four-year-old son Bill lived in the back twenty feet of the store.

---

1. Dana Close Jennings, *Free Ice Water: The Story of Wall Drug* (Aberdeen, South Dakota: North Plains Press, 1969), p. 26.

Source: This case was prepared at the University of South Dakota. Reprinted by permission. Distributed by the Intercollegiate Case Clearing House, Soldiers Field, Boston, Mass. 02163. All rights reserved to the contributors. Printed in the U.S.A.

Wall in 1931 is ably described by Dana Close Jennings in his book about Wall Drug entitled *Free Ice Water*.[2]

Wall, then: a huddle of poor wooden buildings, many unpainted, housing some 300 desperate souls; a 19th century depot and wooden water tank; dirt (or mud) streets; few trees; a stop on the railroad, it wasn't even that on the highway. US 16 and 14 went right on by, as did the tourists speeding between the Badlands and the Black Hills. There was nothing in Wall to stop for.

The drugstore and the town of Wall did not prosper until Dorothy Hustead conceived the idea of placing an advertising sign on the highway to advertise free ice water. Ted put the sign up and cars were turning off at Wall to go to the drugstore before he got back to the store. This turning point in the history of Wall Drug took place on a blazing hot Sunday afternoon in the summer of 1936.

Ted recognized the value of the signs and began putting them up all along the highways leading to Wall. In an article in *Good Housekeeping* in 1951, the Husteads' signs were called "the most ingenious and irresistible system of signs ever devised."[3]

During World War II, Wall Drug signs began to be put up by servicemen from South Dakota who were familiar with the sign advertising in South Dakota. Later some servicemen wrote back requesting signs. During World War II one appeared in Paris: "Wall Drug Store 4,278 miles (6,951 kilometers)." They later appeared in many places, including the 38th parallel in Korea, the North and South Pole areas, and Vietnam jungle trails. These signs led to news stories and publicity which further increased the notoriety of the store.

The sales and size of Wall Drug have grown spectacularly since the 1940s. From 1931 until 1941 the building was rented and was on the west side of Main Street. In 1941 an old lodge hall, which acted as the gymnasium in Wasta (15 miles west of Wall), was bought and moved to become the new Wall Drug. It was placed on the east side of Main across the street from the original store.

When World War II ended, tourist travel greatly increased and the Wall Drug signs brought so many people into Wall Drug that the Husteads claim they were embarrassed because the facilities were not large enough. There were no modern restrooms even. Sales in the 1940s after the war were from $150,000 to $200,000 per year.

In 1951 Bill Hustead, the son of Ted and Dorothy, now a pharmacy graduate of South Dakota State College at Brookings, joined his father in the store. In 1953 Wall Drug was expanded into a former storeroom to the south. This became the Western Clothing Room. In 1954 they built an outside store on the south of the Western Clothing Room. This was accompanied by a

2. Ibid., p. 26.
3. Ibid., p. 42.

30 percent increase in business. In 1956 a self-service cafe was added on the north side of the store. In the early 1950s sales were in the $300,000 per year range and by the early 1960s had climbed to $500,000.

In the early 1960s Ted and his son Bill began seriously thinking of moving Wall Drug to the highway. The original Highway 16 ran by the north side of Wall, about two blocks from the store. It was later moved to run by the south side of Wall, also about two blocks from the drugstore. In the late 1950s and early 1960s a new highway was built running by the south side of Wall paralleling the other highway. Ted and Bill Hustead were considering building an all new Wall Drug along with a gasoline filling station alongside the new highway just where the interchange at Wall was located.

They decided to build the gasoline station first, and did so. It is called Wall Auto Livery. When the station was finished they decided to hold up on the new store, and then decided to continue expanding the old store in downtown Wall. This was a fortunate decision, since soon after that the new interstate highway replaced the former new highway and the new interchange ran through the site of the proposed new Wall Drug.

Since they decided to stay in their present site in 1963 a new fireproof construction coffee shop was added where the present soda fountain is on the front just north of the main store.

In 1964 a new kitchen, again of fireproof construction, was added just in back of the cafe and main store. In 1964 and 1965 offices and the new pharmacy were opened on the second floor over the kitchen.

In 1968 the back dining room and backyard across the alley were added. This was followed in 1971 with the Art Gallery Dining Room.

By the late 1960s and early 1970s annual sales volume went to $1,000,000.

In 1971 the Husteads bought the theater that bordered their store on the south. They ran it as a theater through 1972. In early 1973 they began construction of a new addition in the old theater location. This is called the "Mall." By the summer of 1973 the north part of the Mall was open for business. The south side was not ready yet. That year the Wall Drug grossed $1,600,000, which was an increase of about 20 percent over 1972. Bill believes the increase was due to their new Mall addition.

The Mall. The development of the Mall represents a distinct change in the development of Wall Drug. All previous development had been financed out of retained earnings or short-term loans. In effect each addition was paid for as it was built or added.

The owners of Wall Drug broke with their previous method of expansion when they built the Mall by borrowing approximately $250,000 for 10 years to finance the Mall and part of 20 large new signs which stand 660 feet from the interstate highway.

During the last half of the 1960s and early 1970s Bill Hustead had thought about and planned the concept of the Mall. The Mall was designed as a town within a large room. The main strolling mall was designed as a main street with each store or shop designed as a two-story, frontier Western building. The Mall is thus like a re-created Western town. Inside the stores various woods are used in building and paneling. Such woods as pine from Custer, South Dakota, American black walnut, gumwood, hackberry, cedar, maple, and oak are among the various woods used. The store fronts are re-creations of building fronts found in old photos of Western towns in the 1880s. Many photos, paintings, and prints line the walls. These shops stock products that are more expensive than the souvenir merchandise found in most other parts of the store. The shops are more like Western boutiques.

The northern part of the Mall was open for business shortly after July 10, 1973. In the fall of 1973, Bill was uncertain as to whether or not to open the south side.

The Store Operation. By the end of 1973 the Husteads were operating Wall Drug and Wall Auto Livery as two separate corporations. Financial statements for 1972 and 1973 may be found in the Exhibits. Within these two corporations are trailer rental and interest income. The theater was operated only until the Mall was built on the theater site. Sales for their corporations were at an all-time high in 1973.

The two corporations are mainly dependent on tourist travel. Wall is a small town of 786 people as of 1970. The economic base of the town is primarily built around the Wall Drug and is dependent on tourist business also.

Wall is situated right on the edge of the Badlands and 52 miles east of Rapid City. For miles in either direction, people in autos have been teased and tantalized by Wall Drug signs. Many have heard of the place through stories in the press, or have heard their parents speak of the Wall Drug. In the summer of 1963, in a traffic count made on the highway going by Wall, 46% were found to be eastbound and 54% were westbound. Of the eastbound traffic, 43% turned off at Wall. Of the westbound traffic, 44% turned off at Wall.

When people arrive at Wall (those westbound usually after driving 40 miles or more through the Badlands) they are greeted by the large Wall Drug sign on the interchange and an 80 foot high, 50 ton statue of a dinosaur. The business district of Wall is one block long and is about three blocks from the interchange. The town has eleven motels and a number of gasoline filling stations.

Cars from many states line the street in front of and several blocks on either side of the drugstore. Tabulation of state licenses from autos and campers parked in front of Wall Drug and in the camper and trailer park one block from Wall Drug on Wednesday, June 4, 8 A.M. and 10 A.M., resulted in the following:

Neighboring States and South Dakota (Nonlocal)	37%
South Dakota, Local County	32
Balance of States and Canada	31

The store occupies 31,217 square feet with 11,918 square feet of storage space and 960 square feet of office.

Wall Drug is more than a store. It is a place of amusement, family entertainment, a gallery of the West, a gallery of South Dakota history, and a place that reflects the heritage of the West. Nostalgia addicts have a field day in the Wall Drug. Children are delighted with animated life-size cowboys singing, a tableau of an Indian camp, a stuffed bucking horse, a six foot rabbit, a stuffed buffalo, old slot machines that pay out a souvenir coin for 10¢, statues of cowboys, a coin operated quick-draw game, and souvenirs by the roomful, which make up some of the attractions.

The food is inexpensive and good, and although as many as 10,000 people might stream through on a good day, the place is air conditioned and comfortable. The dining rooms are decorated with beautiful wood paneling, paintings of Western art are displayed, and Western music plays. One can dine on buffalo burgers, roast beef or steak, 5¢ coffee or select wine, beer, or a "Jack Daniels" from the rustic, but beautiful, American walnut bar.

Wall Drug does most of its business during the summer months. Sales for June 1973 were $258,000; July, $423,000; and August, $414,500. April ran about $30,000 and May, $100,000. September and October are fair months when late tourists and hunters travel through.

About one-fourth of the sales in Wall Drug is food, plus about 5% to 10% for beverages and the soda fountain. (This varies with the weather.) About 10% to 15% is jewelry, 15% clothing and hats, 35% to 40% for souvenirs, and 5% to 10% for drugs, drug sundries, and prescriptions.

The store is manned by a crew of about 150 people, 45 of whom are college girls and 15 to 20 college boys who work there in the summer. Student help is housed in homes that have been bought and made into dormitory apartments for these young people. There is a modern swimming pool for their use also. The clerks are trained to be courteous, informed, and pleasant.

Merchandise Ordering. The inventory in Wall Drug varies from around $300,000 in the summer peak to a low around $80,000 at the end of the year. Orders for the following summer season begin being placed in the preceding fall. Orders begin arriving in December, but most arrive in January, February, March, and April. Many large souvenir companies postdate their invoices until July and August. Each year brings new offerings from souvenir companies and other suppliers. Much of the purchasing is done by Bill and/or Ted, who admit they rely on trusted salesmen of these houses to advise them on purchasing. Many of these companies have supplied Wall Drug for 20 years or so. Wall Drug generally buys directly from the producers or importers in most cases. This is true of their photo supplies and clothing also.

Years ago, much of what Wall Drug bought and sold was imported or made in the East. In recent years much of the merchandise is United States made and much more is made locally and regionally. The Indian reservations now have small production firms and individuals who make much handicraft which is sold through Wall Drug. Examples of such firms are Sioux Pottery, Badlands Pottery, Sioux Moccasin, and Milk Camp Industries.

Bill Hustead relies a great deal on his department managers for buying help. The manager of the jewelry, for instance, will determine on the basis of last year's orders and her experience with customer reaction and demand how much to order for the next season. All ordering is centered through Bill and Ted.

Promotion. Over the years Wall Drug has relied greatly on many roadside signs to bring people to the store. By 1968 there were about 3,000 signs displayed along highways and roads in all 50 states. Two men and a truck service signs in South Dakota and adjoining states. However, many signs are put up by volunteers. The store gives away about 14,000 6″ × 8″ signs and 3,000 8″ × 22″ signs a year to people who request them, and these people place them all over the world. These are plastic signs and will stand the weather. Many people will send a photo back showing the Wall Drug sign displayed in some unusual place. These photos are then posted in the store.

In time Wall Drug became noted enough to be considered newsworthy, and articles about Ted Hustead and Wall Drug began appearing. In the late 1950s *Redbook Magazine* carried a story which was later picked up and condensed in *Reader's Digest*. Since then the number of newspapers and magazines carrying feature stories or referring to Wall Drug has increased greatly. Examples are:

National Enquirer, November 11, 1973
Grit, October 28, 1973
Las Vegas Review-Journal, September 22, 1973
Senior Scholastic Magazine, October 4, 1973, p. 11
Congressional Record, September 11, 1973, S16269
Wall Street Journal, September 5, 1973
Omaha World-Herald, May 15, 1972
Elsevier (Dutch magazine), February 12, 1972
A Cleveland daily paper, May 16, 1971
The New York Times, Sunday, January 31, 1971
Rapid City Journal, April 12, 1970
Oshkosh, Wisconsin, *Daily Northwestern*, August 2, 1969
Sunday Picture Magazine, Minneapolis Tribune, September 21, 1969
America Illustrated, USIA in Poland and Russia
Ojai Valley News and Oaks Gazette, August 14, 1968
Chicago Tribune, Norman Vincent Peale's syndicated column, "Confident Living," October 8, 1966
Norman Vincent Peale's book, *You Can If You Think You Can*, p. 34
San Francisco Examiner, February 12, 1966
Women's Wear Daily, September 16, 1966
Coronet Magazine, April, 1964

Cleveland, Ohio, *The Plain Dealer*, date not known

In the mid 1960s during President Lyndon Johnson's administration, Congress passed the Highway Beautification Act reducing the number of roadside signs. South Dakota businesses that depend on tourists use outdoor advertising extensively, and Wall Drug was a well known user of signs. The Husteads were concerned with the threatened loss of signs.

Bill and Ted believed the news stories helped to compensate for the threatened loss of signs as would their sign give-away referred to earlier. Bill and Ted also decided that they must gain as much visibility and notoriety as possible, and to help achieve this they began using unusual advertising means. They began taking small ads in *The Village Voice* in New York City's Greenwich Village, advertising 5¢ coffee and 49¢ breakfast at Wall Drug and animal health remedies. This brought a telephone call and some letter inquiries. It also brought an article in the *Voice* and perhaps attracted other media. This article in the *New York Times* and other notoriety led to Bill's appearance on Garry Moore's television program "To Tell the Truth."

For a while the Wall Drug was advertised in the London undeground (subway). As a result, the BBC called and taped a twenty-minute interview on the telephone with Ted Hustead. Also, many English newspapers carried stories about Wall Drug because of the signs in the London Underground trains.

Wall Drug is also advertised in the Paris Metro (subway) in the English language, and on the dock in Amsterdam where people board sightseeing canal boats.

The Husteads have been preparing for the time when all signs would have to come down along highways in the United States. In the meantime, they have invested in new signs to be seen the required 660 feet back from the highway. There is concern that these will be knocked out by new federal legislation at any time.

Another strategy has been devised by Ted and Bill to gain the attention of motorists driving through South Dakota. This is a reciprocal favor with motels and campgrounds. Wall Drug has two brochures printed which are: 1. *Motel Guide for South Dakota*, and 2. *South Dakota Campground Directory of Privately Owned and Operated Campgrounds and Trailer Parks*. Over 200,000 of these guides are given away to Wall Drug patrons each summer. The Husteads believe each of these motels and campgrounds will reciprocate by displaying a sign on their premises for Wall Drug. This plan is in its infancy at present. Bill and Ted also plan to put up signs to be seen when people turn off the interstate at many of the exits east and west of Wall.

Finance. Until December 1973 all expansion was financed with internally generated funds supplemented with short-term borrowing. The first long-term debt was a 10-year, $250,000 loan in the form of a real estate mortgage taken on December 3, 1973 to fund the construction of the Mall. Payments on this loan, including 8% interest, will be about $34,000 in 1974 and $37,000 annually from 1975 through 1983.

In the winter of 1973 Bill must place orders for the tourist season of 1974. Should he buy light or buy heavy? What should he do with the Mall? Part of it remains unfinished.

Supplies have been purchased, but to finish means using more of the borrowed money and stocking these new stores.

Decisions to purchase inventory must be made several months before each tourist season. Seasonal billings on purchases provide much of the financing needed for the temporary inventory expansion. Obviously a cash problem could occur if a large inventory was left unsold at the end of any tourist season. This potential problem is aggravated by the fixed payments due on the long-term loan.

Discussion Questions

1. What is this firm's Master Strategy?
2. Should the Husteads invest heavily in stock for the summer of 1974?
   a. What are the objectives of this decision?
   b. What are Wall Drug's current strengths and weaknesses relative to this question?
   c. What are Wall Drug's current related threats and opportunities?
   d. What alternatives does Wall Drug have?
   e. Evaluate each of these alternatives.
   f. What is your decision?
3. Should the Husteads continue to expand Wall Drug?
   a. What are the objectives of this decision?
   b. What are Wall Drug's current strengths and weaknesses relative to this question?
   c. What are Wall Drug's current related threats and opportunities?
   d. What alternatives does Wall Drug have?
   e. Evaluate each of these alternatives.
   f. What is your decision?
4. How should the firm advertise?
   a. What are the objectives of this decision?
   b. What are Wall Drug's current strengths and weaknesses relative to this question?
   c. What are Wall Drug's current related threats and opportunities?
   d. What alternatives does Wall Drug have?
   e. Evaluate each of these alternatives.
   f. What is your decision?
5. Is a new Master Strategy for the firm desirable? Why or why not? If yes, what changes should be made to the current Master Strategy?
6. What policies should be changed and how?
7. What impact is the energy crisis likely to have on the Husteads' decisions?

Exhibit 1.1   Wall Drug Store, Inc. Balance Sheets

ASSETS

	December 31, 1973	1972
Current Assets		
Cash on hand	$ 1,037	$ 946
Cash in bank	2,450	138
Investment in commercial paper, at cost	70,000	-
Accounts receivable-trade	12,121	7,183
Accounts receivable-officers and employees	4,300	3,323
Accounts receivable-income tax refund	-	19,824
Inventories	144,013	86,890
Accrued interest receivable	463	-
Prepaid insurance	9,455	9,068
Total current assets	243,839	127,372
Investment and Other Assets		
Bonds, at cost	1,675	1,675
Organization cost, at cost	972	972
Total investments and other assets	2,647	2,647
Property, Plant and Equipment, at cost		
Land	70,454	50,079
Buildings, building improvements and parking lot improvements	692,488	527,456
Equipment, furniture and fixtures	366,651	303,108
	1,129,593	880,643
Less-accumulated depreciation	427,866	369,743
Depreciated cost of fixed assets	701,727	510,900
Goodwill, at cost	31,386	31,386
	$ 979,599	$672,305

The accompanying notes are an integral part of
these financial statements.

Exhibit 1.1 (Continued)

LIABILITIES AND STOCKHOLDERS' EQUITY

	December 31, 1973	1972
Current Liabilities		
Notes payable-Wall Auto Livery, Inc.	$ 20,000	$ 50,000
Notes payable-bank	-	20,000
Current maturities of long-term debt	20,058	-
Accounts payable-trade	22,709	30,979
Income taxes payable	11,161	-
Accrued taxes payable	25,880	18,457
Profit-sharing contribution payable	30,542	18,231
Accrued payroll and bonuses	40,073	28,559
Accrued interest payable	2,573	255
Total current liabilities	172,996	166,481
Long-Term Debt		
Real estate mortgage payable	232,742	-
Contract for deed payable	11,200	-
Total long-term debt	243,942	-
Stockholders' Equity		
Preferred stock, $100 par value, 4%, cumulative, non-voting, 1,000 shares authorized, 300 shares outstanding	30,000	30,000
Common stock, $100 par value, Class A, 500 shares authorized, 480 shares outstanding	48,000	48,000
Common stock, $100 par value, Class B, non-voting, 4,500 shares authorized, 400 shares outstanding	40,000	40,000
Retained earnings	444,661	387,824
Total stockholders' equity	562,661	505,824
	$979,599	$672,305

| | Years ended December 31, | |
	1973	1972
Net sales	$1,606,648	$1,335,932
Cost of goods sold	805,827	687,613
Gross profit	800,821	648,319
General and administrative expenses	690,461	577,767
Income from operations	110,360	70,552
Interest income	2,946	188
Rental income	3,647	4,248
Trailer park income	6,020	4,600
Theatre income	-	5,197
Gain on sale of assets	176	4,286
Other income	747	902
	123,896	89,973
Other deductions		
Interest	19,735	4,072
Theatre expense	-	2,689
Trailer park expense	4,223	3,433
Loss on sale of assets	-	1,674
Loss on demolition of theatre building	-	13,860
	23,958	25,728
Income before income taxes	99,938	64,245
Provision for income tax-current year	40,701	20,176
Net income	59,237	44,069
Retained earnings		
Beginning	387,824	343,755
	447,061	387,824
Dividends paid	2,400	-
Ending	$ 444,661	$ 387,824
Earnings per share	$ 65.95	$ 48.71

The accompanying notes are an integral part of
these financial statements.

Exhibit 1.3 Wall Drug Store, Inc. Statements of Changes in Financial Position

	Years ended December 31,	
	1973	1972
Financial resources were provided by		
Net income	$ 59,237	$ 44,069
Add income charges not affecting working capital in the period—		
Depreciation	58,723	43,862
Demolition loss on theatre building	-	13,860
Working capital provided by operations	117,960	101,791
Proceeds from borrowings	264,000	-
Basis of property and equipment sold	625	2,750
Total resources provided	382,585	104,541
Financial resources were used for		
Acquisition of land	21,000	5,799
Acquisition of building	165,031	149,924
Acquisition of equipment and signs	64,144	50,636
Reduction in long term debt	20,058	-
Dividends paid	2,400	-
Total resources used	272,633	206,359
Increase (decrease) in working capital	109,952	(101,818)
Working capital		
Beginning	(39,109)	62,709
Ending	$ 70,843	$ (39,109)
Increase (decrease) in components of working capital		
Current assets		
Cash	$ 2,403	$ (1,850)
Investment in commercial paper	70,000	-
Marketable securities	-	(59,375)
Accounts receivable-trade and other	(13,909)	684
Inventories	57,123	7,204
Other current assets-net	850	(3,650)
	116,467	(56,987)
Current liabilities		
Note payable-Banks and others	(50,000)	70,000
Current maturities of long-term debt	20,058	-
Accounts payable-trade	(8,270)	12,891
Income tax payable	11,161	(32,272)
Other current and accrued liabilities-net	33,566	(5,788)
	6,515	44,831
Increase (decrease) in working capital	$109,952	$(101,818)

The accompanying notes are an integral part of
these financial statements.

Exhibit 1.4 Wall Drug Store, Inc. Notes to Financial Statements

Note 1 Summary of Accounting Policies

Accounting Method—The corporation uses the accrual method of accounting for income tax and financial statement purposes.

Inventories—Inventories are generally valued at the lower of cost or market on a first-in, first-out basis computed under retail method.

Fixed Assets—Fixed assets are stated at cost. Depreciation is calculated under the straight-line method, 150% declining balance method, and 200% declining balance method. The same depreciation methods are used for financial and tax purposes. The useful lives selected for the assets are as follows: Buildings and building improvements, 15 to 40 years; parking lot, 8 years; and furniture, fixtures and equipment, 5 to 10 years. The provision for depreciation for 1973 of $58,723 and 1972 of $43,862 was charged to operations.

Repairs and maintenance costs are generally charged to expense at the time the expenditure is incurred. When an asset is sold or retired, its cost and related depreciation are removed from the accounts and a gain or loss is recognized on the difference between the proceeds of disposition and the undepreciated cost as the case may be. When an asset is traded in a like exchange, the cost and related depreciation are removed from the accounts and the undepreciated cost is capitalized as a part of the cost of the asset acquired.

Income Taxes—The provision for income taxes is based on the elements of income and expense, as reported in the statement of income. Investment tax credits are accounted for on the "flow-through" method, which recognizes the benefits in the year in which the assets which give rise to the credit are placed in service.

Note 2 Long-Term Debt

The real estate mortgage is an 8% mortgage dated December 3, 1973 and due October 1, 1983. The mortgage is to be paid in annual installments of principal and interest as follows:

10-1-74	$34,035.28
10-1-75 and thereafter	$37,257.50

Note 2 Long-Term Debt Continued

The drugstore in downtown Wall is pledged as security on this real estate mortgage.

The contract for deed payable is a 7% contract for deed, dated January 16, 1973 and is due January 16, 1978. The contract is to be paid in annual installments of $2,800 plus interest. This contract is for the purchase of approximately 202 acres of land which is the security for the contract for deed.

Note 3 Profit-Sharing Plan

The company has a profit-sharing plan for all full time employees who meet the qualification requirements. The company contributed $30,542 in 1973 and $18,231 in 1972 to the profit-sharing trust.

Exhibit 1.5 Wall Auto Livery, Inc. Balance Sheets

ASSETS

	December 31,	
	1973	1972
Current Assets		
Cash on hand	$ 100	$ 100
Cash in bank	14,590	19,916
Marketable securities, at cost	58,715	-
Notes receivable-Wall Drug Store, Inc.	20,000	50,000
Accounts receivable-trade	1,967	8,205
Credit cards	2,010	
Miscellaneous receivables	-	75
Inventory, at lower of cost (FIFO) or market	8,462	9,261
Prepaid insurance	1,557	1,469
Accrued interest receivable	729	247
Total current assets	108,130	89,274
Property and Equipment		
Land	7,367	7,367
Buildings	103,133	103,133
Equipment	26,297	26,076
	136,797	136,576
Less-accumulated depreciation	57,685	52,549
Depreciated cost of fixed assets	79,112	84,027
	$187,242	$173,301

LIABILITIES AND STOCKHOLDERS' EQUITY

	1973	1972
Current Liabilities		
Current maturity of long-term debt	$ 5,000	$ 5,000
Accounts payable-trade	754	5,696
Income taxes payable	7,286	2,774
Accrued profit-sharing contribution	2,666	2,446
Accrued payroll and sales taxes	840	756
Accrued interest payable	125	250
Total current liabilities	16,671	16,922
Long-Term Debt		
Note payable-non-interest bearing contract payable to F.M. Cheny maturing March 1, 1976	5,000	5,000
Note payable-6% to Perpetual National Life Insurance Company maturing in annual installments of $5,000 plus interest	-	5,000
Total long-term debt	5,000	10,000
Stockholders' Equity		
Common stock, $100 par value, 2,000 shares authorized, 444 shares outstanding	44,400	44,400
Retained earnings	121,171	101,979
Total stockholders' equity	165,571	146,379
	$187,242	$173,301

The accompanying notes are an integral part
of these financial statements.

	Years ended December 31,	
	1973	1972
Net sales	$191,969	$172,195
Inventories-beginning of year	9,261	9,467
Purchases	132,698	124,399
Freight	35	-
	141,994	133,866
Inventories-end of year	8,462	9,261
Cost of goods sold	133,532	124,605
Gross profit	58,437	47,590
General and administrative expense	44,568	41,443
Income from operations	13,851	6,147
Interest income	5,441	2,436
Rental income	17,917	15,440
Miscellaneous income	-	1,434
	37,209	25,457
Other deductions		
Interest expense	510	775
Rent expense-depreciation	3,005	3,128
	3,515	3,903
Income before federal income tax	33,694	21,554
Provision for income taxes	14,502	7,574
Net income	19,192	13,980
Retained earnings		
Beginning	101,979	87,999
Ending	$121,171	$101,979
Earnings per share	$ 43.23	$ 31.49

The accompanying notes are an integral part
of these financial statements.

Exhibit 1.7   Wall Auto Livery, Inc. Statements of Changes in Financial Position

	Years ended December 31,	
	1973	1972
Financial resources were provided by		
Net income	$ 19,192	$ 13,980
Add income charges not affecting working capital in the period—		
Depreciation	5,137	5,390
Working capital provided by operations	24,329	19,370
Financial resources were used for		
Acquisition of equipment	221	3,310
Reduction of long-term debt	5,000	5,000
Total resources used	5,221	8,310
Increase in working capital	19,108	11,060
Working capital		
Beginning of year	72,352	61,292
End of year	$ 91,460	$ 72,352
Increase (decrease) in components of working capital		
Current assets		
Cash	$ (5,326)	$ 15,394
Marketable securities	58,715	(58,087)
Notes receivable	(30,000)	50,000
Accounts receivable	(6,238)	3,371
Credit cards	2,010	–
Miscellaneous receivables	(75)	(57)
Inventory	(799)	(206)
Prepaid insurance	88	73
Accrued interest receivable	482	40
	18,857	10,528
Current liabilities		
Accounts payable-trade	(4,942)	1,064
Income taxes payable	4,512	(1,925)
Other current and accrued liabilities	179	329
	(251)	(532)
Increase in working capital	$ 19,108	$ 11,060

The accompanying notes are an integral part of
these financial statements.

2/A Note on Alternative Energy Sources*

James M. Higgins

Several alternative energy sources have been identified. These are presented in Figure 2.1. This figure also notes the various major types of demand placed on these alternative energy supplies. In this note the perceived futures of the major potential energy sources are examined, and, in addition, the factors which bring about this view are noted. The key to most of the perceived futures is the price competitiveness of the various sources. A final comment is made on the nature of energy demand.

Fossil Fuels. What must be recognized with respect to fossil fuels is that their supply is limited, some more than others, of course. Oil and natural gas are extremely limited, with most predictions indicating that all known existing supplies will be depleted by the year 2005. And while additional quantities will certainly be discovered, their costs relative to the costs of alternative sources are expected to cause them to become unattractive alternatives. Modern petroleum exploration and extraction are expensive operations. The technology required to create synthetic supplies is lacking, at least on a cost-benefit, price competitive basis. Coal offers the greatest long-range fossil fuel promise of energy independence for the United States. Estimates are that a 200-year supply to meet all energy needs is available beneath the surface of our 50 states. But the least costly and the best quality coal reserves have already been mined. Furthermore, the technologies required for converting coal into more desirable fuels such as gas are presently lacking, on the cost competitive basis. However, significant strides have been made in granulating coal in order to make it burn cleaner as a primary heating fuel and progress is being made in converting coal into synthetic gas. One central problem is how to power transportation vehicles. With oil quickly diminishing, a new power source is desperately needed.

Natural gas, the crux of the United States' energy problems, became a problem largely because of U.S. government energy policies. Gas prices were regulated to unbelievably low rates, rates reflective of abundance such as existed when the rates were first instituted. As a result of these artificially depressed prices, some of the larger users, such as utilities, have consumed enormous amounts of natural gas and have become—unfortunately—overly dependent on natural gas. And, while further decreasing supplies, these low prices kept drillers from seeking new supplies.

*To be used with Cases 3 and 4.

Nuclear Energy. Nuclear fission (the power created by splitting the atom) was once the promised solution to the energy problem. But its high costs combined with its unattractive environmental aspects, i.e., increased background radiation and the inability to safely store nuclear wastes, have led to a decrease of interest in fission as a panacea. The fear of a nuclear accident, the probability of which could only be increased with the addition of more nuclear reactors, has added to the disenchantment. An additional environmental problem has been the damage to the environment's water as cooling water for the reactors is discharged into local water supply areas. Even with breeder reactors which create more nuclear fuel than they consume, the cost has become prohibitive. Finally, uranium, the fuel of normal fission processes, is in extremely short supply. Nuclear fusion, the fusing of atoms, creates tremendous energy. But the technology has yet to be developed which could harness this energy, and the costs of future development have become astronomical.

Wind Energy. One of the more promising energy sources is the wind. Across the Great Plains and in the mountains, the winds blow almost continuously. Wind can generate electricity which can be employed for any number of purposes including heating and cooling as well as electrical energy provision. Significant strides have been made in improving the efficiency of windmills, and the future of these as a major source of energy appears to depend heavily on the development of technology in competitive sources. And, as with solar energy, key problems are storage and distribution. There simply is no adequate storage system for large quantities of electrical energy. Nor is there a satisfactory system for transferring electrical energy across the country. Energy created in the Great Plains by windmills could not now be transferred to states in the Midwest, East, or South where such energy might be needed.

Geothermal Energy. Geothermal energy, or energy from the earth, is highly promising in theory since the earth's core is molten and if properly tapped could furnish a seemingly inexhaustible supply of energy. However, current technology prohibits employing this source to such an advanced degree. Current applications have largely been limited to using surface or near surface hot spots as sources of steam, either for direct heat or to generate electricity.

Tides and the Ocean. Several methods of employing tidal power and ocean currents as a means of generating electrical energy have been suggested, but these projected systems are largely in the very early development stages.

Solar Energy. Solar energy can be used in two primary ways: first, to provide electricity, and, second, to heat or cool buildings. In many ways, solar energy is inexhaustible and can be found just about everywhere. Unfortunately,

Figure 2.1 Overview of Energy Supply and Demand

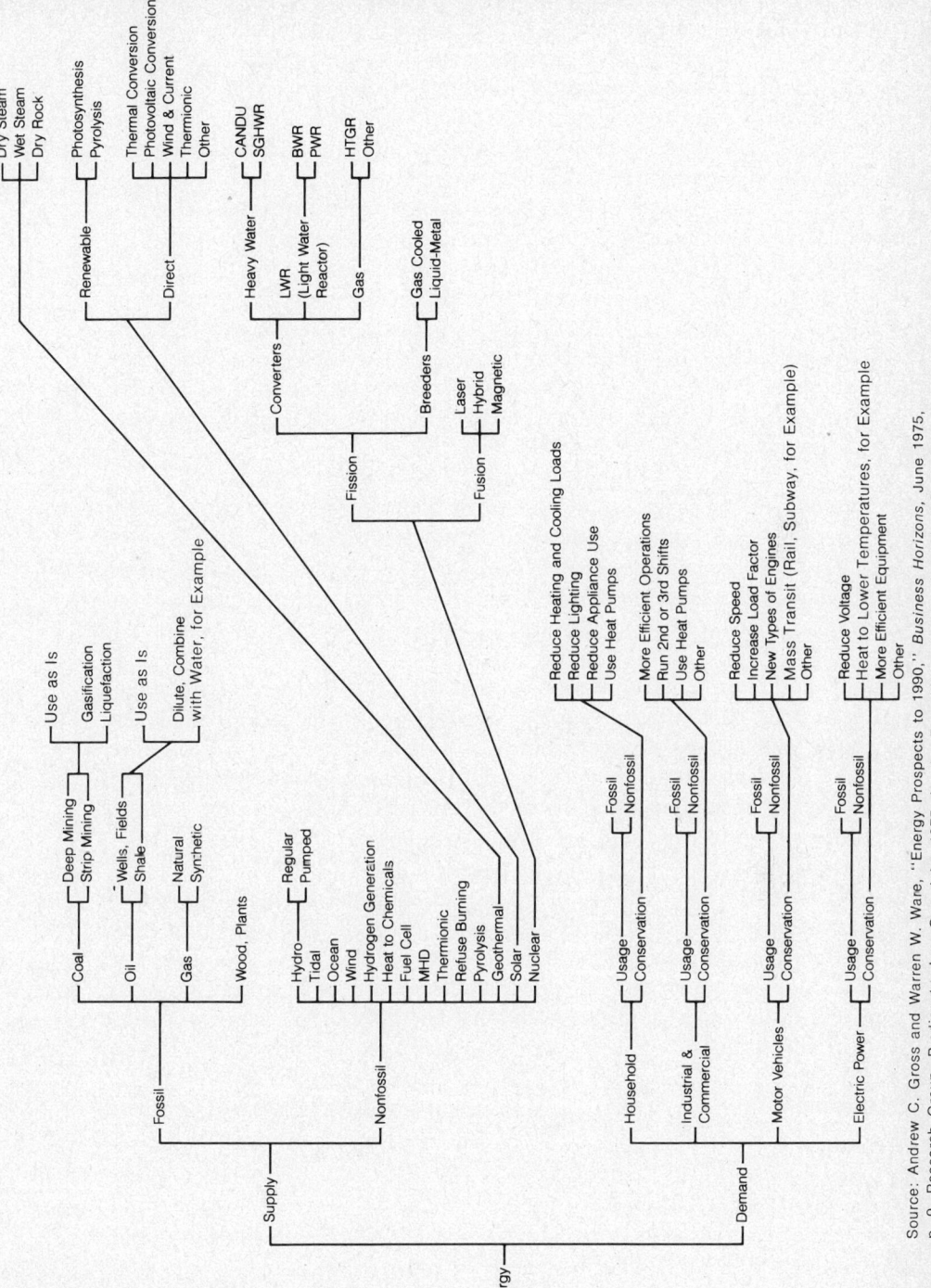

Source: Andrew C. Gross and Warren W. Ware, "Energy Prospects to 1990," *Business Horizons*, June 1975, p. 9. Research Group, Predicasts, Inc. Copyright, 1975, by the Foundation for the School of Business at Indiana University. Reprinted by permission.

problems do exist. Certain portions of this country and others do not receive much sunlight. And unfortunately, solar energy cannot be stored for long periods of time or hauled to deficient areas as can conventional fuels. One hope for transporting solar electrical energy appears to be in large solar power stations whose practical development will probably not reach fruition before 1986.[1] Presently, solar energy must be used within a short distance from the surface receiving sunlight, such as the area beneath the roof of a building. But the biggest problem associated with solar energy is the high cost of gathering the energy. A large portion of a rooftop must be covered with special materials or devices to capture the sunlight for heating or air conditioning. And expensive collection equipment is necessary for converting solar energy into electricity. However, it is rapidly becoming price competitive for purposes of heating and cooling when compared to fossil fuels. Furthermore, because of the rising prices of our normal energy sources, solar energy production has been able to compete with present fuels in certain situations. It is at least price competitive with large utility company generated electricity for the purpose of heating a home.[2]

Technology and Energy. Any number of additional energy sources have been suggested, and, with a significant technological breakthrough, they could easily supplant the major sources as envisioned. Each of the major sources' contributions could be dramatically changed if a major technological innovation were to occur.

Energy and the Environment. Continually, these two considerations appear to be at odds with one another. Besides well-publicized problems encountered with nuclear energy resources, all of the fossil fuels pose serious pollution problems, although those created by natural gas are minimal. The environmental consequences of the less advanced energy generation systems when employed on a large scale are virtually unknown.

Seller Concentration. The major petroleum companies are not just petroleum companies. They are energy companies. Most of the larger firms have invested in competing energy sources. Importantly, these sources include gas, oil shale, coal, uranium, and tar sands,[3] but little interest has been shown by the giants of the industry in less traditional energy sources such as the sun, wind, or tidal sources.

Government Interest Areas. The federal government's interest—i.e., where

1. Edmund Faltermayer, "Solar Energy Is Here, but It's Not Yet Utopia," *Fortune*, February 1976, p. 103.
2. ABC Evening News, December 29, 1976.
3. Bruce Natschert, Abraham Gerber, and Irwin M. Stelzer, *Competition in the Energy Markets* (National Economic Research Associates, Inc., 1970).

Table 2.1   Share of All Energy Used in the United States in 1977, 1985

	1977	1985
Oil	46%	43%
Natural Gas	28	21
Coal	18	23
Hydroelectric	5	4
Nuclear	3	8
Solar Geothermal		
Synthetic Oil and Gas	—	1

Source: Federal Energy Administration, as quoted in "Winter's Legacy: Step-Up in Search for Fuel Supplies," *U.S. News & World Report,* February 21, 1977, p. 19.

it budgets its money—is focused on traditional energy resources although solar energy and wind energy have received substantial budget increases in recent years. ERDA, the Energy Research and Development Administration, the government's energy research agency, reflects the interests of its primary subsystem component, the former Atomic Energy Commission, more than it does any other energy source.

Demand. Decreasing demand would accomplish the same end as increasing

Table 2.2   U.S. Energy Demand

	1970	1980	1990
Motor vehicle demand			
Passenger car equivalent (millions)	166	246	337
Millions of BTUs/Passenger car equivalent	74.7	66.7	60.5
Motor vehicle demand (quadrillions of BTUs)	12.40	16.40	20.40
Household demand			
Households (millions)	63.4	77	91
Millions of BTUs/Household	137.2	129.9	120.9
Household demand (quadrillions of BTUs)	8.70	10.00	11.00
Electric power demand			
Industrial production index (63 = 100)	139	218	310
Trillions of BTUs/Industrial production index	115.5	144.5	183.8
Electric power production (quadrillions of BTUs)	16.05	31.50	57.00
Industrial demand			
GNP (billions 1970 $)	976	1,451	2,110
Thousands of BTUs/1970 $ GNP	30.9	28.1	24.1
Industrial demand (quadrillions of BTUs)	30.15	40.80	50.80
Total demand (quadrillions of BTUs)	67.30	98.70	139.20

Source: Andrew C. Gross and Warren W. Ware, "Energy Prospects to 1990," *Business Horizons,* June 1975, p. 9. Research Group, Predicasts, Inc. Copyright, 1975, by the Foundation for the School of Business at Indiana University. Reprinted by permission.

2/A Note on Alternative Energy Sources

supply, but the task is not an easy one. American industry, American transportation, and America's homes all depend upon energy. Low prices and extensive marketing have created an almost insatiable demand for energy. And the conversion process combined with transmission accounts fully for 50 percent of the raw energy consumed. Much could be done to improve these inefficiencies. Such inefficiencies are prominent in the internal combustion engine which propels some 100 million automobiles across our nation.

Table 2.3   U.S. Energy Supply

	1970	1980	1990
Coal			
Production (millions of metric tons)	522	715	1,000
Quadrillions of BTUs	14.05	19.25	26.90
Crude petroleum			
Production (thousands of b/d)	10,800	13,370	16,600
Quadrillions of BTUs	21.95	27.15	33.70
Natural gas			
Production (billions of cubic meters)	532	690	730
Quadrillions of BTUs	23.90	27.90	29.50
Nonhydrocarbon sources			
Hydroelectric	248	360	475
Nuclear	22	495	2,205
Other	—	35	320
Total nonhydrocarbon (billions of kilowatt-hours)	270	890	3,000
Quadrillions of BTUs	2.85	9.40	31.65
Total domestic production (quadrillions of BTUs)	62.75	83.70	121.75
Percent domestic demand	93.2	84.8	87.2
Surplus (deficit) (quadrillions of BTUs)	—4.55	—15.00	—17.95

Source: Andrew C. Gross and Warren W. Ware, "Energy Prospects to 1990," *Business Horizons,* June 1975, p. 11. Research Group, Predicasts, Inc. Copyright, 1975, by the Foundation for the School of Business at Indiana University. Reprinted by permission.

3/Solar Enterprises Incorporated (SEI)— A Solar Energy Company*

James M. Higgins

The Solar Energy Industry

The use of sunlight for energy is an idea that is gaining acceptance for both its primary areas of application. In producing heat or cooling (buildings), two methodologies may be found: passive systems and active systems. Passive systems have been in use for years. These systems rely on architectural design, e.g., the use of huge south windows and special insulating materials, to heat a home. Active systems involve more complex sunlight collectors and storage facilities. Numerous applications of the latter may now be found. Included are several schools, a Burger King restaurant in New Jersey, banks, small manufacturers, office buildings, a post office in Pennsylvania, and numerous homes across the country. More than 4,000 swimming pools, mostly in the Southwest, are heated by sunlight. With regard to converting sunlight into electricity, the technology is lagging, but, nonetheless, several firms and many individuals are employing this process. The U.S. Forest Service has what is claimed to be the first solar-powered outhouse. Solar cells are used to convert sunlight into electricity to run the flush toilet pump system. The solar equipment was felt to be less expensive than running power lines up the mountain.

Many large firms have been experimenting with harnessing sunlight since the early days of the space program. Few have an actual product to sell, and most of the companies presently selling equipment are small. Sales of the industry probably did not exceed $175 million per year for 1977.

The Processes. Solar energy heating and cooling units consist mainly of large aluminum or alloy sheets, painted black to absorb the sun's heat and covered with glass to hold warmth. Either air or water (or other liquid) is piped under these sheets to collect the heat and cool the metal. The heated air or water is then transferred to storage units and stored until needed. The hot water may be stored in underground or basement tanks, while the hot air is used to heat rocks which will store the heat. At present, solar energy has been used more for space heating and hot water heating applications than for electrical applications or air conditioning. Most solar contractors and designers say it is prudent to set a goal of obtaining 60 to 70 percent of one's

*This is a disguised case. Also, see Case 2 before beginning.

heating requirements from the sun; therefore, a back-up furnace is necessary in most cases.

Solar generating units for electricity involve the use of photovoltaic cells. These cells are composed of two thin layers of materials; one of these is a semiconducting material such as silicon, and the other is a metal such as aluminum or silver. The sunlight stimulates the flow of electrons to generate a current that is drawn off in wires. Even though the price of solar generated electricity has decreased from $200 to $17 a watt, it is still too expensive for general use. Another method of generating electricity is to employ large magnifying parabolic surfaces to reflect and concentrate heat on a water container and then use a conventional steam boiler electrical generator.

Federal Government Interest. In 1973 the total expenditure for solar research and development by the federal government was less than $4 million. The 1977 fiscal budget included expenditures of $160 million. The Energy Research and Development Administration (ERDA) spent $100 million in 1977 on solar programs. And while there are rumors of billion-dollar appropriations in a few years, solar energy has not been financed to the degree that other programs have. For example, even if $1 billion were forthcoming, this is less than the federal government spends to build one 500 megawatt nuclear breeder plant. Most of the solar money is being used on demonstrations of solar heating and cooling systems and on research.

HUD has issued grants for the installation of solar units in new and existing dwellings, as well as grants to contractors using solar heating in commercial buildings. Other government agencies have also shown interest. As one government spokesman explains, "We're priming the pump with these programs. We're letting people see what these units look like, how they work, and we're helping the industry get on its feet." Another party disagrees, "Much of the government money, moreover, has gone not to the small inventors and entrepreneurs who have done much of the innovating and taken most of the risk, but to large corporations schooled in research grantsmanship. The country, in short, may be getting another pork barrel." This authority feels that some federally financed research is needed, but actually less glamorous action is required to ensure the success of the solar energy industry. Several states already have enacted tax laws favoring the use of solar systems. In Florida, a 1974 law requires builders to make all new homes adaptable to solar water heaters. One activist recommends that zoning laws be amended at local levels to protect the sun rights of solar system users. He states that the government's responsibility, which is being accepted to a certain degree, is to "prosecute the fraudulent operators who are said to be moving into solar energy, and to help set standards that will enable a purchaser of a solar system to know what he is getting."

Future Outlook. ERDA projects that by 1985 solar energy will provide 0.8

percent of America's total energy needs and that this figure will rise to 7 percent by the year 2000. Arthur D. Little, Inc. estimates that the market for solar systems could reach $1.3 billion in 1985. Unless competitive energy sources increase substantially in price, solar energy companies must reduce the payback period if they are to seriously challenge for a large portion of the market. There are three possible ways that costs may be reduced: using cheaper materials, redesigning collectors to gather more BTUs, or combining an electric-powered heat pump with the collectors. A new solar panel developed by scientists and engineers at the Massachusetts Institute of Technology *may* cut heating costs in half. The new panel apparently eliminates the need for storage tanks and the plumbing used in conventional solar heating systems. The storage unit is in the collector itself. This decreases the cost of installation as the job is finished at a point where previously the job was only half completed. Production units are not yet available.

The Massachusetts Institute of Technology has also introduced a converter to be used with solar cells to produce energy cheaper than by conventional methods. This converter is expected to be on the market soon. The new converter solves the cost problem by increasing the intensity of the sunlight through the use of mirrors which concentrate sunlight on the solar cells and thereby reducing the number of cells required and the total cost. Intensive photovoltaic research is being carried out by numerous firms.

Solar Enterprises Incorporated (SEI)

In 1975, Mike Newman and a group of solar enthusiasts became interested in organizing a solar management and marketing company. They approached Dr. Henri Metzger, director of the Solar Energy Project at Southwestern State University, for the rights to the solar energy system that Metzger had designed for the federal government. SEI, which is located in Phoenix, Arizona, views itself as "a systems company devoted to the development and marketing of solar energy systems."

The SEI Product. SEI sells the components of a complete system for solar space and hot water heating. This system is a supplement to a normal forced air heating system. The system is based on over thirty years of experimentation and thirteen years of actual application. In 1965, Metzger installed a solar energy system in his home in Flagstaff as a supplement to conventional heating systems. The SEI system operates as follows: Solar collectors on the roof heat the air, and fans force the hot air to a storage container—a rock-filled cylinder where the heat is stored. When warmth is needed, air from the rooms in the building is circulated directly from the collectors into the room air ducting. On cloudy days or at night, air is circulated from the storage cylinder through the room air ducting. If solar heat is not available, the system automatically activates the standby conventional system. The SEI system includes air collectors, air handlers, and automatic system controllers. A hot water heating system is also available for residential and light commercial applications. It uses the SEI air collector, an air to water heat exchanger, and an 80-gallon storage tank. SEI's system differs from most others because air rather than liquid is used as the heat transfer medium. This system has several advantages over its fluid competition. The cost is usually less because this system is simpler and easier to adapt to conventional heating systems. Recent tests of liquid systems have uncovered corrosion and wear problems which do not exist in the air system. The air system requires almost no maintenance as compared to the fluid system. SEI claims its system is safer as it cannot be damaged by freezing or boiling, cannot cause water damage to buildings, and uses tempered glass to resist breakage. The SEI collector is warranted for ten years if the collector is installed according to SEI specifications. This warranty does not include glass breakage. The air handling modules and automatic controller are guaranteed for only one year. SEI's testing programs follow the procedures recommended by the National Bureau of Standards and others that are used in the industry. Results indicate that SEI is the leading firm in cost effectiveness for space heating applications. The SEI system can reduce normal fuel consumption by as much as 80 percent. It has a longer life than liquid systems. It has been in operation for thirteen years in Dr. Metzger's home and shows little sign of wear.

SEI is a marketing, management, and engineering corporation. Components for the system are made by several different sources. The collectors are made by Westchester Manufacturing Company, which does most of the product engineering. When Newman was asked why he chose Westchester, he explained, "Making refrigerators requires the capability of handling metal, glass and insulation—the same components that go into solar collectors. We want absolute control over costs and we get it through this approach to production. We let experienced and efficient manufacturers make the product. We tried our own plant here in Phoenix, but the labor was too inefficient. These people here are not factory oriented. We are thinking of having a plant in Kansas City where you have third generation factory workers." A Phoenix, Arizona, company which specializes in solar controls supplies the control systems.

Distribution. SEI has warehouses in New Jersey and Phoenix to store completely assembled collectors. SEI ships the equipment from stock in one of its warehouses directly to distributor warehouses. "We tried installing them ourselves, but we decided to leave that to the experts." SEI is more oriented toward service than toward production. It is organized as a research and development, systems engineering, and marketing firm. SEI had only 22 employees in December, 1977. SEI is continuing research and development.

Marketing. SEI concentrates on the building industry rather than the consumer to promote its product. This includes selling to builders with large numbers of homes to build. SEI systems are sold only through the best and most established wholesale distributors and factory authorized dealers. This way the firm can benefit from the established heating and cooling distributors' reputation. SEI avoids solar energy conferences. Newman observes, "I don't think the major builders buy heating equipment there." He further states, "We want to be thought of as just another product in the normal channels, not an exotic newcomer." This approach seems to appeal to builders who frequently resist changes in previously successful systems. As one dealer explains, "SEI is simply selling a system to heat an installation."

SEI provides factory training in applications engineering, sales, installation, and services to its distributors. It also provides specific instruction manuals, which few other companies have available. By the end of 1977, SEI had forty distributors and eighty outlets. Their marketing is concentrated in those geographic areas where the economics of applications offer the firm a sales

---

Figure 3.1   Solar Enterprises Inc. Distribution and Marketing Plan

SEI views its responsibilities as:

1. Developing reps, distributors, and dealers
2. Marketing product at corporate level to national accounts, government, and foreign customers
3. Developing and implementing marketing programs
4. Providing technical support, training, and sales assistance to channel members

SEI asks its manufacturers' representatives to:

1. Promote product to architects, engineers, and owners
2. Develop distributors and dealers
3. Provide technical support to above
4. Process orders from above

SEI requires its distributors to:

1. Maintain local inventory
2. Promote sales to installers

SEI requires its installing dealers to:

1. Promote and install product for:
   Owners
   Developers
   General contractors
2. Work in residential, commercial and industrial fields

SEI asks its industrial representatives to:

1. Promote product to industrial accounts
2. Act as technical advisor on general energy conservation
3. Process orders from industrial accounts

Figure 3.2 Essential Considerations of Distributor Marketing Program

Part I. Target Market and Economic Analysis
Distributor
Distributor markets
Utilities covering distributor market area for each:
   fuel type, cost, availability, projected cost increases
Distributor market building starts next 12 months:
   residential, commercial, institutional, governmental
Available tax incentives
Physical solar radiation in area
Distributor's marketing efforts
   Targeted dealers by quarter
   Sales force size, growth rate
Sales literature package
   Engineering manual, sales brochures, installation manuals,
   price lists, advertising program, etc.
Distribution agreement

Part II. Market Introduction, Training
Press release
Distributor training in Phoenix
Distributor training at distributor's location
Dealer program
Local advertising program
Program evaluation
Assistance services

Part III. Marketing Plan
Sales quotas
Shipping dates
Special advertising/promotional actions

advantage. Presently, distributors are located in 23 states. Dealers service the SEI product. All must be factory trained at the SEI home office in Phoenix.

SEI offers support to its dealers and representatives by providing a comprehensive advertising and promotional program. The SEI regional marketing managers help the distributor choose and coordinate a program for his particular market situation. An example of the distributor marketing implementation program is discussed on succeeding pages. Their program offers the following services:

1. publicity releases
2. shared local advertising
3. national advertising
4. inquiry response programs
5. promotion materials and display packages

The firm will prepare news releases announcing the distributor's association with SEI and any SEI installations in the area. It will match every dollar spent by a distributor for local advertising up to 2 percent of the first $50,000 in shipments. Thereafter, SEI will match up to 1 percent of annual subsequent shipments. SEI also will provide ads for local media and yellow pages advertising. The firm conducts a national advertising program based on professional market surveys and media selection aimed at reaching decision makers, engineers, architects, lenders, builders, lawmakers, and owners.

The firm operates inquiry response programs. SEI not only sends the inquirer the name and address of the nearest distributor, but it also sends the nearest distributor complete details so that he may follow up the prospective buyer. At nominal costs, SEI will provide general and technical promotional materials—slide presentations, system description brochures, article reprints, applications engineering manuals, and trade show displays. Finally, to back up its advertising and promotional campaign, SEI provides field services and system engineering departments. SEI's market is both industrial/commercial and the home market, although it concentrates on the latter. The home building market has had its problems in recent years, especially with regard to the decrease in housing starts resulting from the downturn in the economy. SEI perceives the industrial market as highly structured through industrial sales representatives, and in 1977 reached an agreement with a large distributor to handle their products in that market. One survey which SEI executives quoted noted that 75 percent of homeowners surveyed would be willing to invest $6,000 in solar heating equipment in order to cut their heating bills by 50 percent. In a Connecticut development project, SEI's units add $4,650 to the cost of a house. SEI concentrates its marketing efforts on those states where fuel costs are highest and where sufficient sunlight is available to make the system attractive. New England and the Midwest are prime targets. Surprisingly, their market is expected to soon include Southern states such as Texas. Normal market price of a solar unit for heating averages around $7,000.

Finance. According to Newman, 1977 was the year of great accomplishment for the firm, since it completed the development and demonstration of an economically competitive and marketable space and hot water heating system, completed the installation of several full-scale development models in commercial and residential buildings, and had revenues from installations which were commercially marketed without governmental aid. Even with incoming revenues, SEI, like most other firms in the industry, lost money in 1977. SEI had a net loss of over $400,000. Newman expects sales of $4.2 million in 1978. The firm believes that they have strong growth potential. Housing starts are increasing, while the production of fossil fuels is decreasing. Newman feels the firm will control ten percent of the predicted billion-dollar market of 1980. The cost of SEI units is high, but surprisingly cost competitive,

Figure 3.3 SEI Income Statement

	1977	1976	(Start Up) 1975
Sales	$889,350		
Revenue from Development		$143,942	
Costs and Expenses			
Cost of Sales	645,620		
Cost for Development		494,273	
Operating Expenses	681,364	211,699	$77,270
Int. Income	(4,605)	(11,201)	(10,923)
Int. Expenses	2,867	1,196	
Total cost and expenses	$1,325,246	$695,967	
Net Gain or Loss	(435,896)	(546,025)	(66,347)
Loss per Common Share	0.05	0.07	0.02

Figure 3.4 SEI Balance Sheet

	1977	1976
Assets		
Current Assets		
Cash	$140,433	$ 24,135
Accounts Receivable	79,686	35,242
Unbilled costs on government contracts	30,395	
Inventories	87,017	112,966
Prepaid Expenses	3,405	5,872
Total current assets	$341,836	$178,215
Property and equipment	58,193	74,838
Other assets	6,369	5,381
Total	$406,398	$258,434
Liabilities and Stockholders' Equity		
Current Mat. of LTD	2,999	4,726
Accounts Payable—trade	179,102	214,621
Acc. Exp.	22,706	56,067
Customer deposits	6,426	23,432
Total current liabilities	$211,233	$298,846
LTD less current mat.	1,769	5,086
Accrued stock option comp.	17,765	
Stockholders' equity		
Common, par value	101,732	76,899
Add. paid-in capital	1,128,170	495,976
Accumulated deficit	(1,054,271)	(618,373)
Total stock equity	$175,631	$ (45,497)
Total	$406,398	$258,434

especially with liquid solar heating systems, and becoming more so every day. Raw materials for collectors cost $3 per square foot of collector. By the time the manufacturer and distributor add their costs, the retail price per square foot on the collector is about $11. Installation brings the cost to $17. The key to selling is payback on the investment. The payback period becomes less and less as the cost of competitive energy sources steadily rises. Some experts feel this cost must fall to $10 per foot before SEI can be truly competitive with alternative energy sources. However, President Carter's proposed tax rebate program for solar units would cut heating payback by two years in most areas, from fourteen to twelve years, perhaps even less.

Competition. Collectors are now being sold by at least seventy companies, ranging from very small entrepreneurships to large well-known firms such as General Electric, Honeywell, Reynolds Metals, and Lennox. Lennox Industries is one of the country's largest producers of conventional cooling and heating systems, and thus is a substantial potential competitor. The largest firms are just now unveiling products to sell—in the past they have been more concerned with research. Newman observes, "SEI has the foremost air solar system. We have competition in the air systems market, but there are maybe only six firms as advanced as we are in solar energy. Of course, SEI competes with all major heating and cooling firms, not just those in solar energy."

Top Management. Mike Newman is the president of SEI. He was formerly a manager of program development for a major research corporation. Newman was the main instigator in forming SEI. Says Newman, "Metzger had the best system. What we did was 'product-ize' it." Adds Metzger, "I had a good system, and he had a business background. We believed that, jointly, we could take it to the marketplace."

Dr. Metzger is one of the foremost authorities on solar heating in the world. He is a leader of the International Solar Energy Society and, as mentioned previously, is director of the Southwestern State University Solar Laboratory.

Neal McNeal, the Director of Marketing, was formerly a marketing analyst for a large consumer products firm. Newman, Metzger, and McNeal are responsible for the marketing program.

Strategy and Management Philosophy. SEI has no written overall strategy, but its stated strategy is to be the "Standard of the Industry." Their main emphasis appears to be on marketing a high quality, low maintenance product. They feel that their proven technology is the foundation for producing better products and for producing them at lower prices. SEI has introduced many industry firsts and wants to remain the standard of the industry. They do not want to play catch-up; instead, they want other firms to try and catch them. Lowering installation costs was emphasized in 1977, as well as seeking to develop an economical solar cooling system. They also plan to put their technology to use for agricultural and industrial applications. 1978 promises an aggressive marketing campaign.

SEI has a good relationship with the building industry because of its lower prices and conventional structure. It does not replace other equipment, it merely adds to market economy. The firm is profit oriented. SEI feels that social responsiveness may be nice, but that builders only understand money. SEI believes that most other solar energy firms are composed of either scientists or engineers or technical people who are less concerned about price than social responsibility. Newman comments, "The consumer is way ahead of government on solar energy. Solar energy is acceptable to the consumer."

Growth. In 1977, SEI experienced substantial growth. In one of the most important steps for solar heating, SEI agreed to provide solar heating for 150 homes in a Connecticut development project. The 1977 and 1978 winters caused a significant increase in demand for the SEI product, and future gas and other heating shortages can only be expected to increase demand.

Discussion Questions

1. What is SEI's Master Strategy?
2. What is SEI's marketing strategy?
3. What are SEI's strengths and weaknesses?
4. What are the current and future threats and opportunities facing SEI?
5. How else should SEI's marketing strategy be changed?
6. How should SEI's Master Strategy be changed?
7. Can SEI compete effectively with the existing large heating and cooling companies or those large companies now diversifying into this market?
8. How effective has this company been at achieving its mission?
9. What must it do in the future to effectively accomplish its mission?

References

Alexander, T. "ERDA's Job Is to Throw Money at the Energy Crisis." *Fortune* July 1976, pp. 152–162.

"Distant Glimmer: Huge Power Stations for Solar Electricity Are Decades in the Future." *Wall Street Journal,* May 28, 1976, pp. 2, 25.

Energy Research and Development Administration. *Program Opportunity Announcement* DSE–75–1.

Faltermeyer, E. Solar Energy Is Here, but It's Not Yet Utopia." *Fortune,* February 1976, pp. 103–106, 114–116.

"A Giant Step for Solar Heating." *Business Week,* October 18, 1976, pp. 99–100.

Higgins, J. Interview with Mike Newman, President, SEI.

"New Solar Panel May Cut Heating System Cost by Half." *Montgomery Advertiser,* November 26, 1976, p. 32.

"The New Business of Harvesting Sunbeams." *Fortune,* February 1976, pp. 107–111.

SEI advertising brochures.

"Solar Heat Lights Up a New Industry." *Business Week,* May 16, 1977, p. 142.

Solar Heating Is Here and Booming." *U.S. News & World Report,"* March 29, 1976, pp. 30–32.

"Solar Unit Produces Cheap Energy, MIT Researchers Claim." *Wall Street Journal,* June 7, 1976, p. 18.

Weaver, K. "The Search for Tomorrow's Power." *National Geographic,* November 1972, pp. 650–681.

4/Sebring-Vanguard, Inc.: The CitiCar

Frederick E. Webster, Jr., and James E. Williams

In February, 1976, a variety of problems faced Mr. Robert Stone, Marketing Manager of Sebring-Vanguard, Inc. (SV). SV manufactured the first mass-produced electric car in the United States, the SV-48 CitiCar. The first Citi-Cars experienced both engineering and production problems, but by 1976 these problems had been largely eliminated. Unfortunately, Consumers Union had purchased one of the early substandard cars, and had issued a damaging evaluation of the CitiCar in the October, 1975 issue of *Consumer Reports*. Mr. Stone believed that this was having far-reaching demoralizing effects on the entire SV dealer organization. In addition, retail sales had slowed. Mr. Stone suspected that many dealers were not pushing the CitiCar and that it was being used primarily as a traffic builder by some dealers for the "big-four" automobile companies. Mr. Stone was therefore considering either expanding his field force to allow better supervision of CitiCar dealers, or changing his dealer organization drastically. Continued product improvements were also planned. Sebring-Vanguard's president, Mr. Robert Beaumont, had set two goals for 1976: cost reduction throughout all phases of the operation and a sales volume sufficient to give SV its first profitable year of operations.

Company Background. Mr. Robert Beaumont, the president of Sebring-Vanguard, Inc., had been involved in electric vehicle development since the late 1960s, and had been instrumental in the development of the Vanguard Coupe, the predecessor of the CitiCar. He eventually attracted the financial backing of wealthy individual investors living in Florida. Sebring-Vanguard, Inc., was formed on May 14, 1973, to manufacture, assemble, and sell electric vehicles (EV's), with its headquarters and only manufacturing facility at Sebring.

On August 9, 1973, the Company entered into an agreement with Vanguard Vehicles, Inc. (Mr. Beaumont was also the president and a stockholder of Vanguard Vehicles, Inc.) to acquire inventories and rights, and to pay royalties for the use of technology and trade names relating to the design, engineering, manufacture, and sale of the Vanguard Coupe. Beginning in August, 1973, SV began recruiting people to develop systems, procedures, and an understanding of the EV industry. Key production and operation posi-

Source: This case was prepared by Dr. James E. Williams, MBA Candidate, under the direction of Professor Frederick E. Webster, Jr., at The Amos Tuck School of Business Administration. Copyright © 1976 by the Trustees of Dartmouth College. All rights reserved. Distributed by the Intercollegiate Case Clearing House, Soldiers Field, Boston, Mass. 02163. All rights reserved to the contributors. Printed in the U.S.A.

tions were soon under the control of competent personnel. The first CitiCar prototype was produced in February, 1974.

In August, 1974, SV was producing 28 CitiCars per week; a year later production had risen to 40 cars per week. The current physical plant was deemed suitable for production of 240 cars per month. Other facilities capable of handling 800 cars per month were available near the present production location. In August, 1975, SV was recognized by Automotive News as the sixth largest manufacturer of cars in the United States. By January, 1976, SV employed a total of 100 people, with 15–20 personnel involved in management or supervision.

Mr. Robert Stone was a 1970 graduate of Dartmouth College. He had been a school teacher for a few years until he became totally absorbed in the electric car concept. He then worked for a Boston insurance company while searching for the right opportunity in the EV industry. He had met Mr. Beaumont in May, 1973 and immediately joined SV as Marketing Manager.

Net sales for the first complete year of operations ending June 30, 1975 amounted to $2.37 million with a net loss from operations of $488,000 or $0.86 per share. These results are compared to net sales of $185,000 and net loss of $651,000 ($1.85 per share) during the startup period of the Company from May, 1973 through June 30, 1974. Financial statements are shown in Exhibits 4.1–4.3. Because of the high element of risk perceived in the SV venture by lending institutions, SV had not been able to borrow money and establish strong banking relationships. All of the stock was privately held by individuals until mid-1975 when International Nickel Company (INCO) purchased 100,000 shares at $3 per share and also acquired warrants to purchase an additional 60,000 shares at an average price of $5.00 by April 30, 1978. As a result of this investment, ESB, Inc., a wholly-owned subsidiary of INCO that manufactured batteries, had contributed technical assistance to SV. As of January, 1976, SV's management believed that there was virtually no chance of raising additional capital by a new equity issue. Debt financing consisted of notes from individual stockholders, notes from banks secured by essentially all SV's equipment and inventory, and long-term financing leaseholds.

During the year ending June 30, 1975, SV had sold an average of 83 vehicles per month. Sales in the last two months of that year had averaged 99 vehicles and during September and October of 1975, SV showed a monthly profit for the first time. It was estimated by management that monthly sales of roughly 150 CitiCars were necessary for profitable operations. The most difficult task facing SV, commented Mr. Beaumont, was "determining our costs of doing business and our break-even level of operations. Due to the rapid fluctuation in the costs of materials and components in an inflationary climate, it is difficult to determine month to month just what our costs were. A number of cost and engineering studies are currently being undertaken to reduce vehicle costs and to increase production efficiency and output."

Exhibit 4.1 Sebring-Vanguard, Inc. Statement of Operations and Accumulated Deficit

	For the Year Ended June 30, 1975	From Inception (May 14, 1973) to June 30, 1974
Net sales	$2,369,683	$185,364
Costs and expenses:		
Cost of products sold	2,319,761	181,624
General and administrative expenses	252,267	129,097
Selling expenses	259,581	44,422
Research and development	25,915	375,197
Pre-operating expenses		107,272
	2,857,524	837,612
Net loss	487,841	652,248
Accumulated deficit:		
Beginning of period	652,248	
End of period	$1,140,089	$652,248
Number of weighted average shares outstanding	564,251	351,661
Net loss per share	$ .86	$ 1.85

The CitiCar. The CitiCar was designed to fulfill the needs of the average urban and suburban driver, with a range of up to 50 miles on one electrical charge for the batteries. The top speed of the car (38 mph) and the acceleration capacity (0–25 mph in 6.2 seconds) were believed to be more than adequate for stop-and-go city driving. Furthermore, the size and maneuverability of the car were considered ideal for parking ease. The 95-inch length and 22-feet turning circle allowed the driver to pull into and out of a standard parking space without using reverse. It could be parked in places where even subcompacts wouldn't fit. The low center of gravity and wide track (63-inch wheelbase) allowed easy handling and safe performance, even on ice and snow. A description of the car is given in Exhibit 4.4 and a price list, including a list of available options, is shown in Exhibit 4.5.

Economy of operation and maintenance were the major reasons for buying a CitiCar, according to a survey of new owners. Whereas city or in-town driving was harsh on more expensive, conventional family cars, SV emphasized the use of the CitiCar as an economical second car for a family, saving the "gas-powered rig" for longer trips.

The CitiCar was able to travel about three miles on each KWH of electricity, costing about 1¢ per mile (depending on local rates) or roughly $6.00 per month. Maintenance requirements were minimal because no tune-ups or

Exhibit 4.2 Sebring-Vanguard, Inc. Balance Sheet

	June 30, 1975	1974
Assets		
Current assets:		
Cash (including $25,094 held in escrow at June 30, 1974)	$ 84,362	$ 48,178
Accounts receivable	135,140	36,639
Inventories	789,761	534,778
Prepaid expenses	81,774	17,096
Total current assets	1,091,037	636,691
Fixed assets, at cost, less accumulated depreciation	188,103	194,212
Organization expenses	15,095	19,407
	$1,294,235	$850,310
Liabilities and Stockholders' Equity		
Current liabilities:		
Notes payable	$ 91,786	$112,355
Accounts payable	$ 442,423	$371,355
Accrued expenses	97,681	84,838
Customer deposits	20,467	25,094
Total current liabilities	652,357	593,642
Notes payable, due after one year	371,966	8,915
Stockholders' equity		
Common stock, $.10 par value—1,000,000 shares authorized, 659,667 and 489,667 issued	65,967	48,967
Capital in excess of par value	1,443,034	950,034
Accumulated deficit	(1,140,089)	(652,248)
	368,912	346,753
Less: Notes receivable from stockholder	(99,000)	(99,000)
Total stockholders' equity	269,912	247,753
Commitments	$1,294,235	$850,310

periodic parts replacements were required as for vehicles with internal combustion engines. Typical maintenance needs involved checking electrical connections to see if they were tight, tire air pressure, and maintaining batteries (charge and water levels). Exhibit 4.6 shows the recommended maintenance schedule necessary for optimal battery life and CitiCar performance. A new set of batteries was required after 400 to 600 complete recharges, or every 15,000 to 20,000 miles, at a cost of approximately $300.

Exhibit 4.3   Sebring-Vanguard, Inc. Statement of Changes in Financial Position

	For the Year Ended June 30, 1975	From Inception (May 14, 1973) to June 30, 1974
Financial resources were provided by:		
Issuance of common stock	$510,000	$999,001
Less: Notes receivable from stockholder		(99,000)
	510,000	900,001
Proceeds from borrowings	405,003	14,860
	915,003	914,861
Financial resources were used for:		
Operations:		
Net loss	487,841	652,248
Charges not affecting working capital:		
Depreciation	55,215	25,419
Amortization	4,312	2,156
Working capital used in operations	428,314	624,673
Purchase of fixed assets	49,106	219,631
Increase in organization expenses		21,563
Reduction in notes payable due after one year	41,952	5,945
	519,372	871,812
Increase in working capital	395,631	43,049
Working capital at beginning of period	43,049	
Working capital at end of period	$438,680	$ 43,049

Analysis of Changes in Working Capital

Increase in current assets:		
Cash	$ 36,184	$ 48,178
Accounts receivable	98,501	36,639
Inventories	254,983	534,778
Prepaid expenses	64,678	17,096
	454,346	636,691
(Increase) decrease in current liabilities:		
Notes payable	20,569	(112,355)
Accounts payable	(71,068)	(371,355)
Accrued expenses	(12,843)	(84,838)
Customer deposits	4,627	(25,094)
	(58,715)	(593,642)
Increase in working capital	$395,631	$ 43,049

In December, 1975, SV made available a variety of kits to dealers to enhance and update their stock of 1975 CitiCars, to make them equivalent to the newer 1976 models. The list of kits available is shown in Exhibit 4.7.

A research and development program had been established to implement design and engineering improvements. For example, the CitiCar would soon have sliding windows rather than sideflaps and a hatchback window. Other recent modifications included a fully automatic battery charger and side rocker panels. Longer-lived batteries which would extend the range of the CitiCar were also being developed by suppliers and were expected to be commercially available by 1979. Plans were also being made to introduce a CitiVan and CitiTruck on a chassis common to the CitiCar.

Mr. Stone believed that the resale value of a used CitiCar should be high due to very little depreciation. "Calculated obsolescence is not our philosophy," he said. "Since nominal maintenance is required, and very few moving parts are present, there is no reason to expect increased maintenance for older cars, as is the case with all contemporary gasoline-powered vehicles. In

---

Exhibit 4.4   The CitiCar

Specifications

Length/95″
Width/55″
Wheelbase/63″
Height/58″
Front Track/43″
Rear Track/44″
Clearance/4½′
Weight/1300 pounds.

Rear Storage/12 Cu. Ft.
Tires/4.80x12, 4 ply rated
Speed/38 mph cruising.

Range/Up to 50 miles
Acceleration/0 to 25—6.2 secs.
　　　　　　0 to 35—19 secs.

Turning Circle/22 ft.
Controller/Vanguard Multivoltage
　speed control.
Motor/Series wound DC 6 HP
Differential/Direct pinion drive.
Suspension/Leaf springs, front & rear.
　4 wheel shock absorbers.
Body/Impact resistant Cycolac® (ABS)
　rust & corrosion proof.
Frame/Rectangular aluminum chassis,
　tubular aluminum body support.
Brakes/Four wheel hydraulic brakes,

parking brake.
Power Source/Eight 6 volt batteries (HD)

Standard Equipment

110 volt on-board built-in charger - high impact urethane bumpers - laminated safety glass windshield - shoulder harness seat belts - head rests - dual speed windshield wiper - windshield washer - emergency flashers - back up light - license plate light - signal lights - side - view mirror - rearview mirror - courtesy light - horn - speedometer/odometer - voltmeter - 4 ply rated tires - wheel covers - vinyl top - custom side windows - side moldings - shock absorbers - custom woodgrain dashboard, inner door straps, 25′ IID extension cord, drip rail moldings, rear carpeting.

Body Colors

Red, yellow, orange, blue, green, and white. Custom colors (to order) available.

Optional Equipment

Radio and antenna - cigar lighter - heater - right sideview mirror - single car trailer (to tow CitiCar) - spare tire and wheel - hydrometer - CitiCar jack - car cover

4/Sebring-Vanguard, Inc.: The CitiCar

(Custom) - flat tire inflator - defroster - fully automatic custom charger - door locks - custom paint (to order). Radial tires - Sebring-Vanguard battery saver caps - white wall tires - tinted glass.

Note: The CitiCar is best suited on roads where the posted speed limit does not exceed 50 MPH. The CitiCar should not be used on Interstate highways.

Limited Warranty

Under normal use, the CitiCar is warranted by Sebring-Vanguard, Inc. for a period of 6 months after purchase by the customer. This warranty applies to all parts of the vehicle found defective in material or workmanship; except for tires and bat- teries, which are warranted separately by their respective manufacturers.

This is a summary of the entire warranty, which is available at your authorized Se- bring-Vanguard, Inc. dealership.

Q. How fast does the CitiCar by Sebring-Vanguard go?
A. The current version, CitiCar/SV-48, cruises at up to 38 miles per hour.

Q. Can the CitiCar be licensed for on-the-road use?
A. The CitiCar complies with most Fed- eral Motor Vehicle Standards appli- cable to that vehicle. Therefore, it should be licensable in all states.

Q. What is the CitiCar designed for?
A. The CitiCar is designed for low speed, short distance driving by housewives, commuters, students, retired persons, etc. Because it has been constructed on a truck chassis the CitiCar is also ideal for such off-road uses as security patrol, in-plant transportation, etc. The CitiCar has been sold as a mes- senger and delivery vehicle and is useful for city meter maids and utility companies.

Q. How far will the CitiCar go before re- charging?
A. The range is up to 50 miles, depend- ing on temperature, terrain, and traffic conditions. Thirty-five miles is a typi- cal range in city driving conditions. Fortunately, the CitiCar does not use energy when stopped at a light or coasting to a stop.

Q. Will the CitiCar fulfill my driving needs?
A. Chances are it will. The average urban and suburban automobile in the United States is driven only 22.6 miles per day. This makes the CitiCar a very practical second or third car for many families.

Q. How does the top speed hold up as the CitiCar is driven during the day?
A. A top speed of 35–38 miles per hour should be attained during all but the last few miles of the charge.

Q. How will the CitiCar handle in snow?
A. Exceptionally well; its low center of gravity plus the rearmounted motor and transaxle provide excellent trac- tion.

Q. What effect do the lights and wiper have on the range of the CitiCar?
A. Owners' experience has shown that there is a decrease of approximately 10% in the CitiCar's range during night operation.

Q. Can the CitiCar be towed?
A. Only for short distances at low speed. We recommend using a trailer when taking the CitiCar on vacation.

Q. How will the CitiCar handle on hills?
A. Very well. Avoid climbing long steep hills as it may cause the CitiCar's

motor to overheat. However, a HOT MOTOR lamp on the dash board will alert the driver of this unlikely occurrence.

Q. Is the CitiCar really pollution free?

A. Electric vehicles are classified as inherently non-polluting vehicles by the U.S. Environmental Agency. The relatively little pollution that is emitted from the power plant is usually far from populated areas and is easier to control than automobile pollution. Of course, many power plants do not burn fossil fuels, and in these cases the CitiCar is virtually pollution-free.

Q. Do electric vehicles indirectly burn just as much fuel as conventional cars via the electric plant?

A. No, because fuel-burning power plants which generate electricity for the CitiCar can operate more efficiently than small internal combustion engines, the CitiCar's actual fuel usage is only a fraction of that of an average sub-compact.

Q. If millions of electric vehicles were used around the country, wouldn't this cause black outs and brown outs?

A. Surprisingly enough, no. Electric vehicles would most likely be recharged at night during off peak periods, when utility companies have sufficient capacity to recharge many millions of electric vehicles. In this way, power plants will operate more efficiently and electric rates may stabilize.

Q. Could the CitiCar be powered by solar energy?

A. Once the people of our country develop the technology to inexpensively convert solar energy into electricity the CitiCar batteries could then be recharged by a solar charging station.

Q. Can electric vehicles be made to go faster and further?

A. Yes, but at a much greater cost. We have designed the CitiCar based on a comprehensive survey that urban traffic moves at an average of 28 miles per hour, and that most 'second cars' are driven only 5–40 miles per day.

Q. Is the CitiCar as safe as the average small car?

A. The CitiCar is equipped with seat and shoulder belts and most other safety equipment required by law. It is constructed on a rugged aluminum chassis and has a tubular aluminum body support structure surrounding the passenger compartment. Because the CitiCar will not be used on interstate highways, the possibility of a high-speed collision is eliminated. We feel that these features and the fact that the CitiCar will be used only in low speed areas make it one of the safest small cars on the road today.

Q. What about insurance?

A. Insurance should be no different from any other compact motor vehicle. In fact, because the CitiCar will be used only at low speeds and for short-distance driving around town, we think rates for this vehicle will someday be less than for cars driven at highway speeds and for possibly hundreds of miles per day.

Q. What makes the CitiCar a good investment?

A. The CitiCar is a good investment because of its low operating costs, low maintenance costs, and anticipated low depreciation.

Q. Will the CitiCar depreciate as fast or as much as a conventional car does?

A. We think not. The CitiCar's frame is constructed of corrosion-resistant aluminum. The body is of rust-proof Cycolac ABS, with the color impregnated throughout the material. Also there is no internal combustion engine with its associated support systems to require repair or replacement. For these reasons, the CitiCar should retain more of its value over a longer period than a conventional car.

Q. How much maintenance does the

CitiCar require?

A. Much less than for a conventional car. The CitiCar has no spark plugs, points, mufflers, radiator, valves, rings, carburetor, antipollution controls, or transmission. The batteries are the most important part of the CitiCar and should be checked weekly. (Consult your owner's manual for correct procedures.)

Q. How much battery maintenance does the CitiCar require?

A. Approximately 15 minutes per week to refill the batteries with distilled water.

Q. How long will the batteries last?

A. With proper care in accordance with the owner's manual, the batteries should last from 12,000 to 18,000 miles, under normal use.

Q. What is the cost to replace a set of batteries?

A. The current suggested retail price of a set of replacement batteries is about $320.00.

Q. How do the CitiCar batteries differ from regular car batteries?

A. These heavy-duty 6-volt batteries are designed for hundreds of recharging cycles, which electric vehicles require.

Q. How will I know when my batteries need recharging?

A. The CitiCar's voltmeter will indicate approximately when a recharge is necessary.

Q. How do I recharge the batteries?

A. The CitiCar is equipped with a built-in on-board charger. The batteries may be recharged by simply plugging the charger cord into any standard 110 volt household outlet.

Q. How long does it take to recharge the batteries?

A. Usually overnight, depending on the state of battery discharge, in turn, depending on daily mileage.

Q. How does the cold weather affect the CitiCar?

A. The efficiency of the batteries de-creases proportionately to the temperature drop. If the batteries are kept in a state of charge during non-use, loss of battery efficiency can be minimized.

Q. How much does an average recharge cost?

A. About 25 cents, depending on local rates. The CitiCar SV-48 will go about three city miles on one KWH of electricity. Consult your local utility company to compute the per mile cost of operating a CitiCar in your area. Also, ask if your utility company sells off-peak electricity at a cheaper rate.

Q. Why not attach a generator or alternator to the CitiCar in such a way that the batteries can be recharged during operation?

A. This has not been shown to be an effective way of increasing range because more energy is required to turn the generator than is won back.

Q. Is there a chance that my CitiCar could run out of charge while on the road?

A. Not very much, unless you have forgotten to recharge the CitiCar the night before. However, if the CitiCar does run out of charge before you return home (perhaps you had to run an unexpected errand at the end of the day), by simply resting for 15 or 20 minutes, the batteries will recharge themselves enough to get you a mile or so further.

Q. Is air-conditioning available?

A. No, this would cause too much of a drain on the batteries. However, because the CitiCar has large side windows and because there is no engine heat to leak into the passenger compartment, air conditioning should not be needed.

Q. Suppose I drive my CitiCar for 20 or 30 miles in the morning: can I charge up the batteries for an hour or so during lunch before going out again in the afternoon?

A. Yes, indeed.

Q. I have to drive thirty miles to work every morning. Could the CitiCar meet my commuting needs?

A. If your employer will find you a place to charge up the CitiCar during the day, you should have enough charge for the return trip in the evening.

Q. Why should I buy a CitiCar instead of a small similarly-priced sub-compact?

A. In addition to the fact that the Citi-Car is a good investment, an electric vehicle is inherently pollution-free and it can be operated independent of the available supplies of gasoline. Energy independence is one of our country's greatest goals and every-one must do his part to help.

Q. Who can service my CitiCar?

A. Any authorized Sebring-Vanguard, Inc. dealer. The CitiCar is designed so simply that many owners will find that they can perform most service tasks themselves. Technical assist-ance is always available through the Customer Service department of Sebring-Vanguard, Inc.

Q. Are replacement parts available?

A. Yes, at any authorized Sebring-Van-guard dealer, or at the Sebring-Vanguard National Service Depart-ment, Sebring, Fla. 33870.

Q. What about the motor?

A. The electric motor is a heavy-duty 3.5 HP series wound G.E. motor, designed to last for many years. Very little maintenance is required.

Q. Where can I buy a CitiCar?

A. At any authorized Sebring-Vanguard, Inc. Sales and Service dealership. Contact the National Sales Office of Sebring-Vanguard for the name of the dealer nearest you.

---

addition, the body of the car is made of high-impact shatter-resistant ABS Cycolac® plastic, the same material used in football helmets, which will not rust, peel, or corrode with age."

The CitiCar complied with practically all federal safety standards. An integral roll-cage-type construction surrounded the passenger compartment. Polyurethane bumpers reinforced with a steel beam protected the front and back of the car. A variety of interlock systems were also included as safety features: a shift interlock prevented the driver from inadvertently shifting into the wrong gear; the parking brake stopped the car and simultaneously shut off the power; and a charger interlock prevented the car from being driven away while still plugged in.

In October, 1975, Consumers Union published their evaluation of the CitiCar in *Consumer Reports* (Appendix 4.1). The CitiCar was rated "not acceptable." Concerning this report, Mr. Stone commented:

Consumer Reports really hurt us. Unfortunately they tested an *early* model which did have substantial problems and was defective in some respects. They wouldn't let us correct the defects under the service and parts warranty. We have a superior product now. The car is much better built and more reliable, especially the controller and the new brakes, and a variety of options are now available that were not earlier.

Exhibit 4.5   Price List for CitiCar and Optional Equipment

Code	Body Style	Sugg. Retail	Dealer
111-DW	CitiCar (Dana Differential)—Convenience & trim pkg., solid state automatic charger, separate accessory battery, vinyl roof, new silent ride drive-train, eight 6-volt 106 min. batteries, 6HP motor, fuel-less heater & defroster system, full doors with locks & sliding windows, carpeting throughout.	$2,988.00	$2,480.00
111-D	Same as 111-DW, except for full doors & sliding windows. Has removable flexible plastic side curtains with locks.	$2,888.00	$2,425.90
111-T	CitiCar (Terrell Differential)—Serial #2780 & prior. Includes Convenience & Trim pkg., door/window locks, Lester charger with timer, 3½ HP motor, vinyl roof, eight 6-volt, 106 minute batteries, carpeting.	$2,738.00	$2,299.90

Colors

Code		Sugg. Retail	Dealer
201	Red		
202	Orange		
203	Yellow		
204	Blue		
206	White		
207	Green		
299	Custom paint with added charge of:	57.00	38.00

Upholstery/Vinyl Roof

Code	
301	White
302	Black

Optional Equipment

Code		Sugg. Retail	Dealer
426	Hatchback, Including Tinted Rear Glass	57.00	38.00
401	Radio/Antenna	57.00	38.00
424	Tinted Glass (Windshield)	27.00	18.00
427	Tinted Glass (Front and Rear)	33.00	22.00
411	Right Side-View Mirror	9.00	6.00
407	Hydrometer	6.00	4.00
405	Spare Tire and Wheel	36.00	24.00
419	Seal n Drive Tire Repair	4.98	4.00
423	Radial Ply Tires (Michelin)	72.00	48.00
412	CitiCar Jack (custom)	18.00	12.00
416	Cigar Lighter	7.50	5.00
418	Battery Saver Caps	58.50	39.00
413	All Weather Car Cover (custom)	48.00	32.00
428	Custom Rally Stripes	27.00	18.00
408	Single Car Tilt Trailer Fully-Equipped		

Prices subject to change without notice. All prices are FOB Sebring, Fla.
Dealer preparation: $35.00 (On Retail Only)
We also have available several demonstrator CitiCars specially discounted at various prices for those interested in requesting a list.

Exhibit 4.6 Maintenance of CitiCar

For your convenience, your vehicle has been designed to give long, reliable service with the simplest and least costly maintenance requirements possible.

You play an important part in maintenance

Only you can make sure that your vehicle regularly receives the care it needs.

Scheduled maintenance services

The following schedule of periodic servicing of your CitiCar should be adhered to closely. Daily, weekly, and monthly maintenance can usually be performed by you, the owner. We strongly recommend that more detailed servicing, at six-month intervals, be performed by an Authorized Sebring-Vanguard dealer. Also, please make every effort to return your CitiCar to the Selling Dealer after sixty days for various required maintenance checks, as your CitiCar's warranty should be protected. If you are located so far from a Vanguard dealer as to make service visits impractical, be sure to make arrangements for equivalent servicing. The last pages of your manual are set aside to maintain a record of all scheduled servicing.

As the following services are not covered by the warranty, you will be charged for the labor, parts, and lubricants used.

Daily

Keep batteries in a constant state of charge.

Weekly or biweekly

Check the water level of each battery. Refill as needed.

Monthly

Clear dirt, if any, from batteries. If pad protectors should deteriorate, or if new batteries are required, pads should be replaced. Tighten all terminal connections. (Do not overtighten.)
Hydrometer reading of batteries.
Check tire pressure and look for excessive wear, cuts or other damage. Tighten wheel nuts.

Two months after purchase

Thorough vehicle check-up.
Change the transaxle fluid—use SAE 90-EP Non-Detergent Mineral Base Oil—11 ounces.

Every two months

Check fluid level in rear axle.

4/Sebring-Vanguard, Inc.: The CitiCar

Six months after purchase and every six months thereafter

Lubricate chassis—two grease fittings in front suspension. Also lubricate door hinges, parking brakes, cable guides, and linkage.

Check level of brake fluid in master cylinder. If brake fluid must be added, use Type-3 Heavy Duty. Check the brake system for possible leakage or worn out pads. Also, check brake lines and hoses for cracks, chafing, deterioration and proper attachment. Replace or repair any defective parts immediately.

Battery voltage check and battery rotation.

Check suspension and steering for damaged, loose or missing parts or parts showing visible signs of extensive wear or lack of lubrication. Defective parts should be replaced by a qualified mechanic without delay.

Check the motor brushes. Replacement of the motor brushes and the K-1 solenoid (in the controller) may be necessary when the batteries are replaced.

Check the manual steering gear for seal leakage around the pitman shaft and housing. If leakage is evident (heavy oil oozing out— not just oily film), it should be corrected immediately.

Clean underbody of road accumulation.

Clean front wheel bearings and make necessary adjustments.

Check controller points.

Every twelve months

Rotate tires.

Change rear axle lubricant.

Repack front wheel bearings.

Equipment safety checks

As an on-going check on the proper working order of the safety related features of your CitiCar, the following areas should be periodically looked at during normal use of the CitiCar. All appropriate replacements, repairs, adjustments, and cleaning of these features should be performed as soon as possible after problems are detected.

A. Safety Belts	H. Horn
B. Windshield Wiper & Washer	I. Parking Brake
C. Steering	J. Brakes
D. Tires	K. Headlights & Taillights
E. Glass Areas	L. All Running Lights
F. Mirrors	M. Underbody
G. Fluid Leaks	N. Shock Absorbers

Source: CitiCar SV-48 1975 Owner's Manual.

Exhibit 4.7

December 4, 1975
Memorandum to: All Sebring-Vanguard Dealers
From: Terry R. Keller, National Parts Manager
Subject: CitiCar update

Kits are now available for many of the improvements incorporated in the CitiCar since the beginning of production. We are sending this bulletin to you so you can select the items you want, to update your stock to make it more appealing to prospective customers. You can choose any or all of these kits. Full instructions will accompany all items you order.

Item Description	Part No.	Dealer Cost	Labor
1. drip moldings 2 @ 3.95	6170-1 & 2	7.90	.4
2. rocker panels—2 @ 12.00	6927 & 8	24.00	.6
3. disc to drum brakes	909	120.00	3.0
4. defroster	941	14.00	1.0
5. heater—Terrell adaption	942	69.50	2.0
6. new Pitman arm	999	15.75	.2
7. Michelin radial tires—4	10161	187.70	.8
8. automatic charger*	10004	259.17	.7
9. circuit breaker**	10420-1	1.50	.1
10. carpeting for rear floor	6550	5.76	.1
11. door locks	908	8.00	.6
12. window locks	1011-2	7.20	.4
13. battery saver caps	987	39.00	.4
14. thicker seat	6616-10	48.60	—
15. heavier cables—3	6062-7	15.57	.6
16. door pull straps—2	6604	2.70	.4
17. external charging plug	6151-6172	9.12	.5
18. white upholstery	10023-11-12	115.74	.8
19. new style parking lights—2	6838	25.44	.2

*allowance for old charger, $70.00
**replace 40A fuse

Sincerely,

Terry R. Keller
National Parts Manager
TRK/cle

The (CU) article implied that safety problems existed because the car had been exempted from federal safety rules which require other cars to withstand low-speed crashes. The CitiCar has been exempted until June 1, 1978, only from those standards covering defrosting systems, antitheft devices, and side door strength. It meets all remaining standards that apply to every passenger car. The above exemptions were allowed by the government to facilitate development of electric vehicles (EV's). The "lifesaving protection" for frontal and side impacts, and rollovers are not yet requirements for any vehicle, but are only proposed amendments to existing legislation.

We've had difficulty combatting the inaccuracies of this report, mainly because nationwide news release of the "findings" by many news services accompanied the issuance of the report. We can effectively fight this deleterious effect only if the local news media around each of our dealerships carry the SV news release "A Report on the Level of Safety Incorporated in the Sebring-Vanguard Electric CitiCar" (Appendix 4.2). We are confident that once the media in a dealer's area are aware of the truth concerning safety, they will allow equal time to the dealer to report the truth about the CitiCar. Mr. Beaumont has written strong letters of encouragement to each dealer to try and keep morale and dealer-support high. Many satisfied owners have written Consumers Union in protest, which is encouraging to us.

The CitiCar is so unique, it's difficult to make comparisons with cars of today, as CU has done. Society has been spoiled to expect high performance, speed, size, and plush comfort. We believe that our society needs the CitiCar to help alleviate ecology, energy, and urban problems facing us today. We are unique in another sense. We are the world's foremost producer of electric vehicles for personal transportation. There is no serious competition. The Elcar, which was also rated by *Consumer Reports,* is an Italian import, and does not have the high quality of workmanship or design that CitiCar does. There is no roll-cage construction for safety; the batteries are automotive which may have only 1/4 the life that CitiCar batteries have; shifting speeds is required while driving; Elcar does not have roll-up windows contrary to the article's claim; and the estimate of 1/2¢ per mile operating cost is based on electricity rates of two years ago. A more current figure is about 1¢ per mile. Finally, the cost of an Elcar is higher—$3,395 for the 35 mph (top speed) version. We expect no serious competition from the major automotive manufacturers. It would take them 10–12 years to make an engineering change and to undertake conceptual re-education of this magnitude.

Mr. Beaumont also added his comments concerning the viability of the Citi-Car:

The most economical, abundant source of energy today for motor-powered personal transportation available today is the lead-acid battery. The EV concept is very consistent with our nation's energy goals. EV's are not dependent on any one (original) source of energy. All they require is to convert that energy—coal, nuclear, geothermal, solar, etc.—to electricity to recharge the lead-acid batteries. We at SV have undertaken a giant educational process. EV's like the CitiCar can now provide a substantial portion of personal transportation almost anywhere in the world.

Pricing. One of the most appealing characteristics of the CitiCar, according to a survey of purchasers, was its price. The CitiCar was originally priced at $2,269, and the "unimproved" 1976 models still in dealer inventories were currently selling for $2,738 plus taxes, freight, and dealer preparation. A price of $2,888 had recently been announced for a new model with a less noisy differential, and a price of $2,988 was announced on February 18, 1976, for a model with several new features including heater and defroster, carpeting, separate accessory battery, new door and latch design, sliding windows, etc., as shown in Exhibit 4.4. (SV management originally felt that a heater was "not essential" for small errands, etc.) Mr. Stone believed that many people felt that electric cars were much more expensive than they actually were.

Dealers were allowed a 16% discount from list price on the car and 33⅓% on all optional accessories. These trade discounts were comparable to those allowed for conventional compact and subcompact cars. For example, American Motors allowed dealers a 12% discount on its Gremlin. Some companies also gave the dealer no more margin on options than they received on the car. However, it should be noted that dealers were allowed higher margins, up to 20% and more, on bigger and more expensive conventional automobiles.

Electric Car Market. It had been estimated by a variety of trade sources and consumer surveys that over 80% of all motor vehicles were operated in urban areas, with average daily usage of under 22 miles at an average speed of 29 mph. Furthermore, SV estimated that the total cost to the consuming public of the gasoline-powered automobile over the last three years had been $410 billion. These costs covered the initial cost of new and used cars, gasoline, interest and insurance expense, depreciation, maintenance, and costs of scrapping and discarding.

"There is hardly a foreign country that has not requested (unsolicited) information in connection with manufacturing and marketing this vehicle," Mr.

Beaumont had said in his testimony before a Congressional subcommittee studying energy research. "What this means is that the world is eagerly awaiting a new form of transportation. If the world can be transformed in a few short years to computer programming of all facets of business, it would seem logical that it shouldn't be difficult to teach the mass market to drive electrically. This market is simply awaiting a product."

Mr. Beaumont estimated that the U.S. government represented a large potential market for electric cars. He had learned that the U.S. General Services Administration Interagency Motor Pool had 70,574 vehicles in use as of September 30, 1975 of which 36,591 were sedans. Agency officials estimated that 10 to 15 percent of these vehicles traveled less than 30 miles per day. Military vehicles were another major potential market. Mr. Beaumont had testified before several subcommittees in the U.S. Senate and House of Representatives considering programs of encouraging electric vehicles research and development.

The only data available concerning the attitudes and socioeconomic backgrounds of consumers in the electric car market had been obtained from a survey of a small number of current CitiCar owners. The results of this survey are presented below. Selected comments from this survey are contained in Appendix 4.3.

CitiCar Owner Survey

Region		Sex	
South	48.2%	Male	60.7%
East	25.9%	Female	39.3%
Midwest	14.8%		
Other	11.1%		

Age		Family Income	
20—30	23.1%	Less than $10,000	10%
30—40	23.1%	$10—20,000	55%
40—50	11.5%	$20—50,000	20%
Over 50	42.3%	Over $50,000	15%

Occupation		Reasons for Purchase	
White collar and		(more than one could be given)	
Professional	54.5%	Economy	88.0%
Blue collar	22.8%	Energy	40.0%
Retired	22.7%	Environment	36.0%

Use	
In town	46.0%
Commute	46.0%
Other	8.0%

Note: 75% of CitiCar owners surveyed were not in the market for a car when they purchased CitiCars.

Dealer Organization. At the beginning of 1976, CitiCar was available to the public from 200 dealers: 84 dealers in the South, 58 in the Midwest, 52 along the East coast (excluding Florida and Georgia), and 6 in the far West. The type of dealer outlet varied considerably. Of the 200 dealers, 110–120 were established automobile agencies franchised for one or more brand names of domestic and imported cars. Ten CitiCar dealers were used-car dealers. The remaining CitiCar dealers covered a broad spectrum of retail outlets: 10–20 golf cart or equipment houses; two bicycle dealers; two or three electric motor repair dealers; two boat dealers; six recreational vehicle and/or mobile home dealers; six battery dealers, selling to golf courses and to industries, and one lawnmower dealer. A few of these dealers had gone into business solely for the purpose of selling CitiCars. Citicar was available to 85–90% of the U.S. population within a 50-mile radius of one of these dealerships.

SV recommended that a dealer keep four to twelve CitiCars in stock (minimum requirement was four cars) depending on the size of his market. Unless the dealer was an already established automobile dealer, SV recommended that he have at least one salesman, an office worker, and a factory-trained serviceman to handle the CitiCar. SV estimated that total initial investment should be within the $10,000 to $35,000 range. No separate franchise fee was required. The only additional requirement was that the dealer send a maintenance person to Sebring for in-plant training to become expert in servicing cars. Room and board during the training was provided by SV. SV used technical literature and newsletters to dealers to keep them abreast of new developments with CitiCar. No SV technical representatives were as yet available for back-up field support.

Although most dealerships conducted business directly with the factory, a distributor in New Jersey had been given the East Coast (north of Georgia) as his exclusive territory. He developed new and existing dealerships, and they were required to order all their CitiCars from the distributor's inventory. The distributorship was allowed a margin of $200 for each car sold. The distributor also became an SV stockholder as part of the agreement with the company. All other new CitiCar dealers were solicited by the National Sales Manager, Robert Balfour, and their orders were processed and shipped from Sebring.

Approximately 1,600 CitiCars had been manufactured by the end of 1975, although half of these were still in the dealers' inventories. Retail sales of the CitiCar (and subsequent reorders from the factory) had slowed tremendously in the past few months. The apparent lack of enthusiasm shown by the dealers was attributed in part to the effect of the *Consumer Reports* article.

Mr. Stone also feared that the established automotive dealers were using CitiCar as a "traffic builder"—to lure curious potential customers into the showroom and then to sell them conventional gasoline-powered cars.

Interviews were conducted by the case writer with two car dealers in the Northeast who had CitiCar franchises (see Appendix 4.4). Both dealers were located near metropolitan areas. Dealer X had sold no CitiCars since he had obtained them in August, 1975. Dealer Y, a much larger dealership, had sold 16 of the 24 ordered since the Spring of 1975.

In order to achieve the sales goal of 150–200 cars per month, Mr. Stone was considering moving away from established car dealerships as a distribution channel for CitiCar, and using other outlets, such as appliance stores and catalog stores (e.g., Montgomery Ward). Other possibilities included the establishment of a direct sales/service force to handle large national or industrial accounts, or to solicit and service local, state, and federal government agencies. Mr. Beaumont, however, was of the opinion that the best approach was to establish as many retail dealers as possible, with a minimum inventory of cars, but to expect that 20 per cent of the dealers would account for 80 per cent of sales. He argued that local availability was the key to sales.

Promotion. SV emphasized the newsworthiness of CitiCar to its dealers and relied heavily on the free publicity gained from automobile magazines, electric industry trade journals, quasi-technical lay periodicals such as *Popular Mechanics* and *Popular Science,* and magazines such as *U.S. News & World Report, Reader's Digest, Wall Street Journal,* and *Family Circle.* In addition, heavy local news media coverage had always been generated in an area when a new CitiCar dealership had opened or following such events as the purchase of CitiCars by police forces, car-rental agencies, universities, and local industries. Editorial columns had discussed CitiCar in the context of public concern for environmental, energy, and transportation problems. Further exposure had been obtained by featuring the CitiCar on national television shows such as "The Mike Douglas Show," "The Price is Right," and "NBC Network News." The CitiCar had also been displayed in automobile shows, parades, and a variety of other public gatherings.

As Mr. Beaumont pointed out in SV's annual report for 1974–75, ". . . the free ride cannot last forever." Therefore, in December, 1975, SV had produced a TV commercial for $500 that it hoped to sell to dealers for $20–$25. The 30-second commercial showed the CitiCar on a revolving pedestal and the voice-over commented on the negative features of a conventional car which the CitiCar did not have. In addition, a cooperative advertising program had been established to help dealers finance the costs of television air time and other advertising expenses. SV planned to allow dealers $25 per car ordered as reimbursement for up to 50% of their media costs. However, no plans for a nationwide mass media campaign had been considered. A variety of promotional aids and point of purchase displays were also available to the dealerships. A listing of these materials and their cost to the dealer is shown in Exhibit 4.8.

The national sales force consisted of Mr. Balfour (the Sales Manager) and

Mr. William Beaumont, brother of SV's president, both of whom had joined the company in late 1974. Mr. Balfour spent most of his time on the road developing new dealers, whereas Mr. William Beaumont was concerned primarily with dealer follow-up via telephone. Until very recently, Mr. Balfour had been the sole salesman for SV and was responsible for the establishment of many new dealerships. Mr. Balfour had been involved with EV's since 1966. He was an author of numerous papers and pamphlets on lightweight vehicles and had been a vice president and sales manager of the major golf cart manufacturer that had produced the Vanguard Sport Coupe.

Exhibit 4.8   Sales Materials

Description	Price*
Single Car Trailer (shipped via common carrier)	$332.00
Exterior 4'x8' Double Face Illuminated Sign	$439.00
Exterior 4'x8' Single Face Illuminated Sign (flush mounting)	$429.00
Special Construction for Centerpost Mounting	$ 33.00 additional
CitiCar illuminated clock/indoor sign 20"x49" single face	$ 98.00

The following is a list of all currently available sales aids. There is a space available for your name and address on the printed materials. Please feel free to contact me if you have any further suggestions for various marketing materials. There is a space available for you to place an order for any sales materials you may need. Mark your needs and return to my attention. An invoice will be sent to you when we mail the materials out.

Description	Price per Minimum Order Quantity*
Answers to Questions and Specifications (revised 2/75)	$25.00 per 1000
8½x10 Color Brochure	$6.00 per 100
"Electric" License Plates	$1.50 each
Electric Vehicle News Subscription	$10.00 per year
Customer Order Form — 2 page	$5.00 per 50
T-Shirt (Give Mother Nature a Break— Buy an Electric CitiCar)	$3.50 each (in quantities of 6 doz.— $3.25 each)

*Signs are shipped freight collect to dealers; prices are subject to change without notice.

Mr. Balfour's major responsibility was to solicit new accounts. He traveled nationwide, with CitiCar in tow on a trailer behind his Ford LTD sedan, giving demonstration rides to prospective dealers and displaying the vehicle at car shows across the country. Mr. Stone described Mr. Balfour as ". . . the last of the great American salesmen, with the bearing and dignity of a senator. He is totally positive and is entirely committed to the EV concept. His enthusiasm is unquenchable. As a result, his credibility level is very high. He has been an inspiration to many of us." The absence of technical representatives and an adequate field sales force made follow-through and support of a fledgling dealership difficult. Some people did feel that Mr. Balfour was too enthusiastic initially and had a tendency to oversell the CitiCar.

In addition to Mr. Balfour's efforts, the New Jersey distributor had one salesman to solicit new accounts. The distributor also helped new dealerships with promotional campaigns.

Promotional efforts of a different nature were being undertaken as well. The environmental and energy problems of the 1970s had prompted the U.S. government to investigate and fund proposed alternatives to existing energy and transportation technologies.

In the autumn of 1975, the Electric Vehicle Research, Development and Demonstration Act of 1975 was passed by the House of Representatives (H.R. 5470), which established a $160 million project over a three-year period whereby "production and use within one year of several thousand electric vehicles designed about *existing* vehicle chassis (as yet unnamed) and then within three years several thousand vehicles would be introduced . . . to insure . . . widespread use." This would allow performance and maintenance standards to be established and an adequate evaluation program of the "electrical concept" to be initiated. Other R & D work would be authorized for control systems, over-all optimal design, and environmental and urban impact. The passage of this bill was believed by SV executives to be partly due to the testimony of Mr. Beaumont, as an expert on electrical vehicle technology.

Mr. Beaumont commented:

If our government will encourage the use of electric vehicles by funding a program, let the funds be made available only to companies with experience and background in small vehicle manufacturing (preferably electric) and/or those companies willing to participate as peripheral component suppliers. We definitely must not squander taxpayers' money on banal and redundant study papers that gather dust in the archives. The net effect of any funding program must be based on providing value for monies expended. What is needed is one company to thrive; then others will most certainly follow.

Mr. Beaumont and SV were planning continued major lobbying efforts to ensure complete passage of the bill and hopefully to ensure favorable dispensation for SV or its suppliers for government contracts. In February of 1976, this legislation was in the Senate Commerce Committee.

**Consumer Reports
Evaluation of the CitiCar**

Two Electric Cars

Electric cars have been marketed without much success since before the turn of the century. In recent years, concern over air pollution caused by the internal combustion engine and the rising cost of gasoline have revived interest in electric cars. CU therefore decided to test the only two electric cars being sold in any volume in this country: the *CitiCar SV-48* and the *Elcar 2000*. We found major safety and operating problems.

The *CitiCar*, made by Sebring-Vanguard, Inc., of Sebring, Fla., cost $2946 delivered to our Auto Test Center in Connecticut. The *Elcar*, an Italian import distributed in the U.S. by Elcar Corp., Elkhart, Ind., cost $3475 delivered.

Conventional passenger cars must conform to certain Federal safety standards. But to spur the development of low-emission vehicles, the Government has granted temporary exemptions from some of those standards to manufacturers of electric cars—with unfortunate results.

Conventional cars must provide life-saving protection to occupants in a 30-mph barrier crash, a 30-mph rollover, and a 20-mph side impact from another car. We believe any such crash would imperil the lives of persons inside these tiny, fragile, plastic-bodied vehicles. A rollover or a severe crash holds the further threat of sulfuric acid pouring from ruptured batteries. (The batteries are under the padded-plywood seat cushion in the *CitiCar* and under the plywood floor in the *Elcar*—both within the passenger compartments.)

There are other obvious hazards no longer tolerated in conventional automobiles. Adjusting the safety belts is discouragingly complicated. Yet the windshield frame in the *CitiCar* is just a few inches in front of the forehead of tall occupants, making the use of shoulder belts especially important. The *Elcar's* safety belts are not much better.

The *CitiCar* has no steering-wheel lock, and the doors cannot be locked. The hinges and latches looked so flimsy that we tied the doors shut before performing any emergency-handling tests. (The *Elcar's* door hardware also looked flimsy, but at least the doors and steering column had locks.)

In both cars, very wide front and rear roof pillars interfere with the driver's view, as do single wipers in the center of the windshields. The spare tires are free to roll around behind the seats and could cause injury in an accident.

The *CitiCar* has a welded-aluminum "roll cage" intended to keep the plastic body from collapsing during a collision; we doubt that it provides as much protection as a well-designed steel body. But steel is heavy, of course, and would make the car even slower than it already is.

The *Elcar* has yet another mark against it: Its suspension is too flimsy to cope with even the low level of performance of which the vehicle is capable. During hard braking tests from 30 mph, the front suspension collapsed, putting an emphatic end to our testing of the *Elcar*.

The manufacturer of the *CitiCar* specifically warns owners that the vehicle should be used only on roads where the speed limit does not exceed 50 mph. The *Elcar* is promoted simply as "perfect on-street transportation for in-town use." But we believe it would be foolhardy to drive either car on any public road. Neither provides anything close to adequate crash protection; and neither handles or accelerates well enough to give us confidence that they're capable of getting out of a tight spot.

CU hopes experiments with electric cars continue. A practical, safe, economical electric car might be just right as a second car limited to short commutes and shopping trips. But neither the *CitiCar* nor the *Elcar* is practical, safe, or economical. We rate both of them Not Acceptable.

On the two pages that follow we report on our tests of these two cars in more detail. However, the results are presented primarily to satisfy the understandable curiosity about electric cars, not as the basis for a rational purchase. The *CitiCar* is a two-seater, 95 inches long and 55 inches wide. Ours weighs 1303 pounds, including a propane heater ($90) for the occupants and a spare tire and wheel ($36). The *Elcar* also is a two-seater, but it is only 84 inches long and 53 inches wide. Ours weighs 1145 pounds.

The *CitiCar's* 3.5-horsepower motor is powered by eight six-volt batteries similar to those used in golf carts. The accelerator pedal actuates a three-way speed control. Step down one notch and a resistor allows a smooth take-off by limiting the amount of voltage to the motor. Depressing the accelerator pedal further feeds 24 volts to the motor. Stepping down on the accelerator pedal all the way supplies 48 volts to the motor for maximum speed. A built-in charger plugs into a household outlet to recharge the batteries.

The *Elcar* has a smaller motor rated at 2.7 hp and powered by eight 12-volt batteries. Its electrical controls are more complicated than the *CitiCar's*. A rotary actuator on a column (much like those in old-time trolley cars) provides three positions: 24 volts, 36 volts, and 48 volts. There's also an accelerator pedal that provides two speeds in each selector position, for a total of six forward speeds. For maximum cruising speed, one flicks a "booster power" toggle switch when in the third selector position. A charger is included in the price of the *Elcar,* but it is not mounted on board. We mounted ours in the rear compartment.

Is Electricity a Cheap Fuel? To test the batteries' endurance, we ran each car repeatedly around a substantially level one-mile course, permitting the car to rest for one minute after each mile and for 15 minutes every half hour.

That cycle was designed to simulate an urban drive with several shopping stops.

With the temperature at about 80°F., the *CitiCar* was able to run 33.6 miles on that cycle and then required 14 kilowatt hours (kwh) to recharge fully. In the New York City area, where a kwh costs nine cents, the energy cost per mile would be 3.7 cents; in some areas, it might be as low as 1.2 cents. By comparison, if the *Honda Civic CVCC* delivered its city mileage of 21 mpg in that same cycle, fuel cost per mile would be about three cents, assuming gasoline at 60 cents a gallon.

The *CitiCar* does not need the oil changes and tune-ups that the *Honda* and other gasoline-burning cars require. However, the *CitiCar* will require a new set of batteries after 400 to 600 recharges, or about 11,000 to 16,000 miles. The batteries would cost about $320, plus labor.

In the same urban shopping cycle, the *Elcar* was able to run 33.2 miles and required 12.8 kwh to recharge the batteries. That figures out at 3.5 cents per mile where electricity costs nine cents per kwh. The *Elcar* would also need new batteries every 11,000 to 16,000 miles. Cost: $250 to $300, plus labor.

Thus, where electricity is relatively expensive, neither electric car would be cheaper to run than the most economical of standard subcompacts.

A Battery of Woes. How well (or, more precisely, how poorly) these cars perform depends a great deal on the outside temperature. For example, during the summer, our *CitiCar's* useful range without rest periods was about 20 miles; but when the temperature fell to 40°F., the batteries needed to be recharged after less than 10 miles. A full charge usually took more than eight hours.

Other factors affect range. Running at top speed (32.5 mph for the *CitiCar*, 30 mph for the *Elcar*) drains batteries relatively quickly. So does driving in hilly country. Because the headlights of both the *CitiCar* and the *Elcar* dimmed to virtual uselessness by the time half the charge had been consumed, you couldn't (or shouldn't) drive these cars more than about 15 miles after dark.

Acceleration was slow. The *CitiCar* required 17.7 seconds to reach 30 mph. The *Elcar* couldn't quite get up to 30 mph on our test track; it took an excruciating 27.5 seconds to reach 29.5 mph, dangerously slow acceleration even for city streets. Hill-climbing ability of both cars was poor.

The handling of these vehicles hardly inspired driver confidence. During sharp steering maneuvers, the *CitiCar* at first plowed straight ahead; then it would suddenly swing its rear end rapidly to and fro. Bumps caused the car to hop sideways, off course; that characteristic was aggravated by the *CitiCar's* violent ride motions, which caused the driver to turn the steering wheel unintentionally.

The breakdown of the *Elcar's* front suspension prevented us from performing formal handling tests on that vehicle. But the *Elcar* felt tippy and directionally unstable during normal driving. As in the *CitiCar*, the steering was very quick and unpredictable.

Our braking tests went no better. The *CitiCar's* nonpower brakes (discs in front, drums in rear) required high pedal effort—about 120 pounds to lock the wheels. From 30 mph, the *CitiCar* stopped in 51 feet with no wheels locked and in 43 feet with all wheels locked and the tires sliding. Directional stability was not good; the car swerved and pulled, generally coming to a stop at about a 45-degree angle from the direction of travel.

The *Elcar*, with its nonpower all-drum brakes, weaved and leaned sharply when braking from 30 mph. During one hard stop, it almost rolled over. When we tried to stop shorter than about 70 feet, the rear axle hopped. Our shortest stop, 47 feet, involved a sharp veer to the left.

Inconvenience, Discomfort. One would imagine that small electric cars would be most useful for short shopping trips in urban and suburban areas. But even here, the *CitiCar* and the *Elcar* fell down. Neither vehicle has a rear opening, so one must fold the seatback forward and load shopping bags through the narrow door openings. In the *CitiCar*, a horizontal bar that supports the seatback obstructs access to the cargo area. And in the *Elcar*, the seatback doesn't stay folded without a prop. Neither car can hold more than a few small packages.

The seats in both cars were too firm and gave inadequate support. In the *Elcar*, the seat cushions can be adjusted both forward and backward. When tall drivers adjusted the *Elcar's* seat all the way back, they found the leg room adequate—but then the steering wheel was too far away. The small brake pedal was too far to the right. Protruding wheel housings limited foot room for the driver and passenger. Entry and exit were difficult.

The seat in the *CitiCar* allows no adjustment. You either fit comfortably or you don't (most CU drivers didn't). Leg room was very tight. The optional propane heater encroached on the passenger's foot room, the steering wheel was too far to the right, and the brake and accelerator pedals were awkwardly high and close. Entry and exit were difficult. The inside mirror not only threatened one's head during entry, but it was distractingly close to the driver's eye.

The *Elcar's* door windows slide horizontally rather than rolling down. They gave adequate protection from the elements. The *CitiCar*, however, has only drafty, flimsy side curtains like those of many early British sports cars.

One might expect an electric car to be quiet. The *CitiCar* and the *Elcar* are quiet only when stopped. At 30 mph on a coarse road, our sound measurements showed the *CitiCar* to be the noisiest vehicle we have tested this year—about as noisy as the *Honda Civic CVCC* was at 60 mph.

The failure of the Elcar's front suspension prevented us from recording that vehicle's noise levels, but the *Elcar* seemed to us at least as noisy inside as the *CitiCar*.

The *CitiCar* felt as if it had no springs at all. The car rode uncomfortably on every type of road surface. The *Elcar's* independent suspension gave a somewhat less painful ride. Even so, the car bobbed busily on all but the smoothest roads.

Miscellaneous Complaints. The Elcar has no fresh-air ventilation system. Even with the windows open, the car was hot and stuffy in the summer. The *Elcar* also lacks a heater or defroster, perhaps a concession to the fact that cold weather makes the car's range impractically short anyway. In its petition for exemption from Federal safety standards, the manufacturer of the *Elcar* claimed that the sliding windows would alleviate fogging—but that proved true only when the car was moving.

What fresh air entered the *CitiCar* came in mainly past the ill-fitting side curtains. In cold weather, the constant draft was unpleasant. A switch labeled "defroster" is a dummy. According to the owner's manual, it's "not functional on most models." The optional propane heater was hard to light and modulate. And it quickly fogged all the windows (one of the products of the heater's combustion is water vapor).

In our opinion, most of the many serious breakdowns that afflicted our *Elcar* were design flaws. Our *Elcar* sat in the shop awaiting parts or undergoing repair for a total of 74 days—more than half the time we owned it—until its virtual demise. The main power fuses for the high speed ranges blew repeatedly for no apparent reason during the 370 miles we drove the car. We had to order replacement fuses from the distributor. Each time a fuse blew, we limped home in low speed range and waited for a new fuse to arrive. Recently, the distributor shipped us a circuit breaker to replace the fuse box—a much-needed improvement scheduled for future production.

At just over 100 miles, a short circuit produced a brilliant flash of light from the headlights, and the wiper went berserk, wiping at a frantic pace. According to the distributor, such short circuits occur occasionally, because of inadequate accessory wiring design. We received a wiring kit to correct the defect.

Loose connections at the main power fuse box resulted in a loud clicking noise from the turn-signal flasher when we tried to charge the batteries. That flasher, incidentally, was another weak component; it had to be replaced twice.

At 210 miles, the differential gears disintegrated during normal driving and the car ground to a halt. The replacement gears lasted another 160 miles before crumbling during our braking tests.

The horn failed when grease from the steering column fouled the switch contacts. A moderate tug on the parking-brake handle caused the parking-brake assembly to break in two. The wiper arm, retained only by a set screw, slipped on its drive shaft. The final blow was the suspension failure mentioned earlier.

Our *CitiCar* never left us completely stranded during the time we owned it, although it gave us some anxious moments, as the diary (on page 243) indicates. The *CitiCar* suffered from fewer defects than the *Elcar*, and most of those were caused by sloppy manufacture rather than by design flaws. However, four defects were serious. After about 125 miles, the warning light for motor overheating went on even though the motor was only normally warm. At 370 miles, a loose wiring connection caused the voltmeter to flicker and the horn to fail. Most serious, the steering wheel retaining nut was very loose, and all the spring fasteners in the front and rear suspension were loose; had those items gone unnoticed, they could have caused an accident.

The Future of Electric Cars. These two electric cars are clearly unsuitable for any normal transportation function. But the main safety and design problems are solvable, either in these cars or in future competitors.

Whether there is any future for the concept of electric cars probably depends on how well they compete in fuel economy and cleanliness with vehicles powered by internal combustion engines. At this point, electric cars are no cheaper to run than such economical compacts as the *Honda Civic CVCC* and the *Volkswagen Rabbit*—at least not where electricity is costly. And, of course, those two subcompacts and others like them are not limited to trips of under 30 miles at speeds of less than 30 mph.

The cleanliness of electric cars is another open question. Electric cars themselves produce no air-fouling emissions. But most of the generating plants that produce the electricity needed to recharge the cars' batteries do produce emissions. Advocates of the electric car maintain that generating plants are more efficient than the internal-combustion engine, and that generating plants can disperse emissions high into the atmosphere, rather than concentrating them in city streets. Others, however, point out that wide use of electric cars might require double or triple the present electrical generating capacity of the country. At this writing, Congress is considering initiating a program, under the authority of the Energy Research and Development Administration, to explore further the feasibility of electric vehicles. Such exploration is obviously required.

Notes from an Auto Tester's Diary

CU's auto testers customarily familiarize themselves with vehicles by driving them to and from work and on errands before and during the formal testing program. Here is how it went with one of CU's testers during a day of driving the CitiCar:

8:00 A.M.: Went out to car, unplugged battery charger, and coiled up the extension cord. Wiped dew off glass with handkerchief. Got in, buckled up with some difficulty. Glass fogged again from my breath. Wiped glass again. Switched on power and stepped gingerly on accelerator. Powertrain screams. Fluttering along at top speed, about 30 mph, with unsteady siren emanating from somewhere below the seat. More window wiping to keep pace with breathing. Fairly smooth road tosses the little plastic box so violently that steering a steady course is difficult.

The scream from the powertrain drops in pitch, and the speedometer needle plummets. Momentary panic—then realize the car is negotiating a slight grade, one I hardly ever noticed in other cars. Car climbs slowly but steadily. Incredulous glances from other motorists. Otherwise, the remainder of the trip to work is uneventful.

5:00 P.M.: Returning from work. Confidence builds. Ignore catcalls. Pleased about all the gasoline I'm saving.

8:05 P.M.: After dinner, daughter asks for a ride to friend's house, three miles away. So far, car has gone just 10 miles to and from work. Should be no problem; manufacturer claims at least 25 miles on full charge. On return trip, decide to detour to cigar store in next town, another five miles, for a total of 21 miles. On the way, car lacks zip. But battery indicator shows plenty of charge left.

8:20 P.M.: Getting dark. Coasting down hill to cigar store, turn on headlights. Buy a magazine, start for home.

8:25 P.M.: With the lights of town behind me, notice only faint orange glow on pavement from headlights. Can hardly see road ahead. Let up on throttle, lights brighten appreciably. Feeling uneasy. Switch off headlights and drive along on parking lights.

8:30 P.M.: Instrument-panel light now dull orange. Car really slowing down. Pull to right as far as possible to let line of cars behind pass.

8:35 P.M.: The car with the red blinker doesn't pass. Police. Park and explain to officer that stopping 10 minutes or so would allow batteries to recover. Officer mumbles to himself, drives off. All power off, waiting.

8:47 P.M.: Apply power. Car leaps forward as if fully rejuvenated. Proceed without headlights, just to be sure.

8:50 P.M.: Spurt of energy lasts only about one mile. Back at the side of the road. Watch mirror for approaching cars; when one comes along, on with emergency flasher for just a few blinks.

9:05 P.M.: Start out again. Progress obviously labored. Creep to a halt after another quarter-mile, at the foot of a small rise.

9:20 P.M.: Patience near end. Only quarter-mile more to go. Two more rest stops needed.

9:45 P.M.: Finally roll down driveway. Driver and batteries both drained.

**A Report on the Level
of Safety Incorporated
in the Sebring-Vanguard
Electric CitiCar**

Energy, air pollution, gas prices—major topics of today—are making millions of people around the country look at the newly discovered advantages of electric cars. In response to the growing needs of the American people, Sebring-Vanguard, Inc. of Sebring, Florida, has developed CitiCar, perhaps the most advanced car on the road today.

CitiCar was designed with more than energy-efficiency, economy, and pollution control in mind. CitiCar may soon be regarded as one of the safest motor vehicles in automotive history.

High vehicle performance is an important factor in the overall safety of the electric CitiCar. CitiCar was designed to become integrated into city and town traffic patterns. The characteristics of electric propulsion are such that the acceleration capabilities of the CitiCar far exceed average traffic requirements. From 0 to 25 mph takes 6.2 seconds. The CitiCar's top speed is 38 mph, which is consistent with speed limit laws in urban and suburban areas. Maneuverability of the CitiCar is exceptional permitting the CitiCar's operator to respond to tight traffic situations. CitiCar has been designed with a high profile and bright body colors to be easily seen. Four-wheel brakes are on all CitiCars, the 1976 version incorporating a newly designed four-wheel Bendix drum brake system. Because of its light weight, the CitiCar's stopping distances meet or exceed those of most other conventional car models available today.

Maximizing crashworthiness in a small lightweight electric car was no easy task for Sebring-Vanguard designers and yet the results may put CitiCar on the top of the list of safety vehicles. To maximize passenger safety without adding excessive weight to the CitiCar, Sebring-Vanguard departed from conventional auto design plans and adapted aircraft technology to this new four-wheel form of personal transportation. CitiCar's frame includes an aircraft aluminum alloy roll-cage body-support structure which totally surrounds the passenger compartment. The body of CitiCar is made of high impact space age plastic called Cycolac ABS, the same material from which football helmets are made. Any Sebring-Vanguard dealer would be happy to demonstrate how tough and resilient this material is.

In testing, and in real life accidents, where front end, rear end, and even broadside collisions occurred, the CitiCar and its passengers have held up admirably. The record should speak for itself: CitiCars have been on the road now for over one year. There are more than 800 in daily use around

Source: Sebring-Vanguard, Inc.

the country and, having clocked an estimated total of three million vehicle miles to date, there have been no fatalities nor injuries more serious than a broken leg. Hit from any conceivable angle, a CitiCar is likely to remain upright due to the strategic placement of 500 lbs. of lead-acid batteries located along the lower center of the car. The CitiCar's widetrack makes for great stability in normal driving conditions and in emergency situations.

While all of the above-mentioned safety features represent a new and effective approach to motor vehicle safety, the superior long-range safety record of the CitiCar will probably be more closely linked to a more important safety feature than those. The National Safety Council reports that most auto fatalities occur at high speeds. Sebring-Vanguard is the first modern auto manufacturer to develop a passenger car with a top speed of under 40 mph, designed for in-town driving in low-speed areas. While all other conventional auto manufacturers, both domestic and imported, are building large and small fragile passenger cars with speed capabilities of 30, 40, and even 50 mph greater than Federal speed limit laws permit, Sebring-Vanguard believes that a responsible car manufacturer should design a car to travel only as fast as that speed at which the car's occupants can be protected in the event of a collision at top speed. For, if a driver is intoxicated or in any other way loses control of his conventional 2500 lb. car, and inadvertently depresses the accelerator pedal, the lives of pedestrians and other motorists in the car's path are threatened.

With a top speed of only 38 mph the likelihood of such massive death and destruction from a CitiCar is largely eliminated. Therefore, CitiCar represents the first serious attempt of a manufacturer to develop a totally safe passenger car no matter at what speed the car is being driven. The success of Sebring-Vanguard's CitiCar demonstrates that passenger protection can be maximized without turning the vehicle into a veritable weapon.

Owner confidence in the high level of safety became evident in the Spring of 1975 when Sebring-Vanguard petitioned to the United States Department of Transportation for an exemption from certain Safety Standards. (It should be noted that all Standards that are in effect were developed based on the design configuration of the conventional automobile.) A total of 45 letters were received by the Department of Transportation unanimously supporting our petition. Most of the letters were from CitiCar customers who indicated that the level of safety in the CitiCar was more than adequate for the type of use that the CitiCar was designed for. Customer letters which are received at Sebring-Vanguard regularly overwhelmingly corroborate this opinion.

Sebring-Vanguard wishes not only to improve public safety from the standpoint of CitiCar passengers, pedestrians, and other motor vehicle operators, but also to improve the quality of life and public safety in our total environment in general. The National Academy of Sciences recently reported that as many as four thousand people a year die from air pollution directly attributed to the conventional gasoline-operated automobile. In spite of federally-mandated pollution control devices, there is good reason to believe that these devices are either disconnected, removed, or do not operate properly on millions of cars around the country, thus eliminating the benefit that these controls were intended for. In contrast, air pollution from power plants generating electricity to recharge CitiCar batteries is significantly less than the air pollution coming from a conventional car on a per mile basis, and it is much easier to further curtail pollution from one power plant than from thousands of individually owned conventional cars. While figures are not yet available, it is now known that the CitiCar's electric motor produces a small amount of ozone which, if reaching the upper atmosphere, may help shield the earth against harmful cancer-causing radiation. Therefore, the widespread use of electric vehicles would not only reduce conventional forms of pollution, but may also add to the earth shield against radiation.

In conclusion, the electric CitiCar represents a lot more than a significant means of reducing America's dependence on foreign oil. CitiCar represents the form personal transportation will take in the future. Someday most commuters, housewives, students, businesses and Government will use this type of vehicle for the "around town" driving which makes up as much as 75% of the driving done in America. The development of Sebring-Vanguard's CitiCar is an important step in that direction and, as this transition in personal transportation occurs, we should witness a gradual improvement in America's traffic safety record and America's environmental quality.

Appendix 4.3　　　　　　　**Owners' Comments on the CitiCar**

We find the speed and range of the CitiCar adequate to handle most errands.

Am satisfied so far but time will be necessary for the car to prove itself.

So ugly it is beautiful.

I love the car, and have done a considerable amount of advertising for your company. Thank you very much!

You have a good thing going and so do we.

Other than a few other (quality) things, I think it is a pretty nice little car.

After sale the dealer seemed indignant because he sold me a car which did not perform. I requested service to repair the car and it has been sitting there for four days without full service performed.

Source: 1975 Survey of Owners Conducted by Sebring-Vanguard, Inc.

Fun and economical, too.

The heater is a $90 ripoff—it's worth about $15 and doesn't turn on the way the instructions say.

Is the CitiCar made to climb hills? I have burned out two fuses already. Our town is all hills.

Car is too expensive for what is offered. Engineering is not the best. Great fun to drive, though—provides great conversational item.

We have heard a great deal about warranty service problems. Mechanics don't want to do warranty repairs because, they say, the factory is too slow in paying them for their work—like five or six months. I might be the one needing warranty service (at some future time).

We wish the range and speed were extended, but we know the cost would be out of our range if you did this.

Salesman was very accommodating. However, seems very unenthusiastic about Citicar. A very negative attitude.

We like it when it is running, but we've had a lot of trouble with it. The dealer has been very nice about it, though—and more cooperative than Sebring-Vanguard. I hope we have the bugs worked out by now.

Appendix 4.4

Summary of Interviews with Two CitiCar Dealers

Dealer X. This dealership was located in a somewhat economically depressed suburb of a metropolitan area. The dealer carried a major domestic automobile franchise as well as several foreign import lines of cars. When the interviewer entered the dealership, no CitiCar or SV advertisements were visible. The CitiCar was in the back of the showroom, relatively obscure in its niche behind a large pillar. Dealer X commented:

I think the concept is great—the electric car is here to stay. I don't mind pioneering, but remember, I'm not the average consumer either. *This* electric car as it is now will never make it without modifications, a lot of the right kind of advertising, and changes in dealer relationships with the factory.

To sum up the product, the CitiCar needs to be made more utilitarian or more sexy. For example, a hatchback for shoppers' convenience; quality locks and lockable windows are needed on the doors. Can you expect shoppers to carry all of their bundles with them while they complete their errands because they can't lock their car? Some customers comment that the interior looks "cheap" —the switches, instruments, etc.—and the seats are really uncomfortable. There's no heater in the models I have. (Note: These were all 1975 models.) I don't mind sideflaps, even in a snowstorm, but again, I'm not the average, middle-income suburbanite, either. Most of these changes will come with time, and the more adventuresome early owners of CitiCar will put up with the inconveniences.

The car will never be a second family car, but rather a third car. It's too small for a family with school-age children. What about taking the kids and their friends to and from Girl Scouts or Little League practice? The only way that the CitiCar will become a second car for families is if mass transportation to and from the inner city becomes more prevalent. The breadwinner drives the CitiCar to and from the mass transit terminal, thus freeing the bigger car for family use.

The CU report hit hard. It's unfortunate that they compared EV's with standard cars, because they *are* different. However, that's exactly what the consuming public will do. Contrary to the implications in the report, the car is very durable. It withstood a 20-mph crash one of my salesmen had with a steel post. We were all impressed.

The best advertising I know of is to get the cars on the road. All of the free press and radio coverage I received when we got the CitiCar in netted me very few inquiries. Most inquiries have come from either passers-by who saw it in the showroom window, or who saw me driving it. Even then, most people are just curious. I've had very few spinoff sales of my regular line because of the CitiCar. Maybe I'm just in a bad marketing area. . . . As to TV advertising, you're selling a concept, not just another car. It would take a lot of money and a variety of approaches for television to be effective.

The margins are satisfactory. There are ways to control your actual margin. It's similar to other cars of the same price range. However, the older salesmen scarcely try to push them, apparently because they have been selling conventional cars for so long, that they don't want to relearn their trade. The younger people seem to take a greater interest in trying to sell the CitiCar.

My big complaint is with the quality of factory support. Don't forget, we sell service as much as we sell cars—50% of my revenue is from service. I've been five months waiting for replacement parts from the factory for the car that was damaged.

How can my salesforce stay motivated and sell a product in good
faith when the necessary factory follow-through is not forthcoming?
And another thing, it's aggravating to put in an order for $600
worth of parts and get a shipment billed for $900, after they throw
in "extras" I didn't want or need.

The way the procedures are set up now, as they iron out problems at the factory, I'm stuck with obsolete cars, updated eventually by us with those "kits." They need to work out a trade-in
allowance system to replace obsolete cars with the improved
versions, rather than requiring dealer on-site modification. They
could do the modifications a lot better at the factory. That would
certainly boost our morale, and should help guarantee customer
service.

The interviewer then chatted with one of the "older salesmen." He said,

How can I do a good job selling these (pointing to a luxurious
"Detroit special") if I try to push those CitiCars? It's like slitting
my own throat. I'm here to sell cars, not to convince people of
their duty to confront the problems facing us today. I could really
lose customers fast. Anyway, it's tough to sell them (the CitiCar)
when they're "tied" to a plug. Sure, gasoline cars are "tied" to gas
pumps, but there are a lot of gas stations conveniently located,
aren't there? The range isn't nearly as good as for a gasoline car
either—that will bug people. No, electrics will never have a chance
against regular cars . . . .

Dealer Y. This dealership was also located near a metropolitan area. It was
a large agency carrying two major makes of U.S. cars. When the interviewer
entered the showroom, the CitiCar was prominently displayed, as were other
SV signs and displays. The general manager for the dealership commented,

We like these little cars, and have been moderately successful
in merchandising them. We've sold two-thirds of our inventory
since we've had them. In addition, it has been an effective traffic
builder for the agency. At first the novelty appeal to the buyer was
overwhelming, and the free advertising brought about by the news
releases was heartening, but all that wears off fast. We've had to
advertise and promote the CitiCar on its merits. It will never replace the gasoline powered car, but will complement it nicely for
city and town use.

We think it's a good buy for the money. The consumer is getting
exactly what's advertised, even for the outdated 1975 models—a
safe, economical, clean car for city use *only*. Any car travelling
at 35 mph on an interstate highway is unsafe.

4/Sebring-Vanguard, Inc.: The CitiCar

The car is very well built. We've had two occasions to observe CitiCars in collisions, resulting only in superficial damage to it, but with expensive repair work required for the other (standard) car involved. The illusion of flimsiness due to the great flexibility of the plastic used in the body was dispelled by these incidents.

We felt that CU was unfair in many aspects of its report. It's my understanding that they tested a defective, early model, rather than one of the new models. The 1976 cars are much improved, and the kits are now available to update the earlier cars as well. Soon, we even expect to see glass windows and other more standard and useful features as CitiCar evolves and becomes more generally accepted. The transportation industry has always been evolutionary, but changes take time.

Margins are never as high as we want them. However, the margins offered by SV are comparable to other cars in the same price range, presenting no real problem to us. I don't think we have a problem with the older salesmen. They sell CitiCars just as other salesmen working for us do.* Obviously though, we have to make comparisons with standard cars concerning economy, comfort, and so forth.

Yes, the CitiCar will require a little more fussiness by the owner— checking cables and adding distilled water periodically and so forth. However, these services can be performed at any garage at a small charge to the owner and labor costs will be minimal compared to standard maintenance required for gasoline engines.

Although the CitiCar is not particularly lucrative now, we think that electric cars are the car of the future for urban use. We firmly believe that the majority of Americans will want to own one, but they don't necessarily want to be the "first ones on the block."

*Note: Excerpt from a customer who purchased a CitiCar from this dealership and responded to the "CitiCar Owner Survey":

Question   Were you treated courteously at the dealership?
Answer   Yes . . . exceptionally accommodating . . . However, seems
            very unenthusiastic about the CitiCar. A very negative
            attitude.

Discussion Questions

1. What is Sebring-Vanguard's current marketing strategy?
2. What are the problems you see with SV's current marketing strategy?
3. What are the strengths and weaknesses of the product itself?
4. What are Sebring-Vanguard's current and future strengths and weaknesses relative to current and future market threats and opportunities?
5. What are these threats and opportuniites?
6. How can Sebring-Vanguard overcome the Consumer's Union report on the car?
7. How many cars must Sebring-Vanguard sell in order to make a profit?
8. What is Sebring-Vanguard's current financial situation?
9. How can Sebring-Vanguard finance future operations?
10. What are the strengths and weaknesses of the top management team?
11. How good are this firm's objectives and its plans to reach those objectives?
12. What is the future of this company?

5/Artisan Industries (B)   Frank C. Barnes

Artisan Industries was a nine-million-dollar-a-year, family-run manufacturer of wooden decorative products.

They were approaching their first fall sales season since last year's successful turnaround under the direction of the new 29-year-old President, Bill Meister. Last fall had begun with a year-to-date loss of $125,000 and, through Meister's actions, had ended with a $390,000 profit. This had been the first profit in several years and capped a challenging 8 months for the new president.

Meister had hired his first man while his father was still president; bringing in 27-year-old Bob Atwood from the local office of a "Big Eight" firm to begin modernizing the accounting system. On June 10th, 1977, Bob was in Bill's office for further, and he hoped final, discussion of plans for this fall season. Artisan's sales were quite seasonal and on June 10th there were about 2 more months during which production would exceed sales. Atwood, concerned with the company's limited capital, proposed a production plan to hold the inventory build-up to $1,600,000, or about twice the level shown on the last full computer listing.

The President, based on his feel for conditions after the successful 1976 season and viewing sales in the first weeks of 1977, believed total sales for this year would really beat Bob's estimate of the same as last year's and reach $9,000,000. But he would like to have stronger support for his opinions; a lot rested on this estimate. If sales were much beyond their plans he could expect to lose most of them and create difficulties with his customers. New customers might even be lost to the competition. Bill was also concerned with developing contingency plans for dealing effectively with the potential over-sold condition. Besides getting more production from the plants at the last minute, there might be good ideas which involved the customers and salesmen. For example, if all orders couldn't be filled, should some be fully shipped and others dropped, or should all be shipped 75–95% complete? Overall in 1976 orders had been shipped 75% complete and during the peak months this had fallen to 50%. Partial shipments might be a way to keep everyone happy. If orders are canceled should they be the ones from the small "mom and pop" stores or the large department stores? The small stores are more dependable customers, but on the other hand large department stores systematically evaluate suppliers on their order completion history. Also the department store buyers must commit funds when they place an order, thus their resources are idle until the order is filled. There are potential

Source: This case was prepared by Frank C. Barnes, Assistant Professor, University of North Carolina at Charlotte. Presented at a Case Workshop and distributed by the Intercollegiate Case Clearing House, Soldiers Field, Boston, Mass. 02163. All rights reserved to the contributors. Printed in the U.S.A.

benefits from good communications, for if you inform the buyer of any delay quickly he can cancel that order and order something he can get. Such sensitivity to the customer's needs could win the company many friends and aid Meister in building a desirable reputation. On the other hand, poor communication could cause the opposite. Meister wondered if there was some way to usefully involve the salesmen, many of whom had left a Sales Representative organization 6 months earlier to work solely for Artisan.

After about mid-August total annual sales were limited to what had been built up in inventory beforehand and production through mid-November. Thus holding back now put a lid on total sales for the season.

If, on the other hand, the sales plan was not reached there could also be serious consequences. Last year after the fall sales period the inventory loan had been paid off for the first time since the 1960s. This had made a very favorable impression on the lending institutions and brought a reduction in the high interest rates (from 12% to 10¼%). They considered Bill a "super-star," with his youth, professional appearance, and modern ideas, and their fears for the Artisan loan were diminishing. Trouble at this time might erase all this and suggest last year was just a fluke.

If sales don't materialize, inventories could be held down by cutting back on production. But Bill believed the plants operate inefficiently during any cutbacks and such moves very likely saved nothing. He held a similar opinion of temporary second shifts. In many past years over-production early in the year had resulted in big layoffs in December and January and in the financial drain of carrying over large inventories. Meister was highly interested in building an effective work environment for people at Artisan, where attitudes were historically poor. The people, workers, and supervision, had little exposure to "professional" managers and had much to learn. The long process had been begun, but a layoff now could undermine all his efforts and, he felt, lose him what little confidence and support he had been able to encourage.

The strategy for this fall was of critical importance to Bill and his hopes for Artisan and his future.

Artisan's History

Artisan Industries is the product of a classical entrepreneur—W. A. (Buddy) Meister. After a variety of attempts at self-employment, such as running a dry-cleaning shop, a food shop, and an appliance store, he began to have some success making wooden toys. One try in 1950 with his father and brothers failed, leaving Buddy with an old tin building and some worn-out equipment.

During the next few years Buddy put his efforts into making a collection of 10 to 15 toys, sold via direct mail, house-to-house, on television, and on the roadside, all without a salesman. One day a visiting gummed-tape salesman offered to take on the line and a pattern of using outside sales reps was established.

The first attempt at a trade show was a last minute entry into the regional gift show 40 miles away. Out of sympathy for Buddy, Artisan was allowed to pay the $25 a week rent after the show. Buddy brought home $3,000 in sales but lacked the money to produce them until a friend offered a loan. The orders were produced in a dirt-floor barn. In the following months, Buddy and his wife drove off to other markets, showing the goods in their motel room.

In 1953 sales reached $15,000; then climbed to $30,000 in 1954, $60,000 in 1955, and $120,000 in 1956. Then in April the plant, or barn, burned down destroying everything. With hardly a delay Buddy jumped into rebuilding and sales continued to double. In 1958, success allowed Artisan to move into a 30,000 square foot building and continue using its 2 old buildings for finishing and shipping. Then in March of 1960 these two burned down. Again Buddy fought back and sales doubled into 1961. The rate of growth slowed to 50% in 1962.

The third and most disastrous fire occurred in February of 1963. The entire main plant was burned to the ground with the exception of the new office, which stood under one foot of water and was damaged by smoke and water. The company was in the middle of manufacturing its show orders and the only thing saved was the inventory in the paint shop. All the jigs were burned and before work could begin new jigs and patterns had to be made. "Only the plant in Spencer, built only a year before, saved us. The entire operation, with the exception of the office, was moved to Spencer, and working three shifts, we were able to keep most of the 200 employees. Many employees worked night and day for approximately six months to help us get on our feet again." Before Christmas of 1963 the company was back in full operation in the main plant.

Sales reached 4 million dollars in 1967 and 8 million in 1972. During that six-year span Buddy's five children reached ages to begin full-time jobs in the company. The youngest, Bill, was last to join. Typical of the youngest, he had it best; having all the "toys" his father could provide. He attended Vanderbilt, where he majored in Business Administration and the "good life." But his good time was at last interrupted by graduation and retirement to Artisan.

Bill wanted no major role in the company but over the next three years found himself getting more involved. Buddy had developed no modern management systems; accounting was ineffective, sales was in the control of outside reps, manufacturing was outdated and unprofessional. The lack of order fit Buddy's style—close personal control and manipulation. As the company problems increased, family conflict intensified. Bill's older brother lost the support of his father and the support of the other side and left. Bill moved up to the role of spokesman for a change.

In early 1975, though sales were booming, the financial situation at Artisan was "tight." A second shift was in operation, though production was generally inefficient. By October sales had slackened and in November, to hold inventories down, layoffs began. Accounts Receivable were worsening and the worried bankers were forcing the company to pay off some of its $2,500,000 loan. The inventory was reduced some and Accounts Payable were allowed to increase. In December the plant was closed for three weeks and $100,000 in cash was raised through a warehouse sale. But in the end, 1975 closed with a loss of over a million dollars.

As 1976 began the sales picture looked bad. Even with the large inventory there was difficulty shipping because it contained the wrong things. But, since it tied up capital, production of salable items was limited. There were more layoffs and shutdowns in January. Some old suppliers cut off the company's credit. In February, under the threat of the local bank calling the loan, Bill and Bob negotiated a new loan with a New York firm. This was composed of an inventory loan with a ceiling of $500,000, an Accounts Receivable loan of up to $1 million, and a long-term loan on the warehouse and real estate of approximately $350,000. "The package was finalized and the funds transferred about one week prior to payment deadline with the Bank. Had we not completed the deal with the other group, there was no way we could have made the $25,000 payment," according to Bill.

As the troubles deepened in the spring, Buddy had few solutions, and worse, blocked Bill's actions. The atmosphere in the company became grim. As Bill put it: "It became a fight between who was going to make decisions about what. Through the spring the conflict between us continued at a heightened pace. The effect was that most people became very nervous because no one understood who was really in control. With the company in the financial condition it was then, the last thing it needed was a power struggle over who should be in charge. So, in April I went to Buddy and explained the situation that the company needed one person who was clearly in authority and in control, that one person would be better than two, and that I felt that he should leave or I should leave. He suggested that since he had gotten there first, I should leave." Bill went to the mountains for good.

But 2 weeks later, under pressure from the lenders, Buddy stepped aside and Bill became the chief executive.

In May 1976 when Bill Meister became President, Artisan was in critical condition. Sales had fallen off dramatically, there had been little profit for 3 years, the number of employees had fallen from 600 to 370, modern management systems existed in no area of the company, and there were few qualified managers. "When I took over, sales were running 50% off and we could not get a line of credit through our suppliers, we were on a cash basis only, inventory was still relatively high, accounts receivable were running over 120 days, manufacturing was without anyone in charge, and the company was sustaining a loss of approximately $10,000 a week. The general situation looked pretty hopeless."

Exhibit 5.1 Organization Chart—Artisan Industries—June 1977

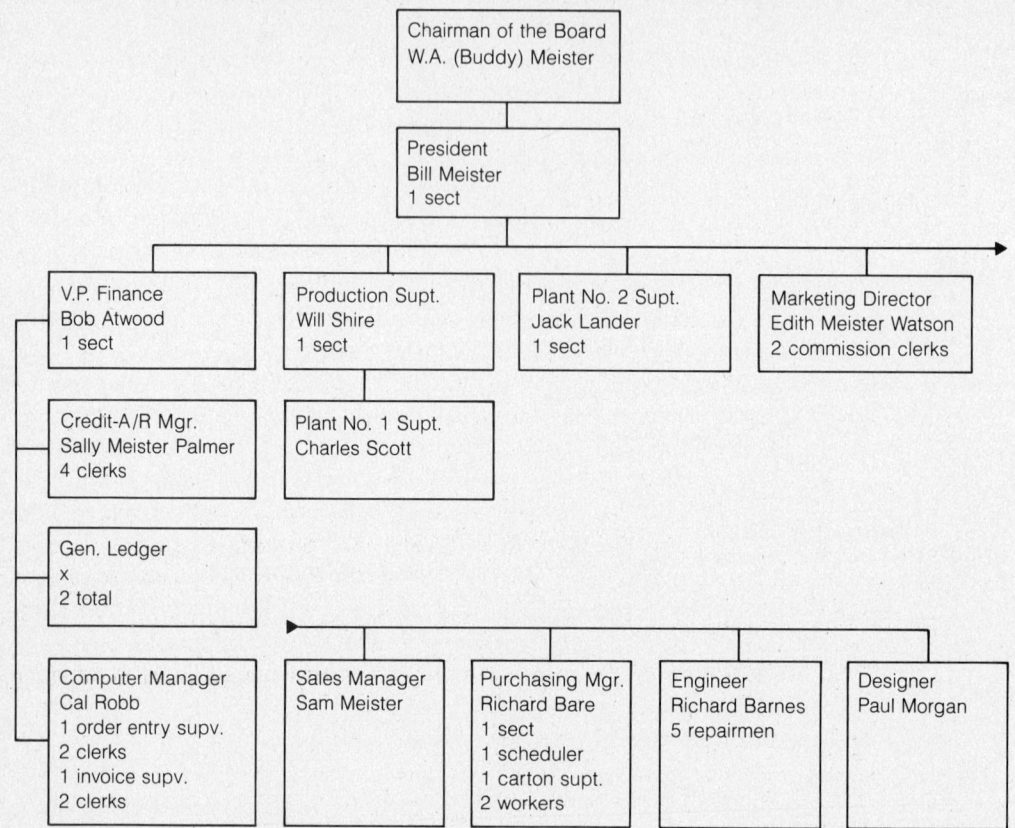

Chairman of the Board
W.A. (Buddy) Meister

President
Bill Meister
1 sect

V.P. Finance
Bob Atwood
1 sect

Production Supt.
Will Shire
1 sect

Plant No. 2 Supt.
Jack Lander
1 sect

Marketing Director
Edith Meister Watson
2 commission clerks

Credit-A/R Mgr.
Sally Meister Palmer
4 clerks

Plant No. 1 Supt.
Charles Scott

Gen. Ledger
x
2 total

Computer Manager
Cal Robb
1 order entry supv.
2 clerks
1 invoice supv.
2 clerks

Sales Manager
Sam Meister

Purchasing Mgr.
Richard Bare
1 sect
1 scheduler
1 carton supt.
2 workers

Engineer
Richard Barnes
5 repairmen

Designer
Paul Morgan

Bill Meister's First Year as President

When Bill became President in May changes began. Although Bill controlled many of the changes, others were the result of actions by his managers or outside forces. By mid-summer of 1976 he had reestablished contact with a business professor he particularly respected at his alma mater and was in regular contact with a management professor at a local school. The small number of trained managers, their lack of experience, and the absence of co-operation among them was a serious handicap to his rebuilding effort. He hoped interaction with the professors would make up for the lack of inside managers to interact with.

Exhibit 5.1 shows the organization chart in June 1977. Buddy moved up to Chairman, but remained around the office. Bill's sister Edith, and Uncle Sam helped in the sales area. Another sister, Sally, worked for Bob Atwood in accounting. A new man, Will Shire, was over production, mainly Plant One. Two long-term men, Charles Scott and Jack Lander, headed the plants. Two other long-term employees were in management: Cal Robb over the computer and Richard Bare over purchasing. A young man, Richard Barnes, had been hired recently for plant engineering. Paul Morgan had been with Artisan about two years in design.

Marketing. The company was one of four making up the wooden decorative products industry. Sales were seasonal, peaking with the Christmas period. Artisan's customers were some 13,000 retail shops which were serviced by outside sales representatives. Regional market shows were an important part of the marketing activity. The product line consisted of over 1,400 items and included almost anything for the customer. The largest item was a tea-cart and the smallest a clothes-pin type desk paper clip. New products were continually coming up; about 100 a year were added to the line. Practically no items were ever dropped. The top one hundred products averaged 5,000 units a year. The first 25 items had doubled the sales units of the next group. Two hundred and fifty sold over 1,000 units. The average wholesale price was $3.75. The top item sold 31,000 units last year for about $75,000 in sales. The 200th had sales over $10,000.

Marketing was the function where Bill wanted to spend most of his time. His father had left this mainly with outsiders, but Bill was determined to put the company in charge of its own marketing. He attended all shows and found out firsthand what was going on. He felt the outside salesmen had let Artisan slide into making anything they could sell easily, regardless of costs and profits.

Bill hired a local young man with good design talent, but little experience,

Exhibit 5.2   Monthly Shipments ($1,000)

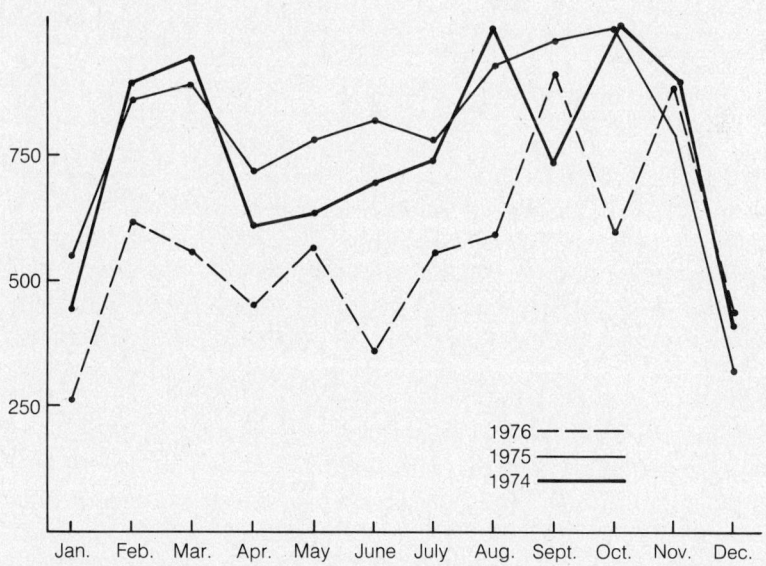

to set up a design department. They soon came up with a new "theme" line of items which became the talk of the industry and Bill planned to try others. He engaged a New York advertising agency for a professional program of advertising in the trade journals and publicity in the newspapers. He produced an artistic catalog with color photographs rather than the dull listing used before.

There had been no price increases in quite awhile, and with the recent inflation Atwood estimated the current sales prices would not yield a profit. In mid-October an immediate price increase appeared imperative if 1976 was to end with a profit. But there was great concern about the advisability of such action in the middle of the major sales season. Also, waiting on new price lists to institute the increase in an ordinary manner would not accomplish a 1976 profit; orders already acknowledged or in-house, but not yet acknowledged, exceeded what could be shipped. In fact, as Bill; his sister Edith from sales; Bob Atwood, the computer manager; Cal Robb; and the university professor met to decide what to do, a 30-page order from one store chain for $221,000 at the old prices sat in front of them. Bob and Cal took the position that no further orders should be acknowledged until the customer had been written that prices were increased and asked to mail a reconfirmation if they still wanted the goods. Edith felt the price increase was very risky and would be very difficult to implement at this time, if even possible. But she had difficulty explaining her views and Bob, with Cal, out-talked her. Bill listened to their arguments as little was accomplished. Only when the consultant added his weight to Edith's views and pointed out the manipulation and lack of good problem-solving did any practical ideas develop.

A 16% price increase was instituted immediately. The orders awaiting acknowledgment were examined that afternoon and on a priority basis the salesmen were called and informed of the necessity of the increase and asked to contact their customers for immediate approval. When possible, and with moderation, orders at the new prices were given priority over those at the old prices. Within a few days the new prices were contributing to profits.

Bill's most aggressive move was to cancel, in November of 1976, the company's long agreement with E. Fudd Associates, a sales representative firm. Accounting for 60% of their sales, Fudd, with 50 salesmen, had handled Artisan's business in about 20 states for many years, and had even lent the company money during the previous December. But Fudd was an old-style "character" much like Buddy—and Bill had been unable to systematically discuss market strategies or improvement ideas with him. Bill felt the 15% commission Fudd was setting could be better used as 10% directly to the salesmen and 5% in a company controlled advertising budget.

Bill had planned to deal with E. Fudd Associates after the first of the year. It would take careful action to break with Fudd and assist any reps wishing to go independent on Artisan's line. But an accidental leak had forced Bill's hand in the middle of the critical sales season. Bill did not back off but broke with Fudd immediately. Fudd countered with suits against Artisan, threats of displacing Artisan's goods with others, claims of tossing Artisan out of major regional market shows, and even withholding back, unpaid commissions on salesmen going with Artisan. Fudd spread rumors of Artisan's impending bankruptcy and sued any salesmen leaving him. Though there were bad moments, Bill held firm and in a few weeks it was over. Bill had gotten all the salesmen he wanted, was lined up for his own space in the critical shows, and the rumors were going against Fudd.

Accounting. With the hiring of Bob Atwood in the fall of 1975, improvement in the accounting systems began, though slowly. By the spring of 1977 the outside Service Bureau had been replaced by a small in-house computer to handle order-entry and invoicing, including an inventory listing.

The small computer system was delivered in January of 1977. Prior to that 85 to 100 thousand dollars a year had been spent for assistance from the Service Bureau. This assistance had been primarily invoicing. After orders were manually checked for accuracy and credit, they went to the Service Bureau where a warehouse picking ticket was prepared. Then after shipment a form went back to initiate the invoice. Besides invoicing, they produced a monthly Statement of Bookings and Shippings which summarized activity by item, customer, and state. The bureau was not involved with Accounts Receivable; aging was a manual process which took 30 days and was possibly only accurate to within $25,000. In 1975 checks had been posted, taking about 3 hours per day, and then forwarded directly to the leader. This had added 3 to 4 days of work for Atwood.

The computer had caused a small management crisis for Bill. Cal Robb and Bob Atwood, neither of whom had any special knowledge or experience with computers, had selected the system they wanted with no help beyond that of computer salesmen. With only verbal arguments and several contract notebooks from the supplier, they pressured Bill for his approval. When he failed to act they saw him as foot-dragging and lacking respect for their opinions. With the counsel of the university consultant, Bill took the unpopular step of sending them back to prepare a proper proposal and timetable. In work with the vendor, several serious omissions were found and corrected, and all agreed the further documentation had been worthwhile. Bill approved the project.

The new system consisted of a 48K "small" computer with a 450-line-per-minute printer—two disc drives with 2 million bytes each, and 7 CRT's. Monthly rental amounted to about $4,000. The software was developed in-house by Robb using basic systems supplied by the vendor at no charge. Robb was the only staff for the computer. He was 36, with a business administration degree with some concentration in accounting from a good state university. Prior to Atwood's hiring he had been controller.

By May, inventory accounting was on the computer. The inventory listings computing EOQs were available but inaccurate. Atwood believed a couple of months of debugging was necessary before computer inventory control

Exhibit 5.3   Financial Statements

Balance Sheets (In thousands of $)

Assets	May 31, 1977	Dec. 31, 1976	May 31, 1976	Dec. 31, 1975	Dec. 31, 1974*	Dec. 31, 1973*	Dec. 31, 1972*	Sept. 30, 1970*	Sept. 30, 1969*
Current Assets									
Cash	111	83	146	97	66	78	69	17	37
Accounts Receivable	552	608	444	693	1,191	1,286	968	911	879
Inventories									
Finished Goods	982	394	537	754	652	652	464	541	576
Work-in-Process	247	247	75	136	551	444	426	367	379
Raw Materials	406	348	352	604	719	547	446	390	252
Supplies	50	41	33	95	79	63	66	83	52
Total Inventories	1,686	1,032	997	1,591	2,003	1,708	1,404	1,382	1,261
Other	37	36	79	256	88	1	1	219	—
Total Current Assets	2,386	1,759	1,666	2,637	3,349	3,073	2,442	2,529	2,177
Property and Equipment	600	616	611	666	745	753	783	844	448
Other Assets	143	86	54	60	731	416	610	163	139
Total	3,129	2,461	2,332	3,365	4,826	4,242	3,836	3,538	2,766
Liabilities									
Current Liabilities									
Accounts Payable	168	228	329	694	543	195	411	467	166
Notes Payable	1,195	643	902	1,222	1,871	1,547	1,040	1,428	1,159
Other	448	375	204	282	131	256	275	377	329
Total Current Liabilities	1,811	1,246	1,435	2,198	2,545	2,098	1,726	2,272	1,654
Longer Term (Adv. from Stockholders)	269	367	651	705	854	593	692	252	226
Stockholders' Equity	1,049	847	245	461	1,426	1,550	1,417	1,012	884

Statements of Income (In thousands)

	Five Months May 31 1977	1976	Five Months May 31 1976	1975	1974*	1973*	1972*	1971**	1970†	1969†
Net Sales	2,769	6,898	2,399	9,441	9,038	8,462	6,992		5,942	5,037
Less Cost of Goods Sold	1,815	4,758	1,921	7,452	7,093	6,145	5,163		4,513	3,676
Gross Profit on Sales	954	2,139	478	1,988	1,945	2,316	1,828		1,428	1,361
Selling and Distribution Expenses	412	992	332	1,370	1,343	1,215	958		682	639
General and Administrative Expenses	306	586	233	897	543	549	429		340	303
Other Income (Expense)	47	(172)	(77)	(909)	(255)	(152)	(215)		(143)	(120)
Income (Loss) before Income Taxes	283	389	(164)	(1,189)	(196)	399	226		263	298

*Prepared by local accountant
**No copy in company files
†Year ending September (909 = Interest expense — 378, write off advance to supplier — 521, write off good will — 77, other — 12.255 = Income — 58 minus interest expense 313. 152 = Income — 93 minus interest expense 245.)

would be possible. The data needed for the EOQ model were all old and inaccurate; lead times, prepared by a consultant years ago, were considered by all to be way off. They and the standards hadn't been studied in 5 to 6 years. For now Atwood felt these listings would be of some help in operating the existing production scheduling system. (EOQ stands for the Economic Order Quantity inventory model.)

By June, invoicing was fully on the computer and the lender had stopped requiring the direct mailing of checks. About 3,000 invoices were prepared each month. The A/R systems, including statements and weekly aging of delinquent accounts, were operational, and about 2,500 statements were being prepared monthly. The controller felt both systems were running well and providing for good control. The computer supplier felt they had been lucky to get the system operational as quickly as they did. (A/R means accounts receivable, A/P means accounts payable.)

Cal expects Inventory Control will be on the computer by February. In another month he will add A/P payroll, and general ledger. Production Control must wait on others' work and input.

Monthly preparation of financial statements had begun in January. Production costing for the statements had been based on historical indices, but Bob reported little resulting error. The statements were out, in typed form, 30 days after the close of the period.

Production. There were 2 plants, roughly identical and 5 miles apart, each with about 60,000 square feet. Kiln dry lumbed, mainly high quality Ponderosa Pine, was inventoried in truck trailers and covered sheds at the rear of the plant. The lumber width, totally random, depended on the tree, and the length was from 8 to 16 feet, in multiples of 2. The thickness started at the lumber mill at 4, 5, or 6 "quarter" ("quarter" meaning ¼ inch, therefore 4 quarters is 1″). By the time it reached the plant it was about ⅛″ less.

The Rough Mill foreman reviewed the batch of production orders he was given about every week and decided on the "panels" the plant would need. A panel is a sheet of wood milled to a desired thickness and with length and width at the desired dimension or some multiple. Clear panels, ones with no knots, can be made from lower grade lumber by cutting out the defects and then gluing these smaller pieces into standard panels. Artisan did no such gluing but cut high quality, clear lumber directly to the desired length and width. The necessary panels would be made-up in the Rough Mill from lumber or from purchased glued panels. Artisan spent about as much on purchased panels as it did on raw lumber, paying about twice as much for a square foot of panel as for a square foot of lumber. Surfacers brought the wood to the desired thickness, the finished dimension plus some excess for later sanding. Rip saws cut the lumber to needed width and cut-off saws took care of the length. About 30 people worked in this area, which had about 12% of the labor cost.

The Plant Superintendent worked with the Machine Room foreman to decide on the sequence in which orders would be processed. Scheduled due-dates for each department were placed on the orders in Production Control but they followed up on the actual flow of orders only if a crisis developed. In the Machine Room 22 workers (17% of the labor cost) shaped panels to the final form. The tools included shapers, molders, routers, and borers. Patterns and jigs lowered the skill requirements, still the highest in the plant. This part of the plant was noisiest and dustiest.

In the third department, Sanding, the parts were sanded by women working mainly at individual stations. There were 24 people here. The sanded components were moved to a nearby temporary storage area on the carts which originated at Machining. It was estimated there were 6 to 8 wooden parts in an average item. In addition there were purchased parts such as turnings and glass or metal parts. Sanding added about 19% of the direct labor to the products.

The Assembly foreman kept an eye on the arrival of all parts for an order. Assembly began when all parts were available. Eighteen people assembled the items using glue, screws, nail guns, or hammer and nails. Jigs assisted the work where possible and usually only one person worked on an order. Fourteen percent of direct labor derived from this step. Little skill was needed and dust and noise weren't a problem.

The assembled items were moved promptly to the separate Finishing area. Here they were dipped by hand into stains and sprayed with several clear coats. After oven-drying they proceeded to Packing. Most were packed individually into cartons made in the company's small plant. Finishing and Packing employed about 50 people and accounted for 34% of direct labor costs. The new 60,000 square foot Finished Goods Warehouse was two miles away.

The labor rates ranged from $2.65 to $5.60 per hour. The average was probably $3.00, with about a dozen people making over $4.00. Factory overhead was about 60% of direct labor. Labor costs as a percent of the wholesale selling price ran about 20%; direct material, 35%. Variable costs totaled about 75%, with about another $1,800,000 in total company fixed costs. There was a three percentage point difference between the plants in labor costs. The capacity of the plant with 150 people working was estimated to be less than $110,000 a week. Indirect labor amounted to about 12% of plant overhead.

Most jobs did not require high skill levels. The average jobs in the Rough Mill and Machine Room, where the skilled jobs were, required no more than 5 weeks to master because the person would usually already have advanced skills. Elsewhere a week was adequate. Everyone but the supervisors and workers considered the work pace quite slow.

Exhibit 5.4   Production Scheduling System

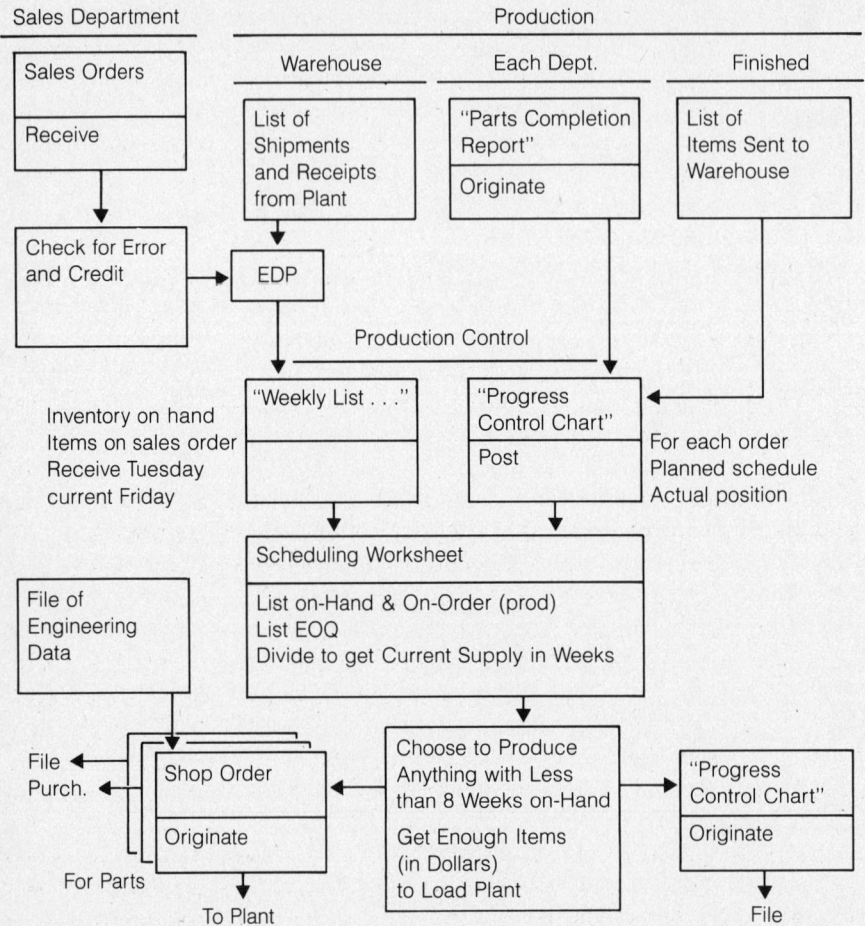

Production Scheduling. The Production Control Department began the scheduling process. Exhibit 5.4 outlines the Production Scheduling System. About every week, sometimes longer, the clerk prepared a batch of production orders for each plant. Several factors determined when a batch of orders was prepared; whether the plants said they needed more work, how sales were doing, what the situation was in the warehouse, etc. The clerk examined the "Weekly Inventory Listing" for items which appeared low and the file of "Progress Control Charts" to see if the items were already on a production order. He converted the information to an available supply in weeks and selected any with less than 8 weeks. If the total of orders gotten this way did not add up to an aggregate amount he had in mind, such as 60 to 100 thousand dollars, he went back through the lists for more things to run.

"Production Sheets," or shop orders, were prepared for each item. These contained a drawing and a list of materials and process steps. The data was already prepared and came from consultant studies several years old. The order contained a date the part was due through each department based on standard lead times, for example, one week in the Rough Mill, 3 days in Machining, etc. The actual work in the plant at the time did not alter lead-times. At the same time a "Progress Control Chart" was prepared for each order. These remained in Production Control to trace the flow of orders.

The batch of orders was then handed to the Plant Superintendent who decided exactly how the items would be run. Daily each department gave Production Control a "Parts Completion Report," listing production from that department—order number, part number, and number produced. The Production Control Clerk posted this information to the "Progress Control Charts." This reporting cycle used to be every two hours. The clerk reported these charts were not actually used to control production progress; they aided in locating an order if a question arose, but one still had to go out on the floor to be sure.

A brief look at the inventory listing for December showed the first 20 items were 23% of the inventory value. The 10th group of 20 items was 2% of inventory; the cumulative value to this point was 82%. The fortieth item had $1,800 in inventory and the two-hundredth $625.

Turning through the notebook for Plant One "Process Control Charts" on one day showed almost 300 open orders, perhaps 30–50% past the due date. Several items had 2 or even 3 different production orders 2 weeks or so apart. The order size appeared to average 200 at most. One in 10 was for more than 250 pieces. Only a couple were for 500 or more, the maximum was 1,000 pieces. The typical items appeared to contain about six parts and each took 3 to 5 processing steps.

The Engineer was trying to estimate standards for new items as they were priced. A quick look at eight of them showed a total of 1800 minutes of set-up time for the eight and a total of 6400 minutes per 100 units of run-time. The set-up times ranged from 100 to 250 minutes for the products, but several of the parts required no set-up in some departments and where there was set-up it amounted to 25 to 50% of the run time for 100. Many parts required less than 30 minutes of processing in a department. The lot size on these ranged from 100 to 200 units; seven were priced around $4.00 and one at $25.00.

Production Problems. Bill feels production efficiency is a major problem. In talks with machinery salesmen and other visitors to the plant over recent years, Bill has come to feel the machinery is generally appropriate. But based on guesses about his competitors he feels his labor costs must be reduced. Earlier attempts to work with the plant superintendents and the various supervisors to systematically improve output met with no success. The supervisors had been unable to identify the needs for change in the plant or to develop the programs for bringing about improvement. To help the supervisors begin to improve their operations, a Weekly Production Meeting was begun in June 1976. At the meeting the supervisors were to examine the total dollar output and total labor cost for each plant for the past week, compare it to the labor percent goal, 16%, set by Bill, and think about what could be done to improve operations for the coming week. Data on department performance was not available. During the first several meetings, the visiting consultant had to provide direction and ideas; the plant superintendent and his supervisors volunteered no ideas about what specifically limited last week's output. Bill reported some discussion of problems began 3 or 4 months later. It was Bill's opinion that this kind of thinking and planning was not required under his father's management. The supervisors in general felt nothing was wrong in the plant and really seemed puzzled at the thought of doing anything except continuing what they had always done.

In March of 1977, after a good deal of thought and search Bill hired 2 young men for the production system. One man, Will Shire, aged 28, was hired to be general superintendent over everyone in production, and the other, Richard Barnes, aged 27, was to be manufacturing engineer. It appeared the plant simply needed good management rather than any single big change that could be brought from the outside. Both of these men were young, college trained, and experienced in a wood industry.

Significant resistance from the old superintendent and most of the supervisors seemed probable. Consequently, the new men were briefed on this problem. As expected, things did not advance smoothly. Even as the new men gained familiarity with the operation no significant changes were observed. The expected complaints and rumors were heavy, and Bill ignored them as best he could. However after three months on the job the complaints still persisted and, more importantly, the new superintendent did not appear to have command of the situation. He had not developed his appraisal of what needed to be done and had no comprehensive plan for improvement. Bill recently received very good evidence that Will had some major difficulties in supervising people. One of the supervisors who did not appear to be a part of the rumor campaign and was conscientiously concerned about the company gave Bill examples of the new man's mistakes. Bill felt he may have made a mistake in hiring Will.

Richard's responsibilities have also been narrowed to more technical tasks. He is supervising the 5 man repair crew, engineering some of the new products, examining the procedures for producing samples of new products and beginning to examine a major redesign of the rough-mill area.

Major Competitor's Production. The major competitor is Sand Crafters, Inc. A managerial person familiar with both operations provided these comments. Demand for Sand Crafters' products exceeded their capacity and this, in the person's opinion, was the main reason Artisan existed. Their sales were somewhat less than Artisan's, they had no debt, and their equipment was described as new. They were located in a small community where the workers were relatively skilled for this kind of business. The work force was primarily white male. The manager characterized the Artisan worker as about ⅔ as good as Sand Crafters. The workers in the third company in the industry were rated as ½. The quality of manufacture of Sand Crafters was considered first, Artisan second, and the third company a close third. Sand Crafters' weakness was in poor engineering of the products and an outdated approach to marketing. Sand Crafters schedules long runs in manufacturing with the objective of having three month's stock of top priority items. They do not use the EOQ Model because they are limited in their work-in-process space.

In describing the Artisan manufacturing system, the person noted that two-thirds of the equipment is idle at any time, and that neither capacity nor optimum production mix have yet been determined. The largest run size he claimed to have seen had been 250. Setup costs he estimated to average $30. He commented that this was the least directed operation he had ever seen, with the slowest pace and the lowest level of knowledge of this type of work. He felt its employees knew only the simple way of doing the job. Only one man in the company, for example, was able to count the board feet of lumber and there was no lumber rule in the plant. He stated that this was a skill that the smallest cabinet shop would have and that it was essential for any kind of usage control.

The Workforce. Bill was greatly interested in the newest concept of management, frequently pointing to the latest book or sending a copy of an article to his managers or anyone with whom he was interacting. The behavioral writings made a lot of sense to him and he was very perceptive of behavioral processes in meetings or situations. The participative management systems and cooperative team environments were ones Bill wanted for Artisan. However he recognized his managers and the workforce were not ready for this yet. His managers manipulated more than cooperated, and the workers were neither skilled nor very productive. When he discussed the workers' desires with the supervisors he was told they wanted a retirement program and higher pay, nothing else. Bill felt this was really what the supervisors themselves wanted.

As a basis for beginning change in this area, an outside consultant conducted an employee attitude survey in May of 1977. All employees in the company were assisted in small groups in completing the written questionnaire. The questionnaire was designed: 1. to find out what they wanted, for example more pay, retirement plans, more or less direction, etc.; 2. to gain insight into the probable impact of participative management moves; 3. to establish benchmarks of employee satisfaction so that changes over time could

Exhibit 5.5 Summary of JDI Scores by Level (Percentile)

Group	No.	Attitude toward:	Coworker	Work	Super-vision	Promo-tion	Pay
Total Company	318		41.2	32.3	40.4	11.1	7.1
Management	7		38.0	39.4	48.0	18.7	15.9
			(35)	(60)	(70)	(80)	(55)
Office	18		45.8	36.6	47.4	6.9	7.7
			(60)	(50)	(65)	(50)	(25)
Supervision	13		46.8	39.2	46.1	16.1	12.2
Plant No. 1 Hourly	141		40.4	31.6	38.4	11.7	6.6
Plant No. 2 Hourly	101		39.8	31.3	42.6	11.0	5.9

be monitored; 4. to develop an objective profile of the workers; and lastly 5. to look for significant differences in attitudes between the various stratifications possible.

The survey included questions developed specifically for this situation as well as a highly regarded attitude instrument, the Job Descriptive Index (JDI). Although the wording is considered simple, many of the workers did not understand such words as "stimulating," "ambitious," or "fascinating," and it became necessary to read the entire questionnaire to them.

The study showed minorities accounted for 80% of the 300 employees; white females were the largest group at 40%. The workforce was 58% female, 57% white, and 39% over 45 years old. As many people have been with the company under 2 years as over 10 years—24%. The pay was only a little above the legal minimum, but many workers felt fortunate to have their jobs. There did not appear to be a "morale" crisis; the 5 JDI measures located the company in about the middle of the norms. The supervisory group was highest in "morale" while management was lowest.

Exhibit 5.5 summarizes the Job Descriptive Index scores. The numbers in parentheses show the norms. The 3-page instrument is not shown here.

They were also questioned about a number of aspects of their work which could be improved. Exhibit 5.6 shows these questions.

Exhibit 5.7 summarizes their views on how important improvement in the more important areas would be to them.

Their expressed view of the organizational climate was relatively good. They claimed to enjoy their work, looked for ways to improve it, and felt expected to do a good job. They especially felt their coworkers were good to work with and felt part of a team. They appeared to like their supervision.

Their views did not suggest need for a different manner of supervision. And they did not respond positively to the suggestions of being more in charge of themselves, did not feel strongly about having more of a say in how things are done, and didn't feel there were too many rules.

The survey revealed no critical problems, differences between groups were not extreme, and the resulting view of the worker was moderate. However the

Exhibit 5.6 Results of Attitude Survey: May, 1977

What is your opinion on the following statements? Do you agree or disagree? Please mark the appropriate box.	Strongly disagree	Disagree	No opinion	Agree	Strongly agree	Mean	St. Dev.
I enjoy taking this test.	3.2	3.8	17.3	44.4	31.3	3.97	.96
My pay is fair for this kind of job.	34.4	35.3	5.4	19.9	5.0	2.26	1.26
My coworkers are good to work with.	2.9	3.5	7.3	49.4	36.9	4.14	.91
My complaints or concerns are heard by management.	12.2	18.4	17.1	39.5	12.8	3.22	1.24
Things are getting better here.	8.3	12.1	23.2	38.9	17.5	3.45	1.16
The supervisors do a poor job.	25.3	39.9	17.2	9.1	8.4	2.35	1.19
I am fortunate to have this job.	3.2	3.8	15.7	48.7	28.5	3.95	.94
Working conditions are bad here.	17.3	41.7	16.3	17.9	6.7	2.55	1.16
I benefit when the company succeeds.	12.4	24.8	16.9	31.3	14.7	3.11	1.28
I have all the chance I wish to improve myself.	11.8	21.4	19.2	31.3	1.63	3.19	1.27
The company is well run.	6.1	18.2	28.1	36.1	11.5	3.29	1.08
Communications are poor.	13.4	27.8	25.2	21.6	12.1	2.91	1.23
I don't get enough direction from my supervisor.	19.6	37.5	20.2	13.1	9.6	2.56	1.22
I enjoy my work.	2.8	2.5	10.1	47.5	37.0	4.13	.90
I look for ways to improve the work I do.	1.0	2.6	8.0	51.4	37.1	4.21	.77
I need more of a chance to manage myself.	8.3	25.2	26.5	26.5	13.4	3.11	1.17
I don't expect to be with the company long.	28.9	30.8	23.6	9.5	7.2	2.35	1.19
Morale is good here.	6.2	15.0	18.0	39.5	21.2	3.55	1.16
Wo all do only what it takes to get by.	32.2	39.7	10.1	12.7	5.2	2.19	1.17
I am concerned about layoffs and losing my job.	9.9	16.9	13.1	32.8	27.4	3.51	1.31
I like the way my supervisor treats me.	4.2	5.1	11.9	42.4	36.3	4.02	1.03
We need a suggestion system.	3.0	7.9	25.6	38.4	25.2	3.75	1.01
I want more opportunity for advancement.	4.02	8.7	17.4	36.1	33.5	3.86	1.10
My supervisor knows me and what I want.	5.1	15.4	18.3	40.5	20.6	3.56	1.13
We are not expected to do a very good job here.	48.2	29.1	4.2	10.2	8.3	2.01	1.30
There are too many rules.	18.1	38.2	21.0	12.6	10.0	2.58	1.21
I feel like part of a team at work.	5.7	6.7	12.4	50.3	24.8	3.82	1.06
The company and my supervisor seek my ideas.	14.2	19.4	24.6	29.1	12.6	3.06	1.25
I can influence dept goals, methods and activities.	9.5	22.0	34.8	25.2	8.5	3.01	1.09
There is too much "family" here.	20.7	24.6	25.2	15.9	13.6	2.77	1.31
This company is good for the community.	2.2	3.5	11.1	36.3	46.5	4.22	.93

Exhibit 5.7 How Important Would Improvement in the Following Things Be to You?

Department	Total Group			
Sex	Male 42.2%	Female 57.7		
Race	White 57.4	Negro 42.5	Other	
Age	Under 25 19.8	26-35 19.8	36-45 21.4	Over 45 39.0
Years with Company	Under 2 23.2	2-5 34.8	6-10 18.5	Over 10 23.5

White Female = 38.7
Black Male = 23.5
Black Female = 19.0
White Male = 18.7

How Important Would Improvement in the Following Things Be To You?	Rank	Very little or not at all	A little	Fairly important	Very important	Extremely important	Mean	St. Dev.
Longer coffee breaks	15	33.7	20.0	16.5	18.1	11.7	2.54	1.41
More holidays	8	19.0	19.0	23.0	23.6	15.4	2.97	1.34
Guaranteed work	2	9.7	3.9	8.7	25.8	51.9	4.06	1.28
Flexibility in hours or days off	10	29.7	11.2	18.2	21.8	19.1	2.89	1.51
More overtime opportunity	17	40.8	14.1	12.4	17.3	15.4	2.52	1.53
Better insurance	6	26.0	8.9	16.1	21.7	27.3	3.15	1.55
Better working conditions	3/4	14.1	10.3	13.8	27.0	34.7	3.58	1.41
Retirement plan	3	12.0	6.5	9.7	18.5	53.2	3.94	1.40
Higher pay	1	3.2	5.4	8.0	19.2	64.1	4.36	1.05
Education refund	16	40.8	14.0	14.4	14.7	16.1	2.51	1.52
Treated more as an individual	7	29.6	8.1	18.2	21.5	22.5	2.99	1.54
Better way to get complaints heard	5	22.3	11.0	13.6	23.3	29.9	3.28	1.53
Better equipment	2/4	16.4	12.1	14.8	23.6	33.1	3.45	1.46
More direction from supervisor	14	33.8	20.0	12.5	18.4	15.4	2.62	1.48
More opportunity to learn and improve self	1/4	14.8	9.8	14.1	26.9	34.4	3.56	1.42
More say in how my department does things	13	37.1	14.5	13.2	18.7	16.5	2.63	1.53
More opportunity to contribute to company success	9	24.5	14.9	18.9	24.2	17.5	2.95	1.44
Better decisions by top management	12	29.8	21.4	14.9	16.2	17.8	2.71	1.48
More information on what's going on	4	16.1	9.7	12.3	29.4	32.6	3.53	1.44
Be more in charge of own self	11	33.3	10.7	16.8	19.7	19.4	2.81	1.54
Other:								

% of Answer

workers were relatively unsophisticated and there was concern they might not have expressed themselves on the instrument.

The Meeting with Bob on June 10th

The last months of 1976 had been very good in spite of fears caused by the price increase and the changes in the sales organization and had resulted in a $390,000 profit. Bob Atwood reported that the original plan for 1977 had been for no major changes—a regrouping, doing as in late 1976, just better. However there was no formal written plan. As actual sales in January and February ran well ahead of the prior year, production was allowed to stay higher than the plan. Bill believed Bob's estimate of sales at 6.5 million dollars was very low. A quite conservative estimate, he felt, was 9.0 million dollars. This level became accepted as the premise for production planning in the first part of the year. But March and April were disappointing and May was only fair. Bill still felt the 9 million was reasonable, as the normal retail sales patterns had been upset by inflation and the fuel crisis. But he recognized the risks and was concerned. He hoped the gift shows in July would settle what 1977 would hold.

On June 10, 1977, Bob Atwood had returned to Bill's office to press for some decision on the inventory level. He wanted Bill to pull back on plans for 1977. As sales had been slower coming in and inventories had increased more than expected, Bob had become increasingly worried. The level on the last full inventory listing prepared about six weeks before stood at $800,000 in wooden goods. The current level was nearer $1,100,000. From a financial perspective Bob was willing to accept a level as high as $1,600,000. But this called for limiting production now. His report dated May 13th (Exhibit 5.8) presented several alternative production levels for the fall, comparing particularly $600,000 and $720,000 per month. The first page of the report showed monthly shipments and order receipts for 1976 and 1977 to-date and production to-date in 1976 and 1977. The second page projected inventories on the basis of several production levels. He advocated a $600,000 per month level.

Bob recommended they immediately cut production and make Richard Bare, the purchasing agent, Production Control Manager with the responsibility for guiding the controlled inventory buildup. Since the desired total inventory level of $1,600,000 was twice the level shown on the last computer listing which included recommended run sizes (EOQs), he felt they could use this part of the computer system as a guide in selectively increasing the inventory. They could double either the Re-Order Points (ROPs) or the lead times in the computer, return the report, and use the new EOQs to double the inventory in a balanced form. Bob felt there had been unnecessary delay in making a decision and was impatient for Bill to put this to rest without further delay.

Exhibit 5.8   Analysis of Production Levels—May 13, 1977

Month	Week	Shipments 1976	Shipments 1977	Order Receipts 1976	Order Receipts 1977	
January	1			60,428	75,517	1.25
	2			210,873	354,705	1.68
	3			176,981	247,592	1.40
	4			329,441	384,532	1.16
Total		267,000	314,000	777,723	1,062,346	1.36
February	1			215,285	143,899	.66
	2			160,996	160,932	.99
	3			230,456	238,577	1.03
	4			168,703	285,378	1.69
Total		616,000	692,000	775,440	832,786	1.06
March	1			155,339	168,217	1.08
	2			124,993	114,936	.91
	3			141,163	122,189	.86
	4			167,915	79,839	.47
Total		554,000	725,000	589,410	485,181	.82
April	1			122,692	116,221	.94
	2			135,976	120,878	.88
	3			88,148	107,590	1.21
	4			157,382	87,861	.56
Total		451,000	432,000	504,298	432,550	1.85
***Year to Date Total		1,888,000	2,163,000	2,646,871	2,808,863	1.06
May	1			107,906	91,791	.85
	2			78,723	88,040	1.11
	3			89,694	114,832	1.28
	4			128,175	112,936	.88
Total		566,000	554,000	404,498	407,599	1.00
June		361,000		756,377		
July		557,000		1,057,604		
August		590,000		1,240,813		
September		922,000		1,753,880		
October		592,000		684,186		
November		896,000		322,049		
December		437,000		157,156		
***Year to Date Total		6,809,000		9,023,434		

Production:	Jan.	Feb.	Mar.	Apr.	May
1976	206,899	428,899	507,589	370,221	348,151
1977	658,306	635,228	762,083	593,246	607,606

Exhibit 5.8 (cont.)

Alternate Production Level

	Order Receipts 1976		Projected Receipts 1977	Less Bad Credit @ 2.4%	Credit Worthy Orders	From Inv. @ 9.5%
Prior	$2,646,871		$2,808,863	($69,496)	$2,739,367	$2,602,398
May	404,498	x .85	343,823	(8,251)	335,572	318,793
June	756,377	x .85	642,920	(15,430)	627,490	596,115
July	1,057,604	x .85	898,963	(21,575)	877,388	833,518
August	1,240,813	x .85	1,054,691	(25,312)	1,029,379	977,910
September	1,753,880	x .85	1,490,798	(35,779)	1,455,019	1,382,268
October	684,186	x .85	581,558	(13,957)	567,601	539,220
November	322,049	x .85	273,741	(6,569)	267,172	253,813
December	157,156	x .85	133,582	(3,205)	130,377	123,858
	$9,023,434		$8,228,939	($199,574)	$8,029,365	$7,627,893

							Optimum
Beginning—May	$1,100,000	$1,100,000	$1,100,000	$1,100,000	$1,100,000	$1,100,000	$1,100,000
May Production	720,000	670,000	620,000	570,000	520,000	470,000	600,000
May Shipments	(318,793)	(318,793)	(318,793)	(318,793)	(318,793)	(318,793)	(318,793)
	1,501,207	1,451,207	1,401,207	1,351,207	1,301,207		1,381,207
June Production	720,000	670,000	620,000	570,000	520,000	470,000	600,000
June Shipments	(596,115)	(596,115)	(596,115)	(596,115)	(596,115)	(596,115)	(596,115)
	1,625,092	1,525,092	1,425,092	1,325,092	1,225,092		1,385,092
July Production	540,000	502,000	452,000	402,000	352,000	302,000	450,000
July Shipments	(833,518)	(833,518)	(833,518)	(833,518)	(833,518)	(833,518)	(833,518)
	1,331,574	1,193,574	1,043,574	893,574	743,574		1,001,574
August Production	720,000	670,000	620,000	570,000	520,000	470,000	600,000
August Shipments	(977,910)	(977,910)	(977,910)	(977,910)	(977,910)	(977,910)	(977,910)
	1,073,664	885,664	685,664	485,664	285,664		623,664
September Production	720,000	670,000	620,000	570,000	520,000	470,000	600,000
September Shipments	(1,382,268)	(1,382,268)	(1,382,268)	(1,382,268)	(1,382,268)	(1,382,268)	(1,382,268)
	411,396	173,396	(76,604)	(326,604)	(576,604)		(158,604)
October Production	720,000	670,000	620,000	570,000	520,000	470,000	600,000
October Shipments	(539,220)	(539,220)	(539,220)	(539,220)	(539,220)	(539,220)	(539,220)
	592,176	304,176	4,176	(295,824)	(595,824)		(97,824)
November Production	720,000	670,000	620,000	570,000	520,000	470,000	600,000
November Shipments	(253,813)	(253,813)	(253,813)	(253,813)	(253,813)	(253,813)	(253,813)
	1,058,363	720,363	370,363	20,363	(329,637)		248,363
December Production	540,000	502,000	452,000	402,000	352,000	302,000	450,000
December Shipments	(123,858)	(123,858)	(123,858)	(123,858)	(123,858)	(123,858)	(123,858)
	1,474,505	1,098,505	698,505	298,505	101,495		574,505

Advantages and Disadvantages

Advantages of $600,000 Production Level:
1. Reduces scope of operation to afford high degree of control.
2. Maintains positive cash flow position for remainder of year.
3. Maintains more liquid corporate position.

5/Artisan Industries (B)

Exhibit 5.8 **(Cont.)**

Disadvantages of $600,000 Production Level:
1. More customer dissatisfaction from possible low service level.
2. Probable lost sales if orders increase.

Advantages of $720,000 Production Level:
1. High service level to accounts.
2. Low probability of decrease in service if orders increase.

Disadvantages of $720,000 Production Level:
1. Risk of inventory buildup.
2. Risk of being in a "lay off" situation if orders do not increase

Note—Funds available on inventory loan *will* support $720,000 level of production.

Assumptions

Order Volume	Order receipts for the remainder of 1977 will be 85 percent of order receipts for the prior year on a dollar to dollar basis.
Orders Not Credit Worthy	.0374 of the dollar volume of orders will not initially clear credit. Of these ⅔ will eventually qualify for shipment via prepayment, etc.
Service Level	A 95 percent service level of order completion will be maintained. All orders will be shipped in month of receipt. Production from plants will be received by the Warehouse prior to orders for shipment.
Production Levels	One week of production will be lost in July and one week of production will be lost in December.

Possible Causes of Sales Decrease

1. Rejection of price increase by wholesale accounts.
2. Rejection of price increase by consumer.
3. Reaction to poor service level of 1976.
4. Loss due to new representation.

Discussion Questions

1. What is the current Master Strategy of this firm?
2. How good is it (i.e., strengths, weaknesses, threats, opportunities vs. strategy)? Why do you feel that way?
3. How would you evaluate the top managers of this organization?
4. Is there teamwork in the management team?
5. What impact did (and do) family relationships have on this firm? What impact might the ultimate disposition of the firm have upon Bill's performance?
6. What do the survey results tell you about this company?
7. What Master Strategy changes do you recommend and why?
8. What operational changes do you recommend and why?
9. What are the evidences of coalition activity?

6/Jones Foundry Company   James M. Higgins

The Jones Foundry Company case is divided into two parts. Part A examines Mr. Morris Hackney's original purchase of Jones Foundry and the conditions he found to exist at the time of purchase. Part B examines the strategy which he has subsequently followed, the actions he has taken, and the condition of the company as it exists in Fall, 1976.

Jones Foundry History

Jones Foundry Company was started by Gibb Jones in 1937. It was one of several foundries that he had owned at one time or another. Gibb, now age 84, is primarily an inventor but has demonstrated that he is also a capable administrator for a small business. Various of his inventions have modernized the foundry industry. It is reported that he has made, and subsequently lost, several small fortunes. In any event, as he progressed in years, he gave each of his three sons a foundry. Of these, Jones Foundry has become the largest, primarily under the guidance of one of Gibb's sons, Jack Jones. Gibb remained at Jones Foundry as an advisor/consultant and is still employed in that capacity today. Jack was a good salesman and was generally recognized as a shrewd businessman. But Jack suddenly died of cancer at the age of 42 in 1969, just as the business had begun to really prosper. The foundry passed to the control of his wife, Betty, with the stipulation that if it floundered, Jack's bank was to assume control and administer the business until a buyer could be found. By mid 1971, it was apparent that the business was not being properly managed. The bank then took control and hired an administrator, a retired plant manager for a major steel company. Until January, 1975, when Mr. Hackney assumed control, the company was run by the administrator.

Jones Foundry and the Foundry Industry

The foundry industry in the Southeast United States where Jones Foundry operates is characterized by a number of large, dominant firms. These firms offer a wide variety of products to their customers, who are also large. Many small firms also exist in the industry, and they survive by offering service and specializing in some particular type of product. Jones Foundry, located in Bessemer, Alabama, near Birmingham, is one of these smaller firms. It produces only ductile steel, i.e., quality flexible steel. Jones forms castings to be

Source: The author wishes to thank Jones Foundry Company, Mrs. Nancy Smith, and especially Mr. Morris Hackney for their cooperation in the preparation of this case.

used by intermediate manufacturers. Like most foundries, Jones melts scrap metal, pours it into molds, and cleans the resultant products. Jones, however, has a largely unique process of heat treatment which it then employs to make the steel more ductile. A few other firms have recently begun using a similar process. Jones Foundry considers its primary market to be the Southeastern states, especially Alabama, Mississippi, Tennessee, and Georgia. Jones has recently begun expanding its sales into the Midwest, however.

The steel foundry industry requires intensive capital investment.[1] Furthermore, the amounts required have been increased by demands from the environmental laws at both state and federal levels. During 1975, return on stockholders' equity for the steel industry fell below the national manufacturing average. Payroll as a percentage of the steel industry's gross revenue fluctuated from a high of 40% in 1970 to a low of 31% in 1974. 1975 found this percentage to be 35.2%. Wide variations in this percentage exist among the various major producers.

The capital requirements for smaller steel foundries are not excessive. Depending upon the types of products, foundries may be opened for as little as $150,000, plus initial operating expenses. The price of labor in the Southeast varies from location to location and with the particular situation found at each foundry.

Part A: The Purchase

Hackney Fence had been and continues to be a major customer of Jones Foundry. Mr. Morris Hackney, one of three Hackneys who owned Hackney Fence Company, had decided to strike out on his own and took the proceeds of the sale of his share of Hackney Fence and purchased what he felt to be a business with significant long range potential. In January, 1975, he purchased 95% of the outstanding stock of Jones Foundry, at that time held by Betty Jones and her three children, for 1.9 million dollars. It should be noted that before Jack Jones had died suddenly, he had been offered over twice the eventual purchase price for the firm. The decision to purchase was made in consideration of the financial statements presented in Exhibits 6.1 and 6.2, the knowledge of the firm gained through business dealings with it, and the belief that the industry was one which could return substantial profits for efficient operation. But once the new owner had begun to actively manage the enterprise, he reports that he became painfully aware that strictly financial information can be misleading. Within a few weeks, Mr. Hackney had uncovered the following conditions.

Top Management/Goals. When Mr. Hackney assumed control, there was

1. Comments in this paragraph are taken from *Standard and Poor's Industry Surveys,* 1976, 2:564–569.

no salesman, no plant manager, no accountant, no goals, no strategy, and no leadership. The bank-appointed administrator was described as incompetent, although "he did have enough sense to raise prices in a favorable economy."

Marketing. The former administrator had not put forth an effort to build a client base. Some of their best customers had left Jones Foundry. No pricing policy existed. Prices were more or less quoted on past experience. But prices had steadily risen during the 1971–1974 period. As a result, customers found the prices to be generally too high. Jones was not getting bids when it quoted prices and no one knew why.

Production. Despite the loss of customers, inventories had continued to grow. Not knowing what the customer wanted nor if he would buy certain products, the former administrator had ordered that previous customer items be manufactured and stored just in case the customer would want them. In the foundry industry, all goods are made to order and raw materials can be obtained almost on a daily basis. Production was inefficient; at least it appeared to be. Other foundries were making the same products, selling them for less, and making a profit. Much of the equipment was old and the work flow was beset with motion problems. No standards existed. The plant was only running three or four days a week.

Finance. The financial statements revealed several areas of concern. See Exhibits 6.1 and 6.2.

Personnel. Several Jones family members had remained with the foundry. A new union agreement was to be negotiated within a year. Productivity, as mentioned, was low. Morale was also low. Half of the foremen had quit during this interim period.

Social Responsibility. Because of the nature of the business and the extreme air pollution common to the Birmingham area due to all of the foundries located there, costly air pollution control equipment appeared inevitable. Because of the number of blacks employed at the foundry, equal employment opportunity was a natural concern. Efforts had been taken to promote blacks to the foreman position.

Information Systems. No reports existed as to weekly sales, labor efficiency in the plant, costs per product, gross margins, position of customer orders in the production process, or accounts receivable by age. The company had no inventory control, had no idea of what molds they had on hand, no job description, and no apparent appreciation for the operating environment.

Exhibit 6.1 Jones Foundry Company, Inc.: Bessemer, Alabama Balance Sheet

Assets

	1969	1970	1971	1972	1973	1974
Current Assets						
Cash	$ 25,714		$124,035	$131,426	$276,541	$ 466,937
Accounts Receivable—Trade	219,216		165,282	188,721	249,071	307,657
Inventory	117,345		163,415	144,970	174,892	281,738
Advances to Employees	853		1,679	191	553	290
Loans Receivable—Officer	103,000					
Loans Receivable—Other	39,221		161,588	159,387	18,786	10,725
Total Current Assets	$505,351		$616,000	$624,697	$719,844	$1,067,348
Fixed Assets						
Land and Buildings	62,454		62,454	62,454	62,454	79,854
Equipment	334,188		346,577	383,911	509,977	583,248
Office Furniture	10,953		12,310	12,791	13,422	13,519
Trucks and Autos, Aircraft	9,866		14,513	8,513	9,195	28,289
Total Fixed Assets	417,461		435,856	467,670	595,049	704,911
Less: Allowance for Depreciation	158,281		219,495	258,690	315,104	370,103
Fixed Assets, Net	259,180		216,361	208,980	279,945	334,807
Total Assets	$764,532		$832,361	$833,677	$999,790	$1,402,156

Liabilities

Current Liabilities

Accounts Payable—Trade	52,981	39,698	71,239	89,174	127,697
Accrued Payroll Taxes	18,504	11,070	13,897	15,203	17,122
Accrued Wages	49,482	54,859	37,513	37,919	53,676
Accrued Corporate Income Taxes	55,293	28,739	1,010	36,758	172,619
Note Payable—Bank	48,980				
Note Payable—Other	25,000				
Total Current Liabilities	$250,243	134,368	123,660	179,056	371,115
Deferred Liabilities					
Notes Payable & Debenture	5,000				
Stockholders' Equity					
Capital Stock	5,000	4,678	4,678	4,519	4,519
Paid in Surplus	685	685	685	685	685
Earned Surplus	503,603	692,629	704,653	815,529	1,025,835
Total Stockholders' Equity	509,288	697,993	710,017	820,733	1,031,040
Total Liabilities	$764,532	$832,361	$833,677	$999,790	$1,402,156

Exhibit 6.2 Jones Foundry Company, Inc.: Income Statement October 1, 1968 to September 30, 1974

	1969	1970	1971	1972	1973	1974
Net Sales	$1,886,810		$2,132,258	$2,242,838	$2,822,165	$3,625,807
Cost of Sales						
Inventory—October 1	55,590		124,544	163,415	144,970	174,892
Raw Materials & Supplies	527,542		608,652	606,099	745,409	1,155,355
Direct Labor	862,959		1,061,964	1,130,515	1,218,507	1,273,330
Freight	23,940		17,280	17,914	21,515	17,234
Utilities	32,782		44,949	50,014	51,799	63,498
Total	1,502,815		1,857,390	1,967,958	2,182,201	2,684,311
Less: Inventory, Sept. 30	117,345		163,415	144,970	174,892	281,738
Cost of Sales	1,385,470		1,693,975	1,822,988	2,007,303	2,402,572
Gross Profit	501,340		438,282	419,850	814,856	1,223,234
Operating Expenses						
Officers' Salaries	100,000		30,503	23,766	25,833	35,070
Advertising	306		1,212	150	423	
Audit & Legal & Directors Fees	1,716		2,900	8,083	71,450	109,968
Bank Charges	56		4	10		
Contract Labor	1,684		1,231			
Contributions	2,960		802	1,847	110	980
Loss on Sale of Assets				1,200		
Depreciation	52,315		41,198	42,213	56,414	55,305
Dues & Subscriptions	2,322		1,660	2,961	3,124	4,530

Employee Medical Expense	3,264	2,064	2,930	2,420	2,125
Insurance	18,138	40,010	37,266	23,978	49,801
Interest	4,972	1,754	1,065	1,138	5,811
Miscellaneous Expense	3,067	1,886	1,049	4,909	5,547
Office Expense	3,891	3,781	4,868	4,586	
Rent	60,000	60,450	60,000	52,000	48,000
Shop Expense	31,486	63,103	86,821	74,487	94,450
Sales & Travel Expense	2,661	3,096	1,223	2,386	1,985
Taxes & Licenses	48,297	64,743	75,718	96,883	96,940
Truck & Auto Expense	12,102	5,367	4,137	7,024	4,858
Data Processing Expense	4,023				
Sales Commissions			2,205	10,427	11,530
Pension Plan Costs	2,930	2,930	43,487	55,878	54,600
Bad Debts			670	32,632	
Consultant Fee	44,203	44,203	6,000	12,000	22,007
Security Guard				2,032	2,760
Total Expenses	353,266	372,906	407,674	540,143	606,274
Net Operating Profit	$ 148,074	$ 65,375	$ 12,176	$ 274,713	$ 616,960
Add: Interest Income and Miscellaneous Income	8,611	1,439	858	5,159	23,459
Net Income (Before Taxes)	156,685	66,815	13,034	279,872	640,420
Provision for Corporate Income Taxes	78,669	28,739	1,010	136,758	312,619
Net Income (After Taxes)	$ 78,016	$ 38,075	$ 12,024	$ 143,114	$ 327,800

Part B: Actions Taken and the Current Situation

Top Management Goals. "We would like to make $500,000 profit before taxes on our current volume ($4,000,000 in sales). We would like to be able to double that volume, run two shifts, modernize the plant, and make this an effective and efficient plant. We target for $80,000 gross sales a week, allowing for $400,000 general and administrative expenses a year."

So spoke Morris Hackney in July, 1976. Having owned the plant for a year and a half, and having suffered through some serious financial situations, Mr. Hackney felt that these were reasonable goals for the next few years. Beyond that time horizon, plant expansion or, more probably, a new plant at another location had been considered.

Morris Hackney, age 44, is the president and general manager of the firm. He is a graduate of the U. S. Naval Academy at Annapolis and has had 17 years of experience in business as part owner of the Hackney Fence Company. Hackney Fence had $28 million in sales in 1974, his last year with the firm. He is on the advisory board of the Birmingham Southern University School of Business. He works occasionally in other civic activities but does not feel he has the time to do very much else. He stays current in the business field by reading *Harvard Business Review, Wall Street Journal, Business Week, Forbes, Fortune,* and various trade journals. He also feels compelled to read a sizable quantity of literature outside the business field in order not to become "stale." He has had no formal management training and his philosophies reflect his reading and experience. As president, he is responsible for sales and administration. He coordinates the functional areas of sales, production, finance, etc. He is also responsible for the hiring of executive personnel, four in number: the plant manager, the salesman, the accountant/administrative manager, and the metallurgist. He makes the capital spending decisions, although those in the above four positions may make recommendations. Beyond these restrictions, he allows those in the four executive positions to make all the decisions. "I let them manage." The first action he took as the new president was to fire the previous bank-appointed administrator, hire a salesman, a plant manager, and an accountant/administrative manager. He instituted budgets, with reports and standards, in late 1975.

Steve Rue, age 29, is the company's only salesman (in addition to Mr. Hackney). He has been in sales "all of his life." He started in retail sales, progressed into direct sales before college. Upon completing a Bachelor of Science in Mechanical Engineering from Mississippi State University, he went to work for Celanese Fibres Corporation as a project engineer, but found the work mentally restraining. He did not want a "limited personality." He transferred to marketing support and design for Celanese, and eventually returned to Mississippi State as Chief Mechanical Engineer in order to go back to school. While he was there, the president of Central Foundry called and offered him a job as sales manager. "During my tenure there I was promoted to

Sales Vice President. I cut overhead by 400% and increased profit from a minus 24% of sales to a plus 4%. Sales grew from 3 million to 7 million in 7 months under my direction. From there I came here in September, 1975." Steve is responsible for increasing sales, both through selling to older customers and through establishing new clients.

Curtis A. Jones, age 46 and no relation to the founder of the company, is the company metallurgist. He also has the additional responsibility of purchasing agent. He has been at the foundry for five years. As the metallurgist, his chief duty is to make certain that the metal which is poured meets customer needs. He determines the exact mixture of raw materials, the chemical properties of the products, and the precise temperature and processes to be used. As an end result, he is in charge of quality control of the final product —he sets the standards. He spends approximately 50% of his time performing duties associated with metallurgy and 50% performing those of purchasing agent. He may occasionally be required to aid in the installation of new equipment, or to design new systems, or fabricate new materials. He is also in charge of physical inventory control but not the decision as to its proper level.

R. Conner Warren, age 32, is the accountant/administrative manager. He has been with the foundry one year. He was formerly employed with Hackney Fence Company as the Control Manager. Prior to that he was an assistant plant manager for the Acondia plant in South Georgia. A former Air Force pilot, he is still active in the Air Force Reserve and is an Auburn University graduate. Warren is in charge of personnel; administrative support services (which include secretarial, information systems, accounting, etc.); and the control of the overall operation. He is responsible for the day to day operation and control of the company, except for sales and the actual manufacturing plant supervision. All of the office staff report directly to him. This includes two secretaries; head bookkeeper, Nancy Smith (formerly Nancy Jones, daughter of Gibb Jones, the founder); and two clerks (one the daughter of Nancy Smith).

The plant manager position is currently vacant. The plant manager was fired in July, 1976. Mr. Hackney reported that the plant manager's position is a vital one, for it is he who is able to make the plant efficient. The plant manager should solve the day-to-day problems which arise. The inefficiency in the plant is believed by Mr. Hackney to be in large part a result of poor plant management (as well as old equipment). Mr. Hackney, Mr. Rue, and Mr. Warren all reported that the previous plant manager could not handle even the simplest of tasks, such as production scheduling. Several customers had been disgruntled because of late delivery. Several incidents were cited where production was delayed because it had not been coordinated or scheduled. In addition, by late March 1976, the labor efficiency system had been finalized and revealed the inefficiency of the operation.

Marketing. Mr. Hackney and Steve indicated that the company followed a two part marketing strategy. First, they sought and found a niche and intended to stay there. They realize that they cannot compete head-on with the dominant foundries, so they do not try. They would not bid, for example, on automobile parts manufacturing castings. They concede those types of contracts to the larger foundries. They feel that being small is an advantage, however. "The larger foundries always abuse some customers. Jones Foundry locates those customers and caters to them for the size of jobs that they could effectively handle." They make them feel important. "We try to keep the delivery on time, the customer informed, and save money if we can. A real asset has been the computer, which, since January, has enabled us to tell every customer exactly where his order is in the production process. Our competitors can't do that! They say, 'we could have it in three weeks,' just like we used to do before we got the computer." Jones views the second phase of this strategy as one of providing service, quality, and price competition with an emphasis on keeping the customer happy. Their major competition, given the size of contracts they are willing to bid on, are the numerous small foundries which are attempting to market in the same way. These smaller foundries could sometimes offer a lower price due to several factors, not the least of which was the inefficiency of the Jones' plant. "If a foundry fails to provide the customer with the desired service, there is always another foundry willing to do so. However, if a foundry keeps the customer satisfied, it is believed that even the lower price would not cause the customer to leave. Customers would not leave because the prices never varied more than 10% (because of the similarities in operation). Depending on the volume of items (recalling that much of the business is special order), the customer would not consider this price variance to be significant if the product was of high quality and could be delivered on time. There are a lot of these foundries, but there is also a lot of business." Jones considered its target market to be those firms with sales under $5 million in the pole line hardware, low voltage pole line, agriculture, fence, hydraulics, and miscellaneous manufacturing businesses. However, they did have some very large customers, EATON, for example. Their attitude towards the bigger companies was, "if they call, we'll give it a try."

One of Mr. Hackney's goals was to improve the client mix. During the recession of 1973–1975 when the foundry took any business it could get and when poor service eroded the customer base, the type of client had changed from those with potential for future business and those who had a future, to those that were onetime purchasers or industries that were phasing out of the economy. Mr. Hackney felt that now that sales were up and a sufficient backlog of customer orders existed (8 weeks from a low of 4 days when he bought the firm) he could begin to weed out some of the less desirable firms.

Jones Foundry now has a pricing policy—only products with absolute gross margin returns of $300 or more will be sold. On many items, prices were negotiated but the information reports printed daily by the computer enabled

Mr. Hackney and Steve Rue to know exactly how low they could go on each item. They receive a contract on 1 of every 10 for which they quote prices.

Seventy-five percent of sales are made either by Mr. Hackney or Steve Rue. The remaining sales are sold through sales representatives. All sales are made through direct contact. Advertising is perceived as having a low return on the cost since there are so many firms and the best differentiation was perceived as being made through personal selling. It takes from six months to two years from the point of initial contact with the customer to the time he takes first delivery.

Mr. Steve Rue expressed one view of his job as follows: "We do four types of molding. Part of my job in sales is not just to get sales per se, but a specific type, so that the production line is balanced between the four types of molding. We try at all times to keep any one line from being shut down. Those of us in sales schedule production by week. It is up to the plant manager to handle the daily scheduling. If the facilities are not loaded properly with job orders, either Mr. Hackney or I must go out and get that particular type of business."

Part of the marketing task is handling customer complaints—this is especially important since the company must cater to customers to keep them. "Moreover, we must be able to respond to a customer's urgent needs, within reason." The feeling is that Jones is in good shape on complaints. "Generally the customer wants a long term relationship because there are always problems with quality with a new foundry as it proceeds through the learning curve on a new product. The foundry also wants a long term relationship. Start ups are expensive and the costs of selling are high. The foundry does not want to have to quote every item." When asked to describe the current sales situation, Steve observed, "In September 1975, the firm's sales were approximately 70% below those of September, 1974. Now (July, 1976) we are back up to the 1974 figures. We have an 8 week backlog. That's what we want. Furthermore, we are in good shape on complaints."

Production. The plant is inefficient according to the foundry's production standards. These standards were set in joint sessions between the supervisors, Mr. Hackney and Mr. Warren. The supervisors feel they should be able to reach the standards but currently are not. Part of the reason for inefficiency is related to plant layout.

Referring to Figure 6.1, the Jones Foundry Plant Layout, scrap metal is loaded into melting pots called cupolas. The scrap is heated in these pots up to 2000°F., and, once molten, it is poured into molds provided by customers in one of two major types of molding processes, i.e., cope and drag molding or matchplate molding. In the molding process, patterns (molds) provided by customers are filled with a special type of sand, which when treated, assumes the shape of the pattern. The pattern is removed and the molten metal is then poured into the sand mold. The type of molding de-

Figure 6.1   Jones Foundry Plant Layout

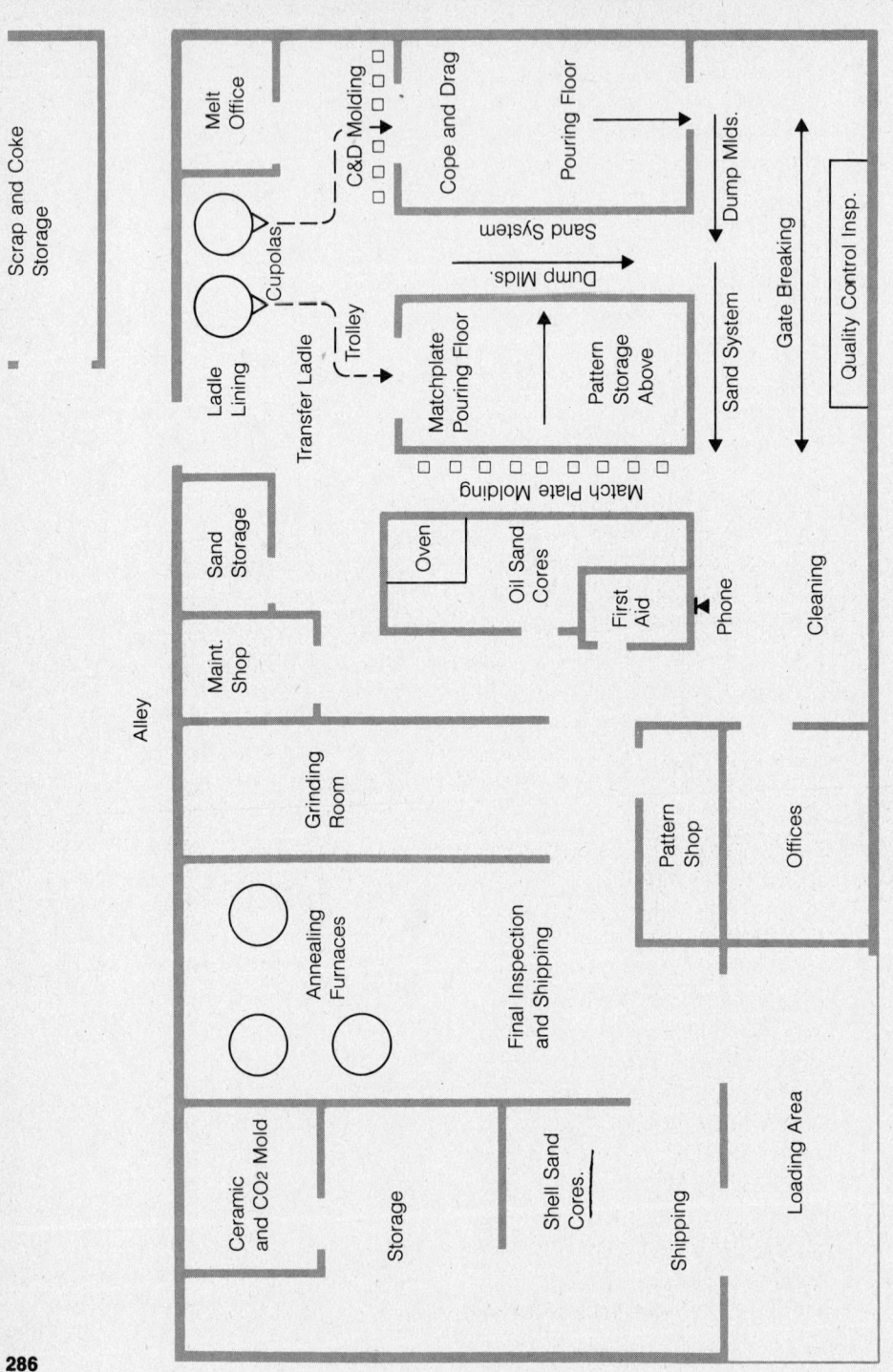

Exhibit 6.3   Jones Foundry Company Balance Sheet

Assets	September 28, 1975	September 26, 1976
Current Assets	$ 283,959	$ 24,598
Cash	241,863	660,143
Accounts Receivable (Net)	224,586	209,877
Inventory	7,638	9,638
Prepaid Insurance and Taxes		108,704
Claim for Income Tax Refund	$ 758,048	$1,012,962
Fixed Assets		
Land and Buildings	481,114	489,628
Plant Equipment	741,481	1,210,455
Office Equipment	17,963	50,694
Trucks and Auto	33,716	35,994
Construction in Progress		29,764
Total	$1,274,276	1,816,537
Less: Allowance for Depreciation	451,378	541,442
Fixed Assets Net	$ 822,897	$1,275,095
Other Assets		
Excess of Cost Over Net Assets	332,080	332,080
Organization Expense	12,384	9,288
Cash Surrender Value—Life Insurance	26,623	
Earnest Money	2,455	
Loans Receivable		34,174
Total Other Assets	373,543	375,542
Total Assets	$1,954,489	$2,663,601

Liabilities and Stockholders' Equity		
Current Liabilities		
Accounts Payable	$ 131,662	$ 317,448
Accrued Wages	21,224	29,979
Accrued Taxes (Other Than Income)	9,348	31,733
Notes Payable (Current Portion)	203,696	196,107
Accrued Income Taxes	289	
Accrued Interest	21,071	25,124
Total Current Liabilities	$ 387,293	$ 600,393
Deferred Liabilities		
Notes Payable	$1,062,045	1,413,810
Subordinated Debentures	300,000	454,500
Total Deferred Liabilities	$1,362,045	$1,868,310
Stockholders' Equity		
Capital Stock	$ 1,000	1,000
Additional Paid in Capital	199,000	199,000
Retained Earnings	5,150	(5,103)
Year to Date Earnings		
Total Stockholders' Equity	$ 205,150	$ 194,896
Total Liabilities and Stockholders' Equity	$1,954,489	$2,663,601

Exhibit 6.4 Jones Foundry Company Income Statement

	October 1, 1974 to September 28, 1975	September 26, 1976
Net Sales	$2,707,999	$3,315,405
Cost of Sales		
Inventory	281,738	224,586
Net Purchases		917,113
Finish and Heat Treating	65,970	
Melting	94,885	316,046
Molding and Pouring	233,567	877,251
Coremaking	47,294	156,171
Annealing	7,009	86,352
Tooling and Inspection	41,846	
Maintenance	45,607	116,062
Production Supervision	12,224	54,898
Raw Material	842,743	
Freight	8,211	
Wages	628,406	
Depreciation	81,275	
Grinding Department		173,262
Shipping		126,585
Local Delivery		8,448
Cost of Sales—Patterns		106,788
Outside Galvanizing		9,347
Total	$2,390,782	$3,172,915
Less: Ending Inventory	224,586	209,877
Cost of Sales	2,116,195	2,963,037
Gross Profit	$ 541,804	$ 352,367
Overhead Expense	567,543	342,062
Operating Loss or Gain	(25,739)	10,305
Other Income	31,178	37,249
Other Expenses		181,259
Net Income (Before Taxes)	5,439	(133,703)
Provision for Income Taxes	289	
Net Income (After Taxes)	$ 5,150	($10,253)
Gross Profit		$ 352,367
General and Administrative		
President	This analysis	57,024
Costing and Reception	not performed	58,650
Accounting	this year.	48,239
Sales		48,773
Technical		129,374
Total General and Administrative		$ 342,062
Operating Income		10,305
Other Income		37,249

Other Expenses

Interest Expense	147,667
Bad Debt Expense	10,667
Sales Commission	18,887
Other Taxes and Misc. Expense	4,035
Total Expenses	181,258
Net Gain (Loss) before Taxes	(133,703)
Provision for Taxes	123,450
Net Gain (Loss)	(10,253)

Exhibit 6.5   Jones Foundry Company, Inc.: Year Ending September 26, 1976

Schedule 1	Amount	Total
Sales		
Sales—Castings	$3,212,190	
Sales—Patterns	116,172	
Sales—Containers	52,084	
Sales—Other	9,394	
Gross Sales		$3,389,841
Returns and Allowances—Castings	51,975	
Returns—Containers	19,279	
Total Returns		71,255
Sales Discounts		3,180
Net Sales		$3,315,405

Schedule 2		
Purchases		
Scrap	$ 370,291	
Coke	225,424	
Foundry Supplies	283,330	
Shipping Containers	38,066	
Total		$ 917,113

Schedule 3		
Other Expenses		
Interest Expense	$ 147,668	
Bad Debt Expense	10,668	
Sales Commission	18,888	
Other Taxes and Expenses	4,036	
Total		$ 181,259

6/Jones Foundry Company

pends on the type of pattern used. In cope and drag molding, 2 molds are pressed together to form one casting. In the matchplate process, a single pattern has impressions on both sides. One side is poured and then the other. Normally this process is done by hand, at 200 molds per shift. Jones Foundry has recently purchased an automated matchplate machine which turns out 800 castings per shift. Once the metal cools, gatebreaking occurs. Gatebreaking is a process of breaking small gates on the mold. The resultant castings are cleaned, i.e., oxidized residue removed by shot blasting with small pellets. Approximately 70% of the castings must be heat treated. Those items requiring heat treating must be moved to the annealing furnace area. The annealing furnaces are large pots. In these pots, the metal is reheated to 1500 degrees, red hot, but not melted. In combination with the chemical properties, this process adds to the ductile strength of the metal. Smaller items, constituting approximately 40% of the castings, after being heat treated go directly to the grinding room. But 60% of the heat treated items, the large castings which protrude above the top of the pot, become oxidized and must be returned to the cleaning area to be shot blasted.

Jones Foundry management recognizes that this is an inappropriate line design, but due to configurations in the plant, they feel that they cannot correct it at this time. In summary, 60% of their castings go from cleaning to annealing and back to cleaning again. Once castings pass through cleaning, they are sent to the grinding room where protrusions are removed. Finally, inspection of the items is made and the items are shipped or temporarily stored and then shipped. Normally, castings are shipped as soon as they complete their final inspection so that the storage is only for perhaps a few hours. Castings would never be stored for longer than one day in the shipping area.

The storage area shown on the plant layout is for scrap since a steel foundry of this type should have only the finished inventory from a few days' output. Scrap iron is melted in the cupolas. Only enough scrap iron is kept in raw materials inventory for the next few days' production. The raw materials can be ordered and will be delivered within a day. If needed, scrap can be picked up in the foundry's own trucks whenever they need it immediately. Therefore, raw material inventories are minimal. The pattern shop is leased to a pattern maker.

The absence of an effective plant manager is perceived as having caused serious problems. Continual scheduling difficulties have been encountered in the plant. Furthermore, various work groups within the plant have argued over priorities and these arguments have led to problems. Production has frequently been late. In Mr. Hackney's words, "The biggest problem is plant operating efficiency. When I get that, then we'll be making money. What needs to be done is for somebody to solve the daily problems that come up. The plant manager must be a knowledgeable person who can help supervise, put out fires, and eventually begin to anticipate problems. This manager must coordinate and motivate superintendents. He should make them comfortable and provide imagination and innovation. He must help the foremen to work out optimum techniques. I can't do this for him. I just don't have the time."

Steve also commented, "One of the most perplexing problems is that of scheduling. I attempt to schedule production in order to help people in the plant. I see this as one of my chief roles. But, even if we schedule properly, we have a problem with the gatebreaking area, the annealing furnace area, but even more importantly we have some very serious problems in terms of ergonomics. By this I mean that we have people going through several motions in the plant which are not necessary. Items are located in the plant within poor reach. People have to make several stooping motions which are not necessary. If we had a better laid out plant with better ergonomic considerations, I think we could make a lot more money. In short, the workers are going through a lot of extra motions that are not necessary. However, we have to recognize that even while we know what our production bottlenecks are, our decision to replace a lot of the equipment in order to have a new plant layout is governed by the available money. There just isn't any." Steve continues, "We have a just horrible scheduling problem. We have to clean before we can heat treat, and then we have to clean again after we heat treat. Most competitors can heat treat and clean; we can't because of the flow, so we have lost a competitive edge in terms of price. Furthermore, gatebreaking is difficult to do here efficiently because of the layout."

Morris Hackney continues his commentary on the plant. "To me to be successful you've got to have labor efficiency. I instituted a labor efficiency system and a cost system so we could get a better grip on what was happening in the plant. The most obvious problem we have had in the plant has been efficiency. My experience has been that if you don't have an efficiency system which measures labor efficiency, the plant may be 60 to 70 to 75% efficient. We reached that point with our labor efficiency system, but improvement stopped. It was then that I realized that the plant manager had to go. We had constant scheduling problems. He just did not organize the work or the work flow."

Mr. Jones, the metallurgist, has his own perceptions of the production system. He indicates that he recognizes the bottlenecks in the plant. He feels that in addition to this problem, they have a problem with quality control. He feels that they have about a 15% rejection rate and that this is high. He feels that 10% is average in the industry. Despite the higher rejection rate, they produce a quality product, and they are able to resolve most of their customers' complaints.

Every single item that is shipped is inspected. Mr. Jones feels that inspection procedures are adequate to catch the problems but that what is needed is controls on the people as the items are being made. The foundry doesn't have them, and he feels that this is where the problem is.

Finance. Referring to their financial problems, Mr. Warren commented, "Our greatest problem right now is cash flow. [Exhibit 6.6 reveals balance sheet comparisons for the 5 quarters.] We started a standard product and cost system in January, 1976, but we operated in all of 1975 without any true picture of what our operating labor efficiency or operating costs were. I suppose we're in the 80–85% efficient range now. I believe that a good accounting system, especially a good standard costing system, is the key to effective management control. We bought the computer and it has enabled us to keep a much tighter rein on cost. We are able daily to know where we are in the plant. We are able to put out daily and monthly labor efficiency reports as a result of the computer."

Mr. Warren continued, "Where we really got in trouble was the $365,000 it cost us to comply with EPA requirements. We had to come up with the cash initially before we could get a Small Business Administration loan. As a result, it put a real crunch on our spending. And as far as I'm concerned it adds not at all to productivity and may eventually force us out of business. If we could have just put that $365,000 into new equipment, we would be able to be price competitive now. But, it was either put the $365,000 in pollution control or they'd close us up. We had to end up absorbing about $165,000 for six months and we managed to get a loan for $200,000 from the Small Business Administration, which came in June. Mr. Hackney originally had $600,000 in the bank, and now that's all gone. You can see that we are in a very tight financial situation."

Accounts receivable are controlled through listings made as a result of the computer. While the computer does not yet automatically age the accounts receivable, this is planned for the near future. The past due amount has begun to decrease over time since March. However, there is a new customer who has approximately $100,000 of the $154,000 shown for July receivables, past due. The firm has had difficulty with getting this individual to pay. "This new customer was given 90 days to pay. Considering our cost of capital is 15%, that 90 day extension of credit cost us three or four thousand dollars. The normal overdue collection procedure is for Nancy, the bookkeeper, to call each of the late firms and others who might not pay on time to indicate to them that their payment is due. If her call is unsuccessful, then I call. Aging receivables by hand is a very long, slow drawn-out process and just wasn't done in the past. But with the computer, this can be accomplished easily. As to exactly who is called, it depends on how long they have been customers and some of their past history. Jones does have some leverage with past due accounts because we hold their patterns (molds) and each pattern costs about $1,000. Jones uses these patterns as collateral against payment. If the firms don't pay, Jones keeps their patterns."

Jones has instituted tight controls on spending. Mr. Warren observes, "I have tried to impress on Mr. Hackney the need to stop spending for new items. We are overextended entirely. Payback on these items takes months. Some items we bought just for 10% loan investment credit. We don't use discounted cash flow concepts because if Morris says buy we have to buy it. What we try to do is tell Morris not to buy."

Exhibit 6.6 Balance Sheet Comparisons

Assets	Sept. 1975	Dec. 1975	March 1976	June 1976	Sept. 1976
Current Assets					
Cash	283,959	121,867	42,795	22,956	24,598
Accounts Receivable	240,956	303,697	443,840	619,614	660,143
Inventory	224,586	185,233	162,510	163,361	209,877
Prepaid Insurance	8,545	11,628	16,100	16,213	9,638
Total Current Assets	758,048	622,426	665,246	822,146	1,012,962
Fixed Assets	822,897	942,236	1,139,630	1,260,899	1,275,095
Other Assets	373,543	355,509	351,855	373,526	375,542
Total Assets	$1,954,489	$1,920,172	$2,156,732	$2,456,572	$2,663,601

Liabilities and Stockholders' Equity

	Sept. 1975	Dec. 1975	March 1976	June 1976	Sept. 1976
Current Liabilities					
Accounts Payable (Trade)	131,662	254,180	222,498	373,568	285,114
Accounts Payable (Other)	—	—	26,907	39,010	35,334
Accrued Wages	21,224	23,634	27,078	30,644	29,979
Notes Payable (Current)	92,163	92,163	294,237	294,237	196,107
Accrued Interest	21,071	11,617	20,054	26,803	25,124
Accrued Income Taxes	289	(47,312)	(53,662)	(47,400)	
Total Current Liabilities	275,760	349,327	568,000	757,965	600,393
Deferred Liabilities	1,473,578	1,423,521	1,449,169	1,551,390	1,868,310
Stockholders' Equity	205,150	147,326	139,562	147,216	194,896
Total	$1,954,489	$1,920,172	$2,156,732	$2,456,572	$ 266,360
Current Ratio	2.75:1	1.78:1	1.17:1	1.08:1	1.7:1
Acid Test Ratio	1.90:1	1.22:1	.86:1	.85:1	1.14:1

Personnel. The company employs in total about 150 people. One hundred forty of these work in the plant. In the plant there is roughly 100% turnover but most of this 100% turnover is represented by individuals who do not stay for more than one day. The company hires about two people per week. The work is very unhealthy, dangerous, and almost thankless. In summertime, the temperature in the foundry may reach 125°. The plant employees are unionized—the International Molders and Allied Workers Union (AFL-CIO CLC Local Union No. 627). All of the floor workers are black. "It is just impossible to get whites to work on the plant floor, which has conditions which the blacks will tolerate." The top pay in the plant goes to the blacks. The whites who work there work in the nonfloor jobs and get paid less. Absenteeism is not a problem and there is a very low level of turnover among those who remain after the first few days.

Jones has a real good safety record and an OSHA inspection in 1975 did not uncover any violations. Jones has much lower workman's compensation payments than the average foundry. Jones has had layoffs only one time in recent history, and that was during the summer of 1975 when sales dropped so drastically. The Union is not perceived as strong or militant. The feeling of the management is "The union does not try to steal you blind and we try to be fair with them." An agreement between Jones Foundry and the union was reached and agreed upon and made effective March 29, 1976 to March 25, 1979. When the contract was negotiated in early 1976, the union brought in a professional negotiator. The company perceived that it was at a disadvantage. The expert knew all the latest legal cases and rulings; Mr. Warren and Mr. Hackney negotiated for the company. It was believed by Mr. Warren that because this expert perceived the dire situation which the organization was in, he was able to press for his demands. That is, the negotiator knew that the company did not want a strike because it did not want to shut down. Therefore, he was able to negotiate a very sizable increase in pay for the individuals in the plant. It amounted to about a $.33 raise per hour per year for three years, plus an increase in fringe benefits, for a total of about $1.27 per hour over the three years. The company has only experienced two grievances through July, 1976. In Table 6.1 a copy of the wages agreed to in the collective bargaining agreement is presented. Tables 6.2 and 6.3 present listings of the insurance and pension provisions respectively, as agreed to under the union contract. The company feels that it has good relations with its union and its employees. No serious problems are envisioned in the future with these people. With regard to the nonunion employees, Mr. Hackney expressed a view that they do not try to eliminate people but rather try to use the people they have better. "As a result of gaining a computer, no one will lose his job." With regard to the standard cost system which was imposed on the plant personnel, there was no perceived resistance to change because the individual supervisors had a chance to participate in developing the standards and individual

Table 6.1 Wages

Section 4.

Classification	3/29/76	3/28/77	3/27/78
Journeymen Molders & Coremakers	$4.66	$5.00	$5.38
Maintenance Mechanics	4.66	5.00	5.38
Inspectors	4.07	4.41	4.79
Cupola Tender	4.07	4.41	4.79
Cupola Tender Helper	3.87	4.21	4.59
Ladle Liner	3.97	4.31	4.69
Furnace Tender Annealing	3.87	4.21	4.59
Muller Operator	3.87	4.21	4.59
Truck Driver	3.87	4.21	4.59
Fork Lift Operator	3.87	4.21	4.59
Grinders	3.87	4.21	4.59
Wheelabrator	4.07	4.41	4.79
Core Setter	3.66	4.00	4.38
Changers	3.87	4.21	4.59
Iron Pourers	3.97	4.31	4.69
Molder & Coreroom Helper	3.62	3.96	4.34
Gate Breaker	3.62	3.96	4.34
Sorter	3.62	3.96	4.34
Cupola Helper	3.62	3.96	4.34
Cupola Charger	3.87	4.21	4.59
Cupola Liner	4.35	4.69	5.07
Cupola Liner Helper	3.87	4.21	4.59
Metal Treater	3.87	4.21	4.59
Ladle Pusher	3.87	4.21	4.59
Sample Catcher	3.77	4.11	4.49
Scrap Burner	3.87	4.21	4.59
Shakeout Man	3.62	3.96	4.34
Laborer	3.10	3.44	3.82

Section 5. Employees who are presently receiving above the scheduled wage rate shall continue to receive their current rate in addition to any scheduled wage increase provided for in this article, until such time the employee makes a permanent job transfer, at which time the employee will receive the rate of the job to which he moves.

workers were glad to know what it is that they were supposed to be doing. Currently these standards are on a department-wide basis, but there is some consideration being given to placing work standards on the individual. Personnel policies have not been written since most employees are affected directly by rules in the union agreement and these are contained therein for each of the individuals to read. Some job descriptions have been begun, but nothing has been written for the plant, as yet.

Table 6.2   Insurance

Section 1.

a. Between the effective date of this contract and March 30, 1977, the total cost of the insurance premium for each covered employee shall be borne equally by the Company and the employee for the benefits provided for in Section 2.
b. Effective March 31, 1977, the total cost of the insurance premium for each covered employee shall be borne 75% by the Company and 25% by the employee for the benefits covered in Section 2.

Section 2.

As a generalization of the principal insurance benefits being provided and as a supplement to the insurance carriers' booklet of scheduled benefits, the following schedule is provided. Benefit levels provided under the Hospitalization and Major Medical programs are not listed in this Agreement.

Type of Insurance	Benefit Level
Life Insurance	$3000
Accidental Death and Dismemberment	$3000
Dependent Life	
(Spouse)	$1000
(Child 14 days to 6 months)	$ 100
(Child 6 months to 19 years)	$1000
Weekly Accident and Sickness	$ 60

Table 6.3   Pension

Section 1. The Pension Plan shall remain in effect for the duration of this Agreement.

Section 2. Subject to qualifications and limitations outlined in the Pension Plan, monthly retirement income shall be computed at the rate of $5 for each year of service after January 1, 1965, up to a maximum of 40 years.

Section 3. The Company agrees that the Pension Plan will be amended and administered in a manner that conforms to the provisions of ERISA.

Section 4. The Company will furnish the Union with the following reports annually:

1. Valuation report of the actuary accompanied by such supporting informations as may be needed.
2. Annual report of the Insurance Company or the corporate trustee of the pension trust fund.
3. Annual D-2 report to the Department of Labor.

Information Systems. At the heart of the Jones Foundry information system is the new Wang Minicomputer which was purchased for approximately $40,000 in early 1976. This machine can run four different programs at the same time. It has external storage capacity, i.e., drums. It has a video display feature as well as a printer. The general feeling of Jones Foundry management is that businesses don't realize the potential of these minicomputers. The following is an example of how effective and important to the organization these can be. Prior to the time the computer was purchased and programmed, whenever a customer called and asked when his order would be ready, the standard reply was three weeks. It could just as well have been six weeks or eight weeks or tomorrow but no one really knew. Now if a customer calls, a daily update sheet is used to tell the customer exactly when the order will be processed. Jones' management believes that this presents a great competitive advantage because other foundries of their size do not have a minicomputer. Furthermore, Jones can tell the exact backlog and can cost every item. This aids in pricing. Every order for each customer by item is placed in the computer. Any clerk can answer a customer question, although Jones still prefers for a salesman to handle customer inquiries. As another example, it used to take Jones three days to extend all of its invoices, now the computer does it in thirty minutes. This frees up a lot of clerical time to be used in analyzing the business as opposed to just keeping records. The payroll used to take Jones four days to prepare. The computer now does this in an hour. Prices and cost margins are printed for every casting, thus aiding the bidding process which must often be performed by phone on a moment's notice.

Standard cost reports and labor efficiency reports are also generated daily. Their future plans are to prepare the financial statements on the computer and completely eliminate the need for any hand bookkeeping except for input to the computer.

Logistics. With respect to logistics, raw materials are ordered on an as-needed basis and very little raw material inventory is stored. The work-in-process material flows through the plant in the manner described previously. Very little finished-goods inventory is stored. With regard to other procurement within the organization, with the exception of the scrap materials, requisitions are filled out and approved by department heads and then the metallurgist purchases these. The metallurgist notifies the requestor when the material arrives. He checks all the invoices against the material and packaging slips and makes certain that he is getting what he pays for. He then sends these to the department. He purchases from established sources, although he will give salesmen a chance to show that they can deliver and that if they succeed at a better price he will give them another chance. They do a monthly periodic inventory for the nonscrap items; no storekeeper is used. Chits are signed for inventory withdrawal. Supplies for the nonproduction areas are kept in cabinets in the offices.

Top Management Philosophy. Morris Hackney has very definite beliefs about how a business should be run. He feels that creativity is the key to success in management. But he also feels that prior to being creative, "You've got to know what you're doing. You can only be creative if you have the data." He feels that you improve your general decision making with experience and therefore your decisions become better with age. He feels that in the foundry business, the president should handle the sales and not the plant. The plant should be run by a plant manager. He perceives that it is important to have good cost control systems. With regard to motivating his management team, Mr. Hackney believes that people at this level are not motivated by money, but he does pay them a bonus in addition to straight salary. He feels that if you get good people in the top positions, money does not really have a big impact, "Money won't make them work any harder. The penalty for not paying them is that they'll leave the foundry." He believes in letting his top people manage. As an example, it was at the recommendation of Connor Warren that Jones Foundry purchased the computer. He believes that you have to "take things one step at a time." While he recognizes many of the problems, he has not been able to solve them all. He feels that the firm just does not have the money to solve all of the problems. "The basis of control is budgets, and we have started budgeting. What you need to do in the sales area is get good clients, clients with a future, and cull out the bad clients. In bad times, you have to take any client you can. Right now times are good, and what we want to do is build a good client base."

Social Responsibilities. In 1975 and 1976 the company was required to install a total of $365,000 in pollution control equipment. As mentioned in the finance section, this has had considerable impact upon the corporate cash flow. Further pollution control equipment expenditures are not anticipated at this time.

Because of concern for equal employment opportunity, half of the company's eight supervisors are now blacks.

With respect to governmental relations, it was pointed out by Connor Warren that approximately ⅓ of his time is spent filling out government required reports, either Federal, State, or Local. The Federal Committee on Paperwork recognizes this as an important cost element. For example, one corporation much larger than Jones, and which reported one hundred million dollars in earnings for 1976, spent 5 million dollars in earnings just reporting to the Federal Government in terms of man hours and paper expenditures. For Jones Foundry, one third of the salary of Warren plus the value of time of clerical people is devoted to such paperwork. A summary of the various reports and their return deadlines is given in Table 6.4.

Table 6.4 Jones Foundry Government Reports and Returns Deadlines

January

20 State and County Use Tax
31 File State Employers Quarterly Income Tax Withholding (A1)
31 File—State Unemployment, Compensation Report
15 Make Estimated Tax Installment
31 Deposit Federal Unemployment Tax—File Quarterly Form
31 941—File OSHA Summary Form 102
31 File Form 940—Employers Annual Federal Unemployment Tax Return
31 Issue Employee W-2's
31 Pay City License Fee

February

28 File Form A-2 & A-3 with State
29 File Form W-3 with Federal Copy of Employees' W-2

March

15 State Franchise Tax Return
15 Make Estimated Tax Installment

April

30 File State Employers' (A-1) Quarterly Tax Withholding
30 File State Unemployment Compensation Report
30 File Quarterly Form 941
20 State and County Use Tax
30 Deposit Federal Unemployment Tax Due

May

30 (1976) File Complete EBS–1

June

15 Make Estimated Tax Installment

July

31 File State Employers (A-1) Quarterly Tax Withholding
31 File State Unemployment Compensation Report
20 State and County Use Tax
31 File Quarterly Form 941
31 Deposit Federal Unemployment Tax Due

August

September

15 Make Estimated Tax Installment
30 State Business License Expires

6/Jones Foundry Company   **299**

October

20 State and County Use Tax
31 Form POGC-1 with Pension Guarantee Benefit Corporation
31 File for County and State License
31 File Quarterly Form 941
31 Deposit Federal Unemployment Tax Due
31 File State Employers (A-1) Quarterly Tax Withholding
31 File State Unemployment Compensation Report

November

15 Auto & Truck Tags

December

15 Federal Corp. Income Tax
15 State Corp. Income Tax
 1 Request New W-4 Forms from Employees

Discussion Questions

Part A

1. How could Mr. Hackney have investigated Jones Foundry before he purchased?
2. Analyze the financial statements in Exhibits 6.1 and 6.2. What does your analysis tell you?
3. What are common problems in a family-owned business?

Part B

1. What are the major problems/opportunities confronting Jones Foundry in each of these areas:

Marketing	Personnel
Production	Top Management
Finance	Information Systems

2. What are Jones' strengths and weaknesses, threats and opportunities related to each of the functional areas mentioned in question 1 above?
3. What are the alternatives in solving these problems or taking advantage of these opportunities?
4. What other problems does the firm face?
5. What impact have social responsibility requirements had on this firm's financial and production capabilities?
6. Discuss the implications that governmental paperwork has for this and other firms.
7. What problems do you see with Jones' pricing policy?
8. Trace the effects of product life cycle on this firm.

7/Pamida Incorporated

Bruce A. Kirchhoff and
Steve Lawrence

[handwritten annotations: - 190 Gibson stores / - 12 small stores carrying beauty aids / - a rack jobbing venture distributing health & beauty aids, soft goods, auto. supplies]

Pamida, a Nebraska Corporation, was founded in 1963 by Jim Witherspoon and Lee Wegener. The company started as two small retail outlets located in Knoxville and Oskaloosa, Iowa and has grown to a discount retail organization with net sales of $241 million for the year ending January 31, 1976. With corporate headquarters located in Omaha, Nebraska, Pamida distributes retail merchandise to its Gibson Discount stores located in mid-America. Most of the stores are located in small communities which are agriculturally based. These communities range in population from eight to twelve thousand. The [handwritten: pop: 8-12K] geographic area served by the organization includes Nebraska, Kansas, Missouri, Illinois, Michigan, Iowa, Wisconsin, Minnesota, North and South Dakota, Wyoming, Montana, and Idaho. Jim Witherspoon, Chairman of the Board and past President, characterizes the company criteria for success as, "involvement of our people in helping create and support the overall company objectives. Through our decentralized management approach we emphasize merchandising, advertising, and people, but we keep in mind that any organization that is well motivated and has an aggressive approach needs ideas, because it is ideas which produce profits, economies, efficiencies, and change." [handwritten: decentralized mgt approach / each store operated as a profit center]

Pamida employs a decentralized management system, with each store operated as a profit center. The store manager is responsible for the operation of his store unit and is compensated by a base salary plus a bonus, calculated on the sales and profits of his individual store.

Pamida's Gibson Discount Centers are divided into three regions, with a manager responsible for each region. Under each regional manager are six district managers who are responsible for 10 to 13 stores. In addition, there are 11 field merchandise supervisors who assist the district managers, thereby increasing the time the district managers are able to spend in the stores.

Besides the 190 full-time Gibson stores, Pamida operates 12 small stores carrying mainly health and beauty aids. None of these stores are operated under the Gibson name. The company also operates a small rack-jobbing venture which distributes health and beauty aids, soft goods, and automotive supplies. These operations account for 6 to 7 percent of sales and, although profitable, no expansion is planned for either.

Pamida is the parent company to its wholly-owned subsidiary Gibson Dis-

Source: Prepared by Steve Lawrence under the supervision of Associate Professor Bruce A. Kirchhoff, for the University of Nebraska at Omaha. Reprinted by permission. Distributed by the Intercollegiate Case Clearing House, Soldiers Field, Boston, Mass. 02163. All rights reserved to the contributors. Printed in the U.S.A.

Table 7.1 Geographic Distribution

State	Number of Stores
Idaho	5
Illinois	18
Iowa	50
Kansas	19
Michigan	1
Minnesota	34
Missouri	15
Montana	3
Nebraska	13
North Dakota	5
South Dakota	10
Wisconsin	9
Wyoming	12
Total	194

count Centers. Pamida buys merchandise and distributes it to Gibson Discount Centers.

Marketing. Pamida's retail outlets are named "Gibson Discount Centers." The right to use this name has been granted by license agreement with H. R. Gibson of Seagoville, Texas, who franchises this name nationally. Pamida pays a relatively small fixed fee for the name which extends to all of the stores presently operated by Pamida. Since the original license agreement was entered into, additional Gibson Discount Centers have been opened by Pamida with the consent of Gibson. However, there is no assurance that this practice will continue. The agreement between Pamida and H. R. Gibson may be terminated by either party on 90 days' written notice. In the agreement, H. R. Gibson retains the right of quality control over any of the products sold by Pamida at any of its Gibson Discount Centers. There are numerous other Gibson licensees in most of the states in which Pamida operates. Pamida's management believes that termination of the agreement with H. R. Gibson would not have a materially adverse effect on the organization.

Pamida's current marketing strategy is to locate Gibson Discount Centers in small, agriculturally oriented communities. In most instances the communities are the county seat. Pamida has found that major retailers have tended not to locate in communities of this size. Thus, the major source of competition for the Gibson Discount Centers are the local drug and variety stores. Most of these communities are too small to support more than one major retail organization. Historically, Pamida's marketing strategy was to locate in towns of between 8 and 10 thousand. When these markets started to become saturated, the company changed its emphasis to include towns between 4 and 12 thousand.

Customers may select from between nine and fourteen thousand nationally advertised brand-name products depending on store size, which ranges from eight to forty thousand square feet. None of the stores sells big-ticket items such as major appliances and furniture. The bulk of store sales dollars is from merchandise with a price of less than five dollars. A breakdown of the merchandise line includes:

1. Soft lines—primarily clothing items
2. Health and beauty aids—includes prescription and nonprescription drugs, as well as personal hygiene products
3. Hardware and appliances—includes basic hardware and small appliances like toasters and blenders
4. Food, candy, cookies, and tobacco
5. Automotive—includes supplies and accessories for automobiles, trucks, and tractors
6. Sporting goods
7. School and pet supplies
8. Jewelry, records, and tapes
9. Housewares
10. Toys

It is management's policy to offer merchandise with quick-selling characteristics at competitive prices. Pamida's pricing policy is to price at or below the manufacturer's suggested retail price, thereby meeting or underselling the local competition. The merchandise line includes items which fall into the necessity, rather than luxury, classification. The primary reason for carrying merchandise with quick-selling characteristics is to maximize inventory turnover. Company policy is to maintain a large in-stock condition, since many rural customers travel long distances to shop at the Gibson Discount Center.

It is Pamida's policy to emphasize cash and carry sales. Pamida's accounts receivable for rack jobbing generally account for less than 2% of sales. Gibson Centers have no accounts receivable. The company does not offer contract

$202.173M - Sales 1975

Exhibit 7.1 Pamida 1975 Sales by Category

Category	Percent	
Soft goods	22.0	*44.47806 M*
Health and beauty aids	16.0	*32.34768*
Hardware and appliances	14.0	*28.30422*
Food, candy, cookies and tobacco	10.0	*20.2173*
Automotive supplies	10.0	*20.2173*
Sporting goods	9.0	*18.19557*
School, pet supplies and misc.	6.0	*12.13038*
Jewelry, records, tapes, cameras	6.0	*12.13038*
Housewares	6.0	*12.13038*
Toys	1.0	*2.02173*

purchase plans and accepts bank credit cards at only one-third of its locations. Stores accepting bank credit cards are those with the larger square footage.

Pamida recently adopted a merchandise line expansion policy. Reflecting this new emphasis, the company assumed operation of the women's and children's clothing departments, which had previously been operated by a lessee. Pamida is also putting pharmacies in all stores over 20,000 square feet.

Property Management. Pamida's Real Estate Development and Construction Department handles the purchase of real estate and the plans for construction of store units. Pamida still owns several of its larger stores, but in the past few years has been using the sale-leaseback method of real estate finance. The sale-leaseback technique was initiated to maximize the amount of capital available for expansion. Prior to 1973, Pamida's policy was to construct and own its facilities, or to lease existing structures. Exhibit 7.2 presents a schedule of property, buildings, and equipment.

Once the decision to build a store is made, the search for a buyer is begun. Usually a buyer is found before construction is started, but many times the store will be constructed regardless of the availability of a buyer. The store will then be sold, at a later date, to an individual or group of investors. Pamida has found that rental rates are generally lower than rates charged in large cities. Rent is based on a percent of sales in 13 leases.

Building construction lasts about 120 days and the store can be fully stocked and ready to open 30 days after construction is complete. The park-

Exhibit 7.2   Schedule of Assets

Classification	Balance at Beginning of Period	Additions at Cost	Retirements or Sales	Transfers	Balance at Close of Period
Year Ended January 31, 1976:					
Land & Improvements	$ 899,000	$ 574,000	$ 87,000		$ 1,436,000
Buildings and Improvement	4,679,000	55,000			4,734,000
Furniture and Equipment	11,571,000	3,051,000	242,000		14,380,000
Automotive	499,000	163,000	45,000		617,000
Lease-hold (improvements)	914,000	579,000	51,000		1,422,000
	$18,562,000	$4,422,000	$375,000		$22,609,000

ing area is generally three times larger than the store space. The cost of trade fixtures (cash registers, display units, etc.) runs $2.50 per square foot.

Management plans call for the addition of approximately 20 stores per year. The company expects to realize this goal through new openings, relocations, and expansions of existing units.

The size of relocations is governed by the population and growth trends of the particular town. New openings are governed by the same criteria. The sites are located primarily in shopping centers, if possible, or near supermarkets as a second alternative.

Advertising. LeRoy Peterson, Director of Corporate Advertising, states, "The goal of the advertising department is to create sales." As a discount store organization, Pamida stresses prices of merchandise in their ads.

Advertising costs run about 2.5% of sales. The choice of advertising media depends on the resources available in the local market. However, the major advertising media are local newspapers, which receive about 70% of total advertising dollars. Approximately 20% of the advertising dollar is spent on direct mailings and shopper publications. The remainder is divided between radio and television time. Between ten and fifteen reprint ads are prepared by corporate advertising each year.

Mr. Peterson indicates that Pamida's advertising policy allows for flexibility at the individual store level. The company allows the local store management to substitute or make price changes to any advertisement layout sent from Omaha. The reason for this policy is to allow the store managers to adjust for local price competition, inventory shortages, and tastes.

Traffic and Warehouse. To facilitate Pamida's in-stock policy, an ordering system called MSI is used. Under MSI, a record of the rate of sale for all merchandise is maintained in an orderbook. Orders are shipped from the Omaha warehouse 72 hours before the merchandise is expected to arrive at the store. The majority of the merchandise is truck shipped within a 400-500 mile radius of the Omaha warehouse.

Approximately 41% of total discount store sales consist of merchandise shipped through the Omaha warehouse. Most of the remaining merchandise is shipped directly from the manufacturer to the individual store. The Omaha warehouse has 260,000 square feet and is believed sufficient to serve approximately 250 stores. Pamida also operates a smaller, 40,000-square-foot warehouse in Omaha which is used as a "flow-through" distribution center. The company has purchased a 22-acre tract of unimproved real estate nearby and tentatively plans to replace the 40,000-square-foot structure in the near future.

The Traffic Department is responsible for the physical movement of goods. This includes both inbound and outbound shipments. Deciding the mode of transportation and the timing of the individual shipments, at the lowest possible cost, is the main objective of this department.

Inbound shipments to the Omaha warehouse are transported 65% by truck, 24% by rail, and 10% by air freight. Outbound shipments to the individual stores are accomplished through use of Pamida's private fleet of 26 tractors and 80 trailers.

Floyd Knutson, Director of Traffic for Pamida, states: "Since the cost of transportation is set in terms of rate structures, rates cannot be bargained, and the savings must be realized in terms of judgments made by this department." Mr. Knutson indicates that these judgments fall into several categories. Some of these cost-saving measures include:

1. Shipping with higher volume, making fewer trips.
2. Use of consolidation points to keep half-empty loads from being transported long distances.
3. More intensive use of the Omaha warehouse so that shipments can be made to the stores at a lower cost and quality checks can be made on bulk shipments from the manufacturer to the warehouse.

Personnel Management. "Although Pamida is a large organization," says Corporate Personnel Director Jack Doyle, "we like to think of it as a family organization." He indicates that the underlying philosophy is to give individuals jobs to be accomplished, requisite responsibility for accomplishment, and then step back and let them perform.

Jim Witherspoon indicated his gratitude for performance by Pamida employees when he donated $1,000,000 of Pamida stock to the Employees' Profit Sharing Plan in 1973. He indicated that the employees had made Pamida what it is today.

Company policy in the area of management training is patterned after a combination of formal and on-the-job training. The formal aspects of the training last for three days. The formal training session takes place at corporate headquarters. The process involves a series of meetings between the new store manager and various executives. Meetings include conference sessions with the following executive level managers:

Personnel
Controller
Payroll
Printing
Advertising
Merchandising (Hard goods, soft goods, and inventory control)
Traffic
At least one corporate officer

Meetings are also held with management personnel in charge of the following areas:

306   7/Pamida Incorporated

Warehouse operations
Daily reports
Purchase reports
Inter-store transfers
Expense reports
Data processing
Store supplies
Accounts payable
Correspondence

The objective of this three-day training session is to give the new manager a working orientation to company operations. After this initial three-day training session the new manager is sent to a store location where he or she works with an older, experienced manager and learns on the job.

Pamida's management feels that since the company is experiencing good growth, management recruitment is important. Pamida recruits store managers from several sources, primarily from other retail chain organizations.

Management evaluation takes place every six months. The process includes all personnel within the organization. The procedure requires a conference between the supervisor and the subordinate. The supervisor evaluates the subordinate using criteria set up by the company (see Management Summary Appraisal, Exhibit 7.3). Mr. Doyle indicates that this process allows for immediate feedback and open and clear communication on and about the subject of the evaluation.

Future Growth. Pamida's current expansion policy was initiated in 1969 in response to trends in population growth. A second factor was the increased consumer acceptance of the discount store format. Many of Pamida's stores were approaching their selling capacity, and in order to maintain historical growth rate in sales volume, the smaller stores were replaced with larger units. The larger units, in already established markets, provided increased sales volume and helped increase Pamida's share of the local market.

Store relocation and expansion within existing markets play an important role in Pamida's overall expansion policy. However, the company continues to search for new markets to be served. The primary criteria for the determination of potential new markets are small mid-American towns with an agri-income base, populations of between eight and twelve thousand, and no other major retail outlet.

Discount Industry. Discount retailing, in its conceptual form, was designated to supply quality merchandise without charging for unneeded services. Industry growth has been rapid and, according to the latest trade statistics, discount department stores are the largest retailers of general merchandise. Many problems have combined to render the thirty-one-billion-dollar industry only mar-

Exhibit 7.3 Pamida Inc.: Criteria for Personnel Evaluation

MANAGEMENT SUMMARY APPRAISAL

Six Month ☐

Special ☐

Date _____

NAME _____ S. S. No. _____

POSITION _____ LOCATION _____

Date of Hire _____ Present Salary _____

Date Last Appraisal _____ Date Last Increase _____

	Unsatisfactory	Satisfactory	Noticeably Satisfactory
A. ATTITUDE			
1. Enthusiasm			
2. Willingness to assume responsibility			
3. Attitude on meeting the public and handling customers			

COMMENTS: _____

B. MANAGERIAL QUALITIES			
1. Aggressiveness			
2. Quickness of his thinking and soundness of his judgment			
3. Alertness			

COMMENTS: _____

This Summary Appraisal is a narative description developed from a detailed analysis of the employee's work.

C. PERFORMANCE   Results: (What has this individual accomplished in measurable results since his last appraisal.)

	This Year	Last Year
Sales		
Gross		
Payroll		
Controlable Expenses		
Net Profit		

COMMENTS: _____

D. PREVIOUS EXPERIENCE WITH OTHER COMPANIES AND JOBS: _____

_____

E. PREVIOUS POSITIONS WITH THIS COMPANY _____

_____

F. METHODS   (How does this person go about getting his job done? How does he organize his work? Where applicable, appraise: 1) Ability to handle people, 2) Selection of people, 3) Training job done, 4) Upgrading of organization, and 5) Development of people.)

_____

_____

Management Summary Appraisal

G. **PERSONAL QUALIFICATIONS** (List only outstanding qualifications either above or below average)

1. General _____

_____

_____

_____

__ _____

2. Strongest Single Qualification _____

_____

3. On what points does this employee need help to overcome his weaknesses _____

_____

H. **POTENTIAL** What is the next step ahead for this individual and does he have further potential beyond next step? If so, outline.

_____

_____

_____

I. **ACTION** (Recommend action for improvement such as Training, Change of attitude, Change in pay, Encouragement, etc.)

☐ LEAVE ON PRESENT JOB _____

    ☐ Put on Probation _____ Until what date? _____

☐ REPLACE: ☐ Promote ☐ Demote to _____ ☐ Transfer to job of same classification

☐ TERMINATE

When should recommended action be taken? _____

J. **CHECK CURRENT STATUS OF THIS INDIVIDUAL**

☐ Immediately Promotable   ☐ Satisfactory

☐ Promotable   ☐ New on Job or with Company

☐ Satisfactory (Potentially Promotable)   ☐ Questionable

     ☐ Unsatisfactory

APPRAISAL MADE BY

Name_____ Title_____

Name_____ Title_____

The performance and personal qualification sections of this report have been discussed with the employee by:

Name_____ Title_____ Date_____

Employee Signature _____ Date Signed _____

7/Pamida Incorporated

Exhibit 7.4 Pamida Inc.: Consolidated Statement of Earnings, 10-Year Summary

	1976*	1975*	1974	1973
Net Sales	241,579,000	202,173,000	158,124,000	133,669,027
Cost of Goods Sold	179,935,000	150,945,000	117,123,000	101,155,192
Gross Margin	61,644,000	51,228,000	41,301,000	32,513,835
Expenses				
Selling	38,303,000	31,105,000	23,425,000	19,039,847
General & Admin.	7,027,000	5,655,000	4,252,000	3,497,494
Interest	1,242,000	1,368,000	1,000,000	768,559
Sum of Expenses	46,572,000	38,128,000	28,667,000	23,305,900
Earnings before Taxes	15,072,000	13,100,000	12,624,000	9,207,935
Taxes on Income	7,400,000	6,475,000	6,235,000	4,270,000
Net Earnings	$7,672,000	$6,625,000	$6,389,000	$4,937,935
Net Earnings per Common & Common Equiv.	.83	.73	.70	.54
Average Common & Common Equiv. Shares & Outstanding	9,265,805	9,134,550	9,149,828	9,145,201

*Changed to LIFO Inventory Costing.

Notes to consolidated statements:
  LIFO Inventory Costing adopted in 1975
  2 for 1 Stock Split May 1972—additional shares also issued in 1972
  2 for 1 Stock Split May 1971
  20 for 1 Stock Split February 1969

ginally profitable for all but the most strongly positioned companies. About half of industry volume is believed to be concentrated in problem companies.

Between the mid-1950s and 1967, industry profits grew rapidly as stores, constructed with adequate parking facilities in growing suburban areas, gained acceptability. However, many chains allowed their merchandise quality to slip, and customer count fell from an average of 39,600 households per store to only 12,000 per store.

Early in its history, the industry chose the chain concept of centralized merchandising as a means of holding down costs and promoting rapid expansion. This was combined with emphasis on selling the most popular items. Centralized buying, however, needed to be supplemented by experienced decision making on the local level, and for many discounters this was not the case. When emphasis on fashion items increased and consumption patterns began to change, it became more difficult to find popular items, and profitability suffered.

1972	1971	1970	1969	1968	1967
104,509,099	79,206,264	62,561,128	43,612,917	28,080,511	19,592,154
77,959,641	59,121,990	46,768,737	33,079,857	21,877,878	15,570,997
26,549,458	20,084,274	15,792,394	10,533,060	6,202,633	4,021,157
17,433,753	13,062,906	9,881,643	6,643,077	4,379,211	2,903,567
	(Combined with Selling)				
664,804	306,499	179,956	102,417	59,599	36,468
96,058,198	72,491,395	56,830,336	39,825,351	26,316,688	18,511,032
8,450,901	6,714,869	5,730,792	3,787,566	1,763,833	1,081,122
3,785,000	2,992,000	2,700,000	1,800,000	718,451	389,448
$4,665,901	$3,719,869	$3,030,792	$1,987,566	$1,045,372	$ 691,674
1.07	.88	1.51	1.04	.55	.36
4,336,410	4,225,312	2,012,489	1,915,780	n/a	n/a
			First Public Offering		

due to 2:1 stock split

Chain economies of scale were late in developing. Few organizations succeeded in garnering substantial market shares in metropolitan areas where department stores and national chains were strong. Image was the main problem. *Image*

The K-Mart division of S. S. Kresge has expanded even more rapidly than the industry since 1962. Yet through careful attention to image building, recognizable values, and fashion business, the company's record of profitability was improved. Today, K-Mart's dominance of the industry is unquestioned. *K-mart dominant in industry*

On a national scale, other former variety store operators, F. W. Woolworth and W. T. Grant, entered the business. But these organizations fell prey to the mistakes of most other discounters, with Grant declaring bankruptcy in early 1976. On the other hand, some smaller regional chains have preserved flexibility in their operations by limiting the geographical dispersion of stores and controlling expansion activities. These organizations have met with success in recent years. *Woolworth Grant fell*

7/Pamida Incorporated

Exhibit 7.5 Pamida Inc.: Consolidated Balance Sheet, 8-Year Summary

	1976*	1975*	1974	1973	1972	1971	1970	1969
Current Assets								
Cash	$ 3,856,000	$1,958,000	$3,972,000	$2,222,160	$ 744,075	$ 599,077	$ 528,127	$ 303,150
Trade Accts Rec (less bad debt allowance)	2,168,000	1,677,000	1,904,000	1,702,713	1,557,659	1,471,891	815,562	536,849
Accounts Receivable (other)	574,000	80,000	165,000	7,029,505	0	0	0	0
Merchandise Inventory	85,211,000	59,286,000	48,378,000	46,960,419	34,309,393	22,019,966	16,000,556	10,181,865
Prepaid Expenses	756,000	794,000	494,000	495,334	277,861	183,628	58,085	15,199
Total Current Assets	92,565,000	63,795,000	54,913,000	58,410,131	36,888,988	24,274,562	17,402,330	11,037,063
Property Building & Equip.	15,378,000	13,125,000	11,859,000	11,068,043	9,918,539	4,765,157	1,984,094	1,198,960
Other Assets	1,353,000	1,094,000	1,029,000	570,195	531,256	224,418	181,274	154,740
Total Assets	109,296,000	78,014,000	67,801,000	70,048,369	47,338,783	29,264,137	19,567,698	12,390,763
Current Liabilities								
Notes Payable to Bank	7,650,000	5,500,000	1,000,000	7,000,000	5,500,000	3,592,335	664,232	871,822
Trade Accounts Payable	25,553,000	10,603,000	10,472,000	14,802,346	8,698,104	4,057,183	3,891,109	3,754,304
Salaries and Wages	675,000	613,000	463,000	706,769	536,750	419,965	353,103	203,891
Taxes Other than Inc. Tax	935,000	821,000	533,000	453,388	493,085	314,208	231,763	154,696
Other Accrued Expenses	2,019,000	1,625,000	1,114,000	942,540	771,718	497,523	338,369	210,094
Taxes on Income	368,000	398,000	2,152,000	1,025,560	1,570,318	1,532,443	1,767,224	1,506,158
Curr. Maturities of LT Debt	639,000	565,000	536,000	225,063	227,517	667,996	553,227	187,770
Total Current Liabilities	37,839,000	20,125,000	16,270,000	25,155,666	17,797,492	11,081,653	7,799,097	6,888,715
Deferred Tax on Income	100,000							
Long Term Debt (Less Curr. Mat.)	14,027,000	7,471,000	7,988,000	8,053,343	7,898,001	2,094,218	1,578,392	720,331
Compensation Deferred	150,000							
Stockholders' Equity	4,567,000	4,567,000	4,567,000	4,565,297	2,140,409	1,057,542	1,009,190	957,890
Additional Paid-in Cap.	12,630,000	12,627,000	12,377,000	12,064,486	4,262,492	4,456,236	2,326,400	—
Retained Earnings	39,983,000	33,224,000	26,599,000	20,209,577	15,240,389	10,574,488	6,854,619	3,823,827
Total Stockholders' Equity	57,180,000	50,418,000	43,543,000	36,839,360	21,643,290	16,088,266	10,190,209	4,781,717
Total Liabilities and Equity	109,296,000	78,014,000	67,801,000	70,048,369	47,338,783	29,264,137	19,567,698	12,390,763

*Changed to LIFO Inventory Costing.

Table 7.2 Consumer Price Index (1967=100)

Year	Nondurables
1974	151.0
1973	132.8
1972	121.7
1971	117.7
1970	114.0
1969	108.9
1968	103.1
1966	98.1

1975   166.3
1976   174.3   *from Handbk of BASIC ECON. STAT. JAN. 1980 Edition*

Source: U.S. Department of Commerce.

Table 7.3 Total Retail Sales (in millions of dollars)

Type of Retailing	1970	1971	1972	1973	1974
All Retailers	375,876	408,850	448,379	503,317	537,782
Nondurable	261,239	177,036	298,720	333,042	370,469
Durable	114,238	131,814	149,659	170,275	167,313
Department Stores	37,295	42,027	46,560	52,292	55,871
Variety Stores	6,959	6,972	7,498	8,212	8,714
Drug & Proprietary	13,366	13,736	14,523	15,474	16,785

Source: U.S. Department of Commerce.

Table 7.4 Retail Sales Index—Discount Stores (1967=100)

Company	1970	1971	1972	1973	1974
Alexander's Inc.	125	138	146	149	151
Ames	226	228	308	337	436
Arlen	—	100	102	106	107
Hecks	189	226	306	397	484
Kings	143	150	165	193	206
Mays	148	154	153	154	151
Pamida	282	383	476	564	720
Vornado	114	119	108	117	128
Wal-Mart	351	618	990	1327	1872
Zayre	164	192	226	241	253

Source: Standard & Poor's.

7/Pamida Incorporated

Table 7.5 Profit Margins—Discount Stores (%)

Company	1970	1971	1972	1973	1974
Alexander's Inc.	7.4	6.8	4.0	4.2	3.8
Ames	6.2	6.7	6.5	5.1	5.1
Arlen	—	4.0	3.7	1.6	—
Hecks	7.8	8.6	8.5	8.4	7.9
Kings	8.2	8.3	7.5	7.0	5.6
Mays	6.6	6.3	5.2	4.5	3.7
Pamida	9.4	9.1	8.2	9.5	8.0
Vornado	4.0	4.1	4.1	3.0	2.6
Wal-Mart	7.9	7.9	7.8	8.2	6.3
Zayre	4.5	4.6	4.3	4.2	2.8

Source: Standard & Poor's.

Table 7.6 Net Income—Discount Stores (1967=100) Millions of Dollars

Company	1970	1971	1972	1973	1974
Alexander's Inc.	219	206	57	39	42
Ames	219	297	326	282	314
Arlen	—	100	96	def.	def.
Hecks	248	337	448	544	567
Kings	152	172	178	200	168
Mays	204	235	161	238	89
Pamida	354	444	470	608	631
Vornado	103	115	106	42	23
Wal-Mart	344	606	956	1,283	1,323
Zayre	90	118	125	107	10

Source: Standard & Poor's.

Table 7.7 Net Income as Percent of Sales—Discount Stores

Company	1970	1971	1972	1973	1974
Alexander's Inc.	2.5	2.1	0.6	0.4	0.4
Ames	3.0	3.5	3.3	2.6	2.2
Arlen	—	1.6	1.5	def.	def.
Hecks	4.2	4.8	4.7	4.4	3.8
Kings	3.9	4.2	4.0	3.8	2.9
Mays	2.4	2.4	1.8	1.5	1.0
Pamida	4.7	4.5	3.7	4.0	3.3
Vornado	1.3	1.5	1.5	0.5	0.3
Wal-Mart	3.7	3.7	3.7	3.7	2.7
Zayre	1.2	1.3	1.1	0.9	0.1

Source: Standard & Poor's.

7/Pamida Incorporated

Table 7.8   Price Earnings Ratios—Discount Stores

Company	High Low	1970	1971	1972	1973	1974
Alexander's	High	17.0	22.9	—	36.5	26.3
	Low	9.5	13.1	23.0	12.5	6.9
Ames	High	11.0	18.5	25.9	12.9	4.6
	Low	4.9	8.0	9.4	3.6	2.2
Arlen	High	—	31.8	44.2	def.	def.
	Low	—	16.5	19.9	def.	def.
Hecks	High	18.0	29.0	28.0	21.3	9.2
	Low	7.0	14.0	14.0	5.2	7.8
Kings	High	11.5	22.4	20.5	12.0	7.0
	Low	6.8	13.4	10.4	4.3	4.3
Mays	High	13.7	17.8	19.7	12.0	9.3
	Low	6.9	10.3	8.2	5.0	4.5
Pamida	High	24.4	35.6	45.6	35.0	8.9
	Low	12.2	19.6	4.0	6.0	3.6
Vornado	High	10.8	13.7	17.9	25.0	15.5
	Low	4.0	9.5	6.7	4.0	7.3
Wal-Mart	High	22.5	43.6	50.0	38.0	21.6
	Low	13.7	13.0	28.2	13.0	7.8
Zayre	High	26.2	22.9	18.5	16.0	—
	Low	12.3	14.6	11.0	2.0	17.9

Source: Standard & Poor's.

Table 7.9   Dividends—Discount Stores (as a percent of earnings)

Company	1970	1971	1972	1973	1974
Alexander's	18.9	21.2	78.9	38.5	34.5
Ames	5.9	5.5	7.3	10.8	9.7
Arlen		No Dividends Declared			
Hecks	8.3	7.1	6.0	6.9	7.2
Kings	23.5	29.2	28.3	27.0	40.3
Mays	27.7	26.8	36.8	45.0	66.7
Pamida		No Dividends Declared			
Vornado		No Dividends Declared			
Wal-Mart	—	—	—	5.0	10.5
Zayre		No Dividends Declared			

Source: Standard & Poor's.

Table 7.10 Capital Expenditures—Discount Stores (in millions of dollars)

Company	1970	1971	1972	1973	1974
Alexander's	11.68	13.16	12.83	7.38	1.50
Ames	1.32	1.13	1.59	1.81	1.26
Arlen	—	139.91	113.71	232.98	—
Kings	0.52	1.37	1.54	1.37	4.99
Hecks	2.59	1.94	3.89	7.19	2.29
Mays	1.43	3.03	3.52	2.64	6.83
Pamida	3.20	5.86	2.03	2.15	2.88
Vornado	16.65	18.06	29.86	33.35	17.95
Wal-Mart	1.64	4.64	4.66	3.52	6.83
Zayre	25.17	23.95	19.17	15.31	9.02

Source: Standard & Poor's.

Table 7.11 Capital Expenditures—Discount Stores (as a percent of gross plant)

Company	1970	1971	1972	1973	1974
Alexander's	12.0	12.0	10.8	6.0	1.2
Ames	30.7	21.1	23.0	20.8	12.7
Arlen	—	23.4	17.7	30.0	—
Hecks	18.5	31.1	26.1	17.3	41.0
Kings	15.9	10.8	18.0	25.0	7.4
Mays	7.9	8.4	8.9	6.3	13.9
Pamida	53.3	49.4	48.4	18.1	21.9
Vornado	7.9	8.3	12.9	12.0	6.6
Wal-Mart	44.1	57.3	31.2	20.4	29.4
Zayre	22.5	18.1	13.6	10.2	5.7

Source: Standard & Poor's.

Table 7.12 Spending Pattern Influences

	1970	1971	1972	1973	1974
Population (millions)	204.9	207.0	208.8	210.4	211.9
Persons Employed (millions)	78.6	79.1	81.7	84.4	85.9
Percent of Population	38.4	38.2	39.1	40.1	40.5
No. of Females Emp. (millions)	29.7	29.9	31.1	32.4	33.4
Percent of Population	14.5	14.4	14.9	15.4	15.3
No. over 25 with HS Education	60.3	62.4	64.7	67.5	70.4
Percent of Population	55.2	56.4	58.2	59.8	61.2
Per-capita Expenditure on Furniture & Equip. (millions)	$193	203	233	261	277
Per-capita Expenditure on Clothing & Footwear	$258	275	302	334	349

Source: Department of Commerce, Bureau of Labor.

Table 7.13 Operating Results of Large Discount Stores
(percent of sales exclude leased departments)

	1969	1970	1971	1972	1973
Number of Firms	43	45	46	47	47
Gross Margin	27.99	27.90	28.37	28.11	28.54
Leased Dept Included	2.68	2.64	1.83	1.40	1.09
Gross Income	30.67	30.54	30.20	29.51	29.63
Total Expense	27.48	28.26	28.08	27.40	27.21
Net Operating Profit	3.19	2.27	2.12	2.11	2.41
Other Inc Deductions	.27	(-.05)	(-.17)	(-.12)	(-.09)
EBIT	3.46	2.22	1.95	1.99	2.32
Taxes	1.67	1.13	1.13	1.28	1.09
Net Earnings	1.79	1.09	.82	.71	1.23

Source: Cornell University.

Table 7.14 Discount Store Population

	1971			1973			1974		
Region	A	B	C	A	B	C	A	B	C
New England	468	1,942	4.00	523	2,714	4.16	535	2,070	3.87
Midatlantic	856	5,972	6.98	959	6,794	7.08	958	7,015	7.32
East No. Central	1,196	5,635	4.71	1,289	6,255	4.85	1,254	6,373	5.08
West No. Central	412	1,615	3.92	510	1,942	3.88	527	2,282	4.33
So. Atlantic	679	2,965	4.38	816	3,673	4.51	851	3,878	4.56
East So. Central	374	1,323	3.54	432	1,405	3.25	471	1,610	3.42
West So. Central	612	2,293	3.75	684	2,581	3.77	726	2,681	3.69
Mountain	248	948	3.82	295	1,092	3.70	320	1,301	4.07
Pacific	628	3,847	6.16	633	4,058	6.18	653	4,196	6.43
Total	5,491	26,540		6,162	29,974		6,295	31,426	
Annual Average			4.58			4.60			4.75

Key
A = Number of Stores
B = Volume (millions of dollars)
C = Per Store Volume (millions of dollars)

Source: *Discount Merchandiser.*

To enhance profitability in the future, many companies will be going back to the basics of the business: emphasizing consumable items with fewer fringe items. A move has begun to switch away from centralized merchandising and to greater regionalized decision-making.[1]

Many discounters have recognized the importance of effective management

1. "Profits Squeezed from Many Operators," *1975-Retailing,* Standard & Poor's, p. R-131.

training and have instituted a restructuring of their management training. Some stores have followed K-Mart's philosophy by letting the manager have profit control of his store. K-Mart generally does not let a management trainee have his first store until he has been with the company at least 10 years.

One recent trend in the industry is expansion into smaller communities where other retail chains have not located. Smaller stores are constructed in these communities, and the move so far has been profitable.

Discussion Questions

1. What are the major characteristics of the industry?
2. What are Pamida's major stated objectives?
3. What has been Pamida's Master Strategy for operating within the industry?
4. What are the major threats/opportunities which the industry will face in the period 1976–1981? How will these affect Pamida?
5. What are the major threats/opportunities facing Pamida in the next five years?
6. What are the strengths and weaknesses of this firm?
7. What does a financial analysis of this firm tell us?
8. What actions should Pamida take to correct its problems and take advantage of its opportunities? With respect to problems, at a minimum, analyze growth, strategy, warehousing policy, future competition, management training, and organization structure–authority distribution.

8/A Note on the Fast Food Industry*

James M. Higgins
and Pep Pilgreen

The fast food industry is a segment of the larger restaurant industry. The restaurant industry in the United States is a multi-billion dollar industry with approximately 255,000 units in operation in 1977. Of this total about 55,000 units were chain units. The total number of restaurant units has remained the same in recent years but the number of chain units has increased substantially.

Industry dollar volume in sales has grown consistently at 9% in recent years and the National Restaurant Association predicts similar growth at least through 1982. Approximately half of this growth will be and has been real. The rest is or will be accounted for by inflated prices. The restaurant industry as a whole has achieved real sales growth in every quarter since 1973 except for two quarters in 1974 when real disposable income fell. Expenditures in restaurants are closely correlated to disposable personal income.

The dominant firms in recent years (in order of 1976 sales) have been McDonald's $2.7 billion; Kentucky Fried Chicken (KFC), $1.2 billion; Burger King, $741 million; and International Dairy Queen, $684 million.

Fast Food Outlook

Several economic and social forces have contributed to the growth in the restaurant industry. Changing life styles are providing more free time, a more mobile society, and a higher education level. Women in the work force, about 45% by 1980, are affecting the life styles of their families. With more money to spend and less time to spend on cooking and cleaning, families are eating out more often (at lunch and at dinner). At the present, one of every three meals are eaten away from home, and by the early 1980s it is estimated that this will become one out of every two. Sixty percent of all lunches are already eaten away from the home. Very importantly, women want to eat in the restaurant. They don't like take-home items, especially for dinners. This has had a very significant impact on KFC's sales since KFC has been primarily a take-home fast food service.

Demographics also favor the industry. The 25 to 44 year old age group will grow at three times the rate of the overall population in the next decade. And this group is the one which spends the most eating out. Its members also have smaller families and a higher disposable income than ever before. Further-

*To be used with "Wendy's International, Inc." (Case 9) and "The Turnaround at Royal Crown Cola" (Case 16), as well as "A Strategic Problem" (Case 10). Certain materials reprinted by permission of Wendy's International, Inc. For those references not cited in Case 8, see "Wendy's International, Inc.: 'Old Fashioned Hamburgers' " (Case 9).

Table 8.1 Total Restaurant Sales and Chain Sales (billions of dollars)

	Total	Franchised Chains	Chains % Total
Est. 1980		16.300	
1976	48.2	12.923	26.8
1975	43.8	11.473	26.2
1974	38.4	10.351	26.9
1973	33.9	8.534	25.2
1972	30.1	6.797	22.6

Source: National Restaurant Association. By permission of Silverman Heller Associates, NYC.

more, the over 55 age group is increasing and members of this group also spend substantial amounts in fast food restaurants. Important to these demographics are the disposable incomes of these two groups, since people spend more on food and in restaurants as disposable income rises. The predictions are that disposable income will continue to rise but at a declining rate. The effect of inflation, higher tax brackets, and social security must be monitored. The strength of the industry also contributes to its growth. Most of the restaurants, particularly the chains, are well financed and managed. Many times a restaurant can fix a meal almost as cheaply as an individual might in his or her own home. Furthermore, fast food chains have not been affected significantly by recession.

Saturation. There is a great deal of evidence that the fast food industry may well be saturated and that unrestrained growth may be over. It is hard to predict something of this sort because no one really knows for sure how many fast food restaurants there are in the U.S. However, the fast food market is approaching the mature stage of the industry life cycle, if it is not already there.

Some analysts believe that saturation has set in and cite recent price cutting in California by KFC as an example of the hard-nosed competition that has started. Others, however, do not feel this way. John DuFon, McDonald's director of financial communications, sees the addition of 3500 new units through the next decade. And John C. Maxwell of Maxwell Associates says: "I've been covering this industry for eight or nine years, and for eight or nine years I've been hearing people say the fast-food industry is saturated."

Almost everyone agrees that saturation is coming (or is already here). The only thing they disagree on is timing. There are signs, however, uncertain as they may be, that some parts of the country already have all the fast food restaurants they can handle. And a chain can be saturated even if a state or the country is not.

A chain is said to be saturated when it can't successfully open a new restaurant without taking sales from another unit of the same chain. In short, saturation is probably more of a local market issue.

To combat the saturation or near saturation of the fast food industry many strategies have been developed in the past few years.

Broader Menus. Many fast food chains are expanding menus to boost sales in existing units. McDonald's, for example, has been trying, with mixed success thus far, to build a breakfast following. Their breakfast effort started with the Egg McMuffin, which was followed by hot cakes and sausage, and scrambled eggs. Breakfast at McDonald's has met with only limited success. Another item McDonald's is trying is fried chicken, which it has been test marketing since 1970 in Dayton, Ohio, and Norfolk, Virginia, while attempting to find a new method of cooking frozen chicken so that it will taste as good as fresh. It is projected that chicken could add as much as 15% to McDonald's sales. This would hurt KFC and others because costs would be lower for buying and handling the frozen meat. McDonald's is also testing salad and soup. McDonald's has recently added sundaes and different types of shakes.

Others are also experimenting with new products. KFC attempted country style ribs, but KFC was caught in a price/cost bind that forced them to drop their ribs. KFC is also testing hamburgers. Hardees has adopted roast beef sandwiches, apparently in an attempt to capture some of Arby's market. Similarly, Arby's has added several different types of sandwiches, and its menu stresses full meals.

Eat-in Dining. Almost all big chains have started adding sit-down dining rooms and extra parking to their new stores as well as making this addition to older ones. Women and men, but especially working women, like to eat out, not take home. Specialty theme restaurants are replacing many less exotic places as the diner becomes more concerned with atmosphere. Arby's and KFC, among others, are moving to expand their sit-down facilities.

New Opportunities. As most fast food customers in the past came from the lunchtime customer, the new market gains (one out of every two meals by the early 1980s) are going to come from the restaurant dinner customer. This movement will require broader menus and places to dine and will also help increase cost, which some observers in the industry feel will cut into the fat profits chains have been making from their operating simplicity. This new area opens up the market for the chains which offer something besides the traditional hamburger. The so-called ethnic chains will benefit from this growth. The restaurants which focus on atmosphere, such as Victoria Station, and are full service chains will probably benefit the most.

Franchise Changes

Two significant trends are present in the area of franchising. First, most franchisers have stopped issuing new franchises. They will, however, grant new sites to older and experienced franchisees. Even the newer franchisees such as Wendy's will grant only groups of franchises to experienced restauranteurs.

Second, there is a definite trend toward accelerating the buying back of franchises. Companies are finding that they can make more money by operating the units themselves. In 1970, 90% of Denny's were franchised. In 1976 only 8% were franchised. According to Verne H. Winchell, Chairman and President of Denny's, Inc., "We felt that we were losing control, and I don't like the feeling of not controlling my own company." And Raymond Danner, President of Shoney's Big Boy Enterprises, Inc., agrees, "It's much more profitable to own the units ourselves. It's a fallacy that you get better supervision from Mom and Pop."

New Locations. One of the major changes has been the location of chains in nontraditional areas such as a Burger King in Times Square and a McDonald's on the fifth floor of Chicago's plush "Water Tower Place." The chains are moving into the big city.

International Market. At least two of the major chains (KFC and McDonald's) have gone to the international market, which seemed to offer an unlimited potential. But inflation, quality control, and other problems have lowered profits in many areas, and both KFC and McDonald's have been forced to close many stores abroad. Not all cultures readily accept American products.

Ethnic Restaurants—New Market Segments. The so-called ethnic restaurants—the pizza, Mexican, and seafood units—have made substantial inroads against the traditional leaders—hamburgers, chicken, and steaks. These restaurants are following the classical market segmentation pattern which accompanies industry maturity. As an example of just how fast this market is growing and just how many firms there are, the Mexican segment has at least the following firms on a national or regional basis: Taco Bell, El Chico, Taco

Table 8.2   Market Share of Fast Food Market (in percentage of sales)

Market Segment	1972	1975	1977*
Chicken	14.9	11.2	9.7
Hamburgers, Franks, Roast Beef, etc.	55.4	55.1	54.2
Pizza	4.4	7.5	8.5
Mexican	1.7	2.2	2.4
Seafood	0.9	2.4	4.1
Pancakes, Waffles	2.6	3.0	3.2
Steak, Full Menu	19.7	18.0	17.2
Sandwich and Other	0.4	0.4	0.6
Total	100.0	100.0	100.0

*Estimated

Source: Standard & Poor's, *Industry Surveys.*

House, Taco Hut, Zanticos (KFC), Pepe's, Pedro's, Taco Casa, Taco John's, Tico Taco, El Palacio, and who knows how many others. Market share information is indicated in Table 8.2. Wendy's has accomplished a similar type of segmentation in focusing on the young adult market, while McDonald's has always focused on young children and families with young children.

Hamburger Chains. Within the restaurant industry there are various sub-

Table 8.3 Restaurant Industry Family Penetration in 8-Week Period (All U.S. Families=100%)

(At least one member of the percent of families shown visited the specified restaurant group at least once in the 8-week period.)

Total Industry	94%
Hamburger	69
Full Menu	30
Ice Cream	25
Pizza	25
Chicken	20
Budget Steak	19
Hotel/Motel	18
Fish	18
Cafeteria	18
Department/Variety Store	16
Other Steak	13
Other Sandwich	10
Donut	10
Mexican	9
Pancake	9
Pie	2

Source: *NRA News*, April, 1977. By permission of Silverman Heller Associates, NYC.

Table 8.4 Hamburger Chains: Comparative Statistics

Average	Hamburger Chains (8/16/76)	Wendy's (12/31/76)
Average Check	$1.45	$2.00
Annual Sales per Unit	$412,724	$511,398
Food Cost per Unit	37.4%	37.0%
Payroll Cost	21.4%	17%
Pre-Tax Profit	12.4%	19.7%
Menu Price Changes in Past Year	7.0%	2.0%
Main Specialty Item	Specialty Burger	Specialty Burger
(% of Sales)	23.1%	62.0%

Source: *Nation's Restaurant News*, 8/16/76, and Wendy's internal documents. By permission of Silverman Heller Associates, NYC.

8/A Note on the Fast Food Industry

Table 8.5 Comparative Statistics

December 31, 1976	Wendy's	Burger King	McDonald's
Average Unit Sales	$511,398	$496,600	$794,000
Average Capital Cost per Unit	310,000	525,000	534,000
Sales per Dollar of Capital Cost	$1.65	$.94	$1.49
Average Square Feet per Unit	2,200	3,000	3,700
Sales per Average Square Foot	232.45	165.53	214.59
Labor Cost/Sales	17%	25%	22%
Food Cost/Sales	37%*	37%	39%

*Beef represented 29% of food cost/sales figure for Wendy's.

Source: Wendy's International, Inc., "A Research Report," prepared for Wendy's by Silverman Heller Associates, NYC.

groups of chain restaurants which sell hamburgers, fish, pizza, etc. With about 12,000 units, the hamburger chains are the largest of the segments. More beef is consumed per capita in the U. S. than all other meats combined. In 1971, 17% was consumed as ground beef, but in 1976 this had moved up to 40%. The 1980 projection is 50 to 60%.

Food Costs. Food costs have been relatively stable, 27% to 36% of sales, depending on the market segment. The price of beef can only be expected to rise. The prices of soft drinks are also expected to continue to rise. Other costs should remain stable through 1979. Wendy's and Taco Bell are two chains that attempt to make everything from the same ingredients. Everything Wendy's sells is a variation on 5 basic products: Chili, fries, Frosty, carbonated beverages, and a square hamburger patty. At Taco Bell everything is a variation on beef, cheese, beans, tortillas, and carbonated beverages. Other chains use more basic items.

Competition. Price competition of those in the same market segment is likely. And as the market matures, more advertising will be necessary to maintain market share. More national advertising will be necessary, and of the fast foods, only McDonald's, Burger King, Pizza Hut, KFC, and Wendy's are

Table 8.6 Comparative Profit Margins

	Church's	Hardee's	McDonald's	Ponderosa	Sambo's	Taco Bell	Wendy's
1976	19.5	8.1	25.4	7.4	17.6	21.8	23.4
1975	16.5	7.0	25.1	6.5	18.5	19.3	22.5
1974	16.8	5.0	24.8	7.2	27.0	17.5	22.2
1973	12.2	6.7	21.6	16.8	27.2	20.2	—
1972	16.8	9.1	21.1	17.4	31.0	21.8	—
1971	18.8	10.6	23.4	18.3	71.3	17.4	—

Source: Standard & Poor's, *Industry Surveys*.

8/A Note on the Fast Food Industry

Table 8.7   Comparative Net Incomes as % of Sales

	Church's	Hardee's	McDonald's	Ponderosa	Sambo's	Taco Bell	Wendy's
1976	8.6	2.2	9.4	2.0	6.1	10.0	10.3
1975	6.9	0.7	9.0	1.4	6.2	8.5	9.3
1974	6.8	0.2	8.6	1.7	12.7	6.9	9.0
1973	4.4	1.6	8.9	8.3	13.1	8.2	—
1972	5.9	2.3	8.8	8.2	33.3	8.4	—
1971	8.4	2.5	9.0	7.9	31.0	5.5	—

Source: Standard & Poor's, *Industry Surveys.*

truly national. National and large regional chains are generating sufficient cash flows to lessen dependence on leases. The number of company owned and managed units is increasing. Menu diversification seems to be a key for most. Couponing, a form of price discounting, has become very popular in the industry. Many see this as a sign of maturity and also of depressed profits and revenues.

9/Wendy's International, Inc.: "Old Fashioned Hamburgers"*

Pep Pilgreen

"Our goal is to dominate the fast food industry," is the ambitious statement of one Wendy's International, Inc. executive. This enthusiasm and confidence is typical of the Dublin, Ohio, hamburger chain started in November, 1969 by R. David Thomas, a former franchisee and vice-president of Kentucky Fried Chicken (KFC). And indeed they may. Wendy's is on its way to becoming the third largest hamburger chain in the U.S. and is closing in on Burger King (No. 2). According to Robert Emerson of Oppenheimer and Company, "Wendy's is going to become Number Two sometime during 1979." Although Thomas has no timetable for growth, he eventually plans to match McDonald's unit for unit.

What is the reason for Wendy's growth in a market which seems to be on the verge of saturation? By ignoring prevailing wisdom, says Thomas, whose chain specializes in hamburgers that appeal to adults, while others are broadening their menus. According to Thomas, "In the food business, you've got a problem if you try to do more than two things." Wendy's two things are a four-inch hamburger patty, square shaped to stick out of the bun, and chili.

R. David Thomas. The man behind the growth of Wendy's is R. David Thomas, who has spent 33 of his 46 years in the fast food business and owns 16.5% of the outstanding shares of common stock. After a stint in the Army where he ran an enlisted man's club, Thomas wound up in Indiana where he met Harland Sanders, "The Colonel," who was trying to sell his chicken recipe to small restaurants. Thomas persuaded the Colonel to drop that idea and open a store selling nothing but chicken with the Colonel's picture out front. "We sold buckets and barrels instead of wings and drumsticks and aimed at the take home market," says Thomas. "We advertised over radio and television, gave away Colonel neckties, and made money like we'd invented it." All of this started in 1954.

Eight years later Thomas was offered a chance to take over an ailing KFC franchise in Columbus, Ohio. After turning those restaurants around to a good

*Students should read "A Note on the Fast Food Industry" (Case 8) before beginning this case.

Source: The author wishes to express his appreciation to Michael Cornette and J. R. Wenzell of Wendy's International and to Wendy's International, Inc. for their assistance in preparing this case. Certain material is reprinted by permission of Wendy's International, Inc.

profit, Thomas sold the franchise back to the parent company in 1968. With the cash generated from the sale he opened his first hamburger restaurant on November 15, 1969, naming it Wendy's after his daughter. "I really couldn't stand the sight of chicken," says Thomas. "I've always been a hamburger man."

With Wendy's, Thomas' aim was to provide a custom made hamburger to the individual customer's taste. His business philosophy was summed up as "first, establish an identity; second, maintain the image; and third, deliver."

Thomas' experience in restaurant operations makes him skeptical of outside experts. "I think it's a big mistake when you let a marketing man come in and run your company when he doesn't know anything about the operation and the product," says Thomas. And Wendy's management structure bears this out. According to Jay Schloemer, Vice President of Marketing, "Every department here is subordinate to operations." Operations sets prices and approves all marketing plans.

The Restaurant and Menu—An Operations Oriented Company

Under the direction of Hank Sherowski, Vice President of Engineering, Wendy's has developed a seventeen-page engineering blueprint for each standard restaurant. All of the buildings have the same interior and exterior decor. The majority are single one-story units constructed on 25,000 square foot sites with parking for 35 to 40 cars. Some stores in downtown areas are of the store front variety with different exteriors in keeping with the location. They all retain the same red, white, and yellow decor and sign, however.

Most of the free standing restaurants have dining room capacity for about 92 persons and a pick-up window for carry out service. The standard decor features Tiffany-style lamps, bentwood chairs, colorful beads, and tabletops printed with reproductions of 19th century advertising. "The seats aren't too comfortable, though," says Thomas, "We don't want customers to stay forever." The restaurants are generally located in urban or heavily populated suburban areas.

Each restaurant offers a uniform limited menu. Hamburgers in three sizes —(single) ¼ pound; (double) ½ pound; and (triple) ¾ pound—are offered with eight condiments and cheese. From these comes Wendy's claim that it offers hamburgers 256 ways. Also included are french fries; chili; Frosty, a dairy dessert; and a limited number of soft drinks and other nonalcoholic beverages. Even though condiments make each hamburger a custom-made product, service is faster at Wendy's than at its competitors. That's because as soon as the cook sees a new car pull into the parking lot a new patty is put on the grill. And they use only fresh beef for hamburgers and chili. If a hamburger goes unsold for two minutes it goes into the chili pot.

Wendy's works hard to keep its quality and uniformity by giving detailed specifications for food products, preparation, and service and with continuing in-service training and field visits. "It used to be that you needed two things for a successful operation: price and a good location. Now the three most important things are quality, service, and cleanliness," quips Thomas. For franchise owners Wendy's makes field visits to review operations and make recommendations. Wendy's Headquarters keeps basically a uniform price throughout the system; however, the charge for the hamburger may vary according to the competition.

The Wendy's "System." Its method of operating, and its building, are interrelated as they are designed to work together. The customer gives his order to the cashier who records it and gives change. The grillman places the hamburgers on the bun, the sandwich maker adds the ordered condiments and wraps the hamburger. Another member gives out the fries, chili, Frosty, and beverage, and the coordinator reviews the order before giving it to the customer.

Most crew members do not move from their station and the whole process averages about 30 seconds to completion. Approximately 15 employees work during rush hours, and this can be lowered at other periods. Wendy's has probably the lowest payroll as a percent of the sales dollar of any firm in the industry, $.15 to $.17 per dollar compared to McDonald's $.22 to $.25. This results from the highly specialized labor.

The "cadillac hamburger," as Mr. Thomas calls it, sells for $.75, which enables Wendy's to collect more per customer than the other chains because the standard hamburger sells for more, even though it is cheaper per ounce to make. From this, Wendy's is able to make more money per unit than Burger King and one of the highest returns on capital in the industry. As Jay Schloemer, the Marketing Vice President, observes, "You have a low inventory, you have low labor costs, you have a small building on a small lot." The result is high sales per customer and per unit, and high profits per customer and per unit. High sales mean more advertising, which means more sales, which means . . . .

Table 9.1   Company Owned Restaurants in Various Cities

Columbus, Ohio	26	Indianapolis, Ind.	12
Cincinnati, Ohio	15	Fort Worth, Tex.	6
Dayton, Ohio	16	Houston, Tex.	12
Toledo, Ohio	9	Dallas, Tex.	9
Atlanta, Ga.	20	Oklahoma City, Ok.	9
Tampa, Sarasota,		Tulsa, Ok.	8
St. Petersburg &		Memphis, Tenn.	10
Clearwater, Fla.	17	Louisville, Ky.	7
Jacksonville, Fla.	11	Syracuse, N.Y.	6

Table 9.2   Wendy's International, Inc.: Revenues, Year Ending December 31

Revenues	1972	1973	1974	1975	1976	1977
Company Owned	98.51%	95.01%	93.99%	92.30%	88.25%	84.61%
Royalties	.45	1.72	3.44	5.01	7.91	11.52
Franchise Fees	.55	1.54	1.62	1.97	2.58	2.42
Interest & Other Income	.49	1.73	.95	.72	1.26	1.44
	100%	100%	100%	100%	100%	100%

Wendy's Restaurants

Company Owned Restaurants. By the end of 1977 Wendy's operated 193 restaurants in 15 multi-county areas around the cities listed in Table 9.1. No franchises are in effect in these markets and there is no indication that franchises will be sold in any of them. Company owned restaurants have contributed the largest part of Wendy's revenue and income in the past as shown in Table 9.2.

Franchised Restaurants. The future of Wendy's is in its franchises because, according to Thomas, "that's where the growth is." In developing his franchises Thomas has used his experience in the industry to avoid some of the pitfalls that ruined other companies. He has concentrated on selling franchise territories rather than single unit franchises, and Wendy's has sold primarily to those with fast food experience and financial strength. Says Thomas, "We would rather work with a few guys who understand the numbers of this business." The company is very proud of its franchise arrangement, and to this date none have been closed.

One of the major franchise owners is Jack C. Massey, a Nashville financier and one of the co-founders of KFC. Massey holds the right to open Wendy's in South Carolina, Louisiana, Southern California, and Massachusetts. "What Thomas has done is to assure himself of a group of mini-chains when the system matures, not a scattering of mom and pop stores," says one competitor.

Wendy's sold its first franchise in 1971 and opened its first franchise restaurant in 1972. By the end of 1977 there were 712 Wendy's restaurants operated by 150 franchise owners in 43 states and Canada. At the end of 1977

Table 9.3   Contribution to Income

Before Taxes	1972	1973	1974	1975	1976
Company Owned	94.3%	83.4%	83.5%	76.4%	57.6%
Royalties	1.3	2.7	10.7	19.2	36.0
Internal Income	4.4	13.9	5.8	4.4	6.4
	100%	100%	100%	100%	100%

individuals in all states except four had been granted franchises, and large areas of many states remain unfranchised. Nearly every major metropolitan area had been sold, however.

Each franchise owner must execute two basic documents. The Development Agreement grants the franchise owner an option to acquire, for a limited period of time, franchises to operate a specified number of Wendy's restaurants within a prescribed geographic area, and prescribes the Technical Assistance Fee ($10,000 per unit, currently) to be paid for each unit opened. Under earlier agreements the Technical Assistance Fee was either $5,000 or $7,500.

In the opinion of company officials franchise fees have not contributed to income before taxes, as they approximate the estimated costs incurred by the company in connection with the opening of franchised restaurants. As long as the Development Agreement is in effect Wendy's cannot grant another franchise in the area. Also, for each new unit opened the franchise owner must sign a new Unit Franchise Agreement giving him exclusive rights to the operation of Wendy's and the use of its trademarks and other rights.

The Unit Franchise Agreement calls for a monthly payment to Wendy's International of 4% of gross sales of all items from the unit, or a minimum of $250.00 per month. The Unit Franchise Agreement generally terminates 20 years after the franchise owner's Franchise Agreement.

Wendy's does not sell, lease, or finance any real estate or equipment to its franchise owners. They do provide advice and approval of site selection, a training program, advertising, and promotional items. Wendy's does not sell fixtures, food, or supplies to its franchise owners, but they have negotiated many national purchasing arrangements with major suppliers which are available if wanted.

Marketing. The sign on the front of each unit reads: "Wendy's Old Fashioned Hamburgers." The name Wendy's was chosen for its identification potential; the theme "Old Fashioned Hamburgers" because it conveyed a natural, home cooked image rather than the artificial, prepared image of many existing chain restaurants.

Wendy's opened its national advertising campaign on April 1, 1977 with its first network television advertising. With a budget of three million dollars

Table 9.4   Restaurants in Operation

	Year Ended December 31,					
	1972	1973	1974	1975	1976	1977
Company Owned	7	17	44	83	151	193
Franchised	2	15	49	169	369	712
Total	9	32	93	252	520	905

the national campaign is only about one-fourth as large as their local advertising budget and is only one-tenth the size of Burger King's 1976 national advertising budget.

"We always knew we were going national," says Vice-President of Marketing, Jay Schloemer. "It was just a matter of getting the market coverage." Management felt that they needed between 650 and 700 stores to get the needed coverage, and they may have close to 1,200 by the end of 1978.

But this is only the beginning of Wendy's national push. Their "Hot 'n Juicy" campaign will grow as the Unit Franchise agreement calls for 1% of gross sales to be contributed to the national campaign and 3% of gross sales to go to local advertising.

Advertising Focuses on a Central Theme. "If you've ever had a dry, chewy hamburger, you're gonna love Wendy's hot and juicy hamburgers. Juicy meat, juicy toppings, and lots of napkins." Fortunes are made on such themes.

There are really only four companies that are truly national chains: McDonald's (3,756 units); KFC (5,055 units); Burger King (1,577 units); and Pizza Hut (2,321 units). By going national Wendy's is bucking the trend in the fast food industry in recent years. Most medium sized chains have chosen to remain regional, so as not to compete with the huge advertising budgets of the major chains. But many feel that Wendy's is indeed a threat to those chains. According to Cyrus C. Wilson, a consultant for Management Horizons, Inc. "Wendy's can build next door to McDonald's and be a great success. Not many fast food operators can do that."

And the people at Wendy's feel the same way. "We are not really worried about the competition at this time, we are just trying to keep up with our own growth."

Wendy's Organization. Wendy's has no organization chart. According to one executive, they really don't need an organization chart because theirs is a company that is operations oriented. "If there was ever an operations minded company, this is the one."

Company Operations. Charles Rioux, Senior Vice President of Company Operations, and his staff are responsible for the growth and operation of all company owned Wendy's restaurants. In 1976 their markets expanded from eight to sixteen, mostly as a result of the acquisition of several franchise areas.

"We don't put any numbers on sales or return on investment or such as that," says Mike Cornette, Administrative Assistant in Company Operations. "All we look for is profitability. It would be impossible to give all the stores the same quota to meet because their markets, locations, and time of service vary so much."

Company Operations divides the United States into eight regions with a regional director and several area directors reporting to the regional director in each. Area directors coordinate the efforts of supervisors who are assigned several restaurants daily to visit.

Franchise Operations. The Franchising Department, under the direction of David Teal, Senior Vice President of Franchising, lends assistance to the franchisees for their daily operations. This includes real estate, purchasing, marketing-management training, on the site assistance with operational and other matters, and selection of local suppliers. Real estate, purchasing, and marketing assistance comes from separate departments within the company. There are at present five regional directors to help Franchise Operations in their eight regions.

Franchise Sales. Graydon Webb, as Vice President of Franchise Sales, is responsible for working with new franchise areas and monitoring the growth and development of current franchise owners.

Training. In 1976 Wendy's Management Institute trained 1,450 managers, management trainees, new franchise owners, and their employees. The basic course is a two week affair with 60% of the time spent in the classroom and the remaining 40% at Columbus area Wendy's restaurants where the students are able to apply the techniques which are taught in the classroom. They also conduct many regional Management Seminars and have a school in Dallas, Texas as well as Dayton, Ohio. Wendy's believes that properly trained employees are the key to good service, product control, and clean, attractive restaurants. All of Wendy's executives are trained in the same seminars as franchisees. This enables them to become familiar with the operations.

Personnel. At the end of 1977 Wendy's employed 7,000 employees, 6,680 of whom worked in the company owned restaurants. Wendy's is not union organized at this time, and they see no organizing in the future. In hiring managers or manager trainees the company looks for people willing to put in a hard six day week and would like it if they had some fast food experience. As for incentives, they feel that the prospect of moving up in the management at Wendy's is incentive enough. "Turnover is high but not above average for this industry."

Wendy's paid out 17 cents of every sales dollar in salaries in 1976. McDonald's paid 22 cents. And they have been able to hold the line on labor costs by promoting the pick-up window, through which 30 to 40% of all sales are generated. As these customers eat off the site they have added savings on dining room and parking space.

Financial Control. Wendy's Controller and Tax Manager, under the direction of Secreary-Treasurer, Ronald E. Musick, is responsible for the preparation of financial data or external reports on company activities, company operation, and for cost control data for each department. In addition, Mr. Musick oversees Wendy's insurance and employee benefit program.

Planning. Planning at Wendy's is performed by the office of Corporate Planning, headed by Vice President of Finance and Chief Financial Officer, William C. Leiter. This office is responsible for short, intermediate, and long range projections on growth, reserve, income, and capital needs; developing capital from brokers, banks, and other sources; and keeping shareholders and the financial community informed as to the progress at Wendy's.

Finance. Wendy's International, Inc.'s financial statement and their accompanying notes for 1977 follow, in Figures 9.1 and 9.2.

Income. Wendy's has shown phenomenal growth in its brief history. This growth was primarily the result of the increasing number of restaurants in operation. As more new restaurants are added, its growth rate will eventually slow, but currently its growth potential is quite large.

Table 9.5   Directors and Executive Officers

Name	Age	Position with Company	Director Continuously Since
R. David Thomas	44	Chairman of the Board of Directors and Chief Executive Officer	1969
Robert L. Barney	40	Director, President and Chief Operating Officer	1969
Ronald E. Musick	36	Director, Secretary and Treasurer	1970
Leonard J. Immke, Jr.	48	Director	1971
Sam Brooks	38	Director	1976
Don M. Hilliker	64	Director	1976
John H. McConnell	54	Director	1976
William C. Leiter	37	Vice President–Finance and Chief Financial Officer	—
Charles Rioux	38	Senior Vice President– Company Operations	—
David L. Teal	29	Senior Vice President– Franchising	—
Graydon D. Webb	29	Vice President– Franchise Sales	—
Jay Schloemer	32	Vice President– Marketing	—
Richard Hill	44	Vice President– Purchasing	—
Henry J. Sherowski	34	Vice President– Engineering	—
H. James Graham	30	Vice President– Real Estate	—

	1977	1976
Revenue:		
Retail operations	$ 96,652,870	$57,926,804
Royalties (Note 1)	13,167,804	5,190,255
Technical assistance fees (Note 1)	2,762,500	1,692,500
Other, principally interest	1,647,972	827,762
	114,231,146	65,637,321
Costs and expenses:		
Cost of sales	53,134,772	32,706,268
Company restaurant operating costs	21,227,820	11,964,105
General and administrative expenses	8,159,564	4,433,673
Depreciation and amortization of property and equipment (Note 1)	2,797,121	1,858,032
Interest	1,943,983	2,001,931
	87,263,260	52,964,009
Income before income taxes	26,967,886	12,673,312
Income taxes (Note 7):		
Federal:		
Current	11,529,700	5,477,400
Deferred	300,300	(8,400)
	11,830,000	5,469,000
State and local	1,076,000	594,000
	12,906,000	6,063,000
Net income	$ 14,061,886	$ 6,610,312
Net income per common and common equivalent share (Note 1)	$2.12	$1.19
Weighted average common and common equivalent shares	6,637,074	5,565,433

The accompanying notes are an integral part of the financial statements.

Assets

	1977	1976
Current assets:		
Cash	$ 1,723,544	$ 858,930
Short-term investments, at cost, which approximates market, including accrued interest	27,635,842	25,678,386
Accounts receivable	2,015,439	1,119,706
Inventories	716,792	433,252
Other	174,661	131,916
Total current assets	32,266,278	28,222,190
Property and equipment, at cost (Notes 1 and 2):		
Buildings	15,550,481	9,172,396
Leasehold improvements	5,183,609	4,384,001
Restaurant equipment	12,150,051	8,165,349
Other equipment	1,988,255	1,081,452
Lease rights	300,709	300,709
Capitalized leases (Note 3)	8,568,600	7,057,600
	43,741,705	30,161,507
Less accumulated depreciation and amortization	6,778,319	4,041,334
	36,963,386	26,120,173
Land	15,009,047	9,751,207
Construction in progress	1,556,442	1,143,710
	53,528,875	37,015,090
Cost in excess of net assets acquired, less amortization of $278,991 and $83,965, respectively (Notes 1 and 8)	5,410,112	5,057,108
Other assets	956,561	1,117,051
	6,366,673	6,174,159
	$92,161,826	$71,411,439

The accompanying notes are an integral part of the financial statements.

Figure 9.2   (Cont.)

Liabilities and Shareholders' Equity

	1977	1976
Current liabilities:		
Accounts payable, trade.	$ 5,229,845	$ 3,546,315
Federal, state and local income taxes.	7,446,888	3,411,735
Accrued expenses.	1,687,437	1,060,404
Current portion, term debt and capitalized lease obligation	1,325,502	961,873
Total current liabilities.	15,689,672	8,980,327
Term debt, net of current portion (Note 2).	9,766,501	9,880,590
Capital lease obligations, net of current portion (Note 3).	6,553,803	5,673,113
	16,320,304	15,553,703
Deferred technical assistance fees (Note 1).	2,155,000	2,035,000
Leases (Note 3)		
Shareholders' equity:		
Common stock, $.10 stated value (Notes 4 and 6):		
Authorized: 12,000,000 shares		
Issued and outstanding:		
6,584,956 shares (6,508,185 in 1976)	658,496	650,819
Capital in excess of stated value	33,828,517	33,100,191
Retained earnings (Note 2).	23,509,837	11,091,399
Total shareholders' equity.	57,996,850	44,842,409
	$92,161,826	$71,411,439

The accompanying notes are an integral part of the financial statements.

Figure 9.3   Wendy's Financial Summary, Four Years Ended December 31

Financial Summary—Eight Years Ended December 31

	1977	1976	1975	1974
Revenues	$114,231,146	$65,637,321	$34,233,583	$13,555,800
Cost of Sales	53,134,772	32,706,268	17,501,392	6,983,055
Operating Expenses	32,184,505	18,255,810	10,260,801	4,003,478
Interest Expense	1,943,983	2,001,931	893,415	394,409
Income Before Income Taxes	26,967,886	12,673,312	5,577,975	2,174,858
Net Income	14,061,886	6,610,312	2,918,875	1,160,125
Earnings Per Share	2.12	1.19	.63	.26
Dividends Per Share	.25	.0075	.0019	.0019
Total Assets	92,161,826	71,411,439	25,904,360	13,028,128
Shareholders' Equity	57,996,850	44,842,409	7,163,129	3,069,157
Number of Shares Outstanding	6,584,956	6,508,185	4,487,630	4,285,490
Pre-Tax Margin	23.6%	19.30%	16.29%	16.04%
Return on Equity (1)	27.4%	28.80%	57.10%	50.00%
Sales—Company-owned and Franchised	425,847,900	187,683,200	74,462,600	24,232,900
Number of Restaurants in Operation	905	520	252	93
Company-owned	193	151	83	44
Franchised	712	369	169	49
Average Annual Revenues of both Company-owned and Franchised Restaurants (2)	609,600	511,400	489,800	429,900

(1) Based on average Equity Employed   (2) Based on weighted average number of days open

The opening of a company owned restaurant has a more pronounced effect on the revenues and expenses than the opening of a franchise unit. The cost of food represents Wendy's largest expense and this cost has fluctuated greatly in the past. This cost stabilized in 1975 and 1976 to about 29% of the cost of sales. However, there is no guarantee that it will stay this way.

As Wendy's develops a new market it incurs certain expenses which do not increase proportionally with the number of restaurants in the area, which has enabled some markets to show increased profitability due to absorption of supervisory and promotional costs by a larger number of units.

Management. The majority of Wendy's management personnel have lengthy experience in the restaurant industry, particularly in franchised chains.

R. David Thomas founded Wendy's in 1969, served as President until 1971, and is currently Chairman of the Board. Mr. Thomas has had a long career in the food service industry, which he began prior to running an Army Officer/NCO Club at age 17. He moved on from there to Vice President of the Hobby Ranch House restaurant chain in Fort Wayne. In 1962 he took over a losing KFC franchise, turned it around the first year and sold it back to the parent for $3 million in 1968. He then became cofounder of Arthur Treacher's Fish & Chips and founded Wendy's in 1969.

Robert L. Barney, too, has spent his entire career in food service, ranging from a steak house operation to KFC, first as General Manager of a franchise, then Area Director, and finally as Vice President of the Midwest Region for the parent KFC. In 1969 he became a franchisee for Arthur Treacher's Fish & Chips and then Vice President of Operations. In July 1971 he joined Wendy's as President and Chief Operating Officer.

Wendy's maintains a very small corporate staff relative to other franchises. Wendy's feels it doesn't need a large one given its multiple unit franchise system.

Future Plans. No major product changes or major changes in services are currently anticipated (March, 1978).

A breakfast menu has been considered, but no action has been taken to further develop this option. Limited additions to the product line have been studied but have thus far been rejected. For now, Wendy's is content to open more restaurants and to encourage its franchisees to do the same.

References

Some comments made by the principals in this case are taken from the following references, but are not individually cited to add realism to the case. Certain information in the tables was also extracted from these sources.

"The Fast Food Stars." *Business Week,* July 11, 1977, pp. 58–59.

"A New Hamburger Chain Built on Hindsight." *Business Week,* September 20, 1976, p. 101.

Silverman, Heller Associates. *Wendy's International, Inc.: A Research Report*, 1977.

"Wendy's Aims to Take Big Bite of Fast Food," *Advertising Age,* March 28, 1977, pp. 24, 72.

"Wendy's, a Unique Strategy for Growth," *Dun's Review,* August 1977, pp. 14–15.

Wendy's International, Inc. Annual Reports, 1976, 1977.

Discussion Questions

1. Just why has Wendy's been so successful?
2. Evaluate the firm's current Master Strategy.
3. What are the implications for future success of its operations orientation?
4. What are the implications for future success of its limited menu?
5. What changes in its Master Strategy would you recommend and why?

10/A Strategic Problem*   James M. Higgins

You and a friend have approximately $100,000 to invest in a business enterprise. You have determined that in your geographic area, the appropriate investment would be some type of eating establishment, preferably a fast food restaurant. You have $30,000 and your associate has $70,000 (both in cash). Your friend is interested in a Mexican fast food establishment or perhaps even a regular sit down type restaurant but with Mexican food. You have essentially no preference as to the type of restaurant. Both of you share the objective of a steady income, with the ultimate idea of establishing your own franchise system within five years, either in the same line of restaurants that you start out in or in some new line. Your friend will manage the everyday operations of the restaurant or restaurants; you will keep your job but help determine the major strategic actions and will probably end up doing the taxes, the licenses, and major planning actions. For example, you will do the break-even analyses and much of the marketing planning. You would like to make as much from your time as you now receive on your job—$40,000 per year. He would like to make at least $25,000 per year for managing the enterprise, plus you both would like a fair return for your capital investment. You would like to keep your personal investments to a minimum. Both of you have good credit ratings. He has about $90,000 in net assets. You have about $40,000 in net assets. Having determined to at least investigate the situation, you have decided to accomplish the following:

1. determine what Mexican fast food franchises are available
2. determine if other nonMexican franchises are available that would be more profitable
3. determine site location(s) and costs
4. determine building costs
5. determine labor costs
6. determine product line
7. determine product prices
8. determine financing structure and costs
9. determine target market
10. determine marketing strategy factors not mentioned above, eg., promotion
11. consider competition
12. determine other relevant factors
13. draw up pro forma income and balance sheets and possibly cash flow sheets for two years of operation

*Students should read "A Note on the Fast Food Industry" (Case 8) and related source materials before beginning this project.

You know that the Small Business Administration has materials related to such endeavors and that many of the franchisors will help you with some of these problems. In addition, some real estate agents in some larger cities specialize in development of commercial properties for fast food franchisees.

11/The U.S. Brewery Industry, 1974*

James M. Higgins

Beer is a mildly bitter, malt-based and hops-flavored alcoholic beverage. Beer is one of man's oldest beverages, having been traced at least to early Mesopotamia, some 6000 years ago. Beer has been identified as part of the cultures of Egypt, Rome, and early China. Until the late sixteenth century, beer was brewed predominantly in homes or monasteries. Today, beer is brewed commercially in most major countries, and, while the taste may vary from country to country, the brewing process is essentially the same. European beers are usually served warm; American beers are normally served cold. Beers today contain three to six percent alcohol. There are three principal types of beer: lager, ale, and bock beer. More than 90 percent of American beer is lager beer, beer fermented using yeast which settles to the bottom of the fermentation vat. Ale is brewed using yeast which rises to the top of the vat, is heavier in consistency, and has more hops than does lager. Bock beer is a heavier, darker, and sweeter beer than lager, brewed using roasted malt. It is normally brewed in late winter for use in early spring. Bock beer is primarily a European phenomenon. Porter and stout are terms used to refer to types of ale.

Of the top ten breweries in 1974, all but one—Miller's, a division of Phillip Morris—is family owned, and Miller's was family owned until it was taken over by Phillip Morris as the result of two large stock purchases in 1969 and 1970. Many family owned breweries have in recent years disappeared from the marketplace. The economies of scale of the large brewery have driven most of the smaller breweries out of business.

The brewing of beer in the United States is profitable, at least for the very large national breweries. At the end of prohibition in 1933, some 750 breweries existed in this country. By 1974, fewer than 60 remained. Of these 60, five might be described as national firms. The others marketed their products only in certain regions of the country. The beer industry is dominated by the few large firms. The large multi-million barrel capacity brewery and its economies of scale when combined with relatively cheap national advertising as opposed to more expensive regional advertising have made the profitable production of beer on a less than national level almost entirely impossible. For example, the difference in production costs per barrel for a national beer such as Budweiser or Schlitz compared to those of a smaller regional firm might be as much as $3 per barrel. Furthermore, the difference in advertising costs per barrel between a national and a regional firm might be as much as $2

*This note is to be used with both the Coors and Miller's cases.

to $3. The combination of these two major factors, plus the distribution of overhead over a larger number of barrels produced, gives the national firm a significant pricing advantage over the smaller firms in the marketplace. Nonetheless, some regionals have managed to survive by employing different strategies than the national firms have utilized. The national firms have essentially sought a high percentage of market share, much of this coming at the expense of the regional brewers. The regional brewers have sought to maintain a loyal local consumer. In 1974, the five largest brewers in order of size by sales dollars were: Anheuser-Busch, Schlitz, Pabst, Coors, and Miller's. Numerous regionals existed. Among these were: Hamm's, Olympia, Schmidt, Heileman's, Lone Star, Falstaff, Carling, and others. Of the national firms, Coors could not truly be called national because Coors is sold in only an eleven state area. It is only because of its high market share that Coors is the fourth largest brewer in the country. Many of the smaller firms disappeared as a result of mergers with the larger firms or acquisition by the larger firms.

Ingredients. The brewing process begins when barley and water are mixed and passed through various germinating and drying processes until malt is created. Water and rice are then added along with hops, and the combination of these ingredients is then brewed or cooked. The hops are removed, and yeast is then added. The resultant product is fermented and aged. The brew is then filtered and subsequently canned or bottled or sold directly in barrels. The canned and bottled items are normally pasteurized. The ingredients utilized may vary. For example, some brewers use more expensive ingredients than do others. But the basic process is shared by all brewers, except for Coors, which does not pasteurize its beer. (See Figure 11.1.) From the brewery, the beer goes to wholesalers (distributors) and warehousers who in turn supply retailers.

During 1972, 1973, and 1974, especially in 1972 and 1974, breweries experienced enormous increases in the prices of their raw materials. The two brewers hardest hit by these price increases were Anheuser-Busch and Coors, because they use only "natural ingredients" and do not use extracts for the various ingredients. Corn prices in 1972 and later in 1974 jumped by as much as 40 percent over the preceding years. Barley prices were perhaps 30 percent higher and rice as much as 50 percent higher. Compounded over three years, but admittedly at lesser rates for some years, these costs left brewers no choice but to raise prices. But they raised prices at a rate which was far less than the increases in cost. As a result, profit margins throughout the industry shrank enormously. Coors was able to avoid some of the difficulties with these price increases because it owns substantial agricultural properties upon which it raises many of its own ingredients. Coors is the most vertically integrated of the brewers. It not only raises most of its own crops, it also makes its own cans.

Competition. In the late 1960s and early 1970s, competition in the brewing industry was especially keen. This competition came about primarily through the use of what has been labelled cutthroat price competition at the retail level. Price competition also existed with distributors of the beer, who were often offered special discounts in what amounted to kickback schemes. These schemes also involved many retailers. Competition also existed in the establishment of market segments and products designed to appeal to those particular segments. (All of the major breweries except Coors sell more than one type of beer in an effort to appeal to these market segments.) The greatest element of competition occurred in the advertising which the various breweries employed. To many persons, beer tastes essentially the same regardless of who brews the beer. Thus, the major effort of the various breweries in their advertising campaigns is to distinguish what is essentially a homogeneous product from other similar products. It is no secret that advertising dollars buy market share, but, strangely, few of the major breweries follow a traditional consumer product strategy. Of the major five breweries, only Miller's has stressed such a strategy. Competition varies from geographic area to geographic area. While one national brewery may be especially strong in one particular geographic area, it may be weak in another. For example, Budweiser has approximately 20 percent of the California market, but has little or no market in several cities controlled by regional brewers. Competition also exists in terms of the containers in which beer is sold. One of the most important innovations has been the 7-ounce, so-called pony-sized, beer bottle or can, which Miller introduced in 1972. The standard 12-ounce size was thought to contain too much beer for many of the less ardent beer drinkers. And some beer always seemed to get warm in the 12-ounce size bottle or can; this does not occur with the 7-ounce size container.

The Big Five Brewers

In recent years, the story of the beer industry has been the story of the five major brewers who some have predicted will eventually control 90 percent of the market. Let us now examine briefly each of these and how each differs from the others.

Anheuser-Busch. In 1957 Anheuser-Busch passed Schlitz in sales and has since remained as the number one seller of beer. In recent years, however, competition has increased and Busch has clearly lost much of its earlier momentum. Yet, Busch's major product, Budweiser, is the undisputed "King of Beers" in that it is the largest selling beer in the entire world. In 1974, August A. "Gussie" Busch, Jr. presided over the Anheuser-Busch empire. The 74-year-old chairman and chief executive had guided the firm for 50 years. He was only the firm's fourth chief executive in its 125 year history. Many attribute Busch's success in the beer business to his phenomenal rapport with his wholesalers. It is anticipated that his son, August A. Busch, III, will replace Gussie as chief executive officer once he retires.

As the largest of the beer producers and one of two firms—the other being Coors—which uses more natural ingredients than the other major breweries, Anheuser-Busch has become responsive to the need for vertical integration. The firm is not only attempting to acquire its own can factories and agricultural lands, but is negotiating long-term pricing and supply agreements with current suppliers of these and other materials. In the past, much of the success of Anheuser-Busch and the other large firms has come as the result of the shake-out which has occurred as smaller regional breweries were forced out of business because they were not economically competitive with the large breweries. Now, Anheuser-Busch is reanalyzing its strategy with regard to competition with its major competitors. Anheuser-Busch has extensively analyzed the market. Busch has one of the more comprehensive and successfully employed computer simulation models in existence. It continually analyzes and reanalyzes impacts on the business of changes in the environment, and the impacts on the environment of changes in strategies. As a result of this extensive research into consumer motivation, as well as recognition of the changing strategies employed by other breweries, Anheuser-Busch has become more aggressive in its own marketing efforts. It has increased its television advertising. It has focused its advertising on the natural ingredients which go into Budweiser, and thus on the high quality of its products. The company has also cut its prices by as much as 20 percent in some markets, attempting to capture a greater percentage of the market. Finally, recognizing that wholesalers are the key to this business and to Anheuser-Busch's success, Busch has created a wholesaler advisory panel which listens to gripes which wholesalers may have. And, despite the increased costs of raw materials, the company has an uncompromising position on quality. It will not sacrifice quality! Anheuser-Busch is one of the few firms which has diversified and receives 10 percent of its income from nonbrewery sources.

Schlitz. 1974 marked the 125th year of the Joseph P. Schlitz brewing company, and for the first time its annual sales exceeded one billion dollars. However, despite a 13.8 percent increase in sales, its earnings declined 11.3 percent. Of the major brewers, Schlitz has had the most difficulty in recent years. The chairman, Robert A. Uihlein, Jr., blames much of the problem on price. Many customers are shifting to the firm's lower profit margin Old Milwaukee beer. Furthermore, Schlitz raised its prices earlier in 1974 than did other brewers, and Uihlein believes that Schlitz lost sales because of this. Uihlein, despite low-profit margin, is reluctant to be the first to raise prices again.

Pabst. In April 1974, Pabst changed its marketing strategy. It dropped its long-standing 1890s theme and shifted instead to emphasizing the quality of its product. Furthermore, it changed its television spots from local to network programs. And, finally, it more aggressively sought to establish better relationships with its wholesalers. As a result, Pabst increased its barrel sales by 9 percent in 1974 compared to 1973. Price increases partially demanded by the increases in cost of raw materials, combined with increased sales, resulted in an 18.3 percent increase in dollar sales in 1974. Earnings for Pabst, as with most of the major brewers in 1974, were down somewhat. These reflected the high cost of raw materials.

Coors. Coors is probably the most unique of the beers because it has a definite mystique about it which no other beer can match. Six-packs of Coors which sold for $1.39 in Denver might be sold for as much as $6.00 in states where Coors is not legally sold. Presidents, kings, and chiefs of state have all been known to hoard Coors as if it were gold. There are two primary differences between Coors and other beers which might affect its taste and thus its popularity. First, Coors is not pasteurized. Second, Coors' ingredients are highly quality controlled and most of them are grown on Coors' own land. Furthermore, Coors is brewed to a very light taste, which seems to be the direction in which consumer preference for most alcoholic beverages is headed. For example, vodka has displaced bourbon as the number one high alcoholic content beverage in the United States.

Coors is the most highly vertically integrated of all the major brewers. Coors has only one brewery, which is located in Golden, Colorado. Coors spends less than one dollar per barrel on advertising while some of its competitors spend three dollars or more per barrel for advertising. Again, the mystique of Coors allows it to spend less for advertising. The firm therefore has a greater profit margin per barrel than any other brewer, almost twice as much as Budweiser—the nearest to them in this category. Coors has only one product and that is Coors. It does not offer a line of beers designed for the different market segments. Coors concentrates its efforts on obtaining high market share. For example, it holds 70 percent of the market in the state of Oklahoma and almost 40 percent of the market in the state of California.

Coors must be refrigerated by the wholesalers and retailers because it is not pasteurized. This extra cost burden does not deter people from wanting to sell Coors, however. Coors cannot remain on the shelf over 30 days. If it does, it must be pulled and destroyed by the retailer. Coors advertising differs from the advertising of most other breweries in that it emphasizes the natural environment and does not particularly emphasize the beer itself. Coors has pioneered in many areas of environmental concern, for example, in originating the aluminum can which is recyclable. Coors has always financed its own expansion internally. It has a very limited amount of long-term debt and is not publicly held. Coors is a family owned business with William K. Coors presiding as chairman, president, and chief executive officer. Coors retained the highest market share of any beer in any of the eleven states in which it was distributed in 1974, except in Texas, where it was not distributed state-wide. Like Anheuser-Busch, Coors receives approximately 10 percent of its annual net sales from nonbrewery operations. Included are brewery by-products, such as cattle feed, and Coors porcelain company. Coors is also the only major brewer with an entirely independent water supply and an entirely independent self-sustaining energy system. Coors is discussed in more depth in the Coors case.

Miller. Miller High Life in 1969 had a very staid image. It was the "Champagne of Bottled Beers." In 1969 and 1970, Philip Morris, the cigarette company, in a diversification effort acquired 100 percent of Miller High Life Beer Company in two large stock purchases. After sizing up the situation for a period of time—approximately a year and a half—Philip Morris replaced Miller's old management with its own cigarette people and changed significantly the strategy which Miller employed. In essence, Philip Morris brought money and consumer marketing knowledge to the brewing industry. It has attempted for all practical purposes to buy market share through substantive advertising. Furthermore, it has segmented the market and produced products and packages aimed at various segments of the market. Since 1970 it has risen from the seventh largest to the fifth largest brewer in the United States. It is expected that the firm may soon pass Coors and become the fourth largest brewer in the United States. Miller has made few profits and in some years has lost money, but it has increased its plant capacity significantly and has grabbed a large share of the market. Philip Morris and the management which leads Miller have recognized that a disproportionately large number of people who had been drinking Miller's were either women or high income individuals who in fact don't consume very much beer. They sought to change the image of the beer. More facts on Miller High Life are contained in the case on Miller Beer.

The Future of the Brewing Industry

In recent years, total sales in the brewing industry have increased by approximately 4 percent per year. Some concern has been expressed that this upward trend cannot continue to occur much longer. Continued high costs of raw materials are of increasing concern. As the number of regional firms diminishes, competition can be expected to increase among the nationals. Some of the top brewers are more vulnerable than others to the increasing competition which Miller's is bringing to the brewing industry. There are indications that Coors is concerned about its regional market appeal. The federal government has from time to time expressed concern over various practices within the brewery industry, particularly those related to pricing. In the past the federal government has even opposed mergers which might further increase the concentration of large firms within the industry.[1]

1. References for this note are found at the conclusion of the Miller case.

Figure 11.1   Major Steps in the Production of Coors Beer

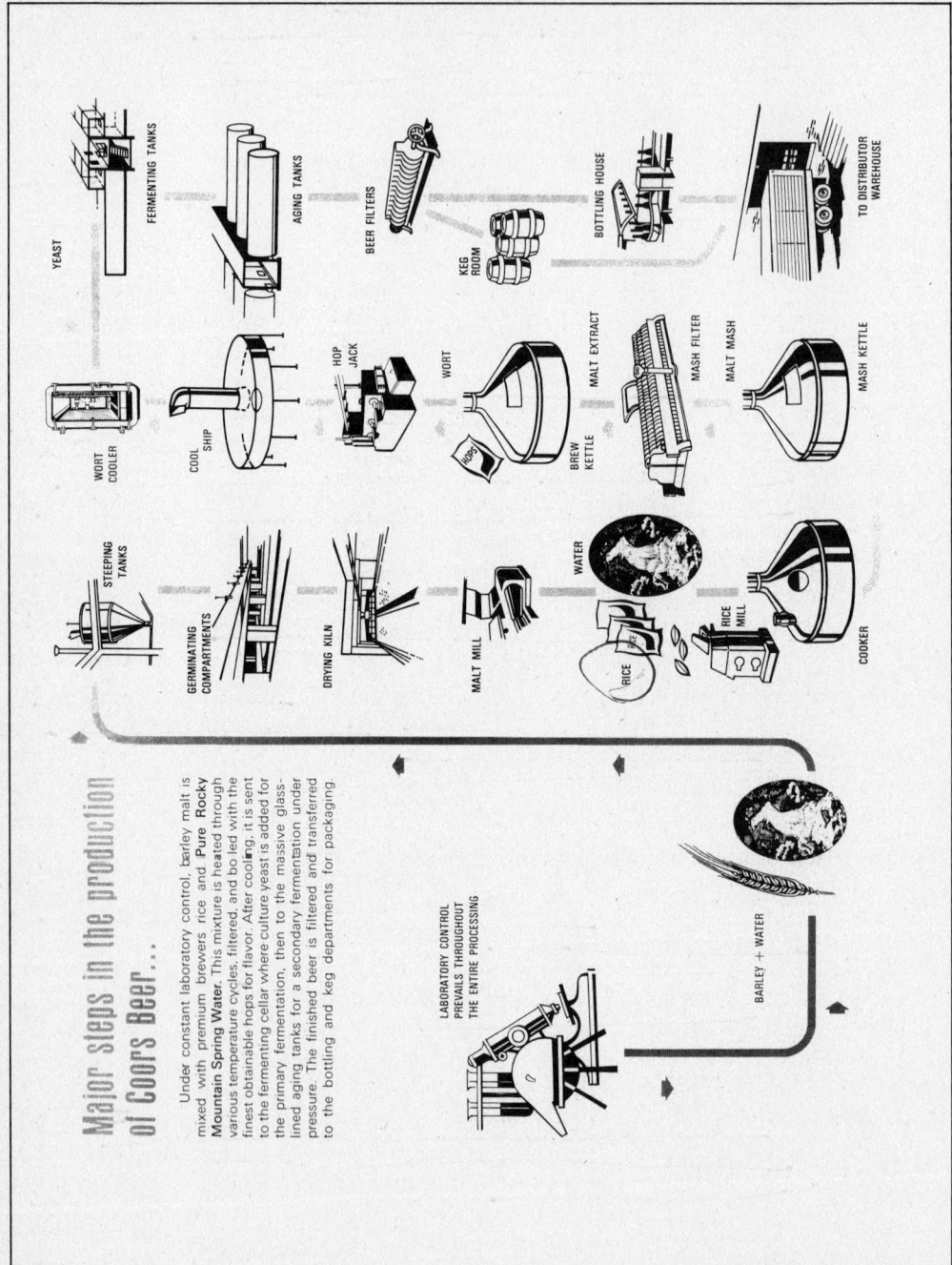

Major steps in the production of Coors Beer...

Under constant laboratory control, barley malt is mixed with premium brewers rice and **Pure Rocky Mountain Spring Water.** This mixture is heated through various temperature cycles, filtered, and boiled with the finest obtainable hops for flavor. After cooling, it is sent to the fermenting cellar where culture yeast is added for the primary fermentation, then to the massive glass-lined aging tanks for a secondary fermentation under pressure. The finished beer is filtered and transferred to the bottling and keg departments for packaging.

Reprinted by permission of Adolph Coors Inc.

Figure 11.2   5-Year Financial Summaries Big Five Breweries

	1974	1973	1972	1971	1970
Barrels Sold (000s omitted)					
Anheuser Busch	34,097	29,887	26,522	24,309	22,202
Schlitz	22,661	21,343	18,906	16,708	15,129
Pabst	14,297	13,128	12,600	11,797	10,517
Miller	9,100	6,900	5,400	5,200	5,150
Coors	12,330	10,947	9,788	8,524	N/A
Sales (Gross) (000s omitted)					
Anheuser Busch	$1,791,863	$1,442,720	$1,273,093	$1,173,476	$1,036,272
Schlitz	1,015,978	892,745	779,359	669,178	594,437
Pabst	558,852	472,548	448,286	416,728	362,682
Miller	403,551	275,860	211,262	204,134	198,479
Coors*	583,683	378,666	330,450	285,912	N/A
Net Income After Taxes (000s omitted)					
Anheuser Busch	64,019	65,577	72,307	71,638	62,549
Schlitz	48,982	53,675	37,539	35,249	29,051
Pabst	18,330	23,827	27,893	25,347	23,283
Miller	6,291	(2,371)	228	1,300	11,409
Coors*	41,051	47,514	48,039	38,408	N/A

*Net of approximately $100,000 in federal and state excise taxes per year.
N/A — Not Available

Introduction

*Mel Linn, Marketing Manager for the Adolph Coors Company, closed the
door to his office and asked the switchboard operator to hold all calls for the
next two hours. He had just met with Bill Coors, President of the privately
owned company and grandson of founder Adolph Coors.*

*After the usual discussion and update regarding day-to-day operations, the
conversation turned to some newly available sales and market share data for
calendar year 1974. Mr. Coors was very pleased with the figures and con-
gratulated Mr. Linn for the part he had played in making it all possible. The
latter had come away from the meeting very happy and somewhat puzzled at
the same time. Although nothing was said directly, it seemed that Mr. Coors
had injected a qualifier into his praise. Mr. Linn felt that he needed some
time to think while memories of the exchange were still fresh in his mind. As
he sat back, his thoughts turned to the market in which Coors was competing
for the customer's favor. He considered the competition and the changes that
he had seen in the market in the past few years. Next his thoughts turned to
those factors unique to Coors.*

The Adolph Coors Company distributes its beer in eleven western states,
in which it holds a dominant average market of 41 percent. From 1966 to
1973 Coors advanced from tenth to fourth in the nation in beer sales.

Distributors attempt to sell their total line to on-premise retails such as
taverns, restaurants, and cocktail lounges. The result is that almost all outlets
that carry Coors on tap also carry it in cans or bottles. This market tactic is
not widely emulated by the competition.

Over the years, the company has built up an impressive list of advantages
over its competitors:

1. The nationwide popularity of Coors beer practically guarantees the company a large market share wherever it chooses to do business.

2. The company employs an extensive marketing network and feedback system. Salespeople and distributors actively seek out new retail clients and
   report to the marketing department every four to six weeks on the state of
   the market.

3. The demand curve for Coors beer is apparently highly price inelastic.
   After holding prices [F.O.B. Golden, Colorado] steady for 27 years, the

Source: Prepared by Professors Jim D. Barnes and William B. Ayars for California State College, Bakers-
field. Reprinted by permission. Distributed by the Intercollegiate Case Clearing House, Soldiers Field,
Boston, Mass. 02163. All rights reserved to the contributors. Printed in the U.S.A.

company had to raise prices twice during 1974 in order to cover increased production costs. These actions have had no noticeable effect on sales.

4. All financing is done internally, so the company is only indirectly subject to the whims of the money market.

5. As prices for liquor and wine rise during inflation, people tend to "trade down" to the less expensive beer. Coors enjoys an advantage here due to its large market share.

6. In a production sense, Coors is almost totally self-sufficient. It manufactures 75 percent of its packaging equipment, 90 percent of its brewing equipment, and all of its malting equipment. Farmers are under contract to grow its own strain of Moravian barley under strictly controlled conditions.[1]

7. The company owns its own can and glass operations. Recycling of used aluminum cans is actively encouraged in advertising copy. The resulting effect on the environment has helped the company's image.

8. Coors has a reputation for innovation. It was the first to use aluminum cans and the first to recycle them. It is the only brewer which does not add chemicals to its beer. It was the first to keep its beer refrigerated from production to retail sale. Currently the company is experimenting with press-in can tabs and a six-pack which is held together with glue (a "stick-pack").

Even though demand for Coors beer exceeds supply nationwide, the company faces stiff competition from Budweiser, Schlitz, Pabst, Miller, and Falstaff within any specific market. Some potential problems are as follows:

1. There is just one brewery. Mr. Coors feels that building one elsewhere might undermine the "Pure Rocky Mountain Spring Water" image which the company has cultivated for 75 years. Also, the policy requiring internal financing is inhibiting.

2. In a marketplace which is becoming oligopolistic, competitors are striving to establish a high degree of brand loyalty. This trend may make it difficult for Coors to expand into new markets, in spite of the existence of untapped markets within its shipping radius which could enable the company to nearly double its size.

3. Coors produces just one brand of beer while some competitors make two or three brands. In a highly segmented market, this could be a disadvantage.

4. Due to stringent quality control requirements and the need for refrigeration during distribution and storage, Coors' costs are generally higher than those of the competition. Therefore, it is reasonable to assume that inflation has hit the company harder than the competition.

1. *Fortune*, November 1972, p. 105.

The Company and Its Marketing Program

Mel Linn mulled over these facts and impressions as he sat in his office pensively sipping coffee and wondering just what Bill Coors had on his mind. Over the years he had come to know Bill quite well due to his openness and informal management style (at his request, every employee calls him Bill). It was not like him to avoid sharing any concern he might have. Temporarily stymied, Mr. Linn's thoughts turned to the company and its marketing mix.

The company has surely come a long way since 1880 when the Coors family became the sole owner of the brewery. In that year, three thousand 31-gallon barrels were produced. With the exceptions of prohibition and the years encompassing the two World Wars, production has increased more or less steadily, culminating in a 1974 figure well in excess of 10 million barrels.

Before the turn of the century, Coors set about development of the finest quality barley in Colorado. The company also began its own malting process, as management felt that perceived variations in flavor, color, and body had to be minimized in order to build a steady clientele. The rice used in the brewing process is an adjunct to the barley malt, contributing to the lightness in body and color. Rice makes the drink less filling than an all-malt beer. Hops are used for flavor and aroma. Only the female blossoms are used. Coors imports 80 percent of its hops from Germany, while 20 percent is grown in Idaho. Coors has contributed over $15 million to this state to help in developing hops. The Rocky Mountain spring water used in the beer is tapped from 60 wells located around the town of Golden. It is biologically pure, contains the proper amount of minerals, and is fresh and cool.

In 1887, a glass company was formed to make beer bottles. Today, the Coors Porcelain Company continues to make bottles, but it is also the largest chemical porcelain plant in the world and the only one in the U.S.

The Coors Container Division was formed in 1954 to produce aluminum beer cans. It is now the largest single metal container plant in the world in spite of the fact that it has not yet achieved the mid-point in the growth planned for 1980. Present production is 100 percent all-aluminum, and every Coors can is marked "All Aluminum—Recycle."

When Adolph Coors died his eldest son, Adolph Jr., assumed control of the brewery. Upon the latter's death in 1970, his second son, William, became president. William's younger brother Joseph is president of Coors Porcelain. In fact, Coors now owns 12 companies, including the largest construction company in Colorado.

In his reflections, it occurred to Mr. Linn that the company is indeed in a strong position in its chosen market. Furthermore, it is sufficiently diversified to provide a strong arsenal of financial strength, should any venture in the beer market turn sour. Mr. Linn's thoughts next turned to the roles played by the marketing mix variables in this success story.

Product. Mr. Linn had earlier stated the "Coors product objective is to produce a beer that is light in body, that has a fresh clean taste, and that has excellent drinkability," the latter being defined as an overall good, appealing taste. The statement seemed to grow out of the company's marketing objective and strategy, which is to obtain and maintain the largest market share in every market it enters and to use an undifferentiated strategy. To elucidate, the company does not segment its markets with respect to age, income, occupation, education, race, or sex, even though it recognizes that most of its beer is consumed by people aged 21 to 35 years.

The following guidelines comprise the product policy:

1. To produce the minimum amount of containers necessary to satisfy target markets, with an emphasis on the most popular 12-ounce aluminum can, thereby cutting costs, increasing efficiency, and raising profits.
2. To make pure aluminum cans which do not impart a metallic taste to the product.
3. To standardize the product in all states, phasing out 11-ounce bottles in favor of the more popular 12-ounce size.
4. To expand plant capacity by 1.5 million barrels per year through internal financing.
5. To expand into other states when the present target markets are satisfied and when there is excess production.
6. To not reduce expenditures on ingredients and quality control. Instead, to cut production, distribution, and promotion costs and still maintain maximum efficiency.

The Coors Company produces a low percentage (3.2) alcoholic content beer and a "repeal" or high percentage beer (3.6 percent alcohol by weight). While all brands lose their freshness and flavor with age, heat, and light, Coors is more vulnerable due to the lack of pasteurizing and chemical additives. Therefore, the company requires that no Coors beer be exposed to light or air until it is opened for consumption.

The following quality control guidelines are enforced:

1. The company has no brew master. Instead, there is a lab which randomly tests the beer in production.
2. A taste panel consisting of 25 people specially trained to identify any taste variation is on duty daily.
3. All packaging is identified by date, time, and assembly line. In this way, any problems which are discovered later may be traced backward.
4. Besides keeping the beer under constant refrigeration, the distributor must clean all taps in on-premise outlets and pull all old beer from retail shelves.

Price. The company's stated pricing objective is to cover all costs and make a reasonable return on investment. (Production cost data and markups are confidential.) Before 1966, twenty percent was thought to be a reasonable markup for each channel member. During that year the Federal Trade Commission filed suit, charging Coors with price fixing. The issue has yet to be resolved; meanwhile, no one in the channel recommends prices.

It will be recalled that Coors very seldom raises F.O.B. Golden prices, and no discounting is practiced. However, channel members are free to set prices and discount within the law.

The company sees its demand curve as being relatively price inelastic, while that of the competition is seen as elastic (elasticity coefficients are not available). This gives Coors considerable flexibility in pricing, which it does not appear to use. Actually, Mr. Linn is unsure just how much pricing flexibility the company does have.

Distribution. Coors does not set sales quotas for its distributors. On the contrary, most of the approximately 170 distributors get their product through a rationing process, as demand exceeds supply. The primary foci in distribution policy are speed and preservation of the "fresh, clean taste and . . . excellent drinkability."

An average distributor moves about 65,000 barrels annually to around 500 retail outlets. He is evaluated by a field salesperson in terms of the percent of outlets that carry Coors in that particular market, whether they carry the full line, servicing conditions, retail relations, and cooler box location. In addition, the distributor is expected to actively feed back market information to the sales representative. He may carry competing brands, but this factor should not interfere with the selling effort. If a distributor violates any policy, the company may drop him; then it helps in selling the business to an approved buyer. Distributor turnover averages two percent annually.

Distributors' route salespersons rotate the beer in each retail outlet in order to minimize aging. Distributors absorb the costs of any dumping, which is seldom necessary (less than one percent annually). If a consumer complains, he is personally called upon by a company salesperson and receives a letter from Bill Coors. If it is legal in that state, the beer is replaced.

The Adolph Coors Company presently distributes the following proportions of beer to outlets in packaging as shown:

Chain Store–Supermarket	20%
Small Grocery Store	15%
Liquor Store	28%
On-Premise Bar or Restaurant	20%
Bowling Alleys	1%
All others	16%

In 1972 the breakdown by package was:

Bottled	20.6%
Canned	67.1%
Draft	12.3%

Coors owns just one distributorship, which is located in Denver and serves as a model and training ground for private distributors. Generally, the maximum credit policy is 15 days for low-risk retailers; otherwise, terms are C.O.D. Occasionally load-to-load credit is extended, where the first load is paid for when the second arrives.

The Denver distributor has directed each of his route salespeople to destroy any beer which is over 60 days old. A route salesperson reports to a distributor sales representative. The latter visits each retail outlet monthly, and he submits a report to the sales manager. Finally, the sales manager sends a summary report to the Golden office.

When hiring salespeople, the Denver distributor presents a slide show giving the company history, philosophy, and objectives and how to be a successful salesperson. Each new route salesperson is thoroughly trained and travels with veteran salespeople before being given a territory. All personnel promotions are from within.

Promotion. There is just one definitive, overall advertising objective: "to maintain and project the corporate image, at the same time present and project the product (beer) in a manner that will promote acceptance and product sales." From this goal emanates a theme of "excellence," which not only pervades the entire Coors organization but also totally disregards promotion campaigns placed in the market by the competition.

Since 1972 the message theme has described the recycling program, which collects any aluminum beverage cans and Coors bottles. The goal is reducing litter and can production costs. During the first two years, Coors paid out more than $8.7 million to the public for aluminum at $.10 per pound. Distributors collect the metal and ship it to an aluminum manufacturer such as Kaiser or Alcoa; these firms in turn ship an appropriate amount of aluminum to Coors. In addition, in 1972, 56 percent of all its bottles were returned to the brewery at either $.01 per bottle or per pound.

Copy concepts never utilize cars, people, food, or "cute" animals; only water and nature. Artwork is executed with clean and clear lines, using cold water complemented by a color scheme that depicts this coolness and freshness. Further, it uses the laws of attention and association, attaching meanings with strong motivational value in addition to its bare functional use value. In this way, aesthetic imagery, emotional meanings, and logical usage fuse together into a product personality.

Media expenditures are matched to each state's population. Ads are never run on Sundays or religious holidays. The media mix and usage rates are as follows:

Television	35%
Radio	25%
Newspapers	15%
Outdoor (being phased out)	15%
Miscellaneous	10%

The company employs no measurements of advertising effectiveness. The budget very nearly reflects a demarketing strategy when compared with the competition: $.70 vs. $4.25–4.75 per barrel.

Bill Coors claims to be at a loss to explain why, in view of these figures, demand so consistently outstrips supply as the production grows ever larger. In fact, the latest production goal is an increase of 1.5 million barrels per year. This would be 12 percent in 1975.

Understanding Beer Drinkers

Mr. Linn wondered if the company had simply been lucky; perhaps Adolph Coors had perpetuated some kind of mystique with which beer drinkers closely identify. Whatever it was, Mr. Linn had earlier thought that he would feel far more comfortable if he at least partially understood it. Thus, it was with ill-disguised enthusiasm that he received a report which described a telephone survey of beer drinkers, undertaken by a group of graduate students at the University of Colorado Business School.

The purpose of the survey was to identify any discrepancies between the attributes that drinkers prefer in their beer, their ability to recall advertising, and the notions of these phenomena held by the Coors marketing department. Furthermore, attempts were made to identify changing consumption patterns from on-premise to off-premise and differences in ad recall between drinkers and nondrinkers. Finally, the survey sought to determine whether brand loyalty was strong enough to generate an evoked set with respect to brand preference.

A stratified random sample of respondents at least 18 years old was drawn from the Denver phone book. (Age was determined by simply asking.) If there was no answer or the respondent would not cooperate, the caller continued down the page column until he found a willing respondent. As it was felt that a majority of beer drinkers are male, the caller first asked to speak with the man of the household.

Execution of the survey generated 66 male and 34 female respondents. Of these, 16 males and 21 females did not drink beer, and 27 of these nondrinkers were over age 35. Among this group, 9 males and 13 females reported that they do not like the taste of beer, while the rest gave a variety of reasons.

Of the 37 nondrinkers, 25 could recall some beer advertising during the past month and 15 of these recalled Coors advertising, mostly on television. Six of the latter group could not remember anything about the ad(s), four remembered something but not the central theme, and five remembered the recycling theme.

Of the beer drinkers, 50 were male and 13 were female. Those over age 35 numbered 31. Exhibit 12.1 breaks down frequency and amount of consumption by sex.

Forty-six percent of the females consume their beer in a tavern, 31 percent consume it at home, and the remainder do so in both locations. In contrast, 80 percent of the males drink at home, 8 percent in a tavern, and 12 percent in both places. Thus, 63 percent of all drinkers consume at home.

Table 12.1   The Brand of Beer Most Often Consumed

Brand	Male	Female
Coors	21	6
Budweiser	8	1
Schlitz	5	1
Olympia	5	1
Michelob	5	1
Hamm's	1	1
Miller	2	1
Old Milwaukee	1	0
Iron City	1	0
No Preference	1	1

The attributes mentioned most often for respondents' "ideal beer" are listed in Exhibit 12.2. Of the 27 who drink Coors beer, 21 felt that Coors matched the attributes of their ideal beer.

Exhibit 12.1   Frequency and Amount of Beer Consumption

Time Span	No. Females	Average Consumption per Interim (Bottles, Cans)
Once per week	4	1.58
1.5 per week	1	
2 per week	2	
Once per month	1	4.38
1.5 per month	3	
Once per two months	1	1
Once per six months	1	1.5
	13	

Time Span	No. Males	Average Consumption
Once per week	7	2.64
1.5–4 per week	17	2.23
5–7 per week	16	3.31
Once per month	4	1.87
Twice per month	3	2.50
4 per six months	2	1.00
Not very often	1	1.00
	50	

12/Adolph Coors Company

Identification of the main purchaser in each household would help to determine the target audience for Coors' advertising, if in the future the company should decide to segment its market. Accordingly, the survey found that 90 percent of the males and 33 percent of the females buy their own Coors. Of these, 63 percent of the males and 33 percent of the females plan their purchases beforehand.

During the past month, 45 of the 63 beer drinkers recalled some advertising. Of these, 23 recalled Coors ads. Ten of the latter group could remember nothing about the ad(s), seven remembered something about Coors but not the central theme, and six remembered the recycling theme.

The survey concluded that beer consumption habits did not differ significantly across age groupings, that a higher percentage of males than females drink beer, and that males drink more frequently. However, there is no apparent difference in the rather low amount consumed at one sitting. Females notwithstanding, the overall trend seems to be toward increasing off-premise consumption.

Of the 63 beer drinkers in the survey, 43 percent most often consumed

Exhibit 12.2 Attributes Mentioned Regarding Respondents' Ideal Beer

Attribute	Males	Females
Light	21	8
Heavy/Strong (European) body	9	1
Not bitter	7	2
Good taste	5	2
Smooth—goes down easily	5	1
Moderate taste (not light, not heavy)	3	–
Foamy	3	–
Not strong taste	3	–
Not too sweet	3	–
Light in color	2	–
Refreshing	1	1
Cold	1	1
Lukewarm	1	–
Wet	–	1
Dry	1	–
Low calorie	1	–
No hops taste	1	–
Draft	1	–
Mellow	1	–
Fresh flavor	1	–
Bitter taste (Mexican beer)	1	–
Noncarbonated	1	–
Carbonated	1	–
Salty	1	–
Not syrupy	1	–
Not giving a full stomach	–	1
No answer	10	3

Exhibit 12.3   Adolph Coors Company and Subsidiaries Four-Year Financial Summary

(In thousands, except per share data)	Fiscal years ended in December			
	1974	1973	1972	1971
Barrels sold	12,330	10,947	9,788	8,524
Summary of Operations:				
Net sales	$466,297	$378,666	$330,450	$285,912
Cost of goods sold	346,855	255,766	212,031	185,075
Marketing, general and administrative	26,700	22,583	20,480	19,273
Research and development	6,066	4,962	3,623	3,096
Other expense (income) – net	3,246	294	(413)	1,645
	382,867	283,605	235,721	209,089
Income from continuing operations before income taxes	83,430	95,061	94,729	76,823
Income taxes	39,167	45,362	46,690	38,415
Income from continuing operations	44,263	49,699	48,039	38,408
Loss from discontinued business	3,212	2,185		
Net income	$ 41,051	$ 47,514	$ 48,039	$ 38,408
Per Share of Common Stock:				
Income from continuing operations	$1.25	$1.40	$1.35	$1.05
Loss from discontinued business	(0.09)	(0.06)		
Net income	$1.16	$1.34	$1.35	$1.05
Shareholders' equity	$10.29	$9.18	$7.86	$6.54
Dividends	$0.048	$0.038	$0.038	$0.029
Average number of outstanding shares of common stock	35,420	35,518	35,631	36,682
Balance Sheet Summary:				
Working capital	$ 45,595	$ 57,820	$ 49,877	$ 41,685
Properties – net	$330,776	$275,019	$225,190	$187,939
Total assets	$484,066	$410,041	$345,111	$287,513
Shareholders' equity	$364,610	$325,271	$279,696	$233,202

Coors. This approximates the 41 percent market share which was documented earlier. When describing ideal beer attributes, the predominant response strongly favored a light beer, which seems to confirm Coors' belief that people prefer a light beer. The belief that beer purchases are mainly planned and executed by the ultimate consumer seems to hold for males but not for females.

Apparently, nondrinkers perceive just as much or more Coors advertising as do drinkers. Perhaps the latter tend to adopt a specific brand and then ignore advertising.

As he reviewed the survey results and conclusions, Mr. Linn suspected that he could extract some new insights into the company's market. He also knew he would be meeting again, very soon, with Bill Coors, as he was due back next Monday from a pleasure trip in Wyoming. Mr. Linn wondered if he had devoted any thought during his vacation to whatever was apparently bothering him. More importantly, Mel Linn was wondering how he should react if Mr. Coors broached the subject during their next meeting. He wondered if it was the advertising strategy per se that was bothering Bill, or if perhaps he was considering further expansion. This latter alternative had been discussed a great deal recently, but the decision to expand the geographic market area had yet to be made. Mel had often pondered the impact that an expansion program would have on his marketing strategy, and his thoughts turned to the alternatives for marketing Coors on an expanded basis.

Discussion Questions

1. Why is Coors successful? What are its strengths, weaknesses?
2. What are the threats, opportunities confronting Coors?
3. If Coors does expand further, what should its strategy be?
4. Given the strengths and weaknesses of the competition, the future beer market, and other relevant factors, what should Coors' Master Strategy be for the next ten years?

13/Miller Brewing Company*

James M. Higgins

In 1970, Philip Morris, Inc. purchased the remaining outstanding shares of Miller Brewing Company, making Miller a wholly owned subsidiary. Philip Morris (PM) began almost immediately to transform the staid and conservative brewing company into an aggressive, consumer product oriented industry giant. To accomplish this end, PM brought in John A. Murphy, the executive vice president in charge of Philip Morris's International Operations, to head the brewing company. Murphy's administrative background was in tobacco, and while that background might seem inappropriate, it was not. PM recognized that beer is essentially a homogeneous product, distinguished primarily as a result of product consumer advertising strategy. PM and Murphy applied to beer those strategies which they had found to be successful with tobacco. Subsequently, Miller became the fastest growing brewer. Between 1970 and 1975, Miller rose from seventh to fourth in sales and passed Pabst to become third in 1976.

Philip Morris Incorporated

Philip Morris Incorporated, is a diversified multinational corporation, with sales exceeding $4 billion in 1976. PM has five main operating divisions: Philip Morris USA, Philip Morris International, Miller Brewing Company, Philip Morris Industrial, and Mission Viejo Company. PM is primarily a cigarette manufacturer and marketer. Its diversification efforts resulted primarily from its concern over the possibilities of imminent action against the cigarette industry by the federal government in response to the Surgeon General's 1964 report linking cancer, heart disease, and other problems with the smoking of cigarettes. Its two major operating divisions, Philip Morris and Philip Morris International, account for 75 percent of Philip Morris's total sales. Both of these operating divisions are tobacco industry related. Philip Morris is an extremely successful marketer of tobacco products. In 1961, PM was the smallest of the six major tobacco companies. It held 9.4 percent of the U.S. cigarette market. In 1976, PM held 25.2 percent of the market. In 1976, it was the second largest of the tobacco companies, trailing only R. J. Reynolds, which held 33.2 percent of the market.

The Industry. R. J. Reynolds and Philip Morris dominate the cigarette industry. Given their large cash flows and their abilities to market their products, there is no reason to believe that their share of the market should decrease.

---

*Certain quotes are made in the case and case note directly from references. Rather than disrupt the continuity of the case with footnotes, references are provided at the end of the case. Students should read "The U.S. Brewery Industry, 1974" (Case 11) before reading this case.

Rather, it is expected that these two will increase their shares of the market, largely at the expense of other major companies. The reason for this is that cigarette sales have grown very, very slowly—less than one percent a year on a compounded basis—in the last fifteen years. As a result, past as well as future growth has been largely at the expense of the other producers. Furthermore, anticipated future federal government and anti-smoking groups' efforts to limit smoking and to convince people not to smoke is anticipated to hold the market steady, if not in fact to reduce it. Also, the number of people in the total population of the United States is not increasing as greatly as it has in the past, and as a result a larger percentage of those persons of smoking age must begin to smoke in order for steady sales growth to be maintained.

Marketing Strategy. Philip Morris recognizes that it operates in a consumer package goods market. In the early 1960s, it developed a strategy for that market, which it still retains in 1976. First, it is not an innovator. This is contrary to the dictum which states that the profitable consumer goods marketer is an innovator. PM waits patiently for competitors to establish a new market, and then moves swiftly into this market with its own products. As a result, PM now has five of the top twenty cigarette brands. Second, it does not usually engage in test marketing, that is, testing brands in a selected number of cities before offering a product nationally. Instead it uses taste test panels in which large numbers of small groups of smokers test the new brand and their reactions are gathered. PM believes that through these test devices rather than through larger test marketing aproaches it can disguise its actions and thus these will not be discovered by competitors. Third, it concentrates on the mass market, avoiding specialty brands which appeal to only a small percentage of the market. Fourth, it encourages its various product groups to develop new brand ideas and new production techniques. Fifth, and probably most importantly, it follows traditional consumer goods marketing strategies. It identifies product market segments, creates products which go into these segments, and then uses massive advertising to buy market share.

PM has made a lot of the right decisions in the past seventeen years. One of their best was the recent introduction of the low tar Merit cigarette in mid-1975. Through 40 million dollars worth of advertising and promotion in the first year, PM was able to sell some 7.4 billion Merit cigarettes ($100 million worth) in 1976. This new brand broke into the top twenty selling brands in one year, an unheard-of success. Furthermore, Merit will begin making money in 1977 for the company. Usually it takes three years at a minimum for a new cigarette to break even. As noted by Joseph F. Cullman, III, the Chairman of the Board, "We are a marketing organization—our success is related to our ability to market and merchandise using consistent and integrated themes aimed at the gross segments of the markets." It should be observed that not only does PM design products for the markets but packages for market segments as well. Much of the success of their number one cigarette, the Marlboro brand, has been attributed to its hard, crush-proof, flip-

Figure 13.1 Philip Morris Incorporated and Consolidated Subsidiaries Five-Year Financial Review

	1976	1975	1974	1973	1972
Summary of Operations:					
Operating Revenues	$ 4,293,782	3,642,414	3,010,961	2,602,498	2,131,224
Cost of Sales:					
Cost of Products Sold	1,966,871	1,656,839	1,290,319	1,060,777	832,890
Federal Excise Taxes	778,161	686,276	619,504	558,947	494,778
Foreign Excise Taxes	381,125	392,127	349,363	334,512	228,151
Operating Income	634,539	492,844	403,585	329,483	287,461
Interest Expense	102,834	99,045	82,741	50,993	37,870
Earnings Before Income Taxes	471,928	360,810	297,502	255,609	229,634
Pre-Tax Profit Margins	11.0%	9.9%	9.9%	9.8%	10.8%
Provision for Income Taxes	$ 206,253	149,172	121,986	106,977	105,168
Net Earnings	265,675	211,638	175,516	148,632	124,466
Primary Earnings Per Common Share	4.47	3.62	3.15	2.71	2.34
Fully Diluted Earnings Per Common Share	4.47	3.62	3.07	2.61	2.18
Dividends Declared Per Common Share	1.150	.925	.775	.674	.631
Weighted Average Shares—Primary	59,408,484	58,442,362	55,649,417	54,804,174	52,999,338
Weighted Average Shares—Fully Diluted	59,408,484	58,442,362	57,339,255	57,315,784	57,265,432
Capital Expenditures	$ 220,173	244,477	215,770	174,665	120,034
Annual Depreciation	64,856	49,853	38,006	30,245	26,576
Property, Plant & Equipment (Gross)	1,323,923	1,129,838	899,810	728,726	571,148
Property, Plant & Equipment (Net)	993,879	851,103	659,520	510,286	373,372
Inventories	1,657,504	1,448,428	1,269,212	1,009,414	801,145
Current Assets	2,005,745	1,788,085	1,557,908	1,245,934	989,708
Working Capital	1,202,224	890,797	725,000	515,347	524,791
Total Assets	3,582,209	3,134,326	2,653,263	2,108,403	1,701,494
Total Debt	1,525,638	1,443,270	1,239,312	947,364	681,000
Stockholders' Equity	1,429,982	1,227,781	974,673	815,028	695,549
Net Earnings Reinvested	197,195	157,102	131,890	111,376	89,894
Common Dividends Declared as % of Net Earnings	25.7%	25.7%	24.8%	25.0%	27.2%
Book Value Per Common Share	$ 23.99	20.63	16.97	14.66	12.55
Market Price of Common Share High-Low	63¼-49¾	59¼-40⅞	61⅜-34⅛	68⅜-48¾	59⅛-33⅞
Closing Price Year-End	61¾	53	48	57⅜	59⅛
Price/Earnings Ratio	13	14	15	21	25
No. of Common Shares—Actual Year-End	59,487,393	59,357,236	57,264,586	55,378,434	54,444,090

Source: Philip Morris Annual Statements. Reprinted by permission of Philip Morris Incorporated.

13/Miller Brewing Company

top box. Merit was successful not just because of its advertising, but because, as PM has recognized, the future growth of the cigarette industry is in low tar cigarettes. PM moved swiftly in following others into that market.

Operating Divisions. Philip Morris has five major operating divisions:

Philip Morris USA. Philip Morris USA is the largest of the operating companies. This company's Marlboro brand is the industry's leader, with the company's new product, Merit, already in the top twenty cigarettes. American Safety Razor is a product division of this company.

Philip Morris International. Philip Morris International sells more than 175 cigarette brands in over 160 countries and territories. It has manufacturing affiliates in 22 countries and licensees in 17 countries and territories. Marlboro sells very well in the international market as well as the American. 1975 was a record year in sales for Philip Morris in Europe and the Middle East and Africa. Major sales efforts are underway in European Economic Community countries, South America, and even in certain Iron Curtain countries.

Miller Brewing Company. Miller Brewing Company has shown a significant increase in market shares in the last five years. Their sales are limited only by insufficient capacity. This problem is being solved by the addition of a 3.3 million barrel brewery in Fulton, New York. Since 1973 Miller has spent more than 250 million dollars on expansion projects to double its capacity. Vertical integration projects are considered important. For example, can making plants are currently under construction at Fort Worth, Texas, and Fulton, New York.

Philip Morris International. Philip Morris International sells more than 175 prised of packaging, paper, and chemical groups. The paper and chemical groups suffered somewhat as a result of the recession, whereas the packaging group has set record levels of profit.

Mission Viejo Company. Mission Viejo has three home building and community development operations. The major of these is in southern California, with small communities located in Denver and Fresno. The southern California operation is very successful, with significant backlogs of home orders at year end.

Miller Brewing Company

When PM took over Miller in 1970, the other brewers laughed and snickered when Murphy, Miller's president, announced that he thought Miller might someday be number one. They are not laughing any more. Miller has risen from the seventh largest to the third largest brewer in sales and is expected to pass Schlitz for the number two position by 1980. Miller's share of the market tripled from 4 to 12 percent since 1972, and its total capacity is expected to be 40 million barrels by 1980—about the same capacity as Anheuser-Busch.

Miller's Marketing Approach. Murphy, the former vice president in charge of Philip Morris's International Corporation, brought to Miller the classic consumer product marketing techniques that had made Philip Morris so successful in the cigarette industry. Murphy and Miller divided up the U.S. beer market into segments, they created new products to meet the demands of these segments, and they created new packages which would appeal to those in these segments. Finally, and most importantly, massive advertising campaigns and promotion efforts were launched to buy high market share. This was unique to the beer industry, with perhaps the exception of Anheuser-Busch. Most of the major breweries in 1970 had only one product and one package and treated beer as a homogeneous entity.

George Weissman, PM's 56-year old vice chairman, feels that tobacco and beer have a great deal in common. They are low-priced pleasure products made from agricultural commodities and are processed and packaged on high-speed machinery. They are advertised in essentially the same ways and are sold to the same customers through similar distribution channels. In fact, "your beer drinker and your cigarette smoker are often the same guy," says Weissman.

Murphy recognized that the 1970 Miller High Life advertising strategy attracted the wrong kind of customers, and not very many of them. He immediately launched an advertising plan which would, as he put it, "attract the real beer drinker." Examples of their advertisements include railroad workers, oil drillers, construction workers, Alaskan pipeline employees, and so forth. The theme of the advertising strategy was hard work, hard play, with beer as the reward. Miller also added a 7-ounce pony bottle in order to attract a large part of the market—those who did not want a full 12 ounces of beer and those who found that 7 ounces of beer stay cold while 12 ounces do not. It is estimated that in 1976 Miller sold 2.5 million barrels of beer in 7-ounce bottles, approximately 15 percent of its total sales volume.

One of the key Miller marketing efforts was the Lite beer which it introduced in 1975. Several new beers have been introduced in recent history in the beer industry, but most have failed. Two other low-caloried beers, similar to Miller's Lite, had also been introduced earlier, but they turned out to be disasters. Miller's Lite succeeded because its advertising campaign emphasized masculinity associated with beer drinking and not just the light-caloried beer. Where other brewers had stressed the fact that their low-caloried beers did not have very many calories, Miller emphasized taste and portrayed masculine images in the drinking of their beer. Their advertising featured many male sports celebrities who pounded home the message that you could get one-third fewer calories and not be as filled and still have a good beer.

Miller next sought to enter another market segment. It is, in 1976, ready to challenge Anheuser's Michelob through the introduction of its own version of Lowenbrau. Through an agreement with Lowenbrau-Munich, Miller will market a domestically brewed Lowenbrau which will sell for an approximately

25 percent higher price than Michelob. Anheuser-Busch's August Busch, III, believes that beer drinkers won't be fooled by a domestic Lowenbrau. Also, Miller tried two or three other beers—Miller Malt, Miller Ale, and Milwaukee Extra. None of the three, however, made it nationwide.

Much of Miller's success is attributed to the fact that it is run by professional managers. These managers were not raised in a family brewing business, as is true of most of the managers of the other major breweries. This allows Miller and its executives to remove much of the conservatism which has dominated the brewery industry.

Finance. Money has been the key to Miller's expansion. In addition to the $227 million that PM paid to acquire the stock, it is estimated that by 1980 Miller will have spent $850 million more on plant expansion. Much of this may have been financed from PM's tobacco profits. While Miller's economies of scale and production of operation are similar to those of other major firms, it is estimated that Miller spends as much as $3 a barrel on advertising, perhaps as much as $6 a barrel on its new Lite beer. The industry average for advertising is much less a barrel. Miller sponsors many sports programs such as the World Series and ABC Monday Night Football, CBS Pro Football, and some professional basketball, as well as several other major events. The heavy expenditures Miller has made and which PM has made in Miller have resulted in a very minimal amount of profits. However, the future for profits looks much, much better as expansion halts and with a probable reduction in other related expenses.

It is alleged that PM is taking much of its cigarette profits and using these to build market share in the beer industry. Robert A. Uihlein, chairman of Schlitz, indicates that he feels that someone will eventually bring a law suit against Miller, "Because it is definitely taking profits from one business and sticking them into another business to gain market share by selling below cost. The law prohibits predatory pricing, and the question now is whether someone might try to interpret it to block what Miller is doing."

The Competition

While the major breweries were caught by surprise by Miller's actions, they quickly began to emulate Miller's marketing strategy. Anheuser-Busch, Schlitz, Coors, and Pabst have all introduced 7-ounce containers. Schlitz has its own Light beer, and Anheuser-Busch began test-marketing its own low-calorie beer in 1976. Advertising has also been increased. In 1975, industry averages rose 17 percent and another 25 percent in 1976. Now, let us examine each of the major brewers to see what major events have transpired since 1974.[1]

Anheuser-Busch. August Busch, III, accepted control of Anheuser-Busch in 1975. Anheuser-Busch has become much more aggressive in its marketing

---

1. For information on the brewing industry prior to 1974 see Case 11.

than it was previously. Busch, like his father, emphasizes the quality of the product and is concerned that Anheuser-Busch continue to make a quality product. It continues to use rice in its beer, whereas most others mix their malt with corn or corn syrup. Busch's profits have been aided since the price of rice dropped 50 percent in 1975. Busch has moved towards a vertical integration strategy in order to be able to assure high quality while maintaining price competitiveness. Its high price, high profit Michelob was successfully introduced into the market and has been contributing substantially to corporate profits. However, a 95-day strike at its plants cut considerably into 1976 profits. A wage agreement was finally reached but not before the strike had done significant damage to Anheuser-Busch's program. Busch gained 4 percent of the California market, taking it directly from Coors, whose market share in California dropped 4 percent.

Schlitz. 1975 and 1976 were not good years for Schlitz. In 1975, Schlitz continued losing momentum because its sales growth rate dropped from 12 to 4 percent, and profits plummeted 42 percent. In 1976, Schlitz's profit picture improved partially as a result of the Anheuser-Busch strike, but a continuation of the reversal of the downward trend does not appear likely at this time. Furthermore, Schlitz was under investigation by the SEC for payments to retailers in alleged kick-back schemes. Robert A. Uihlein died suddenly in November, 1976.

Pabst. Pabst has momentum, but some question its ability to continue sales increases in the long run. Pabst is considered to be the most conservative of the big brewers and has the least ambitious expansion plans of any of the major brewers. And while it has a strong balance sheet, it does not appear to be particularly interested in any aggressive consumer market product strategy. Furthermore, its Red, White and Blue and Andeker beers—its new products—have not been very successful. Some have suggested that Pabst may be vulnerable to acquisition. Both a food company and a tobacco company have shown interest in acquiring Pabst.

Coors. Coors decided to begin to market on a national basis in 1975. Coors does not want to go national but feels that it must in order to survive. Bill Coors, president, says "I think we've got a good enough beer to assure ourselves 20 to 25 percent of the national beer market." Coors had only 8.2 percent of the national market in 1975, while Anheuser-Busch controlled 24 percent of the market. It is clear that Coors is counting on its mystique and charisma. And it is clear that it does indeed have mystique. Former President Ford, former Secretary of State Henry Kissinger, and Clint Eastwood are all known to gulp Coors. That is precious and free advertising. But Coors is vulnerable because of its high market share. Coors has at least a 35 percent market share in any state in which it is sold state-wide. It has a 28 percent operating margin on net sales, the industry's highest, and its return per barrel has averaged almost $9 in the past three years, roughly double that of Anheuser-

Figure 13.2 7-Year Financial Summaries Big Five Breweries

	1976	1975	1974	1973	1972	1971	1970
Barrels Sold* (000s omitted)							
Anheuser-Busch	29,051	35,196	34,097	29,887	26,522	24,309	22,202
Schlitz	23,279	22,661	21,343	18,906	16,708	16,708	15,129
Miller	18,400	12,900	9,100	6,900	5,400	5,200	5,150
Pabst	17,037	15,669	14,297	13,128	12,600	11,797	10,517
Coors	13,545	11,860	12,330	10,947	9,788	8,524	N/A
Sales (Gross) (000s omitted)							
Anheuser-Busch	1,752,998	2,036,687	1,791,863	1,442,720	1,273,093	1,173,476	1,036,272
Schlitz	1,214,662	1,130,439	1,015,978	892,745	779,359	669,178	594,437
Miller	982,810	658,268	403,551	275,860	211,262	204,134	198,479
Pabst	752,654	665,291	558,852	472,548	448,286	416,728	362,682
Coors†	722,966	633,422	583,683	378,666	330,450	285,912	N/A
Net Income after Taxes (000s omitted)							
Anheuser-Busch	55,433	84,723	64,019	65,577	72,307	71,638	62,549
Schlitz	49,947	30,896	48,982	53,675	37,539	35,249	29,051
Miller	76,056	28,628	6,291	(2,371)	228	1,300	11,409
Pabst	32,444	20,695	18,330	23,827	27,893	25,347	23,283
Coors	76,461	59,520	41,051	47,514	48,039	38,408	N/A

* One Barrel equals 34 gallons.
† Net for 1970-1973.
Source: Annual Statements.

Busch, the next highest. But Coors too has had some rough times in recent years. Anheuser-Busch took 4 percent of its California market share in 1976. Then in January 1976 the Supreme Court upheld a Federal Trade Commission decision which in effect required Coors to let distributors sell its beer wherever the law will allow, not just where Coors wanted it to be sold. Publicly, Coors received bad publicity when Bill's brother Joseph was embarrassed as the Senate Commerce Committee vetoed his nomination to the board of the Corporation for Public Broadcasting. And the Equal Employment Opportunity Commission filed a suit against Coors, saying it discriminated against minorities. Finally, Coors, in order to pay for taxes on the family inheritance from the original Adolph Coors estate, had to go public—that is, it had to sell stock for the first time. However, this venture was extremely successful, raising a great deal of money for the firm. Coors' expansion plans are impressive. It anticipates that it will increase capacity at least a million barrels a year until reaching 25 million barrels. Coors plans to move slowly eastward with its beer. Current plans call for expansion to Arkansas, Nebraska, and Missouri, as well as Montana and the state of Washington, with expansion already occurring in other parts of Texas to which they had not previously marketed. Finally, Coors has considered changing its advertising appeal somewhat—concentrating more on the beer and less on the environment and other aesthetic aspects of life. Coors' strategy is summarized by Bill Coors, "If we need to sell more beer, all we do is expand our market."

Other Firms to Watch. In late 1976, the Olympia Brewing Company purchased Lone Star Brewing Company of Texas, making it the sixth largest brewer in the country. With its Hamm's and Olympia labels already covering the Midwest, East and West, Olympia may indeed become a formidable competitor. It is difficult to tell at this time whether or not Olympia will be able to satisfactorily sell three different beer brands, as if it were one nationally known brewer. However, the Lone Star brewery will be used as was the Hamm's brewery upon acquisition to brew Olympia beer. Thus it appears that Olympia is attempting to go national with its primary label—Olympia. Furthermore, the Lone Star plant had a very modern brewery as well as $2.5 million in annual profits. The Lone Star brewery has plenty of room for expansion and a million and a half barrel capacity. It is not clear where Olympia plans to expand to next, but the Northeast or Southeast are the only areas in which Olympia does not now have a major brewery. Of course, Olympia could attempt to go national through distribution only and not through using currently existing distribution systems or an acquired brewery, but this seems a less likely and more risky choice. However, the number of breweries available to acquire in these areas is very limited. Although, certainly, a couple of breweries located in the Northeast have been losing money in recent years and might be the target for Olympia's expansion plan.

Another brewer to watch is G. Heileman Brewing Company of LaCrosse, Wisconsin. Where other regional brewers have failed, it prospers with a multi-regional strategy. Heileman has acquired seven breweries since 1959 and currently ranks as 8th among the industry's producers. Heileman has strong central management and recognizes the advantages of consolidation with regard to finances, planning, and brewing. Importantly, marketing is left separate. It does not attempt to promote national labels. Rather, it retains the original brand names of the breweries that it has acquired and operates individual and separate regional advertising campaigns aimed at local loyalties and tastes. Heileman's strategy is directed by Russell G. Cleary, chairman and president and chief executive officer. He feels that regional operators can compete against the majors but that they must not go national because in that market they cannot hope to compete successfully. Cleary feels that the regionals are much better off attacking on their home ground than they are attempting to go nation-wide where they are unknown and where great amounts of advertising dollars would have to be spent to introduce their products. Heileman markets eight brands and none is marketed or distributed in a larger area than four states. Heileman has been quite sucessful in Minneapolis–St. Paul. The company's Schmidt Brand is No. 1 in that market. In Milwaukee, its Blatz beer ranks as fourth but has been growing at 21 percent a year. Its Drewery's beer is third in Detroit and Cleveland; and Sterling ranks first in Indiana, Kentucky, Tennessee, and Alabama. In order to maintain these sales, however, it has been forced to spend $1.69 per barrel for advertising, whereas the national industry average is $1 per barrel.

Figure 13.3 Wholesale Commodity Prices 1967 = 100

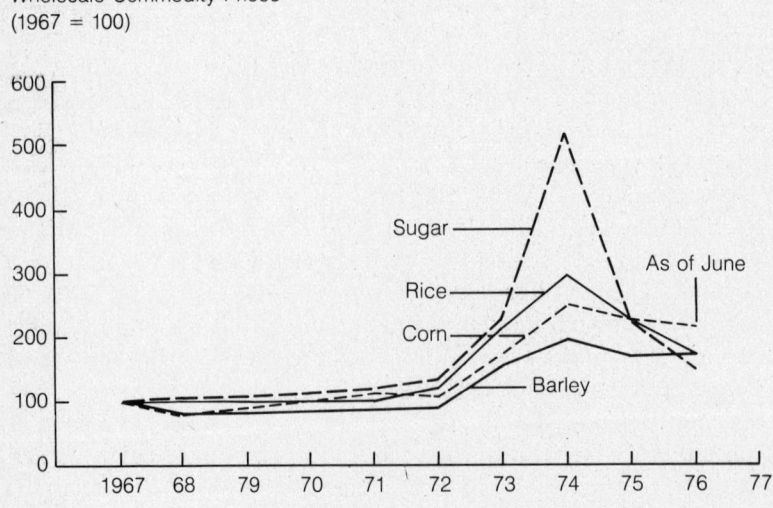

Wholesale Commodity Prices
(1967 = 100)

Source: Standard and Poor's. Reprinted by permission.

Carling, a subsidiary of Rothman's Pall Mall Ltd. of Canada, is expected to infuse large amounts of cash into its U.S. operations of Carling Beer. At one time, Carling was number four in sales in the industry. Now it has slipped to 11th. The primary diagnosis was that Carling lacked aggressive marketing management. To turn this around, the parent Canadian holding company has turned over decentralized management to its American division, allowing them to spend more on marketing in an attempt to regain previous shares of the market. Carling now markets, among others, Black Label, Colt 45, Malt Duck, and National Premium beers. It has new management and feels that it is headed in the right direction. It divested itself of one inefficient plant and shifted production of each of its beers closer to its market, thus avoiding expensive distribution and transportation costs and saving a great deal of money. While Carling has not turned it around as yet, it has stopped the decline and is hoping now to build profits.

Industry Factors

Expansion in capacity is expected by almost all of the majors. Definite overcapacity exists in the market, but much of this is in inefficient and uneco-

Figure 13.4   Beer Container Prices: Wholesale Price Index 1967 = 100

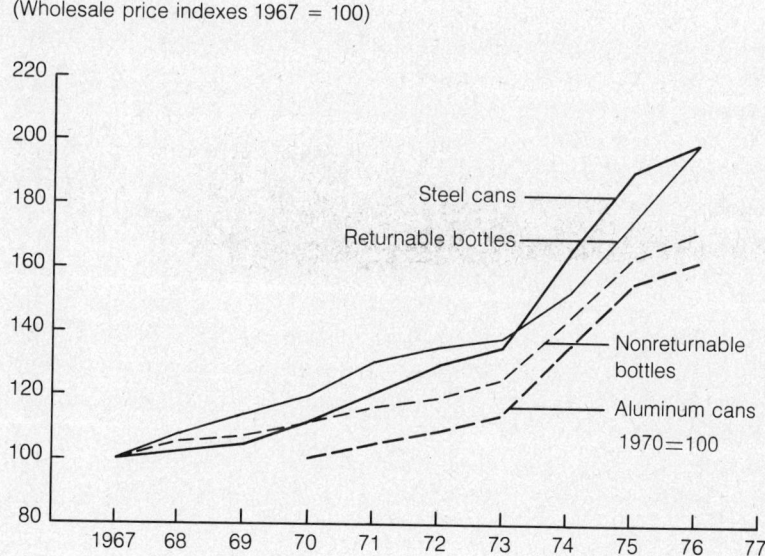

Beer Container Prices
(Wholesale price indexes 1967 = 100)

Source: Standard and Poor's. Reprinted by permission.

Figure 13.5 U.S. Consumption of Beverages
(Units: Total, 1,000,000 Gals.; per Capita, 1 Gal.)

U.S. consumption of beverages
(Units: total, 1,000,000 gals., per capita, 1 gal.)

Year	Wines Total	Wines Per Capita	Beer Total	Beer Per Capita	Distilled Spirits Total	Distilled Spirits Per Capita	Total Alcoholic Total	Total Alcoholic Per Capita	Soft Drinks Total	Soft Drinks Per Capita
1975	361	1.70	4,597	21.5	423	1.98	5,381	25.28	6,690	31.4
1974	343	1.62	4,470	20.9	417	1.97	5,280	24.69	6,690	31.6
R1973	338	1.61	4,239	19.8	404	1.93	4,981	23.74	6,690	31.9
1972	327	1.57	4,053	19.5	393	1.89	4,773	22.96	6,300	30.3
1971	296	1.43	3,918	18.6	381	1.85	4,595	22.28	5,925	28.7
1970	256	1.26	3,771	18.7	370	1.84	4,397	21.68	5,513	27.0
1969	223	1.11	3,593	17.2	362	1.80	4,178	20.71	5,213	25.9
1968	205	1.03	3,443	16.7	345	1.73	3,993	19.98	4,950	24.8
1967	197	0.99	3,313	16.8	325	1.64	3,835	19.38	4,650	23.6
1966	187	0.95	3,219	16.1	309	1.58	3,715	18.96	4,365	22.3

R - Revised.
Source: *The Liquor Handbook*.

Source: Standard and Poor's. Reprinted by permission.

nomical operation of small barrel capacity plants of the regional firms, many of which have been or will be driven out of business. The cost to increase capacity depends upon whether it is an addition or an entirely new plant. Estimates are that it costs $20 per barrel to add on to an existing plant and as much as $40 to $50 per barrel to build a new brewery. Total industry capacity is expected to increase by 30 percent by 1980. Most majors are attempting to increase vertical integration, believing that millions can be saved by processing their own cans or supplying their own basic ingredients. Increased competition as well as increasing costs dropped after tax margins of the larger brewers fell from 6 percent in 1971 to 3.5 percent in 1975. During that same period, return on equity fell from 15 percent to 10 percent for the larger brewers. It should be noted, however, that beer drinking was not extremely affected by the recession. Thus, while in such times people may not drink extra beer, they still drink beer. Raw material prices decreased significantly in late 1975 and 1976. Profit margins increased somewhat as costs were lowered.

Continuing Government Interest in the Brewing Industry. The Securities and Exchange Commission, the Treasury Department, and the Justice De-

Figure 13.6   Beer Production and Consumption

Year	Production Total Thous. of Bbls.		% for Packaging	% for Draught	Per capita Consumption (Gals.)
		Tax-Paid Withdrawals			
1974	156,180	145,464	88	12	20.9
1973	148,602	138,468	87	13	19.8
1972	141,280	131,812	87	13	19.5
1971	137,480	127,397	86	14	18.6
1970	133,123	121,860	86	14	18.7
1969	127,311	116,271	85	15	17.2
1968	122,408	111,416	84	16	16.7
1967	116,551	106,974	84	16	16.8
1966	113,037	104,262	83	17	16.1
1965	108,222	100,421	82	18	16.0

Source: Standard and Poor's. Reprinted by permission.

partment are currently investigating possible layoffs and kickback schemes used by brewers to entice retailers and wholesalers to buy their brand. Regional brewers have claimed that it is a result of these schemes plus intentional underpricing often below cost that has driven them out of business. With regard to this latter factor—predatory pricing—Pearl beer has brought suit against Anheuser-Busch and Schlitz, claiming that as a result of their predatory pricing, its share of the Texas market fell from 23 percent in 1966 to 6 percent in 1976. The brewing industry is also being investigated by the Federal Trade Commission, and a three year study, while completed, has not yet been released. The Justice Department is said to be especially concerned about the growing concentration in this industry, and it is anticipated that further investigation of this concentration will occur. Grand juries have investigated predatory pricing and kickback schemes.

The Industry Future. The industry grew only slightly over 2.2 percent in 1975 and 2.1 percent in 1976. Future projections of the age group that most consumes beer, i.e., the 18 to 34 age group, indicate that this group will diminish as a total percentage of the population in the near future. The beer industry has had two consecutive years of 10 percent or more price increases in retail prices. Consumer spending for soft drinks rose significantly, and is expected to continue to rise, during the same time period in which beer rose less than spectacularly. As a result of the decrease of the relative percentage of the 18 to 34 age beer group, it is expected that beer makers will attempt to appeal to those who traditionally do not drink beer. Furthermore, it is expected that diversification will become a very important concern to most brewers. This will probably be patterned after those efforts of Anheuser-

Table 13.1 Major Products

Anheuser-Busch	Budweiser, Michelob, Busch Bavarian
Schlitz	Schlitz, Schlitz Light, Schlitz Malt Liquor, Old Milwaukee
Pabst	Pabst Blue Ribbon; Red, White and Blue; Andeker
Miller	Miller High Life, Lite, Lowenbrau
Coors	Coors

Table 13.2 Market Share

	1976	1975
Anheuser-Busch	19.1	23.4
Schlitz	16.0	15.7
Pabst	11.3	10.5
Miller	12.2	8.6
Coors	11.0	8.3
	69.6	66.5

Source: Annual statements.

Table 13.3 Capacity (1976)

	Millions of Barrels	Number of Plants
Anheuser-Busch	39	10
Schlitz	27	8
Pabst	19	5
Miller	17	4
Coors	13	1*

*The world's largest single brewery.
Source: Annual statements.

Busch and Coors. Anheuser-Busch, for example, owns the St. Louis Cardinals baseball team and several amusement parks throughout the country. August Busch, III, states that he doubts that price competition will come since none of his competitors have much to gain by such action.

Consumption varies widely with geographic area. The data suggest that in certain parts of the country, consumers could be convinced to buy more beer. As much as a 50 percent difference in consumption existed in 1974 between the highest and the lowest geographic areas of the country with regard to consumption. Furthermore, Olympia and Coors, which were having national sized beer sales and are regional producers, can in fact acquire more beer drinkers perhaps through their mystique if they do indeed expand into new areas. One factor expected to increase total sales for brewers is the increased sale of by-products, such as cattle feeds. Another market area for beer is women. As one of the studies indicates, only 25 percent of today's beer is consumed by women. Note, however, that ten years ago only 15 percent was consumed by women. Competition can be expected to continue and to increase from such other areas as wines, soft drinks, and distilled spirits.

The Future of Miller

The question confronting Miller is the exact content of its strategies for the future. A successful strategy has obviously been found, but the question remains, can it continue to succeed in the future. Increased competition, increased expansion by two or more of the major regional brewers—especially Coors, Olympia, and Heileman—may put a halt to Miller's success. Furthermore, some question exists as to whether or not Miller can maintain its market share without continuing to employ large volumes of cash. Many recall that Carling was supported by its Canadian parent, with large volumes of cash enabling it to move from 53rd to 4th in sales volume by 1960. But when the cash stopped, so did volume. Carling currently languishes in 11th place. Government investigations pose significant potential threats. And August Busch, III, wryly and succinctly summarizing the future observes, "Tell Miller to bring lots of money."

References

"Adolph Coors Company." Information brochure from Adolph Coors Company, Golden, Colorado.

Anheuser Busch, Incorporated: *Annual Report,* for 1975, 1976.

"The Brewers Weep over Inflated Costs." *Business Week,* August 18, 1975, pp. 28–29.

"Carling's Plan to Put the Bubbles Back in Sales." *Business Week,* August 9, 1976, p. 63.

Coors Annual Report, for 1975, 1976.

Ehrbar, A. F. "Why There's No Yeast in Brewer's Stocks." *Fortune,* November 1975, pp. 91–93.

"A Family Brewer Gets Swallowed." *Business Week,* May 5, 1975, p. 39.

"Hot on the Scent of Payoffs at Home." *Business Week,* March 8, 1976, pp. 49–50.

"How Miller Won a Market Slot for Lite Beer." *Business Week,* October 13, 1975, pp. 116–118.

"Beverages: Basic Analysis." *Standard & Poor's Industry Surveys* (Standard & Poor's Corporation, New York). October 28, 1976, pp. B62–B64.

Joseph Schlitz Brewing Company Annual Report, for 1971, 1972, 1973, 1974, 1975, and 1976.

"Make Way for Miller." *Forbes,* May 15, 1976, pp. 45–47.

"Off Coors." *Forbes,* June 1, 1976, pp. 60–61.

Olympia Brewing Company Annual Report, for 1975, 1976.

Pabst Brewing Company Annual Report, for 1971, 1972, 1973, 1974, 1975, and 1976.

Philip Morris Incorporated Annual Statement, for 1971, 1972, 1973, 1974, 1975, and 1976.

"Philip Morris: The Hot Hands in Cigarettes." *Business Week,* December 6, 1976, pp. 60–64.

"Prospects Are Heady for the Top Brewers." *Business Week,* May 19, 1975, pp. 106–108.

"A Regional Brewer That Wasn't Gobbled Up." *Business Week,* October 13, 1975, p. 118.

"A Struggle to Stay First in Brewing." *Business Week,* March 24, 1973, pp. 42–49.

"Turmoil among the Brewers: Miller's Fast Growth Upsets the Beer Industry." *Business Week,* November 8, 1976, pp. 58–67.

"Vodka: Achieving a New High." *Business Week,* September 20, 1976, pp. 103–104.

"Why Coors Finally Had to Take Public Money." *Business Week,* September 22, 1975, pp. 54, 56.

Discussion Questions

1. What is Philip Morris's Master Strategy?
2. What is Miller's Master Strategy?
3. Why has Miller been so successful? Just how successful is Miller relative to other major brewers?
4. What are the major threats which Miller faces in the future?
5. What must Miller do to continue to be successful in the future? Why?

14/Vail Associates at Beaver Creek

James M. Higgins
and Harvey H. Sundel

Vail Ski Area is one of the most successful winter ski areas in the world. During the 1965–1966 skiing season, just four years after its inception in 1962, Vail became the largest single ski area in Colorado based on the number of lift tickets sold, a position which it maintained up through and including the 1975–1976 skiing season. Many movie and television stars, professional athletes, and politicians have residences in Vail. It is extremely popular with the so-called "jet setters." During the 1974–1975 and the 1975–1976 skiing seasons, Vail received considerable national attention as Gerald Ford, then President of the United States, made Vail his winter vacation home.

In the 1970–1971 skiing season, Vail sold 415,600 lift tickets. In the 1975–1976 season, Vail sold 1,015,000 lift tickets. This growth was unprecedented, but not unanticipated. In 1972, Vail Associates Inc., the primary developer and owner of the Vail Ski Area, after considering several alternatives, chose to exercise a purchase option for some 2,200 acres of land located approximately nine miles west of Vail in an area known as Beaver Creek. This acreage was contiguous with some of the finest remaining potential ski area mountain terrain in the country. It was Vail Associates' intention to develop a ski area complex on the acquired land in order to meet increasing demand for skiing trails. Most of the actual ski trails would be on land leased from the U.S. Forest Service. Accommodations and other ski complex facilities would be constructed on Vail owned property. Beaver Creek had been selected as a sight for some of the events for the 1976 Olympics which were to be held in Colorado, subject to voter approval. Little opposition to the proposed ski area was raised, and the firm seemed headed for a profitable venture. However, environmentalists launched a strong and taxing campaign against the proposed Beaver Creek project, and Vail Associates found that the operating environment had become much more hostile than they had anticipated.

The Skiing Industry, 1972

Skiing had been introduced into the United States before the turn of the century, but had failed to attract much interest due to several constraining factors. However, through increased skier mobility resulting from improved air travel and better highways, improved and appealing equipment, increased media attention on the sport, and the promotional efforts of the industry, skiing finally became a popular sport in the 1960s. Based on estimates of those factors considered relevant to the growth of the industry—leisure time,

Source: The authors wish to express their thanks to Vail Associates for their assistance in providing information for use in this case.

discretionary income, population growth, improved ski equipment, and the increased availability of areas—skiing was expected to continue its growth throughout the 1970s.

Lift ticket sales, i.e., sales of tickets to ride the ski lifts which take skiers up the skiing mountain, are greatest in the Rocky Mountain states. The West, the East, and the Midwest trail the mountain states in that order. The quality of skiing is primarily a function of snow depth and composition. One reason the Rocky Mountain states prevail in sales over the other geographic areas of the country is the dryness of their snow. Most skiers prefer dry snow, i.e., "powder," to the wetter, heavier, and harder to ski snow of the other areas. In choosing a potential ski area, years of snow depth measurement as well as composition analysis are necessary. Furthermore, the average temperature of the area must be considered, not only in terms of being cold enough to provide sufficient snow, but also such that the temperature is not too cold. Skiers do not particularly enjoy extremely cold or windy weather, factors which have hurt several ski areas. Depth is important because the best skiing occurs when rocks, tree stumps, and dirt do not surface through the snow and cause the skier to fall. The frequency of snow fall is also important because a ski trail can be "skiied off," i.e., the surface snow removed on the less protected or more heavily skiied areas. Finally, a ski area must have adequate terrain to satisfy all types of skiers—the beginner, the intermediate, and the expert. Beaver Creek met all of these criteria.

Ski areas may be classified into two primary types: destination and single day usage. Destination areas have accommodations at the site for those who do not wish to travel between their residence and the ski area daily. Daily use areas do not have accommodations at the site and are used primarily by those skiers who are able to drive to the ski area without much difficulty. Vail is primarily a destination or resort ski area, although approximately 33% of its ski lift tickets are purchased by single day use skiers. Beaver Creek would have a similar usage pattern. Most of the major ski areas in Colorado and in the United States are destination areas. A ski area must be situated extremely close to a major city and have easy access in order for it to sell a substantial number of lift tickets if it does not provide overnight accommodations.

However, just providing accommodations is not sufficient to assure success. The typical resort skier demands a large number of "après ski" (after ski) activities, including gourmet restaurants, lounges, saunas, swimming pools, tennis courts (enclosed), and nightclub entertainment. Furthermore, the quality of the accommodations is extremely important since skiers tend to be financially able to afford and therefore demand high quality accommodations.

A third classification of ski areas exists. These areas are primarily weekend usage areas which employ only rope tows as ski lifts, as opposed to the more sophisticated chair lifts and gondolas of the daily use and resort areas.

The rope tow areas exist primarily in locations where less snow is available and where the population is such that larger skiing facilities are not economically sound.

Vail: History and Current Situation

Vail ski area was developed by Peter Seibert, an aggressive, hard working, entrepreneurial ski enthusiast. For years, Seibert had sought the perfect mountain, finally finding it at Vail in 1957. He and three friends quickly bought 500 acres at the bottom of the mountain for $55,000. Limited partnerships were sold in Vail Associates Inc., another 630 acres were acquired, a 30-year U.S. Forest Service permit was obtained for the use of the mountain itself, and houses were constructed. In December 1962, Vail's gondola ski lift was opened, the first gondola in the United States, and Vail was in operation. Vail was an immediate success, becoming profitable in 1967. But it was not without its problems. Expansion was a major concern of Vail Associates. Lift capacity was increased by opening a new area of the same mountain—Vail at Lionshead; additional acreage west of Vail at Meadow Mountain was purchased; and several fixed structure investments were made, i.e., condominiums, a second gondola, restaurants, and ski lifts. A severe drain on both cash and profits resulted. Seibert realized that he was in need of additional managerial talent and in 1970 hired first a new vice president, Robert Nott, and then a new president, Dick Peterson, who was then a partner in a major national CPA firm. Peterson immediately employed a retrenchment strategy emphasizing Vail's strong points—ski area management primarily—and instituted a cost efficiency program to put Vail back on its financial feet. Importantly, he employed sound personnel policies, especially motivational compensation programs, to induce his subordinate managers to carry out his programs. Earnings and profits immediately rose.

Vail had four operating departments in 1972: mountain, ski school, food services, and real estate. The mountain division sold ski lift tickets, operated the lifts, groomed the trails—Vail is known for its well-groomed trails—maintained facilities, and would construct new facilities when necessary. The Vail ski school was the largest in the world and contributed substantially to Vail revenues. The food services division operated four restaurants on Vail Mountain, not only providing the company with revenue, but providing skiers with a vital service. The real estate department was a unique feature of Vail Associates. Through this department Vail Associates controlled much of the real estate in and around Vail Village. They were thus able to maintain strict building codes preserving the Alpine village look of the resort. Furthermore, the sale of real estate accounted for a substantial portion of Vail's total revenues—approximately 30%. In 1972, Vail Associates had only 200 acres remaining for sale in Vail itself. Vail Associates also had two functional departments, finance and marketing.

Vail Associates developed five-year goals and plans to reach these goals in its planning committee. Cash flow statements were an integral part of these plans. Vail had established broad goals of profit and growth in the leisure industry, real estate development, and related activities. Diversification had been considered.

Vail Associates at Beaver Creek—The Decision to Purchase

As a result of the planning process, diversification had been considered for the following alternatives:

1. Additional Ski Operations
   Either through acquisition, development, or as a management service to other areas.
2. A Warm Weather Resort Operation
   In order to offset the cyclical nature of the skiing industry and in order to insure revenues in the event that inadequate snow fall were to occur.
3. Summer Programs at Vail
   To offset cyclical revenues, especially to aid hotels and restaurants. Conventions and other traditional resort area customers were sought. This program would stress golf, hiking, mountain beauty, and so forth.
4. Other Leisure Time Products and Services

Vail Associates had contemplated both strengths and weaknesses and threats and opportunities with regard to each of these options.

In August 1972, Vail Associates purchased for $4,600,000 the 2,200 acres of land at Beaver Creek on which it held options. Payment included $415,000 down with $1,020,000 payable at 7% over five years and $3,165,000 payable at 5% over ten years. Options on the property had cost Vail Associates $184,000.

The decision to purchase had been made based on several factors but primarily as the result of the area's need for increased skier capacity. Vail had anticipated continued growth through increased numbers in both destination and single use skiers. By 1977, Vail Associates estimated that Vail Mountain would be filled to capacity and that additional lifts on that mountain were impractical. The Alpine Events for the 1976 Olympics were to be conducted at Beaver Creek, thus providing national advertising for the new ski area without significant cost to Vail Associates. Eventually Vail hoped to make the Beaver Creek complex one of the most exclusive in the world. They hoped to combine the Meadow Mountain ski area with Beaver Creek via ski lifts and thus to create an enormously large ski complex. Several other developers had purchased large holdings of land in the Beaver Creek vicinity. Vail Associates estimated that the total cost of the Beaver Creek project would approach $25 million. Since local groups had been contacted and involved in the planning process and since the U.S. Forest Service seemed amenable to the project and was expected to issue a permit by June of 1973, the project appeared to be imminently probable. No organized opposition existed to the project, but the possibility existed that the Olympics would not receive voter approval in the November election since strong opposition to the Olympics had been organized. Construction on the first four lifts was scheduled to begin in the summer of 1974, with the area to open that fall.

Mounting Opposition to the Beaver Creek Project

In the November election, Colorado's electorate decisively voted against holding the 1976 Olympics in their state. This defeat for Beaver Creek was only the beginning of a long series of actions which were to require the formulation of a strategy by Vail Associates to cope with an increasingly hostile operating environment. Environmentalist groups continually pressured the decision-making state and federal authorities to prohibit the project. And while the Forest Service continued to support the project, it had, as of September 1974, not issued a ski area permit. Other federal agencies and state agencies were far from supportive.

In September 1974, the Vail Associates Planning Committee met to consider the alternatives available to the company with respect to meeting the challenges to their Beaver Creek project.[1] The company's staff had prepared several memoranda describing the problems confronting the company's efforts. Since Vail Associates had no intention of cancelling the project, the formulation of a proper strategy was imperative. In the following paragraphs, their problems are summarized.

Problems

1. Project Size:
   Environmentalists focused on the size of the Beaver Creek development as the primary reason for their opposition. They observed that the four planned dwelling unit developments—Vail Associates Beaver Creek plus Benchmark, Eagle/Vail, and Arrowhead at Vail—would result in a peak ski day population of 40,000 people. The air quality of the valley, the water quality of the valley, and the destruction of wild life habitat which would result were cited as the destructive results of a development of this size. They observed that as a result of the current developments at Vail these same consequences had occurred in that portion of the valley. The poor air quality was frequently referred to.

2. U.S. Forest Service Environmental Impact Statement:
   The National Environmental Protection Act, often referred to as the National Environmental Policy Act, requires that federal agencies carefully scrutinize their decisions for the impact these might have upon the

---

1. Several meetings of the committee were necessary before a strategy was fully formulated.

environment. The environmentalist groups, the press—especially Denver's newspapers—and state agencies had been extremely critical of the Forest Service's environmental impact statement for the Beaver Creek project. One reporter for the *Rocky Mountain News* had called the U.S. Forest Service the "nation's biggest land developer." This reporter labelled the Forest Service report as "shallow" and described the Forest Service as having "shunned" its duty. These comments were considered to be typical of those to be found in the press. Environmentalists were expressing similar views and the Colorado State Planning Division had concluded that the issuance of a permit by the Forest Service would be illegal since they had not, in the planning agency's opinion, adequately satisfied the requirements of the National Environmental Policy Act.

3. Governor Vanderhoof:
    The Governor of the State of Colorado, John Vanderhoof, was expected to request the U.S. Forest Service to further delay its issuance of a permit to Vail Associates. An announcement to this effect was anticipated within a few days. There was considerable discussion as to whether or not the state could prevent the issuance of a permit. With respect to the right of the Forest Service to issue the permit as a federal and therefore legally more powerful entity, there was no question—the state had no authority to intervene. But with respect to the legality of the issuance regarding satisfaction of the National Environmental Policy Act, the state could possibly bring suit to prevent the issuance of the permit. Furthermore, the state could take action under this same act to prohibit development by questioning air pollution and water pollution standards.

4. The Colorado Resident:
    The Colorado resident may be characterized as a lover of mountain beauty and, while many of these individuals are skiers, maintaining the wilderness in its natural state is of equal importance to them. Furthermore, fewer people ski than are perceived to be concerned about preserving the natural environment. Their support of the opposition to the Beaver Creek project could possibly play an important role in the final government decision.

Anticipated Actions. Several anticipated actions may occur, for which Vail Associates feels that it needs to be prepared. Consideration has been given to each of the following, although differing probabilities are assigned to each.

1. The U.S. Forest Service report will probably have to be rewritten. The impact statement was based on only the Vail Associates development and not the others anticipated for the Beaver Creek area. In addition, certain key factors such as energy impact were omitted.

2. With an impending election, Governor Vanderhoof's actions are difficult to predict. However, his opponent, Richard Lamm, if elected, would be certain to attempt to delay or entirely prohibit the project since he is an avowed conservationist.

3. It has been rumored that the state's Planning Division may seek a moratorium on all ski area development.
4. There is a strong possibility that if the project is approved by the state, it will ask for a reduction in scope of the project.
5. It is anticipated that the governor's office will call meetings of the interested parties in order to reach an amenable agreement. These may or may not be open to the public.
6. Concern exists that even if the U.S. Forest Service does rework its impact statement, it may not be found to be acceptable to the state, and then the problems which exist now will not have been solved. Furthermore, even if a permit is granted, the state may take legal action against Beaver Creek, the Forest Service, or both.
7. It is estimated that the further delay of construction of the Beaver Creek project could last as long as two to three years.
8. The Colorado laws related to land use, while vague, are receiving significant attention and may be further delineated by the state legislature. The exact impact on Beaver Creek is difficult to estimate. However, the general mood of the legislature appears to favor increasing control of land use.
9. The various environmental groups opposing the project appear to be gaining strength. They are well organized and are lobbying strongly. They are receiving a great deal of support from the press.
10. The new project is viewed as a "Plastic Bavaria II" by many people—referring to the Bavarian theme of Vail Village and its expected duplication at Beaver Creek.
11. Many Coloradans feel that the tourists which will come to the project do not appreciate the destruction of the valley which will occur. More importantly, they come only for a few days and do not have to live with the consequences.

Discussion Questions

1. What are Vail Associates' alternatives for diversification?
2. Why do you feel that Vail Associates chose Beaver Creek over other alternatives?
3. What are the problems and/or threats facing Vail Associates with regard to Beaver Creek?
4. What would be your strategy for coping with the problems confronting Vail Associates' Beaver Creek project? Why?
5. Evaluate the impact of your strategy on major constituents.

15/A Note on the Soft Drink Industry

James M. Higgins

The soft drink industry is a mature industry with five major firms. In 1976, these firms had sales as follows (in millions of dollars): Coca Cola $3,032.8, PepsiCo $2,727.5, Royal Crown $282.0, Seven-Up $233.3, and Dr Pepper $151.8. In the following pages, several major factors that affect soft drink sales now and will in the future are reviewed. Among the most important of these are demographic factors. Other changes are occurring within the industry, some of which could lead to significant gains or losses in firm viability. These are also reviewed. Finally, the strategy of Coca Cola is discussed as a contrast to that of Royal Crown, discussed in the case which follows. Three major soft drink submarkets exist: fountains, retail stores, and vending machines. The strategy of each company must deal with these submarkets.

Demographic Impacts

The soft drink industry is approaching a period of declining sales in the United States because of changes in population demographics. Soft drink sales are greatest in the 13–24 age group. In 1977, 49 million United States citizens were in that age group. By 1985, only 45 million will be in that age group. On the average, in 1977, 823 cans of soft drinks were consumed per person in the 13–24 age bracket. The average number of cans consumed for all ages is 547. Thus the loss of 4 million consumers in that age group means that some 3.3 billion fewer cans will be sold in 1985 than in 1977 (unless per can consumption can be increased).

But while the U.S. market is losing its 13–24 year olds, the rest of the world is experiencing a population boom. By the year 2000, half the people in the world will be younger than 25. Many, if not most, of these individuals will not have sufficient discretionary income to purchase soft drinks, but even if just ten percent were to have such income, a large potential market would exist. Furthermore, large income markets such as the Middle East remain virtually untapped. And substantial markets in Russia and China remain undeveloped. Coca Cola and PepsiCo have taken actions to serve these markets. North American markets also offer substantial potential as supermarket sales, which account for 55 percent of all U.S. sales, are not well developed in other countries. Furthermore, the evidence indicates that as urbanization occurs and as sophistication levels increase, sales go up. These factors are considered to be especially important in South America, where both events are occurring. However, foreign markets are not without their problems. Changing currency exchange rates and instability of governments are continual areas of concern. Most production facilities are owned by foreign nationals, so that expropriation is not as serious a threat as it might be to a manufacturing organization.

U.S. Industry Trends

In the United States, other industry trends are evident. Powdered soft drink sales rose from $200 million in 1974 to $700 million in 1976. Much of this increase was at the expense of canned or bottled soft drinks. As a result, Coca Cola has entered into this market. However, the powdered drink market is firmly controlled by Kool Aid, Wyler's, and Hawaiian Punch brands.

Sales to major fast food chains and restaurants are of increasing importance. Sales to these enterprises not only increase directly, but also indirectly, by providing advertising. Coca Cola now dominates this market with sales to McDonald's, Burger King, and Pizza Inn. Concern has been expressed by soft drink industry spokesmen that as fast food enterprises and restaurant chains seek to become more competitive, they may integrate backward and produce their own soft drinks. Some fast food operations and restaurant chains have already taken this course of action.

Diversification efforts seem to be increasing within the industry as firms become aware of industry maturity; increasing competition from beer, wine, liquor, and other beverages; and the shrinking U.S. market. Some firms are more vulnerable to these factors than others. Of the major five firms in the industry, Dr Pepper, Coca Cola, and Seven-Up depend more on soft drink revenues than do Royal Crown and PepsiCo. (See Table 15.1.)

Competition is increasing in the total beverage industry. (See earlier note on the brewing industry.) Beer, wine, and liquor sales as well as the sales of nonalcoholic, non–"soft drink" beverages are increasing. As a result, soft drink sales have suffered. These product lines are also in the mature stage and as a result many of these firms are pursuing similar intensive advertising and diversification strategies.

In the last five years, intensive advertising, which normally characterizes a mature industry, has occurred in the soft drink industry. All five of the major firms have attempted to gain market share through extensive and expensive advertising. PepsiCo, Seven-Up, and Dr Pepper have been the primary beneficiaries of these campaigns. Coca Cola and Royal Crown both lost sales to these three firms. Also characterizing the industry during this time period has been the introduction of new products. Diet drinks have been an especially important growth product for all of the firms in the industry. Other factors affecting the industry include the following:

Table 15.1   1976 Soft Drink Beverage Sales as a Percent of Sales

Company	Sales (millions)	Beverage Sales as % of Total
Coca Cola	3,032.8	95
PepsiCo	2,727.5	46
Royal Crown	282.0	76
Seven-Up	233.3	93
Dr Pepper	151.8	100

1. Cola still leads the market with 64 percent of the soft drink market.
2. Southern or "Sunbelt" states have the highest consumption of soft drinks.
3. Hot drinks are the fastest growing segment, with an average annual increase of 11.5 percent from 1972–1975 and with a 16.8 percent increase in 1975.

The Coca Cola Strategy

Coca Cola has long been the giant of the industry. As the industry leader, it is the primary target of the other firms' actions. In 1977, Coca Cola's strategy to counteract those environmental factors which it perceives as threats or to take advantage of those it perceives as opportunities included the following:

1. A major attack on foreign markets. Foreign markets currently account for 44 percent of Coke's sales and 55 percent of its profits.
2. More diversification in the United States. As an example, Coke obtained Taylor Wine Company for $90 million in 1976. Additional similar acquisitions are planned.
3. A major expansion of its Foods Division. Currently this division is a major producer of orange juice, coffee, and tea.
4. A major shift in U.S. advertising for Coke. The attempt here is to maintain the loyalty of consumers once they reach the age of 24.
5. Continued new product development. The soft drink line is not complete, and Coke is soon going to introduce five new fruit flavor drinks under its Hi-C brand.

In support of these efforts Coke has restructured its foreign operations, creating three separate divisions, each headed by a vice president. Coke is pressing hard to establish an operation in Russia, but PepsiCo is far ahead of Coke in this market, with one plant already in operation and four more scheduled for production soon. Coke is also negotiating to regain its lost Middle East sales. Recent talks with Arab leaders suggest that Coke will soon begin sales to this rich market. Coke lost this market when the Arabs retaliated against Coke for selling to Israel by ousting Coke from all Arab countries.

Coke constantly tests new products and is now actively seeking acquisitions. Coke's new theme, "Coke adds life," focuses on showing more older people in commercials in order to sustain consumer interest in older ages.

In summary, Coke has a multi-faceted strategy. Only a few of the major components have been reviewed here, but the strategy seems clear. Full speed ahead on all fronts.

References

"Beverage Briefs." Robinson Humphrey, Atlanta, July 19, 1976.
"Beverages." *Standard & Poor's Industry Surveys,* October 28, 1976.
"The Graying of the Soft Drink Industry." *Business Week*, May 23, 1977, pp. 68–72.

Table 15.2 Consumption of Soft Drinks by Company

Consumption of soft drinks by company

	1970 Million Cases	1970 % Market	1971 Million Cases	1971 % Market	1972 Million Cases	1972 % Market	1973 Million Cases	1973 % Market	1974 Million Cases	1974 % Market	1975 Million Cases	1975 % Market	1974-75 % Chng.
Coca-Cola Co.													
Coca-Cola	1045.0	28.4	1070.0	27.1	1125.0	26.8	1190.0	26.7	1180.0	26.5	1170.0	26.2	− 0.8
Sprite	65.0	1.8	71.0	1.8	81.0	1.9	95.0	2.1	105.0	2.4	115.3	2.6	+ 9.8
Tab	49.0	1.3	66.0	1.7	85.0	2.0	97.0	2.2	100.0	2.2	115.0	2.6	+15.0
Mr. PiBB					5.0	0.1	15.0	0.3	23.0	0.5	37.5	0.8	+63.0
Fresca	46.0	1.3	52.0	1.3	48.0	1.1	44.0	1.0	38.0	0.9	35.0	0.8	− 7.9
Others	71.0	1.9	85.0	2.1	95.0	2.3	100.0	2.3	100.0	2.2	100.0	2.3	—
Total	1276.0	34.7	1344.0	34.0	1439.0	34.3	1541.0	34.6	1546.0	34.7	1572.8	35.3	+ 1.7
PepsiCo, Inc.													
Pepsi-Cola	625.0	17.0	687.0	17.4	735.0	17.5	777.4	17.4	780.0	17.5	778.0	17.4	− 0.3
Diet Pepsi	40.0	1.1	52.0	1.3	58.0	1.4	60.3	1.4	68.0	1.5	75.0	1.7	+10.3
Mountain Dew	34.0	0.9	35.7	0.9	35.0	0.8	42.0	0.9	47.0	1.0	56.0	1.3	+19.1
Teem	14.0	0.4	14.0	0.4	14.0	0.3	14.8	0.3	14.0	0.3	13.5	0.3	− 3.6
Pepsi Light											2.0	0.1	—
Others	15.0	0.4	15.0	0.4	15.0	0.4	16.0	0.4	15.8	0.4	15.0	0.3	− 5.1
Total	728.0	19.8	803.7	20.4	857.0	20.4	910.5	20.4	924.8	20.7	939.5	21.1	+ 1.6
Seven-Up Co.													
7-Up	257.6	7.0	271.4	6.9	289.6	6.9	317.7	7.1	311.3	7.0	295.5	6.6	− 5.1
Sugar Free 7-Up	6.5	0.1	8.4	0.2	10.1	0.2	12.7	0.3	27.3	0.6	43.6	1.0	+59.7
Howdy Flavors	3.0	0.1	2.3	—	1.8	0.1	1.4	—	1.5	—	1.4	—	− 6.6
Total	267.1	7.2	282.1	7.1	301.5	7.2	331.8	7.4	340.1	7.6	340.5	7.6	+ 0.1
Dr Pepper Co.													
Dr Pepper	135.2	3.7	147.7	3.7	180.0	4.3	208.7	4.7	216.0	4.8	217.0	4.9	+ 0.5
Sugar Free Dr Pepper	5.0	0.1	7.2	0.2	11.0	0.3	14.8	0.3	18.0	0.4	28.0	0.6	+55.6
Total	140.2	3.8	154.9	3.9	191.0	4.6	223.5	5.0	234.0	5.2	245.0	5.5	+ 4.7
Royal Crown Cola Co.													
Royal Crown	142.0	3.8	153.0	3.9	165.0	3.9	165.0	3.9	150.0	3.4	153.0	3.4	+ 2.0
Diet Rite Cola	36.0	1.0	42.0	1.0	44.0	1.0	42.0	0.9	34.0	0.8	36.0	0.8	+ 5.9
Nehi & Others	45.0	1.2	46.0	1.2	49.0	1.2	53.0	1.2	56.0	1.2	51.0	1.2	− 8.9
Total	223.0	6.0	241.0	6.1	258.0	6.1	268.0	6.0	240.0	5.4	240.0	5.4	—
Total (5 companies)	2634.3	71.5	2825.7	71.5	3046.5	72.6	3274.8	73.4	3284.9	73.6	3337.8	74.9	+ 1.6
Others	1040.7	28.5	1124.3	28.5	1153.5	27.4	1185.2	26.6	1175.1	26.4	1122.2	25.1	− 4.5
Grand Total	3675.0	100.0	3950.0	100.0	4200.0	100.0	4460.0	100.0	4460.0	100.0	4460.0	100.0	—

Sources: John C. Maxwell, Jr.; Wheat First Securities, Inc.; and *Beverage Industry*.

Source: "Beverages," *Standard & Poor's Industry Surveys*, October 28, 1976, p. B71. Reprinted by permission.

James M. Higgins

In the late 1960s and early 1970s, Royal Crown Cola had followed a strategy of attempting to compete directly with Coca Cola and Pepsico, including the introduction of new products to compete with these firms' new products. Royal Crown had also followed a program of diversification, investing in several nonbeverage or non–soft drink enterprises. By January 1, 1975, when Donald A. McMahon assumed the presidency of Royal Crown, this strategy had resulted in Royal Crown (5.4%) slipping from third in market share to fourth, behind the Coca Cola Co. (34.7%), PepsiCo (20.7%), and the Seven-Up Co. (7.6%), with the Dr Pepper Co. (5.2%) a close fifth place. (Royal Crown Cola trailed the lead brands of the other four firms.) Furthermore, several of its diversification efforts had become unprofitable. Finally, despite increased sales, profits lagged. McMahon set out to change all of that, and by year end 1976, had altered Royal Crown's marketing strategy to one of emphasizing strengths and avoiding head-on confrontations and new product competition with the larger firms; had divested the firm of its less profitable enterprises; had initiated and directed the firm's acquisition of Arby's, the roast beef, fast food service chain; and had instituted a belt tightening program. As a result, both profits and sales rose dramatically in both 1975 and 1976.

Royal Crown Cola: January 1, 1975

The following paragraphs summarize briefly the situation which President McMahon found as he surveyed Royal Crown upon becoming corporate president, January 1, 1975. Before becoming RC's president, McMahon had been president of Baker Industries, Inc., for five years and before that had been president of The Monroe Calculator Company and corporate vice president of its parent, Litton Industries, Inc.

Products. Royal Crown Cola Co. is primarily engaged in the sale of soft drinks, including: Royal Crown Cola (RC), Diet Rite, Nehi-fruit flavors, Par-t-Pak, and Upper 10. Royal Crown also markets Adams and Texsun fruit juices. In addition, it owns several enterprises engaged in the production of home decorating items and furniture.

Competition. The soft drink industry is a mature industry and competition is intense. The other four of the five major firms in the industry all engage in intensive consumer product advertising campaigns, all of which have been successful in recent years. Coca Cola frequently introduces new products into

Source: The author wishes to thank Royal Crown Cola Co. for its assistance with this case. Certain portions of this case contain copyrighted material reprinted with the permission of the Royal Crown Cola Co.

the market. The others do so occasionally too. The national economy has been in a recession for the past two years, but is now beginning to move forward. The price of raw materials has hurt industry profits as costs have risen and consumption has dropped below expected levels as the result of increased prices at the retail level. The industry, in 1969, suffered through a ban on cyclamates, which had been an important ingredient in diet drinks. Of the competition, Dr Pepper is the only firm that is not diversified, although diversification is not really stressed by any of the competitors except Pepsi-Co. Competition with the basic product comes from all drinks, including alcoholic and powdered. Much of the expected growth in soft drinks is anticipated to come in the diet market. Consumption of soft drinks increased 34 percent from 1972 to 1975. Competition existed in packaging, with the larger bottle sizes increasing in popularity. Competition in the other product lines is not as intense. Fewer dominant firms exist in either of the other major product areas. The weak national economy had a large impact on the home decor firms in 1974–1975.

Soft Drink Marketing/Production. From 1964 to 1974, no fewer than eight different advertising campaigns have attempted to sell RC Cola, among these the immemorable, "RC—It's Right for You," and "Tastes Easy on the Syrup, Easy on the Gas." Further, much of the advertising budget has been employed in introducing new products, many of which have been total failures or have met with little success: among these are Gatorade, Flair, RC With a Twist of Lemon, and Sugar Free RC. The larger bottles of RC and the other soft drinks in their product lines were selling well. These included the 32 and 64 oz. sizes. The franchised bottler network was virtually in shambles as little or no attention had been paid to these vital links to the market. Many of these firms had been less than enchanted with the constant flow of new products, consequently many of the franchisers did not adopt some of the new products, making national marketing efforts unsuccessful. Little corporate help was offered franchisers in the way of promotions.

Management Structure. Communication and action channels were perceived as unnecessarily cumbersome. Corporate headquarters were in Columbus, Georgia.

Foreign Operations. As part of the expansion strategy, RC had moved heavily into the franchising of foreign bottling operations.

Finance. Among other problems, RC was overly dependent on expensive, short term debt. While sales were increasing, profits per share had not grown correspondingly and had even decreased in 1974.

The Turnaround Strategy

McMahon undertook to change what he viewed as inappropriate. During 1975 and 1976, he directed Royal Crown Cola Co. to take the following actions, and/or the following events transpired:

1. Advertising would emphasize RC and Diet Rite, the company's best sellers. The advertising budget doubled in two years from $10 million to $21 million.

2. A new advertising campaign for RC ("Me and my RC") would be created, employed, and maintained. Diet Rite received a new distinctive red packaging. A new "No, No—Yes, Yes" Diet Rite commercial theme was adopted.

3. The number of products in the soft drink line would be reduced and new products would not be introduced. Over time, this policy might be changed to allow for exceptional new products.

4. Head-on competition with the two major firms in the soft drink industry would not be the company's plan of action. Rather, the firm would emphasize those market areas such as New York and Los Angeles where the firm was already strong. McMahon felt the company should spend less time trying to catch up and more time selling the product.

5. Franchisers would be supported and their support would in turn be sought. A program of personal visitation by McMahon was undertaken. Each month 15 to 20 franchisers would be visited by top management. Cash, and lots of it, was used to help franchisers promote RC products. Extensive promotions were undertaken in grocery stores under the "Rack Up 76" theme.

6. Nonperforming franchisers were eliminated.

7. Foreign expansion was halted, and the management restructured.

8. Long term debt was substituted for the short term debt.

9. Costs were cut. New budgeting procedures were employed.

10. The company moved its headquarters to Atlanta, Georgia.

11. Losers and marginal diversification investments were divested. Included were a furniture factory, an unprofitable porcelain operation, a bathtub enclosure business, a porcelain sculpture producer, and a lower priced lamp company.

12. Carefully, new diversification efforts would be undertaken.

13. Top management was restructured. Approximately 50 top and middle managers left the firm in the move to Atlanta. In sum, over 90 percent of top management was either shifted or released.

14. Comprehensive, strategic, and operational planning were employed.

15. New additional accounting control programs were instituted. Four distinct operating divisions were created: Soft Drink, Fast Food, Citrus, and Home Decor.

16. Capital expenditures would be increased to support the soft drink program.

The Arby's Acquisition

On November 1, 1976, Royal Crown Cola Co. completed a two part purchase through which, for $18 million, it acquired 100 percent of the outstanding stock of Arby's Inc., the leading national roast beef sandwich chain of fast food restaurants, with 522 franchised and 46 company-owned restaurants throughout the United States. McMahon comments, "The soft drink industry is large, old, and mature, while the fast food industry is still growing." Arby's had had financial problems in recent years, filing for reorganization in 1971 under the Federal Bankruptcy Act, Chapter XI. However, RC reports pretax income of $3.8 million for Arby's in 1976. McMahon intends to expand substantially the number of Arby's, both company-owned and franchised.

One of the keys to the future success of Arby's is the increased seating capacity which will be found in all new Arby's, in RC-owned Arby's, and in older franchised Arby's which choose to expand. Estimates are that by increasing seating capacity from the current 20 to 80, the average sales per unit will increase from $400,000 per year to $700,000.

Arby's stores also provide a sales outlet for RC Cola. While growth is projected to be approximately 3.5 percent per year in the soft drink industry, growth is projected at 15 percent annually for the fast food industry for the next 10 years. RC estimates that by 1980, 30 percent of corporate income, or $130 million, will come from Arby's. Vital to this anticipated income is the increased selection of sandwiches which Arby's had undertaken in recent years. Thus, in addition to roast beef, consumers may find ham and club sandwiches as well as several varieties of beef sandwiches and several additional menu items such as slaw, potatoes, and desserts. (See "A Note on the Fast Food Industry," Case 8.)

Results. In both 1975 and 1976, RC reported both record sales and record earnings. Earnings per share increased dramatically. In 1976, all divisions of the firm showed profit improvement compared to 1975. Record case sales of all soft drink products occurred in 1976. Despite the Arby's acquisition, total borrowings amount to only 17 percent of stockholders' equity as of December 31, 1976. For further results, and a view of the current (December, 1976) situation, see Exhibits 16.1 through 16.9.

The Future

Corporate objectives include the following:

1. 12–15% earnings growth
2. 10% revenue growth
3. Increased dividends in line with earnings
4. 25% return on capital from each division

During the 1977 operating year, capital expenditures are estimated at $29 million, with approximately $17 million designated for the expansion of Arby's

**Exhibit 16.1   Net Sales and Operating Profit by Line of Business
Royal Crown Cola Co. and Subsidiaries***

	1976	1975	1974	1973	1972
			Year Ended December 31		
Net sales:					
Soft drink	$169,358	$159,032	$133,560	$112,376	$111,089
Citrus	46,304	43,342	36,165	34,333	34,741
Home decor	59,868	55,077	53,463	48,658	45,572
Fast food	6,465	0	0	0	0
Total net sales	281,995	257,451	223,188	195,367	191,402
Cost of sales	152,379	145,530	136,910	112,256	111,102
Gross profit	129,616	111,921	86,278	83,111	80,300
Marketing, administrative and other expenses	96,371	84,336	70,222	60,862	58,304
Operating profit:					
Soft drink	20,137	19,192	7,238	13,202	12,800
Citrus	5,793	4,553	4,999	4,043	3,718
Home decor	6,604	3,840	3,819	5,004	5,478
Fast food	711	0	0	0	0
Total operating profit	33,245	27,585	16,056	22,249	21,996
Interest expense	(883)	(1,588)	(2,075)	(643)	(385)
Other income (expense), net	749	(303)	1,990	1,915	1,431
Income before income taxes	33,111	25,694	15,971	23,521	23,042
Provision for income taxes	15,820	12,400	7,750	11,300	11,300
Net income	17,291	13,294	8,221	12,221	11,742
Average shares outstanding	8,064,941	8,049,891	8,031,391	7,994,265	7,938,440
Per average share:					
Net income	$ 2.14	1.65	1.02	1.53	1.48
Cash dividends declared	.76	.68	.64	.61	.56½

*In thousands of dollars except share data.

Exhibit 16.2   Recent Operating Summary (in thousands of dollars)

	1976	1975	1974	1973	1972	1971	1970
Net sales	281,995	257,451	223,188	195,367	191,402	166,919	153,512
Cost of sales	152,379	145,530	136,910	112,256	111,102	92,615	85,682
Gross profit	129,616	111,921	86,278	83,111	80,300	74,304	67,830
Marketing, administrative, and other expenses	96,371	84,336	70,222	60,861	58,304	56,190	52,217
Operating profit	33,245	27,585	16,056	22,250	21,996	18,114	15,613
Other income (expense), net	(134)	(1,891)	(85)	1,271	1,046	771	285
Income before income taxes	33,111	25,694	15,971	23,521	23,042	18,885	15,898
Provision for income taxes	15,820	12,400	7,750	11,300	11,300	9,100	8,282
Net income	17,291	13,294	8,221	12,221	11,742	9,785	7,606
Per average share outstanding:							
Net income	$2.14	$1.65	$1.02	$1.53	$1.48	$1.26	$ .98
Cash dividends declared	.76	.68	.64	.61	.56½	.54½	.54

CONSOLIDATED BALANCE SHEETS
Royal Crown Cola Co. and Subsidiaries

In thousands of dollars	December 31	
ASSETS	1976	1975
Current assets:		
Cash..	$ 2,648	1,537
Receivables less allowance for doubtful accounts:		
1976—$1,313; 1975—$1,193..	29,735	32,567
Inventories:		
Products finished and in process....................................	14,792	16,251
Materials and supplies...	16,633	14,969
Prepaid expenses..	3,474	2,060
Total current assets...	67,282	67,384
Investments and other assets...	3,067	3,597
Property, plant and equipment:		
Land...	3,548	2,631
Buildings..	23,294	18,683
Production equipment...	34,498	30,388
Delivery equipment...	24,422	19,415
	85,762	71,117
Less accumulated depreciation.......................................	36,758	32,734
	49,004	38,383
Goodwill..	11,766	3,198
	$131,119	112,562

See notes to consolidated financial statements.

In thousands of dollars	December 31	
LIABILITIES AND STOCKHOLDERS' EQUITY	1976	1975
Current liabilities:		
Current portion of long-term debt.......................................	$ 1,655	1,619
Dividends payable..	1,615	1,451
Accounts payable...	11,584	13,300
Accrued expenses..	7,686	8,001
Accrued income taxes..	1,914	5,569
Total current liabilities..	24,454	29,940
Long-term debt...	13,584	2,905
Deferred income taxes and deferred credits........................	5,078	3,088
Stockholders' Equity		
Preferred stock at no par:		
authorized 3,000,000 shares; none issued		
Common stock at $1 par:		
authorized 12,000,000 shares;		
issued and outstanding: 1976—8,075,216	8,075	
1975—8,059,016............................		8,059
Capital in excess of par...	8,291	8,093
Retained earnings..	71,637	60,477
Total stockholders' equity...	88,003	76,629
	$131,119	112,562

See notes to consolidated financial statements.

**Exhibit 16.4   Consolidated Statements of Changes in Financial Position
Royal Crown Cola Co. and Subsidiaries**

CONSOLIDATED STATEMENTS OF CHANGES IN FINANCIAL POSITION
Royal Crown Cola Co. and Subsidiaries

In thousands of dollars	Year Ended December 31	
	1976	1975
SOURCE OF WORKING CAPITAL		
From operations:		
Net income	$17,291	13,294
Depreciation and amortization	8,754	7,975
Deferred income taxes	1,774	(339)
Tax benefit of preacquisition operating		
loss carry-forward of Arby's	382	
Total from operations	28,201	20,930
Increase (decrease) in long-term debt	10,166	(1,025)
Disposals of property, plant and equipment	637	1,138
Decrease (increase) in other assets	772	(88)
Common stock issued	214	207
	39,990	21,162
APPLICATION OF WORKING CAPITAL		
Dividends	6,131	5,474
Additions to property, plant and equipment	15,435	8,762
Noncurrent tangible assets less noncurrent		
liabilities of Arby's	3,772	
Increase in goodwill	8,990	
Decrease (increase) in deferred credits	278	(219)
	34,606	14,017
Increase in working capital	$ 5,384	7,145
INCREASE (DECREASE) IN WORKING CAPITAL BY COMPONENT		
Cash	$ 1,111	(2,107)
Receivables	(2,832)	4,286
Inventories	205	(1,139)
Prepaid expenses	1,414	927
Notes payable and current long-term debt	(36)	13,964
Accounts and dividends payable	1,552	(1,086)
Accrued expenses	315	(2,180)
Accrued income taxes	3,655	(5,520)
Net increase in working capital	5,384	7,145
Working capital at beginning of year	37,444	30,299
Working capital at end of year	$42,828	37,444

See notes to consolidated financial statements.

company-owned restaurants. The national economy is still sluggish but is generally improving. Growth is expected for all four operating division industries. The winter of 1977 reduced anticipated citrus crops, but this is not expected to have a very detrimental impact on 1977 citrus revenues, as 1977 was projected to be an unusually large citrus crop year. In February, 1977, RC agreed to purchase the assets of the RC franchise operations in Dallas, Houston, and San Antonio in order to strengthen its position in a growing market. Current projections call for 125 new Arby's restaurants to be opened in 1977, both company-owned and franchised. Currently, one out of every three meals is eaten away from home. This is expected to grow to one in every two in a few years. Bottlers are apparently very pleased with McMahon's personal interest in their operations. The Coca Cola Co. has averaged 22.8 percent return on capital for the last five years—the best in the industry. Royal Crown, as second best, has averaged 18.7 percent.

On March 7, 1977 the United States Food and Drug Administration proposed suspension of authority to use saccharin in foods and beverages because of its cancer causing potential. During 1976, sales of beverages containing

Exhibit 16.5 A Diversified Consumer Products Company

| | Percent of Total | |
	Sales	Profit
Soft Drink	60	61
Fast Food	2	2
Citrus	17	17
Home Decor	21	20

Principal Brands

RC Cola	Texsun
Diet Rite	Couroc Serving Trays
Nehi	Frederick Cooper Lamps
Arby's	Hoyne Mirrors
Adams	Athens Furniture
Structural and	
National Picture Frames	

Financial Highlights ($ Millions)

	1976	1975	1974	Compound Annual Growth Rate 1974-1976
Net Sales	$281,995	257,451	223,188	+12%
Net Income	17,291	13,294	8,221	+45%
Earnings per Share	2.14	1.65	1.02	+45%
Dividends Declared	6,131	5,474	5,140	+ 9%
Stockholders' Equity	88,003	76,629	68,602	+13%
Return on Average Equity	21.0	18.3	12.2	+31%

saccharin represented approximately 17 percent of RC soft drink volume. In addition, the use of plastic bottles, an apparent industry trend, appears headed for stiff government and environmentalist opposition. RC has not pushed a plastic bottle program, but Coca Cola and PepsiCo have.

References

Baer, B. "The Soft Drink Industry." *Industry Review,* March 1976.

"Beverage Briefs." Robinson Humphrey, Atlanta, September 1976.

"Beverages." *Standard and Poor's Industry Survey.* Standard & Poor's Corporation, New York, pp. B-61–B-72, October 28, 1976.

Internal reports. Royal Crown Cola Company.

Royal Crown Cola Company Annual Report, for 1971, 1972, 1973, 1974, 1975, and 1976.

"The Royal Crown Cola Gets a Lot More Fizz." *Business Week,* March 14, 1977, pp. 84–85.

Discussion Questions

1. Evaluate Royal Crown's Turnaround Strategy.
2. How does Royal Crown's Master Strategy compare with the Coca Cola

Exhibit 16.6   Soft Drink ($ Millions)

	1976	1975	1974	Compound Annual Growth 1974-1976
Sales	169.4	159.0	133.6	13%
Operating Profit	20.1	19.2	7.2	67%
Operating Margin (%)	11.9	12.1	5.4	

Soft Drink 1976 Highlights

Record sales and profits
Greatest case volume increase since 1968
80% of bottlers in 64 oz. package
Record bottler participation in programs
Advertising and promotion dollars up 21%

Soft Drink

270 U.S. bottlers
65 bottlers overseas
15 company-owned plants
Third largest cola
Fourth largest diet drink
Approximately 5% of food store market
57% of volume in returnables

Exhibit 16.7 Citrus ($ Millions)

	1976	1975	1974	Compound Annual Growth 1974-1976
Sales	46.3	43.3	36.2	13%
Operating Profit	5.8	4.5	5.0	9%
Operating Margin (%)	12.5	10.4	13.8	

Citrus

4th Largest Citrus Processor
Adams 30% of Volume—70% Private Label
Texsun 50% of Sales in State of Texas
In 11 of 19 Major Markets Served
  Texsun Brand Is Number One

Exhibit 16.8 Home Decor ($ Millions)

	1976	1975	1974	Compound Annual Growth 1974-1976
Sales	59.9	55.1	53.5	6%
Operating Profit	6.6	3.8	3.8	32%
Operating Margin (%)	11.0	6.9	7.1	

Home Decor

Hoyne Industries – A leading mirror company
Frederick Cooper Lamps – Prestige decorator
  design lamps
Couroc – Quality hand inlaid serving trays
Athens Furniture – Middle priced bedroom
  furniture and accent pieces
Structural Industries – Picture frames
  and framed graphics

Company's Master Strategy (see "A Note on the Soft Drink Industry," Case 15, and "The Coca Cola Company—Part A," Case 17). How are they the same? Different? Why?

3. Was the Arby's purchase a sound move? Why? Why not?
4. What actions can any of the soft drink companies take on the saccharin ban?
5. What should RC's Master Strategy be in the future? Why? What should be its strategy for Royal Crown Cola? Why?

Exhibit 16.9   Arby's

	1976	1975	1974	Compound Annual Growth 1974-1976
Sales (Millions)*	$24.7	$17.7	$13.0	37%
Pre-Tax	3.8	2.9	1.7	49%
System Wide Sales	209.0	175.0	153.0	17%

*Fiscal year ended 10/31

Number of Restaurants

	1976	1975
Company-Owned	46	41
Franchise	522	460
Number of Franchisees	110	110

1976 Performance—Company-Owned Units

Average company-owned unit sales—$498 thousand
Sales for comparable units—up 22.5%
Customer count for comparable units—up 11.3%
Average customer check $2.25—up from $2.06
Overall price increase of 5%
46 company-owned restaurants in

Ohio	Pennsylvania
Tennessee	New Jersey
Florida	Michigan

Comparison to Industry

	Sales per Unit (in Thousands $)
McDonald's	$790
Burger King	560
Wendy's	510
Arby's	400
Hardee's	335
Burger Chef	325
Church's	300
KFC	290
Pizza Hut	180
A&W	155

17/The Coca-Cola Company—Part A: A Brief History

R. V. Coone

Coca-Cola was originated in Atlanta, Georgia, in 1886, by a pharmacist and druggist, Dr. John S. Pemberton. It has been said that Dr. Pemberton first produced the syrup for Coca-Cola in a three-legged pot in his back yard. The first sales for this new product occurred at Jacobs' pharmacy soda fountain on May 8, 1886, in the heart of Atlanta.

Dr. Pemberton's bookkeeper, Frank M. Robinson, suggested the name, "Coca-Cola," for the new product and wrote it out in the Spencerian script as we now see it on Coca-Cola bottles. However, the first advertising for the product was a simple block lettered sign hung to the awning of Jacobs' Drug Store. The first newspaper ad for Coca-Cola appeared on May 29, 1886, in the *Atlanta Journal* and invited Atlantans to try the "new and popular soda fountain drink" and proclaimed that Coca-Cola was "Delicious and Refreshing," a theme that is still echoed today.

For the remaining eight months of 1886, sales averaged 13 drinks per day, not a very auspicious beginning for a product whose sales now average more than 214,000,000 drinks a day. Those initial sales were confined to the city of Atlanta, and it was not until 1887 that Dr. Pemberton began to think about extending the sale of his product beyond the confines of the southern city. However, he did not fully realize the importance of the beverage he had created, and, being in need of funds due to ill health, he assigned a two-thirds interest, including the sole right to produce the syrup, to two Atlanta friends for $1,200. Subsequent to this, and only four months before he died, Dr. Pemberton and his son Charles accepted $500 for all remaining rights to the product. These rights were acquired by Asa G. Candler, a native of Villa Rica, Georgia, who had come to Atlanta 15 years before from Cartersville, Georgia. Mr. Candler became the second personality associated with the still relatively unknown product, but before long he had bought additional rights and soon he had acquired complete control. Mr. Candler later estimated that the sole ownership of the company had cost him $2,300.

Mr. Candler had a flair for merchandising, and by 1892 the sales of Coca-Cola syrup had increased almost ten-fold. In view of this, Mr. Candler disposed of his drug business; and with his brother, Attorney John S. Candler, F. M. Robinson, and two other friends, he formed a Georgia Corporation, The Coca-Cola Company, with capital stock of $100,000. To protect the product, the trademark, "Coca-Cola," first used in the marketplace in 1886, was registered in the United States Patent Office on January 31, 1893, and has been renewed periodically as required since then. By 1895, three years

Source: Certain materials are reproduced by permission of The Coca-Cola Company, Inc.

after The Coca-Cola Company had been launched, Asa G. Candler announced in his annual report to stockholders: "Coca-Cola is now drunk in every state and territory in the United States."

Until this time most of the Coca-Cola expansion efforts had been centered around the booming soda fountain sales. Large scale bottling of Coca-Cola only became possible in 1899 when Benjamin F. Thomas and Joseph B. Whitehead secured from Mr. Candler the exclusive right to bottle and sell the beverage in practically the entire United States. They opened their first bottling plant in Chattanooga, Tennessee, in 1899; and a second plant in Atlanta, Georgia, the following year. They enlisted the financial assistance of John T. Lupton and assessed their situation. Realizing their inability to cover the entire country with bottling plants, they began to seek out competent individuals in communities who would establish bottling operations. In return for their willingness to invest the necessary time and capital in the venture, these individuals were given defined geographic areas in which to develop a market and sell Coca-Cola. Such was the genesis of today's locally owned and operated Coca-Cola bottling industry, a significant factor in the development of the current widespread distribution of Coca-Cola.

In 1919, The Coca-Cola Company was sold by the Candler interest to Ernest Woodruff, an Atlanta banker, and a group he had organized for $25,000,000. Soon thereafter the business was re-incorporated as a Delaware corporation and its common stock placed on public sale for $40 per share.

Robert Winship Woodruff was elected President of The Coca-Cola Company in 1923. This youthful, vigorous, 33-year-old son of Ernest envisioned Coca-Cola being within arm's reach of anyone who desired it, even on an international basis. To give tangible form to his vision, he organized a Foreign Sales Department in 1926; and by changing the distribution method of the syrup to concentrate for all syrup being processed overseas, transportation costs were reduced substantially and overseas sales started to rise rapidly. In addition, he emphasized product quality and defined quality standards for every phase of the bottling operation. He also instigated a remarkable advertising campaign and threw his marketing expertise and force behind the bottle, the package which could travel anywhere. By the end of 1928, five years after Woodruff became President, the sale of Coca-Cola in bottles had increased by 65 percent and for the first time bottle sales exceeded sales at the soda fountain, a situation which still exists today.

Robert Woodruff's leadership brought Coca-Cola to unrivaled height in commercial enterprise. He retired in 1955 but has continued to provide his brand of leadership to the business as a Director and Chairman of the Board's Finance Committee. The further development of The Coca-Cola Company is discussed later in the case.

Sales Innovations

Concepts accepted as commonplace in modern merchandising were revolutionary when Woodruff took over as President. The Coca-Cola Company developed the innovative six-bottle carton which came into use during the early 20s to allow the customer additional ease in bringing home more Coca-Cola. By 1928, when bottle sales topped fountain sales, the carton was accepted as one of the industry's most potent merchandising tools. The carton was joined by another revolutionary merchandiser in 1929, the metal, open top cooler from which Coca-Cola could be served ice cold at the retail outlet. Progressively, the cooler for vending the drink was improved with mechanical refrigeration and automatic coin control to the degree that now factories, offices, and many other institutions have become outlets where Coke can be enjoyed on the spot from self-service vending machines.

Other innovations include a distinctive glass for Coca-Cola, adopted as standard in 1929, much like the trademark bottle, which served to advertise the product. Currently this glass is used in thousands of soda fountains throughout the world, and its use has been extended further by a large 12-ounce size.

The Chicago World Fair of 1933 triggered the introduction of automatic fountain dispensers where syrup and carbonated water were mixed at the time the drink was served. By 1937, the automatic dispenser had become an important adjunct at the fountain, and improved models of this item are in current use across the land.

Promotion and Advertisement

Few firms have enjoyed the success that Coca-Cola has realized from its numerous themes and slogans. "The Pause That Refreshes," which appeared in *The Saturday Evening Post* in February, 1929, had a lasting impact. It was the descendant of a long line of great slogans such as: the oldest, Dr. Pemberton's "Delicious and Refreshing" in 1886; "Thirst Knows No Season" in 1922; "It Had To Be Good To Get Where It Is" in 1925; and "Around The Corner From Anywhere" in 1927. A few of the many to follow often re-echoed the refreshing idea: "It's The Refreshing Thing To Do"—1936; "Global High-Sign"—1944; "Sign Of Good Taste"—1957; "Be Really Refreshed"—1959. The highly successful "Things Go Better With Coke" was introduced in 1963. "It's The Real Thing," first used in 1942, was expanded in 1969, and supported a whole new merchandising stance for the product during the 70s.

Down through the years advertising for Coca-Cola has constantly changed with the trends of the times. However, the overriding concept has always been one of refreshment, highlighting the pleasant things of life with distinctive themes that were acceptable anywhere. The 1886 block lettered, oil cloth sign that was hung to the awning of Jacobs' Drug Store soon gave way to more pleasing types of advertising for the outside and interior of the store, to painted walls, and to newspapers. Then leading magazines reflected in impressive four-color ads the image of the drink's quality and distinction. In 1925, nationwide use of the 24-sheet outdoor posters began, and the electrical spectacular arose illuminating crossroads of the world from London's Piccadilly Circus to Tokyo's Ginza.

In the mid-1920s, radio became a forceful medium of communications, and it continues today to be a large segment of the merchandising mix for Coca-Cola.

In point-of-sale advertising for the four million worldwide outlets, Coke is unsurpassed. The quality and quantity of materials to identify the point where the drink is available and to assist the dealer in moving the product have continued to expand year by year.

Edgar Bergen and his dummy, Charlie McCarthy, were the first stars to appear on network television for Coke in 1950. Use of this marvelous electronic advertising medium grew swiftly to giant proportions and remains so today.

In 1970, Coke received a face lift which gave it a new look. As the new look became familiar to consumers, they saw a design that symbolized the way they identified Coca-Cola, one which was a bright bold red with the trademark underscored by a dramatic curve, which is a visual adaption of the distinctive bottle shape. The new look for Coke was largely a matter of style in order to maintain its leadership in the marketplace. Coke needed a strong identity and a style that would fit the tempo of the times, yet it had to retain its familiarity as an old and trusted friend with its great heritage intact.

From 1900–1950, the challenge was to spread Coca-Cola and make it the best known drink in the soft drink business. "The Pause that Refreshes" campaign was instrumental in accomplishing this because it offered many suggestions for occasions the consumer could enjoy Coke. It got across the fact that anytime was a good time to "Pause and Refresh" with ice cold Coca-Cola. The staying power of this campaign was incredible, but changes in the marketplace and challenges from competitors caused the company to revitalize its advertising. To accomplish this, the account was moved to McCann-Erickson, Inc.

McCann-Erickson realized they had their job cut out for them, and in their search for a suitable refrain to reflect the new look for Coke, they recorded several themes for radio, one of which was "Things go better with Coke." It tested well and, in addition, it was a logical follow-up campaign to "The Pause that Refreshes" because it told people what would happen after the pause. Essentially, it said that life would go better with Coke. In January of 1962, a rough television commercial featuring the line, "Things go better with Coke," was tested, and it also did extremely well. After much refinement the phrase, "Things go better" emerged in 1963 as the next official phase in advertising for Coke in the United States

By the winter of 1964–65, with the penetration of the above theme about as high as was possible, it was decided to relax the discipline of one sight, one sound, in order to tailor the message to various groups. It was determined to use television as an all-family medium, radio to appeal primarily to younger people, and print (magazines, outdoor signs, etc.) to make sure that the sensory appeal of Coca-Cola—its sparkle, its color, its thirst quenching, refreshing look—would stay topmost throughout America.

As successful as "Things go better with Coke" was as an advertising campaign, The Coca-Cola Company realized that in today's market nobody could afford to stand pat for long. It was time for a new campaign that would be not only right for the product, Coca-Cola, but one which met the challenges of competitors head-on with a statement of truth—for Coca-Cola is the real thing. The line "It's the real thing" was first used for Coca-Cola in 1938, and, by 1942, it was being used extensively in radio programs sponsored by The Coca-Cola Company. "It's the real thing" was introduced in all media in October 1969, and was managed through a series of phases planned to keep the basic selling message constantly fresh.

In 1973, a series of commercials was released which further expanded the theme. These were aptly called "short story" commercials. They portrayed not only situations which communicated product messages but situations that helped viewers and listeners to remember those simple moments of enjoyment they may have experienced. The "Look up, America" series of commercials was aired in 1974, which further expanded the theme of "It's the real thing."

In May 1976, a totally new advertising campaign for Coke was introduced which positioned the brand as the soft drink for all occasions. Themed, "Coke Adds Life to . . . ," the new campaign heavily emphasized that all of the markets for Coke are comprised of the young and the young-at-heart. This campaign replaced the "It's the real thing" advertising. "Coke Adds Life" continues, like all its predecessor campaigns, to stress the traditional refreshment message for Coca-Cola and gives emphasis to the product's position with food, fun, and leisure.

Lessons of Leadership

J. Paul Austin, Chairman of The Coca-Cola Company, is a man who wastes little time. This becomes obvious when one speaks to him. His answers are short and to the point. That he is a man of action also becomes obvious when one considers his career. Mr. Austin joined The Coca-Cola Company in 1949 as an attorney. In 1962, he became President. By 1966, he was the Chief Executive Officer, and in 1970, he became Chairman.

Few top executives among America's largest organizations have advanced so rapidly. Additionally, few companies can match the pace of The Coca-Cola Company's phenomenal growth under Mr. Austin's leadership. In 1962, when he became President, sales were $567 million, and earnings per share (adjusted for subsequent splits) were 85 cents. In 1977, sales were $3.5 billion with profits at $326 million or $2.67 per share.

The following is a question and answer interview conducted by the editor of *Nation's Business* in June, 1976, with Mr. Austin on some of the do's and don'ts of running a global company.

Question:
The Coca-Cola Company is one of the world's greatest franchisers. You're dependent on bottling companies that are franchisees. How do you keep them working hard?

By giving them the opportunity to build good businesses. Being in business for yourself is one of the biggest motivators there is.

When a franchise system is in the hands of competent, motivated individuals, it is the greatest distribution system there is.

Question:
What can the company do when a competitor is gaining in a territory assigned to an uncompetitive franchisee?

In cases like that, we send in so-called combat teams of a half-dozen topflight fixer-uppers. The team helps the franchisee get reoriented. Once franchisees are shown how to operate efficiently, nine out of ten of them do.

Here in the United States, a contract between The Coca-Cola Company and a franchisee has a provision—with good reason—whereby the contract can be eliminated. On the other hand, if a franchisee operates well, the franchise is in perpetuity. It is handed down through the generations.

Our franchisees abroad have a cooperative marketing program which spells out clearly what resources we and the bottlers assign to reach mutually agreed upon goals.

Question:
How has The Coca-Cola Company maintained such good public relations for so long?

I'll give you a definition of good public relations: Getting caught in the act of doing something good.

Obviously, we've had good public relations people who are helpful in shaping our ideas and advising us in advance of certain things to avoid doing. Also, we have a rule: Don't tell lies.

Question:
What are some of the other rules the company abides by?

Our basic policy is to be a good citizen wherever we are.

Being a good citizen in, for example, Kansas City, involves many things. Showing an interest in the community. Working on hospital drives. Joining the Chamber of Commerce and other good organizations. Running a good business. On and on, the list can go.

We are impeccably accurate in paying our taxes—all kinds of taxes—at home and abroad. We staff our operations in the U.S. and abroad with people of high moral standards. Our people are gentlemen and ladies, and we don't have to write down the things for them to do. They already know.

At the same time, they are tough operators.

Question:
The Coca-Cola Company has a good record of innovation in marketing and management. Why?

We select our marketing people with special care. We want motivated people, people with professional pride. Because they are motivated, I don't have to go around giving pep talks. If I did, I don't think anything would happen.

The Coca-Cola Company has always had esprit de corps.

I think I can claim that we have more than kept up with the pack in marketing.

We go strong for training and retraining of all personnel. To improve our training programs, we bought the Sterling Institute in Washington, D. C., several years ago. Sterling has the best technology and electronics equipment for teaching all sorts of employees to do all sorts of jobs. We set out to find the best company and to buy it, and we did.

Question:
How about technical innovation?

The Coca-Cola Company is far advanced in computer efficiency, and that's something a lot of companies can't honestly say. We intend to stay ahead.

We have too many innovations in equipment and process design to list. They go back to the 19th century.

Of course, it is well-known that several designers have said the shape of the bottle for Coke is just about perfect.

The company came up with the world's first six-pack. We have some of the original cartons in our company museum, and they aren't so different from six-pack cartons used today. This means they must have been pretty good to begin with.

Years ago, we sold Coke syrup in wooden barrels. Some bottlers got the idea of cutting the barrels in half, filling them with ice, and selling cooled Coca-Cola. That was the first machine for Coke, you might say. That ended when we went into metal barrels.

More recently we have come up with the technology for getting protein from various sources. We use the protein in a new nutritive beverage we call Samson. We've test-marketed Samson abroad, and it is a handsome success.

We expect to sell Samson in many countries where the people may not have quite the right diet. They may need more protein, and Samson definitely will supplement their diets in this respect. We also expect to sell Samson in certain areas in the United States.

One of the best sources of protein, by the way, is whey. In processing milk into cheese, what's left is whey. If the whey were dumped in streams and rivers, it would pollute them. Through our Aqua-Chem subsidiary, we purify the whey, making use of the protein it contains. This process turns a potential pollutant into a protein source to be incorporated in product formulations.

Question:
Your company owes only about $10 million in long-term debt. How can a $3 billion-a-year company get by on such tiny debt?
The large portion of our bottlers are self-financed. They own their own businesses, so The Coca-Cola Company never has to put out enormous amounts of money.
This is the nature of the franchise system, although I must admit some other franchisers owe huge sums.

Question:
However, The Coca-Cola Company has done some big league diversifying, hasn't it? What has been acquired?
We are pleased with all of our lines. I'll just quickly list them: Minute Maid frozen concentrate citrus juices; Hi-C fruit drinks; Duncan Foods, with several fine lines including coffees and teas; and Aqua-Chem, a water conditioning firm. And, of course, we have Tab, Fresca, Sprite, and several other soft drinks, which come in many different sizes and types of containers.[1]

Question:
You are directly producing in 138 countries, which is the world's record for a company. How do you keep track of so much in so many places?
We have divided the company into eight profit centers: soft drink operations in the U.S.; Canada; Latin America; Europe; Africa; the Far East; our citrus, fruit drink, coffee, and tea operations in the Foods Division; and Aqua-Chem.
Annual budgets are a key element of control. Every year, each profit center prepares a budget and sends it to our Atlanta headquarters for study and consolidation. We cut and fit each, then take them to the Board of Directors for approval.
By controlling budgets and money, we maintain control over this far-flung company. We are in almost as many countries as there are in the United Nations.

Question:
How do you keep Coca-Cola the same, whether it is bottled in Uganda or in the company's hometown, Atlanta?
We have the technology to, as we call it, bring any kind of water down to neutral. In other words, water treated in this fashion has no effect on the unique taste of Coke syrup used in bottling Coca-Cola. Purity of water is absolute.

1. In addition, The Coca-Cola Company has since acquired wine companies, as noted later in the case.

Question:
What would you do if you learned that a big operation like Mar-
riotte or McDonald's planned to sell another cola drink and stop
selling Coke?

What we try to do is mend our fences in advance. We maintain
the best possible customer relations. We have trained people
who are ready to help our customers in their business. We don't
just sell them syrup and walk out of the shop. We make real contributions to our customers' companies.

Question:
The soft drink business is a hot one competitively. Hasn't Pepsi
gotten ahead of Coke in sales in food stores?

In supermarkets, they have grown closer to our level. But, when
you throw in all the other food stores, that statement won't stand
up. Coca-Cola is ahead.

Increasing the percentage of business a company does in a
more mature market like the United States is difficult. I don't mean
there is no growth. I mean growth is particularly hard to come by.
We've been in business for a long time and we're still growing.

We recently established some working relationships with the
Soviet Union. A group of our technicians went over to discuss
building a plant for the production of instant tea. The benefit to
the Soviet Union would be to have the convenience of instant tea.
You know, the Soviets drink a lot of tea.[2]

Question:
Throwaway containers, which the company makes use of along
with returnable bottles, have come in for a lot of criticism. Do
you see any new developments in throwaway container technology?

We are in a program with a chemical company to market a
plastic bottle that has all of the pluses of plastics but is one that
can be recycled. What you do is pick up used bottles, reduce
them to powder, and form the powder into a new bottle. We are
in commercial production and marketing in Providence, Rhode
Island. And we are exceeding our budget sales substantially.

2. In March, 1977, The Coca-Cola Company signed an agreement with
the Organizing Committee for the 1980 Moscow Olympics naming the
company the exclusive soft drink supplier for the Games. Another agreement signed with the Soviet Trading Organizations, Sojuzplodoimport and
Technopromimport, provides for the producton and sale of Fanta soft
drinks in the Soviet Union.

The instant tea project continues under development, and a whey plant
is being established in the U.S.S.R. to produce protein from cheese whey.

The company also is collaborating with the U.S.S.R. Ministry of Food
Industry and the Ministry of Meat and Dairy Industry on a number of
research and other projects.

Figure 17.1 Coca-Cola International's Organizational Structure, 1978

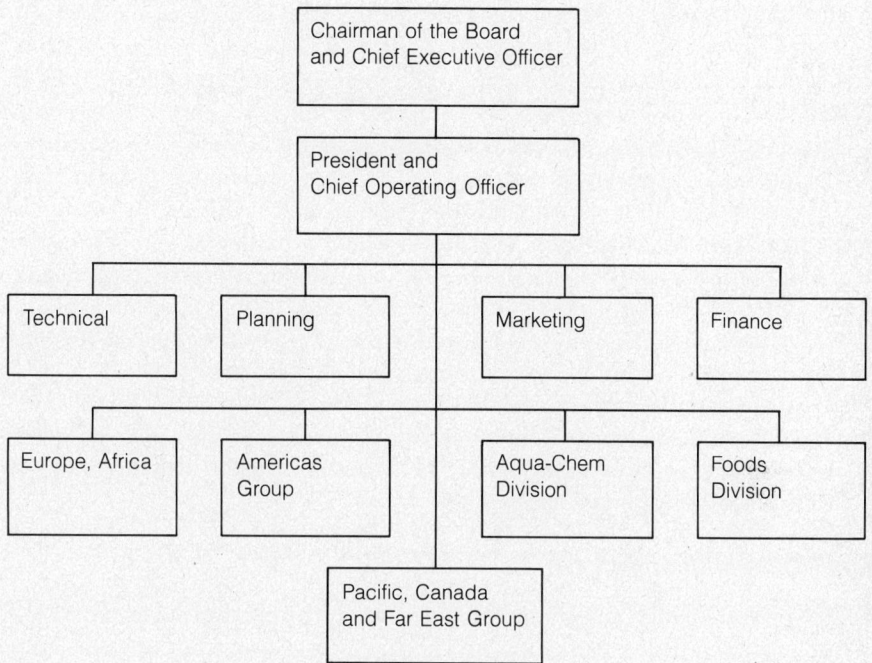

Soft Drink Operations

The Coca-Cola Company is the world's leading manufacturer of soft drink beverages, principally Coca-Cola. To effectively administer and operate a vast network of businesses, the company primarily employs the franchise method of distribution. The parent organization produces the basic ingredients of syrup, concentrate, and beverage bases for Coca-Cola and the company's other soft drinks and sells these to more than 1,400 bottlers in over 135 countries.

These bottling plants, with few exceptions, are owned and operated by independent businessmen who are native to the area or country in which they are located. By contract with The Coca-Cola Company, the local businesses are authorized to bottle and sell Coca-Cola and other soft drinks within certain territorial boundaries and other conditions that insure the highest standards of quality and uniformity.

The independent bottler provides the required capital investments for land, buildings, machinery and equipment, trucks, bottles, and cases that are necessary to operate the business. Most other supplies are purchased from indigenous sources where possible, often creating new supply industries and areas of employment within the local economy.

In addition to the above, the company also actively engages in management guidance to help insure the profitable growth of the bottler's business, thus enhancing the value of the franchise. The management counseling covers a broad spectrum of business experience such as quality control, marketing, advertising, engineering, and financial and personnel training.

The company's operations are managed by geographical subdivisions primarily known as divisions, regions, and districts, each with its own resident manager who is responsible for operations within a particular area(s), country, or group of countries. In addition to maintaining division, region, and district offices, the company also owns and operates syrup, concentrate, and beverage base manufacturing plants, as well as a few bottling plants. Despite field decentralization and the need for programs indigenous to a specific locale, there is a certain degree of uniformity in the methods used to market the products around the world. This uniformity is achieved through a program of management services coordinated by The Coca-Cola Company's headquarters offices in Atlanta, Georgia.

The ABC's of Distribution

Other innovations have also made their debut in the ever waged battle to increase efficiency in the marketing of The Coca-Cola Company's increasingly varied products. The proliferation of product sizes and types created several difficult distribution problems; namely: out of stock conditions on the route and thus in the outlets, rationing of products, and a high return of undelivered goods to the plant.

In an attempt to overcome these problems, the company advised the testing of several approaches.

Specialized Routing. Bottlers would put only Coca-Cola on one truck, all allied products on another—or possibly all home market products on one truck, and cold drinks on another. This reduced some of the problems but did not eliminate them—so another method was tried.

Advance Selling. This method simply involves securing orders prior to the route delivery. There are two modes of implementing this method, each complementing the other:

On-Premise Advance Salesman. The salesman visits his outlets in advance, solicits sales, and records orders. At the end of the day he sends all his invoices to the dispatcher for future delivery.

Tel-Sell. This method consists of telephoning predetermined locations or outlets on preselected days and soliciting orders. It is used primarily for low volume outlets. At the end of the day the tel-seller sends all orders to the dispatcher for future delivery.

The dispatcher at the end of the day totals his orders for each route for the following day and thus knows how much of each product to place on each route truck.

Diversification and Integration

Until the mid-50s, Coca-Cola was the company's one product, and it could be purchased in the familiar 6½-ounce bottle or in a glass at the fountain. By 1954, changing consumer habits and preferences dictated a wider choice in packaging adaptable to the family's greater mobility, larger rate of consumption, and desire for convenience. As a result, to the 6½-ounce bottle size were added larger sizes; 10-, 12-, and 26-ounce bottles and, in a few years, still another, a 16-ounce size was filling yet another market segment need.

Another method of dispensing Coca-Cola, called "Pre-Mix," was put into use in 1954. Through this mode, the finished beverage could be prepared in bulk in the bottling plant and delivered to outlets where equipment automatically refrigerated and dispensed it in cups. This method placed Coke in many more types of outlets, such as, where paper cups were more suitable than bottles, or where there was no water connection for "Post-Mix" dispensing at fountains.

Packaging of Coca-Cola in cans began in 1955, although for several years the Armed Forces overseas enjoyed this package exclusively. However, by 1959, the civilian consumer began to see Coke in 12-ounce flat-top cans on the market shelves. By 1961, as consumers increased demands for greater convenience, the company began to test market no-deposit, no-return bottles similar in design to the distinctively shaped returnable bottle. Convenience likewise led to the development, in 1964, of lift-top cans and bottle crowns, thus eliminating the once indispensable opener.

Soft drink history was made in 1969 with the announcement of experiments with a plastic bottle for Coke. A larger 16-ounce can appeared. Resealable crowns for bottles boosted the convenience feature as the 1970s began. Bottle sizes grew to 32, 48, and 64 ounces and comparable metric sizes. One-way glass, plastic and plastic encased bottles were introduced.

Innovative packaging is a way of life at The Coca-Cola Company, always striving to present Coca-Cola in a most pleasing package consistent with its distinctive quality.

During the late 50s and following the initiation of diversification of packages for Coca-Cola, several new soft drinks were added for distribution by the local bottlers. In 1960, the Fanta line of flavored soft drinks was expanded to national markets. Sprite, a lemon-lime specialty drink arrived nationally the following year. The company's first low-calorie beverage, TAB, was introduced in 1963 and was joined in national markets by a second low-calorie, citrus-flavored drink, Fresca, in 1966. A line of mixers under the trademark of Santiba bowed in during 1970, and during 1972, Mr. PIBB, a blended beverage, was placed on the market.

Other diversifications took place beginning with the company's purchase in 1960 of the Minute Maid Corporation. With this acquisition, the company entered the citrus beverage markets. Through Tenco, a division of Minute Maid, it became one of the world's largest producers of private label instant coffee and tea. By merger with Duncan Foods Company in 1964, the company became one of the leading coffee importing, processing, and marketing firms in the country. Extending beyond the beverage industry, the company acquired Aqua-Chem, Inc., in 1970. It manufactures water pollution control equipment, seawater desalters, and packaged steam and hot water generators.

In 1975, the company acquired Coca-Cola Bottling Company (Thomas), Inc., Coca-Cola Bottling Works (Thomas), Inc. and Coca-Cola Bottling Works (3rd), Inc. This was the last parent bottler acquisition, begun 50 years previously.

On October 29, 1976, the company entered into an agreement and Plan of Merger with The Taylor Wine Company, Inc., and on January 21, 1977, Taylor Wine Company, Inc. became a wholly-owned subsidiary of The Coca-Cola Company. Additional actions have been taken with regard to forming a wine group. Sterling Vinyards of Napa Valley, California, was acquired in August, 1977, and Gonzales & Co., Inc., which operates Monterey Vinyard of Gonzales, California, was acquired in November, 1977.

Foods Division

In August 1967, by action of the Board of Directors of The Coca-Cola Company, the international beverage firm's Foods Division was created. Headquartered in Houston, Texas, the new division brought together two separate divisions of The Coca-Cola Company: Minute Maid Company, world leader in frozen fruit juices and fruit drinks; and Duncan Foods Company, roaster and marketer of prominent regional coffee brands and allied products.

The booming frozen concentrate industry is young in relation to how time is measured in the food industry. The future developers of Minute Maid Frozen Concentrated Orange Juice were working on a powdered orange juice for the Army Quartermaster Corps in 1945. When the war ended, that company turned its attention to perfecting the product in frozen concentrate form instead. As a result, this company was the first to offer a fresh frozen orange juice to the American consumer.

By the late 1940s, Minute Maid Orange Juice had grown into a multi-million dollar factor in the food business. In 1954, the Minute Maid Company acquired Snow Crop Frozen Concentrates and Hi-C Fruit Drinks from Clinton Foods. Today, Hi-C is the leading brand in its field, and Snow Crop Orange Juice is a best seller in the many marketing centers where it is available.

The Foods Division owns or leases some 35,000 acres of groves in Florida's noted citrus belt. These groves supply about one-third of the company's raw material needs. Of the yield from the company groves, 80 percent goes into the processing of concentrate and 20 percent is marketed as fresh fruit.

While the Foods Division processes and markets a variety of citrus and other fruit juices, ades, and drinks, the mainstay of the concentrate family is orange juice. To support this operation the company maintains three processing plants in Florida and one in California, plus can manufacturing plants in New Jersey and Indiana.

The gathering and processing season for citrus extends through six months of the year. It can be seen how important large-capacity, efficient warehousing facilities are to the concentrate industry. It is also obvious that strict temperature control is a must for frozen concentrates right up to the moment the retail shopper lifts the can out of the frozen foods cabinet.

Hi-C Fruit Drinks that are displayed in unrefrigerated areas of the store also start out as a solidly-frozen fruit base containing concentrated fruit juice, natural fruit flavor, Vitamin C, and coloring. This base is placed in 55 gallon drums, shipped in a frozen state, in which it remains until reconstituted according to the strict Hi-C formula to meet local demand. This rigid quality control is what gives Hi-C Fruit Drinks the natural flavor that is responsible for their unquestioned leadership in the fruit drink field.

The histories of the Foods Division's leading coffee brands dip considerably into the past. The Maryland Club brand had its beginnings in a one-man roasting operation that was started in Houston, Texas, in 1917. The Butter-Nut brand developed from a Government Post Trader's enterprise which started in Central Nebraska in 1864.

Distribution of coffee brands is regional in nature, conforming generally to the location of processing plants. Maryland Club, roasted in Houston, Texas, is sold in seven South Central and Southwestern states. Butter-Nut, produced at plants in Nebraska and California, is distributed in the Midwest, West, and parts of the Southeast. Three other Foods Division brands enjoy strong franchises in localized markets: Admiration, popular in Texas and Louisiana; Thomas J. Webb, distributed in greater Chicago; and Huggins Gourmet "Mocha Java," sold in the big Southern California market.

Aqua-Chem, Inc.

This company subsidiary is a pollution fighter. It is a pioneer and leader of a vital, highly technical, and curiously twentieth century industry, which like the exploration of space represents a new frontier for mankind. Technology is the business of Aqua-Chem, Inc. Trying the untried, perfecting the promising design, Aqua-Chem, Inc. through three decades has developed the widest capability for dealing with the varied pollution problems of any company in the field.

A world which is now facing up to the damage it has done to its environment finds Aqua-Chem, Inc. a leading source of equipment which can pro-

The Coca-Cola Company and Subsidiaries
Consolidated Statements of Profit and Loss

	YEAR ENDED DECEMBER 31,	
	1977	**1976**
Net sales..................................	**$3,559,878,282**	$3,094,523,628
Cost of goods sold.........................	**2,009,700,447**	1,728,960,485
GROSS PROFIT..........................	**1,550,177,835**	1,365,563,143
Selling, administrative and general expenses....	**957,072,552**	837,857,757
OPERATING PROFIT.....................	**593,105,283**	527,705,386
Other income.............................	**42,871,486**	47,052,697
	635,976,769	574,758,083
Less other deductions......................	**30,634,018**	29,232,022
PROFIT BEFORE TAXES ON INCOME......	**605,342,751**	545,526,061
Provision for taxes on income................	**279,123,000**	254,809,937
NET PROFIT.............................	**$ 326,219,751**	$ 290,716,124
Net profit per share of common stock.........................	**$2.67**	$2.38

Consolidated Statements of Earned Surplus

	YEAR ENDED DECEMBER 31,	
	1977	**1976**
Balance at January 1:		
The Coca-Cola Company and Subsidiaries	**$1,266,268,875**	$1,096,716,913
The Taylor Wine Company, Inc...............		40,365,750
Adjusted balance at January 1................		1,137,082,663
Net profit for the year......................	**326,219,751**	290,716,124
Dividends paid in cash:		
The Coca-Cola Company (per share— 1977, $1.54; 1976, $1.325)...............	**188,170,329**	158,787,031
The Taylor Wine Company, Inc., prior to combination............................		2,742,881
BALANCE AT DECEMBER 31	**$1,404,318,297**	$1,266,268,875

See Notes to Consolidated Financial Statements

Exhibit 17.2   The Coca-Cola Company and Subsidiaries
Consolidated Statements of Changes in Financial Position

	YEAR ENDED DECEMBER 31,	
	1977	1976
SOURCE OF WORKING CAPITAL		
From operations:		
Net profit for year............................	$326,219,751	$290,716,124
Add charges not requiring outlay of working		
capital during the year:		
Provision for depreciation....................	81,082,646	71,303,981
Deferred income taxes......................	17,466,913	14,457,232
Other.......................................	21,249,112	13,720,164
TOTAL FROM OPERATIONS................	446,018,422	390,197,501
Increase in long-term debt........................	5,905,048	0
Disposals of property, plant and equipment..........	16,711,101	15,816,450
Proceeds from exercise of stock options............	764,880	840,049
Tax benefit from optioned shares sold..............	154,200	224,900
	469,553,651	407,078,900
APPLICATION OF WORKING CAPITAL		
Cash dividends:		
The Coca-Cola Company.......................	188,170,329	158,787,031
The Taylor Wine Company, Inc...................	0	2,742,881
Additions to property, plant and equipment..........	260,913,663	184,721,607
Increase in marketable securities—non-current	30,151,162	11,950,177
Increase in miscellaneous investments.............	1,908,711	18,780,132
Decrease in long-term debt......................	0	1,201,691
Other.......................................	9,814,858	25,933
	490,958,723	378,209,452
INCREASE (DECREASE) IN WORKING		
CAPITAL...............................	(21,405,072)	28,869,448
Working capital at beginning of year...............	520,793,699	491,924,251
WORKING CAPITAL AT END OF YEAR.......	$499,388,627	$520,793,699
INCREASE (DECREASE) IN WORKING		
CAPITAL, BY COMPONENTS		
Cash...	$ 46,687,391	$ 19,155,073
Marketable securities............................	(62,246,148)	(43,331,433)
Trade accounts receivable........................	38,191,881	48,077,146
Inventories....................................	35,948,411	49,008,664
Prepaid expenses...............................	2,385,713	3,350,171
Notes payable.................................	(1,646,876)	(724,783)
Current maturities of long-term debt...............	536,809	(3,402,147)
Accounts payable and accrued accounts....	(56,845,421)	(62,751,461)
Accrued taxes—including taxes on income..........	(24,416,832)	19,488,218
INCREASE (DECREASE) IN WORKING		
CAPITAL...............................	$ (21,405,072)	$ 28,869,448

See Notes to Consolidated Financial Statements

The Coca-Cola Company and Subsidiaries

Assets

	DECEMBER 31,	
	1977	**1976**
CURRENT:		
Cash....................................	**$ 149,633,047**	$ 102,945,656
Marketable securities—1977, at cost		
(approximates market price); 1976 at		
market price (cost, $260,883,168).........	**198,219,118**	260,465,266
Trade accounts receivable (less allowance—		
1977, $7,218,909; 1976, $6,984,611).......	**275,508,790**	237,316,909
Inventories...............................	**432,966,578**	397,018,167
Prepaid expenses.........................	**31,922,307**	29,536,594
TOTAL CURRENT ASSETS............	**1,088,249,840**	1,027,282,592
MARKETABLE SECURITIES—at cost		
(approximates market price).................	**68,392,434**	38,241,272
MISCELLANEOUS INVESTMENTS AND		
OTHER ASSETS...........................	**94,849,109**	92,940,398
PROPERTY, PLANT AND EQUIPMENT:		
Land and improvements....................	**82,183,631**	71,744,181
Buildings................................	**396,088,541**	324,474,794
Machinery and equipment..................	**743,205,844**	656,454,914
Containers...............................	**185,665,467**	158,905,503
	1,407,143,483	1,211,579,392
Less allowance for depreciation.............	**535,048,473**	485,447,525
	872,095,010	726,131,867
FORMULAE, TRADE-MARKS, GOODWILL		
AND CONTRACT RIGHTS.................	**100,338,015**	94,908,059
	$2,223,924,408	$1,979,504,188

See Notes to Consolidated Financial Statements

Exhibit 17.3 Continued

Liabilities

	DECEMBER 31,	
	1977	1976
CURRENT:		
Notes payable.............................$	37,281,226	$ 35,634,350
Current maturities of long-term debt.........	4,615,549	5,152,358
Accounts payable and accrued accounts......	390,832,357	333,986,936
Accrued taxes—including taxes on income....	156,132,081	131,715,249
TOTAL CURRENT LIABILITIES........	588,861,213	506,488,893
LONG-TERM DEBT..........................	13,762,022	7,856,974
DEFERRED INCOME TAXES.................	64,092,379	46,625,466
CAPITAL STOCK AND SURPLUS:		
Common stock—no par value;		
authorized 140,000,000 shares;		
(issued: 1977, 122,604,113 shares;		
1976, 122,574,406 shares).......	61,679,271	61,664,367
Capital surplus...........................	106,564,726	105,964,326
Earned surplus..........................	1,404,318,297	1,266,268,875
	1,572,562,294	1,433,897,568
Less treasury stock—at cost		
(1977, 401,338 shares; 1976, 401,958 shares)	15,353,500	15,364,713
	1,557,208,794	1,418,532,855
	$2,223,924,408	$1,979,504,188

See Notes to Consolidated Financial Statements

vide good water from bad water, eliminate pollutants from industrial effluents, and virtually eliminate air pollution from industrial processing and solid waste disposal.

All of which gives rise to the question—why did The Coca-Cola Company, a leader in the beverage business, acquire Aqua-Chem, Inc., an industrial firm known for its packaged boilers, seawater desalters, and water treatment systems?

Diversification? No, not just for the sake of diversification at least.

Aqua-Chem, Inc., offered The Coca-Cola Company a unique opportunity, and J. Paul Austin, Chairman of the Board of The Coca-Cola Company, explained why in an interview which appeared in *Forbes,* July 15, 1970, shortly after the acquisition: "The Coca-Cola Company already is in the water business," said Austin. "Water is what carries our product, and the water condition in this country is deteriorating. Aqua-Chem, Inc., was the leader in the technology of water. For The Coca-Cola Company to use its resources to bolster a company that is one of the leaders in anti-pollution was a logical approach to take."

Aqua-Chem, Inc., is divided into two major divisions: Water Technologies Division and Cleaver-Brooks Division.

The Water Technologies Division is responsible for all seawater desalting systems and fresh water pollution control systems. This division also operates a subsidiary, Aqua-Chem Pty, Ltd., of Australia.

Established in 1931, the Cleaver-Brooks Division is the world's leading producer of packaged steam and hot water generators. The division operates a Mexican joint venture subsidiary, Cleaver-Brooks de Mexico, and a wholly owned subsidiary, Cleaver-Brooks of Canada, Ltd.

Included with the two major divisions of Aqua-Chem, Inc. are the Environmental Technologies Division—responsible for the development of solid waste disposal systems—and the universal Water Softener Division, which manufactures and sells a complete line of industrial and consumer water softeners.

In addition to its own manufacturing and administrative facilities, the company has six foreign licensees, who manufacture equipment to Aqua-Chem, Inc.'s specifications. The company also maintains a worldwide network of 65 distributors, servicing 80 countries.

Financial Matters

The Coca-Cola Company's Annual Report for 1977 follows in Exhibits 17.1–17.3.

As Coca-Cola looks toward the future there is a shadow on the horizon. Today within the U.S. there are 49 million prime consumers of soft drinks, persons between the ages of 13 and 24. On the average each member of this group consumes 823 cans of soft drinks annually. By 1985, there will be approximately 4 million fewer persons in this age group, which will shrink soft drinks annual sales by some 3.3 billion cans.

Although The Coca-Cola Company claims not to be disturbed by this reduction in a key segment of its market, there is mounting evidence that it is adjusting its huge marketing capabilities to compensate for this core market shrinkage. Some of the strategic actions being contemplated at the company's Atlanta headquarters are:

1. Increase Coke's share of foreign markets by developing and implementing its foreign operations much more effectively and efficiently.
2. Enlarge its Houston-based Foods Division to the extent that revenues can be raised from a current 600 million to 1 billion within the next five years.
3. Slowly transfer some of the emphasis in U.S. Coca-Cola advertising to include the more mature age groups. The company's aim is to retain their Coke consumers after they have reached their 24th birthday.

The Coca-Cola Company occupies the number one position in the soft drink business. There are certain potential problems which it must overcome, such as a saccharin ban and fluctuating sugar prices. Nevertheless, the company's sales and earnings far exceed its nearest competition and its superb expertise in marketing its diversified products on a global basis will undoubtedly give the company a decisive business edge in the future.

References

"The ABC's of Distribution in the 70s, Refresher USA." The Coca-Cola Company, April–June 1973.

"Aqua-Chem, Inc., Pollution Fighters," Information Brochure, November 1972. The Coca-Cola Company. (Atlanta, Georgia.)

"The Chronicle of Coca Cola since 1886," Information Brochure, January 1974. The Coca-Cola Company. (Atlanta, Georgia.)

"The Coca-Cola Company, a Brief Profile of a Worldwide Business." The Coca-Coca Company, June 6, 1977.

The Coca-Cola Company and Subsidiaries Annual Report for 1976.

"The Coca-Cola Company Foods Division," Information Brochure, The Coca-Cola Company.

"The Graying of the Soft Drink Industry." *Business Week*, May 23, 1977, pp. 68–72.

"A New Look for Coca-Cola, a Synopsis of the 70s." The Coca-Cola Company.

"A Successful Formula for Company Growth." *Nation's Business*, June 1976. Reprinted by The Coca-Cola Company.

Discussion Questions

1. Why has The Coca-Cola Company been so successful?
2. How does its history affect its current Master Strategy?

3. Based on the information available, what apears to be the current Master Strategy for this organization?
4. Evaluate this strategy for necessary changes.
5. How does the entrepreneurial leader guide this firm?

17/The Coca-Cola Company —Part B: Shaping the Role of Corporate Planning

James M. Higgins

It was Henry Norman's first day as Director of Corporate Strategic Planning for The Coca-Cola Company. He had selected the proper spot on the wall for his prize Marlin and had decided to keep the chair which came with his new office instead of replacing it with the chair from his old office. Feeling more settled and at ease, he reflected on his objectives for his department and how he hoped to accomplish them.

The Corporate Strategic Planning Office at The Coca-Cola Company consisted of only three people, as opposed to that in General Electric for example, which had approximately 100 staff members. Yet, the Corporate Planner at The Coca-Cola Company and his staff wielded considerable influence within the company because this office was responsible for reviewing and advising the Chief Operating Officer (COO), the President of The Coca-Cola Company, as to the soundness of operating group and divisional strategic objectives and plans. In addition, Corporate Planning (CP) initiated investigations of strategic problem areas, areas of interest to the COO, and was responsible for coordinating the strategic issues management efforts of the firm. Reporting directly to the COO, CP helped shape the future direction of the company's organization. But as Henry considered the past activities of the department, he was convinced that CP needed to become more active in formulating corporate strategy and fulfilling its company defined role. He felt that his predecessor, who had just retired, had been very good at identifying problems, but that solution to these problems had just not materialized. Henry felt that his most important task would be to provide the operating managers and the COO with solutions in terms of well defined strategies.

Under each of the three major operating groups—the American Group, the Pacific Group, and the Europe-African Group—were small planning staffs at the division level. Similar units existed in the Foods Division and the Aqua-Chem Division. For example, the Coca-Cola USA Division, a member of the American Group, had a seven member planning department. It was from this department that Henry had been promoted to Corporate Planning. Henry had had seven years experience in this department. Upon completion of his MBA at Harvard University, he spent two years as a lieutenant in a project office of the Army Material Command and joined The Coca-Cola Company as a District Manager in the Bottler Sales field force. His undergraduate degree had been in Industrial Management from the Georgia Institute of Tech-

Source: The author wishes to express his thanks to Marion B. Glover, Jr. of The Coca-Cola Company and The Coca-Cola Company for assisting in the development of this case.

nology. Henry had served as Director of the USA Planning Office for the past three years.

Henry's Objectives and Plan of Action

Henry's thoughts turned to the objectives which he hoped to accomplish. Some were immediate results that he felt were necessary; others were more long range in nature.

First, he felt that his most vital role was to assist the president in establishing objectives and in formulating strategies to reach those objectives. Since he was already familiar with domestic operations, he would concentrate on the major ten to twenty foreign operations of the 135 countries in which the company operated. Once he was familiar with the total operation he would be better able to advise as to objectives and strategies.

Given the limited size of his department, he believed that providing planning direction to all of the company could best be accomplished through a planned course of action. First, he would establish a planning perspective throughout the company, including renewal of the annual strategic planning exercise. Second, he would need therefore to assist the group and division planners in strategic planning. Everyone had been spending too much time on budgeting, on financial planning, on getting the numbers right and acceptable, but too little time on determining group and division direction, primarily strategic objectives and plans to reach those objectives. Third, where necessary, either because of strategic issues or as the result of COO interest or in order to further group and division interest in planning, he would initiate white paper studies on various strategic problems. Fourth, he would institute a program of management by objectives throughout the company, just as he had assisted in establishing for Coca-Cola USA the previous year. Next, he concluded that he must establish and maintain a rapport with the group and division managers. He summarized that if he could be of genuine assistance to them, he could aid the corporation in accomplishing its objectives. He had already met with the three soft drink group vice presidents, and they had indicated a strong need for his assistance. He believed that they were sincere. Indeed, they did need his department's assistance because the company faced some severe challenges in the next few months.

Next, he noted to himself that he had to sell his programs and teach others in the company how to sell their programs. Further, he would help sell to the COO those programs which he felt that the company should adopt. The COO reserved the right to make all strategic decisions in conjunction with the CEO, the Chairman of the Board. As Henry recalled previous experiences in attempting to have programs implemented, he realized that where presentations were weak the subject programs were simply not adopted, no matter how good the proposed action might actually have been. He saw his function as assisting all the major parties involved, trying to get each to see the others' needs and perspectives.

His thoughts turned to the strategic planning process at the company. Traditionally there had been a bottom up approach, with virtually all managers submitting strategic proposals for refinement by the CP. This program, known as the "Soft Approach" had been adopted at the recommendation of the Stanford Research Institute. Experience had proven the system to be unwieldy, and Henry was certain that the CP should request only a few strategic issues and objectives from the key profit centers. As part of policy, the company was to have an annual planning exercise in which the various divisions, the CP, and eventually the groups submitted strategic plans for review by the COO and possibly the Operating Committee, which was composed of the three soft drink group presidents, the presidents of the Foods Division and Aqua-Chem, and the corporate vice presidents of Marketing, Finance, Personnel, Planning (CP), and Technical. In the last two years, this process had been set aside because of various crises which had occurred. The function of the Operating Committee was to recommend to the president what actions should be taken on strategic proposals. The COO retained the decision prerogative, however. Normally, decisions were made in separate meetings with only the operating manager involved. The Operating Committee did not concern itself with the detailed operations of groups and divisions. Intermediate and operational plans were left to the group and division managers. Only strategic decisions which involved several divisions and crossed group lines were brought before the committee.

Henry wanted to insure that the Operating Committee reviewed the Strategic Plans annually and was already planning for the spring's submissions. He felt that this process was vital on an annual basis because it allowed resource managers to vent their full feelings, to get them out in the open. By challenging proposals with all major parties present, the president and his staff were less likely to adopt unfavorable proposals or similarly less likely to adopt favorable strategic alternatives. Further, by placing planning on an annual basis as opposed to the sporadic and random pattern which had existed in the last two years, Henry felt the company would move more systematically toward its objectives.

Corporate Objectives and Problems

As Henry reflected on the company's desires to increase its profit each year, at least at the level of the past years (12%), the enormous challenge of his job became apparent. To accomplish this objective would require the addition of profits of a size equal to that of two major divisions. And it was he who must assist in putting into effect these objectives and others established by the COO and CEO.

The CEO preferred to personally pursue some of the actions necessary to increase profits. For example, he practiced personal diplomacy in efforts to gain access to the potentially lucrative markets of the Mideast, Russia, and China. The CP really had very little input to this strategic action. The CEO would also occasionally make other strategic decisions, for example, determining new businesses for the company. Henry thought that this was appropriate since the CEO had great vision with respect to these kinds of decisions. But for the current group heads and division managers, Henry knew that he must provide advice to the COO as to what could be accomplished and how, with the existing businesses.

Henry considered this an extremely difficult challenge. Because of the size of the firm, a 12% increase was of enormous proportions. And because of the increased competition and continual Federal intervention such as that from the Food and Drug Administration on saccharin, the task was not an easy one.

Having worked with Coca-Cola USA managers to establish numerous objectives in the past, Henry concluded that this year the total MBO program would be based on four to six key objectives for each of the managers at each level and that they should determine what were the most important, subject to corporate headquarters approval, of course. (It was the CP's responsibility to summarize lower level submissions for the COO's review.) Naturally, appropriate objectives would be necessary for sales, market share, and profits. Other objectives relative to each individual situation would be considered.

Henry was concerned with reaching the 12% profit increase objective. He felt that selling the major product line, Coca-Cola, was absolutely necessary in order to reach this objective. However, the strength of the USA operation had to be the franchisees, the bottlers. Henry felt that it was the bottlers who had made Coke the most successful consumer product of the century. The bottlers had to sell the products. The Coca-Cola Company through advertising pulls the customer in, but so does the local franchiser. Further, push strategies only work where bottlers support them. Henry had determined that the central focus of the company domestic strategy should be on supporting the bottlers in their efforts to sell Coke and in turn winning their support. After all, Coke was the main product. It was the main source of profits. But he felt that the company should also pursue new products, for example, the conversion of Hi-C to a soft drink.

Turning his attention to the foreign situation, he had already concluded from his previous meetings with the group vice presidents that many of their problems were operational in nature, yet of such a size that they took on strategic consequence. That is, he felt that if enough plants could be built and financed, and distribution arranged, many foreign operations would have no trouble meeting the profit objectives. However, the company would have to develop a plan to insure that these events occurred. Foreign nations posed special problems, and these would require a great deal of attention. Distribution, for example, was extremely difficult in many developing nations, which often had inadequate transportation systems. Marketing posed another problem where communications media were not of the type that U.S. corporations were used to employing. Furthermore, capital formation in developing nations was often a function of government and not in the realm of free enterprise. Finally, the various political and social customs proved to be obstacles in many situations. He was not sure exactly what his recommended actions would be, but forthcoming visits to the major overseas operations could hopefully provide some indications of appropriate measures.

Numerous strategic issues plagued the industry. Within the past few months, the company had faced these problems: The acryonitrile plastic bottle was reported to contain carcinogens; saccharin, the only artificial sweetener currently approved for diet drinks, the fastest growing segment of the market, was considered carcinogenic; the South African racial situation and the related social responsibility issues of selling soft drinks there was a matter of controversy; an FTC case attacked the validity of exclusive territories for bottlers; and state and federal bills were attempting to place deposits on non-returnable containers.

Often, the company's plan had been to wait and see what developed, although certain contingency strategies had been prepared in the event, for example, that the federal government were to take any of several courses of action with respect to saccharin. Henry felt that this was appropriate. "You have to know what the government is going to do before you can comply," he thought.

Shaping the Future

Henry was as yet undecided on the exact actions he wanted to take and those he wanted the company to investigate, but he had formed objectives and a strategy for the near future in any event. He was pleased with his staff. Paul Smith had ten years of foreign experience, and Ann Moss had five years in the financial aspects of planning; so he felt that among the three of them, they would have no problem with the technical aspects of their job. It was coming up with the right strategies to reach corporate objectives that concerned him. 1978 was going to be a challenging year.

Discussion Questions

1. What is the role of the corporate planner at The Coca-Cola Company?
2. How does this role differ from that portrayed in the text with respect to GE?
3. What types of qualifications should this individual have at The Coca-Cola Company?
4. What are the major challenges which this individual faces in fulfilling the job's demands?
5. What are the major challenges which he must meet through his office for The Coca-Cola Company? (You may wish to consult Part A again.)
6. What would be your objectives and plan of action if you were Henry Norman? Why? What do you think of his objectives and plans of action; i.e. what is your evaluation of them?

James M. Higgins and
Robert J. Eichenlaub

HMH Company Inc. was organized in 1953 to publish *Playboy* magazine. In 1959, Playboy Clubs International (PCI) was organized as a subsidiary of HMH and entered into the restaurant-nightclub industry. Subsequently, HMH, which later became Playboy Enterprises, Inc. (PEI), diversified into hotels, additional clubs, other magazines, and several limited product and service investment areas. While sales of the first issue of *Playboy* amounted to approximately $30,000, PEI now has sales of $200 million per year. At the center of this empire reigns Hugh Hefner, founder, majority stockholder, and Chairman of the Board. The PEI case is divided into two parts. In Part A, the history of PEI through June, 1975 is reviewed. In Part B, the actions taken by PEI in response to the problems with which it was confronted in June, 1975 are indicated. Supplementary financial data are also presented.

Playboy's History—Hugh Hefner

Hugh Marston Hefner, Playboy Enterprises' founder and majority stockholder, was raised in the city of Chicago. He once summarized his formative years as follows:

My father and mother gave us intellectual freedom and we were taught to ask questions and come to our own conclusions, but they imposed rigid Protestant fundamentalist ethics on us. There was no drinking, no smoking, no swearing, no going to movies on Sunday. Worst of all was their attitude toward sex, which they considered a horrid thing never to be mentioned. This led to serious conflicts when I entered high school . . . . I was very introverted, and this became one of the most difficult periods of my life. So I withdrew into fantasies.

This puritanical background was later to have an important impact on the magazine industry.

After serving two years in the Army, Hefner obtained an undergraduate degree at the University of Illinois. He is remembered by his classmates as an indifferent student—a psychology major and contributor of cartoons to the campus humor magazine. Soon after he graduated in 1949, at the age of 22, he married his high school sweetheart, Millie Williams. In order to support

Source: Certain material in this case is reprinted with the special permission of Playboy Enterprises, Inc. The authors wish to thank Lee Gottlieb and Ann Connor of *Playboy* for their assistance in obtaining information for this case.

his family, Hefner worked as a personnel specialist for a carton printing company. He soon became dissatisfied because of his employer's discriminatory hiring practices and quit. He then attempted to sell a comic-strip about a college student, Fred Frat. This also failed. He next decided to enroll for one semester of graduate work in psychology at Northwestern University. He then became employed for sixty dollars a week as a copywriter in the advertising department of *Esquire,* a men's literary magazine. He left *Esquire* in 1952 after they refused to give him a five dollar cost of living increase when the magazine moved its headquarters to New York City. However, these events did not diminish Hefner's determination. It occurred to Hefner that by altering *Esquire's* format and adding photographs of female nudes, he would have an extremely salable product. The result was *Playboy* magazine.

"Once this idea hit me," Hefner later stated, "I began to work on
it with everything I had, and for the first time in my life I felt free.
It was like a mission—to publish a magazine that would thumb its
nose at all the restrictions that had bound me."

The first issue of *Playboy* was assembled in Hefner's Chicago apartment with the aid of a free-lance art director named Art Paul. To draw attention to his first edition, Hefner bought a nude photograph of Marilyn Monroe from a calendar company for $200. Marilyn became the magazine's first "Playmate of the Month," a unique three-page foldout female nude presented in a tasteful manner which was to symbolize the *Playboy* female—the girl next door. Hefner combined this photograph, some jokes, some cartoons, a few secondhand literary properties, and his own prose for his first edition. The first issue went to press in October 1953, financed by $10,000 raised through the sale of stock to Hefner's friends and $600 he had obtained through hocking his own possessions. Hefner did not put a date on this edition because he was not sure there would be another. This first edition sold 55,000 copies at fifty cents each, and the magazine became an overnight success. By the fourth issue, the magazine was solvent, and Hefner was able to open an office in downtown Chicago. As the magazine's circulation and profits grew, maintaining an "image" became important. When he founded *Playboy,* Hefner adopted a worldlywise male rabbit in evening clothes, surrounded by a host of admiring female bunnies as its trademark. This is the picture that Hefner has tried to project of himself and, more importantly, of *Playboy* readers.

Hefner's daughter, Christie, was born in 1953. His son, David, was born in 1955. Hefner was separated from his wife in 1957 and subsequently was divorced in 1959.

To aid in maintaining the *Playboy* image, in 1959 the company purchased a $400,000 54-room Chicago near North house which is referred to as "the mansion." Hefner lived in this mansion until 1971, when the company purchased a 29-room castle-mansion in suburban Los Angeles. The Chicago mansion serves as a home for about 24 bunnies; also numerous public and charitable events are staged there. Both mansions are luxuriously furnished with all of the latest electronic equipment for listening and viewing pleasure.

During the 1960s Hefner often stayed inside the Chicago mansion for weeks, sometimes months. This created a problem in getting approval for items to be included in the magazine. Often *Playboy* executives had to transport photographs and stories between the mansion and the Chicago offices. Despite these inconveniences, the circulation of *Playboy* was growing at a record pace. If one single characteristic could describe Hefner during these times, it would be the adjective *driven*. He often worked through the night, averaging 20 work hours per day for many consecutive days.

In 1970 Hefner had his own private jet constructed, a DC9. This he referred to as the "Big Bunny." It was the most opulent, best-equipped, and most expensive private plane in the world. Its exterior was completely painted black, except for *Playboy's* white-rabbit emblem on the tail. The interior of the aircraft was decorated as lavishly as Hefner's mansion. Included were costly electronic equipment, plush and costly furniture, and other necessary accommodations for a "playboy." Despite criticism that the plane was just an extravagant plaything for himself, Hefner believed it provided an effective aerial advertisement for his product. In addition, it was calculated to turn a sizable profit for *Playboy*. Hefner utilized the aircraft to make a number of trips to Africa and Europe. In addition, it was used as his commuter transportation from Chicago to California and the new mansion often referred to as "Playboy Mansion West." This abode consisted of a five-and-a-half-acre estate.

In 1970 Hefner stated that a person should not feel guilty about earning money and then spending it. He did not want anyone to forget that all the time he was spending his money, he was developing what he refers to as "a strong social conscience." His main objective was to set a high standard of comfort and living and bring the rest of the world up to it. Throughout the history of *Playboy*, Hefner has maintained his position of final authority. However, his policy of living up to the *Playboy* image has sometimes made it difficult to have major decisions made quickly. Some of Hefner's friends believe that the real world he created is far more complicated than the fantasy one he invented. It is the real world Hefner has admitted he has trouble coping with. He once stated to his friends that when the magazine surpassed the one million circulation mark, he lost all sense of it as a business enterprise. He has also made no secret of the fact that the business part of the enterprise bores him.

One of the most important aspects of the growth of *Playboy* and its acceptance has been Hefner's magazine concept. This was summarized in monthly installments in the magazine, known as "The Playboy Philosophy." The philosophy required 26 issues and a quarter of a million words to express fully. Hefner's thesis was that United States society had too long and too rigorously suppressed good, healthy heterosexuality. Since its growth had been stunted, Hefner believed, all sorts of perversions flourished in its place. Hefner claimed that the villain behind America's sexual problems was organized religion. He stated that people must not be afraid or ashamed of sex and that sex is not necessarily limited to marriage. Such is Hefner's philosophy, the magazine's philosophy, and the philosophy of all Playboy enterprises. The hotels, clubs, resorts, and other assets of the enterprise evolved from this philosophy. Hefner and others feel that *Playboy* came along at just the right time, that is, when the United States was on the verge of a sexual revolution. Hefner believes his women (bunnies) became symbols of disobedience, a triumph of sexuality and an end of Puritanism. He felt that nowhere else in the world had sex been placed in such a demeaning position as in the United States. It was a sexual revolution which Hefner sold to the United States. Hefner believed that at the time he started to sell his revolution a great many of the traditional social and moral values of our society were changing and that *Playboy* was the first to reflect those changes. Hefner offered an alternate lifestyle with a more permissive, more play-and-pleasure orientation. He felt people were getting less of a sense of identity out of their jobs and placing more importance on what they did during their leisure time. In essence, *Playboy* came along and offered a new set of ethical values for the "urban" society. The editorial message in *Playboy* came through loud and clear: Enjoy yourself.

Several important ingredients differentiated *Playboy* from its early competition. The quality of *Playboy*'s photographs and literary material were significantly better than those in other "men's" magazines. The featuring of nude female women, and especially the three page centerfold, were also unique and served to create a rapidly increasing following. *Playboy*'s cartoons and jokes were also instrumental in creating a market. Hefner was an important contributor to the overall quality image, personally inspecting photographs with a magnifying glass. *Playboy* interviews with celebrities, political, and athletic figures have contributed to the *Playboy* success story, as have the *Playboy* editorials on the changing values in the society. *Playboy* has continued to stress not only sex, as do other men's magazines, but "the full scope of interests of the contemporary male."

Playboy Enterprises 1953-1975

Since its inception in 1953, Hefner's empire has grown extensively. His company has pursued not only expansion of its publishing efforts with new magazines, but has also ventured into movies, television, hotels, records, books, personal items, and other diversifications. These endeavors are grouped together under major divisions: The Publishing Group; Playboy

Clubs and Hotels; The Entertainment Group; and Other Operations. All have had a singular dependency upon the Playboy Rabbit emblem and the *Playboy* image.

The Publishing Group

Within the publishing group, several magazines have been attempted, but only two currently play an important role.

Playboy. In 1953 HMH Publishing Company was organized to publish *Playboy* magazine. In its first two years of existence, *Playboy*'s circulation climbed to 500,000 copies a month, only 300,000 behind Hefner's old employer, *Esquire*. During this time *Playboy* was able to start attracting noted authors, maintain its "Playmate of the Month" series, and was able to increase its overall prestige. Hefner observed, "We've given the young city guy a real identification with the magazine by giving him what he wants. I've always edited on the assumption that my tastes are pretty much like those of our readers. As I develop, so will the magazine." By 1960 Hefner had a publishing giant on his hands; a circulation exceeding 1,000,000; and more than $2,300,000 in advertising revenue. Hefner was now a wealthy man, with an estimated personal worth of more than $1,000,000. Through the 1960s and early 1970s the magazine dominated its market. Most competitors, old and new, were unable to dent the circulation growth of the magazine. By 1974 *Playboy*'s circulation of domestic and foreign editions was up to 6.5 million. In 1975 its circulation averaged 5,967,000. While newsstand sales declined, subscription sales rose to record highs.

Advertising in *Playboy* has always been closely tied to the adult fun editorial slant of the magazine. Many advertisers have prepared special ads for *Playboy*. The magazine will not carry ads for hair restorers, toupees, and weight-reducing aids. In other words, anything that might give the millions of male readers concern about loss of youth, vitality, and their "playboy" image is rejected. The policy has also been to refuse ads aimed at women. *Playboy* has always been fighting a barrier that makes future advertising expansion difficult. Although it has remained less racy than some of its competitors, most banks, mutual funds, and insurance companies balk at advertising in the magazine.

Playboy is published in various geographical advertising editions within the United States, all of which contain the same editorial material but vary in advertising copy carried. Table 18.1A shows the amount of advertising revenues in the stated years.

In 1961 Hefner published a biweekly magazine called *Show Business Illustrated*. Like *Playboy,* it was to offer status, romance, and girls. Its objective was to complement *Playboy*. The magazine folded after nine issues with an estimated loss of $2 million. The editorial director of *Show Business*

Table 18.1A   Playboy Magazine Gross Advertising Revenues Fiscal 1964-1975

Year Ended June 30	Nr. of Advertising Pages Carried	Gross Advertising	Average per Advert. Page	Net Advertising Revenue
1975	840.12	$37,595,000	$44,746	$32,027,000
1974	922.02	40,343,000	43,755	34,884,000
1973	916.29	39,432,000	43,034	34,063,000
1972	753.61	36,610,000	38,431	31,089,000
1971	907.15	33,149,000	36,542	28,532,000
1970		32,369,000		
1969		29,508,000		
1968		22,173,000		
1967		19,502,000		
1966		14,437,000		
1965		10,419,000		
1964		7,247,000		

Source: Playboy Annual Statements and 1975 10-K.

Illustrated blamed the death of the magazine on Hefner. He stated, "one problem, pure and simple, was Hefner wanted us to run a lot of smut showing nude showgirls in Las Vegas and of footage cut out of European films by the censors. We just wouldn't do it." *Trump* was another publishing effort which failed. *VIP,* another effort, is distributed to keyholders of The Playboy Club. In 1971, the company's name was changed from HMH Publishing Company Inc. to Playboy Enterprises, Inc.

Oui Magazine. *Oui* was first conceived as a way for Playboy to combat the competition of the European-based *Penthouse* magazine, a growing threat to the Playboy monopoly. *Oui* was created to appeal to the market segment interested in the more international subject matter and increased nudism of *Penthouse*. A French publisher had developed a successful men's magazine called *Lui*, patterned closely after *Playboy*. Playboy wanted to be the first with an English version. However, *Oui* had problems at the very start. But Playboy moved decisively to put *Oui* on the right track. Two experienced *Playboy* editors were shifted to *Oui*. Since then, the magazine's circulation has grown steadily and seems to have a chance for a profitable career as sort of a *Playboy,* Jr. In December 1974 the circulation of *Oui* declined slightly, due to a twenty-five cent increase in price. Circulation for the first half of 1975 averaged 1,302,000 copies per month, compared with 1,542,000 copies during the same period of 1974.

The Book Division. PEI has also engaged in the operation of the Playboy Book Club. The Club provides for the manufacture and sale of Playboy wall and desk calendars, the publication of hard cover books, magazine-size soft cover books, and rack-size paperback books.

Boarts International, Inc. A book exporting firm, Boarts has contributed profit to PEI, but its sales decreased in 1975.

Playboy (Foreign Editions). PEI has entered into agreements with companies in Germany, Italy, France, and Japan to publish editions of *Playboy* in those countries. A Brazilian version began publishing in May, 1975. While the total revenue from foreign editions is at this time limited, it will increase substantially as the volume of foreign sales increases.

Playboy Clubs and Hotels (Leisure Activities)

Clubs. In 1959 *Playboy* printed an article about a club in Chicago which employed scantily clad waitresses and had an exclusive membership which could be purchased along with a key to the premises. The response to this *Playboy* article was great, and Hefner realized the potential for his own company. Hefner subsequently established the first of his Playboy Clubs. The theme of these clubs was that for twenty-five dollars, any tired businessman with an acceptable credit rating could obtain a key which would admit him to any of the Clubs. He would be able to refresh himself with good food, drink, entertainment, all priced at $1.50 per item, and be able to observe the female form of his waitress, dressed in a scant bunny costume. The Chicago Club, the first club, became an instant success. By 1962 the Chicago Club had 106,000 key holders who bought much more food and drink than were bought at many of the other top clubs in Chicago.

Based on this success, Hefner quickly expanded, adding clubs in the cities of Miami, Los Angeles, and St. Louis. Hefner then spent four million dollars remodeling a seven-story building for the New York Club. All clubs had the same basic floor plans on each of four or five floors. From a profit standpoint, the emphasis was on alcholic beverage sales. The number of clubs and their memberships continued to grow, and by 1965, 450,000 men spent $11 million for membership keys. By 1971, clubs were in these United States cities: Chicago, Miami, New Orleans, St. Louis, New York, Phoenix, Detroit, Kansas City, Baltimore, Cincinnati, Los Angeles, Atlanta, San Francisco, Boston, and Denver. Clubs were also to be found in Montreal and London. The clubs had become famous for "mass merchandising a champagne atmosphere at beer prices." The clubs were able to offer good value for the money, a reassuring uniformity of layout and product, and a tight control of quality and operations from a central headquarters. At a time when most nightclubs had priced themselves out of the middle-class market, Playboy keyholders could buy dinner and an evening's entertainment in plush surroundings for themselves and their dates for $20. The club system revolved around the Playboy key, which served as a status symbol to the owner and as a charge card. No money changed hands at a Playboy Club, except for tips. Some club facilities were owned by the company, while others were leased.

The offices for obtaining entertainment were centralized in Chicago. The clubs were able to buy entertainment on a wholesale basis to fill the four rooms in the standard layout of each club. Playboy was able to pay their entertainers less than the market wage because the clubs could offer an entertainer close to a year of solid work. Playboy utilized the benefits of exposure on a national circuit and steady employment as powerful persuaders. In 1966 Playboy charged a $2.50 cover charge for a typical show. In a normal month the cover fees alone yielded over $300,000, which paid for the talent and left a significant contribution to profit.

Central control was utilized in other areas of the clubs also. For example, meats were purchased from a Chicago purveyor who adhered to rigid specifications. Managers filed monthly reports to headquarters itemizing outlays for each product in five general categories. Liquor costs, which were generally regulated by minimum wholesale prices set up by state law, were determined by daily empty bottle counts. Even the hiring of the "bunny" waitresses was strictly controlled. All applicants were carefully screened. The bunnies were made to feel that they were in show business with dressing rooms, wardrobe mistresses, and hairdressers. They had a bunny mother to supervise them, and they were forbidden to date the patrons. Hefner had even hired a detective service to circulate its operatives incognito to attempt to entice the bunnies to break the rules. Hefner claimed his main reason for strict rules was that if a scandal hit pertaining to a bunny, the puritans would try to close the clubs. Hefner, in commenting on the success of his clubs in 1966, stated, "During the late 1950s the nightclub business was murdered by television. Much of our success is our ability to provide something you can't get on TV or in your own home."

Playboy clubs eventually expanded to Europe, establishing clubs with gaming (gambling) facilities in London (1966), Manchester (1972), and Portsmouth (1973), England. These clubs proved highly successful despite the depression in the English economy and the failure of similar English establishments. In 1972, Playboy acquired the Clermont Club of London, a private gaming facility open only to members of the Clermont Club.

In the later 1960s, however, business began sagging in the United States clubs. Playboy executives partially blamed this on the poor location of the clubs. Some were located in the decaying city cores. Some executives stated that they recognized the club idea was somewhat contradictory to the lifestyle extolled by the magazine from the very start. *Playboy* encouraged the easy mingling of the sexes, but the Playboy Clubs discouraged it. Strict rules made bunnies unavailable, and the crowd at the clubs was predominantly male. Singles bars down the streets, where women were available, were cutting into club attendance. Competition for Playboy Clubs comes from all of the major leisure activities including restaurants, lounges, movies, theaters, sports, television, and so forth. Several gaming houses complete with those clubs in England.

By 1973 the Playboy Clubs Division had sales totaling $33.3 million and had pre-tax profits of 67 percent or $5.3 million. However, these impressive figures were only due to the runaway success of Playboy's British casinos.

The company's fifteen domestic clubs operated in the red. Playboy top executives conceded that the overall club operation has "long neglected" the marketing side of its business.

Beginning in January 1972, a major program was initiated to remodel and relocate a number of the clubs. Clubs in Chicago, Miami, Los Angeles, Detroit, Phoenix, and Montreal were moved or remodeled. Clubs in New Orleans, Kansas City, and St. Louis were closed for new site selection, or until franchisees could be found. Beginning in 1974, the club in New York underwent extensive renovation at an estimated cost of $2,800,000. Renovation at the Cincinnati Club cost approximately $830,000. It was hoped that these changes would once again bring in the record volume of crowds. Also, in 1975 Playboy transferred the operational and administrative controls over its clubs and hotels to its management team in England. It was felt that their successful efforts with the British casinos could be applied to the whole operation. Playboy also adopted the policy of franchising clubs and even hotels. Earlier, all hotels and all but three of the clubs (St. Louis, Baltimore, and Boston) had been owned by the company.

Hotels. In 1968 when *Playboy* magazine was continuing its outstanding growth in both sales and profits, Hefner ordered further diversification. He wanted the Playboy name on hotels. The company's first purchase, a resort hotel Ocho Rios in Jamaica, was a success, at least immediately after its purchase. Playboy next acquired "Playboy Plaza" in Miami for $13.8 million and "Playboy Towers" in Chicago. The latter is contiguous with corporate headquarters in the former Palmolive Building at 919 North Michigan Avenue. Continuing expansion, Playboy built two resort hotels on its own, a $14 million, 356-room hotel at Lake Geneva, Wisconsin, and a 674-room hotel at Great Gorge, in Sussex County, New Jersey. However, the hotels did not enjoy the success which PEI had envisioned. While the Jamaica Hotel continued to be profitable, the others dwindled. Playboy executives stated that the Towers had been poorly managed resulting in unrealistic pricing, overstaffing, and widespread inefficiency. The Great Gorge Hotel cost $30 million, half again more than its budgeted price, and Playboy was forced to borrow $15 million (at three percent interest plus the prime rate)to complete it. By 1973, two years after it was built, this hotel was still struggling to bring its occupancy rate to a break-even level of 60 percent. Break-even rates vary for hotels, but 66 percent is a commonly required occupancy for larger hotels. By the end of 1975 the Great Gorge Hotel had operating losses totaling $6 million. Playboy executives stated that the hotel suffered from its isolated location 50 miles west of New York and competition from better-established resorts in the nearby mountains. Playboy operated the Playboy Plaza Hotel in Miami Beach for four years, incurring losses approaching $6 million. Playboy sold the Plaza in 1974 for $13.5 million; and if the new owner defaults on his mortgage payments, Playboy is liable for $4 million

Table 18.2A Occupancy and Room Rates—Playboy Hotels

Year Ended June 30	Great Gorge Average Rm. Rate	Great Gorge Average Occupancy	Lake Geneva Average Rm. Rate	Lake Geneva Average Occupancy
1975	$35.24	52.1%	$32.79	54.1%
1974	32.77	53.7	30.50	59.8
1973	31.87	52.3	28.54	61.7

Year Ended June 30	Jamaica Average Rm. Rate	Jamaica Average Occupancy	Chicago Towers Average Rm. Rate	Chicago Towers Average Occupancy
1975	$34.68	56.0%	$29.30	57.9%
1974	29.88	72.0	26.80	68.1
1973	28.41	69.0	25.00	66.5

Table 18.3A Hotel Acquisition and Room Expansion

Year	Hotel	No. of Rms. Each	Total No. Rms.
1965	Jamaica	200	200
1968	Lake Geneva, Wis.	296	496
1970	Plaza, Miami Beach	450	946
1970	Towers, Chicago	320	1,266
1971	Lake Geneva (Add.)	60	1,326
1972	Great Gorge, N.J.	674	2,000

Table 18.4A Playboy Clubs—Selected Revenues

Year	Keys Sold	Revenues from Sales of Keys	Net Revenues from Annual Keyholder Payments
1975	113,000	$2,542,000	$5,831,000
1974	146,000	3,351,000	5,941,000
1973	141,000	3,338,000	4,954,000
1972	133,500	3,144,000	3,170,000
1971	76,700	2,172,000	3,145,000

Source: Playboy Annual Statements and 1975 10-K.

in debt. The Plaza was located in South Central Miami Beach, while the newer hotels and the night life had moved to North Miami Beach.

In 1975 agreements were made with foreign investors to franchise hotels in Tokyo, in Costa Rica, and in Pangkor Luat near Kuala Lumpur, Malaysia. All but the Chicago hotel are resort hotels. Competition for the hotels comes primarily from other resort hotels. However, the Chicago hotel competes with several other hotels in the Chicago area.

Other Operations

Playboy Sales, Inc. The sale of miscellaneous personal accessory items bearing the Playboy trademark is the responsibility of Playboy Sales, Inc. Such products range from tie clasps bearing the bunny insignia to bunny tail wall plaques.

Entertainment Group

Playboy Productions. Playboy has entered into the movie and television production fields. The movies "The Naked Ape" and "Macbeth," two expensive productions, were financial failures. From 1970 to 1975 Playboy lost $6.2 million in movie making, while passing up the chance to participate in such box office successes as "Jaws" and "Deliverance." Although not fully abandoning the full length productions, Playboy has switched its movie efforts to producing 90-minute made-for-television movies, in an attempt to make this division profitable. Playboy, in 1959 and 1960, had its own late night television talk show. This venture also failed to gain much public interest. Many blamed Hefner, host of the show, for its failure. They claimed his image as a sophisticated playboy was lacking. Occasionally over the years, Playboy has presented TV specials related to its own activities such as "Bunny of the Year" contests. Among the 90-minute TV movies produced in 1975 was "Beyond This Place There Be Dragons," starring Fred MacMurray. Another was "The Great Niagara" with Richard Boone.

Records. Despite continuing losses in record and music publishing, Playboy Records in 1975 did earn its first Gold Record for one of its productions. Also during this year the record distribution was expanded into the international market. While none of the artists or records promoted thus far by Playboy have enjoyed much success, the company tries to maintain an appealing variety of albums for the contemporary market. Much promotion effort during the past few years has been invested in the records and albums sung by Barbi Benton, who has been Hefner's companion during the same period. Hamilton, Joe Frank, and Reynolds also recorded for the Playboy label and were responsible for Playboy's first gold record.

Limited Interests. Other smaller investments are in such activities as product marketing research. In this endeavor Playboy's College Marketing and Research Corporation provides a network of student representatives engaged in product sampling and promotional events for companies wishing to reach the college market. In addition to providing model agencies in Chicago and Los Angeles, Playboy also maintains a Los Angeles based subsidiary which provides limousine service. Just in the initial stages, insurance policies and hospital plans, underwritten by an insurance company, offered to Playboy keyholders and magazine readers, may prove to be a reliable source of income.

Table 18.5A Playboy Subsidiaries

Name of Company	Jurisdiction of Incorporation	Percent Ownership by Immediate Parent
Playboy Enterprises, Inc. (parent)	Delaware	
Boarts International, Inc.	New York	100%
Boarts International, Inc.	Delaware	100%
College Marketing & Research Corp.	Indiana	100%
Playboy Book Club, Inc.	Delaware	100%
Playboy Clubs International, Inc.	Delaware	100%
Bolark Corporation	Delaware	100%
Stockholm Playboy Club, Inc.	Michigan	100%
The Cincinnati Penthouse Club, Inc.	Ohio	100%
Club Land Development Corp.	Delaware	100%
Hoteles Espanoles, Financiacion Construcciones, S.A.	Spain	100% *
IMCO, Inc.	Delaware	100%
International Playboy Company (Quebec) Limited	Quebec	100%
Jamaica Playboy Club, Inc.	Delaware	100%
Play-Key, Inc.	Florida	100%
Play-Key of Kansas City, Inc.	Delaware	100%
Playboy Club of Atlanta, Inc.	Georgia	100%
Playboy Club of Denver, Inc.	Delaware	100%
Playboy Club of Hollywood, Inc.	Delaware	100%
Playboy Club of Lake Geneva, Inc.	Delaware	100%
Playboy of Lyons, Inc.	Wisconsin	100%
Playboy Club of London Limited	United Kingdom	100% †
The Clermont Club Limited	United Kingdom	100%
Cromford Club Limited	United Kingdom	80%
Parade Casinos Limited	United Kingdom	80%
Playboy Club of Louisiana, Inc.	Louisiana	100%
Playboy Club of New York, Inc.	New York	100%
Playboy Club of Phoenix, Inc.	Delaware	100%
Playboy Club of San Francisco, Inc.	Delaware	100%
Playboy Hotel of Chicago, Inc.	Delaware	100%
Playboy Hotel of Florida, Inc.	Delaware	100%
Playboy of Sussex, Inc.	Delaware	100%
Playboy Preferred, Inc.	Illinois	100%
Equinox Marketing Services, Inc.	Delaware	100%
Playboy Land Development, Inc.	Delaware	100%
Realton Inc.	Delaware	100%
Playboy Limousine Inc.	Delaware	100%
Playboy Models, Inc.	Illinois	100%
Playboy Records, Inc.	Delaware	100%
After Dark Music, Inc.	Delaware	100%
Playboy Music Publishing Company	Delaware	100%
Playboy Productions, Inc.	Delaware	100%
Playboy Properties, Inc.	Delaware	100%
Playboy Publications, Inc.	Delaware	100%
Playboy Sales, Inc.	Delaware	100%
Playboy Sales (Overseas) Limited	Delaware	100%
Playboy Theater of New York, Inc.	Delaware	100%
Steelton, Inc.	Delaware	100%

*5% of stock held by a United Kingdom resident as nominee of Playboy Clubs International, Inc.
†75% of stock held in trust by United Kingdom residents for benefit of Playboy Clubs International, Inc. pursuant to certain requirements of Gaming Board of Great Britain.

Other Past Interests. Playboy has held jazz festivals, owned movie theaters (still owns one in NYC), and ventured into bookmaking in England.

Subsidiaries

Table 18.5A indicates the corporate subsidiaries of the company as of August 31, 1975. The accounts of all the subsidiaries are included in the foregoing financial statements. Indented names are subsidiaries of the company under which they are indented. (Table 18.5A is on page 437.)

The Magazine Industry

During the 1960s and early 1970s, the magazine industry underwent a dramatic change. The dominant magazines such as *Life, Look,* and *The Saturday Evening Post* were unable to make a profit and were discontinued by their publishers. Television was an important determinant of their demise since television provided action news accompanied by sound as well as action packed movies and movie-like television series with well known stars. Furthermore, these former giants of the magazine industry had considered their markets to include just about anyone who could read. But the rising costs of paper, printing, and distribution which were passed on to their mass market consumers eventually served to alienate many of them. As a result, the magazines which were aimed at a specific segment of the market and provided subject matter which could not be found on television became the dominant magazine form. Of the mass market magazines, only *Reader's Digest* and *T.V. Guide* have survived, partly because neither is truly a mass market medium, but rather appeals to a very large segment of the total market.

Magazines face competition from television, radio, newspapers, circulars, and other forms of advertising media. During the 1960s and early 1970s, television dominated the advertising industry. Magazines are sold in two primary ways—newsstand and subscriptions. Similar forms of newsstand wholesaling are followed throughout the industry. Actual printing is routinely subcontracted.

Magazines depend on both advertising and magazine sales revenues for profits. Each requires a separate and competitive pricing policy. Production costs have risen significantly in recent years. Paper prices and mailing costs were very high for 1975 as compared to 1971. (Representative advertising rates and circulations are presented in Part B.)

Competition for Playboy

Penthouse. The fastest growing men's magazine in the early 1970s was *Penthouse.* It now threatens *Playboy* leadership in circulation. An Ameri-

Exhibit 18.1A   Ten Year Financial Summary

The consolidated statements of earnings of Playboy Enterprises, Inc. for the ten years ended June 30, 1971 have been examined by Lybrand, Ross Bros. & Montgomery, independent certified public accountants, whose opinion with reference thereto, which is based in part on a report of other independent certified public accountants, is included elsewhere in this Prospectus. The statements should be read in conjunction with other financial statements and notes thereto also appearing in the Prospectus.

(in thousands except per share amounts)

Years Ended June 30, (Note 1)

	1962	1963	1964	1965	1966	1967	1968	1969	1970	1971
Net sales and revenues:										
Playboy magazine:										
Circulation	$ 6,042	$ 7,781	$12,574	$16,560	$21,128	$24,943	$30,793	$ 35,680	$ 40,154	$ 45,234
Advertising	3,830	5,108	6,156	8,237	12,102	16,253	18,601	25,030	27,908	28,532
Clubs and hotels	7,648	10,375	10,765	19,042	24,893	27,312	32,943	40,563	43,235	47,611
Other	505	616	924	2,265	4,180	5,453	6,769	7,215	8,266	10,209
	18,025	23,880	30,419	46,104	62,303	73,961	89,106	108,488	119,563	131,586
Cost of sales and operating expenses:										
Playboy magazine	6,983	8,954	12,530	16,365	22,086	27,323	33,496	41,586	44,824	47,843
Clubs and hotels	4,730	8,353	8,199	15,021	18,282	20,616	25,462	30,996	33,553	38,569
Other	465	513	769	1,981	3,937	4,892	5,537	7,004	8,339	8,439
	12,178	17,820	21,498	33,367	44,305	52,831	64,495	79,586	86,716	94,851
Gross profit	5,847	6,060	8,921	12,737	17,998	21,130	24,611	28,902	32,847	36,735
Selling, general and administrative expenses	3,205	3,458	4,365	5,573	7,125	8,663	10,444	11,806	14,516	17,139
Earnings from operations	2,642	2,602	4,556	7,164	10,873	12,467	14,167	17,096	18,331	19,596
Other expenses (income):										
Interest, principally on long-term debt (Note 2)	131	370	248	383	464	517	621	652	615	1,074
Other, net	(17)	(9)	(9)	539	671	(69)	(250)	4	(130)	121
	114	361	239	922	1,135	448	371	656	485	1,195
Earnings before income taxes and minority interest	2,528	2,241	4,317	6,242	9,738	12,019	13,796	16,440	17,846	18,401
Provision for income taxes (Note 3):										
Currently payable	1,355	901	1,840	2,762	4,299	5,235	5,808	6,918	8,268	7,907
Deferred	122	308	330	301	409	530	1,105	1,829	1,315	1,266
	1,477	1,209	2,170	3,063	4,708	5,765	6,913	8,747	9,583	9,173
Earnings before loss on discontinued operations and minority interest	1,051	1,032	2,147	3,179	5,030	6,254	6,883	7,693	8,263	9,228
Loss on discontinued magazine ("Show Business Illustrated")	926									
Minority interest	209	(20)	115	72	292	321	104	106	98	7
Net earnings	(84)	1,052	2,032	3,107	4,738	5,933	6,779	7,587	8,165	9,221
Less dividends on preferred stock					1	2	4	6	8	10
Net earnings applicable to common stock	$ (84)	$ 1,052	$ 2,032	$ 3,107	$ 4,737	$ 5,931	$ 6,775	$ 7,581	$ 8,157	$ 9,211
Average number of common shares outstanding (Note 4)	8,805	8,785	8,769	8,743	8,720	8,720	8,683	8,565	8,570	8,647
Earnings per share of common stock (Notes 4 and 5)	$(.01)	$.12	$.23	$.36	$.54	$.68	$.78	$.89	$.95	$1.07

Source: Prospectus, Playboy Enterprises, Inc., Common Stock, 1971.

can, Bob Guccione, after several years of publishing in England, started the American edition of *Penthouse* in September 1969. It first appeared as a *Playboy* imitator and was successful with the aid of extensive advance advertising. The first issue sold some 235,000, compared to *Playboy's* circulation of over 5 million. By the end of 1970, *Penthouse's* sales topped 500,000. Thereafter, circulation kept climbing, reaching 4 million by mid-1975. Guccione, referring to his success in entering a market usually well defended by *Playboy,* stated, *"Playboy* stopped growing editorially, intellectually, culturally ten years ago. Then we came along and were a lot hungrier." He maintains that *Penthouse* prints more realistic and sexier photographs than *Playboy*. *Penthouse* was the first to display certain parts of the female body. *Penthouse* has a two-page centerfold—"Pet of the Month."

One of the major features of the *Penthouse* product is the letters to the advisor. This section invites readers to share their own sexual exploits and has created much interest with readers. Although *Playboy* has addressed such letters on a lower key in an effort to maintain its sophisticated image, Guccione expanded them even further. He started a separate magazine, *Forum,* to publish the overflow of these letters received. The *Forum* has proven to be a successful investment.

To interest the female, Guccione initiated *Viva.* This was another monthly magazine, but this time aimed at the sexually liberated female market. It featured, along with articles slanted toward women, photographs of partly undraped males. However, Guccione has not concentrated on male nudes as has *Playgirl,* the female counterpart to *Playboy* and *Penthouse*. This is because Guccione hopes to keep *Viva* in drugstores and grocery stores—two key markets. Continuing with the company's expansion, *Penthouse* also has started four book clubs and "Evelyn Rainbird Ltd," which specializes in the mail order sale of sexual aids.

Not every venture Guccione has started has been successful. In November 1969, Guccione initiated a Penthouse Club in London. Some of the investment dollars came from the profits of *Penthouse* and *Forum*. Since both magazines at that time were still trying to prove themselves, it was a risky investment. The Club turned into a financial disaster. It was hoped that it would be able to cut into the profits obtained by *Playboy's* London Club. However, the Club ran into legal trouble and ended up losing over $2.6 million by 1974. It has been the profits from magazines which has enabled the Club to remain in operation. It has also been reported that his casino venture in association with hotel interests in Yugoslavia was unprofitable. Finally, some estimates indicate that *Viva* may be operating in the red.

Penthouse rose to success essentially by following the strategy of its rival, *Playboy*. The similarities of the magazines seem to extend further to their owners. Guccione, like Hefner, always appears in public accompanied by women, mostly runs the operations from his apartment where he will stay inside for

Table 18.6A   Average Paid Circulation

6-Month Period Ending	Penthouse ABC Circ.	Index	Playboy ABC Circ.	Index	Oui ABC Circ.	Index
December 1972	2,217,207	100	6,977,966	100	—	—
June 1973	3,132,561	141	6,669,911	96	1,508,021	100
December 1973	3,786,016	171	6,503,261	93	1,583,615	105
June 1974	3,809,164	172	6,426,885	92	1,542,369	103
December 1974	4,000,147	180	6,125,330	88	1,339,106	89
June 1975	4,003,619	181	5,808,159	83	1,302,390	86

Year						
1971			5,794,000			
1970			5,349,000			
1969			5,315,000			
1968			4,988,000			
1967			4,145,000			
1966			3,520,000			
1965			2,823,000			
1964			2,188,000			

Source: Playboy Annual Statements and Penthouse advertising brochure.

days. Messengers go back and forth all day between the apartment and the *Penthouse* offices. Some say that these similarities were emphasized by Guccione and aided his jump to popularity. In December 1972, *Penthouse*'s circulation was 2,217,000. *Playboy*'s circulation was 6,977,966. By June 1975, *Penthouse*'s circulation had increased to 4,003,000. *Playboy's* circulation had fallen to 5,701,000. *Oui's* circulation stood at 1,302,000.

Gallery. Another imitator of the Playboy style is *Gallery*. With its first issue in 1972, it carried a cover identical in arrangement and type face to *Playboy*'s. The imitation continues with the "Gallery Interview," and a foldout for the *Gallery* girl of the month. The main reason for such imitation is that editor James Spurlock served three years with *Playboy*. In addition, *Gallery*'s staff offices are set up opposite *Playboy* editorial headquarters in Chicago. However, *Gallery* has not been a financial success. Its 1975 volume was estimated at between 700,000 and 750,000 issues per month.

Hustler. Another threat to Playboy's empire is *Hustler,* an up-and-coming magazine in the men's market. The owner, Larry Flynt, also owns Hustler Clubs in Ohio (Akron, Cincinnati, Cleveland, Columbus, Dayton, and Toledo). The clubs are somewhat different than the "proper" Playboy Clubs. The main difference is the bikini-clad females, who are allowed to chat with customers. These girls do not have a formal training program. They are just encouraged to be friendly and listen to the customers' problems.

Flynt stated, "The trouble with most nightclubs is that unless you are offering gourmet food or great entertainment, the novelty of your place soon wears off. The secret of my places is the girls. That's what the customers come to see. The difference between us and the Playboy Clubs is that we are smaller and so we don't have a huge overhead, and the Playboy Clubs forbid the girls to sit and drink with the customers, while we encourage it. But they are forbidden to date the customers." Circulation was estimated at 2.5 million for June 1975.

The Women's Magazine Market. A market which Playboy Enterprises has not yet ventured into is that of female readers. The leader in this market for women's magazines is *Cosmopolitan*. The philosophy of this magazine conflicts with that of *Playboy*. Its editorials often criticize the *Playboy* man-dominated world and propose a philosophy of woman's self-expression and self-fulfillment.

It is this type of change in thinking towards social order that some have said will be the downfall of *Playboy*. With the advent of the 1970s, a growing sentiment for female independence contrasted sharply with the traditional view of a male-dominated world. By 1975 the number of women becoming "sexually liberated" was quickly increasing and thus enlarging the market for "women's" magazines. The top three magazines which were capitalizing on this new sexual freedom in 1975 were *Cosmopolitan* (approximate circulation 2 million), *Playgirl* (approximate circulation 1 million), and *Penthouse*'s *Viva* (approximate circulation 300,000).

Cosmopolitan has been successful. However, it has held male nudity to a minimum. This allows the magazine to sell in supermarkets and drugstores, where 83 percent of its sales are made. On the other hand, *Playgirl,* which utilizes photographs of nude men as its main selling point, immediately was successful in 1973, starting with a 1.5 million circulation. *Viva* has remained between the two in the use of nudity. However, it has remained third in circulation.

Playboy Management

Hefner reigns supreme over his kingdom. He tried decision decentralization, but "it just did not work out. Some guys just didn't want the responsibility." Hefner has always driven himself, but has relaxed somewhat in recent years, no longer working 20 hours a day. Victor A. Lownes, senior vice-president and long time friend of Hefner's, commented that at one point, "Hefner lost interest in *Playboy* for a while. He wanted to run everything, yet delegate authority—and at the same time he neglected to make key decisions. Company performance showed it." An anonymous former executive reported, "It [the problems] starts at the top with Hefner. He's in, he's out, he's a bottleneck. You never know what he's going to do.

Decisions at *Playboy* often aren't based on normal business considerations. Hefner or another top guy will get excited about something, and they'll plunge ahead without even taking out a pencil. If you don't go along, you're put down as a negativist who can't be trusted." At the very least, severe delays occurred in top decisions with Hefner living in Los Angeles and the *Playboy* headquarters being in Chicago. The Office of the President was reorganized in early 1975 to include seven key individuals, Hefner and six top aides: Richard S. Rosenzweig, Executive Vice-President, Publishing Group; Victor A. Lownes, President, Leisure Activities; Donald S. Lewis, Senior Vice-President, Finance and Administration; Harvey Markowitz, Vice-President, Entertainment Group; Donald L. Parker, Vice-President, Planning and Development; and Robert S. Preuss, Senior Vice-President, Corporate Projects. All of these executives had been with *Playboy* for over five years except for Mr. Lewis, who possessed broad executive experience gained in several firms, and Mr. Parker, who also had considerable experience.

Finance. For three consecutive quarters, ending December 31, 1974, March 31, 1975, and June 30, 1975, PEI lost money. Revenues from *Playboy* were down. Several losers in the investment portfolio could be found.

Hotels. The book value of the hotels is $55 million, or one-third of PEI's total assets in June, 1975. In the last five fiscal years, the hotels have lost $14.4 million, $6 million by the Playboy Plaza (Miami) and over $6 million by the Great Gorge (New Jersey), which apparently suffers from its remote location from any major city (50 miles from New York) and the competition from better established hotels in the Catskills and Pocono Mountains. One hotel chain executive noted that the Great Gorge Hotel would be lucky to sell for $20 million. Furthermore, it has high debt and an unusually high interest rate.

Clubs. Without the $3.2 million pretax profit from the clubs in England, the clubs would have shown a significant loss. Despite downward trends in the total nightclub business, reinvestments have been made.

Movies. Over the past five fiscal years, Playboy has lost $6.2 million in movie production.

Records. The firm has continued to lose money.

Other Financial Problems. Cash flow was impaired and Playboy's line of credit was weakened in 1975 when the First National Bank of Chicago withdrew two lines of credit totaling $6.5 million. Bank officials were worried about a possible drug investigation of PEI. (The investigation failed to indicate any wrongdoing on the part of Playboy or its chief executives and was later dropped.) Playboy retains a single line of credit of $1.5 million, half of which had been borrowed by June 30, 1975.

Playboy failed to obtain a $12–15 million loan to buy back the 2.6 million publicly held shares in order to go private, a move seemingly designed to cut outside control and reduce outgoing dividend cash flows. These shares could have been obtained at a bargain price. The shares initially sold to investors at $23.50 in 1971, dropped to $2.25 in 1975.

The Internal Revenue Service was taking an aggressive position on disallowing several million in deductions taken on the two Playboy mansions and The Big Bunny (the DC9 aircraft). Concern has been expressed by PEI over increases in expenses relative to revenues.

Additional problems and supportive information related to the above problems may be found by examining the various exhibits to this case.

Personnel. PEI employs approximately 4,400 full-time employees. Of these 3,370 are engaged in the operation and supervision of Playboy Clubs and hotels and 1,030 are engaged in the publication of *Playboy* magazine and the company's other activities. Approximately 1,350 of the total employees are represented by labor unions. Employees at ten of the Playboy Clubs are covered by a single labor agreement subject to local modifications. This contract expires in 1977. Other union employees are covered by agreements at individual locations. No material interruptions of services or activities have occurred due to any labor disagreements or individual employment disputes. Turnover is perceived as low for the industry. In 1975 free coffee was served to Chicago headquarters personnel. Numerous other fringe benefits exist with regards to employment at Playboy. However, seven of the fourteen corporate officers listed in the 1975 financial report are new. Some have compared top management at Playboy to a revolving door.

The Drug Problem. In December 1974, the national press carried reports that federal investigators were probing drug use at the Playboy mansions in Chicago and Los Angeles. The resulting publicity led to the resignation of the company's two outside directors.

In addition, in January 1975, Bobbie Arnstein, Mr. Hefner's 34-year-old executive secretary who was out on bond while appealing a 15-year conditional sentence for conspiracy to distribute cocaine, was found dead in a North Side Chicago hotel. An apparent suicide, her death stirred up fresh ammunition for those opposing the Playboy life.

When news of the drug investigation and death was published, there was concern that some advertisers might be frightened away for fear of also gaining bad publicity. However, to combat any such feelings, Mr. Hefner tried to present himself as a victim of federal harassment. He charged that Miss Arnstein's death had been caused by overzealous prosecutors who were trying to harass her into giving evidence against him.

Exhibit 18.2A Playboy Enterprises, Inc. and Subsidiaries Consolidated Statements of Changes in Financial Position (For the Years Ended June 30, 1975 and 1974)

	1975	1974
Sources of Funds:		
Operations:		
Net earnings	$ 1,096,000	$ 5,949,000
Depreciation and amortization	6,740,000	7,032,000
Deferred income taxes and investment credit	1,415,000	1,473,000
Recoverable income taxes (Note H)	(5,218,000)	
Deferred subscription income	3,859,000	(58,000)
Other	95,000	(369,000)
Funds provided from operations	7,987,000	14,027,000
Working capital derived from sale of Playboy Plaza Hotel, net of mortgage debt retired of $12,041,000 (Note M)		1,696,000
Completion and release of films	931,000	684,000
	$ 8,918,000	$ 16,407,000
Application of Funds:		
Additions to property, plant and equipment	$ 6,782,000	$ 7,955,000
Reduction of long-term debt	499,000	801,000
Cash dividends (Note J)	707,000	1,109,000
Miscellaneous investments	295,000	504,000
Purchase of 167,800 treasury shares		1,077,000
Other, net	1,978,000	1,084,000
Increase (decrease) in working capital	(1,343,000)	3,877,000
	$ 8,918,000	$ 16,407,000
Changes in Working Capital Components:		
Cash	$ 2,262,000	$ 391,000
Receivables	(6,767,000)	2,375,000
Inventories	2,057,000	1,493,000
Other current assets	93,000	1,235,000
Notes payable and current maturities of long-term debt	(1,512,000)	(1,531,000)
Accounts payable and accrued expenses	2,337,000	(1,249,000)
Income taxes	187,000	1,163,000
Increase (decrease) in working capital	$ (1,343,000)	$ 3,877,000

The accompanying notes are an integral part of the financial statements.

Source: 1975 Annual Statement.

Exhibit 18.3A   Summary of Operations (in Thousands except per Share Amounts)

	1971	1972	1973	1974	1975
Summary of Operations					
Net sales and revenues	$131,586	$159,450	$190,011	$204,268	$197,734
Cost of sales and operating expenses	94,851	119,165	148,241	169,837	171,562
Gross profit	36,735	40,285	41,770	34,431	26,172
Selling, general and administrative expenses	17,139	19,150	18,609	21,521	21,897
Interest expense	1,073	2,211	2,843	3,028	2,496
Other (income) expense, net	122	(476)	21	(917)	(270)
	18,334	20,885	21,473	23,632	24,123
Earnings before income taxes	18,401	19,400	20,297	10,799	2,049
Provision for income taxes	9,180	8,801	9,039	4,850	953
Net earnings	$ 9,221	$ 10,599	$ 11,258	$ 5,949	$ 1,096
Common shares outstanding					
Average	8,647	9,161	9,408	9,276	9,211
Per share of common stock					
Net earnings	$1.07	$1.16	$1.20	$.64	$.12
Cash dividends declared	.11 3/7	.12	.12	.12	.12
Year-End Position					
Total assets	$115,513	$148,866	$160,599	$154,552	$158,704
Total liabilities	70,637	81,578	83,610	73,800	77,563
Net working capital	10,070	7,510	18,205	22,082	20,739
Net worth	44,876	67,288	76,989	80,752	81,141
Common shares outstanding					
Year-end	8,745	9,398	9,379	9,211	9,211
Book value per share	$5.13	$7.16	$8.21	$8.77	$8.81

Source: 1975 Annual Statement.

Exhibit 18.4A   Five Year Financial Statement (in Thousands)

	1971	1972	1973	1974	1975
Net Sales and Revenues					
Publishing Group					
PLAYBOY magazine	$ 73,766	$ 83,103	$ 87,377	$ 86,321	$ 86,332
OUI magazine	—	—	9,267	13,660	12,722
Other publishing	5,290	8,508	11,523	13,030	13,558
Total publishing	79,056	91,611	108,167	113,011	112,612
Leisure Activities Group					
Clubs	29,012	29,244	33,281	38,342	39,856
Hotels	18,599	31,263	39,922	40,663	32,801
Total leisure activities	47,611	60,507	73,203	79,005	72,657
Entertainment Group					
Motion-picture and TV productions	—	—	1,270	2,880	1,604
Records and music publishing	—	83	121	101	780
Total entertainment	—	83	1,391	2,981	2,384
Other Operations	4,919	7,249	7,250	9,271	10,081
	$131,586	$159,450	$190,011	$204,268	$197,734
Earnings before Income Taxes					
Publishing Group					
PLAYBOY magazine	$ 16,785	$ 18,782	$ 21,918	$ 14,235	$ 8,467
OUI magazine	—	—	983	(351)	(2,278)
Other publishing	1,132	881	1,056	(170)	(307)
Total publishing	17,917	19,663	23,957	13,714	5,882
Leisure Activities Group					
Clubs (1)	3,166	3,178	5,324	5,911	3,195
Hotels (2)	(1,708)	(2,143)	(3,479)	(3,321)	(3,779)
Total leisure activities	1,458	1,035	1,845	2,590	(584)
Entertainment Group					
Motion-picture and TV productions	—	(299)	(2,585)	(2,269)	(1,102)
Records and music publishing	—	(150)	(2,067)	(2,393)	(1,219)
Total entertainment	—	(449)	(4,652)	(4,662)	(2,321)
Other Operations	(974)	(849)	(853)	(843)	(928)
	$ 18,401	$ 19,400	$ 20,297	$ 10,799	$ 2,049

(1) The earnings figures for Clubs include earnings from the operations of the United Kingdom Clubs and gaming facilities. For information reflecting the relative after-tax profitability of these operations, see Note B to the Consolidated Financial Statements.

(2) In May 1974 the company sold its Miami Beach, Florida, Resort Hotel to outside interests. The Hotel had been acquired in August 1970. The figures shown above for Hotels include operating losses sustained by the Miami Beach Hotel (before intra-company allocations) of approximately $1,955,000, $1,203,000, $1,531,000 and $1,232,000 for each of the fiscal years 1971, 1972, 1973 and 1974.

Source: 1975 Annual Statement.

18A/Playboy Enterprises, Inc.—Part A

Exhibit 18.5A Earnings before Taxes

Year	Total Corporate	Playboy Magazine	Playboy Clubs	Playboy Hotels	Other Businesses
1975	$ 2,049,000	8,467,000	3,195,000	(3,779,000)	(5,834,000)
1974	10,799,000	14,235,000	5,911,000	(3,321,000)	(6,026,000)
1973	20,297,000	21,918,000	5,324,000	(3,479,000)	(3,466,000)
1972	19,400,000	18,782,000	3,178,000	(2,143,000)	(417,000)
1971	18,393,000	16,785,000	3,166,000	(1,708,000)	158,000
1970	17,748,000	15,632,000	3,392,000	39,000	(1,217,000)
1969	16,335,000	13,659,000	3,133,000	144,000	(496,000)

Source: Playboy Annual Statements.

Exhibit 18.6A 10-Year Financial Summary

Years	Net Sales and Revenues	Earnings Before Income Taxes	Provision for Income Taxes	Net Earnings	Earnings Per Share
1974	$204,268,366	$10,798,634	$4,849,385	$ 5,949,249	$ .64
1973	190,011,187	20,297,372	9,039,320	11,258,052	1.20
1972	159,449,913	19,399,662	8,800,701	10,598,961	1.16
1971	131,586,891	18,393,351	9,172,703	9,220,648	1.07
1970	119,562,955	17,748,082	9,583,553	8,164,529	.95
1969	108,488,343	16,334,773	8,747,471	7,587,302	.89
1968	89,106,230	13,692,662	6,913,409	6,779,253	.78
1967	73,961,330	11,698,095	5,764,893	5,933,202	.68
1966	62,302,834	9,446,278	4,707,961	4,738,317	.54
1965	46,104,069	6,170,888	3,063,643	3,107,245	.36

Source: Playboy Annual Statements.

Exhibit 18.7A Playboy Enterprises, Inc. and Subsidiaries Consolidated Balance Sheets June 30, 1975, 1974, 1973, 1972, 1971

Assets	1975	1974	1973	1972	1971
Cash	$10,307,000	$ 8,045,000	$ 7,654,344	$ 4,079,423	$ 3,264,324
Receivables (net of allowances)	16,482,000	23,249,000	20,874,087	19,268,438	15,087,669
Inventories	18,155,000	16,098,000	14,605,133	9,792,383	9,728,841
Other current assets	7,844,000	7,751,000	6,515,685	5,318,157	3,240,877
Total current assets	$52,788,000	$55,143,000	$49,649,249	$38,458,401	$31,321,711
Property, Plant & Equipment, at cost					
Land	4,894,000	4,750,000	5,807,641	5,794,570	5,530,739
Buildings & improvements	71,465,000	70,473,000	80,178,878	76,652,430	41,371,279
Furniture & equipment	27,697,000	25,881,000	25,221,006	24,567,023	16,057,688
Leasehold improvements	10,647,000	9,568,000	8,461,607	7,535,053	5,489,705
Aircraft	5,959,000	5,908,000	5,863,507	5,846,828	5,830,375
Construction in process	1,161,000	757,000	519,082	53,593	20,140,196
	$121,823,000	$117,337,000	$126,051,721	$120,449,497	$94,419,982
Less accumulated depreciation & amortization	31,355,000	27,233,000	24,230,209	19,588,805	15,234,436
	$90,468,000	$90,104,000	$101,821,512	$100,860,692	$79,185,546
Excess of cost over equity in net assets of subsidiaries acquired, less amortization	2,998,000	3,087,000	3,174,100	3,445,557	2,386,624
Recoverable income taxes	6,298,000	1,080,000	—	—	—
Other assets & deferred charges	6,152,000	5,138,000	5,954,069	6,101,412	2,618,708
	$158,704,000	$154,552,000	$160,598,930	$148,866,062	$115,512,589

Source: Playboy Annual Statements.

Exhibit 18.7A   Continued

	1975	1974	1973	1972	1971
Liabilities					
Current maturities of long-term debt	$ 506,000	$ 844,000	$ 813,440	$ 1,164,928	$ 915,999
Notes payable	3,350,000	1,500,000		4,215,000	550,000
Accounts payable	11,699,000	14,169,000	13,189,662	11,574,146	10,321,933
Accrued expenses	7,081,000	6,948,000	6,678,709	6,451,815	4,511,756
Income taxes					
Currently payable	4,740,000	4,393,000	6,301,379	4,080,148	2,520,453
Payable in future	4,673,000	5,207,000	4,462,400	3,462,031	2,431,811
Total current liabilities	$32,049,000	$33,061,000	$31,445,590	$30,948,068	$21,251,952
Long-term debt	17,185,000	17,684,000	30,525,688	31,968,534	34,116,662
Deferred subscription income	14,882,000	11,023,000	11,081,100	10,601,962	10,019,004
Deferred income taxes and investment credit	13,447,000	12,032,000	10,558,510	8,059,865	5,249,064
Shareholders' Equity					
Capital shares:					
Preferred, 4% cumulative, $1 par value, redemption value $1.03; authorized, issued and outstanding 241,914 shares				241,914	241,914
Common, $1 par value; authorized 15,000,000 shares, issued and outstanding 9,410,939 shares	9,411,000	9,411,000	9,410,939	9,397,639	8,744,617
Capital in excess of par value	12,372,000	12,372,000	12,371,655	12,293,755	
Retained earnings	60,696,000	60,307,000	55,466,755	45,354,325	35,889,376
	$ 82,479,000	$ 82,090,000	$ 77,249,349	$ 67,287,633	$ 44,875,907
Less cost of common shares in treasury	1,338,000	1,338,000	261,307	—	—
Total shareholders' equity	$ 81,141,000	$ 80,752,000	$ 76,988,042	$ 67,287,633	$ 44,875,907
	$158,704,000	$154,552,000	$160,598,930	$148,866,062	$115,512,589

Source: Playboy Annual Statements.

Discussion Questions

1. How did PEI become successful?
2. What is PEI's Master Strategy in 1975?
3. What are the major problems PEI faces at the end of this case? What opportunities does PEI have?
4. How would you solve PEI's major problems? How would you take advantage of their opportunities?
5. Evaluate, using the strategy matrix (Chapter 3), each of PEI's major diversification efforts at the time of acquisition or inception. Evaluate their major current (1975) diversification efforts in a similar manner. What actions should they take on these various investments (see GE's three types of strategies in Chapter 3).
6. What influence has Hugh Hefner's management style had on PEI?

18B/Playboy Enterprises, Inc.—Part B: FY 1976–December 1977

James M. Higgins and
Robert J. Eichenlaub

Immediate Actions Taken

Reorganization. In mid-1975 Hugh Hefner seemed to take more interest in turning around corporate fortunes. He observed that *Playboy* had been a victim of the economy. The economy was going through a combination of recession and inflation. As a result *Playboy* had been affected greatly, particularly in the leisure market segment of the operation. Inflation had affected the magazine as well because of the tremendous increase in production costs, especially paper. Hefner also added that during its great growth period in the 1960s, Playboy suffered from some of the results of growing pains in terms of upper and middle management. As suggested earlier, he announced plans for a major reorganization. The company was reorganized into a group of divisions with a division head in charge of each major activity. In essence, Hefner attempted to look at the whole Playboy Enterprises more from a profit point of view and tried to better coordinate the empire. Lower level managers, such as those in the clubs, will now be allowed to respond to local markets.

An Office of the President was created, consisting of Mr. Hefner and six department heads. The committee would make operating decisions, a function formerly centered in Robert Preuss, executive vice-president. Departments which had reported to Mr. Preuss would be consolidated under five divisions. The office of the president would be eventually replaced by a new president and chief operating officer, who would replace Mr. Hefner.

Research and Development. A new marketing approach was to be utilized. Rather than jump directly into projects (such as the hotels in the 1960s), market testing and specific plans would be accomplished first. Hefner stated that additional publications for Playboy Enterprises still have vast opportunities, especially a *Playboy* counterpart for the woman's market.

Marketing. Increased advertising for Playboy was undertaken, including television advertisements by Playmates of the Month. New approaches were taken to key activities including vacation trips. The Playboy name was quietly removed from its Great Gorge and Chicago hotels, primarily in order to attract businessmen whose bosses and wives were felt to be prohibiting them from coming to Playboy hotels to prevent their "chasing bunnies" instead of working. An attempt was made to infuse new vitality

Source: Certain material in this case is reprinted with the special permission of Playboy Enterprises, Inc.

into *Playboy* by broadening its content appeal to "more practical life-style situations."

Financial. Economy measures were implemented for all phases of the operation. For example, PEI reduced its headquarters force by 20 percent, to 800 employees. The staff of Hefner's Chicago mansion was reduced from 50 persons to only 12. In addition, the famous Playboy DC9 jet aircraft was sold.

Oui's budget was cut substantially. Some clubs were closed. Franchises were sought for many of the clubs. The price of soft drinks to employees doubled. Coffee is no longer free to employees in Chicago, saving over $50,000 a year. Muzak was eliminated. Employees travel less and no longer in first class. Exotic plants were eliminated in the headquarters building. Fewer parties were given. Hefner took a 25 percent cut in pay from $308,-000 to $220,350.

Editorial Policy. Playboy announced that its policy is to compete, but not by catering to prurience and sensationalism. Playboy feels that there is a growing resistance to blatant pornography.

Subsequent Actions

In April 1976, Hefner announced he was planning to turn over the title of President to an outsider who would be Chief Operating Officer as well. Hefner would remain as Chairman of the Board and Chief Executive Officer. A search was begun for a replacement.

In September 1976, Playboy announced that Derick J. Daniels, 47, was appointed President of PEI. Daniels had risen through the editorial ranks and had become President of Knight News Service, Inc. This marked the first time anyone other than Hefner had held the presidency.

Despite Playboy's financial condition, the new president was optimistic. Daniels claimed, "I am confident that the Presidency of Playboy Enterprises offers the most significant challenge of my career. PEI is a unique company with real potential for further profitable growth. I look forward to working closely with Mr. Hefner in maximizing that potential in fields that run from domestic publishing to the development of new foreign markets for PEI's products and services."

A five-man executive committee was appointed to report to Daniels and the seven-man Office of the President was abolished. Of the six top men who had formally reported to Hefner, all but Preuss remained. The other five composed the new executive committee.

Hefner refused his 1976 dividends of $797,000. Thus dividend payments amounted to $308,000.

1976 in Review

Most of the results of the actions taken are to be found in the financial statements and other exhibits included at the end of this case. However, a few of the results include the following:

Publishing

Playboy. Circulation has increased. Advertising pages per issue have increased, consecutively, for six straight months. A new editorial "On the Scene" was added. *Playboy*'s newsstand price was raised to $1.50, with the two year-end holiday issues (December & January) going to $2.00, effective in September, 1976. Subscriptions to *Playboy* were raised from $10 to $12 on the same effective date. Special efforts have been taken to broaden *Playboy*'s distribution through chain stores, with emphasis on supermarkets. *Playboy*'s covers are being redesigned to ensure open display at all outlets. Increased editorial diversity regarding sex, religion, and politics will occur. Jimmy Carter (who became United States President) was interviewed in the November, 1976 issue which was a sellout at over 6 million copies. Profits rose substantially. *Penthouse,* beginning late in 1975, started to outsell *Playboy* on the newsstands. Unofficial sources indicate that *Playboy* has approximately 40 percent more advertising pages than does *Penthouse.*

Oui. The newsstand prices were raised to $1.50, with the two holiday issues raised to $2.00. A new (and cheaper) printing process was employed without a loss in quality. Circulation stabilized. The magazine is now in the black.

Playboy Book Division. The book club achieved its highest sales and second-highest profits in its history during fiscal year 1976. In addition, the club is now firmly entrenched as the third-largest book club in the United States. During 1976, it broadened its base to include other than *Playboy* magazine readers by acquiring Wyden Press imprint.

Foreign Language Editions of Playboy. In fiscal year 1976, the five foreign language ediitons of *Playboy* more than doubled their circulation. The total circulation was over 1,500,000 copies per month. Since the magazines are published under license agreements that required no investment by Playboy Enterprises, the royalties have proven to be an important source of profit.

An example of their overseas success is illustrated by the Japanese edition. After just thirteen issues, the magazine was selling 800,000 copies. It required four years for the original English-language version to reach that mark.

In addition to the present five foreign editions (Italy, Brazil, France, Germany, and Japan) *Playboy* concluded a license agreement to produce and distribute a sixth version in Spanish. This edition, *Caballero con demejor de Playboy* (*Gentleman with the Best of Playboy*), started in November, 1976 and is distributed in Mexico, throughout Central America, and in Colombia and Venezuela. Spain and the Philippines are targets for the future.

Playboy Clubs and Hotels

The new management team focused on programs of maximum profit and eliminated the less profitable activities. As a result the clubs did show some improvement in fiscal year 1976, but problems remained. It was decided that even with extensive renovation some of the clubs would not be able to offer a profitable return on investment. Playboy clubs in New Orleans, Kansas City, Montreal, Atlanta, and San Francisco are currently closed. The Atlanta club, while being renovated, was damaged by fire and may not be reopened. The greatest successes were in the British gaming clubs, which accounted for $8 million in profit. The United States clubs lost over $4 million.

In 1976, 81,000 keys were sold for $1,717,000. Annual keyholder payments amounted to $5,208,000. As of June 30, 1976, 729,000 keys are outstanding. Since historically keyholder interest declines over time, renewed efforts are made to sell keys each year. In December, 1976, a Playboy Club was opened in Tokyo. This was a franchised club as opposed to a PEI-owned operation. Franchising now appears to be the future of new clubs since this offers Playboy an opportunity to produce acceptable cash flows without investment. Playboy ceased publication of *VIP* magazine in 1976.

Playboy is considering expansion of its casino interests to Atlantic City, New Jersey.

Playboy marketed a prepaid key vacation plan for blocks of times over a multi-year period at Great Gorge and tested other promotional programs. Response to the key vacations was good and may be expanded to Lake Geneva. Playboy hotels recorded a $5,704,000 loss before taxes in 1976. This loss was approximately two million greater than the loss in 1975. Average occupancy rates and room rates for 1976 are shown in Table 18.1B.

Table 18.1B Occupancy and Room Rates—Playboy Hotels

	Occupancy	Room Rate
Great Gorge	48.8%	$36.18
Lake Geneva	55.2	34.32
Jamaica	49.4	36.94
Chicago Towers	50.4	29.63

Dropping the Playboy name from the hotels did not seem to help. The name has been reemployed. Because of the substantial capital investments in the hotels, PEI is exploring alternatives to this venture.

Entertainment Group

Playboy Productions was responsible for "The Minstrel Man," which appeared on CBS-TV early in 1977. Its "International Bunny of the Year Pageant" has proved to be popular. Playboy Records had several hit singles and substantially increased sales. Mickey Gilley was especially prominent in the Country and Western field, winning several major awards for his songs. Barbi Benton's records have also sold well.

Other Operations

Playtique. Another activity of Playboy Enterprises has been the "Playtique," opened in August 1976. It is a retail store in the Playboy Building in Chicago dealing in clothes and music items. It offers a unique mix of designer sportswear for young women, one-of-a-kind items of jewelry, accessories for men and women, and a large selection of albums and tapes. This first store is a test for a possible chain operation.

Exhibit 18.1B   Quarterly Summaries Sept. 30, 1975–Sept. 30, 1976

	Sept 30, 1975	Dec 31, 1975	Mar 31, 1976	Jun 30, 1976	Sep 30, 1976
Sales	$47,837,000	$51,314,000	$47,206,000	$51,447,000	$57,044,000
Earnings before Income Taxes	2,013,000	1,646,000	1,190,000	1,953,000	8,847,000
Net Earnings	899,000	659,000	406,000	95,000	3,768,000
Net Earnings per share	0.10	0.07	0.04	0.01	0.41

	Sept 30, 1974	Dec 31, 1974	Mar 31, 1975	Jun 30, 1975
Sales	$52,389,000	$51,945,000	$46,058,000	$47,342,000
Earnings before Income Taxes	4,636,000	(667,000)	(724,000)	(1,196,000)
Net Earnings	2,480,000	(357,000)	(387,000)	(640,000)
Net Earnings per share	0.27	(0.04)	(0.04)	(0.07)

Source: Playboy Quarterly Statements.

Financial

The First Quarter (FY 1977) Report to Shareholders reported that Playboy was finalizing negotations with four banks for $2 million in unsecured open line credit each. Short term debt had been reduced by $2 million.

Summary

After viewing the substantial improvement in financial performance for 1976 versus 1975, Hugh Hefner remarked,

While we are by no means satisfied with our rate of improvement, we nevertheless are pleased by our ability to report increased earnings. It is heartening as well to realize that our profit improvement was made possible because of the diversification the company has engaged in over the years.

Exhibit 18.2B Newsstand Purchases—Selected Magazines

	Total Circulation	Newsstand Sales	% Total Circulation
Playboy	5,405,443	3,554,253	65.8
Penthouse	4,367,973	4,040,375	92.5
Oui	1,258,734	1,173,314	93.2
Playgirl*	1,006,755	927,371	92.1
Gallery†	900,000	800,000	88.8
Cosmopolitan	2,214,655	2,105,391	95.1
Mademoiselle	873,686	502,522	57.5
Seventeen	1,450,105	908,054	62.6
Vogue	770,954	393,097	51.0
Harper's Bazaar	540,339	268,540	49.7
Glamour	1,855,835	867,936	46.8
House Beautiful	840,629	314,604	37.4
Good Housekeeping	5,312,449	1,575,940	29.7
House & Garden	1,159,197	333,753	28.8
Redbook	4,574,495	1,056,242	23.1
Ladies Home Journal	6,080,058	1,129,502	18.6
McCalls	6,511,891	1,010,010	15.5
Esquire	1,079,253	116,925	10.8
New York	365,268	37,018	10.1
New Yorker	491,684	48,109	9.8
Newsweek	3,012,945	296,138	9.8
Better Homes & Gardens	8,093,646	717,267	8.9
TV Guide	20,249,384	12,083,966	59.7
Readers Digest	18,164,833	1,326,600	7.3
American Home	2,500,813	176,500	7.1
Time	4,522,776	300,289	6.6
U.S. News & World Report	2,056,991	75,236	3.7
Sports Illustrated	2,310,879	76,583	3.3

Source: ABC Fas-Fax June 30, 1976.
*ABC Magazine Publishers Statement.
†Editor's Estimate.

Exhibit 18.3B Comparative Advertising Information

Publication	Estab-lished	Freq'cy	Advertising Rates*		Printing Specs.			Price of Subscription	Circulation
			Bl & Wh	4-Color	Col†	Width‡	Depth		
Playboy (Men's Magazine)	1953	Monthly	$30,800	$42,590	3	32	140	$10.00	5,808,159
Oui (Men's Magazine)	1972	Monthly	9,450	14,875	2	32	140	10.00	1,302,390
VIP (Men's Int)	1964	Bi-Monthly	8,950	9,950	3	27	140	1.00	940,000
Penthouse (Men's Magazine)	1969	Monthly	15,000	25,000	3	27	140	8.00	4,003,619
Penthouse Forum (Human Relations)	1971	Monthly	—	—	2	26	98	10.00	241,900
Gallery (Men's Magazine)	1972	Monthly	3,185	4,780	3	26	136	15.00	750,000**
Cosmopolitan (Woman's Magazine)	1886	Monthly	9,680	12,980	3	27	143	15.00	2,014,208
Time (Current News)	1923	Weekly	29,975	46,460	3	27	140	18.00	4,388,471
Newsweek (Current News)	1933	Weekly	20,875	32,565	3	27	140	19.50	2,917,982
True (Men's Magazine)	1937	Monthly	3,500	5,250	3	27	143	7.00	931,537

*BW; one time black and white; 4C, four color page rate; rates effective April 1, 1976.

†Column length given in agate lines (14 lines equals 1 inch).

‡Column width given in nonpareils (12 nonpareils equals 1 inch).

**Estimated by authors.

Source: 1976 *Ayers Directory of Publications.*

Exhibit 18.4B Ratios for Playboy Enterprises, Inc.

	1971	1972	1973	1974	1975	1976
Liquidity Ratios						
Current Ratio	1.47	1.32	1.58	1.66	1.65	1.81
Acid-Test Ratio	1.02	.95	1.11	1.18	1.08	1.36
Cash Velocity	6.09	5.61	5.42	5.23	5.70	4.39
Inv to Net Working Capital	.97	1.15	.80	.73	.88	.55
Leverage Ratios						
Debt to Equity	1.57	1.20	1.09	.91	.96	.92
Current Liability to Net Worth	.47	.44	.41	.41	.39	.40
Activity Ratios						
Net Working Capital Turnover	13.06	16.27	10.43	9.25	9.53	7.39
Average Collection Period	41.33	43.02	39.60	41.00	30.02	35.75
Equity Capital Turnover	2.93	2.37	2.47	2.53	2.44	2.39
Total Capital Turnover	1.14	1.08	1.18	1.32	1.25	1.24
Profitability Ratios						
Gross Operating Margin	.28	.25	.22	.19	.13	.14
Net Operating Margin	.139	.122	.107	.053	.010	.026
Sales Margin	.070	.066	.059	.029	.006	.010
Return on Capital	.205	.157	.146	.074	.014	.025
Net Profit on Working Capital	.916	1.082	.618	.269	.053	.077

Source: Computed from annual statements.

Discussion Questions

1. Evaluate PEI's turnaround strategy.
2. What should PEI's Master Strategy be for the future? What should be divested?
3. How should *Playboy* magazine be marketed in the future? Why?
4. What other diversification efforts might be suitable for PEI?

References[1]

ABC Fas-Fax, June 30, 1976.

"An Ailing Playboy Gets a New Manager." *Business Week,* September 27, 1976, pp. 30–31.

"Big Problems for Playboy's Empire." *Business Week,* April 13, 1974, p. 74.

Correspondence with Public Relations Director, *Playboy* and *Penthouse*; Editor of *Gallery;* and Editorial Assistants of *Cosmopolitan* and *Playgirl.*

Crain, R. "A Conversation with Hugh Hefner." *Advertising Age,* July 1975, p. 26.

Davidson, B. "Czar of the Bunny Empire." *Saturday Evening Post,* April 28, 1962, p. 72.

"For Young City Guys." *Newsweek,* November 7, 1955, p. 68.

"Gonzalez, A. F., Jr. "Upstart Captain of Skindustry." *MBA,* September 1976, p. 19.

"The Happy Hustler." *Dun's Review,* November 1974, p. 91.

1. Several of the comments and statements made in the cases are taken directly from the above references. These quotations are not footnotes in the text but are referenced here.

Exhibit 18.5B Playboy: Advertising Information

Circulation

Year	Average Circulation per Month during First Six Months	Average Circulation per Month during Second Six Months	Semi-Annual Single Copy	Semi-Annual Single Copy
1976	5,405,400	—	66	34
1975	5,808,200	5,701,000	70	30
1974	6,426,900	6,125,300	76	24
1973	6,669,900	6,503,300	76	24
1972	6,614,000	6,978,000	78	22
1971	5,908,200	6,400,600	76	24

Advertising

Year Ended June 30	Number of Advertising Pages Carried	Gross Advertising	Average per Advertising Page	Net Advertising Revenues
1976	776.21	$33,981,000	$43,778	$29,075,000
1975	840.18	37,595,000	44,746	32,027,000
1974	922.02	40,343,000	43,755	34,884,000
1973	916.29	39,432,000	43,034	34,063,000
1972	952.61	36,610,000	38,431	31,089,000

Advertising and Circulation

Issues with Which Rates and Circulation Base Became Effective	Circulation Base	Black and White		Four-Color	
		Rate	Rate per Thousand Copies	Rate	Rate per Thousand Copies
January 1976	5,400,000	$29,125	$5.39	$40,745	$7.54
April 1975	6,000,000	32,340	5.39	45,250	7.54
July 1972	6,000,000	30,800	5.13	42,950	7.16
October 1971	5,250,000	27,500	5.24	38,950	7.42

Source: 1976 10-K.

Howard, N. A. "Woes of Playboy Empire Continuing to Mount." *Advertising Age,* January 20, 1975, p. 62.

———. "Playboy's President Search Has Deadline of June 30." *Advertising Age,* April 1976, p. 82.

Klein, R., and J. Lainy. "Playboy's Slide." *Wall Street Journal,* April 13, 1976, p. 1.

"Playboy after Hefner." *Dun's Review,* February 1974, p. 45.

Playboy Enterprises, Inc. *Annual Reports,* 1972, 1973, 1974, 1975, and 1976.

Playboy Enterprises, Inc. *Annual Report to the Securities and Exchange Commission,* 10-K, June 30, 1975 and 1976.

"Playboy Holds Key to Night Club Success." *Business Week,* June 25, 1966, p. 89.

"Playboy Interview: Hugh M. Hefner." *Playboy,* January 1974, p. 66.

Playboy Stock Prospectus, 1971.

Ross, I. "Skin-Deep Profits for the Man in Gold Chains." *Fortune,* January 1975, p. 101.

Assets

	1976	1975
Cash...	$ 14,914,000	$ 10,307,000
Receivables (Note C).......................................	19,645,000	16,482,000
Inventories (Notes A and D)................................	14,850,000	18,155,000
Other current assets.......................................	10,536,000	7,844,000
Total current assets....................................	59,945,000	52,788,000
Property, plant and equipment, at cost (Notes A and E)		
Land...	4,868,000	4,894,000
Buildings and improvements...............................	74,225,000	71,465,000
Furniture and equipment..................................	29,810,000	27,697,000
Leasehold improvements...................................	11,161,000	10,647,000
Aircraft...	—	5,959,000
Construction in process...................................	—	1,161,000
	120,064,000	121,823,000
Less accumulated depreciation and amortization..............	34,667,000	31,355,000
	85,397,000	90,468,000
Excess of cost over equity in net assets of subsidiaries acquired, less amortization (Note A)....................................	2,909,000	2,998,000
Recoverable income taxes (Note I)...........................	3,165,000	6,298,000
Other assets and deferred charges (Notes A and F).............	7,854,000	6,152,000
	$159,270,000	$158,704,000

Liabilities

	1976	1975
Current maturities of long-term debt (Note H)....................	$ 535,000	$ 506,000
Notes payable (Note G)......................................	1,500,000	3,350,000
Accounts payable...	14,012,000	11,699,000
Accrued expenses..	8,027,000	7,081,000
Income taxes (Note I)		
Currently payable..	5,656,000	4,740,000
Payable in future..	3,459,000	4,673,000
Total current liabilities..................................	33,189,000	32,049,000
Long-term debt (Note H).....................................	16,593,000	17,185,000
Deferred subscription income (Note A).......................	14,934,000	14,882,000
Deferred income taxes and investment credit (Notes A and I)......	11,662,000	13,447,000
Commitments and contingencies (Notes E, I, L and M)		

Shareholders' Equity

	1976	1975
Common stock, $1 par value; authorized 15,000,000 shares, issued 9,410,939 shares (Note J)	9,411,000	9,411,000
Capital in excess of par value.................................	12,372,000	12,372,000
Retained earnings...	62,447,000	60,696,000
	84,230,000	82,479,000
Less cost of 200,000 shares in treasury.......................	1,338,000	1,338,000
	82,892,000	81,141,000
	$159,270,000	$158,704,000

The accompanying notes are an integral part of the financial statements.

Exhibit 18.7B   Summary of Operations

	1972	1973	1974	1975	1976
Net Sales and Revenues					
Publishing					
PLAYBOY magazine..................	$ 83,103	$ 87,377	$ 86,321	$ 86,332	$ 78,889
OUI magazine......................	—	9,267	13,660	12,722	13,412
Other publishing...................	8,508	11,523	13,030	13,558	13,953
Total publishing................	91,611	108,167	113,011	112,612	106,254
Playboy Clubs International					
Clubs............................	29,244	33,281	38,342	39,856	48,402
Hotels...........................	31,263	39,922	40,663	32,801	29,410
Total PCI.......................	60,507	73,203	79,005	72,657	77,812
Entertainment					
Motion-picture and TV productions...	—	1,270	2,880	1,604	957
Records and music publishing......	83	121	101	780	2,000
Total entertainment.............	83	1,391	2,981	2,384	2,957
Other Operations...................	7,249	7,250	9,271	10,081	10,781
	$159,450	$190,011	$204,268	$197,734	$197,804
Earnings Before Income Taxes					
Publishing					
PLAYBOY magazine..................	$ 18,782	$ 21,918	$ 14,235	$ 8,467	$ 3,595
OUI magazine......................	—	983	(351)	(2,278)	200
Other publishing...................	881	1,056	(170)	(307)	758
Total publishing................	19,663	23,957	13,714	5,882	4,553
Playboy Clubs International					
Clubs (1)........................	3,178	5,324	5,911	3,195	9,150
Hotels (2).......................	(2,143)	(3,479)	(3,321)	(3,779)	(5,704)
Total PCI.......................	1,035	1,845	2,590	(584)	3,446
Entertainment					
Motion-picture and TV productions...	(299)	(2,585)	(2,269)	(1,102)	(933)
Records and music publishing......	(150)	(2,067)	(2,393)	(1,219)	(1,787)
Total entertainment.............	(449)	(4,652)	(4,662)	(2,321)	(2,720)
Other Operations...................	(849)	(853)	(843)	(928)	(195)
	$ 19,400	$ 20,297	$ 10,799	$ 2,049	$ 5,084

(1) The earnings figures for Clubs include earnings from the operations of the United Kingdom Clubs and gaming facilities. For information reflecting the relative after-tax profitability of these operations, see Note B to the consolidated financial statements.

(2) In May 1974, the company sold its Miami Beach, Florida, Resort Hotel to outside interests. The Hotel had been acquired in August 1970. The figures shown above for Hotels include operating losses sustained by the Miami Beach Hotel (before intracompany allocations) of approximately $1,203,000, $1,531,000 and $1,232,000 for each of the fiscal years 1972, 1973 and 1974.

	1976	1975
Sources of Funds		
Operations		
Net earnings..	$ 2,059,000	$ 1,096,000
Depreciation and amortization...........................	6,654,000	6,740,000
Deferred income taxes and investment credit...............	(1,785,000)	1,415,000
Recoverable income taxes (Note I).......................	3,133,000	(5,218,000)
Deferred subscription income............................	52,000	3,859,000
Other...	(253,000)	95,000
Funds provided from operations.....................	9,860,000	7,987,000
Proceeds from sale of aircraft (Note E).......................	4,225,000	—
Completion and release of films............................	472,000	931,000
	$ 14,557,000	$ 8,918,000
Application of Funds		
Additions to property, plant and equipment...................	$ 5,187,000	$ 6,782,000
Reduction of long-term debt...............................	592,000	499,000
Cash dividends (Note K)...................................	308,000	707,000
Investments, primarily condominium and town-house project (Note F).......................................	1,622,000	295,000
Other, net...	831,000	1,978,000
Increase (decrease) in working capital......................	6,017,000	(1,343,000)
	$ 14,557,000	$ 8,918,000
Changes in Working Capital Components		
Cash..	$ 4,607,000	$ 2,262,000
Receivables...	3,163,000	(6,767,000)
Inventories..	(3,305,000)	2,057,000
Other current assets.....................................	2,692,000	93,000
Notes payable and current maturities of long-term debt........	1,821,000	(1,512,000)
Accounts payable and accrued expenses....................	(3,259,000)	2,337,000
Income taxes..	298,000	187,000
Increase (decrease) in working capital......................	$ 6,017,000	$ (1,343,000)

The accompanying notes are an integral part of the financial statements.

Source: 1976 Annual Report.

19/Sterling County Hospital

Ed D. Roach and
B. C. Bizzell

Except for the larger metropolitan hospitals, hospitals historically
have been managed by a board of trustees composed of prominent
civic leaders who generously contribute one hour or so of their
time per month to oversee an operation they do not understand.
They contribute kindness, rather than management . . . If management in hospitals is to become something other than a titular activity, a power structure must be established whereby management
personnel with hospital savvy will be given the responsibility of
resolving: (a) the patient services to be provided by the hospital;
(b) the price that the patients will be charged for those services,
and (c) the administration of activities that will bring actual results
into conformity with those desired objectives . . .[1]

Ray G. Wasyluka

History of Sterling County Hospital

Sterling County Hospital was first conceived in 1926 by a group of civic-
minded individuals of Sterling, Texas. Lacking funds, this group convinced
the city commission to sell the city-owned power system for $150,000 to
build and furnish the facility. The land where the hospital structure was
erected was donated by a local citizen. On December 14, 1929, the hospital
opened its doors with 28 beds and an operating room to serve the city of
Sterling. At that time it was known as Sterling City Hospital, since Sterling
actually owned the facility.

As the city grew the demand for more facilities became more apparent.
In 1938, two floors were added to the back wing to increase the bed capacity
to approximately 50. Then in 1951, a three-story wing was added to the
east side of the main structure. This expansion doubled the patient bed
capacity to 100 and included a new surgical suite. It also allowed the former
surgical facilities to be converted and remodeled for obstetrics.

Expansion continued in 1954 when a minor program added 10 beds, a
recovery room, a doctors' lounge and locker room, and dining and food

Source: Prepared at Stephen F. Austin State University based on a student project done by Jean-Pierre
H. Guitton, James H. Holder, Gloria J. Page, and Laura L. Spurlin in the senior author's graduate course
in Administrative Policy. Copyright 1975 by Ed D. Roach and B. G. Bizzell. Presented at a case workshop and distributed by the Intercollegiate Case Clearing House, Soldiers Field, Boston, Massachusetts
02163. All rights reserved to the contributor. Printed in the U.S.A.

1. Ray G. Wasyluka, "New Blood for Tired Hospitals," *Management of Health Organizations* (A *Harvard Business Review* Reprint Series), p. 25. The article originally appeared
in the *Harvard Business Review*, September-October 1973.

storage facilities. Then in 1964 another major expansion project added a wing across the south. This wing contained 66 more beds on a complete second floor and a partial third floor. At the completion of this project the hospital contained 132 beds. During this phase of expansion, administration and business facilities, radiology, laboratory, and emergency facilities were established and/or improved on the ground floor.

On June 12, 1967, the Texas Legislature established the Sterling County Hospital District by passing bill #1011. The county judge of Sterling County then called for an election to allow the voters to establish and pass the Sterling County Hospital District and to assume the full responsibility of the operations of the hospital, including all assets and liabilities.

The vote was affirmative, and on May 6, 1968, ownership of the hospital changed from the city of Sterling to Sterling County. It was at this point that the name was changed from Sterling City Hospital to Sterling County Hospital. Sterling County Hospital is governed by a seven-member board elected by the voters of Sterling County. Of these seven members, four are elected one year and three the next to ensure that there are always experienced members on the board.

Board Composition. At the time of this case, the Sterling County board was composed of the following members:

Fred Jones, age 48. Owner of his own small manufacturing firm. Originally appointed to board to finish the term of a physician who resigned to form the competing hospital.

Joseph Wilson, age 53. Owner of fuel distribution firm and active in church as well as board. Has served for two terms.

Phillip Dobbs, age 55. Active in various agricultural interests. Has served on board longer than any other member.

Angela Teague, age 51. Wife of a wealthy local rancher and farmer.

Dr. Robert Williams, age 58. Local physician who has a private family practice. Wife is also a physician. Was on original board in 1968 but was off board, by choice, for two years.

Raymond Whittaker, age 76. Owner of construction company. Served on board until 1973 when he was defeated by Dr. Harrison Kramer, age 35. Professor at the local university.

Cecil Stevenson, age 43. Owner of several agricultural interests, including a retail establishment that serves the local agricultural economy.

The legislative act creating the hospital district also created a separate taxing entity. The revenue received from the taxpayers is separate from taxes collected from either the city or the county. Under the legislative action, there is a maximum of $.75 per $100 valuation of property. The hospital currently is taxing at $.40 per $100. Should the board desire to tax at a rate greater than $.75, it would first have to obtain legislative approval.

On October 1, 1968, additional property was purchased by the district for future expansion projects. The board also authorized and purchased a lot across from Sterling County Hospital for additional parking facilities. Currently, the hospital is engaged in a $2.3 million expansion project. This project will add 52 beds and bring the total rated capacity to between 160 and 170 beds. The reason that the 52-bed expansion does not bring the total to over 180 is that some of the beds in the older area are "nonconforming beds." They are nonconforming in that state laws governing square footage needed for a room with two patients have changed since those rooms were constructed. These rooms are to be converted to single-bed private rooms.

Sterling County Hospital recently acquired some new property for future expansion purposes, bringing the total present acreage of hospital property to approximately 4.2 acres.[2]

Stated Objectives of Sterling County Hospital

The stated objectives of Sterling County Hospital as spelled out in Sterling County Hospital's employee handbook are as follows:

To recognize man's unique composition of body and soul and man's basic right to life. Sterling County's concept of total care, therefore, embraces the physical, emotional, spiritual, social and economic needs of each patient.

To affirm that the primary objective of our health services is to relieve suffering and to promote and restore health in a Christian manner which demands competence, mercy, and respect.

To generate and cultivate a source of allied health manpower by orienting and supporting personnel development in the areas of individual skills, knowledges and attitudes.

To participate in the development of health services that are relevant to the total community needs by meaningful area-wide and regional planning and in a partnership for health concept.

Sterling County Hospital's Administrators: Past and Present

Webber Davis. To gain an accurate picture of the administrative past of Sterling County Hospital, it is desirable to start with the administration of Webber Davis. Webber Davis came to Sterling County Hospital in September of 1967 from a large hospital in Dallas. Because of his experience in the hospital field, the board found Davis to be a valuable asset as the hospital made the transition from a city-owned to a county-owned facility.

Employees and members of the hospital board have stated that Mr. Davis was "an efficient administrator." When he arrived at Sterling Hospital, there were no organization chart and no job descriptions, and in general

2. Sterling City is a community of approximately 25,000 people.

there existed an organization that could be characterized as highly informal (with resulting poor communication channels, both up and down). Davis immediately began to develop written job descriptions; also, he organized the hospital and departments as shown in the organization chart in Figure 19.1. Then he developed policy and procedure manuals for each department with the goal being to increase the efficiency of operations.

Next, Davis attacked the problem of in-house communication. Davis visited almost daily with the different doctors in their private lounge. It was in informal meetings such as these that he became fully aware of their problems and gained a deeper insight into the type of medical supplies and equipment that they deemed important.

Davis established an easy style of professional communication with the Sterling County Hospital Board. He accepted their policy of holding the administrator totally responsible for the operation of Sterling County Hospital.[3] Davis spent many hours in conference with the board gathering from them the information needed to direct Sterling County on a growth path to offer ever-better service to the community.

It was in the area of employee-management communications that Webber Davis was apparently unable to fully achieve his desires. Employees who worked under his direction appeared to have great admiration for him as a man and as an administrator, but many comments were offered such as: "Mr. Davis was a great guy; he just didn't have quite enough time to listen and talk with us."

Rift between the Physicians and the Board. Around 1970, a group of physicians practicing at Sterling County became convinced that Sterling needed an entirely new hospital facility. These doctors and a group of followers in the community obtained enough support to bring their proposal to the attention of the voters of Sterling County. This proposal called for the building of an entirely new ultra-modern hospital facility in a geographic location other than where the present hospital stands. A hospital architectural firm studied the area and recommended that the facility be located outside the city proper because of the narrow and highly congested streets that emergency vehicles were forced to use. This proposal further called for the closing of Sterling County Hospital or its conversion to a nursing home. The Sterling County Hospital Board was opposed to this proposal. When formally presented to the people of Sterling, the voters defeated the proposal by a substantial majority.

The defeat of the new hospital project brought an extremely delicate management problem into Webber Davis's life. He was caught between a few very forceful and vocal physicians who were thoroughly dissatisfied

3. Over the years, the Sterling County Hospital Board has more or less followed the practice of making recommendations to the administrator; but it is, according to statements by some board members, up to the administrator as to whether to implement the policy. On large and/or expensive proposals, the administrator presents ideas to the board and then acts according to their votes.

Figure 19.1   Organization Chart for Sterling County Hospital

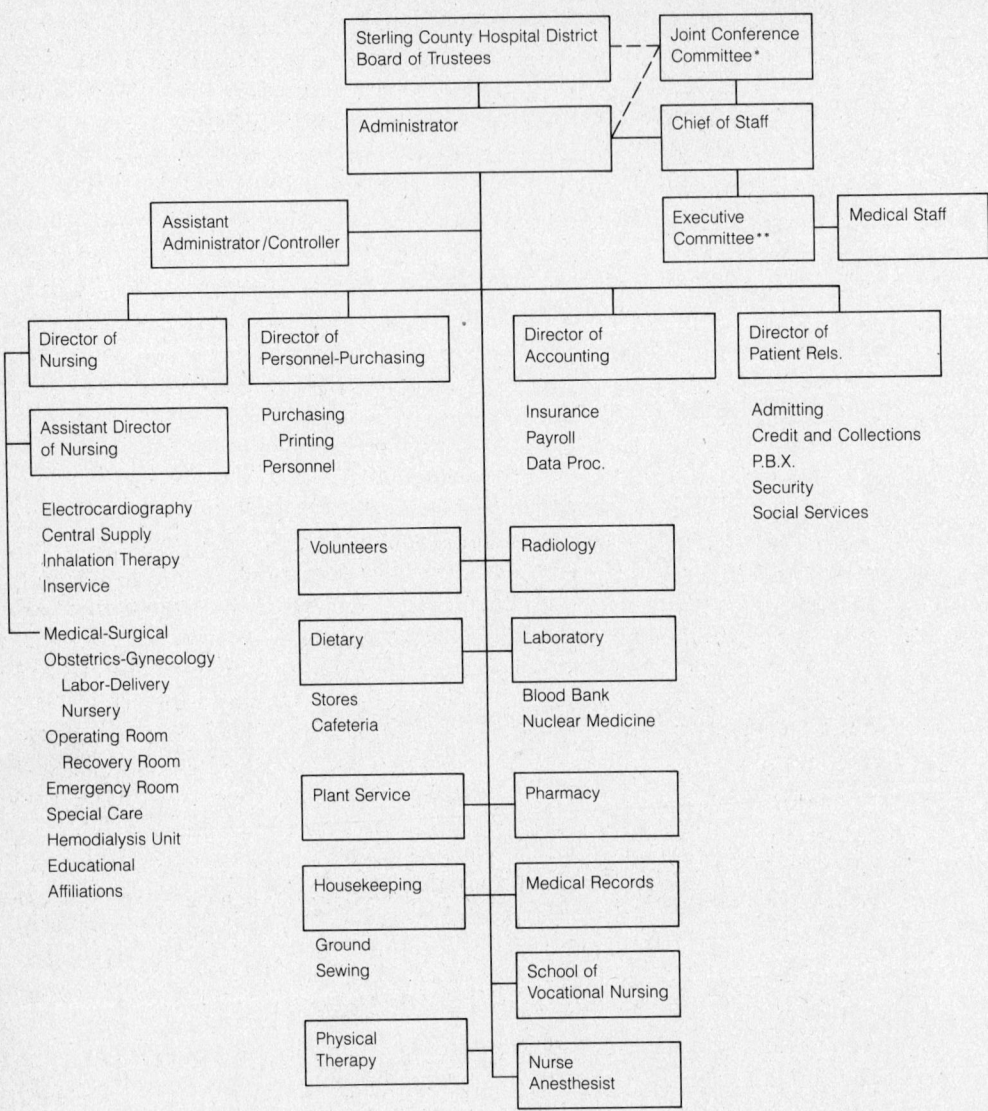

* Joint Conference Committee: This committee is made up of the three offices of the board of directors—The chairman, vice-chairman and secretary—and three physicians from the medical staff—one of which is the chief of staff.

** Executive Committee: This committee is made up of the heads of the various departments of the hospital, ie surgery, radiology, etc.

with the outcome of the election and just as vocal and perhaps an even more forceful hospital board.

The group of dissatisfied physicians sought out and received the support of Medical Corporation. Medical Corporation is an organization that specializes in hospital management and in this case actually did the groundwork, i.e., obtaining land, needed permits for construction, financing, etc., for the group of physicians who were to become the owners of the new private hospital in Sterling (this facility was completed in early 1975).

The Sterling County Hospital Board apparently was fully aware of the action that was taking place, i.e., the physicians' plans for a new, privately funded hospital, and they exerted pressure in the only area of their total control—in the direction of Webber Davis, administrator. Evidently the pressure of the situation became more frustrating than Davis could tolerate because he finally accepted an offer from a larger hospital in a major city in Texas.

James Dula. Upon receiving notification that Davis was resigning, the board immediately began to search for a new administrator. From some twenty résumés submitted for consideration, and with Davis's assistance, the field was narrowed to five. Of these five, one informed the board that he had just accepted a job and would be unable to give further consideration to the Sterling Hospital position.

It was during this period of time that Webber Davis met and became acquainted with James Dula at a hospital administrator's conference. Davis informed Dula of the opening and that the board was interviewing that week. Dula asked Davis to help him contact the board and get an interview. The board granted Dula an interview late on Friday evening and the next day made final financial arrangements to hire him.

James Dula came to Sterling County Hospital from St. Mary's Hospital in Austin. The Board of Directors was impressed with his qualifications and his professional abilities as is evidenced by the "rapid manner in which he was hired." In addition to his professional qualifications, it was a definite advantage, from the board's point of view, that James Dula could be moved quickly to Sterling.

James Dula's administrative position at Sterling County Hospital "just never solidified." Whereas Davis had established lines of communication with the doctors and the board members and had at least attempted to communicate with the employees at the hospital, Dula "closed his office door and did not seriously attempt to bring the factions together." One board member stated that Dula had a serious problem: "He just could not make a decision."

James Dula's administrative philosophy was that each department was a business entity and the department head was totally responsible for its actions. In the opinion of one board member, this policy could have worked, except for two facts:

First, the department heads had little administrative experience, and second, Dula did not give his department heads the needed support of his business knowledge.

In analyzing the administration of James Dula it is of interest to note the format for most board meetings and the expectations of the board members of the hospital administrator at these meetings. The board typically meets once each month. During these meetings, the directors usually review the monthly financial statement, entertain comments and questions from guests, evaluate proposals submitted by the administrator, and transact any and all responsibilities with which they have been entrusted by the voters.

The financial statements are obviously an important input to the directors' evaluation of the hospital's performance. Members of the board related that after James Dula assumed control, there were instances (several meetings) where the directors were either not furnished financial statements, or they were given these statements at the beginning of the meeting with no time to study their contents. One board member stated, "We could have been ruined if we hadn't caught on to his inefficiency." Another board member observed:

The principal complaint of the board was Mr. Dula's inability to answer questions concerning the operations of the hospital. He believed his department heads were responsible for these questions.

Another expression of dissatisfaction with Dula concerned his apparent over-concern with small items and a seeming lack of appreciation of some of the more important matters. One interesting example related by an official of the hospital concerned his ordering of several thousand pencils—"a necessary item, but perhaps not in that quantity," this official observed—while not being able to account for a large quantity of missing bed sheets.

James Dula also had what the board believed to be an over-concern for the collection of statistics. These statistics were generally compiled from within the hospital and then compared either to industry-wide or large city hospital statistics. The board believed that the total good accomplished by these statistical studies was extremely small. The board felt, in effect, that the time spent on these studies was misallocated.

The Case of Ms. Underwood, Director of Nursing. A problem that is common to the hospital industry is that of attracting and keeping efficient, qualified personnel, e.g., nurses, aides, orderlies, etc. The director of nursing, as can be observed from the previously presented organization chart, is responsible for the supervision of these personnel; and turnover took perhaps a greater toll among these groups at Sterling County than one might have expected.

Ms. Underwood was a well-qualified professional nurse, according to hospital officials. However, she was by nature a very domineering individual. She showed little respect for those working below her and as a result morale was expectedly low. Ms. Underwood's view of her job responsibilities is very interesting. One physician alleged that she could very seldom be found on any floor doing anything that resembled common nursing procedures. This physician indicated that he once observed to Ms. Underwood:

Ms. Underwood, I never see you on the floor . . . I never see you
in the emergency room! You are never there! In fact I never see
you in your uniform.

Her rationale for not appearing on the floor was that she was busy with her paperwork. On several occasions, Ms. Underwood used her dominant personality to "completely dominate Mr. Dula," in the words of one hospital employee. An example of her ability to "take control" is related by a Sterling County physician:

Drug control has been and will always be a problem around a
hospital facility. Ordinarily, all hard or addictive or dangerous drugs
are kept locked in the pharmacy department on the first floor.
About the only exception to this is a drug such as adrenaline or
some other life-saving drug that might be needed in just a moment's
notice. This type of drug is then kept in a very limited quantity
right on the floor.
    Ms. Underwood discovered, in some medical journal, a new
cart that could be kept on each floor. This cart could be stocked
out of the pharmacy and in essence would be a small pharmacy
which could be located on each floor.
    In theory, it is a good idea. However, the drawbacks far outweigh
the benefits. First of all, drug inventory would be difficult to compute; second, hard drugs would be more readily accessible to dis-
honest individuals; and third (and probably most important of all),
if you as a doctor needed an injection immediately for a patient, you
would still have to hunt for the nurse who had the key to the cart.
    If we hadn't found out about her plans when we did, Ms. Under-
wood would have had those $1,100 carts on each floor.

Recruitment of Panamanian Nurses. As has been previously noted, nursing turnover was a problem, and now the new hospital was being constructed. Ms. Underwood was held directly responsible for the recruiting of nurses. She decided (what information her decision was based upon is not known) that the only real solution to the present and future problem of nurse turnover was to recruit nurses from the Panama. After having discussed the plan with James Dula, it was decided that she should go to Panama for the purpose of recruiting approximately 50 nurses. One of the board members gives the following account of the board reaction to this move:

It was brought to the attention of the Board of Directors at a Board meeting by Mr. Dula and Ms. Underwood that a possibility existed for obtaining needed nurses for Sterling County hospital by making a contract with a firm which supplied Panamanian nurses in the United States. The Board listened to Mr. Dula's and Ms. Underwood's proposal and made the following statement: "The Board feels that it is not wise to proceed with this matter at the present since it is not known if (1) the nurses would have a good command of English; (2) if they would be properly trained; (3) if they would have any difficulty finding living accommodations in the city of Sterling once they arrived, and, (4) how the community would react to a number of foreign-born nurses in the community."

The Board thought that the item had been dropped until one day I was having a conversation with an individual who at the time was a neighbor of James Dula. He asked me what I knew about the 50 Panamanian nurses coming into the hospital. I told him that I knew nothing of this matter. I contacted other board members and asked them what they knew about it. None of them knew anything. A meeting was arranged between the Executive Committee of the Board and myself and Mr. Dula to discuss this matter.

Mr. Dula took the position that, "Yes, Ms. Underwood has gone to Panama to recruit nurses"; that, "Yes, she has made a contract with 50 of these girls to bring them to Sterling City to practice"; that "She felt that they were highly qualified." The Board questioned Mr. Dula in the relationship to the fact that the Board had given him a direct order not to bring the nurses into the city until he had cleared it first with the Board of Directors. Mr. Dula's position was that he, as chief executive officer of the hospital, had the authority and the responsibility to staff the hospital and that he did this under this staffing authority in the sense that he felt that the nurses were needed. The Board reacted rather unfavorably to Mr. Dula's direct countermand of its order and began seeking solutions as to what could be done to prevent the 50 nurses from coming. The end result was that the original contracts were voided by accepting only 5 of the nurses who were originally scheduled to come into the hospital to practice. The other 45 did not come.

One hospital official observed that the five Panamanian nurses who did come to Sterling County Hospital "are working out well and more nurses may be imported in the future; but if the board had not taken quick and decisive action, the problem could have exploded into one involving the entire community."

James Dula left Sterling County Hospital at the end of 1974. Looking back upon the unfortunate events which began with the hiring of Dula and continued throughout his administration, one board member (himself elected to the board after the hiring of Dula) gave his assessment as to how it had all begun:

No one on the board really remembers (or will admit) exactly how Dula was hired. Actually, I think they hired his wife. At any rate, the Board had interviewed several people to be the Administrator of Sterling County Hospital replacing Mr. Davis. Mr. Davis had indicated that a Mr. Dula would also like to interview for the job and that he had not known Mr. Dula personally, but that he was impressed with the man upon meeting him. Mr. Dula was contacted; he made an immediate trip to Sterling City from Austin, where he was at that time living. He came to Sterling City and met the then Board of Directors along with Mrs. Dula.

The Board was relatively impressed with Mr. Dula, but they were extremely impressed with Mrs. Dula, as she has a rather gracious personality, is very outgoing and is a definite asset to any community in which she would live. In retrospect, some of the Board members indicated later that they felt like the hiring was of Mrs. Dula and not so much of Mr. Dula.

A rather personal opinion is that Mrs. Dula is the driving force behind her husband.

The board began looking toward replacing James Dula before he was notified that he would not be continued as administrator of Sterling County Hospital. Mr. Dula apparently became aware that this was going on, or at least had a suspicion that this was going on and called one of the directors at his home one evening about 10:30 p.m. rather upset, wanting to know if the board was indeed looking for a replacement for him. This director observes:

I informed Mr. Dula that this was indeed the fact, that the Board was dissatisfied with his performance, and that they were in the process of looking for a replacement. At the time of this conversation with Mr. Dula, the Board had interviewed three people—two of whom had indicated that they were interested in the position, but no commitment had been made to anyone.

During the month of November of 1974, the Board reached an informal agreement with Mr. Wilber Page, who was at that time the Administrator of Pine Haven Hospital in Forsythe (a nearby city approximately the same size of Sterling City). Mr. Page agreed to come to Sterling County Hospital as its Administrator on the first of January 1975.

The Board immediately contacted Mr. Dula and informed him that they were giving him, in essence, a 90-day notice of termination of employment and asked that he resign. Mr. Dula did resign with the stipulation that he would be paid for 90 days from the first of November, 1974. This meant that there would be a one-month overlap between Mr. Page and Mr. Dula. For the month of January, Mr. Dula was given his month's salary and was requested not to return to the hospital.

The Executive Committee of the Board met with Mr. Dula, Ms.

Underwood, and Mr. Albert Smith (Dula's controller) around mid-November of 1974, and informed all three people at that time that they would not be continued in their positions after the first of January, with the exception of Mr. Dula, who was given 90-day notice rather than a 60-day notice.

Mr. Smith took this information very graciously indicating that he was probably tired of the job anyway; Ms. Underwood was extremely upset and tendered her resignation immediately.

Wilber Page. Mr. Page was one of the administrators who had been given consideration when James Dula was originally hired. However, he informed the board at that time that he would not be able to consider the position because Pine Haven Hospital (in Forsythe) was undergoing an expansion program; and he felt that he should retain his position there. When the second opportunity presented itself, Page decided to accept the position under the following conditions (as related by a member of the Sterling Board of Directors):

Mr. Page, as a part of the general agreement in accepting this position, insisted that he review all department heads and make a choice as to those he wished to retain and to have those he wished replaced. He insisted, and it was readily agreed upon by the Board of Directors, that he be able to bring Mr. Fredrik Thomas to Sterling County Hospital from Memorial Hospital in Forsythe. Mr. Thomas would act as Page's assistant administrator as well as the controller of the hospital. Mr. Page also indicated that he would not accept Ms. Underwood as director of nursing at Sterling County and said that he would either bring someone from Forsythe with him or would replace her with someone on the staff at Sterling County Hospital.

Mr. Page came to Sterling City and discussed this matter with several people in the hospital and decided that Ms. Jean Holder was ideally suited to be director of nursing and indicated to the Board that he would like Ms. Underwood not to be in her position when he arrived.

Before assuming her position as director of nursing, Ms. Jean Holder had been performing general nursing duties. A breakdown of the nurses under Ms. Holder is shown in Table 19.1.

As Mr. Page took control at the beginning of the year (1974), Ms. Holder (as did the other department heads) adopted one of Wilber Page's "ground-rule" policies. This is the policy of an open administrative door. To quote Mr. Page:

In my fifteen years of hospital administration, I have always had, and I have here, an open-door policy. I have no employee that is not important. Any employee in this building can come in this office, sit down in one of those chairs, and talk to me about any problem that he might have.

Wilber Page hired as his controller, as noted above, Mr. Fredrik Thomas. In addition to his duties as controller, Thomas serves as assistant administrator and is also in charge of purchasing. The occupancy of this latter position is the result of the resignation of the former director of purchasing.

Table 19.1   Nurses at Sterling County Hospital

Category	Number
Registered Nurses	11
Licensed Vocational Nurses	28
Graduate Nurses	10
Graduate Vocational Nurses	2
Nursing Technician—2	2
Nursing Technician—1	1
Nurses Aid 4th Class	3
Nurses Aid 1, 2, 3rd Class	65
Ward Clerks	21
Total	143

[handwritten margin notes: "don't have qualified skill staff", "no professional degree, train on the job 3 yrs., more technical, doesn't involve them detail, more focus on biological parts, lack on sound & spiritual", "graduate already, join the hospital training pro", "minimal train"]

Table 19.2   Comparative Salary Expense

Department	May 1974	May 1975
General Administration	$12,597.74	$14,272.05
Accounting	2,653.77	2,407.08
Data Processing	4,762.83	3,963.69
Communications	1,130.34	1,275.05
Dietary	10,540.15	11,793.14
Housekeeping	9,552.42	10,792.56
Plant Maintenance	3,033.41	2,900.42
Nursing Service	51,101.74	51,657.97
OB-GYN-Delivery	8,332.35	6,751.29
Nursery	3,914.66	2,386.38
Intensive Care	4,285.24	4,894.79
Operating Room	7,176.18	7,567.66
Recovery Room	528.68	546.21
Central Supply	2,218.48	1,370.81
Renal Dialysis	430.00	419.13
Emergency Room	5,155.69	5,204.50
Laboratory	8,102.80	7,071.71
EKG	1,596.74	1,448.35
X-Ray	6,052.74	6,499.95
Pharmacy	2,460.18	3,077.37
Anesthesiology	7,070.09	5,746.02
Inhalation Therapy	2,489.98	2,869.36
Physical Therapy	1,453.59	1,889.52
Medical Records	2,358.07	2,054.04
Ambulance Service	9,076.89	9,519.48
Total	$168,074.76	$168,378.53

Page decided not to hire another director of purchasing but to absorb the job among his department heads, Fredrik Thomas, and himself. This action resulted in the "saving of the salary of the former director of purchasing." The work load of several other positions that opened has been absorbed to further save the hospital salary expense. A comparative salary expense listing is given in Table 19.2

In evaluating the short tenure of Wilber Page at Sterling County Hospital, several board members, doctors, and employees comment, "We have a fine administrator in Mr. Page." Another comment describing Page is as follows:

He is fully aware of the construction process of the new wing. He constantly keeps in touch with the contractors and keeps the board fully informed. When the board issues a directive he does not "put it off." He immediately begins with the project (whether large or small).

His organization is one of total control; while maintaining a highly departmentalized structure, his success stems from staffing those positions with highly competent individuals and in giving them his complete professional support.

He is also fully aware of the future medical needs of the community. The hospital currently is engaged in a project of physician recruitment which will upgrade the medical service of Sterling County Hospital to an all-time high.

All is not "sweetness and light" for Sterling County Hospital, its board, and its new administrator, however. With the opening of the new hospital early in 1975, interorganizational rivalries began to evidence themselves. Apparent ill-will exists between some board members and staff members of Sterling County Hospital and the group of physicians who left Sterling County to form the new Medical Center. Some of these physicians still treat a limited number of patients at Sterling County Hospital, e.g., those who are taken to the emergency room at Sterling County and then ask for a particular physician.

Typical of the problems found by the new administrator is the following:

Dr. X's phone bill was running upwards of $250 per month. Upon checking the numbers called, it was found that Dr. X was using the Sterling County Hospital phone for his own private business e.g., to call his stockbroker. Wilber Page's action was to have the telephone removed and he explained it to the doctor on the basis of cost avoidance on the part of the hospital.

Dr. X, a radiologist who operated his practice originally out of Sterling County Hospital and was a leader in the new hospital movement, now works as the staff radiologist at the new doctors' hospital and has his offices there.

Exhibit 19.1   Sterling County Hospital District Balance Sheet, May 31, 1975

Assets	Current Year Month Ended May 1975	Last Year Month Ended May 1974
Current Assets		
Cash and Certificates of Deposit	$ 506,904.81	$ 928,105.08
Accounts Receivable	1,128,584.07	969,833.12
Allowance for Bad Debts	(374,873.80)	(214,881.14)
Allowance for Medicare Adjustment	(117,387.64)	(115,370.14)
Other Receivables	19,855.06	4,437.14
Inventories	146,780.48	118,003.27
Prepaid Expenses	27,827.84	9,503.23
Total Current Assets	$1,337,690.82	$1,699,630.56
Other Assets		
U.S. Gov't Bond—Social Security	$ –0–	$ 6,000.00
Work in Progress—New Wing	1,510,508.84	41,621.00
Fixed Assets—Cost		
Land and Parking Lot	$ 91,090.90	$ 91,090.90
Hospital Facilities	2,614,186.42	2,356,101.64
Ambulance and Equipment	40,985.71	38,512.10
Accumulated Depreciation	(1,272,984.10)	(950,938.16)
Total Fixed Assets	$1,473,278.93	$1,534,766.48
Total Assets	$4,321,478.59	$3,282,018.04

Liabilities and Fund Balance		
Current Liabilities		
Accounts Payable	$ 204,100.30	$ 176,247.34
Note Payable	50,000.00	—
Construction Contracts Payable	261,709.41	—
Payroll and Accrued Liabilities	55,900.30	74,010.57
Due Medicare and Medicaid	(9,773.05)	5,694.65
Other Liabilities	777.11	(12,977.17)
Current Portion—Long Term Debt	40,000.00	45,000.00
Total Current Liabilities	$ 602,714.07	$ 287,975.39
Deferred Income	$ 93,790.00	$ 93,790.00
Long Term Debt—Less Portion Classified as Current Liability	$1,415,000.00	$ 450,000.00
Total Liabilities	$2,111,504.07	$ 831,765.39
Fund Balance	$2,209,974.52	$2,450,252.65
Total Liabilities and Fund Balance	$4,321,478.59	$3,282,018.04

Exhibit 19.2   Sterling County Hospital District Revenue and Expenses, May 1975

Department	Revenue	Expenses	Profit
Medical and Surgical	$103,722.50	$ 54,587.38	$ 49,135.12
OB-GYN & Delivery Room	10,773.51	6,905.18	3,868.33
Nursery	840.00	2,439.65	(1,599.65)
Intensive Care Unit	6,500.00	5,126.23	1,373.77
Operating Room	13,030.00	9,802.84	3,227.16
Recovery Room	2,935.00	552.57	2,382.43
Central Service	21,169.76	10,256.75	10,913.01
Renal Dialysis	1,950.00	777.84	1,172.16
Emergency Room	8,458.08	5,807.05	2,651.03
ER Coverage Physician Fees	420.00	1,600.00	(1,180.00)
Laboratory	30,820.55	21,656.45	9,164.10
E. K. G. ⇒ electro-cardiogram	4,008.00	2,924.31	1,083.69
X-Ray & Nuclear Medicine	23,843.10	12,430.53	11,412.57
Pharmacy	34,683.60	16,955.14	17,728.46
Anesthesiology 麻醉	8,980.00	6,274.87	2,705.13
Inhalation Therapy	14,273.75	4,243.41	10,030.34
Physical Therapy	2,709.50	2,184.39	525.11
Ambulance	6,832.50	10,887.30	(4,054.80)
Total	$295,949.85	$175,411.89	$120,537.96

Provisions for Bad Debts & Charity	(27,914.29)
Medicare Contractual Adjustments	(17,652.98)
Employee Discounts & Other Expenses	(7,598.06)
Depreciation	(8,606.24)
General Services & Fiscal Administration Expenses	(111,455.51)
Tax Revenue	7,206.87
Cafeteria	8,646.90
Recovery of Bad Debts	2,232.83
Other Income	29,161.79
Net Profit (Loss)	($ 5,440.73)

Discussion Questions

1. What are the functions of a Board of Directors?
2. Did Sterling's Board of Directors properly discharge their functions?
3. What additional policies should they have had?
4. What differences in Board actions might have occurred if this had been a more profit-oriented organization?
5. What are the leadership styles of the three administrators? How do these styles affect results?
6. Discuss the role of hospital administrator (top manager) as an integrator.
7. What should Sterling's Master Strategy be? Why?

20/Edwards, Kimball, & Hall, CPAs: Marketing of Professional Services

Frederick E. Webster, Jr.
and Frank Brown

As Pete Ford, a manager in the firm of Edwards, Kimball, and Hall (EK&H), one of the "Big Eight" accounting firms, returned to his office after a series of conversations with several colleagues, he pondered his new assignment. Pete had recently transferred into the San Francisco office and had been given responsibility for coordinating the office's practice development (PD) effort. Practice development was the term applied by EK&H and other "Big Eight" firms to the firm's program of increasing their chargeable hours through expansion of the firm's practice. PD was a firm-wide program within EK&H with a goal of five percent annual growth in chargeable hours. The San Francisco office had been lagging the national growth goal and was considerably behind other offices which had exceeded this goal. Pete Ford had been responsible for PD in his previous assignment in the firm's Hartford office, which had achieved results well above average. Considerable debate had taken place throughout the firm concerning responsibility for PD among staff members at various levels and what sort of priority it should receive in discharging daily responsibilities. Pete knew that many staff members were negatively disposed in their approach to PD, but he felt that there were many possible explanations for their negative attitudes, not all of which he understood. It was his assigned responsibility to develop an effective PD program within the San Francisco office, and he wondered what steps to take next.

EK&H was a large international accounting firm with approximately 60 domestic offices and 175 other locations throughout the rest of the world. Each of these offices operated in a semiautonomous manner under the direction of the partner in charge of that office. Matters which affected the worldwide operations of the firm were reviewed by the Policy Committee and appropriate action recommended.

The San Francisco office of EK&H was staffed by 148 professional people, 10 partners, 35 managers, 33 senior accountants, and 70 staff accountants. A person was usually promoted to senior accountant status after three or four years with the firm. Similar to other accounting firms, EK&H experienced roughly 20 to 25 percent turnover each year among the staff, mostly at the

Source: Prepared by Professor Frederick E. Webster, Jr., and Frank Brown, Research Assistant, and made possible by the cooperation of a firm which wishes to remain anonymous. Note: This is a hypothetical case study and no attempt has been made to adhere to any state rules or regulations regarding the "marketing of professional services." Those that practice in such states must understand the state rules thoroughly and adhere to them. Copyright © 1975 by the Trustees of Dartmouth College, The Amos Tuck School of Business Administration. Distributed by the Intercollegiate Case Clearing House, Soldiers Field, Boston, Mass. 02163. All rights reserved to the contributors. Printed in the U.S.A.

advanced staff accountant and young senior accountant levels. Staff members at all levels from staff accountants to partners-in-charge maintained contact with clients.

In addition to its auditing services, EK&H offered tax advisory services and management advisory (that is, consulting) services (MAS). Tax and MAS each yielded about 15 percent of the firm's annual revenues. Each office had at least one partner and several other staff members in tax and MAS. MAS competence was focused primarily in electronic data processing, inventory control, management information systems, and related areas of administrative control. Many of the larger offices also had industry specialists in small business, hospital administration, governmental agency management, and other areas, depending on the composition of the local business community served. The San Francisco office, for example, had industry specialists in over a dozen areas including electronics, architecture and engineering, banking, and wine producing. The local partner-in-charge was responsible for developing the industry specialist program in his office. Exhibit 20.1 shows the areas in which the firm had designated a lead Industry Specialist Partner.

During the mid-1970s, a number of events came about which directly affected the firm's growth and stimulated a renewed interest in practice development. Due to economic recession, growth of client companies had abated, and with it the growth in audit fees. Beyond the decreased growth, there was additional pressure by the companies to reduce present audit expenses. The depressed economy also produced a smaller number of public offerings and led to a reduced number of growing companies needing the services of a national or international auditor. These factors had combined to reduce the pool of available new work for the Big Eight and thus increase the competition for it.

The Practice Development Task Force

To meet this challenge, in 1973 a Practice Development Task Force consisting of five partners was established. Its purpose was to examine the firm's present PD effort and to develop a plan which would serve as a PD guideline for the local offices. As a result of this study, a target of a sustained five percent growth per year in the firm's chargeable hours was established. It was felt that this figure was a reasonable one for the firm to achieve and still maintain control over the quality of its service. If annual chargeable hours grew faster than five percent, the Task Force judged that it would be difficult to maintain the quality of the professional staff. Over the long run, the reputation of the firm could suffer.

In addition to the desire to increase the firm's annual chargeable hours, there was another reason why new sources of revenue had to be secured each year. Of the firm's total chargeable hours, approximately seventy percent were recorded by the auditing staff and fifteen percent each by the consulting and tax groups. Fifteen to twenty percent of the audit and tax work was non-recurring, while almost all of the consulting work was nonrecurring. Thus, just to stay even with last year's chargeable hours, the firm needed to regenerate thirty percent of its chargeable hours each year.

Improved earnings also required that existing client relationships be maintained, for two reasons. First, when a new client was obtained, it was understood that EK&H would bear the start-up costs of learning the client's accounting and control systems. These one-time costs could be as much as thirty percent of the annual audit fee. Thus, it was necessary to maintain the client's business if this investment was to be recouped. Secondly, as the relationship developed over time, EK&H could perform the annual audit with less staff time. Therefore, as the client company grew and required more audit services, or as hourly billing rates increased, the total cost of the annual audit for an established client might not increase as greatly as for a newer client.

In addition to establishing a growth objective, the report of the PD Task Force also recommended other steps to improve practice development efforts, all of which had been implemented. A permanent PD Task Force was established, consisting of five senior partners. This group had a rotating chairman. A practice development manual was prepared, and this was the basis for a series of seminar experiences, as well as a handbook to be used by all staff members. It included sections on:

Practice Development Organization
Maintaining and Developing a Practice Development Program
Providing Quality Service
Improving Proposal Acceptance Percentage
Improving Community Image
Use of Firm Periodicals
Professional Development

Appendix 20A contains material from the manual outlining the scope of practice development.

Working closely with the PD Task Force was the senior partner responsible for Professional Development. Within a year the firm had arranged for the production of a series of videotapes, some using professional actors, available to local offices as part of their PD training activities. These tapes reviewed the basic principles of PD as found in the Practice Development Manual and also presented case examples of successful PD effort.

AICPA Professional Standards

Public accounting firms practice their profession under a very rigid set of professional standards and ethics. Among the most restrictive of these is Rule 502 of the Ethics Bylaws of the American Institute of Certified Public

Accountants (AICPA) pertaining to advertising and solicitation (see Exhibit 20.2). As shown in the exhibit, advertising or solicitation in any manner is forbidden. A particularly onerus restriction is the inability of a firm or an individual to specify competence in an area. For example, a tax specialist is not allowed to indicate that specialization on a business card, and the international services of EK&H cannot be displayed in any public manner. Once an individual solicits information concerning the firm and its specialties, this information can be brought out. Within the profession these restrictions are generally agreed to mean that the firm can actively promote itself only by building and maintaining its reputation and by its professional conduct. Because of these restrictions, many people in the firm felt at a loss as to how they might further promote their firm and remain within the code of conduct. In addition, most states have similar and in some cases more stringent rules relating to advertising and solicitation.

The Development of PD at the Hartford Office

Since Pete Ford had helped to develop a successful PD program in Hartford, it was felt he could apply his experience in helping the San Francisco office with its effort. As Pete reflected on this prior experience, he remembered the rocky road which characterized the initiation of PD in the Hartford office. First, there had been a flurry of activity generating lists of potential clients. This was followed by a series of educational office functions which everyone felt compelled to attend. Many people became discouraged by all the activity without any clearcut plan or direction. After a while, attendance at PD meetings dropped off noticeably. It was then that Pete sat down with one of the Hartford senior accountants, Ross Land, and discussed the program with him. During the conversation, Ross had explained the desire of many of the staff accountants and senior accountants to participate in the PD program, but he complained, "We don't know where we fit in." Most were too inexperienced to have developed a wide range of business contacts. They were typically very busy on audits and were really pressed for time to attend PD meetings.

Pete had agreed with most of what Ross had said, but he explained that the younger accountants' business contacts would develop over time. Although the young accountants should maintain old friendships such as college classmates, the responsibility for this type of PD work falls more heavily on the partners and managers. On the other hand, the staff accountants and senior accountants were in a much better position to identify opportunities with existing clients as they performed the audit and demonstrated the expertise of EK&H. As the staff member advanced from staff accountant through the ranks to partner, day-to-day-contact with the client was replaced by more general discussions with a wide variety of people.

As Pete Ford had considered various means of stimulating interest in PD in the Hartford office, he had developed the idea of forming a number of PD task groups around certain industries or accounting issues. Only those people interested in the topic would join, and they would be directed by a senior accountant or manager who had already acquired expertise in the area. This type of program would accomplish several objectives. First, those people interested in PD in general could participate. Next, people with an interest in a specific subject or industry could acquire an expertise in it under the tutelage of a knowledgeable person. Finally, the office would benefit from the development of technical competence as well as PD information. Several groups were soon formed and seemed to work quite well. These groups carried on seminars with the local industry specialists and members of other local professional groups (i.e., lawyers and bankers). Before long, some tangible results from this activity had appeared. In one case, one of the staff accountants had recognized an opportunity for consulting work at a local hospital, as the result of an earlier presentation by a hospital specialist at one of these group meetings. The hospital industry specialist had met with the hospital administrator to explain EK&H's expertise in this area and a consulting contract resulted. In another instance, seminars on tax matters with a group of local attorneys had resulted in one of these attorneys suggesting EK&H to his client as a firm knowledgeable in his tax matters.

Within a year after the Hartford PD program had been developed, the office had acquired several new accounts for audit work, and additional business had been received in the tax and consulting groups as well. There seemed to be a reasonable level of familiarity with the practice development manual among the staff. The partners and managers sought to find ways to make existing clients aware of the full range of services offered and attempted to maintain a year-round relationship with them and develop a full service approach. Many clients had been unaware of the full services provided by EK&H.

San Francisco Office

In many respects the San Francisco area was similar to Hartford. There were a number of universities in the area and a large number of banks and insurance companies, some of which were among the largest in the world. The area just to the south of the city was the location of many high-technology companies, particularly those engaged in the manufacture of integrated circuits and other electronic components.

Since there had not been a formal PD coordinator in the past, Pete found it difficult to estimate how much had been done previously to develop these industries. After some digging, he discovered that lists had been drawn up of the prominent industries in the area and the important members of each sector. But it appeared that the effort had stopped there, without ever making use of the information. Several of the office's staff had spoken to groups at local universities, but their primary motivation had been to stimulate career interest in accounting and EK&H.

Industry was under considerable economic and legal pressure at this time to comply with new laws, take advantage of tax programs, and trim costs wherever possible. The wage and price freeze, tax reform act, changes in inventory valuation methods, pension reform acts, and an increasing public demand for more accurate and fuller disclosure, brought about by several well publicized stock frauds, had generated a host of opportunities for the office, in Pete Ford's opinion. He knew that a substantial number of calls had been received in the past several months from clients, attorneys, bankers, and nonclients asking about these new pressures and how they would affect a company's financial picture. Although this provided an excellent opportunity to demonstrate EK&H's expertise and generate professional contacts, Pete discovered that the office had merely answered the inquiries and had not seized the opportunity to set up joint seminars and speaking engagements. Without any formal program, many of these opportunities were lost.

As he reviewed the situation in San Francisco, Pete was particularly concerned about the senior accountant and his attitude towards PD. In Pete's mind, the senior was one of the key elements in the PD effort, especially with existing clients. The senior accountant was the one with day-to-day client contact and represented EK&H to the client. He was clearly in the best position to spot consulting opportunities. Furthermore, the senior was a major influence upon the attitudes of the staff accountants toward PD. If he insisted on examining every opportunity for new work, this would influence those working with him. Since a senior could work on anywhere from a few to as many as twenty accounts, his impact on the junior staff could be very significant.

The new staff accountants, with a turnover rate of twenty to twenty-five percent each year, represented a special problem in motivation. Many of these young people recognized that they would very likely not be around to secure the benefits of their PD efforts. Since PD was not seen by them as a very significant part of their performance evaluation, they saw little incentive to spend time on it.

To get a better perspective on the senior accountants' thoughts about PD, Pete made a point to talk with several of them about PD. In his first conversation, with Arthur Hanes, Pete attempted to understand what PD means to the senior accountant. Arthur had some definite thoughts on the issue and talked quite a bit.

At present it is very difficult for me to identify with PD. They say that it means more money for the firm and therefore more manager and partner openings, but it's years before we ever see that. At my level it's even difficult to feel the impact of gaining or losing a client. I can see why the partners are so concerned about it because it's money in their pocket, but for me after spending 50-60 hours a week directing 10 audits, it's difficult to appreciate a reward that's five years away at best.

Pete had asked Arthur if he knew how much of EK&H's billings had to be regenerated each year just to stay even. Art confessed he didn't and was surprised at the high percentage necessary.

In his next interview with another senior, Andy Waters, the conversation took a different tack and focused upon Andy's experience with the client and his overall involvement.

I agree with some of the things Arthur has said, but there's another issue which is equally troublesome to me. We're told to make recommendations to client management about ways they could improve their business, but we never find out what happens, even from our own managers and partners. I'd like to feel that I'm helping a client and get some feedback on it. This also goes for the staff accountants who bounce around from one audit to another, and never see a full audit through, only their portion. Last year I made a recommendation to a client that he consider a computerized inventory control system. I didn't find out until eight months later, on the next audit, that he had taken my advice and that our consulting group was doing the work. Now how can I have a proprietary interest in a client or our firm, when no one has the courtesy to tell me what's going on?

Like Arthur Hanes, Andy Waters did not realize how large a portion of EK&H's revenues had to be replaced each year.

A third interview with Mitchell Sands revealed some underlying animosity between the consulting group and the audit group. Mitchell had worked on several occasions with the office's consulting people and had had several experiences which dampened his enthusiasm for them:

First of all, they don't have to worry about collecting their bills. Because of this, they're not as careful about their time budget as they would be if they had the accounts receivable problem. Then there's the case where they blow the job or the final product shows no immediate tangible benefits. Right now, I've got a client who's about to throw me out the door for something I didn't do. There's no way that I'm going to mention our consulting services in that client's presence for a long time. There are some people in that consulting group that I wouldn't want near any of my clients and I have told my manager and the other seniors that. I'm evaluated on my technical competence, my meeting the budget, and my ability not to get a client all teed off at us. PD never enters my evaluation. Maybe it should, but the fact is it doesn't. Right now there's a lot of pressure to meet the budget. Audit fees have gone up 30% in the past few years and clients are screaming. Not only are their audit requirements increasing, but they cost more. I have to watch my people like a hawk if I'm going to meet my time constraints. My staff people don't have an extra five minutes to investigate a consulting opportunity. If they took every one, they'd be over the budget in a week. Neither they nor I are going to waste time on PD if it doesn't pay off.

Finally, Pete was talking with another manager, Leonard Morrissey, about his assignment and his attitudes toward PD. Leonard had been involved in the firm's internal education program and had taught a practice development session. Leonard had observed:

I'm not so sure it's something we can teach, Pete. It's really an "awareness" of the client's business, of the community, of the firm's resources. I don't buy this business about there being no incentive to do any PD work. The person on the job has the opportunity to seek out an area of management concern and recommend action. He or she has the opportunity to work with a specialist and broaden their business experiences. There are ample rewards available for a self starter, someone looking to better himself.

The final dimension of Pete Ford's thinking involved the policy makers of the firm, the partners and the senior managers who set the overall framework and environment for practice development. Throughout the firm there were partners and managers who had opposed the idea of PD and especially their role in it. They felt that they were professional accountants and not salesmen, something they felt PD was trying to make of them. Some had strong opinions that the firm had no business expanding into fields other than auditing as they might compromise their professional independence. They also pointed out the opportunity for conflicts of interest where they might be auditing the results of their consulting or tax work.

In the process of transferring from Hartford to San Francisco, Pete Ford had visited the national offices and had found an opportunity while there to talk with one of the firm's more experienced partners, Jack Hughes, about the approach that EK&H had taken to practice development. Jack Hughes had just returned from a four-week executive seminar at a leading graduate school of business, and marketing management was one of the subjects studied. He had made an observation which had stuck in Pete's mind:

You know, Pete, practice development is our polite word for marketing, a word that is suspect under AICPA Rule 502. But marketing is a lot more than selling. I don't think our firm recognizes that yet. We still treat PD as salesmanship and I think something more is called for. That's not my worry, though. That's what we created the PD Task Force for. Let them know if you have any new ideas after you've got your feet on the ground in San Francisco.

As Pete settled back into his chair and thought about it all, he became worried. The senior accountants must be deeply involved in PD. This was the key group for developing existing client billings. He knew many of them wanted to get involved and help, but at the same time they wanted some recognition and involvement in the work which they help obtain. One staff accountant's response rung in his ear: "I'd like to get involved, but I don't know where to go." Pete wondered how he could develop a PD program which would not only involve the senior and staff accountants, but one which would also appeal to the firm's managers and partners. The PD Task Force had visited San Francisco several weeks earlier and had left a summary of the suggestions they had heard made. Some of these are extracted in Exhibit 20.3. He knew that the national office wanted to support PD at the local level in every possible manner, but he still felt rather as if he had been left alone, and he wondered what kind of support he should be asking for.

Appendix 20A	Excerpts from the EK&H
	Practice Development Manual

Edwards, Kimball, and Hall is a personal service institution which exists because it meets a social need. It serves the stockholder by independently and objectively reporting on the integrity of financial statements. It serves management through constructive advice on financial and other business problems. It serves the public accounting profession by actively participating in the efforts to maintain high ethical standards and raise the competency of the entire profession. It serves the public generally by providing leadership in accounting thought and in the development of financial reporting on a meaningful basis.

The reputation of Edwards, Kimball, and Hall has been built up over the years through the combined efforts of many people. Each, according to his talents, has helped to create the image that the public has of EK&H. This image is that of a firm possessing certain fundamental characteristics—integrity, objectivity, independence and ability.

Our ability to maintain and strengthen this image is based, in large part, on our future growth because no business can stand still. Growth is *essential* to the maintenance of the vigor and vitality of the practice. It is *essential* to attracting into the firm the topflight people who are just *entering* the profession. It is essential to the esprit de corp of our *existing* organization.

This manual has been prepared to serve as a ready reference source of techniques, approaches and resources which have been (or can be) successfully applied to develop, maintain and enhance the firm's image as the leading public accounting firm in the United States and throughout the world. As such, this manual is intended to serve as a guide to assist each office in its efforts to be the leading firm in its own respective business community as well as to contribute to the stature and growth of the firm and of its staff.

In order to accomplish these objectives, each office must decide how it can best apply the techniques contained in this manual.

It is intended that this manual (and future additions to it) be a valuable reference source responsive to changing demands and needs. Each partner and manager should feel personally responsible to offer constructive suggestions and furnish new ideas which can be incorporated into the manual for use by all of the offices. Such suggestions and ideas should be communicated promptly to the Chairman or any other member of the Practice Development Task Force.

Practice Development Concepts

The firm's stature, our future growth and the development of our staff is totally dependent on our ability to *demonstrate* that we are a firm of highly qualified professionals dedicated to providing excellent service to our clients, the public, our communities and our profession. Therefore, activities directed toward improving and maintaining our stature, and toward expanding our practice must be extremely broad in nature to assure that we:

—Render distinguished client service,
—Develop and maintain a high professional, business,
      and civic "community profile," and
—Capitalize on opportunities to be of service.

These are discussed in more detail below:

Render Distinguished Service. Simply stated, the reason for providing distinguished client service of the highest professional quality is to assure that we not only retain our existing clients, but also create opportunities to provide more service—for them and for others! In order to render this distinguished service, we must maintain a highly qualified staff and take the necessary steps to understand our clients' goals and objectives; to be aware of their problems and opportunities; and to properly apply the firm's total resources to their solution.

Maintain a High Profile. To be a leader in any community, the firm as well as *each* member of our staff must be recognized as an active and qualified participant in the community. We must make sure that *all* of the business, professional, civic and public community is aware that we are highly skilled professionals with an extensive array of resources dedicated to those we serve. This requires a "display of energy" by each member of the staff because the firm's reputation is based on our collective efforts. This *must* be done to assure that we are considered when any organization requires the professional services we can provide.

Capitalize on Opportunities. We must always be alert for opportunities to be of service and when an opportunity presents itself, we must always "put our best foot forward" whether it be for an existing client, a prospective client or a public forum—we must *always* be the best choice. This requires an entrepreneurial state of mind, a highly tailored approach and a skillful application of our resources in order to achieve the desired results.

Responsibility for Expanding the Firm's Image

In the broadest sense, *every* staff member has direct, day-to-day responsibility for expanding and maintaining the firm's practice by applying the concepts discussed above. In this regard, it may be helpful to review some specific responsibilities as they relate to each individual within the firm, the practice offices, and the National Office. These responsibilities are as follows.

Individual Responsibilities. For his personal development and the development of the firm, *each* staff member (from the partners to the youngest staff assistant) must assume, in varying degrees, personal responsibility for expanding the firm's practice. Each partner is, of course, directly responsible for carrying out the specific activities outlined below for the practice offices. Other staff members are also responsible for rendering distinguished client service, and, to the extent determined by each office, for other practice development activities. Each staff member has the responsibility of offering constructive suggestions or other material which he believes might assist the efforts of his office or the firm.

Practice Office Responsibilities. The responsibilities of the practice offices can best be described as "front line." This is where the greatest opportunities exist, where the bulk of our resources exist, where the greatest continuing contact opportunities exist, where short and long range practice development plans are developed, and where day-to-day activities are carried out. In addition to having responsibility for successfully applying the practice development concepts outlined above, each practice office also has the responsibility to provide support to the National Office and other practice offices, and to offer suggestions regarding practice development activities to the National Office and/or to the Practice Development Task Force.

National Office Responsibilities. The responsibilities of the National Office include such things as:

National level relations with professional organizations, industry groups, federal agencies and the press
Industry specialist activities
Professional development programs
Publications
Furnishing support to the practice offices
Monitoring practice office activities

Support Activities. There are many resources throughout the firm which are available to assist each practice office in their practice development activities. It is expected that each office will recognize that our firm functions best as a firm-wide team and will appropriately use these resources; these resources include expertise on tax matters, electronic data processing, and a variety of other management consulting services; publications available from National Headquarters (the monthly newsletter, tax guides, books authored by staff members, etc.); industry specialists who can help prepare proposals, are available for public speaking engagements, and can provide special industry information; and the Practice Development Task Force itself for:

Distribution of new ideas, approaches and techniques
Assistance in establishing practice development programs
Over-all communications regarding practice development
    activities
Examples of proposals

It is important to remember that there are many resources available and that they should be appropriately *used* to assure the maximum effectiveness of our practice development activities.

Summary

Practice Development:
1. Is both expanding service to existing clients and obtaining new clients.
2. Is everyone's job—it is a vital part of every professional person.
3. Is a continuous activity.
4. Benefits our clients, the firm and the individual.
    a. Each person on our staff must be dedicated to serving his clients— helping them achieve their objectives better.
    b. Each person on our staff must become well known in the professional, business and civic communities—there are many, many ways.
5. Means we must:
    a. Provide the highest quality service,
    b. Have a top-flight professional staff, and
    c. Be leaders in the profession—in all ways.

Exhibit 20.1   The National Industry Specialists in EK&H

The firm has designated an Industry Specialist Partner for each of the industries listed below. An effort is being made to author Specialized Industry Practice Volumes in as many fields as possible so that they can be used as practice development aids as well as for general technical reference. All of the firm's offices should consult with the lead industry specialist on proposals, ongoing work and practice development plans.

Extractive Industries

Financial Institutions
  Banks
  Insurance
  Investment Companies
  Savings and Loan Associations
  Security Dealers

Industrial and Other Commercial
  Entertainment
  Food Products
  Real Estate
  Steel

Public Services
  Hospital and Medical
  Environmental Protection and Social Measurement
  Nonprofit Organizations
  Public Utilities
  State and Local Governments
  Urban Affairs

Service
  Advertising
  Law Firms
  Litigation Support
  Small Business

Transportation
  Railroads
  Steamships
  Trucking
    Household goods moving and warehousing
    General commodity hauling

Exhibit 20.2   AICPA Professional Standards Relating to Solicitation and Advertising

---

Rule 502—Solicitation and advertising. A member shall not seek to obtain
clients by solicitation. Advertising is a form of solicitation and is prohibited.

Interpretations under Rule 502—Solicitation and advertising.

502-1—Announcements. Publication in a newspaper, magazine or similar
medium of an announcement or what is technically known as a "card"
is prohibited. Also prohibited is the issuance of a press release regarding
firm mergers, opening of new offices, change of address or admission
of new partners.
    Announcements of such changes may be mailed to clients and indivi-
duals with whom professional contacts are maintained, such as lawyers
and bankers. Such announcements should be dignified and should not
refer to fields of specialization.

20/Edwards, Kimball, & Hall, CPAs   **491**

502-2—Office premises. Listing of the firm name in lobby directories of office buildings and on entrance doors solely for the purpose of enabling interested parties to locate an office is permissible. The listing should be in good taste and modest in size.

The indication of a specialty such as "income tax" in such listing constitutes advertising.

502-3—Directories: telephone, classified and trade association. A listing in a telephone, trade association, membership or other classified directory shall not:

1. Appear in a box or other form of display, or in a type or style which differentiates it from other listings in the same directory.
2. Appear in more than one place in the same classified directory.
3. Appear under a heading other than "Certified Public Accountant" or "Public Accountant" where the directory is classified by type of business occupation or service.
4. Be included in the yellow pages or business section of a telephone directory unless the member maintains a bona fide office in the geographic area covered. Determination of what constitutes an "area" shall be made by referring to the positions taken by state CPA societies in the light of local conditions.

Such listing may:

1. Include the firm name, partners' names, professional title (CPA), address and telephone number.
2. Be included under both the geographical and alphabetical section where the directory includes such sections.

502-4—Business stationery. A member's stationery should be in keeping with the dignity of the profession and not list any specialty.

The stationery may include the firm name, address and telephone number, names of partners, names of deceased partners and their years of service, names of professional staff when preceded by a line to separate them from the partners, and cities in which other offices and correspondents or associates are located. Membership in the Institute or state CPA society or associated group of CPA firms whose name does not indicate a specialty may also be shown. In the case of multi-office firms, it is suggested that the words "offices in other principal cities" (or other appropriate wording) be used instead of a full list of offices. Also it is preferable to list only the names of partners resident in the office for which the stationery is used.

502-5—Business cards. Business cards may be used by partners, sole practitioners, and staff members. They should be in good taste and should be limited to the name of the person presenting the card, his firm name, address and telephone number(s), the words "Certified Public Accountant(s)," or "CPA" and such words as "partner," "manager" or "consultant" but without any specialty designation.

Members not in the practice of public accounting may use the title "Certified Public Accountant" or "CPA" but shall not do so when engaged in sales promotion, selling, or similar activities.

502-6—Help-wanted advertisements. A member shall not include his name in help-wanted or situations-wanted display advertising on his own behalf or that of others in any publication. In display advertising, the use of a telephone number, address, or newspaper box number is permissible.

In classified advertisements other than display, the member's name should not appear in boldface type, capital letters or in any other manner which tends to distinguish the name from the body of the advertisement.

502-7—Firm publications. Newsletters, bulletins, house organs, recruiting brochures and other firm literature on accounting and related business subjects prepared and distributed by a firm for the information of its staff and clients serve a useful purpose. The distribution of such material outside the firm must be properly controlled and should be restricted to clients and individuals with whom professional contacts are maintained, such as lawyers and bankers. Copies may also be supplied to job applicants, to students considering employment interviews, to non-clients who specifically request them and to educational institutions.

If requests for multiple copies are received and granted, the member and his firm are responsible for any distribution by the party to whom they are issued.

502-8—Newsletters and publications prepared by others. A member shall not permit newsletters, tax booklets or similar publications to be imprinted with his firm's name if they have not been prepared by his firm.

502-9—Responsibility for publisher's promotional efforts. It is the responsibility of a member to see that the publisher or others who promote distribution of his writing observe the boundaries of professional dignity and make no claims that are not truthful and in good taste. The promotion may indicate the author's background including, for example, his education, professional society affiliations and the name of his firm, the title of his position and principal activities therein. Subjective designations or statements whch proclaim the author as an expert in any specialty may not be used. Repetition of credits in a series of articles in the public press could be construed to be a violation of Rule 502.

502-10—Statements and information to the public press. A member shall not directly or indirectly cultivate publicity which advertises his or his firm's professional attainments or services. He may respond factually when approached by the press for information concerning his firm, but he should not use press inquiries as a means of aggrandizing himself or his firm or of advertising professional attainments or services. When interviewed by a writer or reporter, he is charged with the knowledge that he cannot control the journalistic use of any information he may give and should notify the reporter of the limitations imposed by professional ethics.

Releases and statements made by members on subjects of public interest which may be reported by the news media, and publicity not initiated by a member, such as that which may result from public service concerning internal matters in a member's firm are prohibited.

502-11—Participation in educational seminars. Participation by members in programs of educational seminars, either in person or through audio-visual techniques, on matters within the field of competence of CPAs is in the public interest and is to be encouraged. Such seminars should not be used as a means of soliciting clients. Therefore, certain restraints must be observed to avoid violation of the spirit of Rule 502, which prohibits solicitation and advertising. For example, a member or his firm should not:

1. Send announcements of a seminar to non-clients or invite them to attend. However, educators may be invited to attend to further their education.
2. Sponsor, or convey the impression that he is sponsoring a seminar which will be attended by non-clients. However, a member or his firm may conduct educational seminars solely for clients and those serving his clients in a professional capacity, such as bankers and lawyers.

In addition, when a seminar is sponsored by others and attended by non-clients, a member or his firm should not:

1. Solicit the opportunity to appear on the program.
2. Permit the distribution of publicity relating to the member or his firm in connection with the seminar except as permitted under Interpretation 502-9.
3. Distribute firm literature which is not directly relevant to a subject being presented on the program by the member or persons connected with his firm.

502-12—Solicitation of former clients. Offers by a member to provide services after a client relationship has been clearly terminated, either by completion of a nonrecurring engagement or by direct action of the client, constitute a violation of Rule 520 prohibiting solicitation.

Source: AICPA Professional Standards. 1974. *Ethics and Bylaws.* pp. 4841–4844. Copyright © 1974 by the American Institute of Certified Public Accountants, Inc.

Exhibit 20.3   Summary of Suggestions Made by the Task Force during San Francisco Office Visits

Action Plan
Accelerate implementation of the office's PD plan by establishing formal and reasonable responsibilities and a time frame for accomplishments. Assign responsibilities and establish dates for completion, and follow-up to see that tasks are accomplished.

Assure that all levels of staff are aware of PD plan.

Consider forming PD related task committees (i.e., alumni, organizations, lawyers, publications, etc.) consisting of managers, seniors, and (in some cases) staff. Develop means to obtain more involvement by all staff levels in PD (e.g., holding periodic all-staff PD meetings).

Consider desirability of increasing tax and MAS department chargeable hour goals for the year ending June 30, 1979 to an amount more closely approximating firmwide averages and develop recruiting plan to obtain the manpower to reach these goals.

Coordinate local PD plan with other nearby offices to insure adequate coverage of all practice areas.

Highlight and pursue short-range achievable PD goals in order to create momentum and enthusiasm for the PD plan.

Schedule PD committee meetings on a regular basis.

Expand the PD program to specifically address the development of MAS work.

Consider developing a portion of the PD plan on an industry basis.

Outside Activities

Consider having informal dinner meetings with bank officers and lawyers to discuss matters of current interest.

Increase visibility in community through establishing contact with lawyers and bankers and by encouraging staff involvement in civic and community organizations.

Effort should be made to locate *decision makers* in the community and organizations to which they belong to assure more effective participation in community activities.

Evaluate adequacy of spending for sponsor/patron events (high profile community activities) and for one-on-one contact with clients and prospects (sporting events, theatre, etc.).

Reevaluate membership priorities at all staff levels to assure adequate coverage of all worthwhile community, professional and industry organizations. Discourage excessive emphasis in one area of community activities which may tend to hinder coverage in other important areas.

Attempt should be made to increase contacts in legal community.

Develop one or two special high profile PD projects to which selected staff can be assigned. Possibilities are: (a) more active involvement in expansion of area international commerce, (b) more active involvement in activities designed to increase the area's attractiveness to business investment, (c) etc.

Local Business Awareness

Develop and/or update target company files for prospective clients in local area.

Become more aware of our competitors and our relative strength within our territory.

Prepare an analysis of geographic areas where business growth (and existing business) might justify specific PD efforts and an eventual EK&H presence.

Subscribe to all major newspapers in the office's practice area.

Communications

Review current distribution of various firm publications and assure that proper coverage is being achieved with clients, alumni, local CPA's, bankers, lawyers, professional acquaintances, friends of the firm.

Encourage staff at all levels to seek speaking engagements before business and community organizations.

Use announcements of promotions of clients and non-clients to make contacts by letters of congratulation.

Conduct seminars for local clients, lawyers and bankers.

Industry Specialization

Consider using the insurance industry specialist group to develop information on and relationships with insurance companies in the area.

Bring out-of-town industry specialists on the scene for proposals and on-site visits to existing clients.

Consider designating managers and specialists in particular industries (real estate, electronics, etc.) and have these managers work with the firm's specialists to develop specific local industry oriented PD plans.

Small Business

Place more emphasis on developing the small business practice and make known our interest in small business.

Take a more critical look at establishing a small business department with one partner assuming responsibility for this group.

Make lawyers and bankers more aware of our interest in small business.

Assign staff and clients of a caliber which would give the small business practice stature within office and community.

Determine the size and profile of the local "small business market" to assist in determining where to direct small business PD efforts.

Discussion Questions

1. What are the objectives of a PD program?
2. What are the constraints within which a PD program must operate (corporate mission, objectives, policies, master strategies)?
3. What are the strengths, weaknesses, threats, and opportunities of the San Francisco office of EK&H?

21/The Coca-Cola Company—Part C: The HI-C Soft Drink Product Introduction

James M. Higgins

Tom Watkins and Lou Holt huddled in Tom's office late one Friday afternoon in January, 1978. It had been a hectic week, but now the evidence was in and a decision had to be made as to whether or not to go nationwide with the new product line. They had reviewed the market situation, the test results of the HI-C brand soft drinks, and the various internal corporate factors to be considered. They felt they had a winner, but uncertainty always loomed, especially after the Foods Division's promising powdered fruit drink had not faired particularly well.

The initial decision to explore the possibilities of employing the HI-C brand on a fruit flavored soft drink had been made several months ago. Since that time Lou Holt, with constant advice from Tom, had carefully planned and directed the new product line's development. As operating managers, the decision was theirs to make. Tom, a Vice President, and Lou, a Director, (both of Coca-Cola U.S.A.) had the full responsibility and authority for this decision. No fruit flavored orange or grape soft drink had ever gained national prominence. But they felt HI-C would.

The Decision to Explore Using HI-C as a Soft Drink Brand

Coca-Cola U.S.A. had been carefully monitoring the beverage industry activities. A maturing industry, increased competition, and new products all posed problems for the dominant firm in the soft drink segment of the industry and the leading firm in the total beverage market. A more complete product line for its bottlers had become an integral part of corporate strategy. (See Case 17, "The Coca-Cola Company—Part B.") Attribute listings of current products and market analysis had suggested that employing the HI-C brand for a soft drink product line could be extremely profitable. The soft drink market is unique in the package goods field in that there are few new product categories developed. Thus, it was believed that the introduction of HI-C as a soft drink would be a major breakthrough for Coca-Cola. Soft drink marketers sell taste and refreshment, and there are few consumer benefits that can be added to a product that will make the product more "palatable." The most recent new product categories in the soft drink market that were clearly different from any of the competitors' were Fresca for Coca-Cola and Mountain Dew for Pepsi. Both of these were introduced in the early

Source: The events described herein, while based in fact, are partly hypothesized according to what would normally be expected of a firm in this situation. Students should read Case 17, Parts A and B on The Coca Cola Company before attempting Part C, presented here as Case 21.

1960s, and there had really been nothing of a breakthrough nature since that time. Most new introductions in the soft drink markets were brands to compete with an established category, for example, Barrelhead Root Beer from Canada Dry and On Tap Root Beer from Pepsi.

Simple observation reveals that: 1. consumption of soft drinks is much greater than for fruit drinks; 2. bottlers have greater access to vending locations than do fruit drink sales organizations; and 3. the traffic in food stores or food markets is much greater in the soft drink section than it is in the fruit drink section.

Since profit potential appeared high, Coca-Cola U.S.A. determined that it should actively pursue the opportunity, having to take into account the possible impact on its existing Fanta fruit-flavored soft drinks and HI-C fruit drinks. Lou Holt was assigned the task of establishing the new product line. He immediately set out to list objectives and actions necessary to reach those objectives. A target date of January 1, 1978 was established for completion of the testing phase. Moving backwards in time, he scheduled the necessary events in logical sequence. Lou conferred constantly with Tom and other staff members. Input sessions were formalized periodically.

While preliminary analyses were being made, the marketing of a powdered soft drink by the Foods Division proved unsuccessful. The powder had contained juice and it was priced above Kool-Aid. As one corporate official noted, "it bombed," notwithstanding the fact that the powder entered the market late. As the result of a policy decision, juice was removed from powders, and once that decision was made, the decision to take juice out of the soft drink followed quite naturally. Since the brand name HI-C implied Vitamin C content, Coke had to comply with Federal requirements for advertising and include vitamin C in the drink. Federal law however prohibited the inclusion of vitamin C in a carbonated drink, and thus the proposed HI-C product line became noncarbonated.

The initial marketing strategy logically would be for the HI-C name to be emphasized since it was already established in powders and fruit drinks. The feeling was that since there had never been an orange or grape drink that had gained national promise, HI-C had the best chance since it would be able to utilize the HI-C name. Lou and Tom and others felt that the soft drink would parallel the known marketing pattern for fruit drinks, but according to one company vice president, the family would be the primary target market. However, various tests would be utilized to determine other markets. Standard product development procedures and marketing tests were initiated, including focus sessions, monadic ratings, ratings versus competition, blind taste tests, and volume and brand image tests. These tests all proved favorable to the HI-C product introduction, and additional target markets were uncovered. A weekend selldown test was performed in a major midwestern city. Results proved favorable.

Several problems developed between Coca-Cola U.S.A. and the Foods

Division with respect to the HI-C development program. Once the test market results revealed a high profit potential for the HI-C soft drink, then arrangements had to be made to alleviate these problems.

The Decision to Introduce the New Product

The test results were in.[1] Lou and Tom next proceeded to formulate a pro forma balance sheet in order to convince themselves of the profitability of the product. A pro forma balance sheet of estimated gallon sales plus profit calculations on gallon sales less Fanta losses revealed that Coca-Cola could expect to make a profit from a corporate perspective, although not necessarily in the immediate future. A decision had to be made as to whether or not to develop a marketing program for the bottlers and the customers.

Later, as Tom mulled over the project, he felt that the sales job could be accomplished. What really bothered him most were the underlying problems which could develop. He began to summarize his feelings towards the HI-C introduction. He wrote them down so that he might think about them later.

HI-C is a brand name with 29 years of heritage behind it. It always has been a juice-containing beverage, high in vitamin C. By introducing a soft drink without juice, we are playing with this heritage, a very large and very profitable business, and we don't know the consequences. We risk not only the potential soft drink business, but also the fruit drink business. Competition is forcing us to roll out without complete testing.

We also face a distribution problem, one product, HI-C from the Foods Division going through warehouses and the other product, HI-C of Coca-Cola U.S.A., going through bottlers. His final sentence echoed his doubts. "We are truly rolling the dice."

Discussion Questions

1. How does the proposed HI-C product fit into the overall corporate strategy? (See Parts A and B on The Coca-Cola Company, Case 17.)
2. Just why would Coca-Cola seek to market such a product?
3. Evaluate the evidence gathered in terms of what decision should be made. Why do you feel that way?
4. What types of problems might arise between Coca-Cola U.S.A. and the Foods Division? How might these be solved?
5. What flavors do you feel should be initiated under the HI-C brand name soft drink? Why?

1. Because of their proprietary nature, the results of the various tests and the pro forma formulations could not be shown. Only information which is available in the business literature or which could be readily surmised has been provided in this case.

6. What would your marketing strategy be and why, assuming you decide to go national with the product in February of 1978. Note, there are two major parties to whom the company must market, the consumer and the bottler.

22/Tacoma Shipbuilding and Drydock Company*

Louis K. Bragaw,
William R. Allen,
and Peter T. Landolt

The Problem

It was a muggy Monday afternoon and the mid-July heat permeated the top floor of the ancient brick building as Walter Arillo paced down the hallway to his office overlooking Puget Sound. He couldn't remember such an extended period of heat and humidity in all his years in the Seattle area. He paused for a moment in front of his office door and read the block letters on the glass: W. Arillo, Overhaul Manager. In the lower right corner was also painted: Mrs. K. Hendricks. His secretary glanced up at the clock when he stepped into the office.

"Well, another four-hour conference, I see."

"Yes, and it seems like the longer they get, the less we get done. Karen, before you leave for the day, will you get Mr. Price on the phone?"

While waiting for his call to Jim Price, the General Manager, Walt glanced out the window at the still Sound and wished, instead, that he were standing in a cold shower.

"Your call."

"Thanks, Karen. See you tomorrow." Walt swung his chair back to the desk and lifted the phone.

"Hello, Jim. Walt here. We just finished another session concerning our current problems with engineering support, and on my way back to the office, the thought struck me that it might be time for a special staff meeting to try and get this mess solved once and for all. From my standpoint, this thing is really significant in terms of results and, quite frankly, our weekly coordination meetings seem to aggravate everybody's problems without finding any solutions."

Walt propped his feet up on the desk as he continued to discuss the matter with the General Manager. They talked at length about the overall importance of engineering responsiveness to the shipyard's needs and about what Walt felt were the possible approaches to take. Mr. Price agreed, finally, that a special agenda staff meeting was needed, and it was set up for the following Thursday morning.

Source: Prepared by Professor Louis K. Bragaw, U.S. Coast Guard Academy, and Asst. Professor William R. Allen, University of Rhode Island, with the collaboration of Mr. Peter T. Landolt. Distributed by the Intercollegiate Case Clearing House, Soldiers Field, Boston, Mass. 02163. All rights reserved to the contributors. Printed in the U.S.A.

*The events depicted in this case are actual; however, the company is fictitious.

"That sounds good to me, Jim. I'll send you my summarization of the problem by Wednesday noon, and I'll ask John Harrington to do the same so you can get engineering's point of view. Also, I'll have Karen type up a list of suggested attendees for this get-together. Hopefully, we'll be able to get back to the kind of efficiencies we enjoyed five years ago! See you Thursday morning."

Company Background

Indeed, five years before in 1970, it was a time of continuing boom and great success for the Tacoma Shipbuilding and Drydock Company. Ideally situated in the protected waters at the head of Puget Sound—yet with easy access to the open sea—the company was virtually surrounded by centers of naval and shipbuilding activity at Bremerton and Seattle. Almost all of TSD's enterprise was supported by ship construction for the U. S. Navy, and with current and potential contracts for some 25 vessels, the immediate future looked very bright. This was the company's heaviest backlog of construction activity since the frantic days of World War II, when the 90-day wonders were launched at intervals of every few weeks.

Several years earlier, in the opening months of the 1960 decade, Tacoma had merged and become one of the large parent divisions of a new defense conglomerate, United Enterprises, Inc. This new corporation structure did not, however, radically alter the shipyard's internal hierarchical organization. The corporate headquarters in New York, which had the final say on all major policy matters, pretty much left the company to run its own successful way. The Board of Directors and corporation V.P.s dealt mainly with matters concerning the overall corporation position, such as facility expansion investment and the broad types of activity of each of the divisions. Tacoma Shipbuilding in the meantime, still dealt directly with the Navy and the government on all contractual matters.

TSD's long-standing reputation was that of being one of the country's leading ship design and fabrication plants. Prior to 1964, the Navy had frequently made the company the design lead for various classes of ships. Being the design lead for a ship class involved considerably more than primary ship construction. First, the company had to generate preliminary design concepts and sell these ideas to the Navy, or take Navy design ideas and develop workable design concepts from them. Once an agreement was reached upon the concepts, the basic hull design was begun. Upon the review of this preliminary design work, a complete set of detailed specifications was written and a contract was made for final detailed design of the ship and all its systems. The detailed design consisted principally of producing all the necessary plans from which the ship would be constructed. In addition, the design lead yard was required to supply the design plans and design support to other shipyards which eventually won construction contracts for the ships of that class.

The lead yard, presumably, would build the lead ship (or name ship) as well as several subsequent ships of the class.

Since the period of World War II, Tacoma's history of design lead work caused a proliferation—not unpredictably—of an extensive engineering design department, which could and did exist quite separately from the ship construction activities of the company. Because of this, the engineering arm had evolved with its own separate chain of command up to the General Manager.[1]

Presenting the Problem

Two days of solid rain had cleared the air, and by Thursday morning the heat-wave was broken over Puget Sound. As he headed toward Conference Room One, Walt Arillo felt quite refreshed and hopeful that this meeting would stimulate action toward solving some of his problems in the yard. After all, he thought, even an operation as complex and cumbersome as a shipyard should be flexible enough to handle day-to-day support requirements when they're needed.

Most of the attendees were already assembled when he stepped into the paneled conference room. John Harrington, the recently appointed Director of Engineering, had arrived just before Walt and greeted him at the door. Dave Garnet, Head of Management Engineering,[2] and Ron Williams, Chief of Design, were sitting at the table facing the door. Dave Lojeski from Industrial Relations and Joe Bell, Manager of Electrical Engineering, were talking at the end of the table with Dick Paulsen from Operations. Walt looked around the room and noted that the only people missing were Jim Price and Harvey Hinchcliff, the Head of Class Project Engineering.

By nine o'clock Jim and Harvey had arrived, and the General Manager called the meeting to order.

"You all know that this special staff meeting has a single item agenda. Basically, we're here to discuss engineering and design support to the yard activities—an area where we seem to be having some critical problems, or at least a major breakdown in our communications. Since Walt Arillo is one of those most immediately affected, I'm turning it right over to him to lay out the facts."

Walt opened the large notebook in front of him on the table.

"Okay, let's review the situation as it stands. About four years ago we completed the last hulls of the American Heritage Class for the Navy. As you all recall, the yard was operating at our peak

1. Exhibit 22.1 shows the company's top level organizational structure in 1964.
2. The primary function of the Management Engineering Department was to provide scientific and engineering approaches to maintaining and improving the professional and management structure and capabilities of the company.

manloading since World War II. Most of our work-force was concentrated in the shipyard, where we had, I believe, about 12,000
construction workers in the union trades. The records show that
the Heritage Class ships were fabricated with a high degree of
efficiency and effectiveness. I remember that rework[3] on these ships
was usually at a bare minimum. My records show that whenever
engineering support was needed in the yard, the usual procedure
was to send a request up to engineering or design where the
problem was given high priority and was solved, most often,
through direct personal liaison with the yard activity. The block
schematic shows the basic simplicity with which our support work
was accomplished.[4] We never really had any major difficulty in
getting these jobs done on time.

"During the past few years, however, it has become increasingly
apparent that our support effectiveness to meet these yard requirements has slipped. Right now, for instance, I find it near impossible
to adhere to close schedules when I have to wait for a morass of
red tape to get ten or eleven signatures on a design plan change
that may be required in the yard. And the costs for these services
seem to have gone out of control. This second chart will give you
an idea of the difference between now and four years ago.[5] What
I need, as overhaul manager, is some guy in engineering who can
be responsible to me for schedules and costs in the support area.
Now, since I've started out here by beating the bushes, maybe Dick
Paulsen, my cohort in the shipyard, has something to add?"

Richard Paulsen, manager of new construction in the shipyard, cleared his
throat.

"I see the problem the same way as Walt. On the new hulls we
are really getting hung up with engineering and design support. I
think the cost problem is partly due to mixing of cross-charges[6] in
the design lead activities. Since the design lead business is forcing
us to support the whole world as well as TSD, Walt's right in saying
that we need tighter control *and* accountability to new construction
and overhaul. And to speed up the response, maybe we should
look closely at our present communications links between the engineers and the building ways."

The General Manager broke in.

3. Rework involves redoing a specific task to correct an error or mistake, or to accommodate a change in plans.
4. See Exhibit 22.2 showing Walt Arillo's version of 1965 support work flow.
5. Exhibit 22.3 shows Walt's outline of 1969 support work flow.
6. Cross-charging is a common and acceptable practice where one department does
work for another department and "cross-charges" the expense to the other department's
contract number. In a large organization it is a complex problem to insure that all charges
are expensed to the proper contracts.

"Okay, what about this communication thing between engineering and the shipyard? Let's hear the engineers' viewpoint. John, what do you think?"

"Well, I have no argument at all that an important part of our job is to support the yard in any way required. However, it seems to me we haven't changed our way of handling the interface since the 'efficient days' of five years ago that Walt's talking about. Ron Williams and Harv Hinchcliff are the design and engineering boys—and they can correct me if I'm wrong—but I see no difference between now and then in the way we're handling yard support."

"That's right," Ron broke in, "we're still processing shipyard requests the same as we always have. As soon as a chit or phone call comes up from the waterfront, the supervisor or design chief in that area gets the right people on the job. Of course, just like all our work, the speed of the job depends on the priority given it. However, I will say that most of our yard requests of the type Walt's referring to get priority right away."

Jim Price interjected again.

"I follow what you're saying, Ron, but what about this 'morass of red tape' that Walt's talking about? Can't we do something about that?"

"Well, as you know, the Navy is particularly sticky about us making any changes to design plans even on small detail matters. Their claim is that the original ship's specs should rule, and since we are the design lead, we should have designed to the specs in the first place. And let's face it, the Navy Supervisor of Shipbuilding[7] *is* responsible for overseeing and verifying all our construction activity. Therefore, any time we run into a design problem, it takes a certain number of authorization signatures even before it goes to the Navy Supervisor for approval. He's not about to approve any change unless it has already gone through our own chain of command first. Quite frankly, I don't see any way we can speed up that operation unless you can convince the Navy that they are holding up the works."

Walt Arillo was beginning to think that maybe this discussion would get bogged down and they would get nowhere again, as in past meetings. He rested his elbows on the table and looked discouragingly at the other faces in the room. The Manager of Class Project Engineering, Harvey Hinchcliff, spoke up.

"Sometimes the engineering and design regulations we have to follow might seem to border on the ridiculous. But let's remember that the Navy customer has every right to expect thoroughness,

7. Most private shipyards doing major shipbuilding for the Navy have a senior Naval officer assigned to the facility to oversee contractual activities.

accuracy, and quality control in our work. As lead yard on these ships, it is our responsibility to insure the proper configuration management[8] in engineering as well as construction."

"All right," Walt said, "Harv and Ron, I agree with you that we in the company have a large responsibility to provide proper engineering under proper controls. But I think you may be missing the point somewhat. What I am saying is fact, and the fact is we are not getting the job done as efficiently as we could. Certainly, that is important to the Navy too. Remember, when I have to overhaul one of these babies, I have a ship's Captain and a whole ship's crew breathing down my neck to make sure the job is getting done right—and on time. They don't really want to know what's hanging up engineering support to the yard; they just want action."

John Harrington spoke again.

"Walt, maybe what you say is true and we have slipped somewhat in efficiency lately. But I don't believe the entire cause of this is the engineering department. In defense of Harvey, Ron, and Joe Bell here, I can't recall in my 26 years in the business a more highly skilled or better educated bunch of engineers and designers than we have right now."

There was silence for a moment, and then Dave Garnet from Management Engineering spoke.

"A thought just struck my mind that might be of value here. Some of you will remember that we did a rather extensive study of the company's organizational structure and manpower a couple of years ago, the results of which were a series of recommendations to the General Manager's staff as to what changes should be made organizationally to improve company operations. Some of these recommendations were implemented; some were not. One of the main areas we hoped to improve in was what we're talking about today, that is, the interface between the skilled trades and the professionals. As it now stands, I believe there are several significant factors which play a part in this problem we are presently experiencing. I would like to suggest a review of our study information to see what we can glean from it. We might at least have a good starting point without reinventing the wheel from two years ago."

"Sounds like you might have a good point, Dave," Jim Price said. "Are there any other suggestions to add to that?"

"If you want," Dave continued, "I'll proceed with checking out the previous data. At the same time, I'd like to get together with Dave Lojeski to establish some background information on the present

8. Configuration Management is the management responsibility to insure the proper physical arrangement of the ship. For a design lead shipyard this responsibility impacts both Engineering (ship design) and Construction (ship fabrication).

status of our work-force. I'm sure this has changed somewhat since two years ago."

"Yes, it has," Dave Lojeski stated. "In fact, I wouldn't be surprised to find that there are some changes that may be quite significant to our problem here."

Walt spoke again.

"One suggestion I have if you are going to pursue this—and I guess it's more of a plea than a suggestion—is that we don't drag this thing out into a full-scale, six-month study. I appreciate the value of thoroughly analyzing the situation; but try and remember we have a real critical problem in the yard. For the good of the company, I don't think we can wait long before taking action to solve it. Jim, I hope you appreciate and support my position on this."

"Yes, I do, Walt. Right now I think what we need is a special ad hoc staff committee to look further into the problem. The committee should consist of the managers of Overhaul, Management Engineering, Design, and Class Engineering. In light of what we just discussed and the urgency of the matter, I want this same group to meet again in about two weeks and I want the committee to come in with some facts and options. Get your people to dig out all the information you feel is pertinent, and have some of your whiz-kids do a little brainstorming. But don't try to beat the thing to death. Harv, you chair the committee and try to devote pretty much full time to it. Feel free to call on any department or general staff area where it is needed. I guess that's it, unless anyone has a particular plug to make at the present time."

No one had any more particulars to add to the meeting.

"Okay, let's meet again two weeks from Monday, same time."

Walt Arillo left the meeting with a ray of hope in his mind that some solid action would result from the ad hoc committee. He felt a little apprehensive about getting bogged down in fruitless details which would not contribute to solving his problems in the shipyard. But he was happy that the General Manager had given rather explicit directions to make the study short and sweet. He looked into the bright sunlight over Puget Sound and headed back to his office to have a cup of coffee and read his morning mail.

Committee Factfinding

Dave Garnet's subsequent meeting a few days later with Dave Lojeski and his industrial relations people uncovered that, indeed, some significant changes had recently taken place within the shipyard manpower environment.

It was common knowledge that as the American Heritage Class shipbuilding boom dropped off with the completion of the fleet of ships authorized by

Congress, the very large and experienced shipyard construction organization at Tacoma was cut way back. Since that time, turnover of personnel greatly increased, and, as the new trade workers came in, they did not possess the skills based on experience that were available in earlier years. The result was that the average general expertise in the shipyard had declined, which placed extra burdens on the workers' supervisors and experienced "old-timers."

In the meantime, Ron Williams took the General Manager's advice and during that week conducted a brainstorming session with some of his top men in design. The consensus of opinion from this meeting was that one of the primary factors contributing to the shipyard support problem was the increased complexity of new ships' systems both in electronics and modern machinery. Many of these new systems had incorporated advanced engineering technology, and this new technology was placing demands for increased—rather than decreased—skill levels in shipyard construction and installation. As the hardware became more sophisticated, the design plans for its incorporation into the ship's hull became more and more complex. New methods of fabrication were required. New types of hull mountings were needed for machines and electronics in order to meet stringent sound attenuation requirements and shock specifications. Much of the new equipment had very tight tolerance for installation, checkout, balancing, cooling, cabling, and power.

On the Wednesday following the special staff meeting, Walt Arillo met in his office with Harvey Hinchcliff, Joe Bell from electrical engineering, and Ron Williams from design. Walt particularly wanted to take in different viewpoints and, hopefully, to round out his perspective of the overall problem. The men recalled that the shipyard historically had been oriented to the trade skills. In the period prior to the mid-1960s, TSD had grown primarily from the trade standpoint with relatively little growth in the engineering arm. Additionally, the interfaces and links of communication between engineering and the construction departments within the company had an interesting duality: that is, formal lines of communication were most often used to initiate action, whereas the carrying out of the actual work was usually done via informal person-to-person interface. This duality of action was made possible mainly because of the high level of trade skills built up during the previous ten years of heavy ship construction activity. In most instances, during this period, the engineering and design inputs to construction could be turned over directly to the trades since supervisory and worker skills were sufficiently high to accommodate them. Under these circumstances there was no need for a close mix of engineering and trade skills at the construction level.

Walt also met informally with Dick Paulsen, Manager of Operations. The two men spent much of their time conducting a close mental examination of their own construction and overhaul departments.

"You know, Dick, last night I was thinking that maybe we can shed more light on this whole situation if we look closely at recent history."

Dick smiled as he dropped two lumps of sugar in his coffee.

"I never exactly figured these waterfront operations to be the company's history departments but yes, you're right. Reading history may certainly be better than reliving it! What did you have in mind?"

"Well, let's go back again to about five years ago. As I pointed out at the staff meeting, we were booming along with a high degree of efficiency in the yard."

"Agreed. So why is five years ago a world-shaking turning point for today's problems?"

"One factor could be that the overhaul business began to grow rapidly just about then with the first major overhauls of the early Heritage Class ships."

"Hells-bells, Walt, we've been overhauling ships at Tacoma for twenty-five years!"

"Yes, but take a closer look at that. Before five years ago, an overhaul was a relatively uncomplicated evolution. You stripped down—or replaced—some machinery; did some riveting, welding, painting, and cleaning; rewired electrical circuits; and installed some updated or replacement systems. But starting with the Heritage Class ships, things began to change.

"First off, these ships were already the most sophisticated, complicated, and 'tightly packed' vessels ever built. Reinstallation of electronic packages and machinery was almost a brand new ball game compared to earlier classes. Equipment mounting and alignment tolerances were much more stringent than in the past. The volume of electrical wiring alone was several times greater than on older ships. And the fact that the Heritage Class ships were not all alike tended to compound the importance of these factors. What I mean is that these differences were great enough to really impact overhaul design."

"Yes, I see what you're driving at," Dick replied. "But let's face it, since some of these overhauls were done by other yards, they must have faced the same problems."

"That's just the point!" Walt exclaimed. "Since TSD was the design lead for the Heritage Class, and since these other yards must have been experiencing the same problems, our design and engineering people had to put out a much greater support effort, not just here but at these other yards as well."

"Okay, now we're getting somewhere. I think you hit on one of the points that should be presented to the staff next week. Because of these factors, design support is now spread pretty thin, relatively, to what it should be. Maybe what we need is an engineering effort dedicated to our overhaul problems. And I could certainly use the same kind of dedicated support in the new construction area."

22/Tacoma Shipbuilding and Drydock Company

"Exactly, Dick. I want to stress the idea that we need dedicated support down here in the yard. It will also be important to point out that this support should be accountable to us for both scheduling and costs. I'll put together a small package of these ideas for Harvey and he can coordinate with information from the other members of the committee. We'll leave it at that for today."

Presenting the Options

Jim Price called the meeting to order in his usual precise manner at nine o'clock sharp, Monday morning.

"In our last go-round we set up a special committee to look into the shipyard support problem in detail. Harvey, since you compiled the data from the other members of the committee, why don't you take over, and we'll take a look at our options."

Harvey Hinchcliff shuffled through a large pile of papers in front of him and pulled out a folder of stapled sheets which he passed to each person at the table.

"Here's a summarization of all the facts uncovered by the ad hoc committee. As we look through this package, the committee members may want to add more details to the discussion.

"The first point to make is that we have unanimous agreement that a serious problem in the engineering/design support area exists, and this problem needs top management action for correction. The committee feels that there is no single cause for the problem, but that there are, rather, a combination of factors which have resulted in the situation we have to deal with. Let's look at the personnel circumstances, for example."

Harvey flipped over to a sheet which contained shipyard manpower statistics compiled by Industrial Relations.[9]

"As you can see, our shipyard experience level has declined during the past several years—due primarily to large turnover of personnel. Although our training programs in the trade skills are going full bore, the fact remains that building complicated ships requires a considerable amount of on-the-job training. When you couple this with the rising level of complexity in both new construction and overhaul work, you can see that it becomes more difficult and more time-consuming for the yard to cope with technical problems."

The ensuing discussion reviewed in detail some of the particular technical problems which had to be faced at the shipyard level.

Harvey continued.

9. See Exhibit 22.4.

"Another major factor to consider is work accountability and the method of charging for work done in the support area. It was pointed out at our last meeting that the nature of the work necessitates a certain amount of cross-charging, especially in overhaul contracts where TSD is the design lead agent and therefore supports both our own and other shipyards. As it stands now, we do not have a foolproof handle on these cost accounts. I talked with the Navy Supervisor and he indicates that the Navy would be very happy to see a more accurate means of accounting for design agent costs."

A lengthy discussion continued reiterating the problems associated with Tacoma's costs and schedules and the importance of meeting all the company's commitments to the contract customer. Walt interjected his feelings about the immediate requirements of the waterfront—it seemed to him for the hundredth time. Finally, after many minutes of heated discussion, Jim Price brought the conference back to the issues at point.

"Before we go any further—which is liable to degenerate the meeting to an argument—let's hear out the rest of the committee's report. Then, maybe, we'll have enough information to make some reasonable decisions. Harvey, go ahead."

"Right. It is imperative to focus our attention on the fact that what we are trying to solve here is the waterfront need for improved responsiveness to get the job done as effectively as possible. The committee feels that probably a new mixture of trade and engineering skills is needed in the yard in light of our present technological environment. The big question is, how do we formulate the required mixture?

"Without attempting to argue the merits or demerits of company structure, I would point out that our present set-up, as you all know, has a very well-delineated hierarchy.[10] It was suggested about two years ago that the company establish a new position of Shipyard Design Manager, and certainly this is one option that could be considered. Such a person would be responsible to New Construction and Overhaul for cost and schedule control (as Walt suggested in our last meeting). But he would still fall under the technical cognizance of John Harrington as Director of Engineering, and he would have temporary control of professional personnel in design and engineering as the need arose.[11] I think we should keep in mind, however, the possible splintering effect that this type of move could have on our engineering organization.

"Another option that is worthy of consideration is to provide resident designers and engineers right in the shipyard departments

10. See Exhibits 22.5 and 22.6 showing existing company organization.
11. See Exhibit 22.7 for organization chart of ad hoc committee's first option.

where supporting services are frequently needed. The committee feels that this would provide professional engineering expertise where it is needed on a full time basis. These personnel would be permanently assigned to the waterfront where they would be able to deal directly with the trades in solving support problems. They would report directly to the departments to which they were attached.[12]

"A final option to look at is the possibility of setting up a completely new department which would deal solely with overhaul and construction engineering problems.[13] The advantages of such a department are quite obvious since you would have an entire spectrum of engineering talent devoted full time to shipyard support, under a single management. In its considerations, the committee felt that this would certainly be the most drastic step to take. From the standpoint of effectiveness it would probably solve the waterfront's problems, but it would also create some new ones. For one thing, it would cause more than just a splintering of engineering— it would, in fact, cause a complete redundancy in many areas of engineering and design, which means dollars. It would also be the most costly operation to set up since you would have to decide on the new organization, arrange for office spaces, steal personnel from present departments or hire new people, and establish exactly what the department's responsibilities would be. In short, this would be a major change and an expensive solution, and the question is, do the benefits outweigh the costs?"

Discussion Questions

1. What is the Master Strategy of the firm?
2. How can the proper organization structure insure mission accomplishment?
3. How would you arrange the organization structure of this firm? Why?

12. See Exhibit 22.8 for the organization chart of this option.
13. See Exhibit 22.9 for the organization chart of this option.

Exhibit 22.1   Management Organization Chart—Level O (1964)
Tacoma Shipbuilding and Drydock Company

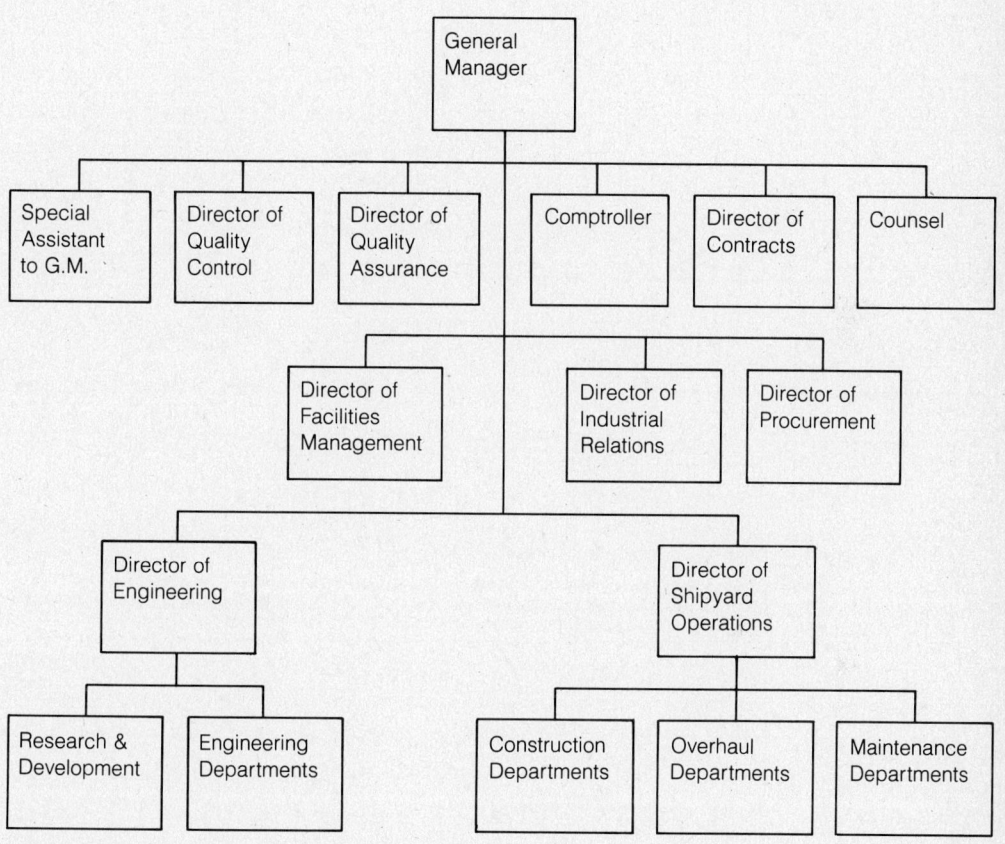

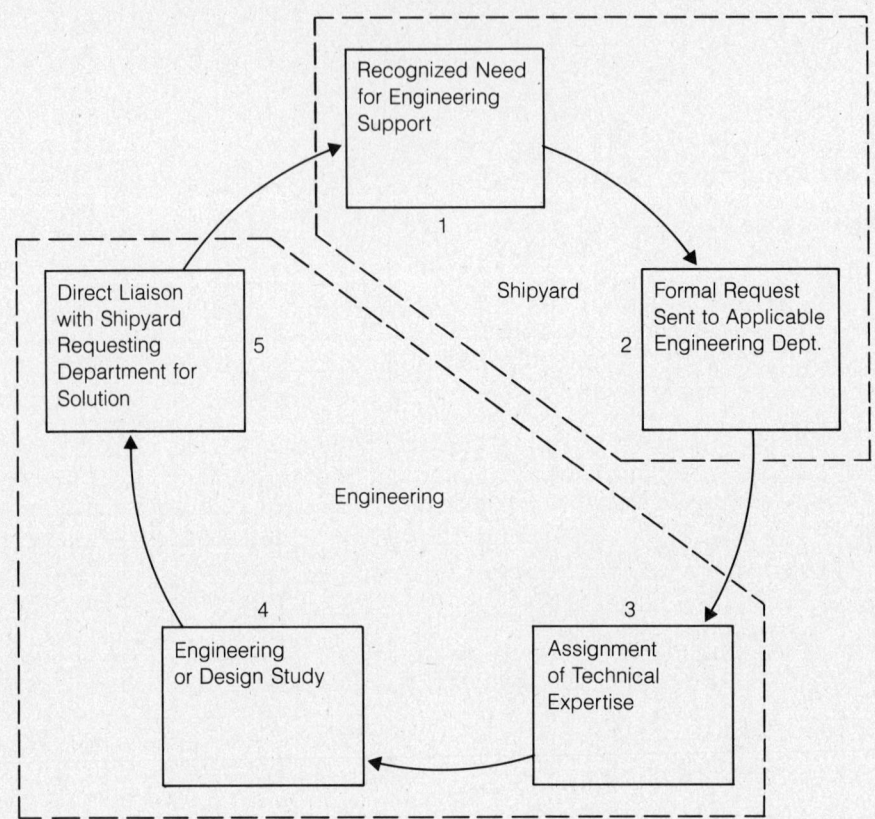

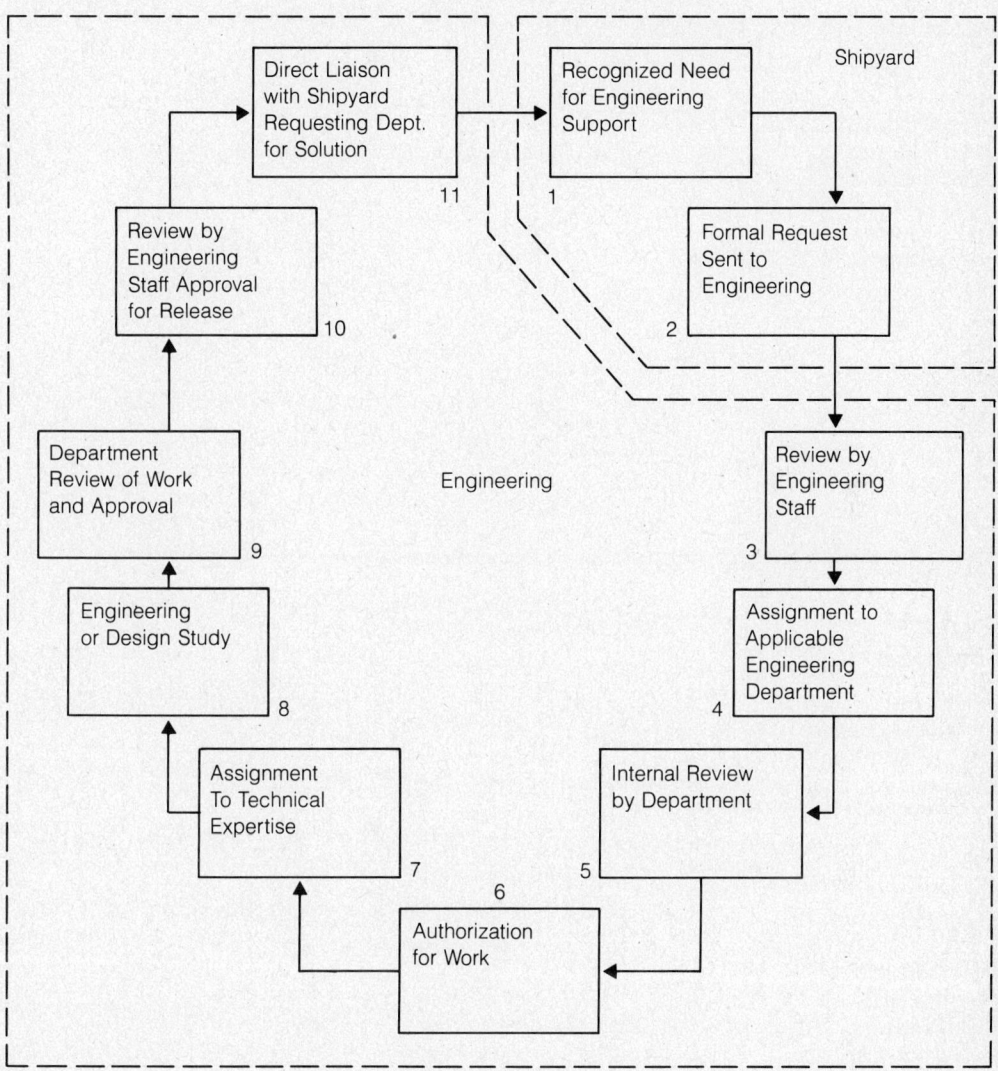

Exhibit 22.4 Tacoma Shipbuilding and Drydock Company Comparison of Shipyard Trade Worker Experience Levels between 1965 and 1969

Part A Number of Workers in Production and Maintenance by Occupational Structure

Structure Level	Years of Experience	Number of Workers 1965	1969
Working Leader	12+	700	710
Specialist	8+	685	611
Skilled Mechanic 1C	10+	820	732
Skilled Mechanic 2C	5	466	255
Skilled Mechanic 3C	4	1,433	445
Skilled Mechanic 4C	3	1,216	609
Semi-skilled Mechanic			
and Learners 6	4	954	667
5	3	727	380
4	2	1,664	629
3	2	1,575	1,175
2	1±	881	921
1	1−	975	980
Totals		11,996	8,114

Part B Breakdown of Years of Experience by Occupational Title

Occupational Title	Average Years of Experience 1965	1969
Painter	7	5
Locomotive Operator	11	11
Transportation Repairman	5	3
Toolmaker	16	15
Inside Machinist (all categories)	8	6
Crane Operator	12	13
Outside Machinist (all categories)	8	6
Service Equipment Repair Machinist	9	8
Maintenance Machinist	7	7
Welding Machine Operator	9	8
R&D Testman	5	4
Test Mechanic	4	4
Dock Crew	8	9
Mechanical Inspector	10	9
Machine Shop Inspector	10	10
Equipment Repairman	6	4
Pipe Machine Operator	6	5
Power Engineer	7	5
Molder	13	12
Foundryman	11	9
Foundry Machine Operator	8	8
Foundry Chipper	5	3
Melter	6	5

Exhibit 22.4 Continued

Occupational Title	Average Years of Experience	
	1965	1969
Coreman	7	5
Foundry Inspector	10	11
Pipefitter	5	4
Silver Brazer	13	9
Hangerman	9	7
Power Bending Machine Operator	9	9
Piping Inspector	8	8
QC Inspector	8	9
Pipecoverer	4	3
Heating Plant Operator	4	4
Pipe Shop Tester	5	6
Outside Electrician	11	10
Electrical Inspector QC	12	12
Electronics Service Engineer	8	6
Electronics Service Calibration Engineer	7	7
Electronics Service Engineer—Fire Control	9	9
Electronics Service Engineer—Sonar	8	7
Electronics Service Engineer—Nuclear	9	9
Electronics Technician	4	5
Electronics Mechanic	4	3
Maintenance Electrician	11	13
Power House Engineer	8	8
Electrical Test Engineer	5	3
Welding Machine Repairman	6	5
Loftsman	14	13
Blacksmith	9	10
Furnaceman	9	7
Plate Shop Mechanic	8	8
Shipfitter	5	4
Chipper/Tank Tester	4	4
Driller	4	3
Welder	11	12
Burner	12	11
Rigger	10	9
Sheet Metal Mechanic	5	5
Structural Inspector QC	11	12
Joiner	7	5
Upholsterer	6	4
Carpenter	14	16
Industrial Radiography Interpreter	6	7
Industrial Radiation Auditor	6	5
Radiography Technician	4	3

Exhibit 22.5 Management Organization Chart—Level O (1969)
Tacoma Shipbuilding and Drydock Company

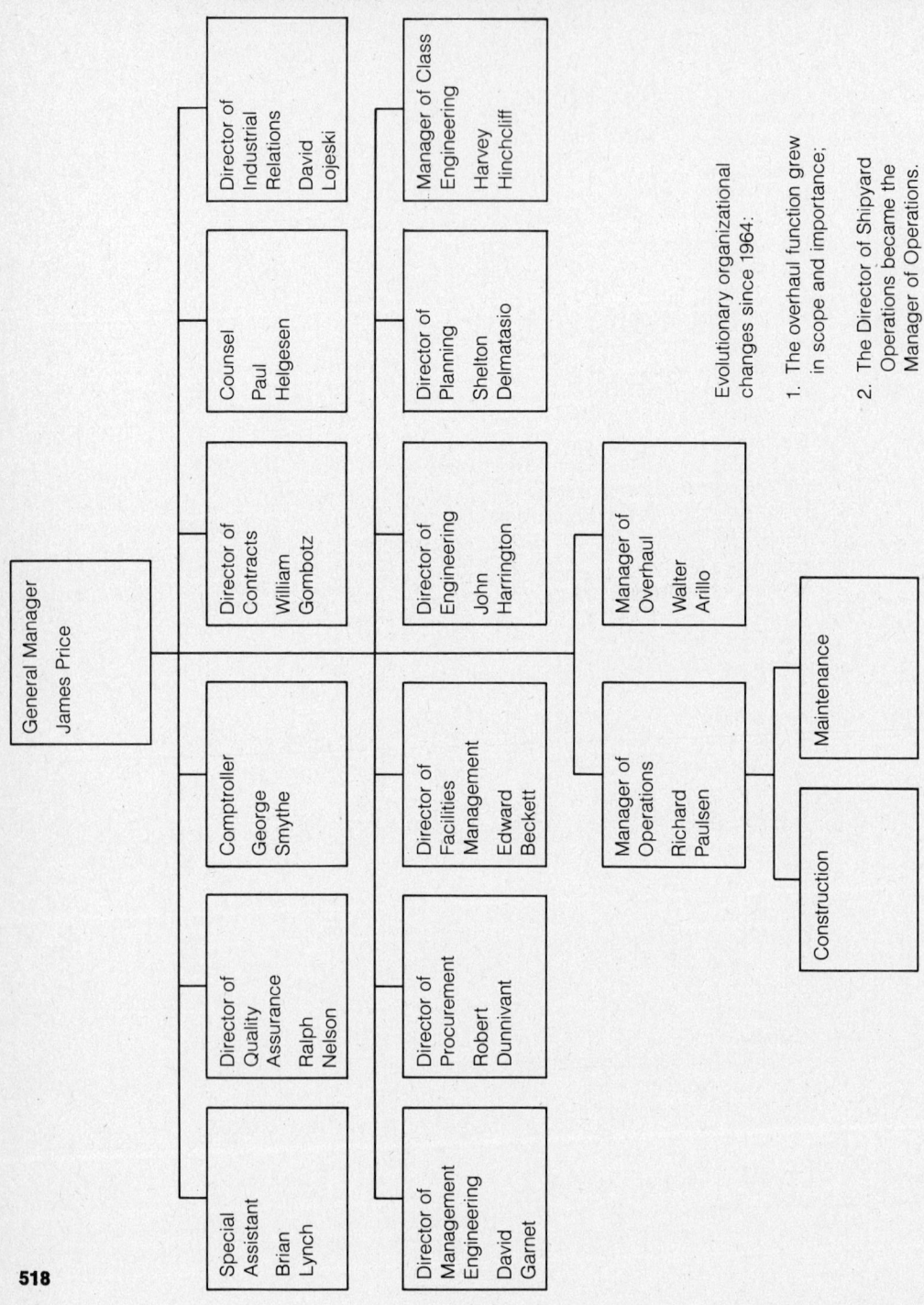

General Manager
James Price

Special Assistant
Brian Lynch

Director of Quality Assurance
Ralph Nelson

Comptroller
George Smythe

Director of Contracts
William Gombotz

Counsel
Paul Helgesen

Director of Industrial Relations
David Lojeski

Director of Management Engineering
David Garnet

Director of Procurement
Robert Dunnivant

Director of Facilities Management
Edward Beckett

Director of Engineering
John Harrington

Director of Planning
Shelton Delmatasio

Manager of Class Engineering
Harvey Hinchcliff

Manager of Overhaul
Walter Arillo

Manager of Operations
Richard Paulsen

Construction

Maintenance

Evolutionary organizational changes since 1964:

1. The overhaul function grew in scope and importance;

2. The Director of Shipyard Operations became the Manager of Operations.

Exhibit 22.6 Management Organization Chart—Level 1 (1969) Engineering Tacoma Shipbuilding and Drydock Company

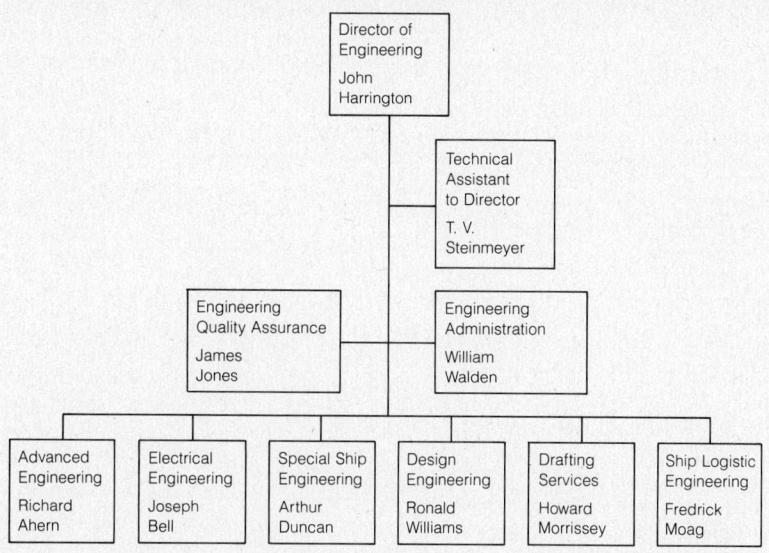

Exhibit 22.7 Organization Chart of Ad Hoc Committee's First Option Tacoma Shipbuilding and Drydock Company

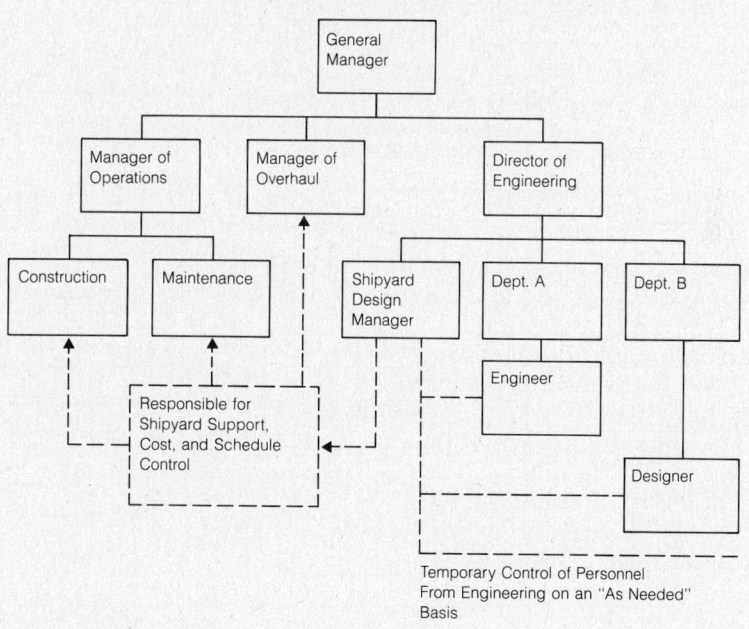

**Exhibit 22.8 Organization Chart of Ad Hoc Committee's Second Option
Tacoma Shipbuilding and Drydock Company**

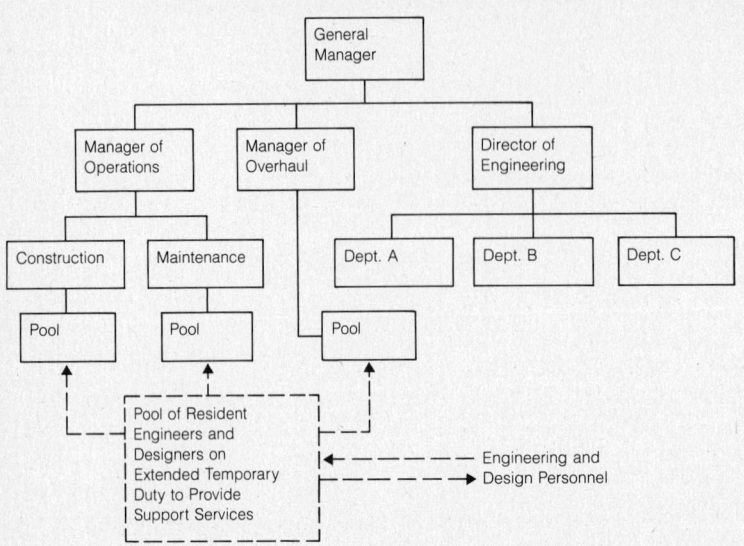

**Exhibit 22.9 Organization Chart of Ad Hoc Committee's Third Option
Tacoma Shipbuilding and Drydock Company**

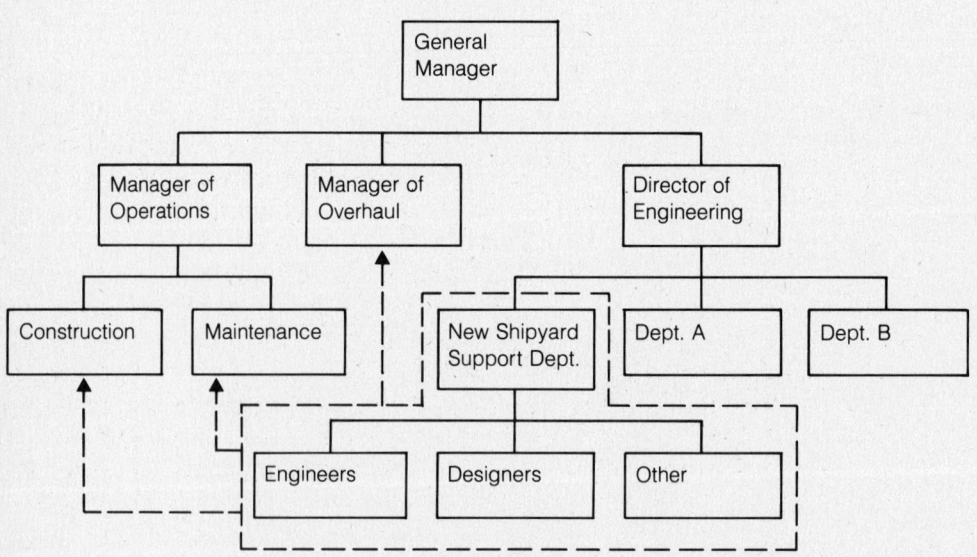

23/Hewlett-Packard Company

Roger M. Atherton and
Dennis M. Crites

Problems of Rapid Growth

In 1972–1973, rapid growth had created significant problems for Hewlett-Packard Company, a leading producer of electronic instruments and a major contender in minicomputers and calculators. Previous efforts to expand sales and market share had been largely successful but had led the company to lower prices, for increased competitiveness; to reduce the percentage spent on research and development, for profitability; and to ease up on credit and payment policies, for the attraction of new customers. Sales and profits had increased substantially, but the company was faced with large increases in inventory, products put into production before they were fully developed, prices set too low to generate sufficient returns, and increased short-term borrowings. For the first time in company history, management had considered converting some of the short-term debt into long-term debt. Chairman David Packard and President William R. Hewlett, who had founded the company in 1939, decided improvements were needed in strategy, structure, and tactics.

A fall 1975 review of these changes is provided for the purpose of analyzing and evaluating the changes made by management and determining whether additional action should be taken.

The Industry

Accelerating rates of technical change, increased competition, and economic uncertainty have made long-range planning and strategic decision-making increasingly complex. The world economic boom of 1972–1973, followed almost immediately by depressed economic conditions, created especially difficult problems for companies in high-technology electronics industry. Recession conditions caused large financial dislocations for many companies accustomed to rapid growth. Some of them decided to reduce expenses by cutting product development. Others increased their research spending in order to be ready for the price cuts and new products that they expected to characterize the next upturn. Since the industry is not capital intensive, a major determinant of growth is the successful development of new products, particularly those which cannot be quickly imitated. This has forced the managers of high-technology companies to make difficult decisions about the probable impact of price changes on sales and profits, and the probable

Source: Prepared by Professors Roger M. Atherton and Dennis M. Crites for the University of Oklahoma. Reprinted by permission. Distributed by the Intercollegiate Case Clearing House, Soldiers Field, Boston, Mass. 02163. All rights reserved to the contributors. Printed in the U.S.A.

effects of research expenditures on growth and on both short-run and long-run profitability.

As *Business Week* has reported, the management of technology—not only in electronics but also in pharmaceuticals, chemicals, and other specialties—is no longer an art but a discipline that is becoming better understood by a growing number of companies. The specialization that once separated an instrument maker from a computer company or a component supplier has largely disappeared, as semiconductor devices have taken on new complexity and instruments have been combined with calculators and computers in an extensive array of specialized systems. Semiconductor companies have integrated forward into end products, and instrument makers have started making their own data-processing equipment. As a result, a large number of potential competitors have entered almost every conceivable product-market segment and niche of high-technology electronics.

An increasingly common tactic used by companies to achieve market dominance is to price new products in relation to manufacturing costs they anticipate will be attained when the product has matured and when economies of scale have been achieved. This puts a premium on obtaining market share early in order to recover development and initial production costs, and to quickly attain sufficient volume to justify the predetermined price. As a result, many of the companies in the industry vigorously pursue strategies designed to achieve both technical and market dominance. This puts a heavy emphasis on innovation and creativity, sensitivity to market and customer needs, skills at finding useful applications of developing technology, and marketing and distribution capabilities to exploit new opportunities and to rapidly obtain dominant market share.

Although the total number of companies competing in this industry is too numerous to permit a comprehensive presentation of their performance, a representative sample is provided in Exhibit 23.1. Sales growth, profit margins, and earnings on net worth are shown.

Hewlett-Packard: A Brief Sketch

Innovative products have been the cornerstone of Hewlett-Packard's growth since 1939, when Hewlett engineered a new type of audio oscillator and, with Packard, created the company in Packard's garage. The product was cheaper and easier to use than competitive products, and it was quickly followed by a family of test instruments based on the same design principles. By the 1950s, they were turning out two dozen new products every year. By 1975, Hewlett-Packard had become one of the giants of the high-technology electronics industry. Annual sales were climbing rapidly toward $1 billion, approximately one-half of which were made to international customers. The company's 29,000 employees were involved in designing, manufacturing, and marketing more than 3,300 products. These included electronic test and

Exhibit 23.1   High-Technology Electronics Industry Companies—Sample Survey

Sales Growth (Percent of Change)

	74-75*	73-74	72-73	71-72
Beckham Instruments	7	21	10	8
Fairchild Camera	—23	10	57	16
General Instrument	—6	—1	34	16
Hewlett-Packard	9	34	38	28
National Semiconductor	11	115	65	58
Raytheon	16	21	9	12
Texas Instruments	—12	22	36	24
Textronix	24	37	21	12
Varian Associates	6	22	18	9

Profit Margin (Percent)

	1975*	1974	1973	1972	1971
Beckham Instruments	4	4	4	3	3
Fairchild Camera	4	7	8	4	d†
General Instrument	2	3	3	3	2
Hewlett-Packard	9	10	8	8	6
National Semiconductor	7	8	4	3	3
Raytheon	3	3	3	3	3
Texas Instruments	5	6	7	5	4
Textronix	8	8	8	7	6
Varian Associates	3	3	3	2	d

Earnings on Net Worth (Percent)

	1975*	1974	1973	1972	1971
Beckham Instruments	10	8	7	6	5
Fairchild Camera	8	17	20	9	d
General Instrument	5	7	9	7	4
Hewlett-Packard	16	18	15	13	10
National Semiconductor	25	35	14	16	12
Raytheon	16	14	13	12	12
Texas Instruments	11	17	18	13	10
Textronix	13	12	11	8	8
Varian Associates	5	5	6	3	d

*Estimated by Value Line.
†d=deficit.
Source: *Value Line Investment Survey* and casewriters' calculations.

measuring instruments and systems; electronic calculators, computers, and computer systems; medical electronic products; electronic instrumentation for chemical analysis; and solid-state components. According to company sources, Hewlett-Packard has remained a people-oriented company with management policies that encourage individual creativity, initiative, and contribution throughout the organization. It has also tried to retain the openness, informality, and unstructured operating procedures that marked the company in its early years. Each individual has been given the freedom and the flexibility to implement work methods and ideas to achieve both personal and company objectives and goals.

Corporate Objectives

When Hewlett-Packard was first formed, Hewlett and Packard formulated many of the management concepts which have since become the formal corporate objectives. As a result of their decision to have a decentralized organization, they believed it desirable to have a set of corporate objectives that would tie the organization more closely together and also ensure that the company as a whole was headed in a common direction. These objectives were first put into writing in 1957. They have been modified occasionally since then to reflect the changing nature of the company's business and environment. The intent and wording of the objectives in 1975 were, according to the founders, remarkably similar to the original versions.

As stated in the introduction to the Hewlett-Packard Statement of Corporate Objectives:

The achievements of an organization are the result of the combined efforts of each individual in the organization working toward common objectives. These objectives should be realistic, should be clearly understood by everyone in the organization, and should reflect the organization's basic character and personality.

The following is a brief description of the Hewlett-Packard objectives in 1975:

1. Profit Objective: To achieve sufficient profit to finance company growth and to provide resources needed to achieve the other corporate objectives.
2. Customer Objective: To provide products and services of the greatest possible value to our customers, thereby gaining and holding their respect and loyalty.
3. Fields of Interest Objective: To enter new fields only when the company's ideas, together with its technical, manufacturing, and marketing skills, assure a needed and profitable contribution to the field.
4. Growth Objective: To let growth be limited only by profits and company ability to develop and produce technical products that satisfy real customer needs.
5. People Objective: To help Hewlett-Packard people share in the company's success, which they make possible; to provide job security based on their performance; to recognize individual achievements; and to insure the personal satisfaction that comes from a sense of accomplishment in their work.

6. Management Objective: To foster initiative and creativity by allowing the individual great freedom of action in attaining well-defined objectives.
7. Citizenship Objective: To honor corporate obligations to society by being an economic, intellectual, and social asset to each nation and each community in which the company operates.

Both Hewlett and Packard have indicated these objectives have served the company well in shaping the company, guiding its growth, and providing the foundation for the company's contribution to technological progress and the betterment of society.

Selected Strategies and Related Policies

Hewlett-Packard's product-market strategy has concentrated on developing quality products which make unique technological contributions and are so far advanced that customers are willing to pay premium prices. Products have been limited to electronic test and measurement and technology related fields. Customer service, both before and after the sale, has been given primary emphasis. The financial strategy has been to use profits, employee stock purchases, and other internally generated funds to finance growth. The firm has avoided long-term debt and resorted to short-term debt only when sales growth exceeded the return on net worth. The growth strategy has been to attain a position of technological strength and leadership by continually developing innovative products and by attracting high caliber and creative people. Motivational strategy has consisted of providing employees with the opportunity to share in the success of the company through high wages, profit-sharing, and stock-purchase plans. The firm has also provided job security by keeping fluctuations in production schedules to a minimum by avoiding consumer-type products and by not making any products exclusively for the government. Managerial strategy has been to practice "management by objective" rather than management by directive; it has used the corporate objectives to provide unity of purpose and given employees the freedom to work toward these goals in ways they determine best for their own area of responsibility. The company has demonstrated its social responsibility by building plants and offices that are attractive and in harmony with the community, by helping to solve community problems, and by contributing both money and time to community projects.

Strategic Situation

The company was fortunate to have entered the electronics industry early, before the rapid growth and expansion had started. Hewlett-Packard's leadership position in instruments has been a major contributor to its success as the company diversified into computers, calculators, and components. In recent years, the original test and measurement instruments have accounted for about half of total sales. Data products, including minicomputers and calculators, brought in 40 percent. Medical electronics, a field entered largely through acquisition, added 10 percent. Analytical instruments counted for an additional 5 percent. The trends in sales and contributions to company profit of these product groups are presented in Exhibit 23.2.

Sales increased 30 percent in fiscal 1972 and almost 40 percent in 1973. At first, this rapid growth was pursued vigorously because the company had been adversely affected by the computer and aerospace downturns in 1970. Earnings declined slightly in fiscal 1971, despite such austere measures as reduced work weeks for everyone, which resulted in company-wide reductions in pay. But the rapidity of the growth in 1972–1973 created problems of a different kind. Inventories and accounts receivable increased substantially. There was an unaccustomed influx of new employees who needed to be trained and absorbed into the company's widely dispersed and decentralized operations. Products were put into production before they were fully developed. Prices were set too low for an adequate return on investment. These problems necessitated a higher level of short-term borrowings. By the end of 1973, these amounted to $118 million, and management considered converting some of the short-term debt to longer-term debt. The company was reluctant to do this because of the uncertain economic conditions. Since the company had policies of keeping employment steady and operating on a pay-as-you-go basis, both Hewlett and Packard believed minimal debt would be more consistent with these policies and the weakening U.S. economy.

Exhibit 23.2   Contributions to Sales and Pre-Tax Profit Margin by Product Groups

	1975*	1974	1973	1972	1971
Sales (Millions of dollars)					
Test, measuring and related items	460.0	442.9	362.3	309.8	264.8
Electronic data products	360.0	325.7	215.2	108.0	63.1
Medical electronic equipment	95.0	76.1	56.6	40.7	30.8
Analytical instrumentation	45.0	39.4	27.2	20.6	16.4
Total	960.0	884.1	661.3	479.1	375.1
Pre-Tax Profit Margin (Percent)					
Test, measuring and related items	14.5	15.1	13.3	14.5	14.3
Electronic data products	18.3	20.7	17.4	19.8	3.3
Medical electronic equipment	11.5	10.0	11.1	14.3	9.7
Analytical instrumentation	8.0	6.1	9.9	10.2	8.5
Total	15.1	16.3	14.3	15.5	11.8

*Estimated by value line in *Value Line Investment Survey*, 1975.
Source: *Value Line Investment Survey*.

In 1973–1974, top management decided to avoid adding long-term debt and to reduce short-term debt by controlling costs, managing assets, and improving profit margins. As Packard made clear to the management at all levels, they had somehow been diverted into seeking market share as an objective. So both he and Hewlett began a year-long campaign to re-emphasize the principles they developed when they began their unique partnership. Clearly, in an industry where much of the competition was pushing for market share, Hewlett-Packard's decision to re-focus on profitability rather than market share presented certain risks. However, according to *Business Week*, neither Hewlett nor Packard saw themselves as risk takers, and their approach was logical for a company that had consistently come up with truly innovative products. Packard toured the divisions to impose this new asset-management discipline. In addition, while other companies dropped prices to boost sales and cut research spending to improve earnings, Hewlett-Packard used quite different tactics. It raised prices by an average of 10 percent over the previous year, and it increased spending on research and development by 20 percent, to an $80 million annual rate. These two strategies were intended to improve company profitability and to slow the rate of growth that had more than doubled sales in the previous three years.

The improvements in 1974 performance compared with 1973 were quite dramatic. During fiscal 1974, inventories and receivables increased about 3 percent while sales grew 34 percent to $884 million. The effect of this better asset control combined with improved earnings resulted in a drop in short-term debt of approximately $77 million. Earnings were up 66 percent to $84 million and were equal to $3.08 per share compared to $1.89 per share. Only 1,000 employees were added compared to 7,000 in the previous year. The improvement continued in fiscal 1975; sales for the first half of fiscal 1975 were up 14 percent to $460 million while profits increased 21 percent to $42 million. However, a *Value Line Investment Survey* estimated that annual sales for 1975 would be up 9 percent to $960 million while profit would increase about 2 percent to $85 million.

The trends in earnings performance are shown in the Ten Year Consolidated Earnings Summary, Exhibit 23.3. Balance sheet effects are shown in the Comparison of 1974 and 1973 Consolidated Financial Positions, Exhibit 23.4. The differences in capital sources and uses are shown in the Consolidated Statement of Changes in 1974 and 1973 Financial Position, Exhibit 23.5.

Both Hewlett and Packard were dismayed that they had been forced to initiate and personally lead the efforts to get the company back on the track. It was particularly disconcerting to them because they believed the issues were fundamental to the basic strategy of the company. They had also had to intervene directly in day-to-day operational management, which was counter to their basic philosophy of a decentralized, product-oriented, and divisionalized organization structure.

Exhibit 23.3 Ten-Year Consolidated Earnings Summary (in Thousands)

Years ended October 31

	1974	1973	1972	1971	1970	1969	1968	1967	1966	1965
Net sales	$884,053	$661,290	$479,077	$375,088	$363,593	$335,690	$277,681	$250,407	$208,263	$167,429
Other income, net	8,732	12,108	3,570	4,202	2,802	541	1,890	827	68	147
Total revenues	892,785	673,398	482,647	379,290	366,395	336,231	279,571	251,234	208,331	167,576
Costs and expenses:										
Cost of goods sold	422,104	312,972	223,690	184,507	173,731	157,364	134,479	122,428	99,421	81,745
Research and development . .	70,685	57,798	44,163	39,426	37,212	31,750	29,282	26,879	22,265	15,877
Marketing, administrative and general	247,232	202,999	138,716	107,822	105,587	90,098	70,890	61,006	52,215	41,742
Interest	8,502	5,057	1,764	1,239	2,212	1,005	728	1,134	766	230
Total costs and expenses . .	748,523	578,826	408,333	332,994	318,742	280,217	235,379	211,447	174,667	139,594
Earnings before taxes on income	144,262	94,572	74,314	46,296	47,653	56,014	44,192	39,787	33,664	27,982
Taxes on income	60,240	43,823	37,064	22,415	24,146	29,977	23,032	19,476	16,470	14,290
Earnings before accounting change	84,022	50,749	37,250	23,881	23,507	26,037	21,160	20,311	17,194	13,692
Accounting change[a]	—	—	1,211	—	—	—	—	—	—	—
Net earnings	$ 84,022	$ 50,749	$ 38,461	$ 23,881	$ 23,507	$ 26,037	$ 21,160	$ 20,311	$ 17,194	$ 13,692
Per share[b]:										
Earnings before accounting change	$3.08	$1.89	$1.40	$ .92	$ .92	$1.03	$ .84	$ .82	$ .70	$ .55
Accounting change	—	—	.05	—	—	—	—	—	—	—
Net earnings	$3.08	$1.89	$1.45	$ .92	$ .92	$1.03	$ .84	$ .82	$ .70	$ .55
Common shares outstanding at year end[b]	27,298	26,816	26,450	26,038	25,649	25,299	25,128	24,863	24,601	24,406

[a] *Cumulative effect on prior years (to October 31, 1971) of change in accounting method used for computing miscellaneous material and labor in inventories. The effect on net earnings and per share amounts in each year prior to 1972, assuming the change in accounting method had been applied retroactively, is insignificant.*

[b] *Based on the shares of common stock outstanding at the end of each year, giving retroactive effect for the 2 for 1 stock split in February, 1970. In 1965 per share amounts are after deducting $292 of dividends on preferred stock.*

HEWLETT-PACKARD COMPANY AND SUBSIDIARIES

Source: 1974 Annual Report.

Exhibit 23.4 Comparison of 1974 and 1973 Consolidated Financial Positions

ASSETS

	1974	1973
	(Thousands)	
CURRENT ASSETS:		
Cash and marketable securities (note 2)	$ 13,828	$ 8,925
Notes and accounts receivable, less provision for losses in collection (1974 - $1,539; 1973 - $1,418)	193,735	187,472
Inventories, at standard cost, which approximates first-in, first-out and average, not in excess of replacement market:		
Finished goods	51,627	51,652
Work in process	82,410	84,687
Raw materials	61,177	52,307
Deposits and prepaid expenses	13,791	10,147
TOTAL CURRENT ASSETS	416,568	395,190
PROPERTY, PLANT AND EQUIPMENT, AT COST (note 1):		
Land	26,566	23,940
Buildings and improvements	128,274	87,961
Machinery and equipment	109,342	94,210
Other	26,846	21,992
Leaseholds and leasehold improvements	10,002	7,056
Construction in progress	41,541	32,493
	342,571	267,652
Accumulated depreciation and amortization	117,709	93,882
	224,862	173,770
OTHER ASSETS AND DEFERRED CHARGES:		
Investment in unconsolidated Japanese affiliate (note 1)	4,391	3,668
Patents and other intangible assets	2,243	2,798
Other	6,317	4,240
	12,951	10,706
	$654,381	$579,666

The accompanying notes are an integral part of these financial statements.

HEWLETT-PACKARD COMPANY AND SUBSIDIARIES

Source: 1974 Annual Report.

Exhibit 23.4   continued

LIABILITIES AND SHAREOWNERS' EQUITY

	1974	1973
	(Thousands)	
CURRENT LIABILITIES:		
Notes payable (note 2)	$ 43,527	$ 94,749
Commercial paper (note 2)	—	25,750
Accounts payable	26,491	36,072
Accrued expenses	74,778	51,471
Federal, foreign and state taxes on income (notes 1 and 3)	34,476	12,745
TOTAL CURRENT LIABILITIES	179,272	220,787
LONG-TERM DEBT, less current portion included in notes		
payable above (1974 - $766; 1973 - $748) (note 2)	2,899	2,182
DEFERRED FEDERAL TAXES ON INCOME — Domestic International		
Sales Corporation (note 1)	14,531	7,500
COMMITMENTS (notes 2 and 8)		

SHAREOWNERS' EQUITY (note 4):
Common stock, par value $1 a share:

	1974	1973		
	(Stated in shares)			
Authorized	40,000,000	40,000,000		
Reserved for:				
Stock option plans	774,892	476,690		
Stock purchase plans	967,697	243,267		
Service award plan	31,130	36,670		
Issued and outstanding	27,298,474	26,815,566	27,298	26,816
Capital in excess of par value			112,157	82,763
Retained earnings			318,224	239,618
TOTAL SHAREOWNERS' EQUITY			457,679	349,197
			$654,381	$579,666

HEWLETT-PACKARD COMPANY AND SUBSIDIARIES

Source: 1974 Annual Report.

For the years ended October 31, 1974 and 1973

	1974	1973
	(Thousands)	
Working capital provided:		
Net earnings	$ 84,022	$ 50,749
Add charges not affecting working capital:		
Depreciation and amortization	31,519	22,917
Deferred federal taxes on income	7,031	5,412
Stock purchase and award plans	5,625	4,169
Other	4,549	522
Working capital provided from operations	132,746	83,769
Proceeds from sale of common stock	23,746	15,483
Proceeds of additional long-term debt	1,277	1,823
Total working capital provided	157,769	101,075
Working capital used:		
Investment in property, plant and equipment	86,327	81,162
Dividends to shareowners	5,416	5,332
Reduction in long-term debt	560	1,558
Increase in equity in unconsolidated Japanese affiliate	723	1,054
Other, net	1,850	4,319
Total working capital used	94,876	93,425
Increase in working capital	62,893	7,650
Working capital at beginning of year	174,403	166,753
Working capital at end of year	$237,296	$174,403
Increase in working capital consisted of:		
Increase (decrease) in current assets:		
Cash and marketable securities	$ 4,903	$ (10,723)
Notes and accounts receivable	6,263	69,057
Inventories	6,568	70,083
Deposits and prepaid expenses	3,644	4,256
	21,378	132,673
Decrease (increase) in current liabilities:		
Notes payable and commercial paper	76,972	(103,201)
Accounts payable and accrued expenses	(13,726)	(26,837)
Federal, foreign and state taxes on income	(21,731)	5,015
	41,515	(125,023)
Increase in working capital	$ 62,893	$ 7,650

The accompanying notes are an integral part of these financial statements.

HEWLETT-PACKARD COMPANY AND SUBSIDIARIES

Source: 1974 Annual Report.

23/Hewlett-Packard Company

Structural Situation

Both men have been personally responsible for many of the company's new products and diversification activities. Since Packard was 65 in 1977 and Hewlett 65 in 1978, both have recognized their retirements might have a substantial impact on the management structure and future success of the company. Some observers suggest that the problems in the early 1970s were the result of Packard's absence while he served in the Defense Department. As of mid-1975, the two men owned about half the company stock and could undoubtedly postpone retirement, but they felt it was very important for them to prepare the organization for an orderly succession. They also wanted to develop an organization structure which could respond more effectively to growth and diversification and would also provide more effective management of day-to-day operations. To accomplish these ends several significant changes were made, shortly before the end of the 1974 fiscal year, in the management structure of the company. The new organization is shown in Exhibit 23.6.

The basic product groups were realigned from four to six. The purpose was to establish a more logical grouping of products and technologies, while creating group organizations of more manageable size and structure. They also established a new level of management to oversee day-to-day operations of the company. This consisted of two executive vice presidents, jointly responsible for operations, and a vice president for corporate administration. These three executives, along with Hewlett and Packard, were set up as an Executive Committee to meet weekly in order to coordinate all phases of the company's operations. This was intended to bring new people into the upper levels of management to build the long-term strength of the company. The new structure was also expected to allow both Hewlett and Packard to devote more time to matters of policy and planning the company's future.

In the new organization, the six product groups each had a general manager, who had responsibility for both domestic and foreign product divisions. The change left intact Hewlett-Packard's basic strategy of approaching established markets through relatively autonomous, product-oriented divisions. In any high-technology operation, according to *Business Week*, a key problem is keeping new-product development focused on the needs of the market rather than on pure research and technological improvements with little market potential. Hewlett-Packard has tried to avoid this by doing most of its research and development at the division level. Of the $70.7 million spent on research and development in 1974, one-sixth was allocated to Corporate R & D and five-sixths was spent by the divisions. Divisions were intentionally kept small to foster open communications and quick responsiveness to their individual market segments. Each product group, in addition to the group general manager, had a sales-service organization serving all the product divisions in the product group. Each product division had its own engineering, manufacturing, personnel, quality, accounting, and marketing functions with

Exhibit 23.6   Hewlett-Packard Corporate Organization, April, 1975

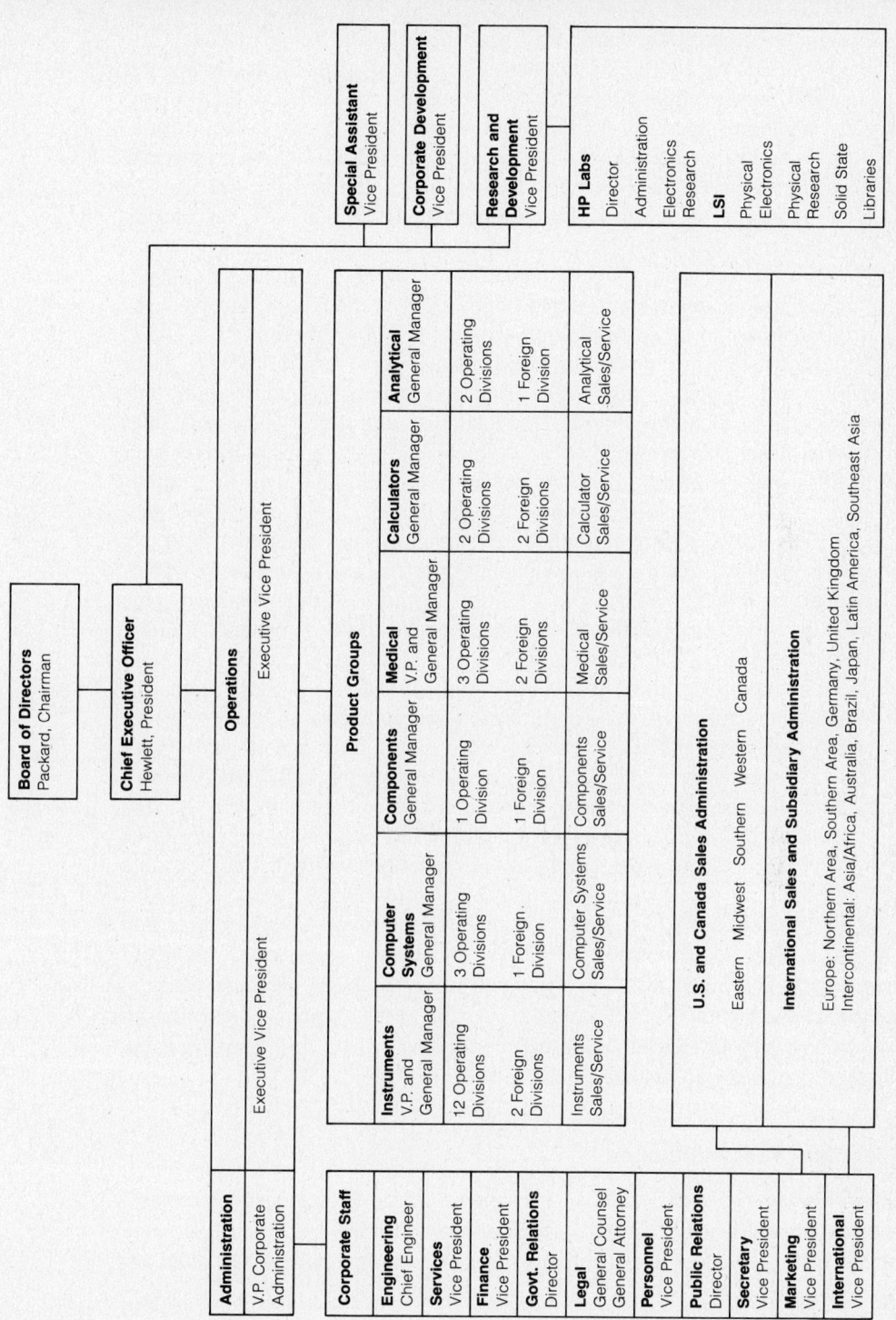

some of the smaller divisions in the same location sharing a functional department between them. Although H-P's divisions had considerable latitude in developing product strategies, they were not allowed to go outside their assigned markets or to borrow money. Even within the limits set by top management, new-product proposals were carefully reviewed at the preliminary investigation stage. The company considered itself conservative in funding projects and expected at least 80 percent of funded projects to be successful. Once development of a new product had been funded, the goal was to get it to the market in a hurry. The company believed that sales lost during development time could not be recovered since, if the technology were available to fill a market need, others could also conceive a product. As a result, both timing and the flexibility to exploit opportunities quickly were considered important reasons for having a multiple-product division structure.

The product-division marketing departments were responsible for order processing and shipping, sales-engineering and contract-administration, service-engineering, technical-writing, publications, and advertising and sales promotion. They also provided sales forecasts and were responsible for recommending and reviewing prices. At the initial pricing this involved a major analysis of the marketplace, competition, profitability, and overall product strategy. The actual selling and customer servicing were handled by the six group organizations. Each division competed for the time of the group's field-sales force. In order to attract the attention of the field-sales engineers, the divisions had to offer extensive marketing support and new product training to these "customers." The broad, growing, and often interacting lines of products frequently resulted in several group sales teams working with one customer. The centralized sales organization was intended to assure that cooperation and communication between sales teams were maintained; Hewlett-Packard wanted customers to feel they were dealing with one company with common policies and services. Confusion and competition were avoided by a clear assignment of sales responsibilities and by organizing the sales force in a way that put primary emphasis on functional rather than product responsibility.

As shown in Exhibit 23.6, both Corporate Research and Development and Corporate Development reported directly to Hewlett. Also, one or both of the founders continued to sit in on annual review sessions for each division. As the 1974 Annual Report pointed out, the restructuring represented an evolutionary step in Hewlett-Packard's continuing growth and diversification, but there had been no changes in basic operating philosophy.

Operating Policy Situation

In addition to the tactics used in implementing the strategic and structural changes already described, there were certain operating policies which were related to the changes. The company's basic operating policy was often referred to by Hewlett-Packard people as "management by objective," and was contrasted with management by directive. Instead of leading and coordinating the organization primarily by factors such as hierarchical authority relationships, detailed rules and regulations, and a tight military-type organization, Hewlett-Packard has chosen to use clearly-stated and agreed-upon objectives. Each individual at every level in the organization has been expected to make plans to achieve the company's broader goals and objectives. After receiving supervisory approval, each individual has been given a wide degree of freedom to work within the limitations imposed by his or her own plans and by the general corporate policies. The purpose has been to offer the greatest possible freedom for individual initiative and contribution. Top management has indicated that this policy has been a major factor in Hewlett-Packard's ability to provide innovative, useful products of high quality and to develop people to accept additional responsibility as the company has grown.

As *Business Week* has suggested, the key to the success of Hewlett-Packard may well be the unusual spirit of corporate loyalty that has permeated the work force, particularly the 1,900 R & D personnel. Even though their individual stock holdings in 1975 were worth some $700 million, Hewlett and Packard still ran an egalitarian company. They drew salaries of only $156,000 each, and few top officers made more than $100,000. The company had distributed $64 million in cash profit-sharing bonuses in the previous five years, and about half the employees were participating in a stock-purchase program. Rather than run the risk of "big" layoffs, Hewlett-Packard has declined to bid on short-run government contracts. It has also avoided getting into product lines where there are wide fluctuations in sales volume, such as in many consumer products. When faced with lean times, inventories have been increased and everyone from Packard on down has worked a reduced work week. This has had the effect of dividing the available jobs among all the employees in contrast to termination or temporarily laying off somewhere between 1,000 and 2,000 people. As a result, Hewlett-Packard has seldom been afflicted with the migrations of people and ideas that many high-technology companies have experienced.

These general policies and the supportive attitudes of managers toward their subordinates were believed to be more important than specific details of the personnel programs. Personnel relations at Hewlett-Packard were considered good only when people demonstrated faith in the motives and integrity of their supervisors and of the company—an example of which was the program of flexible working hours. Under flexi-time, most people at Hewlett-Packard have been allowed to work and leave within two-hour "windows." Employees could arrive within a two-hour period at the beginning of the day and leave after completing eight hours of work. In addition, individuals could vary their starting times from day to day. Hewlett-Packard has not had time clocks for many years. The company's trust in the individual was believed to be the key to the program's success. Both Hewlett and Packard have suggested that people are the essence of their organization, for people determine the character and strength of the company. As Packard has frequently said, "Motivation is the difference between a championship ball team and an ordinary ball team." The question recently posed by *Business Week* is whether the players will stay motivated when their two coaches are no longer with the team.

Discussion Questions

1. What is the Master Strategy of this firm?
2. What organization structure would you recommend for this firm? Why?
3. What problems other than structure do you see in this case?
4. How would you solve the problems you see in this case? Why?

References

"Hewlett-Packard: Where Slower Growth Is Smarter Management." *Business Week,* July 9, 1975, pp. 50–58.

Hewlett, William R. In a three-hour lecture-discussion with students and faculty of the College of Business Administration, University of Oklahoma, April 23, 1975. Sponsored by the Student Business Association.

Value Line Investment Survey. October 10 and November 21, 1975. Arnold Bernhard & Co.

24/Seabrook Oil Company

Robert McGlashan and
William V. Rice

On February 10, 1975, the general manager of the fuel products marketing Southeast division of the Seabrook Oil Company was seated in his office together with the division's transportation and administrative services managers. The general manager's concern was evident. He proceeded to explain that the recent truck accident involving the spill of a large quantity of diesel fuel was resulting in more serious consequences than had originally been anticipated. A telephone call from a state agency to Seabrook had made this quite clear. A decision had to be made regarding the actions which the company proposed to take in this situation.

Company Operations

Seabrook Oil Company is a completely integrated oil company, involving exploration, production, refining, and marketing. In the fuel products marketing part of the company's marketing operations there are three divisions: Midwest, Southeast, and Northeast, headquartered in Wichita, Kansas, Birmingham, Alabama, and Cleveland, Ohio, respectively. A partial organization chart is shown in Exhibit 24.1. The corporate administrative services office shown in the chart provides services in the areas of insurance, public relations, tax, personnel, data processing, safety, environmental affairs, purchasing, and internal audit. The administrative services section of the Southeast fuel products marketing division provides accounting, legal, personnel, and office services for the division.

The company has been profitable, as evidenced by the summary income data in Table 24.1 for the years 1970 to 1974.

The fuel products marketing sector of the company transports refined products from district terminals to service stations and other similar destinations primarily by means of tractor-trailer units. Ordinarily the tractors are leased and the trailers are company-owned.

The Accident

On the night of February 4, 1975, a Seabrook Oil Company tractor-trailer combination carrying 7,000 gallons of number two diesel fuel ran off the road and overturned on a state highway near a small town in a Southeastern

Source: Prepared by Robert McGlashan, Associate Professor of Management, and William V. Rice, Assistant Professor of Economics and Management, for the University of Houston at Clear Lake City. Distributed by the Intercollegiate Case Clearing House, Soldiers Field, Boston, Mass. 02163. All rights reserved to the contributors. Printed in the U.S.A.

Exhibit 24.1   Seabrook Oil Company: Partial Organization Chart

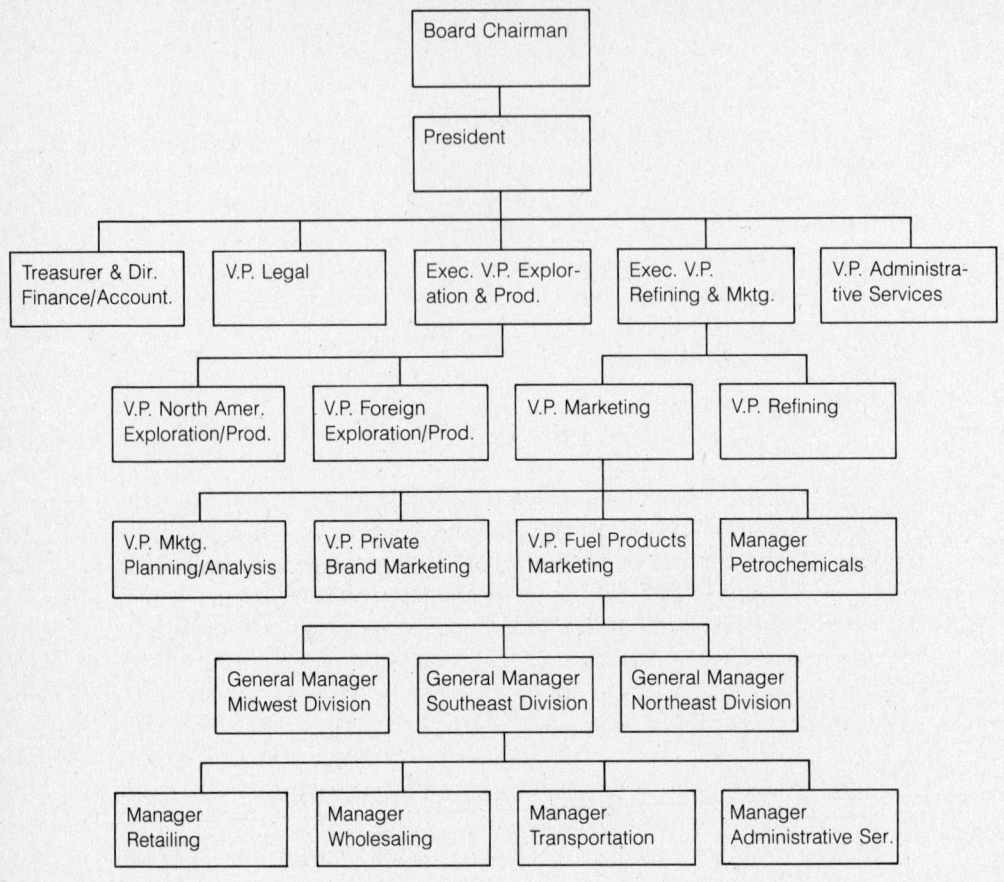

Source: Company organization manual.

Table 24.1   Seabrook Oil Company Summary Income Statement (Expressed in Millions of Dollars)

	1970	1971	1972	1973	1974
Operating Revenues	516	575	653	824	1,440
Other Income	0	5	4	4	16
Cost of Sales and Operating Expenses	376	424	491	594	1,035
Depreciation, Depletion, and Amortization	64	66	75	79	120
Income before Interest, Federal Income Taxes and Outside Stockholders' Interest	76	90	91	155	301

state. The driver was severely injured and was taken to a local hospital for treatment. The tractor-trailer rig was damaged beyond repair, although there was no fire. No third party or other vehicle was involved in the accident. The tractor had been leased from Perrin Truck Rental. Seabrook Oil Company owned the trailer. The district transportation supervisor was contacted regarding the accident. He was asked by a Seabrook corporate office property and casualty insurance department representative to visit the accident scene and determine if the trailer tank had ruptured. This action was thought necessary because of the tough stance the state had been taking on any type of pollution or oil spill. The transportation supervisor was also requested to establish a fire guard at the accident scene and to employ foam or water if the accident constituted a fire hazard.

The following morning, the transportation supervisor reported that there was no fire hazard problem and no pollution problem, so far as he had been able to determine in the poor light on the previous night. He indicated that the fuel that had been spilled had been soaked up by the ground. The transportation supervisor was requested to call the company's insurance carrier and advise them of the accident and employee injury and to have the auto accident and Employer's First Report of Injury reports prepared and distributed. Since Seabrook did not insure auto collision and there were no third parties involved in the accident, the insurance carrier's involvement was limited to the workmen's compensation claim; therefore, a claims adjustor did not visit the accident scene.

The driver of the transport, speaking from his hospital bed, said that as he was rounding a curve, the lights on the tractor went out, he lost control of the rig and flipped into the ditch by the side of the road. A quick investigation showed that the tractor had been in a Perrin truck stop several times immediately prior to the accident, to have the lights repaired. In fact, on the day of the accident, the tractor had been released from the shop following this type of repair.

The Aftermath

On February 7, Seabrook's property and casualty insurance department received a call from a representative of the State Fish and Game Commission. The representative stated that he expected Seabrook to take steps to clean up the pollution caused by the tractor-trailer accident. He said that inspection showed that the entire 7,000 gallons of number two diesel fuel had entered a roadside drainage ditch, drained into a creek, then into a small private lake, and was possibly approaching a local reservoir. A representative of the State Department of Pollution Control made a similar request for clean-up on the same day as the Fish and Game Commission.

At this point, the U.S. Environmental Protection Agency had not been contacted regarding the spill. This agency administers and enforces federal laws and regulations in the area of water pollution, among others, and formulates control strategies for states and localities. Their regulations call for immediate notification of cases of water pollution. State pollution control agencies also require immediate notification.

Inspection by company and state officials revealed that an area of 20 acres of the private lake was affected. It contained a large number of trees and was covered by water hyacinths. All observers noted that it would be virtually impossible to move any kind of equipment into the area except for small hand tools. In addition, the area was infested with alligators and snakes. Apparently a heavy rain which had occurred on February 6 had washed the fuel from the drainage ditch into the private lake.

If the company assumes responsibility for the clean-up, there is a very definite question as to whether their insurance coverage will apply. The company had never faced a similar incident involving pollution containment and had no procedures to handle the situation.

In addition, the company faces potential fines of $10,000 per day from the date of occurrence until the date of notification to the proper governmental authorities, $5,000 per day from the date of notification to the state until date of completion of clean-up, possible class action by area residents, possible claim for punitive damages brought by the state, possible claim from Perrin for the loss of their tractor, and the trailer and product loss.

Seabrook management feels the possibility exists that Perrin Truck Rental could be held responsible for all claims and losses incurred by Seabrook as a result of this accident. In any event, the three people seated in the general manager's office had to decide what the company's recommended course of action should be.

Discussion Questions

1. What are the problems?
2. What should this firm have had that it did not have?
3. What corrective and preventive actions would you take?

25/One Month at Simplan

James M. Higgins

Simplan History

Simplan Manufacturing commenced operations in 1952. It was organized principally by three men, David Harrison, A. T. Watson, Sr., and Herman Wilson, all owners of other businesses in Fort Withdrawal. Their principal aim in beginning an apparel manufacturing company in this town of 1,000 was to provide jobs for the local people. Cotton and corn farming had been the base of the town's economy. Conditions were such that both crops were becoming less profitable, causing many farmers to either move from the area or convert their lands to timber and/or cattle farming. By either action the result for Fort Withdrawal was less employment and less dependable income. Timber and cattle farming along with the other businesses in the area provided basic employment for most of the men. Women, however, had very few employment opportunities available, and most were not employed. The town's merchants noticed that the needle trade industry was moving out of the East and that contract sewing was becoming a major industry in the southern states. The Cut-Make-Trim (CMT) business was a major employer of women. It required a relatively small capital outlay per job provided, and the opportunity for securing contracts looked very bright. Mr. Harrison, Mr. Watson, and Mr. Wilson realized that if their own business concerns were to remain viable, some type of income-producing concern must come to Fort Withdrawal. They organized Simplan with their own money and that of other local investors. A modest building was rented and used equipment was purchased. Although the original investment was small, it represented a significant risk for the investors.

The three men had no experience in apparel manufacturing, so they hired Mr. Ralph Murphy to manage the operation of the plant. Mr. Murphy had many years experience in all phases of apparel manufacturing. The original officers of Simplan were: President, David Harrison; Vice-president, Herman Wilson; Secretary and Treasurer, A. T. Watson, Sr.; Production Manager, Ralph Murphy. Ralph Murphy hired his ex sister-in-law as Supervisor and his brother, Michael Murphy, as mechanic.

The early years of Simplan were difficult. Any type of contractual work was accepted. Simplan manufactured everything from Army shirts to Davy Crockett hats. The original building was expanded in 1956, and additional equipment was purchased. Employment through 1958 never exceeded 150 persons. Profits were used to finance growth over these first years. Nine-

Source: The author wishes to express his appreciation for the cooperation of Simplan Manufacturing Company for aiding in the development of this case. This case is presented with Simplan's permission. This is a disguised case.

teen fifty-eight marked a turning point for Simplan. Harold Steinberg, a former pajama salesman for Center Pajama Company, organized his own sales company, Executive Pajamas, and was looking for a producer for his goods. Through a mutual acquaintance, Mr. Steinberg met Mr. Harrison, and Simplan began producing for Executive. Executive was immediately successful and made large productivity demands on Simplan. Soon Executive was Simplan's only contract. Executive was so successful that Simplan was hard pressed to keep up with its requirements.

The original building was expanded again in 1961, and again in 1963. Also in 1963, one of the main departments, the cutting department, was moved to a newly acquired building in Fruitwood, a slightly larger town 15 miles from Fort Withdrawal. Ralph Murphy hired another brother, Mr. Charlie Murphy, to manage this facility. In 1965, another building, located in downtown Fruitwood, was purchased and a second sewing operation was begun.

The operations portion of the expanded company was largely in the hands of Ralph Murphy, who continued to manage in the same way that he had when the company was in its infancy. He found it extremely difficult to allow authority to pass to any subordinates. During the expansion period, Michael Murphy was promoted to Plant Manager in Fort Withdrawal. Several men were hired to manage the Fruitwood sewing plant, but none were successful prior to 1970. It was believed that Ralph Murphy was difficult to get along with and that plant management was weak as a result.

In 1967, one of David Harrison's sons, Tommie, graduated from college and began working for Simplan. His job duties included industrial engineering and personnel management. With the help of an outside consulting firm, he established a formal training program for new sewing machine operators and worked at overhauling the piece rate system. In 1968, his other son, Phil, joined Simplan, working with Ralph Murphy for a year and a half. In 1970, Phil became the plant manager of the Fruitwood Plant.

1969 and 1970 were disastrous for Simplan. Union organizers called an unfair labor practice strike in 1969. About 169 (or 35%) of the then work force left their jobs. After a long and somewhat bitter strike, a representation election was held in June, 1970. The union won by 2 votes. Negotiations started and a contract was signed in March, 1971. Executive Pajamas was forced by the strike into producing its own goods. Just a month prior to the contract signing, Executive opened its first plant. While Executive still purchases some items from Simplan, by 1974, Simplan's production for Executive was almost stopped. In 1974, Phil Harrison became President of Simplan as his father began moving toward retirement. A. T. Watson, Jr., became Secretary-Treasurer as his father took a decreasing role in the business.

In the period from 1974–1977 the search for new contracts proved to be difficult. The apparel industry as a whole was in a recession, and Simplan had little experience in obtaining contracts due to its long absence from the market. The association with Executive had caused Simplan to become specialized in the production of men's sleepwear. Its equipment could be used for other products, but the employees could not adapt to other products readily. Production management and supervision proved not to be adaptable and responsive in meeting the requirements of new products. Many new contracts were tried during the period from 1974–1977. These included jog suits, ladies' blouses, knit children's tops, and jumpsuits. One contract with a major shirt company for men's sleepwear proved to be successful and still continues.

In 1975, the management of Simplan realized that in order to remain a viable company, it needed its own sales organization. Tommie Harrison assumed responsibility for this project and began the division known as Men's PJ's. A salesman, Samuel Casmier, was hired, and Simplan set up offices in New York City. Mr. Casmier began calling on the large department stores and the chain stores which had buying offices in New York.

Simplan's sales grew steadily during the two year period, 1975 through 1977. Men's PJ's obtained a large share of the expensive men's pajamas market. Additionally, due to the demise of another producer in the summer of 1977, Men's PJ's entered the high priced boxer shorts market.

After Phil Harrison became President, David Harrison served as an advisor and Co-Chairman of the Board of Directors until his death in June, 1976. In 1976, Al Richards was hired to assume the duties formerly held by Tommie Harrison in the areas of engineering and personnel. In April, 1977, Charlie Murphy was forceably retired. His duties were assumed by Phil Harrison and by Al Richards.

In January 1977, Phil Harrison, Tommie Harrison, and Al Richards began work on MBA degrees at a nearby university. This action was prompted by Phil Harrison's realization that Simplan's management badly needed improvement in practically all areas. The course work greatly affected all three men's attitudes about management. The need for personnel motivation and for formalizing company objectives and a business strategy was realized.

Current Industry Background

Apparel manufacturing as an industry suffers from a poor public image. It is thought of, and is, a low paying industry and one that lays off its employees frequently. Even the largest of the manufacturers have been unable to offer pay and benefits equal to other industries. Contract apparel is one of the easiest manufacturing industries to enter. The capital investment is low, and almost any building is suitable for a sewing plant. For these reasons, many manufacturers have failed due to a lack of sufficient capital to sustain the business through difficult times. Entry is made more difficult today because of government regulations. Most of the cost involved in apparel maufacturing is in labor. Technology and automation have not made many changes in the garment industry in the last 50 years. Anything more difficult to make than an undershirt is still manufactured about as it was in 1930. The cutting of the cloth and the sewing requires hand and eye coordination not yet replaced by machines.

Currently the greatest problem facing apparel manufacturers is the rising cost of U.S. labor caused by the continual rising of the minimum wage. When the U.S. legislated a minimum wage of $2.30 (1977), $2.65 (1978), $2.90 (1979), $3.10 (1980), $3.35 (1981), compared to the 37¢ per hour wage of a skilled Korean sewing machine operator, it is easy to see why no U.S. manufacturer can be competitive price wise. There is no difference in the machinery and related technologies used in the two countries. Thus rising imports threaten all apparel manufacturers, but especially smaller ones. Thus virtually no U.S. producer makes a cheap line of sleep wear. Even medium priced lines are mostly manufactured overseas.

The men's nightwear portion of the apparel industry was for many years a stable segment. Men's notch collar pajamas were the principal product, and little variation was required. Through the late fifties and into the sixties more variations in style and trim were introduced. New products were tried, but few were successful. Pajamas are currently manufactured in three basic styles: notch collar, surplice, and middy. The variation in trims available is almost infinite. The biggest changes in sleepwear have come from loungewear products. With the increase in the leisure time of Americans in the late 1960s, most in the apparel industry felt that garments to meet the requirements of leisure activities were needed. Many items were tried; some were successful for a short period, but most were not. Robes currently are big sellers especially for Christmas and Father's Day gifts. Each year, new trim variations to robes are offered for the Christmas season. The basic styles are still the same. The most successful new style in robes in recent years has been the "hooded monk."

Pajamas and robes are products in the mature stage of their product life cycles. Formerly, industry members felt that the demand for these items would increase only with the increase in population. However, some now feel that due to the rising cost of energy, people are not heating their homes as well at night. As a result, it is believed that pajama and robe usage will increase. This theory is partly substantiated by the higher demand for flannel pajamas and velour robes experienced in 1975, 1976, and 1977.

Additional factors contribute to the future of this industry. One is the increasing use of medical facilities. Another is the increasing percentage of older people in the population. Older people wear pajamas and robes more than do younger portions of the population. For these reasons, the future of men's sleepwear may be improving.

Simplan, Fall, 1977

Marketing. Since the organization of the Men's PJ's sales division, Simplan has marketed its products in two ways. The first is through contracts with a sales organization which actually markets the goods. The second is through Men's PJ's.

In a marketing audit performed as the result of a Fall, 1977 course at the university, Simplan's management identified four markets in which they were competing for contractual work. (Contract work differs from work done for Men's PJ's. A contractee in the "Cut-Make-Trim" business does not actually own the goods that he is making. The contractor buys the piece goods and contracts for the labor needed to produce the apparel. Once the garments are complete, Simplan bills the contractor for the labor involved. In producing for its own sales organization, Simplan must buy the piece goods—a considerable cash outlay—make the product, and then market the goods before any incoming cash flow may be realized. Obviously, a large amount of Simplan's cash is tied up in inventory in such operations.)

For contractual work the four markets identified were:

1. National Sales Organizations—these are firms such as Executive Pajama Company. They buy piece goods, contract for the actual making of the goods, then sell them to their customers, which may be large department stores, individual men's shops, chain stores, or other outlets. This is the largest of the three markets, but it is a shrinking one because these organizations are becoming more vertically integrated. The contracts which they do give are for peak season overloads which their own plants cannot handle or for work that is so difficult for them to accomplish that production with any efficiency in their own plants is unlikely. Simplan feels that the business in this market segment is not desirable and is becoming less so. Many of the contractors for this market have either gone out of business or have been bought out by one of the sales organizations. In the view of Simplan's top management, the amount of contract work in this market has decreased to the point that there is only one other contractor with which Simplan competes in price and design features. It was for this reason that the Men's PJ's operation was begun. Management felt that the national sales organization market would not support Simplan at a profitable level again.

2. The second major market was that of the Major Brand Distributors. This market is composed of major independent shirt brands such as Arrow, Munsingwear, Enro, Manhattan, as well as chain brands such as Ward's, Sears, and Penny's. During the marketing survey, it became evident that growth potential existed in this segment because some of the shirt companies listed above were not carrying pajamas but were interested in their potential. Some of these firms are presently making pajamas but find that pajamas do not fit well with their shirt production systems and are therefore considering contracting their pajamas requirements. Simplan's management feels that some economies of scale could be offered to these companies. Their requirements would not justify a separate facility within

their own company, but Simplan could simply handle their requirements with others at a more efficient rate.

3. The third market consisted of the Major Apparel Buying Syndicates. These are stores or chains that pool their buying power by purchasing together. There are two segments of this market, the first are the small men's haberdashery shops that handle only quality merchandise. These syndicates handle quality products that are Simplan's forte. But the total requirements of these stores are comparatively small. The second part of this segment is composed of discount houses and chains. These groups have huge requirements but are very price sensitive. They are willing to accept a standardized product for a lower price rather than pay for any styling uniqueness. These groups are increasingly going to foreign countries for their needs. The only work they currently contract in the United States is for spot requirements or a very few high-line products. Top management feels that this market offers Simplan little. In the first segment, the market is small with many styling variations; and in the second, Simplan is not able to compete with the price of foreign labor.

4. A fourth market was also being considered, and that was the U.S. Government. But this would of course create a whole new set of problems. Nonetheless, Simplan had submitted a bid on one very large export contract as a subcontractor.

Men's PJ's. The formation of Men's PJ's had occurred in 1975, and Tommie and Phil Harrison felt that the contract business was slowly dying in this country due to the vertical integration of sales companies and foreign competitors for contract work. They realized that to form a sales organization was a major step for a company as small as Simplan. They began by hiring a salesman with an established reputation in the New York garment district. Samuel Casmier had been sales manager for a large national shirt company. He had many contacts and friends developed through the years, and he was able to begin making calls and getting buyers into the showroom immediately. However, several months passed before he had his first large sale. His sales have continually grown, and he is currently on target with the forecasts made for the first five years of Men's PJ's. In addition to the New York office, four manufacturer's representatives are employed on a commission basis in several areas of the country. These men carry other men's furnishings items and operate on their own. They show the Men's PJ's line with other men's clothing goods. Some have been successful and others have not. The major customers of Men's PJ's are the highest quality department stores based or having buying offices in New York City. Men's PJ's has been most successful in the highest priced segment of the pajama industry. This is largely due to the demise of a major competitor and to Simplan's ability to produce a product of exceptional quality and features. Also Men's PJ's introduced in the fall of 1977 a line of boxer shorts in the highest quality range.

Demand for these shorts has exceeded Simplan's ability to produce them. The decision to make the shorts was prompted by customers of Men's PJ's requesting the goods. This action caused Simplan's top management to reconsider its product/service niche, as will be discussed later. As a rule, Men's PJ's does not introduce new products on the market. Those items and styles in general acceptance by the market make up PJ's line. If a particular customer asks for a particular item, Men's PJ's may try to make it. Usually market research is not done in any phase of apparel manufacturing. Men's PJ's attempts to offer a standard high- to moderate-priced full line of men's sleepwear and related items such as robes. These are the products that were produced for Executive for many years and which Simplan believes it is best at making. The price range is generally $25.00 to $40.00 retail.

Information as to the size of the pajama market or Men's PJ's share of it is not available. Pajama production and sales are usually counted with shirts; in the various industry statistical sources figures are not meaningful. A recent *Daily News Record* showed that each consumer bought .3 pair of pajamas annually and that equal amounts are sold to men and to women buying for men. This article indicated that over 60% of the pajamas purchased were purchased in department stores or men's shops. The sales of pajamas are fairly constant nationwide. From this article, it appears that Men's PJ's is selling in the largest segment of the market, the department stores.

Product Line (made for Men's PJ's only)

1. Pajamas
   a. Notch collar—The standard button men's pajama is offered with elastic or drawstring pant and a huge variety of trim options.
   b. Surplice—A variation of pajama that has no collar, three button front, usually a warm weather item, often made with short legged pants and a variety of offered trims.
   c. Middy—A pullover pajama top with no buttons, long or short sleeves, short legged or long, and a variety of trims.
   d. Classic—This pajama features double needle seaming, single needle sleeve head, has 16 stitches per inch, is usually made of 100% cotton or other high quality cloth, and is very expensive.

2. Robes
   a. Karate—A collarless wraparound, belted, rather short robe, offered in many trims and fabrics, considered a young man's robe.
   b. Notch collar—A traditional collared robe with long sleeves, offered with many trims, fabrics, and lengths.
   c. Shawl—Another traditional styled robe, has a collar that extends down the front giving a "shawl" look, offered with a variety of trims, fabrics, and lengths.
   d. Monk—A hooded, long robe, usually made of heavy velour.

3. Niteshirts—Long pullover shirt-type garments, made in any fabric, most popular in flannel and for the Christmas season.
4. Jumpsuits—A one-piece outerwear garment, made in several fabrics, with varying sleeve treatments.
5. Shorts—Men's boxer shorts, top quality, full cut and trim fit styles only.

Financial Structure. The ownership structure of Simplan consists of 482,500 shares of common stock outstanding. These shares are held by eleven individuals, eight of whom belong to members of the A. T. Watson and David Harrison families. These two families hold 83% of the outstanding stock. The stock is not traded regularly. The last transaction was in 1974 and was between family members.

The owners have selected to operate under Subchapter "S" of the U.S. tax code. The Simplan dividend policy has been to pay out only enough dividends per share to cover the owners' tax burdens. All additional earnings have been used to finance needed expansions over the years. This policy was adequate until the establishment of the Men's PJ's sales division.

As part of the decision to enter direct sales, management determined that the effort should be financed through:

1. Internally generated funds from the continuing contract production.
2. Credit terms available from the piece goods and materials suppliers.
3. Borrowed capital from one local bank.
4. An accounts receivable factoring arrangement with a major Atlanta bank.
5. Additional stock investment capital when and if required.

The first four sources have provided adequate finances and are expected to continue to do so in the near future.

Cash flow forecasting and budgeting have been initiated and currently serve as valued management tools. Monthly performance statements are prepared and used as management tools to detect problems and point out profits and losses. All of these statements are used to keep creditor banks informed of the company's condition at any point in time. Men's PJ's and Simplan Manufacturing are profit centers. Overhead is allocated. Men's PJ's did not make money in 1975–1976 but began to make money in 1977.

The continued growth of the company's sales division will require changes in the financial structure. As growth takes place, Phil and Tommie feel that stockholder equity must be increased to support sales. If profits are adequate, the increase could result from that source. Should profits lag, the necessity for additional investor capital will be realized. One of the biggest financial problems is that sales fluctuate, causing cash flow problems. Generally sales are up in September, October, and November; begin to go down in December; go down in January and February; are high in March, April, and May; and go down in June, July, and August. The fluctuations in employment are of great concern to top management because of the low morale which results and because of the relearning which must occur as operators

Table 25.1 Inventories and Income Information, 1968–1977 Fiscal Year Ending May 31

	1968	1969	1970	1971	1972
Sales	$1,839,860.52	$2,013,397.43	$1,714,978.51	$1,722,502.51	$2,248,454.36
Inventories					
Materials	$ 11,749.43	$ 18,130.51	$ 23,127.82	$ 21,558.52	$
In Process	19,943.74	15,414.79	30,120.50	23,308.80	50,159.31
Fin. Goods					
Total	$ 31,693.17	$ 33,545.30	$ 53,248.32	$ 44,867.32	$ 50,159.31
Net Income	$ 73,045.71	$ 5,913.47	$ (3,460.80)	$ 63,169.55	$ 246,045.84

	1973	1974	1975	1976	1977
Sales	$2,294,721.05	$2,607,189.01	$2,034,945.73	$2,237,027.33	$3,233,312.75
Inventories					
Materials	$ 43,466.60	$	$ 41,515.89	$ 125,768.75	$ 232,531.00
In Process		54,969.75	10,088.83	146,251.99	72,259.29
Fin. Goods				128,081.95	282,589.18
Total	$ 43,466.60	$ 54,969.75	$ 51,604.72	$ 400,102.69	$ 587,379.47
Net Income	$ 221,654.77	$ 98,961.05	$ 73,648.52	$ (72,627.71)	$ 94,722.21

Table 25.2 Balance Sheet Information 1968–1977 Fiscal Year Ending May 31

	1968	1969	1970	1971	1972
Current Assets	$202,058.96	$171,990.50	$142,878.86	$151,814.68	$ 219,290.16
Total Assets	$431,643.65	$418,765.39	$359,370.88	$346,699.02	$ 437,041.54
Current Liab.	$206,859.25	$214,933.98	$105,252.30	$106,526.39	$ 126,168.07
Total Liab.	$217,413.24	$222,746.51	$166,812.80	$119,921.39	$ 142,743.07
Capital	$214,230.41	$196,018.88	$192,558.08	$226,777.63	$ 294,298.47

	1973	1974	1975	1976	1977
Current Assets	$221,654.77	$296,307.79	$148,149.28	$548,988.36	$ 774,223.94
Total Assets	$475,376.25	$564,700.05	$415,951.49	$850,909.04	$1,044,864.62
Current Liab.	$154,638.61	$238,321.36	$ 46,519.28	$264,231.54	$ 401,364.38
Total Liab.	$174,393.61	$261,256.36	$ 72,634.28	$533,820.54	$ 633,053.91
Capital	$300,982.64	$303,443.69	$343,317.21	$317,088.50	$ 411,810.71

become reaccustomed to the work schedule and new materials each time they come back to work.

Organization. The Company at the present has no formal organization chart, but if one existed, it would look like that presented in Figure 25.1. With respect to past organization structures, for many years Mr. Ralph Murphy was Vice-President of Manufacturing and all responsibility for manufacturing rested with him. Upon his leaving the company, his duties were assumed by Phil Harrison and to a lesser extent by Al Richards. Currently all management within the company involved with manufacturing reports to the President. Phil has been considering having another Vice President of Manufacturing—Al Richards, but his concern is that the position failed once, and he is not sure if he wants to relinquish that much authority to someone again. Phil Harrison feels this is a problem needing immediate attention. He feels that all his time is consumed by the day-to-day operations problems, and none is being spent on organizational planning and directing the total operation.

Facilities and Operation. The plant facilities of Simplan appear cluttered and unorganized. The original plant in Fort Withdrawal has been expanded four times and, as a result, the layout does not best suit the current production flow. The Fruitwood sewing plant is a converted two-story retail store on the main street of the town. It suffers from a lack of employee parking space and of a loading dock.

Machinery in both plants is laid out according to operations. The first step is cutting, the second is sewing. All cutting is accomplished in Fruitwood. All sewing is done according to the division of labor. Thus, an operator may sew only one part—for example, a leg—all day long. All sewing equipment is well maintained and reasonably up to date. Some automated equipment is in use, but in general little is available and most of what exists does not work well in a variety operation such as Simplan's.

Figure 25.1 Simplan Organization Structure

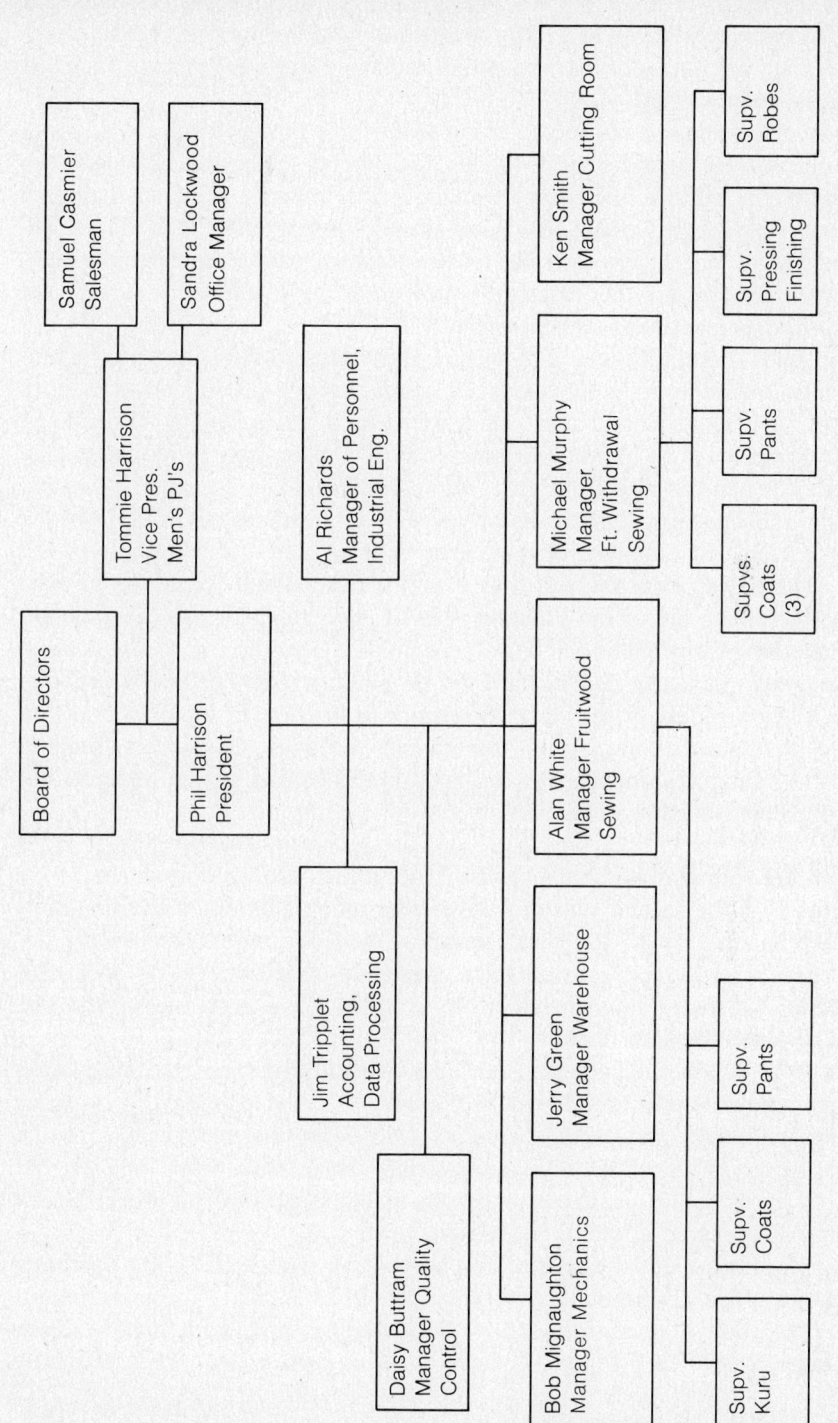

551

Goods made in Fruitwood are transported to Fort Withdrawal for pressing and boxing. After the pressing and boxing, all goods go across the street to the company's warehouse. The warehouse is a converted cotton warehouse, but with the addition of lighting, heating, and steel storage racks, it serves its purpose well.

The cutting room was once a sewing plant for a now defunct company. A high-rise storage area for piece goods with metal racks was added to the building. The cutting operation throughout the industry is much the same now as it has always been. New methods for cutting cloth have been conceived but are not widely used. Several systems for pattern and marker making are in general use, but Simplan is not using these although management has looked at one of the systems recently.

Phil and Tommie believe that one of the worst problems in their manufacturing operation is the movement of goods through production. All goods are cut in Fruitwood and must be trucked to a sewing plant. If made in Fruitwood, they must be trucked again to Fort Withdrawal. Inside the plants, the work is handled numerous times through each of the operations: cutting, sewing, and finishing. Only a major revision or overhaul would correct the flow problems of Simplan. Management believes that the condition of the Fort Withdrawal plant is such that a major expenditure would be unwise, as the remaining life of the building is not long enough to pay the expense. Ultimate long-range plans call for a consolidated operation in a new facility. But the costs of a new facility may be prohibitive. Another major problem is the cyclical nature of the work as mentioned previously. Simplan hopes to secure government contracts to smooth out the work flow. Also, Simplan hopes to offer pricing incentives to major brand contractors in order to encourage them to build inventories in the off season.

Personnel. Simplan's nonmanagement personnel are unionized. In 1977, Simplan is in the second year of a three-year union contract. All union matters are handled by Al Richards. Relations with the union officials are described as friendly and cordial. Each grievance is believed to be given full attention. Currently union membership is 55% of the total employed. The state in which Simplan operates is a 'right to work law" state.

In 1975 Simplan experienced a wildcat strike protesting the termination of an employee. After arbitration, the union was ordered to pay all expenses of the arbitration and excess manufacturing costs incurred because of the illegal strike. The contract has a no-strike clause, and union officials did not use every means available to get the strikers to return to work. Union leaders disappeared after the settlement.

Simplan uses manual dexterity and perception tests in selecting operating employees. The application has been weighted to indicate the most retainable prospects. A standardized form for reference and work history check has been made. Each Plant Manager does his own hiring. They normally

Table 25.3 Employment Information 1972–1977

	1972	1973	1974	1975	1976	1977
New Hires	231	305	409	133	177	148
Terminations	N/A*	433	451	136	368	288
Total Employees as of May 31	236	269	401	172	201	164

*Not applicable.

hire on the basis of the dexterity and perception tests and as the result of a standardized personal interview with the applicant.

Personnel rules for absenteeism, seniority, vacations, and so on, are defined in the company policy manual, or are normally dealt with in the union contract. Individual plant managers are allowed a great deal of leeway in the actual application of the rules. Each plant, for personnel matters, is managed somewhat autonomously. There is no ongoing program to involve the employees in the operation of the plants. There is no established motivational program nor are there clear lines of communication between employees and management, other than union channels. Some members of management will talk with employees, who often bring problems to these individuals in an informal manner.

In 1970, Simplan began a four day, nine and a half hour per day work schedule. Management believes that this has been a very successful move. Absenteeism for 1977 has remained below 3.5% company wide, even during peak seasons. This is much better than the industry average. The work schedule is credited with this improved position.

Employee turnover remains a problem despite several turnover strategies employed by management. Currently four or five people are hired before one will stay. This is a costly problem but one common in sewing industries. Management feels that employee turnover will always be a problem due to the boring nature of the sewing operator's job, the relatively low pay of the industry, and the low regard for the sewing operator's job held by the general public. All sewing operators are paid on a piece-rate basis. For the variety of garments produced and short-run requirements that have existed, this system has caused some problems. Management is trying to devise a more motivating system but is not experiencing much success. This is another problem common to the industry. The piece-rate system is based upon a standard that will yield an earnings incentive. Some exceptional operators make very good money for the local economy. Except for mechanics and first-line supervisors, employees paid by the hour are all within the same earnings ranges as the operators. Mechanics and supervisors are paid at a significantly higher rate. Employee benefits include: paid hospital insurance, four paid holidays, and two weeks paid vacation per year. These benefits do not accrue until one year of employment is reached. Supervisors have two weeks sick leave in addition to the other benefits. There are no stock options, retirement, or disability provisions available to the employees. Performance appraisals are not used at Simplan, nor are managerial, sales, or supervisory performance objectives established. Promotion from operator to supervisor is an uncertain process but is normally based on perceived operator proficiency.

Supervisors. The first line supervisors of Simplan are all promoted machine operators. Some have less than a high school education. None have ever had any formal supervisory training. They were trained at Simplan, on the job, by an older, experienced supervisor. For the difficulties they encounter daily, the management of Simplan believes that the supervisors perform well. They are well motivated, dedicated, and for the most part, reasonably competent. The part of their job where most need improvement is in the area of human relations. These supervisors came up through the ranks by hard work and effort and most do not understand workers who are poorly motivated or lackadaisical. Several supervisors have recently retired and several others are reaching that age. Most of Simplan's supervisors are young and untrained. Management feels that their supervisors represent the company to the employees and that a program to train the supervisors in human relations would pay in the long run. This training is now more important than ever with the number of relatively new supervisors in the company. All supervisors are white in the work force that is 50% black. There exists a problem of communication between the black employees and the white supervisors.

Information Systems. Simplan began using a minicomputer in 1972. All financial statements as well as payroll checks are prepared by the computer. These statements include: monthly and year-to-date Profit and Loss Statements, a weekly General Condition Statement, a General Ledger Summary, a weekly Expense Summary, a Sales Service Register, and a Weekly Employee Savings Plan Report. In addition to these financial records, the computer is used to maintain piece goods and finished stock inventories. Also, several personnel reports are computerized. These include attendance, operator efficiency, and time spent at average for piece rate operators. The piece rate compensation system has been computerized in its initial steps. Management feels that the computer is a tool which is not being fully utilized. Reports identifying turnover and absence to specific sections of each plant are planned. Reports showing the profit yielded by each department and product are desired, but the exact method to accomplish this end has not been determined. Thus while individual efficiency is known, the exact costs of decisions by department are not known.

The Management Team. Ken Smith, age 29, Cutting Room Manager, has been with Simplan two years. He took over from Charlie Murphy at his retirement and has performed better than anyone expected. He likes his job and is liked by his employees. His major handicap is his lack of experience and his lack of management training. He is motivated and conscientious but does become agitated when circumstances are hectic. He is learning to plan and execute his plans. He generally allows his employees a certain amount of freedom in their job until they prove they cannot handle it. This is a sharp contrast to his predecessor. Management feels that the Cutting Room has improved in performance and morale as Ken has improved in his ability.

Alan White, age 30, Fruitwood Sewing Plant Manager, was the assistant Cutting Room Manager for four years. He has been the Fruitwood Sewing Plant Manager for two years. Alan's total management experience has been with Simplan. His prior work experience was in heavy equipment parts and mechanics and the U.S. Navy. Alan's performance in his present job is perceived by management as very good. Under his direction the Fruitwood Plant has had good efficiency of production and good morale. In that location there has been a history of many union grievances, but these have subsided in the last year. Although Alan has never attended college or had any management training other than on the job, he is believed to practice good management procedures. He communicates well with his employees and is approachable. Alan's major problem, and one that he is aware of, is that he sometimes tolerates inferior job performance from some employees.

Michael Murphy, age 53, Fort Withdrawal Sewing Plant Manager, began with Simplan in 1952 as a mechanic. In 1961, he became Plant Manager. His strong points are his ability to schedule the flow of work through his plant and to keep track of the variety of work in process as it travels through the plant. Through long years of experience Michael has learned how to make almost anything and what equipment is needed. In the view of management, the major problem that Michael has is the difficulty he experiences communicating with anyone because of his soft-spoken and jumbled speech characteristics. At the same time he encourages feedback from none of his employees and only some of his supervisors. This results in misunderstandings in the plant. In spite of this, Michael gets the job done, and because of his experience is considered a valuable man. The most serious question in his regard is that he is known to have a serious personal problem that is beginning to affect his job performance. How he felt about his brother, Ralph Murphy, leaving Simplan under strained circumstances is not known.

Al Richards, age 30, Personnel Manager and Industrial Engineer, has been at Simplan a year and a half. Prior to that he held several management positions with a carpet yarn dyeing plant in Fruitwood. He is a college graduate, an ex–Air Force officer, and is currently working on his MBA. While in the Air Force and in his previous job, Al participated in several management seminars and management courses. At Simplan, Al sets all piece rates and works on job methods, setting up production lines and other industrial engineering functions. In Personnel he has worked on developing the hiring done by the Plant Managers and assisting them in personnel problems.

He handles all communications with the union. Al is frequently called upon for various unrelated duties, such as filling in for Plant Managers, taking inventories, or working on developing new products.

Jerry Green, age 44, Finished Goods Warehouse and Shipping Manager, joined Simplan in 1967, after working several years for civil service in Mobile, Alabama. He was promoted to his current position in 1968 and is very capable in his job. He is faced with few personnel problems and has a very good rapport with all personnel under his supervision.

Jim Triplett, age 30, Office Manager and Computer Program/Supervisor, joined Simplan in 1971 to learn the office manager's job and replace the long-time manager, who was nearing retirement. He filled the office manager position in 1973 after converting the basic payroll, accountant, and personnel systems to a minimum card-based computer system. The computer system was upgraded and improved and is scheduled for another upgrading within the next year. His service is highly valued by top management and his job performance has been far above average.

Tommie Harrison, age 33, Vice President Sales, Men's PJ's Division, joined Simplan after graduation from college in 1966 and worked in engineering and employee training until 1970. He assumed the added duties of union negotiator and arbitrator at that time. In May 1975, he changed his duties to the Men's PJ's Division. His work with training and engineering generally remained unattended until Al Richards joined the company in 1976. Phil and Al feel that Tommie has the unique gift of getting to the core of a problem and devising a most effective solution. They feel that he can see a person for what he truly is and can instill that desire to please in the people around him. They also feel that total leadership ability he possesses is unknown to him and is currently not being used to its fullest.

Phil Harrison, age 35, President, joined Simplan in 1968 after four and one half years service with the U.S. Air Force as an administrative officer. He worked with Mr. Ralph Murphy in production for one and a half years before taking over the management of the Fruitwood Sewing Plant in 1970. After three years he was named Vice President of Administration and served as the assistant to his father, David Harrison, Sr. In 1974, he was named President after David Harrison, Sr., retired from day-to-day management. Phil believes that he has a feel for the manufacturing operation and the accounting areas. He has limited training in dealing with and motivating people. He feels that his leadership needs improvement in these areas: setting definable objectives, properly communicating to his subordinate managers, and integrating company efforts. He feels that he must structure the company in such a manner that he is not tied down to the day-to-day activities so that he can devote sufficient time and attention to planning, integrating, and forecasting.

Simplan's Future

Management's intention since 1975 has been to gradually shift all production to support of the Men's PJ's sales division as these sales grew. In performing the marketing audit, it became apparent that additional potential for contract work existed in the Major Brand Distributors Market. Phil, Tommie, and Al felt that staying in contractual work offered Simplan greater protection in several ways. The first is that in time of recession the impact would be less if outlets for production were more diversified. Second, if Men's PJ's experienced severe difficulties in sales, Simplan would be out of business. Third, staying in contractual work would help Simplan to become bigger, thus realizing some economics of scale. Fourth, contractual work could make a contribution to profits. A break-even analysis for Simplan was performed; it indicated that at the current product mix, 80,000 dozen or $2.6 million in sales was needed annually for the company to break even.

In September, 1977, Phil, Tommie, and Al assembled to review the various studies that they had performed while working on their MBAs: the break-even analysis, the marketing audit, and the management audit—the latter having included a considerable amount of financial analysis. They recalled that one of their professors had stressed that one of the most important decisions of an organization was to determine exactly what business it was in and what customer need it wanted to satisfy. It was upon this question that the future of Simplan depended. The 1978 summer season was only a few months away, and a decision had to be made as to exactly what the future master strategy was to be. All three concluded that Simplan needed the contract business, and that in fact what the firm had to offer, above all else, was contract labor, for whoever needed it. They weren't really sure as to how much sales they should establish as an objective or exactly what plant efficiency to expect, but they decided to play it by ear. They did, however, tentatively establish the following objectives.

Short-run Objectives (in Order of Importance)

1. Operate with a gross profit on sales of more than 5% from manufacturing operations.
2. Provide required labor to produce Simplan sales division products.
3. Work with current contracts to secure continuous year-round stable production.
4. Provide employee training programs to increase productivity and value of each employee.
5. Provide year-round employment for between 400 and 500 employees in present facilities.
6. Sales growth of not less than 10% per year.

7. Begin selection and training process to replace retiring first-line supervision.
8. Develop more meaningful and effective information system.

Long-run Objectives

1. Upgrade employees through education and hiring policies and practices.
2. Plan future production facilities to provide necessary capacity as needed.
3. Become the recognized leader in the manufacture of better made men's sleep wear, boxer shorts, and other apparel products.

Short-run Objectives (Which Go Hand and Hand with the Company's Objectives)

1. Keep present contracts happy with product and service provided.
2. Command highest price possible by providing best service available.
3. Negotiate contracts to provide year-round production and employment for labor forces.
4. Obtain additional contracts in order to reach company growth goals.

Policies Established

1. Contact and negotiate with established quality accounts only.
2. Contract for jobs of $100,000 or more, and then only if either we are making the product offered or there is an option available for year-round production of approximately $750,000.
3. Quite often work is offered that Simplan is not equipped to perform or that doesn't fit in with the production flow. This type of work should be refused.

Management feels that securing new accounts is not an overnight situation. The President may or may not make the first contact with the prospect. Reputation in contractual work is critical. Simplan believes it has a good reputation for quality and reliability, thus some accounts seek Simplan's assistance. However, after first contact is made, there will be a period of negotiation and planning before the actual "sale" or contract is consummated. During this negotiation the President's aim is to present Simplan as competent and cooperative while attempting to secure the best price possible and a mix of work that insures orderly production.

Implementation

The annual marketing plan is highly informal. The company president knows the needs of the company and carries a loose plan in his mind for keeping the plants working. Sewing contractual work is largely a system of contacts. The president stays in contact with the current accounts and attempts to keep a regular flow of work so that production can be organized. He contacts possible accounts whenever he feels there may be a chance for business with a company.

The time spent in seeking new accounts is not directed specifically at any of the three markets. It is largely a matter of what is known to be available and working to secure it.

There is limited information available for marketing control. Sales data by accounts for any period of time is available. Cost of any item can be calculated but is not determined for each unit produced. Effectiveness and earnings of each piece-rated employee are monitored daily.

The largest problem in information for planning is the lack of industry data. Men's sleepwear is usually accounted for in shirt sales. Information about the industry is largely observed or impressions of trends made by knowledgeable people in the industry. Surveys, statistical data, and records for men's sleepwear are not kept by anyone in private business or governmental agencies.

One Month at Simplan

By late November, 1977, the men's shorts line had attracted interest from virtually all major department stores. The high priced boxer short had literally captured the market. Its high quality relative to others in the market made it very attractive. Samuel was receiving more orders for Christmas than could possibly be filled. Phil, Tommie, and Al huddled in Phil's office late one Monday morning, wondering if they should attempt to meet this surging demand. Tommie had been on the phone all morning with Samuel, and the sizes of the orders were almost unbelievable, and certainly unexpected.

Tommie summarized his view, "Two major department stores have indicated that if we can meet their Christmas and 'After Christmas Sale' demands, they'll give us all of their business for the entire year. It would mean as much as $1 million in sales. I say that we should do it, no matter what it costs. If we get them this Christmas, we'll get them for all of next year as well, and maybe for several years to come."

Al, who had been steadily assuming the duties associated with managing the total production operation observed, "We have the production capacity, and we can set the lines, but, as you know, every time we change it costs us money. We don't really know how much but a lot. We lose cutting room time, we lose sewing skills as they begin each project. Not only that but . . ."

"Yes, but just how much can we lose? I tell you that we're talking about millions," Tommie interrupted.

Phil noted, "We have already had problems with Ken. We have changed the schedule for his operation twice in the last two weeks, and he is very upset. He claims that he loses 3 days every time he changes products. With 18 people in there, it gets to be expensive."

Al interrupted, "The learning curve on new products costs us, costs us a lot. We have to set up new equipment arrangements too."

The discussion continued for several minutes. Finally, it was obvious that they were getting nowhere. Phil sat back in his chair, with the decisive look that Tommie and Al had come to know. Tommie, who had as much decision authority as Phil, recognized that his brother was right, and so the meeting adjourned. They would try to fill the orders as they came.

Friday, the 2nd of December, Samuel called and reported that one of their new customers, a New York department store, wanted 2,000 dozen pajamas in six days. Phil and Tommie conferred. They were already paying overtime. Additionally, air freight would have to be used. This would raise their costs to way above their price to the customer. Still, a large sales order could be forthcoming. They decided to tell the customer to look elsewhere.

On Tuesday, the 6th, Alan, the Fruitwood plant manager, called Phil. The conversation began, "Phil, you know, you've got to do something about Gary. [Gary was the head mechanic of Fruitwood.] He's so moody and he often just refuses to work. We especially need him now with the changeover, which, as you know, causes more machine problems." Phil thought for a minute before replying. Gary was eccentric. So were the rest of the Dudleys. The mechanic could make or break a plant. And, it was a tough job. Gary was adequate—not really super, but adequate—and replacements were hard if not impossible to find. On the other hand, the last two plant managers had remained with Simplan for only a few months, and Phil felt that they both had left because of Gary and also because of Ralph Murphy. Alan was a good manager, and Phil didn't want to lose him.

"O.K. Alan, let me give this some thought," Phil hung up. He was now convinced more than ever that human relations training was necessary. He would mention it to Al and Tommie. That same day while visiting the Fruitwood plant, Phil overheard two supervisors discussing one of the piece-rate operators who had been continually letting her threads out (spacing them wider than they should be), but they didn't know what to do about it. She was able to get almost twice her normal piece rate this way.

On Wednesday, the 7th, Al reported that Michael had come to work with the smell of alcohol on his breath. His problem was getting worse. This was the second time this month. Phil had been reluctant to approach Michael about his problem. Michael was a nice man, and he seemed to be well liked by his subordinates. But the problem was only going to get worse. Michael naturally was insecure, having seen his brother, Ralph, terminated after so many years with the company. Phil recalled just how that decision had weighed on his mind. But productivity had noticeably improved at both plants, as had morale. Ralph had been a disruptive force for many years. And, despite several attempts by both Tommie and Phil to talk to Ralph on an adult to adult level, Ralph had continued to be critical of everyone and everything, treating everyone like a child, seeing the worst in everything. Just at that moment, Tommie came in.

"Phil, we'll be out of elastic in two days. We've sewn through it all with these huge orders, and Michael says the manufacturer can't make it fast enough to keep up with our demands." Phil was immediately on the phone attempting to locate more elastic.

On Friday, the 9th, Samuel called. In a panic-stricken voice, he reported that one of their major customers had given them an ultimatum. Either get their order for their December 26th After Christmas Sale or forget the $1 million dollars in sales for next year. Tommie, Phil, and Al conferred for only a few minutes. The decision seemed obvious. Phil called Alan and Al talked with Michael. Alan next informed Ken. Ken was less than pleased. He spoke in a dejected voice, "You know my people's morale is very low. We just get started on one project, get it laid out and then Phil changes it. We lose three days every time. You know?" "Yeah, I know," Alan replied, "but Phil says we got to do it, so we got to do it."

On Tuesday, the 13th, Phil received a call from Cougar Unlimited's president. Cougar Unlimted was a newly organized firm which was interested in hiring Simplan to make a very low quality athletic short for them. Arrangements were made for the three top men in Cougar to visit Simplan in late December. Later that day, sufficient elastic had been obtained to get them through Christmas.

On Saturday, December 17, Jerry, the warehouse manager, was hurriedly putting together a shipment. Two of his warehousemen were absent. They had reported in by phone with severe headaches. Two other workers were very disgruntled. "Yeah, we know what kind of headache they have," snickered one. The other replied, "I'll bet ya they didn't get it from drinking no soda pop either." The first workman walked over to Jerry. "Jerry, can you show me which of these orders should be pulled first?" Jerry knew that the worker should know, but then, he'd always had to tell him.

On Monday, the 19th, Sandra, the Office Manager, received a rush order from Tommie. She asked Nancy, one of the clerks, to hunt down the invoice and bring it to her. Sandra was already involved in another project. Nancy looked displeased but had apparently assumed the task. However, a few minutes later, Nancy returned, announcing, "I just can't seem to find it anywhere. Besides, I'm too busy." Sandra glared at her. Just how many times had this happened in the past few months? she wondered as she began to hunt for the invoice.

On Wednesday, Alan and Michael inadvertently met outside Phil's office. The conversation eventually encompassed their supervisors. Both agreed that Simplan's supervisors were reluctant to accept responsibility. "They keep coming to me, asking me what should be done," Alan remarked, "and they should know."

On Tuesday, the 20th, Al reported that operator efficiency was falling drastically. Tommie and Phil agreed. They had all been through the plants and the continuous hum which earmarked efficient production had been replaced by the klackity-klack of individual machines. While the piece rates uses were scientifically and quite laboriously determined, there was room for slack, and the operators could string their work out over time, making a little more money but principally costing Simplan through benefits. The cutting room employees were not on the piece rate, and when they saw that no more goods were to be cut, their pace slowed to that of a snail. Given the current accounting system, it was impossible to tell just how much efficiency had dropped. Clearly the continual changes were one primary cause though.

Later that day Phil sat refiguring the foreign export underwear contract figures. He had received a phone call from the prime federal contractor that afternoon, indicating that they would get the contract. Phil was glad. Now they could expect anywhere from $800,000 to $2 million in sales on this operation. As he reviewed the proposed contract, he wondered just how much Simplan should have charged to perform this work. They had added 4% to estimated costs, including estimated overhead, but he wondered just how much the traffic would or could bear. He called in Al and Tommie and announced the good news. Phil then commented "This, our first government contract will, as you know, Al, require us to do an awful lot of record keeping that we haven't done before, and I want you to look into that. We will of course have to have an affirmative action program. The prime contractor is sending us a copy of theirs to use as an example. I also want you to look into whatever act it is that might enable us to get some tax credit if we hire the hard core unemployed. Also, we will have to go back to the five-day work week because of the Davis-Bacon Act."

On Wednesday, the 21st, one of the supervisors complained to Michael that Bob, the mechanic manager, had, as usual, gotten angry over the increased number of machine breakdowns. He had refused to fix two or three of the operators' machines until "he was good and ready." Michael knew that this was a recurring problem. Bob was, however, a very good mechanic. Michael, Phil, and Al were all aware that this type of problem existed, but Michael had not taken any action and neither had anyone else. Michael told the supervisor that he would talk with Phil about it.

On Thursday, the 22nd, one of the professors from the University visited with Phil and Al at Phil's request. Phil was by this time convinced that a training program in human relations was necessary for the supervisors; for the plant, warehouse, and cutting room managers; and for the mechanics. A program on transactional analysis was agreed upon. In addition, an employee attitude survey would be performed. The survey was to indicate certain questions that Phil wanted asked plus certain questions that the professor felt were necessary for proper construction of the program in terms of attacking problem areas. Exhibit 25.1 shows selected summary results.

Exhibit 25.1   Selected Results from Questionnaires Administered to Simplan Employees

Two behaviorally oriented questionnaires were administered to all employees, except managers. Operators' responses were summarized by supervisor, and supervisor's responses were summarized by manager. One questionnaire employed a four-point Likert scaling, the other a five-point Likert scaling. The first questionnaire related primarily to organizational climate measures, the second to extrinsic types of factors in the company (extrinsic to the job). Included in the first and second questionnaires were questions related to motivation through recognition—recognition for performance and recognition for existence—that is, did the supervisor or manager involved show concern for the respondent as a human being. Careful attention had to be given to the wording of questions and responses since many of the employees had not finished a high school education.

The surveys revealed an absence of communication through the chain of command, a lack of recognition for good performance or existence (on the part of some supervisors), general satisfaction with supervision, a definite tendency for leniency on the part of some supervisors and managers, an expressed desire to retain the four-day work week, considerable inattention to quality of work by supervisors, and alienation with respect to the company's overall actions.

On January 5th, 1978, the monthly income statements were received from accounting, and, as Phil and Tommie analyzed these and the balance sheets, they began to wonder just what had gone wrong. They had lost $40,000 in December, the entire amount that they had made since June 1, when their fiscal year began. With sales so high, they wondered how they could have improved Simplan's performance.

Discussion Questions

1. Evaluate this organization's situation, its current Master Strategy, its top management, and its planning actions.
2. What does the section entitled "One Month at Simplan" tell you about this company?
3. Just what has occurred to cause difficulties for this firm in terms of implementing its Master Strategy?
4. What can be done to improve this firm's current Master Strategy?
5. What can be done to improve this firm's implementation of its strategy?
6. What can be done to improve human relations in this firm, and how do human relations in this firm affect its performance?

Presson S. Shane

The Mesabi Range in Minnesota has long been a source of industrial strength for the United States because of its rich deposits of iron ore. The red hematites (Fe_2O_3) of the western Mesabi were the original attraction, but as these deposits were consumed, attention turned to the poorer taconite deposits which are predominant in the eastern Mesabi. The iron content of taconite is black magnetite (Fe_3O_4) so, although the ore is not rich enough for direct charge into blast furnaces, the magnetic characteristics of the desired iron oxide make it economically recoverable for processing into pellets that can be charged to blast furnaces. Indeed, the production capacity of blast furnaces operated on all-pellet charges is about double that which was possible before this technology was developed.

Silver Bay, Minnesota on the northwest shore of Lake Superior, the largest fresh water lake in the United States, was built to process a taconite deposit about 45 miles away at Babbitt. The location on the lake was important because great quantities of water are used in the processing. A railroad carries two 150-car trains of ore per day from the Babbitt mine to the Silver Bay processing plant. Eighty percent of the 3,200 residents in Silver Bay are members of families employed by Reserve Mining Company, which built the plant there in 1955. The plant has been expanded since it was first built, and the total investment in facilities is now about $350 million. The present production of about 11 million tons of pellets per year shows a profit of $20 million per year (after taxes) for an annual return on the total investment of about 6%.

The Environmental Protection Agency and the Minnesota Pollution Control Agency have charged Reserve with violation of the Federal Water Pollution Control Act as amended in 1970—WPC 15 (a) (4), (c) (16) and (c) (2). Air discharges from the plant have been said to violate Minnesota Regulations APC 5, 6, and 17. The essence of the complaints against Reserve is that the plant discharges, via air and water, minute amphibole fibers. The air discharge is said to constitute a hazard as far away as the eastern shore of Wisconsin, and the water discharge is said to have rendered a major part of Lake Superior hazardous. Specifically, for instance, 200,000 people in the Silver Bay to Duluth area utilize the Lake Superior water, containing substantial quantities of amphibole fibers, for drinking purposes. Exposure to similar fibers under certain conditions can cause asbestosis, mesothelioma, and cancer of the lung, larynx, and gastrointestinal tract. Extensive court hearings (with recourse to expert opinions) have been com-

Source: Prepared by Professor Presson S. Shane. The assistance of officials of the American Iron and Steel Institute and of the Environmental Protection Agency in preparing this case is gratefully acknowledged. Distributed by the Intercollegiate Case Clearing House, Soldiers Field, Boston, Mass. 02163. All rights reserved to the contributors. Printed in U.S.A.

pleted, and the 8th U.S. Circuit Court of Appeals expects to hear the case in the winter of 1974–75 unless agreement is reached before then. Reserve has proposed to build a land disposal site near Lax Lake and to make plant changes which will reduce the air discharge while improving pellet quality— all at a cost said by Reserve to be $243 million.

Taconite operations are important to the state of Minnesota. In 1969–70 there were 9,600 direct jobs related thereto in power, supply, and service industries. Reserve Mining employed 3,000 of the 9,600 directly employed persons. The Minnesota Legislature passed in 1964 a bill that guarantees not to change the tax on taconite before 1989. The Babbitt deposits have an estimated life of 40 more years at the present rate of operation. The total taxes paid to the state of Minnesota by Reserve and its related industries and services are about $8 million per year.

The Technology

Taconite is a hard, gray rock in which are found particles of magnetite, a black oxide of iron which is magnetic and has the approximate oxygen content designated as Fe_3O_4. The deposits of taconite near Babbitt, Minnesota are sufficiently near the surface to permit their being taken from open pits. The taconite is crushed to a nominal 4" size and hauled along the Reserve railroad line to Silver Bay at a rate of about 90,000 tons per day.

At Silver Bay the crushing operation is continued in order to free the particles of iron oxide for recovery and molding into pellets. A series of crushers, rod mills, ball mills, and magnetic separators are operated in processing the water slurry of ore. Two million tons of water are taken from Lake Superior each day (and returned) in the processing. The low-iron tailings are discharged back into the lake in the direction of a trough about 500 feet deep a few miles offshore. The discharge stream comprises the tailings, and the finest fraction, about 1½ % solids, forms a dense current which flows toward the bottom of the lake. The magnetically recovered particles are the concentrate, which is compressed to a cake with 10% moisture. It is then mixed with bentonite, which is a cohesive agent, and rolled into green pellets about ⅜ inch in diameter. The pellets are hardened by heating to 2350°F and are then ready for loading into ore boats at Silver Bay for the trip to the blast furnaces in Cleveland, Youngstown, Ashland, etc. The typical chemical analysis of the pellets as shipped is shown in Table 26.1.

The trade pays for pellets on the basis of iron content, which is described in terms of iron units; an iron unit is 1% iron in a ton of ore. A typical price might be $0.30 per iron unit, which would make the selling price of pellets with the foregoing analysis:

$$0.30 \times 60.6 = \$18.18/\text{ton}$$

The operating costs (no depreciation, depletion taxes, royalties, or ad-

Table 26.1 Chemical Analysis of Pellets

	% by Weight
Fe	60.6
SiO_2	8.6
MgO	0.5
Al_2O_3	0.5
CaO	0.5
Water	2.8
Other	balance

Table 26.2 Approximate Operating Costs

	$ per Ton of Pellets
Mining at Babbitt	2.50
Transport to Silver Bay	0.50
Crushing	1.00
Concentrating	2.00
Pelletizing	2.50

ministration included) for the Reserve operation might approximate, delivered at Silver Bay dock, those found in Table 26.2.

The Industry

The steel industry enjoyed another capacity production year in 1974 after operating at capacity in 1973 and shipping 107 million tons of steel. 1974's output is profitable, too, in contrast to the depressed period of 1970 when the average industry sales price was $232 per ton with a profit of $6.40 per ton.[1] Nineteen seventy-three results were $277.00 and $12.44, respectively. Furthermore, the low-priced foreign steel which accounted for 17% of domestic consumption in 1970 had been reduced to 13% in 1973. Two successive devaluations of the dollar had teamed with rampant inflation abroad to make the landed cost of foreign steel 25% above the price of domestic production in 1974. How long this situation might prevail is uncertain since the 1974 contract with the United Steelworkers Union provides for about a 40% increase in labor costs over the next three years. Scrap steel prices, fuel prices, and new facilities costs are all headed higher, too. The industry showed an average of 7.4% return on stockholders' equity in the 1960s versus a low of 4.1% in 1970 and a value of 9.0% in 1973.

Republic Steel and Armco Steel, each of which owns 50% of Reserve Mining Company, are the 4th and the 5th largest steel companies in the United States. Some recent statistics are shown in Table 26.3.

1. Data from American Iron and Steel Institute.

Table 26.3   Recent Information on Parent Firms

	Employees	Tons of Steel Shipped in 1972	No. of Blast Furnaces	% of Ore from Reserve
Republic	41,000	7.3 million	16	70
Armco	50,000	5.5 million	6	82

Minnesota supplies the United States with about 37% of its iron (ore and pellets), and about 20% of Minnesota's production is accounted for by Reserve Mining Company. The United States now imports about 30% of its iron ore, principally from Canada.

Generally, the outlook for the steel industry is guardedly optimistic in contrast to the pessimism which prevailed from 1955 through 1970. The industry is operating near its maximum capacity and an expansion of 7% or so of capacity is in progress for completion over the next few years. The new capacity is requiring substantially more capital than existing capacity, and financing the new investment is a major concern. Further increases in steel prices will probably be made, and there is concern about the impact that this may have on consumption.

Health

The health hazards on which the plaintiffs have based their charges are related to the fine dust-like particles that are dispersed into the air and discharged in the stream of tailings that is pumped into Lake Superior. The introduction of these particles is said to constitute a threat to health since amosite asbestos, a generic term, is a known human carcinogen, and the principal component in the Babbitt taconite tailings falls within the amosite description. Several thousand people breathe the air which has the dust in it, and at least 200,000 drink Lake Superior water, which has particles in it.

Asbestos is a general term for a number of hydrated silicates that, when crushed or processed, separate into flexible fibers made up of fibrils. Amosite is a nonmineralogical term for certain minerals in the cummingtonite-grunerite range in which the most abundant silicate present is:

$$(MgFe)Si_8O_{22}(OH)_2$$

Amosite is a range of mineral compositions that overlaps cummingtonite-grunerite. Experts agree that the morphology, crystallography, and chemistry of the cummingtonite-grunerites is identical to that of amosite asbestos.

The carcinogenic impact of amosite asbestos on humans is indicated by statistics which indicate that 45 to 50% of asbestos workers die of cancer versus 15 to 20% of the general population. Two studies by Dr. Selikoff and Dr. Hammond, which are generally recognized by all disputants as authorita-

Table 26.4 Related Research

A. 932 amosite-asbestos insulation workers employed in New Jersey at some time during the 1-1-43 to 12-31-71 period:

		Incidence of Cancer Death	
No. of men	Period of Employment	Actual in This Group	Expected If This Group "Normal"
278	less than 3 months	13	3.5
321	3 to 11 months	15	3 to 4
333	1 year or more	45	4

B. 17,800 men working on insulation

	Incidence of Cancer Death	
Period	Actual in This Group	Expected If This Group "Normal"
First 20 years	211	179
After 20 years	271	60

In addition, in the "after-20-years" period there were 73 deaths attributed to asbestosis and 72 to mesothelioma in the group of insulation workers, whereas no deaths due to these causes would be expected in the "normal" population.

tive, have been cited to show the vulnerability of asbestos[2] workers to cancer (see Table 26.4).[3]

The health issues in this study are broad and complex. The latent impact —perhaps twenty years after exposure—is a factor. The allegation that ingestion (as in drinking water) is different in its health impact than inhalation has been made. Too, it has been theorized that those persons who have been drinking the contested water for 15 years and who have died should contain fibers in their bodies if the health hazard is great. The results of the tissue studies which were designed to determine if Duluth residents have additional fibers in their systems were inconclusive. No statistically significant increase in fiber content of the tissue was found. The presence of fibers (derived from the Silver Bay operations) in water and air is not in dispute. Typical values:

Duluth drinking water—12.5 million fibers per liter

Silver Bay air—2,000 to one million fibers per cubic meter. (Current OSHA limit of nonhazardous fibers is five million fibers per cubic meter.)

2. Asbestos workers normally are in close proximity to asbestos, often in confined, dusty spaces where exposure occurs by inhalation throughout the work day.
3. The lung cancer death rate for native-born American men who are not regular cigarette smokers is about 26 per 100,000 men per year and 180 per 100,000 per year for regular cigarette smokers. See *The Consumers Union Report on Smoking and The Public Interest,* Consumers Union, 1963, p. 35.

Reserve

The Reserve Mining Company is a wholly owned subsidiary of Armco Steel (4th largest U.S. Steel producer) and Republic Steel (5th largest U.S. steel producer), which each own one-half of Reserve. Reserve was created to develop the taconite deposits near Babbitt, and the Silver Bay facility was built in 1953 after operating licenses approved by state and federal agencies had been granted in 1947. Environmental hearings had been conducted in Duluth, St. Paul, and Silver Bay before construction began and before the licenses had been granted. The off-shore trough in the lake was viewed as an appropriate disposal site. Dust control at the operation was deemed to be good enough to constitute a goal which competitors tried to achieve in their own facilities.

Reserve has now been operating for seventeen years and achieved the present rate of operations in 1960. The annual profit is about $20 million on the shipment of 11 million tons of pellets to the two owners. The total investment over the years has been about $350 million. Due to the fact that Armco and Republic have used their own financial stability to support this subsidiary and have been its only customers, they have capitalized Reserve with a debt to equity ratio of 3.0 and never used Reserve profits to pay back the debt to themselves. (The steel industry's debt to equity ratio is about 0.4.) The annual return on the cumulative total investment is thus about 5.7%; the annual return on equity is thus about 23%.

Some industry data from *Fortune's* 500 Largest Industrial Companies, May 1974, as to financial status are shown in Table 26.5.

Reserve has proposed that, if allowed to continue operating in the interim, it will construct and operate an on-land disposal area for the tailings. This would be in the lower Lax Lake area, and virtually no fibrous material would be carried into Lake Superior by the returning water stream. Too, dust control will be improved, although the exact concentration of the fibrous material that might, from time to time, reach the atmosphere is not guaranteed. Reserve estimates the capital cost of these additions to be $243 million and the construction time to be 3 to 5 years. Reserve points out that this outlay will permanently impair the economic viability of Reserve, Armco, and Republic. Further, Reserve indicates that if this proposal is not accepted by

Table 26.5 Percent Return on Stockholders' Equity

	1972	1973
Armco (55th in U.S. sales in 1973)	6.9	9.4
Republic (73rd in U.S. sales in 1973)	4.1	7.8
Mining industry median	10.1	16.1
Metal manufacturing industry median	6.9	9.3
All industries median	10.3	12.4

the plaintiffs, it will continue to respond to the complaints in the courts where it is confident of sustaining its operation in its present state.

The Problem

As the regional director of the Environmental Protection Agency's enforcement arm you wryly recall what you, when you were only "one of the boys," regarded as pusillanimous action by the regional directors under whom you were serving. However, each of them is still alive and well and continuing to fight the war for a cleaner environment! The Silver Bay case is your first big battle after less than ten months as a regional director. Would the loss of your first major battle destroy your career? Putting aside such thoughts, you reaffirm your determination to recommend what is going to be best for America over the long haul. Various thoughts flood into your mind:

1. EPA's honeymoon with Congress and, to some extent, with the public is over. It is essential that EPA prove itself to be constructive if it is to avoid ruinous budget cuts which might emasculate the agency.

2. Americans seem to be very fickle about their environment. No one seems to be willing to have *his* plant shut down and *his* job terminated. And in this inflationary time anti-pollution investments seem to be a scapegoat that is being blamed by many. Wasn't it only a few weeks ago that the President of the U.S. was asked at a press conference if he thought the country was heading into a depression?

3. Why can't the medical people and the scientists be more certain in their analysis of the data? Are they just passing the buck to me?

4. The young people in my office are not very much help. They don't seem to really dig in on the assignments that I have given them. They talk bravely, but they don't pass me much ammunition, and they know that it's *my* neck that is on the line.

5. EPA is an executive agency which is charged with protection of the citizenry against environmental health hazards. An important precedent, one way or the other, may emerge from this contest and may have a major impact on EPA's future.

6. My boss in Washington is not much help either. He doesn't know what it's like out here in Minnesota. For instance, he needs my recommendations by next Tuesday and has limited me to 800 words on this complex matter. He's already told me that I have only three choices and, he wants persuasive arguments for my recommendation to:
   a. Accept the Reserve offer.
   b. Reject the Reserve offer.
   c. Reject the Reserve offer and propose action that will be more attractive to both Reserve and EPA.

Discussion Questions

1. What would you do if you were the regional director of EPA? Why?
2. How do personal values enter into this decision?

James M. Higgins

On October 2, 1975, W. T. Grant, at that time the seventeenth largest selling retailer in the United States,[1] filed for bankruptcy under Chapter XI of the Federal Bankruptcy Act. The question is why? As recently as 1969, W. T. Grant's return on equity was 14.4 percent. What were the causes which resulted in the rapid financial collapse of this firm?

The Industry

Success in the retail chain store industry is a function of many variables, the absence of any one of which can lead to significant performance problems. The major variables are image, size, merchandising, location, management skills at both the top management levels and at the store level, store manager motivation, financial resources, and control. Let us now examine each of these factors in more detail.

Image: A firm must know to whom it is attempting to sell and it must know what it is attempting to sell. More importantly, those to whom it is attempting to sell must know what the company stands for and what it sells. K Mart and Woolco, for example, are readily identified for their discount store appeal. Sears, Penney's, and Ward's are clearly large department stores, with Sears being especially known for its service. A part of this image involves store layout. K Mart, for example, uses the same layout in each of its stores.

Size: Both the number of stores in a chain and the size of each of these stores are important factors in success. The absolute number of stores owned by any one chain enables it to be price competitive, primarily by cutting out the middlemen, i.e., wholesalers, and often by producing their own brands of goods. Store sizes vary in the industry as do strategies in this regard.

Merchandising: Successful merchandising depends upon advertisements, promotions, image, price, location, and products. Such factors as store logos play an important role in bringing in customers.

Location: In order to be successful, a store must be located near potential customers. The cost of locations is especially important to the discount type stores that generally try to avoid the high rent shopping centers and prefer to build their own stores apart from others.

Management Skills: At the top management level, strategic decisions must be carefully made. Policies related to price, credit, inventory, cost, etc. must be sound. At the store level, experienced and well trained managers are vital.

Store Manager Motivation: The store manager makes or breaks the com-

1. "The Fifty Largest Retailing Companies," *Fortune*, July 1975, p. 122.

pany. He must be given some reason to make it, rather than to break it.

Financial Resources: A high and balanced cash flow is especially important. A sound credit rating and the moderate use of leverage are found in the more successful firms.

Control: Cost, price, inventory, sales per square foot, financial leverage, purchasing, store reporting, and certain other factors must be scrutinized carefully by top management. While store managers generally receive a great deal of autonomy, they must be controlled.

Growth characterized the retail chain store industry throughout the late 1960s and early 1970s. Sears, Penney's, Wards, Woolworth (Woolco), S.S. Kresge (K Mart), and Grant's all engaged in substantial expansion programs during this time frame. (See Table 27.1.) Late during this period, some concern was expressed that the saturation point was being reached in some geographical areas with respect to the number of competitive stores.

The W. T. Grant Company

The first W. T. Grant store was opened in 1906 in Lynn, Massachusetts. The W. T. Grant Company was incorporated in Delaware on November 27, 1937, in order to consolidate three exisiting Grant corporations. Grant's was primarily a northeastern variety chain store operation until the 1960s when it began to expand rapidly into other parts of the United States. As of January 30, 1975, Grant's had five subsidiaries: Zeller's Ltd of Canada (51 percent ownership); W. T. Grant Financial Corporation; Jones and Presnell Studios, Inc.; Granjewel Jewelers and Distributors Inc.; and G.I.S. Merchandising Corporation. Grant's had 1,152 stores in 42 states, five regional freight distribution centers in New Jersey, California, Georgia, Connecticut, and Indiana; a fashion and import distribution facility in Jersey City, New Jersey; and four freight consolidation centers located in Florida, North Carolina, New Jersey, and Pennsylvania. 1,002 of their stores were located in shopping centers, many anchored by their store. Grant's operated thirty service centers under the name of Bradford, with ten of these serving as central depots for receiving and pretesting the major appliances.

Changes in Management. After serving as President and Chairman of the Board of Directors since the company's inception in 1906, William T. Grant retired on June 30, 1966 at the age of 90 years. His successor as Chairman of the Board was a member of the Board of Directors and a former company President, 1952–1959, Edward Staley. Together with Louis Lustenberger, who had become company President in 1958, Mr. Staley attempted to continue company operations along the lines established by the retiring founder. An expansion program, which primarily focused on increasing the number of stores, begun in 1963 under Mr. Lustenberger's guidance, continued without any changes until February 1, 1968, when Mr. Richard Mayer replaced Mr.

Lustenberger as President of the company. Mr. Mayer increased substantially the rate of expansion and continued this tactic until he was replaced by Harry Pierson in 1973, who was subsequently replaced by Mr. James Kendrick in September, 1974. Former company directors have indicated that Mr. Staley was highly authoritarian, made most of the major decisions himself, and surrounded himself with people who would accept his mandates. It is reported that he became even more authoritarian as company fortunes waned. A company joke reported that a major factor in becoming a director was how fast you could say yes. As a note of interest, Mr. Staley was Mr. Grant's brother-in-law, and as Mr. Grant became less active in the company, he ceded much of his power to Mr. Staley. Under several titles, Mr. Staley in effect ran the company from 1952 to 1974. As early as 1971, however, Mr. Lustenberger and Raymond Folger (director and past president) unsuccessfully attempted to force a change in the company's direction. The continued deterioration of the company's performance eventually caused the directors to insist on a change in management. Mr. Kendrick (former vice president of sales and former director) was elected, effective in September, 1974, as President and Chairman of the Board and Chief Executive Officer because of his proven merchandising and sales promotion ability. Mr. Kendrick had previously been Mr. Lustenberger's choice to succeed him as President in 1968 but was rejected, some say because he was not a "Staley Man," and was therefore in effect exiled to Grant's Canadian subsidiary, Zeller's Ltd. By the time Kendrick took over, Grant's was heavily in debt and the company's banks were assuming a major management role. The banks wanted a top flight merchandiser to replace Mr. Kendrick, and in April, 1975, Mr. Robert Anderson, a former Vice President with Sears, became the President and Chief Executive Officer of Grant's.

The Decline as Revealed in Major Plans and Policies

Let us now view W. T. Grant in terms of some of its major plans and policies. These cut across several years but most occur late in the 1970–1974 time frame.

Growth. An expansion program began under the guidance of Mr. Lustenberger in 1963. From 1963 to 1973 the company opened 612 stores and expanded 91 others. Through 1969, the expansion program fared quite well, with profits keeping pace with expansion. As Grant's top management observed their own successes up to 1968 and the successes of their major competitors, they decided to step up their expansion program. As Mr. Mayer surveyed the retailing scene in 1968, he made these observations: 1. Sales of higher-cost durable goods (not heretofore a Grant forte) such as televisions, air conditioners, furniture, and major appliances, were on the increase. 2. Major competitors were obtaining a larger profit margin by selling private label goods. Hoping to capitalize on these areas, Mr. Mayer established the

Table 27.1   W. T. Grant Co. Number of Stores Open as of January 31

Year	No. of Stores Open
1975	1,152
1974	1,189
1973	1,208
1972	1,168
1971	1,116
1970	1,095
1969	1,092
1968	1,086

Source: W. T. Grant Annual Statements.

goal of developing Grant's as a "one stop family shopping store." Mr. Mayer, who considered this as an extension of the soft goods line they had previously carried, commented: "Today, we like to refer to ourselves as promotional department stores. Our new stores are being built larger than they were in the past, and the inventory is more varied." This change in strategy caused considerable dissension within the company over whether Grant's should go the discount route (like K Mart) or the full service retailer route (like J. C. Penney or Sears). The company compromised, and in the words of one Grant executive, "took a position between the two and thus consequently stood for nothing."

To accommodate the expanded lines of merchandise, such as automotive services, food service facilities, major appliances, home entertainment items, full garden shops, and a complete furniture assortment, Grant's utilized different store sizes depending upon location and volume. While in 1966 new stores were typically smaller than 50,000 square feet, in 1971 the smallest of the three standard sizes was 60,000 square feet. The mid-sized store was 120,000 square feet and the superstore (for "Grant Country or City" stores) was 180,000 square feet. Remodeling and enlarging of profitable existing stores which were in good locations were also included in the expansion program. The goal was to double the square footage in the average store.

In 1968, 80 percent of Grant's stores were located in shopping centers. From 1968 to 1972, the bulk of the new stores were built in community centers or small shopping strips where there would be minimal competition from other major retail chains. Grant's was sometimes forced to accept less than desirable locations because of its poor performance. Developers seek high sales/profit firms for their projects. To hold down construction costs (and also because of limited competition), frills, such as carpeting, were not used in furnishing the stores. In 1973, Grant's new store program centered on its larger Grant City stores, which were full-time family service stores. These ranged in size from 55,000 square feet for smaller towns to 187,000 square feet where Grant's was co-anchoring major shopping malls with retailers like

Sears. The continued increased rate of expansion from 1969 to 1973 (396 stores were opened) put Grant's in the number two spot among major merchandisers with respect to the total square footage of store space added in the 1971–1972 time frame. Grant's peaked in size with approximately 1,250 stores in 1973. Due to a restrained building program and continued closings of mostly older, less profitable stores, the number of stores declined to 1,075 in April of 1975.

Product Mix and Image. During the company's early years and even into the mid to late sixties, Grant's merchandise mix included nearly all soft goods. The new merchandise mix included appliances, home furnishings, sporting goods, and the like. While Grant's had modified its product lines, it did not engage in a major effort to change the image to coincide with the new products. Customers were unaware of Grant's new product lines and its private brand merchandise. The broadening of the product line was seemingly accomplished as a "me too" reaction to seeing other firms successfully selling these items. The company, by default, fell into a gap where it offered neither low prices (like a discounter) nor good service (like Sears). Evidence indicated a lack of customer identification with the new merchandising efforts and expanded product lines. Many asked, "What is a Bradford TV set?" The product mix offered varied with store size. A policy on company image was never clarified and considerable dissension was evident within the company in the early seventies over the issue of going discount or full service. Store layouts were determined by the company's real estate department.

Decentralized Decision Making. Grant's delegated considerable authority to its local store managers. They were allowed to order up to 80 percent of their own inventory and price the merchandise as they wished. This latter policy led to price competition between local Grant stores. Managers also forwarded invoices to headquarters for payment.

Inventory. Grant's policy was to balance the annual percentage change in sales and the percentage change in inventory. From 1965 to 1969, inventory increased 47 percent compared to a 44 percent increase in sales. However, subsequently, Grant's suffered excessive inventory buildup. During the period 1970–1974, inventory levels increased 73 percent, while sales increased by only 48 percent. Although the inventory level was reduced 10 percent in 1974, an accompanying 5 percent decline in sales negated any real gain. Inventory turnover rates went from 94 days in 1966 to 119 days in 1974.

Credit. To help sell slow moving, high priced items, the company undertook a massive credit promotion program in the late 1960s. This program was stressed in the early 1970s. The credit granting program was controlled by each store. Credit checking was left to each store. Each store kept its own credit records, and all payments were made to the stores. A minimum payment of $1 per month was required of a customer ($10 is a common cash industry payment minimum). Payments were made in cash.

Pricing. Another attempt to bolster sagging sales in 1972 was the institution of a limited discount program. However, the company did not establish any kind of a "discount image" and "even if people did buy the discounted items, they left the rest of the goods to collect dust."

Control and Information Systems. By early 1975 several factors became evident. Inventory levels were not considered by several members of top management to be completely accurate. Buyers frequently relied on vendors to keep them posted on inventory needs. No central reports were available which indicated how much of what was selling. No purchasing budget existed. Purchases were not related to sales in any systematic fashion. Some buyers were apparently buying in order to justify their existence, and in the rush to fill new stores, merchandise was bought almost without regard to season, style, etc. Policy had prevented the use of markdowns because it reduced operating margin.

Improper reporting of delinquent accounts was known to be occurring. Repossessions were often made without being entered on store records or the customer's accounts credited. Often, merchandise was just written off after a period of time without any major effort to collect accounts receivable. The time allowed to write off bad debts fluctuated. Purchase invoices were being received late from the stores. The internal audit department never had more than 26 auditors. It usually had less. Indications were that some kickbacks may have been involved in site locations.

Personnel. Compensation for employees in most jobs was generally higher than for competitors. The corporation insisted on training its own store managers. However, the training program was unable to grow as rapidly as the requirement for new managers.

New Store Profitability. Several new stores had failed to show a profit as quickly as had been anticipated. However, company policy indicated that, since five years are usually necessary for a new store to begin contributing, no corrective action was required.

Managerial Motivation. An interesting scheme for encouraging store managers to meet credit quotas was labeled the "Steak and Beans" program. This was a negative incentive program based on indignities. Store managers might be hit in the face with a custard pie, have their ties cut in half, be forced to push peanuts with their noses, or be forced to run around stores backwards. Another feature of the program was nonpromotion to larger stores.

Finance. Grants had leased many of its stores. Commitments to leases existed everywhere stores had been closed. In 1973, Grants expended $85 million for store leases. In December 1974, uncancellable leases were estimated at over $450 million. Dividends were suspended in the summer of 1974 for the first time in the company's history. $92 million of the 1974 loss of $177 million resulted from bad debts write-offs. An additional $63 million was included as allowance for doubtful accounts. Debt increased rapidly in the

Table 27.2 Income and Sales Comparisons (Year Ended January 31, Following Year)

Year	Net Sales (Millions)	Earned per Share
1974	$1,762.0	$(12.74)*
1973	1,849.8	.76
1972	1,644.7	2.49
1971	1,374.8	2.25
1970	1,254.1	2.64
1969	1,210.9	2.99
1968	1,096.2	2.71
1967	979.5	2.58
1966	920.2	2.50
1965	839.7	2.54

Source: W. T. Grant Annual Reports.
*Dividends omitted since August 27, 1974.

early 1970s, especially short term debt, as the company lost its ability to float the less expensive long term debt. Grant's, 1974, had the highest leverage ratio of any major merchandiser.

Innovative Accounting Practices. A special account, the 1517 account, was maintained. Vendors were deliberately overbilling Grant's with Grant's permission. The funds were usually called by Grant's in the fourth quarter to purchase Christmas goods. Also, such actions made fourth quarter profits look better than they really were. Some suspicions have arisen that possible buyer kickbacks were involved in this fund.

Until January, 1975, when it changed its accounting policies, Grant's recognized as income all finance charges billed to customers at date of sale, i.e., months prior to possible collection. This practice was not in accordance with the AICPA guidelines on recognition of such revenues. Consequently, income was highly overstated. In January, 1975, past financial statements were revised to reflect this.

The Effort to Turn Around the Company Fortunes. When Mr. Kendrick assumed the position as Chairman of the Board in September of 1974, his first action was to go public with the financial condition of the firm. For the 9-month period ending October 31, 1974, Grant's reported a $22 million loss. The company followed up with a restatement of earnings for the entire year. This revealed the company had lost $177 million, with $92 million of the loss resulting from writing off bad debts.

Mr. Kendrick identified three priorities when he took over. First, a marketing plan encompassing merchandising, operational, and promotional strategies replaced the previous singular emphasis on growth. Secondly, he sought to improve intramanagement communications so the lower echelon personnel and store managers would level with top management. Lastly, a commitment to selling merchandise instead of operating a financial scheme (such as

Table 27.3 Selected Information—Summary of Operations (in Thousands)

As of January 30	1975	1974	1973	1972	1971
Sales	$1,761,952	$1,849,802	$1,644,747	$1,374,812	$1,254,131
Concession Income	4,238	3,971	3,753	3,439	4,985
Total Income	$1,766,190	$1,853,773	$1,648,500	$1,378,351	$1,259,116
Cost of Merchandise Sold Buying and Occupancy Costs	$1,303,267	$1,282,945	$1,125,261	$ 931,238	$ 843,192
Selling, General and Admin. Exp.	$ 540,953	$ 540,230	$ 476,280	$ 411,225	$ 363,853
Store Closing Expense	24,000				
Net Credit Expense (Income)	161,467	5,972	(13,801)	(21,633)	(13,085)
Other Interest Expenses	37,771	18,082	6,165	5,272	1,526
Total Expenses	$ 764,191	$ 564,284	$ 468,644	$ 394,864	$ 352,294
Gross Margin	(301,268)	6,544	54,595	52,149	63,630
Other Income	3,376	2,996	918	1,270	1,214
Earnings before Taxes and Equity in Unconsolidated Subsidiaries	$ (297,892)*	$ 9,540*	$ 55,513*	$ 53,419*	$ 64,844*
		4,564**	61,089**	60,592**	71,282**
Provision for Taxes	(117,486)	3,289	25,664	25,745	32,604
Equity in Subsidiaries	3,086	4,651	5,116	3,951	4,175
Net Earnings (Loss)	$ (177,340)*	$ 10,902*	$ 34,965*	$ 31,625*	$ 36,415*
		8,429**	37,787**	35,212**	39,577**
Dividends on Preferred Stock	280	293	335	346	395
Net Earnings w/r Common Stock	$ (177,620)	$ 10,609	$ 34,630	$ 31,279	$ 36,020
Net Earnings per Common Share (Loss)	(12.74)*	.76*	2.49*	2.25*	2.64*
		.59**	2.70**	2.51**	2.87**

*/**Where two figures appear for the same line item, the single asterisk (*) indicates that these were taken from the 1974 Annual Report (as of January 30, 1975) and reflect certain accounting changes. Those with a double asterisk (**) were taken from the 1973 Annual Report and do not reflect these changes. Both figures are shown for contrast.

Source: W. T. Grant Annual Reports, 1974 and 1973.

Table 27.4 Selected Information: Balance Sheet (in Thousands of Dollars)

	1975	1974	1973	1972	1971
Cash and Securities	79,642	45,951	30,943	49,851	34,009
Customers' Installment	309,968*	521,319*	468,582*	408,301*	358,428*
Accounts Net	—	598,799**	542,751**	477,324**	419,731**
Total Current Assets	924,781*	1,044,689*	979,876**	831,229**	719,182**
Merchandise Inventories	407,357	450,637	399,533	298,676	260,492
Working Capital	174,875	383,631	315,346	327,011	235,128
Total Assets	1,082,267*	1,194,987*	1,110,698**	944,670**	807,628**
Short Term Debt	600,000	453,097	390,034	237,741	246,420
Long Term Debt (including current portion)	217,336	220,336	126,627	128,432	32,301
Retained Earnings	—	248,461**	261,153**	244,508**	230,435**
	37,674*	219,471*	299,691*	215,867*	205,381*
Net Worth	147,652*	331,444*	334,339**	325,745**	302,036**
Total Current Liabilities	749,906*	661,058*	633,067**	475,577**	459,000**

*Adjusted for 1974 accounting changes.
**Not adjusted for 1974 accounting changes.

Source: W.T. Grant Annual Reports.

the credit program designed to move high priced, slow-moving goods). His intention was to return to the basic, staple merchandise on which Grant's had built its reputation. He also acknowledged the inventory buildup of big ticket items, began changing the merchandise mix, and planned to reduce Grant's 70 percent reliance on private brands. By early 1975, only 40 percent of the company's sales volume was private label goods.

To get a firm grasp on the company's condition, Mr. Kendrick established six task forces to study credit operations, overhead costs, organization structure, the expansion program, computer payroll, and cash management systems. He also hired an outside consultant to study Grant's finances.

Two key points in Kendrick's plan to save Grant's included cutting costs and generating a cash flow. To accomplish this, inventories had to be reduced and sales had to be increased. Unfortunately, a lack of customer identification existed with regard to the company's products. Grant's also possessed an inability to continue low-cost financing. With Grant's heavily in debt with a number of banks, the banks began pushing for a super-hot merchandiser who could cut away enough deadwood and streamline the company to insure its survival. In April of 1975, Mr. Anderson, whose salary for several years was guaranteed by Grant's banks, got his chance to turn the company around.

One of Mr. Anderson's first moves was to drop the major appliance and furniture line since a study indicated people did not want to buy that kind of merchandise at Grant's. He also looked at the effects of overexpansion and the inventory buildup that resulted. He discovered warehouses which were less than 10 percent stocked and stores which were arranged to stress men's apparel when studies indicated most of the store's shoppers were women. He took action to correct these problems. He also cut the number of stores drastically, attempted to find out how much inventory the company had (it was found to be understated by $70 million on the day of bankruptcy), and attempted to create a new image based on the old Northeastern concentration of stores. But, alas, on October 2, 1975, Grant's filed for bankruptcy. Some say it should not have, at least not under Chapter XI.

Table 27.5 Miscellaneous Information

	1975	1974	1973	1972	1971
Current Ratio	1.2	1.6	1.5	1.7	1.5
Common Stock Price Range					
High	11⅝	41	48⅝	70⅝	54⅞
Low	1½	9⅝	34¾	41½	26⅞
Number of Stores					
Beginning of year	1,189	1,208	1,168	1,116	1,095
Opened	44	77	92	83	65
Closed	81	96	52	31	44
End of Year	1,152	1,189	1,208	1,168	1,116

Source: W. T. Grant Annual Reports, 1970–1974.

Table 27.6 Selected Notes from 1974 Financial Statements

Short-Term Borrowing

The following relates to aggregate short-term borrowings ($ in thousands):

	52 weeks ended January 30, 1975	Year ended January 31, 1974
Maximum amount outstanding at any month end	$602,905	$518,871
Average daily amount outstanding	539,880	465,204
Weighed average daily interest rate	11.74%	8.55%

Leases and Contingencies

The estimated net present value of the net fixed minimum rental commitments for all noncancellable financing leases are summarized below ($ in thousands):

	Range of Interest Rates Used	Present Value January 30, 1975	January 31, 1974
Real Estate	2.53% to 11.94%	$386,778	$431,442
Less Subleases	2.62% to 11.94%	9,355	7,610
Net Real Estate		377,423	423,832
Equipment	7.36% to 8.04%	28,695	34,465
		$406,118	$458,297

Source: W. T. Grant Annual Report, 1974, Notes 4 and 12, respectively.

References

"All Is Not Well in the War Room." *Fortune,* November 1975, p. 25.

Bleiberg, R. M. "Grant's Tomb? A Lasting Monument to Failure Would Be Worse." *Barrons,* December 9, 1974, p. 7.

"The Fifty Largest Retailing Companies." *Fortune,* July 1975, pp. 100–122.

"Grant Managers Risk Pie in Face for a Failure." *Wall Street Journal,* February 4, 1977.

"Grant's Chief Reached the Top on Credit." *New York Times,* March 3, 1968, p. 3, Section III.

"Grant's Great Collapse." *Newsweek,* October 13, 1975, p. 81.

"Grant's Tomb." *Newsweek,* February 23, 1977, p. 29.

"Great What—Is—It." *Forbes,* January 15, 1970, p. 15.

"How W. T. Grant Lost $175 Million Last Year." *Business Week,* February 24, 1975, pp. 74–76.

"Investigating the Collapse of W. T. Grant." *Business Week*, July 19, 1976, pp. 60–62.

"It's Get Tough Time at W. T. Grant." *Business Week,* October 19, 1974, p. 46.

"Look to the Malls While Staying with Strips." *Chain Store Age,* November 1972, p. 26.

Slom, S. H. "Grant Is Pressing $25 Million Law Suit on Alleged Kickback Tied to Real Estate." *Wall Street Journal,* June 15, 1976.

————. "Grant Testimony Shows It Lacked Curbs on Budget, Credit and Had Internal Woes." *Wall Street Journal,* February 4, 1977.

W. T. Grant. *Annual Report.* New York: W. T. Grant Co., Inc., 1971, 1972, 1973, and 1974.

Discussion Questions

1. What were the major factors which led to Grant's collapse?
2. What could Grant's directors have done to have prevented the catastrophe? What is the role of the Board of Directors? Did Grant's board members fulfill their roles?
3. What were Grant's strengths and weaknesses, threats and opportunities in 1970? What should its Master Strategy have been in 1970? Why?
4. Evaluate the performances of the various top management teams.
5. What role did coalitions play in Grant's downfall?

28/New York City's Financial Crisis in 1975

David J. Springate

Part I

Charles Sanford, executive vice-president of Banker's Trust, was charged with arranging the prospectus for a New York City bond issue. On Thursday, February 27, 1975, he was informed by the bank's counsel, White & Case, that according to requirements of a New York State law regarding tax anticipation notes the bank must be able to certify the amount of tax revenues anticipated up to the last day of the month in which borrowing was to take place. In accordance with that requirement, no legal opinion relating to the financial viability of the prospectus could be rendered by the firm. The figures available from the city comptroller's office were for January 30, 1975, and the borrowing was to take place February 28, 1975.

An attempt to resolve this issue took place that evening in the office of the New York City Comptroller, Harrison J. Goldin. At the meeting representatives of the two primary underwriters, Chase Manhattan Bank, NA and Banker's Trust, attempted to work with Mr. Goldin to obtain the needed information. Their preliminary investigations related to the manner in which New York City had been keeping its books. When ultimately brought to the public's attention, the resulting effect of their findings and of the disclosures was the total undermining of individual and institutional investor confidence in the city's ability to meet its fiscal obligations.

Background. As is a well-known fact, New York City was the largest city in the United States, with a population in excess of eight million people. A lesser known fact is that 14% of these people were dependent upon welfare and other related social programs for a large portion of their incomes. The expenditures for these programs were, to a great degree, fixed in advance. In a rough sense they might be compared to part of a private company's fixed overhead costs. To a very large degree the city depended on revenue inflows to generate the needed income from these prescribed outflows.

Mr. Goldin was aware of the state laws requiring a balanced budget, or at the very least, the need to show a clearly articulated time table when accumulating debt. In order to effect legal compliance, each borrowing made by the city had to be tied to tangible anticipated revenues. It was the anticipated amounts and associated due dates that became a central political issue and a prime focus of subsequent investigations into the city's fiscal problems.

Borrowings of any magnitude, be they corporate or municipal, are usually

Source: This case authored by David J. Springate, Southern Methodist University, from published sources. Distributed by the Intercollegiate Case Clearing House, Soldiers Field, Boston, Mass. 02163. All rights reserved to the contributors. Printed in the U.S.A.

Table 28.1 New York City's Fiscal Pie

	1966	1974
Total Budget	$3,804 million	$10,249 million
Education and Libraries	23.7%	21.8 %
Health Services	12.4%	8.5 %
Social Services	18.7%	28.8 %
Public Safety	11.4%	9.7 %
Pension Funds	5.7%	7.7 %
Debt Redemption	12.5%	7.0 %
Debt Service	2.0%	4.15%
Other	13.6%	12.6 %
	100 %	100 %

Source: *Fortune*, August 1975, p. 147. Reprinted by permission of *Fortune* Magazine; © 1975 Time Inc.

financed by a multiplicity of sources. The borrowings of New York City were no exception. Over the years the city had financed its debt through sales to individuals and institutions—ranging geographically from Spokane to Miami Beach and from Hong Kong to London. In addition, many prestigious financial institutions located in the city itself had participated. The consequences of any New York City fiscal crisis would thus be immediately far-reaching.

Proceeds from these many borrowings were put to use in a wide range of areas (see Table 28.1). If radical surgery was to be performed on the city's services in order to preserve its fiscal integrity, it would be necessary, according to some, to investigate the effect of the elimination of any one of the multitude of services provided by the city and determine its ensuing socioeconomic implications. (This line of argument is pursued further in Part II of the case.)

One of the arguments later put forth by the city as an explanation for its fiscal plight was that some of the expenditures that the city must make were the result of legislative mandate. To at least some extent the city appeared to have a basis for making the argument. For example, the city's welfare expenditure was federally mandated. Medicare was prescribed by state law. The city's debt service was also a legal obligation. Further, it is a well known fact that New York City paid the highest welfare subsidies in the United States. This situation caused a large scale migration of the less affluent to the city over the last ten years. Prior to 1969 the state legislature attempted to limit this migration by imposing strict residency requirements. Fifteen months was the period for welfare eligibility. However this requirement was declared unconstitutional by the Supreme Court of the United States in *Shapiro vs. Thompson* in 1969. The strict requirement was said to have a "chilling effect" on the individual right to travel from state to state. Today this decision is sometimes referred to as "the case that sank New York City."

A Crisis and Its Genesis. As the crisis built up, Mr. Goldin wondered what steps might be taken in order to place the city in better financial condition. The banks and other large lending institutions threatened to stop lending, much of the public refused to buy debt, and the state and federal governments initially contended that New York City should take care of its own problems.

In attempting to get at the heart of the problems plaguing the city budget, Mr. Goldin uncovered the following facts.

On March 31st, 1958, then Mayor of New York Robert Wagner signed Executive Order No. 49, which allowed city employees the right to join unions and to bargain collectively. This act later played an essential role in helping the reelection cause of John Lindsay in the mayoral election of 1965. Lindsay acquiesced to union demands for very high wage and pension benefits in order to maintain essential city services threatened by a municipal workers' strike. His acquiescence won him popular support in the election and was instrumental in paving the way for the practice of using paid-in investment funds for the payment of retirement benefits, rather than the standard practice of dispersing funds from earnings achieved as a result of prudent investment.

On June 18, 1971, then Governor Nelson Rockefeller signed an amendment to the state municipal financing law which enabled the city to borrow based upon anticipated revenues (Mr. Goldin's problem in early 1975). Through the years, in order to balance the budget according to state law, city leaders used the statute to borrow against anticipated revenues. These anticipated revenues were what the city's bankers ultimately came to question. New York State law specifically required any borrowing be tied to actual future revenues due the city. The amounts claimed as anticipated revenues were later alleged to have been manipulated. The team of bankers and attorneys working with Mayor Abraham Beame and Comptroller Goldin uncovered only $86 million in anticipated revenues available for borrowing. In contrast, city officials had claimed on January 30 that $600 million was available. An investigation revealed that over a period of years city officials had anticipated revenues on property that had not produced taxes for twenty years or more. It was shortly after this that the leading financiers refused to lend more to the city and thereby threw the city into a financial turmoil.

However, the city's descent into financial chaos began at least in 1964 when the state legislature amended the state Local Finance Law. The amendment allowed city officials to use the capital budget to meet current non-capital needs. Instead of requiring politically painful budget cuts the amended section also permitted officials to use the capital budget to borrow money for current expenses. In short, the law, as amended, allowed New York City officials to violate the time-honored financial axiom that one should not finance short-term needs with long-term debt.

Mayor Wagner immediately put the benefit of this amendment to use and placed $26 million of expense items in his 1964–65 capital budget. The Citizen's Budget Commission estimates that between 1965 and 1975 a total of

$2.7 billion in expense items was placed into the city's capital budget at an added interest cost of $250 million. This added interest became a major factor in the city's massive debt service. In 1976 it was projected to consume 14 cents out of every expense budget dollar. This is more than the city spent at the time for police, fire, the City University, sanitation, and the environment combined.[1]

In addition to this practice of transferring expense dollars into the capital budget the city began to close budget deficits by issuing short-term notes. These short-term notes were secured by anticipated revenues. (See Table 28.5 for short-term debt summary). A legislative change in 1965 relaxed many of the constraints that had previously been placed on any borrowing against anticipated revenues. In prior years RANs (Revenue Anticipation Notes) could be issued against uncollected state and federal aid due for that fiscal year; however, the RANs could not exceed the amount of aid actually collected during the prior year. In some years during the 1950s and early 1960s, the city issued no RANs at all, but when it did, these legal constraints helped to assure that they were virtually always paid off by year-end.

The new enactment made two substantial changes. It did away with the old requirements that borrowings against aid be related to the prior year's collections. Instead, it allowed the city to borrow against the Mayor's own estimate of state and federal aid applicable to the current year's budget and left open the question of how the notes would be repaid if the estimates turned out to be overly optimistic. The new law allowed the city to borrow, for the first time, against certain taxes and fees that, while owed, were not scheduled for payment during the year. With the relaxation of these legislative constraints, the city's short-term debt rose from $526 million in 1965 to a massive $5.7 billion by February, 1975.

An additional practice entered into in years close to 1975 was the negotiation of the budget deficit between the various political factions in the state legislature. For example, if the city determined that it would have a $100 million deficit, when asking the state for financial aid it might negotiate the deficit down to, say, $50 million. The theory here was that the legislature might be more willing to give $50 million in aid but less receptive to a request of $100 million. The city would subsequently justify the lower deficit by discovering more tax revenue than was originally anticipated.

During John Lindsay's first term as mayor, the city's fiscal health benefited from a flourishing local economy which was a microcosm of the general economic boom occurring across the United States. As a result of this situation the city's property tax base continued to expand upward with an office-building boom occurring at the end of the decade. Between 1965 and 1969, while the city's population remained stable, there were an additional 220,000 jobs created in the city; one-third of those jobs came in the city government. The

1. See "Going Broke the New York Way," Fortune, August 1975, p. 146–147.

city's welfare bill also increased during this period. From 1965 to 1969 the number of New Yorkers on welfare increased from 500,000 to one million.[2]

The nationwide recession of 1970 affected New York City. There was a net loss of 53,000 jobs in that year alone. However, while 53,000 jobs was the net loss for the city over all, there continued to be a net rise in municipal employment. This rise began to cause larger and larger budget deficits, but the true size of the deficits was disguised by the sale of large amounts of revenue-anticipation notes. In 1970, year-end borrowings against these funds totaled some $720 million. By 1976 it had not been determined what the true size of these deficits were. It is doubtful whether they will ever be determined.

Once this pattern of borrowing began, it was difficult to stop. Revenues used to pay off the maturing notes had to be replaced with new borrowings. The only way to break this chain would have been to make budget appropriations to pay off the ever increasing debt. However, such appropriations would have meant cutting funds allocated elsewhere or raising additional revenues through tax increases.

By year-end 1971, borrowings against state and federal receivables rose to around $965 million.

The downturn in the city's economy in 1970 appears in retrospect not to have been cyclical, as was the downturn in the national economy. Rather it was the beginning of a prevailing trend. Even with the city government's payroll expanding every year since 1969, the city incurred a net loss of jobs, both public and private, in every year since 1969—a cumulative total of more than 700,000 by 1976. By comparison, in the United States as a whole, over this same period, nonagricultural jobs, that is manufacturing and service jobs or the types performed in urban areas, increased by 7%. Furthermore, this job loss tended to erode the city's tax base through the flight of businesses to localities that offered a more favorable tax environment.

Additionally, there was a decrease in state and federal aid to the city. State and federal aid peaked in 1968 and thereafter began a slow decline. Even though these two occurrences brought about a decrease in revenues, the budget rose another 40% during Mayor Lindsay's second term in office.

Part II

[In this part of the case some of the less factual data is discussed. Issues that may be important are raised.]

The Issue of Responsibility. As Mr. Sanford of Banker's Trust discovered along with the rest of New York's bankers, the city's bookkeeping was not an accurate reflection of what was actually taking place, but encompassed a series of maneuvers an independent auditor would not have certified. Among them: (1) the placing of $564 million of expense items in the city's capital budget;

---

2. "Going Broke," *Fortune*, p. 147.

(2) the mid-1975 ending by the city of transit fare subsidies for school children and the elderly, pretending the need would disappear or that the State or Federal Government would bail the city out; (3) the City Council's arbitrary freeing of "revenues" of $148.6 million by, among other things, postponing the statutory repayment of $96 million to the "rainy-day" fund; (4) the announcement by city officials of a deficit, leaving the State to close it; (5) the approval by city officials of a one-year roll-over of the $308 million in budget notes issued to cover the 1970–71 budget deficit.

To many, such actions are reprehensible. They would say, it is Scarlett O'Hara's attitude of worrying tomorrow about troubles of today. Were a corporation to use these procedures, rather than a municipality, some critics point out, the corporate comptroller or treasurer would most probably be serving a jail sentence.

On the other hand, the issue can be seen to be two-sided. Had the politicians not been concerned with the humanistic needs of the city, there could have been grave consequences. A city of eight million people, densely urbanized and highly competitive, needs to have essential services provided and social order maintained. In might be said that no civilization was ever judged on how it kept its books. Rather, looking at history, the contribution of a society to the world and to the generations can be viewed as having come mostly from its major cities. These contributions range from the architecture that was Greece to the culture that is Paris.

Some observers have said the French have given up much to preserve tradition. Not in 700 years have the French people been victorious in battle. Yet it has always been clear that surrender was a lesser price than the destruction of France's monuments. Observers might ask, is dedication to the preservation of a way of life, not to some but for all, a reprehensible action? In mid-1975 some very high executives in New York banks did not appear ready to condemn on the issue.

National and International Implications of Default. What were the consequences the United States might have expected from a default of New York to pay its bond obligations? Between 1968 and 1975 the value of the U.S. dollar fell 17% on the international money market. The supply-and-demand forces dictated that without fixed exchange rates, the U.S. dollar was worth less. Although at the outset this may have looked bad for the U.S., it may, in fact, have been a boon to the U.S. gross national product. When the dollar was worth less, exports ultimately increased.

Similarly, if New York City were to default and markets to recognize this as a weakness in the U.S. currency, these market forces would effectively devaluate the dollar by some percentage. A decreased value of the dollar would presumably be a benefit to the U.S. economy at least with respect to exports. On the other hand, capital flows to the U.S. might be affected adversely.

On the national side, although default might have done little to the everyday lives of the average American outside New York, it would have its effects. The savings of a great many individuals would have been out of reach until New York again became solvent, and the U.S. Banking System would probably require some booster aid from the Federal Reserve Board. The city itself might have had to reduce the payroll by some 30,000. Services such as garbage collection and health care would probably have been reduced, while the City University would likely have instituted a tuition system.[3] Each of these actions would likely have produced severe consequences. In an area as densely populated as Manhattan, reduced garbage collection might foster disease by allowing scavengers such as rats to roam the streets looking for available food. With the reduction of health centers, emergency facilities would likely be eliminated and the unemployment rate go up. Ending free tuition at New York's City University would deprive many of the opportunity for an education.

The worst effect might have been unemployment. Reducing the city payroll by many workers could have left the police and fire departments with dangerously low levels of protection. Day care centers would likely have closed. Mothers might have had to stop work to care for the young. At worst, they would have left little children alone and uncared for. The level of unemployment might have reached 20%. Although welfare would have increased, the tax base would likely have decreased, perhaps by $100 million each month.

Effects of a New York City Default on the Capital Markets. Approximately 14,000 banks outside of New York City held $100 billion in municipal obligations, and, while only a modest share of that sum was in New York issues, a New York default could conceivably have reduced the entire municipal market to tatters. The dire state of the municipal bond market in mid-1975 can be capsulized by the fact that in the months of July through August investors began to make it known to the market that the tax-exempt attractiveness of municipal securities was beginning to lose its appeal. In this time period, interest rates on AAA rated corporate bonds were relatively stabilized at around 8.8% while interest rates on municipal bonds soared from a July figure of 6.95% to a mid-October figure of 7.7%.

There were also rumblings among the treasurers of the many firms that kept their corporate funds tied up in certificates of deposit (C.D.s) in the New York banks. Treasurers began to funnel funds out of New York banks and place them into C.D.s in local or regional banks, or into other monetary instruments. Spreads in the C.D. market for many of the regional banks narrowed significantly, from ¾% in mid-1974 to a late 1975 level of about ⅛ of 1% above the going rate for the large Manhattan banks. Some regionals reported that they were selling C.D.s at par with or even slightly below rates paid in New York City. In late 1975 New York City banks had about

---

3. Such a system was, in fact, instituted in 1976.

Table 28.2   Vulnerability of the Banks (in Billions of $)

	12 Large New York Banks	All Commercial Banks
Total Municipal Holdings	8.0	100.4
New York City and MAC*	2.0	NA
New York State Paper	1.5	NA
Unguaranteed Real Estate Loans	7.6	123.8
Real Estate Investment Trust Loans	4.0	12.0
Airline Loans	1.0	1.9
Loans to W.T. Grant Company	0.4	0.7
Equity Capital	9.5	1.4
Loan Loss Reserves	1.8	0.5

*The Municipal Assistance Corporation was formed in June 1974 by the state to handle all of New York City's financial debt transactions. It was intended to make the city's debt more secure.

Source: *Business Week*, October 20, 1975, p. 95. Reprinted from the October 20, 1975, issue of *Business Week* by special permission. © 1975 by McGraw-Hill, Inc. All rights reserved.

Table 28.3   Money That New York Needed to Raise, December 1975–June 1976* (in Billions of $)

	New York City	New York State
December	.45	.25
January	.90	.10
February	.33	.07
March	.52	.33
April	—	.95
May	.25	.85
June	.36	.99
Total	2.81	3.54

*Excludes any possible borrowing by the Municipal Assistance Corporation.

Source: *Business Week*, October 20, 1975, p. 100. Reprinted from the October 20, 1975, issue of *Business Week* by spcial permission. © 1975 by McGraw-Hill, Inc. All rights reserved.

$30 billion of C.D.'s outstanding. They could not be easily absorbed by the regional banks if there were to be a mass switch.

The city's default would also have been felt throughout the municipal bond market generally, although just what that effect was would be hard to specify. In late 1975 Detroit and Philadelphia paid one or two percentage points above their usual market rates on their municipal bond issues. The market vanished completely for low-grade offerings.

The following tables are intended to demonstrate (1) the vulnerability of the New York banks and of all commercial banks in relation to their respective holdings (Table 28.2); (2) the amount of funds needed to be raised by the city between December of 1975 and June of 1976 (Table 28.3); and

Table 28.4   Ten Cities to Watch

	Bond Rating	Comments (Mid to Late 1975)
Boston	A	State may default on $120 million in housing bonds in December
Buffalo	Baa	Insufficient tax base, $20 million short-term debt, sagging credit rating
Cleveland	A	$140 million in short-term debt, stagnating tax base in inner city
Detroit	Baa	Old central city with economy near stagnation
Hoboken	Ba	An old city with a weak tax base
Newark	Baa 1	Sagging economy, weak tax base, decaying inner city
Jersey City	Baa	Deteriorating economy, static tax base
Philadelphia	A	Has made progress in rebuilding, but has chronic budget problems
Wilmington	A1	Bonds well rated, but city is old, economy lags, will likely scrape by
Yonkers	Baa	$40 million short-term debt; averted default on Nov. 14 with loan from New York State

Source: *Newsweek*, November 10, 1975, p. 25.

(3) the financial plight of ten other major cities in the United States (Table 28.4). The last table demonstrates that the financial crisis experienced by New York City is not a unique possibility. Other American cities may also succumb.

Shockwaves. Analysts predicted that a New York default would have caused three immediate monetary tremors in the market. These tremors were of indeterminate severity.

1. Some depositors, both individual and corporate, would have decided to turn their deposits into cash. Such a move would have had the effect of shrinking bank reserves and total bank assets. The Fed could have offset this effect with open market purchase of treasury bills which would have:
   a. directly given the banks new reserves if they were the ones who sold the bills, or
   b. indirectly given the banks reserves if their customers sold the bills and deposited the proceeds.
2. Corporate treasurers could have pulled their C.D. money out of New York, thus reducing bank reserves. The Fed would have been able to offset this tremor by opening the discount window to those banks losing C.D.s. This, to some extent, would have reassured corporate treasurers and therefore diminished the C.D. run.
3. Some individual investors and companies might have decided to deposit their funds abroad. To the extent these funds were deposited with Euro-

dollar banks the money could have been loaned back to the home office and the transaction would have had no monetary effect. If the money were deposited in foreign banks, U.S. banking would have lost reserves, but once again, the Fed could have offset this reserve drain by open-market purchases of Treasury bills.

Most analysts felt that the Fed could have stopped a bank panic. But the Fed could really have exercised no control over interest rates. A New York bankruptcy would have increased investor uncertainty. Risk averters as they are, investors would have demanded higher interest rates.

Another uncertainty was the extent to which the public would move its money around. A New York default would likely have meant that both the lender and the investor would not be as aggressive as in the past. This in turn would have tended to slow down economic growth and increase any dichotomy within a two-tier credit market. Only the best credit risks would have been able to borrow money; or if an individual or firm were not a prime rate borrower, they would have paid dearly to obtain needed funds. In sum, default would have made capital much shorter in the economy.

There were those who felt that the effect of a New York default occurred in 1975 even though a legal default did not. In June New York was effectively locked out of the capital markets. Others, however, felt that if New York went bankrupt there would have resulted harsh national and international implications. The latter group felt default would have led to the reality of the domino theory. One event would have been the cause of many others. As N.Y. defaulted there would be bank defaults, which in turn would lead to corporate insolvency. This in turn would create individual loss of liquidity, resulting in a series of bankruptcies. The Federal Reserve had indicated its willingess to lend to banks troubled as a result of a New York collapse. This, however, did not fully take into account nonmember and foreign banking organizations.

A Legal Note. The U.S. bankruptcy laws carried no provision that appeared to allow New York City to put itself through or be put through an orderly bankruptcy. Chapter IX of the Federal Bankruptcy Act, entitled Municipal Debt Adjustment, provided for submission to the Court of a plan for recomposition of a municipality's debt. While this out in and of itself may have seemed uncomplicated, there were certain conditions that must have been fulfilled.

1. A petition for recomposition of debts must have been accepted by not less than 51% of all creditors in writing.
2. A list of all creditors with a description of their claims must have been filed in the court.
3. If the plan included a reassessment scheme (i.e. an increase in property taxes), then a list of all owners who have been affected by such a scheme

must have been filed, and such owners were entitled to a hearing upon request.

4. When a plan was accepted by at least two-thirds of the aggregate amount of claims by all classes affected by the plan, it could be confirmed.
5. In the carrying out of the plan, the order of the court putting it into effect could not interfere with:
    a. any of the political or governmental powers of the petitioner, and
    b. any of the property or revenues of the petitioner necessary for essential governmental purposes.
6. Any plan must have included a condensed statement of all outstanding obligations and the names and addresses of the holders of those obligations.

Considering New York's situation, it would have been quite onerous on the city to have to obtain majority approval of any plan from its creditors and to identify its creditors. This latter task would have been virtually impossible in the city's case because the majority of the notes and bonds were of the bearer type. (This means that there was a good possibility that they were not in the hands of the original buyer. These notes and bonds were traded over the counter and it is quite likely that a change of ownership could have taken place several times over the life of the note or bond.)

In order to alleviate New York City from this heavy burden, then President Ford proposed new bankruptcy legislation which included the following points:

1. Approval of a majority of the creditors would not be required.
2. Submission of a "good-faith" plan to restructure the city's debt was necessary.
3. Submission of a plan for balancing the city's budget within a reasonable length of time was also necessary.

President Ford's proposed legislation applied only to cities over one million in population.

Additionally, the proposed legislation would have allowed suppliers of products and services to have top claim on the city's resources. Coming in behind the holders of city contracts would have been the general bondholders and holders of special paper such as Big MAC issues that had a call on specific sources or revenues. If, after the implementation of a plan for reorganization, the city was still short of operating needs, the judge or referee would also have been empowered to issue special debt certificates, giving them priority for repayment ahead of all other outstanding notes and bonds.

Part III

[This part of the case attempts to fulfill an updating function for the reader.]

In early December of 1975, after much political haggling, Congress passed legislation which provided financial aid for New York City. In brief, the aid package contained the following characteristics:

1. A $2.5 billion line of credit was extended over a three-year period.
2. A condition of this aid was that the city would present a balanced budget at the end of fiscal 1978.
3. The city declared a moratorium on its interest payments on certain of its debt obligations—most notably the moral obligation bonds that were backed by nothing but the city's promise to pay.
4. The city agreed to adhere to strict cost-accounting concepts when determining its budgets for future years.
5. The city agreed to make a good-faith effort to cut current expenditures—specifically in the area of employment.
6. The city agreed to present an integrated plan for accomplishing the above tasks and make quarterly reports to the U.S. Treasury Department.

The fifth characteristic above may prove most difficult to meet, for it entails politically painful decision-making. It essentially mandates layoffs of public employees.

The success or failure of this aid package was unknown as of mid 1976. One factor that tended to show that the plan might fail, however, was that as of April 1976 the city was projecting a 1976 budget deficit of approximately $600 million rather than the approximate $300 million deficit it had originally projected under its submitted plan for 1976.[4] Whatever the ultimate fate of the aid package, one fact remains clear: the critical choices between absolute fiscal integrity and fulfilling the governmental purpose of providing essential services for its citizens will remain with New York City and many other municipalities throughout the country.

Table 28.5 New York City's Short-Term Debt (in Millions of Dollars, Cumulative)

	1966	1974
BANs	$325	$ 950
TANs	400	1,250
RANs (Federal Aid)	400	1,700
RANs (State Aid)	400	2,750
RANs (Other)	480	3,000
Budget Notes	490	3,400
Other	500	3,400

Source: *Fortune*, August 1975, p. 149. Reprinted by permission of *Fortune* Magazine; © 1975 Time Inc.

All figures are shown as of the year-end, June 30, 1974. If the market had not vanished in March 1975, the total at the end of fiscal 1975 would have been close to $6 billion. Tax anticipation notes (TANs) and revenue anticipation notes (RANs) are backed by uncollected revenues from various sources; the proceeds are used mainly for operating expenses. Bond anticipation notes (BANs) have mainly financed housing construction. Since the mid-1960s the city rolled over issues of BANs at higher and higher interest rates while waiting for long-term rates to drop before converting the notes to bonds.

4. *Wall Street Journal*, April 24, 1976.

Table 28.6 Municipal Expenditures for Basic Services (Dollars per Capita, 1973)

	Education	Police	Fire
Baltimore	250	67	38
Boston	255	85	50
Chicago	270	75	25
Denver	225	40	30
Detroit	210	75	25
Los Angeles	245	77	30
New York City	295	70	35
Philadelphia	270	75	20
San Francisco	247	65	40
Washington, D. C.	340	125	40

Source: *Fortune*, August 1975, p. 149. Reprinted by permission of *Fortune* Magazine; © 1975 Time Inc.

Exhibit 28.1 He Predicted New York's Woes—in 1908

One of the snappier lines in President Ford's October 29 speech was his charge that New York City's officials "have proved in the past that they will not face up to the city's massive network of pressure groups as long as any alternative is available."

Mr. Ford is by no means the first to express discontent with the way the big city handled its financial affairs. Nearly 190 years ago the New York state legislature was demanding a detailed statement of the city's debt in an effort to control its pellmell growth. A state assemblyman, identified by The New York Herald of Jan. 23, 1877, only as Mr. Morissey, introduced the resolution, at the same time voicing a complaint that "in the past it has been impossible to get at the figures with any degree of accuracy."

But perhaps the most damning indictment of the city was put forth by one Edgar J. Levey in 1908. Today with many of his predictions about to be realized at last, Mr. Levey's pamphlet "New York City's Progress Towards Bankruptcy" may be on its way to becoming a classic of its kind.

Much of what Levey wrote does not sound especially original today. And he tended toward understatement, as when he reluctantly concluded that "the indifferent attitude of the vast body of our electorate towards the really vital questions of municipal government . . . reacts against the rather weak efforts at economy which have been made from time to time by our city officials." But this was 1908.

The timing of Levey's pamphlet is of interest, for as he wrote the city had operated under its relatively new, five-borough structure for only a decade. Although corruption in municipal administration was widely deplored, the general prognosis for the city was guardedly optimistic. Even so, municipal finances were sufficiently precarious that Governor Hughes appointed a Joint Legislative Committee to look into them. It was in response to an invitation from committee member Martin Saxe that Levey, a former official in the city comptroller's office, responded with his prophetic little pamphlet.

To set a benchmark for his criticisms, Levey noted that between 1898 and 1908 the population of New York City had increased by 35%, from 3,272,000 to 4,423,000. The writer didn't see why operating costs should increase ratably with the population, but for the sake of argument he was prepared to accept increases in expenditures no more than 35%. But what did Levey find?

Of 28 categories in the municipal budget, there was only one—the Police Department—which had remained within the 35% ceiling. Debt service was up 189%, the Board of City Records was up 207%, the College of the City of New York was up 182% and appropriations for libraries were up a whopping 425%. This last item led Mr. Levey to a cautious criticism of Andrew Carnegie's gift of $5 million for city libraries. "Munificent as it was," Levey wrote, "the Carnegie gift looms very small in comparison with the burden which its acceptance placed upon the taxpayers."

Having demonstrated that the city's rate of expenditure was about three times its rate of population growth, Levey found cause for special concern in two areas. He was distressed that debt service was far outrunning population growth, which he tended to equate with productivity, and that the trend in excessive municipal spending was increasing rather than diminishing. "As smaller American cities have suffered in the past," he wrote, "so will New York surely suffer in the future, unless this increase in expenditure is sharply checked."

Mr. Levey offered no specific timetable for doomsday, but he anticipated that a causative factor would be a collapse of the city's tax base. Problems of access to the suburbs, he felt, had enabled landlords to pass on the burden of increased taxation to tenants, but this situation was bound to change. "The completion of the Hudson tunnels . . . will render enormous tracts of land in New Jersey available for housing accommodation for those working in New York, and the excessive taxes of the metropolis will no longer be recoverable by excessive rents."

The term "pressure group" had not been coined when Levey wrote, but even in 1908 he saw lobbies as a threat to municipal solvency. Examination of the city's new bond issues, he declared, showed the effectivenss of what he called "the highly interested few." The city's teachers represented "by force of their numbers and . . . effective organization . . . the most powerful lobby ever witnessed in this State. . . ."

As Levey saw it, no one represented the interests of the taxpayer, who was left to finance the projects enacted for the special interest groups. Yet he was critical of the city's voters for allowing this to take place and emphatic that the city's electorate must share responsibility.

As Levey held out no magic cure for New York's ills, he included some advice which might have received more attention than it did. "When a city is growing as rapidly in wealth and population as New York," he wrote, "the temptation to incur expenditures for any ends that seem good in themselves is generally irresistible, and the tendency is to refrain as long as possible from fixing any limit to the incurring of new obligations. But no community, however rich, can defy forever the operation of financial laws."

Let's hear it for Edgar J. Levey!

Source: John M. Taylor, *Wall Street Journal,* November 10, 1975. Reprinted with permission of The Wall Street Journal, © Dow Jones & Company, Inc., 1975. All rights reserved.

Discussion Questions

1. What are the factors which lead up to the New York City crisis? Which of the factors were realistically within the control of New York City, i.e., which factors could they have prevented from so severely affecting them?
2. What role did the federal government play in the New York City crisis?
3. What role did unions play in the New York City crisis?
4. What role did politicians play in the New York City crisis?
5. What could have been done to prevent this crisis? By whom?
6. Why is control so difficult in commonweal and service organizations?
7. What can New York do to correct its situation?
8. What lessons can be learned from the New York experience by: individuals, companies, other cities, the federal government?

29/Expropriation of Alcan's Bauxite Mining Subsidiary

J. Frederick Truitt

Part C

Alcan Aluminium Ltd. in early 1971 was the largest exporter of primary aluminum in the world. The Montreal-based company was truly a multinational enterprise, with subsidiaries that spanned the globe. Because of constant expansion of foreign activities, Alcan had smelters in 9 countries, fabricating operations in 33, and markets for its output in more than 100 countries by the end of 1970.

History. Alcan has traditionally had ties with Aluminum Company of America (Alcoa). Alcoa, Alcan's parent company, was forced to relinquish its holdings in Canada due to federal anti-trust legislation in 1928, and these holdings later became Alcan Aluminium. In 1928 Alcoa accounted for 90 percent of all North American aluminum production, and in 1970 it was still the largest aluminum company in the world. Alcan's first president was Edward K. Davis, brother of a former Alcoa chairman. The current Alcan president, Nathaniel Davis, followed his father into the presidency in 1947.

For decades after its beginning in 1928, Alcan confined its operations to Canada and the production of raw materials. Its sole operation consisted of producing ingots in its huge Canadian smelters and shipping them south to fabricator customers in the U.S. During the 1950's, however, Alcan's U.S. market for primary aluminum products started to shrink. U.S. customers began vertical integration backwards by expanding their own primary production capacity. In 1961 Alcan entered into a joint venture with three U.S. companies to build a hot-rolling mill in Oswego, New York. This mill was to provide an outlet for Alcan's ingot production and to supply the partners' fabricating plants with low-cost aluminum sheet. The partners' interest in the aluminum business waned in depressed market conditions, and in 1963 Alcan bought out their holdings in the Oswego mill. After further plant purchases in the U.S. Alcan formed a U.S. subsidiary, then Cleveland based Alcan Aluminum Corporation, to run these plants. Alcan's vertical integration forward into fabrication continued, and in the five years preceding 1971 a total of $824 million was spent on new plants, equipment, and acquisitions mostly for fabrication.

Source: Prepared at the Graduate School of Business, University of Washington. Copyright © 1974 by J. Frederick Truitt. Distributed by the Intercollegiate Case Clearing House, Soldiers Field, Boston, Mass. 02163. All rights reserved to the contributors. Printed in the U.S.A. The case as presented here represents Parts C, D, and E. Parts A and B have been deleted.

Exhibit 29.1   Alcan Revenues by Origin, 1961–70
          Alcan Consolidated Sales and Operating Revenues

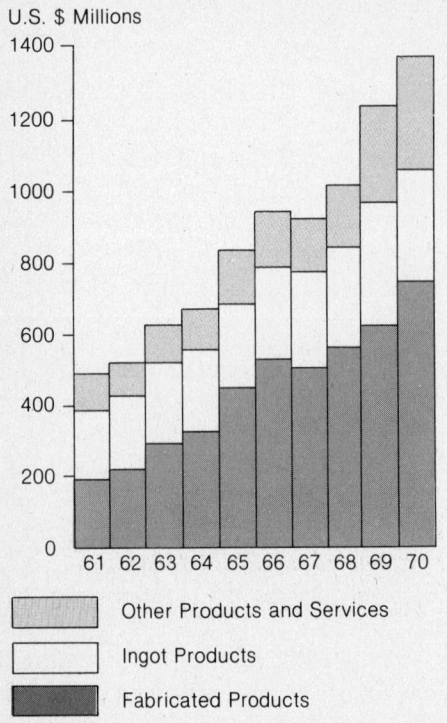

U.S. $ Millions

Other Products and Services

Ingot Products

Fabricated Products

Source: Alcan Aluminium Ltd., Annual Report, 1971, p. 6.

The big U.S. aluminum producers learned the basic lesson years before Alcan: If you get into the aluminum business, you have to go all the way. Turning out aluminum ingots is not enough, because potentially greater profits lie in the forward- and backward-integrated aluminum operation. 1970 and the few years preceding 1970 were years of extensive "catch up" investment for Alcan, and the company had been forced into aggressive marketing operations to support its expansion.

Geographic Locations

Bauxite. In 1970 Alcan and its associated companies were engaged in bauxite development work in nine countries and on every continent except North America. In the aluminum industry as a whole, strenuous development of

Exhibit 29.2   Alcan Profit by Source, 1961–70

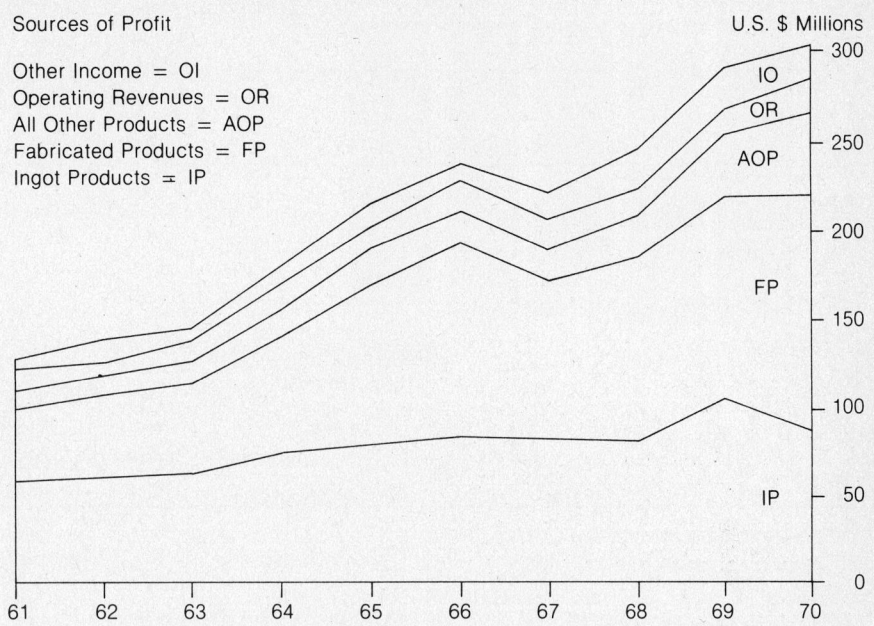

Source: Alcan Aluminium Ltd., Annual Report, 1971, p. 6.

bauxite and alumina sources were the norm in 1970. In that year Alcan's total alumina requirements were about 3.1 million tons for its own smelters and contractual commitments. Bauxite, the basic ore from which alumina is made, contains from 40 to 60 percent aluminum oxide or alumina. Thus it requires about four tons of high-grade bauxite to produce two tons of alumina, which in turn will yield one ton of aluminum metal when smelted. Therefore bauxite requirements for Alcan were around 6.2 million tons in 1970.

Bauxite mining operations are of course located where there are major reserves. Guyana in early 1971 was Alcan's traditional source of bauxite, and in 1970 supplied about 25 percent of Alcan's bauxite requirements. Guyana in the early 1950's supplied 100 percent of Alcan's needs, but Alcan has since developed other sources. In fact, increased mining costs due to deeper mines and the greater weight of over-burden would have made the Guyana operation economically unfeasible before 1970 had it not been for Alcan's development of methods to produce a specialty product, known as calcined bauxite, from some of the low-iron-content ore found on the

29/Expropriation of Alcan's Bauxite Mining Subsidiary   **601**

Exhibit 29.3 Alcan Consolidated Sources of Metal Grade Bauxite

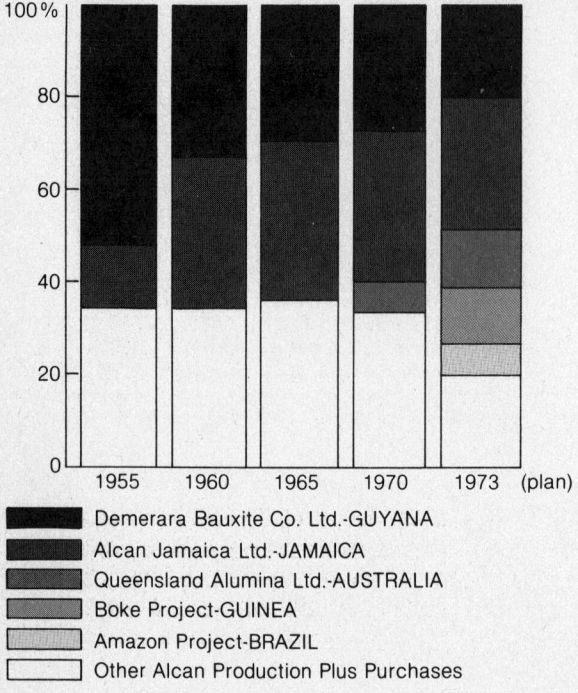

Demerara Bauxite Co. Ltd.-GUYANA
Alcan Jamaica Ltd.-JAMAICA
Queensland Alumina Ltd.-AUSTRALIA
Boke Project-GUINEA
Amazon Project-BRAZIL
Other Alcan Production Plus Purchases

Source: Alcan Aluminium Ltd., Annual Report, 1970, p. 18.

Guyana site. This product, of which the Guyana mine had a virtual world monopoly in 1971, was sold directly to the refractory and abrasive industries, and so did not enter into Alcan's aluminum-processing operations. Calcined bauxite, higher in value than regular metal-grade bauxite which is made into alumina, accounted for 36 percent of the total sales revenue in 1970 for Alcan's Guyana subsidiary, the Demerara Bauxite Company.

Jamaica is another major source of bauxite for Alcan. In 1970 about 35 percent of Alcan's bauxite needs came from Alcan's wholly owned subsidiary there. Australia is another important source of bauxite, supplying 5 percent of Alcan's needs in 1970. The rest of Alcan's bauxite was supplied through purchases or other production sources.

Alcan's bauxite development plans in 1971 included reserves in several countries. Bauxite exploration work was going on in Australia, where the company had extensive mining rights. In the Republic of Guinea, West Africa, construction was proceeding on a new bauxite development which was

Exhibit 29.4 Alcan Aluminium, Ltd.: Ten-Year Summary

Alcan Aluminium Limited

A Ten-Year Summary

All years prior to 1970 have been restated in U.S. dollars for comparative purposes.

Operating Data *(in thousands of tons)*	1961	1962	1963	1964	1965	1966	1967	1968	1969	1970
Aluminum sales by consolidated subsidiaries										
Ingot and ingot products	429	471	531	508	503	561	563	614	742	655
Fabricated products	242	259	331	354	490	554	541	606	621	691
Total	671	730	862	862	993	1,115	1,104	1,220	1,363	1,346
Fabricated products sales by all subsidiary and related companies	346	370	497	590	663	724	703	805	870	930
Production of primary aluminum										
Canada	569	596	626	740	728	788	878	873	969	903
Subsidiary and related companies outside Canada	171	194	214	245	269	286	521	588	724	827
Consolidated Income Statement Items *(in millions of U.S. dollars)*										
Revenues										
Sales of aluminum ingot and ingot products	184	194	215	219	224	251	249	271	342	321
Sales of aluminum fabricated products	218	231	301	333	461	523	514	560	611	723
Sales of all other products	34	32	47	64	79	90	96	119	217	261
Operating revenues	56	52	53	60	63	63	60	57	58	63
Equity in net income of companies 50% owned	4	3	3	3	3	3	6	6	9	10
Other income	4	9	6	8	8	7	8	16	14	11
	500	521	625	687	838	937	933	1,029	1,251	1,389
Income before income taxes	51	64	64	99	119	132	107	133	152	129
Income taxes	24	30	29	45	56	58	44	59	65	54
Minority interests and Alcan preferred dividends	5	4	6	7	8	6	6	5	7	7
Extraordinary gains	—	—	—	—	—	11	—	—	—	9
Net income for common stock	22	30	29	47	55	79	57	69	80	77
Consolidated Balance Sheet Items *(in millions of U.S. dollars)*										
Working capital	207	219	275	277	308	306	399	322	381	440
Property, plant and equipment (net)	945	944	944	938	1,003	1,043	1,074	1,085	1,130	1,223
Investments in companies owned 50% or less	48	54	56	62	57	58	116	155	175	167
Long-term debt	558	562	547	520	575	566	676	608	668	751
Deferred income taxes	134	133	136	137	138	146	150	148	144	150
Minority interests	78	78	78	78	82	82	81	84	92	112
Shareholders' equity	448	460	533	561	591	643	709	744	802	840
Total assets	1,355	1,378	1,439	1,464	1,584	1,662	1,822	1,864	2,044	2,213
Per Share of Common Stock *(in U.S. dollars)*										
Net income (after preferred dividends but before extraordinary gains)	0.73	0.96	0.94	1.52	1.77	2.18	1.76	2.12	2.42	2.08
Extraordinary gains	—	—	—	—	—	0.36	—	—	—	0.27
Net income (including extraordinary gains)	0.73	0.96	0.94	1.52	1.77	2.54	1.76	2.12	2.42	2.35
Dividends paid	0.60	0.60	0.60	0.65	0.82	0.92	1.00	1.02	1.12	1.20
Cash generation	2.50	2.82	2.96	3.61	4.06	4.69	4.15	4.58	4.85	5.30
Book value	14.60	14.97	15.39	16.26	17.22	18.85	20.23	21.33	22.67	23.82
Other Statistics										
Capital expenditures (in millions of U.S. dollars)	79	62	65	67	133	113	176	136	156	185
Cash generation (in millions of U.S. dollars)	77	87	93	115	129	148	136	150	162	177
Return on average equity (as a percentage)	4.9	6.5	6.1	9.0	10.0	11.4	8.8	9.7	10.6	9.7
Number of common stock shareholders at year end (thousands)	54	54	51	50	52	57	67	73	72	76
Number of employees at year end (thousands)	47	50	53	54	60	64	63	61	62	67

37

Source: Alcan Aluminium Ltd., Annual Report, 1970, p. 37.

29/Expropriation of Alcan's Bauxite Mining Subsidiary

to become one of the largest in the world. Alcan in 1971 had a 27 percent share in that project, along with a consortium of other North American and European producers. In Brazil Alcan had confirmed high-grade bauxite reserves of major significance, and commencement of construction on a new bauxite project was planned for 1971 in that area.

Alumina. Alcan's alumina facilities traditionally had been located in Canada, where its main smelters were located. Alumina production is the middle stage in the conversion of bauxite to aluminum metal. In the late 1950's and the 1960's, Alcan built additional alumina plants in Jamaica, Guyana, and Australia. In 1970 Alcan's 3.1 million tons of alumina requirements were filled as follows: 40 percent from Canadian plants, 38 percent from Jamaican plants, 11 percent from the Guyana alumina plant, 8 percent from its Australian source and 3 percent from other sources. The Australian source consisted of Alcan's share in the Gladstone aluminum plant, which in 1972 was to have a capacity of 2,240 tons, making it the largest alumina plant in the world.

Alcan estimated that a new plant for alumina processing would be required in 1976 to serve expanding smelter capacity. Studies up to 1971 indicated that Europe would be the most economical sight for the proposed plant.

Smelting. This stage of production yields primary aluminum metal and requires huge amounts of electricity. Western Canada provided Alcan with a cheap source of hydroelectric power for smelters located in Canada.

In 1970 primary aluminum output by all Alcan subsidiary and related companies reached a total of 1,730,00 tons (contrasted to 1,693 tons in 1969). Aluminum Company of Canada's 903,000-ton production was 120,000 tons below scheduled output because of a major strike at the Kitimat smelter in British Columbia. Increased production outside Canada occurred primarily in smelting facilities located in Australia, India, and Norway. After the Kitimat strike was settled, Alcan's Canadian smelters went back into production at about 8 percent below rated capacity of 1,035,000 tons per year.

An additional 170,000 tons of smelter capacity is scheduled to become operational by mid 1973; 134,000 tons of this additional capacity will be in the U.K., and the rest in Australia, India, and Brazil.

Alcan also owned part interest in other smelting operations throughout the world. In Norway Alcan in 1971 owned one-half interest in a 285,000 ton facility. Alcan owned one-half interest in a Japanese company with smelting capacity of 250,000 in 1971. Alcan held minority interests in smelter companies in Sweden and Spain.

Fabricating Operations. In mid 1970 Alcan's total effective fabricating capacity reached one million tons per year. Because there are great economies of scale in sheet-mill operation, Alcan's six-year building program which culminated in 1970 had resulted in mills larger in size than required to meet the current market demand. In early 1971 Alcan's fabricating sheet mills were operating at only 65 percent of capacity.

Fabrication involves forming aluminum metal into sheets, extrusions, and insulated wire and cable in Alcan's operations. These are Alcan's end products, to be sold in its various markets. Sheet mills are located with proximity to markets in mind. Alcan in early 1971 owned four major integrated sheet-mill systems strategically located in Canada, the U.S., the U.K., and Germany. Alcan's huge New York fabricating complex was one of the largest and most modern in the world, capable of turning out cold-rolled sheets at 8,000 feet per minute, believed at the time to be the fastest speed for aluminum or any metal in the world.

Alcan's facilities in Canada in 1971 processed molten metal directly from smelters, which allowed good cost savings. In the U.K., Alcan's 1970 merger with James Booth Aluminum resulted in a 75 percent equity interest in Alcan-Booth industries for Alcan, and allowed the rationalization of the fabrication complex there. Germany and the other related European mills too were modernized and technologically updated. Alcan also owned in 1971 fabricating operations on a small scale in Italy, Nigeria, South Africa, Mexico, Venezuela, Brazil, Thailand, Malaysia, Japan, and Australia. In Japan and Brazil the mills were integrated with small smelters.

Sales

In 1970 Alcan experienced a disappointment in sales. In the U.S. the economic recession in 1970 was compounded by excess capacity in the aluminum industry as a whole, which resulted in strong price competition. Trends in other markets reflected the inclusion of more fabricated products in Alcan's sales mix, which helped to bolster sales in these areas. For example, the merger in the U.K. with James Booth Industries boosted 1970 aluminum shipments by some 26,000 tons because of the creation of enlarged fabrication facilities.

In dollar terms, as illustrated in Exhibits 29.1 and 29.2, total revenues from all sales and operating sources in 1970 were $1,368 million, an increase of $140 million or 11 percent over 1969. Of the increase, more than $100 million arose in semi-fabricated and finished goods. Sales of aluminum ingots showed a revenue decline of 6 percent to $321 million due to a drop in tonnage. Revenues from other products and services (magnesium and other non-aluminum metals, bauxite and chemical products, houses, power sales and shipping services, etc.) rose by $50 million to $324 million.

In 1970 Alcan achieved a milestone in its campaign to diversify away from dependence on production of primary aluminum products; for the first time semi-fabricated and finished products exceeded sales of ingots in tonnage. In 1970 ingot sales were at 655,000 tons, while semi-fabricated and

Table 29.1   Alcan Aluminium Ltd. Consolidated Sales of Aluminum in 1000 Tons

	1967	1968	1969	1970
Canada	130	150	152	160
U. S.	332	393	399	357
U. K.	172	174	191	222
EEC	102	121	158	168
All Others	368	382	463	439
Totals	1104	1220	1363	1346

Source: Alcan Aluminium Ltd., Annual Report, 1970, p. 8.

finished products amounted to 691,000 tons. In 1970 actual sales were under forecasts, mainly because direct ingot sales to customers were down. Thus the value of fabricating expansion was demonstrated to Alcan, as its finished and semi-fabricated products provided protection by maintaining sales levels in the recession.

Financial Position and Strategy

As can be seen in Exhibit 29.4, Alcan's net income fell in 1970 to $2.08 per share, against $2.42 per share in 1969. This was blamed on declining markets for aluminum because of a general business recession. Further cost burdens were the strike at one of Alcan's major Canadian smelting complexes, and the upward revaluation of the Canadian dollar. In the years before 1970 Alcan had continually borne the cost of expanding its fabrication facilities and marketing position, which also caused huge capital expenditures.

By the end of 1970 Alcan's program for the expansion of its fabrication facilities had nearly been completed. Future conditions seemed to indicate that a soft market in aluminum would be Alcan's major problem. Declining market prices caused by overcapacity were not the only problem ahead in 1971. The full expense of rationalizing the U.K. operations was to be borne in 1971, and by the end of 1970 Alcan's operations in Guyana were placed under a cloud by government demands for participation.

Alcan felt that it could rely on several competitive advantages in the future. First its source of cheap hydroelectric power for its Canadian smelters was one cost advantage, especially in the face of rising ecological concern that increased power costs to other producers. Secondly an encouraging factor was its achievement of a balance in its primary and fabricated metal production and markets. The third factor was Alcan's worldwide geographic diversification. Recognizing that the aluminum industry had been characterized by cyclical growth, Alcan felt that this geographic spread would soften impact of the cycles.

Part D

The Demerara Bauxite Company, Ltd. (Demba) was formally expropriated by the government of Guyana on July 14, 1971, following an eight-month period of negotiations. Demba was a wholly-owned subsidiary of Alcan Aluminium, Ltd., a Canadian corporation headquartered in Montreal. The following discussion describes Demba's operations in Guyana and records the major events in the negotiations and expropriation of Demba.

Demba. Demba employed about 5000 workers in its operations at Mackenzie, 65 miles south of Georgetown on the Demerara River. Demba's industrial complex included a bauxite-processing plant for the manufacture of alumina. The plant processed crude bauxite ore from deposits which were mined by walking draglines and bucket-wheel excavators. The ore was shipped to Mackenzie over the company's 85-mile rail system. Demba products were loaded onto shallow draft vessels which transported the products down the Demerara and across to Chacaramus Bay in Trinidad where they were transshipped to large bulk carriers. Demba exported annually about 1,000,000 tons of metallurgical-grade bauxite, 500,000 tons of calcined bauxite, and 300,000 tons of alumina. In 1968 Alcan made additional investments of $100 million in Demba to enlarge facilities and to build a bridge across the Demerara to exploit deposits on its west bank.

Alcan Policies. Alcan, since its formation in 1928, had depended on the Guyana mining operations for its bauxite requirements. As recently as the early 1950's Guyana supplied 100 percent of Alcan's bauxite needs. But since then Alcan had been continually seeking other sources of bauxite, and by 1970 Guyana supplied only about 25 percent of Alcan's total bauxite requirement, and was projected by Alcan to supply even less in the future as new deposits elsewhere were expanded. In fact, the mines would have been too costly for Alcan to operate long before 1970, because of increasing costs due to the inreasing depth of the mines and the increasing weight of overburden, had it not been for the presence of a special grade of ore with low iron content enabling it to be made into calcined bauxite. The Guyana mine had a virtual world monopoly on the product. Alcan did not smelt calcined bauxite into aluminum, but rather calcined bauxite was sold directly to the refractory and abrasive industries. Calcined bauxite was more valuable than regular bauxite, and thus sustained the mining operation.

Another factor that may have affected Alcan's reactions to the nationalization was the state of the aluminum industry in 1971. All aluminum producers were experiencing soft markets due to an oversupply of aluminum on the market. Cut-throat pricing and voluntary cutbacks in production were employed by the industry in response to the soft market. Thus there was no shortage of bauxite for Alcan at the time of the nationalization.

Guyanization. Early in 1970 the government of Guyana embarked on a policy of Guyanization. This included demands for increased participation by Guyanese citizens in the ownership and management of foreign enterprises and limitations on the number of foreign employees that could be brought into Guyana to take jobs. Government officials expressed the view that foreign interests should no longer continue to play as predominant a role as heretofore in key sectors of the country's economy. Concurrent with the announcement of the new policy, the government announced that it would soon begin talks with the two bauxite mining firms in Guyana, Alcan's Demerara Bauxite Co. and the Reynolds Aluminum subsidiary, aimed at acquiring "meaningful participation" in their operations in Guyana.

Formal notification of Guyana's intention to negotiate government participation in Demerara Bauxite Company came to Demba early in November. The Guyana government position hardened suddenly on Saturday, November 28, when four non-negotiable terms of participation were announced to Demba.

The government took many actions in 1970 towards furthering its Guyanization policies. In Georgetown, it acquired controlling interest in a prominent importing and merchandising concern. It established a new design to further involve Guyana's citizens in their economy. The government also nationalized a major newspaper in Georgetown. It was clear in 1970 that the government was intent on implementing its stated policy.

Negotiations. Negotiations between the Alcan Aluminium Company and the government of Guyana began December 8, 1971. As the negotiations progressed the government continually hardened its stance, and meaningful participation came to be defined much more definitely in a number of non-negotiable points set out by the government. These were: (1) Majority control of the company's assets; (2) evaluation of the assets for compensation purposes at their book value as of December 31, 1969; and (3) payment of compensation to Alcan out of future after-tax profits of the company.

In January of 1971 Forbes Burnham spoke about the proposed participation in New York. Burnham, enroute to a conference in Singapore, stated that Guyana would "pursue relentlessly the policy of owning and controlling our natural resources." Burnham further stated that the negotiated settlement with Alcan would be retroactive to January 1, 1971. Burnham went on to couch the takeover in more emotional terms. He said that although he had heard Alcan could break him, "It is better to be broken by a corporation like Alcan than to be broken by your own people." The alternative to Guyana controlling directly her natural resources, he said, was to "continue to be recipients of handouts, which is the most dehumanizing experience." Burnham ended his speech by telling enthusiastic listeners to join as black men in Guyana's struggle by working for Guyana.

Throughout February the negotiations between Guyana and Alcan were deadlocked on the question of compensation in return for Guyana's majority interest. Alcan countered Guyana's points by demanding a cash payment for its interests, suggesting that Guyana go to the World Bank to finance it. Alcan also was trying to obtain a commitment from the government that present mining operations would not be expanded in the future. Alcan announced late in February that it had failed to get what it considered satisfactory terms for the takeover. At the same time Forbes Burnham announced that Guyana might no longer be satisfied with only majority interest in the ownership of Demba.

On March 1 the Parliament of Guyana passed legislation enabling the takeover of Demba. However, this legislation did not make clear how or when Guyana would acquire Alcan's bauxite interests. Alcan was to remain in control of Demba's operation until an order-in-council had been issued by the government. After March 1 it became clear that any future Alcan involvement in the subsidiary after the nationalization would be only of a technical nature.

On June 17 negotiations between Guyanese representatives and the Royal Trust Company of Montreal began in Montreal. The negotiations concerned a trust deed governing the Alcan retirement income and life insurance plan for its employees, then administered by Royal Trust. Guyana sought to have the funds which were held in trust turned over to the state. Guyana also announced plans of establishing a successor trust to be free of government control. Guyana successively obtained a commitment to deliver the funds.

Finally on July 14 an order-in-council nationalizing the subsidiary went into effect. The final settlement was for $53.5 million (U.S.) as compensation for the nationalization. This figure was arrived at as equivalent to the book value of Demba's assets as of December 31, 1969. Alcan said that this was under the true value of the company as the assets had been written down for tax purposes. Alcan said its total investment over 50 years of operation totaled $150 million. Compensation payments were to be made over a 20-year period with interest at 6 percent per year. The first payment was projected to be in the vicinity of $5 million, not to be paid until after the end of 1972. Agreement was reached for the transfer of Royal Trust's funds. The funds totaled $4.5 million, and were to be repatriated to Guyana within a few months of the nationalization.

After Nationalization. Patterson Thompson, the new chairman of the renamed company—Guybau, short for Guyana Bauxite Company—explained that several important problems contributed to a difficult start for the newly acquired government corporation. These problems included an exodus of former managers, run-down equipment, lack of spare parts, negligible working capital, and marketing difficulties. To help combat the latter, Guybau first appointed Gerald Metals Ltd. of London, a U.S.-owned corporation, as marketing agent. On January 1, 1972, however, Phillipp Brothers A.G. of

Switzerland became worldwide marketing agents for the company's entire production for an initial period of three years. Distribution was hampered by losing Alcan's transshipment facilities at Trinidad, but this problem was overcome by sending ever larger shipments out of Mackenzie.

Despite these problems and a worldwide slump in metals prices, Guyana's bauxite exports earned revenue of $67.5 million in 1971, compared with $69 million in 1970. Guyana actively searched out new markets: diplomatic relations were established with the U.S.S.R., and China was encouraged to establish a permanent trade mission in Georgetown. Peking bought 50,000 tons in 1972, and in return set up a textile factory and rendered other technical assistance to Guyana. The Yugoslav government was also keen to co-operate in developing the bauxite industry.

In 1971 profits were $7 million. Production consisted of 1,024,646 long tons of metal-grade bauxite; 621,333 tons of calcined refractory-grade bauxite; and 305,230 tons of calcined alumina. Production objectives in 1972 for total bauxite products were set at over 2 million tons.

Part E

Prime Minister Forbes Burnham, in explaining to the Guyanese nation on Tuesday why his government had to take over the Demerara Bauxite Company, said that the company and its parent, Alcan, displayed much contempt and arrogance for the government and people of this country during the negotiations.

Mr. Burnham said that when taken as a whole the company's representative showed a "kind of arrogance and lack of concern with the realities in Guyana. One wonders that the controllers of such vast wealth as ALCAN possesses, can be so insensitive to the aspirations of developing nations."

Following is the full text of Mr. Burnham's address,[1] delivered at the National Park on Republic Day:

A year ago today Guyana became the first Co-operative Republic in the world. A year ago today we made a pledge—that pledge was that as a Nation we would work for the economic emancipation of our country, we would work to make the little man a real man.

Sacrifice. Few of us, if any, doubted that sacrifices would be demanded, that obstacles would have to be surmounted, that difficulties would have to be overcome—obstacles and difficulties from within and from without, some arising from the very nature of our history—social and economic—others as a result of the efforts of those who see in an egalitarian society, a threat to their entrenched positions and their vested interests.

Last year saw us survive. It saw us take positive steps to reform

1. This speech by Prime Minister Forbes Burnham appeared in the *Guyana Graphic,* Thursday, February 25, 1971.

and change the bases of our fiscal system. It saw the strengthening and expansion of the co-operative sector. It saw, above all, the beginning of a national self-help project in which every section, every group, every race in Guyana has been involved, a project which when completed, it is expected by the 31st of December, 1971, will be a testimony to the grit, determination and self-reliance of our Guyanese people.

The last year marked, above all, our set determination to own and control our God-given resources. As I said at the 13th Annual Conference of the People's National Congress on Sunday, the 5th of April, 1970, "The Hinterland as we all know, contains the greatest part of our national resources, especially in forests and minerals. In the exploration of these, especially of the latter, we are prepared to enter in consortia with foreign investors but only on certain conditions, and one such condition henceforth will be that government alone or government and co-operatives hold in each case no less than 51 per cent of the equity. We must own and control the exploitation of our resources. We have seen in Guyana and in other underdeveloped countries foreign-owned extractive industries prosper while the native population remained poor and destitute. We must now get the large share of the cake, otherwise what is the difference between Guyana and a colony? What shall we tell our children when they ask us to explain the gaping holes in the earth whence rich minerals have been won? You tell me.

Terms. It was in this context and against this background that on the 9th of November, 1970, in a letter, we invited the Demerara Bauxite Company, a wholly owned subsidiary of the giant multi-national Canadian-based company—ALCAN—to sit around the table to negotiate terms of a new relationship with Guyana. This new relationship was to be in harmony with the policy supported by the sovereign people of Guyana and in keeping with various United Nations resolutions.

Demba has been extracting bauxite in Guyana since 1917 and according to Mr. Nathaniel Davis, the president of Alcan, is the oldest and largest bauxite undertaking owned by Alcan. At this stage it is apposite to note that Alcan in 1969 deployed the equivalent of G$5 billion worth of assets and had an income of over G$2.6 billion, or over five times the Gross Domestic Product of Guyana.

Also, let us observe that on the calculation most favourable to Alcan's generosity, Guyana over the last fifty odd years received less than 3% of the profits accruing from the exploitation of her bauxite.

The discussions with respect to our participation in the Demba operations were fixed by agreement to commence on Monday, 7 December, 1970.

On Saturday, the 28th of November, 1970, I announced the

government's intention to acquire majority control of these operations and had dispatched to the Company's President a letter to that effect. There were set out the principles which we considered fundamental and described as non-negotiable. The contents of the communication which were made public by Alcan on Monday, 30 November 1970, are now well known and stated that—

1. Government's participation shall be a majority one.
2. Participation would be by means of purchase of a share of the assets of the Company.
3. The value of such assets shall be no greater than that given by the Company as the written-down book value for income tax purposes on the 31 of December, 1969, with additions of value during 1970 not by revaluations or reappraisals.
4. The Government will pay for its share of the assets out of future profits of the joint undertaking after tax.
5. The Government's majority holding shall confer on Government the control which inheres in such majority holding.
6. The agreement finally arrived at between the Company and Government shall be deemed to take effect from 1st of January, 1971.

Apart from these, all other terms including the exact size of the majority holding were negotiable. This we made clear and sought to ascertain the special areas of concern to Demba, the satisfaction of which would conduce to a mutually acceptable and therefore amicable agreement and outcome.

But this was not to be. Demba's first counter-proposal made on Tuesday, the 15th of December, was that the government of Guyana should raise a loan from the World Bank for expanding the production of calcined ore and put it into the new entity as equity. Alcan would then put all of Demba's assets into that entity, part of these assets to represent Alcan's equity, the rest to be an interest-bearing loan to be repaid in installments—presumably annual. These installments were to be chargeable against cash generation and before tax. Alcan desired freedom from exchange control and from withholding tax and proposed that it should appoint the Chief Executive Officer of the new Company.

Unacceptable. This proposal was obviously unacceptable for at least three reasons. First is premised the Government's having to pay in advance for participation; second, repayment for assets was to be before tax and third, Alcan's right to appoint the Chief Executive Officer meant that it should in fact control the operations of the new entity. Further, in discussions, the representatives of Alcan and Demba explained that it was intended that the former should be majority share holders. This proposal was rejected but was followed eventually on the 9th of February, 1971, by another, the main points of which may be summarised thus:

1. That a new company would be formed after the Govern-

ment had agreed in advance to commit the new entity to Alcan's scheme for the expansion of calcined bauxite and after the Government had undertaken to provide the $50 million needed for that scheme.

2. That the new company would be capitalised at $100 in $1 shares, 50 to the Government and 50 to Alcan. The company later conceded 51 to the Government and 49 to Alcan.

3. The existing assets of Demba (approx. $100m) would be put in as a fully interest-bearing loan at current commercial rates.

4. The new entity and its shareholders should not be subject to any Income Tax, Corporation Tax, Property Tax, Withholding Tax, Import Duty, Export Duty, Royalty or any Guyana Tax or Impost, nor any Exchange Control restriction with respect to any interest, dividends or fee for its shareholders.

5. That if the Government should sign with any other bauxite producer an agreement containing any single term more favourable than the corresponding term reached with Alcan, the agreement with Alcan would be changed to include the more favourable term.

What did these mean?

1. They meant that there could be no agreement unless the government first found the sum of $50m to put in the new Company to finance an expansion scheme over which it would have no control, or unless we gave an understanding to provide such a sum.

Commercial Rate.

2. The February proposals meant that Alcan would in effect eat its cake and have it. She would be repaid the sum of $100m (estimated book value of Demba by the Company) with interest at a commercial rate. During the period of repayment she would hold 49% of the equity and share in the profits.

   When the loan had been completely repaid, Alcan would still retain a share of 49% in an enterprise now expanded to about $150 million to which Alcan would have contributed no capital. This particular proposal would be well paralleled if, upon the obtaining of a mortgage from a loan company to purchase a house, one had to agree not only to repay the loan but to give the lender half share in the house as well.

3. Another implication of the proposals was that the government would have placed a large area of the country's economy and fiscal system beyond the scope of its own power. This was an attempt to seek to enjoy the benefits of our country while being immune from its laws.

4. The measures meant that we would be restricted in our

dealings with any other bauxite producer, since Alcan would exercise a kind of veto over our dealings with other bauxite interests.

Added to this, the method of repayment suggested by Alcan was not out of future profits after tax, but from cash generation.

The effect of this would be to leave the new company in a position where it was unable to hold any cash for future expansion. All future expansion would have to be done by the Government's obtaining loans. Here one sees Alcan's intention to bleed the industry.

These are not the only objectionable features of the Alcan proposals but they are the most obnoxious.

Taken as a whole, they show a kind of arrogance and lack of concern with the realities in Guyana. One wonders that the controllers of such vast wealth as Alcan possesses, can be so insensitive to the aspirations of developing nations.

What was clear was that Alcan, Demba's parent, was not prepared to invest further money in the enterprise; that the much advertised expansion in alumina production announced on the 21st of September, 1969, was not to be; that any expansion was to be exclusively in calcined ore production financed entirely by government and that the undertaking given by the President of Alcan in 1966, to me in Montreal to construct an aluminum smelter, if reasonably priced power were to be available, was never seriously given or intended.

There were, subsequently, some slight changes to the proposal of the 9th of February, but none of these was of any substance or calculated to alter the original.

It is informative to note that last year Demba undertook to provide a loan to match one from the Canadian Government to ensure a proper water supply to the Mackenzie area where thousands exist under threat of typhoid. This year Demba says that the new entity will have to meet the undertaking. My Government will not toady, will not beg. We will provide the money where Demba has defaulted for the people, the chattels so far as Demba is concerned, are entitled at least to a wholesome water supply.

The final proposal by Alcan and the callous attitude on water by Demba are in keeping with the latter's well-known tradition at Mackenzie. It is a tradition of prejudice, discrimination, segregation, intolerance and a recognition of workers' rights only as a last resort after strikes and stoppages. It bespeaks a basic contempt for the Guyanese people.

Foreign Control. But let us cast our eyes across the world. Even in relatively developed countries governments have been moving to protect their resources from exclusive foreign exploitation. Australia, and even Canada, whose corporate citizen Alcan is, have in the last year proposed measures to limit the degree of foreign control of their mineral resources. The developing or poor and underdeveloped nations like ours in Asia, Africa and Latin America faced with unrepentant and arrogantly short-sighted exploiters are more and more taking control of their resources. Colonialists and exploitative institutions have to be dismantled before we can start on the journey from poverty to prosperity.

In our present circumstances, in the circumstances of what I have narrated, what shall we do? What steps shall we take? We have suffered insolence with calm. We have turned the other cheek. Because ours is a tiny nation, we have been kicked and spat upon. We do not count for human. Those who have with impunity exploited us in the past would deny us the right to what is ours.

Shall we continue bound hand and foot? Shall we be second-class citizens and despised even in our own land? Shall we be content to feast on the crumbs? Will we choose to live on our knees? I ask you . . . you.

It seems to me that there is no alternative to our saying and meaning "thus far and no further." We have offered peace and reason and been met with unreason. We have offered partnership and have been threatened with continued domination. Our choice is between being men or being mice.

Your government therefore proposes to introduce in Parliament this week a measure to nationalise with reasonable compensation the bauxite complex at Mackenzie. I believe, nay I know, that in this step we have the overwhelming support of the Guyanese nation, irrespective of political loyalty or orientation.

We, like all the newly independent countries, have been bequeathed the rotten colonial heritage of shame, frustration, emptiness and self-pity. We, the citizens of Guyana did not make the old Guyana. We inherited it. Together we shall change it. We accept the duty and the challenge. Despite what the servitors of Imperialism may consider, it is a source of considerable strength to know that the present action of the government enjoys the strong support of the overwhelming majority of the Guyanese people and of their political leaders.

We all are aware that no country can be transformed overnight. But we will begin with the control of one of the main and decisive factors in our economy. Today we declare the first major and concrete act of economic independence, the taking over of the Demerara Bauxite Company at Mackenzie. No one in Guyana with good sense will oppose it, for it is the will of the vast majority of the people. There can be no turning back.

And let me say that in this move we have no quarrel with the friendly Canadian Government; no quarrel with the friendly Canadian nation or with the Canadian people; only with the system which Alcan epitomises and Demba illustrates.

Comrades at Christianburg-Wismar-Mackenzie, you, in particular, are in the vanguard of our struggle for economic freedom. Be assured that Guyana recognizes with gratitude the part you are called upon to play. The whole country, the whole world watches your response and is anxious to learn from you the lessons of heroism, of discipline, of solidarity, of self-reliance which you are destined to teach. Without lacking appreciation of the other sections I want to tell the Guyanese supervisory staff, particularly the foremen and general foremen, that all who work in the industry have paid tribute to your very important role in management and your mastery through intelligence and experience of your varied operations and processes. Your country relies on you to work with a greater sense of purpose in the future for material rewards that are no less than you now enjoy.

Social Relations. I want to assure you that the government will allow all those systems and procedures suitable to the industry and its operations to continue and will expect them to improve with time. You will continue to work in a business enterprise using business methods. However, the change of ownership will mean a change in the social relations of the industry. Not only will the technical management staff and foremen have the opportunity of using their initiative, of real authority—collective and individual— but all ranks of members through their representatives and through their union will be afforded the opportunity to play a part as of right in the decision making bodies and processes of the enterprise.

It is natural that at a moment like this as we stand on the verge of a radical change, the workers and other Guyanese should, while confident of success, express certain anxieties. The govern- ment has fortunately made arrangements which are designed to smooth over and reduce the effect of the temporary dislocations and disturbances that are so common in these situations and that must be expected.

All those of any nationality who elect to remain on the job will be paid as usual; their jobs, their livelihood and their welfare, are the government's first and most important consideration.

Challenges. A most important factor in meeting the challenges that lie ahead is, of course, the attitude and performance of the workers.

The complaints and irritations caused in the past by the Canadian company's callous indifference to the needs and welfare of the Guyanese workers must give way to determination to keep the company operating.

Indeed, the nation depends on the workers at this critical period to display a degree of enthusiasm, to show a resolution to suc- ceed, and to rise to a level of efficiency well beyond the normal call of duty.

We must remember that there is nothing in this world that Alcan would enjoy more than to see the chimneys at Mackenzie stop bellowing smoke. They must, they shall be disappointed.

The comparatively few jobs which Guyanese already at Mackenzie and other Guyanese in training cannot immediately fill in the likely event of the departure of non-Guyanese staff have already been identified and steps are being taken to fill them, if necessary.

Ample Provision. Vital supplies used to keep the company in operation, many of which should long ago have been produced in Guyana, but have been imported into the country by Alcan, will of course be maintained.

Any businessman will tell you that any major company must have Working Capital to provide financing for the pay roll, the purchase of supplies and to meet other day-to-day operational expenses. The amount of working capital required has long ago been calculated and the government has made ample provision for supply of the necessary sums of money.

It would be foolish to deny that during the period of transition and until the new bauxite company is fully operational there will be a strain placed on the country's financial resources. Should this involve some hardship, it is the price that we must be prepared to pay for the profits that will accrue later.

It is no secret that Guyana's bauxite was transported from Guyana to the buyer in ships either owned or chartered by the Aluminum Company of Canada. We have also thought about these ships not being available and we are making alternative arrangements.

Great Myths. One of the great myths that Alcan has always attempted to promote is that without them Guyana's bauxite and alumina cannot be sold.

Already two European countries have indicated a positive wish to buy well over half of our total output and no difficulty is anticipated in disposing of the remainder.

Comrades! By nationalising Demba we are asserting our manhood as a nation, our confidence in ourselves, in our people, because it is the ordinary man, the worker—manual or intellectual—who can conceive and make the things that support a nation.

In nationalising Demba, I place the fate of our nation in the hands of the people. If you, the people, will take as natural the wrath of the former masters because we refuse to give up what is rightfully ours, if you trust your own strength, our strength and our own creative genius, we shall succeed.

Direct Relevance. These events have a direct relevance to the celebration of the first anniversary of the Co-operative Republic. The economic content of the Co-operative Republic is nothing more nor less than the Co-operative Sector, in alliance with the public sector and government's majority ownership of participating enterprises. The shape of the economy of the Co-operative Republic, our chosen form of socialism in Guyana, is clear for everyone to see.

Unity Call. When I called for Unity on New Year's Day, 1971, it was no mere idle slogan. It was a serious invitation to all men, women and young people to join the struggle for a new society. My call for unity was not, and is not, a question of routine or a kind of holiday toast. The programme of reconstruction of the economy and the building of our form of socialism against the opposition of our erstwhile masters offers us a concrete material base for internal unity and social peace.

Long live national unity; Long live the Co-operative Republic of Guyana.

Discussion Questions

1. What can a firm such as Alcan effectively do to counteract expropriation?
2. Devise a realistic strategy for coping with this problem in most countries.
3. What policies would guide those managers in the field to implement the strategy you derived in question 2 above?

Index